P9-BUI-135

Collins
Robert
French-English
English-French
Dictionary

HarperCollins Publishers
Westerhill Road
Bishopbriggs
Glasgow
G64 2QT
Great Britain

Fourth Edition 2011

Reprint 10 9 8 7

ISBN 978-0-00-742781-9

www.collinslanguage.com

HarperCollins Publishers Ltd
2 Bloor Street East, 20th Floor
Toronto, Ontario
Canada M4W 1A8

www.collinsdictionaries.ca

A catalogue record for this book is
available from the British Library

Typeset by Davidson Publishing
Solutions, Glasgow

Printed in America by OPM

Pierre-Henri Cousin
Lorna Sinclair Knight
Lesley Robertson

CONTRIBUTORS
Claude Nimmo, Philippe Patry,
Hélène Lewis, Elisabeth Campbell,
Renée Birks, Jean-François Allain,
Christine Penman, Sabine Citron,
Catherine E. Love, Jennifer Baird,
Stewart C. Russell, Wendy Lee,
Callum Brines, Jill Williams,
Laurent Jouet, Phyllis Buchanan

EDITOR
Genevieve Gerrard

EDITORIAL MANAGEMENT
Gaëlle Amiot-Cadey

SERIES EDITOR
Rob Scriven

Acknowledgements
We would like to thank those
authors and publishers who kindly
gave permission for copyright
material to be used in the Collins
Word Web. We would also like to
thank Times Newspapers Ltd for
providing valuable data.

Table des matières

Contents

Introduction

You may be starting French for the first time, or you may wish to extend your knowledge of the language. Perhaps you want to read and study French books, newspapers and magazines, or perhaps simply have a conversation with French speakers. Whatever the reason, whether you're a student, a tourist or want to use French for business, this is the ideal book to help you understand and communicate. This modern, user-friendly dictionary gives priority to everyday vocabulary and the language of current affairs, business, computing and tourism, and, as in all Collins dictionaries, the emphasis is firmly placed on contemporary language and expressions.

How to use the dictionary
Below you will find an outline of how information is presented in your dictionary. Our aim is to give you the maximum amount of detail in the clearest and most helpful way.

Entries
A typical entry in your dictionary will be made up of the following elements:

Phonetic transcription
Phonetics appear in square brackets immediately after the headword. They are shown using the International Phonetic Alphabet (IPA), and a complete list of the symbols used in this system can be found on pages x and xi.

Grammatical information
All words belong to one of the following parts of speech: noun, verb, adjective, adverb, pronoun, article, conjunction, preposition.

Nouns can be singular or plural and, in French, masculine or feminine. Verbs can be transitive, intransitive, reflexive or impersonal. Parts of speech appear in *italics* immediately after the phonetic spelling of the headword. The gender of the translation appears in *italics* immediately following the key element of the translation.

Often a word can have more than one part of speech. Just as the English word **chemical** can be an adjective or a noun, the French word **rose** can be an adjective ("pink") or a feminine noun ("rose"). In the same way the verb **to walk** is sometimes transitive, ie it takes an object ("to walk the dog") and sometimes intransitive, ie it doesn't take an object ("to walk to school"). To help you find the meaning you are looking for quickly and for clarity of presentation, the different part of speech categories are separated by a right facing triangle ▷.

Meaning divisions

Most words have more than one meaning. Take, for example, **punch** which can be, amongst other things, a blow with the fist or an object used for making holes. Other words are translated differently depending on the context in which they are used. The transitive verb **to roll up**, for example, can be translated by "rouler" or "retrousser" depending on what it is you are rolling up. To help you select the most appropriate translation in every context, entries are divided according to meaning. Different meanings are introduced by an "indicator" in *italics* and in brackets. Thus, the examples given above will be shown as follows:

> **punch** n (*blow*) coup m de poing; (*tool*) poinçon m
> **roll up** vt (*carpet, cloth, map*) rouler; (*sleeves*) retrousser

Likewise, some words can have a different meaning when used to talk about a specific subject area or field. For example, **bishop**, which we generally use to mean a high-ranking clergyman, is also the name of a chess piece. To show English speakers which translation to use, we have added "subject field labels" in *italics*, starting with a capital letter, and in brackets, in this case (*Chess*):

> **bishop** n évêque m; (*Chess*) fou m

Field labels are often shortened to save space. You will find a complete list of abbreviations used in the dictionary on pages viii and ix.

Translations

Most English words have a direct translation in French and vice versa, as shown in the examples given above. Sometimes, however, no exact equivalent exists in the target language. In such cases we have given an approximate equivalent, indicated by the sign ≈. An example is **National Insurance**, the French equivalent of which is "Sécurité Sociale". There is no exact equivalent since the systems of the two countries are quite different:

> **National Insurance** n (*Brit*) ≈ Sécurité Sociale

On occasion it is impossible to find even an approximate equivalent. This may be the case, for example, with the names of types of food:

> **mince pie** n *sorte de tarte aux fruits secs*

Here the translation (which doesn't exist) is replaced by an explanation. For increased clarity the explanation, or "gloss", is shown in *italics*.

It is often the case that a word, or a particular meaning of a word, cannot be translated in isolation. The translation of **Dutch**, for example, is "hollandais(e), neérlandais(e)". However, the phrase **to go Dutch** is rendered by "partager les frais".

Even an expression as simple as **washing powder** needs a separate translation since it translates as "lessive (en poudre)", not "poudre à laver". This is where your dictionary will prove to be particularly informative and useful since it contains an abundance of compounds, phrases and idiomatic expressions.

Levels of formality and familiarity

In English you instinctively know when to say "I don't have any money" and when to say "I'm broke" or "I'm a bit short of cash". When you are trying to understand someone who is speaking French, however, or when you yourself try to speak French, it is important to know what is polite and what is less so, and what you can say in a relaxed situation but not in a formal context. To help you with this, on the French–English side we have added the label (*inf*) to show that a French meaning or expression is colloquial, while those meanings or expressions which are vulgar are given an exclamation mark (*inf!*), warning you they can cause serious offence. Note also that on the English–French side, translations which are vulgar are followed by an exclamation mark in brackets.

Keywords

Words labelled in the text as KEYWORDS, such as **be** and **do** or their French equivalents **être** and **faire**, have been given special treatment because they form the basic elements of the language. This extra help will ensure that you know how to use these complex words with confidence.

Cultural information

Entries which appear distinguished in the text by a column of dots explain aspects of culture in French and English-speaking countries. Subject areas covered include politics, education, media and national festivals, for example **Assemblée nationale**, **baccalauréat**, **BBC** and **Hallowe'en**.

Abréviations

Abbreviations

abréviation	*ab(b)r*	abbreviation
adjectif, locution adjectivale	*adj*	adjective, adjectival phrase
administration	*Admin*	administration
adverbe, locution adverbiale	*adv*	adverb, adverbial phrase
agriculture	*Agr*	agriculture
anatomie	*Anat*	anatomy
architecture	*Archit*	architecture
article défini	*art déf*	definite article
article indéfini	*art indéf*	indefinite article
automobile	*Aut(o)*	the motor car and motoring
aviation, voyages aériens	*Aviat*	flying, air travel
biologie	*Bio(l)*	biology
botanique	*Bot*	botany
anglais britannique	*Brit*	British English
chimie	*Chem*	chemistry
cinéma	*Ciné, Cine*	cinema
commerce, finance, banque	*Comm*	commerce, finance, banking
informatique	*Comput*	computing
conjonction	*conj*	conjunction
construction	*Constr*	building
nom utilisé comme adjectif	*cpd*	compound element
cuisine	*Culin*	cookery
article défini	*def art*	definite article
déterminant: article; adjectif démonstratif *ou* indéfini etc	*dét*	determiner: article, demonstrative etc
économie	*Écon, Econ*	economics
électricité, électronique	*Élec, Elec*	electricity, electronics
en particulier	*esp*	especially
exclamation, interjection	*excl*	exclamation, interjection
féminin	*f*	feminine
langue familière (! emploi vulgaire)	*fam(!)*	colloquial usage (! particularly offensive)
emploi figuré	*fig*	figurative use
(verbe anglais) dont la particule est inséparable	*fus*	(phrasal verb) where the particle is inseparable
généralement	*gén, gen*	generally
géographie, géologie	*Géo, Geo*	geography, geology
géométrie	*Géom, Geom*	geometry
langue familière (! emploi vulgaire)	*inf(!)*	colloquial usage (! particularly offensive)
infinitif	*infin*	infinitive
informatique	*Inform*	computing
invariable	*inv*	invariable
irrégulier	*irrég, irreg*	irregular
domaine juridique	*Jur*	law

Abréviations

Abbreviations

grammaire, linguistique	*Ling*	grammar, linguistics
masculin	*m*	masculine
mathématiques, algèbre	*Math*	mathematics, calculus
médecine	*Méd, Med*	medical term, medicine
masculin *ou* féminin	*m/f*	masculine *or* feminine
domaine militaire, armée	*Mil*	military matters
musique	*Mus*	music
nom	*n*	noun
navigation, nautisme	*Navig, Naut*	sailing, navigation
nom *ou* adjectif numéral	*num*	numeral noun *or* adjective
	o.s.	oneself
péjoratif	*péj, pej*	derogatory, pejorative
photographie	*Phot(o)*	photography
physiologie	*Physiol*	physiology
pluriel	*pl*	plural
politique	*Pol*	politics
participe passé	*pp*	past participle
préposition	*prép, prep*	preposition
pronom	*pron*	pronoun
psychologie, psychiatrie	*Psych*	psychology, psychiatry
temps du passé	*pt*	past tense
quelque chose	*qch*	
quelqu'un	*qn*	
religion, domaine ecclésiastique	*Rel*	religion
	sb	somebody
enseignement, système scolaire et universitaire	*Scol*	schooling, schools and universities
singulier	*sg*	singular
	sth	something
subjonctif	*sub*	subjunctive
sujet (grammatical)	*su(b)j*	(grammatical) subject
superlatif	*superl*	superlative
techniques, technologie	*Tech*	technical term, technology
télécommunications	*Tél, Tel*	telecommunications
télévision	*TV*	television
typographie	*Typ(o)*	typography, printing
anglais des USA	*US*	American English
verbe (auxiliaire)	*vb (aux)*	(auxiliary) verb
verbe intransitif	*vi*	intransitive verb
verbe transitif	*vt*	transitive verb
zoologie	*Zool*	zoology
marque déposée	®	registered trademark
indique une équivalence culturelle	≈	introduces a cultural equivalent

Transcription phonétique

## Consonnes		## Consonants
poupée	p	puppy
bombe	b	baby
tente thermal	t	tent
dinde	d	daddy
coq qui képi	k	cork kiss chord
gag bague	g	gag guess
sale ce nation	s	so rice kiss
zéro rose	z	cousin buzz
tache chat	ʃ	sheep sugar
gilet juge	ʒ	pleasure beige
	tʃ	church
	dʒ	judge general
fer phare	f	farm raffle
valve	v	very rev
	θ	thin maths
	ð	that other
lent salle	l	little ball
rare rentrer	R	
	r	rat rare
maman femme	m	mummy comb
non nonne	n	no ran
agneau vigne	ɲ	
	ŋ	singing bank
hop!	h	hat reheat
yeux paille pied	j	yet
nouer oui	w	wall bewail
huile lui	ɥ	
	x	loch

## Divers		## Miscellaneous
pour l'anglais: le "r" final se prononce en liaison devant une voyelle	ʳ	in English transcription: final "r" can be pronounced before a vowel
pour l'anglais: précède la syllabe accentuée	'	in French wordlist: no liaison before aspirate "h"

NB: p, b, t, d, k, g sont suivis d'une aspiration en anglais.
p, b, t, d, k, g are not aspirated in French.

En règle générale, la prononciation est donnée entre crochets après chaque entrée. Toutefois, du côté anglais-français et dans le cas des expressions composées de deux ou plusieurs mots non réunis par un trait d'union et faisant l'objet d'une entrée séparée, la prononciation doit être cherchée sous chacun des mots constitutifs de l'expression en question.

Phonetic transcription

Voyelles

Vowels

ici vie lyrique	i iː	heel bead
	ɪ	hit pity
jouer été	e	
lait jouet merci	ɛ	set tent
plat amour	a æ	bat apple
bas pâte	ɑ ɑː	after car calm
	ʌ	fun cousin
le premier	ə	over above
beurre peur	œ	
peu deux	ø əː	urgent fern work
or homme	ɔ	wash pot
mot eau gauche	o ɔː	born cork
genou roue	u	full hook
	uː	boom shoe
rue urne	y	

Diphtongues

Diphthongs

	ɪə	beer tier
	ɛə	tear fair there
	eɪ	date plaice day
	aɪ	life buy cry
	au	owl foul now
	əu	low no
	ɔɪ	boil boy oily
	uə	poor tour

Nasales

Nasal vowels

matin plein	ɛ̄
brun	œ̄
sang an dans	ɑ̄
non pont	ɔ̄

NB: La mise en équivalence de certains sons n'indique qu'une ressemblance approximative.

The pairing of some vowel sounds only indicates approximate equivalence.

In general, we give the pronunciation of each entry in square brackets after the word in question. However, on the English-French side, where the entry is composed of two or more unhyphenated words, each of which is given elsewhere in this dictionary, you will find the pronunciation of each word in its alphabetical position.

French verb forms

1 Present participle **2** Past participle **3** Present **4** Imperfect **5** Future **6** Conditional
7 Present subjunctive **8** Impératif

acquérir **1** acquérant **2** acquis **3** acquiers, acquérons, acquièrent **4** acquérais **5** acquerrai **7** acquière

ALLER **1** allant **2** allé **3** vais, vas, va, allons, allez, vont **4** allais **5** irai **6** irais **7** aille

asseoir **1** asseyant **2** assis **3** assieds, asseyons, asseyez, asseyent **4** asseyais **5** assiérai **7** asseye

atteindre **1** atteignant **2** atteint **3** atteins, atteignons **4** atteignais **7** atteigne

AVOIR **1** ayant **2** eu **3** ai, as, a, avons, avez, ont **4** avais **5** aurai **6** aurais **7** aie, aies, ait, ayons, ayez, aient

battre **1** battant **2** battu **3** bats, bat, battons **4** battais **7** batte

boire **1** buvant **2** bu **3** bois, buvons, boivent **4** buvais **7** boive

bouillir **1** bouillant **2** bouilli **3** bous, bouillons **4** bouillais **7** bouille

conclure **1** concluant **2** conclu **3** conclus, concluons **4** concluais **7** conclue

conduire **1** conduisant **2** conduit **3** conduis, conduisons **4** conduisais **7** conduise

connaître **1** connaissant **2** connu **3** connais, connaît, connaissons **4** connaissais **7** connaisse

coudre **1** cousant **2** cousu **3** couds, cousons, cousez, cousent **4** cousais **7** couse

courir **1** courant **2** couru **3** cours, courons **4** courais **5** courrai **7** coure

couvrir **1** couvrant **2** couvert **3** couvre, couvrons **4** couvrais **7** couvre

craindre **1** craignant **2** craint **3** crains, craignons **4** craignais **7** craigne

croire **1** croyant **2** cru **3** crois, croyons, croient **4** croyais **7** croie

croître **1** croissant **2** crû, crue, crus, crues **3** croîs, croissons **4** croissais **7** croisse

cueillir **1** cueillant **2** cueilli **3** cueille, cueillons **4** cueillais **5** cueillerai **7** cueille

devoir **1** devant **2** dû, due, dus, dues **3** dois, devons, doivent **4** devais **5** devrai **7** doive

dire **1** disant **2** dit **3** dis, disons, dites, disent **4** disais **7** dise

dormir **1** dormant **2** dormi **3** dors, dormons **4** dormais **7** dorme

écrire **1** écrivant **2** écrit **3** écris, écrivons **4** écrivais **7** écrive

ÊTRE **1** étant **2** été **3** suis, es, est, sommes, êtes, sont **4** étais **5** serai **6** serais **7** sois, sois, soit, soyons, soyez, soient

FAIRE **1** faisant **2** fait **3** fais, fais, fait, faisons, faites, font **4** faisais **5** ferai **6** ferais **7** fasse

falloir **2** fallu **3** faut **4** fallait **5** faudra **7** faille

FINIR **1** finissant **2** fini **3** finis, finis, finit, finissons, finissez, finissent **4** finissais **5** finirai **6** finirais **7** finisse

fuir **1** fuyant **2** fui **3** fuis, fuyons, fuient **4** fuyais **7** fuie

joindre **1** joignant **2** joint **3** joins, joignons **4** joignais **7** joigne

lire **1** lisant **2** lu **3** lis, lisons **4** lisais **7** lise

luire **1** luisant **2** lui **3** luis, luisons **4** luisais **7** luise

maudire **1** maudissant **2** maudit **3** maudis, maudissons **4** maudissait **7** maudisse

mentir **1** mentant **2** menti **3** mens, mentons **4** mentais **7** mente

mettre **1** mettant **2** mis **3** mets, mettons **4** mettais **7** mette

mourir **1** mourant **2** mort **3** meurs, mourons, meurent **4** mourais **5** mourrai **7** meure

naître **1** naissant **2** né **3** nais, naît, naissons **4** naissais **7** naisse

offrir **1** offrant **2** offert **3** offre, offrons **4** offrais **7** offre

PARLER **1** parlant **2** parlé **3** parle, parles, parle, parlons, parlez, parlent **4** parlais, parlais, parlait, parlions, parliez, parlaient **5** parlerai, parleras, parlera, parlerons,

parlerez, parleront **6** parlerais, parlerais,
parlerait, parlerions, parleriez, parleraient
7 parle, parles, parle, parlions, parliez,
parlent **8** parle! parlons! parlez!

partir **1** partant **2** parti **3** pars, partons
4 partais **7** parte

plaire **1** plaisant **2** plu **3** plais, plaît,
plaisons **4** plaisais **7** plaise

pleuvoir **1** pleuvant **2** plu **3** pleut, pleuvent
4 pleuvait **5** pleuvra **7** pleuve

pourvoir **1** pourvoyant **2** pourvu
3 pourvois, pourvoyons, pourvoient
4 pourvoyais **7** pourvoie

pouvoir **1** pouvant **2** pu **3** peux, peut,
pouvons, peuvent **4** pouvais **5** pourrai
7 puisse

prendre **1** prenant **2** pris **3** prends,
prenons, prennent **4** prenais **7** prenne

prévoir *like* **voir** **5** prévoirai

RECEVOIR **1** recevant **2** reçu **3** reçois,
reçois, reçoit, recevons, recevez, reçoivent
4 recevais **5** recevrai **6** recevrais **7** reçoive

RENDRE **1** rendant **2** rendu **3** rends, rends,
rend, rendons, rendez, rendent **4** rendais
5 rendrai **6** rendrais **7** rende

résoudre **1** résolvant **2** résolu **3** résous,
résout, résolvons **4** résolvais **7** résolve

rire **1** riant **2** ri **3** ris, rions **4** riais **7** rie

savoir **1** sachant **2** su **3** sais, savons, savent

4 savais **5** saurai **7** sache **8** sache! sachons!
sachez!

servir **1** servant **2** servi **3** sers, servons
4 servais **7** serve

sortir **1** sortant **2** sorti **3** sors, sortons
4 sortais **7** sorte

souffrir **1** souffrant **2** souffert **3** souffre,
souffrons **4** souffrais **7** souffre

suffire **1** suffisant **2** suffi **3** suffis, suffisons
4 suffisais **7** suffise

suivre **1** suivant **2** suivi **3** suis, suivons
4 suivais **7** suive

taire **1** taisant **2** tu **3** tais, taisons **4** taisais
7 taise

tenir **1** tenant **2** tenu **3** tiens, tenons,
tiennent **4** tenais **5** tiendrai **7** tienne

vaincre **1** vainquant **2** vaincu **3** vaincs,
vainc, vainquons **4** vainquais **7** vainque

valoir **1** valant **2** valu **3** vaux, vaut, valons
4 valais **5** vaudrai **7** vaille

venir **1** venant **2** venu **3** viens, venons,
viennent **4** venais **5** viendrai **7** vienne

vivre **1** vivant **2** vécu **3** vis, vivons **4** vivais
7 vive

voir **1** voyant **2** vu **3** vois, voyons, voient
4 voyais **5** verrai **7** voie

vouloir **1** voulant **2** voulu **3** veux, veut,
voulons, veulent **4** voulais **5** voudrai
7 veuille **8** veuillez!

Les nombres

Numbers

un (une)	1	one
deux	2	two
trois	3	three
quatre	4	four
cinq	5	five
six	6	six
sept	7	seven
huit	8	eight
neuf	9	nine
dix	10	ten
onze	11	eleven
douze	12	twelve
treize	13	thirteen
quatorze	14	fourteen
quinze	15	fifteen
seize	16	sixteen
dix-sept	17	seventeen
dix-huit	18	eighteen
dix-neuf	19	nineteen
vingt	20	twenty
vingt et un (une)	21	twenty-one
vingt-deux	22	twenty-two
trente	30	thirty
quarante	40	forty
cinquante	50	fifty
soixante	60	sixty
soixante-dix	70	seventy
soixante-et-onze	71	seventy-one
soixante-douze	72	seventy-two
quatre-vingts	80	eighty
quatre-vingt-un (-une)	81	eighty-one
quatre-vingt-dix	90	ninety
cent	100	a hundred, one hundred
cent un (une)	101	a hundred and one
deux cents	200	two hundred
deux cent un (une)	201	two hundred and one
quatre cents	400	four hundred
mille	1000	a thousand
cinq mille	5000	five thousand
un million	1000000	a million

Les nombres

premier (première), 1er (1ère)
deuxième, 2e or 2ème
troisième, 3e or 3ème
quatrième, 4e or 4ème
cinquième, 5e or 5ème
sixième, 6e or 6ème
septième
huitième
neuvième
dixième
onzième
douzième
treizième
quartorzième
quinzième
seizième
dix-septième
dix-huitième
dix-neuvième
vingtième
vingt-et-unième
vingt-deuxième
trentième
centième
cent-unième
millième

Numbers

first, 1st
second, 2nd
third, 3rd
fourth, 4th
fifth, 5th
sixth, 6th
seventh
eighth
ninth
tenth
eleventh
twelfth
thirteenth
fourteenth
fifteenth
sixteenth
seventeenth
eighteenth
nineteenth
twentieth
twenty-first
twenty-second
thirtieth
hundredth
hundred-and-first
thousandth

L'heure

The time

quelle heure est-il?
  il est ...

what time is it?
  it's ...

minuit	midnight, twelve p.m.
une heure (du matin)	one o'clock (in the morning), one (a.m.)
une heure cinq	five past one
une heure dix	ten past one
une heure et quart	a quarter past one, one fifteen
une heure vingt-cinq	twenty-five past one, one twenty-five
une heure et demie,	half-past one,
une heure trente	one thirty
deux heures moins vingt-cinq,	twenty-five to two,
une heure trente-cinq	one thirty-five
deux heures moins vingt,	twenty to two,
une heure quarante	one forty
deux heures moins le quart,	a quarter to two,
une heure quarante-cinq	one forty-five
deux heures moins dix,	ten to two,
une heure cinquante	one fifty
midi	twelve o'clock, midday, noon
deux heures (de l'après-midi),	two o'clock (in the afternoon),
quatorze heures	two (p.m.)
sept heures (du soir),	seven o'clock (in the evening),
dix-sept heures	seven (p.m.)

à quelle heure?
à minuit
à sept heures

(at) what time?
at midnight
at seven o'clock

dans vingt minutes
il y a un quart d'heure

in twenty minutes
fifteen minutes ago

La date

aujourd'hui	today
demain	tomorrow
après-demain	the day after tomorrow
hier	yesterday
avant-hier	the day before yesterday
la veille	the day before, the previous day
le lendemain	the next *or* following day
le matin	morning
le soir	evening
ce matin	this morning
ce soir	this evening
cet après-midi	this afternoon
hier matin	yesterday morning
hier soir	yesterday evening
demain matin	tomorrow morning
demain soir	tomorrow evening
dans la nuit du samedi au dimanche	during Saturday night, during the night of Saturday to Sunday
il viendra samedi	he's coming on Saturday
le samedi	on Saturdays
tous les samedis	every Saturday
samedi passé *ou* dernier	last Saturday
samedi prochain	next Saturday
samedi en huit	a week on Saturday
samedi en quinze	a fortnight *or* two weeks on Saturday
du lundi au samedi	from Monday to Saturday
tous les jours	every day
une fois par semaine	once a week
une fois par mois	once a month
deux fois par semaine	twice a week
il y a une semaine *ou* huit jours	a week ago
il y a quinze jours	a fortnight *or* two weeks ago
l'année passée *ou* dernière	last year
dans deux jours	in two days
dans huit jours *ou* une semaine	in a week
dans quinze jours	in a fortnight *or* two weeks
le mois prochain	next month
l'année prochaine	next year

quel jour sommes-nous?	*what day is it?*
le 1er/24 octobre 2007	the 1st/24th of October 2007, October 1st/24th 2007
en 2007	in 2007
mille neuf cent quatre-vingt seize	nineteen ninety-six
44 av. J.-C.	44 BC
14 apr. J.-C.	14 AD
au XIXe (siècle)	in the nineteenth century
dans les années trente	in the thirties
il était une fois ...	once upon a time ...

The date

a [a] *vb voir* **avoir**

 MOT-CLÉ

à [a] (*à* + *le* = **au**, *à* + *les* = **aux**) *prép* **1** (*endroit, situation*) at, in; **être à Paris/au Portugal** to be in Paris/Portugal; **être à la maison/à l'école** to be at home/at school; **à la campagne** in the country; **c'est à 10 m/km/à 20 minutes (d'ici)** it's 10 m/km/20 minutes away
2 (*direction*) to; **aller à Paris/au Portugal** to go to Paris/Portugal; **aller à la maison/à l'école** to go home/to school; **à la campagne** to the country
3 (*temps*): **à 3 heures/minuit** at 3 o'clock/midnight; **au printemps** in the spring; **au mois de juin** in June; **à Noël/Pâques** at Christmas/Easter; **au départ** at the start, at the outset; **à demain/la semaine prochaine!** see you tomorrow/next week!; **visites de 5 heures à 6 heures** visiting from 5 to *ou* till 6 o'clock
4 (*attribution, appartenance*) to; **le livre est à Paul/à lui/à nous** this book is Paul's/his/ours; **donner qch à qn** to give sth to sb; **un ami à moi** a friend of mine; **c'est à moi de le faire** it's up to me to do it
5 (*moyen*) with; **se chauffer au gaz** to have gas heating; **à bicyclette** on a *ou* by bicycle; **à pied** on foot; **à la main/machine** by hand/machine; **à la télévision/la radio** on television/the radio

6 (*provenance*) from; **boire à la bouteille** to drink from the bottle
7 (*caractérisation, manière*): **l'homme aux yeux bleus** the man with the blue eyes; **à la russe** the Russian way; **glace à la framboise** raspberry ice cream
8 (*but, destination*): **tasse à café** coffee cup; **maison à vendre** house for sale; **je n'ai rien à lire** I don't have anything to read; **à bien réfléchir ...** thinking about it ..., on reflection ...; **problème à régler** problem to sort out
9 (*rapport, évaluation, distribution*): **100 km/unités à l'heure** 100 km/units per *ou* an hour; **payé à l'heure** paid by the hour; **cinq à six** five to six
10 (*conséquence, résultat*): **à ce qu'il prétend** according to him; **à leur grande surprise** much to their surprise; **à nous trois nous n'avons pas su le faire** we couldn't do it even between the three of us; **ils sont arrivés à quatre** four of them arrived (together)

abaisser [abese] *vt* to lower, bring down; (*manette*) to pull down; (*fig*) to debase; to humiliate; **s'abaisser** *vi* to go down; (*fig*) to demean o.s.; **s'~ à faire/à qch** to stoop *ou* descend to doing/to sth

abandon [abɑ̃dɔ̃] *nm* abandoning; deserting; giving up; withdrawal; surrender; relinquishing; (*fig*) lack of constraint; relaxed pose *ou* mood; **être à l'~** to be in a state of neglect; **laisser à l'~** to abandon

abandonner [abɑ̃dɔne] *vt* (*personne*) to leave, abandon, desert; (*projet, activité*) to abandon, give up; (*Sport*) to retire *ou* withdraw from; (*Inform*) to abort; (*céder*) to surrender, relinquish; **s'abandonner** *vi* to let o.s. go; **s'~ à** (*paresse, plaisirs*) to give o.s. up to; **~ qch à qn** to give sth up to sb

abasourdir [abazurdir] *vt* to stun, stagger

abat-jour [abaʒur] *nm inv* lampshade

abats [aba] *vb voir* **abattre** ▷ *nmpl* (*de bœuf, porc*) offal *sg* (*Brit*), entrails (*US*); (*de volaille*) giblets

abattement [abatmɑ̃] *nm* (*physique*) enfeeblement; (*moral*) dejection, despondency; (*déduction*) reduction; **~ fiscal** ≈ tax allowance

abattoir [abatwar] *nm* abattoir (*Brit*), slaughterhouse

abattre [abatr] *vt* (*arbre*) to cut down, fell; (*mur, maison*) to pull down; (*avion, personne*) to shoot down; (*animal*) to shoot, kill; (*fig: physiquement*) to wear out, tire out; (*: moralement*) to demoralize; **s'abattre** *vi* to crash down; **ne pas se laisser ~** to keep one's spirits up, not to let things get one down; **s'~ sur** (*pluie*) to beat down on; (*: coups, injures*) to rain down on; **~ ses cartes** (*aussi fig*) to lay one's cards on the table; **~ du travail** *ou* **de la besogne** to get through a lot of work

abbaye [abei] *nf* abbey

abbé [abe] *nm* priest; (*d'une abbaye*) abbot; **M l'~** Father

abcès [apsɛ] *nm* abscess

abdiquer [abdike] *vi* to abdicate ▷ *vt* to renounce, give up

abdominal, e, -aux [abdɔminal, -o] *adj* abdominal ▷ *nmpl* **faire des ~** to do sit-ups

abeille [abɛj] *nf* bee

aberrant, e [aberɑ̃, ɑ̃t] *adj* absurd

aberration [aberasjɔ̃] *nf* aberration

abêtir [abetiʀ] *vt* to make morons (*ou a moron*) of

abîme [abim] *nm* abyss, gulf

abîmer [abime] *vt* to spoil, damage; **s'abîmer** *vi* to get spoilt *ou* damaged; (*fruits*) to spoil; (*tomber*) to sink, founder; **s'~ les yeux** to ruin one's eyes *ou* eyesight

ablation [ablasjɔ̃] *nf* removal

aboiement [abwamɑ̃] *nm* bark, barking *no pl*

abois [abwa] *nmpl*: **aux ~** at bay

abolir [abɔliʀ] *vt* to abolish

abominable [abɔminabl] *adj* abominable

abondance [abɔ̃dɑ̃s] *nf* abundance; (*richesse*) affluence; **en ~** in abundance

abondant, e [abɔ̃dɑ̃, -ɑ̃t] *adj* plentiful, abundant, copious

abonder [abɔ̃de] *vi* to abound, be plentiful; **~ en** to be full of, abound in; **~ dans le sens de qn** to concur with sb

abonné, e [abɔne] *nm/f* subscriber; season ticket holder ▷ *adj*: **être ~ à un journal** to subscribe to *ou* have a subscription to a periodical; **être ~ au téléphone** to be on the (tele)phone

abonnement [abɔnmɑ̃] *nm* subscription; (*pour transports en commun, concerts*) season ticket

abonner [abɔne] *vt*: **s'abonner à** to subscribe to, take out a subscription to

abord [abɔʀ] *nm*: **être d'un ~ facile** to be approachable; **être d'un ~ difficile** (*personne*) to be unapproachable; (*lieu*) to be hard to reach *ou* difficult to get to; **de prime ~, au premier ~** at first sight, initially; **abords** *nmpl* (*environs*) surroundings; **d'~** *adv* first; **tout d'~** first of all

abordable [abɔʀdabl] *adj* (*personne*) approachable; (*marchandise*) reasonably priced; (*prix*) affordable, reasonable

aborder [abɔʀde] *vi* to land ▷ *vt* (*sujet, difficulté*) to tackle; (*personne*) to approach; (*rivage etc*) to reach; (*Navig: attaquer*) to board; (: *heurter*) to collide with

aboutir [abutiʀ] *vi* (*négociations etc*) to succeed; (*abcès*) to come to a head; **~ à/dans/sur** to end up at/in/on; **n'~ à rien** to come to nothing

aboyer [abwaje] *vi* to bark

abréger [abʀeʒe] *vt* (*texte*) to shorten, abridge; (*mot*) to shorten, abbreviate; (*réunion, voyage*) to cut short, shorten

abreuver [abʀœve] *vt* to water; (*fig*): **~ qn de** to shower *ou* swamp sb with; (*injures etc*) to shower sb with; **s'abreuver** *vi* to drink

abreuvoir [abʀœvwaʀ] *nm* watering place

abréviation [abʀevjasjɔ̃] *nf* abbreviation

abri [abʀi] *nm* shelter; **être à l'~** to be under cover; **se mettre à l'~** to shelter; **à l'~ de** sheltered from; (*danger*) safe from

abricot [abʀiko] *nm* apricot

abriter [abʀite] *vt* to shelter; (*loger*) to accommodate; **s'abriter** *vi* to shelter, take cover

abrupt, e [abʀypt] *adj* sheer, steep; (*ton*) abrupt

abruti, e [abʀyti] *adj* stunned, dazed ▷ *nm/f* (*fam*) idiot, moron; **~ de travail** overworked

absence [apsɑ̃s] *nf* absence; (*Méd*) blackout; **en l'~ de** in the absence of; **avoir des ~s** to have mental blanks

absent, e [apsɑ̃, -ɑ̃t] *adj* absent; (*chose*) missing, lacking; (*distrait: air*) vacant, faraway ▷ *nm/f* absentee

absenter [apsɑ̃te]: **s'absenter** *vi* to take time off work; (*sortir*) to leave, go out

absolu, e [apsɔly] *adj* absolute; (*caractère*) rigid, uncompromising ▷ *nm* (*Philosophie*): **l'~** the Absolute; **dans l'~** in the absolute, in a vacuum

absolument [apsɔlymɑ̃] *adv* absolutely

absorbant, e [apsɔʀbɑ̃, -ɑ̃t] *adj* absorbent; (*tâche*) absorbing, engrossing

absorber [apsɔʀbe] *vt* to absorb; (*gén Méd: manger, boire*) to take; (*Écon: firme*) to take over, absorb

abstenir [apstəniʀ]: **s'abstenir** *vi* (*Pol*) to abstain; **s'~ de qch/de faire** to refrain from sth/from doing

abstraction [apstʀaksjɔ̃] *nf* abstraction; **faire ~ de** to set *ou* leave aside; **~ faite de ...** leaving aside ...

abstrait, e [apstʀɛ, -ɛt] *adj* abstract ▷ *nm*: **dans l'~** in the abstract

absurde [apsyʀd] *adj* absurd ▷ *nm* absurdity; (*Philosophie*): **l'~** absurd; **par l'~** ad absurdio

abus [aby] *nm* (*excès*) abuse, misuse; (*injustice*) abuse; **~ de confiance** breach of trust; (*détournement de fonds*) embezzlement; **il y a de l'~!** (*fam*) that's a bit much!

abuser [abyze] *vi* to go too far, overstep the mark ▷ *vt* to deceive, mislead; **s'abuser** *vi* (*se méprendre*) to be mistaken; **~ de** *vt* (*force, droit*) to misuse; (*alcool*) to take to excess; (*violer, duper*) to take advantage of

abusif, -ive [abyzif, -iv] *adj* exorbitant; (*punition*) excessive; (*pratique*) improper

acabit [akabi] *nm*: **du même ~** of the same type

académie [akademi] *nf* (*société*) learned society; (*école: d'art, de danse*) academy; (*Art: nu*) nude; (*Scol: circonscription*) ≈ regional education authority; **l'A~ (française)** the French Academy; *see note*

acajou [akaʒu] *nm* mahogany

acariâtre [akarjɑtr] *adj* sour(-tempered)
(*Brit*), cantankerous

accablant, e [akablɑ̃, -ɑ̃t] *adj* (*chaleur*)
oppressive; (*témoignage, preuve*)
overwhelming

accablement [akabləmɑ̃] *nm* deep
despondency

accabler [akable] *vt* to overwhelm,
overcome; (*témoignage*) to condemn, damn;
~ **qn d'injures** to heap *ou* shower abuse on
sb; ~ **qn de travail** to overwork sb; **accablé
de dettes/soucis** weighed down with debts/
cares

accalmie [akalmi] *nf* lull

accaparer [akapare] *vt* to monopolize;
(*travail etc*) to take up (all) the time *ou*
attention of

accéder [aksede]: ~ **à** *vt* (*lieu*) to reach; (*fig:
pouvoir*) to accede to; (: *poste*) to attain;
(*accorder: requête*) to grant, accede to

accélérateur [akseleratœr] *nm* accelerator

accélération [akselerasjɔ̃] *nf* speeding up;
acceleration

accélérer [akselere] *vt* (*mouvement, travaux*) to
speed up ▷ *vi* (*Auto*) to accelerate

accent [aksɑ̃] *nm* accent; (*inflexions expressives*)
tone (of voice); (*Phonétique, fig*) stress; **aux ~s
de** (*musique*) to the strains of; **mettre l'~ sur**
(*fig*) to stress; ~ **aigu/grave/circonflexe**
acute/grave/circumflex accent

accentuer [aksɑ̃tɥe] *vt* (*Ling: orthographe*) to
accent; (: *phonétique*) to stress, accent; (*fig*) to
accentuate, emphasize; (: *effort, pression*) to
increase; **s'accentuer** *vi* to become more
marked *ou* pronounced

acceptation [akseptasjɔ̃] *nf* acceptance

accepter [aksepte] *vt* to accept; (*tolérer*):
~ **que qn fasse** to agree to sb doing; ~ **de
faire** to agree to do

accès [akse] *nm* (*à un lieu, Inform*) access; (*Méd*)
attack; (: *de toux*) fit; (*de fièvre*) bout ▷ *nmpl*
(*routes etc*) means of access, approaches; **d'~
facile/malaisé** easily/not easily accessible;
facile d'~ easy to get to; **donner ~ à** (*lieu*) to
give access to; (*carrière*) to open the door to;

avoir ~ **auprès de qn** to have access to sb; **l'~
aux quais est interdit aux personnes non
munies d'un billet** ticket-holders only on
platforms, no access to platforms without a
ticket; ~ **de colère** fit of anger; ~ **de joie** burst
of joy

accessible [aksesibl] *adj* accessible;
(*personne*) approachable; (*livre, sujet*): ~ **à qn**
within the reach of sb; (*sensible*): ~ **à la pitié/
l'amour** open to pity/love

accessoire [akseswar] *adj* secondary, of
secondary importance; (*frais*) incidental
▷ *nm* accessory; (*Théât*) prop

accident [aksidɑ̃] *nm* accident; **par ~** by
chance; ~ **de parcours** mishap; ~ **de la route**
road accident; ~ **du travail** accident at work;
industrial injury *ou* accident; ~**s de terrain**
unevenness of the ground

accidenté, e [aksidɑ̃te] *adj* damaged *ou*
injured (in an accident); (*relief, terrain*)
uneven; hilly

accidentel, le [aksidɑ̃tɛl] *adj* accidental

acclamation [aklamasjɔ̃] *nf:* **par ~** (*vote*) by
acclamation; **acclamations** *nfpl* cheers,
cheering *sg*

acclamer [aklame] *vt* to cheer, acclaim

acclimater [aklimate] *vt* to acclimatize;
s'acclimater *vi* to become acclimatized

accolade [akɔlad] *nf* (*amicale*) embrace;
(*signe*) brace; **donner l'~ à qn** to embrace sb

accommodant, e [akɔmɔdɑ̃, -ɑ̃t] *adj*
accommodating, easy-going

accommoder [akɔmɔde] *vt* (*Culin*) to
prepare; (*points de vue*) to reconcile; ~ **qch à**
(*adapter*) to adapt sth to; **s'accommoder de** to
put up with; (*se contenter de*) to make do with;
s'~ à (*s'adapter*) to adapt to

accompagnateur, -trice [akɔ̃paɲatœr,
-tris] *nm/f* (*Mus*) accompanist; (*de voyage*)
guide; (*de voyage organisé*) courier; (*d'enfants*)
accompanying adult

accompagner [akɔ̃paɲe] *vt* to accompany,
be *ou* go *ou* come with; (*Mus*) to accompany;
s'accompagner de to bring, be accompanied by

accompli, e [akɔ̃pli] *adj* accomplished

accomplir [akɔ̃plir] *vt* (*tâche, projet*) to carry
out; (*souhait*) to fulfil; **s'accomplir** *vi* to be
fulfilled

accord [akɔr] *nm* (*entente, convention, Ling*)
agreement; (*entre des styles, tons etc*) harmony;
(*consentement*) agreement, consent; (*Mus*)
chord; **donner son ~** to give one's
agreement; **mettre deux personnes d'~** to
make two people come to an agreement,
reconcile two people; **se mettre d'~** to come
to an agreement (with each other); **être d'~**
to agree; **être d'~ avec qn** to agree with sb;
d'~! OK!, right!; **d'un commun ~** of one
accord; ~ **parfait** (*Mus*) tonic chord

accordéon [akɔrdeɔ̃] *nm* (*Mus*) accordion

accorder [akɔrde] *vt* (*faveur, délai*) to grant;
(*attribuer*): ~ **de l'importance/de la valeur à**

qch to attach importance/value to sth;
(*harmoniser*) to match; (*Mus*) to tune;
s'accorder vi to get on together; (*être d'accord*)
to agree; (*couleurs, caractères*) to go together,
match; (*Ling*) to agree; **je vous accorde
que ...** I grant you that ...

accoster [akɔste] vt (*Navig*) to draw alongside;
(*personne*) to accost ▷ vi (*Navig*) to berth

accotement [akɔtmɑ̃] nm (*de route*) verge
(*Brit*), shoulder; **~ stabilisé/non stabilisé**
hard shoulder/soft verge ou shoulder

accouchement [akuʃmɑ̃] nm delivery,
(child)birth; (*travail*) labour (*Brit*), labor (*US*);
~ à terme delivery at (full) term; **~ sans
douleur** natural childbirth

accoucher [akuʃe] vi to give birth, have a
baby; (*être en travail*) to be in labour (*Brit*) ou
labor (*US*) ▷ vt to deliver; **~ d'un garçon** to
give birth to a boy

accoucheur [akuʃœʀ] nm: **(médecin) ~**
obstetrician

accouder [akude]: **s'accouder** vi: **s'~ à/
contre** to rest one's elbows on/against/
on; **accoudé à la fenêtre** leaning on the
windowsill

accoudoir [akudwaʀ] nm armrest

accoupler [akuple] vt to couple; (*pour la
reproduction*) to mate; **s'accoupler** vi to mate

accourir [akuʀiʀ] vi to rush ou run up

accoutrement [akutʀəmɑ̃] nm (*péj*) getup
(*Brit*), outfit

accoutumance [akutymɑ̃s] nf (*gén*)
adaptation; (*Méd*) addiction

accoutumé, e [akutyme] adj (*habituel*)
customary, usual; **comme à l'~e** as is
customary ou usual

accoutumer [akutyme] vt: **~ qn à qch/faire**
to accustom sb to sth/to doing;
s'accoutumer à to get accustomed ou used to

accréditer [akʀedite] vt (*nouvelle*) to
substantiate; **~ qn (auprès de)** to accredit
sb (to)

accroc [akʀo] nm (*déchirure*) tear; (*fig*) hitch,
snag; **sans ~** without a hitch; **faire un ~ à**
(*vêtement*) to make a tear in, tear; (*fig: règle etc*)
to infringe

accrochage [akʀɔʃaʒ] nm hanging (up);
hitching (up); (*Auto*) (minor) collision; (*Mil*)
encounter, engagement; (*dispute*) clash,
brush

accrocher [akʀɔʃe] vt (*suspendre*): **~ qch à** to
hang sth up (on); (*attacher: remorque*) to hitch
sth (up) to; (*heurter*) to catch; to hit; (*déchirer*):
~ qch (à) to catch sth (on); (*Mil*) to engage;
(*fig*) to catch, attract ▷ vi to stick, get stuck;
(*fig: pourparlers etc*) to hit a snag; (*plaire: disque
etc*) to catch on; **s'accrocher** vi (*se disputer*)
to have a clash ou brush; (*ne pas céder*) to hold
one's own, hang on in (*fam*); **il a accroché
ma voiture** he bumped into my car; **s'~ à**
(*rester pris à*) to catch on; (*agripper, fig*) to hang
on ou cling to

accroissement [akʀwasmɑ̃] nm increase

accroître [akʀwatʀ] vt, **s'accroître** vi to
increase

accroupir [akʀupiʀ]: **s'accroupir** vi to squat,
crouch (down)

accru, e [akʀy] pp de **accroître**

accueil [akœj] nm welcome; (*endroit*)
reception (desk); (: *dans une gare*) information
kiosk; **comité/centre d'~** reception
committee/centre

accueillant, e [akœjɑ̃, -ɑ̃t] adj welcoming,
friendly

accueillir [akœjiʀ] vt to welcome; (*aller chercher*)
to meet, collect; (*loger*) to accommodate

acculer [akyle] vt: **~ qn à** ou **contre** to drive
sb back against; **~ qn dans** to corner sb in;
~ qn à (*faillite*) to drive sb to the brink of

accumuler [akymyle] vt to accumulate,
amass; **s'accumuler** vi to accumulate; to
pile up

accusation [akyzasjɔ̃] nf (*gén*) accusation;
(*Jur*) charge; (*partie*): **l'~** the prosecution;
mettre en ~ to indict; **acte d'~** bill of
indictment

accusé, e [akyze] nm/f accused; (*prévenu(e)*)
defendant ▷ nm: **~ de réception**
acknowledgement of receipt

accuser [akyze] vt to accuse; (*fig*) to
emphasize, bring out; (: *montrer*) to show;
s'accuser vi (*s'accentuer*) to become more
marked; **~ qn de** to accuse sb of; (*Jur*) to
charge sb with; **~ qn/qch de qch** (*rendre
responsable*) to blame sb/sth for sth; **s'~ de
qch/d'avoir fait qch** to admit sth/having
done sth; to blame o.s. for sth/for having
done sth; **~ réception de** to acknowledge
receipt of; **~ le coup** (*aussi fig*) to be visibly
affected

acerbe [asɛʀb] adj caustic, acid

acéré, e [aseʀe] adj sharp

acharné, e [aʃaʀne] adj (*lutte, adversaire*)
fierce, bitter; (*travail*) relentless, unremitting

acharner [aʃaʀne]: **s'acharner** vi: **s'~ sur** to
go at fiercely, hound; **s'~ contre** to set o.s.
against; to dog, pursue; (*malchance*) to hound;
s'~ à faire to try doggedly to do; to persist in
doing

achat [aʃa] nm buying *no pl*; (*article acheté*)
purchase; **faire l'~ de** to buy, purchase; **faire
des ~s** to do some shopping, buy a few things

acheminer [aʃmine] vt (*courrier*) to forward,
dispatch; (*troupes*) to convey, transport; (*train*)
to route; **s'~ vers** to head for

acheter [aʃte] vt to buy, purchase; (*soudoyer*)
to buy, bribe; **~ qch à** (*marchand*) to buy ou
purchase sth from; (*ami etc: offrir*) to buy sth
for; **~ à crédit** to buy on credit

acheteur, -euse [aʃtœʀ, -øz] nm/f buyer;
shopper; (*Comm*) buyer; (*Jur*) vendee,
purchaser

achever [aʃ(ə)ve] vt to complete, finish;
(*blessé*) to finish off; **s'achever** vi to end

acide [asid] *adj* sour, sharp; *(ton)* acid, biting; *(Chimie)* acid(ic) ▷ *nm* acid

acidulé, e [asidyle] *adj* slightly acid; **bonbons ~s** acid drops *(Brit)*, = lemon drops *(US)*

acier [asje] *nm* steel; **~ inoxydable** stainless steel

aciérie [asjeʀi] *nf* steelworks *sg*

acné [akne] *nf* acne

acolyte [akɔlit] *nm (péj)* associate

acompte [akɔ̃t] *nm* deposit; *(versement régulier)* instalment; *(sur somme due)* payment on account; *(sur salaire)* advance; **un ~ de 10 euros** 10 euros on account

à-côté [akote] *nm* side-issue; *(argent)* extra

à-coup [aku] *nm (du moteur)* (hic)cough; *(fig)* jolt; **sans ~s** smoothly; **par ~s** by fits and starts

acoustique [akustik] *nf (d'une salle)* acoustics *pl*; *(science)* acoustics *sg* ▷ *adj* acoustic

acquéreur [akeʀœʀ] *nm* buyer, purchaser; **se porter/se rendre ~ de qch** to announce one's intention to purchase/to purchase sth

acquérir [akeʀiʀ] *vt* to acquire; *(par achat)* to purchase, acquire; *(valeur)* to gain; *(résultats)* to achieve; **ce que ses efforts lui ont acquis** what his efforts have won *ou* gained (for) him

acquis, e [aki, -iz] *pp de* **acquérir** ▷ *nm* (accumulated) experience; *(avantage)* gain ▷ *adj (achat)* acquired; *(valeur)* gained; *(résultats)* achieved; **être ~ à** *(plan, idée)* to be in full agreement with; **son aide nous est ~e** we can count on *ou* be sure of his help; **tenir qch pour ~** to take sth for granted

acquit [aki] *vb voir* **acquérir** ▷ *nm (quittance)* receipt; **pour ~** received; **par ~ de conscience** to set one's mind at rest

acquitter [akite] *vt (Jur)* to acquit; *(facture)* to pay, settle; **s'~ de** to discharge; *(promesse, tâche)* to fulfil *(Brit)*, fulfill *(US)*, carry out

âcre [ɑkʀ] *adj* acrid, pungent

acrobate [akʀɔbat] *nm/f* acrobat

acrobatie [akʀɔbasi] *nf (art)* acrobatics *sg*; *(exercice)* acrobatic feat; **~ aérienne** aerobatics *sg*

acte [akt] *nm* act, action; *(Théât)* act; **actes** *nmpl (compte-rendu)* proceedings; **prendre ~ de** to note, take note of; **faire ~ de présence** to put in an appearance; **faire ~ de candidature** to submit an application; **~ d'accusation** charge *(Brit)*, bill of indictment; **~ de baptême** baptismal certificate; **~ de mariage/naissance** marriage/birth certificate; **~ de vente** bill of sale

acteur [aktœʀ] *nm* actor

actif, -ive [aktif, -iv] *adj* active ▷ *nm (Comm)* assets *pl*; *(Ling)* active (voice); *(fig)*: **avoir à son ~** to have to one's credit; **actifs** *nmpl* people in employment; **~ toxique** toxic asset; **mettre à son ~** to add to one's list of achievements; **l'~ et le passif** assets and liabilities; **prendre une part active à qch** to take an active part in sth; **population active** working population

action [aksjɔ̃] *nf (gén)* action; *(Comm)* share; **une bonne/mauvaise ~** a good/an unkind deed; **mettre en ~** to put into action; **passer à l'~** to take action; **sous l'~ de** under the effect of; **l'~ syndicale** (the) union action; **un film d'~** an action film *ou* movie; **~ en diffamation** libel action; **~ de grâce(s)** *(Rel)* thanksgiving

actionnaire [aksjɔnɛʀ] *nm/f* shareholder

actionner [aksjɔne] *vt* to work; *(mécanisme)* to activate; *(machine)* to operate

activer [aktive] *vt* to speed up; *(Chimie)* to activate; **s'activer** *vi (s'affairer)* to bustle about; *(se hâter)* to hurry up

activité [aktivite] *nf* activity; **en ~** *(volcan)* active; *(fonctionnaire)* in active life; *(militaire)* on active service

actrice [aktʀis] *nf* actress

actualiser [aktɥalize] *vt* to actualize; *(mettre à jour)* to bring up to date

actualité [aktɥalite] *nf (d'un problème)* topicality; *(événements)*: **l'~** current events; **les ~s** *(Ciné, TV)* the news; **l'~ politique/sportive** the political/sports *ou* sporting news; **les ~s télévisées** the television news; **d'~** topical

actuel, le [aktɥɛl] *adj (présent)* present; *(d'actualité)* topical; *(non virtuel)* actual; **à l'heure ~le** at this moment in time, at the moment

actuellement [aktɥɛlmɑ̃] *adv* at present, at the present time

acuité [akɥite] *nf* acuteness

acuponcteur, acupuncteur [akypɔ̃ktœʀ] *nm* acupuncturist

acuponcture, acupuncture [akypɔ̃ktyʀ] *nf* acupuncture

adaptateur, -trice [adaptatœʀ, -tʀis] *nm/f* adapter

adapter [adapte] *vt* to adapt; **s'~ (à)** *(personne)* to adapt (to); *(: objet, prise etc)* to apply (to); **~ qch à** *(approprier)* to adapt sth to (fit); **~ qch sur/dans/à** *(fixer)* to fit sth on/into/to

additif [aditif] *nm* additional clause; *(substance)* additive; **~ alimentaire** food additive

addition [adisjɔ̃] *nf* addition; *(au café)* bill

additionner [adisjɔne] *vt* to add (up); **s'additionner** *vi* to add up; **~ un produit d'eau** to add water to a product

adepte [adɛpt] *nm/f* follower

adéquat, e [adekwa(t), at] *adj* appropriate, suitable

adhérent, e [adeʀɑ̃, -ɑ̃t] *nm/f (de club)* member

adhérer [adeʀe] *vi (coller)* to adhere, stick; **~ à** *(coller)* to adhere *ou* stick to; *(se rallier à: parti, club)* to join; to be a member of; *(: opinion, mouvement)* to support

adhésif, -ive [adezif, -iv] *adj* adhesive, sticky; **ruban ~** sticky *ou* adhesive tape ▷ *nm* adhesive

adhésion [adezjɔ̃] nf (à un club) joining; membership; (à une opinion) support

adieu, x [adjø] excl goodbye ▷ nm farewell; **dire ~ à qn** to say goodbye ou farewell to sb; **dire ~ à qch** (renoncer) to say ou wave goodbye to sth

adjectif [adʒɛktif] nm adjective; **~ attribut** adjectival complement; **~ épithète** attributive adjective

adjoindre [adʒwɛ̃dʀ] vt: **~ qch à** to attach sth to; (ajouter) to add sth to; **~ qn à** (personne) to appoint sb as an assistant to; (comité) to appoint sb to, attach sb to; **s'adjoindre** vt (collaborateur etc) to take on, appoint

adjoint, e [adʒwɛ̃, -wɛ̃t] pp de **adjoindre** ▷ nm/f assistant; **~ au maire** deputy mayor; **directeur ~** assistant manager

adjudant [adʒydɑ̃] nm (Mil) warrant officer; **~-chef** ≈ warrant officer 1st class (Brit), ≈ chief warrant officer (US)

adjuger [adʒyʒe] vt (prix, récompense) to award; (lors d'une vente) to auction (off); **s'adjuger** vt to take for o.s.; **adjugé!** (vendu) gone!, sold!

adjurer [adʒyʀe] vt: **~ qn de faire** to implore ou beg sb to do

admettre [admɛtʀ] vt (visiteur, nouveau-venu) to admit, let in; (candidat: Scol) to pass; (Tech: gaz, eau, air) to admit; (tolérer) to allow, accept; (reconnaître) to admit, acknowledge; (supposer) to suppose; **j'admets que ...** I admit that ...; **je n'admets pas que tu fasses cela** I won't allow you to do that; **admettons que ...** let's suppose that ...; **admettons** let's suppose so

administrateur, -trice [administʀatœʀ, -tʀis] nm/f (Comm) director; (Admin) administrator; **~ délégué** managing director; **~ judiciaire** receiver

administration [administʀasjɔ̃] nf administration; **l'A~** ≈ the Civil Service

administrer [administʀe] vt (firme) to manage, run; (biens, remède, sacrement etc) to administer

admirable [admiʀabl] adj admirable, wonderful

admirateur, -trice [admiʀatœʀ, -tʀis] nm/f admirer

admiration [admiʀasjɔ̃] nf admiration; **être en ~ devant** to be lost in admiration before

admirer [admiʀe] vt to admire

admis, e [admi, -iz] pp de **admettre**

admissible [admisibl] adj (candidat) eligible; (comportement) admissible, acceptable; (Jur) receivable

admission [admisjɔ̃] nf admission; **tuyau d'~** intake pipe; **demande d'~** application for membership; **service des ~s** admissions

ADN sigle m (= acide désoxyribonucléique) DNA

adolescence [adɔlesɑ̃s] nf adolescence

adolescent, e [adɔlesɑ̃, -ɑ̃t] nm/f adolescent, teenager

adonner [adɔne]: **s'adonner à** vt (sport) to devote o.s. to; (boisson) to give o.s. over to

adopter [adɔpte] vt to adopt; (projet de loi etc) to pass

adoptif, -ive [adɔptif, -iv] adj (parents) adoptive; (fils, patrie) adopted

adorable [adɔʀabl] adj adorable

adorer [adɔʀe] vt to adore; (Rel) to worship

adosser [adose] vt: **~ qch à** ou **contre** to stand sth against; **s'~ à** ou **contre** to lean with one's back against; **être adossé à** ou **contre** to be leaning with one's back against

adoucir [adusiʀ] vt (goût, température) to make milder; (avec du sucre) to sweeten; (peau, voix, eau) to soften; (caractère, personne) to mellow; (peine) to soothe, allay; **s'adoucir** vi to become milder; to soften; (caractère) to mellow

adresse [adʀɛs] nf (voir adroit) skill, dexterity; (domicile, Inform) address; **à l'~ de** (pour) for the benefit of; **~ électronique** email address; **~ Web** web address

adresser [adʀese] vt (lettre: expédier) to send; (: écrire l'adresse sur) to address; (injure, compliments) to address; **~ qn à un docteur/ bureau** to refer ou send sb to a doctor/an office; **~ la parole à qn** to speak ou address sb; **s'adresser à** (parler à) to speak to, address; (s'informer auprès de) to go and see, go and speak to; (: bureau) to enquire at; (livre, conseil) to be aimed at

adroit, e [adʀwa, -wat] adj (joueur, mécanicien) skilful (Brit), skillful (US), dext(e)rous; (politicien etc) shrewd, skilled

ADSL sigle m (= asymmetrical digital subscriber line) ADSL, broadband; **avoir l'~** to have broadband

adulte [adylt] nm/f adult, grown-up ▷ adj (personne, attitude) adult, grown-up; (chien, arbre) fully-grown, mature; **l'âge ~** adulthood; **formation/film pour ~s** adult training/film

adultère [adyltɛʀ] adj adulterous ▷ nm/f adulterer/adulteress ▷ nm (acte) adultery

advenir [advəniʀ] vi to happen; **qu'est-il advenu de ...?** what has become of ...?; **quoi qu'il advienne** whatever befalls ou happens

adverbe [advɛʀb] nm adverb; **~ de manière** adverb of manner

adversaire [advɛʀsɛʀ] nm/f (Sport, gén) opponent, adversary; (Mil) adversary, enemy

adverse [advɛʀs] adj opposing

aération [aeʀasjɔ̃] nf airing; (circulation de l'air) ventilation; **conduit d'~** ventilation shaft; **bouche d'~** air vent

aérer [aeʀe] vt to air; (fig) to lighten; **s'aérer** vi to get some (fresh) air

aérien, ne [aeʀjɛ̃, -ɛn] adj (Aviat) air cpd, aerial; (câble, métro) overhead; (fig) light; **compagnie ~ne** airline (company); **ligne ~ne** airline

aérobic [aeʀɔbik] nf aerobics sg

aérogare [aeʀɔgaʀ] nf airport (buildings); (en ville) air terminal

aéroglisseur [aeʀɔglisœʀ] nm hovercraft

Aéronavale [aeʀɔnaval] *nf* ≈ Fleet Air Arm (Brit); ≈ Naval Air Force (US)

aérophagie [aeʀɔfaʒi] *nf* (*Méd*) wind, aerophagia (*Méd*); **il fait de l'~** he suffers from abdominal wind

aéroport [aeʀɔpɔʀ] *nm* airport; **~ d'embarquement** departure airport

aéroporté, e [aeʀɔpɔʀte] *adj* airborne, airlifted

aérosol [aeʀɔsɔl] *nm* aerosol

affable [afabl] *adj* affable

affaiblir [afebliʀ] *vt* to weaken; **s'affaiblir** *vi* to weaken, grow weaker; (*vue*) to grow dim

affaire [afɛʀ] *nf* (*problème, question*) matter, (*criminelle, judiciaire*) case; (*scandaleuse etc*) affair; (*entreprise*) business; (*marché, transaction*) (business) deal, (piece of) business *no pl*; (*occasion intéressante*) good deal; **affaires** *nfpl* affairs; (*activité commerciale*) business *sg*; (*effets personnels*) things, belongings; **~s de sport** sports gear; **tirer qn/se tirer d'~** to get sb/o.s. out of trouble; **ceci fera l'~** this will do (nicely); **avoir ~ à** (*comme adversaire*) to be faced with; (*en contact*) to be dealing with; **tu auras ~ à moi!** (*menace*) you'll have me to contend with!; **c'est une ~ de goût/d'argent** it's a question *ou* matter of taste/money; **c'est l'~ d'une minute/heure** it'll only take a minute/an hour; **ce sont mes ~s** (*cela me concerne*) that's my business; **occupe-toi de tes ~s!** mind your own business!; **toutes ~s cessantes** forthwith; **les ~s étrangères** (*Pol*) foreign affairs

affairer [afeʀe]: **s'affairer** *vi* to busy o.s., bustle about

affaisser [afese]: **s'affaisser** *vi* (*terrain, immeuble*) to subside, sink; (*personne*) to collapse

affaler [afale]: **s'affaler** *vi*: **s'~ dans/sur** to collapse *ou* slump into/onto

affamé, e [afame] *adj* starving, famished

affectation [afɛktasjɔ̃] *nf* (*voir affecter*) allotment; appointment; posting; (*voir affecté*) affectedness

affecter [afɛkte] *vt* (*émouvoir*) to affect, move; (*feindre*) to affect, feign; (*telle ou telle forme etc*) to take on, assume; **~ qch à** to allocate *ou* allot sth to; **~ qn à** to appoint sb to; (*diplomate*) to post sb to; **~ qch de** (*de coefficient*) to modify sth by

affectif, -ive [afɛktif, -iv] *adj* emotional, affective

affection [afɛksjɔ̃] *nf* affection; (*mal*) ailment; **avoir de l'~ pour** to feel affection for; **prendre en ~** to become fond of

affectionner [afɛksjɔne] *vt* to be fond of

affectueusement [afɛktyøzmɑ̃] *adv* affectionately

affectueux, -euse [afɛktyø, -øz] *adj* affectionate

affermir [afɛʀmiʀ] *vt* to consolidate, strengthen

affichage [afiʃaʒ] *nm* billposting, billsticking; (*électronique*) display; "**~ interdit**" "stick no bills", "billsticking prohibited"; **~ à cristaux liquides** liquid crystal display, LCD; **~ numérique** *ou* **digital** digital display

affiche [afiʃ] *nf* poster; (*officielle*) (public) notice; (*Théât*) bill; **être à l'~** (*Théât*) to be on; **tenir l'~** to run

afficher [afiʃe] *vt* (*affiche*) to put up, post up; (*réunion*) to put up a notice about; (*électroniquement*) to display; (*fig*) to exhibit, display; **s'afficher** *vi* (*péj*) to flaunt o.s.; (*électroniquement*) to be displayed; "**défense d'~**" "no bill posters"

affilée [afile]: **d'~** *adv* at a stretch

affiler [afile] *vt* to sharpen

affilier [afilje] *vt*: **s'affilier à** to become affiliated to

affiner [afine] *vt* to refine; **s'affiner** *vi* to become (more) refined

affirmatif, -ive [afiʀmatif, -iv] *adj* affirmative ▷ *nf*: **répondre par l'affirmative** to reply in the affirmative; **dans l'affirmative** (*si oui*) if (the answer is) yes …; if he does (*ou* you do *etc*) …

affirmation [afiʀmasjɔ̃] *nf* assertion

affirmer [afiʀme] *vt* (*prétendre*) to maintain, assert; (*autorité etc*) to assert; **s'affirmer** *vi* to assert o.s.; to assert itself

affligé, e [afliʒe] *adj* distressed, grieved; **~ de** (*maladie, tare*) afflicted with

affliger [afliʒe] *vt* (*peiner*) to distress, grieve

affluence [aflyɑ̃s] *nf* crowds *pl*; **heures d'~** rush hour *sg*; **jours d'~** busiest days

affluent [aflyɑ̃] *nm* tributary

affluer [aflye] *vi* (*secours, biens*) to flood in, pour in; (*sang*) to rush, flow

affolant, e [afɔlɑ̃, -ɑ̃t] *adj* terrifying

affolement [afɔlmɑ̃] *nm* panic

affoler [afɔle] *vt* to throw into a panic; **s'affoler** *vi* to panic

affranchir [afʀɑ̃ʃiʀ] *vt* to put a stamp *ou* stamps on; (*à la machine*) to frank (Brit), meter (US); (*esclave*) to enfranchise, emancipate; (*fig*) to free, liberate; **s'affranchir de** to free o.s. from; **machine à ~** franking machine, postage meter

affranchissement [afʀɑ̃ʃismɑ̃] *nm* franking (Brit), metering (US); freeing; (*Postes: prix payé*) postage; **tarifs d'~** postage rates

affréter [afʀete] *vt* to charter

affreux, -euse [afʀø, -øz] *adj* dreadful, awful

affront [afʀɔ̃] *nm* affront

affrontement [afʀɔ̃tmɑ̃] *nm* (*Mil, Pol*) clash, confrontation

affronter [afʀɔ̃te] *vt* to confront, face; **s'affronter** to confront each other

affubler [afyble] *vt* (*péj*): **~ qn de** to rig *ou* deck sb out in; (*surnom*) to attach to sb

affût [afy] *nm* (*de canon*) gun carriage; **à l'~ (de)** (*gibier*) lying in wait (for); (*fig*) on the look-out (for)

affûter [afyte] vt to sharpen, grind

Afghanistan [afganistã] nm: **l'~** Afghanistan

afin [afɛ̃]: **~ que** conj so that, in order that; **~ de faire** in order to do, so as to do

africain, e [afʁikɛ̃, -ɛn] adj African ▷ nm/f: **A~, e** African

Afrique [afʁik] nf: **l'~** Africa; **l'~ australe/du Nord/du Sud** southern/North/South Africa

agacer [agase] vt to pester, tease; (involontairement) to irritate, aggravate; (aguicher) to excite, lead on

âge [ɑʒ] nm age; **quel ~ as-tu?** how old are you?; **une femme d'un certain ~** a middle-aged woman, a woman who is getting on (in years); **bien porter son ~** to wear well; **prendre de l'~** to be getting on (in years), grow older; **limite d'~** age limit; **dispense d'~** special exemption from age limit; **le troisième ~** (personnes âgées) senior citizens; (période) retirement; **l'~ ingrat** the awkward ou difficult age; **~ légal** legal age; **~ mental** mental age; **l'~ mûr** maturity, middle age; **~ de raison** age of reason

âgé, e [ɑʒe] adj old, elderly; **~ de 10 ans** 10 years old

agence [aʒɑ̃s] nf agency, office; (succursale) branch; **~ immobilière** estate agent's (office), real estate office (US); **~ matrimoniale** marriage bureau; **~ de placement** employment agency; **~ de publicité** advertising agency; **~ de voyages** travel agency

agencer [aʒɑ̃se] vt to put together; (local) to arrange, lay out

agenda [aʒɛ̃da] nm diary; **~ électronique** PDA

agenouiller [aʒ(ə)nuje]: **s'agenouiller** vi to kneel (down)

agent, e [aʒɑ̃, ɑ̃t] nm/f (aussi: **~(e) de police**) policeman/policewoman; (Admin) official, officer; (fig: élément, facteur) agent; **~ d'assurances** insurance broker; **~ de change** stockbroker; **~ commercial** sales representative; **~ immobilier** estate agent (Brit), realtor (US); **~ (secret)** (secret) agent

agglomération [aglɔmeʁasjɔ̃] nf town; (Auto) built-up area; **l'~ parisienne** the urban area of Paris

aggloméré [aglɔmeʁe] nm (bois) chipboard; (pierre) conglomerate

aggraver [agʁave] vt to worsen, aggravate; (Jur: peine) to increase; **s'aggraver** vi to worsen; **~ son cas** to make one's case worse

agile [aʒil] adj agile, nimble

agir [aʒiʁ] vi (se comporter) to behave, act; (faire quelque chose) to act, take action; (avoir de l'effet) to act; **il s'agit de** it's a matter ou question of; (ça traite de) it is about; (il importe que): **il s'agit de faire** we (ou you etc) must do; **de quoi s'agit-il?** what is it about?

agitation [aʒitasjɔ̃] nf (hustle and) bustle; (trouble) agitation, excitement; (politique) unrest, agitation

agité, e [aʒite] adj (remuant) fidgety, restless; (trouble) agitated, perturbed; (journée) hectic; (mer) rough; (sommeil) disturbed, broken

agiter [aʒite] vt (bouteille, chiffon) to shake; (bras, mains) to wave; (préoccuper, exciter) to trouble, perturb; **s'agiter** vi to bustle about; (dormeur) to toss and turn; (enfant) to fidget; (Pol) to grow restless; **"~ avant l'emploi"** "shake before use"

agneau, x [aɲo] nm lamb; (toison) lambswool

agonie [agɔni] nf mortal agony, death pangs pl; (fig) death throes pl

agrafe [agʁaf] nf (de vêtement) hook, fastener; (de bureau) staple; (Méd) clip

agrafer [agʁafe] vt to fasten; to staple

agrafeuse [agʁaføz] nf stapler

agrandir [agʁɑ̃diʁ] vt (magasin, domaine) to extend, enlarge; (trou) to enlarge, make bigger; (Photo) to enlarge, blow up; **s'agrandir** vi (ville, famille) to grow, expand; (trou, écart) to get bigger

agrandissement [agʁɑ̃dismɑ̃] nm extension; enlargement; (photographie) enlargement

agréable [agʁeabl] adj pleasant, nice

agréé, e [agʁee] adj: **concessionnaire ~** registered dealer; **magasin ~** registered dealer('s)

agréer [agʁee] vt (requête) to accept; **~ à** vt to please, suit; **veuillez ~, Monsieur/ Madame, mes salutations distinguées** (personne nommée) yours sincerely; (personne non nommée) yours faithfully

agrégation [agʁegasjɔ̃] nf highest teaching diploma in France; see note

agrégé, e [agʁeʒe] nm/f holder of the agrégation

agrément [agʁemɑ̃] nm (accord) consent, approval; (attraits) charm, attractiveness; (plaisir) pleasure; **voyage d'~** pleasure trip

agrémenter [agʁemɑ̃te] vt: **~ (de)** to embellish (with), adorn (with)

agresser [agʁese] vt to attack

agresseur [agʁesœʁ] nm aggressor, attacker; (Pol, Mil) aggressor

agressif, -ive [agʁesif, -iv] adj aggressive

agricole [agʁikɔl] adj agricultural, farm cpd

agriculteur, -trice [agʁikyltœʁ, -tʁis] nm/f farmer

agriculture [agʀikyltyʀ] *nf* agriculture; farming

agripper [agʀipe] *vt* to grab, clutch; *(pour arracher)* to snatch, grab; **s'~ à** to cling (on) to, clutch, grip

agroalimentaire [agʀɔalimɑ̃tɛʀ] *adj* farming *cpd* ▷ *nm* farm-produce industry; **l'~** agribusiness

agrumes [agʀym] *nmpl* citrus fruit(s)

aguerrir [ageʀiʀ] *vt* to harden; **s'~ (contre)** to become hardened (to)

aguets [agɛ]: **aux ~** *adv*: **être aux ~** to be on the look-out

aguicher [agiʃe] *vt* to entice

ahuri, e [ayʀi] *adj (stupéfait)* flabbergasted; *(idiot)* dim-witted

ai [ɛ] *vb voir* **avoir**

aide [ɛd] *nm/f* assistant ▷ *nf* assistance, help; *(secours financier)* aid; **à l'~ de** with the help *ou* aid of; **aller à l'~ de** qn to go to sb's aid, go to help sb; **venir en ~ à** qn to help sb, come to sb's assistance; **appeler (qn) à l'~** to call for help (from sb); **à l'~!** help!; **~ de camp** *nm* aide-de-camp; **~ comptable** *nm* accountant's assistant; **~ électricien** *nm* electrician's mate; **~ familiale** *nf* mother's help, ≈ home help; **~ judiciaire** *nf* legal aid; **~ de laboratoire** *nm/f* laboratory assistant; **~ ménagère** *nf* ≈ home help (Brit) *ou* helper (US); **~ sociale** *nf (assistance)* state aid; **~ soignant, e** *nm/f* auxiliary nurse; **~ technique** *nf* ≈ VSO (Brit), ≈ Peace Corps (US)

aide-éducateur, -trice [ɛdmedykatœʀ, tʀis] *nm/f* classroom assistant

aide-mémoire [ɛdmemwaʀ] *nm inv* memoranda pages *pl*; *(key facts)* handbook

aider [ede] *vt* to help; **~ à qch** to help (towards); **~ qn à faire qch** to help sb to do sth; **s'~ de** *(se servir de)* to use, make use of

aide-soignant, e [ɛdswaɲɑ̃, ɑ̃t] *nm/f* auxiliary nurse

aie *etc* [ɛ] *vb voir* **avoir**

aïe [aj] *excl* ouch!

aïeul, e [ajœl] *nm/f* grandparent, grandfather/grandmother; *(ancêtre)* forebear

aïeux [ajø] *nmpl* grandparents; forebears, forefathers

aigle [egl] *nm* eagle

aigre [ɛgʀ] *adj* sour, sharp; *(fig)* sharp, cutting; **tourner à l'~** to turn sour

aigre-doux, -douce [ɛgʀədu, -dus] *adj (fruit)* bitter-sweet; *(sauce)* sweet and sour

aigreur [ɛgʀœʀ] *nf* sourness, sharpness; **~s d'estomac** heartburn *sg*

aigrir [egʀiʀ] *vt (personne)* to embitter; *(caractère)* to sour; **s'aigrir** *vi* to become embittered; *(lait etc)* to turn sour

aigu, ë [egy] *adj (objet, arête)* sharp, pointed; *(son, voix)* high-pitched, shrill; *(note)* high(-pitched); *(douleur, intelligence)* acute, sharp

aiguille [egɥij] *nf* needle; *(de montre)* hand; **~ à tricoter** knitting needle

aiguiller [egɥije] *vt (orienter)* to direct; *(Rail)* to shunt

aiguilleur [egɥijœʀ] *nm*: **~ du ciel** air traffic controller

aiguillon [egɥijɔ̃] *nm (d'abeille)* sting; *(fig)* spur, stimulus

aiguillonner [egɥijɔne] *vt* to spur *ou* goad on

aiguiser [egize] *vt* to sharpen, grind; *(fig)* to stimulate; *(: esprit)* to sharpen; *(: sens)* to excite

ail [aj] *nm* garlic

aile [ɛl] *nf* wing; *(de voiture)* wing (Brit), fender (US); **battre de l'~** *(fig)* to be in a sorry state; **voler de ses propres ~s** to stand on one's own two feet; **~ libre** hang-glider

aileron [ɛlʀɔ̃] *nm (de requin)* fin; *(d'avion)* aileron

ailier [elje] *nm (Sport)* winger

aille *etc* [aj] *vb voir* **aller**

ailleurs [ajœʀ] *adv* elsewhere, somewhere else; **partout/nulle part ~** everywhere/nowhere else; **d'~** *adv (du reste)* moreover, besides; **par ~** *adv (d'autre part)* moreover, furthermore

aimable [ɛmabl] *adj* kind, nice; **vous êtes bien ~** that's very nice *ou* kind of you, how kind (of you)

aimant¹ [ɛmɑ̃] *nm* magnet

aimant², e [ɛmɑ̃, -ɑ̃t] *adj* loving, affectionate

aimer [eme] *vt* to love; *(d'amitié, affection, par goût)* to like; *(souhait)*: **j'aimerais ...** I would like ...; **s'aimer** to love each other; to like each other; **je n'aime pas beaucoup Paul** I don't like Paul much, I don't care much for Paul; **~ faire qch** to like doing sth, like to do sth; **j'aime faire du ski** I like skiing; **je t'aime** I love you; **aimeriez-vous que je vous accompagne?** would you like me to come with you?; **j'aimerais (bien) m'en aller** I should (really) like to go; **bien ~ qn/qch** to like sb/sth; **j'aime mieux Paul (que Pierre)** I prefer Paul (to Pierre); **j'aime mieux ou autant vous dire que** I may as well tell you that; **j'aimerais autant ou mieux y aller maintenant** I'd sooner *ou* rather go now; **j'aime assez aller au cinéma** I quite like going to the cinema

aine [ɛn] *nf* groin

aîné, e [ene] *adj* elder, older; *(le plus âgé)* eldest, oldest ▷ *nm/f* eldest child *ou* one, oldest boy *ou* son/girl *ou* daughter; **aînés** *nmpl (fig: anciens)* elders; **il est mon ~ (de 2 ans)** he's (2 years) older than me, he's (2 years) my senior

ainsi [ɛ̃si] *adv (de cette façon)* like this, in this way, thus; *(ce faisant)* thus, so; **~ que** *(comme)* (just) as; *(et aussi)* as well as; **pour ~ dire** so to speak, as it were; **~ donc** and so; **~ soit-il** (Rel) so be it; **et ~ de suite** and so on (and so forth)

air [ɛʀ] *nm* air; *(mélodie)* tune; *(expression)* look, air; *(atmosphère, ambiance)*: **dans l'~** in the air *(fig)*; **prendre de grands ~s (avec qn)** to give o.s. airs (with sb); **en l'~** (up) into the air; **tirer en l'~** to fire shots in the air; **paroles/menaces en l'~** empty words/threats; **prendre l'~** to get some (fresh) air; *(avion)* to take off; **avoir l'~** *(sembler)* to look, appear; **avoir l'~ triste** to look *ou* seem sad; **avoir l'~ de qch** to look like sth; **avoir l'~ de faire** to look as though one is doing, appear to be doing; **courant d'~** draught *(Brit)*, draft *(US)*; **le grand ~** the open air; **mal de l'~** air-sickness; **tête en l'~** scatterbrain; **~ comprimé** compressed air; **~ conditionné** air-conditioning

airbag [ɛʀbag] *nm* airbag

aisance [ɛzɑ̃s] *nf* ease; *(Couture)* easing, freedom of movement; *(richesse)* affluence; **être dans l'~** to be well-off *ou* affluent

aise [ɛz] *nf* comfort ▷ *adj*: **être bien ~ de/que** to be delighted to/that; **aises** *nfpl*: **aimer ses ~s** to like one's (creature) comforts; **prendre ses ~s** to make o.s. comfortable; **frémir d'~** to shudder with pleasure; **être à l'~** *ou* **à son ~** to be comfortable; *(pas embarrassé)* to be at ease; *(financièrement)* to be comfortably off; **se mettre à l'~** to make o.s. comfortable; **être mal à l'~** *ou* **à son ~** to be uncomfortable; *(gêné)* to be ill at ease; **mettre qn à l'~** to put sb at his *(ou* her) ease; **mettre qn mal à l'~** to make sb feel ill at ease; **à votre ~** please yourself, just as you like; **en faire à son ~** to do as one likes; **en prendre à son ~ avec qch** to be free and easy with sth, do as one likes with sth

aisé, e [eze] *adj* easy; *(assez riche)* well-to-do, well-off

aisselle [ɛsɛl] *nf* armpit

ait [ɛ] *vb voir* **avoir**

ajonc [aʒɔ̃] *nm* gorse *no pl*

ajourner [aʒuʀne] *vt (réunion)* to adjourn; *(décision)* to defer, postpone; *(candidat)* to refer; *(conscrit)* to defer

ajouter [aʒute] *vt* to add; **~ à** *(accroître)* to add to; **s'~ à** to add to; **~ que** to add that; **~ foi à** to lend *ou* give credence to

ajusté, e [aʒyste] *adj*: **bien ~** *(robe etc)* close-fitting

ajuster [aʒyste] *vt (régler)* to adjust; *(vêtement)* to alter; *(arranger)*: **~ sa cravate** to adjust one's tie; *(coup de fusil)* to aim; *(cible)* to aim at; *(adapter)*: **~ qch à** to fit sth to

alarme [alaʀm] *nf* alarm; **donner l'~** to give *ou* raise the alarm; **jeter l'~** to cause alarm

alarmer [alaʀme] *vt* to alarm; **s'alarmer** *vi* to become alarmed

alarmiste [alaʀmist] *adj* alarmist

Albanie [albani] *nf*: **l'~** Albania

album [albɔm] *nm* album; **~ à colorier** colouring book; **~ de timbres** stamp album

albumine [albymin] *nf* albumin; **avoir** *ou* **faire de l'~** to suffer from albuminuria

alcool [alkɔl] *nm*: **l'~** alcohol; **un ~** a spirit, a brandy; **bière sans ~** non-alcoholic *ou*

alcohol-free beer; **~ à brûler** methylated spirits *(Brit)*, wood alcohol *(US)*; **~ à 90°** surgical spirit; **~ camphré** camphorated alcohol; **~ de prune** *etc* plum *etc* brandy

alcoolique [alkɔlik] *adj*, *nm/f* alcoholic

alcoolisé, e [alkɔlize] *adj* alcoholic; **une boisson non ~e** a soft drink

alcoolisme [alkɔlism] *nm* alcoholism

alcootest®, alcotest® [alkotɛst] *nm (objet)* Breathalyser®; *(test)* breath-test; **faire subir l'alco(o)test à qn** to Breathalyse® sb

aléas [alea] *nmpl* hazards

aléatoire [aleatwaʀ] *adj* uncertain; *(Inform, Statistique)* random

alentour [alɑ̃tuʀ] *adv* around (about); **alentours** *nmpl* surroundings; **aux ~s de** in the vicinity *ou* neighbourhood of, around about; *(temps)* around about

alerte [alɛʀt] *adj* agile, nimble; *(style)* brisk, lively ▷ *nf* alert; warning; **donner l'~** to give the alert; **à la première ~** at the first sign of trouble *ou* danger; **~ à la bombe** bomb scare

alerter [alɛʀte] *vt* to alert

algèbre [alʒɛbʀ] *nf* algebra

Alger [alʒe] *n* Algiers

Algérie [alʒeʀi] *nf*: **l'~** Algeria

algérien, ne [alʒeʀjɛ̃, -ɛn] *adj* Algerian ▷ *nm/f*: **A~, ne** Algerian

algue [alg] *nf* seaweed *no pl*; *(Bot)* alga

alibi [alibi] *nm* alibi

aliéné, e [aljene] *nm/f* insane person, lunatic *(péj)*

aligner [aliɲe] *vt* to align, line up; *(idées, chiffres)* to string together; *(adapter)*: **~ qch sur** to bring sth into alignment with; **s'aligner** *vi (soldats etc)* to line up; **s'~ sur** *(Pol)* to align o.s. with

aliment [alimɑ̃] *nm* food; **~ complet** whole food

alimentaire [alimɑ̃tɛʀ] *adj* food *cpd*; *(péj: besogne)* done merely to earn a living; **produits ~s** foodstuffs, foods

alimentation [alimɑ̃tasjɔ̃] *nf* feeding; *(en eau etc, de moteur)* supplying, supply; *(commerce)* food trade; *(produits)* groceries *pl*; *(régime)* diet; *(Inform)* feed; **~ (générale)** (general) grocer's; **~ de base** staple diet; **~ en feuilles/en continu/en papier** form/stream/sheet feed

alimenter [alimɑ̃te] *vt* to feed; *(Tech)*: **~ (en)** to supply (with), feed (with); *(fig)* to sustain, keep going

alinéa [alinea] *nm* paragraph; **"nouvel ~"** "new line"

aliter [alite]: **s'aliter** *vi* to take to one's bed; **infirme alité** bedridden person *ou* invalid

allaiter [alete] *vt (femme)* to (breast-)feed, nurse; *(animal)* to suckle; **~ au biberon** to bottle-feed

allant [alɑ̃] *nm* drive, go

alléchant, e [aleʃɑ̃, -ɑ̃t] *adj* tempting, enticing

allécher [aleʃe] *vt*: ~ **qn** to make sb's mouth water; to tempt sb, entice sb

allée [ale] *nf* (*de jardin*) path; (*en ville*) avenue, drive; ~**s et venues** comings and goings

allégé, e [aleʒe] *adj* (*yaourt etc*) low-fat

alléger [aleʒe] *vt* (*voiture*) to make lighter; (*chargement*) to lighten; (*souffrance*) to alleviate, soothe

allègre [alɛɡʀ] *adj* lively, jaunty (*Brit*); (*personne*) gay, cheerful

alléguer [alege] *vt* to put forward (as proof *ou* an excuse)

Allemagne [almaɲ] *nf*: **l'~** Germany; **l'~ de l'Est/Ouest** East/West Germany; **l'~ fédérale (RFA)** the Federal Republic of Germany (FRG)

allemand, e [almɑ̃, -ɑ̃d] *adj* German ▷ *nm* (*Ling*) German ▷ *nm/f*: **A~, e** German; **A~ de l'Est/l'Ouest** East/West German

aller [ale] *nm* (*trajet*) outward journey; (*billet*): ~ **(simple)** single (*Brit*) *ou* one-way ticket; ~ **(et) retour (AR)** (*trajet*) return trip *ou* journey (*Brit*), round trip (*US*); (*billet*) return (*Brit*) *ou* round-trip (*US*) ticket ▷ *vi* (*gén*) to go; ~ **à** (*convenir*) to suit; (*forme, pointure etc*) to fit; **cela me va** (*couleur*) that suits me; (*vêtement*) that suits me; that fits me; (*projet, disposition*) that suits me, that's fine *ou* OK by me; ~ **à la chasse/pêche** to go hunting/fishing; ~ **avec** (*couleurs, style etc*) to go (well) with; **je vais le faire/me fâcher** I'm going to do it/to get angry; ~ **voir/chercher qn** to go and see/look for sb; **comment allez-vous?** how are you?; **comment ça va?** how are you?; (*affaires etc*) how are things?; **ça va?** — **oui (ça va)!** how are things? — fine!; **pour** ~ **à** how do I get to; **ça va (comme ça)** that's fine (as it is); **il va bien/mal** he's well/ not well, he's fine/ill; **ça va bien/mal** (*affaires etc*) it's going well/not going well; **tout va bien** everything's fine; **ça ne va pas!** (*mauvaise humeur etc*) that's not on!, hey, come on!; **ça ne va pas sans difficultés** it's not without difficulties; ~ **mieux** to be better; **il y va de leur vie** their lives are at stake; **se laisser** ~ to let o.s. go; **s'en aller** *vi* (*partir*) to be off, go, leave; (*disparaître*) to go away; ~ **jusqu'à** to go as far as; **ça va de soi, ça va sans dire** that goes without saying; **tu y vas un peu fort** you're going a bit (too) far; **allez!** go on!; come on!; **allons!** come now!; **allons-y!** let's go!; **allez, au revoir!** right *ou* OK then, bye-bye!

allergie [alɛʀʒi] *nf* allergy

allergique [alɛʀʒik] *adj* allergic; ~ **à** allergic to

alliage [aljaʒ] *nm* alloy

alliance [aljɑ̃s] *nf* (*Mil, Pol*) alliance; (*mariage*) marriage; (*bague*) wedding ring; **neveu par** ~ nephew by marriage

allier [alje] *vt* (*métaux*) to alloy; (*Pol, gén*) to ally; (*fig*) to combine; **s'allier** *vi* to become allies; (*éléments, caractéristiques*) to combine; **s'~ à** to become allied to *ou* with

allô [alo] *excl* hullo, hallo

allocation [alɔkasjɔ̃] *nf* allowance; ~ **(de) chômage** unemployment benefit; ~ **(de) logement** rent allowance; ~**s familiales** ≈ child benefit *no pl*; ~**s de maternité** maternity allowance

allocution [alɔkysjɔ̃] *nf* short speech

allonger [alɔ̃ʒe] *vt* to lengthen, make longer; (*étendre: bras, jambe*) to stretch (out); (*sauce*) to spin out, make go further; **s'allonger** *vi* to get longer; (*se coucher*) to lie down, stretch out; ~ **le pas** to hasten one's step(s)

allouer [alwe] *vt*: ~ **qch à** to allocate sth to, allot sth to

allumage [alymaʒ] *nm* (*Auto*) ignition

allume-cigare [alymsigaʀ] *nm inv* cigar lighter

allumer [alyme] *vt* (*lampe, phare, radio*) to put *ou* switch on; (*pièce*) to put *ou* switch the light(s) on in; (*feu, bougie, cigare, pipe, gaz*) to light; (*chauffage*) to put on; **s'allumer** *vi* (*lumière, lampe*) to come *ou* go on; ~ **(la lumière** *ou* **l'électricité)** to put on the light

allumette [alymɛt] *nf* match; (*morceau de bois*) matchstick; (*Culin*): ~ **au fromage** cheese straw; ~ **de sûreté** safety match

allure [alyʀ] *nf* (*vitesse*) speed; (*: à pied*) pace; (*démarche*) walk; (*maintien*) bearing; (*aspect, air*) look; **avoir de l'~** to have style; **à toute** ~ at full speed

allusion [a(l)lyzjɔ̃] *nf* allusion; (*sous-entendu*) hint; **faire** ~ **à** to allude *ou* refer to; to hint at

⬤ MOT-CLÉ

alors [alɔʀ] *adv* **1** (*à ce moment-là*) then, at that time; **il habitait alors à Paris** he lived in Paris at that time; **jusqu'alors** up till *ou* until then
2 (*par conséquent*) then; **tu as fini? alors je m'en vais** have you finished? I'm going then
3 (*expressions*): **alors? quoi de neuf?** well *ou* so? what's new?; **et alors?** so (what)?; **ça alors!** (well) really!
▷ *conj*: **alors que 1** (*au moment où*) when, as; **il est arrivé alors que je partais** he arrived as I was leaving
2 (*tandis que*) whereas, while; **alors que son frère travaillait dur, lui se reposait** while his brother was working hard, HE would rest
3 (*bien que*) even though; **il a été puni alors qu'il n'a rien fait** he was punished, even though he had done nothing
4 (*pendant que*) while, when; **alors qu'il était à Paris, il a visité ...** while *ou* when he was in Paris, he visited ...

alouette [alwɛt] *nf* (sky)lark

alourdir [aluʀdiʀ] *vt* to weigh down, make heavy; **s'alourdir** *vi* to grow heavy *ou* heavier

aloyau [alwajo] *nm* sirloin

Alpes [alp] *nfpl*: **les** ~ the Alps

alphabet [alfabɛ] *nm* alphabet; (*livre*) ABC (book), primer

alphabétique [alfabetik] *adj* alphabetic(al); **par ordre ~** in alphabetical order

alphabétiser [alfabetize] *vt* to teach to read and write; (*pays*) to eliminate illiteracy in

alpinisme [alpinism] *nm* mountaineering, climbing

alpiniste [alpinist] *nm/f* mountaineer, climber

Alsace [alzas] *nf*: **l'~** Alsace

alsacien, ne [alzasjɛ̃, -ɛn] *adj* Alsatian ▷ *nm/f*: **A~, ne** Alsatian

altérer [altere] *vt* (*faits, vérité*) to falsify, distort; (*qualité*) to debase, impair; (*données*) to corrupt; (*donner soif à*) to make thirsty; **s'altérer** *vi* to deteriorate; to spoil

altermondialisme [altɛʀmɔ̃djalism] *nm* anti-globalism

altermondialiste [altɛʀmɔ̃djalist] *adj, nm/f* anti-globalist

alternateur [altɛʀnatœʀ] *nm* alternator

alternatif, -ive [altɛʀnatif, -iv] *adj* alternating ▷ *nf* alternative

alternative *nf* (*choix*) alternative

alternativement [altɛʀnativmɑ̃] *adv* alternately

alterner [altɛʀne] *vt* to alternate ▷ *vi*: **~ (avec)** to alternate (with); **(faire) ~ qch avec qch** to alternate sth with sth

Altesse [altɛs] *nf* Highness

altitude [altityd] *nf* altitude, height; **à 1000 m d'~** at a height *ou* an altitude of 1000 m; **en ~** at high altitudes; **perdre/prendre de l'~** to lose/gain height; **voler à haute/ basse ~** to fly at a high/low altitude

alto [alto] *nm* (*instrument*) viola ▷ *nf* (*contr*)alto

aluminium [alyminjɔm] *nm* aluminium (Brit), aluminum (US)

amabilité [amabilite] *nf* kindness; **il a eu l'~ de** he was kind *ou* good enough to

amadouer [amadwe] *vt* to coax, cajole; (*adoucir*) to mollify, soothe

amaigrir [amegʀiʀ] *vt* to make thin *ou* thinner

amaigrissant, e [amegʀisɑ̃, -ɑ̃t] *adj*: **régime ~** slimming (Brit) *ou* weight-reduction (US) diet

amalgame [amalgam] *nm* amalgam; (*fig: de gens, d'idées*) hotch-potch, mixture

amande [amɑ̃d] *nf* (*de l'amandier*) almond; (*de noyau de fruit*) kernel; **en ~** (*yeux*) almond *cpd*, almond-shaped

amandier [amɑ̃dje] *nm* almond (tree)

amant [amɑ̃] *nm* lover

amarrer [amaʀe] *vt* (Navig) to moor; (*gén*) to make fast

amas [amɑ] *nm* heap, pile

amasser [amase] *vt* to amass; **s'amasser** *vi* to pile up, accumulate; (*foule*) to gather

amateur [amatœʀ] *nm* amateur; **en ~** (*péj*) amateurishly; **musicien/sportif ~** amateur musician/sportsman; **~ de musique/sport** *etc* music/sport *etc* lover

amazone [amazon] *nf* horsewoman; **en ~** side-saddle

ambassade [ɑ̃basad] *nf* embassy; (*mission*): **en ~** on a mission; **l'~ de France** the French Embassy

ambassadeur, -drice [ɑ̃basadœʀ, -dʀis] *nm/f* ambassador/ambassadress

ambiance [ɑ̃bjɑ̃s] *nf* atmosphere; **il y a de l'~** everyone's having a good time

ambiant, e [ɑ̃bjɑ̃, -ɑ̃t] *adj* (*air, milieu*) surrounding; (*température*) ambient

ambigu, ë [ɑ̃bigy] *adj* ambiguous

ambitieux, -euse [ɑ̃bisjø, -øz] *adj* ambitious

ambition [ɑ̃bisjɔ̃] *nf* ambition

ambulance [ɑ̃bylɑ̃s] *nf* ambulance

ambulancier, -ière [ɑ̃bylɑ̃sje, -jɛʀ] *nm/f* ambulanceman/woman (Brit), paramedic (US)

ambulant, e [ɑ̃bylɑ̃, -ɑ̃t] *adj* travelling, itinerant

âme [am] *nf* soul; **rendre l'~** to give up the ghost; **bonne ~** (*aussi ironique*) kind soul; **un joueur/tricheur dans l'~** a gambler/cheat through and through; **~ sœur** kindred spirit

amélioration [ameljɔʀasjɔ̃] *nf* improvement

améliorer [ameljɔʀe] *vt* to improve; **s'améliorer** *vi* to improve, get better

aménager [amenaʒe] *vt* (*agencer: espace, local*) to fit out; (: *terrain*) to lay out; (: *quartier, territoire*) to develop; (*installer*) to fix up, put in; **ferme aménagée** converted farmhouse

amende [amɑ̃d] *nf* fine; **mettre à l'~** to penalize; **faire ~ honorable** to make amends

amener [am(ə)ne] *vt* to bring; (*causer*) to bring about; (*baisser: drapeau, voiles*) to strike; **s'amener** *vi* (*fam*) to show up, turn up; **~ qn à qch/à faire** to lead sb to sth/to do

amenuiser [amənɥize]: **s'amenuiser** *vi* to dwindle; (*chances*) to grow slimmer, lessen

amer, amère [amɛʀ] *adj* bitter

américain, e [ameʀikɛ̃, -ɛn] *adj* American ▷ *nm* (Ling) American (English) ▷ *nm/f*: **A~, e** American; **en vedette ~e** as a special guest (star)

Amérique [ameʀik] *nf* America; **l'~ centrale** Central America; **l'~ latine** Latin America; **l'~ du Nord** North America; **l'~ du Sud** South America

amertume [amɛʀtym] *nf* bitterness

ameublement [amœblamɑ̃] *nm* furnishing; (*meubles*) furniture; **articles d'~** furnishings; **tissus d'~** soft furnishings, furnishing fabrics

ameuter [amøte] *vt* (*badauds*) to draw a crowd of; (*peuple*) to rouse, stir up

ami, e [ami] *nm/f* friend; (*amant/maîtresse*) boyfriend/girlfriend ▷ *adj*: **pays/groupe ~** friendly country/group; **être (très) ~ avec qn**

to be (very) friendly with sb; **être ~ de l'ordre** to be a lover of order; **un ~ des arts** a patron of the arts; **un ~ des chiens** a dog lover; **petit ~/petite ~e** (*fam*) boyfriend/girlfriend

amiable [amjabl]: **à l'~** *adv* (*Jur*) out of court; (*gén*) amicably

amiante [amjɑ̃t] *nm* asbestos

amical, e, -aux [amikal, -o] *adj* friendly ▷ *nf* (*club*) association

amicalement [amikalmɑ̃] *adv* in a friendly way; (*formule épistolaire*) regards

amidon [amidɔ̃] *nm* starch

amincir [amɛ̃siʀ] *vt* (*objet*) to thin (down); **s'amincir** *vi* to get thinner *ou* slimmer; **~ qn** to make sb thinner *ou* slimmer; (*vêtement*) to make sb look slimmer

amincissant, e [amɛ̃sisɑ̃, -ɑ̃t] *adj* slimming; **régime ~** diet; **crème ~e** slimming cream

amiral, -aux [amiral, -o] *nm* admiral

amitié [amitje] *nf* friendship; **prendre en ~** to take a liking to; **faire** *ou* **présenter ses ~s à qn** to send sb one's best wishes; **~s** (*formule épistolaire*) (with) best wishes

ammoniaque [amɔnjak] *nf* ammonia (water)

amnistie [amnisti] *nf* amnesty

amoindrir [amwɛ̃dʀiʀ] *vt* to reduce

amollir [amɔliʀ] *vt* to soften

amonceler [amɔ̃s(ə)le] *vt* to pile *ou* heap up; **s'amonceler** to pile *ou* heap up; (*fig*) to accumulate

amont [amɔ̃]: **en ~** *adv* upstream; (*sur une pente*) uphill; **en ~ de** *prép* upstream from; uphill from, above

amorce [amɔʀs] *nf* (*sur un hameçon*) bait; (*explosif*) cap; (*tube*) primer; (: *contenu*) priming; (*fig*: *début*) beginning(s), start

amorcer [amɔʀse] *vt* to bait; to prime; (*commencer*) to begin, start

amorphe [amɔʀf] *adj* passive, lifeless

amortir [amɔʀtiʀ] *vt* (*atténuer*: *choc*) to absorb, cushion; (*bruit, douleur*) to deaden; (*Comm*: *dette*) to pay off, amortize; (: *mise de fonds, matériel*) to write off; **~ un abonnement** to make a season ticket pay (for itself)

amortisseur [amɔʀtisœʀ] *nm* shock absorber

amour [amuʀ] *nm* love; (*liaison*) love affair, love; (*statuette etc*) cupid; **un ~ de** a lovely little; **faire l'~** to make love

amouracher [amuʀaʃe]: **s'amouracher de** *vt* (*péj*) to become infatuated with

amoureux, -euse [amuʀø, -øz] *adj* (*regard, tempérament*) amorous; (*vie, problèmes*) love *cpd*; (*personne*): **être ~ (de qn)** to be in love (with sb) ▷ *nm/f* lover ▷ *nmpl* courting couple(s); **tomber ~ de qn** to fall in love with sb; **être ~ de qch** to be passionately fond of sth; **un ~ de la nature** a nature lover

amour-propre (*pl* **amours-propres**) [amuʀpʀɔpʀ] *nm* self-esteem, pride

amovible [amɔvibl] *adj* removable, detachable

ampère [ɑ̃pɛʀ] *nm* amp(ere)

amphithéâtre [ɑ̃fiteɑtʀ] *nm* amphitheatre; (*d'université*) lecture hall *ou* theatre

ample [ɑ̃pl] *adj* (*vêtement*) roomy, ample; (*gestes, mouvement*) broad; (*ressources*) ample; **jusqu'à plus ~ informé** (*Admin*) until further details are available

amplement [ɑ̃pləmɑ̃] *adv* amply; **~ suffisant** ample, more than enough

ampleur [ɑ̃plœʀ] *nf* scale, size; (*de dégâts, problème*) extent, magnitude

amplificateur [ɑ̃plifikatœʀ] *nm* amplifier

amplifier [ɑ̃plifje] *vt* (*son, oscillation*) to amplify; (*fig*) to expand, increase

ampoule [ɑ̃pul] *nf* (*électrique*) bulb; (*de médicament*) phial; (*aux mains, pieds*) blister

ampoulé, e [ɑ̃pule] *adj* (*péj*) pompous, bombastic

amputer [ɑ̃pyte] *vt* (*Méd*) to amputate; (*fig*) to cut *ou* reduce drastically; **~ qn d'un bras/pied** to amputate sb's arm/foot

amusant, e [amyzɑ̃, -ɑ̃t] *adj* (*divertissant, spirituel*) entertaining, amusing; (*comique*) funny, amusing

amuse-gueule [amyzgœl] *nm inv* appetizer, snack

amusement [amyzmɑ̃] *nm* (*voir amusé*) amusement; (*voir amuser*) entertaining, amusing; (*jeu etc*) pastime, diversion

amuser [amyze] *vt* (*divertir*) to entertain, amuse; (*égayer, faire rire*) to amuse; (*détourner l'attention de*) to distract; **s'amuser** *vi* (*jouer*) to amuse o.s., play; (*se divertir*) to enjoy o.s., have fun; (*fig*) to mess around; **s'~ de qch** (*trouver comique*) to find sth amusing; **s'~ avec** *ou* **de qn** (*duper*) to make a fool of sb

amygdale [amidal] *nf* tonsil; **opérer qn des ~s** to take sb's tonsils out

an [ɑ̃] *nm* year; **être âgé de** *ou* **avoir 3 ans** to be 3 (years old); **en l'an 1980** in the year 1980; **le jour de l'an, le premier de l'an, le nouvel an** New Year's Day

analogique [analɔʒik] *adj* (*Logique*: *raisonnement*) analogical; (*calculateur, montre etc*) analogue; (*Inform*) analog

analogue [analɔg] *adj*: **~ (à)** analogous (to), similar (to)

analphabète [analfabɛt] *nm/f* illiterate

analyse [analiz] *nf* analysis; (*Méd*) test; **faire l'~ de** to analyse; **une ~ approfondie** an in-depth analysis; **en dernière ~** in the last analysis; **avoir l'esprit d'~** to have an analytical turn of mind; **~ grammaticale** grammatical analysis, parsing (*Scol*)

analyser [analize] *vt* to analyse; (*Méd*) to test

ananas [anana(s)] *nm* pineapple

anarchie [anaʀʃi] *nf* anarchy

anatomie [anatɔmi] *nf* anatomy

ancêtre [ɑ̃sɛtʀ] *nm/f* ancestor; (*fig*): **l'~ de** the forerunner of

anchois [ɑ̃ʃwa] *nm* anchovy

ancien, ne [ɑ̃sjɛ̃, -ɛn] *adj* old; (*de jadis, de l'antiquité*) ancient; (*précédent, ex-*) former, old; (*par l'expérience*) senior ▷ *nm* (*mobilier ancien*): **l'~** antiques *pl* ▷ *nm/f* (*dans une tribu etc*) elder; **un ~ ministre** a former minister; **mon ~ne voiture** my previous car; **être plus ~ que qn dans une maison** to have been in a firm longer than sb; (*dans la hiérarchie*) to be senior to sb in a firm; **~ combattant** ex-serviceman; **~ (élève)** (*Scol*) ex-pupil (*Brit*), alumnus (*US*)

anciennement [ɑ̃sjɛnmɑ̃] *adv* formerly

ancienneté [ɑ̃sjɛnte] *nf* oldness; antiquity; (*Admin*) (length of) service; (*privilèges obtenus*) seniority

ancre [ɑ̃kʀ] *nf* anchor; **jeter/lever l'~** to cast/ weigh anchor; **à l'~** at anchor

ancrer [ɑ̃kʀe] *vt* (*Constr: câble etc*) to anchor; (*fig*) to fix firmly; **s'ancrer** *vi* (*Navig*) to (cast) anchor

Andorre [ɑ̃dɔʀ] *nf* Andorra

andouille [ɑ̃duj] *nf* (*Culin*) *sausage made of chitterlings*; (*fam*) clot, nit

âne [ɑn] *nm* donkey, ass; (*péj*) dunce, fool

anéantir [aneɑ̃tiʀ] *vt* to annihilate, wipe out; (*fig*) to obliterate, destroy; (*déprimer*) to overwhelm

anémie [anemi] *nf* anaemia

anémique [anemik] *adj* anaemic

ânerie [ɑnʀi] *nf* stupidity; (*parole etc*) stupid *ou* idiotic comment *etc*

anesthésie [anɛstezi] *nf* anaesthesia; **sous ~** under anaesthetic; **~ générale/locale** general/local anaesthetic; **faire une ~ locale à qn** to give sb a local anaesthetic

ange [ɑ̃ʒ] *nm* angel; **être aux ~s** to be over the moon; **~ gardien** guardian angel

angélus [ɑ̃ʒelys] *nm* angelus; (*cloches*) evening bells *pl*

angine [ɑ̃ʒin] *nf* sore throat, throat infection; **~ de poitrine** angina (pectoris)

anglais, e [ɑ̃glɛ, -ɛz] *adj* English ▷ *nm* (*Ling*) English ▷ *nm/f*: **A-, e** Englishman/woman; **les A-** the English; **filer à l'~e** to take French leave; **à l'~e** (*Culin*) boiled

angle [ɑ̃gl] *nm* angle; (*coin*) corner; **~ droit/ obtus/aigu/mort** right/obtuse/acute/dead angle

Angleterre [ɑ̃glətɛʀ] *nf*: **l'~** England

anglo... [ɑ̃glɔ] *préfixe* Anglo-, anglo(-)

anglophone [ɑ̃glɔfɔn] *adj* English-speaking

angoisse [ɑ̃gwas] *nf*: **l'~** anguish *no pl*

angoissé, e [ɑ̃gwase] *adj* anguished; (*personne*) distressed

angoisser [ɑ̃gwase] *vt* to harrow, cause anguish to ▷ *vi* to worry, fret

anguille [ɑ̃gij] *nf* eel; **~ de mer** conger (eel); **il y a ~ sous roche** (*fig*) there's something going on, there's something beneath all this

anicroche [anikʀɔʃ] *nf* hitch, snag

animal, e, -aux [animal, -o] *adj, nm* animal; **~ domestique/sauvage** domestic/wild animal

animateur, -trice [animatœʀ, -tʀis] *nm/f* (*de télévision*) host; (*de music-hall*) compère; (*de groupe*) leader, organizer; (*Ciné: technicien*) animator

animation [animasjɔ̃] *nf* (*voir animé*) busyness; liveliness; (*Ciné: technique*) animation; **animations** *nfpl* (*activité*) activities; **centre d'~** ≈ community centre

animé, e [anime] *adj* (*rue, lieu*) busy; lively; (*conversation, réunion*) lively, animated; (*opposé à inanimé, aussi Ling*) animate

animer [anime] *vt* (*ville, soirée*) to liven up, enliven; (*mettre en mouvement*) to drive; (*stimuler*) to drive, impel; **s'animer** *vi* to liven up, come to life

anis [ani(s)] *nm* (*Culin*) aniseed; (*Bot*) anise

ankyloser [ɑ̃kiloze]: **s'ankyloser** *vi* to get stiff

anneau, x [ano] *nm* (*de rideau, bague*) ring; (*de chaîne*) link; (*Sport*): **exercices aux ~x** ring exercises

année [ane] *nf* year; **souhaiter la bonne ~ à qn** to wish sb a Happy New Year; **tout au long de l'~** all year long; **d'une ~ à l'autre** from one year to the next; **d'~ en ~** from year to year; **l'~ scolaire/fiscale** the school/tax year

annexe [anɛks] *adj* (*problème*) related; (*document*) appended; (*salle*) adjoining ▷ *nf* (*bâtiment*) annex(e); (*de document, ouvrage*) annex, appendix; (*jointe à une lettre, un dossier*) enclosure

anniversaire [anivɛʀsɛʀ] *nm* birthday; (*d'un événement, bâtiment*) anniversary ▷ *adj*: **jour ~** anniversary

annonce [anɔ̃s] *nf* announcement; (*signe, indice*) sign; (*aussi*: **~ publicitaire**) advertisement; (*Cartes*) declaration; **~ personnelle** personal message; **les petites ~s** the small *ou* classified ads

annoncer [anɔ̃se] *vt* to announce; (*être le signe de*) to herald; (*Cartes*) to declare; **je vous annonce que ...** I wish to tell you that ...; **s'annoncer bien/difficile** *vi* to look promising/difficult; **~ la couleur** (*fig*) to lay one's cards on the table

annonceur, -euse [anɔ̃sœʀ, -øz] *nm/f* (*TV, Radio: speaker*) announcer; (*publicitaire*) advertiser

annuaire [anɥɛʀ] *nm* yearbook, annual; **~ téléphonique** (telephone) directory, phone book

annuel, le [anɥɛl] *adj* annual, yearly

annuité [anɥite] *nf* annual instalment

annulation [anylasjɔ̃] *nf* cancellation; annulment; quashing, repeal

annuler [anyle] *vt* (*rendez-vous, voyage*) to cancel, call off; (*mariage*) to annul; (*jugement*) to quash (*Brit*), repeal (*US*); (*résultats*) to declare void; (*Math, Physique*) to cancel out; **s'annuler** to cancel each other out

anodin, e [anɔdɛ̃, -in] *adj* harmless; (*sans importance*) insignificant, trivial

anonymat [anɔnima] *nm* anonymity;
garder l'~ to remain anonymous
anonyme [anɔnim] *adj* anonymous; *(fig)*
impersonal
anorak [anɔrak] *nm* anorak
anorexie [anɔrɛksi] *nf* anorexia
anormal, e, -aux [anɔrmal, -o] *adj*
abnormal; *(insolite)* unusual, abnormal
ANPE *sigle f* (= *Agence nationale pour l'emploi)* national
employment agency *(functions include job creation)*
anse [ɑ̃s] *nf* handle; *(Géo)* cove
antan [ɑ̃tɑ̃]: **d'~** of yesteryear, of long ago
antarctique [ɑ̃tarktik] *adj* Antarctic ▷ *nm*:
l'A~ the Antarctic; **le cercle A~** the Antarctic
Circle; **l'océan A~** the Antarctic Ocean
antécédent [ɑ̃tesedɑ̃] *nm* *(Ling)* antecedent;
antécédents *nmpl* *(Méd etc)* past history *sg*; **~s
professionnels** record, career to date
antenne [ɑ̃tɛn] *nf* *(de radio, télévision)* aerial;
(d'insecte) antenna, feeler; *(poste avancé)*
outpost; *(petite succursale)* sub-branch; **sur l'~**
on the air; **passer à/avoir l'~** to go/be on the
air; **deux heures d'~** two hours'
broadcasting time; **hors ~** off the air;
~ chirurgicale *(Mil)* advance surgical unit;
~ parabolique satellite dish
antérieur, e [ɑ̃terjœr] *adj* *(d'avant)* previous,
earlier; *(de devant)* front; **~ à** prior *ou* previous
to; **passé/futur ~** *(Ling)* past/future anterior
anti... [ɑ̃ti] *préfixe* anti...
antialcoolique [ɑ̃tialkɔlik] *adj* anti-alcohol;
ligue ~ temperance league
antiatomique [ɑ̃tiatɔmik] *adj*: **abri ~** fallout
shelter
antibiotique [ɑ̃tibjɔtik] *nm* antibiotic
antibrouillard [ɑ̃tibrujar] *adj*: **phare ~** fog
lamp
anticipation [ɑ̃tisipasjɔ̃] *nf* anticipation;
(Comm) payment in advance; **par ~** in
anticipation, in advance; **livre/film d'~**
science fiction book/film
anticipé, e [ɑ̃tisipe] *adj* *(règlement, paiement)*
early, in advance; *(joie etc)* anticipated, early;
avec mes remerciements ~s thanking you
in advance *ou* anticipation
anticiper [ɑ̃tisipe] *vt* *(événement, coup)* to
anticipate, foresee; *(paiement)* to pay *ou* make
in advance ▷ *vi* to look *ou* think ahead; *(en
racontant)* to jump ahead; *(prévoir)* to
anticipate: **~ sur** to anticipate
anticonceptionnel, le [ɑ̃tikɔ̃sɛpsjɔnɛl] *adj*
contraceptive
anticorps [ɑ̃tikɔr] *nm* antibody
antidote [ɑ̃tidɔt] *nm* antidote
antigel [ɑ̃tiʒɛl] *nm* antifreeze
antihistaminique [ɑ̃tiistaminik] *nm*
antihistamine
antillais, e [ɑ̃tijɛ, -ɛz] *adj* West Indian,
Caribbean ▷ *nm/f*: **A~, e** West Indian,
Caribbean
Antilles [ɑ̃tij] *nfpl*: **les ~** the West Indies; **les
Grandes/Petites ~** the Greater/Lesser Antilles

antilope [ɑ̃tilɔp] *nf* antelope
antimite, antimites [ɑ̃timit] *adj, nm*:
(produit) ~(s) mothproofer, moth repellent
antimondialisation [ɑ̃timɔ̃djalizasjɔ̃] *nf*
anti-globalization
antipathique [ɑ̃tipatik] *adj* unpleasant,
disagreeable
antipelliculaire [ɑ̃tipelikylɛr] *adj*
anti-dandruff
antipodes [ɑ̃tipɔd] *nmpl* *(Géo)*: **les ~** the
antipodes; *(fig)*: **être aux ~ de** to be the
opposite extreme of
antiquaire [ɑ̃tikɛr] *nm/f* antique dealer
antique [ɑ̃tik] *adj* antique; *(très vieux)*
ancient, antiquated
antiquité [ɑ̃tikite] *nf* *(objet)* antique; **l'A~**
Antiquity; **magasin/marchand d'~s**
antique shop/dealer
antirabique [ɑ̃tirabik] *adj* rabies *cpd*
antirouille [ɑ̃tiruj] *adj inv* anti-rust *cpd*;
peinture ~ antirust paint; **traitement ~**
rustproofing
antisémite [ɑ̃tisemit] *adj* anti-Semitic
antiseptique [ɑ̃tisɛptik] *adj, nm* antiseptic
antiviral, e, -aux [ɑ̃tiviral, -o] *adj* *(Méd)*
antiviral
antivirus [ɑ̃tivirys] *nm* *(Inform)* antivirus
(program)
antivol [ɑ̃tivɔl] *adj, nm*: **(dispositif) ~**
antitheft device; *(pour vélo)* padlock
antre [ɑ̃tr] *nm* den, lair
anxiété [ɑ̃ksjete] *nf* anxiety
anxieux, -euse [ɑ̃ksjø, -øz] *adj* anxious,
worried; **être ~ de faire** to be anxious to do
AOC *sigle f* (= *Appellation d'origine contrôlée)*
guarantee of quality of wine; see note

> ◈ **AOC**
> ◈
> ◈ AOC ("appellation d'origine contrôlée") is
> ◈ the highest French wine classification. It
> ◈ indicates that the wine meets strict
> ◈ requirements concerning vineyard of
> ◈ origin, type of grape, method of
> ◈ production and alcoholic strength.

août [u(t)] *nm* August; *voir aussi* **juillet;
Assomption**
apaiser [apeze] *vt* *(colère)* to calm, quell,
soothe; *(faim)* to appease, assuage; *(douleur)*
to soothe; *(personne)* to calm (down), pacify;
s'apaiser *vi* *(tempête, bruit)* to die down,
subside; *(personne)* to calm down
apanage [apanaʒ] *nm*: **être l'~ de** to be the
privilege *ou* prerogative of
aparté [aparte] *nm* *(Théât)* aside; *(entretien)*
private conversation; **en ~** *adv* in an aside
(Brit); *(entretien)* in private
apathique [apatik] *adj* apathetic
apatride [apatrid] *nm/f* stateless person
apercevoir [apɛrsəvwar] *vt* to see;
s'apercevoir de *vt* to notice; **s'~ que** to

notice that; **sans s'en ~** without realizing *ou* noticing

aperçu, e [apɛʀsy] *pp de* **apercevoir** ▷ *nm* (*vue d'ensemble*) general survey; (*intuition*) insight

apéritif, -ive [apeʀitif, -iv] *adj* which stimulates the appetite ▷ *nm* (*boisson*) aperitif; (*réunion*) (pre-lunch *ou* -dinner) drinks *pl*; **prendre l'~** to have drinks (before lunch *ou* dinner) *ou* an aperitif

à-peu-près [apøpʀɛ] *nm inv* (*péj*) vague approximation

apeuré, e [apœʀe] *adj* frightened, scared

aphte [aft] *nm* mouth ulcer

apiculture [apikyltyʀ] *nf* beekeeping, apiculture

apitoyer [apitwaje] *vt* to move to pity; **~ qn sur qn/qch** to move sb to pity for sb/over sth; **s'~ (sur qn/qch)** to feel pity *ou* compassion (for sb/over sth)

aplanir [aplaniʀ] *vt* to level; (*fig*) to smooth away, iron out

aplatir [aplatiʀ] *vt* to flatten; **s'aplatir** *vi* to become flatter; (*écrasé*) to be flattened; (*fig*) to lie flat on the ground; (: *fam*) to fall flat on one's face; (: *péj*) to grovel

aplomb [aplɔ̃] *nm* (*équilibre*) balance, equilibrium; (*fig*) self-assurance; (: *péj*) nerve; **d'~** *adv* steady; (*Constr*) plumb

APN *sigle m* (= *appareil photo(graphique) numérique*) digital camera

apogée [apɔʒe] *nm* (*fig*) peak, apogee

apologie [apɔlɔʒi] *nf* praise; (*Jur*) vindication

a posteriori [apɔsteʀjɔʀi] *adv* after the event, with hindsight, a posteriori

apostrophe [apɔstʀɔf] *nf* (*signe*) apostrophe; (*appel*) interpellation

apostropher [apɔstʀɔfe] *vt* (*interpeller*) to shout at, address sharply

apothéose [apɔteoz] *nf* pinnacle (of achievement); (*Mus etc*) grand finale

apôtre [apotʀ] *nm* apostle, disciple

apparaître [apaʀɛtʀ] *vi* to appear ▷ *vb copule* to appear, seem

apparat [apaʀa] *nm*: **tenue/dîner d'~** ceremonial dress/dinner

appareil [apaʀɛj] *nm* (*outil, machine*) piece of apparatus, device; (*électrique etc*) appliance; (*politique, syndical*) machinery; (*avion*) (aero) plane (*Brit*), (air)plane (*US*), aircraft (*inv*); (*téléphonique*) telephone; (*dentier*) brace (*Brit*), braces (*US*); **~ digestif/reproducteur** digestive/reproductive system *ou* apparatus; **l'~ productif** the means of production; **qui est à l'~?** who's speaking?; **dans le plus simple ~** in one's birthday suit; **~ (photo)** camera; **~ numérique** digital camera

appareiller [apaʀeje] *vi* (*Navig*) to cast off, get under way ▷ *vt* (*assortir*) to match up

appareil photo (*pl* **appareils photos**) [apaʀɛjfɔto] *nm* camera

apparemment [apaʀamɑ̃] *adv* apparently

apparence [apaʀɑ̃s] *nf* appearance; **malgré les ~s** despite appearances; **en ~** apparently, seemingly

apparent, e [apaʀɑ̃, -ɑ̃t] *adj* visible; (*évident*) obvious; (*superficiel*) apparent; **coutures ~es** topstitched seams; **poutres ~es** exposed beams

apparenté, e [apaʀɑ̃te] *adj*: **~ à** related to; (*fig*) similar to

apparition [apaʀisjɔ̃] *nf* appearance; (*surnaturelle*) apparition; **faire son ~** to appear

appartement [apaʀtəmɑ̃] *nm* flat (*Brit*), apartment (*US*)

appartenir [apaʀtəniʀ]: **~ à** *vt* to belong to; (*faire partie de*) to belong to, be a member of; **il lui appartient de** it is up to him to

apparu, e [apaʀy] *pp de* **apparaître**

appât [apɑ] *nm* (*Pêche*) bait; (*fig*) lure, bait

appâter [apɑte] *vt* (*hameçon*) to bait; (*poisson, fig*) to lure, entice

appauvrir [apovʀiʀ] *vt* to impoverish; **s'appauvrir** *vi* to grow poorer, become impoverished

appel [apɛl] *nm* call; (*nominal*) roll call; (: *Scol*) register; (*Mil: recrutement*) call-up; (*Jur*) appeal; **faire ~ à** (*invoquer*) to appeal to; (*avoir recours à*) to call on; (*nécessiter*) to call for, require; **faire** *ou* **interjeter ~** (*Jur*) to appeal, lodge an appeal; **faire l'~** to call the roll; (*Scol*) to call the register; **indicatif d'~** call sign; **numéro d'~** (*Tél*) number; **produit d'~** (*Comm*) loss leader; **sans ~** (*fig*) final, irrevocable; **~ d'air** in-draught; **~ d'offres** (*Comm*) invitation to tender; **faire un ~ de phares** to flash one's headlights; **~ (téléphonique)** (tele)phone call

appelé [ap(ə)le] *nm* (*Mil*) conscript

appeler [ap(ə)le] *vt* to call; (*Tél*) to call, ring; (*faire venir: médecin etc*) to call, send for; (*fig: nécessiter*) to call for, demand; **~ au secours** to call for help; **~ qn à l'aide** *ou* **au secours** to call to sb to help; **~ qn à un poste/des fonctions** to appoint sb to a post/assign duties to sb; **être appelé à** (*fig*) to be destined to; **~ qn à comparaître** (*Jur*) to summon sb to appear; **en ~ à** to appeal to; **s'appeler** *vi*: **elle s'appelle Gabrielle** her name is Gabrielle, she's called Gabrielle; **comment vous appelez-vous?** what's your name?; **comment ça s'appelle?** what is it *ou* that called?; **être appelé à** (*fig*) to be destined to

appendice [apɛ̃dis] *nm* appendix

appendicite [apɛ̃disit] *nf* appendicitis

appentis [apɑ̃ti] *nm* lean-to

appesantir [apəzɑ̃tiʀ]: **s'appesantir** *vi* to grow heavier; **s'~ sur** (*fig*) to dwell at length on

appétissant, e [apetisɑ̃, -ɑ̃t] *adj* appetizing, mouth-watering

appétit [apeti] *nm* appetite; **couper l'~ à qn** to take away sb's appetite; **bon ~!** enjoy your meal!

applaudir [aplodiʀ] *vt* to applaud ▷ *vi* to applaud, clap; **~ à** *vt* (*décision*) to applaud, commend

applaudissements [aplodismɑ̃] nmpl applause sg, clapping sg

application [aplikasjɔ̃] nf application; (d'une loi) enforcement; **mettre en ~** to implement

applique [aplik] nf wall lamp

appliquer [aplike] vt to apply; (loi) to enforce; (donner: gifle, châtiment) to give; **s'appliquer** vi (élève etc) to apply o.s.; **~ à** (loi, remarque) to apply to; **s'~ à faire qch** to apply o.s. to doing sth, take pains to do sth; **s'~ sur** (coïncider avec) to fit over

appoint [apwɛ̃] nm (extra) contribution ou help; **avoir/faire l'~** (en payant) to have/give the right change ou money; **chauffage d'~** extra heating

appointements [apwɛ̃tmɑ̃] nmpl salary sg, stipend

apport [apɔʀ] nm supply; (argent, biens etc) contribution

apporter [apɔʀte] vt to bring; (preuve) to give, provide; (modification) to make; (remarque) to contribute, add

apposer [apoze] vt to append; (sceau etc) to affix

appréciable [apʀesjabl] adj (important) appreciable, significant

apprécier [apʀesje] vt to appreciate; (évaluer) to estimate, assess; **j'~ais que tu ...** I should appreciate (it) if you ...

appréhender [apʀeɑ̃de] vt (craindre) to dread; (arrêter) to apprehend; **~ que** to fear that; **~ de faire** to dread doing

appréhension [apʀeɑ̃sjɔ̃] nf apprehension

apprendre [apʀɑ̃dʀ] vt to learn; (événement, résultats) to learn of, hear of; **~ qch à qn** (informer) to tell sb (of) sth; (enseigner) to teach sb sth; **tu me l'apprends!** that's news to me!; **~ à faire qch** to learn to do sth; **~ à qn à faire qch** to teach sb to do sth

apprenti, e [apʀɑ̃ti] nm/f apprentice; (fig) novice, beginner

apprentissage [apʀɑ̃tisaʒ] nm learning; (Comm, Scol: période) apprenticeship; **école** ou **centre d'~** training school ou centre; **faire l'~ de qch** (fig) to be initiated into sth

apprêté, e [apʀete] adj (fig) affected

apprêter [apʀete] vt to dress, finish; **s'apprêter** vi: **s'~ à qch/à faire qch** to prepare for sth/for doing sth

appris, e [apʀi, -iz] pp de **apprendre**

apprivoiser [apʀivwaze] vt to tame

approbation [apʀɔbasjɔ̃] nf approval; **digne d'~** (conduite, travail) praiseworthy, commendable

approchant, e [apʀɔʃɑ̃, -ɑ̃t] adj similar, close; **quelque chose d'~** something similar

approche [apʀɔʃ] nf approaching; (arrivée, attitude) approach; **approches** nfpl (abords) surroundings; **à l'~ du bateau/de l'ennemi** as the ship/enemy approached ou drew near; **l'~ d'un problème** the approach to a problem; **travaux d'~** (fig) manoeuvrings

approcher [apʀɔʃe] vi to approach, come near ▷ vt to approach, come close to; (rapprocher): **~ qch (de qch)** to bring ou put ou move sth near (to sth); **~ de** vt (lieu, but) to draw near to; (quantité, moment) to approach; **s'approcher de** to approach, go ou come near ou move near to; **approchez-vous** come ou go nearer

approfondir [apʀɔfɔ̃diʀ] vt to deepen; (question) to go further into; **sans ~** without going too deeply into it

approprié, e [apʀɔpʀije] adj: **~ (à)** appropriate (to), suited (to)

approprier [apʀɔpʀije] vt (adapter) adapt; **s'approprier** vt to appropriate, take over; **s'~ en** to stock up with

approuver [apʀuve] vt to agree with; (autoriser: loi, projet) to approve, pass; (trouver louable) to approve of; **je vous approuve entièrement/ne vous approuve pas** I agree with you entirely/don't agree with you; **lu et approuvé** (read and) approved

approvisionner [apʀɔvizjɔne] vt to supply; (compte bancaire) to pay funds into; **~ qn en** to supply sb with; **s'approvisionner** vi: **s'~ dans un certain magasin/au marché** to shop in a certain shop/at the market; **s'~ en** to stock up with

approximatif, -ive [apʀɔksimatif, -iv] adj approximate, rough; (imprécis) vague

appt abr = **appartement**

appui [apɥi] nm support; **prendre ~ sur** to lean on; (objet) to rest on; **point d'~** fulcrum; (fig) something to lean on; **à l'~ de** (pour prouver) in support of; **à l'~** adv to support one's argument; **l'~ de la fenêtre** the windowsill, the window ledge

appui-tête, appuie-tête [apɥitɛt] nm inv headrest

appuyer [apɥije] vt (poser): **~ qch sur/contre/à** to lean ou rest sth on/against/on; (soutenir: personne, demande) to support, back (up) ▷ vi: **~ sur** (bouton) to press, push; (mot, détail) to stress, emphasize; **~ sur le frein** to brake, to apply the brakes; **s'appuyer sur** vt (chose: peser sur) to rest (heavily) on, press against; to lean on; (compter sur) to rely on; **s'~ sur qn** to lean on sb; **~ contre** (toucher: mur, porte) to lean ou rest against; **~ à droite** ou **sur sa droite** to bear (to the) right; **~ sur le champignon** to put one's foot down

âpre [ɑpʀ] adj acrid, pungent; (fig) harsh; (lutte) bitter; **~ au gain** grasping, greedy

après [apʀe] prép after ▷ adv afterwards; **deux heures ~** two hours later; **~ qu'il est parti/avoir fait** after he left/having done; **courir ~ qn** to run after sb; **crier ~ qn** to shout at sb; **être toujours ~ qn** (critiquer etc) to be always on at sb; **~ quoi** after which; **d'~** prép (selon) according to; **d'~ lui** according to him; **d'~ moi** in my opinion; **~ coup** adv after the event, afterwards; **~ tout** adv (au fond) after all; **et (puis) ~?** so what?

après-demain [apʀɛdmɛ̃] adv the day after tomorrow

après-guerre [apʀɛgɛʀ] nm post-war years pl; **d'~** adj post-war

après-midi [apʀɛmidi] nm ou f inv afternoon

après-rasage [apʀɛʀazaʒ] nm inv after-shave

après-shampooing [apʀɛʃɑ̃pwɛ̃] nm inv conditioner

après-ski [apʀɛski] nm inv (chaussure) snow boot; (moment) après-ski

après-soleil [apʀɛsɔlɛj] adj inv after-sun cpd ▷ nm after-sun cream ou lotion

à-propos [apʀɔpo] nm (d'une remarque) aptness; **faire preuve d'~** to show presence of mind, do the right thing; **avec ~** suitably, aptly

apte [apt] adj: **~ à qch/faire qch** capable of sth/doing sth; **~ (au service)** (Mil) fit (for service)

aquarelle [akwaʀɛl] nf (tableau) watercolour (Brit), watercolor (US); (genre) watercolo(u)rs pl, aquarelle

aquarium [akwaʀjɔm] nm aquarium

arabe [aʀab] adj Arabic (désert, cheval) Arabian; (nation, peuple) Arab ▷ nm (Ling) Arabic ▷ nm/f: **A~** Arab

Arabie [aʀabi] nf: **l'~** Arabia; **l'~ Saoudite ou Séoudite** Saudi Arabia

arachide [aʀaʃid] nf groundnut (plant); (graine) peanut, groundnut

araignée [aʀeɲe] nf spider; **~ de mer** spider crab

arbitraire [aʀbitʀɛʀ] adj arbitrary

arbitre [aʀbitʀ] nm (Sport) referee; (: Tennis, Cricket) umpire; (fig) arbiter, judge; (Jur) arbitrator

arbitrer [aʀbitʀe] vt to referee; to umpire; to arbitrate

arborer [aʀbɔʀe] vt to bear, display; (avec ostentation) to sport

arbre [aʀbʀ] nm tree; (Tech) shaft; **~ à cames** (Auto) camshaft; **~ fruitier** fruit tree; **~ généalogique** family tree; **~ de Noël** Christmas tree; **~ de transmission** (Auto) driveshaft

arbuste [aʀbyst] nm small shrub, bush

arc [aʀk] nm (arme); (Géom) arc; (Archit) arch; **~ de cercle** arc of a circle; **en ~ de cercle** adj semi-circular

arcade [aʀkad] nf arch(way); **~s** arcade sg, arches; **~ sourcilière** arch of the eyebrows

arcanes [aʀkan] nmpl mysteries

arc-boutant (pl **arcs-boutants**) [aʀkbutɑ̃] nm flying buttress

arceau, x [aʀso] nm (métallique etc) hoop

arc-en-ciel (pl **arcs-en-ciel**) [aʀkɑ̃sjɛl] nm rainbow

arche [aʀʃ] nf arch; **~ de Noé** Noah's Ark

archéologie [aʀkeɔlɔʒi] nf arch(a)eology

archéologue [aʀkeɔlɔg] nm/f arch(a)eologist

archet [aʀʃɛ] nm bow

archevêque [aʀʃəvɛk] nm archbishop

archi... [aʀʃi] préfixe (très) dead, extra

archipel [aʀʃipɛl] nm archipelago

architecte [aʀʃitɛkt] nm architect

architecture [aʀʃitɛktyʀ] nf architecture

archive [aʀʃiv] nf file

archives [aʀʃiv] nfpl (collection) archives

arctique [aʀktik] adj Arctic ▷ nm: **l'A~** the Arctic; **le cercle A~** the Arctic Circle; **l'océan A~** the Arctic Ocean

ardemment [aʀdamɑ̃] adv ardently, fervently

ardent, e [aʀdɑ̃, -ɑ̃t] adj (soleil) blazing; (fièvre) raging; (amour) ardent, passionate; (prière) fervent

ardeur [aʀdœʀ] nf blazing heat; (fig) fervour, ardour

ardoise [aʀdwaz] nf slate

ardu, e [aʀdy] adj (travail) arduous; (problème) difficult; (pente) steep, abrupt

arène [aʀɛn] nf arena; (fig): **l'~ politique** the political arena; **arènes** nfpl bull-ring sg

arête [aʀɛt] nf (de poisson) bone; (d'une montagne) ridge; (Géom etc) edge (where two faces meet)

argent [aʀʒɑ̃] nm (métal) silver; (monnaie) money; (couleur) silver; **en avoir pour son ~** to get value for money; **gagner beaucoup d'~** to earn a lot of money; **~ comptant** (hard) cash; **~ de poche** pocket money; **~ liquide** ready money, (ready) cash

argenté, e [aʀʒɑ̃te] adj silver(y); (métal) silver-plated

argenterie [aʀʒɑ̃tʀi] nf silverware; (en métal argenté) silver plate

argentin, e [aʀʒɑ̃tɛ̃, -in] adj Argentinian, Argentine ▷ nm/f: **A~, e** Argentinian, Argentine

Argentine [aʀʒɑ̃tin] nf: **l'~** Argentina, the Argentine

argentique [aʀʒɑ̃tik] adj (appareil photo) film cpd

argile [aʀʒil] nf clay

argot [aʀgo] nm slang; see note

ARGOT

Argot was the term originally used to describe the jargon of the criminal underworld, characterized by colourful images and distinctive intonation and designed to confuse the outsider. Some French authors write in argot and so have helped it spread and grow. More generally, the special vocabulary used by any social or professional group is also known as argot.

argotique [aʀgɔtik] adj slang cpd; (très familier) slangy

argument [aʀgymɑ̃] nm argument

argumentaire [aʀgymɑ̃tɛʀ] *nm* list of sales points; (*brochure*) sales leaflet

argumenter [aʀgymɑ̃te] *vi* to argue

argus [aʀgys] *nm* guide to second-hand car etc prices

aride [aʀid] *adj* arid

aristocratie [aʀistɔkʀasi] *nf* aristocracy

aristocratique [aʀistɔkʀatik] *adj* aristocratic

arithmétique [aʀitmetik] *adj* arithmetic(al) ▷ *nf* arithmetic

armateur [aʀmatœʀ] *nm* shipowner

armature [aʀmatyʀ] *nf* framework; (*de tente etc*) frame; (*de corset*) bone; (*de soutien-gorge*) wiring

arme [aʀm] *nf* weapon; (*section de l'armée*) arm; **armes** *nfpl* weapons, arms; (*blason*) (coat of) arms; **les ~s** (*profession*) soldiering *sg*; **à ~s égales** on equal terms; **en ~s** up in arms; **passer par les ~s** to execute (by firing squad); **prendre/présenter les ~s** to take up/present arms; **se battre à l'~ blanche** to fight with blades; **~ à feu** firearm; **~s de destruction massive** weapons of mass destruction

armée [aʀme] *nf* army; **~ de l'air** Air Force; **l'~ du Salut** the Salvation Army; **~ de terre** Army

armement [aʀməmɑ̃] *nm* (*matériel*) arms *pl*, weapons *pl*; (: *d'un pays*) arms *pl*, armament; (*action d'équiper: d'un navire*) fitting out; **~s nucléaires** nuclear armaments; **course aux ~s** arms race

armer [aʀme] *vt* to arm; (*arme à feu*) to cock; (*appareil photo*) to wind on; **~ qch de** to fit sth with; (*renforcer*) to reinforce sth with; **~ qn de** to arm *ou* equip sb with; **s'armer de** to arm o.s. with

armistice [aʀmistis] *nm* armistice; **l'A~** ≈ Remembrance (*Brit*) *ou* Veterans (*US*) Day

armoire [aʀmwaʀ] *nf* (*tall*) cupboard; (*penderie*) wardrobe (*Brit*), closet (*US*); **~ à pharmacie** medicine chest

armoiries [aʀmwaʀi] *nfpl* coat of arms *sg*

armure [aʀmyʀ] *nf* armour *no pl*, suit of armour

armurier [aʀmyʀje] *nm* gunsmith; (*Mil, d'armes blanches*) armourer

arnaque [aʀnak] (*fam*) *nf* swindling; **c'est de l'~** it's daylight robbery

arnaquer [aʀnake] (*fam*) *vt* to do (*fam*), swindle; **se faire ~** to be had (*fam*) *ou* done

arobase [aʀɔbaz] *nf* (*Inform*) "at" symbol, @; **"paul ~ société point fr"** "paul at société dot fr"

aromates [aʀɔmat] *nmpl* seasoning *sg*, herbs (and spices)

aromathérapie [aʀɔmateʀapi] *nf* aromatherapy

aromatisé, e [aʀɔmatize] *adj* flavoured

arôme [aʀom] *nm* aroma; (*d'une fleur etc*) fragrance

arpenter [aʀpɑ̃te] *vt* to pace up and down

arpenteur [aʀpɑ̃tœʀ] *nm* land surveyor

arqué, e [aʀke] *adj* arched; (*jambes*) bow *cpd*, bandy

arrache-pied [aʀaʃpje]: **d'~** *adv* relentlessly

arracher [aʀaʃe] *vt* to pull out; (*page etc*) to tear off, tear out; (*déplanter: légume, herbe, souche*) to pull up; (*bras etc: par explosion*) to blow off; (: *par accident*) to tear off; **s'arracher** *vt* (*article très recherché*) to fight over; **~ qch à qn** to snatch sth from sb; (*fig*) to wring sth out of sb, wrest sth from sb; **~ qn à** (*solitude, rêverie*) to drag sb out of; (*famille etc*) to tear *ou* wrench sb away from; **se faire ~ une dent** to have a tooth out *ou* pulled (*US*); **s'~ de** (*lieu*) to tear o.s. away from; (*habitude*) to force o.s. out of

arraisonner [aʀɛzɔne] *vt* to board and search

arrangeant, e [aʀɑ̃ʒɑ̃, -ɑ̃t] *adj* accommodating, obliging

arrangement [aʀɑ̃ʒmɑ̃] *nm* arrangement

arranger [aʀɑ̃ʒe] *vt* to arrange; (*réparer*) to fix, put right; (*régler*) to settle, sort out; (*convenir à*) to suit, be convenient for; **cela m'arrange** that suits me (fine); **s'arranger** *vi* (*se mettre d'accord*) to come to an agreement *ou* arrangement; (*s'améliorer: querelle, situation*) to be sorted out; (*se débrouiller*): **s'~ pour que ...** to arrange things so that ...; **je vais m'~** I'll manage; **ça va s'~** it'll sort itself out; **s'~ pour faire** to make sure that *ou* see to it that one can do

arrestation [aʀɛstasjɔ̃] *nf* arrest

arrêt [aʀɛ] *nm* stopping; (*de bus etc*) stop; (*Jur*) judgment, decision; (*Football*) save; **arrêts** *nmpl* (*Mil*) arrest *sg*; **être à l'~** to be stopped, have come to a halt; **rester** *ou* **tomber en ~ devant** to stop short in front of; **sans ~** without stopping, non-stop; (*fréquemment*) continually; **~ d'autobus** bus stop; **~ facultatif** request stop; **~ de mort** capital sentence; **~ de travail** stoppage (of work)

arrêté, e [aʀete] *adj* (*idées*) firm, fixed ▷ *nm* order, decree; **~ municipal** ≈ bylaw, byelaw

arrêter [aʀete] *vt* to stop; (*chauffage etc*) to turn off, switch off; (*Comm: compte*) to settle; (*Couture: point*) to fasten off; (*fixer: date etc*) to appoint, decide on; (*criminel, suspect*) to arrest; **s'arrêter** *vi* to stop; (*s'interrompre*) to stop o.s.; **~ de faire** to stop doing; **arrête de te plaindre** stop complaining; **ne pas ~ de faire** to keep on doing; **s'~ de faire** to stop doing; **s'~ sur** (*choix, regard*) to fall on

arrhes [aʀ] *nfpl* deposit *sg*

arrière [aʀjɛʀ] *nm* back; (*Sport*) fullback ▷ *adj inv*: **siège/roue ~** back *ou* rear seat/wheel; **arrières** *nmpl* (*fig*): **protéger ses ~s** to protect the rear; **à l'~** *adv* behind, at the back; **en ~** *adv* behind; (*regarder*) back, behind; (*tomber, aller*) backwards; **en ~ de** *prép* behind

arriéré, e [aʀjeʀe] *adj* (*péj*) backward ▷ *nm* (*d'argent*) arrears *pl*

arrière-goût [aʀjɛʀgu] *nm* aftertaste

arrière-grand-mère (*pl* **arrière-grand-mères**) [aʀjɛʀɡʀɑ̃mɛʀ] *nf* great-grandmother

arrière-grand-père (*pl* **arrière-grands-pères**) [aʀjɛʀɡʀɑ̃pɛʀ] *nm* great-grandfather

arrière-pays [aʀjɛʀpei] *nm inv* hinterland

arrière-pensée [aʀjɛʀpɑ̃se] *nf* ulterior motive; (*doute*) mental reservation

arrière-plan [aʀjɛʀplɑ̃] *nm* background; **à l'~** in the background; **d'~** *adj* (*Inform*) background *cpd*

arrière-saison [aʀjɛʀsezɔ̃] *nf* late autumn

arrière-train [aʀjɛʀtʀɛ̃] *nm* hindquarters *pl*

arrimer [aʀime] *vt* (*cargaison*) to stow; (*fixer*) to secure, fasten securely

arrivage [aʀivaʒ] *nm* consignment

arrivée [aʀive] *nf* arrival; (*ligne d'arrivée*) finish; **~ d'air/de gaz** air/gas inlet; **courrier à l'~** incoming mail; **à mon ~** when I arrived

arriver [aʀive] *vi* to arrive; (*survenir*) to happen, occur; **j'arrive!** (I'm) just coming!; **il arrive à Paris à 8 h** he gets to *ou* arrives in Paris at 8; **~ à destination** to arrive at one's destination; **~ à** (*atteindre*) to reach; **~ à (faire) qch** (*réussir*) to manage (to do) sth; **~ à échéance** to fall due; **en ~ à faire ...** to end up doing ..., get to the point of doing ...; **il arrive que ...** it happens that ...; **il lui arrive de faire ...** he sometimes does ...

arriviste [aʀivist] *nm/f* go-getter

arrobase [aʀɔbaz] *nf* (*Inform*) @, 'at' sign

arrogance [aʀɔɡɑ̃s] *nf* arrogance

arrogant, e [aʀɔɡɑ̃, -ɑ̃t] *adj* arrogant

arrondir [aʀɔ̃diʀ] *vt* (*forme, objet*) to round; (*somme*) to round off; **s'arrondir** *vi* to become round(ed); **~ ses fins de mois** to supplement one's pay

arrondissement [aʀɔ̃dismɑ̃] *nm* (*Admin*) ≈ district

arroser [aʀoze] *vt* to water; (*victoire etc*) to celebrate (over a drink); (*Culin*) to baste

arrosoir [aʀozwaʀ] *nm* watering can

arsenal, -aux [aʀsənal, -o] *nm* (*Navig*) naval dockyard; (*Mil*) arsenal; (*fig*) gear, paraphernalia

art [aʀ] *nm* art; **avoir l'~ de faire** (*fig: personne*) to have a talent for doing; **les ~s** the arts; **livre/critique d'~** art book/ critic; **objet d'~** objet d'art; **~ dramatique** dramatic art; **~s martiaux** martial arts; **~s et métiers** applied arts and crafts; **~s ménagers** home economics *sg*; **~s plastiques** plastic arts

artère [aʀtɛʀ] *nf* (*Anat*) artery; (*rue*) main road

arthrite [aʀtʀit] *nf* arthritis

artichaut [aʀtiʃo] *nm* artichoke

article [aʀtikl] *nm* article; (*Comm*) item, article; **faire l'~** (*Comm*) to do one's sales spiel; **faire l'~ de** (*fig*) to sing the praises of; **à l'~ de la mort** at the point of death; **~ défini/indéfini** definite/indefinite article; **~ de fond** (*Presse*) feature article; **~s de bureau** office equipment; **~s de voyage** travel goods *ou* items

articulation [aʀtikylasjɔ̃] *nf* articulation; (*Anat*) joint

articuler [aʀtikyle] *vt* to articulate; **s'articuler (sur)** *vi* (*Anat, Tech*) to articulate (with); **s'~ autour de** (*fig*) to centre around *ou* on, turn on

artifice [aʀtifis] *nm* device, trick

artificiel, le [aʀtifisjɛl] *adj* artificial

artisan [aʀtizɑ̃] *nm* artisan, (self-employed) craftsman; **l'~ de la victoire/du malheur** the architect of victory/of the disaster

artisanal, e, -aux [aʀtizanal, -o] *adj* of *ou* made by craftsmen; (*péj*) cottage industry *cpd*, unsophisticated; **de fabrication ~e** home-made

artisanat [aʀtizana] *nm* arts and crafts *pl*

artiste [aʀtist] *nm/f* artist; (*Théât, Mus*) artist, performer; (*: de variétés*) entertainer

artistique [aʀtistik] *adj* artistic

as *vb* [a] *voir* **avoir** ▷ *nm* [as] ace

ascendance [asɑ̃dɑ̃s] *nf* (*origine*) ancestry; (*Astrologie*) ascendant

ascendant, e [asɑ̃dɑ̃, -ɑ̃t] *adj* upward ▷ *nm* influence; **ascendants** *nmpl* ascendants

ascenseur [asɑ̃sœʀ] *nm* lift (*Brit*), elevator (*US*)

ascension [asɑ̃sjɔ̃] *nf* ascent; (*de montagne*) climb; **l'A~** (*Rel*) the Ascension; (*: jour férié*) Ascension (Day); *see note*; **(île de) l'A~** Ascension Island

▓ L'ASCENSION

The *fête de l'Ascension* is a public holiday in France. It always falls on a Thursday, usually in May. Many French people take the following Friday off work too and enjoy a long weekend.

aseptisé, e [aseptize] (*péj*) *adj* sanitized

asiatique [azjatik] *adj* Asian, Asiatic ▷ *nm/f*: **A~** Asian

Asie [azi] *nf*: **l'~** Asia

asile [azil] *nm* (*refuge*) refuge, sanctuary; (*Pol*): **droit d'~** (political) asylum; (*pour malades, vieillards etc*) home; **accorder l'~ politique à qn** to grant *ou* give sb political asylum; **chercher/trouver ~ quelque part** to seek/find refuge somewhere

aspect [aspɛ] *nm* appearance, look; (*fig*) aspect, side; (*Ling*) aspect; **à l'~ de** at the sight of

asperge [aspɛʀʒ] *nf* asparagus *no pl*

asperger [aspɛʀʒe] *vt* to spray, sprinkle

aspérité [asperite] *nf* excrescence, protruding bit (of rock *etc*)

asphalte [asfalt] *nm* asphalt

asphyxier [asfiksje] *vt* to suffocate, asphyxiate; (*fig*) to stifle; **mourir asphyxié** to die of suffocation *ou* asphyxiation

aspirateur [aspiʀatœʀ] *nm* vacuum cleaner, hoover®; **passer l'~** to vacuum

aspirer [aspire] *vt* (*air*) to inhale; (*liquide*) to suck (up); (*appareil*) to suck *ou* draw up; **~ à** *vt* to aspire to

aspirine [aspirin] *nf* aspirin

assagir [asaʒir] *vt*, **s'assagir** *vi* to quieten down, settle down

assaillir [asajir] *vt* to assail, attack; **~ qn de** (*questions*) to assail *ou* bombard sb with

assainir [asenir] *vt* to clean up; (*eau, air*) to purify

assaisonnement [asɛzɔnmɑ̃] *nm* seasoning

assaisonner [asɛzɔne] *vt* to season; **bien assaisonné** highly seasoned

assassin [asasɛ̃] *nm* murderer; assassin

assassiner [asasine] *vt* to murder; (*esp Pol*) to assassinate

assaut [aso] *nm* assault, attack; **prendre d'~** to (take by) storm, assault; **donner l'~ (à)** to attack; **faire ~ de** (*rivaliser*) to vie with *ou* rival each other in

assécher [asefe] *vt* to drain

assemblage [asɑ̃blaʒ] *nm* (*action*) assembling; (*Menuiserie*) joint; **un ~ de** (*fig*) a collection of; **langage d'~** (*Inform*) assembly language

assemblée [asɑ̃ble] *nf* (*réunion*) meeting; (*public, assistance*) gathering; assembled people; (*Pol*) assembly; (*Rel*): **l'~ des fidèles** the congregation; **l'A~ nationale (AN)** the (French) National Assembly; *see note*

⁂ **ASSEMBLÉE NATIONALE**

The *Assemblée nationale* is the lower house of the French Parliament, the upper house being the "Sénat". It is housed in the Palais Bourbon in Paris. Its members, or "députés", are elected every five years.

assembler [asɑ̃ble] *vt* (*joindre, monter*) to assemble, put together; (*amasser*) to gather (together), collect (together); **s'assembler** *vi* to gather, collect

assener, asséner [asene] *vt*: **~ un coup à qn** to deal sb a blow

assentiment [asɑ̃timɑ̃] *nm* assent, consent; (*approbation*) approval

asseoir [aswar] *vt* (*malade, bébé*) to sit up; (*personne debout*) to sit down; (*autorité, réputation*) to establish; **s'asseoir** *vi* to sit (o.s.) up; to sit (o.s.) down; **faire ~ qn** to ask sb to sit down; **asseyez-vous!, assieds-toi!** sit down!; **~ qch sur** to build sth on; (*appuyer*) to base sth on

assermenté, e [asɛrmɑ̃te] *adj* sworn, on oath

asservir [asɛrvir] *vt* to subjugate, enslave

assez [ase] *adv* (*suffisamment*) enough, sufficiently; (*passablement*) rather, quite, fairly; **~!** enough!, that'll do!; **~/pas ~ cuit** well enough done/underdone; **est-il ~ fort/rapide?** is he strong/fast enough?; **il est passé ~ vite** he went past rather *ou* quite

fairly fast; **~ de pain/livres** enough *ou* sufficient bread/books; **vous en avez ~?** have you got enough?; **en avoir ~ de qch** (*en être fatigué*) to have had enough of sth; **j'en ai ~ -!** I've had enough!; **travailler ~** to work (hard) enough

assidu, e [asidy] *adj* assiduous, painstaking; (*régulier*) regular; **~ auprès de qn** attentive towards sb

assied *etc* [asje] *vb voir* **asseoir**

assiéger [asjeʒe] *vt* to besiege, lay siege to; (*foule, touristes*) to mob, besiege

assiérai *etc* [asjere] *vb voir* **asseoir**

assiette [asjɛt] *nf* plate; (*contenu*) plate(ful); (*équilibre*) seat; (*de colonne*) seating; (*de navire*) trim; **il n'est pas dans son ~** he's not feeling quite himself; **~ à dessert** dessert *ou* side plate; **~ anglaise** assorted cold meats; **~ creuse** (soup) dish, soup plate; **~ de l'impôt** basis of (tax) assessment; **~ plate** (dinner) plate

assigner [asine] *vt*: **~ qch à** to assign *ou* allot sth to; (*valeur, importance*) to attach sth to; (*somme*) to allocate sth to; (*limites*) to set *ou* fix sth to; (*cause, effet*) to ascribe *ou* attribute sth to; **~ qn à** (*affecter*) to assign sb to; **~ qn à résidence** (*Jur*) to give sb a compulsory order of residence

assimiler [asimile] *vt* to assimilate, absorb; (*comparer*): **~ qch/qn à** to liken *ou* compare sth/sb to; **s'assimiler** *vi* (*s'intégrer*) to be assimilated *ou* absorbed; **ils sont assimilés aux infirmières** (*Admin*) they are classed as nurses

assis, e [asi, -iz] *pp de* **asseoir** ▷ *adj* sitting (down), seated ▷ *nf* (*Constr*) course; (*Géo*) stratum (*pl* -a); (*fig*) basis (*pl* bases), foundation; **~ en tailleur** sitting cross-legged

assises [asiz] *nfpl* (*Jur*) assizes; (*congrès*) (annual) conference

assistance [asistɑ̃s] *nf* (*public*) audience; (*aide*) assistance; **porter** *ou* **prêter ~ à qn** to give sb assistance; **A~ publique (AP)** *public health service*; **enfant de l'A~ (publique)** child in care; **~ technique** technical aid

assistant, e [asistɑ̃, -ɑ̃t] *nm/f* assistant; (*d'université*) probationary lecturer; **les assistants** *nmpl* (*auditeurs etc*) those present; **~e sociale** social worker

assisté, e [asiste] *adj* (*Auto*) power assisted; **~ par ordinateur** computer-assisted; **direction ~e** power steering ▷ *nm/f* person receiving aid from the State

assister [asiste] *vt* to assist; **~ à** *vt* (*scène, événement*) to witness; (*conférence*) to attend, be (present) at; (*spectacle, match*) to be at, see

association [asɔsjasjɔ̃] *nf* association; (*Comm*) partnership; **~ d'idées/images** association of ideas/images

associé, e [asɔsje] *nm/f* associate; (*Comm*) partner

associer [asɔsje] vt to associate; **~ qn à** (profits) to give sb a share of; (affaire) to make sb a partner in; (joie, triomphe) to include sb in; **~ qch à** (joindre, allier) to combine sth with; **s'associer** vi to join together; (Comm) to form a partnership ▷ vt (collaborateur) to take on (as a partner); **s'~ à** (couleurs, qualités) to be combined with; (opinions, joie de qn) to share in; **s'~ à** ou **avec qn pour faire** to join (forces) ou join together with sb to do

assoiffé, e [aswafe] adj thirsty; (fig): **~ de** (sang) thirsting for; (gloire) thirsting after

assombrir [asɔ̃bʀiʀ] vt to darken; (fig) to fill with gloom; **s'assombrir** vi to darken; (devenir nuageux, fig: visage) to cloud over; (fig) to become gloomy

assommer [asɔme] vt (étourdir, abrutir) to knock out, stun; (fam: ennuyer) to bore stiff

Assomption [asɔ̃psjɔ̃] nf: **l'~** the Assumption; see note

⁂ **L'ASSOMPTION**

⁂ The fête de l'Assomption, more commonly
⁂ known as "le 15 août" is a national
⁂ holiday in France. Traditionally, large
⁂ numbers of holidaymakers leave home
⁂ on 15 August, frequently causing chaos
⁂ on the roads.

assorti, e [asɔʀti] adj matched, matching; **fromages/légumes ~s** assorted cheeses/vegetables; **~ à** matching; **~ de** accompanied with; (conditions, conseils) coupled with; **bien/mal ~** well/ill-matched

assortiment [asɔʀtimã] nm (choix) assortment, selection; (harmonie de couleurs, formes) arrangement; (Comm: lot, stock) selection

assortir [asɔʀtiʀ] vt to match; **s'assortir** vi to go well together, match; **~ qch à** to match sth with; **~ qch de** to accompany sth with; **s'~ de** to be accompanied by

assoupi, e [asupi] adj dozing, sleeping; (fig) (be)numbed; (sens) dulled

assoupir [asupiʀ]: **s'assoupir** vi (personne) to doze off; (sens) to go numb

assouplir [asupliʀ] vt to make supple, soften; (membres, corps) to limber up, make supple; (fig) to relax; (: caractère) to make more flexible; **s'assouplir** vi to soften; to limber up; to relax; to become more flexible

assouplissant [asuplisã] nm (fabric) softener

assourdir [asuʀdiʀ] vt (bruit) to deaden, muffle; (bruit) to deafen

assouvir [asuviʀ] vt to satisfy, appease

assujettir [asyʒetiʀ] vt to subject, subjugate; (fixer: planches, tableau) to fix securely; **~ qn à** (règle, impôt) to subject sb to

assumer [asyme] vt (fonction, emploi) to assume, take on; (accepter: conséquence, situation) to accept

assurance [asyʀãs] nf (certitude) assurance; (confiance en soi) (self-)confidence; (contrat) insurance (policy); (secteur commercial) insurance; **prendre une ~ contre** to take out insurance ou an insurance policy against; **~ contre l'incendie** fire insurance; **~ contre le vol** insurance against theft; **société d'~**, **compagnie d'~s** insurance company; **~ au tiers** third party insurance; **~ maladie (AM)** health insurance; **~ tous risques** comprehensive insurance; **~s sociales (AS)** ≈ National Insurance (Brit), ≈ Social Security (US)

assurance-vie (pl **assurances-vie**) [asyʀãsvi] nf life assurance ou insurance

assuré, e [asyʀe] adj (réussite, échec, victoire etc) certain, sure; (démarche, voix) assured; (pas) steady, (self-)confident; (certain): **~ de** confident of; (Assurances) insured ▷ nm/f insured (person); **~ social** ≈ member of the National Insurance (Brit) ou Social Security (US) scheme

assurément [asyʀemã] adv assuredly, most certainly

assurer [asyʀe] vt (Comm) to insure; (stabiliser) to steady, stabilize; (victoire etc) to ensure, make certain; (frontières, pouvoir) to make secure; (service, garde) to provide, operate; **~ qch à qn** (garantir) to secure ou guarantee sth for sb; (certifier) to assure sb of sth; **~ à qn que** to assure sb that; **je vous assure que non/si** I assure you that that is not the case/is the case; **~ qn de** to assure sb of; **~ ses arrières** (fig) to be sure one has something to fall back on; **s'assurer (contre)** vi (Comm) to insure o.s. (against); **s'~ de/que** (vérifier) to make sure of/that; **s'~ (de)** (aide de qn) to secure; **s'~ sur la vie** to take out life insurance; **s'~ le concours/la collaboration de qn** to secure sb's aid/collaboration

assureur [asyʀœʀ] nm insurance agent; (société) insurers pl

asthmatique [asmatik] adj, nm/f asthmatic

asthme [asm] nm asthma

asticot [astiko] nm maggot

astiquer [astike] vt to polish, shine

astre [astʀ] nm star

astreignant, e [astʀɛɲã, -ãt] adj demanding

astreindre [astʀɛ̃dʀ] vt: **~ qn à qch** to force sth upon sb; **~ qn à faire** to compel ou force sb to do; **s'~ à** to compel ou force o.s. to

astrologie [astʀɔlɔʒi] nf astrology

astronaute [astʀɔnot] nm/f astronaut

astronomie [astʀɔnɔmi] nf astronomy

astuce [astys] nf shrewdness, astuteness; (truc) trick, clever way; (plaisanterie) wisecrack

astucieux, -euse [astysjø, -øz] adj shrewd, clever, astute

atelier [atəlje] nm workshop; (de peintre) studio

athée [ate] adj atheistic ▷ nm/f atheist

Athènes [atɛn] n Athens

a

athlète [atlɛt] nm/f (Sport) athlete; (costaud) muscleman

athlétisme [atletism] nm athletics sg; **faire de l'~** to do athletics; **tournoi d'~** athletics meeting

atlantique [atlɑ̃tik] adj Atlantic ▷ nm: **l'(océan) A~** the Atlantic (Ocean)

atlas [atlas] nm atlas

atmosphère [atmɔsfɛʀ] nf atmosphere

atome [atom] nm atom

atomique [atɔmik] adj atomic, nuclear; (usine) nuclear; (nombre, masse) atomic

atomiseur [atɔmizœʀ] nm atomizer

atout [atu] nm trump; (: plus fort) trump card; **"~ pique/trèfle"** "spades/clubs are trumps"

âtre [ɑtʀ] nm hearth

atroce [atʀɔs] adj atrocious, horrible

attabler [atable]: **s'attabler** vi to sit down at (the) table; **s'~ à la terrasse** to sit down (at a table) on the terrace

attachant, e [ataʃɑ̃, -ɑ̃t] adj engaging, likeable

attache [ataʃ] nf clip, fastener; (fig) tie; **attaches** nfpl (relations) connections; **à l'~** (chien) tied up

attacher [ataʃe] vt to tie up; (étiquette) to attach, tie on; (ceinture) to fasten; (souliers) to do up ▷ vi (poêle, riz) to stick; **s'attacher** (robe etc) to do up; **s'~ à** (par affection) to become attached to; **s'~ à faire qch** to endeavour to do sth; **~ qch à** to tie ou fasten ou attach sth to; **~ qn** (fig: lier) to attach sb to; **~ du prix/de l'importance à** to attach great value/attach importance to

attaque [atak] nf attack; (cérébrale) stroke; (d'épilepsie) fit; **être/se sentir d'~** to be/feel on form; **~ à main armée** armed attack

attaquer [atake] vt to attack; (en justice) to sue, bring an action against; (travail) to tackle, set about ▷ vi to attack; **s'attaquer à** vt (personne) to attack; (épidémie, misère) to tackle, attack

attardé, e [atarde] adj (passants) late; (enfant) backward; (conceptions) old-fashioned

attarder [atarde]: **s'attarder** vi (sur qch, en chemin) to linger; (chez qn) to stay on

atteindre [atɛ̃dʀ] vt to reach; (blesser) to hit; (contacter) to reach, contact, get in touch with; (émouvoir) to affect

atteint, e [atɛ̃, -ɛ̃t] pp de **atteindre** ▷ adj (Méd): **être ~ de** to be suffering from ▷ nf attack; **hors d'~e** out of reach; **porter ~e à** to strike a blow at, undermine

atteler [atle] vt (cheval, bœufs) to hitch up; (wagons) to couple; **s'atteler à** (travail) to buckle down to

attelle [atɛl] nf splint

attenant, e [atnɑ̃, -ɑ̃t] adj: **~ (à)** adjoining

attendant [atɑ̃dɑ̃]: **en ~** adv (dans l'intervalle) meanwhile, in the meantime

attendre [atɑ̃dʀ] vt to wait for; (être destiné ou réservé à) to await, be in store for ▷ vi to wait; **je n'attends plus rien (de la vie)** I expect nothing more (from life); **attendez que je réfléchisse** wait while I think; **s'~ à (ce que)** (escompter) to expect (that); **je ne m'y attendais pas** I didn't expect that; **ce n'est pas ce à quoi je m'attendais** that's not what I expected; **attendez-moi, s'il vous plaît** wait for me, please; **~ un enfant** to be expecting a baby; **~ de pied ferme** to wait determinedly; **~ de faire/d'être** to wait until one does/is; **~ que** to wait until; **attendez qu'il vienne** wait until he comes; **~ qch de, ~ qch de** to expect sth of; **faire ~ qn** to keep sb waiting; **se faire ~** to keep people (ou us etc) waiting; **en attendant** adv voir **attendant**

attendrir [atɑ̃dʀiʀ] vt to move (to pity); (viande) to tenderize; **s'~ (sur)** to be moved ou touched (by)

attendrissant, e [atɑ̃dʀisɑ̃, -ɑ̃t] adj moving, touching

attendu, e [atɑ̃dy] pp de **attendre** ▷ adj (événement) long-awaited; (prévu) expected ▷ nm: **~s** reasons adduced for a judgment; **~ que** conj considering that, since

attentat [atɑ̃ta] nm (contre une personne) assassination attempt; (contre un bâtiment) attack; **~ à la bombe** bomb attack; **~ à la pudeur** (exhibitionnisme) indecent exposure no pl; (agression) indecent assault no pl; **~ suicide** suicide bombing

attente [atɑ̃t] nf wait; (espérance) expectation; **contre toute ~** contrary to (all) expectations

attenter [atɑ̃te]: **~ à** vt (liberté) to violate; **~ à la vie de qn** to make an attempt on sb's life; **~ à ses jours** to make an attempt on one's life

attentif, -ive [atɑ̃tif, -iv] adj (auditeur) attentive; (soin) scrupulous; (travail) careful; **~ à** paying attention to; (devoir) mindful of; **~ à faire** careful to do

attention [atɑ̃sjɔ̃] nf attention; (prévenance) attention, thoughtfulness no pl; **mériter ~** to be worthy of attention; **à l'~ de** for the attention of; **porter qch à l'~ de qn** to bring sth to sb's attention; **attirer l'~ de qn sur qch** to draw sb's attention to sth; **faire ~ (à)** to be careful (of); **faire ~ (à ce) que** to be ou make sure that; **~!** careful!, watch!, watch out!; **~ à la voiture!** watch out for that car!; **~, si vous ouvrez cette lettre** (sanction) just watch out, if you open that letter; **~, respectez les consignes de sécurité** be sure to observe the safety instructions

attentionné, e [atɑ̃sjɔne] adj thoughtful, considerate

atténuer [atenɥe] vt (douleur) to alleviate, ease; (couleurs) to soften; (diminuer) to lessen; (amoindrir) to mitigate the effects of; **s'atténuer** vi to ease; (violence etc) to abate

atterrer [ateʀe] vt to dismay, appal

atterrir [ateʀiʀ] vi to land

atterrissage [aterisaʒ] *nm* landing; ~ **sur le ventre/sans visibilité/forcé** belly/blind/ forced landing

attestation [atɛstasjɔ̃] *nf* certificate, testimonial; ~ **médicale** doctor's certificate

attester [atɛste] *vt* to testify to, vouch for; (*démontrer*) to attest, testify to; ~ **que** to testify that

attirail [atiraj] *nm* gear; (*péj*) paraphernalia

attirant, e [atirɑ̃, -ɑ̃t] *adj* attractive, appealing

attirer [atire] *vt* to attract; (*appâter*) to lure, entice; ~ **qn dans un coin/vers soi** to draw sb into a corner/towards one; ~ **l'attention de qn** to attract sb's attention; ~ **l'attention de qn sur qch** to draw sb's attention to sth; ~ **des ennuis à qn** to make trouble for sb; **s'~ des ennuis** to bring trouble upon o.s., get into trouble

attiser [atize] *vt* (*feu*) to poke (up), stir up; (*fig*) to fan the flame of, stir up

attitré, e [atitre] *adj* qualified; (*agréé*) accredited, appointed

attitude [atityd] *nf* attitude; (*position du corps*) bearing

attouchements [atuʃmɑ̃] *nmpl* touching *sg*; (*sexuels*) fondling *sg*, stroking *sg*

attraction [atraksjɔ̃] *nf* attraction; (*de cabaret, cirque*) number

attrait [atrɛ] *nm* appeal, attraction; (*plus fort*) lure; **attraits** *nmpl* attractions; **éprouver de l'~ pour** to be attracted to

attrape-nigaud [atrapnigo] *nm* con

attraper [atrape] *vt* to catch; (*habitude, amende*) to get, pick up; (*fam: duper*) to con, take in (*Brit*); **se faire ~** (*fam*) to be told off

attrayant, e [atrɛjɑ̃, -ɑ̃t] *adj* attractive

attribuer [atribɥe] *vt* (*prix*) to award; (*rôle, tâche*) to allocate, assign; (*imputer*): ~ **qch à** to attribute sth to, ascribe sth to, put sth down to; **s'attribuer** *vt* (*s'approprier*) to claim for o.s.

attribut [atriby] *nm* attribute; (*Ling*) complement

attrister [atriste] *vt* to sadden; **s'~ de qch** to be saddened by sth

attroupement [atrupmɑ̃] *nm* crowd, mob

attrouper [atrupe]: **s'attrouper** *vi* to gather

au [o] *prép voir* **à**

aubaine [obɛn] *nf* godsend; (*financière*) windfall; (*Comm*) bonanza

aube [ob] *nf* dawn, daybreak; (*Rel*) alb; **à l'~** at dawn *ou* daybreak; **à l'~ de** (*fig*) at the dawn of

aubépine [obepin] *nf* hawthorn

auberge [obɛrʒ] *nf* inn; ~ **de jeunesse** youth hostel

aubergine [obɛrʒin] *nf* aubergine (*Brit*), eggplant (*US*)

aubergiste [obɛrʒist] *nm/f* inn-keeper, hotel-keeper

aucun, e [okœ̃, -yn] *adj, pron* no; (*positif*) any ▷ *pron* none; (*positif*) any(one); **il n'y a ~ livre** there isn't any book, there is no book; **je n'en vois ~ qui ...** I can't see any which ..., I (can)

see none which ...; ~ **homme** no man; **sans ~ doute** without any doubt; **sans ~e hésitation** without hesitation; **plus qu'~ autre** more than any other; **il le fera mieux qu'~ de nous** he'll do it better than any of us; **plus qu'~ de ceux qui ...** more than any of those who ...; **en ~e façon** in no way at all; ~ **des deux** neither of the two; ~ **d'entre eux** none of them; **d'~s** (*certains*) some

aucunement [okynmɑ̃] *adv* in no way, not in the least

audace [odas] *nf* daring, boldness; (*péj*) audacity; **il a eu l'~ de ...** he had the audacity to ...; **vous ne manquez pas d'~!** you're not lacking in nerve *ou* cheek!

audacieux, -euse [odasjø, -øz] *adj* daring, bold

au-delà [od(ə)la] *adv* beyond ▷ *nm*: **l'~** the hereafter; ~ **de** *prép* beyond

au-dessous [odsu] *adv* underneath; below; ~ **de** *prép* under(neath), below; (*limite, somme etc*) below, under; (*dignité, condition*) below

au-dessus [odsy] *adv* above; ~ **de** *prép* above

au-devant [od(ə)vɑ̃]: ~ **de** *prép*: **aller ~ de** (*personne, danger*) to go (out) and meet; (*souhaits de qn*) to anticipate

audience [odjɑ̃s] *nf* audience; (*Jur: séance*) hearing; **trouver ~ auprès de** to arouse much interest among, get the (interested) attention of

audimat® [odimat] *nm* (*taux d'écoute*) ratings *pl*

audio-visuel, le [odjɔvizɥɛl] *adj* audio-visual ▷ *nm* (*équipement*) audio-visual aids *pl*; (*méthodes*) audio-visual methods *pl*; **l'~** radio and television

auditeur, -trice [oditœr, -tris] *nm/f* (*à la radio*) listener; (*à une conférence*) member of the audience, listener; ~ **libre** unregistered student (*attending lectures*), auditor (*US*)

audition [odisjɔ̃] *nf* (*ouïe, écoute*) hearing; (*Jur: de témoins*) examination; (*Mus, Théât*: *épreuve*) audition

auditoire [oditwar] *nm* audience

auge [oʒ] *nf* trough

augmentation [ogmɑ̃tasjɔ̃] *nf* (*action*) increasing; raising; (*résultat*) increase; ~ (**de salaire**) rise (in salary) (*Brit*), (pay) raise (*US*)

augmenter [ogmɑ̃te] *vt* to increase; (*salaire, prix*) to increase, raise, put up; (*employé*) to increase the salary of, give a (salary) rise (*Brit*) *ou* (pay) raise (*US*) to ▷ *vi* to increase; ~ **de poids/volume** to gain (in) weight/volume

augure [ogyr] *nm* soothsayer, oracle; **de bon/ mauvais ~** of good/ill omen

augurer [ogyre] *vt*: ~ **qch de** to foresee sth (coming) from *ou* out of; ~ **bien de** to augur well for

aujourd'hui [oʒurdɥi] *adv* today; ~ **en huit/ quinze** a week/two weeks today, a week/two weeks from now; **à dater** *ou* **partir d'~** from today('s date)

aumône [omon] *nf* alms *sg* (*pl inv*); **faire l'~**

(**à qn**) to give alms (to sb); **faire l'~ de qch à qn** (*fig*) to favour sb with sth

aumônier [omonje] *nm* chaplain

auparavant [oparavã] *adv* before(hand)

auprès [opRε]: **~ de** *prép* next to, close to; (*recourir, s'adresser*) to; (*en comparaison de*) compared with, next to; (*dans l'opinion de*) in the opinion of

auquel [okεl] *pron voir* **lequel**

aura *etc* [ɔRa] *vb voir* **avoir**

aurai *etc* [ɔRe] *vb voir* **avoir**

auréole [ɔReɔl] *nf* halo; (*tache*) ring

aurons *etc* [ɔRɔ̃] *vb voir* **avoir**

aurore [ɔRɔR] *nf* dawn, daybreak; **~ boréale** northern lights *pl*

ausculter [ɔskylte] *vt* to sound

aussi [osi] *adv* (*également*) also, too; (*de comparaison*) ▷ *conj* therefore, consequently; **~ fort que** as strong as; **moi ~** me too; **lui ~** (*sujet*) he too; (*objet*) him too; **~ bien que** (*de même que*) as well as

aussitôt [osito] *adv* straight away, immediately; **~ que** as soon as; **~ envoyé** as soon as it is (*ou* was) sent; **~ fait** no sooner done

austère [ostεR] *adj* austere; (*sévère*) stern

austral, e [ɔstRal] *adj* southern; **l'océan A~** the Antarctic Ocean; **les Terres A~es** Antarctica

Australie [ostRali] *nf*: **l'~** Australia

australien, ne [ɔstRaljẽ, -εn] *adj* Australian ▷ *nm/f*: **A~, ne** Australian

autant [otã] *adv* so much; **je ne savais pas que tu la détestais ~** I didn't know you hated her so much; (*comparatif*): **~ (que)** as much (as); (*nombre*) as many (as); **~ (de)** so much (*ou* many); as much (*ou* many); **n'importe qui aurait pu en faire ~** anyone could have done the same *ou* as much; **~ partir** we (*ou* you *etc*) may as well leave; **~ ne rien dire** best not say anything; **~ dire que ...** one might as well say that ...; **fort ~ que courageux** as strong as he is brave; **pour ~** for all that; **il n'est pas découragé pour ~** he isn't discouraged for all that; **pour ~ que** *conj* assuming, as long as; **d'~** *adv* accordingly, in proportion; **d'~ plus/mieux (que)** all the more/the better (since)

autel [otεl] *nm* altar

auteur [otœR] *nm* author; **l'~ de cette remarque** the person who said that; **droit d'~** copyright

authenticité [ɔtãtisite] *nf* authenticity

authentique [otãtik] *adj* authentic, genuine

auto [oto] *nf* car; **~s tamponneuses** bumper cars, dodgems

autobiographie [ɔtɔbjɔgRafi] *nf* autobiography

autobronzant [ɔtɔbRɔ̃zã] *nm* self-tanning cream (*or lotion etc*)

autobus [ɔtɔbys] *nm* bus

autocar [ɔtɔkaR] *nm* coach

autochtone [ɔtɔktɔn] *nm/f* native

autocollant, e [ɔtɔkɔlã, -ãt] *adj* self-adhesive; (*enveloppe*) self-seal ▷ *nm* sticker

auto-couchettes [ɔtɔkuʃεt] *adj inv*: **train ~** car sleeper train, motorail® train (*Brit*)

autocuiseur [ɔtɔkwizœR] *nm* (*Culin*) pressure cooker

autodéfense [ɔtɔdefãs] *nf* self-defence; **groupe d'~** vigilante committee

autodidacte [ɔtɔdidakt] *nm/f* self-taught person

auto-école [ɔtɔekɔl] *nf* driving school

autographe [ɔtɔgRaf] *nm* autograph

automate [ɔtɔmat] *nm* (*robot*) automaton; (*machine*) (automatic) machine

automatique [ɔtɔmatik] *adj* automatic ▷ *nm*: **l'~** (*Tél*) = direct dialling

automatiquement [ɔtɔmatikmã] *adv* automatically

automatiser [ɔtɔmatize] *vt* to automate

automne [ɔtɔn] *nm* autumn (*Brit*), fall (*US*)

automobile [ɔtɔmɔbil] *adj* motor *cpd* ▷ *nf* (motor) car; **l'~** motoring; (*industrie*) the car *ou* automobile (*US*) industry

automobiliste [ɔtɔmɔbilist] *nm/f* motorist

autonome [ɔtɔnɔm] *adj* autonomous

autonomie [ɔtɔnɔmi] *nf* autonomy; (*Pol*) self-government, autonomy; **~ de vol** range

autopsie [ɔtɔpsi] *nf* post-mortem (examination), autopsy

autoradio [otoRadjo] *nf* car radio

autorisation [ɔtɔRizasjɔ̃] *nf* permission, authorization; (*papiers*) permit; **donner à qn l'~ de** to give sb permission to, authorize sb to; **avoir l'~ de faire** to be allowed *ou* have permission to do, be authorized to do

autorisé, e [ɔtɔRize] *adj* (*opinion, sources*) authoritative; (*permis*): **~ à faire** authorized *ou* permitted to do; **dans les milieux ~s** in official circles

autoriser [ɔtɔRize] *vt* to give permission for, authorize; (*fig*) to allow (of), sanction; **~ qn à faire** to give permission to sb to do, authorize sb to do

autoritaire [ɔtɔRitεR] *adj* authoritarian

autorité [ɔtɔRite] *nf* authority; **faire ~** to be authoritative; **~s constituées** constitutional authorities

autoroute [otoRut] *nf* motorway (*Brit*), expressway (*US*); **~ de l'information** (*Inform*) information superhighway

---

▨ **AUTOROUTE**

▨ Motorways in France, indicated by blue
▨ road signs with the letter A followed by a
▨ number, are toll roads. The speed limit is
▨ 130 km/h (110 km/h when it is raining).
▨ At the tollgate, the lanes marked 'réservé'
▨ and with an orange 't' are reserved for
▨ people who subscribe to 'télépéage', an
▨ electronic payment system.

auto-stop [otostɔp] nm: l'~ hitch-hiking; **faire de l'~** to hitch-hike; **prendre qn en ~** to give sb a lift

auto-stoppeur, -euse [ɔtostɔpœʀ, -øz] nm/f hitch-hiker, hitcher (Brit)

autour [otuʀ] adv around; **~ de** prép around; (environ) around, about; **tout ~** adv all around

 MOT-CLÉ

autre [otʀ] adj 1 (différent) other, different; **je préférerais un autre verre** I'd prefer another ou a different glass; **d'autres verres** different glasses; **se sentir autre** to feel different; **la difficulté est autre** the difficulty is ou lies elsewhere

2 (supplémentaire) other; **je voudrais un autre verre d'eau** I'd like another glass of water

3: **autre chose** something else; **autre part** somewhere else; **d'autre part** on the other hand

▷ pron 1: **un autre** another (one); **nous/vous autres** us/you; **d'autres** others; **l'autre** the other (one); **les autres** the others; (autrui) others; **l'un et l'autre** both of them; **ni l'un ni l'autre** neither of them; **se détester l'un l'autre/les uns les autres** to hate each other ou one another; **d'une semaine/minute à l'autre** from one week/minute ou moment to the next; (incessamment) any week/minute ou moment now; **de temps à autre** from time to time; **entre autres** (personnes) among others; (choses) among other things

2 (expressions): **j'en ai vu d'autres** I've seen worse; **à d'autres!** pull the other one!

autrefois [otʀəfwa] adv in the past

autrement [otʀəmɑ̃] adv differently; (d'une manière différente) in another way; (sinon) otherwise; **je n'ai pas pu faire ~** I couldn't do anything else, I couldn't do otherwise; **~ dit** in other words; (c'est-à-dire) that is to say

Autriche [otʀiʃ] nf: l'~ Austria

autrichien, ne [otʀiʃjɛ̃, -ɛn] adj Austrian ▷ nm/f: A~, ne Austrian

autruche [otʀyʃ] nf ostrich; **faire l'~** (fig) to bury one's head in the sand

autrui [otʀɥi] pron others

auvent [ovɑ̃] nm canopy

aux [o] prép voir **à**

auxiliaire [oksiljɛʀ] adj, nm/f auxiliary

auxquels, auxquelles [okɛl] pron voir **lequel**

avachi, e [avaʃi] adj limp, flabby; (chaussure, vêtement) out-of-shape; (personne): **~ sur qch** slumped on ou across sth

aval [aval] nm (accord) endorsement, backing; (Géo): **en ~** downstream, downriver; (sur une pente) downhill; **en ~ de** downstream ou downriver from; downhill from

avalanche [avalɑ̃ʃ] nf avalanche; **~ poudreuse** powder snow avalanche

avaler [avale] vt to swallow

avance [avɑ̃s] nf (de troupes etc) advance; (progrès) progress; (d'argent) advance; (opposé à retard) lead; being ahead of schedule; **avances** nfpl overtures; (amoureuses) advances; **une ~ de 300 m/4 h** (Sport) a 300 m/4 hour lead; **(être) en ~** (to be) early; (sur un programme) (to be) ahead of schedule; **on n'est pas en ~!** we're kind of late!; **être en ~ sur qn** to be ahead of sb; **d'~, à l'~, par ~** in advance; **~ (du) papier** (Inform) paper advance

avancé, e [avɑ̃se] adj advanced; (travail etc) well on, well under way; (fruit, fromage) overripe ▷ nf projection; overhang; **il est ~ pour son âge** he is advanced for his age

avancement [avɑ̃smɑ̃] nm (professionnel) promotion; (de travaux) progress

avancer [avɑ̃se] vi to move forward, advance; (projet, travail) to make progress; (être en saillie) to overhang; to project; (montre, réveil) to be fast; (: d'habitude) to gain ▷ vt to move forward, advance; (argent) to advance; (montre, pendule) to put forward; (faire progresser: travail etc) to advance, move on; **s'avancer** vi to move forward, advance; (fig) to commit o.s.; (faire saillie) to overhang; to project; **j'avance (d'une heure)** I'm (an hour) fast

avant [avɑ̃] prép before ▷ adv: **trop/plus ~** too far/further forward ▷ adj inv: **siège/roue ~** front seat/wheel ▷ nm (d'un véhicule, bâtiment) front; (Sport: joueur) forward; **~ qu'il parte/de partir** before he leaves/leaving; **~ qu'il (ne) pleuve** before it rains (ou rained); **~ tout** (surtout) above all; (à l'avant) in the front; à l'~ (dans un véhicule) in (the) front; **en ~** adv (se pencher, tomber) forward(s); **partir en ~** to go on ahead; **en ~ de** prép in front of; **aller de l'~** to steam ahead (fig), make good progress

avantage [avɑ̃taʒ] nm advantage; (Tennis): **~ service/dehors** advantage ou van (Brit) ou ad (US) in/out; **tirer ~ de** to take advantage of; **vous auriez à faire** you would be well-advised to do, it would be to your advantage to do; **à l'~ de qn** to sb's advantage; **être à son ~** to be at one's best; **~s en nature** benefits in kind; **~s sociaux** fringe benefits

avantager [avɑ̃taʒe] vt (favoriser) to favour; (embellir) to flatter

avantageux, -euse [avɑ̃taʒø, -øz] adj (prix) attractive; (intéressant) attractively priced; (portrait, coiffure) flattering; **conditions avantageuses** favourable terms

avant-bras [avɑ̃bʀa] nm inv forearm

avant-coureur [avɑ̃kuʀœʀ] adj inv (bruit etc) precursory; **signe ~** advance indication ou sign

avant-dernier, -ière [avɑ̃dɛʀnje, -jɛʀ] adj, nm/f next to last, last but one

avant-goût [avɑ̃gu] nm foretaste

avant-hier [avɑ̃tjɛʀ] adv the day before yesterday

avant-première [avɑ̃pʀəmjɛʀ] nf (de film) preview; **en ~** as a preview, in a preview showing

avant-projet [avɑ̃pʀɔʒɛ] nm preliminary draft

avant-propos [avɑ̃pʀɔpo] nm foreword

avant-veille [avɑ̃vɛj] nf: **l'~** two days before

avare [avaʀ] adj miserly, avaricious ▷ nm/f miser; **~ de compliments** stingy ou sparing with one's compliments

avarié, e [avaʀje] adj (viande, fruits) rotting, going off (Brit); (Navig: navire) damaged

avaries [avaʀi] nfpl (Navig) damage sg

avec [avɛk] prép with; (à l'égard de) to(wards), with ▷ adv (fam) with it (ou him etc); **~ habileté/lenteur** skilfully/slowly; **~ eux/ces maladies** with them/these diseases; **~ ça** (malgré ça) for all that; **et ~ ça?** (dans un magasin) anything ou something else?

avenant, e [avnɑ̃, -ɑ̃t] adj pleasant ▷ nm (Assurances) additional clause; **à l'~** adv in keeping

avènement [avɛnmɑ̃] nm (d'un roi) accession, succession; (d'un changement) advent; (d'une politique, idée) coming

avenir [avniʀ] nm: **l'~** the future; **à l'~** in future; **sans ~** with no future, without a future; **carrière/politicien d'~** career/ politician with prospects ou a future

aventure [avɑ̃tyʀ] nf: **l'~** adventure; **une ~** an adventure; (amoureuse) an affair; **partir à l'~** to go off in search of adventure; (au hasard) to go where one's fancy takes one; **roman/film d'~** adventure story/film

aventurer [avɑ̃tyʀe] vt (somme, réputation, vie) to stake; (remarque, opinion) to venture; **s'aventurer** vi to venture; **s'~ à faire qch** to venture into sth

aventureux, -euse [avɑ̃tyʀø, -øz] adj adventurous, venturesome; (projet) risky, chancy

avenue [avny] nf avenue

avérer [aveʀe]: **s'avérer** vr: **s'~ faux/coûteux** to prove (to be) wrong/expensive

averse [avɛʀs] nf shower

averti, e [avɛʀti] adj (well-)informed

avertir [avɛʀtiʀ] vt: **~ qn (de qch/que)** to warn sb (of sth/that); (renseigner) to inform sb (of sth/that); **~ qn de ne pas faire qch** to warn sb not to do sth

avertissement [avɛʀtismɑ̃] nm warning

avertisseur [avɛʀtisœʀ] nm horn, siren; **~ (d'incendie)** (fire) alarm

aveu, x [avø] nm confession; **passer aux ~x** to make a confession; **de l'~ de** according to

aveugle [avœgl] adj blind ▷ nm/f blind person; **les ~s** the blind; **test en (double) ~** (double) blind test

aveuglément [avœglemɑ̃] adv blindly

aveugler [avœgle] vt to blind

aviateur, -trice [avjatœʀ, -tʀis] nm/f aviator, pilot

aviation [avjasjɔ̃] nf (secteur commercial) aviation; (sport, métier de pilote) flying; (Mil) air force; **terrain d'~** airfield; **~ de chasse** fighter force

avide [avid] adj eager; (péj) greedy, grasping; **~ de** (sang etc) thirsting for; **~ d'honneurs/ d'argent** greedy for honours/money; **~ de connaître/d'apprendre** eager to know/ learn

avilir [aviliʀ] vt to debase

avion [avjɔ̃] nm (aero)plane (Brit), (air)plane (US); **aller (quelque part) en ~** to go (somewhere) by plane, fly (somewhere); **par ~** by airmail; **~ de chasse** fighter; **~ de ligne** airliner; **~ à réaction** jet (plane)

aviron [aviʀɔ̃] nm oar; (sport): **l'~** rowing

avis [avi] nm opinion; (notification) notice; (Comm): **~ de crédit/débit** credit/debit advice; **à mon ~** in my opinion; **je suis de votre ~** I share your opinion, I am of your opinion; **être d'~ que** to be of the opinion that; **changer d'~** to change one's mind; **sauf ~ contraire** unless you hear to the contrary; **sans ~ préalable** without notice; **jusqu'à nouvel ~** until further notice; **~ de décès** death announcement

avisé, e [avize] adj sensible, wise; **être bien/ mal ~ de faire** to be well-/ill-advised to do

aviser [avize] vt (voir) to notice, catch sight of; (informer): **~ qn de/que** to advise ou inform ou notify sb of/that ▷ vi to think about things, assess the situation; **nous ~ons sur place** we'll work something out once we're there; **s'~ de qch/que** to become suddenly aware of sth/that; **s'~ de faire** to take it into one's head to do

avocat, e [avɔka, -at] nm/f (Jur) ≈ barrister (Brit), lawyer; (fig) advocate, champion ▷ nm (Culin) avocado (pear); **se faire l'~ du diable** to be the devil's advocate; **l'~ de la défense/ partie civile** the counsel for the defence/ plaintiff; **~ d'affaires** business lawyer; **~ général** assistant public prosecutor

avoine [avwan] nf oats pl

⊙ **MOT-CLÉ**

avoir [avwaʀ] nm assets pl, resources pl; (Comm) credit; **avoir fiscal** tax credit
▷ vt **1** (posséder) to have; **elle a deux enfants/ une belle maison** she has (got) two children/a lovely house; **il a les yeux bleus** he has (got) blue eyes; **vous avez du sel?** do you have any salt?; **avoir du courage/de la patience** to be brave/patient

2 (éprouver): **qu'est-ce que tu as?, qu'as-tu?** what's wrong?, what's the matter?; **avoir de la peine** to be ou feel sad; voir aussi **faim, peur** etc

3 (âge, dimensions) to be; **il a 3 ans** he is 3 (years old); **le mur a 3 mètres de haut** the wall is 3 metres high

4 (*fam: duper*) to do, have; **on vous a eu!** you've been done *ou* had!; (*fait une plaisanterie*) we *ou* they had you there

5: **en avoir contre qn** to have a grudge against sb; **en avoir assez** to be fed up; **j'en ai pour une demi-heure** it'll take me half an hour; **n'avoir que faire de qch** to have no use for sth

6 (*obtenir, attraper*) to get; **j'ai réussi à avoir mon train** I managed to get *ou* catch my train; **j'ai réussi à avoir le renseignement qu'il me fallait** I managed to get (hold of) the information I needed

▷ *vb aux* **1** to have; **avoir mangé/dormi** to have eaten/slept; **hier je n'ai pas mangé** I didn't eat yesterday

2 (*avoir +à +infinitif*): **avoir à faire qch** to have to do sth; **vous n'avez qu'à lui demander** you only have to ask him; **tu n'as pas à me poser des questions** it's not for you to ask me questions

▷ *vb impers* **1**: **il y a** (+*singulier*) there is; (+*pluriel*) there are; **il y avait du café/des gâteaux** there was coffee/there were cakes; **qu'y-a-t-il?, qu'est-ce qu'il y a?** what's the matter?, what is it?; **il doit y avoir une explication** there must be an explanation; **il n'y a qu'à ...** we (*ou* you *etc*) will just have to ...; **il ne peut y en avoir qu'un** there can only be one

2 (*temporel*): **il y a 10 ans** 10 years ago; **il y a 10 ans/longtemps que je le connais** I've known him for 10 years/a long time; **il y a 10 ans qu'il est arrivé** it's 10 years since he arrived

avoisiner [avwazine] *vt* to be near *ou* close to; (*fig*) to border on *ou* verge on

avortement [avɔrtəmɑ̃] *nm* abortion

avorter [avɔrte] *vi* (*Méd*) to have an abortion; (*fig*) to fail; **faire ~** to abort; **se faire ~** to have an abortion

avoué, e [avwe] *adj* avowed ▷ *nm* (*Jur*) ≈ solicitor (*Brit*), lawyer

avouer [avwe] *vt* (*crime, défaut*) to confess (to) ▷ *vi* (*se confesser*) to confess; (*admettre*) to admit; **~ avoir fait/que** to admit *ou* confess to having done/that; **~ que oui/non** to admit that that is so/not so

avril [avril] *nm* April; *voir aussi* **juillet**

axe [aks] *nm* axis (*pl* axes); (*de roue etc*) axle; **dans l'~ de** directly in line with; (*fig*) main line; **~ routier** trunk road (*Brit*), main road, highway (*US*)

axer [akse] *vt*: **~ qch sur** to centre sth on

ayons *etc* [ɛjɔ̃] *vb voir* **avoir**

azote [azɔt] *nm* nitrogen

baba [baba] *adj inv*: **en être ~** (*fam*) to be flabbergasted ▷ *nm*: **~ au rhum** rum baba

babines [babin] *nfpl* chops

babiole [babjɔl] *nf* (*bibelot*) trinket; (*vétille*) trifle

bâbord [babɔr] *nm*: **à** *ou* **par ~** to port, on the port side

baby-foot [babifut] *nm inv* table football

baby-sitting [babisitiŋ] *nm* baby-sitting; **faire du ~** to baby-sit

bac [bak] *nm* (*Scol*) = **baccalauréat**; (*bateau*) ferry; (*récipient*) tub; (*: Photo etc*) tray; (*: Industrie*) tank; **~ à glace** ice-tray; **~ à légumes** vegetable compartment *ou* rack

baccalauréat [bakalɔrea] *nm* ≈ A-levels *pl* (*Brit*), ≈ high school diploma (*US*); *see note*

BACCALAURÉAT

The *baccalauréat* or "bac" is the school-leaving examination taken at a French "lycée" at the age of 18; it marks the end of seven years' secondary education. Several subject combinations are available, although in all cases a broad range is studied. Successful candidates can go on to university, if they so wish.

bâche [baʃ] *nf* tarpaulin, canvas sheet

bachelier, -ière [baʃəlje, -jɛr] *nm/f* holder of the *baccalauréat*

bâcler [bakle] *vt* to botch (up)

badaud, e [bado, -od] *nm/f* idle onlooker
badigeonner [badiʒɔne] *vt* to distemper; to
colourwash; (*péj: barbouiller*) to daub; (*Méd*) to
paint
badiner [badine] *vi*: **~ avec qch** to treat sth
lightly; **ne pas ~ avec qch** not to trifle with sth
baffe [baf] *nf* (*fam*) slap, clout
baffle [bafl] *nm* baffle (board)
bafouer [bafwe] *vt* to deride, ridicule
bafouiller [bafuje] *vi, vt* to stammer
bâfrer [bafʀe] *vi, vt* to guzzle, gobble
bagage [bagaʒ] *nm*: **~s** luggage *sg*, baggage *sg*;
(*connaissances*) background, knowledge; **faire
ses ~s** to pack (one's bags); **~ littéraire** (stock
of) literary knowledge; **~ à main** hand-
luggage
bagarre [bagaʀ] *nf* fight, brawl; **il aime la ~**
he loves a fight, he likes fighting
bagarrer [bagaʀe]: **se bagarrer** *vi* to (have a)
fight
bagatelle [bagatɛl] *nf* trifle, trifling sum (*ou*
matter)
bagne [baɲ] *nm* penal colony; **c'est le ~** (*fig*)
it's forced labour
bagnole [baɲɔl] *nf* (*fam*) car, wheels *pl* (*Brit*)
bagout [bagu] *nm* glibness; **avoir du ~** to
have the gift of the gab
bague [bag] *nf* ring; **~ de fiançailles**
engagement ring; **~ de serrage** clip
baguette [bagɛt] *nf* stick; (*cuisine chinoise*)
chopstick; (*de chef d'orchestre*) baton; (*pain*) stick
of (French) bread; (*Constr: moulure*) beading;
mener qn à la ~ to rule sb with a rod of iron;
~ magique magic wand; **~ de sourcier**
divining rod; **~ de tambour** drumstick
baie [bɛ] *nf* (*Géo*) bay; (*fruit*) berry; **~ (vitrée)**
picture window
baignade [bɛɲad] *nf* (*action*) bathing; (*bain*)
bathe; (*endroit*) bathing place; **"~ interdite"**
"no bathing"
baigner [bɛɲe] *vt* (*bébé*) to bath ▷ *vi*: **~ dans
son sang** to lie in a pool of blood; **~ dans la
brume** to be shrouded in mist; **se baigner** *vi*
to go swimming *ou* bathing; (*dans une
baignoire*) to have a bath; **ça baigne!** (*fam*)
everything's great!
baignoire [bɛɲwaʀ] *nf* bath (tub); (*Théât*)
ground-floor box
bail, baux [baj, bo] *nm* lease; **donner** *ou*
prendre qch à ~ to lease sth
bâillement [bajmã] *nm* yawn
bâiller [baje] *vi* to yawn; (*être ouvert*) to gape
bâillonner [bajɔne] *vt* to gag
bain [bɛ] *nm* (*dans une baignoire, Photo, Tech*)
bath; (*dans la mer, une piscine*) swim; **costume
de ~** bathing costume (*Brit*), swimsuit;
prendre un ~ to have a bath; **se mettre
dans le ~** (*fig*) to get into (the way of) it *ou*
things; **~ de bouche** mouthwash; **~ de foule**
walkabout; **~ moussant** bubble bath; **~ de
pieds** footbath; (*au bord de la mer*) paddle; **~ de
siège** hip bath; **~ de soleil** sunbathing *no pl*;

prendre un ~ de soleil to sunbathe; **~s de
mer** sea bathing *sg*; **~s(-douches)
municipaux** public baths
bain-marie (*pl* **bains-marie**) [bɛmaʀi] *nm*
double boiler; **faire chauffer au ~** (*boîte etc*)
to immerse in boiling water
baiser [beze] *nm* kiss ▷ *vt* (*main, front*) to kiss;
(*fam!*) to screw (!)
baisse [bes] *nf* fall, drop; (*Comm*): **"~ sur la
viande"** "meat prices down"; **en ~** (*cours,
action*) falling; **à la ~** downwards
baisser [bese] *vt* to lower; (*radio, chauffage*) to
turn down; (*Auto: phares*) to dip (*Brit*), lower
(*US*) ▷ *vi* to fall, drop, go down; (*vue, santé*) to
fail, dwindle; **se baisser** *vi* to bend down
bal [bal] *nm* dance; (*grande soirée*) ball;
~ costumé/masqué fancy-dress/masked
ball; **~ musette** dance (*with accordion
accompaniment*)
balade [balad] (*fam*) *nf* (*à pied*) walk, stroll;
(*en voiture*) drive; **faire une ~** to go for a walk
ou stroll; to go for a drive
balader [balade] (*fam*) *vt* (*traîner*) to trail
around; **se balader** *vi* to go for a walk *ou*
stroll; to go for a drive
baladeur [baladœʀ] *nm* personal stereo,
Walkman®; **~ numérique** MP3 player
balafre [balafʀ] *nf* gash, slash; (*cicatrice*) scar
balai [balɛ] *nm* broom, brush; (*Auto: de essuie-
glace*) blade; (*Mus: de batterie etc*) brush;
donner un coup de ~ to give the floor a
sweep; **~ mécanique** carpet sweeper
balai-brosse (*pl* **balais-brosses**) [balɛbʀɔs]
nm (long-handled) scrubbing brush
balance [balãs] *nf* (*à plateaux*) scales *pl*; (*de
précision*) balance; (*Comm, Pol*): **~ des comptes
ou paiements** balance of payments; (*signe*):
la B~ Libra, the Scales; **être de la B~** to be
Libra; **~ commerciale** balance of trade; **~ des
forces** balance of power; **~ romaine**
steelyard
balancer [balãse] *vt* to swing; (*lancer*) to
fling, chuck; (*renvoyer, jeter*) to chuck out ▷ *vi*
to swing; **se balancer** *vi* to swing; (*bateau*)
to rock; (*branche*) to sway; **se ~ de qch** (*fam*)
not to give a toss about sth
balançoire [balãswaʀ] *nf* swing; (*sur pivot*)
seesaw
balayer [baleje] *vt* (*feuilles etc*) to sweep up,
brush up; (*pièce, cour*) to sweep; (*chasser*) to
sweep away *ou* aside; (*radar*) to scan; (: *phares*)
to sweep across
balayeur, -euse [balɛjœʀ, -øz] *nm/f* road
sweeper ▷ *nf* (*engin*) road sweeper
balbutier [balbysje] *vi, vt* to stammer
balcon [balkɔ̃] *nm* balcony; (*Théât*) dress
circle
Bâle [bal] *n* Basle *ou* Basel
Baléares [baleaʀ] *nfpl*: **les ~** the Balearic
Islands, the Balearics
baleine [balɛn] *nf* whale; (*de parapluie*) rib;
(*de corset*) bone

balise [baliz] *nf* (*Navig*) beacon, (marker) buoy; (*Aviat*) runway light, beacon; (*Auto, Ski*) sign, marker

baliser [balize] *vt* to mark out (with beacons *ou* lights *etc*)

balivernes [balivɛʀn] *nfpl* twaddle *sg* (*Brit*), nonsense *sg*

ballant, e [balɑ̃, -ɑ̃t] *adj* dangling

balle [bal] *nf* (*de fusil*) bullet; (*de sport*) ball; (*du blé*) chaff; (*paquet*) bale; (*fam: franc*) franc; ~ **perdue** stray bullet

ballerine [bal(ə)ʀin] *nf* (*danseuse*) ballet dancer; (*chaussure*) pump, ballet shoe

ballet [balɛ] *nm* ballet; (*fig*): ~ **diplomatique** diplomatic to-ings and fro-ings

ballon [balɔ̃] *nm* (*de sport*) ball; (*jouet, Aviat, de bande dessinée*) balloon; (*de vin*) glass; (*d'essai* (*météorologique*) pilot balloon; (*fig*) feeler(s); ~ **de football** football; ~ **d'oxygène** oxygen bottle

ballot [balo] *nm* bundle; (*péj*) nitwit

ballottage [balɔtaʒ] *nm* (*Pol*) second ballot

ballotter [balɔte] *vi* to roll around; (*bateau etc*) to toss ▷ *vt* to shake *ou* throw about; to toss; **être ballotté entre** (*fig*) to be shunted between; (: *indécis*) to be torn between

balnéaire [balneɛʀ] *adj* seaside *cpd*; **station** ~ seaside resort

balourd, e [baluʀ, -uʀd] *adj* clumsy ▷ *nm/f* clodhopper

balustrade [balystʀad] *nf* railings *pl*, handrail

bambin [bɑ̃bɛ̃] *nm* little child

bambou [bɑ̃bu] *nm* bamboo

ban [bɑ̃] *nm* round of applause, cheer; **être/mettre au ~ de** to be outlawed/to outlaw from; **le ~ et l'arrière-ban de sa famille** every last one of his relatives; ~**s (de mariage)** banns, bans

banal, e [banal] *adj* banal, commonplace; (*péj*) trite; **four/moulin** ~ village oven/mill

banalité [banalite] *nf* banality; (*remarque*) truism, trite remark

banane [banan] *nf* banana; (*sac*) waist-bag, bum-bag

banc [bɑ̃] *nm* seat, bench; (*de poissons*) shoal; ~ **des accusés** dock; ~ **d'essai** (*fig*) testing ground; ~ **de sable** sandbank; ~ **des témoins** witness box; ~ **de touche** dugout

bancaire [bɑ̃kɛʀ] *adj* banking; (*chèque, carte*) bank *cpd*

bancal, e [bɑ̃kal] *adj* wobbly; (*personne*) bow-legged; (*fig: projet*) shaky

bandage [bɑ̃daʒ] *nm* bandaging; (*pansement*) bandage; ~ **herniaire** truss

bande [bɑ̃d] *nf* (*de tissu etc*) strip; (*Méd*) bandage; (*motif, dessin*) stripe; (*Ciné*) film; (*Radio, groupe*) band; (*péj*): **une** ~ **de** a bunch *ou* crowd of; **par la** ~ in a roundabout way; **donner de la** ~ to list; **faire** ~ **à part** to keep to o.s.; ~ **dessinée (BD)** strip cartoon (*Brit*), comic strip; ~ **magnétique** magnetic tape;

~ **passante** (*Inform*) bandwidth; ~ **perforée** punched tape; ~ **de roulement** (*de pneu*) tread; ~ **sonore** sound track; ~ **de terre** strip of land; ~ **Velpeau**® (*Méd*) crêpe bandage

bande-annonce (*pl* **bandes-annonces**) [bɑ̃danɔ̃s] *nf* (*Ciné*) trailer

bandeau, x [bɑ̃do] *nm* headband; (*sur les yeux*) blindfold; (*Méd*) head bandage

bander [bɑ̃de] *vt* (*blessure*) to bandage; (*muscle*) to tense; (*arc*) to bend ▷ *vi* (*fam!*) to have a hard on (!); ~ **les yeux à qn** to blindfold sb

banderole [bɑ̃dʀɔl] *nf* banderole; (*dans un défilé etc*) streamer

bandit [bɑ̃di] *nm* bandit

banditisme [bɑ̃ditism] *nm* violent crime, armed robberies *pl*

bandoulière [bɑ̃duljɛʀ] *nf*: **en** ~ (slung *ou* worn) across the shoulder

Bangladesh [bɑ̃glade∫] *nm*: **le** ~ Bangladesh

banlieue [bɑ̃ljø] *nf* suburbs *pl*; **quartiers de** ~ suburban areas; **trains de** ~ commuter trains

banlieusard, e [bɑ̃ljøzaʀ, -aʀd] *nm/f* suburbanite

bannière [banjɛʀ] *nf* banner

bannir [baniʀ] *vt* to banish

banque [bɑ̃k] *nf* bank; (*activités*) banking; ~ **des yeux/du sang** eye/blood bank; ~ **d'affaires** merchant bank; ~ **de dépôt** deposit bank; ~ **de données** (*Inform*) data bank; ~ **d'émission** bank of issue

banqueroute [bɑ̃kʀut] *nf* bankruptcy

banquet [bɑ̃kɛ] *nm* (*de club*) dinner; (*de noces*) reception; (*d'apparat*) banquet

banquette [bɑ̃kɛt] *nf* seat

banquier [bɑ̃kje] *nm* banker

banquise [bɑ̃kiz] *nf* ice field

baptême [batɛm] *nm* (*sacrement*) baptism; (*cérémonie*) christening; baptism; (*d'un navire*) launching; (*d'une cloche*) consecration, dedication; ~ **de l'air** first flight

baptiser [batize] *vt* to christen; to baptize; to launch; to consecrate, dedicate

baquet [bakɛ] *nm* tub, bucket

bar [baʀ] *nm* bar; (*poisson*) bass

baraque [baʀak] *nf* shed; (*fam*) house; ~ **foraine** fairground stand

baraqué, e [baʀake] (*fam*) *adj* well-built, hefty

baraquements [baʀakmɑ̃] *nmpl* huts (*for refugees, workers etc*)

baratin [baʀatɛ̃] *nm* (*fam*) smooth talk, patter

baratiner [baʀatine] *vt* to chat up

barbant, e [baʀbɑ̃, -ɑ̃t] *adj* (*fam*) deadly (boring)

barbare [baʀbaʀ] *adj* barbaric ▷ *nm/f* barbarian

barbarie [baʀbaʀi] *nf* barbarism; (*cruauté*) barbarity

barbe [baʀb] *nf* beard; (**au nez et**) **à la** ~ **de qn** (*fig*) under sb's very nose; **la** ~**!** (*fam*) damn it!; **quelle** ~**!** (*fam*) what a drag *ou* bore!; ~ **à papa** candy-floss (*Brit*), cotton candy (*US*)

barbelé [barbəle] *adj, nm*: **(fil de fer)** ~ barbed wire *no pl*
barber [barbe] *vt (fam)* to bore stiff
barbiturique [barbityrik] *nm* barbiturate
barboter [barbɔte] *vi* to paddle, dabble ▷ *vt (fam)* to filch
barbouiller [barbuje] *vt* to daub; *(péj: écrire, dessiner)* to scribble; **avoir l'estomac barbouillé** to feel queasy *ou* sick
barbu, e [barby] *adj* bearded
barda [barda] *nm (fam)* kit, gear
barder [barde] *vt (Culin: rôti, volaille)* to bard ▷ *vi (fam)*: **ça va ~** sparks will fly
barème [barɛm] *nm (Scol)* scale; *(liste)* table; **~ des salaires** salary scale
baril [baril)] *nm (tonneau)* barrel; *(de poudre)* keg
bariolé, e [barjɔle] *adj* many-coloured, rainbow-coloured
baromètre [barɔmɛtr] *nm* barometer; **~ anéroïde** aneroid barometer
baron [barɔ̃] *nm* baron
baronne [barɔn] *nf* baroness
baroque [barɔk] *adj (Art)* baroque; *(fig)* weird
barque [bark] *nf* small boat
barquette [barkɛt] *nf* small boat-shaped tart; *(récipient: en aluminium)* tub; *(: en bois)* basket; *(pour repas)* tray; *(pour fruits)* punnet
barrage [baraʒ] *nm* dam; *(sur route)* roadblock, barricade; **~ de police** police roadblock
barre [bar] *nf (de fer etc)* rod; *(Navig)* helm; *(écrite)* line, stroke; *(Danse)* barre; *(niveau)*: **la livre a franchi la ~ des 1,70 euros** the pound has broken the 1.70 euros barrier; *(Jur)*: **comparaître à la ~** to appear as a witness; **être à** *ou* **tenir la ~** *(Navig)* to be at the helm; **coup de ~** *(fig)*: **c'est le coup de ~!** it's daylight robbery!; **j'ai le coup de ~!** I'm all in!; **~ fixe** *(Gym)* horizontal bar; **~ de mesure** *(Mus)* bar line; **~ à mine** crowbar; **~s parallèles/asymétriques** *(Gym)* parallel/asymmetric bars
barreau, x [baro] *nm* bar; *(Jur)*: **le ~** the Bar
barrer [bare] *vt (route etc)* to block; *(mot)* to cross out; *(chèque)* to cross *(Brit)*; *(Navig)* to steer; **se barrer** *vi (fam)* to clear off
barrette [barɛt] *nf (pour cheveux)* (hair) slide *(Brit) ou* clip *(US)*; *(broche)* brooch
barricader [barikade] *vt* to barricade; **se barricader** *vi*: **se ~ chez soi** *(fig)* to lock o.s. in
barrière [barjɛr] *nf* fence; *(obstacle)* barrier; *(porte)* gate; **la Grande B~** the Great Barrier Reef; **~ de dégel** *(Admin: on roadsigns)* no heavy vehicles — road liable to subsidence due to thaw; **~s douanières** trade barriers
barrique [barik] *nf* barrel, cask
bar-tabac [bartaba] *nm* bar *(which sells tobacco and stamps)*
bas, basse [ba, bas] *adj* low; *(action)* low, ignoble ▷ *nm (vêtement)* stocking; *(partie inférieure)*: **le ~ de** the lower part *ou* foot *ou* bottom of ▷ *nf (Mus)* bass ▷ *adv* low; *(parler)* softly; **plus ~** lower down; more softly; *(dans un texte)* further on, below; **la tête ~e** with lowered head; *(fig)* with head hung low; **avoir la vue ~e** to be short-sighted; **au ~ mot** at the lowest estimate; **enfant en ~ âge** infant, young child; **en ~** down below; *(d'une liste, d'un mur etc)* at *(ou* to) the bottom; *(dans une maison)* downstairs; **en ~ de** at the bottom of; **de ~ en haut** upwards; from the bottom to the top; **des hauts et des ~** ups and downs; **un ~ de laine** *(fam: économies)* money under the mattress *(fig)*; **mettre ~** *vi (animal)* to give birth; **à ~ la dictature!** down with dictatorship!; **~ morceaux** *(viande)* cheap cuts
basané, e [bazane] *adj (teint)* tanned, bronzed; *(foncé: péj)* swarthy
bas-côté [bakote] *nm (de route)* verge *(Brit)*, shoulder *(US)*; *(d'église)* (side) aisle
bascule [baskyl] *nf*: **(jeu de)** ~ seesaw; **(balance à)** ~ scales *pl*; **fauteuil à** ~ rocking chair; **système à** ~ tip-over device; rocker device
basculer [baskyle] *vi* to fall over, topple (over); *(benne)* to tip up ▷ *vt (aussi:* **faire ~**) to topple over; *(contenu)* to tip out; *(benne)* tip up
base [baz] *nf* base; *(Pol)*: **la ~** the rank and file, the grass roots; *(fondement, principe)* basis *(pl* bases); **jeter les ~s de** to lay the foundations of; **à la ~ de** *(fig)* at the root of; **sur la ~ de** *(fig)* on the basis of; **de ~** basic; **à ~ de café** *etc* coffee *etc* based; **~ de données** *(Inform)* database; **~ de lancement** launching site
baser [baze] *vt*: **~ qch sur** to base sth on; **se ~ sur** *(données, preuves)* to base one's argument on; **être basé à/dans** *(Mil)* to be based at/in
bas-fond [bafɔ̃] *nm (Navig)* shallow; **bas-fonds** *nmpl (fig)* dregs
basilic [bazilik] *nm (Culin)* basil
basket [baskɛt], **basket-ball** [baskɛtbol] *nm* basketball
baskets [baskɛt] *nfpl (chaussures)* trainers *(Brit)*, sneakers *(US)*
basque [bask] *adj, nm (Ling)* Basque ▷ *nm/f*: **B~** Basque; **le Pays ~** the Basque country
basse [bas] *adj voir* **bas** ▷ *nf (Mus)* bass
basse-cour *(pl* **basses-cours)** [baskur] *nf* farmyard; *(animaux)* farmyard animals
bassin [basɛ̃] *nm (cuvette)* bowl; *(pièce d'eau)* pond, pool; *(de fontaine, Géo)* basin; *(Anat)* pelvis; *(portuaire)* dock; **~ houiller** coalfield
bassine [basin] *nf* basin; *(contenu)* bowl, bowlful
basson [basɔ̃] *nm* bassoon
bas-ventre [bavɑ̃tr] *nm* (lower part of the) stomach
bat [ba] *vb voir* **battre**
bataille [bataj] *nf* battle; *(rixe)* fight; **en ~** *(en travers)* at an angle; *(en désordre)* awry; **elle avait les cheveux en ~** her hair was a mess; **~ rangée** pitched battle

bâtard, e [batar, -ard] *adj* (*enfant*) illegitimate; (*fig*) hybrid ▷ *nm/f* illegitimate child, bastard (*péj*) ▷ *nm* (*Boulangerie*) ≈ Vienna loaf; **chien ~** mongrel

bateau, x [bato] *nm* boat; (*grand*) ship ▷ *adj inv* (*banal, rebattu*) hackneyed; **~ de pêche/à moteur/à voiles** fishing/motor/sailing boat

bateau-mouche [batomuʃ] *nm* (*passenger*) pleasure boat (*on the Seine*)

bâti, e [bati] *adj* (*terrain*) developed ▷ *nm* (*armature*) frame; (*Couture*) tacking; **bien ~** (*personne*) well-built

batifoler [batifɔle] *vi* to frolic *ou* lark about

bâtiment [batimɑ̃] *nm* building; (*Navig*) ship, vessel; (*industrie*): **le ~** the building trade

bâtir [batir] *vt* to build; (*Couture*: *jupe, ourlet*) to tack; **fil à ~** (*Couture*) tacking thread

bâtisse [batis] *nf* building

bâton [batɔ̃] *nm* stick; **mettre des ~s dans les roues à qn** to put a spoke in sb's wheel; **à ~s rompus** informally; **parler à ~s rompus** to chat about this and that; **~ de rouge (à lèvres)** lipstick; **~ de ski** ski stick

bats [ba] *vb voir* **battre**

battage [bataʒ] *nm* (*publicité*) (hard) plugging

battant, e [batɑ̃, -ɑ̃t] *vb voir* **battre** ▷ *adj*: **pluie ~e** lashing rain ▷ *nm* (*de cloche*) clapper; (*de volets*) shutter, flap; (*de porte*) side; (*fig*: *personne*) fighter; **porte à double ~** double door; **tambour ~** briskly

battement [batmɑ̃] *nm* (*de cœur*) beat; (*intervalle*) interval (*between classes, trains etc*); **~ de paupières** blinking *no pl* (*of eyelids*); **un ~ de 10 minutes, 10 minutes de ~** 10 minutes to spare

batterie [batri] *nf* (*Mil, Élec*) battery; (*Mus*) drums *pl*, drum kit; **~ de cuisine** kitchen utensils *pl*; (*casseroles etc*) pots and pans *pl*; **une ~ de tests** a string of tests

batteur [batœr] *nm* (*Mus*) drummer; (*appareil*) whisk

battre [batr] *vt* to beat; (*pluie, vagues*) to beat *ou* lash against; (*œufs etc*) to beat up, whisk; (*blé*) to thresh; (*cartes*) to shuffle; (*passer au peigne fin*) to scour ▷ *vi* (*cœur*) to beat; (*volets etc*) to bang, rattle; **se battre** *vi* to fight; **~ la mesure** to beat time; **~ en brèche** (*Mil*: *mur*) to batter; (*fig*: *théorie*) to demolish; (: *institution etc*) to attack; **~ son plein** to be at its height, be going full swing; **~ pavillon britannique** to fly the British flag; **~ des mains** to clap one's hands; **~ des ailes** to flap its wings; **~ de l'aile** (*fig*) to be in a bad way *ou* in bad shape; **~ la semelle** to stamp one's feet; **~ en retraite** to beat a retreat

baume [bom] *nm* balm

bavard, e [bavar, -ard] *adj* (very) talkative; gossipy

bavarder [bavarde] *vi* to chatter; (*indiscrètement*) to gossip; (: *révéler un secret*) to blab

bave [bav] *nf* dribble; (*de chien etc*) slobber, slaver (*Brit*), drool (*US*); (*d'escargot*) slime

baver [bave] *vi* to dribble; (*chien*) to slobber, slaver (*Brit*), drool (*US*); (*encre, couleur*) to run; **en ~** (*fam*) to have a hard time (of it)

baveux, -euse [bavø, -øz] *adj* dribbling; (*omelette*) runny

bavoir [bavwar] *nm* (*de bébé*) bib

bavure [bavyr] *nf* smudge; (*fig*) hitch; (*policière etc*) blunder

bayer [baje] *vi*: **~ aux corneilles** to stand gaping

bazar [bazar] *nm* general store; (*fam*) jumble

bazarder [bazarde] *vt* (*fam*) to chuck out

BCBG *sigle adj* (= *bon chic bon genre*) smart and trendy, ≈ preppy

BD *sigle f* = **bande dessinée**; (= *base de données*) DB

bd *abr* = **boulevard**

béant, e [beɑ̃, -ɑ̃t] *adj* gaping

béat, e [bea, -at] *adj* showing open-eyed wonder; (*sourire etc*) blissful

béatitude [beatityd] *nf* bliss

beau, bel, belle, beaux [bo, bɛl] *adj* beautiful, lovely; (*homme*) handsome ▷ *nf* (*Sport*) decider ▷ *adv*: **il fait ~** the weather's fine ▷ *nm*: **avoir le sens du ~** to have an aesthetic sense; **le temps est au ~** the weather is set fair; **un ~ geste** (*fig*) a fine gesture; **un ~ salaire** a good salary; **un ~ gâchis/rhume** a fine mess/nasty cold; **en faire/dire de belles** to do/say (some) stupid things; **le ~ monde** high society; **~ parleur** smooth talker; **~ jour** one (fine) day; **de plus belle** more than ever, even more; **bel et bien** well and truly; (*vraiment*) really (and truly); **le plus ~ c'est que ...** the best of it is that ...; **c'est du ~!** that's great, that is!; **on a ~ essayer** however hard *ou* no matter how hard we try; **il a ~ jeu de protester** *etc* it's easy for him to protest *etc*; **faire le ~** (*chien*) to sit up and beg

 MOT-CLÉ

beaucoup [boku] *adv* **1** a lot; **il boit beaucoup** he drinks a lot; **il ne boit pas beaucoup** he doesn't drink much *ou* a lot

2 (*suivi de plus, trop etc*) much, a lot, far; **il est beaucoup plus grand** he is much *ou* a lot *ou* far taller; **c'est beaucoup plus cher** it's a lot *ou* much more expensive; **il a beaucoup plus de temps que moi** he has much *ou* a lot more time than me; **il y a beaucoup plus de touristes ici** there are a lot *ou* many more tourists here; **beaucoup trop vite** much too fast; **il fume beaucoup trop** he smokes far too much

3: **beaucoup de** (*nombre*) many, a lot of; (*quantité*) a lot of; **pas beaucoup de** (*nombre*) not many, not a lot of; (*quantité*) not much, not a lot of; **beaucoup d'étudiants/de touristes** a lot *ou* many students/tourists; **beaucoup de courage** a lot of courage; **il n'a**

pas beaucoup d'argent he hasn't got much *ou* a lot of money; **il n'y a pas beaucoup de touristes** there aren't many *ou* a lot of tourists

4: de beaucoup by far

▷ *pron*: **beaucoup le savent** lots of people know that

beau-fils (*pl* **beaux-fils**) [bofis] *nm* son-in-law; (*remariage*) stepson

beau-frère (*pl* **beaux-frères**) [bofʀɛʀ] *nm* brother-in-law

beau-père (*pl* **beaux-pères**) [bopɛʀ] *nm* father-in-law; (*remariage*) stepfather

beauté [bote] *nf* beauty; **de toute ~** beautiful; **en ~** *adv* with a flourish, brilliantly; **finir qch en ~** to complete sth brilliantly

beaux-arts [bozaʀ] *nmpl* fine arts

beaux-parents [bopaʀɑ̃] *nmpl* wife's/husband's family, in-laws

bébé [bebe] *nm* baby

bec [bɛk] *nm* beak, bill; (*de plume*) nib; (*de cafetière etc*) spout; (*de casserole etc*) lip; (*d'une clarinette etc*) mouthpiece; (*fam*) mouth; **clouer le ~ à qn** (*fam*) to shut sb up; **ouvrir le ~** (*fam*) to open one's mouth; **~ de gaz** (*street*) gaslamp; **~ verseur** pouring lip

bécane [bekan] *nf* (*fam*) bike

bec-de-lièvre (*pl* **becs-de-lièvre**) [bɛkdə ljɛvʀ] *nm* harelip

bêche [bɛʃ] *nf* spade

bêcher [beʃe] *vt* (*terre*) to dig; (*personne*: *critiquer*) to slate; (: *snober*) to look down on

bécoter [bekɔte]: **se bécoter** *vi* to smooch

becqueter [bɛkte] *vt* (*fam*) to eat

bedaine [bədɛn] *nf* paunch

bedonnant, e [bədɔnɑ̃, -ɑ̃t] *adj* paunchy, potbellied

bée [be] *adj*: **bouche ~** gaping

beffroi [befʀwa] *nm* belfry

bégayer [begeje] *vt*, *vi* to stammer

bègue [bɛg] *nm/f*: **être ~** to have a stammer

beige [bɛʒ] *adj* beige

beignet [bɛɲɛ] *nm* fritter

bel [bɛl] *adj m voir* **beau**

bêler [bele] *vi* to bleat

belette [bəlɛt] *nf* weasel

belge [bɛlʒ] *adj* Belgian ▷ *nm/f*: **B~** Belgian; *see note*

◈ **FÊTE NATIONALE BELGE**

◈ The *fête nationale belge*, on 21 July, marks
◈ the day in 1831 when Leopold of
◈ Saxe-Coburg Gotha was crowned King
◈ Leopold I.

Belgique [bɛlʒik] *nf*: **la ~** Belgium

bélier [belje] *nm* ram; (*engin*) (battering) ram; (*signe*): **le B~** Aries, the Ram; **être du B~** to be Aries

belle [bɛl] *adj voir* **beau** ▷ *nf* (*Sport*): **la ~** the decider

belle-fille (*pl* **belles-filles**) [bɛlfij] *nf* daughter-in-law; (*remariage*) stepdaughter

belle-mère (*pl* **belles-mères**) [bɛlmɛʀ] *nf* mother-in-law; (*remariage*) stepmother

belle-sœur (*pl* **belles-sœurs**) [bɛlsœʀ] *nf* sister-in-law

belliqueux, -euse [belikø, -øz] *adj* aggressive, warlike

belvédère [bɛlvedɛʀ] *nm* panoramic viewpoint (*or small building there*)

bémol [bemɔl] *nm* (*Mus*) flat

bénédiction [benediksjɔ̃] *nf* blessing

bénéfice [benefis] *nm* (*Comm*) profit; (*avantage*) benefit; **au ~ de** in aid of

bénéficier [benefisje] *vi*: **~ de** to enjoy; (*profiter*) to benefit by *ou* from; (*obtenir*) to get, be given

bénéfique [benefik] *adj* beneficial

Benelux [benelyks] *nm*: **le ~** Benelux, the Benelux countries

bénévole [benevɔl] *adj* voluntary, unpaid

bénin, -igne [benɛ̃, -iɲ] *adj* minor, mild; (*tumeur*) benign

bénir [beniʀ] *vt* to bless

bénit, e [beni, -it] *adj* consecrated; **eau ~e** holy water

benjamin, e [bɛ̃ʒamɛ̃, -in] *nm/f* youngest child; (*Sport*) under-13

benne [bɛn] *nf* skip; (*de téléphérique*) (cable) car; **~ basculante** tipper (Brit), dump *ou* dumper truck; **~ à ordures** (*amovible*) skip

BEP *sigle m* (= *Brevet d'études professionnelles*) school-leaving diploma, taken at approx. 18 years

béquille [bekij] *nf* crutch; (*de bicyclette*) stand

berceau, x [bɛʀso] *nm* cradle, crib

bercer [bɛʀse] *vt* to rock, cradle; (*musique etc*) to lull; **~ qn de** (*promesses etc*) to delude sb with

berceur, -euse [bɛʀsœʀ, -øz] *adj* soothing ▷ *nf* (*chanson*) lullaby

berceuse *nf* lullaby

béret [beʀɛ], **béret basque** [beʀɛbask] *nm* beret

berge [bɛʀʒ] *nf* bank

berger, -ère [bɛʀʒe, -ɛʀ] *nm/f* shepherd/shepherdess; **~ allemand** (*chien*) alsatian (dog) (Brit), German shepherd (dog) (US)

Berlin [bɛʀlɛ̃] *n* Berlin; **~-Est/-Ouest** East/West Berlin

berlingot [bɛʀlɛ̃go] *nm* (*emballage*) carton (*pyramid shaped*); (*bonbon*) lozenge

berlue [bɛʀly] *nf*: **j'ai la ~** I must be seeing things

Bermudes [bɛʀmyd] *nfpl*: **les (îles) ~** Bermuda

Berne [bɛʀn] *n* Bern

berner [bɛʀne] *vt* to fool

besogne [bəzɔɲ] *nf* work *no pl*, job

besoin [bəzwɛ̃] *nm* need; (*pauvreté*): **le ~** need, want; **le ~ d'argent/de gloire** the need for money/glory; **~s (naturels)** nature's needs; **faire ses ~s** to relieve o.s.; **avoir ~ de qch/**

faire qch to need sth/to do sth; **il n'y a pas ~ de (faire)** there is no need to (do); **au ~, si ~ est** if need be; **pour les ~s de la cause** for the purpose in hand; **être dans le ~** to be in need *ou* want

bestial, e, -aux [bɛstjal, -o] *adj* bestial, brutish ▷ *nmpl* cattle

bestiole [bɛstjɔl] *nf* (tiny) creature

bétail [betaj] *nm* livestock, cattle *pl*

bête [bɛt] *nf* animal; (*bestiole*) insect, creature ▷ *adj* stupid, silly; **les ~s** (the animals; **chercher la petite ~** to nit-pick; **~ noire** pet hate, bugbear (*Brit*); **~ sauvage** wild beast; **~ de somme** beast of burden

bêtement [bɛtmã] *adv* stupidly; **tout ~** quite simply

bêtise [betiz] *nf* stupidity; (*action, remarque*) stupid thing (to say *ou* do); (*bonbon*) type of mint sweet (*Brit*) *ou* candy (*US*); **faire/dire une ~** to do/say something stupid

béton [betɔ̃] *nm* concrete; **(en)** ~ (*fig: alibi, argument*) cast iron; **~ armé** reinforced concrete; **~ précontraint** prestressed concrete

bétonnière [betɔnjɛʀ] *nf* cement mixer

betterave [bɛtʀav] *nf* (*rouge*) beetroot (*Brit*), beet (*US*); **~ fourragère** mangel-wurzel; **~ sucrière** sugar beet

beugler [bøgle] *vi* to low; (*péj: radio etc*) to blare ▷ *vt* (*péj: chanson etc*) to bawl out

Beur [bœʀ] *adj, nm/f see note*

beurre [bœʀ] *nm* butter; **mettre du ~ dans les épinards** (*fig*) to add a little to the kitty; **~ de cacao** cocoa butter; **~ noir** brown butter (sauce)

beurrer [bœʀe] *vt* to butter

beurrier [bœʀje] *nm* butter dish

beuverie [bœvʀi] *nf* drinking session

bévue [bevy] *nf* blunder

Beyrouth [beʀut] *n* Beirut

biais [bjɛ] *nm* (*moyen*) device, expedient; (*aspect*) angle; (*bande de tissu*) piece of cloth cut on the bias; **en ~, de ~** (*obliquement*) at an angle; (*fig*) indirectly; **par le ~ de** by means of

biaiser [bjeze] *vi* (*fig*) to sidestep the issue

bibelot [biblo] *nm* trinket, curio

biberon [bibʀɔ̃] *nm* (feeding) bottle; **nourrir au ~** to bottle-feed

bible [bibl] *nf* bible

bibliobus [biblijɔbys] *nm* mobile library van

bibliographie [biblijɔgʀafi] *nf* bibliography

bibliothécaire [biblijɔtekɛʀ] *nm/f* librarian

bibliothèque [biblijɔtɛk] *nf* library; (*meuble*) bookcase; **~ municipale** public library

bic® [bik] *nm* Biro®

bicarbonate [bikaʀbɔnat] *nm*: **~ (de soude)** bicarbonate of soda

biceps [bisɛps] *nm* biceps

biche [biʃ] *nf* doe

bichonner [biʃɔne] *vt* to groom

bicolore [bikɔlɔʀ] *adj* two-coloured (*Brit*), two-colored (*US*)

bicoque [bikɔk] *nf* (*péj*) shack, dump

bicyclette [bisiklɛt] *nf* bicycle

bide [bid] *nm* (*fam: ventre*) belly; (*Théât*) flop

bidet [bidɛ] *nm* bidet

bidon [bidɔ̃] *nm* can ▷ *adj inv* (*fam*) phoney

bidonville [bidɔ̃vil] *nm* shanty town

bidule [bidyl] *nm* (*fam*) thingamajig

 MOT-CLÉ

bien [bjɛ̃] *nm* **1** (*avantage, profit*): **faire le bien** to do good; **faire du bien à qn** to do sb good; **ça fait du bien de faire** it does you good to do; **dire du bien de** to speak well of; **c'est pour son bien** it's for his own good; **changer en bien** to change for the better; **le bien public** the public good; **vouloir du bien à qn** (*vouloir aider*) to have sb's (best) interests at heart; **je te veux du bien** (*pour mettre en confiance*) I don't wish you any harm **2** (*possession, patrimoine*) possession, property; **son bien le plus précieux** his most treasured possession; **avoir du bien** to have property; **biens (de consommation** *etc*) (consumer *etc*) goods; **biens durables** (consumer) durables **3** (*moral*): **le bien** good; **distinguer le bien du mal** to tell good from evil
▷ *adv* **1** (*de façon satisfaisante*) well; **elle travaille/mange bien** she works/eats well; **aller** *ou* **se porter bien** to be well; **croyant bien faire, je/il ...** thinking I/he was doing the right thing, I/he ...; **tiens-toi bien!** (*assieds-toi correctement*) sit up straight!; (*debout*) stand up straight!; (*sois sage*) behave yourself!; (*prépare-toi*) wait for it! **2** (*valeur intensive*) quite; **bien jeune** quite young; **bien assez** quite enough; **bien mieux** (very) much better; **bien du temps/des gens** quite a time/a number of people; **j'espère bien y aller** I do hope to go; **je veux bien le faire** (*concession*) I'm quite willing to do it; **il faut bien le faire** it has to be done; **il y a bien deux ans** at least two years ago; **cela fait bien deux ans que je ne l'ai pas vu** I haven't seen him for at least *ou* a good two years; **il semble bien que** it really seems that; **peut-être bien** it could well be; **aimer bien** to like; **Paul est bien venu, n'est-ce pas?** Paul HAS come, hasn't he?; **où peut-il**

bien être passé? where on earth can he have got to?

3 (*conséquence, résultat*): **si bien que** with the result that; **on verra bien** we'll see; **faire bien de ...** to be right to ...

▷ *excl* right!, OK!, fine!; **eh bien!** well!; **(c'est) bien fait!** it serves you (*ou* him *etc*) right!; **bien sûr!, bien entendu!** certainly!, of course!

▷ *adj inv* **1** (*en bonne forme, à l'aise*): **je me sens bien, je suis bien** I feel fine; **je ne me sens pas bien, je ne suis pas bien** I don't feel well; **on est bien dans ce fauteuil** this chair is very comfortable

2 (*joli, beau*) good-looking; **tu es bien dans cette robe** you look good in that dress

3 (*satisfaisant*) good; **elle est bien, cette maison/secrétaire** it's a good house/she's a good secretary; **c'est très bien (comme ça)** it's fine (like that); **ce n'est pas si bien que ça** it's not as good *ou* great as all that; **c'est bien?** is that all right?

4 (*moralement*) right; (*: personne*) good, nice; (*respectable*) respectable; **ce n'est pas bien de ...** it's not right to ...; **elle est bien, cette femme** she's a nice woman, she's a good sort; **des gens bien** respectable people

5 (*en bons termes*): **être bien avec qn** to be on good terms with sb

bien-aimé, e [bjɛ̃neme] *adj, nm/f* beloved
bien-être [bjɛ̃nɛtʀ] *nm* well-being
bienfaisance [bjɛ̃fəzɑ̃s] *nf* charity
bienfait [bjɛ̃fɛ] *nm* act of generosity, benefaction; (*de la science etc*) benefit
bienfaiteur, -trice [bjɛ̃fɛtœʀ, -tʀis] *nm/f* benefactor/benefactress
bien-fondé [bjɛ̃fɔ̃de] *nm* soundness
bien que [bjɛ̃k] *conj* although
bienséant, e [bjɛ̃seɑ̃, -ɑ̃t] *adj* proper, seemly
bientôt [bjɛ̃to] *adv* soon; **à ~** see you soon
bienveillant, e [bjɛ̃vɛjɑ̃, -ɑ̃t] *adj* kindly
bienvenu, e [bjɛ̃vny] *adj* welcome ▷ *nm/f:* **être le ~/la ~e** to be welcome ▷ *nf:* **souhaiter la ~e à** to welcome; **~e à** welcome to
bière [bjɛʀ] *nf* (*boisson*) beer; (*cercueil*) bier; **~ blonde** lager; **~ brune** brown ale (*Brit*), dark beer (*US*); **~ (à la) pression** draught beer
biffer [bife] *vt* to cross out
bifteck [biftɛk] *nm* steak
bifurquer [bifyʀke] *vi* (*route*) to fork; (*véhicule*) to turn off
bigarré, e [bigaʀe] *adj* multicoloured (*Brit*), multicolored (*US*); (*disparate*) motley
bigorneau, x [bigɔʀno] *nm* winkle
bigot, e [bigo, -ɔt] (*péj*) *adj* bigoted ▷ *nm/f* bigot
bigoudi [bigudi] *nm* curler
bijou, x [biʒu] *nm* jewel
bijouterie [biʒutʀi] *nf* (*magasin*) jeweller's (shop) (*Brit*), jewelry store (*US*); (*bijoux*)

jewellery, jewelry
bijoutier, -ière [biʒutje, -jɛʀ] *nm/f* jeweller (*Brit*), jeweler (*US*)
bikini [bikini] *nm* bikini
bilan [bilɑ̃] *nm* (*Comm*) balance sheet(s); (*annuel*) end of year statement; (*fig*) (*net*) outcome; (*: de victimes*) toll; **faire le ~ de** to assess; to review; **déposer son ~** to file a bankruptcy statement; **~ de santé** (*Méd*) check-up; **~ social** *statement of a firm's policies towards its employees*
bile [bil] *nf* bile; **se faire de la ~** (*fam*) to worry o.s. sick
bilieux, -euse [biljø, -øz] *adj* bilious; (*fig: colérique*) testy
bilingue [bilɛ̃g] *adj* bilingual
billard [bijaʀ] *nm* billiards *sg*; (*table*) billiard table; **c'est du ~** (*fam*) it's a cinch; **passer sur le ~** (*fam*) to have an (*ou* one's) operation; **~ électrique** pinball
bille [bij] *nf* ball; (*du jeu de billes*) marble; (*de bois*) log; **jouer aux ~s** to play marbles
billet [bijɛ] *nm* (*aussi:* **~ de banque**) (bank) note; (*de cinéma, de bus etc*) ticket; (*courte lettre*) note; **~ à ordre** *ou* **de commerce** (*Comm*) promissory note, IOU; **~ d'avion/de train** plane/train ticket; **~ circulaire** round-trip ticket; **~ doux** love letter; **~ de faveur** complimentary ticket; **~ de loterie** lottery ticket; **~ de quai** platform ticket; **~ électronique** e-ticket
billetterie [bijɛtʀi] *nf* ticket office; (*distributeur*) ticket dispenser; (*Banque*) cash dispenser
billion [biljɔ̃] *nm* billion (*Brit*), trillion (*US*)
billot [bijo] *nm* block
bimensuel, le [bimɑ̃sɥɛl] *adj* bimonthly, twice-monthly
binette [binɛt] *nf* (*outil*) hoe
bio [bjo] *adj* (*fam: = biologique*) (*produits, aliments*) organic
bio... [bjo] *préfixe* bio...
biocarburant [bjɔkaʀbyʀɑ̃] *nm* biofuel
biochimie [bjɔʃimi] *nf* biochemistry
biodiversité [bjɔdivɛʀsite] *nf* biodiversity
bioéthique [bjɔetik] *nf* bioethics *sg*
biographie [bjɔgʀafi] *nf* biography
biologie [bjɔlɔʒi] *nf* biology
biologique [bjɔlɔʒik] *adj* biological; (*produits, aliments*) organic
biologiste [bjɔlɔʒist] *nm/f* biologist
biométrie *nf* biometrics
biotechnologie [bjɔtɛknɔlɔʒi] *nf* biotechnology
bioterrorisme [bjɔtɛʀɔʀism] *nm* bioterrorism
bioterroriste [bjɔtɛʀɔʀist] *nm/f* bioterrorist
Birmanie [biʀmani] *nf:* **la ~** Burma
bis, e [*adj* bi, *adj*, *nf* biz, *adv*, *excl*, *nm* bis] *adj* (*couleur*) greyish brown ▷ *adv:* **12 ~ 12a** *ou* A ▷ *excl*, *nm* encore ▷ *nf* (*baiser*) kiss; (*vent*) North wind; **faire une** *ou* **la ~e à qn** to kiss

sb; **grosses ~es (de)** (sur lettre) love and kisses (from)

bisannuel, le [bizanɥɛl] adj biennial

biscornu, e [biskɔrny] adj crooked; (bizarre) weird(-looking)

biscotte [biskɔt] nf toasted bread (sold in packets)

biscuit [biskɥi] nm biscuit (Brit), cookie (US); (gâteau) sponge cake; **~ à la cuiller** sponge finger

bise [biz] adj f, nf voir **bis**

bisexuel, le [bisɛksɥɛl] adj, nm/f bisexual

bisou [bizu] nm (fam) kiss

bissextile [bisɛkstil] adj: **année ~** leap year

bistouri [bisturi] nm lancet

bistro, bistrot [bistro] nm bistro, café

bitume [bitym] nm asphalt

bizarre [bizar] adj strange, odd

blafard, e [blafar, -ard] adj wan

blague [blag] nf (propos) joke; (farce) trick; **sans ~!** no kidding!; **~ à tabac** tobacco pouch

blaguer [blage] vi to joke ▷ vt to tease

blaireau, x [blɛro] nm (Zool) badger; (brosse) shaving brush

blairer [blɛre] vt: **je ne peux pas le ~** I can't bear ou stand him

blâme [blɑm] nm blame; (sanction) reprimand

blâmer [blɑme] vt (réprouver) to blame; (réprimander) to reprimand

blanc, blanche [blɑ̃, blɑ̃ʃ] adj white; (non imprimé) blank; (innocent) pure ▷ nm/f white, white man/woman ▷ nm (couleur) white; (linge) **le ~** whites pl; (espace non écrit) blank; (aussi: **~ d'œuf**) (egg-)white; (aussi: **~ de poulet**) breast, white meat; (aussi: **vin ~**) white wine ▷ nf (Mus) minim (Brit), half-note (US); (fam: drogue) smack; **d'une voix blanche** in a toneless voice; **aux cheveux ~s** white-haired; **le ~ de l'œil** the white of the eye; **laisser en ~** to leave blank; **chèque en ~** blank cheque; **à ~** adv (chauffer) white-hot; (tirer, charger) with blanks; **saigner à ~** to bleed white; **~ cassé** off-white

blancheur [blɑ̃ʃœr] nf whiteness

blanchir [blɑ̃ʃir] vt (gén) to whiten; (linge, fig: argent) to launder; (Culin) to blanch; (fig: disculper) to clear ▷ vi to grow white; (cheveux) to go white; **blanchi à la chaux** whitewashed

blanchisserie [blɑ̃ʃisri] nf laundry

blason [blɑzɔ̃] nm coat of arms

blasphème [blasfɛm] nm blasphemy

blazer [blazɛr] nm blazer

blé [ble] nm wheat; **~ en herbe** wheat on the ear; **~ noir** buckwheat

bled [blɛd] nm (péj) hole; (en Afrique du Nord): **le ~** the interior

blême [blɛm] adj pale

blessant, e [blesɑ̃, -ɑ̃t] adj hurtful

blessé, e [blese] adj injured ▷ nm/f injured person, casualty; **un ~ grave, un grand ~** a seriously injured ou wounded person

blesser [blese] vt to injure; (délibérément: Mil etc) to wound; (souliers etc, offenser) to hurt; **se blesser** to injure o.s.; **se ~ au pied** etc to injure one's foot etc

blessure [blesyr] nf (accidentelle) injury; (intentionnelle) wound

bleu, e [blø] adj blue; (bifteck) very rare ▷ nm (couleur) blue; (novice) greenhorn; (contusion) bruise; (vêtement: aussi: **~s**) overalls pl (Brit), coveralls pl (US); **avoir une peur ~e** to be scared stiff; **zone ~e** ≈ restricted parking area; **fromage ~** blue cheese; **au ~** (Culin) au bleu; **~ (de lessive)** ≈ blue bag; **~ de méthylène** (Méd) methylene blue; **~ marine/nuit/roi** navy/midnight/royal blue

bleuet [bløɛ] nm cornflower

bleuté, e [bløte] adj blue-shaded

blinder [blɛ̃de] vt to armour (Brit), armor (US); (fig) to harden

bloc [blɔk] nm (de pierre etc, Inform) block; (de papier à lettres) pad; (ensemble) group, block; **serré à ~** tightened right down; **en ~** as a whole; wholesale; **faire ~** to unite; **~ opératoire** operating ou theatre block; **~ sanitaire** toilet block; **~ sténo** shorthand notebook

blocage [blɔkaʒ] nm (voir bloquer) blocking; jamming; (des prix) freezing; (Psych) hang-up

bloc-notes (pl **blocs-notes**) [blɔknɔt] nm note pad

blocus [blɔkys] nm blockade

blog, blogue [blɔg] nm blog

blogging [blɔgiŋ] nm blogging

bloguer [blɔge] vi to blog

blond, e [blɔ̃, -ɔ̃d] adj fair; (plus clair) blond; (sable, blés) golden ▷ nm/f fair-haired ou blond man/woman; **~ cendré** ash blond

bloquer [blɔke] vt (passage) to block; (pièce mobile) to jam; (crédits, compte) to freeze; (personne, négociations etc) to hold up; (regrouper) to group; **~ les freins** to jam on the brakes

blottir [blɔtir]: **se blottir** vi to huddle up

blouse [bluz] nf overall

blouson [bluzɔ̃] nm blouson (jacket); **~ noir** (fig) ≈ rocker

blue-jean [bludʒin], **blue-jeans** [bludʒins] nm jeans

bluff [blœf] nm bluff

bluffer [blœfe] vi, vt to bluff

bobard [bɔbar] nm (fam) tall story

bobine [bɔbin] nf (de fil) reel; (de machine à coudre) spool; (de machine à écrire) ribbon; (Élec) coil; (~ d'allumage) (Auto) coil; **~ de pellicule** (Photo) roll of film

bobo [bobo] abr m/f (= bourgeois bohème) boho

bocal, -aux [bɔkal, -o] nm jar

bock [bɔk] nm (beer) glass; (contenu) glass of beer

body [bɔdi] nm body(suit); (Sport) leotard

bœuf (pl **bœufs**) [bœf, bø] nm ox; (Culin) beef; (Mus: fam) jam session

bof [bɔf] excl (fam: indifférence) don't care!,

meh; (*pas terrible*) nothing special

bogue [bog] *nf* (*Bot*) husk ▷ *nm* (*Inform*) bug

bohème [bɔɛm] *adj* happy-go-lucky, unconventional

bohémien, ne [bɔemjɛ̃, -ɛn] *adj* Bohemian ▷ *nm/f* gipsy

boire [bwar] *vt* to drink; (*s'imprégner de*) to soak up; **~ un coup** to have a drink

bois [bwa] *vb voir* **boire** ▷ *nm* wood; (*Zool*) antler; (*Mus*): **les ~** the woodwind; **de ~, en ~** wooden; **~ vert** green wood; **~ mort** deadwood; **~ de lit** bedstead

boisé, e [bwaze] *adj* woody, wooded

boisson [bwasɔ̃] *nf* drink; **pris de ~** drunk, intoxicated; **~s alcoolisées** alcoholic beverages *ou* drinks; **~s non alcoolisées** soft drinks

boîte [bwat] *nf* box; (*fam: entreprise*) firm, company; **aliments en ~** canned *ou* tinned (*Brit*) foods; **~ à gants** glove compartment; **~ à musique** musical box; **~ à ordures** dustbin (*Brit*), trash can (*US*); **~ aux lettres** letter box, mailbox (*US*); (*Inform*) mailbox; **~ crânienne** cranium; **~ d'allumettes** box of matches; (*vide*) matchbox; **~ de conserve** can *ou* tin (*Brit*) (of food); **~ de nuit** night club; **~ de sardines/petits pois** can *ou* tin (*Brit*) of sardines/peas; **mettre qn en ~** (*fam*) to have a laugh at sb's expense; **~ de vitesses** gear box; **~ noire** (*Aviat*) black box; **~ postale (BP)** PO box; **~ vocale** voice mail

boiter [bwate] *vi* to limp; (*fig*) to wobble; (*raisonnement*) to be shaky

boîtier [bwatje] *nm* case; (*d'appareil photo*) body; **~ de montre** watch case

boive *etc* [bwav] *vb voir* **boire**

bol [bɔl] *nm* bowl; (*contenu*): **un ~ de café** *etc* a bowl of coffee *etc*; **un ~ d'air** a breath of fresh air; **en avoir ras le ~** (*fam*) to have had a bellyful; **avoir du ~** (*fam*) to be lucky

bolide [bɔlid] *nm* racing car; **comme un ~** like a rocket

bombardement [bɔ̃baʀdəmɑ̃] *nm* bombing

bombarder [bɔ̃baʀde] *vt* to bomb; **~ qn de** (*cailloux, lettres*) to bombard sb with; **~ qn directeur** to thrust sb into the director's seat

bombe [bɔ̃b] *nf* bomb; (*atomiseur*) (aerosol) spray; (*Équitation*) riding cap; **faire la ~** (*fam*) to go on a binge; **~ atomique** atomic bomb; **~ à retardement** time bomb

bombé, e [bɔ̃be] *adj* rounded; (*mur*) bulging; (*front*) domed; (*route*) steeply cambered

bomber [bɔ̃be] *vi* to bulge; (*route*) to camber ▷ *vt*: **~ le torse** to swell out one's chest

 MOT-CLÉ

bon, bonne [bɔ̃, bɔn] *adj* **1** (*agréable, satisfaisant*) good; **un bon repas/restaurant** a good meal/restaurant; **être bon en maths** to be good at maths

2 (*charitable*): **être bon (envers)** to be good (to), to be kind (to); **vous êtes trop bon** you're too kind

3 (*correct*) right; **le bon numéro/moment** the right number/moment

4 (*souhaits*): **bon anniversaire!** happy birthday!; **bon courage!** good luck!; **bon séjour!** enjoy your stay!; **bon voyage!** have a good trip!; **bon week-end!** have a good weekend!; **bonne année!** happy New Year!; **bonne chance!** good luck!; **bonne fête!** happy holiday!; **bonne nuit!** good night!

5 (*approprié*): **bon à/pour** fit to/for; **bon à jeter** fit for the bin; **c'est bon à savoir** that's useful to know; **à quoi bon (...)?** what's the point *ou* use (of ...)?

6 (*intensif*): **ça m'a pris deux bonnes heures** it took me a good two hours; **un bon nombre de** a good number of

7: **bon enfant** *adj inv* accommodating, easy-going; **bonne femme** (*péj*) woman; **de bonne heure** early; **bon marché** *adj inv, adv* cheap; **bon mot** witticism; **pour faire bon poids ...** to make up for it ...; **bon sens** common sense; **bon vivant** jovial chap; **bonnes œuvres** charitable works, charities; **bonne sœur** nun

▷ *nm* **1** (*billet*) voucher; (*aussi*: **bon cadeau**) gift voucher; **bon de caisse** cash voucher; **bon d'essence** petrol coupon; **bon à tirer** pass for press; **bon du Trésor** Treasury bond

2: **avoir du bon** to have its good points; **il y a du bon dans ce qu'il dit** there's some sense in what he says; **pour de bon** for good

▷ *nm/f*: **un bon à rien** a good-for-nothing

▷ *adv*: **il fait bon** it's *ou* the weather is fine; **sentir bon** to smell good; **tenir bon** to stand firm; **juger bon de faire ...** to think fit to do ...

▷ *excl* right!, good!; **ah bon?** really?; **bon, je reste** right, I'll stay; *voir aussi* **bonne**

bonbon [bɔ̃bɔ̃] *nm* (boiled) sweet

bonbonne [bɔ̃bɔn] *nf* demijohn; carboy

bond [bɔ̃] *nm* leap; (*d'une balle*) rebound, ricochet; **faire un ~** to leap in the air; **d'un seul ~** in one bound, with one leap; **~ en avant** (*fig: progrès*) leap forward

bondé, e [bɔ̃de] *adj* packed (full)

bondir [bɔ̃diʀ] *vi* to leap; **~ de joie** (*fig*) to jump for joy; **~ de colère** (*fig*) to be hopping mad

bonheur [bɔnœʀ] *nm* happiness; **avoir le ~ de** to have the good fortune to; **porter ~ (à qn)** to bring (sb) luck; **au petit ~** haphazardly; **par ~** fortunately

bonhomie [bɔnɔmi] *nf* good-naturedness

bonhomme [bɔnɔm] (*pl* **bonshommes** [bɔ̃zɔm]) *nm* fellow ▷ *adj* good-natured; **un vieux ~** an old chap; **aller son ~ de chemin** to carry on in one's own sweet way; **~ de neige** snowman

bonifier [bɔnifje]: **se bonifier** vi to improve
boniment [bɔnimɑ̃] nm patter no pl
bonjour [bɔ̃ʒuʀ] excl, nm hello; (selon l'heure) good morning (ou afternoon); **donner** ou **souhaiter le ~ à qn** to bid sb good morning ou afternoon; **c'est simple comme ~!** it's easy as pie!
bonne [bɔn] adj f voir **bon** ▷ nf (domestique) maid; **~ à toute faire** general help; **~ d'enfant** nanny
bonnement [bɔnmɑ̃] adv: **tout ~** quite simply
bonnet [bɔnɛ] nm bonnet, hat; (de soutien-gorge) cup; **~ d'âne** dunce's cap; **~ de bain** bathing cap; **~ de nuit** nightcap
bonsoir [bɔ̃swaʀ] excl good evening
bonté [bɔ̃te] nf kindness no pl; **avoir la ~ de** to be kind ou good enough to
bonus [bɔnys] nm (Assurances) no-claims bonus; (de DVD) extras pl
bord [bɔʀ] nm (de table, verre, falaise) edge; (de rivière, lac) bank; (de route) side; (de vêtement) edge, border; (de chapeau) brim; (monter) à **~** (to go) on board; **jeter par-dessus ~** to throw overboard; **le commandant de ~/les hommes du ~** the ship's master/crew; **du même ~** (fig) of the same opinion; **au ~ de la mer/route** at the seaside/roadside; **être au ~ des larmes** to be on the verge of tears; **virer de ~** (Navig) to tack; **sur les ~s** (fig) slightly; **de tous ~s** on all sides; **~ du trottoir** kerb (Brit), curb (US)
bordeaux [bɔʀdo] nm Bordeaux ▷ adj inv maroon
bordel [bɔʀdɛl] nm brothel; (fam!) bloody (Brit) ou goddamn (US) mess (!) ▷ excl hell!
bordelais, e [bɔʀdəlɛ, -ɛz] adj of ou from Bordeaux
border [bɔʀde] vt (être le long de) to line, border; (garnir): **~ qch de** to line sth with; to trim sth with; (qn dans son lit) to tuck up
bordereau, x [bɔʀdəʀo] nm docket, slip
bordure [bɔʀdyʀ] nf border; (sur un vêtement) trim(ming), border; **en ~ de** on the edge of
borgne [bɔʀɲ] adj one-eyed; **hôtel ~** shady hotel; **fenêtre ~** obstructed window
borne [bɔʀn] nf boundary stone; (aussi: **~ kilométrique**) kilometre-marker, ≈ milestone; **bornes** nfpl (fig) limits; **dépasser les ~s** to go too far; **sans ~(s)** boundless
borné, e [bɔʀne] adj narrow; (obtus: personne) narrow-minded
borner [bɔʀne] vt (délimiter) to limit; (limiter) to confine; **se ~ à faire** (se contenter de) to content o.s. with doing; (se limiter à) to limit o.s. to doing
bosniaque [bɔznjak] adj Bosnian ▷ nm/f: **B~** Bosnian
Bosnie-Herzégovine [bɔzniɛʀzegɔvin] nf Bosnia-Herzegovina
bosquet [bɔskɛ] nm copse (Brit), grove

bosse [bɔs] nf (de terrain etc) bump; (enflure) lump; (du bossu, du chameau) hump; **avoir la ~ des maths** etc (fam) to have a gift for maths etc; **il a roulé sa ~** (fam) he's been around
bosser [bɔse] vi (fam) to work; (: dur) to slave (away), slog (hard) (Brit)
bossu, e [bɔsy] nm/f hunchback
botanique [bɔtanik] nf botany ▷ adj botanic(al)
botte [bɔt] nf (soulier) (high) boot; (Escrime) thrust; (gerbe): **~ de paille** bundle of straw; **~ de radis/d'asperges** bunch of radishes/asparagus; **~s de caoutchouc** wellington boots
botter [bɔte] vt to put boots on; (donner un coup de pied à) to kick; (fam): **ça me botte** I fancy that
bottin® [bɔtɛ̃] nm directory
bottine [bɔtin] nf ankle boot
bouc [buk] nm goat; (barbe) goatee; **~ émissaire** scapegoat
boucan [bukɑ̃] nm din, racket
bouche [buʃ] nf mouth; **une ~ à nourrir** a mouth to feed; **les ~s inutiles** the non-productive members of the population; **faire du ~ à ~ à qn** to give sb the kiss of life (Brit), give sb mouth-to-mouth resuscitation; **de ~ à oreille** confidentially; **pour la bonne ~** (pour la fin) till last; **faire venir l'eau à la ~** to make one's mouth water; **cousu!** mum's the word!; **rester ~ bée** to stand open-mouthed; **~ d'aération** air vent; **~ de chaleur** hot air vent; **~ d'égout** manhole; **~ d'incendie** fire hydrant; **~ de métro** métro entrance
bouché, e [buʃe] adj (flacon etc) stoppered; (temps, ciel) overcast; (carrière) blocked; (péj: personne) thick; (trompette) muted; **avoir le nez ~** to have a blocked(-up) nose; **c'est un secteur ~** there's no future in that area; **l'évier est ~** the sink's blocked
bouchée [buʃe] nf mouthful; **ne faire qu'une ~ de** (fig) to make short work of; **pour une ~ de pain** (fig) for next to nothing; **~s à la reine** chicken vol-au-vents
boucher [buʃe] nm butcher ▷ vt (pour colmater) to stop up; (trou) to fill up; (obstruer) to block (up); **se boucher** vi (tuyau etc) to block up, get blocked up; **j'ai le nez bouché** my nose is blocked; **se ~ le nez** to hold one's nose
bouchère [buʃɛʀ] nf butcher
boucherie [buʃʀi] nf butcher's (shop); (métier) butchery; (fig) slaughter, butchery
bouche-trou [buʃtʀu] nm (fig) stop-gap
bouchon [buʃɔ̃] nm (en liège) cork; (autre matière) stopper; (de tube) tops; (fig: embouteillage) holdup; (Pêche) float; **~ doseur** measuring cap
boucle [bukl] nf (forme, figure, aussi Inform) loop; (objet) buckle; **~ (de cheveux)** curl; **~ d'oreille** earring
bouclé, e [bukle] adj (cheveux) curly; (tapis) uncut

boucler [bukle] vt (fermer: ceinture etc) to fasten; (: magasin) to shut; (terminer) to finish off; (: circuit) to complete; (budget) to balance; (enfermer) to shut away; (: condamné) to lock up; (: quartier) to seal off ▷ vi to curl; **faire ~** (cheveux) to curl; **~ la boucle** (Aviat) to loop the loop

bouclier [buklije] nm shield

bouddhiste [budist] nm/f Buddhist

bouder [bude] vi to sulk ▷ vt (chose) to turn one's nose up at; (personne) to refuse to have anything to do with

boudin [budɛ̃] nm (Culin): **~ (noir)** black pudding; (Tech) roll; **~ blanc** white pudding

boue [bu] nf mud

bouée [bwe] nf buoy; (de baigneur) rubber ring; **~ (de sauvetage)** lifebuoy; (fig) lifeline

boueux, -euse [bwø, -øz] adj muddy ▷ nm (fam) refuse (Brit) ou garbage (US) collector

bouffe [buf] nf (fam) grub, food

bouffée [bufe] nf (de cigarette) puff; **une ~ d'air pur** a breath of fresh air; **~ de chaleur** (gén) blast of hot air; (Méd) hot flush (Brit) ou flash (US); **~ de fièvre/de honte** flush of fever/shame; **~ d'orgueil** fit of pride

bouffer [bufe] vi (fam) to eat; (Couture) to puff out ▷ vt (fam) to eat

bouffi, e [bufi] adj swollen

bougeoir [buʒwaR] nm candlestick

bougeotte [buʒɔt] nf: **avoir la ~** to have the fidgets

bouger [buʒe] vi to move; (dent etc) to be loose; (changer) to alter; (agir) to stir; (s'activer) to get moving ▷ vt to move; **les prix/les couleurs n'ont pas bougé** prices/colours haven't changed; **se bouger** (fam) to move (oneself)

bougie [buʒi] nf candle; (Auto) spark(ing) plug

bougon, ne [bugɔ̃, -ɔn] adj grumpy

bougonner [bugɔne] vi, vt to grumble

bouillabaisse [bujabɛs] nf type of fish soup

bouillant, e [bujɑ̃, -ɑ̃t] adj (qui bout) boiling; (très chaud) boiling (hot); (fig: ardent) hot-headed; **~ de colère** etc seething with anger etc

bouillie [buji] nf gruel; (de bébé) cereal; **en ~** (fig) crushed

bouillir [bujiR] vi to boil ▷ vt (aussi: **faire ~**: Culin) to boil; **~ de colère** etc to seethe with anger etc

bouilloire [bujwaR] nf kettle

bouillon [bujɔ̃] nm (Culin) stock no pl; (bulles, écume) bubble; **~ de culture** culture medium

bouillonner [bujɔne] vi to bubble; (fig: idées) to bubble up; (torrent) to foam

bouillotte [bujɔt] nf hot-water bottle

boulanger, -ère [bulɑ̃ʒe, -ɛR] nm/f baker ▷ nf (femme du boulanger) baker's wife

boulangerie [bulɑ̃ʒRi] nf bakery, baker's (shop); (commerce) bakery; **~ industrielle** bakery

boulangerie-pâtisserie (pl **boulangeries-pâtisseries**) [bulɑ̃ʒRipatisRi] nf baker's and confectioner's (shop)

boule [bul] nf (gén) ball; (de pétanque) bowl; (de machine à écrire) golf ball; **roulé en ~** curled up in a ball; **se mettre en ~** (fig) to fly off the handle, blow one's top; **perdre la ~** (fig: fam) to go off one's rocker; **~ de gomme** (bonbon) gum(drop), pastille; **~ de neige** snowball; **faire ~ de neige** (fig) to snowball

bouleau, x [bulo] nm (silver) birch

bouledogue [buldɔg] nm bulldog

boulet [bulɛ] nm (aussi: **~ de canon**) cannonball; (de bagnard) ball and chain; (charbon) (coal) nut

boulette [bulɛt] nf (de viande) meatball

boulevard [bulvaR] nm boulevard

bouleversant, e [bulvɛRsɑ̃, -ɑ̃t] adj (récit) deeply distressing; (nouvelle) shattering

bouleversement [bulvɛRsəmɑ̃] nm (politique, social) upheaval

bouleverser [bulvɛRse] vt (émouvoir) to overwhelm; (causer du chagrin à) to distress; (pays, vie) to disrupt; (papiers, objets) to turn upside down, upset

boulimie [bulimi] nf bulimia; compulsive eating

boulimique [bulimik] adj bulimic

boulon [bulɔ̃] nm bolt

boulot¹ [bulo] nm (fam: travail) work

boulot², te [bulo, -ɔt] adj plump, tubby

boum [bum] nm bang ▷ nf (fam) party

bouquet [bukɛ] nm (de fleurs) bunch (of flowers), bouquet; (de persil etc) bunch; (parfum) bouquet; (fig) crowning piece; **c'est le ~!** that's the last straw!; **~ garni** (Culin) bouquet garni

bouquin [bukɛ̃] nm (fam) book

bouquiner [bukine] vi (fam) to read

bouquiniste [bukinist] nm/f bookseller

bourbeux, -euse [buRbø, -øz] adj muddy

bourbier [buRbje] nm (quag)mire

bourde [buRd] nf (erreur) howler; (gaffe) blunder

bourdon [buRdɔ̃] nm bumblebee

bourdonner [buRdɔne] vi to buzz; (moteur) to hum

bourg [buR] nm small market town (ou village)

bourgeois, e [buRʒwa, -waz] adj (péj) ≈ (upper) middle class; bourgeois; (maison etc) very comfortable ▷ nm/f (autrefois) burgher

bourgeoisie [buRʒwazi] nf ≈ upper middle classes pl; bourgeoisie; **petite ~** middle classes

bourgeon [buRʒɔ̃] nm bud

Bourgogne [buRgɔɲ] nf: **la ~** Burgundy ▷ nm: **bourgogne** Burgundy (wine)

bourguignon, ne [buRgiɲɔ̃, -ɔn] adj of ou from Burgundy, Burgundian; **bœuf ~** bœuf bourguignon

bourlinguer [buRlɛ̃ge] vi to knock ~~ ~ ~t a lot, get around a lot

bourrade [buʀad] nf shove, thump

bourrage [buʀaʒ] nm (papier) jamming; ~ **de crâne** brainwashing; (Scol) cramming

bourrasque [buʀask] nf squall

bourratif, -ive [buʀatif, -iv] (fam) adj filling, stodgy

bourré, e [buʀe] adj (rempli): ~ **de** crammed full of; (fam: ivre) pickled, plastered

bourreau, x [buʀo] nm executioner; (fig) torturer; ~ **de travail** workaholic, glutton for work

bourrelet [buʀlɛ] nm draught (Brit) ou draft (US) excluder; (de peau) fold ou roll (of flesh)

bourrer [buʀe] vt (pipe) to fill; (poêle) to pack; (valise) to cram (full); ~ **de** to cram (full) with, stuff with; ~ **de coups** to hammer blows on, pummel; ~ **le crâne à qn** to pull the wool over sb's eyes; (endoctriner) to brainwash sb

bourrique [buʀik] nf (âne) ass

bourru, e [buʀy] adj surly, gruff

bourse [buʀs] nf (subvention) grant; (porte-monnaie) purse; **sans ~ délier** without spending a penny; **la B~** the Stock Exchange; ~ **du travail** ≈ trades union council (regional headquarters)

boursier, -ière [buʀsje, -jɛʀ] adj (Comm) Stock Market cpd ▷ nm/f (Scol) grant-holder

boursoufler [buʀsufle] vt to puff up, bloat; **se boursoufler** vi (visage) to swell ou puff up; (peinture) to blister

bous [bu] vb voir **bouillir**

bousculade [buskylad] nf (hâte) rush; (poussée) crush

bousculer [buskyle] vt to knock over; (heurter) to knock into; (fig) to push, rush

bouse [buz] nf: ~ **(de vache)** (cow) dung no pl (Brit), manure no pl

bousiller [buzije] vt (fam) to wreck

boussole [busɔl] nf compass

bout [bu] vb voir **bouillir** ▷ nm bit; (extrémité: d'un bâton etc) tip; (: d'une ficelle, table, rue, période) end; **au ~ de** at the end of, after; **au ~ du compte** at the end of the day; **pousser qn à ~** to push sb to the limit (of his patience); **venir à ~ de** to manage to finish (off) ou overcome; ~ **à ~** end to end; **à tout ~ de champ** at every turn; **d'un ~ à l'autre, de ~ en ~** from one end to the other; **à ~ portant** at point-blank range; **un ~ de chou** (enfant) a little tot; ~ **d'essai** (Ciné etc) screen test; ~ **filtre** filter tip

boutade [butad] nf quip, sally

boute-en-train [butɑ̃tʀɛ̃] nm inv live wire (fig)

bouteille [butɛj] nf bottle; (de gaz butane) cylinder

boutique [butik] nf shop (Brit), store (US); (de grand couturier, de mode) boutique

bouton [butɔ̃] nm (de vêtement, électrique etc) button; (Bot) bud; (sur la peau) spot; (de porte) knob; ~ **de manchette** cuff-link; ~ **d'or** buttercup

boutonner [butɔne] vt to button up, do up;

se boutonner to button one's clothes up

boutonnière [butɔnjɛʀ] nf buttonhole

bouton-pression (pl **boutons-pression**) [butɔ̃pʀesjɔ̃] nm press stud, snap fastener

bouture [butyʀ] nf cutting; **faire des ~s** to take cuttings

bovin, e [bɔvɛ̃, -in] adj bovine ▷ nm: ~**s** cattle pl

bowling [boliŋ] nm (tenpin) bowling; (salle) bowling alley

box [bɔks] nm lock-up (garage); (de salle, dortoir) cubicle; (d'écurie) loose-box; (aussi: ~-**calf**) box calf; **le ~ des accusés** the dock

boxe [bɔks] nf boxing

boxeur [bɔksœʀ] nm boxer

boyaux [bwajo] nmpl (viscères) entrails, guts

BP sigle f = **boîte postale**

bracelet [bʀaslɛ] nm bracelet

braconnier [bʀakɔnje] nm poacher

brader [bʀade] vt to sell off, sell cheaply

braderie [bʀadʀi] nf clearance sale; (par des particuliers) ≈ car boot sale (Brit), ≈ garage sale (US); (magasin) discount store; (sur marché) cut-price (Brit) ou cut-rate (US) stall

braguette [bʀagɛt] nf fly, flies pl (Brit), zipper (US)

brailler [bʀaje] vi to bawl, yell ▷ vt to bawl out, yell out

braire [bʀɛʀ] vi to bray

braise [bʀɛz] nf embers pl

brancard [bʀɑ̃kaʀ] nm (civière) stretcher; (bras, perche) shaft

brancardier [bʀɑ̃kaʀdje] nm stretcher-bearer

branchages [bʀɑ̃ʃaʒ] nmpl branches, boughs

branche [bʀɑ̃ʃ] nf branch; (de lunettes) side(-piece)

branché, e [bʀɑ̃ʃe] adj (fam) switched-on, trendy ▷ nm/f (fam) trendy

brancher [bʀɑ̃ʃe] vt to connect (up); (en mettant la prise) to plug in; ~ **qn/qch sur** (fig) to get sb/sth launched onto

brandir [bʀɑ̃diʀ] vt (arme) to brandish, wield; (document) to flourish, wave

branle [bʀɑ̃l] nm: **mettre en ~** to set swinging; **donner le ~ à** to set in motion

branle-bas [bʀɑ̃lba] nm inv commotion

braquer [bʀake] vi (Auto) to turn (the wheel) ▷ vt (revolver etc): ~ **qch sur** to aim sth at, point sth at; (mettre en colère): ~ **qn** to antagonize sb, put sb's back up; ~ **son regard sur** to fix one's gaze on; **se braquer** vi: **se ~ (contre)** to take a stand (against)

bras [bʀa] nm arm; (de fleuve) branch ▷ nmpl (fig: travailleurs) labour sg (Brit), labor sg (US), hands; ~ **dessus ~ dessous** arm in arm; **à ~ raccourcis** with fists flying; **à tour de ~** with all one's might; **baisser les ~** to give up; **se retrouver avec qch sur les ~** (fam) to be landed with sth; ~ **droit** (fig) right hand man; ~ **de fer** arm-wrestling; **une partie de ~ de fer** (fig) a trial of strength; ~ **de levier**

lever arm; **~ de mer** arm of the sea, sound

brasier [bʀɑzje] *nm* blaze, (blazing) inferno; *(fig)* inferno

bras-le-corps [bʀɑlkɔʀ]: **à ~** *adv* (a)round the waist

brassard [bʀasaʀ] *nm* armband

brasse [bʀas] *nf* (*nage*) breast-stroke; (*mesure*) fathom; **~ papillon** butterfly(-stroke)

brassée [bʀase] *nf* armful; **une ~ de** *(fig)* a number of

brasser [bʀase] *vt* (*bière*) to brew; (*remuer*: *salade*) to toss; (*: cartes*) to shuffle; *(fig)* to mix; **~ l'argent/les affaires** to handle a lot of money/ business

brasserie [bʀasʀi] *nf* (*restaurant*) bar (*selling food*), brasserie; (*usine*) brewery

brave [bʀav] *adj* (*courageux*) brave; (*bon, gentil*) good, kind

braver [bʀave] *vt* to defy

bravo [bʀavo] *excl* bravo! ▷ *nm* cheer

bravoure [bʀavuʀ] *nf* bravery

break [bʀɛk] *nm* (*Auto*) estate car (*Brit*), station wagon (*US*)

brebis [bʀəbi] *nf* ewe; **~ galeuse** black sheep

brèche [bʀɛʃ] *nf* breach, gap; **être sur la ~** *(fig)* to be on the go

bredouille [bʀəduj] *adj* empty-handed

bredouiller [bʀəduje] *vi, vt* to mumble, stammer

bref, brève [bʀɛf, bʀɛv] *adj* short, brief ▷ *adv* in short ▷ *nf* (*voyelle*) short vowel; (*information*) brief news item; **d'un ton ~** sharply, curtly; **en ~** in short, in brief; **à ~ délai** shortly

Brésil [bʀezil] *nm*: **le ~** Brazil

brésilien, ne [bʀeziljɛ̃, -ɛn] *adj* Brazilian ▷ *nm/f*: **B~, ne** Brazilian

Bretagne [bʀətaɲ] *nf*: **la ~** Brittany

bretelle [bʀətɛl] *nf* (*de fusil etc*) sling; (*de vêtement*) strap; (*d'autoroute*) slip road (*Brit*), entrance *ou* exit ramp (*US*); **bretelles** *nfpl* (*pour pantalon*) braces (*Brit*), suspenders (*US*); **~ de contournement** (*Auto*) bypass; **~ de raccordement** (*Auto*) access road

breton, ne [bʀətɔ̃, -ɔn] *adj* Breton ▷ *nm* (*Ling*) Breton ▷ *nm/f*: **B~, ne** Breton

breuvage [bʀœvaʒ] *nm* beverage, drink

brève [bʀɛv] *adj f, nf voir* **bref**

brevet [bʀəvɛ] *nm* diploma, certificate; **~ d'apprentissage** certificate of apprenticeship; **~ (des collèges)** *school certificate, taken at approx. 16 years*; **~ (d'invention)** patent

breveté, e [bʀəvte] *adj* patented; (*diplômé*) qualified

bribes [bʀib] *nfpl* bits, scraps; (*d'une conversation*) snatches; **par ~** piecemeal

bricolage [bʀikɔlaʒ] *nm*: **le ~** do-it-yourself (jobs); (*péj*) patched-up job

bricole [bʀikɔl] *nf* (*babiole, chose insignifiante*) trifle; (*petit travail*) small job

bricoler [bʀikɔle] *vi* to do odd jobs; (*en amateur*) to do DIY jobs; (*passe-temps*) to potter about ▷ *vt* (*réparer*) to fix up; (*mal réparer*) to tinker with; (*trafiquer: voiture etc*) to doctor, fix

bricoleur, -euse [bʀikɔlœʀ, -øz] *nm/f* handyman/woman, DIY enthusiast

bride [bʀid] *nf* bridle; (*d'un bonnet*) string, tie; **à ~ abattue** flat out, hell for leather; **tenir en ~** to keep in check; **lâcher la ~ à, laisser la ~ sur le cou à** to give free rein to

bridé, e [bʀide] *adj*: **yeux ~s** slit eyes

bridge [bʀidʒ] *nm* (*Cartes*) bridge

brièvement [bʀijɛvmã] *adv* briefly

brigade [bʀigad] *nf* (*Police*) squad; (*Mil*) brigade

brigadier [bʀigadje] *nm* (*Police*) ≈ sergeant; (*Mil*) bombardier; corporal

brigandage [bʀigãdaʒ] *nm* robbery

briguer [bʀige] *vt* to aspire to; (*suffrages*) to canvass

brillamment [bʀijamã] *adv* brilliantly

brillant, e [bʀijã, -ãt] *adj* brilliant; (*remarquable*) bright; (*luisant*) shiny, shining ▷ *nm* (*diamant*) brilliant

briller [bʀije] *vi* to shine

brimer [bʀime] *vt* to harass; to bully

brin [bʀɛ̃] *nm* (*de laine, ficelle etc*) strand; (*fig*): **un ~ de** a bit of; **un ~ mystérieux** *etc* (*fam*) a weeny bit mysterious *etc*; **~ d'herbe** blade of grass; **~ de muguet** sprig of lily of the valley; **~ de paille** wisp of straw

brindille [bʀɛ̃dij] *nf* twig

brio [bʀijo] *nm* brilliance; (*Mus*) brio; **avec ~** brilliantly, with panache

brioche [bʀijɔʃ] *nf* brioche (bun); (*fam: ventre*) paunch

brique [bʀik] *nf* brick; (*de lait*) carton; (*fam*) 10 000 francs ▷ *adj inv* brick red

briquer [bʀike] *vt* (*fam*) to polish up

briquet [bʀikɛ] *nm* (cigarette) lighter

brise [bʀiz] *nf* breeze

briser [bʀize] *vt* to break; **se briser** *vi* to break

britannique [bʀitanik] *adj* British ▷ *nm/f*: **B~** Briton, British person; **les B~s** the British

brocante [bʀɔkãt] *nf* (*objets*) secondhand goods *pl*, junk; (*commerce*) secondhand trade; junk dealing

brocanteur, -euse [bʀɔkãtœʀ, -øz] *nm/f* junk shop owner; junk dealer

broche [bʀɔʃ] *nf* brooch; (*Culin*) spit; (*fiche*) spike, peg; (*Méd*) pin; **à la ~** spit-roasted, roasted on a spit

broché, e [bʀɔʃe] *adj* (*livre*) paper-backed; (*tissu*) brocaded

brochet [bʀɔʃɛ] *nm* pike *inv*

brochette [bʀɔʃɛt] *nf* (*ustensile*) skewer; (*plat*) kebab; **~ de décorations** row of medals

brochure [bʀɔʃyʀ] *nf* pamphlet, brochure, booklet

broder [bʀɔde] *vt* to embroider ▷ *vi*: **~ (sur des faits ou une histoire)** to embroider the facts

broderie [bʀɔdʀi] nf embroidery

broncher [bʀɔ̃ʃe] vi: **sans ~** without flinching, without turning a hair

bronches [bʀɔ̃ʃ] nfpl bronchial tubes

bronchite [bʀɔ̃ʃit] nf bronchitis

bronze [bʀɔ̃z] nm bronze

bronzer [bʀɔ̃ze] vt to tan ▷ vi to get a tan; **se bronzer** to sunbathe

brosse [bʀɔs] nf brush; **donner un coup de ~ à qch** to give sth a brush; **coiffé en ~** with a crewcut; **~ à cheveux** hairbrush; **~ à dents** toothbrush; **~ à habits** clothesbrush

brosser [bʀɔse] vt (nettoyer) to brush; (fig: tableau etc) to paint; to draw; **se brosser** vt, vi to brush one's clothes; **se ~ les dents** to brush one's teeth; **tu peux te ~!** (fam) you can sing for it!

brouette [bʀuet] nf wheelbarrow

brouhaha [bʀuaa] nm hubbub

brouillard [bʀujaʀ] nm fog; **être dans le ~** (fig) to be all at sea

brouille [bʀuj] nf quarrel

brouiller [bʀuje] vt (œufs, message) to scramble; (idées) to mix up; to confuse; (Radio) to cause interference to; (: délibérément) to jam; (rendre trouble) to cloud; (désunir: amis) to set at odds; **se brouiller** vi (ciel, vue) to cloud over; (détails) to become confused; **se ~ (avec)** to fall out (with); **~ les pistes** to cover one's tracks; (fig) to confuse the issue

brouillon, ne [bʀujɔ̃, -ɔn] adj (sans soin) untidy; (qui manque d'organisation) disorganized, unmethodical ▷ nm (first) draft; **cahier de ~** rough (work) book; **(papier) ~** rough paper

broussailles [bʀusaj] nfpl undergrowth sg

broussailleux, -euse [bʀusajø, -øz] adj bushy

brousse [bʀus] nf: **la ~** the bush

brouter [bʀute] vt to graze on ▷ vi to graze; (Auto) to judder

broutille [bʀutij] nf trifle

broyer [bʀwaje] vt to crush; **~ du noir** to be down in the dumps

bru [bʀy] nf daughter-in-law

brugnon [bʀynɔ̃] nm nectarine

bruiner [bʀɥine] vb impers: **il bruine** it's drizzling, there's a drizzle

bruire [bʀɥiʀ] vi (eau) to murmur; (feuilles, étoffe) to rustle

bruit [bʀɥi] nm: **un ~** a noise, a sound; (fig: rumeur) a rumour (Brit), a rumor (US); **le ~** noise; **pas/trop de ~** no/too much noise; **sans ~** without a sound, noiselessly; **faire du ~** to make a noise; **~ de fond** background noise

bruitage [bʀɥitaʒ] nm sound effects pl

brûlant, e [bʀylɑ̃, -ɑ̃t] adj burning (hot); (liquide) boiling (hot); (regard) fiery; (sujet) red-hot

brûlé, e [bʀyle] adj (fig: démasqué) blown; (: homme politique etc) discredited ▷ nm: **odeur de ~** smell of burning

brûle-pourpoint [bʀylpuʀpwɛ̃]: **à ~** adv point-blank

brûler [bʀyle] vt to burn; (eau bouillante) to scald; (consommer: électricité, essence) to use; (feu rouge, signal) to go through (without stopping) ▷ vi to burn; (jeu): **tu brûles** you're getting warm ou hot; **se brûler** to burn o.s.; (s'ébouillanter) to scald o.s.; **se ~ la cervelle** to blow one's brains out; **~ les étapes** to make rapid progress; (aller trop vite) to cut corners; **~ (d'impatience) de faire qch** to burn with impatience to do sth, be dying to do sth

brûlure [bʀylyʀ] nf (lésion) burn; (sensation) burning no pl, burning sensation; **~s d'estomac** heartburn sg

brume [bʀym] nf mist

brumeux, -euse [bʀymø, -øz] adj misty; (fig) hazy

brumisateur [bʀymizatœʀ] nm atomizer

brun, e [bʀœ̃, -yn] adj (gén, bière) brown; (cheveux, personne, tabac) dark; **elle est ~e** she's got dark hair ▷ nm (couleur) brown ▷ nf (cigarette) cigarette made of dark tobacco; (bière) = brown ale, ≈ stout

brunch [bʀœntʃ] nm brunch

brunir [bʀyniʀ] vi: **se brunir** to get a tan ▷ vt to tan

brushing [bʀœʃiŋ] nm blow-dry

brusque [bʀysk] adj (soudain) abrupt, sudden; (rude) abrupt, brusque

brusquer [bʀyske] vt to rush

brut, e [bʀyt] adj raw, crude, rough; (diamant) uncut; (soie, minéral, données) raw; (Comm) gross ▷ nf brute; **(champagne) ~** brut champagne; **(pétrole) ~** crude (oil)

brutal, e, -aux [bʀytal, -o] adj brutal

brutaliser [bʀytalize] vt to handle roughly, manhandle

Bruxelles [bʀysɛl] n Brussels

bruyamment [bʀɥijamɑ̃] adv noisily

bruyant, e [bʀɥijɑ̃, -ɑ̃t] adj noisy

bruyère [bʀɥijɛʀ] nf heather

BTS sigle m (= Brevet de technicien supérieur) vocational training certificate taken at end of two-year higher education course

bu, e [by] pp de **boire**

buccal, e, -aux [bykal, -o] adj: **par voie ~e** orally

bûche [byʃ] nf log; **prendre une ~** (fig) to come a cropper (Brit), fall flat on one's face; **~ de Noël** Yule log

bûcher [byʃe] nm (funéraire) pyre; bonfire; (supplice) stake ▷ vi (fam: étudier) to swot (Brit), grind (US), slave (away) ▷ vt to swot up (Brit), cram, slave away at

bûcheron [byʃʀɔ̃] nm woodcutter

bûcheur, -euse [byʃœʀ, -øz] nm/f (fam: étudiant) swot (Brit), grind (US)

budget [bydʒɛ] nm budget

buée [bɥe] nf (sur une vitre) mist; (de l'haleine) steam

buffet [byfɛ] nm (meuble) sideboard; (de réception) buffet; ~ **(de gare)** (station) buffet, snack bar

buffle [byfl] nm buffalo

buis [bui] nm box tree; (bois) box(wood)

buisson [buisɔ̃] nm bush

buissonnière [buisɔnjɛʀ] adj f: **faire l'école** ~ to play truant (Brit), skip school

bulbe [bylb] nm (Bot, Anat) bulb; (coupole) onion-shaped dome

Bulgarie [bylgaʀi] nf: **la** ~ Bulgaria

bulle [byl] adj, nm: **(papier)** ~ manil(l)a paper ▷ nf bubble; (de bande dessinée) balloon; (papale) bull; ~ **de savon** soap bubble

bulletin [byltɛ̃] nm (communiqué, journal) bulletin; (papier) form; (: de bagages) ticket; (Scol) report; ~ **d'informations** news bulletin; ~ **de naissance** birth certificate; ~ **de salaire** pay slip; ~ **de santé** medical bulletin; ~ **(de vote)** ballot paper; ~ **météorologique** weather report

bureau, x [byʀo] nm (meuble) desk; (pièce, service) office; ~ **de change** (foreign) exchange office ou bureau; ~ **d'embauche** ≈ job centre; ~ **d'études** design office; ~ **de location** box office (Brit), lost and found (US); ~ **des objets trouvés** lost property office (Brit), lost and found (US); ~ **de placement** employment agency; ~ **de poste** post office; ~ **de tabac** tobacconist's (shop), smoke shop (US); ~ **de vote** polling station

bureaucratie [byʀokʀasi] nf bureaucracy

burin [byʀɛ̃] nm cold chisel; (Art) burin

burlesque [byʀlɛsk] adj ridiculous; (Littérature) burlesque

bus vb [by] voir **boire** ▷ nm [bys] (véhicule, aussi Inform) bus

busqué, e [byske] adj: **nez** ~ hook(ed) nose

buste [byst] nm (Anat) chest; (: de femme) bust; (sculpture) bust

but [by] vb voir **boire** ▷ nm (cible) target; (fig) goal, aim; (Football etc) goal; **de** ~ **en blanc** point-blank; **avoir pour** ~ **de faire** to aim to do; **dans le** ~ **de** with the intention of

butane [bytan] nm butane; (domestique) calor gas® (Brit), butane

buté, e [byte] adj stubborn, obstinate ▷ nf (Archit) abutment; (Tech) stop

buter [byte] vi: ~ **contre** ou **sur** to bump into; (trébucher) to stumble against ▷ vt to antagonize; **se buter** vi to get obstinate, dig in one's heels

butin [bytɛ̃] nm booty, spoils pl; (d'un vol) loot

butiner [bytine] vi (abeilles) to gather nectar

butte [byt] nf mound, hillock; **être en** ~ **à** to be exposed to

buvais etc [byvɛ] vb voir **boire**

buvard [byvaʀ] nm blotter

buvette [byvɛt] nf refreshment room ou stall; (comptoir) bar

buveur, -euse [byvœʀ, -øz] nm/f drinker

C

c' [s] pron voir **ce**

CA sigle m = **chiffre d'affaires**; **conseil d'administration**; **corps d'armée** ▷ sigle f = **chambre d'agriculture**

ça [sa] pron (pour désigner) this; (: plus loin) that; (comme sujet indéfini) it; **ça m'étonne que** it surprises me that; **ça va?** how are you?; how are things?; (d'accord?) OK?, all right?; **où ça?** where's that?; **pourquoi ça?** why's that?; **qui ça?** who's that?; **ça alors!** (désapprobation) well!, really!; (étonnement) heavens!; **c'est ça** that's right; **ça y est** that's it

çà [sa] adv: **çà et là** here and there

cabane [kaban] nf hut, cabin

cabaret [kabaʀɛ] nm night club

cabas [kabɑ] nm shopping bag

cabillaud [kabijo] nm cod inv

cabine [kabin] nf (de bateau) cabin; (de plage) (beach) hut; (de piscine etc) cubicle; (de camion, train) cab; (d'avion) cockpit; ~ **(d'ascenseur)** lift cage; ~ **d'essayage** fitting room; ~ **de projection** projection room; ~ **spatiale** space capsule; ~ **(téléphonique)** call ou (tele)phone box, (tele)phone booth

cabinet [kabinɛ] nm (petite pièce) closet; (de médecin) surgery (Brit), office (US); (de notaire etc) office; (: clientèle) practice; (Pol) cabinet; (d'un ministre) advisers pl; **cabinets** nmpl (w.-c.) toilet sg; ~ **d'affaires** business consultants' (bureau), business partnership; ~ **de toilette** toilet; ~ **de travail** study

câble [kabl] *nm* cable; **le ~** (TV) cable television, cablevision (US)

cabosser [kabɔse] *vt* to dent

cabrer [kabʀe]: **se cabrer** *vi* (*cheval*) to rear up; (*avion*) to nose up; (*fig*) to revolt, rebel; to jib

cabriole [kabʀijɔl] *nf* caper; (*gymnastique etc*) somersault

cacahuète [kakaɥɛt] *nf* peanut

cacao [kakao] *nm* cocoa (powder); (*boisson*) cocoa

cache [kaʃ] *nm* mask, card (*for masking*) ▷ *nf* hiding place

cache-cache [kaʃkaʃ] *nm*: **jouer à ~** to play hide-and-seek

cachemire [kaʃmiʀ] *nm* cashmere ▷ *adj*: **dessin ~** paisley pattern; **le C~** Kashmir

cache-nez [kaʃne] *nm inv* scarf, muffler

cacher [kaʃe] *vt* to hide, conceal; **~ qch à qn** to hide ou conceal sth from sb; **se cacher** *vi* (*volontairement*) to hide; (*être caché*) to be hidden ou concealed; **il ne s'en cache pas** he makes no secret of it

cachet [kaʃɛ] *nm* (*comprimé*) tablet; (*sceau: du roi*) seal; (: *de la poste*) postmark; (*rétribution*) fee; (*fig*) style, character

cacheter [kaʃte] *vt* to seal; **vin cacheté** vintage wine

cachette [kaʃɛt] *nf* hiding place; **en ~** on the sly, secretly

cachot [kaʃo] *nm* dungeon

cachotterie [kaʃɔtʀi] *nf* mystery; **faire des ~s** to be secretive

cactus [kaktys] *nm* cactus

cadavre [kadavʀ] *nm* corpse, (dead) body

Caddie® [kadi] *nm* (*supermarket*) trolley (*Brit*), (*grocery*) cart (US)

cadeau, x [kado] *nm* present, gift; **faire un ~ à qn** to give sb a present ou gift; **faire ~ de qch à qn** to make a present of sth to sb, give sb sth as a present

cadenas [kadna] *nm* padlock

cadence [kadɑ̃s] *nf* (*Mus*) cadence; (: *rythme*) rhythm; (*de travail etc*) rate; **cadences** *nfpl* (*en usine*) production rate *sg*; **en ~** rhythmically; in time

cadet, te [kadɛ, -ɛt] *adj* younger; (*le plus jeune*) youngest ▷ *nm/f* youngest child ou one, youngest boy ou son/girl ou daughter; **il est mon ~ de deux ans** he's two years younger than me, he's two years my junior; **les ~s** (*Sport*) the minors (15–17 years); **le ~ de mes soucis** the least of my worries

cadran [kadʀɑ̃] *nm* dial; **~ solaire** sundial

cadre [kadʀ] *nm* frame; (*environnement*) surroundings *pl*; (*limites*) scope ▷ *nm/f* (*Admin*) managerial employee, executive ▷ *adj*: **loi ~** outline ou blueprint law; **~ moyen/supérieur** (*Admin*) middle/senior management employee, junior/senior executive; **rayer qn des ~s** to discharge sb; to dismiss sb; **dans le ~ de** (*fig*) within the framework ou context of

cadrer [kadʀe] *vi*: **~ avec** to tally ou correspond with ▷ *vt* (*Ciné, Photo*) to frame

cafard [kafaʀ] *nm* cockroach; **avoir le ~** to be down in the dumps, be feeling low

café [kafe] *nm* coffee; (*bistro*) café ▷ *adj inv* coffee *cpd*; **~ crème** coffee with cream; **~ au lait** white coffee; **~ noir** black coffee; **~ en grains** coffee beans; **~ en poudre** instant coffee; **~ liégeois** coffee ice cream with whipped cream

cafétéria [kafeteʀja] *nf* cafeteria

café-tabac *nm* tobacconist's or newsagent's also serving coffee and spirits

cafetière [kaftjɛʀ] *nf* (*pot*) coffee-pot

cafouiller [kafuje] *vi* to get in a shambles; (*machine etc*) to work in fits and starts

cage [kaʒ] *nf* cage; **~ (des buts)** goal; **en ~** in a cage, caged up ou in; **~ d'ascenseur** lift shaft; **~ d'escalier** (stair)well; **~ thoracique** rib cage

cageot [kaʒo] *nm* crate

cagibi [kaʒibi] *nm* shed

cagnotte [kaɲɔt] *nf* kitty

cagoule [kagul] *nf* cowl; hood; (*Ski etc*) cagoule; (*passe-montagne*) balaclava

cahier [kaje] *nm* notebook; (*Typo*) signature; (*revue*) journal; **~ de revendications/doléances** list of claims/grievances; **~ de brouillons** rough book, jotter; **~ des charges** specification; **~ d'exercices** exercise book

cahot [kao] *nm* jolt, bump

caïd [kaid] *nm* big chief, boss

caille [kaj] *nf* quail

cailler [kaje] *vi* (*lait*) to curdle; (*sang*) to clot; (*fam*) to be cold

caillot [kajo] *nm* (blood) clot

caillou, x [kaju] *nm* (little) stone

caillouteux, -euse [kajutø, -øz] *adj* stony; pebbly

Caire [kɛʀ] *nm*: **le ~** Cairo

caisse [kɛs] *nf* box; (*où l'on met la recette*) cashbox; (: *machine*) till; (*où l'on paye*) cash desk (*Brit*), checkout counter; (: *au supermarché*) checkout; (*de banque*) cashier's desk; (*Tech*) case, casing; **faire sa ~** (*Comm*) to count the takings; **~ claire** (*Mus*) side ou snare drum; **~ éclair** express checkout; **~ enregistreuse** cash register; **~ d'épargne (CE)** savings bank; **~ noire** slush fund; **~ de retraite** pension fund; **~ de sortie** checkout; *voir* **grosse**

caissier, -ière [kesje, -jɛʀ] *nm/f* cashier

cajoler [kaʒɔle] *vt* to wheedle, coax; to surround with love and care, make a fuss of

cake [kɛk] *nm* fruit cake

calandre [kalɑ̃dʀ] *nf* radiator grill; (*machine*) calender, mangle

calanque [kalɑ̃k] *nf* rocky inlet

calcaire [kalkɛʀ] *nm* limestone ▷ *adj* (*eau*) hard; (*Géo*) limestone *cpd*

calciné, e [kalsine] *adj* burnt to ashes

calcul [kalkyl] nm calculation; **le ~** (Scol) arithmetic; **~ différentiel/intégral** differential/integral calculus; **~ mental** mental arithmetic; **~ (biliaire)** (gall)stone; **~ (rénal)** (kidney) stone; **d'après mes ~s** by my reckoning

calculateur [kalkylatœʀ] nm, **calculatrice** [kalkylatʀis] nf calculator

calculer [kalkyle] vt to calculate, work out, reckon; (combiner) to calculate; **~ qch de tête** to work sth out in one's head

calculette [kalkylɛt] nf (pocket) calculator

cale [kal] nf (de bateau) hold; (en bois) wedge, chock; **~ sèche** ou **de radoub** dry dock

calé, e [kale] adj (fam) clever, bright

caleçon [kalsɔ̃] nm (d'homme) boxer shorts; (de femme) leggings; **~ de bain** bathing trunks pl

calembour [kalɑ̃buʀ] nm pun

calendrier [kalɑ̃dʀije] nm calendar; (fig) timetable

calepin [kalpɛ̃] nm notebook

caler [kale] vt to wedge, chock up; **~ (son moteur/véhicule)** to stall (one's engine/vehicle); **se ~ dans un fauteuil** to make o.s. comfortable in an armchair ▷ vi (moteur, véhicule) to stall

calfeutrer [kalføtʀe] vt to (make) draughtproof (Brit) ou draftproof (US); **se calfeutrer** vi to make o.s. snug and comfortable

calibre [kalibʀ] nm (d'un fruit) grade; (d'une arme) bore, calibre (Brit), caliber (US); (fig) calibre, caliber

califourchon [kalifuʀʃɔ̃]: **à ~** adv astride; **à ~ sur** astride, straddling

câlin, e [kɑlɛ̃, -in] adj cuddly, cuddlesome; (regard, voix) tender

câliner [kaline] vt to fondle, cuddle

calmant [kalmɑ̃] nm tranquillizer, sedative; (contre la douleur) painkiller

calme [kalm] adj calm, quiet ▷ nm calm(ness), quietness; **sans perdre son ~** without losing one's cool ou calmness; **~ plat** (Navig) dead calm

calmer [kalme] vt to calm (down); (douleur, inquiétude) to ease, soothe; **se calmer** vi to calm down

calomnie [kalɔmni] nf slander; (écrite) libel

calomnier [kalɔmnje] vt to slander; to libel

calorie [kalɔʀi] nf calorie

calotte [kalɔt] nf (coiffure) skullcap; (gifle) slap; **la ~** (péj: clergé) the cloth, the clergy; **~ glaciaire** icecap

calquer [kalke] vt to trace; (fig) to copy exactly

calvaire [kalvɛʀ] nm (croix) wayside cross, calvary; (souffrances) suffering, martyrdom

calvitie [kalvisi] nf baldness

camarade [kamaʀad] nm/f friend, pal; (Pol) comrade

camaraderie [kamaʀadʀi] nf friendship

Cambodge [kɑ̃bɔdʒ] nm: **le ~** Cambodia

cambouis [kɑ̃bwi] nm dirty oil ou grease

cambrer [kɑ̃bʀe] vt to arch; **se cambrer** vi to arch one's back; **~ la taille** ou **les reins** to arch one's back

cambriolage [kɑ̃bʀijɔlaʒ] nm burglary

cambrioler [kɑ̃bʀijɔle] vt to burgle (Brit), burglarize (US)

cambrioleur, -euse [kɑ̃bʀijɔlœʀ, -øz] nm/f burglar

camelote [kamlɔt] (fam) nf rubbish, trash, junk

caméra [kameʀa] nf (Ciné, TV) camera; (d'amateur) cine-camera

Cameroun [kamʀun] nm: **le ~** Cameroon

caméscope® [kameskɔp] nm camcorder

camion [kamjɔ̃] nm lorry (Brit), truck; (plus petit, fermé) van; (charge): **~ de sable/cailloux** lorry-load (Brit) ou truck-load of sand/stones; **~ de dépannage** breakdown (Brit) ou tow (US) truck

camion-citerne (pl **camions-citernes**) [kamjɔ̃sitɛʀn] nm tanker

camionnette [kamjɔnɛt] nf (small) van

camionneur [kamjɔnœʀ] nm (entrepreneur) haulage contractor (Brit), trucker (US); (chauffeur) lorry (Brit) ou truck driver; van driver

camisole [kamizɔl] nf: **~ (de force)** straitjacket

camomille [kamɔmij] nf camomile; (boisson) camomile tea

camoufler [kamufle] vt to camouflage; (fig) to conceal, cover up

camp [kɑ̃] nm camp; (fig) side; **~ de nudistes/vacances** nudist/holiday camp; **~ de concentration** concentration camp

campagnard, e [kɑ̃paɲaʀ, -aʀd] adj country cpd ▷ nm/f countryman/woman

campagne [kɑ̃paɲ] nf country, countryside; (Mil, Pol, Comm) campaign; **en ~** (Mil) in the field; **à la ~** in/to the country; **faire ~ pour** to campaign for; **~ électorale** election campaign; **~ de publicité** advertising campaign

camper [kɑ̃pe] vi to camp ▷ vt (chapeau etc) to pull ou put on firmly; (dessin) to sketch; **se ~ devant** to plant o.s. in front of

campeur, -euse [kɑ̃pœʀ, -øz] nm/f camper

camping [kɑ̃piŋ] nm camping; **(terrain de) ~** campsite, camping site; **faire du ~** to go camping; **faire du ~ sauvage** to camp rough

camping-car [kɑ̃piŋkaʀ] nm camper, motorhome (US)

camping-gaz® [kɑ̃piŋgaz] nm inv camp(ing) stove

Canada [kanada] nm: **le ~** Canada

canadien, ne [kanadjɛ̃, -ɛn] adj Canadian ▷ nm/f: **C~, ne** Canadian ▷ nf (veste) fur-lined jacket

canaille [kanaj] nf (péj) scoundrel; (populace) riff-raff ▷ adj raffish, rakish

canal, -aux [kanal, -o] *nm* canal; (*naturel*, TV) channel; (*Admin*): **par le ~ de** through (the medium of), via; **~ de distribution/ télévision** distribution/television channel; **~ de Panama/Suez** Panama/ Suez Canal

canalisation [kanalizasjɔ̃] *nf* (*tuyau*) pipe

canaliser [kanalize] *vt* to canalize; (*fig*) to channel

canapé [kanape] *nm* settee, sofa; (*Culin*) canapé, open sandwich

canard [kanaʀ] *nm* duck; (*fam: journal*) rag

canari [kanaʀi] *nm* canary

cancans [kɑ̃kɑ̃] *nmpl* (*malicious*) gossip *sg*

cancer [kɑ̃sɛʀ] *nm* cancer; (*signe*): **le C~** Cancer, the Crab; **être du C~** to be Cancer; **il a un ~** he has cancer

cancre [kɑ̃kʀ] *nm* dunce

candeur [kɑ̃dœʀ] *nf* ingenuousness

candidat, e [kɑ̃dida, -at] *nm/f* candidate; (*à un poste*) applicant, candidate

candidature [kɑ̃didatyʀ] *nf* (*Pol*) candidature; (*à poste*) application; **poser sa ~** to submit an application, apply; **poser sa ~ à un poste** to apply for a job; **~ spontanée** unsolicited job application

candide [kɑ̃did] *adj* ingenuous, guileless, naïve

cane [kan] *nf* (*female*) duck

caneton [kantɔ̃] *nm* duckling

canette [kanɛt] *nf* (*de bière*) (flip-top) bottle; (*de machine à coudre*) spool

canevas [kanva] *nm* (*Couture*) canvas (for tapestry work); (*fig*) framework, structure

caniche [kaniʃ] *nm* poodle

canicule [kanikyl] *nf* scorching heat; midsummer heat, dog days *pl*

canif [kanif] *nm* penknife, pocket knife

canin, e [kanɛ̃, -in] *adj* canine ▷ *nf* canine (tooth), eye tooth

caniveau, x [kanivo] *nm* gutter

canne [kan] *nf* (*walking*) stick; **~ à pêche** fishing rod; **~ à sucre** sugar cane; **les ~s blanches** (*les aveugles*) the blind

cannelle [kanɛl] *nf* cinnamon

canoë [kanɔe] *nm* canoe; (*sport*) canoeing; **~ (kayak)** kayak

canon [kanɔ̃] *nm* (*arme*) gun; (*Hist*) cannon; (*d'une arme: tube*) barrel; (*fig*) model; (*Mus*) canon ▷ *adj*: **droit ~** canon law; **~ rayé** rifled barrel

canot [kano] *nm* boat, ding(h)y; **~ pneumatique** rubber *ou* inflatable ding(h)y; **~ de sauvetage** lifeboat

canotier [kanɔtje] *nm* boater

cantatrice [kɑ̃tatʀis] *nf* (*opera*) singer

cantine [kɑ̃tin] *nf* canteen; (*réfectoire d'école*) dining hall

cantique [kɑ̃tik] *nm* hymn

canton [kɑ̃tɔ̃] *nm* district (*consisting of several communes*); *see note*; (*en Suisse*) canton

see note

❀ CANTON

❀
❀ A French *canton* is the administrative
❀ division represented by a councillor in
❀ the "Conseil général". It comprises a
❀ number of "communes" and is, in turn,
❀ a subdivision of an "arrondissement".
❀ In Switzerland the *cantons* are the 23
❀ autonomous political divisions which
❀ make up the Swiss confederation.

cantonade [kɑ̃tɔnad]: **à la ~** *adv* to everyone in general; (*crier*) from the rooftops

cantonner [kɑ̃tɔne] *vt* (*Mil*) to billet (*Brit*), quarter; to station; **se ~ dans** to confine o.s. to

cantonnier [kɑ̃tɔnje] *nm* roadmender

canular [kanylaʀ] *nm* hoax

caoutchouc [kautʃu] *nm* rubber; **~ mousse** foam rubber; **en ~** rubber *cpd*

CAP *sigle m* (= *Certificat d'aptitude professionnelle*) *vocational training certificate taken at secondary school*

cap [kap] *nm* (*Géo*) cape; (*promontoire*) headland; (*fig*) hurdle; (*tournant*) watershed; (*Navig*): **changer de ~** to change course; **mettre le ~ sur** to head *ou* steer for; **doubler** *ou* **passer le ~** (*fig*) to get over the worst; **Le C~** Cape Town; **le ~ de Bonne Espérance** the Cape of Good Hope; **le ~ Horn** Cape Horn; **les îles du C~ Vert** (*aussi*: **le C~-Vert**) the Cape Verde Islands

capable [kapabl] *adj* able, capable; **~ de qch/ faire** capable of sth/doing; **il est ~ d'oublier** he could easily forget; **spectacle ~ d'intéresser** show likely to be of interest

capacité [kapasite] *nf* (*compétence*) ability; (*Jur, Inform, d'un récipient*) capacity; **~ (en droit)** *basic legal qualification*

cape [kap] *nf* cape, cloak; **rire sous ~** to laugh up one's sleeve

CAPES [kapɛs] *sigle m* (= *Certificat d'aptitude au professorat de l'enseignement du second degré*) *secondary teaching diploma*; *see note*

❀ CAPES

❀
❀ The French CAPES ("certificat d'aptitude
❀ au professorat de l'enseignement du
❀ second degré") is a competitive
❀ examination sat by prospective
❀ secondary school teachers after the
❀ "licence". Successful candidates become
❀ fully qualified teachers ("professeurs
❀ certifiés").

capillaire [kapilɛʀ] *adj* (*soins, lotion*) hair *cpd*; (*vaisseau etc*) capillary; **artiste ~** hair artist *ou* designer

capitaine [kapitɛn] *nm* captain; **~ des pompiers** fire chief (*Brit*), fire marshal (*US*); **~ au long cours** master mariner

capital, e, -aux [kapital, -o] *adj (œuvre)* major; *(question, rôle)* fundamental; *(Jur)* capital ▷ *nm* capital; *(fig)* stock; asset ▷ *nf (ville)* capital; *(lettre)* capital (letter); **d'une importance ~e** of capital importance; **capitaux** *nmpl (fonds)* capital *sg*, money *sg*; **les sept péchés capitaux** the seven deadly sins; **peine ~e** capital punishment; **~ (social)** authorized capital; **~ d'exploitation** working capital

capitalisme [kapitalism] *nm* capitalism

capitaliste [kapitalist] *adj, nm/f* capitalist

capitonné, e [kapitɔne] *adj* padded

caporal, -aux [kapɔral, -o] *nm* lance corporal

capot [kapo] *nm (Auto)* bonnet *(Brit)*, hood *(US)*

capote [kapɔt] *nf (de voiture)* hood *(Brit)*, top *(US)*; *(de soldat)* greatcoat; **~ (anglaise)** *(fam)* rubber, condom

capoter [kapɔte] *vi* to overturn; *(négociations)* to founder

câpre [kɑpr] *nf* caper

caprice [kapris] *nm* whim, caprice; passing fancy; **caprices** *nmpl (de la mode etc)* vagaries; **faire un ~** to throw a tantrum; **faire des ~s** to be temperamental

capricieux, -euse [kaprisjø, -øz] *adj (fantasque)* capricious; whimsical; *(enfant)* temperamental

Capricorne [kaprikɔrn] *nm*: **le ~** Capricorn, the Goat; **être du ~** to be Capricorn

capsule [kapsyl] *nf (de bouteille)* cap; *(amorce)* primer; cap; *(Bot etc, spatiale)* capsule

capter [kapte] *vt (ondes radio)* to pick up; *(eau)* to harness; *(fig)* to win, capture

captivant, e [kaptivɑ̃, -ɑ̃t] *adj* captivating

captivité [kaptivite] *nf* captivity; **en ~** in captivity

capturer [kaptyre] *vt* to capture, catch

capuche [kapyʃ] *nf* hood

capuchon [kapyʃɔ̃] *nm* hood; *(de stylo)* cap, top

capucine [kapysin] *nf (Bot)* nasturtium

caquet [kake] *nm*: **rabattre le ~ à qn** to bring sb down a peg or two

caqueter [kakte] *vi (poule)* to cackle; *(fig)* to prattle

car [kar] *nm* coach *(Brit)*, bus ▷ *conj* because, for; **~ de police** police van; **~ de reportage** broadcasting *ou* radio van

carabine [karabin] *nf* carbine, rifle; **~ à air comprimé** airgun

caractère [karaktɛr] *nm (gén)* character; **en ~s gras** in bold type; **en petits ~s** in small print; **en ~s d'imprimerie** in block capitals; **avoir du ~** to have character; **avoir bon/mauvais ~** to be good-/ill-natured *ou* tempered; **~ de remplacement** wild card *(Inform)*; **~s/seconde (cps)** characters per second (cps)

caractériel, le [karaktɛrjɛl] *adj (enfant)* (emotionally) disturbed ▷ *nm/f* problem child; **troubles ~s** emotional problems

caractérisé, e [karakterize] *adj*: **c'est une grippe/de l'insubordination ~e** it is a clear(-cut) case of flu/insubordination

caractériser [karakterize] *vt* to characterize; **se ~ par** to be characterized *ou* distinguished by

caractéristique [karakteristik] *adj, nf* characteristic

carafe [karaf] *nf* decanter; *(pour eau, vin ordinaire)* carafe

caraïbe [karaib] *adj* Caribbean; **les Caraïbes** *nfpl* the Caribbean (Islands); **la mer des C~s** the Caribbean Sea

carambolage [karɑ̃bɔlaʒ] *nm* multiple crash, pileup

caramel [karamɛl] *nm (bonbon)* caramel, toffee; *(substance)* caramel

carapace [karapas] *nf* shell

caravane [karavan] *nf* caravan

caravaning [karavaniŋ] *nm* caravanning; *(emplacement)* caravan site

carbone [karbɔn] *nm* carbon; *(feuille)* carbon, sheet of carbon paper; *(double)* carbon (copy)

carbonique [karbɔnik] *adj*: **gaz ~** carbon dioxide; **neige ~** dry ice

carbonisé, e [karbɔnize] *adj* charred; **mourir ~** to be burned to death

carburant [karbyrɑ̃] *nm (motor)* fuel

carburateur [karbyratœr] *nm* carburettor

carcan [karkɑ̃] *nm (fig)* yoke, shackles *pl*

carcasse [karkas] *nf* carcass; *(de véhicule etc)* shell

cardiaque [kardjak] *adj* cardiac, heart *cpd* ▷ *nm/f* heart patient; **être ~** to have a heart condition

cardigan [kardigɑ̃] *nm* cardigan

cardiologue [kardjɔlɔg] *nm/f* cardiologist, heart specialist

carême [karɛm] *nm*: **le C~** Lent

carence [karɑ̃s] *nf* incompetence, inadequacy; *(manque)* deficiency; **~ vitaminique** vitamin deficiency

caresse [karɛs] *nf* caress

caresser [karɛse] *vt* to caress; *(animal)* to stroke, fondle; *(fig: projet, espoir)* to toy with

cargaison [kargɛzɔ̃] *nf* cargo, freight

cargo [kargo] *nm* cargo boat, freighter; **~ mixte** cargo and passenger ship

caricature [karikatyr] *nf* caricature; *(politique etc)* (satirical) cartoon

carie [kari] *nf*: **la ~ (dentaire)** tooth decay; **une ~** a bad tooth

carillon [karijɔ̃] *nm (d'église)* bells *pl*; *(de pendule)* chimes *pl*; *(de porte)*: **~ (électrique)** (electric) door chime *ou* bell

caritatif, -ive [karitatif, -iv] *adj* charitable

carnassier, -ière [karnasje, -jɛr] *adj* carnivorous ▷ *nm* carnivore

carnaval [karnaval] *nm* carnival

carnet [karnɛ] *nm (calepin)* notebook; *(de tickets, timbres etc)* book; *(d'école)* school report; *(journal intime)* diary; **~ d'adresses** address book; **~ de chèques** cheque book (*Brit*), checkbook (*US*); **~ de commandes** order book; **~ de notes** (*Scol*) (school) report; **~ à souches** counterfoil book

carotte [kaʀɔt] *nf* (*aussi fig*) carrot

carpette [kaʀpɛt] *nf* rug

carré, e [kaʀe] *adj* square; (*fig: franc*) straightforward ▷ *nm* (*de terrain, jardin*) patch, plot; (*Navig: salle*) wardroom; (*Math*)-square; **~ blanc** (*TV*) "adults only" symbol; (*Cartes*): **~ d'as/de rois** four aces/kings; **élever un nombre au ~** to square a number; **mètre/ kilomètre ~** square metre/kilometre; **~ de soie** silk headsquare *ou* headscarf; **~ d'agneau** loin of lamb

carreau, x [kaʀo] *nm* (*en faïence etc*) (floor) tile; (*au mur*) (wall) tile; (*window*) pane; (*motif*) check, square; (*Cartes: couleur*) diamonds *pl*; (: *carte*) diamond; **tissu à ~x** checked fabric; **papier à ~x** squared paper

carrefour [kaʀfuʀ] *nm* crossroads *sg*

carrelage [kaʀlaʒ] *nm* tiling; (*sol*) (tiled) floor

carrelet [kaʀlɛ] *nm* (*poisson*) plaice

carrément [kaʀemɑ̃] *adv* (*franchement*) straight out, bluntly; (*sans détours, sans hésiter*) straight; (*nettement*) definitely; (*intensif*) completely; **c'est ~ impossible** it's completely impossible; **il l'a ~ mis à la porte** he threw him straight out

carrière [kaʀjɛʀ] *nf* (*de roches*) quarry; (*métier*) career; **militaire de ~** professional soldier; **faire ~ dans** to make one's career in

carrossable [kaʀɔsabl] *adj* suitable for (motor) vehicles

carrosse [kaʀɔs] *nm* (horse-drawn) coach

carrosserie [kaʀɔsʀi] *nf* body, bodywork *no pl* (*Brit*); (*activité, commerce*) coachwork (*Brit*), (*car*) body manufacturing; **atelier de ~** (*pour réparations*) body shop, panel beaters' (yard) (*Brit*)

carrure [kaʀyʀ] *nf* build; (*fig*) stature, calibre

cartable [kaʀtabl] *nm* (*d'écolier*) satchel, (school)bag

carte [kaʀt] *nf* (*de géographie*) map; (*marine, du ciel*) chart; (*de fichier, d'abonnement etc, à jouer*) card; (*au restaurant*) menu; (*aussi*: **~ postale**) (post)card; (*aussi*: **~ de visite**) (visiting) card; **avoir/donner ~ blanche** to have/give carte blanche *ou* a free hand; **tirer les ~s à qn** to read sb's cards; **jouer aux ~s** to play cards; **jouer ~s sur table** (*fig*) to put one's cards on the table; **à la ~** (*au restaurant*) à la carte; **~ à circuit imprimé** printed circuit; **~ à puce** smartcard, chip and PIN card; **~ bancaire** cash card; **C~ Bleue®** debit card; **~ de crédit** credit card; **~ de fidélité** loyalty card; **la ~ des vins** the wine list; **~ d'état-major** ≈ Ordnance (*Brit*) *ou* Geological (*US*) Survey map; **~ d'identité** identity card; **la ~ grise** (*Auto*) ≈ the (car) registration document; **~ jeune** young person's railcard; **~ mémoire** (*d'appareil photo numérique*) memory card; **~**

perforée punch(ed) card; **~ routière** road map; **~ de séjour** residence permit; **~ SIM** SIM card; **~ téléphonique** phonecard; **la ~ verte** (*Auto*) the green card

carter [kaʀtɛʀ] *nm* (*Auto: d'huile*) sump (*Brit*), oil pan (*US*); (: *de la boîte de vitesses*) casing; (*de bicyclette*) chain guard

carton [kaʀtɔ̃] *nm* (*matériau*) cardboard; (*boîte*) (cardboard) box; (*d'invitation*) invitation card; (*Art*) sketch; cartoon; **en ~** cardboard *cpd*; **faire un ~** (*au tir*) to have a go at the rifle range; to score a hit; **~ (à dessin)** portfolio

carton-pâte [kaʀtɔ̃pɑt] *nm* pasteboard; **de ~** (*fig*) cardboard *cpd*

cartouche [kaʀtuʃ] *nf* cartridge; (*de cigarettes*) carton

cas [kɑ] *nm* case; **faire peu de ~/grand ~ de** to attach little/great importance to; **ne faire aucun ~ de** to take no notice of; **le ~ échéant** if need be; **en aucun ~** on no account, under no circumstances (whatsoever); **au ~ où** in case; **dans ce ~** in that case; **en ~ de** in case of, in the event of; **en ~ de besoin** if need be; **en ~ d'urgence** in an emergency; **en ce ~** in that case; **en tout ~** in any case, at any rate; **~ de conscience** matter of conscience; **~ de force majeure** case of absolute necessity; (*Assurances*) act of God; **~ limite** borderline case; **~ social** social problem

casanier, -ière [kazanje, -jɛʀ] *adj* stay-at-home

cascade [kaskad] *nf* waterfall, cascade; (*fig*) stream, torrent

cascadeur, -euse [kaskadœʀ, -øz] *nm/f* stuntman/girl

case [kɑz] *nf* (*hutte*) hut; (*compartiment*) compartment; (*pour le courrier*) pigeonhole; (*d'échiquier*) square; (*sur un formulaire, de mots croisés*) box

caser [kaze] (*fam*) *vt* (*mettre*) to put; (*loger*) to put up; (*péj*) to find a job for; to marry off; **se caser** *vi* (*se marier*) to settle down; (*trouver un emploi*) to find a (steady) job

caserne [kazɛʀn] *nf* barracks

cash [kaʃ] *adv*: **payer ~** to pay cash down

casier [kazje] *nm* (*à journaux etc*) rack; (*de bureau*) filing cabinet; (: *à cases*) set of pigeonholes; (*case*) compartment; (*pour courrier*) pigeonhole; (: *à clef*) locker; (*Pêche*) lobster pot; **~ à bouteilles** bottle rack; **~ judiciaire** police record

casino [kazino] *nm* casino

casque [kask] *nm* helmet; (*chez le coiffeur*) (hair-)dryer; (*pour audition*) (head-)phones *pl*, headset; **les C~s bleus** the UN peacekeeping force

casquette [kaskɛt] *nf* cap

cassant, e [kasɑ̃, -ɑ̃t] *adj* brittle; (*fig*) brusque, abrupt

cassation [kasasjɔ̃] *nf*: **se pourvoir en ~** to lodge an appeal; **recours en ~** appeal to the Supreme Court

casse [kɑs] nf (pour voitures): **mettre à la** ~ to scrap, send to the breakers (Brit); (dégâts): **il y a eu de la** ~ there were a lot of breakages; (Typo): **haut/bas de** ~ upper/lower case

casse-cou [kɑsku] adj inv daredevil, reckless; **crier** ~ **à qn** to warn sb (against a risky undertaking)

casse-croûte [kɑskrut] nm inv snack

casse-noisettes [kɑsnwazɛt], **casse-noix** [kɑsnwa] nm inv nutcrackers pl

casse-pieds [kɑspje] adj, nm/f inv (fam): **il est** ~, **c'est un** ~ he's a pain (in the neck)

casser [kɑse] vt to break; (Admin: gradé) to demote; (Jur) to quash; (Comm): ~ **les prix** to slash prices; **se casser** vi to break; (fam) to go, leave ▷ vt: ~ **les pieds à qn** (fam: irriter) to get on sb's nerves; **se ~ la jambe/une jambe** to break one's leg/a leg; **se ~ la tête** (fam) to go to a lot of trouble; **à tout** ~ fantastic, brilliant; **se ~ net** to break clean off

casserole [kɑsrɔl] nf saucepan; **à la** ~ (Culin) braised

casse-tête [kɑstɛt] nm inv (fig) brain teaser; (difficultés) headache (fig)

cassette [kɑsɛt] nf (bande magnétique) cassette; (coffret) casket; ~ **numérique** digital compact cassette; ~ **vidéo** video

casseur [kɑsœr] nm hooligan; rioter

cassis [kɑsis] nm blackcurrant; (de la route) dip, bump

cassoulet [kɑsulɛ] nm sausage and bean hotpot

cassure [kɑsyr] nf break, crack

castor [kɑstɔr] nm beaver

castrer [kɑstre] vt (mâle) to castrate; (femelle) to spay; (cheval) to geld; (chat, chien) to doctor (Brit), fix (US)

catalogue [katalɔg] nm catalogue

cataloguer [katalɔge] vt to catalogue, list; (péj) to put a label on

catalyseur [katalizœr] nm catalyst

catalytique [katalitik] adj catalytic; **pot** ~ catalytic converter

catastrophe [katastrɔf] nf catastrophe, disaster; **atterrir en** ~ to make an emergency landing; **partir en** ~ to rush away

catch [katʃ] nm (all-in) wrestling

catéchisme [kateʃism] nm catechism

catégorie [kategɔri] nf category; (Boucherie): **morceaux de première/deuxième** ~ prime/ second cuts

catégorique [kategɔrik] adj categorical

cathédrale [katedral] nf cathedral

catholique [katɔlik] adj, nm/f (Roman) Catholic; **pas très** ~ a bit shady ou fishy

catimini [katimini]: **en** ~ adv on the sly, on the quiet

cauchemar [koʃmar] nm nightmare

cause [koz] nf cause; (Jur) lawsuit, case; brief; **faire** ~ **commune avec qn** to take sides with sb; **être** ~ **de** to be the cause of; **à** ~ **de** because of, owing to; **pour** ~ **de** on account of; owing

to; **(et) pour** ~ and for (a very) good reason; **être en** ~ (intérêts) to be at stake; (personne) to be involved; (qualité) to be in question; **mettre en** ~ to implicate; to call into question; **remettre en** ~ to challenge, call into question; **c'est hors de** ~ it's out of the question; **en tout état de** ~ in any case

causer [koze] vt to cause ▷ vi to chat, talk

causerie [kozri] nf talk

causette [kozɛt] nf: **faire la** ou **un brin de** ~ to have a chat

caution [kosjɔ̃] nf guarantee, security; deposit; (Jur) bail (bond); (fig) backing, support; **payer la** ~ **de qn** to stand bail for sb; **se porter** ~ **pour qn** to stand security for sb; **libéré sous** ~ released on bail; **sujet à** ~ unconfirmed

cautionner [kosjɔne] vt to guarantee; (soutenir) to support

cavalcade [kavalkad] nf (fig) stampede

cavalier, -ière [kavalje, -jɛr] adj (désinvolte) offhand ▷ nm/f rider; (au bal) partner ▷ nm (Échecs) knight; **faire ~ seul** to go it alone; **allée** ou **piste cavalière** riding path

cave [kav] nf cellar; (cabaret) (cellar) nightclub ▷ adj: **yeux ~s** sunken eyes; **joues ~s** hollow cheeks

caveau, x [kavo] nm vault

caverne [kavɛrn] nf cave

CCP sigle m = **compte chèque postal**

CD sigle m (= chemin départemental) secondary road, = B road (Brit); (= compact disc) CD; (= comité directeur) steering committee

CD-ROM [sederɔm] nm inv (= Compact Disc Read Only Memory) CD-Rom

CE sigle f (= Communauté européenne) EC; (Comm) = **caisse d'épargne** ▷ sigle m (Industrie) = **comité d'entreprise**; (Scol) = **cours élémentaire**

MOT-CLÉ

ce, cette [sə, sɛt] (devant nm **cet** + voyelle ou h aspiré) (pl **ces**) adj dém (proximité) this; these pl; (non-proximité) that; those pl; **cette maison(-ci/là)** this/that house; **cette nuit** (qui vient) tonight; (passée) last night
▷ pron **1**: **c'est** it's, it is; **c'est petit/grand/un livre** it's ou it is small/big/a book; **c'est un peintre** he's ou he is a painter; **ce sont des peintres** they're ou they are painters; **c'est le facteur** etc (à la porte) it's the postman etc; **qui est-ce?** who is it?; (en désignant) who is he/she?; **qu'est-ce?** what is it?; **c'est toi qui lui as parlé** it was you who spoke to him
2: **c'est que**: **c'est qu'il est lent/qu'il n'a pas faim** the fact is, he's slow/he's not hungry
3 (expressions): **c'est ça** (correct) that's it, that's right; **c'est toi qui le dis!** that's what YOU say!; voir aussi **c'est-à-dire** voir **-ci**; **est-ce que**; **n'est-ce pas**

4: ce qui, ce que what; **ce qui me plaît, c'est sa franchise** what I like about him *ou* her is his *ou* her frankness; *(chose qui):* **il est bête, ce qui me chagrine** he's stupid, which saddens me; **tout ce qui bouge** everything that *ou* which moves; **tout ce que je sais** all I know; **ce dont j'ai parlé** what I talked about; **ce que c'est grand!** it's so big!

ceci [səsi] *pron* this

cécité [sesite] *nf* blindness

céder [sede] *vt* to give up ▷ *vi (pont, barrage)* to give way; *(personne)* to give in; **~ à** to yield to, give in to

cédérom [sederɔm] *nm* CD-ROM

CEDEX [sedɛks] *sigle m (= courrier d'entreprise à distribution exceptionnelle)* accelerated postal service for bulk users

cédille [sedij] *nf* cedilla

cèdre [sɛdʀ] *nm* cedar

CEI *sigle f (= Communauté des États indépendants)* CIS

ceinture [sɛtyʀ] *nf* belt; *(taille)* waist; *(fig)* ring; belt; circle; **~ de sauvetage** lifebelt *(Brit)*, life preserver *(US)*; **~ de sécurité** safety *ou* seat belt; **~ (de sécurité) à enrouleur** inertia reel seat belt; **~ verte** green belt

cela [s(ə)la] *pron* that; *(comme sujet indéfini)* it; **~ m'étonne que** it surprises me that; **quand/où ~?** when/where (was that)?

célèbre [selɛbʀ] *adj* famous

célébrer [selebʀe] *vt* to celebrate; *(louer)* to extol

céleri [sɛlʀi] *nm:* **~(-rave)** celeriac; **~ (en branche)** celery

célibat [seliba] *nm* celibacy, bachelor/spinsterhood

célibataire [selibatɛʀ] *adj* single, unmarried ▷ *nm/f* bachelor/unmarried *ou* single woman; **mère ~** single *ou* unmarried mother

celle, celles [sɛl] *pron voir* **celui**

cellier [selje] *nm* storeroom

cellule [selyl] *nf (gén)* cell; **~ (photo-électrique)** electronic eye; **~ souche** stem cell

cellulite [selylit] *nf* cellulite

 MOT-CLÉ

celui, celle [səlɥi, sɛl] *(mpl* **ceux**, *fpl* **celles)** *pron* **1: celui-ci/là, celle-ci/là** this one/that one; **ceux-ci, celles-ci** these (ones); **ceux-là, celles-là** those (ones); **celui de mon frère** my brother's; **celui du salon/du dessous** the one in *(ou* from) the lounge/below
2: celui qui bouge the one which *ou* that moves; *(personne)* the one who moves; **celui que je vois** the one (which *ou* that) I see; *(personne)* the one (whom) I see; **celui dont je parle** the one I'm talking about
3 *(valeur indéfinie):* **celui qui veut** whoever wants

cendre [sɑ̃dʀ] *nf* ash; **~s** *(d'un foyer)* ash(es), cinders; *(volcaniques)* ash *sg; (d'un défunt)* ashes; **sous la ~** *(Culin)* in (the) embers

cendrier [sɑ̃dʀije] *nm* ashtray

cène [sɛn] *nf:* **la ~** (Holy) Communion; *(Art)* the Last Supper

censé, e [sɑ̃se] *adj:* **être ~ faire** to be supposed to do

censeur [sɑ̃sœʀ] *nm (Scol)* deputy head *(Brit)*, vice-principal *(US); (Ciné, Pol)* censor

censure [sɑ̃syʀ] *nf* censorship

censurer [sɑ̃syʀe] *vt (Ciné, Presse)* to censor; *(Pol)* to censure

cent [sɑ̃] *num* a hundred, one hundred; **pour ~ (%)** per cent (%); **faire les ~ pas** to pace up and down ▷ *nm (US, Canada, partie du euro etc)* cent

centaine [sɑ̃tɛn] *nf:* **une ~ (de)** about a hundred, a hundred or so; *(Comm)* a hundred; **plusieurs ~s (de)** several hundred; **des ~s (de)** hundreds (of)

centenaire [sɑ̃tnɛʀ] *adj* hundred-year-old ▷ *nm/f* centenarian ▷ *nm (anniversaire)* centenary; *(monnaie)* cent

centième [sɑ̃tjɛm] *num* hundredth

centigrade [sɑ̃tigʀad] *nm* centigrade

centilitre [sɑ̃tilitʀ] *nm* centilitre *(Brit)*, centiliter *(US)*

centime [sɑ̃tim] *nm* centime; **~ d'euro** euro cent

centimètre [sɑ̃timɛtʀ] *nm* centimetre *(Brit)*, centimeter *(US); (ruban)* tape measure, measuring tape

central, e, -aux [sɑ̃tʀal, -o] *adj* central ▷ *nm:* **~ (téléphonique)** (telephone) exchange ▷ *nf* power station; **~e d'achat** *(Comm)* central buying service; **~e électrique/nucléaire** electric/nuclear power station; **~e syndicale** group of affiliated trade unions

centre [sɑ̃tʀ] *nm* centre *(Brit)*, center *(US)*; **~ commercial/sportif/culturel** shopping/sports/arts centre; **~ aéré** outdoor centre; **~ d'appels** call centre; **~ d'apprentissage** training college; **~ d'attraction** centre of attraction; **~ de gravité** centre of gravity; **~ de loisirs** leisure centre; **~ d'enfouissement des déchets** landfill site; **~ hospitalier** hospital complex; **~ de tri** *(Postes)* sorting office; **~s nerveux** *(Anat)* nerve centres

centre-ville *(pl* **centres-villes)** [sɑ̃tʀəvil] *nm* town centre *(Brit)* ou center *(US)*, downtown (area) *(US)*

centuple [sɑ̃typl] *nm:* **le ~ de qch** a hundred times sth; **au ~** a hundredfold

cep [sɛp] *nm (vine)* stock

cèpe [sɛp] *nm (edible)* boletus

cependant [s(ə)pɑ̃dɑ̃] *adv* however, nevertheless

céramique [seʀamik] *adj* ceramic ▷ *nf* ceramic; *(art)* ceramics *sg*

cercle [sɛʀkl] *nm* circle; *(objet)* band, hoop; **décrire un ~** *(avion)* to circle; *(projectile)* to

describe a circle; **~ d'amis** circle of friends;
~ de famille family circle; **~ vicieux** vicious
circle

ercueil [sɛrkœj] nm coffin

éréale [sereal] nf cereal

érémonie [seremɔni] nf ceremony; **sans ~**
(*inviter, manger*) informally; **cérémonies** nfpl
(*péj*) fuss sg, to-do sg

erf [sɛr] nm stag

erfeuil [sɛrfœj] nm chervil

erf-volant [sɛrvɔlɑ̃] nm kite; **jouer au ~** to
fly a kite

erise [səriz] nf cherry

erisier [sərizje] nm cherry (tree)

erner [sɛrne] vt (*Mil etc*) to surround; (*fig:
problème*) to delimit, define

ernes [sɛrn] nfpl (dark) rings, shadows
(under the eyes)

ertain, e [sɛrtɛ̃, -ɛn] adj certain; (*sûr*): **~ (de/
que)** certain ou sure (of/ that); **d'un ~ âge**
past one's prime, not so young; **un ~ temps**
(quite) some time; **sûr et ~** absolutely
certain; **un ~ Georges** someone called
Georges; **~s** pron some

ertainement [sɛrtɛnmɑ̃] adv (*probablement*)
most probably ou likely; (*bien sûr*) certainly, of
course

ertes [sɛrt] adv (*sans doute*) admittedly; (*bien
sûr*) of course; indeed (yes)

ertificat [sɛrtifika] nm certificate; **C~
d'études (primaires)** former school leaving
certificate (taken at the end of primary education); **C~
de fin d'études secondaires** school leaving
certificate

ertifier [sɛrtifje] vt to certify, guarantee; **~ à
qn que** to assure sb that, guarantee to sb
that; **~ qch à qn** to guarantee sth to sb

ertitude [sɛrtityd] nf certainty

erveau, x [sɛrvo] nm brain; **~ électronique**
electronic brain

ervelas [sɛrvəla] nm saveloy

ervelle [sɛrvɛl] nf (*Anat*) brain; (*Culin*)
brain(s); **se creuser la ~** to rack one's brains

CES sigle m (= Collège d'enseignement secondaire)
≈ (junior) secondary school (*Brit*), ≈ junior
high school (*US*)

ces [se] adj dém voir **ce**

esse [sɛs]: **sans ~** adv (*tout le temps*)
continually, constantly; (*sans interruption*)
continuously; **il n'avait de ~ que** he would
not rest until

esser [sese] vt to stop ▷ vi to stop, cease; **~ de
faire** to stop doing; **faire ~** (*bruit, scandale*) to
put a stop to

essez-le-feu [seselfø] nm inv ceasefire

c'est-à-dire [sɛtadir] adv that is (to say);
(*demander de préciser*): **~?** what does that mean?;
~ que ... (*en conséquence*) which means that ...;
(*manière d'excuse*) well, in fact ...

cet [sɛt] adj dém voir **ce**

ceux [sø] pron voir **celui**

CFC sigle mpl (= chlorofluorocarbures) CFC

CFDT sigle f (= Confédération française démocratique
du travail) trade union

CGT sigle f (= Confédération générale du travail) trade
union

chacun, e [ʃakœ̃, -yn] pron each; (*indéfini*)
everyone, everybody

chagrin, e [ʃagrɛ̃, -in] adj morose ▷ nm grief,
sorrow; **avoir du ~** to be grieved ou sorrowful

chagriner [ʃagrine] vt to grieve, distress;
(*contrarier*) to bother, worry

chahut [ʃay] nm uproar

chahuter [ʃayte] vt to rag, bait ▷ vi to make
an uproar

chaîne [ʃɛn] nf chain; (*Radio, TV*: stations)
channel; (*Inform*) string; **chaînes** nfpl (*liens,
asservissement*) fetters, bonds; **travail à la ~**
production line work; **réactions en ~** chain
reactions; **faire la ~** to form a (human)
chain; **~ alimentaire** food chain;
~ compacte music centre; **~ d'entraide**
mutual aid association; **~ (haute-fidélité** ou
hi-fi) hi-fi system; **~ (de montage** ou **de
fabrication)** production ou assembly line;
~ (de montagnes) (mountain) range; **~ de
solidarité** solidarity network; **~ (stéréo** ou
audio) stereo (system)

chaînette [ʃɛnɛt] nf (small) chain

chair [ʃɛr] nf flesh ▷ adj: (*couleur*) **~** flesh-
coloured; **avoir la ~ de poule** to have goose
pimples ou goose flesh; **bien en ~** plump,
well-padded; **en ~ et en os** in the flesh; **~ à
saucisse** sausage meat

chaire [ʃɛr] nf (*d'église*) pulpit; (*d'université*)
chair

chaise [ʃɛz] nf chair; **~ de bébé** high chair;
~ électrique electric chair; **~ longue**
deckchair

châle [ʃɑl] nm shawl

chaleur [ʃalœr] nf heat; (*fig: d'accueil*)
warmth; fire, fervour (*Brit*), fervor (*US*); heat;
en ~ (*Zool*) on heat

chaleureux, -euse [ʃalœrø, -øz] adj warm

chaloupe [ʃalup] nf launch; (*de sauvetage*)
lifeboat

chalumeau, x [ʃalymo] nm blowlamp (*Brit*),
blowtorch

chalutier [ʃalytje] nm trawler; (*pêcheur*)
trawlerman

chamailler [ʃamaje]: **se chamailler** vi to
squabble, bicker

chambouler [ʃɑ̃bule] vt to disrupt, turn
upside down

chambre [ʃɑ̃br] nf bedroom; (*Tech*) chamber;
(*Pol*) chamber, house; (*Jur*) court; (*Comm*)
chamber; federation; **faire ~ à part** to sleep
in separate rooms; **stratège/alpiniste en ~**
armchair strategist/mountaineer; **~ à un lit/
deux lits** single/twin-bedded room; **~ pour
une/deux personne(s)** single/double room;
~ d'accusation court of criminal appeal;
~ d'agriculture (CA) body responsible for the
agricultural interests of a département; **~ à air**

(de pneu) (inner) tube; **~ d'amis** spare *ou* guest room; **~ de combustion** combustion chamber; **~ de commerce et d'industrie (CCI)** chamber of commerce and industry; **~ à coucher** bedroom; **la C~ des députés** the Chamber of Deputies, ≈ the House (of Commons) *(Brit)*, ≈ the House of Representatives *(US)*; **~ forte** strongroom; **~ froide** *ou* **frigorifique** cold room; **~ à gaz** gas chamber; **~ d'hôte** ≈ bed and breakfast *(in private home)*; **~ des machines** engine-room; **~ des métiers (CM)** *chamber of commerce for trades*; **~ meublée** bedsit(ter) *(Brit)*, furnished room; **~ noire** *(Photo)* dark room

chambrer [ʃɑ̃bʀe] *vt (vin)* to bring to room temperature

chameau, x [ʃamo] *nm* camel

chamois [ʃamwa] *nm* chamois ▷ *adj*: **(couleur) ~** fawn, buff

champ [ʃɑ̃] *nm (aussi Inform)* field; *(Photo: aussi:* **dans le ~)** in the picture; **prendre du ~** to draw back; **laisser le ~ libre à qn** to leave sb a clear field; **~ d'action** sphere of operation(s); **~ de bataille** battlefield; **~ de courses** racecourse; **~ d'honneur** field of honour; **~ de manœuvre** *(Mil)* parade ground; **~ de mines** minefield; **~ de tir** shooting *ou* rifle range; **~ visuel** field of vision

champagne [ʃɑ̃paɲ] *nm* champagne

champêtre [ʃɑ̃pɛtʀ] *adj* country *cpd*, rural

champignon [ʃɑ̃piɲɔ̃] *nm* mushroom; *(terme générique)* fungus; *(fam: accélérateur)* accelerator, gas pedal *(US)*; **~ de couche** *ou* **de Paris** button mushroom; **~ vénéneux** toadstool, poisonous mushroom

champion, ne [ʃɑ̃pjɔ̃, -ɔn] *adj, nm/f* champion

championnat [ʃɑ̃pjɔna] *nm* championship

chance [ʃɑ̃s] *nf*: **la ~** luck; **une ~** a stroke *ou* piece of luck *ou* good fortune; *(occasion)* a lucky break; **chances** *nfpl (probabilités)* chances; **avoir de la ~** to be lucky; **il a des ~s de gagner** he has a chance of winning; **il y a de fortes ~s pour que Paul soit malade** it's highly probable that Paul is ill; **bonne ~!** good luck!; **encore une ~ que tu viennes!** it's lucky you're coming!; **je n'ai pas de ~** I'm out of luck; *(toujours)* I never have any luck; **donner sa ~ à qn** to give sb a chance

chanceler [ʃɑ̃sle] *vi* to totter

chancelier [ʃɑ̃səlje] *nm (allemand)* chancellor; *(d'ambassade)* secretary

chanceux, -euse [ʃɑ̃sø, -øz] *adj* lucky, fortunate

chandail [ʃɑ̃daj] *nm* (thick) jumper *ou* sweater

Chandeleur [ʃɑ̃dlœʀ] *nf*: **la ~** Candlemas

chandelier [ʃɑ̃dəlje] *nm* candlestick; *(à plusieurs branches)* candelabra

chandelle [ʃɑ̃dɛl] *nf* (tallow) candle; *(Tennis)*: **faire une ~** to lob; *(Aviat)*: **monter en ~** to

climb vertically; **tenir la ~** to play gooseberry; **dîner aux ~s** candlelight dinner

change [ʃɑ̃ʒ] *nm (Comm)* exchange; **opérations de ~** (foreign) exchange transactions; **contrôle des ~s** exchange control; **gagner/perdre au ~** to be better/worse off (for it); **donner le ~ à qn** *(fig)* to lead sb up the garden path

changement [ʃɑ̃ʒmɑ̃] *nm* change; **~ de vitesse** *(dispositif)* gears *pl*; *(action)* gear change

changer [ʃɑ̃ʒe] *vt (modifier)* to change, alter; *(remplacer, Comm, rhabiller)* to change ▷ *vi* to change, alter; **se changer** *vi* to change (o.s.); **~ de** *(remplacer: adresse, nom, voiture etc)* to change one's; **~ de train** to change trains; **~ d'air** to get a change of air; **~ de couleur/direction** to change colour/direction; **~ d'avis, ~ d'idée** to change one's mind; **~ de place avec qn** to change places with sb; **~ de vitesse** *(Auto)* to change gear; **~ qn/qch de place** to move sb/sth to another place; **~ (de bus etc)** to change (buses *etc*); **~ qch en** to change sth into

chanson [ʃɑ̃sɔ̃] *nf* song

chant [ʃɑ̃] *nm* song; *(art vocal)* singing; *(d'église)* hymn; *(de poème)* canto; *(Tech)*: **posé de** *ou* **sur ~** placed edgeways; **~ de Noël** Christmas carol

chantage [ʃɑ̃taʒ] *nm* blackmail; **faire du ~** to use blackmail; **soumettre qn à un ~** to blackmail sb

chanter [ʃɑ̃te] *vt, vi* to sing; **~ juste/faux** to sing in tune/out of tune; **si cela lui chante** *(fam)* if he feels like it *ou* fancies it

chanteur, -euse [ʃɑ̃tœʀ, -øz] *nm/f* singer; **~ de charme** crooner

chantier [ʃɑ̃tje] *nm* (building) site; *(sur une route)* roadworks *pl*; **mettre en ~** to start work on; **~ naval** shipyard

chantilly [ʃɑ̃tiji] *nf voir* **crème**

chantonner [ʃɑ̃tɔne] *vi, vt* to sing to oneself, hum

chanvre [ʃɑ̃vʀ] *nm* hemp

chaparder [ʃapaʀde] *vt* to pinch

chapeau, x [ʃapo] *nm* hat; *(Presse)* introductory paragraph; **~!** well done!; **~ melon** bowler hat; **~ mou** trilby; **~x à roues** hub caps

chapelet [ʃaplɛ] *nm (Rel)* rosary; *(fig)*: **un ~ de** a string of; **dire son ~** to tell one's beads

chapelle [ʃapɛl] *nf* chapel; **~ ardente** chapel of rest

chapelure [ʃaplyʀ] *nf* (dried) breadcrumbs *pl*

chapiteau, x [ʃapito] *nm (Archit)* capital; *(de cirque)* marquee, big top

chapitre [ʃapitʀ] *nm* chapter; *(fig)* subject, matter; **avoir voix au ~** to have a say in the matter

chaque [ʃak] *adj* each, every; *(indéfini)* every

char [ʃaʀ] *nm (à foin etc)* cart, waggon;

(*de carnaval*) float; ~ **(d'assaut)** tank; ~ **à voile** sand yacht

charabia [ʃaʀabja] *nm* (*péj*) gibberish, gobbledygook (Brit)

charade [ʃaʀad] *nf* riddle; (*mimée*) charade

charbon [ʃaʀbɔ̃] *nm* coal; ~ **de bois** charcoal

charcuterie [ʃaʀkytʀi] *nf* (*magasin*) pork butcher's shop and delicatessen; (*produits*) cooked pork meats *pl*

charcutier, -ière [ʃaʀkytje, -jɛʀ] *nm/f* pork butcher

chardon [ʃaʀdɔ̃] *nm* thistle

charge [ʃaʀʒ] *nf* (*fardeau*) load; (*explosif, Élec, Mil, Jur*) charge; (*rôle, mission*) responsibility; **charges** *nfpl* (*du loyer*) service charges; **à la ~ de** (*dépendant de*) dependent upon, supported by; (*aux frais de*) chargeable to, payable by; **j'accepte, à - de revanche** I accept, provided I can do the same for you (in return) one day; **prendre en ~** to take charge of; (*véhicule*) to take on; (*dépenses*) to take care of; **~ utile** (*Auto*) live load; (*Comm*) payload; **~s sociales** social security contributions

chargé, e [ʃaʀʒe] *adj* (*voiture, animal, personne*) laden; (*fusil, batterie, caméra*) loaded; (*occupé: emploi du temps, journée*) busy, full; (*estomac*) heavy, full; (*langue*) furred; (*décoration, style*) heavy, ornate ▷ *nm*: **~ d'affaires** chargé d'affaires; **~ de cours** = lecturer; **~ de** (*responsable de*) responsible for

chargement [ʃaʀʒəmɑ̃] *nm* (*action*) loading; charging; (*objets*) load

charger [ʃaʀʒe] *vt* (*voiture, fusil, caméra*) to load; (*batterie*) to charge ▷ *vi* (*Mil etc*) to charge; **se - de** *vt* to see to, take care of; **~ qn de qch/faire qch** to give sb the responsibility for sth/of doing sth; to put sb in charge of sth/doing sth; **se - de faire qch** to take it upon o.s. to do sth

chariot [ʃaʀjo] *nm* trolley; (*charrette*) waggon; **~ élévateur** fork-lift truck

charité [ʃaʀite] *nf* charity; **faire la ~** to give to charity; to do charitable works; **faire la ~ à** to give (something) to; **fête/vente de ~** fête/ sale in aid of charity

charmant, e [ʃaʀmɑ̃, -ɑ̃t] *adj* charming

charme [ʃaʀm] *nm* charm; **charmes** *nmpl* (*appas*) charms; **c'est ce qui en fait le ~** that is its attraction; **faire du ~** to be charming, turn on the charm; **aller ou se porter comme un ~** to be in the pink

charmer [ʃaʀme] *vt* to charm; **je suis charmé de ...** I'm delighted to ...

charnel, le [ʃaʀnɛl] *adj* carnal

charnière [ʃaʀnjɛʀ] *nf* hinge; (*fig*) turning- point

charnu, e [ʃaʀny] *adj* fleshy

charpente [ʃaʀpɑ̃t] *nf* frame(work); (*fig*) structure, framework; (*carrure*) build, frame

charpentier [ʃaʀpɑ̃tje] *nm* carpenter

charpie [ʃaʀpi] *nf*: **en ~** (*fig*) in shreds *ou* ribbons

charrette [ʃaʀɛt] *nf* cart

charrier [ʃaʀje] *vt* to carry (along); to cart, carry ▷ *vi* (*fam*) to exaggerate

charrue [ʃaʀy] *nf* plough (Brit), plow (US)

charter [tʃaʀtœʀ] *nm* (*vol*) charter flight; (*avion*) charter plane

chasse [ʃas] *nf* hunting; (*au fusil*) shooting; (*poursuite*) chase; (*aussi*: **~ d'eau**) flush; **la - est ouverte** the hunting season is open; **la - est fermée** it is the close (Brit) *ou* closed (US) season; **aller à la ~** to go hunting; **prendre en ~, donner la - à** to give chase to; **tirer la ~ (d'eau)** to flush the toilet, pull the chain; **~ aérienne** aerial pursuit; **~ à courre** hunting; **~ à l'homme** manhunt; **~ gardée** private hunting grounds *pl*; **~ sous-marine** underwater fishing

chasse-neige [ʃasnɛʒ] *nm inv* snowplough (Brit), snowplow (US)

chasser [ʃase] *vt* to hunt; (*expulser*) to chase away *ou* out, drive away *ou* out; (*dissiper*) to chase *ou* sweep away; to dispel, drive away

chasseur, -euse [ʃasœʀ, -øz] *nm/f* hunter ▷ *nm* (*avion*) fighter; (*domestique*) page (boy), messenger (boy); **~ d'images** roving photographer; **~ de têtes** (*fig*) headhunter; **~s alpins** mountain infantry

châssis [ʃasi] *nm* (*Auto*) chassis; (*cadre*) frame; (*de jardin*) cold frame

chat' [ʃa] *nm* cat; **~ sauvage** wildcat

chat² [tʃat] *nm* (*Internet: salon*) chat room; (*conversation*) chat

châtaigne [ʃatɛɲ] *nf* chestnut

châtaignier [ʃatɛɲe] *nm* chestnut (tree)

châtain [ʃatɛ̃] *adj inv* chestnut (brown); (*personne*) chestnut-haired

château, x [ʃato] *nm* (*forteresse*) castle; (*résidence royale*) palace; (*manoir*) mansion; **~ d'eau** water tower; **~ fort** stronghold, fortified castle; **~ de sable** sand castle

châtier [ʃatje] *vt* to punish, castigate; (*fig: style*) to polish, refine

châtiment [ʃatimɑ̃] *nm* punishment, castigation; **~ corporel** corporal punishment

chaton [ʃatɔ̃] *nm* (*Zool*) kitten; (*Bot*) catkin; (*de bague*) bezel; stone

chatouiller [ʃatuje] *vt* to tickle; (*l'odorat, le palais*) to titillate

chatouilleux, -euse [ʃatujø, -øz] *adj* ticklish; (*fig*) touchy, over-sensitive

chatoyer [ʃatwaje] *vi* to shimmer

châtrer [ʃatʀe] *vt* (*mâle*) to castrate; (*femelle*) to spay; (*cheval*) to geld; (*chat, chien*) to doctor (Brit), fix (US); (*fig*) to mutilate

chatte [ʃat] *nf* (she-)cat

chatter [tʃate] *vi* (*Internet*) to chat

chaud, e [ʃo, -od] *adj* (*gén*) warm; (*très chaud*) hot; (*fig: félicitations*) hearty; (*discussion*) heated; **il fait ~** it's warm; it's hot; **manger ~** to have something hot to eat; **avoir ~** to be warm; to be hot; **tenir ~** to keep hot; **ça me**

tient ~ it keeps me warm; **tenir au ~** to keep in a warm place; **rester au ~** to stay in the warm

chaudière [ʃodjɛʀ] nf boiler

chaudron [ʃodʀɔ̃] nm cauldron

chauffage [ʃofaʒ] nm heating; **~ au gaz/à l'électricité/au charbon** gas/electric/solid fuel heating; **~ central** central heating; **~ par le sol** underfloor heating

chauffard [ʃofaʀ] nm (péj) reckless driver; road hog; (après un accident) hit-and-run driver

chauffe-eau [ʃofo] nm inv water heater

chauffer [ʃofe] vt to heat ▷ vi to heat up, warm up; (trop chauffer: moteur) to overheat; **se chauffer** vi (se mettre en train) to warm up; (au soleil) to warm o.s.

chauffeur [ʃofœʀ] nm driver; (privé) chauffeur; **voiture avec/sans ~** chauffeur-driven/self-drive car; **~ de taxi** taxi driver

chaume [ʃom] nm (du toit) thatch; (tiges) stubble

chaumière [ʃomjɛʀ] nf (thatched) cottage

chaussée [ʃose] nf road(way); (digue) causeway

chausse-pied [ʃospje] nm shoe-horn

chausser [ʃose] vt to put on; (enfant) to put shoes on; (soulier) to fit; **~ du 38/42** to take size 38/42; **~ grand/bien** to be big-/well-fitting; **se chausser** to put one's shoes on

chaussette [ʃosɛt] nf sock

chausson [ʃosɔ̃] nm (de bébé) bootee; **~ (aux pommes)** (apple) turnover

chaussure [ʃosyʀ] nf shoe; (commerce): **la ~** the shoe industry ou trade; **~s basses** flat shoes; **~s montantes** ankle boots; **~s de ski** ski boots

chauve [ʃov] adj bald

chauve-souris (pl chauves-souris) [ʃovsuʀi] nf bat

chauvin, e [ʃovɛ̃, -in] adj chauvinistic; jingoistic

chaux [ʃo] nf lime; **blanchi à la ~** whitewashed

chavirer [ʃaviʀe] vi to capsize, overturn

chef [ʃɛf] nm head, leader; (patron) boss; (de cuisine) chef; **au premier ~** extremely, to the nth degree; **de son propre ~** on his ou her own initiative; **général/commandant en ~** general-/commander-in-chief; **~ d'accusation** (Jur) charge, count (of indictment); **~ d'atelier** (shop) foreman; **~ de bureau** head clerk; **~ de clinique** senior hospital lecturer; **~ d'entreprise** company head; **~ d'équipe** team leader; **~ d'état** head of state; **~ de famille** head of the family; **~ de file** (de parti etc) leader; **~ de gare** station master; **~ d'orchestre** conductor (Brit), leader (US); **~ de rayon** department(al) supervisor; **~ de service** departmental head

chef-d'œuvre (pl chefs-d'œuvre) [ʃɛdœvʀ] nm masterpiece

chef-lieu (pl chefs-lieux) [ʃɛfljø] nm county town

chemin [ʃəmɛ̃] nm path; (itinéraire, direction, trajet) way; **en ~, ~ faisant** on the way; **~ de fer** railway (Brit), railroad (US); **par ~ de fer** by rail; **les ~s de fer** the railways (Brit), the railroad (US); **~ de terre** dirt track

cheminée [ʃəmine] nf chimney; (à l'intérieur) chimney piece, fireplace; (de bateau) funnel

cheminement [ʃəminmɑ̃] nm progress; course

cheminot [ʃəmino] nm railwayman (Brit), railroad worker (US)

chemise [ʃəmiz] nf shirt; (dossier) folder; **~ de nuit** nightdress

chemisier [ʃəmizje] nm blouse

chenal, -aux [ʃənal, -o] nm channel

chêne [ʃɛn] nm oak (tree); (bois) oak

chenil [ʃənil] nm kennels pl

chenille [ʃənij] nf (Zool) caterpillar; (Auto) caterpillar track; **véhicule à ~s** tracked vehicle, caterpillar

chèque [ʃɛk] nm cheque (Brit), check (US); **faire/toucher un ~** to write/cash a cheque; **par ~** by cheque; **~ barré/sans provision** crossed (Brit) /bad cheque; **~ en blanc** blank cheque; **~ au porteur** cheque to bearer; **~ postal** post office cheque, ≈ giro cheque (Brit); **~ de voyage** traveller's cheque

chéquier [ʃekje] nm cheque book (Brit), checkbook (US)

cher, -ère [ʃɛʀ] adj (aimé) dear; (coûteux) expensive, dear ▷ adv: **coûter/payer ~** to cost/pay a lot ▷ nf: **la bonne chère** good food; **cela coûte ~** it's expensive, it costs a lot of money; **mon ~, ma chère** my dear

chercher [ʃɛʀʃe] vt to look for; (gloire etc) to seek; **~ des ennuis/la bagarre** to be looking for trouble/a fight; **aller ~** to go for, go and fetch; **~ à faire** to try to do

chercheur, -euse [ʃɛʀʃœʀ, -øz] nm/f researcher, research worker; **~ de** seeker of; hunter of; **~ d'or** gold digger

chère [ʃɛʀ] adj f, nf voir **cher**

chéri, e [ʃeʀi] adj beloved, dear; **(mon) ~** darling

chérir [ʃeʀiʀ] vt to cherish

cherté [ʃɛʀte] nf: **la ~ de la vie** the high cost of living

chétif, -ive [ʃetif, -iv] adj puny, stunted

cheval, -aux [ʃəval, -o] nm horse; (Auto): **~ (vapeur) (CV)** horsepower no pl; **50 chevaux (au frein)** 50 brake horsepower, 50 b.h.p.; **10 chevaux (fiscaux)** 10 horsepower (for tax purposes); **faire du ~** to ride; **à ~** on horseback; **à ~ sur** astride, straddling; (fig) overlapping; **~ d'arçons** vaulting horse; **~ à bascule** rocking horse; **~ de bataille** charger; (fig) hobby-horse; **~ de course** race horse; **chevaux de bois** (des manèges) wooden (fairground) horses; (manège) merry-go-round

chevalet [ʃəvalɛ] *nm* easel

chevalier [ʃəvalje] *nm* knight; **~ servant** escort

chevalière [ʃəvaljɛʀ] *nf* signet ring

chevalin, e [ʃəvalɛ̃, -in] *adj* of horses, equine; (*péj*) horsy; **boucherie ~e** horse-meat butcher's

chevaucher [ʃəvoʃe] *vi* (*aussi*: **se ~**) to overlap (each other) ▷ *vt* to be astride, straddle

chevaux [ʃəvo] *nmpl voir* **cheval**

chevelu, e [ʃəvly] *adj* with a good head of hair, hairy (*péj*)

chevelure [ʃəvlyʀ] *nf* hair *no pl*

chevet [ʃəvɛ] *nm*: **au ~ de qn** at sb's bedside; **lampe de ~** bedside lamp

cheveu, x [ʃəvø] *nm* hair ▷ *nmpl* (*chevelure*) hair *sg*; **avoir les ~x courts/en brosse** to have short hair/a crew cut; **se faire couper les ~x** to get *ou* have one's hair cut; **tiré par les ~x** (*histoire*) far-fetched

cheville [ʃəvij] *nf* (*Anat*) ankle; (*de bois*) peg; (*pour enfoncer une vis*) plug; **être en ~ avec qn** to be in cahoots with sb; **~ ouvrière** (*fig*) kingpin

chèvre [ʃɛvʀ] *nf* (she-)goat; **ménager la ~ et le chou** to try to please everyone

chevreau, x [ʃəvʀo] *nm* kid

chèvrefeuille [ʃɛvʀəfœj] *nm* honeysuckle

chevreuil [ʃəvʀœj] *nm* roe deer *inv*; (*Culin*) venison

chevronné, e [ʃəvʀɔne] *adj* seasoned, experienced

MOT-CLÉ

chez [ʃe] *prép* **1** (*à la demeure de*) at; (: *direction*) to; **chez qn** at/to sb's house *ou* place; **je suis chez moi** I'm at home; **je rentre chez moi** I'm going home; **allons chez Nathalie** let's go to Nathalie's

2 (+*profession*) at; (: *direction*) to; **chez le boulanger/dentiste** at *ou* to the baker's/dentist's

3 (*dans le caractère, l'œuvre de*) in; **chez les renards/Racine** in foxes/Racine; **chez ce poète** in this poet's work; **chez les Français** among the French; **chez lui, c'est un devoir** for him, it's a duty

▷ *nm inv*: **mon chez moi/ton chez toi** *etc* my/your *etc* home *ou* place; **c'est ce que je préfère chez lui** that's what I like best about him

4 (*à l'entreprise de*): **il travaille chez Renault** he works for Renault, he works at Renault('s)

chez-soi [ʃeswa] *nm inv* home

chic [ʃik] *adj inv* chic, smart; (*généreux*) nice, decent ▷ *nm* stylishness; **avoir le ~ de** *ou* **pour** to have the knack of *ou* for; **de ~** *adv* off the cuff; **~!** great!, terrific!

chicane [ʃikan] *nf* (*obstacle*) zigzag; (*querelle*) squabble

chicaner [ʃikane] *vi* (*ergoter*): **~ sur** to quibble about

chiche [ʃiʃ] *adj* (*mesquin*) niggardly, mean; (*pauvre*) meagre (*Brit*), meager (*US*) ▷ *excl* (*en réponse à un défi*) you're on!; **tu n'es pas ~ de lui parler!** you wouldn't (dare) speak to her!

chichis [ʃiʃi] *nmpl* (*fam*) fuss *sg*

chicorée [ʃikɔʀe] *nf* (*café*) chicory; (*salade*) endive; **~ frisée** curly endive

chien [ʃjɛ̃] *nm* dog; (*de pistolet*) hammer; **temps de ~** rotten weather; **vie de ~** dog's life; **couché en ~ de fusil** curled up; **~ d'aveugle** guide dog; **~ de chasse** gun dog; **~ de garde** guard dog; **~ policier** police dog; **~ de race** pedigree dog; **~ de traîneau** husky

chiendent [ʃjɛ̃dɑ̃] *nm* couch grass

chien-loup (*pl* **chiens-loups**) [ʃjɛ̃lu] *nm* wolfhound

chienne [ʃjɛn] *nf* (she-)dog, bitch

chier [ʃje] *vi* (*fam!*) to crap (!), shit (!); **faire ~ qn** (*importuner*) to bug sb; (*causer des ennuis à*) to piss sb around (!); **se faire ~** (*s'ennuyer*) to be bored rigid

chiffon [ʃifɔ̃] *nm* (piece of) rag

chiffonner [ʃifɔne] *vt* to crumple, crease; (*tracasser*) to concern

chiffre [ʃifʀ] *nm* (*représentant un nombre*) figure; numeral; (*montant, total*) total, sum; (*d'un code*) code, cipher; **~s romains/arabes** roman/arabic figures *ou* numerals; **en ~s ronds** in round figures; **écrire un nombre en ~s** to write a number in figures; **~ d'affaires** (*CA*) turnover; **~ de ventes** sales figures

chiffrer [ʃifʀe] *vt* (*dépense*) to put a figure to, assess; (*message*) to (en)code, cipher ▷ *vi*: **~ à, se ~ à** to add up to

chignon [ʃiɲɔ̃] *nm* chignon, bun

Chili [ʃili] *nm*: **le ~** Chile

chilien, ne [ʃiljɛ̃, -ɛn] *adj* Chilean ▷ *nm/f*: **C~, ne** Chilean

chimie [ʃimi] *nf* chemistry

chimiothérapie [ʃimjoteʀapi] *nf* chemotherapy

chimique [ʃimik] *adj* chemical; **produits ~s** chemicals

chimpanzé [ʃɛ̃pɑ̃ze] *nm* chimpanzee

Chine [ʃin] *nf*: **la ~** China; **la ~ libre, la république de ~** the Republic of China, Nationalist China (*Taiwan*)

chine [ʃin] *nm* rice paper; (*porcelaine*) china (vase)

chinois, e [ʃinwa, -waz] *adj* Chinese; (*fig: péj*) pernickety, fussy ▷ *nm* (*Ling*) Chinese ▷ *nm/f*: **C~, e** Chinese

chiot [ʃjo] *nm* pup(py)

chiper [ʃipe] *vt* (*fam*) to pinch

chipoter [ʃipɔte] *vi* (*manger*) to nibble; (*ergoter*) to quibble, haggle

chips [ʃips] *nfpl* (*aussi*: **pommes ~**) crisps (*Brit*), (potato) chips (*US*)

chiquenaude [ʃiknod] *nf* flick, flip

chirurgical, e, -aux [ʃiRyRʒikal, -o] *adj* surgical

chirurgie [ʃiRyRʒi] *nf* surgery; ~ **esthétique** cosmetic *ou* plastic surgery

chirurgien, ne [ʃiRyRʒjɛ̃] *nm/f* surgeon; ~ **dentiste** dental surgeon

chlore [klɔR] *nm* chlorine

choc [ʃɔk] *nm* (*heurt*) impact; shock; (*collision*) crash; (*moral*) shock; (*affrontement*) clash ▷ *adj*: **prix** ~ amazing *ou* incredible price/ prices; **de** ~ (*troupe, traitement*) shock *cpd*; (*patron etc*) high-powered; ~ **opératoire/ nerveux** post-operative/nervous shock; ~ **en retour** return shock; (*fig*) backlash

chocolat [ʃɔkɔla] *nm* chocolate; (*boisson*) (hot) chocolate; ~ **chaud** hot chocolate; ~ **à cuire** cooking chocolate; ~ **au lait** milk chocolate; ~ **en poudre** drinking chocolate

chœur [kœR] *nm* (*chorale*) choir; (*Opéra, Théât*) chorus; (*Archit*) choir, chancel; **en** ~ in chorus

choisir [ʃwaziR] *vt* to choose; (*entre plusieurs*) to choose, select; ~ **de faire qch** to choose *ou* opt to do sth

choix [ʃwa] *nm* choice; selection; **avoir le** ~ to have the choice; **je n'avais pas le** ~ I had no choice; **de premier** ~ (*Comm*) class *ou* grade one; **de** ~ choice *cpd*, selected; **au** ~ as you wish *ou* prefer; **de mon/son** ~ of my/his *ou* her choosing

chômage [ʃomaʒ] *nm* unemployment; **mettre au** ~ to make redundant, put out of work; **être au** ~ to be unemployed *ou* out of work; ~ **partiel** short-time working; ~ **structurel** structural unemployment; ~ **technique** lay-offs *pl*

chômeur, -euse [ʃomœR, -øz] *nm/f* unemployed person, person out of work

chope [ʃɔp] *nf* tankard

choper [ʃɔpe] (*fam*) *vt* (*objet, maladie*) to catch

choquer [ʃɔke] *vt* (*offenser*) to shock; (*commotionner*) to shake (up)

choral, e [kɔRal] *adj* choral ▷ *nf* choral society, choir

chorale [kɔRal] *nf* choir

choriste [kɔRist] *nm/f* choir member; (*Opéra*) chorus member

chose [ʃoz] *nf* thing ▷ *nm* (*fam: machin*) thingamajig ▷ *adj inv*: **être/se sentir tout** ~ (*bizarre*) to be/feel a bit odd; (*malade*) to be/feel out of sorts; **dire bien des** ~**s à qn** to give sb's regards to sb; **parler de** ~(**s**) **et d'autre(s)** to talk about one thing and another; **c'est peu de** ~ it's nothing much

chou, x [ʃu] *nm* cabbage ▷ *adj inv* cute; **mon petit** ~ (my) sweetheart; **faire** ~ **blanc** to draw a blank; **feuille de** ~ (*fig: journal*) rag; ~ **à la crème** cream bun (*made of choux pastry*); ~ **de Bruxelles** Brussels sprout

chouchou, te [ʃuʃu, -ut] *nm/f* (*Scol*) teacher's pet

choucroute [ʃukRut] *nf* sauerkraut; ~ **garnie** sauerkraut with cooked meats and potatoes

chouette [ʃwɛt] *nf* owl ▷ *adj* (*fam*) great, smashing

chou-fleur (*pl* **choux-fleurs**) [ʃuflœR] *nm* cauliflower

choyer [ʃwaje] *vt* to cherish; to pamper

chrétien, ne [kRetjɛ̃, -ɛn] *adj, nm/f* Christian

Christ [kRist] *nm*: **le** ~ Christ; **christ** (*crucifix etc*) figure of Christ; **Jésus** ~ Jesus Christ

christianisme [kRistjanism] *nm* Christianity

chrome [kRom] *nm* chromium; (*revêtement*) chrome, chromium

chromé, e [kRome] *adj* chrome-plated, chromium-plated

chronique [kRɔnik] *adj* chronic ▷ *nf* (*de journal*) column, page; (*historique*) chronicle; (*Radio, TV*): **la** ~ **sportive/théâtrale** the sports/theatre review; **la** ~ **locale** local news and gossip

chronologique [kRɔnɔlɔʒik] *adj* chronological

chronomètre [kRɔnɔmɛtR] *nm* stopwatch

chronométrer [kRɔnɔmetRe] *vt* to time

chrysanthème [kRizɑ̃tɛm] *nm* chrysanthemum

⬥ **CHRYSANTHÈME**

⬥ Chrysanthemums are strongly
⬥ associated with funerals in France, and
⬥ therefore should not be given as gifts.

chuchotement [ʃyʃɔtmɑ̃] *nm* whisper

chuchoter [ʃyʃɔte] *vt, vi* to whisper

chut *excl* [ʃyt] sh!

chute [ʃyt] *nf* fall; (*de bois, papier: déchet*) scrap; **la** ~ **des cheveux** hair loss; **faire une** ~ **(de 10 m)** to fall (10 m); ~**s de pluie/neige** rain/ snowfalls; ~ **(d'eau)** waterfall; ~ **du jour** nightfall; ~ **libre** free fall; ~ **des reins** small of the back

Chypre [ʃipR] *nm/f* Cyprus

-ci, ci- [si] *adv voir* **par**; **ci-contre**; **ci-joint** *etc* ▷ *adj dém*: **ce garçon-~/-là** this/that boy; **ces femmes-~/-là** these/those women

cible [sibl] *nf* target

ciboulette [sibulɛt] *nf* (small) chive

cicatrice [sikatRis] *nf* scar

cicatriser [sikatRize] *vt* to heal; **se cicatriser** to heal (up), form a scar

ci-contre [sikɔ̃tR] *adv* opposite

ci-dessous [sidəsu] *adv* below

ci-dessus [sidəsy] *adv* above

cidre [sidR] *nm* cider

Cie *abr* (= *compagnie*) Co

ciel [sjɛl] *nm* sky; (*Rel*) heaven; **ciels** *nmpl* (*Peinture etc*) skies; **cieux** *nmpl* sky *sg*, skies; (*Rel*) heaven *sg*; **à** ~ **ouvert** open-air; (*mine*) opencast; **tomber du** ~ (*arriver à l'improviste*) to appear out of the blue; (*être stupéfait*) to be unable to believe one's eyes; **C~!** good heavens!; ~ **de lit** canopy

cierge [sjɛʁʒ] nm candle; ~ **pascal** Easter candle

cieux [sjø] nmpl voir **ciel**

cigale [sigal] nf cicada

cigare [sigaʁ] nm cigar

cigarette [sigaʁɛt] nf cigarette; ~ **(à) bout filtre** filter cigarette

ci-gît [siʒi] adv here lies

cigogne [sigɔɲ] nf stork

ci-inclus, e [siɛ̃kly, -yz] adj, adv enclosed

ci-joint, e [siʒwɛ̃, -ɛ̃t] adj, adv enclosed; (to email) attached; **veuillez trouver** ~ please find enclosed or attached

cil [sil] nm (eye)lash

cime [sim] nf top; (montagne) peak

ciment [simɑ̃] nm cement; ~ **armé** reinforced concrete

cimetière [simtjɛʁ] nm cemetery; (d'église) churchyard; ~ **de voitures** scrapyard

cinéaste [sineast] nmf film-maker

cinéma [sinema] nm cinema; **aller au** ~ to go to the cinema ou pictures ou movies; ~ **d'animation** cartoon (film)

cinématographique [sinematɔgʁafik] adj film cpd, cinema cpd

cinglant, e [sɛ̃glɑ̃, -ɑ̃t] adj (propos, ironie) scathing, biting; (échec) crushing

cinglé, e [sɛ̃gle] adj (fam) crazy

cinq [sɛ̃k] num five

cinquantaine [sɛ̃kɑ̃tɛn] nf: **une** ~ **(de)** about fifty; **avoir la** ~ (âge) to be around fifty

cinquante [sɛ̃kɑ̃t] num fifty

cinquantenaire [sɛ̃kɑ̃tnɛʁ] adj, nm/f fifty-year-old

cinquième [sɛ̃kjɛm] num fifth ▷ nf (Scol) year 8 (Brit), seventh grade (US)

cintre [sɛ̃tʁ] nm coat-hanger; (Archit) arch; **plein** ~ semicircular arch

cintré, e [sɛ̃tʁe] adj curved; (chemise) fitted, slim-fitting

cirage [siʁaʒ] nm (shoe) polish

circonflexe [siʁkɔ̃flɛks] adj: **accent** ~ circumflex accent

circonscription [siʁkɔ̃skʁipsjɔ̃] nf district; ~ **électorale** (d'un député) constituency; ~ **militaire** military area

circonscrire [siʁkɔ̃skʁiʁ] vt to define, delimit; (incendie) to contain; (propriété) to mark out; (sujet) to define

circonstance [siʁkɔ̃stɑ̃s] nf circumstance; (occasion) occasion; **œuvre de** ~ occasional work; **air de** ~ fitting air; **tête de** ~ appropriate demeanour (Brit) ou demeanor (US); ~**s atténuantes** mitigating circumstances

circuit [siʁkɥi] nm (trajet) tour, (round) trip; (Élec, Tech) circuit; ~ **automobile** motor circuit; ~ **de distribution** distribution network; ~ **fermé** closed circuit; ~ **intégré** integrated circuit

circulaire [siʁkylɛʁ] adj, nf circular

circulation [siʁkylasjɔ̃] nf circulation; (Auto): **la** ~ (the) traffic; **bonne/mauvaise** ~ good/bad circulation; **mettre en** ~ to put into circulation

circuler [siʁkyle] vi (véhicules) to drive (along); (passants) to walk along; (train etc) to run; (sang, devises) to circulate; **faire** ~ (nouvelle) to spread (about), circulate; (badauds) to move on

cire [siʁ] nf wax; ~ **à cacheter** sealing wax

ciré [siʁe] nm oilskin

cirer [siʁe] vt to wax, polish

cirque [siʁk] nm circus; (arène) amphitheatre (Brit), amphitheater (US); (Géo) cirque; (fig: désordre) chaos, bedlam; (: chichis) carry-on; **quel** ~! what a carry-on!

cisaille [sizaj], **cisailles** nf(pl) (gardening) shears pl

ciseau, x [sizo] nm: ~ **(à bois)** chisel ▷ nmpl (paire de ciseaux) (pair of) scissors; **sauter en** ~**x** to do a scissors jump; ~ **à froid** cold chisel

ciseler [sizle] vt to chisel, carve

citadin, e [sitadɛ̃, -in] nm/f city dweller ▷ adj town cpd, city cpd, urban

citation [sitasjɔ̃] nf (d'auteur) quotation; (Jur) summons sg; (Mil: récompense) mention

cité [site] nf town; (plus grande) city; ~ **ouvrière** (workers') housing estate; ~ **universitaire** students' residences pl

citer [site] vt (un auteur) to quote (from); (nommer) to name; (Jur) to summon; ~ **(en exemple)** (personne) to hold up (as an example); **je ne veux** ~ **personne** I don't want to name names

citerne [sitɛʁn] nf tank

citoyen, ne [sitwajɛ̃, -ɛn] nm/f citizen

citron [sitʁɔ̃] nm lemon; ~ **pressé** (fresh) lemon juice; ~ **vert** lime

citronnade [sitʁɔnad] nf still lemonade

citrouille [sitʁuj] nf pumpkin

civet [sivɛ] nm stew; ~ **de lièvre** jugged hare; ~ **de lapin** rabbit stew

civière [sivjɛʁ] nf stretcher

civil, e [sivil] adj (Jur, Admin, poli) civil; (non militaire) civilian ▷ nm civilian; **en** ~ in civilian clothes; **dans le** ~ in civilian life

civilisation [sivilizasjɔ̃] nf civilization

clair, e [klɛʁ] adj light; (chambre) light, bright; (eau, son, fig) clear ▷ adv: **voir** ~ to see clearly ▷ nm: **mettre au** ~ (notes etc) to tidy up; **tirer qch au** ~ to clear sth up, clarify sth; **bleu** ~ light blue; **pour être** ~ so as to make it plain; **y voir** ~ (comprendre) to understand, see; **le plus** ~ **de son temps/argent** the better part of his time/money; **en** ~ (non codé) in clear; ~ **de lune** moonlight

clairement [klɛʁmɑ̃] adv clearly

clairière [klɛʁjɛʁ] nf clearing

clairon [klɛʁɔ̃] nm bugle

claironner [klɛʁɔne] vt (fig) to trumpet, shout from the rooftops

clairsemé, e [klɛʁsəme] adj sparse

clairvoyant, e [klɛʁvwajɑ̃, -ɑ̃t] adj perceptive, clear-sighted

clandestin, e [klɑ̃dɛstɛ̃, -in] *adj* clandestine, covert; (*Pol*) underground, clandestine; (*travailleur, immigration*) illegal; **passager ~** stowaway

clapier [klapje] *nm* (rabbit) hutch

clapoter [klapɔte] *vi* to lap

claque [klak] *nf* (*gifle*) slap; (*Théât*) claque ▷ *nm* (*chapeau*) opera hat

claquer [klake] *vi* (*drapeau*) to flap; (*porte*) to bang, slam; (*fam: mourir*) to snuff it; (*coup de feu*) to ring out ▷ *vt* (*porte*) to slam, bang; (*doigts*) to snap; (*fam: dépenser*) to blow; **elle claquait des dents** her teeth were chattering; **être claqué** (*fam*) to be dead tired; **se ~ un muscle** to pull *ou* strain a muscle

claquettes [klakɛt] *nfpl* tap-dancing *sg*; (*chaussures*) flip-flops

clarinette [klarinɛt] *nf* clarinet

clarté [klarte] *nf* lightness, brightness; (*d'un son, de l'eau*) clearness; (*d'une explication*) clarity

classe [klɑs] *nf* class; (*Scol: local*) class(room); (: *leçon*) class; (: *élèves*) class, form; **1ère/2ème ~** 1st/2nd class; **un (soldat de) deuxième ~** (*Mil: armée de terre*) = private (soldier); (: *armée de l'air*) = aircraftman (*Brit*), = airman basic (*US*); **de ~** luxury *cpd*; **faire ses ~s** (*Mil*) to do one's (recruit's) training; **faire la ~** (*Scol*) to be a *ou* the teacher; to teach; **aller en ~** to go to school; **aller en ~ verte/de neige/de mer** to go to the countryside/skiing/to the seaside with the school; **~ préparatoire** *class which prepares students for the Grandes Écoles entry exams; see note*; **~ sociale** social class; **~ touriste** economy class

⬥ **CLASSES PRÉPARATOIRES**

⬥ *Classes préparatoires* are the two years of
⬥ intensive study which coach students for
⬥ the competitive entry examinations to
⬥ the "grandes écoles". These extremely
⬥ demanding courses follow the
⬥ "baccalauréat" and are usually done at a
⬥ "lycée". Schools which provide such
⬥ classes are more highly regarded than
⬥ those which do not.

classement [klɑsmɑ̃] *nm* classifying; filing; grading; closing; (*rang: Scol*) place; (: *Sport*) placing; (*liste: Scol*) class list (in order of merit); (: *Sport*) placings *pl*; **premier au ~ général** (*Sport*) first overall

classer [klɑse] *vt* (*idées, livres*) to classify; (*papiers*) to file; (*candidat, concurrent*) to grade; (*personne: juger: péj*) to rate; (*Jur: affaire*) to close; **se ~ premier/dernier** to come first/last; (*Sport*) to finish first/last

classeur [klɑsœr] *nm* (*cahier*) file; (*meuble*) filing cabinet; **~ à feuillets mobiles** ring binder

classique [klɑsik] *adj* (*sobre: coupe etc*)

classic(al), classical; (*habituel*) standard, classic ▷ *nm* classic; classical author; **études ~s** classical studies, classics

clause [kloz] *nf* clause

clavecin [klav(ə)sɛ̃] *nm* harpsichord

clavicule [klavikyl] *nf* clavicle, collarbone

clavier [klavje] *nm* keyboard

clé, clef [kle] *nf* key; (*Mus*) clef; (*de mécanicien*) spanner (*Brit*), wrench (*US*) ▷ *adj*: **problème/position ~** key problem/position; **mettre sous ~** to place under lock and key; **prendre la ~ des champs** to run away, make off; **prix ~s en main** (*d'une voiture*) on-the-road price; (*d'un appartement*) price with immediate entry; **~ de sol/de fa/d'ut** treble/bass/alto clef; **livre/film** *etc* **à ~** book/film *etc* in which real people are depicted under fictitious names; **à la ~** (*à la fin*) at the end of it all; **~ anglaise** = clé à molette; **~ de contact** ignition key; **~ à molette** adjustable spanner (*Brit*) *ou* wrench, monkey wrench; **~ USB** USB key; **~ de voûte** keystone

clément, e [klemɑ̃, -ɑ̃t] *adj* (*temps*) mild; (*indulgent*) lenient

clerc [klɛr] *nm*: **~ de notaire** *ou* **d'avoué** lawyer's clerk

clergé [klɛrʒe] *nm* clergy

cliché [kliʃe] *nm* (*fig*) cliché; (*Photo*) negative; print; (*Typo*) (printing) plate; (*Ling*) cliché

client, e [klijɑ̃, -ɑ̃t] *nm/f* (*acheteur*) customer, client; (*d'hôtel*) guest, patron; (*du docteur*) patient; (*de l'avocat*) client

clientèle [klijɑ̃tɛl] *nf* (*du magasin*) customers *pl*, clientèle; (*du docteur, de l'avocat*) practice; **accorder sa ~ à** to give one's custom to; **retirer sa ~ à** to take one's business away from

cligner [kliɲe] *vi*: **~ des yeux** to blink (one's eyes); **~ de l'œil** to wink

clignotant [kliɲɔtɑ̃] *nm* (*Auto*) indicator

clignoter [kliɲɔte] *vi* (*étoiles etc*) to twinkle; (*lumière: à intervalles réguliers*) to flash; (: *vaciller*) to flicker; (*yeux*) to blink

climat [klima] *nm* climate

climatisation [klimatizasjɔ̃] *nf* air conditioning

climatisé, e [klimatize] *adj* air-conditioned

clin d'œil [klɛ̃dœj] *nm* wink; **en un ~** in a flash

clinique [klinik] *adj* clinical ▷ *nf* nursing home, (private) clinic

clinquant, e [klɛ̃kɑ̃, -ɑ̃t] *adj* flashy

clip [klip] *nm* (*pince*) clip; (*boucle d'oreille*) clip-on; (**vidéo**) **~** pop (*ou* promotional) video

cliquer [klike] *vi* (*Inform*) to click; **~ deux fois** to double-click ▷ *vt* to click; **~ sur** to click on

cliqueter [klikte] *vi* to clash; (*ferraille, clefs, monnaie*) to jangle, jingle; (*verres*) to chink

clochard, e [klɔʃar, -ard] *nm/f* tramp

cloche [klɔʃ] *nf* (*d'église*) bell; (*fam*) clot; (*chapeau*) cloche (hat); **~ à fromage** cheese-cover

cloche-pied [klɔʃpje]: **à ~** adv on one leg, hopping (along)

clocher [klɔʃe] nm church tower; (en pointe) steeple ▷ vi (fam) to be ou go wrong; **de ~** (péj) parochial

cloison [klwazɔ̃] nf partition (wall); **~ étanche** (fig) impenetrable barrier, brick wall (fig)

cloître [klwatR] nm cloister

cloîtrer [klwatRe] vt: **se cloîtrer** to shut o.s. away; (Rel) to enter a convent ou monastery

clonage [klɔnaʒ] nm cloning

clone [klon] nm clone

cloner [klone] vt to clone

cloque [klɔk] nf blister

clore [klɔR] vt to close; **~ une session** (Inform) to log out

clos, e [klo, -oz] pp de **clore** ▷ adj voir **maison; huis; vase** ▷ nm (enclosed) field

clôture [klotyR] nf closure, closing; (barrière) enclosure, fence

clôturer [klotyRe] vt (terrain) to enclose, close off; (festival, débats) to close

clou [klu] nm nail; (Méd) boil; **clous** nmpl **= passage clouté; pneus à ~s** studded tyres; **le ~ du spectacle** the highlight of the show; **~ de girofle** clove

clouer [klue] vt to nail down (ou up); (fig): **~ sur/contre** to pin to/against

clown [klun] nm clown; **faire le ~** (fig) to clown (about), play the fool

club [klœb] nm club

CMU sigle f (= couverture maladie universelle) system of free health care for those on low incomes

CNRS sigle m (= Centre national de la recherche scientifique) ≈ SERC (Brit), ≈ NSF (US)

coaguler [kɔagyle] vi, vt, **se coaguler** vi (sang) to coagulate

coasser [kɔase] vi to croak

cobaye [kɔbaj] nm guinea-pig

coca® [kɔka] nm Coke®

cocaïne [kɔkain] nf cocaine

cocasse [kɔkas] adj comical, funny

coccinelle [kɔksinɛl] nf ladybird (Brit), ladybug (US)

cocher [kɔʃe] nm coachman ▷ vt to tick off; (entailler) to notch

cochère [kɔʃɛR] adj f voir **porte**

cochon, ne [kɔʃɔ̃, -ɔn] nm pig ▷ nm/f (péj: sale) (filthy) pig; (: méchant) swine ▷ adj (fam) dirty, smutty; **~ d'Inde** guinea-pig; **~ de lait** (Culin) sucking pig

cochonnerie [kɔʃɔnRi] nf (fam: saleté) filth; (: marchandises) rubbish, trash

cocktail [kɔktɛl] nm cocktail; (réception) cocktail party

coco [kɔko] nm voir **noix;** (fam) bloke (Brit), dude (US)

cocorico [kɔkɔRiko] excl, nm cock-a-doodle-do

cocotier [kɔkɔtje] nm coconut palm

cocotte [kɔkɔt] nf (en fonte) casserole; **ma ~** (fam) sweetie (pie); **~ (minute)**® pressure cooker; **~ en papier** paper shape

cocu [kɔky] nm cuckold

code [kɔd] nm code ▷ adj: **phares ~s** dipped lights; **se mettre en ~(s)** to dip (Brit) ou dim (US) one's (head)lights; **~ à barres** bar code; **~ de caractère** (Inform) character code; **~ civil** Common Law; **~ machine** machine code; **~ pénal** penal code; **~ postal** (numéro) postcode (Brit), zip code (US); **~ de la route** highway code; **~ secret** cipher

cœur [kœR] nm heart; (Cartes: couleur) hearts pl; (: carte) heart; (Culin): **~ de laitue/d'artichaut** lettuce/artichoke heart; (fig): **~ du débat** heart of the debate; **~ de l'été** height of summer; **~ de la forêt** depths pl of the forest; **affaire de ~** love affair; **avoir bon ~** to be kind-hearted; **avoir mal au ~** to feel sick; **contre ou sur son ~** to one's breast; **opérer qn à ~ ouvert** to perform open-heart surgery on sb; **recevoir qn à ~ ouvert** to welcome sb with open arms; **parler à ~ ouvert** to open one's heart; **de tout son ~** with all one's heart; **avoir le ~ gros ou serré** to have a heavy heart; **en avoir le ~ net** to be clear in one's own mind (about it); **par ~** by heart; **de bon ~** willingly; **avoir à ~ de faire** to be very keen to do; **cela lui tient à ~** that's (very) close to his heart; **prendre les choses à ~** to take things to heart; **à ~ joie** to one's heart's content; **être de tout ~ avec qn** to be (completely) in accord with sb

coffre [kɔfR] nm (meuble) chest; (coffre-fort) safe; (d'auto) boot (Brit), trunk (US); **avoir du ~** (fam) to have a lot of puff

coffre-fort (pl **coffres-forts**) [kɔfRəfɔR] nm safe

coffret [kɔfRɛ] nm casket; **~ à bijoux** jewel box

cognac [kɔɲak] nm brandy, cognac

cogner [kɔɲe] vi to knock, bang; **se cogner** vi to bump o.s.; **se ~ contre** to knock ou bump into; **se ~ la tête** to bang one's head

cohérent, e [kɔeRɑ̃, -ɑ̃t] adj coherent, consistent

cohorte [kɔɔRt] nf troop

cohue [kɔy] nf crowd

coi, coite [kwa, kwat] adj: **rester ~** to remain silent

coiffe [kwaf] nf headdress

coiffé, e [kwafe] adj: **bien/mal ~** with tidy/ untidy hair; **~ d'un béret** wearing a beret; **~ en arrière** with one's hair brushed ou combed back; **~ en brosse** with a crew cut

coiffer [kwafe] vt (fig: surmonter) to cover, top; **~ qn** to do sb's hair; **~ qn d'un béret** to put a beret on sb; **se coiffer** vi to do one's hair; to put on a ou one's hat

coiffeur, -euse [kwafœR, -øz] nm/f hairdresser ▷ nf (table) dressing table

coiffure [kwafyR] nf (cheveux) hairstyle, hairdo; (chapeau) hat, headgear no pl; (art): **la ~** hairdressing

coin [kwɛ̃] nm corner; (pour graver) die; (pour coincer) wedge; (poinçon) hallmark; **l'épicerie du ~** the local grocer; **dans le ~** (aux alentours) in the area, around about; (habiter) locally; **je ne suis pas du ~** I'm not from here; **au ~ du feu** by the fireside; **du ~ de l'œil** out of the corner of one's eye; **regard en ~** side(ways) glance; **sourire en ~** half-smile

coincé, e [kwɛse] adj stuck, jammed; (fig: inhibé) inhibited, with hang-ups

coincer [kwɛse] vt to jam; (fam) to catch (out); to nab; **se coincer** vi to get stuck ou jammed

coïncidence [kɔɛ̃sidɑ̃s] nf coincidence

coïncider [kɔɛ̃side] vi: **~ (avec)** to coincide (with); (correspondre: témoignage etc) to correspond ou tally (with)

coing [kwɛ̃] nm quince

col [kɔl] nm (de chemise) collar; (encolure, cou) neck; (de montagne) pass; **~ roulé** polo-neck; **~ de l'utérus** cervix

colère [kɔlɛʀ] nf anger; **une ~** a fit of anger; **être en ~ (contre qn)** to be angry (with sb); **mettre qn en ~** to make sb angry; **se mettre en ~ contre qn** to get angry with sb; **se mettre en ~** to get angry

coléreux, -euse [kɔleʀø, -øz], **colérique** [kɔleʀik] adj quick-tempered, irascible

colifichet [kɔlifiʃɛ] nm trinket

colimaçon [kɔlimasɔ̃] nm: **escalier en ~** spiral staircase

colin [kɔlɛ̃] nm hake

colique [kɔlik] nf diarrhoea (Brit), diarrhea (US); (douleurs) colic (pains pl); (fam: personne ou chose ennuyeuse) pain

colis [kɔli] nm parcel; **par ~ postal** by parcel post

collaborateur, -trice [kɔlabɔʀatœʀ, -tʀis] nm/f (aussi Pol) collaborator; (d'une revue) contributor

collaborer [kɔ(l)labɔʀe] vi to collaborate; (aussi: **~ à**) to collaborate on; (revue) to contribute to

collant, e [kɔlɑ̃, -ɑ̃t] adj sticky; (robe etc) clinging, skintight; (péj) clinging ▷ nm (bas) tights pl; (de danseur) leotard

collation [kɔlasjɔ̃] nf light meal

colle [kɔl] nf glue; (à papiers peints) (wallpaper) paste; (devinette) teaser, riddle; (Scol fam) detention; **~ forte** superglue®

collecte [kɔlɛkt] nf collection; **faire une ~** to take up a collection

collectif, -ive [kɔlɛktif, -iv] adj collective; (visite, billet etc) group cpd ▷ nm: **~ budgétaire** mini-budget (Brit), mid-term budget; **immeuble ~** block of flats

collection [kɔlɛksjɔ̃] nf collection; (Édition) series; **pièce de ~** collector's item; **faire (la) ~ de** to collect; **(toute) une ~ de ...** (fig) a (complete) set of ...

collectionner [kɔlɛksjɔne] vt (tableaux, timbres) to collect

collectionneur, -euse [kɔlɛksjɔnœʀ, -øz] nm/f collector

collectivité [kɔlɛktivite] nf group; **la ~** the community, the collectivity; **les ~s locales** local authorities

collège [kɔlɛʒ] nm (école) (secondary) school; see note; (assemblée) body; **~ électoral** electoral college

> ● **COLLÈGE**
>
> ● A collège is a state secondary school for children between 11 and 15 years of age. Pupils follow a national curriculum which prescribes a common core along with several options. Schools are free to arrange their own timetable and choose their own teaching methods. Before leaving this phase of their education, students are assessed by examination and course work for their "brevet des collèges".

collégien, ne [kɔleʒjɛ̃, -ɛn] nm/f secondary school pupil (Brit), high school student (US)

collègue [kɔ(l)lɛg] nm/f colleague

coller [kɔle] vt (papier, timbre) to stick (on); (affiche) to stick up; (appuyer, placer contre): **~ son front à la vitre** to press one's face to the window; (enveloppe) to stick down; (morceaux) to stick ou glue together; (Inform) to paste; (fam: mettre, fourrer) to stick, shove; (Scol fam) to keep in, give detention to ▷ vi (être collant) to be sticky; (adhérer) to stick; **~ qch sur** to stick (ou paste ou glue) sth on(to); **~ à** to stick to; (fig) to cling to; **être collé à un examen** (fam) to fail an exam

collet [kɔlɛ] nm (piège) snare, noose; (cou): **prendre qn au ~** to grab sb by the throat; **~ monté** adj inv straight-laced

collier [kɔlje] nm (bijou) necklace; (de chien, Tech) collar; **~ (de barbe), barbe en ~** narrow beard along the line of the jaw; **~ de serrage** choke collar

collimateur [kɔlimatœʀ] nm: **être dans le ~** (fig) to be in the firing line; **avoir qn/qch dans le ~** (fig) to have sb/sth in one's sights

colline [kɔlin] nf hill

collision [kɔlizjɔ̃] nf collision, crash; **entrer en ~ (avec)** to collide (with)

colloque [kɔlɔk] nm colloquium, symposium

collyre [kɔliʀ] nm (Méd) eye lotion

colmater [kɔlmate] vt (fuite) to seal off; (brèche) to plug, fill in

colombe [kɔlɔ̃b] nf dove

Colombie [kɔlɔ̃bi] nf: **la ~** Colombia

colon [kɔlɔ̃] nm settler; (enfant) boarder (in children's holiday camp)

colonel [kɔlɔnɛl] nm colonel; (de l'armée de l'air) group captain

colonie [kɔlɔni] nf colony; **~ (de vacances)** holiday camp (for children)

colonne [kɔlɔn] *nf* column; **se mettre en ~ par deux/quatre** to get into twos/fours; **en ~ par deux** in double file; **~ de secours** rescue party; **~ (vertébrale)** spine, spinal column

colorant [kɔlɔrɑ̃] *nm* colo(u)ring

colorer [kɔlɔʀe] *vt* to colour (*Brit*), color (*US*); **se colorer** *vi* to turn red; to blush

colorier [kɔlɔʀje] *vt* to colo(u)r (in); **album à ~** colouring book

coloris [kɔlɔʀi] *nm* colo(u)r, shade

colporter [kɔlpɔʀte] *vt* to peddle

colza [kɔlza] *nm* rape(seed)

coma [kɔma] *nm* coma; **être dans le ~** to be in a coma

combat [kɔ̃ba] *vb voir* **combattre** ▷ *nm* fight; fighting *no pl*; **~ de boxe** boxing match; **~ de rues** street fighting *no pl*; **~ singulier** single combat

combattant [kɔ̃batɑ̃] *vb voir* **combattre** ▷ *nm* combatant; (*d'une rixe*) brawler; **ancien ~** war veteran

combattre [kɔ̃batʀ] *vi* to fight ▷ *vt* to fight; (*épidémie, ignorance*) to combat, fight against

combien [kɔ̃bjɛ̃] *adv* (*quantité*) how much; (*nombre*) how many; (*exclamatif*) how; **~ de** how much; (*nombre*) how many; **~ de temps** how long, how much time; **c'est ~?, ça fait ~?** how much is it?; **~ coûte/pèse ceci?** how much does this cost/weigh?; **vous mesurez ~?** what size are you?; **ça fait ~ en largeur?** how wide is that?; **on est le ~ aujourd'hui?** (*fam*) what's the date today?

combinaison [kɔ̃binezɔ̃] *nf* combination; (*astuce*) device, scheme; (*de femme*) slip; (*d'aviateur*) flying suit; (*de plongée*) wetsuit; (*bleu de travail*) boilersuit (*Brit*), coveralls *pl* (*US*)

combine [kɔ̃bin] *nf* trick; (*péj*) scheme, fiddle (*Brit*)

combiné [kɔ̃bine] *nm* (*aussi*: **~ téléphonique**) receiver; (*Ski*) combination (event); (*vêtement de femme*) corselet

combiner [kɔ̃bine] *vt* to combine; (*plan, horaire*) to work out, devise

comble [kɔ̃bl] *adj* (*salle*) packed (full) ▷ *nm* (*du bonheur, plaisir*) height; **combles** *nmpl* (*Constr*) attic *sg*, loft *sg*; **de fond en ~** from top to bottom; **pour ~ de malchance** to cap it all; **c'est le ~!** that beats everything!, that takes the biscuit! (*Brit*); **sous les ~s** in the attic

combler [kɔ̃ble] *vt* (*trou*) to fill in; (*besoin, lacune*) to fill; (*déficit*) to make good; (*satisfaire*) to gratify, fulfil (*Brit*), fulfill (*US*); **~ qn de joie** to fill sb with joy; **~ qn d'honneurs** to shower sb with honours

combustible [kɔ̃bystibl] *adj* combustible ▷ *nm* fuel

comédie [kɔmedi] *nf* comedy; (*fig*) playacting *no pl*; **jouer la ~** (*fig*) to put on an act; **faire une ~** (*fig*) to make a fuss; **la C~ française** *see note*; **~ musicale** musical

 COMÉDIE FRANÇAISE

Founded in 1680 by Louis XIV, the *Comédie française* is the French national theatre. The company is subsidized by the state and mainly performs in the Palais Royal in Paris, tending to concentrate on classical French drama.

comédien, ne [kɔmedjɛ̃, -ɛn] *nm/f* actor/actress; (*comique*) comedy actor/actress, comedian/comedienne; (*fig*) sham

comestible [kɔmɛstibl] *adj* edible; **comestibles** *nmpl* foods

comique [kɔmik] *adj* (*drôle*) comical; (*Théât*) comic ▷ *nm* (*artiste*) comic, comedian; **le ~ de qch** the funny *ou* comical side of sth

comité [kɔmite] *nm* committee; **petit ~** select group; **~ directeur** management committee; **~ d'entreprise (CE)** works council; **~ des fêtes** festival committee

commandant [kɔmɑ̃dɑ̃] *nm* (*gén*) commander, commandant; (*Mil: grade*) major; (*armée de l'air*) squadron leader; (*Navig*) captain; **~ (de bord)** (*Aviat*) captain

commande [kɔmɑ̃d] *nf* (*Comm*) order; (*Inform*) command; **commandes** *nfpl* (*Aviat etc*) controls; **passer une ~ (de)** to put in an order (for); **sur ~** to order; **à distance** remote control; **véhicule à double ~** vehicle with dual controls

commandement [kɔmɑ̃dmɑ̃] *nm* command; (*ordre*) command, order; (*Rel*) commandment

commander [kɔmɑ̃de] *vt* (*Comm*) to order; (*diriger, ordonner*) to command; **~ à** (*Mil*) to command; (*contrôler, maîtriser*) to have control over; **~ à qn de faire** to command *ou* order sb to do

commando [kɔmɑ̃do] *nm* commando (squad)

MOT-CLÉ

comme [kɔm] *prép* **1** (*comparaison*) like; **tout comme son père** just like his father; **fort comme un bœuf** as strong as an ox; **joli comme tout** ever so pretty

2 (*manière*) like; **faites-le comme ça** do it like this, do it this way; **comme ça ou cela on n'aura pas d'ennuis** that way we won't have any problems; **comme ci, comme ça** so-so, middling; **comment ça va? — comme ça** how are things? — OK; **comme on dit** as they say

3 (*en tant que*) as a; **donner comme prix** to give as a prize; **travailler comme secrétaire** to work as a secretary

4: **comme quoi** (*d'où il s'ensuit que*) which shows that; **il a écrit une lettre comme quoi il …** he's written a letter saying that …

5: **comme il faut** *adv* properly

▷ *adj* (*correct*) proper, correct
▷ *conj* **1** (*ainsi que*) as; **elle écrit comme elle parle** she writes as she talks; **comme si** as if **2** (*au moment où, alors que*) 'as; **il est parti comme j'arrivais** he left as I arrived **3** (*parce que, puisque*) as, since; **comme il était en retard, il ...** as he was late, he ...
▷ *adv*: **comme il est fort/c'est bon!** he's so strong/it's so good!; **il est malin comme c'est pas permis** he's as smart as anything

commémorer [kɔmemɔʀe] *vt* to commemorate

commencement [kɔmɑ̃smɑ̃] *nm* beginning, start, commencement; **commencements** *nmpl* (*débuts*) beginnings

commencer [kɔmɑ̃se] *vt* to begin, start, commence ▷ *vi* to begin, start, commence; **~ à** *ou* **de faire** to begin *ou* start doing; **~ par qch** to begin with sth; **~ par faire qch** to begin by doing sth

comment [kɔmɑ̃] *adv* how; **~?** (*que dites-vous*) (I beg your) pardon?; **~! what!** ▷ *nm*: **le ~ et le pourquoi** the whys and wherefores; **et ~!** and how!; **~ donc!** of course!; **~ faire?** how will we do it?; **~ se fait-il que ...?** how is it that ...?

commentaire [kɔmɑ̃tɛʀ] *nm* comment; remark; **~ (de texte)** (*Scol*) commentary; **~ sur image** voice-over

commenter [kɔmɑ̃te] *vt* (*jugement, événement*) to comment (up)on; (*Radio, TV*): **match, manifestation**) to cover, give a commentary on

commérages [kɔmeʀaʒ] *nmpl* gossip *sg*

commerçant, e [kɔmɛʀsɑ̃, -ɑ̃t] *adj* commercial; trading; (*rue*) shopping *cpd*; (*personne*) commercially-shrewd ▷ *nm/f* shopkeeper, trader

commerce [kɔmɛʀs] *nm* (*activité*) trade, commerce; (*boutique*) business; **le petit ~** small shop owners *pl*, small traders *pl*; **faire ~ de** to trade in; (*fig: péj*) to trade on; **chambre de ~** Chamber of Commerce; **livres de ~** (*account*) books; **vendu dans le ~** sold in the shops; **vendu hors-~** sold directly to the public; **~ en** *ou* **de gros/détail** wholesale/retail trade; **~ électronique** e-commerce; **~ équitable** fair trade; **~ intérieur/extérieur** home/foreign trade

commercial, e, -aux [kɔmɛʀsjal, -o] *adj* commercial, trading; (*péj*) commercial ▷ *nm*: **les commerciaux** the commercial people

commercialiser [kɔmɛʀsjalize] *vt* to market

commère [kɔmɛʀ] *nf* gossip

commettre [kɔmɛtʀ] *vt* to commit; **se commettre** *vi* to compromise one's good name

commis¹ [kɔmi] *nm* (*de magasin*) (shop) assistant (*Brit*), sales clerk (*US*); (*de banque*) clerk; **~ voyageur** commercial traveller (*Brit*) *ou* traveler (*US*)

commis², e [kɔmi, -iz] *pp de* **commettre**

commissaire [kɔmisɛʀ] *nm* (*de police*) ≈ (police) superintendent (*Brit*), ≈ (police) captain (*US*); (*de rencontre sportive etc*) steward; **~ du bord** (*Navig*) purser; **~ aux comptes** (*Admin*) auditor

commissaire-priseur (*pl* **commissaires-priseurs**) [kɔmisɛʀpʀizœʀ] *nm* (official) auctioneer

commissariat [kɔmisaʀja] *nm*: **~ (de police)** police station; (*Admin*) commissionership

commission [kɔmisjɔ̃] *nf* (*comité, pourcentage*) commission; (*message*) message; (*course*) errand; **commissions** *nfpl* (*achats*) shopping *sg*; **~ d'examen** examining board

commode [kɔmɔd] *adj* (*pratique*) convenient, handy; (*facile*) easy; (*air, personne*) easy-going; (*personne*): **pas ~** awkward (to deal with) ▷ *nf* chest of drawers

commodité [kɔmɔdite] *nf* convenience

commotion [kɔmosjɔ̃] *nf*: **~ (cérébrale)** concussion

commotionné, e [kɔmosjɔne] *adj* shocked, shaken

commun, e [kɔmœ̃, -yn] *adj* common; (*pièce*) communal, shared; (*réunion, effort*) joint ▷ *nf* (*Admin*) commune, ≈ district; (: *urbaine*) ≈ borough; **communs** *nmpl* (*bâtiments*) outbuildings; **cela sort du ~** it's out of the ordinary; **le ~ des mortels** the common run of people; **sans ~e mesure** incomparable; **être ~ à** (*chose*) to be shared by; **en ~** (*faire*) jointly; **mettre en ~** to pool, share; **peu ~** unusual; **d'un ~ accord** of one accord; with one accord

communauté [kɔmynote] *nf* community; (*Jur*): **régime de la ~** communal estate settlement

commune [kɔmyn] *adj f, nf* voir **commun**

communicatif, -ive [kɔmynikatif, -iv] *adj* (*personne*) communicative; (*rire*) infectious

communication [kɔmynikasjɔ̃] *nf* communication; **~ (téléphonique)** (telephone) call; **avoir la ~ (avec)** to get *ou* be through (to); **vous avez la ~** you're through; **donnez-moi la ~ avec** put me through to; **mettre qn en ~ avec qn** (*en contact*) to put sb in touch with sb; (*au téléphone*) to connect sb with sb; **~ interurbaine** long-distance call; **~ en PCV** reverse charge (*Brit*) *ou* collect (*US*) call; **~ avec préavis** personal call

communier [kɔmynje] *vi* (*Rel*) to receive communion; (*fig*) to be united

communion [kɔmynjɔ̃] *nf* communion

communiquer [kɔmynike] *vt* (*nouvelle, dossier*) to pass on, convey; (*maladie*) to pass on; (*peur etc*) to communicate; (*chaleur, mouvement*) to transmit ▷ *vi* to communicate; **~ avec** (*salle*) to communicate with; **se ~ à** (*se propager*) to spread to

communisme [kɔmynism] *nm* communism

communiste [kɔmynist] *adj, nm/f* communist

commutateur [kɔmytatœr] nm (Élec) (change-over) switch, commutator

compact, e [kɔ̃pakt] adj (dense) dense; (appareil) compact

compagne [kɔ̃paɲ] nf companion

compagnie [kɔ̃paɲi] nf (firme, Mil) company; (groupe) gathering; (présence): **la ~ de qn** sb's company; **homme/femme de ~** escort; **tenir ~ à qn** to keep sb company; **fausser ~ à qn** to give sb the slip, slip ou sneak away from sb; **en ~ de** in the company of; **Dupont et ~, Dupont et Cie** Dupont and Company, Dupont and Co; **~ aérienne** airline (company)

compagnon [kɔ̃paɲɔ̃] nm companion; (autrefois: ouvrier) craftsman; journeyman

comparable [kɔ̃parabl] adj: **~ (à)** comparable (to)

comparaison [kɔ̃parɛzɔ̃] nf comparison; (métaphore) simile; **en ~ (de)** in comparison (with); **par ~ (à)** by comparison (with)

comparaître [kɔ̃parɛtr] vi: **~ (devant)** to appear (before)

comparer [kɔ̃pare] vt to compare; **~ qch/qn à** ou **et** (pour choisir) to compare sth/sb with ou and; (: pour établir une similitude) to compare sth/sb to ou and

compartiment [kɔ̃partimã] nm compartment

comparution [kɔ̃parysjɔ̃] nf appearance

compas [kɔ̃pa] nm (Géom) (pair of) compasses pl; (Navig) compass

compatible [kɔ̃patibl] adj compatible; **~ (avec)** compatible (with)

compatir [kɔ̃patir] vi: **~ (à)** to sympathize (with)

compatriote [kɔ̃patrijɔt] nm/f compatriot, fellow countryman/woman

compensation [kɔ̃pãsasjɔ̃] nf compensation; (Banque) clearing; **en ~** in ou as compensation

compenser [kɔ̃pãse] vt to compensate for, make up for

compère [kɔ̃pɛr] nm accomplice; fellow musician ou comedian etc

compétence [kɔ̃petãs] nf competence

compétent, e [kɔ̃petã, -ãt] adj (apte) competent, capable; (Jur) competent

compétition [kɔ̃petisjɔ̃] nf (gén) competition; (Sport: épreuve) event; **la ~** competitive sport; **être en ~ avec** to be competing with; **la ~ automobile** motor racing

complainte [kɔ̃plɛ̃t] nf lament

complaire [kɔ̃plɛr]: **se complaire** vi: **se ~ dans/parmi** to take pleasure in/in being among

complaisance [kɔ̃plɛzãs] nf kindness; (péj) indulgence; (: fatuité) complacency; **attestation de ~** certificate produced to oblige a patient etc; **pavillon de ~** flag of convenience

complaisant, e [kɔ̃plɛzã, -ãt] vb voir **complaire** ▷ adj (aimable) kind; obliging; (péj) accommodating; (: fat) complacent

complément [kɔ̃plemã] nm complement; (reste) remainder; (Ling) complement; **~ d'information** (Admin) supplementary ou further information; **~ d'agent** agent; **~ (d'objet) direct/indirect** direct/indirect object; **~ (circonstanciel) de lieu/temps** adverbial phrase of place/time; **~ de nom** possessive phrase

complémentaire [kɔ̃plemãtɛr] adj complementary; (additionnel) supplementary

complet, -ète [kɔ̃plɛ, -ɛt] adj complete; (plein: hôtel etc) full ▷ nm (aussi: **~-veston**) suit; **pain ~** wholemeal bread; **au (grand) ~** all together

complètement [kɔ̃plɛtmã] adv (en entier) completely; (absolument: fou, faux etc) absolutely; (à fond: étudier etc) fully, in depth

compléter [kɔ̃plete] vt (porter à la quantité voulue) to complete; (augmenter: connaissances, études) to complement, supplement; (: garde-robe) to add to; **se compléter** vi (personnes) to complement one another; (collection etc) to become complete

complexe [kɔ̃plɛks] adj complex ▷ nm (Psych) complex, hang-up; (bâtiments): **~ hospitalier/industriel** hospital/industrial complex

complexé, e [kɔ̃plɛkse] adj mixed-up, hung-up

complication [kɔ̃plikasjɔ̃] nf complexity, intricacy; (difficulté, ennui) complication; **complications** nfpl (Méd) complications

complice [kɔ̃plis] nm accomplice

complicité [kɔ̃plisite] nf complicity

compliment [kɔ̃plimã] nm (louange) compliment; **compliments** nmpl (félicitations) congratulations

compliqué, e [kɔ̃plike] adj complicated, complex, intricate; (personne) complicated

compliquer [kɔ̃plike] vt to complicate; **se compliquer** vi (situation) to become complicated; **se ~ la vie** to make life difficult ou complicated for o.s

complot [kɔ̃plo] nm plot

comportement [kɔ̃pɔrtəmã] nm behaviour (Brit), behavior (US); (Tech: d'une pièce, d'un véhicule) behavio(u)r, performance

comporter [kɔ̃pɔrte] vt (consister en) to consist of, be composed of, comprise; (être équipé de) to have; (impliquer) to entail, involve; **se comporter** vi to behave; (Tech) to behave, perform

composant [kɔ̃pozã] nm component, constituent

composé, e [kɔ̃poze] adj (visage, air) studied; (Bio, Chimie, Ling) compound ▷ nm (Chimie, Ling) compound; **~ de** made up of

composer [kɔ̃poze] vt (musique, texte) to compose; (mélange, équipe) to make up; (faire partie de) to make up, form; (Typo) to (type)set ▷ vi (Scol) to sit ou do a test; (transiger) to come to terms; **se ~ de** to be composed of, be made up of; **~ un numéro** (au téléphone) to dial a number

compositeur, -trice [kɔ̃pozitœR, -tRis] nm/f (Mus) composer; (Typo) compositor, typesetter

composition [kɔ̃pozisjɔ̃] nf composition; (Scol) test; (Typo) (type)setting, composition; **de bonne ~** (accommodant) easy to deal with; **amener qn à ~** to get sb to come to terms; **~ française** (Scol) French essay

composter [kɔ̃poste] vt to date-stamp; (billet) to punch

◈ **COMPOSTER**

◈ In France you have to punch your ticket
◈ on the platform to validate it before
◈ getting onto the train.

compote [kɔ̃pɔt] nf stewed fruit no pl; **~ de pommes** stewed apples

compréhensible [kɔ̃pReãsibl] adj comprehensible; (attitude) understandable

compréhensif, -ive [kɔ̃pReãsif, -iv] adj understanding

comprendre [kɔ̃pRãdR] vt to understand; (se composer de) to comprise, consist of; (inclure) to include; **se faire ~** to make o.s. understood; to get one's ideas across; **mal ~** to misunderstand

compresse [kɔ̃pRɛs] nf compress

compression [kɔ̃pResjɔ̃] nf compression; (d'un crédit etc) reduction

comprimé, e [kɔ̃pRime] adj: **air ~** compressed air ▷ nm tablet

comprimer [kɔ̃pRime] vt to compress; (fig: crédit etc) to reduce, cut down

compris, e [kɔ̃pRi, -iz] pp de **comprendre** ▷ adj (inclus) included; **~?** understood?, is that clear?; **~ entre** (situé) contained between; **la maison ~e/non ~e, y/non ~ la maison** including/excluding the house; **service ~** service (charge) included; **100 euros tout ~** 100 euros all inclusive ou all-in

compromettre [kɔ̃pRɔmɛtR] vt to compromise

compromis [kɔ̃pRɔmi] vb voir **compromettre** ▷ nm compromise

comptabilité [kɔ̃tabilite] nf (activité, technique) accounting, accountancy; (d'une société: comptes) accounts pl, books pl; (: service) accounts office ou department; **~ à partie double** double-entry book-keeping

comptable [kɔ̃tabl] nm/f accountant ▷ adj accounts cpd, accounting

comptant [kɔ̃tã] adv: **payer ~** to pay cash; **acheter ~** to buy for cash

compte [kɔ̃t] nm count, counting; (total, montant) count, (right) number; (bancaire, facture) account; **comptes** nmpl accounts, books; (fig) explanation sg; **ouvrir un ~** to open an account; **rendre des ~s à qn** (fig) to be answerable to sb; **faire le ~ de** to count up, make a count of; **tout ~ fait** on the whole; **à ce ~-là** (dans ce cas) in that case; (à ce train-là) at that rate; **en fin de ~** (fig) all things considered, weighing it all up; **au bout du ~** in the final analysis; **à bon ~** at a favourable price; (fig) lightly; **avoir son ~** (fig: en avoir assez) to have had it; **s'en tirer à bon ~** to get off lightly; **pour le ~ de** on behalf of; **pour son propre ~** for one's own benefit; **sur le ~ de qn** (à son sujet) about sb; **travailler à son ~** to work for oneself; **mettre qch sur le ~ de qn** (le rendre responsable) to attribute sth to sb; **prendre qch à son ~** to take responsibility for sth; **trouver son ~ à qch** to do well out of sth; **régler un ~** (s'acquitter de qch) to settle an account; (se venger) to get one's own back; **rendre ~ (à qn) de qch** to give (sb) an account of sth; **rendre des ~s à qn** (fig) to be answerable to sb; **tenir ~ de** to take sth into account; **~ tenu de** taking into account; **~ en banque** bank account; **~ chèque(s)** current account; **~ chèque postal (CCP)** Post Office account; **~ client** (sur bilan) accounts receivable; **~ courant (CC)** current account; **~ de dépôt** deposit account; **~ d'exploitation** operating account; **~ fournisseur** (sur bilan) accounts payable; **~ à rebours** countdown; **~ rendu** account, report; (de film, livre) review; voir aussi **rendre**

compte-gouttes [kɔ̃tgut] nm inv dropper

compter [kɔ̃te] vt to count; (facturer) to charge for; (avoir à son actif, comporter) to have; (prévoir) to allow, reckon; (tenir compte de, inclure) to include; (penser, espérer) to expect; **~ réussir/revenir** to expect to succeed/return ▷ vi to count; (être économe) to economize; (être non négligeable) to count, matter; (valoir): **~ pour** to count for; (figurer): **~ parmi** to be ou rank among; **~ sur** to count (up)on; **~ avec qch/qn** to reckon with ou take account of sth/sb; **~ sans qch/qn** to reckon without sth/sb; **sans ~ que** besides which; **à ~ du 10 janvier** (Comm) (as) from 10th January

compteur [kɔ̃tœR] nm meter; **~ de vitesse** speedometer

comptine [kɔ̃tin] nf nursery rhyme

comptoir [kɔ̃twaR] nm (de magasin) counter; (de café) counter, bar; (colonial) trading post

compulser [kɔ̃pylse] vt to consult

comte, comtesse [kɔ̃t, kɔ̃tɛs] nm/f count/countess

con, ne [kɔ̃, kɔn] adj (fam!) bloody (Brit) ou damned stupid (!)

concéder [kɔ̃sede] vt to grant; (défaite, point) to concede; **~ que** to concede that

concentré [kɔ̃sãtRe] nm concentrate; **~ de tomates** tomato purée

concentrer [kɔ̃sɑ̃tʀe] vt to concentrate; **se concentrer** vi to concentrate

concept [kɔ̃sɛpt] nm concept

conception [kɔ̃sɛpsjɔ̃] nf conception; (d'une machine etc) design

concerner [kɔ̃sɛʀne] vt to concern; **en ce qui me concerne** as far as I am concerned; **en ce qui concerne ceci** as far as this is concerned, with regard to this

concert [kɔ̃sɛʀ] nm concert; **de ~** adv in unison; together; (décider) unanimously

concerter [kɔ̃sɛʀte] vt to devise; **se concerter** vi (collaborateurs etc) to put our (ou their etc) heads together, consult (each other)

concession [kɔ̃sesjɔ̃] nf concession

concessionnaire [kɔ̃sesjɔnɛʀ] nm/f agent, dealer

concevoir [kɔ̃s(ə)vwaʀ] vt (idée, projet) to conceive (of); (méthode, plan d'appartement, décoration etc) to plan, design; (comprendre) to understand; (enfant) to conceive; **maison bien/mal conçue** well-/badly-designed ou -planned house

concierge [kɔ̃sjɛʀʒ] nm/f caretaker; (d'hôtel) head porter

conciliabules [kɔ̃siljabyl] nmpl (private) discussions, confabulations (Brit)

concilier [kɔ̃silje] vt to reconcile; **se ~ qn/l'appui de qn** to win sb over/sb's support

concis, e [kɔ̃si, -iz] adj concise

concitoyen, ne [kɔ̃sitwajɛ̃, -ɛn] nm/f fellow citizen

concluant, e [kɔ̃klyɑ̃, -ɑ̃t] vb voir **conclure** ▷ adj conclusive

conclure [kɔ̃klyʀ] vt to conclude; (signer: accord, pacte) to enter into; (déduire): **~ qch de qch** to deduce sth from sth; **~ à l'acquittement** to decide in favour of an acquittal; **~ au suicide** to come to the conclusion (ou (Jur) to pronounce) that it is a case of suicide; **~ un marché** to clinch a deal; **j'en conclus que** from that I conclude that

conclusion [kɔ̃klyzjɔ̃] nf conclusion; **conclusions** nfpl (Jur) submissions; findings; **en ~** in conclusion

conçois [kɔ̃swa], **conçoive** etc [kɔ̃swav] vb voir **concevoir**

concombre [kɔ̃kɔ̃bʀ] nm cucumber

concorder [kɔ̃kɔʀde] vi to tally, agree

concourir [kɔ̃kuʀiʀ] vi (Sport) to compete; **~ à** vt (effet etc) to work towards

concours [kɔ̃kuʀ] vb voir **concourir** ▷ nm competition; (Scol) competitive examination; (assistance) aid, help; **recrutement par voie de ~** recruitment by (competitive) examination; **apporter son ~ à** to give one's support to; **~ de circonstances** combination of circumstances; **~ hippique** horse show; voir **hors-concours**

concret, -ète [kɔ̃kʀɛ, -ɛt] adj concrete

concrétiser [kɔ̃kʀetize] vt to realize; **se concrétiser** vi to materialize

conçu, e [kɔ̃sy] pp de **concevoir**

concubinage [kɔ̃kybinaʒ] nm (Jur) cohabitation

concurrence [kɔ̃kyʀɑ̃s] nf competition; **jusqu'à ~ de** up to; **faire ~ à** to be in competition with; **~ déloyale** unfair competition

concurrent, e [kɔ̃kyʀɑ̃, -ɑ̃t] adj competing ▷ nm/f (Sport, Écon etc) competitor; (Scol) candidate

condamner [kɔ̃dɑne] vt (blâmer) to condemn; (Jur) to sentence; (porte, ouverture) to fill in, block up; (malade) to give up (hope for); (obliger): **~ qn à qch/à faire** to condemn sb to sth/to do; **~ qn à deux ans de prison** to sentence sb to two years' imprisonment; **~ qn à une amende** to impose a fine on sb

condensation [kɔ̃dɑ̃sasjɔ̃] nf condensation

condenser [kɔ̃dɑ̃se]: **se condenser** vi to condense

condisciple [kɔ̃disipl] nm/f school fellow, fellow student

condition [kɔ̃disjɔ̃] nf condition; **conditions** nfpl (tarif, prix) terms; (circonstances) conditions; **sans ~** adj unconditional ▷ adv unconditionally; **sous ~ que** on condition that; **à ~ de ou que** provided that; **en bonne ~** in good condition; **mettre en ~** (Sport etc) to get fit; (Psych) to condition (mentally); **~s de vie** living conditions

conditionnel, le [kɔ̃disjɔnɛl] adj conditional ▷ nm conditional (tense)

conditionnement [kɔ̃disjɔnmɑ̃] nm (emballage) packaging; (fig) conditioning

conditionner [kɔ̃disjɔne] vt (déterminer) to determine; (Comm: produit) to package; (fig: personne) to condition; **air conditionné** air conditioning; **réflexe conditionné** conditioned reflex

condoléances [kɔ̃dɔleɑ̃s] nfpl condolences

conducteur, -trice [kɔ̃dyktœʀ, -tʀis] adj (Élec) conducting ▷ nm/f (Auto etc) driver; (d'une machine) operator ▷ nm (Élec etc) conductor

conduire [kɔ̃dɥiʀ] vt (véhicule, passager) to drive; (délégation, troupeau) to lead; **se conduire** vi to behave; **~ vers/à** to lead towards/to; **~ qn quelque part** to take sb somewhere; to drive sb somewhere

conduite [kɔ̃dɥit] nf (en auto) driving; (comportement) behaviour (Brit), behavior (US); (d'eau, de gaz) pipe; **sous la ~ de** led by; **~ forcée** pressure pipe; **~ à gauche** left-hand drive; **~ intérieure** saloon (car)

cône [kon] nm cone; **en forme de ~** cone-shaped

confection [kɔ̃fɛksjɔ̃] nf (fabrication) making; (Couture): **la ~** the clothing industry, the rag trade (fam); **vêtement de ~** ready-to-wear ou off-the-peg garment

confectionner [kɔ̃fɛksjɔne] vt to make

conférence [kɔ̃feʀɑ̃s] nf (exposé) lecture; (pourparlers) conference; **~ de presse** press conference; **~ au sommet** summit (conference)

conférencier, -ière [kɔ̃feRɑ̃sje, -jɛR] nm/f lecturer

confesser [kɔ̃fese] vt to confess; **se confesser** vi (Rel) to go to confession

confession [kɔ̃fesjɔ̃] nf confession; (culte: catholique etc) denomination

confetti [kɔ̃feti] nm confetti no pl

confiance [kɔ̃fjɑ̃s] nf (en l'honnêteté de qn) confidence, trust; (en la valeur de qch) faith; **avoir ~ en** to have confidence ou faith in, trust; **faire ~ à** to trust; **en toute ~** with complete confidence; **de ~** trustworthy, reliable; **mettre qn en ~** to win sb's trust; **vote de ~** (Pol) vote of confidence; **inspirer ~ à** to inspire confidence in; **~ en soi** self-confidence; voir **question**

confiant, e [kɔ̃fjɑ̃, -ɑ̃t] adj confident; trusting

confidence [kɔ̃fidɑ̃s] nf confidence

confidentiel, le [kɔ̃fidɑ̃sjɛl] adj confidential

confier [kɔ̃fje] vt: **~ à qn** (objet en dépôt, travail etc) to entrust to sb; (secret, pensée) to confide to sb; **se ~ à qn** to confide in sb

confins [kɔ̃fɛ̃] nmpl: **aux ~ de** on the borders of

confirmation [kɔ̃fiRmasjɔ̃] nf confirmation

confirmer [kɔ̃fiRme] vt to confirm; **~ qn dans une croyance/ses fonctions** to strengthen sb in a belief/his duties

confiserie [kɔ̃fizRi] nf (magasin) confectioner's ou sweet shop (Brit), candy store (US); **confiseries** nfpl (bonbons) confectionery sg, sweets, candy no pl

confisquer [kɔ̃fiske] vt to confiscate

confit, e [kɔ̃fi, -it] adj: **fruits ~s** crystallized fruits ▷ nm: **~ d'oie** potted goose

confiture [kɔ̃fityR] nf jam; **~ d'oranges** (orange) marmalade

conflit [kɔ̃fli] nm conflict

confondre [kɔ̃fɔ̃dR] vt (jumeaux, faits) to confuse, mix up; (témoin, menteur) to confound; **se confondre** vi to merge; **se ~ en excuses** to offer profuse apologies, apologize profusely; **~ qch/qn avec qch/qn d'autre** to mistake sth/sb for sth/sb else

confondu, e [kɔ̃fɔ̃dy] pp de **confondre** ▷ adj (stupéfait) speechless, overcome; **toutes catégories ~es** taking all categories together

conforme [kɔ̃fɔRm] adj: **~ à** (en accord avec: loi, règle) in accordance with, in keeping with; (identique à) true to; **copie certifiée ~** (Admin) certified copy; **~ à la commande** as per order

conformément [kɔ̃fɔRmemɑ̃] adv: **~ à** in accordance with

conformer [kɔ̃fɔRme] vt: **~ qch à** to model sth on; **se ~ à** to conform to

confort [kɔ̃fɔR] nm comfort; **tout ~** (Comm) with all mod cons (Brit) ou modern conveniences

confortable [kɔ̃fɔRtabl] adj comfortable

confrère [kɔ̃fRɛR] nm colleague; fellow member

confronter [kɔ̃fRɔ̃te] vt to confront; (textes) to compare, collate

confus, e [kɔ̃fy, -yz] adj (vague) confused; (embarrassé) embarrassed

confusion [kɔ̃fyzjɔ̃] nf (voir confus) confusion; embarrassment; (voir confondre) confusion; mixing up; (erreur) confusion; **~ des peines** (Jur) concurrency of sentences

congé [kɔ̃ʒe] nm (vacances) holiday; (arrêt de travail) time off no pl, leave no pl; (Mil) leave no pl; (avis de départ) notice; **en ~** on holiday; off (work); on leave; **semaine/jour de ~** week/day off; **prendre ~ de qn** to take one's leave of sb; **donner son ~ à** to hand ou give in one's notice to; **~ de maladie** sick leave; **~ de maternité** maternity leave; **~s payés** paid holiday ou leave

congédier [kɔ̃ʒedje] vt to dismiss

congélateur [kɔ̃ʒelatœR] nm freezer, deep freeze

congeler [kɔ̃ʒ(ə)le] vt to freeze; **les produits congelés** frozen foods; **se congeler** vi to freeze

congestion [kɔ̃ʒɛstjɔ̃] nf congestion; **~ cérébrale** stroke; **~ pulmonaire** congestion of the lungs

congestionner [kɔ̃ʒɛstjɔne] vt to congest; (Méd) to flush

Congo [kɔ̃go] nm: **le ~** (pays, fleuve) the Congo

congrès [kɔ̃gRɛ] nm congress

conifère [kɔnifɛR] nm conifer

conjecture [kɔ̃ʒɛktyR] nf conjecture, speculation no pl

conjoint, e [kɔ̃ʒwɛ̃, -wɛ̃t] adj joint ▷ nm/f spouse

conjonction [kɔ̃ʒɔ̃ksjɔ̃] nf (Ling) conjunction

conjonctivite [kɔ̃ʒɔ̃ktivit] nf conjunctivitis

conjoncture [kɔ̃ʒɔ̃ktyR] nf circumstances pl; **la ~ (économique)** the economic climate ou situation

conjugaison [kɔ̃ʒygɛzɔ̃] nf (Ling) conjugation

conjuguer [kɔ̃ʒyge] vt (Ling) to conjugate; (efforts etc) to combine

conjuration [kɔ̃ʒyRasjɔ̃] nf conspiracy

conjurer [kɔ̃ʒyRe] vt (sort, maladie) to avert; (implorer): **~ qn de faire qch** to beseech ou entreat sb to do sth

connaissance [kɔnɛsɑ̃s] nf (savoir) knowledge no pl; (personne connue) acquaintance; (conscience) consciousness; **connaissances** nfpl knowledge no pl; **être sans ~** to be unconscious; **perdre/reprendre ~** to lose/regain consciousness; **à ma/sa ~** to (the best of) my/his knowledge; **faire ~ avec qn** ou **la ~ de qn** (rencontrer) to meet sb; (apprendre à connaître) to get to know sb; **avoir ~ de** to be aware of; **prendre ~ de** (document etc) to peruse; **en ~ de cause** with full knowledge of the facts; **de ~** (personne, visage) familiar

connaisseur, -euse [kɔnɛsœR, -øz] nm/f connoisseur ▷ adj expert

connaître [kɔnɛtR] vt to know; (éprouver) to experience; (avoir: succès) to have; to enjoy;

~ **de nom/vue** to know by name/sight; **se connaître** *vi* to know each other; *(soi-même)* to know o.s.; **ils se sont connus à Genève** they (first) met in Geneva; **s'y ~ en qch** to know about sth

connecter [kɔnɛkte] *vt* to connect; **se ~ à Internet** to log onto the Internet

connerie [kɔnʀi] *nf (fam)* (bloody) stupid *(Brit)* ou damn-fool *(US)* thing to do ou say

connexion [kɔnɛksjɔ̃] *nf* connection

connu, e [kɔny] *pp de* **connaître** ▷ *adj (célèbre)* well-known

conquérir [kɔ̃keʀiʀ] *vt* to conquer, win

conquête [kɔ̃kɛt] *nf* conquest

consacrer [kɔ̃sakʀe] *vt (Rel)* to consecrate; **~ qch (à)** to consecrate sth (to); *(fig: usage etc)* to sanction, establish; *(employer)*: **~ qch à** to devote ou dedicate sth to; **se ~ à qch/faire** to dedicate ou devote o.s. to sth/doing

conscience [kɔ̃sjɑ̃s] *nf* conscience; *(perception)* consciousness; **avoir/prendre ~ de** to be/ become aware of; **perdre/reprendre ~** to lose/regain consciousness; **avoir bonne/ mauvaise ~** to have a clear/guilty conscience; **en (toute) ~** in all conscience

consciencieux, -euse [kɔ̃sjɑ̃sjø, -øz] *adj* conscientious

conscient, e [kɔ̃sjɑ̃, -ɑ̃t] *adj* conscious; **~ de** aware ou conscious of

conscrit [kɔ̃skʀi] *nm* conscript

consécutif, -ive [kɔ̃sekytif, -iv] *adj* consecutive; **~ à** following upon

conseil [kɔ̃sɛj] *nm (avis)* piece of advice, advice *no pl; (assemblée)* council; *(expert)*: **~ en recrutement** recruitment consultant ▷ *adj:* **ingénieur-~** engineering consultant; **tenir ~** to hold a meeting; to deliberate; **donner un ~** ou **des ~s à qn** to give sb (a piece of) advice; **demander ~ à qn** to ask sb's advice; **prendre ~ (auprès de qn)** to take advice (from sb); **~ d'administration (CA)** board (of directors); **~ de classe** *(Scol)* meeting of teachers, parents and class representatives to discuss pupils' progress; **~ de discipline** disciplinary committee; **~ général** regional council; *see note;* **~ de guerre** court-martial; **le ~ des ministres** ≈ the Cabinet; **~ municipal (CM)** town council; **~ régional** *regional board of elected representatives;* **~ de révision** recruitment ou draft *(US)* board

> ◈ **CONSEIL GÉNÉRAL**
>
> ◈ Each "département" of France is run by
> ◈ a *Conseil général*, whose remit covers
> ◈ personnel, transport infrastructure,
> ◈ housing, school grants and economic
> ◈ development. The council is made up of
> ◈ "conseillers généraux", each of whom
> ◈ represents a "canton" and is elected for
> ◈ a six-year term. Half of the council's
> ◈ membership are elected every three years.

conseiller¹ [kɔ̃seje] *vt (personne)* to advise; *(méthode, action)* to recommend, advise; **~ qch à qn** to recommend sth to sb; **~ à qn de faire qch** to advise sb to do sth

conseiller², -ière [kɔ̃seje, -ɛʀ] *nm/f* adviser; **~ général** regional councillor; **~ matrimonial** marriage guidance counsellor; **~ municipal** town councillor; **~ d'orientation** *(Scol)* careers adviser *(Brit)*, (school) counselor *(US)*

consentement [kɔ̃sɑ̃tmɑ̃] *nm* consent

consentir [kɔ̃sɑ̃tiʀ] *vt*: **~ (à qch/faire)** to agree ou consent (to sth/to doing); **~ qch à qn** to grant sb sth

conséquence [kɔ̃sekɑ̃s] *nf* consequence, outcome; **conséquences** *nfpl* consequences, repercussions; **en ~** *(donc)* consequently; *(de façon appropriée)* accordingly; **ne pas tirer à ~** to be unlikely to have any repercussions; **sans ~** unimportant; **de ~** important

conséquent, e [kɔ̃sekɑ̃, -ɑ̃t] *adj* logical, rational; *(fam: important)* substantial; **par ~** consequently

conservateur, -trice [kɔ̃sɛʀvatœʀ, -tʀis] *adj* conservative ▷ *nm/f (Pol)* conservative; *(de musée)* curator ▷ *nm (pour aliments)* preservative

conservatoire [kɔ̃sɛʀvatwaʀ] *nm* academy; *(Écologie)* conservation area

conserve [kɔ̃sɛʀv] *nf (gén pl)* canned ou tinned *(Brit)* food; **~s de poisson** canned ou tinned *(Brit)* fish; **en ~** canned, tinned *(Brit)*; **de ~** *(ensemble)* in concert; *(naviguer)* in convoy

conserver [kɔ̃sɛʀve] *vt (faculté)* to retain, keep; *(habitude)* to keep up; *(amis, livres)* to keep; *(préserver, Culin)* to preserve; **se conserver** *vi (aliments)* to keep; **"~ au frais"** "store in a cool place"

considérable [kɔ̃sideʀabl] *adj* considerable, significant, extensive

considération [kɔ̃sideʀasjɔ̃] *nf* consideration; *(estime)* esteem, respect; **considérations** *nfpl (remarques)* reflections; **prendre en ~** to take into consideration ou account; **ceci mérite ~** this is worth considering; **en ~ de** given, because of

considérer [kɔ̃sideʀe] *vt* to consider; *(regarder)* to consider, study; **~ qch comme** to regard sth as

consigne [kɔ̃siɲ] *nf (Comm)* deposit; *(de gare)* left luggage (office) *(Brit)*, checkroom *(US)*; *(punition: Scol)* detention; *(: Mil)* confinement to barracks; *(ordre, instruction)* instructions *pl*; **~ automatique** left-luggage locker; **~s de sécurité** safety instructions

consigner [kɔ̃siɲe] *vt (note, pensée)* to record; *(marchandises)* to deposit; *(punir: Mil)* to confine to barracks; *(: élève)* to put in detention; *(Comm)* to put a deposit on

consistant, e [kɔ̃sistɑ̃, -ɑ̃t] *adj* thick; solid

consister [kɔ̃siste] *vi*: **~ en/dans/à faire** to consist of/in/in doing

consœur [kɔ̃sœʀ] nf (lady) colleague; fellow member

console [kɔ̃sɔl] nf console; ~ **graphique** ou **de visualisation** (*Inform*) visual display unit, VDU; ~ **de jeux** games console

consoler [kɔ̃sɔle] vt to console; **se** ~ **(de qch)** to console o.s. (for sth)

consolider [kɔ̃sɔlide] vt to strengthen, reinforce; (*fig*) to consolidate; **bilan consolidé** consolidated balance sheet

consommateur, -trice [kɔ̃sɔmatœʀ, -tʀis] nm/f (*Écon*) consumer; (*dans un café*) customer

consommation [kɔ̃sɔmasjɔ̃] nf (*Écon*) consumption; (*Jur*) consummation; (*boisson*) drink; ~ **aux 100 km** (*Auto*) (fuel) consumption per 100 km, ≈ miles per gallon (mpg), ≈ gas mileage (US); **de** ~ (*biens, société*) consumer cpd

consommer [kɔ̃sɔme] vt (*personne*) to eat ou drink, consume; (*voiture, usine, poêle*) to use, consume; (*Jur: mariage*) to consummate ▷ vi (*dans un café*) to (have a) drink

consonne [kɔ̃sɔn] nf consonant

conspirer [kɔ̃spiʀe] vi to conspire, plot; ~ **à** (*tendre à*) to conspire to

constamment [kɔ̃stamɑ̃] adv constantly

constant, e [kɔ̃stɑ̃, -ɑ̃t] adj constant; (*personne*) steadfast ▷ nf constant

constat [kɔ̃sta] nm (*d'huissier*) certified report (by bailiff); (*de police*) report; (*observation*) (observed) fact, observation; (*affirmation*) statement; ~ **(à l'amiable)** (*jointly agreed*) *statement for insurance purposes*; ~ **d'échec** acknowledgement of failure

constatation [kɔ̃statasjɔ̃] nf noticing; certifying; (*remarque*) observation

constater [kɔ̃state] vt (*remarquer*) to note, notice; (*Admin, Jur: attester*) to certify; (*dégâts*) to note; ~ **que** (*dire*) to state that

consterner [kɔ̃stɛʀne] vt to dismay

constipé, e [kɔ̃stipe] adj constipated; (*fig*) stiff

constitué, e [kɔ̃stitɥe] adj: ~ **de** made up ou composed of; **bien** ~ of sound constitution; well-formed

constituer [kɔ̃stitɥe] vt (*comité, équipe*) to set up, form; (*dossier, collection*) to put together, build up; (*éléments, parties: composer*) to make up, constitute; (*représenter, être*) to constitute; **se** ~ **prisonnier** to give o.s. up; **se** ~ **partie civile** *to bring an independent action for damages*

constitution [kɔ̃stitysjɔ̃] nf setting up; building up; (*composition*) composition, make-up; (*santé, Pol*) constitution

constructeur [kɔ̃stʀyktœʀ] nm/f manufacturer, builder

constructif, -ive [kɔ̃stʀyktif, -iv] adj (*positif*) constructive

construction [kɔ̃stʀyksjɔ̃] nf construction, building

construire [kɔ̃stʀɥiʀ] vt to build, construct; **se construire** vi: **l'immeuble s'est** **construit très vite** the building went up ou was built very quickly

consul [kɔ̃syl] nm consul

consulat [kɔ̃syla] nm consulate

consultant, e [kɔ̃syltɑ̃, -ɑ̃t] adj, nm consultant

consultation [kɔ̃syltasjɔ̃] nf consultation; **consultations** nfpl (*Pol*) talks; **être en** ~ (*délibération*) to be in consultation; (*médecin*) to be consulting; **aller à la** ~ (*Méd*) to go to the surgery (*Brit*) ou doctor's office (US); **heures de** ~ (*Méd*) surgery (*Brit*) ou office (US) hours

consulter [kɔ̃sylte] vt to consult ▷ vi (*médecin*) to hold surgery (*Brit*), be in (the office) (US); **se consulter** vi to confer

consumer [kɔ̃syme] vt to consume; **se consumer** vi to burn; **se** ~ **de chagrin/ douleur** to be consumed with sorrow/grief

contact [kɔ̃takt] nm contact; **au** ~ **de** (*air, peau*) on contact with; (*gens*) through contact with; **mettre/couper le** ~ (*Auto*) to switch on/off the ignition; **entrer en** ~ (*fils, objets*) to come into contact, make contact; **se mettre en** ~ **avec** (*Radio*) to make contact with; **prendre** ~ **avec** (*relation d'affaires, connaissance*) to get in touch ou contact with

contacter [kɔ̃takte] vt to contact, get in touch with

contagieux, -euse [kɔ̃taʒjø, -øz] adj infectious; (*par le contact*) contagious

contaminer [kɔ̃tamine] vt (*par un virus*) to infect; (*par des radiations*) to contaminate

conte [kɔ̃t] nm tale; ~ **de fées** fairy tale

contempler [kɔ̃tɑ̃ple] vt to contemplate, gaze at

contemporain, e [kɔ̃tɑ̃pɔʀɛ̃, -ɛn] adj, nm/f contemporary

contenance [kɔ̃tnɑ̃s] nf (*d'un récipient*) capacity; (*attitude*) bearing, attitude; **perdre** ~ to lose one's composure; **se donner une** ~ to give the impression of composure; **faire bonne** ~ **(devant)** to put on a bold front (in the face of)

conteneur [kɔ̃tnœʀ] nm container; ~ **(de bouteilles)** bottle bank

contenir [kɔ̃t(ə)niʀ] vt to contain; (*avoir une capacité de*) to hold; **se contenir** vi (*se retenir*) to control o.s. ou one's emotions, contain o.s.

content, e [kɔ̃tɑ̃, -ɑ̃t] adj pleased, glad; ~ **de** pleased with; **je serais** ~ **que tu ...** I would be pleased if you ...

contenter [kɔ̃tɑ̃te] vt to satisfy, please; (*envie*) to satisfy; **se** ~ **de** to content o.s. with

contentieux [kɔ̃tɑ̃sjø] nm (*Comm*) litigation; (: *service*) litigation department; (*Pol etc*) contentious issues pl

contenu, e [kɔ̃t(ə)ny] pp de **contenir** ▷ nm (*d'un bol*) contents pl; (*d'un texte*) content

conter [kɔ̃te] vt to recount, relate; **en** ~ **de belles à qn** to tell tall stories to sb

contestable [kɔ̃tɛstabl] adj questionable

contestation [kɔ̃tɛstasjɔ̃] nf questioning,

contesting; (Pol): **la ~** anti-establishment activity, protest

conteste [kɔ̃tɛst]: **sans ~** adv unquestionably, indisputably

contester [kɔ̃tɛste] vt to question, contest ▷ vi (Pol: gén) to rebel (against established authority), protest

contexte [kɔ̃tɛkst] nm context

contigu, ë [kɔ̃tigy] adj: **~ (à)** adjacent (to)

continent [kɔ̃tinɑ̃] nm continent

continu, e [kɔ̃tiny] adj continuous; **faire la journée ~e** to work without taking a full lunch break; (courant) **~ direct** current, DC

continuel, le [kɔ̃tinɥɛl] adj (qui se répète) constant, continual; (continu) continuous

continuer [kɔ̃tinɥe] vt (travail, voyage etc) to continue (with), carry on (with), go on with; (prolonger: alignement, rue) to continue ▷ vi (pluie, vie, bruit) to continue, go on; (voyageur) to go on; **se continuer** vi to carry on; **~ à** ou **de faire** to go on ou continue doing

contorsionner [kɔ̃tɔʁsjɔne]: **se contorsionner** vi to contort o.s., writhe about

contour [kɔ̃tuʁ] nm outline, contour; **contours** nmpl (d'une rivière etc) windings

contourner [kɔ̃tuʁne] vt to bypass, walk ou drive round; (difficulté) to get round

contraceptif, -ive [kɔ̃tʁasɛptif, -iv] adj, nm contraceptive

contraception [kɔ̃tʁasɛpsjɔ̃] nf contraception

contracté, e [kɔ̃tʁakte] adj (muscle) tense, contracted; (personne: tendu) tense, tensed up; **article ~** (Ling) contracted article

contracter [kɔ̃tʁakte] vt (muscle etc) to tense, contract; (maladie, dette, obligation) to contract; (assurance) to take out; **se contracter** vi (métal, muscles) to contract

contractuel, le [kɔ̃tʁaktɥɛl] adj contractual ▷ nm/f (agent) traffic warden; (employé) contract employee

contradiction [kɔ̃tʁadiksjɔ̃] nf contradiction

contradictoire [kɔ̃tʁadiktwaʁ] adj contradictory, conflicting; **débat ~** (open) debate

contraignant, e [kɔ̃tʁɛɲɑ̃, -ɑ̃t] vb voir **contraindre** ▷ adj restricting

contraindre [kɔ̃tʁɛ̃dʁ] vt: **~ qn à faire** to force ou compel sb to do

contraint, e [kɔ̃tʁɛ̃, -ɛ̃t] pp de **contraindre** ▷ nf constraint

contraire [kɔ̃tʁɛʁ] adj, nm opposite; **~ à** contrary to; **au ~** adv on the contrary

contrarier [kɔ̃tʁaʁje] vt (personne) to annoy, bother; (fig) to impede; (projets) to thwart, frustrate

contrariété [kɔ̃tʁaʁjete] nf annoyance

contraste [kɔ̃tʁast] nm contrast

contrat [kɔ̃tʁa] nm contract; (fig: accord, pacte) agreement; **~ de travail** employment contract

contravention [kɔ̃tʁavɑ̃sjɔ̃] nf (infraction): **~ à** contravention of; (amende) fine; (PV pour stationnement interdit) parking ticket; **dresser ~ à** (automobiliste) to book; to write out a parking ticket for

contre [kɔ̃tʁ] prép against; (en échange) (in exchange) for; **par ~** on the other hand

contrebande [kɔ̃tʁəbɑ̃d] nf (trafic) contraband, smuggling; (marchandise) contraband, smuggled goods pl; **faire la ~ de** to smuggle

contrebandier, -ière [kɔ̃tʁəbɑ̃dje, -jɛʁ] nm/f smuggler

contrebas [kɔ̃tʁəbɑ]: **en ~** adv (down) below

contrebasse [kɔ̃tʁəbɑs] nf (double) bass

contrecarrer [kɔ̃tʁəkaʁe] vt to thwart

contrecœur [kɔ̃tʁəkœʁ]: **à ~** adv (be) grudgingly, reluctantly

contrecoup [kɔ̃tʁəku] nm repercussions pl; **par ~** as an indirect consequence

contredire [kɔ̃tʁədiʁ] vt (personne) to contradict; (témoignage, assertion, faits) to refute; **se contredire** vi to contradict o.s.

contrée [kɔ̃tʁe] nf region; land

contrefaçon [kɔ̃tʁəfasɔ̃] nf forgery; **~ de brevet** patent infringement

contrefaire [kɔ̃tʁəfɛʁ] vt (document, signature) to forge, counterfeit; (personne, démarche) to mimic; (dénaturer: sa voix etc) to disguise

contre-indication [kɔ̃tʁɛ̃dikasjɔ̃] (pl **contre-indications**) nf (Méd) contra-indication; **"~ en cas d'eczéma"** "should not be used by people with eczema"

contre-indiqué, e [kɔ̃tʁɛ̃dike] adj (Méd) contraindicated; (déconseillé) unadvisable, ill-advised

contre-jour [kɔ̃tʁəʒuʁ]: **à ~** adv against the light

contremaître [kɔ̃tʁəmɛtʁ] nm foreman

contrepartie [kɔ̃tʁəparti] nf compensation; **en ~** in compensation; in return

contre-pied [kɔ̃tʁəpje] nm (inverse, opposé): **le ~ de ...** the exact opposite of ...; **prendre le ~ de** to take the opposing view of; to take the opposite course to; **prendre qn à ~** (Sport) to wrong-foot sb

contre-plaqué [kɔ̃tʁəplake] nm plywood

contrepoids [kɔ̃tʁəpwa] nm counterweight, counterbalance; **faire ~** to act as a counterbalance

contrepoison [kɔ̃tʁəpwazɔ̃] nm antidote

contrer [kɔ̃tʁe] vt to counter

contresens [kɔ̃tʁəsɑ̃s] nm (erreur) misinterpretation; (mauvaise traduction) mistranslation; (absurdité) nonsense no pl; **à ~** adv the wrong way

contretemps [kɔ̃tʁətɑ̃] nm hitch, contretemps; **à ~** adv (Mus) out of time; (fig) at an inopportune moment

contrevenir [kɔ̃tʁəvniʁ]: **~ à** vt to contravene

contribuable [kɔ̃tʁibɥabl] nm/f taxpayer

contribuer [kɔ̃tribɥe]: ~ **à** vt to contribute towards

contribution [kɔ̃tribysjɔ̃] nf contribution; **les ~s** (bureaux) the tax office; **mettre à ~** to call upon; **~s directes/indirectes** direct/indirect taxation

contrôle [kɔ̃trol] nm checking no pl, check; supervision; monitoring; (test) test, examination; **perdre le ~ de son véhicule** to lose control of one's vehicle; **~ des changes** (Comm) exchange controls; **~ continu** (Scol) continuous assessment; **~ d'identité** identity check; **~ des naissances** birth control; **~ des prix** price control

contrôler [kɔ̃trole] vt (vérifier) to check; (surveiller: opérations) to supervise; (: prix) to monitor, control; (maîtriser, Comm: firme) to control; **se contrôler** vi to control o.s.

contrôleur, -euse [kɔ̃trolœr, -øz] nm/f (de train) (ticket) inspector; (de bus) (bus) conductor/tress; **~ de la navigation aérienne, ~ aérien** air traffic controller; **~ financier** financial controller

contrordre [kɔ̃trɔrdr] nm counter-order, countermand; **sauf ~** unless otherwise directed

controversé, e [kɔ̃trɔvɛrse] adj (personnage, question) controversial

contusion [kɔ̃tyzjɔ̃] nf bruise, contusion

convaincre [kɔ̃vɛ̃kr] vt: **~ qn (de qch)** to convince sb (of sth); **~ qn (de faire)** to persuade sb (to do); **~ qn de** (Jur: délit) to convict sb of

convalescence [kɔ̃valesɑ̃s] nf convalescence; **maison de ~** convalescent home

convenable [kɔ̃vnabl] adj suitable; (décent) acceptable, proper; (assez bon) decent, acceptable; adequate, passable

convenance [kɔ̃vnɑ̃s] nf: **à ma/votre ~** to my/your liking; **convenances** nfpl proprieties

convenir [kɔ̃vnir] vi to be suitable; **~ à** to suit; **il convient de** it is advisable to; (bienséant) it is right ou proper to; **~ de** (bien-fondé de qch) to admit (to), acknowledge; (date, somme etc) to agree upon; **~ que** (admettre) to admit that, acknowledge the fact that; **~ de faire qch** to agree to do sth; **il a été convenu que** it has been agreed that; **comme convenu** as agreed

convention [kɔ̃vɑ̃sjɔ̃] nf convention; **conventions** nfpl (convenances) convention sg, social conventions; **de ~** conventional; **~ collective** (Écon) collective agreement

conventionné, e [kɔ̃vɑ̃sjɔne] adj (Admin) applying charges laid down by the state

convenu, e [kɔ̃vny] pp de **convenir** ▷ adj agreed

conversation [kɔ̃vɛrsasjɔ̃] nf conversation; **avoir de la ~** to be a good conversationalist

convertir [kɔ̃vɛrtir] vt: **~ qn (à)** to convert sb (to); **~ qch en** to convert sth into; **se ~ (à)** to be converted (to)

conviction [kɔ̃viksjɔ̃] nf conviction

convienne etc [kɔ̃vjɛn] vb voir **convenir**

convier [kɔ̃vje] vt: **~ qn à** (dîner etc) to (cordially) invite sb to; **~ qn à faire** to urge sb to do

convive [kɔ̃viv] nm/f guest (at table)

convivial, e [kɔ̃vivjal] adj (Inform) user-friendly

convocation [kɔ̃vɔkasjɔ̃] nf (voir convoquer) convening, convoking; summoning; invitation; (document) notification to attend; summons sg

convoi [kɔ̃vwa] nm (de voitures, prisonniers) convoy; (train) train; **~ (funèbre)** funeral procession

convoiter [kɔ̃vwate] vt to covet

convoquer [kɔ̃vɔke] vt (assemblée) to convene, convoke; (subordonné, témoin) to summon; (candidat) to ask to attend; **~ qn (à)** (réunion) to invite sb to attend

convoyeur [kɔ̃vwajœr] nm (Navig) escort ship; **~ de fonds** security guard

cookie [kuki] nm (Inform) cookie

coopération [kɔɔperasjɔ̃] nf co-operation; (Admin): **la C~** = Voluntary Service Overseas (Brit) ou the Peace Corps (US) (done as alternative to military service)

coopérer [kɔɔpere] vi: **~ (à)** to co-operate (in)

coordonné, e [kɔɔrdɔne] adj coordinated ▷ nf (Ling) coordinate clause; **coordonnés** nmpl (vêtements) coordinates; **coordonnées** nfpl (Math) coordinates; (détails personnels) address, phone number, schedule etc; whereabouts

coordonner [kɔɔrdɔne] vt to coordinate

copain, copine [kɔpɛ̃, kɔpin] nm/f mate (Brit), pal; (petit ami) boyfriend; (petite amie) girlfriend ▷ adj: **être ~ avec** to be pally with

copeau, x [kɔpo] nm shaving; (de métal) turning

copie [kɔpi] nf copy; (Scol) script, paper; exercise; **~ certifiée conforme** certified copy; **~ papier** (Inform) hard copy

copier [kɔpje] vt, vi to copy; **~ coller** (Inform) copy and paste; **~ sur** to copy from

copieur [kɔpjœr] nm (photo)copier

copieux, -euse [kɔpjø, -øz] adj copious, hearty

copine [kɔpin] nf voir **copain**

copropriété [kɔprɔprijete] nf co-ownership, joint ownership; **acheter en ~** to buy on a co-ownership basis

coq [kɔk] nm cockerel, rooster ▷ adj inv (Boxe): **poids ~** bantamweight; **~ de bruyère** grouse; **~ du village** (fig: péj) ladykiller; **~ au vin** coq au vin

coq-à-l'âne [kɔkalan] nm inv abrupt change of subject

coque [kɔk] nf (de noix, mollusque) shell; (de bateau) hull; **à la ~** (Culin) (soft-)boiled

coquelicot [kɔkliko] nm poppy

coqueluche [kɔklyʃ] nf whooping-cough;

(fig): **être la ~ de qn** to be sb's flavour of the month

coquet, te [kɔkɛ, -ɛt] *adj* appearance-conscious; *(joli)* pretty; *(logement)* smart, charming

coquetier [kɔk(ə)tje] *nm* egg-cup

coquillage [kɔkijaʒ] *nm (mollusque)* shellfish *inv*; *(coquille)* shell

coquille [kɔkij] *nf* shell; *(Typo)* misprint; **~ de beurre** shell of butter; **~ d'œuf** *adj (couleur)* eggshell; **~ de noix** nutshell; **~ St Jacques** scallop

coquin, e [kɔkɛ̃, -in] *adj* mischievous, roguish; *(polisson)* naughty ▷ *nm/f (péj)* rascal

cor [kɔʀ] *nm (Mus)* horn; *(Méd)*: **~ (au pied)** corn; **réclamer à ~ et à cri** to clamour for; **~ anglais** cor anglais; **~ de chasse** hunting horn

corail, -aux [kɔʀaj, -o] *nm* coral *no pl*

Coran [kɔʀɑ̃] *nm*: **le ~** the Koran

corbeau, x [kɔʀbo] *nm* crow

corbeille [kɔʀbɛj] *nf* basket; *(Inform)* recycle bin; *(Bourse)*: **la ~ =** the floor (of the Stock Exchange); **~ de mariage** *(fig)* wedding presents *pl*; **~ à ouvrage** work-basket; **~ à pain** breadbasket; **~ à papier** waste paper basket *ou* bin

corbillard [kɔʀbijaʀ] *nm* hearse

corde [kɔʀd] *nf* rope; *(de violon, raquette, d'arc)* string; *(trame)*: **la ~** the thread; *(Athlétisme, Auto)*: **la ~** the rails *pl*; **les ~s** *(Boxe)* the ropes; **les (instruments à) ~s** *(Mus)* the strings, the stringed instruments; **semelles de ~** rope soles; **tenir la ~** *(Athlétisme, Auto)* to be in the inside lane; **tomber des ~s** to rain cats and dogs; **tirer sur la ~** to go too far; **la ~ sensible** the right chord; **usé jusqu'à la ~** threadbare; **~ à linge** washing *ou* clothes line; **~ lisse** (climbing) rope; **~ à nœuds** knotted climbing rope; **~ raide** tightrope; **~ à sauter** skipping rope; **~s vocales** vocal cords

cordée [kɔʀde] *nf (d'alpinistes)* rope, roped party

cordialement [kɔʀdjalmɑ̃] *adv* cordially, heartily; *(formule épistolaire)* (kind) regards

cordon [kɔʀdɔ̃] *nm* cord, string; **~ sanitaire/ de police** sanitary/police cordon; **~ littoral** sandbank, sandbar; **~ ombilical** umbilical cord

cordonnerie [kɔʀdɔnʀi] *nf* shoe repairer's *ou* mender's (shop)

cordonnier [kɔʀdɔnje] *nm* shoe repairer *ou* mender, cobbler

Corée [kɔʀe] *nf*: **la ~** Korea; **la ~ du Sud/du Nord** South/North Korea; **la République (démocratique populaire) de ~** the (Democratic People's) Republic of Korea

coriace [kɔʀjas] *adj* tough

corne [kɔʀn] *nf* horn; *(de cerf)* antler; *(de la peau)* callus; **~ d'abondance** horn of plenty; **~ de brume** *(Navig)* foghorn

cornée [kɔʀne] *nf* cornea

corneille [kɔʀnɛj] *nf* crow

cornemuse [kɔʀnəmyz] *nf* bagpipes *pl*; **joueur de ~** piper

cornet [kɔʀnɛ] *nm (paper) cone*; *(de glace)* cornet, cone; **~ à pistons** cornet

corniche [kɔʀniʃ] *nf (de meuble, neigeuse)* cornice; *(route)* coast road

cornichon [kɔʀniʃɔ̃] *nm* gherkin

Cornouailles [kɔʀnwaj] *nf(pl)* Cornwall

corporation [kɔʀpɔʀasjɔ̃] *nf* corporate body; *(au Moyen-Âge)* guild

corporel, le [kɔʀpɔʀɛl] *adj* bodily; *(punition)* corporal; **soins ~s** care *sg* of the body

corps [kɔʀ] *nm (gén)* body; *(cadavre)* (dead) body; **à son ~ défendant** against one's will; **à ~ perdu** headlong; **perdu ~ et biens** lost with all hands; **prendre ~** to take shape; **faire ~ avec** to be joined to; to form one body with; **~ d'armée (CA)** army corps; **~ de ballet** corps de ballet; **~ constitués** *(Pol)* constitutional bodies; **le ~ consulaire (CC)** the consular corps; **~ à ~** *adv* hand-to-hand ▷ *nm* clinch; **le ~ du délit** *(Jur)* corpus delicti; **le ~ diplomatique (CD)** the diplomatic corps; **le ~ électoral** the electorate; **le ~ enseignant** the teaching profession; **~ étranger** *(Méd)* foreign body; **~ expéditionnaire** task force; **~ de garde** guardroom; **~ législatif** legislative body; **le ~ médical** the medical profession

corpulent, e [kɔʀpylɑ̃, -ɑ̃t] *adj* stout *(Brit)*, corpulent

correct, e [kɔʀɛkt] *adj (exact)* accurate, correct; *(bienséant, honnête)* correct; *(passable)* adequate

correcteur, -trice [kɔʀɛktœʀ, -tʀis] *nm/f (Scol)* examiner, marker; *(Typo)* proofreader

correction [kɔʀɛksjɔ̃] *nf (voir corriger)* correction; marking; *(voir correct)* correctness; *(rature, surcharge)* correction, emendation; *(coups)* thrashing; **~ sur écran** *(Inform)* screen editing; **~ des épreuves** proofreading

correctionnel, le [kɔʀɛksjɔnɛl] *adj (Jur)*: **tribunal ~ =** criminal court

correspondance [kɔʀɛspɔ̃dɑ̃s] *nf* correspondence; *(de train, d'avion)* connection; **ce train assure la ~ avec l'avion de 10 heures** this train connects with the 10 o'clock plane; **cours par ~** correspondence course; **vente par ~** mail-order business

correspondant, e [kɔʀɛspɔ̃dɑ̃, -ɑ̃t] *nm/f* correspondent; *(Tél)* person phoning *(ou* being phoned)

correspondre [kɔʀɛspɔ̃dʀ] *vi (données, témoignages)* to correspond, tally; *(chambres)* to communicate; **~ à** to correspond to; **~ avec qn** to correspond with sb

corrida [kɔʀida] *nf* bullfight

corridor [kɔʀidɔʀ] *nm* corridor, passage

corrigé [kɔʀiʒe] *nm (Scol: d'exercice)* correct version; fair copy

corriger [kɔriʒe] vt (devoir) to correct, mark; (texte) to correct, emend; (erreur, défaut) to correct, put right; (punir) to thrash; ~ **qn de** (défaut) to cure sb of; **se ~ de** to cure o.s. of

corroborer [kɔrɔbɔre] vt to corroborate

corrompre [kɔrɔ̃pr] vt (dépraver) to corrupt; (acheter: témoin etc) to bribe

corruption [kɔrypsjɔ̃] nf corruption; (de témoins) bribery

corsage [kɔrsaʒ] nm (d'une robe) bodice; (chemisier) blouse

corsaire [kɔrsɛr] nm pirate, corsair; privateer

corse [kɔrs] adj Corsican ▷ nm/f: **C~** Corsican ▷ nf: **la C~** Corsica

corsé, e [kɔrse] adj vigorous; (café etc) full-flavoured (Brit) ou -flavored (US); (goût) full; (sauce) spicy; (problème) tough, tricky

corset [kɔrsɛ] nm corset; (d'une robe) bodice; ~ **orthopédique** surgical corset

cortège [kɔrtɛʒ] nm procession

cortisone [kɔrtizɔn] nf (Méd) cortisone

corvée [kɔrve] nf chore, drudgery no pl; (Mil) fatigue (duty)

cosmétique [kɔsmetik] nm (pour les cheveux) hair-oil; (produit de beauté) beauty care product

cosmopolite [kɔsmɔpɔlit] adj cosmopolitan

cossu, e [kɔsy] adj opulent-looking, well-to-do

costaud, e [kɔsto, -od] adj strong, sturdy

costume [kɔstym] nm (d'homme) suit; (de théâtre) costume

costumé, e [kɔstyme] adj dressed up

cote [kɔt] nf (en Bourse etc) quotation; quoted value; (d'un cheval): **la ~ de** the odds pl on; (d'un candidat etc) rating; (mesure: sur une carte) spot height; (sur un croquis) dimension; (de classement) (classification) mark; reference number; **avoir la ~** to be very popular; **inscrit à la ~** quoted on the Stock Exchange; **~ d'alerte** danger ou flood level; **~ mal taillée** (fig) compromise; **~ de popularité** popularity rating

coté, e [kɔte] adj: **être ~** to be listed ou quoted; **être ~ en Bourse** to be quoted on the Stock Exchange; **être bien/mal ~** to be highly/poorly rated

côte [kot] nf (rivage) coast(line); (pente) slope; (: sur une route) hill; (Anat) rib; (d'un tricot, tissu) rib, ribbing no pl; **~ à ~** adv side by side; **la C~ (d'Azur)** the (French) Riviera; **la C~ d'Ivoire** the Ivory Coast; **~ de porc** pork chop

côté [kote] nm (gén) side; (direction) way, direction; **de chaque ~ (de)** on each side of; **de tous les ~s** from all directions; **de quel ~ est-il parti?** which way ou in which direction did he go?; **de ce/de l'autre ~** this/the other way; **d'un ~ ... de l'autre ~ ...** (alternative) on (the) one hand ... on the other (hand) ...; **du ~ de** (provenance) from; (direction) towards; **du ~ de Lyon** (proximité) near Lyons;

du ~ gauche on the left-hand side; **de ~** adv (regarder) sideways; on one side; to one side, aside; **laisser de ~** to leave on one side; **mettre de ~** to put aside, put on one side; **mettre de l'argent de ~** to save some money; **de mon ~** (quant à moi) for my part; **à ~** adv (right) nearby; (voisins) next door; (d'autre part) besides; **à ~ de** beside; next to; (fig) in comparison to; **à ~ (de la cible)** off target, wide (of the mark); **être aux ~s de** to be by the side of

coteau, x [kɔto] nm hill

Côte d'Ivoire [kotdivwar] nf: **la ~** Côte d'Ivoire, the Ivory Coast

côtelette [kotlɛt] nf chop

côtier, -ière [kotje, -jɛr] adj coastal

cotisation [kɔtizasjɔ̃] nf subscription, dues pl; (pour une pension) contributions pl

cotiser [kɔtize] vi: **~ (à)** to pay contributions (to); (à une association) to subscribe (to); **se cotiser** vi to club together

coton [kɔtɔ̃] nm cotton; **~ hydrophile** cotton wool (Brit), absorbent cotton (US)

Coton-Tige® [kɔtɔ̃tiʒ] nm cotton bud

côtoyer [kotwaje] vt to be close to; (rencontrer) to rub shoulders with; (longer) to run alongside; (fig: friser) to be bordering ou verging on

cou [ku] nm neck

couchant [kuʃɑ̃] adj: **soleil ~** setting sun

couche [kuʃ] nf (strate: gén, Géo) layer, stratum (pl -a); (de peinture, vernis) coat; (de poussière, crème) layer; (de bébé) nappy (Brit), diaper (US); **~ d'ozone** ozone layer; **couches** nfpl (Méd) confinement sg; **~s sociales** social levels ou strata

couché, e [kuʃe] adj (étendu) lying down; (au lit) in bed

coucher [kuʃe] nm (du soleil) setting ▷ vt (personne) to put to bed; (: loger) to put up; (objet) to lay on its side; (écrire) to inscribe, couch ▷ vi (dormir) to sleep, spend the night; **~ avec qn** to sleep with sb, go to bed with sb; **se coucher** vi (pour dormir) to go to bed; (pour se reposer) to lie down; (soleil) to set, go down; **à prendre avant le ~** (Méd) take at night ou before going to bed; **~ de soleil** sunset

couchette [kuʃɛt] nf couchette; (de marin) bunk; (pour voyageur, sur bateau) berth

coucou [kuku] nm cuckoo ▷ excl peek-a-boo

coude [kud] nm (Anat) elbow; (de tuyau, de la route) bend; **~ à ~** adv shoulder to shoulder, side by side

coudre [kudr] vt (bouton) to sew on; (robe) to sew (up) ▷ vi to sew

couenne [kwan] nf (de lard) rind

couette [kwɛt] nf duvet; **couettes** nfpl (cheveux) bunches

couffin [kufɛ̃] nm Moses basket; (straw) basket

couler [kule] vi to flow, run; (fuir: stylo, récipient) to leak; (nez) to run; (sombrer: bateau)

to sink ▷ vt (cloche, sculpture) to cast; (bateau)
to sink; (faire échouer: personne) to bring down,
ruin; (: passer): **~ une vie heureuse** to enjoy a
happy life; **se ~ dans** (interstice etc) to slip into;
faire ~ (eau) to run; **faire ~ un bain** to run a
bath; **il a coulé une bielle** (Auto) his big end
went; **~ de source** to follow on naturally; **~ à
pic** to sink ou go straight to the bottom

couleur [kulœʀ] nf colour (Brit), color (US);
(Cartes) suit; **couleurs** nfpl (du teint) colo(u)r
sg; **les ~s** (Mil) the colo(u)rs; **en ~s** (film) in
colo(u)r; **télévision en ~s** colo(u)r television;
de ~ (homme, femme: vieilli) colo(u)red; **sous ~
de** on the pretext of; **de quelle ~** of what
colo(u)r

couleuvre [kulœvʀ] nf grass snake

coulisse [kulis] nf (Tech) runner; **coulisses**
nfpl (Théât) wings; (fig): **dans les ~s** behind
the scenes; **porte à ~** sliding door

coulisser [kulise] vi to slide, run

couloir [kulwaʀ] nm corridor, passage;
(d'avion) aisle; (de bus) gangway; (: sur la route)
bus lane; (Sport: de piste) lane; (Géo) gully;
~ aérien air corridor ou lane; **~ de navigation**
shipping lane

coup [ku] nm (heurt, choc) knock; (affectif)
blow, shock; (agressif) blow; (avec arme à feu)
shot; (de l'horloge) chime; stroke; (Sport: golf)
stroke; (tennis) shot; blow; (fam: fois) time;
(Échecs) move; **~ de coude/genou** nudge
(with the elbow)/ with the knee; **à ~s de
hache/marteau** (hitting) with an axe/a
hammer; **~ de tonnerre** clap of thunder;
~ de sonnette ring of the bell; **~ de crayon/
pinceau** stroke of the pencil/brush; **donner
un ~ de balai** to give the floor a sweep, sweep
up; **donner un ~ de chiffon** to go round with
the duster; **avoir le ~** (fig) to have the knack;
être dans le/hors du ~ to be/not to be in on
it; (à la page) to be hip ou trendy; **du ~** as a
result; **boire un ~** to have a drink; **d'un seul
~** (subitement) suddenly; (à la fois) at one go; in
one blow; **du premier ~** first time ou go, at the
first attempt; **du
même ~** at the same time; **à ~ sûr** definitely,
without fail; **après ~** afterwards; **~ sur ~** in
quick succession; **être sur un ~** to be on to
something; **sur le ~** outright; **sous le ~ de**
(surprise etc) under the influence of; **tomber
sous le ~ de la loi** to constitute a statutory
offence; **à tous les ~s** every time; **tenir le ~**
to hold out; **il a raté son ~** he missed his
turn; **pour le ~** for once; **~ bas** (fig): **donner
un ~ bas à qn** to hit sb below the belt; **~ de
chance** stroke of luck; **~ de chapeau** (fig) pat
on the back; **~ de couteau** stab (of a knife);
~ dur hard blow; **~ d'éclat** (great) feat;
~ d'envoi kick-off; **~ d'essai** first attempt;
~ d'état coup d'état; **~ de feu** shot; **~ de filet**
(Police) haul; **~ de foudre** love at first
sight; **~ fourré** stab in the back; **~ franc** free
kick; **~ de frein** (sharp) braking no pl; **~ de

fusil rifle shot; **~ de grâce** coup de grâce;
~ du lapin (Auto) whiplash; **~ de main**:
donner un coup de main à qn to give sb a
(helping) hand; **~ de maître** master stroke;
~ d'œil glance; **~ de pied** kick; **~ de poing**
punch; **~ de soleil** sunburn no pl; **~ de
sonnette** ring of the bell; **~ de téléphone**
phone call; **~ de tête** (fig) (sudden) impulse;
~ de théâtre (fig) dramatic turn of events; **~
de tonnerre** clap of thunder; **~ de vent** gust
of wind; **en ~ de vent** (rapidement) in a tearing
hurry

coupable [kupabl] adj guilty; (pensée) guilty,
culpable ▷ nm/f (gén) culprit; (Jur) guilty
party; **~ de** guilty of

coupe [kup] nf (verre) goblet; (à fruits) dish;
(Sport) cup; (de cheveux, de vêtement) cut;
(graphique, plan) (cross) section; **être sous la ~
de** to be under the control of; **faire des ~s
sombres dans** to make drastic cuts in

coupe-papier [kuppapje] nm inv paper knife

couper [kupe] vt to cut; (retrancher) to cut
(out), take out; (route, courant) to cut off;
(appétit) to take away; (fièvre) to take down,
reduce; (vin, cidre) to blend; (: à table) to dilute
(with water) ▷ vi to cut; (prendre un raccourci) to
take a short-cut; (Cartes: diviser le paquet) to
cut; (: avec l'atout) to trump; **se couper** vi (se
blesser) to cut o.s.; (en témoignant etc) to give o.s.
away; **~ l'appétit à qn** to spoil sb's appetite;
~ la parole à qn to cut sb short; **~ les vivres à
qn** to cut off sb's vital supplies; **~ le contact
ou l'allumage** (Auto) to turn off the ignition;
~ les ponts avec qn to break with sb; **se faire
~ les cheveux** to have ou get one's hair cut;
nous avons été coupés we've been cut off

couple [kupl] nm couple; **~ de torsion** torque

couplet [kuplɛ] nm verse

coupole [kupɔl] nf dome; cupola

coupon [kupɔ̃] nm (ticket) coupon; (de tissu)
remnant; roll

coupon-réponse (pl coupons-réponses)
[kupɔ̃ʀepɔ̃s] nm reply coupon

coupure [kupyʀ] nf cut; (billet de banque) note;
(de journal) cutting; **~ de courant** power cut

cour [kuʀ] nf (de ferme, jardin) (court)yard;
(d'immeuble) back yard; (Jur, royale) court; **faire
la ~ à qn** to court sb; **~ d'appel** appeal court
(Brit), appellate court (US); **~ d'assises** court
of assizes, ≈ Crown Court (Brit); **~ de
cassation** final court of appeal; **~ des
comptes** (Admin) revenue court; **~ martiale**
court-martial; **~ de récréation** (Scol)
playground, schoolyard

courage [kuʀaʒ] nm courage, bravery

courageux, -euse [kuʀaʒø, -øz] adj brave,
courageous

couramment [kuʀamã] adv commonly;
(parler) fluently

courant, e [kuʀã, -ãt] adj (fréquent) common;
(Comm, gén: normal) standard; (en cours)
current ▷ nm current; (fig) movement;

(: *d'opinion*) trend; **être au ~ (de)** (*fait, nouvelle*) to know (about); **mettre qn au ~ (de)** (*fait, nouvelle*) to tell sb (about); (*nouveau travail etc*) to teach sb the basics (of), brief sb (about); **se tenir au ~ (de)** (*techniques etc*) to keep o.s. up-to-date (on); **dans le ~ de** (*pendant*) in the course of; **~ octobre** *etc* in the course of October *etc*; **le 10 ~** (*Comm*) the 10th inst.; **~ d'air** draught (*Brit*), draft (*US*); **~ électrique** (electric) current, power

courbature [kuʀbatyʀ] *nf* ache

courbe [kuʀb] *adj* curved ▷ *nf* curve; **~ de niveau** contour line

courber [kuʀbe] *vt* to bend; **~ la tête** to bow one's head; **se courber** *vi* (*branche etc*) to bend, curve; (*personne*) to bend (down)

coureur, -euse [kuʀœʀ, -øz] *nm/f* (*Sport*) runner (*ou* driver); (*péj*) womanizer/ manhunter; **~ cycliste/automobile** racing cyclist/driver

courge [kuʀʒ] *nf* (*Bot*) gourd; (*Culin*) marrow

courgette [kuʀʒɛt] *nf* courgette (*Brit*), zucchini (*US*)

courir [kuʀiʀ] *vi* (*gén*) to run; (*se dépêcher*) to rush; (*fig: rumeurs*) to go round; (*Comm: intérêt*) to accrue ▷ *vt* (*Sport: épreuve*) to compete in; (*risque*) to run; (*danger*) to face; **~ les cafés/bals** to do the rounds of the cafés/ dances; **le bruit court que** the rumour is going round that; **par les temps qui courent** at the present time; **~ après qn** to run after sb, chase (after) sb; **laisser ~** to let things alone; **faire ~ qn** to make sb run around (all over the place); **tu peux (toujours) ~!** you've got a hope!

couronne [kuʀɔn] *nf* crown; (*de fleurs*) wreath, circlet; **~ (funéraire *ou* mortuaire)** (funeral) wreath

courons [kuʀɔ̃], **courrai** *etc* [kuʀe] *vb voir* **courir**

courriel [kuʀjɛl] *nm* email

courrier [kuʀje] *nm* mail, post; (*lettres à écrire*) letters *pl*; (*rubrique*) column; **qualité ~** letter quality; **long/moyen ~** *adj* (*Aviat*) long-/ medium-haul; **~ du cœur** problem page; **~ électronique** electronic mail, email; **est-ce que j'ai du ~?** are there any letters for me?

courroie [kuʀwa] *nf* strap; (*Tech*) belt; **~ de transmission/de ventilateur** driving/ fan belt

courrons *etc* [kuʀɔ̃] *vb voir* **courir**

cours [kuʀ] *vb voir* **courir** ▷ *nm* (*leçon*) class; (: *particulier*) lesson; (*série de leçons*) course; (*cheminement*) course; (*écoulement*) flow; (*avenue*) walk; (*Comm: de devises*) rate; (: *de denrées*) price; (*Bourse*) quotation; **donner libre ~ à** to give free expression to; **avoir ~** (*monnaie*) to be legal tender; (*fig*) to be current; (*Scol*) to have a class *ou* lecture; **en ~** (*année*) current; (*travaux*) in progress; **en ~ de route** on the way; **au ~ de** in the course of,

during; **le ~ du change** the exchange rate; **~ d'eau** waterway; **~ élémentaire (CE)** 2nd and 3rd years of primary school; **~ moyen (CM)** 4th and 5th years of primary school; **~ préparatoire** ≈ infants' class (*Brit*), ≈ 1st grade (*US*); **~ du soir** night school

course [kuʀs] *nf* running; (*Sport: épreuve*) race; (*trajet: du soleil*) course; (: *d'un projectile*) flight; (: *d'une pièce mécanique*) travel; (*excursion*) outing; climb; (*d'un taxi, autocar*) journey, trip; (*petite mission*) errand; **courses** *nfpl* (*achats*) shopping *sg*; (*Hippisme*) races; **faire les** *ou* **ses ~s** to go shopping; **jouer aux ~s** to bet on the races; **à bout de ~** (*épuisé*) exhausted; **~ automobile** car race; **~ de côte** (*Auto*) hill climb; **~ par étapes** *ou* **d'étapes** race in stages; **~ d'obstacles** obstacle race; **~ à pied** walking race; **~ de vitesse** sprint; **~s de chevaux** horse racing

court, e [kuʀ, kuʀt] *adj* short ▷ *adv* short ▷ *nm*: **~ (de tennis)** (tennis) court; **tourner ~** to come to a sudden end; **couper ~ à** to cut short; **à ~ de** short of; **prendre qn de ~** to catch sb unawares; **pour faire ~** briefly, to cut a long story short; **ça fait ~** that's not very long; **tirer à la ~e paille** to draw lots; **faire la ~e échelle à qn** to give sb a leg up; **~ métrage** (*Ciné*) short (film)

court-circuit (*pl* **courts-circuits**) [kuʀsiʀkɥi] *nm* short-circuit

courtier, -ière [kuʀtje, -jɛʀ] *nm/f* broker

courtiser [kuʀtize] *vt* to court, woo

courtois, e [kuʀtwa, -waz] *adj* courteous

courtoisie [kuʀtwazi] *nf* courtesy

couru, e [kuʀy] *pp de* **courir** ▷ *adj* (*spectacle etc*) popular; **c'est ~ (d'avance)!** (*fam*) it's a safe bet!

cousais *etc* [kuze] *vb voir* **coudre**

couscous [kuskus] *nm* couscous

cousin, e [kuzɛ̃, -in] *nm/f* cousin ▷ *nm* (*Zool*) mosquito; **~ germain** first cousin

coussin [kusɛ̃] *nm* cushion; **~ d'air** (*Tech*) air cushion

cousu, e [kuzy] *pp de* **coudre** ▷ *adj*: **~ d'or** rolling in riches

coût [ku] *nm* cost; **le ~ de la vie** the cost of living

coûtant [kutɑ̃] *adj m*: **au prix ~** at cost price

couteau, x [kuto] *nm* knife; **~ à cran d'arrêt** flick-knife; **~ de cuisine** kitchen knife; **~ à pain** bread knife; **~ de poche** pocket knife

coûter [kute] *vt* to cost ▷ *vi* to cost; **~ à qn** to cost sb a lot; **~ cher** to be expensive; **~ cher à qn** (*fig*) to cost sb dear *ou* dearly; **combien ça coûte?** how much is it?, what does it cost?; **coûte que coûte** at all costs

coûteux, -euse [kutø, -øz] *adj* costly, expensive

coutume [kutym] *nf* custom; **de ~** usual, customary

couture [kutyʀ] *nf* sewing; (*profession*) dress-making; (*points*) seam

couturier [kutyʀje] nm fashion designer, couturier

couturière [kutyʀjɛʀ] nf dressmaker

couvée [kuve] nf brood, clutch

couvent [kuvɑ̃] nm (de sœurs) convent; (de frères) monastery; (établissement scolaire) convent (school)

couver [kuve] vt to hatch; (maladie) to be sickening for ▷ vi (feu) to smoulder (Brit), smolder (US); (révolte) to be brewing; **~ qn/ qch des yeux** to look lovingly at sb/sth; (convoiter) to look longingly at sb/sth

couvercle [kuvɛʀkl] nm lid; (de bombe aérosol etc, qui se visse) cap, top

couvert, e [kuvɛʀ, -ɛʀt] pp de couvrir ▷ adj (ciel) overcast; (coiffé d'un chapeau) wearing a hat ▷ nm place setting; (place à table) place; (au restaurant) cover charge; **couverts** nmpl place settings; (ustensiles) cutlery sg; **~ de** covered with ou in; **bien ~** (habillé) well wrapped up; **mettre le ~** to lay the table; **à ~** under cover; **sous le ~ de** under the shelter of; (fig) under cover of

couverture [kuvɛʀtyʀ] nf (de lit) blanket; (de bâtiment) roofing; (de livre, fig: d'un espion etc, Assurances) cover; (Presse) coverage; **de ~** (lettre etc) covering; **~ chauffante** electric blanket

couveuse [kuvøz] nf (à poules) sitter, brooder; (de maternité) incubator

couvre-feu, x [kuvʀəfø] nm curfew

couvre-lit [kuvʀəli] nm bedspread

couvreur [kuvʀœʀ] nm roofer

couvrir [kuvʀiʀ] vt to cover; (dominer, étouffer: voix, pas) to drown out; (erreur) to cover up; (Zool: s'accoupler à) to cover; **se couvrir** (ciel) to cloud over; (s'habiller) to cover up, wrap up; (se coiffer) to put on one's hat; (par une assurance) to cover o.s.; **se ~ de** (fleurs, boutons) to become covered in

cow-boy [koboj] nm cowboy

crabe [kʀab] nm crab

cracher [kʀaʃe] vi to spit ▷ vt to spit out; (fig: lave etc) to belch (out); **~ du sang** to spit blood

crachin [kʀaʃɛ̃] nm drizzle

crack [kʀak] nm (intellectuel) whiz kid; (sportif) ace; (poulain) hot favourite (Brit) ou favorite (US)

craie [kʀɛ] nf chalk

craindre [kʀɛ̃dʀ] vt to fear, be afraid of; (être sensible à: chaleur, froid) to be easily damaged by; **~ de/que** to be afraid of/that; **je crains qu'il (ne) vienne** I am afraid he may come

crainte [kʀɛ̃t] nf fear; **de ~ de/que** for fear of/ that

craintif, -ive [kʀɛ̃tif, -iv] adj timid

cramoisi, e [kʀamwazi] adj crimson

crampe [kʀɑ̃p] nf cramp; **~ d'estomac** stomach cramp; **j'ai une ~ à la jambe** I've got cramp in my leg

crampon [kʀɑ̃pɔ̃] nm (de semelle) stud; (Alpinisme) crampon

cramponner [kʀɑ̃pɔne]: **se cramponner** vi: **se ~ (à)** to hang ou cling on (to)

cran [kʀɑ̃] nm (entaille) notch; (de courroie) hole; (courage) guts pl; **~ d'arrêt/de sûreté** safety catch; **~ de mire** bead

crâne [kʀɑn] nm skull

crâner [kʀɑne] vi (fam) to swank, show off

crapaud [kʀapo] nm toad

crapule [kʀapyl] nf villain

craquement [kʀakmɑ̃] nm crack, snap; (du plancher) creak, creaking no pl

craquer [kʀake] vi (bois, plancher) to creak; (fil, branche) to snap; (couture) to come apart, burst; (fig: accusé) to break down, fall apart; (: être enthousiasmé) to go wild ▷ vt: **une allumette** to strike a match; **j'ai craqué** (fam) I couldn't resist it

crasse [kʀas] nf grime, filth ▷ adj (fig: ignorance) crass

crasseux, -euse [kʀasø, øz] adj filthy

cravache [kʀavaʃ] nf (riding) crop

cravate [kʀavat] nf tie

crawl [kʀol] nm crawl; **dos -é** backstroke

crayon [kʀɛjɔ̃] nm pencil; (de rouge à lèvres etc) stick, pencil; **écrire au ~** to write in pencil; **~ à bille** ball-point pen; **~ de couleur** crayon; **~ optique** light pen

crayon-feutre (pl **crayons-feutres**) [kʀɛjɔ̃føtʀ] nm felt(-tip) pen

créancier, -ière [kʀeɑ̃sje, -jɛʀ] nm/f creditor

création [kʀeasjɔ̃] nf creation

créature [kʀeatyʀ] nf creature

crèche [kʀɛʃ] nf (de Noël) crib; see note; (garderie) crèche, day nursery

CRÈCHE

In France the Christmas crib (crèche) usually contains figurines representing a miller, a wood-cutter and other villagers as well as the Holy Family and the traditional cow, donkey and shepherds. The Three Wise Men are added to the nativity scene at Epiphany (6 January, Twelfth Night).

crédit [kʀedi] nm (gén) credit; **crédits** nmpl funds; **acheter à ~** to buy on credit ou on easy terms; **faire ~ à qn** to give sb credit; **~ municipal** pawnshop; **~ relais** bridging loan

créditer [kʀedite] vt: **~ un compte (de)** to credit an account (with)

crédule [kʀedyl] adj credulous, gullible

créer [kʀee] vt to create; (Théât: pièce) to produce (for the first time); (: rôle) to create

crémaillère [kʀemajɛʀ] nf (Rail) rack; (tige crantée) trammel; **direction à ~** (Auto) rack and pinion steering; **pendre la ~** to have a house-warming party

crématoire [kʀematwaʀ] adj: **four ~** crematorium

crème [kʀɛm] nf cream; (entremets) cream dessert ▷ adj inv cream; **un (café)** ~ = a white coffee; ~ **anglaise** (egg) custard; ~ **chantilly** whipped cream, crème Chantilly; ~ **fouettée** whipped cream; ~ **glacée** ice cream; ~ **à raser** shaving cream; ~ **solaire** sun cream

crémerie [kʀɛmʀi] nf dairy; (tearoom) teashop

crémeux, -euse [kʀɛmø, -øz] adj creamy

créneau, x [kʀeno] nm (de fortification) crenel(le); (fig, aussi Comm) gap, slot; (Auto): **faire un** ~ to reverse into a parking space (between cars alongside the kerb)

crêpe [kʀɛp] nf (galette) pancake ▷ nm (tissu) crêpe; (de deuil) black mourning crêpe; (ruban) black armband (ou hatband ou ribbon); **semelle (de)** ~ crêpe sole; ~ **de Chine** crêpe de Chine

crêpé, e [kʀepe] adj (cheveux) backcombed

crêperie [kʀepʀi] nf pancake shop ou restaurant

crépiter [kʀepite] vi to sputter, splutter, crackle

crépu, e [kʀepy] adj frizzy, fuzzy

crépuscule [kʀepyskyl] nm twilight, dusk

cresson [kʀesɔ̃] nm watercress

crête [kʀɛt] nf (de coq) comb; (de vague, montagne) crest

creuser [kʀøze] vt (trou, tunnel) to dig; (sol) to dig a hole in; (bois) to hollow out; (fig) to go (deeply) into; **ça creuse** that gives you a real appetite; **se ~ (la cervelle)** to rack one's brains

creux, -euse [kʀø, -øz] adj hollow ▷ nm hollow; (fig: sur graphique etc) trough; **heures creuses** slack periods; (électricité, téléphone) off-peak periods; **le ~ de l'estomac** the pit of the stomach; **avoir un ~** (fam) to be hungry

crevaison [kʀəvɛzɔ̃] nf puncture, flat

crevasse [kʀəvas] nf (dans le sol) crack, fissure; (de glacier) crevasse; (de la peau) crack

crevé, e [kʀəve] adj (fam: fatigué) shattered (Brit), exhausted

crever [kʀəve] vt (papier) to tear, break; (tambour, ballon) to burst ▷ vi (pneu) to burst; (automobiliste) to have a puncture (Brit) ou a flat (tire) (US); (abcès, outre, nuage) to burst (open); (fam) to die; **cela lui a crevé un œil** it blinded him in one eye; ~ **l'écran** to have real screen presence

crevette [kʀəvɛt] nf: ~ **(rose)** prawn; ~ **grise** shrimp

cri [kʀi] nm cry, shout; (d'animal: spécifique) cry, call; **à grands ~s** at the top of one's voice; **c'est le dernier ~** (fig) it's the latest fashion

criant, e [kʀijɑ̃, -ɑ̃t] adj (injustice) glaring

criard, e [kʀijaʀ, -aʀd] adj (couleur) garish, loud; (voix) yelling

crible [kʀibl] nm riddle; (mécanique) screen, jig; **passer qch au ~** to put sth through a riddle; (fig) to go over sth with a fine-tooth comb

criblé, e [kʀible] adj: ~ **de** riddled with

cric [kʀik] nm (Auto) jack

crier [kʀije] vi (pour appeler) to shout, cry (out); (de peur, de douleur etc) to scream, yell; (fig: grincer) to squeal, screech ▷ vt (ordre, injure) to shout (out), yell (out); **sans ~ gare** without warning; ~ **grâce** to cry for mercy; ~ **au secours** to shout for help

crime [kʀim] nm crime; (meurtre) murder

criminel, le [kʀiminɛl] adj criminal ▷ nm/f criminal; murderer; ~ **de guerre** war criminal

crin [kʀɛ̃] nm (de cheval) hair no pl; (fibre) horsehair; **à tous ~s, à tout ~** diehard, out-and-out

crinière [kʀinjɛʀ] nf mane

crique [kʀik] nf creek, inlet

criquet [kʀikɛ] nm grasshopper

crise [kʀiz] nf crisis (pl crises); (Méd) attack; (: d'épilepsie) fit; ~ **cardiaque** heart attack; ~ **de foi** crisis of belief; **avoir une ~ de foie** to have really bad indigestion; ~ **de nerfs** attack of nerves; **piquer une ~ de nerfs** to go hysterical

crisper [kʀispe] vt to tense; (poings) to clench; **se crisper** to tense; to clench; (personne) to get tense

crisser [kʀise] vi (neige) to crunch; (tissu) to rustle; (pneu) to screech

cristal, -aux [kʀistal, -o] nm crystal; **crystaux** nmpl (objets) crystal(ware) sg; ~ **de plomb** (lead) crystal; ~ **de roche** rock-crystal; **cristaux de soude** washing soda sg

cristallin, e [kʀistalɛ̃, -in] adj crystal-clear ▷ nm (Anat) crystalline lens

critère [kʀitɛʀ] nm criterion (pl -ia)

critiquable [kʀitikabl] adj open to criticism

critique [kʀitik] adj critical ▷ nm/f (de théâtre, musique) critic ▷ nf criticism; (Théât etc: article) review; **la ~** (activité) criticism; (personnes) the critics pl

critiquer [kʀitike] vt (dénigrer) to criticize; (évaluer, juger) to assess, examine (critically)

croasser [kʀɔase] vi to caw

croate [kʀɔat] adj Croatian ▷ nm (Ling) Croat, Croatian ▷ nm/f: **C~** Croat, Croatian

Croatie [kʀɔasi] nf: **la ~** Croatia

croc [kʀo] nm (dent) fang; (de boucher) hook

croc-en-jambe (pl crocs-en-jambe) [kʀɔkɑ̃ʒɑ̃b] nm: **faire un ~ à qn** to trip sb up

croche [kʀɔʃ] nf (Mus) quaver (Brit), eighth note (US); **double ~** semiquaver (Brit), sixteenth note (US)

croche-pied [kʀɔʃpje] nm = **croc-en-jambe**

crochet [kʀɔʃɛ] nm hook; (clef) picklock; (détour) detour; (Boxe): ~ **du gauche** left hook; (Tricot: aiguille) crochet hook; (: technique) crochet; **crochets** nmpl (Typo) square brackets; **vivre aux ~s de qn** to live ou sponge off sb

crochu, e [kʀɔʃy] adj hooked; claw-like

crocodile [kʀɔkɔdil] nm crocodile

croire [kʀwaʀ] vt to believe; ~ **qn honnête** to

believe sb (to be) honest; **se ~ fort** to think one is strong; **~ que** to believe ou think that; **vous croyez?** do you think so?; **~ être/faire** to think one is/does; **~ à**, **~ en** to believe in

croîs etc [kʀwa] vb voir **croître**

croisade [kʀwazad] nf crusade

croisé, e [kʀwaze] adj (veston) double-breasted ▷ nm (guerrier) crusader ▷ nf (fenêtre) window, casement; **~e d'ogives** intersecting ribs; **à la ~e des chemins** at the crossroads

croisement [kʀwazmã] nm (carrefour) crossroads sg; (Bio) crossing; (: résultat) crossbreed

croiser [kʀwaze] vt (personne, voiture) to pass; (route) to cross, cut across; (Bio) to cross ▷ vi (Navig) to cruise; **~ les jambes/bras** to cross one's legs/ fold one's arms; **se croiser** vi (personnes, véhicules) to pass each other; (routes) to cross, intersect; (lettres) to cross (in the post); (regards) to meet; **se ~ les bras** (fig) to fold one's arms, to twiddle one's thumbs

croisière [kʀwazjɛʀ] nf cruise; **vitesse de ~** (Auto etc) cruising speed

croissance [kʀwasãs] nf growing, growth; **troubles de la ~** growing pains; **maladie de ~** growth disease; **~ économique** economic growth

croissant, e [kʀwasã, -ãt] vb voir **croître** ▷ adj growing; rising ▷ nm (à manger) croissant; (motif) crescent; **~ de lune** crescent moon

croître [kʀwatʀ] vi to grow; (lune) to wax

croix [kʀwa] nf cross; **en ~** adj, adv in the form of a cross; **la C~ Rouge** the Red Cross

croque-madame [kʀɔkmadam] nm inv toasted cheese sandwich with a fried egg on top

croque-monsieur [kʀɔkməsjø] nm inv toasted ham and cheese sandwich

croquer [kʀɔke] vt (manger) to crunch; (: fruit) to munch; (dessiner) to sketch ▷ vi to be crisp ou crunchy; **chocolat à ~** plain dessert chocolate

croquis [kʀɔki] nm sketch

cross [kʀɔs], **cross-country** [kʀɔskuntʀi] (pl **cross(-countries)**) nm cross-country race ou run; cross-country racing ou running

crosse [kʀɔs] nf (de fusil) butt; (de revolver) grip; (d'évêque) crook, crosier; (de hockey) hockey stick

crotte [kʀɔt] nf droppings pl; **~!** (fam) damn!

crotté, e [kʀɔte] adj muddy, mucky

crottin [kʀɔtɛ̃] nm dung, manure; (fromage) (small round) cheese (made of goat's milk)

crouler [kʀule] vi (s'effondrer) to collapse; (être délabré) to be crumbling

croupe [kʀup] nf croup, rump; **en ~** pillion

croupir [kʀupiʀ] vi to stagnate

croustillant, e [kʀustijã, -ãt] adj crisp; (fig) spicy

croûte [kʀut] nf crust; (du fromage) rind; (de vol-au-vent) case; (Méd) scab; **en ~** (Culin) in pastry, in a pie; **~ aux champignons** mushrooms on toast; **~ au fromage** cheese

on toast no pl; **~ de pain** (morceau) crust (of bread); **~ terrestre** earth's crust

croûton [kʀutɔ̃] nm (Culin) crouton; (bout du pain) crust, heel

croyable [kʀwajabl] adj believable, credible

croyant, e [kʀwajã, -ãt] vb voir **croire** ▷ adj: **être/ne pas être ~** to be/not to be a believer ▷ nm/f believer

CRS sigle fpl (= Compagnies républicaines de sécurité) state security police force ▷ sigle m member of the CRS

cru, e [kʀy] pp de **croire** ▷ adj (non cuit) raw; (lumière, couleur) harsh; (description) crude; (paroles, langage: franc) blunt; (: grossier) crude ▷ nm (vignoble) vineyard; (vin) wine ▷ nf (d'un cours d'eau) swelling, rising; **de son (propre) ~** (fig) of his own devising; **monter à ~** to ride bareback; **du ~** local; **en ~** in spate; **un grand ~** a great vintage; **jambon ~** Parma ham

crû [kʀy] pp de **croître**

cruauté [kʀyote] nf cruelty

cruche [kʀyʃ] nf pitcher, (earthenware) jug

crucifix [kʀysifi] nm crucifix

crucifixion [kʀysifiksjɔ̃] nf crucifixion

crudité [kʀydite] nf crudeness no pl; harshness no pl; **crudités** nfpl (Culin) selection of raw vegetables

crue [kʀy] nf (inondation) flood; voir aussi **cru**

cruel, le [kʀyɛl] adj cruel

crus, crûs etc [kʀy] vb voir **croire**; **croître**

crustacés [kʀystase] nmpl shellfish

Cuba [kyba] nm: **le ~** Cuba

cubain, e [kybɛ̃, -ɛn] adj Cuban ▷ nm/f: **C~, e** Cuban

cube [kyb] nm cube; (jouet) brick, building block; **gros ~** powerful motorbike; **mètre ~** cubic metre; **2 au ~ = 8** 2 cubed is 8; **élever au ~** to cube

cueillette [kœjɛt] nf picking; (quantité) crop, harvest

cueillir [kœjiʀ] vt (fruits, fleurs) to pick, gather; (fig) to catch

cuiller, cuillère [kɥijɛʀ] nf spoon; **~ à café** coffee spoon; (Culin) ≈ teaspoonful; **~ à soupe** soup spoon; (Culin) ≈ tablespoonful

cuillerée [kɥijʀe] nf spoonful; (Culin): **~ à soupe/café** tablespoonful/teaspoonful

cuir [kɥiʀ] nm leather; (avant tannage) hide; **~ chevelu** scalp

cuire [kɥiʀ] vt: **(faire) ~** (aliments) to cook; (au four) to bake; (poterie) to fire ▷ vi to cook; (picoter) to smart, sting, burn; **bien cuit** well done; **trop cuit** overdone; **pas assez cuit** underdone; **cuit à point** medium done; done to a turn

cuisant, e [kɥizã, -ãt] vb voir **cuire** ▷ adj (douleur) smarting, burning; (fig: souvenir, échec) bitter

cuisine [kɥizin] nf (pièce) kitchen; (art culinaire) cookery, cooking; (nourriture) cooking, food; **faire la ~** to cook

cuisiné, e [kɥizine] *adj:* **plat** ~ ready-made meal *ou* dish

cuisiner [kɥizine] *vt* to cook; *(fam)* to grill ▷ *vi* to cook

cuisinier, -ière [kɥizinje, -jɛʀ] *nm/f* cook ▷ *nf (poêle)* cooker; **cuisinière électrique/à gaz** electric/gas cooker

cuisse [kɥis] *nf (Anat)* thigh; *(Culin)* leg

cuisson [kɥisɔ̃] *nf* cooking; *(de poterie)* firing

cuit, e [kɥi, -it] *pp de* **cuire** ▷ *nf (fam):* **prendre une** – to get plastered *ou* smashed

cuivre [kɥivʀ] *nm* copper; **les ~s** *(Mus)* the brass; **~ rouge** copper; **~ jaune** brass

cul [ky] *nm (fam!)* arse *(Brit)* (!), ass *(US)* (!), bum *(Brit)*; **~ de bouteille** bottom of a bottle

culbute [kylbyt] *nf* somersault; *(accidentelle)* tumble, fall

culminant, e [kylminɑ̃, -ɑ̃t] *adj:* **point ~** highest point; *(fig)* height, climax

culminer [kylmine] *vi* to reach its highest point; to tower

culot [kylo] *(fam) nm (d'ampoule)* cap; *(effronterie)* cheek, nerve

culotte [kylɔt] *nf (de femme)* panties *pl,* knickers *pl (Brit)*; *(d'homme)* underpants *pl*; *(pantalon)* trousers *pl (Brit),* pants *pl (US)*; **~ de cheval** riding breeches *pl*

culpabilité [kylpabilite] *nf* guilt

culte [kylt] *adj:* **livre/film** ~ cult film/book ▷ *nm (religion)* religion; *(hommage, vénération)* worship; *(protestant)* service

cultivateur, -trice [kyltivatœʀ, -tʀis] *nm/f* farmer

cultivé, e [kyltive] *adj (personne)* cultured, cultivated

cultiver [kyltive] *vt* to cultivate; *(légumes)* to grow, cultivate

culture [kyltyʀ] *nf* cultivation; growing; *(connaissances etc)* culture; **(champs de) ~s** land(s) under cultivation; **les ~s intensives** intensive farming; **~ physique** physical training

culturel, le [kyltyʀɛl] *adj* cultural

culturisme [kyltyʀism] *nm* body-building

cumin [kymɛ̃] *nm (Culin)* cumin

cumuler [kymyle] *vt (emplois, honneurs)* to hold concurrently; *(salaires)* to draw concurrently; *(Jur: droits)* to accumulate

cupide [kypid] *adj* greedy, grasping

cure [kyʀ] *nf (Méd)* course of treatment; *(Rel)* cure, ≈ living; presbytery, ≈ vicarage; **faire une ~ de fruits** to go on a fruit cure *ou* diet; **faire une ~ thermale** to take the waters; **n'avoir ~ de** to pay no attention to; **~ d'amaigrissement** slimming course; **~ de repos** rest cure; **~ de sommeil** sleep therapy *no pl*

curé [kyʀe] *nm* parish priest; **M le ~** ≈ Vicar

cure-dent [kyʀdɑ̃] *nm* toothpick

cure-pipe [kyʀpip] *nm* pipe cleaner

curer [kyʀe] *vt* to clean out; **se ~ les dents** to pick one's teeth

curieusement [kyʀjøzmɑ̃] *adv* oddly

curieux, -euse [kyʀjø, -øz] *adj (étrange)* strange, curious; *(indiscret)* curious, inquisitive; *(intéressé)* inquiring, curious ▷ *nmpl (badauds)* onlookers, bystanders

curiosité [kyʀjozite] *nf* curiosity, inquisitiveness; *(objet)* curio(sity); *(site)* unusual feature *ou* sight

curriculum vitae [kyʀikylɔmvite] *nm inv* curriculum vitae

curseur [kyʀsœʀ] *nm (Inform)* cursor; *(de règle)* slide; *(de fermeture-éclair)* slider

cutané, e [kytane] *adj* cutaneous, skin *cpd*

cuti-réaction [kytiʀeaksjɔ̃] *nf (Méd)* skin-test

cuve [kyv] *nf* vat; *(à mazout etc)* tank

cuvée [kyve] *nf* vintage

cuvette [kyvɛt] *nf (récipient)* bowl, basin; *(du lavabo)* (wash)basin; *(des w.-c.)* pan; *(Géo)* basin

CV *sigle m (Auto)* = **cheval vapeur**; *(Admin)* = **curriculum vitae**

cyanure [sjanyʀ] *nm* cyanide

cybercafé [sibɛʀkafe] *nm* Internet café

cyberespace [sibɛʀɛspas] *nm* cyberspace

cybernaute [sibɛʀnot] *nm/f* Internet user

cyclable [siklabl] *adj:* **piste ~** cycle track

cycle [sikl] *nm* cycle; *(Scol):* **premier/second ~ ≈** middle/upper school *(Brit),* ≈ junior/senior high school *(US)*

cyclisme [siklism] *nm* cycling

cycliste [siklist] *nm/f* cyclist ▷ *adj* cycle *cpd*; **coureur ~** racing cyclist

cyclomoteur [siklomɔtœʀ] *nm* moped

cyclone [siklon] *nm* hurricane

cygne [siɲ] *nm* swan

cylindre [silɛ̃dʀ] *nm* cylinder; **moteur à 4 ~s en ligne** straight-4 engine

cylindrée [silɛ̃dʀe] *nf (Auto)* (cubic) capacity; **une (voiture de) grosse ~** a big-engined car

cymbale [sɛ̃bal] *nf* cymbal

cynique [sinik] *adj* cynical

cystite [sistit] *nf* cystitis

d

d' *prép, art voir* **de**

dactylo [daktilo] *nf* (*aussi*: **~graphe**) typist; (*aussi*: **~graphie**) typing, typewriting

dactylographier [daktilɔgʀafje] *vt* to type (out)

dada [dada] *nm* hobby-horse

daigner [deɲe] *vt* to deign

daim [dɛ̃] *nm* (fallow) deer *inv*; (*peau*) buckskin; (*cuir suédé*) suede

dalle [dal] *nf* slab; (*au sol*) paving stone, flag(stone); **que ~** nothing at all, damn all (Brit)

daltonien, ne [daltɔnjɛ̃, -ɛn] *adj* colour-blind (Brit), color-blind (US)

dam [dam] *nm*: **au grand ~ de** much to the detriment (*ou* annoyance) of

dame [dam] *nf* lady; (*Cartes, Échecs*) queen; **dames** *nfpl* (*jeu*) draughts *sg* (Brit), checkers *sg* (US); **les (toilettes des) ~s** the ladies' (toilets); **~ de charité** benefactress; **~ de compagnie** lady's companion

damner [dɑne] *vt* to damn

dancing [dɑ̃siŋ] *nm* dance hall

Danemark [danmaʀk] *nm*: **le ~** Denmark

danger [dɑ̃ʒe] *nm* danger; **mettre en ~** (*personne*) to put in danger; (*projet, carrière*) to jeopardize; **être en ~** (*personne*) to be in danger; **être en ~ de mort** to be in peril of one's life; **être hors de ~** to be out of danger

dangereux, -euse [dɑ̃ʒʀø, -øz] *adj* dangerous

danois, e [danwa, -waz] *adj* Danish ⊳ *nm* (*Ling*) Danish ⊳ *nm/f*: **D~, e** Dane

⊙ **MOT-CLÉ**

dans [dɑ̃] *prép* **1** (*position*) in; (*à l'intérieur de*) inside; **c'est dans le tiroir/le salon** it's in the drawer/lounge; **dans la boîte** in *ou* inside the box; **marcher dans la ville/la rue** to walk about the town/along the street; **je l'ai lu dans le journal** I read it in the newspaper; **être dans les meilleurs** to be among *ou* one of the best
2 (*direction*) into; **elle a couru dans le salon** she ran into the lounge; **monter dans une voiture/le bus** to get into a car/on to the bus
3 (*provenance*) out of, from; **je l'ai pris dans le tiroir/salon** I took it out of *ou* from the drawer/lounge; **boire dans un verre** to drink out of *ou* from a glass
4 (*temps*) in; **dans deux mois** in two months, in two months' time
5 (*approximation*) about; **dans les 20 euros** about 20 euros

danse [dɑ̃s] *nf*: **la ~** dancing; (*classique*) (ballet) dancing; **une ~** a dance; **~ du ventre** belly dancing

danser [dɑ̃se] *vi, vt* to dance

danseur, -euse [dɑ̃sœʀ, -øz] *nm/f* ballet dancer; (*au bal etc*) dancer; (: *cavalier*) partner; **~ de claquettes** tap-dancer; **en danseuse** (*à vélo*) standing on the pedals

dard [daʀ] *nm* sting (*organ*)

date [dat] *nf* date; **faire ~** to mark a milestone; **de longue ~** *adj* longstanding; **~ de naissance** date of birth; **~ limite** deadline; (*d'un aliment*: *aussi*: **~ limite de vente**) sell-by date

dater [date] *vt, vi* to date; **~ de** to date from, go back to; **à ~ de** (as) from

datte [dat] *nf* date

dauphin [dofɛ̃] *nm* (*Zool*) dolphin; (*du roi*) dauphin; (*fig*) heir apparent

davantage [davɑ̃taʒ] *adv* more; (*plus longtemps*) longer; **~ de** more; **~ que** more than

⊙ **MOT-CLÉ**

de, d' [də, d] (*de + le* = **du**, *de + les* = **des**) *prép* **1** (*appartenance*) of; **le toit de la maison** the roof of the house; **la voiture d'Elisabeth/de mes parents** Elisabeth's/my parents' car
2 (*provenance*) from; **il vient de Londres** he comes from London; **de Londres à Paris** from London to Paris; **elle est sortie du cinéma** she came out of the cinema
3 (*moyen*) with; **je l'ai fait de mes propres mains** I did it with my own two hands
4 (*caractérisation, mesure*) un mur de brique/ bureau d'acajou a brick wall/mahogany desk; **un billet de 10 euros** a 10 euro note; **une pièce de 2 m de large** *ou* **large de 2 m** a room 2 m wide, a 2m-wide room; **un bébé de 10 mois** a 10-month-old baby; **12 mois de**

crédit/travail 12 months' credit/work; **elle est payée 20 euros de l'heure** she's paid 20 euros an hour ou per hour; **augmenter de 10 euros** to increase by 10 euros; **trois jours de libres** three free days, three days free; **un verre d'eau** a glass of water; **il mange de tout** he'll eat anything

5 (rapport) from; **de quatre à six** from four to six

6 (cause): **mourir de faim** to die of hunger; **rouge de colère** red with fury

7 (vb +de +infin) to; **il m'a dit de rester** he told me to stay

8 (de la part de): **estimé de ses collègues** respected by his colleagues

9 (en apposition): **cet imbécile de Paul** that idiot Paul; **le terme de franglais** the term "franglais"

▷ art **1** (phrases affirmatives) some (souvent omis); **du vin, de l'eau, des pommes** (some) wine, (some) water, (some) apples; **des enfants sont venus** some children came; **pendant des mois** for months

2 (phrases interrogatives et négatives) any; **a-t-il du vin?** has he got any wine?; **il n'a pas de pommes/d'enfants** he hasn't (got) any apples/children, he has no apples/children

dé [de] nm (à jouer) die ou dice; (aussi: **dé à coudre**) thimble; **dés** nmpl (jeu) (game of) dice; **un coup de dés** a throw of the dice; **couper en dés** (Culin) to dice

dealer [dilœʀ] nm (fam) (drug) pusher

déambuler [deãbyle] vi to stroll about

débâcle [debɑkl] nf rout

déballer [debale] vt to unpack

débandade [debãdad] nf scattering; (déroute) rout

débarbouiller [debaʀbuje] vt to wash; **se débarbouiller** vi to wash (one's face)

débarcadère [debaʀkadɛʀ] nm landing stage (Brit), wharf

débardeur [debaʀdœʀ] nm docker, stevedore; (maillot) slipover; (pour femme) vest top; (pour homme) sleeveless top

débarquer [debaʀke] vt to unload, land ▷ vi to disembark; (fig) to turn up

débarras [debaʀɑ] nm (pièce) lumber room; (placard) junk cupboard; (remise) outhouse; **bon ~!** good riddance!

débarrasser [debaʀase] vt to clear ▷ vi (enlever le couvert) to clear away; **~ qn de** (vêtements, paquets) to relieve sb of; (habitude, ennemi) to rid sb of; **qch de** (fouillis etc) to clear sth of; **se débarrasser de** vt to get rid of; to rid o.s. of

débat [deba] vb voir **débattre** ▷ nm discussion, debate; **débats** nmpl (Pol) proceedings, debates

débattre [debatʀ] vt to discuss, debate; **se débattre** vi to struggle

débaucher [deboʃe] vt (licencier) to lay off, dismiss; (salarié d'une autre entreprise) to poach; (entraîner) to lead astray, debauch; (inciter à la grève) to incite

débile [debil] adj weak, feeble; (fam: idiot) dim-witted ▷ nm/f: **~ mental, e** mental defective

débit [debi] nm (d'un liquide, fleuve) (rate of) flow; (d'un magasin) turnover (of goods); (élocution) delivery; (bancaire) debit; **avoir un ~ de 10 euros** to be 10 euros in debit; **~ de boissons** drinking establishment; **~ de tabac** tobacconist's (shop) (Brit), tobacco ou smoke shop (US)

débiter [debite] vt (compte) to debit; (liquide, gaz) to yield, produce, give out; (couper: bois, viande) to cut up; (vendre) to retail; (péj: paroles etc) to come out with, churn out

débiteur, -trice [debitœʀ, -tʀis] nm/f debtor ▷ adj in debit; (compte) debit cpd

déblayer [debleje] vt to clear; **~ le terrain** (fig) to clear the ground

débloquer [debloke] vt (frein, fonds) to release; (prix, crédits) to free ▷ vi (fam) to talk rubbish

déboires [debwaʀ] nmpl setbacks

déboiser [debwaze] vt to clear of trees; (région) to deforest; **se déboiser** vi (colline, montagne) to become bare of trees

déboîter [debwate] vt (Auto) to pull out; **se ~ le genou** etc to dislocate one's knee etc

débonnaire [deboneʀ] adj easy-going, good-natured

débordé, e [debɔʀde] adj: **être ~ de** (travail, demandes) to be snowed under with

déborder [debɔʀde] vi to overflow; (lait etc) to boil over ▷ vt (Mil, Sport) to outflank; **~ (de) qch** (dépasser) to extend beyond sth; **~ de** (joie, zèle) to be brimming over with ou bursting with

débouché [debuʃe] nm (pour vendre) outlet; (perspective d'emploi) opening; (sortie): **au ~ de la vallée** where the valley opens out (onto the plain)

déboucher [debuʃe] vt (évier, tuyau etc) to unblock; (bouteille) to uncork, open ▷ vi: **~ de** to emerge from, come out of; **~ sur** to come out onto; to open out onto; (fig) to arrive at, lead up to; (études) to lead on to

débourser [debuʀse] vt to pay out, lay out

déboussoler [debusole] vt to disorientate, disorient

debout [dəbu] adv: **être ~** (personne) to be standing, stand; (: levé, éveillé) to be up (and about); (chose) to be upright; **être encore ~** (fig: en état) to be still going; to be still standing; to be still up; **mettre qn ~** to get sb to his feet; **mettre qch ~** to stand sth up; **se mettre ~** to get up (on one's feet); **se tenir ~** to stand; **~!** stand up!; (du lit) get up!; **cette histoire ne tient pas ~** this story doesn't hold water

déboutonner [debutone] vt to undo, unbutton; **se déboutonner** vi to come undone ou unbuttoned

débraillé, e [debraje] *adj* slovenly, untidy

débrancher [debrãʃe] *vt* (*appareil électrique*) to unplug; (*téléphone, courant électrique*) to disconnect, cut off

débrayage [debrεjaʒ] *nm* (*Auto*) clutch; (: *action*) disengaging the clutch; (*grève*) stoppage; **faire un double ~** to double-declutch

débrayer [debreje] *vi* (*Auto*) to declutch, disengage the clutch; (*cesser le travail*) to stop work

débris [debri] *nm* (*fragment*) fragment ▷ *nmpl* (*déchets*) pieces, debris *sg*; rubbish *sg* (*Brit*), garbage *sg* (*US*); **des ~ de verre** bits of glass

débrouillard, e [debrujar, -ard] *adj* smart, resourceful

débrouiller [debruje] *vt* to disentangle, untangle; (*fig*) to sort out, unravel; **se débrouiller** *vi* to manage; **débrouillez-vous** you'll have to sort things out yourself

début [deby] *nm* beginning, start; **débuts** *nmpl* beginnings; (*de carrière*) début *sg*; **faire ses ~s** to start out; **au ~** in *ou* at the beginning, at first; **au ~ de** at the beginning *ou* start of; **dès le ~** from the start; **~ juin** in early June

débutant, e [debytã, -ãt] *nm/f* beginner, novice

débuter [debyte] *vi* to begin, start; (*faire ses débuts*) to start out

deçà [dəsa]: **en ~ de** *prép* this side of; **en ~** *adv* on this side

décadence [dekadãs] *nf* decadence; decline

décaféiné, e [dekafeine] *adj* decaffeinated, caffeine-free

décalage [dekalaʒ] *nm* move forward *ou* back; shift forward *ou* back; (*écart*) gap; (*désaccord*) discrepancy; **~ horaire** time difference (between time zones), time-lag

décaler [dekale] *vt* (*dans le temps: avancer*) to bring forward; (: *retarder*) to put back; (*changer de position*) to shift forward *ou* back; **~ de 10 cm** to move forward *ou* back by 10 cm; **~ de deux heures** to bring *ou* move forward two hours; to put back two hours

décalquer [dekalke] *vt* to trace; (*par pression*) to transfer

décamper [dekãpe] *vi* to clear out *ou* off

décaper [dekape] *vt* to strip; (*avec abrasif*) to scour; (*avec papier de verre*) to sand

décapiter [dekapite] *vt* to behead; (*par accident*) to decapitate; (*fig*) to cut the top off; (: *organisation*) to remove the top people from

décapotable [dekapɔtabl] *adj* convertible

décapsuleur [dekapsylœr] *nm* bottle-opener

décarcasser [dekarkase] *vt*: **se ~ pour qn/ pour faire qch** (*fam*) to slog one's guts out for sb/to do sth

décédé, e [desede] *adj* deceased

décéder [desede] *vi* to die

déceler [desle] *vt* to discover, detect; (*révéler*) to indicate, reveal

décembre [desãbr] *nm* December; *voir aussi* **juillet**

décemment [desamã] *adv* decently

décennie [deseni] *nf* decade

décent, e [desã, -ãt] *adj* decent

déception [desεpsjɔ̃] *nf* disappointment

décerner [deserne] *vt* to award

décès [desε] *nm* death, decease; **acte de ~** death certificate

décevant, e [desvã, -ãt] *adj* disappointing

décevoir [des(ə)vwar] *vt* to disappoint

déchaîner [deʃene] *vt* (*passions, colère*) to unleash; (*rires etc*) to give rise to, arouse; **se déchaîner** *vi* to be unleashed; (*rires*) to burst out; (*se mettre en colère*) to fly into a rage; **se ~ contre qn** to unleash one's fury on sb

déchanter [deʃãte] *vi* to become disillusioned

décharge [deʃarʒ] *nf* (*dépôt d'ordures*) rubbish tip *ou* dump; (*électrique*) electrical discharge; (*salve*) volley of shots; **à la ~ de** in defence of

décharger [deʃarʒe] *vt* (*marchandise, véhicule*) to unload; (*Élec*) to discharge; (*arme: neutraliser*) to unload; (: *faire feu*) to discharge, fire; **~ qn de** (*responsabilité*) to relieve sb of, release sb from; **~ sa colère (sur)** to vent one's anger (on); **~ sa conscience** to unburden one's conscience; **se ~ dans** (*se déverser*) to flow into; **se ~ d'une affaire sur qn** to hand a matter over to sb

décharné, e [deʃarne] *adj* bony, emaciated, fleshless

déchausser [deʃose] *vt* (*personne*) to take the shoes off; (*skis*) to take off; **se déchausser** *vi* to take off one's shoes; (*dent*) to come *ou* work loose

déchéance [deʃeãs] *nf* (*déclin*) degeneration, decay, decline; (*chute*) fall

déchet [deʃε] *nm* (*de bois, tissu etc*) scrap; (*perte: gén Comm*) wastage, waste; **déchets** *nmpl* (*ordures*) refuse *sg*, rubbish *sg* (*Brit*), garbage *sg* (*US*); **~s nucléaires** nuclear waste; **~s radioactifs** radioactive waste

déchiffrer [deʃifre] *vt* to decipher

déchiqueter [deʃikte] *vt* to tear *ou* pull to pieces

déchirant, e [deʃirã, -ãt] *adj* heart-breaking, heart-rending

déchirement [deʃirmã] *nm* (*chagrin*) wrench, heartbreak; (*gén pl: conflit*) rift, split

déchirer [deʃire] *vt* to tear, rip; (*mettre en morceaux*) to tear up; (*pour ouvrir*) to tear off; (*arracher*) to tear out; (*fig*) to tear apart; **se déchirer** *vi* to tear, rip; **se ~ un muscle/ tendon** to tear a muscle/tendon

déchirure [deʃiryr] *nf* (*accroc*) tear, rip; **~ musculaire** torn muscle

déchoir [deʃwar] *vi* (*personne*) to lower o.s., demean o.s.; **~ de** to fall from

déchu, e [deʃy] *pp de* **déchoir** ▷ *adj* fallen; (*roi*) deposed

décidé, e [deside] adj (personne, air) determined; **c'est ~** it's decided; **être ~ à faire** to be determined to do

décidément [desidemã] adv undoubtedly; really

décider [deside] vt: **~ qch** to decide on sth; **~ de faire/que** to decide to do/that; **~ qn (à faire qch)** to persuade ou induce sb (to do sth); **~ de qch** to decide upon sth; (chose) to determine sth; **se décider** vi (personne) to decide, make up one's mind; (problème, affaire) to be resolved; **se ~ à qch** to decide on sth; **se ~ à faire** to decide ou make up one's mind to do; **se ~ pour qch** to decide on ou in favour of sth

décimal, e, -aux [desimal, -o] adj, nf decimal

décimètre [desimetʀ] nm decimetre (Brit), decimeter (US); **double ~** (20 cm) ruler

décisif, -ive [desizif, -iv] adj decisive; (qui l'emporte): **le facteur/l'argument ~** the deciding factor/argument

décision [desizjɔ̃] nf decision; (fermeté) decisiveness, decision; **prendre une ~** to make a decision; **prendre la ~ de faire** to take the decision to do; **emporter** ou **faire la ~** to be decisive

déclaration [deklaʀasjɔ̃] nf declaration; registration; (discours: Pol etc) statement; (compte rendu) report; **fausse ~** misrepresentation; **~ (d'amour)** declaration; **~ de décès** registration of death; **~ de guerre** declaration of war; **~ (d'impôts)** statement of income, tax declaration, ≈ tax return; **~ (de sinistre)** (insurance) claim; **~ de revenus** statement of income; **faire une ~ de vol** to report a theft

déclarer [deklaʀe] vt to declare, announce; (revenus, employés, marchandises) to declare; (décès, naissance) to register; (vol etc: à la police) to report; **rien à ~** nothing to declare; **se déclarer** vi (feu, maladie) to break out; **~ la guerre** to declare war

déclencher [deklãʃe] vt (mécanisme etc) to release; (sonnerie) to set off, activate; (attaque, grève) to launch; (provoquer) to trigger off; **se déclencher** vi to release itself; (sonnerie) to go off

déclic [deklik] nm trigger mechanism; (bruit) click

décliner [dekline] vi to decline ▷ vt (invitation) to decline, refuse; (responsabilité) to refuse to accept; (nom, adresse) to state; (Ling) to decline; **se décliner** (Ling) to decline

décocher [dekɔʃe] vt to hurl; (flèche, regard) to shoot

décoiffer [dekwafe] vt: **~ qn** to mess up sb's hair; to take sb's hat off; **je suis toute décoiffée** my hair is in a real mess; **se décoiffer** vi to take off one's hat

déçois etc [deswa], **déçoive** etc [deswav] vb voir **décevoir**

décollage [dekɔlaʒ] nm (Aviat, Écon) takeoff

décoller [dekɔle] vt to unstick ▷ vi (avion) to take off; (projet, entreprise) to take off, get off the ground; **se décoller** vi to come unstuck

décolleté, e [dekɔlte] adj low-necked, low-cut; (femme) wearing a low-cut dress ▷ nm low neck(line); (épaules) (bare) neck and shoulders; (plongeant) cleavage

décolorer [dekɔlɔʀe] vt (tissu) to fade; (cheveux) to bleach, lighten; **se décolorer** vi to fade; **se faire ~ les cheveux** to have one's hair bleached

décombres [dekɔ̃bʀ] nmpl rubble sg, debris sg

décommander [dekɔmãde] vt to cancel; (invités) to put off; **se décommander** vi to cancel, cry off

décomposé, e [dekɔ̃poze] adj (pourri) decomposed; (visage) haggard, distorted

décompte [dekɔ̃t] nm deduction; (facture) breakdown (of an account), detailed account

déconcerter [dekɔ̃sɛʀte] vt to disconcert, confound

déconfit, e [dekɔ̃fi, -it] adj crestfallen, downcast

décongeler [dekɔ̃ʒ(ə)le] vt to thaw (out)

déconner [dekɔne] vi (fam!: en parlant) to talk (a load of) rubbish (Brit) ou garbage (US); (: faire des bêtises) to muck about; **sans ~** no kidding

déconseiller [dekɔ̃seje] vt: **~ qch (à qn)** to advise (sb) against sth; **~ à qn de faire** to advise sb against doing; **c'est déconseillé** it's not advised ou advisable

décontracté, e [dekɔ̃tʀakte] adj relaxed, laid-back (fam)

décontracter [dekɔ̃tʀakte] vt, **se décontracter** vi to relax

déconvenue [dekɔ̃vny] nf disappointment

décor [dekɔʀ] nm décor; (paysage) scenery; **décors** nmpl (Théât) scenery sg, decor sg; (Ciné) set sg; **changement de ~** (fig) change of scene; **entrer dans le ~** (fig) to run off the road; **en ~ naturel** (Ciné) on location

décorateur, -trice [dekɔʀatœʀ, -tʀis] nm/f (interior) decorator; (Ciné) set designer

décoration [dekɔʀasjɔ̃] nf decoration

décorer [dekɔʀe] vt to decorate

décortiquer [dekɔʀtike] vt to shell; (riz) to hull; (fig: texte) to dissect

découcher [dekuʃe] vi to spend the night away

découdre [dekudʀ] vt (vêtement, couture) to unpick, take the stitching out of; (bouton) to take off; **se découdre** vi to come unstitched; (bouton) to come off; **en ~** (fig) to fight, do battle

découler [dekule] vi: **~ de** to ensue ou follow from

découper [dekupe] vt (papier, tissu etc) to cut up; (volaille, viande) to carve; (détacher: manche, article) to cut out; **se ~ sur** (ciel, fond) to stand out against

décourager [dekuraʒe] vt to discourage, dishearten; (dissuader) to discourage, put off; **se décourager** vi to lose heart, become discouraged; **~ qn de faire/de qch** to discourage sb from doing/from sth, put sb off doing/sth

décousu, e [dekuzy] pp de **découdre** ▷ adj unstitched; (fig) disjointed, disconnected

découvert, e [dekuvɛʀ, -ɛʀt] pp de **découvrir** ▷ adj (tête) bare, uncovered; (lieu) open, exposed ▷ nm (bancaire) overdraft ▷ nf discovery; **à ~** adv (Mil) exposed, without cover; (fig) openly ▷ adj (Comm) overdrawn; **à visage ~** openly; **aller à la ~e de** to go in search of; **faire la ~e de** to discover

découvrir [dekuvʀiʀ] vt to discover; (apercevoir) to see; (enlever ce qui couvre ou protège) to uncover; (montrer, dévoiler) to reveal; **se découvrir** vi (chapeau) to take off one's hat; (se déshabiller) to take something off; (au lit) to uncover o.s.; (ciel) to clear; **se ~ des talents** to find hidden talents in o.s.

décret [dekʀɛ] nm decree

décréter [dekʀete] vt to decree; (ordonner) to order

décrié, e [dekʀije] adj disparaged

décrire [dekʀiʀ] vt to describe; (courbe, cercle) to follow, describe

décrocher [dekʀɔʃe] vt (dépendre) to take down; (téléphone) to take off the hook; (: pour répondre): **~ (le téléphone)** to pick up ou lift the receiver; (fig: contrat etc) to get, land ▷ vi (fam: abandonner) to drop out; (cesser d'écouter) to switch off; **se décrocher** vi (tableau, rideau) to fall down

décroître [dekʀwatʀ] vi to decrease, decline diminish

décrypter [dekʀipte] vt to decipher

déçu, e [desy] pp de **décevoir** ▷ adj disappointed

décupler [dekyple] vt, vi to increase tenfold

dédaigner [dedɛɲe] vt to despise, scorn; (négliger) to disregard, spurn; **~ de faire** to consider it beneath one to do, not deign to do

dédaigneux, -euse [dedɛɲø, -øz] adj scornful, disdainful

dédain [dedɛ̃] nm scorn, disdain

dédale [dedal] nm maze

dedans [dədɑ̃] adv inside; (pas en plein air) indoors, inside ▷ nm inside; **au ~** on the inside; inside; **en ~** (vers l'intérieur) inwards; voir aussi **là**

dédicacer [dedikase] vt: **~ (à qn)** to sign (for sb), autograph (for sb), inscribe (to sb)

dédier [dedje] vt to dedicate; **~ à** to dedicate to

dédire [dediʀ]: **se dédire** vi to go back on one's word; (se rétracter) to retract, recant

dédommagement [dedɔmaʒmɑ̃] nm compensation

dédommager [dedɔmaʒe] vt: **~ qn (de)** to compensate sb (for); (fig) to repay sb (for)

dédouaner [dedwane] vt to clear through customs

dédoubler [deduble] vt (classe, effectifs) to split (into two); (couverture etc) to unfold; (manteau) to remove the lining of; **~ un train/ les trains** to run a relief train/additional trains; **se dédoubler** vi (Psych) to have a split personality

déduire [dedɥiʀ] vt: **~ qch (de)** (ôter) to deduct sth (from); (conclure) to deduce ou infer sth (from)

déesse [deɛs] nf goddess

défaillance [defajɑ̃s] nf (syncope) blackout; (fatigue) (sudden) weakness no pl; (technique) fault, failure; (morale etc) weakness; **~ cardiaque** heart failure

défaillir [defajiʀ] vi to faint; to feel faint; (mémoire etc) to fail

défaire [defɛʀ] vt (installation, échafaudage) to take down, dismantle; (paquet etc, nœud, vêtement) to undo; (bagages) to unpack; (ouvrage) to undo, unpick; (cheveux) to take out; **se défaire** vi to come undone; **se ~ de** vt (se débarrasser de) to get rid of; (se séparer de) to part with; **~ le lit** (pour changer les draps) to strip the bed; (pour se coucher) to turn back the bedclothes

défait, e [defɛ, -ɛt] pp de **défaire** ▷ adj (visage) haggard, ravaged ▷ nf defeat

défalquer [defalke] vt to deduct

défaut [defo] nm (moral) fault, failing, defect; (d'étoffe, métal) fault, flaw, defect; (manque, carence): **~ de** lack of; shortage of; (Inform) bug; **~ de la cuirasse** (fig) chink in the armour (Brit) ou armor (US); **en ~** at fault; in the wrong; **prendre qn en ~** to catch sb out; **faire ~** (manquer) to be lacking; **à ~** adv failing that; **à ~ de** for lack ou want of; **par ~** (Jur) in his (ou her etc) absence

défavorable [defavɔʀabl] adj unfavourable (Brit), unfavorable (US)

défavoriser [defavɔʀize] vt to put at a disadvantage

défection [defɛksjɔ̃] nf defection, failure to give support ou assistance; failure to appear; **faire ~** (d'un parti etc) to withdraw one's support, leave

défectueux, -euse [defɛktɥø, -øz] adj faulty, defective

défendre [defɑ̃dʀ] vt to defend; (interdire) to forbid; **~ à qn qch/de faire** to forbid sb sth/to do; **il est défendu de cracher** spitting (is) prohibited ou is not allowed; **c'est défendu** it is forbidden; **se défendre** vi to defend o.s.; **il se défend** (fig) he can hold his own; **ça se défend** (fig) it holds together; **se ~ de/contre** (se protéger) to protect o.s. from/against; **se ~ de** (se garder de) to refrain from; (nier): **se ~ de vouloir** to deny wanting

défense [defɑ̃s] nf defence (Brit), defense (US); (d'éléphant etc) tusk; **ministre de la ~** Minister of Defence (Brit), Defence Secretary;

la ~ **nationale** defence, the defence of the realm (Brit); **la ~ contre avions** anti-aircraft defence; **"~ de fumer/cracher"** "no smoking/spitting", "smoking/spitting prohibited"; **prendre la ~ de qn** to stand up for sb; **~ des consommateurs** consumerism

déférer [defere] vt (Jur) to refer; **~ à** vt (requête, décision) to defer to; **~ qn à la justice** to hand sb over to justice

déferler [defɛʀle] vi (vagues) to break; (fig) to surge

défi [defi] nm (provocation) challenge; (bravade) defiance; **mettre qn au ~ de faire qch** to challenge sb to do sth; **relever un ~** to take up ou accept a challenge; **lancer un ~ à qn** to challenge sb; **sur un ton de ~** defiantly

déficit [defisit] nm (Comm) deficit; (Psych etc: manque) defect; **~ budgétaire** budget deficit; **être en ~** to be in deficit

déficitaire [defisitɛʀ] adj (année, récolte) bad; **entreprise/budget** ~ business/budget in deficit

défier [defje] vt (provoquer) to challenge; (fig) to defy, brave; **se ~ de** (se méfier de) to distrust, mistrust; **~ qn de faire** to challenge ou defy sb to do sth; **~ qn à** to challenge sb to; **~ toute comparaison/concurrence** to be incomparable/unbeatable

défigurer [defigyʀe] vt to disfigure; (boutons etc) to mar ou spoil (the looks of); (fig: œuvre) to mutilate, deface

défilé [defile] nm (Géo) (narrow) gorge ou pass; (soldats) parade; (manifestants) procession, march; **un ~ de** (voitures, visiteurs etc) a stream of

défiler [defile] vi (troupes) to march past; (sportifs) to parade; (manifestants) to march; (visiteurs) to pour, stream; **faire ~ un document** (Inform) to scroll a document; **se défiler** vi (se dérober) to slip away, sneak off; faire ~ (bande, film) to put on; (Inform) to scroll; **il s'est défilé** (fam) he wriggled out of it

définir [definiʀ] vt to define

définitif, -ive [definitif, -iv] adj (final) final, definitive; (pour longtemps) permanent, definitive; (sans appel) final, definite ▷ nf: **en définitive** eventually; (somme toute) when all is said and done

définitivement [definitivmɑ̃] adv definitively; permanently; definitely

défoncer [defɔ̃se] vt (caisse) to stave in; (porte) to smash in ou down; (lit, fauteuil) to burst (the springs of); (terrain, route) to rip ou plough up; **se défoncer** vi (se donner à fond) to give it all one's got

déformer [defɔʀme] vt to put out of shape; (corps) to deform; (pensée, fait) to distort; **se déformer** vi to lose its shape

défouler [defule]: **se défouler** vi (Psych) to work off one's tensions, release one's pent-up feelings; (gén) to unwind, let off steam

défraîchir [defreʃiʀ]: **se défraîchir** vi to fade; to become shop-soiled

défricher [defʀiʃe] vt to clear (for cultivation)

défunt, e [defœ̃, -œ̃t] adj: **son ~ père** his late father ▷ nm/f deceased

dégagé, e [degaʒe] adj (route, ciel) clear; (ton, air) casual, jaunty; **sur un ton ~** casually

dégagement [degaʒmɑ̃] nm emission; freeing; clearing; (espace libre) clearing; passage; clearance; (Football) clearance; **voie de ~** slip road; **itinéraire de ~** alternative route (to relieve traffic congestion)

dégager [degaʒe] vt (exhaler) to give off, emit; (délivrer) to free, extricate; (Mil: troupes) to relieve; (désencombrer) to clear; (isoler, mettre en valeur) to bring out; (crédits) to release; **se dégager** vi (odeur) to emanate, be given off; (passage, ciel) to clear; **~ qn de** (engagement, parole etc) to release ou free sb from; **se ~ de** (fig: engagement etc) to get out of; (: promesse) to go back on

dégarnir [degaʀniʀ] vt (vider) to empty, clear; **se dégarnir** vi to empty; to be cleaned out ou cleared; (tempes, crâne) to go bald

dégâts [dega] nmpl damage sg; **faire des ~** to damage

dégel [deʒɛl] nm thaw; (fig: des prix etc) unfreezing

dégeler [deʒle] vt to thaw (out); (fig) to unfreeze ▷ vi to thaw (out); **se dégeler** vi (fig) to thaw out

dégénérer [deʒeneʀe] vi to degenerate; (empirer) to go from bad to worse; (devenir): **~ en** to degenerate into

dégingandé, e [deʒɛ̃gɑ̃de] adj gangling, lanky

dégivrer [deʒivʀe] vt (frigo) to defrost; (vitres) to de-ice

dégonflé, e [degɔ̃fle] adj (pneu) flat; (fam) chicken ▷ nm/f chicken

dégonfler [degɔ̃fle] vt (pneu, ballon) to let down, deflate ▷ vi (désenfler) to go down; **se dégonfler** vi (fam) to chicken out

dégouliner [deguline] vi to trickle, drip; **~ de** to be dripping with

dégourdi, e [deguʀdi] adj smart, resourceful

dégourdir [deguʀdiʀ] vt to warm (up); **se ~ (les jambes)** to stretch one's legs

dégoût [degu] nm disgust, distaste

dégoûtant, e [degutɑ̃, -ɑ̃t] adj disgusting

dégoûté, e [degute] adj disgusted; **~ de** sick of

dégoûter [degute] vt to disgust; **cela me dégoûte** I find this disgusting ou revolting; **~ qn de qch** to put sb off sth; **se ~ de** to get ou become sick of

dégrader [degʀade] vt (Mil: officier) to degrade; (abîmer) to damage, deface; (avilir) to degrade, debase; **se dégrader** vi (relations, situation) to deteriorate

dégrafer [degʀafe] vt to unclip, unhook, unfasten

degré [dəgʀe] nm degree; (d'escalier) step; **brûlure au 1er/2ème ~** 1st/2nd degree burn; **équation du 1er/2ème ~** linear/quadratic equation; **le premier ~** (Scol) primary level; **alcool à 90 ~s** surgical spirit; **vin de 10 ~s** 10° wine (on Gay-Lussac scale); **par ~(s)** adv by degrees, gradually

dégressif, -ive [degresif, -iv] adj on a decreasing scale, degressive; **tarif ~** decreasing rate of charge

dégringoler [degʀɛ̃gɔle] vi to tumble (down); (fig: prix, monnaie etc) to collapse

dégrossir [degʀosiʀ] vt (bois) to trim; (fig) to work out roughly; (: personne) to knock the rough edges off

déguenillé, e [dɛgnije] adj ragged, tattered

déguerpir [degɛʀpiʀ] vi to clear off

dégueulasse [degœlas] adj (fam) disgusting

dégueuler [degœle] vi (fam) to puke, throw up

déguisement [degizmɑ̃] nm disguise; (habits: pour s'amuser) fancy dress; (: pour tromper) disguise

déguiser [degize] vt to disguise; **se déguiser (en)** vi (se costumer) to dress up (as); (pour tromper) to disguise o.s. (as)

dégustation [degystasjɔ̃] nf tasting; (de fromages etc) sampling; savouring (Brit), savoring (US); (séance): **~ de vin(s)** wine-tasting

déguster [degyste] vt (vins) to taste; (fromages etc) to sample; (savourer) to enjoy, savour (Brit), savor (US)

dehors [dəɔʀ] adv outside; (en plein air) outdoors, outside ▷ nm outside ▷ nmpl (apparences) appearances, exterior sg; **mettre ou jeter ~** to throw out; **au ~** outside; (en apparence) outwardly; **au ~ de** outside; **de ~** from outside; **en ~** outside; outwards; **en ~ de** apart from

déjà [deʒa] adv already; (auparavant) before, already; **as-tu ~ été en France?** have you been to France before?; **c'est ~ pas mal** that's not too bad (at all); **c'est ~ quelque chose** (at least) it's better than nothing; **quel nom, ~?** what was the name again?

déjeuner [deʒœne] vi to (have) lunch; (le matin) to have breakfast ▷ nm lunch; (petit déjeuner) breakfast; **~ d'affaires** business lunch

déjouer [deʒwe] vt to elude, to foil, thwart

delà [dəla] adv: **par ~**, **en ~ (de)**, **au ~ (de)** beyond

délabrer [delabʀe]: **se délabrer** vi to fall into decay, become dilapidated

délacer [delase] vt (chaussures) to undo, unlace

délai [dele] nm (attente) waiting period; (sursis) extension (of time); (temps accordé: aussi: **~s**) time limit; **sans ~** without delay; **à bref ~** shortly, very soon; at short notice; **dans les ~s** within the time limit; **un ~ de 30 jours** a period of 30 days; **comptez un ~ de livraison de 10 jours** allow 10 days for delivery

délaisser [delese] vt (abandonner) to abandon, desert; (négliger) to neglect

délasser [delase] vt (reposer) to relax; (divertir) to divert, entertain; **se délasser** vi to relax

délavé, e [delave] adj faded

délayer [deleje] vt (Culin) to mix (with water etc); (peinture) to thin down; (fig) to pad out, spin out

delco® [dɛlko] nm (Auto) distributor; **tête de ~** distributor cap

délecter [delɛkte]: **se délecter** vi: **se ~ de** to revel ou delight in

délégué, e [delege] adj delegated ▷ nm/f delegate; representative; **ministre ~ à** minister with special responsibility for

déléguer [delege] vt to delegate

délibéré, e [delibeʀe] adj (conscient) deliberate; (déterminé) determined, resolute; **de propos ~** (à dessein, exprès) intentionally

délibérer [delibeʀe] vi to deliberate

délicat, e [delika, -at] adj delicate; (plein de tact) tactful; (attentionné) thoughtful; (exigeant) fussy, particular; **procédés peu ~s** unscrupulous methods

délicatement [delikatmɑ̃] adv delicately; (avec douceur) gently

délice [delis] nm delight

délicieux, -euse [delisjø, -øz] adj (au goût) delicious; (sensation, impression) delightful

délimiter [delimite] vt (terrain) to delimit, demarcate

délinquance [delɛ̃kɑ̃s] nf criminality; **~ juvénile** juvenile delinquency

délinquant, e [delɛ̃kɑ̃, -ɑ̃t] adj, nm/f delinquent

délirant, e [deliʀɑ̃, -ɑ̃t] adj (Méd: fièvre) delirious; (imagination) frenzied; (fam: déraisonnable) crazy

délirer [deliʀe] vi to be delirious; **tu délires!** (fam) you're crazy!

délit [deli] nm (criminal) offence; **~ de droit commun** violation of common law; **~ de fuite** failure to stop after an accident; **~ d'initiés** insider dealing ou trading; **~ de presse** violation of the press laws

délivrer [delivʀe] vt (prisonnier) to (set) free, release; (passeport, certificat) to issue; **~ qn de** (ennemis) to set sb free from, deliver ou free sb from; (fig) to rid sb of

déloger [deloʒe] vt (locataire) to turn out; (objet coincé, ennemi) to dislodge

déloyal, e, -aux [delwajal, -o] adj (personne, conduite) disloyal; (procédé) unfair

deltaplane® [dɛltaplan] nm hang-glider

déluge [delyʒ] nm (biblique) Flood, Deluge; (grosse pluie) downpour, deluge; (grand nombre): **~ de** flood of

déluré, e [delyʀe] adj smart, resourceful; (péj) forward, pert

demain [d(ə)mɛ̃] adv tomorrow; **~ matin/soir** tomorrow morning/evening; **~ midi** tomorrow at midday; **à ~!** see you tomorrow!

demande [d(ə)mɑ̃d] *nf* (*requête*) request; (*revendication*) demand; (*Admin, formulaire*) application; (*Écon*): **la ~** demand; **"~s d'emploi"** "situations wanted"; **à la ~ générale** by popular request; **~ en mariage** (marriage) proposal; **faire sa ~ (en mariage)** to propose (marriage); **~ de naturalisation** application for naturalization; **~ de poste** job application

demandé, e [d(ə)mɑ̃de] *adj* (*article etc*): **très ~** (very) much in demand

demander [d(ə)mɑ̃de] *vt* to ask for; (*question: date, heure, chemin*) to ask; (*requérir, nécessiter*) to require, demand; **~ qch à qn** to ask sb for sth, ask sb sth; **ils demandent deux secrétaires et un ingénieur** they're looking for two secretaries and an engineer; **~ la main de qn** to ask for sb's hand (in marriage); **~ pardon à qn** to apologize to sb; **~ à** *ou* **de voir/faire** to ask to see/ask if one can do; **~ à qn de faire** to ask sb to do; **~ que/pourquoi** to ask that/why; **se ~ si/pourquoi** *etc* to wonder if/why *etc*; (*sens purement réfléchi*) to ask o.s. if/why *etc*; **on vous demande au téléphone** you're wanted on the phone, there's someone for you on the phone; **il me demande que ça** that's all he wants; **je ne demande pas mieux** I'm asking nothing more; **il ne demande qu'à faire** all he wants is to do

demandeur, -euse [dəmɑ̃dœr, -øz] *nm/f*: **~ d'asile** asylum-seeker; **~ d'emploi** job-seeker

démangeaison [demɑ̃ʒɛzɔ̃] *nf* itching; **avoir des ~s** to be itching

démanger [demɑ̃ʒe] *vi* to itch; **la main me démange** my hand is itching; **l'envie** *ou* **ça me démange de faire** I'm itching to do

démanteler [demɑ̃tle] *vt* to break up; to demolish

démaquillant [demakijɑ̃] *nm* make-up remover

démaquiller [demakije] *vt*: **se démaquiller** to remove one's make-up

démarche [demarʃ] *nf* (*allure*) gait, walk; (*intervention*) step; approach; (*fig: intellectuelle*) thought processes *pl*; approach; **faire** *ou* **entreprendre des ~s** to take action; **faire des ~s auprès de qn** to approach sb; **faire les ~s nécessaires (pour obtenir qch)** to take the necessary steps (to obtain sth)

démarcheur, -euse [demarʃœr, -øz] *nm/f* (*Comm*) door-to-door salesman/woman; (*Pol etc*) canvasser

démarque [demark] *nf* (*Comm: d'un article*) mark-down

démarrage [demaraʒ] *nm* starting *no pl*, start; **~ en côte** hill start

démarrer [demare] *vt* to start up ▷ *vi* (*conducteur*) to start (up); (*véhicule*) to move off; (*travaux, affaire*) to get moving; (*coureur: accélérer*) to pull away

démarreur [demarœr] *nm* (*Auto*) starter

démêlant, e [demelɑ̃, -ɑ̃t] *adj*: **baume ~, crème ~e** (hair) conditioner ▷ *nm* conditioner

démêler [demele] *vt* to untangle, disentangle

démêlés [demele] *nmpl* problems

déménagement [demenaʒmɑ̃] *nm* (*du point de vue du locataire etc*) move; (: *du déménageur*) removal (Brit), moving (US); **entreprise/camion de ~** removal (Brit) *ou* moving (US) firm/van

déménager [demenaʒe] *vt* (*meubles*) to (re)move ▷ *vi* to move (house)

déménageur [demenaʒœr] *nm* removal man (Brit), (furniture) mover (US); (*entrepreneur*) furniture remover

démener [demne]: **se démener** *vi* to thrash about; (*fig*) to exert o.s.

dément, e [demɑ̃, -ɑ̃t] *vb voir* **démentir** ▷ *adj* (*fou*) mad (Brit), crazy; (*fam*) brilliant, fantastic

démentiel, le [demɑ̃sjɛl] *adj* insane

démentir [demɑ̃tir] *vt* (*nouvelle, témoin*) to refute; (*faits etc*) to belie, refute; **~ que** to deny that; **ne pas se ~** not to fail, keep up

démerder [demɛrde]: **se démerder** *vi* (*fam!*) to bloody well manage for o.s.

démesuré, e [deməzyre] *adj* immoderate, disproportionate

démettre [demɛtr] *vt*: **~ qn de** (*fonction, poste*) to dismiss sb from; **se ~ (de ses fonctions)** to resign (from) one's duties; **se ~ l'épaule** *etc* to dislocate one's shoulder *etc*

demeurant [dəmœrɑ̃]: **au ~** *adv* for all that

demeure [dəmœr] *nf* residence; **dernière ~** (*fig*) last resting place; **mettre qn en ~ de faire** to enjoin *ou* order sb to do; **à ~** *adv* permanently

demeurer [d(ə)mœre] *vi* (*habiter*) to live; (*séjourner*) to stay; (*rester*) to remain; **en ~ là** (*personne*) to leave it at that; (: *choses*) to be left at that

demi, e [dəmi] *adj* half; **et ~, trois heures/bouteilles et ~es** three and a half hours/bottles, three hours/bottles and a half ▷ *nm* (*bière: = 0.25 litre*) ≈ half-pint; (*Football*) half-back; **il est 2 heures et ~** it's half past 2; **il est midi et ~** it's half past 12; **~ de mêlée/d'ouverture** (*Rugby*) scrum/fly half; **à ~** *adv* half-; **ouvrir à ~** to half-open; **faire les choses à ~** to do things by halves; **à la ~e** (*heure*) on the half-hour

demi-cercle [dəmisɛrkl] *nm* semicircle; **en ~** *adj* semicircular ▷ *adv* in a semicircle

demi-douzaine [dəmiduzɛn] *nf* half-dozen, half a dozen

demi-finale [dəmifinal] *nf* semifinal

demi-frère [dəmifrɛr] *nm* half-brother

demi-heure [dəmijœr] *nf*: **une ~** a half-hour, half an hour

demi-journée [dəmiʒurne] *nf* half-day, half a day

demi-litre [dəmilitʀ] *nm* half-litre (*Brit*), half-liter (*US*), half a litre *ou* liter

demi-livre [dəmilivʀ] *nf* half-pound, half a pound

demi-mot [dəmimo]: **à ~** *adv* without having to spell things out

demi-pension [dəmipɑ̃sjɔ̃] *nf* half-board; **être en ~** (*Scol*) to take school meals

demi-pensionnaire [dəmipɑ̃sjɔnɛʀ] *nm/f*: **être ~** to take school lunches

demi-place [dəmiplas] *nf* half-price; (*Transports*) half-fare

démis, e [demi, -iz] *pp de* **démettre** ▷ *adj* (*épaule etc*) dislocated

demi-sel [dəmisɛl] *adj inv* slightly salted

demi-sœur [dəmisœʀ] *nf* half-sister

démission [demisjɔ̃] *nf* resignation; **donner sa ~** to give *ou* hand in one's notice, hand in one's resignation

démissionner [demisjɔne] *vi* (*de son poste*) to resign, give *ou* hand in one's notice

demi-tarif [dəmitaʀif] *nm* half-price; (*Transports*) half-fare; **voyager à ~** to travel half-fare

demi-tour [dəmituʀ] *nm* about-turn; **faire un ~** (*Mil etc*) to make an about-turn; **faire ~** to turn (and go) back; (*Auto*) to do a U-turn

démocratie [demɔkʀasi] *nf* democracy; **~ populaire/libérale** people's/liberal democracy

démocratique [demɔkʀatik] *adj* democratic

démodé, e [demɔde] *adj* old-fashioned

demoiselle [d(ə)mwazɛl] *nf* (*jeune fille*) young lady; (*célibataire*) single lady, maiden lady; **~ d'honneur** bridesmaid

démolir [demɔliʀ] *vt* to demolish; (*fig: personne*) to do for

démon [demɔ̃] *nm* demon, fiend; evil spirit; (*enfant turbulent*) devil, demon; **le ~ du jeu/des femmes** a mania for gambling/women; **le D~** the Devil

démonstration [demɔ̃stʀasjɔ̃] *nf* demonstration; (*aérienne, navale*) display

démonté, e [demɔ̃te] *adj* (*fig*) raging, wild

démonter [demɔ̃te] *vt* (*machine etc*) to take down, dismantle; (*pneu, porte*) to take off; (*cavalier*) to throw, unseat; (*fig: personne*) to disconcert; **se démonter** *vi* (*meuble*) to be dismantled, be taken to pieces; (*personne*) to lose countenance

démontrer [demɔ̃tʀe] *vt* to demonstrate, show

démordre [demɔʀdʀ] *vi* (*aussi:* **ne pas ~ de**) to refuse to give up, stick to

démouler [demule] *vt* (*gâteau*) to turn out

démuni, e [demyni] *adj* (*sans argent*) impoverished; **~ de** without, lacking in

démunir [demyniʀ] *vt*: **~ qn de** to deprive sb of; **se ~ de** to part with, give up

dénaturer [denatyʀe] *vt* (*goût*) to alter (completely); (*pensée, fait*) to distort, misrepresent

dénicher [denife] *vt* (*fam*) ▷ *vt* (*objet*) to unearth; (*restaurant etc*) to discover

dénier [denje] *vt* to deny; **~ qch à qn** to deny sb sth

dénigrer [denigʀe] *vt* to denigrate, run down

dénivellation [denivelasjɔ̃] *nf*, **dénivellement** [denivɛlmɑ̃] *nm* difference in level; (*pente*) ramp; (*creux*) dip

dénombrer [denɔ̃bʀe] *vt* (*compter*) to count; (*énumérer*) to enumerate, list

dénomination [denɔminasjɔ̃] *nf* designation, appellation

dénommé, e [denɔme] *adj*: **le ~ Dupont** the man by the name of Dupont

dénoncer [denɔ̃se] *vt* to denounce; **se dénoncer** *vi* to give o.s. up, come forward

dénouement [denumɑ̃] *nm* outcome, conclusion; (*Théât*) dénouement

dénouer [denwe] *vt* to unknot, undo

dénoyauter [denwajote] *vt* to stone; **appareil à ~** stoner

denrée [dɑ̃ʀe] *nf* commodity; (*aussi:* **~ alimentaire**) food(stuff)

dense [dɑ̃s] *adj* dense

densité [dɑ̃site] *nf* denseness; (*Physique*) density

dent [dɑ̃] *nf* tooth; **avoir/garder une ~ contre qn** to have/hold a grudge against sb; **se mettre qch sous la ~** to eat sth; **être sur les ~s** to be on one's last legs; **faire ses ~s** to teethe, cut (one's) teeth; **en ~s de scie** serrated; (*irrégulier*) jagged; **avoir les ~s longues** (*fig*) to be ruthlessly ambitious; **~ de lait/sagesse** milk/wisdom tooth

dentaire [dɑ̃tɛʀ] *adj* dental; **cabinet ~** dental surgery; **école ~** dental school

dentelé, e [dɑ̃tle] *adj* jagged, indented

dentelle [dɑ̃tɛl] *nf* lace *no pl*

dentier [dɑ̃tje] *nm* denture

dentifrice [dɑ̃tifʀis] *adj, nm*: (**pâte**) **~** toothpaste; **eau ~** mouthwash

dentiste [dɑ̃tist] *nm/f* dentist

dentition [dɑ̃tisjɔ̃] *nf* teeth *pl*, dentition

dénuder [denyde] *vt* to bare; **se dénuder** (*personne*) to strip

dénué, e [denɥe] *adj*: **~ de** lacking in; (*intérêt*) devoid of

dénuement [denɥmɑ̃] *nm* destitution

déodorant [deɔdɔʀɑ̃] *nm* deodorant

déontologie [deɔ̃tɔlɔʒi] *nf* code of ethics; (*professionnelle*) (professional) code of practice

dépannage [depanaʒ] *nm*: **service/camion de ~** (*Auto*) breakdown service/truck

dépanner [depane] *vt* (*voiture, télévision*) to fix, repair; (*fig*) to bail out, help out

dépanneuse [depanøz] *nf* breakdown lorry (*Brit*), tow truck (*US*)

dépareillé, e [depaʀeje] *adj* (*collection, service*) incomplete; (*gant, volume, objet*) odd

départ [depaʀ] *nm* leaving *no pl*, departure; (*Sport*) start; (*sur un horaire*) departure; **à son ~** when he left; **au ~** (*au début*) initially, at the start; **courrier au ~** outgoing mail; **la veille de son ~** the day before he leaves/left

départager [depaʀtaʒe] *vt* to decide between

département [depaʀtəmɑ̃] *nm* department; *see note*

⬡ **DÉPARTEMENTS**
⬡
⬡ France is divided into 96 administrative
⬡ units called *départements*. These local
⬡ government divisions are headed by a
⬡ state-appointed 'préfet', and
⬡ administered by an elected 'Conseil
⬡ général'. *Départements* are usually named
⬡ after northern geographical features
⬡ such as rivers or mountain ranges.

dépassé, e [depase] *adj* superseded, outmoded; *(fig)* out of one's depth

dépasser [depase] *vt* (*véhicule, concurrent*) to overtake; *(endroit)* to pass, go past; *(somme, limite)* to exceed; *(fig: en beauté etc)* to surpass, outshine; *(être en saillie sur)* to jut out above *(ou* in front of); *(dérouter):* **cela me dépasse** it's beyond me ▷ *vi* (*Auto*) to overtake; *(jupon)* to show; **se dépasser** *vi* to excel o.s.

dépaysé, e [depeize] *adj* disoriented

dépaysement [depeizmɑ̃] *nm* disorientation; change of scenery

dépecer [depəse] *vt* (*boucher*) to joint, cut up; *(animal)* to dismember

dépêche [depɛʃ] *nf* dispatch; **~ (télégraphique)** telegram, wire

dépêcher [depeʃe] *vt* to dispatch; **se dépêcher** *vi* to hurry; **se ~ de faire qch** to hasten to *ou* be quick (in order) to do sth

dépeindre [depɛ̃dʀ] *vt* to depict

dépendance [depɑ̃dɑ̃s] *nf* (*interdépendance*) dependence *no pl*, dependency; *(bâtiment)* outbuilding

dépendre [depɑ̃dʀ] *vt* (*tableau*) to take down; **~ de** *vt* to depend on, to be dependent on; *(appartenir)* to belong to; **ça dépend** it depends

dépens [depɑ̃] *nmpl:* **aux ~ de** at the expense of

dépense [depɑ̃s] *nf* spending *no pl*, expense, expenditure *no pl*; *(fig)* consumption; *(de temps, de forces)* expenditure; **pousser qn à la ~** to make sb incur an expense; **~ physique** (physical) exertion; **~s de fonctionnement** revenue expenditure; **~s d'investissement** capital expenditure; **~s publiques** public expenditure

dépenser [depɑ̃se] *vt* to spend; *(gaz, eau)* to use; *(fig)* to expend, use up; **se dépenser** *vi* (*se fatiguer*) to exert o.s.

dépensier, -ière [depɑ̃sje, -jɛʀ] *adj:* **il est ~** he's a spendthrift

dépérir [depeʀiʀ] *vi* (*personne*) to waste away; *(plante)* to wither

dépêtrer [depetʀe] *vt:* **se ~ de** (*situation*) to extricate o.s. from

dépeupler [depœple] *vt* to depopulate; **se dépeupler** *vi* to become depopulated

dépilatoire [depilatwaʀ] *adj* depilatory, hair-removing; **crème ~** hair-removing *ou* depilatory cream

dépister [depiste] *vt* to detect; *(Méd)* to screen; *(voleur)* to track down; *(poursuivants)* to throw off the scent

dépit [depi] *nm* vexation, frustration; **en ~ de** *prép* in spite of; **en ~ du bon sens** contrary to all good sense

dépité, e [depite] *adj* vexed, frustrated

déplacé, e [deplase] *adj* (*propos*) out of place, uncalled-for; **personne ~e** displaced person

déplacement [deplasmɑ̃] *nm* moving; shifting; transfer; *(voyage)* trip, travelling *no pl* (*Brit*), traveling *no pl* (*US*); **en ~** away (on a trip); **~ d'air** displacement of air; **~ de vertèbre** slipped disc

déplacer [deplase] *vt* (*table, voiture*) to move, shift; *(employé)* to transfer, move; **se déplacer** *vi* (*objet*) to move; *(organe*) to become displaced; *(personne: bouger)* to move, walk; (*: voyager*) to travel ▷ *vt:* **se ~ une vertèbre** to slip a disc

déplaire [deplɛʀ] *vi:* **ceci me déplaît** I don't like this, I dislike this; **il cherche à nous ~** he's trying to displease us *ou* be disagreeable to us; **se ~ quelque part** to dislike it *ou* be unhappy somewhere

déplaisant, e [deplezɑ̃, -ɑ̃t] *vb voir* **déplaire** ▷ *adj* disagreeable, unpleasant

dépliant [deplijɑ̃] *nm* leaflet

déplier [deplije] *vt* to unfold; **se déplier** *vi* (*parachute*) to open

déplorer [deplɔʀe] *vt* (*regretter*) to deplore; *(pleurer sur*) to lament

déployer [deplwaje] *vt* (*table*) to open out, spread; *(Mil)* to deploy; *(montrer)* to display, exhibit

déporter [depɔʀte] *vt* (*Pol*) to deport; *(dévier)* to carry off course; **se déporter** *vi* (*voiture*) to swerve

déposer [depoze] *vt* (*gén: mettre, poser*) to lay down, put down, set down; *(à la banque, à la consigne*) to deposit; *(caution*) to put down; *(passager*) to drop (off), set down; *(démonter: serrure, moteur*) to take out; (*: rideau*) to take down; *(roi*) to depose; *(Admin: faire enregistrer*) to file; *(marque*) to register; *(plainte*) to lodge ▷ *vi* to form a sediment *ou* deposit; *(Jur):* **~ (contre)** to testify *ou* give evidence (against); **se déposer** *vi* to settle; **~ son bilan** (*Comm*) to go into (voluntary) liquidation

dépositaire [depoziteʀ] *nm/f* (*Jur*) depository; *(Comm)* agent; **~ agréé** authorized agent

déposition [depozisjɔ̃] *nf* (*Jur*) deposition, statement

dépôt [depo] *nm* (*à la banque, sédiment*) deposit; *(entrepôt, réserve*) warehouse, store; *(gare*) depot; *(prison*) cells *pl*; **~ d'ordures** rubbish

(Brit) ou garbage (US) dump, tip (Brit); ~ **de bilan** (voluntary) liquidation; ~ **légal** registration of copyright

dépotoir [depɔtwaʀ] nm dumping ground, rubbish (Brit) ou garbage (US) dump; ~ **nucléaire** nuclear (waste) dump

dépouiller [depuje] vt (animal) to skin; (spolier) to deprive of one's possessions; (documents) to go through, peruse; ~ **qn/qch de** to strip sb/sth of; ~ **le scrutin** to count the votes

dépourvu, e [depuʀvy] adj: ~ **de** lacking in, without; **au** ~ adv: **prendre qn au** ~ to catch sb unawares

déprécier [depʀesje] vt to reduce the value of; **se déprécier** vi to depreciate

dépression [depʀesjɔ̃] nf depression; ~ **(nerveuse)** (nervous) breakdown

déprimant, e [depʀimɑ̃, -ɑ̃t] adj depressing

déprimer [depʀime] vt to depress

 MOT-CLÉ

depuis [dəpɥi] prép **1** (point de départ dans le temps) since; **il habite Paris depuis 1983/l'an dernier** he has been living in Paris since 1983/last year; **depuis quand?** since when?; **depuis quand le connaissez-vous?** how long have you known him?; **depuis lors** since then

2 (temps écoulé) for; **il habite Paris depuis cinq ans** he has been living in Paris for five years; **je le connais depuis trois ans** I've known him for three years; **depuis combien de temps êtes-vous ici?** how long have you been here?

3 (lieu): **il a plu depuis Metz** it's been raining since Metz; **elle a téléphoné depuis Valence** she rang from Valence

4 (quantité, rang) from; **depuis les plus petits jusqu'aux plus grands** from the youngest to the oldest

▷ adv (temps) since (then); **je ne lui ai pas parlé depuis** I haven't spoken to him since (then); **depuis que** conj (ever) since; **depuis qu'il m'a dit ça** (ever) since he said that to me

député, e [depyte] nm/f (Pol) deputy, ≈ Member of Parliament (Brit), ≈ Congressman/woman (US)

députer [depyte] vt to delegate; ~ **qn auprès de** to send sb (as a representative) to

déraciner [deʀasine] vt to uproot

dérailler [deʀaje] vi (train) to be derailed, go off ou jump the rails; (fam) to be completely off the track; **faire** ~ to derail

déraisonner [deʀɛzɔne] vi to talk nonsense, rave

dérangement [deʀɑ̃ʒmɑ̃] nm (gêne, déplacement) trouble; (gastrique etc) disorder; (mécanique) breakdown; **en** ~ (téléphone) out of order

déranger [deʀɑ̃ʒe] vt (personne) to trouble, bother, disturb; (projets) to disrupt, upset; (objets, vêtements) to disarrange; **se déranger** to put o.s. out; (se déplacer) to (take the trouble to) come (ou go) out; **surtout ne vous dérangez pas pour moi** please don't put yourself out on my account; **est-ce que cela vous dérange si …?** do you mind if …?; **ça te dérangerait de faire …?** would you mind doing …?; **ne vous dérangez pas** don't go to any trouble; don't disturb yourself

déraper [deʀape] vi (voiture) to skid; (personne, semelles, couteau) to slip; (fig: économie etc) to go out of control

dérégler [deʀegle] vt (mécanisme) to put out of order, cause to break down; (estomac) to upset; **se dérégler** vi to break down, go wrong

dérider [deʀide] vt: **se dérider** vi to cheer up

dérision [deʀizjɔ̃] nf derision; **tourner en** ~ to deride; **par** ~ in mockery

dérisoire [deʀizwaʀ] adj derisory

dérive [deʀiv] nf (de dériveur) centre-board; **aller à la** ~ (Navig, fig) to drift; ~ **des continents** (Géo) continental drift

dérivé, e [deʀive] adj derived ▷ nm (Ling) derivative; (Tech) by-product ▷ nf (Math) derivative

dériver [deʀive] vt (Math) to derive; (cours d'eau etc) to divert ▷ vi (bateau) to drift; ~ **de** to derive from

dermatologue [dɛʀmatɔlɔg] nm/f dermatologist

dernier, -ière [dɛʀnje, -jɛʀ] adj (dans le temps, l'espace) last; (le plus récent: gén avant n) latest, last; (final, ultime: effort) final; (échelon, grade) top, highest ▷ nm (étage) top floor; **lundi/le mois** ~ last Monday/month; **du** ~ **chic** extremely smart; **le** ~ **cri** the last word (in fashion); **les** ~**s honneurs** the last tribute; **le** ~ **soupir, rendre le** ~ **soupir** to breathe one's last; **en** ~ adv last; **ce** ~, **cette dernière** the latter

dernièrement [dɛʀnjɛʀmɑ̃] adv recently

dérobé, e [deʀɔbe] adj (porte) secret, hidden; **à la** ~**e** surreptitiously

dérober [deʀɔbe] vt to steal; (cacher): ~ **qch à (la vue de) qn** to conceal ou hide sth from sb('s view); **se dérober** vi (s'esquiver) to slip away; (fig) to shy away; **se** ~ **sous** (s'effondrer) to give way beneath; **se** ~ **à** (justice, regards) to hide from; (obligation) to shirk

dérogation [deʀɔgasjɔ̃] nf (special) dispensation

déroger [deʀɔʒe]: ~ **à** vt to go against, depart from

dérouiller [deʀuje] vt: **se** ~ **les jambes** to stretch one's legs (fig)

déroulement [deʀulmɑ̃] nm (d'une opération etc) progress

dérouler [deʀule] vt (ficelle) to unwind; (papier) to unroll; **se dérouler** vi to unwind;

to unroll, come unrolled; (avoir lieu) to take place; (se passer) to go; **tout s'est déroulé comme prévu** everything went as planned

dérouter [derute] vt (avion, train) to reroute, divert; (étonner) to disconcert, throw (out)

derrière [dɛʀjɛʀ] adv, prép behind ▷ nm (d'une maison) back; (postérieur) behind, bottom; **les pattes de ~** the back legs, the hind legs; **par ~** from behind; (fig) in an underhand way, behind one's back

des [de] art voir **de**

dès [dɛ] prép from; **~ que** conj as soon as; **~ à présent** here and now; **~ son retour** as soon as he was (ou is) back; **~ réception** upon receipt; **~ lors** adv from then on; **~ lors que** conj from the moment (that)

désabusé, e [dezabyze] adj disillusioned

désaccord [dezakɔʀ] nm disagreement

désaccordé, e [dezakɔʀde] adj (Mus) out of tune

désaffecté, e [dezafɛkte] adj disused

désagréable [dezagreabl] adj unpleasant, disagreeable

désagréger [dezagreʒe]: **se désagréger** vi to disintegrate, break up

désagrément [dezagremɑ̃] nm annoyance, trouble no pl

désaltérer [dezaltere] vt: **se désaltérer** to quench one's thirst; **ça désaltère** it's thirst-quenching, it quenches your thirst

désapprobateur, -trice [dezapʀɔbatœʀ, -tʀis] adj disapproving

désapprouver [dezapʀuve] vt to disapprove of

désarmant, e [dezaʀmɑ̃, -ɑ̃t] adj disarming

désarroi [dezaʀwa] nm helplessness, disarray

désastre [dezastʀ] nm disaster

désastreux, -euse [dezastʀø, -øz] adj disastrous

désavantage [dezavɑ̃taʒ] nm disadvantage; (inconvénient) drawback, disadvantage

désavantager [dezavɑ̃taʒe] vt to put at a disadvantage

descendre [desɑ̃dʀ] vt (escalier, montagne) to go (ou come) down; (valise, paquet) to take ou get down; (étagère etc) to lower; (fam: abattre) to shoot down; (:boire) to knock back ▷ vi to go (ou come) down; (passager: s'arrêter) to get out, alight; (niveau, température) to go ou come down, fall, drop; (marée) to go out; **~ à pied/ en voiture** to walk/drive down, go down on foot/by car; **~ de** (famille) to be descended from; **~ du train** to get out of ou off the train; **~ d'un arbre** to climb down from a tree; **~ de cheval** to dismount, get off one's horse; **~ à l'hôtel** to stay at a hotel; **~ dans la rue** (manifester) to take to the streets; **~ en ville** to go into town, go down town

descente [desɑ̃t] nf descent, going down; (chemin) way down; (Ski) downhill (race); **au milieu de la ~** halfway down; **freinez dans les ~s** use the brakes going downhill; **~ de lit** bedside rug; **~ (de police)** (police) raid

description [dɛskʀipsjɔ̃] nf description

désemparé, e [dezɑ̃paʀe] adj bewildered, distraught; (bateau, avion) crippled

désemplir [dezɑ̃pliʀ] vi: **ne pas ~** to be always full

déséquilibre [dezekilibʀ] nm (position): **être en ~** to be unsteady; (fig: des forces, du budget) imbalance; (Psych) unbalance

déséquilibré, e [dezekilibʀe] nm/f (Psych) unbalanced person

déséquilibrer [dezekilibʀe] vt to throw off balance

désert, e [dezɛʀ, -ɛʀt] adj deserted ▷ nm desert

déserter [dezɛʀte] vi, vt to desert

désertique [dezɛʀtik] adj desert cpd; (inculte) barren, empty

désespéré, e [dezɛspeʀe] adj desperate; (regard) despairing; **état ~** (Méd) hopeless condition

désespérer [dezɛspeʀe] vt to drive to despair; **se désespérer** vi to despair; **~ de** to despair of

désespoir [dezɛspwaʀ] nm despair; **être ou faire le ~ de qn** to be the despair of sb; **en ~ de cause** in desperation

déshabiller [dezabije] vt to undress; **se déshabiller** vi to undress (o.s.)

déshérité, e [dezeʀite] adj disinherited ▷ nm/f: **les ~s** (pauvres) the underprivileged, the deprived

déshériter [dezeʀite] vt to disinherit

déshonneur [dezɔnœʀ] nm dishonour (Brit), dishonor (US), disgrace

déshydraté, e [dezidʀate] adj dehydrated

desiderata [deziderata] nmpl requirements

désigner [dezine] vt (montrer) to point out, indicate; (dénommer) to denote, refer to; (nommer: candidat etc) to name, appoint

désinfectant, e [dezɛ̃fɛktɑ̃, -ɑ̃t] adj, nm disinfectant

désinfecter [dezɛ̃fɛkte] vt to disinfect

désintégrer [dezɛ̃tegʀe] vt to break up; **se désintégrer** vi to disintegrate

désintéressé, e [dezɛ̃teʀese] adj (généreux, bénévole) disinterested, unselfish

désintéresser [dezɛ̃teʀese] vt: **se désintéresser (de)** to lose interest (in)

désintoxication [dezɛ̃tɔksikasjɔ̃] nf treatment for alcoholism (ou drug addiction); **faire une cure de ~** to have ou undergo treatment for alcoholism (ou drug addiction)

désinvolte [dezɛ̃vɔlt] adj casual, off-hand

désinvolture [dezɛ̃vɔltyʀ] nf casualness

désir [deziʀ] nm wish; (fort, sensuel) desire

désirer [deziʀe] vt to want, wish for; (sexuellement) to desire; **je désire ...** (formule de politesse) I would like ...; **il désire que tu l'aides** he would like ou he wants you to help

him; **~ faire** to want *ou* wish to do; **ça laisse
à ~** it leaves something to be desired
désister [deziste]: **se désister** *vi* to stand
down, withdraw
désobéir [dezɔbeir] *vi*: **~ (à qn/qch)** to
disobey (sb/sth)
désobéissant, e [dezɔbeisɑ̃, -ɑ̃t] *adj*
disobedient
désobligeant, e [dezɔbliʒɑ̃, -ɑ̃t] *adj*
disagreeable, unpleasant
désodorisant [dezɔdɔrizɑ̃] *nm* air freshener,
deodorizer
désœuvré, e [dezœvre] *adj* idle
désolé, e [dezɔle] *adj* (*paysage*) desolate; **je
suis ~** I'm sorry
désoler [dezɔle] *vt* to distress, grieve; **se
désoler** *vi* to be upset
désopilant, e [dezɔpilɑ̃, -ɑ̃t] *adj* screamingly
funny, hilarious
désordonné, e [dezɔrdɔne] *adj* untidy,
disorderly
désordre [dezɔrdr] *nm* disorder(liness),
untidiness; (*anarchie*) disorder; **désordres**
nmpl (Pol) disturbances, disorder *sg*; **en ~** in a
mess, untidy
désorienté, e [dezɔrjɑ̃te] *adj* disorientated;
(*fig*) bewildered
désormais [dezɔrmɛ] *adv* in future, from
now on
désosser [dezɔse] *vt* to bone
desquels, desquelles [dekɛl] *prép + pron voir*
lequel
desséché, e [deseʃe] *adj* dried up
dessécher [deseʃe] *vt* (*terre, plante*) to dry out,
parch; (*peau*) to dry out; (*volontairement:
aliments etc*) to dry, dehydrate; (*fig: cœur*) to
harden; **se dessécher** *vi* to dry out; (*peau,
lèvres*) to go dry
dessein [desɛ̃] *nm* design; **dans le ~ de** with
the intention of; **à ~** intentionally,
deliberately
desserrer [desere] *vt* to loosen; (*frein*) to
release; (*poing, dents*) to unclench; (*objets
alignés*) to space out; **ne pas ~ les dents** not to
open one's mouth
dessert [desɛr] *vb voir* **desservir** ▷ *nm*
dessert, pudding
desserte [desɛrt] *nf* (*table*) side table;
(*transport*): **la ~ du village est assurée par
autocar** there is a coach service to the
village; **chemin** *ou* **voie de ~** service road
desservir [desɛrvir] *vt* (*ville, quartier*) to serve;
(: *voie de communication*) to lead into; (*vicaire:
paroisse*) to serve; (*nuire à: personne*) to do a
disservice to; (*débarrasser*): **~ (la table)** to clear
the table
dessin [desɛ̃] *nm* (*œuvre, art*) drawing; (*motif*)
pattern, design; (*contour*) (out)line; **le ~
industriel** draughtsmanship (Brit),
draftsmanship (US); **~ animé** cartoon (film);
~ humoristique cartoon
dessinateur, -trice [desinatœr, -tris] *nm/f*

drawer; (*de bandes dessinées*) cartoonist;
(*industriel*) draughtsman (Brit), draftsman
(US); **dessinatrice de mode** fashion
designer
dessiner [desine] *vt* to draw; (*concevoir:
carrosserie, maison*) to design; (*robe: taille*) to
show off; **se dessiner** *vi* (*forme*) to be
outlined; (*fig: solution*) to emerge
dessous [d(ə)su] *adv* underneath, beneath
▷ *nm* underside; (*étage inférieur*): **les voisins
du ~** the downstairs neighbours ▷ *nmpl* (*sous-
vêtements*) underwear *sg*; (*fig*) hidden aspects;
en ~ underneath; below; (*fig: en catimini*) slyly,
on the sly; **par ~** underneath; below; **de ~ le
lit** from under the bed; **au-~** *adv* below; **au-~
de** *prép* below; (*peu digne de*) beneath; **au-~ de
tout** the (absolute) limit; **avoir le ~** to get the
worst of it
dessous-de-plat [dəsudpla] *nm inv* tablemat
dessus [d(ə)sy] *adv* on top; (*collé, écrit*) on it
▷ *nm* top; (*étage supérieur*): **les
voisins/l'appartement du ~** the upstairs
neighbours/flat; **en ~** above; **par ~** *adv* over it
▷ *prép* over; **au-~** above; **au-~ de** above; **avoir/
prendre le ~** to have/get the upper hand;
reprendre le ~ to get over it; **bras ~ bras
dessous** arm in arm; **sens ~ dessous** upside
down; *voir* **ci-**; **là-**
dessus-de-lit [dəsydli] *nm inv* bedspread
destin [dɛstɛ̃] *nm* fate; (*avenir*) destiny
destinataire [dɛstinatɛr] *nm/f* (*Postes*)
addressee; (*d'un colis*) consignee; (*d'un mandat*)
payee; **aux risques et périls du ~** at owner's
risk
destination [dɛstinasjɔ̃] *nf* (*lieu*) destination;
(*usage*) purpose; **à ~ de** (*avion etc*) bound for;
(*voyageur*) bound for, travelling to
destinée [dɛstine] *nf* fate; (*existence, avenir*)
destiny
destiner [dɛstine] *vt*: **~ qn à** (*poste, sort*) to
destine sb for; **~ qn/qch à** (*prédestiner*) to mark
sb/sth out for; **qch à** (*envisager d'affecter*) to
intend to use sth for; **~ qch à qn** (*envisager de
donner*) to intend sb to have sth, intend to
give sth to sb; (*adresser*) to intend sth for sb;
se ~ à l'enseignement to intend to become
a teacher; **être destiné à** (*sort*) to be destined
to + *verbe*; (*usage*) to be intended *ou* meant for;
(*sort*) to be in store for
destruction [dɛstryksjɔ̃] *nf* destruction
désuet, -ète [desɥɛ, -ɛt] *adj* outdated,
outmoded
détachant [detaʃɑ̃] *nm* stain remover
détachement [detaʃmɑ̃] *nm* detachment;
(*fonctionnaire, employé*): **être en ~** to be on
secondment (Brit) *ou* a posting
détacher [detaʃe] *vt* (*enlever*) to detach,
remove; (*délier*) to untie; (*Admin*): **~ qn
(auprès de *ou* à)** to post sb (to), send sb on
secondment (to) (Brit); (*Mil*) to detail;
(*vêtement: nettoyer*) to remove the stains from;
se détacher *vi* (*se séparer*) to come off; (*page*)

to come out; (*se défaire*) to come undone; (*Sport*) to pull ou break away; (*se délier: chien, prisonnier*) to break loose; **se ~ sur** to stand out against; **se ~ de** (*se désintéresser*) to grow away from

détail [detaj] *nm* detail; (*Comm*) **le ~** retail; **prix de ~** retail price; **au ~** *adv* (*Comm*) retail; (: *individuellement*) separately; **donner le ~ de** to give a detailed account of; (*compte*) to give a breakdown of; **en ~** in detail

détaillant, e [detajɑ̃, -ɑ̃t] *nm/f* retailer

détaillé, e [detaje] *adj* (*récit, plan, explications*) detailed; (*facture*) itemized

détailler [detaje] *vt* (*Comm*) to sell retail; to sell separately; (*expliquer*) to explain in detail; to detail; (*examiner*) to look over, examine

détaler [detale] *vi* (*lapin*) to scamper off; (*fam: personne*) to make off, scarper (*fam*)

détartrant [detartrɑ̃] *nm* descaling agent (*Brit*), scale remover

détaxer [detakse] *vt* (*réduire*) to reduce the tax on; (*ôter*) to remove the tax on

détecter [detɛkte] *vt* to detect

détective [detɛktiv] *nm* detective; **~ (privé)** private detective ou investigator

déteindre [detɛ̃dʀ] *vi* to fade; (*au lavage*) to run; **~ sur** (*vêtement*) to run into; (*fig*) to rub off on

détendre [detɑ̃dʀ] *vt* (*fil*) to slacken, loosen; (*personne, atmosphère, corps, esprit*) to relax; (: *situation*) to relieve; **se détendre** *vi* (*ressort*) to lose its tension; (*personne*) to relax

détenir [det(ə)niʀ] *vt* (*fortune, objet, secret*) to be in possession of; (*prisonnier*) to detain; (*record*) to hold; **~ le pouvoir** to be in power

détente [detɑ̃t] *nf* relaxation; (*Pol*) détente; (*d'une arme*) trigger; (*d'un athlète qui saute*) spring

détention [detɑ̃sjɔ̃] *nf* (*de fortune, objet, secret*) possession; (*captivité*) detention; (*de record*) holding; **~ préventive** (pre-trial) custody

détenu, e [det(ə)ny] *pp de* **détenir** ▷ *nm/f* prisoner

détergent [detɛʀʒɑ̃] *nm* detergent

détériorer [deteʀjɔʀe] *vt* to damage; **se détériorer** *vi* to deteriorate

déterminé, e [detɛʀmine] *adj* (*résolu*) determined; (*précis*) specific, definite

déterminer [detɛʀmine] *vt* (*fixer*) to determine; (*décider*): **~ qn à faire** to decide sb to do; **se ~ à faire** to make up one's mind to do

déterrer [deteʀe] *vt* to dig up

détestable [detɛstabl] *adj* foul, detestable

détester [detɛste] *vt* to hate, detest

détonner [detɔne] *vi* (*Mus*) to go out of tune; (*fig*) to clash

détour [detuʀ] *nm* detour; (*tournant*) bend, curve; (*fig: subterfuge*) roundabout means; **ça vaut le ~** it's worth the trip; **sans ~** (*fig*) plainly

détourné, e [detuʀne] *adj* (*sentier, chemin, moyen*) roundabout

détournement [detuʀnəmɑ̃] *nm* diversion, rerouting; **~ d'avion** hijacking; **~ (de fonds)** embezzlement ou misappropriation (of funds); **~ de mineur** corruption of a minor

détourner [detuʀne] *vt* to divert; (*avion*) to divert, reroute; (: *par la force*) to hijack; (*yeux, tête*) to turn away; (*de l'argent*) to embezzle, misappropriate; **se détourner** *vi* to turn away; **~ la conversation** to change the subject; **~ qn de son devoir** to divert sb from his duty; **~ l'attention (de qn)** to distract ou divert (sb's) attention

détracteur, -trice [detʀaktœʀ, -tʀis] *nm/f* disparager, critic

détraquer [detʀake] *vt* to put out of order; (*estomac*) to upset; **se détraquer** *vi* to go wrong

détrempé, e [detʀɑ̃pe] *adj* (*sol*) sodden, waterlogged

détresse [detʀɛs] *nf* distress; **en ~** (*avion etc*) in distress; **appel/signal de ~** distress call/signal

détriment [detʀimɑ̃] *nm*: **au ~ de** to the detriment of

détritus [detʀitys] *nmpl* rubbish *sg*, refuse *sg*, garbage *sg* (*US*)

détroit [detʀwa] *nm* strait; **le ~ de Bering** ou **Behring** the Bering Strait; **le ~ de Gibraltar** the Straits of Gibraltar; **le ~ du Bosphore** the Bosphorus; **le ~ de Magellan** the Strait of Magellan, the Magellan Strait

détromper [detʀɔ̃pe] *vt* to disabuse; **se détromper** *vi*: **détrompez-vous** don't believe it

détruire [detʀɥiʀ] *vt* to destroy; (*fig: santé, réputation*) to ruin; (*documents*) to shred

dette [dɛt] *nf* debt; **~ publique** ou **de l'État** national debt

DEUG [døg] *sigle m* = **Diplôme d'études universitaires générales** *see note*

> ### DEUG
>
> French students sit their DEUG ('diplôme d'études universitaires générales') after two years at university. They can then choose to leave university altogether, or go on to study for their 'licence'. The certificate specifies the student's major subject and may be awarded with distinction.

deuil [dœj] *nm* (*perte*) bereavement; (*période*) mourning; (*chagrin*) grief; **porter le ~** to wear mourning; **prendre le/être en ~** to go into/be in mourning

deux [dø] *num* two; **les ~** both; **ses ~ mains** both his hands, his two hands; **à ~ pas** a short distance away; **tous les ~ mois** every two months, every other month; **~ fois** twice

deuxième [døzjɛm] *num* second

deuxièmement [døzjɛmmɑ̃] *adv* secondly, in the second place

deux-pièces [døpjɛs] *nm inv* (*tailleur*) two-piece (suit); (*de bain*) two-piece (swimsuit); (*appartement*) two-roomed flat (*Brit*) *ou* apartment (US)

deux-points *nm inv* colon *sg*

deux-roues [døʀu] *nm inv* two-wheeled vehicle

devais *etc* [dəvɛ] *vb voir* **devoir**

dévaler [devale] *vt* to hurtle down

dévaliser [devalize] *vt* to rob, burgle

dévaloriser [devalɔʀize] *vt* to reduce the value of; **se dévaloriser** *vi* to depreciate

dévaluation [devaluasjɔ̃] *nf* depreciation; (*Écon: mesure*) devaluation

devancer [d(ə)vɑ̃se] *vt* to be ahead of; (*distancer*) to get ahead of; (*arriver avant*) to arrive before; (*prévenir*) to anticipate; **~ l'appel** (*Mil*) to enlist before call-up

devant [d(ə)vɑ̃] *vb voir* **devoir** ▷ *adv* in front; (*à distance: en avant*) ahead ▷ *prép* in front of; (*en avant*) ahead of; (*avec mouvement: passer*) past; (*fig*) before, in front of; (*: face à*) faced with, in the face of; (*: vu*) in view of ▷ *nm* front; **prendre les ~s** to make the first move; **de ~** (*roue, porte*) front; **les pattes de ~** the front legs, the forelegs; **par ~** (*boutonner*) at the front; (*entrer*) the front way; **par-~ notaire** in the presence of a notary; **aller au-~ de qn** to go out to meet sb; **aller au-~ de** (*désirs de qn*) to anticipate; **aller au-~ des ennuis** *ou* **difficultés** to be asking for trouble

devanture [d(ə)vɑ̃tyʀ] *nf* (*façade*) (shop) front; (*étalage*) display; (*vitrine*) (shop) window

déveine [devɛn] *nf* rotten luck *no pl*

développement [dev(ə)lɔpmɑ̃] *nm* development; **pays en voie de ~** developing countries

développer [dev(ə)lɔpe] *vt* to develop; **se développer** *vi* to develop

devenir [dəv(ə)niʀ] *vi* to become; **~ instituteur** to become a teacher; **que sont-ils devenus?** what has become of them?

dévergondé, e [devɛʀgɔ̃de] *adj* wild, shameless

déverser [devɛʀse] *vt* (*liquide*) to pour (out); (*ordures*) to tip (out); **se ~ dans** (*fleuve, mer*) to flow into

dévêtir [devetiʀ] *vt*, **se dévêtir** *vi* to undress

devez [dəve] *vb voir* **devoir**

déviation [devjasjɔ̃] *nf* deviation; (*Auto*) diversion (*Brit*), detour (US); **~ de la colonne** (**vertébrale**) curvature of the spine

devienne *etc* [dəvjɛn] *vb voir* **devenir**

dévier [devje] *vt* (*fleuve, circulation*) to divert; (*coup*) to deflect ▷ *vi* to veer (off course); (**faire**) **~** (*projectile*) to deflect; (*véhicule*) to push off course

devin [dəvɛ̃] *nm* soothsayer, seer

deviner [d(ə)vine] *vt* to guess; (*prévoir*) to foretell, foresee; (*apercevoir*) to distinguish

devinette [d(ə)vinɛt] *nf* riddle

devis [d(ə)vi] *nm* estimate, quotation; **~ descriptif/estimatif** detailed/preliminary estimate

dévisager [deviʒaʒe] *vt* to stare at

devise [dəviz] *nf* (*formule*) motto, watchword; (*Écon: monnaie*) currency; **devises** *nfpl* (*argent*) currency *sg*

deviser [dəvize] *vi* to converse

dévisser [devise] *vt* to unscrew, undo; **se dévisser** *vi* to come unscrewed

dévoiler [devwale] *vt* to unveil

devoir [d(ə)vwaʀ] *nm* duty; (*Scol*) piece of homework, homework *no pl*; (**: en classe**) exercise ▷ *vt* (*argent, respect*): **~ qch (à qn)** to owe (sb) sth; **combien est-ce que je vous dois?** how much do I owe you?; (*suivi de l'infinitif: obligation*): **il doit le faire** he has to do it, he must do it; (**: fatalité**): **cela devait arriver un jour** it was bound to happen; (**: intention**): **il doit partir demain** he is due to leave tomorrow; (**: probabilité**): **il doit être tard** it must be late; **se faire un ~ de faire qch** to make it one's duty to do sth; **~s de vacances** homework set for the holidays; **se ~ de faire qch** to be duty bound to do sth; **je devrais faire** I ought to *ou* should do; **tu n'aurais pas dû** you ought not to have *ou* shouldn't have; **comme il se doit** (*comme il faut*) as is right and proper

dévolu, e [devɔly] *adj*: **~ à** allotted to ▷ *nm*: **jeter son ~ sur** to fix one's choice on

dévorer [devɔʀe] *vt* to devour; (*feu, soucis*) to consume; **~ qn/qch des yeux** *ou* **du regard** (*fig*) to eye sb/sth intently; (**: convoitise**) to eye sb/sth greedily

dévot, e [devo, -ɔt] *adj* devout, pious ▷ *nm/f* devout person; **un faux ~** a falsely pious person

dévotion [devosjɔ̃] *nf* devoutness; **être à la ~ de qn** to be totally devoted to sb; **avoir une ~ pour qn** to worship sb

dévoué, e [devwe] *adj* devoted

dévouement [devumɑ̃] *nm* devotion, dedication

dévouer [devwe]: **se dévouer** *vi* (*se sacrifier*): **se ~ (pour)** to sacrifice o.s. (for); (*se consacrer*): **se ~ à** to devote o.s. *ou* dedicate o.s. to

dévoyé, e [devwaje] *adj* delinquent

devrai *etc* [dəvʀe] *vb voir* **devoir**

dézipper [dezipe] *vt* (*Inform*) to unzip

diabète [djabɛt] *nm* diabetes *sg*

diabétique [djabetik] *nm/f* diabetic

diable [djabl] *nm* devil; **une musique du ~** an unholy racket; **il fait une chaleur du ~** it's fiendishly hot; **avoir le ~ au corps** to be the very devil

diabolo [djabɔlo] *nm* (*jeu*) diabolo; (*boisson*) lemonade and fruit cordial; **~-(-menthe)** lemonade and mint cordial

diagnostic [djagnɔstik] *nm* diagnosis *sg*

diagnostiquer [djagnɔstike] *vt* to diagnose

diagonal, e, -aux [djagɔnal, -o] *adj, nf* diagonal; **en ~e** diagonally; **lire en ~e** (*fig*) to skim through

diagramme [djagʀam] *nm* chart, graph

dialecte [djalɛkt] *nm* dialect

dialogue [djalɔg] *nm* dialogue; **~ de sourds** dialogue of the deaf

diamant [djamɑ̃] *nm* diamond

diamètre [djamɛtʀ] *nm* diameter

diapason [djapazɔ̃] *nm* tuning fork; (*fig*): **être/se mettre au ~ (de)** to be/get in tune (with)

diaphragme [djafʀagm] *nm* (*Anat, Photo*) diaphragm; (*contraceptif*) diaphragm, cap; **ouverture du ~** (*Photo*) aperture

diapo [djapo], **diapositive** [djapozitiv] *nf* transparency, slide

diarrhée [djaʀe] *nf* diarrhoea (*Brit*), diarrhea (*US*)

dictateur [diktatœʀ] *nm* dictator

dictature [diktatyʀ] *nf* dictatorship

dictée [dikte] *nf* dictation; **prendre sous ~** to take down (*sth dictated*)

dicter [dikte] *vt* to dictate

dictionnaire [diksjɔnɛʀ] *nm* dictionary; **~ géographique** gazetteer

dicton [diktɔ̃] *nm* saying, dictum

dièse [djɛz] *nm* (*Mus*) sharp

diesel [djezɛl] *nm, adj inv* diesel

diète [djɛt] *nf* (*jeûne*) starvation diet; (*régime*) diet; **être à la ~** to be on a diet

diététique [djetetik] *nf* dietetics *sg* ⊳ *adj*: **magasin ~** health food shop (*Brit*) *ou* store (*US*)

dieu, x [djø] *nm* god; **D~** God; **le bon D~** the good Lord; **mon D~!** good heavens!

diffamation [difamasjɔ̃] *nf* slander; (*écrite*) libel; **attaquer qn en ~** to sue sb for slander (*ou* libel)

différé [difeʀe] *adj* (*Inform*): **traitement ~** batch processing; **crédit ~** deferred credit ⊳ *nm* (*TV*): **en ~** (pre-)recorded

différemment [difeʀamɑ̃] *adv* differently

différence [difeʀɑ̃s] *nf* difference; **à la ~ de** unlike

différencier [difeʀɑ̃sje] *vt* to differentiate; **se différencier** *vi* (*organisme*) to become differentiated; **se ~ de** to differentiate o.s. from; (*être différent*) to differ from

différend [difeʀɑ̃] *nm* difference (of opinion), disagreement

différent, e [difeʀɑ̃, -ɑ̃t] *adj* (*dissemblable*) different; **~ de** different from; **~s objets** different *ou* various objects; **à ~es reprises** on various occasions

différer [difeʀe] *vt* to postpone, put off ⊳ *vi*: **~ (de)** to differ (from); **~ de faire** (*tarder*) to delay doing

difficile [difisil] *adj* difficult; (*exigeant*) hard to please, difficult (to please); **faire le** *ou* **la ~** to be hard to please, be difficult

difficilement [difisilmɑ̃] *adv* (*marcher,*

s'expliquer etc) with difficulty; **~ lisible/ compréhensible** difficult *ou* hard to read/ understand

difficulté [difikylte] *nf* difficulty; **en ~** (*bateau, alpiniste*) in trouble *ou* difficulties; **avoir de la ~ à faire** to have difficulty (in) doing

difforme [difɔʀm] *adj* deformed, misshapen

diffuser [difyze] *vt* (*chaleur, bruit, lumière*) to diffuse; (*émission, musique*) to broadcast; (*nouvelle, idée*) to circulate; (*Comm: livres, journaux*) to distribute

digérer [diʒeʀe] *vt* (*personne*) to digest; (*: machine*) to process; (*fig: accepter*) to stomach, put up with

digestif, -ive [diʒestif, -iv] *adj* digestive ⊳ *nm* (after-dinner) liqueur

digestion [diʒestjɔ̃] *nf* digestion

digne [diɲ] *adj* dignified; **~ de** worthy of; **~ de foi** trustworthy

dignité [diɲite] *nf* dignity

digue [dig] *nf* dike, dyke; (*pour protéger la côte*) sea wall

dilapider [dilapide] *vt* to squander, waste; (*détourner: biens, fonds publics*) to embezzle, misappropriate

dilemme [dilem] *nm* dilemma

dilettante [diletɑ̃t] *nm/f* dilettante; **en ~** in a dilettantish way

diligence [diliʒɑ̃s] *nf* stagecoach, diligence; (*empressement*) despatch; **faire ~** to make haste

diluer [dilɥe] *vt* to dilute

diluvien, ne [dilyvjɛ̃, -ɛn] *adj*: **pluie ~ne** torrential rain

dimanche [dimɑ̃ʃ] *nm* Sunday; **le ~ des Rameaux/de Pâques** Palm/Easter Sunday; *voir aussi* **lundi**

dimension [dimɑ̃sjɔ̃] *nf* (*grandeur*) size; (*gén pl: cotes, Math: de l'espace*) dimension; (*dimensions*) dimensions

diminué, e [diminɥe] *adj* (*personne: physiquement*) run-down; (*: mentalement*) less alert

diminuer [diminɥe] *vt* to reduce, decrease; (*ardeur etc*) to lessen; (*personne: physiquement*) to undermine; (*dénigrer*) to belittle ⊳ *vi* to decrease, diminish

diminutif [diminytif] *nm* (*Ling*) diminutive; (*surnom*) pet name

diminution [diminysjɔ̃] *nf* decreasing, diminishing

dinde [dɛ̃d] *nf* turkey; (*femme stupide*) goose

dindon [dɛ̃dɔ̃] *nm* turkey

dîner [dine] *nm* dinner ⊳ *vi* to have dinner; **~ d'affaires/de famille** business/family dinner

dingue [dɛ̃g] *adj* (*fam*) crazy

dinosaure [dinɔzɔʀ] *nm* dinosaur

diplomate [diplɔmat] *adj* diplomatic ⊳ *nm* diplomat; (*fig: personne habile*) diplomatist; (*Culin: gâteau*) dessert made of sponge cake, candied fruit and custard, ≈ trifle (*Brit*)

diplomatie [diplɔmasi] nf diplomacy
diplôme [diplom] nm diploma certificate; (*examen*) (diploma) examination; **avoir des ~s** to have qualifications
diplômé, e [diplome] adj qualified
dire [diʀ] nm: **au ~ de** according to; **leurs ~s** what they say ▷ vt to say; (*secret, mensonge*) to tell; **~ l'heure/la vérité** to tell the time/the truth; **dis pardon/merci** say sorry/thank you; **~ qch à qn** to tell sb sth; **~ à qn qu'il fasse** ou **de faire** to tell sb to do; **~ que** to say that; **on dit que** they say that; **comme on dit** as they say; **on dirait que** it looks (ou sounds *etc*) as though; **on dirait du vin** you'd ou one would think it was wine; **que dites-vous de** (*penser*) what do you think of; **si cela lui dit** if he feels like it, if he fancies it; **cela ne me dit rien** that doesn't appeal to me; **à vrai ~** truth to tell; **pour ainsi ~** so to speak; **cela va sans ~** that goes without saying; **dis donc!, dites donc!** (*pour attirer l'attention*) hey!; (*au fait*) by the way; **et ~ que ...** and to think that ...; **ceci** ou **cela dit** that being said; (*à ces mots*) whereupon; **c'est dit, voilà qui est dit** so that's settled; **il n'y a pas à ~** there's no getting away from it; **c'est ~ si ...** that just shows that ...; **c'est beaucoup/peu ~** that's saying a lot/not saying much; **se dire** vi (*à soi-même*) to say to oneself; (*se prétendre*) **se ~ malade** *etc* to say (that) one is ill *etc*; **ça se dit ... en anglais** that is ... in English; **ça ne se dit pas** (*impoli*) you shouldn't say that; (*pas en usage*) you don't say that; **cela ne se dit pas comme ça** you don't say it like that; **se ~ au revoir** to say goodbye (to each other)
direct, e [diʀɛkt] adj direct ▷ nm (*train*) through train; **en ~** (*émission*) live; **train/ bus ~** express train/bus
directement [diʀɛktəmɑ̃] adv directly
directeur, -trice [diʀɛktœʀ, -tʀis] nm/f (*d'entreprise*) director; (*de service*) manager/eress; (*d'école*) head(teacher) (Brit), principal (US); **comité ~** management ou steering committee; **~ général** general manager; **~ de thèse** ≈ PhD supervisor
direction [diʀɛksjɔ̃] nf (*d'entreprise*) management; conducting; supervision; (*Auto*) steering; (*sens*) direction; **sous la ~ de** (*Mus*) conducted by; **en ~ de** (*avion, train, bateau*) for; **"toutes ~s"** (*Auto*) "all routes"
dirent [diʀ] vb voir **dire**
dirigeant, e [diʀiʒɑ̃, -ɑ̃t] adj managerial; (*classes*) ruling ▷ nm/f (*d'un parti etc*) leader; (*d'entreprise*) manager, member of the management
diriger [diʀiʒe] vt (*entreprise*) to manage, run; (*véhicule*) to steer; (*orchestre*) to conduct; (*recherches, travaux*) to supervise, be in charge of; (*braquer: regard, arme*): **~ sur** (*arme*) to point ou level ou aim at; (*fig: critiques*): **~ contre** to aim at; **~ son regard sur** to look in the direction of; **se diriger** vi (*s'orienter*) to find

one's way; **se ~ vers** ou **sur** to make ou head for
dis [di], **disais** *etc* [dizɛ] vb voir **dire**
discernement [disɛʀnəmɑ̃] nm discernment, judgment
discerner [disɛʀne] vt to discern, make out
discipline [disiplin] nf discipline
discipliner [disipline] vt to discipline; (*cheveux*) to control
discontinu, e [diskɔ̃tiny] adj intermittent; (*bande: sur la route*) broken
discontinuer [diskɔ̃tinɥe] vi: **sans ~** without stopping, without a break
discordant, e [diskɔʀdɑ̃, -ɑ̃t] adj discordant; conflicting
discothèque [diskɔtɛk] nf (*disques*) record collection; (: *dans une bibliothèque*): **~ (de prêt)** record library; (*boîte de nuit*) disco(thèque)
discours [diskuʀ] nm speech; **~ direct/ indirect** (Ling) direct/indirect ou reported speech
discret, -ète [diskʀɛ, -ɛt] adj discreet; (*fig: musique, style, maquillage*) unobtrusive; (: *endroit*) quiet
discrétion [diskʀesjɔ̃] nf discretion; **à la ~ de qn** at sb's discretion; in sb's hands; **à ~** (*boisson etc*) unlimited, as much as one wants
discrimination [diskʀiminasjɔ̃] nf discrimination; **sans ~** indiscriminately
disculper [diskylpe] vt to exonerate
discussion [diskysjɔ̃] nf discussion
discutable [diskytabl] adj (*contestable*) doubtful; (*à débattre*) debatable
discuté, e [diskyte] adj controversial
discuter [diskyte] vt (*contester*) to question, dispute; (*débattre: prix*) to discuss ▷ vi to talk; (*protester*) to argue; **~ de** to discuss
dise *etc* [diz] vb voir **dire**
diseuse [dizøz] nf: **~ de bonne aventure** fortune-teller
disgracieux, -euse [disgʀasjø, -øz] adj ungainly, awkward
disjoindre [disʒwɛ̃dʀ] vt to take apart; **se disjoindre** vi to come apart
disjoncteur [disʒɔ̃ktœʀ] nm (Élec) circuit breaker
disloquer [dislɔke] vt (*membre*) to dislocate; (*chaise*) to dismantle; (*troupe*) to disperse; **se disloquer** vi (*parti, empire*) to break up; (*meuble*) to come apart; **se ~ l'épaule** to dislocate one's shoulder
disons *etc* [dizɔ̃] vb voir **dire**
disparaître [dispaʀɛtʀ] vi to disappear; (*à la vue*) to vanish, disappear; to be hidden ou concealed; (*être manquant*) to go missing, disappear; (*se perdre: traditions etc*) to die out; (*personne: mourir*) to die; **faire ~** (*objet, tache, trace*) to remove; (*personne, douleur*) to get rid of
disparition [dispaʀisjɔ̃] nf disappearance; **espèce en voie de ~** endangered species
disparu, e [dispaʀy] pp de **disparaître** ▷ nm/f missing person; (*défunt*) departed; **être porté ~** to be reported missing

dispensaire [dispɑ̃sɛʀ] nm community clinic
dispenser [dispɑ̃se] vt (donner) to lavish, bestow; (exempter): **~ qn de** to exempt sb from; **se ~ de** vt to avoid, get out of
disperser [dispɛʀse] vt to scatter; (fig: son attention) to dissipate; **se disperser** vi to scatter; (fig) to dissipate one's efforts
disponibilité [disponibilite] nf availability; (Admin): **être en ~** to be on leave of absence; **disponibilités** nfpl (Comm) liquid assets
disponible [disponibl] adj available
dispos [dispo] adj m: **(frais et) ~** fresh (as a daisy)
disposé, e [dispoze] adj (d'une certaine manière) arranged, laid-out; **bien/mal ~** (humeur) in a good/bad mood; **bien/mal ~ pour** ou **envers qn** well/badly disposed towards sb; **~ à** (prêt à) willing ou prepared to
disposer [dispoze] vt (arranger, placer) to arrange; (inciter): **~ qn à qch/faire qch** to dispose ou incline sb towards sth/to do sth ▷ vi: **vous pouvez ~** you may leave; **~ de** vt to have (at one's disposal); **se ~ à faire** to prepare to do, be about to do
dispositif [dispozitif] nm device; (fig) system, plan of action; set-up; (d'un texte de loi) operative part; **~ de sûreté** safety device
disposition [dispozisjɔ̃] nf (arrangement) arrangement, layout; (humeur) mood; (tendance) tendency; **dispositions** nfpl (mesures) steps, measures; (préparatifs) arrangements; (de loi, testament) provisions; (aptitudes) bent sg, aptitude sg; **prendre ses ~s** to make arrangements; **avoir des ~s pour la musique** etc to have a special aptitude for music etc; **à la ~ de qn** at sb's disposal; **je suis à votre ~** I am at your service
disproportionné, e [dispʀɔpɔʀsjɔne] adj disproportionate, out of all proportion
dispute [dispyt] nf quarrel, argument
disputer [dispyte] vt (match) to play; (combat) to fight; (course) to run; **se disputer** vi to quarrel, have a quarrel; (match, combat, course) to take place; **~ qch à qn** to fight with sb for ou over sth
disquaire [diskɛʀ] nm/f record dealer
disqualifier [diskalifje] vt to disqualify; **se disqualifier** vi to bring discredit on o.s.
disque [disk] nm (Mus) record; (Inform) disk, disc; (forme, pièce) disc; (Sport) discus; **~ compact** compact disc; **~ compact interactif** CD-I®; **~ dur** hard disk; **~ d'embrayage** (Auto) clutch plate; **~ laser** compact disc; **~ de stationnement** parking disc; **~ système** system disk
disquette [diskɛt] nf floppy disk, diskette
disséminer [disemine] vt to scatter; (troupes: sur un territoire) to disperse
disséquer [diseke] vt to dissect
dissertation [disɛʀtasjɔ̃] nf (Scol) essay
dissimuler [disimyle] vt to conceal; **se dissimuler** vi to conceal o.s.; to be concealed

dissipé, e [disipe] adj (indiscipliné) unruly
dissiper [disipe] vt to dissipate; (fortune) to squander, fritter away; **se dissiper** vi (brouillard) to clear, disperse; (doutes) to disappear, melt away; (élève) to become undisciplined ou unruly
dissolvant, e [disɔlvɑ̃, -ɑ̃t] vb voir **dissoudre** ▷ nm (Chimie) solvent; **~ (gras)** nail polish remover
dissonant, e [disɔnɑ̃, -ɑ̃t] adj discordant
dissoudre [disudʀ] vt, **se dissoudre** vi to dissolve
dissuader [disɥade] vt, **~ qn de faire/de qch** to dissuade sb from doing/from sth
dissuasion [disɥazjɔ̃] nf dissuasion; **force de ~** deterrent power
distance [distɑ̃s] nf distance; (fig: écart) gap; **à ~** at ou from a distance; (fig: écart) gap; **à ~** at ou from a distance; (mettre en marche, commander) by remote control; **(situé) à ~** (Inform) remote; **tenir qn à ~** to keep sb at a distance; **se tenir à ~** to keep one's distance; **à une ~ de 10 km, à 10 km de ~** 10 km away, at a distance of 10 km; **à deux ans de ~** with a gap of two years; **prendre ses ~s** to space out; **garder ses ~s** to keep one's distance; **tenir la ~** (Sport) to cover the distance, last the course; **~ focale** (Photo) focal length
distancer [distɑ̃se] vt to outdistance, leave behind
distant, e [distɑ̃, -ɑ̃t] adj (réservé) distant, aloof; (éloigné) distant, far away; **~ de** (lieu) far away ou a long way from; **de 5 km (d'un lieu)** 5 km away (from a place)
distendre [distɑ̃dʀ] vt, **se distendre** vi to distend
distillerie [distilʀi] nf distillery
distinct, e [distɛ̃(kt), distɛ̃kt] adj distinct
distinctement [distɛ̃ktəmɑ̃] adv distinctly
distinctif, -ive [distɛ̃ktif, -iv] adj distinctive
distingué, e [distɛ̃ge] adj distinguished
distinguer [distɛ̃ge] vt to distinguish; **se distinguer** vi (s'illustrer) to distinguish o.s.; (différer): **se ~ (de)** to distinguish o.s. ou be distinguished (from)
distraction [distʀaksjɔ̃] nf (manque d'attention) absent-mindedness; (oubli) lapse (in concentration ou attention); (détente) diversion, recreation; (passe-temps) distraction, entertainment
distraire [distʀɛʀ] vt (déranger) to distract; (divertir) to entertain, divert; (détourner: somme d'argent) to divert, misappropriate; **se distraire** vi to amuse ou enjoy o.s.
distrait, e [distʀɛ, -ɛt] pp de **distraire** ▷ adj absent-minded
distrayant, e [distʀɛjɑ̃, -ɑ̃t] vb voir **distraire** ▷ adj entertaining
distribuer [distʀibɥe] vt to distribute; to hand out; (Cartes) to deal (out); (courrier) to deliver
distributeur [distʀibytœʀ] nm (Auto, Comm) distributor; (automatique) (vending)

machine; **~ de billets** (*Rail*) ticket machine; (*Banque*) cash dispenser

distribution [distʀibysjɔ̃] *nf* distribution; (*postale*) delivery; (*choix d'acteurs*) casting; **circuits de ~** (*Comm*) distribution network; **~ des prix** (*Scol*) prize giving

dit, e [di, dit] *pp de* **dire** ▷ *adj* (*fixé*): **le jour ~** the arrangèd day; (*surnommé*): **X, ~ Pierrot** X, known as ou called Pierrot

dites [dit] *vb voir* **dire**

divaguer [divage] *vi* to ramble; (*malade*) to rave

divan [divɑ̃] *nm* divan

diverger [diveʀʒe] *vi* to diverge

divers, e [divɛʀ, -ɛʀs] *adj* (*varié*) diverse, varied; (*différent*) different, various; (**frais**) **~** (*Comm*) sundries, miscellaneous (expenses); **"~"** (*rubrique*) "miscellaneous"; **~es personnes** various ou several people

diversifier [diveʀsifje] *vt*, **se diversifier** *vi* to diversify

diversité [diveʀsite] *nf* diversity, variety

divertir [diveʀtiʀ] *vt* to amuse, entertain; **se divertir** *vi* to amuse ou enjoy o.s.

divertissement [diveʀtismɑ̃] *nm* entertainment; (*Mus*) divertimento, divertissement

divin, e [divɛ̃, -in] *adj* divine; (*fig: excellent*) heavenly, divine

diviser [divize] *vt* (*gén, Math*) to divide; (*morceler, subdiviser*) to divide (up), split (up); **se ~ en** to divide into; **~ par** to divide by

division [divizjɔ̃] *nf* (*gén*) division; **~ du travail** (*Écon*) division of labour

divorce [divɔʀs] *nm* divorce

divorcé, e [divɔʀse] *nm/f* divorcee

divorcer [divɔʀse] *vi* to get a divorce, get divorced; **~ de** ou **d'avec qn** to divorce sb

divulguer [divylge] *vt* to disclose, divulge

dix [di, dis, diz] *num* ten

dix-huit [dizɥit] *num* eighteen

dix-huitième [dizɥitjɛm] *num* eighteenth

dixième [dizjɛm] *num* tenth

dix-neuf [diznœf] *num* nineteen

dix-neuvième [diznœvjɛm] *num* nineteenth

dix-sept [disɛt] *num* seventeen

dix-septième [disɛtjɛm] *num* seventeenth

dizaine [dizɛn] *nf* (10) ten; (*environ 10*): **une ~ (de)** about ten, ten or so

do [do] *nm* (*note*) C; (*en chantant la gamme*) do(h)

docile [dɔsil] *adj* docile

dock [dɔk] *nm* dock; (*hangar, bâtiment*) warehouse

docker [dɔkɛʀ] *nm* docker

docteur, e [dɔktœʀ] *nm/f* doctor; **~ en médecine** doctor of medicine

doctorat [dɔktɔʀa] *nm*: **~ (d'Université)** ≈ doctorate; **~ d'État** ≈ PhD; **~ de troisième cycle** ≈ doctorate

doctoresse [dɔktɔʀɛs] *nf* lady doctor

doctrine [dɔktʀin] *nf* doctrine

document [dɔkymɑ̃] *nm* document

documentaire [dɔkymɑ̃tɛʀ] *adj, nm* documentary

documentaliste [dɔkymɑ̃talist] *nm/f* archivist; (*Presse, TV*) researcher

documentation [dɔkymɑ̃tasjɔ̃] *nf* documentation, literature; (*Presse, TV: service*) research

documenter [dɔkymɑ̃te] *vt*: **se ~ (sur)** to gather information ou material (on ou about)

dodo [dodo] *nm*: **aller faire ~** to go to beddy-byes

dodu, e [dody] *adj* plump

dogue [dɔg] *nm* mastiff

doigt [dwa] *nm* finger; **à deux ~s de** within an ace (*Brit*) ou an inch of; **un ~ de lait/ whisky** a drop of milk/whisky; **désigner** ou **montrer du ~** to point at; **au ~ et à l'œil** to the letter; **connaître qch sur le bout du ~** to know sth backwards; **mettre le ~ sur la plaie** (*fig*) to find the sensitive spot; **~ de pied** toe

doigté [dwate] *nm* (*Mus*) fingering; (*fig: habileté*) diplomacy, tact

doit *etc* [dwa] *vb voir* **devoir**

doléances [dɔleɑ̃s] *nfpl* complaints; (*réclamations*) grievances

dollar [dɔlaʀ] *nm* dollar

domaine [dɔmɛn] *nm* estate, property; (*fig*) domain, field; **tomber dans le ~ public** (*livre etc*) to be out of copyright; **dans tous les ~s** in all areas

domestique [dɔmɛstik] *adj* domestic ▷ *nm/f* servant, domestic

domestiquer [dɔmɛstike] *vt* to domesticate; (*vent, marées*) to harness

domicile [dɔmisil] *nm* home, place of residence; **à ~** at home; **élire ~ à** to take up residence in; **sans ~ fixe** of no fixed abode; **~ conjugal** marital home; **~ légal** domicile; **livrer à ~** to deliver

domicilié, e [dɔmisilje] *adj*: **être ~ à** to have one's home in ou at

dominant, e [dɔminɑ̃, -ɑ̃t] *adj* dominant; (*plus important: opinion*) predominant ▷ *nf* (*caractéristique*) dominant characteristic; (*couleur*) dominant colour

dominer [dɔmine] *vt* to dominate; (*passions etc*) to control, master; (*sujet*) to master; (*surpasser*) to outclass, surpass; (*surplomber*) to tower above, dominate ▷ *vi* to be in the dominant position; **se dominer** *vi* to control o.s.

domino [dɔmino] *nm* domino; **dominos** *nmpl* (*jeu*) dominoes *sg*

dommage [dɔmaʒ] *nm* (*préjudice*) harm, injury; (*dégâts, pertes*) damage *no pl*; **c'est ~ de faire/que** it's a shame ou pity to do/that; **quel ~!, c'est ~!** what a pity ou shame!; **~s corporels** physical injury

dommages-intérêts [dɔmaʒ(əz)ɛ̃teʀɛ] *nmpl* damages

dompter [dɔ̃(p)te] *vt* to tame

dompteur, -euse [dɔ̃tœʀ, -øz] nm/f trainer; (de lion) lion tamer

DOM-ROM [dɔmʀɔm], **DOM-TOM** [dɔmtɔm] sigle m ou mpl (= Département(s) et Régions/Territoire(s) d'outre-mer) French overseas departments and regions; see note

DOM-TOM, ROM ET COM

There are four "Départements d'outre-mer" or DOMs: Guadeloupe, Martinique, La Réunion and French Guyana. They are run in the same way as metropolitan "départements" and their inhabitants are French citizens. In administrative terms they are also "Régions", and in this regard are also referred to as "ROM" (Régions d'outre-mer).

The term "DOM-TOM" is still commonly used, but the term "Territoire d'outre-mer" has been superseded by that of "Collectivité d'outre-mer" (COM). The COMs include French Polynesia, Wallis-and-Futuna, New Caledonia and polar territories. They are independent, but each is supervised by a representative of the French government.

don [dɔ̃] nm (cadeau) gift; (charité) donation; (aptitude) gift, talent; **avoir des ~s pour** to have a gift ou talent for; **faire ~ de** to make a gift of; **~ en argent** cash donation; **elle a le ~ de m'énerver** she's got a knack of getting on my nerves

donc [dɔ̃k] conj therefore, so; (après une digression) so, then; (intensif): **voilà ~ la solution** so there's the solution; **je disais ~ que ...** as I was saying, ...; **venez ~ dîner à la maison** do come for dinner; **allons ~!** come now!; **faites ~** go ahead

donjon [dɔ̃ʒɔ̃] nm keep

donné, e [dɔne] adj (convenu: lieu, heure) given; (pas cher) very cheap; **données** nfpl (Math, Inform, gén) data; **c'est ~** it's a gift; **étant ~ que ...** given that ...

données [dɔne] nfpl data

donner [dɔne] vt to give; (vieux habits etc) to give away; (spectacle) to put on; (film) to show; **~ qch à qn** to give sb sth, give sth to sb; **~ sur** (fenêtre, chambre) to look (out) onto; **~ dans** (piège etc) to fall into; **faire ~ l'infanterie** (Mil) to send in the infantry; **~ l'heure à qn** to tell sb the time; **~ le ton** (fig) to set the tone; **~ à penser/entendre que ...** to make one think/give one to understand that ...; **ça donne soif/faim** it makes you (feel) thirsty/hungry; **se ~ à fond (à son travail)** to give one's all (to one's work); **se ~ du mal ou de la peine (pour faire qch)** to go to a lot of trouble (to do sth); **s'en ~ à cœur joie** (fam) to have a great time (of it)

dont [dɔ̃] pron relatif **1** (appartenance: objets) whose, of which; (appartenance: êtres animés) whose; **la maison dont le toit est rouge** the house the roof of which is red, the house whose roof is red; **l'homme dont je connais la sœur** the man whose sister I know **2** (parmi lesquel(le)s): **deux livres, dont l'un est ...** two books, one of which is ...; **il y avait plusieurs personnes, dont Gabrielle** there were several people, among them Gabrielle; **10 blessés, dont 2 grièvement** 10 injured, 2 of them seriously **3** (complément d'adjectif, de verbe): **le fils dont il est si fier** the son he's so proud of; **le pays dont il est originaire** the country he's from; **ce dont je parle** what I'm talking about; **la façon dont il l'a fait** the way (in which) he did it

dopage [dɔpaʒ] nm (Sport) drug use; (de cheval) doping

doré, e [dɔʀe] adj golden; (avec dorure) gilt, gilded

dorénavant [dɔʀenavɑ̃] adv from now on, henceforth

dorer [dɔʀe] vt (cadre) to gild; (faire) ~ (Culin) to brown; (: gâteau) to glaze; **se ~ au soleil** to sunbathe; **~ la pilule à qn** to sugar the pill for sb

dorloter [dɔʀlɔte] vt to pamper, cosset (Brit); **se faire ~** to be pampered ou cosseted

dormir [dɔʀmiʀ] vi to sleep; (être endormi) to be asleep; **~ à poings fermés** to sleep very soundly

dortoir [dɔʀtwaʀ] nm dormitory

dorure [dɔʀyʀ] nf gilding

dos [do] nm back; (de livre) spine; **"voir au ~"** "see over"; **robe décolletée dans le ~** low-backed dress; **de ~** from the back, from behind; **~ à ~** back to back; **sur le ~** on one's back; **à ~ de chameau** riding on a camel; **avoir bon ~** to be a good excuse; **se mettre qn à ~** to turn sb against one

dosage [dozaʒ] nm mixture

dose [doz] nf (Méd) dose; **forcer la ~** (fig) to overstep the mark

doser [doze] vt to measure out; (mélanger) to mix in the correct proportions; (fig) to expend in the right amounts ou proportions; to strike a balance between; **il faut savoir ~ ses efforts** you have to be able to pace yourself

dossard [dosaʀ] nm number (worn by competitor)

dossier [dosje] nm (renseignements, fichier) file; (enveloppe) folder, file; (de chaise) back; (Presse) feature; (Inform) folder; **un ~ scolaire** a school report; **le ~ social/monétaire** (fig) the social/financial question; **~ suspendu** suspension file

dot [dɔt] nf dowry

doter [dɔte] vt: **~ qn/qch de** to equip sb/sth with

douane [dwan] nf (poste, bureau) customs pl; (taxes) (customs) duty; **passer la ~** to go through customs; **en ~** (marchandises, entrepôt) bonded

douanier, -ière [dwanje, -jɛʀ] adj customs cpd ▷ nm customs officer

double [dubl] adj, adv double ▷ nm (2 fois plus): **le ~ (de)** twice as much (ou many) (as), double the amount (ou number) (of); (autre exemplaire) duplicate, copy; (sosie) double; (Tennis) doubles sg; **voir ~** to see double; **en ~ (exemplaire)** in duplicate; **faire ~ emploi** to be redundant; **à ~ sens** with a double meaning; **à ~ tranchant** two-edged; **~ carburateur** twin carburettor; **à ~s commandes** dual-control; **~ messieurs/ mixte** men's/mixed doubles sg; **~ toit** (de tente) fly sheet; **~ vue** second sight

double-cliquer [dubl(ə)klike] vi (Inform) to double-click

doubler [duble] vt (multiplier par 2) to double; (vêtement) to line; (dépasser) to overtake, pass; (film) to dub; (acteur) to stand in for ▷ vi to double, increase twofold; **se ~ de** to be coupled with; **~ (la classe)** (Scol) to repeat a year; **~ un cap** (Navig) to round a cape; (fig) to get over a hurdle

doublure [dublyʀ] nf lining; (Ciné) stand-in

douce [dus] adj f voir **doux**

douceâtre [dusɑtʀ] adj sickly sweet

doucement [dusmɑ̃] adv gently; (à voix basse) softly; (lentement) slowly

doucereux, -euse [dusʀø, -øz] adj (péj) sugary

douceur [dusœʀ] nf softness; sweetness; (de climat) mildness; (de quelqu'un) gentleness; **douceurs** nfpl (friandises) sweets (Brit), candy sg (US); **en ~** gently

douche [duʃ] nf shower; **douches** nfpl shower room sg; **prendre une ~** to have ou take a shower; **~ écossaise** (fig); **~ froide** (fig) let-down

doucher [duʃe] vt: **~ qn** to give sb a shower; (mouiller) to drench sb; (fig) to give sb a telling-off; **se doucher** vi to have ou take a shower

doudoune [dudun] nf padded jacket; (fam) boob

doué, e [dwe] adj gifted, talented; **~ de** endowed with; **être ~ pour** to have a gift for

douille [duj] nf (Élec) socket; (de projectile) case

douillet, te [dujɛ, -ɛt] adj cosy; (péj: à la douleur) soft

douleur [dulœʀ] nf pain; (chagrin) grief, distress; **ressentir des ~s** to feel pain; **il a eu la ~ de perdre son père** he suffered the grief of losing his father

douloureux, -euse [duluʀø, -øz] adj painful

doute [dut] nm doubt; **sans ~** adv no doubt;

(probablement) probably; **sans nul** ou **aucun ~** without (a) doubt; **hors de ~** beyond doubt; **nul ~ que** there's no doubt that; **mettre en ~** to call into question; **mettre en ~ que** to question whether

douter [dute] vt to doubt; **~ de** vt (allié, sincérité de qn) to have (one's) doubts about, doubt; (résultat, réussite) to be doubtful of; **~ que** to doubt whether ou if; **j'en doute** I have my doubts; **se ~ de qch/que** to suspect sth/that; **je m'en doutais** I suspected as much; **il ne se doutait de rien** he didn't suspect a thing

douteux, -euse [dutø, -øz] adj (incertain) doubtful; (discutable) dubious, questionable; (péj) dubious-looking

Douvres [duvʀ] n Dover

doux, douce [du, dus] adj (lisse, moelleux, pas vif: couleur, non calcaire: eau) soft; (sucré, agréable) sweet; (peu fort: moutarde etc, clément: climat) mild; (pas brusque) gentle; **en douce** (partir etc) on the quiet

douzaine [duzɛn] nf (12) dozen; (environ 12): **une ~ (de)** a dozen or so, twelve or so

douze [duz] num twelve

douzième [duzjɛm] num twelfth

doyen, ne [dwajɛ̃, -ɛn] nm/f (en âge, ancienneté) most senior member; (de faculté) dean

dragée [dʀaʒe] nf sugared almond; (Méd) (sugar-coated) pill

dragon [dʀagɔ̃] nm dragon

draguer [dʀage] vt (rivière: pour nettoyer) to dredge; (: pour trouver qch) to drag; (fam) to try and pick up, chat up (Brit) ▷ vi (fam) to try and pick sb up, chat sb up (Brit)

dramatique [dʀamatik] adj dramatic; (tragique) tragic ▷ nf (TV) (television) drama

dramaturge [dʀamatyʀʒ] nm dramatist, playwright

drame [dʀam] nm (Théât) drama; (catastrophe) drama, tragedy; **~ familial** family drama

drap [dʀa] nm (de lit) sheet; (tissu) woollen fabric; **~ de plage** beach towel

drapeau, x [dʀapo] nm flag; **sous les ~x** with the colours (Brit) ou colors (US), in the army

drap-housse (pl **draps-housses**) [dʀaus] nm fitted sheet

dresser [dʀese] vt (mettre vertical, monter: tente) to put up, erect; (fig: liste, bilan, contrat) to draw up; (animal) to train; **se dresser** vi (falaise, obstacle) to stand; (avec grandeur, menace) to tower (up); (personne) to draw o.s. up; **~ l'oreille** to prick up one's ears; **~ la table** to set ou lay the table; **~ qn contre qn d'autre** to set sb against sb else; **~ un procès-verbal** ou **une contravention à qn** to book sb

drogue [dʀɔg] nf drug; **la ~** drugs pl; **~ dure/ douce** hard/soft drugs pl

drogué, e [dʀɔge] nm/f drug addict

droguer [dʀɔge] *vt* (*victime*) to drug; (*malade*) to give drugs to; **se droguer** *vi* (*aux stupéfiants*) to take drugs; (*péj: de médicaments*) to dose o.s. up

droguerie [dʀɔgʀi] *nf* ≈ hardware shop (*Brit*) *ou* store (*US*)

droguiste [dʀɔgist] *nm* ≈ keeper (*ou* owner) of a hardware shop *ou* store

droit, e [dʀwa, dʀwat] *adj* (*non courbe*) straight; (*vertical*) upright, straight; (*fig: loyal, franc*) upright, straight(forward); (*opposé à gauche*) right, right-hand ▷ *adv* straight ▷ *nm* (*prérogative, Boxe*) right; (*taxe*) duty, tax; (*: d'inscription*) fee; (*lois, branche*): **le ~** law ▷ *nf* (*Pol*) right (wing); (*ligne*) straight line; **~ au but** *ou* **au fait/cœur** straight to the point/heart; **avoir le ~ de** to be allowed to; **avoir ~ à** to be entitled to; **être en ~ de** to have a *ou* the right to; **faire ~ à** to grant, accede to; **être dans son ~** to be within one's rights; **à bon ~** (*justement*) with good reason; **de quel ~?** by what right?; **à qui de ~** to whom it may concern; **à ~e** on the right; (*direction*) (to the) right; **à ~e de** to the right of; **de ~e, sur votre ~e** on your right; (*Pol*) right-wing; **~ d'auteur** copyright; **~s d'auteur** royalties; **avoir ~ de cité (dans)** (*fig*) to belong (to); **~ coutumier** common law; **~ de regard** right of access *ou* inspection; **~ de réponse** right to reply; **~ de visite** (*right of*) access; **~ de vote** (right to) vote; **~s d'auteur** royalties; **~s de douane** customs duties; **~s de l'homme** human rights; **~s d'inscription** enrolment *ou* registration fees

droitier, -ière [dʀwatje, -jɛʀ] *nm/f* right-handed person ▷ *adj* right-handed

droiture [dʀwatyʀ] *nf* uprightness, straightness

drôle [dʀol] *adj* (*amusant*) funny, amusing; (*bizarre*) funny, peculiar; **un ~ de ...** (*bizarre*) a strange *ou* funny ...; (*intensif*) an incredible ..., a terrific ...

drôlement [dʀolmɑ̃] *adv* funnily; peculiarly; (*très*) terribly, awfully; **il fait ~ froid** it's awfully cold

dromadaire [dʀɔmadɛʀ] *nm* dromedary

dru, e [dʀy] *adj* (*cheveux*) thick, bushy; (*pluie*) heavy ▷ *adv* (*pousser*) thickly; (*tomber*) heavily

du [dy] *art voir* **de** ▷ *prép+dét* = **de + le**

dû, due [dy] *pp de* **devoir** ▷ *adj* (*somme*) owing, owed; (*: venant à échéance*) due; (*causé par*): **dû à** due to ▷ *nm* due; (*somme*) dues *pl*

duc [dyk] *nm* duke

duchesse [dyʃɛs] *nf* duchess

dûment [dymɑ̃] *adv* duly

dune [dyn] *nf* dune

Dunkerque [dœ̃kɛʀk] *n* Dunkirk

duo [dɥo] *nm* (*Mus*) duet; (*fig: couple*) duo, pair

dupe [dyp] *nf* dupe ▷ *adj*: (**ne pas**) **être ~ de** (not) to be taken in by

duplex [dypleks] *nm* (*appartement*) split-level apartment, duplex; (*TV*): **émission en ~** link-up

duplicata [dyplikata] *nm* duplicate

duquel [dykɛl] *prép + pron voir* **lequel**

dur, e [dyʀ] *adj* (*pierre, siège, travail, problème*) hard; (*lumière, voix, climat*) harsh; (*sévère*) hard, harsh; (*cruel*) hard(-hearted); (*porte, col*) stiff; (*viande*) tough ▷ *adv* hard ▷ *nf*: **à la ~e** rough; **mener la vie ~e à qn** to give sb a hard time ▷ *nm* (*fam: meneur*) tough nut; **~ d'oreille** hard of hearing

durant [dyʀɑ̃] *prép* (*au cours de*) during; (*pendant*) for; **~ des mois, des mois ~** for months

durcir [dyʀsiʀ] *vt, vi* to harden; **se durcir** *vi* to harden

durée [dyʀe] *nf* length; (*d'une pile etc*) life; (*déroulement: des opérations etc*) duration; **pour une ~ illimitée** for an unlimited length of time; **de courte ~** (*séjour, répit*) brief, short-term; **de longue ~** (*effet*) long-term; **pile de longue ~** long-life battery

durement [dyʀmɑ̃] *adv* harshly

durer [dyʀe] *vi* to last

dureté [dyʀte] *nf* (*voir dur*) hardness; harshness; stiffness; toughness

durit® [dyʀit] *nf* (*car radiator*) hose

duvet [dyvɛ] *nm* down; (**sac de couchage en**) **~** down-filled sleeping bag

DVD *sigle m* (= *digital versatile disc*) DVD

dynamique [dinamik] *adj* dynamic

dynamisme [dinamism] *nm* dynamism

dynamite [dinamit] *nf* dynamite

dynamo [dinamo] *nf* dynamo

dyslexie [disleksi] *nf* dyslexia, word blindness

e

eau, x [o] *nf* water ▷ *nfpl* (*Méd*) waters;
prendre l'~ (*chaussure etc*) to leak, let in water;
prendre les ~x to take the waters; **faire ~** to
leak; **tomber à l'~** (*fig*) to fall through; **à l'~
de rose** slushy, sentimental; **~ bénite** holy
water; **~ de Cologne** eau de Cologne;
~ courante running water; **~ distillée**
distilled water; **~ douce** fresh water;
~ gazeuse sparkling (mineral) water;
~ de Javel bleach; **~ lourde** heavy water;
~ minérale mineral water; **~ oxygénée**
hydrogen peroxide; **~ plate** still water; **~ de
pluie** rainwater; **~ salée** salt water; **~ de
toilette** toilet water; **~x ménagères** dirty
water (*from washing up etc*); **~x territoriales**
territorial waters; **~x usées** liquid waste
eau-de-vie [odvi] (*pl* **eaux-de-vie**) *nf* brandy
eau-forte [ofɔʀt] (*pl* **eaux-fortes**) *nf* etching
ébahi, e [ebai] *adj* dumbfounded,
flabbergasted
ébattre [ebatʀ]: **s'ébattre** *vi* to frolic
ébaucher [eboʃe] *vt* to sketch out, outline;
(*fig*): **~ un sourire/geste** to give a hint of a
smile/make a slight gesture; **s'ébaucher** *vi*
to take shape
ébène [eben] *nf* ebony
ébéniste [ebenist] *nm* cabinetmaker
éberlué, e [ebɛʀlɥe] *adj* astounded,
flabbergasted
éblouir [ebluiʀ] *vt* to dazzle
éborgner [ebɔʀɲe] *vt*: **~ qn** to blind sb in
one eye

éboueur [ebwœʀ] *nm* dustman (*Brit*),
garbage man (*US*)
ébouillanter [ebujɑ̃te] *vt* to scald; (*Culin*) to
blanch; **s'ébouillanter** *vi* to scald o.s.
éboulement [ebulmɑ̃] *nm* falling rocks *pl*,
rock fall; (*amas*) heap of boulders *etc*
ébouler [ebule]: **s'ébouler** *vi* to crumble,
collapse
éboulis [ebuli] *nmpl* fallen rocks
ébouriffé, e [eburife] *adj* tousled, ruffled
ébranler [ebrɑ̃le] *vt* to shake; (*rendre instable*:
mur, santé) to weaken; **s'ébranler** *vi* (*partir*) to
move off
ébrécher [ebreʃe] *vt* to chip
ébriété [ebrijete] *nf*: **en état d'~** in a state of
intoxication
ébrouer [ebrue]: **s'ébrouer** *vi* (*souffler*) to
snort; (*s'agiter*) to shake o.s.
ébruiter [ebrɥite] *vt*, **s'ébruiter** *vi* to spread
ébullition [ebylisjɔ̃] *nf* boiling point; **en ~**
boiling; (*fig*) in an uproar
écaille [ekaj] *nf* (*de poisson*) scale; (*de coquillage*)
shell; (*matière*) tortoiseshell; (*de roc etc*) flake
écailler [ekaje] *vt* (*poisson*) to scale; (*huître*) to
open; **s'écailler** *vi* to flake *ou* peel (off)
écarlate [ekaʀlat] *adj* scarlet
écarquiller [ekaʀkije] *vt*: **~ les yeux** to stare
wide-eyed
écart [ekaʀ] *nm* gap; (*embardée*) swerve; (*saut*)
sideways leap; (*fig*) departure, deviation;
à l'~ *adv* out of the way; **à l'~ de** *prép* away
from; (*fig*) out of; **faire un ~** (*voiture*) to
swerve; **faire le grand ~** (*Danse, Gymnastique*)
to do the splits; **~ de conduite**
misdemeanour
écarté, e [ekaʀte] *adj* (*lieu*) out-of-the-way,
remote; (*ouvert*): **les jambes ~es** legs apart;
les bras ~s arms outstretched
écarter [ekaʀte] *vt* (*séparer*) to move apart,
separate; (*éloigner*) to push back, move away;
(*ouvrir*: *bras, jambes*) to spread, open; (*: rideau*)
to draw (back); (*éliminer*: *candidat, possibilité*) to
dismiss; (*Cartes*) to discard; **s'écarter** *vi* to
part; (*personne*) to move away; **s'~ de** to
wander from
écervelé, e [esɛʀvəle] *adj* scatterbrained,
featherbrained
échafaud [eʃafo] *nm* scaffold
échafaudage [eʃafodaʒ] *nm* scaffolding; (*fig*)
heap, pile
échafauder [eʃafode] *vt* (*plan*) to construct
échalote [eʃalɔt] *nf* shallot
échancrure [eʃɑ̃kryʀ] *nf* (*de robe*) scoop
neckline; (*de côte, arête rocheuse*) indentation
échange [eʃɑ̃ʒ] *nm* exchange; **en ~** in
exchange; **en ~ de** in exchange *ou* return for;
libre ~ free trade; **~ de lettres/politesses/
vues** exchange of letters/civilities/views; **~s
commerciaux** trade; **~s culturels** cultural
exchanges
échanger [eʃɑ̃ʒe] *vt*: **~ qch (contre)** to
exchange sth (for)

échangeur [eʃɑ̃ʒœʀ] nm (Auto) interchange

échantillon [eʃɑ̃tijɔ̃] nm sample

échappement [eʃapmɑ̃] nm (Auto) exhaust; ~ **libre** cutout

échapper [eʃape]: **~ à** vt (gardien) to escape (from); (punition, péril) to escape; **~ à qn** (détail, sens) to escape sb; (objet qu'on tient: aussi: **~ des mains de qn**) to slip out of sb's hands; **laisser ~** to let fall; (cri etc) to let out; **s'échapper** vi to escape; **l'~ belle** to have a narrow escape

écharde [eʃaʀd] nf splinter (of wood)

écharpe [eʃaʀp] nf scarf; (de maire) sash; (Méd) sling; **avoir le bras en ~** to have one's arm in a sling; **prendre en ~** (dans une collision) to hit sideways on

échasse [eʃas] nf stilt

échassier [eʃasje] nm wader

échauffer [eʃofe] vt (métal, moteur) to overheat; (fig: exciter) to fire, excite; **s'échauffer** vi (Sport) to warm up; (discussion) to become heated

échéance [eʃeɑ̃s] nf (d'un paiement: date) settlement date; (: somme due) financial commitment(s); (fig) deadline; **à brève/ longue ~** adj short-/long-term ▷ adv in the short/long term

échéant [eʃeɑ̃]: **le cas ~** adv if the case arises

échec [eʃɛk] nm failure; (Échecs): **~ et mat/au roi** checkmate/check; **échecs** nmpl (jeu) chess sg; **mettre en ~** to put in check; **tenir en ~** to hold in check; **faire ~ à** to foil, thwart

échelle [eʃɛl] nf ladder; (fig, d'une carte) scale; **à l'~ de** on the scale of; **sur une grande/ petite ~** on a large/small scale; **faire la courte ~ à qn** to give sb a leg up; **~ de corde** rope ladder

échelon [eʃ(ə)lɔ̃] nm (d'échelle) rung; (Admin) grade

échelonner [eʃ(ə)lɔne] vt to space out, spread out; **(versement) échelonné** (payement) by instalments

échevelé, e [eʃəvle] adj tousled, dishevelled; (fig) wild, frenzied

échine [eʃin] nf backbone, spine

échiquier [eʃikje] nm chessboard

écho [eko] nm echo; **échos** nmpl (potins) gossip sg, rumours; (Presse: rubrique) "news in brief"; **rester sans ~** (suggestion etc) to come to nothing; **se faire l'~ de** to repeat, spread about

échographie [ekɔgʀafi] nf ultrasound (scan); **passer une ~** to have a scan

échoir [eʃwaʀ] vi (dette) to fall due; (délais) to expire; **~ à** vt to fall to

échouer [eʃwe] vi to fail; (débris etc: sur la plage) to be washed up; (aboutir: personne dans un café etc) to arrive ▷ vt (bateau) to ground; **s'échouer** vi to run aground

échu, e [eʃy] pp de **échoir** ▷ adj due, mature

éclabousser [eklabuse] vt to splash; (fig) to tarnish

éclair [eklɛʀ] nm (d'orage) flash of lightning, lightning no pl; (Photo: de flash) flash; (fig) flash, spark; (gâteau) éclair

éclairage [eklɛʀaʒ] nm lighting

éclaircie [eklɛʀsi] nf bright ou sunny interval

éclaircir [eklɛʀsiʀ] vt to lighten; (fig: mystère) to clear up; (point) to clarify; (Culin) to thin (down); **s'éclaircir** vi (ciel) to brighten up, clear; (cheveux) to go thin; (situation etc) to become clearer; **s'~ la voix** to clear one's throat

éclaircissement [eklɛʀsismɑ̃] nm clearing up, clarification

éclairer [eklɛʀe] vt (lieu) to light (up); (personne: avec une lampe de poche etc) to light the way for; (fig: instruire) to enlighten; (: rendre compréhensible) to shed light on ▷ vi: **~ mal/ bien** to give a poor/good light; **s'éclairer** vi (phare, rue) to light up; (situation etc) to become clearer; **s'~ à la bougie/l'électricité** to use candlelight/have electric lighting

éclaireur, -euse [eklɛʀœʀ, -øz] nm/f (scout) (boy) scout/(girl) guide ▷ nm (Mil) scout; **partir en ~** to go off to reconnoitre

éclat [ekla] nm (de bombe, de verre) fragment; (du soleil, d'une couleur etc) brightness, brilliance; (d'une cérémonie) splendour; (scandale): **faire un ~** to cause a commotion; **action d'~** outstanding action; **voler en ~s** to shatter; **des ~s de verre** broken glass; flying glass; **~ de rire** burst ou roar of laughter; **~ de voix** shout

éclatant, e [eklatɑ̃, -ɑ̃t] adj brilliant, bright; (succès) resounding; (revanche) devastating

éclater [eklate] vi (pneu) to burst; (bombe) to explode; (guerre, épidémie) to break out; (groupe, parti) to break up; **~ de rire/en sanglots** to burst out laughing/sobbing

éclipse [eklips] vt to eclipse; **s'éclipser** vi to slip away

éclore [eklɔʀ] vi (œuf) to hatch; (fleur) to open (out)

écluse [eklyz] nf lock

écœurant, e [ekœʀɑ̃, -ɑ̃t] adj sickening; (gâteau etc) sickly

écœurer [ekœʀe] vt: **~ qn** (nourriture) to make sb feel sick; (fig: conduite, personne) to disgust sb

école [ekɔl] nf school; **aller à l'~** to go to school; **faire ~** to collect a following; **les grandes ~s** prestige university-level colleges with competitive entrance examinations; **~ maternelle** nursery school; see note; **~ primaire** primary (Brit) ou grade (US) school; **~ secondaire** secondary (Brit) ou high (US) school; **~ privée/ publique/élémentaire** private/state/ elementary school; **~ de dessin/danse/ musique** art/dancing/music school; **~ hôtelière** catering college; **~ normale (d'instituteurs) (ENI)** primary school teachers' training college; **~ normale supérieure (ENS)** grande école for training secondary school teachers; **~ de secrétariat** secretarial college

ÉCOLE MATERNELLE

Nursery school (kindergarten) (*l'école maternelle*) is publicly funded in France and, though not compulsory, is attended by most children between the ages of three and six. Statutory education begins with primary (grade) school (*l'école primaire*) and is attended by children between the ages of six and 10 or 11.

écolier, -ière [ekɔlje, -jɛʀ] *nm/f* schoolboy/girl

écologie [ekɔlɔʒi] *nf* ecology; (*sujet scolaire*) environmental studies *pl*

écologique [ekɔlɔʒik] *adj* ecological; environment-friendly

écologiste [ekɔlɔʒist] *nm/f* ecologist; environmentalist

éconduire [ekɔ̃dɥiʀ] *vt* to dismiss

économe [ekɔnɔm] *adj* thrifty ▷ *nm/f* (*de lycée etc*) bursar (Brit), treasurer (US)

économie [ekɔnɔmi] *nf* (*vertu*) economy, thrift; (*gain: d'argent, de temps etc*) saving; (*science*) economics *sg*; (*situation économique*) economy; **économies** *nfpl* (*pécule*) savings; **faire des ~s** to save up; **une ~ de temps/d'argent** a saving in time/of money; **~ dirigée** planned economy; **~ de marché** market economy

économique [ekɔnɔmik] *adj* (*avantageux*) economical; (*Écon*) economic

économiser [ekɔnɔmize] *vt, vi* to save

économiseur [ekɔnɔmizœʀ] *nm*: **~ d'écran** (Inform) screen saver

écoper [ekɔpe] *vi* to bale out; (*fig*) to cop it; **~ (de)** *vt* to get

écorce [ekɔʀs] *nf* bark; (*de fruit*) peel

écorcher [ekɔʀʃe] *vt* (*animal*) to skin; (*égratigner*) to graze; **~ une langue** to speak a language brokenly; **s'~ le genou** *etc* to scrape *ou* graze one's knee *etc*

écorchure [ekɔʀʃyʀ] *nf* graze

écossais, e [ekɔsɛ, -ɛz] *adj* Scottish, Scots; (*whisky, confiture*) Scotch; (*écharpe, tissu*) tartan ▷ *nm* (Ling) Scots; (: *gaélique*) Gaelic; (*tissu*) tartan (cloth) ▷ *nm/f*: **É~, e** Scot, Scotsman/woman; **les É~** the Scots

Écosse [ekɔs] *nf*: **l'~** Scotland

écosser [ekɔse] *vt* to shell

écoulement [ekulmɑ̃] *nm* (*de faux billets*) circulation; (*de stock*) selling

écouler [ekule] *vt* to dispose of; **s'écouler** *vi* (*eau*) to flow (out); (*foule*) to drift away; (*jours, temps*) to pass (by)

écourter [ekuʀte] *vt* to curtail, cut short

écoute [ekut] *nf* (Navig: *cordage*) sheet; (Radio, TV): **temps d'~** (listening *ou* viewing) time; **heure de grande ~** peak listening *ou* viewing time; **prendre l'~** to tune in; **rester à l'~ (de)** to stay tuned in (to); **~s téléphoniques** phone tapping *sg*

écouter [ekute] *vt* to listen to; **s'écouter** (*malade*) to be a bit of a hypochondriac; **si je m'écoutais** if I followed my instincts

écouteur [ekutœʀ] *nm* (Tél) receiver; **écouteurs** *nmpl* (*casque*) headphones, headset *sg*

écoutille [ekutij] *nf* hatch

écran [ekʀɑ̃] *nm* screen; (Inform) screen, VDU; **~ de fumée/d'eau** curtain of smoke/water; **porter à l'~** (Ciné) to adapt for the screen; **le petit ~** television, the small screen; **~ total** sunblock

écrasant, e [ekʀazɑ̃, -ɑ̃t] *adj* overwhelming

écraser [ekʀaze] *vt* to crush; (*piéton*) to run over; (Inform) to overwrite; **se faire ~** to be run over; **écrase(-toi)!** shut up!; **s'~ (au sol)** *vi* to crash; **s'~ contre** to crash into

écrémé, e [ekʀeme] *adj* (*lait*) skimmed

écrevisse [ekʀəvis] *nf* crayfish *inv*

écrier [ekʀije]: **s'écrier** *vi* to exclaim

écrin [ekʀɛ̃] *nm* case, box

écrire [ekʀiʀ] *vt, vi* to write ▷ *vi*: **ça s'écrit comment?** how is it spelt?; **~ à qn** to write and tell sb that; **s'écrire** *vi* to write to one another

écrit, e [ekʀi, -it] *pp de* **écrire** ▷ *adj*: **bien/mal ~** well/badly written ▷ *nm* document; (*examen*) written paper; **par ~** in writing

écriteau, x [ekʀito] *nm* notice, sign

écriture [ekʀityʀ] *nf* writing; (Comm) entry; **écritures** *nfpl* (Comm) accounts, books; **l'É~ (sainte), les É~s** the Scriptures

écrivain [ekʀivɛ̃] *nm* writer

écrou [ekʀu] *nm* nut

écrouer [ekʀue] *vt* to imprison; (*provisoirement*) to remand in custody

écrouler [ekʀule]: **s'écrouler** *vi* to collapse

écru, e [ekʀy] *adj* (*toile*) raw, unbleached; (*couleur*) off-white, écru

écueil [ekœj] *nm* reef; (*fig*) pitfall; stumbling block

éculé, e [ekyle] *adj* (*chaussure*) down-at-heel; (*fig: péj*) hackneyed

écume [ekym] *nf* foam; (Culin) scum; **~ de mer** meerschaum

écumer [ekyme] *vt* (Culin) to skim; (*fig*) to plunder ▷ *vi* (*mer*) to foam; (*fig*) to boil with rage

écumoire [ekymwaʀ] *nf* skimmer

écureuil [ekyʀœj] *nm* squirrel

écurie [ekyʀi] *nf* stable

écusson [ekysɔ̃] *nm* badge

écuyer, -ère [ekɥije, -ɛʀ] *nm/f* rider

eczéma [ɛgzema] *nm* eczema

édenté, e [edɑ̃te] *adj* toothless

EDF *sigle f* (= *Électricité de France*) national electricity company

édifice [edifis] *nm* building, edifice

édifier [edifje] *vt* to build, erect; (*fig*) to edify

Édimbourg [edɛ̃buʀ] *n* Edinburgh

éditer [edite] *vt* (*publier*) to publish; (: *disque*) to produce; (*préparer: texte, Inform: annuɛ er*) to edit

éditeur, -trice [editœr, -tris] nm/f publisher; editor; ~ **de textes** (Inform) text editor

édition [edisjɔ̃] nf editing no pl; (série d'exemplaires) edition; (industrie du livre): l'~ publishing; ~ **sur écran** (Inform) screen editing

édredon [edrədɔ̃] nm eiderdown, comforter (US)

éducateur, -trice [edykatœr, -tris] nm/f teacher; (en école spécialisée) instructor; ~ **spécialisé** specialist teacher

éducatif, -ive [edykatif, -iv] adj educational

éducation [edykasjɔ̃] nf education; (familiale) upbringing; (manières) (good) manners pl; **bonne/mauvaise** ~ good/bad upbringing; **sans** ~ bad-mannered, ill-bred; l'É-**(nationale)** ≈ the Department for Education; ~ **permanente** continuing education; ~ **physique** physical education

édulcorant [edylkɔrɑ̃] nm sweetener

éduquer [edyke] vt to educate; (élever) to bring up; (faculté) to train; **bien/mal éduqué** well/badly brought up

effacé, e [efase] adj (fig) retiring, unassuming

effacer [efase] vt to erase, rub out; (bande magnétique) to erase; (Inform: fichier, fiche) to delete; **s'effacer** vi (inscription etc) to wear off; (pour laisser passer) to step aside; ~ **le ventre** to pull one's stomach in

effarant, e [efarɑ̃, -ɑ̃t] adj alarming

effarer [efare] vt to alarm

effaroucher [efaruʃe] vt to frighten ou scare away; (personne) to alarm

effectif, -ive [efɛktif, -iv] adj real; effective ▷ nm (Mil) strength; (Scol) total number of pupils, size; ~**s** numbers, strength sg; (Comm) manpower sg; **réduire l'~ de** to downsize

effectivement [efɛktivmɑ̃] adv effectively; (réellement) actually, really; (en effet) indeed

effectuer [efɛktɥe] vt (opération, mission) to carry out; (déplacement, trajet) to make, complete; (mouvement) to execute, make; **s'effectuer** vi to be carried out

efféminé, e [efemine] adj effeminate

effervescent, e [efɛrvesɑ̃, -ɑ̃t] adj (cachet, boisson) effervescent; (fig) agitated, in a turmoil

effet [efɛ] nm (résultat, artifice) effect; (impression) impression; (Comm) bill; (Jur: d'une loi, d'un jugement): **avec** ~ **rétroactif** applied retrospectively; **effets** nmpl (vêtements etc) things; ~ **de style/couleur/lumière** stylistic/colour/lighting effect; ~**s de voix** dramatic effects with one's voice; **faire** ~ (médicament) to take effect; **faire de l'**~ (médicament, menace) to have an effect, be effective; (impressionner) to make an impression; **faire bon/mauvais** ~ **sur qn** to make a good/bad impression on sb; **sous l'**~ **de** under the effect of; **donner de l'**~ **à une**

balle (Tennis) to put some spin on a ball; **à cet** ~ to that end; **en** ~ indeed; ~ **(de commerce)** bill of exchange; ~ **de serre** greenhouse effect; ~**s spéciaux** (Ciné) special effects

efficace [efikas] adj (personne) efficient; (action, médicament) effective

efficacité [efikasite] nf efficiency; effectiveness

effilocher [efilɔʃe]: **s'effilocher** vi to fray

efflanqué, e [eflɑ̃ke] adj emaciated

effleurer [eflœre] vt to brush (against); (sujet) to touch upon; (idée, pensée): ~ **qn** to cross sb's mind

effluves [eflyv] nmpl exhalation(s)

effondrer [efɔ̃dre]: **s'effondrer** vi to collapse

efforcer [efɔrse]: **s'efforcer de** vt: **s'**~ **de faire** to try hard to do

effort [efɔr] nm effort; **faire un** ~ to make an effort; **faire tous ses** ~**s** to try one's hardest; **faire l'**~ **de ...** to make the effort to ...; **sans** ~ adj effortless ▷ adv effortlessly; ~ **de mémoire** attempt to remember; ~ **de volonté** effort of will

effraction [efraksjɔ̃] nf breaking-in; **s'introduire par** ~ **dans** to break into

effrayant, e [efrejɑ̃, -ɑ̃t] adj frightening, fearsome; (sens affaibli) dreadful

effrayer [efreje] vt to frighten, scare; (rebuter) to put off; **s'effrayer (de)** vi to be frightened ou scared (by)

effréné, e [efrene] adj wild

effriter [efrite]: **s'effriter** vi to crumble; (monnaie) to be eroded; (valeurs) to slacken off

effroi [efrwa] nm terror, dread no pl

effronté, e [efrɔ̃te] adj insolent

effroyable [efrwajabl] adj horrifying, appalling

effusion [efyzjɔ̃] nf effusion; **sans** ~ **de sang** without bloodshed

égal, e, -aux [egal, -o] adj (identique, ayant les mêmes droits) equal; (plan: surface) even, level; (constant: vitesse) steady; (équitable) even ▷ nm/f equal; **être** ~ **à** (prix, nombre) to be equal to; **ça m'est** ~ it's all the same to me, I don't mind; it doesn't matter to me, I don't mind; **c'est** ~, ... all the same, ...; **sans** ~ matchless, unequalled; **à l'**~ **de** (comme) just like; **d'**~ **à** ~ as equals

également [egalmɑ̃] adv equally; evenly; steadily; (aussi) too, as well

égaler [egale] vt to equal

égaliser [egalize] vt (sol, salaires) to level (out); (chances) to equalize ▷ vi (Sport) to equalize

égalité [egalite] nf equality; evenness, steadiness; (Math) identity; **être à** ~ **(de points)** to be level; ~ **de droits** equality of rights; ~ **d'humeur** evenness of temper

égard [egar] nm: ~**s** nmpl consideration sg; **à cet** ~ in this respect; **à certains** ~**s/tous** ~**s** in certain respects/all respects; **eu** ~ **à** in view of; **par** ~ **pour** out of consideration for; **sans**

~ pour without regard for; **à l'~ de** *prép* towards; (*en ce qui concerne*) concerning, as regards

égarement [egaʀmɑ̃] *nm* distraction; aberration

égarer [egaʀe] *vt* (*objet*) to mislay; (*moralement*) to lead astray; **s'égarer** *vi* to get lost, lose one's way; (*objet*) to go astray; (*fig: dans une discussion*) to wander

égayer [egeje] *vt* (*personne*) to amuse; (: *remonter*) to cheer up; (*récit, endroit*) to brighten up, liven up

églantine [eglɑ̃tin] *nf* wild *ou* dog rose

églefin [egləfɛ̃] *nm* haddock

église [egliz] *nf* church; **aller à l'~** to go to church

égoïsme [egɔism] *nm* selfishness, egoism

égoïste [egɔist] *adj* selfish, egoistic ▷ *nm/f* egoist

égorger [egɔʀʒe] *vt* to cut the throat of

égosiller [egozije]: **s'égosiller** *vi* to shout o.s. hoarse

égout [egu] *nm* sewer; **eaux d'~** sewage

égoutter [egute] *vt* (*linge*) to wring out; (*vaisselle, fromage*) to drain ▷ *vi* to drip; **s'égoutter** *vi* to drip

égouttoir [egutwaʀ] *nm* draining board; (*mobile*) draining rack

égratigner [egʀatiɲe] *vt* to scratch; **s'égratigner** *vi* to scratch o.s.

égratignure [egʀatiɲyʀ] *nf* scratch

Égypte [eʒipt] *nf*: **l'~** Egypt

égyptien, ne [eʒipsjɛ̃, -ɛn] *adj* Egyptian ▷ *nm/f*: **É-, ne** Egyptian

eh [e] *excl* hey!; **eh bien** well

éhonté, e [eɔ̃te] *adj* shameless, brazen (Brit)

éjecter [eʒɛkte] *vt* (*Tech*) to eject; (*fam*) to kick *ou* chuck out

élaborer [elabɔʀe] *vt* to elaborate; (*projet, stratégie*) to work out; (*rapport*) to draft

élan [elɑ̃] *nm* (*Zool*) elk, moose; (*Sport: avant le saut*) run up; (*de véhicule*) momentum; (*fig: de tendresse etc*) surge; **prendre son ~/de l'~** to take a run up/gather speed; **perdre son ~** to lose one's momentum

élancé, e [elɑ̃se] *adj* slender

élancement [elɑ̃smɑ̃] *nm* shooting pain

élancer [elɑ̃se]: **s'élancer** *vi* to dash, hurl o.s.; (*fig: arbre, clocher*) to soar (upwards)

élargir [elaʀʒiʀ] *vt* to widen; (*vêtement*) to let out; (*Jur*) to release; **s'élargir** *vi* to widen; (*vêtement*) to stretch

élastique [elastik] *adj* elastic ▷ *nm* (*de bureau*) rubber band; (*pour la couture*) elastic *no pl*

électeur, -trice [elɛktœʀ, -tʀis] *nm/f* elector, voter

élection [elɛksjɔ̃] *nf* election; **élections** *nfpl* (*Pol*) election(s); **sa terre/patrie d'~** the land/ country of one's choice; **~ partielle** ≈ by-election; **~s législatives/présidentielles** general/presidential election *sg*; *see note*

électorat [elɛktɔʀa] *nm* electorate

électricien, ne [elɛktʀisjɛ̃, -ɛn] *nm/f* electrician

électricité [elɛktʀisite] *nf* electricity; **allumer/éteindre l'~** to put on/off the light; **~ statique** static electricity

électrique [elɛktʀik] *adj* electric(al)

électrocuter [elɛktʀɔkyte] *vt* to electrocute

électroménager [elɛktʀomenaʒe] *adj*: **appareils ~s** domestic (electrical) appliances ▷ *nm*: **l'~** household appliances

électronique [elɛktʀonik] *adj* electronic ▷ *nf* (*science*) electronics *sg*

électrophone [elɛktʀofɔn] *nm* record player

élégance [elegɑ̃s] *nf* elegance

élégant, e [elegɑ̃, -ɑ̃t] *adj* elegant; (*solution*) neat, elegant; (*attitude, procédé*) courteous, civilized

élément [elemɑ̃] *nm* element; (*pièce*) component, part; **éléments** *nmpl* elements

élémentaire [elemɑ̃tɛʀ] *adj* elementary; (*Chimie*) elemental

éléphant [elefɑ̃] *nm* elephant; **~ de mer** elephant seal

élevage [el(ə)vaʒ] *nm* breeding; (*de bovins*) cattle breeding *ou* rearing; (*ferme*) cattle farm; **truite d'~** farmed trout

élévation [elevasjɔ̃] *nf* (*gén*) elevation; (*voir élever*) raising; (*voir s'élever*) rise

élevé, e [el(ə)ve] *adj* (*prix, sommet*) high; (*fig: noble*) elevated; **bien/mal ~** well-/ill-mannered

élève [elɛv] *nm/f* pupil; **~ infirmière** student nurse

élever [el(ə)ve] *vt* (*enfant*) to bring up, raise; (*bétail, volaille*) to breed; (*abeilles*) to keep; (*hausser: taux, niveau*) to raise; (*fig: âme, esprit*) to elevate; (*édifier: monument*) to put up, erect; **s'élever** *vi* (*avion, alpiniste*) to go up; (*niveau, température, aussi: cri etc*) to rise; (*survenir: difficultés*) to arise; **s'~ à** (*frais, dégâts*) to amount to, add up to; **s'~ contre** to rise up against; **~ la voix** to raise one's voice; **~ une protestation/critique** to raise a protest/ make a criticism; **~ qn au rang de** to raise *ou* elevate sb to the rank of; **~ un nombre au carré/au cube** to square/cube a number

éleveur, -euse [el(ə)vœʀ, -øz] *nm/f* stock breeder

élimé, e [elime] *adj* worn (thin), threadbare

éliminatoire [eliminatwaʀ] *adj* eliminatory; (*Sport*) disqualifying ▷ *nf* (*Sport*) heat

éliminer [elimine] vt to eliminate

élire [eliʀ] vt to elect; **~ domicile à** to take up residence in ou at

elle [ɛl] pron (sujet) she; (: chose) it; (complément) her; it; **~s** (sujet) they; (complément) them; **~-même** herself; itself; **~s-mêmes** themselves; voir **il**

élocution [elɔkysjɔ̃] nf delivery; **défaut d'~** speech impediment

éloge [elɔʒ] nm praise gen no pl; **faire l'~ de** to praise

élogieux, -euse [elɔʒjø, -øz] adj laudatory, full of praise

éloigné, e [elwaɲe] adj distant, far-off; (parent) distant

éloignement [elwaɲmɑ̃] nm removal; putting off; estrangement; (fig: distance) distance

éloigner [elwaɲe] vt (objet): **~ qch (de)** to move ou take sth away (from); (personne): **~ qn (de)** to take sb away ou remove sb (from); (échéance) to put off, postpone; (soupçons, danger) to ward off; **s'éloigner (de)** vi (personne) to go away (from); (véhicule) to move away (from); (affectivement) to become estranged (from)

élu, e [ely] pp de **élire** ▷ nm/f (Pol) elected representative

éluder [elyde] vt to evade

Élysée [elize] nm: **(le palais de) l'~** the Élysée palace; see note; **les Champs ~s** the Champs Élysées

émacié, e [emasje] adj emaciated

émail, -aux [emaj, -o] nm enamel

e-mail [imɛl] nm email; **envoyer qch par ~** to email sth

émaillé, e [emaje] adj enamelled; (fig): **~ de** dotted with

émanciper [emɑ̃sipe] vt to emancipate; **s'émanciper** vi (fig) to become emancipated ou liberated

émaner [emane]: **~ de** vt to emanate from; (Admin) to proceed from

emballage [ɑ̃balaʒ] nm wrapping; packing; (papier) wrapping; (carton) packaging

emballer [ɑ̃bale] vt to wrap (up); (dans un carton) to pack (up); (fig: fam) to thrill (to bits); **s'emballer** vi (moteur) to race; (cheval) to bolt; (fig: personne) to get carried away

embarcadère [ɑ̃baʀkadɛʀ] nm landing stage (Brit), pier

embarcation [ɑ̃baʀkasjɔ̃] nf (small) boat, (small) craft inv

embardée [ɑ̃baʀde] nf swerve; **faire une ~** to swerve

embarquement [ɑ̃baʀkəmɑ̃] nm embarkation; (de marchandises) loading; (de passagers) boarding

embarquer [ɑ̃baʀke] vt (personne) to embark; (marchandise) to load; (fam) to cart off; (: arrêter) to nick ▷ vi (passager) to board; (Navig) to ship water; **s'embarquer** vi to board; **s'~ dans** (affaire, aventure) to embark upon

embarras [ɑ̃baʀa] nm (obstacle) hindrance; (confusion) embarrassment; (ennuis): **être dans l'~** to be in a predicament ou an awkward position; (gêne financière) to be in difficulties; **~ gastrique** stomach upset; **vous n'avez que l'~ du choix** the only problem is choosing

embarrassant, e [ɑ̃baʀasɑ̃, -ɑ̃t] adj cumbersome; embarrassing; awkward

embarrasser [ɑ̃baʀase] vt (encombrer) to clutter (up); (gêner) to hinder, hamper; (fig) to cause embarrassment; to put in an awkward position; **s'embarrasser de** vi to burden o.s. with

embauche [ɑ̃boʃ] nf hiring; **bureau d'~** labour office

embaucher [ɑ̃boʃe] vt to take on, hire; **s'embaucher comme** vi to get (o.s.) a job as

embaumer [ɑ̃bome] vt to embalm; (parfumer) to fill with its fragrance; **~ la lavande** to be fragrant with (the scent of) lavender

embellie [ɑ̃beli] nf bright spell, brighter period

embellir [ɑ̃beliʀ] vt to make more attractive; (une histoire) to embellish ▷ vi to grow lovelier ou more attractive

embêtant, e [ɑ̃bɛtɑ̃, -ɑ̃t] adj annoying

embêtement [ɑ̃bɛtmɑ̃] nm problem, difficulty; **embêtements** nmpl trouble sg

embêter [ɑ̃bɛte] vt to bother; **s'embêter** vi (s'ennuyer) to be bored; **ça m'embête** it bothers me; **il ne s'embête pas!** (ironique) he does all right for himself!

emblée [ɑ̃ble]: **d'~** adv straightaway

embobiner [ɑ̃bɔbine] vt (enjôler): **~ qn** to get round sb

emboîter [ɑ̃bwate] vt to fit together; **s'emboîter dans** to fit into; **s'~ (l'un dans l'autre)** to fit together; **~ le pas à qn** to follow in sb's footsteps

embonpoint [ɑ̃bɔ̃pwɛ̃] nm stoutness (Brit), corpulence; **prendre de l'~** to grow stout (Brit) ou corpulent

embouchure [ɑ̃buʃyʀ] nf (Géo) mouth; (Mus) mouthpiece

embourber [ɑ̃buʀbe]: **s'embourber** vi to get stuck in the mud; (fig): **s'~ dans** to sink into

embourgeoiser [ɑ̃buʀʒwaze]: **s'embourgeoiser** vi to adopt a middle-class outlook

embouteillage [ābutɛjaʒ] *nm* traffic jam, (traffic) holdup (Brit)

emboutir [ābutiʀ] *vt* (Tech) to stamp; (heurter) to crash into, ram

embranchement [ābʀɑ̃ʃmɑ̃] *nm* (routier) junction; (classification) branch

embraser [ābʀaze]: **s'embraser** *vi* to flare up

embrasser [ābʀase] *vt* to kiss; (sujet, période) to embrace, encompass; (carrière) to embark on; (métier) to go in for, take up; **~ du regard** to take in (with eyes); **s'embrasser** *vi* to kiss (each other)

embrasure [ābʀazyʀ] *nf*: **dans l'~ de la porte** in the door(way)

embrayage [ābʀɛjaʒ] *nm* clutch

embrayer [ābʀeje] *vi* (Auto) to let in the clutch ▷ *vt* (fig: affaire) to set in motion; **~ sur qch** to begin on sth

embrocher [ābʀɔʃe] *vt* to (put on a) spit (ou skewer)

embrouiller [ābʀuje] *vt* (fils) to tangle (up); (fiches, idées, personne) to muddle up; **s'embrouiller** *vi* to get in a muddle

embruns [ābʀœ̃] *nmpl* sea spray *sg*

embryon [ābʀijɔ̃] *nm* embryo

embûches [ābyʃ] *nfpl* pitfalls, traps

embué, e [ābɥe] *adj* misted up; **yeux ~s de larmes** eyes misty with tears

embuscade [ābyskad] *nf* ambush; **tendre une ~ à** to lay an ambush for

éméché, e [emeʃe] *adj* tipsy, merry

émeraude [em(ə)ʀod] *nf* emerald ▷ *adj inv* emerald-green

émerger [emɛʀʒe] *vi* to emerge; (faire saillie, aussi fig) to stand out

émeri [em(ə)ʀi] *nm*: **toile** *ou* **papier ~** emery paper

émerveillement [emɛʀvejmɑ̃] *nm* wonderment

émerveiller [emɛʀveje] *vt* to fill with wonder; **s'émerveiller de** to marvel at

émettre [emɛtʀ] *vt* (son, lumière) to give out, emit; (message etc: Radio) to transmit; (billet, timbre, emprunt, chèque) to issue; (hypothèse, avis) to voice, put forward; (vœu) to express ▷ *vi* to broadcast; **~ sur ondes courtes** to broadcast on short wave

émeus etc [emø] *vb* voir **émouvoir**

émeute [emøt] *nf* riot

émietter [emjete] *vt* (pain, terre) to crumble; (fig) to split up, disperse; **s'émietter** *vi* (pain, terre) to crumble

émigrer [emigʀe] *vi* to emigrate

émincer [emɛ̃se] *vt* (Culin) to slice thinly

éminent, e [eminɑ̃, -ɑ̃t] *adj* distinguished

émission [emisjɔ̃] *nf* (voir émettre) emission; (d'un message) transmission; (de billet, timbre, emprunt, chèque) issue; (Radio, TV) programme, broadcast

emmagasiner [āmagazine] *vt* to (put into) store; (fig) to store up

emmanchure [āmɑ̃ʃyʀ] *nf* armhole

emmêler [āmele] *vt* to tangle (up); (fig) to muddle up; **s'emmêler** *vi* to get into a tangle

emménager [āmenaʒe] *vi* to move in; **~ dans** to move into

emmener [ām(ə)ne] *vt* to take (with one); (comme otage, capture) to take away; **~ qn au cinéma** to take sb to the cinema

emmerder [āmɛʀde] (fam!) *vt* to bug, bother; **s'emmerder** *vi* (s'ennuyer) to be bored stiff; **je t'emmerde!** to hell with you!

emmitoufler [āmitufle] *vt* to wrap up (warmly); **s'emmitoufler** *vi* to wrap (o.s.) up (warmly)

émoi [emwa] *nm* (agitation, effervescence) commotion; (trouble) agitation; **en ~** (sens) excited, stirred

émoticone [emɔticon] *nm* (Inform) smiley

émotif, -ive [emɔtif, -iv] *adj* emotional

émotion [emosjɔ̃] *nf* emotion; **avoir des ~s** (fig) to get a fright; **donner des ~s à** to give a fright to; **sans ~** without emotion, coldly

émousser [emuse] *vt* to blunt; (fig) to dull

émouvoir [emuvwaʀ] *vt* (troubler) to stir, affect; (toucher, attendrir) to move; (indigner) to rouse; (effrayer) to disturb, worry; **s'émouvoir** *vi* to be affected; to be moved; to be roused; to be disturbed *ou* worried

empailler [āpaje] *vt* to stuff

empaqueter [āpakte] *vt* to pack up

emparer [āpaʀe]: **s'emparer de** *vt* (objet) to seize, grab; (comme otage, Mil) to seize; (peur etc) to take hold of

empâter [āpate]: **s'empâter** *vi* to thicken out

empêchement [āpɛʃmɑ̃] *nm* (unexpected) obstacle, hitch

empêcher [āpeʃe] *vt* to prevent; **~ qn de faire** to prevent *ou* stop sb (from) doing; **~ que qch (n')arrive/qn (ne) fasse** to prevent sth from happening/sb doing; **il n'empêche que** nevertheless, be that as it may; **il n'a pas pu s'~ de rire** he couldn't help laughing

empereur [āpʀœʀ] *nm* emperor

empester [āpeste] *vt* (lieu) to stink out ▷ *vi* to stink, reek; **~ le tabac/le vin** to stink *ou* reek of tobacco/wine

empêtrer [āpetʀe] *vt*: **s'empêtrer dans** (fils etc, aussi fig) to get tangled up in

emphase [āfaz] *nf* pomposity, bombast; **avec ~** pompously

empiéter [āpjete]: **~ sur** *vt* to encroach upon

empiffrer [āpifʀe]: **s'empiffrer** *vi* (péj) to stuff o.s.

empiler [āpile] *vt* to pile (up), stack (up); **s'empiler** *vi* to pile up

empire [āpiʀ] *nm* empire; (fig) influence; **style E~** Empire style; **sous l'~ de** in the grip of

empirer [āpiʀe] *vi* to worsen, deteriorate

emplacement [āplasmɑ̃] *nm* site; **sur l'~ de** on the site of

emplette [āplɛt] *nf*: **faire l'~ de** to purchase; **emplettes** shopping *sg*; **faire des ~s** to go shopping

emplir [ɑ̃pliʀ] vt to fill; **s'emplir (de)** vi to fill (with)

emploi [ɑ̃plwa] nm use; (Comm, Écon): **l'~** employment; (poste) job, situation; **d'~ facile** easy to use; **le plein ~** full employment; **mode d'~** directions for use; **~ du temps** timetable, schedule

employé, e [ɑ̃plwaje] nm/f employee; **~ de bureau/banque** office/bank employee ou clerk; **~ de maison** domestic (servant)

employer [ɑ̃plwaje] vt (outil, moyen, méthode, mot) to use; (ouvrier, main-d'œuvre) to employ; **s'~ à qch/à faire** to apply ou devote o.s. to sth/to doing

employeur, -euse [ɑ̃plwajœʀ, -øz] nm/f employer

empocher [ɑ̃pɔʃe] vt to pocket

empoigner [ɑ̃pwaɲe] vt to grab; **s'empoigner** (fig) to have a row ou set-to

empoisonner [ɑ̃pwazɔne] vt to poison; (empester: air, pièce) to stink out; (fam): **~ qn** to drive sb mad; **s'empoisonner** to poison o.s.; **~ l'atmosphère** (aussi fig) to poison the atmosphere; (aussi: **il nous empoisonne l'existence**) he's the bane of our life

emporté, e [ɑ̃pɔʀte] adj (personne, caractère) fiery

emporter [ɑ̃pɔʀte] vt to take (with one); (en dérobant ou enlevant, emmener: blessés, voyageurs) to take away; (entraîner) to carry away ou along; (arracher) to tear off; (rivière, vent) to carry away; (Mil: position) to take; (avantage, approbation) to win; **s'emporter** vi (de colère) to fly into a rage, lose one's temper; **la maladie qui l'a emporté** the illness which caused his death; **l'~** to gain victory; **l'~ (sur)** to get the upper hand (of); (méthode etc) to prevail (over); **boissons à ~** take-away drinks; **plats à ~** take-away meals

empreint, e [ɑ̃pʀɛ̃, -ɛ̃t] adj: **~ de** marked with; tinged with ▷ nf (de pied, main) print; (fig) stamp, mark; **~e (digitale)** fingerprint; **~e écologique** carbon footprint

empressé, e [ɑ̃pʀese] adj attentive; (péj) overanxious to please, overattentive

empressement [ɑ̃pʀesmɑ̃] nm eagerness

empresser [ɑ̃pʀese]: **s'empresser** vi: **s'~ auprès de qn** to surround sb with attentions; **s'~ de faire** to hasten to do

emprise [ɑ̃pʀiz] nf hold, ascendancy; **sous l'~ de** under the influence of

emprisonnement [ɑ̃pʀizɔnmɑ̃] nm imprisonment

emprisonner [ɑ̃pʀizɔne] vt to imprison, jail

emprunt [ɑ̃pʀœ̃] nm borrowing no pl, loan (from debtor's point of view); (Ling etc) borrowing; **nom d'~** assumed name; **~ d'État** government ou state loan; **~ public à 5%** 5% public loan

emprunté, e [ɑ̃pʀœ̃te] adj (fig) ill-at-ease, awkward

emprunter [ɑ̃pʀœ̃te] vt to borrow; (itinéraire)

to take, follow; (style, manière) to adopt, assume

ému, e [emy] pp de **émouvoir** ▷ adj excited; (gratitude) touched; (compassion) moved

 MOT-CLÉ

en [ɑ̃] prép **1** (endroit, pays) in; (direction) to; **habiter en France/ville** to live in France/town; **aller en France/ville** to go to France/town

2 (moment, temps) in; **en été/juin** in summer/June; **en 3 jours/20 ans** in 3 days/20 years

3 (moyen) by; **en avion/taxi** by plane/taxi

4 (composition) made of; **c'est en verre/coton/laine** it's (made of) glass/cotton/wool; **en métal/plastique** made of metal/plastic; **un collier en argent** a silver necklace; **en deux volumes/une pièce** in two volumes/one piece

5 (description, état): **une femme (habillée) en rouge** a woman (dressed) in red; **peindre qch en rouge** to paint sth red; **en T/étoile** T-/star-shaped; **en chemise/chaussettes** in one's shirt sleeves/socks; **en soldat** as a soldier; **en civil** in civilian clothes; **cassé en plusieurs morceaux** broken into several pieces; **en réparation** being repaired, under repair; **en vacances** on holiday; **en bonne santé** healthy, in good health; **en deuil** in mourning; **le même en plus grand** the same but ou only bigger

6 (avec gérondif) while; on; **en dormant** while sleeping, as one sleeps; **en sortant** on going out, as he etc went out; **sortir en courant** to run out; **en apprenant la nouvelle, il s'est évanoui** he fainted at the news ou when he heard the news

7 (matière): **fort en math** good at maths; **expert en** expert in

8 (conformité): **en tant que** as; **en bon politicien, il ...** good politician that he is, he ..., like a good ou true politician, he ...; **je te parle en ami** I'm talking to you as a friend ▷ pron **1** (indéfini): **j'en ai/veux** I have/want some; **en as-tu?** have you got any?; **il n'y en a pas** there isn't ou aren't any; **je n'en veux pas** I don't want any; **j'en ai deux** I've got two; **combien y en a-t-il?** how many (of them) are there?; **j'en ai assez** I've got enough (of it ou them); **j'en ai marre** I've had enough; **où en étais-je?** where was I?

2 (provenance) from there; **j'en viens** I've come from there

3 (cause): **il en est malade/perd le sommeil** he is ill/can't sleep because of it

4 (de la part de): **elle en est aimée** she is loved by him (ou them etc)

5 (complément de nom, d'adjectif, de verbe): **j'en connais les dangers** I know its ou the dangers; **j'en suis fier/ai besoin** I am proud of it/need it; **il en est ainsi** ou **de même pour moi** it's the same for me, same here

ENA [ena] *sigle f* (= *École nationale d'administration*) *grande école for training civil servants*

encadrement [ɑ̃kadrəmɑ̃] *nm* framing; training; (*de porte*) frame; **~ du crédit** credit restrictions

encadrer [ɑ̃kadre] *vt* (*tableau, image*) to frame; (*fig: entourer*) to surround; (*personnel, soldats etc*) to train; (*Comm: crédit*) to restrict

encaissé, e [ɑ̃kese] *adj* (*vallée*) steep-sided; (*rivière*) with steep banks

encaisser [ɑ̃kese] *vt* (*chèque*) to cash; (*argent*) to collect; (*fig: coup, défaite*) to take

encart [ɑ̃kar] *nm* insert; **~ publicitaire** publicity insert

en-cas [ɑ̃ka] *nm inv* snack

encastré, e [ɑ̃kastre] *adj* (*four, baignoire*) built-in

enceinte [ɑ̃sɛ̃t] *adj f:* **~ (de six mois)** (six months) pregnant ▷ *nf* (*mur*) wall; (*espace*) enclosure; **~ (acoustique)** speaker

encens [ɑ̃sɑ̃] *nm* incense

encercler [ɑ̃serkle] *vt* to surround

enchaîner [ɑ̃ʃene] *vt* to chain up; (*mouvements, séquences*) to link (together) ▷ *vi* to carry on

enchanté, e [ɑ̃ʃɑ̃te] *adj* (*ravi*) delighted; (*ensorcelé*) enchanted; **~ (de faire votre connaissance)** pleased to meet you, how do you do?

enchantement [ɑ̃ʃɑ̃tmɑ̃] *nm* delight; (*magie*) enchantment; **comme par ~** as if by magic

enchère [ɑ̃ʃer] *nf* bid; **faire une ~** to (make a) bid; **mettre/vendre aux ~s** to put up for (sale by)/sell by auction; **les ~s montent** the bids are rising; **faire monter les ~s** (*fig*) to raise the bidding

enchevêtrer [ɑ̃ʃvetre] *vt* to tangle (up)

enclencher [ɑ̃klɑ̃ʃe] *vt* (*mécanisme*) to engage; (*fig: affaire*) to set in motion; **s'enclencher** *vi* to engage

enclin, e [ɑ̃klɛ̃, -in] *adj:* **~ à qch/à faire** inclined ou prone to sth/to do

enclos [ɑ̃klo] *nm* enclosure; (*clôture*) fence

enclume [ɑ̃klym] *nf* anvil

encoche [ɑ̃kɔʃ] *nf* notch

encoignure [ɑ̃kɔɲyr] *nf* corner

encolure [ɑ̃kɔlyr] *nf* (*tour de cou*) collar size; (*col, cou*) neck

encombrant, e [ɑ̃kɔ̃brɑ̃, -ɑ̃t] *adj* cumbersome, bulky

encombre [ɑ̃kɔ̃br] *nm:* **sans ~** *adv* without mishap *ou* incident

encombrement [ɑ̃kɔ̃brəmɑ̃] *nm* (*d'un lieu*) cluttering (up); (*d'un objet: dimensions*) bulk; **être pris dans un ~** to be stuck in a traffic jam

encombrer [ɑ̃kɔ̃bre] *vt* to clutter (up); (*gêner*) to hamper; **s'encombrer de** *vi* (*bagages etc*) to load *ou* burden o.s. with; **~ le passage** to block *ou* obstruct the way

encontre [ɑ̃kɔ̃tr] **à l'~ de** *prép* against, counter to

encore [ɑ̃kɔr] *adv* **1** (*continuation*) still; **il y travaille encore** he's still working on it; **pas encore** not yet

2 (*de nouveau*) again; **j'irai encore demain** I'll go again tomorrow; **encore une fois** (once) again

3 (*en plus*) more; **encore un peu de viande?** a little more meat?; **encore un effort** one last effort; **encore deux jours** two more days

4 (*intensif*) even, still; **encore plus fort/mieux** even louder/better, louder/better still; **hier encore** even yesterday; **non seulement ..., mais encore ...** not only ..., but also ...; **encore!** (*insatisfaction*) not again!; **quoi encore?** what now?

5 (*restriction*) even so *ou* then, only; **encore pourrais-je le faire si ...** even so, I might be able to do it if ...; **si encore** if only; **encore que** *conj* although

encouragement [ɑ̃kuraʒmɑ̃] *nm* encouragement; (*récompense*) incentive

encourager [ɑ̃kuraʒe] *vt* to encourage; **~ qn à faire qch** to encourage sb to do sth

encourir [ɑ̃kurir] *vt* to incur

encrasser [ɑ̃krase] *vt* to foul up; (*Auto etc*) to soot up

encre [ɑ̃kr] *nf* ink; **~ de Chine** Indian ink; **~ indélébile** indelible ink; **~ sympathique** invisible ink

encrier [ɑ̃krije] *nm* inkwell

encroûter [ɑ̃krute] **s'encroûter** *vi* (*fig*) to get into a rut, get set in one's ways

encyclopédie [ɑ̃siklɔpedi] *nf* encyclopaedia (*Brit*), encyclopedia (*US*)

endetter [ɑ̃dete] *vt*, **s'endetter** *vi* to get into debt

endiablé, e [ɑ̃djable] *adj* furious; (*enfant*) boisterous

endimanché, e [ɑ̃dimɑ̃ʃe] *adj* in one's Sunday best

endive [ɑ̃div] *nf* chicory *no pl*

endoctriner [ɑ̃dɔktrine] *vt* to indoctrinate

endommager [ɑ̃dɔmaʒe] *vt* to damage

endormi, e [ɑ̃dɔrmi] *pp de* **endormir** ▷ *adj* (*personne*) asleep; (*fig: indolent, lent*) sluggish; (*engourdi: main, pied*) numb

endormir [ɑ̃dɔrmir] *vt* to put to sleep; (*chaleur etc*) to send to sleep; (*Méd: dent, nerf*) to anaesthetize; (*fig: soupçons*) to allay; **s'endormir** *vi* to fall asleep, go to sleep

endosser [ɑ̃dose] *vt* (*responsabilité*) to take, shoulder; (*chèque*) to endorse; (*uniforme, tenue*) to put on, don

endroit [ɑ̃drwa] *nm* place; (*localité*): **les gens de l'~** the local people; (*opposé à l'envers*) right side; **à cet ~** in this place; **à l'~** right side out; the right way up; (*vêtement*) the right way out; **à l'~ de** *prép* regarding, with regard to; **par ~s** in places; (*objet posé*) the right way round

enduire [ɑ̃dɥiʀ] vt to coat; **~ qch de** to coat sth with

enduit, e [ɑ̃dɥi, -it] pp de **enduire** ▷ nm coating

endurance [ɑ̃dyʀɑ̃s] nf endurance

endurant, e [ɑ̃dyʀɑ̃, -ɑ̃t] adj tough, hardy

endurcir [ɑ̃dyʀsiʀ] vt (physiquement) to toughen; (moralement) to harden; **s'endurcir** vi (physiquement) to become tougher; (moralement) to become hardened

endurer [ɑ̃dyʀe] vt to endure, bear

énergétique [enɛʀʒetik] adj (ressources etc) energy cpd; (aliment) energizing

énergie [enɛʀʒi] nf (Physique) energy; (Tech) power; (fig: physique) energy; (: morale) vigour, spirit; **~ éolienne/solaire** wind/solar power

énergique [enɛʀʒik] adj energetic; vigorous; (mesures) drastic, stringent

énervant, e [enɛʀvɑ̃, -ɑ̃t] adj irritating, annoying

énervé, e [enɛʀve] adj nervy, on edge; (agacé) irritated

énerver [enɛʀve] vt to irritate, annoy; **s'énerver** vi to get excited, get worked up

enfance [ɑ̃fɑ̃s] nf (âge) childhood; (fig) infancy; (enfants) children pl; **c'est l'~ de l'art** it's child's play; **petite ~** infancy; **souvenir/ami d'~** childhood memory/ friend; **retomber en ~** to lapse into one's second childhood

enfant [ɑ̃fɑ̃] nm/f child; **~ adoptif/naturel** adopted/natural child; **bon ~** adj good-natured, easy-going; **~ de chœur** nm (Rel) altar boy; **~ prodige** child prodigy; **~ unique** only child

enfantillage [ɑ̃fɑ̃tijaʒ] nm (péj) childish behaviour no pl

enfantin, e [ɑ̃fɑ̃tɛ̃, -in] adj childlike; (péj) childish; (langage) children's cpd

enfer [ɑ̃fɛʀ] nm hell; **allure/bruit d'~** horrendous speed/noise

enfermer [ɑ̃fɛʀme] vt to shut up; (à clef, interner) to lock up; **s'enfermer** to shut o.s. away; **s'~ à clé** to lock o.s. in; **s'~ dans la solitude/le mutisme** to retreat into solitude/silence

enfiévré, e [ɑ̃fjevʀe] adj (fig) feverish

enfiler [ɑ̃file] vt (vêtement): **~ qch** to slip sth on, slip into sth; (insérer): **~ qch dans** to stick sth into; (rue, couloir) to take; (perles) to string; (aiguille) to thread; **s'enfiler dans** vi to disappear into

enfin [ɑ̃fɛ̃] adv at last; (en énumérant) lastly; (de restriction, résignation) still; (eh bien) well; (pour conclure) in a word; (somme toute) after all

enflammer [ɑ̃flame] vt to set fire to; (Méd) to inflame; **s'enflammer** vi to catch fire; (Méd) to become inflamed

enflé, e [ɑ̃fle] adj swollen; (péj: style) bombastic, turgid

enfler [ɑ̃fle] vi to swell (up); **s'enfler** vi to swell

enfoncer [ɑ̃fɔ̃se] vt (clou) to drive in; (faire pénétrer): **~ qch dans** to push (ou drive) sth into; (forcer: porte) to break open; (: plancher) to cause to cave in; (défoncer: côtes etc) to smash; (fam: surpasser) to lick, beat (hollow) ▷ vi (dans la vase etc) to sink in; (sol, surface porteuse) to give way; **s'enfoncer** vi to sink; **s'~ dans** to sink into; (forêt, ville) to disappear into; **~ un chapeau sur la tête** to cram ou jam a hat on one's head; **~ qn dans la dette** to drag sb into debt

enfouir [ɑ̃fwiʀ] vt (dans le sol) to bury; (dans un tiroir etc) to tuck away; **s'enfouir dans/sous** to bury o.s. in/under

enfourcher [ɑ̃fuʀʃe] vt to mount; **~ son dada** (fig) to get on one's hobby-horse

enfreindre [ɑ̃fʀɛ̃dʀ] vt to infringe, break

enfuir [ɑ̃fɥiʀ]: **s'enfuir** vi to run away ou off

enfumer [ɑ̃fyme] vt to smoke out

engageant, e [ɑ̃gaʒɑ̃, -ɑ̃t] adj attractive, appealing

engagement [ɑ̃gaʒmɑ̃] nm taking on, engaging; starting; investing; (promesse) commitment; (Mil: combat) engagement; (: recrutement) enlistment; (Sport) entry; **prendre l'~ de faire** to undertake to do; **sans ~** (Comm) without obligation

engager [ɑ̃gaʒe] vt (embaucher) to take on; (: artiste) to engage; (commencer) to start; (lier) to bind, commit; (impliquer, entraîner) to involve; (investir) to invest, lay out; (faire intervenir) to engage; (Sport: concurrents, chevaux) to enter; (introduire: clé) to insert; (inciter): **~ qn à faire** to urge sb to do; (faire pénétrer): **~ qch dans** to insert sth into; **~ qn à qch** to urge sth on sb; **s'engager** vi to get taken on; (Mil) to enlist; (promettre, politiquement) to commit o.s.; (débuter: conversation etc) to start (up); **s'~ à faire** to undertake to do; **s'~ dans** (rue, passage) to turn into, enter; (s'emboîter) to engage ou fit into; (fig: affaire, discussion) to enter into, embark on

engelures [ɑ̃ʒlyʀ] nfpl chilblains

engendrer [ɑ̃ʒɑ̃dʀe] vt to father; (fig) to create, breed

engin [ɑ̃ʒɛ̃] nm machine; (outil) instrument; (Auto) vehicle; (péj) gadget; (Aviat: avion) aircraft inv; (: missile) missile; **~ blindé** armoured vehicle; **~ (explosif)** (explosive) device; **~s (spéciaux)** missiles

englober [ɑ̃glɔbe] vt to include

engloutir [ɑ̃glutiʀ] vt to swallow up; (fig: dépenses) to devour; **s'engloutir** vi to be engulfed

engoncé, e [ɑ̃gɔ̃se] adj: **~ dans** cramped in

engorger [ɑ̃gɔʀʒe] vt to obstruct, block; **s'engorger** vi to become blocked

engouement [ɑ̃gumɑ̃] nm (sudden) passion

engouffrer [ɑ̃gufʀe] vt to swallow up, devour; **s'engouffrer dans** to rush into

engourdir [ɑ̃guʀdiʀ] vt to numb; (fig) to dull, blunt; **s'engourdir** vi to go numb

engrais [ɑ̃gʀɛ] nm manure; **~ (chimique)** (chemical) fertilizer; **~ organique/ inorganique** organic/inorganic fertilizer

engraisser [ɑ̃gʀese] vt to fatten (up); (terre: fertiliser) to fertilize ▷ vi (péj) to get fat(ter)

engrenage [ɑ̃gʀənaʒ] nm gears pl, gearing; (fig) chain

engueuler [ɑ̃gœle] vt (fam) to bawl at ou out

enhardir [ɑ̃aʀdiʀ]: **s'enhardir** vi to grow bolder

énigme [enigm] nf riddle

enivrer [ɑ̃nivʀe] vt: **s'enivrer** to get drunk; **s'~ de** (fig) to become intoxicated with

enjambée [ɑ̃ʒɑ̃be] nf stride; **d'une ~** with one stride

enjamber [ɑ̃ʒɑ̃be] vt to stride over; (pont etc) to span, straddle

enjeu, x [ɑ̃ʒø] nm stakes pl

enjôler [ɑ̃ʒole] vt to coax, wheedle

enjoliver [ɑ̃ʒolive] vt to embellish

enjoliveur [ɑ̃ʒolivœʀ] nm (Auto) hub cap

enjoué, e [ɑ̃ʒwe] adj playful

enlacer [ɑ̃lase] vt (étreindre) to embrace, hug; (lianes) to wind round, entwine

enlaidir [ɑ̃lediʀ] vt to make ugly ▷ vi to become ugly

enlèvement [ɑ̃lɛvmɑ̃] nm removal; (rapt) abduction, kidnapping; **l'~ des ordures ménagères** refuse collection

enlever [ɑ̃l(ə)ve] vt (ôter: gén) to remove; (: vêtement, lunettes) to take off; (: Méd: organe) to remove; (emporter: ordures etc) to collect, take away; (kidnapper) to abduct, kidnap; (obtenir: prix, contrat) to win; (Mil: position) to take; (morceau de piano etc) to execute with spirit ou brio; (prendre): **~ qch à qn** to take sth (away) from sb; **s'enlever** vi (tache) to come out ou off; **la maladie qui nous l'a enlevé** (euphémisme) the illness which took him from us

enliser [ɑ̃lize]: **s'enliser** vi to sink, get stuck; (dialogue etc) to get bogged down

enneigé, e [ɑ̃neʒe] adj snowy; (col) snowed-up; (maison) snowed-in

ennemi, e [ɛnmi] adj hostile; (Mil) enemy cpd ▷ nm/f enemy; **être ~ de** to be strongly averse ou opposed to

ennui [ɑ̃nɥi] nm (lassitude) boredom; (difficulté) trouble no pl; **avoir des ~s** to have problems; **s'attirer des ~s** to cause problems for o.s.

ennuyer [ɑ̃nɥije] vt to bother; (lasser) to bore; **s'ennuyer** vi to be bored; (s'ennuyer de: regretter) to miss; **si cela ne vous ennuie pas** if it's no trouble to you

ennuyeux, -euse [ɑ̃nɥijø, -øz] adj boring, tedious; (agaçant) annoying

énoncé [enɔ̃se] nm terms pl; wording; (Ling) utterance

énoncer [enɔ̃se] vt to say, express; (conditions) to set out, lay down, state

enorgueillir [ɑ̃nɔʀgœjiʀ]: **s'enorgueillir de** vt to pride o.s. on; to boast

énorme [enɔʀm] adj enormous, huge

énormément [enɔʀmemɑ̃] adv enormously, tremendously; **~ de neige/gens** an enormous amount of snow/number of people

énormité [enɔʀmite] nf enormity, hugeness; (propos) outrageous remark

enquérir [ɑ̃keʀiʀ]: **s'enquérir de** vt to inquire about

enquête [ɑ̃kɛt] nf (de journaliste, de police) investigation; (judiciaire, administrative) inquiry; (sondage d'opinion) survey

enquêter [ɑ̃kete] vi to investigate; to hold an inquiry; (faire un sondage): **~ (sur)** to do a survey (on), carry out an opinion poll (on)

enquiers, enquière etc [ɑ̃kjɛʀ] vb voir **enquérir**

enquiquiner [ɑ̃kikine] vt to rile, irritate

enraciné, e [ɑ̃ʀasine] adj deep-rooted

enragé, e [ɑ̃ʀaʒe] adj (Méd) rabid, with rabies; (furieux) furiously angry; (fig) fanatical; **~ de** wild about

enrageant, e [ɑ̃ʀaʒɑ̃, -ɑ̃t] adj infuriating

enrager [ɑ̃ʀaʒe] vi to be furious, be in a rage; **faire ~ qn** to make sb wild with anger

enrayer [ɑ̃ʀeje] vt to check, stop; **s'enrayer** vi (arme à feu) to jam

enregistrement [ɑ̃ʀ(ə)ʒistʀəmɑ̃] nm recording; (Admin) registration; **~ des bagages** (à l'aéroport) baggage check-in; **~ magnétique** tape-recording

enregistrer [ɑ̃ʀ(ə)ʒistʀe] vt (Mus) to record; (Inform) to save; (remarquer, noter) to note, record; (Comm: commande) to note, enter; (fig: mémoriser) to make a mental note of; (Admin) to register; (aussi: **faire ~**: bagages: par train) to register; (: à l'aéroport) to check in

enrhumé, e [ɑ̃ʀyme] adj: **il est ~** he has a cold

enrhumer [ɑ̃ʀyme]: **s'enrhumer** vi to catch a cold

enrichir [ɑ̃ʀiʃiʀ] vt to make rich(er); (fig) to enrich; **s'enrichir** vi to get rich(er)

enrober [ɑ̃ʀobe] vt: **~ qch de** to coat sth with; (fig) to wrap sth up in

enrôler [ɑ̃ʀole] vt to enlist; **s'enrôler (dans)** vi to enlist (in)

enrouer [ɑ̃ʀwe]: **s'enrouer** vi to go hoarse

enrouler [ɑ̃ʀule] vt (fil, corde) to wind (up); **s'enrouler** to coil up; **~ qch autour de** to wind sth (a)round

ensanglanté, e [ɑ̃sɑ̃glɑ̃te] adj covered with blood

enseignant, e [ɑ̃sɛɲɑ̃, -ɑ̃t] adj teaching ▷ nm/f teacher

enseigne [ɑ̃sɛɲ] nf sign ▷ nm: **~ de vaisseau** lieutenant; **à telle ~ que** so much so that; **être logés à la même ~** (fig) to be in the same boat; **~ lumineuse** neon sign

enseignement [ɑ̃sɛɲ(ə)mɑ̃] nm teaching; (Admin) education; **~ ménager** home economics; **~ primaire** primary (Brit) ou

grade school (US) education; **~ secondaire** secondary (Brit) ou high school (US) education
enseigner [āsɛɲe] vt, vi to teach; **~ qch à qn/à qn que** to teach sb sth/sb that
ensemble [āsābl] adv together ▷ nm (assemblage, Math) set; (totalité): **l'~ du/de la** the whole ou entire; (vêtements) outfit; (vêtement féminin) ensemble, suit; (unité, harmonie) unity; (résidentiel) housing development; **aller ~** to go together; **impression/idée d'~** overall ou general impression/idea; **dans l'~** (en gros) on the whole; **dans son ~** overall, in general; **~ vocal/musical** vocal/musical ensemble
ensemencer [āsmāse] vt to sow
ensevelir [āsəvlir] vt to bury
ensoleillé, e [āsɔleje] adj sunny
ensommeillé, e [āsɔmeje] adj sleepy, drowsy
ensorceler [āsɔrsəle] vt to enchant, bewitch
ensuite [āsɥit] adv then, next; (plus tard) afterwards, later; **~ de quoi** after which
ensuivre [āsɥivr]: **s'ensuivre** vi to follow, ensue; **il s'ensuit que ...** it follows that ...; **et tout ce qui s'ensuit** and all that goes with it
entaille [ātaj] nf (encoche) notch; (blessure) cut; **se faire une ~** to cut o.s.
entamer [ātame] vt (pain, bouteille) to start; (hostilités, pourparlers) to open; (fig: altérer) to make a dent in; to damage
entasser [ātase] vt (empiler) to pile up, heap up; (tenir à l'étroit) to cram together; **s'entasser** vi (s'amonceler) to pile up; to cram; **s'~ dans** to cram into
entendre [ātādr] vt to hear; (comprendre) to understand; (vouloir dire) to mean; (vouloir): **~ être obéi/que** to intend ou mean to be obeyed/that; **j'ai entendu dire que** I've heard (it said) that; **je suis heureux de vous l'~ dire** I'm pleased to hear you say it; **~ parler de** to hear of; **laisser ~ que, donner à ~ que** to let it be understood that; **~ raison** to see sense, listen to reason; **qu'est-ce qu'il ne faut pas ~!** whatever next!; **j'ai mal entendu** I didn't catch what was said; **je vous entends très mal** I can hardly hear you; **s'entendre** vi (sympathiser) to get on; (se mettre d'accord) to agree; **s'~ à qch/à faire** (être compétent) to be good at sth/doing; **ça s'entend** (est audible) it's audible; **je m'entends** I mean; **entendons-nous!** let's be clear what we mean
entendu, e [ātādy] pp de **entendre** ▷ adj (réglé) agreed; (au courant: air) knowing; **étant ~ que** since (it's understood ou agreed that); **(c'est) ~** all right, agreed; **c'est ~** (concession) all right, granted; **bien ~** of course
entente [ātāt] nf (entre amis, pays) understanding, harmony; (accord, traité) agreement, understanding; **à double ~** (sens) with a double meaning
entériner [āterine] vt to ratify, confirm
enterrement [ātermā] nm burying;

(cérémonie) funeral, burial; (cortège funèbre) funeral procession
enterrer [ātere] vt to bury
entêtant, e [ātetā, -āt] adj heady
en-tête [ātet] nm heading; (de papier à lettres) letterhead; **papier à ~** headed notepaper
entêté, e [ātete] adj stubborn
entêter [ātete]: **s'entêter** vi: **s'~ (à faire)** to persist (in doing)
enthousiasme [ātuzjasm] nm enthusiasm; **avec ~** enthusiastically
enthousiasmer [ātuzjasme] vt to fill with enthusiasm; **s'~ (pour qch)** to get enthusiastic (about sth)
enthousiaste [ātuzjast] adj enthusiastic
enticher [ātife]: **s'enticher de** vt to become infatuated with
entier, -ière [ātje, -jɛr] adj (non entamé, en totalité) whole; (total, complet: satisfaction etc) complete; (fig: caractère) unbending, averse to compromise ▷ nm (Math) whole; **en ~** totally; in its entirety; **se donner tout ~ à qch** to devote o.s. completely to sth; **lait ~** full-cream milk; **pain ~** wholemeal bread; **nombre ~** whole number
entièrement [ātjɛrmā] adv entirely, completely, wholly
entonner [ātɔne] vt (chanson) to strike up
entonnoir [ātɔnwar] nm (ustensile) funnel; (trou) shell-hole, crater
entorse [ātɔrs] nf (Méd) sprain; (fig): **~ à la loi/au règlement** infringement of the law/rule; **se faire une ~ à la cheville/au poignet** to sprain one's ankle/wrist
entortiller [ātɔrtije] vt (envelopper): **~ qch dans/avec** to wrap sth in/with; (enrouler): **~ qch autour de** to twist ou wind sth (a)round; (fam): **~ qn** to get (a)round sb; (: duper) to hoodwink sb (Brit), trick sb; **s'entortiller dans** vi (draps) to roll o.s. up in; (fig: réponses) to get tangled up in
entourage [āturaʒ] nm circle; (famille) family (circle); (d'une vedette etc) entourage; (ce qui enclôt) surround
entouré, e [āture] adj (recherché, admiré) popular; **~ de** surrounded by
entourer [āture] vt to surround; (apporter son soutien à) to rally round; **~ de** to surround with; (trait) to encircle with; **s'entourer de** vi to surround o.s. with; **s'~ de précautions** to take all possible precautions
entracte [ātrakt] nm interval
entraide [ātrɛd] nf mutual aid ou assistance
entrain [ātrē] nm spirit; **avec ~** (répondre, travailler) energetically; **faire qch sans ~** to do sth half-heartedly ou without enthusiasm
entraînement [ātrɛnmā] nm training; (Tech): **~ à chaîne/galet** chain/wheel drive; **manquer d'~** to be unfit; **~ par ergots/friction** (Inform) tractor/friction feed
entraîner [ātrene] vt (tirer: wagons) to pull; (charrier) to carry ou drag along; (Tech) to drive;

(*emmener: personne*) to take (off); (*mener à l'assaut, influencer*) to lead; (*Sport*) to train; (*impliquer*) to entail; (*causer*) to lead to, bring about; **~ qn à faire** (*inciter*) to lead sb to do; **s'entraîner** *vi* (*Sport*) to train; **s'~ à qch/à faire** to train o.s. for sth/to do

entraîneur [ɑ̃tʀɛnœʀ] *nm/f* (*Sport*) coach, trainer ▷ *nm* (*Hippisme*) trainer

entraver [ɑ̃tʀave] *vt* (*circulation*) to hold up; (*action, progrès*) to hinder, hamper

entre [ɑ̃tʀ] *prép* between; (*parmi*) among(st); **l'un d'~ eux/nous** one of them/us; **le meilleur d'~ eux/nous** the best of them/us; **ils préfèrent rester ~ eux** they prefer to keep to themselves; **~ autres (choses)** among other things; **~ nous, ...** between ourselves ..., between you and me ...; **ils se battent ~ eux** they are fighting among(st) themselves

entrebâillé, e [ɑ̃tʀəbaje] *adj* half-open, ajar

entrechoquer [ɑ̃tʀəʃɔke]: **s'entrechoquer** *vi* to knock *ou* bang together

entrecôte [ɑ̃tʀəkot] *nf* entrecôte *ou* rib steak

entrecouper [ɑ̃tʀəkupe] *vt*, **~ qch de** to intersperse sth with; **un récit/voyage de** to interrupt a story/journey with; **s'entrecouper** *vi* (*traits, lignes*) to cut across each other

entrecroiser [ɑ̃tʀəkʀwaze] *vt*, **s'entrecroiser** *vi* to intertwine

entrée [ɑ̃tʀe] *nf* entrance; (*accès: au cinéma etc*) admission; (*billet*) (admission) ticket; (*Culin*) first course; (*Comm: de marchandises*) entry; (*Inform*) entry, input; **entrées** *nfpl*: **avoir ses ~s chez** *ou* **auprès de** to be a welcome visitor to; **d'~** from the outset; **erreur d'~** input error; **"~ interdite"** "no admittance *ou* entry"; **~ des artistes** stage door; **~ en matière** introduction; **~ principale** main entrance; **~ en scène** entrance; **~ de service** service entrance

entrefaites [ɑ̃tʀəfɛt]: **sur ces ~** *adv* at this juncture

entrefilet [ɑ̃tʀəfilɛ] *nm* (*article*) paragraph, short report

entrejambes [ɑ̃tʀəʒɑ̃b] *nm inv* crotch

entrelacer [ɑ̃tʀəlase] *vt*, **s'entrelacer** *vi* to intertwine

entremêler [ɑ̃tʀəmele] *vt*: **~ qch de** to (inter) mingle sth with

entremets [ɑ̃tʀəmɛ] *nm* (cream) dessert

entremise [ɑ̃tʀəmiz] *nf* intervention; **par l'~ de** through

entreposer [ɑ̃tʀəpoze] *vt* to store, put into storage

entrepôt [ɑ̃tʀəpo] *nm* warehouse

entreprenant, e [ɑ̃tʀəpʀənɑ̃, -ɑ̃t] *vb voir* **entreprendre** ▷ *adj* (*actif*) enterprising; (*trop galant*) forward

entreprendre [ɑ̃tʀəpʀɑ̃dʀ] *vt* (*se lancer dans*) to undertake; (*commencer*) to begin *ou* start (upon); (*personne*) to buttonhole; **~ qn sur un**

sujet to tackle sb on a subject; **~ de faire** to undertake to do

entrepreneur, -euse [ɑ̃tʀəpʀənœʀ] *nm/f*: **~ (en bâtiment)** (building) contractor; **~ de pompes funèbres** funeral director, undertaker

entrepris, e [ɑ̃tʀəpʀi, -iz] *pp de* **entreprendre** ▷ *nf* (*société*) firm, business; (*action*) undertaking, venture

entrer [ɑ̃tʀe] *vi* to go (*ou* come) in, enter ▷ *vt* (*Inform*) to input, enter; (*faire*) **~ qch dans** to get sth into; **~ dans** (*gén*) to enter; (*pièce*) to go (*ou* come) into, enter; (*club*) to join; (*heurter*) to run into; (*partager: vues, craintes de qn*) to share; (*être une composante de*) to go into; (*faire partie de*) to form part of; **~ au couvent** to enter a convent; **~ à l'hôpital** to go into hospital; **~ dans le système** (*Inform*) to log in; **~ en fureur** to become angry; **~ en ébullition** to start to boil; **~ en scène** to come on stage; **laisser ~ qn/qch** to let sb/sth in; **faire ~** (*visiteur*) to show in

entresol [ɑ̃tʀəsɔl] *nm* entresol, mezzanine

entre-temps [ɑ̃tʀətɑ̃] *adv* meanwhile, (in the) meantime

entretenir [ɑ̃tʀət(ə)niʀ] *vt* to maintain; (*amitié*) to keep alive; (*famille, maîtresse*) to support, keep; **~ qn (de)** to speak to sb (about); **s'entretenir (de)** to converse (about); **~ qn dans l'erreur** to let sb remain in ignorance

entretien [ɑ̃tʀətjɛ̃] *nm* maintenance; (*discussion*) discussion, talk; (*pour un emploi*) interview; **frais d'~** maintenance charges

entrevoir [ɑ̃tʀəvwaʀ] *vt* (*à peine*) to make out; (*brièvement*) to catch a glimpse of

entrevu, e [ɑ̃tʀəvy] *pp de* entrevoir ▷ *nf* meeting; (*audience*) interview

entrouvert, e [ɑ̃tʀuvɛʀ, -ɛʀt] *adj* half-open

énumérer [enymeʀe] *vt* to list, enumerate

envahir [ɑ̃vaiʀ] *vt* to invade; (*inquiétude, peur*) to come over

envahissant, e [ɑ̃vaisɑ̃, -ɑ̃t] *adj* (*péj: personne*) interfering, intrusive

enveloppe [ɑ̃v(ə)lɔp] *nf* (*de lettre*) envelope; (*Tech*) casing; outer layer; (*crédits*) budget; **mettre sous ~** to put in an envelope; **~ autocollante** self-seal envelope; **~ budgétaire** budget; **~ à fenêtre** window envelope

envelopper [ɑ̃v(ə)lɔpe] *vt* to wrap; (*fig*) to envelop, shroud; **s'~ dans un châle/une couverture** to wrap o.s. in a shawl/blanket

envenimer [ɑ̃vnime] *vt* to aggravate; **s'envenimer** *vi* (*plaie*) to fester; (*situation, relations*) to worsen

envergure [ɑ̃vɛʀgyʀ] *nf* (*d'un oiseau, avion*) wingspan; (*fig: étendue*) scope; (: *valeur*) calibre

enverrai *etc* [ɑ̃veʀe] *vb voir* envoyer

envers [ɑ̃vɛʀ] *prép* towards, to ▷ *nm* other side; (*d'une étoffe*) wrong side; **à l'~**

(verticalement) upside down; *(pull)* back to front; *(vêtement)* inside out; **~ et contre tous** *ou* **tout** against all opposition

envie [ãvi] *nf (sentiment)* envy; *(souhait)* desire, wish; *(filet de peau)* hangnail; **avoir ~ de** to feel like; *(désir plus fort)* to want; **avoir ~ de faire** to feel like doing; to want to do; **avoir ~ que** to wish that; **donner à qn l'~ de faire** to make sb want to do; **cette glace me fait ~** I fancy some of that ice cream

envier [ãvje] *vt* to envy; **~ qch à qn** to envy sb sth; **n'avoir rien à ~ à** to have no cause to be envious of

envieux, -euse [ãvjø, -øz] *adj* envious

environ [ãvirɔ̃] *adv:* **~ 3 h/2 km, 3 h/2km ~** (around) or so *ou* to 3 o'clock/2 km, 3 o'clock/2 km or so; *voir aussi* **environs**

environnant, e [ãvirɔnã, -ãt] *adj* surrounding

environnement [ãvirɔnmã] *nm* environment

environs [ãvirɔ̃] *nmpl* surroundings; **aux ~ de** around

envisager [ãvizaʒe] *vt (examiner, considérer)* to contemplate, view; *(avoir en vue)* to envisage; **~ de faire** to consider doing

envoi [ãvwa] *nm* sending; *(paquet)* parcel, consignment; **~ contre remboursement** *(Comm)* cash on delivery

envoler [ãvɔle]: **s'envoler** *vi (oiseau)* to fly away *ou* off; *(avion)* to take off; *(papier, feuille)* to blow away; *(fig)* to vanish (into thin air)

envoûter [ãvute] *vt* to bewitch

envoyé, e [ãvwaje] *nm/f (Pol)* envoy; *(Presse)* correspondent; **~ spécial** special correspondent ▷ *adj:* **bien ~** *(remarque, réponse)* well-aimed

envoyer [ãvwaje] *vt* to send; *(lancer)* to hurl, throw; **~ une gifle/un sourire à qn** to aim a blow/flash a smile at sb; **~ les couleurs** to run up the colours; **~ chercher** to send for; **~ par le fond** *(bateau)* to send to the bottom; **~ promener qn** *(fam)* to send sb packing; **~ un SMS à qn** to text sb

épagneul, e [epaɲœl] *nm/f* spaniel

épais, se [epɛ, -ɛs] *adj* thick

épaisseur [epɛsœr] *nf* thickness

épancher [epãʃe] *vt* to give vent to; **s'épancher** *vi* to open one's heart; *(liquide)* to pour out

épanouir [epanwir]: **s'épanouir** *vi (fleur)* to bloom, open out; *(visage)* to light up; *(fig: se développer)* to blossom (out); *(: mentalement)* to open up

épargne [eparɲ] *nf* saving; **l'~-logement** property investment

épargner [eparɲe] *vt* to save; *(ne pas tuer ou endommager)* to spare ▷ *vi* to save; **~ qch à qn** to spare sb sth

éparpiller [eparpije] *vt* to scatter; *(pour répartir)* to disperse; *(fig: efforts)* to dissipate; **s'éparpiller** *vi* to scatter; *(fig)* to dissipate one's efforts

épars, e [epar, -ars] *adj (maisons)* scattered; *(cheveux)* sparse

épatant, e [epatã, -ãt] *adj (fam)* super, splendid

épater [epate] *vt (fam)* to amaze; *(impressionner)* to impress

épaule [epol] *nf* shoulder

épauler [epole] *vt (aider)* to back up, support; *(arme)* to raise (to one's shoulder) ▷ *vi* to (take) aim

épaulette [epolɛt] *nf (Mil, d'un veston)* epaulette; *(de combinaison)* shoulder strap

épave [epav] *nf* wreck

épée [epe] *nf* sword

épeler [ep(ə)le] *vt* to spell

éperdu, e [eperdy] *adj (personne)* overcome; *(sentiment)* passionate; *(fuite)* frantic

éperon [eprɔ̃] *nm* spur

épervier [epervje] *nm (Zool)* sparrowhawk; *(Pêche)* casting net

épi [epi] *nm (de blé, d'orge)* ear; *(de maïs)* cob; **~ de cheveux** tuft of hair; **stationnement/se garer en ~** parking/to park at an angle to the kerb

épice [epis] *nf* spice

épicé, e [epise] *adj* highly spiced, spicy; *(fig)* spicy

épicer [epise] *vt* to spice; *(fig)* to add spice to

épicerie [episri] *nf (magasin)* grocer's shop; *(denrées)* groceries *pl*; **~ fine** delicatessen (shop)

épicier, -ière [episje, -jɛr] *nm/f* grocer

épidémie [epidemi] *nf* epidemic

épiderme [epiderm] *nm* skin, epidermis

épier [epje] *vt* to spy on, watch closely; *(occasion)* to look out for

épilepsie [epilɛpsi] *nf* epilepsy

épiler [epile] *vt (jambes)* to remove the hair from; *(sourcils)* to pluck; **s'~ les jambes** to remove the hair from one's legs; **s'~ les sourcils** to pluck one's eyebrows; **se faire ~** to get unwanted hair removed; **crème à ~** hair-removing *ou* depilatory cream; **pince à ~** eyebrow tweezers

épilogue [epilɔg] *nm (fig)* conclusion, dénouement

épiloguer [epilɔge] *vi:* **~ sur** to hold forth on

épinards [epinar] *nmpl* spinach *sg*

épine [epin] *nf* thorn, prickle; *(d'oursin etc)* spine, prickle; **~ dorsale** backbone

épineux, -euse [epinø, -øz] *adj* thorny, prickly

épingle [epɛ̃gl] *nf* pin; **tirer son ~ du jeu** to play one's game well; **tiré à quatre ~s** well turned-out; **monter qch en ~** to build sth up, make a thing of sth *(fam)*; **~ à chapeau** hatpin; **~ à cheveux** hairpin; **virage en ~ à cheveux** hairpin bend; **~ de cravate** tie pin; **~ de nourrice** *ou* **de sûreté** *ou* **double** safety pin, nappy *(Brit)* *ou* diaper *(US)* pin

épingler [epɛ̃gle] *vt (badge, décoration):* **~ qch sur** to pin sth on(to); *(Couture: tissu, robe)* to

pin together; (*fam*) to catch, nick
pique [epik] *adj* epic
pisode [epizɔd] *nm* episode; **film/roman à ~s** serialized film/novel, serial
pisodique [epizɔdik] *adj* occasional
ploré, e [eplɔʀe] *adj* in tears, tearful
pluche-légumes [eplyʃlegym] *nm inv* potato peeler
plucher [eplyʃe] *vt* (*fruit, légumes*) to peel; (*comptes, dossier*) to go over with a fine-tooth comb
pluchures [eplyʃyʀ] *nfpl* peelings
ponge [epɔ̃ʒ] *nf* sponge; **passer l'~ (sur)** (*fig*) to let bygones be bygones (with regard to); **jeter l'~** (*fig*) to throw in the towel; **~ métallique** scourer
ponger [epɔ̃ʒe] *vt* (*liquide*) to mop *ou* sponge up; (*surface*) to sponge; (*fig: déficit*) to soak up, absorb; **s'~ le front** to mop one's brow
popée [epɔpe] *nf* epic
poque [epɔk] *nf* (*de l'histoire*) age, era; (*de l'année, la vie*) time; **d'~** *adj* (*meuble*) period *cpd*; **à cette ~** at this (*ou* that) time *ou* period; **faire ~** to make history
poumoner [epumɔne]: **s'époumoner** *vi* to shout (*ou* sing) o.s. hoarse
pouse [epuz] *nf* wife
pouser [epuze] *vt* to marry; (*fig: idées*) to espouse; (: *forme*) to fit
poussenter [epuste] *vt* to dust
poustouflant, e [epustuflɑ̃, -ɑ̃t] *adj* staggering, mind-boggling
pouvantable [epuvɑ̃tabl] *adj* appalling, dreadful
pouvantail [epuvɑ̃taj] *nm* (*à moineaux*) scarecrow; (*fig*) bog(e)y; bugbear
pouvante [epuvɑ̃t] *nf* terror; **film d'~** horror film
pouvanter [epuvɑ̃te] *vt* to terrify
poux [epu] *nm* husband ▷ *nmpl:* **les ~** the (married) couple, the husband and wife
prendre [epʀɑ̃dʀ]: **s'éprendre de** *vt* to fall in love with
preuve [epʀœv] *nf* (*d'examen*) test; (*malheur, difficulté*) trial, ordeal; (*Photo*) print; (*Typo*) proof; (*Sport*) event; **à l'~ des balles/du feu** (*vêtement*) bulletproof/fireproof; **à toute ~** unfailing; **mettre à l'~** to put to the test; **~ de force** trial of strength; (*fig*) showdown; **~ de résistance** test of resistance; **~ de sélection** (*Sport*) heat
pris, e [epʀi, -iz] *vb voir* **éprendre** ▷ *adj:* **~ de** in love with
prouvant, e [epʀuvɑ̃, -ɑ̃t] *adj* trying
prouver [epʀuve] *vt* (*tester*) to test; (*mettre à l'épreuve*) to put to the test; (*marquer, faire souffrir*) to afflict, distress; (*ressentir*) to experience
prouvette [epʀuvɛt] *nf* test tube
EPS *sigle f* (= Éducation physique et sportive) ≈ PE
puisé, e [epɥize] *adj* exhausted; (*livre*) out of print

épuisement [epɥizmɑ̃] *nm* exhaustion; **jusqu'à ~ des stocks** while stocks last
épuiser [epɥize] *vt* (*fatiguer*) to exhaust, wear *ou* tire out; (*stock, sujet*) to exhaust; **s'épuiser** *vi* to wear *ou* tire o.s. out, exhaust o.s.; (*stock*) to run out
épuisette [epɥizɛt] *nf* landing net; shrimping net
épurer [epyʀe] *vt* (*liquide*) to purify; (*parti, administration*) to purge; (*langue, texte*) to refine
équateur [ekwatœʀ] *nm* equator; **(la république de) l'É~** Ecuador
équation [ekwasjɔ̃] *nf* equation; **mettre en ~** to equate; **~ du premier/second degré** simple/quadratic equation
équerre [ekɛʀ] *nf* (*à dessin*) (set) square; (*pour fixer*) brace; **en ~** at right angles; **à l'~, d'~** straight; **double ~** T-square
équilibre [ekilibʀ] *nm* balance; (*d'une balance*) equilibrium; **~ budgétaire** balanced budget; **garder/perdre l'~** to keep/lose one's balance; **être en ~** to be balanced; **mettre en ~** to make steady; **avoir le sens de l'~** to be well-balanced
équilibré, e [ekilibʀe] *adj* (*fig*) well-balanced, stable
équilibrer [ekilibʀe] *vt* to balance; **s'équilibrer** *vi* (*poids*) to balance; (*fig: défauts etc*) to balance each other out
équipage [ekipaʒ] *nm* crew; **en grand ~** in great array
équipe [ekip] *nf* team; (*bande: parfois péj*) bunch; **travailler par ~s** to work in shifts; **travailler en ~** to work as a team; **faire ~ avec** to team up with; **~ de chercheurs** research team; **~ de secours** *ou* **de sauvetage** rescue team
équipé, e [ekipe] *adj* (*cuisine etc*) equipped, fitted(-out) ▷ *nf* escapade; **bien/mal ~** well-/poorly-equipped
équipement [ekipmɑ̃] *nm* equipment; **équipements** *nmpl* amenities, facilities; installations; **biens/dépenses d'~** capital goods/expenditure; **ministère de l'É~** department of public works; **~s sportifs/collectifs** sports/community facilities *ou* resources
équiper [ekipe] *vt* to equip; (*voiture, cuisine*) to equip, fit out; **~ qn/qch de** to equip sb/sth with; **s'équiper** *vi* (*sportif*) to equip o.s., kit o.s. out
équipier, -ière [ekipje, -jɛʀ] *nm/f* team member
équitable [ekitabl] *adj* fair
équitation [ekitasjɔ̃] *nf* (horse-)riding; **faire de l'~** to go (horse-)riding
équivalent, e [ekivalɑ̃, -ɑ̃t] *adj, nm* equivalent
équivaloir [ekivalwaʀ]: **~ à** *vt* to be equivalent to; (*représenter*) to amount to
équivoque [ekivɔk] *adj* equivocal, ambiguous; (*louche*) dubious ▷ *nf* ambiguity

érable [eʀabl] *nm* maple

érafler [eʀafle] *vt* to scratch; **s'~ la main/les jambes** to scrape *ou* scratch one's hand/legs

éraflure [eʀaflyʀ] *nf* scratch

éraillé, e [eʀaje] *adj* (*voix*) rasping, hoarse

ère [ɛʀ] *nf* era; **en l'an 1050 de notre ~** in the year 1050 A.D.

érection [eʀɛksjɔ̃] *nf* erection

éreinter [eʀɛ̃te] *vt* to exhaust, wear out; (*fig: critiquer*) to slate; **s'~ (à faire qch/à qch)** to wear o.s. out (doing sth/with sth)

ériger [eʀiʒe] *vt* (*monument*) to erect; **~ qch en principe/loi** to make sth a principle/law; **s'~ en critique (de)** to set o.s. up as a critic (of)

ermite [ɛʀmit] *nm* hermit

éroder [eʀɔde] *vt* to erode

érotique [eʀɔtik] *adj* erotic

errer [eʀe] *vi* to wander

erreur [eʀœʀ] *nf* mistake, error; (*Inform*) error; (*morale*): **~s** *nfpl* errors; **être dans l'~** to be wrong; **induire qn en ~** to mislead sb; **par ~** by mistake; **sauf ~** unless I'm mistaken; **faire ~** to be mistaken; **~ de date** mistake in the date; **~ de fait** error of fact; **~ d'impression** (*Typo*) misprint; **~ judiciaire** miscarriage of justice; **~ de jugement** error of judgment; **~ matérielle** *ou* **d'écriture** clerical error; **~ tactique** tactical error

érudit, e [eʀydi, -it] *adj* erudite, learned ▷ *nm/f* scholar

éruption [eʀypsjɔ̃] *nf* eruption, (*cutanée*) outbreak; (: *boutons*) rash; (*fig: de joie, colère, folie*) outburst

es [ɛ] *vb voir* **être**

ès [ɛs] *prép*: **licencié ès lettres/sciences** ≈ Bachelor of Arts/Science; **docteur ès lettres** ≈ doctor of philosophy

ESB *sigle f* (= *encéphalopathie spongiforme bovine*) BSE

escabeau, x [ɛskabo] *nm* (*tabouret*) stool; (*échelle*) stepladder

escadron [ɛskadʀɔ̃] *nm* squadron

escalade [ɛskalad] *nf* climbing *no pl*; (*Pol etc*) escalation

escalader [ɛskalade] *vt* to climb, scale

escale [ɛskal] *nf* (*Navig: durée*) call; (: *port*) port of call; (*Aviat*) stop(over); **faire ~ à** (*Navig*) to put in at, call in at; (*Aviat*) to stop over at; **~ technique** refuelling stop; **vol sans ~** nonstop flight

escalier [ɛskalje] *nm* stairs *pl*; **dans l'~** *ou* **les ~s** on the stairs; **descendre l'~** *ou* **les ~s** to go downstairs; **~ mécanique** *ou* **roulant** escalator; **~ de secours** fire escape; **~ de service** backstairs; **~ à vis** *ou* **en colimaçon** spiral staircase

escamoter [ɛskamɔte] *vt* (*esquiver*) to get round, evade; (*faire disparaître*) to conjure away; (*dérober: portefeuille etc*) to snatch; (*train d'atterrissage*) to retract; (*mots*) to miss out

escapade [ɛskapad] *nf*: **faire une ~** to go on a jaunt; (*s'enfuir*) to run away *ou* off

escargot [ɛskaʀgo] *nm* snail

escarpé, e [ɛskaʀpe] *adj* steep

escarpin [ɛskaʀpɛ̃] *nm* flat(-heeled) shoe

escient [esjɑ̃] *nm*: **à bon ~** advisedly

esclaffer [ɛsklafe]: **s'esclaffer** *vi* to guffaw

esclandre [ɛsklɑ̃dʀ] *nm* scene, fracas

esclavage [ɛsklavaʒ] *nm* slavery

esclave [ɛsklav] *nm/f* slave; **être ~ de** (*fig*) to be a slave of

escompte [ɛskɔ̃t] *nm* discount

escompter [ɛskɔ̃te] *vt* (*Comm*) to discount; (*espérer*) to expect, reckon upon; **~ que** to reckon *ou* expect that

escorte [ɛskɔʀt] *nf* escort; **faire ~ à** to escort

escorter [ɛskɔʀte] *vt* to escort

escouade [ɛskwad] *nf* squad; (*fig: groupe de personnes*) group

escrime [ɛskʀim] *nf* fencing; **faire de l'~** to fence

escrimer [ɛskʀime]: **s'escrimer** *vi*: **s'~ à faire** to wear o.s. out doing

escroc [ɛskʀo] *nm* swindler, con-man

escroquer [ɛskʀɔke] *vt*: **~ qn (de qch)/qch à qn** to swindle sb (out of sth)/sth out of sb

escroquerie [ɛskʀɔkʀi] *nf* swindle

espace [ɛspas] *nm* space; **~ publicitaire** advertising space; **~ vital** living space

espacer [ɛspase] *vt* to space out; **s'espacer** *vi* (*visites etc*) to become less frequent

espadon [ɛspadɔ̃] *nm* swordfish *inv*

espadrille [ɛspadʀij] *nf* rope-soled sandal

Espagne [ɛspaɲ] *nf*: **l'~** Spain

espagnol, e [ɛspaɲɔl] *adj* Spanish ▷ *nm* (*Ling*) Spanish ▷ *nm/f*: **E~, e** Spaniard

espèce [ɛspɛs] *nf* (*Bio, Bot, Zool*) species *inv*; (*gén: sorte*) sort, kind, type; (*péj*): **~ de maladroit/de brute!** you clumsy oaf/you brute!; **espèces** *nfpl* (*Comm*) cash *sg*; (*Rel*) species; **de toute ~** of all kinds *ou* sorts; **en l'~** *adv* in the case in point; **payer en ~s** to pay (in) cash; **cas d'~** individual case; **l'~ humaine** humankind

espérance [ɛspeʀɑ̃s] *nf* hope; **~ de vie** life expectancy

espérer [ɛspeʀe] *vt* to hope for; **j'espère (bien)** I hope so; **~ que/faire** to hope that/to do; **~ en** to trust in

espiègle [ɛspjɛgl] *adj* mischievous

espion, ne [ɛspjɔ̃, -ɔn] *nm/f* spy; **avion ~** spy plane

espionnage [ɛspjɔnaʒ] *nm* espionage, spying; **film/roman d'~** spy film/novel

espionner [ɛspjɔne] *vt* to spy (up)on

esplanade [ɛsplanad] *nf* esplanade

espoir [ɛspwaʀ] *nm* hope; **l'~ de qch/de faire qch** the hope of sth/of doing sth; **avoir bon ~ que ...** to have high hopes that ...; **garder l'~ que ...** to remain hopeful that ...; **dans l'~ de/que** in the hope of/that; **reprendre ~** not to lose hope; **un ~ de la boxe/du ski** one of boxing's/skiing's hopefuls, one of the hopes of boxing/skiing; **sans ~** *adj* hopeless

esprit [ɛspʀi] nm (pensée, intellect) mind; (humour, ironie) wit; (mentalité, d'une loi etc, fantôme etc) spirit; **l'~ d'équipe/de compétition** team/competitive spirit; **faire de l'~** to try to be witty; **reprendre ses ~s** to come to; **perdre l'~** to lose one's mind; **avoir bon/mauvais ~** to be of a good/bad disposition; **avoir l'~ à faire qch** to have a mind to do sth; **avoir l'~ critique** to be critical; **~ de contradiction** contrariness; **~ de corps** esprit de corps; **~ de famille** family loyalty; **l'~ malin** (le diable) the Evil One; **~s chagrins** fault-finders

esquimau, de, x [ɛskimo, -od] adj Eskimo ▷ nm (Ling) Eskimo; (glace): **E-®** ice lolly (Brit), popsicle (US) ▷ nm/f: **E~, de** Eskimo; **chien ~** husky

esquinter [ɛskɛ̃te] vt (fam) to mess up; **s'esquinter** vi: **s'~ à faire qch** to knock o.s. out doing sth

esquisse [ɛskis] nf sketch; **l'~ d'un sourire/ changement** a hint of a smile/of change

esquisser [ɛskise] vt to sketch; **s'esquisser** vi (amélioration) to begin to be detectable; **~ un sourire** to give a hint of a smile

esquiver [ɛskive] vt to dodge; **s'esquiver** vi to slip away

essai [ese] nm trying; (tentative) attempt, try; (de produit) testing; (Rugby) try; (Littérature) essay; **essais** nmpl (Auto) trials; **à l'~** on a trial basis; **mettre à l'~** to put to the test; **~ gratuit** (Comm) free trial

essaim [esɛ̃] nm swarm

essayer [eseje] vt (gén) to try; (vêtement, chaussures) to try (on); (restaurant, méthode, voiture) to try (out) ▷ vi to try; **~ de faire** to try ou attempt to do; **s'~ à faire** to try one's hand at doing; **essayez un peu!** (menace) just you try!

essence [esɑ̃s] nf (de voiture) petrol (Brit), gas(oline) (US); (extrait de plante, Philosophie) essence; (espèce: d'arbre) species inv; **prendre de l'~** to get (some) petrol ou gas; **par ~** (essentiellement) essentially; **~ de citron/rose** lemon/rose oil; **~ sans plomb** unleaded petrol; **~ de térébenthine** turpentine

essentiel, le [esɑ̃sjɛl] adj essential ▷ nm: **l'~ d'un discours/d'une œuvre** the essence of a speech/work of art; **emporter l'~** to take the essentials; **c'est l'~** (ce qui importe) that's the main thing; **l'~ de** (la majeure partie) the main part of

essieu, x [esjø] nm axle

essor [esɔʀ] nm (de l'économie etc) rapid expansion; **prendre son ~** (oiseau) to fly off

essorer [esɔʀe] vt (en tordant) to wring (out); (par la force centrifuge) to spin-dry; (salade) to spin; (: en secouant) to shake dry

essoreuse [esɔʀøz] nf mangle, wringer; (à tambour) spin-dryer

essoufflé, e [esufle] adj out of breath, breathless

essouffler [esufle] vt to make breathless; **s'essouffler** vi to get out of breath; (fig: économie) to run out of steam

essuie-glace [esɥiglas] nm windscreen (Brit) ou windshield (US) wiper

essuyer [esɥije] vt to wipe; (fig: subir) to suffer; **s'essuyer** (après le bain) to dry o.s.; **~ la vaisselle** to dry up, dry the dishes

est [ɛ] vb voir **être** ▷ nm [ɛst]: **l'~** the east ▷ adj inv east; (région) east(ern); **à l'~** in the east; (direction) to the east, east(wards); **à l'~ de** (to the) east of; **les pays de l'E~** the eastern countries

estampe [ɛstɑ̃p] nf print, engraving

est-ce que [ɛskə] adv: **~ c'est cher/c'était bon?** is it expensive/was it good?; **quand est-ce qu'il part?** when does he leave?, when is he leaving?; **où est-ce qu'il va?** where's he going?; voir aussi **que**

esthéticienne [ɛstetisjɛn] nf beautician

esthétique [ɛstetik] adj (sens, jugement) aesthetic; (beau) attractive, aesthetically pleasing ▷ nf aesthetics sg; **l'~ industrielle** industrial design

estimation [ɛstimasjɔ̃] nf valuation; assessment; (chiffre) estimate; **d'après mes ~s** according to my calculations

estime [ɛstim] nf esteem, regard; **avoir de l'~ pour qn** to think highly of sb

estimer [ɛstime] vt (respecter) to esteem, hold in high regard; (expertiser: bijou) to value; (évaluer: coût etc) to assess, estimate; (penser): **~ que/être** to consider that/o.s. to be; **s'estimer** vi: **s'~ satisfait/hevreux** to feel satisfied/happy; **j'estime la distance à 10 km** I reckon the distance to be 10 km

estival, e, -aux [ɛstival, -o] adj summer cpd; **station ~e** (summer) holiday resort

estivant, e [ɛstivɑ̃, -ɑ̃t] nm/f (summer) holiday-maker

estomac [ɛstɔma] nm stomach; **avoir mal à l'~** to have stomach ache; **avoir l'~ creux** to have an empty stomach

estomaqué, e [ɛstɔmake] adj flabbergasted

estomper [ɛstɔ̃pe] vt (Art) to shade off; (fig) to blur, dim; **s'estomper** vi (sentiments) to soften; (contour) to become blurred

estrade [ɛstʀad] nf platform, rostrum

estragon [ɛstʀagɔ̃] nm tarragon

estuaire [ɛstɥɛʀ] nm estuary

et [e] conj and; **et lui?** what about him?; **et alors?, et (puis) après?** so what?; (ensuite) and then?

étable [etabl] nf cowshed

établi, e [etabli] adj established ▷ nm (work) bench

établir [etabliʀ] vt (papiers d'identité, facture) to make out; (liste, programme) to draw up; (gouvernement, artisan etc: aider à s'installer) to set up, establish; (entreprise, atelier, camp) to set up; (réputation, usage, fait, culpabilité, relations) to establish; (Sport: record) to set; **s'établir** vi (se *faire: entente etc)* to be established; **s'~ (à son compte)** to set up in business; **s'~ à/près de** to settle in/near

établissement [etablismɑ̃] *nm* making out; drawing up; setting up, establishing, *(entreprise, institution)* establishment; **~ de crédit** credit institution; **~ hospitalier** hospital complex; **~ industriel** industrial plant, factory; **~ scolaire** school, educational establishment

étage [etaʒ] *nm (d'immeuble)* storey (Brit), story (US), floor; *(de fusée)* stage; *(Géo: de culture, végétation)* level; **au 2ème ~** on the 2nd (Brit) *ou* 3rd (US) floor; **à l'~** upstairs; **maison à deux ~s** two-storey *ou* -story house; **c'est à quel ~?** what floor is it on?; **de bas ~** *adj* low-born; *(médiocre)* inferior

étagère [etaʒɛʀ] *nf (rayon)* shelf; *(meuble)* shelves *pl*, set of shelves

étai [etɛ] *nm* stay, prop

étain [etɛ̃] *nm* tin; *(Orfèvrerie)* pewter *no pl*

étais *etc* [etɛ] *vb voir* **être**

étal [etal] *nm* stall

étalage [etalaʒ] *nm* display; *(vitrine)* display window; **faire ~ de** to show off, parade

étaler [etale] *vt (carte, nappe)* to spread (out); *(peinture, liquide)* to spread; *(échelonner: paiements, dates, vacances)* to spread, stagger; *(exposer: marchandises)* to display; *(richesses, connaissances)* to parade; **s'étaler** *vi (liquide)* to spread out; *(fam)* to fall flat on one's face, come a cropper (Brit); **s'~ sur** *(paiements etc)* to be spread over

étalon [etalɔ̃] *nm (mesure)* standard; *(cheval)* stallion; **l'~-or** the gold standard

étanche [etɑ̃ʃ] *adj (récipient, aussi fig)* watertight; *(montre, vêtement)* waterproof; **~ à l'air** airtight

étancher [etɑ̃ʃe] *vt (liquide)* to stop (flowing); **~ sa soif** to quench *ou* slake one's thirst

étang [etɑ̃] *nm* pond

étant [etɑ̃] *vb voir* **être**; **donné**

étape [etap] *nf* stage; *(lieu d'arrivée)* stopping place; *(: Cyclisme)* staging point; **faire ~ à** to stop off at; **brûler les ~s** *(fig)* to cut corners

état [eta] *nm (Pol, condition)* state; *(d'un article d'occasion etc)* condition, state; *(liste)* inventory, statement; *(condition: professionnelle)* profession, trade; *(: sociale)* status; **en bon/mauvais ~** in good/poor condition; **en ~ (de marche)** in (working) order; **remettre en ~** to repair; **hors d'~** out of order; **être en ~/hors d'~ de faire** to be in a state/in no fit state to do; **en tout ~ de cause** in any event; **être dans tous ses ~s** to be in a state; **faire ~ de** *(alléguer)* to put forward; **en ~ d'arrestation** under arrest; **~ de grâce** *(Rel)* state of grace; *(fig)* honeymoon period; **en ~ de grâce** *(fig)* inspired; **en ~ d'ivresse** under the influence of drink; **~ de choses** *(situation)* state of affairs; **l'É~** the State; **~ civil** civil status; *(bureau)* registry office (Brit); **~ d'esprit** frame

of mind; **~ des lieux** inventory of fixtures; **~ de santé** state of health; **~ de siège/d'urgence** state of siege/emergency; **~ de veille** *(Psych)* waking state; **~s d'âme** moods; **les É~s barbaresques** the Barbary States; **les É~s du Golfe** the Gulf States; **~s de service** service record *sg*

étatiser [etatize] *vt* to bring under state control

état-major *(pl* **états-majors)** [etamaʒɔʀ] *nm (Mil)* staff; *(d'un parti etc)* top advisers *pl*; *(d'une entreprise)* top management

États-Unis [etazyni] *nmpl*: **les ~ (d'Amérique)** the United States (of America)

étau, x [eto] *nm* vice (Brit), vise (US)

étayer [eteje] *vt* to prop *ou* shore up; *(fig)* to back up

etc. [ɛtseteʀa] *adv* etc

et cætera, et cetera [ɛtseteʀa], **etc.** *adv* et cetera, and so on, etc

été [ete] *pp de* **être** ▷ *nm* summer; **en ~** in summer

éteindre [etɛ̃dʀ] *vt (lampe, lumière, radio, chauffage)* to turn *ou* switch off; *(cigarette, incendie, bougie)* to put out, extinguish; *(Jur: dette)* to extinguish; **s'éteindre** *vi* to go off; *(feu, lumière)* to go out; *(mourir)* to pass away

éteint, e [etɛ̃, -ɛ̃t] *pp de* **éteindre** ▷ *adj (fig)* lacklustre, dull; *(volcan)* extinct; **tous feux ~s** *(Auto: rouler)* without lights

étendard [etɑ̃daʀ] *nm* standard

étendre [etɑ̃dʀ] *vt (appliquer: pâte, liquide)* to spread; *(déployer: carte etc)* to spread out; *(sur un fil: lessive, linge)* to hang up *ou* out; *(bras, jambes, par terre: blessé)* to stretch out; *(diluer)* to dilute, thin; *(fig: agrandir)* to extend; *(fam: adversaire)* to floor; **s'étendre** *vi (augmenter, se propager)* to spread; *(terrain, forêt etc)*: **s'~ jusqu'à/de ... à** to stretch as far as/from ... to; **s'~ (sur)** *(s'allonger)* to stretch out (upon); *(se coucher)* to lie down (on); *(fig: expliquer)* to elaborate *ou* enlarge (upon)

étendu, e [etɑ̃dy] *adj* extensive ▷ *nf (d'eau, de sable)* stretch, expanse; *(importance)* extent

éternel, le [etɛʀnɛl] *adj* eternal; **les neiges ~les** perpetual snow

éterniser [etɛʀnize]: **s'éterniser** *vi* to last for ages; *(personne)* to stay for ages

éternité [etɛʀnite] *nf* eternity; **il y a** *ou* **ça fait une ~ que** it's ages since; **de toute ~** from time immemorial; **ça a duré une ~** it lasted for ages

éternuement [etɛʀnymɑ̃] *nm* sneeze

éternuer [etɛʀnɥe] *vi* to sneeze

êtes [ɛt(z)] *vb voir* **être**

Éthiopie [etjɔpi] *nf*: **l'~** Ethiopia

éthique [etik] *adj* ethical ▷ *nf* ethics *sg*

ethnie [ɛtni] *nf* ethnic group

éthylisme [etilism] *nm* alcoholism

étiez [etje] *vb voir* **être**

étinceler [etɛ̃s(ə)le] *vi* to sparkle

étincelle [etɛ̃sɛl] *nf* spark

étiqueter [etikte] vt to label

étiquette [etiket] vb voir **étiqueter** ▷ nf label; (protocole): **l'~** etiquette

étirer [etire] vt to stretch; (ressort) to stretch out; **s'étirer** vi (personne) to stretch; (convoi, route): **s'~ sur** to stretch out over

étoffe [etof] nf material, fabric; **avoir l'~ d'un chef** etc to be cut out to be a leader etc; **avoir de l'~** to be a forceful personality

étoffer [etofe] vt to flesh out; **s'étoffer** vi to fill out

étoile [etwal] nf star ▷ adj: **danseuse** ou **danseur ~** leading dancer; **la bonne/ mauvaise ~ de qn** sb's lucky/unlucky star; **à la belle ~** (out) in the open; **~ filante** shooting star; **~ de mer** starfish; **~ polaire** pole star

étoilé, e [etwale] adj starry

étonnant, e [etɔnã, -ãt] adj surprising

étonnement [etɔnmã] nm surprise, amazing; **à mon grand ~ ...** to my great surprise ou amazement ...

étonner [etɔne] vt to surprise, amaze; **s'étonner que/de** to be surprised that/at; **cela m'~ait (que)** (j'en doute) I'd be (very) surprised (if)

étouffant, e [etufã, -ãt] adj stifling

étouffé, e [etufe] adj (asphyxié) suffocated; (assourdi: cris, rires) smothered ▷ nf: **à l'~e** (Culin: poisson, légumes) steamed; (: viande) braised

étouffer [etufe] vt to suffocate; (bruit) to muffle; (scandale) to hush up ▷ vi to suffocate; (avoir trop chaud; aussi fig) to feel stifled; **s'étouffer** vi (en mangeant etc) to choke; **on étouffe** it's stifling

étourderie [eturdəri] nf (caractère) absent-mindedness no pl; (faute) thoughtless blunder; **faute d'~** careless mistake

étourdi, e [eturdi] adj (distrait) scatterbrained, heedless

étourdir [eturdir] vt (assommer) to stun, daze; (griser) to make dizzy ou giddy

étourdissement [eturdismã] nm dizzy spell

étourneau, x [eturno] nm starling

étrange [etrãʒ] adj strange

étranger, -ère [etrãʒe, -ɛr] adj foreign; (pas de la famille, non familier) strange ▷ nm/f foreigner; stranger ▷ nm: **l'~** foreign countries; **à l'~** abroad; **de l'~** from abroad; **~ à** (mal connu) unfamiliar to; (sans rapport) irrelevant to

étrangler [etrãgle] vt to strangle; (fig: presse, libertés) to stifle; **s'étrangler** vi (en mangeant etc) to choke; (se resserrer) to make a bottleneck

⬤ **MOT-CLÉ**

être [etr] nm being; **être humain** human being

▷ vb copule 1 (état, description) to be; **il est**

instituteur he is ou he's a teacher; **vous êtes grand/intelligent/fatigué** you are ou you're tall/clever/tired

2 (+à: appartenir) to be; **le livre est à Paul** the book is Paul's ou belongs to Paul; **c'est à moi/ eux** it is ou it's mine/theirs

3 (+de: provenance): **il est de Paris** he is from Paris; (appartenance: 000): **il est des nôtres** he is one of us

4 (date): **nous sommes le 10 janvier** it's the 10th of January (today)

▷ vi to be; **je ne serai pas ici demain** I won't be here tomorrow

▷ vb aux 1 to have; to be; **être arrivé/allé** to have arrived/gone; **il est parti** he has left, he has gone

2 (forme passive) to be; **être fait par** to be made by; **il a été promu** he has been promoted

3 (+à +inf: obligation, but): **c'est à réparer** it needs repairing; **c'est à essayer** it should be tried; **il est à espérer que ...** it is ou it's to be hoped that ...

▷ vb impers 1: **il est** avec adjectif it is; **il est impossible de le faire** it's impossible to do it

2 (heure, date): **il est 10 heures** it is ou it's 10 o'clock

3 (emphatique): **c'est moi** it's me; **c'est à lui de le faire** it's up to him to do it; voir aussi **est-ce que**; **n'est-ce pas**; **c'est-à-dire**; **ce**

étreindre [etrẽdr] vt to clutch, grip; (amoureusement, amicalement) to embrace; **s'étreindre** to embrace

étrenner [etrene] vt to use (ou wear) for the first time

étrennes [etren] nfpl (cadeaux) New Year's present; (gratifications) ≈ Christmas box sg, ≈ Christmas bonus

étrier [etrije] nm stirrup

étriqué, e [etrike] adj skimpy

étroit, e [etrwa, -wat] adj narrow; (vêtement) tight; (fig: serré: liens, collaboration) close, tight; **à l'~** cramped; **d'esprit** narrow-minded

étude [etyd] nf studying; (ouvrage, rapport, Mus) study; (de notaire: bureau) office; (: charge) practice; (Scol: salle de travail) study room; **études** nfpl (Scol) studies; **être à l'~** (projet etc) to be under consideration; **faire des ~s (de droit/médecine)** to study (law/medicine); **~s secondaires/supérieures** secondary/higher education; **~ de cas** case study; **~ de faisabilité** feasibility study; **~ de marché** (Écon) market research

étudiant, e [etydjã, -ãt] adj, nm/f student

étudier [etydje] vt, vi to study

étui [etyi] nm case

étuve [etyv] nf steamroom; (appareil) sterilizer

étuvée [etyve]: **à l'~** adv braised

eu, eue [y] pp de **avoir**

euh [ø] excl er

euro [øʀo] nm euro

Euroland [øʀolɑ̃d] nm Euroland

Europe [øʀɔp] nf: **l'~** Europe; **l'~ centrale** Central Europe; **l'~ verte** European agriculture

européen, ne [øʀɔpeɛ̃, -ɛn] adj European ▷ nm/f: **E~, ne** European

eus etc [y] vb voir **avoir**

eux [ø] pron (sujet) they; (objet) them; **~, ils ont fait ...** THEY did ...

évacuer [evakɥe] vt (salle, région) to evacuate, clear; (occupants, population) to evacuate; (toxine etc) to evacuate, discharge

évader [evade]: **s'évader** vi to escape

évaluer [evalɥe] vt (expertiser) to assess, evaluate; (juger approximativement) to estimate

évangile [evɑ̃ʒil] nm gospel; (texte de la Bible): **É~** Gospel; **ce n'est pas l'É~** (fig) it's not gospel

évanouir [evanwiʀ]: **s'évanouir** vi to faint, pass out; (disparaître) to vanish, disappear

évanouissement [evanwismɑ̃] nm (syncope) fainting fit; (Méd) loss of consciousness

évaporer [evapɔʀe]: **s'évaporer** vi to evaporate

évasé, e [evaze] adj (jupe etc) flared

évasif, -ive [evazif, -iv] adj evasive

évasion [evazjɔ̃] nf escape; **littérature d'~** escapist literature; **~ des capitaux** (Écon) flight of capital; **~ fiscale** tax avoidance

évêché [eveʃe] nm (fonction) bishopric; (palais) bishop's palace

éveil [evɛj] nm awakening; **être en ~** to be alert; **mettre qn en ~, donner l'~ à qn** to arouse sb's suspicions; **activités d'~** early-learning activities

éveillé, e [eveje] adj awake; (vif) alert, sharp

éveiller [eveje] vt to (a)waken; (soupçons etc) to arouse; **s'éveiller** vi to (a)waken; (fig) to be aroused

événement [evɛnmɑ̃] nm event

éventail [evɑ̃taj] nm fan; (choix) range; **en ~** fanned out; fan-shaped

éventaire [evɑ̃tɛʀ] nm stall, stand

éventer [evɑ̃te] vt (secret, complot) to uncover; (avec un éventail) to fan; **s'éventer** vi (parfum, vin) to go stale

éventualité [evɑ̃tɥalite] nf eventuality; possibility; **dans l'~ de** in the event of; **parer à toute ~** to guard against all eventualities

éventuel, le [evɑ̃tɥɛl] adj possible

éventuellement [evɑ̃tɥɛlmɑ̃] adv possibly

évêque [evɛk] nm bishop

évertuer [evɛʀtɥe]: **s'évertuer** vi: **s'~ à faire** to try very hard to do

éviction [eviksjɔ̃] nf ousting, supplanting; (de locataire) eviction

évidemment [evidamɑ̃] adv (bien sûr) of course; (certainement) obviously

évidence [evidɑ̃s] nf obviousness; (fait) obvious fact; **se rendre à l'~** to bow before the evidence; **nier l'~** to deny the evidence;

à l'~ evidently; **de toute ~** quite obviously ou evidently; **en ~** conspicuous; **être en ~** to be clearly visible; **mettre en ~** (fait) to highlight

évident, e [evidɑ̃, -ɑ̃t] adj obvious, evident; **ce n'est pas ~** (cela pose des problèmes) it's not (all that) straightforward, it's not as simple as all that

évider [evide] vt to scoop out

évier [evje] nm (kitchen) sink

évincer [evɛ̃se] vt to oust, supplant

éviter [evite] vt to avoid; **~ de faire/que qch ne se passe** to avoid doing/sth happening; **~ qch à qn** to spare sb sth

évolué, e [evɔlɥe] adj advanced; (personne) broad-minded

évoluer [evɔlɥe] vi (enfant, maladie) to develop; (situation, moralement) to evolve, develop; (aller et venir: danseur etc) to move about, circle

évolution [evɔlysjɔ̃] nf development; evolution; **évolutions** nfpl movements

évoquer [evɔke] vt to call to mind, evoke; (mentionner) to mention

ex- [ɛks] préfixe ex-; **son ~mari** her ex-husband; **son ~femme** his ex-wife

exact, e [ɛgza(kt), ɛgzakt] adj (précis) exact, accurate, precise; (correct) correct; (ponctuel) punctual; **l'heure ~e** the right ou exact time

exactement [ɛgzaktəmɑ̃] adv exactly, accurately, precisely; correctly; (c'est cela même) exactly

exagéré, e [ɛgzaʒeʀe] adj (prix etc) excessive

exagérer [ɛgzaʒeʀe] vt to exaggerate ▷ vi (abuser) to go too far; (dépasser les bornes) to overstep the mark; (déformer les faits) to exaggerate; **s'exagérer qch** to exaggerate sth

exalter [ɛgzalte] vt (enthousiasmer) to excite, elate; (glorifier) to exalt

examen [ɛgzamɛ̃] nm examination; (Scol) exam, examination; **à l'~** (dossier, projet) under consideration; (Comm) on approval; **~ blanc** mock exam(ination); **~ de la vue** sight test; **~ médical** (medical) examination; (analyse) test

examinateur, -trice [ɛgzaminatœʀ, -tʀis] nm/f examiner

examiner [ɛgzamine] vt to examine

exaspérant, e [ɛgzaspeʀɑ̃, -ɑ̃t] adj exasperating

exaspérer [ɛgzaspeʀe] vt to exasperate; (aggraver) to exacerbate

exaucer [ɛgzose] vt (vœu) to grant, fulfil; **~ qn** to grant sb's wishes

excédent [ɛksedɑ̃] nm surplus; **en ~** surplus; **payer 60 euros d'~** (de bagages) to pay 60 euros excess baggage; **~ de bagages** excess baggage; **~ commercial** trade surplus

excéder [ɛksede] vt (dépasser) to exceed; (agacer) to exasperate; **excédé de fatigue** exhausted; **excédé de travail** worn out with work

excellent, e [ɛksɛlɑ̃, -ɑ̃t] *adj* excellent

excentrique [ɛksɑ̃tʀik] *adj* eccentric; *(quartier)* outlying ▷ *nm/f* eccentric

excepté, e [ɛksɛpte] *adj, prép*: **les élèves ~s**, **~ les élèves** except for *ou* apart from the pupils; **~ si/quand** except if/when; **~ que** except that

exception [ɛksɛpsjɔ̃] *nf* exception; **faire ~** to be an exception; **faire une ~** to make an exception; **sans ~** without exception; **à l'~ de** except for, with the exception of; **d'~** *(mesure, loi)* special, exceptional

exceptionnel, le [ɛksɛpsjɔnɛl] *adj* exceptional; *(prix)* special

exceptionnellement [ɛksɛpsjɔnɛlmɑ̃] *adv* exceptionally; *(par exception)* by way of an exception, on this occasion

excès [ɛksɛ] *nm* surplus ▷ *nmpl* excesses; **à l'~** *(méticuleux, généreux)* to excess; **avec ~** to excess; **sans ~** in moderation; **tomber dans l'~ inverse** to go to the opposite extreme; **~ de langage** immoderate language; **~ de pouvoir** abuse of power; **faire des ~** to overindulge; **~ de vitesse** speeding *no pl*, exceeding the speed limit; **~ de zèle** overzealousness *no pl*

excessif, -ive [ɛksesif, -iv] *adj* excessive

excitant, e [ɛksitɑ̃, -ɑ̃t] *adj* exciting ▷ *nm* stimulant

excitation [ɛksitasjɔ̃] *nf* *(état)* excitement

exciter [ɛksite] *vt* to excite; *(café etc)* to stimulate; **s'exciter** *vi* to get excited; **~ qn à** *(révolte etc)* to incite sb to

exclamation [ɛksklamasjɔ̃] *nf* exclamation

exclamer [ɛksklame]: **s'exclamer** *vi* to exclaim

exclu, e [ɛkskly] *adj*: **il est/n'est pas ~ que ...** it's out of the question/not impossible that ...

exclure [ɛksklyʀ] *vt* *(faire sortir)* to expel; *(ne pas compter)* to exclude, leave out; *(rendre impossible)* to exclude, rule out

exclusif, -ive [ɛksklyzif, -iv] *adj* exclusive; **avec la mission exclusive/dans le but ~ de ...** with the sole mission/aim of ...; **agent ~** sole agent

exclusion [ɛksklyzjɔ̃] *nf* expulsion; **à l'~ de** with the exclusion *ou* exception of

exclusivité [ɛksklyzivite] *nf* exclusiveness; *(Comm)* exclusive rights *pl*; **film passant en ~ à** film showing only at

excursion [ɛkskyʀsjɔ̃] *nf* *(en autocar)* excursion, trip; *(à pied)* walk, hike; **faire une ~** to go on an excursion *ou* a trip; to go on a walk *ou* hike

excuse [ɛkskyz] *nf* excuse; **excuses** *nfpl* *(regret)* apology *sg*, apologies; **faire des ~s** to apologize; **faire ses ~s** to offer one's apologies; **mot d'~** *(Scol)* note from one's parent(s) *(to explain absence etc)*; **lettre d'~s** letter of apology

excuser [ɛkskyze] *vt* to excuse; **~ qn de qch** *(dispenser)* to excuse sb from sth; **s'excuser**

(de) to apologize (for); **"excusez-moi"** "I'm sorry"; *(pour attirer l'attention)* "excuse me"; **se faire ~** to ask to be excused

exécrable [ɛgzekʀabl] *adj* atrocious

exécuter [ɛgzekyte] *vt* *(prisonnier)* to execute; *(tâche etc)* to execute, carry out; *(Mus: jouer)* to perform, execute; *(Inform)* to run; **s'exécuter** *vi* to comply

exécutif, -ive [ɛgzekytif, -iv] *adj, nm* *(Pol)* executive

exécution [ɛgzekysjɔ̃] *nf* execution; carrying out; **mettre à ~** to carry out

exemplaire [ɛgzɑ̃plɛʀ] *adj* exemplary ▷ *nm* copy

exemple [ɛgzɑ̃pl] *nm* example; **par ~** for instance, for example; *(valeur intensive)* really!; **sans ~** *(bêtise, gourmandise etc)* unparalleled; **donner l'~** to set an example; **prendre ~ sur** to take as a model; **à l'~ de** just like; **pour l'~** *(punir)* as an example

exempt, e [ɛgzɑ̃, -ɑ̃t] *adj*: **~ de** *(dispensé de)* exempt from; *(sans)* free from; **~ de taxes** tax-free

exercer [ɛgzɛʀse] *vt* *(pratiquer)* to exercise, practise; *(faire usage de: prérogative)* to exercise; *(effectuer: influence, contrôle, pression)* to exert; *(former)* to exercise, train; **s'exercer** *vi* *(médecin)* to be in practice; *(sportif, musicien)* to practise; *(se faire sentir: pression etc)*: **s'~ (sur *ou* contre)** to be exerted (on); **s'~ à faire qch** to train o.s. to do sth

exercice [ɛgzɛʀsis] *nm* practice; exercising; *(tâche, travail)* exercise; *(Comm, Admin: période)* accounting period; **l'~** *(sportive etc)* exercise; *(Mil)* drill; **en ~** *(juge)* in office; *(médecin)* practising; **dans l'~ de ses fonctions** in the discharge of his duties; **~s d'assouplissement** limbering-up (exercises)

exhaustif, -ive [ɛgzostif, -iv] *adj* exhaustive

exhiber [ɛgzibe] *vt* *(montrer: papiers, certificat)* to present, produce; *(péj)* to display, flaunt; **s'exhiber** *vi* *(personne)* to parade; *(exhibitionniste)* to expose o.s.

exhibitionniste [ɛgzibisjɔnist] *nm/f* exhibitionist

exhorter [ɛgzɔʀte] *vt*: **~ qn à faire** to urge sb to do

exigeant, e [ɛgziʒɑ̃, -ɑ̃t] *adj* demanding; *(péj)* hard to please

exigence [ɛgziʒɑ̃s] *nf* demand, requirement

exiger [ɛgziʒe] *vt* to demand, require

exigu, ë [ɛgzigy] *adj* cramped, tiny

exil [ɛgzil] *nm* exile; **en ~** in exile

exiler [ɛgzile] *vt* to exile; **s'exiler** *vi* to go into exile

existence [ɛgzistɑ̃s] *nf* existence; **dans l'~** in life

exister [ɛgziste] *vi* to exist; **il existe un/des** there is a/are (some)

exonérer [ɛgzɔneʀe] *vt*: **~ de** to exempt from

exorbitant, e [ɛgzɔʀbitɑ̃, -ɑ̃t] *adj* exorbitant

exorbité, e [ɛgzɔrbite] *adj*: **yeux ~s** bulging eyes

exotique [ɛgzɔtik] *adj* exotic; **yaourt aux fruits ~s** tropical fruit yoghurt

expatrier [ɛkspatrije] *vt* (*argent*) to take *ou* send out of the country; **s'expatrier** to leave one's country

expectative [ɛkspɛktativ] *nf*: **être dans l'~** to be waiting to see

expédient [ɛkspedjɑ̃] *nm* (*parfois péj*) expedient; **vivre d'~s** to live by one's wits

expédier [ɛkspedje] *vt* (*lettre, paquet*) to send; (*troupes, renfort*) to dispatch; (*péj: travail etc*) to dispose of, dispatch

expéditeur, -trice [ɛkspeditœr, -tris] *nm/f* (*Postes*) sender

expédition [ɛkspedisjɔ̃] *nf* sending; (*scientifique, sportive, Mil*) expedition; **~ punitive** punitive raid

expérience [ɛksperjɑ̃s] *nf* (*de la vie, des choses*) experience; (*scientifique*) experiment; **avoir de l'~** to have experience, be experienced; **avoir l'~ de** to have experience of; **faire l'~ de qch** to experience sth; **~ de chimie/d'électricité** chemical/electrical experiment

expérimenté, e [ɛksperimɑ̃te] *adj* experienced

expérimenter [ɛksperimɑ̃te] *vt* (*machine, technique*) to test out, experiment with

expert, e [ɛkspɛr, -ɛrt] *adj*: **~ en** expert in ▷ *nm* (*spécialiste*) expert; **~ en assurances** insurance valuer

expert-comptable (*pl* **experts-comptables**) [ɛkspɛrkɔ̃tabl] *nm* ≈ chartered (*Brit*) *ou* certified public (*US*) accountant

expertise [ɛkspɛrtiz] *nf* valuation; assessment; valuer's (*ou* assessor's) report; (*Jur*) (forensic) examination

expertiser [ɛkspɛrtize] *vt* (*objet de valeur*) to value; (*voiture accidentée etc*) to assess damage to

expier [ɛkspje] *vt* to expiate, atone for

expirer [ɛkspire] *vi* (*prendre fin, littéraire: mourir*) to expire; (*respirer*) to breathe out

explicatif, -ive [ɛksplikatif, -iv] *adj* (*mot, texte, note*) explanatory

explication [ɛksplikasjɔ̃] *nf* explanation; (*discussion*) discussion; (*dispute*) argument; **~ de texte** (*Scol*) critical analysis (of a text)

explicite [ɛksplisit] *adj* explicit

expliquer [ɛksplike] *vt* to explain; **~ (à qn) comment/que** to point out *ou* explain (to sb) how/that; **s'expliquer** (*se faire comprendre: personne*) to explain o.s.; (*se disputer*) to have it out; (*comprendre*): **je m'explique son retard/ absence** I understand his lateness/absence; **son erreur s'explique** one can understand his mistake; **s'~ avec qn** (*discuter*) to explain o.s. to sb

exploit [ɛksplwa] *nm* exploit, feat

exploitant [ɛksplwatɑ̃] *nm/f*: **~ (agricole)** farmer

exploitation [ɛksplwatasjɔ̃] *nf* exploitation; (*d'une entreprise*) running; (*entreprise*): **~ agricole** farming concern

exploiter [ɛksplwate] *vt* (*personne, don*) to exploit; (*entreprise, ferme*) to run, operate; (*mine*) to exploit, work

explorer [ɛksplɔre] *vt* to explore

exploser [ɛksploze] *vi* to explode, blow up; (*engin explosif*) to go off; (*fig: joie, colère*) to burst out, explode; (: *personne: de colère*) to explode, flare up; **faire ~** (*bombe*) to explode, detonate; (*bâtiment, véhicule*) to blow up

explosif, -ive [ɛksplozif, -iv] *adj, nm* explosive

explosion [ɛksplozjɔ̃] *nf* explosion; **~ de joie/ colère** outburst of joy/rage; **~ démographique** population explosion

exportateur, -trice [ɛksportatœr, -tris] *adj* export *cpd*, exporting ▷ *nm* exporter

exportation [ɛksportasjɔ̃] *nf* (*action*) exportation; (*produit*) export

exporter [ɛksporte] *vt* to export

exposant [ɛkspozɑ̃] *nm* exhibitor; (*Math*) exponent

exposé, e [ɛkspoze] *nm* (*écrit*) exposé; (*oral*) talk ▷ *adj*: **~ au sud** facing south, with a southern aspect; **bien ~** well situated; **très ~** very exposed

exposer [ɛkspoze] *vt* (*montrer: marchandise*) to display; (: *peinture*) to exhibit, show; (*parler de: problème, situation*) to explain, expose, set out; (*mettre en danger, orienter, Photo: maison etc*) to expose; **~ qn/qch à** to expose sb/sth to; **~ sa vie** to risk one's life; **s'exposer à** (*soleil, danger*) to expose o.s. to; (*critiques, punition*) to lay o.s. open to

exposition [ɛkspozisjɔ̃] *nf* (*voir exposer*) displaying; exhibiting; explanation, exposition; (*voir exposé*) aspect, situation; (*manifestation*) exhibition; (*Photo*) exposure; (*introduction*) exposition

exprès¹ [ɛksprɛ] *adv* (*délibérément*) on purpose; (*spécialement*) specially; **faire ~ de faire qch** to do sth on purpose

exprès², -esse [ɛksprɛs] *adj* (*ordre, défense*) express, formal ▷ *adj inv, adv* (*Postes: lettre, colis*) express; **envoyer qch en ~** to send sth express

express [ɛksprɛs] *adj, nm*: (**café**) **~** espresso; (**train**) **~** fast train

expressément [ɛksprɛsemɑ̃] *adv* expressly, specifically

expressif, -ive [ɛksprɛsif, -iv] *adj* expressive

expression [ɛksprɛsjɔ̃] *nf* expression; **réduit à sa plus simple ~** reduced to its simplest terms; **liberté/moyens d'~** freedom/means of expression; **~ toute faite** set phrase

exprimer [ɛksprime] *vt* (*sentiment, idée*) to express; (*faire sortir: jus, liquide*) to press out; **s'exprimer** *vi* (*personne*) to express o.s.

exproprier [ɛksproprije] *vt* to buy up (*ou* buy

the property of) by compulsory purchase,
expropriate

expulser [ɛkspylse] vt *(d'une salle, d'un groupe)*
to expel; *(locataire)* to evict; *(Football)* to send off

exquis, e [ɛkski, -iz] adj *(gâteau, parfum,
élégance)* exquisite; *(personne, temps)* delightful

extase [ɛkstɑz] nf ecstasy; **être en ~** to be in
raptures

extasier [ɛkstɑzje]: **s'extasier** vi: **s'~ sur** to
go into raptures over

extension [ɛkstɑ̃sjɔ̃] nf *(d'un muscle, ressort)*
stretching; *(Méd)*: **à l'~** in traction; *(fig)*
extension; expansion

exténuer [ɛkstenɥe] vt to exhaust

extérieur, e [ɛksterjœʁ] adj *(de dehors: porte,
mur etc)* outer, outside; *(: commerce, politique)*
foreign; *(: influences, pressions)* external; *(au
dehors: escalier, w.-c.)* outside; *(apparent: calme,
gaieté etc)* outer ▷ nm *(d'une maison, d'un récipient
etc)* outside, exterior; *(d'une personne:
apparence)* exterior; *(d'un pays, d'un groupe social)*:
l'~ the outside world; **à l'~** *(dehors)* outside;
(fig: à l'étranger) abroad

extérieurement [ɛksterjœʁmɑ̃] adv *(de
dehors)* on the outside; *(en apparence)* on the
surface

exterminer [ɛkstɛʁmine] vt to exterminate,
wipe out

externat [ɛkstɛʁna] nm day school

externe [ɛkstɛʁn] adj external, outer ▷ nm/f
(Méd) non-resident medical student, extern
(US); *(Scol)* day pupil

extincteur [ɛkstɛ̃ktœʁ] nm *(fire)*
extinguisher

extinction [ɛkstɛ̃ksjɔ̃] nf extinction; *(Jur:
d'une dette)* extinguishment; **~ de voix** *(Méd)*
loss of voice

extorquer [ɛkstɔʁke] vt *(de l'argent, un
renseignement)*: **~ qch à qn** to extort sth
from sb

extra [ɛkstʁa] adj inv first-rate; *(fam)*
fantastic; *(marchandises)* top-quality ▷ nm inv
extra help ▷ préfixe extra(-)

extrader [ɛkstʁade] vt to extradite

extraire [ɛkstʁɛʁ] vt to extract; **~ qch de** to
extract sth from

extrait, e [ɛkstʁɛ, -ɛt] pp de **extraire** ▷ nm
(de plante) extract; *(de film, livre)* extract,
excerpt; **~ de naissance** birth certificate

extraordinaire [ɛkstʁaɔʁdinɛʁ] adj
extraordinary; *(Pol, Admin: mesures etc)*
special; **ambassadeur ~** ambassador
extraordinary; **assemblée ~** extraordinary
meeting; **par ~** by some unlikely chance

extravagant, e [ɛkstʁavagɑ̃, -ɑ̃t] adj
(personne, attitude) extravagant; *(idée)* wild

extraverti, e [ɛkstʁavɛʁti] adj extrovert

extrême [ɛkstʁɛm] adj, nm extreme; *(intensif)*:
d'une ~ simplicité/brutalité extremely
simple/brutal; **d'un ~ à l'autre** from one
extreme to another; **à l'~** in the extreme; **à l'~
rigueur** in the absolute extreme

extrêmement [ɛkstʁɛmmɑ̃] adv extremely

extrême-onction (pl **extrêmes-onctions**)
[ɛkstʁɛmɔ̃ksjɔ̃] nf *(Rel)* last rites pl, Extreme
Unction

Extrême-Orient [ɛkstʁɛmɔʁjɑ̃] nm: **l'~** the
Far East

extrémité [ɛkstʁemite] nf *(bout)* end;
(situation) straits pl, plight; *(geste désespéré)*
extreme action; **extrémités** nfpl *(pieds et
mains)* extremities; **à la dernière ~** *(à l'agonie)*
on the point of death

exubérant, e [ɛgzybeʁɑ̃, -ɑ̃t] adj exuberant

exutoire [ɛgzytwaʁ] nm outlet, release

F, f [ɛf] *nm inv* F, f ▷ *abr* = **féminin**; (= *franc*) fr.;
(= *Fahrenheit*) F; (= *frère*) Br(o).; (= *femme*) W;
(*appartement*): **un F2/F3** a 2-/3-roomed flat
(Brit) *ou* apartment (US); **F comme François**
F for Frederick (Brit) *ou* Fox (US)

fa [fa] *nm inv* (Mus) F; (*en chantant la gamme*) fa

fable [fabl] *nf* fable; (*mensonge*) story, tale

fabricant, e [fabʀikɑ̃, ɑ̃t] *nm/f*
manufacturer, maker

fabrication [fabʀikasjɔ̃] *nf* manufacture,
making

fabrique [fabʀik] *nf* factory

fabriquer [fabʀike] *vt* to make;
(*industriellement*) to manufacture, make;
(*construire: voiture*) to manufacture, build;
(: *maison*) to build; (*fig: inventer: histoire, alibi*) to
make up; (*fam*): **qu'est-ce qu'il fabrique?**
what is he up to?; **~ en série** to mass-produce

fabulation [fabylasjɔ̃] *nf* (Psych) fantasizing

fac [fak] *abr f* (*fam: Scol: = faculté*) Uni (Brit: *fam*)
= college (US)

façade [fasad] *nf* front, façade; (*fig*) façade

face [fas] *nf* face; (*fig: aspect*) side ▷ *adj*: **le
côté ~** heads; **perdre/sauver la ~** to lose/save
face; **regarder qn en ~** to look sb in the face;
la maison/le trottoir d'en ~ the house/
pavement opposite; **en ~ de** *prép* opposite;
(*fig*) in front of; **de ~** *adv* from the front; face
on; **~ à** *prép* facing; (*fig*) faced with, in the
face of; **faire ~ à** to face; **faire ~ à la
demande** (Comm) to meet the demand; **~ à ~**
adv facing each other ▷ *nm inv* encounter

fâché, e [faʃe] *adj* angry; (*désolé*) sorry

fâcher [faʃe] *vt* to anger; **se fâcher** *vi* to get
angry; **se ~ avec** (*se brouiller*) to fall out with

fâcheux, -euse [faʃø, -øz] *adj* unfortunate,
regrettable

facile [fasil] *adj* easy; (*accommodant: caractère*)
easy-going

facilement [fasilmɑ̃] *adv* easily

facilité [fasilite] *nf* easiness; (*disposition, don*)
aptitude; (*moyen, occasion, possibilité*): **il a la ~
de rencontrer les gens** he has every
opportunity to meet people; **facilités** *nfpl*
(*possibilités*) facilities; (Comm) terms; **~s de
crédit** credit terms; **~s de paiement** easy
terms

faciliter [fasilite] *vt* to make easier

façon [fasɔ̃] *nf* (*manière*) way; (*d'une robe etc*)
making-up; cut; (: *main-d'œuvre*) labour (Brit),
labor (US); (*imitation*): **châle ~ cachemire**
cashmere-style shawl; **façons** *nfpl* (*péj*) fuss
sg; **faire des ~s** (*péj: être affecté*) to be affected;
(: *faire des histoires*) to make a fuss; **de quelle ~?**
(in) what way?; **sans ~** *adv* without fuss ▷ *adj*
unaffected; **non merci, sans ~** no thanks,
honestly; **d'une autre ~** in another way; **en
aucune ~** in no way; **de ~ à so as to**; **de ~ à ce
que, de (telle) ~ que** so that; **de toute ~**
anyway, in any case; **(c'est une) ~ de parler**
it's a way of putting it; **travail à ~** tailoring

façonner [fasɔne] *vt* (*fabriquer*) to
manufacture; (*travailler: matière*) to shape,
fashion; (*fig*) to mould, shape

facteur, -trice [faktœʀ, -tʀis] *nm/f*
postman/woman (Brit), mailman/woman
(US) ▷ *nm* (Math, *gén*: *élément*) factor;
~ d'orgues organ builder; **~ de pianos** piano
maker; **~ rhésus** rhesus factor

factice [faktis] *adj* artificial

faction [faksjɔ̃] *nf* (*groupe*) faction; (*Mil*)
guard *ou* sentry (duty); watch; **en ~** on guard;
standing watch

facture [faktyʀ] *nf* (*à payer: gén*) bill; (: Comm)
invoice; (*d'un artisan, artiste*) technique,
workmanship

facturer [faktyʀe] *vt* to invoice

facultatif, -ive [fakyltatif, -iv] *adj* optional;
(*arrêt de bus*) request *cpd*

faculté [fakylte] *nf* (*intellectuelle, d'université*)
faculty; (*pouvoir, possibilité*) power

fade [fad] *adj* insipid

fagot [fago] *nm* (*de bois*) bundle of sticks

faible [fɛbl] *adj* weak; (*voix, lumière, vent*) faint;
(*élève, copie*) poor; (*rendement, intensité, revenu
etc*) low ▷ *nm* weak point; (*pour quelqu'un*)
weakness, soft spot; **~ d'esprit**
feeble-minded

faiblesse [fɛbles] *nf* weakness

faiblir [feblir] *vi* to weaken; (*lumière*) to dim;
(*vent*) to drop

faïence [fajɑ̃s] *nf* earthenware *no pl*; (*objet*)
piece of earthenware

faignant, e [fɛɲɑ̃, -ɑ̃t] *nm/f* = **fainéant, e**

faille [faj] *vb voir* **falloir** ▷ *nf* (*Géo*) fault; (*fig*) flaw, weakness

faillir [fajiʀ] *vi*: **j'ai failli tomber/lui dire** I almost *ou* nearly fell/told him; **~ à une promesse/un engagement** to break a promise/an agreement

faillite [fajit] *nf* bankruptcy; (*échec: d'une politique etc*) collapse; **être en ~** to be bankrupt; **faire ~** to go bankrupt

faim [fɛ̃] *nf* hunger; (*fig*): **~ d'amour/de richesse** hunger *ou* yearning for love/wealth; **avoir ~** to be hungry; **rester sur sa ~** (*aussi fig*) to be left wanting more

fainéant, e [fɛneɑ̃, -ɑ̃t] *nm/f* idler, loafer

 MOT-CLÉ

faire [fɛʀ] *vt* **1** (*fabriquer, être l'auteur de*) to make; (*produire*) to produce; (*construire: maison, bateau*) to build; **faire du vin/une offre/un film** to make wine/an offer/a film; **faire du bruit** to make a noise

2 (*effectuer: travail, opération*) to do; **que faites-vous?** (*quel métier etc*) what do you do?; (*quelle activité: au moment de la question*) what are you doing?; **que faire?** what are we going to do?, what can be done (about it)?; **faire la lessive/le ménage** to do the washing/the housework

3 (*études*) to do; (*sport, musique*) to play; **faire du droit/du français** to do law/French; **faire du rugby/piano** to play rugby/the piano; **faire du cheval/du ski** to go riding/skiing

4 (*visiter*): **faire les magasins** to go shopping; **faire l'Europe** to tour *ou* do Europe

5 (*distance*): **faire du 50 (à l'heure)** to do 50 (km an hour); **nous avons fait 1000 km en 2 jours** we did *ou* covered 1000 km in 2 days

6 (*simuler*): **faire le malade/l'ignorant** to act the invalid/the fool

7 (*transformer, avoir un effet sur*): **faire de qn un frustré/avocat** to make sb frustrated/a lawyer; **ça ne me fait rien** (*m'est égal*) I don't care *ou* mind; (*me laisse froid*) it has no effect on me; **ça ne fait rien** it doesn't matter; **faire que** (*impliquer*) to mean that

8 (*calculs, prix, mesures*): **deux et deux font quatre** two and two are *ou* make four; **ça fait 10 m/15 euros** it's 10 m/15 euros; **je vous le fais 10 euros** I'll let you have it for 10 euros; **je fais du 40** I take a size 40

9 (*vb +de*): **qu'a-t-il fait de sa valise/de sa sœur?** what has he done with his case/his sister?

10: **ne faire que**: **il ne fait que critiquer** (*sans cesse*) all he (ever) does is criticize; (*seulement*) he's only criticizing

11 (*dire*) to say; **vraiment? fit-il** really? he said

12 (*maladie*) to have; **faire du diabète/de la tension** to have diabetes *sg*/high blood pressure

▷ *vi* **1** (*agir, s'y prendre*) to act, do; **il faut faire vite** we (*ou* you *etc*) must act quickly; **comment a-t-il fait pour?** how did he manage to?; **faites comme chez vous** make yourself at home; **je n'ai pas pu faire autrement** there was nothing else I could do

2 (*paraître*) to look; **faire vieux/démodé** to look old/old-fashioned; **ça fait bien** it looks good; **tu fais jeune dans cette robe** that dress makes you look young(er)

3 (*remplaçant un autre verbe*) to do; **il ne casse pas comme je l'ai fait** don't break it as I did; **je peux le voir? — faites!** can I see it? — please do!; **remets-le en place — je viens de le faire** put it back in its place — I just have (done)

▷ *vb impers* **1**: **il fait beau** *etc* the weather is fine *etc*; *voir aussi* **jour**; **froid** *etc*

2 (*temps écoulé, durée*): **ça fait deux ans qu'il est parti** it's two years since he left; **ça fait deux ans qu'il y est** he's been there for two years

▷ *vb aux* **1**: **faire** (*+infinitif: action directe*) to make; **faire tomber/bouger qch** to make sth fall/move; **faire démarrer un moteur/chauffer de l'eau** to start up an engine/heat some water; **cela lui fait dormir** it makes you sleep; **faire travailler les enfants** to make the children work *ou* get the children to work; **il m'a fait traverser la rue** he helped me to cross the road

2 (*indirectement, par un intermédiaire*): **faire réparer qch** to get *ou* have sth repaired; **faire punir les enfants** to have the children punished; **il m'a fait ouvrir la porte** he got me to open the door

se faire *vi* **1** (*vin, fromage*) to mature

2 (*être convenable*): **cela se fait beaucoup/ne se fait pas** it's done a lot/not done

3 (*+nom ou pron*): **se faire une jupe** to make o.s. a skirt; **se faire des amis** to make friends; **se faire du souci** to worry; **se faire des illusions** to delude o.s.; **se faire beaucoup d'argent** to make a lot of money; **il ne s'en fait pas** he doesn't worry

4 (*+adj: devenir*): **se faire vieux** to be getting old; (*délibérément*): **se faire beau** to do o.s. up

5: **se faire à** (*s'habituer*) to get used to; **je n'arrive pas à me faire à la nourriture/au climat** I can't get used to the food/climate

6 (*+infinitif*): **se faire examiner la vue/opérer** to have one's eyes tested/have an operation; **se faire couper les cheveux** to get one's hair cut; **il va se faire tuer/punir** he's going to get himself killed/get (himself) punished; **il s'est fait aider** he got somebody to help him; **il s'est fait aider par Simon** he got Simon to help him; **se faire faire un vêtement** to get a garment made for o.s.

7 (*impersonnel*): **comment se fait-il/faisait-il que?** how is it/was it that?; **il peut se faire que nous utilisions ...** it's possible that we could use ...

faire-part [fɛʀpaʀ] *nm inv* announcement (*of birth, marriage etc*)

faisable [fəzabl] *adj* feasible

faisan, e [fəzɑ̃, -an] *nm/f* pheasant

faisandé, e [fəzɑ̃de] *adj* high (*bad*); (*fig péj*) corrupt, decadent

faisceau, x [feso] *nm* (*de lumière etc*) beam; (*de branches etc*) bundle

faisons [fəzɔ̃] *vb voir* **faire**

fait¹ [fɛ] *vb voir* **faire** ▷ *nm* (*événement*) event, occurrence; (*réalité, donnée*) fact; **le ~ que/de manger** the fact that/of eating; **être le ~ de** (*causé par*) to be the work of; **être au ~ (de)** to be informed (of); **mettre qn au ~** to inform sb, put sb in the picture; **au ~** (*à propos*) by the way; **en venir au ~** to get to the point; **de ~** *adj* (*opposé à: de droit*) de facto ▷ *adv* in fact; **du ~ de ceci/qu'il a menti** because of ou on account of this/his having lied; **de ce ~** therefore, for this reason; **en ~** in fact; **en ~ de repas** by way of a meal; **prendre ~ et cause pour qn** to support sb, side with sb; **prendre qn sur le ~** to catch sb in the act; **dire à qn son ~** to give sb a piece of one's mind; **hauts ~s** (*exploits*) exploits; **~ d'armes** feat of arms; **~ divers** (*short*) news item; **les ~s et gestes de qn** sb's actions ou doings

fait², e [fɛ, fɛt] *pp de* **faire** ▷ *adj* (*mûr: fromage, melon*) ripe; (*maquillé: yeux*) made-up; (*vernis: ongles*) painted, polished; **un homme ~** a grown man; **tout(e) ~(e)** (*préparé à l'avance*) ready-made; **c'en est ~ de notre tranquillité** that's the end of our peace; **c'est bien ~ (pour lui ou eux etc)** it serves him (ou them *etc*) right

faîte [fɛt] *nm* top; (*fig*) pinnacle, height

faites [fɛt] *vb voir* **faire**

faitout [fɛtu] *nm* stewpot

falaise [falɛz] *nf* cliff

falloir [falwaʀ] *vb impers*: **il faut faire les lits** we (*ou you etc*) have to ou must make the beds; **il faut que je fasse les lits** I have to ou must make the beds; **il a fallu qu'il parte** he had to leave; **il faudrait qu'elle rentre** she should come ou go back, she ought to come ou go back; **il faut faire attention** you have to be careful; **il me faudrait 100 euros** I would need 100 euros; **il doit ~ du temps** that must take time; **il vous faut tourner à gauche après l'église** you have to turn left past the church; **nous avons ce qu'il (nous) faut** we have what we need; **il faut qu'il ait oublié** he must have forgotten; **il a fallu qu'il l'apprenne** he would have to hear about it; **il ne fallait pas** (*pour remercier*) you shouldn't have (done); **que faut-il faire!** (it) takes some doing! ▷ *vi*: **s'en falloir**: **il s'en est fallu de 10 euros/5 minutes** we (*ou they etc*) were 10 euros short/5 minutes late (*ou* early); **il s'en faut de beaucoup qu'il soit …** he is far from being …; **il s'en est fallu de peu que cela n'arrive** it very nearly happened; **ou peu**

s'en faut or just about, or as good as; **comme il faut** *adj* proper ▷ *adv* properly

falsifier [falsifje] *vt* to falsify

famé, e [fame] *adj*: **mal ~** disreputable, of ill repute

famélique [famelik] *adj* half-starved

fameux, -euse [famø, -øz] *adj* (*illustre: parfois péj*) famous; (*bon: repas, plat etc*) first-rate, first-class; (*intensif*): **un ~ problème** *etc* a real problem *etc*; **pas ~** not great, not much good

familial, e, -aux [familjal, -o] *adj* family *cpd* ▷ *nf* (*Auto*) family estate car (*Brit*), station wagon (*US*)

familiarité [familjaʀite] *nf* familiarity; informality; **familiarités** *nfpl* familiarities; **~ avec** (*sujet, science*) familiarity with

familier, -ière [familje, -jɛʀ] *adj* (*connu, impertinent*) familiar; (*atmosphère*) informal, friendly; (*Ling*) informal, colloquial ▷ *nm* regular (*visitor*)

famille [famij] *nf* family; **il a de la ~ à Paris** he has relatives in Paris

famine [famin] *nf* famine

fana [fana] *adj, nm/f* (*fam*) = **fanatique**

fanatique [fanatik] *adj*: **~ (de)** fanatical (about) ▷ *nm/f* fanatic

fanatisme [fanatism] *nm* fanaticism

faner [fane]: **se faner** *vi* to fade

fanfare [fɑ̃faʀ] *nf* (*orchestre*) brass band; (*musique*) fanfare; **en ~** (*avec bruit*) noisily

fanfaron, ne [fɑ̃faʀɔ̃, -ɔn] *nm/f* braggart

fantaisie [fɑ̃tezi] *nf* (*spontanéité*) fancy, imagination; (*caprice*) whim; extravagance; (*Mus*) fantasia ▷ *adj*: **bijou (de) ~** (piece of) costume jewellery (*Brit*) ou jewelry (*US*); **pain (de) ~** fancy bread

fantaisiste [fɑ̃tezist] *adj* (*péj*) unorthodox, eccentric ▷ *nm/f* (*de music-hall*) variety artist *ou* entertainer

fantasme [fɑ̃tasm] *nm* fantasy

fantasque [fɑ̃task] *adj* whimsical, capricious; fantastic

fantastique [fɑ̃tastik] *adj* fantastic

fantôme [fɑ̃tom] *nm* ghost, phantom

faon [fɑ̃] *nm* fawn (*deer*)

FAQ *abr f* (= *foire aux questions*) FAQ *pl* (= *frequently asked questions*)

farce [faʀs] *nf* (*viande*) stuffing; (*blague*) (practical) joke; (*Théât*) farce; **faire une ~ à qn** to play a (practical) joke on sb; **~s et attrapes** jokes and novelties

farcir [faʀsiʀ] *vt* (*viande*) to stuff; (*fig*): **~ qch de** to stuff sth with; **se farcir** (*fam*): **je me suis farci la vaisselle** I've got stuck ou landed with the washing-up

fardeau, x [faʀdo] *nm* burden

farder [faʀde] *vt* to make up; (*vérité*) to disguise; **se farder** to make o.s. up

farfelu, e [faʀfəly] *adj* wacky (*fam*), hare-brained

farine [faʀin] *nf* flour; **~ de blé** wheatflour; **~ de maïs** cornflour (*Brit*), cornstarch (*US*);

~ lactée (*pour bouillie*) baby cereal

farineux, -euse [faʀinø, -øz] *adj* (*sauce, pomme*) floury ▷ *nmpl* (*aliments*) starchy foods

farouche [faʀuʃ] *adj* shy, timid; (*sauvage*) savage, wild; (*violent*) fierce

fart [faʀt] *nm* (ski) wax

fascicule [fasikyl] *nm* volume

fascination [fasinasjɔ̃] *nf* fascination

fasciner [fasine] *vt* to fascinate

fascisme [faʃism] *nm* fascism

fasse *etc* [fas] *vb voir* **faire**

faste [fast] *nm* splendour (*Brit*), splendor (*US*) ▷ *adj*: **c'est un jour ~** it's his (*ou* our *etc*) lucky day

fastidieux, -euse [fastidjø, -øz] *adj* tedious, tiresome

fastueux, -euse [fastɥø, -øz] *adj* sumptuous, luxurious

fatal, e [fatal] *adj* fatal; (*inévitable*) inevitable

fatalité [fatalite] *nf* (*destin*) fate; (*coïncidence*) fateful coincidence; (*caractère inévitable*) inevitability

fatidique [fatidik] *adj* fateful

fatigant, e [fatigɑ̃, -ɑ̃t] *adj* tiring; (*agaçant*) tiresome

fatigue [fatig] *nf* tiredness, fatigue; (*détérioration*) fatigue; **les ~s du voyage** the wear and tear of the journey

fatigué, e [fatige] *adj* tired

fatiguer [fatige] *vt* to tire, make tired; (*Tech*) to put a strain on, strain; (*fig: agacer*) to annoy ▷ *vi* (*moteur*) to labour (*Brit*), labor (*US*), strain; **se fatiguer** *vi* to get tired; to tire o.s. (out); **se ~ à faire qch** to tire o.s. out doing sth

fatras [fatʀɑ] *nm* jumble, hotchpotch

faubourg [fobuʀ] *nm* suburb

fauché, e [foʃe] *adj* (*fam*) broke

faucher [foʃe] *vt* (*herbe*) to cut; (*champs, blés*) to reap; (*fig*) to cut down; (*véhicule*) to mow down; (*fam: voler*) to pinch, nick

faucille [fosij] *nf* sickle

faucon [fokɔ̃] *nm* falcon, hawk

faudra *etc* [fodʀa] *vb voir* **falloir**

faufiler [fofile] *vt* to tack, baste; **se faufiler** *vi*: **se ~ dans** to edge one's way into; **se ~ parmi/entre** to thread one's way among/between

faune [fon] *nf* (*Zool*) wildlife, fauna; (*fig péj*) set, crowd ▷ *nm* faun; **~ marine** marine (animal) life

faussaire [foseʀ] *nm/f* forger

fausse [fos] *adj f voir* **faux**

faussement [fosmɑ̃] *adv* (*accuser*) wrongly, wrongfully; (*croire*) falsely, erroneously

fausser [fose] *vt* (*objet*) to bend, buckle; (*fig*) to distort; **~ compagnie à qn** to give sb the slip

faut [fo] *vb voir* **falloir**

faute [fot] *nf* (*erreur*) mistake, error; (*péché, manquement*) misdemeanour; (*Football etc*) offence; (*Tennis*) fault; (*responsabilité*): **par la ~ de** through the fault of, because of; **c'est de sa/ma ~** it's his/my fault; **être en ~** to be in

the wrong; **prendre qn en ~** to catch sb out; **~ de** (*temps, argent*) for *ou* through lack of; **~ de mieux** for want of anything ou something better; **sans ~** *adv* without fail; **~ de frappe** typing error; **~ d'inattention** careless mistake; **~ d'orthographe** spelling mistake; **~ professionnelle** professional misconduct *no pl*

fauteuil [fotœj] *nm* armchair; **~ à bascule** rocking chair; **~ club** (big) easy chair; **~ d'orchestre** seat in the front stalls (*Brit*) *ou* the orchestra (*US*); **~ roulant** wheelchair

fauteur [fotœʀ] *nm*: **~ de troubles** trouble-maker

fautif, -ive [fotif, -iv] *adj* (*incorrect*) incorrect, inaccurate; (*responsable*) at fault, in the wrong; (*coupable*) guilty ▷ *nm/f* culprit; **il se sentait ~** he felt guilty

fauve [fov] *nm* wildcat; (*peintre*) Fauve ▷ *adj* (*couleur*) fawn

faux¹ [fo] *nf* scythe

faux², fausse [fo, fos] *adj* (*inexact*) wrong; (*piano, voix*) out of tune; (*falsifié: billet*) fake, forged; (*sournois, postiche*) false ▷ *adv* (*Mus*) out of tune ▷ *nm* (*copie*) fake, forgery; (*opposé au vrai*): **le ~** falsehood; **le ~ numéro/la fausse clé** the wrong number/key; **faire fausse route** to go the wrong way; **faire ~ bond à qn** to let sb down; **~ ami** (*Ling*) faux ami; **~ col** detachable collar; **~ départ** (*Sport, fig*) false start; **~ frais** *nmpl* extras, incidental expenses; **~ frère** (*fig péj*) false friend; **~ mouvement** awkward movement; **~ nez** false nose; **~ nom** assumed name; **~ pas** tripping *no pl*; (*fig*) faux pas; **faire un ~ pas** to trip; (*fig*) to make a faux pas; **~ témoignage** (*délit*) perjury; **fausse alerte** false alarm; **fausse clé** skeleton key; **fausse couche** (*Méd*) miscarriage; **fausse joie** vain joy; **fausse note** wrong note

faux-filet [fofilɛ] *nm* sirloin

faux-monnayeur [fomɔnɛjœʀ] *nm* counterfeiter, forger

faveur [favœʀ] *nf* favour (*Brit*), favor (*US*); **traitement de ~** preferential treatment; **à la ~ de** under cover of; (*grâce à*) thanks to; **en ~ de** in favo(u)r of

favorable [favɔʀabl] *adj* favo(u)rable

favori, te [favɔʀi, -it] *adj, nm/f* favo(u)rite

favoriser [favɔʀize] *vt* to favour (*Brit*), favor (*US*)

fax [faks] *nm* fax

faxer [fakse] *vt* to fax

FB *abr* (= *franc belge*) BF, FB

fébrile [febʀil] *adj* feverish, febrile; **capitaux ~s** (*Écon*) hot money

fécond, e [fekɔ̃, -ɔ̃d] *adj* fertile

féconder [fekɔ̃de] *vt* to fertilize

fécondité [fekɔ̃dite] *nf* fertility

fécule [fekyl] *nf* potato flour

féculent [fekylɑ̃] *nm* starchy food

fédéral, e, -aux [fedeʀal, -o] *adj* federal

fée [fe] *nf* fairy

féerique [feʀik] *adj* magical, fairytale *cpd*

feignant, e [fɛɲɑ̃, -ɑ̃t] *nm/f* = **fainéant, e**

feindre [fɛ̃dʀ] *vt* to feign ▷ *vi* to dissemble; **~ de faire** to pretend to do

feint, e [fɛ̃, fɛ̃t] *pp de* **feindre** ▷ *adj* feigned ▷ *nf* (Sport: escrime) feint; (: Football, Rugby) dummy (Brit), fake (US); (fam: ruse) sham

fêler [fele] *vt* to crack

félicitations [felisitasjɔ̃] *nfpl* congratulations

féliciter [felisite] *vt*: **~ qn (de)** to congratulate sb (on)

félin, e [felɛ̃, -in] *adj* feline ▷ *nm* (big) cat

fêlure [felyʀ] *nf* crack

femelle [fəmɛl] *adj* (aussi Élec, Tech) female ▷ *nf* female

féminin, e [feminɛ̃, -in] *adj* feminine; (sexe) female; (équipe, vêtements etc) women's; (parfois péj: homme) effeminate ▷ *nm* (Ling) feminine

féministe [feminist] *adj, nf* feminist

femme [fam] *nf* woman; (épouse) wife; **être très ~** to be very much a woman; **devenir ~** to attain womanhood; **~ d'affaires** businesswoman; **~ de chambre** chambermaid; **~ fatale** femme fatale; **~ au foyer** housewife; **~ d'intérieur** (real) homemaker; **~ de ménage** domestic help, cleaning lady; **~ du monde** society woman; **~ -objet** sex object; **~ de tête** determined, intellectual woman

fémur [femyʀ] *nm* femur, thighbone

fendre [fɑ̃dʀ] *vt* (couper en deux) to split; (fissurer) to crack; (fig: traverser) to cut through; to push one's way through; **se fendre** *vi* to crack

fenêtre [f(ə)nɛtʀ] *nf* window; **~ à guillotine** sash window

fenouil [fənuj] *nm* fennel

fente [fɑ̃t] *nf* (fissure) crack; (de boîte à lettres etc) slit

féodal, e, -aux [feɔdal, -o] *adj* feudal

fer [fɛʀ] *nm* iron; (de cheval) shoe; **fers** *nmpl* (Méd) forceps; **mettre aux ~s** (enchaîner) to put in chains; **au ~ rouge** with a red-hot iron; **santé/main de ~** iron constitution/hand; **~ à cheval** horseshoe; **en ~ à cheval** (fig) horseshoe-shaped; **~ forgé** wrought iron; **~ à friser** curling tongs; **~ de lance** spearhead; **~ (à repasser)** iron; **~ à souder** soldering iron

ferai *etc* [fəʀe] *vb voir* **faire**

fer-blanc [fɛʀblɑ̃] *nm* tin(plate)

férié, e [feʀje] *adj*: **jour ~** public holiday

ferions *etc* [fəʀjɔ̃] *vb voir* **faire**

ferme [fɛʀm] *adj* firm ▷ *adv* (travailler etc) hard; (discuter) ardently ▷ *nf* (exploitation) farm; (maison) farmhouse; **tenir ~** to stand firm

fermé, e [fɛʀme] *adj* closed, shut; (gaz, eau etc) off; (fig: personne) uncommunicative; (: milieu) exclusive

fermenter [fɛʀmɑ̃te] *vi* to ferment

fermer [fɛʀme] *vt* to close, shut; (cesser l'exploitation de) to close down, shut down; (eau, lumière, électricité, robinet) to turn off; (aéroport, route) to close ▷ *vi* to close, shut; (magasin: définitivement) to close down, shut down; **se fermer** *vi* (yeux) to close, shut; (fleur, blessure) to close up; **~ à clef** to lock; **~ au verrou** to bolt; **~ les yeux (sur qch)** (fig) to close one's eyes (to sth); **se ~ à** (pitié, amour) to close one's heart ou mind to

fermeté [fɛʀməte] *nf* firmness

fermeture [fɛʀmətyʀ] *nf* closing; shutting; closing ou shutting down; putting ou turning off; (dispositif) catch; fastening, fastener; **heure de ~** (Comm) closing time; **jour de ~** (Comm) day on which the shop (etc) is closed; **~ éclair® ou à glissière** zip (fastener) (Brit), zipper; *voir* **fermer**

fermier, -ière [fɛʀmje, -jɛʀ] *nm/f* farmer ▷ *nf* (femme de fermier) farmer's wife ▷ *adj*: **beurre/cidre ~** farm butter/cider

fermoir [fɛʀmwaʀ] *nm* clasp

féroce [feʀɔs] *adj* ferocious, fierce

ferons *etc* [fəʀɔ̃] *vb voir* **faire**

ferraille [feʀaj] *nf* scrap iron; **mettre à la ~** to scrap; **bruit de ~** clanking

ferrer [feʀe] *vt* (cheval) to shoe; (chaussure) to nail; (canne) to tip; (poisson) to strike

ferronnerie [feʀɔnʀi] *nf* ironwork; **~ d'art** wrought iron work

ferroviaire [feʀɔvjɛʀ] *adj* rail *cpd*, railway *cpd* (Brit), railroad *cpd* (US)

ferry [feʀe], **ferry-boat** [feʀebot] *nm* ferry

fertile [fɛʀtil] *adj* fertile; **~ en incidents** eventful, packed with incidents

féru, e [feʀy] *adj*: **~ de** with a keen interest in

fervent, e [fɛʀvɑ̃, -ɑ̃t] *adj* fervent

fesse [fɛs] *nf* buttock; **les ~s** the bottom *sg*, the buttocks

fessée [fese] *nf* spanking

festin [fɛstɛ̃] *nm* feast

festival [fɛstival] *nm* festival

festivités [fɛstivite] *nfpl* festivities, merrymaking *sg*

festoyer [fɛstwaje] *vi* to feast

fêtard, e [fɛtaʀ, fɛtaʀ, aʀd] *(fam) nm/f (péj)* high liver, merrymaker

fête [fɛt] *nf* (religieuse) feast; (publique) holiday; (en famille etc) celebration; (réception) party; (kermesse) fête, fair, festival; (du nom) feast day, name day; **faire la ~** to live it up; **faire ~ à qn** to give sb a warm welcome; **se faire une ~ de** to look forward to; to enjoy; **ça va être sa ~!** (fam) he's going to get it!; **jour de ~** holiday; **les ~s (de fin d'année)** the festive season; **la salle/le comité des ~s** the village hall/festival committee; **la ~ des Mères/Pères** Mother's/Father's Day; **~ de charité** charity fair ou fête; **~ foraine** (fun)fair; **la ~ de la musique** see note; **~ mobile** movable feast (day); **la F~ Nationale** the national holiday

fêter [fete] *vt* to celebrate; (*personne*) to have a
celebration for

feu¹ [fø] *adj inv*: ~ **son père** his late father

feu², x [fø] *nm* (*gén*) fire; (*signal lumineux*) light;
(*de cuisinière*) ring; (*sensation de brûlure*) burning
(sensation); **feux** *nmpl* fire *sg*; (*Auto*) (traffic)
lights; **tous ~x éteints** (*Navig, Auto*) without
lights; **au ~!** (*incendie*) fire!; **à ~ doux/vif** over a
slow/brisk heat; **à petit ~** (*Culin*) over a gentle
heat; (*fig*) slowly; **faire ~** to fire; **ne pas faire
long ~** (*fig*) not to last long; **commander le ~**
(*Mil*) to give the order to (open) fire; **tué au ~**
(*Mil*) killed in action; **mettre à ~** (*fusée*) to fire
off; **pris entre deux ~x** caught in the
crossfire; **en ~** on fire; **être tout ~ tout
flamme (pour)** (*passion*) to be aflame with
passion (for); (*enthousiasme*) to be fired with
enthusiasm (for); **prendre ~** to catch fire;
mettre le ~ à to set fire to, set on fire; **faire
du ~** to make a fire; **avez-vous du ~?** (*pour
cigarette*) have you (got) a light?; **~ rouge/
vert/orange** (*Auto*) red/green/amber (*Brit*) *ou*
yellow (US) light; **donner le ~ vert à qch/qn**
(*fig*) to give sth/sb the go-ahead *ou* green
light; **~ arrière** (*Auto*) rear light; **~ d'artifice**
firework; (*spectacle*) fireworks *pl*; **~ de camp**
campfire; **~ de cheminée** chimney fire; **~ de
joie** bonfire; **~ de paille** (*fig*) flash in the pan;
~x de brouillard (*Auto*) fog lights *ou* lamps;
~x de croisement (*Auto*) dipped (*Brit*) *ou*
dimmed (US) headlights; **~x de position**
(*Auto*) sidelights; **~x de route** (*Auto*)
headlights (on full (*Brit*) *ou* high (US) beam);
~x de stationnement parking lights

feuillage [fœjaʒ] *nm* foliage, leaves *pl*

feuille [fœj] *nf* (*d'arbre*) leaf; **~ (de papier)**
sheet (of paper); **rendre ~ blanche** (*Scol*) to
give in a blank paper; **~ de calcul**
spreadsheet; **~ d'or/de métal** gold/metal
leaf; **~ de chou** (*péj: journal*) rag; **~ d'impôts**
tax form; **~ de maladie** medical expenses
claim form; **~ morte** dead leaf; **~ de paye,
~ de paie** pay slip; **~ de présence** attendance
sheet; **~ de température** temperature chart;
~ de vigne (*Bot*) vine leaf; (*sur statue*) fig leaf;
~ volante loose sheet

feuillet [fœjɛ] *nm* leaf, page

feuilleté, e [fœjte] *adj* (*Culin*) flaky; (*verre*)
laminated; **pâte ~** flaky pastry

feuilleter [fœjte] *vt* (*livre*) to leaf through

feuilleton [fœjtɔ̃] *nm* serial

feutre [føtʀ] *nm* felt; (*chapeau*) felt hat; (*stylo*)
felt-tip(ped pen)

feutré, e [føtʀe] *adj* feltlike; (*pas, voix,
atmosphère*) muffled

fève [fɛv] *nf* broad bean; (*dans la galette des
Rois*) charm (*hidden in cake eaten on Twelfth Night*)

février [fevʀije] *nm* February; *voir aussi* **juillet**

FF *abr* (= *franc français*) FF

FFF *abr* = **Fédération française de football**

fiable [fjabl] *adj* reliable

fiançailles [fjɑ̃saj] *nfpl* engagement *sg*

fiancé, e [fjɑ̃se] *nm/f* fiancé/fiancée ▷ *adj*:
être ~ (à) to be engaged (to)

fiancer [fjɑ̃se]: **se fiancer** *vi*: **se ~ (avec)** to
become engaged (to)

fibre [fibʀ] *nf* fibre, fiber (US); **avoir la ~
paternelle/militaire** to be a born father/
soldier; **~ optique** optical fibre *ou* fiber; **~ de
verre** fibreglass (*Brit*), fiberglass (US), glass
fibre *ou* fiber

ficeler [fis(ə)le] *vt* to tie up

ficelle [fisɛl] *nf* string *no pl*; (*morceau*) piece *ou*
length of string; (*pain*) stick of French bread;
ficelles *nfpl* (*fig*) strings; **tirer sur la ~** (*fig*) to
go too far

fiche [fiʃ] *nf* (*carte*) (index) card; (*formulaire*)
form; (*Élec*) plug; **~ de paye** pay slip;
~ signalétique (*Police*) identification card;
~ technique data sheet, specification *ou*
spec sheet

ficher [fiʃe] *vt* (*dans un fichier*) to file; (*: Police*) to
put on file; (*fam: faire*) to do; (*: donner*) to give;
(*: mettre*) to stick *ou* shove; (*planter*): **~ qch
dans** to stick *ou* drive sth into; **~ qn à la
porte** (*fam*) to chuck sb out; **fiche(-moi) le
camp** (*fam*) clear off; **fiche-moi la paix** (*fam*)
leave me alone; **se ~ dans** (*s'enfoncer*) to get
stuck in, embed itself in; **se ~ de** (*fam: rire de*)
to make fun of; (*être indifférent à*) not to care
about

fichier [fiʃje] *nm* (*gén, Inform*) file; (*à cartes*)
card index; **~ actif** *ou* **en cours d'utilisation**
(*Inform*) active file; **~ d'adresses** mailing list;
~ d'archives (*Inform*) archive file; **~ joint**
(*Inform*) attachment

fichu, e [fiʃy] *pp de* **ficher** ▷ *adj* (*fam: fini,
inutilisable*) bust, done for; (*: intensif*)
wretched, darned ▷ *nm* (*foulard*) (head)scarf;
être ~ de to be capable of; **mal ~** feeling
lousy; useless; **bien ~** great

fictif, -ive [fiktif, -iv] *adj* fictitious

fiction [fiksjɔ̃] *nf* fiction; (*fait imaginé*)
invention

fidèle [fidɛl] *adj*: **~ (à)** faithful (to) ▷ *nm/f* (*Rel*):
les ~s the faithful; (*à l'église*) the congregation

fidélité [fidelite] *nf* (*d'un conjoint*) fidelity,
faithfulness; (*d'un ami, client*) loyalty

fier¹ [fje]: **se ~ à** *vt* to trust

fier², fière [fjɛʀ] *adj* proud; **~ de** proud of;
avoir fière allure to cut a fine figure

fierté [fjɛʀte] *nf* pride

fièvre [fjɛvʀ] *nf* fever; **avoir de la ~/39 de ~** to
have a high temperature/a temperature of
39°C; **~ typhoïde** typhoid fever

fiévreux, -euse [fjevʀø, -øz] *adj* feverish

figé, e [fiʒe] adj (manières) stiff; (société) rigid; (sourire) set

figer [fiʒe] vt to congeal; (fig: personne) to freeze, root to the spot; **se figer** vi to congeal; (personne) to freeze; (institutions etc) to become set, stop evolving

fignoler [fiɲɔle] vt to put the finishing touches to

figue [fig] nf fig

figuier [figje] nm fig tree

figurant, e [figyʀɑ̃, -ɑ̃t] nm/f (Théât) walk-on; (Ciné) extra

figure [figyʀ] nf (visage) face; (image, tracé, forme, personnage) figure; (illustration) picture, diagram; **faire ~ de** to look like; **faire bonne ~** to put up a good show; **faire triste ~** to be a sorry sight; **~ de rhétorique** figure of speech

figuré, e [figyʀe] adj (sens) figurative

figurer [figyʀe] vi to appear ▷ vt to represent; **se ~ que** to imagine that; **figurez-vous que ...** would you believe that ...?

fil [fil] nm (brin, fig: d'une histoire) thread; (du téléphone) cable, wire; (textile de lin) linen; (d'un couteau: tranchant) edge; **au ~ des années** with the passing of the years; **au ~ de l'eau** with the stream ou current; **de ~ en aiguille** one thing leading to another; **ne tenir qu'à un ~** (vie, réussite etc) to hang by a thread; **donner du ~ à retordre à qn** to make life difficult for sb; **coup de ~** (fam) phone call; **donner/recevoir un coup de ~** to make/get a phone call; **~ à coudre** (sewing) thread ou yarn; **~ dentaire** dental floss; **~ électrique** electric wire; **~ de fer** wire; **~ de fer barbelé** barbed wire; **~ à pêche** fishing line; **~ à plomb** plumb line; **~ à souder** soldering wire

filament [filamɑ̃] nm (Élec) filament; (de liquide) trickle, thread

filandreux, -euse [filɑ̃dʀø, -øz] adj stringy

filature [filatyʀ] nf (fabrique) mill; (policière) shadowing no pl, tailing no pl; **prendre qn en ~** to shadow ou tail sb

file [fil] nf line; (Auto) lane; **~ (d'attente)** queue (Brit), line (US); **prendre la ~** to join (the end of) the queue ou line; **prendre la ~ de droite** (Auto) to move into the right-hand lane; **se mettre en ~** to form a line; (Auto) to get into lane; **stationner en double ~** (Auto) to double-park; **à la ~** adv (d'affilée) in succession; (à la suite) one after another; **à la ou en ~ indienne** in single file

filer [file] vt (tissu, toile, verre) to spin; (dérouler: câble etc) to pay ou let out; (prendre en filature) to shadow, tail; (fam: donner): **~ qch à qn** to slip sb sth ▷ vi (bas, maille, liquide, pâte) to run; (aller vite) to fly past ou by; (fam: partir) to make off; **~ à l'anglaise** to take French leave; **~ doux** to behave o.s., toe the line; **~ un mauvais coton** to be in a bad way

filet [filɛ] nm net; (Culin) fillet; (d'eau, de sang) trickle; **tendre un ~** (police) to set a trap; **~ (à**

bagages) (Rail) luggage rack; **~ (à provisions)** string bag

filial, e, -aux [filjal, -o] adj filial ▷ nf (Comm) subsidiary; affiliate

filière [filjɛʀ] nf (carrière) path; **passer par la ~** to go through the (administrative) channels; **suivre la ~** to work one's way up (through the hierarchy)

filiforme [filifɔʀm] adj spindly; threadlike

filigrane [filigʀan] nm (d'un billet, timbre) watermark; **en ~** (fig) showing just beneath the surface

fille [fij] nf girl; (opposé à fils) daughter; **vieille ~** old maid; **~ de joie** prostitute; **~ de salle** waitress

fillette [fijɛt] nf (little) girl

filleul [fijœl] nm/f godchild, godson/goddaughter

film [film] nm (pour photo) (roll of) film; (œuvre) film, picture, movie; (couche) film; **~ muet/parlant** silent/talking picture ou movie; **~ alimentaire** clingfilm; **~ d'amour/d'animation/d'horreur** romantic/animated/horror film; **~ comique** comedy; **~ policier** thriller

filon [filɔ̃] nm vein, lode; (fig) lucrative line, money-spinner

fils [fis] nm son; **~ de famille** moneyed young man; **~ à papa** (péj) daddy's boy

filtre [filtʀ] nm filter; **"~ ou sans ~?"** (cigarettes) "tipped or plain?"; **~ à air** air filter

filtrer [filtʀe] vt to filter; (fig: candidats, visiteurs) to screen ▷ vi to filter (through)

fin¹ [fɛ̃] nf end; **fins** nfpl (but) ends; **à (la) ~ mai**, **~ mai** at the end of May; **en ~ de semaine** at the end of the week; **prendre ~** to come to an end; **toucher à sa ~** to be drawing to a close; **mettre ~ à** to put an end to; **mener à bonne ~** to bring to a successful conclusion; **à cette ~** to this end; **à toutes ~s utiles** for your information; **à la ~** in the end, eventually; **en ~ de compte** in the end; **sans ~** adj endless ▷ adv endlessly; **~ de non-recevoir** (Jur, Admin) objection; **~ de section** (de ligne d'autobus) (fare) stage

fin², e [fɛ̃, fin] adj (papier, couche, fil) thin; (cheveux, poudre, pointe, visage) fine; (taille) neat, slim; (esprit, remarque) subtle; shrewd ▷ adv (moudre, couper) finely ▷ nm: **vouloir jouer au plus ~** (avec qn) to try to outsmart sb ▷ nf (alcool) liqueur brandy; **c'est ~!** (ironique) how clever!; **~ prêt/soûl** quite ready/drunk; **un ~ gourmet** a gourmet; **un ~ tireur** a crack shot; **avoir la vue/l'ouïe ~e** to have keen eyesight/hearing, have sharp eyes/ears; **or/linge/vin ~** fine gold/linen/wine; **le ~ fond de** the very depths of; **le ~ mot de** the real story behind; **la ~e fleur de** the flower of; **une ~e mouche** (fig) a sly customer; **~es herbes** mixed herbs

final, e [final] adj, nf final ▷ nm (Mus) finale; **quarts de ~e** quarter finals; **8èmes/16èmes**

de ~e 2nd/1st round (*in 5 round knock-out competition*)

finalement [finalmã] *adv* finally, in the end; (*après tout*) after all

finance [finãs] *nf* finance; **finances** *nfpl* (*situation financière*) finances; (*activités financières*) finance *sg*; **moyennant ~** for a fee *ou* consideration

financer [finãse] *vt* to finance

financier, -ière [finãsje, -jɛʀ] *adj* financial ▷ *nm* financier

finaud, e [fino, -od] *adj* wily

finesse [finɛs] *nf* thinness; (*raffinement*) fineness; neatness, slimness; (*subtilité*) subtlety; shrewdness; **finesses** *nfpl* (*subtilités*) niceties; finer points

fini, e [fini] *adj* finished; (*Math*) finite; (*intensif*): **un menteur ~** a liar through and through ▷ *nm* (*d'un objet manufacturé*) finish

finir [finiʀ] *vt* to finish ▷ *vi* to finish, end; **~ quelque part** to end up finish somewhere; **~ de faire** to finish doing; (*cesser*) to stop doing; **~ par faire** to end *ou* finish up doing; **il finit par m'agacer** he's beginning to get on my nerves; **~ en pointe/tragédie** to end in a point/in tragedy; **en ~ avec** to be *ou* have done with; **à n'en plus ~** (*route, discussions*) never-ending; **il va mal ~** he will come to a bad end; **c'est bientôt fini?** (*reproche*) have you quite finished?

finition [finisjõ] *nf* finishing; (*résultat*) finish

finlandais, e [fēlãdɛ, -ɛz] *adj* Finnish ▷ *nm/f*: **F~, e** Finn

Finlande [fēlãd] *nf*: **la ~** Finland

finnois, e [finwa, -waz] *adj* Finnish ▷ *nm* (*Ling*) Finnish

fiole [fjɔl] *nf* phial

fioul [fjul] *nm* fuel oil

firme [fiʀm] *nf* firm

fis [fi] *vb voir* **faire**

fisc [fisk] *nm* tax authorities *pl*, ≈ Inland Revenue (*Brit*), ≈ Internal Revenue Service (*US*)

fiscal, e, -aux [fiskal, -o] *adj* tax *cpd*, fiscal

fiscalité [fiskalite] *nf* tax system; (*charges*) taxation

fissure [fisyʀ] *nf* crack

fissurer [fisyʀe] *vt* to crack; **se fissurer** *vi* to crack

fiston [fistõ] *nm* (*fam*) son, lad

fit [fi] *vb voir* **faire**

fixation [fiksasjõ] *nf* fixing; (*attache*) fastening; setting; (*de ski*) binding; (*Psych*) fixation

fixe [fiks] *adj* fixed; (*emploi*) steady, regular ▷ *nm* (*salaire*) basic salary; (*téléphone*) landline; **à heure ~** at a set time; **menu à prix ~** set menu

fixé, e [fikse] *adj* (*heure, jour*) appointed; **être ~ (sur)** (*savoir à quoi s'en tenir*) to have made up one's mind (about); to know for certain (about)

fixer [fikse] *vt* (*attacher*): **~ qch (à/sur)** to fix *ou* fasten sth (to/onto); (*déterminer*) to fix, set; (*Chimie, Photo*) to fix; (*regarder*) to stare at, look hard at; **se fixer** (*s'établir*) to settle down; **~ son choix sur qch** to decide on sth; **se ~ sur** (*attention*) to focus on

flacon [flakõ] *nm* bottle

flageoler [flaʒɔle] *vi* to have knees like jelly

flageolet [flaʒɔlɛ] *nm* (*Mus*) flageolet; (*Culin*) dwarf kidney bean

flagrant, e [flagʀã, -ãt] *adj* flagrant, blatant; **en ~ délit** in the act, in flagrante delicto

flair [flɛʀ] *nm* sense of smell; (*fig*) intuition

flairer [flɛʀe] *vt* (*humer*) to sniff (at); (*détecter*) to scent

flamand, e [flamã, -ãd] *adj* Flemish ▷ *nm* (*Ling*) Flemish ▷ *nm/f*: **F~, e** Fleming; **les F~s** the Flemish

flamant [flamã] *nm* flamingo

flambant [flãbã] *adv*: **~ neuf** brand new

flambé, e [flãbe] *adj* (*Culin*) flambé ▷ *nf* blaze; (*fig*) flaring-up, explosion

flambeau, x [flãbo] *nm* (flaming) torch; **se passer le ~** (*fig*) to hand down the (*ou* a) tradition

flambée [flãbe] *nf* (*feu*) blaze; (*Comm*): **~ des prix** (sudden) shooting up of prices

flamber [flãbe] *vi* to blaze (up) ▷ *vt* (*poulet*) to singe; (*aiguille*) to sterilize

flamboyer [flãbwaje] *vi* to blaze (up); (*fig*) to flame

flamme [flam] *nf* flame; (*fig*) fire, fervour; **en ~s** on fire, ablaze

flan [flã] *nm* (*Culin*) custard tart *ou* pie

flanc [flã] *nm* side; (*Mil*) flank; **à ~ de colline** on the hillside; **prêter le ~ à** (*fig*) to lay o.s. open to

flancher [flãʃe] *vi* (*cesser de fonctionner*) to fail, pack up; (*armée*) to quit

flanelle [flanɛl] *nf* flannel

flâner [flɑne] *vi* to stroll

flânerie [flɑnʀi] *nf* stroll

flanquer [flãke] *vt* to flank; (*fam: mettre*) to chuck, shove; (: *jeter*): **~ par terre/à la porte** to fling to the ground/chuck out; (: *donner*): **~ la frousse à qn** to put the wind up sb, give sb an awful fright

flaque [flak] *nf* (*d'eau*) puddle; (*d'huile, de sang etc*) pool

flash (*pl* **flashes**) [flaʃ] *nm* (*Photo*) flash; **~ (d'information)** newsflash

flasque [flask] *adj* flabby ▷ *nf* (*flacon*) flask

flatter [flate] *vt* to flatter; (*caresser*) to stroke; **se ~ de qch** to pride o.s. on sth

flatterie [flatʀi] *nf* flattery

flatteur, -euse [flatœʀ, -øz] *adj* flattering ▷ *nm/f* flatterer

fléau, x [fleo] *nm* scourge, curse; (*de balance*) beam; (*pour le blé*) flail

flèche [flɛʃ] *nf* arrow; (*de clocher*) spire; (*de grue*) jib; (*trait d'esprit, critique*) shaft; **monter en ~** (*fig*) to soar, rocket; **partir en ~** (*fig*) to be off like a shot; **à ~ variable** (avion) swing-wing *cpd*

fléchette [fleʃɛt] *nf* dart; **fléchettes** *nfpl* (jeu) darts *sg*

fléchir [fleʃiʀ] *vt* (corps, genou) to bend; (fig) to sway, weaken ▷ *vi* (poutre) to sag, bend; (fig) to weaken, flag; (: baisser: prix) to fall off

flemmard, e [flemaʀ, -aʀd] *nm/f* lazybones *sg*, loafer

flemme [flɛm] *nf* (fam): **j'ai la ~ de le faire** I can't be bothered

flétrir [fletʀiʀ] *vt* to wither; (stigmatiser) to condemn (in the most severe terms); **se flétrir** *vi* to wither

fleur [flœʀ] *nf* flower; (d'un arbre) blossom; **être en ~** (arbre) to be in blossom; **tissu à ~s** flowered *ou* flowery fabric; **la (fine) ~ de** (fig) the flower of; **être ~ bleue** to be soppy *ou* sentimental; **à ~ de terre** just above the ground; **faire une ~ à qn** to do sb a favour (Brit) *ou* favor (US); **~ de lis** fleur-de-lis

fleuri, e [flœʀi] *adj* (jardin) in flower *ou* bloom; surrounded by flowers; (fig: style, tissu, papier) flowery; (: teint) glowing

fleurir [flœʀiʀ] *vi* (rose) to flower; (arbre) to blossom; (fig) to flourish ▷ *vt* (tombe) to put flowers on; (chambre) to decorate with flowers

fleuriste [flœʀist] *nm/f* florist

fleuve [flœv] *nm* river; **roman-~** saga; **discours-~** interminable speech

flexible [flɛksibl] *adj* flexible

flic [flik] *nm* (fam: péj) cop

flipper *nm* [flipœʀ] pinball (machine) ▷ *vi* [flipe] (fam: être déprimé) to feel down, be on a downer; (: être exalté) to freak out

flirter [flœʀte] *vi* to flirt

flocon [flɔkɔ̃] *nm* flake; (de laine etc: boulette) flock; **~s d'avoine** oat flakes, porridge oats

flopée [flɔpe] *nf*: **une ~ de** loads of

floraison [flɔʀɛzɔ̃] *nf* flowering; blossoming; flourishing; *voir* **fleurir**

flore [flɔʀ] *nf* flora

florissant, e [flɔʀisɑ̃, -ɑ̃t] *vb voir* **fleurir** ▷ *adj* (économie) flourishing; (santé, teint, mine) blooming

flot [flo] *nm* flood, stream; (marée) flood tide; **flots** *nmpl* (de la mer) waves; **être à ~** (Navig) to be afloat; (fig) to be on an even keel; **à ~s** (couler) in torrents; **entrer à ~** to stream *ou* pour in

flottant, e [flɔtɑ̃, -ɑ̃t] *adj* (vêtement) loose(-fitting); (cours, barème) floating

flotte [flɔt] *nf* (Navig) fleet; (fam: eau) water; (: pluie) rain

flottement [flɔtmɑ̃] *nm* (fig) wavering, hesitation; (Écon) floating

flotter [flɔte] *vi* to float; (nuage, odeur) to drift; (drapeau) to fly; (vêtements) to hang loose ▷ *vb impers* (fam: pleuvoir): **il flotte** it's raining ▷ *vt* to float; **faire ~** to float

flotteur [flɔtœʀ] *nm* float

flou, e [flu] *adj* fuzzy, blurred; (fig) woolly (Brit), vague; (non ajusté: robe) loose(-fitting)

fluctuation [flyktɥasjɔ̃] *nf* fluctuation

fluet, te [flyɛ, -ɛt] *adj* thin, slight; (voix) thin

fluide [flɥid] *adj* fluid; (circulation etc) flowing freely ▷ *nm* fluid; (force) (mysterious) power

fluor [flyɔʀ] *nm* fluorine; **dentifrice au ~** fluoride toothpaste

fluorescent, e [flyɔʀesɑ̃, -ɑ̃t] *adj* fluorescent

flûte [flyt] *nf* (aussi: **~ traversière**) flute; (verre) flute glass; (pain) (thin) baguette; **petite ~** piccolo; **~! drat it!**; **~ (à bec)** recorder; **~ de Pan** panpipes *pl*

flux [fly] *nm* incoming tide; (écoulement) flow; **le ~ et le reflux** the ebb and flow

FM *sigle f* (= frequency modulation) FM

foc [fɔk] *nm* jib

foi [fwa] *nf* faith; **sous la ~ du serment** under *ou* on oath; **ajouter ~ à** to lend credence to; **faire ~** (prouver) to be evidence; **digne de ~** reliable; **sur la ~ de** on the word *ou* strength of; **être de bonne/mauvaise ~** to be in good faith/not to be in good faith; **ma ~!** well!

foie [fwa] *nm* liver; **~ gras** foie gras; **crise de ~** stomach upset

foin [fwɛ̃] *nm* hay; **faire les ~s** to make hay; **faire du ~** (fam) to kick up a row

foire [fwaʀ] *nf* fair; (fête foraine) (fun) fair; (fig: désordre, confusion) bear garden; **~ aux questions** (Internet) frequently asked questions; **faire la ~** to whoop it up; **~ (exposition)** trade fair

fois [fwa] *nf* time; **une/deux ~** once/twice; **trois/vingt ~** three/twenty times; **deux ~ deux** twice two; **deux/quatre ~ plus grand (que)** twice/four times as big (as); **une ~** (passé) once; (futur) sometime; **une (bonne) ~ pour toutes** once and for all; **encore une ~** again, once more; **il était une ~** once upon a time; **une ~ que c'est fait** once it's done; **une ~ parti** once he (ou I etc) had left; **des ~** (parfois) sometimes; **si des ~...** (fam) if ever ...; **non mais des ~!** (fam) (now) look here!; **à la ~** (ensemble) (all) at once; **à la ~ grand et beau** both tall and handsome

foison [fwazɔ̃] *nf*: **une ~ de** an abundance of; **à ~** *adv* in plenty

foisonner [fwazɔne] *vi* to abound; **~ en** *ou* **de** to abound in

fol [fɔl] *adj m voir* **fou**

folie [fɔli] *nf* (d'une décision, d'un acte) madness, folly; (état) madness, insanity; (acte) folly; **la ~ des grandeurs** delusions of grandeur; **faire des ~s** (en dépenses) to be extravagant

folklorique [fɔlklɔʀik] *adj* folk *cpd*; (fam) weird

folle [fɔl] *adj f, nf voir* **fou**

follement [fɔlmɑ̃] *adv* (très) madly, wildly

foncé, e [fɔ̃se] *adj* dark; **bleu ~** dark blue

foncer [fɔ̃se] *vt* to make darker; (Culin: moule etc) to line ▷ *vi* to go darker; (fam: aller vite) to tear *ou* belt along; **~ sur** to charge at

foncier, -ière [fɔ̃sje, -jɛʀ] *adj* (honnêteté etc)

basic, fundamental; (*malhonnêteté*) deep-rooted; (*Comm*) real estate *cpd*

fonction [fɔ̃ksjɔ̃] *nf* (*rôle*, *Math*, *Ling*) function; (*emploi*, *poste*) post, position; **fonctions** *nfpl* (*professionnelles*) duties; **entrer en ~s** to take up one's post *ou* duties; to take up office; **voiture de ~** company car; **être ~ de** (*dépendre de*) to depend on; **en ~ de** (*par rapport à*) according to; **faire ~ de** to serve as; **la ~ publique** the state *ou* civil (*Brit*) service

fonctionnaire [fɔ̃ksjɔnɛʀ] *nm/f* state employee *ou* official; (*dans l'administration*) ≈ civil servant (*Brit*)

fonctionner [fɔ̃ksjɔne] *vi* to work, function; (*entreprise*) to operate, function; **faire ~** to work, operate

fond [fɔ̃] *nm voir aussi* **fonds**; (*d'un récipient, trou*) bottom; (*d'une salle, scène*) back; (*d'un tableau, décor*) background; (*opposé à la forme*) content; (*petite quantité*): **un ~ de verre** a drop; (*Sport*): **le ~** long distance (running); **course/épreuve de ~** long-distance race/trial; **au ~ de** at the bottom of; at the back of; **aller au ~ des choses** to get to the root of things; **le ~ de sa pensée** his (*ou* her) true thoughts *ou* feelings; **sans ~** *adj* bottomless; **envoyer par le ~** (*Navig*: *couler*) to sink, scuttle; **à ~** *adv* (*connaître, soutenir*) thoroughly; (*appuyer, visser*) right down *ou* home; **à ~ (de train)** *adv* (*fam*) full tilt; **dans le ~, au ~** *adv* (*en somme*) basically, really; **de ~ en comble** *adv* from top to bottom; **~ sonore** background noise; background music; **~ de teint** foundation

fondamental, e, -aux [fɔ̃damɑ̃tal, -o] *adj* fundamental

fondant, e [fɔ̃dɑ̃, -ɑ̃t] *adj* (*neige*) melting; (*poire*) that melts in the mouth; (*chocolat*) fondant

fondateur, -trice [fɔ̃datœʀ, -tʀis] *nm/f* founder; **membre ~** founder (*Brit*) *ou* founding (*US*) member

fondation [fɔ̃dasjɔ̃] *nf* founding; (*établissement*) foundation; **fondations** *nfpl* (*d'une maison*) foundations; **travail de ~** foundation works *pl*

fondé, e [fɔ̃de] *adj* (*accusation etc*) well-founded ▷ *nm*: **~ de pouvoir** authorized representative; **mal ~** unfounded; **être ~ à croire** to have grounds for believing *ou* good reason to believe

fondement [fɔ̃dmɑ̃] *nm* (*derrière*) behind; **fondements** *nmpl* foundations; **sans ~** *adj* (*rumeur etc*) groundless, unfounded

fonder [fɔ̃de] *vt* to found; (*fig*): **~ qch sur** to base sth on; **se ~ sur** (*personne*) to base o.s. on; **~ un foyer** (*se marier*) to set up home

fonderie [fɔ̃dʀi] *nf* smelting works *sg*

fondre [fɔ̃dʀ] *vt* (*aussi*: **faire ~**) to melt; (*dans l'eau*: *sucre, sel*) to dissolve; (*fig*: *mélanger*) to merge, blend ▷ *vi* (*à la chaleur*) to melt; to dissolve; (*fig*) to melt away; (*se précipiter*): **~ sur** to swoop down on; **se fondre** *vi* (*se*

combiner, *se confondre*) to merge into each other; to dissolve; **~ en larmes** to dissolve into tears

fonds [fɔ̃] *nm* (*de bibliothèque*) collection; (*Comm*): **~ (de commerce)** business; (*fig*): **~ de probité** *etc* fund of integrity *etc* ▷ *nmpl* (*argent*) funds; **à ~ perdus** *adv* with little or no hope of getting the money back; **être en ~** to be in funds; **mise de ~** investment, (capital) outlay; **F~ monétaire international (FMI)** International Monetary Fund (IMF); **~ de roulement** *nm* float

fondu, e [fɔ̃dy] *adj* (*beurre, neige*) melted; (*métal*) molten ▷ *nm* (*Ciné*): **~ (enchaîné)** dissolve ▷ *nf* (*Culin*) fondue

font [fɔ̃] *vb voir* **faire**

fontaine [fɔ̃tɛn] *nf* fountain; (*source*) spring

fonte [fɔ̃t] *nf* melting; (*métal*) cast iron; **la ~ des neiges** the (spring) thaw

foot [fut], **football** [futbol] *nm* football, soccer

footballeur, -euse [futbolœʀ, -øz] *nm/f* footballer (*Brit*), football *ou* soccer player

footing [futiŋ] *nm* jogging; **faire du ~** to go jogging

for [fɔʀ] *nm*: **dans** *ou* **en son ~ intérieur** in one's heart of hearts

forain, e [fɔʀɛ̃, -ɛn] *adj* fairground *cpd* ▷ *nm* (*marchand*) stallholder; (*acteur etc*) fairground entertainer

forçat [fɔʀsa] *nm* convict

force [fɔʀs] *nf* strength; (*puissance*: *surnaturelle etc*) power; (*Physique, Mécanique*) force; **forces** *nfpl* (*physiques*) strength *sg*; (*Mil*) forces; (*effectifs*): **d'importantes ~s de police** large contingents of police; **avoir de la ~** to be strong; **être à bout de ~** to have no strength left; **à la ~ du poignet** (*fig*) by the sweat of one's brow; **à ~ de faire** by dint of doing; **arriver en ~** (*nombreux*) to arrive in force; **cas de ~ majeure** case of absolute necessity; (*Assurances*) act of God; **~ de la nature** natural force; **de ~** *adv* forcibly, by force; **de toutes mes/ses ~s** with all my/his strength; **par la ~** using force; **par la ~ des choses/d'habitude** by force of circumstances/habit; **à toute ~** (*absolument*) at all costs; **faire ~ de rames/voiles** to ply the oars/cram on sail; **être de ~ à faire** to be up to doing; **de première ~** first class; **la ~ armée** (*les troupes*) the army; **~ d'âme** fortitude; **~ de frappe** strike force; **~ d'inertie** force of inertia; **la ~ publique** the authorities responsible for public order; **~s d'intervention** (*Mil, Police*) peace-keeping force *sg*; **dans la ~ de l'âge** in the prime of life; **les ~s de l'ordre** the police

forcé, e [fɔʀse] *adj* forced; (*bain*) unintended; (*inévitable*): **c'est ~!** it's inevitable!, it HAS to be!

forcément [fɔʀsemɑ̃] *adv* necessarily, inevitably; (*bien sûr*) of course; **pas ~** not necessarily

forcené, e [fɔʀsəne] *adj* frenzied ▷ *nm/f* maniac

forcer [fɔʀse] *vt* (*contraindre*): ~ **qn à faire** to force sb to do; (*porte, serrure, plante*) to force; (*moteur, voix*) to strain ▷ *vi* (*Sport*) to overtax o.s.; **se** - **à faire qch** to force o.s. to do sth; ~ **la dose/ l'allure** to overdo it/increase the pace; ~ **l'attention/le respect** to command attention/ respect; ~ **la consigne** to bypass orders

forcir [fɔʀsiʀ] *vi* (*grossir*) to broaden out; (*vent*) to freshen

forer [fɔʀe] *vt* to drill, bore

forestier, -ière [fɔʀɛstje, -jɛʀ] *adj* forest *cpd*

forêt [fɔʀɛ] *nf* forest; **Office National des F-s** (*Admin*) ≈ Forestry Commission (*Brit*), ≈ National Forest Service (*US*); **la F- Noire** the Black Forest

forfait [fɔʀfɛ] *nm* (*Comm*) fixed *ou* set price; all-in deal *ou* price; (*crime*) infamy; **déclarer** ~ to withdraw; **gagner par** ~ to win by a walkover; **travailler à** ~ to work for a lump sum

forfaitaire [fɔʀfetɛʀ] *adj* set; inclusive

forge [fɔʀʒ] *nf* forge, smithy

forger [fɔʀʒe] *vt* to forge; (*fig: personnalité*) to form; (*prétexte*) to contrive, make up

forgeron [fɔʀʒəʀɔ̃] *nm* (black)smith

formaliser [fɔʀmalize]: **se formaliser** *vi*: **se** ~ **(de)** to take offence (at)

formalité [fɔʀmalite] *nf* formality; **simple** ~ mere formality

format [fɔʀma] *nm* size; **petit** ~ small size; (*Photo*) 35 mm (film)

formater [fɔʀmate] *vt* (*disque*) to format; **non formaté** unformatted

formation [fɔʀmasjɔ̃] *nf* forming; (*éducation*) training; (*Mus*) group; (*Mil, Aviat, Géo*) formation; **la** ~ **permanente** *ou* **continue** continuing education; **la** ~ **professionnelle** vocational training

forme [fɔʀm] *nf* (*gén*) form; (*d'un objet*) shape, form; **formes** *nfpl* (*bonnes manières*) proprieties; (*d'une femme*) figure *sg*; **en** ~ **de poire** pear-shaped, in the shape of a pear; **sous** ~ **de** in the form of; in the guise of; **sous** ~ **de cachets** in the form of tablets; **être en** (**bonne** *ou* **pleine**) ~, **avoir la** ~ (*Sport etc*) to be on form; **en bonne et due** ~ in due form; **pour la** ~ for the sake of form; **sans autre** ~ **de procès** (*fig*) without further ado; **prendre** ~ to take shape

formel, le [fɔʀmɛl] *adj* (*preuve, décision*) definite, positive; (*logique*) formal

formellement [fɔʀmɛlmɑ̃] *adv* (*interdit*) strictly; (*absolument*) positively

former [fɔʀme] *vt* (*gén*) to form; (*éduquer: soldat, ingénieur etc*) to train; **se former** *vi* to form; to train

formidable [fɔʀmidabl] *adj* tremendous

formulaire [fɔʀmylɛʀ] *nm* form

formule [fɔʀmyl] *nf* (*gén*) formula; (*formulaire*) form; (*expression*) phrase; **selon la** ~

consacrée as one says; ~ **de politesse** polite phrase; (*en fin de lettre*) letter ending

formuler [fɔʀmyle] *vt* (*émettre: réponse, vœux*) to formulate; (*expliciter: sa pensée*) to express

fort, e [fɔʀ, fɔʀt] *adj* strong; (*intensité, rendement*) high, great; (*corpulent*) large; (*doué*): **être** ~ (**en**) to be good (at) ▷ *adv* (*serrer, frapper*) hard; (*sonner*) loud(ly); (*beaucoup*) greatly, very much; (*très*) very ▷ *nm* (*édifice*) fort; (*point fort*) strong point, forte; (*gén pl: personne, pays*): **le** ~, **les** ~**s** the strong; **c'est un peu** ~! it's a bit much!; **à plus** -**e raison** even more so, all the more reason; **avoir** ~ **à faire avec qn** to have a hard job with sb; **se faire** ~ **de faire** to claim one can do; ~ **bien/peu** very well/few; **au plus** ~ **de** (*au milieu de*) in the thick of, at the height of; -**e tête** rebel

forteresse [fɔʀtəʀɛs] *nf* fortress

fortifiant [fɔʀtifjɑ̃] *nm* tonic

fortifier [fɔʀtifje] *vt* to strengthen, fortify; (*Mil*) to fortify; **se fortifier** *vi* (*personne, santé*) to grow stronger

fortiori [fɔʀtjɔʀi]: **à** ~ *adv* all the more so

fortuit, e [fɔʀtɥi, -it] *adj* fortuitous, chance *cpd*

fortune [fɔʀtyn] *nf* fortune; **faire** ~ to make one's fortune; **de** ~ *adj* makeshift; (*compagnon*) chance *cpd*

fortuné, e [fɔʀtyne] *adj* wealthy, well-off; **forum de discussion** (*Internet*) message board

forum [fɔʀɔm] *nm* forum

fosse [fos] *nf* (*grand trou*) pit; (*tombe*) grave; **la** ~ **aux lions/ours** the lions' den/bear pit; ~ **commune** common *ou* communal grave; ~ (**d'orchestre**) (orchestra) pit; ~ **à purin** cesspit; ~ **septique** septic tank; ~**s nasales** nasal fossae

fossé [fose] *nm* ditch; (*fig*) gulf, gap

fossette [fosɛt] *nf* dimple

fossile [fosil] *nm* fossil ▷ *adj* fossilized, fossil *cpd*

fossoyeur [foswajœʀ] *nm* gravedigger

fou, fol, folle [fu, fɔl] *adj* mad, crazy; (*déréglé etc*) wild, erratic; (*mèche*) stray; (*herbe*) wild; (*fam: extrême, très grand*) terrific, tremendous ▷ *nm/f* madman/woman ▷ *nm* (*du roi*) jester, fool; (*Échecs*) bishop; ~ **à lier**, ~ **furieux** (**folle furieuse**) raving mad; **être** ~ **de** to be mad *ou* crazy about; (*chagrin, joie, colère*) to be wild with; **faire le** ~ to play *ou* act the fool; **avoir le** ~ **rire** to have the giggles

foudre [fudʀ] *nf*: **la** ~ lightning; **foudres** *nfpl* (*fig: colère*) wrath *sg*

foudroyant, e [fudʀwajɑ̃, -ɑ̃t] *adj* devastating; (*progrès*) lightning *cpd*; (*succès*) stunning; (*maladie, poison*) violent

foudroyer [fudʀwaje] *vt* to strike down; ~ **qn du regard** to look daggers at sb; **il a été foudroyé** he was struck by lightning

fouet [fwɛ] *nm* whip; (*Culin*) whisk; **de plein** ~ *adv* (*se heurter*) head on

fouetter [fwete] vt to whip; (*crème*) to whisk

fougère [fuʒɛʀ] nf fern

fougue [fug] nf ardour (*Brit*), ardor (*US*), spirit

fougueux, -euse [fugø, -øz] adj fiery, ardent

fouille [fuj] nf search; **fouilles** nfpl (*archéologiques*) excavations; **passer à la ~** to be searched

fouiller [fuje] vt to search; (*creuser*) to dig; (: *archéologue*) to excavate; (*approfondir: étude etc*) to go into ▷ vi (*archéologue*) to excavate; **~ dans/parmi** to rummage in/among

fouillis [fuji] nm jumble, muddle

fouiner [fwine] vi (*péj*): **~ dans** to nose around *ou* about in

foulard [fulaʀ] nm scarf

foule [ful] nf crowd; **la ~** crowds pl; **une ~ de** masses of; **venir en ~** to come in droves

foulée [fule] nf stride; **dans la ~ de** on the heels of

fouler [fule] vt to press; (*sol*) to tread upon; **se fouler** vi (*fam*) to overexert o.s.; **se ~ la cheville** to sprain one's ankle; **ne pas se ~** not to overexert o.s.; **il ne se foule pas** he doesn't put himself out; **~ aux pieds** to trample underfoot

foulure [fulyʀ] nf sprain

four [fuʀ] nm oven; (*de potier*) kiln; (*Théât: échec*) flop; **allant au ~** ovenproof

fourbe [fuʀb] adj deceitful

fourbu, e [fuʀby] adj exhausted

fourche [fuʀʃ] nf pitchfork; (*de bicyclette*) fork

fourchette [fuʀʃɛt] nf fork; (*Statistique*) bracket, margin

fourgon [fuʀgɔ̃] nm van; (*Rail*) wag(g)on; **~ mortuaire** hearse

fourgonnette [fuʀgɔnɛt] nf (delivery) van

fourmi [fuʀmi] nf ant; **avoir des ~s dans les jambes/mains** to have pins and needles in one's legs/hands

fourmilière [fuʀmiljɛʀ] nf ant-hill; (*fig*) hive of activity

fourmiller [fuʀmije] vi to swarm; **~ de** to be teeming with, be swarming with

fournaise [fuʀnɛz] nf blaze; (*fig*) furnace, oven

fourneau, x [fuʀno] nm stove

fournée [fuʀne] nf batch

fourni, e [fuʀni] adj (*barbe, cheveux*) thick; (*magasin*): **bien ~ (en)** well stocked (with)

fournir [fuʀniʀ] vt to supply; (*preuve, exemple*) to provide, supply; (*effort*) to put in; **~ qch à qn** to supply sth to sb, supply *ou* provide sb with sth; **~ qn en** (*Comm*) to supply sb with; **se ~ chez** to shop at

fournisseur, -euse [fuʀnisœʀ, -øz] nm/f supplier; (*Internet*): **~ d'accès à Internet** (Internet) service provider, ISP

fourniture [fuʀnityʀ] nf supply(ing); **fournitures** nfpl supplies; **~s de bureau** office supplies, stationery; **~s scolaires** school stationery

fourrage [fuʀaʒ] nm fodder

fourré, e [fuʀe] adj (*bonbon, chocolat*) filled; (*manteau, botte*) fur-lined ▷ nm thicket

fourrer [fuʀe] vt (*fam*) to stick, shove; **~ qch dans** to stick *ou* shove sth into; **se ~ dans/ sous** to get into/under; **se ~ dans** (*une mauvaise situation*) to land o.s. in

fourre-tout [fuʀtu] nm inv (*sac*) holdall; (*péj*) junk room (*ou* cupboard); (*fig*) rag-bag

fourrière [fuʀjɛʀ] nf pound

fourrure [fuʀyʀ] nf fur; (*sur l'animal*) coat; **manteau/col de ~** fur coat/collar

fourvoyer [fuʀvwaje]: **se fourvoyer** vi to go astray, stray; **se ~ dans** to stray into

foutre [futʀ] vt (*fam!*) = **ficher**

foutu, e [futy] adj (*fam!*) = **fichu**

foyer [fwaje] nm (*de cheminée*) hearth; (*fig*) seat, centre; (*famille*) family; (*domicile*) home; (*local de réunion*) (social) club; (*résidence*) hostel; (*salon*) foyer; (*Optique, Photo*) focus; **lunettes à double ~** bi-focal glasses

fracas [fʀaka] nm din; crash

fracassant, e [fʀakasɑ̃, -ɑ̃t] adj (*succès*) sensational, staggering

fracasser [fʀakase] vt to smash; **se fracasser contre** *ou* **sur** to crash against

fraction [fʀaksjɔ̃] nf fraction

fractionner [fʀaksjone] vt to divide (up), split (up)

fracture [fʀaktyʀ] nf fracture; **~ du crâne** fractured skull; **~ de la jambe** broken leg

fracturer [fʀaktyʀe] vt (*coffre, serrure*) to break open; (*os, membre*) to fracture; **se ~ le crâne** to fracture one's skull

fragile [fʀaʒil] adj fragile, delicate; (*fig*) frail

fragilité [fʀaʒilite] nf fragility

fragment [fʀagmɑ̃] nm (*d'un objet*) fragment, piece; (*d'un texte*) passage, extract

fraîche [fʀɛʃ] adj f voir **frais**

fraîcheur [fʀɛʃœʀ] nf coolness; (*d'un aliment*) freshness; voir **frais**

fraîchir [fʀɛʃiʀ] vi to get cooler; (*vent*) to freshen

frais, fraîche [fʀɛ, fʀɛʃ] adj (*air, eau, accueil*) cool; (*petit pois, œufs, nouvelles, couleur, troupes*) fresh; **le voilà ~!** he's in a (right) mess! ▷ adv (*récemment*) newly, fresh(ly); **il fait ~** it's cool; **servir ~** chill before serving, serve chilled ▷ nm: **mettre au ~** to put in a cool place; **prendre le ~** to take a breath of cool air ▷ nmpl (*débours*) expenses; (*Comm*) costs; charges; **faire des ~** to spend; to go to a lot of expense; **faire les ~ de** to bear the brunt of; **faire les ~ de la conversation** (*parler*) to do most of the talking; (*en être le sujet*) to be the topic of conversation; **il en a été pour ses ~** he could have spared himself the trouble; **rentrer dans ses ~** to recover one's expenses; **~ de déplacement** travel(ling) expenses; **~ d'entretien** upkeep; **~ généraux** overheads; **~ de scolarité** school fees, tuition (*US*)

fraise [fʀɛz] nf strawberry; (*Tech*) countersink (bit); (*de dentiste*) drill; **~ des bois** wild strawberry

framboise [fʀɑ̃bwaz] nf raspberry

franc, franche [fʀɑ̃, fʀɑ̃ʃ] adj (personne) frank, straightforward; (visage) open; (net: refus, couleur) clear; (: coupure) clean; (intensif) downright; (exempt): **~ de port** post free, postage paid; (zone, port) free; (boutique) duty-free ▷ adv: **parler ~** to be frank ou candid ▷ nm franc

français, e [fʀɑ̃sɛ, -ɛz] adj French ▷ nm (Ling) French ▷ nm/f: **F~, e** Frenchman/woman; **les F~** the French

France [fʀɑ̃s] nf: **la ~** France; **en ~** in France; **~ 2, ~ 3** public-sector television channels; see note

franche [fʀɑ̃ʃ] adj f voir **franc**

franchement [fʀɑ̃ʃmɑ̃] adv frankly; clearly; (nettement) definitely; (tout à fait) downright ▷ excl well, really!; voir **franc**

franchir [fʀɑ̃ʃiʀ] vt (obstacle) to clear, get over; (seuil, ligne, rivière) to cross; (distance) to cover

franchise [fʀɑ̃ʃiz] nf frankness; (douanière, d'impôt) exemption; (Assurances) excess; (Comm) franchise; **~ de bagages** baggage allowance

franc-maçon (pl **francs-maçons**) [fʀɑ̃masɔ̃] nm Freemason

franco [fʀɑ̃ko] adv (Comm): **~ (de port)** postage paid

francophone [fʀɑ̃kɔfɔn] adj French-speaking ▷ nm/f French speaker

franc-parler [fʀɑ̃paʀle] nm inv outspokenness; **avoir son ~** to speak one's mind

frange [fʀɑ̃ʒ] nf fringe; (cheveux) fringe (Brit), bangs (US)

frangipane [fʀɑ̃ʒipan] nf almond paste

franquette [fʀɑ̃kɛt]: **à la bonne ~** adv without any fuss

frappant, e [fʀapɑ̃, -ɑ̃t] adj striking

frappé, e [fʀape] adj (Culin) iced; **~ de panique** panic-stricken; **~ de stupeur** thunderstruck, dumbfounded

frapper [fʀape] vt (lieu) to hit, strike; (étonner) to strike; (monnaie) to strike, stamp; **se frapper** vi (s'inquiéter) to get worked up; **~ à la porte** to knock at the door; **~ dans ses mains** to clap one's hands; **~ du poing sur** to bang one's fist on; **~ un grand coup** (fig) to strike a blow; **frappé de stupeur** dumbfounded

frasques [fʀask] nfpl escapades; **faire des ~** to get up to mischief

fraternel, le [fʀatɛʀnɛl] adj brotherly, fraternal

fraternité [fʀatɛʀnite] nf brotherhood

fraude [fʀod] nf fraud; (Scol) cheating; **passer qch en ~** to smuggle sth in (ou out); **~ fiscale** tax evasion

frauder [fʀode] vi, vt to cheat; **~ le fisc** to evade paying tax(es)

frauduleux, -euse [fʀodylø, -øz] adj fraudulent

frayer [fʀeje] vt to open up, clear ▷ vi to spawn; (fréquenter): **~ avec** to mix ou associate with; **se ~ un passage dans** to clear o.s. a path through, force one's way through

frayeur [fʀejœʀ] nf fright

fredonner [fʀədɔne] vt to hum

freezer [fʀizœʀ] nm freezing compartment

frein [fʀɛ̃] nm brake; **mettre un ~ à** (fig) to put a brake on, check; **sans ~** (sans limites) unchecked; **~ à main** handbrake; **~ moteur** engine braking; **~s à disques** disc brakes; **~s à tambour** drum brakes

freiner [fʀene] vi to brake ▷ vt (progrès etc) to check

frêle [fʀɛl] adj frail, fragile

frelon [fʀəlɔ̃] nm hornet

frémir [fʀemiʀ] vi (de froid, de peur) to shudder, shiver; (de colère) to shake; (de joie, feuillage) to quiver; (eau) to (begin to) bubble

frêne [fʀɛn] nm ash (tree)

frénétique [fʀenetik] adj frenzied, frenetic

fréquemment [fʀekamɑ̃] adv frequently

fréquent, e [fʀekɑ̃, -ɑ̃t] adj frequent

fréquentation [fʀekɑ̃tasjɔ̃] nf frequenting; seeing; **fréquentations** nfpl (relations) company sg; **avoir de mauvaises ~s** to be in with the wrong crowd, keep bad company

fréquenté, e [fʀekɑ̃te] adj: **très ~** (very) busy; **mal ~** patronized by disreputable elements

fréquenter [fʀekɑ̃te] vt (lieu) to frequent; (personne) to see; **se fréquenter** to see a lot of each other

frère [fʀɛʀ] nm brother ▷ adj: **partis/pays ~s** sister parties/countries

fresque [fʀɛsk] nf (Art) fresco

fret [fʀɛ(t)] nm freight

frétiller [fʀetije] vi to wriggle; to quiver; **~ de la queue** to wag its tail

fretin [fʀətɛ̃] nm: **le menu ~** the small fry

friable [fʀijabl] adj crumbly

friand, e [fʀijɑ̃, -ɑ̃d] adj: **~ de** very fond of ▷ nm (Culin) small minced-meat (Brit) ou ground-meat (US) pie; (: sucré) small almond cake; **~ au fromage** cheese puff

friandise [fʀijɑ̃diz] nf sweet

fric [fʀik] nm (fam) cash, bread

friche [fʀiʃ]: **en ~** adj, adv (lying) fallow

friction [fʀiksjɔ̃] nf (massage) rub, rub-down; (chez le coiffeur) scalp massage; (Tech, fig) friction

frictionner [fʀiksjɔne] vt to rub (down); to massage

frigidaire® [fʀiʒidɛʀ] nm refrigerator

frigide [fʀiʒid] adj frigid

frigo [fʀigo] nm (= frigidaire) fridge

frigorifique [fʀigɔʀifik] adj refrigerating

frileux, -euse [fʀilø, -øz] adj sensitive to (the) cold; (fig) overcautious

frime [fʀim] nf (fam): **c'est de la ~** it's all put on; **pour la ~** just for show

frimer [fʀime] vi (fam) ▷ vi to show off

frimousse [fʀimus] nf (sweet) little face

fringale [fʀɛ̃gal] nf (fam): **avoir la ~** to be ravenous

fringant, e [fʀɛ̃gɑ̃, -ɑ̃t] adj dashing

fringues [fʀɛ̃g] nfpl (fam) clothes, gear no pl

fripé, e [fʀipe] adj crumpled

fripon, ne [fʀipɔ̃, -ɔn] adj roguish, mischievous ▷ nm/f rascal, rogue

fripouille [fʀipuj] nf scoundrel

frire [fʀiʀ] vt (aussi: **faire ~**) ▷ vi to fry

frisé, e [fʀize] adj (cheveux) curly; (personne) curly-haired ▷ nf: (**chicorée**) **-e** curly endive

frisson [fʀisɔ̃], **frissonnement** [fʀisɔnmɑ̃] nm (de froid) shiver; (de peur) shudder; quiver

frissonner [fʀisɔne] vi (de fièvre, froid) to shiver; (d'horreur) to shudder; (feuilles) to quiver

frit, e [fʀi, fʀit] pp de **frire** ▷ adj fried ▷ nf: (**pommes**) **-es** chips (Brit), French fries

friteuse [fʀitøz] nf chip pan (Brit); **~ électrique** deep (fat) fryer

friture [fʀityʀ] nf (huile) (deep) fat; (plat): **~ (de poissons)** fried fish; (Radio) crackle, crackling no pl; **fritures** nfpl (aliments frits) fried food sg

frivole [fʀivɔl] adj frivolous

froid, e [fʀwa, fʀwad] adj cold ▷ nm cold; (absence de sympathie) coolness no pl; **il fait ~** it's cold; **avoir ~** to be cold; **prendre ~** to catch a chill ou cold; **à ~** adv (démarrer) (from) cold; (**pendant**) **les grands ~s** (in) the depths of winter, (during) the cold season; **jeter un ~** (fig) to cast a chill; **être en ~ avec** to be on bad terms with; **battre ~ à qn** to give sb the cold shoulder

froidement [fʀwadmɑ̃] adv (accueillir) coldly; (décider) coolly

froideur [fʀwadœʀ] nf coolness no pl

froisser [fʀwase] vt to crumple (up), crease; (fig) to hurt, offend; **se froisser** vi to crumple, crease; (personne) to take offence (Brit) ou offense (US); **se ~ un muscle** to strain a muscle

frôler [fʀole] vt to brush against; (projectile) to skim past; (fig) to come very close to, come within a hair's breadth of

fromage [fʀɔmaʒ] nm cheese; **~ blanc** soft white cheese; **~ de tête** pork brawn

froment [fʀɔmɑ̃] nm wheat

froncer [fʀɔ̃se] vt to gather; **~ les sourcils** to frown

frondaisons [fʀɔ̃dezɔ̃] nfpl foliage sg

front [fʀɔ̃] nm forehead, brow; (Mil, Météorologie, Pol) front; **avoir le ~ de faire** to have the effrontery to do; **de ~** adv (se heurter) head-on; (rouler) together (2 or 3 abreast);

(simultanément) at once; **faire ~ à** to face up to; **~ de mer** (sea) front

frontalier, -ière [fʀɔ̃talje, -jɛʀ] adj border cpd, frontier cpd ▷ nm/f: (**travailleurs**) **~s** workers who cross the border to go to work, commuters from across the border

frontière [fʀɔ̃tjɛʀ] nf (Géo, Pol) frontier, border; (fig) frontier, boundary

frotter [fʀɔte] vi to rub, scrape ▷ vt to rub; (pour nettoyer) to rub (up); (: avec une brosse: pommes de terre, plancher) to scrub; **~ une allumette** to strike a match; **se ~ à qn** to cross swords with sb; **se ~ à qch** to come up against sth; **se ~ les mains** (fig) to rub one's hands (gleefully)

fructifier [fʀyktifje] vi to yield a profit; **faire ~** to turn to good account

fructueux, -euse [fʀyktɥø, -øz] adj fruitful; profitable

frugal, e, -aux [fʀygal, -o] adj frugal

fruit [fʀɥi] nm fruit gen no pl; **~s de mer** (Culin) seafood(s); **~s secs** dried fruit sg

fruité, e [fʀɥite] adj (vin) fruity

fruitier, -ière [fʀɥitje, -jɛʀ] adj: **arbre ~** fruit tree ▷ nm/f fruiterer (Brit), fruit merchant (US)

fruste [fʀyst] adj unpolished, uncultivated

frustrer [fʀystʀe] vt to frustrate; (priver): **~ qn de qch** to deprive sb of sth

FS abr (= franc suisse) FS, SF

fuel [fjul], **fuel-oil** [fjulɔjl] nm fuel oil; (pour chauffer) heating oil

fugace [fygas] adj fleeting

fugitif, -ive [fyʒitif, -iv] adj (lueur, amour) fleeting; (prisonnier etc) runaway ▷ nm/f fugitive, runaway

fugue [fyg] nf (d'un enfant) running away no pl; (Mus) fugue; **faire une ~** to run away, abscond

fuir [fɥiʀ] vt to flee from; (éviter) to shun ▷ vi to run away; (gaz, robinet) to leak

fuite [fɥit] nf flight; (écoulement) leak, leakage; (divulgation) leak; **être en ~** to be on the run; **mettre en ~** to put to flight; **prendre la ~** to take flight

fulgurant, e [fylgyʀɑ̃, -ɑ̃t] adj lightning cpd, dazzling

fulminer [fylmine] vi: **~ (contre)** to thunder forth (against)

fumé, e [fyme] adj (Culin) smoked; (verre) tinted ▷ nf smoke; **partir en ~e** to go up in smoke

fumer [fyme] vi to smoke; (liquide) to steam ▷ vt to smoke; (terre, champ) to manure

fûmes [fym] vb voir **être**

fumet [fymɛ] nm aroma

fumeur, -euse [fymœʀ, -øz] nm/f smoker; (**compartiment**) **~s** smoking compartment

fumeux, -euse [fymø, -øz] adj (péj) woolly (Brit), hazy

fumier [fymje] nm manure

fumiste [fymist] nm (ramoneur) chimney sweep ▷ nm/f (péj: paresseux) shirker; (charlatan) phoney

funèbre [fynɛbʀ] *adj* funeral *cpd*; (*fig*) doleful; funereal

funérailles [fyneʀaj] *nfpl* funeral *sg*

funeste [fynɛst] *adj* disastrous; deathly

fur [fyʀ]: **au ~ et à mesure** *adv* as one goes along; **au ~ et à mesure que** as; **au ~ et à mesure de leur progression** as they advance (*ou* advanced)

furet [fyʀɛ] *nm* ferret

fureter [fyʀ(ə)te] *vi* (*péj*) to nose about

fureur [fyʀœʀ] *nf* fury; (*passion*): ~ **de** passion for; **être en ~** to be infuriated; **faire ~** to be all the rage

furibond, e [fyʀibɔ̃, -ɔ̃d] *adj* livid, absolutely furious

furie [fyʀi] *nf* fury; (*femme*) shrew, vixen; **en ~** (*mer*) raging

furieux, -euse [fyʀjø, -øz] *adj* furious

furoncle [fyʀɔ̃kl] *nm* boil

furtif, -ive [fyʀtif, -iv] *adj* furtive

fus [fy] *vb voir* **être**

fusain [fyzɛ̃] *nm* (*Bot*) spindle-tree; (*Art*) charcoal

fuseau, x [fyzo] *nm* (*pantalon*) (ski-)pants *pl*; (*pour filer*) spindle; **en ~** (*jambes*) tapering; (*colonne*) bulging; **~ horaire** time zone

fusée [fyze] *nf* rocket; **~ éclairante** flare

fuser [fyze] *vi* (*rires etc*) to burst forth

fusible [fyzibl] *nm* (*Élec*: *fil*) fuse wire; (: *fiche*) fuse

fusil [fyzi] *nm* (*de guerre, à canon rayé*) rifle, gun; (*de chasse, à canon lisse*) shotgun, gun; **~ à deux coups** double-barrelled rifle *ou* shotgun; **~ sous-marin** spear-gun

fusillade [fyzijad] *nf* gunfire *no pl*, shooting *no pl*; (*combat*) gun battle

fusiller [fyzije] *vt* to shoot; **~ qn du regard** to look daggers at sb

fusil-mitrailleur (*pl* **fusils-mitrailleurs**) [fyzimitʀajœʀ] *nm* machine gun

fusionner [fyzjɔne] *vi* to merge

fut [fy] *vb voir* **être**

fût [fy] *vb voir* **être** ▷ *nm* (*tonneau*) barrel, cask; (*de canon*) stock; (*d'arbre*) bole, trunk; (*de colonne*) shaft

futé, e [fyte] *adj* crafty; **Bison ~®** TV and radio traffic monitoring service

futile [fytil] *adj* (*inutile*) futile; (*frivole*) frivolous

futur, e [fytyʀ] *adj, nm* future; **son ~ époux** her husband-to-be; **au ~** (*Ling*) in the future

fuyant, e [fɥijɑ̃, -ɑ̃t] *vb voir* **fuir** ▷ *adj* (*regard etc*) evasive; (*lignes etc*) receding; (*perspective*) vanishing

fuyard, e [fɥijaʀ, -aʀd] *nm/f* runaway

Gabon [gabɔ̃] *nm*: **le ~** Gabon

gâcher [gaʃe] *vt* (*gâter*) to spoil, ruin; (*gaspiller*) to waste; (*plâtre*) to temper; (*mortier*) to mix

gâchis [gaʃi] *nm* (*désordre*) mess; (*gaspillage*) waste *no pl*

gadoue [gadu] *nf* sludge

gaffe [gaf] *nf* (*instrument*) boat hook; (*fam*: *erreur*) blunder; **faire ~** (*fam*) to watch out

gage [gaʒ] *nm* (*dans un jeu*) forfeit; (*fig*: *de fidélité*) token; **gages** *nmpl* (*salaire*) wages; (*garantie*) guarantee *sg*; **mettre en ~** to pawn; **laisser en ~** to leave as security

gageure [gaʒyʀ] *nf*: **c'est une ~** it's attempting the impossible

gagnant, e [gaɲɑ̃, -ɑ̃t] *adj*: **billet/numéro ~** winning ticket/number ▷ *adv*: **jouer ~** (*aux courses*) to be bound to win ▷ *nm/f* winner

gagne-pain [gaɲpɛ̃] *nm inv* job

gagner [gaɲe] *vt* (*concours, procès, pari*) to win; (*somme d'argent, revenu*) to earn; (*aller vers, atteindre*) to reach; (*s'emparer de*) to overcome; (*envahir*) to spread to; (*se concilier*): **~ qn** to win sb over ▷ *vi* to win; (*fig*) to gain; **~ du temps/de la place** to gain time/save space; **~ sa vie** to earn one's living; **~ du terrain** (*aussi fig*) to gain ground; **~ qn de vitesse** to outstrip sb; (*aussi fig*): **~ à faire** (*s'en trouver bien*) to be better off doing; **il y gagne** it's in his interest, it's to his advantage

gai, e [ge] *adj* cheerful; (*livre, pièce de théâtre*) light-hearted; (*un peu ivre*) merry

gaiement [gemɑ̃] *adv* cheerfully

gaieté [gete] *nf* cheerfulness; **gaietés** *nfpl* (*souvent ironique*) delights; **de ~ de cœur** with a light heart

gaillard, e [gajaʀ, -aʀd] *adj* (*robuste*) sprightly; (*grivois*) bawdy, ribald ▷ *nm/f* (*strapping*) fellow/wench

gain [gɛ̃] *nm* (*revenu*) earnings *pl*; (*bénéfice: gén pl*) profits *pl*; (*au jeu: gén pl*) winnings *pl*; (*fig: de temps, place*) saving; (: *avantage*) benefit; (: *lucre*) gain; **avoir ~ de cause** to win the case; (*fig*) to be proved right; **obtenir ~ de cause** (*fig*) to win out

gaine [gen] *nf* (*corset*) girdle; (*fourreau*) sheath; (*de fil électrique etc*) outer covering

gala [gala] *nm* official reception; **soirée de ~** gala evening

galant, e [galɑ̃, -ɑ̃t] *adj* (*courtois*) courteous, gentlemanly; (*entreprenant*) flirtatious, gallant; (*aventure, poésie*) amorous; (*scène, rendez-vous*) romantic; **en ~e compagnie** (*homme*) with a lady friend; (*femme*) with a gentleman friend

galère [galɛʀ] *nf* galley

galérer [galere] *vi* (*fam*) to work hard, slave (away)

galerie [galʀi] *nf* gallery; (*Théât*) circle; (*de voiture*) roof rack; (*fig: spectateurs*) audience; **~ marchande** shopping mall; **~ de peinture** (*private*) art gallery

galet [galɛ] *nm* pebble; (*Tech*) wheel; **galets** *nmpl* pebbles, shingle *sg*

galette [galɛt] *nf* (*gâteau*) flat pastry cake; (*crêpe*) savoury pancake; **la ~ des Rois** *cake traditionally eaten on Twelfth Night*

░ **GALETTE DES ROIS**
░
░ A *galette des Rois* is a cake eaten on
░ Twelfth Night containing a figurine.
░ The person who finds it is the king
░ (or queen) and gets a paper crown. They
░ then choose someone else to be their
░ queen (or king).

galipette [galipɛt] *nf* somersault; **faire des ~s** to turn somersaults

Galles [gal] *nfpl*: **le pays de ~** Wales

gallois, e [galwa, -waz] *adj* Welsh ▷ *nm* (*Ling*) Welsh ▷ *nm/f*: **G~, e** Welshman(-woman)

galon [galɔ̃] *nm* (*Mil*) stripe; (*décoratif*) piece of braid; **prendre du ~** to be promoted

galop [galo] *nm* gallop; **au ~** at a gallop; **~ d'essai** (*fig*) trial run

galoper [galɔpe] *vi* to gallop

galopin [galɔpɛ̃] *nm* urchin, ragamuffin

gambader [gɑ̃bade] *vi* (*animal, enfant*) to leap about

gamin, e [gamɛ̃, -in] *nm/f* kid ▷ *adj* mischievous, playful

gamme [gam] *nf* (*Mus*) scale; (*fig*) range

gammé, e [game] *adj*: **croix ~e** swastika

gang [gɑ̃g] *nm* (*de criminels*) gang

gant [gɑ̃] *nm* glove; **prendre des ~s** (*fig*) to handle the situation with kid gloves; **relever le ~** (*fig*) to take up the gauntlet; **~ de crin** massage glove; **~ de toilette** (*face*) flannel (*Brit*), face cloth; **~s de boxe** boxing gloves; **~s de caoutchouc** rubber gloves

garage [gaʀaʒ] *nm* garage; **~ à vélos** bicycle shed

garagiste [gaʀaʒist] *nm/f* (*propriétaire*) garage owner; (*mécanicien*) garage mechanic

garantie [gaʀɑ̃ti] *nf* guarantee, warranty; (*gage*) security, surety; (**bon de**) **~** guarantee *ou* warranty slip; **~ de bonne exécution** performance bond

garantir [gaʀɑ̃tiʀ] *vt* to guarantee; (*protéger*): **~ de** to protect from; **je vous garantis que** I can assure you that; **garanti pure laine/2 ans** guaranteed pure wool/for 2 years

garce [gaʀs] *nf* (*péj*) bitch

garçon [gaʀsɔ̃] *nm* boy; (*célibataire*): **vieux ~** bachelor; (*jeune homme*) boy, lad; (*aussi*: **~ de café**) waiter; **~ boucher/coiffeur** butcher's/hairdresser's assistant; **~ de courses** messenger; **~ d'écurie** stable lad; **~ manqué** tomboy

garçonnière [gaʀsɔnjɛʀ] *nf* bachelor flat

garde [gaʀd] *nm* (*de prisonnier*) guard; (*de domaine etc*) warden; (*soldat, sentinelle*) guardsman ▷ *nf* guarding; looking after; (*soldats, Boxe, Escrime*) guard; (*faction*) watch; (*d'une arme*) hilt; (*Typo: aussi*: **page** *ou* **feuille de ~**) flyleaf; (: *collée*) endpaper; **de ~** *adj, adv* on duty; **monter la ~** to stand guard; **être sur ses ~s** to be on one's guard; **mettre en ~** to warn; **mise en ~** warning; **prendre ~ (à)** to be careful (of); **avoir la ~ des enfants** (*après divorce*) to have custody of the children; **~ champêtre** *nm* rural policeman; **~ du corps** *nm* bodyguard; **~ d'enfants** *nf* child minder; **~ forestier** *nm* forest warden; **~ mobile** *nm, nf* mobile guard; **~ des Sceaux** *nm* ≈ Lord Chancellor (*Brit*), ≈ Attorney General (*US*); **~ à vue** *nf* (*Jur*) ≈ police custody

garde-à-vous [gaʀdavu] *nm inv*: **être/se mettre au ~** to be at/stand to attention; **~ (fixe)!** (*Mil*) attention!

garde-barrière (*pl* **gardes-barrière(s)**) [gaʀdəbaʀjɛʀ] *nm/f* level-crossing keeper

garde-boue [gaʀdəbu] *nm inv* mudguard

garde-chasse (*pl* **gardes-chasse(s)**) [gaʀdəʃas] *nm* gamekeeper

garde-malade (*pl* **gardes-malade(s)**) [gaʀdəmalad] *nf* home nurse

garde-manger [gaʀdəmɑ̃ʒe] *nm inv* (*boîte*) meat safe; (*placard*) pantry, larder

garder [gaʀde] *vt* (*conserver*) to keep; (: *sur soi: vêtement, chapeau*) to keep on; (*surveiller: enfants*) to look after; (: *immeuble, lieu, prisonnier*) to guard; **se garder** *vi* (*aliment: se conserver*) to keep; **se ~ de faire** to be careful not to do; **~ le lit/la chambre** to stay in bed/indoors; **~ le silence** to keep silent *ou* quiet; **~ la ligne** to keep one's figure; **~ à vue** to keep in custody; **pêche/chasse gardée** private fishing/ hunting (ground)

garderie [gaʀdəʀi] *nf* day nursery, crèche

garde-robe [gaʀdəʀɔb] *nf* wardrobe

gardien, ne [gaʀdjɛ̃, -ɛn] *nm/f* (*garde*) guard; (*de prison*) warder; (*de domaine, réserve*) warden; (*de musée etc*) attendant; (*de phare, cimetière*) keeper; (*d'immeuble*) caretaker; (*fig*) guardian; **~ de but** goalkeeper; **~ de nuit** night watchman; **~ de la paix** policeman

gare [gaʀ] *nf* (*railway*) station, train station (US) ▷ *excl*: **~ à ...** mind ...!, watch out for ...!; **~ à ne pas ...** mind you don't ...; **~ à toi!** watch out!; **sans crier ~** without warning; **~ maritime** harbour station; **~ routière** bus station; (*de camions*) haulage (Brit) *ou* trucking (US) depot; **~ de triage** marshalling yard

garer [gaʀe] *vt* to park; **se garer** *vi* to park; (*pour laisser passer*) to draw into the side

gargariser [gaʀgaʀize]: **se gargariser** *vi* to gargle; **se ~ de** (*fig*) to revel in

gargote [gaʀgɔt] *nf* cheap restaurant, greasy spoon (*fam*)

gargouille [gaʀguj] *nf* gargoyle

gargouiller [gaʀguje] *vi* (*estomac*) to rumble; (*eau*) to gurgle

garnement [gaʀnəmã] *nm* rascal, scallywag

garni, e [gaʀni] *adj* (*plat*) served with vegetables (*and chips, pasta or rice*) ▷ *nm* (*appartement*) furnished accommodation *no pl* (Brit) *ou* accommodations *pl* (US)

garnison [gaʀnizɔ̃] *nf* garrison

garniture [gaʀnityʀ] *nf* (*Culin*: *légumes*) vegetables *pl*; (: *persil etc*) garnish; (: *farce*) filling; (*décoration*) trimming; (*protection*) fittings *pl*; **~ de cheminée** mantelpiece ornaments *pl*; **~ de frein** (*Auto*) brake lining; **~ intérieure** (*Auto*) interior trim; **~ périodique** sanitary towel (Brit) *ou* napkin (US)

gars [gɑ] *nm* lad; (*type*) guy

Gascogne [gaskɔɲ] *nf*: **la ~** Gascony; **le golfe de ~** the Bay of Biscay

gas-oil [gazɔjl] *nm* diesel oil

gaspiller [gaspije] *vt* to waste

gastronome [gastʀɔnɔm] *nm/f* gourmet

gastronomie [gastʀɔnɔmi] *nf* gastronomy

gastronomique [gastʀɔnɔmik] *adj* gastronomic; **menu ~** gourmet menu

gâteau, x [gɑto] *nm* cake ▷ *adj inv* (*fam*: *trop indulgent*): **papa-/maman-~** doting father/ mother; **~ d'anniversaire** birthday cake; **~ de riz** rice pudding; **~ sec** biscuit

gâter [gɑte] *vt* to spoil; **se gâter** *vi* (*dent, fruit*) to go bad; (*temps, situation*) to change for the worse

gâterie [gɑtʀi] *nf* little treat

gâteux, -euse [gɑtø, -øz] *adj* senile

gauche [goʃ] *adj* left, left-hand; (*maladroit*) awkward, clumsy ▷ *nf* (*Pol*) left (wing); **le bras ~** the left arm; **le côté ~** the left-hand

side; (*Boxe*) left; **à ~** on the left; (*direction*) (to the) left; **à ~ de** (on *ou* to the) left of; **à la ~ de** to the left of; **sur votre ~** on your left; **de ~** (*Pol*) left-wing

gaucher, -ère [goʃe, -ɛʀ] *adj* left-handed

gauchiste [goʃist] *adj, nm/f* leftist

gaufre [gofʀ] *nf* (*pâtisserie*) waffle; (*de cire*) honeycomb

gaufrette [gofʀɛt] *nf* wafer

gaulois, e [golwa, -waz] *adj* Gallic; (*grivois*) bawdy ▷ *nm/f*: **G~, e** Gaul

gaver [gave] *vt* to force-feed; (*fig*): **~ de** to cram with, fill up with; (*personne*): **se ~ de** to stuff o.s. with

gaz [gaz] *nm inv* gas; **mettre les ~** (*Auto*) to put one's foot down; **chambre/masque à ~** gas chamber/mask; **~ en bouteille** bottled gas; **~ butane** Calor gas® (Brit), butane gas; **~ carbonique** carbon dioxide; **~ hilarant** laughing gas; **~ lacrymogène** tear gas; **~ naturel** natural gas; **~ de ville** town gas (Brit), manufactured domestic gas; **ça sent le ~** I can smell gas, there's a smell of gas

gaze [gaz] *nf* gauze

gazer [gaze] *vt* to gas ▷ *vi* (*fam*) to be going *ou* working well

gazette [gazɛt] *nf* news sheet

gazeux, -euse [gazø, -øz] *adj* gaseous; (*eau*) sparkling; (*boisson*) fizzy

gazoduc [gazodyk] *nm* gas pipeline

gazon [gazɔ̃] *nm* (*herbe*) turf, grass; (*pelouse*) lawn

gazouiller [gazuje] *vi* (*oiseau*) to chirp; (*enfant*) to babble

GDF *sigle m* (= *Gaz de France*) national gas company

geai [ʒɛ] *nm* jay

géant, e [ʒeã, -ãt] *adj* gigantic, giant; (*Comm*) giant-size ▷ *nm/f* giant

geindre [ʒɛ̃dʀ] *vi* to groan, moan

gel [ʒɛl] *nm* frost; (*de l'eau*) freezing; (*fig*: *des salaires, prix*) freeze; freezing; (*produit de beauté*) gel; **~ douche** shower gel

gélatine [ʒelatin] *nf* gelatine

gelé, e [ʒəle] *adj* frozen ▷ *nf* jelly; (*gel*) frost; **~ blanche** hoarfrost, white frost

geler [ʒ(ə)le] *vt, vi* to freeze; **il gèle** it's freezing

gélule [ʒelyl] *nf* (*Méd*) capsule

gelures [ʒəlyʀ] *nfpl* frostbite *sg*

Gémeaux [ʒemo] *nmpl*: **les ~** Gemini, the Twins; **être des ~** to be Gemini

gémir [ʒemiʀ] *vi* to groan, moan

gênant, e [ʒenã, -ãt] *adj* (*objet*) awkward, in the way; (*histoire, personne*) embarrassing

gencive [ʒãsiv] *nf* gum

gendarme [ʒãdaʀm] *nm* gendarme

gendarmerie [ʒãdaʀməʀi] *nf* military police force in countryside and small towns; their police station or barracks

gendre [ʒãdʀ] *nm* son-in-law

gêné, e [ʒene] *adj* embarrassed; (*dépourvu d'argent*) short (of money)

gêner [ʒene] vt (incommoder) to bother; (encombrer) to hamper; (bloquer le passage) to be in the way of; (déranger) to bother; (embarrasser): ~ **qn** to make sb feel ill-at-ease; **se gêner** to put o.s. out; **ne vous gênez pas!** (ironique) go right ahead!, don't mind me!; **je vais me ~!** (ironique) why should I care?

général, e, -aux [ʒeneral, -o] adj, nm general ▷ nf: **(répétition) ~e** final dress rehearsal; **en ~** usually, in general; **à la satisfaction ~e** to everyone's satisfaction

généralement [ʒeneralmã] adv generally

généraliser [ʒeneralize] vt, vi to generalize; **se généraliser** vi to become widespread

généraliste [ʒeneralist] nm/f (Méd) general practitioner, GP

génération [ʒenerasjõ] nf generation

généreux, -euse [ʒenerø, -øz] adj generous

générique [ʒenerik] adj generic ▷ nm (Ciné, TV) credits pl, credit titles pl

générosité [ʒenerozite] nf generosity

genêt [ʒ(ə)nɛ] nm (Bot) broom no pl

génétique [ʒenetik] adj genetic ▷ nf genetics sg

Genève [ʒ(ə)nɛv] n Geneva

génial, e, -aux [ʒenjal, -o] adj of genius; (fam: formidable) fantastic, brilliant

génie [ʒeni] nm genius; (Mil): **le ~** the Engineers pl; **avoir du ~** to have genius; **~ civil** civil engineering; **~ génétique** genetic engineering

genièvre [ʒənjɛvr] nm (Bot) juniper (tree); (boisson) Dutch gin; **grain de ~** juniper berry

génisse [ʒenis] nf heifer; **foie de ~** ox liver

génital, e, -aux [ʒenital, -o] adj genital; **les parties ~es** the genitals

génois, e [ʒenwa, -waz] adj Genoese ▷ nf (gâteau) ≈ sponge cake

genou, x [ʒ(ə)nu] nm knee; **à ~x** on one's knees; **se mettre à ~x** to kneel down

genre [ʒãr] nm (espèce, sorte) kind, type, sort; (allure) manner; (Ling) gender; (Art) genre; (Zool etc) genus; **se donner du ~** to give o.s. airs; **avoir bon ~** to look a nice sort; **avoir mauvais ~** to be coarse-looking; **ce n'est pas son ~** it's not like him

gens [ʒã] nmpl (f in some phrases) people pl; **les ~ d'Église** the clergy; **les ~ du monde** society people; **~ de maison** domestics

gentil, le [ʒãti, -ij] adj kind; (enfant: sage) good; (sympa: endroit etc) nice; **c'est très ~ à vous** it's very kind ou good ou nice of you

gentillesse [ʒãtijɛs] nf kindness

gentiment [ʒãtimã] adv kindly

géo abr (= géographie) geography

géographie [ʒeografi] nf geography

geôlier [ʒolje] nm jailer

géologie [ʒeɔlɔʒi] nf geology

géomètre [ʒeɔmɛtr] nm: **(arpenteur-)~** (land) surveyor

géométrie [ʒeɔmetri] nf geometry; **à ~ variable** (Aviat) swing-wing

géométrique [ʒeɔmetrik] adj geometric

géranium [ʒeranjom] nm geranium

gérant, e [ʒerã, -ãt] nm/f manager/manageress; **~ d'immeuble** managing agent

gerbe [ʒɛrb] nf (de fleurs, d'eau) spray; (de blé) sheaf; (fig) shower, burst

gercé, e [ʒɛrse] adj chapped

gerçure [ʒɛrsyr] nf crack

gérer [ʒere] vt to manage

germain, e [ʒɛrmɛ̃, -ɛn] adj: **cousin ~** first cousin

germe [ʒɛrm] nm germ

germer [ʒɛrme] vi to sprout; (semence, aussi fig) to germinate

Ghana [gana] nm: **le ~** Ghana

ghetto [geto] nm ghetto

gibet [ʒibɛ] nm gallows pl

gibier [ʒibje] nm (animaux) game; (fig) prey

giboulée [ʒibule] nf sudden shower

gicler [ʒikle] vi to spurt, squirt

gifle [ʒifl] nf slap (in the face)

gifler [ʒifle] vt to slap (in the face)

gigantesque [ʒigãtɛsk] adj gigantic

gigogne [ʒigɔɲ] adj: **lits ~s** truckle (Brit) ou trundle (US) beds; **tables/poupées ~s** nest of tables/dolls

gigot [ʒigo] nm leg (of mutton ou lamb)

gigoter [ʒigɔte] vi to wriggle (about)

gilet [ʒilɛ] nm waistcoat; (pull) cardigan; (de corps) vest; **~ pare-balles** bulletproof jacket; **~ de sauvetage** life jacket

gin [dʒin] nm gin; **~-tonic** gin and tonic

gingembre [ʒɛ̃ʒãbr] nm ginger

girafe [ʒiraf] nf giraffe

giratoire [ʒiratwar] adj: **sens ~** roundabout

girofle [ʒirɔfl] nm: **clou de ~** clove

girouette [ʒirwɛt] nf weather vane ou cock

gitan, e [ʒitã, -an] nm/f gipsy

gîte [ʒit] nm (maison) home; (abri) shelter; (du lièvre) form; **~ (rural)** (country) holiday cottage ou apartment, gîte (self-catering accommodation in the country)

givre [ʒivr] nm (hoar) frost

givré, e [ʒivre] adj covered in frost; (fam: fou) nuts; **citron ~/orange ~e** lemon/orange sorbet (served in fruit skin)

glace [glas] nf ice; (crème glacée) ice cream; (verre) sheet of glass; (miroir) mirror; (de voiture) window; **glaces** nfpl (Géo) ice sheets, ice sg; **de ~** (fig: accueil, visage) frosty, icy; **rester de ~** to remain unmoved

glacé, e [glase] adj (mains, vent, pluie) freezing; (lac) frozen; (boisson) iced

glacer [glase] vt to freeze; (boisson) to chill, ice; (gâteau) to ice (Brit), frost (US); (papier, tissu) to glaze; (fig): ~ **qn** (intimider) to chill sb; (fig) to make sb's blood run cold

glacial, e [glasjal] adj icy

glacier [glasje] nm (Géo) glacier; (marchand) ice-cream maker

glacière [glasjɛʀ] nf icebox

glaçon [glasɔ̃] nm icicle; (pour boisson) ice cube

glaïeul [glajœl] nm gladiola

glaise [glez] nf clay

gland [glɑ̃] nm (de chêne) acorn; (décoration) tassel; (Anat) glans

glande [glɑ̃d] nf gland

glander [glɑ̃de] vi (fam) to fart around (Brit) (!), screw around (US) (!)

glauque [glok] adj dull blue-green

glissade [glisad] nf (par jeu) slide; (chute) slip; (dérapage) skid; **faire des ~s** to slide

glissant, e [glisɑ̃, -ɑ̃t] adj slippery

glissement [glismɑ̃] nm sliding; (fig) shift; ~ **de terrain** landslide

glisser [glise] vi (avancer) to glide ou slide along; (coulisser, tomber) to slide; (déraper) to slip; (être glissant) to be slippery ▷ vt to slip; ~ **qch sous/dans/à** to slip sth under/into/to; ~ **sur** (fig: détail etc) to skate over; **se ~ dans/ entre** to slip into/between

global, e, -aux [glɔbal, -o] adj overall

globe [glɔb] nm globe; **sous ~** under glass; ~ **oculaire** eyeball; **le ~ terrestre** the globe

globule [glɔbyl] nm (du sang): ~ **blanc/rouge** white/red corpuscle

globuleux, -euse [glɔbylø, -øz] adj: **yeux ~** protruding eyes

gloire [glwaʀ] nf glory; (mérite) distinction, credit; (personne) celebrity

glorieux, -euse [glɔʀjø, -øz] adj glorious

gloussement [glusmɑ̃] nm (de poule) cluck; (rire) chuckle

glousser [gluse] vi to cluck; (rire) to chuckle

glouton, ne [glutɔ̃, -ɔn] adj gluttonous, greedy

gluant, e [glyɑ̃, -ɑ̃t] adj sticky, gummy

glucose [glykoz] nm glucose

glycine [glisin] nf wisteria

GO sigle fpl (= grandes ondes) LW ▷ sigle m (= gentil organisateur) title given to leaders on Club Méditerranée holidays; extended to refer to easy-going leader of any group

go [go]: **tout de go** adv straight out

goal [gol] nm goalkeeper

gobelet [gɔblɛ] nm (en métal) tumbler; (en plastique) beaker; (à dés) cup

gober [gɔbe] vt to swallow

godasse [gɔdas] nf (fam) shoe

godet [gɔde] nm pot; (Couture) unpressed pleat

goéland [gɔelɑ̃] nm (sea)gull

goélette [gɔelɛt] nf schooner

gogo [gɔgo] nm (péj) mug, sucker; **à ~** adv galore

goguenard, e [gɔgnaʀ, -aʀd] adj mocking

goinfre [gwɛ̃fʀ] nm glutton

golf [gɔlf] nm (jeu) golf; (terrain) golf course; ~ **miniature** crazy ou miniature golf

golfe [gɔlf] nm gulf; (petit) bay; **le ~ d'Aden** the Gulf of Aden; **le ~ de Gascogne** the Bay of Biscay; **le ~ du Lion** the Gulf of Lions; **le ~ Persique** the Persian Gulf

gomme [gɔm] nf (à effacer) rubber (Brit), eraser; (résine) gum; **boule** ou **pastille de ~** throat pastille

gommer [gɔme] vt (effacer) to rub out (Brit), erase; (enduire de gomme) to gum

gond [gɔ̃] nm hinge; **sortir de ses ~s** (fig) to fly off the handle

gondoler [gɔ̃dɔle]: **se gondoler** vi to warp, buckle; (fam: rire) to hoot with laughter; to be in stitches

gonflé, e [gɔ̃fle] adj swollen; (ventre) bloated; **il est ~** (fam: courageux) he's got some nerve; (impertinent) he's got a nerve

gonfler [gɔ̃fle] vt (pneu, ballon) to inflate, blow up; (nombre, importance) to inflate ▷ vi (pied etc) to swell (up); (Culin: pâte) to rise

gonfleur [gɔ̃flœʀ] nm air pump

gonzesse [gɔ̃zɛs] nf (fam) chick, bird (Brit)

goret [gɔʀɛ] nm piglet

gorge [gɔʀʒ] nf (Anat) throat; (poitrine) breast; (Géo) gorge; (rainure) groove; **avoir mal à la ~** to have a sore throat; **avoir la ~ serrée** to have a lump in one's throat

gorgé, e [gɔʀʒe] adj: ~ **de** filled with; (eau) saturated with ▷ nf mouthful; (petite) sip; (grande) gulp; **boire à petites/grandes ~es** to take little sips/big gulps

gorille [gɔʀij] nm gorilla; (fam) bodyguard

gosier [gozje] nm throat

gosse [gɔs] nm/f kid

goudron [gudʀɔ̃] nm (asphalte) tar(mac) (Brit), asphalt; (du tabac) tar

goudronner [gudʀɔne] vt to tar(mac) (Brit), asphalt

gouffre [gufʀ] nm abyss, gulf

goujat [guʒa] nm boor

goulot [gulo] nm neck; **boire au ~** to drink from the bottle

goulu, e [guly] adj greedy

gourd, e [guʀ, guʀd] adj numb (with cold); (fam) oafish

gourde [guʀd] nf (récipient) flask; (fam) (clumsy) clot ou oaf ▷ adj oafish

gourdin [guʀdɛ̃] nm club, bludgeon

gourer [guʀe] (fam): **se gourer** vi to boob

gourmand, e [guʀmɑ̃, -ɑ̃d] adj greedy

gourmandise [guʀmɑ̃diz] nf greed; (bonbon) sweet (Brit), piece of candy (US)

gourmet [guʀmɛ] nm epicure

gourmette [guʀmɛt] nf chain bracelet

gousse [gus] nf (de vanille etc) pod; ~ **d'ail** clove of garlic

goût [gu] nm taste; (fig: appréciation) taste, liking; **le (bon) ~** good taste; **de bon ~** in good taste, tasteful; **de mauvais ~** in bad taste, tasteless; **avoir bon/mauvais ~** (aliment) to taste nice/nasty; (*personne*) to have good/bad taste; **avoir du/manquer de ~** to have/lack taste; **avoir du ~ pour** to have a liking for; **prendre ~ à** to develop a taste *ou* a liking for

goûter [gute] *vt* (*essayer*) to taste; (*apprécier*) to enjoy ▷ *vi* to have (afternoon) tea ▷ *nm* (afternoon) tea; **~ à** to taste, sample; **~ de** to have a taste of; **~ d'enfants/d'anniversaire** children's tea/birthday party; **je peux ~?** can I have a taste?

goutte [gut] *nf* drop; (*Méd*) gout; (*alcool*) nip (Brit), tot (Brit), drop (US); **gouttes** *nfpl* (*Méd*) drops; **~ à ~** *adv* a drop at a time; **tomber ~ à ~** to drip

goutte-à-goutte [gutagut] *nm inv* (*Méd*) drip; **alimenter ~** to drip-feed

gouttelette [gutlɛt] *nf* droplet

gouttière [gutjɛr] *nf* gutter

gouvernail [guvɛrnaj] *nm* rudder; (*barre*) helm, tiller

gouvernant, e [guvɛrnɑ̃, -ɑ̃t] *adj* ruling *cpd* ▷ *nf* housekeeper; (*d'un enfant*) governess

gouvernement [guvɛrnəmɑ̃] *nm* government

gouverner [guvɛrne] *vt* to govern; (*diriger*) to steer; (*fig*) to control

grâce [grɑs] *nf* (*charme*, Rel) grace; (*faveur*) favour; (*Jur*) pardon; **grâces** *nfpl* (Rel) grace *sg*; **de bonne/mauvaise ~** with (a) good/bad grace; **dans les bonnes ~s de qn** in favour with sb; **faire ~ à qn de qch** to spare sb sth; **rendre ~(s) à** to give thanks to; **demander ~** to beg for mercy; **droit de ~** right of reprieve; **recours en ~** plea for pardon; **~ à** *prép* thanks to

gracier [grasje] *vt* to pardon

gracieux, -euse [grasjø, -øz] *adj* (*charmant, élégant*) graceful; (*aimable*) gracious, kind; **à titre ~** free of charge

grade [grad] *nm* (Mil) rank; (Scol) degree; **monter en ~** to be promoted

gradin [gradɛ̃] *nm* (*dans un théâtre*) tier; (*de stade*) step; **gradins** *nmpl* (*de stade*) terracing *no pl* (Brit), standing area; **en ~s** terraced

gradué, e [gradɥe] *adj* (*exercices*) graded (for difficulty); (*thermomètre*) graduated; **verre ~** measuring jug

graduel, le [gradɥɛl] *adj* gradual; progressive

graduer [gradɥe] *vt* (*effort etc*) to increase gradually; (*règle, verre*) to graduate

graffiti [grafiti] *nmpl* graffiti

grain [grɛ̃] *nm* (*gén*) grain; (*de chapelet*) bead; (*Navig*) squall; (*averse*) heavy shower; (*fig: petite quantité*): **un ~ de** a touch of; **~ de beauté** beauty spot; **~ de café** coffee bean; **~ de poivre** peppercorn; **~ de poussière** speck of dust; **~ de raisin** grape

graine [grɛn] *nf* seed; **mauvaise ~** (*mauvais sujet*) bad lot; **une ~ de voyou** a hooligan in the making

graissage [grɛsaʒ] *nm* lubrication, greasing

graisse [grɛs] *nf* fat; (*lubrifiant*) grease; **~ saturée** saturated fat

graisser [grese] *vt* to lubricate, grease; (*tacher*) to make greasy

graisseux, -euse [grɛsø, -øz] *adj* greasy; (*Anat*) fatty

grammaire [gramɛr] *nf* grammar

grammatical, e, -aux [gramatikal, -o] *adj* grammatical

gramme [gram] *nm* gramme

grand, e [grɑ̃, grɑ̃d] *adj* (*haut*) tall; (*gros, vaste, large*) big, large; (*long*) long; (*plus âgé*) big; (*adulte*) grown-up; (*important, brillant*) great ▷ *adv*: **~ ouvert** wide open; **un ~ buveur** a heavy drinker; **~ homme** a great man; **son ~ frère** his big *ou* older brother; **avoir ~ besoin de** to be in dire *ou* desperate need of; **il est ~ temps de** it's high time to; **il est assez ~ pour** he's big *ou* old enough to; **voir ~** to think big; **en ~** on a large scale; **au ~ air** in the open (air); **les ~s blessés/brûlés** the severely injured/burned; **de ~ matin** at the crack of dawn; **~ écart** splits *pl*; **~ ensemble** housing scheme; **~ jour** broad daylight; **~ livre** (Comm) ledger; **~ magasin** department store; **~ malade** very sick person; **~ public** general public; **~e personne** grown-up; **~e surface** hypermarket, superstore; **~es écoles** *prestige university-level colleges with competitive entrance examinations; see note*; **~es lignes** (Rail) main lines; **~es vacances** summer holidays (Brit) *ou* vacation (US)

▓▓ **GRANDES ÉCOLES**
▓
▓ The *grandes écoles* are highly-respected
▓ institutes of higher education which
▓ train students for specific careers.
▓ Students who have spent two years after
▓ the 'baccalauréat' in the 'classes
▓ préparatoires' are recruited by
▓ competitive entry examination. The
▓ prestigious *grandes écoles* have a strong
▓ corporate identity and tend to furnish
▓ France with its intellectual,
▓ administrative and political élite.

grand-chose [grɑ̃ʃoz] *nm/f inv*: **pas ~** not much

Grande-Bretagne [grɑ̃dbrətaɲ] *nf*: **la ~** (Great) Britain; **en ~** in (Great) Britain

grandeur [grɑ̃dœr] *nf* (*dimension*) size; (*fig: ampleur, importance*) magnitude; (: *gloire, puissance*) greatness; **~ nature** life-size

grandiose [grɑ̃djoz] *adj* (*paysage, spectacle*) imposing

grandir [grɑ̃dir] *vi* (*enfant, arbre*) to grow; (*bruit, hostilité*) to increase, grow ▷ *vt*: **~ qn** (*vêtement, chaussure*) to make sb look taller; (*fig*) to make sb grow in stature

grand-mère (*pl* **grand(s)-mères**) [grɑ̃mɛr] *nf* grandmother

grand-messe [gʀɑ̃mɛs] *nf* high mass
grand-peine [gʀɑ̃pɛn]: **à ~** *adv* with (great) difficulty
grand-père (*pl* **grands-pères**) [gʀɑ̃pɛʀ] *nm* grandfather
grand-route [gʀɑ̃ʀut] *nf* main road
grands-parents [gʀɑ̃paʀɑ̃] *nmpl* grandparents
grange [gʀɑ̃ʒ] *nf* barn
granit, granite [gʀanit] *nm* granite
graphique [gʀafik] *adj* graphic ▷ *nm* graph
grappe [gʀap] *nf* cluster; **~ de raisin** bunch of grapes
gras, se [gʀɑ, gʀɑs] *adj* (*viande, soupe*) fatty; (*personne*) fat; (*surface, main, cheveux*) greasy; (*terre*) sticky; (*toux*) loose, phlegmy; (*rire*) throaty; (*plaisanterie*) coarse; (*crayon*) soft-lead; (*Typo*) bold ▷ *nm* (*Culin*) fat; **faire la ~se matinée** to have a lie-in (*Brit*), sleep late; **matière ~se** fat (content)
grassement [gʀɑsmɑ̃] *adv* (*généreusement*): **~ payé** handsomely paid; (*grossièrement: rire*) coarsely
grassouillet, te [gʀasujɛ, -ɛt] *adj* podgy, plump
gratifiant, e [gʀatifjɑ̃, -ɑ̃t] *adj* gratifying, rewarding
gratin [gʀatɛ̃] *nm* (*Culin*) cheese- (*ou* crumb-) topped dish; (: *croûte*) topping; **au ~** au gratin; **tout le ~ parisien** all the best people of Paris
gratiné [gʀatine] *adj* (*Culin*) au gratin; (*fam*) hellish ▷ *nf* (*soupe*) onion soup au gratin
gratis [gʀatis] *adv, adj* free
gratitude [gʀatityd] *nf* gratitude
gratte-ciel [gʀatsjɛl] *nm inv* skyscraper
gratte-papier [gʀatpapje] *nm inv* (*péj*) penpusher
gratter [gʀate] *vt* (*frotter*) to scrape; (*enlever: avec un outil*) to scrape off; (*avec un ongle: bras, bouton*) to scratch; (*enlever avec un ongle*) to scratch off ▷ *vi* (*irriter*) to be scratchy; (*démanger*) to itch; **se gratter** to scratch o.s.
gratuit, e [gʀatɥi, -ɥit] *adj* (*entrée*) free; (*billet*) free, complimentary; (*fig*) gratuitous
gravats [gʀava] *nmpl* rubble *sg*
grave [gʀav] *adj* (*dangereux: maladie, accident*) serious, bad; (*sérieux: sujet, problème*) serious, grave; (*personne, air*) grave, solemn; (*voix, son*) deep, low-pitched ▷ *nm* (*Mus*) low register; **ce n'est pas ~!** it's all right, don't worry; **blessé ~** seriously injured person
gravement [gʀavmɑ̃] *adv* seriously; badly; (*parler, regarder*) gravely
graver [gʀave] *vt* (*plaque, nom*) to engrave; (*CD, DVD*) to burn; (*fig*): **~ qch dans son esprit/sa mémoire** to etch sth in one's mind/memory
graveur [gʀavœʀ] *nm* engraver; **~ de CD/ DVD** CD/DVD burner *or* writer
gravier [gʀavje] *nm* (loose) gravel *no pl*
gravillons [gʀavijɔ̃] *nmpl* gravel *sg*, loose chippings *ou* gravel

gravir [gʀaviʀ] *vt* to climb (up)
gravité [gʀavite] *nf* (*de maladie, d'accident*) seriousness; (*de sujet, problème*) gravity; (*Physique*) gravity
graviter [gʀavite] *vi* to revolve; **~ autour de** to revolve around
gravure [gʀavyʀ] *nf* engraving; (*reproduction*) print; plate
gré [gʀe] *nm*: **à son ~** *adj* to his liking ▷ *adv* as he pleases; **au ~ de** according to, following; **contre le ~ de qn** against sb's will; **de son (plein) ~** of one's own free will; **de ~ ou de force** whether one likes it or not; **de bon ~** willingly; **bon ~ mal ~** like it or not; willy-nilly; **de ~ à ~** (*Comm*) by mutual agreement; **savoir (bien) ~ à qn de qch** to be (most) grateful to sb for sth
grec, grecque [gʀɛk] *adj* Greek; (*classique: vase etc*) Grecian ▷ *nm* (*Ling*) Greek ▷ *nm/f*: **G~, G~que** Greek
Grèce [gʀɛs] *nf*: **la ~** Greece
greffe [gʀɛf] *nf* (*Bot, Méd: de tissu*) graft; (*Méd: d'organe*) transplant ▷ *nm* (*Jur*) office
greffer [gʀefe] *vt* (*Bot, Méd: tissu*) to graft; (*Méd: organe*) to transplant
greffier [gʀefje] *nm* clerk of the court
grêle [gʀɛl] *adj* (*very*) thin ▷ *nf* hail
grêler [gʀele] *vb impers*: **il grêle** it's hailing ▷ *vt*: **la région a été grêlée** the region was damaged by hail
grêlon [gʀɛlɔ̃] *nm* hailstone
grelot [gʀəlo] *nm* little bell
grelotter [gʀəlɔte] *vi* (*trembler*) to shiver
grenade [gʀənad] *nf* (*explosive*) grenade; (*Bot*) pomegranate; **~ lacrymogène** teargas grenade
grenadine [gʀənadin] *nf* grenadine
grenat [gʀəna] *adj inv* dark red
grenier [gʀənje] *nm* (*de maison*) attic; (*de ferme*) loft
grenouille [gʀənuj] *nf* frog
grès [gʀɛ] *nm* (*roche*) sandstone; (*poterie*) stoneware
grésiller [gʀezije] *vi* to sizzle; (*Radio*) to crackle
grève [gʀɛv] *nf* (*d'ouvriers*) strike; (*plage*) shore; **se mettre en/faire ~** to go on/be on strike; **~ bouchon** partial strike (*in key areas of a company*); **~ de la faim** hunger strike; **~ perlée** go-slow (*Brit*), slowdown (*US*); **~ sauvage** wildcat strike; **~ de solidarité** sympathy strike; **~ surprise** lightning strike; **~ sur le tas** sit down strike; **~ tournante** strike by rota; **~ du zèle** work-to-rule (*Brit*), slowdown (*US*)
gréviste [gʀevist] *nm/f* striker
gribouiller [gʀibuje] *vt* to scribble, scrawl ▷ *vi* to doodle
grièvement [gʀijɛvmɑ̃] *adv* seriously
griffe [gʀif] *nf* claw; (*fig*) signature; (: *d'un couturier, parfumeur*) label, signature
griffer [gʀife] *vt* to scratch

griffonner [gʀifɔne] vt to scribble

grignoter [gʀiɲɔte] vt (personne) to nibble at; (souris) to gnaw at ▷ vi to nibble

gril [gʀil] nm steak ou grill pan

grillade [gʀijad] nf grill

grillage [gʀijaʒ] nm (treillis) wire netting; (clôture) wire fencing

grille [gʀij] nf (portail) (metal) gate; (clôture) railings pl; (d'égout) (metal) grate; (fig) grid

grille-pain [gʀijpɛ̃] nm inv toaster

griller [gʀije] vt (aussi: **faire ~**: pain) to toast; (: viande) to grill (Brit), broil (US); (: café) to roast; (châtaignes) to roast; (fig: ampoule etc) to burn out, blow; **~ un feu rouge** to jump the lights (Brit), run a stoplight (US) ▷ vi (brûler) to be roasting

grillon [gʀijɔ̃] nm (Zool) cricket

grimace [gʀimas] nf grimace; (pour faire rire): **faire des ~s** to pull ou make faces

grimper [gʀɛ̃pe] vi, vt to climb ▷ nm: **le ~** (Sport) rope-climbing; **~ à/sur** to climb (up)/ climb onto

grincer [gʀɛ̃se] vi (porte, roue) to grate; (plancher) to creak; **~ des dents** to grind one's teeth

grincheux, -euse [gʀɛ̃ʃø, -øz] adj grumpy

grippe [gʀip] nf flu, influenza; **avoir la ~** to have (the) flu; **prendre qn/qch en ~** (fig) to take a sudden dislike to sb/sth; **~ aviaire** bird flu; **~ porcine** swine flu

grippé, e [gʀipe] adj: **être ~** to have (the) flu; (moteur) to have seized up (Brit) ou jammed

gris, e [gʀi, gʀiz] adj grey (Brit), gray (US); (ivre) tipsy ▷ nm (couleur) grey (Brit), gray (US); **il fait ~** it's a dull ou grey day; **faire ~e mine** to look miserable ou morose; **faire ~e mine à qn** to give sb a cool reception

grisaille [gʀizɑj] nf greyness (Brit), grayness (US), dullness

griser [gʀize] vt to intoxicate; **se ~ de** (fig) to become intoxicated with

grisonner [gʀizɔne] vi to be going grey (Brit) ou gray (US)

grisou [gʀizu] nm firedamp

grive [gʀiv] nf (Zool) thrush

grivois, e [gʀivwa, -waz] adj saucy

Groenland [gʀɔɛnlɑ̃d] nm: **le ~** Greenland

grogner [gʀɔɲe] vi to growl; (fig) to grumble

grognon, ne [gʀɔɲɔ̃, -ɔn] adj grumpy, grouchy

groin [gʀwɛ̃] nm snout

grommeler [gʀɔmle] vi to mutter to o.s.

gronder [gʀɔ̃de] vi (canon, moteur, tonnerre) to rumble; (animal) to growl; (fig: révolte) to be brewing ▷ vt to scold; **se faire ~** to get a telling-off

groom [gʀum] nm page, bellhop (US)

gros, se [gʀo, gʀos] adj big, large; (obèse) fat; (problème, quantité) great; (travaux, dégâts) extensive; (large: trait, fil) thick; (rhume, averse) heavy ▷ adv: **risquer/gagner ~** to risk/win a lot ▷ nm/f fat man/woman ▷ nm (Comm): **le ~** the wholesale business; **écrire ~** to write in big letters; **prix de ~** wholesale price; **par ~ temps/~se mer** in rough weather/heavy seas; **le ~ de** the main body of; (du travail etc) the bulk of; **en avoir ~ sur le cœur** to be upset; **en ~** roughly; (Comm) wholesale; **~ intestin** large intestine; **~ lot** jackpot; **~ mot** swearword, vulgarity; **~ œuvre** shell (of building); **~ plan** (Photo) close-up; **~ porteur** wide-bodied aircraft, jumbo (jet); **~ sel** cooking salt; **~ titre** headline; **~se caisse** big drum

groseille [gʀozɛj] nf: **~ (rouge)/(blanche)** red/white currant; **~ à maquereau** gooseberry

grosse [gʀos] adj f voir **gros** ▷ nf (Comm) gross

grossesse [gʀosɛs] nf pregnancy; **~ nerveuse** phantom pregnancy

grosseur [gʀosœʀ] nf size; fatness; (tumeur) lump

grossier, -ière [gʀosje, -jɛʀ] adj coarse; (insolent) rude; (dessin) rough; (travail) roughly done; (imitation, instrument) crude; (évident: erreur) gross

grossièrement [gʀosjɛʀmɑ̃] adv (vulgairement) coarsely; (sommairement) roughly; crudely; (en gros) roughly

grossièreté [gʀosjɛʀte] nf coarseness; rudeness; (mot): **dire des ~s** to use coarse language

grossir [gʀosiʀ] vi (personne) to put on weight; (fig) to grow, get bigger; (rivière) to swell ▷ vt to increase; (exagérer) to exaggerate; (au microscope) to magnify, enlarge; (vêtement): **~ qn** to make sb look fatter

grossiste [gʀosist] nm/f wholesaler

grosso modo [gʀosomɔdo] adv roughly

grotesque [gʀɔtɛsk] adj (extravagant) grotesque; (ridicule) ludicrous

grotte [gʀɔt] nf cave

grouiller [gʀuje] vi (foule) to mill about; (fourmis) to swarm about; **~ de** to be swarming with

groupe [gʀup] nm group; **cabinet de ~** group practice; **médecine de ~** group practice; **~ électrogène** generator; **~ de parole** support group; **~ de pression** pressure group; **~ sanguin** blood group; **~ scolaire** school complex

groupement [gʀupmɑ̃] nm grouping; (groupe) group; **~ d'intérêt économique (GIE)** = trade association

grouper [gʀupe] vt to group; (ressources, moyens) to pool; **se grouper** vi to get together

grue [gʀy] nf crane; **faire le pied de ~** (fam) to hang around (waiting), kick one's heels (Brit)

grumeaux [gʀymo] nmpl (Culin) lumps

GSM [ʒeɛsɛm] nm, adj GSM

guenilles [gənij] nfpl rags

guenon [gənɔ̃] nf female monkey

guépard [gepaʀ] nm cheetah

guêpe [gɛp] nf wasp

guêpier [gepje] *nm* (*fig*) trap

guère [gɛʀ] *adv* (*avec adjectif, adverbe*): **ne ... ~**
hardly; (*avec verbe: pas beaucoup*): **ne ... ~**
(*tournure négative*) much; (*pas souvent*) hardly
ever; (*very*) long; **il n'y a ~ que/de** there's
hardly anybody (*ou* anything) but/hardly
any; **ce n'est ~ difficile** it's hardly difficult;
nous n'avons ~ de temps we have hardly
any time

guéridon [geʀidɔ̃] *nm* pedestal table

guérilla [geʀija] *nf* guerrilla warfare

guérillero [geʀijeʀo] *nm* guerrilla

guérir [geʀiʀ] *vt* (*personne, maladie*) to cure;
(*membre, plaie*) to heal ▷ *vi* (*personne, malade*) to
recover, be cured; (*maladie*) to be cured; (*plaie,
chagrin, blessure*) to heal; **~ de** to be cured of,
recover from; **~ qn de** to cure sb of

guérison [geʀizɔ̃] *nf* (*de maladie*) curing; (*de
membre, plaie*) healing; (*de malade*) recovery

guérisseur, -euse [geʀisœʀ, -øz] *nm/f*
healer

guerre [gɛʀ] *nf* war; (*méthode*): **~ atomique/
de tranchées** atomic/trench warfare *no pl*;
en ~ at war; faire la ~ à to wage war against;
de ~ lasse (*fig*) tired of fighting *ou* resisting;
de bonne ~ fair and square; **~ civile/
mondiale** civil/world war; **~ froide/sainte**
cold/holy war; **~ d'usure** war of attrition

guerrier, -ière [gɛʀje, -jɛʀ] *adj* warlike
▷ *nm/f* warrior

guet [gɛ] *nm*: **faire le ~** to be on the watch *ou*
look-out

guet-apens (*pl* **guets-apens**) [gɛtapɑ̃] *nm*
ambush

guetter [gete] *vt* (*épier*) to watch (intently);
(*attendre*) to watch (out) for; (: *pour surprendre*)
to be lying in wait for

gueule [gœl] *nf* (*d'animal*) mouth; (*fam: visage*)
mug; (: *bouche*) gob (!), mouth; **ta ~!** (*fam*) shut
up!; **avoir la ~ de bois** (*fam*) to have a
hangover, be hung over

gueuler [gœle] *vi* (*fam*) to bawl

gueuleton [gœltɔ̃] *nm* (*fam*) blowout (Brit),
big meal

gui [gi] *nm* mistletoe

guichet [giʃɛ] *nm* (*de bureau, banque*) counter,
window; (*d'une porte*) wicket, hatch; **les ~s** (*à
la gare, au théâtre*) the ticket office; **jouer à ~s
fermés** to play to a full house

guide [gid] *nm* (*personne*) guide; (*livre*)
guide(book) ▷ *nf* (*fille scout*) (girl) guide (Brit),
girl scout (US); **guides** *nfpl* (*d'un cheval*) reins

guider [gide] *vt* to guide

guidon [gidɔ̃] *nm* handlebars *pl*

guignol [giɲɔl] *nm* ≈ Punch and Judy show;
(*fig*) clown

guillemets [gijmɛ] *nmpl*: **entre ~** in inverted
commas *ou* quotation marks; **~ de répétition**
ditto marks

guillotiner [gijɔtine] *vt* to guillotine

guindé, e [gɛ̃de] *adj* (*personne, air*) stiff,
starchy; (*style*) stilted

Guinée [gine] *nf*: **la (République de) ~** (the
Republic of) Guinea

guirlande [giʀlɑ̃d] *nf* (*fleurs*) garland; (*de
papier*) paper chain; **~ lumineuse** lights *pl*,
fairy lights *pl* (Brit); **~ de Noël** tinsel *no pl*

guise [giz] *nf*: **à votre ~** as you wish *ou* please;
en ~ de by way of

guitare [gitaʀ] *nf* guitar

Guyane [gɥijan] *nf*: **la ~** Guyana; **la ~
(française)** (French) Guiana

gym [ʒim] *nf* (*exercices*) gym

gymnase [ʒimnɑz] *nm* gym(nasium)

gymnaste [ʒimnast] *nm/f* gymnast

gymnastique [ʒimnastik] *nf* gymnastics *sg*;
(*au réveil etc*) keep-fit exercises *pl*; **~ corrective**
remedial gymnastics

gynécologie [ʒinekɔlɔʒi] *nf* gynaecology
(Brit), gynecology (US)

gynécologique [ʒinekɔlɔʒik] *adj*
gynaecological (Brit), gynecological (US)

gynécologue [ʒinekɔlɔg] *nm/f* gynaecologist
(Brit), gynecologist (US)

h

get into the habit of doing sth; **perdre une ~** to get out of a habit; **d'~** usually; **comme d'~** as usual; **par ~** out of habit

habitué, e [abitɥe] *adj*: **être ~ à** to be used *ou* accustomed to ▷ *nm/f* (*de maison*) regular visitor; (*client*) regular (customer)

habituel, le [abitɥɛl] *adj* usual

habituer [abitɥe] *vt*: **~ qn à** to get sb used to; **s'habituer à** to get used to

hache ['aʃ] *nf* axe

hacher ['aʃe] *vt* (*viande*) to mince (*Brit*), grind (*US*); (*persil*) to chop; **~ menu** to mince *ou* grind finely; to chop finely

hachis ['aʃi] *nm* mince *no pl* (*Brit*), hamburger meat (*US*); **~ de viande** minced (*Brit*) *ou* ground (*US*) meat; **hachis Parmentier** ≈ shepherd's pie

hachisch ['aʃiʃ] *nm* hashish

hachoir ['aʃwaʀ] *nm* chopper; (*meat*) mincer (*Brit*) *ou* grinder (*US*); (*planche*) chopping board

hagard, e ['agaʀ, -aʀd] *adj* wild, distraught

haie ['ɛ] *nf* hedge; (*Sport*) hurdle; (*fig: rang*) line, row; **200 m ~s** 200 m hurdles; **~ d'honneur** guard of honour

haillons ['ajɔ̃] *nmpl* rags

haine ['ɛn] *nf* hatred

haïr ['aiʀ] *vt* to detest, hate; **se haïr** to hate each other

hâlé, e ['ɑle] *adj* (sun)tanned, sunburnt

haleine [alɛn] *nf* breath; **perdre ~** to get out of breath; **à perdre ~** until one is gasping for breath; **avoir mauvaise ~** to have bad breath; **reprendre ~** to get one's breath back; **hors d'~** out of breath; **tenir en ~** (*attention*) to hold spellbound; (*en attente*) to keep in suspense; **de longue ~** *adj* long-term

haleter ['alte] *vi* to pant

hall ['ol] *nm* hall

halle ['al] *nf* (covered) market; **halles** *nfpl* (*d'une grande ville*) central food market *sg*

hallucinant, e [alysinɑ̃, -ɑ̃t] *adj* staggering

hallucination [alysinasjɔ̃] *nf* hallucination

halte ['alt] *nf* stop, break; (*escale*) stopping place; (*Rail*) halt ▷ *excl* stop!; **faire halte** to stop

haltère [altɛʀ] *nm* (*à boules, disques*) dumbbell, barbell; (**poids et**) **~s** (*activité*) weightlifting *sg*

haltérophilie [alteʀofili] *nf* weightlifting

hamac ['amak] *nm* hammock

hamburger ['ɑ̃buʀɡœʀ] *nm* hamburger

hameau, x ['amo] *nm* hamlet

hameçon [amsɔ̃] *nm* (fish) hook

hamster ['amstɛʀ] *nm* hamster

hanche ['ɑ̃ʃ] *nf* hip

hand-ball ['ɑ̃dbal] *nm* handball

handicapé, e ['ɑ̃dikape] *adj* disabled, handicapped ▷ *nm/f* handicapped person; **handicapé mental/physique** mentally/ physically handicapped person; **~ moteur** person with a movement disorder

hangar ['ɑ̃ɡaʀ] *nm* shed; (*Aviat*) hangar

hanneton ['antɔ̃] *nm* cockchafer

hanter ['ɑ̃te] *vt* to haunt

habile [abil] *adj* skilful; (*malin*) clever

habileté [abilte] *nf* skill, skilfulness; cleverness

habillé, e [abije] *adj* dressed; (*chic*) dressy; (*Tech*): **~ de** covered with; encased in

habillement [abijmɑ̃] *nm* clothes *pl*; (*profession*) clothing industry

habiller [abije] *vt* to dress; (*fournir en vêtements*) to clothe; (*couvrir*) to cover; **s'habiller** *vi* to dress (o.s.); (*se déguiser, mettre des vêtements chic*) to dress up; **s'~ de/en** to dress in/dress up as; **s'~ chez/à** to buy one's clothes from/at

habit [abi] *nm* outfit; **habits** *nmpl* (*vêtements*) clothes; **~ (de soirée)** evening dress; (*pour homme*) tails *pl*; **prendre l'~** (*Rel: entrer en religion*) to enter (holy) orders

habitant, e [abitɑ̃, -ɑ̃t] *nm/f* inhabitant; (*d'une maison*) occupant, occupier; **loger chez l'~** to stay with the locals

habitation [abitasjɔ̃] *nf* living; (*demeure*) residence, home; (*maison*) house; **~s à loyer modéré (HLM)** low-rent, state-owned housing, ≈ council flats (*Brit*), ≈ public housing units (*US*)

habiter [abite] *vt* to live in; (*sentiment*) to dwell in ▷ *vi*: **~ à/dans** to live in *ou* at/in; **~ chez** *ou* **avec qn** to live with sb; **~ 16 rue Montmartre** to live at number 16 rue Montmartre; **~ rue Montmartre** to live in rue Montmartre

habitude [abityd] *nf* habit; **avoir l'~ de faire** to be in the habit of doing; (*expérience*) to be used to doing; **avoir l'~ des enfants** to be used to children; **prendre l'~ de faire qch** to

'hantise ['ɑ̃tiz] *nf* obsessive fear

'happer ['ape] *vt* to snatch; (*train etc*) to hit

'haras ['aʀɑ] *nm* stud farm

'harassant, e ['aʀasɑ̃, -ɑ̃t] *adj* exhausting

'harcèlement ['aʀsɛlmɑ̃] *nm* harassment;
~ **sexuel** sexual harassment

'harceler ['aʀsəle] *vt* (*Mil, Chasse*) to harass,
harry; (*importuner*) to plague; **harceler qn de
questions** to plague sb with questions

'hardi, e ['aʀdi] *adj* bold, daring

'hareng ['aʀɑ̃] *nm* herring; **hareng saur**
kipper, smoked herring

'hargne ['aʀɲ] *nf* aggressivity, aggressiveness

'hargneux, -euse ['aʀɲø, -øz] *adj* (*propos,
personne*) belligerent, aggressive; (*chien*) fierce

'haricot ['aʀiko] *nm* bean; ~ **blanc/rouge**
haricot/kidney bean; ~ **vert** French (*Brit*) *ou*
green bean

harmonica [aʀmɔnika] *nm* mouth organ

harmonie {aʀmɔni} *nf* harmony

harmonieux, -euse [aʀmɔnjø, -øz] *adj*
harmonious; (*couleurs, couple*) well-matched

'harnacher ['aʀnaʃe] *vt* to harness

'harnais ['aʀnɛ] *nm* harness

'harpe ['aʀp] *nf* harp

'harponner ['aʀpɔne] *vt* to harpoon; (*fam*) to
collar

'hasard ['azaʀ] *nm*: **le ~** chance, fate; **un ~** a
coincidence; (*aubaine, chance*) a stroke of luck;
au ~ (*sans but*) aimlessly; (*à l'aveuglette*) at
random, haphazardly; **par ~** by chance;
comme par ~ as if by chance; **à tout ~** (*en
espérant trouver ce qu'on cherche*) on the off
chance; (*en cas de besoin*) just in case

'hasarder ['azaʀde] *vt* (*mot*) to venture; (*fortune*)
to risk; **se ~ à faire** to risk doing, venture to do

'hâte ['ɑt] *nf* haste; **à la ~** hurriedly, hastily;
en ~ posthaste, with all possible speed; **avoir
~ de** to be eager *ou* anxious to

'hâter ['ɑte] *vt* to hasten; **se 'hâter** to hurry;
se ~ de to hurry *ou* hasten to

'hâtif, -ive ['ɑtif, -iv] *adj* (*travail*) hurried;
(*décision*) hasty; (*légume*) early

'hausse ['os] *nf* rise, increase; (*de fusil*)
backsight adjuster; **à la ~** upwards; **en ~**
rising; **être en ~** to be going up

'hausser ['ose] *vt* to raise; ~ **les épaules** to
shrug (one's shoulders); **se ~ sur la pointe des
pieds** to stand (up) on tiptoe *ou* tippy-toe (*US*)

'haut, e ['o, 'ot] *adj* high; (*grand*) tall; (*son, voix*)
high(-pitched) ▷ *adv* high ▷ *nm* top (part);
de 3 m de ~, ~ de 3 m 3 m high, 3 m in height;
en ~e montagne high up in the mountains;
en ~ lieu in high places; **à ~e voix, (tout) ~**
aloud, out loud; **des ~s et des bas** ups and
downs; **du ~ de** from the top of; **tomber de ~**
to fall from a height; (*fig*) to have one's hopes
dashed; **dire qch bien ~** to say sth plainly;
prendre qch de (très) ~ to react haughtily to
sth; **traiter qn de ~** to treat sb with disdain;
de ~ en bas from top to bottom; downwards;
~ **en couleur** (*chose*) highly coloured;

(*personne*): **un personnage ~ en couleur** a
colourful character; **plus ~** higher up,
further up; (*dans un texte*) above; (*parler*)
louder; **en ~** up above; (*être/aller*) at (*ou* to)
the top; (*dans une maison*) upstairs; **en ~ de** at the
top of; ~ **les mains!** hands up!, stick 'em up!;
la ~e couture/coiffure haute couture/
coiffure; ~ **débit** (*Inform*) broadband; **~e
fidélité** hi-fi, high fidelity; **la ~e finance**
high finance; **~e trahison** high treason

'hautain, e ['otɛ̃, -ɛn] *adj* (*personne, regard*)
haughty

'hautbois ['obwɑ] *nm* oboe

'haut-de-forme (*pl* **'hauts-de-forme**)
['odfɔʀm] *nm* top hat

'hauteur ['otœʀ] *nf* height; (*Géo*) height, hill;
(*fig*) loftiness; haughtiness; **à ~ de** up to (the
level of); **à ~ des yeux** at eye level; **à la ~ de** (*sur la
même ligne*) level with; by; (*fig: tâche, situation*)
equal to; **à la ~** (*fig*) up to it, equal to the task

'haut-fourneau (*pl* **'hauts-fourneaux**)
['ofuʀno] *nm* blast *ou* smelting furnace

'haut-le-cœur ['olkœʀ] *nm inv* retch, heave

'haut-parleur (*pl* **'haut-parleurs**) ['opaʀlœʀ]
nm (loud)speaker

'havre ['avʀ] *nm* haven

Hawaï [awai] *n* Hawaii; **les îles ~** the
Hawaiian Islands

'Haye ['ɛ] *n*: **la ~** the Hague

'hayon ['ɛjɔ̃] *nm* tailgate

hebdo [ɛbdo] *nm* (*fam*) weekly

hebdomadaire [ɛbdɔmadɛʀ] *adj, nm* weekly

hébergement [ebɛʀʒəmɑ̃] *nm*
accommodation, lodging; taking in

héberger [ebɛʀʒe] *vt* (*touristes*) to
accommodate, lodge; (*amis*) to put up;
(*réfugiés*) to take in

hébergeur [ebɛʀʒœʀ] *nm* (*Internet*) host

hébété, e [ebete] *adj* dazed

hébreu, x [ebʀø] *adj m, nm* Hebrew

Hébrides [ebʀid] *nf*: **les ~** the Hebrides

hécatombe [ekatɔ̃b] *nf* slaughter

hectare [ɛktaʀ] *nm* hectare, 10,000 square
metres

'hein ['ɛ̃] *excl* eh?; (*sollicitant l'approbation*): **tu
m'approuves, ~?** so I did the right thing
then?; **Paul est venu, ~?** Paul came, did he?;
que fais-tu, ~? hey! what are you doing?

'hélas ['elas] *excl* alas! ▷ *adv* unfortunately

'héler ['ele] *vt* to hail

hélice [elis] *nf* propeller

hélicoptère [elikɔptɛʀ] *nm* helicopter

helvétique [elvetik] *adj* Swiss

hématome [ematom] *nm* haematoma

hémicycle [emisikl] *nm* semicircle; (*Pol*): **l'~**
the benches (in French parliament)

hémisphère [emisfɛʀ] *nm*: ~ **nord/sud**
northern/southern hemisphere

hémorragie [emɔʀaʒi] *nf* bleeding *no pl*,
haemorrhage (*Brit*), hemorrhage (*US*);
~ **cérébrale** cerebral haemorrhage;
~ **interne** internal bleeding *ou* haemorrhage

hémorroïdes [emɔrɔid] *nfpl* piles, haemorrhoids (Brit), hemorrhoids (US)

'hennir ['enir] *vi* to neigh, whinny

'hennissement ['enismɑ̃] *nm* neighing, whinnying

hépatite [epatit] *nf* hepatitis, liver infection

herbe [ɛrb] *nf* grass; (Culin, Méd) herb; **~s de Provence** mixed herbs; **en ~** unripe; (fig) budding; **touffe/brin d'~** clump/blade of grass

herbicide [ɛrbisid] *nm* weed-killer

herboriste [ɛrbɔrist] *nm/f* herbalist

'hère ['ɛr] *nm:* **pauvre ~** poor wretch

héréditaire [erediter] *adj* hereditary

'hérisser ['erise] *vt:* **~ qn** (fig) to ruffle sb; **se 'hérisser** *vi* to bristle, bristle up

'hérisson ['erisɔ̃] *nm* hedgehog

héritage [eritaʒ] *nm* inheritance; (fig: coutumes, système) heritage; (: legs) legacy; **faire un (petit) ~** to come into (a little) money

hériter [erite] *vi:* **~ de qch (de qn)** to inherit sth (from sb); **~ de qn** to inherit sb's property

héritier, -ière [eritje, -jɛr] *nm/f* heir/heiress

hermétique [ɛrmetik] *adj* (à l'air) airtight; (à l'eau) watertight; (fig: écrivain, style) abstruse; (: visage) impenetrable

hermine [ɛrmin] *nf* ermine

'hernie ['ɛrni] *nf* hernia

héroïne [erɔin] *nf* heroine; (drogue) heroin

héroïque [erɔik] *adj* heroic

'héron ['erɔ̃] *nm* heron

'héros ['ero] *nm* hero

hésitant, e [ezitɑ̃, -ɑ̃t] *adj* hesitant

hésitation [ezitasjɔ̃] *nf* hesitation

hésiter [ezite] *vi:* **~ (à faire)** to hesitate (to do); **~ sur qch** to hesitate over sth

hétéroclite [eterɔklit] *adj* heterogeneous; (objets) sundry

hétérogène [eterɔʒɛn] *adj* heterogeneous

hétérosexuel, le [eterɔsɛkɥɛl] *adj* heterosexual

'hêtre ['ɛtr] *nm* beech

heure [œr] *nf* hour; (Scol) period; (moment, moment fixé) time; **c'est l'~** it's time; **pourriez-vous me donner l'~, s'il vous plaît?** could you tell me the time, please?; **quelle ~ est-il?** what time is it?; **2 ~s (du matin)** 2 o'clock (in the morning); **à la bonne ~!** (parfois ironique) splendid!; **être à l'~** to be on time; (montre) to be right; **le bus passe à l'~** the bus runs on the hour; **mettre à l'~** to set right; **100 km à l'~** ≈ 60 miles an ou per hour; **à toute ~** at any time; **24 ~s sur 24** round the clock, 24 hours a day; **à l'~ qu'il est** at this time (of day); (fig) now; **à l'~ actuelle** at the present time; **sur l'~** at once; **pour l'~** for the time being; **d'~ en ~** from one hour to the next; (régulièrement) hourly; **d'une ~ à l'autre** from hour to hour; **à une ~ avancée (de la nuit)** at a late hour (of the night); **de bonne ~** early; **deux ~s de marche/travail** two hours' walking/work; **une ~ d'arrêt** an hour's break ou stop; **~ d'été** summer time

(Brit), daylight saving time (US); **~ de pointe** rush hour; (téléphone) peak period; **~s de bureau** office hours; **~s supplémentaires** overtime *sg*

heureusement [œrøzmɑ̃] *adv* (par bonheur) fortunately, luckily; **~ que ...** it's a good job that ..., fortunately ...

heureux, -euse [œrø, -øz] *adj* happy; (chanceux) lucky, fortunate; (judicieux) felicitous, fortunate; **être ~ de qch** to be pleased ou happy about sth; **être ~ de faire/que** to be pleased ou happy to do/that; **s'estimer ~ de qch/que** to consider o.s. fortunate with sth/that; **encore ~ que ...** just as well that ...

'heurt ['œr] *nm* (choc) collision; **'heurts** *nmpl* (fig) clashes

'heurter ['œrte] *vt* (mur) to strike, hit; (personne) to collide with; (fig) to go against, upset; **se 'heurter** (couleurs, tons) to clash; **se ~ à** to collide with; (fig) to come up against; **~ qn de front** to clash head-on with sb

hexagone [ɛgzagɔn] *nm* hexagon; **l'H~** (la France) France (because of its roughly hexagonal shape)

hiberner [ibɛrne] *vi* to hibernate

'hibou, x ['ibu] *nm* owl

'hideux, -euse ['idø, -øz] *adj* hideous

hier [jɛr] *adv* yesterday; **~ matin/soir/midi** yesterday morning/evening/lunchtime; **toute la journée d'~** all day yesterday; **toute la matinée d'~** all yesterday morning

'hiérarchie ['jerarʃi] *nf* hierarchy

'hi-fi ['ifi] *nf inv* hi-fi

hilare [ilar] *adj* mirthful

hindou, e [ɛ̃du] *adj* Hindu ▷ *nm/f:* **H~, e** Hindu; (Indien) Indian

hippique [ipik] *adj* equestrian, horse *cpd;* **un club ~** a riding centre; **un concours ~** a horse show

hippisme [ipism] *nm* (horse-)riding

hippodrome [ipodrom] *nm* racecourse

hippopotame [ipopotam] *nm* hippopotamus

hirondelle [irɔ̃dɛl] *nf* swallow

hirsute [irsyt] *adj* (personne) hairy; (barbe) shaggy; (tête) tousled

'hisser ['ise] *vt* to hoist, haul up; **se 'hisser sur** to haul o.s. up onto

histoire [istwar] *nf* (science, événements) history; (anecdote, récit, mensonge) story; (affaire) business *no pl;* (chichis: gén pl) fuss *no pl;* **histoires** *nfpl* (ennuis) trouble *sg;* **l'~ de France** French history, the history of France; **l'~ sainte** biblical history; **~ géo** humanities *pl;* **une ~ de** (fig) a question of

historique [istɔrik] *adj* historical; (important) historic ▷ *nm* (exposé, récit): **faire l'~ de** to give the background to

'hit-parade ['itparad] *nm:* **le ~** the charts

hiver [ivɛr] *nm* winter; **en ~** in winter

hivernal, e, -aux [ivɛrnal, -o] *adj* (de l'hiver) winter *cpd;* (comme en hiver) wintry

hiverner [ivɛrne] *vi* to winter

HLM *sigle m ou f* (= *habitations à loyer modéré*) low-rent, state-owned housing; **un(e)** ~ ≈ a council flat (*ou* house) (Brit); ≈ a public housing unit (US)

'**hobby** ['ɔbi] *nm* hobby

'**hocher** ['ɔʃe] *vt*: ~ **la tête** to nod; (*signe négatif ou dubitatif*) to shake one's head

'**hochet** ['ɔʃe] *nm* rattle

'**hockey** ['ɔkɛ] *nm*: ~ (**sur glace/gazon**) (ice/field) hockey

'**hold-up** ['ɔldœp] *nm inv* hold-up

'**hollandais, e** ['ɔlɑ̃dɛ, -ɛz] *adj* Dutch ▷ *nm* (*Ling*) Dutch ▷ *nm/f*: '**Hollandais, e** Dutchman/woman; **les 'Hollandais** the Dutch

'**Hollande** ['ɔlɑ̃d] *nf*: **la** ~ Holland ▷ *nm*: '**hollande** (*fromage*) Dutch cheese

'**homard** ['ɔmar] *nm* lobster

homéopathique [ɔmeɔpatik] *adj* homoeopathic

homicide [ɔmisid] *nm* murder ▷ *nm/f* murderer/eress; ~ **involontaire** manslaughter

hommage [ɔmaʒ] *nm* tribute; **hommages** *nmpl*: **présenter ses ~s** to pay one's respects; **rendre** ~ **à** to pay tribute *ou* homage to; **en ~ de** as a token of; **faire** ~ **de qch à qn** to present sb with sth

homme [ɔm] *nm* man; (*espèce humaine*): **l'**~ man, mankind; ~ **d'affaires** businessman; ~ **des cavernes** caveman; ~ **d'Église** churchman, clergyman; ~ **d'État** statesman; ~ **de loi** lawyer; ~ **de main** hired man; ~ **de paille** stooge; ~ **politique** politician; **l'**~ **de la rue** the man in the street; ~ **à tout faire** odd-job man

homme-grenouille (*pl* **hommes-grenouilles**) [ɔmgrənuj] *nm* frogman

homogène [ɔmɔʒɛn] *adj* homogeneous

homologue [ɔmɔlɔg] *nm/f* counterpart, opposite number

homologué, e [ɔmɔlɔge] *adj* (*Sport*) officially recognized, ratified; (*tarif*) authorized

homonyme [ɔmɔnim] *nm* (*Ling*) homonym; (*d'une personne*) namesake

homosexuel, le [ɔmɔsɛksɥel] *adj* homosexual

'**Hong-Kong** ['ɔ̃gkɔ̃g] *n* Hong Kong

'**Hongrie** ['ɔ̃gri] *nf*: **la** ~ Hungary

'**hongrois, e** ['ɔ̃grwa, -waz] *adj* Hungarian ▷ *nm* (*Ling*) Hungarian ▷ *nm/f*: '**Hongrois, e** Hungarian

honnête [ɔnɛt] *adj* (*intègre*) honest; (*juste, satisfaisant*) fair

honnêtement [ɔnɛtmɑ̃] *adv* honestly

honnêteté [ɔnɛtte] *nf* honesty

honneur [ɔnœr] *nm* honour; (*mérite*): **l'**~ **lui revient** the credit is his; **à qui ai-je l'**~? to whom have I the pleasure of speaking?; "**j'ai l'**~ **de ...**" "I have the honour of ..."; **en l'**~ **de** (*personne*) in honour of; (*événement*) on the occasion of; **faire** ~ **à** (*engagements*) to honour; (*famille, professeur*) to be a credit to; (*fig: repas etc*) to do justice to; **être à l'**~ to be in the place of honour; **être en** ~ to be in favour; **membre d'**~ honorary member; **table d'**~ top table

honorable [ɔnɔrabl] *adj* worthy, honourable; (*suffisant*) decent

honoraire [ɔnɔrɛr] *adj* honorary; **honoraires** *nmpl* fees; **professeur** ~ professor emeritus

honorer [ɔnɔre] *vt* to honour; (*estimer*) to hold in high regard; (*faire honneur à*) to do credit to; ~ **qn de** to honour sb with; **s'honorer de** to pride o.s. upon

honorifique [ɔnɔrifik] *adj* honorary

'**honte** ['ɔ̃t] *nf* shame; **avoir** ~ **de** to be ashamed of; **faire** ~ **à qn** to make sb (feel) ashamed

'**honteux, -euse** ['ɔ̃tø, -øz] *adj* ashamed; (*conduite, acte*) shameful, disgraceful

hôpital, -aux [ɔpital, -o] *nm* hospital; **où est l'**~ **le plus proche?** where is the nearest hospital?

'**hoquet** ['ɔkɛ] *nm* hiccough; **avoir le** ~ to have (the) hiccoughs

'**hoqueter** ['ɔkte] *vi* to hiccough

horaire [ɔrɛr] *adj* hourly ▷ *nm* timetable, schedule; **horaires** *nmpl* (*heures de travail*) hours; ~ **flexible** *ou* **mobile** *ou* **à la carte** *ou* **souple** flex(i)time

horizon [ɔrizɔ̃] *nm* horizon; (*paysage*) landscape, view; **sur l'**~ on the skyline *ou* horizon

horizontal, e, -aux [ɔrizɔtal, -o] *adj* horizontal ▷ *nf*: **à l'**~**e** on the horizontal

horloge [ɔrlɔʒ] *nf* clock; **l'**~ **parlante** the speaking clock; ~ **normande** grandfather clock; ~ **physiologique** biological clock

horloger, -ère [ɔrlɔʒe, -ɛr] *nm/f* watchmaker; clockmaker

'**hormis** ['ɔrmi] *prép* save

horoscope [ɔrɔskɔp] *nm* horoscope

horreur [ɔrœr] *nf* horror; **avoir** ~ **de** to loathe, detest; **quelle** ~! how awful!; **avoir** ~ **de** to loathe ou detest

horrible [ɔribl] *adj* horrible

horrifier [ɔrifje] *vt* to horrify

horripiler [ɔripile] *vt* to exasperate

'**hors** ['ɔr] *prép* except (for); ~ **de** out of; ~ **ligne** (*Inform*) off line; ~ **pair** outstanding; ~ **de propos** inopportune; ~ **série** (*sur mesure*) made-to-order; (*exceptionnel*) exceptional; ~ **service (HS)**, ~ **d'usage** out of service; **être** ~ **de soi** to be beside o.s.

'**hors-bord** ['ɔrbɔr] *nm inv* outboard motor; (*canot*) speedboat (with outboard motor)

'**hors-d'œuvre** ['ɔrdœvr] *nm inv* hors d'œuvre

'**hors-jeu** ['ɔrʒø] *nm inv* being offside *no pl*

'**hors-la-loi** ['ɔrlalwa] *nm inv* outlaw

hors-taxe ['ɔrtaks] *adj* (*sur une facture, prix*) excluding VAT; (*boutique, marchandises*) duty-free

hortensia [ɔrtɑ̃sja] *nm* hydrangea

hospice [ɔspis] *nm* (*de vieillards*) home; (*asile*) hospice

hospitalier, -ière [ɔspitalje, -jɛr] *adj* (*accueillant*) hospitable; (*Méd: service, centre*) hospital *cpd*

hospitaliser [ɔspitalize] *vt* to take (*ou* send) to hospital, hospitalize

hospitalité [ɔspitalite] nf hospitality

hostie [ɔsti] nf host; (Rel)

hostile [ɔstil] adj hostile

hostilité [ɔstilite] nf hostility; **hostilités** nfpl hostilities

hôte [ot] nm (maître de maison) host; (client) patron; (fig) inhabitant, occupant ⊳ nm/f (invité) guest; **~ payant** paying guest

hôtel [otɛl] nm hotel; **aller à l'~** to stay in a hotel; **~ (particulier)** (private) mansion; **~ de ville** town hall

HÔTELS

There are six categories of hotel in France, from zero ('non classé') to four stars and luxury four stars ('quatre étoiles luxe'). Prices include VAT but not breakfast. In some towns, guests pay a small additional tourist tax, the 'taxe de séjour'.

hôtelier, -ière [otəlje, -jɛʀ] adj hotel cpd ⊳ nm/f hotelier, hotel-keeper

hôtellerie [otɛlʀi] nf (profession) hotel business; (auberge) inn

hôtesse [otɛs] nf hostess; **~ de l'air** flight attendant; **~ (d'accueil)** receptionist

hotte ['ɔt] nf (panier) basket (carried on the back); (de cheminée) hood; **~ aspirante** cooker hood

houblon ['ublɔ̃] nm (Bot) hop; (pour la bière) hops pl

houille ['uj] nf coal; **~ blanche** hydroelectric power

houle ['ul] nf swell

houleux, -euse ['ulø, -øz] adj heavy, swelling; (fig) stormy, turbulent

hourra ['uʀa] nm cheer ⊳ excl hurrah!

houspiller ['uspije] vt to scold

housse ['us] nf cover; (pour protéger provisoirement) dust cover; (pour recouvrir à neuf) loose ou stretch cover; **~ (penderie)** hanging wardrobe

houx ['u] nm holly

hovercraft [ɔvœʀkʀaft] nm hovercraft

hublot ['yblo] nm porthole

huche ['yʃ] nf: **~ à pain** bread bin

huer ['ɥe] vt to boo; (hibou, chouette) to hoot

huile [ɥil] nf oil; (Art) oil painting; (fam) bigwig; **mer d'~** (très calme) glassy sea, sea of glass; **faire tache d'~** (fig) to spread; **~ d'arachide** groundnut oil; **~ essentielle** essential oil; **~ de foie de morue** cod-liver oil; **~ de ricin** castor oil; **~ solaire** suntan oil; **~ de table** salad oil

huiler [ɥile] vt to oil

huileux, -euse [ɥilø, -øz] adj oily

huis [ɥi] nm: **à ~ clos** in camera

huissier [ɥisje] nm usher; (Jur) ≈ bailiff

huit ['ɥi(t)] num eight; **samedi en ~** a week on Saturday; **dans ~ jours** in a week('s time)

huitaine ['ɥiten] nf: **une ~ de** about eight, eight or so; **une ~ de jours** a week or so

huitième ['ɥitjɛm] num eighth

huître [ɥitʀ] nf oyster

humain, e [ymɛ̃, -ɛn] adj human; (compatissant) humane ⊳ nm human (being)

humanitaire [ymanitɛʀ] adj humanitarian

humanité [ymanite] nf humanity

humble [œ̃bl] adj humble

humecter [ymɛkte] vt to dampen; **s'~ les lèvres** to moisten one's lips

humer ['yme] vt (parfum) to inhale; (pour sentir) to smell

humeur [ymœʀ] nf mood; (tempérament) temper; (irritation) bad temper; **de bonne/ mauvaise ~** in a good/bad mood; **être d'~ à faire qch** to be in the mood for doing sth

humide [ymid] adj (linge) damp; (main, yeux) moist; (climat, chaleur) humid; (saison, route) wet

humilier [ymilje] vt to humiliate; **s'~ devant qn** to humble o.s. before sb

humilité [ymilite] nf humility, humbleness

humoristique [ymɔʀistik] adj humorous; humoristic

humour [ymuʀ] nm humour; **avoir de l'~** to have a sense of humour; **~ noir** sick humour

huppé, e ['ype] adj crested; (fam) posh

hurlement ['yʀləmã] nm howling no pl, howl; yelling no pl, yell

hurler ['yʀle] vi to howl, yell; (fig: vent) to howl; (: couleurs etc) to clash; **~ à la mort** (chien) to bay at the moon

hurluberlu [yʀlybɛʀly] nm (péj) crank ⊳ adj cranky

hutte ['yt] nf hut

hybride [ibʀid] adj hybrid

hydratant, e [idʀatɑ̃, -ɑ̃t] adj (crème) moisturizing

hydraulique [idʀolik] adj hydraulic

hydravion [idʀavjɔ̃] nm seaplane, hydroplane

hydrogène [idʀɔʒɛn] nm hydrogen

hydroglisseur [idʀoglisœʀ] nm hydroplane

hyène [jɛn] nf hyena

hygiène [iʒjɛn] nf hygiene; **~ intime** personal hygiene

hygiénique [iʒjenik] adj hygienic

hymne [imn] nm hymn; **~ national** national anthem

hyperlien [ipɛʀljɛ̃] nm (Inform) hyperlink

hypermarché [ipɛʀmaʀʃe] nm hypermarket

hypermétrope [ipɛʀmetʀɔp] adj long-sighted

hypertension [ipɛʀtɑ̃sjɔ̃] nf high blood pressure, hypertension

hypertexte [ipɛʀtɛkst] nm (Inform) hypertext

hypnose [ipnoz] nf hypnosis

hypnotiser [ipnotize] vt to hypnotize

hypnotiseur [ipnotizœʀ] nm hypnotist

hypocrisie [ipɔkʀizi] nf hypocrisy

hypocrite [ipɔkʀit] adj hypocritical ⊳ nm/f hypocrite

hypothèque [ipɔtɛk] nf mortgage

hypothèse [ipɔtɛz] nf hypothesis; **dans l'~ où** assuming that

hystérique [isteʀik] adj hysterical

iceberg [isbɛʀɡ] *nm* iceberg

ici [isi] *adv* here; **jusqu'~** as far as this; (*temporel*) until now; **d'~ là** by then; **d'~ demain** by tomorrow; (*en attendant*) in the meantime; **d'~ peu** before long

icône [ikon] *nf* (*aussi Inform*) icon

idéal, e, -aux [ideal, -o] *adj* ideal ▷ *nm* ideal; (*système de valeurs*) ideals *pl*

idéaliste [idealist] *adj* idealistic ▷ *nm/f* idealist

idée [ide] *nf* idea; (*illusion*): **se faire des ~s** to imagine things, get ideas into one's head; **avoir dans l'~ que** to have an idea that; **mon ~, c'est que ...** I suggest that ..., I think that ...; **à l'~ de/que** at the idea of/that, at the thought of/that; **je n'ai pas la moindre ~** I haven't the faintest idea; **avoir ~ que** to have an idea that; **avoir des ~s larges/étroites** to be broad-/narrow-minded; **venir à l'~ de qn** to occur to sb; **en voilà des ~s!** the very idea!; **~ fixe** idée fixe, obsession; **~s noires** black *ou* dark thoughts; **~s reçues** accepted ideas *ou* wisdom

identifiant [idɑ̃tifjɑ̃] *nm* (*Inform*) login

identifier [idɑ̃tifje] *vt* to identify; **~ qch/qn à** to identify sth/sb with; **s'identifier** *vi*: **s'~ avec** *ou* **à qn/qch** (*héros etc*) to identify with sb/sth

identique [idɑ̃tik] *adj*: **~ (à)** identical (to)

identité [idɑ̃tite] *nf* identity; **~ judiciaire** (*Police*) ≈ Criminal Records Office

idiot, e [idjo, idjɔt] *adj* idiotic ▷ *nm/f* idiot

idiotie [idjɔsi] *nf* idiocy; (*propos*) idiotic remark

idole [idɔl] *nf* idol

if [if] *nm* yew

igloo [iglu] *nm* igloo

ignare [iɲaʀ] *adj* ignorant

ignoble [iɲɔbl] *adj* vile

ignorant, e [iɲɔʀɑ̃, -ɑ̃t] *adj* ignorant ▷ *nm/f*: **faire l'~** to pretend one doesn't know; **~ de** ignorant of, not aware of; **~ en** ignorant of, knowing nothing of

ignorer [iɲɔʀe] *vt* (*ne pas connaître*) not to know, be unaware *ou* ignorant of; (*être sans expérience de: plaisir, guerre etc*) not to know about, have no experience of; (*bouder: personne*) to ignore; **j'ignore comment/si** I do not know how/if; **~ que** to be unaware that, not to know that; **je n'ignore pas que ...** I'm not forgetting that ..., I'm not unaware that ...; **je l'ignore** I don't know

il [il] *pron* he; (*animal, chose, en tournure impersonnelle*) it, NB: *en anglais les navires et les pays sont en général assimilés aux femelles, et les bébés aux choses, si le sexe n'est pas spécifié;* **ils** they; **il neige** it's snowing; **Pierre est-il arrivé?** has Pierre arrived?; **il a gagné** he won; *voir aussi* **avoir**

île [il] *nf* island; **les Î~s** the West Indies; **l'~ de Beauté** Corsica; **l'~ Maurice** Mauritius; **les ~s anglo-normandes** the Channel Islands; **les ~s Britanniques** the British Isles; **les ~s Cocos** *ou* **Keeling** the Cocos *ou* Keeling Islands; **les ~s Cook** the Cook Islands; **les ~s Scilly** the Scilly Isles, the Scillies; **les ~s Shetland** the Shetland Islands, Shetland; **les ~s Sorlingues = les îles Scilly**; **les ~s Vierges** the Virgin Islands

illégal, e, -aux [ilegal, -o] *adj* illegal, unlawful (*Admin*)

illégitime [ileʒitim] *adj* illegitimate; (*optimisme, sévérité*) unjustified, unwarranted

illettré, e [iletʀe] *adj, nm/f* illiterate

illimité, e [ilimite] *adj* (*immense*) boundless, unlimited; (*congé, durée*) indefinite, unlimited

illisible [ilizibl] *adj* illegible; (*roman*) unreadable

illogique [ilɔʒik] *adj* illogical

illumination [ilyminasjɔ̃] *nf* illumination, floodlighting; (*inspiration*) flash of inspiration; **illuminations** *nfpl* illuminations, lights

illuminer [ilymine] *vt* to light up; (*monument, rue: pour une fête*) to illuminate; (*au moyen de projecteurs*) floodlight; **s'illuminer** *vi* to light up

illusion [ilyzjɔ̃] *nf* illusion; **se faire des ~s** to delude o.s.; **faire ~** to delude *ou* fool people; **~ d'optique** optical illusion

illusionniste [ilyzjɔnist] *nm/f* conjuror

illustration [ilystʀasjɔ̃] *nf* illustration; (*d'un ouvrage: photos*) illustrations *pl*

illustre [ilystʀ] *adj* illustrious, renowned

illustré, e [ilystʀe] *adj* illustrated ▷ *nm*

illustrated magazine; (*pour enfants*) comic
illustrer [ilystʀe] *vt* to illustrate; **s'illustrer**
to become famous, win fame
îlot [ilo] *nm* small island, islet; (*de maisons*)
block; (*petite zone*): **un ~ de verdure** an island
of greenery, a patch of green
ils [il] *pron* they
image [imaʒ] *nf* (*gén*) picture; (*comparaison,
ressemblance, Optique*) image; **~ de** picture *ou*
image of; **~ d'Épinal** (*social*) stereotype; **~ de
marque** brand image; (*d'une personne*)
(public) image; (*d'une entreprise*) corporate
image; **~ pieuse** holy picture
imagé, e [imaʒe] *adj* (*texte*) full of imagery;
(*langage*) colourful
imaginaire [imaʒinɛʀ] *adj* imaginary
imagination [imaʒinasjɔ̃] *nf* imagination;
(*chimère*) fancy, imagining; **avoir de l'~** to be
imaginative, have a good imagination
imaginer [imaʒine] *vt* to imagine; (*croire*):
qu'allez-vous ~ là? what on earth are you
thinking of?; (*inventer: expédient, mesure*) to
devise, think up; **s'imaginer** *vt* (*se figurer:
scène etc*) to imagine, picture; **s'~ à 60 ans** to
picture *ou* imagine o.s. at 60; **s'~ que** to
imagine that; **s'~ pouvoir faire qch** to think
one can do sth; **j'imagine qu'il a voulu
plaisanter** I suppose he was joking; **~ de
faire** (*se mettre dans l'idée de*) to dream up the
idea of doing
imbattable [ɛ̃batabl] *adj* unbeatable
imbécile [ɛ̃besil] *adj* idiotic ▷ *nm/f* idiot;
(*Méd*) imbecile
imbécillité [ɛ̃besilite] *nf* idiocy; imbecility;
idiotic action (*ou* remark *etc*)
imbiber [ɛ̃bibe] *vt*: **~ qch de** to moisten *ou*
wet sth with; **s'imbiber de** to become
saturated with; **imbibé(e) d'eau** (*chaussures,
étoffe*) saturated; (*terre*) waterlogged
imbu, e [ɛ̃by] *adj*: **~ de** full of; **~ de soi-même/
sa supériorité** full of oneself/one's
superiority
imbuvable [ɛ̃byvabl] *adj* undrinkable
imitateur, -trice [imitatœʀ, -tʀis] *nm/f* (*gén*)
imitator; (*Music-Hall: d'une personnalité*)
impersonator
imitation [imitasjɔ̃] *nf* imitation; (*de
personnalité*) impersonation; **sac ~ cuir** bag in
imitation *ou* simulated leather; **à l'~ de** in
imitation of
imiter [imite] *vt* to imitate; (*personne*) to
imitate, impersonate; (*contrefaire: signature,
document*) to forge, copy; (*ressembler à*) to look
like; **il se leva et je l'imitai** he got up and I
did likewise
immaculé, e [imakyle] *adj* spotless,
immaculate; **l'I~e Conception** (*Rel*) the
Immaculate Conception
immangeable [ɛ̃mɑ̃ʒabl] *adj* inedible,
uneatable
immatriculation [imatrikylasjɔ̃] *nf*
registration

immatriculer [imatrikyle] *vt* to register;
faire/se faire ~ to register; **voiture
immatriculée dans la Seine** car with a
Seine registration (number)
immédiat, e [imedja, -at] *adj* immediate
▷ *nm*: **dans l'~** for the time being; **dans le
voisinage ~** in the immediate vicinity
immédiatement [imedjatmɑ̃] *adv*
immediately
immense [imɑ̃s] *adj* immense
immerger [imɛʀʒe] *vt* to immerse,
submerge; (*câble etc*) to lay under water;
(*déchets*) to dump at sea; **s'immerger** *vi* (*sous-
marin*) to dive, submerge
immeuble [imœbl] *nm* building ▷ *adj* (*Jur*)
immovable, real; **~ locatif** block of rented
flats (*Brit*), rental building (*US*); **~ de rapport**
investment property
immigration [imigʀasjɔ̃] *nf* immigration
immigré, e [imigʀe] *nm/f* immigrant
imminent, e [iminɑ̃, -ɑ̃t] *adj* imminent,
impending
immiscer [imise]: **s'immiscer** *vi*: **s'~ dans** to
interfere in *ou* with
immobile [imɔbil] *adj* still, motionless; (*pièce
de machine*) fixed; (*fig*) unchanging; **rester/se
tenir ~** to stay/keep still
immobilier, -ière [imɔbilje, -jɛʀ] *adj*
property *cpd*, in real property ▷ *nm*: **l'~** the
property *ou* the real estate business
immobiliser [imɔbilize] *vt* (*gén*) to
immobilize; (*circulation, véhicule, affaires*) to
bring to a standstill; **s'immobiliser** (*personne*)
to stand still; (*machine, véhicule*) to come to a
halt *ou* a standstill
immonde [imɔ̃d] *adj* foul; (*sale: ruelle, taudis*)
squalid
immoral, e, -aux [imɔʀal, -o] *adj* immoral
immortel, le [imɔʀtɛl] *adj* immortal ▷ *nf*
(*Bot*) everlasting (flower)
immuable [imɥabl] *adj* (*inébranlable*)
immutable; (*qui ne change pas*) unchanging;
(*personne*): **~ dans ses convictions**
immoveable (in one's convictions)
immunisé, e [im(m)ynize] *adj*: **~ contre**
immune to
immunité [imynite] *nf* immunity;
~ diplomatique diplomatic immunity;
~ parlementaire parliamentary
privilege
impact [ɛ̃pakt] *nm* impact; **point d'~** point of
impact
impair, e [ɛ̃pɛʀ] *adj* odd ▷ *nm* faux pas,
blunder; **numéros ~s** odd numbers

impardonnable [ɛ̃paʀdɔnabl] *adj*
unpardonable, unforgivable; **vous êtes ~ d'avoir fait cela** it's unforgivable of you to have done that

imparfait, e [ɛ̃paʀfɛ, -ɛt] *adj* imperfect ⊳ *nm* (*Ling*) imperfect (tense)

impartial, e, -aux [ɛ̃paʀsjal, -o] *adj* impartial, unbiased

impasse [ɛ̃pas] *nf* dead-end, cul-de-sac; (*fig*) deadlock; **être dans l'~** (*négociations*) to have reached deadlock; **~ budgétaire** budget deficit

impassible [ɛ̃pasibl] *adj* impassive

impatience [ɛ̃pasjɑ̃s] *nf* impatience

impatient, e [ɛ̃pasjɑ̃, -ɑ̃t] *adj* impatient; **~ de faire qch** keen *ou* impatient to do sth

impatienter [ɛ̃pasjɑ̃te] *vt* to irritate, annoy; **s'impatienter** *vi* to get impatient; **s'~ de/ contre** to lose patience at/with, grow impatient at/with

impeccable [ɛ̃pekabl] *adj* faultless, impeccable; (*propre*) spotlessly clean; (*chic*) impeccably dressed; (*fam*) smashing

impensable [ɛ̃pɑ̃sabl] *adj* (*événement hypothétique*) unthinkable; (*événement qui a eu lieu*) unbelievable

imper [ɛ̃pɛʀ] *nm* (*imperméable*) mac

impératif, -ive [ɛ̃peʀatif, -iv] *adj* imperative; (*Jur*) mandatory ⊳ *nm* (*Ling*) imperative; **impératifs** *nmpl* (*exigences: d'une fonction, d'une charge*) requirements; (*de la mode*) demands

impératrice [ɛ̃peʀatʀis] *nf* empress

imperceptible [ɛ̃pɛʀsɛptibl] *adj* imperceptible

impérial, e, -aux [ɛ̃peʀjal, -o] *adj* imperial ⊳ *nf* upper deck; **autobus à ~e** double-decker bus

impérieux, -euse [ɛ̃peʀjø, -øz] *adj* (*caractère, ton*) imperious; (*obligation, besoin*) pressing, urgent

impérissable [ɛ̃peʀisabl] *adj* undying, imperishable

imperméable [ɛ̃pɛʀmeabl] *adj* waterproof; (*Géo*) impermeable; (*fig*): **~ à** impervious to ⊳ *nm* raincoat; **~ à l'air** airtight

impertinent, e [ɛ̃pɛʀtinɑ̃, -ɑ̃t] *adj* impertinent

imperturbable [ɛ̃pɛʀtyʀbabl] *adj* (*personne*) imperturbable; (*sang-froid*) unshakeable; **rester ~** to remain unruffled

impétueux, -euse [ɛ̃petɥø, -øz] *adj* fiery

impitoyable [ɛ̃pitwajabl] *adj* pitiless, merciless

implanter [ɛ̃plɑ̃te] *vt* (*usine, industrie, usage*) to establish; (*colons etc*) to settle; (*idée, préjugé*) to implant; **s'implanter dans** *vi* to be established in; to settle in; to become implanted in

impliquer [ɛ̃plike] *vt* to imply; **~ qn (dans)** to implicate sb (in)

impoli, e [ɛ̃pɔli] *adj* impolite, rude

impopulaire [ɛ̃pɔpylɛʀ] *adj* unpopular

importance [ɛ̃pɔʀtɑ̃s] *nf* importance; (*de somme*) size; (*de retard*): **avoir de l'~** to be important; **sans ~** unimportant; **d'~** important, considerable; **quelle ~?** what does it matter?

important, e [ɛ̃pɔʀtɑ̃, -ɑ̃t] *adj* important; (*en quantité: somme, retard*) considerable, sizeable; (: *gamme, dégâts*) extensive; (*péj: airs, ton*) self-important ⊳ *nm*: **l'~** the important thing

importateur, -trice [ɛ̃pɔʀtatœʀ, -tʀis] *adj* importing ⊳ *nm/f* importer; **pays ~ de blé** wheat-importing country

importation [ɛ̃pɔʀtasjɔ̃] *nf* import; introduction; (*produit*) import

importer [ɛ̃pɔʀte] *vt* (*Comm*) to import; (*maladies, plantes*) to introduce ⊳ *vi* (*être important*) to matter; **~ à qn** to matter to sb; **il importe de** it is important to; **il importe qu'il fasse** he must do, it is important that he should do; **peu m'importe** (*je n'ai pas de préférence*) I don't mind; (*je m'en moque*) I don't care; **peu importe** it doesn't matter; **peu importe (que)** it doesn't matter (if); **peu importe le prix** never mind the price; *voir aussi* **n'importe**

importun, e [ɛ̃pɔʀtœ̃, -yn] *adj* irksome, importunate; (*arrivée, visite*) inopportune, ill-timed ⊳ *nm* intruder

importuner [ɛ̃pɔʀtyne] *vt* to bother

imposable [ɛ̃pozabl] *adj* taxable

imposant, e [ɛ̃pozɑ̃, -ɑ̃t] *adj* imposing

imposer [ɛ̃poze] *vt* (*taxer*) to tax; (*Rel*): **~ les mains** to lay on hands; **~ qch à qn** to impose sth on sb; **s'imposer** *vi* (*être nécessaire*) to be imperative; (*montrer sa proéminence*) to stand out, emerge; (*artiste: se faire connaître*) to win recognition, come to the fore; **en ~** to be imposing; **s'~ à qn** to impress; **s'~ comme** to emerge as; **s'~ par** to win recognition through; **ça s'impose** it's essential, it's vital

impossibilité [ɛ̃pɔsibilite] *nf* impossibility; **être dans l'~ de faire** to be unable to do, find it impossible to do

impossible [ɛ̃pɔsibl] *adj* impossible ⊳ *nm*: **l'~** the impossible; **~ à faire** impossible to do; **il m'est ~ de le faire** it is impossible for me to do it, I can't possibly do it; **faire l'~ (pour que)** to do one's utmost (so that); **si, par ~ ...** if, by some miracle ...

imposteur [ɛ̃pɔstœʀ] *nm* impostor

impôt [ɛ̃po] *nm* tax; (*taxes*) taxation, taxes *pl*; **impôts** *nmpl* (*contributions*) (income) tax *sg*; **payer 1000 euros d'~s** to pay 1,000 euros in tax; **~ direct/indirect** direct/indirect tax; **~ sur le chiffre d'affaires** corporation tax (*Brit*) *ou* corporate (*US*) tax; **~ foncier** land tax; **~ sur la fortune** wealth tax; **~ sur les plus-values** capital gains tax; **~ sur le revenu** income tax; **~ sur le RPP** personal income tax; **~ sur les sociétés** tax on companies; **~s locaux** rates, local taxes (*US*), ≈ council tax (*Brit*)

impotent, e [ɛ̃pɔtɑ̃, -ɑ̃t] *adj* disabled

impraticable [ɛ̃pratikabl] *adj* (*projet*) impracticable, unworkable; (*piste*) impassable

imprécis, e [ɛ̃presi, -iz] *adj* (*contours, souvenir*) imprecise, vague; (*tir*) inaccurate, imprecise

imprégner [ɛ̃preɲe] *vt* (*tissu, tampon*): ~ **(de)** to soak *ou* impregnate (with); (*lieu, air*): ~ **(de)** to fill (with); (*amertume, ironie*) to pervade; **s'imprégner de** *vi* to become impregnated with; to be filled with; (*fig*) to absorb

imprenable [ɛ̃prǝnabl] *adj* (*forteresse*) impregnable; **vue** ~ unimpeded outlook

impresario [ɛ̃presarjo] *nm* manager, impresario

impression [ɛ̃presjɔ̃] *nf* impression; (*d'un ouvrage, tissu*) printing; (*Photo*) exposure; **faire bonne/mauvaise** ~ to make a good/bad impression; **donner une ~ de/l' ~ que** to give the impression of/that; **avoir l' ~ de/que** to have the impression of/that; **faire** ~ to make an impression; **~s de voyage** impressions of one's journey

impressionnant, e [ɛ̃presjɔnɑ̃, -ɑ̃t] *adj* (*imposant*) impressive; (*bouleversant*) upsetting

impressionner [ɛ̃presjɔne] *vt* (*frapper*) to impress; (*troubler*) to upset; (*Photo*) to expose

imprévisible [ɛ̃previzibl] *adj* unforeseeable; (*réaction, personne*) unpredictable

imprévoyant, e [ɛ̃prevwajɑ̃, -ɑ̃t] *adj* lacking in foresight; (*en matière d'argent*) improvident

imprévu, e [ɛ̃prevy] *adj* unforeseen, unexpected ▷ *nm* (*incident*) unexpected incident; **l'~** the unexpected; **des vacances pleines d'~** holidays full of surprises; **en cas d'~** if anything unexpected happens; **sauf ~** unless anything unexpected crops up

imprimante [ɛ̃primɑ̃t] *nf* (*Inform*) printer; ~ **à bulle d'encre** bubblejet printer; ~ **à jet d'encre** ink-jet printer; ~ **à laser** laser printer; ~ **(ligne par) ligne** line printer; ~ **à marguerite** daisy-wheel printer

imprimé [ɛ̃prime] *nm* (*formulaire*) printed form; (*Postes*) printed matter *no pl*; (*tissu*) printed fabric; **un ~ à fleurs/pois** (*tissu*) a floral/polka-dot print

imprimer [ɛ̃prime] *vt* to print; (*Inform*) to print (out); (*apposer: visa, cachet*) to stamp; (*empreinte etc*) to imprint; (*publier*) to publish; (*communiquer: mouvement, impulsion*) to impart, transmit

imprimerie [ɛ̃primri] *nf* printing; (*établissement*) printing works *sg*; (*atelier*) printing house, printery

imprimeur [ɛ̃primœr] *nm* printer; **~-éditeur/-libraire** printer and publisher/ bookseller

impromptu, e [ɛ̃prɔ̃pty] *adj* impromptu; (*départ*) sudden

impropre [ɛ̃prɔpr] *adj* inappropriate; ~ **à** unsuitable for

improviser [ɛ̃prɔvize] *vt, vi* to improvize; **s'improviser** (*secours, réunion*) to be

improvized; **s'~ cuisinier** to (decide to) act as cook; ~ **qn cuisinier** to get sb to act as cook

improviste [ɛ̃prɔvist]: **à l'~** *adv* unexpectedly, without warning

imprudence [ɛ̃prydɑ̃s] *nf* (*d'une personne, d'une action*) carelessness *no pl*; (*d'une remarque*) imprudence *no pl*; act of carelessness; (*ooo*) foolish *ou* unwise action; **commettre une ~** to do something foolish

imprudent, e [ɛ̃prydɑ̃, -ɑ̃t] *adj* (*conducteur, geste, action*) careless; (*remarque*) unwise, imprudent; (*projet*) foolhardy

impudent, e [ɛ̃pydɑ̃, -ɑ̃t] *adj* impudent

impudique [ɛ̃pydik] *adj* shameless

impuissant, e [ɛ̃pɥisɑ̃, -ɑ̃t] *adj* helpless; (*sans effet*) ineffectual; (*sexuellement*), impotent ▷ *nm* impotent man; ~ **à faire qch** powerless to do sth

impulsif, -ive [ɛ̃pylsif, -iv] *adj* impulsive

impulsion [ɛ̃pylsjɔ̃] *nf* (*Élec, instinct*) impulse; (*élan, influence*) impetus

impunément [ɛ̃pynemɑ̃] *adv* with impunity

inabordable [inabɔrdabl] *adj* (*lieu*) inaccessible; (*cher*) prohibitive

inacceptable [inaksɛptabl] *adj* unacceptable

inaccessible [inaksesibl] *adj* inaccessible; (*objectif*) unattainable; (*insensible*): ~ **à** impervious to

inachevé, e [inaʃve] *adj* unfinished

inactif, -ive [inaktif, -iv] *adj* inactive, idle; (*remède*) ineffective; (*Bourse: marché*) slack

inadapté, e [inadapte] *adj* (*Psych: adulte, enfant*) maladjusted ▷ *nm/f* (*péj: adulte: asocial*) misfit; ~ **à** not adapted to, unsuited to

inadéquat, e [inadekwa, wat] *adj* inadequate

inadmissible [inadmisibl] *adj* inadmissible

inadvertance [inadvɛrtɑ̃s]: **par ~** *adv* inadvertently

inaltérable [inalterabl] *adj* (*matière*) stable; (*fig*) unchanging; ~ **à** unaffected by; **couleur ~ (au lavage/à la lumière)** fast colour/fade-resistant colour

inanimé, e [inanime] *adj* (*matière*) inanimate; (*évanoui*) unconscious; (*sans vie*) lifeless

inanition [inanisjɔ̃] *nf*: **tomber d'~** to faint with hunger (and exhaustion)

inaperçu, e [inapɛrsy] *adj*: **passer ~** to go unnoticed

inapte [inapt] *adj*: ~ **à** incapable of; (*Mil*) unfit for

inattaquable [inatakabl] *adj* (*Mil*) unassailable; (*texte, preuve*) irrefutable

inattendu, e [inatɑ̃dy] *adj* unexpected ▷ *nm*: **l'~** the unexpected

inattentif, -ive [inatɑ̃tif, -iv] *adj* inattentive; ~ **à** (*dangers, détails*) heedless of

inattention [inatɑ̃sjɔ̃] *nf* inattention; (*inadvertance*): **une minute d'~** a minute of inattention, a minute's carelessness; **par ~** inadvertently; **faute d'~** careless mistake

inauguration [inɔgyRasjɔ̃] nf unveiling; opening; **discours/cérémonie d'~** inaugural speech/ceremony

inaugurer [inɔgyRe] vt (monument) to unveil; (exposition, usine) to open; (fig) to inaugurate

inavouable [inavwabl] adj (bénéfices) undisclosable; (honteux) shameful

incalculable [ɛ̃kalkylabl] adj incalculable; **un nombre ~ de** countless numbers of

incandescence [ɛ̃kɑ̃desɑ̃s] nf incandescence; **en ~** incandescent, white-hot; **porter à ~** to heat white-hot; **lampe/manchon à ~** incandescent lamp/(gas) mantle

incapable [ɛ̃kapabl] adj incapable; **~ de faire** incapable of doing; (empêché) unable to do

incapacité [ɛ̃kapasite] nf (incompétence) incapability; (Jur: impossibilité) incapacity; **être dans l'~ de faire** to be unable to do; **~ permanente/de travail** permanent/industrial disablement; **~ électorale** ineligibility to vote

incarcérer [ɛ̃kaRseRe] vt to incarcerate, imprison

incarné, e [ɛ̃kaRne] adj incarnate; (ongle) ingrown

incarner [ɛ̃kaRne] vt to embody, personify; (Théât) to play; (Rel) to incarnate; **s'incarner dans** vi (Rel) to be incarnate in

incassable [ɛ̃kasabl] adj unbreakable

incendiaire [ɛ̃sɑ̃djɛR] adj incendiary; (fig: discours) inflammatory ▷ nm/f fire-raiser, arsonist

incendie [ɛ̃sɑ̃di] nm fire; **~ criminel** arson no pl; **~ de forêt** forest fire

incendier [ɛ̃sɑ̃dje] vt (mettre le feu à) to set fire to, set alight; (brûler complètement) to burn down

incertain, e [ɛ̃sɛRtɛ̃, -ɛn] adj uncertain; (temps) uncertain, unsettled; (imprécis: contours) indistinct, blurred

incertitude [ɛ̃sɛRtityd] nf uncertainty

incessamment [ɛ̃sesamɑ̃] adv very shortly

incident [ɛ̃sidɑ̃] nm incident; **~ de frontière** border incident; **~ de parcours** minor hitch ou setback; **~ technique** technical difficulties pl, technical hitch

incinérer [ɛ̃sineRe] vt (ordures) to incinerate; (mort) to cremate

incisif, -ive [ɛ̃sizif, -iv] adj incisive, cutting ▷ nf incisor

inciter [ɛ̃site] vt: **~ qn à (faire) qch** to prompt ou encourage sb to do sth; (à la révolte etc) to incite sb to do sth

incivilité [ɛ̃sivilite] nf (grossièreté) incivility; **incivilités** nfpl antisocial behaviour sg

inclinable [ɛ̃klinabl] adj (dossier etc) tilting; **siège à dossier ~** reclining seat

inclinaison [ɛ̃klinɛzɔ̃] nf (déclivité: d'une route etc) incline; (: d'un toit) slope; (état penché: d'un mur) lean; (: de la tête) tilt; (: d'un navire) list

inclination [ɛ̃klinasjɔ̃] nf (penchant)

inclination, tendency; **montrer de l'~ pour les sciences etc** to show an inclination for the sciences etc; **~s égoïstes/altruistes** egoistic/altruistic tendencies; **~ de (la) tête** nod (of the head); **~ de buste** bow

incliner [ɛ̃kline] vt (bouteille) to tilt; (tête) to incline; (inciter): **~ qn à qch/à faire** to encourage sb towards sth/to do ▷ vi: **~ à qch/à faire** (tendre à, pencher pour) to incline towards sth/to do, tend towards sth/to do; **s'incliner** vi (route) to slope; (toit) to be sloping; **s'~ (devant)** to bow (before)

inclure [ɛ̃klyR] vt to include; (joindre à un envoi) to enclose; **jusqu'au 10 mars inclus** until 10th March inclusive

inclus, e [ɛ̃kly, -yz] pp de **inclure** ▷ adj included; (joint à un envoi) enclosed; (compris: frais, dépense) included; (Math: ensemble): **~ dans** included in; **jusqu'au troisième chapitre ~** up to and including the third chapter; **jusqu'au 10 mars ~** until 10th March inclusive

incognito [ɛ̃kɔɲito] adv incognito ▷ nm: **garder l'~** to remain incognito

incohérent, e [ɛ̃kɔeRɑ̃, -ɑ̃t] adj (comportement) inconsistent; (geste, langage, texte) incoherent

incollable [ɛ̃kɔlabl] adj (riz) that does not stick; (fam: personne): **il est ~** he's got all the answers

incolore [ɛ̃kɔlɔR] adj colourless

incommoder [ɛ̃kɔmɔde] vt (chaleur, odeur): **~ qn** to bother ou inconvenience sb; (embarrasser) to make sb feel uncomfortable ou ill at ease

incomparable [ɛ̃kɔ̃paRabl] adj not comparable; (inégalable) incomparable, matchless

incompatible [ɛ̃kɔ̃patibl] adj incompatible

incompétent, e [ɛ̃kɔ̃petɑ̃, -ɑ̃t] adj (ignorant) inexpert; (incapable) incompetent, not competent

incomplet, -ète [ɛ̃kɔ̃plɛ, -ɛt] adj incomplete

incompréhensible [ɛ̃kɔ̃pReɑ̃sibl] adj incomprehensible

incompris, e [ɛ̃kɔ̃pRi, -iz] adj misunderstood

inconcevable [ɛ̃kɔ̃svabl] adj (conduite etc) inconceivable; (mystère) incredible

inconciliable [ɛ̃kɔ̃siljabl] adj irreconcilable

inconditionnel, le [ɛ̃kɔ̃disjɔnɛl] adj unconditional; (partisan) unquestioning ▷ nm/f (partisan) unquestioning supporter

inconfort [ɛ̃kɔ̃fɔR] nm lack of comfort, discomfort

inconfortable [ɛ̃kɔ̃fɔRtabl] adj uncomfortable

incongru, e [ɛ̃kɔ̃gRy] adj unseemly; (remarque) incongruous, incongruous

inconnu, e [ɛ̃kɔny] adj unknown; (sentiment, plaisir) new, strange ▷ nm/f stranger; unknown person (ou artist etc) ▷ nm: **l'~** the unknown ▷ nf (Math) unknown; (fig) unknown factor

inconsciemment [ɛ̃kɔ̃sjamɑ̃] adv
unconsciously

inconscient, e [ɛ̃kɔ̃sjɑ̃, -ɑ̃t] adj unconscious;
(irréfléchi) thoughtless, reckless; (sentiment)
subconscious ▷ nm (Psych): **l'~** the
subconscious, the unconscious; **~ de**
unaware of

inconsidéré, e [ɛ̃kɔ̃sidere] adj ill-considered

inconsistant, e [ɛ̃kɔ̃sistɑ̃, -ɑ̃t] adj flimsy,
weak; (crème etc) runny

inconsolable [ɛ̃kɔ̃sɔlabl] adj inconsolable

incontestable [ɛ̃kɔ̃tɛstabl] adj
unquestionable, indisputable

incontinent, e [ɛ̃kɔ̃tinɑ̃, -ɑ̃t] adj (Méd)
incontinent ▷ adv (tout de suite) forthwith

incontournable [ɛ̃kɔ̃turnabl] adj
unavoidable

incontrôlable [ɛ̃kɔ̃trolabl] adj unverifiable;
(irrépressible) uncontrollable

inconvenant, e [ɛ̃kɔ̃vnɑ̃, -ɑ̃t] adj unseemly,
improper

inconvénient [ɛ̃kɔ̃venjɑ̃] nm (d'une situation,
d'un projet) disadvantage, drawback; (d'un
remède, changement etc) risk, inconvenience; **si
vous n'y voyez pas d'~** if you have no
objections; **y a-t-il un ~ à …?** (risque) isn't
there a risk in …?; (objection) is there any
objection to …?

incorporer [ɛ̃kɔrpɔre] vt: **~ (à)** to mix in
(with); (paragraphe etc): **~ (dans)** to
incorporate (in); (territoire, immigrants): **~
(dans)** to incorporate (into); (Mil: appeler) to
recruit, call up; (: affecter): **~ qn dans** to enlist
sb into; **il a très bien su s'~ à notre groupe**
he was very easily incorporated into our
group

incorrect, e [ɛ̃kɔrɛkt] adj (impropre,
inconvenant) improper; (défectueux) faulty;
(inexact) incorrect; (impoli) impolite; (déloyal)
underhand

incorrigible [ɛ̃kɔriʒibl] adj incorrigible

incrédule [ɛ̃kredyl] adj incredulous; (Rel)
unbelieving

increvable [ɛ̃krəvabl] adj (pneu) puncture-
proof; (fam) tireless

incriminer [ɛ̃krimine] vt (personne) to
incriminate; (action, conduite) to bring under
attack; (bonne foi, honnêteté) to call into
question; **livre/article incriminé** offending
book/article

incroyable [ɛ̃krwajabl] adj incredible,
unbelievable

incruster [ɛ̃kryste] vt (Art): **~ qch dans/qch
de** to inlay sth into/sth with; (radiateur etc) to
coat with scale ou fur; **s'incruster** vi (invité) to
take root; (radiateur etc) to become coated
with scale ou fur; **s'~ dans** (corps étranger,
caillou) to become embedded in

inculpé, e [ɛ̃kylpe] nm/f accused

inculper [ɛ̃kylpe] vt: **~ (de)** to charge (with)

inculquer [ɛ̃kylke] vt: **~ qch à** to inculcate
sth in, instil into

inculte [ɛ̃kylt] adj uncultivated; (esprit, peuple)
uncultured; (barbe) unkempt

Inde [ɛ̃d] nf: **l'~** India

indécent, e [ɛ̃desɑ̃, -ɑ̃t] adj indecent

indéchiffrable [ɛ̃deʃifrabl] adj indecipherable

indécis, e [ɛ̃desi, -iz] adj (par nature)
indecisive; (perplexe) undecided

indéfendable [ɛ̃defɑ̃dabl] adj indefensible

indéfini, e [ɛ̃defini] adj (imprécis, incertain)
undefined; (illimité, Ling) indefinite

indéfiniment [ɛ̃definimɑ̃] adv indefinitely

indéfinissable [ɛ̃definisabl] adj indefinable

indélébile [ɛ̃delebil] adj indelible

indélicat, e [ɛ̃delika, -at] adj tactless;
(malhonnête) dishonest

indemne [ɛ̃dɛmn] adj unharmed

indemniser [ɛ̃dɛmnize] vt: **~ qn (de)** to
compensate sb (for); **se faire ~** to get
compensation

indemnité [ɛ̃dɛmnite] nf (dédommagement)
compensation no pl; (allocation) allowance;
~ de licenciement redundancy payment;
~ de logement housing allowance;
~ parlementaire = MP's (Brit) ou
Congressman's (US) salary

indépendamment [ɛ̃depɑ̃damɑ̃] adv
independently; **~ de** independently of;
(abstraction faite de) irrespective of; (en plus de)
over and above

indépendance [ɛ̃depɑ̃dɑ̃s] nf independence;
~ matérielle financial independence

indépendant, e [ɛ̃depɑ̃dɑ̃, -ɑ̃t] adj
independent; **~ de** independent of; **chambre
~e** room with private entrance; **travailleur ~**
self-employed worker

indescriptible [ɛ̃dɛskriptibl] adj
indescribable

indésirable [ɛ̃dezirabl] adj undesirable

indestructible [ɛ̃dɛstryktibl] adj
indestructible; (marque, impression) indelible

indétermination [ɛ̃determinasjɔ̃] nf
indecision, indecisiveness

indéterminé, e [ɛ̃determine] adj (date, cause,
nature) unspecified; (forme, longueur, quantité)
indeterminate; indeterminable

index [ɛ̃dɛks] nm (doigt) index finger; (d'un
livre etc) index; **mettre à l'~** to blacklist

indexé, e [ɛ̃dɛkse] adj (Écon): **~ (sur)** index-
linked (to)

indicateur [ɛ̃dikatœr] nm (Police) informer;
(livre) guide; (: liste) directory; (Tech) gauge;
indicator; (Écon) indicator ▷ adj: **poteau ~**
signpost; **tableau ~** indicator (board); **~ des
chemins de fer** railway timetable; **~ de
direction** (Auto) indicator; **~ immobilier**
property gazette; **~ de niveau** level, gauge;
~ de pression pressure gauge; **~ de rues**
street directory; **~ de vitesse** speedometer

indicatif, -ive [ɛ̃dikatif, -iv] adj: **à titre ~** for
(your) information ▷ nm (Ling) indicative;
(d'une émission) theme ou signature tune; (Tél)
dialling code (Brit), area code (US); **~ d'appel**

(*Radio*) call sign; **quel est l'~ de ...** what's the code for ...?

indication [ɛ̃dikasjɔ̃] *nf* indication; (*renseignement*) information *no pl*; **indications** *nfpl* (*directives*) instructions; **~ d'origine** (*Comm*) place of origin

indice [ɛ̃dis] *nm* (*marque, signe*) indication, sign; (*Police: lors d'une enquête*) clue; (*Jur: présomption*) piece of evidence; (*Science, Écon, Tech*) index; (*Admin*) grading; rating; **~ du coût de la vie** cost-of-living index; **~ inférieur** subscript; **~ d'octane** octane rating; **~ des prix** price index; **~ de traitement** salary grading; **~ de protection** (sun protection) factor

indicible [ɛ̃disibl] *adj* inexpressible

indien, ne [ɛ̃djɛ̃, -ɛn] *adj* Indian ▷ *nm/f*: **I~, ne** (*d'Amérique*) Native American; (*d'Inde*) Indian

indifféremment [ɛ̃diferamɑ̃] *adv* (*sans distinction*) equally; indiscriminately

indifférence [ɛ̃diferɑ̃s] *nf* indifference

indifférent, e [ɛ̃diferɑ̃, -ɑ̃t] *adj* (*peu intéressé*) indifferent; **~ à** (*insensible à*) indifferent to, unconcerned about; (*peu intéressant pour*) indifferent to; immaterial to; **ça m'est ~ (que ...)** it doesn't matter to me (whether ...); **elle m'est ~e** I am indifferent to her

indigence [ɛ̃diʒɑ̃s] *nf* poverty; **être dans l'~** to be destitute

indigène [ɛ̃diʒɛn] *adj* native, indigenous; (*de la région*) local ▷ *nm/f* native

indigeste [ɛ̃diʒɛst] *adj* indigestible

indigestion [ɛ̃diʒɛstjɔ̃] *nf* indigestion *no pl*; **avoir une ~** to have indigestion

indigne [ɛ̃diɲ] *adj*: **~ (de)** unworthy (of)

indigner [ɛ̃diɲe] *vt* to make indignant; **s'indigner (de/contre)** *vi* to be (*ou* become) indignant (at)

indiqué, e [ɛ̃dike] *adj* (*date, lieu*) given, appointed; (*adéquat*) appropriate, suitable; (*conseillé*) advisable; (*remède, traitement*) appropriate

indiquer [ɛ̃dike] *vt* (*désigner*): **~ qch/qn à qn** to point sth/sb out to sb; (*faire connaître: médecin, restaurant*) to tell sb of sth/sb; (*pendule, aiguille*) to show; (*étiquette, plan*) to show, indicate; (*faire connaître: médecin, lieu*): **~ qch/qn à qn** to tell sb of sth/sb; (*renseigner sur*) to point out, tell; (*déterminer: date, lieu*) to give, state; (*dénoter*) to indicate, point to; **~ du doigt** to point out; **~ de la main** to indicate with one's hand; **~ du regard** to glance towards *ou* in the direction of; **pourriez-vous m'~ les toilettes/l'heure?** could you direct me to the toilets/tell me the time?

indirect, e [ɛ̃dirɛkt] *adj* indirect

indiscipliné, e [ɛ̃disipline] *adj* undisciplined; (*fig*) unmanageable

indiscret, -ète [ɛ̃diskrɛ, -ɛt] *adj* indiscreet

indiscutable [ɛ̃diskytabl] *adj* indisputable

indispensable [ɛ̃dispɑ̃sabl] *adj* indispensable, essential; **~ à qn/pour faire qch** essential for sb/to do sth

indisposé, e [ɛ̃dispoze] *adj* indisposed, unwell

indisposer [ɛ̃dispoze] *vt* (*incommoder*) to upset; (*déplaire à*) to antagonize

indistinct, e [ɛ̃distɛ̃, -ɛkt] *adj* indistinct

indistinctement [ɛ̃distɛ̃ktəmɑ̃] *adv* (*voir, prononcer*) indistinctly; (*sans distinction*) without distinction, indiscriminately

individu [ɛ̃dividy] *nm* individual

individuel, le [ɛ̃dividɥɛl] *adj* (*gén*) individual; (*opinion, livret, contrôle, avantages*) personal; **chambre ~le** single room; **maison ~le** detached house; **propriété ~le** personal *ou* private property

indolore [ɛ̃dɔlɔr] *adj* painless

indomptable [ɛ̃dɔ̃tabl] *adj* untameable; (*fig*) invincible, indomitable

Indonésie [ɛ̃dɔnezi] *nf*: **l'~** Indonesia

indu, e [ɛ̃dy] *adj*: **à une heure ~e** at some ungodly hour

induire [ɛ̃dɥir] *vt*: **~ qch de** to induce sth from; **~ qn en erreur** to lead sb astray, mislead sb

indulgent, e [ɛ̃dylʒɑ̃, -ɑ̃t] *adj* (*parent, regard*) indulgent; (*juge, examinateur*) lenient

industrialisé, e [ɛ̃dystrijalize] *adj* industrialized

industrie [ɛ̃dystri] *nf* industry; **~ automobile/textile** car/textile industry; **~ du spectacle** entertainment business

industriel, le [ɛ̃dystrijɛl] *adj* industrial; (*produit industriellement: pain etc*) mass-produced, factory-produced ▷ *nm* industrialist; (*fabricant*) manufacturer

inébranlable [inebrɑ̃labl] *adj* (*masse, colonne*) solid; (*personne, certitude, foi*) steadfast, unwavering

inédit, e [inedi, -it] *adj* (*correspondance etc*) (hitherto) unpublished; (*spectacle, moyen*) novel, original; (*film*) unreleased

ineffaçable [inefasabl] *adj* indelible

inefficace [inefikas] *adj* (*remède, moyen*) ineffective; (*machine, employé*) inefficient

inégal, e, -aux [inegal, -o] *adj* unequal; (*irrégulier*) uneven

inégalable [inegalabl(ə)] *adj* matchless

inégalé, e [inegale] *adj* (*record*) unmatched, unequalled; (*beauté*) unrivalled

inégalité [inegalite] *nf* inequality; unevenness *no pl*; **~ de deux hauteurs** difference *ou* disparity between two heights; **~s de terrain** uneven ground

inépuisable [inepɥizabl] *adj* inexhaustible

inerte [inɛrt] *adj* (*immobile*) lifeless; (*apathique*) passive, inert; (*Physique, Chimie*) inert

inespéré, e [inɛspere] *adj* unhoped-for, unexpected

inestimable [inɛstimabl] *adj* priceless; (*fig: bienfait*) invaluable

inévitable [inevitabl] *adj* unavoidable; (*fatal, habituel*) inevitable

inexact, e [inɛgzakt] *adj* inaccurate, inexact; (*non ponctuel*) unpunctual

inexcusable [inεkskyzabl] *adj* inexcusable, unforgivable

inexplicable [inεksplikabl] *adj* inexplicable

in extremis [inεkstremis] *adv* at the last minute ▷ *adj* last-minute; (*testament*) death bed *cpd*

infaillible [ēfajibl] *adj* infallible; (*instinct*) infallible, unerring

infâme [ēfɑm] *adj* vile

infarctus [ēfarktys] *nm*: ~ **(du myocarde)** coronary (thrombosis)

infatigable [ēfatigabl] *adj* tireless, indefatigable

infect, e [ēfεkt] *adj* revolting; (*repas, vin*) revolting, foul; (*personne*) obnoxious; (*temps*) foul

infecter [ēfεkte] *vt* (*atmosphère, eau*) to contaminate; (*Méd*) to infect; **s'infecter** *vi* to become infected ou septic

infection [ēfεksjɔ̃] *nf* infection; (*puanteur*) stench

inférieur, e [ēferjœr] *adj* lower; (*en qualité, intelligence*) inferior ▷ *nm/f* inferior; ~ **à** (*somme, quantité*) less ou smaller than; (*moins bon que*) inferior to; (*tâche: pas à la hauteur de*) unequal to

infernal, e, -aux [ēfεrnal, -o] *adj* (*insupportable: chaleur, rythme*) infernal; (*enfant*) horrid; (*méchanceté, complot*) diabolical

infidèle [ēfidεl] *adj* unfaithful; (*Rel*) infidel

infiltrer [ēfiltre]: **s'infiltrer** *vi*: **s'~ dans** to penetrate into; (*liquide*) to seep into; (*fig: noyauter*) to infiltrate

infime [ēfim] *adj* minute, tiny; (*inférieur*) lowly

infini, e [ēfini] *adj* infinite ▷ *nm* infinity; **à l'~** (*Math*) to infinity; (*discourir*) ad infinitum, endlessly; (*agrandir, varier*) infinitely; (*à perte de vue*) endlessly (into the distance)

infiniment [ēfinimɑ̃] *adv* infinitely; ~ **grand/petit** (*Math*) infinitely great/infinitesimal

infinité [ēfinite] *nf*: **une ~ de** an infinite number of

infinitif, -ive [ēfinitif, -iv] *adj, nm* infinitive

infirme [ēfirm] *adj* disabled ▷ *nm/f* disabled person; ~ **de guerre** war cripple; ~ **du travail** industrially disabled person

infirmerie [ēfirməri] *nf* sick bay

infirmier, -ière [ēfirmje, -jεr] *nm/f* nurse ▷ *adj*: **élève ~** student nurse; **infirmière chef** sister; **infirmière diplômée** registered nurse; **infirmière visiteuse** visiting nurse, ≈ district nurse (*Brit*)

infirmité [ēfirmite] *nf* disability

inflammable [ēflamabl] *adj* (in)flammable

inflation [ēflasjɔ̃] *nf* inflation; ~ **rampante/galopante** creeping/galloping inflation

infliger [ēfliʒe] *vt*: ~ **qch (à qn)** to inflict sth (on sb); (*amende, sanction*) to impose sth (on sb)

influençable [ēflyɑ̃sabl] *adj* easily influenced

influence [ēflyɑ̃s] *nf* influence; (*d'un médicament*) effect

influencer [ēflyɑ̃se] *vt* to influence

influent, e [ēflyɑ̃, -ɑ̃t] *adj* influential

informateur, -trice [ēfɔrmatœr, -tris] *nm/f* informant

informaticien, ne [ēfɔrmatisjē, -εn] *nm/f* computer scientist

information [ēfɔrmasjɔ̃] *nf* (*renseignement*) piece of information; (*Presse, TV: nouvelle*) item of news; (*diffusion de renseignements, Inform*) information; (*Jur*) inquiry, investigation; **informations** *nfpl* (*TV*) news *sg*; **voyage d'~** fact-finding trip; **agence d'~** news agency; **journal d'~** quality (*Brit*) ou serious newspaper

informatique [ēfɔrmatik] *nf* (*technique*) data processing; (*science*) computer science ▷ *adj* computer *cpd*

informatiser [ēfɔrmatize] *vt* to computerize

informe [ēfɔrm] *adj* shapeless

informer [ēfɔrme] *vt*: ~ **qn (de)** to inform sb (of) ▷ *vi* (*Jur*): ~ **contre qn/sur qch** to initiate inquiries about sb/sth; **s'informer (sur)** to inform o.s. (about); **s'~ (de qch/si)** to inquire ou find out (about sth/whether ou if)

infos [ēfo] *nfpl* (= *informations*) news

infraction [ēfraksjɔ̃] *nf* offence; ~ **à** violation ou breach of; **être en ~** to be in breach of the law

infranchissable [ēfrɑ̃ʃisabl] *adj* impassable; (*fig*) insuperable

infrarouge [ēfraruʒ] *adj, nm* infrared

infrastructure [ēfrastryktyr] *nf* (*d'une route etc*) substructure; (*Aviat, Mil*) ground installations *pl*; (*Écon: touristique etc*) facilities *pl*

infuser [ēfyze] *vt* (*aussi*: **faire ~**: *thé*) to brew; (: *tisane*) to infuse ▷ *vi* to brew; to infuse; **laisser ~** (to leave) to brew

infusion [ēfyzjɔ̃] *nf* (*tisane*) infusion, herb tea

ingénier [ēʒenje]: **s'ingénier** *vi*: **s'~ à faire** to strive to do

ingénierie [ēʒeniri] *nf* engineering

ingénieur [ēʒenjœr] *nm* engineer; ~ **agronome/chimiste** agricultural/chemical engineer; ~ **conseil** consulting engineer; ~ **du son** sound engineer

ingénieux, -euse [ēʒenjø, -øz] *adj* ingenious, clever

ingénu, e [ēʒeny] *adj* ingenuous, artless ▷ *nf* (*Théât*) ingénue

ingérer [ēʒere]: **s'ingérer** *vi*: **s'~ dans** to interfere in

ingrat, e [ēgra, -at] *adj* (*personne*) ungrateful; (*sol*) poor; (*travail, sujet*) arid, thankless; (*visage*) unprepossessing

ingrédient [ēgredjɑ̃] *nm* ingredient

ingurgiter [ēgyrʒite] *vt* to swallow; **faire ~ qch à qn** to make sb swallow sth; (*fig: connaissances*) to force sth into sb

inhabitable [inabitabl] *adj* uninhabitable

inhabité, e [inabite] *adj* (*régions*) uninhabited; (*maison*) unoccupied

inhabituel, le [inabitɥɛl] *adj* unusual

inhibition [inibisjɔ̃] *nf* inhibition

inhumain, e [inymɛ̃, -ɛn] *adj* inhuman

inhumation [inymasjɔ̃] *nf* interment, burial

inhumer [inyme] *vt* to inter, bury

inimaginable [inimaʒinabl] *adj* unimaginable

ininterrompu, e [inɛ̃terɔ̃py] *adj* (*file, série*) unbroken; (*flot, vacarme*) uninterrupted, non-stop; (*effort*) unremitting, continuous; (*suite, ligne*) unbroken

initial, e, -aux [inisjal, -o] *adj, nf* initial; **initiales** *nfpl* initials

initialiser [inisjalize] *vt* to initialize

initiation [inisjasjɔ̃] *nf* initiation; **~ à** introduction to

initiative [inisjativ] *nf* initiative; **prendre l'~ de qch/de faire** to take the initiative for sth/of doing; **avoir de l'~** to have initiative, show enterprise; **esprit/qualités d'~** spirit/qualities of initiative; **à ou sur l'~ de qn** on sb's initiative; **de sa propre ~** on one's own initiative

initier [inisje] *vt* to initiate; **~ qn à** to initiate sb into; (*faire découvrir: art, jeu*) to introduce sb to; **s'initier à** *vi* (*métier, profession, technique*) to become initiated into

injecté, e [ɛ̃ʒɛkte] *adj:* **yeux ~s de sang** bloodshot eyes

injecter [ɛ̃ʒɛkte] *vt* to inject

injection [ɛ̃ʒɛksjɔ̃] *nf* injection; **à ~** (*Auto*) fuel injection *cpd*

injure [ɛ̃ʒyR] *nf* insult, abuse *no pl*

injurier [ɛ̃ʒyRje] *vt* to insult, abuse

injurieux, -euse [ɛ̃ʒyRjø, -øz] *adj* abusive, insulting

injuste [ɛ̃ʒyst] *adj* unjust, unfair

injustice [ɛ̃ʒystis] *nf* injustice

inlassable [ɛ̃lɑsabl] *adj* tireless, indefatigable

inné, e [ine] *adj* innate, inborn

innocent, e [inɔsɑ̃, -ɑ̃t] *adj* innocent ▷ *nm/f* innocent person; **faire l'~** to play *ou* come the innocent

innocenter [inɔsɑ̃te] *vt* to clear, prove innocent

innombrable [inɔ̃bRabl] *adj* innumerable

innommable [inɔmabl] *adj* unspeakable

innover [inɔve] *vi:* **~ en matière d'art** to break new ground in the field of art

inoccupé, e [inɔkype] *adj* unoccupied

inodore [inɔdɔR] *adj* (*gaz*) odourless; (*fleur*) scentless

inoffensif, -ive [inɔfɑ̃sif, -iv] *adj* harmless, innocuous

inondation [inɔ̃dasjɔ̃] *nf* flooding *no pl*; (*torrent, eau*) flood

inonder [inɔ̃de] *vt* to flood; (*fig*) to inundate, overrun; **~ de** (*fig*) to flood *ou* swamp with

inopiné, e [inɔpine] *adj* unexpected, sudden

inopportun, e [inɔpɔRtœ̃, -yn] *adj* ill-timed, untimely; inappropriate; (*moment*) inopportune

inoubliable [inublijabl] *adj* unforgettable

inouï, e [inwi] *adj* unheard-of, extraordinary

inox [inɔks] *adj, nm* (= *inoxydable*) stainless (steel)

inqualifiable [ɛ̃kalifjabl] *adj* unspeakable

inquiet, -ète [ɛ̃kjɛ, -ɛt] *adj* (*par nature*) anxious; (*momentanément*) worried; **~ de qch/au sujet de qn** worried about sth/sb

inquiétant, e [ɛ̃kjetɑ̃, -ɑ̃t] *adj* worrying, disturbing

inquiéter [ɛ̃kjete] *vt* to worry, disturb; (*harceler*) to harass; **s'inquiéter** to worry, become anxious; **s'~ de** to worry about; (*s'enquérir de*) to inquire about

inquiétude [ɛ̃kjetyd] *nf* anxiety; **donner de l'~ ou des ~s à** to worry; **avoir de l'~ ou des ~s au sujet de** to feel anxious *ou* worried about

insaisissable [ɛ̃sezisabl] *adj* (*fugitif, ennemi*) elusive; (*différence, nuance*) imperceptible

insalubre [ɛ̃salybR] *adj* unhealthy, insalubrious

insatisfait, e [ɛ̃satisfɛ, -ɛt] *adj* (*non comblé*) unsatisfied; (: *passion, envie*) unfulfilled; (*mécontent*) dissatisfied

inscription [ɛ̃skRipsjɔ̃] *nf* (*sur un mur, écriteau etc*) inscription; (*à une institution: voir s'inscrire*) enrolment; registration

inscrire [ɛ̃skRiR] *vt* (*marquer: sur son calepin etc*) to note *ou* write down; (: *sur un mur, une affiche etc*) to write; (: *dans la pierre, le métal*) to inscribe; (*mettre: sur une liste, un budget etc*) to put down; (*enrôler: soldat*) to enlist; **~ qn à** (*club, école etc*) to enrol sb at; **s'inscrire** (*pour une excursion etc*) to put one's name down; **s'~ (à)** (*club, parti*) to join; (*université*) to register *ou* enrol (at); (*examen, concours*) to register *ou* enter (for); **s'~ dans** (*se situer: négociations etc*) to come within the scope of; **s'~ en faux contre** to deny (strongly); (*Jur*) to challenge

insecte [ɛ̃sɛkt] *nm* insect

insecticide [ɛ̃sɛktisid] *nm* insecticide

insensé, e [ɛ̃sɑ̃se] *adj* insane, mad

insensibiliser [ɛ̃sɑ̃sibilize] *vt* to anaesthetize; (*à une allergie*) to desensitize; **~ à qch** (*fig*) to cause to become insensitive to sth

insensible [ɛ̃sɑ̃sibl] *adj* (*nerf, membre*) numb; (*dur, indifférent*) insensitive; (*imperceptible*) imperceptible

inséparable [ɛ̃sepaRabl] *adj:* **~ (de)** inseparable (from) ▷ *nmpl:* **~s** (*oiseaux*) lovebirds

insigne [ɛ̃siɲ] *nm* (*d'un parti, club*) badge ▷ *adj* distinguished; **insignes** *nmpl* (*d'une fonction*) insignia *pl*

insignifiant, e [ɛ̃siɲifjɑ̃, -ɑ̃t] *adj* insignificant; (*somme, affaire, détail*) trivial, insignificant

insinuer [ɛ̃sinɥe] *vt* to insinuate, imply; **s'insinuer dans** *vi* to seep into; (*fig*) to worm one's way into, creep into

insipide [ɛ̃sipid] *adj* insipid

insister [ɛ̃siste] *vi* to insist; *(s'obstiner)* to keep on; ~ **sur** *(détail, note)* to stress; ~ **pour qch/ pour faire qch** to be insistent about sth/ about doing sth

insolation [ɛ̃sɔlasjɔ̃] *nf* (Méd) sunstroke *no pl*; *(ensoleillement)* period of sunshine

insolent, e [ɛ̃sɔlɑ̃, -ɑ̃t] *adj* insolent

insolite [ɛ̃sɔlit] *adj* strange, unusual

insomnie [ɛ̃sɔmni] *nf* insomnia *no pl*, sleeplessness *no pl*; **avoir des ~s** to sleep badly, suffer from insomnia

insonoriser [ɛ̃sɔnɔʀize] *vt* to soundproof

insouciant, e [ɛ̃susjɑ̃, -ɑ̃t] *adj* carefree; *(imprévoyant)* heedless; ~ **du danger** heedless of (the) danger

insoumis, e [ɛ̃sumi, -iz] *adj* *(caractère, enfant)* rebellious, refractory; *(contrée, tribu)* unsubdued; (Mil: *soldat*) absent without leave ▷ *nm* (Mil: *soldat*) absentee

insoupçonnable [ɛ̃supsɔnabl] *adj* unsuspected; *(personne)* above suspicion

insoupçonné, e [ɛ̃supsɔne] *adj* unsuspected

insoutenable [ɛ̃sutnabl] *adj* *(argument)* untenable; *(chaleur)* unbearable

inspecter [ɛ̃spɛkte] *vt* to inspect

inspecteur, -trice [ɛ̃spɛktœʀ, -tʀis] *nm/f* inspector; *(des assurances)* assessor; ~ **d'Académie** (regional) director of education; ~ **(de l'enseignement) primaire** primary school inspector; ~ **des finances** ≈ tax inspector (Brit), ≈ Internal Revenue Service agent (US); ~ **(de police)** (police) inspector

inspection [ɛ̃spɛksjɔ̃] *nf* inspection

inspirer [ɛ̃spiʀe] *vt (gén)* to inspire ▷ *vi* *(aspirer)* to breathe in; **s'inspirer de** *(artiste)* to draw one's inspiration from; *(tableau)* to be inspired by; ~ **qch à qn** *(œuvre, projet, action)* to inspire sb with sth; *(dégoût, crainte, horreur)* to fill sb with sth; **ça ne m'inspire pas** I'm not keen on the idea

instable [ɛ̃stabl] *adj* *(meuble, équilibre)* unsteady; *(population, temps)* unsettled; *(paix, régime, caractère)* unstable

installation [ɛ̃stalasjɔ̃] *nf* *(mise en place)* installation; putting in ou up; fitting out; settling in; *(appareils etc)* fittings *pl*, installations *pl*; **installations** *nfpl* installations; *(industrielles)* plant *sg*; *(de sport, dans un camping)* facilities; **l'~ électrique** wiring

installer [ɛ̃stale] *vt (loger)*: ~ **qn** to get sb settled, install sb; *(asseoir, coucher)* to settle (down); *(placer)* to put, place; *(meuble)* to put in; *(rideau, étagère, tente)* to put up; *(gaz, électricité etc)* to put in, install; *(appartement)* to fit out; *(aménager)*: ~ **une salle de bains dans une pièce** to fit out a room with a bathroom suite; **s'installer** *vi (s'établir: artisan, dentiste etc)* to set o.s. up; *(se loger)*: **s'~ à l'hôtel/chez qn** to move into a hotel/in with sb; *(emménager)* to settle in; *(sur un siège, à un emplacement)* to settle (down); (fig: *maladie, grève)* to take a firm hold ou grip

instance [ɛ̃stɑ̃s] *nf* (Jur: *procédure)* (legal) proceedings *pl*; (Admin: *autorité)* authority; **instances** *nfpl* *(prières)* entreaties; **affaire en** ~ matter pending; **courrier en** ~ mail ready for posting; **être en** ~ **de divorce** to be awaiting a divorce; **train en** ~ **de départ** train on the point of departure; **tribunal de première** ~ court of first instance; **en seconde** ~ on appeal

instant [ɛ̃stɑ̃] *nm* moment, instant; **dans un** ~ in a moment; **à l'** ~ this instant; **je l'ai vu à l'** ~ I've just this minute seen him, I saw him a moment ago; **à l'** ~ **(même) où** at the (very) moment that ou when, (just) as; **à chaque** ~, **à tout** ~ at any moment; constantly; **pour l'** ~ for the moment, for the time being; **par** ~**s** at times; **de tous les** ~**s** perpetual; **dès l'** ~ **où** ou **que** ... from the moment when ..., since that moment when ...

instantané, e [ɛ̃stɑ̃tane] *adj* *(lait, café)* instant; *(explosion, mort)* instantaneous ▷ *nm* snapshot

instar [ɛ̃staʀ]: **à l'** ~ **de** *prép* following the example of, like

instaurer [ɛ̃stɔʀe] *vt* to institute; *(couvre-feu)* to impose; **s'instaurer** *vi* to set o.s. up; *(collaboration, paix etc)* to be established; *(doute)* to set in

instinct [ɛ̃stɛ̃] *nm* instinct; **d'** ~ *(spontanément)* instinctively; ~ **grégaire** herd instinct; ~ **de conservation** instinct of self-preservation

instinctivement [ɛ̃stɛ̃ktivmɑ̃] *adv* instinctively

instit [ɛ̃stit] *(fam)* *nm/f* (primary school) teacher

instituer [ɛ̃stitɥe] *vt* to establish, institute; **s'~ défenseur d'une cause** to set o.s up as defender of a cause

institut [ɛ̃stity] *nm* institute; ~ **de beauté** beauty salon; ~ **médico-légal** mortuary; **I~ universitaire de technologie (IUT)** ≈ Institute of technology

instituteur, -trice [ɛ̃stitytœʀ, -tʀis] *nm/f* (primary (Brit) ou grade (US) school) teacher

institution [ɛ̃stitysjɔ̃] *nf* institution; *(collège)* private school; **institutions** *nfpl* *(structures politiques et sociales)* institutions

instructif, -ive [ɛ̃stʀyktif, -iv] *adj* instructive

instruction [ɛ̃stʀyksjɔ̃] *nf* *(enseignement, savoir)* education; (Jur) (preliminary) investigation and hearing; *(directive)* instruction; (Admin: *document)* directive; **instructions** *nfpl* instructions; *(mode d'emploi)* directions, instructions; ~ **civique** civics *sg*; ~ **primaire/publique** primary/public education; ~ **religieuse** religious instruction; ~ **professionnelle** vocational training

instruire [ɛ̃stʀɥiʀ] *vt* *(élèves)* to teach; *(recrues)* to train; (Jur: *affaire)* to conduct the investigation for; **s'instruire** to educate o.s.; **s'~ auprès de qn de qch** *(s'informer)* to find sth out from sb; ~ **qn de qch** (informer) to inform ou advise sb of sth; ~ **contre qn** (Jur) to investigate sb

instruit, e [ɛ̃stʀųi, -it] pp de **instruire** ▷ adj educated

instrument [ɛ̃stʀymɑ̃] nm instrument; ~ **à cordes/vent** stringed/wind instrument; ~ **de mesure** measuring instrument; ~ **de musique** musical instrument; ~ **de travail** (working) tool

insu [ɛ̃sy] nm: **à l'~ de qn** without sb knowing

insubmersible [ɛ̃sybmɛʀsibl] adj unsinkable

insuffisant, e [ɛ̃syfizɑ̃, -ɑ̃t] adj (en quantité) insufficient; (en qualité: élève, travail) inadequate; (sur une copie) poor

insulaire [ɛ̃sylɛʀ] adj island cpd; (attitude) insular

insuline [ɛ̃sylin] nf insulin

insulte [ɛ̃sylt] nf insult

insulter [ɛ̃sylte] vt to insult

insupportable [ɛ̃sypɔʀtabl] adj unbearable

insurger [ɛ̃syʀʒe]: **s'insurger** vi: **s'~ (contre)** to rise up ou rebel (against)

insurmontable [ɛ̃syʀmɔ̃tabl] adj (difficulté) insuperable; (aversion) unconquerable

insurrection [ɛ̃syʀɛksjɔ̃] nf insurrection, revolt

intact, e [ɛ̃takt] adj intact

intangible [ɛ̃tɑ̃ʒibl] adj intangible; (principe) inviolable

intarissable [ɛ̃taʀisabl] adj inexhaustible

intégral, e, -aux [ɛ̃tegʀal, -o] adj complete ▷ nf (Math) integral; (œuvres complètes) complete works; **texte ~** unabridged version; **bronzage ~** all-over suntan

intégralement [ɛ̃tegʀalmɑ̃] adv in full, fully

intégralité [ɛ̃tegʀalite] nf (d'une somme, d'un revenu) whole (ou full) amount; **dans son ~** in its entirety

intégrant, e [ɛ̃tegʀɑ̃, -ɑ̃t] adj: **faire partie ~e** to be an integral part of, be part and parcel of

intègre [ɛ̃tegʀ] adj perfectly honest, upright

intégrer [ɛ̃tegʀe] vt: ~ **qch à** ou **dans** to integrate sth into; **s'intégrer** vr: **s'~ à** ou **dans** to become integrated into; **bien s'~** to fit in

intégrisme [ɛ̃tegʀism] nm fundamentalism

intellectuel, le [ɛ̃telɛktɥɛl] adj, nm/f intellectual; (péj) highbrow

intelligence [ɛ̃teliʒɑ̃s] nf intelligence; (compréhension): **l'~ de** the understanding of; (complicité): **regard d'~** glance of complicity, meaningful ou knowing look; (accord): **vivre en bonne ~ avec qn** to be on good terms with sb; **intelligences** nfpl (Mil, fig) secret contacts; **être d'~** to have an understanding, ~ **artificielle** artificial intelligence (A.I.)

intelligent, e [ɛ̃teliʒɑ̃, -ɑ̃t] adj intelligent; (capable): ~ **en affaires** competent in business

intelligible [ɛ̃teliʒibl] adj intelligible

intempéries [ɛ̃tɑ̃peʀi] nfpl bad weather sg

intempestif, -ive [ɛ̃tɑ̃pestif, -iv] adj untimely

intenable [ɛ̃tnabl] adj unbearable

intendant, e [ɛ̃tɑ̃dɑ̃, -ɑ̃t] nm/f (Mil) quartermaster; (Scol) bursar; (d'une propriété) steward

intense [ɛ̃tɑ̃s] adj intense

intensif, -ive [ɛ̃tɑ̃sif, -iv] adj intensive; **cours ~** crash course; ~ **en main-d'œuvre** labour-intensive; ~ **en capital** capital-intensive

intenter [ɛ̃tɑ̃te] vt: ~ **un procès contre** ou **à qn** to start proceedings against sb

intention [ɛ̃tɑ̃sjɔ̃] nf intention; (Jur) intent; **avoir l'~ de faire** to intend to do, have the intention of doing; **dans l'~ de faire qch** with a view to doing sth; **à l'~ de** prép for; (renseignement) for the benefit ou information of; (film, ouvrage) aimed at; **à cette ~** with this aim in view; **sans ~** unintentionally; **faire qch sans mauvaise ~** to do sth without ill intent; **agir dans une bonne ~** to act with good intentions

intentionné, e [ɛ̃tɑ̃sjɔne] adj: **bien ~** well-meaning ou -intentioned; **mal ~** ill-intentioned

interactif, -ive [ɛ̃teʀaktif, -iv] adj (aussi Inform) interactive

intercalaire [ɛ̃teʀkalɛʀ] adj, nm: (feuillet) ~ insert; (fiche) ~ divider

intercaler [ɛ̃teʀkale] vt to insert; **s'intercaler entre** vi to come in between; to slip in between

intercepter [ɛ̃teʀsepte] vt to intercept; (lumière, chaleur) to cut off

interchangeable [ɛ̃teʀʃɑ̃ʒabl] adj interchangeable

interclasse [ɛ̃teʀklas] nm (Scol) break (between classes)

interdiction [ɛ̃teʀdiksjɔ̃] nf ban; ~ **de faire qch** ban on doing sth; ~ **de séjour** (Jur) order banning ex-prisoner from frequenting specified places; ~ **de fumer** no smoking

interdire [ɛ̃teʀdiʀ] vt to forbid; (Admin: stationnement, meeting, passage) to ban, prohibit; (: journal, livre) to ban; ~ **qch à qn** to forbid sb sth; ~ **à qn de faire** to forbid sb to do, prohibit sb from doing; (empêchement) to prevent ou preclude sb from doing; **s'interdire qch** vi (éviter) to refrain ou abstain from sth; (se refuser): **il s'interdit d'y penser** he doesn't allow himself to think about it

interdit, e [ɛ̃teʀdi, -it] pp de **interdire** ▷ adj (stupéfait) taken aback; (défendu) forbidden, prohibited ▷ nm interdict, prohibition; **film ~ aux moins de 18/12 ans** ≈ 18-/12A-rated film; **sens ~** one way; **stationnement ~** no parking; ~ **de chéquier** having cheque book facilities suspended; ~ **de séjour** subject to an "interdiction de séjour"

intéressant, e [ɛ̃teʀesɑ̃, -ɑ̃t] adj interesting; (avantageux) attractive; **faire l'~** to draw attention to o.s.

intéressé, e [ɛ̃terese] adj (parties) involved, concerned; (amitié, motifs) self-interested ▷ nm: **l'~** the interested party; **les ~s** those concerned ou involved

intéresser [ɛ̃terese] vt (captiver) to interest; (toucher) to be of interest ou concern to; (Admin: concerner) to affect, concern; (Comm: travailleur) to give a share in the profits to; (: partenaire) to interest (in the business); **s'intéresser à** vi to take an interest in, be interested in; **~ qn à qch** to get sb interested in sth

intérêt [ɛ̃terɛ] nm (aussi Comm) interest; (égoïsme) self-interest; **porter de l'~ à qn** to take an interest in sb; **agir par ~** to act out of self-interest; **avoir des ~s dans** (Comm) to have a financial interest ou a stake in; **avoir ~ à faire** to do well to do; **tu as ~ à accepter** it's in your interest to accept; **tu as ~ à te dépêcher** you'd better hurry; **il y a ~ à ...** it would be a good thing to ...; **~ composé** compound interest

intérieur, e [ɛ̃terjœr] adj (mur, escalier, poche) inside; (commerce, politique) domestic; (cour, calme, vie) inner; (navigation) inland ▷ nm (d'une maison, d'un récipient etc) inside; (d'un pays, aussi: décor, mobilier) interior; (Pol): **l'I~** (the Department of) the Interior, ≈ the Home Office (Brit); **à l'~ (de)** inside; (fig) within; **de l'~** (fig) from the inside; **en ~** (Ciné) in the studio; **vêtement d'~** indoor garment

intérieurement [ɛ̃terjœrmɑ̃] adv inwardly

intérim [ɛ̃terim] nm (période) interim period; (travail) temping; **agence d'~** temping agency; **assurer l'~ (de)** to deputize (for); **président par ~** interim president; **travailler en ~, faire de l'~** to temp

intérimaire [ɛ̃terimɛr] adj (directeur, ministre) acting; (secrétaire, personnel) temporary, interim ▷ nm/f (secrétaire etc) temporary, temp (Brit); (suppléant) deputy

interlocuteur, -trice [ɛ̃terlɔkytœr, -tris] nm/f speaker; (Pol): **valable representative**; **son ~** the person he ou she was speaking to

interloquer [ɛ̃terlɔke] vt to take aback

intermède [ɛ̃termɛd] nm interlude

intermédiaire [ɛ̃termedjɛr] adj intermediate; middle; half-way; (solution) temporary ▷ nm/f intermediary; (Comm) middleman; **sans ~** directly; **par l'~ de** through

interminable [ɛ̃terminabl] adj never-ending

intermittence [ɛ̃termitɑ̃s] nf: **par ~** intermittently, sporadically

internat [ɛ̃terna] nm (Scol) boarding school

international, e, -aux [ɛ̃ternasjɔnal, -o] adj, nm/f international

internaute [ɛ̃ternot] nm/f Internet user

interne [ɛ̃tɛrn] adj internal ▷ nm/f (Scol) boarder; (Méd) houseman (Brit), intern (US)

interner [ɛ̃tɛrne] vt (Pol) to intern; (Méd) to confine to a mental institution

Internet [ɛ̃tɛrnɛt] nm: **l'~** the Internet

interpeller [ɛ̃tɛrpele] vt (appeler) to call out to; (apostropher) to shout at; (Police) to take in for questioning; (Pol) to question; (concerner) to concern; **s'interpeller** vi to exchange insults

interphone [ɛ̃tɛrfɔn] nm intercom; (d'immeuble) entry phone

interposer [ɛ̃tɛrpoze] vt to interpose; **s'interposer** vi to intervene; **par personnes interposées** through a third party

interprétation [ɛ̃tɛrpretasjɔ̃] nf interpretation

interprète [ɛ̃tɛrprɛt] nm/f interpreter; (porte-parole) spokesman

interpréter [ɛ̃tɛrprete] vt to interpret; (jouer) to play; (chanter) to sing

interrogateur, -trice [ɛ̃terɔgatœr, -tris] adj questioning, inquiring ▷ nm/f (Scol) (oral) examiner

interrogatif, -ive [ɛ̃terɔgatif, -iv] adj (Ling) interrogative

interrogation [ɛ̃terɔgasjɔ̃] nf question; (Scol) (written ou oral) test

interrogatoire [ɛ̃terɔgatwar] nm (Police) questioning no pl; (Jur, aussi fig) cross-examination, interrogation

interroger [ɛ̃terɔʒe] vt to question; (Inform) to search; (Scol: candidat) to test; **~ qn (sur qch)** to question sb (about sth); **~ qn du regard** to look questioningly at sb, give sb a questioning look; **s'~ sur qch** to ask o.s. about sth, ponder (about) sth

interrompre [ɛ̃terɔ̃pr] vt (gén) to interrupt; (travail, voyage) to break off, interrupt; (négociations) to break off; (match) to stop; **s'interrompre** vi to break off

interrupteur [ɛ̃teryptœr] nm switch

interruption [ɛ̃terypsjɔ̃] nf interruption; (pause) break; **sans ~** without a break; **~ de grossesse** termination of pregnancy; **~ volontaire de grossesse** voluntary termination of pregnancy, abortion

intersection [ɛ̃tersɛksjɔ̃] nf intersection

interstice [ɛ̃terstis] nm crack, slit

interurbain [ɛ̃teryrbɛ̃] nm (Tél) long-distance call service ▷ adj long-distance

intervalle [ɛ̃terval] nm (espace) space; (de temps) interval; **dans l'~** in the meantime; **à deux jours d'~** two days apart; **à ~s rapprochés** at close intervals; **par ~s** at intervals

intervenir [ɛ̃tervənir] vi (gén) to intervene; (survenir) to take place; (faire une conférence) to give a talk ou lecture; **~ auprès de/en faveur de qn** to intervene with/on behalf of sb; **la police a dû ~** police had to step in ou intervene; **les médecins ont dû ~** the doctors had to operate

intervention [ɛ̃tervɑ̃sjɔ̃] nf intervention; (conférence) talk, paper; (discours) speech; **~ (chirurgicale)** operation

intervertir [ɛ̃tɛʀvɛʀtiʀ] *vt* to invert (the order of), reverse

interview [ɛ̃tɛʀvju] *nf* interview

interviewer [ɛ̃tɛʀvjuve] *vt* to interview ▷ *nm* [ɛ̃tɛʀvjuvœʀ] (*journaliste*) interviewer

intestin, e [ɛ̃tɛstɛ̃, -in] *adj* internal ▷ *nm* intestine; ~ **grêle** small intestine

intime [ɛ̃tim] *adj* intimate; (*vie, journal*) private; (*convictions*) inmost; (*dîner, cérémonie*) held among friends, quiet ▷ *nm/f* close friend; **un journal** ~ a diary

intimider [ɛ̃timide] *vt* to intimidate

intimité [ɛ̃timite] *nf* intimacy; (*vie privée*) privacy; private life; **dans l'**~ in private; (*sans formalités*) with only a few friends, quietly

intitulé [ɛ̃tityle] *nm* title

intolérable [ɛ̃tɔleʀabl] *adj* intolerable

intox [ɛ̃tɔks] (*fam*) *nf* brainwashing

intoxication [ɛ̃tɔksikasjɔ̃] *nf* poisoning *no pl*; (*toxicomanie*) drug addiction; (*fig*) brainwashing; ~ **alimentaire** food poisoning

intoxiquer [ɛ̃tɔksike] *vt* to poison; (*fig*) to brainwash; **s'intoxiquer** to poison o.s.

intraduisible [ɛ̃tʀadɥizibl] *adj* untranslatable; (*fig*) inexpressible

intraitable [ɛ̃tʀɛtabl] *adj* inflexible, uncompromising

intranet [ɛ̃tʀanɛt] *nm* intranet

intransigeant, e [ɛ̃tʀɑ̃ziʒɑ̃, -ɑ̃t] *adj* intransigent; (*morale, passion*) uncompromising

intransitif, -ive [ɛ̃tʀɑ̃zitif, -iv] *adj* (*Ling*) intransitive

intrépide [ɛ̃tʀepid] *adj* dauntless, intrepid

intrigue [ɛ̃tʀig] *nf* intrigue; (*scénario*) plot

intriguer [ɛ̃tʀige] *vi* to scheme ▷ *vt* to puzzle, intrigue

intrinsèque [ɛ̃tʀɛ̃sɛk] *adj* intrinsic

introduction [ɛ̃tʀɔdyksjɔ̃] *nf* introduction; **paroles/chapitre d'**~ introductory words/ chapter; **lettre/mot d'**~ letter/note of introduction

introduire [ɛ̃tʀɔdɥiʀ] *vt* to introduce; (*visiteur*) to show in; (*aiguille, clef*): ~ **qch dans** to insert ou introduce sth into; (*personne*): ~ **à qch** to introduce to sth; (: *présenter*): ~ **qn à qn/dans un club** to introduce sb to sb/to a club; **s'introduire** *vi* (*techniques, usages*) to be introduced; **s'**~ **dans** to gain entry into; (*dans un groupe*) to get o.s. accepted into; (*eau, fumée*) to get into; ~ **au clavier** to key in

introuvable [ɛ̃tʀuvabl] *adj* which cannot be found; (*Comm*) unobtainable

introverti, e [ɛ̃tʀɔvɛʀti] *nm/f* introvert

intrus, e [ɛ̃tʀy, -yz] *nm/f* intruder

intrusion [ɛ̃tʀyzjɔ̃] *nf* intrusion; (*ingérence*) interference

intuition [ɛ̃tɥisjɔ̃] *nf* intuition; **avoir une** ~ to have a feeling; **avoir l'**~ **de qch** to have an intuition of sth; **avoir l'**~ **que** to have intuition

inusable [inyzabl] *adj* hard-wearing

inusité, e [inyzite] *adj* rarely used

inutile [inytil] *adj* useless; (*superflu*) unnecessary

inutilement [inytilmɑ̃] *adv* needlessly

inutilisable [inytilizabl] *adj* unusable

invalide [ɛ̃valid] *adj* disabled ▷ *nm/f*: ~ **de guerre** disabled ex-serviceman; ~ **du travail** industrially disabled person

invariable [ɛ̃vaʀjabl] *adj* invariable

invasion [ɛ̃vazjɔ̃] *nf* invasion

invectiver [ɛ̃vɛktive] *vt* to hurl abuse at ▷ *vi*: ~ **contre** to rail against

invendable [ɛ̃vɑ̃dabl] *adj* unsaleable, unmarketable

invendu, e [ɛ̃vɑ̃dy] *adj* unsold ▷ *nm* return; **invendus** *nmpl* unsold goods

inventaire [ɛ̃vɑ̃tɛʀ] *nm* inventory; (*Comm*: *liste*) stocklist; (: *opération*) stocktaking *no pl*; (*fig*) survey; **faire un** ~ to make an inventory; (*Comm*) to take stock; **faire** *ou* **procéder à l'**~ to take stock

inventer [ɛ̃vɑ̃te] *vt* to invent; (*subterfuge*) to devise, invent; (*histoire, excuse*) to make up, invent; ~ **de faire** to hit on the idea of doing

inventeur, -trice [ɛ̃vɑ̃tœʀ, -tʀis] *nm/f* inventor

inventif, -ive [ɛ̃vɑ̃tif, -iv] *adj* inventive

invention [ɛ̃vɑ̃sjɔ̃] *nf* invention; (*imagination, inspiration*) inventiveness

inverse [ɛ̃vɛʀs] *adj* (*ordre*) reverse; (*sens*) opposite; (*rapport*) inverse ▷ *nm* reverse; inverse; **l'**~ the opposite; **dans l'ordre** ~ in the reverse order; **en proportion** ~ in inverse proportion; **dans le sens** ~ **des aiguilles d'une montre** anti-clockwise; **en sens** ~ in (ou from) the opposite direction; **à l'**~ conversely

inversement [ɛ̃vɛʀsəmɑ̃] *adv* conversely

inverser [ɛ̃vɛʀse] *vt* to reverse, invert; (*Élec*) to reverse

investigation [ɛ̃vɛstigasjɔ̃] *nf* investigation, inquiry

investir [ɛ̃vɛstiʀ] *vt* to invest; ~ **qn de** (*d'une fonction, d'un pouvoir*) to vest ou invest sb with; **s'investir** *vi* (*Psych*) to involve o.s.; ~ **qn de** vest ou invest sb with; **s'**~ **dans** to put a lot into

investissement [ɛ̃vɛstismɑ̃] *nm* investment; (*Psych*) involvement

investiture [ɛ̃vɛstityʀ] *nf* investiture; (*à une élection*) nomination

invétéré, e [ɛ̃veteʀe] *adj* (*habitude*) ingrained; (*bavard, buveur*) inveterate

invisible [ɛ̃vizibl] *adj* invisible; (*fig*: *personne*) not available

invitation [ɛ̃vitasjɔ̃] *nf* invitation; **à/sur l'**~ **de qn** at/on sb's invitation; **carte/lettre d'**~ invitation card/letter

invité, e [ɛ̃vite] *nm/f* guest

inviter [ɛ̃vite] *vt* to invite; ~ **qn à faire qch** to invite sb to do sth; (*chose*) to induce ou tempt sb to do sth

invivable [ɛ̃vivabl] *adj* unbearable, impossible

involontaire [ɛ̃vɔlɔ̃tɛʀ] *adj* (*mouvement*)

involuntary; (*insulte*) unintentional; (*complice*) unwitting

invoquer [ɛ̃vɔke] *vt* (*Dieu, muse*) to call upon, invoke; (*prétexte*) to put forward (as an excuse); (*témoignage*) to call upon; (*loi, texte*) to refer to; **~ la clémence de qn** to beg sb ou appeal to sb for clemency

invraisemblable [ɛ̃vʀɛsɑ̃blabl] *adj* (*fait, nouvelle*) unlikely, improbable; (*bizarre*) incredible

iode [jɔd] *nm* iodine

irai *etc* [iʀe] *vb voir* **aller**

Irak [iʀak] *nm*: **l'~** Iraq ou Irak

irakien, ne [iʀakjɛ̃, -ɛn] *adj* Iraqi ⊳ *nm/f*: **I~, ne** Iraqi

Iran [iʀɑ̃] *nm*: **l'~** Iran

iranien, ne [iʀanjɛ̃, -ɛn] *adj* Iranian ⊳ *nm* (*Ling*) Iranian ⊳ *nm/f*: **I~, ne** Iranian

irascible [iʀasibl] *adj* short-tempered, irascible

irions *etc* [iʀjɔ̃] *vb voir* **aller**

iris [iʀis] *nm* iris

irlandais, e [iʀlɑ̃dɛ, -ɛz] *adj, nm* (*Ling*) Irish ⊳ *nm/f*: **I~, e** Irishman/woman; **les I~** the Irish

Irlande [iʀlɑ̃d] *nf*: **l'~** (*pays*) Ireland; **la République d'~** the Irish Republic, the Republic of Ireland, Eire; **l'~ du Nord** Northern Ireland, Ulster; **~ du Sud** Southern Ireland, Irish Republic, Eire; **la mer d'~** the Irish Sea

ironie [iʀɔni] *nf* irony

ironique [iʀɔnik] *adj* ironical

ironiser [iʀɔnize] *vi* to be ironical

irons *etc* [iʀɔ̃] *vb voir* **aller**

irradier [iʀadje] *vi* to radiate ⊳ *vt* to irradiate

irraisonné, e [iʀezɔne] *adj* irrational, unreasoned

irrationnel, le [iʀasjɔnɛl] *adj* irrational

irréalisable [iʀealizabl] *adj* unrealizable; (*projet*) impracticable

irrécupérable [iʀekypeʀabl] *adj* unreclaimable, beyond repair; (*personne*) beyond redemption ou recall

irréductible [iʀedyktibl] *adj* indomitable, implacable; (*Math: fraction, équation*) irreducible

irréel, le [iʀeɛl] *adj* unreal

irréfléchi, e [iʀeflefi] *adj* thoughtless

irrégularité [iʀegylaʀite] *nf* irregularity; (*de travail, d'effort, de qualité*) unevenness *no pl*

irrégulier, -ière [iʀegylje, -jɛʀ] *adj* irregular; (*surface, rythme, écriture*) uneven, irregular; (*travail, effort, qualité*) uneven; (*élève, athlète*) erratic

irrémédiable [iʀemedjabl] *adj* irreparable

irremplaçable [iʀɑ̃plasabl] *adj* irreplaceable

irréparable [iʀepaʀabl] *adj* beyond repair, irreparable; (*fig*) irreparable

irréprochable [iʀepʀɔfabl] *adj* irreproachable, beyond reproach; (*tenue, toilette*) impeccable

irrésistible [iʀezistibl] *adj* irresistible;

(*preuve, logique*) compelling; (*amusant*) hilarious

irrésolu, e [iʀezɔly] *adj* irresolute

irrespectueux, -euse [iʀɛspɛktɥø, -øz] *adj* disrespectful

irrespirable [iʀɛspiʀabl] *adj* unbreathable; (*fig*) oppressive, stifling

irresponsable [iʀɛspɔ̃sabl] *adj* irresponsible

irriguer [iʀige] *vt* to irrigate

irritable [iʀitabl] *adj* irritable

irriter [iʀite] *vt* (*agacer*) to irritate, annoy; (*Méd: enflammer*) to irritate; **s'~ contre qn/de qch** to get annoyed ou irritated with sb/at sth

irruption [iʀypsjɔ̃] *nf* irruption *no pl*; **faire ~ dans** to burst into; **faire ~ chez qn** to burst in on sb

Islam [islam] *nm*: **l'~** Islam

islamique [islamik] *adj* Islamic

islamiste [islamist] *adj, nm/f* Islamic

islamophobie *nf* Islamophobia

Islande [islɑ̃d] *nf*: **l'~** Iceland

isolant, e [izɔlɑ̃, -ɑ̃t] *adj* insulating; (*insonorisant*) soundproofing ⊳ *nm* insulator

isolation [izɔlasjɔ̃] *nf* insulation; **~ thermique** thermal insulation; **~ acoustique** soundproofing

isolé, e [izɔle] *adj* isolated; (*Élec*) insulated; (*contre le froid*) insulated

isoler [izɔle] *vt* to isolate; (*prisonnier*) to put in solitary confinement; (*ville*) to cut off, isolate; (*Élec*) to insulate; (*contre le froid*) to insulate; **s'isoler** *vi* to isolate o.s.

isoloir [izɔlwaʀ] *nm* polling booth

Israël [isʀaɛl] *nm*: **l'~** Israel

israélien, ne [isʀaeljɛ̃, -ɛn] *adj* Israeli ⊳ *nm/f*: **I~, ne** Israeli

israélite [isʀaelit] *adj* Jewish; (*dans l'Ancien Testament*) Israelite ⊳ *nm/f*: **I~** Jew/Jewess; Israelite

issu, e [isy] *adj*: **~ de** (*né de*) descended from; (*fig: résultant de*) stemming from ⊳ *nf* (*ouverture, sortie*) exit; (*solution*) way out, solution; (*dénouement*) outcome; **à l'~e de** at the conclusion ou close of; **rue sans ~e, voie sans ~e** dead end, no through road (*Brit*), no outlet (*US*); **~e de secours** emergency exit

Italie [itali] *nf*: **l'~** Italy

italien, ne [italjɛ̃, -ɛn] *adj* Italian ⊳ *nm* (*Ling*) Italian ⊳ *nm/f*: **I~, ne** Italian

italique [italik] *nm*: **en ~(s)** in italics

itinéraire [itineʀɛʀ] *nm* itinerary, route; **~ bis** alternative route

IUT *sigle m* = **Institut universitaire de technologie**

IVG *sigle f* (= *interruption volontaire de grossesse*) abortion

ivoire [ivwaʀ] *nm* ivory

ivre [ivʀ] *adj* drunk; **~ de** (*colère*) wild with; (*bonheur*) drunk ou intoxicated with; **~ mort** dead drunk

ivresse [ivʀɛs] *nf* drunkenness; (*euphorie*) intoxication

ivrogne [ivʀɔɲ] *nm/f* drunkard

J

j' [ʒ] *pron voir* **je**

jacasser [ʒakase] *vi* to chatter

jacinthe [ʒasɛ̃t] *nf* hyacinth; **~ des bois** bluebell

jadis [ʒadis] *adv* in times past, formerly

jaillir [ʒajiʀ] *vi* (*liquide*) to spurt out, gush out; (*lumière*) to flood out; (*fig*) to rear up; (*cris, réponses*) to burst out

jais [ʒɛ] *nm* jet; (**d'un noir**) **de ~** jet-black

jalousie [ʒaluzi] *nf* jealousy; (*store*) (venetian) blind

jaloux, -ouse [ʒalu, -uz] *adj* jealous; **être ~ de qn/qch** to be jealous of sb/sth

jamaïquain, e [ʒamaikɛ̃, -ɛn] *adj* Jamaican ▷ *nm/f*: **J~, e** Jamaican

Jamaïque [ʒamaik] *nf*: **la ~** Jamaica

jamais [ʒamɛ] *adv* never; (*sans négation*) ever; **ne ... ~** never; **~ de la vie!** never!; **si ... ~** if ever ...; **à (tout) ~, pour ~** for ever, for ever and ever; **je ne suis ~ allé en Espagne** I've never been to Spain

jambe [ʒɑ̃b] *nf* leg; **à toutes ~s** as fast as one's legs can carry one

jambon [ʒɑ̃bɔ̃] *nm* ham

jambonneau, x [ʒɑ̃bɔno] *nm* knuckle of ham

jante [ʒɑ̃t] *nf* (wheel) rim

janvier [ʒɑ̃vje] *nm* January; *voir aussi* **juillet**

Japon [ʒapɔ̃] *nm*: **le ~** Japan

japonais, e [ʒapɔnɛ, -ɛz] *adj* Japanese ▷ *nm* (*Ling*) Japanese ▷ *nm/f*: **J~, e** Japanese

japper [ʒape] *vi* to yap, yelp

jaquette [ʒakɛt] *nf* (*de cérémonie*) morning coat; (*de femme*) jacket; (*de livre*) dust cover, (dust) jacket

jardin [ʒaʀdɛ̃] *nm* garden; **~ d'acclimatation** zoological gardens *pl*; **~ botanique** botanical gardens *pl*; **~ d'enfants** nursery school; **~ potager** vegetable garden; **~ public** (public) park, public gardens *pl*; **~s suspendus** hanging gardens; **~ zoologique** zoological gardens

jardinage [ʒaʀdinaʒ] *nm* gardening

jardiner [ʒaʀdine] *vi* to garden, do some gardening

jardinier, -ière [ʒaʀdinje, -jɛʀ] *nm/f* gardener ▷ *nf* (*de fenêtre*) window box; **jardinière d'enfants** nursery school teacher; **jardinière (de légumes)** (*Culin*) mixed vegetables

jargon [ʒaʀgɔ̃] *nm* (*charabia*) gibberish; (*publicitaire, scientifique etc*) jargon

jarret [ʒaʀɛ] *nm* back of knee; (*Culin*) knuckle, shin

jarretelle [ʒaʀtɛl] *nf* suspender (*Brit*), garter (*US*)

jarretière [ʒaʀtjɛʀ] *nf* garter

jaser [ʒaze] *vi* to chatter, prattle; (*indiscrètement*) to gossip

jatte [ʒat] *nf* basin, bowl

jauge [ʒoʒ] *nf* (*capacité*) capacity, tonnage; (*instrument*) gauge; **~ (de niveau) d'huile** (*Auto*) dipstick

jaune [ʒon] *adj, nm* yellow ▷ *nm/f* Asiatic; (*briseur de grève*) blackleg ▷ *adv* (*fam*): **rire ~** to laugh on the other side of one's face; **~ d'œuf** (egg) yolk

jaunir [ʒoniʀ] *vi, vt* to turn yellow

jaunisse [ʒonis] *nf* jaundice

Javel [ʒavɛl] *nf voir* **eau**

javelot [ʒavlo] *nm* javelin; (*Sport*): **faire du ~** to throw the javelin

J.-C. *abr* = **Jésus-Christ**

je, j' [ʒə, ʒ] *pron* I

jean [dʒin] *nm* jeans *pl*

Jésus-Christ [ʒezykʀi(st)] *n* Jesus Christ; **600 avant/après ~** 600 B.C./A.D.

jet¹ [ʒɛ] *nm* (*lancer: action*) throwing *no pl*; (*résultat*) throw; (*jaillissement: d'eaux*) jet; (*de sang*) spurt; (*de tuyau*) nozzle; (*fig*): **premier ~** (*ébauche*) rough outline; **arroser au ~** to hose; **d'un (seul) ~** (*d'un seul coup*) in one (*ou* at) one go; **du premier ~** at the first attempt *ou* shot; **~ d'eau** spray; (*fontaine*) fountain

jet² [dʒɛt] *nm* (*avion*) jet

jetable [ʒətabl] *adj* disposable

jetée [ʒəte] *nf* jetty; (*grande*) pier

jeter [ʒəte] *vt* (*gén*) to throw; (*se défaire de*) to throw away *ou* out; (*son, lueur etc*) to give out; **~ qch à qn** to throw sth to sb; (*de façon agressive*) to throw sth at sb; (*Navig*): **~ l'ancre** to cast anchor; **~ un coup d'œil (à)** to take a look (at); **~ les bras en avant/la tête en arrière** to throw one's arms forward/one's head back(ward); **~ l'effroi parmi** to spread fear among; **~ un sort à qn** to cast a spell on sb; **~ qn dans la misère** to reduce sb to poverty; **~ qn dehors/en prison** to throw sb out/into prison; **~ l'éponge** (fig) to throw in the towel; **~ des fleurs à qn** (fig) to say lovely things to sb; **la pierre à qn** (accuser, blâmer) to accuse sb; **se ~ sur** to throw o.s. onto; **se ~ dans** (fleuve) to flow into; **se ~ par la fenêtre** to throw o.s. out of the window; **se ~ à l'eau** (fig) to take the plunge

jeton [ʒətɔ̃] nm (au jeu) counter; (de téléphone) token; **~s de présence** (director's) fees

jette etc [ʒɛt] vb voir**jeter**

jeu, x [ʒø] nm (divertissement, Tech: d'une pièce) play; (défini par des règles, Tennis: partie, Football etc: façon de jouer) game; (Théât etc) acting; (fonctionnement) working, interplay; (série d'objets, jouet) set; (Cartes) hand; (au casino): **le ~** gambling; **cacher son ~** (fig) to keep one's cards hidden, conceal one's hand; **c'est un ~ d'enfant!** (fig) it's child's play!; **en ~** at stake; at work; (Football) in play; **remettre en ~** to throw in; **entrer/mettre en ~** to come/bring into play; **par ~** (pour s'amuser) for fun; **d'entrée de ~** (tout de suite, dès le début) from the outset; **entrer dans le ~/le ~ de qn** (fig) to play the game/sb's game; **jouer gros ~** to play for high stakes; **se piquer/se prendre au ~** to get excited over/get caught up in the game; **~ d'arcade** video game; **~ de boules** game of bowls; (endroit) bowling pitch; (boules) set of bowls; **~ de cartes** card game; (paquet) pack of cards; **~ de construction** building set; **~ d'échecs** chess set; **~ d'écritures** (Comm) paper transaction; **~ électronique** electronic game; **de hasard** game of chance; **~ de mots** pun; **le ~ de l'oie** snakes and ladders sg; **~ d'orgue(s)** organ stop; **~ de patience** puzzle; **~ de physionomie** facial expressions pl; **~ de société** board game; **~ télévisé** television quiz; **~ vidéo** video game; **~x de lumière** lighting effects; **J~x olympiques (JO)** Olympic Games

jeudi [ʒødi] nm Thursday; **~ saint** Maundy Thursday; voir aussi **lundi**

jeun [ʒœ̃]: **à ~** adv on an empty stomach; **être à ~** to have eaten nothing; **rester à ~** not to eat anything

jeune [ʒœn] adj young ▷ adv: **faire/s'habiller ~** to look/dress young; **les ~s** young people, the young; **~ fille** nf girl; **~ homme** nm young man; **~ loup** nm (Pol, Écon) young go-getter; **~ premier** leading man; **~s gens** nmpl young people; **~s mariés** nmpl newly weds

jeûne [ʒøn] nm fast

jeunesse [ʒœnɛs] nf youth; (aspect) youthfulness; (jeunes) young people pl, youth

joaillerie [ʒɔajʀi] nf jewel trade; jewellery (Brit), jewelry (US)

joaillier, -ière [ʒɔaje, -jɛʀ] nm/f jeweller

(Brit), jeweler (US)

jogging [dʒɔgiŋ] nm jogging; (survêtement) tracksuit (Brit), sweatsuit (US); **faire du ~** to go jogging, jog

joie [ʒwa] nf joy

joindre [ʒwɛ̃dʀ] vt to join; **~ qch à** (à une lettre) to enclose sth with; (contacter) to contact, get in touch with; **~ un fichier à un mail** (Inform) to attach a file to an email; **~ les mains/talons** to put one's hands/heels together; **~ les deux bouts** (fig: du mois) to make ends meet; **se joindre** (mains etc) to come together; **se ~ à qn** to join sb; **se ~ à qch** to join in sth

joint, e [ʒwɛ̃, -ɛ̃t] pp de **joindre** ▷ adj: **~ (à)** (lettre, paquet) attached (to), enclosed (with); **pièce ~e** (de lettre) enclosure; (de mail) attachment ▷ nm joint; (ligne) join; (de ciment etc) pointing no pl; **chercher/trouver le ~** (fig) to look for/come up with the answer; **~ de cardan** cardan joint; **~ de culasse** cylinder head gasket; **~ de robinet** washer; **~ universel** universal joint

joker [ʒɔkɛʀ] nm (Cartes) joker; (Inform): **(caractère) ~** wild card

joli, e [ʒɔli] adj pretty, attractive; **une ~e somme/situation** a nice little sum/ situation; **un ~ gâchis** etc a nice mess etc; **c'est du ~!** (ironique) that's very nice!; **tout ça, c'est bien ~ mais ...** that's all very well but ...

jonc [ʒɔ̃] nm (bot)rush; (bague, bracelet) band

jonction [ʒɔ̃ksjɔ̃] nf joining; **(point de) ~** (de routes) junction; (de fleuves) confluence; **opérer une ~** (Mil etc) to rendez-vous

jongleur, -euse [ʒɔ̃glœʀ, -øz] nm/f juggler

jonquille [ʒɔ̃kij] nf daffodil

Jordanie [ʒɔʀdani] nf: **la ~** Jordan

joue [ʒu] nf cheek; **mettre en ~** to take aim at

jouer [ʒwe] vt (partie, carte, coup, Mus: morceau) to play; (somme d'argent, réputation) to stake, wager; (pièce, rôle) to perform; (film) to show; (simuler: sentiment) to affect, feign ▷ vi to play; (Théât, Ciné) to act, perform; (au casino) to gamble; (bois, porte: se voiler) to warp; (clef, pièce: avoir du jeu) to be loose; (entrer ou être en jeu) to come into play, come into it; **~ sur** (miser) to gamble on; **~ de** (Mus) to play; **~ du couteau/des coudes** to use knives/one's elbows; **~ à** (jeu, sport, roulette) to play; **~ au héros** to act ou play the hero; **~ avec** (risquer) to gamble with; **se ~ de** (difficultés) to make light of; **se ~ de qn** to deceive ou dupe sb; **~ un tour à qn** to play a trick on sb; **~ la comédie** (fig) to put on an act, put it on; **~ aux courses** to back horses, bet on horses; **~ à la baisse/ hausse** (Bourse) to play for a fall/rise; **~ serré** to play a close game; **~ de malchance** to be dogged with ill-luck; **~ sur les mots** to play with words; **à toi/nous de ~** it's your/our go ou turn; **bien joué!** well done!; **on joue Hamlet au théâtre X** Hamlet is on at the X theatre

jouet [ʒwɛ] nm toy; **être le ~ de** (illusion etc) to be the victim of

joueur, -euse [ʒwœʀ, -øz] nm/f player ▷ adj (enfant, chat) playful; **être beau/mauvais ~** to be a good/bad loser

joufflu, e [ʒufly] adj chubby(-cheeked)

joug [ʒu] nm yoke

jouir [ʒwiʀ] vi (sexe: fam) to come ▷ vt: **~ de** to enjoy

jouissance [ʒwisɑ̃s] nf pleasure; (Jur) use

joujou [ʒuʒu] nm (fam) toy

jour [ʒuʀ] nm day; (opposé à la nuit) day, daytime; (clarté) daylight; (fig: aspect): **sous un ~ favorable/nouveau** in a favourable/ new light; (ouverture) opening; (Couture) openwork no pl; **de ~** (crème, service) day cpd; **travailler de ~** to work during the day; **voyager de ~** to travel by day; **au ~ le ~** from day to day; **de nos ~s** these days, nowadays; **tous les ~** every day; **de ~ en ~** day by day; **d'un ~ à l'autre** from one day to the next; **du ~ au lendemain** overnight; **il fait ~** it's daylight; **en plein ~** in broad daylight; **au ~** in daylight; **au petit ~** at daybreak; **au grand ~** (fig) in the open; **mettre au ~** to disclose, uncover; **être à ~** to be up to date; **mettre à ~** to bring up to date, update; **mise à ~** updating; **donner le ~ à** to give birth to; **voir le ~** to be born; **se faire ~** (fig) to become clear; **~ férié** public holiday; **le ~ J** D-day; **~ ouvrable** working day

journal, -aux [ʒuʀnal, -o] nm (news)paper; (personnel) journal; (intime) diary; **~ de bord** log; **~ de mode** fashion magazine; **le J~ officiel (de la République française) (JO)** bulletin giving details of laws and official announcements; **~ parlé/télévisé** radio/ television news sg

journalier, -ière [ʒuʀnalje, -jɛʀ] adj daily; (banal) everyday ▷ nm day labourer

journalisme [ʒuʀnalism] nm journalism

journaliste [ʒuʀnalist] nm/f journalist

journée [ʒuʀne] nf day; **la ~ continue** the 9 to 5 working day (with short lunch break)

journellement [ʒuʀnɛlmɑ̃] adv (tous les jours) daily; (souvent) every day

joyau, x [ʒwajo] nm gem, jewel

joyeux, -euse [ʒwajø, -øz] adj joyful, merry; **~ Noël!** Merry ou Happy Christmas!; **joyeuses Pâques!** Happy Easter!; **~ anniversaire!** many happy returns!

jubiler [ʒybile] vi to be jubilant, exult

jucher [ʒyʃe] vt: **~ qch sur** to perch sth (up)on ▷ vi (oiseau): **~ sur** to perch (up)on; **se ~ sur** to perch o.s. (up)on

judas [ʒyda] nm (trou) spy-hole

judiciaire [ʒydisjɛʀ] adj judicial

judicieux, -euse [ʒydisjø, -øz] adj judicious

judo [ʒydo] nm judo

juge [ʒyʒ] nm judge; **~ d'instruction** examining (Brit) ou committing (US) magistrate; **~ de paix** justice of the peace;

~ de touche linesman

jugé [ʒyʒe]: **au ~** adv by guesswork

jugement [ʒyʒmɑ̃] nm judgment; (Jur: au pénal) sentence; (: au civil) decision; **~ de valeur** value judgment

jugeote [ʒyʒɔt] nf (fam) gumption

juger [ʒyʒe] vt to judge; (estimer) to consider ▷ nm: **au ~** by guesswork; **~ qn/qch satisfaisant** to consider sb/sth (to be) satisfactory; **~ que** to think ou consider that; **~ bon de faire** to consider it a good idea to do, see fit to do; **~ de** vt to judge; **jugez de ma surprise** imagine my surprise

juif, -ive [ʒɥif, -iv] adj Jewish ▷ nm/f: **J~, ive** Jew/Jewess ou Jewish woman

juillet [ʒɥijɛ] nm July; **le premier ~** the first of July (Brit), July first (US); **le deux/onze ~** the second/eleventh of July, July second/ eleventh; **il est venu le 5 ~** he came on 5th July ou July 5th; **en ~** in July; **début/fin ~** at the beginning/end of July; see note

○ LE 14 JUILLET

Le 14 juillet is a national holiday in France and commemorates the storming of the Bastille during the French Revolution. Throughout the country there are celebrations, which feature parades, music, dancing and firework displays. In Paris a military parade along the Champs-Élysées is attended by the President.

juin [ʒɥɛ̃] nm June; voir aussi **juillet**

jumeau, -elle, x [ʒymo, -ɛl] adj, nm/f twin; **maisons jumelles** semidetached houses

jumelage [ʒymlaʒ] nm twinning

jumeler [ʒymle] vt to twin; **roues jumelées** double wheels; **billets de loterie jumelés** double series lottery tickets; **pari jumelé** double bet

jumelle [ʒymɛl] adj f, nf voir **jumeau** ▷ vb voir **jumeler**

jument [ʒymɑ̃] nf mare

jungle [ʒɔ̃gl] nf jungle

jupe [ʒyp] nf skirt

jupon [ʒypɔ̃] nm waist slip ou petticoat

juré, e [ʒyʀe] nm/f juror ▷ adj: **ennemi ~** sworn ou avowed enemy

jurer [ʒyʀe] vt (obéissance etc) to swear, vow ▷ vi (dire des jurons) to swear, curse; (dissoner): **~ (avec)** to clash (with); (s'engager): **~ de faire/ que** to swear ou vow to do/that; (affirmer): **~ que** to swear ou vouch that; **~ de qch** (s'en porter garant) to swear to sth; **ils se jurent que par lui** they swear by him; **je vous jure!** honestly!

juridique [ʒyʀidik] adj legal

juron [ʒyʀɔ̃] nm curse, swearword

jury [ʒyʀi] nm (Jur) jury; (Art, Sport) panel of judges; (Scol) board (of examiners), jury

jus [ʒy] nm juice; (de viande) gravy, (meat) juice; **~ de fruits** fruit juice; **~ de raisin/tomates** grape/tomato juice

jusque [ʒysk]: **jusqu'à** prép (endroit) as far as, (up) to; (moment) until, till; (limite) up to; **~ sur/dans** up to, as far as; (y compris) even on/in; **~ vers** until about; **jusqu'à ce que** conj until; **~-là** (temps) until then; (espace) up to there; **jusqu'ici** (temps) until now; (espace) up to here; **jusqu'à présent** ou **maintenant** until now, so far; **jusqu'où?** how far?

justaucorps [ʒystokɔʀ] nm inv (Danse, Sport) leotard

juste [ʒyst] adj (équitable) just, fair; (légitime) just, justified; (exact, vrai) right; (pertinent) apt; (étroit, insuffisant) tight; (insuffisant) on the short side ▷ adv right; tight; (chanter) in tune; (seulement) just; **~ assez/au-dessus** just enough/above; **pouvoir tout ~ faire** to be only just able to do; **au ~** exactly, actually; **comme de ~** of course, naturally; **le ~ milieu** the happy medium; **c'était ~** it was a close thing; **à ~ titre** rightfully

justement [ʒystəmɑ̃] adv rightly; justly; (précisément) just, precisely; **c'est ~ ce qu'il fallait faire** that's just ou precisely what needed doing

justesse [ʒystɛs] nf (précision) accuracy; (d'une remarque) aptness; (d'une opinion) soundness; **de ~** only just, by a narrow margin

justice [ʒystis] nf (équité) fairness, justice; (Admin) justice; **rendre la ~** to dispense justice; **traduire en ~** to bring before the courts; **obtenir ~** to obtain justice; **rendre ~ à qn** to do sb justice; **se faire ~** to take the law into one's own hands; (se suicider) to take one's life

justicier, -ière [ʒystisje, -jɛʀ] nm/f judge, righter of wrongs

justificatif, -ive [ʒystifikatif, -iv] adj (document etc) supporting ▷ nm supporting proof; **pièce justificative** written proof

justifier [ʒystifje] vt to justify; **~ de** vt to prove; **non justifié** unjustified; **justifié à droite/gauche** ranged right/left

juteux, -euse [ʒytø, -øz] adj juicy

juvénile [ʒyvenil] adj young, youthful

K

K, k [kɑ] nm inv K, k ▷ abr (= kilo) kg; **K comme Kléber** K for King

K 7 [kasɛt] nf cassette

kaki [kaki] adj inv khaki

kangourou [kɑ̃guʀu] nm kangaroo

karaté [kaʀate] nm karate

karting [kaʀtiŋ] nm go-carting, karting

kascher [kaʃɛʀ] adj inv kosher

kayak [kajak] nm kayak; **faire du ~** to go kayaking

képi [kepi] nm kepi

kermesse [kɛʀmɛs] nf bazaar, (charity) fête; village fair

kidnapper [kidnape] vt to kidnap

kilo [kilo] nm kilo

kilogramme [kilɔgʀam] nm kilogramme (Brit), kilogram (US)

kilométrage [kilɔmetʀaʒ] nm number of kilometres travelled, = mileage

kilomètre [kilɔmetʀ] nm kilometre (Brit), kilometer (US); **~-heure** kilometres per hour

kilométrique [kilɔmetʀik] adj (distance) in kilometres; **compteur ~** = mileage indicator

kinésithérapeute [kineziteʀapøt] nm/f physiotherapist

kiosque [kjɔsk] nm kiosk, stall; (Tél etc) telephone and/or videotext information service; **~ à journaux** newspaper kiosk

kir [kiʀ] nm kir (white wine with blackcurrant liqueur)

kit [kit] nm kit; **~ piéton** ou **mains libres** hands-free kit; **en ~** in kit form

kiwi [kiwi] *nm* (*Zool*) kiwi; (*Bot*) kiwi (fruit)
klaxon [klaksɔn] *nm* horn
klaxonner [klaksɔne] *vi, vt* to hoot (*Brit*),
  honk (one's horn) (*US*)
km *abr* (= *kilomètre*) km
km/h *abr* (= *kilomètres/heure*) km/h, kph
K.-O. [kao] *adj inv* shattered, knackered
Kosovo [kɔsɔvo] *nm*: **le ~** Kosovo
Koweit, Kuweit [kɔwɛt] *nm*: **le ~** Kuwait,
  Koweit
k-way® [kawɛ] *nm* (lightweight nylon)
  cagoule
kyste [kist] *nm* cyst

l' [l] *art déf voir* **le**
la [la] *art déf, pron voir* **le** ▷ *nm* (*Mus*) A; (*en
  chantant la gamme*) la
là [la] *adv voir aussi* **-ci; celui** there; (*ici*) here;
  (*dans le temps*) then; **est-ce que Catherine est
  là?** is Catherine there (*ou* here)?; **elle n'est
  pas là** she isn't here; **c'est là que** this is
  where; **là où** where; **de là** (*fig*) hence; **par là**
  (*fig*) by that; **tout est là** (*fig*) that's what it's
  all about
là-bas [labɑ] *adv* there
label [label] *nm* stamp, seal
labeur [labœʀ] *nm* toil *no pl*, toiling *no pl*
labo [labo] *nm* (= *laboratoire*) lab
laboratoire [labɔʀatwaʀ] *nm* laboratory;
  ~ de langues/d'analyses language/
  (medical) analysis laboratory
laborieux, -euse [labɔʀjø, -øz] *adj* (*tâche*)
  laborious; **classes laborieuses** working
  classes
labour [labuʀ] *nm* ploughing *no pl* (*Brit*),
  plowing *no pl* (*US*); **labours** *nmpl* (*champs*)
  ploughed fields; **cheval de ~** plough- *ou* cart-
  horse; **bœuf de ~** ox
labourer [labuʀe] *vt* to plough (*Brit*), plow
  (*US*); (*fig*) to make deep gashes *ou* furrows in
labyrinthe [labiʀɛ̃t] *nm* labyrinth, maze
lac [lak] *nm* lake; **le ~ Léman** Lake Geneva;
  les Grands L~s the Great Lakes; *voir aussi*
  lacs
lacer [lase] *vt* to lace *ou* do up
lacérer [laseʀe] *vt* to tear to shreds

lacet [lasɛ] nm (de chaussure) lace; (de route) sharp bend; (piège) snare; **chaussures à ~s** lace-up ou lacing shoes

lâche [laʃ] adj (poltron) cowardly; (desserré) loose, slack; (morale, mœurs) lax ▷ nm/f coward

lâcher [laʃe] nm (de ballons, oiseaux) release ▷ vt to let go of; (ce qui tombe, abandonner) to drop; (oiseau, animal: libérer) to release, set free; (fig: mot, remarque) to let slip, come out with; (Sport: distancer) to leave behind ▷ vi (fil, amarres) to break, give way; (freins) to fail; **~ les amarres** (Navig) to cast off (the moorings); **~ prise** to let go

lâcheté [laʃte] nf cowardice; (bassesse) lowness

lacrymogène [lakrimɔʒɛn] adj: **grenade/gaz ~** tear gas grenade/tear gas

lacté, e [lakte] adj milk cpd

lacune [lakyn] nf gap

là-dedans [ladadã] adv inside (there), in it; (fig) in that

là-dessous [ladsu] adv underneath, under there; (fig) behind that

là-dessus [ladsy] adv on there; (fig: sur ces mots) at that point; (: à ce sujet) about that

ladite [ladit] adj voir **ledit**

lagune [lagyn] nf lagoon

là-haut [lao] adv up there

laïc [laik] adj, nm/f = **laïque**

laid, e [lɛ, lɛd] adj ugly; (fig: acte) mean, cheap

laideur [lɛdœʀ] nf ugliness no pl; (fig: d'un acte) meanness no pl

lainage [lɛnaʒ] nm (vêtement) woollen garment; (étoffe) woollen material

laine [lɛn] nf wool; **~ peignée** worsted (wool); **~ à tricoter** knitting wool; **~ de verre** glass wool; **~ vierge** new wool

laïque [laik] adj lay, civil; (Scol) state cpd (as opposed to private and Roman Catholic) ▷ nm/f layman(-woman)

laisse [lɛs] nf (de chien) lead, leash; **tenir en ~** to keep on a lead ou leash

laisser [lese] vt to leave ▷ vb aux: **~ qn faire** to let sb do; **se ~ exploiter** to let o.s. be exploited; **se ~ aller** to let o.s. go; **~ qn tranquille** to let ou leave sb alone; **laisse-toi faire** let me (ou him) do it; **rien ne laisse penser que ...** there is no reason to think that ...; **cela ne laisse pas de surprendre** nonetheless it is surprising

laisser-aller [leseale] nm carelessness, slovenliness

laissez-passer [lesepase] nm inv pass

lait [lɛ] nm milk; **frère/sœur de ~** foster brother/sister; **~ écrémé/entier/concentré/condensé** skimmed/full-fat/condensed/evaporated milk; **~ en poudre** powdered milk, milk powder; **~ de chèvre/vache** goat's/cow's milk; **~ maternel** mother's milk; **~ démaquillant/de beauté** cleansing/beauty lotion

laitage [lɛtaʒ] nm dairy product

laiterie [lɛtʀi] nf dairy

laitier, -ière [letje, -jɛʀ] adj dairy cpd ▷ nm/f milkman/dairywoman

laiton [lɛtɔ̃] nm brass

laitue [lety] nf lettuce

laïus [lajys] nm (péj) spiel

lambeau, x [lãbo] nm scrap; **en ~x** in tatters, tattered

lambris [lãbʀi] nm panelling no pl

lame [lam] nf blade; (vague) wave; (lamelle) strip; **~ de fond** ground swell no pl; **~ de rasoir** razor blade

lamelle [lamɛl] nf (lame) small blade; (morceau) sliver; (de champignon) gill; **couper en ~s** to slice thinly

lamentable [lamãtabl] adj (déplorable) appalling; (pitoyable) pitiful

lamenter [lamãte]: **se lamenter** vi: **se ~ (sur)** to moan (over)

lampadaire [lãpadɛʀ] nm (de salon) standard lamp; (dans la rue) street lamp

lampe [lãp] nf lamp; (Tech) valve; **~ à alcool** spirit lamp; **~ à pétrole** oil lamp; **~ à bronzer** sunlamp; **~ de poche** torch (Brit), flashlight (US); **~ à souder** blowlamp; **~ témoin** warning light; **~ halogène** halogen lamp

lampion [lãpjɔ̃] nm Chinese lantern

lance [lãs] nf spear; **~ d'arrosage** garden hose; **~ à eau** water hose; **~ d'incendie** fire hose

lancée [lãse] nf: **être/continuer sur sa ~** to be under way/keep going

lancement [lãsmã] nm launching no pl, launch; **offre de ~** introductory offer

lance-pierres [lãspjɛʀ] nm inv catapult

lancer [lãse] nm (Sport) throwing no pl, throw; (Pêche) rod and reel fishing ▷ vt to throw; (émettre, projeter) to throw out, send out; (produit, fusée, bateau, artiste) to launch; (injure) to hurl, fling; (proclamation, mandat d'arrêt) to issue; (emprunt) to float; (moteur) to send roaring away; **~ qch à qn** to throw sth to sb; (de façon agressive) to throw sth at sb; **~ un cri ou un appel** to shout ou call out; **se lancer** vi (prendre de l'élan) to build up speed; (se précipiter): **se ~ sur ou contre** to rush at; **se ~ dans** (discussion) to launch into; (aventure) to embark on; (les affaires, la politique) to go into; **~ du poids** nm putting the shot

lancinant, e [lãsinã, -ãt] adj (regrets etc) haunting; (douleur) shooting

landau [lãdo] nm (Brit) pram (Brit), baby carriage (US)

lande [lãd] nf moor

langage [lãgaʒ] nm language; **~ d'assemblage** (Inform) assembly language; **~ du corps** body language; **~ évolué/machine** (Inform) high-level/machine language; **~ de programmation** (Inform) programming language

langouste [lãgust] nf crayfish inv

langoustine [lãgustin] nf Dublin Bay prawn

langue [lãg] nf (Anat, Culin) tongue; (Ling) language; (bande): **~ de terre** spit of land; **tirer la ~ (à)** to stick out one's tongue (at);

donner sa ~ au chat to give up, give in; **de ~ française** French-speaking; **~ de bois** officialese; **~ maternelle** native language, mother tongue; **~ verte** slang; **~s vivantes** modern languages

langueur [lɑ̃gœʀ] *nf* languidness

languir [lɑ̃giʀ] *vi* to languish; *(conversation)* to flag; **se languir** *vi* to be languishing; **faire ~ qn** to keep sb waiting

lanière [lanjɛʀ] *nf (de fouet)* lash; *(de valise, bretelle)* strap

lanterne [lɑ̃tɛʀn] *nf (portable)* lantern; *(électrique)* light, lamp; *(de voiture)* (side)light; **~ rouge** *(fig)* tail-ender; **~ vénitienne** Chinese lantern

laper [lape] *vt* to lap up

lapidaire [lapidɛʀ] *adj* stone *cpd*; *(fig)* terse

lapin [lapɛ̃] *nm* rabbit; *(peau)* rabbitskin; *(fourrure)* cony; **coup du ~** rabbit punch; **poser un ~ à qn** to stand sb up; **~ de garenne** wild rabbit

Laponie [laponi] *nf*: **la ~** Lapland

laps [laps] *nm*: **~ de temps** space of time, time *no pl*

laque [lak] *nf (vernis)* lacquer; *(brute)* shellac; *(pour cheveux)* hair spray ▷ *nm* lacquer; piece of lacquer ware

laquelle [lakɛl] *pron voir* **lequel**

larcin [laʀsɛ̃] *nm* theft

lard [laʀ] *nm (graisse)* fat; *(bacon)* (streaky) bacon

lardon [laʀdɔ̃] *nm (Culin)* piece of chopped bacon; *(fam: enfant)* kid

large [laʀʒ] *adj* wide; broad; *(fig)* generous ▷ *adv*: **calculer/voir ~** to allow extra/think big ▷ *nm (largeur)*: **5 m de ~** 5 m wide *ou* in width; *(mer)*: **le ~** the open sea; **en ~** *adv* sideways; **au ~ de** off; **~ d'esprit** broadminded; **ne pas en mener ~** to have one's heart in one's boots

largement [laʀʒəmɑ̃] *adv* widely; *(de loin)* greatly; *(amplement, au minimum)* easily; *(sans compter: donner etc)* generously; **c'est ~ suffisant** that's ample

largesse [laʀʒɛs] *nf* generosity; **largesses** *nfpl (dons)* liberalities

largeur [laʀʒœʀ] *nf (qu'on mesure)* width; *(impression visuelle)* wideness, width; breadth; *(d'esprit)* broadness

larguer [laʀge] *vt* to drop; *(fam: se débarrasser de)* to get rid of; **~ les amarres** to cast off (the moorings)

larme [laʀm] *nf* tear; *(fig)*: **une ~ de** a drop of; **en ~s** in tears; **pleurer à chaudes ~s** to cry one's eyes out, cry bitterly

larmoyer [laʀmwaje] *vi (yeux)* to water; *(se plaindre)* to whimper

larvé, e [laʀve] *adj (fig)* latent

laryngite [laʀɛ̃ʒit] *nf* laryngitis

las, lasse [lɑ, lɑs] *adj* weary

laser [lazɛʀ] *nm*: **(rayon)** laser (beam); **chaîne** *ou* **platine ~** compact disc (player);

disque ~ compact disc

lasse [lɑs] *adj f voir* **las**

lasser [lɑse] *vt* to weary, tire; **se ~ de** to grow weary *ou* tired of

latéral, e, -aux [lateʀal, -o] *adj* side *cpd*, lateral

latin, e [latɛ̃, -in] *adj* Latin ▷ *nm (Ling)* Latin ▷ *nm/f*: **L~, e** Latin; **j'y perds mon ~** it's all Greek to me

latitude [latityd] *nf* latitude; *(fig)*: **avoir la ~ de faire** to be left free *ou* be at liberty to do; **à 48° de ~ Nord** at latitude 48° North; **sous toutes les ~s** *(fig)* world-wide, throughout the world

latte [lat] *nf* lath, slat; *(de plancher)* board

lauréat, e [lɔʀea, -at] *nm/f* winner

laurier [lɔʀje] *nm (Bot)* laurel; *(Culin)* bay leaves *pl*; **lauriers** *nmpl (fig)* laurels

lavable [lavabl] *adj* washable

lavabo [lavabo] *nm* washbasin; **lavabos** *nmpl* toilet *sg*

lavage [lavaʒ] *nm* washing *no pl*, wash; **~ d'estomac/d'intestin** stomach/intestinal wash; **~ de cerveau** brainwashing *no pl*

lavande [lavɑ̃d] *nf* lavender

lave [lav] *nf* lava *no pl*

lave-linge [lavlɛ̃ʒ] *nm inv* washing machine

laver [lave] *vt* to wash; *(tache)* to wash off; *(fig: affront)* to avenge; **se laver** *vi* to have a wash, wash; **se ~ les mains/dents** to wash one's hands/clean one's teeth; **~ la vaisselle/le linge** to wash the dishes/clothes; **~ qn de** *(accusation)* to clear sb of

laverie [lavʀi] *nf*: **~ (automatique)** launderette

lavette [lavɛt] *nf (chiffon)* dish cloth; *(brosse)* dish mop; *(fam: homme)* wimp, drip

laveur, -euse [lavœʀ, -øz] *nm/f* cleaner

lave-vaisselle [lavvɛsɛl] *nm inv* dishwasher

lavoir [lavwaʀ] *nm* wash house; *(bac)* washtub; *(évier)* sink

laxatif, -ive [laksatif, -iv] *adj, nm* laxative

layette [lɛjɛt] *nf* layette

 MOT-CLÉ

le, l', la [lə, l, la] *(pl* **les**) *art déf* **1** the; **le livre/la pomme/l'arbre** the book/the apple/the tree; **les étudiants** the students

2 *(noms abstraits)*: **le courage/l'amour/la jeunesse** courage/love/youth

3 *(indiquant la possession)*: **se casser la jambe** *etc* to break one's leg *etc*; **levez la main** put your hand up; **avoir les yeux gris/le nez rouge** to have grey eyes/a red nose

4 *(temps)*: **le matin/soir** in the morning/evening; mornings/evenings; **le jeudi** *etc (d'habitude)* on Thursdays *etc*; *(ce jeudi-là etc)* on (the) Thursday; **nous venons le 3 décembre** *(parlé)* we're coming on the 3rd of December *ou* on December the 3rd; *(écrit)* we're coming (on) 3rd *ou* 3 December

5 (*distribution, évaluation*) a, an; **trois euros le mètre/kilo** three euros a *ou* per metre/kilo; **le tiers/quart de** a third/quarter of
▷ *pron* **1** (*personne: mâle*) him; (: *femelle*) her; (: *pluriel*) them; **je le/la/les vois** I can see him/her/them
2 (*animal, chose: singulier*) it; (: *pluriel*) them; **je le** (*ou* **la**) **vois** I can see it; **je les vois** I can see them
3 (*remplaçant une phrase*): **je ne le savais pas** I didn't know (about it); **il était riche et ne l'est plus** he was once rich but no longer is

lécher [leʃe] *vt* to lick; (*laper: lait, eau*) to lick *ou* lap up; (*finir, polir*) to over-refine; **~ les vitrines** to go window-shopping; **se ~ les doigts/lèvres** to lick one's fingers/lips

lèche-vitrines [lɛʃvitʀin] *nm inv*: **faire du ~** to go window-shopping

leçon [ləsɔ̃] *nf* lesson; **faire la ~** to teach; **faire la ~ à** (*fig*) to give a lecture to; **~s de conduite** driving lessons; **~s particulières** private lessons *ou* tuition *sg* (*Brit*)

lecteur, -trice [lɛktœʀ, -tʀis] *nm/f* reader; (*d'université*) (foreign language) assistant (*Brit*), (foreign) teaching assistant (*US*) ▷ *nm* (*Tech*): **~ de cassettes** cassette player; **~ de disquette(s)** disk drive; **~ de CD/DVD** (*Inform*: *d'ordinateur*) CD/DVD drive; (*de salon*) CD/DVD player; **~ MP3** MP3 player

lecture [lɛktyʀ] *nf* reading

ledit [lədi], **ladite** [ladit] (*mpl* **lesdits**) [ledi] (*fpl* **lesdites**) [ledit] *adj* the aforesaid

légal, e, -aux [legal, -o] *adj* legal

légaliser [legalize] *vt* to legalize

légalité [legalite] *nf* legality, lawfulness; **être dans/sortir de la ~** to be within/step outside the law

légendaire [leʒɑ̃dɛʀ] *adj* legendary

légende [leʒɑ̃d] *nf* (*mythe*) legend; (*de carte, plan*) key, legend; (*de dessin*) caption

léger, -ère [leʒe, -ɛʀ] *adj* light; (*bruit, retard*) slight; (*boisson, parfum*) weak; (*couche, étoffe*) thin; (*superficiel*) thoughtless; (*volage*) free and easy; (*peu sérieux*) flighty; (*peu important*) lightweight; **blessé ~** slightly injured person; **à la légère** *adv* (*parler, agir*) rashly, thoughtlessly

légèrement [leʒɛʀmɑ̃] *adv* (*s'habiller, bouger*) lightly; thoughtlessly, rashly; **~ plus grand** slightly bigger; **manger ~** to eat a light meal

légèreté [leʒɛʀte] *nf* lightness; thoughtlessness; (*d'une remarque*) flippancy

législatif, -ive [leʒislatif, -iv] *adj* legislative; **législatives** *nfpl* general election *sg*

légitime [leʒitim] *adj* (*Jur*) lawful, legitimate; (*enfant*) legitimate; (*fig*) rightful, legitimate; **en état de ~ défense** in self-defence

legs [lɛg] *nm* legacy

léguer [lege] *vt*: **~ qch à qn** (*Jur*) to bequeath sth to sb; (*fig*) to hand sth down *ou* pass sth on to sb

légume [legym] *nm* vegetable; **~s verts** green vegetables; **~s secs** pulses

lendemain [lɑ̃dmɛ̃] *nm*: **le ~** the next *ou* following day; **le ~ matin/soir** the next *ou* following morning/evening; **le ~ de** the day after; **au ~ de** in the days following; in the wake of; **penser au ~** to think of the future; **sans ~** short-lived; **de beaux ~s** bright prospects; **des ~s qui chantent** a rosy future

lent, e [lɑ̃, lɑ̃t] *adj* slow

lentement [lɑ̃tmɑ̃] *adv* slowly

lenteur [lɑ̃tœʀ] *nf* slowness *no pl*; **lenteurs** *nfpl* (*actions, décisions lentes*) slowness *sg*

lentille [lɑ̃tij] *nf* (*Optique*) lens *sg*; (*Bot*) lentil; **~ d'eau** duckweed; **~s de contact** contact lenses

léopard [leɔpaʀ] *nm* leopard

lèpre [lɛpʀ] *nf* leprosy

◯ **MOT-CLÉ**

lequel, laquelle [ləkɛl, lakɛl] (*mpl* **lesquels**, *fpl* **lesquelles**) (*à + lequel* = **auquel**, *de + lequel* = **duquel**) *pron* **1** (*interrogatif*) which, which one; **lequel des deux?** which one?
2 (*relatif: personne: sujet*) who; (: *objet, après préposition*) whom; (: *sujet: possessif*) whose; (: *chose*) which; **je l'ai proposé au directeur, lequel est d'accord** I suggested it to the director, who agrees; **la femme à laquelle j'ai acheté mon chien** the woman from whom I bought my dog; **le pont sur lequel nous sommes passés** the bridge (over) which we crossed; **un homme sur la compétence duquel on peut compter** a man whose competence one can count on
▷ *adj*: **auquel cas** in which case

les [le] *art déf, pron voir* **le**

lesbienne [lɛsbjɛn] *nf* lesbian

lesdits [ledi], **lesdites** [ledit] *adj voir* **ledit**

léser [leze] *vt* to wrong; (*Méd*) to injure

lésiner [lezine] *vi*: **ne pas ~ sur les moyens** (*pour mariage etc*) to push the boat out

lésion [lezjɔ̃] *nf* lesion, damage *no pl*; **~s cérébrales** brain damage

lesquels, lesquelles [lekɛl] *pron voir* **lequel**

lessive [lesiv] *nf* (*poudre*) washing powder; (*linge*) washing *no pl*, wash; (*opération*) washing *no pl*; **faire la ~** to do the washing

lessiver [lesive] *vt* to wash; (*fam: fatiguer*) to tire out, exhaust

lest [lɛst] *nm* ballast; **jeter** *ou* **lâcher du ~** (*fig*) to make concessions

leste [lɛst] *adj* (*personne, mouvement*) sprightly, nimble; (*désinvolte: manières*) offhand; (*osé: plaisanterie*) risqué

lettre [lɛtʀ] *nf* letter; **lettres** *nfpl* (*étude, culture*) literature *sg*; (*Scol*) arts (subjects); **à la ~** (*au sens propre*) literally; (*ponctuellement*) to the letter; **en ~s majuscules** *ou* **capitales** in capital letters, in capitals; **en toutes ~s** in words, in full; **~ de change** bill of exchange; **~ piégée** letter bomb; **~ de voiture (aérienne)** (air) waybill, (air) bill of lading; **~s de noblesse** pedigree

leucémie [løsemi] *nf* leukaemia

 MOT-CLÉ

leur [lœʀ] *adj poss* their; **leur maison** their house; **leurs amis** their friends; **à leur approche** as they came near; **à leur vue** at the sight of them
▷ *pron* **1** (*objet indirect*) (to) them; **je leur ai dit la vérité** I told them the truth; **je le leur ai donné** I gave it to them, I gave them it
2 (*possessif*): **le(la) leur, les leurs** theirs

leurre [lœʀ] *nm* (*appât*) lure; (*fig*) delusion; (*: piège*) snare

leurrer [lœʀe] *vt* to delude, deceive

leurs [lœʀ] *adj voir* **leur**

levain [ləvɛ̃] *nm* leaven; **sans ~** unleavened

levé, e [ləve] *adj*: **être ~** to be up ▷ *nm*: **~ de terrain** land survey; **à mains ~es** (*vote*) by a show of hands; **au pied ~** at a moment's notice

levée [ləve] *nf* (*Postes*) collection; (*Cartes*) trick; **~ de boucliers** general outcry; **~ du corps** *collection of the body from house of the deceased, before funeral*; **~ d'écrou** release from custody; **~ de terre** levee; **~ de troupes** levy

lever [ləve] *vt* (*vitre, bras etc*) to raise; (*soulever de terre, supprimer: interdiction, siège*) to lift; (*: difficulté*) to remove; (*séance*) to close; (*impôts, armée*) to levy; (*Chasse: lièvre*) to start; (*: perdrix*) to flush; (*fam: fille*) to pick up ▷ *vi* (*Culin*) to rise ▷ *nm*: **au ~** on getting up; **se lever** *vi* to get up; (*soleil*) to rise; (*jour*) to break; (*brouillard*) to lift; **levez-vous!, lève-toi!** stand up!, get up!; **ça va se ~** (*temps*) it's going to clear up; **~ du jour** daybreak; **~ du rideau** (*Théât*) curtain; **~ de rideau** (*pièce*) curtain raiser; **~ de soleil** sunrise

levier [ləvje] *nm* lever; **faire ~ sur** to lever up (*ou* off); **~ de changement de vitesse** gear lever

lèvre [lɛvʀ] *nf* lip; **lèvres** *nfpl* (*d'une plaie*) edges; **petites/grandes ~s** labia minora/ majora; **du bout des ~s** half-heartedly

lévrier [levʀije] *nm* greyhound

levure [ləvyʀ] *nf* yeast; **~ chimique** baking powder

lexique [lɛksik] *nm* vocabulary, lexicon; (*glossaire*) vocabulary

lézard [lezaʀ] *nm* lizard; (*peau*) lizard skin

lézarde [lezaʀd] *nf* crack

liaison [ljɛzɔ̃] *nf* (*rapport*) connection, link; (*Rail, Aviat etc*) link; (*relation: d'amitié*) friendship; (*: d'affaires*) relationship; (*: amoureuse*) affair; (*Culin, Phonétique*) liaison; **entrer/être en ~ avec** to get/be in contact with; **~ radio** radio contact; **~ (de transmission de données)** (*Inform*) data link

liane [ljan] *nf* creeper

liant, e [ljɑ̃, -ɑ̃t] *adj* sociable

liasse [ljas] *nf* wad, bundle

Liban [libɑ̃] *nm*: **le ~** (the) Lebanon

libanais, e [libanɛ, -ɛz] *adj* Lebanese ▷ *nm/f*: **L~, e** Lebanese

libeller [libele] *vt* (*chèque, mandat*): **~ (au nom de)** to make out (to); (*lettre*) to word

libellule [libelyl] *nf* dragonfly

libéral, e, -aux [liberal, -o] *adj, nm/f* liberal; **les professions ~es** liberal professions

libérer [libere] *vt* (*délivrer*) to free, liberate; (*: moralement, Psych*) to liberate; (*relâcher: prisonnier*) to release; (*: soldat*) to discharge; (*dégager: gaz, cran d'arrêt*) to release; (*Écon: échanges commerciaux*) to ease restrictions on; **se libérer** *vi* (*de rendez-vous*) to get out of previous engagements, try and be free; **~ qn de** (*liens, dette*) to free sb from; (*promesse*) to release sb from

liberté [libɛʀte] *nf* freedom; (*loisir*) free time; **libertés** *nfpl* (*privautés*) liberties; **mettre/être en ~** to set/be free; **en ~ provisoire/ surveillée/conditionnelle** on bail/ probation/parole; **~ d'association** right of association; **~ de conscience** freedom of conscience; **~ du culte** freedom of worship; **~ d'esprit** independence of mind; **~ d'opinion** freedom of thought; **~ de la presse** freedom of the press; **~ de réunion** right to hold meetings; **~ syndicale** union rights *pl*; **~s individuelles** personal freedom *sg*; **~s publiques** civil rights

libraire [libʀɛʀ] *nm/f* bookseller

librairie [libʀɛʀi] *nf* bookshop

libre [libʀ] *adj* free; (*route*) clear; (*place etc*) vacant, free; (*fig: propos, manières*) open; (*ligne*) not engaged; (*Scol*) non-state, private and Roman Catholic (*as opposed to "laïque"*); **de ~** (*place*) free; **~ de qch/de faire** free from sth/to do; **vente ~** (*Comm*) unrestricted sale; **~ arbitre** free will; **~ concurrence** free-market economy; **~ entreprise** free enterprise

libre-échange [libʀeʃɑ̃ʒ] *nm* free trade

libre-service [libʀəsɛʀvis] *nm inv* (*magasin*) self-service store; (*restaurant*) self-service restaurant

Libye [libi] *nf*: **la ~** Libya

licence [lisɑ̃s] *nf* (*permis*) permit; (*diplôme*) (first) degree; *see note*; (*liberté*) liberty; (*poétique, orthographique*) licence (*Brit*), license

(US); (des mœurs) licentiousness; ~ **ès lettres/
en droit** arts/law degree

◈ **LICENCE**
◈
◈ After the "DEUG", French university
◈ students undertake a third year of study
◈ to complete their *licence*. This is roughly
◈ equivalent to a bachelor's degree in Britain.

licencié, e [lisɑ̃sje] *nm/f* (*Scol*): ~ **ès lettres/
en droit** = Bachelor of Arts/Law, arts/law
graduate; (*Sport*) permit-holder
licenciement [lisɑ̃simɑ̃] *nm* dismissal;
redundancy; laying off *no pl*
licencier [lisɑ̃sje] *vt* (*renvoyer*) to dismiss;
(*débaucher*) to make redundant; to lay off
licite [lisit] *adj* lawful
lie [li] *nf* dregs *pl*, sediment
lié, e [lje] *adj*: **très ~ avec** (*fig*) very friendly
with *ou* close to; ~ **par** (*serment, promesse*)
bound by; **avoir partie ~e (avec qn)** to be
involved (with sb)
Liechtenstein [liʃtɛnʃtajn] *nm*: **le ~**
Liechtenstein
liège [ljɛʒ] *nm* cork
lien [ljɛ̃] *nm* (*corde, fig: affectif, culturel*) bond;
(*rapport*) link, connection; (*analogie*) link; ~ **de
parenté** family tie; ~ **hypertexte** hyperlink
lier [lje] *vt* (*attacher*) to tie up; to link
up; (*fig: unir, engager*) to bind; (*Culin*) to
thicken; ~ **qch à** (*attacher*) to tie sth to;
(*associer*) to link sth to; ~ **conversation (avec)**
to strike up a conversation (with); **se ~ avec**
to make friends with; ~ **connaissance avec**
to get to know
lierre [ljɛʀ] *nm* ivy
liesse [ljɛs] *nf*: **être en ~** to be jubilant
lieu, x [ljø] *nm* place; **lieux** *nmpl* (*locaux*)
premises; (*endroit: d'un accident etc*) scene *sg*;
en ~ sûr in a safe place; **en haut ~** in high
places; **vider** *ou* **quitter les ~x** to leave the
premises; **arriver/être sur les ~x** to arrive/
be on the scene; **en premier ~** in the
first place; **en dernier ~** lastly; **avoir ~** to take
place; **avoir ~ de faire** to have grounds *ou*
good reason for doing; **tenir ~ de** to take the
place of; (*servir de*) to serve as; **donner ~ à** to
give rise to, give cause for; **au ~ de** instead of;
au ~ qu'il y aille instead of him going;
~ **commun** commonplace; ~ **géométrique**
locus; ~ **de naissance** place of birth
lieu-dit (*pl* **lieux-dits**) [ljødi] *nm* locality
lieutenant [ljøtnɑ̃] *nm* lieutenant; ~ **de
vaisseau** (*Navig*) lieutenant
lièvre [ljɛvʀ] *nm* hare; (*coureur*) pacemaker;
lever un ~ (*fig*) to bring up a prickly subject
ligament [ligamɑ̃] *nm* ligament
ligne [liɲ] *nf* (*gén*) line; (*Transports: liaison*)
service; (*: trajet*) route; (*silhouette*) figure;
garder la ~ to keep one's figure; **en ~** (*Inform*)
online; **en ~ droite** as the crow flies; **"à la ~"**

"new paragraph"; **entrer en ~ de compte** to
be taken into account; to come into it; ~ **de
but/médiane** goal/halfway line; ~
d'arrivée/de départ finishing/starting line;
~ **de conduite** course of action; ~ **directrice**
guiding line; ~ **fixe** (*Tél*) fixed line (phone);
~ **d'horizon** skyline; ~ **de mire** line of sight;
~ **de touche** touchline
ligné, e [liɲe] *adj*: **papier** ~ ruled paper ▷ *nf*
(*race, famille*) line, lineage; (*postérité*)
descendants *pl*
ligoter [ligɔte] *vt* to tie up
ligue [lig] *nf* league
liguer [lige]: **se liguer** *vi* to form a league; **se ~
contre** (*fig*) to combine against
lilas [lila] *nm* lilac
limace [limas] *nf* slug
limande [limɑ̃d] *nf* dab
lime [lim] *nf* (*Tech*) file; (*Bot*) lime; ~ **à ongles**
nail file
limer [lime] *vt* (*bois, métal*) to file (down);
(*ongles*) to file; (*fig: prix*) to pare down
limier [limje] *nm* (*Zool*) bloodhound;
(*détective*) sleuth
limitation [limitasjɔ̃] *nf* limitation,
restriction; **sans ~ de temps** with no time
limit; ~ **des naissances** birth control; ~ **de
vitesse** speed limit
limite [limit] *nf* (*de terrain*) boundary; (*partie ou
point extrême*) limit; **dans la ~ de** within the
limits of; **à la ~** (*au pire*) if the worst comes (*ou*
came) to the worst; **sans ~s** (*bêtise, richesse,
pouvoir*) limitless, boundless; **vitesse/charge**
~ maximum speed/load; **cas** ~ borderline
case; **date** ~ deadline; **date** ~ **de vente/
consommation** sell-by/best-before date;
prix ~ upper price limit; ~ **d'âge** maximum
age, age limit
limiter [limite] *vt* (*restreindre*) to limit,
restrict; (*délimiter*) to border, form the
boundary of; **se ~ (à qch/à faire)** (*personne*) to
limit *ou* confine o.s. (to sth/to doing sth); **se ~
à** (*chose*) to be limited to
limitrophe [limitʀɔf] *adj* border *cpd*; ~ **de**
bordering on
limoger [limɔʒe] *vt* to dismiss
limon [limɔ̃] *nm* silt
limonade [limɔnad] *nf* lemonade (*Brit*),
(lemon) soda (*US*)
lin [lɛ̃] *nm* (*Bot*) flax; (*tissu, toile*) linen
linceul [lɛ̃sœl] *nm* shroud
linge [lɛ̃ʒ] *nm* (*serviettes etc*) linen; (*pièce de tissu*)
cloth; (*aussi*: ~ **de corps**) underwear; (*aussi*:
~ **de toilette**) towel; (*lessive*) washing; ~ **sale**
dirty linen
lingerie [lɛ̃ʒʀi] *nf* lingerie, underwear
lingot [lɛ̃go] *nm* ingot
linguistique [lɛ̃gɥistik] *adj* linguistic ▷ *nf*
linguistics *sg*
lion, ne [ljɔ̃, ljɔn] *nm/f* lion/lioness; (*signe*): **le
L~** Leo, the Lion; **être du L~** to be Leo; ~ **de
mer** sea lion

lionceau, x [ljɔ̃so] nm lion cub

liqueur [likœʀ] nf liqueur

liquidation [likidasjɔ̃] nf (vente) sale, liquidation; (Comm) clearance (sale); **~ judiciaire** compulsory liquidation

liquide [likid] adj liquid ▷ nm liquid; (Comm): **en ~** in ready money ou cash; **je n'ai pas de ~** I haven't got any cash

liquider [likide] vt (société, biens, témoin gênant) to liquidate; (compte, problème) to settle; (Comm: articles) to clear, sell off

liquidités [likidite] nfpl (Comm) liquid assets

lire [liʀ] nf (monnaie) lira ▷ vt, vi to read; **~ qch à qn** to read sth (out) to sb

lis vb [li] voir **lire** ▷ nm [lis] = **lys**

Lisbonne [lizbɔn] n Lisbon

lisible [lizibl] adj legible; (digne d'être lu) readable

lisière [lizjɛʀ] nf (de forêt) edge; (de tissu) selvage

lisons [lizɔ̃] vb voir **lire**

lisse [lis] adj smooth

lisseur [lisœʀ] nm straighteners pl

liste [list] nf list; (Inform) listing; **faire la ~ de** to list, make out a list of; **~ d'attente** waiting list; **~ civile** civil list; **~ électorale** electoral roll; **~ de mariage** wedding (present) list; **~ noire** hit list

listing [listiŋ] nm (Inform) printout; **qualité ~** draft quality

lit [li] nm (gén) bed; **petit ~, ~ à une place** single bed; **grand ~, ~ à deux places** double bed; **faire son ~** to make one's bed; **aller/se mettre au ~** to go to/get into bed; **chambre avec un grand ~** room with a double bed; **prendre le ~** to take to one's bed; **d'un premier ~** (Jur) of a first marriage; **~ de camp** camp bed (Brit), cot (US); **~ d'enfant** cot (Brit), crib (US)

literie [litʀi] nf bedding; (linge) bedding, bedclothes pl

litière [litjɛʀ] nf litter

litige [litiʒ] nm dispute; **en ~** in contention

litre [litʀ] nm litre; (récipient) litre measure

littéraire [literɛʀ] adj literary ▷ nm/f arts student; **elle est très ~** she's very literary

littéral, e, -aux [literal, -o] adj literal

littérature [literatyʀ] nf literature

littoral, e, -aux [litɔral, -o] adj coastal ▷ nm coast

liturgie [lityʀʒi] nf liturgy

livide [livid] adj livid, pallid

livraison [livʀɛzɔ̃] nf delivery; **~ à domicile** home delivery (service)

livre [livʀ] nm book; (imprimerie etc): **le ~** the book industry ▷ nf (poids, monnaie) pound; **traduire qch à ~ ouvert** to translate sth off the cuff ou at sight; **~ blanc** official report (on war, natural disaster etc, prepared by independent body); **~ de bord** (Navig) logbook; **~ de comptes** account(s) book; **~ de cuisine** cookery book (Brit), cookbook; **~ de messe** mass ou prayer book; **~ d'or** visitors' book;

~ de poche paperback (small and cheap); **~ sterling** pound sterling; **~ verte** green pound

livré, e [livʀe] nf livery ▷ adj: **~ à** (l'anarchie etc) given over to; **~ à soi-même** left to oneself ou one's own devices

livrer [livʀe] vt (Comm) to deliver; (otage, coupable) to hand over; (secret, information) to give away; **se ~ à** (se confier) to confide in; (se rendre) to give o.s. up to; (s'abandonner à: débauche etc) to give o.s. up ou over to; (faire: pratiques, actes) to indulge in; (travail) to be engaged in, engage in; (: sport) to practise; (: enquête) to carry out; **~ bataille** to give battle

livret [livʀɛ] nm booklet; (d'opéra) libretto; **~ de caisse d'épargne** (savings) bank-book; **~ de famille** (official) family record book; **~ scolaire** (school) report book

livreur, -euse [livʀœʀ, -øz] nm/f delivery boy ou man/girl ou woman

local, e, -aux [lɔkal, -o] adj local ▷ nm (salle) premises pl ▷ nmpl premises

localiser [lɔkalize] vt (repérer) to locate, place; (limiter) to localize, confine

localité [lɔkalite] nf locality

locataire [lɔkatɛʀ] nm/f tenant; (de chambre) lodger

location [lɔkasjɔ̃] nf (par le locataire) renting; (par l'usager: de voiture etc) hiring (Brit), renting (US); (par le propriétaire) renting out, letting, hiring out (Brit); (de billets, places) booking; (bureau) booking office; **"~ de voitures"** "car hire (Brit) ou rental (US)"; **habiter en ~** to live in rented accommodation; **prendre une ~ (pour les vacances)** to rent a house etc (for the holidays)

locomotive [lɔkɔmɔtiv] nf locomotive, engine; (fig) pacesetter, pacemaker

locution [lɔkysjɔ̃] nf phrase

loge [lɔʒ] nf (Théât: d'artiste) dressing room; (: de spectateurs) box; (de concierge, franc-maçon) lodge

logement [lɔʒmɑ̃] nm flat (Brit), apartment (US); accommodation no pl (Brit), accommodations pl (US); (Pol, Admin): **le ~** housing; **chercher un ~** to look for a flat ou apartment, look for accommodation(s); **construire des ~s bon marché** to build cheap housing sg; **crise du ~** housing shortage; **~ de fonction** (Admin) company flat ou apartment, accommodation(s) provided with one's job

loger [lɔʒe] vt to accommodate ▷ vi to live; **être logé, nourri** to have board and lodging; **se loger; trouver à se ~** to find accommodation; **se ~ dans** (balle, flèche) to lodge itself in

logeur, -euse [lɔʒœʀ, -øz] nm/f landlord/landlady

logiciel [lɔʒisjɛl] nm (Inform) piece of software

logique [lɔʒik] adj logical ▷ nf logic; **c'est ~** it stands to reason

logis [lɔʒi] nm home; abode, dwelling

logo [lɔgo], **logotype** [lɔgɔtip] nm logo

loi [lwa] nf law; **faire la ~** to lay down the law; **les ~s de la mode** (fig) the dictates of fashion; **proposition de ~** (private member's) bill; **projet de ~** (government) bill

loin [lwɛ̃] adv far; (dans le temps: futur) a long way off; (: passé) a long time ago; **plus ~** further; **moins ~ (que)** not as far (as); **~ de** far from; **~ d'ici** a long way from here; **pas ~ de 100 euros** not far off 100 euros; **au ~** far off; **de ~** adv from a distance; (fig: de beaucoup) by far; **il vient de ~** he's come a long way; he comes from a long way away; **de ~ en ~** here and there; (de temps en temps) (every) now and then; **~ de là** (au contraire) far from it

lointain, e [lwɛ̃tɛ̃, -ɛn] adj faraway, distant; (dans le futur, passé) distant, far-off; (cause, parent) remote, distant ▷ nm: **dans le ~** in the distance

loir [lwaR] nm dormouse

Loire [lwaR] nf: **la ~** the Loire

loisir [lwaziR] nm: **heures de ~** spare time; **loisirs** nmpl (temps libre) leisure sg; (activités) leisure activities; **avoir le ~ de faire** to have the time ou opportunity to do; **(tout) à ~** (prenant son temps) at leisure; (autant qu'on le désire) at one's pleasure

londonien, ne [lɔ̃dɔnjɛ̃, -ɛn] adj London cpd, of London ▷ nm/f: **L~, ne** Londoner

Londres [lɔ̃dR] n London

long, longue [lɔ̃, lɔ̃g] adj long ▷ adv: **en savoir ~** to know a great deal ▷ nm: **de 3 m de ~** 3 m long, 3 m in length ▷ nf: **à la longue** in the end; **faire ~ feu** to fizzle out; **ne pas faire ~ feu** not to last long; **au ~ cours** (Navig) ocean cpd, ocean-going; **de longue date** adj long-standing; **longue durée** adj long-term; **de longue haleine** adj long-term; **être ~ à faire** to take a long time to do; **en ~** adv lengthwise, lengthways; **(tout) le ~ de** (all) along; **tout au ~ de** (année, vie) throughout; **de ~ en large** (marcher) to and fro, up and down; **en ~ et en large** (fig) in every detail

longer [lɔ̃ʒe] vt to go (ou walk ou drive) along(side); (mur, route) to border

longiligne [lɔ̃ʒilin] adj long-limbed

longitude [lɔ̃ʒityd] nf longitude; **à 45° de ~ ouest** at 45° longitude west

longtemps [lɔ̃tɑ̃] adv (for) a long time, (for) long; **ça ne va pas durer ~** it won't last long; **avant ~** before long; **pour/pendant ~** for a long time; **je n'en ai pas pour ~** I shan't be long; **mettre ~ à faire** to take a long time to do; **il en a pour ~** he'll be a long time; **il y a ~ que je travaille** I have been working (for) a long time; **il n'y a pas ~ que je l'ai rencontré** it's not long since I met him

longue [lɔ̃g] adj f voir **long** ▷ nf: **à la ~** in the end

longuement [lɔ̃gmɑ̃] adv (longtemps: parler, regarder) for a long time; (en détail: expliquer, raconter) at length

longueur [lɔ̃gœR] nf length; **longueurs** nfpl (fig: d'un film etc) tedious parts; **sur une ~ de 10 km** for ou over 10 km; **en ~** adv lengthwise, lengthways; **tirer en ~** to drag on; **à ~ de journée** all day long; **d'une ~ (gagner)** by a length; **~ d'onde** wavelength

longue-vue [lɔ̃gvy] nf telescope

look [luk] (fam) nm look, image

lopin [lɔpɛ̃] nm: **~ de terre** patch of land

loque [lɔk] nf (personne) wreck; **loques** nfpl (habits) rags; **être** ou **tomber en ~s** to be in rags

loquet [lɔkɛ] nm latch

lorgner [lɔRne] vt to eye; (fig: convoiter) to have one's eye on

lors [lɔR]: **~ de** prép (au moment de) at the time of; (pendant) during; **~ même que** even though

lorsque [lɔRsk] conj when, as

losange [lɔzɑ̃ʒ] nm diamond; (Géom) lozenge; **en ~** diamond-shaped

lot [lo] nm (part) share; (de loterie) prize; (fig: destin) fate, lot; (Comm, Inform) batch; **le gros ~** the jackpot; **~ de consolation** consolation prize

loterie [lɔtRi] nf lottery; (tombola) raffle; **L~ nationale** French national lottery

loti, e [lɔti] adj: **bien/mal ~** well-/badly off, lucky/unlucky

lotion [losjɔ̃] nf lotion; **~ après rasage** after-shave (lotion); **~ capillaire** hair lotion

lotissement [lɔtismɑ̃] nm (groupe de maisons, d'immeubles) housing development; (parcelle) (building) plot, lot

loto [lɔto] nm lotto

lotte [lɔt] nf (Zool: de rivière) burbot; (: de mer) monkfish

louable [lwabl] adj (appartement, garage) rentable; (action, personne) praiseworthy, commendable

louange [lwɑ̃ʒ] nf: **à la ~ de** in praise of; **louanges** nfpl praise sg

loubar, loubard [lubaR] nm (fam) lout

louche [luʃ] adj shady, fishy, dubious ▷ nf ladle

loucher [luʃe] vi to squint; (fig): **~ sur** to have one's (beady) eye on

louer [lwe] vt (maison: propriétaire) to let, rent (out); (: locataire) to rent; (voiture etc: entreprise) to hire out (Brit), rent (out); (locataire) to hire (Brit), rent; (réserver) to book; (faire l'éloge de) to praise; **"à ~"** "to let" (Brit), "for rent" (US); **~ qn de** to praise sb for; **se ~ de** to congratulate o.s. on

loup [lu] nm wolf; (poisson) bass; (masque) (eye) mask; **jeune ~** young go-getter; **~ de mer** (marin) old seadog

loupe [lup] nf magnifying glass; **~ de noyer** burr walnut; **à la ~** (fig) in minute detail

louper [lupe] *vt* (*fam: manquer*) to miss; (*: gâcher*) to mess up, bungle; (*examen*) to flunk

lourd, e [lur, lurd] *adj* heavy; (*chaleur, temps*) sultry; (*fig: personne, style*) heavy-handed
▷ *adv*: **peser ~** to be heavy; **~ de** (*menaces*) charged with; (*conséquences*) fraught with; **artillerie/industrie ~e** heavy artillery/industry

lourdaud, e [lurdo, -od] *adj* clumsy

lourdement [lurdəmã] *adv* heavily; **se tromper ~** to make a big mistake

lourdeur [lurdœr] *nf* heaviness; **~ d'estomac** indigestion *no pl*

loutre [lutr] *nf* otter; (*fourrure*) otter skin

louveteau, x [luvto] *nm* (*Zool*) wolf-cub; (*scout*) cub (scout)

louvoyer [luvwaje] *vi* (*Navig*) to tack; (*fig*) to hedge, evade the issue

loyal, e, -aux [lwajal, -o] *adj* (*fidèle*) loyal, faithful; (*fair-play*) fair

loyauté [lwajote] *nf* loyalty, faithfulness; fairness

loyer [lwaje] *nm* rent; **~ de l'argent** interest rate

lu, e [ly] *pp de* lire

lubie [lybi] *nf* whim, craze

lubrifiant [lybrifjã] *nm* lubricant

lubrifier [lybrifje] *vt* to lubricate

lubrique [lybrik] *adj* lecherous

lucarne [lykarn] *nf* skylight

lucide [lysid] *adj* (*conscient*) lucid; (*accidenté*) conscious; (*perspicace*) clear-headed

lucratif, -ive [lykratif, -iv] *adj* lucrative; profitable; **à but non ~** non profit-making

lueur [lɥœr] *nf* (*chatoyante*) glimmer *no pl*; (*métallique, mouillée*) gleam *no pl*; (*rougeoyante*) glow *no pl*; (*pâle*) faint light; (*fig*) spark; (*: d'espérance*) glimmer, gleam

luge [lyʒ] *nf* sledge (*Brit*), sled (*US*); **faire de la ~** to sledge (*Brit*), sled (*US*), toboggan

lugubre [lygybr] *adj* gloomy; dismal

 MOT-CLÉ

lui [lɥi] *pp de* luire
▷ *pron* **1** (*objet indirect: mâle*) (to) him; (*: femelle*) (to) her; (*: chose, animal*) (to) it; **je lui ai parlé** I have spoken to him (*ou* to her); **il lui a offert un cadeau** he gave him (*ou* her) a present; **je le lui ai donné** I gave it to him (*ou* her)
2 (*après préposition, comparatif: personne*) him; (*: chose, animal*) it; **elle est contente de lui** she is pleased with him; **je la connais mieux que lui** I know her better than he does; I know her better than him; **cette voiture est à lui** this car belongs to him, this is HIS car; **c'est à lui de jouer** it's his turn *ou* go
3 (*sujet, forme emphatique*) he; **lui, il est à Paris** HE is in Paris; **c'est lui qui l'a fait** HE did it

4 (*objet, forme emphatique*) him; **c'est lui que j'attends** I'm waiting for HIM
5: **lui-même** himself; itself

luire [lɥir] *vi* (*gén*) to shine, gleam; (*surface mouillée*) to glisten; (*reflets chauds, cuivrés*) to glow

lumière [lymjɛr] *nf* light; **lumières** *nfpl* (*d'une personne*) knowledge *sg*, wisdom *sg*; **à la ~ de** by the light of; (*fig: événements*) in the light of; **fais de la ~** let's have some light, give us some light; **faire (toute) la ~ sur** (*fig*) to clarify (completely); **mettre en ~** (*fig*) to highlight; **du jour/soleil** day/sunlight

luminaire [lyminɛr] *nm* lamp, light

lumineux, -euse [lyminø, -øz] *adj* (*émettant de la lumière*) luminous; (*éclairé*) illuminated; (*ciel, journée, couleur*) bright; (*relatif à la lumière: rayon etc*) of light, light *cpd*; (*fig: regard*) radiant

lunatique [lynatik] *adj* whimsical, temperamental

lundi [lœdi] *nm* Monday; **on est ~** it's Monday; **le ~ 20 août** Monday 20th August; **il est venu ~** he came on Monday; **le(s) ~(s)** on Mondays; **à ~!** see you (on) Monday!; **~ de Pâques** Easter Monday; **~ de Pentecôte** Whit Monday (*Brit*)

lune [lyn] *nf* moon; **pleine/nouvelle ~** full/new moon; **être dans la ~** (*distrait*) to have one's head in the clouds; **~ de miel** honeymoon

lunette [lynɛt] *nf*: **~s** *nfpl* glasses, spectacles; (*protectrices*) goggles; **~ d'approche** telescope; **~ arrière** (*Auto*) rear window; **~s noires** dark glasses; **~s de soleil** sunglasses

lus *etc* [ly] *vb voir* lire

lustre [lystr] *nm* (*de plafond*) chandelier; (*fig: éclat*) lustre

lustrer [lystre] *vt*: **~ qch** (*faire briller*) to make sth shine; (*user*) to make sth shiny

lut [ly] *vb voir* lire

luth [lyt] *nm* lute

lutin [lytɛ̃] *nm* imp, goblin

lutte [lyt] *nf* (*conflit*) struggle; (*Sport*): **la ~** wrestling; **de haute ~** after a hard-fought struggle; **~ des classes** class struggle; **~ libre** (*Sport*) all-in wrestling

lutter [lyte] *vi* to fight, struggle; (*Sport*) to wrestle

luxe [lyks] *nm* luxury; **un ~ de** (*détails, précautions*) a wealth of; **de ~** *adj* luxury *cpd*

Luxembourg [lyksãbur] *nm*: **le ~** Luxembourg

luxembourgeois, e [lyksãburʒwa, -waz] *adj* of *ou* from Luxembourg ▷ *nm/f*: **L~, e** inhabitant *ou* native of Luxembourg

luxer [lykse] *vt*: **se ~ l'épaule** to dislocate one's shoulder

luxueux, -euse [lyksɥø, -øz] *adj* luxurious

luxure [lyksyr] *nf* lust

luxuriant, e [lyksyrjã, -ãt] *adj* luxuriant, lush

ycée [lise] nm (state) secondary (Brit) ou high (US) school; **~ technique** technical secondary ou high school; *see note*

ycéen, ne [liseɛ̃, -ɛn] nm/f secondary school pupil

yon [ljɔ̃] n Lyons

yophilisé, e [ljɔfilize] adj (café) freeze-dried

yrique [liʀik] adj lyrical; (Opéra) lyric; **artiste ~** opera singer; **comédie ~** comic opera; **théâtre ~** opera house (for light opera)

ys [lis] nm lily

m

M, m [ɛm] nm inv M, m ▷ abr = **majeur**; **masculin**; **mètre**; **Monsieur**; (= million) M; **M comme Marcel** M for Mike

m' [m] pron voir **me**

ma [ma] adj poss voir **mon**

macaron [makaʀɔ̃] nm (gâteau) macaroon; (insigne) (round) badge

macaroni [makaʀɔni] nm, **macaronis** nmpl macaroni sg; **~(s) au gratin** macaroni cheese (Brit), macaroni and cheese (US)

Macédoine [masedwan] nf Macedonia

macédoine [masedwan] nf: **~ de fruits** fruit salad; **~ de légumes** mixed vegetables pl

macérer [maseʀe] vi, vt to macerate; (dans du vinaigre) to pickle

mâcher [maʃe] vt to chew; **ne pas ~ ses mots** not to mince one's words; **~ le travail à qn** (fig) to spoon-feed sb, do half sb's work for him

machin [maʃɛ̃] nm (fam) thingamajig, thing; (personne): **M~(e)** nm(f) what's-his(ou her)-name

machinal, e, -aux [maʃinal, -o] adj mechanical, automatic

machinalement [maʃinalmmɑ̃] adv mechanically, automatically

machination [maʃinasjɔ̃] nf scheming, frame-up

machine [maʃin] nf machine; (locomotive; de navire etc) engine; (fig: rouages) machinery; (fam: personne): **M~** what's-her-name; **faire ~ arrière** (Navig) to go astern; (fig) to backpedal; **~ à laver/coudre/tricoter** washing/sewing/knitting machine; **~ à écrire** typewriter; **~ à sous** fruit machine; **~ à vapeur** steam engine

macho [matʃo] *(fam) nm* male chauvinist

mâchoire [mɑʃwaʀ] *nf* jaw; **~ de frein** brake shoe

mâchonner [mɑʃɔne] *vt* to chew (at)

maçon [masɔ̃] *nm* bricklayer; *(constructeur)* builder

maçonnerie [masɔnʀi] *nf (murs: de brique)* brickwork; (: *de pierre)* masonry, stonework; *(activité)* bricklaying; building; **~ de béton** concrete

maculer [makyle] *vt* to stain; *(Typo)* to mackle

Madagascar [madagaskaʀ] *nf* Madagascar

Madame [madam] *(pl* **Mesdames)** [medam] *nf*: **~ X** Mrs X; **occupez-vous de ~/Monsieur/Mademoiselle** please serve this lady/gentleman/(young) lady; **bonjour ~/Monsieur/Mademoiselle** good morning; *(ton déférent)* good morning Madam/Sir/Madam; *(le nom est connu)* good morning Mrs X/Mr X/Miss X; **~/Monsieur/Mademoiselle!** *(pour appeler)* excuse me!; *(ton déférent)* Madam/Sir/Miss!; **~/Monsieur/Mademoiselle** *(sur lettre)* Dear Madam/Sir/Madam; **chère ~/cher Monsieur/chère Mademoiselle** Dear Mrs X/Mr X/Miss X; **~ la Directrice** the director; the manageress; the head teacher; **Mesdames** Ladies; **mesdames, mesdemoiselles, messieurs** ladies and gentlemen

madeleine [madlɛn] *nf* madeleine, ≈ sponge finger cake

Mademoiselle [madmwazɛl] *(pl* **Mesdemoiselles)** [medmwazɛl] *nf* Miss; *voir aussi* **Madame**

Madère [madɛʀ] *nf* Madeira ▷ *nm*: **madère** Madeira (wine)

Madrid [madʀid] *n* Madrid

magasin [magazɛ̃] *nm (boutique)* shop; *(entrepôt)* warehouse; *(d'arme, appareil photo)* magazine; **en ~** *(Comm)* in stock; **faire les ~s** to go (a)round the shops, do the shops; **~ d'alimentation** grocer's (shop) *(Brit)*, grocery store *(US)*

⬡ MAGASINS

French shops are usually open from 9am to noon and from 2pm to 7pm. Most shops are closed on Sunday and some do not open on Monday. In bigger towns and shopping centres, most shops are open throughout the day.

magazine [magazin] *nm* magazine

Maghreb [magʀɛb] *nm*: **le ~** the Maghreb, North(-West) Africa

maghrébin, e [magʀebɛ̃, -in] *adj* of ou from the Maghreb, North African ▷ *nm/f*: **M~, e** North African, Maghrebi

magicien, ne [maʒisjɛ̃, -ɛn] *nm/f* magician

magie [maʒi] *nf* magic; **~ noire** black magic

magique [maʒik] *adj (occulte)* magic; *(fig)* magical

magistral, e, -aux [maʒistʀal, -o] *adj (œuvre adresse)* masterly; *(ton)* authoritative; *(gifle etc)* sound, resounding; *(ex cathedra)*: **enseignement ~** lecturing, lectures *pl*; **cours ~** lecture

magistrat [maʒistʀa] *nm* magistrate

magnat [magna] *nm* tycoon, magnate

magnétique [maɲetik] *adj* magnetic

magnétiser [maɲetize] *vt* to magnetize; *(fig)* to mesmerize, hypnotize

magnétophone [maɲetɔfɔn] *nm* tape recorder; **~ à cassettes** cassette recorder

magnétoscope [maɲetɔskɔp] *nm*: **~ (à cassette)** video (recorder)

magnifique [maɲifik] *adj* magnificent

magot [mago] *nm (argent)* pile (of money); *(économies)* nest egg

magouille [maguj] *nf (fam)* scheming

magret [magʀɛ] *nm*: **~ de canard** duck breast

mai [mɛ] *nm* May; *see note*; *voir aussi* **juillet**

⬡ LE PREMIER MAI

Le premier mai is a public holiday in France and commemorates the trades union demonstrations in the United States in 1886 when workers demanded the right to an eight-hour working day. Sprigs of lily of the valley are traditionally exchanged. *Le 8 mai* is also a public holiday and commemorates the surrender of the German army to Eisenhower on 7 May, 1945. It is marked by parades of ex-servicemen and ex-servicewomen in most towns. The social upheavals of May and June 1968, with their student demonstrations, workers' strikes and general rioting, are usually referred to as "les événements de mai 68". De Gaulle's Government survived, but reforms in education and a move towards decentralization ensued.

maigre [mɛgʀ] *adj* (very) thin, skinny; *(viande)* lean; *(fromage)* low-fat; *(végétation)* thin, sparse; *(fig)* poor, meagre, skimpy ▷ *adv*: **faire ~** not to eat meat; **jours ~s** days of abstinence, fish days

maigreur [mɛgʀœʀ] *nf* thinness

maigrir [megʀiʀ] *vi* to get thinner, lose weight ▷ *vt*: **~ qn** *(vêtement)* to make sb look slim(mer); **~ de 2 kilos** to lose 2 kilos

mail [mɛl] *nm* email

maille [maj] *nf (boucle)* stitch; *(ouverture)* hole (in the mesh); **avoir ~ à partir avec qn** to have a brush with sb; **~ à l'endroit/à l'envers** knit one/purl one; *(boucle)* plain/purl stitch

aillet [majɛ] nm mallet

aillon [majɔ̃] nm link

aillot [majo] nm (aussi: ~ de corps) vest; (de danseur) leotard; (de sportif) jersey; ~ de **bain** swimming ou bathing (Brit) costume, swimsuit; (d'homme) (swimming ou bathing (Brit)) trunks pl; ~ **deux pièces** two-piece swimsuit, bikini; ~ **jaune** yellow jersey

ain [mɛ̃] nf hand; **la ~ dans la ~** hand in hand; **à deux ~s** with both hands; **à une ~** with one hand; **à la ~** (tenir, avoir) in one's hand; (faire, tricoter etc) by hand; **se donner la ~** to hold hands; **donner ou tendre la ~ à qn** to hold out one's hand to sb; **se serrer la ~** to shake hands; **serrer la ~ à qn** to shake hands with sb; **sous la ~** to ou at hand; **haut les ~s!** hands up!; **à ~ levée** (Art) freehand; **à ~s levées** (voter) with a show of hands; **attaque à ~ armée** armed attack; **à ~ droite/gauche** to the right/left; **à remettre en ~s propres** to be delivered personally; **de première ~** (renseignement) first-hand; (Comm: voiture etc) with only one previous owner; **faire ~ basse sur** to help o.s. to; **mettre la dernière ~ à** to put the finishing touches to; **mettre la ~ à la pâte** (fig) to lend a hand; **avoir/passer la ~** (Cartes) to lead/hand over the lead; **s'en laver les ~s** (fig) to wash one's hands of it; **se faire/perdre la ~** to get one's hand in/lose one's touch; **avoir qch bien en ~** to have got the hang of sth; **en un tour de ~** (fig) in the twinkling of an eye; ~ **courante** handrail

ain-d'œuvre [mɛ̃dœvR] nf manpower, labour (Brit), labor (US)

ain-forte [mɛ̃fɔRt] nf: **prêter ~ à qn** to come to sb's assistance

ainmise [mɛ̃miz] nf seizure; (fig): **avoir la ~ sur** to have a grip ou stranglehold on

ains-libres [mɛ̃libR] adj inv (téléphone, kit) hands-free

aint, e [mɛ̃, mɛ̃t] adj many a; **~s** many; **à ~es reprises** time and (time) again

aintenant [mɛ̃tnɑ̃] adv now; (actuellement) nowadays

aintenir [mɛ̃tniR] vt (retenir, soutenir) to support; (contenir: foule etc) to keep in check, hold back; (conserver) to maintain, uphold; (affirmer) to maintain; **se maintenir** vi (paix, temps) to hold; (prix) to keep steady; (préjugé) to persist; (malade) to remain stable

maintien [mɛ̃tjɛ̃] nm maintaining, upholding; (attitude) bearing; ~ **de l'ordre** maintenance of law and order

maire [mɛR] nm mayor

mairie [meRi] nf (bâtiment) town hall; (administration) town council

mais [mɛ] conj but; ~ **non!** of course not!; ~ **enfin** but after all; (indignation) look here!; ~ **encore?** is that all?

maïs [mais] nm maize (Brit), corn (US)

maison [mɛzɔ̃] nf (bâtiment) house; (chez-soi) home; (Comm) firm; (famille): **ami de la ~**

friend of the family ▷ adj inv (Culin) home-made; (: au restaurant) made by the chef; (Comm) in-house, own; (fam) first-rate; **à la ~** at home; (direction) home; ~ **d'arrêt** (short-stay) prison; ~ **centrale** ≈ prison; ~ **close** brothel; ~ **de correction** ≈ remand home (Brit), ≈ reformatory (US); ~ **de la culture** ≈ arts centre; ~ **des jeunes** ≈ youth club; ~ **mère** parent company; ~ **de passe** = **maison close**; ~ **de repos** convalescent home; ~ **de retraite** old people's home; ~ **de santé** mental home

maisonnée [mɛzɔne] nf household, family

maisonnette [mɛzɔnɛt] nf small house

maître, -esse [mɛtR, mɛtRɛs] nm/f master/mistress; (Scol) teacher, schoolmaster(-mistress) ▷ nm (peintre etc) master; (titre): **M~ (M^e)** Maître, term of address for lawyers etc ▷ nf (amante) mistress ▷ adj (principal, essentiel) main; **maison de ~** family seat; **être ~ de** (soi-même, situation) to be in control of; **se rendre ~ de** (pays, ville) to gain control of; (situation, incendie) to bring under control; **être passé ~ dans l'art de** to be a (past) master in the art of; **une maîtresse femme** a forceful woman; ~ **d'armes** fencing master; ~ **auxiliaire (MA)** (Scol) temporary teacher; ~ **chanteur** blackmailer; ~ **de chapelle** choirmaster; ~ **de conférences** ≈ senior lecturer (Brit), ≈ assistant professor (US); ~/**maîtresse d'école** teacher, schoolmaster/-mistress; ~ **d'hôtel** (domestique) butler; (d'hôtel) head waiter; ~ **de maison** host; ~ **nageur** lifeguard; ~ **d'œuvre** (Constr) project manager; ~ **d'ouvrage** (Constr) client; ~ **queux** chef; **maîtresse de maison** hostess; (ménagère) housewife

maîtrise [metRiz] nf (aussi: ~ **de soi**) self-control, self-possession; (habileté) skill, mastery; (suprématie) mastery, command; (diplôme) ≈ master's degree; see note; (chefs d'équipe) supervisory staff

🔹 **MAÎTRISE**

🔹 The maîtrise is a French degree which is
🔹 awarded to university students if they
🔹 successfully complete two more years'
🔹 study after the "DEUG". Students
🔹 wishing to go on to do research or to take
🔹 the "agrégation" must hold a maîtrise.

maîtriser [metRize] vt (cheval, incendie) to (bring under) control; (sujet) to master; (émotion) to control, master; **se maîtriser** to control o.s.

majestueux, -euse [maʒɛstɥø, -øz] adj majestic

majeur, e [maʒœR] adj (important) major; (Jur) of age; (fig) adult ▷ nm/f (Jur) person who has come of age ou attained his (ou her) majority

▷ *nm* (*doigt*) middle finger; **en ~e partie** for the most part; **la ~e partie de** most of

majoration [maʒɔRasjɔ̃] *nf* increase

majorer [maʒɔRe] *vt* to increase

majoritaire [maʒɔRitɛR] *adj* majority *cpd*; **système/scrutin ~** majority system/ballot

majorité [maʒɔRite] *nf* (*gén*) majority; (*parti*) party in power; **en ~** composé *etc*) mainly; **avoir la ~** to have the majority

majuscule [maʒyskyl] *adj, nf*: **(lettre) ~** capital (letter)

mal, maux [mal, mo] *nm* (*opposé au bien*) evil; (*tort, dommage*) harm; (*douleur physique*) pain, ache; (*maladie*) illness, sickness no *pl*; (*difficulté, peine*) trouble; (*souffrance morale*) pain ▷ *adv* badly ▷ *adj*: **c'est ~ (de faire)** it's bad *ou* wrong (to do); **être ~ (à l'aise)** to be uncomfortable; **être ~ avec qn** to be on bad terms with sb; **être au plus ~** (*malade*) to be very bad; (*brouillé*) to be at daggers drawn; **il comprend ~** he has difficulty in understanding; **il a ~ compris** he misunderstood; **se sentir** *ou* **se trouver ~** to feel ill *ou* unwell; **~ tourner** to go wrong; **dire/penser du ~ de** to speak/think ill of; **ne vouloir de ~ à personne** to wish nobody any ill; **il n'a rien fait de ~** he has done nothing wrong; **avoir du ~ à faire qch** to have trouble doing sth; **se donner du ~ pour faire qch** to go to a lot of trouble to do sth; **ne voir aucun ~ à** to see no harm in, see nothing wrong in; **craignant ~ faire** fearing he *etc* was doing the wrong thing; **sans penser** *ou* **songer à ~** without meaning any harm; **faire du ~ à qn** to hurt sb; to harm sb; **se faire ~** to hurt o.s.; **se faire ~ au pied** to hurt one's foot; **ça fait ~** it hurts; **j'ai ~ (ici)** it hurts (here); **j'ai ~ au dos** my back aches, I've got a pain in my back; **avoir ~ à la tête/à la gorge** to have a headache/a sore throat; **avoir ~ aux dents/à l'oreille** to have toothache/earache; **avoir le ~ de l'air** to be airsick; **avoir le ~ du pays** to be homesick; **~ de mer** seasickness; **~ de la route** carsickness; **~ en point** *adj inv* in a bad state; **maux de ventre** stomach ache *sg*; *voir aussi* **cœur**

malade [malad] *adj* ill, sick; (*poitrine, jambe*) bad; (*plante*) diseased; (*fig: entreprise, monde*) ailing ▷ *nm/f* invalid, sick person; (*à l'hôpital etc*) patient; **tomber ~** to fall ill; **être ~ du cœur** to have heart trouble *ou* a bad heart; **grand ~** seriously ill person; **~ mental** mentally sick *ou* ill person

maladie [maladi] *nf* (*spécifique*) disease, illness; (*mauvaise santé*) illness, sickness; (*fig: manie*) mania; **être rongé par la ~** to be wasting away (through illness); **~ d'Alzheimer** Alzheimer's disease; **~ de peau** skin disease

maladif, -ive [maladif, -iv] *adj* sickly; (*curiosité, besoin*) pathological

maladresse [maladRɛs] *nf* clumsiness no *pl*; (*gaffe*) blunder

maladroit, e [maladRwa, -wat] *adj* clumsy

malaise [malɛz] *nm* (*Méd*) feeling of faintness; feeling of discomfort; (*fig*) uneasiness, malaise; **avoir un ~** to feel faint *ou* dizzy

malaisé, e [maleze] *adj* difficult

Malaisie [malɛzi] *nf*: **la ~** Malaysia; **la péninsule de ~** the Malay Peninsula

malaria [malaRja] *nf* malaria

malaxer [malakse] *vt* (*pétrir*) to knead; (*mêler*) to mix

malbouffe [malbuf] *nf* (*fam*): **la ~** junk food

malchance [malʃɑ̃s] *nf* misfortune, ill luck no *pl*; **par ~** unfortunately; **quelle ~!** what bad luck!

malchanceux, -euse [malʃɑ̃sø, -øz] *adj* unlucky

mâle [mɑl] *adj* (*Élec, Tech*) male; (*viril: voix, traits*) manly ▷ *nm* male

malédiction [malediksjɔ̃] *nf* curse

malencontreux, -euse [malɑ̃kɔ̃tRø, -øz] *adj* unfortunate, untoward

malentendant, e [malɑ̃tɑ̃dɑ̃, -ɑ̃t] *nm/f*: **les ~s** the hard of hearing

malentendu [malɑ̃tɑ̃dy] *nm* misunderstanding; **il y a eu un ~** there's been a misunderstanding

malfaçon [malfasɔ̃] *nf* fault

malfaisant, e [malfəzɑ̃, -ɑ̃t] *adj* evil, harmful

malfaiteur [malfɛtœR] *nm* lawbreaker, criminal; (*voleur*) burglar, thief

malfamé, e [malfame] *adj* disreputable, of ill repute

malgache [malgaʃ] *adj* Malagasy, Madagascan ▷ *nm* (*Ling*) Malagasy ▷ *nm/f*: **M~** Malagasy, Madagascan

malgré [malgRe] *prép* in spite of, despite; **~ tout** *adv* in spite of everything

malhabile [malabil] *adj* clumsy

malheur [malœR] *nm* (*situation*) adversity, misfortune; (*événement*) misfortune; (: *plus fort*) disaster, tragedy; **par ~** unfortunately; **quel ~!** what a shame *ou* pity!; **faire un ~** (*fam: un éclat*) to do something desperate; (: *avoir du succès*) to be a smash hit

malheureusement [malœRøzmɑ̃] *adv* unfortunately

malheureux, -euse [malœRø, -øz] *adj* (*triste*) unhappy, miserable; (*infortuné, regrettable*) unfortunate; (*malchanceux*) unlucky; (*insignifiant*) wretched ▷ *nm/f* (*infortuné, misérable*) poor soul; (*indigent, miséreux*) unfortunate creature; **les ~** the destitute; **avoir la main malheureuse** (*au jeu*) to be unlucky; (*tout casser*) to be ham-fisted

malhonnête [malɔnɛt] *adj* dishonest

malhonnêteté [malɔnɛtte] *nf* dishonesty; rudeness no *pl*

malice [malis] *nf* mischievousness; (*méchanceté*): **par ~** out of malice *ou* spite; **sans ~** guileless

malicieux, -euse [malisjø, -øz] *adj* mischievous

malin, -igne [malɛ̃, -iɲ] (*f gén* **maline**) *adj* (*futé*) smart, shrewd; (: *sourire*) knowing; (*Méd, influence*) malignant; **faire le ~** to show off; **éprouver un ~ plaisir à** to take malicious pleasure in

malingre [malɛ̃gʀ] *adj* puny

malle [mal] *nf* trunk; (*Auto*): **~ (arrière)** boot (*Brit*), trunk (*US*)

mallette [malɛt] *nf* (*valise*) (small) suitcase; (*aussi*: **~ de voyage**) overnight case; (*pour documents*) attaché case

malmener [malməne] *vt* to manhandle; (*fig*) to give a rough ride to

malodorant, e [malɔdɔʀɑ̃, -ɑ̃t] *adj* foul-smelling

malotru [malɔtʀy] *nm* lout, boor

malpoli, e [malpɔli] *nm/f* rude individual ▷ *adj* impolite

malpropre [malpʀɔpʀ] *adj* (*personne, vêtement*) dirty; (*travail*) slovenly; (*histoire, plaisanterie*) unsavoury (*Brit*), unsavory (*US*), smutty; (*malhonnête*) dishonest

malsain, e [malsɛ̃, -ɛn] *adj* unhealthy

malt [malt] *nm* malt; **pur ~** (*whisky*) malt (whisky)

Malte [malt] *nf* Malta

maltraiter [maltʀete] *vt* (*brutaliser*) to manhandle, ill-treat; (*critiquer, éreinter*) to slate (*Brit*), roast

malveillance [malvejɑ̃s] *nf* (*animosité*) ill will; (*intention de nuire*) malevolence; (*Jur*) malicious intent *no pl*

malversation [malvɛʀsasjɔ̃] *nf* embezzlement, misappropriation (of funds)

mal-vivre [malvivʀ] *nm inv* malaise

maman [mamɑ̃] *nf* mum(my) (*Brit*), mom (*US*)

mamelle [mamɛl] *nf* teat

mamelon [mamlɔ̃] *nm* (*Anat*) nipple; (*colline*) knoll, hillock

mamie [mami] *nf* (*fam*) granny

mammifère [mamifɛʀ] *nm* mammal

mammouth [mamut] *nm* mammoth

manche [mɑ̃ʃ] *nf* (*de vêtement*) sleeve; (*d'un jeu, tournoi*) round; (*Géo*): **la M~** the (English) Channel ▷ *nm* (*d'outil, casserole*) handle; (*de pelle, pioche etc*) shaft; (*de violon, guitare*) neck; (*fam*) clumsy oaf; **faire la ~** to pass the hat; **~ à air** (*Aviat*) wind-sock; **à ~s courtes/longues** short-/long-sleeved; **~ à balai** *nm* broomstick; (*Aviat, Inform*) joystick *m inv*

manchette [mɑ̃ʃɛt] *nf* (*de chemise*) cuff; (*coup*) forearm blow; (*titre*) headline

manchot [mɑ̃ʃo] *nm* one-armed man; armless man; (*Zool*) penguin

mandarine [mɑ̃daʀin] *nf* mandarin (orange), tangerine

mandat [mɑ̃da] *nm* (*postal*) postal *ou* money order; (*d'un député etc*) mandate; (*procuration*) power of attorney, proxy; (*Police*) warrant; **~ d'amener** summons *sg*; **~ d'arrêt** warrant

for arrest; **~ de dépôt** committal order; **~ de perquisition** (*Police*) search warrant

mandataire [mɑ̃datɛʀ] *nm/f* (*représentant, délégué*) representative; (*Jur*) proxy

manège [manɛʒ] *nm* riding school; (*à la foire*) roundabout (*Brit*), merry-go-round; (*fig*) game, ploy; **faire un tour de ~** to go for a ride on a *ou* the roundabout *etc*; **~ (de chevaux de bois)** roundabout (*Brit*), merry-go-round

manette [manɛt] *nf* lever, tap; **~ de jeu** (*Inform*) joystick

mangeable [mɑ̃ʒabl] *adj* edible, eatable

mangeoire [mɑ̃ʒwaʀ] *nf* trough, manger

manger [mɑ̃ʒe] *vt* to eat; (*ronger: rouille etc*) to eat into *ou* away; (*utiliser, consommer*) to eat up ▷ *vi* to eat; **donner à ~** (*à enfant*) to feed

mangeur, -euse [mɑ̃ʒœʀ, -øz] *nm/f* eater

mangue [mɑ̃g] *nf* mango

maniable [manjabl] *adj* (*outil*) handy; (*voiture, voilier*) easy to handle; manoeuvrable (*Brit*), maneuverable (*US*); (*fig: personne*) easily influenced, manipulable

maniaque [manjak] *adj* (*pointilleux, méticuleux*) finicky, fussy; (*atteint de manie*) suffering from a mania ▷ *nm/f* (*méticuleux*) fusspot; (*fou*) maniac

manie [mani] *nf* mania; (*tic*) odd habit; **avoir la ~ de** to be obsessive about

manier [manje] *vt* to handle; **se manier** *vi* (*fam*) to get a move on

maniéré, e [manjeʀe] *adj* affected

manière [manjɛʀ] *nf* (*façon*) way, manner; (*genre, style*) style; **manières** *nfpl* (*attitude*) manners; (*chichis*) fuss *sg*; **de ~ à** so as to; **de telle ~ que** in such a way that; **de cette ~** in this way *ou* manner; **d'une ~ générale** generally speaking, as a general rule; **de toute ~** in any case; **d'une certaine ~** in a (certain) way; **faire des ~s** to put on airs; **employer la ~ forte** to use strong-arm tactics

manif [manif] *nf* (*manifestation*) demo

manifestant, e [manifɛstɑ̃, -ɑ̃t] *nm/f* demonstrator

manifestation [manifɛstasjɔ̃] *nf* (*de joie, mécontentement*) expression, demonstration; (*symptôme*) outward sign; (*fête etc*) event; (*Pol*) demonstration

manifeste [manifɛst] *adj* obvious, evident ▷ *nm* manifesto

manifester [manifɛste] *vt* (*volonté, intentions*) to show, indicate; (*joie, peur*) to express, show ▷ *vi* (*Pol*) to demonstrate; **se manifester** *vi* (*émotion*) to show *ou* express itself; (*difficultés*) to arise; (*symptômes*) to appear; (*témoin etc*) to come forward

manigance [manigɑ̃s] *nf* scheme

manigancer [manigɑ̃se] *vt* to plot, devise

manipulation [manipylasjɔ̃] *nf* handling; (*Pol, génétique*) manipulation

manipuler [manipyle] *vt* to handle; (*fig*) to manipulate

manivelle [manivɛl] nf crank

mannequin [mankɛ̃] nm (*Couture*) dummy; (*Mode*) model

manœuvre [manœvʀ] nf (*gén*) manoeuvre (*Brit*), maneuver (*US*) ▷ nm (*ouvrier*) labourer (*Brit*), laborer (*US*)

manœuvrer [manœvʀe] vt to manoeuvre (*Brit*), maneuver (*US*); (*levier, machine*) to operate; (*personne*) to manipulate ▷ vi to manoeuvre *ou* maneuver

manoir [manwaʀ] nm manor *ou* country house

manque [mɑ̃k] nm (*insuffisance*): ~ **de** lack of; (*vide*) emptiness, gap; (*Méd*) withdrawal; **manques** nmpl (*lacunes*) faults, defects; **par ~ de** for want of; **~ à gagner** loss of profit *ou* earnings; **être en état de ~** to suffer withdrawal symptoms

manqué [mɑ̃ke] adj failed; **garçon ~** tomboy

manquer [mɑ̃ke] vi (*faire défaut*) to be lacking; (*être absent*) to be missing; (*échouer*) to fail ▷ vt to miss ▷ vb impers: **il (nous) manque encore 10 euros** we are still 10 euros short; **il manque des pages (au livre)** there are some pages missing *ou* some pages are missing (from the book); **l'argent qui leur manque** the money they need *ou* are short of; **le pied/la voix lui manqua** he missed his footing/his voice failed him; **~ à qn** (*absent etc*): **il/cela me manque** I miss him/that; **~ à** vt (*règles etc*) to be in breach of, fail to observe; **~ de** vt to lack; (*Comm*) to be out of (stock of); **ne pas ~ de faire**, **je ne ~ai pas de le lui dire** I'll be sure to tell him; **~ (de) faire**, **il a manqué (de) se tuer** he very nearly got killed; **il ne manquerait plus qu'il fasse** all we need now is for him to do; **je n'y manquerai pas** leave it to me, I'll definitely do it

mansarde [mɑ̃saʀd] nf attic

mansardé, e [mɑ̃saʀde] adj: **chambre ~e** attic room

manteau, x [mɑ̃to] nm coat; **~ de cheminée** mantelpiece; **sous le ~** (*fig*) under cover

manucure [manykyʀ] nf manicurist

manuel, le [manɥɛl] adj manual ▷ nm/f manually gifted pupil (*as opposed to intellectually gifted*) ▷ nm (*ouvrage*) manual, handbook

manufacture [manyfaktyʀ] nf (*établissement*) factory; (*fabrication*) manufacture

manufacturé, e [manyfaktyʀe] adj manufactured

manuscrit, e [manyskʀi, -it] adj handwritten ▷ nm manuscript

manutention [manytɑ̃sjɔ̃] nf (*Comm*) handling; (*local*) storehouse

mappemonde [mapmɔ̃d] nf (*plane*) map of the world; (*sphère*) globe

maquereau, x [makʀo] nm (*Zool*) mackerel inv; (*fam*: proxénète) pimp

maquette [makɛt] nf (*d'un décor, bâtiment, véhicule*) (scale) model; (*Typo*) mockup; (: *d'une page illustrée, affiche*) paste-up; (: *prêt à la reproduction*) artwork

maquillage [makijaʒ] nm making up; faking; (*produits*) make-up

maquiller [makije] vt (*personne, visage*) to make up; (*truquer: passeport, statistique*) to fake; (: *voiture volée*) to do over (*respray etc*); **se maquiller** vi to make o.s. up

maquis [maki] nm (*Géo*) scrub; (*fig*) tangle; (*Mil*) maquis, underground fighting *no pl*

maraîcher, -ère [maʀeʃe, maʀeʃɛʀ] adj: **cultures maraîchères** market gardening *sg* ▷ nm/f market gardener

marais [maʀɛ] nm marsh, swamp; **~ salant** saltworks

marasme [maʀasm] nm (*Pol, Écon*) stagnation, sluggishness; (*accablement*) dejection, depression

marathon [maʀatɔ̃] nm marathon

maraudeur, -euse [maʀodœʀ, -øz] nm/f marauder; prowler

marbre [maʀbʀ] nm (*pierre, statue*) marble; (*d'une table, commode*) marble top; (*Typo*) stone, bed; **rester de ~** to remain stonily indifferent

marc [maʀ] nm (*de raisin, pommes*) marc; **~ de café** coffee grounds *pl ou* dregs *pl*

marchand, e [maʀʃɑ̃, -ɑ̃d] nm/f shopkeeper, tradesman(-woman); (*au marché*) stallholder; (*spécifique*): **~ de cycles/tapis** bicycle/carpet dealer; **~ de charbon/vins** coal/wine merchant ▷ adj: **prix/valeur ~(e)** market price/value; **qualité ~e** standard quality; **~ en gros/au détail** wholesaler/retailer; **~ de biens** real estate agent; **~ de canons** (*péj*) arms dealer; **~ de couleurs** ironmonger (*Brit*), hardware dealer (*US*); **~ de fruits** fruiterer (*Brit*), fruit seller (*US*); **~/e de journaux** newsagent; **~/e de légumes** greengrocer (*Brit*), produce dealer (*US*); **~/e de poisson** fishmonger (*Brit*), fish seller (*US*); **~/e de(s) quatre-saisons** costermonger (*Brit*), street vendor (selling fresh fruit and vegetables); **~ de sable** (*fig*) sandman; **~ de tableaux** art dealer

marchander [maʀʃɑ̃de] vt (*article*) to bargain *ou* haggle over; (*éloges*) to be sparing with ▷ vi to bargain, haggle

marchandise [maʀʃɑ̃diz] nf goods *pl*, merchandise *no pl*

marche [maʀʃ] nf (*d'escalier*) step; (*activité*) walking; (*promenade, trajet, allure*) walk; (*démarche*) walk, gait; (*Mil etc, Mus*) march; (*fonctionnement*) running; (*progression*) progress; (*des événements*) course; **à une heure de ~** an hour's walk (away); **ouvrir/fermer la ~** to lead the way/bring up the rear; **dans le sens de la ~** (*Rail*) facing the engine; **en ~** (*monter etc*) while the vehicle is moving *ou* in motion; **mettre en ~** to start; **remettre qch en ~** to set *ou* start sth going again; **se mettre en ~** (*personne*) to get moving; (*machine*) to start; **être en état de ~** to be in working order; **~ arrière** (*Auto*) reverse (gear);

faire ~ arrière (Auto) to reverse; (fig) to backtrack, back-pedal; **~ à suivre** (correct) procedure; (sur notice) (step by step) instructions pl

marché [maʁʃe] nm (lieu, Comm, Écon) market; (ville) trading centre; (transaction) bargain, deal; **par-dessus le ~** into the bargain; **faire son ~** to do one's shopping; **mettre le ~ en main à qn** to tell sb to take it or leave it; **~ au comptant** (Bourse) spot market; **~ aux fleurs** flower market; **~ noir** black market; **faire du ~ noir** to buy and sell on the black market; **~ aux puces** flea market; **~ à terme** (Bourse) forward market; **~ du travail** labour market

marchepied [maʁʃəpje] nm (Rail) step; (Auto) running board; (fig) stepping stone

marcher [maʁʃe] vi to walk; (Mil) to march; (aller: voiture, train, affaires) to go; (prospérer) to go well; (fonctionner) to work, run; (fam: consentir) to go along, agree; (: croire naïvement) to be taken in; **~ sur** to walk on; (mettre le pied sur) to step on ou in; (Mil) to march upon; **~ dans** (herbe etc) to walk in ou on; (flaque) to step in; **faire ~ qn** (pour rire) to pull sb's leg; (pour tromper) to lead sb up the garden path

marcheur, -euse [maʁʃœʁ, -øz] nm/f walker

mardi [maʁdi] nm Tuesday; **M~ gras** Shrove Tuesday; voir aussi **lundi**

mare [maʁ] nf pond; (flaque) pool; **~ de sang** pool of blood

marécage [maʁekaʒ] nm marsh, swamp

marécageux, -euse [maʁekaʒø, -øz] adj marshy, swampy

maréchal, -aux [maʁeʃal, -o] nm marshal; **~ des logis** (Mil) sergeant

maréchal-ferrant (pl **maréchaux-ferrants**) [maʁeʃalferɑ̃, maʁeʃo-] nm blacksmith

marée [maʁe] nf tide; (poissons) fresh (sea) fish; **~ haute/basse** high/low tide; **~ montante/descendante** rising/ebb tide; **~ noire** oil slick

marelle [maʁɛl] nf: **(jouer à) la ~** (to play) hopscotch

margarine [maʁɡaʁin] nf margarine

marge [maʁʒ] nf margin; **en ~** in the margin; **en ~ de** (fig) on the fringe of; (en dehors de) cut off from; (qui se rapporte à) connected with; **~ bénéficiaire** profit margin, mark-up; **~ de sécurité** safety margin

marginal, e, -aux [maʁʒinal, -o] adj marginal ▷ nm/f (original) eccentric; (déshérité) dropout

marguerite [maʁɡəʁit] nf marguerite, (oxeye) daisy; (d'imprimante) daisy-wheel

mari [maʁi] nm husband

mariage [maʁjaʒ] nm (union, état, fig) marriage; (noce) wedding; **~ civil/religieux** registry office (Brit) ou civil/church wedding; **un ~ de raison/d'amour** a marriage of convenience/a love match; **~ blanc** unconsummated marriage; **~ en blanc** white wedding

marié, e [maʁje] adj married ▷ nm/f (bride) groom/bride; **les ~s** the bride and groom; **les (jeunes) ~s** the newly-weds

marier [maʁje] vt to marry; (fig) to blend; **se ~ (avec)** to marry, get married (to); (fig) to blend (with)

marin, e [maʁɛ̃, -in] adj sea cpd, marine ▷ nm sailor ▷ nf navy; (Art) seascape; (couleur) navy (blue); **avoir le pied ~** to be a good sailor; (garder son équilibre) to have one's sea legs; **~e de guerre** navy; **~e marchande** merchant navy; **~e à voiles** sailing ships pl

marine [maʁin] adj f, nf voir **marin** ▷ adj inv navy (blue) ▷ nm (Mil) marine

mariner [maʁine] vi, vt to marinate, marinade

marionnette [maʁjɔnɛt] nf puppet

maritalement [maʁitalmɑ̃] adv: **vivre ~** to live together (as husband and wife)

maritime [maʁitim] adj sea cpd, maritime; (ville) coastal, seaside; (droit) shipping, maritime

mark [maʁk] nm mark

marmelade [maʁməlad] nf (compote) stewed fruit, compote; **~ d'oranges** (orange) marmalade; **en ~** (fig) crushed (to a pulp)

marmite [maʁmit] nf (cooking-)pot

marmonner [maʁmɔne] vt, vi to mumble, mutter

marmot [maʁmo] nm (fam) brat

marmotter [maʁmɔte] vt (prière) to mumble, mutter

Maroc [maʁɔk] nm: **le ~** Morocco

marocain, e [maʁɔkɛ̃, -ɛn] adj Moroccan ▷ nm/f: **M~, e** Moroccan

maroquinerie [maʁɔkinʁi] nf (industrie) leather craft; (commerce) leather shop; (articles) fine leather goods pl

marquant, e [maʁkɑ̃, -ɑ̃t] adj outstanding

marque [maʁk] nf mark; (Sport, Jeu) score; (Comm: de nourriture) brand; (: de voiture, produits manufacturés) make; (: de disques) label; (insigne: d'une fonction) badge; (fig): **~ d'affection** token of affection; **~ de joie** sign of joy; **à vos ~s!** (Sport) on your marks!; **de ~** adj (Comm) brand-name cpd; proprietary; (fig) high-class; (: personnage, hôte) distinguished; **produit de ~** quality product; **~ déposée** registered trademark; **~ de fabrique** trademark; **une grande ~ de vin** a well-known brand of wine

marquer [maʁke] vt to mark; (inscrire) to write down; (bétail) to brand; (Sport: but etc) to score; (: joueur) to mark; (accentuer: taille etc) to emphasize; (manifester: refus, intérêt) to show ▷ vi (événement, personnalité) to stand out, be outstanding; (Sport) to score; **~ qn de son influence/empreinte** to have an influence/leave its impression on sb; **~ un temps d'arrêt** to pause momentarily; **~ le pas** (fig) to mark time; **il a marqué ce jour-là d'une pierre blanche** that was a red-letter day for him; **~ les points** (tenir la marque) to keep the score

marqueterie [markɛtri] nf inlaid work, marquetry

marquis, e [marki, -iz] nm/f marquis ou marquess/marchioness ▷ nf (auvent) glass canopy ou awning

marraine [marɛn] nf godmother; (d'un navire, d'une rose etc) namer

marrant, e [marɑ̃, -ɑ̃t] adj (fam) funny

marre [mar] adv (fam): **en avoir ~ de** to be fed up with

marrer [mare]: **se marrer** vi (fam) to have a (good) laugh

marron, ne [marɔ̃, -ɔn] nm (fruit) chestnut ▷ adj inv brown ▷ adj (péj) crooked; (: faux) bogus; **~s glacés** marrons glacés

marronnier [marɔnje] nm chestnut (tree)

mars [mars] nm March; voir aussi **juillet**

◈ LA MARSEILLAISE

The Marseillaise has been France's national anthem since 1879. The words of the "Chant de guerre de l'armée du Rhin", as the song was originally called, were written to an anonymous tune by an army captain called Rouget de Lisle in 1792. Adopted as a marching song by the Marseille battalion, it was finally popularized as the Marseillaise.

Marseille [marsɛj] n Marseilles

marsouin [marswɛ̃] nm porpoise

marteau, x [marto] nm hammer; (de porte) knocker; **~ pneumatique** pneumatic drill; **être ~** (fam) to be nuts

marteau-piqueur (pl marteaux-piqueurs) [martopikœr] nm pneumatic drill

marteler [martəle] vt to hammer; (mots, phrases) to rap out

martien, ne [marsjɛ̃, -ɛn] adj Martian, of ou from Mars

martyr, e [martir] nm/f martyr ▷ adj martyred; **enfants ~s** battered children

martyre [martir] nm martyrdom; (fig: sens affaibli) agony, torture; **souffrir le ~** to suffer agonies

martyriser [martirize] vt (Rel) to martyr; (fig) to bully; (: enfant) to batter

marxiste [marksist] adj, nm/f Marxist

mascara [maskara] nm mascara

masculin, e [maskylɛ̃, -in] adj masculine; (sexe, population) male; (équipe, vêtements) men's; (viril) manly ▷ nm masculine

masochiste [mazɔʃist] adj masochistic ▷ nm/f masochist

masque [mask] nm mask; **~ de beauté** face pack; **~ à gaz** gas mask; **~ de plongée** diving mask

masquer [maske] vt (cacher: porte, goût) to hide, conceal; (dissimuler: vérité, projet) to mask, obscure

massacre [masakr] nm massacre, slaughter;

jeu de ~ (fig) wholesale slaughter

massacrer [masakre] vt to massacre, slaughter; (fig: adversaire) to slaughter; (: texte etc) to murder

massage [masaʒ] nm massage

masse [mas] nf mass; (péj): **la ~** the masses pl; (Élec) earth; (maillet) sledgehammer; **masses** nfpl masses; **une ~ de, des ~s de** (fam) masses ou loads of; **en ~** adv (en bloc) in bulk; (en foule) en masse ▷ adj (exécutions, production) mass cpd; **~ monétaire** (Écon) money supply; **~ salariale** (Comm) wage(s) bill

masser [mase] vt (assembler: gens) to gather; (pétrir) to massage; **se masser** vi (foule) to gather

masseur, -euse [masœr, -øz] nm/f (personne) masseur(-euse) ▷ nm (appareil) massager

massif, -ive [masif, -iv] adj (porte) solid, massive; (visage) heavy, large; (bois, or) solid; (dose) massive; (déportations etc) mass cpd ▷ nm (montagneux) massif; (de fleurs) clump, bank; **le M~ Central** the Massif Central

massue [masy] nf club, bludgeon ▷ adj inv: **argument ~** sledgehammer argument

mastic [mastik] nm (pour vitres) putty; (pour fentes) filler

mastiquer [mastike] vt (aliment) to chew, masticate; (fente) to fill; (vitre) to putty

mat, e [mat] adj (couleur, métal) mat(t); (bruit, son) dull ▷ adj inv (Échecs): **être ~** to be checkmate

mât [mɑ] nm (Navig) mast; (poteau) pole, post

match [matʃ] nm match; **~ nul** draw, tie (US); **faire ~ nul** to draw (Brit), tie (US); **~ aller** first leg; **~ retour** second leg, return match

matelas [matla] nm mattress; **~ pneumatique** air bed ou mattress; **~ à ressorts** spring ou interior-sprung mattress

matelassé, e [matlase] adj padded; (tissu) quilted

matelot [matlo] nm sailor, seaman

mater [mate] vt (personne) to bring to heel, subdue; (révolte) to put down; (fam) to watch, look at

matérialiser [materjalize]: **se matérialiser** vi to materialize

matérialiste [materjalist] adj materialistic ▷ nm/f materialist

matériau, x [materjo] nm material; **matériaux** nmpl material(s); **~x de construction** building materials

matériel, le [materjɛl] adj material; (organisation, aide, obstacle) practical; (fig: péj: personne) materialistic ▷ nm equipment no pl; (de camping etc) gear no pl; (Inform) hardware; **il n'a pas le temps ~ de le faire** he doesn't have the time (needed) to do it; **~ d'exploitation** (Comm) plant; **~ roulant** rolling stock

maternel, le [maternɛl] adj (amour, geste) motherly, maternal; (grand-père, oncle) maternal ▷ nf (aussi: **école ~le**) (state) nursery school

maternité [matɛrnite] *nf (établissement)*
maternity hospital; *(état de mère)*
motherhood, maternity; *(grossesse)*
pregnancy; **congé de ~** maternity leave
mathématique [matematik] *adj*
mathematical
mathématiques [matematik] *nfpl*
mathematics *sg*
maths [mat] *nfpl* maths *(Brit)*, math *(US)*
matière [matjɛr] *nf (Physique)* matter; *(Comm,
Tech)* material; matter *no pl; (fig: d'un livre etc)*
subject matter, material; *(Scol)* subject; **en ~
de** as regards; **donner ~ à** to give cause to;
~ plastique plastic; **~s fécales** faeces; **~s
grasses** fat (content) *sg*; **~s premières** raw
materials
Matignon [matiɲɔ̃] *nm:* (**l'hôtel) ~** the French
Prime Minister's residence; *see note*

◈ **HÔTEL MATIGNON**
◈
◈ The *hôtel Matignon* is the Paris office and
◈ residence of the French Prime Minister.
◈ By extension, the term "Matignon" is
◈ often used to refer to the Prime Minister
◈ and his or her staff.

matin [matɛ̃] *nm, adv* morning; **le ~** *(pendant le
matin)* in the morning; **demain/hier/
dimanche ~** tomorrow/yesterday/Sunday
morning; **tous les ~s** every morning; **le
lendemain ~** (the) next morning; **du ~ au
soir** from morning till night; **une heure du
~** one o'clock in the morning; **de grand** *ou*
bon ~ early in the morning
matinal, e, -aux [matinal, -o] *adj (toilette,
gymnastique)* morning *cpd; (de bonne heure)*
early; **être ~** *(personne)* to be up early;
(: habituellement) to be an early riser
matinée [matine] *nf* morning; *(spectacle)*
matinée, afternoon performance
matou [matu] *nm* tom(cat)
matraque [matrak] *nf (de malfaiteur)* cosh
(Brit), club; *(de policier)* truncheon *(Brit)*, billy
(US)
matricule [matrikyl] *nf (aussi:* **registre ~)**
roll, register ▷ *nm (aussi:* **numéro ~:** *Mil)*
regimental number; *(: Admin)* reference
number
matrimonial, e, -aux [matrimɔnjal, -o] *adj*
marital, marriage *cpd*
maudire [modir] *vt* to curse
maudit, e [modi, -it] *adj (fam: satané)*
blasted, confounded
maugréer [mogree] *vi* to grumble
maussade [mosad] *adj (air, personne)* sullen;
(ciel, temps) gloomy
mauvais, e [mɔvɛ, -ɛz] *adj* bad; *(méchant,
malveillant)* malicious, spiteful; *(faux):* **le ~
numéro** the wrong number ▷ *nm:* **le ~** the
bad side ▷ *adv:* **il fait ~** the weather is bad;
sentir ~ to have a nasty smell, smell bad *ou*

nasty; **la mer est ~e** the sea is rough;
~ coucheur awkward customer; **~ coup** *(fig)*
criminal venture; **~ garçon** tough; **~ pas**
tight spot; **~ plaisant** hoaxer; **~e
plaisanterie** nasty trick; **~ traitements** ill
treatment *sg*; **~ joueur** bad loser; **~e herbe**
weed; **~e langue** gossip, scandalmonger
(Brit); **~e passe** difficult situation; *(période)*
bad patch; **~e tête** rebellious *ou* headstrong
customer
mauve [mov] *adj (couleur)* mauve ▷ *nf (Bot)*
mallow
maux [mo] *nmpl voir* **mal**
maximal, e, -aux [maksimal, -o] *adj*
maximal
maximum [maksimɔm] *adj, nm* maximum;
atteindre un/son ~ to reach a/his peak; **au ~**
adv (le plus possible) to the full; as much as one
can; *(tout au plus)* at the (very) most *ou*
maximum; **faire le ~** to do one's level best
mayonnaise [majɔnɛz] *nf* mayonnaise
mazout [mazut] *nm (fuel)* oil; **chaudière/
poêle à ~** oil-fired boiler/stove
me, m' [mə, m] *pron (direct: téléphoner, attendre
etc)* me; *(indirect: parler, donner etc)* (to) me;
(réfléchi) myself
mec [mek] *nm (fam)* guy, bloke *(Brit)*
mécanicien, ne [mekanisjɛ̃, -ɛn] *nm/f*
mechanic; *(Rail)* (train *ou* engine) driver;
~ navigant *ou* **de bord** *(Aviat)* flight engineer
mécanique [mekanik] *adj* mechanical ▷ *nf
(science)* mechanics *sg; (technologie)*
mechanical engineering; *(mécanisme)*
mechanism; engineering; works *pl*; **ennui ~**
engine trouble *no pl*; **s'y connaître en ~** to be
mechanically minded; **~ hydraulique**
hydraulics *sg*; **~ ondulatoire** wave
mechanics *sg*
mécanisme [mekanism] *nm* mechanism;
~ des taux de change exchange rate
mechanism
méchamment [meʃamɑ̃] *adv* nastily,
maliciously; spitefully; viciously
méchanceté [meʃɑ̃ste] *nf (d'une personne, d'une
parole)* nastiness, maliciousness,
spitefulness; *(parole, action)* nasty *ou* spiteful
ou malicious remark *(ou* action); **dire des ~s à
qn** to say spiteful things to sb
méchant, e [meʃɑ̃, -ɑ̃t] *adj* nasty, malicious,
spiteful; *(enfant: pas sage)* naughty; *(animal)*
vicious; *(avant le nom: péjorative)* nasty
mèche [meʃ] *nf (de lampe, bougie)* wick; *(d'un
explosif)* fuse; *(Méd)* pack, dressing; *(de
vilebrequin, perceuse)* bit; *(de dentiste)* drill; *(de
fouet)* lash; *(de cheveux)* lock; **se faire faire des
~s** *(chez le coiffeur)* to have highlights put in
one's hair, have one's hair streaked; **vendre
la ~** to give the game away; **de ~ avec** in
league with
méchoui [meʃwi] *nm whole sheep barbecue*
méconnaissable [mekɔnɛsabl] *adj*
unrecognizable

n

méconnaître [mekɔnɛtʀ] *vt* (*ignorer*) to be unaware of; (*mésestimer*) to misjudge

mécontent, e [mekɔ̃tã, -ãt] *adj*: **~ (de)** (*insatisfait*) discontented *ou* dissatisfied *ou* displeased (with); (*contrarié*) annoyed (at) ▷ *nm/f* malcontent, dissatisfied person

mécontentement [mekɔ̃tãtmã] *nm* dissatisfaction, discontent, displeasure; (*irritation*) annoyance

Mecque [mɛk] *nf*: **la ~** Mecca

médaille [medaj] *nf* medal

médaillon [medajɔ̃] *nm* (*portrait*) medallion; (*bijou*) locket; (*Culin*) médaillon; **en ~** *adj* (*carte etc*) inset

médecin [medsɛ̃] *nm* doctor; **~ du bord** (*Navig*) ship's doctor; **~ généraliste** general practitioner, GP; **~ légiste** forensic scientist (*Brit*), medical examiner (*US*); **~ traitant** family doctor, GP

médecine [medsin] *nf* medicine; **~ générale** general medicine; **~ infantile** paediatrics *sg* (*Brit*), pediatrics *sg* (*US*); **~ légale** forensic medicine; **~ préventive** preventive medicine; **~ du travail** occupational *ou* industrial medicine; **~s parallèles** *ou* **douces** alternative medicine

média [medja] *nmpl*: **les ~** the media

médiatique [medjatik] *adj* media *cpd*

médiatisé, e [medjatize] *adj* reported in the media; **ce procès a été très ~** (*péj*) this trial was turned into a media event

médical, e, -aux [medikal, -o] *adj* medical; **visiteur** *ou* **délégué ~** medical rep *ou* representative; **passer une visite ~e** to have a medical

médicament [medikamã] *nm* medicine, drug

médiéval, e, -aux [medjeval, -o] *adj* medieval

médiocre [medjɔkʀ] *adj* mediocre, poor

médire [mediʀ] *vi*: **~ de** to speak ill of

médisance [medizãs] *nf* scandalmongering *no pl* (*Brit*), mud-slinging *no pl*; (*propos*) piece of scandal *ou* malicious gossip

méditer [medite] *vt* (*approfondir*) to meditate on, ponder (over); (*combiner*) to meditate ▷ *vi* to meditate; **~ de faire** to contemplate doing, plan to do

Méditerranée [mediteʀane] *nf*: **la (mer) ~** the Mediterranean (Sea)

méditerranéen, ne [mediteʀaneɛ̃, -ɛn] *adj* Mediterranean ▷ *nm/f*: **M~, ne** Mediterranean

méduse [medyz] *nf* jellyfish

meeting [mitiŋ] *nm* (*Pol, Sport*) rally, meeting; **~ d'aviation** air show

méfait [mefɛ] *nm* (*faute*) misdemeanour, wrongdoing; **méfaits** *nmpl* (*ravages*) ravages, damage *sg*

méfiance [mefjãs] *nf* mistrust, distrust

méfiant, e [mefjã, -ãt] *adj* mistrustful, distrustful

méfier [mefje]: **se méfier** *vi* to be wary; (*faire attention*) to be careful; **se ~ de** *vt* to mistrust, distrust, be wary of; to be careful about

méga-octet [megaɔktɛ] *nm* megabyte

mégarde [megaʀd] *nf*: **par ~** (*accidentellement*) accidentally; (*par erreur*) by mistake

mégère [meʒɛʀ] *nf* (*péj: femme*) shrew

mégot [mego] *nm* cigarette end *ou* butt

meilleur, e [mejœʀ] *adj, adv* better; (*valeur superlative*) best ▷ *nm*: **le ~** (*celui qui ...*) the best (one); (*ce qui ...*) the best ▷ *nf*: **la ~e** the best (one); **le ~ des deux** the better of the two; **il fait ~ qu'hier** it's better weather than yesterday; **de ~e heure** earlier; **~ marché** cheaper

mél [mɛl] *nm* email

mélancolie [melãkɔli] *nf* melancholy, gloom

mélancolique [melãkɔlik] *adj* melancholy, gloomy

mélange [melãʒ] *nm* (*opération*) mixing; blending; (*résultat*) mixture; blend; **sans ~** unadulterated

mélanger [melãʒe] *vt* (*substances*) to mix; (*vins, couleurs*) to blend; (*mettre en désordre, confondre*) to mix up, muddle (up); **se mélanger** (*liquides, couleurs*) to blend, mix

mélasse [melas] *nf* treacle, molasses *sg*

mêlée [mele] *nf* (*bataille, cohue*) mêlée, scramble; (*lutte, conflit*) tussle, scuffle; (*Rugby*) scrum(mage)

mêler [mele] *vt* (*substances, odeurs, races*) to mix; (*embrouiller*) to muddle (up), mix up; **se mêler** *vi* to mix; (*se joindre, s'allier*) to mingle; **se ~ à** (*personne*) to join; (*s'associer à*) to mix with; (: *odeurs etc*) to mingle with; **se ~ de** (*personne*) to meddle with, interfere in; **mêle-toi de tes affaires!** mind your own business!; **~ à** *ou* **avec** *ou* **de** to mix with; to mingle with; **~ qn à** (*affaire*) to get sb mixed up *ou* involved in

mélodie [melɔdi] *nf* melody

mélodieux, -euse [melɔdjø, -øz] *adj* melodious, tuneful

melon [məlɔ̃] *nm* (*Bot*) (honeydew) melon; (*aussi*: **chapeau ~**) bowler (hat); **~ d'eau** watermelon

membre [mãbʀ] *nm* (*Anat*) limb; (*personne, pays, élément*) member ▷ *adj* member *cpd*; **être ~ de** to be a member of; **~ (viril)** (male) organ

mémé [meme] *nf* (*fam*) granny; (: *vieille femme*) old dear

 MOT-CLÉ

même [mɛm] *adj* **1** (*avant le nom*) same; **en même temps** at the same time; **ils ont les mêmes goûts** they have the same *ou* similar tastes

2 (*après le nom: renforcement*): **il est la loyauté même** he is loyalty itself; **ce sont ses paroles/celles-là même** they are his very words/the very ones

▷ *pron*: **le (la) même** the same one

▷ *adv* **1** (*renforcement*): **il n'a même pas pleuré** he didn't even cry; **même lui l'a dit** even HE said it; **ici même** at this very place; **même si** even if

2: **à même** (000): **à même la bouteille** straight from the bottle; **à même la peau** next to the skin; **être à même de faire** to be in a position to do, be able to do; **mettre qn à même de faire** to enable sb to do

3: **de même** likewise; **faire de même** to do likewise *ou* the same; **lui de même** so does (*ou* did *ou* is) he; **de même que** just as; **il en va de même pour** the same goes for

mémo [memo] (*fam*) *nm* memo

mémoire [memwaʀ] *nf* memory ▷ *nm* (*Admin, Jur*) memorandum; (*Scol*) dissertation, paper; **avoir la ~ des visages/chiffres** to have a (good) memory for faces/figures; **n'avoir aucune ~** to have a terrible memory; **avoir de la ~** to have a good memory; **à la ~ de** to the *ou* in memory of; **pour ~** *adv* for the record; **de ~** *adv* from memory; **de ~ d'homme** in living memory; **mettre en ~** (*Inform*) to store; **~ morte** read-only memory, ROM; **~ vive** random access memory, RAM

mémoires [memwaʀ] *nmpl* memoirs

mémorable [memɔʀabl] *adj* memorable

menace [mənas] *nf* threat; **~ en l'air** empty threat

menacer [mənase] *vt* to threaten; **~ qn de qch/de faire qch** to threaten sb with sth/to do sth

ménage [menaʒ] *nm* (*travail*) housekeeping, housework; (*couple*) (married) couple; (*famille, Admin*) household; **faire le ~** to do the housework; **faire des ~s** to work as a cleaner (*in private homes*); **monter son ~** to set up house; **se mettre en ~ (avec)** to set up house (with); **heureux en ~** happily married; **faire bon ~ avec** to get on well with; **~ de poupée** doll's kitchen set; **~ à trois** love triangle

ménagement [menaʒmã] *nm* care and attention; **ménagements** *nmpl* (*égards*) consideration *sg*, attention *sg*

ménager¹ [menaʒe] *vt* (*traiter avec mesure*) to handle with tact; (*: traiter considérément*) to treat considerately; (*utiliser*) to use with care; (*: avec économie*) to use sparingly; (*prendre soin de*) to take (great) care of, look after; (*organiser*) to arrange; (*installer*) to put in; to make; **se ménager** to look after o.s.; **~ qch à qn** (*réserver*) to have sth in store for sb

ménager², -ère [menaʒe, -ɛʀ] *adj* household *cpd*, domestic ▷ *nf* (*femme*) housewife; (*couverts*) canteen (*of cutlery*)

mendiant, e [mãdjã, -ãt] *nm/f* beggar

mendier [mãdje] *vi* to beg ▷ *vt* to beg (for); (*fig: éloges, compliments*) to fish for

mener [məne] *vt* to lead; (*enquête*) to conduct; (*affaires*) to manage, conduct, run ▷ *vi*: **~ (à la marque)** to lead, be in the lead; **~ à/dans** (*emmener*) to take to/into; **~ qch à bonne fin** *ou* **à terme** *ou* **à bien** to see sth through (to a successful conclusion), complete sth successfully

meneur, -euse [mənœʀ, -øz] *nm/f* leader; (*péj: agitateur*) ringleader; **~ d'hommes** born leader; **~ de jeu** host, quizmaster (*Brit*)

méningite [menɛ̃ʒit] *nf* meningitis *no pl*

ménopause [menopoz] *nf* menopause

menotte [mənɔt] *nf* (*langage enfantin*) handie; **menottes** *nfpl* handcuffs; **passer les ~ à** to handcuff

mensonge [mãsɔ̃ʒ] *nm*: **le ~** lying *no pl*; **un ~** a lie

mensonger, -ère [mãsɔ̃ʒe, -ɛʀ] *adj* false

mensualité [mãsɥalite] *nf* (*somme payée*) monthly payment; (*somme perçue*) monthly salary

mensuel, le [mãsɥɛl] *adj* monthly ▷ *nm/f* (*employé*) employee paid monthly ▷ *nm* (*Presse*) monthly

mensurations [mãsyʀasjɔ̃] *nfpl* measurements

mental, e, -aux [mãtal, -o] *adj* mental

mentalité [mãtalite] *nf* mentality

menteur, -euse [mãtœʀ, -øz] *nm/f* liar

menthe [mãt] *nf* mint; **~ (à l'eau)** peppermint cordial

mention [mãsjɔ̃] *nf* (*note*) note, comment; (*Scol*): **~ (très) bien/passable** (*very*) *good/satisfactory* pass; **faire ~ de** to mention; **"rayer la ~ inutile"** "delete as appropriate"

mentionner [mãsjɔne] *vt* to mention

mentir [mãtiʀ] *vi* to lie

menton [mãtɔ̃] *nm* chin

menu, e [məny] *adj* (*mince*) slim, slight; (*petit*) tiny; (*frais, difficulté*) minor ▷ *adv* (*couper, hacher*) very fine ▷ *nm* menu; **par le ~** (*raconter*) in minute detail; **~ touristique** popular *ou* tourist menu; **~e monnaie** small change

menuiserie [mənɥizʀi] *nf* (*travail*) joinery, carpentry; (*d'amateur*) woodwork; (*local*) joiner's workshop; (*ouvrages*) woodwork *no pl*

menuisier [mənɥizje] *nm* joiner, carpenter

méprendre [mepʀãdʀ]: **se méprendre** *vi*: **se ~ sur** to be mistaken about

mépris, e [mepʀi, -iz] *pp de* **méprendre** ▷ *nm* (*dédain*) contempt, scorn; (*indifférence*): **le ~ de** contempt *ou* disregard for; **au ~ de** regardless of, in defiance of

méprisable [mepʀizabl] *adj* contemptible, despicable

méprisant, e [mepʀizã, -ãt] *adj* contemptuous, scornful

méprise [mepʀiz] *nf* mistake, error; (*malentendu*) misunderstanding

mépriser [mepʀize] *vt* to scorn, despise; (*gloire, danger*) to scorn, spurn

mer [mɛʀ] *nf* sea; (*marée*) tide; **~ fermée** inland sea; **en ~** at sea; **prendre la ~** to put out to sea; **en haute** *ou* **pleine ~** off shore, on the open sea; **la ~ Adriatique** the Adriatic

(Sea); **la ~ des Antilles** ou **des Caraïbes** the Caribbean (Sea); **la ~ Baltique** the Baltic (Sea); **la ~ Caspienne** the Caspian Sea; **la ~ de Corail** the Coral Sea; **la ~ Égée** the Aegean (Sea); **la ~ Ionienne** the Ionian Sea; **la ~ Morte** the Dead Sea; **la ~ Noire** the Black Sea; **la ~ du Nord** the North Sea; **la ~ Rouge** the Red Sea; **la ~ des Sargasses** the Sargasso Sea; **les ~s du Sud** the South Seas; **la ~ Tyrrhénienne** the Tyrrhenian Sea

mercenaire [mɛʀsənɛʀ] *nm* mercenary, hired soldier

mercerie [mɛʀsəʀi] *nf* (*Couture*) haberdashery (*Brit*), notions *pl* (*US*); (*boutique*) haberdasher's (shop) (*Brit*), notions store (*US*)

merci [mɛʀsi] *excl* thank you ▷ *nf*: **à la ~ de qn/qch** at sb's mercy/the mercy of sth; **~ beaucoup** thank you very much; **~ de** ou **pour** thank you for; **sans ~** *adj* merciless ▷ *adv* mercilessly

mercredi [mɛʀkʀədi] *nm* Wednesday; **~ des Cendres** Ash Wednesday; *voir aussi* **lundi**

mercure [mɛʀkyʀ] *nm* mercury

merde [mɛʀd] (*fam!*) *nf* shit (!) ▷ *excl* (bloody) hell (!)

mère [mɛʀ] *nf* mother ▷ *adj inv* mother *cpd*; **~ célibataire** single parent, unmarried mother; **~ de famille** housewife, mother

merguez [mɛʀgɛz] *nf* spicy North African sausage

méridional, e, -aux [meʀidjɔnal, -o] *adj* southern; (*du midi de la France*) Southern (French) ▷ *nm/f* Southerner

meringue [məʀɛ̃g] *nf* meringue

mérite [meʀit] *nm* merit; **avoir du ~** (**à faire qch**) to deserve credit (for doing sth); **le ~ (de ceci) lui revient** the credit (for this) is his

mériter [meʀite] *vt* to deserve; **~ de réussir** to deserve to succeed; **il mérite qu'on fasse ... ** he deserves people to do ...

merlan [mɛʀlɑ̃] *nm* whiting

merle [mɛʀl] *nm* blackbird

merveille [mɛʀvɛj] *nf* marvel, wonder; **faire ~** ou **des ~s** to work wonders; **à ~** perfectly, wonderfully

merveilleux, -euse [mɛʀvɛjø, -øz] *adj* marvellous, wonderful

mes [me] *adj poss voir* **mon**

mésange [mezɑ̃ʒ] *nf* tit(mouse); **~ bleue** bluetit

mésaventure [mezavɑ̃tyʀ] *nf* misadventure, misfortune

Mesdames [medam] *nfpl voir* **Madame**

Mesdemoiselles [medmwazɛl] *nfpl voir* **Mademoiselle**

mesquin, e [mɛskɛ̃, -in] *adj* mean, petty

mesquinerie [mɛskinʀi] *nf* meanness *no pl*, pettiness *no pl*; (*procédé*) mean trick

message [mesaʒ] *nm* message; **~ d'erreur** (*Inform*) error message; **~ électronique** (*Inform*) email; **~ publicitaire** ad, advertisement; **~ téléphoné** telegram dictated by telephone; **~ SMS** text message

messager, -ère [mesaʒe, -ɛʀ] *nm/f* messenger

messagerie [mesaʒʀi] *nf*: **~s aériennes/ maritimes** air freight/shipping service *sg*; (*Internet*): **~ électronique** electronic mail, email; **~s de presse** press distribution service; **~ instantanée** instant messenger, IM; **~ rose** *lonely hearts and contact service on videotext*; **~ vocale** voice mail

messe [mɛs] *nf* mass; **aller à la ~** to go to mass; **~ de minuit** midnight mass; **faire des ~s basses** (*fig, péj*) to mutter

Messieurs [mesjø] *nmpl voir* **Monsieur**

mesure [məzyʀ] *nf* (*évaluation, dimension*) measurement; (*étalon, récipient, contenu*) measure; (*Mus: cadence*) time, tempo; (: *division*) bar; (*retenue*) moderation; (*disposition*) measure, step; **unité/système de ~** unit/system of measurement; **sur ~** (*costume*) made-to-measure; (*fig*) personally adapted; **à la ~ de** (*fig: personne*) worthy of; (*chambre etc*) on the same scale as; **dans la ~ où** insofar as, inasmuch as; **dans une certaine ~** to some ou a certain extent; **à ~ que** as; **en ~** (*Mus*) in time ou tempo; **être en ~ de** to be in a position to; **dépasser la ~** (*fig*) to overstep the mark

mesurer [məzyʀe] *vt* to measure; (*juger*) to weigh up, assess; (*limiter*) to limit, ration; (*modérer: ses paroles etc*) to moderate; (*proportionner*): **~ qch à** to match sth to, gear sth to; **se ~ avec** to have a confrontation with; to tackle; **il mesure 1 m 80** he's 1 m 80 tall

met [mɛ] *vb voir* **mettre**

métal, -aux [metal, -o] *nm* metal

métallique [metalik] *adj* metallic

météo [meteo] *nf* (*bulletin*) (weather) forecast; (*service*) ≈ Met Office (*Brit*), ≈ National Weather Service (*US*)

météorologie [meteɔʀɔlɔʒi] *nf* (*étude*) meteorology; (*service*) ≈ Meteorological Office (*Brit*), ≈ National Weather Service (*US*)

méthode [metɔd] *nf* method; (*livre, ouvrage*) manual, tutor

méticuleux, -euse [metikylø, -øz] *adj* meticulous

métier [metje] *nm* (*profession: gén*) job; (: *manuel*) trade; (: *artisanal*) craft; (*technique, expérience*) (acquired) skill ou technique; (*aussi*: **~ à tisser**) (weaving) loom; **être du ~** to be in the trade ou profession

métis, se [metis] *adj, nm/f* half-caste, half-breed

métrage [metʀaʒ] *nm* (*de tissu*) length; (*Ciné*) footage, length; **long/moyen/court ~** feature ou full-length/medium-length/short film

mètre [mɛtʀ] *nm* metre (*Brit*), meter (*US*); (*règle*) (metre ou meter) rule; (*ruban*) tape measure; **~ carré/cube** square/cubic metre ou meter

métrique [metʀik] *adj* metric ▷ *nf* metrics *sg*

métro [metʀo] nm underground (Brit), subway (US)

métropole [metʀɔpɔl] nf (capitale) metropolis; (pays) home country

mets [mɛ] nm dish ⊳ vb voir **mettre**

metteur [metœʀ] nm: ~ **en scène** (Théât) producer; (Ciné) director; ~ **en ondes** (Radio) producer

⬤ MOT-CLÉ

mettre [mɛtʀ] vt **1** (placer) to put; **mettre en bouteille/en sac** to bottle/put in bags ou sacks; **mettre qch à la poste** to post sth (Brit), mail sth (US); **mettre en examen (pour)** to charge (with) (Brit), indict (for) (US); **mettre une note gaie/amusante** to inject a cheerful/an amusing note; **mettre qn debout/assis** to help sb up ou to their feet/help sb to sit down

2 (vêtements: revêtir) to put on; (: porter) to wear; **mets ton gilet** put your cardigan on; **je ne mets plus mon manteau** I no longer wear my coat

3 (faire fonctionner: chauffage, électricité) to put on; (: réveil, minuteur) to set; (installer: gaz, eau) to put in, lay on; **mettre en marche** to start up

4 (consacrer): **mettre du temps/deux heures à faire qch** to take time/two hours to do sth; **y mettre du sien** to pull one's weight

5 (noter, écrire) to say, put (down); **qu'est-ce qu'il a mis sur la carte?** what did he say ou write on the card?; **mettez au pluriel ...** put ... into the plural

6 (supposer): **mettons que ...** let's suppose ou say that ...

7 (faire + vb): **faire mettre le gaz/l'électricité** to have gas/electricity put in ou installed

se mettre vi **1** (se placer): **vous pouvez vous mettre là** you can sit (ou stand) there; **où ça se met?** where does it go?; **se mettre au lit** to get into bed; **se mettre au piano** to sit down at the piano; **se mettre à l'eau** to get into the water; **se mettre de l'encre sur les doigts** to get ink on one's fingers

2 (s'habiller): **se mettre en maillot de bain** to get into ou put on a swimsuit; **n'avoir rien à se mettre** to have nothing to wear

3 (dans rapports): **se mettre bien/mal avec qn** to get on the right/wrong side of sb; **se mettre qn à dos** to get on sb's bad side; **se mettre avec qn** (prendre parti) to side with sb; (faire équipe) to team up with sb; (en ménage) to move in with sb

4: **se mettre à** to begin, start; **se mettre à faire** to begin ou start doing ou to do; **se mettre au piano** to start learning the piano; **se mettre au régime** to go on a diet; **se mettre au travail/à l'étude** to get down to work/one's studies; **il est temps de s'y mettre** it's time we got down to it ou got on with it

meuble [mœbl] nm (objet) piece of furniture; (ameublement) furniture no pl ⊳ adj (terre) loose, friable; (Jur): **biens** ~**s** movables

meublé [mœble] nm (pièce) furnished room; (appartement) furnished flat (Brit) ou apartment (US)

meubler [mœble] vt to furnish; (fig): ~ **qch (de)** to fill sth (with); **se meubler** to furnish one's house

meuf [mœf] nf (fam) woman

meugler [møgle] vi to low, moo

meule [møl] nf (à broyer) millstone; (à aiguiser) grindstone; (à polir) buff wheel; (de foin, blé) stack; (de fromage) round

meunier, -ière [mønje, -jɛʀ] nm miller ⊳ nf miller's wife ⊳ adj f (Culin) meunière

meurs etc [mœʀ] vb voir **mourir**

meurtre [mœʀtʀ] nm murder

meurtrier, -ière [mœʀtʀije, -jɛʀ] adj (arme, épidémie, combat) deadly; (accident) fatal; (carrefour, route) lethal; (fureur, instincts) murderous ⊳ nm/f murderer(-ess) ⊳ nf (ouverture) loophole

meurtrir [mœʀtʀiʀ] vt to bruise; (fig) to wound

meurtrissure [mœʀtʀisyʀ] nf bruise; (fig) scar

meus etc [mœ] vb voir **mouvoir**

meute [møt] nf pack

mexicain, e [mɛksikɛ̃, -ɛn] adj Mexican ⊳ nm/f: **M~, e** Mexican

Mexico [mɛksiko] n Mexico City

Mexique [mɛksik] nm: **le ~** Mexico

mi [mi] nm (Mus) E; (en chantant la gamme) mi

mi... [mi] préfixe half(-), mid-; **à la ~nvier** in mid-January; **à ~mbes/-corps** (up ou down) to the knees/waist; **à ~uteur/-pente** halfway up (ou down)/up (ou down) the hill

miauler [mjole] vi to miaow

mi-bas [miba] nm inv knee-length sock

miche [miʃ] nf round ou cob loaf

mi-chemin [miʃmɛ̃]: **à ~** adv halfway, midway

mi-clos, e [miklo, -kloz] adj half-closed

micro [mikʀo] nm mike, microphone; (Inform) micro; ~ **cravate** lapel mike

microbe [mikʀɔb] nm germ, microbe

micro-onde [mikʀɔɔ̃d] nf: **four à ~s** microwave oven

micro-ordinateur [mikʀɔɔʀdinatœʀ] nm microcomputer

microscope [mikʀɔskɔp] nm microscope; **au ~** under ou through the microscope

microscopique [mikʀɔskɔpik] adj microscopic

midi [midi] nm (milieu du jour) midday, noon; (moment du déjeuner) lunchtime; (sud) south; (: de la France): **le M~** the South (of France), the Midi; **à ~** at 12 (o'clock) ou midday ou noon; **tous les ~** every lunchtime; **le repas de ~** lunch; **en plein ~** (right) in the middle of the day; (sud) facing south

mie [mi] nf inside (of the loaf)

miel [mjɛl] nm honey; **être tout ~** (fig) to be all sweetness and light

mielleux, -euse [mjelø, -øz] adj (péj: personne) sugary, syrupy

mien, ne [mjɛ̃, mjɛn] adj, pron: **le (la) ~(ne), les ~s** mine; **les ~s** (ma famille) my family

miette [mjɛt] nf (de pain, gâteau) crumb; (fig: de la conversation etc) scrap; **en ~s** (fig) in pieces ou bits

 MOT-CLÉ

mieux [mjø] adv **1** (d'une meilleure façon): **mieux (que)** better (than); **elle travaille/mange mieux** she works/eats better; **aimer mieux** to prefer; **j'attendais mieux de vous** I expected better of you; **elle va mieux** she is better; **de mieux en mieux** better and better **2** (de la meilleure façon) best; **ce que je sais le mieux** what I know best; **les livres les mieux faits** the best made books **3** (intensif): **vous feriez mieux de faire ...** you would be better to do ...; **crier à qui mieux mieux** to try to shout each other down ▷ adj **1** (plus à l'aise, en meilleure forme) better; **se sentir mieux** to feel better **2** (plus satisfaisant) better; **c'est mieux ainsi** it's better like this; **c'est le mieux des deux** it's the better of the two; **le/la mieux, les mieux** the best; **demandez-lui, c'est le mieux** ask him, it's the best thing **3** (plus joli) better-looking; (plus gentil) nicer; **il est mieux que son frère** (plus beau) he's better-looking than his brother; (plus gentil) he's nicer than his brother; **il est mieux sans moustache** he looks better without a moustache **4**: **au mieux** at best; **au mieux avec** on the best of terms with; **pour le mieux** for the best; **qui mieux est** even better, better still ▷ nm **1** (progrès) improvement **2**: **de mon/ton mieux** as best I/you can (ou could); **faire de son mieux** to do one's best; **du mieux qu'il peut** the best he can; **faute de mieux** for lack ou want of anything better, failing anything better

mièvre [mjɛvʀ] adj sickly sentimental

mignon, ne [miɲɔ̃, -ɔn] adj sweet, cute

migraine [migʀɛn] nf headache; (Méd) migraine

mijoter [miʒɔte] vt to simmer; (préparer avec soin) to cook lovingly; (affaire, projet) to plot, cook up ▷ vi to simmer

mil [mil] num = **mille**

milieu, x [miljø] nm (centre) middle; (fig) middle course ou way; (aussi: **juste ~**) happy medium; (Bio, Géo) environment; (entourage social) milieu; (familial) background; circle; (pègre): **le ~** the underworld; **au ~ de** in the middle of; **au beau** ou **en plein ~ (de)** right in the middle (of); **~ de terrain** (Football: joueur) midfield player; (: joueurs) midfield

militaire [militɛʀ] adj military, army cpd ▷ nm serviceman; **service ~** military service

militant, e [militɑ̃, -ɑ̃t] adj, nm/f militant

militer [milite] vi to be a militant; **~ pour/ contre** to militate in favour of/against

mille [mil] num a ou one thousand ▷ nm (mesure): **~ (marin)** nautical mile; **mettre dans le ~** to hit the bull's-eye; (fig) to be bang on (target)

millefeuille [milfœj] nm cream ou vanilla slice

millénaire [milenɛʀ] nm millennium ▷ adj thousand-year-old; (fig) ancient

mille-pattes [milpat] nm inv centipede

millésimé, e [milezime] adj vintage cpd

millet [mijɛ] nm millet

milliard [miljaʀ] nm milliard, thousand million (Brit), billion (US)

milliardaire [miljaʀdɛʀ] nm/f multimillionaire (Brit), billionaire (US)

millier [milje] nm thousand; **un ~ (de)** a thousand or so, about a thousand; **par ~s** in (their) thousands, by the thousand

milligramme [miligram] nm milligramme (Brit), milligram (US)

millimètre [milimɛtʀ] nm millimetre (Brit), millimeter (US)

million [miljɔ̃] nm million; **deux ~s de** two million; **riche à ~s** worth millions

millionnaire [miljɔnɛʀ] nm/f millionaire

mime [mim] nm/f (acteur) mime(r); (imitateur) mimic ▷ nm (art) mime, miming

mimer [mime] vt to mime; (singer) to mimic, take off

mimique [mimik] nf (funny) face; (signes) gesticulations pl, sign language no pl

minable [minabl] adj (personne) shabby(-looking); (travail) pathetic

mince [mɛ̃s] adj thin; (personne, taille) slim, slender; (fig: profit, connaissances) slight, small; (: prétexte) weak ▷ excl: **~ (alors)!** darn it!

minceur [mɛ̃sœʀ] nf thinness; (d'une personne) slimness, slenderness

mincir [mɛ̃siʀ] vi to get slimmer ou thinner

mine [min] nf (physionomie) expression, look; (extérieur) exterior, appearance; (de crayon) lead; (gisement, exploitation, explosif) mine; **mines** nfpl (péj) simpering airs; **les M~s** (Admin) the national mining and geological service, the government vehicle testing department; **avoir bonne ~** (personne) to look well; (ironique) to look an utter idiot; **avoir mauvaise ~** to look unwell; **faire ~ de faire** to make a pretence of doing; **ne pas payer de ~** to be not much to look at; **~ de rien** adv with a casual air; although you wouldn't think so; **~ de charbon** coal mine; **~ à ciel ouvert** opencast (Brit) ou open-air (US) mine

miner [mine] vt (saper) to undermine, erode; (Mil) to mine

minerai [minʀɛ] nm ore

minéral, e, -aux [mineʀal, -o] *adj* mineral; (*Chimie*) inorganic ▷ *nm* mineral

minéralogique [mineʀalɔʒik] *adj* mineralogical; **plaque** ~ number (*Brit*) *ou* license (*US*) plate; **numéro** ~ registration (*Brit*) *ou* license (*US*) number

minet, te [mine, -ɛt] *nm/f* (*chat*) pussy-cat; (*péj*) young trendy

mineur, e [minœʀ] *adj* minor ▷ *nm/f* (*Jur*) minor ▷ *nm* (*travailleur*) miner; (*Mil*) sapper; ~ **de fond** face worker

miniature [minjatyʀ] *adj, nf* miniature

minibus [minibys] *nm* minibus

mini-cassette [minikasɛt] *nf* cassette (recorder)

minier, -ière [minje, -jɛʀ] *adj* mining

mini-jupe [miniʒyp] *nf* mini-skirt

minimal, e, -aux [minimal, -o] *adj* minimum

minime [minim] *adj* minor, minimal ▷ *nm/f* (*Sport*) junior

minimiser [minimize] *vt* to minimize; (*fig*) to play down

minimum [minimɔm] *adj, nm* minimum; **au** ~ at the very least; ~ **vital** (*salaire*) living wage; (*niveau de vie*) subsistence level

ministère [ministɛʀ] *nm* (*cabinet*) government; (*département*) ministry (*Brit*), department; (*Rel*) ministry; ~ **public** (*Jur*) Prosecution, State Prosecutor

ministre [ministʀ] *nm* minister (*Brit*), secretary; (*Rel*) minister; ~ **d'État** senior minister *ou* secretary

Minitel® [minitɛl] *nm* videotext terminal and service

minoritaire [minɔʀitɛʀ] *adj* minority *cpd*

minorité [minɔʀite] *nf* minority; **être en** ~ to be in the *ou* a minority; **mettre en** ~ (*Pol*) to defeat

minuit [minɥi] *nm* midnight

minuscule [minyskyl] *adj* minute, tiny ▷ *nf*: (**lettre**) ~ small letter

minute [minyt] *nf* minute; (*Jur*: *original*) minute, draft ▷ *excl* just a minute!, hang on!; **à la** ~ (*présent*) (just) this instant; (*passé*)

there and then; **entrecôte** *ou* **steak** ~ minute steak

minuter [minyte] *vt* to time

minuterie [minytʀi] *nf* time switch

minutieux, -euse [minysjø, -øz] *adj* (*personne*) meticulous; (*inspection*) minutely detailed; (*travail*) requiring painstaking attention to detail

mirabelle [miʀabɛl] *nf* (*fruit*) (cherry) plum; (*eau-de-vie*) plum brandy

miracle [miʀakl] *nm* miracle

mirage [miʀaʒ] *nm* mirage

mire [miʀ] *nf* (*d'un fusil*) sight; (*TV*) test card; **point de** ~ target; (*fig*) focal point; **ligne de** ~ line of sight

miroir [miʀwaʀ] *nm* mirror

miroiter [miʀwate] *vi* to sparkle, shimmer; **faire** ~ **qch à qn** to paint sth in glowing colours for sb, dangle sth in front of sb's eyes

mis, e [mi, miz] *pp de* **mettre** ▷ *adj* (*couvert, table*) set, laid; (*personne*): **bien** ~ well dressed ▷ *nf* (*argent*: *au jeu*) stake; (*tenue*) clothing; attire; **être de** ~**e** to be acceptable *ou* in season; ~**e en bouteilles** bottling; ~**e en examen** charging, indictment; ~**e à feu** blast-off; ~**e de fonds** capital outlay; ~**e à jour** (*Inform*) update; ~**e à mort** kill; ~**e à pied** (*d'un employé*) suspension; lay-off; ~**e sur pied** (*d'une affaire, entreprise*) setting up; ~**e en plis** set; ~**e au point** (*Photo*) focusing; (*fig*) clarification; ~**e à prix** reserve (*Brit*) *ou* upset price; ~**e en scène** production

mise [miz] *adj f, nf voir* **mis**

miser [mize] *vt* (*enjeu*) to stake, bet; ~ **sur** *vt* (*cheval, numéro*) to bet on; (*fig*) to bank *ou* count on

misérable [mizeʀabl] *adj* (*lamentable, malheureux*) pitiful, wretched; (*pauvre*) poverty-stricken; (*insignifiant, mesquin*) miserable ▷ *nm/f* wretch; (*miséreux*) poor wretch

misère [mizɛʀ] *nf* (*pauvreté*) (extreme) poverty, destitution; **misères** *nfpl* (*malheurs*) woes, miseries; (*ennuis*) little troubles; **être dans la** ~ to be destitute *ou* poverty-stricken; **salaire de** ~ starvation wage; **faire des** ~**s à qn** to torment sb; ~ **noire** utter destitution, abject poverty

missile [misil] *nm* missile

mission [misjɔ̃] *nf* mission; **partir en** ~ (*Admin, Pol*) to go on an assignment

missionnaire [misjɔnɛʀ] *nm/f* missionary

mit [mi] *vb voir* **mettre**

mité, e [mite] *adj* moth-eaten

mi-temps [mitɑ̃] *nf inv* (*Sport*: *période*) half; (: *pause*) half-time; **à** ~ *adj, adv* part-time

miteux, -euse [mitø, -øz] *adj* seedy, shabby

mitigé, e [mitiʒe] *adj* (*conviction, ardeur*) lukewarm; (*sentiments*) mixed

mitonner [mitɔne] *vt* (*préparer*) to cook with loving care; (*fig*) to cook up quietly

mitoyen, ne [mitwajɛ̃, -ɛn] *adj* (*mur*)

common, party *cpd*; **maisons ~nes** semi-detached houses; (*plus de deux*) terraced (*Brit*) *ou* row (*US*) houses

mitrailler [mitʀaje] *vt* to machine-gun; (*fig: photographier*) to snap away at; ~ **qn de** to pelt *ou* bombard sb with

mitraillette [mitʀajɛt] *nf* submachine gun

mitrailleuse [mitʀajøz] *nf* machine gun

mi-voix [mivwa]: **à ~** *adv* in a low *ou* hushed voice

mixage [miksaʒ] *nm* (*Ciné*) (sound) mixing

mixer, mixeur [miksœʀ] *nm* (*Culin*) (food) mixer

mixte [mikst] *adj* (*gén*) mixed; (*Scol*) mixed, coeducational; **à usage ~** dual-purpose; **cuisinière ~** combined gas and electric cooker; **équipe ~** combined team

mixture [mikstyʀ] *nf* mixture; (*fig*) concoction

MJC *sigle f* (= *maison des jeunes et de la culture*) community arts centre and youth club

Mlle (*pl* **Mlles**) *abr* = **Mademoiselle**

MM *abr* = **Messieurs** *voir* **Monsieur**

Mme (*pl* **Mmes**) *abr* = **Madame**

mobile [mɔbil] *adj* mobile; (*amovible*) loose, removable; (*pièce de machine*) moving; (*élément de meuble etc*) movable ▷ *nm* (*motif*) motive; (*œuvre d'art*) mobile; (*Physique*) moving object *ou* body; **(téléphone) ~** mobile (phone) (*Brit*), cell (phone) (*US*)

mobilier, -ière [mɔbilje, -jɛʀ] *adj* (*Jur*) personal ▷ *nm* (*meubles*) furniture; **valeurs mobilières** transferable securities; **vente mobilière** sale of personal property *ou* chattels

mobiliser [mɔbilize] *vt* (*Mil, gén*) to mobilize

mobylette® [mɔbilɛt] *nf* moped

mocassin [mɔkasɛ̃] *nm* moccasin

moche [mɔʃ] *adj* (*fam: laid*) ugly; (: *mauvais, méprisable*) rotten

modalité [mɔdalite] *nf* form, mode; **modalités** *nfpl* (*d'un accord etc*) clauses, terms; **~s de paiement** methods of payment

mode [mɔd] *nf* fashion; (*commerce*) fashion trade *ou* industry ▷ *nm* (*manière*) form, mode, method; (*Ling*) mood; (*Inform, Mus*) mode; **travailler dans la ~** to be in the fashion business; **à la ~** fashionable, in fashion; **~ dialogué** (*Inform*) interactive *ou* conversational mode; **~ d'emploi** directions *pl* (for use); **~ de paiement** method of payment; **~ de vie** way of life

modèle [mɔdɛl] *adj* model ▷ *nm* model; (*qui pose: de peintre*) sitter; (*type*) type; (*gabarit, patron*) pattern; **~ courant** *ou* **de série** (*Comm*) production model; **~ déposé** registered design; **~ réduit** small-scale model

modeler [mɔdle] *vt* (*Art*) to model, mould; (*vêtement, érosion*) to mould, shape; **~ qch sur/ d'après** to model sth on

modem [mɔdɛm] *nm* (*Inform*) modem

modéré, e [mɔdeʀe] *adj, nm/f* moderate

modérer [mɔdeʀe] *vt* to moderate; **se modérer** *vi* to restrain o.s

moderne [mɔdɛʀn] *adj* modern ▷ *nm* (*Art*) modern style; (*ameublement*) modern furniture

moderniser [mɔdɛʀnize] *vt* to modernize

modeste [mɔdɛst] *adj* modest; (*origine*) humble, lowly

modestie [mɔdɛsti] *nf* modesty; **fausse ~** false modesty

modifier [mɔdifje] *vt* to modify, alter; (*Ling*) to modify; **se modifier** *vi* to alter

modique [mɔdik] *adj* (*salaire, somme*) modest

modiste [mɔdist] *nf* milliner

module [mɔdyl] *nm* module

moelle [mwal] *nf* marrow; (*fig*) pith, core; **~ épinière** spinal chord

moelleux, -euse [mwalø, -øz] *adj* soft; (*au goût, à l'ouïe*) mellow; (*gracieux, souple*) smooth; (*gâteau*) light and moist

mœurs [mœʀ] *nfpl* (*morale*) morals; (*manières*) manners; (*pratiques sociales*) habits; (*mode de vie*) life style *sg*; (*d'une espèce animale*) behaviour *sg* (*Brit*), behavior *sg* (*US*); **femme de mauvaises ~** loose woman; **passer dans les ~** to become the custom; **contraire aux bonnes ~** contrary to proprieties

mohair [mɔɛʀ] *nm* mohair

moi [mwa] *pron* me; (*emphatique*): **~, je ...** for my part, I ..., I myself ...; **c'est ~ qui l'ai fait** I did it, it was me who did it; **apporte-le-~** bring it to me; **à ~ mine**; (*dans un jeu*) my turn ▷ *nm inv* (*Psych*) ego, self; **à ~!** (*à l'aide*) help (me)!

moi-même [mwamɛm] *pron* myself; (*emphatique*) I myself

moindre [mwɛ̃dʀ] *adj* lesser; lower; **le (la) ~, les ~s** the least; the slightest; **le (la) ~ de** the least of; **c'est la ~ des choses** it's nothing at all

moine [mwan] *nm* monk, friar

moineau, x [mwano] *nm* sparrow

⊙ **MOT-CLÉ**

moins [mwɛ̃] *adv* **1** *comparatif*; **moins (que)** less (than); **moins grand que** less tall than, not as tall as; **il a trois ans de moins que moi** he's three years younger than me; **il est moins intelligent que moi** he's not as clever as me, he's less clever than me; **moins je travaille, mieux je me porte** the less I work, the better I feel

2 *superlatif*; **le moins** (the) least; **c'est ce que j'aime le moins** it's what I like (the) least; **le(la) moins doué(e)** the least gifted; **au moins, du moins** at least; **pour le moins** at the very least

3: **moins de** (*quantité*) less (than); (*nombre*) fewer (than); **moins de sable/d'eau** less sand/water; **moins de livres/gens** fewer books/people; **moins de deux ans** less than

two years; **moins de midi** not yet midday
4: **de moins, en moins** (000): **100 euros/3
jours de moins** 100 euros/3 days less; **trois
livres en moins** three books fewer; three
books too few; **de l'argent en moins** less
money; **le soleil en moins** but for the sun,
minus the sun; **de moins en moins** less and
less; **en moins de deux** in a flash *ou* a trice
5: **à moins de, à moins que** unless; **à moins
de faire** unless we do (*ou* he does *etc*); **à
moins que tu ne fasses** unless you do; **à
moins d'un accident** barring any accident
▷ *prép*: **quatre moins deux** four minus two;
dix heures moins cinq five to ten; **il fait
moins cinq** it's five (degrees) below
(freezing), it's minus five; **il est moins cinq**
it's five to
▷ *nm* (*signe*) minus sign

mois [mwa] *nm* month; (*salaire, somme dû*)
(monthly) pay *ou* salary; **treizième ~,
double ~** extra month's salary
moisi, e [mwazi] *adj* mouldy (*Brit*), moldy
(*US*) ▷ *nm* mould, mold, mildew;
odeur de ~ musty smell
moisir [mwazir] *vi* to go mouldy (*Brit*) *ou*
moldy (*US*); (*fig*) to rot; (*personne*) to hang
about ▷ *vt* to make mouldy *ou* moldy
moisissure [mwazisyr] *nf* mould *no pl* (*Brit*),
mold *no pl* (*US*)
moisson [mwasɔ̃] *nf* harvest; (*époque*)
harvest (time); (*fig*): **faire une ~ de** to gather
a wealth of
moissonner [mwasɔne] *vt* to harvest, reap;
(*fig*) to collect
moissonneur, -euse [mwasɔnœr, -øz] *nm/f*
harvester, reaper ▷ *nf* (*machine*) harvester
moissonneuse *nf* (*machine*) harvester
moite [mwat] *adj* (*peau, mains*) sweaty, sticky;
(*atmosphère*) muggy
moitié [mwatje] *nf* half; (*épouse*): **sa ~** his
better half; **la ~ de** half; **la ~ de** half (of),
the amount (*ou* number) of; **la ~ du temps/des
gens** half the time/the people; **à la ~ de**
halfway through; **~ moins grand** half as
tall; **~ plus long** half as long again, longer by
half; **à ~** half (*avant le verbe*), half- (*avant
l'adjectif*); **à ~ prix** (at) half price, half-price;
de ~ by half; **~ ~** half-and-half
moka [mɔka] *nm* (*café*) mocha coffee; (*gâteau*)
mocha cake
mol [mɔl] *adj m voir* **mou**
molaire [mɔlɛr] *nf* molar
molester [mɔlɛste] *vt* to manhandle, maul
(about)
molle [mɔl] *adj f voir* **mou**
mollement [mɔlmɑ̃] *adv* softly; (*péj*:
travailler) sluggishly; (*protester*) feebly
mollet [mɔlɛ] *nm* calf ▷ *adj m*: **œuf ~** soft-
boiled egg
molletonné, e [mɔltɔne] *adj* (*gants etc*)
fleece-lined

mollir [mɔlir] *vi* (*jambes*) to give way; (*Navig*:
vent) to drop, die down; (*fig*: *personne*) to relent;
(: *courage*) to fail, flag; (*substance*) to go soft
mollusque [mɔlysk] *nm* (*Zool*) mollusc; (*fig*:
personne) lazy lump
môme [mom] *nm/f* (*fam*: *enfant*) brat; (: *fille*)
bird (*Brit*), chick
moment [mɔmɑ̃] *nm* moment; (*occasion*):
profiter du ~ to take (advantage of) the
opportunity; **ce n'est pas le ~** this is not the
right time; **à un certain ~** at some point; **à
un ~ donné** at a certain point; **d'un ~ à
l'autre** any time (now); **du ~ où** *ou* **que**
seeing that, since; **n'avoir pas un ~ à soi** not
to have a minute to oneself
momentané, e [mɔmɑ̃tane] *adj* temporary,
momentary
momentanément [mɔmɑ̃tanemɑ̃] *adv* for a
moment, for a while
momie [mɔmi] *nf* mummy
mon [mɔ̃], **ma** [ma] (*pl* **mes**) [me] *adj poss* my
Monaco [mɔnako] *nm*: **le ~** Monaco
monarchie [mɔnarʃi] *nf* monarchy
monastère [mɔnastɛr] *nm* monastery
monceau, x [mɔ̃so] *nm* heap
mondain, e [mɔ̃dɛ̃, -ɛn] *adj* (*soirée, vie*) society
cpd; (*obligations*) social; (*peintre, écrivain*)
fashionable; (*personne*) society *cpd* ▷ *nm/f*
society man/woman, socialite ▷ *nf*: **la M-e,
la police ~e** the vice squad
monde [mɔ̃d] *nm* world; (*personnes mondaines*):
le ~ (high) society; (*milieu*): **être du même ~**
to move in the same circles; (*gens*): **il y a du ~**
(*beaucoup de gens*) there are a lot of people;
(*quelques personnes*) there are some people; **y
a-t-il du ~ dans le salon?** is there anybody in
the lounge?; **beaucoup/peu de ~** many/few
people; **le meilleur** *etc* **du ~** the best *etc* in
the world; **mettre au ~** to bring into the
world; **pas le moins du ~** not in the least; **se
faire un ~ de qch** to make a great deal of fuss
about sth; **tour du ~** round-the-world trip;
homme/femme du ~ society man/woman
mondial, e, -aux [mɔ̃djal, -o] *adj* (*population*)
world *cpd*; (*influence*) world-wide
mondialement [mɔ̃djalmɑ̃] *adv* throughout
the world
mondialisation [mɔ̃djalizasjɔ̃] *nf*
globalization; (*d'une technique*) global
application; (*d'un conflit*) global spread
monégasque [mɔnegask] *adj* Monegasque,
of *ou* from Monaco ▷ *nm/f*: **M-** Monegasque
monétaire [mɔnetɛr] *adj* monetary

moniteur, -trice [mɔnitœʀ, -tʀis] *nm/f* (*Sport*) instructor/instructress; (*de colonie de vacances*) supervisor ▷ *nm* (*écran*) monitor; ~ **cardiaque** cardiac monitor; ~ **d'auto-école** driving instructor

monnaie [mɔnɛ] *nf* (*pièce*) coin; (*Écon: gén: moyen d'échange*) currency; (*petites pièces*): **avoir de la ~** to have (some) change; **faire de la ~** to get (some) change; **avoir/faire la ~ de 20 euros** to have change of/get change for 20 euros; **faire** *ou* **donner la ~ de 20 euros** to give sb change for 20 euros, change 20 euros for sb; **rendre à qn la ~ (sur 20 euros)** to give sb the change (out ou out of 20 euros); **servir de ~ d'échange** (*fig*) to be used as a bargaining counter *ou* as bargaining counters; **payer en ~ de singe** to fob (sb) off with empty promises; **c'est ~ courante** it's a common occurrence; ~ **légale** legal tender

monnayer [mɔneje] *vt* to convert into cash; (*talent*) to capitalize on

monologue [mɔnɔlɔg] *nm* monologue, soliloquy; ~ **intérieur** stream of consciousness

monologuer [mɔnɔlɔge] *vi* to soliloquize

monopole [mɔnɔpɔl] *nm* monopoly

monotone [mɔnɔtɔn] *adj* monotonous

Monsieur [məsjø] (*pl* **Messieurs**) [mesjø] *nm* (*titre*) Mr; (*homme quelconque*): **un/le monsieur** a/the gentleman; ~, ... (*en tête de lettre*) Dear Sir, ...; *voir aussi* **Madame**

monstre [mɔstʀ] *nm* monster ▷ *adj* (*fam: effet, publicité*) massive; **un travail** ~ a fantastic amount of work; an enormous job; ~ **sacré** superstar

monstrueux, -euse [mɔstʀyø, -øz] *adj* monstrous

mont [mɔ̃] *nm*: **par ~s et par vaux** up hill and down dale; **le M~ Blanc** Mont Blanc; ~ **de Vénus** mons veneris

montage [mɔtaʒ] *nm* putting up; (*d'un bijou*) mounting, setting; (*d'une machine etc*) assembly; (*Photo*) photomontage; (*Ciné*) editing; ~ **sonore** sound editing

montagnard, e [mɔtaɲaʀ, -aʀd] *adj* mountain *cpd* ▷ *nm/f* mountain-dweller

montagne [mɔtaɲ] *nf* (*cime*) mountain; (*région*): **la** ~ the mountains *pl*; **la haute** ~ the high mountains; **les ~s Rocheuses** the Rocky Mountains, the Rockies; **~s russes** big dipper *sg*, switchback *sg*

montagneux, -euse [mɔtaɲø, -øz] *adj* mountainous; (*basse montagne*) hilly

montant, e [mɔ̃tɑ̃, -ɑ̃t] *adj* (*mouvement, marée*) rising; (*chemin*) uphill; (*robe, corsage*) high-necked ▷ *nm* (*somme, total*) (sum) total, (total) amount; (*de fenêtre*) upright; (*de lit*) post

monte-charge [mɔ̃tʃaʀʒ] *nm inv* goods lift, hoist

montée [mɔte] *nf* rising, rise; (*escalade*) ascent, climb; (*chemin*) way up; (*côte*) hill; **au milieu de la** ~ halfway up; **le moteur chauffe dans les ~s** the engine overheats

going uphill

Monténégro [mɔtenegʀo] *nm*: **le ~** Montenegro

monter [mɔte] *vt* (*escalier, côte*) to go (*ou* come) up; (*valise, paquet*) to take (*ou* bring) up; (*cheval*) to mount; (*femelle*) to serve; (*étagère*) to raise; (*tente, échafaudage*) to put up; (*machine*) to assemble; (*bijou*) to mount, set; (*Couture*) to sew on; (: *manche*) to set in; (*Ciné*) to edit; (*Théât*) to put on, stage; (*société, coup etc*) to set up; (*fournir, équiper*) to equip ▷ *vi* to go (*ou* come) up; (*avion, voiture*) to climb, go up, rise; (*chemin, niveau, température, voix, prix*) to go up, rise; (*brouillard, bruit*) to rise, come up; (*passager*) to get on; (*à cheval*): ~ **bien/mal** to ride well/badly; ~ **à cheval** to get on *ou* mount a horse; (*faire du cheval*) to ride (a horse); ~ **à bicyclette** to get on *ou* mount a bicycle, to (ride a) bicycle; ~ **à pied/en voiture** to walk/ drive up, go up on foot/by car; ~ **dans le train/l'avion** to get into the train/plane, board the train/plane; ~ **sur** to climb up onto; ~ **sur** *ou* **à un arbre/une échelle** to climb (up) a tree/ladder; ~ **à bord** to (get on) board; ~ **à la tête de qn** to go to sb's head; ~ **sur les planches** to go on the stage; ~ **en grade** to be promoted; **se monter** (*s'équiper*) to equip o.s., get kitted out (*Brit*); **se ~ à** (*frais etc*) to add up to, come to; ~ **qn contre qn** to set sb against sb; ~ **la tête à qn** to give sb ideas

montgolfière [mɔgɔlfjɛʀ] *nf* hot-air balloon

montre [mɔtʀ] *nf* watch; (*ostentation*): **pour la** ~ for show; ~ **en main** exactly, to the minute; **faire ~ de** to show, display; **contre là** ~ (*Sport*) against the clock; ~ **de plongée** diver's watch

Montréal [mɔʀeal] *n* Montreal

montre-bracelet (*pl* **montres-bracelets**) [mɔtʀəbʀaslɛ] *nf* wrist watch

montrer [mɔtʀe] *vt* to show; **se montrer** to appear; ~ **qch à qn** to show sb sth; ~ **qch du doigt** to point to sth, point one's finger at sth; **se ~ intelligent** to prove (to be) intelligent

monture [mɔtyʀ] *nf* (*bête*) mount; (*d'une bague*) setting; (*de lunettes*) frame

monument [mɔnymɑ̃] *nm* monument; ~ **aux morts** war memorial

moquer [mɔke]: **se ~ de** *vt* to make fun of, laugh at; (*fam: se désintéresser de*) not to care about; (*tromper*): **se ~ de qn** to take sb for a ride

moquerie [mɔkʀi] *nf* mockery *no pl*

moquette [mɔkɛt] *nf* fitted carpet, wall-to-wall carpeting *no pl*

moqueur, -euse [mɔkœʀ, -øz] *adj* mocking

moral, e, -aux [mɔʀal, -o] *adj* moral ▷ *nm* morale ▷ *nf* (*conduite*) morals *pl* (*règles*), moral code, ethic; (*valeurs*) moral standards *pl*, morality; (*science*) ethics *sg*, moral philosophy; (*conclusion: d'une fable etc*) moral;

au ~, sur le plan ~ morally; **avoir le ~** (*fam*) to be in good spirits; **avoir le ~ à zéro** to be really down; **faire la ~e à** to lecture, preach at

moralité [mɔralite] *nf* (*d'une action, attitude*) morality; (*conduite*) morals *pl*; (*conclusion, enseignement*) moral

morceau, x [mɔrso] *nm* piece, bit; (*d'une œuvre*) passage, extract; (*Mus*) piece; (*Culin: de viande*) cut; (*de sucre*) lump; **mettre en ~x** to pull to pieces *ou* bits; **manger un ~** to have a bite (to eat)

morceler [mɔrsəle] *vt* to break up, divide up

mordant, e [mɔrdã, -ãt] *adj* (*ton, remarque*) scathing, cutting; (*froid*) biting ▷ *nm* (*dynamisme, énergie*) spirit; (*fougue*) bite, punch

mordiller [mɔrdije] *vt* to nibble at, chew at

mordre [mɔrdr] *vt* to bite; (*lime, vis*) to bite into ▷ *vi* (*poisson*) to bite; **~ dans** to bite into; **~ sur** (*fig*) to go over into, overlap into; **~ à qch** (*comprendre, aimer*) to take to; **~ à l'hameçon** to bite, rise to the bait

mordu, e [mɔrdy] *pp de* **mordre** ▷ *adj* (*amoureux*) smitten ▷ *nm/f* enthusiast; **un ~ du jazz/de la voile** a jazz/sailing fanatic *ou* buff

morfondre [mɔrfɔ̃dr]: **se morfondre** *vi* to mope

morgue [mɔrg] *nf* (*arrogance*) haughtiness; (*lieu: de la police*) morgue; (: *à l'hôpital*) mortuary

morne [mɔrn] *adj* (*personne, visage*) glum, gloomy; (*temps, vie*) dismal, dreary

morose [mɔroz] *adj* sullen, morose; (*marché*) sluggish

mors [mɔr] *nm* bit

morse [mɔrs] *nm* (*Zool*) walrus; (*Tél*) Morse (code)

morsure [mɔrsyr] *nf* bite

mort¹ [mɔr] *nf* death; **se donner la ~** to take one's own life; **de ~** (*silence, pâleur*) deathly; **blessé à ~** (*accident, blessure*) fatal; **à la vie, à la ~** for better, for worse; **~ clinique** brain death; **~ subite du nourrisson, ~ au berceau** cot death

mort² [mɔr, mɔrt] *pp de* **mourir** ▷ *adj* dead ▷ *nm/f* (*défunt*) dead man/woman; (*victime*): **il y a eu plusieurs ~s** several people were killed, there were several killed ▷ *nm* (*Cartes*) dummy; **~ ou vif** dead or alive; **~ de peur/ fatigue** frightened to death/dead tired; **~s et blessés** casualties; **faire le ~** to play dead; (*fig*) to lie low

mortalité [mɔrtalite] *nf* mortality, death rate

mortel, le [mɔrtɛl] *adj* (*poison etc*) deadly, lethal; (*accident, blessure*) fatal; (*silence, ennemi*) deadly; (*Rel: danger, frayeur, péché*) mortal; (*fig: froid*) deathly; (: *ennui, soirée*) deadly (boring) ▷ *nm/f* mortal

mortier [mɔrtje] *nm* (*gén*) mortar

mort-né, e [mɔrne] *adj* (*enfant*) stillborn; (*fig*) abortive

mortuaire [mɔrtɥer] *adj* funeral *cpd*; **avis ~s** death announcements, intimations; **chapelle ~** mortuary chapel; **couronne ~** (funeral) wreath; **domicile ~** house of the deceased; **drap ~** pall

morue [mɔry] *nf* (*Zool*) cod *inv*; (*Culin: salée*) salt-cod

mosaïque [mɔzaik] *nf* (*Art*) mosaic; (*fig*) patchwork

Moscou [mɔsku] *n* Moscow

mosquée [mɔske] *nf* mosque

mot [mo] *nm* word; (*message*) line, note; (*bon mot etc*) saying; **le ~ de la fin** the last word; **~ à ~** *adj, adv* word for word; **~ pour ~** word for word, verbatim; **sur** *ou* **à ces ~s** with these words; **en un ~** in a word; **à ~s couverts** in veiled terms; **prendre qn au ~** to take sb at his word; **se donner le ~** to send the word round; **avoir son ~ à dire** to have a say; **~ d'ordre** watchword; **~ de passe** password; **~s croisés** crossword (puzzle) *sg*

motard [mɔtar] *nm* biker; (*policier*) motorcycle cop

motel [mɔtɛl] *nm* motel

moteur, -trice [mɔtœr, -tris] *adj* (*Anat, Physiol*) motor; (*Tech*) driving; (*Auto*): **à 4 roues motrices** 4-wheel drive ▷ *nm* engine, motor; (*fig*) mover, mainspring; **à ~** power-driven, motor *cpd*; **~ à deux temps** two-stroke engine; **~ à explosion** internal combustion engine; **~ à réaction** jet engine; **~ de recherche** search engine; **~ thermique** heat engine

motif [mɔtif] *nm* (*cause*) motive; (*décoratif*) design, pattern, motif; (*d'un tableau*) subject, motif; (*Mus*) figure, motif; **motifs** *nmpl* (*Jur*) grounds *pl*; **sans ~** *adj* groundless

motivation [mɔtivasjɔ̃] *nf* motivation

motiver [mɔtive] *vt* (*justifier*) to justify, account for; (*Admin, Jur, Psych*) to motivate

moto [mɔto] *nf* (*motor*)bike; **~ verte** *ou* **de trial** trail (*Brit*) *ou* dirt (*US*) bike

motocyclette [mɔtɔsiklɛt] *nf* motorbike, motorcycle

motocycliste [mɔtɔsiklist] *nm/f* motorcyclist

motorisé, e [mɔtɔrize] *adj* (*troupe*) motorized; (*personne*) having one's own transport

motrice [mɔtris] *adj f voir* **moteur**

motte [mɔt] *nf*: **~ de terre** lump of earth, clod (of earth); **~ de gazon** turf, sod; **~ de beurre** lump of butter

mou, mol, molle [mu, mɔl] *adj* soft; (*péj: visage, traits*) flabby; (: *geste*) limp; (: *personne*) sluggish; (: *résistance, protestations*) feeble ▷ *nm* (*homme mou*) wimp; (*abats*) lights *pl*, lungs *pl*; (*de la corde*) avoir du ~ to be slack; **donner du ~** to slacken, loosen; **avoir les jambes molles** to be weak at the knees

mouche [muʃ] *nf* fly; (*Escrime*) button; (*de taffetas*) patch; **prendre la ~** to go into a huff; **faire ~** to score a bull's-eye

moucher [muʃe] vt (enfant) to blow the nose of; (chandelle) to snuff (out); **se moucher** vi to blow one's nose

moucheron [muʃʀɔ̃] nm midge

mouchoir [muʃwaʀ] nm handkerchief, hanky; ~ **en papier** tissue, paper hanky

moudre [mudʀ] vt to grind

moue [mu] nf pout; **faire la** ~ to pout; (fig) to pull a face

mouette [mwɛt] nf (sea)gull

moufle [mufl] nf (gant) mitt(en); (Tech) pulley block

mouillé, e [muje] adj wet

mouiller [muje] vt (humecter) to wet, moisten; (tremper): ~ **qn/qch** to make sb/sth wet; (Culin: ragoût) to add stock ou wine to; (couper, diluer) to water down; (mine etc) to lay ▷ vi (Navig) to lie ou be at anchor; **se mouiller** to get wet; (fam: prendre des risques) to commit o.s.; to get (o.s.) involved; ~ **l'ancre** to drop ou cast anchor

moulant, e [mulɑ̃, -ɑ̃t] adj figure-hugging

moule [mul] vb voir **moudre** ▷ nf (mollusque) mussel ▷ nm (creux, Culin) mould (Brit), mold (US); (modèle plein) cast; ~ **à gâteau** nm cake tin (Brit) ou pan (US); ~ **à gaufre** nm waffle iron; ~ **à tarte** nm pie ou flan dish

moulent [mul] vb voir **moudre; mouler**

mouler [mule] vt (brique) to mould (Brit), mold (US); (statue) to cast; (visage, bas-relief) to make a cast of; (lettre) to shape with care; (vêtement) to hug, fit closely round; ~ **qch sur** (fig) to model sth on

moulin [mulɛ̃] nm mill; (fam) engine; ~ **à café** coffee mill; ~ **à eau** watermill; ~ **à légumes** (vegetable) shredder; ~ **à paroles** (fig) chatterbox; ~ **à poivre** pepper mill; ~ **à prières** prayer wheel; ~ **à vent** windmill

moulinet [mulinɛ] nm (de treuil) winch; (de canne à pêche) reel; (mouvement): **faire des ~s avec qch** to whirl sth around

moulinette® [mulinɛt] nf (vegetable) shredder

moulu, e [muly] pp de **moudre** ▷ adj (café) ground

mourant, e [muʀɑ̃, -ɑ̃t] vb voir **mourir** ▷ adj dying ▷ nm/f dying man/woman

mourir [muʀiʀ] vi to die; (civilisation) to die out; ~ **assassiné** to be murdered; ~ **de froid/faim/vieillesse** to die of exposure/hunger/old age; ~ **de faim/d'ennui** (fig) to be starving/be bored to death; ~ **d'envie de faire** to be dying to do; **s'ennuyer à** ~ to be bored to death

mousse [mus] nf (Bot) moss; (de savon) lather; (écume: sur eau, bière) froth, foam; (: shampooing) lather; (de champagne) bubbles pl; (Culin) mousse; (en caoutchouc etc) foam ▷ nm (Navig) ship's boy; **bain de** ~ bubble bath; **bas** ~ stretch stockings; **balle** ~ rubber ball; ~ **carbonique** (fire-fighting) foam; ~ **de nylon** nylon foam; (tissu) stretch nylon; ~ **à raser** shaving foam

mousseline [muslin] nf (Textiles) muslin;

chiffon; **pommes** ~ (Culin) creamed potatoes

mousser [muse] vi (bière, détergent) to foam; (savon) to lather

mousseux, -euse [musø, -øz] adj (chocolat) frothy; (eau) foamy, frothy; (vin) sparkling ▷ nm: (vin) ~ sparkling wine

mousson [musɔ̃] nf monsoon

moustache [mustaʃ] nf moustache; **moustaches** nfpl (d'animal) whiskers pl

moustachu, e [mustaʃy] adj with a moustache

moustiquaire [mustikɛʀ] nf (rideau) mosquito net; (chassis) mosquito screen

moustique [mustik] nm mosquito

moutarde [mutaʀd] nf mustard ▷ adj inv mustard(-coloured)

mouton [mutɔ̃] nm (Zool, péj) sheep inv; (peau) sheepskin; (Culin) mutton

mouvement [muvmɑ̃] nm (gen, aussi: mécanisme) movement; (ligne courbe) contours pl; (fig: tumulte, agitation) activity, bustle; (: impulsion) impulse; reaction; (geste) gesture; (Mus: rythme) tempo; **avoir un bon** ~ to make a nice gesture; **en** ~ in motion; on the move; **mettre qch en** ~ to set sth in motion, set sth going; ~ **d'humeur** fit ou burst of temper; ~ **d'opinion** trend of (public) opinion; **le ~ perpétuel** perpetual motion

mouvementé, e [muvmɑ̃te] adj (vie, poursuite) eventful; (réunion) turbulent

mouvoir [muvwaʀ] vt (levier, membre) to move; (machine) to drive; **se mouvoir** vi to move

moyen, ne [mwajɛ̃, -ɛn] adj average; (tailles, prix) medium; (de grandeur moyenne) medium-sized ▷ nm (façon) means sg, way ▷ nf average; (Statistique) mean; (Scol: à l'examen) pass mark; (Auto) average speed; **moyens** nmpl (capacités) means; **très ~** (résultats) pretty poor; **je n'en ai pas les ~s** I can't afford it; **au ~ de** by means of; **y a-t-il ~ de …?** is it possible to …?; **can one …?**; **par quel ~?** how?, which way?, by which means?; **par tous les ~s** by every possible means, every possible way; **avec les ~s du bord** (fig) with what's available ou what comes to hand; **employer les grands ~s** to resort to drastic measures; **par ses propres ~s** all by oneself; **en ~ne** on (an) average; **faire la ~ne** to work out the average; ~ **de locomotion/d'expression** means of transport/expression; ~ **âge** Middle Ages; ~ **de transport** means of transport; ~**ne d'âge** average age; ~**ne entreprise** (Comm) medium-sized firm

moyennant [mwajɛnɑ̃] prép (somme) for; (service, conditions) in return for; (travail, effort) with

Moyen-Orient [mwajɛnɔʀjɑ̃] nm: **le** ~ the Middle East

moyeu, x [mwajø] nm hub

MSF sigle mpl = **Médecins sans frontières**

MST sigle f (= maladie sexuellement transmissible) STD (= sexually transmitted disease)

mû, mue [my] *pp de* **mouvoir**

muer [mɥe] *vi* (*oiseau, mammifère*) to moult (*Brit*), molt (*US*); (*serpent*) to slough (its skin); (*jeune garçon*): **il mue** his voice is breaking; **se ~ en** to transform into

muet, te [mɥɛ, -ɛt] *adj* dumb; (*fig*): **~ d'admiration** *etc* speechless with admiration *etc*; (*joie, douleur, Ciné*) silent; (*Ling: lettre*) silent, mute; (*carte*) blank ▷ *nm/f* mute ▷ *nm*: **le ~** (*Ciné*) the silent cinema *ou* (*esp US*) movies

mufle [myfl] *nm* muzzle; (*goujat*) boor ▷ *adj* boorish

mugir [myʒiʀ] *vi* (*bœuf*) to bellow; (*vache*) to low, moo; (*fig*) to howl

muguet [mygɛ] *nm* (*Bot*) lily of the valley; (*Méd*) thrush

mule [myl] *nf* (*Zool*) (she-)mule

mulet [mylɛ] *nm* (*Zool*) (he-)mule; (*poisson*) mullet

multinational, e, -aux [myltinasjɔnal, -o] *adj, nf* multinational

multiple [myltipl] *adj* multiple, numerous; (*varié*) many, manifold ▷ *nm* (*Math*) multiple

multiplication [myltiplikasjɔ̃] *nf* multiplication

multiplier [myltiplije] *vt* to multiply; **se multiplier** *vi* to multiply; (*fig: personne*) to be everywhere at once

municipal, e, -aux [mynisipal, -o] *adj* (*élections, stade*) municipal; (*conseil*) town *cpd*; **piscine/bibliothèque ~e** public swimming pool/library

municipalité [mynisipalite] *nf* (*corps municipal*) town council, corporation; (*commune*) town, municipality

munir [myniʀ] *vt*: **~ qn/qch de** to equip sb/sth with; **se ~ de** to provide o.s. with

munitions [mynisjɔ̃] *nfpl* ammunition *sg*

mur [myʀ] *nm* wall; (*fig*) stone *ou* brick wall; **faire le ~** (*interne, soldat*) to jump the wall; **~ du son** sound barrier

mûr, e [myʀ] *adj* ripe; (*personne*) mature ▷ *nf* (*de la ronce*) blackberry; (*du mûrier*) mulberry

muraille [myʀɑj] *nf* (high) wall

mural, e, -aux [myʀal, -o] *adj* wall *cpd* ▷ *nm* (*Art*) mural

mûre [myʀ] *nf* blackberry

muret [myʀɛ] *nm* low wall

mûrir [myʀiʀ] *vi* (*fruit, blé*) to ripen; (*abcès, furoncle*) to come to a head; (*fig: idée, personne*) to mature; (*projet*) to develop ▷ *vt* (*fruit, blé*) to ripen; (*personne*) to (make) mature; (*pensée, projet*) to nurture

murmure [myʀmyʀ] *nm* murmur; **murmures** *nmpl* (*plaintes*) murmurings, mutterings

murmurer [myʀmyʀe] *vi* to murmur; (*se plaindre*) to mutter, grumble

muscade [myskad] *nf* (*aussi*: **noix (de) ~**) nutmeg

muscat [myska] *nm* (*raisin*) muscat grape; (*vin*) muscatel (wine)

muscle [myskl] *nm* muscle

musclé, e [myskle] *adj* (*personne, corps*) muscular; (*fig: politique, régime etc*) strong-arm *cpd*

museau, x [myzo] *nm* muzzle; (*Culin*) brawn

musée [myze] *nm* museum; (*de peinture*) art gallery

museler [myzle] *vt* to muzzle

muselière [myzəljɛʀ] *nf* muzzle

musette [myzɛt] *nf* (*sac*) lunch bag ▷ *adj inv* (*orchestre etc*) accordion *cpd*

musical, e, -aux [myzikal, -o] *adj* musical

music-hall [myzikol] *nm* (*salle*) variety theatre; (*genre*) variety

musicien, ne [myzisjɛ̃, -ɛn] *adj* musical ▷ *nm/f* musician

musique [myzik] *nf* music; (*fanfare*) band; **faire de la ~** to make music; (*jouer d'un instrument*) to play an instrument; **~ de chambre** chamber music; **~ de fond** background music

⬥ **FÊTE DE LA MUSIQUE**

The *Fête de la Musique* is a music festival which takes place every year on 21 June. Throughout France, local musicians perform free of charge in parks, streets and squares.

musulman, e [myzylmɑ̃, -an] *adj, nm/f* Moslem, Muslim

mutation [mytasjɔ̃] *nf* (*Admin*) transfer; (*Bio*) mutation

muter [myte] *vt* (*Admin*) to transfer, move

mutilé, e [mytile] *nm/f* disabled person (*through loss of limbs*); **~ de guerre** disabled ex-serviceman; **grand ~** severely disabled person

mutiler [mytile] *vt* to mutilate, maim; (*fig*) to mutilate, deface

mutin, e [mytɛ̃, -in] *adj* (*enfant, air, ton*) mischievous, impish ▷ *nm/f* (*Mil, Navig*) mutineer

mutinerie [mytinʀi] *nf* mutiny

mutisme [mytism] *nm* silence

mutuel, le [mytɥɛl] *adj* mutual ▷ *nf* mutual benefit society

myope [mjɔp] *adj* short-sighted

myosotis [mjɔzɔtis] *nm* forget-me-not

myrtille [miʀtij] *nf* blueberry, bilberry (*Brit*)

mystère [mistɛʀ] *nm* mystery

mystérieux, -euse [misteʀjø, -øz] *adj* mysterious

mystifier [mistifje] *vt* to fool, take in; (*tromper*) to mystify

mythe [mit] *nm* myth

mythologie [mitɔlɔʒi] *nf* mythology

n [n]

n' [n] *adv voir* **ne**

nacre [nakʀ] *nf* mother-of-pearl

nage [naʒ] *nf* swimming; (*manière*) style of swimming, stroke; **traverser/s'éloigner à la ~** to swim across/away; **en ~** bathed in sweat; **~ indienne** sidestroke; **~ libre** freestyle; **~ papillon** butterfly

nageoire [naʒwaʀ] *nf* fin

nager [naʒe] *vi* to swim; (*fig: ne rien comprendre*) to be all at sea; **~ dans** to be swimming in; (*vêtements*) to be lost in; **~ dans le bonheur** to be overjoyed

nageur, -euse [naʒœʀ, -øz] *nm/f* swimmer

naguère [nagɛʀ] *adv* (*il y a peu de temps*) not long ago; (*autrefois*) formerly

naïf, -ïve [naif, naiv] *adj* naïve

nain, e [nɛ̃, nɛn] *adj, nm/f* dwarf

naissance [nɛsɑ̃s] *nf* birth; **donner ~ à** to give birth to; (*fig*) to give rise to; **prendre ~** to originate; **aveugle de ~** born blind; **Français de ~** French by birth; **à la ~ des cheveux** at the roots of the hair; **lieu de ~** place of birth

naître [nɛtʀ] *vi* to be born; (*conflit, complications*): **~ de** to arise from, be born out of; **~ à** (*amour, poésie*) to awaken to; **je suis né en 1960** I was born in 1960; **il naît plus de filles que de garçons** there are more girls born than boys; **faire ~** (*fig*) to give rise to, arouse

naïveté [naivte] *nf* naivety

nana [nana] *nf* (*fam: fille*) bird (*Brit*), chick

nantir [nɑ̃tiʀ] *vt*: **~ qn de** to provide sb with; **les nantis** (*péj*) the well-to-do

nappe [nap] *nf* tablecloth; (*fig*) sheet; (*de pétrole, gaz*) layer; **~ de mazout** oil slick; **~ (phréatique)** water table

napperon [napʀɔ̃] *nm* table-mat; **~ individuel** place mat

narcodollars [naʀkodɔlaʀ] *nmpl* drug money *no pl*

narguer [naʀge] *vt* to taunt

narine [naʀin] *nf* nostril

narquois, e [naʀkwa, -waz] *adj* derisive, mocking

natal, e [natal] *adj* native

natalité [natalite] *nf* birth rate

natation [natasjɔ̃] *nf* swimming; **faire de la ~** to go swimming (*regularly*)

natif, -ive [natif, -iv] *adj* native

nation [nasjɔ̃] *nf* nation; **les N~s unies (NU)** the United Nations (UN)

national, e, -aux [nasjɔnal, -o] *adj* national ▷ *nf*: (**route**) **~e** ≈ A road (*Brit*), ≈ state highway (*US*); **obsèques ~es** state funeral

nationaliser [nasjɔnalize] *vt* to nationalize

nationalisme [nasjɔnalism] *nm* nationalism

nationalité [nasjɔnalite] *nf* nationality; **de ~ française** of French nationality

natte [nat] *nf* (*tapis*) mat; (*cheveux*) plait

naturaliser [natyʀalize] *vt* to naturalize; (*empailler*) to stuff

nature [natyʀ] *nf* nature ▷ *adj, adv* (*Culin*) plain, without seasoning or sweetening; (*café, thé: sans lait*) black; (*: sans sucre*) without sugar; (*yaourt*) natural; **payer en ~** to pay in kind; **peint d'après ~** painted from life; **être de ~ à faire qch** (*propre à*) to be the sort of thing (*ou* person) to do sth; **~ morte** still-life

naturel, le [natyʀɛl] *adj* natural ▷ *nm* naturalness; (*caractère*) disposition, nature; (*autochtone*) native; (*aussi*: **au ~**: *Culin*) in water; in its own juices

naturellement [natyʀɛlmɑ̃] *adv* naturally; (*bien sûr*) of course

naufrage [nofʀaʒ] *nm* (*ship*)wreck; (*fig*) wreck; **faire ~** to be shipwrecked

nauséabond, e [nozeabɔ̃, -ɔ̃d] *adj* foul, nauseous

nausée [noze] *nf* nausea; **avoir la ~** to feel sick; **avoir des ~s** to have waves of nausea, feel nauseous *ou* sick

nautique [notik] *adj* nautical, water *cpd*; **sports ~s** water sports

naval, e [naval] *adj* naval; (*industrie*) shipbuilding

navet [navɛ] *nm* turnip; (*péj: film*) third-rate film

navette [navɛt] *nf* shuttle; (*en car etc*) shuttle (service); **faire la ~ (entre)** to go to and fro (between), shuttle (between); **~ spatiale** space shuttle

navigateur [navigatœʀ] *nm* (*Navig*) seafarer, sailor; (*Aviat*) navigator; (*Inform*) browser

navigation [navigasjɔ̃] *nf* navigation, sailing; (*Comm*) shipping; **compagnie de ~**

shipping company; ~ **spatiale** space navigation

naviguer [navige] *vi* to navigate, sail; ~ **sur Internet** to browse the Internet

navire [naviʀ] *nm* ship; ~ **de guerre** warship; ~ **marchand** merchantman

navrer [navʀe] *vt* to upset, distress; **je suis navré (de/de faire/que)** I'm so sorry (for/for doing/that)

ne, n' [nə, n] *adv voir* **pas**; **plus**; **jamais** *etc*; (*sans valeur négative: non traduit*): **c'est plus loin que je ne le croyais** it's further than I thought

né, e [ne] *pp de* **naître**; **né en 1960** born in 1960; **née Scott** née Scott; **né(e) de ... et de ...** son/daughter of ... and of ...; **né d'une mère française** having a French mother; **né pour commander** born to lead ▷ *adj*: **un comédien né** a born comedian

néanmoins [neãmwɛ̃] *adv* nevertheless, yet

néant [neã] *nm* nothingness; **réduire à ~** to bring to nought; (*espoir*) to dash

nécessaire [neseseʀ] *adj* necessary ▷ *nm* necessary; (*sac*) kit; **faire le ~** to do the necessary; **n'emporter que le strict ~** to take only what is strictly necessary; ~ **de couture** sewing kit; ~ **de toilette** toilet bag; ~ **de voyage** overnight bag

nécessité [nesesite] *nf* necessity; **se trouver dans la ~ de faire qch** to find it necessary to do sth; **par ~** out of necessity

nécessiter [nesesite] *vt* to require

nécrologique [nekʀɔlɔʒik] *adj*: **article ~** obituary; **rubrique ~** obituary column

nectar [nɛktaʀ] *nm* nectar

néerlandais, e [neɛʀlãdɛ, -ɛz] *adj* Dutch, of the Netherlands ▷ *nm* (*Ling*) Dutch ▷ *nm/f*: **N~, e** Dutchman/woman; **les N~** the Dutch

nef [nɛf] *nf* (*d'église*) nave

néfaste [nefast] *adj* (*nuisible*) harmful; (*funeste*) ill-fated

négatif, -ive [negatif, iv] *adj* negative ▷ *nm* (*Photo*) negative

négligé, e [neglize] *adj* (*en désordre*) slovenly ▷ *nm* (*tenue*) negligee

négligeable [neglizabl] *adj* insignificant, negligible

négligent, e [neglizã, -ãt] *adj* careless; (*Jur etc*) negligent

négliger [neglize] *vt* (*épouse, jardin*) to neglect; (*tenue*) to be careless about; (*avis, précautions*) to disregard, overlook; ~ **de faire** to fail to do, not bother to do; **se négliger** to neglect o.s

négoce [negɔs] *nm* trade

négociant, e [negɔsjã, jãt] *nm/f* merchant

négociation [negɔsjasjɔ̃] *nf* negotiation; **~s collectives** collective bargaining *sg*

négocier [negɔsje] *vi*, *vt* to negotiate

nègre [nɛgʀ] *nm* (*péj*) Negro; (*péj*: *écrivain*) ghost writer ▷ *adj* (*péj*) Negro

neige [nɛʒ] *nf* snow; **battre les œufs en ~** (*Culin*) to whip *ou* beat the egg whites until

stiff; ~ **carbonique** dry ice; ~ **fondue** (*par terre*) slush; (*qui tombe*) sleet; ~ **poudreuse** powdery snow

neiger [neʒe] *vi* to snow

nénuphar [nenyfaʀ] *nm* water-lily

néon [neɔ̃] *nm* neon

néo-zélandais, e [neozelãdɛ, -ɛz] *adj* New Zealand *cpd* ▷ *nm/f*: **N~, e** New Zealander

Népal [nepal] *nm*: **le ~** Nepal

nerf [nɛʀ] *nm* nerve; (*fig*) spirit; (: *forces*) stamina; **nerfs** *nmpl* nerves; **être** *ou* **vivre sur les ~s** to live on one's nerves; **être à bout de ~s** to be at the end of one's tether; **passer ses ~s sur qn** to take it out on sb

nerveux, -euse [nɛʀvø, -øz] *adj* nervous; (*cheval*) highly-strung; (*irritable*) touchy, nervy; (*voiture*) nippy, responsive; (*tendineux*) sinewy

nervosité [nɛʀvozite] *nf* nervousness; (*émotivité*) excitability, tenseness

nervure [nɛʀvyʀ] *nf* (*de feuille*) vein; (*Archit, Tech*) rib

n'est-ce pas [nɛspa] *adv* isn't it?, won't you? *etc* (*selon le verbe qui précède*); **c'est bon, ~?** it's good, isn't it?; **il a peur, ~?** he's afraid, isn't he?; ~ **que c'est bon?** don't you think it's good?; **lui, ~, il peut se le permettre** he, of course, can afford to do that, can't he?

net, nette [nɛt] *adj* (*sans équivoque, distinct*) clear; (*photo*) sharp; (*évident*) definite; (*amélioration, différence*) marked, distinct; (*propre*) neat, clean; (*Comm*: *prix, salaire, poids*) net ▷ *adv* (*refuser*) flatly ▷ *nm*: **mettre au ~** to copy out; **s'arrêter ~** to stop dead; **la lame a cassé ~** the blade snapped clean through; **faire place nette** to make a clean sweep; ~ **d'impôt** tax free

Net [nɛt] *nm* (*Internet*): **le ~** the Net

netiquette [nɛtikɛt] *nf* netiquette

nettement [nɛtmã] *adv* (*distinctement*) clearly; (*évidemment*) definitely; (*incontestablement*) decidedly; (*avec comparatif, superlatif*): ~ **mieux** definitely *ou* clearly better

netteté [nɛtte] *nf* clearness

nettoyage [netwajaʒ] *nm* cleaning; ~ **à sec** dry cleaning

nettoyer [netwaje] *vt* to clean; (*fig*) to clean out

neuf¹ [nœf] *num* nine

neuf², neuve [nœf, nœv] *adj* new ▷ *nm*: **repeindre à ~** to redecorate; **remettre à ~** to do up (as good as new), refurbish; **n'acheter que du ~** to buy everything new; **quoi de ~?** what's new?

neutre [nøtʀ] *adj*, *nm* (*Ling*) neuter

neuve [nœv] *adj f voir* **neuf**

neuvième [nœvjɛm] *num* ninth

neveu, x [nəvø] *nm* nephew

névrosé, e [nevʀoze] *adj*, *nm/f* neurotic

New York [njujɔʀk] *n* New York

nez [ne] *nm* nose; **rire au ~ de qn** to laugh in sb's face; **avoir du ~** to have flair; **avoir le ~**

fin to have foresight; **~ à - avec** face to face with; **à vue de ~** roughly

ni [ni] *conj:* **ni ... ni** neither ... nor; **je n'aime ni les lentilles ni les épinards** I like neither lentils nor spinach; **il n'a dit ni oui ni non** he didn't say either yes or no; **elles ne sont venues ni l'une ni l'autre** neither of them came; **il n'a rien vu ni entendu** he didn't see or hear anything

niais, e [nje, -ɛz] *adj* silly, thick

niche [niʃ] *nf* (*du chien*) kennel; (*de mur*) recess, niche; (*farce*) trick

nicher [niʃe] *vi* to nest; **se ~ dans** (*personne: se blottir*) to snuggle into; (: *se cacher*) to hide in; (*objet*) to lodge itself in

nid [ni] *nm* nest; (*fig: repaire etc*) den, lair; **~ d'abeilles** (*Couture, Textile*) honeycomb stitch; **~ de poule** pothole

nièce [njɛs] *nf* niece

nier [nje] *vt* to deny

nigaud, e [nigo, -od] *nm/f* booby, fool

Nil [nil] *nm:* **le ~** the Nile

n'importe [nɛ̃pɔʀt] *adv:* **~!** no matter!; **~ qui/quoi/où** anybody/anything/anywhere; **~ quoi!** (*fam: désapprobation*) what rubbish!; **~ quand** any time; **~ quel/quelle** any; **~ lequel/laquelle** any (one); **~ comment** (*sans soin*) carelessly; **~ comment, il part ce soir** he's leaving tonight in any case

niveau, x [nivo] *nm* level; (*des élèves, études*) standard; **au ~ de** at the level of; (*personne*) on a level with; **de ~ (avec)** level (with); **le ~ de la mer** sea level; **~ (à bulle)** spirit level; **~ (d'eau)** water level; **~ de vie** standard of living

niveler [nivle] *vt* to level

NN *abr* (= *nouvelle norme*) *revised standard of hotel classification*

noble [nɔbl] *adj* noble; (*de qualité: métal etc*) precious ▷ *nm/f* noble(man/-woman)

noblesse [nɔbles] *nf* (*classe sociale*) nobility; (*d'une action etc*) nobleness

noce [nɔs] *nf* wedding; (*gens*) wedding party (*ou* guests *pl*); **il l'a épousée en secondes ~s** she was his second wife; **faire la ~** (*fam*) to go on a binge; **~s d'or/d'argent/de diamant** golden/silver/diamond wedding

nocif, -ive [nɔsif, -iv] *adj* harmful, noxious

nocturne [nɔktyʀn] *adj* nocturnal ▷ *nf* (*Sport*) floodlit fixture; (*d'un magasin*) late opening

Noël [nɔɛl] *nm* Christmas; **la (fête de) ~** Christmas time

nœud [nø] *nm* (*de corde, du bois, Navig*) knot; (*ruban*) bow; (*fig: liens*) bond, tie; (: *d'une question*) crux; (*Théât etc*): **le ~ de l'action** the web of events; **~ coulant** noose; **~ gordien** Gordian knot; **~ papillon** bow tie

noir, e [nwaʀ] *adj* black; (*obscur, sombre*) dark ▷ *nm/f* black man/woman ▷ *nm:* **dans le ~** in the dark ▷ *nf* (*Mus*) crotchet (*Brit*), quarter note (*US*); **il fait ~** it is dark; **au ~** *adv* (*acheter,*

vendre) on the black market; **travail au ~** moonlighting; **travailler au ~** to work on the side

noircir [nwaʀsiʀ] *vt, vi* to blacken

noisette [nwazɛt] *nf* hazelnut; (*morceau: de beurre etc*) small knob ▷ *adj* (*yeux*) hazel

noix [nwa] *nf* walnut; (*fam*) twit; (*Culin*): **une ~ de beurre** a knob of butter; **à la ~** (*fam*) worthless; **~ de cajou** cashew nut; **~ de coco** coconut; **~ muscade** nutmeg; **~ de veau** (*Culin*) round fillet of veal

nom [nɔ̃] *nm* name; (*Ling*) noun; **connaître qn de ~** to know sb by name; **au ~ de** in the name of; **~ d'une pipe** *ou* **d'un chien!** (*fam*) for goodness' sake!; **~ de Dieu!** (*fam!*) bloody hell! (*Brit*), my God!; **~ commun/propre** common/proper noun; **~ composé** (*Ling*) compound noun; **~ déposé** trade name; **~ d'emprunt** assumed name; **~ de famille** surname; **~ de fichier** file name; **~ de jeune fille** maiden name

nomade [nɔmad] *adj* nomadic ▷ *nm/f* nomad

nombre [nɔ̃bʀ] *nm* number; **venir en ~** to come in large numbers; **depuis ~ d'années** for many years; **ils sont au ~ de trois** there are three of them; **au ~ de mes amis** among my friends; **sans ~** countless; (**bon**) **~ de** (*beaucoup, plusieurs*) a (large) number of; **~ premier/entier** prime/whole number

nombreux, -euse [nɔ̃bʀø, -øz] *adj* many, numerous; (*avec nom sg: foule etc*) large; **peu ~** few; small; **de ~ cas** many cases

nombril [nɔ̃bʀi(l)] *nm* navel

nommer [nɔme] *vt* (*baptiser*) to name, give a name to; (*qualifier*) to call; (*mentionner*) to name, give the name of; (*élire*) to appoint, nominate; **se nommer; il se nomme Pascal** his name's Pascal, he's called Pascal

non [nɔ̃] *adv* (*réponse*) no; (*suivi d'un adjectif, adverbe*) not; **Paul est venu, ~?** Paul came, didn't he?; **répondre ou dire que ~** to say no; **~ pas que** not that; **~ plus: moi non plus** neither do I, I don't either; **je préférerais que ~** I would prefer not; **il se trouve que ~** perhaps not; **je pense que ~** I don't think so; **~ mais!** well really!; **~ mais des fois!** you must be joking!; **~ alcoolisé** non-alcoholic; **~ loin/seulement** not far/only

nonante [nɔnɑ̃t] *num* (*Belgique, Suisse*) ninety

nonchalant, e [nɔ̃ʃalɑ̃, -ɑ̃t] *adj* nonchalant, casual

non-fumeur, -euse [nɔ̃fymœʀ, øz] *nm/f* non-smoker

non-sens [nɔ̃sɑ̃s] *nm* absurdity

nord [nɔʀ] *nm* North ▷ *adj* northern; north; **au ~** (*situation*) in the north; (*direction*) to the north; **au ~ de** north of, to the north of; **perdre le ~** to lose one's way (*fig*)

nord-africain, e [nɔʀafʀikɛ̃, -ɛn] *adj* North-African ▷ *nm/f:* **Nord-Africain, e** North African

nord-est [nɔʀɛst] *nm* North-East

nord-ouest [nɔʀwɛst] *nm* North-West
normal, e, -aux [nɔʀmal, -o] *adj* normal
▷ *nf*: **la ~e** the norm, the average; **c'est tout à fait ~** it's perfectly natural; **vous trouvez ça ~?** does it seem right to you?
normalement [nɔʀmalmɑ̃] *adv* (*en général*) normally; (*comme prévu*): **~, il le fera demain** he should be doing it tomorrow, he's supposed to do it tomorrow
normand, e [nɔʀmɑ̃, -ɑ̃d] *adj* (*de Normandie*) Norman ▷ *nm/f*: **N~, e** (*de Normandie*) Norman
Normandie [nɔʀmɑ̃di] *nf*: **la ~** Normandy
norme [nɔʀm] *nf* norm; (*Tech*) standard
Norvège [nɔʀvɛʒ] *nf*: **la ~** Norway
norvégien, ne [nɔʀveʒjɛ̃, -ɛn] *adj* Norwegian ▷ *nm* (*Ling*) Norwegian ▷ *nm/f*: **N~, ne** Norwegian
nos [no] *adj poss voir* **notre**
nostalgie [nɔstalʒi] *nf* nostalgia
nostalgique [nɔstalʒik] *adj* nostalgic
notable [nɔtabl] *adj* notable, noteworthy; (*marqué*) noticeable, marked ▷ *nm* prominent citizen
notaire [nɔtɛʀ] *nm* notary; solicitor
notamment [nɔtamɑ̃] *adv* in particular, among others
note [nɔt] *nf* (*écrite, Mus*) note; (*Scol*) mark (Brit), grade; (*facture*) bill; **prendre des ~s** to take notes; **prendre ~ de** to note; (*par écrit*) to note, write down; **dans la ~** exactly right; **forcer la ~** to exaggerate; **une ~ de tristesse/ de gaieté** a sad/happy note; **~ de service** memorandum
noté, e [nɔte] *adj*: **être bien/mal ~** (*employé etc*) to have a good/bad record
noter [nɔte] *vt* (*écrire*) to write down, note; (*remarquer*) to note, notice; (*Scol, Admin: donner une appréciation: devoir*) to mark, give a grade to; **notez bien que ...** (please) note that ...
notice [nɔtis] *nf* summary, short article; (*brochure*): **~ explicative** explanatory leaflet, instruction booklet
notifier [nɔtifje] *vt*: **~ qch à qn** to notify sb of sth, notify sth to sb
notion [nosjɔ̃] *nf* notion, idea; **notions** *nfpl* (*rudiments*) rudiments
notoire [nɔtwaʀ] *adj* widely known; (*en mal*) notorious; **le fait est ~** the fact is common knowledge
notre, nos [nɔtʀ(ə), no] *adj poss* our
nôtre [notʀ] *adj* *ours* ▷ *pron*: **le/la ~** ours; **les ~s** ours; (*alliés etc*) our own people; **soyez des ~s** join us
nouer [nwe] *vt* to tie, knot; (*fig: alliance etc*) to strike up; **~ la conversation** to start a conversation; **se nouer** *vi*: **c'est là où l'intrigue se noue** it's at that point that the strands of the plot come together; **ma gorge se noua** a lump came to my throat
noueux, -euse [nwø, -øz] *adj* gnarled
nouille [nuj] *nf* (*fam*) noodle (Brit), fathead; **nouilles** *nfpl* (*pâtes*) noodles; pasta *sg*

nourrice [nuʀis] *nf* ≈ child-minder; (*autrefois*) wet-nurse
nourrir [nuʀiʀ] *vt* to feed; (*fig: espoir*) to harbour, nurse; **logé nourri** with board and lodging; **~ au sein** to breast-feed; **se ~ de légumes** to live on vegetables
nourrissant, e [nuʀisɑ̃, -ɑ̃t] *adj* nourishing, nutritious
nourrisson [nuʀisɔ̃] *nm* (*unweaned*) infant
nourriture [nuʀityʀ] *nf* food
nous [nu] *pron* (*sujet*) we; (*objet*) us
nous-mêmes [numɛm] *pron* ourselves
nouveau, nouvel, -elle, x [nuvo, -ɛl] *adj* new; (*original*) novel ▷ *nm/f* new pupil (*ou* employee) ▷ *nm*: **il y a du ~** there's something new ▷ *nf* (*piece of*) news *sg*; (*Littérature*) short story; **nouvelles** *nfpl* (*Presse, TV*) news *sg*; **de ~, à ~** again; **je suis sans nouvelles de lui** I haven't heard from him; **Nouvel An** New Year; **~ venu, nouvelle venue** newcomer; **~x mariés** newly-weds; **nouvelle vague** new wave
nouveau-né, e [nuvone] *nm/f* newborn (baby)
nouveauté [nuvote] *nf* novelty; (*chose nouvelle*) innovation, something new; (*Comm*) new film (*ou* book *ou* creation *etc*)
nouvel *adj m*, **nouvelle** *adj f, nf* [nuvɛl] *voir* **nouveau**
Nouvelle-Calédonie [nuvɛlkaledɔni] *nf*: **la ~** New Caledonia
nouvellement [nuvɛlmɑ̃] *adv* (*arrivé etc*) recently, newly
Nouvelle-Zélande [nuvɛlzelɑ̃d] *nf*: **la ~** New Zealand
novembre [nɔvɑ̃bʀ] *nm* November; *see note*; *voir aussi* **juillet**

> ⚜ **LE 11 NOVEMBRE**
>
> ⚜ *Le 11 novembre* is a public holiday in France
> ⚜ and commemorates the signing of the
> ⚜ armistice, near Compiègne, at the end of
> ⚜ the First World War.

novice [nɔvis] *adj* inexperienced ▷ *nm/f* novice
noyade [nwajad] *nf* drowning *no pl*
noyau, x [nwajo] *nm* (*de fruit*) stone; (*Bio, Physique*) nucleus; (*Élec, Géo, fig: centre*) core; (*fig: d'artistes etc*) group; (*: de résistants etc*) cell
noyauter [nwajote] *vt* (*Pol*) to infiltrate
noyer [nwaje] *nm* walnut (tree); (*bois*) walnut ▷ *vt* to drown; (*fig*) to flood; to submerge; (*Auto: moteur*) to flood; **se noyer** to be drowned, drown; (*suicide*) to drown o.s.; **~ son chagrin** to drown one's sorrows; **~ le poisson** to duck the issue
nu, e [ny] *adj* (*membres*) naked, bare; (*chambre, fil, plaine*) bare ▷ *nm* (*Art*) nude; **le nu intégral** total nudity; **tout nu** stark naked; **se mettre nu** to strip; **mettre à nu** to bare

nuage [nɥaʒ] *nm* cloud; **être dans les ~s** (*distrait*) to have one's head in the clouds; **~ de lait** drop of milk

nuageux, -euse [nɥaʒø, -øz] *adj* cloudy

nuance [nɥɑ̃s] *nf* (*de couleur, sens*) shade; **il y a une ~ (entre)** there's a slight difference (between); **une ~ de tristesse** a tinge of sadness

nuancer [nɥɑ̃se] *vt* (*pensée, opinion*) to qualify

nucléaire [nykleɛʀ] *adj* nuclear ▷ *nm*: **le ~** nuclear power

nudiste [nydist] *adj, nm/f* nudist

nuée [nɥe] *nf*: **une ~ de** a cloud *ou* host *ou* swarm of

nues [ny] *nfpl*: **tomber des ~** to be taken aback; **porter qn aux ~** to praise sb to the skies

nuire [nɥiʀ] *vi* to be harmful; **~ à** to harm, do damage to

nuisible [nɥizibl] *adj* harmful; **(animal) ~** pest

nuit [nɥi] *nf* night; **payer sa ~** to pay for one's overnight accommodation; **il fait ~** it's dark; **cette ~** (*hier*) last night; (*aujourd'hui*) tonight; **de ~** (*vol, service*) night *cpd*; **~ blanche** sleepless night; **~ de noces** wedding night; **~ de Noël** Christmas Eve

nul, nulle [nyl] *adj* (*aucun*) no; (*minime*) nil, non-existent; (*non valable*) null; (*péj*) useless, hopeless ▷ *pron* none, no one; **résultat ~, match ~** draw; **nulle part** *adv* nowhere

nullement [nylmɑ̃] *adv* by no means

nullité [nylite] *nf* nullity; (*péj*) hopelessness; (: *personne*) hopeless individual, nonentity

numérique [nymeʀik] *adj* numerical; (*Inform, TV*: *affichage, son, télévision*) digital

numéro [nymeʀo] *nm* number; (*spectacle*) act, turn; (*Presse*) issue, number; **faire** *ou* **composer un ~** to dial a number; **~ d'identification personnel** personal identification number (PIN); **~ d'immatriculation** *ou* **minéralogique** *ou* **de police** registration (Brit) *ou* license (US) number; **~ de téléphone** (tele)phone number; **~ vert** ≈ Freefone® number (Brit), ≈ toll-free number (US)

numéroter [nymeʀɔte] *vt* to number

nu-pieds [nypje] *nm inv* sandal ▷ *adj inv* barefoot

nuque [nyk] *nf* nape of the neck

nu-tête [nytɛt] *adj inv* bareheaded

nutritif, -ive [nytʀitif, -iv] *adj* (*besoins, valeur*) nutritional; (*aliment*) nutritious, nourishing

nylon [nilɔ̃] *nm* nylon

oasis [ɔazis] *nf ou m* oasis

obéir [ɔbeiʀ] *vi* to obey; **~ à** to obey; (*moteur, véhicule*) to respond to

obéissance [ɔbeisɑ̃s] *nf* obedience

obéissant, e [ɔbeisɑ̃, -ɑ̃t] *adj* obedient

obèse [ɔbɛz] *adj* obese

obésité [ɔbezite] *nf* obesity

objecter [ɔbʒɛkte] *vt* (*prétexter*) to plead, put forward as an excuse; **~ qch à** (*argument*) to put forward sth against; **~ (à qn) que** to object (to sb) that

objecteur [ɔbʒɛktœʀ] *nm*: **~ de conscience** conscientious objector

objectif, -ive [ɔbʒɛktif, -iv] *adj* objective ▷ *nm* (*Optique, Photo*) lens *sg*; (*Mil: fig*) objective; **~ grand angulaire/à focale variable** wide-angle/zoom lens

objection [ɔbʒɛksjɔ̃] *nf* objection; **~ de conscience** conscientious objection

objectivité [ɔbʒɛktivite] *nf* objectivity

objet [ɔbʒɛ] *nm* (*chose*) object; (*d'une discussion, recherche*) subject; **être** *ou* **faire l'~ de** (*discussion*) to be the subject of; (*soins*) to be given *ou* shown; **sans ~** *adj* purposeless; (*sans fondement*) groundless; **~ d'art** objet d'art; **~s personnels** personal items; **~s de toilette** toiletries; **~s trouvés** lost property *sg* (Brit), lost-and-found *sg* (US); **~s de valeur** valuables

obligation [ɔbligasjɔ̃] *nf* obligation; (*gén pl*: *devoir*) duty; (*Comm*) bond, debenture; **sans ~ d'achat** with no obligation (to buy); **être**

dans l'~ de faire to be obliged to do; **avoir l'~ de faire** to be under an obligation to do; **~s familiales** family obligations *ou* responsibilities; **~s militaires** military obligations *ou* duties

obligatoire [ɔbligatwaʀ] *adj* compulsory, obligatory

obligatoirement [ɔbligatwaʀmɑ̃] *adv* compulsorily; *(fatalement)* necessarily; *(fam: sans aucun doute)* inevitably

obligé, e [ɔbliʒe] *adj (redevable):* **être très ~ à qn** to be most obliged to sb; *(contraint):* **je suis (bien) ~ (de le faire)** I have to (do it); *(nécessaire: conséquence)* necessary; **c'est ~!** it's inevitable

obligeance [ɔbliʒɑ̃s] *nf:* **avoir l'~ de** to be kind *ou* good enough to

obligeant, e [ɔbliʒɑ̃, -ɑ̃t] *adj* obliging; kind

obliger [ɔbliʒe] *vt (contraindre):* **~ qn à faire** to force *ou* oblige sb to do; *(Jur: engager)* to bind; *(rendre service à)* to oblige; **je suis bien obligé (de le faire)** I have to (do it)

oblique [ɔblik] *adj* oblique; **regard ~** sidelong glance; **en ~** *adv* diagonally

obliquer [ɔblike] *vi:* **~ vers** to turn off towards

oblitérer [ɔblitere] *vt (timbre-poste)* to cancel; *(Méd: canal, vaisseau)* to obstruct

obnubiler [ɔbnybile] *vt* to obsess

obscène [ɔpsɛn] *adj* obscene

obscur, e [ɔpskyʀ] *adj (sombre)* dark; *(fig: raisons)* obscure; *(: sentiment, malaise)* vague; *(: personne, vie)* humble, lowly

obscurcir [ɔpskyʀsiʀ] *vt* to darken; *(fig)* to obscure; **s'obscurcir** *vi* to grow dark

obscurité [ɔpskyʀite] *nf* darkness; **dans l'~** in the dark, in darkness; *(anonymat, médiocrité)* in obscurity

obsédé, e [ɔpsede] *nm/f* fanatic; **~(e) sexuel(le)** sex maniac

obséder [ɔpsede] *vt* to obsess, haunt

obsèques [ɔpsɛk] *nfpl* funeral *sg*

observateur, -trice [ɔpsɛʀvatœʀ, -tʀis] *adj* observant, perceptive ▷ *nm/f* observer

observation [ɔpsɛʀvasjɔ̃] *nf* observation; *(d'un règlement etc)* observance; *(commentaire)* observation, remark; *(reproche)* reproof; **en ~** *(Méd)* under observation

observatoire [ɔpsɛʀvatwaʀ] *nm* observatory; *(lieu élevé)* observation post, vantage point

observer [ɔpsɛʀve] *vt (regarder)* to observe, watch; *(examiner)* to examine; *(scientifiquement, aussi: règlement, jeûne etc)* to observe; *(surveiller)* to watch; *(remarquer)* to observe, notice; **faire ~ qch à qn** *(dire)* to point out sth to sb; **s'observer** *vi (se surveiller)* to keep a check on o.s.

obsession [ɔpsesjɔ̃] *nf* obsession; **avoir l'~ de** to have an obsession with

obstacle [ɔpstakl] *nm* obstacle; *(Équitation)* jump, hurdle; **faire ~ à** *(lumière)* to block out;

(projet) to hinder, put obstacles in the path of; **~s antichars** tank defences

obstiné, e [ɔpstine] *adj* obstinate

obstiner [ɔpstine]: **s'obstiner** *vi* to insist, dig one's heels in; **s'~ à faire** to persist (obstinately) in doing; **s'~ sur qch** to keep working at sth, labour away at sth

obstruer [ɔpstʀye] *vt* to block, obstruct; **s'obstruer** *vi* to become blocked

obtenir [ɔptəniʀ] *vt* to obtain, get; *(total)* to arrive at, reach; *(résultat)* to achieve, obtain; **~ de pouvoir faire** to obtain permission to do; **~ qch à qn** to obtain sth for sb; **~ de qn qu'il fasse** to get sb to agree to do(ing)

obturateur [ɔptyʀatœʀ] *nm (Photo)* shutter; **~ à rideau** focal plane shutter

obus [ɔby] *nm* shell; **~ explosif** high-explosive shell; **~ incendiaire** incendiary device, fire bomb

occasion [ɔkazjɔ̃] *nf (aubaine, possibilité)* opportunity; *(circonstance)* occasion; *(Comm: article non neuf)* secondhand buy; *(: acquisition avantageuse)* bargain; **à plusieurs ~s** on several occasions; **à la première ~** at the first *ou* earliest opportunity; **avoir l'~ de faire** to have the opportunity to do; **être l'~ de** to occasion, give rise to; **à l'~** *adv* sometimes, on occasions; *(un jour)* some time; **à l'~ de** on the occasion of; **d'~** *adj, adv* secondhand

occasionnel, le [ɔkazjɔnɛl] *adj (fortuit)* chance *cpd*; *(non régulier)* occasional; *(: travail)* casual

occasionnellement [ɔkazjɔnɛlmɑ̃] *adv* occasionally, from time to time

occasionner [ɔkazjɔne] *vt* to cause, bring about; **~ qch à qn** to cause sb sth

occident [ɔksidɑ̃] *nm:* **l'O~** the West

occidental, e, -aux [ɔksidɑ̃tal, -o] *adj* western; *(Pol)* Western ▷ *nm/f* Westerner

occupation [ɔkypasjɔ̃] *nf* occupation; **l'O~** the Occupation (of France)

occupé, e [ɔkype] *adj (Mil, Pol)* occupied; *(personne: affairé, pris)* busy; *(esprit: absorbé)* occupied; *(place, sièges)* taken; *(toilettes)* engaged; **la ligne est ~e** the line's engaged (Brit) *ou* busy (US)

occuper [ɔkype] *vt* to occupy; *(poste, fonction)* to hold; *(main-d'œuvre)* to employ; **s'~ à (à qch)** to occupy o.s. *ou* keep o.s. busy (with sth); **s'~ de** *(être responsable de)* to be in charge of; *(se charger de: affaire)* to take charge of, deal with; *(: clients etc)* to attend to; *(s'intéresser à, pratiquer: politique etc)* to be involved in; **ça occupe trop de place** it takes up too much room

occurrence [ɔkyʀɑ̃s] *nf:* **en l'~** in this case

océan [ɔseɑ̃] *nm* ocean; **l'~ Indien** the Indian Ocean

octante [ɔktɑ̃t] *num (Belgique, Suisse)* eighty

octet [ɔktɛ] *nm* byte

octobre [ɔktɔbʀ] *nm* October; *voir aussi* **juillet**

octroyer [ɔktʀwaje] *vt:* **~ qch à qn** to grant sth to sb, grant sb sth

oculiste [ɔkylist] *nm/f* eye specialist, oculist
odeur [ɔdœʀ] *nf* smell
odieux, -euse [ɔdjø, -øz] *adj* odious, hateful
odorant, e [ɔdɔʀɑ̃, -ɑ̃t] *adj* sweet-smelling, fragrant
odorat [ɔdɔʀa] *nm* (sense of) smell; **avoir l'~ fin** to have a keen sense of smell
œil [œj] (*pl* **yeux**) [jø] *nm* eye; **avoir un ~ poché ou au beurre noir** to have a black eye; **à l'~** (*fam*) for free; **à l'~ nu** with the naked eye; **tenir qn à l'~** to keep an eye ou a watch on sb; **avoir l'~ à** to keep an eye on; **faire de l'~ à qn** to make eyes at sb; **voir qch d'un bon/mauvais ~** to view sth in a favourable/ an unfavourable light; **à l'~ vif** with a lively expression; **à mes/ses yeux** in my/his eyes; **de ses propres yeux** with his own eyes; **fermer les yeux (sur)** (*fig*) to turn a blind eye (to); **les yeux fermés** (*aussi fig*) with one's eyes shut; **ouvrir l'~** (*fig*) to keep one's eyes open ou an eye out; **fermer l'~** to get a moment's sleep; **pour ~, dent pour dent** an eye for an eye, a tooth for a tooth; **pour les beaux yeux de qn** (*fig*) for love of sb; **~ de verre** glass eye
œillères [œjɛʀ] *nfpl* blinkers (Brit), blinders (US); **avoir des ~** (*fig*) to be blinkered, wear blinders
œillet [œjɛ] *nm* (Bot) carnation; (*trou*) eyelet
œuf [œf] *nm* egg; **étouffer dans l'~** to nip in the bud; **~ à la coque/dur/mollet** boiled/hard-boiled/soft-boiled egg; **~ au plat/poché** fried/poached egg; **~s brouillés** scrambled eggs; **~ de Pâques** Easter egg; **à repriser** darning egg
œuvre [œvʀ] *nf* (*tâche*) task, undertaking; (*ouvrage achevé, livre, tableau etc*) work; (*ensemble de la production artistique*) works *pl*; (*organisation charitable*) charity ▷ *nm* (*d'un artiste*) works *pl*; (*Constr*): **le gros ~** the shell; **œuvres** *nfpl* (*actes*) deeds, works; **être/se mettre à l'~** to be at/get (down) to work; **mettre en ~** (*moyens*) to make use of; (*plan, loi, projet etc*) to implement; **~ d'art** work of art; **bonnes ~s** good works ou deeds; **~s de bienfaisance** charitable works
offense [ɔfɑ̃s] *nf* (*affront*) insult; (Rel: *péché*) transgression, trespass
offenser [ɔfɑ̃se] *vt* to offend, hurt; (*principes, Dieu*) to offend against; **s'offenser de** *vi* to take offence (Brit) ou offense (US) at
offert, e [ɔfɛʀ, -ɛʀt] *pp de* **offrir**
office [ɔfis] *nm* (*charge*) office; (*agence*) bureau, agency; (Rel) service ▷ *nm ou f* (*pièce*) pantry; **faire ~ de** to act as; to do duty as; **d'~** *adv* automatically; **bons ~s** (Pol) good offices; **~ du tourisme** tourist office
officiel, le [ɔfisjɛl] *adj, nm/f* official
officier [ɔfisje] *nm* officer ▷ *vi* (Rel) to officiate; **~ de l'état-civil** registrar; **~ ministériel** member of the legal profession; **~ de police** = police officer

officieux, -euse [ɔfisjø, -øz] *adj* unofficial
offrande [ɔfʀɑ̃d] *nf* offering
offre [ɔfʀ] *vb voir* **offrir** ▷ *nf* offer; (*aux enchères*) bid; (Admin: *soumission*) tender; (Écon): **l'~ et la demande** supply and demand; **~ d'emploi** job advertised; **"~s d'emploi"** "situations vacant"; **~ publique d'achat (OPA)** takeover bid; **~s de service** offer of service
offrir [ɔfʀiʀ] *vt*: **~ (à qn)** to offer (to sb); (*faire cadeau*) to give (to sb); **s'offrir** *vi* (*se présenter: occasion, paysage*) to present itself ▷ *vt* (*se payer: vacances, voiture*) to treat o.s. to; **~ (à qn) de faire qch** to offer to do sth (for sb); **~ à boire à qn** (*chez soi*) to offer sb a drink; **je vous offre un verre** I'll buy you a drink; **s'~ à faire qch** to offer ou volunteer to do sth; **s'~ comme guide/en otage** to offer one's services as (a) guide/offer o.s. as (a) hostage; **s'~ aux regards** (*personne*) to expose o.s. to the public gaze
offusquer [ɔfyske] *vt* to offend; **s'offusquer de** to take offence (Brit) ou offense (US) at, be offended by
OGM *sigle m* (= *organisme génétiquement modifié*) GMO
oie [wa] *nf* (Zool) goose; **~ blanche** (*fig*) young innocent
oignon [ɔɲɔ̃] *nm* (Culin) onion; (*de tulipe etc: bulbe*) bulb; (Méd) bunion; **ce ne sont pas tes ~s** (*fam*) that's none of your business
oiseau, x [wazo] *nm* bird; **~ de proie** bird of prey
oisif, -ive [wazif, -iv] *adj* idle ▷ *nm/f* (*péj*) man/lady of leisure
oléoduc [ɔleɔdyk] *nm* (oil) pipeline
olive [ɔliv] *nf* (Bot) olive ▷ *adj inv* olive-green
olivier [ɔlivje] *nm* olive (tree); (*bois*) olive (wood)
OLP *sigle f* (= *Organisation de libération de la Palestine*) PLO
olympique [ɔlɛ̃pik] *adj* Olympic
ombragé, e [ɔ̃bʀaʒe] *adj* shaded, shady
ombrageux, -euse [ɔ̃bʀaʒø, -øz] *adj* (*cheval*) skittish, nervous; (*personne*) touchy, easily offended
ombre [ɔ̃bʀ] *nf* (*espace non ensoleillé*) shade; (*ombre portée, tache*) shadow; **à l'~** in the shade; (*fam: en prison*) behind bars; **à l'~ de** in the shade of; (*tout près de, fig*) in the shadow of; **tu me fais de l'~** you're in my light; **ça nous donne de l'~** it gives us (some) shade; **il n'y a pas l'~ d'un doute** there's not the shadow of a doubt; **dans l'~** in the shade; (*fig*) in the dark; **vivre dans l'~** (*fig*) to live in obscurity; **laisser dans l'~** (*fig*) to leave in the dark; **~ à paupières** eye shadow; **~ portée** shadow; **~s chinoises** (*spectacle*) shadow show *sg*
ombrelle [ɔ̃bʀɛl] *nf* parasol, sunshade
omelette [ɔmlɛt] *nf* omelette; **~ baveuse** runny omelette; **~ au fromage/au jambon** cheese/ham omelette; **~ aux herbes** omelette with herbs; **~ norvégienne** baked Alaska

omettre [ɔmɛtʀ] vt to omit, leave out; ~ **de faire** to fail ou omit to do
omnibus [ɔmnibys] nm slow ou stopping train
omoplate [ɔmɔplat] nf shoulder blade

🔵 MOT-CLÉ

on [ɔ̃] pron 1 (indéterminé) you, one; **on peut le faire ainsi** you ou one can do it like this, it can be done like this; **on dit que ...** they say that ..., it is said that ..
2 (quelqu'un): **on les a attaqués** they were attacked; **on vous demande au téléphone** there's a phone call for you, you're wanted on the phone; **on frappe à la porte** someone's knocking at the door
3 (nous) we; **on va y aller demain** we're going tomorrow
4 (les gens) they; **autrefois, on croyait ...** they used to believe ..
5: **on ne peut plus** adv: **on ne peut plus stupide** as stupid as can be

oncle [ɔ̃kl] nm uncle
onctueux, -euse [ɔ̃ktɥø, -øz] adj creamy, smooth; (fig) smooth, unctuous
onde [ɔ̃d] nf (Physique) wave; **sur l'~** on the waters; **sur les ~s** on the radio; **mettre en ~s** to produce for the radio; **~ de choc** shock wave; **~s courtes (OC)** short wave sg; **petites ~s (PO)**, **~s moyennes (OM)** medium wave sg; **grandes ~s (GO)**, **~s longues (OL)** long wave sg; **~s sonores** sound waves
ondée [ɔ̃de] nf shower
on-dit [ɔ̃di] nm inv rumour
onduler [ɔ̃dyle] vi to undulate; (cheveux) to wave
onéreux, -euse [ɔneʀø, -øz] adj costly; **à titre ~** in return for payment
ongle [ɔ̃gl] nm (Anat) nail; **manger** ou **ronger ses ~s** to bite one's nails; **se faire les ~s** to do one's nails .
ont [ɔ̃] vb voir **avoir**
ONU [ɔny] sigle f (= Organisation des Nations unies) UN(O)
onze [ɔ̃z] num eleven
onzième [ɔ̃zjɛm] num eleventh
OPA sigle f = offre publique d'achat
opaque [ɔpak] adj (vitre, verre) opaque; (brouillard, nuit) impenetrable
opéra [ɔpeʀa] nm opera; (édifice) opera house
opérateur, -trice [ɔpeʀatœʀ, -tʀis] nm/f operator; **~ (de prise de vues)** cameraman
opération [ɔpeʀasjɔ̃] nf operation; (Comm) dealing; **salle/table d'~** operating theatre/table; **~ de sauvetage** rescue operation; **~ à cœur ouvert** open-heart surgery no pl
opératoire [ɔpeʀatwaʀ] adj (manœuvre, méthode) operating; (choc etc) post-operative
opérer [ɔpeʀe] vt (Méd) to operate on; (faire, exécuter) to carry out, make ▷ vi (remède: faire

effet) to act, work; (procéder) to proceed; (Méd) to operate; **s'opérer** vi (avoir lieu) to occur, take place; **se faire ~** to have an operation; **se faire ~ des amygdales/du cœur** to have one's tonsils out/a heart operation
opérette [ɔpeʀɛt] nf operetta, light opera
ophtalmologie [ɔftalmɔlɔʒi] nf ophthalmology
opiner [ɔpine] vi: **~ de la tête** to nod assent ▷ vt: **~ à** to consent to
opinion [ɔpinjɔ̃] nf opinion; **l'~ (publique)** public opinion; **avoir bonne/mauvaise ~ de** to have a high/low opinion of
opportun, e [ɔpɔʀtœ̃, -yn] adj timely, opportune; **en temps ~** at the appropriate time
opportuniste [ɔpɔʀtynist] adj, nm/f opportunist
opposant, e [ɔpozɑ̃, -ɑ̃t] adj opposing ▷ nm/f opponent
opposé, e [ɔpoze] adj (direction, rive) opposite; (faction) opposing; (couleurs) contrasting; (opinions, intérêts) conflicting; (contre): **~ à** opposed to, against ▷ nm: **l'~** the other ou opposite side (ou direction); (contraire) the opposite; **être ~ à** to be opposed to; **à l'~ (fig)** on the other hand; **à l'~ de** on the other ou opposite side from; (fig) contrary to, unlike
opposer [ɔpoze] vt (meubles, objets) to place opposite each other; (personnes, armées, équipes) to oppose; (couleurs, termes, tons) to contrast; (comparer: livres, avantages) to contrast; **~ qch à** (comme obstacle, défense) to set sth against; (comme objection) to put sth forward against; (en contraste) to set sth opposite; to match sth with; **s'opposer** vi (équipes) to confront each other; (opinions) to conflict; (couleurs, styles) to contrast; **s'~ à** (interdire, empêcher) to oppose; (tenir tête à) to rebel against; **sa religion s'y oppose** it's against his religion; **s'~ à ce que qn fasse** to be opposed to sb's doing
opposition [ɔpozisjɔ̃] nf opposition; **par ~** in contrast; **par ~ à** as opposed to, in contrast with; **entrer en ~ avec** to come into conflict with; **être en ~ avec** (idées, conduite) to be at variance with; **faire ~ à un chèque** to stop a cheque
oppressant, e [ɔpʀesɑ̃, -ɑ̃t] adj oppressive
oppresser [ɔpʀese] vt to oppress; **se sentir oppressé** to feel breathless
oppression [ɔpʀesjɔ̃] nf oppression; (malaise) feeling of suffocation
opprimer [ɔpʀime] vt (asservir: peuple, faibles) to oppress; (étouffer: liberté, opinion) to suppress, stifle; (chaleur etc) to suffocate, oppress
opter [ɔpte] vi: **~ pour** to opt for; **~ entre** to choose between
opticien, ne [ɔptisjɛ̃, -ɛn] nm/f optician
optimisme [ɔptimism] nm optimism
optimiste [ɔptimist] adj optimistic ▷ nm/f optimist

option [ɔpsjɔ̃] nf option; (Auto: supplément) optional extra; **matière à ~** (Scol) optional subject (Brit), elective (US); **prendre une ~ sur** to take (out) an option on; **~ par défaut** (Inform) default (option)

optique [ɔptik] adj (nerf) optic; (verres) optical ▷ nf (Photo: lentilles etc) optics pl; (science, industrie) optics sg; (fig: manière de voir) perspective

opulent, e [ɔpylɑ̃, -ɑ̃t] adj wealthy, opulent; (formes, poitrine) ample, generous

or [ɔʀ] nm gold ▷ conj now, but; **d'or** (fig) golden; **en or** gold cpd; (occasion) golden; **un mari/enfant en or** a treasure; **une affaire en or** (achat) a real bargain; (commerce) a gold mine; **plaqué or** gold-plated; **or noir** black gold; **il croyait gagner or il a perdu** he was sure he would win and yet he lost

orage [ɔʀaʒ] nm (thunder)storm

orageux, -euse [ɔʀaʒø, -øz] adj stormy

oral, e, -aux [ɔʀal, -o] adj (déposition, promesse) oral, verbal; (Méd): **par voie ~e** by mouth, orally ▷ nm (Scol) oral

orange [ɔʀɑ̃ʒ] adj inv, nf orange; **~ sanguine** blood orange; **~ pressée** freshly-squeezed orange juice

orangé, e [ɔʀɑ̃ʒe] adj orangey, orange-coloured

orangeade [ɔʀɑ̃ʒad] nf orangeade

oranger [ɔʀɑ̃ʒe] nm orange tree

orateur [ɔʀatœʀ] nm speaker; orator

orbite [ɔʀbit] nf (Anat) (eye-)socket; (Physique) orbit; **mettre sur ~** to put into orbit; (fig) to launch; **dans l'~ de** (fig) within the sphere of influence of

Orcades [ɔʀkad] nfpl: **les ~** the Orkneys, the Orkney Islands

orchestre [ɔʀkɛstʀ] nm orchestra; (de jazz, danse) band; (places) stalls pl (Brit), orchestra (US)

orchestrer [ɔʀkɛstʀe] vt (Mus) to orchestrate; (fig) to mount, stage-manage

orchidée [ɔʀkide] nf orchid

ordinaire [ɔʀdinɛʀ] adj ordinary; (coutumier: maladresse etc) usual; (de tous les jours) everyday; (modèle, qualité) standard; (péj: commun) common ▷ nm ordinary; (menus) everyday fare ▷ nf (essence) ≈ two-star (petrol) (Brit), ≈ regular (gas) (US); **d'~** usually, normally; **à l'~** usually, ordinarily; **comme à l'~** as usual

ordinateur [ɔʀdinatœʀ] nm computer; **mettre sur ~** to computerize, put on computer; **~ de bureau** desktop computer; **~ individuel** ou **personnel** personal computer; **~ portable** laptop (computer)

ordonnance [ɔʀdɔnɑ̃s] nf organization; (groupement, disposition) layout; (Méd) prescription; (Jur) order; (Mil) orderly, batman (Brit); **d'~** (Mil) regulation cpd; **officier d'~** aide-de-camp

ordonné, e [ɔʀdɔne] adj tidy, orderly; (Math) ordered ▷ nf (Math) Y-axis, ordinate

ordonner [ɔʀdɔne] vt (agencer) to organize, arrange; (: meubles, appartement) to lay out, arrange; (donner un ordre): **~ à qn de faire** to order sb to do; (Math) (to arrange in) order; (Rel) to ordain; (Méd) to prescribe; (Jur) to order; **s'ordonner** vi (faits) to organize themselves

ordre [ɔʀdʀ] nm (gén) order; (propreté et soin) orderliness, tidiness; (association professionnelle, honorifique) association; (Comm): **à l'~ de** payable to; (nature): **d'~ pratique** of a practical nature; **ordres** nmpl (Rel) holy orders; **avoir de l'~** to be tidy ou orderly; **mettre en ~** to tidy (up), put in order; **mettre bon ~ à** to put to rights, sort out; **procéder par ~** to take things one at a time; **par ~ alphabétique/d'importance** in alphabetical order/in order of importance; **être aux ~s de qn/sous les ~s de qn** to be at sb's disposal/under sb's command; **rappeler qn à l'~** to call sb to order; **jusqu'à nouvel ~** until further notice; **dans le même ~ d'idées** in this connection; **par ~ d'entrée en scène** in order of appearance; **un ~ de grandeur** some idea of the size (ou amount); **de premier ~** first-rate; **~ de grève** strike call; **~ du jour** (d'une réunion) agenda; (Mil) order of the day; **à l'~ du jour** on the agenda; (fig) topical; (Mil: citer) in dispatches; **~ de mission** (Mil) orders pl; **~ public** law and order; **~ de route** marching orders pl

ordure [ɔʀdyʀ] nf filth no pl; (propos, écrit) obscenity, (piece of) filth; **ordures** nfpl (balayures, déchets) rubbish sg, refuse sg; **~s ménagères** household refuse

oreille [ɔʀɛj] nf (Anat) ear; (de marmite, tasse) handle; (Tech: d'un écrou) wing; **avoir de l'~** to have a good ear (for music); **avoir l'~ fine** to have good ou sharp ears; **l'~ basse** crestfallen, dejected; **se faire tirer l'~** to take a lot of persuading; **dire qch à l'~ de qn** to have a word in sb's ear (about sth)

oreiller [ɔʀeje] nm pillow

oreillons [ɔʀejɔ̃] nmpl mumps sg

ores [ɔʀ]: **d'~ et déjà** adv already

orfèvrerie [ɔʀfɛvʀəʀi] nf (art, métier) goldsmith's (ou silversmith's) trade; (ouvrage) (silver ou gold) plate

organe [ɔʀgan] nm organ; (véhicule, instrument) instrument; (voix) voice; (porte-parole) representative, mouthpiece; **~s de commande** (Tech) controls; **~s de transmission** (Tech) transmission system sg

organigramme [ɔʀganigʀam] nm (hiérarchique, structure) organization chart; (des opérations) flow chart

organique [ɔʀganik] adj organic

organisateur, -trice [ɔʀganizatœʀ, -tʀis] nm/f organizer

organisation [ɔʀganizasjɔ̃] nf organization; **O~ des Nations unies (ONU)** United Nations (Organization) (UN, UNO); **O~**

mondiale de la santé (OMS) World Health Organization (WHO); **O~ du traité de l'Atlantique Nord (OTAN)** North Atlantic Treaty Organization (NATO)

organiser [ɔʀganize] vt to organize; (*mettre sur pied: service etc*) to set up; **s'organiser** vi to get organized

organisme [ɔʀganism] nm (*Bio*) organism; (*corps humain*) body; (*Admin, Pol etc*) body, organism

organiste [ɔʀganist] nm/f organist

orgasme [ɔʀgasm] nm orgasm, climax

orge [ɔʀʒ] nf barley

orgue [ɔʀg] nm organ; **orgues** nfpl organ sg; **~ de Barbarie** barrel *ou* street organ

orgueil [ɔʀgœj] nm pride

orgueilleux, -euse [ɔʀgœjø, -øz] adj proud

Orient [ɔʀjã] nm: **l'~** the East, the Orient

oriental, e, -aux [ɔʀjãtal, -o] adj (*langue, produit*) oriental, eastern; (*frontière*) eastern ▷ nm/f: **O~, e** Oriental

orientation [ɔʀjãtasjõ] nf positioning; adjustment; (*de recherches*) orientation; direction; (*d'une maison etc*) aspect; (*d'un journal*) leanings pl; **avoir le sens de l'~** to have a (good) sense of direction; **course d'~** orienteering exercise; **~ professionnelle** careers advice *ou* guidance; (*service*) careers advisory service

orienté, e [ɔʀjãte] adj (*fig: article, journal*) slanted; **bien/mal ~** (*appartement*) well/badly positioned; **~ au sud** facing south, with a southern aspect

orienter [ɔʀjãte] vt (*situer*) to position; (*placer, disposer: pièce mobile*) to adjust, position; (*tourner: antenne etc*) to direct, turn; (*voyageur, touriste, recherches*) to direct; (*fig: élève*) to orientate; **s'orienter** vi (*se repérer*) to find one's bearings; **s'~ vers** (*fig*) to turn towards

origan [ɔʀigã] nm oregano

originaire [ɔʀiʒinɛʀ] adj original; **être ~ de** (*pays, lieu*) to be a native of; (*provenir de*) to originate from; to be native to

original, e, -aux [ɔʀiʒinal, -o] adj original; (*bizarre*) eccentric ▷ nm/f (*fam: excentrique*) eccentric; (*: fantaisiste*) joker ▷ nm (*document etc, Art*) original; (*dactylographie*) top copy

origine [ɔʀiʒin] nf origin; (*d'un message, appel téléphonique*) source; (*d'une révolution, réussite*) root; **origines** nfpl (*d'une personne*) origins; **d'~** (*pays*) of origin; (*pneus etc*) original; (*bureau postal*) dispatching; **d'~ française** of French origin; **dès l'~** at *ou* from the outset; **à l'~** originally; **avoir son ~ dans** to have its origins in, originate in

originel, le [ɔʀiʒinɛl] adj original

orme [ɔʀm] nm elm

ornement [ɔʀnəmã] nm ornament; (*fig*) embellishment, adornment; **~s sacerdotaux** vestments

orner [ɔʀne] vt to decorate, adorn; **~ qch de** to decorate sth with

ornière [ɔʀnjɛʀ] nf rut; (*fig*): **sortir de l'~** (*routine*) to get out of the rut; (*impasse*) to get out of a spot

orphelin, e [ɔʀfəlɛ̃, -in] adj orphan(ed) ▷ nm/f orphan; **~ de père/mère** fatherless/motherless

orphelinat [ɔʀfəlina] nm orphanage

orteil [ɔʀtɛj] nm toe; **gros ~** big toe

orthographe [ɔʀtɔgʀaf] nf spelling

ortie [ɔʀti] nf (stinging) nettle; **~ blanche** white dead-nettle

os [ɔs] nm bone; **sans os** (*Boucherie*) off the bone, boned; **os à moelle** marrowbone

osciller [ɔsile] vi (*pendule*) to swing; (*au vent etc*) to rock; (*Tech*) to oscillate; (*fig*): **~ entre** to waver *ou* fluctuate between

osé, e [oze] adj daring, bold

oseille [ozɛj] nf sorrel

oser [oze] vi, vt to dare; **~ faire** to dare (to) do

osier [ozje] nm (*Bot*) willow; **d'~, en ~** wicker(work) cpd

ossature [ɔsatyʀ] nf (*Anat: squelette*) frame, skeletal structure; (*: du visage*) bone structure; (*fig*) framework

osseux, -euse [ɔsø, -øz] adj bony; (*tissu, maladie, greffe*) bone cpd

ostensible [ɔstãsibl] adj conspicuous

otage [ɔtaʒ] nm hostage; **prendre qn comme ~** to take sb hostage

OTAN [ɔtã] sigle f (= *Organisation du traité de l'Atlantique Nord*) NATO

otarie [ɔtaʀi] nf sea-lion

ôter [ote] vt to remove; (*soustraire*) to take away; **~ qch à qn** to take sth (away) from sb; **~ qch de** to remove sth from; **six ôté de dix égale quatre** six from ten equals *ou* is four

otite [ɔtit] nf ear infection

ou [u] conj or; **ou ... ou** either ... or; **ou bien** or (else)

○ MOT-CLÉ

où [u] pron relatif **1** (*position, situation*) where, that (*souvent omis*); **la chambre où il était** the room (that) he was in, the room where he was; **la ville où je l'ai rencontré** the town where I met him; **la pièce d'où il est sorti** the room he came out of; **le village d'où je viens** the village I come from; **les villes par où il est passé** the towns he went through **2** (*temps, état*) that (*souvent omis*); **le jour où il est parti** the day (that) he left; **au prix où c'est** at the price it is
▷ adv **1** (*interrogation*) where; **où est-il/va-t-il?** where is he/is he going?; **par où?** which way?; **d'où vient que ...?** how come ...?
2 (*position*) where; **je sais où il est** I know where he is; **où que l'on aille** wherever you go

ouate [wat] nf cotton wool (Brit), cotton (US); (*bourre*) padding, wadding; **~ (hydrophile)** cotton wool (Brit), (absorbent) cotton (US)

oubli [ubli] *nm* (*acte*): **l'~ de** forgetting; (*trou de mémoire*) lapse of memory; (*étourderie*) forgetfulness *no pl*; (*négligence*) omission, oversight; (*absence de souvenirs*) oblivion; **~ de soi** self-effacement, self-negation; **tomber dans l'~** to sink into oblivion

oublier [ublije] *vt* (*gén*) to forget; (*ne pas voir: erreurs etc*) to miss; (*ne pas mettre: virgule, nom*) to leave out, forget; (*laisser quelque part: chapeau etc*) to leave behind; **s'oublier** *vi* to forget o.s.; (*enfant, animal*) to have an accident (*euphemism*); **~ l'heure** to forget (about) the time

oubliettes [ublijet] *nfpl* dungeon *sg*; (**jeter**) **aux ~** (*fig*) to put) completely out of mind

ouest [wɛst] *nm* west ▷ *adj inv* west; (*région*) western; **à l'~** in the west; (*direction*) (to the) west, westwards; **à l'~ de** (to the) west of; **vent d'~** westerly wind

ouf [uf] *excl* phew!

oui [wi] *adv* yes; **répondre (par) ~** to answer yes; **mais ~, bien sûr** yes, of course; **je pense que ~** I think so; **pour un ~ ou pour un non** for no apparent reason

ouï-dire ['widir] *nm*: **par ~** *adv* by hearsay

ouïe [wi] *nf* hearing; **ouïes** *nfpl* (*de poisson*) gills; (*de violon*) sound-hole *sg*

ouragan [uragɑ̃] *nm* hurricane; (*fig*) storm

ourlet [urlɛ] *nm* hem; (*de l'oreille*) rim; **faire un ~ à** to hem

ours [urs] *nm* bear; **~ brun/blanc** brown/polar bear; **~ marin** fur seal; **~ mal léché** uncouth fellow; **~ (en peluche)** teddy (bear)

oursin [ursɛ̃] *nm* sea urchin

ourson [ursɔ̃] *nm* (bear-)cub

ouste [ust] *excl* hop it!

outil [uti] *nm* tool

outiller [utije] *vt* (*ouvrier, usine*) to equip

outrage [utraʒ] *nm* insult; **faire subir les derniers ~s à** (*femme*) to ravish; **~ aux bonnes mœurs** (*Jur*) outrage to public decency; **~ à magistrat** (*Jur*) contempt of court; **~ à la pudeur** (*Jur*) indecent behaviour *no pl*

outrager [utraʒe] *vt* to offend gravely; (*fig: contrevenir à*) to outrage, insult

outrance [utrɑ̃s] *nf* excessiveness *no pl*, excess; **à ~** *adv* excessively, to excess

outre [utr] *nf* goatskin, water skin ▷ *prép* besides ▷ *adv*: **passer ~** to carry on regardless; **passer ~ à** to disregard, take no notice of; **en ~** besides, moreover; **~ que** apart from the fact that; **~ mesure** to excess; (*manger, boire*) immoderately

outre-Atlantique [utratlɑ̃tik] *adv* across the Atlantic

outre-Manche [utrəmɑ̃ʃ] *adv* across the Channel

outre-mer [utrəmɛr] *adv* overseas; **d'~** overseas

outrepasser [utrəpɑse] *vt* to go beyond, exceed

ouvert, e [uvɛr, -ɛrt] *pp de* **ouvrir** ▷ *adj* open; (*robinet, gaz etc*) on; **à bras ~s** with open arms

ouvertement [uvɛrtəmɑ̃] *adv* openly

ouverture [uvɛrtyr] *nf* opening; (*Mus*) overture; (*Pol*): **l'~ the** widening of the political spectrum; (*Photo*): **~ (du diaphragme)** aperture; **ouvertures** *nfpl* (*propositions*) overtures; **~ d'esprit** open-mindedness; **heures d'~** (*Comm*) opening hours; **jours d'~** (*Comm*) days of opening

ouvrable [uvrabl] *adj*: **jour ~** working day, weekday; **heures ~s** business hours

ouvrage [uvraʒ] *nm* (*tâche, de tricot etc, Mil*) work *no pl*; (*objet: Couture, Art*) (piece of) work; (*texte, livre*) work; **panier ou corbeille à ~** work basket; **~ d'art** (*Génie Civil*) bridge or tunnel etc

ouvragé, e [uvraʒe] *adj* finely embroidered (*ou worked ou carved*)

ouvre-boîte, ouvre-boîtes [uvrəbwat] *nm inv* tin (*Brit*) *ou* can opener

ouvre-bouteille, ouvre-bouteilles [uvrə butɛj] *nm inv* bottle-opener

ouvreuse [uvrøz] *nf* usherette

ouvrier, -ière [uvrije, -jɛr] *nm/f* worker ▷ *nf* (*Zool*) worker (bee) ▷ *adj* working-class; (*problèmes, conflit*) industrial; (*mouvement*) labour *cpd* (*Brit*), labor *cpd* (*US*); (*revendications*) workers'; **classe ouvrière** working class; **~ agricole** farmworker; **~ qualifié** skilled worker; **~ spécialisé (OS)** semiskilled worker; **~ d'usine** factory worker

ouvrir [uvrir] *vt* (*gén*) to open; (*brèche, passage*) to open up; (*commencer l'exploitation de, créer*) to open (up); (*eau, électricité, chauffage, robinet*) to turn on; (*Méd: abcès*) to open ▷ *vi* to open up; to open up; (*Cartes*): **~ à trèfle** to open in clubs; **s'ouvrir** *vi* to open; **s'~ à** (*art etc*) to open one's mind to; **s'~ à qn (de qch)** to open one's heart to sb (about sth); **s'~ les veines** to slash *ou* cut one's wrists; **~ sur** to open onto; **~ l'appétit à qn** to whet sb's appetite; **~ des horizons** to open up new horizons; **~ l'esprit** to broaden one's horizons; **~ une session** (*Inform*) to log in

ovaire [ovɛr] *nm* ovary

ovale [ɔval] *adj* oval

OVNI [ɔvni] *sigle m* (= *objet volant non identifié*) UFO

oxyder [ɔkside]: **s'oxyder** *vi* to become oxidized

oxygéné, e [ɔksiʒene] *adj*: **eau ~e** hydrogen peroxide; **cheveux ~s** bleached hair

oxygène [ɔksiʒɛn] *nm* oxygen; (*fig*): **cure d'~** fresh air cure

ozone [ozon] *nm* ozone; **trou dans la couche d'~** hole in the ozone layer

P

pacifique [pasifik] *adj* (*personne*) peaceable; (*intentions, coexistence*) peaceful ⊳ *nm*: **le P~, l'océan P~** the Pacific (Ocean)

pack [pak] *nm* pack

pacotille [pakɔtij] *nf* (*péj*) cheap junk *pl*; **de ~** cheap

PACS [paks] *sigle m* (= *pacte civil de solidarité*) ≈ civil partnership

pacser [pakse]: **se pacser** *vi* ≈ to form a civil partnership

pacte [pakt] *nm* pact, treaty

pagaie [pagɛ] *nf* paddle

pagaille [pagaj] *nf* mess, shambles *sg*; **il y en a en ~** there are loads of them

pagayer [pageje] *vi* to paddle

page [paʒ] *nf* page; (*passage: d'un roman*) passage ⊳ *nm* page (boy); **mettre en ~s** to make up (into pages); **mise en ~** layout; **à la ~** (*fig*) up-to-date; **~ d'accueil** (*Inform*) home page; **~ blanche** blank page; **~ de garde** endpaper; **~ Web** (*Inform*) web page

païen, ne [pajɛ̃, -ɛn] *adj, nm/f* pagan, heathen

paillasson [pajasɔ̃] *nm* doormat

paille [paj] *nf* straw; (*défaut*) flaw; **être sur la ~** to be ruined; **~ de fer** steel wool

paillette [pajɛt] *nf* speck, flake; **paillettes** *nfpl* (*décoratives*) sequins, spangles; **lessive en ~s** soapflakes *pl*

pain [pɛ̃] *nm* (*substance*) bread; (*unité*) loaf (of bread); (*morceau*): **~ de cire** *etc* bar of wax *etc*; (*Culin*): **~ de poisson/légumes** fish/vegetable loaf; **petit ~** (bread) roll; **~ bis/complet** brown/wholemeal (*Brit*) *ou* wholewheat (*US*) bread; **~ de campagne** farmhouse bread; **~ d'épice** ≈ gingerbread; **~ grillé** toast; **~ de mie** sandwich loaf; **~ perdu** French toast; **~ de seigle** rye bread; **~ de sucre** sugar loaf; **~ au chocolat** pain au chocolat; **~ aux raisins** currant pastry

pair, e [pɛʀ] *adj* (*nombre*) even ⊳ *nm* peer; **aller de ~ (avec)** to go hand in hand *ou* together (with); **au ~** (*Finance*) at par; **valeur au ~** par value; **jeune fille au ~** au pair

paire [pɛʀ] *nf* pair; **une ~ de lunettes/ tenailles** a pair of glasses/pincers; **faire la ~: les deux font la paire** they are two of a kind

paisible [pezibl] *adj* peaceful, quiet

paître [pɛtʀ] *vi* to graze

paix [pɛ] *nf* peace; (*fig*) peacefulness, peace; **faire la ~ avec** to make peace with; **avoir la ~** to have peace (and quiet); **fiche-lui la ~!** (*fam*) leave him alone!

Pakistan [pakistɑ̃] *nm*: **le ~** Pakistan

palace [palas] *nm* luxury hotel

palais [palɛ] *nm* palace; (*Anat*) palate; **le P~ Bourbon** *the seat of the French National Assembly*; **le P~ de l'Élysée** the Élysée Palace; **~ des expositions** exhibition centre; **le P~ de Justice** the Law Courts *pl*

pâle [pal] *adj* pale; (*fig*): **une ~ imitation** a pale imitation; **bleu ~** pale blue; **~ de colère** white *ou* pale with anger

Palestine [palɛstin] *nf*: **la ~** Palestine

palet [palɛ] *nm* disc; (*Hockey*) puck

paletot [palto] *nm* (short) coat

palette [palɛt] *nf* (*de peintre*) palette; (*de produits*) range

pâleur [pɑlœʀ] *nf* paleness

palier [palje] *nm* (*d'escalier*) landing; (*fig*) level, plateau; (: *phase stable*) levelling (*Brit*) *ou* leveling (*US*) off, new level; (*Tech*) bearing; **nos voisins de ~** our neighbo(u)rs across the landing (*Brit*) *ou* the hall (*US*); **en ~** *adv* level; **par ~s** in stages

pâlir [paliʀ] *vi* to turn *ou* go pale; (*couleur*) to fade; **faire ~ qn** (*de jalousie*) to make sb green (with envy)

palissade [palisad] *nf* fence

pallier [palje] *vt*: **~ à** *vt* to offset, make up for

palmarès [palmaʀɛs] *nm* record (of achievements); (*Scol*) prize list; (*Sport*) list of winners

palme [palm] *nf* (*Bot*) palm leaf; (*symbole*) palm; (*de plongeur*) flipper; **~s (académiques)** *decoration for services to education*

palmé, e [palme] *adj* (*pattes*) webbed

palmier [palmje] *nm* palm tree; (*gâteau*) *heart-shaped biscuit made of flaky pastry*

pâlot, te [palo, -ɔt] *adj* pale, peaky

palourde [paluʀd] *nf* clam

palper [palpe] *vt* to feel, finger

palpitant, e [palpitɑ̃, -ɑ̃t] *adj* thrilling, gripping

palpiter [palpite] vi (*cœur, pouls*) to beat; (: *plus fort*) to pound, throb; (*narines, chair*) to quiver

paludisme [palydism] nm malaria

pamphlet [pɑ̃flɛ] nm lampoon, satirical tract

pamplemousse [pɑ̃pləmus] nm grapefruit

pan [pɑ̃] nm section, piece; (*côté: d'un prisme, d'une tour*) side, face ▷ excl bang!; ~ **de chemise** shirt tail; ~ **de mur** section of wall

panache [panaʃ] nm plume; (*fig*) spirit, panache

panaché, e [panaʃe] adj: **œillet** ~ variegated carnation; **glace** ~**e** mixed ice cream; **salade** ~**e** mixed salad ▷ nm (*bière*) shandy

pancarte [pɑ̃kaʀt] nf sign, notice; (*dans un défilé*) placard

pancréas [pɑ̃kʀeɑs] nm pancreas

pandémie [pɑ̃demi] nf pandemic

pané, e [pane] adj fried in breadcrumbs

panier [panje] nm basket; (*à diapositives*) magazine; **mettre au** ~ to chuck away; ~ **de crabes: c'est un panier de crabes** (*fig*) they're constantly at one another's throats; ~ **percé** (*fig*) spendthrift; ~ **à provisions** shopping basket; ~ **à salade** (*Culin*) salad shaker; (*Police*) paddy wagon, police van

panier-repas (*pl* **paniers-repas**) [panjeʀ(ə) pɑ] nm packed lunch

panique [panik] adj panicky ▷ nf panic

paniquer [panike] vi to panic

panne [pan] nf (*d'un mécanisme, moteur*) breakdown; **être/tomber en** ~ to have broken down/break down; **être en** ~ **d'essence** ou **en** ~ **sèche** to have run out of petrol (*Brit*) ou gas (*US*); **mettre en** ~ (*Navig*) to bring to; ~ **d'électricité** ou **de courant** power ou electrical failure

panneau, x [pano] nm (*écriteau*) sign, notice; (*de boiserie, de tapisserie etc*) panel; **tomber dans le** ~ (*fig*) to walk into the trap; ~ **d'affichage** notice (*Brit*) ou bulletin (*US*) board; ~ **électoral** board for election poster; ~ **indicateur** signpost; ~ **publicitaire** hoarding (*Brit*), billboard (*US*); ~ **de signalisation** roadsign; ~ **solaire** solar panel

panoplie [panɔpli] nf (*jouet*) outfit; (*d'armes*) display; (*fig*) array

panorama [panɔʀama] nm (*vue*) all-round view, panorama; (*peinture*) panorama; (*fig: étude complète*) complete overview

panse [pɑ̃s] nf paunch

pansement [pɑ̃smɑ̃] nm dressing, bandage; ~ **adhésif** sticking plaster (*Brit*), bandaid® (*US*)

panser [pɑ̃se] vt (*plaie*) to dress, bandage; (*bras*) to put a dressing on, bandage; (*cheval*) to groom

pantacourt [pɑ̃takuʀ] nm cropped trousers pl

pantalon [pɑ̃talɔ̃] nm trousers pl (*Brit*), pants pl (*US*), pair of trousers ou pants; ~ **de ski** ski pants pl

panthère [pɑ̃tɛʀ] nf panther

pantin [pɑ̃tɛ̃] nm (*jouet*) jumping jack; (*péj: personne*) puppet

pantois [pɑ̃twa] adj m: **rester** ~ to be flabbergasted

pantoufle [pɑ̃tufl] nf slipper

paon [pɑ̃] nm peacock

papa [papa] nm dad(dy)

pape [pap] nm pope

paperasse [papʀas] nf (*péj*) bumf no pl, papers pl; forms pl

paperasserie [papʀasʀi] nf (*péj*) red tape no pl; paperwork no pl

papeterie [papɛtʀi] nf (*fabrication du papier*) paper-making (industry); (*usine*) paper mill; (*magasin*) stationer's (shop (*Brit*)); (*articles*) stationery

papetier, -ière [paptje, -jɛʀ] nm/f paper-maker; stationer

papi [papi] nm (*fam*) granddad

papier [papje] nm paper; (*feuille*) sheet ou piece of paper; (*article*) article; (*écrit officiel*) document; **papiers** nmpl (*aussi*: ~**s d'identité**) (identity) papers; **sur le** ~ (*théoriquement*) on paper; **noircir du** ~ to write page after page; ~ **couché/glacé** art/glazed paper; ~ **(d') aluminium** aluminium (*Brit*) ou aluminum (*US*) foil, tinfoil; ~ **d'Arménie** incense paper; ~ **bible** India ou bible paper; ~ **de brouillon** rough ou scrap paper; ~ **bulle** manil(l)a paper; ~ **buvard** blotting paper; ~ **calque** tracing paper; ~ **carbone** carbon paper; ~ **collant** Sellotape® (*Brit*), Scotch tape® (*US*), sticky tape; ~ **en continu** continuous stationery; ~ **à dessin** drawing paper; ~ **d'emballage** wrapping paper; ~ **gommé** gummed paper; ~ **hygiénique** ou **(de) toilette** toilet paper; ~ **journal** newsprint; (*pour emballer*) newspaper; ~ **à lettres** writing paper, notepaper; ~ **mâché** papier-mâché; ~ **machine** typing paper; ~ **peint** wallpaper; ~ **pelure** India paper; ~ **à pliage accordéon** fanfold paper; ~ **de soie** tissue paper; ~ **thermique** thermal paper; ~ **de tournesol** litmus paper; ~ **de verre** sandpaper

papillon [papijɔ̃] nm butterfly; (*fam: contravention*) (parking) ticket; (*Tech: écrou*) wing ou butterfly nut; ~ **de nuit** moth

papillote [papijɔt] nf (*pour cheveux*) curlpaper; (*de gigot*) (paper) frill; **en** ~ cooked in tinfoil

papoter [papɔte] vi to chatter

paquebot [pakbo] nm liner

pâquerette [pakʀɛt] nf daisy

Pâques [pak] nm, nfpl Easter; **faire ses** ~ to do one's Easter duties; **l'île de** ~ Easter Island

> ● **PÂQUES**
>
> ● In France, Easter eggs are said to be
> ● brought by the Easter bells or *cloches de*
> ● *Pâques* which fly from Rome and drop
> ● them in people's gardens.

paquet [pakɛ] nm packet; (*colis*) parcel; (*ballot*) bundle; (*dans négociations*) package (deal); (fig: tas): **~ de** pile ou heap of; **paquets** nmpl (bagages) bags; **mettre le ~** (fam) to give one's all; **~ de mer** big wave

paquet-cadeau (pl **paquets-cadeaux**) [pakɛkado] nm gift-wrapped parcel

par [paʀ] prép by; **finir** etc **~** to end etc with; **~ amour** out of love; **passer ~ Lyon/la côte** to go via ou through Lyons/along by the coast; **~ la fenêtre** (jeter, regarder) out of the window; **trois ~ jour/personne** three ou per day/head; **deux ~ deux** two at a time; (marcher etc) in twos; **où?** which way?; **~ ici** this way; (dans le coin) round here; **~-ci, ~-là** here and there; **~ temps de pluie** in wet weather

parabolique [paʀabɔlik] adj parabolic; **antenne ~** satellite dish

parachever [paʀaʃve] vt to perfect

parachute [paʀaʃyt] nm parachute

parachutiste [paʀaʃytist] nm/f parachutist; (Mil) paratrooper

parade [paʀad] nf (spectacle, défilé) parade; (Escrime, Boxe) parry; (ostentation): **faire ~ de** to display, show off; (défense, riposte): **trouver la ~ à une attaque** to find the answer to an attack; **de ~** adj ceremonial; (superficiel) superficial, outward

paradis [paʀadi] nm heaven, paradise; **P~ terrestre** (Rel) Garden of Eden; (fig) heaven on earth

paradoxe [paʀadɔks] nm paradox

paraffine [paʀafin] nf paraffin; paraffin wax

parages [paʀaʒ] nmpl (Navig) waters; **dans les ~ (de)** in the area ou vicinity (of)

paragraphe [paʀagʀaf] nm paragraph

paraître [paʀɛtʀ] vb copule to seem, look, appear ▷ vi to appear; (être visible) to show; (Presse, Édition) to be published, come out, appear; (briller) to show ▷ vb impers: **il paraît que** it seems ou appears that; **il me paraît que** it seems to me that; **il paraît absurde de** it seems absurd to; **il ne paraît pas son âge** he doesn't look his age; **~ en justice** to appear before the court(s); **~ en scène/en public/à l'écran** to appear on stage/in public/on the screen

parallèle [paʀalɛl] adj parallel; (police, marché) unofficial; (société, énergie) alternative ▷ nm (comparaison): **faire un ~ entre** to draw a parallel between; (Géo) parallel ▷ nf parallel (line); **en ~** in parallel; **mettre en ~** (choses opposées) to compare; (choses semblables) to parallel

paralyser [paʀalize] vt to paralyze

paramédical, e, -aux [paʀamedikal, -o] adj paramedical; **personnel ~** paramedics pl, paramedical workers pl

paraphrase [paʀafʀaz] nf paraphrase

parapluie [paʀaplɥi] nm umbrella; **~ atomique** ou **nucléaire** nuclear umbrella; **~ pliant** telescopic umbrella

parasite [paʀazit] nm parasite ▷ adj (Bot, Bio) parasitic(al); **parasites** nmpl (Tél) interference sg

parasol [paʀasɔl] nm parasol, sunshade

paratonnerre [paʀatɔnɛʀ] nm lightning conductor

paravent [paʀavɑ̃] nm folding screen; (fig) screen

parc [paʀk] nm (public) park, gardens pl; (de château etc) grounds pl; (pour le bétail) pen, enclosure; (d'enfant) playpen; (Mil: entrepôt) depot; (ensemble d'unités) stock; (de voitures etc) fleet; **~ d'attractions** amusement park; **~ automobile** (d'un pays) number of cars on the roads; **~ à huîtres** oyster bed; **~ à thème** theme park; **~ national** national park; **~ naturel** nature reserve; **~ de stationnement** car park; **~ zoologique** zoological gardens pl

parcelle [paʀsɛl] nf fragment, scrap; (de terrain) plot, parcel

parce que [paʀskə] conj because

parchemin [paʀʃəmɛ̃] nm parchment

parcmètre [paʀkmɛtʀ], **parcomètre** [paʀkɔmɛtʀ] nm parking meter

parcourir [paʀkuʀiʀ] vt (trajet, distance) to cover; (article, livre) to skim ou glance through; (lieu) to go all over, travel up and down; (frisson, vibration) to run through; **~ des yeux** to run one's eye over

parcours [paʀkuʀ] vb voir **parcourir** ▷ nm (trajet) journey; (itinéraire) route; (Sport: terrain) course; (: tour) round; run; lap; **~ du combattant** assault course

par-dessous [paʀdəsu] prép, adv under(neath)

pardessus [paʀdəsy] nm overcoat

par-dessus [paʀdəsy] prép over (the top of) ▷ adv over (the top); **~ le marché** on top of it all; **~ tout** above all; **en avoir ~ la tête** to have had enough

par-devant [paʀdəvɑ̃] prép in the presence of, before ▷ adv at the front; (passer) round the front

pardon [paʀdɔ̃] nm forgiveness no pl ▷ excl (excuses) (I'm) sorry; (pour interpeller etc) excuse me; **demander ~ à qn (de)** to apologize to sb (for); **je vous demande ~** I'm sorry; (pour interpeller) excuse me; (demander de répéter) (I beg your) pardon?; **pardon?** (Brit), **pardon me?** (US)

pardonner [paʀdɔne] vt to forgive; **~ qch à qn** to forgive sb for sth; **qui ne pardonne pas** (maladie, erreur) fatal

paré, e [paʀe] adj ready, prepared

pare-balles [paʀbal] adj inv bulletproof

pare-brise [paʀbʀiz] nm inv windscreen (Brit), windshield (US)

pare-chocs [paʀʃɔk] nm inv bumper (Brit), fender (US)

pare-feu [paʀfø] nm inv (de foyer) fireguard; (Inform) firewall ▷ adj inv

pareil, le [paʀɛj] adj (identique) the same, alike; (similaire) similar; (tel): **un courage/livre ~** such courage/a book, courage/a book like this; **de ~s livres** such books ▷ adv:

p

habillés ~ dressed the same (way), dressed alike; **faire** ~ to do the same (thing); **j'en veux un** ~ I'd like one just like it; **rien de** ~ no (ou any) such thing, nothing (ou anything) like it; **ses** ~**s** one's fellow men; one's peers; **ne pas avoir son (sa)** ~**(le)** to be second to none; ~ **à** the same as; similar to; **sans** ~ unparalleled, unequalled; **c'est du** ~ **au même** it comes to the same thing, it's six of one and half-a-dozen (of the other); **en** ~ **cas** in such a case; **rendre la** ~**le à qn** to pay sb back in his own coin

parent, e [paʀɑ̃, -ɑ̃t] *nm/f:* **un/une** ~**/e** a relative *ou* relation ▷ *adj:* **être** ~ **de** to be related to; **parents** *nmpl* (*père et mère*) parents; (*famille, proches*) relatives, relations; ~ **unique** lone parent; ~**s par alliance** relatives *ou* relations by marriage; ~**s en ligne directe** blood relations

parenté [paʀɑ̃te] *nf* (*lien*) relationship; (*personnes*) relatives *pl*, relations *pl*

parenthèse [paʀɑ̃tɛz] *nf* (*ponctuation*) bracket, parenthesis; (*Math*) bracket; (*digression*) parenthesis, digression; **ouvrir/ fermer la** ~ to open/close brackets; **entre** ~**s** in brackets; (*fig*) incidentally

parer [paʀe] *vt* to adorn; (*Culin*) to dress, trim; (*éviter*) to ward off; ~ **à** (*danger*) to ward off; (*inconvénient*) to deal with; **se** ~ **de** (*fig: qualité, titre*) to assume; ~ **à toute éventualité** to be ready for every eventuality; ~ **au plus pressé** to attend to what's most urgent

paresse [paʀɛs] *nf* laziness

paresseux, -euse [paʀɛsø, -øz] *adj* lazy; (*fig*) slow, sluggish ▷ *nm* (*Zool*) sloth

parfaire [paʀfɛʀ] *vt* to perfect, complete

parfait, e [paʀfɛ, -ɛt] *pp de* **parfaire** ▷ *adj* perfect ▷ *nm* (*Ling*) perfect (tense); (*Culin*) parfait ▷ *excl* fine, excellent

parfaitement [paʀfɛtmɑ̃] *adv* perfectly ▷ *excl* (most) certainly

parfois [paʀfwa] *adv* sometimes

parfum [paʀfœ̃] *nm* (*produit*) perfume, scent; (*odeur: de fleur*) scent, fragrance; (: *de tabac, vin*) aroma; (*goût: de glace, milk-shake*) flavour (*Brit*), flavor (*US*)

parfumé, e [paʀfyme] *adj* (*fleur, fruit*) fragrant; (*papier à lettres etc*) scented; (*femme*) wearing perfume *ou* scent, perfumed; (*aromatisé*): ~ **au café** coffee-flavoured (*Brit*) *ou* -flavored (*US*)

parfumer [paʀfyme] *vt* (*odeur, bouquet*) to perfume; (*mouchoir*) to put scent *ou* perfume on; (*crème, gâteau*) to flavour (*Brit*), flavor (*US*); **se parfumer** to put on (some) perfume *ou* scent; (*d'habitude*) to use perfume *ou* scent

parfumerie [paʀfymʀi] *nf* (*commerce*) perfumery; (*produits*) perfumes; (*boutique*) perfume shop (*Brit*) *ou* store (*US*)

pari [paʀi] *nm* bet, wager; (*Sport*) bet; ~ **mutuel urbain (PMU)** system of betting on horses

parier [paʀje] *vt* to bet; **j'aurais parié que si/ non** I'd have said he (*ou* you *etc*) would/ wouldn't

Paris [paʀi] *n* Paris

parisien, ne [paʀizjɛ̃, -ɛn] *adj* Parisian; (*Géo, Admin*) Paris *cpd* ▷ *nm/f:* **P**~, **ne** Parisian

parité [paʀite] *nf* parity; ~ **de change** (*Écon*) exchange parity; (*Pol*): ~ **hommes-femmes** balanced representation of men and women

parjure [paʀʒyʀ] *nm* (*faux serment*) false oath, perjury; (*violation de serment*) breach of oath, perjury ▷ *nm/f* perjurer

parking [paʀkiŋ] *nm* (*lieu*) car park (*Brit*), parking lot (*US*)

parlant, e [paʀlɑ̃, -ɑ̃t] *adj* (*fig*) graphic, vivid; (: *comparaison, preuve*) eloquent; (*Ciné*) talking ▷ *adv:* **généralement** ~ generally speaking

parlement [paʀləmɑ̃] *nm* parliament; **le P~ européen** the European Parliament

parlementaire [paʀləmɑ̃tɛʀ] *adj* parliamentary ▷ *nm/f* (*député*) ≈ Member of Parliament (*Brit*) *ou* Congress (*US*); parliamentarian; (*négociateur*) negotiator, mediator

parlementer [paʀləmɑ̃te] *vi* (*ennemis*) to negotiate, parley; (*s'entretenir, discuter*) to argue at length, have lengthy talks

parler [paʀle] *nm* speech; dialect ▷ *vi* to speak, talk; (*avouer*) to talk; ~ (**à qn**) **de** to talk *ou* speak (to sb) about; ~ **pour qn** (*intercéder*) to speak for sb; ~ **en l'air** to say the first thing that comes into one's head; ~ **le/en français** to speak French/in French; ~ **affaires** to talk business; ~ **en dormant/du nez** to talk in one's sleep/through one's nose; **sans** ~ **de** (*fig*) not to mention, to say nothing of; **tu parles!** you must be joking!; (*bien sûr*) you bet!; **n'en parlons plus!** let's forget it!

parloir [paʀlwaʀ] *nm* (*d'une prison, d'un hôpital*) visiting room; (*Rel*) parlour (*Brit*), parlor (*US*)

parmi [paʀmi] *prép* among(st)

paroi [paʀwa] *nf* wall; (*cloison*) partition; ~ **rocheuse** rock face

paroisse [paʀwas] *nf* parish

parole [paʀɔl] *nf* (*faculté*): **la** ~ speech; (*mot, promesse*) word; (*Rel*): **la bonne** ~ the word of God; **paroles** *nfpl* (*Mus*) words, lyrics; **tenir** ~ to keep one's word; **avoir la** ~ to have the floor; **n'avoir qu'une** ~ to be true to one's word; **donner la** ~ **à qn** to hand over to sb; **prendre la** ~ to speak; **demander la** ~ to ask for permission to speak; **perdre la** ~ to lose the power of speech; (*fig*) to lose one's tongue; **je le crois sur** ~ I'll take his word for it, I'll take him at his word; **temps de** ~ (*TV, Radio etc*) discussion time; **ma** ~! my word!, good heavens!; ~ **d'honneur** word of honour (*Brit*) *ou* honor (*US*)

parquer [paʀke] *vt* (*voiture, matériel*) to park; (*bestiaux*) to pen (in *ou* up); (*prisonniers*) to pack in

parquet [paʀke] *nm* (*parquet*) floor; (*Jur: bureau*) public prosecutor's office; **le** ~ **(général)** (*magistrats*) ≈ the Bench

parrain [paʀɛ̃] nm godfather; (d'un navire) namer; (d'un nouvel adhérent) sponsor, proposer

parrainer [paʀene] vt (nouvel adhérent) to sponsor, propose; (entreprise) to promote, sponsor

pars [paʀ] vb voir **partir**

parsemer [paʀsəme] vt (feuilles, papiers) to be scattered over; **~ qch de** to scatter sth with

part [paʀ] vb voir **partir** ▷ nf (qui revient à qn) share; (fraction, partie) part; (de gâteau, fromage) portion; (Finance) (non-voting) share; **prendre ~ à** (débat etc) to take part in; (soucis, douleur de qn) to share in; **faire ~ de qch à qn** to announce sth to sb, inform sb of sth; **pour ma ~** as for me, as far as I'm concerned; **à ~ entière** adj full; **de la ~ de** (au nom de) on behalf of; (donné par) from; **c'est de la ~ de qui?** (au téléphone) who's calling ou speaking (please)?; **de toute(s) ~(s)** from all sides ou quarters; **de ~ et d'autre** on both sides, on either side; **de ~ en ~** right through; **d'une ~ ... d'autre ~** on the one hand ... on the other hand; **d'autre ~** (de plus) moreover; **nulle/autre/quelque ~** nowhere/elsewhere/somewhere; **à ~** adv separately; (de côté) aside ▷ prép apart from, except for ▷ adj exceptional, special; **pour une large** ou **bonne ~** to a great extent; **prendre qch en bonne/mauvaise ~** to take sth well/badly; **faire la ~ des choses** to make allowances; **faire la ~ du feu** (fig) to cut one's losses; **faire la ~ (trop) belle à qn** to give sb more than his (ou her) share

partage [paʀtaʒ] nm voir **partager** sharing (out), share-out; sharing; dividing up; (Pol: de suffrages) share; **recevoir qch en ~** to receive sth as one's share (ou lot); **sans ~** undivided

partager [paʀtaʒe] vt to share; (distribuer, répartir) to share (out); (morceler, diviser) to divide (up); **se partager** vt (héritage etc) to share between themselves (ou ourselves etc)

partance [paʀtɑ̃s]: **en ~** adv outbound, due to leave; **en ~ pour** (bound) for

partenaire [paʀtənɛʀ] nm/f partner; **~s sociaux** management and workforce

parterre [paʀtɛʀ] nm (de fleurs) (flower) bed, border; (Théât) stalls pl

parti [paʀti] nm (Pol) party; (décision) course of action; (personne à marier) match; **tirer ~ de** to take advantage of, turn to good account; **prendre le ~ de faire** to make up one's mind to do, resolve to do; **prendre le ~ de qn** to stand up for sb, side with sb; **prendre ~ (pour/contre)** to take sides ou a stand (for/against); **prendre son ~ de** to come to terms with; **~ pris** bias

partial, e, -aux [paʀsjal, -o] adj biased, partial

participant, e [paʀtisipɑ̃, -ɑ̃t] nm/f participant; (à un concours) entrant; (d'une société) member

participation [paʀtisipasjɔ̃] nf participation; (financière) contribution; sharing; (Comm) interest; **la ~ aux bénéfices** profit-sharing; **la ~ ouvrière** worker participation; **"avec la ~ de ..."** "featuring ..."

participer [paʀtisipe]: **~ à** vt (course, réunion) to take part in; (profits etc) to share in; (frais etc) to contribute to; (entreprise: financièrement) to cooperate in; (chagrin, succès de qn) to share (in); **~ de** vt to partake of

particularité [paʀtikylaʀite] nf particularity; (distinctive) characteristic, feature

particulier, -ière [paʀtikylje, -jɛʀ] adj (personnel, privé) private; (étrange) peculiar, odd; (spécial) special, particular; (caractéristique) characteristic, distinctive; (spécifique) particular ▷ nm (individu: Admin) private individual; **"~ vend ..."** (Comm) "for sale privately ...", "for sale by owner ..." (US); **~ à** peculiar to; **en ~** adv (surtout) in particular, particularly; (à part) separately; (en privé) in private

particulièrement [paʀtikyljɛʀmɑ̃] adv particularly

partie [paʀti] nf (gén) part; (profession, spécialité) field, subject; (Jur etc: protagonistes) party; (de cartes, tennis etc) game; (fig: lutte, combat) struggle, fight; **une ~ de campagne/de pêche** an outing in the country/a fishing party ou trip; **en ~** adv partly, in part; **faire ~ de** to belong to; (chose) to be part of; **prendre qn à ~** to take sb to task; (malmener) to set on sb; **en grande ~** largely, in the main; **ce n'est que ~ remise** it will be for another time ou the next time; **avoir ~ liée avec qn** to be in league with sb; **~ civile** (Jur) party claiming damages in a criminal case

partiel, le [paʀsjɛl] adj partial ▷ nm (Scol) class exam

partir [paʀtiʀ] vi (gén) to go; (quitter) to go, leave; (s'éloigner) to go ou drive etc) away ou off; (moteur) to start; (pétard) to go off; (bouchon) to come out; (bouton) to come off; (tache) to go, come out; **~ de** (lieu: quitter) to leave; (: commencer à) to start from; (date) to run ou start from; **~ pour/à** (lieu, pays etc) to leave for/go off to; **à ~ de** from

partisan, e [paʀtizɑ̃, -an] nm/f partisan; (d'un parti, régime etc) supporter ▷ adj (lutte, querelle) partisan, one-sided; **être ~ de qch/faire** to be in favour (Brit) ou favor (US) of sth/doing

partition [paʀtisjɔ̃] nf (Mus) score

partout [paʀtu] adv everywhere; **~ où il allait** everywhere ou wherever he went; **trente ~** (Tennis) thirty all

paru [paʀy] pp de **paraître**

parure [paʀyʀ] nf (bijoux etc) finery no pl; jewellery no pl (Brit), jewelry no pl (US); (assortiment) set

parution [paʀysjɔ̃] nf publication, appearance

parvenir [paʀvəniʀ]: **~ à** vt (atteindre) to reach; (obtenir, arriver à) to attain; (réussir): **~ à faire** to manage to do, succeed in doing; **faire ~ qch à qn** to have sth sent to sb

 MOT-CLÉ

pas¹ [pɑ] adv **1** (en corrélation avec ne, non etc) not; **il ne pleure pas** (habituellement) he does not ou doesn't cry; (maintenant) he's not ou isn't crying; **je ne mange pas de viande** I don't ou do not eat meat; **il n'a pas pleuré/ne pleurera pas** he did not ou didn't/will not ou won't cry; **ils n'ont pas de voiture/d'enfants** they haven't got a car/any children, they have no car/children; **il m'a dit de ne pas le faire** he told me not to do it; **non pas que ...** not that ..
2 (employé sans ne etc): **pas moi** not me, not I, I don't (ou can't etc); **elle travaille, (mais) lui pas** ou **pas lui** she works but he doesn't ou does not; **une pomme pas mûre** an apple which isn't ripe; **pas plus tard qu'hier** only yesterday; **pas du tout** not at all; **pas de sucre, merci** no sugar, thanks; **ceci est à vous ou pas?** is this yours or not?, is this yours or isn't it?
3: **pas mal** (joli: personne, maison) not bad; **pas mal fait** not badly done ou made; **comment ça va? — pas mal** how are things? — not bad; **pas mal de** quite a lot of

pas² [pɑ] nm (démarche) tread; (enjambée, Danse, fig: étape) step; (bruit) (foot)step; (trace) footprint; (allure, mesure) pace; (d'un cheval) walk; (Tech: de vis, d'écrou) thread; **~ à ~** step by step; **au ~** at a walking pace; **de ce ~** (à l'instant même) straightaway, at once; **marcher à grands ~** to stride along; **mettre qn au ~** to bring sb to heel; **au ~ de gymnastique/de course** at a jog trot/at a run; **à ~ de loup** stealthily; **faire les cent ~** to pace up and down; **faire les premiers ~** to make the first move; **retourner** ou **revenir sur ses ~** to retrace one's steps; **se tirer d'un mauvais ~** to get o.s. out of a tight spot; **sur le ~ de la porte** on the doorstep; **le ~ de Calais** (détroit) the Straits pl of Dover; **~ de porte** (fig) key money

passage [pɑsaʒ] nm (fait de passer) voir **passer**; (lieu, prix de la traversée, extrait de livre etc) passage; (chemin) way; (itinéraire): **sur le ~ du cortège** along the route of the procession; **"laissez/n'obstruez pas le ~"** "keep clear/do not obstruct"; **au ~** (en passant) as I (ou he etc) went by; **de ~** (touristes) passing through; (amants etc) casual; **~ clouté** pedestrian crossing; **"~ interdit"** "no entry"; **~ à niveau** level (Brit) ou grade (US) crossing; **"~ protégé"** right of way over secondary road(s) on your right;

~ souterrain subway (Brit), underpass; **~ à tabac** beating-up; **~ à vide** (fig) bad patch

passager, -ère [pɑsaʒe, -ɛʀ] adj passing; (hôte) short-stay cpd; (oiseau) migratory ▷ nm/f passenger; **~ clandestin** stowaway

passant, e [pɑsɑ̃, -ɑ̃t] adj (rue, endroit) busy ▷ nm/f passer-by ▷ nm (pour ceinture etc) loop; **en ~: remarquer qch en passant** to notice sth in passing

passe [pɑs] nf (Sport, magnétique) pass; (Navig) channel ▷ nm (passe-partout) master ou skeleton key; **être en ~ de faire** to be on the way to doing; **être dans une mauvaise ~** (fig) to be going through a bad patch; **être dans une bonne ~** (fig) to be in a healthy situation; **~ d'armes** (fig) heated exchange

passé, e [pɑse] adj (événement, temps) past; (dernier: semaine etc) last; (couleur, tapisserie) faded; (précédent): **dimanche ~** last Sunday ▷ prép after ▷ nm past; (Ling) past (tense); **il est ~ midi** ou **midi ~** it's gone (Brit) ou past twelve; **~ de mode** out of fashion; **~ composé** perfect (tense); **~ simple** past historic

passe-partout [pɑspaʀtu] nm inv master ou skeleton key ▷ adj inv all-purpose

passeport [pɑspɔʀ] nm passport

passer [pɑse] vi (se rendre, aller) to go; (voiture, piétons: défiler) to pass (by), go by; (faire une halte rapide: facteur, laitier etc) to come, call; (: pour rendre visite) to call ou drop in; (courant, air, lumière, franchir un obstacle etc) to get through; (accusé, projet de loi): **~ devant** to come before; (film, émission) to be on; (temps, jours) to pass, go by; (liquide, café) to go through; (être digéré, avalé) to go down; (couleur, papier) to fade; (mode) to die out; (douleur) to pass, go away; (Cartes) to pass; (Scol): **~ dans la classe supérieure** to go up (to the next class); (devenir): **~ président** to be appointed ou become president ▷ vt (frontière, rivière etc) to cross; (douane) to go through; (examen) to sit, take; (visite médicale etc) to have; (journée, temps) to spend; (donner): **~ qch à qn** (sel etc) to pass sth to sb; (prêter) to lend sb sth; (lettre, message) to pass sth on to sb; (tolérer) to let sb get away with sth; (transmettre): **~ qch à qn** to pass sth on to sb; (enfiler: vêtement) to slip on; (faire entrer, mettre): **(faire) ~ qch dans/par** to get sth into/through; (café) to pour the water on; (film, soupe) to strain; (film, pièce) to show, put on; (disque) to play, put on; (commande) to place; (marché, accord) to agree on; (tolérer): **~ qch à qn** to let sb get away with sth; **se passer** vi (avoir lieu: scène, action) to take place; (se dérouler: entretien etc) to go; (arriver): **que s'est-il passé?** what happened?; (s'écouler: semaine etc) to pass, go by; **se ~ de** vt to go ou do without; **se ~ les mains sous l'eau/de l'eau sur le visage** to put one's hands under the tap/run water over one's face; **en passant** in passing; **~ par** to go through; **passez devant/par ici** go in front/

this way; **~ sur** vt (faute, détail inutile) to pass over; **~ dans les mœurs/l'usage** to become the custom/normal usage; **~ avant qch/qn** (fig) to come before sth/sb; **~ un coup de fil à qn** (fam) to give sb a ring; **laisser ~** (air, lumière, personne) to let through; (occasion) to let slip, miss; (erreur) to overlook; **faire ~** (message) to get over ou across; **faire ~ à qn le goût de qch** to cure sb of his (ou her) taste for sth; **~ à la radio/fouille** to be X-rayed/searched; **~ à la radio/télévision** to be on the radio/on television; **~ à table** to sit down to eat; **~ au salon** to go through to ou into the sitting room; **~ son tour** to miss one's turn; **~ à l'opposition** to go over to the opposition; **~ aux aveux** to confess, make a confession; **~ à l'action** to go into action; **~ pour riche** to be taken for a rich man; **il passait pour avoir** he was said to have; **faire ~ qn/qch pour** to make sb/sth out to be; **passe encore de le penser, mais de le dire!** it's one thing to think it, but to say it!; **passons!** let's say no more (about it); **et j'en passe!** and that's not all!; **~ en seconde, ~ la seconde** (Auto) to change into second; **~ qch en fraude** to smuggle sth in (ou out); **~ la main par la portière** to stick one's hand out of the door; **~ le balai/l'aspirateur** to sweep up/hoover; **~ commande/la parole à qn** to hand over to sb; **je vous passe M. X** (je vous mets en communication avec lui) I'm putting you through to Mr X; (je lui passe l'appareil) here is Mr X, I'll hand you over to Mr X; **je vous passe M. Dupont** (je vous mets en communication avec lui) I'm putting you through to Mr Dupont; (je lui passe l'appareil) here is Mr Dupont, I'll hand you over to Mr Dupont; **~ prendre** to (come and) collect

passerelle [pɑsʀɛl] nf footbridge; (de navire, avion) gangway; (Navig): **~ (de commandement)** bridge

passe-temps [pɑstɑ̃] nm inv pastime

passible [pasibl] adj: **~ de** liable to

passif, -ive [pasif, -iv] adj passive ▷ nm (Ling) passive; (Comm) liabilities pl

passion [pasjɔ̃] nf passion; **avoir la ~ de** to have a passion for; **fruit de la ~** passion fruit

passionnant, e [pasjɔnɑ̃, -ɑ̃t] adj fascinating

passionné, e [pasjɔne] adj (personne, tempérament) passionate; (description, récit) impassioned ▷ nm/f: **c'est un ~ d'échecs** he's a chess fanatic; **être ~ de** ou **pour qch** to have a passion for sth

passionner [pasjɔne] vt (personne) to fascinate, grip; (débat, discussion) to inflame; **se ~ pour** to take an avid interest in; to have a passion for

passoire [paswaʀ] nf sieve; (à légumes) colander; (à thé) strainer

pastèque [pastɛk] nf watermelon

pasteur [pastœʀ] nm (protestant) minister, pastor

pasteurisé, e [pastœʀize] adj pasteurized

pastille [pastij] nf (à sucer) lozenge, pastille; (de papier etc) (small) disc; **~s pour la toux** cough drops ou lozenges

patate [patat] nf spud; **~ douce** sweet potato

patauger [patoʒe] vi (pour s'amuser) to splash about; (avec effort) to wade about; (fig) to flounder; **~ dans** (en marchant) to wade through

pâte [pɑt] nf (à tarte) pastry; (à pain) dough; (à frire) batter; (substance molle) paste; cream; **pâtes** nfpl (macaroni etc) pasta sg; **fromage à ~ dure/molle** hard/soft cheese; **~ d'amandes** almond paste, marzipan; **~ brisée** shortcrust (Brit) ou pie crust (US) pastry; **~ à choux/feuilletée** choux/puff ou flaky (Brit) pastry; **~ de fruits** crystallized fruit no pl; **~ à modeler** modelling clay, Plasticine® (Brit); **~ à papier** paper pulp

pâté [pate] nm (charcuterie: terrine) pâté; (tache) ink blot; (de sable) sandpie; **~ (en croûte)** ≈ meat pie; **~ de foie** liver pâté; **~ de maisons** block (of houses)

pâtée [pate] nf mash, feed

patente [patɑ̃t] nf (Comm) trading licence (Brit) ou license (US)

paternel, le [patɛʀnɛl] adj (amour, soins) fatherly; (ligne, autorité) paternal

pâteux, -euse [patø, -øz] adj thick; pasty; **avoir la bouche** ou **langue pâteuse** to have a furred (Brit) ou coated tongue

pathétique [patetik] adj pathetic, moving

patience [pasjɑ̃s] nf patience; **être à bout de ~** to have run out of patience; **perdre/prendre ~** to lose one's/have patience

patient, e [pasjɑ̃, -ɑ̃t] adj, nm/f patient

patienter [pasjɑ̃te] vi to wait

patin [patɛ̃] nm skate; (sport) skating; (de traîneau, luge) runner; (pièce de tissu) cloth pad (used as slippers to protect polished floor); **~ (de frein)** brake block; **~s (à glace)** (ice) skates; **~s à roulettes** roller skates

patinage [patinaʒ] nm skating; **~ artistique/de vitesse** figure/speed skating

patiner [patine] vi to skate; (embrayage) to slip; (roue, voiture) to spin; **se patiner** vi (meuble, cuir) to acquire a sheen, become polished

patineur, -euse [patinœʀ, -øz] nm/f skater

patinoire [patinwaʀ] nf skating rink, (ice) rink

pâtir [patiʀ]: **~ de** vt to suffer because of

pâtisserie [patisʀi] nf (boutique) cake shop; (métier) confectionery; (à la maison) pastry- ou cake-making, baking; **pâtisseries** nfpl (gâteaux) pastries, cakes

pâtissier, -ière [patisje, -jɛʀ] nm/f pastrycook; confectioner

patois [patwa] nm dialect, patois

patraque [patʀak] (fam) adj peaky, off-colour

patrie [patʀi] nf homeland

patrimoine [patʀimwan] nm inheritance, patrimony; (culture) heritage; **~ génétique** ou **héréditaire** genetic inheritance

patriotique [patrijɔtik] *adj* patriotic
patron, ne [patrɔ̃, -ɔn] *nm/f* (*chef*) boss, manager(-ess); (*propriétaire*) owner, proprietor(-tress); (*employeur*) employer; (*Méd*) = senior consultant; (*Rel*) patron saint ▷ *nm* (*Couture*) pattern; **~ de thèse** supervisor (of postgraduate thesis)
patronat [patrɔna] *nm* employers *pl*
patronner [patrɔne] *vt* to sponsor, support
patrouille [patruj] *nf* patrol
patte [pat] *nf* (*jambe*) leg; (*pied: de chien, chat*) paw; (: *d'oiseau*) foot; (*languette*) strap; (: *de poche*) flap; (*favoris*): **~s (de lapin)** (short) sideburns; **à ~s d'éléphant** *adj* (*pantalon*) flared; **~s de mouche** (*fig*) spidery scrawl *sg*; **~s d'oie** (*fig*) crow's feet
pâturage [patyraʒ] *nm* pasture
paume [pom] *nf* palm
paumé, e [pome] *nm/f* (*fam*) drop-out
paumer [pome] *vt* (*fam*) to lose
paupière [popjɛr] *nf* eyelid
pause [poz] *nf* (*arrêt*) break; (*en parlant, Mus*) pause; **~ de midi** lunch break
pauvre [povr] *adj* poor ▷ *nm/f* poor man/ woman; **les ~s** the poor; **~ en calcium** low in calcium
pauvreté [povrəte] *nf* (*état*) poverty; **pauvreté énergétique** fuel poverty
pavaner [pavane]: **se pavaner** *vi* to strut about
pavé, e [pave] *adj* (*cour*) paved; (*rue*) cobbled ▷ *nm* (*bloc*) paving stone; cobblestone; (*pavage*) paving; (*bifteck*) slab of steak; (*fam: livre*) hefty tome; **être sur le ~** (*sans domicile*) to be on the streets; (*sans emploi*) to be out of a job; **~ numérique** (*Inform*) keypad
pavillon [pavijɔ̃] *nm* (*de banlieue*) small (detached) house; (*kiosque*) lodge; pavilion; (*d'hôpital*) ward; (*Mus: de cor etc*) bell; (*Anat: de l'oreille*) pavilion, pinna; (*Navig*) flag; **~ de complaisance** flag of convenience
pavoiser [pavwaze] *vt* to deck with flags ▷ *vi* to put out flags; (*fig*) to rejoice, exult
pavot [pavo] *nm* poppy
payant, e [pɛjɑ̃, -ɑ̃t] *adj* (*spectateurs etc*) paying; (*billet*) that you pay for, to be paid for; (*fig: entreprise*) profitable; (*effort*) which pays off; **c'est ~** you have to pay, there is a charge
paye [pɛj] *nf* pay, wages *pl*
payer [peje] *vt* (*créancier, employé, loyer*) to pay; (*achat, réparations, fig: faute*) to pay for ▷ *vi* to pay; (*métier*) to be well-paid, pay; (*effort, tactique etc*) to pay off; **être bien/mal payé** to be well/badly paid; **il me l'a fait ~ 10 euros** he charged me 10 euros for it; **~ qn de** (*ses*

efforts, peines) to reward sb for; **~ qch à qn** to buy sth for sb, buy sb sth; **ils nous ont payé le voyage** they paid for our trip; **~ de sa personne** to give of oneself; **~ d'audace** to act with great daring; **~ cher qch** to pay dear(ly) for sth; **cela ne paie pas de mine** it doesn't look much; **se ~ qch** to buy o.s. sth; **se ~ de mots** to shoot one's mouth off; **se ~ la tête de qn** to take the mickey out of sb (Brit), make a fool of sb; (*duper*) to take sb for a ride
pays [pei] *nm* (*territoire, habitants*) country, land; (*région*) region; (*village*) village; **du ~** *adj* local; **le ~ de Galles** Wales
paysage [peizaʒ] *nm* landscape
paysan, ne [peizɑ̃, -an] *nm/f* countryman/- woman; farmer; (*péj*) peasant ▷ *adj* (*rural*) country *cpd*; (*agricole*) farming, farmers'
Pays-Bas [peiba] *nmpl*: **les ~** the Netherlands
PC *sigle m* (*Pol*) = **parti communiste**; (*Inform*: = *personal computer*) PC; (= *prêt conventionné*) *type of loan for house purchase*; (*Constr*) = **permis de construire**; (*Mil*) = **poste de commandement**
PDA *sigle m* (= *personal digital assistant*) PDA
PDG *sigle m* = **président directeur général**
péage [peaʒ] *nm* toll; (*endroit*) tollgate; **pont à ~** toll bridge
peau, x [po] *nf* skin; (*cuir*): **gants de ~** leather gloves; **être bien/mal dans sa ~** to be at ease/ill-at-ease; **se mettre dans la ~ de qn** to put o.s. in sb's place *ou* shoes; **faire ~ neuve** (*se renouveler*) to change one's image; **~ de chamois** (*chiffon*) chamois leather, shammy; **~ d'orange** orange peel
Peau-Rouge [poruʒ] *nm/f* Red Indian, red skin
péché [peʃe] *nm* sin; **~ mignon** weakness
pêche [pɛʃ] *nf* (*sport, activité*) fishing; (*poissons pêchés*) catch; (*fruit*) peach; **aller à la ~** to go fishing; **avoir la ~** (*fam*) to be on (top) form; **~ à la ligne** (*en rivière*) angling; **~ sous-marine** deep-sea fishing
pécher [peʃe] *vi* (*Rel*) to sin; (*fig: personne*) to err; (: *chose*) to be flawed; **~ contre la bienséance** to break the rules of good behaviour
pêcher [peʃe] *nm* peach tree ▷ *vi* to go fishing; (*en rivière*) to go angling ▷ *vt* (*attraper*) to catch, land; (*chercher*) to fish for; **~ au chalut** to trawl
pécheur, -eresse [peʃœr, peʃrɛs] *nm/f* sinner
pêcheur [peʃœr] *nm voir* **pêcher** fisherman; (*à la ligne*) angler; **~ de perles** pearl diver
pécule [pekyl] *nm* savings *pl*, nest egg; (*d'un détenu*) earnings *pl* (*paid on release*)
pédagogie [pedagɔʒi] *nf* educational methods *pl*, pedagogy
pédagogique [pedagɔʒik] *adj* educational; **formation ~** teacher training
pédale [pedal] *nf* pedal; **mettre la ~ douce** to soft-pedal

pédalo [pedalo] *nm* pedalo, pedal-boat
pédant, e [pedã, -ãt] *adj* (*péj*) pedantic ▷ *nm/f* pedant
pédestre [pedɛstʁ] *adj*: **tourisme ~** hiking; **randonnée ~** (*activité*) rambling; (*excursion*) ramble; **sentier ~** pedestrian footpath
pédiatre [pedjatʁ] *nm/f* paediatrician (*Brit*), pediatrician *ou* pediatrist (*US*), child specialist
pédicure [pedikyʁ] *nm/f* chiropodist
pègre [pɛgʁ] *nf* underworld
peignais *etc* [pɛɲɛ] *vb voir* **peindre**
peigne [pɛɲ] *vb voir* **peindre**; **peigner** ▷ *nm* comb
peigner [pɛɲe] *vt* to comb (the hair of); **se peigner** *vi* to comb one's hair
peignoir [pɛɲwaʁ] *nm* dressing gown; **~ de bain** bathrobe; **~ de plage** beach robe
peindre [pɛdʁ] *vt* to paint; (*fig*) to portray, depict
peine [pɛn] *nf* (*affliction*) sorrow, sadness *no pl*; (*mal, effort*) trouble *no pl*, effort; (*difficulté*) difficulty; (*punition, châtiment*) punishment; (*Jur*) sentence; **faire de la ~ à qn** to distress *ou* upset sb; **prendre la ~ de faire** to go to the trouble of doing; **se donner de la ~** to make an effort; **ce n'est pas la ~ de faire** there's no point in doing; **se donner de la ~** to make an effort; **ce n'est pas la ~ que vous fassiez** there's no point (in) your doing; **avoir de la ~** to be sad; **avoir de la ~ à faire** to have difficulty doing; **donnez-vous** *ou* **veuillez-vous donner la ~ d'entrer** please do come in; **c'est ~ perdue** it's a waste of time (and effort); **à ~** *adv* scarcely, hardly, barely; **à ~ ... que** hardly ... than, no sooner ... than; **c'est à ~ si ...** it's (*ou* it was) a job to ...; **sous ~:** **sous peine d'être puni** for fear of being punished; **défense d'afficher sous ~ d'amende** billposters will be fined; **~ capitale** capital punishment; **~ de mort** death sentence *ou* penalty
peiner [pene] *vi* to work hard; to struggle; (*moteur, voiture*) to labour (*Brit*), labor (*US*) ▷ *vt* to grieve, sadden
peintre [pɛtʁ] *nm* painter; **~ en bâtiment** house painter, painter and decorator; **~ d'enseignes** signwriter
peinture [pɛtyʁ] *nf* painting; (*couche de couleur, couleur*) paint; (*surfaces peintes: aussi:* **~s**) paintwork; **je ne peux pas le voir en ~** I can't stand the sight of him; **~ mate/brillante** matt/gloss paint; "**~ fraîche**" "wet paint"
péjoratif, -ive [peʒɔʁatif, -iv] *adj* pejorative, derogatory
Pékin [pekɛ̃] *n* Beijing
pelage [pəlaʒ] *nm* coat, fur
pêle-mêle [pɛlmɛl] *adv* higgledy-piggledy
peler [pəle] *vt, vi* to peel
pèlerin [pɛlʁɛ̃] *nm* pilgrim
pèlerinage [pɛlʁinaʒ] *nm* (*voyage*) pilgrimage; (*lieu*) place of pilgrimage, shrine

pelle [pɛl] *nf* shovel; (*d'enfant, de terrassier*) spade; **~ à gâteau** cake slice; **~ mécanique** mechanical digger
pellicule [pelikyl] *nf* film; **pellicules** *nfpl* (*Méd*) dandruff *sg*
pelote [pəlɔt] *nf* (*de fil, laine*) ball; (*d'épingles*) pin cushion; **~ basque** pelota
peloton [pəlɔtɔ̃] *nm* (*groupe: de personnes*) group; (: *de pompiers, gendarmes*) squad; (: *Sport*) pack; (*de laine*) ball; **~ d'exécution** firing squad
pelotonner [pəlɔtɔne]: **se pelotonner** *vi* to curl (o.s.) up
pelouse [pəluz] *nf* lawn; (*Hippisme*) spectating area inside racetrack
peluche [pəlyʃ] *nf* (bit of) fluff; **animal en ~** soft toy, fluffy animal; **chien/lapin en ~** fluffy dog/rabbit
pelure [pəlyʁ] *nf* peeling, peel *no pl*; **~ d'oignon** onion skin
pénal, e, -aux [penal, -o] *adj* penal
pénalité [penalite] *nf* penalty
penaud, e [pəno, -od] *adj* sheepish, contrite
penchant [pãʃã] *nm*: **un ~ à faire/à qch** a tendency to do/to sth; **un ~ pour qch** a liking *ou* fondness for sth
pencher [pãʃe] *vi* to tilt, lean over ▷ *vt* to tilt; **se pencher** *vi* to lean over; (*se baisser*) to bend down; **se ~ sur** to bend over; (*fig: problème*) to look into; **se ~ au dehors** to lean out; **~ pour** to be inclined to favour (*Brit*) *ou* favor (*US*)
pendaison [pãdɛzɔ̃] *nf* hanging
pendant, e [pãdã, -ãt] *adj* hanging (out); (*Admin, Jur*) pending ▷ *nm* counterpart; matching piece ▷ *prép* (*au cours de*) during; (*indique la durée*) for; **faire ~ à** to match; to be the counterpart of; **~ que** while; **~s d'oreilles** drop *ou* pendant earrings
pendentif [pãdãtif] *nm* pendant
penderie [pãdʁi] *nf* wardrobe; (*placard*) walk-in cupboard
pendre [pãdʁ] *vt, vi* to hang; **se ~ (à)** (*se suicider*) to hang o.s. (on); **~ à** to hang (down) from; **~ qch à** (*mur*) to hang sth (up) on; (*plafond*) to hang sth (up) from; **se ~ à** (*se suspendre*) to hang from
pendule [pãdyl] *nf* clock ▷ *nm* pendulum
pénétrer [penetʁe] *vi* to come *ou* get in ▷ *vt* to penetrate; **~ dans** to enter; (*froid, projectile*) to penetrate; (: *air, eau*) to come into, get into; (*mystère, secret*) to fathom; **se ~ de qch** to get sth firmly set in one's mind
pénible [penibl] *adj* (*astreignant*) hard; (*affligeant*) painful; (*personne, caractère*) tiresome; **il m'est ~ de ...** I'm sorry to ...
péniblement [penibləmã] *adv* with difficulty
péniche [peniʃ] *nf* barge; **~ de débarquement** landing craft *inv*
pénicilline [penisilin] *nf* penicillin
péninsule [penɛ̃syl] *nf* peninsula
pénis [penis] *nm* penis

pénitence [penitɑ̃s] nf (repentir) penitence; (peine) penance; (punition, châtiment) punishment; **mettre un enfant en ~** ≈ to make a child stand in the corner; **faire ~** to do a penance

pénitencier [penitɑ̃sje] nm prison, penitentiary (US)

pénombre [penɔ̃br] nf (faible clarté) half-light; (obscurité) darkness

pensée [pɑ̃se] nf thought; (démarche, doctrine) thinking no pl; (Bot) pansy; **se représenter qch par la ~** to conjure up a mental picture of sth; **en ~** in one's mind

penser [pɑ̃se] vi to think ▷ vt to think; (concevoir: problème, machine) to think out; **~ à** (prévoir) to think of; (songer à: ami, vacances) to think of ou about; (réfléchir à: problème, offre): **~ à qch** to think about sth, think sth over; **~ à faire qch** to think of doing sth; **~ faire qch** to be thinking of doing sth, intend to do sth; **faire ~ à** to remind one of; **n'y pensons plus** let's forget it; **vous n'y pensez pas!** don't let it bother you!; **sans ~ à mal** without meaning any harm; **je le pense aussi** I think so too; **je pense que oui/non** I think so/don't think so

pensif, -ive [pɑ̃sif, -iv] adj pensive, thoughtful

pension [pɑ̃sjɔ̃] nf (allocation) pension; (prix du logement) board and lodging, bed and board; (maison particulière) boarding house; (hôtel) guesthouse, hotel; (école) boarding school; **prendre ~ chez** to take board and lodging at; **prendre qn en ~** to take sb (in) as a lodger; **mettre en ~** to send to boarding school; **~ alimentaire** (d'étudiant) living allowance; (de divorcée) maintenance allowance; alimony; **~ complète** full board; **~ de famille** boarding house, guesthouse; **~ de guerre/d'invalidité** war/disability pension

pensionnaire [pɑ̃sjɔnɛr] nm/f (Scol) boarder; guest

pensionnat [pɑ̃sjɔna] nm boarding school

pente [pɑ̃t] nf slope; **en ~** adj sloping

Pentecôte [pɑ̃tkot] nf: **la ~** Whitsun (Brit), Pentecost; (dimanche) Whitsunday (Brit); **lundi de ~** Whit Monday (Brit)

pénurie [penyri] nf shortage; **~ de main-d'œuvre** undermanning

pépé [pepe] nm (fam) grandad

pépin [pepɛ̃] nm (Bot: graine) pip; (fam: ennui) snag, hitch; (: parapluie) brolly (Brit), umbrella

pépinière [pepinjɛr] nf nursery; (fig) nest, breeding-ground

perçant, e [pɛrsɑ̃, -ɑ̃t] adj (vue, regard, yeux) sharp, keen; (cri, voix) piercing, shrill

percée [pɛrse] nf (trouée) opening; (Mil, Comm, fig) breakthrough; (Sport) break

perce-neige [pɛrsənɛʒ] nm ou f inv snowdrop

percepteur [pɛrsɛptœr] nm tax collector

perception [pɛrsɛpsjɔ̃] nf perception; (d'impôts etc) collection; (bureau) tax (collector's) office

percer [pɛrse] vt to pierce; (ouverture etc) to make; (mystère, énigme) to penetrate ▷ vi to come through; (réussir) to break through; **~ une dent** to cut a tooth

perceuse [pɛrsøz] nf drill; **~ à percussion** hammer drill

percevoir [pɛrsəvwar] vt (distinguer) to perceive, detect; (taxe, impôt) to collect; (revenu, indemnité) to receive

perche [pɛrʃ] nf (Zool) perch; (bâton) pole; **~ à son** (sound) boom

percher [pɛrʃe] vt to perch; **~ qch sur** to perch sth on; **se percher** vi (oiseau) to perch

perchoir [pɛrʃwar] nm perch; (fig) presidency of the French National Assembly

perçois etc [pɛrswa] vb voir **percevoir**

percolateur [pɛrkɔlatœr] nm percolator

perçu, e [pɛrsy] pp de **percevoir**

percussion [pɛrkysjɔ̃] nf percussion

percuter [pɛrkyte] vt to strike; (véhicule) to crash into ▷ vi: **~ contre** to crash into

perdant, e [pɛrdɑ̃, -ɑ̃t] nm/f loser ▷ adj losing

perdre [pɛrdr] vt to lose; (gaspiller: temps, argent) to waste; (: occasion) to waste, miss; (personne: moralement etc) to ruin ▷ vi to lose; (sur une vente etc) to lose out; (récipient) to leak; **se perdre** vi (s'égarer) to get lost, lose one's way; (fig: se gâter) to go to waste; (disparaître) to disappear, vanish; **il ne perd rien pour attendre** it can wait, it'll keep; **je me suis perdu** (et je le suis encore) I'm lost; (et je ne le suis plus) I got lost

perdrix [pɛrdri] nf partridge

perdu, e [pɛrdy] pp de **perdre** ▷ adj (enfant, cause, objet) lost; (isolé) out-of-the-way; (Comm: emballage) non-returnable; (récolte etc) ruined; (malade): **il est ~** there's no hope left for him; **à vos moments ~s** in your spare time

père [pɛr] nm father; **pères** nmpl (ancêtres) forefathers; **de ~ en fils** from father to son; **~ de famille** father; family man; **mon ~** (Rel) Father; **le ~ Noël** Father Christmas

perfection [pɛrfɛksjɔ̃] nf perfection; **à la ~** adv to perfection

perfectionné, e [pɛrfɛksjɔne] adj sophisticated

perfectionner [pɛrfɛksjɔne] vt to improve, perfect; **se ~ en anglais** to improve one's English

perforer [pɛrfɔre] vt to perforate, punch a hole ou holes in; (ticket, bande, carte) to punch

performant, e [pɛrfɔrmɑ̃, -ɑ̃t] adj (Écon: produit, entreprise) high-return cpd; (Tech): **très ~** (appareil, machine) high-performance cpd

perfusion [pɛrfyzjɔ̃] nf perfusion; **faire une ~ à qn** to put sb on a drip

péricliter [periklite] vi to go downhill

péril [peril] nm peril; **au ~ de sa vie** at the risk of his life; **à ses risques et ~s** at his (ou her) own risk

périmé, e [peʀime] adj (out)dated; (Admin) out-of-date, expired

périmètre [peʀimɛtʀ] nm perimeter

période [peʀjɔd] nf period

périodique [peʀjɔdik] adj (phases) periodic; (publication) periodical; (Math: fraction) recurring ▷ nm periodical; **garniture** ou **serviette** ~ sanitary towel (Brit) ou napkin (US)

péripéties [peʀipesi] nfpl events, episodes

périphérique [peʀifeʀik] adj (quartiers) outlying; (Anat, Tech) peripheral; (station de radio) operating from a neighbouring country ▷ nm (Inform) peripheral; (Auto): (boulevard) ~ ring road (Brit), beltway (US)

périple [peʀipl] nm journey

périr [peʀiʀ] vi to die, perish

périssable [peʀisabl] adj perishable

perle [pɛʀl] nf pearl; (de plastique, métal, sueur) bead; (personne, chose) gem, treasure; (erreur) gem, howler

permanence [pɛʀmanɑ̃s] nf permanence; (local) (duty) office, strike headquarters; (service des urgences) emergency service; (Scol) study room; **assurer une** ~ (service public, bureaux) to operate ou maintain a basic service; **être de** ~ to be on call ou duty; **en** ~ adv (toujours) permanently; (continûment) continuously

permanent, e [pɛʀmanɑ̃, -ɑ̃t] adj permanent; (spectacle) continuous; (armée, comité) standing ▷ nf perm ▷ nm/f (d'un syndicat, parti) paid official

perméable [pɛʀmeabl] adj (terrain) permeable; ~ à (fig) receptive ou open to

permettre [pɛʀmɛtʀ] vt to allow, permit; ~ à **qn de faire/qch** to allow sb to do/sth; **se** ~ **de faire qch** to take the liberty of doing sth; **permettez!** excuse me!

permis, e [pɛʀmi, -iz] pp de **permettre** ▷ nm permit, licence (Brit), license (US); ~ **de chasse** hunting permit; ~ **(de conduire)** (driving) licence (Brit), (driver's) license (US); ~ **de construire** planning permission (Brit), building permit (US); ~ **d'inhumer** burial certificate; ~ **poids lourds** ≈ HGV (driving) licence (Brit), ≈ class E (driver's) license (US); ~ **de séjour** residence permit; ~ **de travail** work permit

permission [pɛʀmisjɔ̃] nf permission; (Mil) leave; (: papier) pass; **en** ~ on leave; **avoir la** ~ **de faire** to have permission to do, be allowed to do

permuter [pɛʀmyte] vt to change around, permutate ▷ vi to change, swap

Pérou [peʀu] nm: **le** ~ Peru

perpétuel, le [pɛʀpetɥɛl] adj perpetual; (Admin etc) permanent; for life

perpétuité [pɛʀpetɥite] nf: **à** ~ adj, adv for life; **être condamné à** ~ to be sentenced to life imprisonment, receive a life sentence

perplexe [pɛʀplɛks] adj perplexed, puzzled

perquisitionner [pɛʀkizisjɔne] vi to carry out a search

perron [peʀɔ̃] nm steps pl (in front of mansion etc)

perroquet [peʀɔkɛ] nm parrot

perruche [peʀyʃ] nf budgerigar (Brit), budgie (Brit), parakeet (US)

perruque [peʀyk] nf wig

persan, e [pɛʀsɑ̃, -an] adj Persian ▷ nm (Ling) Persian

persécuter [pɛʀsekyte] vt to persecute

persévérer [pɛʀsevere] vi to persevere; ~ **à croire que** to continue to believe that

persiennes [pɛʀsjɛn] nfpl (slatted) shutters

persil [pɛʀsi] nm parsley

Persique [pɛʀsik] adj: **le golfe** ~ the (Persian) Gulf

persistant, e [pɛʀsistɑ̃, -ɑ̃t] adj persistent; (feuilles) evergreen; **à feuillage** ~ evergreen

persister [pɛʀsiste] vi to persist; ~ **à faire qch** to persist in doing sth

personnage [pɛʀsɔnaʒ] nm (notable) personality; figure; (individu) character, individual; (Théât: de roman, film) character; (Peinture) figure

personnalité [pɛʀsɔnalite] nf personality; (personnage) prominent figure

personne [pɛʀsɔn] nf person ▷ pron nobody, no one; (avec négation en anglais) anybody, anyone; **personnes** nfpl people pl; **il n'y a** ~ there's nobody in ou there, there isn't anybody in ou there; **10 euros par** ~ 10 euros per person ou a head; **en** ~ personally, in person; ~ **âgée** elderly person; ~ **à charge** (Jur) dependent; ~ **morale** ou **civile** (Jur) legal entity

personnel, le [pɛʀsɔnɛl] adj personal; (égoïste: personne) selfish, self-centred; (idée, opinion): **j'ai des idées ~les à ce sujet** I have my own ideas about that ▷ nm personnel, staff; **service du** ~ personnel department

personnellement [pɛʀsɔnɛlmɑ̃] adv personally

perspective [pɛʀspɛktiv] nf (Art) perspective; (vue, coup d'œil) view; (point de vue) viewpoint, angle; (chose escomptée, envisagée) prospect; **en** ~ in prospect

perspicace [pɛʀspikas] adj clear-sighted, gifted with ou showing insight

perspicacité [pɛʀspikasite] nf insight, perspicacity

persuader [pɛʀsɥade] vt: ~ **qn (de/de faire)** to persuade sb (of/to do); **j'en suis persuadé** I'm quite sure ou convinced (of it)

persuasif, -ive [pɛʀsɥazif, -iv] adj persuasive

perte [pɛʀt] nf loss; (de temps) waste; (fig: morale) ruin; **pertes** nfpl losses; **à** ~ (Comm) at a loss; **à** ~ **de vue** as far as the eye can (ou could) see; (fig) interminably; **en pure** ~ for absolutely nothing; **courir à sa** ~ to be on the road to ruin; **être en** ~ **de vitesse** (fig) to be losing momentum; **avec** ~ **et fracas**

forcibly; ~ **de chaleur** heat loss; ~ **sèche** dead loss; **~s blanches** (vaginal) discharge sg

pertinemment [pɛʀtinamɑ̃] adv to the point; (savoir) perfectly well, full well

pertinent, e [pɛʀtinɑ̃, -ɑ̃t] adj (remarque) apt, pertinent, relevant; (analyse) discerning, judicious

perturbation [pɛʀtyʀbasjɔ̃] nf (dans un service public) disruption; (agitation, trouble) perturbation; ~ **(atmosphérique)** atmospheric disturbance

perturber [pɛʀtyʀbe] vt to disrupt; (Psych) to perturb, disturb

pervers, e [pɛʀvɛʀ, -ɛʀs] adj perverted, depraved; (malfaisant) perverse

pervertir [pɛʀvɛʀtiʀ] vt to pervert

pesant, e [pəzɑ̃, -ɑ̃t] adj heavy; (fig: présence) burdensome ▷ nm: **valoir son ~ de** to be worth one's weight in

pèse-personne [pɛzpɛʀsɔn] nm (bathroom) scales pl

peser [pəze] vt to weigh; (considérer, comparer) to weigh up ▷ vi to be heavy; (fig: avoir de l'importance) to carry weight; ~ **sur** (levier, bouton) to press, push; (fig: accabler) to lie heavy on; (: influencer) to influence; ~ **à qn** to weigh heavy on sb

pessimisme [pesimism] nm pessimism

pessimiste [pesimist] adj pessimistic ▷ nm/f pessimist

peste [pɛst] nf plague; (fig) pest, nuisance

pester [pɛste] vi: ~ **contre** to curse

pétale [petal] nm petal

pétanque [petɑ̃k] nf type of bowls; see note

pétarader [petaʀade] vi to backfire

pétard [petaʀ] nm (feu d'artifice) banger (Brit), firecracker; (de cotillon) cracker; (Rail) detonator

péter [pete] vi (fam: casser, sauter) to burst; to bust; (fam!) to fart (!)

pétillant, e [petijɑ̃, -ɑ̃t] adj (eau) sparkling

pétiller [petije] vi (flamme, bois) to crackle; (mousse, champagne) to bubble; (pierre, métal) to glisten; (yeux) to sparkle; (fig): ~ **d'esprit** to sparkle with wit

petit, e [pəti, -it] adj (gén) small; (avec nuance affective) little; (main, objet, colline, en âge: enfant) small, little; (mince, fin: personne, taille, pluie) (voyage) short, little; (bruit etc) faint, slight; (mesquin) mean; (peu important) minor ▷ nm/f (petit enfant) little one, child; **petits** nmpl (d'un animal) young pl; **faire des** **~s** to have kittens (ou puppies etc); **en ~** in miniature; **mon ~** son; little one; **ma ~e** dear; little one; **le petit** little thing; **la classe des ~s** the infant class; **pour ~s et grands** for children and adults; **les tout-~s** the little ones, the tiny tots; ~ **à** ~ bit by bit, gradually; **~(e) ami/e** boyfriend/girlfriend; **les ~es annonces** the small ads; ~ **déjeuner** breakfast; ~ **doigt** little finger; **le** ~ **écran** the small screen; ~ **four** petit four; ~ **pain** (bread) roll; **~e monnaie** small change; **~e vérole** smallpox; **~s pois** petit pois pl, garden peas; **~es gens** people of modest means

petite-fille (pl **petites-filles**) [pətitfij] nf granddaughter

petit-fils (pl **petits-fils**) [pətifis] nm grandson

pétition [petisjɔ̃] nf petition; **faire signer une** ~ to get up a petition

petits-enfants [pətizɑ̃fɑ̃] nmpl grandchildren

petit-suisse (pl **petits-suisses**) [pətisɥis] nm small individual pot of cream cheese

pétrin [petʀɛ̃] nm kneading-trough; (fig): **dans le** ~ in a jam ou fix

pétrir [petʀiʀ] vt to knead

pétrole [petʀɔl] nm oil; (aussi: ~ **lampant:** pour lampe, réchaud etc) paraffin (Brit), kerosene (US)

pétrolier, -ière [petʀɔlje, -jɛʀ] adj oil cpd; (pays) oil-producing ▷ nm (navire) oil tanker; (financier) oilman; (technicien) petroleum engineer

P et T sigle fpl = **postes et télécommunications**

 MOT-CLÉ

peu [pø] adv **1** (modifiant verbe, adjectif, adverbe): **il boit peu** he doesn't drink (very) much; **il est peu bavard** he's not very talkative; **peu avant/après** shortly before/afterwards; **pour peu qu'il fasse** if he should do, if by any chance he does

2 (modifiant nom): **peu de: peu de gens/d'arbres** few ou not (very) many people/trees; **il a peu d'espoir** he hasn't (got) much hope, he has little hope; **pour peu de temps** for (only) a short while; **à peu de frais** for very little cost

3: peu à peu little by little; **à peu près** just about, more or less; **à peu près 10 kg/10 euros** approximately 10 kg/10 euros

▷ nm **1: le peu de gens qui** the few people who; **le peu de sable qui** what little sand, the little sand which

2: un peu a little; **un petit peu** a little bit; **un peu d'espoir** a little hope; **elle est un peu bavarde** she's rather talkative; **un peu plus de** slightly more than; **un peu moins de** slightly less than; (avec pluriel) slightly fewer than; **pour un peu il ...**, **un peu plus et il ...** he very nearly ou all but ...; **essayez un peu!** have a go!, just try it!

▷ pron: **peu le savent** few know (it); **avant ou**

sous peu shortly, before long; **depuis peu** for a short ou little while; (*au passé*) a short ou little while ago; **de peu** (only) just; **c'est peu de chose** it's nothing; **il est de peu mon cadet** he's just a little ou bit younger than me

peuple [pœpl] *nm* people; (*masse*): **un ~ de vacanciers** a crowd of holiday-makers; **il y a du ~** there are a lot of people

peupler [pœple] *vt* (*pays, région*) to populate; (*étang*) to stock; (*hommes, poissons*) to inhabit; (*fig: imagination, rêves*) to fill; **se peupler** *vi* (*ville, région*) to become populated; (*fig: s'animer*) to fill (up), be filled

peuplier [pœplije] *nm* poplar (tree)

peur [pœʀ] *nf* fear; **avoir ~ (de/de faire/que)** to be frightened ou afraid (of/of doing/that); **prendre ~** to take fright; **faire ~ à** to frighten; **de ~ de/que** for fear of/that; **j'ai ~ qu'il ne soit trop tard** I'm afraid it might be too late; **j'ai ~ qu'il (ne) vienne (pas)** I'm afraid he may (not) come

peureux, -euse [pœʀø, -øz] *adj* fearful, timorous

peut [pø] *vb voir* **pouvoir**

peut-être [pøtɛtʀ] *adv* perhaps, maybe; **~ que** perhaps, maybe; **bien qu'il fera/est** he may well do/be

phare [faʀ] *nm* (*en mer*) lighthouse; (*d'aéroport*) beacon; (*de véhicule*) headlight, headlamp (*Brit*) ▷ *adj*: **produit ~** leading product; **se mettre en ~s, mettre ses ~s** to put on one's headlights; **~s de recul** reversing (*Brit*) ou back-up (*US*) lights

pharmacie [faʀmasi] *nf* (*science*) pharmacology; (*magasin*) chemist's (*Brit*), pharmacy; (*officine*) dispensary; (*produits*) pharmaceuticals *pl*; (*armoire*) medicine chest ou cupboard, first-aid cupboard

pharmacien, ne [faʀmasjɛ̃, -ɛn] *nm/f* pharmacist, chemist (*Brit*)

phénomène [fenɔmɛn] *nm* phenomenon; (*monstre*) freak

philatélie [filateli] *nf* philately, stamp collecting

philosophe [filɔzɔf] *nm/f* philosopher ▷ *adj* philosophical

philosophie [filɔzɔfi] *nf* philosophy

phobie [fɔbi] *nf* phobia

phonétique [fɔnetik] *adj* phonetic ▷ *nf* phonetics *sg*

phoque [fɔk] *nm* seal; (*fourrure*) sealskin

phosphorescent, e [fɔsfɔʀesɑ̃, -ɑ̃t] *adj* luminous

photo [fɔto] *nf* (*photographie*) photo ▷ *adj*: **appareil/pellicule ~** camera/film; **en ~** in ou on a photo; **prendre en ~** to take a photo of; **aimer la/faire de la ~** to like taking/take photos; **~ en couleurs** colour photo; **~ d'identité** passport photo

photocopie [fɔtokɔpi] *nf* (*procédé*) photocopying; (*document*) photocopy

photocopier [fɔtokɔpje] *vt* to photocopy

photocopieur [fɔtokɔpjœʀ] *nm*, **photocopieuse** [fɔtokɔpjøz] *nf* (photo) copier

photographe [fɔtɔgʀaf] *nm/f* photographer

photographie [fɔtɔgʀafi] *nf* (*procédé, technique*) photography; (*cliché*) photograph; **faire de la ~** to do photography as a hobby; (*comme métier*) to be a photographer

photographier [fɔtɔgʀafje] *vt* to photograph, take

phrase [fʀɑz] *nf* (*Ling*) sentence; (*propos, Mus*) phrase; **phrases** *nfpl* (*péj*) flowery language *sg*

physicien, ne [fizisjɛ̃, -ɛn] *nm/f* physicist

physionomie [fizjɔnɔmi] *nf* face; (*d'un paysage etc*) physiognomy

physique [fizik] *adj* physical ▷ *nm* physique ▷ *nf* physics *sg*; **au ~** physically

physiquement [fizikmɑ̃] *adv* physically

piailler [pjaje] *vi* to squawk

pianiste [pjanist] *nm/f* pianist

piano [pjano] *nm* piano; **~ à queue** grand piano

pianoter [pjanɔte] *vi* to tinkle away (at the piano); (*tapoter*): **~ sur** to drum one's fingers on

pic [pik] *nm* (*instrument*) pick(axe); (*montagne*) peak; (*Zool*) woodpecker; **à ~** *adv* vertically; (*fig: tomber, arriver*) just at the right time; **couler à ~** (*bateau*) to go straight down; **~ à glace** ice pick

pichet [piʃɛ] *nm* jug

picorer [pikɔʀe] *vt* to peck

picoter [pikɔte] *vt* (*oiseau*) to peck ▷ *vi* (*irriter*) to smart, prickle

pie [pi] *nf* magpie; (*fig*) chatterbox ▷ *adj inv*: **cheval ~** piebald; **vache ~** black and white cow

pièce [pjɛs] *nf* (*d'un logement*) room; (*Théât*) play; (*de mécanisme, machine*) part; (*de monnaie*) coin; (*Couture*) patch; (*document*) document; (*de drap, fragment, d'une collection*) piece; (*de bétail*) head; **mettre en ~s** to smash to pieces; **deux euros ~** two euros each; **vendre à la ~** to sell separately ou individually; **travailler/payer à la ~** to do piecework/pay piece rate; **de toutes ~s**: **c'est inventé de toutes pièces** it's a complete fabrication; **un maillot une ~** a one-piece swimsuit; **un deux-~s cuisine** a two-room(ed) flat (*Brit*) ou apartment (*US*) with kitchen; **tout d'une ~** (*personne: franc*) blunt; (: *sans souplesse*) inflexible; **~ à conviction** exhibit; **~ d'eau** ornamental lake ou pond; **~ d'identité**: **avez-vous une pièce d'identité?** have you got any (means of) identification?; **~ jointe** (*Inform*) attachment; **~ montée** tiered cake; **~ de rechange** spare (part); **~ de résistance** pièce de résistance; (*plat*) main dish; **~s détachées** spares, (spare) parts; **en ~s détachées** (*à monter*) in kit form; **~s justificatives** supporting documents

pied [pje] *nm* foot; (*de verre*) stem; (*de table*) leg; (*de lampe*) base; (*plante*) footing; **~s nus** barefoot; **à ~** on foot; **à ~ sec** without getting one's feet wet; **à ~ d'œuvre** ready to start (work); **au ~ de la lettre** literally; **au ~ levé** at a moment's notice; **de ~ en cap** from head to foot; **en ~** (*portrait*) full-length; **avoir ~** to be able to touch the bottom, not to be out of one's depth; **avoir le ~ marin** to be a good sailor; **perdre ~** to lose one's footing; (*fig*) to get out of one's depth; **sur ~** (*Agr*) on the stalk, uncut; (*debout, rétabli*) up and about; **mettre sur ~** (*entreprise*) to set up; **mettre à ~** to suspend; to lay off; **mettre qn au ~ du mur** to get sb with his (*ou* her) back to the wall; **sur le ~ de guerre** ready for action; **sur un ~ d'égalité** on an equal footing; **sur ~ d'intervention** on stand-by; **faire du ~ à qn** (*prévenir*) to give sb a (warning) kick; (*galamment*) to play footsie with sb; **mettre les ~s quelque part** to set foot somewhere; **faire des ~s et des mains** (*fig*) to move heaven and earth, pull out all the stops; **c'est le ~!** (*fam*) it's brilliant!; **mettre les ~s dans le plat** (*fam*) to put one's foot in it; **il se débrouille comme un ~** (*fam*) he's completely useless; **se lever du bon ~/du ~ gauche** to get out of bed on the right/wrong side; **~ de lit** footboard; **~ de nez:** **faire un pied de nez à** to thumb one's nose at; **~ de vigne** vine

pied-noir (*pl* **pieds-noirs**) [pjenwaʀ] *nm* Algerian-born Frenchman

piège [pjɛʒ] *nm* trap; **prendre au ~** to trap

piéger [pjeʒe] *vt* (*animal, fig*) to trap; (*avec une bombe*) to booby-trap; **lettre/voiture piégée** letter-/car-bomb

piercing [pjɛʀsiŋ] *nm* piercing

pierre [pjɛʀ] *nf* stone; **première ~** (*d'un édifice*) foundation stone; **mur de ~s sèches** drystone wall; **faire d'une ~ deux coups** to kill two birds with one stone; **~ à briquet** flint; **~ fine** semiprecious stone; **~ ponce** pumice stone; **~ de taille** freestone *no pl*; **~ tombale** tombstone, gravestone; **~ de touche** touchstone

pierreries [pjɛʀʀi] *nfpl* gems, precious stones

piétiner [pjetine] *vi* (*trépigner*) to stamp (one's foot); (*marquer le pas*) to stand about; (*fig*) to be at a standstill ▷ *vt* to trample on

piéton, ne [pjetɔ̃, -ɔn] *nm/f* pedestrian ▷ *adj* pedestrian *cpd*

piétonnier, -ière [pjetɔnje, -jɛʀ] *adj* pedestrian *cpd*

pieu, x [pjø] *nm* (*piquet*) post; (*pointu*) stake; (*fam: lit*) bed

pieuvre [pjœvʀ] *nf* octopus

pieux, -euse [pjø, -øz] *adj* pious

piffer [pife] *vt* (*fam*): **je ne peux pas le ~** I can't stand him

pigeon [piʒɔ̃] *nm* pigeon; **~ voyageur** homing pigeon

piger [piʒe] *vi* (*fam*) to get it ▷ *vt* (*fam*) to get, understand

pigiste [piʒist] *nm/f* (*typographe*) typesetter on piecework; (*journaliste*) freelance journalist (*paid by the line*)

pignon [piɲɔ̃] *nm* (*de mur*) gable; (*d'engrenage*) cog(wheel), gearwheel; (*graine*) pine kernel; **avoir ~ sur rue** (*fig*) to have a prosperous business

pile [pil] *nf* (*tas, pilier*) pile; (*Élec*) battery ▷ *adj*: **le côté ~ tails** ▷ *adv* (*net, brusquement*) dead; (*à temps, à point nommé*) just at the right time; **à deux heures ~** at two on the dot; **jouer à ~ ou face** to toss up (for it); **~ ou face?** heads or tails?

piler [pile] *vt* to crush, pound

pilier [pilje] *nm* (*colonne, support*) pillar; (*personne*) mainstay; (*Rugby*) prop (forward)

piller [pije] *vt* to pillage, plunder, loot

pilote [pilɔt] *nm* pilot; (*de char, voiture*) driver ▷ *adj* pilot *cpd*; **usine/ferme ~** experimental factory/farm; **~ de chasse/d'essai/de ligne** fighter/test/airline pilot; **~ de course** racing driver

piloter [pilɔte] *vt* (*navire*) to pilot; (*avion*) to fly; (*automobile*) to drive; (*fig*): **~ qn** to guide sb round

pilule [pilyl] *nf* pill; **prendre la ~** to be on the pill; **~ du lendemain** morning-after pill

piment [pimɑ̃] *nm* (*Bot*) pepper, capsicum; (*fig*) spice, piquancy; **~ rouge** (*Culin*) chilli

pimenté, e [pimɑ̃te] *adj* (*plat*) hot and spicy

pimpant, e [pɛ̃pɑ̃, -ɑ̃t] *adj* spruce

pin [pɛ̃] *nm* pine (tree); (*bois*) pine(wood)

pinard [pinaʀ] *nm* (*fam*) (cheap) wine, plonk (Brit)

pince [pɛ̃s] *nf* (*outil*) pliers *pl*; (*de homard, crabe*) pincer, claw; (*Couture: pli*) dart; **~ à sucre/glace** sugar/ice tongs *pl*; **~ à épiler** tweezers *pl*; **~ à linge** clothes peg (Brit) *ou* pin (US); **~ universelle** (universal) pliers *pl*; **~s de cycliste** bicycle clips

pincé, e [pɛ̃se] *adj* (*air*) stiff; (*mince: bouche*) pinched ▷ *nf*: **une ~e de** a pinch of

pinceau, x [pɛ̃so] *nm* (paint)brush

pincer [pɛ̃se] *vt* to pinch; (*Mus: cordes*) to pluck; (*Couture*) to dart, put darts in; (*fam*) to nab; **se ~ le doigt** to squeeze *ou* nip one's finger; **se ~ le nez** to hold one's nose

pinède [pinɛd] *nf* pinewood, pine forest

pingouin [pɛ̃gwɛ̃] *nm* penguin

ping-pong [piŋpɔ̃g] *nm* table tennis

pingre [pɛ̃gʀ] *adj* niggardly

pinson [pɛ̃sɔ̃] *nm* chaffinch

pintade [pɛ̃tad] *nf* guinea-fowl

pioche [pjɔʃ] *nf* pickaxe

piocher [pjɔʃe] *vt* to dig up (with a pickaxe); (*fam*) to swot (Brit) *ou* grind (US) at; **~ dans** to dig into

pion, ne [pjɔ̃, pjɔn] *nm/f* (*Scol: péj*) student paid to supervise schoolchildren ▷ *nm* (*Échecs*) pawn; (*Dames*) piece, draught (Brit), checker (US)

pionnier [pjɔnje] *nm* pioneer

pipe [pip] nf pipe; **fumer la** ou **une** ~ to smoke a pipe; ~ **de bruyère** briar pipe

pipeau, x [pipo] nm (reed-)pipe

piquant, e [pikɑ̃, -ɑ̃t] adj (barbe, rosier etc) prickly; (saveur, sauce) hot, pungent; (fig: description, style) racy; (: mordant, caustique) biting ▷ nm (épine) thorn, prickle; (de hérisson) quill, spine; (fig) spiciness, spice

pique [pik] nf (arme) pike; (fig): **envoyer** ou **lancer des ~s à qn** to make cutting remarks to sb ▷ nm (Cartes: couleur) spades pl; (: carte) spade

pique-nique [piknik] nm picnic

pique-niquer [piknike] vi to (have a) picnic

piquer [pike] vt (percer) to prick; (Méd) to give an injection to; (: animal blessé etc) to put to sleep; (insecte, fumée, ortie) to sting; (moustique) to bite; (: poivre) to burn; (: froid) to bite; (Couture) to machine (stitch); (intérêt etc) to arouse; (fam: prendre) to pick up; (: voler) to pinch; (: arrêter) to nab; (planter): ~ **qch dans** to stick sth into; (fixer): ~ **qch à** ou **sur** to pin sth onto ▷ vi (oiseau, avion) to go into a dive; (saveur) to be pungent; to be sour; **se piquer** (avec une aiguille) to prick o.s.; (se faire une piqûre) to inject o.s.; (se vexer) to get annoyed; **se ~ de faire** to pride o.s. on doing; ~ **sur** to swoop down on; to head straight for; ~ **du nez** (avion) to go into a nose-dive; ~ **une tête** (plonger) to dive headfirst; ~ **un galop/un cent mètres** to break into a gallop/put on a sprint; ~ **une crise** to throw a fit; ~ **au vif** (fig) to sting

piquet [pikɛ] nm (pieu) post, stake; (de tente) peg; **mettre un élève au ~** to make a pupil stand in the corner; ~ **de grève** (strike) picket; ~ **d'incendie** fire-fighting squad

piqûre [pikyʀ] nf (d'épingle) prick; (d'ortie) sting; (de moustique) bite; (Méd) injection, shot (US); (Couture) (straight) stitch; straight stitching; (de ver) hole; (tache) (spot of) mildew; **faire une ~ à qn** to give sb an injection

pirate [piʀat] adj pirate cpd ▷ nm pirate; (fig: escroc) crook, shark; (Inform) hacker; ~ **de l'air** hijacker

pirater [piʀate] vi (Inform) to hack ▷ vt (Inform) to hack into

pire [piʀ] adj (comparatif).worse; (superlatif): **le (la)** ~ ... the worst ... ▷ nm: **le ~ (de)** the worst (of); **au ~** (at the very) worst

pis [pi] nm (de vache) udder; (pire): **le ~** the worst ▷ adj, adv worse; **qui ~ est** what is worse; **au ~ aller** if the worst comes to the worst, at worst; **de mal en ~** from bad to worse

piscine [pisin] nf (swimming) pool; ~ **couverte** indoor (swimming) pool

pissenlit [pisɑ̃li] nm dandelion

pistache [pistaʃ] nf pistachio (nut)

piste [pist] nf (d'un animal, sentier) track, trail; (indice) lead; (de stade, de magnétophone) track; (de cirque) ring; (de danse) floor; (de patinage)

rink; (de ski) run; (Aviat) runway; ~ **cavalière** bridle path; ~ **cyclable** cycle track, bikeway (US); ~ **sonore** sound track

pistolet [pistolɛ] nm (arme) pistol, gun; (à peinture) spray gun; ~ **à bouchon/air comprimé** popgun/airgun; ~ **à eau** water pistol

pistolet-mitrailleur [pl **pistolets-mitrailleurs**] [pistolɛmitʀajœʀ] nm submachine gun

piston [pistɔ̃] nm (Tech) piston; (Mus) valve; (fig: appui) string-pulling; **avoir du ~** (fam) to have friends in the right places

pistonner [pistɔne] vt (candidat) to pull strings for

piteux, -euse [pitø, -øz] adj pitiful, sorry (avant le nom); **en ~ état** in a sorry state

pitié [pitje] nf pity; **sans ~** adj pitiless, merciless; **faire ~** to inspire pity; **il me fait ~** I pity him, I feel sorry for him; **avoir ~ de** (compassion) to pity, feel sorry for; (merci) to have pity ou mercy on; **par ~!** for pity's sake!

pitoyable [pitwajabl] adj pitiful

pitre [pitʀ] nm clown

pitrerie [pitʀəʀi] nf tomfoolery no pl

pittoresque [pitɔʀɛsk] adj picturesque; (expression, détail) colourful (Brit), colorful (US)

pivot [pivo] nm (d'une dent) post

pivoter [pivɔte] vi (fauteuil) to swivel; (porte) to revolve; ~ **sur ses talons** to swing round

pizza [pidza] nf pizza

PJ sigle f (= police judiciaire) ≈ CID (Brit), ≈ FBI (US) ▷ sigle fpl (= pièces jointes) encl

placard [plakaʀ] nm (armoire) cupboard; (affiche) poster, notice; (Typo) galley; ~ **publicitaire** display advertisement

place [plas] nf (emplacement, situation, classement) place; (de ville, village) square; (Écon): ~ **financière/boursière** money/stock market; (espace libre) room, space; (de parking) space; (siège: de train, cinéma, voiture) seat; (prix: au cinéma etc) price; (: dans un bus, taxi) fare; (emploi) job; **en ~** (mettre) in its place; **de ~ en ~, par ~s** here and there, in places; **sur ~** on the spot; **faire ~ à** to give way to; **faire de la ~ à** to make room for; **ça prend de la ~** it takes up a lot of room ou space; **prendre ~** to take one's place; **remettre qn à sa ~** to put sb in his (ou her) place; **ne pas rester en place** to be always on the go; **à la ~ de** in place of, instead of; **à votre ~ ...** if I were you ...; **se mettre à la ~ de qn** to put o.s. in sb's place ou in sb's shoes; **une quatre ~s** (Auto) a four-seater; **il y a 20 ~s assises/debout** there are 20 seats/there is standing room for 20; ~ **forte** fortified town; ~ **d'honneur** place (ou seat) of honour (Brit) ou honor (US)

placé, e [plase] adj (Hippisme) placed; **haut ~** (fig) high-ranking; **être bien/mal ~** to be well/badly placed; (spectateur) to have a good/ bad seat; **être bien/mal ~ pour faire** to be in/not to be in a position to do; **il est bien ~ pour le savoir** he is in a position to know

placement [plasmã] *nm* placing; (*Finance*) investment; **agence** *ou* **bureau de ~** employment agency

placer [plase] *vt* to place, put; (*convive, spectateur*) to seat; (*capital, argent*) to place, invest; (*dans la conversation*) to put *ou* get in; **~ qn chez** to get sb a job at (*ou* with); **se ~ au premier rang** to go and stand (*ou* sit) in the first row

plafond [plafõ] *nm* ceiling

plage [plaʒ] *nf* beach; (*station*) (seaside) resort; (*fig*) band, bracket; (*de disque*) track, band; **~ arrière** (*Auto*) parcel *ou* back shelf

plagiat [plaʒja] *nm* plagiarism

plaid [plɛd] *nm* (tartan) car rug, lap robe (US)

plaider [plede] *vi* (*avocat*) to plead; (*plaignant*) to go to court, litigate ▷ *vt* to plead; **~ pour** (*fig*) to speak for

plaidoyer [pledwaje] *nm* (*Jur*) speech for the defence (*Brit*) *ou* defense (US); (*fig*) plea

plaie [plɛ] *nf* wound

plaignant, e [plɛɲã, -ãt] *vb voir* **plaindre** ▷ *nm/f* plaintiff

plaindre [plɛ̃dʀ] *vt* to pity, feel sorry for; **se plaindre** *vi* (*gémir*) to moan; (*protester, rouspéter*): **se ~ (à qn) (de)** to complain (to sb) (about); (*souffrir*): **se ~ de** to complain of

plaine [plɛn] *nf* plain

plain-pied [plɛ̃pje]: **de ~** *adv* at street-level; (*fig*) straight; **de ~ (avec)** on the same level (as)

plaint, e [plɛ̃, -ɛ̃t] *pp de* **plaindre** ▷ *nf* (*gémissement*) moan, groan; (*doléance*) complaint; **porter ~e** to lodge a complaint

plaire [plɛʀ] *vi* to be a success, be successful; to please; **~ à**: **cela me plaît** I like it; **ça plaît beaucoup aux jeunes** it's very popular with young people; **essayer de ~ à qn** (*en étant serviable etc*) to try and please sb; **elle plaît aux hommes** she's a success with men, men like her; **se ~ quelque part** to like being somewhere, like it somewhere; **se ~ à faire** to take pleasure in doing; **ce qu'il vous plaira** what(ever) you like *ou* wish; **s'il vous plaît, s'il te plaît** please

plaisance [plɛzãs] *nf* (*aussi*: **navigation de ~**) (pleasure) sailing, yachting

plaisant, e [plɛzã, -ãt] *adj* pleasant; (*histoire, anecdote*) amusing

plaisanter [plɛzãte] *vi* to joke ▷ *vt* (*personne*) to tease, make fun of; **pour ~** for a joke; **on ne plaisante pas avec cela** that's no joking matter; **tu plaisantes!** you're joking *ou* kidding!

plaisanterie [plɛzãtʀi] *nf* joke; joking *no pl*

plaise *etc* [plɛz] *vb voir* **plaire**

plaisir [plezɪʀ] *nm* pleasure; **faire ~ à qn** (*délibérément*) to be nice to sb, please sb; (*cadeau, nouvelle etc*): **ça me fait ~** I'm delighted *ou* very pleased with this; **j'espère que ça te fera ~** I hope you'll like it; **prendre ~ à/à faire** to take pleasure in/in doing; **j'ai le ~ de ...** it is with great pleasure that I ...; **M. et Mme X ont le ~ de vous faire part de ...** M. and Mme X are pleased to announce ...; **se faire un ~ de faire qch** to be (only too) pleased to do sth; **faites-moi le ~ de ...** would you mind ..., would you be kind enough to ...; **à ~** freely; for the sake of it; **au ~ (de vous revoir)** (I hope) to see you again; **pour le** *ou* **pour son** *ou* **par ~** for pleasure

plaît [plɛ] *vb voir* **plaire**

plan, e [plã, -an] *adj* flat ▷ *nm* plan; (*Géom*) plane; (*fig*) level, plane; (*Ciné*) shot; **au premier/second ~** in the foreground/middle distance; **à l'arrière ~** in the background; **mettre qch au premier ~** (*fig*) to consider sth to be of primary importance; **sur le ~ sexuel** sexually, as far as sex is concerned; **laisser/rester en ~** to abandon/be abandoned; **~ d'action** plan of action; **~ directeur** (*Écon*) master plan; **~ d'eau** lake; pond; **~ de travail** work-top, work surface; **~ de vol** (*Aviat*) flight plan

planche [plãʃ] *nf* (*pièce de bois*) plank, (wooden) board; (*illustration*) plate; (*de salades, radis, poireaux*) bed; (*d'un plongeoir*) (diving) board; **les ~s** (*Théât*) the boards; **en ~** *adj* wooden; **faire la ~** (*dans l'eau*) to float on one's back; **avoir du pain sur la ~** to have one's work cut out; **~ à découper** chopping board; **~ à dessin** drawing board; **~ à pain** breadboard; **~ à repasser** ironing board; **~ (à roulettes)** (*planche*) skateboard; (*sport*) skateboarding; **~ de salut** (*fig*) sheet anchor; **~ à voile** (*planche*) windsurfer, sailboard; (*sport*) windsurfing

plancher [plãʃe] *nm* floor; (*planches*) floorboards *pl*; (*fig*) minimum level ▷ *vi* to work hard

planer [plane] *vi* (*oiseau, avion*) to glide; (*fumée, vapeur*) to float, hover; (*drogué*) to be (on a) high; (*fam: rêveur*) to have one's head in the clouds; **~ sur** (*fig: danger*) to hang over; to hover above

planète [planɛt] *nf* planet

planeur [plancɛr] *nm* glider

planification [planifikasjõ] *nf* (economic) planning

planifier [planifje] *vt* to plan

planning [planiŋ] *nm* programme (*Brit*), program (US), schedule; **~ familial** family planning

planque [plãk] *nf* (*fam: combine, filon*) cushy (*Brit*) *ou* easy number; (: *cachette*) hideout

plant [plã] *nm* seedling, young plant

plante [plãt] *nf* plant; **~ d'appartement** house *ou* pot plant; **~ du pied** sole (of the foot); **~ verte** house plant

planter [plãte] *vt* (*plante*) to plant; (*enfoncer*) to hammer *ou* drive in; (*tente*) to put up, pitch; (*drapeau, échelle, décors*) to put up; (*fam: mettre*) to dump; (: *abandonner*): **~ là** to ditch; **se planter** *vi* (*fam: se tromper*) to get it wrong;

(ordinateur) to crash; **~ qch dans** to hammer *ou* drive sth into; to stick sth into; **se ~ dans** to sink into; to get stuck in; **se ~ devant** to plant o.s. in front of

plantureux, -euse [plãtyʀø, -øz] *adj (repas)* copious, lavish; *(femme)* buxom

plaque [plak] *nf* plate; *(de verre)* sheet; *(de verglas, d'eczéma)* patch; *(dentaire)* plaque; *(avec inscription)* plaque; **~ (minéralogique** *ou* **de police** *ou* **d'immatriculation)** number *(Brit)* *ou* license *(US)* plate; **~ de beurre** slab of butter; **~ chauffante** hotplate; **~ de chocolat** bar of chocolate; **~ de cuisson** hob; **~ d'identité** identity disc; **~ tournante** *(fig)* centre *(Brit)*, center *(US)*

plaqué, e [plake] *adj:* **~ or/argent** gold-/silver-plated ▷ *nm:* **~ or/argent** gold/silver plate; **~ acajou** with a mahogany veneer

plaquer [plake] *vt (bijou)* to plate; *(bois)* to veneer; *(aplatir)*: **~ qch sur/contre** to make sth stick *ou* cling to; *(Rugby)* to bring down; *(fam: laisser tomber)* to drop, ditch; **se ~ contre** to flatten o.s. against; **~ qn contre** to pin sb to

plaquette [plaket] *nf* tablet; *(de chocolat)* bar; *(de beurre)* slab, packet; *(livre)* small volume; *(Méd: de pilules, gélules)* pack, packet; **~ de frein** *(Auto)* brake pad

plastique [plastik] *adj* plastic ▷ *nm* plastic ▷ *nf* plastic arts *pl*; *(d'une statue)* modelling

plastiquer [plastike] *vt* to blow up

plat, e [pla, -at] *adj* flat; *(fade: vin)* flat-tasting, insipid; *(personne, livre)* dull; *(style)* flat, dull ▷ *nm (récipient, Culin)* dish; *(d'un repas)* course; **le premier ~** the first course; *(partie plate)*: **le ~ de la main** the flat of the hand; *(: d'une route)* flat *(part)*; **à ~ ventre** *adv* face down; *(tomber)* flat on one's face; **à ~** *adj (pneu, batterie)* flat; *(fam: fatigué)* dead beat, tired out; **~ cuisiné** pre-cooked meal *(ou* dish); **~ du jour** dish of the day; **~ principal** *ou* **de résistance** main course; **~s préparés** convenience food(s)

platane [platan] *nm* plane tree

plateau, x [plato] *nm (support)* tray; *(d'une table)* top; *(d'une balance)* pan; *(Géo)* plateau; *(de tourne-disques)* turntable; *(Ciné)* set; *(TV):* **nous avons deux journalistes sur le ~ ce soir** we have two journalists with us tonight; **~ à fromages** cheeseboard

plate-bande *(pl* **plates-bandes)** [platbãd] *nf* flower bed

plate-forme *(pl* **plates-formes)** [platfɔʀm] *nf* platform; **~ de forage/pétrolière** drilling/oil rig

platine [platin] *nm* platinum ▷ *nf (d'un tourne-disque)* turntable; **~ disque/cassette** record/cassette deck; **~ laser** *ou* **compact-disc** compact disc (player)

plâtre [plɑtʀ] *nm (matériau)* plaster; *(statue)* plaster statue; *(Méd)* (plaster) cast; **plâtres** *nmpl* plasterwork *sg*; **avoir un bras dans le ~** to have an arm in plaster

plein, e [plɛ̃, -ɛn] *adj* full; *(porte, roue)* solid; *(chienne, jument)* big (with young) ▷ *nm:* **faire le ~ (d'essence)** to fill up (with petrol *(Brit)* *ou* gas *(US))* ▷ *prép:* **avoir de l'argent ~ les poches** to have loads of money; **~ de** full of; **avoir les mains ~es** to have one's hands full; **à ~es mains** *(ramasser)* in handfuls; *(empoigner)* firmly; **à ~ régime** at maximum revs; *(fig)* at full speed; **à ~ temps** full-time; **en ~ air** in the open air; **jeux en ~ air** outdoor games; **en ~e mer** on the open sea; **en ~ soleil** in direct sunlight; **en ~ nuit/rue** in the middle of the night/street; **en ~ milieu** right in the middle; **en ~ jour** in broad daylight; **les ~s** the downstrokes *(in handwriting)*; **faire le ~ des voix** to get the maximum number of votes possible; **en ~ sur** right on; **en avoir ~ le dos** *(fam)* to have had it up to here

pleurer [plœʀe] *vi* to cry; *(yeux)* to water ▷ *vt* to mourn (for); **~ sur** *vt* to lament (over), bemoan; **~ de rire** to laugh till one cries

pleurnicher [plœʀniʃe] *vi* to snivel, whine

pleurs [plœʀ] *nmpl:* **en ~** in tears

pleut [plø] *vb voir* **pleuvoir**

pleuvait *etc* [pløvɛ] *vb voir* **pleuvoir**

pleuvoir [pløvwaʀ] *vb impers* to rain ▷ *vi (fig):* **~ (sur)** *(coups)* to rain down; *(critiques, invitations)* to shower down; **il pleut** it's raining; **il pleut des cordes** *ou* **à verse** *ou* **à torrents** it's pouring (down), it's raining cats and dogs

pli [pli] *nm* fold; *(de jupe)* pleat; *(de pantalon)* crease; *(aussi:* **faux ~)** crease; *(enveloppe)* envelope; *(lettre)* letter; *(Cartes)* trick; **prendre le ~ de faire** to get into the habit of doing; **ça ne fait pas un ~!** don't you worry!; **~ d'aisance** inverted pleat

pliant, e [plijã, -ãt] *adj* folding ▷ *nm* folding stool, campstool

plier [plije] *vt* to fold; *(pour ranger)* to fold up; *(table pliante)* to fold down; *(genou, bras)* to bend ▷ *vi* to bend; *(fig)* to yield; **se ~ à** to submit to; **~ bagages** *(fig)* to pack up (and go)

plinthe [plɛ̃t] *nf* skirting board

plisser [plise] *vt (chiffonner: papier, étoffe)* to crease; *(rider: yeux)* to screw up; *(front)* to furrow, wrinkle; *(: bouche)* to pucker; *(jupe)* to put pleats in; **se plisser** *vi (vêtement, étoffe)* to crease

plomb [plɔ̃] *nm (métal)* lead; *(d'une cartouche)* (lead) shot; *(Pêche)* sinker; *(sceau)* (lead) seal; *(Élec)* fuse; **de ~** *(soleil)* blazing; **sans ~** *(essence)* unleaded; **sommeil de ~** heavy *ou* very deep sleep; **mettre à ~** to plumb

plombage [plɔ̃baʒ] *nm (de dent)* filling

plomberie [plɔ̃bʀi] *nf* plumbing

plombier [plɔ̃bje] *nm* plumber

plonge [plɔ̃ʒ] *nf:* **faire la ~** to be a washer-up *(Brit)* *ou* dishwasher *(person)*

plongeant, e [plɔ̃ʒã, -ãt] *adj (vue)* from above; *(tir, décolleté)* plunging

plongée [plɔ̃ʒe] nf (Sport) diving no pl; (: sans scaphandre) skin diving; (de sous-marin) submersion, dive; **en ~** (sous-marin) submerged; (prise de vue) high angle; **~ sous-marine** diving

plongeoir [plɔ̃ʒwaʀ] nm diving board

plongeon [plɔ̃ʒɔ̃] nm dive

plonger [plɔ̃ʒe] vi to dive ▷ vt: **~ qch dans** to plunge sth into; **~ dans un sommeil profond** to sink straight into a deep sleep; **~ qn dans l'embarras** to throw sb into a state of confusion; **se ~ dans** (études, lecture) to bury ou immerse o.s. in

plongeur, -euse [plɔ̃ʒœʀ, -øz] nm/f diver; (de café) washer-up (Brit), dishwasher (person)

ployer [plwaje] vt to bend ▷ vi to bend; (plancher) to sag

plu [ply] pp de **plaire**; **pleuvoir**

pluie [plɥi] nf rain; (averse, ondée): **une ~ brève** a shower; (fig): **~ de** shower of; **une ~ fine** fine rain; **retomber en ~** to shower down; **sous la ~** in the rain

plume [plym] nf feather; (pour écrire) (pen) nib; (fig) pen; **dessin à la ~** pen and ink drawing

plupart [plypaʀ]: **la ~** pron the majority, most (of them); **la ~ des** most, the majority of; **la ~ du temps/d'entre nous** most of the time/of us; **pour la ~** adv for the most part, mostly

pluriel [plyʀjɛl] nm plural; **au ~** in the plural

plus¹ [ply] vb voir **plaire**

⊙ MOT-CLÉ

plus² [ply] adv **1** (forme négative): **ne … plus** no more, no longer; **je n'ai plus d'argent** I've got no more money ou no money left; **il ne travaille plus** he's no longer working, he doesn't work any more

2 [ply, plyz] (+voyelle: comparatif) more, …+er; (superlatif): **le plus** the most, the …+est; **plus grand/intelligent (que)** bigger/more intelligent (than); **le plus grand/ intelligent** the biggest/most intelligent; **tout au plus** at the very most

3 [plys, plyz] (+voyelle: davantage) more; **il travaille plus (que)** he works more (than); **plus il travaille, plus il est heureux** the more he works, the happier he is; **plus de pain** more bread; **plus de 10 personnes/ trois heures/quatre kilos** more than ou over 10 people/three hours/four kilos; **trois heures de plus que** three hours more than; **plus de minuit** after ou past midnight; **de plus** what's more, moreover; **il a trois ans de plus que moi** he's three years older than me; **trois kilos en plus** three kilos more; **en plus de** in addition to; **de plus en plus** more and more; **en plus de cela …** what is more …; **plus ou moins** more or less; **ni plus ni moins** no more, no less; **sans plus** (but) no

more than that, (but) that's all; **qui plus est** what is more
▷ prép [plys]: **quatre plus deux** four plus two

plusieurs [plyzjœʀ] adj, pron several; **ils sont ~** there are several of them

plus-value [plyvaly] nf (d'un bien) appreciation; (bénéfice) capital gain; (budgétaire) surplus

plut [ply] vb voir **plaire**; **pleuvoir**

plutôt [plyto] adv rather; **je ferais ~ ceci** I'd rather ou sooner do this; **fais ~ comme ça** try this way instead; **~ que (de) faire** rather than ou instead of doing

pluvieux, -euse [plyvjø, -øz] adj rainy, wet

PME sigle fpl (= petites et moyennes entreprises) small businesses

PMU sigle m (= pari mutuel urbain) (café) betting agency; see note

⊛ PMU
⊛
⊛ The PMU ("pari mutuel urbain") is a
⊛ Government-regulated network of
⊛ betting counters run from bars
⊛ displaying the PMU sign. Punters buy
⊛ fixed-price tickets predicting winners or
⊛ finishing positions in horse races. The
⊛ traditional bet is the "tiercé", a triple bet,
⊛ although other multiple bets ("quarté"
⊛ and so on) are becoming increasingly
⊛ popular.

PNB sigle m (= produit national brut) GNP

pneu [pnø] nm (de roue) tyre (Brit), tire (US); (message) letter sent by pneumatic tube

pneumonie [pnømɔni] nf pneumonia

poche [pɔʃ] nf pocket; (déformation): **faire une/des ~(s)** to bag; (sous les yeux) bag, pouch; (Zool) pouch ▷ nm (livre de poche) (pocket-size) paperback; **de ~** pocket cpd; **en être de sa ~** to be out of pocket; **c'est dans la ~** it's in the bag; **argent de ~** pocket money

pocher [pɔʃe] vt (Culin) to poach; (Art) to sketch ▷ vi (vêtement) to bag

pochette [pɔʃɛt] nf (de timbres) wallet, envelope; (d'aiguilles etc) case; (sac: de femme) clutch bag, purse; (: d'homme) bag; (sur veston) breast pocket; (mouchoir) breast pocket handkerchief; **~ d'allumettes** book of matches; **~ de disque** record sleeve; **~ surprise** lucky bag

podcast [pɔdkast] nm (Inform) podcast

podcaster [pɔdkaste] vi (Inform) to podcast

poêle [pwal] nm stove ▷ nf: **~ (à frire)** frying pan

poème [pɔɛm] nm poem

poésie [pɔezi] nf (poème) poem; (art): **la ~** poetry

poète [pɔɛt] nm poet; (fig) dreamer ▷ adj poetic

poids [pwɑ] nm weight; (Sport) shot; **vendre au ~** to sell by weight; **de ~** adj (argument etc) weighty; **perdre/prendre du ~** to lose/put on weight; **faire le ~** (fig) to measure up; **~ plume/mouche/coq/moyen** (Boxe) feather/fly/bantam/middleweight; **~ et haltères** weight lifting sg; **~ lourd** (Boxe) heavyweight; (camion: aussi: **PL**) (big) lorry (Brit), truck (US); (: Admin) large goods vehicle (Brit), truck (US); **~ mort** dead weight; **~ utile** net weight

poignant, e [pwaɲɑ̃, -ɑ̃t] adj poignant, harrowing

poignard [pwaɲaʀ] nm dagger

poignarder [pwaɲaʀde] vt to stab, knife

poigne [pwaɲ] nf grip; (fig) firm-handedness; **à ~** firm-handed; **avoir de la ~** (fig) to rule with a firm hand

poignée [pwaɲe] nf (de sel etc, fig) handful; (de couvercle, porte) handle; **~ de main** handshake

poignet [pwaɲɛ] nm (Anat) wrist; (de chemise) cuff

poil [pwal] nm (Anat) hair; (de pinceau, brosse) bristle; (de tapis, tissu) strand; (pelage) coat; (ensemble des poils): **avoir du ~ sur la poitrine** to have hair(s) on one's chest, have a hairy chest; **à ~** adj (fam) starkers; **au ~** adj (fam) hunky-dory; **de tout ~** of all kinds; **être de bon/mauvais ~** to be in a good/bad mood; **~ à gratter** itching powder

poilu, e [pwaly] adj hairy

poinçon [pwɛ̃sɔ̃] nm awl; bodkin; (marque) hallmark

poinçonner [pwɛ̃sɔne] vt (marchandise) to stamp; (bijou etc) to hallmark; (billet, ticket) to punch, clip

poing [pwɛ̃] nm fist; **coup de ~** punch; **dormir à ~s fermés** to sleep soundly

point [pwɛ̃] nm (marque, signe) spot; (: de ponctuation) full stop, period (US); (: moment, de score etc, fig: question) point; (endroit) spot; (Couture, Tricot) stitch ▷ adv = **pas**; **ne ... ~** not (at all); **faire le ~** (Navig) to take a bearing; (fig) to take stock (of the situation); **faire le ~ sur** to review; **en tout ~** in every respect; **sur le ~ de faire** (just) about to do; **au ~ que, à tel ~ que** so much so that; **mettre au ~** (mécanisme, procédé) to develop; (appareil photo) to focus; (affaire) to settle; **à ~** (Culin) just right; (: viande) medium; **à ~ (nommé)** just at the right time; **~ de croix/tige/chaînette** (Couture) cross/stem/chain stitch; **~ mousse/jersey** (Tricot) garter/stocking stitch; **~ de départ/d'arrivée/d'arrêt** departure/arrival/stopping point; **~ chaud** (Mil, Pol) hot spot; **~ de chute** landing place; (fig) stopping-off point; **deux ~s** colon; **~ (de côté)** stitch (pain); **~ culminant** summit; (fig) height, climax; **~ d'eau** spring, water point; **~ d'exclamation** exclamation mark; **~ faible** weak spot; **~ final** full stop, period (US); **~ d'interrogation** question mark; **~ mort** (Finance) break-even point; **au ~ mort** (Auto) in neutral; (affaire, entreprise) at a standstill; **~ noir** (sur le visage) blackhead; (Auto) accident black spot; **~ de non-retour** point of no return; **~ de repère** landmark; (dans le temps) point of reference; **~ de vente** retail outlet; **~ de vue** viewpoint; (fig: opinion) point of view; **du ~ de vue de** from the point of view of; **~s cardinaux** points of the compass, cardinal points; **~s de suspension** suspension points

pointe [pwɛ̃t] nf point; (de la côte) headland; (allusion) sally; (clou) tack; (fig): **une ~ d'ail/d'accent** a touch ou hint of garlic/of an accent; **pointes** nfpl (Danse) points, point shoes; **être à la ~ de** (fig) to be in the forefront of; **faire ou pousser une ~ jusqu'à ...** to press on as far as ...; **sur la ~ des pieds** on tiptoe; **en ~** adv (tailler) into a point ▷ adj pointed, tapered; **de ~** adj (technique etc) leading; (vitesse) maximum, top; **heures/jours de ~** peak hours/days; **faire du 180 en ~** (Auto) to have a top ou maximum speed of 180; **faire des ~s** (Danse) to dance on points; **~ d'asperge** asparagus tip; **~ de courant** surge (of current); **~ de vitesse** burst of speed

pointer [pwɛ̃te] vt (cocher) to tick off; (employés etc) to check in; (diriger: canon, longue-vue, doigt): **~ vers qch, ~ sur qch** to point at sth; (Mus: note) to dot ▷ vi (employé) to clock in ou on; (pousses) to come through; (jour) to break; **~ les oreilles** (chien) to prick up its ears

pointeur, -euse [pwɛ̃tœʀ, -øz] nf timeclock ▷ nm (Inform) cursor

pointillé [pwɛ̃tije] nm (trait) dotted line; (Art) stippling no pl

pointilleux, -euse [pwɛ̃tijø, -øz] adj particular, pernickety

pointu, e [pwɛ̃ty] adj pointed; (clou) sharp; (voix) shrill; (analyse) precise

pointure [pwɛ̃tyʀ] nf size

point-virgule (pl **points-virgules**) [pwɛ̃viʀgyl] nm semi-colon

poire [pwaʀ] nf pear; (fam: péj) mug; **~ électrique** (pear-shaped) switch; **~ à injections** syringe

poireau, x [pwaʀo] nm leek

poireauter [pwaʀote] vi (fam) to hang about (waiting)

poirier [pwaʀje] nm pear tree; (Sport): **faire le ~** to do a headstand

pois [pwa] nm (Bot) pea; (sur une étoffe) dot, spot; **à ~** (cravate etc) spotted, polka-dot cpd; **~ chiche** chickpea; **~ de senteur** sweet pea; **~ cassés** split peas

poison [pwazɔ̃] nm poison

poisse [pwas] nf rotten luck

poisseux, -euse [pwasø, -øz] adj sticky

poisson [pwasɔ̃] nm fish gen inv; (Astrol): **les P~s** (signe) Pisces, the Fish; **être des P~s** to be Pisces; **pêcher ou prendre du ~ ou des ~s** to fish; **~ d'avril** April fool; (blague) April fool's day trick; see note; **~ rouge** goldfish

poissonnerie [pwasɔnʀi] nf fishmonger's
(Brit), fish store (US)

poissonnier, -ière [pwasɔnje, -jɛʀ] nm/f
fishmonger (Brit), fish merchant (US) ▷ nf
(ustensile) fish kettle

poitrine [pwatʀin] nf (Anat) chest; (seins)
bust, bosom; (Culin) breast; **~ de bœuf** brisket

poivre [pwavʀ] nm pepper; **~ en grains/
moulu** whole/ground pepper; **~ de cayenne**
cayenne (pepper); **~ et sel** adj (cheveux)
pepper-and-salt

poivron [pwavʀɔ̃] nm pepper, capsicum;
~ vert/rouge green/red pepper

polaire [pɔlɛʀ] adj polar

polar [pɔlaʀ] (fam) nm detective novel

pôle [pol] nm (Géo, Élec) pole; **le ~ Nord/Sud**
the North/South Pole; **~ d'attraction** (fig)
centre of attraction

poli, e [pɔli] adj polite; (lisse) smooth;
polished

police [pɔlis] nf police; (discipline): **assurer la
~ de** ou **dans** to keep order in; **peine de
simple ~** sentence given by a magistrates' or police
court; **~ (d'assurance)** (insurance) policy;
~ (de caractères) (Typo, Inform) font, typeface;
~ judiciaire (PJ) ≈ Criminal Investigation
Department (CID) (Brit), ≈ Federal Bureau of
Investigation (FBI) (US); **~ des mœurs** ≈ vice
squad; **~ secours** ≈ emergency services pl
(Brit), ≈ paramedics pl (US)

policier, -ière [pɔlisje, -jɛʀ] adj police cpd
▷ nm policeman; (aussi: **roman ~**) detective
novel

polio [pɔljo] nf (aussi: **~myélite**) polio ▷ nm/f
(aussi: **~myélitique**) polio patient ou case

poliomyélite [pɔljɔmjelit] nf poliomyelitis

poliomyélitique [pɔljɔmjelitik] nm/f polio
patient ou case

polir [pɔliʀ] vt to polish

polisson, ne [pɔlisɔ̃, -ɔn] adj naughty

politesse [pɔlites] nf politeness; **politesses**
nfpl (exchange of) courtesies; **rendre une ~ à
qn** to return sb's favour (Brit) ou favor (US)

politicien, ne [pɔlitisjɛ̃, -ɛn] adj political
▷ nm/f (péj) politician

politique [pɔlitik] adj political ▷ nf (science,
activité) politics sg; (principes, tactique) policy,
policies pl ▷ nm (politicien) politician;
~ étrangère/intérieure foreign/domestic
policy

politiquement [pɔlitikmɑ̃] adv politically;
~ correct politically correct

pollen [pɔlɛn] nm pollen

polluant, e [pɔlɥɑ̃, -ɑ̃t] adj polluting ▷ nm
polluting agent, pollutant; **non ~** non-
polluting

polluer [pɔlɥe] vt to pollute

pollution [pɔlysjɔ̃] nf pollution

polo [pɔlo] nm (sport) polo; (tricot) polo shirt

Pologne [pɔlɔɲ] nf: **la ~** Poland

polonais, e [pɔlɔnɛ, -ɛz] adj Polish ▷ nm
(Ling) Polish ▷ nm/f: **P~, e** Pole

poltron, ne [pɔltʀɔ̃, -ɔn] adj cowardly

polycopier [pɔlikɔpje] vt to duplicate

Polynésie [pɔlinezi] nf: **la ~** Polynesia; **la ~
française** French Polynesia

polyvalent, e [pɔlivalɑ̃, -ɑ̃t] adj (vaccin)
polyvalent; (personne) versatile; (rôle) varied;
(salle) multi-purpose ▷ nm ≈ tax inspector

pommade [pɔmad] nf ointment, cream

pomme [pɔm] nf (Bot) apple; (boule décorative)
knob; (pomme de terre): **steak ~s (frites)** steak
and chips (Brit) ou (French) fries (US); **tomber
dans les ~s** (fam) to pass out; **~ d'Adam**
Adam's apple; **~s allumettes** French fries
(thin-cut); **~ d'arrosoir** (sprinkler) rose; **~ de
pin** pine ou fir cone; **~ de terre** potato; **~s
vapeur** boiled potatoes

pommeau, x [pɔmo] nm (boule) knob; (de
selle) pommel

pommette [pɔmɛt] nf cheekbone

pommier [pɔmje] nm apple tree

pompe [pɔ̃p] nf pump; (faste) pomp (and
ceremony); **~ à eau/essence** water/petrol
pump; **~ à huile** oil pump; **~ à incendie** fire
engine (apparatus); **~s funèbres** undertaker's
sg, funeral parlour sg (Brit), mortician's sg (US)

pomper [pɔ̃pe] vt to pump; (évacuer) to pump
out; (aspirer) to pump up; (absorber) to soak up
▷ vi to pump

pompeux, -euse [pɔ̃pø, -øz] adj pompous

pompier [pɔ̃pje] nm fireman ▷ adj m (style)
pretentious, pompous

pompiste [pɔ̃pist] nm/f petrol (Brit) ou gas
(US) pump attendant

poncer [pɔ̃se] vt to sand (down)

ponctuation [pɔ̃ktɥasjɔ̃] nf punctuation

ponctuel, le [pɔ̃ktɥɛl] adj (à l'heure, Tech)
punctual; (fig: opération etc) one-off, single;
(scrupuleux) punctilious, meticulous

pondéré, e [pɔ̃deʀe] adj level-headed,
composed

pondre [pɔ̃dʀ] vt to lay; (fig) to produce ▷ vi
to lay

poney [pɔnɛ] nm pony

pont [pɔ̃] nm bridge; (Auto): **~ arrière/avant**
rear/front axle; (Navig) deck; **faire le ~** to
take the extra day off; see note; **faire un ~ d'or
à qn** to offer sb a fortune to take a job;
~ aérien airlift; **~ basculant** bascule bridge;
~ d'envol flight deck; **~ élévateur** hydraulic
ramp; **~ de graissage** ramp (in garage); **~ à
péage** tollbridge; **~ roulant** travelling crane;
~ suspendu suspension bridge; **~ tournant**
swing bridge; **P~s et Chaussées** highways
department

⁂ **FAIRE LE PONT**

The expression "faire le pont" refers to the practice of taking a Monday or Friday off to make a long weekend if a public holiday falls on a Tuesday or Thursday. The French commonly take an extra day off work to give four consecutive days' holiday at "l'Ascension", "le 14 juillet" and le "15 août".

pont-levis (pl ponts-levis) [pɔ̃lvi] nm drawbridge

pop [pɔp] adj inv pop ▷ nm: **le ~** pop (music)

populace [pɔpylas] nf (péj) rabble

populaire [pɔpylɛʀ] adj popular; (manifestation) mass cpd, of the people; (milieux, clientèle) working-class; (Ling: mot etc) used by the lower classes (of society)

popularité [pɔpylaʀite] nf popularity

population [pɔpylasjɔ̃] nf population; **~ active/agricole** working/farming population

populeux, -euse [pɔpylø, -øz] adj densely populated

porc [pɔʀ] nm (Zool) pig; (Culin) pork; (peau) pigskin

porcelaine [pɔʀsəlɛn] nf (substance) porcelain, china; (objet) piece of china(ware)

porc-épic (pl porcs-épics) [pɔʀkepik] nm porcupine

porche [pɔʀʃ] nm porch

porcherie [pɔʀʃəʀi] nf pigsty

pore [pɔʀ] nm pore

porno [pɔʀno] adj porno ▷ nm porn

port [pɔʀ] nm (Navig) harbour (Brit), harbor (US), port; (ville, Inform) port; (de l'uniforme etc) wearing; (pour lettre) postage; (pour colis, aussi: posture) carriage; **~ de commerce/de pêche** commercial/fishing port; **arriver à bon ~** to arrive safe and sound; **~ d'arme** (Jur) carrying of a firearm; **~ d'attache** (Navig) port of registry; (fig) home base; **~ d'escale** port of call; **~ franc** free port; **~ payé** postage paid

portable [pɔʀtabl] adj (vêtement) wearable; (portatif) portable; (téléphone) mobile (Brit), cell(phone) (US) ▷ nm (Inform) laptop (computer); (téléphone) mobile (phone) (Brit), cell(phone) (US)

portail [pɔʀtaj] nm gate; (de cathédrale) portal

portant, e [pɔʀtɑ̃, -ɑ̃t] adj (murs) structural, supporting; (roues) running; **bien/mal ~ in** good/bad health

portatif, -ive [pɔʀtatif, -iv] adj portable

porte [pɔʀt] nf door; (de ville, forteresse, Ski) gate; (de cathédrale) portal; **mettre à la ~** to throw out; **prendre la ~** to leave, go away; **à ma/sa ~** (tout près) on my/his (ou her) doorstep; **~ (d'embarquement)** (Aviat) (departure) gate; **~ d'entrée** front door; **~ à ~** nm door-to-door selling; **~ de secours** emergency exit; **~ de service** service entrance

porté, e [pɔʀte] adj: **être ~ à faire qch** to be apt to do sth, tend to do sth; **être ~ sur qch** to be partial to sth

porte-avions [pɔʀtavjɔ̃] nm inv aircraft carrier

porte-bagages [pɔʀtbagaʒ] nm inv luggage rack (ou basket etc)

porte-bonheur [pɔʀtbɔnœʀ] nm inv lucky charm

porte-clefs [pɔʀtəkle] nm inv key ring

porte-documents [pɔʀtdɔkymɑ̃] nm inv attaché ou document case

portée [pɔʀte] nf (d'une arme) range; (fig: importance) impact, import; (: capacités) scope, capability; (de chatte etc) litter; (Mus) stave, staff; **à/hors de ~ (de)** within/out of reach (of); **à ~ de (la) main** within (arm's) reach; **à ~ de voix** within earshot; **à la ~ de qn** (fig) at sb's level, within sb's capabilities; **à la ~ de toutes les bourses** to suit every pocket, within everyone's means

porte-fenêtre (pl portes-fenêtres) [pɔʀtəfənɛtʀ] nf French window

portefeuille [pɔʀtəfœj] nm wallet; (Pol, Bourse) portfolio; **faire un lit en ~** to make an apple-pie bed

portemanteau, x [pɔʀtmɑ̃to] nm coat rack; (cintre) coat hanger

porte-monnaie [pɔʀtmɔnɛ] nm inv purse

porte-parole [pɔʀtpaʀɔl] nm inv spokesperson

porter [pɔʀte] vt (charge ou sac etc, aussi: fœtus) to carry; (sur soi: vêtement, barbe, bague) to wear; (fig: responsabilité etc) to bear, carry; (inscription, marque, titre, patronyme: arbre: fruits, fleurs) to bear; (coup) to deal; (attention) to turn; (jugement) to pass; (apporter): **~ qch quelque part/à qn** to take sth somewhere/to sb; (inscrire): **~ qch sur** to put sth down on; to enter sth in ▷ vi (voix, regard, canon) to carry; (coup, argument) to hit home; **se porter** vi (se sentir): **se ~ bien/mal** to be well/unwell; (aller): **se ~ vers** to go towards; **~ sur** (peser) to rest on; (accent) to fall on; (conférence etc) to concern; (heurter) to strike; **être porté à faire** to be apt ou inclined to do; **elle portait le nom de Rosalie** she was called Rosalie; **~ qn au pouvoir** to bring sb to power; **~ bonheur à qn** to bring sb luck; **~ qn à croire** to lead sb to believe; **~ son âge** to look one's age; **~ un toast** to drink a toast; **~ de l'argent au crédit d'un compte** to credit an account with some money; **se ~ partie civile to** associate in a court action with the public prosecutor; **se ~ garant de qch** to guarantee sth, vouch for sth; **se ~ candidat à la députation ≈** to stand for Parliament (Brit), ≈ run for Congress (US); **se faire ~ malade** to report sick; **~ la main à son chapeau** to raise one's hand to one's hat; **~ son effort sur** tô direct one's efforts towards; **~ un fait à la connaissance de qn** to bring a fac... sb's attention ou notice

p

porteur, -euse [pɔʀtœʀ, -øz] adj (Comm) strong, promising; (nouvelle, chèque etc) ▷ **être ~ de** to be the bearer of ▷ nm/f (de messages) bearer ▷ nm (de bagages) porter; (Comm: de chèque) bearer; (: d'actions) holder; (avion) **gros ~** wide-bodied aircraft, jumbo (jet)

porte-voix [pɔʀtəvwa] nm inv megaphone, loudhailer (Brit)

portier [pɔʀtje] nm doorman, commissionnaire (Brit)

portière [pɔʀtjɛʀ] nf door

portillon [pɔʀtijɔ̃] nm gate

portion [pɔʀsjɔ̃] nf (part) portion, share; (partie) portion, section

porto [pɔʀto] nm port (wine)

portrait [pɔʀtʀɛ] nm portrait; (photographie) photograph; (fig): **elle est le ~ de sa mère** she's the image of her mother

portrait-robot [pɔʀtʀeʀobo] nm Identikit® ou Photo-fit® (Brit) picture

portuaire [pɔʀtɥɛʀ] adj port cpd, harbour cpd (Brit), harbor cpd (US)

portugais, e [pɔʀtɥgɛ, -ɛz] adj Portuguese ▷ nm (Ling) Portuguese ▷ nm/f: **P~, e** Portuguese

Portugal [pɔʀtygal] nm: **le ~** Portugal

pose [poz] nf (de moquette) laying; (de rideaux, papier peint) hanging; (attitude, d'un modèle) pose; (Photo) exposure

posé, e [poze] adj calm, unruffled

poser [poze] vt (déposer): **~ qch (sur)/qn à** to put sth down/drop sb at; (placer): **~ qch sur/quelque part** to put sth on/somewhere; (installer: moquette, carrelage) to lay; (rideaux, papier peint) to hang; (Math: chiffre) to put (down); (question) to ask; (principe, conditions) to lay ou set down; (problème) to formulate; (difficulté) to pose; (personne: mettre en valeur) to give standing to ▷ vi (modèle) to pose; to sit; **se poser** vi (oiseau, avion) to land; (question) to arise; **se ~ en** to pass o.s off as, pose as; **~ son ou un regard sur qn/qch** to turn one's gaze on sb/sth; **~ sa candidature à un poste** to apply for a post; (Pol) to put o.s up for election

positif, -ive [pozitif, -iv] adj positive

position [pozisjɔ̃] nf position; **prendre ~** (fig) to take a stand

posologie [pozɔlɔʒi] nf directions pl for use, dosage

posséder [posede] vt to own, possess; (qualité, talent) to have, possess; (bien connaître: métier, langue) to have mastered, have a thorough knowledge of; (sexuellement, aussi: suj: colère) to possess; (fam: duper) to take in

possession [posesjɔ̃] nf ownership no pl; possession; (aussi: **être/entrer en/prendre ~ de qch** to be in/take possession of sth

possibilité [posibilite] nf possibility; **possibilités** nfpl (moyens) means; (potentiel) potential sg; **avoir la ~ de faire** to be in a position to do; to have the opportunity to do

possible [posibl] adj possible; (projet, entreprise) feasible ▷ nm: **faire son ~** to do all one can, do one's utmost; **(ce n'est) pas ~!** impossible!; **le plus/moins de livres ~** as many/few books as possible; **le plus vite ~** as quickly as possible; **dès que ~** as soon as possible; **gentil** etc **au ~** as nice etc as it is possible to be

postal, e, -aux [postal, -o] adj postal, post office cpd; **sac ~** mailbag, postbag

poste¹ [post] nf (service) post, postal service; (administration, bureau) post office; **mettre à la ~** to post; **~ restante (PR)** nf poste restante (Brit), general delivery (US); **postes** nfpl post office sg; **P~s télécommunications et télédiffusion (PTT)** postal and telecommunications service; **agent** ou **employé des ~s** post office worker

poste² [post] nm (fonction, Mil) post; (Tél) extension; (de radio etc) set; (de budget) item; **~ de commandement (PC)** (Mil etc) headquarters; **~ de contrôle** checkpoint; **~ de douane** customs post; **~ émetteur** transmitting set; **~ d'essence** filling station; **~ d'incendie** fire point; **~ de péage** tollgate; **~ de pilotage** cockpit, flight deck; **~ (de police)** police station; **~ de radio** radio set; **~ de secours** first-aid post; **~ de télévision** television set; **~ de travail** work station

poster vt [poste] to post ▷ nm [pɔstɛʀ] poster; **se poster** to position o.s

postérieur, e [posteʀjœʀ] adj (date) later; (partie) back ▷ nm (fam) behind

posthume [postym] adj posthumous

postulant, e [postylɑ̃, -ɑ̃t] nm/f (candidat) applicant; (Rel) postulant

postuler [postyle] vt (emploi) to apply for, put in for ▷ vi: **~ à ou pour un emploi** to apply for a job

posture [postyʀ] nf posture, position; (fig) position

pot [po] nm (en verre) jar; (en terre) pot; (en plastique, carton) carton; (en métal) tin; (fam: chance) luck; **avoir du ~** to be lucky; **boire ou prendre un ~** (fam) to have a drink; **petit ~ (pour bébé)** (jar of) baby food; **découvrir le ~ aux roses** to find out what's been going on; **~ catalytique** catalytic converter; **~ (de chambre)** (chamber)pot; **~ d'échappement** exhaust pipe; **~ de fleurs** plant pot, flowerpot; (plante) pot plant; **à tabac** tobacco jar

potable [pɔtabl] adj (fig: boisson) drinkable; (: travail, devoir) decent; **eau (non) ~** (not) drinking water

potage [pɔtaʒ] nm soup

potager, -ère [pɔtaʒe, -ɛʀ] adj (plante) edible, vegetable cpd; **(jardin) ~** kitchen ou vegetable garden

pot-au-feu [pɔtofø] nm inv (beef) stew; (viande) stewing beef ▷ adj (fam: personne) stay-at-home

pot-de-vin (pl **pots-de-vin**) [podvɛ̃] nm bribe

pote [pɔt] nm (fam) mate (Brit), pal

poteau, x [pɔto] nm post; **~ de départ/ arrivée** starting/finishing post; **~ (d'exécution)** execution post, stake; **~ indicateur** signpost; **~ télégraphique** telegraph pole; **~x (de but)** goal-posts

potelé, e [pɔtle] adj plump, chubby

potence [pɔtɑ̃s] nf gallows sg; **en ~** T-shaped

potentiel, le [pɔtɑ̃sjɛl] adj, nm potential

poterie [pɔtʀi] nf (fabrication) pottery; (objet) piece of pottery

potier, -ière [pɔtje, jɛʀ] nm/f potter

potins [pɔtɛ̃] nmpl gossip sg

potiron [pɔtiʀɔ̃] nm pumpkin

pou, x [pu] nm louse

poubelle [pubɛl] nf (dust)bin

pouce [pus] nm thumb; **se tourner** ou **se rouler les ~s** (fig) to twiddle one's thumbs; **manger sur le ~** to eat on the run, snatch something to eat

poudre [pudʀ] nf powder; (fard) (face) powder; (explosif) gunpowder; **en ~: café en poudre** instant coffee; **savon en ~** soap powder; **lait en ~** dried ou powdered milk; **~ à canon** gunpowder; **~ à éternuer** sneezing powder; **~ à récurer** scouring powder; **~ de riz** face powder

poudreux, -euse [pudʀø, -øz] adj dusty; (neige) powdery, powder cpd

poudrier [pudʀije] nm (powder) compact

pouffer [pufe] vi: **~ (de rire)** to burst out laughing

poulailler [pulaje] nm henhouse; (Théât): **le ~** the gods sg

poulain [pulɛ̃] nm foal; (fig) protégé

poule [pul] nf (Zool) hen; (Culin) (boiling) fowl; (Sport) (round-robin) tournament; (Rugby) group; (fam) bird (Brit), chick, broad (US); (prostituée) tart; **~ d'eau** moorhen; **~ mouillée** coward; **~ pondeuse** laying hen, layer; **~ au riz** chicken and rice

poulet [pulɛ] nm chicken; (fam) cop

poulie [puli] nf pulley

pouls [pu] nm pulse; (Anat): **prendre le ~ de qn** to take sb's pulse

poumon [pumɔ̃] nm lung; **~ d'acier** ou **artificiel** iron ou artificial lung

poupe [pup] nf stern; **en ~** astern

poupée [pupe] nf doll; **jouer à la ~** to play with one's doll (ou dolls); **de ~** (très petit): **jardin de ~** doll's garden, pocket-handkerchief-sized garden

pouponnière [pupɔnjɛʀ] nf crèche, day nursery

pour [puʀ] prép for ▷ nm: **le ~ et le contre** the pros and cons; **~ faire** (so as) to do, in order to do; **~ avoir fait** for having done; **~ que** so that, in order that; **fermé ~ (cause de) travaux** closed for refurbishment ou alterations; **c'est ~ ça que ...** that's why ...; **~ quoi faire?** what for?; **~ moi** (à mon avis, pour ma part) for

my part, personally; **~ riche qu'il soit** rich though he may be; **~ 20 euros d'essence** 20 euros' worth of petrol; **~ cent** per cent; **~ ce qui est de** as for; **y être ~ quelque chose** to have something to do with it

pourboire [puʀbwaʀ] nm tip

pourcentage [puʀsɑ̃taʒ] nm percentage; **travailler au ~** to work on commission

pourchasser [puʀʃase] vt to pursue

pourparlers [puʀpaʀle] nmpl talks, negotiations; **être en ~ avec** to be having talks with

pourpre [puʀpʀ] adj crimson

pourquoi [puʀkwa] adv, conj why ▷ nm inv: **le ~ (de)** the reason (for)

pourrai etc [puʀe] vb voir **pouvoir**

pourri, e [puʀi] adj rotten; (roche, pierre) crumbling; (temps, climat) filthy, foul ▷ nm: **sentir le ~** to smell rotten

pourriel [puʀjɛl] nm (Inform) spam

pourrir [puʀiʀ] vi to rot; (fruit) to go rotten ou bad; (fig: situation) to deteriorate ▷ vt to rot; (fig: corrompre: personne) to corrupt; (: gâter: enfant) to spoil thoroughly

pourriture [puʀityʀ] nf rot

pourrons etc [puʀɔ̃] vb voir **pouvoir**

poursuite [puʀsɥit] nf pursuit, chase; **poursuites** nfpl (Jur) legal proceedings; **(course) ~** track race; (fig) chase

poursuivre [puʀsɥivʀ] vt to pursue, chase (after); (relancer) to hound, harry; (obséder) to haunt; (Jur) to bring proceedings against, prosecute; (: au civil) to sue; (but) to strive towards; (voyage, études) to carry on with, continue ▷ vi to carry on, go on; **se poursuivre** vi to go on, continue

pourtant [puʀtɑ̃] adv yet; **mais ~** but nevertheless, but even so; **c'est ~ facile** (and) yet it's easy

pourtour [puʀtuʀ] nm perimeter

pourvoir [puʀvwaʀ] nm (Comm) supply ▷ vt: **~ qch/qn de** to equip sth/sb with ▷ vi: **~ à** to provide for; (emploi) to fill; **se pourvoir** vi (Jur): **se ~ en cassation** to take one's case to the Court of Appeal

pourvoyeur, -euse [puʀvwajœʀ, -øz] nm/f supplier

pourvu, e [puʀvy] pp de **pourvoir** ▷ adj: **~ de** equipped with; **~ que** conj (si) provided that, so long as; (espérons que) let's hope (that)

pousse [pus] nf growth; (bourgeon) shoot

poussé, e [puse] adj sophisticated, advanced; (moteur) souped-up

poussée [puse] nf thrust; (coup) push; (Méd: d'acné) eruption; (fig: prix) upsurge

pousser [puse] vt to push; (acculer) to drive sb to do sth; (moteur, voiture) to drive hard; (émettre: cri etc) to give; (stimuler: élève) to urge on; to drive hard; (poursuivre: études, discussion) to carry on; (inciter): **~ qn à faire qch** (inciter) to urge ou press sb to do sth; (acculer) ▷ vi to push; (croître) to grow; (aller): **~ plus loin** to push on a bit further; **se pousser** vi to move over; **faire ~** (*plante*) to grow; **~ le dévouement** *etc* **jusqu'à ...** to take devotion *etc* as far as ...

poussette [puset] nf (*voiture d'enfant*) pushchair (*Brit*), stroller (*US*)

poussière [pusjɛʀ] nf dust; (*grain*) speck of dust; **et des ~s** (*fig*) and a bit; **~ de charbon** coaldust

poussiéreux, -euse [pusjeʀø, -øz] adj dusty

poussin [pusɛ̃] nm chick

poutre [putʀ] nf beam; (*en fer, ciment armé*) girder; **~s apparentes** exposed beams

 MOT-CLÉ

pouvoir [puvwaʀ] nm power; (*Pol: dirigeants*): **le pouvoir** those in power; **les pouvoirs publics** the authorities; **avoir pouvoir de faire** (*autorisation*) to have (the) authority to do; (*droit*) to have the right to do; **pouvoir absolu** absolute power; **pouvoir absorbant** absorbency; **pouvoir d'achat** purchasing power; **pouvoir calorifique** calorific value
▷ vb semi-aux **1** (*être en état de*) can, be able to; **je ne peux pas le réparer** I can't *ou* I am not able to repair it; **déçu de ne pas pouvoir le faire** disappointed not to be able to do it
2 (*avoir la permission*) can, may, be allowed to; **vous pouvez aller au cinéma** you can *ou* may go to the pictures
3 (*probabilité, hypothèse*) may, might, could; **il a pu avoir un accident** he may *ou* might *ou* could have had an accident; **il aurait pu le dire!** he might *ou* could have said (so)!
4 (*expressions*): **tu ne peux pas savoir!** you have no idea!; **tu peux le dire!** you can say that again!
▷ vb impers may, might, could; **il peut arriver que** it may *ou* might *ou* could happen that; **il pourrait pleuvoir** it might rain
▷ vt **1** can, be able to; **j'ai fait tout ce que j'ai pu** I did all I could; **je n'en peux plus** (*épuisé*) I'm exhausted; (*à bout*) I can't take any more
2 (*vb +adj ou adv comparatif*): **je me porte ou ne peux mieux** I'm absolutely fine, I couldn't be better; **elle est ou ne peut plus gentille** she couldn't be nicer, she's as nice as can be
se pouvoir vi: **il se peut que** it may *ou* might be that; **cela se pourrait** that's quite possible

prairie [pʀeʀi] nf meadow

praline [pʀalin] nf (*bonbon*) sugared almond; (*au chocolat*) praline

praticable [pʀatikabl] adj (*route etc*) passable, practicable; (*projet*) practicable

pratiquant, e [pʀatikɑ̃, -ɑ̃t] adj practising (*Brit*), practicing (*US*) ▷ nm/f (*regular*) churchgoer

pratique [pʀatik] nf practice ▷ adj practical; (*commode: horaire etc*) convenient; (: *outil*)

handy, useful; **dans la ~** in (actual) practice; **mettre en ~** to put into practice

pratiquement [pʀatikmɑ̃] adv (*dans la pratique*) in practice; (*pour ainsi dire*) practically, virtually

pratiquer [pʀatike] vt to practise (*Brit*), practice (*US*); (*l'équitation, la pêche*) to go in for; (*le golf, football*) to play; (*appliquer: méthode, théorie*) to apply; (*intervention, opération*) to carry out; (*ouverture, abri*) to make ▷ vi (*Rel*) to be a churchgoer

pré [pʀe] nm meadow

préalable [pʀealabl] adj preliminary; **condition ~ (de)** precondition (for), prerequisite (for); **sans avis ~** without prior *ou* previous notice; **au ~** first, beforehand

préambule [pʀeɑ̃byl] nm preamble; (*fig*) prelude; **sans ~** straight away

préau, x [pʀeo] nm (*d'une cour d'école*) covered playground; (*d'un monastère, d'une prison*) inner courtyard

préavis [pʀeavi] nm notice; **~ de congé** notice; **communication avec ~** (*Tél*) personal *ou* person-to-person call

précaution [pʀekosjɔ̃] nf precaution; **avec ~** cautiously; **prendre des** *ou* **ses ~s** to take precautions; **par ~** as a precaution; **pour plus de ~** to be on the safe side; **~s oratoires** carefully phrased remarks

précédemment [pʀesedamɑ̃] adv before, previously

précédent, e [pʀesedɑ̃, -ɑ̃t] adj previous ▷ nm precedent; **sans ~** unprecedented; **le jour ~** the day before, the previous day

précéder [pʀesede] vt to precede; (*marcher ou rouler devant*) to be in front of; (*arriver avant*) to get ahead of

précepteur, -trice [pʀesɛptœʀ, -tʀis] nm/f (*private*) tutor

prêcher [pʀeʃe] vt, vi to preach

précieux, -euse [pʀesjø, -øz] adj precious; (*collaborateur, conseils*) invaluable; (*style, écrivain*) précieux, precious

précipice [pʀesipis] nm drop, chasm; (*fig*) abyss; **au bord du ~** at the edge of the precipice

précipitamment [pʀesipitamɑ̃] adv hurriedly, hastily

précipitation [pʀesipitasjɔ̃] nf (*hâte*) haste; **~s (atmosphériques)** precipitation sg

précipité, e [pʀesipite] adj (*respiration*) fast; (*pas*) hurried; (*départ*) hasty

précipiter [pʀesipite] vt (*faire tomber*): **~ qn/ qch du haut de** to throw *ou* hurl sb/sth off *ou* from; (*hâter: marche*) to quicken; (: *départ*) to hasten; **se précipiter** vi (*événements*) to move faster; (*respiration*) to speed up; **se ~ sur/vers** to rush at/towards; **se ~ au-devant de qn** to throw o.s. before sb

précis, e [pʀesi, -iz] adj precise; (*tir, mesures*) accurate, precise; **à 4 heures ~es** at 4 o'clock sharp ▷ nm handbook

précisément [pResizemɑ̃] adv precisely; **ma vie n'est pas ~ distrayante** my life is not exactly entertaining

préciser [pResize] vt (expliquer) to be more specific about, clarify; (spécifier) to state, specify; **se préciser** vi to become clear(er)

précision [pResizjɔ̃] nf precision; accuracy; (détail) point ou detail (made clear or to be clarified); **précisions** nfpl further details

précoce [pRekɔs] adj early; (enfant) precocious; (calvitie) premature

préconçu, e [pRekɔ̃sy] adj preconceived

préconiser [pRekɔnize] vt to advocate

prédécesseur [pRedesesœR] nm predecessor

prédilection [pRedileksjɔ̃] nf: **avoir une ~ pour** to be partial to; **de ~** favourite (Brit), favorite (US)

prédire [pRediR] vt to predict

prédominer [pRedɔmine] vi to predominate; (avis) to prevail

préface [pRefas] nf preface

préfecture [pRefEktyR] nf prefecture; see note; **~ de police** police headquarters

préférable [pRefeRabl] adj preferable

préféré, e [pRefeRe] adj, nm/f favourite (Brit), favorite (US)

préférence [pRefeRɑ̃s] nf preference; **de ~** preferably; **de** ou **par ~ à** in preference to, rather than; **donner la ~ à** to give preference to sb; **par ordre de ~** in order of preference; **obtenir la ~ sur** to have preference over

préférer [pRefeRe] vt: **~ qn/qch (à)** to prefer sb/sth (to), like sb/sth better (than); **~ faire** to prefer to do; **je préférerais du thé** I would rather have tea, I'd prefer tea

préfet [pRefE] nm prefect; **~ de police** = Chief Constable (Brit), = Police Commissioner (US)

préhistorique [pReistɔRik] adj prehistoric

préjudice [pRezydis] nm (matériel) loss; (moral) harm no pl; **porter ~ à** to harm, be detrimental to; **au ~ de** at the expense of

préjugé [pRezyze] nm prejudice; **avoir un ~ contre** to be prejudiced against; **bénéficier d'un ~ favorable** to be viewed favourably

préjuger [pRezyze] : **~ de** vt to prejudge

prélasser [pRelase] : **se prélasser** vi to lounge

prélèvement [pRelEvmɑ̃] nm (montant) deduction; withdrawal; **faire un ~ de sang** to take a blood sample

prélever [pRelve] vt (échantillon) to take; **~ (sur)** (argent) to deduct (from); (: sur son compte) to withdraw (from)

prématuré, e [pRematyRe] adj premature; (retraite) early ▷ nm premature baby

premier, -ière [pRəmje, -jɛR] adj first; (rang) front; (branche, marche, grade) bottom; (fig: fondamental) basic; prime; (en importance) first, foremost ▷ nm (premier étage) first (Brit) ou second (US) floor ▷ nf (Auto) first (gear); (Rail, Aviat etc) first class; (Scol) year 12 (Brit), eleventh grade (US); (Théât) first night; (Ciné) première; (exploit) first; **au ~ abord** at first sight; **au** ou **du ~ coup** at the first attempt ou go; **de ~ ordre** first-class, first-rate; **de première qualité, de ~ choix** best ou top quality; **de première importance** of the highest importance; **de première nécessité** absolutely essential; **le ~ venu** the first person to come along; **jeune ~** leading man; **le ~ de l'an** New Year's Day; **enfant du ~ lit** child of a first marriage; **en ~ lieu** in the first place; **~ âge** (d'un enfant) the first three months (of life); **P~ Ministre** Prime Minister

premièrement [pRəmjɛRmɑ̃] adv firstly

prémonition [pRemɔnisjɔ̃] nf premonition

prémunir [pRemyniR]: **se prémunir** vi: **~ contre** to protect o.s. from, guard against

prenant, e [pRənɑ̃, -ɑ̃t] vb voir **prendre** ▷ adj absorbing, engrossing

prénatal, e [pRenatal] adj (Méd) antenatal; (allocation) maternity cpd

prendre [pRɑ̃dR] vt to take; (repas) to have; (aller chercher) to get, fetch; (se procurer) to get; (réserver: place) to book; (acquérir: du poids, de la valeur) to put on, gain; (malfaiteur, poisson) to catch; (passager) to pick up; (personnel, aussi: couleur, goût) to take on; (locataire) to take in; (traiter: enfant, problème) to handle; (voix, ton) to put on; (prélever: pourcentage, argent) to take off; (ôter): **~ qch à** to take sth from; (coincer): **se ~ les doigts dans** to get one's fingers caught in ▷ vi (liquide, ciment) to set; (greffe, vaccin) to take; (mensonge) to be successful; (feu: foyer) to go; (: incendie) to start; (allumette) to light; (se diriger): **~ à gauche** to turn (to the) left; **~ froid** to catch cold; **~ son origine** ou **sa source** (mot, rivière) to have its source; **~ qn pour** to take sb for; **se ~ pour** to think one is; **~ sur soi de faire qch** to take it upon o.s. to do sth; **~ qn en sympathie/horreur** to get to like/ loathe sb; **à tout ~** all things considered; **s'en ~ à** (agresser) to set about; (passer sa colère sur) to take it out on; (critiquer) to attack; (remettre en question) to challenge; **se ~ d'amitié/ d'affection pour** to befriend/become fond of; **s'y ~** (procéder) to set about it; **s'y ~ à l'avance** to see to it in advance; **s'y ~ à deux fois** to try twice, make two attempts

preneur [pRənœR] nm: **être ~** to be willing to buy; **trouver ~** to find a buyer

preniez [pRənje] vb voir **prendre**

prenne etc [pʀɛn] vb voir **prendre**

prénom [pʀenɔ̃] nm first name

préoccupation [pʀeɔkypasjɔ̃] nf (souci) concern; (idée fixe) preoccupation

préoccuper [pʀeɔkype] vt (tourmenter, tracasser) to concern; (absorber, obséder) to preoccupy; **se ~ de qch** to be concerned about sth; to show concern about sth

préparatifs [pʀepaʀatif] nmpl preparations

préparation [pʀepaʀasjɔ̃] nf preparation; (Scol) piece of homework

préparer [pʀepaʀe] vt to prepare; (café, repas) to make; (examen) to prepare for; (voyage, entreprise) to plan; **se préparer** vi (orage, tragédie) to brew, be in the air; **se ~ (à qch/à faire)** to prepare (o.s.) ou get ready (for sth/to do); **~ qch à qn** (surprise etc) to have sth in store for sb; **~ qn à qch** (nouvelle etc) to prepare sb for sth

prépondérant, e [pʀepɔ̃deʀɑ̃, -ɑ̃t] adj major, dominating; **voix ~e** casting vote

préposé, e [pʀepoze] adj: **~ à** in charge of ▷ nm/f (gén: employé) employee; (Admin: facteur) postman/woman (Brit), mailman/woman (US); (de la douane etc) official; (de vestiaire) attendant

préposition [pʀepozisjɔ̃] nf preposition

près [pʀɛ] adv near, close; **~ de** prép near (to), close to; (environ) nearly, almost; **~ d'ici** near here; **de ~** adv closely; **à cinq kg ~** to within about five kg; **à cela ~ que** apart from the fact that; **je ne suis pas ~ de lui pardonner** I'm nowhere near ready to forgive him; **on n'est pas à un jour ~** one day (either way) won't make any difference, we're not going to quibble over the odd day; **il n'est pas à 10 minutes ~** he can spare 10 minutes

présage [pʀezaʒ] nm omen

présager [pʀezaʒe] vt (prévoir) to foresee; (annoncer) to portend

presbyte [pʀɛsbit] adj long-sighted (Brit), far-sighted (US)

presbytère [pʀɛsbiteʀ] nm presbytery

prescription [pʀɛskʀipsjɔ̃] nf (instruction) order, instruction; (Méd, Jur) prescription

prescrire [pʀɛskʀiʀ] vt to prescribe; **se prescrire** vi (Jur) to lapse

présence [pʀezɑ̃s] nf presence; (au bureau etc) attendance; **en ~** face to face; **en ~ de** in (the) presence of; (fig) in the face of; **faire acte de ~** to put in a token appearance; **~ d'esprit** presence of mind

présent, e [pʀezɑ̃, -ɑ̃t] adj, nm present; (Admin, Comm): **la ~e lettre/loi** this letter/law ▷ nm/f: **les ~s** (personnes) those present ▷ nf (Comm: lettre): **la ~e** this letter; **à ~** now, at present; **dès à ~** here and now; **jusqu'à ~** up till now, until now; **à ~ que** now that

présentation [pʀezɑ̃tasjɔ̃] nf presentation; (de nouveau venu) introduction; (allure) appearance; **faire les ~s** to do the introductions

présenter [pʀezɑ̃te] vt to present; (invité, candidat) to introduce; (félicitations, condoléances) to offer; (montrer: billet, pièce d'identité) to show, produce; (faire inscrire: candidat) to put forward; (soumettre) to submit; **~ qn à** to introduce sb to ▷ vi: **~ mal/bien** to have an unattractive/a pleasing appearance; **se présenter** vi (sur convocation) to report, come; (se faire connaître) to come forward; (à une élection) to stand; (occasion) to arise; **se ~ à un examen** to sit an exam; **se ~ bien/mal** to look good/not too good; **je vous présente Nadine** this is Nadine

préservatif [pʀezeʀvatif] nm condom, sheath

préserver [pʀezeʀve] vt: **~ de** (protéger) to protect from; (sauver) to save from

président [pʀezidɑ̃] nm (Pol) president; (d'une assemblée, Comm) chairman; **~ directeur général (PDG)** chairman and managing director (Brit), chairman and president (US); **~ du jury** (Jur) foreman of the jury; (d'examen) chief examiner

présidentiel, le [pʀezidɑ̃sjɛl] adj presidential; **présidentielles** nfpl presidential election(s)

présider [pʀezide] vt to preside over; (dîner) to be the guest of honour (Brit) ou honor (US) at; **~ à** vt to direct; to govern

présomptueux, -euse [pʀezɔ̃ptɥø, -øz] adj presumptuous

presque [pʀɛsk] adv almost, nearly; **~ rien** hardly anything; **~ pas** hardly (at all); **~ pas de** hardly any; **personne, ou ~** next to nobody, hardly anyone; **la ~ totalité (de)** almost ou nearly all

presqu'île [pʀɛskil] nf peninsula

pressant, e [pʀesɑ̃, -ɑ̃t] adj urgent; (personne) insistent; **se faire ~** to become insistent

presse [pʀɛs] nf press; (affluence): **heures de ~** busy times; **sous ~** gone to press; **mettre sous ~** to send to press; **avoir une bonne/mauvaise ~** to have a good/bad press; **~ féminine** women's magazines pl; **~ d'information** quality newspapers pl

pressé, e [pʀese] adj in a hurry; (air) hurried; (besogne) urgent ▷ nm: **aller au plus ~** to see to first things first; **être ~ de faire qch** to be in a hurry to do sth; **orange ~e** freshly squeezed orange juice

pressentiment [pʀesɑ̃timɑ̃] nm foreboding, premonition

pressentir [pʀesɑ̃tiʀ] vt to sense; (prendre contact avec) to approach

presse-papiers [pʀɛspapje] nm inv paperweight

presser [pʀese] vt (fruit, éponge) to squeeze; (interrupteur, bouton) to press, push; (allure, affaire) to speed up; (débiteur etc) to press; **~ qn de faire** to urge ou press sb to do ▷ vi to be urgent; **se presser** vi (se hâter) to hurry (up); (se grouper) to crowd; **rien ne presse**

there's no hurry; **se ~ contre qn** to squeeze up against sb; **le temps presse** there's not much time; **~ le pas** to quicken one's step; **~ qn entre ses bras** to squeeze sb tight

pressing [pʀɛsiŋ] *nm* (*repassage*) steam-pressing; (*magasin*) dry-cleaner's

pression [pʀɛsjɔ̃] *nf* pressure; (*bouton*) press stud (*Brit*), snap fastener; (*fam: bière*) draught beer; **faire ~ sur** to put pressure on; **sous ~** pressurized, under pressure; (*fig*) keyed up; **~ artérielle** blood pressure

prestance [pʀɛstɑ̃s] *nf* presence, imposing bearing

prestataire [pʀɛstatɛʀ] *nm/f* person receiving benefits; (*Comm*): **~ de services** provider of services

prestation [pʀɛstasjɔ̃] *nf* (*allocation*) benefit; (*d'une assurance*) cover *no pl*; (*d'une entreprise*) service provided; (*d'un joueur, artiste*) performance; **~ de serment** taking the oath; **~ de service** provision of a service; **~s familiales** ≈ child benefit

prestidigitateur, -trice [pʀɛstidiʒitatœʀ, -tʀis] *nm/f* conjurer

prestige [pʀɛstiʒ] *nm* prestige

prestigieux, -euse [pʀɛstiʒjø, -øz] *adj* prestigious

présumer [pʀezyme] *vt*: **~ que** to presume *ou* assume that; **~ de** to overrate; **~ qn coupable** to presume sb guilty

prêt, e [pʀɛ, pʀɛt] *adj* ready ▷ *nm* lending *no pl*; (*somme prêtée*) loan; **~ à faire** ready to do; **~ à tout** ready for anything; **~ sur gages** pawnbroking *no pl*

prêt-à-porter (*pl* **prêts-à-porter**) [pʀɛtapɔʀte] *nm* ready-to-wear *ou* off-the-peg (*Brit*) clothes *pl*

prétendre [pʀetɑ̃dʀ] *vt* (*affirmer*): **~ que** to claim that; (*avoir l'intention de*): **~ faire qch** to mean *ou* intend to do sth; **~ à** *vt* (*droit, titre*) to lay claim to

prétendu, e [pʀetɑ̃dy] *adj* (*supposé*) so-called

prétentieux, -euse [pʀetɑ̃sjø, -øz] *adj* pretentious

prétention [pʀetɑ̃sjɔ̃] *nf* pretentiousness; (*exigence, ambition*) claim; **sans ~** unpretentious

prêter [pʀete] *vt* (*livres, argent*): **~ qch (à)** to lend sth (to); (*supposer*): **~ à qn** (*caractère, propos*) to attribute to sb ▷ *vi*: **se prêter** (*tissu, cuir*) to give; **~ à** (*commentaires etc*) to be open to, give rise to; **se ~ à** to lend o.s. (*ou* itself) to; (*manigances etc*) to go along with; **~ assistance à** to give help to; **~ attention** to pay attention; **~ serment** to take the oath; **~ l'oreille** to listen

prétexte [pʀetɛkst] *nm* pretext, excuse; **sous aucun ~** on no account; **sous (le) ~ que/de** on the pretext that/of

prétexter [pʀetɛkste] *vt* to give as a pretext *ou* an excuse

prêtre [pʀɛtʀ] *nm* priest

preuve [pʀœv] *nf* proof; (*indice*) proof, evidence *no pl*; **jusqu'à ~ du contraire** until proved otherwise; **faire ~ de** to show; **faire ses ~s** to prove o.s. (*ou* itself); **~ matérielle** material evidence

prévaloir [pʀevalwaʀ] *vi* to prevail; **se ~ de** *vt* to take advantage of; (*tirer vanité de*) to pride o.s. on

prévenant, e [pʀevnɑ̃, -ɑ̃t] *adj* thoughtful, kind

prévenir [pʀevniʀ] *vt* (*éviter: catastrophe etc*) to avoid, prevent; (*anticiper: désirs, besoins*) to anticipate; **~ qn (de)** (*avertir*) to warn sb (about); (*informer*) to tell *ou* inform sb (about); **~ qn contre** (*influencer*) to prejudice sb against

préventif, -ive [pʀevɑ̃tif, -iv] *adj* preventive

prévention [pʀevɑ̃sjɔ̃] *nf* prevention; (*préjugé*) prejudice; (*Jur*) custody, detention; **~ routière** road safety

prévenu, e [pʀevny] *nm/f* (*Jur*) defendant, accused

prévision [pʀevizjɔ̃] *nf*: **~s** predictions; (*météorologiques, économiques*) forecast *sg*; **en ~ de** in anticipation of; **~s météorologiques** *ou* **du temps** weather forecast *sg*

prévoir [pʀevwaʀ] *vt* (*deviner*) to foresee; (*s'attendre à*) to expect, reckon on; (*prévenir*) to anticipate; (*organiser: voyage etc*) to plan; (*préparer, réserver*) to allow; **prévu pour quatre personnes** designed for four people; **prévu pour 10 h** scheduled for 10 o'clock; **comme prévu** as planned

prévoyant, e [pʀevwajɑ̃, -ɑ̃t] *vb voir* **prévoir** ▷ *adj* gifted with (*ou* showing) foresight, far-sighted

prévu, e [pʀevy] *pp de* **prévoir**

prier [pʀije] *vi* to pray ▷ *vt* (*Dieu*) to pray to; (*implorer*) to beg; (*demander*): **~ qn de faire** to ask sb to do; (*inviter*): **~ qn à dîner** to invite sb to dinner; **se faire ~** to need coaxing *ou* persuading; **je vous en prie** (*allez-y*) please do; (*de rien*) don't mention it; **je vous prie de faire** please (would you) do

prière [pʀijɛʀ] *nf* prayer; (*demande instante*) plea, entreaty; "**~ de faire ...**" "please do ..."

primaire [pʀimɛʀ] *adj* primary; (*péj: personne*) simple-minded; (: *idées*) simplistic ▷ *nm* (*Scol*) primary education

prime [pʀim] *nf* (*bonification*) bonus; (*subside*) allowance; (*Comm: cadeau*) free gift; (*Assurances, Bourse*) premium ▷ *adj*: **de ~ abord** at first glance; **~ de risque** danger money *no pl*; **~ de transport** travel allowance

primer [pʀime] *vt* (*l'emporter sur*) to prevail over; (*récompenser*) to award a prize to ▷ *vi* to dominate, prevail

primeur [pʀimœʀ] *nf*: **avoir la ~ de** to be the first to hear (*ou* see etc); **primeurs** *nfpl* (*fruits, légumes*) early fruits and vegetables; **marchand de ~** greengrocer (*Brit*), produce dealer (*US*)

primevère [pʀimvɛʀ] nf primrose
primitif, -ive [pʀimitif, -iv] adj primitive; *(originel)* original ▷ nm/f primitive
primordial, e, -aux [pʀimɔʀdjal, -o] adj essential, primordial
prince [pʀɛ̃s] nm prince; ~ **charmant** Prince Charming; ~ **de Galles** nm inv *(tissu)* check cloth; ~ **héritier** crown prince
princesse [pʀɛ̃sɛs] nf princess
principal, e, -aux [pʀɛ̃sipal, -o] adj principal, main ▷ nm *(Scol)* head (teacher) *(Brit)*, principal *(US)*; *(essentiel)* main thing ▷ nf *(Ling)*: **(proposition) -e** main clause
principe [pʀɛ̃sip] nm principle; **partir du ~ que** to work on the principle *ou* assumption that; **pour le ~** on principle, for the sake of it; **de ~** adj *(hostilité)* automatic; *(accord)* in principle; **par ~** on principle; **en ~** *(habituellement)* as a rule; *(théoriquement)* in principle
printemps [pʀɛ̃tɑ̃] nm spring; **au ~** in spring
priorité [pʀijɔʀite] nf priority; *(Auto)*: **avoir la ~ (sur)** to have right of way (over); ~ **à droite** right of way to vehicles coming from the right; **en ~** as a (matter of) priority
pris, e [pʀi, pʀiz] pp de **prendre** ▷ adj *(place)* taken; *(billets)* sold; *(journée, mains)* full; *(personne)* busy; *(crème, ciment)* set; *(Méd: enflammé)*: **avoir le nez/la gorge ~(e)** to have a stuffy nose/a bad throat; *(saisi)*: **être ~ de peur/de fatigue/de panique** to be stricken with fear/overcome with fatigue/panic-stricken
prise [pʀiz] nf *(d'une ville)* capture; *(Pêche, Chasse)* catch; *(de judo ou catch, point d'appui ou pour empoigner)* hold; *(Élec: fiche)* plug; *(: femelle)* socket; *(: au mur)* point; **en ~** *(Auto)* in gear; **être aux ~s avec** to be grappling with; to be battling with; **lâcher ~** to let go; **donner ~ à** *(fig)* to give rise to; **avoir ~ sur qn** to have a hold over sb; ~ **en charge** *(taxe)* pick-up charge; *(par la sécurité sociale)* undertaking to reimburse costs; ~ **de contact** initial meeting, first contact; ~ **de courant** power point; ~ **d'eau** water (supply) point; tap; ~ **multiple** adaptor; ~ **d'otages** hostage-taking; ~ **à partie** *(Jur)* action against a judge; ~ **péritel** SCART socket; ~ **de sang** blood test; ~ **de son** sound recording; ~ **de tabac** pinch of snuff; ~ **de terre** earth; ~ **de vue** *(photo)* shot; *(action)*: ~ **de vue(s)** filming, shooting
priser [pʀize] vt *(tabac, héroïne)* to take; *(estimer)* to prize, value ▷ vi to take snuff
prison [pʀizɔ̃] nf prison; **aller/être en ~** to go to/be in prison *ou* jail; **faire de la ~** to serve time; **être condamné à cinq ans de ~** to be sentenced to five years' imprisonment *ou* five years in prison
prisonnier, -ière [pʀizɔnje, -jɛʀ] nm/f prisoner ▷ adj captive; **faire qn ~** to take sb prisoner
prit [pʀi] vb voir **prendre**

privé, e [pʀive] adj private; *(en punition)*: **tu es ~ de télé!** no TV for you!; *(dépourvu)*: ~ **de** without, lacking; **en ~** *(Comm)* private sector; **en ~**, **dans le ~** in private
priver [pʀive] vt: ~ **qn de** to deprive sb of; **se ~ de** to go *ou* do without; **ne pas se ~ de faire** not to refrain from doing
privilège [pʀivilɛʒ] nm privilege
prix [pʀi] nm *(valeur)* price; *(récompense, Scol)* prize; **mettre à ~** to set a reserve *(Brit)* ou upset *(US)* price on; **au ~ fort** at a very high price; **acheter qch à ~ d'or** to pay a (small) fortune for sth; **hors de ~** exorbitantly priced; **à aucun ~** not at any price; **à tout ~** at all costs; **grand ~** *(Sport)* Grand Prix; ~ **d'achat/de vente/de revient** purchasing/selling/cost price; ~ **conseillé** manufacturer's recommended price (MRP)
probable [pʀɔbabl] adj likely, probable
probablement [pʀɔbabləmɑ̃] adv probably
probant, e [pʀɔbɑ̃, -ɑ̃t] adj convincing
problème [pʀɔblɛm] nm problem
procédé [pʀɔsede] nm *(méthode)* process; *(comportement)* behaviour no pl *(Brit)*, behavior no pl *(US)*
procéder [pʀɔsede] vi to proceed; *(moralement)* to behave; ~ **à** vt to carry out
procès [pʀɔsɛ] nm *(Jur)* trial; *(: poursuites)* proceedings pl; **être en ~ avec** to be involved in a lawsuit with; **faire le ~ de qn/qch** *(fig)* to put sb/sth on trial; **sans autre forme de ~** without further ado
processus [pʀɔsesys] nm process
procès-verbal, -aux [pʀɔsevɛʀbal, -o] nm *(constat)* statement; *(aussi:* **PV***)*: **avoir un ~** to get a parking ticket; to be booked; *(de réunion)* minutes pl
prochain, e [pʀɔʃɛ̃, -ɛn] adj next; *(proche: départ, arrivée)* impending; near ▷ nm fellow man; **la ~e fois/semaine ~e** next time/week; **à la ~e!** *(fam)*: **à la ~e fois** see you!, till the next time!; **un ~ jour** (some day) soon
prochainement [pʀɔʃɛnmɑ̃] adv soon, shortly
proche [pʀɔʃ] adj nearby; *(dans le temps)* imminent; close at hand; *(parent, ami)* close; **proches** nmpl *(parents)* close relatives, next of kin; *(amis)*: **l'un de ses ~s** one of those close to him *(ou* her); **être ~ (de)** to be near, be close (to); **de ~ en ~** gradually
proclamer [pʀɔklame] vt to proclaim; *(résultat d'un examen)* to announce
procuration [pʀɔkyʀasjɔ̃] nf proxy; power of attorney; **voter par ~** to vote by proxy
procurer [pʀɔkyʀe] vt *(fournir)*: ~ **qch à qn** to get *ou* obtain sth for sb; *(causer: plaisir etc)*: ~ **qch à qn** to bring *ou* give sb sth; **se procurer** vt to get
procureur [pʀɔkyʀœʀ] nm public prosecutor; ~ **général** public prosecutor (in appeal court)
prodige [pʀɔdiʒ] nm *(miracle, merveille)* marvel, wonder; *(personne)* prodigy

prodiguer [prɔdige] vt (argent, biens) to be lavish with; (soins, attentions): ~ **qch à qn** to lavish sth on sb

producteur, -trice [prɔdyktœr, -tris] adj: ~ **de blé** wheat-producing; (Ciné): **société productrice** film ou movie company ▷ nm/f producer

productif, -ive [prɔdyktif, -iv] adj productive

production [prɔdyksjɔ̃] nf (gén) production; (rendement) output; (produits) products pl, goods pl; (œuvres): **la ~ dramatique du XVIIe siècle** the plays of the 17th century

productivité [prɔdyktivite] nf productivity

produire [prɔdɥir] vt, vi to produce; **se produire** vi (acteur) to perform, appear; (événement) to happen, occur

produit, e [prɔdɥi, -it] pp de **produire** ▷ nm (gén) product; ~ **chimique** chemical; ~ **d'entretien** cleaning product; ~ **national brut (PNB)** gross national product (GNP); ~ **net** net profit; ~ **pour la vaisselle** washing-up (Brit) ou dish-washing (US) liquid; ~ **des ventes** income from sales; ~**s agricoles** farm produce sg; ~**s alimentaires** foodstuffs; ~**s de beauté** beauty products, cosmetics

prof [prɔf] nm (fam: = professeur) teacher; professor; lecturer

profane [prɔfan] adj (Rel) secular; (ignorant, non initié) uninitiated ▷ nm/f layman

proférer [prɔfere] vt to utter

professeur, e [prɔfesœr] nm/f teacher; (titulaire d'une chaire) professor; ~ **(de faculté)** (university) lecturer

profession [prɔfesjɔ̃] nf (libérale) profession; (gén) occupation; **faire ~ de** (opinion, religion) to profess; **de ~** by profession; **"sans ~"** "unemployed", (femme mariée) "housewife"

professionnel, le [prɔfesjɔnɛl] adj professional ▷ nm/f professional; (ouvrier qualifié) skilled worker

profil [prɔfil] nm profile; (d'une voiture) line, contour; **de ~** in profile

profit [prɔfi] nm (avantage) benefit, advantage; (Comm, Finance) profit; **au ~ de** in aid of; **tirer ou retirer ~ de** to profit from; **mettre à ~** to take advantage of; to turn to good account; ~**s et pertes** (Comm) profit and loss(es)

profitable [prɔfitabl] adj (utile) beneficial; (lucratif) profitable

profiter [prɔfite] vi: ~ **de** (situation, occasion) to take advantage of; (vacances, jeunesse etc) to make the most of; ~ **de ce que ...** to take advantage of the fact that ...; ~ **à** to be of benefit to, benefit; to be profitable to

profond, e [prɔfɔ̃, -ɔ̃d] adj deep; (méditation, mépris) profound; **peu ~** (eau, vallée, puits) shallow; (coupure) superficial; **au plus ~ de** in the depths of, at the (very) bottom of; **la France ~e** the heartlands of France

profondément [prɔfɔ̃demɑ̃] adv deeply; profoundly; **il dort ~** he is sound asleep

profondeur [prɔfɔ̃dœr] nf depth; **l'eau a quelle ~?** how deep is the water?

progéniture [prɔʒenityr] nf offspring inv

programme [prɔgram] nm programme (Brit), program (US); (TV, Radio) program(me)s pl; (Scol) syllabus, curriculum; (Inform) program; **au ~ de ce soir** (TV) among tonight's program(me)s

programmer [prɔgrame] vt (TV, Radio) to put on, show; (organiser, prévoir: émission) to schedule; (Inform) to program

programmeur, -euse [prɔgramœr, -øz] nm/f (computer) programmer

progrès [prɔgrɛ] nm progress no pl; **faire des/être en ~** to make/be making progress

progresser [prɔgrese] vi to progress; (troupes etc) to make headway ou progress

progressif, -ive [prɔgresif, -iv] adj progressive

prohiber [prɔibe] vt to prohibit, ban

proie [prwa] nf prey no pl; **être la ~ de** to fall prey to; **être en ~ à** (doutes, sentiment) to be prey to; (douleur, mal) to be suffering

projecteur [prɔʒɛktœr] nm projector; (de théâtre, cirque) spotlight

projectile [prɔʒɛktil] nm missile; (d'arme) projectile, bullet (ou shell etc)

projection [prɔʒɛksjɔ̃] nf projection; (séance) showing; **conférence avec ~s** lecture with slides (ou a film)

projet [prɔʒɛ] nm plan; (ébauche) draft; **faire des ~s** to make plans; ~ **de loi** bill

projeter [prɔʒte] vt (envisager) to plan; (film, photos) to project; (passer) to show; (ombre, lueur) to throw, cast, project; (jeter) to throw up (ou off ou out); ~ **de faire qch** to plan to do sth

prolétaire [prɔletɛr] adj, nm/f proletarian

prolongation [prɔlɔ̃gasjɔ̃] nf extension; **prolongements** nmpl (fig) repercussions, effects; **dans le ~ de** running on from

prolonger [prɔlɔ̃ʒe] vt (débat, séjour) to prolong; (délai, billet, rue) to extend; (chose) to be a continuation ou an extension of; **se prolonger** vi to go on

promenade [prɔmnad] nf walk (ou drive ou ride); **faire une ~** to go for a walk; **une ~ (à pied)/en voiture/à vélo** a walk/drive/ (bicycle) ride

promener [prɔmne] vt (personne, chien) to take out for a walk; (fig) to carry around; to trail round; (doigts, regard): ~ **qch sur** to run sth over; **se promener** vi (à pied) to go for (ou be out for) a walk; (en voiture) to go for (ou be out for) a drive; (fig): **se ~ sur** to wander over

promesse [prɔmɛs] nf promise; ~ **d'achat** commitment to buy

promettre [prɔmɛtr] vt to promise ▷ vi (récolte, arbre) to look promising; (enfant, musicien) to be promising; **se ~ de faire** to resolve ou mean to do; ~ **à qn de faire** to promise sb that one will do

promiscuité [prɔmiskɥite] *nf* crowding; lack of privacy

promontoire [prɔmɔ̃twar] *nm* headland

promoteur, -trice [prɔmɔtœr, -tris] *nm/f* (*instigateur*) instigator, promoter; **~ (immobilier)** property developer (*Brit*), real estate promoter (*US*)

promotion [prɔmosjɔ̃] *nf* (*avancement*) promotion; (*Scol*) year (*Brit*), class; **en ~** (*Comm*) on promotion, on (special) offer

promouvoir [prɔmuvwar] *vt* to promote

prompt, e [prɔ̃, prɔ̃t] *adj* swift, rapid; (*intervention, changement*) sudden; **~ à faire qch** quick to do sth

prôner [prone] *vt* (*louer*) to laud, extol; (*préconiser*) to advocate, commend

pronom [prɔnɔ̃] *nm* pronoun

prononcer [prɔnɔ̃se] *vt* (*son, mot, jugement*) to pronounce; (*dire*) to utter; (*discours*) to deliver ▷ *vi* (*Jur*) to deliver *ou* give a verdict; **~ bien/ mal** to have good/poor pronunciation; **se prononcer** *vi* to be pronounced; **se ~ (sur)** (*se décider*) to reach a decision (on *ou* about), give a verdict (on); **se ~ contre** to come down against; **ça se prononce comment?** how do you pronounce this?

prononciation [prɔnɔ̃sjasjɔ̃] *nf* pronunciation

pronostic [prɔnɔstik] *nm* (*Méd*) prognosis; (*fig: aussi:* **~s**) forecast

propagande [prɔpagɑ̃d] *nf* propaganda; **faire de la ~ pour qch** to plug *ou* push sth

propager [prɔpaʒe] *vt* to spread; **se propager** *vi* to spread; (*Physique*) to be propagated

prophète [prɔfɛt], **prophétesse** [prɔfetɛs] *nm/f* prophet(ess)

prophétie [prɔfesi] *nf* prophecy

propice [prɔpis] *adj* favourable (*Brit*), favorable (*US*)

proportion [prɔpɔrsjɔ̃] *nf* proportion; **il n'y a aucune ~ entre le prix demandé et le prix réel** the asking price bears no relation to the real price; **à ~ de** proportionally to, in proportion to; **en ~ (de)** in proportion (to); **hors de ~** out of proportion; **toute(s) ~(s) gardée(s)** making due allowance(s)

propos [prɔpo] *nm* (*paroles*) talk *no pl*, remark; (*intention, but*) intention, aim; (*sujet*): **à quel ~?** what about?; **à ~ de** about, regarding; **à tout ~** for no reason at all; **à ce ~** on that subject, in this connection; **à ~** *adv* by the way; (*opportunément*) (just) at the right moment; **hors de ~, mal à ~** *adv* at the wrong moment

proposer [prɔpoze] *vt* (*loi, motion*) to propose; (*suggérer*): **~ qch (à qn)/de faire** to suggest sth (to sb)/doing, propose sth (to sb)/to do; (*offrir*): **~ qch à qn/de faire** to offer sb sth/to do; (*candidat*) to nominate, put forward; **se ~ (pour faire)** to offer one's services (to do); **se ~ de faire** to intend *ou* propose to do

proposition [prɔpozisjɔ̃] *nf* suggestion; proposal; offer; (*Ling*) clause; **sur la ~ de** at the suggestion of; **~ de loi** private bill

propre [prɔpr] *adj* clean; (*net*) neat, tidy; (*qui ne salit pas: chien, chat*) house-trained; (: *enfant*) toilet-trained; (*fig: honnête*) honest; (*possessif*) own; (*sens*) literal; (*particulier*): **~ à** peculiar to, characteristic of; (*approprié*): **~ à** suitable *ou* appropriate for; (*de nature à*): **~ à faire** likely to do, that will do ▷ *nm*: **recopier au ~** to make a fair copy of; (*particularité*): **le ~ de** the peculiarity of, the distinctive feature of; **au ~** (*Ling*) literally; **appartenir à qn en ~** to belong to sb (exclusively); **~ à rien** *nm/f* (*péj*) good-for-nothing

proprement [prɔprəmɑ̃] *adv* (*avec propreté*) cleanly; neatly, tidily; **à ~ parler** strictly speaking; **le village ~ dit** the actual village, the village itself

propreté [prɔprəte] *nf* cleanliness, cleanness; neatness, tidiness

propriétaire [prɔprijetɛr] *nm/f* owner; (*d'hôtel etc*) proprietor(-tress), owner; (*pour le locataire*) landlord(-lady); **~ (immobilier)** house-owner; householder; **~ récoltant** grower; **~ (terrien)** landowner

propriété [prɔprijete] *nf* (*droit*) ownership; (*objet, immeuble etc*) property *gen no pl*; (*villa*) residence, property; (*terres*) property *gen no pl*, land *gen no pl*; (*qualité, Chimie, Math*) property; (*correction*) appropriateness, suitability; **~ artistique et littéraire** artistic and literary copyright; **~ industrielle** patent rights *pl*

propulser [prɔpylse] *vt* (*missile*) to propel; (*projeter*) to hurl, fling

proroger [prɔrɔʒe] *vt* to put back, defer; (*prolonger*) to extend; (*assemblée*) to adjourn, prorogue

proscrire [prɔskrir] *vt* (*bannir*) to banish; (*interdire*) to ban, prohibit

prose [proz] *nf* prose (*style*)

prospecter [prɔspɛkte] *vt* to prospect; (*Comm*) to canvass

prospectus [prɔspɛktys] *nm* (*feuille*) leaflet; (*dépliant*) brochure, leaflet

prospère [prɔspɛr] *adj* prosperous; (*santé, entreprise*) thriving, flourishing

prospérer [prɔspere] *vi* to thrive

prosterner [prɔstɛrne]: **se prosterner** *vi* to bow low, prostrate o.s

prostituée [prɔstitɥe] *nf* prostitute

prostitution [prɔstitysjɔ̃] *nf* prostitution

protecteur, -trice [prɔtɛktœr, -tris] *adj* protective; (*air, ton: péj*) patronizing ▷ *nm/f* (*défenseur*) protector; (*des arts*) patron

protection [prɔtɛksjɔ̃] *nf* protection; (*d'un personnage influent: aide*) patronage; **écran de ~** protective screen; **~ civile** state-financed civilian rescue service; **~ maternelle et infantile (PMI)** social service concerned with child welfare

protéger [prɔteʒe] *vt* to protect; (*aider, patronner: personne, arts*) to be a patron of;

(: *carrière*) to further; **se ~ de/contre** to protect o.s. from

protège-slip [pʀɔtɛʒslip] *nm* panty liner

protéine [pʀɔtein] *nf* protein

protestant, e [pʀɔtɛstã, -ãt] *adj, nm/f* Protestant

protestation [pʀɔtɛstasjɔ̃] *nf* (*plainte*) protest; (*déclaration*) protestation, profession

protester [pʀɔtɛste] *vi*: **~ (contre)** to protest (against *ou* about); **~ de** (*son innocence, sa loyauté*) to protest

prothèse [pʀɔtɛz] *nf* artificial limb, prosthesis; **~ dentaire** (*appareil*) denture; (*science*) dental engineering

protocole [pʀɔtɔkɔl] *nm* protocol; (*fig*) etiquette; **~ d'accord** draft treaty; **~ opératoire** (*Méd*) operating procedure

proue [pʀu] *nf* bow(s *pl*), prow

prouesse [pʀuɛs] *nf* feat

prouver [pʀuve] *vt* to prove

provenance [pʀɔvnãs] *nf* origin; (*de mot, coutume*) source; **avion en ~ de** plane (arriving) from

provenir [pʀɔvniʀ]: **~ de** *vt* to come from; (*résulter de*) to be due to, be the result of

proverbe [pʀɔvɛʀb] *nm* proverb

province [pʀɔvɛ̃s] *nf* province

proviseur [pʀɔvizœʀ] *nm* ≈ head (teacher) (*Brit*), ≈ principal (*US*)

provision [pʀɔvizjɔ̃] *nf* (*réserve*) stock, supply; (*avance*: à un avocat, avoué) retainer, retaining fee; (*Comm*) funds *pl* (in account); reserve; **provisions** *nfpl* (*vivres*) provisions, food *no pl*; **faire ~ de** to stock up with; **placard** *ou* **armoire à ~s** food cupboard

provisoire [pʀɔvizwaʀ] *adj* temporary; (*Jur*) provisional; **mise en liberté ~** release on bail

provisoirement [pʀɔvizwaʀmã] *adv* temporarily, for the time being

provocant, e [pʀɔvɔkã, -ãt] *adj* provocative

provoquer [pʀɔvɔke] *vt* (*défier*) to provoke; (*causer*) to cause, bring about; (: *curiosité*) to arouse, give rise to; (: *aveux*) to prompt, elicit; (*inciter*): **~ qn à** to incite sb to

proxénète [pʀɔksenɛt] *nm* procurer

proximité [pʀɔksimite] *nf* nearness, closeness, proximity; (*dans le temps*) imminence, closeness; **à ~** near *ou* close by; **à ~ de** near (to), close to

prudemment [pʀydamã] *adv* (*voir prudent*) carefully; cautiously; prudently; wisely, sensibly

prudence [pʀydãs] *nf* carefulness; caution; prudence; **avec ~** carefully; cautiously; wisely; **par (mesure de) ~** as a precaution

prudent, e [pʀydã, -ãt] *adj* (*pas téméraire*) careful, cautious, prudent; (: *en général*) safety-conscious; (*sage, conseillé*) wise, sensible; (*réservé*) cautious; **c'est plus ~** it's wiser; **ce n'est pas ~** it's risky; it's not sensible; **soyez ~** take care, be careful

prune [pʀyn] *nf* plum

pruneau, x [pʀyno] *nm* prune

prunelle [pʀynɛl] *nf* pupil; (*œil*) eye; (*Bot*) sloe; (*eau de vie*) sloe gin

prunier [pʀynje] *nm* plum tree

PS *sigle m* = **parti socialiste**; (= *post-scriptum*) PS

psaume [psom] *nm* psalm

pseudonyme [psødɔnim] *nm* (*gén*) fictitious name; (*d'écrivain*) pseudonym, pen name; (*de comédien*) stage name

psychanalyse [psikanaliz] *nf* psychoanalysis

psychiatre [psikjatʀ] *nm/f* psychiatrist

psychiatrique [psikjatʀik] *adj* psychiatric; (*hôpital*) mental, psychiatric

psychique [psiʃik] *adj* psychological

psychologie [psikɔlɔʒi] *nf* psychology

psychologique [psikɔlɔʒik] *adj* psychological

psychologue [psikɔlɔg] *nm/f* psychologist; **être ~** (*fig*) to be a good psychologist

pu [py] *pp de* **pouvoir**

puanteur [pɥãtœʀ] *nf* stink, stench

pub [pyb] *nf* (*fam*: = *publicité*): **la ~** advertising

public, -ique [pyblik] *adj* public; (*école, instruction*) state *cpd*; (*scrutin*) open ▷ *nm* public; (*assistance*) audience; **en ~** in public; **le grand ~** the general public

publicitaire [pyblisitɛʀ] *adj* advertising *cpd*; (*film, voiture*) publicity *cpd*; (*vente*) promotional ▷ *nm* adman; **rédacteur ~** copywriter

publicité [pyblisite] *nf* (*méthode, profession*) advertising; (*annonce*) advertisement; (*révélations*) publicity

publier [pyblije] *vt* to publish; (*nouvelle*) to publicize, make public

publipostage [pyblipostaʒ] *nm* mailshot, (mass) mailing

publique [pyblik] *adj f voir* **public**

puce [pys] *nf* flea; (*Inform*) chip; **carte à ~** smart card; (**marché aux) ~s** flea market *sg*; **mettre la ~ à l'oreille de qn** to give sb something to think about

pudeur [pydœʀ] *nf* modesty

pudique [pydik] *adj* (*chaste*) modest; (*discret*) discreet

puer [pɥe] (*péj*) *vi* to stink ▷ *vt* to stink of, reek of

puéricultrice [pɥeʀikyltʀis] *nf* ≈ paediatric nurse

puéril, e [pɥeʀil] *adj* childish

puis [pɥi] *vb voir* **pouvoir** ▷ *adv* (*ensuite*) then; (*dans une énumération*) next; (*en outre*): **et ~** and (then); **et ~ (après ou quoi?)** so (what?)

puiser [pɥize] *vt*: **~ (dans)** to draw (from); **~ dans qch** to dip into sth

puisque [pɥisk] *conj* since; (*valeur intensive*): **~ je te le dis!** I'm telling you!

puissance [pɥisãs] *nf* power; **en ~** *adj* potential; **deux (à la) ~ cinq** two to the power (of) five

puissant, e [pɥisã, -ãt] *adj* powerful

P

puisse etc [pɥis] vb voir **pouvoir**
puits [pɥi] nm well; **~ artésien** artesian well;
~ de mine mine shaft; **~ de science** fount of
knowledge
pull [pyl], **pull-over** [pylɔvœʀ] nm sweater,
jumper (Brit)
pulluler [pylyle] vi to swarm; (fig: erreurs) to
abound, proliferate
pulpe [pylp] nf pulp
pulvérisateur [pylveʀizatœʀ] nm spray
pulvériser [pylveʀize] vt (solide) to pulverize;
(liquide) to spray; (fig: anéantir: adversaire) to
pulverize; (: record) to smash, shatter;
(: argument) to demolish
punaise [pynɛz] nf (Zool) bug; (clou) drawing
pin (Brit), thumb tack (US)
punch [pɔ̃ʃ] nm (boisson) punch [pœnʃ] (Boxe)
punching ability; (fig) punch
punir [pyniʀ] vt to punish; **~ qn de qch** to
punish sb for sth
punition [pynisjɔ̃] nf punishment
pupille [pypij] nf (Anat) pupil ▷ nm/f (enfant)
ward; **~ de l'État** child in care; **~ de la Nation**
war orphan
pupitre [pypitʀ] nm (Scol) desk; (Rel) lectern;
(de chef d'orchestre) rostrum; **~ de commande**
control panel
pur, e [pyʀ] adj pure; (vin) undiluted; (whisky)
neat; (intentions) honourable (Brit), honorable
(US) ▷ nm (personne) hard-liner; **en ~e perte**
fruitlessly, to no avail; **c'est de la folie ~e** it's
sheer madness
purée [pyʀe] nf: **~ (de pommes de terre)**
= mashed potatoes pl; **~ de marrons**
chestnut purée; **~ de pois** (fig) peasoup(er)
purement [pyʀmɑ̃] adv purely
purgatoire [pyʀgatwaʀ] nm purgatory
purger [pyʀʒe] vt (radiateur) to flush (out),
drain; (circuit hydraulique) to bleed; (Méd, Pol) to
purge; (Jur: peine) to serve
purin [pyʀɛ̃] nm liquid manure
pur-sang [pyʀsɑ̃] nm inv thoroughbred,
pure-bred
pus [py] vb voir **pouvoir** ▷ nm pus
putain [pytɛ̃] nf (fam!) whore (!); **ce/cette ~**
de ... this bloody (Brit) ou goddamn (US) ... (!)
puzzle [pœzl] nm jigsaw (puzzle)
PV sigle m = procès-verbal
pyjama [piʒama] nm pyjamas pl (Brit),
pajamas pl (US)
pyramide [piʀamid] nf pyramid
Pyrénées [piʀene] nfpl: **les ~** the Pyrenees

q

QI sigle m (= quotient intellectuel) IQ
quadragénaire [kadʀaʒenɛʀ] nm/f (de
quarante ans) forty-year-old; (de quarante à
cinquante ans) man/woman in his/her forties
quadriller [kadʀije] vt (papier) to mark out in
squares; (Police: ville, région etc) to keep under
tight control, be positioned throughout
quadruple [k(w)adʀypl] nm: **le ~ de** four
times as much as
quadruplés, -ées [k(w)adʀyple] nm/fpl
quadruplets, quads
quai [ke] nm (de port) quay; (de gare) platform;
(de cours d'eau, canal) embankment; **être à ~**
(navire) to be alongside; (train) to be in the
station; **le Q~ d'Orsay** offices of the French
Ministry for Foreign Affairs; **le Q~ des Orfèvres**
central police headquarters
qualification [kalifikasjɔ̃] nf qualification
qualifié, e [kalifje] adj qualified; (main
d'œuvre) skilled
qualifier [kalifje] vt to qualify; (appeler):
~ qch/qn de to describe sth/sb as; **se**
qualifier vi (Sport) to qualify; **être qualifié**
pour to be qualified for
qualité [kalite] nf quality; (titre, fonction)
position; **en ~ de** in one's capacity as; **ès ~s** in
an official capacity; **avoir ~ pour** to have
authority to; **de ~** adj quality cpd; **rapport**
~-prix value (for money)
quand [kɑ̃] conj, adv when; **~ je serai riche**
when I'm rich; **~ même** (cependant, pourtant)
nevertheless; (tout de même) all the same;

~ même, il exagère! really, he overdoes it!;
~ bien même even though

quant [kɑ̃]: **~ à** prép (pour ce qui est de) as for, as
to; (au sujet de) regarding

quant-à-soi [kɑ̃taswa] nm: **rester sur son ~**
to remain aloof

quantité [kɑ̃tite] nf quantity, amount;
(Science) quantity; (grand nombre): **une** ou **des
~(s) de** a great deal of; a lot of; **en grande ~** in
large quantities; **en ~s industrielles** in vast
amounts; **du travail en ~** a great deal of
work; **~ de** many

quarantaine [kaʀɑ̃tɛn] nf (isolement)
quarantine; (âge): **avoir la ~** to be around
forty; (nombre): **une ~ (de)** forty or so, about
forty; **mettre en ~** to put into quarantine;
(fig) to send to Coventry (Brit), ostracize

quarante [kaʀɑ̃t] num forty

quart [kaʀ] nm (fraction) quarter; (surveillance)
watch; (partie): **un ~ de poulet/fromage** a
chicken quarter/a quarter of a cheese; **un ~
de beurre** a quarter kilo of butter, ≈ a half
pound of butter; **un ~ de vin** a quarter litre of
wine; **une livre un ~** ou **et ~** one and a quarter
pounds; **le ~ de** a quarter of; **~ d'heure**
quarter of an hour; **deux heures et** ou **un ~**
(a) quarter past two, (a) quarter after two
(US); **il est le ~** it's (a) quarter past ou after
(US); **une heure moins le ~** (a) quarter to
one, (a) quarter of one (US); **il est moins le ~**
it's (a) quarter to one; **être de/prendre le ~** to
keep/take the watch; **~ de tour** quarter turn;
au ~ de tour (fig) straight off; **~s de finale**
(Sport) quarter finals

quartier [kaʀtje] nm (de ville) district, area;
(de bœuf, de la lune) quarter; (de fruit, fromage)
piece; **quartiers** nmpl (Mil, Blason) quarters;
cinéma/salle de ~ local cinema/hall; **avoir ~
libre** (fig: être libre) (Mil) to have leave from
barracks; **ne pas faire de ~** to spare no one,
give no quarter; **~ commerçant/résidentiel**
shopping/residential area; **~ général (QG)**
headquarters (HQ)

quartz [kwaʀts] nm quartz

quasi [kazi] adv almost, nearly ▷ préfixe:
~-certitude near certainty

quasiment [kazimɑ̃] adv almost, (very)
nearly; **~ jamais** hardly ever

quatorze [katɔʀz] num fourteen

quatorzième [katɔʀzjɛm] num fourteenth

quatre [katʀ] num four; **à ~ pattes** on all
fours; **tiré à ~ épingles** dressed up to the
nines; **faire les ~ cent coups** to be a bit wild;
se mettre en ~ pour qn to go out of one's
way for sb; **~ à ~** (monter, descendre) four at a
time; **à ~ mains** (jouer) four-handed

quatre-vingt-dix [katʀəvɛ̃dis] num ninety

quatre-vingts [katʀəvɛ̃] num eighty

quatre-vingt-un num eighty-one

quatrième [katʀijɛm] num fourth ▷ nf (Scol)
year 9 (Brit), eighth grade (US)

quatuor [kwatɥɔʀ] nm quartet(te)

🔵 **MOT-CLÉ**

que [kə] conj **1** (introduisant complétive) that; **il
sait que tu es là** he knows (that) you're here;
je veux que tu acceptes I want you to accept;
il a dit que oui he said he would (ou it was etc)
2 (reprise d'autres conjonctions): **quand il
rentrera et qu'il aura mangé** when he gets
back and (when) he has eaten; **si vous y allez
ou que vous …** if you go there or if you …
3 (en tête de phrase: hypothèse, souhait etc): **qu'il le
veuille ou non** whether he likes it or not; **qu'il
fasse ce qu'il voudra!** let him do as he pleases!
4 (but): **tenez-le qu'il ne tombe pas** hold it
so (that) it doesn't fall
5 (après comparatif) than; as; voir aussi **plus;
aussi; autant** etc
6 (seulement): **ne … que** only; **il ne boit que
de l'eau** he only drinks water
7 (temps): **elle venait à peine de sortir qu'il
se mit à pleuvoir** she had just gone out
when it started to rain, no sooner had she
gone out than it started to rain; **il y a quatre
ans qu'il est parti** it is four years since he
left, he left four years ago
▷ adv (exclamation): **qu'il** ou **qu'est-ce qu'il
est bête/court vite!** he's so silly!/he runs so
fast!; **que de livres!** what a lot of books!
▷ pron **1** (relatif: personne) whom; (: chose) that,
which; **l'homme que je vois** the man
(whom) I see; **le livre que tu vois** the book
(that ou which) you see; **un jour que
j'étais …** a day when I was …
2 (interrogatif) what; **que fais-tu?, qu'est-ce
que tu fais?** what are you doing?; **qu'est-ce
que c'est?** what is it?, what's that?; **que
faire?** what can one do?; **que préfères-tu,
celui-ci** ou **celui-là?** which (one) do you
prefer, this one or that one?

Québec [kebɛk] n (ville) Quebec ▷ nm: **le ~**
Quebec (Province)

québécois, e [kebekwa, -waz] adj Quebec
cpd ▷ nm (Ling) Quebec French ▷ nm/f: **Q~, e**
Quebecois, Quebec(k)er

🔵 **MOT-CLÉ**

quel, quelle [kɛl] adj **1** (interrogatif: personne)
who; (: chose) what; which; **quel est cet
homme?** who is this man?; **quel est ce
livre?** what is this book?; **quel livre/
homme?** what book/man?; (parmi un certain
choix) which book/man?; **quels acteurs
préférez-vous?** which actors do you prefer?;
dans quels pays êtes-vous allé? which ou
what countries did you go to?
2 (exclamatif): **quelle surprise/coïncidence!**
what a surprise/coincidence!
3: quel(le) que soit le coupable whoever is
guilty; **quel que soit votre avis** whatever
your opinion (may be)

quelconque [kɛlkɔ̃k] *adj* (*médiocre*: *repas*) indifferent, poor; (*sans attrait*) ordinary, plain; (*indéfini*): **un ami/prétexte ~** some friend/pretext or other; **un livre ~ suffira** any book will do; **pour une raison ~** for some reason (or other)

🔵 **MOT-CLÉ**

quelque [kɛlk] *adj* **1** (*au singulier*) some; (*au pluriel*) a few, some; (*tournure interrogative*) any; **quelque espoir** some hope; **il a quelques amis** he has a few *ou* some friends; **a-t-il quelques amis?** does he have any friends?; **les quelques livres qui** the few books which; **20 kg et quelque(s)** a bit over 20 kg; **il habite à quelque distance d'ici** he lives some distance *ou* way (away) from here **2**: **quelque ... que** whatever, whichever; **quelque livre qu'il choisisse** whatever (*ou* whichever) book he chooses; **par quelque temps qu'il fasse** whatever the weather **3**: **quelque chose** something; (*tournure interrogative*) anything; **quelque chose d'autre** something else; anything else; **y être pour quelque chose** to have something to do with it; **faire quelque chose à qn** to have an effect on sb, do something to sb; **quelque part** somewhere; anywhere; **en quelque sorte** as it were ▷ *adv* **1** (*environ*): **quelque 100 mètres** some 100 metres **2**: **quelque peu** rather, somewhat

quelquefois [kɛlkəfwa] *adv* sometimes
quelques-uns, -unes [kɛlkəzœ̃, -yn] *pron* some, a few; **~ des lecteurs** some of the readers
quelqu'un [kɛlkœ̃] *pron* someone, somebody; (*tournure interrogative ou négative +*) anyone *ou* anybody; **~ d'autre** someone *ou* somebody else; anybody else
quémander [kemɑ̃de] *vt* to beg for
qu'en dira-t-on [kɑ̃diratɔ̃] *nm inv*: **le ~** gossip, what people say
querelle [kəʀɛl] *nf* quarrel; **chercher ~ à qn** to pick a quarrel with sb
quereller [kəʀele]: **se quereller** *vi* to quarrel
qu'est-ce que [kɛskə] *vb + conj voir* **que**
qu'est-ce qui [kɛski] *vb + conj voir* **qui**
question [kɛstjɔ̃] *nf* (*gén*) question; (*fig*) matter; issue; **il a été ~ de** we (*ou* they) spoke about; **il est ~ de les emprisonner** there's talk of them being jailed; **c'est une ~ de temps** it's a matter *ou* question of time; **de quoi est-il ~?** what is it about?; **il n'en est pas ~** there's no question of it; **en ~** in question; **hors de ~** out of the question; **je ne me suis jamais posé la ~** I've never thought about it; **(re)mettre en ~** (*autorité, science*) to question; **poser la ~ de confiance** (*Pol*) to ask for a vote of confidence; **~ piège** (*d'apparence facile*) trick question; (*pour nuire*) loaded question; **~ subsidiaire** tiebreaker

questionnaire [kɛstjɔnɛʀ] *nm* questionnaire
questionner [kɛstjɔne] *vt* to question
quête [kɛt] *nf* (*collecte*) collection; (*recherche*) quest, search; **faire la ~** (*à l'église*) to take the collection; (*artiste*) to pass the hat round; **se mettre en ~ de qch** to go in search of sth
quetsche [kwɛtʃ] *nf* damson
queue [kø] *nf* tail; (*fig*: *du classement*) bottom; (*: de poêle*) handle; (*: de fruit, feuille*) stalk; (*: de train, colonne, file*) rear; (*file*: *de personnes*) queue (*Brit*), line (*US*); **en ~ (de train)** at the rear (of the train); **faire la ~** to queue (up) (*Brit*), line up (*US*); **se mettre à la ~** to join the queue *ou* line; **histoire sans ~ ni tête** cock and bull story; **à la ~ leu leu** in single file; (*fig*) one after the other; **~ de cheval** ponytail; **~ de poisson**: **faire une queue de poisson à qn** (*Auto*) to cut in front of sb; **finir en ~ de poisson** (*film*) to come to an abrupt end

🔵 **MOT-CLÉ**

qui [ki] *pron* **1** (*interrogatif*: *personne*) who; (*avec préposition*) whom; (*chose, animal*) which, that; (*interrogatif indirect*: *sujet*): **je me demande ~ est là?** I wonder who is there?; (*objet*): **elle ne sait à ~ se plaindre** she doesn't know who to complain to *ou* to whom to complain; (*: chose*): **qu'est-ce ~ est sur la table?** what is on the table?; **~ est-ce ~ who?**; **~ est-ce que?** who?; **à ~ est ce sac?** whose bag is this?; **à ~ parlais-tu?** who were you talking to?, to whom were you talking?; **chez ~ allez-vous?** whose house are you going to? **2** (*relatif*: *personne*) who; (*+prép*) whom; **l'ami de ~ je vous ai parlé** the friend I told you about; **la dame chez ~ je suis allé** the lady whose house I went to **3** (*sans antécédent*): **amenez ~ vous voulez** bring who you like; **~ que ce soit** whoever it may be

quiche [kiʃ] *nf* quiche; **~ lorraine** quiche Lorraine
quiconque [kikɔ̃k] *pron* (*celui qui*) whoever, anyone who; (*n'importe qui, personne*) anyone, anybody
quiétude [kjetyd] *nf* (*d'un lieu*) quiet, tranquillity; (*d'une personne*) peace (of mind), serenity; **en toute ~** in complete peace; (*mentale*) with complete peace of mind
quille [kij] *nf* bowling, skittle (*Brit*); (*Navig*: *d'un bateau*) keel; **(jeu de) ~s** skittles *sg* (*Brit*), bowling (*US*)
quincaillerie [kɛ̃kajʀi] *nf* (*ustensiles, métier*) hardware, ironmongery (*Brit*); (*magasin*) hardware shop *ou* store (*US*), ironmonger's (*Brit*)
quincaillier, -ière [kɛ̃kaje, -jɛʀ] *nm/f* hardware dealer, ironmonger (*Brit*)
quinquagénaire [kɛ̃kazenɛʀ] *nm/f* (*de cinquante ans*) fifty-year old; (*de cinquante à soixante ans*) man/woman in his/her fifties

quinquennat [kɛ̃kena] nm five year term of office (of French President)

quintal, -aux [kɛ̃tal, -o] nm quintal (100 kg)

quinte [kɛ̃t] nf: ~ **(de toux)** coughing fit

quintuple [kɛ̃typl] nm: **le ~ de** five times as much as

quintuplés, -ées [kɛ̃typle] nm/fpl quintuplets, quins

quinzaine [kɛ̃zɛn] nf: **une ~ (de)** about fifteen, fifteen or so; **une ~ (de jours)** (deux semaines) a fortnight (Brit), two weeks; **~ publicitaire** ou **commerciale** (two-week) sale

quinze [kɛ̃z] num fifteen; **demain en ~ a** fortnight (Brit) ou two weeks tomorrow; **dans ~ jours** in a fortnight('s time) (Brit), in two weeks(' time)

quinzième [kɛ̃zjɛm] num fifteenth

quittance [kitɑ̃s] nf (reçu) receipt; (facture) bill

quitte [kit] adj: **être ~ envers qn** to be no longer in sb's debt; (fig) to be quits with sb; **être ~ de** (obligation) to be clear of; **en être ~ à bon compte** to have got off lightly; **~ à faire** even if it means doing; **~ ou double** (jeu) double or quits; (fig): **c'est du ~ ou double** it's a big risk

quitter [kite] vt to leave; (espoir, illusion) to give up; (vêtement) to take off; **se quitter** vi (couples, interlocuteurs) to part; **ne quittez pas** (au téléphone) hold the line; **ne pas ~ qn d'une semelle** to stick to sb like glue

qui-vive [kiviv] nm inv: **être sur le ~** to be on the alert

quoi [kwa] pron interrog what; **~ de neuf?** what's new?; **~?** (qu'est-ce que tu dis?) what?; (avec prép): **à ~ tu penses?** what are you thinking about?; **de ~ parlez-vous?** what are you talking about?; **à ~ bon?** what's the use? ▷ pron rel: **as-tu de ~ écrire?** do you have anything to write with?; **il n'a pas de ~ se l'acheter** he can't afford it, he hasn't got the money to buy it; **il y a de ~ être fier** that's something to be proud of; **il n'y a pas de ~** (please) don't mention it; **il n'y a pas de ~ rire** there's nothing to laugh about ▷ pron (locutions): **~ qu'il arrive** whatever happens; **~ qu'il en soit** be that as it may; **~ que ce soit** anything at all; **en ~ puis-je vous aider?** how can I help you?; **et puis ~ encore!** what(ever) next!; **~ faire?** what's to be done?; **sans ~** (ou sinon) otherwise ▷ excl what!

quoique [kwak] conj (al)though

quote-part [kɔtpaʀ] nf share

quotidien, ne [kɔtidjɛ̃, -ɛn] adj (journalier) daily; (banal) ordinary, everyday ▷ nm (journal) daily (paper); (vie quotidienne) daily life, day-to-day existence; **les grands ~s** the big (national) dailies

quotidiennement [kɔtidjɛnmɑ̃] adv daily, every day

r

R, r abr = **route; rue**

rab [ʀab], **rabiot** [ʀabjo] (fam) nm (nourriture) extra, more; **est-ce qu'il y a du ~?** are there any seconds?

rabâcher [ʀabɑʃe] vi to harp on ▷ vt to keep on repeating

rabais [ʀabɛ] nm reduction, discount; **au ~** at a reduction ou discount

rabaisser [ʀabese] vt (rabattre: prix) to reduce; (dénigrer) to belittle

Rabat [ʀaba(t)] n Rabat

rabat-joie [ʀabaʒwa] nm/f inv killjoy (Brit), spoilsport

rabattre [ʀabatʀ] vt (couvercle, siège) to pull down; (col) to turn down; (couture) to stitch down; (gibier) to drive; (somme d'un prix) to deduct, take off; (orgueil, prétentions) to humble; (Tricot) to decrease; (déduire) to reduce; **se rabattre** vi (bords, couvercle) to fall shut; (véhicule, coureur) to cut in; **se ~ sur** (accepter) to fall back on

rabbin [ʀabɛ̃] nm rabbi

râblé, e [ʀɑble] adj broad-backed, stocky

rabot [ʀabo] nm plane

rabougri, e [ʀabugʀi] adj stunted

rabrouer [ʀabʀue] vt to snub, rebuff

racaille [ʀakɑj] nf (péj) rabble, riffraff

raccommoder [ʀakɔmɔde] vt to mend, repair; (chaussette etc) to darn; (fam: réconcilier: amis, ménage) to bring together again; **se ~ (avec)** (fam) to patch it up (with)

raccompagner [Rakɔ̃paɲe] vt to take ou see back

raccord [Rakɔʀ] nm link; ~ **de maçonnerie** pointing no pl; ~ **de peinture** join; (retouche) touch-up

raccorder [Rakɔʀde] vt to join (up), link up; (pont etc) to connect, link; **se ~ à** to join up with; (fig: se rattacher à) to tie in with; ~ **au réseau du téléphone** to connect to the telephone service

raccourci [Rakuʀsi] nm short cut; **en ~** in brief

raccourcir [Rakuʀsiʀ] vt to shorten ▷ vi (vêtement) to shrink; (jours) to grow shorter, draw in

raccrocher [RakRɔʃe] vt (tableau, vêtement) to hang back up; (récepteur) to put down; (fig: affaire) to save ▷ vi (Tél) to hang up, ring off; **se ~ à** vt to cling to, hang on to; **ne raccrochez pas** (Tél) hold on, don't hang up

race [Ras] nf race; (d'animaux, fig: espèce) breed; (ascendance, origine) stock, race; **de ~** adj purebred, pedigree

rachat [Raʃa] nm buying; (du même objet) buying back; redemption; atonement

racheter [Raʃte] vt (article perdu) to buy another; (davantage): ~ **du lait/trois œufs** to buy more milk/another three eggs ou three more eggs; (après avoir vendu) to buy back; (d'occasion) to buy; (Comm: part, firme) to buy up; (: pension, rente) to redeem; (Rel: pécheur) to redeem; (: péché) to atone for, expiate; (mauvaise conduite, oubli, défaut) to make up for; **se racheter** (Rel) to redeem o.s.; (gén) to make amends, make up for it

racial, e, -aux [Rasjal, -o] adj racial

racine [Rasin] nf root; (fig: attache) roots pl; ~ **carrée/cubique** square/cube root; **prendre ~** (fig) to take root; to put down roots

racisme [Rasism] nm racism

raciste [Rasist] adj, nm/f racist

racket [Rakɛt] nm racketeering no pl

raclée [Rakle] nf (fam) hiding, thrashing

racler [Rakle] vt (os, plat) to scrape; (tache, boue) to scrape off; (fig: instrument) to scrape on; (chose: frotter contre) to scrape (against); **se ~ la gorge** to clear one's throat

racoler [Rakɔle] vt (attirer: prostituée) to solicit; (: parti, marchand) to tout for; (attraper) to pick up

racontars [Rakɔ̃taʀ] nmpl stories, gossip sg

raconter [Rakɔ̃te] vt: ~ (**à qn**) (décrire) to relate (to sb), tell (sb) about; (dire) to tell (sb); ~ **une histoire** to tell a story

racorni, e [Rakɔʀni] adj hard(ened)

radar [RadaR] nm radar; **système ~** radar system; **écran ~** radar screen

rade [Rad] nf (natural) harbour; **en ~ de Toulon** in Toulon harbour; **rester en ~** (fig) to be left stranded

radeau, x [Rado] nm raft; ~ **de sauvetage** life raft

radiateur [RadjatœR] nm radiator, heater; (Auto) radiator; ~ **électrique/à gaz** electric/gas heater ou fire

radiation [Radjasjɔ̃] nf (d'un nom etc) striking off no pl; (Physique) radiation

radical, e, -aux [Radikal, -o] adj radical ▷ nm (Ling) stem; (Math) root sign; (Pol) radical

radier [Radje] vt to strike off

radieux, -euse [Radjø, -øz] adj (visage, personne) radiant; (journée, soleil) brilliant, glorious

radin, e [Radɛ̃, -in] adj (fam) stingy

radio [Radjo] nf radio; (Méd) X-ray ▷ nm (personne) radio operator; **à la ~** on the radio; **avoir la ~** to have a radio; **passer à la ~** to be on the radio; **se faire faire une ~/une ~ des poumons** to have an X-ray/a chest X-ray

radioactif, -ive [Radjɔaktif, -iv] adj radioactive

radiocassette [Radjɔkasɛt] nf cassette radio

radiodiffuser [Radjɔdifyze] vt to broadcast

radiographie [Radjɔgʀafi] nf radiography; (photo) X-ray photograph, radiograph

radiophonique [Radjɔfɔnik] adj radio cpd; **programme/émission/jeu ~** radio programme/broadcast/game

radio-réveil [Radjɔʀevɛj] (pl **radios-réveils**) nm radio alarm (clock)

radis [Radi] nm radish; ~ **noir** horseradish no pl

radoter [Radɔte] vi to ramble on

radoucir [Radusiʀ]: **se radoucir** vi (se réchauffer) to become milder; (se calmer) to calm down; to soften

rafale [Rafal] nf (vent) gust of wind; (de balles, d'applaudissements) burst; ~ **de mitrailleuse** burst of machine-gun fire

raffermir [RafɛʀmiR] vt, **se raffermir** vi (tissus, muscle) to firm up; (fig) to strengthen

raffiner [Rafine] vt to refine

raffinerie [RafinRi] nf refinery

raffoler [Rafɔle]: ~ **de** vt to be very keen on

rafistoler [Rafistɔle] vt (fam) to patch up

rafle [Rafl] nf (de police) roundup, raid

rafler [Rafle] vt (fam) to swipe, nick

rafraîchir [RafʀeʃiR] vt (atmosphère, température) to cool (down); (aussi: **mettre à ~**) to chill; (air, eau) to freshen up; (: boisson) to refresh; (fig: rénover) to brighten up ▷ vi: **mettre du vin/une boisson à ~** to chill wine/a drink; **se rafraîchir** to grow cooler; (en se lavant) to freshen up; (personne: en buvant etc) to refresh o.s.; ~ **la mémoire à qn** to refresh sb's memory

rafraîchissant, e [Rafʀeʃisɑ̃, -ɑ̃t] adj refreshing

rafraîchissement [Rafʀeʃismɑ̃] nm cooling; (boisson) cool drink; **rafraîchissements** nmpl (boissons, fruits etc) refreshments

rage [Raʒ] nf (Méd): **la ~** rabies; (fureur) rage, fury; **faire ~** to rage; ~ **de dents** (raging) toothache

ragot [Rago] *nm (fam)* malicious gossip *no pl*

ragoût [Ragu] *nm (plat)* stew

raide [Rɛd] *adj (tendu)* taut, tight; *(escarpé)* steep; *(droit: cheveux)* straight; *(ankylosé, dur, guindé)* stiff; *(fam: cher)* steep, stiff; *(: sans argent)* flat broke; *(osé, licencieux)* daring ▷ *adv (en pente)* steeply; **~ mort** stone dead

raideur [Rɛdœr] *nf* steepness; *(rigidité)* stiffness; **avec ~** *(répondre)* stiffly, abruptly

raidir [Redir] *vt (muscles)* to stiffen; *(câble)* to pull taut, tighten; **se raidir** *vi* to stiffen; to become taut; *(personne: se crisper)* to tense up; *(: se préparer moralement)* to brace o.s.; *(fig: devenir intransigeant)* to harden

raie [Rɛ] *nf (Zool)* skate, ray; *(rayure)* stripe; *(des cheveux)* parting

raifort [Refɔr] *nm* horseradish

rail [Raj] *nm (barre d'acier)* rail; *(chemins de fer)* railways *pl* (Brit), railroads *pl* (US); **les ~s** *(la voie ferrée)* the rails, the track *sg*; **par ~** by rail; **~ conducteur** live *ou* conductor rail

railler [Raje] *vt* to scoff at, jeer at

rainure [Renyr] *nf* groove; slot

raisin [Rezɛ̃] *nm (aussi: **~s**)* grapes *pl*; *(variété)*: **~ blanc/noir** white *(ou* green)/black grape; **~ muscat** muscat grape; **~s secs** raisins

raison [Rezɔ̃] *nf* reason; **avoir ~** to be right; **donner ~ à qn** *(personne)* to agree with sb; *(fait)* to prove sb right; **avoir ~ de qn/qch** to get the better of sb/sth; **se faire une ~** to learn to live with it; **perdre la ~** to become insane; *(fig)* to take leave of one's senses; **recouvrer la ~** to come to one's senses; **ramener qn à la ~** to make sb see sense; **demander ~ à qn de** *(affront etc)* to demand satisfaction from sb for; **entendre ~** to listen to reason, see reason; **plus que de ~** too much, more than is reasonable; **~ de plus** all the more reason; **à plus forte ~** all the more so; **sans ~** for no reason; **en ~ de** *(à cause de)* because of; *(à proportion de)* in proportion to; **à ~ de** at the rate of; **~ d'État** reason of state; **~ d'être** raison d'être; **~ sociale** corporate name

raisonnable [Rezɔnabl] *adj* reasonable, sensible

raisonnement [Rezɔnmɑ̃] *nm* reasoning; arguing; argument

raisonner [Rezɔne] *vi (penser)* to reason; *(argumenter, discuter)* to argue ▷ *vt (personne)* to reason with; *(attitude: justifier)* to reason out; **se raisonner** to reason with oneself

rajeunir [Raʒœnir] *vt (coiffure, robe):* **~ qn** to make sb look younger; *(cure etc)* to rejuvenate; *(fig: rafraîchir)* to brighten up; *(: moderniser)* to give a new look to; *(: en recrutant)* to inject new blood into ▷ *vi (personne)* to become *(ou* look) younger; *(entreprise, quartier)* to be modernized

rajouter [Raʒute] *vt (commentaire)* to add; **~ du sel/un œuf** to add some more salt/another egg; **~ que** to add that; **en ~** to lay it on thick

rajuster [Raʒyste] *vt (vêtement)* to straighten, tidy; *(salaires)* to adjust; *(machine)* to readjust; **se rajuster** to tidy ou straighten o.s. up

ralenti [Ralɑ̃ti] *nm:* **au ~** *(Ciné)* in slow motion; *(fig)* at a slower pace; **tourner au ~** *(Auto)* to tick over, idle

ralentir [Ralɑ̃tir] *vt, vi*, **se ralentir** *vi* to slow down

râler [Rɑle] *vi* to groan; *(fam)* to grouse, moan (and groan)

rallier [Ralje] *vt (rassembler)* to rally; *(rejoindre)* to rejoin; *(gagner à sa cause)* to win over; **se ~ à** *(avis)* to come over ou round to

rallonge [Ralɔ̃ʒ] *nf (de table)* (extra) leaf; *(argent etc)* extra *no pl*; *(Élec)* extension (cable *ou* flex); *(fig: de crédit etc)* extension

rallonger [Ralɔ̃ʒe] *vt* to lengthen

rallye [Rali] *nm* rally; (Pol) march

ramassage [Ramasaʒ] *nm:* **~ scolaire** school bus service

ramassé, e [Ramase] *adj (trapu)* squat, stocky; *(concis: expression etc)* compact

ramasser [Ramase] *vt (objet tombé ou par terre: fam)* to pick up; *(recueillir: copies, ordures)* to collect; *(récolter)* to gather; *(: pommes de terre)* to lift; **se ramasser** *vi (sur soi-même)* to huddle up; to crouch

ramassis [Ramasi] *nm (péj: de voyous)* bunch; *(: de choses)* jumble

rambarde [Rɑ̃bard] *nf* guardrail

rame [Ram] *nf (aviron)* oar; *(de métro)* train; *(de papier)* ream; **~ de haricots** bean support; **faire force de ~s** to row hard

rameau, x [Ramo] *nm (small)* branch; *(fig)* branch; **les R~x** (Rel) Palm Sunday *sg*

ramener [Ramne] *vt* to bring back; *(reconduire)* to take back; *(rabattre: couverture, visière)*: **~ qch sur** to pull sth back over; **~ qch à** *(réduire à, Math)* to reduce sth to; **~ qn à la vie/raison** to bring sb back to life/bring sb to his *(ou* her) senses; **se ramener** *vi (fam)* to roll ou turn up; **se ~ à** *(se réduire à)* to come ou boil down to

ramer [Rame] *vi* to row

ramollir [Ramɔlir] *vt* to soften; **se ramollir** *vi (os, tissus)* to get *(ou* go) soft; *(beurre, asphalte)* to soften

ramoner [Ramɔne] *vt (cheminée)* to sweep; *(pipe)* to clean

rampe [Rɑ̃p] *nf (d'escalier)* banister(s *pl*); *(dans un garage, d'un terrain)* ramp; (Théât): **la ~** the footlights *pl*; *(lampes: lumineuse, de balisage)* floodlights *pl*; **passer la ~** *(toucher le public)* to get across to the audience; **~ de lancement** launching pad

ramper [Rɑ̃pe] *vi (reptile, animal)* to crawl; *(plante)* to creep

rancard [Rɑ̃kar] *nm (fam)* date; tip

rancart [Rɑ̃kar] *nm:* **mettre au ~** *(article, projet)* to scrap; *(personne)* to put on the scrapheap

rance [Rɑ̃s] *adj* rancid

r

rancœur [ʀɑ̃kœʀ] nf rancour (Brit), rancor (US), resentment

rançon [ʀɑ̃sɔ̃] nf ransom; (fig): **la ~ du succès** etc the price of success etc

rancune [ʀɑ̃kyn] nf grudge, rancour (Brit), rancor (US); **garder ~ à qn (de qch)** to bear sb a grudge (for sth); **sans ~!** no hard feelings!

rancunier, -ière [ʀɑ̃kynje, -jɛʀ] adj vindictive, spiteful

randonnée [ʀɑ̃dɔne] nf ride; (à pied) walk, ramble; (en montagne) hike, hiking no pl; **la ~** (activité) hiking, walking; **une ~ à cheval** a pony trek

rang [ʀɑ̃] nm (rangée) row; (de perles) row, string, rope; (grade, condition sociale, classement) rank; **rangs** nmpl (Mil) ranks; **se mettre en ~s/sur un ~** to get into ou form rows/a line; **sur trois ~s** (lined up) three deep; **se mettre en ~s par quatre** to form fours ou rows of four; **se mettre sur les ~s** (fig) to get into the running; **au premier ~** in the first row; (fig) ranking first; **rentrer dans le ~** to get into line; **au ~ de** (au nombre de) among (the ranks of); **avoir ~ de** to hold the rank of

rangé, e [ʀɑ̃ʒe] adj (vie) well-ordered; (sérieux: personne) orderly, steady

rangée [ʀɑ̃ʒe] nf row

ranger [ʀɑ̃ʒe] vt (classer, grouper) to order, arrange; (mettre à sa place) to put away; (voiture dans la rue) to park; (mettre de l'ordre dans) to tidy up; (arranger, disposer: en cercle etc) to arrange; (fig: classer): **~ qn/qch parmi** to rank sb/sth among; **se ranger** vi (se placer, se disposer: autour d'une table etc) to take one's place, sit round; (véhicule, conducteur: s'écarter) to pull over ou in; (: s'arrêter) to stop; (piéton) to step aside; (s'assagir) to settle down; **se ~ à** (avis) to come round to, fall in with

ranimer [ʀanime] vt (personne évanouie) to bring round; (revigorer: forces, courage) to restore; (réconforter: troupes etc) to kindle new life in; (douleur, souvenir) to revive; (feu) to rekindle

rap [ʀap] nm rap (music)

rapace [ʀapas] nm bird of prey ▷ adj (péj) rapacious, grasping; **~ diurne/nocturne** diurnal/nocturnal bird of prey

râpe [ʀɑp] nf (Culin) grater; (à bois) rasp

râper [ʀɑpe] vt (Culin) to grate; (gratter, râcler) to rasp

rapetisser [ʀaptise] vt: **~ qch** to shorten sth; to make sth look smaller ▷ vi, **se rapetisser** vi to shrink

rapide [ʀapid] adj fast; (prompt: intelligence, coup d'œil, mouvement) quick ▷ nm express (train); (de cours d'eau) rapid

rapidement [ʀapidmɑ̃] adv fast; quickly

rapiécer [ʀapjese] vt to patch in

rappel [ʀapɛl] nm (d'un ambassadeur, Mil) recall; (Théât) curtain call; (Méd: vaccination) booster; (Admin: de salaire) back pay no pl; (d'une aventure, d'un nom) reminder; (de limitation de vitesse: sur écriteau) speed limit sign (reminder); (Tech) return; (Navig) sitting out; (Alpinisme: aussi: **~ de corde**) abseiling no pl; roping down no pl; abseil; **à l'ordre** call to order

rappeler [ʀaple] vt (pour faire revenir, retéléphoner) to call back; (ambassadeur, Mil) to recall; (acteur) to call back (onto the stage); (faire se souvenir): **~ qch à qn** to remind sb of sth; **se rappeler** vt (se souvenir de) to remember, recall; **~ qn à la vie** to bring sb back to life; **~ qn à la décence** to recall sb to a sense of decency; **ça rappelle la Provence** it's reminiscent of Provence, it reminds you of Provence; **se ~ que...** to remember that...

rapport [ʀapɔʀ] nm (compte rendu) report; (profit) yield, return; revenue; (lien, analogie) relationship; (corrélation) connection; (proportion: Math, Tech) ratio; **rapports** nmpl (entre personnes, pays) relations; **avoir ~ à** to have something to do with, concern; **être en ~ avec** (idée de corrélation) to be related to; **être/se mettre en ~ avec qn** to be/get in touch with sb; **par ~ à** (comparé à) in relation to; (à propos de) with regard to; **sous tous (les) ~s** in all respects; **~s (sexuels)** (sexual) intercourse sg; **~ qualité-prix** value (for money)

rapporter [ʀapɔʀte] vt (rendre, ramener) to bring back; (apporter davantage) to bring more; (Couture) to sew on; (investissement) to yield; (: activité) to bring in; (relater) to report; (Jur: annuler) to revoke ▷ vi (investissement) to give a good return ou yield; (: activité) to be very profitable; (péj: moucharder) to tell; **~ qch à** (fig: rattacher) to relate sth to; **se ~ à** (correspondre à) to relate to; **s'en ~ à** to rely on

rapporteur, -euse [ʀapɔʀtœʀ, -øz] nm/f (de procès, commission) reporter; (péj) telltale ▷ nm (Géom) protractor

rapprochement [ʀapʀɔʃmɑ̃] nm (réconciliation: de nations, familles) reconciliation; (analogie, rapport) parallel

rapprocher [ʀapʀɔʃe] vt (chaise d'une table): **~ qch (de)** to bring sth closer (to); (deux objets) to bring closer together; (réunir: ennemis, partis etc) to bring together; (comparer) to establish a parallel between; **se rapprocher** vi to draw closer ou nearer; (fig: familles, pays) to come together; to come closer together; **se ~ de** to come closer to; (présenter une analogie avec) to be close to

rapt [ʀapt] nm abduction

raquette [ʀakɛt] nf (de tennis) racket; (de ping-pong) bat; (à neige) snowshoe

rare [ʀɑʀ] adj rare; (main-d'œuvre, denrées) scarce; (cheveux, herbe) sparse; **il est ~ que** it's rare that, it's unusual that; **se faire ~** to become scarce; (fig: personne) to make oneself scarce

rarement [ʀɑʀmɑ̃] adv rarely, seldom

ras, e [ʀɑ, ʀɑz] adj (tête, cheveux) close-cropped; (poil, herbe) short; (mesure, cuillère) level ▷ *adv* short; **faire table ~e** to make a clean sweep; **en ~e campagne** in open country; **à ~ bords** to the brim; **au ~ de** level with; **en avoir ~ le bol** (*fam*) to be fed up; **~ du cou** *adj* (*pull, robe*) crew-neck

rasade [ʀazad] *nf* glassful

raser [ʀɑze] *vt* (*barbe, cheveux*) to shave off; (*menton, personne*) to shave; (*fam: ennuyer*) to bore; (*démolir*) to raze (to the ground); (*frôler*) to graze, skim; **se raser** to shave; (*fam*) to be bored (to tears)

rasoir [ʀazwaʀ] *nm* razor; **~ électrique** electric shaver *ou* razor; **~ mécanique** *ou* **de sûreté** safety razor

rassasier [ʀasazje] *vt* to satisfy; **être rassasié** (*dégoûté*) to be sated; to have had more than enough

rassemblement [ʀasɑ̃bləmɑ̃] *nm* (*groupe*) gathering; (*Pol*) union; association; (*Mil*): **le ~** parade

rassembler [ʀasɑ̃ble] *vt* (*réunir*) to assemble, gather; (*regrouper, amasser: documents, notes*) to gather together, collect; **se rassembler** *vi* to gather; **ses idées/ses esprits/son courage** to collect one's thoughts/gather one's wits/screw up one's courage

rassis, e [ʀasi, -iz] *adj* (*pain*) stale

rassurer [ʀasyʀe] *vt* to reassure; **se rassurer** *vi* to be reassured; **rassure-toi** don't worry

rat [ʀa] *nm* rat; **~ d'hôtel** hotel thief; **~ musqué** muskrat

rate [ʀat] *nf* female rat; (*Anat*) spleen

raté, e [ʀate] *adj* (*tentative*) unsuccessful, failed ▷ *nm/f* (*personne*) failure ▷ *nm* misfiring *no pl*

râteau, x [ʀɑto] *nm* rake

rater [ʀate] *vi* (*ne pas partir: coup de feu*) to fail to go off; (*affaire, projet etc*) to go wrong, fail ▷ *vt* (*cible, train, occasion*) to miss; (*démonstration, plat*) to spoil; (*examen*) to fail; **~ son coup** to fail, not to bring it off

ration [ʀasjɔ̃] *nf* ration; (*fig*) share; **~ alimentaire** food intake

ratisser [ʀatise] *vt* (*allée*) to rake; (*feuilles*) to rake up; (*armée, police*) to comb; **~ large** to cast one's net wide

RATP *sigle f* (= *Régie autonome des transports parisiens*) Paris transport authority

rattacher [ʀataʃe] *vt* (*animal, cheveux*) to tie up again; (*incorporer: Admin etc*): **~ qch à** to join sth to, unite sth with; (*relier*): **~ qch à** to link sth with, relate sth to; (: *lier*): **~ qn à** to bind *ou* tie sb to; **se ~ à** (*fig: avoir un lien avec*) to be linked (*ou* connected) with

rattrapage [ʀatʀapaʒ] *nm* (*Scol*) remedial classes *pl*; (*Écon*) catching up

rattraper [ʀatʀape] *vt* (*fugitif*) to recapture; (*retenir, empêcher de tomber*) to catch (hold of); (*atteindre, rejoindre*) to catch up with; (*réparer: erreur*) to make up for; **se rattraper** *vi* (*regagner: du temps*) to make up for lost time; (: *de l'argent etc*) to make good one's losses;

(*réparer une gaffe etc*) to make up for it; **se ~ (à)** (*se raccrocher*) to stop o.s. falling (by catching hold of); **~ son retard/le temps perdu** to make up (for) lost time

rature [ʀatyʀ] *nf* deletion, erasure

rauque [ʀok] *adj* raucous; (*voix*) hoarse

ravages [ʀavaʒ] *nmpl* ravages; **faire des ~** to wreak havoc; (*fig: séducteur*) to break hearts

ravaler [ʀavale] *vt* (*mur, façade*) to restore; (*déprécier*) to lower; (*avaler de nouveau*) to swallow again; **sa colère/son dégoût** to stifle one's anger/swallow one's distaste

ravi, e [ʀavi] *adj* delighted; **être ~ de/que** to be delighted with/that

ravigoter [ʀavigɔte] *vt* (*fam*) to buck up

ravin [ʀavɛ̃] *nm* gully, ravine

ravir [ʀaviʀ] *vt* (*enchanter*) to delight; (*enlever*): **~ qch à qn** to rob sb of sth; **à ~** *adv* delightfully, beautifully; **être beau ~ à ~** to be ravishingly beautiful

raviser [ʀavize]: **se raviser** *vi* to change one's mind

ravissant, e [ʀavisɑ̃, -ɑ̃t] *adj* delightful

ravisseur, -euse [ʀavisœʀ, -øz] *nm/f* abductor, kidnapper

ravitaillement [ʀavitɑjmɑ̃] *nm* resupplying; refuelling; (*provisions*) supplies *pl*; **aller au ~** to go for fresh supplies; **~ en vol** (*Aviat*) in-flight refuelling

ravitailler [ʀavitɑje] *vt* (*en vivres, munitions*) to provide with fresh supplies; (*véhicule*) to refuel; **se ravitailler** *vi* to get fresh supplies

raviver [ʀavive] *vt* (*feu*) to rekindle, revive; (*douleur*) to revive; (*couleurs*) to brighten up

rayé, e [ʀeje] *adj* (*à rayures*) striped; (*éraflé*) scratched

rayer [ʀeje] *vt* (*érafler*) to scratch; (*barrer*) to cross *ou* score out; (*d'une liste: radier*) to cross *ou* strike off

rayon [ʀejɔ̃] *nm* (*de soleil etc*) ray; (*Géom*) radius; (*de roue*) spoke; (*étagère*) shelf; (*de grand magasin*) department; (*fig: domaine*) responsibility, concern; (*de ruche*) (honey) comb; **dans un ~ de** within a radius of; **rayons** *nmpl* (*radiothérapie*) radiation; **~ d'action** range; **~ de braquage** (*Auto*) turning circle; **~ laser** laser beam; **~ de soleil** sunbeam, ray of sunlight *ou* sunshine; **~s X** X-rays

rayonnement [ʀejɔnmɑ̃] *nm* radiation; (*fig: éclat*) radiance; (*influence: d'une culture*) influence

rayonner [ʀejɔne] *vi* (*chaleur, énergie*) to radiate; (*fig: émotion*) to shine forth; (: *visage, personne*) to be radiant; (*avenues, axes*) to radiate; (*touriste*) to go touring (*from one base*)

rayure [ʀejyʀ] *nf* (*motif*) stripe; (*éraflure*) scratch; (*rainure, d'un fusil*) groove; **à ~s** striped

raz-de-marée [ʀɑdmaʀe] *nm inv* tidal wave

ré [ʀe] *nm* (*Mus*) D; (*en chantant la gamme*) re

réacteur [ʀeaktœʀ] *nm* jet engine; **~ nucléaire** nuclear reactor

réaction [Reaksjɔ̃] nf reaction; **par ~** jet-propelled; **avion/moteur à ~** jet (plane)/jet engine; **~ en chaîne** chain reaction

réadapter [Readapte] vt to readjust; (Méd) to rehabilitate; **se ~ (à)** vi to readjust (to)

réagir [ReaʒiR] vi to react

réalisateur, -trice [RealizatœR, -tRis] nm/f (TV, Ciné) director

réalisation [Realizasjɔ̃] nf carrying out, realization; fulfilment; achievement; (Ciné) production; (œuvre) work, work; (création) creation; **en cours de ~** under way

réaliser [Realize] vt (projet, opération) to carry out, realize; (rêve, souhait) to realize, fulfil; (exploit) to achieve; (achat, vente) to make; (film) to produce; (se rendre compte de, Comm: bien, capital) to realize; **se réaliser** vi to be realized

réaliste [Realist] adj realistic; (peintre, roman) realist ▷ nm/f realist

réalité [Realite] nf reality; **en ~** in (actual) fact; **dans la ~** in reality; **~ virtuelle** virtual reality

réanimation [Reanimasjɔ̃] nf resuscitation; **service de ~** intensive care unit

rébarbatif, -ive [RebaRbatif, -iv] adj forbidding; (style) off-putting (Brit), crabbed

rebattu, e [Rebaty] adj hackneyed

rebelle [Rebɛl] nm/f rebel ▷ adj (troupes) rebel; (enfant) rebellious; (mèche etc) unruly; **~ à qch** unamenable to sth; **~ à faire** unwilling to do

rebeller [Rebele]: **se rebeller** vi to rebel

rebondi, e [Rebɔ̃di] adj (ventre) rounded; (joues) chubby, well-rounded

rebondir [Rebɔ̃diR] vi (ballon: au sol) to bounce; (: contre un mur) to rebound; (fig: procès, action, conversation) to get moving again, be suddenly revived

rebondissement [Rebɔ̃dismɑ̃] nm new development

rebord [RebɔR] nm edge; **le ~ de la fenêtre** the windowsill

rebours [RebuR]: **à ~** adv the wrong way

rebrousser [RebRuse] vt (cheveux, poils) to brush back, brush up; **~ chemin** to turn back

rebut [Reby] nm: **mettre au ~** to scrap, discard

rebutant, e [Rebytɑ̃, -ɑ̃t] adj (travail, démarche) off-putting, disagreeable

rebuter [Rebyte] vt to put off

récalcitrant, e [Rekalsitʀɑ̃, -ɑ̃t] adj refractory, recalcitrant

recaler [Rekale] vt (Scol) to fail

récapituler [Rekapityle] vt to recapitulate; (résumer) to sum up

receler [Rəsəle] vt (produit d'un vol) to receive; (malfaiteur) to harbour; (fig) to conceal

receleur, -euse [RəsəlœR, -øz] nm/f receiver

récemment [Resamɑ̃] adv recently

recensement [Rəsɑ̃smɑ̃] nm census; inventory

recenser [Rəsɑ̃se] vt (population) to take a census of; (inventorier) to make an inventory of; (dénombrer) to list

récent, e [Resɑ̃, -ɑ̃t] adj recent

récépissé [Resepise] nm receipt

récepteur, -trice [ReseptœR, -tRis] adj receiving ▷ nm receiver; **~ (de radio)** radio set ou receiver

réception [Resepsjɔ̃] nf receiving no pl; (d'une marchandise, commande) receipt; (accueil) reception, welcome; (bureau) reception (desk); (réunion mondaine) reception, party; (pièces) reception rooms pl; (Sport: après un saut) landing; (du ballon) catching no pl; **jour/heures de ~** day/hours for receiving visitors (ou students etc)

réceptionniste [Resepsjɔnist] nm/f receptionist

recette [Rəsɛt] nf (Culin) recipe; (fig) formula, recipe; (Comm) takings pl; (Admin: bureau) tax ou revenue office; **recettes** nfpl (Comm: rentrées) receipts; **faire ~** (spectacle, exposition) to be a winner

receveur, -euse [RəsəvœR, -øz] nm/f (des contributions) tax collector; (des postes) postmaster/mistress; (d'autobus) conductor/conductress; (Méd: de sang, organe) recipient

recevoir [RəsəvwaR] vt to receive; (lettre, prime) to receive, get; (client, patient, représentant) to see; (jour, soleil: pièce) to get; (Scol: candidat) to pass ▷ vi to receive visitors; to give parties; to see patients etc; **se recevoir** vi (athlète) to land; **~ qn à dîner** to invite sb to dinner; **il reçoit de huit à 10** he's at home from eight to 10, he will see visitors from eight to 10; (docteur, dentiste etc) he sees patients from eight to 10; **être reçu** (à un examen) to pass; **être bien/mal reçu** to be well/badly received

rechange [Rəʃɑ̃ʒ]: **de ~** adj (pièces, roue) spare; (fig: solution) alternative; **des vêtements de ~** a change of clothes

réchapper [Reʃape]: **~ de** ou **à** vt (accident, maladie) to come through; **va-t-il en ~?** is he going to get over it?, is he going to come through (it)?

recharge [RəʃaRʒ] nf refill

rechargeable [RəʃaRʒabl] adj (stylo etc) refillable; rechargeable

recharger [RəʃaRʒe] vt (camion, fusil, appareil photo) to reload; (briquet, stylo) to refill; (batterie) to recharge

réchaud [Reʃo] nm (portable) stove, plate-warmer

réchauffer [Reʃofe] vt (plat) to reheat; (mains, personne) to warm; **se réchauffer** vi (température) to get warmer; (personne) to warm o.s. (up); **se ~ les doigts** to warm (up) one's fingers

rêche [Rɛʃ] adj rough

recherche [RəʃɛRʃ] nf (action): **la ~ de** the search for; (raffinement) affectedness, studied elegance; (scientifique etc): **la ~** research;

recherches *nfpl* (*de la police*) investigations; (*scientifiques*) research *sg*; **être/se mettre à la ~ de** to be/go in search of

recherché, e [RəʃɛRʃe] *adj* (*rare, demandé*) much sought-after; (*entouré: acteur, femme*) in demand; (*raffiné*) studied, affected; (*tenue*) elegant

rechercher [RəʃɛRʃe] *vt* (*objet égaré, personne*) to look for, search for; (*témoins, coupable, main-d'œuvre*) to look for; (*causes d'un phénomène, nouveau procédé*) to try to find; (*bonheur etc, l'amitié de qn*) to seek; "**~ et remplacer**" (*Inform*) "find and replace"

rechigner [Rəʃiɲe] *vi*: **~ (à)** to balk (at)

rechute [Rəʃyt] *nf* (*Méd*) relapse; (*dans le péché, le vice*) lapse; **faire une ~** to have a relapse

récidiver [Residive] *vi* to commit a second (*ou* subsequent) offence; (*fig*) to do it again

récif [Resif] *nm* reef

récipient [Resipjɑ̃] *nm* container

réciproque [Resiprɔk] *adj* reciprocal ⊳ *nf*: **la ~** (*l'inverse*) the converse

récit [Resi] *nm* (*action de narrer*) telling; (*conte, histoire*) story

récital [Resital] *nm* recital

réciter [Resite] *vt* to recite

réclamation [Reklamasjɔ̃] *nf* complaint; **réclamations** *nfpl* (*bureau*) complaints department *sg*

réclame [Reklam] *nf*: **la ~** advertising; **une ~** an ad(vertisement), an advert (*Brit*); **faire de la ~ (pour qch/qn)** to advertise (sth/sb); **article en ~** special offer

réclamer [Reklame] *vt* (*aide, nourriture etc*) to ask for; (*revendiquer: dû, part, indemnité*) to claim, demand; (*nécessiter*) to demand, require ⊳ *vi* to complain; **se ~ de** to give as one's authority; to claim filiation with

réclusion [Reklyzjɔ̃] *nf* imprisonment; **~ à perpétuité** life imprisonment

recoin [Rəkwɛ̃] *nm* nook, corner; (*fig*) hidden recess

reçois *etc* [Rəswa] *vb voir* **recevoir**

récolte [Rekɔlt] *nf* harvesting, gathering; (*produits*) harvest, crop; (*fig*) crop, collection; (*: d'observations*) findings

récolter [Rekɔlte] *vt* to harvest, gather (in); (*fig*) to get

recommandé [Rəkɔmɑ̃de] *nm* (*méthode etc*) recommended; (*Postes*): **en ~** by registered mail

recommander [Rəkɔmɑ̃de] *vt* to recommend; (*qualités etc*) to commend; (*Postes*) to register; **~ qch à qn** to recommend sth to sb; **~ à qn de faire** to recommend sb to do; **~ qn auprès de qn** *ou* **à qn** to recommend sb to sb; **il est recommandé de faire ...** it is recommended that one does ...; **se ~ à qn** to commend o.s. to sb; **se ~ de qn** to give sb's name as a reference

recommencer [Rəkɔmɑ̃se] *vt* (*reprendre: lutte, séance*) to resume, start again; (*refaire: travail, explications*) to start afresh, start (over) again;

(*récidiver: erreur*) to make again ⊳ *vi* to start again; (*récidiver*) to do it again; **~ à faire** to start doing again; **ne recommence pas!** don't do that again!

récompense [Rekɔ̃pɑ̃s] *nf* reward; (*prix*) award; **recevoir qch en ~** to get sth as a reward, be rewarded with sth

récompenser [Rekɔ̃pɑ̃se] *vt*: **~ qn (de** *ou* **pour)** to reward sb (for)

réconcilier [Rekɔ̃silje] *vt* to reconcile; **~ qn avec qn** to reconcile sb with sb; **~ qn avec qch** to reconcile sb to sth; **se réconcilier (avec)** to be reconciled (with)

reconduire [Rəkɔ̃dɥiR] *vt* (*raccompagner*) to take *ou* see back; (*: à la porte*) to show out; (*: à son domicile*) to see home, take home; (*Jur, Pol: renouveler*) to renew

réconfort [Rekɔ̃fɔR] *nm* comfort

réconforter [Rekɔ̃fɔRte] *vt* (*consoler*) to comfort; (*revigorer*) to fortify

reconnaissance [Rəkɔnɛsɑ̃s] *nf* (*action de reconnaître*) recognition; acknowledgement; (*gratitude*) gratitude, gratefulness; (*Mil*) reconnaissance, recce; **en ~** (*Mil*) on reconnaissance; **~ de dette** acknowledgement of a debt, IOU

reconnaissant, e [Rəkɔnɛsɑ̃, -ɑ̃t] *vb voir* **reconnaître** ⊳ *adj* grateful; **je vous serais ~ de bien vouloir** I should be most grateful if you would (kindly)

reconnaître [RəkɔnɛtR] *vt* to recognize; (*Mil: lieu*) to reconnoitre; (*Jur: enfant, dette, droit*) to acknowledge; **~ que** to admit *ou* acknowledge that; **~ qn/qch à** (*l'identifier grâce à*) to recognize sb/sth by; **~ à qn: je lui reconnais certaines qualités** I recognize certain qualities in him; **se ~ quelque part** (*s'y retrouver*) to find one's way around (a place)

reconnu, e [R(ə)kɔny] *pp de* **reconnaître** ⊳ *adj* (*indiscuté, connu*) recognized

reconstituant, e [Rəkɔ̃stitɥɑ̃, -ɑ̃t] *adj* (*régime*) strength-building ⊳ *nm* tonic, pick-me-up

reconstituer [Rəkɔ̃stitɥe] *vt* (*monument ancien*) to recreate, build a replica of; (*fresque, vase brisé*) to piece together, reconstitute; (*événement, accident*) to reconstruct; (*fortune, patrimoine*) to rebuild; (*Bio: tissus etc*) to regenerate

reconstruction [Rəkɔ̃stRyksjɔ̃] *nf* rebuilding, reconstruction

reconstruire [Rəkɔ̃stRɥiR] *vt* to rebuild, reconstruct

reconvertir [Rəkɔ̃vɛRtiR] *vt* (*usine*) to reconvert; (*personnel, troupes etc*) to redeploy; **se ~ dans** (*un métier, une branche*) to move into, be redeployed into

record [RəkɔR] *nm, adj* record; **~ du monde** world record

recoupement [Rəkupmɑ̃] *nm*: **faire un ~** *ou* **des ~s** to cross-check; **par ~** by cross-checking

r

recouper [Rəkupe] vt (tranche) to cut again; (vêtement) to recut ▷ vi (Cartes) to cut again; **se recouper** vi (témoignages) to tie ou match up

recourber [Rəkurbe] vt (branche, tige de métal) to bend; **se recourber** vi to curve (up), bend (up)

recourir [Rəkurir] vi (courir de nouveau) to run again; (refaire une course) to race again; **~ à** vt (ami, agence) to turn ou appeal to; (force, ruse, emprunt) to resort to, have recourse to

recours [Rəkur] vb voir **recourir** ▷ nm (Jur) appeal; **avoir ~ à = recourir à**; **en dernier ~** as a last resort; **sans ~** final; with no way out; **~ en grâce** plea for clemency (ou pardon)

recouvrer [Rəkuvre] vt (vue, santé etc) to recover, regain; (impôts) to collect; (créance) to recover

recouvrir [Rəkuvrir] vt (couvrir à nouveau) to re-cover; (couvrir entièrement: aussi fig) to cover; (cacher, masquer) to conceal, hide; **se recouvrir** (se superposer) to overlap

récréation [Rekreasjɔ̃] nf recreation, entertainment; (Scol) break

récrier [Rekrije]: **se récrier** vi to exclaim

récriminations [Rekriminasjɔ̃] nfpl remonstrations, complaints

recroqueviller [Rəkrɔkvije]: **se recroqueviller** vi (feuilles) to curl ou shrivel up; (personne) to huddle up

recru, e [Rəkry] adj: **~ de fatigue** exhausted ▷ nf recruit

recrudescence [Rəkrydesɑ̃s] nf fresh outbreak

recruter [Rəkryte] vt to recruit

rectangle [Rɛktɑ̃gl] nm rectangle

rectangulaire [Rɛktɑ̃gylɛr] adj rectangular

rectificatif, -ive [Rɛktifikatif, -iv] adj corrected ▷ nm correction

rectifier [Rɛktifje] vt (tracé, virage) to straighten; (calcul, adresse) to correct; (erreur, faute) to rectify, put right

rectiligne [Rɛktilin] adj straight; (Géom) rectilinear

recto [Rɛkto] nm front (of a sheet of paper); **~ verso** on both sides (of the page)

reçu, e [Rəsy] pp de **recevoir** ▷ adj (candidat) successful; (admis, consacré) accepted ▷ nm (Comm) receipt

recueil [Rəkœj] nm collection

recueillir [Rəkœjir] vt to collect; (voix, suffrages) to win; (accueillir: réfugiés, chat) to take in; **se recueillir** vi to gather one's thoughts; to meditate

recul [Rəkyl] nm retreat, recession; (déclin) decline; (éloignement) distance; (d'arme à feu) recoil, kick; **avoir un mouvement de ~** to recoil, start back; **prendre du ~** to stand back; **être en ~** to be on the decline; **avec le ~** with the passing of time, in retrospect

reculé, e [Rəkyle] adj remote

reculer [Rəkyle] vi to move back, back away; (Auto) to reverse, back (up); (fig: civilisation,

épidémie) to (be on the) decline; (: se dérober) to shrink back ▷ vt to move back; (véhicule) to reverse, back (up); (fig: possibilités, limites) to extend; (: date, décision) to postpone; **~ devant** (danger, difficulté) to shrink from; **~ pour mieux sauter** (fig) to postpone the evil day

reculons [Rəkylɔ̃]: **à ~** adv backwards

récupérer [Rekypere] vt (rentrer en possession de) to recover, get back; (: forces) to recover; (déchets etc) to salvage (for reprocessing); (remplacer: journée, heures de travail) to make up; (délinquant etc) to rehabilitate; (Pol) to bring into line ▷ vi to recover

récurer [Rekyre] vt to scour; **poudre à ~** scouring powder

reçus etc [Rəsy] vb voir **recevoir**

récuser [Rekyze] vt to challenge; **se récuser** to decline to give an opinion

recycler [Rəsikle] vt (Scol) to reorientate; (employés) to retrain; (matériau) to recycle; **se recycler** vi to retrain; to go on a retraining course

rédacteur, -trice [Redaktœr, -tris] nm/f (journaliste) writer; subeditor; (d'ouvrage de référence) editor, compiler; **~ en chef** chief editor; **~ publicitaire** copywriter

rédaction [Redaksjɔ̃] nf writing; (rédacteurs) editorial staff; (bureau) editorial office(s); (Scol: devoir) essay, composition

redemander [Rədmɑ̃de] vt (renseignement) to ask again for; (nourriture): **~ de** to ask for more (ou another); (objet prêté): **~ qch** to ask for sth back

redescendre [Rədesɑ̃dr] vi (à nouveau) to go back down; (après la montée) to go down (again) ▷ vt (pente etc) to go down

redevance [Rədvɑ̃s] nf (Tél) rental charge; (TV) licence (Brit) ou license (US) fee

rédiger [Redize] vt to write; (contrat) to draw up

redire [Rədir] vt to repeat; **trouver à ~ à** to find fault with

redonner [Rədɔne] vt (restituer) to give back, return; (du courage, des forces) to restore

redoubler [Rəduble] vi (tempête, violence) to intensify, get even stronger ou fiercer etc; (Scol) to repeat a year ▷ vt (Scol: classe) to repeat; (Ling: lettre) to double; **le vent redouble de violence** the wind is blowing twice as hard; **~ de patience/prudence** to be doubly patient/careful

redoutable [Rədutabl] adj formidable, fearsome

redouter [Rədute] vt to fear; (appréhender) to dread; **~ de faire** to dread doing

redressement [Rədrɛsmɑ̃] nm (économique) recovery; (de l'économie etc) putting right; **maison de ~** reformatory; **~ fiscal** repayment of back taxes

redresser [Rədrese] vt (arbre, mât) to set upright, right; (pièce tordue) to straighten out; (Aviat, Auto) to straighten up; (situation, *économie*) to put right; **se redresser** vi (*objet penché*) to right itself; to straighten up; (*personne*) to sit (*ou* stand) up; to sit (*ou* stand) up straight; (*fig: pays, situation*) to recover; **~ (les roues)** (*Auto*) to straighten up

réduction [Redyksjɔ̃] nf reduction; **en ~** adv in miniature, scaled-down

réduire [RedɥiR] vt (*gén, Culin, Math*) to reduce; (*prix, dépenses*) to cut, reduce; (*carte*) to scale down, reduce; (*Méd: fracture*) to set; **~ qn/qch à** to reduce sb/sth to; **se ~ à** (*revenir à*) to boil down to; **se ~ en** (*se transformer en*) to be reduced to; **en être réduit à** to be reduced to

réduit, e [Redɥi, -it] pp de **réduire** ▷ adj (*prix, tarif, échelle*) reduced; (*mécanisme*) scaled-down; (*vitesse*) reduced ▷ nm tiny room; recess

rééducation [Reedykasjɔ̃] nf (*d'un membre*) re-education; (*de délinquants, d'un blessé*) rehabilitation; **~ de la parole** speech therapy; **centre de ~** physiotherapy *ou* physical therapy (US) centre

réel, le [Reɛl] adj real ▷ nm: **le ~** reality

réellement [Reɛlmã] adv really

réexpédier [Reɛkspedje] vt (*à l'envoyeur*) to return, send back; (*au destinataire*) to send on, forward

refaire [RəfɛR] vt (*faire de nouveau, recommencer*) to do again; (*sport*) to take up again; (*réparer, restaurer*) to do up; **se refaire** vi (*en argent*) to make up one's losses; **se ~ une santé** to recuperate; **se ~ à qch** (*se réhabituer à*) to get used to sth again

réfection [Refɛksjɔ̃] nf repair; **en ~** under repair

réfectoire [RefɛktwaR] nm refectory

référence [RefeRɑ̃s] nf reference; **références** nfpl (*recommandations*) reference sg; **faire ~ à** to refer to; **ouvrage de ~** reference work; **ce n'est pas une ~** (*fig*) that's no recommendation

référer [RefeRe]: **se ~ à** vt to refer to; **en ~ à qn** to refer the matter to sb

refermer [RəfɛRme] vt to close again, shut again; **se refermer** vi (*porte*) to close *ou* shut (again)

refiler [Rəfile] vt (*fam*): **~ qch à qn** to palm (*Brit*) *ou* fob sth off on sb; to pass sth on to sb

réfléchi, e [Refleʃi] adj (*caractère*) thoughtful; (*action*) well-thought-out; (*Ling*) reflexive; **c'est tout ~** my mind's made up

réfléchir [RefleʃiR] vt to reflect ▷ vi to think; **~ à** *ou* **sur** to think about; **c'est tout réfléchi** my mind's made up

reflet [Rəflɛ] nm reflection; (*sur l'eau etc*) sheen *no pl*, glint; **reflets** nmpl gleam sg

refléter [Rəflete] vt to reflect; **se refléter** vi to be reflected

réflexe [Reflɛks] adj, nm reflex; **~ conditionné** conditioned reflex

réflexion [Refleksjɔ̃] nf (*de la lumière etc, pensée*) reflection; (*fait de penser*) thought; (*remarque*)

remark; **réflexions** nfpl (*méditations*) thought sg, reflection sg; **sans ~** without thinking; **~ faite, à la ~, après ~** on reflection; **délai de ~** cooling-off period; **groupe de ~** think tank

réflexologie [Refleksɔlɔʒi] nf reflexology

refluer [Rəflye] vi to flow back; (*foule*) to surge back

reflux [Rəfly] nm (*de la mer*) ebb; (*fig*) backward surge

réforme [RefɔRm] nf reform; (*Mil*) declaration of unfitness for service; discharge (*on health grounds*); (*Rel*): **la R~** the Reformation

réformer [RefɔRme] vt to reform; (*Mil: recrue*) to declare unfit for service; (*: soldat*) to discharge, invalid out; (*matériel*) to scrap

refouler [Rəfule] vt (*envahisseurs*) to drive back, repulse; (*liquide, larmes*) to force back; (*fig*) to suppress; (*Psych: désir, colère*) to repress

refrain [Rəfrɛ̃] nm (*Mus*) refrain, chorus; (*air, fig*) tune

réfréner, refréner [Refrene, Rəfrene] vt to curb, check

réfrigérateur [RefRiʒeRatœR] nm refrigerator; **~-congélateur** fridge-freezer

refroidir [RəfRwadiR] vt to cool; (*fig*) to have a cooling effect on; (*fam*) to do in ▷ vi to cool (down); **se refroidir** vi (*prendre froid*) to catch a chill; (*temps*) to get cooler *ou* colder; (*fig: ardeur*) to cool (off)

refroidissement [RəfRwadismã] nm cooling; (*grippe etc*) chill

refuge [Rəfyʒ] nm refuge; (*pour piétons*) (traffic) island; **demander ~ à qn** to ask sb for refuge

réfugié, e [Refyʒje] adj, nm/f refugee

réfugier [Refyʒje]: **se réfugier** vi to take refuge

refus [Rəfy] nm refusal; **ce n'est pas de ~** I won't say no, it's very welcome

refuser [Rəfyze] vt to refuse; (*Scol: candidat*) to fail ▷ vi to refuse; (*personne*) to put off; **~ qch à qn/de faire** to refuse sb sth/to do; **~ du monde** to have to turn people away; **se ~ à qch** *ou* **à faire qch** to refuse to do sth; **il ne se refuse rien** he doesn't stint himself; **se ~ à qn** to refuse sb

réfuter [Refyte] vt to refute

regagner [Rəgaɲe] vt (*argent, faveur*) to win back; (*lieu*) to get back to; **~ le temps perdu** to make up for lost time; **~ du terrain** to regain ground

regain [Rəgɛ̃] nm (*herbe*) second crop of hay; (*renouveau*): **~ de qch** renewed sth

régal [Regal] nm treat; **un ~ pour les yeux** a pleasure *ou* delight to look at

régaler [Regale] vt: **~ qn** to treat sb to a delicious meal; **~ qn de** to treat sb to; **se régaler** vi to have a delicious meal; (*fig*) to enjoy o.s

regard [RəgaR] nm (*coup d'œil*) look, glance; (*expression*) look (in one's eye); **parcourir/ menacer du ~** to cast an eye over/look threateningly at; **au ~ de** (*loi, morale*) from the point of view of; **en ~** (*vis à vis*) opposite; **en ~ de** in comparison with

regardant, e [ʀəgaʀdɑ̃, -ɑ̃t] *adj*: **très/peu ~ (sur)** quite fussy/very free (about); (*économe*) very tight-fisted/quite generous (with)

regarder [ʀəgaʀde] *vt* (*examiner, observer, lire*) to look at; (*film, télévision, match*) to watch; (*envisager: situation, avenir*) to view; (*considérer: son intérêt etc*) to be concerned with; (*être orienté vers*): **~ (vers)** to face; (*concerner*) to concern ▷ *vi* to look; **~ à** *vt* (*dépense, qualité, détails*) to be fussy with *ou* over; **~ à faire** to hesitate to do; **dépenser sans ~** to spend freely; **ne pas ~ à la dépense** to spare no expense; **~ qn/qch comme** to regard sb/sth as; **~ (qch) dans le dictionnaire** to look (sth up) in the dictionary; **~ par la fenêtre** to look out of the window; **cela me regarde** it concerns me, it's my business

régie [ʀeʒi] *nf* (*Comm, Industrie*) state-owned company; (*Théât, Ciné*) production; (*Radio, TV*) control room; **la ~ de l'État** state control

regimber [ʀəʒɛ̃be] *vi* to balk, jib

régime [ʀeʒim] *nm* (*Pol Géo*) régime; (*Admin: carcéral, fiscal etc*) system; (*Méd*) diet; (*Tech*) (engine) speed; (*fig*) rate, pace; (*de bananes, dattes*) bunch; **se mettre au/suivre un ~** to go on/be on a diet; **~ sans sel** salt-free diet; **à bas/haut ~** (*Auto*) at low/high revs; **à plein ~** flat out, at full speed; **~ matrimonial** marriage settlement

régiment [ʀeʒimɑ̃] *nm* (*Mil: unité*) regiment; (*fig: fam*): **un ~ de** an army of; **un copain de ~** a pal from military service *ou* (one's) army days

région [ʀeʒjɔ̃] *nf* region; **la ~ parisienne** the Paris area

régional, e, -aux [ʀeʒjɔnal, -o] *adj* regional

régir [ʀeʒiʀ] *vt* to govern

régisseur [ʀeʒisœʀ] *nm* (*d'un domaine*) steward; (*Ciné, TV*) assistant director; (*Théât*) stage manager

registre [ʀeʒistʀ] *nm* (*livre*) register; logbook; ledger; (*Mus, Ling*) register; (*d'orgue*) stop; **~ de comptabilité** ledger; **~ de l'état civil** register of births, marriages and deaths

réglage [ʀeglaʒ] *nm* (*d'une machine*) adjustment; (*d'un moteur*) tuning

réglé, e [ʀegle] *adj* well-ordered; stable, steady; (*papier*) ruled; (*arrangé*) settled

règle [ʀegl] *nf* (*instrument*) ruler; (*loi, prescription*) rule; **règles** *nfpl* (*Physiol*) period *sg*; **avoir pour ~ de** to make it a rule that *ou* to; **en ~** (*papiers d'identité*) in order; **être/se mettre en ~** to be/put o.s. straight with the authorities; **en ~ générale** as a (general) rule; **être la ~** to be the rule; **être de ~** to be usual; **~ à calcul** slide rule; **~ de trois** (*Math*) rule of three

règlement [ʀeglɑ̃mɑ̃] *nm* settling; (*paiement*) settlement; (*arrêté*) regulation; (*règles, statuts*) regulations *pl*, rules *pl*; **~ à la commande** cash with order; **~ de compte(s)** settling of scores; **~ en espèces/par chèque** payment in cash/by cheque; **~ intérieur** (*Scol*) school rules *pl*; (*Admin*) by-laws *pl*; **~ judiciaire** compulsory liquidation

réglementaire [ʀegləmɑ̃tɛʀ] *adj* conforming to the regulations; (*tenue, uniforme*) regulation *cpd*

réglementation [ʀegləmɑ̃tasjɔ̃] *nf* regulation, control; (*règlements*) regulations *pl*

réglementer [ʀegləmɑ̃te] *vt* to regulate, control

régler [ʀegle] *vt* (*mécanisme, machine*) to regulate, adjust; (*moteur*) to tune; (*thermostat etc*) to set, adjust; (*emploi du temps etc*) to organize, plan; (*question, conflit, facture, dette*) to settle; (*fournisseur*) to settle up with, pay; (*papier*) to rule; **~ qch sur** to model sth on; **~ son compte** to sort sb out, settle sb; **~ un compte** to settle a score with sb

réglisse [ʀeglis] *nf ou m* liquorice; **bâton de ~** liquorice stick

règne [ʀɛɲ] *nm* (*d'un roi etc, fig*) reign; (*Bio*): **le ~ végétal/animal** the vegetable/animal kingdom

régner [ʀeɲe] *vi* (*roi*) to rule, reign; (*fig*) to reign

regorger [ʀəgɔʀʒe] *vi* to overflow; **~ de** to overflow with, be bursting with

regret [ʀəgʀɛ] *nm* regret; **à ~** with regret; **avec ~** regretfully; **sans ~** with no regrets; **être au ~ de devoir/ne pas pouvoir faire** to regret to have to/that one is unable to do; **j'ai le ~ de vous informer que ...** I regret to inform you that ...

regrettable [ʀəgʀɛtabl] *adj* regrettable

regretter [ʀəgʀɛte] *vt* to regret; (*personne*) to miss; **~ d'avoir fait** to regret doing; **~ que** to regret that, be sorry that; **non, je regrette** no, I'm sorry

regrouper [ʀəgʀupe] *vt* (*grouper*) to group together; (*contenir*) to include, comprise; **se regrouper** *vi* to gather (together)

régulier, -ière [ʀegylje, -jɛʀ] *adj* (*gén*) regular; (*vitesse, qualité*) steady; (*répartition, pression*) even; (*Transports: ligne, service*) scheduled, regular; (*légal, réglementaire*) lawful, in order; (*fam: correct*) straight, on the level

régulièrement [ʀegyljɛʀmɑ̃] *adv* regularly; steadily; evenly; normally

rehausser [ʀəose] *vt* (*relever*) to heighten, raise; (*fig: souligner*) to set off, enhance

rein [ʀɛ̃] *nm* kidney; **reins** *nmpl* (*dos*) back *sg*; **avoir mal aux ~s** to have backache; **~ artificiel** kidney machine

reine [ʀɛn] *nf* queen

reine-claude [ʀɛnklod] *nf* greengage

réinscriptible [ʀeɛ̃skʀiptibl] *adj* (*CD, DVD*) rewritable

réinsertion [ʀeɛ̃sɛʀsjɔ̃] *nf* (*de délinquant*) reintegration, rehabilitation

réintégrer [ReɛɛtegRe] vt (lieu) to return to; (fonctionnaire) to reinstate

rejaillir [RəʒajiR] vi to splash up; **~ sur** to splash up onto; (fig: scandale) to rebound on; (: gloire) to be reflected on; to fall upon

rejet [Rəʒɛ] nm (action, aussi Méd) rejection; (Poésie) enjambement, rejet; (Bot) shoot

rejeter [Rəʒte] vt (relancer) to throw back; (vomir) to bring ou throw up; (écarter) to reject; (déverser) to throw out, discharge; (reporter): **~ un mot à la fin d'une phrase** to transpose a word to the end of a sentence; **se ~ sur qch** (accepter faute de mieux) to fall back on sth; **~ la tête/les épaules en arrière** to throw one's head/pull one's shoulders back; **~ la responsabilité de qch sur qn** to lay the responsibility for sth at sb's door

rejoindre [RəʒwɛdR] vt (famille, régiment) to rejoin, return to; (lieu) to get (back) to; (route etc) to meet, join; (rattraper) to catch up (with); **se rejoindre** vi to meet; **je te rejoins au café** I'll see ou meet you at the café

réjouir [RəʒwiR] vt to delight; **se réjouir** vi to be delighted; **se ~ de qch/de faire** to be delighted about sth to do; **se ~ que** to be delighted that

réjouissances [Reʒwisãs] nfpl (joie) rejoicing sg; (fête) festivities, merry-making sg

relâche [Rəlɑʃ]: **faire ~** vi (navire) to put into port; (Ciné) to be closed; **c'est le jour de ~** (Ciné) it's closed today; **sans ~** adv without respite ou a break

relâché, e [Rəlɑʃe] adj loose, lax

relâcher [Rəlɑʃe] vt (ressort, prisonnier) to release; (étreinte, cordes) to loosen; (discipline) to relax ▷ vi (Navig) to put into port; **se relâcher** vi to loosen; (discipline) to become slack ou lax; (élève etc) to slacken off

relais [Rəlɛ] nm (Sport): **course de ~** relay (race); (Radio, TV) relay; (intermédiaire) go-between; **équipe de ~** shift team; (Sport) relay team; **prendre le ~ (de)** to take over (from); **~ de poste** post house, coaching inn; **~ routier** = transport café (Brit), = truck stop (US)

relancer [Rəlãse] vt (balle) to throw back (again); (moteur) to restart; (fig) to boost, revive; (personne): **~ qn** to pester sb; to get on to sb again

relatif, -ive [Rəlatif, -iv] adj relative

relation [Rəlasjõ] nf (récit) account, report; (rapport) relation(ship); (connaissance) acquaintance; **relations** nfpl (rapports) relations; relationship; (connaissances) connections; **être/entrer en ~(s) avec** to be in contact ou be dealing/get in contact with; **mettre qn en ~(s) avec** to put sb in touch with; **~s internationales** international relations; **~s publiques** public relations; **~s (sexuelles)** sexual relations, (sexual) intercourse sg

relaxer [Rəlakse] vt to relax; (Jur) to discharge; **se relaxer** vi to relax

relayer [Rəleje] vt (collaborateur, coureur etc) to relieve, take over from; (Radio, TV) to relay; **se relayer** vi (dans une activité) to take it in turns

reléguer [Rəlege] vt to relegate; **~ au second plan** to push into the background

relent [Rəlã], **relents** nm(pl) stench sg

relevé, e [Rəlve] adj (bord de chapeau) turned-up; (manches) rolled-up; (fig: style) elevated; (: sauce) highly-seasoned ▷ nm (lecture) reading; (de cotes) plotting; (liste) statement; list; (facture) account; **~ bancaire** ou **de compte** bank statement; **~ d'identité bancaire (RIB)** (bank) account number

relève [Rəlɛv] nf (personne) relief; (équipe) relief team (ou troops etc); **prendre la ~** to take over

relever [Rəlve] vt (statue, meuble) to stand up again; (personne tombée) to help up; (vitre, plafond, niveau de vie) to raise; (pays, économie, entreprise) to put back on its feet; (col) to turn up; (style, conversation) to elevate; (plat, sauce) to season; (sentinelle, équipe) to relieve; (souligner: fautes, points) to pick out; (constater: traces etc) to find, pick up; (répliquer à: remarque) to react to, reply to; (: défi) to accept, take up; (noter: adresse etc) to take down, note; (: plan) to sketch; (: cotes etc) to plot; (compteur) to read; (ramasser: cahiers, copies) to collect, take in ▷ vi (jupe, bord) to ride up; **~ de** (maladie) to be recovering from; (être du ressort de) to be a matter for; (Admin: dépendre de) to come under; (fig) to pertain to; **se relever** vi (se remettre debout) to get up; (fig): **se ~ (de)** to recover (from); **~ qn de** (vœux) to release sb from; (fonctions) to relieve sb of; **~ la tête** to look up; to hold up one's head

relief [Rəljɛf] nm relief; (de pneu) tread pattern; **reliefs** nmpl (restes) remains; **en ~** in relief; (photographie) three-dimensional; **mettre en ~** (fig) to bring out, highlight

relier [Rəlje] vt to link up; (livre) to bind; **~ qch à** to link sth to; **livre relié cuir** leather-bound book

religieux, -euse [Rəliʒjø, -øz] adj religious ▷ nm monk ▷ nf nun; (gâteau) cream bun

religion [Rəliʒjõ] nf religion; (piété, dévotion) faith; **entrer en ~** to take one's vows

relire [RəliR] vt (à nouveau) to reread, read again; (vérifier) to read over; **se relire** to read through what one has written

reliure [RəljyR] nf binding; (art, métier): **la ~** book-binding

relooker [Rəluke] vt: **~ qn** to give sb a makeover

reluire [RəlɥiR] vi to gleam

remanier [Rəmanje] vt to reshape, recast; (Pol) to reshuffle

remarquable [Rəmarkabl] adj remarkable

remarque [Rəmark] nf remark; (écrite) note

remarquer [Rəmarke] vt (voir) to notice; (dire): **~ que** to remark that; **se ~** to be noticeable; **se faire ~** to draw attention to o.s.; **faire ~ (à qn) que** to point out (to sb) that; **faire ~ qch (à qn)** to point sth out (to sb); **remarquez, ...** mark you, ..., mind you, ...

rembourrer [ʀɑ̃buʀe] vt to stuff; (dossier, vêtement, souliers) to pad

remboursement [ʀɑ̃buʀsəmɑ̃] nm (de dette, d'emprunt) repayment; (de frais) refund; **envoi contre ~** cash on delivery

rembourser [ʀɑ̃buʀse] vt to pay back, repay; (frais, billet etc) to refund; **se faire ~** to get a refund

remède [ʀəmɛd] nm (médicament) medicine; (traitement, fig) remedy, cure; **trouver un ~ à** (Méd, fig) to find a cure for

remémorer [ʀəmemɔʀe]: **se remémorer** vt to recall, recollect

remerciements [ʀəmɛʀsimɑ̃] nmpl thanks; **(avec) tous mes ~** (with) grateful ou many thanks

remercier [ʀəmɛʀsje] vt to thank; (congédier) to dismiss; **~ qn de/d'avoir fait** to thank sb for/for having done; **non, je vous remercie** no thank you

remettre [ʀəmɛtʀ] vt (vêtement): **~ qch** to put sth back on, put sth on again; (replacer): **~ qch quelque part** to put sth back somewhere; (ajouter): **~ du sel/un sucre** to add more salt/another lump of sugar; (rétablir: personne): **~ qn** to set sb back on his (ou her) feet; (rendre, restituer): **~ qch à qn** to give sth back to sb, return sth to sb; (donner, confier: paquet, argent): **~ qch à qn** to hand sth over to sb, deliver sth to sb; (prix, décoration): **~ qch à qn** (donner: lettre, clé etc) to hand over sth to sb, (: prix, décoration) to present sb with sth; (ajourner): **~ qch (à)** to postpone sth ou put sth off (until); **se remettre** vi to get better, recover; **se ~ de** to recover from, get over; **s'en ~ à** to leave it (up) to; **se ~ à faire/qch** to start doing/sth again; **~ un pendule à l'heure** to put a clock right; **~ un moteur/une machine en marche** to get an engine/a machine going again; **~ en état/en ordre** to repair/sort out; **~ en cause/question** to challenge/question again; **~ sa démission** to hand in one's notice; **~ qch à neuf** to make sth as good as new; **~ qn à sa place** (fig) to put sb in his (ou her) place

remis, e [ʀəmi, -iz] pp de **remettre** ▷ nf delivery; presentation; (rabais) discount; (local) shed; **~e en marche/en ordre** starting up again/sorting out; **~e en cause/question** calling into question/challenging; **~e de fonds** remittance; **~e en jeu** (Football) throw-in; **~e à neuf** restoration; **~e de peine** remission of sentence; **~e des prix** prize-giving

remontant [ʀəmɔ̃tɑ̃] nm tonic, pick-me-up

remonte-pente [ʀəmɔ̃tpɑ̃t] nm ski lift, (ski) tow

remonter [ʀəmɔ̃te] vi (à nouveau) to go back up; (à cheval) to remount; (après une descente) to go up (again); (prix, température) to go up again; (en voiture) to get back in; (jupe) to ride up ▷ vt (pente) to go up; (fleuve) to sail (ou swim etc) up; up; (manches, pantalon) to roll up; (col) to turn up; (niveau, limite) to raise; (fig: personne) to buck up; (moteur, meuble) to put back together, reassemble; (garde-robe etc) to renew, replenish; (montre, mécanisme) to wind up; **~ le moral à qn** to raise sb's spirits; **~ à** (dater de) to date ou go back to; **~ en voiture** to get back into the car

remontrance [ʀəmɔ̃tʀɑ̃s] nf reproof, reprimand

remontrer [ʀəmɔ̃tʀe] vt (montrer de nouveau): **~ qch (à qn)** to show sth again (to sb); (fig): **en ~ à** to prove one's superiority over

remords [ʀəmɔʀ] nm remorse no pl; **avoir des ~** to feel remorse, be conscience-stricken

remorque [ʀəmɔʀk] nf trailer; **prendre/être en ~** to tow/be on tow; **être à la ~** (fig) to tag along (behind)

remorquer [ʀəmɔʀke] vt to tow

remorqueur [ʀəmɔʀkœʀ] nm tug(boat)

remous [ʀəmu] nm (d'un navire) (back)wash no pl; (de rivière) swirl, eddy pl; (fig) stir sg

remparts [ʀɑ̃paʀ] nmpl walls, ramparts

remplaçant, e [ʀɑ̃plasɑ̃, -ɑ̃t] nm/f replacement, substitute, stand-in; (Théât) understudy; (Scol) supply (Brit) ou substitute (US) teacher

remplacement [ʀɑ̃plasmɑ̃] nm replacement; (job) replacement work no pl; (suppléance: Scol) supply (Brit) ou substitute (US) teacher; **assurer le ~ de qn** (remplaçant) to stand in ou substitute for sb; **faire des ~s** (professeur) to do supply ou substitute teaching; (médecin) to do locum work; (secrétaire) to temp

remplacer [ʀɑ̃plase] vt to replace; (prendre temporairement la place de) to stand in for; (tenir lieu de) to take the place of, act as a substitute for; **~ qch/qn par** to replace sth/sb with

rempli, e [ʀɑ̃pli] adj (emploi du temps) full, busy; **~ de** full of, filled with

remplir [ʀɑ̃pliʀ] vt to fill (up); (questionnaire) to fill out ou up; (obligations, fonction, condition) to fulfil; **se remplir** vi to fill up; **~ qch de** to fill sth with

remporter [ʀɑ̃pɔʀte] vt (marchandise) to take away; (fig) to win, achieve

remuant, e [ʀəmyɑ̃, -ɑ̃t] adj restless

remue-ménage [ʀəmymenaʒ] nm inv commotion

remuer [ʀəmye] vt to move; (café, sauce) to stir ▷ vi to move; (fig: opposants) to show signs of unrest; **se remuer** vi to move; (se démener) to stir o.s.; (fam: s'activer) to get a move on

rémunérer [ʀemyneʀe] vt to remunerate, pay

renard [ʀənaʀ] nm fox

renchérir [ʀɑ̃ʃeʀiʀ] vi to become more expensive; (fig): **~ (sur)** (en paroles) to add something (to)

rencontre [Rɑ̃kɔ̃tR] nf (de cours d'eau) confluence; (de véhicules) collision; (entrevue, congrès, match etc) meeting; (imprévue) encounter; **faire la ~ de qn** to meet sb; **aller à la ~ de qn** to go and meet sb; **amours de ~** casual love affairs

rencontrer [Rɑ̃kɔ̃tRe] vt to meet; (mot, expression) to come across; (difficultés) to meet with; **se rencontrer** vi to meet; (véhicules) to collide

rendement [Rɑ̃dmɑ̃] nm (d'un travailleur, d'une machine) output; (d'une culture, d'un champ) yield; (d'un investissement) return; **à plein ~** at full capacity

rendez-vous [Rɑ̃devu] nm (rencontre) appointment; (: d'amoureux) date; (lieu) meeting place; **donner ~ à qn** to arrange to meet sb; **recevoir sur ~** to have an appointment system; **fixer un ~ à qn** to give sb an appointment; **avoir/prendre ~ (avec)** to have/make an appointment (with); **prendre ~ chez le médecin** to make an appointment with the doctor; **~ spatial** ou **orbital** docking (in space)

rendre [Rɑ̃dR] vt (livre, argent etc) to give back, return; (otages, visite, politesse, invitation, Jur: verdict) to return; (honneurs) to pay; (sang, aliments) to bring up; (sons: instrument) to produce, make; (exprimer, traduire) to render; (jugement) to pronounce, render; (faire devenir): **~ qn célèbre/qch possible** to make sb famous/sth possible; **se rendre** vi (capituler) to surrender, give o.s. up; (aller): **se ~ quelque part** to go somewhere; **se ~ à** (arguments etc) to bow to; (ordres) to comply with; **se ~ compte de qch** to realize sth; **~ la vue/la santé à qn** to restore sb's sight/health; **~ la liberté à qn** to set sb free; **~ la monnaie** to give change; **se ~ insupportable/malade** to become unbearable/make o.s. ill

rênes [Rɛn] nfpl reins

renfermé, e [Rɑ̃fɛRme] adj (fig) withdrawn ▷ nm: **sentir le ~** to smell stuffy

renfermer [Rɑ̃fɛRme] vt to contain; **se renfermer (sur soi-même)** to withdraw into o.s

renflouer [Rɑ̃flue] vt to refloat; (fig) to set back on its (ou his/her etc) feet (again)

renfoncement [Rɑ̃fɔ̃smɑ̃] nm recess

renforcer [Rɑ̃fɔRse] vt to reinforce; **~ qn dans ses opinions** to confirm sb's opinion

renfort [Rɑ̃fɔR]: **~s** nmpl reinforcements; **en ~** as a back-up; **à grand ~ de** with a great deal of

renfrogné, e [Rɑ̃fRɔɲe] adj sullen, scowling

rengaine [Rɑ̃gɛn] nf (péj) old tune

renier [Rənje] vt (parents) to disown, repudiate; (engagements) to go back on; (foi) to renounce

renifler [Rənifle] vi to sniff ▷ vt (tabac) to sniff up; (odeur) to sniff

renne [Rɛn] nm reindeer inv

renom [Rənɔ̃] nm reputation; (célébrité) renown; **vin de grand ~** celebrated ou highly renowned wine

renommé, e [R(ə)nɔme] adj celebrated, renowned ▷ nf fame

renoncer [Rənɔ̃se] vi: **~ à** vt to give up; **~ à faire** to give up the idea of doing; **j'y renonce!** I give up!

renouer [Rənwe] vt (cravate etc) to retie; (fig: conversation, liaison) to renew, resume; **~ avec** (tradition) to revive; (habitude) to take up again; **~ avec qn** to take up with sb again

renouvelable [R(ə)nuvlabl] adj (contrat, bail, énergie) renewable; (expérience) which can be renewed

renouveler [Rənuvle] vt to renew; (exploit, méfait) to repeat; **se renouveler** vi (incident) to recur, happen again, be repeated; (cellules etc) to be renewed ou replaced; (artiste, écrivain) to try something new

renouvellement [R(ə)nuvɛlmɑ̃] nm renewal; recurrence

rénover [Renɔve] vt (immeuble) to renovate, do up; (meuble) to restore; (enseignement) to reform; (quartier) to redevelop

renseignement [Rɑ̃sɛɲmɑ̃] nm information no pl, piece of information; (Mil) intelligence no pl; **prendre des ~s sur** to make inquiries about, ask for information about; **(guichet des) ~s** information desk; **(service des) ~s** (Brit) directory inquiries (Tél) information (US); **service de ~s** (Mil) intelligence service; **les ~s généraux** ≈ the secret police

renseigner [Rɑ̃sɛɲe] vt: **~ qn (sur)** to give information to sb (about); **se renseigner** vi to ask for information, make inquiries

rentabilité [Rɑ̃tabilite] nf profitability; cost-effectiveness; (d'un investissement) return; **seuil de ~** break-even point

rentable [Rɑ̃tabl] adj profitable; cost-effective

rente [Rɑ̃t] nf income; (pension) pension; (titre) government stock ou bond; **~ viagère** life annuity

rentrée [Rɑ̃tRe] nf: **~ (d'argent)** cash no pl coming in; **la ~ (des classes** ou **scolaire)** the start of the new school year; **la ~ (parlementaire)** the reopening ou reassembly of parliament; see note; **faire sa ~** (artiste, acteur) to make a comeback

RENTRÉE

La rentrée (des classes) in September each year has wider connotations than just the start of the new school year. It is also the time when political and social life pick up again after the long summer break, and so marks an important point in the French calendar.

rentrer [Rɑ̃tRe] vi (entrer de nouveau) to go (ou come) back in; (entrer) to go (ou come) in;

(*revenir chez soi*) to go (*ou* come) (back) home; (*air, clou: pénétrer*) to go in; (*revenu, argent*) to come in ▷ *vt* (*foins*) to bring in; (*véhicule*) to put away; (*chemise dans pantalon etc*) to tuck in; (*griffes*) to draw in; (*train d'atterrissage*) to raise; (*fig: larmes, colère etc*) to hold back; ~ **le ventre** to pull in one's stomach; ~ **dans** to go (*ou* come) back into; to go (*ou* come) into; (*famille, patrie*) to go back *ou* return to; (*heurter*) to crash into; (*appartenir à*) to be included in; (: *catégorie etc*) to fall into; ~ **dans l'ordre** to get back to normal; ~ **dans ses frais** to recover one's expenses (*ou* initial outlay)

renverse [ʀɑ̃vɛʀs]: **à la** ~ *adv* backwards

renverser [ʀɑ̃vɛʀse] *vt* (*faire tomber: chaise, verre*) to knock over, overturn; (*piéton*) to knock down; (*liquide, contenu*) to spill, upset; (*retourner: verre, image*) to turn upside down, invert; (: *ordre des mots etc*) to reverse; (*fig: gouvernement etc*) to overthrow; (*stupéfier*) to bowl over, stagger; **se renverser** *vi* (*verre, vase*) to fall over; (*contenu*) to spill; **se** ~ **(en arrière)** to lean back; ~ **la tête/le corps (en arrière)** to tip one's head back/throw oneself back; ~ **la vapeur** (*fig*) to change course

renvoi [ʀɑ̃vwa] *nm* (*d'employé*) dismissal; return; reflection; postponement; (*d'élève*) expulsion; (*référence*) cross-reference; (*éructation*) belch

renvoyer [ʀɑ̃vwaje] *vt* to send back; (*congédier*) to dismiss; (*Tennis*) to return; (*élève: définitivement*) to expel; (*lumière*) to reflect; (*son*) to echo; (*ajourner*): ~ **qch (à)** to postpone sth (until); ~ **qch à qn** (*rendre*) to return sth to sb; ~ **qn à** (*fig*) to refer sb to

repaire [ʀəpɛʀ] *nm* den

répandre [ʀepɑ̃dʀ] *vt* (*renverser*) to spill; (*étaler, diffuser*) to spread; (*lumière*) to shed; (*chaleur, odeur*) to give off; **se répandre** *vi* to spill; to spread; **se** ~ **en** (*injures etc*) to pour out

répandu, e [ʀepɑ̃dy] *pp de* **répandre** ▷ *adj* (*opinion, usage*) widespread

réparateur, -trice [ʀepaʀatœʀ, -tʀis] *nm/f* repairer

réparation [ʀepaʀasjɔ̃] *nf* repairing *no pl*, repair; **en** ~ (*machine etc*) under repair; **demander à qn** ~ **de** (*offense etc*) to ask sb to make amends for

réparer [ʀepaʀe] *vt* to repair; (*fig: offense*) to make up for, atone for; (: *oubli, erreur*) to put right

repartie [ʀəpaʀti] *nf* retort; **avoir de la** ~ to be quick at repartee

repartir [ʀəpaʀtiʀ] *vi* to set off again; (*voyageur*) to leave again; (*fig*) to get going again, pick up again; ~ **à zéro** to start from scratch (again)

répartir [ʀepaʀtiʀ] *vt* (*pour attribuer*) to share out; (*pour disperser, disposer*) to divide up; (*poids, chaleur*) to distribute; (*étaler: dans le temps*): ~ **sur** to spread over; (*classer, diviser*): ~ **en** to

divide into, split up into; **se répartir** *vt* (*travail, rôles*) to share out between themselves

répartition [ʀepaʀtisjɔ̃] *nf* sharing out; dividing up; (*des richesses etc*) distribution

repas [ʀəpa] *nm* meal; **à l'heure des** ~ at mealtimes

repassage [ʀəpasaʒ] *nm* ironing

repasser [ʀəpase] *vi* to come (*ou* go) back ▷ *vt* (*vêtement, tissu*) to iron; (*examen*) to retake, resit; (*film*) to show again; (*lame*) to sharpen; (*leçon, rôle: revoir*) to go over (again); (*plat, pain*): ~ **qch à qn** to pass sth back to sb

repêcher [ʀəpeʃe] *vt* (*noyé*) to recover the body of, fish out; (*fam: candidat*) to pass (*by inflating marks*); to give a second chance to

repentir [ʀəpɑ̃tiʀ] *nm* repentance; **se repentir** *vi* to repent; **se** ~ **d'avoir fait qch** (*regretter*) to regret having done sth

répercussions [ʀepɛʀkysjɔ̃] *nfpl* repercussions

répercuter [ʀepɛʀkyte] *vt* (*réfléchir, renvoyer: son, voix*) to reflect; (*faire transmettre: consignes, charges etc*) to pass on; **se répercuter** *vi* (*bruit*) to reverberate; (*fig*): **se** ~ **sur** to have repercussions on

repère [ʀəpɛʀ] *nm* mark; (*monument etc*) landmark; (**point de**) ~ point of reference

repérer [ʀəpeʀe] *vt* (*erreur, connaissance*) to spot; (*abri, ennemi*) to locate; **se repérer** *vi* to get one's bearings; **se faire** ~ to be spotted

répertoire [ʀepɛʀtwaʀ] *nm* (*liste*) (alphabetical) list; (*carnet*) index notebook; (*Inform*) directory; (*de carnet*) thumb index; (*indicateur*) directory, index; (*d'un théâtre, artiste*) repertoire

répéter [ʀepete] *vt* to repeat; (*préparer: leçon*) ▷ *aussi vi* to learn, go over; (*Théât*) to rehearse; **se répéter** (*redire*) to repeat o.s.; (*se reproduire*) to be repeated, recur

répétition [ʀepetisjɔ̃] *nf* repetition; (*Théât*) rehearsal; **répétitions** *nfpl* (*leçons*) private coaching *sg*; **armes à** ~ repeater weapons; ~ **générale** final dress rehearsal

répit [ʀepi] *nm* respite; **sans** ~ without letting up

replier [ʀəplije] *vt* (*rabattre*) to fold down *ou* over; **se replier** *vi* (*armée*) to withdraw, fall back; **se** ~ **sur soi-même** to withdraw into oneself

réplique [ʀeplik] *nf* (*repartie, fig*) reply; (*objection*) retort; (*Théât*) line; (*copie*) replica; **donner la** ~ **à** to play opposite; **sans** ~ *adj* no-nonsense; irrefutable

répliquer [ʀeplike] *vi* to reply; (*avec impertinence*) to answer back; (*riposter*) to retaliate

répondeur [ʀepɔ̃dœʀ] *nm*: ~ **(automatique)** (*Tél*) answering machine

répondre [ʀepɔ̃dʀ] *vi* to answer, reply; (*freins, mécanisme*) to respond; ~ **à** *vt* to reply to, answer; (*avec impertinence*): ~ **à qn** to answer sb back; (*invitation, convocation*) to reply to;

(affection, salut) to return; (provocation: mécanisme etc) to respond to; (correspondre à: besoin) to answer; (: conditions) to meet; (: description) to match; **~ que** to answer ou reply that; **~ de** to answer for

réponse [ʀepɔ̃s] nf answer, reply; **avec ~ payée** (Postes) reply-paid, post-paid (US); **avoir ~ à tout** to have an answer for everything; **en ~ à** in reply to; **carte-/ bulletin-~** reply card/slip

reportage [ʀəpɔʀtaʒ] nm (bref) report; (écrit: documentaire) story; article; (en direct) commentary; (genre, activité): **le ~** reporting

reporter[1] [ʀəpɔʀtɛʀ] nm reporter

reporter[2] [ʀəpɔʀte] vt (total): **~ qch sur** to carry sth forward ou over to; (ajourner): **~ qch (à)** to postpone sth (until); (transférer): **~ qch sur** to transfer sth to; **se ~ à** (époque) to think back to; (document) to refer to

repos [ʀəpo] nm rest; (fig) peace (and quiet); (mental) peace of mind; (Mil): **~!** (stand) at ease!; **en ~** at rest; **au ~** at rest; (soldat) at ease; **de tout ~** safe; **ce n'est pas de tout ~!** it's no picnic!

reposant, e [ʀ(ə)pozã, -ãt] adj restful; (sommeil) refreshing

reposer [ʀəpoze] vt (verre, livre) to put down; (rideaux, carreaux) to put back; (délasser) to rest; (problème) to reformulate ▷ vi (liquide, pâte) to settle, rest; **laisser ~** (pâte) to leave to stand; (personne): **ici repose ...** here lies ...; **~ sur** to be built on; (fig) to rest on; **se reposer** vi to rest; **se ~ sur qn** to rely on sb

repoussant, e [ʀəpusã, -ãt] adj repulsive

repousser [ʀəpuse] vi to grow again ▷ vt to repel, repulse; (offre) to turn down, reject; (tiroir, personne) to push back; (différer) to put back

reprendre [ʀəpʀɑ̃dʀ] vt (prisonnier, ville) to recapture; (objet prêté, donné) to take back; (chercher): **je viendrai te ~ à 4 h** I'll come and fetch you at 4; (se resservir de): **~ du pain/un œuf** to take (ou eat) more bread/another egg; (Comm: article usagé) to take back; to take in part exchange; (firme, entreprise) to take over; (travail, promenade) to resume; (emprunter: argument, idée) to take up, use; (refaire: article etc) to go over again; (jupe etc) to alter; (émission, pièce) to put on again; (réprimander) to tell off; (corriger) to correct ▷ vi (classes, pluie) to start (up) again; (activités, travaux, combats) to resume, start (up) again; (affaires, industrie) to pick up; (dire): **reprit-il** he went on; **se reprendre** (se ressaisir) to recover, pull o.s. together; **s'y ~** to make another attempt; **~ des forces** to recover one's strength; **~ courage** to take new heart; **~ ses habitudes/sa liberté** to get back into one's old habits/regain one's freedom; **~ la route** to resume one's journey, set off again; **~ connaissance** to come to, regain consciousness; **~ haleine** ou **son souffle** to

get one's breath back; **~ la parole** to speak again

représailles [ʀəpʀezaj] nfpl reprisals, retaliation sg

représentant, e [ʀəpʀezɑ̃tɑ̃, -ɑ̃t] nm/f representative

représentation [ʀəpʀezɑ̃tasjɔ̃] nf representation; (spectacle) performing; (symbole, image) representation; (spectacle) performance; (Comm): **la ~** commercial travelling; sales representation; **frais de ~** (d'un diplomate) entertainment allowance

représenter [ʀəpʀezɑ̃te] vt to represent; **se représenter** vt (se figurer) to imagine; to visualize ▷ vi: **se ~ à** (Pol) to stand ou run again at; (Scol) to resit

répression [ʀepʀesjɔ̃] nf voir **réprimer** suppression; repression; (Pol): **la ~** repression; **mesures de ~** repressive measures

réprimer [ʀepʀime] vt (émotions) to suppress; (peuple etc) repress

repris, e [ʀəpʀi, -iz] pp de **reprendre** ▷ nm: **~ de justice** ex-prisoner, ex-convict

reprise [ʀəpʀiz] nf (recommencement) resumption; (économique) recovery; (TV) repeat; (Ciné) rerun; (Boxe etc) round; (Auto) acceleration no pl; (Comm) trade-in, part exchange; (de location) sum asked for any extras or improvements made to the property; (raccommodage) darn; mend; **la ~ des hostilités** the resumption of hostilities; **à plusieurs ~s** on several occasions, several times

repriser [ʀəpʀize] vt (chaussette, lainage) to darn; (tissu) to mend; **aiguille/coton à ~** darning needle/thread

reproche [ʀəpʀɔʃ] nm (remontrance) reproach; **ton/air de ~** reproachful tone/look; **faire des ~s à qn** to reproach sb; **faire ~ à qn de qch** to reproach sb for sth; **sans ~(s)** beyond ou above reproach

reprocher [ʀəpʀɔʃe] vt: **~ qch à qn** to reproach ou blame sb for sth; **~ qch à** (machine, théorie) to have sth against; **se ~ qch/d'avoir fait qch** to blame o.s for sth/for doing sth

reproduction [ʀəpʀɔdyksjɔ̃] nf reproduction; **~ interdite** all rights (of reproduction) reserved

reproduire [ʀəpʀɔdɥiʀ] vt to reproduce; **se reproduire** vi (Bio) to reproduce; (recommencer) to recur, re-occur

réprouver [ʀepʀuve] vt to reprove

reptile [ʀɛptil] nm reptile

repu, e [ʀəpy] adj satisfied, sated

république [ʀepyblik] nf republic; **R~ arabe du Yémen** Yemen Arab Republic; **R~ Centrafricaine** Central African Republic; **R~ de Corée** South Korea; **R~ dominicaine** Dominican Republic; **R~ d'Irlande** Irish Republic, Eire; **R~ populaire de Chine** People's Republic of China; **R~ populaire**

démocratique de Corée Democratic People's Republic of Korea; **R~ populaire du Yémen** People's Democratic Republic of Yemen

répugnant, e [ʀepyɲɑ̃, -ɑ̃t] *adj* repulsive, loathsome

répugner [ʀepyɲe]: **~ à** *vt*: **~ à qn** to repel *ou* disgust sb; **~ à faire** to be loath *ou* reluctant to do

réputation [ʀepytasjɔ̃] *nf* reputation; **avoir la ~ d'être …** to have a reputation for being …; **connaître qn/qch de ~** to know sb/ sth by repute; **de ~ mondiale** world-renowned

réputé, e [ʀepyte] *adj* renowned; **être ~ pour** to have a reputation for, be renowned for

requérir [ʀəkeʀiʀ] *vt* (*nécessiter*) to require, call for; (*au nom de la loi*) to call upon; (*Jur: peine*) to call for, demand

requête [ʀəkɛt] *nf* request, petition; (*Jur*) petition

requin [ʀəkɛ̃] *nm* shark

requis, e [ʀəki, -iz] *pp de* **requérir** ▷ *adj* required

RER *sigle m* (= *Réseau express régional*) Greater Paris high-speed train service

rescapé, e [ʀɛskape] *nm/f* survivor

rescousse [ʀɛskus] *nf*: **aller à la ~ de qn** to go to sb's aid *ou* rescue; **appeler qn à la ~** to call on sb for help

réseau, x [ʀezo] *nm* network

réservation [ʀezɛʀvasjɔ̃] *nf* reservation; booking

réserve [ʀezɛʀv] *nf* (*retenue*) reserve; (*entrepôt*) storeroom; (*restriction, aussi: d'Indiens*) reservation; (*de pêche, chasse*) preserve; (*restrictions*): **faire des ~s** to have reservations; **officier de ~** reserve officer; **sous toutes ~s** with all reserve; (*dire*) with reservations; **sous ~ de** subject to; **sans ~** *adv* unreservedly; **en ~** in reserve; **de ~** (*provisions etc*) in reserve

réservé, e [ʀezɛʀve] *adj* (*discret*) reserved; (*chasse, pêche*) private; **~ à** *ou* **pour** reserved for

réserver [ʀezɛʀve] *vt* (*gén*) to reserve; (*chambre, billet etc*) to book, reserve; (*mettre de côté, garder*): **~ qch pour** *ou* **à** to keep *ou* save sth for; **~ qch à qn** to reserve *ou* (book) sth for sb; (*fig: destiner*) to have sth in store for sb; **se ~ le droit de faire** to reserve the right to do

réservoir [ʀezɛʀvwaʀ] *nm* tank

résidence [ʀezidɑ̃s] *nf* residence; **~ principale/secondaire** main/second home; **~ universitaire** hall of residence (*Brit*), dormitory (*US*); **(en) ~ surveillée** (under) house arrest

résidentiel, le [ʀezidɑ̃sjɛl] *adj* residential

résider [ʀezide] *vi*: **~ à** *ou* **dans** *ou* **en** to reside in; **~ dans** (*fig*) to lie in

résidu [ʀezidy] *nm* residue *no pl*

résigner [ʀezine] *vt* to relinquish, resign; **se résigner** *vi*: **se ~ (à qch/à faire)** to resign o.s. (to sth/to doing)

résilier [ʀezilje] *vt* to terminate

résistance [ʀezistɑ̃s] *nf* resistance; (*de réchaud, bouilloire: fil*) element

résistant, e [ʀezistɑ̃, -ɑ̃t] *adj* (*personne*) robust, tough; (*matériau*) strong, hard-wearing ▷ *nm/f* (*patriote*) Resistance worker *ou* fighter

résister [ʀeziste] *vi* to resist; **~ à** *vt* (*assaut, tentation*) to resist; (*effort, souffrance*) to withstand; (*matériau, plante*) to withstand, stand up to; (*personne: désobéir à*) to stand up to, oppose

résolu, e [ʀezɔly] *pp de* **résoudre** ▷ *adj* (*ferme*) resolute; **être ~ à qch/faire** to be set upon sth/doing

résolution [ʀezɔlysjɔ̃] *nf* solving; (*fermeté, décision, Inform*) resolution; (*d'un problème*) solution; **prendre la ~ de** to make a resolution to

résolvais *etc* [ʀezɔlve] *vb voir* **résoudre**

résonner [ʀezɔne] *vi* (*cloche, pas*) to reverberate, resound; (*salle*) to be resonant; **~ de** to resound with

résorber [ʀezɔʀbe]: **se résorber** *vi* (*Méd*) to be resorbed; (*fig*) to be absorbed

résoudre [ʀezudʀ] *vt* to solve; **~ qn à faire qch** to get sb to make up his (*ou* her) mind to do sth; **~ de faire** to resolve to do; **se ~ à faire** to bring o.s. to do

respect [ʀɛspɛ] *nm* respect; **tenir en ~** to keep at bay; **présenter ses ~s à qn** to pay one's respects to sb

respecter [ʀɛspɛkte] *vt* to respect; **faire ~** to enforce; **le lexicographe qui se respecte** (*fig*) any self-respecting lexicographer

respectueux, -euse [ʀɛspɛktɥø, -øz] *adj* respectful; **~ de** respectful of

respiration [ʀɛspiʀasjɔ̃] *nf* breathing *no pl*; **faire une ~ complète** to breathe in and out; **retenir sa ~** to hold one's breath; **~ artificielle** artificial respiration

respirer [ʀɛspiʀe] *vi* to breathe; (*fig: se reposer*) to get one's breath, have a break; (: *être soulagé*) to breathe again ▷ *vt* to breathe (in), inhale; (*manifester: santé, calme etc*) to exude

resplendir [ʀɛsplɑ̃diʀ] *vi* to shine; (*fig*): **~ (de)** to be radiant (with)

responsabilité [ʀɛspɔ̃sabilite] *nf* responsibility; (*légale*) liability; **refuser la ~ de** to deny responsibility (*ou* liability) for; **prendre ses ~s** to assume responsibility for one's actions; **~ civile** civil liability; **~ pénale/morale/collective** criminal/ moral/collective responsibility

responsable [ʀɛspɔ̃sabl] *adj* responsible ▷ *nm/f* (*personne coupable*) person responsible; (*du ravitaillement etc*) person in charge; (*de parti, syndicat*) official; **~ de** responsible for; (*légalement: de dégâts etc*) liable for; (*chargé de*) in charge of, responsible for

resquiller [ʀɛskije] *vi* (*au cinéma, au stade*) to get in on the sly; (*dans le train*) to fiddle a free ride

ressaisir [RəseziR]: **se ressaisir** vi to regain one's self-control; (*équipe sportive*) to rally

ressasser [Rəsase] vt (*remâcher*) to keep turning over; (*redire*) to keep trotting out

ressemblance [Rəsɑ̃blɑ̃s] nf (*visuelle*) resemblance, similarity, likeness; (:*Art*) likeness; (*analogie, trait commun*) similarity

ressemblant, e [Rəsɑ̃blɑ̃, -ɑ̃t] adj (*portrait*) lifelike, true to life

ressembler [Rəsɑ̃ble]: **~ à** vt to be like, resemble; (*visuellement*) to look like; **se ressembler** vi to be (ou look) alike

ressemeler [Rəsəmle] vt to (re)sole

ressentiment [Rəsɑ̃timɑ̃] nm resentment

ressentir [Rəsɑ̃tiR] vt to feel; **se ~ de** to feel (ou show) the effects of

resserrer [RəseRe] vt (*pores*) to close; (*nœud, boulon*) to tighten (up); (*fig: liens*) to strengthen; **se resserrer** vi (*route, vallée*) to narrow; (*liens*) to strengthen; **se ~ (autour de)** to draw closer (around), to close in (on)

resservir [RəseRviR] vt to do ou serve again ▷ vt: **~ qch (à qn)** to serve sth up again (to sb); **~ de qch (à qn)** to give (sb) a second helping of sth; **~ qn (d'un plat)** to give sb a second helping of (a dish); **se ~ de** (*plat*) to take a second helping of; (*outil etc*) to use again

ressort [RəsɔR] vb voir **ressortir** ▷ nm (*pièce*) spring; (*force morale*) spirit; (*recours*): **en dernier ~** as a last resort; (*compétence*): **être du ~ de** to fall within the competence of

ressortir [RəsɔRtiR] vi to go (ou come) out (again); (*contraster*) to stand out; **se ~ de** (*résulter de*): **il ressort de ceci que** it emerges from this that; **~ à** (*Jur*) to come under the jurisdiction of; (*Admin*) to be the concern of; **faire ~** (*fig: souligner*) to bring out

ressortissant, e [RəsɔRtisɑ̃, -ɑ̃t] nm/f national

ressource [RəsuRs] nf: **avoir la ~ de** to have the possibility of; **ressources** nfpl resources; (*fig*) possibilities; **leur seule ~ était de** the only course open to them was to; **~s d'énergie** energy resources

ressusciter [Resysite] vt to resuscitate, restore to life; (*fig*) to revive, bring back ▷ vi to rise (from the dead); (*fig: pays*) to come back to life

restant, e [Restɑ̃, -ɑ̃t] adj remaining ▷ nm: **le ~ (de)** the remainder (of); **un ~ de** (*de trop*) some leftover; (*fig: vestige*) a remnant ou last trace of

restaurant [RestɔRɑ̃] nm restaurant; **manger au ~** to eat out; **~ d'entreprise** staff canteen ou cafeteria (US); **~ universitaire (RU)** university refectory ou cafeteria (US)

restauration [RestɔRasjɔ̃] nf restoration; (*hôtellerie*) catering; **~ rapide** fast food

restaurer [RestɔRe] vt to restore; **se restaurer** vi to have something to eat

reste [Rest] nm (*restant*): **le ~ (de)** the rest (of); (*de trop*): **un ~ (de)** some leftover; (*vestige*): **un**

~ de a remnant ou last trace of; (*Math*) remainder; **restes** nmpl leftovers; (*d'une cité etc, dépouille mortelle*) remains; **avoir du temps de ~** to have time to spare; **ne voulant pas être en ~** not wishing to be outdone; **partir sans attendre** ou **demander son ~** (*fig*) to leave without waiting to hear more; **du ~, au ~** adv besides, moreover; **pour le ~, quant au ~** adv as for the rest

rester [Reste] vi (*dans un lieu, un état, une position*) to stay, remain; (*subsister*) to remain, be left; (*durer*) to last, live on ▷ vb impers: **il reste du pain/deux œufs** there's some bread/there are two eggs left (over); **il reste du temps/10 minutes** there's some time/there are 10 minutes left; **il me reste assez de temps** I have enough time left; **il ne me reste plus qu'à ...** I've just got to ...; **voilà tout ce qui (me) reste** that's all I've got left; **ce qui reste à faire** what remains to be done; **ce qui me reste à faire** what remains for me to do; **(il) reste à savoir/établir si ...** it remains to be seen/established if ou whether ...; **il n'en reste pas moins que ...** the fact remains that ..., it's nevertheless a fact that ...; **en ~ à** (*stade, menaces*) to go no further than, only go as far as; **restons-en là** let's leave it at that; **~ sur une impression** to retain an impression; **y ~**: **il a failli y rester** he nearly met his end

restituer [Restitɥe] vt (*objet, somme*): **~ qch (à qn)** to return ou restore sth (to sb); (*énergie*) to release; (*son*) to reproduce

restreindre [RestRɛdR] vt to restrict, limit; **se restreindre** (*dans ses dépenses etc*) to cut down; (*champ de recherches*) to narrow

restriction [Restriksjɔ̃] nf restriction; (*condition*) qualification; **restrictions** nfpl (*mentales*) reservations; **sans ~** adv unreservedly

résultat [Rezylta] nm result; (*conséquence*) outcome no pl, result; (*d'élection etc*) results pl; **résultats** nmpl (*d'une enquête*) findings; **~s sportifs** sports results

résulter [Rezylte]: **~ de** vt to result from, be the result of; **il résulte de ceci que ...** the result of this is that ...

résumé [Rezyme] nm summary, résumé; **faire le ~ de** to summarize; **en ~** adv in brief; (*pour conclure*) to sum up

résumer [Rezyme] vt (*texte*) to summarize; (*récapituler*) to sum up; (*fig*) to epitomize, typify; **se résumer** vi (*personne*) to sum up (one's ideas); **se ~ à** to come down to

résurrection [RezyRɛksjɔ̃] nf resurrection; (*fig*) revival

rétablir [RetabliR] vt to restore, re-establish; (*personne: traitement*): **~ qn** to restore sb to health, help sb recover; (*Admin*): **~ qn dans son emploi/ses droits** to reinstate sb in his post/restore sb's rights; **se rétablir** vi (*guérir*) to recover; (*silence, calme*) to return, be restored; (*Gym etc*) **se ~ (sur)** to pull o.s. up (onto)

rétablissement [retablismɑ̃] *nm* restoring; (*guérison*) recovery; pull-up

retaper [rətape] *vt* (*maison, voiture etc*) to do up; (*fam: revigorer*) to buck up; (*redactylographier*) to retype

retard [rətaʀ] *nm* (*d'une personne attendue*) lateness *no pl*; (*sur l'horaire, un programme, une échéance*) delay; (*fig: scolaire, mental etc*) backwardness; **être en ~ (pays)** to be backward; (*dans paiement, travail*) to be behind; **en ~ (de deux heures)** (two hours) late; **désolé d'être en ~** sorry I'm late; **avoir un ~ de deux km** (*Sport*) to be two km behind; **rattraper son ~** to catch up; **avoir du ~** to be late; (*sur un programme*) to be behind (schedule); **prendre du ~** (*train, avion*) to be delayed; (*montre*) to lose (time); **sans ~** *adv* without delay; **~ à l'allumage** (*Auto*) retarded spark; **~ scolaire** backwardness at school

retardataire [rətaʀdatɛʀ] *adj* late; (*enfant, idées*) backward ▷ *nm/f* latecomer; backward child

retardement [rətaʀdəmɑ̃]: **à ~** *adj* delayed action *cpd*; **bombe à ~** time bomb

retarder [rətaʀde] *vt* to delay; (*sur un horaire*): **~ qn (d'une heure)** to delay sb (an hour); (*sur un programme*): **~ qn (de trois mois)** to set sb back *ou* delay sb (three months); (*départ, date*): **~ qch (de deux jours)** to put sth back (two days), delay sth (for *ou* by two days); (*horloge*) to put back ▷ *vi* (*montre*) to be slow; (*: habituellement*) to lose (time); **je retarde (d'une heure)** I'm (an hour) slow

retenir [rətniʀ] *vt* (*garder, retarder*) to keep, detain; (*maintenir: objet qui glisse, fig: colère, larmes, rire*) to hold back; (*: objet suspendu*) to hold; (*: chaleur, odeur*) to retain; (*fig: empêcher d'agir*): **~ qn (de faire)** to hold sb back (from doing); (*se rappeler*) to retain; (*réserver*) to reserve; (*accepter*) to accept; (*prélever*): **~ qch (sur)** to deduct sth (from); **se retenir** *vi* (*euphémisme*) to hold on; (*se raccrocher*): **se ~ à** to hold onto; (*se contenir*): **se ~ de faire** to restrain o.s. from doing; **~ son souffle** *ou* **haleine** to hold one's breath; **~ qn à dîner** to ask sb to stay for dinner; **je pose trois et je retiens deux** put down three and carry two

retentir [rətɑ̃tiʀ] *vi* to ring out; (*salle*): **~ de** to ring *ou* resound with; **~ sur qn** (*fig*) to have an effect upon

retentissant, e [rətɑ̃tisɑ̃, -ɑ̃t] *adj* resounding; (*fig*) impact-making

retentissement [rətɑ̃tismɑ̃] *nm* (*retombées*) repercussions *pl*; effect, impact

retenu, e [rətny] *pp de* **retenir** ▷ *adj* (*place*) reserved; (*personne: empêché*) held up; (*propos: contenu, discret*) restrained ▷ *nf* (*prélèvement*) deduction; (*Math*) number to carry over; (*Scol*) detention; (*modération*) (self-)restraint; (*réserve*) reserve, reticence; (*Auto*) tailback

réticence [retisɑ̃s] *nf* reticence *no pl*, reluctance *no pl*; **sans ~** without hesitation

réticent, e [retisɑ̃, -ɑ̃t] *adj* reticent, reluctant

rétine [retin] *nf* retina

retiré, e [rətiʀe] *adj* (*solitaire*) secluded; (*éloigné*) remote

retirer [rətiʀe] *vt* (*argent, plainte*) to withdraw; (*vêtement, lunettes*) to take off, remove; (*enlever*): **~ qch à qn** to take sth from sb; (*extraire*): **~ qn/qch de** to take sb away from/ sth out of, remove sb/sth from; (*reprendre: bagages, billets*) to collect, pick up; **~ des avantages de** to derive advantages from; **se retirer** *vi* (*partir, reculer*) to withdraw; (*prendre sa retraite*) to retire; **se ~ de** to withdraw from; to retire from

retombées [rətɔ̃be] *nfpl* (*radioactives*) fallout *sg*; (*fig*) fallout; spin-offs

retomber [rətɔ̃be] *vi* (*à nouveau*) to fall again; (*rechuter*): **~ malade/dans l'erreur** to fall ill again/fall back into error; (*atterrir: après un saut etc*) to land; (*tomber, redescendre*) to fall back; (*pendre*) to fall, hang (down); (*échoir*): **~ sur qn** to fall on sb

rétorquer [retɔʀke] *vt*: **~ (à qn) que** to retort (to sb) that

retouche [rətuʃ] *nf* touching up *no pl*; (*sur vêtement*) alteration; **faire une ~** *ou* **des ~s à** to touch up

retoucher [rətuʃe] *vt* (*photographie, tableau*) to touch up; (*texte, vêtement*) to alter

retour [rətuʀ] *nm* return; **au ~** (*en arrivant*) when we (*ou* they *etc*) get (*ou* got) back; (*en route*) on the way back; **pendant le ~** on the way *ou* journey back; **à mon/ton ~** on my/ your return; **au ~ de** on the return of; **être de ~ (de)** to be back (from); **de ~ à .../chez moi** back at .../back home; **quand serons-nous de ~?** when do we get back? **en ~** *adv* in return; **par ~ du courrier** by return of post; **par un juste ~ des choses** by a favourable twist of fate; **match ~** return match; **~ en arrière** (*Ciné*) flashback; (*mesure*) backward step; **~ de bâton** kickback; **~ de chariot** carriage return; **~ à l'envoyeur** (*Postes*) return to sender; **~ de flamme** backfire; **~ (automatique) à la ligne** (*Inform*) wordwrap; **~ de manivelle** (*fig*) backfire; **~ offensif** renewed attack; **~ aux sources** (*fig*) return to basics

retourner [rətuʀne] *vt* (*dans l'autre sens: matelas, crêpe*) to turn (over); (*: caisse*) to turn upside down; (*: sac, vêtement*) to turn inside out; (*fig: argument*) to turn back; (*en remuant: terre, sol, foin*) to turn over; (*émouvoir: personne*) to shake; (*renvoyer, restituer*): **~ qch à qn** to return sth to sb ▷ *vi* (*aller, revenir*): **~ quelque part/à** to go back *ou* return somewhere/to; **~ à** (*état, activité*) to return to, go back to; **se retourner** *vi* to turn over; (*tourner la tête*) to turn round; **s'en ~** to go back; **se ~ contre**

(fig) to turn against; **savoir de quoi il retourne** to know what it is all about; **~ sa veste** *(fig)* to turn one's coat; **~ en arrière** *ou* **sur ses pas** to turn back, retrace one's steps; **~ aux sources** to go back to basics

retrait [ʀətʀɛ] *nm (d'argent)* withdrawal; collection; *(rétrécissement)* shrinkage; **en ~** *adj* set back; **écrire en ~** to indent; **~ du permis (de conduire)** disqualification from driving *(Brit)*, revocation of driver's license *(US)*

retraite [ʀətʀɛt] *nf (d'une armée, Rel, refuge)* retreat; *(d'un employé)* retirement; *(revenu)* (retirement) pension; **être/mettre à la ~** to be retired/pension off *ou* retire; **prendre sa ~** to retire; **~ anticipée** early retirement; **~ aux flambeaux** torchlight tattoo

retraité, e [ʀətʀete] *adj* retired *▷ nm/f* (old age) pensioner

retrancher [ʀətʀɑ̃ʃe] *vt (passage, détails)* to take out, remove; *(nombre, somme)*: **~ qch de** to take *ou* deduct sth from; *(couper)* to cut off; **se ~ derrière/dans** to entrench o.s. behind/in; *(fig)* to take refuge behind/in

retransmettre [ʀətʀɑ̃smɛtʀ] *vt (Radio)* to broadcast, relay; *(TV)* to show

rétrécir [ʀetʀesiʀ] *vt (vêtement)* to take in *▷ vi* to shrink; **se rétrécir** *vi (route, vallée)* to narrow

rétribution [ʀetʀibysjɔ̃] *nf* payment

rétro [ʀetʀo] *adj inv* old-style *▷ nm (rétroviseur)* (rear-view) mirror; **la mode ~** the nostalgia vogue

rétrograde [ʀetʀɔɡʀad] *adj* reactionary, backward-looking

rétroprojecteur [ʀetʀopʀɔʒɛktœʀ] *nm* overhead projector

rétrospectif, -ive [ʀetʀɔspɛktif, -iv] *adj, nf (Art)* retrospective; *(Ciné)* season, retrospective

rétrospectivement [ʀetʀɔspɛktivmɑ̃] *adv* in retrospect

retrousser [ʀətʀuse] *vt* to roll up; *(fig: nez)* to wrinkle; *(: lèvres)* to curl

retrouvailles [ʀətʀuvaj] *nfpl* reunion *sg*

retrouver [ʀətʀuve] *vt (fugitif, objet perdu)* to find; *(occasion)* to find again; *(calme, santé)* to regain; *(reconnaître: expression, style)* to recognize; *(revoir)* to see again; *(rejoindre)* to meet (again), join; **se retrouver** *vi* to meet; *(s'orienter)* to find one's way; **se ~ quelque part** to find o.s. somewhere; to end up somewhere; **se ~ seul/sans argent** to find o.s. alone/with no money; **se ~ dans** *(calculs, dossiers, désordre)* to make sense of it; **s'y ~** *(y voir clair)* to make sense of it; *(rentrer dans ses frais)* to break even

rétroviseur [ʀetʀɔvizœʀ] *nm* (rear-view) mirror

réunion [ʀeynjɔ̃] *nf* bringing together; joining; *(séance)* meeting

réunir [ʀeyniʀ] *vt (convoquer)* to call together; *(rassembler)* to gather together; *(inviter: amis, famille)* to have round, have in; *(cumuler: qualités etc)* to combine; *(rapprocher: ennemis)* to bring together (again), reunite; *(rattacher: parties)* to join (together); **se réunir** *vi (se rencontrer)* to meet; *(s'allier)* to unite

réussi, e [ʀeysi] *adj* successful

réussir [ʀeysiʀ] *vi* to succeed, be successful; *(à un examen)* to pass; *(plante, culture)* to thrive, do well *▷ vt* to make a success of; to bring off; **~ à faire** to succeed in doing; **~ à qn** to go right for sb; *(être bénéfique à)* to agree with sb; **le travail/le mariage lui réussit** work/married life agrees with him

réussite [ʀeysit] *nf* success; *(Cartes)* patience

revaloir [ʀəvalwaʀ] *vt*: **je vous revaudrai cela** I'll repay you some day; *(en mal)* I'll pay you back for this

revanche [ʀəvɑ̃ʃ] *nf* revenge; *(sport)* revenge match; **prendre sa ~ (sur)** to take one's revenge (on); **en ~** *(par contre)* on the other hand; *(en compensation)* in return

rêve [ʀɛv] *nm* dream; *(activité psychique)*: **le ~** dreaming; **de ~** dream *cpd*; **faire un ~** to have a dream; **~ éveillé** daydreaming *no pl*, daydream

revêche [ʀəvɛʃ] *adj* surly, sour-tempered

réveil [ʀevɛj] *nm (d'un dormeur)* waking up *no pl*; *(fig)* awakening; *(pendule)* alarm (clock); **au ~** when I *(ou you etc)* wake *(ou woke)* up, on waking (up); **sonner le ~** *(Mil)* to sound the reveille

réveille-matin [ʀevɛjmatɛ̃] *nm inv* alarm clock

réveiller [ʀeveje] *vt (personne)* to wake up; *(fig)* to awaken, revive; **se réveiller** *vi* to wake up; *(fig)* to be revived, reawaken

réveillon [ʀevɛjɔ̃] *nm* Christmas Eve; *(de la Saint-Sylvestre)* New Year's Eve; Christmas Eve *(ou New Year's Eve)* party *ou* dinner

réveillonner [ʀevɛjɔne] *vi* to celebrate Christmas Eve *(ou New Year's Eve)*

révélateur, -trice [ʀevelatœʀ, -tʀis] *adj*: **~ (de qch)** revealing (sth) *▷ nm (Photo)* developer

révéler [ʀevele] *vt (gén)* to reveal; *(divulguer)* to disclose, reveal; *(dénoter)* to reveal, show; *(faire connaître au public)*: **~ qn/qch** to make sb/sth widely known, bring sb/sth to the public's notice; **se révéler** *vi* to be revealed, reveal itself; **se ~ facile/faux** to prove (to be) easy/false; **se ~ cruel/un allié sûr** to show o.s. to be cruel/a trustworthy ally

revenant, e [ʀəvnɑ̃, -ɑ̃t] *nm/f* ghost

revendeur, -euse [ʀəvɑ̃dœʀ, -øz] *nm/f (détaillant)* retailer; *(d'occasions)* secondhand dealer; *(de drogue)* (drug-)dealer

revendication [ʀəvɑ̃dikasjɔ̃] *nf* claim, demand; **journée de ~** day of action (in support of one's claims)

revendiquer [ʀəvɑ̃dike] *vt* to claim, demand; *(responsabilité)* to claim *▷ vi* to agitate in favour of one's claims

r

revendre [Rəvɑ̃dR] *vt* (*d'occasion*) to resell; (*détailler*) to sell; (*vendre davantage de*): ~ **du sucre/un foulard/deux bagues** to sell more sugar/another scarf/another two rings; **à** ~ *adv* (*en abondance*) to spare

revenir [RəvniR] *vi* to come back; (*Culin:*) **faire** ~ to brown; (*coûter*): ~ **cher/à 100 euros** (**à qn**) to cost (sb) a lot/100 euros; ~ **à** (*reprendre: études, projet*) to return to, go back to; (*équivaloir à*) to amount to; ~ **à qn** (*rumeur, nouvelle*) to get back to sb, reach sb's ears; (*part, honneur*) to come back to sb; ~ **de** (*fig: maladie, étonnement*) to recover from; ~ **sur** (*question, sujet*) to go back over; (*engagement*) to go back on; ~ **à la charge** to return to the attack; ~ **à soi** to come round; **n'en pas** ~: **je n'en reviens** I can't get over it; ~ **sur ses pas** to retrace one's steps; **cela revient à dire que/au même** it amounts to saying that/to the same thing; ~ **de loin** (*fig*) to have been at death's door

revenu, e [Rəvny] *pp de* **revenir** ▷ *nm* income; (*de l'État*) revenue; (*d'un capital*) yield; **revenus** *nmpl* income *sg*; ~ **national brut** gross national income

rêver [Reve] *vi, vt* to dream; (*rêvasser*) to (day) dream; ~ **de** (*voir en rêve*) to dream of *ou* about; ~ **de qch/de faire** to dream of sth/of doing; ~ **à** to dream of

réverbère [ReverbER] *nm* street lamp *ou* light

réverbérer [Reverbere] *vt* to reflect

révérence [Reverɑ̃s] *nf* (*vénération*) reverence; (*salut: d'homme*) bow; (*: de femme*) curtsey

rêverie [Revri] *nf* daydreaming *no pl*, daydream

revers [RəvER] *nm* (*de feuille, main*) back; (*d'étoffe*) wrong side; (*de pièce, médaille*) back, reverse; (*Tennis, Ping-Pong*) backhand; (*de veston*) lapel; (*de pantalon*) turn-up; (*fig: échec*) setback; ~ **de fortune** reverse of fortune; **d'un** ~ **de main** with the back of one's hand; **le** ~ **de la médaille** (*fig*) the other side of the coin; **prendre à** ~ (*Mil*) to take from the rear

revêtement [Rəvεtmɑ̃] *nm* (*de paroi*) facing; (*des sols*) flooring; (*de chaussée*) surface; (*de tuyau etc: enduit*) coating

revêtir [RəvεtiR] *vt* (*habit*) to don, put on; (*prendre: importance, apparence*) to take on; ~ **qn de** to dress sb in; (*fig*) to endow *ou* invest sb with; ~ **qch de** to cover sth with; (*fig*) to cloak sth in; ~ **d'un visa** to append a visa to

rêveur, -euse [RεvœR, -øz] *adj* dreamy ▷ *nm/f* dreamer

revient [Rəvjɛ̃] *vb voir* **revenir** ▷ *nm:* **prix de** ~ cost price

revigorer [RəvigoRe] *vt* (*air frais*) to invigorate, brace up; (*repas, boisson*) to revive, buck up

revirement [RəviRmɑ̃] *nm* change of mind; (*d'une situation*) reversal

réviser [Revize] *vt* (*texte, Scol: matière*) to revise; (*comptes*) to audit; (*machine, installation, moteur*) to overhaul, service; (*Jur: procès*) to review

révision [Revizjɔ̃] *nf* revision; auditing *no pl*; (*de voiture*) overhaul, servicing *no pl*; review; **conseil de** ~ (*Mil*) recruiting board; **faire ses** ~**s** (*Scol*) to do one's revision (*Brit*), revise (*Brit*), review (*US*); **la** ~ **des 10 000 km** (*Auto*) the 10,000 km service

revivre [RəvivR] *vi* (*reprendre des forces*) to come alive again; (*traditions*) to be revived ▷ *vt* (*épreuve, moment*) to relive; **faire** ~ (*mode, institution, usage*) to bring back to life

revoir [RəvwaR] *vt* to see again; (*réviser*) to revise (*Brit*), review (*US*) ▷ *nm:* **au** ~ goodbye; **dire au** ~ **à qn** to say goodbye to sb; **se revoir** (*amis*) to meet (again), see each other again

révoltant, e [Revɔltɑ̃, -ɑ̃t] *adj* revolting, appalling

révolte [Revɔlt] *nf* rebellion, revolt

révolter [Revɔlte] *vt* to revolt, outrage; **se révolter** *vi:* **se** ~ (**contre**) to rebel (against); **se** ~ (**à**) to be outraged (by)

révolu, e [Revɔly] *adj* past; (*Admin*): **âgé de 18 ans** ~**s** over 18 years of age; **après trois ans** ~**s** when three full years have passed

révolution [Revɔlysjɔ̃] *nf* revolution; **être en** ~ (*pays etc*) to be in revolt; **la** ~ **industrielle** the industrial revolution

révolutionnaire [RevɔlysjɔnεR] *adj, nm/f* revolutionary

revolver [RevɔlvεR] *nm* gun; (*à barillet*) revolver

révoquer [Revɔke] *vt* (*fonctionnaire*) to dismiss, remove from office; (*arrêt, contrat*) to revoke

revu, e [Rəvy] *pp de* **revoir** ▷ *nf* (*inventaire, examen*) review; (*Mil: défilé*) review, march past; (*: inspection*) inspection, review; (*périodique*) review, magazine; (*pièce satirique*) revue; (*de music-hall*) variety show; **passer en** ~ to review, inspect; (*fig: mentalement*) to review, to go through; ~ **de (la) presse** press review

rez-de-chaussée [Redʃose] *nm inv* ground floor

RF *sigle f* = **République française**

Rhin [Rɛ̃] *nm:* **le** ~ the Rhine

rhinocéros [RinɔseRɔs] *nm* rhinoceros

Rhône [Ron] *nm:* **le** ~ the Rhone

rhubarbe [RybaRb] *nf* rhubarb

rhum [Rɔm] *nm* rum

rhumatisme [Rymatism] *nm* rheumatism *no pl*

rhume [Rym] *nm* cold; ~ **de cerveau** head cold; **le** ~ **des foins** hay fever

ri [Ri] *pp de* **rire**

riant, e [Rjɑ̃, -ɑ̃t] *vb voir* **rire** ▷ *adj* smiling, cheerful; (*campagne, paysage*) pleasant

ricaner [Rikane] *vi* (*avec méchanceté*) to snigger; (*bêtement, avec gêne*) to giggle

riche [Riʃ] *adj* (*gén*) rich; (*personne, pays*) rich, wealthy; ~ **en** rich in; ~ **de** full of; rich in

richesse [Riʃɛs] nf wealth; (fig: de sol, musée etc) richness; **richesses** nfpl (ressources, argent) wealth sg; (fig: trésors) treasures; ~ **en vitamines** high vitamin content

ricochet [Rikɔʃɛ] nm rebound; bounce; **faire** ~ to rebound, bounce; (fig) to rebound; **faire des ~s** to skip stones; **par** ~ adv on the rebound; (fig) as an indirect result

rictus [Riktys] nm grin, (snarling) grimace

ride [Rid] nf wrinkle; (fig) ripple

rideau, x [Rido] nm curtain; **tirer/ouvrir les ~x** to draw/open the curtains; ~ **de fer** metal shutter; (Pol): **le ~ de fer** the Iron Curtain

rider [Ride] vt to wrinkle; (fig) to ripple, ruffle the surface of; **se rider** vi to become wrinkled

ridicule [Ridikyl] adj ridiculous ▷ nm ridiculousness no pl; **le ~** ridicule; (travers: gén pl) absurdities pl; **tourner en** ~ to ridicule

ridiculiser [Ridikylize] vt to ridicule; **se ridiculiser** vi to make a fool of o.s

MOT-CLÉ

rien [Rjɛ̃] pron **1**: (ne)... **rien** nothing; (tournure négative) anything; **qu'est-ce que vous avez?** — **rien** what have you got? — nothing; **il n'a rien dit/fait** he said/did nothing, he hasn't said/done anything; **n'avoir peur de rien** to be afraid ou frightened of nothing, not to be afraid ou frightened of anything; **il n'a rien** (n'est pas blessé) he's all right; **ça ne fait rien** it doesn't matter; **il n'y est pour rien** he's got nothing to do with it
2 (quelque chose): **a-t-il jamais rien fait pour nous?** has he ever done anything for us?
3: **rien de**: **rien d'intéressant** nothing interesting; **rien d'autre** nothing else; **rien du tout** nothing at all; **il n'a rien d'un champion** he's no champion, there's nothing of the champion about him
4: **rien que** just, only; nothing but; **rien que pour lui faire plaisir** only ou just to please him; **rien que la vérité** nothing but the truth; **rien que cela** that alone
▷ excl: **de rien!** not at all!, don't mention it!; **il n'en est rien!** nothing of the sort!; **rien à faire!** it's no good!, it's no use!
▷ nm: **un petit rien** (cadeau) a little something; **des riens** trivia pl; **un rien de** a hint of; **en un rien de temps** in no time at all; **avoir peur d'un rien** to be frightened of the slightest thing

rieur, -euse [RjœR, -øz] adj cheerful

rigide [Riʒid] adj stiff; (fig) rigid; (moralement) strict

rigole [Rigɔl] nf (conduit) channel; (filet d'eau) rivulet

rigoler [Rigɔle] vi (rire) to laugh; (s'amuser) to have (some) fun; (plaisanter) to be joking ou kidding

rigolo, rigolote [Rigɔlo, -ɔt] adj (fam) funny ▷ nm/f comic; (péj) fraud, phoney

rigoureusement [RiguRøzmɑ̃] adv rigorously; ~ **vrai/interdit** strictly true/forbidden

rigoureux, -euse [RiguRø, -øz] adj (morale) rigorous, strict; (personne) stern, strict; (climat, châtiment) rigorous, harsh, severe; (interdiction, neutralité) strict; (preuves, analyse, méthode) rigorous

rigueur [RigœR] nf rigour (Brit), rigor (US); strictness; harshness; **"tenue de soirée de ~"** "evening dress (to be worn)"; **être de ~** to be the usual thing, be the rule; **à la ~** at a pinch; possibly; **tenir ~ à qn de qch** to hold sth against sb

rillettes [Rijet] nfpl ≈ potted meat sg (made from pork or goose)

rime [Rim] nf rhyme; **n'avoir ni ~ ni raison** to have neither rhyme nor reason

rinçage [Rɛ̃saʒ] nm rinsing (out); (opération) rinse

rincer [Rɛ̃se] vt to rinse; (récipient) to rinse out; **se ~ la bouche** to rinse one's mouth out

ring [Riŋ] nm (boxing) ring; **monter sur le ~** (aussi fig) to enter the ring; (: faire carrière de boxeur) to take up boxing

ringard, e [Rɛ̃gaR, -aRd] adj (péj) old-fashioned

rions [Rjɔ̃] vb voir **rire**

riposter [Ripɔste] vi to retaliate ▷ vt: ~ **que** to retort that; ~ **à** vt to counter; to reply to

ripper [Ripe] vt (Inform) to rip

rire [RiR] vi to laugh; (se divertir) to have fun; (plaisanter) to joke ▷ nm laugh; **le ~** laughter; ~ **de** vt to laugh at; **se** ~ to make light of; **tu veux ~!** you must be joking!; ~ **aux éclats/aux larmes** to roar with laughter/laugh until one cries; ~ **jaune** to force oneself to laugh; ~ **sous cape** to laugh up one's sleeve; ~ **au nez de qn** to laugh in sb's face; **pour** ~ (pas sérieusement) for a joke ou a laugh

risée [Rize] nf: **être la ~ de** to be the laughing stock of

risible [Rizibl] adj laughable, ridiculous

risque [Risk] nm risk; **le ~** danger; **l'attrait du ~** the lure of danger; **prendre des ~s** to take risks; **à ses ~s et périls** at his own risk; **au ~ de** at the risk of; ~ **d'incendie** fire risk; ~ **calculé** calculated risk

risqué, e [Riske] adj risky; (plaisanterie) risqué, daring

risquer [Riske] vt to risk; (allusion, question) to venture, hazard; **tu risques qu'on te renvoie** you risk being dismissed; **ça ne risque rien** it's quite safe; ~ **de**: **il risque de se tuer** he could get ou risks getting himself killed; **il a risqué de se tuer** he almost got himself killed; **ce qui risque de se produire** what might ou could well happen; **il ne risque pas de recommencer** there's no chance of him doing that again; **se risquer**:

se ~ dans (s'aventurer) to venture into; **se ~ à faire** (tenter) to dare to do; **~ le tout pour le tout** to risk the lot

rissoler [Risɔle] vi, vt: (faire) ~ to brown

ristourne [Risturn] nf rebate; discount

rite [Rit] nm rite; (fig) ritual

rivage [Rivaʒ] nm shore

rival, e, -aux [Rival, -o] adj, nm/f rival; **sans ~** adj unrivalled

rivaliser [Rivalize] vi: **~ avec** to rival, vie with; (être comparable) to hold its own against, compare with; **~ avec qn de** (élégance etc) to vie with ou rival sb in

rivalité [Rivalite] nf rivalry

rive [Riv] nf shore; (de fleuve) bank

riverain, e [Rivʀɛ̃, -ɛn] adj riverside cpd; lakeside cpd; roadside cpd ▷ nm/f riverside (ou lakeside) resident; (d'une route) local ou roadside resident

rivet [Rivɛ] nm rivet

rivière [Rivjɛʀ] nf river; **~ de diamants** diamond rivière

rixe [Riks] nf brawl, scuffle

riz [Ri] nm rice; **~ au lait** ≈ rice pudding

rizière [Rizjɛʀ] nf paddy field

RMI sigle m (= revenu minimum d'insertion) ≈ income support (Brit), ≈ welfare (US)

RN sigle f = **route nationale**

robe [Rɔb] nf dress; (de juge, d'ecclésiastique) robe; (de professeur) gown; (pelage) coat; **~ de soirée/de mariée** evening/wedding dress; **~ de baptême** christening robe; **~ de chambre** dressing gown; **~ de grossesse** maternity dress

robinet [Rɔbinɛ] nm tap (Brit), faucet (US); **~ du gaz** gas tap; **~ mélangeur** mixer tap

robot [Rɔbo] nm robot; **~ de cuisine** food processor

robuste [Rɔbyst] adj robust, sturdy

robustesse [Rɔbystɛs] nf robustness, sturdiness

roc [Rɔk] nm rock

rocade [Rɔkad] nf (Auto) bypass

rocaille [Rɔkaj] nf (pierres) loose stones pl; (terrain) rocky ou stony ground; (jardin) rockery, rock garden ▷ adj (style) rocaille

roche [Rɔʃ] nf rock

rocher [Rɔʃe] nm rock; (Anat) petrosal bone

rocheux, -euse [Rɔʃø, -øz] adj rocky; **les (montagnes) Rocheuses** the Rockies, the Rocky Mountains

rock [Rɔk], **rock and roll** [Rɔkɛnʀɔl] nm (musique) rock(-'n'-roll); (danse) rock

rodage [Rɔdaʒ] nm running in (Brit), breaking in (US); **en ~** (Auto) running ou breaking in

roder [Rɔde] vt (moteur, voiture) to run in (Brit), break in (US); **~ un spectacle** to iron out the initial problems of a show

rôder [Rɔde] vi to roam ou wander about; (de façon suspecte) to lurk (about ou around)

rôdeur, -euse [Rɔdœʀ, -øz] nm/f prowler

rogne [Rɔɲ] nf: **être en ~** to be mad ou in a temper; **se mettre en ~** to get mad ou in a temper

rogner [Rɔɲe] vt to trim; (fig) to whittle down; **~ sur** (fig) to cut down ou back on

rognons [Rɔɲɔ̃] nmpl kidneys

roi [Rwa] nm king; **les R~s mages** the Three Wise Men, the Magi; **le jour** ou **la fête des R~s, les R~s** Twelfth Night; see note

◈ **FÊTE DES ROIS**

◈ The 'fête des Rois' is celebrated on 6 January.
◈ Figurines representing the Three Wise
◈ Men are traditionally added to the
◈ Christmas crib ('crèche') and people eat
◈ 'galette des Rois', a flat cake in which a
◈ porcelain charm ('la fève') is hidden.
◈ Whoever finds the charm is king or
◈ queen for the day and can choose a
◈ partner.

rôle [Rol] nm role; (contribution) part

rollers [Rɔlœʀ] nmpl Rollerblades®

romain, e [Rɔmɛ̃, -ɛn] adj Roman ▷ nm/f: **R~, e** Roman ▷ nf (Culin) cos (lettuce)

roman, e [Rɔmɑ̃, -an] adj (Archit) Romanesque; (Ling) Romance cpd, Romanic ▷ nm novel; **~ d'amour** love story; **~ d'espionnage** spy novel ou story; **~ noir** thriller; **~ policier** detective novel

romance [Rɔmɑ̃s] nf ballad

romancer [Rɔmɑ̃se] vt to romanticize

romancier, -ière [Rɔmɑ̃sje, -jɛʀ] nm/f novelist

romanesque [Rɔmanɛsk] adj (fantastique) fantastic; (amours, aventures) storybook cpd; (sentimental: personne) romantic; (Littérature) novelistic

roman-feuilleton (pl **romans-feuilletons**) [Rɔmɑ̃fœjtɔ̃] nm serialized novel

romanichel, le [Rɔmaniʃɛl] nm/f gipsy

romantique [Rɔmɑ̃tik] adj romantic

romarin [Rɔmaʀɛ̃] nm rosemary

Rome [Rɔm] n Rome

rompre [Rɔ̃pʀ] vt to break; (entretien, fiançailles) to break off ▷ vi (fiancés) to break it off; **se rompre** vi to break; (Méd) to burst, rupture; **se ~ les os** ou **le cou** to break one's neck; **~ avec** to break with; **à tout ~** adv wildly; **applaudir à tout ~** to bring down the house, applaud wildly; **~ la glace** (fig) to break the ice; **rompez (les rangs)!** (Mil) dismiss!, fall out!

rompu, e [Rɔ̃py] pp de **rompre** ▷ adj (fourbu) exhausted, worn out; **~ à** with wide experience of; inured to

ronce [Rɔ̃s] nf (Bot) bramble branch; (Menuiserie): **~ de noyer** burr walnut; **ronces** nfpl brambles, thorns

ronchonner [Rɔ̃ʃɔne] vi (fam) to grouse, grouch

rond, e [Rɔ̃, Rɔ̃d] adj round; (joues, mollets) well-rounded; (fam: ivre) tight; (sincère, décidé): **être ~ en affaires** to be on the level in business, do an honest deal ▷ nm (cercle) ring; (fam: sou): **je n'ai plus un ~** I haven't a penny left ▷ nf (gén: de surveillance) rounds pl, patrol; (danse) round (dance); (Mus) semibreve (Brit), whole note (US) ▷ adv: **tourner ~** (moteur) to run smoothly; **ça ne tourne pas ~** (fig) there's something not quite right about it; **pour faire un compte ~** to make (it) a round figure, to round (it) off; **avoir le dos ~** to be round-shouldered; **en ~** (s'asseoir, danser) in a ring; **à la ~e** (alentour): **à 10 km à la ~e** for 10 km round; (à chacun son tour): **passer qch à la ~e** to pass sth (a)round; **faire des ~s de jambe** to bow and scrape; **~ de serviette** napkin ring

rondelet, te [Rɔ̃dlε, -εt] adj plump; (fig: somme) tidy; (: bourse) well-lined, fat

rondelle [Rɔ̃dεl] nf (Tech) washer; (tranche) slice, round

rondement [Rɔ̃dmɑ̃] adv (avec décision) briskly; (loyalement) frankly

rondin [Rɔ̃dɛ̃] nm log

rond-point (pl ronds-points) [Rɔ̃pwɛ̃] nm roundabout (Brit), traffic circle (US)

ronflant, e [Rɔ̃flɑ̃, -ɑ̃t] adj (péj) high-flown, grand

ronflement [Rɔ̃fləmɑ̃] nm snore, snoring no pl

ronfler [Rɔ̃fle] vi to snore; (moteur, poêle) to hum; (: plus fort) to roar

ronger [Rɔ̃ʒe] vt to gnaw (at); (vers, rouille) to eat into; **~ son frein** to champ (at) the bit; (fig): **se ~ de souci, se ~ les sangs** to worry o.s. sick, fret; **se ~ les ongles** to bite one's nails

rongeur, -euse [Rɔ̃ʒœR, -øz] nm/f rodent

ronronner [Rɔ̃Rɔne] vi to purr

rosace [Rozas] nf (vitrail) rose window, rosace; (motif: de plafond etc) rose

rosbif [Rɔsbif] nm: **du ~** roasting beef; (cuit) roast beef; **un ~** a joint of (roasting) beef

rose [Roz] nf rose; (vitrail) rose window ▷ adj pink; **~ bonbon** adj inv candy pink; **~ des vents** compass card

rosé, e [Roze] adj pinkish; (vin) **~ rosé** (wine)

roseau, x [Rozo] nm reed

rosée [Roze] adj f voir **rosé** ▷ nf dew; **goutte de ~** dewdrop

rosette [Rozεt] nf rosette (gen of the Légion d'honneur)

rosier [Rozje] nm rosebush, rose tree

rosse [Rɔs] nf (péj: cheval) nag ▷ adj nasty, vicious

rossignol [Rɔsiɲɔl] nm (Zool) nightingale; (crochet) picklock

rot [Ro] nm belch; (de bébé) burp

rotatif, -ive [Rɔtatif, -iv] adj rotary ▷ nf rotary press

rotation [Rɔtasjɔ̃] nf rotation; (fig) rotation, swap-around; (renouvellement) turnover; **par ~** on a rota (Brit) ou rotation (US) basis; **~ des**

cultures crop rotation; **~ des stocks** stock turnover

roter [Rɔte] vi (fam) to burp, belch

rôti [Roti] nm: **du ~** roasting meat; (cuit) roast meat; **un ~ de bœuf/porc** a joint of beef/pork

rotin [Rɔtɛ̃] nm rattan (cane); **fauteuil en ~** cane (arm)chair

rôtir [RotiR] vt (aussi: **faire ~**) to roast ▷ vi to roast; **se ~ au soleil** to bask in the sun

rôtisserie [RotisRi] nf (restaurant) steakhouse; (comptoir, magasin) roast meat counter (ou shop); (traiteur) roast meat shop

rôtissoire [RotiswaR] nf (roasting) spit

rotule [Rɔtyl] nf kneecap, patella

roturier, -ière [RɔtyRje, -jɛR] nm/f commoner

rouage [Rwaʒ] nm cog(wheel), gearwheel; (de montre) part; (fig) cog; **rouages** nmpl (fig) internal structure sg; **les ~s de l'État** the wheels of State

roucouler [Rukule] vi to coo; (fig: péj) to warble; (: amoureux) to bill and coo

roue [Ru] nf wheel; **faire la ~** (paon) to spread ou fan its tail; (Gym) to do a cartwheel; **descendre en ~ libre** to freewheel ou coast down; **pousser à la ~** to put one's shoulder to the wheel; **grande ~** (à la foire) big wheel; **~ à aubes** paddle wheel; **~ dentée** cogwheel; **~ de secours** spare wheel

roué, e [Rwe] adj wily

rouer [Rwe] vt: **~ qn de coups** to give sb a thrashing

rouge [Ruʒ] adj, nm/f red ▷ nm red; (fard) rouge; (vin) **~ red wine; passer au ~** (signal) to go red; (automobiliste) to go through a red light; **porter au ~** (métal) to bring to red heat; **sur la liste ~** (Tél) ex-directory (Brit), unlisted (US); **~ de honte/colère** red with shame/ anger; **se fâcher tout/voir ~** to blow one's top/see red; **~ à joue** blusher; **~ (à lèvres)** lipstick

rouge-gorge [RuʒgɔRʒ] nm robin (redbreast)

rougeole [Ruʒɔl] nf measles sg

rougeoyer [Ruʒwaje] vi to glow red

rouget [Ruʒε] nm mullet

rougeur [RuʒœR] nf redness; (du visage) red face; **rougeurs** nfpl (Méd) red blotches

rougir [RuʒiR] vi to turn red; (de honte, timidité) to blush, flush; (de plaisir, colère) to flush; (fraise, tomate) to go ou turn red; (ciel) to redden

rouille [Ruj] adj inv rust-coloured, rusty ▷ nf rust; (Culin) spicy (Provençal) sauce served with fish dishes

rouillé, e [Ruje] adj rusty

rouiller [Ruje] vt to rust ▷ vi to rust, go rusty; **se rouiller** vi to rust; (fig: mentalement) to become rusty; (: physiquement) to grow stiff

roulant, e [Rulɑ̃, -ɑ̃t] adj (meuble) on wheels; (surface, trottoir, tapis) moving; **matériel ~** (Rail) rolling stock; **escalier ~** = escalator; **personnel ~** (Rail) train crews pl

rouleau, x [Rulo] *nm* (*de papier, tissu, pièces de monnaie, Sport*) roll; (*de machine à écrire*) roller, platen; (*à mise en plis, à peinture, vague*) roller; **être au bout du ~** (*fig*) to be at the end of the line; **~ compresseur** steamroller; **~ à pâtisserie** rolling pin; **~ de pellicule** roll of film

roulement [Rulmɑ̃] *nm* (*bruit*) rumbling *no pl*, rumble; (*rotation*) rotation; turnover; (*: de capitaux*) circulation; **par ~** on a rota (*Brit*) *ou* rotation (*US*) basis; **~ (à billes)** ball bearings *pl*; **~ de tambour** drum roll; **~ d'yeux** roll(ing) of the eyes

rouler [Rule] *vt* to roll; (*papier, tapis*) to roll up; (*Culin: pâte*) to roll out; (*fam: duper*) to do, con ▷ *vi* (*bille, boule*) to roll; (*voiture, train*) to go, run; (*automobiliste*) to drive; (*cycliste*) to ride; (*bateau*) to roll; (*tonnerre*) to rumble, roll; (*dégringoler*): **~ en bas de** to roll down; **~ sur** (*conversation*) to turn on; **se ~ dans** (*boue*) to roll in; (*couverture*) to roll o.s. (up) in; **~ dans la farine** (*fam*) to con; **~ les épaules/hanches** to sway one's shoulders/wiggle one's hips; **~ les "r"** to roll one's r's; **~ sur l'or** to be rolling in money, be rolling in it; **~ (sa bosse)** to go places

roulette [Rulɛt] *nf* (*de table, fauteuil*) castor; (*de dentiste*) drill; (*de pâtissier*) pastry wheel; (*jeu*): **la ~** roulette; **à ~s** on castors; **la ~ russe** Russian roulette; **ça a marché comme sur des ~s** (*fam*) it went off very smoothly

roulis [Ruli] *nm* roll(ing)

roulotte [Rulɔt] *nf* caravan

roumain, e [Rumɛ̃, -ɛn] *adj* Rumanian, Romanian ▷ *nm* (*Ling*) Rumanian, Romanian ▷ *nm/f*: **R~, e** Rumanian, Romanian

Roumanie [Rumani] *nf*: **la ~** Rumania, Romania

rouquin, e [Rukɛ̃, -in] *nm/f* (*péj*) redhead

rouspéter [Ruspete] *vi* (*fam*) to moan, grouse

rousse [Rus] *adj f voir* **roux**

roussir [Rusir] *vt* to scorch ▷ *vi* (*feuilles*) to go *ou* turn brown; (*Culin*): **faire ~** to brown

route [Rut] *nf* road; (*fig: chemin*) way; (*itinéraire, parcours*) route; (*fig: voie*) road, path; **par (la) ~** by road; **il y a trois heures de ~** it's a three-hour ride *ou* journey; **en ~** *adv* on the way; **en ~!** let's go!; **en cours de ~** en route; **mettre en ~** to start up; **se mettre en ~** to set off; **faire ~ vers** to head towards; **faire fausse ~** (*fig*) to be on the wrong track; **~ nationale (RN)** ≈ A-road (*Brit*), ≈ state highway (*US*)

routier, -ière [Rutje, -jɛR] *adj* road *cpd* ▷ *nm* (*camionneur*) (long-distance) lorry (*Brit*) *ou* truck driver; (*restaurant*) ≈ transport café (*Brit*), ≈ truck stop (*US*); (*scout*) ≈ rover; (*cycliste*) road racer ▷ *nf* (*voiture*) touring car; **vieux ~** old stager; **carte routière** road map

routine [Rutin] *nf* routine; **visite/contrôle de ~** routine visit/check

routinier, -ière [Rutinje, -jɛR] *adj* (*péj: travail*) humdrum, routine; (*: personne*) addicted to routine

rouvrir [RuvRiR] *vt, vi* to reopen, open again; **se rouvrir** *vi* (*blessure*) to open up again

roux, rousse [Ru, Rus] *adj* red; (*personne*) red-haired ▷ *nm/f* redhead ▷ *nm* (*Culin*) roux

royal, e, -aux [Rwajal, -o] *adj* royal; (*fig*) fit for a king, princely; blissful; thorough

royaume [Rwajom] *nm* kingdom; (*fig*) realm; **le ~ des cieux** the kingdom of heaven

Royaume-Uni [Rwajomyni] *nm*: **le ~** the United Kingdom

royauté [Rwajote] *nf* (*dignité*) kingship; (*régime*) monarchy

ruban [Rybɑ̃] *nm* (*gén*) ribbon; (*pour ourlet, couture*) binding; (*de télescripteur etc*) tape; (*d'acier*) strip; **~ adhésif** adhesive tape; **~ carbone** carbon ribbon

rubéole [Rybeɔl] *nf* German measles *sg*, rubella

rubis [Rybi] *nm* ruby; (*Horlogerie*) jewel; **payer ~ sur l'ongle** to pay cash on the nail

rubrique [RybRik] *nf* (*titre, catégorie*) heading, rubric; (*Presse: article*) column

ruche [Ryʃ] *nf* hive

rude [Ryd] *adj* (*barbe, toile*) rough; (*métier, tâche*) hard, tough; (*climat*) severe, harsh; (*bourru*) harsh, rough; (*fruste: manières*) rugged, tough; (*fam: fameux*) jolly good; **être mis à ~ épreuve** to be put through the mill

rudement [Rydmɑ̃] *adv* (*tomber, frapper*) hard; (*traiter, reprocher*) harshly; (*fam: très*) terribly; (*: beaucoup*) terribly hard

rudimentaire [Rydimɑ̃tɛR] *adj* rudimentary, basic

rudiments [Rydimɑ̃] *nmpl* rudiments; basic knowledge *sg*; basic principles; **avoir des ~ d'anglais** to have a smattering of English

rudoyer [Rydwaje] *vt* to treat harshly

rue [Ry] *nf* street; **être/jeter qn à la ~** to be on the streets/throw sb out onto the street

ruée [Rɥe] *nf* rush; **la ~ vers l'or** the gold rush

ruelle [Rɥɛl] *nf* alley(way)

ruer [Rɥe] *vi* (*cheval*) to kick out; **se ruer** *vi*: **se ~ sur** to pounce on; **se ~ vers/dans/hors de** to rush *ou* dash towards/into/out of; **~ dans les brancards** to become rebellious

rugby [Rygbi] *nm* rugby (football); **~ à treize/quinze** rugby league/union

rugir [RyʒiR] *vi* to roar

rugueux, -euse [Rygø, -øz] *adj* rough

ruine [Rɥin] *nf* ruin; **ruines** *nfpl* ruins; **tomber en ~** to fall into ruin(s)

ruiner [Rɥine] *vt* to ruin

ruineux, -euse [Rɥinø, -øz] *adj* terribly expensive to buy (*ou* run), ruinous; extravagant

ruisseau, x [Rɥiso] *nm* stream, brook; (*caniveau*) gutter; (*fig*): **~x de larmes/sang** floods of tears/streams of blood

ruisseler [ʀɥisle] *vi* to stream; ~ **(d'eau)** to be streaming (with water); ~ **de lumière** to stream with light

rumeur [ʀymœʀ] *nf* (*bruit confus*) rumbling; hubbub *no pl*; (*protestation*) murmur(ing); (*nouvelle*) rumour (*Brit*), rumor (*US*)

ruminer [ʀymine] *vt* (*herbe*) to ruminate; (*fig*) to ruminate on *ou* over, chew over ▷ *vi* (*vache*) to chew the cud, ruminate

rupture [ʀyptyʀ] *nf* (*de câble, digue*) breaking; (*de tendon*) rupture, tearing; (*de négociations etc*) breakdown; (*de contrat*) breach; (*dans continuité*) break; (*séparation, désunion*) break-up, split; **en ~ de ban** at odds with authority; **en ~ de stock** (*Comm*) out of stock

rural, e, -aux [ʀyʀal, -o] *adj* rural, country *cpd* ▷ *nmpl*: **les ruraux** country people

ruse [ʀyz] *nf*: **la ~** cunning, craftiness; (*pour tromper*) trickery; **une ~** a trick, a ruse; **par ~** by trickery

rusé, e [ʀyze] *adj* cunning, crafty

russe [ʀys] *adj* Russian ▷ *nm* (*Ling*) Russian ▷ *nm/f*: **R~** Russian

Russie [ʀysi] *nf*: **la ~** Russia; **la ~ blanche** White Russia; **la ~ soviétique** Soviet Russia

rustine [ʀystin] *nf* repair patch (*for bicycle inner tube*)

rustique [ʀystik] *adj* rustic; (*plante*) hardy

rustre [ʀystʀ] *nm* boor

rutilant, e [ʀytilɑ̃, -ɑ̃t] *adj* gleaming

rythme [ʀitm] *nm* rhythm; (*vitesse*) rate; (: *de la vie*) pace, tempo; **au ~ de 10 par jour** at the rate of 10 a day

rythmé, e [ʀitme] *adj* rhythmic(al)

S

s' [s] *pron voir* **se**

SA *sigle f* = **société anonyme**; (= *Son Altesse*) HH

sa [sa] *adj possessif voir* **son**

sable [sabl] *nm* sand; ~**s mouvants** quicksand(s)

sablé [sable] *adj* (*allée*) sandy ▷ *nm* shortbread biscuit; **pâte ~e** (*Culin*) shortbread dough

sabler [sable] *vt* to sand; (*contre le verglas*) to grit; ~ **le champagne** to drink champagne

sablier [sablije] *nm* hourglass; (*de cuisine*) egg timer

sablonneux, -euse [sablɔnø, -øz] *adj* sandy

saborder [sabɔʀde] *vt* (*navire*) to scuttle; (*fig*) to wind up, shut down

sabot [sabo] *nm* clog; (*de cheval, bœuf*) hoof; ~ **(de Denver)** (wheel) clamp; ~ **de frein** brake shoe

saboter [sabɔte] *vt* (*travail, morceau de musique*) to botch, make a mess of; (*machine, installation, négociation etc*) to sabotage

sac [sak] *nm* bag; (*à charbon etc*) sack; (*pillage*) sack(ing); **mettre à ~** to sack; ~ **à provisions/ de voyage** shopping/travelling bag; ~ **de couchage** sleeping bag; ~ **à dos** rucksack; ~ **à main** handbag; ~ **de plage** beach bag

saccadé, e [sakade] *adj* jerky; (*respiration*) spasmodic

saccager [sakaʒe] *vt* (*piller*) to sack, lay waste; (*dévaster*) to create havoc in, wreck

saccharine [sakaʀin] *nf* saccharin(e)

sacerdoce [sasɛʀdɔs] *nm* priesthood; (*fig*) calling, vocation

S

sache etc [saʃ] vb voir **savoir**
sachet [saʃɛ] nm (small) bag; (de lavande, poudre, shampooing) sachet; **thé en ~s** tea bags; **~ de thé** tea bag; **du potage en ~** packet soup
sacoche [sakɔʃ] nf (gén) bag; (de bicyclette) saddlebag; (du facteur) (post)bag; (d'outils) toolbag
sacquer [sake] vt (fam: candidat, employé) to sack; (: réprimander, mal noter) to plough
sacre [sakʀ] nm coronation; consecration
sacré, e [sakʀe] adj sacred; (fam: satané) blasted; (: fameux): **un ~ ...** a heck of a ...; (Anat) sacral
sacrement [sakʀəmã] nm sacrament; **les derniers ~s** the last rites
sacrifice [sakʀifis] nm sacrifice; **faire le ~ de** to sacrifice
sacrifier [sakʀifje] vt to sacrifice; **~ à** vt to conform to; **se sacrifier** to sacrifice o.s.; **articles sacrifiés** (Comm) items sold at rock-bottom ou give-away prices
sacristie [sakʀisti] nf sacristy; (culte protestant) vestry
sadique [sadik] adj sadistic ▷ nm/f sadist
safran [safʀã] nm saffron
sage [saʒ] adj wise; (enfant) good ▷ nm wise man; sage
sage-femme [saʒfam] nf midwife
sagesse [saʒɛs] nf wisdom
Sagittaire [saʒitɛʀ] nm: **le ~** Sagittarius, the Archer; **être du ~** to be Sagittarius
Sahara [saaʀa] nm: **le ~** the Sahara (Desert); **le ~ occidental** (pays) Western Sahara
saignant, e [sɛɲã, -ãt] adj (viande) rare; (blessure, plaie) bleeding
saignée [seɲe] nf (Méd) bleeding no pl, bloodletting no pl; (Anat): **la ~ du bras** the bend of the arm; (fig: Mil) heavy losses pl; (: prélèvement) savage cut
saigner [seɲe] vi to bleed ▷ vt to bleed; (animal) to bleed to death; **~ qn à blanc** (fig) to bleed sb white; **~ du nez** to have a nosebleed
saillie [saji] nf (sur un mur etc) projection; (trait d'esprit) witticism; (accouplement) covering, serving; **faire ~** to project, stick out; **en ~, formant ~** projecting, overhanging
saillir [sajiʀ] vi to project, stick out; (veine, muscle) to bulge ▷ vt (Élevage) to cover, serve
sain, e [sɛ̃, sɛn] adj healthy; (dents, constitution) healthy, sound; (lectures) wholesome; **~ et sauf** safe and sound, unharmed; **~ d'esprit** sound in mind, sane
saindoux [sɛ̃du] nm lard
saint, e [sɛ̃, sɛ̃t] adj holy; (fig) saintly ▷ nm/f saint; **la S~e Vierge** the Blessed Virgin
Saint-Esprit [sɛ̃tɛspʀi] nm: **le ~** the Holy Spirit ou Ghost
sainteté [sɛ̃tte] nf holiness; saintliness
Saint-Sylvestre [sɛ̃silvɛstʀ] nf: **la ~** New Year's Eve
sais etc [sɛ] vb voir **savoir**
saisie [sezi] nf seizure; **à la ~** (texte) being keyed; **~ (de données)** (data) capture

saisir [seziʀ] vt to take hold of, grab; (fig: occasion) to seize; (comprendre) to grasp; (entendre) to get, catch; (émotions) to take hold of, come over; (Inform) to capture, keyboard; (Culin) to fry quickly; (Jur: biens, publication) to seize; (: juridiction): **un tribunal d'une affaire** to submit ou refer a case to a court; **se ~ de** vt to seize; **être saisi** (frappé de) to be overcome
saisissant, e [sezisã, -ãt] adj startling, striking; (froid) biting
saison [sezɔ̃] nf season; **la belle/mauvaise ~** the summer/winter months; **être de ~** to be in season; **en/hors ~** in/out of season; **haute/basse/morte ~** high/low/slack season; **la ~ des pluies/des amours** the rainy/mating season
saisonnier, -ière [sezɔnje, -jɛʀ] adj seasonal ▷ nm (travailleur) seasonal worker; (vacancier) seasonal holidaymaker
sait [sɛ] vb voir **savoir**
salade [salad] nf (Bot) lettuce etc (generic term); (Culin) (green) salad; (fam: confusion) tangle, muddle; **salades** nfpl (fam): **raconter des ~s** to tell tales (fam); **haricots en ~** bean salad; **~ composée** mixed salad; **~ de concombres** cucumber salad; **~ de fruits** fruit salad; **~ niçoise** salade niçoise; **~ russe** Russian salad; **~ de tomates** tomato salad; **~ verte** green salad
saladier [saladje] nm (salad) bowl
salaire [salɛʀ] nm (annuel, mensuel) salary; (hebdomadaire, journalier) pay, wages pl; (fig) reward; **~ de base** basic salary (ou wage); **~ de misère** starvation wage; **~ minimum interprofessionnel de croissance (SMIC)** index-linked guaranteed minimum wage
salami [salami] nm salami no pl, salami sausage
salarié, e [salaʀje] adj salaried; wage-earning ▷ nm/f salaried employee; wage-earner
salaud [salo] nm (fam!) sod (!), bastard (!)
sale [sal] adj dirty, filthy; (fig: mauvais: avant le nom) nasty
salé, e [sale] adj (liquide, saveur, mer, goût) salty; (Culin: amandes, beurre etc) salted; (: gâteaux) savoury; (fig: grivois) spicy, juicy; (: note, facture) steep, stiff ▷ nm (porc salé) salt pork; **petit ~** = boiling bacon
saler [sale] vt to salt
saleté [salte] nf (état) dirtiness; (crasse) dirt, filth; (tache etc) dirt no pl, something dirty, dirty mark; (fig: tour) filthy trick; (: chose sans valeur) rubbish no pl; (: obscénité) filth no pl; (: microbe etc) bug; **vivre dans la ~** to live in squalor
salière [saljɛʀ] nf saltcellar
salin, e [salɛ̃, -in] adj saline ▷ nf saltworks sg
salir [saliʀ] vt to (make) dirty; (fig) to soil the reputation of; **se salir** vi to get dirty
salissant, e [salisã, -ãt] adj (tissu) which shows the dirt; (métier) dirty, messy

salle [sal] nf room; (d'hôpital) ward; (de restaurant) dining room; (d'un cinéma) auditorium; (: public) audience; **faire ~ comble** to have a full house; **~ d'armes** (pour l'escrime) arms room; **~ d'attente** waiting room; **~ de bain(s)** bathroom; **~ de bal** ballroom; **~ de cinéma** cinema; **~ de classe** classroom; **~ commune** (d'hôpital) ward; **~ de concert** concert hall; **~ de consultation** consulting room (Brit), office (US); **~ de danse** dance hall; **~ de douches** shower-room; **~ d'eau** shower-room; **~ d'embarquement** (à l'aéroport) departure lounge; **~ d'exposition** showroom; **~ de jeux** games room; (pour enfants) playroom; **~ des machines** engine room; **~ à manger** dining room; (mobilier) dining room suite; **~ obscure** cinema (Brit), movie theater (US); **~ d'opération** (d'hôpital) operating theatre; **~ des professeurs** staffroom; **~ de projection** film theatre; **~ de séjour** living room; **~ de spectacle** theatre, cinema; **~ des ventes** saleroom

salon [salɔ̃] nm lounge, sitting room; (mobilier) lounge suite; (exposition) exhibition, show; (mondain, littéraire) salon; **~ de coiffure** hairdressing salon; **~ de discussion** (Inform) chatroom; **~ de thé** tearoom

salope [salɔp] nf (fam!) bitch (!)

saloperie [salɔpʀi] nf (fam!) filth no pl; (action) dirty trick; (chose sans valeur) rubbish no pl

salopette [salɔpɛt] nf dungarees pl; (d'ouvrier) overall(s)

salsifis [salsifi] nm salsify, oyster plant

salubre [salybʀ] adj healthy, salubrious

saluer [salɥe] vt (pour dire bonjour, fig) to greet; (pour dire au revoir) to take one's leave; (Mil) to salute

salut [saly] nm (sauvegarde) safety; (Rel) salvation; (geste) wave; (parole) greeting; (Mil) salute ▷ excl (fam: pour dire bonjour) hi (there); (: pour dire au revoir) see you!, bye!

salutations [salytasjɔ̃] nfpl greetings; **recevez mes ~ distinguées** ou **respectueuses** yours faithfully

samedi [samdi] nm Saturday; voir aussi **lundi**

SAMU [samy] sigle m (= service d'assistance médicale d'urgence) ≈ ambulance (service) (Brit), ≈ paramedics (US)

sanction [sɑ̃ksjɔ̃] nf sanction; (fig) penalty; **prendre des ~s contre** to impose sanctions on

sanctionner [sɑ̃ksjɔne] vt (loi, usage) to sanction; (punir) to punish

sandale [sɑ̃dal] nf sandal; **~s à lanières** strappy sandals

sandwich [sɑ̃dwitʃ] nm sandwich; **pris en ~** sandwiched

sang [sɑ̃] nm blood; **en ~** covered in blood; **jusqu'au ~** (mordre, pincer) till the blood comes; **se faire du mauvais ~** to fret, get in a state

sang-froid [sɑ̃fʀwa] nm calm, sangfroid; **garder/perdre/reprendre son ~** to keep/ lose/regain one's cool; **de ~** in cold blood

sanglant, e [sɑ̃glɑ̃, -ɑ̃t] adj bloody, covered in blood; (combat) bloody; (fig: reproche, affront) cruel

sangle [sɑ̃gl] nf strap; **sangles** nfpl (pour lit etc) webbing sg

sanglier [sɑ̃glije] nm (wild) boar

sanglot [sɑ̃glo] nm sob

sangloter [sɑ̃glɔte] vi to sob

sangsue [sɑ̃sy] nf leech

sanguin, e [sɑ̃gɛ̃, -in] adj blood cpd; (fig) fiery ▷ nf blood orange; (Art) red pencil drawing

sanguinaire [sɑ̃ginɛʀ] adj (animal, personne) bloodthirsty; (lutte) bloody

sanitaire [sanitɛʀ] adj health cpd; **sanitaires** nmpl (salle de bain et w.-c.) bathroom sg; **installation/appareil ~** bathroom plumbing/appliance

sans [sɑ̃] prép without; **~ qu'il s'en aperçoive** without him ou his noticing; **~ scrupules** unscrupulous; **~ manches** sleeveless; **un pull ~ manches** a sleeveless jumper; **~ faute** without fail; **~ arrêt** without a break; **~ ça** (fam) otherwise

sans-abri [sɑ̃zabʀi] nmpl homeless

sans-emploi [sɑ̃zɑ̃plwa] nm/f inv unemployed person; **les ~** the unemployed

sans-gêne [sɑ̃ʒɛn] adj inv inconsiderate ▷ nm inv (attitude) lack of consideration

santé [sɑ̃te] nf health; **avoir une ~ de fer** to be bursting with health; **être en bonne ~** to be in good health, be healthy; **boire à la ~ de qn** to drink (to) sb's health; **"à la ~ de"** "here's to"; **à ta** ou **votre ~!** cheers!; **service de ~** (dans un port etc) quarantine service; **la ~ publique** public health

saoudien, ne [saudjɛ̃, -ɛn] adj Saudi (Arabian) ▷ nm/f: **S~, ne** Saudi (Arabian)

saoul, e [su, sul] adj = **soûl, e**

saper [sape] vt to undermine, sap; **se saper** vi (fam) to dress

sapeur-pompier [sapœʀpɔ̃pje] nm fireman

saphir [safiʀ] nm sapphire; (d'électrophone) needle, sapphire

sapin [sapɛ̃] nm fir (tree); (bois) fir; **~ de Noël** Christmas tree

sarcastique [saʀkastik] adj sarcastic

sarcler [saʀkle] vt to weed

Sardaigne [saʀdɛɲ] nf: **la ~** Sardinia

sardine [saʀdin] nf sardine; **~s à l'huile** sardines in oil

SARL [saʀl] sigle f (= société à responsabilité limitée) ≈ plc (Brit), ≈ Inc. (US)

sarrasin [saʀazɛ̃] nm buckwheat

sas [sas] nm (de sous-marin, d'engin spatial) airlock; (d'écluse) lock

satané, e [satane] adj (fam) confounded

satellite [satelit] nm satellite; **pays ~** satellite country

satin [satɛ̃] nm satin

satire [satiʀ] nf satire; **faire la ~ to** satirize

satirique [satiʀik] adj satirical

satisfaction [satisfaksjɔ̃] nf satisfaction; **à ma grande ~** to my great satisfaction; **obtenir ~** to obtain ou get satisfaction; **donner ~ (à)** to give satisfaction (to)

satisfaire [satisfɛʁ] vt to satisfy; **se satisfaire de** to be satisfied ou content with; **~ à** vt (engagement) to fulfil; (revendications, conditions) to meet, satisfy

satisfaisant, e [satisfəzɑ̃, -ɑ̃t] vb voir **satisfaire** ▷ adj (acceptable) satisfactory; (qui fait plaisir) satisfying

satisfait, e [satisfɛ, -ɛt] pp de **satisfaire** ▷ adj satisfied; **~ de** happy ou satisfied with

saturer [satyʁe] vt to saturate; **~ qn/qch de** to saturate sb/sth with

sauce [sos] nf sauce; (avec un rôti) gravy; **en ~** in a sauce; **~ blanche** white sauce; **~ chasseur** sauce chasseur; **~ tomate** tomato sauce

saucière [sosjɛʁ] nf sauceboat; gravy boat

saucisse [sosis] nf sausage

saucisson [sosisɔ̃] nm (slicing) sausage; **~ à l'ail** garlic sausage

sauf[1] [sof] prép except; **~ si** (à moins que) unless; **~ avis contraire** unless you hear to the contrary; **~ empêchement** barring (any) problems; **~ erreur** if I'm not mistaken; **~ imprévu** unless anything unforeseen arises, barring accidents

sauf[2], sauve [sof, sov] adj unharmed, unhurt; (fig: honneur) intact, saved; **laisser la vie sauve à qn** to spare sb's life

sauge [soʒ] nf sage

saugrenu, e [sogʁəny] adj preposterous, ludicrous

saule [sol] nm willow (tree); **~ pleureur** weeping willow

saumon [somɔ̃] nm salmon inv ▷ adj inv salmon (pink)

saumure [somyʁ] nf brine

saupoudrer [supudʁe] vt: **~ qch de** to sprinkle sth with

saur [sɔʁ] adj m: **hareng ~** smoked ou red herring, kipper

saurai etc [sɔʁe] vb voir **savoir**

saut [so] nm jump; (discipline sportive) jumping; **faire un ~** to (make a) jump ou leap; **faire un ~ chez qn** to pop over to sb's (place); **au ~ du lit** on getting out of bed; **~ en hauteur/longueur** high/long jump; **~ à la corde** skipping; **~ de page/ligne** (Inform) page/line break; **~ en parachute** parachuting no pl; **~ à la perche** pole vaulting; **~ à l'élastique** bungee jumping; **~ périlleux** somersault

saute [sot] nf: **~ de vent/température** sudden change of wind direction/in the temperature; **avoir des ~s d'humeur** to have sudden changes of mood

sauter [sote] vi to jump, leap; (exploser) to blow up, explode; (: fusibles) to blow; (se rompre) to snap, burst; (se détacher) to pop out

(ou off) ▷ vt to jump (over), leap (over); (fig: omettre) to skip, miss (out); **faire ~** to blow up; to burst open; (Culin) to sauté; **~ à pieds joints/à cloche-pied** to make a standing jump/to hop; **~ en parachute** to make a parachute jump; **~ à la corde** to skip; **~ de joie** to jump for joy; **~ de colère** to be hopping with rage ou hopping mad; **~ au cou de qn** to fly into sb's arms; **~ sur une occasion** to jump at an opportunity; **~ aux yeux** to be quite obvious; **~ au plafond** (fig) to hit the roof

sauterelle [sotʁɛl] nf grasshopper

sautiller [sotije] vi (oiseau) to hop; (enfant) to skip

sauvage [sovaʒ] adj (gén) wild; (peuplade) savage; (farouche) unsociable; (barbare) wild, savage; (non officiel) unauthorized, unofficial; **faire du camping ~** to camp in the wild ▷ nm/f savage; (timide) unsociable type, recluse

sauve [sov] adj f voir **sauf**

sauvegarde [sovgaʁd] nf safeguard; **sous la ~ de** under the protection of; **disquette/ fichier de ~** (Inform) backup disk/file

sauvegarder [sovgaʁde] vt to safeguard; (Inform: enregistrer) to save; (: copier) to back up

sauve-qui-peut [sovkipø] nm inv stampede, mad rush ▷ excl run for your life!

sauver [sove] vt to save; (porter secours à) to rescue; (récupérer) to salvage, rescue; **se sauver** vi (s'enfuir) to run away; (fam: partir) to be off; **~ qn de** to save sb from; **~ la vie à qn** to save sb's life; **~ les apparences** to keep up appearances

sauvetage [sovtaʒ] nm rescue; **~ en montagne** mountain rescue; **ceinture de ~** lifebelt (Brit), life preserver (US); **brassière ou gilet de ~** lifejacket (Brit), life preserver (US)

sauveteur [sovtœʁ] nm rescuer

sauvette [sovɛt]: **à la ~** adv (vendre) without authorization; (se marier etc) hastily, hurriedly; **vente à la ~** (unauthorized) street trading, (street) peddling

sauveur [sovœʁ] nm saviour (Brit), savior (US)

savais etc [save] vb voir **savoir**

savamment [savamɑ̃] adv (avec érudition) learnedly; (habilement) skilfully, cleverly

savant, e [savɑ̃, -ɑ̃t] adj scholarly, learned; (calé) clever ▷ nm scientist; **animal ~** performing animal

saveur [savœʁ] nf flavour (Brit), flavor (US); (fig) savour (Brit), savor (US)

savoir [savwaʁ] vt to know; (être capable de): **il sait nager** he knows how to swim, he can swim ▷ nm knowledge; **se savoir** vi (être connu) to be known; **se ~ malade/incurable** to know that one is ill/incurably ill; **il est petit: tu ne peux pas ~!** you won't believe how small he is!; **vous n'êtes pas sans ~ que** you are not ou will not be unaware of the fact that; **je crois ~ que ...**

I believe that ..., I think I know that ...; **je n'en sais rien** I (really) don't know; **à ~ (que)** that is, namely; **faire ~ qch à qn** to let sb know sth, inform sb about sth; **pas que je sache** not as far as I know; **sans le ~** *adv* unknowingly, unwittingly; **en ~ long** to know a lot

savon [savɔ̃] *nm* (*produit*) soap; (*morceau*) bar *ou* tablet of soap; (*fam*): **passer un ~ à qn** to give sb a good dressing-down

savonner [savɔne] *vt* to soap

savonnette [savɔnɛt] *nf* bar of soap

savons [savɔ̃] *vb voir* **savoir**

savourer [savuʀe] *vt* to savour (*Brit*), savor (*US*)

savoureux, -euse [savuʀø, -øz] *adj* tasty; (*fig: anecdote*) spicy, juicy

saxo [saksɔ], **saxophone** [saksɔfɔn] *nm* sax(ophone)

scabreux, -euse [skabʀø, -øz] *adj* risky; (*indécent*) improper, shocking

scandale [skɑ̃dal] *nm* scandal; **faire un ~** (*scène*) to make a scene; (*Jur*) create a disturbance; **faire ~** to scandalize people; **au grand ~ de ...** to the great indignation of ...

scandaleux, -euse [skɑ̃dalø, -øz] *adj* scandalous, outrageous

scandinave [skɑ̃dinav] *adj* Scandinavian ▷ *nm/f*: **S-** Scandinavian

Scandinavie [skɑ̃dinavi] *nf*: **la ~** Scandinavia

scaphandre [skafɑ̃dʀ] *nm* (*de plongeur*) diving suit; (*de cosmonaute*) spacesuit; **~ autonome** aqualung

scarabée [skaʀabe] *nm* beetle

scarlatine [skaʀlatin] *nf* scarlet fever

scarole [skaʀɔl] *nf* endive

sceau, x [so] *nm* seal; (*fig*) stamp, mark; **sous le ~ du secret** under the seal of secrecy

scélérat, e [selera, -at] *nm/f* villain, blackguard ▷ *adj* villainous, blackguardly

sceller [sele] *vt* to seal

scénario [senaʀjo] *nm* (*Ciné*) screenplay, script; (: *idée, plan*) scenario; (*fig*) pattern; scenario

scène [sɛn] *nf* (*gén*) scene; (*estrade, fig: théâtre*) stage; **entrer en ~** to come on stage; **mettre en ~** (*Théât*) to stage; (*Ciné*) to direct; (*fig*) to present, introduce; **sur le devant de la ~** (*en pleine actualité*) in the forefront; **porter à la ~** to adapt for the stage; **faire une ~ (à qn)** to make a scene (with sb); **~ de ménage** domestic fight *ou* scene

sceptique [sɛptik] *adj* sceptical ▷ *nm/f* sceptic

schéma [ʃema] *nm* (*diagramme*) diagram, sketch; (*fig*) outline

schématique [ʃematik] *adj* diagrammatic(al), schematic; (*fig*) oversimplified

sciatique [sjatik] *adj*: **nerf ~** sciatic nerve ▷ *nf* sciatica

scie [si] *nf* saw; (*fam: rengaine*) catch-tune; (: *personne*) bore; **~ à bois** wood saw; **~ circulaire** circular saw; **~ à découper** fretsaw; **~ à métaux** hacksaw; **~ sauteuse** jigsaw

sciemment [sjamɑ̃] *adv* knowingly, wittingly

science [sjɑ̃s] *nf* science; (*savoir*) knowledge; (*savoir-faire*) art, skill; **~s économiques** economics; **~s humaines/sociales** social sciences; **~s naturelles** (*Scol*) natural science *sg*, biology *sg*; **~s po** political science *ou* studies *pl*

science-fiction [sjɑ̃sfiksjɔ̃] *nf* science fiction

scientifique [sjɑ̃tifik] *adj* scientific ▷ *nm/f* (*savant*) scientist; (*étudiant*) science student

scier [sje] *vt* to saw; (*retrancher*) to saw off

scierie [siʀi] *nf* sawmill

scinder [sɛ̃de] *vt*, **se scinder** *vi* to split (up)

scintiller [sɛ̃tije] *vi* to sparkle; (*étoile*) to twinkle

scission [sisjɔ̃] *nf* split

sciure [sjyʀ] *nf*: **~ (de bois)** sawdust

sclérose [skleʀoz] *nf* sclerosis; (*fig*) ossification; **~ en plaques (SEP)** multiple sclerosis (MS)

scolaire [skɔlɛʀ] *adj* school *cpd*; (*péj*) schoolish; **l'année ~** the school year; (*à l'université*) the academic year; **en âge ~** of school age

scolariser [skɔlaʀize] *vt* to provide with schooling (*ou* schools)

scolarité [skɔlaʀite] *nf* schooling; **frais de ~** school fees (*Brit*), tuition (*US*)

scooter [skutɛʀ] *nm* (motor) scooter

score [skɔʀ] *nm* score; (*électoral etc*) result

scorpion [skɔʀpjɔ̃] *nm* (*signe*): **le S-** Scorpio, the Scorpion; **être du S-** to be Scorpio

scotch [skɔtʃ] *nm* (*whisky*) scotch, whisky; **S-®** (*adhésif*) Sellotape® (*Brit*), Scotch tape® (*US*)

scout, e [skut] *adj, nm* scout

script [skʀipt] *nm* (*écriture*) printing; (*Ciné*) (shooting) script

scrupule [skʀypyl] *nm* scruple; **être sans ~s** to be unscrupulous; **se faire un ~ de qch** to have scruples *ou* qualms about doing sth

scruter [skʀyte] *vt* to scrutinize, search; (*l'obscurité*) to peer into; (*motifs, comportement*) to examine, scrutinize

scrutin [skʀytɛ̃] *nm* (*vote*) ballot; (*ensemble des opérations*) poll; **~ proportionnel/majoritaire** election on a proportional/majority basis; **~ à deux tours** poll with two ballots *ou* rounds; **~ de liste** list system

sculpter [skylte] *vt* to sculpt; (*érosion*) to carve

sculpteur [skyltœʀ] *nm* sculptor

sculpture [skyltyʀ] *nf* sculpture; **~ sur bois** wood carving

SDF *sigle m* (= *sans domicile fixe*) homeless person; **les ~** the homeless

🔘 **MOT-CLÉ**

se, s' [sə, s] *pron* **1** (*emploi réfléchi*) oneself;
(*: masc*) himself; (*: fém*) herself; (*: sujet non
humain*) itself; (*: pl*) themselves; **se voir
comme l'on est** to see o.s. as one is; **se
savonner** to soap o.s.
2 (*réciproque*) one another, each other; **ils
s'aiment** they love one another *ou* each
other
3 (*passif*): **cela se répare facilement** it is
easily repaired
4 (*possessif*): **se casser la jambe/se laver les
mains** to break one's leg/wash one's hands

séance [seɑ̃s] *nf* (*d'assemblée, récréative*)
meeting, session; (*de tribunal*) sitting,
session; (*musicale, Ciné, Théât*) performance;
ouvrir/lever la ~ to open/close the meeting;
~ tenante forthwith

seau, x [so] *nm* bucket, pail; **~ à glace** ice
bucket

sec, sèche [sɛk, sɛʃ] *adj* dry; (*raisins, figues*)
dried; (*cœur, personne*) insensible; hard, cold;
(*maigre, décharné*) spare, lean; (*réponse, ton*)
sharp, curt; (*démarrage*) sharp, sudden ▷ *nm*:
tenir au ~ to keep in a dry place ▷ *adv* hard;
(*démarrer*) sharply; **boire ~** to be a heavy
drinker; **je le bois ~** I drink it straight *ou*
neat; **à pied ~** without getting one's feet wet;
à ~ *adj* (*puits*) dried up; (*à court d'argent*) broke

sécateur [sekatœR] *nm* secateurs *pl* (Brit),
shears *pl*, pair of secateurs *ou* shears

sèche [sɛʃ] *adj f voir* **sec** ▷ *nf* (*fam*) cigarette,
fag (Brit)

sèche-cheveux [sɛʃʃøvø] *nm inv* hair-drier

sèche-linge [sɛʃlɛ̃ʒ] *nm inv* tumble dryer

sèchement [sɛʃmɑ̃] *adv* (*frapper etc*) sharply;
(*répliquer etc*) drily, sharply

sécher [seʃe] *vt* to dry; (*dessécher: peau, blé*) to
dry (out); (*: étang*) to dry up; (*bois*) to season;
(*fam: classe, cours*) to skip, miss ▷ *vi* to dry; to
dry out; to dry up; (*fam: candidat*) to be
stumped; **se sécher** (*après le bain*) to dry o.s.

sécheresse [sɛʃʀɛs] *nf* dryness; (*absence de
pluie*) drought

séchoir [seʃwaR] *nm* drier

second, e [səgɔ̃, -ɔ̃d] *adj* second ▷ *nm*
(*assistant*) second in command; (*étage*) second
floor (Brit), third floor (US); (*Navig*) first mate
▷ *nf* second; (*Scol*) = year 11 (Brit), = tenth
grade (US); (*Aviat, Rail etc*) second class; **en ~**
(*en second rang*) in second place; **voyager en ~e**
to travel second-class; **doué de ~e vue**
having (the gift of) second sight; **trouver
son ~ souffle** (*Sport, fig*) to get one's second
wind; **être dans un état ~** to be in a daze (*ou*
trance); **de ~e main** second-hand

secondaire [səgɔ̃dɛR] *adj* secondary

seconder [səgɔ̃de] *vt* to assist; (*favoriser*) to back

secouer [səkwe] *vt* to shake; (*passagers*) to
rock; (*traumatiser*) to shake (up); **se secouer**

(*chien*) to shake itself; (*fam: se démener*) to
shake o.s. up; **~ la poussière d'un tapis** to
shake the dust off a carpet; **~ la tête** to shake
one's head

secourir [səkuRiR] *vt* (*aller sauver*) to (go and)
rescue; (*prodiguer des soins à*) to help, assist;
(*venir en aide à*) to assist, aid

secourisme [səkuRism] *nm* (*premiers soins*)
first aid; (*sauvetage*) life saving

secouriste [səkuRist] *nm/f* first-aid worker

secours [səkuR] *vb voir* **secourir** ▷ *nm* help,
aid, assistance ▷ *nmpl* aid *sg*; **cela lui a été
d'un grand ~** this was a great help to him;
au ~! help!; **appeler au ~** to shout *ou* call for
help; **appeler qn à son ~** to call sb to one's
assistance; **porter ~ à qn** to give sb
assistance, help sb; **les premiers ~** first aid
sg; **le ~ en montagne** mountain rescue

⬢ **ÉQUIPES DE SECOURS**

⬢ Emergency phone numbers can be
⬢ dialled free from public phones. For the
⬢ police ('la police') dial 17; for medical
⬢ services ('le SAMU') dial 15; for the fire
⬢ brigade ('les sapeurs pompiers'), dial 18.

secousse [səkus] *nf* jolt, bump; (*électrique*)
shock; (*fig: psychologique*) jolt, shock;
~ sismique *ou* **tellurique** earth tremor

secret, -ète [səkRɛ, -ɛt] *adj* secret; (*fig:
renfermé*) reticent, reserved ▷ *nm* secret;
(*discrétion absolue*): **le ~** secrecy; **en ~** in secret,
secretly; **au ~** in solitary confinement; **~ de
fabrication** trade secret; **~ professionnel**
professional secrecy

secrétaire [səkReteR] *nm/f* secretary ▷ *nm*
(*meuble*) writing desk, secretaire;
~ d'ambassade embassy secretary; **~ de
direction** private *ou* personal secretary;
~ d'État = junior minister; **~ général (SG)**
Secretary-General; (*Comm*) company
secretary; **~ de mairie** town clerk;
~ médicale medical secretary; **~ de
rédaction** sub-editor

secrétariat [s(ə)kRetaRja] *nm* (*profession*)
secretarial work; (*bureau: d'entreprise, d'école*)
(secretary's) office; (*: d'organisation
internationale*) secretariat; (*Pol etc: fonction*)
secretaryship, office of Secretary

secteur [sɛktœR] *nm* sector; (*Admin*) district;
(*Élec*): **branché sur le ~** plugged into the
mains (supply); **fonctionne sur pile et ~**
battery or mains operated; **le ~ privé/public**
(*Écon*) the private/public sector; **le ~
primaire/tertiaire** the primary/tertiary
sector

section [sɛksjɔ̃] *nf* section; (*de parcours
d'autobus*) fare stage; (*Mil: unité*) platoon;
~ rythmique rhythm section

sectionner [sɛksjɔne] *vt* to sever; **se
sectionner** *vi* to be severed

sécu [seky] nf (fam: = sécurité sociale) ≈ dole (Brit), ≈ Welfare (US)

séculaire [sekylɛʀ] adj secular; (très vieux) age-old

sécuriser [sekyʀize] vt to give a sense of security to

sécurité [sekyʀite] nf (absence de troubles) security; (absence de danger) safety; **impression de** ~ sense of security; **la** ~ **internationale** international security; **système de** ~ security (ou safety) system; **être en** ~ to be safe; **la** ~ **de l'emploi** job security; **la** ~ **routière** road safety; **la** ~ **sociale** ≈ (the) Social Security (Brit), ≈ (the) Welfare (US)

sédentaire [sedɑ̃tɛʀ] adj sedentary

séduction [sedyksjɔ̃] nf seduction; (charme, attrait) appeal, charm

séduire [sedɥiʀ] vt to charm; (femme: abuser de) to seduce; (chose) to appeal to

séduisant, e [sedɥizɑ̃, -ɑ̃t] vb voir **séduire** ▷ adj (femme) seductive; (homme, offre) very attractive

ségrégation [segʀegasjɔ̃] nf segregation

seigle [sɛgl] nm rye

seigneur [sɛɲœʀ] nm lord; **le S~** the Lord

sein [sɛ̃] nm breast; (entrailles) womb; **au ~ de** prép (équipe, institution) within; (flots, bonheur) in the midst of; **donner le** ~ **à** (bébé) to feed (at the breast); to breast-feed; **nourrir au** ~ to breast-feed

séisme [seism] nm earthquake

seize [sɛz] num sixteen

seizième [sɛzjɛm] num sixteenth

séjour [seʒuʀ] nm stay; (pièce) living room

séjourner [seʒuʀne] vi to stay

sel [sɛl] nm salt; (fig) wit; (piquant) spice; ~ **de cuisine/de table** cooking/table salt; ~ **gemme** rock salt; ~**s de bain** bathsalts

sélection [seleksjɔ̃] nf selection; **faire/ opérer une** ~ **parmi** to make a selection from among; **épreuve de** ~ (Sport) trial (for selection); ~ **naturelle** natural selection; ~ **professionnelle** professional recruitment

sélectionner [seleksjɔne] vt to select

self [sɛlf] nm (fam) self-service

self-service [sɛlfsɛʀvis] adj self-service ▷ nm self-service (restaurant); (magasin) self-service shop

selle [sɛl] nf saddle; **selles** nfpl (Méd) stools; **aller à la** ~ (Méd) to have a bowel movement; **se mettre en** ~ to mount, get into the saddle

seller [sele] vt to saddle

sellette [sɛlɛt] nf: **être sur la** ~ to be on the carpet (fig)

selon [səlɔ̃] prép according to; (en se conformant à) in accordance with; ~ **moi** as I see it; ~ **que** according to, depending on whether

semaine [səmɛn] nf week; (salaire) week's wages ou pay, weekly wages ou pay; **en** ~ during the week, on weekdays; **à la petite** ~ from day to day; **la** ~ **sainte** Holy Week

semblable [sɑ̃blabl] adj similar; (de ce genre): **de** ~**s mésaventures** such mishaps ▷ nm fellow creature ou man; ~ **à** similar to, like

semblant [sɑ̃blɑ̃] nm: **un** ~ **de vérité** a semblance of truth; **faire** ~ **(de faire)** to pretend (to do)

sembler [sɑ̃ble] vb copule to seem ▷ vb impers: **il semble (bien) que/inutile de** it (really) seems ou appears that/useless to; **il me semble (bien) que** it (really) seems to me that, I (really) think that; **il me semble le connaître** I think ou I've a feeling I know him; ~ **être** to seem to be; **comme bon lui semble** as he sees fit; **me semble-t-il, à ce qu'il me semble** it seems to me, to my mind

semelle [səmɛl] nf sole; (intérieure) insole, inner sole; **battre la** ~ to stamp one's feet (to keep them warm); (fig) to hang around (waiting); ~**s compensées** platform soles

semence [səmɑ̃s] nf (graine) seed; (clou) tack

semer [səme] vt to sow; (: éparpiller) to scatter; (: confusion) to spread; (fam: poursuivants) to lose, shake off; ~ **la discorde parmi** to sow discord among; **semé de** (difficultés) riddled with

semestre [səmɛstʀ] nm half-year; (Scol) semester

séminaire [seminɛʀ] nm seminar; (Rel) seminary

semi-remorque [səmiʀəmɔʀk] nf trailer ▷ nm articulated lorry (Brit), semi(trailer) (US)

semoule [səmul] nf semolina; ~ **de riz** ground rice

sempiternel, le [sɛ̃pitɛʀnɛl] adj eternal, never-ending

sénat [sena] nm senate; see note

◈ **SÉNAT**

◈ The *Sénat* is the upper house of the French
◈ parliament and is housed in the Palais du
◈ Luxembourg in Paris. One-third of its
◈ members, "sénateurs" are elected for a
◈ nine-year term every three years by an
◈ electoral college consisting of the
◈ "députés" and other elected
◈ representatives. The *Sénat* has a wide
◈ range of powers but can be overridden by
◈ the lower house, the "Assemblée
◈ nationale" in case of dispute.

sénateur [senatœʀ] nm senator

Sénégal [senegal] nm: **le** ~ Senegal

sens [sɑ̃s] vb voir **sentir** ▷ nm [sɑ̃s] (Physiol, instinct) sense; (signification) meaning, sense; (direction) direction, way ▷ nmpl (sensualité) senses; **reprendre ses** ~ to regain consciousness; **avoir le** ~ **des affaires/de la mesure** to have business sense/a sense of moderation; **ça n'a pas de** ~ that doesn't make (any) sense; **en dépit du bon** ~

contrary to all good sense; **tomber sous le ~** to stand to reason, be perfectly obvious; **en un ~, dans un ~** in a way; **en ce ~ que** in the sense that; **à mon ~** to my mind; **dans le ~ des aiguilles d'une montre** clockwise; **dans le ~ contraire des aiguilles d'une montre** anticlockwise; **dans le ~ de la longueur/largeur** lengthways/widthways; **dans le ~ mauvais ~** (aller) the wrong way; in the wrong direction; **bon ~** good sense; **~ commun** common sense; **~ dessus dessous** upside down; **~ interdit, ~ unique** one-way street

sensass [sɑ̃sas] adj (fam) fantastic

sensation [sɑ̃sasjɔ̃] nf sensation; **faire ~** to cause a sensation, create a stir; **à ~** (péj) sensational

sensationnel, le [sɑ̃sasjɔnɛl] adj sensational, fantastic

sensé, e [sɑ̃se] adj sensible

sensibiliser [sɑ̃sibilize] vt to sensitize; **~ qn (à)** to make sb sensitive (to)

sensibilité [sɑ̃sibilite] nf sensitivity; (affectivité, émotivité) sensitivity, sensibility

sensible [sɑ̃sibl] adj sensitive; (aux sens) perceptible; (appréciable: différence, progrès) appreciable, noticeable; (quartier) problem cpd; **~ à** sensitive to

sensiblement [sɑ̃sibləmɑ̃] adv (notablement) appreciably, noticeably; (à peu près) **ils ont ~ le même poids** they weigh approximately the same

sensiblerie [sɑ̃sibləri] nf sentimentality; squeamishness

sensuel, le [sɑ̃sɥɛl] adj (personne) sensual; (musique) sensuous

sentence [sɑ̃tɑ̃s] nf (jugement) sentence; (adage) maxim

sentier [sɑ̃tje] nm path

sentiment [sɑ̃timɑ̃] nm feeling; (conscience, impression): **avoir le ~ de/que** to be aware of/ have the feeling that; **recevez mes ~s respectueux** (personne nommée) yours sincerely; (personne non nommée) yours faithfully; **faire du ~** (péj) to be sentimental; **si vous me prenez par les ~s** if you appeal to my feelings

sentimental, e, -aux [sɑ̃timɑ̃tal, -o] adj sentimental; (vie, aventure) love cpd

sentinelle [sɑ̃tinɛl] nf sentry; **en ~** standing guard; (soldat: en faction) on sentry duty

sentir [sɑ̃tir] vt (par l'odorat) to smell; (par le goût) to taste; (au toucher, fig) to feel; (répandre une odeur de) to smell of; (: ressemblance) to smell like; (avoir la saveur de) to taste of; to taste like; (fig: dénoter, annoncer) to be indicative of; to smack of; to foreshadow ▷ vi to smell; **~ mauvais** to smell bad; **se ~ bien** to feel good; **se ~ mal** (être indisposé) to feel unwell ou ill; **se ~ le courage/la force de faire** to feel brave/strong enough to do; **ne plus se ~ de joie** to be beside o.s. with joy; **il**

ne peut pas le ~ (fam) he can't stand him; **je ne me sens pas bien** I don't feel well

séparation [separasjɔ̃] nf separation; (cloison) division, partition; **~ de biens** division of property (in marriage settlement); **~ de corps** legal separation

séparé, e [separe] adj (appartements, pouvoirs) separate; (époux) separated; **~ de** separate from; separated from

séparément [separemɑ̃] adv separately

séparer [separe] vt (gén) to separate; (désunir: divergences etc) to divide; to drive apart; (: différences, obstacles) to stand between; (détacher): **~ qch de** to pull sth (off) from; (dissocier) to distinguish between; (diviser): **~ qch par** to divide sth (up) with; **~ une pièce en deux** to divide a room into two; **se séparer** vi (époux) to separate, part; (prendre congé: amis etc) to part, leave each other; (adversaires) to separate; (se diviser: route, tige etc) to divide; (se détacher): **se ~ (de)** to split off (from); to come off; **se ~ de** (époux) to separate ou part from; (employé, objet personnel) to part with

sept [sɛt] num seven

septante [sɛptɑ̃t] num (Belgique, Suisse) seventy

septembre [sɛptɑ̃br] nm September; voir aussi **juillet**

septennat [sɛptena] nm seven-year term (of office)

septentrional, e, -aux [sɛptɑ̃trijɔnal, -o] adj northern

septicémie [sɛptisemi] nf blood poisoning, septicaemia

septième [sɛtjɛm] num seventh; **être au ~ ciel** to be on cloud nine

septique [sɛptik] adj: **fosse ~** septic tank

sépulture [sepyltyr] nf burial; (tombeau) burial place, grave

séquelles [sekɛl] nfpl after-effects; (fig) aftermath sg; consequences

séquestrer [sekɛstre] vt (personne) to confine illegally; (biens) to impound

serai etc [səre] vb voir **être**

serbe [sɛrb] adj Serbian ▷ nm (Ling) Serbian ▷ nm/f

Serbie [sɛrbi] nf: **la ~** Serbia

serein, e [sərɛ̃, -ɛn] adj serene; (jugement) dispassionate

serez [səre] vb voir **être**

sergent [sɛrʒɑ̃] nm sergeant

série [seri] nf (de questions, d'accidents, TV) series inv; (de clés, casseroles, outils) set; (catégorie: Sport) rank; class; **en ~** in quick succession; (Comm) mass cpd; **de ~** adj (voiture) standard; **hors ~** (Comm) custom-built; (fig) outstanding; **imprimante ~** (Inform) serial printer; **soldes de fin de ~s** end of line special offers; **~ noire** (crime) thriller ▷ nf (suite de malheurs) run of bad luck

sérieusement [serjøzmɑ̃] adv seriously; reliably; responsibly; **il parle ~** he's serious, he means it; **~?** are you serious?, do you mean it?

sérieux, -euse [seʀjø, -øz] adj serious; (élève, employé) reliable, responsible; (client, maison) reliable, dependable; (offre, proposition) genuine, serious; (grave, sévère) serious, solemn; (maladie, situation) serious, grave; (important) considerable ⊳ nm seriousness; (d'une entreprise etc) reliability; **ce n'est pas ~** (raisonnable) that's not on; **garder son ~** to keep a straight face; **manquer de ~** not to be very responsible (ou reliable); **prendre qch/qn au ~** to take sth/sb seriously

serin [səʀɛ̃] nm canary

seringue [səʀɛ̃g] nf syringe

serions etc [səʀjɔ̃] vb voir **être**

serment [seʀmɑ̃] nm (juré) oath; (promesse) pledge, vow; **prêter ~** to take the ou an oath; **faire le ~ de** to take a vow to, swear to; **sous ~** on ou under oath

sermon [seʀmɔ̃] nm sermon; (péj) sermon, lecture

séronégatif, -ive [seʀonegatif, -iv] adj HIV negative

séropositif, -ive [seʀopozitif, -iv] adj HIV positive

serpent [seʀpɑ̃] nm snake; **~ à sonnettes** rattlesnake; **~ monétaire (européen)** (European) monetary snake

serpenter [seʀpɑ̃te] vi to wind

serpillière [seʀpijɛʀ] nf floorcloth

serre [seʀ] nf (Agr) greenhouse; **serres** nfpl (griffes) claws, talons; **~ chaude** hothouse; **~ froide** unheated greenhouse

serré, e [seʀe] adj (tissu) closely woven; (réseau) dense; (écriture) close; (habits) tight; (fig: lutte, match) tight, close-fought; (passagers etc) (tightly) packed; (café) strong ⊳ adv: **jouer ~** to play it close, play a close game; **écrire ~** to write a cramped hand; **avoir la gorge ~e** to have a lump in one's throat; **avoir le cœur ~** to have a heavy heart

serrer [seʀe] vt (tenir) to grip ou hold tight; (comprimer, coincer) to squeeze; (poings, mâchoires) to clench; (vêtement) to be too tight for; to fit tightly; (rapprocher) to close up, move closer together; (ceinture, nœud, frein, vis) to tighten ⊳ vi: **~ à droite** to keep to the right; to move into the right-hand lane; **se serrer** (se rapprocher) to squeeze up; **se ~ contre qn** to huddle up to sb; **se ~ les coudes** to stick together, back one another up; **se ~ la ceinture** to tighten one's belt; **la main à qn** to shake sb's hand; **~ qn dans ses bras** to hug sb, clasp sb in one's arms; **la gorge à qn** (chagrin) to bring a lump to sb's throat; **~ les dents** to clench ou grit one's teeth; **~ qn de près** to follow close behind sb; **~ le trottoir** to hug the kerb; **~ sa droite** to keep well to the right; **~ la vis à qn** to crack down harder on sb; **~ les rangs** to close ranks

serrure [seʀyʀ] nf lock

serrurier [seʀyʀje] nm locksmith

sers, sert [sɛʀ] vb voir **servir**

servante [sɛʀvɑ̃t] nf (maid) servant

serveur, -euse [sɛʀvœʀ, -øz] nm/f waiter/waitress ⊳ nm (Inform) server ⊳ adj: **centre ~** (Inform) service centre

serviable [sɛʀvjabl] adj obliging, willing to help

service [sɛʀvis] nm (gén) service; (série de repas): **premier ~** first sitting; (pourboire) service (charge); (assortiment de vaisselle) set, service; (linge de table) set; (bureau: de la vente etc) department, section; (travail): **pendant le ~** on duty; **services** nmpl (travail, Écon) services, inclusive/exclusive of service; **faire le ~** to serve; **être en ~ chez qn** (domestique) to be in sb's service; **être au ~ de** (patron, patrie) to be in the service of; **être au ~ de qn** (collaborateur, voiture) to be at sb's service; **porte de ~** tradesman's entrance; **rendre ~ à** to help; **il aime rendre ~** he likes to help; **rendre un ~ à qn** to do sb a favour; (objet): **s'avérer utile** to come in useful ou handy for sb; **heures de ~** hours of duty; **être de ~** to be on duty; **reprendre du ~** to get back into action; **avoir 25 ans de ~** to have completed 25 years' service; **être/mettre en ~** to be in/put into service ou operation; **~ compris/non compris** service included/not included; **hors ~** not in use; out of order; **~ à thé/café** tea/coffee set ou service; **~ après-vente (SAV)** after-sales service; **en ~ commandé** on an official assignment; **~ funèbre** funeral service; **~ militaire** military service; see note; **~ d'ordre** police (ou stewards) in charge of maintaining order; **~s publics** public services, (public) utilities; **~s secrets** secret service sg; **~s sociaux** social services

S

serviette [sɛʀvjɛt] nf (de table) (table) napkin, serviette; (de toilette) towel; (porte-documents) briefcase; ~ **éponge** terry towel; ~ **hygiénique** sanitary towel

servir [sɛʀviʀ] vt (gén) to serve; (dîneur: au restaurant) to wait on; (client: au magasin) to serve, attend to; (fig: aider): ~ **qn** to aid sb; to serve sb's interests; to stand sb in good stead; (Comm: rente) to pay ▷ vi (Tennis) to serve; (Cartes) to deal; (être militaire) to serve; ~ **qch à qn** to serve sb with sth, help sb to sth; **qu'est-ce que je vous sers?** what can I get you?; **se servir** vi (prendre d'un plat) to help o.s.; (s'approvisionner): **vous êtes servi?** are you being served?; **sers-toi!** help yourself!; **se ~ chez** to shop at; **se ~ de** (plat) to help o.s. to; (voiture, outil, relations) to use; ~ **à qn** (diplôme, livre) to be of use to sb; **ça m'a servi pour faire** it was useful to me when I did; I used it to do; ~ **à qch/à faire** (outil etc) to be used for sth/for doing; **ça peut** – it may come in handy; **à quoi cela sert-il (de faire)?** what's the use (of doing)?; **ça ne sert à rien** it's no use; ~ **(à qn) de ...** to serve as ... (for sb); ~ **à dîner (à qn)** to serve dinner (to sb)

serviteur [sɛʀvitœʀ] nm servant

ses [se] adj possessif voir **son**

set [sɛt] nm set; (napperon) placemat; ~ **de table** set of placemats

seuil [sœj] nm doorstep; (fig) threshold; **sur le ~ de la maison** in the doorway of his house, on his doorstep; **au ~ de** (fig) on the threshold or brink or edge of; ~ **de rentabilité** (Comm) breakeven point

seul, e [sœl] adj (sans compagnie) alone; (avec nuance affective: isolé) lonely; (unique): **un ~ livre** only one book, a single book; **le ~ livre** the only book; ~ **ce livre, ce livre ~** this book alone, only this book; **d'un ~ coup** (soudainement) all at once; (à la fois) at one blow ▷ adv (vivre) alone, on one's own; **parler tout** ~ to talk to oneself; **faire qch (tout)** ~ to do sth (all) on one's own or (all) by oneself ▷ nm, nf: **il en reste un(e) ~(e)** there's only one left; **pas un(e) ~(e)** not a single; **à lui (tout)** ~ single-handed, on his own; ~ **à** ~ in private; **se sentir** ~ to feel lonely

seulement [sœlmɑ̃] adv only; (pas davantage): ~ **cinq, cinq** ~ only five; (exclusivement): ~ **eux** only them, them alone; (pas avant): ~ **hier/à 10h** only yesterday/at 10 o'clock; (mais, toutefois): **il consent,** ~ **il demande des garanties** he agrees, only he wants guarantees; **non ~ ... mais aussi** or **encore** not only ... but also

sève [sɛv] nf sap

sévère [seveʀ] adj severe

sévices [sevis] nmpl (physical) cruelty sg, ill treatment sg

sévir [seviʀ] vi (punir) to use harsh measures, crack down; (fléau) to rage, be rampant; ~ **contre** (abus) to deal ruthlessly with, crack down on

sevrer [səvʀe] vt to wean; (fig): ~ **qn de** to deprive sb of

sexe [sɛks] nm sex; (organe mâle) member

sexuel, le [sɛksɥɛl] adj sexual; **acte** ~ sex act

seyant, e [sɛjɑ̃, -ɑ̃t] adj becoming

shampooing [ʃɑ̃pwɛ̃] nm shampoo; **se faire un** ~ to shampoo one's hair; ~ **colorant** (colour) rinse; ~ **traitant** medicated shampoo

Shetland [ʃɛtlɑ̃d] n: **les îles** ~ the Shetland Islands, Shetland

shopping [ʃɔpiŋ] nm: **faire du** ~ to go shopping

short [ʃɔʀt] nm (pair of) shorts pl

 MOT-CLÉ

si [si] nm (Mus) B; (en chantant la gamme) ti ▷ adv **1** (oui) yes; **"Paul n'est pas venu"** — **"si!"** "Paul hasn't come" — "Yes he has!"; **je vous assure que si** I assure you he did/she is etc
2 (tellement) so; **si gentil/rapidement** so kind/fast; **(tant et) si bien que** so much so that; **si rapide qu'il soit** however fast he may be
▷ conj if; **si tu veux** if you want; **je me demande si** I wonder if or whether; **si j'étais toi** if I were you; **si seulement** if only; **si ce n'est** apart from; **une des plus belles, si ce n'est la plus belle** one of the most beautiful, if not THE most beautiful; **s'il est aimable, eux par contre ...** while or whereas he's nice, they (on the other hand) ...

Sicile [sisil] nf: **la** ~ Sicily

sida [sida] nm (= syndrome immuno-déficitaire acquis) AIDS sg

sidéré, e [sideʀe] adj staggered

sidérurgie [sideʀyʀʒi] nf steel industry

siècle [sjɛkl] nm century; (époque): **le ~ des lumières/de l'atome** the age of enlightenment/atomic age; (Rel): **le** ~ the world

siège [sjɛʒ] nm seat; (d'entreprise) head office; (d'organisation) headquarters pl; (Mil) siege; **lever le** ~ to raise the siege; **mettre le ~ devant** to besiege; **présentation par le** ~ (Méd) breech presentation; ~ **avant/arrière** (Auto) front/back seat; ~ **baquet** bucket seat; ~ **social** registered office

siéger [sjeʒe] vi (assemblée, tribunal) to sit; (résider, se trouver) to lie, be located

sien, ne [sjɛ̃, sjɛn] pron: **le(la) ~(ne), les ~s(-nes)** (d'un homme) his; (d'une femme) hers; (d'une chose) its; **y mettre du** ~ to pull one's weight; **faire des ~nes** (fam) to be up to one's (usual) tricks; **les ~s** (sa famille) one's family

sieste [sjɛst] nf (afternoon) snooze or nap, siesta; **faire la** ~ to have a snooze or nap

sifflement [siflǝmɑ̃] nm whistle, whistling no pl; wheezing no pl; hissing no pl

siffler [sifle] vi (gén) to whistle; (avec un sifflet) to blow (on) one's whistle; (en respirant) to wheeze; (serpent, vapeur) to hiss ▷ vt (chanson) to whistle; (chien etc) to whistle for; (fille) to whistle at; (pièce, orateur) to hiss, boo; (faute) to blow one's whistle at; (fin du match, départ) to blow one's whistle for; (fam: verre, bouteille) to guzzle, knock back (Brit)

sifflet [siflɛ] nm whistle; **sifflets** nmpl (de mécontentement) whistles, boos; **coup de ~** whistle

siffloter [siflɔte] vi, vt to whistle

sigle [sigl] nm acronym, (set of) initials pl

signal, -aux [siɲal, -o] nm (signe convenu, appareil) signal; (indice, écriteau) sign; **donner le ~ de** to give the signal for; **~ d'alarme** alarm signal; **~ d'alerte/de détresse** warning/distress signal; **~ horaire** time signal; **~ optique/sonore** warning light/ sound; visual/acoustic signal; **signaux (lumineux)** (Auto) traffic signals; **signaux routiers** road signs; (lumineux) traffic lights

signalement [siɲalmɑ̃] nm description, particulars pl

signaler [siɲale] vt to indicate; to announce; (vol, perte) to report; (personne: faire un signe) to signal; (être l'indice de) to indicate; (faire remarquer): **qch à qn/à qn que** to point out sth to sb/to sb that; (appeler l'attention sur): **~ qn à la police** to bring sb to the notice of the police; **se ~ par** to distinguish o.s. by; **se ~ à l'attention de qn** to attract sb's attention

signature [siɲatyʀ] nf signature; (action) signing

signe [siɲ] nm sign; (Typo) mark; **ne pas donner ~ de vie** to give no sign of life; **c'est bon ~** it's a good sign; **c'est ~ que** it's a sign that; **faire un ~ de la main/tête** to give a sign with one's hand/shake one's head; **faire ~ à qn** (fig: contacter) to get in touch with sb; **faire ~ à qn d'entrer** to motion (to) sb to come in; **en ~ de** as a sign ou mark of; **le ~ de la croix** the sign of the Cross; **~ de ponctuation** punctuation mark; **~ du zodiaque** sign of the zodiac; **~s particuliers** distinguishing marks

signer [siɲe] vt to sign; **se signer** vi to cross o.s

significatif, -ive [siɲifikatif, -iv] adj significant

signification [siɲifikasjɔ̃] nf meaning

signifier [siɲifje] vt (vouloir dire) to mean, signify; (faire connaître): **~ qch (à qn)** to make sth known (to sb); (Jur): **~ qch à qn** to serve notice of sth on sb

silence [silɑ̃s] nm silence; (Mus) rest; **garder le ~ (sur qch)** to keep silent (about sth), say nothing (about sth); **passer sous ~** to pass over (in silence); **réduire au ~** to silence

silencieux, -euse [silɑ̃sjø, -øz] adj quiet, silent ▷ nm silencer (Brit), muffler (US)

silex [silɛks] nm flint

silhouette [silwɛt] nf outline, silhouette; (lignes, contour) outline; (figure) figure

silicium [silisjɔm] nm silicon; **plaquette de ~** silicon chip

sillage [sijaʒ] nm wake; (fig) trail; **dans le ~ de** (fig) in the wake of

sillon [sijɔ̃] nm (d'un champ) furrow; (de disque) groove

sillonner [sijɔne] vt (creuser) to furrow; (traverser) to criss-cross, cross

simagrées [simagʀe] nfpl fuss sg; airs and graces

similaire [similɛʀ] adj similar

similicuir [similikɥiʀ] nm imitation leather

similitude [similityd] nf similarity

simple [sɛ̃pl] adj (gén) simple; (non multiple) single; **simples** nmpl (Méd) medicinal plants; **~ messieurs/dames** nm (Tennis) men's/ ladies' singles sg; **un ~ particulier** an ordinary citizen; **une ~ formalité** a mere formality; **cela varie du ~ au double** it can double, it can double the price etc; **dans le plus ~ appareil** in one's birthday suit; **~ course** adj single; **~ d'esprit** nm/f simpleton; **~ soldat** private

simplicité [sɛ̃plisite] nf simplicity; **en toute ~** quite simply

simplifier [sɛ̃plifje] vt to simplify

simulacre [simylakʀ] nm enactment; (péj): **un ~ de** a pretence of, a sham

simuler [simyle] vt to sham, simulate

simultané, e [simyltane] adj simultaneous

sincère [sɛ̃sɛʀ] adj sincere; genuine; heartfelt; **mes ~s condoléances** my deepest sympathy

sincèrement [sɛ̃sɛʀmɑ̃] adv sincerely; genuinely

sincérité [sɛ̃seʀite] nf sincerity; **en toute ~** in all sincerity

sine qua non [sinekwanɔn] adj: **condition ~** indispensable condition

Singapour [sɛ̃gapuʀ] nm Singapore

singe [sɛ̃ʒ] nm monkey; (de grande taille) ape

singer [sɛ̃ʒe] vt to ape, mimic

singeries [sɛ̃ʒʀi] nfpl antics; (simagrées) airs and graces

singulariser [sɛ̃gylaʀize] vt to mark out; **se singulariser** vi to call attention to o.s.

singularité [sɛ̃gylaʀite] nf peculiarity

singulier, -ière [sɛ̃gylje, -jɛʀ] adj remarkable, singular; (Ling) singular ▷ nm singular

sinistre [sinistʀ] adj sinister; (intensif): **un ~ imbécile** an incredible idiot ▷ nm (incendie) blaze; (catastrophe) disaster; (Assurances) damage (giving rise to a claim)

sinistré, e [sinistʀe] adj disaster-stricken ▷ nm/f disaster victim

sinon [sinɔ̃] conj (autrement, sans quoi) otherwise, or else; (sauf) except, other than; (si ce n'est) if not

sinueux, -euse [sinɥø, -øz] adj winding; (fig) tortuous

S

sinus [sinys] *nm* (*Anat*) sinus; (*Géom*) sine

sinusite [sinyzit] *nf* sinusitis, sinus infection

siphon [sifɔ̃] *nm* (*tube, d'eau gazeuse*) siphon; (*d'évier etc*) U-bend

sirène [siʀɛn] *nf* siren; ~ **d'alarme** fire alarm; (*pendant la guerre*) air-raid siren

sirop [siʀo] *nm* (*à diluer: de fruit etc*) syrup, cordial (*Brit*); (*boisson*) fruit drink; (*pharmaceutique*) syrup, mixture; ~ **de menthe** mint syrup *ou* cordial; ~ **contre la toux** cough syrup *ou* mixture

siroter [siʀɔte] *vt* to sip

sismique [sismik] *adj* seismic

site [sit] *nm* (*paysage, environnement*) setting; (*d'une ville etc: emplacement*) site; ~ (**pittoresque**) beauty spot; **~s touristiques** places of interest; **~s naturels/historiques** natural/historic sites; ~ **web** (*Inform*) website

sitôt [sito] *adv*: ~ **parti** as soon as he *etc* had left; ~ **après** straight after; **pas de** ~ not for a long time; ~ (**après**) **que** as soon as

situation [sitɥasjɔ̃] *nf* (*gén*) situation; (*d'un édifice, d'une ville*) situation, position; (*emplacement*) location; **être en** ~ **de faire qch** to be in a position to do sth; ~ **de famille** marital status

situé, e [sitɥe] *adj*: **bien** ~ well situated, in a good location; ~ **à/près de** situated at/near

situer [sitɥe] *vt* to site, situate; (*en pensée*) to set, place; **se situer** *vi*: **se** ~ **à/près de** to be situated at/near

six [sis] *num* six

sixième [sizjɛm] *num* sixth ▷ *nf*: **en** ~ (*Scol: classe*) year 7 (*Brit*), sixth grade (*US*)

skaï® [skaj] *nm* ≈ Leatherette®

skate [sket], **skate-board** [sketbɔʀd] *nm* (*sport*) skateboarding; (*planche*) skateboard

ski [ski] *nm* (*objet*) ski; (*sport*) skiing; **faire du** ~ to ski; ~ **alpin** Alpine skiing; ~ **court** short ski; ~ **évolutif** short ski method; ~ **de fond** cross-country skiing; ~ **nautique** water-skiing; ~ **de piste** downhill skiing; ~ **de randonnée** cross-country skiing

skier [skje] *vi* to ski

skieur, -euse [skjœʀ, -øz] *nm/f* skier

slip [slip] *nm* (*sous-vêtement*) underpants *pl*, pants *pl* (*Brit*), briefs *pl*; (*de bain: d'homme*) trunks *pl*; (*: du bikini*) (bikini) briefs *pl*

slogan [slɔgɑ̃] *nm* slogan

Slovaquie [slɔvaki] *nf*: **la** ~ Slovakia

SMIC [smik] *sigle m* = **salaire minimum interprofessionnel de croissance** *see note*

  SMIC

  In France, the *SMIC* ("salaire minimum interprofessionnel de croissance") is the minimum hourly rate which workers over the age of 18 must legally be paid. It is index-linked and is raised each time the cost of living rises by 2 per cent.

smicard, e [smikaʀ, -aʀd] *nm/f* minimum wage earner

smoking [smɔkiŋ] *nm* dinner *ou* evening suit

SMS *sigle m* (= *short message service*) (*service*) SMS; (*message*) text (message)

SNC *abr* = **service non compris**

SNCF *sigle f* (= *Société nationale des chemins de fer français*) French railways

snob [snɔb] *adj* snobbish ▷ *nm/f* snob

snobisme [snɔbism] *nm* snobbery, snobbishness

sobre [sɔbʀ] *adj* (*personne*) temperate, abstemious; (*élégance, style*) restrained, sober; ~ **de** (*gestes, compliments*) sparing of

sobriquet [sɔbʀikɛ] *nm* nickname

social, e, -aux [sɔsjal, -o] *adj* social

socialisme [sɔsjalism] *nm* socialism

socialiste [sɔsjalist] *adj, nm/f* socialist

société [sɔsjete] *nf* society; (*d'abeilles, de fourmis*) colony; (*sportive*) club; (*Comm*) company; **la bonne** ~ polite society; **se plaire dans la** ~ **de** to enjoy the society of; **l'archipel de la S**~ the Society Islands; **la** ~ **d'abondance/de consommation** affluent/consumer society; ~ **par actions** joint stock company; ~ **anonyme (SA)** ≈ limited company (Ltd) (*Brit*), ≈ incorporated company (Inc.) (*US*); ~ **d'investissement à capital variable (SICAV)** = investment trust (*Brit*), ≈ mutual fund (*US*); ~ **à responsabilité limitée (SARL)** *type of limited liability company* (*with non-negotiable shares*); ~ **savante** learned society; ~ **de services** service company

sociologie [sɔsjɔlɔʒi] *nf* sociology

socle [sɔkl] *nm* (*de colonne, statue*) plinth, pedestal; (*de lampe*) base

socquette [sɔkɛt] *nf* ankle sock

sœur [sœʀ] *nf* sister; (*religieuse*) nun, sister; ~ **Élisabeth** (*Rel*) Sister Elizabeth; ~ **de lait** foster sister

soi [swa] *pron* oneself; **en** ~ (*intrinsèquement*) in itself; **cela va de** ~ that *ou* it goes without saying, it stands to reason

soi-disant [swadizɑ̃] *adj inv* so-called ▷ *adv* supposedly

soie [swa] *nf* silk; (*de porc, sanglier: poil*) bristle

soierie [swaʀi] *nf* (*industrie*) silk trade; (*tissu*) silk

soif [swaf] *nf* thirst; (*fig*): ~ **de** thirst *ou* craving for; **avoir** ~ to be thirsty; **donner** ~ **à qn** to make sb thirsty

soigné, e [swaɲe] *adj* (*tenue*) well-groomed, neat; (*travail*) careful, meticulous; (*fam*) whopping; stiff

soigner [swaɲe] *vt* (*malade, maladie: docteur*) to treat; (*: infirmière, mère*) to nurse, look after; (*blessé*) to tend; (*travail, détails*) to take care over; (*jardin, chevelure, invités*) to look after

soigneux, -euse [swaɲø, -øz] *adj* (*propre*) tidy, neat; (*méticuleux*) painstaking, careful; ~ **de** careful with

soi-même [swamɛm] *pron* oneself

soin [swɛ̃] nm (application) care; (propreté, ordre) tidiness, neatness; (responsabilité): **le ~ de qch** the care of sth; **soins** nmpl (à un malade, blessé) treatment sg, medical attention sg; (attentions, prévenance) care and attention sg; (hygiène) care sg; **~s de la chevelure/de beauté** hair/beauty care; **~s du corps/ ménage** care of one's body/the home; **avoir ou prendre ~ de** to take care of, look after; **avoir ou prendre ~ de faire** to take care to do; **faire qch avec (grand) ~** to do sth (very) carefully; **sans ~** adj careless; untidy; **les premiers ~s** first aid sg; **aux bons ~s de** c/o, care of; **être aux petits ~s pour qn** to wait on sb hand and foot, see to sb's every need; **confier qn aux ~s de qn** to hand sb over to sb's care

soir [swaʀ] nm, adv evening; **le ~** in the evening(s); **ce ~** this evening, tonight; **à ce ~!** see you this evening (ou tonight)!; **la veille au ~** the previous evening; **sept/dix heures du ~** seven in the evening/ten at night; **le repas/journal du ~** the evening meal/ newspaper; **dimanche ~** Sunday evening; **hier ~** yesterday evening; **demain ~** tomorrow evening, tomorrow night

soirée [swaʀe] nf evening; (réception) party; **donner en ~** (film, pièce) to give an evening performance of

soit [swa] vb voir **être** ▷ conj (à savoir) namely, to wit; (ou): **~ ... ~** either ... or ▷ adv so be it, very well; **~ un triangle ABC** let ABC be a triangle; **~ que ... ~ que ou ou que** whether ... or whether

soixantaine [swasɑ̃tɛn] nf: **une ~ (de)** sixty or so, about sixty; **avoir la ~ (âge)** to be around sixty

soixante [swasɑ̃t] num sixty

soixante-dix [swasɑ̃tdis] num seventy

soja [sɔʒa] nm soya; (graines) soya beans pl; **germes de ~** beansprouts

sol [sɔl] nm ground; (de logement) floor; (revêtement) flooring no pl; (territoire, Agr, Géo) soil; (Mus) G; (: en chantant la gamme) so(h)

solaire [sɔlɛʀ] adj (énergie etc) solar; (crème etc) sun cpd

soldat [sɔlda] nm soldier; **S~ inconnu** Unknown Warrior ou Soldier; **~ de plomb** tin ou toy soldier

solde [sɔld] nf pay ▷ nm (Comm) balance; **soldes** nmpl ou nfpl (Comm) sales; (articles) sale goods; **à la ~ de qn** (péj) in sb's pay; **~ créditeur/débiteur** credit/debit balance; **~ à payer** balance outstanding; **en ~** at sale price; **aux ~s** at the sales

solder [sɔlde] vt (compte) to settle; (marchandise) to sell at sale price, sell off; **se ~ par** (fig) to end in; **article soldé (à) 10 euros** item reduced to 10 euros

sole [sɔl] nf sole inv (fish)

soleil [sɔlɛj] nm sun; (lumière) sun(light); (temps ensoleillé) sun(shine); (feu d'artifice) Catherine wheel; (d'acrobate) grand circle; (Bot) sunflower; **il y a ou il fait du ~** it's sunny; **au ~** in the sun; **en plein ~** in full sun; **le ~ levant/couchant** the rising/setting sun; **le ~ de minuit** the midnight sun

solennel, le [sɔlanɛl] adj solemn; ceremonial

solfège [sɔlfɛʒ] nm rudiments pl of music; (exercices) ear training no pl

solidaire [sɔlidɛʀ] adj: **être ~s** (personnes) to show solidarity, stick ou stick together; (pièces mécaniques) interdependent; (Jur: engagement) binding on all parties; (: débiteurs) jointly liable; **être ~ de** (collègues) to stand by; (mécanisme) to be bound up with, be dependent on

solidarité [sɔlidaʀite] nf (entre personnes) solidarity; (de mécanisme, phénomènes) interdependence; **par ~ (avec)** (cesser le travail etc) in sympathy (with)

solide [sɔlid] adj solid; (mur, maison, meuble) solid, sturdy; (connaissances, argument) sound; (personne) robust, sturdy; (estomac) strong ▷ nm solid; **avoir les reins ~s** (fig) to be in a good financial position; to have sound financial backing

soliste [sɔlist] nm/f soloist

solitaire [sɔlitɛʀ] adj (sans compagnie) solitary, lonely; (isolé) solitary, isolated, lone; (lieu) lonely ▷ nm/f (ermite) recluse; (fig: ours) loner ▷ nm (diamant, jeu) solitaire

solitude [sɔlityd] nf loneliness; (paix) solitude

solive [sɔliv] nf joist

solliciter [sɔlisite] vt (personne) to appeal to; (emploi, faveur) to seek; (moteur) to prompt; (occupations, attractions etc): **~ qn** to appeal to sb's curiosity etc, to entice sb; to make demands on sb's time; **~ qn de faire** to appeal to sb ou request sb to do

sollicitude [sɔlisityd] nf concern

soluble [sɔlybl] adj (sucre, cachet) soluble; (problème etc) soluble, solvable

solution [sɔlysjɔ̃] nf solution; **~ de continuité** gap, break; **~ de facilité** easy way out

solvable [sɔlvabl] adj solvent

sombre [sɔ̃bʀ] adj dark; (fig) dark, gloomy; (sinistre) awful, dreadful

sombrer [sɔ̃bʀe] vi (bateau) to sink, go down; **~ corps et biens** to go down with all hands; **~ dans** (misère, désespoir) to sink into

sommaire [sɔmɛʀ] adj (simple) basic; (expéditif) summary ▷ nm summary; **faire le ~ de** to make a summary of, summarize; **exécution ~** summary execution

sommation [sɔmasjɔ̃] nf (Jur) summons sg; (avant de faire feu) warning

somme [sɔm] nf (Math) sum; (fig) amount; (argent) sum, amount ▷ nm: **faire un ~** to have a (short) nap; **faire la ~ de** to add up; **en ~, ~ toute** adv all in all

sommeil [sɔmɛj] nm sleep; **avoir ~** to be sleepy; **avoir le ~ léger** to be a light sleeper; **en ~** (fig) dormant

S

sommeiller [sɔmeje] vi to doze; (fig) to lie
dormant

sommer [sɔme] vt: ~ **qn de faire** to
command ou order sb to do; (Jur) to summon
sb to do

sommes [sɔm] vb voir **être** voir aussi **somme**

sommet [sɔme] nm top; (d'une montagne)
summit, top; (fig: de la perfection, gloire) height;
(Géom: d'angle) vertex; (conférence) summit
(conference)

sommier [sɔmje] nm bed base, bedspring
(US); (Admin: registre) register; ~ **à ressorts**
(interior sprung) divan base (Brit), box spring
(US); ~ **à lattes** slatted bed base

somnambule [sɔmnɑ̃byl] nm/f sleepwalker

somnifère [sɔmnifɛʀ] nm sleeping drug;
(comprimé) sleeping pill ou tablet

somnoler [sɔmnɔle] vi to doze

somptueux, -euse [sɔptɥø, -øz] adj
sumptuous; (cadeau) lavish

son¹ [sɔ̃], **sa** [sa] (pl **ses**) [se] adj possessif
(antécédent humain mâle) his; (: femelle) her;
(: valeur indéfinie) one's, his/her; (: non humain)
its; voir **il**

son² [sɔ̃] nm sound; (de blé etc) bran; ~ **et
lumière** adj inv son et lumière

sondage [sɔ̃daʒ] nm (de terrain) boring,
drilling; (de mer, atmosphère) sounding; probe;
(enquête) survey, sounding out of opinion;
~ **(d'opinion)** (opinion) poll

sonde [sɔ̃d] nf (Navig) lead ou sounding line;
(Météorologie) sonde; (Méd) probe; catheter;
(d'alimentation) feeding tube; (Tech) borer,
driller; (de forage, sondage) drill; (pour fouiller etc)
probe; ~ **à avalanche** pole (for probing snow and
locating victims); ~ **spatiale** probe

sonder [sɔ̃de] vt (Navig) to sound; (atmosphère,
plaie, bagages etc) to probe; (Tech) to bore, drill;
(fig: personne) to sound out; (: opinion) to probe;
~ **le terrain** (fig) to see how the land lies

songe [sɔ̃ʒ] nm dream

songer [sɔ̃ʒe] vi to dream; ~ **à** (rêver à) to think
over, muse over; (penser à) to think of;
(envisager) to contemplate, think of, consider;
~ **que** to consider that; to think that

songeur, -euse [sɔ̃ʒœʀ, -øz] adj pensive; **ça
me laisse** ~ that makes me wonder

sonnant, e [sɔnɑ̃, -ɑ̃t] adj: **en espèces ~es et
trébuchantes** in coin of the realm; **à huit
heures ~es** on the stroke of eight

sonné, e [sɔne] adj (fam) cracked; (passé): **il
est midi** ~ it's gone twelve; **il a quarante
ans bien ~s** he's well into his forties

sonner [sɔne] vi (retentir) to ring; (donner une
impression) to sound ▷ vt (cloche) to ring; (glas,
tocsin) to sound; (portier, infirmière) to ring for;
(messe) to ring the bell for; (fam: choc, coup) to
knock out; ~ **du clairon** to sound the bugle;
~ **bien/mal/creux** to sound good/bad/
hollow; ~ **faux** (instrument) to sound out of
tune; (rire) to ring false; ~ **les heures** to strike
the hours; **minuit vient de** ~ midnight has

just struck; ~ **chez qn** to ring sb's doorbell,
ring at sb's door

sonnerie [sɔnʀi] nf (son) ringing; (sonnette)
bell; (mécanisme d'horloge) striking
mechanism; (de portable) ringtone;
~ **d'alarme** alarm bell; ~ **de clairon** bugle
call

sonnette [sɔnɛt] nf bell; ~ **d'alarme** alarm
bell; ~ **de nuit** night-bell

sono [sɔno] nf (= sonorisation) PA (system);
(d'une discothèque) sound system

sonore [sɔnɔʀ] adj (voix) sonorous, ringing;
(salle, métal) resonant; (ondes, film, signal)
sound cpd; (Ling) voiced; **effets ~s** sound
effects

sonorisation [sɔnɔʀizasjɔ̃] nf (équipement: de
salle de conférences) public address system, P.A.
system; (: de discothèque) sound system

sonorité [sɔnɔʀite] nf (de piano, violon) tone;
(de voix, mot) sonority; (d'une salle) resonance;
acoustics pl

sont [sɔ̃] vb voir **être**

sophistiqué, e [sɔfistike] adj sophisticated

sorbet [sɔʀbɛ] nm water ice, sorbet

sorcellerie [sɔʀsɛlʀi] nf witchcraft no pl,
sorcery no pl

sorcier, -ière [sɔʀsje, -jɛʀ] nm/f sorcerer/
witch ou sorceress ▷ adj: **ce n'est pas** ~ (fam)
it's as easy as pie

sordide [sɔʀdid] adj (lieu) squalid; (action) sordid

sornettes [sɔʀnɛt] nfpl twaddle sg

sort [sɔʀ] vb voir **sortir** ▷ nm (fortune, destinée)
fate; (condition, situation) lot; (magique): **jeter
un** ~ to cast a spell; **un coup du** ~ a blow
dealt by fate; **le ~ en est jeté** the die is cast;
tirer au ~ to draw lots; **tirer qch au** ~ to
draw lots for sth

sorte [sɔʀt] vb voir **sortir** ▷ nf sort, kind; **une
~ de** a sort of; **de la** ~ in that way; **en
quelque** ~ in a way; **de** ~ **à** so as to, in order
to; **de (telle) ~ que, en ~ que** (de manière que)
so that; (si bien que) so much so that; **faire en
~ que** to see to it that

sortie [sɔʀti] nf (issue) way out, exit; (Mil)
sortie; (fig: verbale) outburst; sally; (: parole
incongrue) odd remark; (d'un gaz, de l'eau) outlet;
(promenade) outing; (le soir: au restaurant etc)
night out; (de produits) export; (de capitaux)
outflow; (Comm: somme): ~**s** items of
expenditure; outgoings; (Inform) output;
(d'imprimante) printout; (Comm: d'un disque)
release; (: d'un livre) publication; (: d'un modèle)
launching; **à sa** ~ as he went out ou left; **à la ~
de l'école/l'usine** (moment) after school/
work; when school/the factory comes out;
(lieu) at the school/factory gates; **à la ~ de ce
nouveau modèle** when this new model
comes (ou came) out, when they bring (ou
brought) out this new model; ~ **de bain**
(vêtement) bathrobe; "~ **de camions**" "vehicle
exit"; ~ **papier** hard copy; ~ **de secours**
emergency exit

sortilège [sɔʀtilɛʒ] nm (magic) spell
sortir [sɔʀtiʀ] vi (gén) to come out; (partir, se promener, aller au spectacle etc) to go out; (bourgeon, plante, numéro gagnant) to come up ▷ vt (gén) to take out; (produit, ouvrage, modèle) to bring out; (fam: dire: boniments, incongruités) to come out with; (Inform) to output; (: sur papier) to print out; (fam: expulser) to throw out ▷ nm: **au ~ de l'hiver/l'enfance** as winter/childhood nears its end; **~ qch de** to take sth out of; **~ qn d'embarras** to get sb out of trouble; **~ avec qn** to be going out with sb; **~ de** (gén) to leave; (endroit) to go (ou come) out of, leave; (rainure etc) to come out of; (maladie) to get over; (époque) to get through; (cadre, compétence) to be outside; (provenir de: famille etc) to come from; **~ de table** to leave the table; **~ du système** (Inform) to log out; **~ de ses gonds** (fig) to fly off the handle; **se ~ de** (affaire, situation) to get out of; **s'en ~** (malade) to pull through; (d'une difficulté etc) to come through all right; to get through, be able to manage
sosie [sɔzi] nm double
sot, sotte [so, sɔt] adj silly, foolish ▷ nm/f fool
sottise [sɔtiz] nf silliness no pl, foolishness no pl; (propos, acte) silly ou foolish thing (to do ou say)
sou [su] nm: **près de ses ~s** tight-fisted; **sans le ~** penniless; **~ à ~** penny by penny; **pas un ~ de bon sens** not a scrap ou an ounce of good sense; **de quatre ~s** worthless
soubresaut [subʀəso] nm (de peur etc) start; (cahot: d'un véhicule) jolt
souche [suʃ] nf (d'arbre) stump; (de carnet) counterfoil (Brit), stub; **dormir comme une ~** to sleep like a log; **de vieille ~** of old stock
souci [susi] nm (inquiétude) worry; (préoccupation) concern; (Bot) marigold; **se faire du ~** to worry; **avoir (le) ~ de** to have concern for; **par ~ de** for the sake of, out of concern for
soucier [susje]: **se ~ de** vt to care about
soucieux, -euse [susjø, -øz] adj concerned, worried; **~ de** concerned about; **peu ~ de/que** caring little about/whether
soucoupe [sukup] nf saucer; **~ volante** flying saucer
soudain, e [sudɛ̃, -ɛn] adj (douleur, mort) sudden ▷ adv suddenly, all of a sudden
Soudan [sudɑ̃] nm: **le ~** Sudan
soude [sud] nf soda
souder [sude] vt (avec fil à souder) to solder; (par soudure autogène) to weld; (fig) to bind ou knit together; to fuse (together); **se souder** vi (os) to knit (together)
soudoyer [sudwaje] vt (péj) to bribe, buy over
soudure [sudyʀ] nf soldering; welding; (joint) soldered joint; weld; **faire la ~** (Comm) to fill a gap; (fig: assurer une transition) to bridge the gap

souffert, e [sufɛʀ, -ɛʀt] pp de **souffrir**
souffle [sufl] nm (en expirant) breath; (en soufflant) puff, blow; (respiration) breathing; (d'explosion, de ventilateur) blast; (du vent) blowing; (fig) inspiration; **retenir son ~** to hold one's breath; **avoir du/manquer de ~** to have a lot of puff/be short of breath; **être à bout de ~** to be out of breath; **avoir le ~ court** to be short-winded; **un ~ d'air** ou **de vent** a breath of air, a puff of wind; **~ au cœur** (Méd) heart murmur
soufflé, e [sufle] adj (Culin) souffléd; (fam: ahuri, stupéfié) staggered ▷ nm (Culin) soufflé
souffler [sufle] vi (gén) to blow; (haleter) to puff (and blow) ▷ vt (feu, bougie) to blow out; (chasser: poussière etc) to blow away; (Tech: verre) to blow; (explosion) to destroy (with its blast); (dire): **~ qch à qn** to whisper sth to sb; (fam: voler): **~ qch à qn** to pinch sth from sb; **~ son rôle à qn** to prompt sb; **ne pas ~ mot** not to breathe a word; **laisser ~ qn** (fig) to give sb a breather
soufflet [suflɛ] nm (instrument) bellows pl; (entre wagons) vestibule; (Couture) gusset; (gifle) slap (in the face)
souffleur, -euse [suflœʀ, -øz] nm/f (Théât) prompter; (Tech) glass-blower
souffrance [sufʀɑ̃s] nf suffering; **en ~** (marchandise) awaiting delivery; (affaire) pending
souffrant, e [sufʀɑ̃, -ɑ̃t] adj unwell
souffre-douleur [sufʀədulœʀ] nm inv whipping boy (Brit), butt, underdog
souffrir [sufʀiʀ] vi to suffer; (éprouver des douleurs) to be in pain ▷ vt to suffer, endure; (supporter) to bear, stand; (admettre: exception etc) to allow ou admit of; **~ de** (maladie, froid) to suffer from; **~ des dents** to have trouble with one's teeth; **ne pas pouvoir ~ qch/qn ...** not to be able to endure ou bear sth/that ...; **elle ne peut pas le ~** she can't stand ou bear him; **faire ~ qn** (personne) to make sb suffer; (: dents, blessure etc) to hurt sb
soufre [sufʀ] nm sulphur (Brit), sulfur (US)
souhait [swɛ] nm wish; **tous nos ~s de** good wishes ou our best wishes for; **tous nos ~s pour la nouvelle année** (our) best wishes for the New Year; **riche à ~** as rich etc as one could wish; **à vos ~s!** bless you!
souhaitable [swɛtabl] adj desirable
souhaiter [swete] vt to wish for; **~ le bonjour à qn** to bid sb good day; **~ la bonne année à qn** to wish sb a happy New Year; **~ que** to hope that; **il est à ~ que** it is to be hoped that
souiller [suje] vt to dirty, soil; (fig) to sully, tarnish
soûl, e [su, sul] adj drunk; (fig): **~ de musique/plaisirs** drunk with music/pleasure ▷ nm: **tout son ~** to one's heart's content
soulagement [sulaʒmɑ̃] nm relief

soulager [sulaʒe] vt to relieve; **~ qn de** to relieve sb of

soûler [sule] vt: **~ qn** to get sb drunk; (boisson) to make sb drunk; (fig) to make sb's head spin ou reel; **se soûler** vi to get drunk; **se ~ de** (fig) to intoxicate o.s with

soulever [sulve] vt to lift; (vagues, poussière) to send up; (peuple) to stir up (to revolt); (enthousiasme) to arouse; (question, débat, protestations, difficultés) to raise; **se soulever** vi (peuple) to rise up; (personne couchée) to lift o.s. up; (couvercle etc) to lift; **cela me soulève le cœur** it makes me feel sick

soulier [sulje] nm shoe; **~s bas** low-heeled shoes; **~s plats/à talons** flat/heeled shoes

souligner [suliɲe] vt to underline; (fig) to emphasize, stress

soumettre [sumɛtʀ] vt (pays) to subject, subjugate; (rebelles) to put down, subdue; **~ qn/qch à** to subject sb/sth to; **~ qch à qn** (projet etc) to submit sth to sb; **se ~ (à)** (se rendre, obéir) to submit (to); **se ~ à** (formalités etc) to submit to; (régime etc) to submit o.s to

soumis, e [sumi, -iz] pp de **soumettre** ▷ adj submissive; **revenus ~ à l'impôt** taxable income

soumission [sumisjɔ̃] nf (voir se soumettre) submission; (docilité) submissiveness; (Comm) tender

soupape [supap] nf valve; **~ de sûreté** safety valve

soupçon [supsɔ̃] nm suspicion; (petite quantité): **un ~ de** a hint ou touch of; **avoir ~ de** to suspect; **au dessus de tout ~** above (all) suspicion

soupçonner [supsɔne] vt to suspect; **~ qn de qch/d'être** to suspect sb of sth/of being

soupçonneux, -euse [supsɔnø, -øz] adj suspicious

soupe [sup] nf soup; **~ au lait** adj inv quick-tempered; **~ à l'oignon/de poisson** onion/fish soup; **~ populaire** soup kitchen

souper [supe] vi to have supper ▷ nm supper; **avoir soupé de** (fam) to be sick and tired of

soupeser [supəze] vt to weigh in one's hand(s), feel the weight of; (fig) to weigh up

soupière [supjɛʀ] nf (soup) tureen

soupir [supiʀ] nm sigh; (Mus) crotchet rest (Brit), quarter note rest (US); **rendre le dernier ~** to breathe one's last; **pousser un ~ de soulagement** to heave a sigh of relief

soupirail, -aux [supiʀaj, -o] nm (small) basement window

soupirer [supiʀe] vi to sigh; **~ après qch** to yearn for sth

souple [supl] adj supple; (col) soft; (fig: règlement, caractère) flexible; (: démarche, taille) lithe, supple

souplesse [suplɛs] nf suppleness; (de caractère) flexibility

source [suʀs] nf (point d'eau) spring; (d'un cours d'eau, fig) source; **prendre sa ~ à/dans** (cours d'eau) to have its source at/in; **tenir qch de bonne ~/de ~ sûre** to have sth on good authority/from a reliable source; **~ thermale/d'eau minérale** hot ou thermal/mineral spring

sourcil [suʀsij] nm (eye)brow

sourciller [suʀsije] vi: **sans ~** without turning a hair ou batting an eyelid

sourd, e [suʀ, suʀd] adj deaf; (bruit, voix) muffled; (couleur) muted; (douleur) dull; (lutte) silent, hidden; (Ling) voiceless ▷ nm/f deaf person; **être ~ à** to be deaf to; **faire la ~e oreille** to turn a deaf ear

sourdine [suʀdin] nf (Mus) mute; **en ~** adv softly, quietly; **mettre une ~ à** (fig) to tone down

sourd-muet, sourde-muette [suʀmɥɛ, suʀdmɥɛt] adj deaf-and-dumb ▷ nm/f deaf-mute

souriant, e [suʀjã, -ãt] vb voir **sourire** ▷ adj cheerful

souricière [suʀisjɛʀ] nf mousetrap; (fig) trap

sourire [suʀiʀ] nm smile ▷ vi to smile; **~ à qn** to smile at sb; (fig: plaire à) to appeal to sb; (: chance) to smile on sb; **faire un ~ à qn** to give sb a smile; **garder le ~** to keep smiling

souris [suʀi] nf (aussi Inform) mouse

sournois, e [suʀnwa, -waz] adj deceitful, underhand

sous [su] prép (gén) under; **~ la pluie/le soleil** in the rain/sunshine; **~ mes yeux** before my eyes; **~ terre** adj, adv underground; **~ vide** adj, adv vacuum-packed; **~ l'influence/l'action de** under the influence of/by the action of; **~ antibiotiques/perfusion** on antibiotics/a drip; **~ cet angle/ce rapport** from this angle/in this respect; **~ peu** adv shortly, before long

sous-bois [subwa] nm inv undergrowth

souscrire [suskʀiʀ]: **~ à** vt to subscribe to

sous-directeur, -trice [sudiʀɛktœʀ, -tʀis] nm/f assistant manager/manageress, submanager/manageress

sous-entendre [suzãtãdʀ] vt to imply, infer

sous-entendu, e [suzãtãdy] adj implied; (Ling) understood ▷ nm innuendo, insinuation

sous-estimer [suzɛstime] vt to underestimate

sous-jacent, e [suʒasã, -ãt] adj underlying

sous-louer [sulwe] vt to sublet

sous-marin, e [sumaʀɛ̃, -in] adj (flore, volcan) submarine; (navigation, pêche, explosif) underwater ▷ nm submarine

sous-officier [suzɔfisje] nm ≈ non-commissioned officer (NCO)

sous-produit [supʀɔdɥi] nm by-product; (fig: péj) pale imitation

sous-pull [supul] nm thin poloneck sweater

soussigné, e [susiɲe] adj: **je ~ I** the undersigned

sous-sol [susɔl] nm basement; (Géo) subsoil

sous-titre [sutitʀ] *nm* subtitle

soustraction [sustʀaksjɔ̃] *nf* subtraction

soustraire [sustʀɛʀ] *vt* to subtract, take away; (*dérober*): **~ qch à qn** to remove sth from sb; **~ qn à** (*danger*) to shield sb from; **se ~ à** (*autorité, obligation, devoir*) to elude, escape from

sous-traitant [sutʀɛtɑ̃] *nm* subcontractor

sous-traiter [sutʀete] *vt, vi* to subcontract

sous-vêtement [suvɛtmɑ̃] *nm* undergarment, item of underwear; **sous-vêtements** *nmpl* underwear *sg*

soutane [sutan] *nf* cassock, soutane

soute [sut] *nf* hold; **~ à bagages** baggage hold

soutenir [sutniʀ] *vt* to support; (*assaut, choc, regard*) to stand up to, withstand; (*intérêt, effort*) to keep up; (*assurer*): **~ que** to maintain that; **se soutenir** (*dans l'eau etc*) to hold o.s. up; (*être soutenable: point de vue*) to be tenable; (*s'aider mutuellement*) to stand by each other; **~ la comparaison avec** to bear *ou* stand comparison with; **~ le regard de qn** to be able to look sb in the face

soutenu, e [sutny] *pp de* **soutenir** ▷ *adj* (*efforts*) sustained, unflagging; (*style*) elevated; (*couleur*) strong

souterrain, e [suteʀɛ̃, -ɛn] *adj* underground; (*fig*) subterranean ▷ *nm* underground passage

soutien [sutjɛ̃] *nm* support; **apporter son ~ à** to lend one's support to; **~ de famille** breadwinner

soutien-gorge (*pl* **soutiens-gorge**) [sutjɛ̃gɔʀʒ] *nm* bra; (*de maillot de bain*) top

soutirer [sutiʀe] *vt*: **~ qch à qn** to squeeze *ou* get sth out of sb

souvenir [suvniʀ] *nm* (*réminiscence*) memory; (*cadeau*) souvenir, keepsake; (*de voyage*) souvenir ▷ *vb*: **se ~ de** *vt* to remember; **se ~ que** to remember that; **garder le ~ de** to retain the memory of; **en ~ de** in memory *ou* remembrance of; **avec mes affectueux/meilleurs ~s, …** with love from, …/ regards, …

souvent [suvɑ̃] *adv* often; **peu ~** seldom, infrequently; **le plus ~** more often than not, most often

souverain, e [suvʀɛ̃, -ɛn] *adj* sovereign; (*fig: mépris*) supreme ▷ *nm/f* sovereign, monarch

soyeux, -euse [swajø, -øz] *adj* silky

soyons *etc* [swajɔ̃] *vb voir* **être**

spacieux, -euse [spasjø, -øz] *adj* spacious; roomy

spaghettis [spageti] *nmpl* spaghetti *sg*

sparadrap [spaʀadʀa] *nm* adhesive *ou* sticking (*Brit*) plaster, bandaid® (*US*)

spatial, e, -aux [spasjal, -o] *adj* (*Aviat*) space *cpd*; (*Psych*) spatial

speaker, ine [spikœʀ, -kʀin] *nm/f* announcer

spécial, e, -aux [spesjal, -o] *adj* special; (*bizarre*) peculiar

spécialement [spesjalmɑ̃] *adv* especially, particularly; (*tout exprès*) specially; **pas ~** not particularly

spécialiser [spesjalize]: **se spécialiser** *vi* to specialize

spécialiste [spesjalist] *nm/f* specialist

spécialité [spesjalite] *nf* speciality; (*Scol*) special field; **~ pharmaceutique** patent medicine

spécifier [spesifje] *vt* to specify, state

spécimen [spesimɛn] *nm* specimen; (*revue etc*) specimen *ou* sample copy

spectacle [spɛktakl] *nm* (*tableau, scène*) sight; (*représentation*) show; (*industrie*) show business, entertainment; **se donner en ~** (*péj*) to make a spectacle *ou* an exhibition of o.s.; **pièce/revue à grand ~** spectacular (play/revue); **au ~ de …** at the sight of …

spectaculaire [spɛktakylɛʀ] *adj* spectacular

spectateur, -trice [spɛktatœʀ, -tʀis] *nm/f* (*Ciné etc*) member of the audience; (*Sport*) spectator; (*d'un événement*) onlooker, witness

spéculer [spekyle] *vi* to speculate; **~ sur** (*Comm*) to speculate in; (*réfléchir*) to speculate on; (*tabler sur*) to bank *ou* rely on

spéléologie [speleɔlɔʒi] *nf* (*étude*) speleology; (*activité*) potholing

sperme [spɛʀm] *nm* semen, sperm

sphère [sfɛʀ] *nf* sphere

spirale [spiʀal] *nf* spiral; **en ~** in a spiral

spirituel, le [spiʀitɥɛl] *adj* spiritual; (*fin, piquant*) witty; **musique ~le** sacred music; **concert ~** concert of sacred music

splendide [splɑ̃did] *adj* splendid, magnificent

sponsoriser [spɔ̃sɔʀize] *vt* to sponsor

spontané, e [spɔ̃tane] *adj* spontaneous

spontanéité [spɔ̃taneite] *nf* spontaneity

sport [spɔʀ] *nm* sport ▷ *adj inv* (*vêtement*) casual; (*fair-play*) sporting; **faire du ~** to do sport; **~ individuel/d'équipe** individual/ team sport; **~ de combat** combative sport; **~s d'hiver** winter sports

sportif, -ive [spɔʀtif, -iv] *adj* (*journal, association, épreuve*) sports *cpd*; (*allure, démarche*) athletic; (*attitude, esprit*) sporting; **les résultats ~s** the sports results

spot [spɔt] *nm* (*lampe*) spot(light); (*annonce*): **~ (publicitaire)** commercial (*break*)

square [skwaʀ] *nm* public garden(s)

squelette [skəlɛt] *nm* skeleton

squelettique [skəletik] *adj* scrawny; (*fig*) skimpy

SRAS [sʀas] *sigle m* (= *syndrome respiratoire aigu sévère*) SARS

Sri Lanka [sʀilɑ̃ka] *nm*: **le ~** Sri Lanka

stabiliser [stabilize] *vt* to stabilize; (*terrain*) to consolidate

stable [stabl] *adj* stable, steady

stade [stad] *nm* (*Sport*) stadium; (*phase, niveau*) stage

stage [staʒ] *nm* training period; (*cours*) training course; (*d'avocat stagiaire*) articles *pl*;

S

~ en entreprise work experience placement; **~ de formation (professionnelle)** vocational (training) course; **~ de perfectionnement** advanced training course

stagiaire [staʒjɛʀ] *nm/f, adj* trainee *(cpd)*

stagner [stagne] *vi* to stagnate

stalle [stal] *nf* stall, box

stand [stɑ̃d] *nm (d'exposition)* stand; *(de foire)* stall; **~ de tir** *(à la foire, Sport)* shooting range; **~ de ravitaillement** pit

standard [stɑ̃daʀ] *adj inv* standard ▷ *nm (type, norme)* standard; *(téléphonique)* switchboard

standardiste [stɑ̃daʀdist] *nm/f* switchboard operator

standing [stɑ̃diŋ] *nm* standing; **de grand ~** luxury; **immeuble de grand ~** block of luxury flats *(Brit)*, condo(minium) *(US)*

starter [staʀtɛʀ] *nm (Auto)* choke; *(Sport: personne)* starter; **mettre le ~** to pull out the choke

station [stasjɔ̃] *nf* station; *(de bus)* stop; *(de villégiature)* resort; *(posture)*: **la ~ debout** standing, an upright posture; **~ balnéaire** seaside resort; **~ de graissage** lubrication bay; **~ de lavage** carwash; **~ de ski** ski resort; **~ de sports d'hiver** winter sports resort; **~ de taxis** taxi rank *(Brit)* ou stand *(US)*; **~ thermale** thermal spa; **~ de travail** workstation

stationnement [stasjɔnmɑ̃] *nm* parking; **zone de ~ interdit** no parking area; **~ alterné** parking on alternate sides

stationner [stasjɔne] *vi* to park

station-service [stasjɔ̃sɛʀvis] *nf* service station

statistique [statistik] *nf (science)* statistics *sg*; *(rapport, étude)* statistic ▷ *adj* statistical; **statistiques** *nfpl (données)* statistics *pl*

statue [staty] *nf* statue

statu quo [statykwo] *nm* status quo

statut [staty] *nm* status; **statuts** *nmpl (Jur, Admin)* statutes

statutaire [statytɛʀ] *adj* statutory

Sté *abr (= société)* soc

steak [stɛk] *nm* steak; **~ haché** hamburger

sténo [steno] *nf (aussi: **~graphie**)* shorthand; **prendre en ~** to take down in shorthand

sténographie [stenografi] *nf* shorthand; **prendre en ~** to take down in shorthand

stéréo *nf (aussi: **~phonie**)* stereo; **émission en ~** stereo broadcast ▷ *adj (aussi: **~phonique**)* stereo

stéréophonie [stereofɔni] *nf* stereo(phony); **émission en ~** stereo broadcast

stéréophonique [stereofɔnik] *adj* stereo(phonic)

stérile [steʀil] *adj* sterile; *(terre)* barren; *(fig)* fruitless, futile

stérilet [steʀilɛ] *nm* coil, loop

stériliser [steʀilize] *vt* to sterilize

stigmates [stigmat] *nmpl* scars, marks; *(Rel)* stigmata *pl*

stimulant, e [stimylɑ̃, -ɑ̃t] *adj* stimulating ▷ *nm (Méd)* stimulant; *(fig)* stimulus, incentive

stimuler [stimyle] *vt* to stimulate

stipuler [stipyle] *vt* to stipulate, specify

stock [stɔk] *nm* stock; **en ~** in stock

stocker [stɔke] *vt* to stock; *(déchets)* to store

stop [stɔp] *nm (Auto: écriteau)* stop sign; *(: signal)* brake-light; *(dans un télégramme)* stop ▷ *excl* stop!; **faire du ~** *(fam)* to hitch(hike)

stopper [stɔpe] *vt* to stop, halt; *(Couture)* to mend ▷ *vi* to stop, halt

store [stɔʀ] *nm* blind; *(de magasin)* shade, awning

strabisme [strabism] *nm* squint(ing)

strapontin [strapɔ̃tɛ̃] *nm* jump ou foldaway seat

Strasbourg [strazbuʀ] *n* Strasbourg

stratégie [strateʒi] *nf* strategy

stratégique [strateʒik] *adj* strategic

stress [strɛs] *nm inv* stress

stressant, e [strɛsɑ̃, -ɑ̃t] *adj* stressful

stresser [strɛse] *vt* to stress, cause stress in; **~ qn** to make sb (feel) tense

strict, e [strikt] *adj* strict; *(tenue, décor)* severe, plain; **son droit le plus ~** his most basic right; **dans la plus ~e intimité** strictly in private; **le ~ nécessaire/minimum** the bare essentials/minimum

strident, e [stridɑ̃, -ɑ̃t] *adj* shrill, strident

strophe [strɔf] *nf* verse, stanza

structure [stryktyʀ] *nf* structure; **~s d'accueil/touristiques** reception/tourist facilities

studieux, -euse [stydjø, -øz] *adj (élève)* studious; *(vacances)* study *cpd*

studio [stydjo] *nm (logement)* studio flat *(Brit)* ou apartment *(US)*; *(d'artiste, TV etc)* studio

stupéfait, e [stypefɛ, -ɛt] *adj* astonished

stupéfiant, e [stypefjɑ̃, -ɑ̃t] *adj (étonnant)* stunning, astonishing ▷ *nm (Méd)* drug, narcotic

stupéfier [stypefje] *vt* to stupefy; *(étonner)* to stun, astonish

stupeur [stypœʀ] *nf (inertie, insensibilité)* stupor; *(étonnement)* astonishment, amazement

stupide [stypid] *adj* stupid; *(hébété)* stunned

stupidité [stypidite] *nf* stupidity *no pl*; *(parole, acte)* stupid thing (to say ou do)

style [stil] *nm* style; **meuble/robe de ~** piece of period furniture/period dress; **~ de vie** lifestyle

stylé, e [stile] *adj* well-trained

styliste [stilist] *nm/f* designer; stylist

stylo [stilo] *nm*: **~ (à encre)** (fountain) pen; **~ (à) bille** ballpoint pen

su, e [sy] *pp de* **savoir** ▷ *nm*: **au su de** with the knowledge of

suave [sɥav] *adj (odeur)* sweet; *(voix)* suave, smooth; *(coloris)* soft, mellow

subalterne [sybaltɛʀn] *adj (employé, officier)*

junior; (*rôle*) subordinate, subsidiary ⊳ *nm/f* subordinate, inferior

subconscient [sypkɔ̃sjɑ̃] *nm* subconscious

subir [sybiʀ] *vt* (*affront, dégâts, mauvais traitements*) to suffer; (*influence, charme*) to be under, be subjected to; (*traitement, opération, châtiment*) to undergo; (*personne*) to suffer, be subjected to

subit, e [sybi, -it] *adj* sudden

subitement [sybitmɑ̃] *adv* suddenly, all of a sudden

subjectif, -ive [sybʒɛktif, -iv] *adj* subjective

subjonctif [sybʒɔ̃ktif] *nm* subjunctive

subjuguer [sybʒyge] *vt* to subjugate

submerger [sybmɛʀʒe] *vt* to submerge; (*foule*) to engulf; (*fig*) to overwhelm

subordonné, e [sybɔʀdɔne] *adj, nm/f* subordinate; **~ à** (*personne*) subordinate to; (*résultats etc*) subject to, depending on

subrepticement [sybʀɛptismɑ̃] *adv* surreptitiously

subside [sypsid] *nm* grant

subsidiaire [sypsidjɛʀ] *adj* subsidiary; **question ~** deciding question

subsister [sybziste] *vi* (*rester*) to remain, subsist; (*vivre*) to live; (*survivre*) to live on

substance [sypstɑ̃s] *nf* substance; **en ~** in substance

substituer [sypstitɥe] *vt*: **~ qn/qch à** to substitute sb/sth for; **se ~ à qn** (*représenter*) to substitute for sb; (*évincer*) to substitute o.s. for sb

substitut [sypstity] *nm* (*Jur*) deputy public prosecutor; (*succédané*) substitute

subterfuge [syptɛʀfyʒ] *nm* subterfuge

subtil, e [syptil] *adj* subtle

subtiliser [syptilize] *vt*: **~ qch (à qn)** to spirit sth away (from sb)

subvenir [sybvəniʀ] *vt*: **~ à** *vt* to meet

subvention [sybvɑ̃sjɔ̃] *nf* subsidy, grant

subventionner [sybvɑ̃sjɔne] *vt* to subsidize

suc [syk] *nm* (*Bot*) sap; (*de viande, fruit*) juice; **~s gastriques** gastric juices

succédané [syksedane] *nm* substitute

succéder [syksede]: **~ à** *vt* (*directeur, roi etc*) to succeed; (*venir après: dans une série*) to follow, succeed; **se succéder** *vi* (*accidents, années*) to follow one another

succès [syksɛ] *nm* success; **avec ~** successfully; **sans ~** unsuccessfully; **avoir du ~** to be a success, be successful; **à ~** successful; **livre à ~** bestseller; **~ de librairie** bestseller; **~ (féminins)** conquests

successeur [syksesœʀ] *nm* successor

successif, -ive [syksesif, -iv] *adj* successive

succession [syksesjɔ̃] *nf* (*série, Pol*) succession; (*Jur: patrimoine*) estate, inheritance; **prendre la ~ de** (*directeur*) to succeed, take over from; (*entreprise*) to take over

succomber [sykɔ̃be] *vi* to die, succumb; (*fig*): **~ à** to succumb to, give way to

succulent, e [sykylɑ̃, -ɑ̃t] *adj* delicious

succursale [sykyʀsal] *nf* branch; **magasin à ~s multiples** chain *ou* multiple store

sucer [syse] *vt* to suck

sucette [sysɛt] *nf* (*bonbon*) lollipop; (*de bébé*) dummy (Brit), comforter, pacifier (US)

sucre [sykʀ] *nm* (*substance*) sugar; (*morceau*) lump of sugar, sugar lump *ou* cube; **~ de canne/betterave** cane/beet sugar; **~ en morceaux/cristallisé/en poudre** lump *ou* cube/granulated/caster sugar; **~ glace** icing sugar (Brit), confectioner's sugar (US); **~ d'orge** barley sugar

sucré, e [sykʀe] *adj* (*produit alimentaire*) sweetened; (*au goût*) sweet; (*péj*) sugary, honeyed

sucrer [sykʀe] *vt* (*thé, café*) to sweeten, put sugar in; **~ qn** to put sugar in sb's tea (*ou* coffee *etc*); **se sucrer** to help o.s. to sugar, have some sugar; (*fam*) to line one's pocket(s)

sucrerie [sykʀəʀi] *nf* (*usine*) sugar refinery; **sucreries** *nfpl* (*bonbons*) sweets, sweet things

sucrier, -ière [sykʀije, -jɛʀ] *adj* (*industrie*) sugar *cpd*; (*région*) sugar-producing ⊳ *nm* (*fabricant*) sugar producer; (*récipient*) sugar bowl *ou* basin

sud [syd] *nm*: **le ~** the south ⊳ *adj inv* south; (*côte*) south, southern; **au ~** (*situation*) in the south; (*direction*) to the south; **au ~ de** (to the) south of

sud-africain, e [sydafʀikɛ̃, -ɛn] *adj* South African ⊳ *nm/f*: **Sud-Africain, e** South African

sud-américain, e [sydameʀikɛ̃, -ɛn] *adj* South American ⊳ *nm/f*: **Sud-Américain, e** South American

sud-est [sydɛst] *nm, adj inv* south-east

sud-ouest [sydwɛst] *nm, adj inv* south-west

Suède [sɥɛd] *nf*: **la ~** Sweden

suédois, e [sɥedwa, -waz] *adj* Swedish ⊳ *nm* (*Ling*) Swedish ⊳ *nm/f*: **S~, e** Swede

suer [sɥe] *vi* to sweat; (*suinter*) to ooze ⊳ *vt* (*fig*) to exude; **~ à grosses gouttes** to sweat profusely

sueur [sɥœʀ] *nf* sweat; **en ~** sweating, in a sweat; **avoir des ~s froides** to be in a cold sweat

suffire [syfiʀ] *vi* (*être assez*): **~ (à qn/pour qch/ pour faire)** to be enough *ou* sufficient (for sb/for sth/to do); (*satisfaire*): **cela lui suffit** he's content with this, this is enough for him; **se suffire** *vi* to be self-sufficient; **cela suffit pour les irriter/qu'ils se fâchent** it's enough to annoy them/for them to get angry; **il suffit d'une négligence/qu'on oublie pour que ...** it only takes one act of carelessness/one only needs to forget for ...; **ça suffit!** that's enough!, that'll do!

suffisamment [syfizamɑ̃] *adv* sufficiently, enough; **~ de** sufficient, enough

suffisant, e [syfizɑ̃, -ɑ̃t] *adj* (*temps, ressources*) sufficient; (*résultats*) satisfactory; (*vaniteux*) self-important, bumptious

suffixe [syfiks] *nm* suffix

suffoquer [syfɔke] *vt* to choke, suffocate; (*stupéfier*) to stagger, astound ▷ *vi* to choke, suffocate; **~ de colère/d'indignation** to choke with anger/indignation

suffrage [syfraʒ] *nm* (Pol: *voix*) vote; (: *méthode*): **~ universel/direct/indirect** universal/direct/indirect suffrage; (*du public etc*) approval *no pl*; **~s exprimés** valid votes

suggérer [sygʒeʀe] *vt* to suggest; **~ que/de faire** to suggest that/doing

suggestion [sygʒɛstjɔ̃] *nf* suggestion

suicide [sɥisid] *nm* suicide ▷ *adj*: **opération ~** suicide mission

suicider [sɥiside]: **se suicider** *vi* to commit suicide

suie [sɥi] *nf* soot

suinter [sɥɛ̃te] *vi* to ooze

suis [sɥi] *vb voir* **être**; **suivre**

suisse [sɥis] *adj* Swiss ▷ *nm* (*bedeau*) ≈ verger ▷ *nm/f*: **S~** Swiss *pl inv* ▷ *nf*: **la S~** Switzerland; **la S~ romande/allemande** French-speaking/German-speaking Switzerland; **~ romand** Swiss French

Suissesse [sɥises] *nf* Swiss (woman *ou* girl)

suite [sɥit] *nf* (*continuation*: d'énumération *etc*) rest, remainder; (: *de feuilleton*) continuation; (: *second film etc sur le même thème*) sequel; (*série*: *de maisons, succès*): **une ~ de** a series *ou* succession of; (*Math*) series *sg*; (*conséquence*) result; (*ordre, liaison logique*) coherence; (*appartement, Mus*) suite; (*escorte*) retinue, suite; **suites** *nfpl* (*d'une maladie etc*) effects; **prendre la ~ de** (*directeur etc*) to succeed, take over from; **donner ~ à** (*requête, projet*) to follow up; **faire ~ à** to follow; (**faisant**) **~ à votre lettre du** further to your letter of the; **sans ~** *adj* incoherent, disjointed ▷ *adv* incoherently, disjointedly; **de ~** *adv* (*d'affilée*) in succession; (*immédiatement*) at once; **par la ~** afterwards, subsequently; **à la ~** *adv* one after the other; **à la ~ de** (*derrière*) behind; (*en conséquence de*) following; **par ~ de** owing to, as a result of; **avoir de la ~ dans les idées** to show great singleness of purpose; **attendre la ~ des événements** to (wait and see) what happens

suivant, e [sɥivɑ̃, -ɑ̃t] *vb voir* **suivre** ▷ *adj* next, following; (*ci-après*): **l'exercice ~** the following exercise ▷ *prép* (*selon*) according to; **~ que** according to whether; **au ~!** next!

suivi, e [sɥivi] *pp de* **suivre** ▷ *adj* (*régulier*) regular; (*Comm: article*) in general production; (*effort, qualité*) consistent; (*cohérent*) coherent ▷ *nm* follow-up; **très/peu ~** (*cours*) well-/poorly-attended; (*mode*) widely/not widely adopted; (*feuilleton etc*) widely/not widely followed

suivre [sɥivʀ] *vt* (*gén*) to follow; (*Scol: cours*) to attend; (: *leçon*) to follow, attend to; (: *programme*) to keep up with; (*Comm: article*) to continue to stock ▷ *vi* to follow; (*élève*:

écouter) to attend, pay attention; (: *assimiler le programme*) to keep up, follow; **se suivre** *vi* (*accidents, personnes, voitures etc*) to follow one after the other; (*raisonnement*) to be coherent; **~ des yeux** to follow with one's eyes; **faire ~** (*lettre*) to forward; **son cours** (*enquête etc*) to run *ou* take its course; **"à ~"** "to be continued"

sujet, te [syʒɛ, -ɛt] *adj*: **être ~ à** (*accidents*) to be prone to; (*vertige etc*) to be liable *ou* subject to ▷ *nm/f* (*d'un souverain*) subject ▷ *nm* subject; **un ~ de dispute/discorde/mécontentement** a cause for argument/dissension/dissatisfaction; **c'est à quel ~?** what is it about?; **avoir ~ de se plaindre** to have cause for complaint; **au ~ de** *prép* about; **~ à caution** *adj* questionable; **~ de conversation** topic *ou* subject of conversation; **~ d'examen** (*Scol*) examination question; examination paper; **~ d'expérience** (*Bio etc*) experimental subject

summum [sɔmɔm] *nm*: **le ~ de** the height of

super [sypɛʀ] *adj inv* great, fantastic ▷ *nm* (= *supercarburant*) ≈ 4-star (Brit), ≈ premium (US)

superbe [sypɛʀb] *adj* magnificent, superb ▷ *nf* arrogance

supercherie [sypɛʀʃəʀi] *nf* trick, trickery *no pl*; (*fraude*) fraud

supérette [sypeʀɛt] *nf* minimarket

superficie [sypɛʀfisi] *nf* (*surface*) area; (*fig*) surface

superficiel, le [sypɛʀfisjɛl] *adj* superficial

superflu, e [sypɛʀfly] *adj* superfluous ▷ *nm*: **le ~** the superfluous

supérieur, e [sypeʀjœʀ] *adj* (*lèvre, étages, classes*) upper; (*plus élevé: température, niveau*): **~ (à)** higher (than); (*meilleur: qualité, produit*): **~ (à)** superior (to); (*excellent, hautain*) superior ▷ *nm/f* superior; **Mère ~e** Mother Superior; **à l'étage ~** on the next floor up; **~ en nombre** superior in number

supériorité [sypeʀjɔʀite] *nf* superiority

superlatif [sypɛʀlatif] *nm* superlative

supermarché [sypɛʀmaʀʃe] *nm* supermarket

superposer [sypɛʀpoze] *vt* to superpose; (*meubles, caisses*) to stack; (*faire chevaucher*) to superimpose; **se superposer** (*images, souvenirs*) to be superimposed; **lits superposés** bunk beds

superproduction [sypɛʀpʀɔdyksjɔ̃] *nf* (*film*) spectacular

superpuissance [sypɛʀpɥisɑ̃s] *nf* superpower

superstitieux, -euse [sypɛʀstisjø, -øz] *adj* superstitious

superviser [sypɛʀvize] *vt* to supervise

supplanter [syplɑ̃te] *vt* to supplant

suppléance [sypleɑ̃s] *nf* (*poste*) supply post (Brit), substitute teacher's post (US)

suppléant, e [sypleɑ̃, -ɑ̃t] *adj* (*juge, fonctionnaire*) deputy *cpd*; (*professeur*) supply *cpd*

(Brit), substitute *cpd* (US) ▷ *nm/f* deputy; (*professeur*) supply *ou* substitute teacher; **médecin** ~ locum

suppléer [syplee] *vt* (*ajouter: mot manquant etc*) to supply, provide; (*compenser: lacune*) to fill in; (: *défaut*) to make up for; (*remplacer: professeur*) to stand in for; (: *juge*) to deputize for; ~ **à** *vt* to make up for; to substitute for

supplément [syplemã] *nm* supplement; **un ~ de travail** extra *ou* additional work; **un ~ de frites** *etc* an extra portion of chips *etc*; **un ~ de 10 euros** a supplement of 10 euros, an extra *ou* additional 10 euros; **ceci est en ~** (*au menu etc*) this is extra, there is an extra charge for this; **le vin est en ~** wine is extra; **payer un ~** to pay an additional charge; **~ d'information** additional information

supplémentaire [syplemãtɛʀ] *adj* additional, further; (*train, bus*) relief *cpd*, extra

supplication [syplikasjɔ̃] *nf* (*Rel*) supplication; **supplications** *nfpl* (*adjurations*) pleas, entreaties

supplice [syplis] *nm* (*peine corporelle*) torture *no pl*; form of torture; (*douleur physique, morale*) torture, agony; **être au ~** to be in agony

supplier [syplije] *vt* to implore, beseech

support [sypɔʀ] *nm* support; (*pour livre, outils*) stand; ~ **audio-visuel** audio-visual aid; ~ **publicitaire** advertising medium

supportable [sypɔʀtabl] *adj* (*douleur, température*) bearable; (*procédé, conduite*) tolerable

supporter[1] [sypɔʀtɛʀ] *nm* supporter, fan

supporter[2] [sypɔʀte] *vt* [sypɔʀte] (*poids, poussée, Sport: concurrent, équipe*) to support; (*conséquences, épreuve*) to bear, endure; (*défauts, personne*) to tolerate, put up with; (*chose: chaleur etc*) to withstand; (*personne: chaleur, vin*) to take

supposer [sypoze] *vt* to suppose; (*impliquer*) to presuppose; **en supposant** *ou* **à ~ que** supposing (that)

suppositoire [sypozitwaʀ] *nm* suppository

suppression [sypʀesjɔ̃] *nf* (*voir supprimer*) removal; deletion; cancellation; suppression

supprimer [sypʀime] *vt* (*cloison, cause, anxiété*) to remove; (*clause, mot*) to delete; (*congés, service d'autobus etc*) to cancel; (*publication, article*) to suppress; (*emplois, privilèges, témoin gênant*) to do away with; **~ qch à qn** to deprive sb of sth

suprême [sypʀɛm] *adj* supreme

 MOT-CLÉ

sur[1] [syʀ] *prép* **1** (*position*) on; (*pardessus*) over; (*au-dessus*) above; **pose-le sur la table** put it on the table; **je n'ai pas d'argent sur moi** I haven't any money on me
2 (*direction*) towards; **en allant sur Paris** going towards Paris; **sur votre droite** on *ou* to your right
3 (*à propos de*) on, about; **un livre/une conférence sur Balzac** a book/lecture on *ou* about Balzac
4 (*proportion, mesures*) out of; by; **un sur 10** one in 10; (*Scol*) one out of 10; **sur 20, deux sont venus** out of 20, two came; **4 m sur 2** 4 m by 2; **avoir accident sur accident** to have one accident after another
5 (*cause*): **sur sa recommandation** on *ou* at his recommendation; **sur son invitation** at his invitation
6: **sur ce** *adv* whereupon; **sur ce, il faut que je vous quitte** and now I must leave you

sur[2]**, e** [syʀ] *adj* sour

sûr, e [syʀ] *adj* sure, certain; (*digne de confiance*) reliable; (*sans danger*) safe; **peu ~** unreliable; **~ de qch** sure *ou* certain of sth; **être ~ de qn** to be sure of sb; **~ et certain** absolutely certain; **~ de soi** self-assured, self-confident; **le plus ~ est de** the safest thing is to

surcharge [syʀʃaʀʒ] *nf* (*de passagers, marchandises*) excess load; (*de détails, d'ornements*) overabundance, excess; (*correction*) alteration; (*Postes*) surcharge; **prendre des passagers en ~** to take on excess *ou* extra passengers; **~ de bagages** excess luggage; **~ de travail** extra work

surcharger [syʀʃaʀʒe] *vt* to overload; (*timbre-poste*) to surcharge; (*décoration*) to overdo

surchoix [syʀʃwa] *adj inv* top-quality

surclasser [syʀklase] *vt* to outclass

surcroît [syʀkʀwa] *nm*: **~ de qch** additional sth; **par ou de ~** moreover; **en ~** in addition

surdité [syʀdite] *nf* deafness; **atteint de ~ totale** profoundly deaf

surélever [syʀelve] *vt* to raise, heighten

sûrement [syʀmã] *adv* reliably; (*sans risques*) safely, securely; (*certainement*) certainly; **~ pas** certainly not

surenchère [syʀãʃɛʀ] *nf* (*aux enchères*) higher bid; (*sur prix fixe*) overbid; (*fig*) overstatement; outbidding tactics *pl*; **~ de violence** build-up of violence; **~ électorale** political (*ou* electoral) one-upmanship

surenchérir [syʀãʃeʀiʀ] *vi* to bid higher; to raise one's bid; (*fig*) to try and outbid each other

surent [syʀ] *vb voir* **savoir**

surestimer [syʀɛstime] *vt* (*tableau*) to overvalue; (*possibilité, personne*) to overestimate

sûreté [syʀte] *nf* (*voir sûr: exactitude: de renseignements etc*) reliability; (*sécurité*) safety; (*d'un geste*) steadiness; (*Jur*) guaranty; surety; **mettre en ~** to put in a safe place; **pour plus de ~** as an extra precaution; to be on the safe side; **la ~ de l'État** State security; **la S~ (nationale)** division of the Ministère de l'Intérieur heading all police forces except the gendarmerie and the Paris préfecture de police

S

surf [sœrf] nm surfing; **faire du ~** to go surfing
surface [syrfas] nf surface; (superficie) surface area; **une grande ~** a supermarket; **faire ~** to surface; **en ~** adv near the surface; (fig) superficially; **la pièce fait 100 m² de ~** the room has a surface area of 100m²; **~ de réparation** (Sport) penalty area; **~ porteuse** ou **de sustentation** (Aviat) aerofoil
surfait, e [syrfɛ, -ɛt] adj overrated
surfer [sœrfe] vi to surf; **~ sur Internet** to surf ou browse the Internet
surgelé, e [syrʒəle] adj (deep-)frozen ▷ nm: **les ~s** (deep-)frozen food
surgir [syrʒir] vi (personne, véhicule) to appear suddenly; (jaillir) to shoot up; (montagne etc) to rise up, loom up; (fig: problème, conflit) to arise
surhumain, e [syrymɛ̃, -ɛn] adj superhuman
sur-le-champ [syrləʃɑ̃] adv immediately
surlendemain [syrlɑ̃dmɛ̃] nm: **le ~ (soir)** two days later (in the evening); **le ~ de** two days after
surmenage [syrmənaʒ] nm overwork; **le ~ intellectuel** mental fatigue
surmener [syrməne] vt, **se surmener** vi to overwork
surmonter [syrmɔ̃te] vt (coupole etc) to surmount, top; (vaincre) to overcome, surmount; (être au-dessus de) to top
surnaturel, le [syrnatyrɛl] adj, nm supernatural
surnom [syrnɔ̃] nm nickname
surnombre [syrnɔ̃br] nm: **être en ~** to be too many (ou one too many)
surpeuplé, e [syrpœple] adj overpopulated
surplace [syrplas] nm: **faire du ~** to mark time
surplomber [syrplɔ̃be] vi to be overhanging ▷ vt to overhang; (dominer) to tower above
surplus [syrply] nm (Comm) surplus; (reste): **~ de bois** wood left over; **au ~** moreover; **~ américains** American army surplus sg
surprenant, e [syrprənɑ̃, -ɑ̃t] vb voir **surprendre** ▷ adj amazing
surprendre [syrprɑ̃dr] vt (étonner, prendre à l'improviste) to amaze, surprise; (secret) to discover; (tomber sur: intrus etc) to catch; (fig) to detect; to chance ou happen upon; (clin d'œil) to intercept; (conversation) to overhear; (orage, nuit etc) to catch out, take by surprise; **~ la vigilance/bonne foi de qn** to catch sb out/betray sb's good faith; **se ~ à faire** to catch ou find o.s. doing
surpris, e [syrpri, -iz] pp de **surprendre** ▷ adj: **~ (de/que)** amazed ou surprised (at/that)
surprise [syrpriz] nf surprise; **faire une ~ à qn** to give sb a surprise; **voyage sans ~s** uneventful journey; **par ~** adv by surprise
surprise-partie [syrprizparti] nf party
sursaut [syrso] nm start, jump; **~ de** (énergie, indignation) sudden fit ou burst of; **en ~** adv with a start

sursauter [syrsote] vi to (give a) start, jump
sursis [syrsi] nm (Jur: gén) suspended sentence; (à l'exécution capitale, aussi fig) reprieve; (Mil): **~ (d'appel** ou **d'incorporation)** deferment; **condamné à cinq mois (de prison) avec ~** given a five-month suspended (prison) sentence
surtaxe [syrtaks] nf surcharge
surtout [syrtu] adv (avant tout, d'abord) above all; (spécialement, particulièrement) especially; **il aime le sport, ~ le football** he likes sport, especially football; **cet été, il a ~ fait de la pêche** this summer he went fishing more than anything (else); **~ pas d'histoires!** no fuss now!; **~, ne dites rien!** whatever you do – don't say anything!; **~ pas!** certainly ou definitely not!; **~ que...** especially as ...
surveillance [syrvejɑ̃s] nf watch; (Police, Mil) surveillance; **sous ~ médicale** under medical supervision; **la ~ du territoire** internal security; voir aussi **DST**
surveillant, e [syrvejɑ̃, -ɑ̃t] nm/f (de prison) warder; (Scol) monitor; (de travaux) supervisor, overseer
surveiller [syrveje] vt (enfant, élèves, bagages) to watch, keep an eye on; (malade) to watch over; (prisonnier, suspect) to keep (a) watch on; (territoire, bâtiment) to (keep) watch over; (travaux, cuisson) to supervise; (Scol: examen) to invigilate; **se surveiller** to keep a check ou watch on o.s.; **~ son langage/sa ligne** to watch one's language/figure
survenir [syrvənir] vi (incident, retards) to occur, arise; (événement) to take place; (personne) to appear, arrive
survêt [syrvɛt], **survêtement** [syrvɛtmɑ̃] nm tracksuit (Brit), sweat suit (US)
survie [syrvi] nf survival; (Rel) afterlife; **équipement de ~** survival equipment; **une ~ de quelques mois** a few more months of life
survivant, e [syrvivɑ̃, -ɑ̃t] vb voir **survivre** ▷ nm/f survivor
survivre [syrvivr] vi to survive; **~ à** vt (accident etc) to survive; (personne) to outlive; **la victime a peu de chance de ~** the victim has little hope of survival
survoler [syrvole] vt to fly over; (fig: livre) to skim through; (: question, problèmes) to skim over
survolté, e [syrvolte] adj (Élec) stepped up, boosted; (fig) worked up
sus [sy(s)]: **en ~ de** prép in addition to, over and above; **en ~** adv in addition; **~ à** excl: **~ au tyran!** at the tyrant! ▷ vb [sy] voir **savoir**
susceptible [sysɛptibl] adj touchy, sensitive; **~ d'amélioration** ou **d'être amélioré** that can be improved, open to improvement; **~ de faire** (capacité) able to do; (probabilité) liable to do
susciter [sysite] vt (admiration) to arouse; (obstacles, ennuis): **~ (à qn)** to create (for sb)
suspect, e [syspɛ(kt), -ɛkt] adj suspicious;

(témoignage, opinions, vin etc) suspect ▷ *nm/f* suspect; **peu ~ de** most unlikely to be suspected of

suspecter [syspɛkte] *vt* to suspect; *(honnêteté de qn)* to question, have one's suspicions about; **~ qn d'être/d'avoir fait qch** to suspect sb of being/having done sth

suspendre [syspɑ̃dʀ] *vt (accrocher: vêtement)*: **~ qch (à)** to hang sth up (on); *(fixer: lustre etc)*: **~ qch à** to hang sth from; *(interrompre, démettre)* to suspend; *(remettre)* to defer; **se ~ à** to hang from

suspendu, e [syspɑ̃dy] *pp de* **suspendre** ▷ *adj (accroché)*: **~ à** hanging on (ou from); *(perché)*: **~ au-dessus de** suspended over; *(Auto)*: **bien/mal ~** with good/poor suspension; **être ~ aux lèvres de qn** to hang upon sb's every word

suspens [syspɑ̃]: **en ~** *adv (affaire)* in abeyance; **tenir en ~** to keep in suspense

suspense [syspɑ̃s] *nm* suspense

suspension [syspɑ̃sjɔ̃] *nf* suspension; deferment; *(Auto)* suspension; *(lustre)* pendant light fitting; **en ~** in suspension, suspended; **~ d'audience** adjournment

sut [sy] *vb voir* **savoir**

suture [sytyʀ] *nf*: **point de ~** stitch

svelte [svɛlt] *adj* slender, svelte

SVP *sigle (= s'il vous plaît)* please

sweat [swit] *nm (fam)* sweatshirt

sweat-shirt [switʃœʀt] *(pl* **sweat-shirts***) nm* sweatshirt

syllabe [silab] *nf* syllable

symbole [sɛ̃bɔl] *nm* symbol

symbolique [sɛ̃bɔlik] *adj* symbolic; *(geste, offrande)* token *cpd*; *(salaire, dommages-intérêts)* nominal

symboliser [sɛ̃bɔlize] *vt* to symbolize

symétrique [simetʀik] *adj* symmetrical

sympa [sɛ̃pa] *adj inv (fam: = sympathique)* nice; friendly; good; **sois ~, prête-le moi** be a pal and lend it to me

sympathie [sɛ̃pati] *nf (inclination)* liking; *(affinité)* fellow feeling; *(condoléances)* sympathy; **accueillir avec ~** *(projet)* to receive favourably; **avoir de la ~ pour qn** to like sb, have a liking for sb; **témoignages de ~** expressions of sympathy; **croyez à toute ma ~** you have my deepest sympathy

sympathique [sɛ̃patik] *adj (personne, figure)* nice, friendly, likeable; *(geste)* friendly; *(livre)* good; *(déjeuner)* nice; *(réunion, endroit)* pleasant, nice

sympathisant, e [sɛ̃patizɑ̃, -ɑ̃t] *nm/f* sympathizer

sympathiser [sɛ̃patize] *vi (voisins etc: s'entendre)* to get on (Brit) *ou* along (US) (well); *(: se fréquenter)* to socialize, see each other; **~ avec** to get on *ou* along (well) with, to see, socialize with

symphonie [sɛ̃fɔni] *nf* symphony

symptôme [sɛ̃ptom] *nm* symptom

synagogue [sinagɔg] *nf* synagogue

syncope [sɛ̃kɔp] *nf (Méd)* blackout; *(Mus)* syncopation; **tomber en ~** to faint, pass out

syndic [sɛ̃dik] *nm* managing agent

syndical, e, -aux [sɛ̃dikal, -o] *adj* (trade-)union *cpd*; **centrale ~e** group of affiliated trade unions

syndicaliste [sɛ̃dikalist] *nm/f* trade unionist

syndicat [sɛ̃dika] *nm (d'ouvriers, employés)* (trade(s)) union; *(autre association d'intérêts)* union, association; **~ d'initiative (SI)** tourist office *ou* bureau; **~ patronal** employers' syndicate, federation of employers; **~ de propriétaires** association of property owners

syndiqué, e [sɛ̃dike] *adj* belonging to a (trade) union; **non ~** non-union

syndiquer [sɛ̃dike]: **se syndiquer** *vi* to form a trade union; *(adhérer)* to join a trade union

synonyme [sinɔnim] *adj* synonymous ▷ *nm* synonym; **~ de** synonymous with

syntaxe [sɛ̃taks] *nf* syntax

synthèse [sɛ̃tɛz] *nf* synthesis; **faire la ~ de** to synthesize

synthétique [sɛ̃tetik] *adj* synthetic

Syrie [siʀi] *nf*: **la ~** Syria

systématique [sistematik] *adj* systematic

système [sistɛm] *nm* system; **le ~ D** resourcefulness; **~ décimal** decimal system; **~ expert** expert system; **~ d'exploitation** *(Inform)* operating system; **~ immunitaire** immune system; **~ métrique** metric system; **~ solaire** solar system

S

t' [t] *pron voir* **te**

ta [ta] *adj poss voir* **ton**

tabac [taba] *nm* tobacco; (*aussi*: **débit** *ou* **bureau de ~**) tobacconist's (shop) ▷ *adj inv*: (**couleur**) **~** buff, tobacco *cpd*; **passer qn à ~** to beat sb up; **faire un ~** (*fam*) to be a big hit; **~ blond/brun** light/dark tobacco; **~ gris** shag; **~ à priser** snuff

tabagisme [tabaʒism] *nm* nicotine addiction; **~ passif** passive smoking

tabasser [tabase] *vt* to beat up

table [tabl] *nf* table; **avoir une bonne ~** to keep a good table; **à ~!** dinner *etc* is ready!; **se mettre à ~** to sit down to eat; (*fig*: *fam*) to come clean; **mettre** *ou* **dresser/desservir la ~** to lay *ou* set/clear the table; **faire ~ rase de** to make a clean sweep of; **~ à repasser** ironing board; **~ basse** coffee table; **~ de cuisson** (*à l'électricité*) hob, hotplate; (*au gaz*) hob, gas ring; **~ d'écoute** wire-tapping set; **~ d'harmonie** sounding board; **~ d'hôte** menu; **~ de lecture** turntable; **~ des matières** (table of) contents *pl*; **~ de multiplication** multiplication table; **~ des négociations** negotiating table; **~ de nuit** *ou* **de chevet** bedside table; **~ d'orientation** viewpoint indicator; **~ ronde** (*débat*) round table; **~ roulante** (tea) trolley (*Brit*), tea wagon (*US*); **~ de toilette** washstand; **~ traçante** (*Inform*) plotter

tableau, x [tablo] *nm* (*Art*) painting; (*reproduction*, *fig*) picture; (*panneau*) board; (*schéma*) table, chart; **~ d'affichage** notice board; **~ de bord** dashboard; (*Aviat*) instrument panel; **~ de chasse** tally; **~ de contrôle** console, control panel; **~ de maître** masterpiece; **~ noir** blackboard

tabler [table] *vi*: **~ sur** to count *ou* bank on

tablette [tablɛt] *nf* (*planche*) shelf; **~ de chocolat** bar of chocolate

tableur [tablœʀ] *nm* (*Inform*) spreadsheet

tablier [tablije] *nm* apron; (*de pont*) roadway; (*de cheminée*) (flue-)shutter

tabou, e [tabu] *adj, nm* taboo

tabouret [tabuʀɛ] *nm* stool

tac [tak] *nm*: **du ~ au ~** tit for tat

tache [taʃ] *nf* (*saleté*) stain, mark; (*Art, de couleur, lumière*) spot; splash, patch; **faire ~ d'huile** to spread, gain ground; **~ de rousseur** *ou* **de son** freckle; **~ de vin** (*sur la peau*) strawberry mark

tâche [tɑʃ] *nf* task; **travailler à la ~** to do piecework

tacher [taʃe] *vt* to stain, mark; (*fig*) to sully, stain; **se tacher** *vi* (*fruits*) to become marked

tâcher [tɑʃe] *vi*: **~ de faire** to try to do, endeavour (*Brit*) *ou* endeavor (*US*) to do

tacheté, e [taʃte] *adj*: **~ de** speckled *ou* spotted with

tacot [tako] *nm* (*péj*: *voiture*) banger (*Brit*), clunker (*US*)

tact [takt] *nm* tact; **avoir du ~** to be tactful, have tact

tactique [taktik] *adj* tactical ▷ *nf* (*technique*) tactics *nsg*; (*plan*) tactic

taie [tɛ] *nf*: **~ (d'oreiller)** pillowslip, pillowcase

taille [taj] *nf* cutting; (*d'arbre*) pruning; (*milieu du corps*) waist; (*hauteur*) height; (*grandeur*) size; **de ~ à faire** capable of doing; **de ~** *adj* sizeable; **quelle ~ faites-vous?** what size are you?

taille-crayon, taille-crayons [tajkʀɛjɔ̃] *nm inv* pencil sharpener

tailler [taje] *vt* (*pierre, diamant*) to cut; (*arbre, plante*) to prune; (*vêtement*) to cut out; (*crayon*) to sharpen; **se tailler** *vt* (*ongles, barbe*) to trim, cut; (*fig*: *réputation*) to gain, win ▷ *vi* (*fam*: *s'enfuir*) to beat it; **~ dans** (*chair, bois*) to cut into; **~ grand/petit** to be on the large/small side

tailleur [tajœʀ] *nm* (*couturier*) tailor; (*vêtement*) suit, costume; **en ~** (*assis*) cross-legged; **~ de diamants** diamond-cutter

taillis [taji] *nm* copse

taire [tɛʀ] *vt* to keep to o.s., conceal ▷ *vi*: **faire ~ qn** to make sb quiet; (*fig*) to silence sb; **se taire** *vi* (*s'arrêter de parler*) to fall silent, stop talking; (*ne pas parler*) to be silent *ou* quiet; (*s'abstenir de s'exprimer*) to keep quiet; (*bruit, voix*) to disappear; **tais-toi!, taisez-vous!** be quiet!

Taiwan [tajwan] *nf* Taiwan

talc [talk] *nm* talc, talcum powder

talent [talɑ̃] *nm* talent; **avoir du ~** to be talented, have talent

talkie-walkie [tɔkiwɔki] *nm* walkie-talkie

taloche [talɔʃ] *nf* (*fam: claque*) slap; (*Tech*) plaster float

talon [talɔ̃] *nm* heel; (*de chèque, billet*) stub, counterfoil (*Brit*); **~s plats/aiguilles** flat/stiletto heels; **être sur les ~s de qn** to be on sb's heels; **tourner les ~s** to turn on one's heel; **montrer les ~s** (*fig*) to show a clean pair of heels

talonner [talɔne] *vt* to follow hard behind; (*fig*) to hound; (*Rugby*) to heel

talus [taly] *nm* embankment; **~ de remblai/déblai** embankment/excavation slope

tambour [tãbuʀ] *nm* (*Mus, also Tech*) drum; (*musicien*) drummer; (*porte*) revolving door(s pl); **sans ~ ni trompette** unobtrusively

tambourin [tãbuʀɛ̃] *nm* tambourine

tambouriner [tãbuʀine] *vi:* **~ contre** to drum against ou on

tamis [tami] *nm* sieve

Tamise [tamiz] *nf:* **la ~** the Thames

tamisé, e [tamize] *adj* (*fig*) subdued, soft

tampon [tãpɔ̃] *nm* (*de coton, d'ouate*) pad; (*aussi:* **~ hygiénique** ou **périodique**) tampon; (*amortisseur, Inform: aussi:* **mémoire ~**) buffer; (*bouchon*) plug, stopper; (*cachet, timbre*) stamp; (*Chimie*) buffer; **~ buvard** blotter; **~ encreur** inking pad; **~ (à récurer)** scouring pad

tamponner [tãpɔne] *vt* (*timbres*) to stamp; (*heurter*) to crash ou ram into; (*essuyer*) to mop up; **se tamponner** (*voitures*) to crash (into each other)

tamponneuse [tãpɔnøz] *adj f:* **autos ~s** dodgems, bumper cars

tandem [tãdɛm] *nm* tandem; (*fig*) duo, pair

tandis [tãdi]: **~ que** *conj* while

tanguer [tãge] *vi* to pitch (and toss)

tanière [tanjɛʀ] *nf* lair, den

tankini [tãkini] *nm* tankini

tanné, e [tane] *adj* weather-beaten

tanner [tane] *vt* to tan

tant [tã] *adv* so much; **~ de** (*sable, eau*) so much; (*gens, livres*) so many; **~ que** *conj* as long as; **~ que** (*comparatif*) as much as; **~ mieux** that's great; (*avec une certaine réserve*) so much the better; **~ mieux pour lui** good for him; **~ pis** too bad; (*conciliant*) never mind; **un ~ soit peu** (*un peu*) a little bit; (*même un peu*) (even) remotely; **~ bien que mal** as well as can be expected; **~ s'en faut** far from it, not by a long way

tante [tãt] *nf* aunt

tantôt [tãto] *adv* (*parfois*): **~ ... ~** now ... now; (*cet après-midi*) this afternoon

taon [tã] *nm* horsefly, gadfly

tapage [tapaʒ] *nm* uproar, din; (*fig*) fuss, row; **~ nocturne** (*Jur*) disturbance of the peace (*at night*)

tapageur, -euse [tapaʒœʀ, -øz] *adj* (*bruyant: enfants etc*) noisy; (*voyant: toilette*) loud, flashy; (*publicité*) obtrusive

tape [tap] *nf* slap

tape-à-l'œil [tapalœj] *adj inv* flashy, showy

taper [tape] *vt* (*personne*) to clout; (*porte*) to bang, slam; (*enfant*) to slap; (*dactylographier*) to type (out); (*Inform*) to key(board); (*fam: emprunter*): **~ qn de 10 euros** to touch sb for 10 euros, cadge 10 euros off sb ▷ *vi* (*soleil*) to beat down; **se taper** *vt* (*fam: travail*) to get landed with; (: *boire, manger*) to down; **~ sur qn** to thump sb; (*fig*) to run sb down; **~ sur qch** (*clou etc*) to hit sth; (*table etc*) to bang on sth; **~ à** (*porte etc*) to knock on; **~ dans** (*se servir*) to dig into; **~ des mains/pieds** to clap one's hands/stamp one's feet; **~ (à la machine)** to type

tapi, e [tapi] *adj:* **~ dans/derrière** (*blotti*) crouching ou cowering in/behind; (*caché*) hidden away in/behind

tapis [tapi] *nm* carpet; (*petit*) rug; (*de table*) cloth; **mettre sur le ~** (*fig*) to bring up for discussion; **aller au ~** (*Boxe*) to go down; **envoyer au ~** (*Boxe*) to floor; **~ roulant** conveyor belt; (*pour piétons*) moving walkway; (*pour bagages*) carousel; **~ de sol** (*de tente*) groundsheet; **~ de souris** (*Inform*) mouse mat

tapisser [tapise] *vt* (*avec du papier peint*) to paper; (*recouvrir*): **~ qch (de)** to cover sth (with)

tapisserie [tapisʀi] *nf* (*tenture, broderie*) tapestry; (: *travail*) tapestry-making; (: *ouvrage*) tapestry work; (*papier peint*) wallpaper; (*fig*): **faire ~** to sit out, be a wallflower

tapissier, -ière [tapisje, -jɛʀ] *nm/f:* **~-décorateur** interior decorator

tapoter [tapɔte] *vt* (*joue, main*) to pat; (*objet*) to tap

taquin, e [takɛ̃, -in] *adj* teasing

taquiner [takine] *vt* to tease

tarabiscoté, e [taʀabiskɔte] *adj* over-ornate, fussy

tard [taʀ] *adv* late; **au plus ~** at the latest; **plus ~** later (on) ▷ *nm:* **sur le ~** (*à une heure avancée*) late in the day; (*vers la fin de la vie*) late in life; **il est trop ~** it's too late

tarder [taʀde] *vi* (*chose*) to be a long time coming; (*personne*): **~ à faire** to delay doing; **il me tarde d'être** I am longing to be; **sans (plus) ~** without (further) delay

tardif, -ive [taʀdif, -iv] *adj* (*heure, repas, fruit*) late; (*talent, goût*) late in developing

taré, e [taʀe] *nm/f* cretin

tarif [taʀif] *nm:* **~ des consommations** price list; **~s postaux/douaniers** postal/customs rates; **~ des taxis** taxi fares; **~ plein/réduit** (*train*) full/reduced fare; (*téléphone*) peak/off-peak rate; **voyager à plein ~/à ~ réduit** to travel at full/reduced fare

tarir [taʀiʀ] *vi* to dry up, run dry ▷ *vt* to dry up

tarte [taʀt] *nf* tart; **~ aux pommes/à la crème** apple/custard tart; **~ Tatin** ≈ apple upside-down tart

tartine [taʀtin] *nf* slice of bread (and butter (ou jam)); **~ de miel** slice of bread and honey; **~ beurrée** slice of bread and butter

tartiner [taʀtine] vt to spread; **fromage à ~** cheese spread

tartre [taʀtʀ] nm (des dents) tartar; (de chaudière) fur, scale

tas [tɑ] nm heap, pile; (fig): **un ~ de** heaps of, lots of; **en ~** in a heap ou pile; **dans le ~** (fig) in the crowd; among them; **formé sur le ~** trained on the job

tasse [tɑs] nf cup; **boire la ~** (en se baignant) to swallow a mouthful; **~ à café/thé** coffee/teacup

tassé, e [tɑse] adj: **bien ~** (café etc) strong

tasser [tɑse] vt (terre, neige) to pack down; (entasser): **~ qch dans** to cram sth into; **se tasser** vi (se serrer) to squeeze up; (s'affaisser) to settle; (personne: avec l'âge) to shrink; (fig) to sort itself out, settle down

tâter [tate] vt to feel; (fig) to try out; **~ de** (prison etc) to have a taste of; **se tâter** (hésiter) to be in two minds; **~ le terrain** (fig) to test the ground

tatillon, ne [tatijɔ̃, -ɔn] adj pernickety

tâtonnement [tatɔnmɑ̃] nm: **par ~s** (fig) by trial and error

tâtonner [tatɔne] vi to grope one's way along; (fig) to grope around (in the dark)

tâtons [tatɔ̃]: **à ~** adv: **chercher/avancer à ~** to grope around for/grope one's way forward

tatouage [tatwaʒ] nm tattooing; (dessin) tattoo

tatouer [tatwe] vt to tattoo

taudis [todi] nm hovel, slum

taule [tol] nf (fam) nick (Brit), jail

taupe [top] nf mole; (peau) moleskin

taureau, x [tɔʀo] nm bull; (signe): **le T~** Taurus, the Bull; **être du T~** to be Taurus

tauromachie [tɔʀɔmaʃi] nf bullfighting

taux [to] nm rate; (d'alcool) level; **~ d'escompte** discount rate; **~ d'intérêt** interest rate; **~ de mortalité** mortality rate

taxe [taks] nf tax; (douanière) duty; **toutes ~s comprises (TTC)** inclusive of tax; **la boutique hors ~s** the duty-free shop; **~ de base** (Tél) unit charge; **~ de séjour** tourist tax; **~ à ou sur la valeur ajoutée (TVA)** value added tax (VAT)

taxer [takse] vt (personne) to tax; (produit) to put a tax on, tax; **~ qn de qch** (qualifier) to call sb sth; (accuser) to accuse sb of sth, tax sb with sth

taxi [taksi] nm taxi; (chauffeur: fam) taxi driver

Tchécoslovaquie [tʃekɔslɔvaki] nf: **la ~** Czechoslovakia

tchèque [tʃɛk] adj Czech ▷ nm (Ling) Czech ▷ nm/f: **T~** Czech; **la République ~** the Czech Republic

Tchétchénie [tʃetʃeni] nf: **la ~** Chechnya

te, t' [tə] pron you; (réfléchi) yourself

technicien, ne [tɛknisjɛ̃, -ɛn] nm/f technician

technico-commercial, e, -aux [tɛknikokɔmɛʀsjal, -o] adj: **agent ~** sales technician

technique [tɛknik] adj technical ▷ nf technique

techniquement [tɛknikmɑ̃] adv technically

techno [tɛkno] nf (fam: Mus): **la (musique) ~** techno (music); (fam) = **technologie**

technologie [tɛknɔlɔʒi] nf technology

technologique [tɛknɔlɔʒik] adj technological

teck [tɛk] nm teak

tee-shirt [tiʃœʀt] nm T-shirt, tee-shirt

teindre [tɛ̃dʀ] vt to dye; **se ~ (les cheveux)** to dye one's hair

teint, e [tɛ̃, tɛ̃t] pp de **teindre** ▷ adj dyed ▷ nm (du visage: permanent) complexion, colouring (Brit), coloring (US); (momentané) colour (Brit), color (US) ▷ nf shade, colour, color; (fig: petite dose): **une ~e de** a hint of; **grand ~** adj inv colourfast; **bon ~** adj inv (couleur) fast; (tissu) colourfast; (personne) staunch, firm

teinté, e [tɛ̃te] adj (verres) tinted; (bois) stained; **~ acajou** mahogany-stained; **~ de** (fig) tinged with

teinter [tɛ̃te] vt (verre) to tint; (bois) to stain; (fig: d'ironie etc) to tinge

teinture [tɛ̃tyʀ] nf dyeing; (substance) dye; (Méd): **~ d'iode** tincture of iodine

teinturerie [tɛ̃tyʀʀi] nf dry cleaner's

teinturier, -ière [tɛ̃tyʀje, -jɛʀ] nm/f dry cleaner

tel, telle [tɛl] adj (pareil) such; (comme): **~ un/des ...** like a/like ...; (indéfini) such-and-such a, given; **venez ~ jour** come on such-and-such a day; (intensif): **un ~/de ~s ...** such (a)/such ...; **rien de ~** nothing like it, no such thing; **~ que** conj like, such as; **~ quel** as it is ou stands (ou was etc)

télé [tele] nf (fam: télévision) TV, telly (Brit); **à la ~** on TV ou telly

télécabine [telekabin] nm, nf (benne) cable car

télécarte [telekaʀt] nf phonecard

téléchargeable [teleʃaʀʒabl] adj downloadable

téléchargement [teleʃaʀʒemɑ̃] nm (action) downloading; (fichier) download

télécharger [teleʃaʀʒe] vt (Inform) to download

télécommande [telekɔmɑ̃d] nf remote control

télécopie [telekɔpi] nf fax, telefax

télécopieur [telekɔpjœʀ] nm fax (machine)

télédistribution [teledistʀibysjɔ̃] nf cable TV

téléférique [teleferik] nm = **téléphérique**

télégramme [telegʀam] nm telegram

télégraphier [telegʀafje] vt to telegraph, cable

téléguider [telegide] vt to operate by remote control, radio-control

téléjournal, -aux [teleʒuʀnal, -o] nm television news magazine programme

télématique [telematik] nf telematics nsg ▷ adj telematic

téléobjectif [teleɔbʒɛktif] nm telephoto lens nsg

télépathie [telepati] nf telepathy

téléphérique [teleferik] *nm* cable-car
téléphone [telefɔn] *nm* telephone; **avoir le ~** to be on the (tele)phone; **au ~** on the phone; **~ arabe** bush telegraph; **~ à carte** cardphone; **~ avec appareil photo** cameraphone; **~ mobile** *ou* **portable** mobile (phone) (*Brit*), cell (phone) (*US*); **~ rouge** hotline; **~ sans fil** cordless (tele)phone
téléphoner [telefɔne] *vt* to telephone ⊳ *vi* to telephone; to make a phone call; **à** to phone, ring up, call up
téléphonie [telefɔni] *nf* telephony
téléphonique [telefɔnik] *adj* (tele)phone *cpd*, phone *cpd*; **cabine ~** call box (*Brit*), (tele) phone box (*Brit*) *ou* booth; **conversation/appel ~** (tele)phone conversation/call
téléréalité [telerealite] *nf* reality TV
télescope [teleskɔp] *nm* telescope
télescoper [teleskɔpe] *vt* to smash up; **se télescoper** (*véhicules*) to concertina, crash into each other
téléscripteur [teleskriptœr] *nm* teleprinter
télésiège [telesjɛʒ] *nm* chairlift
téléski [teleski] *nm* ski-tow; **~ à archets** T-bar tow; **~ à perche** button lift
téléspectateur, -trice [telespɛktatœr, -tris] *nm/f* (television) viewer
télétravail *nm* telecommuting
télévente [televɑ̃t] *nf* telesales
téléviseur [televizœr] *nm* television set
télévision [televizjɔ̃] *nf* television; (**poste de**) **~** television (set); **avoir la ~** to have a television; **à la ~** on television; **~ numérique** digital TV; **~ par câble/satellite** cable/satellite television
télex [telɛks] *nm* telex
telle [tɛl] *adj f voir* **tel**
tellement [tɛlmɑ̃] *adv* (*tant*) so much; (*si*) so; **~ plus grand (que)** so much bigger (than); **~ de** (*sable, eau*) so much; (*gens, livres*) so many; **il s'est endormi ~ il était fatigué** he was so tired (that) he fell asleep; **pas ~** not really; **pas ~ fort/lentement** not (all) that strong/slowly; **il ne mange pas ~** he doesn't eat (all that) much
téméraire [temerɛr] *adj* reckless, rash
témérité [temerite] *nf* recklessness, rashness
témoignage [temwaɲaʒ] *nm* (*Jur: déclaration*) testimony *no pl*, evidence *no pl*; (: *faits*) evidence *no pl*; (*gén: rapport, récit*) account; (*fig: d'affection etc*) token, mark; (*geste*) expression
témoigner [temwaɲe] *vt* (*manifester: intérêt, gratitude*) to show ⊳ *vi* (*Jur*) to testify, give evidence; **~ que** to testify that; (*fig: démontrer*) to reveal that, testify to the fact that; **~ de** *vt* (*confirmer*) to bear witness to, testify to
témoin [temwɛ̃] *nm* witness; (*fig*) testimony; (*Sport*) baton; (*Constr*) telltale ⊳ *adj* control *cpd*, test *cpd*; **le fait que ...** (as) witness the fact that ...; **appartement-~** show flat (*Brit*), model apartment (*US*); **être ~ de** (*voir*) to

witness; **prendre à ~** to call to witness; **~ à charge** witness for the prosecution; **~ de connexion** (*Inform*) cookie; **T~ de Jehovah** Jehovah's Witness; **~ de moralité** character reference; **~ oculaire** eyewitness
tempe [tɑ̃p] *nf* (*Anat*) temple
tempérament [tɑ̃peramɑ̃] *nm* temperament, disposition; (*santé*) constitution; **à ~** (*vente*) on deferred (payment) terms; (*achat*) by instalments, hire purchase *cpd*; **avoir du ~** to be hot-blooded
température [tɑ̃peratyr] *nf* temperature; **prendre la ~ de** to take the temperature of; (*fig*) to gauge the feeling of; **avoir** *ou* **faire de la ~** to be running *ou* have a temperature
tempéré, e [tɑ̃pere] *adj* temperate
tempête [tɑ̃pɛt] *nf* storm; **~ de sable/neige** sand/snowstorm; **vent de ~** gale
temple [tɑ̃pl] *nm* temple; (*protestant*) church
temporaire [tɑ̃pɔrɛr] *adj* temporary
temps [tɑ̃] *nm* (*atmosphérique*) weather; (*durée*) time; (*époque*) time, times *pl*; (*Ling*) tense; (*Mus*) beat; (*Tech*) stroke; **un ~ de chien** (*fam*) rotten weather; **quel ~ fait-il?** what's the weather like?; **il fait beau/mauvais ~** the weather is fine/bad; **avoir le ~/tout le ~/ juste le ~** to have time/plenty of time/just enough time; **les ~ changent/sont durs** times are changing/hard; **avoir fait son ~** (*fig*) to have had its (*ou* his *etc*) day; **en ~ de paix/guerre** in peacetime/wartime; **en ~ utile** *ou* **voulu** in due time *ou* course; **ces derniers ~** lately; **dans quelque ~** in a (little) while; **de ~ en ~, de ~ à autre** from time to time, now and again; **en même ~** at the same time; **à ~** (*partir, arriver*) in time; **à ~ complet, à plein ~** *adv, adj* full-time; **à ~ partiel, à mi-~** *adv, adj* part-time; **dans le ~** at one time; **de tout ~** always; **du ~ que** at the time when, in the days when; **dans le** *ou* **du** *ou* **au ~ où** at the time when; **pendant ce ~** in the meantime; **~ d'accès** (*Inform*) access time; **~ d'arrêt** pause, halt; **~ libre** free *ou* spare time; **~ mort** (*Sport*) stoppage (time); (*Comm*) slack period; **~ partagé** (*Inform*) time-sharing; **~ réel** (*Inform*) real time
tenable [tənabl] *adj* bearable
tenace [tənas] *adj* tenacious, persistent
tenailler [tənaje] *vt* (*fig*) to torment, torture
tenailles [tənaj] *nfpl* pincers
tenais *etc* [t(ə)nɛ] *vb voir* **tenir**
tenancier, -ière [tənɑ̃sje, -jɛr] *nm/f* (*d'hôtel, de bistro*) manager/manageress
tenant, e [tənɑ̃, -ɑ̃t] *adj f voir* **séance** ⊳ *nm/f* (*Sport*): **~ du titre** title-holder ⊳ *nm*: **d'un seul ~** in one piece; **les ~s et les aboutissants** (*fig*) the ins and outs
tendance [tɑ̃dɑ̃s] *nf* (*opinions*) leanings *pl*, sympathies *pl*; (*inclination*) tendency; (*évolution*) trend; **à la hausse/baisse** upward/downward trend; **avoir ~ à** have a tendency to, tend to

tendeur [tɑ̃dœʀ] nm (de vélo) chain-adjuster; (de câble) wire-strainer; (de tente) runner; (attache) elastic strap

tendre [tɑ̃dʀ] adj (viande, légumes) tender; (bois, roche, couleur) soft; (affectueux) tender, loving ▷ vt (élastique, peau) to stretch, draw tight; (corde) to tighten; (muscle) to tense; (donner): ~ **qch à qn** to hold sth out to sb; (offrir) to offer sb sth; (piège) to set, lay; (tapisserie): **tendu de soie** hung with silk, with silk hangings; **se tendre** vi (corde) to tighten; (relations) to become strained; ~ **à qch/à faire** to tend towards sth/to do; ~ **l'oreille** to prick up one's ears; ~ **la main/le bras** to hold out one's hand/stretch out one's arm; ~ **la perche à qn** (fig) to throw sb a line

tendrement [tɑ̃dʀəmɑ̃] adv tenderly, lovingly

tendresse [tɑ̃dʀɛs] nf tenderness; **tendresses** nfpl (caresses etc) tenderness no pl, caresses

tendu, e [tɑ̃dy] pp de **tendre** ▷ adj (corde) tight; (muscles) tensed; (relations) strained

ténèbres [tenɛbʀ] nfpl darkness nsg

teneur [tənœʀ] nf content, substance; (d'une lettre) terms pl, content; ~ **en cuivre** copper content

tenir [təniʀ] vt to hold; (magasin, hôtel) to run; (promesse) to keep ▷ vi to hold; (neige, clou) to last; (survivre) to survive; **se tenir** vi (avoir lieu) to be held, take place; (être: personne) to stand; **se ~ droit** to stand up (ou sit up) straight; **bien se ~** to behave well; **se ~ à qch** to hold on to sth; **s'en ~ à qch** to confine o.s. to sth; to stick to sth; ~ **à** (personne, objet) to be attached to, care about (ou for); (réputation) to care about; (avoir pour cause) to be due to, stem from; ~ **à faire** to want to do, be keen to do; ~ **à ce que qn fasse qch** to be anxious that sb should do sth; ~ **de** vt to partake of; (ressembler à) to take after; **ça ne tient qu'à lui** it is entirely up to him; ~ **qn pour** to take sb for; ~ **qch de qn** (histoire) to have heard ou learnt sth from sb; (qualité, défaut) to have inherited ou got sth from sb; ~ **dans** to fit into; ~ **compte de qch** to take sth into account; ~ **les comptes** to keep the books; ~ **un rôle** to play a part; ~ **de la place** to take up space ou room; ~ **l'alcool** to be able to hold a drink; ~ **le coup** to hold out; ~ **bon** to stand ou hold fast; ~ **trois jours/deux mois** (résister) to hold out ou last three days/two months; ~ **au chaud/à l'abri** to keep hot/under shelter ou cover; **un manteau qui tient chaud** a warm coat; ~ **prêt** to have ready; ~ **sa langue** (fig) to hold one's tongue; **tiens (ou tenez), voilà le stylo** there's the pen!; **tiens, Alain!** look, here's Alain!; **tiens?** (surprise) really?; **tiens-toi bien!** (pour informer) brace yourself!, take a deep breath!

tennis [tenis] nm tennis; (aussi: **court de ~**) tennis court ▷ nmpl ou fpl (aussi: **chaussures de ~**) tennis ou gym shoes; ~ **de table** table tennis

tennisman [tenisman] nm tennis player

tension [tɑ̃sjɔ̃] nf tension; (fig: des relations, de la situation) tension; (: concentration, effort) strain; (Méd) blood pressure; **faire** ou **avoir de la ~** to have high blood pressure; ~ **nerveuse/raciale** nervous/racial tension

tentation [tɑ̃tasjɔ̃] nf temptation

tentative [tɑ̃tativ] nf attempt, bid; ~ **d'évasion** escape bid; ~ **de suicide** suicide attempt

tente [tɑ̃t] nf tent; ~ **à oxygène** oxygen tent

tenter [tɑ̃te] vt (éprouver, attirer) to tempt; (essayer): ~ **qch/de faire** to attempt ou try sth/to do; **être tenté de** to be tempted to; ~ **sa chance** to try one's luck

tenture [tɑ̃tyʀ] nf hanging

tenu, e [təny] pp de **tenir** ▷ adj (maison, comptes): **bien** ~ well-kept; (obligé): ~ **de faire** under an obligation to do ▷ nf (action de tenir) running; keeping; holding; (vêtements) clothes pl, gear; (allure) dress no pl, appearance; (comportement) manners pl, behaviour (Brit), behavior (US); (d'une maison) upkeep; **être en** ~**e** to be dressed (up); **se mettre en** ~**e** to dress (up); **en grande** ~**e** in full dress; **en petite** ~**e** scantily dressed ou clad; **avoir de la** ~**e** to have good manners; (journal) to have a high standard; ~**e de combat** combat gear ou dress; ~**e de pompier** fireman's uniform; ~**e de route** (Auto) road-holding; ~**e de soirée** evening dress; ~**e de sport/voyage** sports/travelling clothes pl ou gear no pl

TER abr m (= Train Express Régional) local train

ter [tɛʀ] adj: **16** ≈ 16b ou B

térébenthine [teʀebɑ̃tin] nf: (**essence de** ~) (oil of) turpentine

tergal® [tɛʀgal] nm Terylene®

terme [tɛʀm] nm term; (fin) end; **être en bons/mauvais** ~**s avec qn** to be on good/bad terms with sb; **vente/achat à** ~ (Comm) forward sale/purchase; **au** ~ **de** at the end of; **en d'autres** ~**s** in other words; **moyen** ~ (solution intermédiaire) middle course; **à court/long** ~ adj short-/long-term ou -range ▷ adv in the short/long term; **à** ~ adj (Méd) full-term ▷ adv sooner or later, eventually; (Méd) at term; **avant** ~ (Méd) ▷ adj premature ▷ adv prematurely; **mettre un** ~ **à** to put an end ou a stop to; **toucher à son** ~ to be nearing its end

terminaison [tɛʀminɛzɔ̃] nf (Ling) ending

terminal, e, -aux [tɛʀminal, -o] adj (partie, phase) final; (Méd) terminal ▷ nm terminal ▷ nf (Scol) ≈ year 13 (Brit), ≈ twelfth grade (US)

terminer [tɛʀmine] vt to end; (travail, repas) to finish; **se terminer** vi to end; **se ~ par** to end with

terne [tɛʀn] adj dull

ternir [tɛʀniʀ] vt to dull; (fig) to sully, tarnish; **se ternir** vi to become dull

terrain [terɛ̃] nm (sol, fig) ground; (Comm: étendue de terre) land no pl; (parcelle) plot (of land); (: à bâtir) site; **sur le ~** (fig) on the field; **~ de football/rugby** football/rugby pitch (Brit) ou field (US); **~ d'atterrissage** landing strip; **~ d'aviation** airfield; **~ de camping** campsite; **un ~ d'entente** an area of agreement; **~ de golf** golf course; **~ de jeu** (pour les petits) playground; (Sport) games field; **~ de sport** sports ground; **~ vague** waste ground no pl

terrasse [teras] nf terrace; (de café) pavement area, terrasse; **à la ~** (café) outside

terrasser [terase] vt (adversaire) to floor, bring down; (maladie etc) to lay low

terre [tɛr] nf (gén, aussi Élec) earth; (substance) soil, earth; (opposé à mer) land no pl; (contrée) land; **terres** nfpl (terrains) lands, land nsg; **travail de la ~** work on the land; **en ~** (pipe, poterie) clay cpd; **mettre en ~** (plante etc) to plant; (personne: enterrer) to bury; **à ou par ~** (mettre, être, s'asseoir) on the ground (ou floor); (jeter, tomber) to the ground, down; **~ à ~** adj inv down-to-earth, matter-of-fact; **la T~ Adélie** Adélie Coast ou Land; **~ de bruyère** (heath-)peat; **~ cuite** earthenware; terracotta; **la ~ ferme** dry land, terra firma; **la T~ de Feu** Tierra del Fuego; **la ~ glaise** clay; **la T~ promise** the Promised Land; **la T~ Sainte** the Holy Land

terreau [terо] nm compost

terre-plein [terplɛ̃] nm platform; (sur chaussée) central reservation

terrer [tere]: **se terrer** vi to hide away; to go to ground

terrestre [terɛstr] adj (surface) earth's, of the earth; (Bot, Zool, Mil) land cpd; (Rel) earthly, worldly

terreur [terœr] nf terror no pl, fear

terrible [teribl] adj terrible, dreadful; (fam: fantastique) terrific; **pas ~** nothing special

terrien, ne [terjɛ̃, -ɛn] adj: **propriétaire ~** landowner ⊳ nm/f countryman/woman, man/woman of the soil; (non martien etc) earthling; (non marin) landsman

terrier [terje] nm burrow, hole; (chien) terrier

terrifier [terifje] vt to terrify

terrine [terin] nf (récipient) terrine; (Culin) pâté

territoire [teritwar] nm territory; **T~ des Afars et des Issas** French Territory of Afars and Issas

terroir [terwar] nm (Agr) soil; (région) region; **accent du ~** country ou rural accent

terroriser [terɔrize] vt to terrorize

terrorisme [terɔrism] nm terrorism

terroriste [terɔrist] nm/f terrorist

tertiaire [tersjɛr] adj tertiary ⊳ nm (Écon) tertiary sector, service industries pl

tertre [tɛrtr] nm hillock, mound

tes [te] adj poss voir **ton**

tesson [tesɔ̃] nm: **~ de bouteille** piece of broken bottle

test [tɛst] nm test; **~ de grossesse** pregnancy test

testament [tɛstamɑ̃] nm (Jur) will; (fig) legacy; (Rel) T~ Testament; **faire son ~** to make one's will

tester [tɛste] vt to test

testicule [tɛstikyl] nm testicle

tétanos [tetanos] nm tetanus

têtard [tɛtar] nm tadpole

tête [tɛt] nf head; (cheveux) hair no pl; (visage) face; (longueur): **gagner d'une (courte) ~** to win by a (short) head; (Football) header; **de ~** adj (wagon etc) front cpd; (concurrent) leading ⊳ adv (calculer) in one's head, mentally; **par ~** (par personne) per person; **se mettre en ~ que** to get it into one's head that; **se mettre en ~ de faire** to take it into one's head to do; **prendre la ~ de qch** to take the lead in sth; **perdre la ~** (fig: s'affoler) to lose one's head; (: devenir fou) to go off one's head; **ça ne va pas, la ~?** (fam) are you crazy?; **tenir ~ à qn** to stand up to ou defy sb; **la ~ en bas** with one's head down; **la ~ la première** (tomber) head-first; **la ~ basse** hanging one's head; **avoir la ~ dure** (fig) to be thickheaded; **faire une ~** (Football) to head the ball; **faire la ~** (fig) to sulk; **en ~** (Sport) in the lead; **à la ~ de** at the head of; **à ~ reposée** in a more leisurely moment; **n'en faire qu'à sa ~** to do as one pleases; **en avoir par-dessus la ~** to be fed up; **en ~ à ~** in private, alone together; **de la ~ aux pieds** from head to toe; **~ d'affiche** (Théât etc) top of the bill; **~ de bétail** head inv of cattle; **~ brûlée** desperado; **~ chercheuse** homing device; **~ d'enregistrement** recording head; **~ d'impression** printhead; **~ de lecture** (playback) head; **~ de ligne** (Transports) start of the line; **~ de liste** (Pol) chief candidate; **~ de mort** skull and crossbones; **~ de pont** (Mil) bridge- ou beachhead; **~ de série** (Tennis) seeded player, seed; **~ de Turc** (fig) whipping boy (Brit), butt; **~ de veau** (Culin) calf's head

tête-à-queue [tɛtakø] nm inv: **faire un ~** to spin round

tête-à-tête [tɛtatɛt] nm inv: **en ~** in private, alone together

téter [tete] vt: **~ (sa mère)** to suck at one's mother's breast, feed

tétine [tetin] nf teat; (sucette) dummy (Brit), pacifier (US)

têtu, e [tety] adj stubborn, pigheaded

texte [tɛkst] nm text; (morceau choisi) passage; (Scol: d'un devoir) subject, topic; **apprendre son ~** (Théât) to learn one's lines; **un ~ de loi** the wording of a law

textile [tɛkstil] adj textile cpd ⊳ nm textile; (industrie) textile industry

Texto® [tɛksto] nm text (message)

texto [tɛksto] (fam) adj word for word

texture [tɛkstyr] nf texture; (fig: d'un texte, livre) feel

TGV sigle m = **train à grande vitesse**
thaïlandais, e [tailɑ̃dɛ, -ɛz] adj Thai ▷ nm/f:
   T~, e Thai
Thaïlande [tailɑ̃d] nf: **la ~** Thailand
thé [te] nm tea; (réunion) tea party; **prendre**
   le ~ to have tea; **~ au lait/citron** tea with
   milk/lemon; **faire le ~** to make the tea
théâtral, e, -aux [teatRal, -o] adj theatrical
théâtre [teatR] nm theatre; (techniques, genre)
   drama, theatre; (activité) stage, theatre;
   (œuvres) plays pl, dramatic works pl; (fig: lieu):
   le ~ de the scene of; (péj) histrionics pl,
   playacting; **faire du ~** (en professionnel) to be
   on the stage; (en amateur) to act; **~ filmé**
   filmed stage productions pl
théière [tejɛR] nf teapot
thème [tɛm] nm theme; (Scol: traduction)
   prose (composition); **~ astral** birth chart
théologie [teɔlɔʒi] nf theology
théorie [teɔRi] nf theory; **en ~** in theory
théorique [teɔRik] adj theoretical
thérapie [teRapi] nf therapy; **~ de groupe**
   group therapy
thermal, e, -aux [tɛRmal, -o] adj thermal;
   station ~e spa; **cure ~e** water cure
thermes [tɛRm] nmpl thermal baths;
   (romains) thermae pl
thermomètre [tɛRmɔmɛtR] nm
   thermometer
thermos® [tɛRmos] nm ou nf: **(bouteille) ~**
   vacuum ou Thermos® flask (Brit) ou bottle (US)
thermostat [tɛRmɔsta] nm thermostat
thèse [tɛz] nf thesis
thon [tɔ̃] nm tuna (fish)
thym [tɛ̃] nm thyme
Tibet [tibɛ] nm: **le ~** Tibet
tibia [tibja] nm shin; (os) shinbone, tibia
TIC sigle fpl (= technologies de l'information et de la
   communication) ICT sg
tic [tik] nm tic, (nervous) twitch; (de langage
   etc) mannerism
ticket [tikɛ] nm ticket; **~ de caisse** till receipt;
   ~ modérateur patient's contribution towards
   medical costs; **~ de quai** platform ticket;
   ~ repas luncheon voucher
tic-tac [tiktak] nm inv tick-tock
tiède [tjɛd] adj (bière etc) lukewarm; (thé, café
   etc) tepid; (bain, accueil, sentiment) lukewarm;
   (vent, air) mild, warm ▷ adv: **boire ~** to drink
   things lukewarm
tiédir [tjediR] vi (se réchauffer) to grow warmer;
   (refroidir) to cool
tien, tienne [tjɛ̃, tjɛn] pron: **le ~ (la ~ne), les**
   ~s (~nes) yours; **à la ~ne!** cheers!
tiens [tjɛ̃] vb, excl voir **tenir**
tierce [tjɛRs] adj f, nf voir **tiers**
tiercé [tjɛRse] nm system of forecast betting giving
   first three horses
tiers, tierce [tjɛR, tjɛRs] adj third ▷ nm (Jur)
   third party; (fraction) third ▷ nf (Mus) third;
   (Cartes) tierce; **une tierce personne** a third
   party; **assurance au ~** third-party insurance;

   le ~ monde the third world; **~ payant** direct
   payment by insurers of medical expenses;
   ~ provisionnel interim payment of tax
tifs [tif] (fam) nmpl hair
tige [tiʒ] nf stem; (baguette) rod
tignasse [tiɲas] nf (péj) shock ou mop of hair
tigre [tigR] nm tiger
tigré, e [tigRe] adj (rayé) striped; (tacheté)
   spotted; (chat) tabby
tigresse [tigRɛs] nf tigress
tilleul [tijœl] nm lime (tree), linden (tree);
   (boisson) lime(-blossom) tea
timbale [tɛ̃bal] nf (metal) tumbler; **timbales**
   nfpl (Mus) timpani, kettledrums
timbre [tɛ̃bR] nm (tampon) stamp; (aussi:
   ~-poste) (postage) stamp; (cachet de la poste)
   postmark; (sonnette) bell; (Mus: de voix,
   instrument) timbre, tone; **~ anti-tabac**
   nicotine patch; **~ dateur** date stamp
timbré, e [tɛ̃bRe] adj (enveloppe) stamped;
   (voix) resonant; (fam: fou) cracked, nuts
timide [timid] adj (emprunté) shy, timid;
   (timoré) timid, timorous
timidement [timidmɑ̃] adv shyly; timidly
timidité [timidite] nf shyness; timidity
tintamarre [tɛ̃tamaR] nm din, uproar
tinter [tɛ̃te] vi to ring, chime; (argent, clés) to
   jingle
tique [tik] nf tick (insect)
tir [tiR] nm (sport) shooting; (fait ou manière de
   tirer) firing no pl; (Football) shot; (rafale) fire;
   (stand) shooting gallery; **~ d'obus/de**
   mitraillette shell/machine gun fire; **~ à**
   l'arc archery; **~ de barrage** barrage fire; **~ au**
   fusil (rifle) shooting; **~ au pigeon** (d'argile)
   clay pigeon shooting
tirage [tiRaʒ] nm (action) printing; (Photo)
   print; (Inform) printout; (de journal) circulation;
   (de livre) (print-)run; edition; (de cheminée)
   draught (Brit), draft (US); (de loterie) draw; (fig:
   désaccord) friction; **~ au sort** drawing lots
tirailler [tiRaje] vt to pull at, tug at; (fig) to
   gnaw at ▷ vi to fire at random
tire [tiR] nf: **vol à la ~** pickpocketing
tiré, e [tiRe] adj (visage, traits) drawn ▷ nm
   (Comm) drawee; **~ par les cheveux** far-
   fetched; **~ à part** off-print
tire-au-flanc [tiRoflɑ̃] nm inv (péj) skiver
tire-bouchon [tiRbuʃɔ̃] nm corkscrew
tirelire [tiRliR] nf moneybox
tirer [tiRe] vt (gén) to pull; (extraire): **~ qch de**
   to take ou pull sth out of; to get sth out of; to
   extract sth from; (tracer: ligne, trait) to draw,
   trace; (fermer: volet, porte, trappe) to pull to,
   close; (: rideau) to draw; (choisir: carte,
   conclusion, aussi Comm: chèque) to draw; (en
   faisant feu: balle, coup) to fire; (: animal) to
   shoot; (journal, livre, photo) to print; (Football:
   corner etc) to take ▷ vi (faire feu) to fire; (faire du
   tir, Football) to shoot; (cheminée) to draw; **se**
   tirer vi (fam) to push off; (aussi: **s'en ~**: éviter le
   pire) to get off; (survivre) to pull through; (se

débrouiller) to manage; ~ **sur** (*corde, poignée*) to pull on ou at; (*faire feu sur*) to shoot ou fire at; (*pipe*) to draw on; (*fig: aboisiner*) to verge ou border on; ~ **six mètres** (*Navig*) to draw six metres of water; ~ **son nom de** to take ou get its name from; ~ **la langue** to stick out one's tongue; **qn de** (*embarras etc*) to help ou get sb out of; ~ **à l'arc/la carabine** to shoot with a bow and arrow/with a rifle; ~ **en longueur** to drag on; ~ **à sa fin** to be drawing to an end; ~ **qch au clair** to clear sth up; ~ **au sort** to draw lots; ~ **parti de** to take advantage of; ~ **profit de** to profit from; ~ **les cartes** to read ou tell the cards

tiret [tiʀɛ] *nm* dash; (*en fin de ligne*) hyphen
tireur [tiʀœʀ] *nm* gunman; (*Comm*) drawer; **bon** ~ good shot; ~ **d'élite** marksman; ~ **de cartes** fortuneteller
tiroir [tiʀwaʀ] *nm* drawer
tiroir-caisse [tiʀwaʀkɛs] *nm* till
tisane [tizan] *nf* herb tea
tisonnier [tizɔnje] *nm* poker
tisser [tise] *vt* to weave
tisserand, e [tisʀɑ̃, -ɑ̃d] *nm/f* weaver
tissu¹ [tisy] *nm* fabric, material, cloth *no pl*; (*fig*) fabric; (*Anat, Bio*) tissue; ~ **de mensonges** web of lies
tissu², e [tisy] *adj*: ~ **de** woven through with
tissu-éponge [tisyepɔ̃ʒ] *nm* (terry) towelling *no pl*
titre [titʀ] *nm* (*gén*) title; (*de journal*) headline; (*diplôme*) qualification; (*Comm*) security; (*Chimie*) titre; **en** ~ (*champion, responsable*) official, recognized; **à juste** ~ with just cause, rightly; **à quel** ~? on what grounds?; **à aucun** ~ on no account; **au même** ~ (**que**) in the same way (as); **au** ~ **de la coopération** *etc* in the name of cooperation *etc*; **à** ~ **d'exemple** as an ou by way of an example; **à** ~ **exceptionnel** exceptionally; **à** ~ **d'information** for (your) information; **à** ~ **gracieux** free of charge; **à** ~ **d'essai** on a trial basis; **à** ~ **privé** in a private capacity; ~ **courant** running head; ~ **de propriété** title deed; ~ **de transport** ticket
tituber [titybe] *vi* to stagger ou reel (along)
titulaire [titylɛʀ] *adj* (*Admin*) appointed, with tenure ▷ *nm/f* (*Admin*) incumbent; (*de permis*) holder; **être** ~ **de** (*diplôme, permis*) to hold
TNT *sigle m* (= *Trinitrotoluène*) TNT ▷ *sigle f* (= *Télévision numérique terrestre*) digital television
toast [tost] *nm* slice ou piece of toast; (*de bienvenue*) (welcoming) toast; **porter un** ~ **à qn** to propose ou drink a toast to sb
toboggan [tɔbɔgɑ̃] *nm* toboggan; (*jeu*) slide; (*Auto*) flyover (*Brit*), overpass (*US*); ~ **de secours** (*Aviat*) escape chute
toc [tɔk] *nm*: **en** ~ imitation *cpd* ▷ *excl*: ~, ~ knock knock
tocsin [tɔksɛ̃] *nm* alarm (bell)
toge [tɔʒ] *nf* toga; (*de juge*) gown

tohu-bohu [tɔybɔy] *nm* (*désordre*) confusion; (*tumulte*) commotion
toi [twa] *pron* you; ~, **tu l'as fait?** did YOU do it?
toile [twal] *nf* (*matériau*) cloth *no pl*; (*bâche*) piece of canvas; (*tableau*) canvas; **grosse** ~ canvas; **de** ou **en** ~ (*pantalon*) cotton; (*sac*) canvas; **tisser sa** ~ (*araignée*) to spin its web; ~ **d'araignée** spider's web; (*au plafond etc*: *à enlever*) cobweb; **la T**~ (*Internet*) the Web; ~ **cirée** oilcloth; ~ **émeri** emery cloth; ~ **de fond** (*fig*) backdrop; ~ **de jute** hessian; ~ **de lin** linen; ~ **de tente** canvas
toilette [twalɛt] *nf* wash; (*s'habiller et se préparer*) getting ready, washing and dressing; (*habits*) outfit; dress *no pl*; **toilettes** *nfpl* toilet *nsg*; **les** ~**s des dames/messieurs** the ladies'/gents' (toilets) (*Brit*), the ladies'/men's (rest)room (*US*); **faire sa** ~ to have a wash, get washed; **faire la** ~ **de** (*animal*) to groom; (*voiture etc*) to clean, wash; (*texte*) to tidy up; **articles de** ~ toiletries; ~ **intime** personal hygiene
toi-même [twamɛm] *pron* yourself
toiser [twaze] *vt* to eye up and down
toison [twazɔ̃] *nf* (*de mouton*) fleece; (*cheveux*) mane
toit [twa] *nm* roof; ~ **ouvrant** sun roof
toiture [twatyʀ] *nf* roof
Tokyo [tɔkjo] *n* Tokyo
tôle [tol] *nf* sheet metal *no pl*; (*plaque*) steel (ou iron) sheet; **tôles** *nfpl* (*carrosserie*) bodywork *nsg* (*Brit*), body *nsg*; panels; ~ **d'acier** sheet steel *no pl*; ~ **ondulée** corrugated iron
tolérable [tɔleʀabl] *adj* tolerable, bearable
tolérant, e [tɔleʀɑ̃, -ɑ̃t] *adj* tolerant
tolérer [tɔleʀe] *vt* to tolerate; (*Admin: hors taxe etc*) to allow
tollé [tɔle] *nm*: **un** ~ (**de protestations**) a general outcry
tomate [tɔmat] *nf* tomato; ~**s farcies** stuffed tomatoes
tombe [tɔ̃b] *nf* (*sépulture*) grave; (*avec monument*) tomb
tombeau, x [tɔ̃bo] *nm* tomb; **à** ~ **ouvert** at breakneck speed
tombée [tɔ̃be] *nf*: **à la** ~ **du jour** ou **de la nuit** at the close of day, at nightfall
tomber [tɔ̃be] *vi* to fall; (*fièvre, vent*) to drop ▷ *vt*: ~ **la veste** to slip off one's jacket; **laisser** ~ (*objet*) to drop; (*personne*) to let down; (*activité*) to give up; **laisse** ~! forget it!; **faire** ~ to knock over; ~ **sur** *vt* (*rencontrer*) to come across; (*attaquer*) to set about; ~ **de fatigue/sommeil** to drop from exhaustion/be falling asleep on one's feet; ~ **à l'eau** (*fig: projet etc*) to fall through; ~ **en panne** to break down; ~ **juste** (*opération, calcul*) to come out right; ~ **en ruine** to fall into ruins; **ça tombe bien/mal** (*fig*) that's come at the right/wrong time; **il est bien/mal tombé** (*fig*) he's been lucky/unlucky
tombola [tɔ̃bɔla] *nf* raffle
tome [tɔm] *nm* volume

t

ton', ta (pl **tes**) [tõ, ta, te] adj poss your

ton² [tõ] nm (gén) tone; (Mus) key; (couleur) shade, tone; (de la voix: hauteur) pitch; **donner le ~** to set the tone; **élever** ou **hausser le ~** to raise one's voice; **de bon ~** in good taste; **si vous le prenez sur ce ~** if you're going to take it like that; **~ sur ~** in matching shades

tonalité [tɔnalite] nf (au téléphone) dialling tone; (Mus) tonality; (: ton) key; (fig) tone

tondeuse [tõdøz] nf (à gazon) (lawn)mower; (du coiffeur) clippers pl; (pour la tonte) shears pl

tondre [tõdʀ] vt (pelouse, herbe) to mow; (haie) to cut, clip; (mouton, toison) to shear; (cheveux) to crop

tongs [tõg] nfpl flip-flops (Brit), thongs (US)

tonifier [tɔnifje] vt (air, eau) to invigorate; (peau, organisme) to tone up

tonique [tɔnik] adj fortifying; (personne) dynamic ▷ nm, nf tonic

tonne [tɔn] nf metric ton, tonne

tonneau, x [tɔno] nm (à vin, cidre) barrel; (Navig) ton; **faire des ~x** (voiture, avion) to roll over

tonnelle [tɔnɛl] nf bower, arbour (Brit), arbor (US)

tonner [tɔne] vi to thunder; (parler avec véhémence): **~ contre qn/qch** to inveigh against sb/sth; **il tonne** it is thundering, there's some thunder

tonnerre [tɔnɛʀ] nm thunder; **coup de ~** (fig) thunderbolt, bolt from the blue; **un ~ d'applaudissements** thunderous applause; **du ~** adj (fam) terrific

tonte [tõt] nf shearing

tonton [tõtõ] nm uncle

tonus [tɔnys] nm energy; (des muscles) tone; (d'une personne) dynamism

top [tɔp] nm: **au troisième ~** at the third stroke ▷ adj: **~ secret** top secret ▷ excl go!

topinambour [tɔpinãbuʀ] nm Jerusalem artichoke

topo [tɔpo] nm (discours, exposé) talk; (fam) spiel

toque [tɔk] nf (de fourrure) fur hat; **~ de jockey/juge** jockey's/judge's cap; **~ de cuisinier** chef's hat

toqué, e [tɔke] adj (fam) touched, cracked

torche [tɔʀʃ] nf torch; **se mettre en ~** (parachute) to candle

torchon [tɔʀʃõ] nm cloth, duster; (à vaisselle) tea towel ou cloth

tordre [tɔʀdʀ] vt (chiffon) to wring; (barre, fig: visage) to twist; **se tordre** vi (barre) to bend; (roue) to twist, buckle; (ver, serpent) to writhe; **se ~ le poignet/la cheville** to twist one's wrist/ankle; **se ~ de douleur/rire** to writhe in pain/be doubled up with laughter

tordu, e [tɔʀdy] pp de **tordre** ▷ adj (fig) warped, twisted; (fig) crazy

tornade [tɔʀnad] nf tornado

torpille [tɔʀpij] nf torpedo

torréfier [tɔʀefje] vt to roast

torrent [tɔʀã] nm torrent, mountain stream; (fig): **un ~ de** a torrent ou flood of; **il pleut à ~s** the rain is lashing down

torsade [tɔʀsad] nf twist; (Archit) cable moulding (Brit) ou molding (US); **un pull à ~s** a cable sweater

torse [tɔʀs] nm chest, (Anat, Sculpture) torso; (poitrine) chest; **~ nu** stripped to the waist

tort [tɔʀ] nm (défaut) fault; (préjudice) wrong no pl; **torts** nmpl (Jur) fault nsg; **avoir ~** to be wrong; **être dans son ~** to be in the wrong; **donner ~ à qn** to lay the blame on sb; (fig) to prove sb wrong; **causer du ~ à** to harm; to be harmful ou detrimental to; **en ~** in the wrong, at fault; **à ~** wrongly; **à ~ ou à raison** rightly or wrongly; **à ~ et à travers** wildly

torticolis [tɔʀtikɔli] nm stiff neck

tortiller [tɔʀtije] vt (corde, mouchoir) to twist; (doigts) to twiddle; (moustache) to twirl; **se tortiller** vi to wriggle, squirm; (en dansant) to wiggle

tortionnaire [tɔʀsjɔnɛʀ] nm torturer

tortue [tɔʀty] nf tortoise; (fig) slowcoach (Brit), slowpoke (US); (d'eau douce) terrapin; (d'eau de mer) turtle

tortueux, -euse [tɔʀtɥø, -øz] adj (rue) twisting; (fig) tortuous

torture [tɔʀtyʀ] nf torture

torturer [tɔʀtyʀe] vt to torture; (fig) to torment

tôt [to] adv early; **~ ou tard** sooner or later; **si ~** so early; (déjà) so soon; **au plus ~** at the earliest, as soon as possible; **plus ~** earlier; **il eut ~ fait de faire ...** he soon did ...

total, e, -aux [tɔtal, -o] adj, nm total; **au ~** in total ou all; (fig) all in all, on the whole; **faire le ~** to work out the total

totalement [tɔtalmã] adv totally, completely

totaliser [tɔtalize] vt to total (up)

totalitaire [tɔtalitɛʀ] adj totalitarian

totalité [tɔtalite] nf: **la ~ de:** la ~ des **élèves** all (of) the pupils; **la ~ de la population/classe** the whole population/class; **en ~** entirely

toubib [tubib] nm (fam) doctor

touchant, e [tuʃã, -ãt] adj touching

touche [tuʃ] nf (de piano, de machine à écrire) key; (de violon) fingerboard; (de télécommande etc) key, button; (de téléphone) button; (Peinture etc) stroke, touch; (fig: de couleur, nostalgie) touch, hint; (Rugby) line-out; (Football: aussi: **remise en ~**) throw-in; (aussi: **ligne de ~**) touch-line; (Escrime) hit; **en ~** in (ou into) touch; **avoir une drôle de ~** to look a sight; **~ de commande/de fonction/de retour** (Inform) control/function/return key; **~ dièse** (de téléphone, clavier) hash key; **~ à effleurement** ou **sensitive** touch-sensitive control ou key

toucher [tuʃe] nm touch ▷ vt to touch; (palper) to feel; (atteindre: d'un coup de feu etc) to hit; (affecter) to touch, affect; (concerner) to concern, affect; (contacter) to reach, contact; (recevoir: récompense) to receive, get; (: salaire) to draw, get; (chèque) to cash; (aborder: problème, *sujet*) to touch on; **au ~** to the touch; by the feel; **se toucher** (*être en contact*) to touch; **~ à** to touch; (*modifier*) to touch, tamper *ou* meddle with; (*traiter de, concerner*) to have to do with, concern; **je vais lui en ~ un mot** I'll have a word with him about it; **~ au but** (*fig*) to near one's goal; **~ à sa fin** to be drawing to a close

touffe [tuf] *nf* tuft

touffu, e [tufy] *adj* thick, dense; (*fig*) complex, involved

toujours [tuʒuʀ] *adv* always; (*encore*) still; (*constamment*) forever; **depuis ~** always; **essaie ~** (you can) try anyway; **pour ~** forever; **~ est-il que** the fact remains that; **~ plus** more and more

toupet [tupɛ] *nm* quiff (*Brit*), tuft; (*fam*) nerve, cheek (*Brit*)

toupie [tupi] *nf* (spinning) top

tour [tuʀ] *nf* tower; (*immeuble*) high-rise block (*Brit*) *ou* building (*US*), tower block (*Brit*); (*Échecs*) castle, rook ▷ *nm* (*excursion: à pied*) stroll, walk; (: *en voiture etc*) run, ride; (: *plus long*) trip; (*Sport: aussi:* **~ de piste**) lap; (*d'être servi ou de jouer etc, tournure, de vis ou clef*) turn; (*de roue etc*) revolution; (*circonférence*): **de 3 m de ~** 3 m round, with a circumference *ou* girth of 3 m; (*Pol: aussi:* **~ de scrutin**) ballot; (*ruse, de prestidigitation, de cartes*) trick; (*de potier*) wheel; (*à bois, métaux*) lathe; **faire le ~ de** to go (a)round; (*fig*) to review; **faire le ~ de l'Europe** to tour Europe; **faire un ~** to go for a walk; (*en voiture etc*) to go for a ride; **faire 2 ~s** to go (a)round twice; (*hélice etc*) to turn *ou* revolve twice; **fermer à double ~** *vi* to double-lock the door; **c'est au ~ de Renée** it's Renée's turn; **à ~ de rôle, ~ à ~** in turn; **à ~ de bras** with all one's strength; (*fig*) non-stop, relentlessly; **~ de taille/tête** *nm* waist/head measurement; **~ de chant** *nm* song recital; **~ de contrôle** *nf* control tower; **la ~ Eiffel** the Eiffel Tower; **le T~ de France** the Tour de France; *see note*; **~ de force** *nm* tour de force; **~ de garde** *nm* spell of duty; **un 33 ~s** an LP; **un 45 ~s** a single; **~ d'horizon** *nm* (*fig*) general survey; **~ de lit** *nm* valance; **~ de main** *nm* dexterity, knack; **en un ~ de main** (as) quick as a flash; **~ de passe-passe** *nm* trick, sleight of hand; **~ de reins** *nm* sprained back

●● **TOUR DE FRANCE**

The *Tour de France* is an annual road race for professional cyclists. It takes about three weeks to complete and is divided into daily stages, or "étapes" of approximately 175km (110 miles) over terrain of varying levels of difficulty. The leading cyclist wears a yellow jersey, the "maillot jaune". The route varies; it is not usually confined to France but always ends in Paris. In addition, there are a number of time trials.

tourbe [tuʀb] *nf* peat

tourbillon [tuʀbijɔ̃] *nm* whirlwind; (*d'eau*) whirlpool; (*fig*) whirl, swirl

tourbillonner [tuʀbijɔne] *vi* to whirl, swirl; (*objet, personne*) to whirl *ou* twirl round

tourelle [tuʀɛl] *nf* turret

tourisme [tuʀism] *nm* tourism; **agence de ~** tourist agency; **avion/voiture de ~** private plane/car; **faire du ~** to go touring; (*en ville*) to go sightseeing

touriste [tuʀist] *nm/f* tourist

touristique [tuʀistik] *adj* tourist *cpd*; (*région*) touristic (*péj*), with tourist appeal

tourment [tuʀmɑ̃] *nm* torment

tourmenter [tuʀmɑ̃te] *vt* to torment; **se tourmenter** *vi* to fret, worry o.s.

tournage [tuʀnaʒ] *nm* (*d'un film*) shooting

tournant, e [tuʀnɑ̃, -ɑ̃t] *adj* (*feu, scène*) revolving; (*chemin*) winding; (*escalier*) spiral *cpd*; (*mouvement*) circling ▷ *nm* (*de route*) bend (*Brit*), curve (*US*); (*fig*) turning point; *voir* **plaque**; **grève**

tournebroche [tuʀnəbʀɔʃ] *nm* roasting spit

tourne-disque [tuʀnədisk] *nm* record player

tournée [tuʀne] *nf* (*du facteur etc*) round; (*d'artiste, politicien*) tour; (*au café*) round (of drinks); **faire la ~ de** to go (a)round

tournemain [tuʀnəmɛ̃]: **en un ~** *adv* in a flash

tourner [tuʀne] *vt* to turn; (*sauce, mélange*) to stir; (*contourner*) to get (a)round; (*Ciné: faire les prises de vues*) to shoot; (*produire*) to make ▷ *vi* to turn; (*moteur*) to run; (*compteur*) to tick away; (*lait etc*) to turn (sour); (*fig: chance, vie*) to turn out; **se tourner** *vi* to turn (a)round; **se ~ vers** to turn to; to turn towards; **bien ~** to turn out well; **mal ~** to go wrong; **~ autour de** to go (a)round; (*planète*) to revolve (a) round; (*péj*) to hang (a)round; **~ autour du pot** (*fig*) to go (a)round in circles; **~ à/en** to turn into; **~ à la pluie/au rouge** to turn rainy/red; **~ en ridicule** to ridicule; **~ le dos à** (*mouvement*) to turn one's back on; (*position*) to have one's back to; **~ court** to come to a sudden end; **se ~ les pouces** to twiddle one's thumbs; **~ la tête** to look away; **~ la tête à qn** (*fig*) to go to sb's head; **~ de l'œil** to pass out; **~ la page** (*fig*) to turn the page

tournesol [tuʀnəsɔl] *nm* sunflower

tournevis [tuʀnəvis] *nm* screwdriver

tourniquet [tuʀnikɛ] *nm* (*pour arroser*) sprinkler; (*portillon*) turnstile; (*présentoir*) revolving stand, spinner; (*Chirurgie*) tourniquet

tournoi [tuʀnwa] *nm* tournament

tournoyer [tuʀnwaje] *vi* (*oiseau*) to wheel (a) round; (*fumée*) to swirl (a)round

tournure [tuʀnyʀ] *nf* (*Ling: syntaxe*) turn of phrase; form; (*d'une phrase*) phrasing; (*évolution*): **la ~ de qch** the way sth is developing; (*aspect*): **la ~ de** the look of; **la ~ des événements** the turn of events; **prendre ~** to take shape; **~ d'esprit** turn *ou* cast of mind

tourte [tuʀt] *nf* pie
tourterelle [tuʀtəʀɛl] *nf* turtledove
tous [*adj* tu, *pron* tus] *adj, pron voir* **tout**
Toussaint [tusɛ̃] *nf*: **la ~** All Saints' Day; *see note*

 TOUSSAINT

La Toussaint, 1 November, or All Saints' Day, is a public holiday in France. People traditionally visit the graves of friends and relatives to lay chrysanthemums on them.

tousser [tuse] *vi* to cough

MOT-CLÉ

tout, e [tu, tut] (*mpl* **tous**, *fpl* **toutes**) *adj* **1**
(*avec article singulier*) all; **tout le lait** all the milk; **toute la nuit** all night, the whole night; **tout le livre** the whole book; **tout un pain** a whole loaf; **tout le temps** all the time, the whole time; **c'est tout le contraire** it's quite the opposite; **c'est toute une affaire** *ou* **histoire** it's quite a business, it's a whole rigmarole
2 (*avec article pluriel*) every; all; **tous les livres** all the books; **toutes les nuits** every night; **toutes les fois** every time; **toutes les trois/deux semaines** every third/other *ou* second week, every three/two weeks; **tous les deux** both *ou* each of us (*ou* them *ou* you); **toutes les trois** all three of us (*ou* them *ou* you)
3 (*sans article*): **à tout âge** at any age; **pour toute nourriture, il avait ...** his only food was ...; **de tous côtés, de toutes parts** from everywhere, from every side
▷ *pron* everything, all; **il a tout fait** he's done everything; **je les vois tous** I can see them all *ou* all of them; **nous y sommes tous allés** all of us went, we all went; **c'est tout** that's all; **en tout** in all; **en tout et pour tout** all in all; **tout ce qu'il sait** all he knows; **c'était tout ce qu'il y a de chic** it was the last word *ou* the ultimate in chic
▷ *nm* whole; **le tout** all of it (*ou* them); **le tout est de ...** the main thing is to ...; **pas du tout** not at all; **elle a tout d'une mère/d'une intrigante** she's a real *ou* true mother/schemer; **du tout au tout** utterly
▷ *adv* **1** (*très, complètement*) very; **tout près** *ou* **à côté** very near; **le tout premier** the very first; **tout seul** all alone; **il était tout rouge** he was really *ou* all red; **parler tout bas** to speak very quietly; **le livre tout entier** the whole book; **tout en haut** right at the top; **tout droit** straight ahead
2: **tout en** while; **tout en travaillant** while working, as he *etc* works
3: **tout d'abord** first of all; **tout à coup** suddenly; **tout à fait** absolutely; **tout à fait!** exactly!; **tout à l'heure** a short while ago;

(*futur*) in a short while, shortly; **à tout à l'heure!** see you later!; **il répondit tout court que non** he just answered no (and that was all); **tout de même** all the same; **tout le monde** everybody; **tout ou rien** all or nothing; **tout simplement** quite simply; **tout de suite** immediately, straight away

toutefois [tutfwa] *adv* however
toutes [tut] *adj, pron voir* **tout**
tout-terrain [tuteʀɛ̃] *adj*: **vélo ~** mountain bike; **véhicule ~** four-wheel drive
toux [tu] *nf* cough
toxicomane [tɔksikɔman] *nm/f* drug addict
toxique [tɔksik] *adj* toxic, poisonous
trac [tʀak] *nm* (*aux examens*) nerves *pl*; (*Théât*) stage fright; **avoir le ~** (*aux examens*) to get an attack of nerves; (*Théât*) to have stage fright; **tout à ~** all of a sudden
tracasser [tʀakase] *vt* to worry, bother; (*harceler*) to harass; **se tracasser** *vi* to worry (o.s.), fret
trace [tʀas] *nf* (*empreintes*) tracks *pl*; (*marques, aussi fig*) mark; (*restes, vestige*) trace; (*indice*) sign; (*aussi*: **suivre à la ~**) to track; **~s de pas** footprints
tracé [tʀase] *nm* (*contour*) line; (*plan*) layout
tracer [tʀase] *vt* to draw; (*mot*) to trace; (*piste*) to open up; (*fig: chemin*) to show
tract [tʀakt] *nm* tract, pamphlet; (*publicitaire*) handout
tractations [tʀaktasjɔ̃] *nfpl* dealings, bargaining *nsg*
tracteur [tʀaktœʀ] *nm* tractor
traction [tʀaksjɔ̃] *nf* traction; (*Gym*) pull-up; **~ avant/arrière** front-wheel/rear-wheel drive; **~ électrique** electric(al) traction *ou* haulage
tradition [tʀadisjɔ̃] *nf* tradition
traditionnel, le [tʀadisjɔnɛl] *adj* traditional
traducteur, -trice [tʀadyktœʀ, -tʀis] *nm/f* translator
traduction [tʀadyksjɔ̃] *nf* translation
traduire [tʀadɥiʀ] *vt* to translate; (*exprimer*) to convey, render; **se ~ par** to find expression in; **~ en français** to translate into French; **~ en justice** to bring before the courts
trafic [tʀafik] *nm* traffic; **~ d'armes** arms dealing; **~ de drogue** drug peddling
trafiquant, e [tʀafikɑ̃, -ɑ̃t] *nm/f* trafficker; (*d'armes*) dealer
trafiquer [tʀafike] *vt* (*péj: vin*) to doctor; (*moteur, document*) to tamper with ▷ *vi* to traffic, be engaged in trafficking
tragédie [tʀaʒedi] *nf* tragedy
tragique [tʀaʒik] *adj* tragic ▷ *nm*: **prendre qch au ~** to make a tragedy out of sth
trahir [tʀaiʀ] *vt* to betray; (*fig*) to give away, reveal; **se trahir** to betray o.s., give o.s. away
trahison [tʀaizɔ̃] *nf* betrayal; (*Jur*) treason
train [tʀɛ̃] *nm* (*Rail*) train; (*allure*) pace; (*fig: ensemble*) set; **être en ~ de faire qch** to be doing sth; **mettre qch en ~** to get sth under

way; **mettre qn en ~** to put sb in good
spirits; **se mettre en ~** (*commencer*) to get
started; (*faire de la gymnastique*) to warm up; **se
sentir en ~** to feel in good form; **aller bon ~**
to make good progress; **~ avant/arrière**
front-wheel/rear-wheel axle unit; **~ à
grande vitesse (TGV)** high-speed train;
~ d'atterrissage undercarriage; **~ autos-
couchettes** car-sleeper train; **~ électrique**
(*jouet*) (electric) train set; **~ de pneus** set of
tyres *ou* tires; **~ de vie** style of living

traîne [tʀɛn] *nf* (*de robe*) train; **être à la ~** to be
in tow; (*en arrière*) to lag behind; (*en désordre*)
to be lying around

traîneau, x [tʀɛno] *nm* sleigh, sledge

traînée [tʀene] *nf* streak, trail; (*péj*) slut

traîner [tʀene] *vt* (*remorque*) to pull; (*enfant,
chien*) to drag *ou* trail along; (*maladie*):
il traîne un rhume depuis l'hiver he has
a cold which has been dragging on since
winter ▷ *vi* (*robe, manteau*) to trail; (*être en
désordre*) to lie around; (*marcher lentement*) to
dawdle (along); (*vagabonder*) to hang about;
(*agir lentement*) to idle about; (*durer*) to drag on;
se traîner *vi* (*ramper*) to crawl along; (*marcher
avec difficulté*) to drag o.s. along; (*durer*) to drag
on; **se ~ par terre** to crawl (on the ground);
~ qn au cinéma to drag sb to the cinema;
~ les pieds to drag one's feet; **~ par terre** to
trail on the ground; **~ en longueur** to drag out

train-train [tʀɛ̃tʀɛ̃] *nm* humdrum routine

traire [tʀɛʀ] *vt* to milk

trait, e [tʀɛ, -ɛt] *pp de* **traire** ▷ *nm* (*ligne*) line;
(*de dessin*) stroke; (*caractéristique*) feature, trait;
(*flèche*) dart, arrow; shaft; **traits** *nmpl* (*du
visage*) features; **d'un ~** (*boire*) in one gulp; **de ~**
adj (*animal*) draught (Brit), draft (US); **avoir ~ à**
to concern; **~ pour** line for line; **~ de
caractère** characteristic, trait; **~ d'esprit**
flash of wit; **~ de génie** brainwave; **~ d'union**
hyphen; (*fig*) link

traitant, e [tʀɛtɑ̃, -ɑ̃t] *adj*: **votre médecin ~**
your usual *ou* family doctor; **shampooing ~**
medicated shampoo; **crème ~e** conditioning
cream, conditioner

traite [tʀɛt] *nf* (*Comm*) draft; (*Agr*) milking;
(*trajet*) stretch; **d'une (seule) ~** without
stopping (once); **la ~ des noirs** the slave trade;
la ~ des blanches the white slave trade

traité [tʀete] *nm* treaty

traitement [tʀɛtmɑ̃] *nm* treatment;
processing; (*salaire*) salary; **suivre un ~** to
undergo treatment; **mauvais ~**
ill-treatment; **~ de données** *ou* **de
l'information** (*Inform*) data processing;
~ hormono-supplétif hormone
replacement therapy; **~ par lots** (*Inform*)
batch processing; **~ de texte** (*Inform*) word
processing; (*logiciel*) word processing package

traiter [tʀete] *vt* (*gén*) to treat; (*Tech:
matériaux*) to process, treat; (*Inform*) to
process; (*affaire*) to deal with, handle;

(*qualifier*): **~ qn d'idiot** to call sb a fool ▷ *vi* to
deal; **~ de** *vt* to deal with; **bien/mal ~** to treat
well/ill-treat

traiteur [tʀɛtœʀ] *nm* caterer

traître, -esse [tʀɛtʀ, -tʀɛs] *adj* (*dangereux*)
treacherous ▷ *nm* traitor; **prendre qn en ~** to
make an insidious attack on sb

trajectoire [tʀaʒɛktwaʀ] *nf* trajectory, path

trajet [tʀaʒɛ] *nm* (*parcours, voyage*) journey;
(*itinéraire*) route; (*fig*) path, course; (*distance à
parcourir*) distance; **il y a une heure de ~** the
journey takes one hour

trame [tʀam] *nf* (*de tissu*) weft; (*fig*)
framework; texture; (*Typo*) screen

tramer [tʀame] *vt* to plot, hatch

trampoline [tʀɑ̃polin], **trampolino**
[tʀɑ̃polino] *nm* trampoline; (*Sport*)
trampolining

tramway [tʀamwɛ] *nm* tram(way); (*voiture*)
tram(car) (Brit), streetcar (US)

tranchant, e [tʀɑ̃ʃɑ̃, -ɑ̃t] *adj* sharp; (*fig:
personne*) peremptory; (: *couleurs*) striking
▷ *nm* (*d'un couteau*) cutting edge; (*de la main*)
edge; **à double ~** (*argument, procédé*) double-
edged

tranche [tʀɑ̃ʃ] *nf* (*morceau*) slice; (*arête*) edge;
(*partie*) section; (*série*) block; (*d'impôts, revenus
etc*) bracket; (*loterie*) issue; **~ d'âge/de
salaires** age/wage bracket; **~ (de silicium)**
wafer

tranché, e [tʀɑ̃ʃe] *adj* (*couleurs*) distinct,
sharply contrasted; (*opinions*) clear-cut,
definite ▷ *nf* trench

trancher [tʀɑ̃ʃe] *vt* to cut, sever; (*fig: résoudre*)
to settle ▷ *vi* to be decisive; (*entre deux choses*)
to settle the argument; **~ avec** to contrast
sharply with

tranquille [tʀɑ̃kil] *adj* calm, quiet; (*enfant,
élève*) quiet; (*rassuré*) easy in one's mind, with
one's mind at rest; **se tenir ~** (*enfant*) to be
quiet; **avoir la conscience ~** to have an easy
conscience; **laisse-moi/laisse-ça ~** leave me/
it alone

tranquillisant, e [tʀɑ̃kilizɑ̃, -ɑ̃t] *adj*
(*nouvelle*) reassuring ▷ *nm* tranquillizer

tranquillité [tʀɑ̃kilite] *nf* quietness, peace
(and quiet); **en toute ~** with complete peace
of mind; **~ d'esprit** peace of mind

transat [tʀɑ̃zat] *nm* deckchair ▷ *nf* = **course
transatlantique**

transborder [tʀɑ̃sbɔʀde] *vt* to tran(s)ship

transcription [tʀɑ̃skʀipsjɔ̃] *nf* transcription

transférer [tʀɑ̃sfeʀe] *vt* to transfer

transfert [tʀɑ̃sfɛʀ] *nm* transfer

transformation [tʀɑ̃sfɔʀmasjɔ̃] *nf* change,
alteration; (*radicale*) transformation; (*Rugby*)
conversion; **transformations** *nfpl* (*travaux*)
alterations; **industries de ~** processing
industries

transformer [tʀɑ̃sfɔʀme] *vt* to change;
(*radicalement*) to transform, alter ("*alter*"
implique un changement moins radical); (*vêtement*)

alter; (*matière première, appartement, Rugby*) to convert; **~ en** to transform into; to turn into; to convert into; **se transformer** vi to be transformed; to alter

transfusion [trɑ̃fyzjɔ̃] nf: **~ sanguine** blood transfusion

transgénique [trɑ̃sʒenik] adj transgenic

transgresser [trɑ̃sgrese] vt to contravene, disobey

transi, e [trɑ̃zi] adj numb (with cold), chilled to the bone

transiger [trɑ̃ziʒe] vi to compromise, come to an agreement; **~ sur** ou **avec qch** to compromise on sth

transistor [trɑ̃zistɔr] nm transistor

transit [trɑ̃zit] nm transit; **de ~** transit cpd; **en ~** in transit

transiter [trɑ̃zite] vi to pass in transit

transitif, -ive [trɑ̃zitif, -iv] adj transitive

transition [trɑ̃zisjɔ̃] nf transition; **de ~** transitional

transitoire [trɑ̃zitwar] adj (*mesure, gouvernement*) transitional, provisional; (*fugitif*) transient

translucide [trɑ̃slysid] adj translucent

transmettre [trɑ̃smɛtr] vt (*passer*): **~ qch à qn** to pass sth on to sb; (*Tech, Tél, Méd*) to transmit; (*TV, Radio: retransmettre*) to broadcast

transmission [trɑ̃smisjɔ̃] nf transmission, passing on; (*Auto*) transmission; **transmissions** nfpl (*Mil*) ≈ signals corps nsg; **~ de données** (*Inform*) data transmission; **~ de pensée** thought transmission

transparent, e [trɑ̃sparɑ̃, -ɑ̃t] adj transparent

transpercer [trɑ̃spɛrse] vt (*froid, pluie*) to go through, pierce; (*balle*) to go through

transpiration [trɑ̃spirasjɔ̃] nf perspiration

transpirer [trɑ̃spire] vi to perspire; (*information, nouvelle*) to come to light

transplantation [trɑ̃splɑ̃tasjɔ̃] nf transplant

transplanter [trɑ̃splɑ̃te] vt (*Méd, Bot*) to transplant; (*personne*) to uproot, move

transport [trɑ̃spɔr] nm transport; (*émotions*): **~ de colère** fit of rage; **~ de joie** transport of delight; **~ de voyageurs/marchandises** passenger/goods transportation; **~s en commun** public transport nsg; **~s routiers** haulage (*Brit*), trucking (*US*)

transporter [trɑ̃spɔrte] vt to carry, move; (*Comm*) to transport, convey; (*fig*): **~ qn (de joie)** to send sb into raptures; **se ~ quelque part** (*fig*) to let one's imagination carry one away (somewhere)

transporteur [trɑ̃spɔrtœr] nm haulage contractor (*Brit*), trucker (*US*)

transvaser [trɑ̃svaze] vt to decant

transversal, e, -aux [trɑ̃svɛrsal, -o] adj transverse, cross(-); (*route etc*) cross-country; (*mur, chemin, rue*) running at right angles;

(*Auto*): **axe ~** main cross-country road (*Brit*) ou highway (*US*); **coupe ~e** cross section

trapèze [trapɛz] nm (*Géom*) trapezium; (*au cirque*) trapeze

trappe [trap] nf (*de cave, grenier*) trap door; (*piège*) trap

trapu, e [trapy] adj squat, stocky

traquenard [traknar] nm trap

traquer [trake] vt to track down; (*harceler*) to hound

traumatiser [tromatize] vt to traumatize

travail, -aux [travaj, -o] nm (*gén*) work; (*tâche, métier*) work no pl, job; (*Écon, Méd*) labour (*Brit*), labor (*US*); (*Inform*) job ▷ nmpl (*de réparation, agricoles etc*) work nsg; (*sur route*) roadworks; (*de construction*) building (work) nsg; **être/entrer en ~** (*Méd*) to be in/go into labour; **être sans ~** (*employé*) to be out of work, be unemployed; **~ d'intérêt général (TIG)** ≈ community service; **~ (au) noir** moonlighting; **~ posté** shiftwork; **travaux des champs** farmwork nsg; **travaux dirigés (TD)** (*Scol*) supervised practical work nsg; **travaux forcés** hard labour nsg; **travaux manuels** (*Scol*) handicrafts; **travaux ménagers** housework nsg; **travaux pratiques (TP)** (*gén*) practical work; (*en laboratoire*) lab work (*Brit*), lab (*US*); **travaux publics (TP)** ≈ public works nsg

travailler [travaje] vi to work; (*bois*) to warp ▷ vt (*bois, métal*) to work; (*pâte*) to knead; (*objet d'art, discipline, fig: influencer*) to work on; **cela le travaille** it is on his mind; **~ la terre** to work the land; **~ son piano** to do one's piano practice; **~ à** to work on; (*fig: contribuer à*) to work towards; **~ à faire** to endeavour (*Brit*) ou endeavor (*US*) to do

travailleur, -euse [travajœr, -øz] adj hardworking ▷ nm/f worker; **~ de force** labourer (*Brit*), laborer (*US*); **~ intellectuel** nonmanual worker; **~ social** social worker; **travailleuse familiale** home help

travailliste [travajist] adj ≈ Labour cpd ▷ nm/f member of the Labour party

travaux [travo] nmpl voir **travail**

travers [travɛr] nm fault, failing; **en ~ (de)** across; **au ~ (de)** through; **de ~** adj (*nez, bouche*) crooked; (*chapeau*) askew ▷ adv sideways; (*fig*) the wrong way; **à ~** through; **regarder de ~** (*fig*) to look askance at; **comprendre de ~** to misunderstand

traverse [travɛrs] nf (*de voie ferrée*) sleeper; **chemin de ~** shortcut

traversée [travɛrse] nf crossing

traverser [travɛrse] vt (*gén*) to cross; (*ville, tunnel, aussi: percer, fig*) to go through; (*ligne, trait*) to run across

traversin [travɛrsɛ̃] nm bolster

travesti [travɛsti] nm (*comme mode de vie*) transvestite; (*artiste de cabaret*) female impersonator, drag artist; (*costume*) fancy dress

trébucher [trebyʃe] vi: **~ (sur)** to stumble (over), trip (over)

trèfle [tʀɛfl] nm (Bot) clover; (Cartes: couleur) clubs pl; (: carte) club; **à quatre feuilles** four-leaf clover

treille [tʀɛj] nf (tonnelle) vine arbour (Brit) ou arbor (US); (vigne) climbing vine

treillis [tʀɛji] nm (métallique) wire-mesh; (toile) canvas; (Mil: tenue) combat uniform; (pantalon) combat trousers pl

treize [tʀɛz] num thirteen

treizième [tʀɛzjɛm] num thirteenth; see note

> ❊ **TREIZIÈME MOIS**
>
> ❊ The treizième mois is an end-of-year bonus
> ❊ roughly corresponding to one month's
> ❊ salary. For many employees it is a
> ❊ standard part of their salary package.

tréma [tʀema] nm diaeresis

tremblement [tʀɑ̃bləmɑ̃] nm trembling no pl, shaking no pl, shivering no pl; **de terre** earthquake

trembler [tʀɑ̃ble] vi to tremble, shake; **de** (froid, fièvre) to shiver ou tremble with; (peur) to shake ou tremble with; **pour qn** to fear for sb

trémousser [tʀemuse]: **se trémousser** vi to jig about, wriggle about

trempe [tʀɑ̃p] nf (fig): **de cette/sa** ~ of this/his calibre (Brit) ou caliber (US)

trempé, e [tʀɑ̃pe] adj soaking (wet), drenched; (Tech): **acier** ~ tempered steel

tremper [tʀɑ̃pe] vt to soak, drench; (aussi: **faire** ~, **mettre à** ~) to soak; (plonger): **~ qch dans** to dip sth in(to) ▷ vi to soak; (fig): **~ dans** to be involved ou have a hand in; **se tremper** vi to have a quick dip; **se faire** ~ to get soaked ou drenched

trempette [tʀɑ̃pɛt] nf: **faire** ~ to go paddling

tremplin [tʀɑ̃plɛ̃] nm springboard; (Ski) ski jump

trentaine [tʀɑ̃tɛn] nf (âge): **avoir la** ~ to be around thirty; **une** ~ **(de)** thirty or so, about thirty

trente [tʀɑ̃t] num thirty; **voir** ~-**six chandelles** (fig) to see stars; **être/se mettre sur son** ~ **et un** to be wearing/put on one's Sunday best; ~-**trois tours** nm long-playing record, LP

trentième [tʀɑ̃tjɛm] num thirtieth

trépidant, e [tʀepidɑ̃, -ɑ̃t] adj (fig: rythme) pulsating; (: vie) hectic

trépied [tʀepje] nm (d'appareil) tripod; (meuble) trivet

trépigner [tʀepiɲe] vi to stamp (one's feet)

très [tʀɛ] adv very; **~ beau/bien** very beautiful/well; **~ critiqué** much criticized; **~ industrialisé** highly industrialized; **j'ai ~ faim** I'm very hungry

trésor [tʀezɔʀ] nm treasure; (Admin) finances pl; (d'une organisation) funds pl; **~ (public) (TP)** public revenue office

trésorerie [tʀezɔʀʀi] nf (fonds) funds pl; (gestion) accounts pl; (bureaux) accounts department; (poste) treasurership; **difficultés de** ~ cash problems, shortage of cash ou funds; **~ générale (TG)** local government finance office

trésorier, -ière [tʀezɔʀje, -jɛʀ] nm/f treasurer

tressaillir [tʀesajiʀ] vi (de peur etc) to shiver, shudder; (de joie) to quiver

tressauter [tʀesote] vi to start, jump

tresse [tʀɛs] nf (de cheveux) braid, plait; (cordon, galon) braid

tresser [tʀese] vt (cheveux) to braid, plait; (fil, jonc) to plait; (corbeille) to weave; (corde) to twist

tréteau, x [tʀeto] nm trestle; **les ~x** (fig: Théât) the boards

treuil [tʀœj] nm winch

trêve [tʀɛv] nf (Mil, Pol) truce; (fig) respite; **sans** ~ unremittingly; **~ de ...** enough of this ...; **les États de la T-** the Trucial States

tri [tʀi] nm (voir trier) sorting (out) no pl; selection; screening; (Inform) sort; (Postes: action) sorting; **faire le** ~ **(de)** to sort out; **le (bureau de)** ~ (Postes) the sorting office

triangle [tʀijɑ̃gl] nm triangle; **~ isocèle/ équilatéral** isosceles/equilateral triangle; **~ rectangle** right-angled triangle

triangulaire [tʀijɑ̃gylɛʀ] adj triangular

tribord [tʀibɔʀ] nm: **à** ~ starboard, on the starboard side

tribu [tʀiby] nf tribe

tribunal, -aux [tʀibynal, -o] nm (Jur) court; (Mil) tribunal; **~ de police/pour enfants** police/juvenile court; **~ d'instance (TI)** ≈ magistrates' court (Brit), ≈ district court (US); **~ de grande instance (TGI)** ≈ High Court (Brit), ≈ Supreme Court (US)

tribune [tʀibyn] nf (estrade) platform, rostrum; (débat) forum; (d'église, de tribunal) gallery; (de stade) stand; **~ libre** (Presse) opinion column

tribut [tʀiby] nm tribute

tributaire [tʀibytɛʀ] adj: **être** ~ **de** to be dependent on; (Géo) to be a tributary of

tricher [tʀiʃe] vi to cheat

tricheur, -euse [tʀiʃœʀ, -øz] nm/f cheat

tricolore [tʀikɔlɔʀ] adj three-coloured (Brit), three-colored (US); (français: drapeau) red, white and blue; (: équipe etc) French

tricot [tʀiko] nm (technique, ouvrage) knitting no pl; (tissu) knitted fabric; (vêtement) jersey, sweater; **~ de corps**, **~ de peau** vest (Brit), undershirt (US)

tricoter [tʀikɔte] vt to knit; **machine/ aiguille à** ~ knitting machine/needle (Brit) ou pin (US)

trictrac [tʀiktʀak] nm backgammon

tricycle [tʀisikl] nm tricycle

triennal, e, -aux [tʀiɛnal, -o] adj (prix, foire, élection) three-yearly; (charge, mandat, plan) three-year

trier [tʀije] vt (classer) to sort (out); (choisir) to select; (visiteurs) to screen; (Postes, Inform, fruits) to sort

trimestre [tʀimɛstʀ] nm (Scol) term; (Comm) quarter

trimestriel, le [tʀimɛstʀijɛl] adj quarterly; (Scol) end-of-term

tringle [tʀɛ̃gl] nf rod

trinquer [tʀɛ̃ke] vi to clink glasses; (fam) to cop it; **à qch/la santé de qn** to drink to sth/sb

triomphe [tʀijɔ̃f] nm triumph; **être reçu/porté en ~** to be given a triumphant welcome/be carried shoulder-high in triumph

triompher [tʀijɔ̃fe] vi to triumph, win; **~ de** to triumph over, overcome

tripes [tʀip] nfpl (Culin) tripe nsg; (fam) guts

triple [tʀipl] adj (à trois éléments) triple; (trois fois plus grand) treble ▷ nm: **le ~ (de)** (comparaison) three times as much (as); **en ~ exemplaire** in triplicate; **~ saut** (Sport) triple jump

tripler [tʀiple] vi, vt to triple, treble, increase threefold

triplés, -ées [tʀiple] nm/fpl triplets

tripoter [tʀipote] vt to fiddle with, finger ▷ vi (fam) to rummage about

triste [tʀist] adj sad; (couleur, temps, journée) dreary; (péj): **~ personnage/affaire** sorry individual/affair; **c'est pas ~!** (fam) it's something else!

tristesse [tʀistɛs] nf sadness

trivial, e, -aux [tʀivjal, -o] adj coarse, crude; (commun) mundane

troc [tʀɔk] nm (Écon) barter; (transaction) exchange, swap

troène [tʀɔɛn] nm privet

trognon [tʀɔɲɔ̃] nm (de fruit) core; (de légume) stalk

trois [tʀwa] num three

troisième [tʀwazjɛm] num third ▷ nf (Scol) year 10 (Brit), ninth grade (US); **le ~ âge** (période de vie) one's retirement years; (personnes âgées) senior citizens pl

trois quarts [tʀwakaʀ] nmpl: **les ~ de** three-quarters of

trombe [tʀɔ̃b] nf waterspout; **des ~s d'eau** a downpour; **en ~** (arriver, passer) like a whirlwind

trombone [tʀɔ̃bɔn] nm (Mus) trombone; (de bureau) paper clip; **~ à coulisse** slide trombone

trompe [tʀɔ̃p] nf (d'éléphant) trunk; (Mus) trumpet, horn; **~ d'Eustache** Eustachian tube; **~s utérines** Fallopian tubes

tromper [tʀɔ̃pe] vt to deceive; (fig: espoir, attente) to disappoint; (vigilance, poursuivants) to elude; **se tromper** vi to make a mistake, be mistaken; **se ~ de voiture/jour** to take the wrong car/get the day wrong; **se ~ de 3 cm/20 euros** to be out by 3 cm/20 euros

tromperie [tʀɔ̃pʀi] nf deception, trickery no pl

trompette [tʀɔ̃pɛt] nf trumpet; **en ~** (nez) turned-up

trompeur, -euse [tʀɔ̃pœʀ, -øz] adj deceptive, misleading

tronc [tʀɔ̃] nm (Bot, Anat) trunk; (d'église) collection box; **~ d'arbre** tree trunk; **~ commun** (Scol) common-core syllabus; **~ de cône** truncated cone

tronçon [tʀɔ̃sɔ̃] nm section

tronçonner [tʀɔ̃sɔne] vt (arbre) to saw up; (pierre) to cut up

tronçonneuse [tʀɔ̃sɔnøz] nf chainsaw

trône [tʀon] nm throne; **monter sur le ~** to ascend the throne

trop [tʀo] adv too; (avec verbe) too much; (aussi: **~ nombreux**) too many; (aussi: **~ souvent**) too often; **~ peu (nombreux)** too few; **~ longtemps** (for) too long; **~ de** (nombre) too many; (quantité) too much; **de ~, en ~: des livres en trop** a few books too many, a few extra books; **du lait en ~** too much milk; **trois livres/cinq euros de ~** three books too many/five euros too much; **ça coûte ~ cher** it's too expensive

tropical, e, -aux [tʀɔpikal, -o] adj tropical

tropique [tʀɔpik] nm tropic; **tropiques** nmpl tropics; **~ du Cancer/Capricorne** Tropic of Cancer/Capricorn

trop-plein [tʀoplɛ̃] nm (tuyau) overflow ou outlet (pipe); (liquide) overflow

troquer [tʀɔke] vt: **~ qch contre** to barter ou trade sth for; (fig) to swap sth for

trot [tʀo] nm trot; **aller au ~** to trot along; **partir au ~** to set off at a trot

trotter [tʀɔte] vi to trot; (fig) to scamper along (ou about)

trotteuse [tʀɔtøz] nf (de montre) second hand

trottinette [tʀɔtinɛt] nf (child's) scooter

trottoir [tʀɔtwaʀ] nm pavement (Brit), sidewalk (US); **faire le ~** (péj) to walk the streets; **~ roulant** moving walkway, travellator

trou [tʀu] nm hole; (fig) gap; (Comm) deficit; **~ d'aération** (air) vent; **~ d'air** air pocket; **~ de mémoire** blank, lapse of memory; **~ noir** black hole; **~ de la serrure** keyhole

troublant, e [tʀublɑ̃, -ɑ̃t] adj disturbing

trouble [tʀubl] adj (liquide) cloudy; (image, photo) blurred; (mémoire) indistinct, hazy; (affaire) shady, murky ▷ adv indistinctly; **voir ~** to have blurred vision ▷ nm (désarroi) distress, agitation; (émoi sensuel) turmoil, agitation; (embarras) confusion; (zizanie) unrest, discord; **troubles** nmpl (Pol) disturbances, troubles, unrest nsg; (Méd) trouble nsg, disorders; **~s de la personnalité** personality problems; **~s de la vision** eye trouble

trouble-fête [tʀubləfɛt] nm/f inv spoilsport

troubler [tʀuble] vt (embarrasser) to confuse, disconcert; (émouvoir) to agitate; to disturb; to perturb; (perturber: ordre etc) to disrupt, disturb; (*liquide*) to make cloudy; (*intriguer*) to bother; **se troubler** vi (*personne*) to become flustered ou confused; **~ l'ordre public** to cause a breach of the peace

trouer [tʀue] vt to make a hole (ou holes) in; (*fig*) to pierce

trouille [tʀuj] nf (*fam*): **avoir la ~** to be scared stiff, be scared out of one's wits

troupe [tʀup] nf (*Mil*) troop; (*groupe*) troop, group; **la ~** (*Mil: l'armée*) the army; (*: les simples soldats*) the troops pl; **~ (de théâtre)** (theatrical) company; **~s de choc** shock troops

troupeau, x [tʀupo] nm (*de moutons*) flock; (*de vaches*) herd

trousse [tʀus] nf case, kit; (*d'écolier*) pencil case; (*de docteur*) instrument case; **aux ~s de** (*fig*) on the heels ou tail of; **~ à outils** toolkit; **~ de toilette** toilet bag

trousseau, x [tʀuso] nm (*de mariée*) trousseau; **~ de clefs** bunch of keys

trouvaille [tʀuvaj] nf find; (*fig: idée, expression etc*) brainwave

trouver [tʀuve] vt to find; (*rendre visite*): **aller/venir ~ qn** to go/come and see sb; **je trouve que** I find ou think that; **~ à boire/critiquer** to find something to drink/criticize; **~ asile/refuge** to find refuge/shelter; **se trouver** vi (*être*) to be; (*être soudain*) to find o.s.; **se ~ être/avoir** to happen to be/have; **il se trouve que** it happens that, it turns out that; **se ~ bien** to feel well; **se ~ mal** to pass out

truand [tʀyɑ̃] nm villain, crook

truander [tʀyɑ̃de] vi (*fam*) to cheat, do ▷ vt: **se faire ~** to be swindled

truc [tʀyk] nm (*astuce*) way, device; (*de cinéma, prestidigitateur*) trick effect; (*chose*) thing; (*machin*) thingumajig, whatsit (*Brit*); **avoir le ~** to have the knack; **c'est pas son** (ou **mon** etc) **~** (*fam*) it's not really his (ou my etc) thing

truelle [tʀyɛl] nf trowel

truffe [tʀyf] nf truffle; (*nez*) nose

truffé, e [tʀyfe] adj (*Culin*) garnished with truffles; **~ de** (*fig: citations*) peppered with; (*fautes*) riddled with; (*pièges*) bristling with

truie [tʀɥi] nf sow

truite [tʀɥit] nf trout inv

truquage [tʀyka3] nm fixing; (*Ciné*) special effects pl

truquer [tʀyke] vt (*élections, serrure, dés*) to fix; (*Ciné*) to use special effects in

TSVP abr (= *tournez s'il vous plaît*) PTO

TTC abr (= *toutes taxes comprises*) inclusive of tax

tu¹ [ty] pron you ▷ nm: **employer le tu** to use the "tu" form

tu², e [ty] pp de **taire**

tuba [tyba] nm (*Mus*) tuba; (*Sport*) snorkel

tube [tyb] nm tube; (*de canalisation, métallique etc*) pipe; (*chanson, disque*) hit song ou record; **~ digestif** alimentary canal, digestive tract; **à ~ essai** test tube

tuberculose [tybɛʀkyloz] nf tuberculosis, TB

tuer [tɥe] vt to kill; **se tuer** (*se suicider*) to kill

o.s.; (*dans un accident*) to be killed; **se ~ au travail** (*fig*) to work o.s. to death

tuerie [tyʀi] nf slaughter no pl, massacre

tue-tête [tytɛt]: **à ~** adv at the top of one's voice

tueur [tɥœʀ] nm killer; **~ à gages** hired killer

tuile [tɥil] nf tile; (*fam*) spot of bad luck, blow

tulipe [tylip] nf tulip

tuméfié, e [tymefje] adj puffy, swollen

tumeur [tymœʀ] nf growth, tumour (*Brit*), tumor (*US*)

tumulte [tymylt] nm commotion, hubbub

tumultueux, -euse [tymyltɥø, -øz] adj stormy, turbulent

tunique [tynik] nf tunic; (*de femme*) smock, tunic

Tunis [tynis] n Tunis

Tunisie [tynizi] nf: **la ~** Tunisia

tunisien, ne [tynizjɛ̃, -ɛn] adj Tunisian ▷ nm/f: **T~, ne** Tunisian

tunnel [tynɛl] nm tunnel; **le ~ sous la Manche** the Channel Tunnel

turbulences [tyʀbylɑ̃s] nfpl (*Aviat*) turbulence sg

turbulent, e [tyʀbylɑ̃, -ɑ̃t] adj boisterous, unruly

turc, turque [tyʀk] adj Turkish; (*w.-c.*) seatless ▷ nm (*Ling*) Turkish ▷ nm/f: **T~, Turque** Turk/Turkish woman; **à la turque** adv (*assis*) cross-legged

turf [tyʀf] nm racing

turfiste [tyʀfist] nm/f racegoer

Turquie [tyʀki] nf: **la ~** Turkey

turquoise [tyʀkwaz] nf, adj inv turquoise

tus etc [ty] vb voir **taire**

tutelle [tytɛl] nf (*Jur*) guardianship; (*Pol*) trusteeship; **sous la ~ de** (*fig*) under the supervision of

tuteur, -trice [tytœʀ, -tʀis] nm/f (*Jur*) guardian; (*de plante*) stake, support

tutoyer [tytwaje] vt: **~ qn** to address sb as "tu"

tuyau, x [tɥijo] nm pipe; (*flexible*) tube; (*fam: conseil*) tip; (*: mise au courant*) gen no pl; **~ d'arrosage** hosepipe; **~ d'échappement** exhaust pipe; **~ d'incendie** fire hose

tuyauterie [tɥijotʀi] nf piping no pl

TVA sigle f (= *taxe à ou sur la valeur ajoutée*) VAT

TVHD abr f (= *télévision haute-définition*) HDTV

tympan [tɛ̃pɑ̃] nm (*Anat*) eardrum

type [tip] nm type; (*personne, chose: représentant*) classic example, epitome; (*fam*) chap, guy ▷ adj typical, standard; **avoir le ~ nordique** to be Nordic-looking

typé, e [tipe] adj ethnic (*euph*)

typique [tipik] adj typical

tyran [tiʀɑ̃] nm tyrant

tyrannique [tiʀanik] adj tyrannical

tzigane [dzigan] adj gipsy, tzigane ▷ nm/f (Hungarian) gipsy, Tzigane

u

UEM sigle f (= Union économique et monétaire) EMU

ulcère [ylsɛʀ] nm ulcer; **~ à l'estomac** stomach ulcer

ulcérer [ylseʀe] vt (Méd) to ulcerate; (fig) to sicken, appal

ultérieur, e [ylteʀjœʀ] adj later, subsequent; **remis à une date ~e** postponed to a later date

ultérieurement [ylteʀjœʀmɑ̃] adv later, subsequently

ultime [yltim] adj final

UMP sigle f (= Union pour un mouvement populaire) political party

 MOT-CLÉ

un, une [œ̃, yn] art indéf a; (devant voyelle) an; **un garçon/vieillard** a boy/an old man; **une fille** a girl
▷ pron one; **l'un des meilleurs** one of the best; **l'un ..., l'autre** (the) one ..., the other; **les uns ..., les autres** some ..., others; **l'un et l'autre** both (of them); **l'un ou l'autre** either (of them); **l'un l'autre, les uns les autres** each other, one another; **pas un seul** not a single one; **un par un** one by one
▷ num one; **une pomme seulement** one apple only, just one apple
▷ nf: **la une** (Presse) the front page

unanime [ynanim] adj unanimous; **ils sont ~s (à penser que)** they are unanimous (in thinking that)

unanimité [ynanimite] nf unanimity; **à l'~** unanimously; **faire l'~** to be approved unanimously

uni, e [yni] adj (ton, tissu) plain; (surface) smooth, even; (famille) close(-knit); (pays) united

unifier [ynifje] vt to unite, unify; (systèmes) to standardize, unify; **s'unifier** vi to become united

uniforme [ynifɔʀm] adj (mouvement) regular, uniform; (surface, ton) even; (objets, maisons) uniform; (fig: vie, conduite) unchanging ▷ nm uniform; **être sous l'~** (Mil) to be serving

uniformiser [ynifɔʀmize] vt to make uniform; (systèmes) to standardize

union [ynjɔ̃] nf union; **~ conjugale** union of marriage; **~ de consommateurs** consumers' association; **~ libre** free love; **vivre en ~ libre** (en concubinage) to cohabit; **U~ européenne** European Union; **l'U~ des Républiques socialistes soviétiques (URSS)** the Union of Soviet Socialist Republics (USSR); **l'U~ soviétique** the Soviet Union

unique [ynik] adj (seul) only; (le même): **un prix/système** ~ a single price/system; (exceptionnel) unique; **ménage à salaire ~** one-salary family; **route à voie ~** single-lane road; **fils/fille ~** only son/daughter, only child; **sens ~** one-way street; **~ en France** the only one of its kind in France

uniquement [ynikmɑ̃] adv only, solely; (juste) only, merely

unir [yniʀ] vt (nations) to unite; (éléments, couleurs) to combine; (en mariage) to unite, join together; **~ qch à** to unite sth with; to combine sth with; **s'unir** vi to unite; (en mariage) to be joined together; **s'~ à** ou **avec** to unite with

unitaire [ynitɛʀ] adj unitary; (Pol) unitarian; **prix ~** unit price

unité [ynite] nf (harmonie, cohésion) unity; (Comm, Mil, de mesure, Math) unit; **~ centrale** central processing unit; **~ de valeur** (university) course, credit

univers [ynivɛʀ] nm universe

universel, le [ynivɛʀsɛl] adj universal; (esprit) all-embracing

universitaire [ynivɛʀsitɛʀ] adj university cpd; (diplôme, études) academic, university cpd ▷ nm/f academic

université [ynivɛʀsite] nf university

urbain, e [yʀbɛ̃, -ɛn] adj urban, city cpd, town cpd; (poli) urbane

urbanisme [yʀbanism] nm town planning

urgence [yʀʒɑ̃s] nf urgency; (Méd etc) emergency; **d'~** adj emergency cpd ▷ adv as a matter of urgency; **en cas d'~** in case of emergency; **service des ~s** emergency service

urgent, e [yʀʒɑ̃, -ɑ̃t] adj urgent

urine [yʀin] nf urine

urinoir [yʀinwaʀ] nm (public) urinal

urne [yʀn] *nf* (*électorale*) ballot box; (*vase*) urn; **aller aux ~s** (*voter*) to go to the polls

urticaire [yʀtikɛʀ] *nf* nettle rash, urticaria

us [ys] *nmpl*: **us et coutumes** (habits and) customs

USA *sigle mpl* (= *United States of America*) USA

usage [yzaʒ] *nm* (*emploi, utilisation*) use; (*coutume*) custom; (*éducation*) (good) manners *pl*, (good) breeding; (*Ling*): **l'~** usage; **faire ~ de** (*pouvoir, droit*) to exercise; **avoir l'~ de** to have the use of; **à l'~** *adv* with use; **à l'~ de** (*pour*) for (use of); **en ~** in use; **hors d'~** out of service; **à ~ interne** (*Méd*) to be taken (internally); **à ~ externe** (*Méd*) for external use only

usagé, e [yzaʒe] *adj* (*usé*) worn; (*d'occasion*) used

usager, -ère [yzaʒe, -ɛʀ] *nm/f* user

usé, e [yze] *adj* worn (down *ou* out *ou* away); ruined; (*banal: argument etc*) hackneyed

user [yze] *vt* (*outil*) to wear down; (*vêtement*) to wear out; (*matière*) to wear away; (*consommer: charbon etc*) to use; (*fig: santé*) to ruin; (*: personne*) to wear out; **s'user** *vi* to wear; (*tissu, vêtement*) to wear out; (*fig*) to decline; **s'~ à la tâche** to wear o.s. out with work; **~ de** *vt* (*moyen, procédé*) to use, employ; (*droit*) to exercise

usine [yzin] *nf* factory; **~ atomique** nuclear power plant; **à gaz** gasworks *sg*; **~ marémotrice** tidal power station

usité, e [yzite] *adj* in common use, common; **peu ~** rarely used

ustensile [ystɑ̃sil] *nm* implement; **~ de cuisine** kitchen utensil

usuel, le [yzɥɛl] *adj* everyday, common

usure [yzyʀ] *nf* wear; worn state; (*de l'usurier*) usury; **avoir qn à l'~** to wear sb down; **~ normale** fair wear and tear

utérus [yteʀys] *nm* uterus, womb

utile [ytil] *adj* useful; **~ à qn/qch** of use to sb/sth

utilisation [ytilizasjɔ̃] *nf* use

utiliser [ytilize] *vt* to use

utilitaire [ytilitɛʀ] *adj* utilitarian; (*objets*) practical ▷ *nm* (*Inform*) utility

utilité [ytilite] *nf* usefulness *no pl*; use; **jouer les ~s** (*Théât*) to play bit parts; **reconnu d'~ publique** state-approved; **c'est d'une grande ~** it's extremely useful; **il n'y a aucune ~ à ...** there's no use in ...; **de peu d'~** of little use *ou* help

utopie [ytɔpi] *nf* (*idée, conception*) utopian idea *ou* view; (*société etc idéale*) utopia

V

va [va] *vb voir* **aller**

vacance [vakɑ̃s] *nf* (*Admin*) vacancy; **vacances** *nfpl* holiday(s) *pl* (Brit), vacation *sg* (US); **les grandes ~s** the summer holidays *ou* vacation; **prendre des/ses ~s** to take a holiday *ou* vacation/one's holiday(s) *ou* vacation; **aller en ~s** to go on holiday *ou* vacation

vacancier, -ière [vakɑ̃sje, -jɛʀ] *nm/f* holidaymaker (Brit), vacationer (US)

vacant, e [vakɑ̃, -ɑ̃t] *adj* vacant

vacarme [vakaʀm] *nm* row, din

vaccin [vaksɛ̃] *nm* vaccine; (*opération*) vaccination

vaccination [vaksinasjɔ̃] *nf* vaccination

vacciner [vaksine] *vt* to vaccinate; (*fig*) to make immune; **être vacciné** (*fig*) to be immune

vache [vaʃ] *nf* (*Zool*) cow; (*cuir*) cowhide ▷ *adj* (*fam*) rotten, mean; **~ à eau** (canvas) water bag; (**manger de la**) **~ enragée** (to go through) hard times; **~ à lait** (*péj*) mug, sucker; **~ laitière** dairy cow; **période des ~s maigres** lean times *pl*, lean period

vachement [vaʃmɑ̃] *adv* (*fam*) damned, really

vacherie [vaʃʀi] *nf* (*fam*) meanness *no pl*; (*action*) dirty trick; (*propos*) nasty remark

vaciller [vasije] *vi* to sway, wobble; (*bougie, lumière*) to flicker; (*fig*) to be failing, falter; **~ dans ses réponses** to falter in one's replies; **~ dans ses résolutions** to waver in one's resolutions

va-et-vient [vaevjɛ̃] nm inv (de pièce mobile) to and fro (ou up and down) movement; (de personnes, véhicules) comings and goings pl, to-ings and fro-ings pl; (Élec) two-way switch

vagabond, e [vagabɔ̃, -ɔ̃d] adj wandering; (imagination) roaming, roving ▷ nm (rôdeur) tramp, vagrant; (voyageur) wanderer

vagabonder [vagabɔ̃de] vi to roam, wander

vagin [vaʒɛ̃] nm vagina

vague [vag] nf wave ▷ adj vague; (regard) faraway; (manteau, robe) loose(-fitting); (quelconque): un ~ bureau/cousin some office/cousin or other ▷ nm: être dans le ~ to be rather in the dark; rester dans le ~ to keep things rather vague; regarder dans le ~ to gaze into space; ~ à l'âme nm vague melancholy; ~ d'assaut nf (Mil) wave of assault; ~ de chaleur nf heatwave; ~ de fond nf ground swell; ~ de froid nf cold spell

vaillant, e [vajɑ̃, -ɑ̃t] adj (courageux) brave, gallant; (robuste) vigorous, hale and hearty; n'avoir plus un sou ~ to be penniless

vaille [vaj] vb voir **valoir**

vain, e [vɛ̃, vɛn] adj vain; en ~ adv in vain

vaincre [vɛ̃kʀ] vt to defeat; (fig) to conquer, overcome

vaincu, e [vɛ̃ky] pp de **vaincre** ▷ nm/f defeated party

vainqueur [vɛ̃kœʀ] nm victor; (Sport) winner ▷ adj m victorious

vais [vɛ] vb voir **aller**

vaisseau, x [vɛso] nm (Anat) vessel; (Navig) ship, vessel; ~ spatial spaceship

vaisselier [vɛsəlje] nm dresser

vaisselle [vɛsɛl] nf (service) crockery; (plats etc à laver) (dirty) dishes pl; faire la ~ to do the washing-up (Brit) ou the dishes

val [val] (pl vaux ou vals) nm valley

valable [valabl] adj valid; (acceptable) decent, worthwhile

valent etc [val] vb voir **valoir**

valet [valɛ] nm valet; (péj) lackey; (Cartes) jack, knave (Brit); ~ de chambre manservant, valet; ~ de ferme farmhand; ~ de pied footman

valeur [valœʀ] nf (gén) value; (mérite) worth, merit; (Comm: titre) security; valeurs nfpl (morales) values; mettre en ~ (bien) to exploit; (terrain, région) to develop; (fig) to highlight; to show off to advantage; avoir de la ~ to be valuable; prendre de la ~ to go up ou gain in value; sans ~ worthless; ~ absolue absolute value; ~ d'échange exchange value; ~ nominale face value; ~s mobilières transferable securities

valide [valid] adj (en bonne santé) fit, well; (indemne) able-bodied, fit; (valable) valid

valider [valide] vt to validate

valions etc [valjɔ̃] vb voir **valoir**

valise [valiz] nf (suit)case; faire sa ~ to pack one's (suit)case; la ~ (diplomatique) the diplomatic bag

vallée [vale] nf valley

vallon [valɔ̃] nm small valley

vallonné, e [valɔne] adj undulating

valoir [valwaʀ] vi (être valable) to hold, apply ▷ vt (prix, valeur, effort) to be worth; (causer): ~ qch à qn to earn sb sth; se valoir to be of equal merit; (péj) to be two of a kind; faire ~ (droits, prérogatives) to assert; (domaine, capitaux) to exploit; faire ~ que to point out that; se faire ~ to make the most of o.s.; à ~ on account; à ~ sur to be deducted from; vaille que vaille somehow or other; cela ne me dit rien qui vaille I don't like the look of it at all; ce climat ne me vaut rien this climate doesn't suit me; ~ la peine to be worth the trouble, be worth it; ~ mieux: il vaut mieux se taire it's better to say nothing; il vaut mieux que je fasse/comme ceci it's better if I do/like this; ça ne vaut rien it's worthless; que vaut ce candidat? how good is this applicant?

valse [vals] nf waltz; c'est la ~ des étiquettes the prices don't stay the same from one moment to the next

valu, e [valy] pp de **valoir**

vandalisme [vɑ̃dalism] nm vandalism

vanille [vanij] nf vanilla; glace à la ~ vanilla ice cream

vanité [vanite] nf vanity

vaniteux, -euse [vanitø, -øz] adj vain, conceited

vanne [van] nf gate; (fam: remarque) dig, (nasty) crack; lancer une ~ à qn to have a go at sb (Brit), knock sb

vannerie [vanʀi] nf basketwork

vantard, e [vɑ̃taʀ, -aʀd] adj boastful

vanter [vɑ̃te] vt to speak highly of, praise; se vanter vi to boast, brag; se ~ de to pride o.s. on; (péj) to boast of

vapeur [vapœʀ] nf steam; (émanation) vapour (Brit), vapor (US), fumes pl; (brouillard, buée) haze; vapeurs nfpl (bouffées) vapours, vapors; à ~ steam-powered, steam cpd; à toute ~ full steam ahead; (fig) at full tilt; renverser la ~ to reverse engines; (fig) to backtrack, backpedal; cuit à la ~ steamed

vaporeux, -euse [vapoʀø, -øz] adj (flou) hazy, misty; (léger) filmy, gossamer cpd

vaporisateur [vapoʀizatœʀ] nm spray

vaporiser [vapoʀize] vt (Chimie) to vaporize; (parfum etc) to spray

varappe [vaʀap] nf rock climbing

vareuse [vaʀøz] nf (blouson) pea jacket; (d'uniforme) tunic

variable [vaʀjabl] adj variable; (temps, humeur) changeable; (Tech: à plusieurs positions etc) adaptable; (Ling) inflectional; (divers: résultats) varied, various ▷ nf (Inform, Math) variable

varice [vaʀis] nf varicose vein

varicelle [vaʀisɛl] nf chickenpox

varié, e [vaʀje] adj varied; (divers) various; hors-d'œuvre ~s selection of hors d'œuvres

varier [vaʀje] *vi* to vary; *(temps, humeur)* to change ▷ *vt* to vary

variété [vaʀjete] *nf* variety; **spectacle de ~s** variety show

variole [vaʀjɔl] *nf* smallpox

Varsovie [vaʀsɔvi] *n* Warsaw

vas [va] *vb voir* **aller**; **~-y!** [vazi] go on!

vase [vaz] *nm* vase ▷ *nf* silt, mud; **en ~ clos** in isolation; **~ de nuit** chamberpot; **~s communicants** communicating vessels

vaseux, -euse [vazø, -øz] *adj* silty, muddy; *(fig: confus)* woolly, hazy; *(: fatigué)* peaky; *(: étourdi)* woozy

vasistas [vazistas] *nm* fanlight

vaste [vast] *adj* vast, immense

vaudrai *etc* [vodʀe] *vb voir* **valoir**

vaurien, ne [voʀjɛ̃, -ɛn] *nm/f* good-for-nothing, guttersnipe

vaut [vo] *vb voir* **valoir**

vautour [votuʀ] *nm* vulture

vautrer [votʀe]: **se ~ dans** *vi* to wallow in; **se ~ sur** to sprawl on

vaux [vo] *pl de* **val** ▷ *vb voir* **valoir**

va-vite [vavit]: **à la ~** *adv* in a rush

VDQS *sigle m* (= *vin délimité de qualité supérieure*) *label guaranteeing quality of wine*

veau, x [vo] *nm* (*Zool*) calf; (*Culin*) veal; *(peau)* calfskin; **tuer le ~ gras** to kill the fatted calf

vécu, e [veky] *pp de* **vivre** ▷ *adj* real(-life)

vedette [vədɛt] *nf* (*artiste etc*) star; *(canot)* patrol boat; *(police)* launch; **avoir la ~** to top the bill, get star billing; **mettre qn en ~** (*Ciné etc*) to give sb the starring role; *(fig)* to push sb into the limelight; **voler la ~ à qn** to steal the show from sb

végétal, e, -aux [veʒetal, -o] *adj* vegetable ▷ *nm* vegetable, plant

végétalien, ne [veʒetaljɛ̃, -ɛn] *adj, nm/f* vegan

végétarien, ne [veʒetaʀjɛ̃, -ɛn] *adj, nm/f* vegetarian

végétation [veʒetasjɔ̃] *nf* vegetation; **végétations** *nfpl* (*Méd*) adenoids

véhicule [veikyl] *nm* vehicle; **~ utilitaire** commercial vehicle

veille [vɛj] *nf* (*garde*) watch; (*Psych*) wakefulness; *(jour)*: **la ~** the day before, the previous day; **la ~ au soir** the previous evening; **la ~ de** the day before; **la ~ de Noël** Christmas Eve; **la ~ du jour de l'An** New Year's Eve; **à la ~ de** on the eve of; **l'état de ~** the waking state

veillée [veje] *nf* (*soirée*) evening; (*réunion*) evening gathering; **~ d'armes** night before combat; *(fig)* vigil; **~ (funèbre)** wake; **~ (mortuaire)** watch

veiller [veje] *vi* (*rester debout*) to stay *ou* sit up; *(ne pas dormir)* to be awake; *(être de garde)* to be on watch; *(être vigilant)* to be watchful ▷ *vt* (*malade, mort*) to watch over, sit up with; **~ à** *vt* to attend to, see to; **~ à ce que** to make sure that, see to it that; **~ sur** *vt* to keep a watch *ou* an eye on

veilleur [vɛjœʀ] *nm*: **~ de nuit** night watchman

veilleuse [vɛjøz] *nf* (*lampe*) night light; *(Auto)* sidelight; *(flamme)* pilot light; **en ~** *adj* (*lampe*) dimmed; *(fig: affaire)* shelved, set aside

veinard, e [venaʀ, -aʀd] *nm/f* (*fam*) lucky devil

veine [vɛn] *nf* (*Anat, du bois etc*) vein; *(filon)* vein, seam; *(fam: chance)*: **avoir de la ~** to be lucky; *(inspiration)* inspiration

véliplanchiste [veliplɑ̃ʃist] *nm/f* windsurfer

vélo [velo] *nm* bike, cycle; **faire du ~** to go cycling

vélomoteur [velomɔtœʀ] *nm* moped

velours [v(ə)luʀ] *nm* velvet; **~ côtelé** corduroy

velouté, e [vəlute] *adj* (*au toucher*) velvety; *(à la vue)* soft, mellow; *(au goût)* smooth, mellow ▷ *nm*: **~ d'asperges/de tomates** cream of asparagus/tomato soup

velu, e [vəly] *adj* hairy

venais *etc* [vənɛ] *vb voir* **venir**

venaison [vənɛzɔ̃] *nf* venison

vendange [vɑ̃dɑ̃ʒ] *nf* (*opération, période: aussi:* **~s**) grape harvest; *(raisins)* grape crop, grapes *pl*

vendanger [vɑ̃dɑ̃ʒe] *vi* to harvest the grapes

vendeur, -euse [vɑ̃dœʀ, -øz] *nm/f* (*de magasin*) shop *ou* sales assistant (*Brit*), sales clerk (*US*); (*Comm*) salesman/woman ▷ *nm* (*Jur*) vendor, seller; **~ de journaux** newspaper seller

vendre [vɑ̃dʀ] *vt* to sell; **~ qch à qn** to sell sb sth; **cela se vend à la douzaine** these are sold by the dozen; **"à ~"** "for sale"

vendredi [vɑ̃dʀədi] *nm* Friday; **V~ saint** Good Friday; *voir aussi* **lundi**

vénéneux, -euse [venenø, -øz] *adj* poisonous

vénérien, ne [veneʀjɛ̃, -ɛn] *adj* venereal

vengeance [vɑ̃ʒɑ̃s] *nf* vengeance *no pl*, revenge *no pl*; *(acte)* act of vengeance *ou* revenge

venger [vɑ̃ʒe] *vt* to avenge; **se venger** *vi* to avenge o.s.; *(par rancune)* to take revenge; **se ~ de qch** to avenge o.s. for sth; **se ~ de qn** to take revenge on sb; **se ~ sur** to wreak vengeance upon; to take revenge on *ou* through; to take it out on

venimeux, -euse [vənimø, -øz] *adj* poisonous, venomous; *(fig: haineux)* venomous, vicious

venin [vənɛ̃] *nm* venom, poison; *(fig)* venom

venir [v(ə)niʀ] *vi* to come; **~ de** to come from; **~ faire: je viens d'y aller/de le voir** I've just been there/seen him; **s'il vient à pleuvoir** if it should rain, if it happens to rain; **en ~ à faire: j'en viens à croire que** I am coming to believe that; **où veux-tu en ~?** what are you getting at?; **il en est venu à mendier** he has been reduced to begging; **en ~ aux mains** to come to blows; **les années/**

générations à ~ the years/generations to come; **il me vient une idée** an idea has just occurred to me; **il me vient des soupçons** I'm beginning to be suspicious; **je te vois ~** I know what you're after; **faire ~** (*docteur, plombier*) to call (out); **d'où vient que ...?** how is it that ...?; **~ au monde** to come into the world

vent [vɑ̃] *nm* wind; **il y a du ~** it's windy; **c'est du ~** it's all hot air; **au ~** to windward; **sous le ~** to leeward; **avoir le ~ debout/arrière** to head into the wind/have the wind astern; **dans le ~** (*fam*) trendy; **prendre le ~** (*fig*) to see which way the wind blows; **avoir ~ de** to get wind of; **contre ~s et marées** come hell or high water

vente [vɑ̃t] *nf* sale; **la ~** (*activité*) selling; (*secteur*) sales *pl*; **mettre en ~** to put on sale; (*objets personnels*) to put up for sale; **~ aux enchères** auction sale; **~ de charité** jumble (*Brit*) *ou* rummage (*US*) sale; **~ par correspondance (VPC)** mail-order selling

venteux, -euse [vɑ̃tø, -øz] *adj* windswept, windy

ventilateur [vɑ̃tilatœr] *nm* fan

ventiler [vɑ̃tile] *vt* to ventilate; (*total, statistiques*) to break down

ventouse [vɑ̃tuz] *nf* (*ampoule*) cupping glass; (*de caoutchouc*) suction pad; (*Zool*) sucker

ventre [vɑ̃tr] *nm* (*Anat*) stomach; (*fig*) belly; **prendre du ~** to be getting a paunch; **avoir mal au ~** to have (a) stomach ache

ventriloque [vɑ̃trilɔk] *nm/f* ventriloquist

venu, e [v(ə)ny] *pp de* **venir** ▷ *adj*: **être mal ~ à** *ou* **de faire** to have no grounds for doing, be in no position to do; **mal ~** ill-timed, unwelcome; **bien ~** timely, welcome ▷ *nf* coming

ver [vɛr] *nm* worm; (*des fruits etc*) maggot; (*du bois*) woodworm *no pl*; **~ blanc** May beetle grub; **~ luisant** glow-worm; **~ à soie** silkworm; **~ solitaire** tapeworm; **~ de terre** earthworm

verbaliser [vɛrbalize] *vi* (*Police*) to book *ou* report an offender; (*Psych*) to verbalize

verbe [vɛrb] *nm* (*Ling*) verb; (*voix*): **avoir le ~ sonore** to have a sonorous tone (of voice); (*expression*): **la magie du ~** the magic of language *ou* the word; (*Rel*): **le V~** the Word

verdâtre [vɛrdɑtr] *adj* greenish

verdict [vɛrdik(t)] *nm* verdict

verdir [vɛrdir] *vi, vt* to turn green

verdure [vɛrdyr] *nf* (*arbres, feuillages*) greenery; (*légumes verts*) green vegetables *pl*, greens *pl*

véreux, -euse [verø, -øz] *adj* worm-eaten; (*malhonnête*) shady, corrupt

verge [vɛrʒ] *nf* (*Anat*) penis; (*baguette*) stick, cane

verger [vɛrʒe] *nm* orchard

verglacé, e [vɛrglase] *adj* icy, iced-over

verglas [vɛrglɑ] *nm* (black) ice

vergogne [vɛrgɔɲ]: **sans ~** *adv* shamelessly

véridique [veridik] *adj* truthful

vérification [verifikasjɔ̃] *nf* checking *no pl*, check; **~ d'identité** identity check

vérifier [verifje] *vt* to check; (*corroborer*) to confirm, bear out; **se vérifier** *vi* to be confirmed *ou* verified

véritable [veritabl] *adj* real; (*ami, amour*) true; **un ~ désastre** an absolute disaster

vérité [verite] *nf* truth; (*d'un portrait*) lifelikeness; (*sincérité*) truthfulness, sincerity; **en ~, à la ~** to tell the truth

verlan [vɛrlɑ̃] *nm* (back) slang; *see note*

▩ **VERLAN**

Verlan is a form of slang popularized in the 1950's. It consists of inverting a word's syllables, the term *verlan* itself coming from "l'envers" ("à l'envers" = back to front). Typical examples are "féca" ("café"), "ripou" ("pourri"), "meuf" ("femme"), and "beur" ("Arabe").

vermeil, le [vɛrmɛj] *adj* bright red, ruby red ▷ *nm* (*substance*) vermeil

vermine [vɛrmin] *nf* vermin *pl*

vermoulu, e [vɛrmuly] *adj* worm-eaten, with woodworm

verni, e [vɛrni] *adj* varnished; glazed; (*fam*) lucky; **cuir ~** patent leather; **souliers ~s** patent (leather) shoes

vernir [vɛrnir] *vt* (*bois, tableau, ongles*) to varnish; (*poterie*) to glaze

vernis [vɛrni] *nm* (*enduit*) varnish; glaze; (*fig*) veneer; **~ à ongles** nail varnish (*Brit*) *ou* polish

vernissage [vɛrnisaʒ] *nm* varnishing; glazing; (*d'une exposition*) preview

vérole [verɔl] *nf* (*variole*) smallpox; (*fam: syphilis*) pox

verrai *etc* [vere] *vb voir* **voir**

verre [vɛr] *nm* glass; (*de lunettes*) lens *sg*; **verres** *nmpl* (*lunettes*) glasses; **boire** *ou* **prendre un ~** to have a drink; **~ à vin/à liqueur** wine/liqueur glass; **~ à dents** tooth mug; **~ dépoli** frosted glass; **~ de lampe** lamp glass *ou* chimney; **~ de montre** watch glass; **~ à pied** stemmed glass; **~s de contact** contact lenses; **~s fumés** tinted lenses

verrerie [vɛrri] *nf* (*fabrique*) glassworks *sg*; (*activité*) glass-making, glass-working; (*objets*) glassware

verrière [vɛrjɛr] *nf* (*grand vitrage*) window; (*toit vitré*) glass roof

verrons *etc* [vɛrɔ̃] *vb voir* **voir**

verrou [vɛru] *nm* (*targette*) bolt; (*fig*) constriction; **mettre le ~** to bolt the door; **mettre qn sous les ~s** to put sb behind bars

verrouillage [vɛrujaʒ] *nm* (*dispositif*) locking mechanism; (*Auto*): **~ central** *ou* **centralisé** central locking

verrouiller [veʀuje] vt to bolt; to lock; (Mil: brèche) to close

verrue [veʀy] nf wart; (plantaire) verruca; (fig) eyesore

vers [veʀ] nm line ▷ nmpl (poésie) verse sg ▷ prép (en direction de) toward(s); (près de) around (about); (temporel) about, around

versant [veʀsɑ̃] nm slopes pl, side

versatile [veʀsatil] adj fickle, changeable

verse [veʀs]: à ~ adv: **il pleut à ~** it's pouring (with rain)

Verseau [veʀso] nm: **le** ~ Aquarius, the water-carrier; **être du** ~ to be Aquarius

versement [veʀsəmɑ̃] nm payment; (sur un compte) deposit, remittance; **en trois ~s** in three instalments

verser [veʀse] vt (liquide, grains) to pour; (larmes, sang) to shed; (argent) to pay; (soldat: affecter): ~ **qn dans** to assign sb to ▷ vi (véhicule) to overturn; (fig): ~ **dans** to lapse into; ~ **sur un compte** to pay into an account

verset [veʀse] nm verse; versicle

version [veʀsjɔ̃] nf version; (Scol) translation (into the mother tongue); **film en ~ originale** film in the original language

verso [veʀso] nm back; **voir au** ~ see over(leaf)

vert, e [veʀ, veʀt] adj green; (vin) young; (vigoureux) sprightly; (cru) forthright ▷ nm green; **dire des ~es (et des pas mûres)** to say some pretty spicy things; **il en a vu des ~es** he's seen a thing or two; ~ **bouteille** adj inv bottle-green; ~ **d'eau** adj inv sea-green; ~ **pomme** adj inv apple-green; **les V~s** (Pol) the Greens

vertèbre [veʀtɛbʀ] nf vertebra

vertement [veʀtəmɑ̃] adv (réprimander) sharply

vertical, e, -aux [veʀtikal, -o] adj, nf vertical; **à la ~e** adv vertically

verticalement [veʀtikalmɑ̃] adv vertically

vertige [veʀtiʒ] nm (peur du vide) vertigo; (étourdissement) dizzy spell; (fig) fever; **ça me donne le** ~ it makes me dizzy; (fig) it makes my head spin ou reel

vertigineux, -euse [veʀtiʒinø, -øz] adj (hausse, vitesse) breathtaking; (altitude, gorge) breathtakingly high (ou deep)

vertu [veʀty] nf virtue; **une** ~ a saint, a paragon of virtue; **avoir la** ~ **de faire** to have the virtue of doing; **en** ~ **de** prép in accordance with

vertueux, -euse [veʀtɥø, -øz] adj virtuous

verve [veʀv] nf witty eloquence; **être en** ~ to be in brilliant form

verveine [veʀven] nf (Bot) verbena, vervain; (infusion) verbena tea

vésicule [vezikyl] nf vesicle; ~ **biliaire** gall-bladder

vessie [vesi] nf bladder

veste [vest] nf jacket; ~ **droite/croisée** single/double-breasted jacket; **retourner sa** ~ (fig) to change one's colours

vestiaire [vestjɛʀ] nm (au théâtre etc) cloakroom; (de stade etc) changing-room (Brit), locker-room (US); (métallique): (**armoire**) ~ locker

vestibule [vestibyl] nm hall

vestige [vestiʒ] nm (objet) relic; (fragment) trace; (fig) remnant, vestige; **vestiges** nmpl (d'une ville) remains; (d'une civilisation, du passé) remnants, relics

vestimentaire [vestimɑ̃tɛʀ] adj (dépenses) clothing; (détail) of dress; (élégance) sartorial; **dépenses ~s** clothing expenditure

veston [vestɔ̃] nm jacket

vêtement [vɛtmɑ̃] nm garment, item of clothing; (Comm): **le** ~ the clothing industry; **vêtements** nmpl clothes; **~s de sport** sportswear sg, sports clothes

vétérinaire [veteʀinɛʀ] adj veterinary ▷ nm/f vet, veterinary surgeon (Brit), veterinarian (US)

vêtir [vetiʀ] vt to clothe, dress; **se vêtir** to dress (o.s.)

veto [veto] nm veto; **droit de** ~ right of veto; **mettre** ou **opposer un** ~ **à** to veto

vêtu, e [vety] pp de **vêtir** ▷ adj: ~ **de** dressed in, wearing; **chaudement** ~ warmly dressed

vétuste [vetyst] adj ancient, timeworn

veuf, veuve [vœf, vœv] adj widowed ▷ nm widower ▷ nf widow

veuille [vœj], **veuillez** etc [vœje] vb voir **vouloir**

veule [vøl] adj spineless

veuve [vœv] adj f, nf voir **veuf**

veux [vø] vb voir **vouloir**

vexant, e [vɛksɑ̃, -ɑ̃t] adj (contrariant) annoying; (blessant) upsetting

vexation [vɛksasjɔ̃] nf humiliation

vexations [vɛksasjɔ̃] nfpl humiliations

vexer [vɛkse] vt to hurt, upset; **se vexer** vi to be offended, get upset

viable [vjabl] adj viable; (économie, industrie etc) sustainable

viaduc [vjadyk] nm viaduct

viager, -ère [vjaʒe, -ɛʀ] adj: **rente viagère** life annuity ▷ nm: **mettre en** ~ to sell in return for a life annuity

viande [vjɑ̃d] nf meat; **je ne mange pas de** ~ I don't eat meat

vibrer [vibʀe] vi to vibrate; (son, voix) to be vibrant; (fig) to be stirred; **faire** ~ to (cause to) vibrate; to stir, thrill

vice [vis] nm vice; (défaut) fault; ~ **caché** (Comm) latent ou inherent defect; ~ **de forme** legal flaw ou irregularity

vichy [viʃi] nm (toile) gingham; (eau) Vichy water; **carottes V~** boiled carrots

vicié, e [visje] adj (air) polluted, tainted; (Jur) invalidated

vicieux, -euse [visjø, -øz] adj (pervers) dirty(-minded); (méchant) nasty; (fautif) incorrect, wrong ▷ nm/f lecher

vicinal, e, -aux [visinal, -o] adj: **chemin** ~ byroad, byway

victime [viktim] nf victim; (d'accident) casualty; **être (la) ~ de** to be the victim of; **être ~ d'une attaque/d'un accident** to suffer a stroke/be involved in an accident

victoire [viktwaʀ] nf victory

victuailles [viktɥaj] nfpl provisions

vidange [vidɑ̃ʒ] nf (d'un fossé, réservoir) emptying; (Auto) oil change; (de lavabo: bonde) waste outlet; **vidanges** nfpl (matières) sewage sg; **faire la ~** (Auto) to change the oil, do an oil change; **tuyau de ~** drainage pipe

vidanger [vidɑ̃ʒe] vt to empty; **faire ~ la voiture** to have the oil changed in one's car

vide [vid] adj empty ⊳ nm (Physique) vacuum; (espace) (empty) space, gap; (sous soi: dans une falaise etc) drop; (futilité, néant) void; **~ de** empty of; (de sens etc) devoid of; **sous ~** adv in a vacuum; **emballé sous ~** vacuum-packed; **regarder dans le ~** to stare into space; **avoir peur du ~** to be afraid of heights; **parler dans le ~** to waste one's breath; **faire le ~** (dans son esprit) to make one's mind go blank; **faire le ~ autour de qn** to isolate sb; **emballé sous ~** vacuum packed; **à ~** adv (sans occupants) empty; (sans charge) unladen; (Tech) without gripping ou being in gear

vidéo [video] nf, adj inv video; **cassette ~** video cassette; **~ inverse** reverse video

vidéoclip [videoklip] nm music video

vidéoclub [videoklœb] nm video club

vidéoconférence [videokɔ̃feʀɑ̃s] nf videoconference

vide-ordures [vidɔʀdyʀ] nm inv (rubbish) chute

vidéothèque [videotɛk] nf video library

vide-poches [vidpɔʃ] nm inv tidy; (Auto) glove compartment

vider [vide] vt to empty; (Culin: volaille, poisson) to gut, clean out; (régler: querelle) to settle; (fatiguer) to wear out; (fam: expulser) to throw out, chuck out; **se vider** vi to empty; **~ les lieux** to quit ou vacate the premises

videur [vidœʀ] nm (de boîte de nuit) bouncer

vie [vi] nf life; **être en ~** to be alive; **sans ~** lifeless; **à ~** for life; **membre à ~** life member; **dans la ~ courante** in everyday life; **avoir la ~ dure** to have nine lives; **to die hard**; **mener la ~ dure à qn** to make life a misery for sb; **que faites-vous dans la ~?** what do you do?

vieil [vjɛj] adj m voir **vieux**

vieillard [vjɛjaʀ] nm old man; **les ~s** old people, the elderly

vieille [vjɛj] adj f, nf voir **vieux**

vieilleries [vjɛjʀi] nfpl old things ou stuff sg

vieillesse [vjɛjɛs] nf old age; (vieillards): **la ~** the old pl, the elderly pl

vieillir [vjejiʀ] vi (prendre de l'âge) to grow old; (population, vin) to age; (doctrine, auteur) to become dated ⊳ vt to age; **il a beaucoup vieilli** he has aged a lot; **se vieillir** to make o.s. older

vieillissement [vjejismɑ̃] nm growing old; ageing

Vienne [vjɛn] n (en Autriche) Vienna

vienne [vjɛn], **viens** etc [vjɛ̃] vb voir **venir**

viens [vjɛ̃] vb voir **venir**

vierge [vjɛʀʒ] adj virgin; (film) blank; (page) clean, blank; (jeune fille): **être ~** to be a virgin ⊳ nf virgin; (signe): **la V~** Virgo, the Virgin; **être de la V~** to be Virgo; **~ de** (sans) free from, unsullied by

Viêtnam, Vietnam [vjɛtnam] nm: **le ~** Vietnam; **le ~ du Nord/du Sud** North/South Vietnam

vietnamien, ne [vjɛtnamjɛ̃, -ɛn] adj Vietnamese ⊳ nm (Ling) Vietnamese ⊳ nm/f: **V~, ne** Vietnamese; **V~, ne du Nord/Sud** North/South Vietnamese

vieux, vieil, vieille [vjø, vjɛj] adj old ⊳ nm/f old man/woman ⊳ nmpl: **les ~** the old, old people; (fam: parents) the old folk ou ones; **un petit ~** a little old man; **mon ~/ma vieille** (fam) old man/girl; **pauvre ~** poor old soul; **prendre un coup de ~** to put years on; **se faire ~** to make o.s. look older; **un ~ de la vieille** one of the old brigade; **~ garçon** nm bachelor; **~ jeu** adj inv old-fashioned; **~ rose** adj inv old rose; **vieil or** adj inv old gold; **vieille fille** nf spinster

vif, vive [vif, viv] adj (animé) lively; (alerte) sharp, quick; (brusque) sharp, brusque; (aigu) sharp; (lumière, couleur) brilliant; (air) crisp; (vent, émotion) keen; (froid) bitter; (fort: regret, déception) great, deep; (vivant): **brûlé ~** burnt alive; **eau vive** running water; **de vive voix** personally; **avoir l'esprit ~** to be quick-witted; **piquer qn au ~** to cut sb to the quick; **tailler dans le ~** to cut into the living flesh; **à ~** (plaie) open; **avoir les nerfs à ~** to be on edge; **sur le ~** (Art) from life; **entrer dans le ~ du sujet** to get to the very heart of the matter

vigne [viɲ] nf (plante) vine; (plantation) vineyard; **~ vierge** Virginia creeper

vigneron [viɲʀɔ̃] nm wine grower

vignette [viɲɛt] nf (motif) vignette; (de marque) manufacturer's label ou seal; (petite illustration) (small) illustration; (Admin) ≈ (road) tax disc (Brit), ≈ license plate sticker (US); (: sur médicament) price label (on medicines for reimbursement by Social Security)

vignoble [viɲɔbl] nm (plantation) vineyard; (vignes d'une région) vineyards pl

vigoureux, -euse [viguʀø, -øz] adj vigorous, robust

vigueur [vigœʀ] nf vigour (Brit), vigor (US); **être/entrer en ~** to be in/come into force; **en ~** current

vil, e [vil] adj vile, base; **à ~ prix** at a very low price

vilain, e [vilɛ̃, -ɛn] adj (laid) ugly; (affaire, blessure) nasty; (pas sage: enfant) naughty ⊳ nm (paysan) villein, villain; **ça va tourner au ~** things are going to turn nasty; **~ mot** bad word

villa [vila] *nf* (detached) house; ~ **en multipropriété** time-share villa

village [vilaʒ] *nm* village; ~ **de toile** tent village; ~ **de vacances** holiday village

villageois, e [vilaʒwa, -waz] *adj* village *cpd* ▷ *nm/f* villager

ville [vil] *nf* town; (*importante*) city; (*administration*): **la** ~ ≈ the Corporation, ≈ the (town) council; **aller en** ~ to go to town; **habiter en** ~ to live in town; ~ **jumelée** twin town; ~ **d'eaux** spa; ~ **nouvelle** new town

villégiature [vileʒjatyʀ] *nf* (*séjour*) holiday; (*lieu*) (holiday) resort

vin [vɛ̃] *nm* wine; **avoir le** ~ **gai/triste** to get happy/miserable after a few drinks; ~ **blanc/ rosé/rouge** white/rosé/red wine; ~ **d'honneur** reception (*with wine and snacks*); ~ **de messe** altar wine; ~ **ordinaire** ou **de table** table wine; ~ **de pays** local wine; *voir aussi* **AOC; VDQS**

vinaigre [vinɛgʀ] *nm* vinegar; **tourner au** ~ (*fig*) to turn sour; ~ **de vin/d'alcool** wine/ spirit vinegar

vinaigrette [vinɛgʀɛt] *nf* vinaigrette, French dressing

vindicatif, -ive [vɛ̃dikatif, -iv] *adj* vindictive

vineux, -euse [vinø, -øz] *adj* win(e)y

vingt [vɛ̃, vɛ̃t] (*2nd pron used when followed by a vowel*) *num* twenty; ~-**quatre heures sur** ~-**quatre** twenty-four hours a day, round the clock

vingtaine [vɛ̃tɛn] *nf*: **une** ~ (**de**) around twenty, twenty or so

vingtième [vɛ̃tjɛm] *num* twentieth

vinicole [vinikɔl] *adj* (*production*) wine *cpd*; (*région*) wine-growing

vins *etc* [vɛ̃] *vb voir* **venir**

vinyle [vinil] *nm* vinyl

viol [vjɔl] *nm* (*d'une femme*) rape; (*d'un lieu sacré*) violation

violacé, e [vjɔlase] *adj* purplish, mauvish

violemment [vjɔlamɑ̃] *adv* violently

violence [vjɔlɑ̃s] *nf* violence; **violences** *nfpl* acts of violence; **faire** ~ **à qn** to do violence to sb; **se faire** ~ to force o.s

violent, e [vjɔlɑ̃, -ɑ̃t] *adj* violent; (*remède*) drastic; (*besoin, désir*) intense, urgent

violer [vjɔle] *vt* (*femme*) to rape; (*sépulture*) to desecrate, violate; (*loi, traité*) to violate

violet, te [vjɔlɛ, -ɛt] *adj, nm* purple, mauve ▷ *nf* (*fleur*) violet

violon [vjɔlɔ̃] *nm* violin; (*dans la musique folklorique etc*) fiddle; (*fam: prison*) lock-up; **premier** ~ first violin; ~ **d'Ingres** (artistic) hobby

violoncelle [vjɔlɔ̃sɛl] *nm* cello

violoniste [vjɔlɔnist] *nm/f* violinist, violin-player; (*folklorique etc*) fiddler

vipère [vipɛʀ] *nf* viper, adder

virage [viʀaʒ] *nm* (*d'un véhicule*) turn; (*d'une route, piste*) bend; (*Chimie*) change in colour (Brit) ou color (US); (*de cuti-réaction*) positive reaction; (*Photo*) toning; (*fig: Pol*) about-turn; **prendre un** ~ to go into a bend, take a bend; ~ **sans visibilité** blind bend

virée [viʀe] *nf* (*courte*) run; (: *à pied*) walk; (*longue*) trip; hike, walking tour

virement [viʀmɑ̃] *nm* (*Comm*) transfer; ~ **bancaire** (bank) credit transfer, ≈ transfer; giro transfer (Brit); ~ **postal** Post office credit transfer, ≈ Girobank® transfer (Brit)

virent [viʀ] *vb voir* **voir**

virer [viʀe] *vt* (*Comm*): ~ **qch** (**sur**) to transfer sth (into); (*Photo*) to tone; (*fam: renvoyer*) to sack, boot out ▷ *vi* to turn; (*Chimie*) to change colour (Brit) ou color (US); (*cuti-réaction*) to come up positive; (*Photo*) to tone; ~ **au bleu** to turn blue; ~ **de bord** to tack; (*fig*) to change tack; ~ **sur l'aile** to bank

virevolter [viʀvɔlte] *vi* to twirl around

virgule [viʀgyl] *nf* comma; (*Math*) point; **quatre** ~ **deux** four point two; ~ **flottante** floating decimal

viril, e [viʀil] *adj* (*propre à l'homme*) masculine; (*énergique, courageux*) manly, virile

virtuel, le [viʀtɥɛl] *adj* potential; (*théorique*) virtual

virtuose [viʀtɥoz] *nm/f* (*Mus*) virtuoso; (*gén*) master

virus [viʀys] *nm* virus

vis *vb* [vi] *voir* **voir; vivre** ▷ *nf* [vis] screw; ~ **à tête plate/ronde** flat-headed/round-headed screw; ~ **platinées** (*Auto*) (contact) points; ~ **sans fin** worm, endless screw

visa [viza] *nm* (*sceau*) stamp; (*validation de passeport*) visa; ~ **de censure** (censor's) certificate

visage [vizaʒ] *nm* face; **à** ~ **découvert** (*franchement*) openly

vis-à-vis [vizavi] *adv* face to face ▷ *nm* person opposite; house *etc* opposite; ~ **de** *prép* opposite; (*fig*) towards, vis-à-vis; **en** ~ facing ou opposite each other; **sans** ~ (*immeuble*) with an open outlook

viscéral, e, -aux [viseʀal, -o] *adj* (*fig*) deep-seated, deep-rooted

visée [vize] *nf* (*avec une arme*) aiming; (*Arpentage*) sighting; **visées** *nfpl* (*intentions*) designs; **avoir des** ~**s sur qn/qch** to have designs on sb/sth

viser [vize] *vi* to aim ▷ *vt* to aim at; (*concerner*) to be aimed ou directed at; (*apposer un visa sur*) to stamp, visa; ~ **à qch/faire** to aim at sth/at doing ou to do

viseur [vizœʀ] *nm* (*d'arme*) sights *pl*; (*Photo*) viewfinder

visibilité [vizibilite] *nf* visibility; **sans** ~ (*pilotage, virage*) blind *cpd*

visible [vizibl] *adj* visible; (*disponible*): **est-il** ~? can he see me?, will he see visitors?

visière [vizjɛʀ] *nf* (*de casquette*) peak; (*qui s'attache*) eyeshade

vision [vizjɔ̃] *nf* vision; (*sens*) (eye)sight, vision; (*fait de voir*): **la** ~ **de** the sight of; **première** ~ (*Ciné*) first showing

visionneuse [vizjɔnøz] nf viewer

visiophone [vizjɔfɔn] nm videophone

visite [vizit] nf visit; (visiteur) visitor; (touristique: d'un musée etc) tour; (Comm: de représentant) call; (expertise, d'inspection) inspection; (médicale, à domicile) visit, call; ~ **médicale** medical examination; (Mil: d'entrée) medicals pl; (: quotidienne) sick parade; ~ **accompagnée ou guidée** guided tour; **faire une ~ à qn** to call on sb, pay sb a visit; **rendre ~ à qn** to visit sb, pay sb a visit; **être en ~ (chez qn)** to be visiting (sb); **avoir de la ~** to have visitors; **heures de ~** (hôpital, prison) visiting hours; **le droit de ~** (Jur: aux enfants) right of access, access; ~ **de douane** customs inspection ou examination; ~ **guidée** guided tour

visiter [vizite] vt to visit; (musée, ville) to visit, go round

visiteur, -euse [vizitœʀ, -øz] nm/f visitor; ~ **des douanes** customs inspector; ~ **médical** medical rep(resentative); ~ **de prison** prison visitor

vison [vizɔ̃] nm mink

visser [vise] vt: ~ **qch** (fixer, serrer) to screw sth on

visuel, le [vizɥɛl] adj visual

vit [vi] vb voir **vivre**; **voir**

vital, e, -aux [vital, -o] adj vital

vitamine [vitamin] nf vitamin

vite [vit] adv (rapidement) quickly, fast; (sans délai) quickly; soon; ~! quick!; **faire ~** (agir rapidement) to act fast; (se dépêcher) to be quick; **ce sera ~ fini** this will soon be finished; **viens ~** come quick(ly)

vitesse [vites] nf speed; (Auto: dispositif) gear; **faire de la ~** to drive fast ou at speed; **prendre qn de ~** to outstrip sb, get ahead of sb; **prendre de la ~** to pick up ou gather speed; **à toute ~** at full ou top speed; **en perte de ~** (avion) losing lift; (fig) losing momentum; **changer de ~** (Auto) to change gear; ~ **acquise** momentum; ~ **de croisière** cruising speed; ~ **de pointe** top speed; ~ **du son** speed of sound; **en ~** quickly

viticole [vitikɔl] adj (industrie) wine cpd; (région) wine-growing

viticulteur [vitikyltœʀ] nm wine grower

vitrage [vitʀaʒ] nm (cloison) glass partition; (toit) glass roof; (rideau) net curtain; **double ~** double glazing

vitrail, -aux [vitʀaj, -o] nm stained-glass window

vitre [vitʀ] nf (window) pane; (de portière, voiture) window

vitré, e [vitʀe] adj glass cpd

vitrer [vitʀe] vt to glaze

vitreux, -euse [vitʀø, -øz] adj vitreous; (terne) glassy

vitrine [vitʀin] nf (devanture) (shop) window; (étalage) display; (petite armoire) display cabinet; **en ~** in the window, on display; ~ **publicitaire** display case, showcase

vivable [vivabl] adj (personne) livable-with; (maison) fit to live in

vivace adj [vivas] (arbre, plante) hardy; (fig) enduring ▷ adv [vivatʃe] (Mus) vivace

vivacité [vivasite] nf (voir vif) liveliness, vivacity; sharpness; brilliance

vivant, e [vivɑ̃, -ɑ̃t] vb voir **vivre** ▷ adj (qui vit) living, alive; (animé) lively; (preuve, exemple) living; (langue) modern ▷ nm: **du ~ de qn** in sb's lifetime; **les ~s et les morts** the living and the dead

vive [viv] adj f voir **vif** ▷ vb voir **vivre** ▷ excl: ~ **le roi!** long live the king!; ~ **les vacances!** hurrah for the holidays!

vivement [vivmɑ̃] adv vivaciously; sharply ▷ excl: ~ **les vacances!** I can't wait for the holidays!, roll on the holidays!

vivier [vivje] nm (au restaurant etc) fish tank; (étang) fishpond

vivifiant, e [vivifjɑ̃, -ɑ̃t] adj invigorating

vivions [vivjɔ̃] vb voir **vivre**

vivoter [vivɔte] vi (personne) to scrape a living, get by; (fig: affaire etc) to struggle along

vivre [vivʀ] vi, vt to live ▷ nm: **le ~ et le logement** board and lodging; **vivres** nmpl provisions, food supplies; **il vit encore** he is still alive; **se laisser ~** to take life as it comes; **ne plus ~** (être anxieux) to live on one's nerves; **il a vécu** (eu une vie aventureuse) he has seen life; **ce régime a vécu** this regime has had its day; **être facile à ~** to be easy to get on with; **faire ~ qn** (pourvoir à sa subsistance) to provide (a living) for sb; ~ **mal** (chichement) to have a meagre existence; ~ **de** (salaire etc) to live on

vlan [vlɑ̃] excl wham!, bang!

VO sigle f (Ciné: = version originale): **voir un film en VO** to see a film in its original language

vocable [vɔkabl] nm term

vocabulaire [vɔkabylɛʀ] nm vocabulary

vocation [vɔkasjɔ̃] nf vocation, calling; **avoir la ~** to have a vocation

vociférer [vɔsifeʀe] vi, vt to scream

vœu, x [vø] nm wish; (à Dieu) vow; **faire ~ de** to take a vow of; **avec tous nos ~x** with every good wish ou our best wishes; **meilleurs ~x** best wishes; (sur une carte) "Season's Greetings"; **~x de bonheur** best wishes for your future happiness; **~x de bonne année** best wishes for the New Year

vogue [vɔg] nf fashion, vogue; **en ~** in fashion, in vogue

voguer [vɔge] vi to sail

voici [vwasi] *prép* (*pour introduire, désigner*) here is; (+*sg*) here are; (+*pl*): **et ~ que ...** and now it (ou he) ...; **il est parti ~ trois ans** he left three years ago; **~ une semaine que je l'ai vue** it's a week since I've seen her; **me ~** here I am; *voir aussi* **voilà**

voie [vwa] *vb voir* **voir** ▷ *nf* way; (*Rail*) track, line; (*Auto*) lane; **par ~ buccale** *ou* **orale** orally; **par ~ rectale** rectally; **suivre la ~ hiérarchique** to go through official channels; **ouvrir/montrer la ~** to open up/show the way; **être en bonne ~** to be shaping *ou* going well; **mettre qn sur la ~** to put sb on the right track; **être en ~ d'achèvement/de rénovation** to be nearing completion/in the process of renovation; **à ~ étroite** narrow-gauge; **à ~ unique** single-track; **route à deux/trois ~s** two-/three-lane road; **par la ~ aérienne/maritime** by air/sea; **~ d'eau** (*Navig*) leak; **~ express** expressway; **~ de fait** (*Jur*) assault (and battery); **~ ferrée** track; railway line (*Brit*), railroad (*US*); **par ~ ferrée** by rail, by railroad; **~ de garage** (*Rail*) siding; **la ~ lactée** the Milky Way; **~ navigable** waterway; **~ prioritaire** (*Auto*) road with right of way; **~ privée** private road; **la ~ publique** the public highway

voilà [vwala] *prép* (*en désignant*) there is; (+*sg*) there are; (+*pl*): **les ~** *ou* **voici** here *ou* there they are; **en ~** *ou* **voici un** here's one, there's one; **voici mon frère et ~ ma sœur** this is my brother and that's my sister; **~** *ou* **voici deux ans** two years ago; **~** *ou* **voici deux ans que** it's two years since; **et ~!** there we are!; **~ tout** that's all; **"~** *ou* **voici"** (*en offrant etc*) "there *ou* here you are"; **tiens! ~ Paul** look! there's Paul

voile [vwal] *nm* veil; (*tissu léger*) net ▷ *nf* sail; (*sport*) sailing; **prendre le ~** to take the veil; **mettre à la ~** to make way under sail; **~ du palais** *nm* soft palate, velum; **~ au poumon** *nm* shadow on the lung

voiler [vwale] *vt* to veil; (*Photo*) to fog; (*fausser: roue*) to buckle; (*: bois*) to warp; **se voiler** *vi* (*lune, regard*) to mist over; (*ciel*) to grow hazy; (*voix*) to become husky; (*roue, disque*) to buckle; (*planche*) to warp; **se ~ la face** to hide one's face

voilier [vwalje] *nm* sailing ship; (*de plaisance*) sailing boat

voilure [vwalyR] *nf* (*de voilier*) sails *pl*; (*d'avion*) aerofoils *pl* (*Brit*), airfoils *pl* (*US*); (*de parachute*) canopy

voir [vwaR] *vi, vt* to see; **se voir**; **se ~ critiquer/transformer** to be criticized/transformed; **cela se voit** (*cela arrive*) it happens; (*c'est visible*) that's obvious, it shows; (*c'est visible*) that's obvious, it shows; **~ à faire qch** to see to it that sth is done; **~ loin** (*fig*) to be far-sighted; **~ venir** (*fig*) to wait and see; **faire ~ qch à qn** to show sb sth; **en faire ~ à qn** (*fig*) to give sb a hard

time; **ne pas pouvoir ~ qn** (*fig*) not to be able to stand sb; **regardez ~** just look; **montrez ~** show (me); **dites ~** tell me; **voyons!** let's see now; (*indignation etc*) come (along) now!; **c'est à ~!** we'll see!; **c'est ce qu'on va ~!** we'll see about that!; **avoir quelque chose à ~ avec** to have something to do with; **ça n'a rien à ~ avec lui** that has nothing to do with him

voire [vwaR] *adv* indeed; nay; or even

voisin, e [vwazɛ̃, -in] *adj* (*proche*) neighbouring (*Brit*), neighboring (*US*); (*contigu*) next; (*ressemblant*) connected ▷ *nm/f* neighbo(u)r; (*de table, de dortoir etc*) person next to me (*ou* him *etc*); **~ de palier** neighbo(u)r across the landing (*Brit*) *ou* hall (*US*)

voisinage [vwazinaʒ] *nm* (*proximité*) proximity; (*environs*) vicinity; (*quartier, voisins*) neighbourhood (*Brit*), neighborhood (*US*); **relations de bon ~** neighbo(u)rly terms

voiture [vwatyR] *nf* car; (*wagon*) coach, carriage; **en ~!** all aboard!; **~ à bras** handcart; **~ d'enfant** pram (*Brit*), baby carriage (*US*); **~ d'infirme** invalid carriage; **~ de course** racing car; **~ de sport** sports car

voix [vwa] *nf* voice; (*Pol*) vote; **la ~ de la conscience/raison** the voice of conscience/reason; **à haute ~** aloud; **à ~ basse** in a low voice; **faire la grosse ~** to speak gruffly; **avoir de la ~** to have a good voice; **rester sans ~** to be speechless; **~ de basse/ténor etc** bass/tenor *etc* voice; **à deux/quatre ~** (*Mus*) in two/four parts; **avoir ~ au chapitre** to have a say in the matter; **mettre aux ~** to put to the vote; **~-off** voice-over

vol [vɔl] *nm* (*mode de locomotion*) flying; (*trajet, voyage, groupe d'oiseaux*) flight; (*mode d'appropriation*) theft, stealing; (*larcin*) theft; **à ~ d'oiseau** as the crow flies; **au ~:** **attraper qch au vol** to catch sth as it flies past; **saisir une remarque au ~** to pick up a passing remark; **prendre son ~** to take flight; **de haut ~** (*fig*) of the highest order; **en ~** in flight; **~ avec effraction** breaking and entering *no pl*, break-in; **~ à l'étalage** shoplifting *no pl*; **~ libre** hang-gliding; **~ à main armée** armed robbery; **~ de nuit** night flight; **~ régulier** scheduled flight; **~ plané** (*Aviat*) glide, gliding *no pl*; **~ à la tire** pickpocketing *no pl*; **~ à voile** gliding

volage [vɔlaʒ] *adj* fickle

volaille [vɔlaj] *nf* (*oiseaux*) poultry *pl*; (*viande*) poultry *no pl*; (*oiseau*) fowl

volant, e [vɔlɑ̃, -ɑ̃t] *adj voir* **feuille** *etc* ▷ *nm* (*d'automobile*) steering wheel; (*de commande*) wheel; (*objet lancé*) shuttlecock; (*jeu*) battledore and shuttlecock; (*bande de tissu*) flounce; (*feuillet détachable*) tear-off portion; **le personnel ~, les ~s** (*Aviat*) the flight staff; **~ de sécurité** (*fig*) reserve, margin, safeguard

volcan [vɔlkɑ̃] *nm* volcano; (*fig: personne*) hothead

V

volée [vɔle] nf (*groupe d'oiseaux*) flight, flock; (*Tennis*) volley; **~ de coups/de flèches** volley of blows/arrows; **à la ~: rattraper à la volée** to catch in midair; **lancer à la ~** to fling about; **semer à la ~** to (sow) broadcast; **à toute ~** (*sonner les cloches*) vigorously; (*lancer un projectile*) with full force; **de haute ~** (*fig*) of the highest order

voler [vɔle] vi (*avion, oiseau, fig*) to fly; (*voleur*) to steal ▷ vt (*objet*) to steal; (*personne*) to rob; **~ en éclats** to smash to smithereens; **~ de ses propres ailes** (*fig*) to stand on one's own two feet; **~ au vent** to fly in the wind; **~ qch à qn** to steal sth from sb; **on m'a volé mon portefeuille** (*Brit*) ou billfold (*US*) has been stolen; **il ne l'a pas volé!** he asked for it!

volet [vɔle] nm (*de fenêtre*) shutter; (*Aviat*) flap; (*de feuillet, document*) section; (*fig: d'un plan*) facet; **trié sur le ~** hand-picked

voleur, -euse [vɔlœʀ, -øz] nm/f thief ▷ adj thieving; **"au ~!"** "stop thief!"

volière [vɔljɛʀ] nf aviary

volley [vɔlɛ], **volley-ball** [vɔlɛbol] nm volleyball

volontaire [vɔlɔ̃tɛʀ] adj (*acte, activité*) voluntary; (*délibéré*) deliberate; (*caractère, personne: décidé*) self-willed ▷ nm/f volunteer

volonté [vɔlɔ̃te] nf (*faculté de vouloir*) will; (*énergie, fermeté*) will(power); (*souhait, désir*) wish; **se servir/boire à ~** to take/drink as much as one likes; **bonne ~** goodwill, willingness; **mauvaise ~** lack of goodwill, unwillingness

volontiers [vɔlɔ̃tje] adv (*de bonne grâce*) willingly; (*avec plaisir*) willingly, gladly; (*habituellement, souvent*) readily, willingly; **"~"** "with pleasure", "I'd be glad to"

volt [vɔlt] nm volt

volte-face [vɔltəfas] nf inv about-turn; (*fig*) about-turn, U-turn; **faire ~** to do an about-turn; to do a U-turn

voltige [vɔltiʒ] nf (*Équitation*) trick riding; (*au cirque*) acrobatics sg; (*Aviat*) (aerial) acrobatics sg; **numéro de haute ~** acrobatic act

voltiger [vɔltiʒe] vi to flutter (about)

volubile [vɔlybil] adj voluble

volume [vɔlym] nm volume; (*Géom: solide*) solid

volumineux, -euse [vɔlyminø, -øz] adj voluminous, bulky

volupté [vɔlypte] nf sensual delight ou pleasure

vomi [vɔmi] nm vomit

vomir [vɔmiʀ] vi to vomit, be sick ▷ vt to vomit, bring up; (*fig*) to belch out, spew out; (*exécrer*) to loathe, abhor

vomissements [vɔmismɑ̃] nmpl (*action*) vomiting no pl; **des ~** vomit sg

vont [vɔ̃] vb voir **aller**

vorace [vɔʀas] adj voracious

vos [vo] adj poss voir **votre**

vote [vɔt] nm vote; **~ par correspondance/procuration** postal/proxy vote; **~ à main levée** vote by show of hands; **~ secret, ~ à bulletins secrets** secret ballot

voter [vɔte] vi to vote ▷ vt (*loi, décision*) to vote for

votre [vɔtʀ] (pl **vos**) [vo] adj poss your

vôtre [votʀ] pron: **le ~, la ~, les ~s** yours; **les ~s** (*fig*) your family ou folks; **à la ~** (*toast*) your (good) health!

voudrai etc [vudʀe] vb voir **vouloir**

voué, e [vwe] adj: **~ à** doomed to, destined for

vouer [vwe] vt: **~ qch à** (*Dieu/un saint*) to dedicate sth to; **sa vie/son temps à** (*étude, cause etc*) to devote one's life/time to; **~ une haine/amitié éternelle à qn** to vow undying hatred/friendship to sb

⊙ **MOT-CLÉ**

vouloir [vulwaʀ] nm: **le bon vouloir de qn** sb's goodwill; sb's pleasure
▷ vt **1** (*exiger, désirer*) to want; **vouloir faire/que qn fasse** to want to do/sb to do; **voulez-vous du thé?** would you like ou do you want some tea?; **vouloir qch à qn** to wish sth for sb; **que me veut-il?** what does he want with me?; **que veux-tu que je te dise?** what do you want me to say?; **sans le vouloir** (*involontairement*) without meaning to, unintentionally; **je voudrais ceci/faire** I would ou I'd like this/to do; **le hasard a voulu que ...** as fate would have it, ...; **la tradition veut que ...** tradition demands that ...; **... qui se veut moderne ...** which purports to be modern

2 (*consentir*): **je veux bien** (*bonne volonté*) I'll be happy to; (*concession*) fair enough, that's fine; **oui, si on veut** (*en quelque sorte*) yes, if you like; **comme tu veux** as you wish; (*en quelque sorte*) if you like; **veuillez attendre** please wait; **veuillez agréer ...** (*formule épistolaire*) yours faithfully

3: **en vouloir** (*être ambitieux*) to be out to win; **en vouloir à qn** to bear sb a grudge; **je lui en veux d'avoir fait ça** I resent his having done that; **s'en vouloir (de)** to be annoyed with o.s. (for); **il en veut à mon argent** he's after my money

4: **vouloir de** to want; **l'entreprise ne veut plus de lui** the firm doesn't want him any more; **elle ne veut pas de son aide** she doesn't want his help

5: **vouloir dire** to mean

voulu, e [vuly] pp de **vouloir** ▷ adj (*requis*) required, requisite; (*délibéré*) deliberate, intentional

vous [vu] pron you; (*objet indirect*) (to) you; (*réfléchi: sg*) yourself; (: pl) yourselves; (*réciproque*) each other ▷ nm: **employer le ~** (*vouvoyer*) to use the "vous" form; **~-même** yourself; **~-mêmes** yourselves

voûte [vut] *nf* vault; **la ~ céleste** the vault of heaven; **~ du palais** (*Anat*) roof of the mouth; **~ plantaire** arch (of the foot)

voûter [vute] *vt* (*Archit*) to arch, vault; **se voûter** *vi* (*dos, personne*) to become stooped

vouvoyer [vuvwaje] *vt*: **~ qn** to address sb as "vous"

voyage [vwajaʒ] *nm* journey, trip; (*fait de voyager*): **le ~** travel(ling); **partir/être en ~** to go off/be away on a journey *ou* trip; **faire un ~** to go on *ou* make a trip *ou* journey; **faire bon ~** to have a good journey; **les gens du ~** travelling people; **~ d'agrément/d'affaires** pleasure/business trip; **~ de noces** honeymoon; **~ organisé** package tour

voyager [vwajaʒe] *vi* to travel

voyageur, -euse [vwajaʒœʀ, -øz] *nm/f* traveller; (*passager*) passenger ▷ *adj* (*tempérament*) nomadic, wayfaring; **~ (de commerce)** commercial traveller

voyant, e [vwajɑ̃, -ɑ̃t] *adj* (*couleur*) loud, gaudy ▷ *nm/f* (*personne qui voit*) sighted person ▷ *nm* (*signal*) (warning) light ▷ *nf* clairvoyant

voyelle [vwajɛl] *nf* vowel

voyons *etc* [vwajɔ̃] *vb voir* **voir**

voyou [vwaju] *nm* lout, hoodlum; (*enfant*) guttersnipe

vrac [vʀak]: **en ~** *adv* loose; (*Comm*) in bulk

vrai, e [vʀɛ] *adj* (*véridique: récit, faits*) true; (*non factice, authentique*) real ▷ *nm*: **le ~** the truth; **à ~ dire** to tell the truth; **il est ~ que** it is true that; **être dans le ~** to be right

vraiment [vʀɛmɑ̃] *adv* really

vraisemblable [vʀɛsɑ̃blabl] *adj* (*plausible*) likely; (*excuse*) plausible; (*probable*) likely, probable

vraisemblablement [vʀɛsɑ̃blabləmɑ̃] *adv* in all likelihood, very likely

vraisemblance [vʀɛsɑ̃blɑ̃s] *nf* likelihood, plausibility; (*romanesque*) verisimilitude; **selon toute ~** in all likelihood

vrille [vʀij] *nf* (*de plante*) tendril; (*outil*) gimlet; (*spirale*) spiral; (*Aviat*) spin

vrombir [vʀɔ̃biʀ] *vi* to hum

VRP *sigle m* (= *voyageur, représentant, placier*) (sales) rep (*fam*)

VTT *sigle m* (= *vélo tout-terrain*) mountain bike

vu¹ [vy] *prép* (*en raison de*) in view of; **vu que** in view of the fact that

vu², e¹ [vy] *pp de* **voir** ▷ *adj*: **bien/mal vu** (*personne*) well/poorly thought of; (*conduite*) good/bad form ▷ *nm*: **au vu et au su de tous** openly and publicly; **ni vu ni connu** what the eye doesn't see …!, no one will be any the wiser; **c'est tout vu** it's a foregone conclusion

vue² [vy] *nf* (*fait de voir*): **la ~ de** the sight of; (*sens, faculté*) (eye)sight; (*panorama, image, photo*) view; (*spectacle*) sight; **vues** *nfpl* (*idées*) views; (*dessein*) designs; **perdre la ~** to lose one's (eye)sight; **perdre de ~** to lose sight of; **à la ~ de tous** in full view of everybody; **hors de ~** out of sight; **à première ~** at first sight; **connaître de ~** to know by sight; **à ~** (*Comm*) at sight; **tirer à ~** to shoot on sight; **à ~ d'œil** *adv* visibly; (*à première vue*) at a quick glance; **avoir ~ sur** to have a view of; **en ~** (*visible*) in sight; (*Comm: célèbre*) in the public eye; **avoir qch en ~** (*intentions*) to have one's sights on sth; **en ~ de faire** with the intention of doing, with a view to doing; **~ d'ensemble** overall view; **~ de l'esprit** theoretical view

vulgaire [vylgɛʀ] *adj* (*grossier*) vulgar, coarse; (*trivial*) commonplace, mundane; (*péj: quelconque*): **de ~s touristes/chaises de cuisine** common tourists/kitchen chairs; (*Bot, Zool: non latin*) common

vulgariser [vylgaʀize] *vt* to popularize

vulnérable [vylneʀabl] *adj* vulnerable

V

W   X

wagon [vagɔ̃] *nm* (*de voyageurs*) carriage; (*de marchandises*) truck, wagon
wagon-lit (*pl* **wagons-lits**) [vagɔ̃li] *nm* sleeper, sleeping car
wagon-restaurant (*pl* **wagons-restaurants**) [vagɔ̃ʀɛstɔʀɑ̃] *nm* restaurant *ou* dining car
wallon, ne [walɔ̃, -ɔn] *adj* Walloon ▷ *nm* (*Ling*) Walloon ▷ *nm/f*: **W~, ne** Walloon
waters [watɛʀ] *nmpl* toilet *sg*, loo *sg* (*Brit*)
watt [wat] *nm* watt
WC [vese] *nmpl* toilet *sg*, lavatory *sg*
Web [wɛb] *nm inv*: **le ~** the (World Wide) Web
webcam [wɛbkam] *nf* webcam
webmaster [-mastœʀ], **webmestre** [-mɛstʀ] *nm/f* webmaster
week-end [wikɛnd] *nm* weekend
western [wɛstɛʀn] *nm* western
whisky (*pl* **whiskies**) [wiski] *nm* whisky
widget [widʒɛt] *nm* (*Inform*) widget
wifi [wifi] *nm inv* wifi
WWW *sigle m* (= *World Wide Web*) WWW

xénophobe [gzenɔfɔb] *adj* xenophobic ▷ *nm/f* xenophobe
xérès [gzeʀɛs] *nm* sherry
xylophone [gzilɔfɔn] *nm* xylophone

y z

y [i] *adv* (*à cet endroit*) there; (*dessus*) on it (*ou* them); (*dedans*) in it (*ou* them) ▷ *pron* (*about ou on ou of*) it (*vérifier la syntaxe du verbe employé*); **j'y pense** I'm thinking about it; **ça y est!** that's it!; *voir aussi* **aller; avoir**

yacht [jɔt] *nm* yacht

yaourt [jauʀt] *nm* yogurt; **~ nature/aux fruits** plain/fruit yogurt

yeux [jø] *nmpl de* **œil**

yoga [jɔga] *nm* yoga

yoghourt [jɔguʀt] *nm* = **yaourt**

yougoslave [jugɔslav] *adj* Yugoslav(ian) ▷ *nm/f:* **Y~** Yugoslav(ian)

Yougoslavie [jugɔslavi] *nf:* **la ~** Yugoslavia; **l'ex-~** the former Yugoslavia

zapper [zape] *vi* to zap

zapping [zapiŋ] *nm:* **faire du ~** to flick through the channels

zébré, e [zebʀe] *adj* striped, streaked

zèbre [zɛbʀ] *nm* (*Zool*) zebra

zélé, e [zele] *adj* zealous

zèle [zɛl] *nm* zeal, diligence, assiduousness; **faire du ~** (*péj*) to be over-zealous

zéro [zeʀo] *nm* zero, nought (*Brit*); **au-dessous de ~** below zero (Centigrade), below freezing; **partir de ~** to start from scratch; **réduire à ~** to reduce to nothing; **trois (buts) à ~** three (goals) to nil

zeste [zɛst] *nm* peel, zest; **un ~ de citron** a piece of lemon peel

zézayer [zezeje] *vi* to have a lisp

zigzag [zigzag] *nm* zigzag

zigzaguer [zigzage] *vi* to zigzag (along)

Zimbabwe [zimbabwe] *nm:* **le ~** Zimbabwe

zinc [zɛ̃g] *nm* (*Chimie*) zinc; (*comptoir*) bar, counter

zipper [zipe] *vt* (*Inform*) to zip

zizanie [zizani] *nf:* **semer la ~** to stir up ill-feeling

zizi [zizi] *nm* (*fam*) willy (*Brit*), peter (*US*)

zodiaque [zɔdjak] *nm* zodiac

zona [zona] *nm* shingles *sg*

zone [zon] *nf* zone, area; (*quartiers pauvres*): **la ~** the slums; **de seconde ~** (*fig*) second-rate; **~ d'action** (*Mil*) sphere of activity; **~ bleue** ≈ restricted parking area; **~ d'extension** *ou* **d'urbanisation** urban development area;

~ **franche** free zone; ~ **industrielle (ZI)**
industrial estate; ~ **piétonne** pedestrian
precinct; ~ **résidentielle** residential area;
~ **tampon** buffer zone
zoo [zoo] *nm* zoo
zoologie [zɔɔlɔʒi] *nf* zoology
zoologique [zɔɔlɔʒik] *adj* zoological
zut [zyt] *excl* dash (it)! (*Brit*), nuts! (*US*)

L'anglais en situation

French in action

Collaborateurs/Contributors

Rose Rociola Daphne Day

Coordination/Coordination

Isobel Gordon

Introduction

The aim of **French in action** is to help you express yourself simply but correctly in fluent, natural French.

The **Sentence builder** section provides hundreds of phrases in which the key elements have been translated, providing an invaluable point of reference when you then construct your own sentences.

The section on correspondence provides practical models of personal and business letters, job applications and CVs, together with examples of standard opening and closing formulae and information on how to address an envelope. This section also offers guidance notes to help the user adapt these models to his/her needs.

A separate section covers fax and e-mail correspondence as well as all the expressions you might need to make different types of phone calls.

We hope you will find **French in action** both relevant and useful and that, used in conjunction with the dictionary, it will improve your understanding and enjoyment of French.

Contents

Introduction

L'anglais en situation a pour objectif de vous aider à vous exprimer en anglais, dans un style simple et naturel.

Dans le **Mémo des tournures essentielles**, vous trouverez des centaines d'expressions anglaises de base, qui vous permettront de construire vos propres phrases dans toutes sortes de contextes.

La partie correspondance contient des modèles de lettres de tous genres, dont vous pourrez vous inspirer pour rédiger à votre tour vos lettres, que ce soit dans un contexte privé ou professionnel. Si vous êtes à la recherche d'un travail, vous y trouverez également des exemples de curriculum vitæ et de lettres de candidature. Pour vous permettre d'adapter ces modèles à vos besoins, nous vous donnons en outre une liste des formules de politesse employées en début et en fin de lettre.

La dernière partie est consacrée à la communication par télécopie, par courrier électronique et par téléphone, et comprend une liste des expressions de base les plus couramment utilisées au téléphone.

L'anglais en situation, complément indispensable de votre dictionnaire, vous permettra de vous exprimer avec aisance dans toutes les situations.

Table des matières

Likes, dislikes and preferences

Saying what you like

J'aime les gâteaux.	I like ...
J'aime que les choses soient à leur place.	I like ...
J'ai bien aimé le film.	I liked ...
J'adore sortir en boîte.	I love ...
Ce que je préfère chez Laurent, c'est son enthousiasme.	What I like most ...
Ce que j'aime par-dessus tout, c'est son sourire.	What I like most of all is ...
La visite des vignobles m'a beaucoup plu.	I very much enjoyed ...
J'ai un faible pour le chocolat.	I've got a weakness for ...
Rien ne vaut un bon café.	You can't beat ...
Rien de tel qu'un bon bain chaud !	There's nothing better than ...
Le couscous est mon plat favori.	My favourite ...
La lecture est une de mes activités préférées.	... one of my favourite ...
Cela ne me déplaît pas de sortir seule.	I don't mind ...

Saying what you dislike

Je n'aime pas le poisson.	I don't like ...
Je n'aime pas beaucoup parler en public.	I'm not very keen on ...
Je ne l'aime pas du tout.	I don't like ... at all.
Cette idée ne m'emballe pas.	I'm not particularly keen on ...
Je déteste la chimie.	I hate ...
J'ai horreur du sport.	I loathe ...
Je ne supporte pas qu'on me mente.	I can't stand ...
Sa façon d'agir ne me plaît pas du tout.	I don't like ... at all.
Ce que je déteste le plus, c'est le repassage.	What I hate most is ...

Saying what you prefer

Je préfère le rock à la musique classique.	I prefer ... to ...
Je préférerais vivre à Paris.	I would rather ...
J'aimerais mieux mourir de faim que de lui demander un service.	I'd sooner ... than ...

Expressing indifference

Ça m'est égal.	It's all the same to me.
Je n'ai pas de préférence.	I have no preference either way.
C'est comme vous voudrez.	As you wish.
Cela n'a aucune importance.	It doesn't matter in the least.
Peu importe.	I don't mind.

Asking what someone likes

Est-ce que vous aimez les frites ?	Do you like ...
Est-ce que vous aimez faire la cuisine ?	Do you like ...
Est-ce que cela vous plaît de vivre en ville ?	Do you like ...
Qu'est-ce que vous préférez : la mer ou la montagne ?	Which do you like better ...
Vous préférez lequel, le rouge ou le noir ?	Which do you prefer ...
Est-ce que vous préférez vivre à la campagne ou en ville ?	Do you prefer ...
Qu'est-ce que vous aimez le plus à la télévision ?	What do you like best ...

Opinions

Asking for opinions

Qu'en pensez-vous ?	What do you think about it?
Que pensez-vous de sa façon d'agir ?	What do you think of ...
Je voudrais savoir ce que vous pensez de son travail.	I'd like to know what you think of ...
J'aimerais connaître votre avis sur ce problème.	I would like to know your views on ...
Est-ce que vous pourriez me donner votre opinion sur cette émission ?	What do you think of ...
Quelle est votre opinion sur la peine de mort ?	What is your opinion on ...
À votre avis, hommes et femmes sont-ils égaux ?	In your opinion ...
Selon vous, faut-il donner plus de liberté aux jeunes ?	In your opinion ...

Expressing opinions

Vous avez raison.	You are right.
Il a tort.	He is wrong.
Il a eu tort de démissionner.	He was wrong to ...
Je pense que ce sera possible.	I think ...
Je crois que c'est un peu prématuré.	I think ...
Je trouve que c'est normal.	I think ...
Personnellement, je pense que c'est trop cher.	Personally, I think that ...
Il me semble que vous vous trompez.	I think ...
J'ai l'impression que ses parents ne la comprennent pas.	I get the impression that ...
Je suis certain qu'il est tout à fait sincère.	I'm sure ...
Je suis sûr que Marc va gagner.	I'm sure ...
Je suis persuadé qu'il y a d'autres solutions.	I am convinced that ...
À mon avis, il n'a pas changé.	In my opinion ...
D'après moi, il a fait une erreur.	In my view ...
Selon moi, c'est impossible.	In my view ...

Being noncommittal

Ça dépend.	It depends.
Tout dépend de ce que vous entendez par là.	It all depends what you mean by ...
Je ne peux pas me prononcer.	I'd rather not express an opinion.
Je n'ai pas d'opinion bien précise à ce sujet.	I have no definite opinion on this.
Je ne me suis jamais posé la question.	I have never thought about it.

Approval and agreement

Je trouve que c'est une excellente idée.	I think it's an excellent idea.
Quelle bonne idée !	What a good idea!
J'ai beaucoup apprécié son article.	I was very impressed by ...
C'est une très bonne chose.	It's a very good thing.
Je trouve que vous avez raison de vous méfier.	I think you're right to ...
Les journaux **ont raison de** publier ces informations.	... are right to ...

Vous avez **bien fait de** laisser vos bagages à la consigne.	You were right to ...
Vous **n'avez pas tort de** critiquer le gouvernement.	You're quite justified in ...
Je partage cette opinion.	I share this view.
Je partage votre inquiétude.	I fully share your ...
Nous sommes favorables à la création d'emplois.	We are in favour of ...
Nous sommes en faveur d'une Europe unie.	We are in favour of ...
Il est exact que c'est un risque à prendre.	It is true that ...
Il est vrai que cette erreur aurait pu être évitée.	It is true that ...
Je suis d'accord avec vous.	I agree with you.
Je suis entièrement d'accord avec toi.	I entirely agree with you.

Disapproval and disagreement

Je trouve qu'il a eu tort d'emprunter autant d'argent.	I think he was wrong to ...
Il est dommage qu'il ait réagi ainsi.	It's a pity that ...
Il est regrettable qu'ils ne nous aient pas prévenus.	It is regrettable that ...
Cette idée **me déplaît profondément.**	I dislike ... intensely.
Je ne supporte pas le mensonge.	I can't stand ...
Nous sommes contre la chasse.	We are against ...
Je refuse cette solution.	I reject ...
Je suis opposé à toute forme de censure.	I am opposed to ...
Je ne partage pas ce point de vue.	I don't share this point of view.
Je suis déçu par son attitude.	I am disappointed by ...
Je suis profondément déçu.	I am deeply disappointed.
Tu n'aurais pas dû lui parler sur ce ton.	You shouldn't have ...
Nous ne pouvons accepter de voir la situation se dégrader.	We can't stand by and ...
De quel droit agit-**il** de la sorte ?	What gives him the right to ...
Je ne suis pas d'accord.	I disagree.
Nous ne sommes pas d'accord avec eux.	We don't agree with ...
Je ne suis absolument pas d'accord avec ce qu'il a dit.	I totally disagree with ...
C'est faux de dire que cette erreur était inévitable.	It is wrong to say that ...
Vous vous trompez !	You're wrong!

Apologies

How to say sorry

Excusez-moi.	Sorry.
Excusez-moi de vous déranger.	Sorry to bother you.
Oh, pardon ! J'ai dû faire un faux numéro.	Oh, sorry!
Je suis désolé de vous avoir réveillé.	I am sorry I ...
Je suis désolé pour tout ce qui s'est passé.	I am sorry about ...
Je vous prie de m'excuser.	I do apologize.
Nous prions nos lecteurs **de bien vouloir excuser** cette omission.	We hope ... will excuse ...

Admitting responsibility

C'est (de) ma faute : j'aurais dû partir plus tôt.	It's my fault, I should have ...
Je n'aurais pas dû me moquer d'elle.	I shouldn't have ...
Nous avons eu tort de ne pas vérifier cette information.	We were wrong not to ...
J'assume seul l'entière responsabilité de cette erreur.	I take full responsibility for ...
Si seulement j'avais préparé ma leçon !	If only I had ...

Disclaiming responsibility

Ce n'est pas (de) ma faute.	It's not my fault.
Ce n'est pas (de) ma faute si nous sommes en retard.	It isn't my fault if ...
Je ne l'ai pas fait exprès.	I didn't do it on purpose.
Je ne pouvais pas faire autrement.	I had no other option.
J'avais pourtant cru comprendre que je pouvais me garer là.	But I thought that ...
J'avais cru bien faire en le prévenant.	I thought I was doing the right thing in ...

Apologizing for being unable to do something

Je regrette, mais ce n'est pas possible.	I'm sorry, but ...
Je suis désolé, mais je ne peux pas vous aider.	I'm sorry, but ...
Il nous est malheureusement impossible d'accéder à votre demande.	Unfortunately, it's impossible for us to ...

Explanations

Causes

Je n'ai rien acheté **parce que** je n'ai pas d'argent.	... because ...
Je suis arrivé en retard **à cause des** embouteillages.	... because of ...
Puisque tu insistes, je rentre dans une semaine.	Since ...
Comme j'habitais près de la bibliothèque, j'y allais souvent.	As ...
J'ai réussi à m'en sortir **grâce au** soutien de . mes amis	... thanks to ...
Je ne pourrai pas venir **car** je n'ai pas fini.	... as ...
Vu la situation actuelle, nous ne pouvons pas nous prononcer.	Given ...
Étant donné la crise, il est difficile de trouver du travail.	Given ...
C'est une rupture d'essieu **qui a provoqué** le déraillement.	It was ... that caused ...
Le théâtre va fermer **faute de** moyens.	... due to lack of ...
Il a donné sa démission **pour des raisons de** santé.	... for ... reasons.
Le projet a été abandonné **en raison de** problèmes juridiques.	... owing to ...
Le malaise des enseignants **est lié à** la difficulté de leur métier.	... is linked to ...
Le problème vient de ce que les gens ont peur des ordinateurs.	The problem is that ...
Le ralentissement des exportations **provient de** la chute de la demande européenne.	... is the result of ...
La haine **résulte de** l'incompréhension.	... results from ...

Consequences

Je dois partir ce soir. Je ne pourrai **donc** pas venir avec vous.	... so ...
La distribution a été améliorée, **de telle sorte que** les lecteurs trouveront leur journal plus tôt.	... so that ...
Le cidre nouveau est très peu fermenté et **par conséquent** très peu alcoolisé.	... consequently ...
Ce manque de concertation **a eu pour conséquence** une duplication inutile de nos efforts.	... has resulted in ...
Voilà pourquoi on s'en souvient.	That's why ...

Comparisons

On peut comparer la télévision **à** une drogue.	... can be compared to ...
C'est une très belle performance **que l'on peut comparer à** celle des meilleurs athlètes.	... which can be compared to ...
Le Centre Pompidou **est souvent comparé à** un paquebot.	... is often compared to ...
Le bruit **était comparable à** celui d'une moto dépourvue de silencieux.	... was comparable to ...
L'Afrique reste un continent sous-peuplé **comparé à** l'Asie.	... compared with ...
Par comparaison avec l'Islande, l'Irlande a un climat tropical.	Compared to ...
Les investissements publicitaires ont connu une légère progression **par rapport à** l'année dernière.	... compared to ...
Cette histoire **ressemble à** un conte de fées.	... is like ...
Il adorait cette campagne qui **lui rappelait** l'Irlande.	... reminded him of ...
Des taux de chômage effrayants, **rappelant ceux** des années 30.	... reminiscent of those ...
Il me fait penser à mon frère.	He reminds me of ...
Le surf des neiges **est l'équivalent** sur neige **de** la planche à roulettes.	... is the equivalent ... of ...
Cette somme **correspond à** six mois de salaire.	... corresponds to ...
C'est la même chose.	It's the same thing.
Cela revient au même.	It comes to the same thing.
Ce disque **n'est ni meilleur ni moins bon que** les autres.	... is no better and no worse than ...

Stressing differences

Aucune catastrophe **ne peut être comparée au** tsunami de 2004.	No ... can compare with ...
On ne peut pas comparer les usines modernes **à** celles où travaillaient nos grands-parents.	... cannot be compared with ...
Les actions de ce groupe **n'ont rien de comparable avec** les agissements des terroristes.	... are in no way comparable to ...
Sa démarche le **différencie de** son frère.	... distinguishes ... from ...
L'histoire des États-Unis **ne ressemble en rien à** la nôtre.	... in no way resembles ...
Il y a des événements bien plus tragiques que de perdre une finale de Coupe d'Europe.	There are worse things than ...
Le gruyère **est meilleur que** le comté.	... is better than ...

Son deuxième film **est moins** réussi **que** le premier.	... is less ... than ...
L'espérance de vie des femmes est de 81 ans, **tandis que** celle des hommes est de 72 ans.	... while ...
Alors que la consommation de vin et de bière diminue, l'eau minérale est un marché en expansion.	While ...

Requests and offers

Requests

Je voudrais trois tartelettes.	I'd like ...
Je voudrais connaître les horaires des trains pour Lille.	I'd like to ...
Pourriez-vous nous donner un coup de main ?	Could you ...
Est-ce que vous pouvez annoncer la bonne nouvelle à Éliane ?	Can you ...
Est-ce que vous pourriez venir me chercher ?	Could you ...
Sois gentille, fais un saut chez le boulanger.	Be an angel ...
Auriez-vous l'amabilité de m'indiquer la sortie ?	Could you please ...
Auriez-vous la gentillesse de nous donner la recette ?	Would you be so kind as to ...
Auriez-vous l'obligeance de me garder ma place ?	Would you be very kind and ...
Puis-je vous demander de m'accorder un instant ?	Could you ...
Merci de bien vouloir patienter.	If you wouldn't mind ...
Est-ce que cela vous dérangerait d'ouvrir la fenêtre ?	Would you mind ...
Je vous serais reconnaissant de me prévenir dès que possible.	I would be grateful if you would ...
Je vous serais reconnaissant de bien vouloir me communiquer votre décision d'ici vendredi.	I would be grateful if you would ...

Offers

Je peux passer vous prendre, **si** vous voulez.	I can ... if ...
Je pourrais vous accompagner.	I could ...
Ça te dirait, une glace ?	Do you fancy ...
Ça vous dirait d'aller faire un tour ?	Would you like to ...
Que diriez-vous d'une balade en forêt ?	How do you fancy ...
Est-ce que vous voulez que j'aille chercher votre voiture ?	Do you want me to ...
Est-ce que vous voulez dîner avec nous un soir ?	Would you like to ...

Advice and suggestions

Asking for advice or suggestions

À ma place, que feriez-vous ?	What would you do, if you were me?
Quel est votre avis sur la question ?	What's your opinion on the matter?
Qu'est-ce que vous me conseillez, les Baléares ou les Canaries ?	Which would you recommend ...
Que me conseillez-vous de faire ?	What would you advise me to do?
Parmi les excursions à faire, laquelle nous conseilleriez-vous ?	... which would you recommend?
Quelle stratégie proposez-vous ?	What ... do you suggest?
Que proposez-vous pour réduire la pollution ?	What, in your opinion, should be done to ...
Qu'est-ce que vous proposez contre le chômage ?	How would you deal with ...

Offering advice or suggestions

À votre place, je me méfierais.	If I were you ...
Si j'étais toi, je ne dirais rien.	If I were you ...
Je peux vous donner un conseil : achetez votre billet à l'avance.	If I may give you a bit of advice ...
Un conseil : lisez le mode d'emploi.	A word of advice ...
Un bon conseil : n'attendez pas le dernier moment pour faire votre réservation.	A useful tip ...
Vous devriez voir un spécialiste.	You should ...
Vous feriez bien de consulter un avocat.	You would do well to ...
Vous feriez mieux d'acheter une nouvelle voiture.	You would do better to ...
Vous pourriez peut-être demander à quelqu'un de vous le traduire.	You could perhaps ...
Vous pourriez montrer un peu plus de compréhension.	You could ...
Pourquoi ne pas lui téléphoner ?	Why don't you ...
Il faudrait peut-être essayer autre chose.	Perhaps we ought to ...
Et si on allait au cinéma ?	How about ...
Je vous propose le 3 mars à 10 h 30.	How about ...
Il vaudrait mieux lui offrir de l'argent qu'un bijou.	It might be better to ...
Il serait préférable d'attendre le résultat.	It would be better to ...

Warnings

Je vous préviens, je ne me laisserai pas faire.	I warn you …
Je te préviens que ça ne sera pas facile.	I'd better warn you that …
N'oubliez pas de conserver le double de votre déclaration d'impôts.	Don't forget to …
Méfiez-vous des apparences.	Remember: appearances can be deceptive.
Surtout, n'y allez **jamais** le samedi.	Whatever you do, don't …
Si tu ne viens pas, **tu risques de** le regretter.	… you risk …

Intentions and desires

Asking what someone intends to do

Qu'est-ce que vous allez faire ?	What are you going to do?
Qu'est-ce que tu vas faire si tu rates ton examen ?	What will you do if …
Qu'allez-vous faire en rentrant? **Avez-vous des projets ?**	What are you going to do … ? Do you have anything planned?
Quels sont vos projets ?	What are your plans?
Est-ce que tu comptes passer tes vacances ici ?	Are you planning to …
Vous comptez rester longtemps ?	Are you planning on …
Que comptez-vous faire de votre collection ?	What are you planning to do with …
Comment comptez-vous faire ?	What are you thinking of doing?
Tu as l'intention de passer des concours ?	Do you intend to …
Songez-vous à refaire un film en Europe ?	Are you thinking of …

Talking about intentions

Je comptais m'envoler pour Ajaccio le 8 juillet.	I was planning to …
Elle prévoit de voyager pendant un an.	She plans to …
Il est prévu de construire un nouveau stade.	There are plans to …
Ils envisagent d'avoir plusieurs enfants.	They are thinking of …
Cette banque **a l'intention de** fermer un grand nombre de succursales.	… intends to …
Je songe à abandonner la politique.	I am thinking of …
J'ai décidé de changer de carrière.	I have decided to …
Je suis décidée à arrêter de fumer.	I have made up my mind to …

Je me suis **décidée à** y aller.	I have decided to ...
C'est décidé, nous partons à la campagne.	That's settled ...
Il n'a jamais été dans nos intentions de lui cacher la vérité.	We never had any intention of ...
Il n'est pas question pour moi **de** renoncer à ce projet.	There is no question of ...

Wishes

Je veux faire du cinéma.	I want to ...
Je voudrais savoir jouer aussi bien que lui.	I'd like to ...
J'aimerais faire du deltaplane.	I'd like to ...
J'aimerais que mes photos soient publiées dans la presse.	I would like ...
J'aurais aimé avoir un frère.	I would have liked to ...
Lionel **voulait à tout prix** partir le soir-même.	... wanted at all costs ...
Nous souhaitons préserver notre indépendance.	We wish to ...
J'espère avoir des enfants.	I hope to ...
Nous espérons que les enfants regarderont cette émission avec leurs parents.	We hope that ...
Vous rêvez de faire le tour du monde ?	Do you dream of ...
Mon rêve serait d'avoir une grande maison.	My dream would be to ...

Obligation

Il faut que je me trouve un logement.	I must ...
Il faut absolument qu'on se revoie avant le 23 !	We really must ...
Si vous allez en Pologne, **vous devez** venir nous voir.	... you must ...
Les auteurs du détournement **ont exigé que** l'avion reparte vers New York.	... demanded that ...
Ça **me force à** faire de l'exercice.	... makes me ...
Une violente crise d'asthme **m'a obligé à** consulter un médecin.	... forced me to ...
Je suis obligé de partir.	I have to ...
Il est obligé de travailler, **il n'a pas le choix.**	He has to ... he has no other option.
On ne peut pas faire autrement que d'accepter.	You have no choice but to ...
L'école **est obligatoire** jusqu'à seize ans.	... is compulsory ...
Il est indispensable de voyager pour comprendre les autres.	It is essential to ...

Permission

Asking for permission

Je peux téléphoner ?	Can I ...
Je peux vous demander quelque chose ?	Can I ...
Est-ce que je peux passer vous dire un petit bonjour tout à l'heure ?	Can I ...
Ça ne vous dérange pas si j'arrive en avance ?	Is it alright if ...
Ça ne vous dérange pas que je fume ?	Do you mind if ...
Est-ce que ça vous dérange si j'ouvre la fenêtre ?	Do you mind if ...
Vous permettez, Madame, **que** je regarde ce qu'il y a dans votre sac ?	Would you mind if ...

Giving permission

(Vous) faites comme vous voulez.	Do as you please.
Allez-y !	Go ahead!
Je n'y vois pas d'inconvénient.	I have nothing against it.
Vous avez le droit de porter plainte.	You have the right to ...

Saying something is not allowed

Je te défends de sortir !	I forbid you to ...
C'est défendu.	It's forbidden.
Il est interdit de fumer dans les toilettes.	... is forbidden.
Le travail des enfants **est formellement interdit par** une convention de l'ONU.	... is strictly forbidden by ...
Défense d'entrer.	No entry.
Stationnement interdit.	No parking.
Interdiction de stationner.	No parking.
C'est interdit.	It's not allowed.
Elle interdit à ses enfants **d'**ouvrir la porte.	She forbids ... to ...
Tu n'as pas le droit.	You're not allowed.
On n'avait pas le droit de manger ni de boire pendant le service.	We weren't allowed to ...
Il n'en est pas question.	That's out of the question.

Certainty, probability and possibility

Certainty

Il est certain qu'il y aura des problèmes.	Undoubtedly …
Il ne fait aucun doute que ce produit connaîtra un réel succès.	There is no doubt that …
Il est évident qu'il traverse une période difficile.	Clearly …
C'est **de toute évidence** la seule chose à faire.	Quite obviously …
Il est indéniable qu'il a eu tort d'agir ainsi.	It is undeniable that …
Je suis sûre que mon frère te plaira.	I am sure that …
Je suis sûr de gagner.	I am sure that I …
Je suis certain que nous sommes sur la bonne voie.	I am certain that …
J'ai la certitude qu'en travaillant avec lui, je ne m'ennuierai pas.	I am sure that …
Je suis persuadé qu'il y a d'autres solutions.	I am convinced that …

Probability

Il est probable que le prix du pétrole va continuer d'augmenter.	… probably …
Le taux d'inflation dépassera **très probablement** les 10 %.	… very probably …
80 % des problèmes de peau sont **sans doute** d'origine psychique.	… undoubtedly …
Ils avaient **sans doute** raison.	… no doubt …
Les travaux **devraient** débuter au mois d'avril.	… should …
Il se pourrait bien qu'ils cherchent à tester nos réactions.	It is quite possible that …
On dirait que tout lui est égal.	It's as if …
Il a dû oublier d'ouvrir les fenêtres.	He must have …

Possibility

C'est possible.	It is possible.
Il est possible que cela coûte plus cher.	That might …
Il n'est pas impossible qu'il soit parti à Paris.	It is not impossible that …
Il se pourrait que l'Amérique ait été découverte par des Chinois.	It is possible that …
Il se peut que ce virus soit particulièrement virulent.	… may …
En quelques mois tout **peut** changer.	… could …
Il a **peut-être** mal compris.	Maybe …
Peut-être que je me trompe.	Perhaps …

Doubt, improbability and impossibility

Doubt

Je ne suis pas sûr que ce soit utile.	I'm not sure …
Je ne suis pas sûre d'y arriver.	I'm not sure I'll …
Je ne suis pas certain d'avoir raison.	I'm not sure I'm …
Il n'est pas certain que cela soit une bonne idée.	I'm not sure that …
Il n'est pas certain qu'un vaccin puisse être mis au point.	I'm not sure that …
Je me demande si nous avons fait beaucoup de progrès dans ce domaine.	I wonder if …
Est-ce sage ? **J'en doute.**	I doubt it.
Il se mit à **douter de** la compétence de son médecin.	… to have doubts about …
Je doute fort qu'il accepte de rester inactif.	I very much doubt …
On ne sait pas exactement ce qui s'est passé.	Nobody knows exactly …

Improbability

Il **ne** changera **probablement pas** d'avis.	… probably won't …
Il est peu probable qu'il reste encore des places.	It is unlikely that …
Ça m'étonnerait qu'ils aient ta pointure.	I'd be surprised if …
Il serait étonnant que tout se passe conformément aux prévisions.	It would be amazing if …
Nous ne risquons pas de nous ennuyer.	There's no danger of …
Elles ne risquent pas d'avoir le prix Nobel d'économie.	They are not likely to …
Il y a peu de chances que le taux de croissance dépasse 1,5 %.	There is not much chance of …

Impossibility

C'est impossible.	It's impossible.
Il n'est pas possible qu'il n'y ait rien à faire.	It is not possible that …
Il est impossible que ces renseignements soient faux.	… cannot …
Il n'y a aucune chance qu'ils viennent à notre secours.	There is no chance of …

Greetings

Bonjour !	Hello!
Bonsoir !	Good evening!
Salut !	Hi!
Comment allez-vous ?	How are you?
Comment ça va ?	How's things?

What to say in reply

Très bien, merci, et vous ?	Fine thanks, and you?
Ça va, et toi ?	Fine thanks, and you?
Super bien !	Great!
On fait aller.	So-so.
Couci-couça.	So-so.

Introductions

Je vous présente Charles.	This is ...
Je vous présente mon amie.	May I introduce ...
Marc ; Laurent	Marc, this is Laurent; Laurent, Marc.
Je ne crois pas que vous vous connaissiez.	I don't believe you know one another.

Replying to an introduction

Enchanté.	Pleased to meet you.
Enchanté or Ravi de faire votre connaissance.	Pleased to meet you.
Salut, moi c'est Dominique.	Hi, I'm ...

Leavetaking

Au revoir !	Goodbye!
Bonne nuit !	Good night!
Salut !	Bye!
Ciao !	See you!
À bientôt !	See you later!
À demain !	See you tomorrow!
À la semaine prochaine !	See you next week!
À jeudi !	See you Thursday!

Best wishes

Bon anniversaire !	Happy Birthday!
Joyeux Noël !	Merry Christmas!
Bonne année !	Happy New Year!
Félicitations !	Congratulations!
Bon voyage !	Safe journey!
Bonne chance !	Good luck!
Bienvenue !	Welcome!
Amusez-vous bien !	Have fun!
Bon appétit !	Enjoy your meal!
(À votre) santé !	Cheers!
Tchin-tchin !	Cheers!

Correspondence

How to address an envelope

On the front

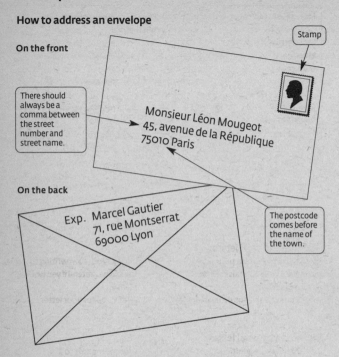

Stamp

There should always be a comma between the street number and street name.

Monsieur Léon Mougeot
45, avenue de la République
75010 Paris

On the back

Exp. Marcel Gautier
71, rue Montserrat
69000 Lyon

The postcode comes before the name of the town.

Common abbreviations used in addresses

av. = avenue	bd = boulevard	Exp. = expéditeur
fg = faubourg	pas. = passage	pl. = place

Standard opening and closing formulae
In personal correspondence

Cher Monsieur	**Je vous envoie mes bien amicales pensées** *(fairly formal)*
Chers Jean et Sylvie	**Bien amicalement**
Chère tante Laure	**Je t'embrasse bien affectueusement**
Mon cher Laurent	**Grosses bises** *(very informal)*

In formal correspondence

Monsieur le Directeur (or le Maire etc) Madame le Directeur	Je vous prie d'agréer, [...], l'assurance de ma considération distinguée
Messieurs Monsieur Madame	Je vous prie d'agréer, [...], l'assurance de mes sentiments distingués or Veuillez accepter, [...], l'expression de mes sentiments distingués
Cher Monsieur Chère Madame	Croyez, [...], à l'expression de mes sentiments les meilleurs

Starting a personal letter

Je te remercie de ta lettre ...
Thanks for your letter ...

J'ai été très content d'avoir de tes nouvelles.
It was lovely to hear from you.

Je suis désolé de ne pas vous avoir répondu plus vite.
I'm sorry I didn't reply sooner.

Starting a formal letter

Suite à ... je vous écris pour ...
Further to ... I am writing to ...

Je vous serais reconnaissant de ...
I would be grateful if you would ...

Je vous prie de ...
Please ...

Nous vous remercions de votre lettre ...
Thank you for your letter ...

Ending a personal letter

Transmettez mes amitiés à ...
Give my regards to ...

Dis bonjour à ... de ma part.
Say hello to ... for me.

... t'embrasse ...
... sends you his love ...

Embrasse ... pour moi.
Give my love to ...

Ending a formal letter

Dans l'attente de votre réponse ...
I look forward to hearing from you ...

Je demeure à votre entière disposition pour toute information complémentaire.
I will be happy to supply any further information you may require.

Je vous remercie dès à présent de ...
Thank you in advance for ...

Thank you letter

Name and address of sender.

The town or city from which the letter is being sent should be included along with the date. The article **le** should be included in the date.

Anne et Cyrille Legendre
25, rue des Grillons
69000 LYON

Lyon, le 24 octobre 2007

Chers oncle et tante,

Le grand jour, c'était il y a presqu'un mois déjà ...
Ce fut une merveilleuse fête et nous étions très heureux
de vous avoir parmi nous.

Nous tenons à vous remercier chaleureusement de votre
gentil cadeau et nous vous inviterons bientôt pour
inaugurer ce superbe service à raclette comme
il se doit.

Vous trouverez aussi ci-joint une photo-souvenir.

Nous vous embrassons tous les deux,

Anne et Cyrille

For alternatives see p20.

Hotel booking

Name and address of letter's recipient.

Jeanne Judon
89, bd des Tertres
75008 PARIS

Hôtel Renoir
15, rue de Beaumanoir
59000 LILLE

Paris, le 3 novembre 2007

Madame ou Monsieur,

For alternatives see p21.

Me rendant à Lille le mois prochain à l'occasion du Salon de l'esthétique, j'aimerais réserver une chambre avec salle de bains pour deux nuits le mercredi 5 et le jeudi 6 décembre 2007.

Je vous saurais gré de me communiquer vos tarifs et de me confirmer que vous avez bien une chambre libre à cette époque.

Je vous prie de croire, Madame, Monsieur, à l'assurance de mes sentiments distingués.

Jeanne Judon

Letter of complaint

M et Mme DAUNAY
La Longue Haie
35135 CHANTEPIE

Hôtel "Au Bon Accueil "
17, rue Nationale
86000 POITIERS

Chantepie, le 29 décembre 2007

Madame, Monsieur,

Mon mari et moi avons passé la nuit du 23 décembre dans votre hôtel, où nous avions préalablement réservé une chambre. Nous tenons à vous faire savoir que nous avons été très déçus par vos services, en particulier par le bruit – nous avons pourtant demandé une chambre calme – et l'impossibilité de se faire servir un petit déjeuner avant notre départ à 6 h 30.

Cet arrêt dans votre hôtel qui devait nous permettre de nous reposer au cours d'un long voyage en voiture n'a fait que nous fatiguer davantage. Sachez que nous prendrons bien soin de déconseiller votre établissement à nos amis.

Je vous prie d'agréer, Madame, Monsieur, mes salutations distinguées.

For alternatives see p21.

Curriculum Vitæ

The words **courriel** or **mél** can also be used.

CURRICULUM VITÆ

LEGUEN Maxime
29, rue de Vannes
35000 RENNES
Tél : 56 02 71 28

29 ans
célibataire
nationalité française

Adresse électronique : mleguen@agriventes.com.fr

EXPÉRIENCE PROFESSIONNELLE

Du 10.3.05 à ce jour :   Adjointe du directeur à l'exportation, Agriventes, Rennes

Du 8.10.03 au 30.1.05 :   Secrétaire de direction, France-Exportations, Cognac

DIPLÔMES

2003 :   Diplôme de secrétaire bilingue, délivré par l'École de commerce de Poitiers

2002 :   Licence de langues étrangères appliquées (anglais et russe), Université de Poitiers – plusieurs mentions

1998 :   Baccalauréat (langues) – mention assez bien

AUTRES RENSEIGNEMENTS

Langues étrangères : anglais et russe (courant), allemand (bonnes connaissances)

Stage d'information dans le cadre de la formation continue, 2005

Permis de conduire

Nombreux voyages en Europe et aux États-Unis

If you have British or American etc qualifications you should use wording such as "**équivalence baccalauréat (3 A-levels), équivalence licence de lettres (BA Hons)**" etc.

Job application

This is appropriate if you are writing to a company. However, if you are writing to the holder of a particular post use the following:
Monsieur (or Madame) le Directeur des ressources humaines
Société GERBAULT etc and begin the letter:
Monsieur le Directeur des ressources humaines,
If you know the name of the person you should use the following:
Monsieur Alain Dupont
Directeur des ressources humaines
Société GERBAULT etc and begin the letter:
Monsieur,

Maxime LEGUEN
29, rue de Vannes
35000 RENNES

Service du Personnel
Société GERBAULT
85, bd de la Liberté
35000 RENNES

Rennes, le 12 juillet 2007

Madame, Monsieur,

Votre annonce parue dans le Monde du 8 juillet concernant un poste d'assistante de direction dans votre service Import-Export m'a particulièrement intéressée.

Mon expérience de quatre ans en tant qu'assistante de direction dans le service d'exportation d'une petite entreprise m'a permis d'acquérir un sens des responsabilités ainsi qu'une grande capacité d'adaptation. Le poste que vous proposez m'intéresse tout particulièrement car j'aimerais beaucoup pouvoir utiliser ma connaissance de la langue et de la culture russe dans le cadre de mon travail.

Je me tiens à votre disposition pour vous apporter de plus amples renseignements sur ma formation et mon expérience.

Je vous prie, Madame, Monsieur, de bien vouloir agréer mes salutations distinguées.

Maxime Leguen

Maxime Leguen
P.J. : CV

= pièces jointes. You should add this if you are enclosing any other information with your letter eg a CV.

Invitation to interview

SOCIÉTÉ GERBAULT

85, bd de la Liberté
35000 RENNES
TÉLÉPHONE : 02 99 45 32 88 • TÉLÉCOPIE : 02 99 45 32 90

Maxime LEGUEN
29, rue de Vannes
35000 RENNES

Rennes, le 19 juillet

Madame,

Votre candidature au poste d'assistante de direction au sein de notre Compagnie a retenu notre attention.

Nous vous proposons, dans le but de faire plus ample connaissance de part et d'autre, de rencontrer :

Monsieur LAURENT

notre Directeur Régional, le 26 juillet prochain, à 9 h, à l'adresse suivante :

2, bd de Lattre de Tassigny
35000 RENNES

Si cette date ne vous convenait pas, vous seriez aimable d'avertir notre secrétariat (Tél : 02 99 45 32 88) afin de convenir d'un autre rendez-vous.

Nous vous prions de croire, Madame, à l'expression de nos sentiments distingués.

Jean Minet
Jean Minet

For alternatives see p21.

Fax

France-Sanitaires S.A.

55, rue de Strasbourg
75012 Paris
Téléphone : 01 63 13 84 20
Télécopie : 01 63 13 84 32

TÉLÉCOPIE

À : Mme Robin

Date : le 7 janvier 2007

De : M. Edmond
Service clientèle

Nombre de pages à suivre : 1

Réf. : Devis pour installation salle de bains.

Madame,

Suite à notre visite d'avant-hier, veuillez trouver ci-joint notre devis pour l'installation d'une salle de bains dans votre appartement. Les prix comprennent la fourniture du matériel ainsi que la main d'oeuvre.

Dans l'attente de votre réponse, je vous prie, Madame, d'agréer l'expression de mes meilleurs sentiments,

Y. Edmond

E-Mail

Sending messages

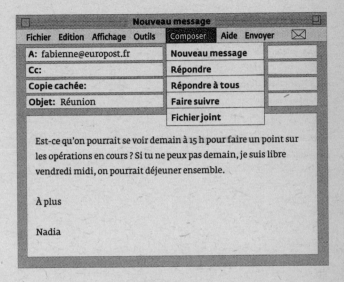

Fichier	File
Édition	Edit
Affichage	View
Outils	Tools
Composer	Compose
Aide	Help
Envoyer	Send
Nouveau message	New
Répondre	Reply to Sender

E-Mail

Receiving messages

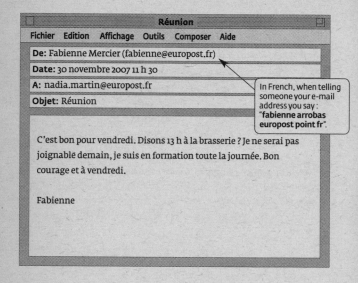

Réunion

Fichier   Edition   Affichage   Outils   Composer   Aide

De: Fabienne Mercier (fabienne@europost.fr)

Date: 30 novembre 2007 11 h 30

A: nadia.martin@europost.fr

Objet: Réunion

In French, when telling someone your e-mail address you say : **"fabienne arrobas europost point fr".**

C'est bon pour vendredi. Disons 13 h à la brasserie ? Je ne serai pas joignable demain, je suis en formation toute la journée. Bon courage et à vendredi.

Fabienne

Répondre à tous	Reply to All
Faire suivre	Forward
Fichier joint	Attachment
À	To
Cc	Cc (carbon copy)
Copie cachée	Bcc (blind carbon copy)
Objet	Subject
De	From
Date	Sent

TELEPHONE

Different types of call

Communication locale/interurbaine.
Je voudrais appeler l'étranger.

Je voudrais appeler Londres en PCV.

Comment est-ce que je peux téléphoner
à l'extérieur ?

Local/national call.
I want to make an international call.

I want to make a reverse charge call (Brit) to a … number or I want to call a … number collect (US).

How do I get an outside line?

Asking for information

Quel est le numéro des renseignements ?

Je voudrais le numéro de la société Europost,
20, rue de la Marelle, à Pierrefitte.
Quel est l'indicatif de la Martinique ?
Quel est le numéro de l'horloge parlante ?

What is the number for directory enquiries (Brit) or directory assistance (US)?

Can you give me the number of …
What is the code for …
What is the number for the speaking clock?

Receiving information

Le numéro que vous avez demandé est
le 01 40 32 37 12. (zéro-un quarante
trente-deux trente-sept douze)
Je regrette, mais il n'y a pas d'abonné
à ce nom.
Le numéro que vous avez demandé est
sur liste rouge.

The number you require is …

I'm sorry, there's no listing under that name.

The number you require is ex-directory (Brit) or unlisted (US).

When your number answers

Je voudrais parler à or Pourrais-je parler à
M. Wolff, s'il vous plaît ?
Pourriez-vous me passer le docteur
Henderson, s'il vous plaît ?
Pourriez-vous me passer le poste 52 64,
s'il vous plaît ?
Je rappellerai dans une demi-heure.
Pourriez-vous lui demander de me rappeler
à son retour ?

Could I speak to …

Could you put me through to …

Can I have extension …

I'll call back in …
Would you ask him to ring me when he gets back?

The switchboard operator speaks

C'est de la part de qui ?	Who shall I say is calling?
Je vous le passe.	I'm putting you through.
J'ai un appel de Tokyo pour Mme Thomson.	I have a call from … for …
J'ai Mlle Martin en ligne.	I've got … on the line.
Le docteur Roberts est en ligne, vous patientez ?	… is on another line. Do you want to wait?
Ne quittez pas.	Please hold.
Ça ne répond pas.	There's no reply.
Voulez-vous laisser un message ?	Would you like to leave a message?

Recorded messages

Le numéro de votre correspondant n'est plus attribué. Veuillez consulter l'annuaire ou votre centre de renseignements.	The number you have dialled has not been recognized. Please consult the directory or directory enquiries.
Le numéro de votre correspondant a changé. Veuillez composer désormais le 33 42 21 70.	The number you have dialled has been changed to …
Par suite de l'encombrement des lignes, votre appel ne peut aboutir. Veuillez rappeler ultérieurement.	All the lines are busy right now. Please try again later.
Bonjour, vous êtes en communication avec le service des ventes. Veuillez patienter, nous allons donner suite à votre appel dans quelques instants.	Hello, you have reached … Please wait, your call will be answered shortly.
Bonjour, vous êtes bien chez M. et Mme Martin. Laissez un message après le bip sonore et nous vous rappellerons dès notre retour. Merci.	Hello, you are through to … Leave a message after the tone and we'll get back to you.

Answering the telephone

Allô, c'est Anne à l'appareil.	Hello, it's … speaking.
C'est moi or lui-même (or elle-même).	Speaking.
Qui est à l'appareil ?	Who's speaking?

When in trouble

Je n'arrive pas à avoir le numéro.	I can't get through.
Leur téléphone est en dérangement.	Their phone is out of order.
Nous avons été coupés.	We have been cut off.
J'ai dû faire un faux numéro.	I must have dialled the wrong number.
La ligne est très mauvaise.	This is a very bad line.

Goûts et préférences

Pour dire ce que l'on aime

I **like** cakes.	J'aime …
I **like** things to be in their proper place.	J'aime que …
I **really liked** the film.	J'ai bien aimé …
I **love** going to clubs.	J'adore …
What I like best about Matthew are his eyes.	Ce que je préfère …
What I enjoy most is an evening with friends.	Ce que j'aime par-dessus tout, c'est …
I **very much enjoyed** the trip to the vineyards.	… m'a beaucoup plu.
I've never tasted **anything better than** this chicken.	… rien … de meilleur que …
I've got a **weakness for** chocolate cakes.	J'ai un faible pour …
You can't beat a good cup of tea.	Rien ne vaut …
There's nothing quite like a nice hot bath!	Rien de tel que …
My favourite dish is lasagne.	… mon … favori.
Reading is **one of my favourite** pastimes.	… une de mes … préférées.
I **don't mind** being alone.	Cela ne me déplaît pas de …

Pour dire ce que l'on n'aime pas

I **don't like** fish.	Je n'aime pas …
I **don't like** him **at all**.	Je ne … aime pas du tout.
I'm **not very keen on** speaking in public.	Je n'aime pas beaucoup …
I'm **not particularly keen on** the idea.	… ne m'emballe pas.
I **hate** chemistry.	Je déteste …
I **loathe** sport.	J'ai horreur du …
I **can't stand** being lied to.	Je ne supporte pas que …
If there's one thing I hate it's ironing.	Ce que je déteste le plus, c'est de …

Préférences

I **prefer** pop **to** classical music.	Je préfère … à …
I **would rather** live in Paris.	Je préférerais …
I'd **rather** starve **than** ask him a favour.	J'aimerais mieux … que de …

Indifférence

It's **all the same to me**.	Ça m'est égal.
I have **no particular preference**.	Je n'ai pas de préférence.
As you like.	C'est comme vous voudrez.

It doesn't matter in the least.	Cela n'a aucune importance.
I don't mind.	Peu importe.

Comment demander à quelqu'un ce qu'il aime

Do you like chocolate?	Est-ce que vous aimez ...
Do you like cooking?	Est-ce que vous aimez ...
Which do you like better: football or cricket?	Qu'est-ce que vous préférez : ...
Which would you rather have: the red one or the black one?	Lequel préférez-vous : ...
Do you prefer living in the town or in the country?	Est-ce que vous préférez ...
What do you like best on television?	Qu'est-ce que vous aimez le plus ...

Opinions

Comment demander l'avis de quelqu'un

What do you think about it?	Qu'en pensez-vous ?
What do you think about divorce?	Que pensez-vous du ...
What do you think of his behaviour?	Que pensez-vous de ...
I'd like to know what you think of his work.	Je voudrais savoir ce que vous pensez de ...
I would like to know your views on this.	J'aimerais connaître votre avis sur ...
What is your opinion on the team's chances of success?	Quelle est votre opinion sur ...
Could you give me your opinion on this proposal?	Est-ce que vous pourriez me donner votre avis sur ...
In your opinion, are men and women equal?	À votre avis ...
In your view, is this the best solution?	Selon vous ...

Comment donner son avis

You are right.	Vous avez raison.
He is wrong.	Il a tort.
He was wrong to resign.	Il a eu tort de ...
I think it ought to be possible.	Je pense que ...

I **think** it's a bit premature.	Je crois que ...
I **think** it's quite natural.	Je trouve que ...
Personally, I think that it's a waste of money.	Personnellement, je pense que ...
I **have the impression that** her parents don't understand her.	J'ai l'impression que ...
I'**m sure** he is completely sincere.	Je suis certain que ...
I'**m convinced that** there are other possibilities.	Je suis persuadé que ...
In my opinion, he hasn't changed.	À mon avis ...
In my view, he's their best player.	Selon moi ...

Comment éviter de donner son avis

It depends.	Ça dépend.
It all depends on what you mean by patriotism.	Tout dépend de ce que vous entendez par ...
I'd rather not express an opinion.	Je préfère ne pas me prononcer.
Actually, I've never thought about it.	À vrai dire, je ne me suis jamais posé la question.

Approbation et accord

I think it's an excellent idea.	Je trouve que c'est une excellente idée.
What a good idea!	Quelle bonne idée !
I **was very impressed by** his speech.	J'ai beaucoup apprécié ...
It's a very good thing.	C'est une très bonne chose.
I think **you're right to** be wary.	Je trouve que vous avez raison de ...
Newspapers **are right to** publish these stories.	... ont raison de ...
You were right to leave your bags in left-luggage.	Vous avez bien fait de ...
Third World countries **rightly believe that** most pollution comes from developed countries.	... estiment à juste titre que ...
You're quite justified in complaining.	Vous avez bien raison de ...
I **share** this view.	Je partage cette opinion.
I **fully share** your concern.	Je partage ...
We **support** the creation of jobs.	Nous sommes favorables à ...
We **are in favour of** a united Europe.	Nous sommes en faveur de ...

It is true that mistakes were made.
I agree with you.
I entirely agree with you.

Il est vrai que ...
Je suis d'accord avec vous.
Je suis entièrement
  d'accord avec toi.

Désapprobation et désaccord

I think he was wrong to borrow so much money.
It's a pity that you didn't tell me.
It is regrettable that they allowed this to happen.
I dislike the idea intensely.

Je trouve qu'il a eu tort de ...
Il est dommage que ...
Il est regrettable que ...
... me déplaît
  profondément.

I can't stand lies.
We are against hunting.
We do not condone violence.
I am opposed to compulsory screening.
I don't share this point of view.

Je ne supporte pas ...
Nous sommes contre ...
Nous ne tolérons pas ...
Je suis opposé au ...
Je ne partage pas ce point
  de vue.

I am disappointed by his attitude.
I am deeply disappointed.
You shouldn't have said that.
What gives him the right to act like this?
I disagree.
We don't agree with them.

Je suis déçu par ...
Je suis profondément déçu.
Tu n'aurais pas dû ...
De quel droit ...
Je ne suis pas d'accord.
Nous ne sommes pas
  d'accord avec ...

I totally disagree with what he said.

Je ne suis absolument pas
  d'accord avec ...

It is not true to say that the disaster was
  inevitable.
You are wrong!

C'est faux de dire que ...

Vous vous trompez !

Excuses

Pour s'excuser
Sorry.
Oh, sorry! I've got the wrong number.
Sorry to bother you.

Excusez-moi.
Oh, pardon !
Excusez-moi de vous
  déranger.

I'm **sorry** I woke you.	Je suis désolé de ...
I'm **terribly sorry about** the misunderstanding.	Je suis navré de ...
I **do apologize.**	Je vous prie de m'excuser.
We **hope** our readers **will excuse** this oversight.	Nous prions ... de bien vouloir excuser ...

En assumant la responsabilité de ce qui s'est passé

It's **my fault; I should have** left earlier.	C'est (de) ma faute : j'aurais dû ...
I **shouldn't have** laughed at her.	Je n'aurais pas dû ...
We **were wrong not to** check this information.	Nous avons eu tort de ne pas ...
I **take full responsibility for** what I did.	J'assume seul l'entière responsabilité de ...
If only I had done my homework!	Si seulement j'avais ...

En niant toute responsabilité

It's **not my fault.**	Ce n'est pas (de) ma faute.
It **isn't my fault if** we're late.	Ce n'est pas (de) ma faute si ...
I **didn't do it on purpose.**	Je ne l'ai pas fait exprès.
I **had no option.**	Je ne pouvais pas faire autrement.
But I thought that it was okay to park here.	J'avais pourtant cru comprendre que ...
I **thought I was doing the right thing in** warning him.	J'avais cru bien faire en ...

En exprimant ses regrets

I'm **sorry, but** it's impossible.	Je regrette, mais ...
I'm **afraid** we're fully booked.	Je regrette, mais ...
Unfortunately we are unable to meet your request.	Il nous est malheureusement impossible de ...

Explications

Causes

I didn't buy anything **because** I had no money.	... parce que ...
I arrived late **because of** the traffic.	... à cause de ...
Since you insist, I'll come again tomorrow.	Puisque ...
As I lived near the library, I used it a lot.	Comme ...
I got through it **thanks to** the support of my friends.	... grâce à ...
Given the present situation, finding a job will be difficult.	Vu ...
Given that there is an economic crisis, it is difficult to find work.	Étant donné ...
Considering how many problems we had, we did well.	Étant donné ...
It was a broken axle **that caused** the derailment.	C'est ... qui a provoqué ...
He resigned **for** health **reasons.**	... pour des raisons de ...
The theatre is closing, **due to lack of** funds.	... faute de ...
The project was abandoned **owing to** legal problems.	... en raison de ...
Many cancers **are linked to** smoking.	... sont dus à ...
The problem is that people are afraid of computers.	Le problème vient de ce que ...
The drop in sales **is the result of** high interest rates.	... est due à ...
The quarrel **resulted from** a misunderstanding.	... a pour origine ...

Conséquences

I have to leave tonight; **so** I can't come with you.	... donc ...
Distribution has been improved **so that** readers now get their newspaper earlier.	... de telle sorte que ...
This cider is fermented for a very short time and is **consequently** low in alcohol.	... par conséquent ...
Our lack of consultation **has resulted in** a duplication of effort.	... a eu pour conséquence ...
That's why they are easy to remember.	Voilà pourquoi ...

Comparaisons

Gambling **can be compared to** a drug.	On peut comparer ... à ...
The gas has a smell **that can be compared to** rotten eggs.	... que l'on peut comparer à ...

The shape of Italy **is often compared to** a boot.	... est souvent comparé à ...
The noise **was comparable to** that of a large motorbike.	... était comparable à ...
Africa is still underpopulated **compared with** Asia.	... comparé à ...
In the UK, the rate of inflation increased slightly **compared to** the previous year.	... par rapport à ...
What is so special about a holiday in Florida **as compared to** one in Spain?	... par rapport à ...
This story **is like** a fairy tale.	... ressemble à ...
He loved this countryside, which **reminded him of** Ireland.	... lui rappelait ...
Frightening levels of unemployment, **reminiscent of those** of the 30s.	... rappelant ceux ...
The snowboard **is the equivalent** on snow **of** the skateboard.	... est l'équivalent ... de ...
This sum **corresponds to** six months' salary.	... correspond à ...
A 'bap'? **It's the same thing as** a bread roll.	C'est la même chose que ...
It comes to the same thing in terms of calories.	Ça revient au même ...
This record **is no better and no worse than** the others.	... n'est ni meilleur ni moins bon que ...

Pour souligner une différence

No catastrophe **can compare with** the tsunami of 2004.	Aucune ... ne peut être comparée à ...
Modern factories **cannot be compared with** those our grandparents worked in.	On ne peut pas comparer ... à ...
The actions of this group **are in no way comparable to** those of terrorists.	... n'ont rien de comparable avec ...
The newspaper reports **differ** on this point.	... divergent ...
The history of the United States **in no way resembles** our own.	... ne ressemble en rien à ...
There are worse things than losing a European cup final.	Il y a des événements bien plus tragiques que ...
This film **is less** interesting **than** his first one.	... est moins ... que ...
Women's life expectancy is 81 years, **while** men's is 72.	... tandis que ...
While the consumption of wine and beer is decreasing, the consumption of bottled water is increasing.	Alors que ...

Demandes et propositions

Demandes

I'd like another beer.	Je voudrais ...
I'd like to know the times of trains to Lille.	Je voudrais ...
Could you give us a hand?	Pourriez-vous ...
Can you tell Eleanor the good news?	Est-ce que vous pouvez ...
Could you please show me the way out?	Auriez-vous l'obligeance de ...
Could I ask you for a few minutes of your time?	Puis-je vous demander de ...
Be an angel, pop to the baker's for me.	Sois gentille ...
If you wouldn't mind waiting for a moment.	Merci de bien vouloir ...
Would you mind opening the window?	Est-ce que cela vous dérangerait de ...
Would you be very kind and save my seat for me?	Auriez-vous l'obligeance de ...
I would be grateful if you could reply as soon as possible.	Je vous serais reconnaissant de ...

Propositions

I can come and pick you up **if** you like.	Je peux ... si ...
I could go with you.	Je pourrais ...
Do you fancy a bit of Stilton?	Ça te dit ...
How about a pear tart?	Que diriez-vous de ...
Would you like to see my photos?	Ça vous dirait de ...
Would you like to have dinner with me one evening?	Est-ce que vous voulez ...
Do you want me to go and get your car?	Est-ce que vous voulez que ...

Conseils et suggestions

Comment demander conseil

What would you do, if you were me?	À ma place, que feriez-vous ?
Would you accept, **if you were me?**	À ma place ...
What's your opinion on this?	Quel est votre avis sur la question ?
What, in your opinion, should be done to reduce pollution?	Que proposez-vous pour ...
What would you advise?	Que me conseillez-vous ?

What would you advise me to do?	Que me conseillez-vous de faire ?
Which would you recommend, Majorca or Ibiza?	Qu'est-ce que vous me conseillez …
If we were to sponsor a player, **who would you recommend?**	… lequel nous conseilleriez-vous ?
What strategy **do you suggest?**	Quelle … proposez-vous ?
How would you deal with unemployment?	Qu'est-ce que vous proposez contre …

Comment donner un conseil

If I were you, I'd be a bit wary.	À votre place …
If I were you I wouldn't say anything.	À ta place …
Take my advice, buy your tickets in advance.	Je vous conseille de …
A word of advice: read the instructions.	Un conseil …
A useful tip: always have some pasta in your cupboard.	Un bon conseil …
As you like languages, **you ought to** study as a translator.	… vous devriez …
You should see a specialist.	Vous devriez …
You would do well to see a solicitor.	Vous feriez bien de …
You would do better to spend the money on a new car.	Vous feriez mieux de …
You could perhaps ask someone to go with you.	Vous pourriez peut-être …
You could try being a little more understanding.	Vous pourriez …
Perhaps you should speak to a plumber about it.	Il faudrait peut-être que …
Perhaps we ought to try a different approach.	Il faudrait peut-être …
Why don't you phone him?	Pourquoi ne pas …
How about renting a video?	Et si on …
How about 3 March at 10.30am?	… ça vous va ?
It might be better to give her money rather than jewellery.	Il vaudrait peut-être mieux …
It would be better to wait a bit.	Il serait préférable de …

Mises en garde

I warn you, I intend to get my own back.	Je vous préviens …
I'd better warn you that he knows you did it.	Mieux vaut que je te prévienne …
Don't forget to keep a copy of your income tax return.	N'oubliez pas de …

Remember: appearances can be deceptive.	Méfiez-vous des apparences.
Beware of buying tickets from touts.	Attention ...
Whatever you do, don't leave your camera in the car.	Surtout, ne ... jamais ...
If you don't book early **you risk** being disappointed.	... tu risques de ...

Intentions et souhaits

Pour demander à quelqu'un ce qu'il compte faire

What are you going to do?	Qu'est-ce que vous allez faire ?
What will you do if you fail your exams?	Qu'est-ce que tu vas faire si ...
What are you going to do when you get back?	Qu'allez-vous faire ...
Do you have anything planned?	Avez-vous des projets ?
Can we expect you next Sunday?	On compte sur vous ...
Are you planning to spend all of the holiday here?	Est-ce que tu comptes ...
Are you planning on staying long?	Vous comptez ...
What are you planning to do with your collection?	Que comptez-vous faire de ...
What are you thinking of doing?	Que comptez-vous faire ?
Do you intend to go into teaching?	Est-ce que tu as l'intention de ...
Are you thinking of making another film in Europe?	Songez-vous à ...

Pour dire ce qu'on a l'intention de faire

I was planning to go to Ajaccio on 8 July.	Je comptais ...
She plans to go to India for a year.	Elle prévoit de ...
There are plans to build a new stadium.	Il est prévu de ...
The bank **intends to** close a hundred branches.	... a l'intention de ...
I am thinking of giving up politics.	Je songe à ...
I have decided to get a divorce.	J'ai décidé de ...
I have made up my mind to stop smoking.	Je suis décidé à ...
We never had any intention of talking to the press.	Il n'a jamais été dans nos intentions de ...
That's settled, we'll go to Florida in May.	C'est décidé ...
For me, living abroad **is out of the question.**	Il n'est pas question ... de ...

Souhaits

I'd like to be able to play as well as him.	Je voudrais ...
I'd like to go hang-gliding.	J'aimerais ...
I would like my photos to be published.	J'aimerais que ...
I would like to have had a brother.	J'aurais aimé ...
I want to act in films.	Je veux ...
Ian **wanted at all costs** to prevent his boss finding out.	... voulait à tout prix ...
We wish to preserve our independence.	Nous souhaitons ...
I hope to have children.	J'espère ...
We hope that children will watch this programme with their parents.	Nous espérons que ...
Do you dream of winning the lottery?	Vous rêvez de...
I dream of having a big house.	Mon rêve serait de ...

Obligation

I must find somewhere to live.	Il faut que je ...
We really must see each other more often!	Il faut absolument qu'on ...
If you're going to Poland, **you must** learn Polish.	... vous devez ...
He **made** his secretary answer all his calls.	... exigeait que ...
My mother **makes me** eat spinach.	... me force à ...
The hijackers **demanded that** the plane fly to New York.	... ont exigé que ...
A serious illness **forced me to** cancel my holiday.	... m'a obligé à ...
He **was obliged to** borrow more and more money.	... a été obligé de ...
Mary **had no choice but to** invite him.	... n'avait pas pu faire autrement que de ...
The only thing you can do is say no.	Tu ne peux pas faire autrement que de ...
Many mothers **have to** work; **they have no other option.**	... sont obligées de ... elles n'ont pas le choix.
She had the baby adopted because **she had no other option.**	... elle ne pouvait pas faire autrement.
School **is compulsory** until the age of sixteen.	... est obligatoire ...
It is essential to know some history, if we are to understand the situation.	Il est indispensable de ...

Permission

Comment demander la permission de faire quelque chose

Can I use the phone?	Je peux ...
Can I ask you something?	Je peux ...
Is it okay if I come now, or is it too early?	Ça ne vous dérange pas si ...
Do you mind if I smoke?	Ça ne vous dérange pas que ...
Do you mind if I open the window?	Est-ce que ça vous dérange si ...
Would you mind if I had a look in your briefcase, madam?	Vous permettez que ...
Could I have permission to leave early?	Est-ce que je peux vous demander la permission de ...

Autorisation

Do as you please.	(Vous) faites comme vous voulez.
Go ahead!	Allez-y !
No, of course I don't mind.	Bien sûr que non.
I have nothing against it.	Je n'y vois pas d'inconvénient.
Pupils **are allowed to** wear what they like.	... ont le droit de ...

Défense

I forbid you to go out!	Je te défends de ...
It's forbidden.	C'est défendu.
Smoking in the toilet **is forbidden.**	Il est interdit de ...
Child labour is **strictly forbidden by** a UN convention.	... formellement interdit par ...
No entry!	Défense d'entrer !
No parking.	Stationnement interdit.
It's not allowed.	C'est interdit.
You are not allowed to swim in the lake.	Il est interdit de ...
We weren't allowed to eat or drink while on duty.	On n'avait pas le droit de ...
That's out of the question.	Il n'en est pas question.

Certitude, probabilité et possibilité

Certitude

Undoubtedly, there will be problems.
There is no doubt that the country's image has suffered.
It's bound to cause trouble.
Clearly the company is in difficulties.
A foreign tourist is **quite obviously** a rare sight here.
It is undeniable that she was partly to blame.
I am sure you will like my brother.
I am sure that I will win.
I'm sure that I won't get bored working with him.
I am certain that we are on the right track.
I am convinced that there are other solutions.

Il est certain que …
Il ne fait aucun doute que …
Cela va sûrement …
Il est évident que …
… de toute évidence …
Il est indéniable que …
Je suis sûre que …
Je suis sûr de …
J'ai la certitude que …
Je suis certain que …
Je suis persuadé que …

Probabilité

The price of petrol will **probably** rise.
Inflation will **very probably** exceed 10%.
It is highly probable that they will abandon the project.
The trend **is likely** to continue.
80% of skin problems **undoubtedly** have psychological origins.
They were **no doubt** right.
The construction work **should** start in April.
He must have forgotten to open the windows.

Il est probable que …
… très probablement …
Il est fort probable que …
Il est probable que …
… sans doute …
… sans doute …
… devrait …
Il a dû …

Possibilité

It's possible.
It is possible that they got your name from the electoral register.
It is not impossible that he has gone to Paris.

That **might be** more expensive.
He may have misunderstood.
This virus **may** be extremely infectious.
It may be that it will take time to achieve peace.
In a few months everything **could** change.
Perhaps I am mistaken.

C'est possible.
Il est possible que …
Il n'est pas impossible que …
Il se peut que …
Il a peut-être …
Il se peut que …
Il se peut que …
… peut …
Peut-être que …

Incertitude, improbabilité et impossibilité

Incertitude

I'm not sure it's useful.	Je ne suis pas sûr que ...
I'm not sure I'll manage.	Je ne suis pas certain de ...
I'm not sure that it's a good idea.	Je ne suis pas sûr que ...
We cannot be sure that the problem will be solved.	Il n'est pas sûr que ...
I very much doubt he'll adapt to not working.	Je doute fort que ...
Is it wise? **I doubt it.**	J'en doute.
He began to **have doubts about** his doctor's competence.	... douter de ...
I wonder if we've made much progress in this area.	Je me demande si ...
There is no guarantee that a vaccine can be developed.	Il n'est pas certain que ...
Nobody knows exactly what happened.	Personne ne sait exactement ...

Improbabilité

He **probably won't** change his mind.	... ne ... probablement pas ...
It is unlikely that there'll be any tickets left.	Il est peu probable que ...
I'd be surprised if they had your size.	Ça m'étonnerait que ...
They are not likely to get the Nobel prize for Economics!	Ils ne risquent pas de ...
There is not much chance the growth rate will exceed 1.5%.	Il y a peu de chances que ...
There's no danger we'll get bored.	Nous ne risquons pas de ...
It would be amazing if everything went according to plan.	Il serait étonnant que ...

Impossibilité

It's impossible.	C'est impossible.
It is not possible for the government to introduce this Bill before the recess.	Il n'est pas possible que ...
This information **cannot be** wrong.	Il est impossible que ...
There is no chance of their helping us.	Il n'y a aucune chance que ...

Salutations

Hello!	Bonjour !
Hi!	Salut !
Good morning!	Bonjour !
Good afternoon!	Bonjour !
Good evening!	Bonsoir !
How's it going?	Comment ça va ?
How's things?	Comment (ça) va ?
How's life?	Comment (ça) va ?
How are you?	Comment allez-vous ?

Réponses

Very well, and you?	Très bien, merci, et vous ?
Fine, thanks.	Bien, merci.
Great!	Super bien !
So-so.	Comme ci comme ça.
Could be worse.	On fait aller.

Présentations

This is Charles.	Je te présente ...
Let me introduce you to my girlfriend.	Je vous présente ...
I'd like you to meet my husband.	Je vous présente ...
I don't believe you know one another.	Je ne crois pas que vous vous connaissiez.

Une fois qu'on a été présenté

Pleased to meet you.	Enchanté.
Hello, how do you do?	Enchanté de faire votre connaissance.
Hi, I'm Jane.	Salut, moi c'est ...

Pour prendre congé

Bye!	Au revoir !
Goodbye!	Au revoir !
Good night!	Bonne nuit !
See you!	Ciao !
See you later!	À tout à l'heure !

See you soon!	À bientôt !
See you tomorrow!	À demain !
See you next week!	À la semaine prochaine !
See you Thursday!	À jeudi !

Vœux et félicitations

Happy Birthday!	Bon anniversaire !
Many happy returns!	Bon anniversaire !
Merry Christmas!	Joyeux Noël !
Happy New Year!	Bonne année !
Happy Anniversary!	Bon anniversaire de mariage !
Congratulations!	Félicitations !
Welcome!	Soyez les bienvenus !
Good luck!	Bonne chance !
Safe journey!	Bon voyage !
Have fun!	Amusez-vous bien !
Get well soon!	Bon rétablissement !
Take care!	Fais bien attention à toi !
Cheers!	(À votre) santé !
Enjoy your meal!	Bon appétit !

Correspondance

La rédaction de l'adresse en Grande-Bretagne

Timbre

Le code postal vient après le nom de la ville ou du département.

Mrs J.M. Mackintosh
129 Strathmore Ave
EDINBURGH
EH11 2AD
UK

La rédaction de l'adresse aux États-Unis

Timbre

MARK SMITH
968 MICHIGAN ST
SEATTLE WA 98060-1024
USA

Le code postal (**zip code**) vient après le nom de la ville et de l'État (en abrégé).

Abréviations couramment employées dans les adresses

Ave = avenue	Dr = drive	Pl = place	Sq = square
Cres = crescent	Gdns = gardens	Rd = road	St = street

Les formes d'adresse et les formules de politesse
Dans les lettres personnelles

Dear Mr and Mrs Roberts	Yours *(assez soutenu)*
Dear Kate and Jeremy	With best wishes
Dear Aunt Jane and Uncle Alan	Love from
Dear Granny	Lots of love from *(familier)*

Dans les lettres d'affaires

Dear Sirs	Yours faithfully
Dear Sir	
Dear Madam	
Dear Sir or Madam	
Dear Professor Meldrum	Yours sincerely
Dear Ms Gilmour	

Pour commencer une lettre personnelle

It was lovely to hear from you.	Cela m'a fait plaisir d'avoir de vos nouvelles.
Thanks for your letter ...	Merci pour ta lettre ...
Sorry I haven't written sooner.	Je suis désolé de ne pas t'avoir écrit plus tôt.

Pour commencer une lettre d'affaires

Thank you for your letter of ...	Je vous remercie de votre lettre du ...
In reply to your letter of ...	En réponse à votre lettre du ...
With reference to ...	Suite à ...
We are writing to you to ...	Nous vous écrivons pour ...
We are pleased to inform you ...	Nous avons le plaisir de vous informer ...
We regret to inform you ...	Nous sommes au regret de vous informer ...

Pour terminer une lettre personnelle

Write soon.	Écris-moi vite.
Give my regards to ...	Transmettez mes amitiés à ...
... sends his/her best wishes.	... me charge de transmettre ses amitiés.
Give my love to ...	Embrasse ... de ma part.

Pour terminer une lettre d'affaires

I look forward to hearing from you.	Dans l'attente de votre réponse.
Thanking you in advance for your help.	En vous remerciant à l'avance pour votre aide.
If you require any further information please do not hesitate to contact me.	N'hésitez pas à me contacter pour toute information complémentaire.

Lettre de remerciement

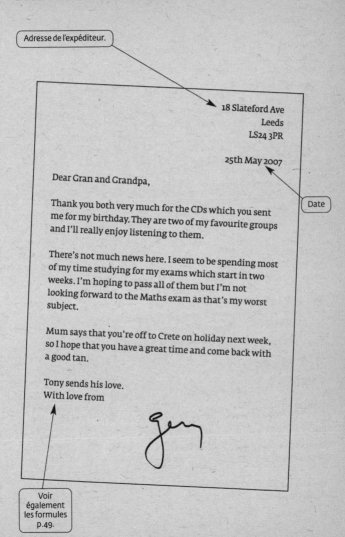

Adresse de l'expéditeur.

18 Slateford Ave
Leeds
LS24 3PR

25th May 2007

Date

Dear Gran and Grandpa,

Thank you both very much for the CDs which you sent me for my birthday. They are two of my favourite groups and I'll really enjoy listening to them.

There's not much news here. I seem to be spending most of my time studying for my exams which start in two weeks. I'm hoping to pass all of them but I'm not looking forward to the Maths exam as that's my worst subject.

Mum says that you're off to Crete on holiday next week, so I hope that you have a great time and come back with a good tan.

Tony sends his love.
With love from

Voir également les formules p.49.

Pour réserver une chambre d'hôtel

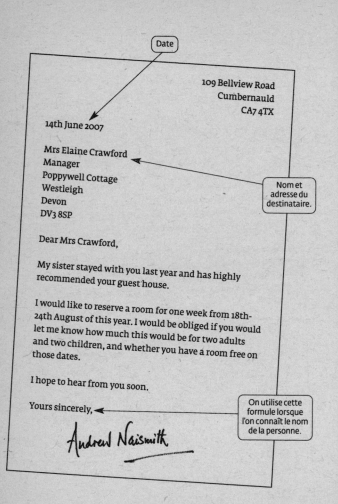

Date

109 Bellview Road
Cumbernauld
CA7 4TX

14th June 2007

Mrs Elaine Crawford
Manager
Poppywell Cottage
Westleigh
Devon
DV3 8SP

Nom et
adresse du
destinataire.

Dear Mrs Crawford,

My sister stayed with you last year and has highly recommended your guest house.

I would like to reserve a room for one week from 18th-24th August of this year. I would be obliged if you would let me know how much this would be for two adults and two children, and whether you have a room free on those dates.

I hope to hear from you soon.

Yours sincerely,

Andrew Naismith

On utilise cette
formule lorsque
l'on connaît le nom
de la personne.

Lettre de réclamation

Voir également les formules p.50.

85 Rush Lane
Triptown
Lancs
LC4 2DT

20th February 2007

Woodpecker Restaurant
145 Main Street
Triptown
Lancs
LC4 3EF

Dear Sir/Madam

I was to have dined in your restaurant last Thursday by way of celebrating my wedding anniversary with my wife and young son but am writing to let you know of our great dissatisfaction.

I had reserved a corner table for two with a view of the lake. However, when we arrived we had to wait for more than 20 minutes for a table and even then, not in the area which I had chosen. There was no highchair for my son as was promised and your staff made no effort whatsoever to accommodate our needs. In fact, they were downright discourteous. Naturally we went elsewhere, and not only have you lost any future custom from me, but I will be sure to advise my friends and colleagues against your establishment.

Yours faithfully

T. Greengage

On utilise cette formule lorsque l'on commence la lettre par **Dear Sir** etc.

Curriculum Vitæ

CURRICULUM VITÆ

Name: Rosalind A. Williamson
Address: 11 North Street, Barnton NE6 2BT
Telephone: 01294 476230
E-mail: rosalind@metalcomp.co.uk
Date of Birth: 18/4/1981
Nationality: British
Marital Status: Single

Pour les diplômes obtenus en France, mettre le nom du diplôme suivi d'une brève description en anglais entre parenthèses.

CAREER

2/05 to date: Sales and Marketing Executive, Metal Company plc, Barnton

11/03-1/05: Marketing Assistant, Metal Company plc

QUALIFICATIONS

1999-2003: University of Newby BA (Hons) Italian with French – 2:1

1992-1999: Barnton Comprehensive School
A-levels: English Literature (D), French (B), Italian (A)
GCSEs: Art, Chemistry, English Language, English Literature, French, German, Italian, Maths

OTHER SKILLS

Computer literate (Word for Windows, Excel, QuarkXPress), good keyboarding skills, full, clean driving licence.

INTERESTS

Travel (have travelled extensively throughout Europe and North Amercia), riding and sailing.

REFEREES

Ms Alice Bluegown
Sales and Marketing Manager
Metal Company plc
Barnton
NE4 3KL

Dr I.O. Sono
Department of Italian
University of Newby
Newby
S13 2RR

Il est d'usage d'indiquer sur son C.V. les noms de deux personnes prêtes à fournir une recommandation à l'employeur potentiel. L'une d'entre elles doit normalement être un ancien employeur, ou, pour les étudiants, un professeur.

Lettre de candidature

11 North Street
Barnton
NE6 2BY

18 August 2007

The Personnel Director
Clifton Manufacturing Ltd
Firebrick House
Clifton
MK45 6RB

Lorsqu'on ignore si le destinataire est un homme ou une femme, il convient d'utiliser la formule ci–contre. Toutefois, si l'on connaît le nom de la personne, on utilise la présentation suivante :
Mrs Lynn Kerr
Personnel Director
Clifton Manufacturing Ltd etc.
Pour commencer votre lettre, la formule à employer est la suivante :
Dear Mrs Kerr

Dear Sir or Madam

With reference to your advertisement in the Guardian of 15 August, I wish to apply for the position of Marketing Manager in your company.

I am currently employed as a Sales and Marketing Executive for the Metal Company in Barnton where my main role is maintaining and developing links with our customers within the UK and producing material for marketing purposes.

I am interested in this position as it offers an opportunity to apply my sales and marketing skills in a new and challenging direction. I enclose my Curriculum Vitae for your consideration. Please do not hesitate to contact me if you require any further details.

Yours faithfully

Rosalind Williamson

Enc.

On utilise cette formule lorsque l'on commence la lettre par **Dear Sir or Madam** etc.

= **enclosures.** On ajoute ceci lorsque l'on joint d'autres pièces à la lettre, un C.V. par exemple.

Pour proposer un entretien

Clifton Manufacturing Ltd.

Firebrick House • Clifton MK45 6RB
Tel: (01367) 345 900 • Fax: (01367) 345 901
E-mail: personnel@cliftman.co.uk

Ref: RW/LK

27 August 2007

Ms Rosalind Williamson
11 North Street
Barnton
NE6 2BT

Dear Ms Williamson

Following your recent application for the position of Marketing Manager, I would like to invite you to attend an interview at the above office on Friday 3 September at 11am.

The interview will be conducted by the Sales and Marketing Director and myself and should last approximately one hour.

If this date does not suit please notify Jane Simpson on extension 3287 to arrange an alternative date.

We look forward to meeting you.

Yours sincerely

Lynn Kerr

Lynn Kerr (Mrs)
Personnel Director

Télécopie

Brown & Sons

Northport Enterprise Park
Birmingham B45 6JH
Tel: 0121 346 3287
Fax: 0121 346 3288
E-mail: orders@brownandsons.co.uk

FAX

To: Emma Scott, Westcott Hotel

Date: 6 November 2007

From: Malcolm Marshall

No. of pages to follow: 1

Re your order of 23 October for 100 tablecloths (Catalogue number 435789), I regret to inform you that these items are currently out of stock.

The next delivery will be in approximately four weeks' time. However, if this delay is unacceptable to you, please can you let me know so that I can cancel the order.

I am sorry for any inconvenience this may cause.

Regards

Malcolm Marshall

Courrier électronique

Envoyer des messages

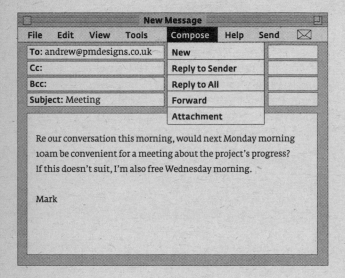

New Message	Nouveau message
File	Fichier
Edit	Édition
View	Affichage
Tools	Outils
Compose	Composer
Help	Aide
Send	Envoyer
New	Nouveau message
Reply to Sender	Répondre

Courrier électronique

Recevoir des messages

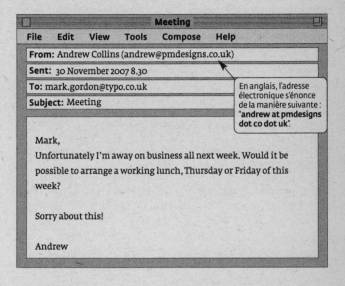

```
┌──────────────────────── Meeting ────────────────────────┐
│ File    Edit    View    Tools    Compose    Help         │
├──────────────────────────────────────────────────────────┤
│ From: Andrew Collins (andrew@pmdesigns.co.uk)            │
├──────────────────────────────────────────────────────────┤
│ Sent:  30 November 2007 8.30                             │
├──────────────────────────────────────────────────────────┤
│ To: mark.gordon@typo.co.uk                               │
├──────────────────────────────────────────────────────────┤
│ Subject: Meeting                                         │
├──────────────────────────────────────────────────────────┤
```

En anglais, l'adresse électronique s'énonce de la manière suivante : **andrew at pmdesigns dot co dot uk**.

Mark,

Unfortunately I'm away on business all next week. Would it be possible to arrange a working lunch, Thursday or Friday of this week?

Sorry about this!

Andrew

Reply to All	Répondre à tous
Forward	Faire suivre
Attachment	Fichier joint
To	À
Cc (carbon copy)	Cc
Bcc (blind carbon copy)	Copie cachée
Subject	Objet
From	De
Sent	Date

Téléphone

Les différents types de communication

Local/national call.

Communication locale/
interurbaine.

I want to make an international call.

Je voudrais appeler l'étranger.

I want to make a reverse charge call (Brit)
to a Paris number ou I want to call a Paris
number collect (US).

Je voudrais appeler ... en PCV.

How do I get an outside line?

Comment est-ce que je peux
téléphoner à l'extérieur ?

Les renseignements

What is the number for directory enquiries
(Brit) ou directory assistance (US)?

Quel est le numéro des
renseignements ?

Can you give me the number of Europost,
20 Cumberland Street, Newquay?

Je voudrais le numéro de ...

What is the code for Martinique?

Quel est l'indicatif de ...

What is the number for the speaking clock?

Quel est le numéro de l'horloge
parlante ?

Réponses

The number you require is 0181-613 3297.
(o-one-eight-one six-one-three
three-two-nine-seven)

Le numéro que vous avez
demandé est le ...

I'm sorry, there's no listing under that name.

Je regrette, mais il n'y a pas
d'abonné à ce nom.

The number you require is ex-directory (Brit)
ou unlisted (US).

Le numéro que vous avez
demandé est sur liste rouge.

Lorsque l'abonné répond

Could I speak to Mr Sanderson, please?

Pourrais-je parler à ...

Could you put me through to Dr Evans, please?

Pourriez-vous me passer ...

Can I have extension 6578, please?

Pourriez-vous me passer
le poste ...

I'll call back in half an hour.

Je rappellerai dans ...

Would you ask him to ring me when he
gets back?

Pourriez-vous lui demander de
me rappeler à son retour ?

Au standard

Who shall I say is calling?	C'est de la part de qui ?
I'm putting you through.	Je vous le passe.
I have a call from Tokyo for Mrs Thomson.	J'ai un appel de … pour …
I've got Miss Martin on the line.	J'ai … en ligne.
Dr Roberts is on another line. Do you want to wait?	… est en ligne, vous patientez ?
Please hold.	Ne quittez pas.
There's no reply.	Ça ne répond pas.
Would you like to leave a message?	Voulez-vous laisser un message ?

Messages enregistrés

The number you have dialled has not been recognized. Please hang up.	Le numéro de votre correspondant n'est plus attribué. Veuillez raccrocher.
The number you have dialled has been changed to 020-7789 0044.	Le numéro de votre correspondant a changé. Veuillez composer désormais le …
All the lines are busy right now. Please try again later.	Par suite de l'encombrement des lignes, votre appel ne peut aboutir. Veuillez rappeler ultérieurement.
Hello, you have reached Sunspot Insurance. Please wait, your call will be answered shortly.	Bonjour, vous êtes en communication avec … Veuillez patienter, nous allons donner suite à votre appel dans quelques instants.
Hello, you are through to Emma and Matthew Hargreaves. Please leave a message after the tone and we'll get back to you. Thanks.	Bonjour, vous êtes bien chez … Laissez un message après le bip sonore et nous vous rappellerons dès notre retour.

Pour répondre au téléphone

Hello, it's Anne speaking.	Allô, c'est … à l'appareil.
Speaking.	C'est moi.
Who's speaking?	Qui est à l'appareil ?

En cas de difficulté

I can't get through.	Je n'arrive pas à avoir le numéro.
Their phone is out of order.	Leur téléphone est en dérangement.
We have been cut off.	Nous avons été coupés.
I must have dialled the wrong number.	J'ai dû faire un faux numéro.
We've got a crossed line.	Il y a quelqu'un d'autre sur la ligne.
This is a very bad line.	La ligne est très mauvaise.

a

A, a¹ [eɪ] n (letter) A, a m; (Scol: mark) A; (Mus) la m; **A for Andrew, A for Able** (US) A comme Anatole; **A shares** npl (Brit Stock Exchange) actions fpl prioritaires

⊙ **KEYWORD**

a² [eɪ, ə] (before vowel and silent h **an**) indef art **1** un(e); **a book** un livre; **an apple** une pomme; **she's a doctor** elle est médecin
2 (instead of the number "one") un(e); **a year ago** il y a un an; **a hundred/thousand** etc **pounds** cent/mille etc livres
3 (in expressing ratios, prices etc): **three a day/week** trois par jour/semaine; **10 km an hour** 10 km à l'heure; **£5 a person** 5£ par personne; **30p a kilo** 30p le kilo

A2 n (Brit: Scol) deuxième partie de l'examen équivalent au baccalauréat
A.A. n abbr (Brit: = Automobile Association) ≈ ACF m; (US: = Associate in/of Arts) diplôme universitaire; (= Alcoholics Anonymous) AA; (= anti-aircraft) AA
A.A.A. n abbr (= American Automobile Association) ≈ ACF m; (Brit) = **Amateur Athletics Association**
aback [ə'bæk] adv: **to be taken ~** être décontenancé(e)
abandon [ə'bændən] vt abandonner ▷ n abandon m; **to ~ ship** évacuer le navire
abate [ə'beɪt] vi s'apaiser, se calmer
abattoir ['æbətwɑːʳ] n (Brit) abattoir m

abbey ['æbɪ] n abbaye f
abbot ['æbət] n père supérieur
abbreviation [əbriːvɪ'eɪʃən] n abréviation f
abdicate ['æbdɪkeɪt] vt, vi abdiquer
abdomen ['æbdəmən] n abdomen m
abduct [æb'dʌkt] vt enlever
aberration [æbə'reɪʃən] n anomalie f; **in a moment of mental ~** dans un moment d'égarement
abide [ə'baɪd] vt souffrir, supporter; **I can't ~ it/him** je ne le supporte pas; **abide by** vt fus observer, respecter
ability [ə'bɪlɪtɪ] n compétence f; capacité f; (skill) talent m; **to the best of my ~** de mon mieux
abject ['æbdʒekt] adj (poverty) sordide; (coward) méprisable; **an ~ apology** les excuses les plus plates
ablaze [ə'bleɪz] adj en feu, en flammes; **~ with light** resplendissant de lumière
able ['eɪbl] adj compétent(e); **to be ~ to do sth** pouvoir faire qch, être capable de faire qch
able-bodied ['eɪbl'bɔdɪd] adj robuste; **~ seaman** (Brit) matelot breveté
ably ['eɪblɪ] adv avec compétence or talent, habilement
abnormal [æb'nɔːməl] adj anormal(e)
aboard [ə'bɔːd] adv à bord ▷ prep à bord de; (train) dans
abode [ə'bəud] n (old) demeure f; (Law): **of no fixed ~** sans domicile fixe
abolish [ə'bɔlɪʃ] vt abolir
abolition [æbə'lɪʃən] n abolition f
aborigine [æbə'rɪdʒɪnɪ] n aborigène m/f
abort [ə'bɔːt] vt (Med) faire avorter; (Comput, fig) abandonner
abortion [ə'bɔːʃən] n avortement m; **to have an ~** se faire avorter
abortive [ə'bɔːtɪv] adj manqué(e)

⊙ **KEYWORD**

about [ə'baut] adv **1** (approximately) environ, à peu près; **about a hundred/thousand** etc environ cent/mille etc, une centaine (de)/un millier (de) etc; **it takes about 10 hours** ça prend environ or à peu près 10 heures; **at about 2 o'clock** vers 2 heures; **I've just about finished** j'ai presque fini
2 (referring to place) çà et là, de-ci de-là; **to run about** courir çà et là; **to walk about** se promener, aller et venir; **is Paul about?** (Brit) est-ce que Paul est là?; **it's about here** c'est par ici, c'est dans les parages; **they left all their things lying about** ils ont laissé traîner toutes leurs affaires
3: **to be about to do sth** être sur le point de faire qch; **I'm not about to do all that for nothing** (inf) je ne vais quand même pas faire tout ça pour rien
4 (opposite): **it's the other way about** (Brit) c'est l'inverse

▷ prep **1** (relating to) au sujet de, à propos de; **a book about London** un livre sur Londres; **what is it about?** de quoi s'agit-il?; **we talked about it** nous en avons parlé; **do something about it!** faites quelque chose!; **what** or **how about doing this?** et si nous faisions ceci?
2 (referring to place) dans; **to walk about the town** se promener dans la ville

above [ə'bʌv] adv au-dessus ▷ prep au-dessus de; (more than) plus de; **mentioned ~** mentionné ci-dessus; **costing ~ £10** coûtant plus de 10 livres; **~ all** par-dessus tout, surtout

aboveboard [ə'bʌv'bɔːd] adj franc/franche, loyal(e); honnête

abrasive [ə'breɪzɪv] adj abrasif(-ive); (fig) caustique, agressif(-ive)

abreast [ə'brest] adv de front; **to keep ~ of** se tenir au courant de

abroad [ə'brɔːd] adv à l'étranger; **there is a rumour ~ that ...** (fig) le bruit court que ...

abrupt [ə'brʌpt] adj (steep, blunt) abrupt(e); (sudden, gruff) brusque

abruptly [ə'brʌptlɪ] adv (speak, end) brusquement

abscess ['æbsɪs] n abcès m

absence ['æbsəns] n absence f; **in the ~ of** (person) en l'absence de; (thing) faute de

absent ['æbsənt] adj absent(e); **~ without leave (AWOL)** (Mil) en absence irrégulière

absentee [æbsən'tiː] n absent(e)

absent-minded ['æbsənt'maɪndɪd] adj distrait(e)

absolute ['æbsəluːt] adj absolu(e)

absolutely [æbsə'luːtlɪ] adv absolument

absolve [əb'zɔlv] vt: **to ~ sb (from)** (sin etc) absoudre qn (de); **to ~ sb from** (oath) délier qn de

absorb [əb'zɔːb] vt absorber; **to be ~ed in a book** être plongé(e) dans un livre

absorbent cotton [əb'zɔːbənt-] n (US) coton m hydrophile

absorbing [əb'zɔːbɪŋ] adj absorbant(e); (book, film etc) captivant(e)

abstain [əb'steɪn] vi: **to ~ (from)** s'abstenir (de)

abstract ['æbstrækt] adj abstrait(e) ▷ n (summary) résumé m ▷ vt [æb'strækt] extraire

absurd [əb'sɜːd] adj absurde

abundance [ə'bʌndəns] n abondance f

abundant [ə'bʌndənt] adj abondant(e)

abuse n [ə'bjuːs] (insults) insultes fpl, injures fpl; (ill-treatment) mauvais traitements mpl; (of power etc) abus m ▷ vt [ə'bjuːz] (insult) insulter; (ill-treat) malmener; (power etc) abuser de; **to be open to ~** se prêter à des abus

abusive [ə'bjuːsɪv] adj grossier(-ière), injurieux(-euse)

abysmal [ə'bɪzməl] adj exécrable; (ignorance etc) sans bornes

abyss [ə'bɪs] n abîme m, gouffre m

AC n abbr (US) = **athletic club**

academic [ækə'demɪk] adj universitaire; (person: scholarly) intellectuel(-le); (pej: issue) oiseux(-euse), purement théorique ▷ n universitaire m/f; **~ freedom** liberté f académique

academic year n (University) année f universitaire; (Scol) année scolaire

academy [ə'kædəmɪ] n (learned body) académie f; (school) collège m; **military/naval ~** école militaire/navale; **~ of music** conservatoire m

accelerate [æk'seləreɪt] vt, vi accélérer

acceleration [ækselə'reɪʃən] n accélération f

accelerator [æk'seləreɪtər] n (Brit) accélérateur m

accent ['æksent] n accent m

accept [ək'sept] vt accepter

acceptable [ək'septəbl] adj acceptable

acceptance [ək'septəns] n acceptation f; **to meet with general ~** être favorablement accueilli par tous

access ['ækses] n accès m ▷ vt (Comput) accéder à; **to have ~ to** (information, library etc) avoir accès à, pouvoir utiliser or consulter; (person) avoir accès auprès de; **the burglars gained ~ through a window** les cambrioleurs sont entrés par une fenêtre

accessible [æk'sesəbl] adj accessible

accessory [æk'sesərɪ] n accessoire m; **toilet accessories** (Brit) articles mpl de toilette; **~ to** (Law) accessoire à

accident ['æksɪdənt] n accident m; (chance) hasard m; **to meet with** or **to have an ~** avoir un accident; **I've had an ~** j'ai eu un accident; **~s at work** accidents du travail; **by ~** (by chance) par hasard; (not deliberately) accidentellement

accidental [æksɪ'dentl] adj accidentel(le)

accidentally [æksɪ'dentəlɪ] adv accidentellement

Accident and Emergency Department n (Brit) service m des urgences

accident insurance n assurance f accident

accident-prone ['æksɪdənt'prəun] adj sujet(te) aux accidents

acclaim [ə'kleɪm] vt acclamer ▷ n acclamations fpl

accommodate [ə'kɔmədeɪt] vt loger, recevoir; (oblige, help) obliger; (car etc) contenir; (adapt): **to ~ one's plans to** adapter ses projets à

accommodating [ə'kɔmədeɪtɪŋ] adj obligeant(e), arrangeant(e)

accommodation, (US) **accommodations** [əkɔmə'deɪʃən(z)] n(pl) logement m; **he's found ~** il a trouvé à se loger; **"~ to let"** (Brit) "appartement or studio etc à louer"; **they have ~ for 500** ils peuvent recevoir 500 personnes, il y a de la place pour 500 personnes; **the hall has seating - for 600** (Brit) la salle contient 600 places assises

accompaniment [əˈkʌmpənɪmənt] n accompagnement m

accompany [əˈkʌmpənɪ] vt accompagner

accomplice [əˈkʌmplɪs] n complice m/f

accomplish [əˈkʌmplɪʃ] vt accomplir

accomplishment [əˈkʌmplɪʃmənt] n (skill: gen pl) talent m; (completion) accomplissement m; (achievement) réussite f

accord [əˈkɔːd] n accord m ⊳ vt accorder; **of his own -** de son plein gré; **with one -** d'un commun accord

accordance [əˈkɔːdəns] n: **in - with** conformément à

according [əˈkɔːdɪŋ]: **- to** prep selon; **- to plan** comme prévu

accordingly [əˈkɔːdɪŋlɪ] adv (appropriately) en conséquence; (as a result) par conséquent

accordion [əˈkɔːdɪən] n accordéon m

account [əˈkaunt] n (Comm) compte m; (report) compte rendu, récit m; **accounts** npl (Comm: records) comptabilité f, comptes; **"- payee only"** (Brit) "chèque non endossable"; **to keep an - of** noter; **to bring sb to - for sth/for having done sth** amener qn à rendre compte de qch/d'avoir fait qch; **by all -s** au dire de tous; **of little -** de peu d'importance; **of no -** sans importance; **on -** en acompte; **to buy sth on -** acheter qch à crédit; **on no -** en aucun cas; **on - of** à cause de; **to take into -**, **take - of** tenir compte de; **account for** vt fus (explain) expliquer, rendre compte de; (represent) représenter; **all the children were -ed for** aucun enfant ne manquait; **four people are still not -ed for** on n'a toujours pas retrouvé quatre personnes

accountable [əˈkauntəbl] adj: **- (for/to)** responsable (de/devant)

accountancy [əˈkauntənsɪ] n comptabilité f

accountant [əˈkauntənt] n comptable m/f

account number n numéro m de compte

accrue [əˈkruː] vi s'accroître; (mount up) s'accumuler; **to -** to s'ajouter à; **-d interest** intérêt couru

accumulate [əˈkjuːmjuleɪt] vt accumuler, amasser ⊳ vi s'accumuler, s'amasser

accuracy [ˈækjurəsɪ] n exactitude f, précision f

accurate [ˈækjurɪt] adj exact(e), précis(e); (device) précis

accurately [ˈækjurɪtlɪ] adv avec précision

accusation [ækjuˈzeɪʃən] n accusation f

accuse [əˈkjuːz] vt: **to - sb (of sth)** accuser qn (de qch)

accused [əˈkjuːzd] n (Law) accusé(e)

accustom [əˈkʌstəm] vt accoutumer, habituer; **to - o.s. to sth** s'habituer à qch

accustomed [əˈkʌstəmd] adj (usual) habituel(le); **to be habitué(e) or accoutumé(e) à**

ace [eɪs] n as m; **within an - of** (Brit) à deux doigts or un cheveu de

ache [eɪk] n mal m, douleur f ⊳ vi (be sore) faire mal, être douloureux(-euse); (yearn); **I've got stomach -** or (US) **a stomach -** j'ai mal à l'estomac; **my head -s** j'ai mal à la tête; **I'm aching all over** j'ai mal partout

achieve [əˈtʃiːv] vt (aim) atteindre; (victory, success) remporter, obtenir; (task) accomplir

achievement [əˈtʃiːvmənt] n exploit m, réussite f; (of aims) réalisation f

acid [ˈæsɪd] adj, n acide (m)

acid rain n pluies fpl acides

acknowledge [əkˈnɔlɪdʒ] vt (also: **- receipt of**) accuser réception de; (fact) reconnaître

acknowledgement [əkˈnɔlɪdʒmənt] n (of letter) accusé m de réception; **acknowledgements** (in book) remerciements mpl

acne [ˈæknɪ] n acné m

acorn [ˈeɪkɔːn] n gland m

acoustic [əˈkuːstɪk] adj acoustique

acoustics [əˈkuːstɪks] n, npl acoustique f

acquaint [əˈkweɪnt] vt: **to - sb with sth** mettre qn au courant de qch; **to be -ed with** (person) connaître; (fact) savoir

acquaintance [əˈkweɪntəns] n connaissance f; **to make sb's -** faire la connaissance de qn

acquire [əˈkwaɪəʳ] vt acquérir

acquisition [ækwɪˈzɪʃən] n acquisition f

acquit [əˈkwɪt] vt acquitter; **to - o.s. well** s'en tirer très honorablement

acre [ˈeɪkəʳ] n acre f (= 4047 m²)

acrid [ˈækrɪd] adj (smell) âcre; (fig) mordant(e)

acrobat [ˈækrəbæt] n acrobate m/f

acronym [ˈækrənɪm] n acronyme m

across [əˈkrɔs] prep (on the other side) de l'autre côté de; (crosswise) en travers de ⊳ adv de l'autre côté; en travers; **to walk - (the road)** traverser (la route); **to run/swim -** traverser en courant/à la nage; **to take sb - the road** faire traverser la route à qn; **a road - the wood** une route qui traverse le bois; **the lake is 12 km -** le lac fait 12 km de large; **- from** en face de; **to get sth - (to sb)** faire comprendre qch (à qn)

acrylic [əˈkrɪlɪk] adj, n acrylique (m)

act [ækt] n acte m, action f; (Theat: part of play) acte; (: of performer) numéro m; (Law) loi f ⊳ vi agir; (Theat) jouer; (pretend) jouer la comédie ⊳ vt (role) jouer, tenir; **- of God** (Law) catastrophe naturelle; **to catch sb in the -** prendre qn sur le fait or en flagrant délit; **it's only an -** c'est du cinéma; **to - Hamlet** (Brit) tenir or jouer le rôle d'Hamlet; **to - the fool** (Brit) faire l'idiot; **to - as** servir de; **it -s as a deterrent** cela a un effet dissuasif; **-ing in my capacity as chairman, I ...** en ma qualité de président, je ...; **act on** vt: **to - on sth** agir sur la base de qch; **act out** vt (event) raconter en mimant; (*fantasies*) réaliser; **act up** (*inf*) *vi* (*person*) se conduire mal; (*knee, back, injury*) jouer des tours; (*machine*) être capricieux(-ieuse)

acting ['æktɪŋ] *adj* suppléant(e), par intérim ▷ *n* (*of actor*) jeu *m*; (*activity*): **to do some ~** faire du théâtre (*or* du cinéma); **he is the ~ manager** il remplace (provisoirement) le directeur

action ['ækʃən] *n* action *f*; (*Mil*) combat(s) *m(pl)*; (*Law*) procès *m*, action en justice ▷ *vt* (*Comm*) mettre en œuvre; **to bring an ~ against sb** (*Law*) poursuivre qn en justice, intenter un procès contre qn; **killed in ~** (*Mil*) tué au champ d'honneur; **out of ~** hors de combat; (*machine etc*) hors d'usage; **to take ~** agir, prendre des mesures; **to put a plan into ~** mettre un projet à exécution

action replay *n* (*Brit TV*) ralenti *m*

activate ['æktɪveɪt] *vt* (*mechanism*) actionner, faire fonctionner; (*Chem, Physics*) activer

active ['æktɪv] *adj* actif(-ive); (*volcano*) en activité; **to play an ~ part in** jouer un rôle actif dans

actively ['æktɪvlɪ] *adv* activement; (*discourage*) vivement

activist ['æktɪvɪst] *n* activiste *m/f*

activity [æk'tɪvɪtɪ] *n* activité *f*

activity holiday *n* vacances actives

actor ['æktəʳ] *n* acteur *m*

actress ['æktrɪs] *n* actrice *f*

actual ['æktjuəl] *adj* réel(le), véritable; (*emphatic use*) lui-même/elle-même

actually ['æktjuəlɪ] *adv* réellement, véritablement; (*in fact*) en fait

acupuncture ['ækjupʌŋktʃəʳ] *n* acuponcture *f*

acute [ə'kjuːt] *adj* aigu(ë); (*mind, observer*) pénétrant(e)

A.D. *adv abbr* (= *Anno Domini*) ap. J.-C. ▷ *n abbr* (*US Mil*) = **active duty**

ad [æd] *n abbr* = **advertisement**

adamant ['ædəmənt] *adj* inflexible

adapt [ə'dæpt] *vt* adapter ▷ *vi*: **to ~ (to)** s'adapter (à)

adaptable [ə'dæptəbl] *adj* (*device*) adaptable; (*person*) qui s'adapte facilement

adapter, adaptor [ə'dæptəʳ] *n* (*Elec*) adaptateur *m*; (*for several plugs*) prise *f* multiple

add [æd] *vt* ajouter; (*figures*: *also*: **to ~ up**) additionner ▷ *vi*: **to ~ to** (*increase*) ajouter à, accroître ▷ *n* (*Internet*): **thanks for the ~** merci pour l'ajout; **add on** *vt* ajouter ▷ *vi* (*fig*): **it doesn't ~ up** cela ne rime à rien; **add up to** *vt fus* (*Math*) s'élever à; (*fig*: *mean*) signifier; **it doesn't ~ up to much** ça n'est pas grand'chose

adder ['ædəʳ] *n* vipère *f*

addict ['ædɪkt] *n* toxicomane *m/f*; (*fig*) fanatique *m/f*; **heroin ~** héroïnomane *m/f*; **drug ~** drogué(e) *m/f*

addicted [ə'dɪktɪd] *adj*: **to be ~ to** (*drink, drugs*) être adonné(e) à; (*fig*: *football etc*) être un(e) fanatique de

addiction [ə'dɪkʃən] *n* (*Med*) dépendance *f*

addictive [ə'dɪktɪv] *adj* qui crée une dépendance

addition [ə'dɪʃən] *n* (*adding up*) addition *f*; (*thing added*) ajout *m*; **in ~** de plus, de surcroît; **in ~ to** en plus de

additional [ə'dɪʃənl] *adj* supplémentaire

additive ['ædɪtɪv] *n* additif *m*

address [ə'drɛs] *n* adresse *f*; (*talk*) discours *m*, allocution *f* ▷ *vt* adresser; (*speak to*) s'adresser à; **my ~ is ...** mon adresse, c'est ...; **form of ~** titre *m*; **what form of ~ do you use for ...?** comment s'adresse-t-on à ...?; **to ~ (o.s. to) sth** (*problem, issue*) aborder qch; **absolute/relative ~** (*Comput*) adresse absolue/relative

address book *n* carnet *m* d'adresses

adept ['ædɛpt] *adj*: **~ at** expert(e) à *or* en

adequate ['ædɪkwɪt] *adj* (*enough*) suffisant(e); (*satisfactory*) satisfaisant(e); **to feel ~ to the task** se sentir à la hauteur de la tâche

adhere [əd'hɪəʳ] *vi*: **to ~ to** adhérer à; (*fig*: *rule, decision*) se tenir à

adhesive [əd'hiːzɪv] *adj* adhésif(-ive) ▷ *n* adhésif *m*

adhesive tape *n* (*Brit*) ruban *m* adhésif; (*US Med*) sparadrap *m*

ad hoc [æd'hɔk] *adj* (*decision*) de circonstance; (*committee*) ad hoc

adjacent [ə'dʒeɪsənt] *adj* adjacent(e), contigu(ë); **~ to** adjacent à

adjective ['ædʒɛktɪv] *n* adjectif *m*

adjoining [ə'dʒɔɪnɪŋ] *adj* voisin(e), adjacent(e), attenant(e) ▷ *prep* voisin de, adjacent à

adjourn [ə'dʒəːn] *vt* ajourner ▷ *vi* suspendre la séance; lever la séance; clore la session; (*go*) se retirer; **to ~ a meeting till the following week** reporter une réunion à la semaine suivante; **they ~ed to the pub** (*Brit inf*) ils ont filé au pub

adjust [ə'dʒʌst] *vt* (*machine*) ajuster, régler; (*prices, wages*) rajuster ▷ *vi*: **to ~ (to)** s'adapter (à)

adjustable [ə'dʒʌstəbl] *adj* réglable

adjustment [ə'dʒʌstmənt] *n* (*of machine*) ajustage *m*, réglage *m*; (*of prices, wages*) rajustement *m*; (*of person*) adaptation *f*

ad-lib [æd'lɪb] *vt, vi* improviser ▷ *n* improvisation *f* ▷ *adv*: **ad lib** à volonté, à discrétion

administer [əd'mɪnɪstəʳ] *vt* administrer; (*justice*) rendre

administration [ədmɪnɪs'treɪʃən] *n* (*management*) administration *f*; (*government*) gouvernement *m*

administrative [əd'mɪnɪstrətɪv] *adj* administratif(-ive)

administrator [əd'mɪnɪstreɪtəʳ] n administrateur(-trice)

admiral ['ædmərəl] n amiral m

Admiralty ['ædmərəltɪ] n (Brit: also: ~ Board) ministère m de la Marine

admiration [ædmə'reɪʃən] n admiration f

admire [əd'maɪəʳ] vt admirer

admirer [əd'maɪərəʳ] n (fan) admirateur(-trice)

admission [əd'mɪʃən] n admission f; (to exhibition, night club etc) entrée f; (confession) aveu m; "~ free", "free ~" "entrée libre"; **by his own** ~ de son propre aveu

admission charge n droits mpl d'admission

admit [əd'mɪt] vt laisser entrer; admettre; (agree) reconnaître, admettre; (crime) reconnaître avoir commis; **"children not ~ted"** "entrée interdite aux enfants"; **this ticket ~s two** ce billet est valable pour deux personnes; **I must ~ that ...** je dois admettre or reconnaître que ...; **admit of** vt fus admettre, permettre; **admit to** vt fus reconnaître, avouer

admittance [əd'mɪtəns] n admission f, (droit m d')entrée f; **"no ~"** "défense d'entrer"

admittedly [əd'mɪtɪdlɪ] adv il faut en convenir

ado [ə'duː] n: **without (any) more ~** sans plus de cérémonies

adolescence [ædəu'lɛsns] n adolescence f

adolescent [ædəu'lɛsnt] adj, n adolescent(e)

adopt [ə'dɔpt] vt adopter

adopted [ə'dɔptɪd] adj adoptif(-ive), adopté(e)

adoption [ə'dɔpʃən] n adoption f

adore [ə'dɔːʳ] vt adorer

adorn [ə'dɔːn] vt orner

Adriatic [eɪdrɪ'ætɪk], **Adriatic Sea** n: **the ~ (Sea)** la mer Adriatique, l'Adriatique f

adrift [ə'drɪft] adv à la dérive; **to come ~** (boat) aller à la dérive; (wire, rope, fastening etc) se défaire

ADSL n abbr (= asymmetric digital subscriber line) ADSL m

adult ['ædʌlt] n adulte m/f ▷ adj (grown-up) adulte; (for adults) pour adultes

adult education n éducation f des adultes

adultery [ə'dʌltərɪ] n adultère m

advance [əd'vɑːns] n avance f ▷ vt avancer ▷ vi s'avancer; **in ~** en avance, d'avance; **to make ~s to sb** (gen) faire des propositions à qn; (amorously) faire des avances à qn; **~ booking** location f; **~ notice**, **~ warning** préavis m; (verbal) avertissement m; **do I need to book in ~?** est-ce qu'il faut réserver à l'avance?

advanced [əd'vɑːnst] adj avancé(e); (Scol: studies) supérieur(e); **~ in years** d'un âge avancé

advantage [əd'vɑːntɪdʒ] n (also Tennis) avantage m; **to take ~ of** (person) exploiter; (opportunity) profiter de; **it's to our ~** c'est

notre intérêt; **it's to our ~ to ...** nous avons intérêt à ...

advent ['ædvənt] n avènement m, venue f; **A~ (Rel)** avent m

adventure [əd'vɛntʃəʳ] n aventure f

adventurous [əd'vɛntʃərəs] adj aventureux(-euse)

adverb ['ædvəːb] n adverbe m

adversary ['ædvəsərɪ] n adversaire m/f

adverse ['ædvəːs] adj adverse; (effect) négatif(-ive); (weather, publicity) mauvais(e); (wind) contraire; **~ to** hostile à; **in ~ circumstances** dans l'adversité

advert ['ædvəːt] n abbr (Brit) = **advertisement**

advertise ['ædvətaɪz] vi faire de la publicité or de la réclame; (in classified ads etc) mettre une annonce ▷ vt faire de la publicité or de la réclame pour; (in classified ads etc) mettre une annonce pour vendre; **to ~ for** (staff) recruter par (voie d')annonce

advertisement [əd'vəːtɪsmənt] n publicité f, réclame f; (in classified ads etc) annonce f

advertiser ['ædvətaɪzəʳ] n annonceur m

advertising ['ædvətaɪzɪŋ] n publicité f

advice [əd'vaɪs] n conseils mpl; (notification) avis m; **a piece of ~** un conseil; **to ask (sb) for ~** demander conseil (à qn); **to take legal ~** consulter un avocat

advisable [əd'vaɪzəbl] adj recommandable, indiqué(e)

advise [əd'vaɪz] vt conseiller; **to ~ sb of sth** aviser or informer qn de qch; **to ~ against sth/doing sth** déconseiller qch/conseiller de ne pas faire qch; **you would be well/ill ~d to go** vous feriez mieux d'y aller/de ne pas y aller, vous auriez intérêt à y aller/à ne pas y aller

adviser, advisor [əd'vaɪzəʳ] n conseiller(-ère)

advisory [əd'vaɪzərɪ] adj consultatif(-ive); **in an ~ capacity** à titre consultatif

advocate n ['ædvəkɪt] (lawyer) avocat (plaidant); (upholder) défenseur m, avocat(e) ▷ vt ['ædvəkeɪt] recommander, prôner; **to be an ~ of** être partisan(e) de

Aegean [iː'dʒiːən] n, adj: **the ~ (Sea)** la mer Égée, l'Égée f

aerial ['ɛərɪəl] n antenne f ▷ adj aérien(ne)

aerobics [ɛə'rəubɪks] n aérobic m

aeroplane ['ɛərəpleɪn] n (Brit) avion m

aerosol ['ɛərəsɔl] n aérosol m

aesthetic [ɪs'θɛtɪk] adj esthétique

afar [ə'fɑːʳ] adv: **from ~** de loin

affair [ə'fɛəʳ] n affaire f; (also: **love ~**) liaison f; aventure f; **affairs** (business) affaires f

affect [ə'fɛkt] vt affecter; (subj: disease) atteindre

affected [ə'fɛktɪd] adj affecté(e)

affection [ə'fɛkʃən] n affection f

affectionate [ə'fɛkʃənɪt] adj affectueux(-euse)

affinity [ə'fɪnɪtɪ] n affinité f

afflict [əˈflɪkt] vt affliger

affluence [ˈæfluəns] n aisance f, opulence f

affluent [ˈæfluənt] adj opulent(e); (person, family, surroundings) aisé(e), riche; **the ~ society** la société d'abondance

afford [əˈfɔːd] vt (goods etc) avoir les moyens d'acheter or d'entretenir; (behaviour) se permettre; (provide) fournir, procurer; **can we ~ a car?** avons-nous de quoi acheter or les moyens d'acheter une voiture?; **I can't ~ the time** je n'ai vraiment pas le temps

affordable [əˈfɔːdəbl] adj abordable

Afghanistan [æfˈɡænɪstæn] n Afghanistan m

afloat [əˈfləʊt] adj à flot ▷ adv: **to stay ~** surnager; **to keep/get a business ~** maintenir à flot/lancer une affaire

afoot [əˈfʊt] adv: **there is something ~** il se prépare quelque chose

afraid [əˈfreɪd] adj effrayé(e); **to be ~ of or to** avoir peur de; **I am ~ that** je crains que + sub; **I'm ~ so/not** oui/non, malheureusement

Africa [ˈæfrɪkə] n Afrique f

African [ˈæfrɪkən] adj africain(e) ▷ n Africain(e)

African-American [ˈæfrɪkənəˈmɛrɪkən] adj afro-américain(e) ▷ n Afro-Américain(e)

after [ˈɑːftəʳ] prep, adv après ▷ conj après que, après avoir or être + pp; **~ dinner** après (le) dîner; **the day ~ tomorrow** après demain; **it's quarter ~ two** (US) il est deux heures et quart; **~ having done/~ he left** après avoir fait/ après son départ; **to name sb ~ sb** donner à qn le nom de qn; **to ask ~ sb** demander des nouvelles de qn; **what/who are you ~?** que/qui cherchez-vous?; **the police are ~ him** la police est à ses trousses; **~ you!** après vous!; **~ all** après tout

after-effects [ˈɑːftərɪfɛkts] npl (of disaster, radiation, drink etc) répercussions fpl; (of illness) séquelles fpl, suites fpl

aftermath [ˈɑːftəmɑːθ] n conséquences fpl; **in the ~ of** dans les mois ou années etc qui suivirent, au lendemain de

afternoon [ˈɑːftəˈnuːn] n après-midi m or f; **good ~!** bonjour!; (goodbye) au revoir!

afters [ˈɑːftəz] n (Brit inf: dessert) dessert m

after-sales service [ɑːftəˈseɪlz-] n service m après-vente, SAV m

after-shave [ˈɑːftəʃeɪv], **after-shave lotion** n lotion f après-rasage

aftersun [ˈɑːftəsʌn], **aftersun cream, aftersun lotion** n après-soleil m inv

afterthought [ˈɑːftəθɔːt] n: **I had an ~** il m'est venu une idée après coup

afterwards [ˈɑːftəwədz], (US) **afterward** [ˈɑːftəwəd] adv après

again [əˈɡɛn] adv de nouveau, encore (une fois); **to do sth ~** refaire qch; **not ... ~** ne ... plus; **~ and ~** à plusieurs reprises; **he's opened it ~** il l'a rouvert, il l'a de nouveau or l'a encore ouvert; **now and ~** de temps à autre

against [əˈɡɛnst] prep contre; (compared to) par rapport à; **~ a blue background** sur un fond bleu; **(as) ~** (Brit) contre

age [eɪdʒ] n âge m ▷ vt, vi vieillir; **what ~ is he?** quel âge a-t-il?; **he is 20 years of ~** il a 20 ans; **under ~** mineur(e); **to come of ~** atteindre sa majorité; **it's been ~s since I saw you** ça fait une éternité que je ne t'ai pas vu

aged [ˈeɪdʒd] adj âgé(e); **~ 10** âgé de 10 ans ▷ npl [ˈeɪdʒɪd]: **the ~** les personnes âgées

age group n tranche f d'âge; **the 40 to 50 ~** la tranche d'âge des 40 à 50 ans

age limit n limite f d'âge

agency [ˈeɪdʒənsɪ] n agence f; **through or by the ~ of** par l'entremise or l'action de

agenda [əˈdʒɛndə] n ordre m du jour; **on the ~** à l'ordre du jour

agent [ˈeɪdʒənt] n agent m; (firm) concessionnaire m

aggravate [ˈæɡrəveɪt] vt (situation) aggraver; (annoy) exaspérer, agacer

aggression [əˈɡrɛʃən] n agression f

aggressive [əˈɡrɛsɪv] adj agressif(-ive)

agile [ˈædʒaɪl] adj agile

agitate [ˈædʒɪteɪt] vt rendre inquiet(-ète) or agité(e) ▷ vi faire de l'agitation (politique); **to ~ for** faire campagne pour

AGM n abbr (= annual general meeting) AG f

ago [əˈɡəʊ] adv: **two days ~** il y a deux jours; **not long ~** il n'y a pas longtemps; **as long ~ as 1960** déjà en 1960; **how long ~?** il y a combien de temps (de cela)?

agony [ˈæɡənɪ] n (pain) douleur f atroce; (distress) angoisse f; **to be in ~** souffrir le martyre

agree [əˈɡriː] vt (price) convenir de ▷ vi: **to ~ with** (person) être d'accord avec; (statements etc) concorder avec; (Ling) s'accorder avec; **to ~ to do** accepter de or consentir à faire; **to ~ to sth** consentir à qch; **to ~ that** (admit) convenir or reconnaître que; **it was ~d that ...** il a été convenu que ...; **they ~ on this** ils sont d'accord sur ce point; **they ~d on going/a price** ils se mirent d'accord pour y aller/sur un prix; **garlic doesn't ~ with me** je ne supporte pas l'ail

agreeable [əˈɡriːəbl] adj (pleasant) agréable; (willing) consentant(e), d'accord; **are you ~ to this?** est-ce que vous êtes d'accord?

agreed [əˈɡriːd] adj (time, place) convenu(e); **to be ~ about sth** être d'accord

agreement [əˈɡriːmənt] n accord m; **in ~** d'accord; **by mutual ~** d'un commun accord

agricultural [æɡrɪˈkʌltʃərəl] adj agricole

agriculture [ˈæɡrɪkʌltʃəʳ] n agriculture f

aground [əˈɡraʊnd] adv: **to run ~** s'échouer

ahead [əˈhɛd] adv en avant; devant; **go right or straight ~** (direction) allez tout droit; **go ~!** (permission) allez-y!; **~ of** devant; (fig: schedule etc) en avance sur; **~ of time** en avance; **they were (right) ~ of us** ils nous précédaient (de peu), ils étaient (juste) devant nous

a

aid [eɪd] n aide f; (device) appareil m ▷ vt aider;
with the ~ of avec l'aide de; **in ~ of** en faveur
de; **to ~ and abet** (Law) se faire le complice de

aide [eɪd] n (person) assistant(e)

AIDS [eɪdz] n abbr (= acquired immune (or immuno-)
deficiency syndrome) SIDA m

ailing ['eɪlɪŋ] adj (person) souffreteux(euse);
(economy) malade

ailment ['eɪlmənt] n affection f

aim [eɪm] vt: **to ~ sth (at)** (gun, camera)
braquer or pointer qch (sur); (missile) lancer
qch (à or contre or en direction de); (remark,
blow) destiner or adresser qch (à) ▷ vi (also: **to
take ~**) viser ▷ n (objective) but m; (skill): **his ~
is bad** il vise mal; **to ~ at** viser; (fig) viser (à);
avoir pour but or ambition; **to ~ to do** avoir
l'intention de faire

aimless ['eɪmlɪs] adj sans but

ain't [eɪnt] (inf) = **am not; aren't; isn't**

air [ɛəʳ] n air m ▷ vt aérer; (idea, grievance, views)
mettre sur le tapis; (knowledge) faire étalage
de ▷ cpd (currents, attack etc) aérien(ne); **to
throw sth into the ~** (ball etc) jeter qch en
l'air; **by ~** par avion; **to be on the ~** (Radio, TV:
programme) être diffusé(e); (: station) émettre

airbag ['ɛəbæg] n airbag m

airbed ['ɛəbed] n (Brit) matelas m
pneumatique

airborne ['ɛəbɔ:n] adj (plane) en vol; (troops)
aéroporté(e); (particles) dans l'air; **as soon as
the plane was ~** dès que l'avion eut décollé

air-conditioned ['ɛəkən'dɪʃənd] adj
climatisé(e), à air conditionné

air conditioning [-kən'dɪʃnɪŋ] n
climatisation f

aircraft ['ɛəkrɑ:ft] n inv avion m

aircraft carrier n porte-avions m inv

airfield ['ɛəfi:ld] n terrain m d'aviation

Air Force n Armée f de l'air

air freshener [-'frɛʃnəʳ] n désodorisant m

airgun ['ɛəgʌn] n fusil m à air comprimé

air hostess (Brit) hôtesse f de l'air

airing cupboard n (Brit) placard qui contient la
chaudière et dans lequel on met le linge à sécher

air letter n (Brit) aérogramme m

airlift ['ɛəlɪft] n pont aérien

airline ['ɛəlaɪn] n ligne aérienne, compagnie
aérienne

airliner ['ɛəlaɪnəʳ] n avion m de ligne

airmail ['ɛəmeɪl] n: **by ~** par avion

air mile n air mile m

airplane ['ɛəpleɪn] n (US) avion m

airport ['ɛəpɔ:t] n aéroport m

air raid n attaque aérienne

airsick ['ɛəsɪk] adj: **to be ~** avoir le mal de l'air

airspace ['ɛəspeɪs] n espace m aérien

airstrip ['ɛəstrɪp] n terrain m d'atterrissage

air terminal n aérogare f

airtight ['ɛətaɪt] adj hermétique

air-traffic controller n aiguilleur m du ciel

airy ['ɛərɪ] adj bien aéré(e); (manners)
dégagé(e)

aisle [aɪl] n (of church: central) allée f centrale;
(: side) nef f latérale, bas-côté m; (in theatre,
supermarket) allée; (on plane) couloir m

aisle seat n place f côté couloir

ajar [ə'dʒɑ:ʳ] adj entrouvert(e)

akin [ə'kɪn] adj: **~ to** semblable à, du même
ordre que

à la carte [ælæ'kɑ:t] adv à la carte

alarm [ə'lɑ:m] n alarme f ▷ vt alarmer

alarm call n coup m de fil pour réveiller;
could I have an ~ at 7 am, please? pouvez-
vous me réveiller à 7 heures, s'il vous plaît?

alarm clock n réveille-matin m inv, réveil m

alarmed [ə'lɑ:md] adj (frightened) alarmé(e);
(protected by an alarm) protégé(e) par un
système d'alarme; **to become ~** prendre
peur

alarming [ə'lɑ:mɪŋ] adj alarmant(e)

alas [ə'læs] excl hélas

Albania [æl'beɪnɪə] n Albanie f

albeit [ɔ:l'bi:ɪt] conj bien que + sub, encore que
+ sub

album ['ælbəm] n album m

alcohol ['ælkəhɔl] n alcool m

alcohol-free ['ælkəhɔlfri:] adj sans alcool

alcoholic [ælkə'hɔlɪk] adj, n alcoolique (m/f)

alcove ['ælkəuv] n alcôve f

ale [eɪl] n bière f

alert [ə'lə:t] adj alerte, vif/vive; (watchful)
vigilant(e) ▷ n alerte f ▷ vt alerter; **to ~ sb (to
sth)** attirer l'attention de qn (sur qch); **to ~
sb to the dangers of sth** avertir qn des
dangers de qch; **on the ~** sur le qui-vive; (Mil)
en état d'alerte

algebra ['ældʒɪbrə] n algèbre m

Algeria [æl'dʒɪərɪə] n Algérie f

Algerian [æl'dʒɪərɪən] adj algérien(ne) ▷ n
Algérien(ne)

Algiers [æl'dʒɪəz] n Alger

alias ['eɪlɪəs] adv alias ▷ n faux nom, nom
d'emprunt

alibi ['ælɪbaɪ] n alibi m

alien ['eɪlɪən] n (from abroad) étranger(-ère);
(from outer space) extraterrestre ▷ adj: **~ (to)**
étranger(-ère) (à)

alienate ['eɪlɪəneɪt] vt aliéner; (subj: person)
s'aliéner

alight [ə'laɪt] adj, adv en feu ▷ vi mettre pied à
terre; (passenger) descendre; (bird) se poser

align [ə'laɪn] vt aligner

alike [ə'laɪk] adj semblable, pareil(le) ▷ adv de
même; **to look ~** se ressembler

alimony ['ælɪmənɪ] n (payment) pension f
alimentaire

alive [ə'laɪv] adj vivant(e); (active) plein(e) de
vie; **~ with** grouillant(e) de; **~ to** sensible à

KEYWORD

all [ɔ:l] adj (singular) tout(e); (plural) tous/
toutes; **all day** toute la journée; **all night**
toute la nuit; **all men** tous les hommes; **all**

five tous les cinq; **all the food** toute la nourriture; **all the books** tous les livres; **all the time** tout le temps; **all his life** toute sa vie ▷ *pron* **1** tout; **I ate it all, I ate all of it** j'ai tout mangé; **all of us went** nous y sommes tous allés; **all of the boys went** tous les garçons y sont allés; **is that all?** c'est tout?; (*in shop*) ce sera tout?

2 (*in phrases*): **above all** surtout, par-dessus tout; **after all** après tout; **at all: not at all** (*in answer to question*) pas du tout; (*in answer to thanks*) je vous en prie!; **I'm not at all tired** je ne suis pas du tout fatigué(e); **anything at all will do** n'importe quoi fera l'affaire; **all in all** tout bien considéré, en fin de compte ▷ *adv*: **all alone** tout(e) seul(e); **it's not as hard as all that** ce n'est pas si difficile que ça; **all the more/the better** d'autant plus/ mieux; **all but** presque, pratiquement; **to be all in** (*Brit inf*) être complètement à plat; **the score is 2 all** le score est de 2 partout

Allah ['ælə] *n* Allah *m*
allegation [ælɪ'geɪʃən] *n* allégation *f*
allege [ə'ledʒ] *vt* alléguer, prétendre; **he is ~d to have said** il aurait dit
alleged [ə'ledʒd] *adj* prétendu(e)
allegedly [ə'ledʒɪdlɪ] *adv* à ce que l'on prétend, paraît-il
allegiance [ə'li:dʒəns] *n* fidélité *f*, obéissance *f*
allergic [ə'lə:dʒɪk] *adj*: **~ to** allergique à; **I'm ~ to penicillin** je suis allergique à la pénicilline
allergy ['ælədʒɪ] *n* allergie *f*
alleviate [ə'li:vɪeɪt] *vt* soulager, adoucir
alley ['ælɪ] *n* ruelle *f*; (*in garden*) allée *f*
alliance [ə'laɪəns] *n* alliance *f*
allied ['ælaɪd] *adj* allié(e)
alligator ['ælɪgeɪtər] *n* alligator *m*
all-in ['ɔ:lɪn] *adj, adv* (*Brit: charge*) tout compris
all-night ['ɔ:l'naɪt] *adj* ouvert(e) *or* qui dure toute la nuit
allocate ['æləkeɪt] *vt* (*share out*) répartir, distribuer; **to ~ sth to** (*duties*) assigner *or* attribuer qch à; (*sum, time*) allouer qch à; **to ~ sth for** affecter qch à
allot [ə'lɔt] *vt* (*share out*) répartir, distribuer; **to ~ sth to** (*time*) allouer qch à; (*duties*) assigner qch à; **in the ~ted time** dans le temps imparti
allotment [ə'lɔtmənt] *n* (*share*) part *f*; (*garden*) lopin *m* de terre (*loué à la municipalité*)
all-out ['ɔ:l'aut] *adj* (*effort etc*) total(e)
allow [ə'lau] *vt* (*practice, behaviour*) permettre, autoriser; (*sum to spend etc*) accorder, allouer; (*sum, time estimated*) compter, prévoir; (*claim, goal*) admettre; (*concede*): **to ~ that** convenir que; **to ~ sb to do** permettre à qn de faire, autoriser qn à faire; **he is ~ed to** ... on lui permet de ...; **smoking is not ~ed** il est interdit de fumer; **we must ~ three days for**

the journey il faut compter trois jours pour le voyage; **allow for** *vt fus* tenir compte de
allowance [ə'lauəns] *n* (*money received*) allocation *f*; (*: from parent etc*) subside *m*; (*: for expenses*) indemnité *f*; (*US: pocket money*) argent *m* de poche; (*Tax*) somme *f* déductible du revenu imposable, abattement *m*; **to make ~s for** (*person*) essayer de comprendre; (*thing*) tenir compte de
alloy ['ælɔɪ] *n* alliage *m*
all right *adv* (*feel, work*) bien; (*as answer*) d'accord
all-rounder [ɔ:l'raundər] *n* (*Brit*): **to be a good ~** être doué(e) en tout
all-time ['ɔ:l'taɪm] *adj* (*record*) sans précédent, absolu(e)
ally ['ælaɪ] *n* allié *m* ▷ *vt* [ə'laɪ]: **to ~ o.s. with** s'allier avec
almighty [ɔ:l'maɪtɪ] *adj* tout(e)-puissant(e); (*tremendous*) énorme
almond ['ɑ:mənd] *n* amande *f*
almost ['ɔ:lməust] *adv* presque; **he ~ fell** il a failli tomber
alone [ə'ləun] *adj, adv* seul(e); **to leave sb ~** laisser qn tranquille; **to leave sth ~** ne pas toucher à qch; **let ~ ...** sans parler de ...; encore moins ...
along [ə'lɔŋ] *prep* le long de ▷ *adv*: **is she coming ~ with us?** vient-il avec nous?; **he was hopping/limping ~** il venait *or* avançait en sautillant/boitant; **~ with** avec, en plus de; (*person*) en compagnie de; **all ~** (*all the time*) depuis le début
alongside [ə'lɔŋ'saɪd] *prep* (*along*) le long de; (*beside*) à côté de ▷ *adv* bord à bord; côte à côte; **we brought our boat ~** (*of a pier, shore etc*) nous avons accosté
aloof [ə'lu:f] *adj* distant(e) ▷ *adv* à distance, à l'écart; **to stand ~** se tenir à l'écart *or* à distance
aloud [ə'laud] *adv* à haute voix
alphabet ['ælfəbet] *n* alphabet *m*
alphabetical [ælfə'betɪkl] *adj* alphabétique; **in ~ order** par ordre alphabétique
alpine ['ælpaɪn] *adj* alpin(e), alpestre; **~ hut** cabane *f or* refuge *m* de montagne; **~ pasture** pâturage *m* (de montagne); **~ skiing** ski alpin
Alps [ælps] *npl*: **the ~** les Alpes *fpl*
already [ɔ:l'redɪ] *adv* déjà
alright ['ɔ:l'raɪt] *adv* (*Brit*) = **all right**
Alsatian [æl'seɪʃən] *adj* alsacien(ne), d'Alsace ▷ *n* Alsacien(ne); (*Brit: dog*) berger allemand
also ['ɔ:lsəu] *adv* aussi
altar ['ɔltər] *n* autel *m*
alter ['ɔltər] *vt, vi* changer
alteration [ɔltə'reɪʃən] *n* changement *m*, modification *f*; **alterations** *npl* (*Sewing*) retouches *fpl*; (*Archit*) modifications *fpl*; **timetable subject to ~** horaires sujets à modifications
alternate *adj* [ɔl'tə:nɪt] alterné(e), alternant(e), alternatif(-ive); (*US*)

= **alternative** ▷ vi ['ɔltəˌneɪt] alterner; **to ~ with** alterner avec; **on ~ days** un jour sur deux, tous les deux jours

alternative [ɔl'tɜːnətɪv] adj (solution, plan) autre, de remplacement; (energy) doux/ douce; (lifestyle) parallèle ▷ n (choice) alternative f; (other possibility) autre possibilité f; ~ **medicine** médecine alternative, médecine douce

alternatively [ɔl'tɜːnətɪvlɪ] adv: ~ **one could** ... une autre or l'autre solution serait de ...

alternator ['ɔltɜːneɪtə'] n (Aut) alternateur m

although [ɔːl'ðəu] conj bien que + sub

altitude ['æltɪtjuːd] n altitude f

alto ['æltəu] n (female) contralto m; (male) haute-contre f

altogether [ɔːltə'ɡɛðə'] adv entièrement, tout à fait; (on the whole) tout compte fait; (in all) en tout; **how much is that ~?** ça fait combien en tout?

aluminium [æljuˈmɪnɪəm], (US) **aluminum** [əˈluːmɪnəm] n aluminium m

always ['ɔːlweɪz] adv toujours

Alzheimer's ['æltshaɪməz], **Alzheimer's disease** n maladie f d'Alzheimer

AM abbr = **amplitude modulation** ▷ n abbr (= Assembly Member) député m au Parlement gallois

am [æm] vb see **be**

a.m. adv abbr (= ante meridiem) du matin

amalgamate [ə'mælɡəmeɪt] vt, vi fusionner

amass [ə'mæs] vt amasser

amateur ['æmətə'] n amateur m ▷ adj (Sport) amateur inv; ~ **dramatics** le théâtre amateur

amateurish ['æmətərɪʃ] adj (pej) d'amateur, un peu amateur

amaze [ə'meɪz] vt stupéfier; **to be ~d (at)** être stupéfait(e) (de)

amazed [ə'meɪzd] adj stupéfait(e)

amazement [ə'meɪzmənt] n surprise f, étonnement m

amazing [ə'meɪzɪŋ] adj étonnant(e), incroyable; (bargain, offer) exceptionnel(le)

Amazon ['æməzən] n (Geo, Mythology) Amazone f ▷ cpd amazonien(ne), de l'Amazone; **the ~ basin** le bassin de l'Amazone; **the ~ jungle** la forêt amazonienne

ambassador [æm'bæsədə'] n ambassadeur m

amber ['æmbə'] n ambre m; **at ~** (Brit Aut) à l'orange

ambiguous [æm'bɪɡjuəs] adj ambigu(ë)

ambition [æm'bɪʃən] n ambition f

ambitious [æm'bɪʃəs] adj ambitieux(-euse)

ambulance ['æmbjuləns] n ambulance f; **call an ~!** appelez une ambulance!

ambush ['æmbuʃ] n embuscade f ▷ vt tendre une embuscade à

amen ['ɑː'mɛn] excl amen

amenable [ə'miːnəbl] adj: ~ **to** (advice etc) disposé(e) à écouter or suivre; ~ **to the law** responsable devant la loi

amend [ə'mɛnd] vt (law) amender; (text) corriger; (habits) réformer ▷ vi s'amender, se corriger; **to make ~s** réparer ses torts, faire amende honorable

amendment [ə'mɛndmənt] n (to law) amendement m; (to text) correction f

amenities [ə'miːnɪtɪz] npl aménagements mpl, équipements mpl

America [ə'mɛrɪkə] n Amérique f

American [ə'mɛrɪkən] adj américain(e) ▷ n Américain(e)

American football n (Brit) football m américain

amiable ['eɪmɪəbl] adj aimable, affable

amicable ['æmɪkəbl] adj amical(e); (Law) à l'amiable

amid [ə'mɪd], **amidst** [ə'mɪdst] prep parmi, au milieu de

amiss [ə'mɪs] adj, adv: **there's something ~** il y a quelque chose qui ne va pas or qui cloche; **to take sth ~** prendre qch mal or de travers

ammonia [ə'məunɪə] n (gas) ammoniac m; (liquid) ammoniaque f

ammunition [æmju'nɪʃən] n munitions fpl; (fig) arguments mpl

amnesty ['æmnɪstɪ] n amnistie f; **to grant an ~** to accorder une amnistie à

amok [ə'mɔk] adv: **to run ~** être pris(e) d'un accès de folie furieuse

among [ə'mʌŋ], **amongst** [ə'mʌŋst] prep parmi, entre

amorous ['æmərəs] adj amoureux(-euse)

amount [ə'maunt] n (sum of money) somme f; (total) montant m; (quantity) quantité f; nombre m ▷ vi: **to ~ to** (total) s'élever à; (be same as) équivaloir à, revenir à; **this ~s to a refusal** cela équivaut à un refus; **the total ~** (of money) le montant total

amp ['æmp], **ampère** ['æmpɛə'] n ampère m; **a 13 ~ plug** une fiche de 13 A

ample ['æmpl] adj ample, spacieux(-euse); (enough): **this is ~** c'est largement suffisant; **to have ~ time/room** avoir bien assez de temps/place, avoir largement le temps/la place

amplifier ['æmplɪfaɪə'] n amplificateur m

amputate ['æmpjuteɪt] vt amputer

Amtrak ['æmtræk] (US) n société mixte de transports ferroviaires interurbains pour voyageurs

amuse [ə'mjuːz] vt amuser; **to ~ o.s. with sth/by doing sth** se divertir avec qch/à faire qch; **to be ~d at** être amusé par; **he was not ~d** il n'a pas apprécié

amusement [ə'mjuːzmənt] n amusement m; (pastime) distraction f

amusement arcade n salle f de jeu

amusement park n parc m d'attractions

amusing [ə'mjuːzɪŋ] adj amusant(e), divertissant(e)

an [æn, ən, n] indef art see **a**

anaemia, (US) **anemia** [ə'niːmɪə] n anémie f

anaemic, (US) **anemic** [ə'niːmɪk] adj anémique

anaesthetic, (US) **anesthetic** [ænɪs'θεtɪk] *adj, n* anesthésique *m*; **under the ~** sous anesthésie; **local/general ~** anesthésie locale/générale

analogue, analog ['ænəlɒg] *adj* (*watch, computer*) analogique

analogy [ə'nælədʒɪ] *n* analogie *f*; **to draw an ~ between** établir une analogie entre

analyse, (US) **analyze** ['ænəlaɪz] *vt* analyser

analysis (*pl* **analyses**) [ə'næləsɪs, -siːz] *n* analyse *f*; **in the last ~** en dernière analyse

analyst ['ænəlɪst] *n* (*political analyst etc*) analyste *m/f*; (US) psychanalyste *m/f*

analyze ['ænəlaɪz] *vt* (US) = **analyse**

anarchist ['ænəkɪst] *n*, *a* anarchiste (*m/f*)

anarchy ['ænəkɪ] *n* anarchie *f*

anatomy [ə'nætəmɪ] *n* anatomie *f*

ancestor ['ænsɪstə*r*] *n* ancêtre *m*, aïeul *m*

anchor ['æŋkə*r*] *n* ancre *f* ▷ *vi* (*also*: **to drop ~**) jeter l'ancre, mouiller ▷ *vt* mettre à l'ancre; (*fig*) **to ~ sth to** fixer qch à; **to weigh ~** lever l'ancre

anchovy ['æntʃəvɪ] *n* anchois *m*

ancient ['eɪnʃənt] *adj* ancien(ne), antique; (*person*) d'un âge vénérable; (*car*) antédiluvien(ne); **~ monument** monument *m* historique

ancillary [æn'sɪlərɪ] *adj* auxiliaire

and [ænd] *conj* et; **~ so on** et ainsi de suite; **try ~ come** tâchez de venir; **come ~ sit here** venez vous asseoir ici; **he talked ~ talked** il a parlé pendant des heures; **better ~ better** de mieux en mieux; **more ~ more** de plus en plus

Andorra [æn'dɔːrə] *n* (principauté *f* d')Andorre *f*

anemia *etc* [ə'niːmɪə] *n* (US) = **anaemia** *etc*

anesthetic [ænɪs'θεtɪk] *n*, *adj* (US) = **anaesthetic**

anew [ə'njuː] *adv* à nouveau

angel ['eɪndʒəl] *n* ange *m*

anger ['æŋgə*r*] *n* colère *f* ▷ *vt* mettre en colère, irriter

angina [æn'dʒaɪnə] *n* angine *f* de poitrine

angle ['æŋgl] *n* angle *m* ▷ *vi*: **to ~ for** (*trout*) pêcher; (*compliments*) chercher, quêter; **from their ~** de leur point de vue

angler ['æŋglə*r*] *n* pêcheur(-euse) à la ligne

Anglican ['æŋglɪkən] *adj*, *n* anglican(e)

angling ['æŋglɪŋ] *n* pêche *f* à la ligne

Anglo- ['æŋgləʊ] *prefix* anglo(-)

angrily ['æŋgrɪlɪ] *adv* avec colère

angry ['æŋgrɪ] *adj* en colère, furieux(-euse); (*wound*) enflammé(e); **to be ~ with sb/at sth** être furieux contre qn/de qch; **to get ~** se fâcher, se mettre en colère; **to make sb ~** mettre qn en colère

anguish ['æŋgwɪʃ] *n* angoisse *f*

animal ['ænɪməl] *n* animal *m* ▷ *adj* animal(e)

animate *vt* ['ænɪmeɪt] animer ▷ *adj* ['ænɪmɪt] animé(e), vivant(e)

animated ['ænɪmeɪtɪd] *adj* animé(e)

animation [ænɪ'meɪʃən] *n* (*of person*) entrain *m*; (*of street, Cine*) animation *f*

aniseed ['ænɪsiːd] *n* anis *m*

ankle ['æŋkl] *n* cheville *f*

ankle socks *npl* socquettes *fpl*

annex ['ænεks] *n* (*Brit: also*: **~e**) annexe *f* ▷ *vt* [ə'nεks] annexer

anniversary [ænɪ'vəːsərɪ] *n* anniversaire *m*

announce [ə'naʊns] *vt* annoncer; (*birth, death*) faire part de; **he ~d that he wasn't going** il a déclaré qu'il n'irait pas

announcement [ə'naʊnsmənt] *n* annonce *f*; (*for births etc: in newspaper*) avis *m* de faire-part; (*: letter, card*) faire-part *m*; **I'd like to make an ~** j'ai une communication à faire

announcer [ə'naʊnsə*r*] *n* (*Radio, TV: between programmes*) speaker(ine); (*: in a programme*) présentateur(-trice)

annoy [ə'nɔɪ] *vt* agacer, ennuyer, contrarier; **to be ~ed (at sth/with sb)** être en colère *or* irrité (contre qch/qn); **don't get ~ed!** ne vous fâchez pas!

annoyance [ə'nɔɪəns] *n* mécontentement *m*, contrariété *f*

annoying [ə'nɔɪɪŋ] *adj* agaçant(e), contrariant(e)

annual ['ænjuəl] *adj* annuel(le) ▷ *n* (*Bot*) plante annuelle; (*book*) album *m*

annually ['ænjuəlɪ] *adv* annuellement

annul [ə'nʌl] *vt* annuler; (*law*) abroger

annum ['ænəm] *n see* **per**

anonymous [ə'nɒnɪməs] *adj* anonyme; **to remain ~** garder l'anonymat

anorak ['ænəræk] *n* anorak *m*

anorexia [ænə'rεksɪə] *n* (*also*: **~ nervosa**) anorexie *f*

anorexic [ænə'rεksɪk] *adj*, *n* anorexique (*m/f*)

another [ə'nʌðə*r*] *adj*: **~ book** (*one more*) un autre livre, encore un livre, un livre de plus; (*a different one*) un autre livre ▷ *pron* un(e) autre, encore un(e), un(e) de plus; **~ drink?** encore un verre?; **in ~ five years** dans cinq ans; *see also* **one**

answer ['ɑːnsə*r*] *n* réponse *f*; (*to problem*) solution *f* ▷ *vi* répondre ▷ *vt* (*reply to*) répondre à; (*problem*) résoudre; (*prayer*) exaucer; **in ~ to your letter** suite à *or* en réponse à votre lettre; **to ~ the phone** répondre (au téléphone); **to ~ the bell** *or* **the door** aller *or* venir ouvrir (la porte); **answer back** *vi* répondre, répliquer; **answer for** *vt fus* répondre de, se porter garant de; (*crime, one's actions*) répondre de; **answer to** *vt fus* (*description*) répondre *or* correspondre à

answerable ['ɑːnsərəbl] *adj*: **~ (to sb/for sth)** responsable (devant qn/de qch); **I am ~ to no-one** je n'ai de comptes à rendre à personne

answering machine ['ɑːnsərɪŋ-] *n* répondeur *m*

answerphone ['ɑːnsəfəʊn] *n* (*esp Brit*) répondeur *m* (téléphonique)

ant [ænt] n fourmi f
antagonism [æn'tægənɪzəm] n
antagonisme m
antagonize [æn'tægənaɪz] vt éveiller
l'hostilité de, contrarier
Antarctic [ænt'ɑːktɪk] adj antarctique,
austral(e) ▷ n: **the ~** l'Antarctique m
antelope ['æntɪləup] n antilope f
antenatal ['æntɪ'neɪtl] adj prénatal(e)
antenatal clinic n service m de consultation
prénatale
antenna (pl **antennae**) [æn'tɛnə, -niː] n
antenne f
anthem ['ænθəm] n motet m; **national ~**
hymne national
anthology [æn'θɔlədʒɪ] n anthologie f
anthrax ['ænθræks] n anthrax m
anthropology [ænθrə'pɔlədʒɪ] n
anthropologie f
anti ['æntɪ] prefix anti-
anti-aircraft ['æntɪ'ɛəkrɑːft] adj
antiaérien(ne)
antibiotic ['æntɪbaɪ'ɔtɪk] adj, n
antibiotique m
antibody ['æntɪbɔdɪ] n anticorps m
anticipate [æn'tɪsɪpeɪt] vt s'attendre à,
prévoir; (wishes, request) aller au devant de,
devancer; **this is worse than I ~d** c'est pire
que je ne pensais; **as ~d** comme prévu
anticipation [æntɪsɪ'peɪʃən] n attente f;
thanking you in ~ en vous remerciant
d'avance, avec mes remerciements anticipés
anticlimax ['æntɪ'klaɪmæks] n déception f
anticlockwise ['æntɪ'klɔkwaɪz] (Brit) adv
dans le sens inverse des aiguilles d'une
montre
antics ['æntɪks] npl singeries fpl
antidepressant ['æntɪdɪ'prɛsnt] n
antidépresseur m
antidote ['æntɪdəut] n antidote m,
contrepoison m
antifreeze ['æntɪfriːz] n antigel m
anti-globalization ['æntɪgləubəlaɪ'zeɪʃən] n
antimondialisation f
antihistamine [æntɪ'hɪstəmɪn] n
antihistaminique m
antiperspirant [æntɪ'pəːspɪrənt] n
déodorant m
antiquated ['æntɪkweɪtɪd] adj vieilli(e),
suranné(e), vieillot(te)
antique [æn'tiːk] n (ornament) objet m d'art
ancien; (furniture) meuble ancien ▷ adj
ancien(ne); (pre-mediaeval) antique
antique dealer n antiquaire m/f
antique shop n magasin m d'antiquités
anti-Semitism ['æntɪ'sɛmɪtɪzəm] n
antisémitisme m
antiseptic [æntɪ'sɛptɪk] adj, n antiseptique (m)
antisocial ['æntɪ'səuʃəl] adj (unfriendly) peu
liant(e), insociable; (against society) antisocial(e)
antiviral ['æntɪvaɪərəl] adj (Med)
antiviral

antivirus [æntɪ'vaɪrəs] adj (Comput) antivirus
inv; **~ software** (logiciel m) antivirus
antlers ['æntləz] npl bois mpl, ramure f
anvil ['ænvɪl] n enclume f
anxiety [æŋ'zaɪətɪ] n anxiété f; (keenness):
~ to do grand désir or impatience f de faire
anxious ['æŋkʃəs] adj (très) inquiet(-ète);
(always worried) anxieux(-euse); (worrying)
angoissant(e); (keen): **~ to do/that** qui tient
beaucoup à faire/à ce que + sub; impatient(e)
de faire/que + sub; **I'm very ~ about you** je me
fais beaucoup de souci pour toi

⊙ **KEYWORD**

any ['ɛnɪ] adj **1** (in questions etc: singular) du, de l',
de la; (: plural) des; **do you have any butter/
children/ink?** avez-vous du beurre/des
enfants/de l'encre?
2 (with negative) de, d'; **I don't have any
money/books** je n'ai pas d'argent/de livres;
without any difficulty sans la moindre
difficulté
3 (no matter which) n'importe quel(le); (each and
every) tout(e), chaque; **choose any book you
like** vous pouvez choisir n'importe quel
livre; **any teacher you ask will tell you**
n'importe quel professeur vous le dira
4 (in phrases): **in any case** de toute façon; **any
day now** d'un jour à l'autre; **at any moment**
à tout moment, d'un instant à l'autre; **at
any rate** en tout cas; **any time** n'importe
quand; **he might come (at) any time** il
pourrait venir n'importe quand; **come (at)
any time** venez quand vous voulez
▷ pron **1** (in questions etc) en; **have you got any?**
est-ce que vous en avez?; **can any of you
sing?** est-ce que parmi vous il y en a qui
savent chanter?
2 (with negative) en; **I don't have any (of
them)** je n'en ai pas, je n'en ai aucun
3 (no matter which one(s)) n'importe lequel (or
laquelle); (anybody) n'importe qui; **take any
of those books (you like)** vous pouvez
prendre n'importe lequel de ces livres
▷ adv **1** (in questions etc): **do you want any more
soup/sandwiches?** voulez-vous encore de la
soupe/des sandwichs?; **are you feeling any
better?** est-ce que vous vous sentez mieux?
2 (with negative): **I can't hear him any more**
je ne l'entends plus; **don't wait any longer**
n'attendez pas plus longtemps

anybody ['ɛnɪbɔdɪ] pron n'importe qui; (in
interrogative sentences) quelqu'un; (in negative
sentences): **I don't see ~** je ne vois personne; **if
~ should phone ...** si quelqu'un téléphone ...
anyhow ['ɛnɪhau] adv quoi qu'il en soit;
(haphazardly) n'importe comment; **do it ~ you
like** faites-le comme vous voulez; **she leaves
things just ~** elle laisse tout traîner; **I shall
go ~** j'irai de toute façon

anyone ['ɛnɪwʌn] pron = **anybody**

anything ['ɛnɪθɪŋ] pron (no matter what) n'importe quoi; (in questions) quelque chose; (with negative) ne ... rien; **I don't want ~** je ne veux rien; **can you see ~?** tu vois quelque chose?; **if ~ happens to me ...** s'il m'arrive quoi que ce soit ...; **you can say ~ you like** vous pouvez dire ce que vous voulez; **~ will do** n'importe quoi fera l'affaire; **he'll eat ~** il mange de tout; **~ else?** (in shop) avec ceci?; **it can cost ~ between £15 and £20** (Brit) ça peut coûter dans les 15 à 20 livres

anytime ['ɛnɪtaɪm] adv (at any moment) d'un moment à l'autre; (whenever) n'importe quand

anyway ['ɛnɪweɪ] adv de toute façon; **~, I couldn't come even if I wanted to** de toute façon, je ne pouvais pas venir même si je le voulais; **I shall go ~** j'irai quand même; **why are you phoning, ~?** au fait, pourquoi tu me téléphones?

anywhere ['ɛnɪwɛəʳ] adv n'importe où; (in interrogative sentences) quelque part; (in negative sentences): **I can't see him ~** je ne le vois nulle part; **can you see him ~?** tu le vois quelque part?; **put the books down ~** pose les livres n'importe où; **~ in the world** (no matter where) n'importe où dans le monde

apart [ə'pɑːt] adv (to one side) à part; de côté; à l'écart; (separately) séparément; **to take/pull ~** démonter; **10 miles/a long way ~** à 10 miles/très éloignés l'un de l'autre; **they are living ~** ils sont séparés; **~ from** prep à part, excepté

apartheid [ə'pɑːteɪt] n apartheid m

apartment [ə'pɑːtmənt] n (US) appartement m, logement m; (room) chambre f

apartment building n (US) immeuble m; maison divisée en appartements

apathy ['æpəθɪ] n apathie f, indifférence f

ape [eɪp] n (grand) singe ▷ vt singer

aperitif [ə'pɛrɪtɪf] n apéritif m

aperture ['æpətʃjuəʳ] n orifice m, ouverture f; (Phot) ouverture (du diaphragme)

APEX ['eɪpɛks] n abbr (Aviat: = advance purchase excursion) APEX m

apex ['eɪpɛks] n sommet m

apologetic [əpɒlə'dʒɛtɪk] adj (tone, letter) d'excuse; **to be very ~ about** s'excuser vivement de

apologize [ə'pɒlədʒaɪz] vi: **to ~ (for sth to sb)** s'excuser (de qch auprès de qn), présenter des excuses (à qn pour qch)

apology [ə'pɒlədʒɪ] n excuses fpl; **to send one's apologies** envoyer une lettre or un mot d'excuse, s'excuser (de ne pas pouvoir venir); **please accept my apologies** vous voudriez bien m'excuser

apostle [ə'pɒsl] n apôtre m

apostrophe [ə'pɒstrəfɪ] n apostrophe f

app n abbr (Comput) = **application**

appal, (US) **appall** [ə'pɔːl] vt consterner, atterrer; horrifier

appalling [ə'pɔːlɪŋ] adj épouvantable; (stupidity) consternant(e); **she's an ~ cook** c'est une très mauvaise cuisinière

apparatus [æpə'reɪtəs] n appareil m, dispositif m; (in gymnasium) agrès mpl

apparel [ə'pærl] n (US) habillement m, confection f

apparent [ə'pærənt] adj apparent(e); **it is ~ that** il est évident que

apparently [ə'pærəntlɪ] adv apparemment

appeal [ə'piːl] vi (Law) faire or interjeter appel ▷ n (Law) appel m; (request) appel; prière f; (charm) attrait m, charme m; **to ~ for** demander (instamment); implorer; **to ~ to** (beg) faire appel à; (be attractive) plaire à; **to ~ to sb for mercy** implorer la pitié de qn, prier or adjurer qn d'avoir pitié; **it doesn't ~ to me** cela ne m'attire pas; **right of ~** droit m de recours

appealing [ə'piːlɪŋ] adj (attractive) attrayant(e); (touching) attendrissant(e)

appear [ə'pɪəʳ] vi apparaître, se montrer; (Law) comparaître; (publication) paraître, sortir, être publié(e); (seem) paraître, sembler; **it would ~ that** il semble que; **to ~ in Hamlet** jouer dans Hamlet; **to ~ on TV** passer à la télé

appearance [ə'pɪərəns] n apparition f; parution f; (look, aspect) apparence f, aspect m; **to put in or make an ~** faire acte de présence; (Theat): **by order of ~** par ordre d'entrée en scène; **to keep up ~s** sauver les apparences; **to all ~s** selon toute apparence

appease [ə'piːz] vt apaiser, calmer

appendices [ə'pɛndɪsiːz] npl of **appendix**

appendicitis [əpɛndɪ'saɪtɪs] n appendicite f

appendix (pl **appendices**) [ə'pɛndɪks, -siːz] n appendice m; **to have one's ~ out** se faire opérer de l'appendicite

appetite ['æpɪtaɪt] n appétit m; **that walk has given me an ~** cette promenade m'a ouvert l'appétit

appetizer ['æpɪtaɪzəʳ] n (food) amuse-gueule m; (drink) apéritif m

applaud [ə'plɔːd] vt, vi applaudir

applause [ə'plɔːz] n applaudissements mpl

apple ['æpl] n pomme f; (also: **~ tree**) pommier m; **it's the ~ of my eye** j'y tiens comme à la prunelle de mes yeux

apple pie n tarte f aux pommes

appliance [ə'plaɪəns] n appareil m; **electrical ~s** l'électroménager m

applicable [ə'plɪkəbl] adj applicable; **the law is ~ from January** la loi entre en vigueur au mois de janvier; **to be ~ to** (relevant) valoir pour

applicant ['æplɪkənt] n: **~ (for)** (Admin: for benefit etc) demandeur(-euse) (de); (for post) candidat(e) (à)

application [æplɪ'keɪʃən] n application f; (for a job, a grant etc) demande f; candidature f;

(*Comput*) application *f*, (*logiciel m*) applicatif *m*;
on ~ sur demande
application form *n* formulaire *m* de
demande
applied [əˈplaɪd] *adj* appliqué(e); **~ arts** *npl*
arts décoratifs
apply [əˈplaɪ] *vt*: **to ~ (to)** (*paint, ointment*)
appliquer (sur); (*law, etc*) appliquer (à) ▷ *vi*:
to ~ to (*ask*) s'adresser à; (*be suitable for, relevant
to*) s'appliquer à, être valable pour; **to ~ (for)**
(*permit, grant*) faire une demande (en vue
d'obtenir); (*job*) poser sa candidature (pour),
faire une demande d'emploi (concernant);
to ~ the brakes actionner les freins, freiner;
to ~ o.s. s'appliquer à
appoint [əˈpɔɪnt] *vt* (*to post*) nommer,
engager; (*date, place*) fixer, désigner
appointment [əˈpɔɪntmənt] *n* (*to post*)
nomination *f*; (*job*) poste *m*; (*arrangement to
meet*) rendez-vous *m*; **to have an ~** avoir un
rendez-vous; **to make an ~ (with)** prendre
rendez-vous (avec); **I'd like to make an ~** je
voudrais prendre rendez-vous; **"~s (vacant)"**
(*Press*) "offres d'emploi"; **by ~** sur rendez-vous
appraisal [əˈpreɪzl] *n* évaluation *f*
appreciate [əˈpriːʃieɪt] *vt* (*like*) apprécier,
faire cas de; (*be grateful for*) être
reconnaissant(e) de; (*assess*) évaluer; (*be
aware of*) comprendre, se rendre compte de
▷ *vi* (*Finance*) prendre de la valeur; **I ~ your
help** je vous remercie pour votre aide
appreciation [əpriːʃiˈeɪʃən] *n* appréciation *f*;
(*gratitude*) reconnaissance *f*; (*Finance*) hausse
f, valorisation *f*
appreciative [əˈpriːʃiətɪv] *adj* (*person*)
sensible; (*comment*) élogieux(-euse)
apprehension [æprɪˈhɛnʃən] *n*
appréhension *f*, inquiétude *f*
apprehensive [æprɪˈhɛnsɪv] *adj*
inquiet(-ète), appréhensif(-ive)
apprentice [əˈprɛntɪs] *n* apprenti *m* ▷ *vt*: **to
be ~d** être en apprentissage chez
apprenticeship [əˈprɛntɪʃɪp] *n*
apprentissage *m*; **to serve one's ~** faire son
apprentissage
approach [əˈprəʊtʃ] *vi* approcher ▷ *vt* (*come
near*) approcher de; (*ask, apply to*) s'adresser à;
(*subject, passer-by*) aborder ▷ *n* approche *f*;
accès *m*, abord *m*; démarche *f* (*auprès de qn*);
(*intellectual*) démarche *f*; **to ~ sb about sth**
aller *or* venir voir qn pour qch
approachable [əˈprəʊtʃəbl] *adj* accessible
appropriate *adj* [əˈprəʊpriɪt] (*tool etc*) qui
convient, approprié(e); (*moment, remark*)
opportun(e) ▷ *vt* [əˈprəʊprieɪt] (*take*)
s'approprier; (*allot*): **to ~ sth for** affecter qch
à; **~ for** *or* **to** approprié à; **it would not be ~
for me to comment** il ne me serait pas
approprié de commenter
approval [əˈpruːvəl] *n* approbation *f*; **to
meet with sb's ~** (*proposal etc*) recueillir
l'assentiment de qn; **on ~** (*Comm*) à l'examen

approve [əˈpruːv] *vt* approuver; **approve of**
vt fus (*thing*) approuver; (*person*): **they don't ~
of her** ils n'ont pas bonne opinion d'elle
approximate [əˈprɔksɪmɪt] *adj*
approximatif(-ive) ▷ *vt* [əˈprɔksɪmeɪt] se
rapprocher de; être proche de
approximately [əˈprɔksɪmətlɪ] *adv*
approximativement
Apr. *abbr* = **April**
apricot [ˈeɪprɪkɔt] *n* abricot *m*
April [ˈeɪprəl] *n* avril *m*; **~ fool!** poisson
d'avril!; *see also* **July**
April Fools' Day *n* le premier avril; *voir article*

❀ **APRIL FOOLS' DAY**

April Fools' Day est le 1er avril, à l'occasion
duquel on fait des farces de toutes sortes.
Les victimes de ces farces sont les "April
fools". Traditionnellement, on n'est
censé faire des farces que jusqu'à midi.

apron [ˈeɪprən] *n* tablier *m*; (*Aviat*) aire *f* de
stationnement
apt [æpt] *adj* (*suitable*) approprié(e); (*able*): **~
(at)** doué(e) (pour); apte (à); (*likely*): **~ to do**
susceptible de faire; ayant tendance à faire
aquarium [əˈkwɛəriəm] *n* aquarium *m*
Aquarius [əˈkwɛəriəs] *n* le Verseau; **to be ~**
être du Verseau
Arab [ˈærəb] *n* Arabe *m/f* ▷ *adj* arabe
Arabia [əˈreɪbiə] *n* Arabie *f*
Arabian [əˈreɪbiən] *adj* arabe
Arabic [ˈærəbɪk] *adj, n* arabe (*m*)
arbitrary [ˈɑːbɪtrərɪ] *adj* arbitraire
arbitration [ɑːbɪˈtreɪʃən] *n* arbitrage *m*; **the
dispute went to ~** le litige a été soumis à
arbitrage
arc [ɑːk] *n* arc *m*
arcade [ɑːˈkeɪd] *n* arcade *f*; (*passage with shops*)
passage *m*, galerie *f*; (*with games*) salle *f* de jeu
arch [ɑːtʃ] *n* arche *f*; (*of foot*) cambrure *f*, voûte
f plantaire ▷ *vt* arquer, cambrer ▷ *adj*
malicieux(-euse) ▷ *prefix*: **~(-)** achevé(e); par
excellence; **pointed ~** ogive *f*
archaeologist [ɑːkɪˈɔlədʒɪst] *n*
archéologue *m/f*
archaeology, (US) **archeology** [ɑːkɪˈɔlədʒɪ]
n archéologie *f*
archbishop [ɑːtʃˈbɪʃəp] *n* archevêque *m*
archeology [ɑːkɪˈɔlədʒɪ] (US) *n* = **archaeology**
archery [ˈɑːtʃərɪ] *n* tir *m* à l'arc
architect [ˈɑːkɪtɛkt] *n* architecte *m*
architectural [ɑːkɪˈtɛktʃərəl] *adj*
architectural(e)
architecture [ˈɑːkɪtɛktʃə*r*] *n* architecture *f*
archive [ˈɑːkaɪv] *n* (*often pl*) archives *fpl*
archives [ˈɑːkaɪvz] *npl* archives *fpl*
Arctic [ˈɑːktɪk] *adj* arctique ▷ *n*: **the ~**
l'Arctique *m*
ardent [ˈɑːdənt] *adj* fervent(e)
are [ɑː*r*] *vb see* **be**

area ['ɛərɪə] n (Geom) superficie f; (zone) région f; (: smaller) secteur m; (in room) coin m; (knowledge, research) domaine m; **the London ~** la région Londonienne

area code (US) n (Tel) indicatif m de zone

arena [ə'ri:nə] n arène f

aren't [ɑ:nt] = are not

Argentina [ɑ:dʒən'ti:nə] n Argentine f

Argentinian [ɑ:dʒən'tɪnɪən] adj argentin(e) ▷ n Argentin(e)

arguably ['ɑ:gjuəblɪ] adv: **it is ~ ...** on peut soutenir que c'est ...

argue ['ɑ:gju:] vi (quarrel) se disputer; (reason) argumenter ▷ vt (debate: case, matter) débattre; **to ~ about sth (with sb)** se disputer (avec qn) au sujet de qch; **to ~ that** objecter or alléguer que, donner comme argument que

argument ['ɑ:gjumənt] n (quarrel) dispute f, discussion f; (reasons) argument m; (debate) discussion, controverse f; **~ for/against** argument pour/contre

argumentative [ɑ:gju'mɛntətɪv] adj ergoteur(-euse), raisonneur(-euse)

Aries ['ɛərɪz] n le Bélier; **to be ~** être du Bélier

arise (pt arose, pp arisen) [ə'raɪz, ə'rəuz, ə'rɪzn] vi survenir, se présenter; **to ~ from** résulter de; **should the need ~** en cas de besoin

aristocrat ['ærɪstəkræt] n aristocrate m/f

arithmetic [ə'rɪθmətɪk] n arithmétique f

ark [ɑ:k] n: **Noah's A~** l'Arche f de Noé

arm [ɑ:m] n bras m ▷ vt armer; **arms** npl (weapons, Heraldry) armes fpl; **~ in ~** bras dessus bras dessous

armaments ['ɑ:məmənts] npl (weapons) armement m

armchair ['ɑ:mtʃɛəʳ] n fauteuil m

armed [ɑ:md] adj armé(e)

armed forces npl: **the ~** les forces armées

armed robbery n vol m à main armée

armour, (US) **armor** ['ɑ:məʳ] n armure f; (also: ~-plating) blindage m; (Mil: tanks) blindés mpl

armoured car, (US) **armored car** ['ɑ:məd-] n véhicule blindé

armpit ['ɑ:mpɪt] n aisselle f

armrest ['ɑ:mrɛst] n accoudoir m

army ['ɑ:mɪ] n armée f

A road n (Brit) ≈ route nationale

aroma [ə'rəumə] n arôme m

aromatherapy [ərəumə'θerəpɪ] n aromathérapie f

arose [ə'rəuz] pt of **arise**

around [ə'raund] adv (tout) autour; (nearby) dans les parages ▷ prep autour de; (near) près de; (fig: about) environ; (: date, time) vers; **is he ~?** est-il dans les parages or là?

arouse [ə'rauz] vt (sleeper) éveiller; (curiosity, passions) éveiller, susciter; (anger) exciter

arrange [ə'reɪndʒ] vt arranger; (programme) arrêter, convenir de ▷ vi: **we have ~d for a** car to pick you up nous avons prévu qu'une voiture vienne vous prendre; **it was ~d that ...** il a été convenu que ..., il a été décidé que ...; **to ~ to do sth** prévoir de faire qch

arrangement [ə'reɪndʒmənt] n arrangement m; **to come to an ~ (with sb)** se mettre d'accord (avec qn); **home deliveries by ~** livraison à domicile sur demande; **arrangements** npl (plans etc) arrangements mpl, dispositions fpl; **I'll make ~s for you to be met** je vous enverrai chercher

array [ə'reɪ] n (of objects) déploiement m, étalage m; (Math, Comput) tableau m

arrears [ə'rɪəz] npl arriéré m; **to be in ~ with one's rent** devoir un arriéré de loyer, être en retard pour le paiement de son loyer

arrest [ə'rɛst] vt arrêter; (sb's attention) retenir, attirer ▷ n arrestation f; **under ~** en état d'arrestation

arrival [ə'raɪvl] n arrivée f; (Comm) arrivage m; (person) arrivant(e); **new ~** nouveau venu/ nouvelle venue; (baby) nouveau-né(e)

arrive [ə'raɪv] vi arriver; **arrive at** vt fus (decision, solution) parvenir à

arrogance ['ærəgəns] n arrogance f

arrogant ['ærəgənt] adj arrogant(e)

arrow ['ærəu] n flèche f

arse [ɑ:s] n (Brit infl) cul m (!)

arson ['ɑ:sn] n incendie criminel

art [ɑ:t] n art m; (craft) métier m; **work of ~** œuvre f d'art; **Arts** npl (Scol) les lettres fpl

art college n école f des beaux-arts

artery ['ɑ:tərɪ] n artère f

art gallery n musée m d'art; (saleroom) galerie f de peinture

arthritis [ɑ:'θraɪtɪs] n arthrite f

artichoke ['ɑ:tɪtʃəuk] n artichaut m; **Jerusalem ~** topinambour m

article ['ɑ:tɪkl] n article m; (Brit Law: training): **articles** npl stage m; **~s of clothing** vêtements mpl

articulate adj [ɑ:'tɪkjulɪt] (person) qui s'exprime clairement et aisément; (speech) bien articulé(e), prononcé(e) clairement ▷ vi [ɑ:'tɪkjulɛt] articuler, parler distinctement ▷ vt articuler

articulated lorry [ɑ:'tɪkjulɛtɪd-] n (Brit) (camion m) semi-remorque m

artificial [ɑ:tɪ'fɪʃəl] adj artificiel(le)

artificial respiration n respiration artificielle

artist ['ɑ:tɪst] n artiste m/f

artistic [ɑ:'tɪstɪk] adj artistique

artistry ['ɑ:tɪstrɪ] n art m, talent m

art school n école f des beaux-arts

⬤ **KEYWORD**

as [æz] conj **1** (time: moment) comme, alors que; (: duration) tandis que; **he came in as I was leaving** il est arrivé comme je partais; **as the years went by** à mesure

que les années passaient; **as from
tomorrow** à partir de demain
2 *(since, because)* comme, puisque; **he left
early as he had to be home by 10** comme il
or puisqu'il devait être de retour avant 10h, il
est parti de bonne heure
3 *(referring to manner, way)* comme; **do as you
wish** faites comme vous voudrez; **as she said**
comme elle disait
▷ *adv* **1** *(in comparisons)*: **as big as** aussi grand
que; **twice as big as** deux fois plus grand
que; **big as it is** si grand que ce soit; **much as
I like them, I ...** je les aime bien, mais je ...;
as much or **many as** autant que; **as much
money/many books as** autant d'argent/de
livres que; **as soon as** dès que
2 *(concerning)*: **as for** or **to that** quant à cela,
pour ce qui est de cela
3: **as if** or **though** comme si; **he looked as if
he was ill** il avait l'air d'être malade; *see also*
long; such; well
▷ *prep (in the capacity of)* en tant que, en qualité
de; **he works as a driver** il travaille comme
chauffeur; **as chairman of the company,
he ...** en tant que président de la société, il ...;
dressed up as a cowboy déguisé en cowboy;
he gave me it as a present il me l'a offert, il
m'en a fait cadeau

a.s.a.p. *abbr* = **as soon as possible**
asbestos [æz'bɛstəs] *n* asbeste *m*, amiante *m*
ascend [ə'sɛnd] *vt* gravir
ascent [ə'sɛnt] *n (climb)* ascension *f*
ascertain [æsə'teɪn] *vt* s'assurer de, vérifier;
établir
ash [æʃ] *n (dust)* cendre *f*; *(also:* **~ tree**) frêne *m*
ashamed [ə'ʃeɪmd] *adj* honteux(-euse),
confus(e); **to be ~ of** avoir honte de; **to be ~
(of o.s.) for having done** avoir honte d'avoir
fait
ashore [ə'ʃɔːʳ] *adv* à terre; **to go ~** aller à terre,
débarquer
ashtray ['æʃtreɪ] *n* cendrier *m*
Ash Wednesday *n* mercredi *m* des Cendres
Asia ['eɪʃə] *n* Asie *f*
Asian ['eɪʃən] *n (from Asia)* Asiatique *m/f*; *(Brit:
from Indian subcontinent)* Indo-Pakistanais(-e)
▷ *adj* asiatique; indo-pakistanais(-e)
aside [ə'saɪd] *adv* de côté; à l'écart ▷ *n*
aparté *m*; **~ from** *prep* à part, excepté
ask [ɑːsk] *vt* demander; *(invite)* inviter; **to ~ sb
sth/to do sth** demander à qn qch/de faire
qch; **to ~ sb the time** demander l'heure à qn;
to ~ sb about sth questionner qn au sujet de
qch; se renseigner auprès de qn au sujet de
qch; **to ~ about the price** s'informer du prix,
se renseigner au sujet du prix; **to ~ (sb) a
question** poser une question (à qn); **to ~ sb
out to dinner** inviter qn au restaurant; **ask
after** *vt fus* demander des nouvelles de; **ask
for** *vt fus* demander; **it's just ~ing for
trouble** or **for it** ce serait chercher des ennuis

asking price ['ɑːskɪŋ-] *n* prix demandé
asleep [ə'sliːp] *adj* endormi(e); **to be ~**
dormir, être endormi; **to fall ~** s'endormir
AS level *n abbr* (= *Advanced Subsidiary level*)
*première partie de l'examen équivalent au
baccalauréat*
asparagus [əs'pærəgəs] *n* asperges *fpl*
aspect ['æspɛkt] *n* aspect *m*; *(direction in which
a building etc faces)* orientation *f*, exposition *f*
aspire [əs'paɪəʳ] *vi*: **to ~ to** aspirer à
aspirin ['æsprɪn] *n* aspirine *f*
ass [æs] *n* âne *m*; *(inf)* imbécile *m/f*; *(US inf!)*
cul *m* (!)
assailant [ə'seɪlənt] *n* agresseur *m*;
assaillant *m*
assassin [ə'sæsɪn] *n* assassin *m*
assassinate [ə'sæsɪneɪt] *vt* assassiner
assassination [əsæsɪ'neɪʃən] *n* assassinat *m*
assault [ə'sɔːlt] *n (Mil)* assaut *m*; *(gen: attack)*
agression *f*; *(Law)*: **~ (and battery)** voies *fpl* de
fait, coups *mpl* et blessures *fpl* ▷ *vt* attaquer;
(sexually) violenter
assemble [ə'sɛmbl] *vt* assembler ▷ *vi*
s'assembler, se rassembler
assembly [ə'sɛmblɪ] *n (meeting)*
rassemblement *m*; *(parliament)* assemblée *f*;
(construction) assemblage *m*
assembly line *n* chaîne *f* de montage
assent [ə'sɛnt] *n* assentiment *m*,
consentement *m* ▷ *vi*: **to ~ (to sth)** donner
son assentiment (à qch), consentir (à qch)
assert [ə'sɜːt] *vt* affirmer, déclarer; établir;
(authority) faire valoir; *(innocence)* protester de;
to ~ o.s. s'imposer
assertion [ə'sɜːʃən] *n* assertion *f*,
affirmation *f*
assess [ə'sɛs] *vt* évaluer, estimer; *(tax,
damages)* établir or fixer le montant de;
(property etc: for tax) calculer la valeur
imposable de; *(person)* juger la valeur de
assessment [ə'sɛsmənt] *n* évaluation *f*,
estimation *f*; *(of tax)* fixation *f*; *(of property)*
calcul *m* de la valeur imposable; *(judgment)*:
~ (of) jugement *m* or opinion *f* (sur)
assessor [ə'sɛsəʳ] *n* expert *m* *(en matière d'impôt
et d'assurance)*
asset ['æsɛt] *n* avantage *m*, atout *m*; *(person)*
atout; **assets** *npl* *(Comm)* capital *m*; avoir(s)
m(pl); actif *m*
assign [ə'saɪn] *vt (date)* fixer, arrêter; **to ~ sth
to** *(task)* assigner qch à; *(resources)* affecter
qch à; *(cause, meaning)* attribuer qch à
assignment [ə'saɪnmənt] *n (task)* mission *f*;
(homework) devoir *m*
assist [ə'sɪst] *vt* aider, assister; *(injured person
etc)* secourir
assistance [ə'sɪstəns] *n* aide *f*, assistance *f*;
secours *mpl*
assistant [ə'sɪstənt] *n* assistant(e),
adjoint(e); *(Brit: also:* **shop ~**) vendeur(-euse)
associate [*adj, n* ə'səʊʃɪɪt, *vb* ə'səʊʃɪeɪt] *adj, n*
associé(e) ▷ *vt* associer ▷ *vi*: **to ~ with sb**

fréquenter qn; **~ director** directeur adjoint;
~d company société affiliée

association [əsəusɪ'eɪʃən] n association f; **in ~ with** en collaboration avec

assorted [ə'sɔːtɪd] adj assorti(e); **in ~ sizes** en plusieurs tailles

assortment [ə'sɔːtmənt] n assortiment m; (of people) mélange m

assume [ə'sjuːm] vt supposer; (responsibilities etc) assumer; (attitude, name) prendre, adopter

assumption [ə'sʌmpʃən] n supposition f, hypothèse f; (of power) assomption f, prise f; **on the ~ that** dans l'hypothèse où; (on condition that) à condition que

assurance [ə'ʃuərəns] n assurance f; **I can give you no ~s** je ne peux rien vous garantir

assure [ə'ʃuə'] vt assurer

asterisk ['æstərɪsk] n astérisque m

asthma ['æsmə] n asthme m

astonish [ə'stɔnɪʃ] vt étonner, stupéfier

astonished [ə'stɔnɪʃt] adj étonné(e); **to be ~ at** être étonné(e) de

astonishing [ə'stɔnɪʃɪŋ] adj étonnant(e), stupéfiant(e); **I find it ~ that ...** je trouve incroyable que ...+sub

astonishment [ə'stɔnɪʃmənt] n (grand) étonnement, stupéfaction f

astound [ə'staund] vt stupéfier, sidérer

astray [ə'streɪ] adv: **to go ~** s'égarer; (fig) quitter le droit chemin; **to lead ~** (morally) détourner du droit chemin; **to go ~ in one's calculations** faire fausse route dans ses calculs

astride [ə'straɪd] adv à cheval ▷ prep à cheval sur

astrology [əs'trɔlədʒɪ] n astrologie f

astronaut ['æstrənɔːt] n astronaute m/f

astronomer [əs'trɔnəmə'] n astronome m

astronomical [æstrə'nɔmɪkl] adj astronomique

astronomy [əs'trɔnəmɪ] n astronomie f

astute [əs'tjuːt] adj astucieux(-euse), malin(-igne)

asylum [ə'saɪləm] n asile m; **to seek political ~** demander l'asile politique

asylum seeker [-siː-kə'] n demandeur(-euse) d'asile

 KEYWORD

at [æt] prep **1** (referring to position, direction) à; **at the top** au sommet; **at home/school** à la maison or chez soi/à l'école; **at the baker's** à la boulangerie, chez le boulanger; **to look at sth** regarder qch
2 (referring to time): **at 4 o'clock** à 4 heures; **at Christmas** à Noël; **at night** la nuit; **at times** par moments, parfois
3 (referring to rates, speed etc) à; **at £1 a kilo** une livre le kilo; **two at a time** deux à la fois; **at 50 km/h** à 50 km/h; **at full speed** à toute vitesse

4 (referring to manner): **at a stroke** d'un seul coup; **at peace** en paix
5 (referring to activity): **to be at work** (in the office etc) être au travail; (working) travailler; **to play at cowboys** jouer aux cowboys; **to be good at sth** être bon en qch
6 (referring to cause): **shocked/surprised/ annoyed at sth** choqué par/étonné de/agacé par qch; **I went at his suggestion** j'y suis allé sur son conseil
7 (@ symbol) arobase f

ate [eɪt] pt of **eat**

atheist ['eɪθɪɪst] n athée m/f

Athens ['æθɪnz] n Athènes

athlete ['æθliːt] n athlète m/f

athletic [æθ'lɛtɪk] adj athlétique

athletics [æθ'lɛtɪks] n athlétisme m

Atlantic [ət'læntɪk] adj atlantique ▷ n: **the ~ (Ocean)** l'(océan m) Atlantique m

atlas ['ætləs] n atlas m

A.T.M. n abbr (= Automated Telling Machine) guichet m automatique

atmosphere ['ætməsfɪə'] n (air) atmosphère f; (fig: of place etc) atmosphère, ambiance f

atom ['ætəm] n atome m

atom bomb n bombe f atomique

atomic [ə'tɔmɪk] adj atomique

atomic bomb n bombe f atomique

atomizer ['ætəmaɪzə'] n atomiseur m

atone [ə'təun] vi: **to ~ for** expier, racheter

atrocious [ə'trəuʃəs] adj (very bad) atroce, exécrable

atrocity [ə'trɔsɪtɪ] n atrocité f

attach [ə'tætʃ] vt (gen) attacher; (document, letter) joindre; (employee, troops) affecter; **to be ~ed to sb/sth** (to like) être attaché à qn/qch; **to ~ a file to an email** joindre un fichier à un e-mail; **the ~ed letter** la lettre ci-jointe

attaché case [ə'tæʃeɪ-] n mallette f, attaché-case m

attachment [ə'tætʃmənt] n (tool) accessoire m; (Comput) fichier m joint; (love): **~ (to)** affection f (pour), attachement m (à)

attack [ə'tæk] vt attaquer; (task etc) s'attaquer à ▷ n attaque f; **heart ~** crise f cardiaque

attacker [ə'tækə'] n attaquant m; agresseur m

attain [ə'teɪn] vt (also: **to ~ to**) parvenir à, atteindre; (knowledge) acquérir

attempt [ə'tɛmpt] n tentative f ▷ vt essayer, tenter; **~ed theft** etc (Law) tentative de vol etc; **to make an ~ on sb's life** attenter à la vie de qn; **he made no ~ to help** il n'a rien fait pour m'aider or l'aider etc

attempted [ə'tɛmptɪd] adj: **~ murder/ suicide** tentative f de meurtre/suicide

attend [ə'tɛnd] vt (course) suivre; (meeting, talk) assister à; (school, church) aller à, fréquenter; (patient) soigner, s'occuper de; **to ~ (up)on** servir; être au service de; **attend to** vt fus (needs, affairs etc) s'occuper de; (customer) s'occuper de, servir

attendance [ə'tɛndəns] *n* (*being present*) présence *f*; (*people present*) assistance *f*

attendant [ə'tɛndənt] *n* employé(e); gardien(ne) ▷ *adj* concomitant(e), qui accompagne *or* s'ensuit

attention [ə'tɛnʃən] *n* attention *f*; **attentions** attentions *fpl*, prévenances *fpl* ▷ *excl* (*Mil*) garde-à-vous!; **at ~** (*Mil*) au garde-à-vous; **for the ~ of** (*Admin*) à l'attention de; **it has come to my ~ that ...** je constate que ...

attentive [ə'tɛntɪv] *adj* attentif(-ive); (*kind*) prévenant(e)

attest [ə'tɛst] *vi*: **to ~ to** témoigner de attester (de)

attic ['ætɪk] *n* grenier *m*, combles *mpl*

attitude ['ætɪtjuːd] *n* (*behaviour*) attitude *f*, manière *f*; (*posture*) pose *f*, attitude; (*view*): **~ (to)** attitude (envers)

attorney [ə'təːnɪ] *n* (US: *lawyer*) avocat *m*; (*having proxy*) mandataire *m*; **power of ~** procuration *f*

Attorney General *n* (*Brit*) ≈ procureur général; (US) ≈ garde *m* des Sceaux, ministre *m* de la Justice

attract [ə'trækt] *vt* attirer

attraction [ə'trækʃən] *n* (*gen pl*: *pleasant things*) attraction *f*, attrait *m*; (*Physics*) attraction; (*fig: towards sb, sth*) attirance *f*

attractive [ə'træktɪv] *adj* séduisant(e), attrayant(e)

attribute *n* ['ætrɪbjuːt] attribut *m* ▷ *vt* [ə'trɪbjuːt]: **to ~ sth to** attribuer qch à

attrition [ə'trɪʃən] *n*: **war of ~** guerre *f* d'usure

aubergine ['əubəʒiːn] *n* aubergine *f*

auburn ['ɔːbən] *adj* auburn *inv*, châtain roux *inv*

auction ['ɔːkʃən] *n* (*also*: **sale by ~**) vente *f* aux enchères ▷ *vt* (*also*: **to sell by ~**) vendre aux enchères; (*also*: **to put up for ~**) mettre aux enchères

auctioneer [ɔːkʃə'nɪər] *n* commissaire-priseur *m*

audible ['ɔːdɪbl] *adj* audible

audience ['ɔːdɪəns] *n* (*people*) assistance *f*, public *m*; (*on radio*) auditeurs *mpl*; (*at theatre*) spectateurs *mpl*; (*interview*) audience *f*

audiovisual [ɔːdɪəu'vɪzjuəl] *adj* audio-visuel(le); **~ aids** supports *or* moyens audiovisuels

audit ['ɔːdɪt] *n* vérification *f* des comptes, apurement *m* ▷ *vt* vérifier, apurer

audition [ɔː'dɪʃən] *n* audition *f* ▷ *vi* auditionner

auditor ['ɔːdɪtər] *n* vérificateur *m* des comptes

auditorium [ɔːdɪ'tɔːrɪəm] *n* auditorium *m*, salle *f* de concert ou de spectacle

Aug. *abbr* = **August**

augur ['ɔːgər] *vt* (*be a sign of*) présager, annoncer ▷ *vi*: **it ~s well** c'est bon signe ou de

bon augure, cela s'annonce bien

August ['ɔːgəst] *n* août *m*; *see also* **July**

august [ɔː'gʌst] *adj* majestueux(-euse), imposant(e)

aunt [ɑːnt] *n* tante *f*

auntie, aunty ['ɑːntɪ] *n diminutive of* **aunt**

au pair ['əu'pɛər] *n* (*also*: **~ girl**) jeune fille *f* au pair

aura ['ɔːrə] *n* atmosphère *f*; (*of person*) aura *f*

auspicious [ɔːs'pɪʃəs] *adj* de bon augure, propice

austerity [ɔs'tɛrɪtɪ] *n* austérité *f*

Australia [ɔs'treɪlɪə] *n* Australie *f*

Australian [ɔs'treɪlɪən] *adj* australien(ne) ▷ *n* Australien(ne)

Austria ['ɔstrɪə] *n* Autriche *f*

Austrian ['ɔstrɪən] *adj* autrichien(ne) ▷ *n* Autrichien(ne)

authentic [ɔː'θɛntɪk] *adj* authentique

author ['ɔːθər] *n* auteur *m*

authoritarian [ɔːθɔrɪ'tɛərɪən] *adj* autoritaire

authoritative [ɔː'θɔrɪtətɪv] *adj* (*account*) digne de foi; (*study, treatise*) qui fait autorité; (*manner*) autoritaire

authority [ɔː'θɔrɪtɪ] *n* autorité *f*; (*permission*) autorisation (formelle); **the authorities** les autorités *fpl*, l'administration *f*; **to have ~ to do sth** être habilité à faire qch

authorize ['ɔːθəraɪz] *vt* autoriser

auto ['ɔːtəu] *n* (US) auto *f*, voiture *f*

autobiography [ɔːtəbaɪ'ɔgrəfɪ] *n* autobiographie *f*

autograph ['ɔːtəgrɑːf] *n* autographe *m* ▷ *vt* signer, dédicacer

automated ['ɔːtəmeɪtɪd] *adj* automatisé(e)

automatic [ɔːtə'mætɪk] *adj* automatique ▷ *n* (*gun*) automatique *m*; (*washing machine*) lave-linge *m* automatique; (*car*) voiture *f* à transmission automatique

automatically [ɔːtə'mætɪklɪ] *adv* automatiquement

automation [ɔːtə'meɪʃən] *n* automatisation *f*

automobile ['ɔːtəməbiːl] *n* (US) automobile *f*

autonomous [ɔː'tɔnəməs] *adj* autonome

autonomy [ɔː'tɔnəmɪ] *n* autonomie *f*

autumn ['ɔːtəm] *n* automne *m*

auxiliary [ɔːg'zɪlɪərɪ] *adj*, *n* auxiliaire (*m/f*)

avail [ə'veɪl] *vt*: **to ~ o.s. of** user de; profiter de ▷ *n*: **to no ~** sans résultat, en vain, en pure perte

availability [əveɪlə'bɪlɪtɪ] *n* disponibilité *f*

available [ə'veɪləbl] *adj* disponible; **every ~ means** tous les moyens possibles *or* à sa (*or* notre *etc*) disposition; **is the manager ~?** est-ce que le directeur peut (me) recevoir?; (*on phone*) pourrais-je parler au directeur?; **to make sth ~ to sb** mettre qch à la disposition de qn

avalanche ['ævəlɑːnʃ] *n* avalanche *f*

Ave. *abbr* = **avenue**

avenge [ə'vɛndʒ] *vt* venger

avenue ['ævənjuː] *n* avenue *f*; (*fig*) moyen *m*

average ['ævərɪdʒ] n moyenne f ▷ adj moyen(ne) ▷ vt (a certain figure) atteindre or faire etc en moyenne; **on ~** en moyenne; **above/below (the) ~** au-dessus/en-dessous de la moyenne; **average out** vi: **to ~ out at** représenter en moyenne, donner une moyenne de

averse [ə'vəːs] adj: **to be ~ to sth/doing** éprouver une forte répugnance envers qch/à faire; **I wouldn't be ~ to a drink** un petit verre ne serait pas de refus, je ne dirais pas non à un petit verre

avert [ə'vəːt] vt (danger) prévenir, écarter; (one's eyes) détourner

aviary ['eɪvɪərɪ] n volière f

avid ['ævɪd] adj avide

avocado [ævə'kɑːdəu] n (Brit: also: **~ pear**) avocat m

avoid [ə'vɔɪd] vt éviter

await [ə'weɪt] vt attendre; **~ing attention/ delivery** (Comm) en souffrance; **long ~ed** tant attendu(e)

awake [ə'weɪk] (pt **awoke** [ə'wəuk] pp **awoken** [ə'wəukən] adj éveillé(e); (fig) en éveil ▷ vt éveiller ▷ vi s'éveiller; **~ to** conscient de; **to be ~** être réveillé(e); **he was still ~** il ne dormait pas encore

awakening [ə'weɪknɪŋ] n réveil m

award [ə'wɔːd] n (for bravery) récompense f; (prize) prix m; (Law: damages) dommages-intérêts mpl ▷ vt (prize) décerner; (Law: damages) accorder

aware [ə'wɛər] adj: **~ of** (conscious) conscient(e) de; (informed) au courant de; **to become ~ of/ that** prendre conscience de/que; se rendre compte de/que; **politically/socially ~** sensibilisé(e) aux or ayant pris conscience des problèmes politiques/sociaux; **I am fully ~ that** je me rends parfaitement compte que

awareness [ə'wɛənɪs] n conscience f, connaissance f; **to develop people's ~ (of)** sensibiliser le public (à)

away [ə'weɪ] adv (au) loin; (movement): **she went ~** elle est partie ▷ adj (not in, not here) absent(e); **far ~** (au) loin; **two kilometres ~** à (une distance de) deux kilomètres, à deux kilomètres de distance; **two hours ~ by car** à deux heures de voiture or de route; **the holiday was two weeks ~** il restait deux semaines jusqu'aux vacances; **~ from** loin de; **he's ~ for a week** il est parti (pour) une semaine; **he's ~ in Milan** il est (parti) à Milan; **to take sth ~ from sb** prendre qch à qn; **to take sth ~ from sth** (subtract) ôter qch de qch; **to work/pedal ~** travailler/pédaller à cœur joie; **to fade ~** (colour) s'estomper; (sound) s'affaiblir

away game n (Sport) match m à l'extérieur

awe [ɔː] n respect mêlé de crainte, effroi mêlé d'admiration

awe-inspiring ['ɔːɪnspaɪərɪŋ], **awesome** ['ɔːsəm] adj impressionnant(e)

awesome ['ɔːsəm] (US) adj (inf: excellent) génial(e)

awful ['ɔːfəl] adj affreux(-euse); **an ~ lot of** énormément de

awfully ['ɔːfəlɪ] adv (very) terriblement, vraiment

awkward ['ɔːkwəd] adj (clumsy) gauche, maladroit(e); (inconvenient) peu pratique; (embarrassing) gênant; **I can't talk just now, it's a bit ~** je ne peux pas parler tout de suite, c'est un peu difficile

awning ['ɔːnɪŋ] n (of tent) auvent m; (of shop) store m; (of hotel etc) marquise f (de toile)

awoke [ə'wəuk] pt of **awake**

awoken [ə'wəukən] pp of **awake**

axe, (US) **ax** [æks] n hache f ▷ vt (employee) renvoyer; (project etc) abandonner; (jobs) supprimer; **to have an ~ to grind** (fig) prêcher pour son saint

axes ['æksiːz] npl of **axis**

axis (pl **axes**) ['æksɪs, -siːz] n axe m

axle ['æksl] n (also: **~-tree**) essieu m

ay, aye [aɪ] excl (yes) oui ▷ n: **the ay(e)s** les oui

azalea [ə'zeɪlɪə] n azalée f

b

compounds) de derrière, à l'arrière; **~ seat/
wheel** (Aut) siège m/roue f arrière inv; **~
payments/rent** arriéré m de paiements/
loyer; **~ garden/room** jardin/pièce sur
l'arrière; **to take a ~ seat** (fig) se contenter
d'un second rôle, être relégué(e) au second
plan ▷ adv (not forward) en arrière; (returned):
he's ~ il est rentré, il est de retour; **when will
you be ~?** quand seras-tu de retour?; **he ran ~**
il est revenu en courant; (restitution): **throw
the ball ~** renvoie la balle; **can I have it ~?**
puis-je le ravoir?, peux-tu me le rendre?;
(again): **he called ~** il a rappelé; **back down** vi
rabattre de ses prétentions; **back on to** vt fus:
the house ~s on to the golf course la
maison donne derrière sur le terrain de golf;
back out vi (of promise) se dédire; **back up** vt
(person) soutenir; (Comput) faire une copie de
sauvegarde de
backache ['bækeɪk] n mal m au dos
backbencher [bæk'bentʃəʳ] (Brit) n membre du
parlement sans portefeuille
backbone ['bækbəʊn] n colonne vertébrale,
épine dorsale; **he's the ~ of the
organization** c'est sur lui que repose
l'organisation
backdate [bæk'deɪt] vt (letter) antidater; **~d
pay rise** augmentation f avec effet rétroactif
back door n porte f de derrière
backfire [bæk'faɪəʳ] vi (Aut) pétarader; (plans)
mal tourner
backgammon ['bækgæmən] n trictrac m
background ['bækgraʊnd] n arrière-plan m;
(of events) situation f, conjoncture f; (basic
knowledge) éléments mpl de base; (experience)
formation f ▷ cpd (noise, music) de fond;
~ reading lecture(s) générale(s) (sur un
sujet); **family ~** milieu familial
backhand ['bækhænd] n (Tennis: also:
~ stroke) revers m
backhander ['bæk'hændəʳ] n (Brit: bribe)
pot-de-vin m
backing ['bækɪŋ] n (fig) soutien m, appui m;
(Comm) soutien (financier); (Mus)
accompagnement m
backlash ['bæklæʃ] n contre-coup m,
répercussion f
backlog ['bæklɒg] n: **~ of work** travail m
en retard
back number n (of magazine etc) vieux
numéro
backpack ['bækpæk] n sac m à dos
backpacker ['bækpækəʳ] n
randonneur(-euse)
back pain n mal m de dos
back pay n rappel m de salaire
backside ['bæksaɪd] n (inf) derrière m,
postérieur m
backslash ['bækslæʃ] n barre oblique
inversée
backstage [bæk'steɪdʒ] adv dans les
coulisses

B, b [bi:] n (letter) B, b m; (Scol: mark) B; (Mus):
B si m; **B for Benjamin**, (US) **B for Baker** B
comme Berthe; **B road** n (Brit Aut) route
départementale
B.A. abbr = **British Academy**; (Scol) = **Bachelor
of Arts**
babble ['bæbl] vi babiller ▷ n babillage m
baby ['beɪbɪ] n bébé m
baby carriage n (US) voiture f d'enfant
baby food n aliments mpl pour bébé(s)
baby-sit ['beɪbɪsɪt] vi garder les enfants
baby-sitter ['beɪbɪsɪtəʳ] n baby-sitter m/f
baby wipe n lingette f (pour bébé)
bachelor ['bætʃələʳ] n célibataire m; **B~ of
Arts/Science (BA/BSc)** ≈ licencié(e) ès or en
lettres/sciences; **B~ of Arts/Science degree
(BA/BSc)** ≈ licence f ès or en lettres/
sciences; voir article
back [bæk] n (of person, horse) dos m; (of hand)
dos, revers m; (of house) derrière m; (of car,
train) arrière m; (of chair) dossier m; (of page)
verso m; (of crowd): **can the people at the ~
hear me properly?** est-ce que les gens du
fond peuvent m'entendre?; (Football)
arrière m; **to have one's ~ to the wall** (fig)
être au pied du mur; **to break the ~ of a job**
(Brit) faire le gros d'un travail; **~ to front** à
l'envers ▷ vt (financially) soutenir
(financièrement); (candidate: also: **~ up**)
soutenir, appuyer; (horse: at races) parier or
miser sur; (car) (faire) reculer ▷ vi reculer;
(car etc) faire marche arrière ▷ adj (in

backstroke ['bækstrəuk] n dos crawlé
backup ['bækʌp] adj (train, plane) supplémentaire, de réserve; (Comput) de sauvegarde ▷ n (support) appui m, soutien m; (Comput: also: ~ file) sauvegarde f
backward ['bækwəd] adj (movement) en arrière; (measure) rétrograde; (person, country) arriéré(e); (shy) hésitant(e); **~ and forward movement** mouvement de va-et-vient
backwards ['bækwədz] adv (move, go) en arrière; (read a list) à l'envers, à rebours; (fall) à la renverse; (walk) à reculons; (in time) en arrière, vers le passé; **to know sth ~** or (US) **~ and forwards** (inf) connaître qch sur le bout des doigts
backwater ['bækwɔ:tə'] n (fig) coin reculé; bled perdu
backyard ['bæk'jɑ:d] n arrière-cour f
bacon ['beɪkən] n bacon m, lard m
bacteria [bæk'tɪərɪə] npl bactéries fpl
bad [bæd] adj mauvais(e); (child) vilain(e); (mistake, accident) grave; (meat, food) gâté(e), avarié(e); **his ~ leg** sa jambe malade; **to go ~** (meat, food) se gâter; (milk) tourner; **to have a ~ time of it** traverser une mauvaise passe; **I feel ~ about it** (guilty) j'ai un peu mauvaise conscience; **~ debt** créance douteuse; **in ~ faith** de mauvaise foi
bade [bæd] pt of **bid**
badge [bædʒ] n insigne m; (of policeman) plaque f; (stick-on, sew-on) badge m
badger ['bædʒə'] n blaireau m ▷ vt harceler
badly ['bædlɪ] adv (work, dress etc) mal; **to reflect ~ on sb** donner une mauvaise image de qn; **~ wounded** grièvement blessé; **he needs it ~** il en a un absolument besoin; **things are going ~** les choses vont mal; **~ off** adj, adv dans la gêne
bad-mannered ['bæd'mænəd] adj mal élevé(e)
badminton ['bædmɪntən] n badminton m
bad-tempered ['bæd'tempəd] adj (by nature) ayant mauvais caractère; (on one occasion) de mauvaise humeur
baffle ['bæfl] vt (puzzle) déconcerter
bag [bæg] n sac m; (of hunter) gibecière f, chasse f ▷ vt (inf: take) empocher; s'approprier; (Tech) mettre en sacs; **~s of** (inf: lots of) des tas de; **to pack one's ~s** faire ses valises or bagages; **~s under the eyes** poches fpl sous les yeux
baggage ['bægɪdʒ] n bagages mpl
baggage allowance n franchise f de bagages
baggage reclaim n (at airport) livraison f de bagages
baggy ['bægɪ] adj avachi(e), qui fait des poches
bagpipes ['bægpaɪps] npl cornemuse f
bail [beɪl] n caution f ▷ vt (prisoner: also:

grant ~ to) mettre en liberté sous caution; (boat: also: ~ **out**) écoper; **to be released on ~** être libéré(e) sous caution; see **bale**; **bail out** vt (prisoner) payer la caution de
bailiff ['beɪlɪf] n huissier m
bait [beɪt] n appât m ▷ vt appâter; (fig: tease) tourmenter
bake [beɪk] vt (faire) cuire au four ▷ vi (bread etc) cuire (au four); (make cakes etc) faire de la pâtisserie
baked beans [beɪkt-] npl haricots blancs à la sauce tomate
baked potato n pomme f de terre en robe des champs
baker ['beɪkə'] n boulanger m
bakery ['beɪkərɪ] n boulangerie f; boulangerie industrielle
baking ['beɪkɪŋ] n (process) cuisson f
baking powder n levure f (chimique)
balance ['bæləns] n équilibre m; (Comm: sum) solde m; (remainder) reste m; (scales) balance f ▷ vt mettre or faire tenir en équilibre; (pros and cons) peser; (budget) équilibrer; (account) balancer; (compensate) compenser, contrebalancer; **~ of trade/payments** balance commerciale/des comptes or paiements; **~ carried forward** solde m à reporter; **~ brought forward** solde reporté; **to ~ the books** arrêter les comptes, dresser le bilan
balanced ['bælənst] adj (personality, diet) équilibré(e); (report) objectif(-ive)
balance sheet n bilan m
balcony ['bælkənɪ] n balcon m; **do you have a room with a ~?** avez-vous une chambre avec balcon?
bald [bɔːld] adj chauve; (tyre) lisse
bale [beɪl] n balle f, ballot m; **bale out** vi (of a plane) sauter en parachute ▷ vt (Naut: water, boat) écoper
ball [bɔːl] n boule f; (football) ballon m; (for tennis, golf) balle f; (dance) bal m; **to play ~** jouer au ballon (or à la balle); (fig) coopérer; **to be on the ~** (fig: competent) être à la hauteur; (: alert) être éveillé(e), être vif/vive; **to start the ~ rolling** (fig) commencer; **the ~ is in their court** (fig) la balle est dans leur camp
ballast ['bæləst] n lest m
ball bearings n roulement m à billes
ballerina [bælə'riːnə] n ballerine f
ballet ['bæleɪ] n ballet m; (art) danse f (classique)
ballet dancer n danseur(-euse) de ballet
ballet shoe n chausson m de danse
balloon [bə'luːn] n ballon m; (in comic strip) bulle f ▷ vi gonfler
ballot ['bælət] n scrutin m
ballot paper n bulletin m de vote
ballpoint ['bɔːlpɔɪnt], **ballpoint pen** n stylo m à bille
ballroom ['bɔːlrum] n salle f de bal

Baltic [ˈbɔːltɪk] *adj, n*: **the ~ (Sea)** la (mer) Baltique

bamboo [bæmˈbuː] *n* bambou *m*

ban [bæn] *n* interdiction *f* ▷ *vt* interdire; **he was ~ned from driving** (*Brit*) on lui a retiré le permis (de conduire)

banana [bəˈnɑːnə] *n* banane *f*

band [bænd] *n* bande *f*; (*at a dance*) orchestre *m*; (*Mil*) musique *f*, fanfare *f*; **band together** *vi* se liguer

bandage [ˈbændɪdʒ] *n* bandage *m*, pansement *m* ▷ *vt* (*wound, leg*) mettre un pansement *or* un bandage sur; (*person*) mettre un pansement *or* un bandage à

Band-Aid® [ˈbændeɪd] *n* (*US*) pansement adhésif

B. & B. *n abbr* = **bed and breakfast**

bandit [ˈbændɪt] *n* bandit *m*

bandy-legged [ˈbændɪˈlɛgɪd] *adj* aux jambes arquées

bang [bæŋ] *n* détonation *f*; (*of door*) claquement *m*; (*blow*) coup (violent) ▷ *vt* frapper (violemment); (*door*) claquer ▷ *vi* détoner; claquer ▷ *adv*: **to be ~ on time** (*Brit inf*) être à l'heure pile; **to ~ at the door** cogner à la porte; **to ~ into sth** se cogner contre qch

Bangladesh [bæŋɡləˈdɛʃ] *n* Bangladesh *m*

Bangladeshi [bæŋɡləˈdɛʃɪ] *adj* du Bangladesh ▷ *n* habitant(e) du Bangladesh

bangle [ˈbæŋɡl] *n* bracelet *m*

bangs [bæŋz] *npl* (*US: fringe*) frange *f*

banish [ˈbænɪʃ] *vt* bannir

banister [ˈbænɪstə*] *n*, **banisters** [ˈbænɪstəz] *npl* rampe *f* (d'escalier)

banjo (*pl* **banjoes** *or* **banjos**) [ˈbændʒəu] *n* banjo *m*

bank [bæŋk] *n* banque *f*; (*of river, lake*) bord *m*, rive *f*; (*of earth*) talus *m*, remblai *m* ▷ *vi* (*Aviat*) virer sur l'aile; (*Comm*): **they ~ with Pitt's** leur banque or banquier est Pitt's; **bank on** *vt fus* miser *or* tabler sur

bank account *n* compte *m* en banque

bank balance *n* solde *m* bancaire

bank card (*Brit*) *n* carte *f* d'identité bancaire

bank charges *npl* (*Brit*) frais *mpl* de banque

banker [ˈbæŋkə*] *n* banquier *m*; **~'s card** (*Brit*) carte *f* d'identité bancaire; **~'s order** (*Brit*) ordre *m* de virement

bank holiday *n* (*Brit*) jour férié (*où les banques sont fermées*); *voir article*

◈ **BANK HOLIDAY**

◈ Le terme *bank holiday* s'applique au
◈ Royaume-Uni aux jours fériés pendant
◈ lesquels banques et commerces sont
◈ fermés. Les principaux *bank holidays* à part
◈ Noël et Pâques se situent au mois de mai
◈ et fin août, et contrairement aux pays de
◈ tradition catholique, ne coïncident pas
◈ nécessairement avec une fête religieuse.

banking [ˈbæŋkɪŋ] *n* opérations *fpl* bancaires; profession *f* de banquier

bank manager *n* directeur *m* d'agence (bancaire)

banknote [ˈbæŋknəut] *n* billet *m* de banque

bank rate *n* taux *m* de l'escompte

bankrupt [ˈbæŋkrʌpt] *n* failli(e) ▷ *adj* en faillite; **to go ~** faire faillite

bankruptcy [ˈbæŋkrʌptsɪ] *n* faillite *f*

bank statement *n* relevé *m* de compte

banner [ˈbænə*] *n* bannière *f*

bannister [ˈbænɪstə*] *n*, **bannisters** [ˈbænɪstəz] *npl* = **banister; banisters**

banquet [ˈbæŋkwɪt] *n* banquet *m*, festin *m*

baptism [ˈbæptɪzəm] *n* baptême *m*

baptize [bæpˈtaɪz] *vt* baptiser

bar [bɑː*] *n* (*pub*) bar *m*; (*counter*) comptoir *m*, bar; (*rod: of metal etc*) barre *f*; (*of window etc*) barreau *m*; (*of chocolate*) tablette *f*, plaque *f*; (*fig: obstacle*) obstacle *m*; (*prohibition*) mesure *f* d'exclusion; (*Mus*) mesure *f* ▷ *vt* (*haggle*); (*window*) munir de barreaux; (*person*) exclure; (*activity*) interdire; **~ of soap** savonnette *f*; **behind ~s** (*prisoner*) derrière les barreaux; **the B~** (*Law*) le barreau; **~ none** sans exception

barbaric [bɑːˈbærɪk] *adj* barbare

barbecue [ˈbɑːbɪkjuː] *n* barbecue *m*

barbed wire [ˈbɑːbd-] *n* fil *m* de fer barbelé

barber [ˈbɑːbə*] *n* coiffeur *m* (pour hommes)

barber's [ˈbɑːbəz], **barber's shop**, (*US*) **barber shop** *n* salon *m* de coiffure (pour hommes); **to go to the ~** aller chez le coiffeur

bar code *n* code *m* à barres, code-barre *m*

bare [bɛə*] *adj* nu(e) ▷ *vt* mettre à nu, dénuder; (*teeth*) montrer; **the ~ essentials** le strict nécessaire

bareback [ˈbɛəbæk] *adv* à cru, sans selle

barefaced [ˈbɛəfeɪst] *adj* impudent(e), effronté(e)

barefoot [ˈbɛəfut] *adj, adv* nu-pieds, (les) pieds nus

barely [ˈbɛəlɪ] *adv* à peine

bargain [ˈbɑːɡɪn] *n* (*transaction*) marché *m*; (*good buy*) affaire *f*, occasion *f* ▷ *vi* (*haggle*) marchander; (*negotiate*) négocier, traiter; **into the ~** par-dessus le marché; **bargain for** *vt fus* (*inf*): **he got more than he ~ed for!** il en a eu pour son argent!

barge [bɑːdʒ] *n* péniche *f*; **barge in** *vi* (*walk in*) faire irruption; (*interrupt talk*) intervenir mal à propos; **barge into** *vt fus* rentrer dans

bark [bɑːk] *n* (*of tree*) écorce *f*; (*of dog*) aboiement *m* ▷ *vi* aboyer

barley [ˈbɑːlɪ] *n* orge *f*

barley sugar *n* sucre *m* d'orge

barmaid [ˈbɑːmeɪd] *n* serveuse *f* (de bar), barmaid *f*

barman [ˈbɑːmən] (*irreg*) *n* serveur *m* (de bar), barman *m*

bar meal *n* repas *m* de bistrot; **to go for a ~** aller manger au bistrot

barn [bɑːn] *n* grange *f*

barometer [bəˈrɒmɪtəʳ] n baromètre m
baron [ˈbærən] n baron m; **the press/oil ~s** les magnats mpl de la presse/du pétrole
baroness [ˈbærənɪs] n baronne f
barracks [ˈbærəks] npl caserne f
barrage [ˈbærɑːʒ] n (Mil) tir m de barrage; (dam) barrage m; (of criticism) feu m
barrel [ˈbærəl] n tonneau m; (of gun) canon m
barren [ˈbærən] adj stérile; (hills) aride
barrette [bæˈrɛt] (US) n barrette f
barricade [bærɪˈkeɪd] n barricade f ▷ vt barricader
barrier [ˈbærɪəʳ] n barrière f; (Brit: also: **crash ~**) rail m de sécurité
barring [ˈbɑːrɪŋ] prep sauf
barrister [ˈbærɪstəʳ] n (Brit) avocat (plaidant); voir article
barrow [ˈbærəu] n (cart) charrette f à bras
bartender [ˈbɑːtɛndəʳ] n (US) serveur m (de bar), barman m
barter [ˈbɑːtəʳ] n échange m, troc m ▷ vt: **to ~ sth for** échanger qch contre
base [beɪs] n base f ▷ vt (troops): **to be ~d at** être basé(e) à; (opinion, belief): **to ~ sth on** baser or fonder qch sur ▷ adj vil(e), bas(se); **coffee-~** à base de café; **a Paris-~d firm** une maison opérant de Paris or dont le siège est à Paris; **I'm ~d in London** je suis basé(e) à Londres
baseball [ˈbeɪsbɔːl] n base-ball m
baseball cap n casquette f de base-ball
Basel [bɑːl] n = **Basle**
basement [ˈbeɪsmənt] n sous-sol m
bases [ˈbeɪsiːz] npl of **basis**; [ˈbeɪsɪz] npl of **base**
bash [bæʃ] vt (inf) frapper, cogner ▷ n: **I'll have a ~ (at it)** (Brit inf) je vais essayer un coup; **~ed in** adj enfoncé(e), défoncé(e); **bash up** vt (inf: car) bousiller; (Brit: person) tabasser
bashful [ˈbæʃful] adj timide; modeste
basic [ˈbeɪsɪk] adj (precautions, rules) élémentaire; (principles, research) fondamental(e); (vocabulary, salary) de base; (minimal) réduit(e) au minimum, rudimentaire
basically [ˈbeɪsɪklɪ] adv (in fact) en fait; (essentially) fondamentalement
basics [ˈbeɪsɪks] npl: **the ~** l'essentiel m
basil [ˈbæzl] n basilic m
basin [ˈbeɪsn] n (vessel, also Geo) cuvette f, bassin m; (Brit: for food) bol m; (: bigger) saladier m; (: also: **wash~**) lavabo m
basis (pl **bases**) [ˈbeɪsɪs, -siːz] n base f; **on a part-time/trial ~** à temps partiel/à l'essai; **on the ~ of what you've said** d'après or compte tenu de ce que vous dites
bask [bɑːsk] vi: **to ~ in the sun** se chauffer au soleil
basket [ˈbɑːskɪt] n corbeille f; (with handle) panier m
basketball [ˈbɑːskɪtbɔːl] n basket-ball m

Basle [bɑːl] n Bâle
Basque [bæsk] adj basque ▷ n Basque m/f; **the ~ Country** le Pays basque
bass [beɪs] n (Mus) basse f
bass drum n grosse caisse f
bassoon [bəˈsuːn] n basson m
bastard [ˈbɑːstəd] n enfant naturel(le), bâtard(e); (inf!) salaud m (!)
bat [bæt] n chauve-souris f; (for baseball etc) batte f; (Brit: for table tennis) raquette f ▷ vt: **he didn't ~ an eyelid** il n'a pas sourcillé or bronché; **off one's own ~** de sa propre initiative
batch [bætʃ] n (of bread) fournée f; (of papers) liasse f; (of applicants, letters) paquet m; (of work) monceau m; (of goods) lot m
bated [ˈbeɪtɪd] adj: **with ~ breath** en retenant son souffle
bath (pl **baths**) [bɑːθ, bɑːðz] n bain m; (bathtub) baignoire f ▷ vt baigner, donner un bain; **to have a ~** prendre un bain; see also **baths**
bathe [beɪð] vi se baigner ▷ vt baigner; (wound) laver
bathing [ˈbeɪðɪŋ] n baignade f
bathing costume, (US) **bathing suit** n maillot m de bain
bathrobe [ˈbɑːθrəub] n peignoir m de bain
bathroom [ˈbɑːθrum] n salle f de bains
baths [bɑːðz] npl (Brit: also: **swimming ~**) piscine f
bath towel n serviette f de bain
bathtub [ˈbɑːθtʌb] n baignoire f
baton [ˈbætən] n bâton m; (Mus) baguette f; (club) matraque f
batter [ˈbætəʳ] vt battre ▷ n pâte f à frire
battered [ˈbætəd] adj (hat, pan) cabossé(e); **~ wife/child** épouse/enfant maltraité(e) or martyr(e)
battery [ˈbætərɪ] n (for torch, radio) pile f; (Aut, Mil) batterie f
battery farming n élevage m en batterie
battle [ˈbætl] n bataille f, combat m ▷ vi battre, lutter; **that's half the ~** (fig) c'est déjà bien; **it's a** or **we're fighting a losing ~** (fig) c'est perdu d'avance, c'est peine perdue
battlefield [ˈbætlfiːld] n champ m de bataille
battleship [ˈbætlʃɪp] n cuirassé m
Bavaria [bəˈvɛərɪə] n Bavière f
bawl [bɔːl] vi hurler, brailler
bay [beɪ] n (of sea) baie f; (Brit: for parking) place f de stationnement; (: for loading) aire f de chargement; (horse) bai(e) m/f; **B~ of Biscay** golfe m de Gascogne; **to hold sb at ~** tenir qn à distance or en échec
bay leaf n laurier m
bazaar [bəˈzɑːʳ] n (shop, market) bazar m; (sale) vente f de charité
BBC n abbr (= British Broadcasting Corporation) office de la radiodiffusion et télévision britannique
B.C. adv abbr (= before Christ) av. J.-C. ▷ abbr (Canada) = **British Columbia**

○ **KEYWORD**

be [biː] (*pt* **was** *or* **were**, *pp* **been**) *aux vb* **1** (*with present participle: forming continuous tenses*): **what are you doing?** que faites-vous?; **they're coming tomorrow** ils viennent demain; **I've been waiting for you for 2 hours** je t'attends depuis 2 heures

2 (*with pp: forming passives*) être; **to be killed** être tué(e); **the box had been opened** la boîte avait été ouverte; **he was nowhere to be seen** on ne le voyait nulle part

3 (*in tag questions*): **it was fun, wasn't it?** c'était drôle, n'est-ce pas?; **he's good-looking, isn't he?** il est beau, n'est-ce pas?; **she's back, is she?** elle est rentrée, n'est-ce pas *or* alors?

4 (*+to +infinitive*): **the house is to be sold** (*necessity*) la maison doit être vendue; (*future*) la maison va être vendue; **he's not to open it** il ne doit pas l'ouvrir; **am I to understand that ...?** dois-je comprendre que ...?; **he was to have come yesterday** il devait venir hier

5 (*possibility, supposition*): **if I were you, I ...** à votre place, je ..., si j'étais vous, je ...

▷ *vb + complement* **1** (*gen*) être; **I'm English** je suis anglais(e); **I'm tired** je suis fatigué(e); **I'm hot/cold** j'ai chaud/froid; **he's a doctor** il est médecin; **be careful/good/quiet!** faites attention/soyez sages/taisez-vous!; **2 and 2 are 4** 2 et 2 font 4

2 (*of health*) aller; **how are you?** comment allez-vous?; **I'm better now** je vais mieux maintenant; **he's fine now** il va bien maintenant; **he's very ill** il est très malade

3 (*of age*) avoir; **how old are you?** quel âge avez-vous?; **I'm sixteen (years old)** j'ai seize ans

4 (*cost*) coûter; **how much was the meal?** combien a coûté le repas?; **that'll be £5, please** ça fera 5 livres, s'il vous plaît; **this shirt is £17** cette chemise coûte 17 livres

▷ *vi* **1** (*exist, occur etc*) être, exister; **the prettiest girl that ever was** la fille la plus jolie qui ait jamais existé; **is there a God?** y a-t-il un dieu?; **be that as it may** quoi qu'il en soit; **so be it** soit

2 (*referring to place*) être, se trouver; **I won't be here tomorrow** je ne serai pas là demain; **Edinburgh is in Scotland** Édimbourg est *or* se trouve en Écosse

3 (*referring to movement*) aller; **where have you been?** où êtes-vous allé(s)?

▷ *impers vb* **1** (*referring to time*) être; **it's 5 o'clock** il est 5 heures; **it's the 28th of April** c'est le 28 avril

2 (*referring to distance*): **it's 10 km to the village** le village est à 10 km

3 (*referring to the weather*) faire; **it's too hot/cold** il fait trop chaud/froid; **it's windy today** il y a du vent aujourd'hui

4 (*emphatic*): **it's me/the postman** c'est moi/le facteur; **it was Maria who paid the bill** c'est Maria qui a payé la note

beach [biːtʃ] *n* plage *f* ▷ *vt* échouer

beacon ['biːkən] *n* (*lighthouse*) fanal *m*; (*marker*) balise *f*; (*also*: **radio ~**) radiophare *m*

bead [biːd] *n* perle *f*; (*of dew, sweat*) goutte *f*; **beads** *npl* (*necklace*) collier *m*

beak [biːk] *n* bec *m*

beaker ['biːkə^r] *n* gobelet *m*

beam [biːm] *n* (*Archit*) poutre *f*; (*of light*) rayon *m*; (*Radio*) faisceau *m* ▷ *vi* rayonner; **to drive on full** *or* **main** *or* (*US*) **high ~** rouler en pleins phares

bean [biːn] *n* haricot *m*; (*of coffee*) grain *m*

beansprouts ['biːnsprauts] *npl* pousses *fpl* *or* germes *mpl* de soja

bear [bɛə^r] (*pt* **bore**, *pp* **borne**) [bɔː^r, bɔːn] *n* ours *m*; (*Stock Exchange*) baissier *m* ▷ *vt* porter; (*endure*) supporter; (*traces, signs*) porter; (*Comm: interest*) rapporter ▷ *vi*: **to ~ right/left** obliquer à droite/gauche, se diriger vers la droite/gauche; **to ~ the responsibility of** assumer la responsabilité de; **to ~ comparison with** soutenir la comparaison avec; **I can't ~ him** je ne peux pas le supporter *or* souffrir; **to bring pressure to ~ on sb** faire pression sur qn; **bear out** *vt* (*theory, suspicion*) confirmer; **bear up** *vi* supporter, tenir le coup; **he bore up well** il a tenu le coup; **bear with** *vt fus* (*sb's moods, temper*) supporter; **~ with me a minute** un moment, s'il vous plaît

beard [bɪəd] *n* barbe *f*

bearded ['bɪədɪd] *adj* barbu(e)

bearer ['bɛərə^r] *n* porteur *m*; (*of passport etc*) titulaire *m/f*

bearing ['bɛərɪŋ] *n* maintien *m*, allure *f*; (*connection*) rapport *m*; (*Tech*): (**ball) bearings** *npl* roulement *m* (à billes); **to take a ~** faire le point; **to find one's ~s** s'orienter

beast [biːst] *n* bête *f*; (*inf: person*) brute *f*

beastly ['biːstlɪ] *adj* infect(e)

beat [biːt] *n* battement *m*; (*Mus*) temps *m*, mesure *f*; (*of policeman*) ronde *f* ▷ *vt, vi* (*pt* **beat**, *pp* **beaten**) battre; **off the ~ en track** hors des chemins *or* sentiers battus; **to ~ it** (*inf*) ficher le camp; **to ~ about the bush** tourner autour du pot; **that ~s everything!** c'est le comble!; **beat down** *vt* (*door*) enfoncer; (*price*) faire baisser; (*seller*) faire descendre ▷ *vi* (*rain*) tambouriner; (*sun*) taper; **beat off** *vt* repousser; **beat up** *vt* (*eggs*) battre; (*inf: person*) tabasser

beating ['biːtɪŋ] *n* raclée *f*

beautiful ['bjuːtɪful] *adj* beau/belle

beautifully ['bjuːtɪflɪ] *adv* admirablement

beauty ['bjuːtɪ] *n* beauté *f*; **the ~ of it is that ...** le plus beau, c'est que ...

beauty parlour, (*US*) **beauty parlor** *n* institut *m* de beauté

beauty salon *n* institut *m* de beauté

beauty spot n (on skin) grain m de beauté; (Brit Tourism) site naturel (d'une grande beauté)

beaver ['biːvə^r] n castor m

became [bɪ'keɪm] pt of **become**

because [bɪ'kɔz] conj parce que; **~ of** prep à cause de

beck [bɛk] n: **to be at sb's ~ and call** être à l'entière disposition de qn

beckon ['bɛkən] vt (also: **~ to**) faire signe (de venir) à

become [bɪ'kʌm] vi devenir; **to ~ fat/thin** grossir/maigrir; **to ~ angry** se mettre en colère; **it became known that** on apprit que; **what has ~ of him?** qu'est-il devenu?

becoming [bɪ'kʌmɪŋ] adj (behaviour) convenable, bienséant(e); (clothes) seyant(e)

bed [bɛd] n lit m; (of flowers) parterre m; (of coal, clay) couche f; (of sea, lake) fond m; **to go to ~** aller se coucher; **bed down** vi se coucher

bed and breakfast n (terms) chambre et petit déjeuner; (place) ≈ chambre f d'hôte; voir article

◈ **BED AND BREAKFAST**

◈ Un bed and breakfast est une petite pension
◈ dans une maison particulière ou une
◈ ferme où l'on peut louer une chambre
◈ avec petit déjeuner compris pour un prix
◈ modique par rapport à ce que l'on paierait
◈ dans un hôtel. Ces établissements sont
◈ communément appelés "B & B", et sont
◈ signalés par une pancarte dans le jardin
◈ ou au-dessus de la porte.

bedclothes ['bɛdkləuðz] npl couvertures fpl et draps mpl

bedding ['bɛdɪŋ] n literie f

bed linen n draps mpl de lit (et taies fpl d'oreillers), literie f

bedraggled [bɪ'drægld] adj dépenaillé(e), les vêtements en désordre

bedridden ['bɛdrɪdn] adj cloué(e) au lit

bedroom ['bɛdrum] n chambre f (à coucher)

bedside ['bɛdsaɪd] n: **at sb's ~** au chevet de qn ▷ cpd (book, lamp) de chevet

bedside lamp n lampe f de chevet

bedside table n table f de chevet

bedsit ['bɛdsɪt], **bedsitter** ['bɛdsɪtə^r] n (Brit) chambre meublée, studio m

bedspread ['bɛdspred] n couvre-lit m, dessus-de-lit m

bedtime ['bɛdtaɪm] n: **it's ~** c'est l'heure de se coucher

bee [biː] n abeille f; **to have a ~ in one's bonnet (about sth)** être obnubilé(e) (par qch)

beech [biːtʃ] n hêtre m

beef [biːf] n bœuf m; **roast ~** rosbif m; **beef up** vt (inf: support) renforcer; (: essay) étoffer

beefburger ['biːfbəːgə^r] n hamburger m

beehive ['biːhaɪv] n ruche f

beeline ['biːlaɪn] n: **to make a ~ for** se diriger tout droit vers

been [biːn] pp of **be**

beer [bɪə^r] n bière f

beer garden n (Brit) jardin m d'un pub (où l'on peut emmener ses consommations)

beet [biːt] n (vegetable) betterave f; (US: also: **red ~**) betterave (potagère)

beetle ['biːtl] n scarabée m, coléoptère m

beetroot ['biːtruːt] n (Brit) betterave f

before [bɪ'fɔː^r] prep (of time) avant; (of space) devant ▷ conj avant que + sub; avant de ▷ adv avant; **~ going** avant de partir; **~ she goes** avant qu'elle (ne) parte; **the week ~** la semaine précédente or d'avant; **I've seen it ~** je l'ai déjà vu; **I've never seen it ~** c'est la première fois que je le vois

beforehand [bɪ'fɔːhænd] adv au préalable, à l'avance

beg [bɛg] vi mendier ▷ vt mendier; (favour) quémander, solliciter; (forgiveness, mercy etc) demander; (entreat) supplier; **to ~ sb to do sth** supplier qn de faire qch; **I ~ your pardon** (apologising) excusez-moi; (: not hearing) pardon?; **that ~s the question of ...** cela soulève la question de ..., cela suppose réglée la question de ...; see also **pardon**

began [bɪ'gæn] pt of **begin**

beggar ['bɛgə^r] n (also: **~man, ~woman**) mendiant(e)

begin [bɪ'gɪn] (pt **began**, pp **begun**) [bɪ'gɪn, -'gæn, -'gʌn] vt, vi commencer; **to ~ doing** or **to do sth** commencer à faire qch; **~ning (from) Monday** à partir de lundi; **I can't ~ to thank you** je ne saurais vous remercier; **to ~ with** d'abord, pour commencer

beginner [bɪ'gɪnə^r] n débutant(e)

beginning [bɪ'gɪnɪŋ] n commencement m, début m; **right from the ~** dès le début

begun [bɪ'gʌn] pp of **begin**

behalf [bɪ'hɑːf] n: **on ~ of**, (US) **in ~ of** (representing) de la part de; au nom de; (for benefit of) pour le compte de; **on my/his ~** de ma/sa part

behave [bɪ'heɪv] vi se conduire, se comporter; (well: also: **~ o.s.**) se conduire bien or comme il faut

behaviour, (US) **behavior** [bɪ'heɪvjə^r] n comportement m, conduite f

behead [bɪ'hɛd] vt décapiter

behind [bɪ'haɪnd] prep derrière; (time) en retard sur; (supporting): **to be ~ sb** soutenir qn ▷ adv derrière; en retard ▷ n derrière m; **~ the scenes** dans les coulisses; **to leave sth ~** (forget) oublier de prendre qch; **to be ~ (schedule) with sth** être en retard dans qch

behold [bɪ'həuld] vt (irreg like: **hold**) apercevoir, voir

beige [beɪʒ] adj beige

Beijing ['beɪ'dʒɪŋ] n Pékin

being ['biːɪŋ] n être m; **to come into ~**
prendre naissance

Beirut [beɪ'ruːt] n Beyrouth

Belarus [belə'rʌs] n Biélorussie f, Bélarus m

belated [bɪ'leɪtɪd] adj tardif(-ive)

belch [beltʃ] vi avoir un renvoi, roter ▷ vt
(also: **~ out**: smoke etc) vomir, cracher

Belgian ['beldʒən] adj belge, de Belgique ▷ n
Belge m/f

Belgium ['beldʒəm] n Belgique f

belie [bɪ'laɪ] vt démentir; (give false impression
of) occulter

belief [bɪ'liːf] n (opinion) conviction f; (trust,
faith) foi f; (acceptance as true) croyance f; **it's
beyond ~** c'est incroyable; **in the ~ that** dans
l'idée que

believe [bɪ'liːv] vt, vi croire, estimer; **to ~ in**
(God) croire en; (ghosts, method) croire à; **I
don't ~ in corporal punishment** je ne suis
pas partisan des châtiments corporels; **he is
~d to be abroad** il serait à l'étranger

believer [bɪ'liːvə'] n (in idea, activity)
partisan(e); **~ in** partisan(e) de; (Rel)
croyant(e)

belittle [bɪ'lɪtl] vt déprécier, rabaisser

bell [bel] n cloche f; (small) clochette f,
grelot m; (on door) sonnette f; (electric)
sonnerie f; **that rings a ~** (fig) cela me
rappelle qch

bellboy ['belbɔɪ], (US) **bellhop** ['belhɔp] n
groom m, chasseur m

belligerent [bɪ'lɪdʒərənt] adj (at war)
belligérant(e); (fig) agressif(-ive)

bellow ['beləʊ] vi (bull) meugler; (person)
brailler ▷ vt (orders) hurler

bell pepper n (esp US) poivron m

belly ['belɪ] n ventre m

belly button (inf) n nombril m

belong [bɪ'lɔŋ] vi: **to ~ to** appartenir à; (club
etc) faire partie de; **this book ~s here** ce livre
va ici, la place de ce livre est ici

belongings [bɪ'lɔŋɪŋz] npl affaires fpl,
possessions fpl; **personal ~** effets personnels

beloved [bɪ'lʌvɪd] adj (bien-)aimé(e), chéri(e)
▷ n bien-aimé(e)

below [bɪ'ləʊ] prep sous, au-dessous de ▷ adv
en dessous; en contre-bas; **see ~** voir plus bas
or plus loin or ci-dessous; **temperatures ~
normal** températures inférieures à la
normale

belt [belt] n ceinture f; (Tech) courroie f ▷ vt
(thrash) donner une raclée à ▷ vi (Brit inf) filer
(à toutes jambes); **industrial ~** zone
industrielle; **belt out** vt (song) chanter à tue-
tête or à pleins poumons; **belt up** (Brit inf)
la boucler

beltway ['beltweɪ] n (US Aut) route f de
ceinture; (: motorway) périphérique m

bemused [bɪ'mjuːzd] adj médusé(e)

bench [bentʃ] n banc m; (in workshop) établi m;
the B~ (Law: judges) la magistrature, la Cour

bend [bend] (pt, pp **bent**) [bent] vt courber;
(leg, arm) plier ▷ vi se courber ▷ n (Brit: in road)
virage m, tournant m; (in pipe, river) coude m;
bend down vi se baisser; **bend over** vi se
pencher

beneath [bɪ'niːθ] prep sous, au-dessous de;
(unworthy of) indigne de ▷ adv dessous,
au-dessous, en bas

benefactor ['benɪfæktə'] n bienfaiteur m

beneficial [benɪ'fɪʃəl] adj: **~ (to)** salutaire
(pour), bénéfique (à)

benefit ['benɪfɪt] n avantage m, profit m;
(allowance of money) allocation f ▷ vt faire du
bien à, profiter à ▷ vi: **he'll ~ from it** cela lui
fera du bien, il y gagnera or s'en trouvera
bien

Benelux ['benɪlʌks] n Bénélux m

benevolent [bɪ'nevələnt] adj bienveillant(e)

benign [bɪ'naɪn] adj (person, smile)
bienveillant(e), affable; (Med) bénin(-igne)

bent [bent] pt, pp of **bend** ▷ n inclination f,
penchant m ▷ adj (wire, pipe) coudé(e); (inf:
dishonest) véreux(-euse); **to be ~ on** être
résolu(e) à

bequest [bɪ'kwest] n legs m

bereaved [bɪ'riːvd] n: **the ~** la famille du
disparu ▷ adj endeuillé(e)

beret ['bereɪ] n béret m

Berlin [bəː'lɪn] n Berlin; **East/West ~** Berlin
Est/Ouest

berm [bəːm] n (US Aut) accotement m

Bermuda [bəː'mjuːdə] n Bermudes fpl

Bern [bəːn] n Berne

berry ['berɪ] n baie f

berserk [bə'səːk] adj: **to go ~** être pris(e)
d'une rage incontrôlable; se déchaîner

berth [bəːθ] n (bed) couchette f; (for ship)
poste m d'amarrage, mouillage m ▷ vi (in
harbour) venir à quai; (at anchor) mouiller; **to
give sb a wide ~** (fig) éviter qn

beseech (pt, pp **besought**) [bɪ'siːtʃ, -'sɔːt] vt
implorer, supplier

beset (pt, pp **beset**) [bɪ'set] vt assaillir ▷ adj:
~ with semé(e) de

beside [bɪ'saɪd] prep à côté de; (compared with)
par rapport à; **that's ~ the point** ça n'a rien à
voir; **to be ~ o.s. (with anger)** être hors de
soi

besides [bɪ'saɪdz] adv en outre, de plus ▷ prep
en plus de; (except) excepté

besiege [bɪ'siːdʒ] vt (town) assiéger; (fig)
assaillir

best [best] adj meilleur(e) ▷ adv le mieux;
the ~ part of (quantity) le plus clair de, la plus
grande partie de; **at ~** au mieux; **to make the
~ of sth** s'accommoder de qch (du mieux que
l'on peut); **to do one's ~** faire de son mieux;
to the ~ of my knowledge pour autant que
je sache; **to the ~ of my ability** du mieux
que je pourrai; **he's not exactly patient at
the ~ of times** il n'est jamais spécialement
patient; **the ~ thing to do is ...** le mieux,
c'est de ...

best-before date n date f de limite d'utilisation or de consommation

best man (irreg) n garçon m d'honneur

bestow [bɪˈstəu] vt accorder; (title) conférer

bestseller [ˈbɛstˈsɛləʳ] n best-seller m, succès m de librairie

bet [bɛt] n pari m ▷ vt, vi (pt, pp **bet** or **betted**) parier; **it's a safe ~** (fig) il y a de fortes chances; **to ~ sb sth** parier qch à qn

betray [bɪˈtreɪ] vt trahir

better [ˈbɛtəʳ] adj meilleur(e) ▷ adv mieux ▷ vt améliorer ▷ n: **to get the ~ of** triompher de, l'emporter sur; **a change for the ~** une amélioration; **I had ~ go** il faut que je m'en aille; **you had ~ do it** vous feriez mieux de le faire; **he thought ~ of it** il s'est ravisé; **to get ~** (Med) aller mieux; (improve) s'améliorer; **that's ~!** c'est mieux!; **~ off** adj plus à l'aise financièrement; (fig): **you'd be ~ off this way** vous vous en trouveriez mieux ainsi, ce serait mieux or plus pratique ainsi

betting [ˈbɛtɪŋ] n paris mpl

betting shop n (Brit) bureau m de paris

between [bɪˈtwiːn] prep entre ▷ adv au milieu, dans l'intervalle; **the road ~ here and London** la route d'ici à Londres; **we only had 5 ~ us** nous n'en avions que 5 en tout

beverage [ˈbɛvərɪdʒ] n boisson f (gén sans alcool)

beware [bɪˈwɛəʳ] vt, vi: **to ~ (of)** prendre garde (à); **"~ of the dog"** "(attention) chien méchant"

bewildered [bɪˈwɪldəd] adj dérouté(e), ahuri(e)

beyond [bɪˈjɔnd] prep (in space, time) au-delà de; (exceeding) au-dessus de ▷ adv au-delà; **~ doubt** hors de doute; **~ repair** irréparable

bias [ˈbaɪəs] n (prejudice) préjugé m, parti pris m; (preference) prévention f

biased, biassed [ˈbaɪəst] adj partial(e), montrant un parti pris; **to be bias(s)ed against** avoir un préjugé contre

bib [bɪb] n bavoir m, bavette f

Bible [ˈbaɪbl] n Bible f

bicarbonate of soda [baɪˈkɑːbənɪt-] n bicarbonate m de soude

biceps [ˈbaɪsɛps] n biceps m

bicker [ˈbɪkəʳ] vi se chamailler

bicycle [ˈbaɪsɪkl] n bicyclette f

bicycle pump n pompe f à vélo

bid [bɪd] n offre f; (at auction) enchère f; (attempt) tentative f ▷ vi (pt, pp **bid**) faire une enchère or offre ▷ vt (pt **bade**) [bæd] (pp **bidden**) [ˈbɪdn] faire une enchère or offre de; **to ~ sb good day** souhaiter le bonjour à qn

bidder [ˈbɪdəʳ] n: **the highest ~** le plus offrant

bidding [ˈbɪdɪŋ] n enchères fpl

bide [baɪd] vt: **to ~ one's time** attendre son heure

bidet [ˈbiːdeɪ] n bidet m

bifocals [baɪˈfəuklz] npl lunettes fpl à double foyer

big [bɪg] adj (in height: person, building, tree) grand(e); (in bulk, amount: person, parcel, box) gros(se); **to do things in a ~ way** faire les choses en grand

Big Apple n voir article

bigheaded [ˈbɪgˈhɛdɪd] adj prétentieux(-euse)

bigot [ˈbɪgət] n fanatique m/f, sectaire m/f

bigoted [ˈbɪgətɪd] adj fanatique, sectaire

bigotry [ˈbɪgətrɪ] n fanatisme m, sectarisme m

big toe n gros orteil

big top n grand chapiteau

bike [baɪk] n vélo m, bécane f

bike lane n piste f cyclable

bikini [bɪˈkiːnɪ] n bikini m

bilateral [baɪˈlætərl] adj bilatéral(e)

bilingual [baɪˈlɪŋgwəl] adj bilingue

bill [bɪl] n note f, facture f; (in restaurant) addition n note f; (Pol) projet m de loi; (US: banknote) billet m (de banque); (notice) affiche f; (of bird) bec m; (Theat): **on the ~** à l'affiche ▷ vt (item) facturer; (customer) remettre la facture à; **may I have the ~ please?** (est-ce que je peux avoir) l'addition, s'il vous plaît?; **put it on my ~** mettez-le sur mon compte; **"post no ~s"** "défense d'afficher"; **to fit** or **fill the ~** (fig) faire l'affaire; **~ of exchange** lettre f de change; **~ of lading** connaissement m; **~ of sale** contrat m de vente

billboard [ˈbɪlbɔːd] (US) n panneau m d'affichage

billet [ˈbɪlɪt] n cantonnement m (chez l'habitant) ▷ vt (troops) cantonner

billfold [ˈbɪlfəuld] n (US) portefeuille m

billiards [ˈbɪljədz] n (jeu m de) billard m

billion [ˈbɪljən] n (Brit) billion m (million de millions); (US) milliard m

bimbo [ˈbɪmbəu] n (inf) ravissante idiote f

bin [bɪn] n boîte f; (Brit: also: **dust~, litter~**) poubelle f; (for coal) coffre m

bind (pt, pp **bound**) [baɪnd, baund] vt attacher; (book) relier; (oblige) obliger, contraindre ▷ *n* (*inf: nuisance*) scie *f*; **bind over** *vt* (*Law*) mettre en liberté conditionnelle; **bind up** *vt* (*wound*) panser; **to be bound up in** (*work, research etc*) être complètement absorbé par, être accroché par; **to be bound up with** (*person*) être accroché à

binding ['baɪndɪŋ] *n* (*of book*) reliure *f* ▷ *adj* (*contract*) qui constitue une obligation

binge [bɪndʒ] *n* (*inf*): **to go on a** ~ faire la bringue

bingo ['bɪŋgəu] *n* sorte de jeu de loto pratiqué dans des établissements publics

binoculars [bɪ'nɔkjuləz] *npl* jumelles *fpl*

biochemistry [baɪə'kemɪstrɪ] *n* biochimie *f*

biodegradable ['baɪəudɪ'greɪdəbl] *adj* biodégradable

biography [baɪ'ɔgrəfɪ] *n* biographie *f*

biological [baɪə'lɔdʒɪkl] *adj* biologique

biology [baɪ'ɔlədʒɪ] *n* biologie *f*

biometric [baɪə'metrɪk] *adj* biométrique

birch [bə:tʃ] *n* bouleau *m*

bird [bə:d] *n* oiseau *m*; (*Brit inf: girl*) nana *f*

bird flu *n* grippe *f* aviaire

bird of prey *n* oiseau *m* de proie

bird's-eye view ['bə:dzaɪ-] *n* vue *f* à vol d'oiseau; (*fig*) vue *f* d'ensemble *or* générale

bird watcher [-wɔtʃə'] *n* ornithologue *m/f* amateur

birdwatching ['bə:dwɔtʃɪŋ] *n* ornithologie *f* (*d'amateur*)

Biro® ['baɪərəu] *n* stylo *m* à bille

birth [bə:θ] *n* naissance *f*; **to give ~ to** donner naissance à, mettre au monde; (*subj: animal*) mettre bas

birth certificate *n* acte *m* de naissance

birth control *n* (*policy*) limitation *f* des naissances; (*methods*) méthode(s) contraceptive(s)

birthday ['bə:θdeɪ] *n* anniversaire *m* ▷ *cpd* (*cake, card etc*) d'anniversaire

birthmark ['bə:θmɑːk] *n* envie *f*, tache *f* de vin

birthplace ['bə:θpleɪs] *n* lieu *m* de naissance

birth rate *n* (taux *m* de) natalité *f*

biscuit ['bɪskɪt] *n* (*Brit*) biscuit *m*; (*US*) petit pain au lait

bisect [baɪ'sɛkt] *vt* couper *or* diviser en deux

bishop ['bɪʃəp] *n* évêque *m*; (*Chess*) fou *m*

bistro ['bi:strəu] *n* petit restaurant *m*, bistrot *m*

bit [bɪt] *pt of* **bite** ▷ *n* morceau *m*; (*Comput*) bit *m*, élément *m* binaire; (*of tool*) mèche *f*; (*of horse*) mors *m*; **a ~ of** un peu de; **a ~ mad/dangerous** un peu fou/risqué; **~ by ~** petit à petit; **to come to ~s** (*break*) tomber en morceaux, se déglinguer; **bring all your ~s and pieces** apporte toutes tes affaires; **to do one's ~** y mettre du sien

bitch [bɪtʃ] *n* (*dog*) chienne *f*; (*inf!*) salope *f* (!), garce *f*

bite [baɪt] *vt, vi* [*pt* **bit**, *pp* **bitten**] [bɪt, 'bɪtn]

mordre; (*insect*) piquer ▷ *n* morsure *f*; (*insect bite*) piqûre *f*; (*mouthful*) bouchée *f*; **let's have a ~ (to eat)** mangeons un morceau; **to ~ one's nails** se ronger les ongles

bitten ['bɪtn] *pp of* **bite**

bitter ['bɪtə'] *adj* amer(-ère); (*criticism*) cinglant(e); (*icy: weather, wind*) glacial(e) ▷ *n* (*Brit: beer*) bière *f* (à forte teneur en houblon); **to the ~ end** jusqu'au bout

bitterness ['bɪtənɪs] *n* amertume *f*; goût amer

bizarre [bɪ'zɑː'] *adj* bizarre

black [blæk] *adj* noir(e) ▷ *n* (*colour*) noir *m*; (*person*): **B~** noir(e) ▷ *vt* (*shoes*) cirer; (*Brit Industry*) boycotter; **to give sb a ~ eye** pocher l'œil à qn, faire un œil au beurre noir à qn; **there it is in ~ and white** (*fig*) c'est écrit noir sur blanc; **to be in the ~** (*in credit*) avoir un compte créditeur; **~ and blue** (*bruised*) couvert(e) de bleus; **black out** *vi* (*faint*) s'évanouir

blackberry ['blækbərɪ] *n* mûre *f*

blackbird ['blækbə:d] *n* merle *m*

blackboard ['blækbɔːd] *n* tableau noir

black coffee *n* café noir

blackcurrant ['blæk'kʌrənt] *n* cassis *m*

blacken ['blækn] *vt* noircir

black ice *n* verglas *m*

blackleg ['blækleg] *n* (*Brit*) briseur *m* de grève, jaune *m*

blacklist ['blæklɪst] *n* liste noire ▷ *vt* mettre sur la liste noire

blackmail ['blækmeɪl] *n* chantage *m* ▷ *vt* faire chanter, soumettre au chantage

black market *n* marché noir

blackout ['blækaut] *n* panne *f* d'électricité; (*in wartime*) black-out *m*; (*TV*) interruption *f* d'émission; (*fainting*) syncope *f*

black pepper *n* poivre noir

black pudding *n* boudin (noir)

Black Sea *n*: **the ~** la mer Noire

black sheep *n* brebis galeuse

blacksmith ['blæksmɪθ] *n* forgeron *m*

black spot *n* (*Aut*) point noir

bladder ['blædə'] *n* vessie *f*

blade [bleɪd] *n* lame *f*; (*of oar*) plat *m*; (*of propeller*) pale *f*; **a ~ of grass** un brin d'herbe

blame [bleɪm] *n* faute *f*, blâme *m* ▷ *vt*: **to ~ sb/sth for sth** attribuer à qn/qch la responsabilité de qch; reprocher qch à qn/qch; **who's to ~?** qui est le fautif *or* coupable *or* responsable?; **I'm not to ~** ce n'est pas ma faute

bland [blænd] *adj* affable; (*taste, food*) doux/douce, fade

blank [blæŋk] *adj* blanc/blanche; (*look*) sans expression, dénué(e) d'expression ▷ *n* espace *m* vide, blanc *m*; (*cartridge*) cartouche *f* à blanc; **his mind was a ~** il avait la tête vide; **we drew a ~** (*fig*) nous n'avons abouti à rien

blanket ['blæŋkɪt] *n* couverture *f*; (*of snow, cloud*) couche *f* ▷ *adj* (*statement, agreement*) global(e), de portée générale; **to give ~ cover** (insurance policy) couvrir tous les risques

blare [blɛəʳ] vi (brass band, horns, radio) beugler

blast [blɑːst] n explosion f; (shock wave) souffle m; (of air, steam) bouffée f ▷ vt faire sauter or exploser ▷ excl (Brit inf) zut!; (at) full ~ (play music etc) à plein volume; **blast off** vi (Space) décoller

blast-off [ˈblɑːstɔf] n (Space) lancement m

blatant [ˈbleɪtənt] adj flagrant(e), criant(e)

blaze [bleɪz] n (fire) incendie m; (flames: of fire, sun etc) embrasement m; (: in hearth) flamme f, flambée f; (fig) flamboiement m ▷ vi (fire) flamber; (fig) flamboyer, resplendir ▷ vt: **to ~ a trail** (fig) montrer la voie; **in a ~ of publicity** à grand renfort de publicité

blazer [ˈbleɪzəʳ] n blazer m

bleach [bliːtʃ] n (also: **household ~**) eau f de Javel ▷ vt (linen) blanchir

bleached [bliːtʃt] adj (hair) oxygéné(e), décoloré(e)

bleachers [ˈbliːtʃəz] npl (US Sport) gradins mpl (en plein soleil)

bleak [bliːk] adj morne, désolé(e); (weather) triste, maussade; (smile) lugubre; (prospect, future) morose

bleat [bliːt] n bêlement m ▷ vi bêler

bled [blɛd] pt, pp of **bleed**

bleed (pt, pp bled) [bliːd, blɛd] vt saigner; (brakes, radiator) purger ▷ vi saigner; **my nose is ~ing** je saigne du nez

bleeper [ˈbliːpəʳ] n (of doctor etc) bip m

blemish [ˈblɛmɪʃ] n défaut m; (on reputation) tache f

blend [blɛnd] n mélange m ▷ vt mélanger ▷ vi (colours etc: also: **~ in**) se mélanger, se fondre, s'allier

blender [ˈblɛndəʳ] n (Culin) mixeur m

bless (pt, pp blessed or blest) [blɛs, blɛst] vt bénir; **to be ~ed with** avoir le bonheur de jouir de or d'avoir; **~ you!** (after sneeze) à tes souhaits!

blessing [ˈblɛsɪŋ] n bénédiction f; (godsend) bienfait m; **to count one's ~s** s'estimer heureux; **it was a ~ in disguise** c'est un bien pour un mal

blew [bluː] pt of **blow**

blight [blaɪt] n (of plants) rouille f ▷ vt (hopes etc) anéantir, briser

blimey [ˈblaɪmɪ] excl (Brit inf) mince alors!

blind [blaɪnd] adj aveugle ▷ n (for window) store m ▷ vt aveugler; **to turn a ~ eye (on** or **to)** fermer les yeux (sur); **the blind** npl les aveugles mpl

blind alley n impasse f

blind corner n (Brit) virage m sans visibilité

blindfold [ˈblaɪndfəuld] n bandeau m ▷ adj, adv les yeux bandés ▷ vt bander les yeux à

blindly [ˈblaɪndlɪ] adv aveuglément

blindness [ˈblaɪndnɪs] n cécité f; (fig) aveuglement m

blind spot n (Aut etc) angle m aveugle; (fig) angle mort

blink [blɪŋk] vi cligner des yeux; (light) clignoter ▷ n: **the TV's on the ~** (inf) la télé ne va pas tarder à nous lâcher

blinkers [ˈblɪŋkəz] npl œillères fpl

bliss [blɪs] n félicité f, bonheur m sans mélange

blister [ˈblɪstəʳ] n (on skin) ampoule f, cloque f; (on paintwork) boursouflure f ▷ vi (paint) se boursoufler, se cloquer

blizzard [ˈblɪzəd] n blizzard m, tempête f de neige

bloated [ˈbləutɪd] adj (face) bouffi(e); (stomach, person) gonflé(e)

blob [blɔb] n (drop) goutte f; (stain, spot) tache f

block [blɔk] n bloc m; (in pipes) obstruction f; (toy) cube m; (of buildings) pâté m (de maisons) ▷ vt bloquer; (fig) faire obstacle à; (Comput) grouper; **the sink is ~ed** l'évier est bouché; **~ of flats** (Brit) immeuble (locatif); **3 ~s from here** à trois rues d'ici; **mental ~** blocage m; **~ and tackle** (Tech) palan m; **block up** vt boucher

blockade [blɔˈkeɪd] n blocus m ▷ vt faire le blocus de

blockage [ˈblɔkɪdʒ] n obstruction f

blockbuster [ˈblɔkbʌstəʳ] n (film, book) grand succès

block capitals npl majuscules fpl d'imprimerie

block letters npl majuscules fpl

blog [blɔg] n blog m, blogue m ▷ vi bloguer

blogger [ˈblɔgəʳ] (inf) n (person) blogueur(-euse) m/f

blogging [ˈblɔgɪŋ] n blogging m

bloke [bləuk] n (Brit inf) type m

blond, blonde [blɔnd] adj, n blond(e)

blood [blʌd] n sang m

blood donor n donneur(-euse) de sang

blood group n groupe sanguin

bloodhound [ˈblʌdhaund] n limier m

blood poisoning n empoisonnement m du sang

blood pressure n tension (artérielle); **to have high/low ~** faire de l'hypertension/l'hypotension

bloodshed [ˈblʌdʃɛd] n effusion f de sang, carnage m

bloodshot [ˈblʌdʃɔt] adj: **~ eyes** yeux injectés de sang

blood sports npl sports mpl sanguinaires

bloodstream [ˈblʌdstriːm] n sang m, système sanguin

blood test n analyse f de sang

bloodthirsty [ˈblʌdθəːstɪ] adj sanguinaire

blood transfusion n transfusion f de sang

blood type n groupe sanguin

blood vessel n vaisseau sanguin

bloody [ˈblʌdɪ] adj sanglant(e); (Brit inf!): **this ~ ...** ce foutu ..., ce putain de ... (!) ▷ adv:

~ strong/good (Brit: inf!) vachement or sacrément fort/bon

bloody-minded ['blʌdɪ'maɪndɪd] *adj* (Brit inf) contrariant(e), obstiné(e)

bloom [bluːm] *n* fleur *f*; (fig) épanouissement *m* ▷ *vi* être en fleur; (fig) s'épanouir; être florissant(e)

blossom ['blɒsəm] *n* fleur(s) *f(pl)* ▷ *vi* être en fleurs; (fig) s'épanouir; **to ~ into** (fig) devenir

blot [blɒt] *n* tache *f* ▷ *vt* tacher; (ink) sécher; **to be a ~ on the landscape** gâcher le paysage; **to ~ one's copy book** (fig) faire un impair; **blot out** *vt* (memories) effacer; (view) cacher, masquer; (nation, city) annihiler

blotchy ['blɒtʃɪ] *adj* (complexion) couvert(e) de marbrures

blotting paper ['blɒtɪŋ-] *n* buvard *m*

blouse [blauz] *n* (feminine garment) chemisier *m*, corsage *m*

blow [bləu] (*pt* blew, *pp* blown) [bluː, bləun] *n* coup *m* ▷ *vi* souffler ▷ *vt* (glass) souffler; (instrument) jouer de; (fuse) faire sauter; **to ~ one's nose** se moucher; **to ~ a whistle** siffler; **to come to ~s** en venir aux coups; **blow away** *vi* s'envoler ▷ *vt* chasser, faire s'envoler; **blow down** *vt* faire tomber, renverser; **blow off** *vi* s'envoler ▷ *vt* (hat) emporter; (ship): **to ~ off course** faire dévier; **blow out** *vi* (fire, flame) s'éteindre; (tyre) éclater; (fuse) sauter; **blow over** *vi* s'apaiser; **blow up** *vi* exploser, sauter ▷ *vt* faire sauter; (tyre) gonfler; (Phot) agrandir

blow-dry ['bləudraɪ] *n* (hairstyle) brushing *m* ▷ *vt* faire un brushing à

blowlamp ['bləulæmp] *n* (Brit) chalumeau *m*

blown [bləun] *pp of* **blow**

blow-out ['bləuaut] *n* (of tyre) éclatement *m*; (Brit: inf: big meal) gueuleton *m*

blowtorch ['bləutɔːtʃ] *n* chalumeau *m*

blue [bluː] *adj* bleu(e); (depressed) triste; **~ film/joke** film *m*/histoire *f* pornographique; **(only) once in a ~ moon** tous les trente-six du mois; **out of the ~** (fig) à l'improviste, sans qu'on s'y attende

bluebell ['bluːbel] *n* jacinthe *f* des bois

blueberry ['bluːbərɪ] *n* myrtille *f*, airelle *f*

bluebottle ['bluːbɒtl] *n* mouche *f* à viande

blue cheese *n* (fromage) bleu *m*

blueprint ['bluːprɪnt] *n* bleu *m*; (fig) projet *m*, plan directeur

blues [bluːz] *npl*: **the ~** (Mus) le blues; **to have the ~** (inf: feeling) avoir le cafard

bluff [blʌf] *vi* bluffer ▷ *n* bluff *m*; (cliff) promontoire *m*, falaise *f* ▷ *adj* (person) bourru(e), brusque; **to call sb's ~** mettre qn au défi d'exécuter ses menaces

blunder ['blʌndəʳ] *n* gaffe *f*, bévue *f* ▷ *vi* faire une gaffe *or* une bévue; **to ~ into sb/sth** buter contre qn/qch

blunt [blʌnt] *adj* (knife) émoussé(e), peu tranchant(e); (pencil) mal taillé(e); (person) brusque, ne mâchant pas ses mots ▷ *vt*

émousser; **~ instrument** (Law) instrument contondant

blur [bləːʳ] *n* (shape): **to become a ~** devenir flou ▷ *vt* brouiller, rendre flou(e)

blurred [bləːd] *adj* flou(e)

blush [blʌʃ] *vi* rougir ▷ *n* rougeur *f*

blusher ['blʌʃəʳ] *n* rouge *m* à joues

blustery ['blʌstərɪ] *adj* (weather) à bourrasques

boar [bɔːʳ] *n* sanglier *m*

board [bɔːd] *n* (wooden) planche *f*; (on wall) panneau *m*; (for chess etc) plateau *m*; (cardboard) carton *m*; (committee) conseil *m*, comité *m*; (in firm) conseil d'administration; (Naut, Aviat): **on ~** à bord ▷ *vt* (ship) monter à bord de; (train) monter dans; **full ~** (Brit) pension complète; **half ~** (Brit) demi-pension *f*; **~ and lodging** chambre *f* avec pension; **with ~ and lodging** logé nourri; **above ~** (fig) régulier(-ère); **across the ~** (fig: adv) systématiquement; (: adj) de portée générale; **to go by the ~** (hopes, principles) être abandonné(e); (be unimportant) compter pour rien, n'avoir aucune importance; **board up** *vt* (door) condamner (au moyen de planches, de tôle)

boarder ['bɔːdəʳ] *n* pensionnaire *m/f*; (Scol) interne *m/f*, pensionnaire

board game *n* jeu *m* de société

boarding card ['bɔːdɪŋ-] *n* (Aviat, Naut) carte *f* d'embarquement

boarding house ['bɔːdɪŋ-] *n* pension *f*

boarding pass ['bɔːdɪŋ-] *n* (Brit) = **boarding card**

boarding school ['bɔːdɪŋ-] *n* internat *m*, pensionnat *m*

board room *n* salle *f* du conseil d'administration

boast [bəust] *vi*: **to ~ (about or of)** se vanter (de) ▷ *vt* s'enorgueillir de ▷ *n* vantardise *f*, sujet *m* d'orgueil or de fierté

boat [bəut] *n* bateau *m*; (small) canot *m*; barque *f*; **to go by ~** aller en bateau; **to be in the same ~** (fig) être logé à la même enseigne

bob [bɒb] *vi* (boat, cork on water: also: **~ up and down**) danser, se balancer ▷ *n* (Brit inf) = **shilling**; **bob up** *vi* surgir or apparaître brusquement

bobby ['bɒbɪ] *n* (Brit inf) = agent *m* (de police)

bobby pin ['bɒbɪ-] *n* (US) pince *f* à cheveux

bobsleigh ['bɒbsleɪ] *n* bob *m*

bode [bəud] *vi*: **to ~ well/ill (for)** être de bon/mauvais augure (pour)

bodily ['bɒdɪlɪ] *adj* corporel(le); (pain, comfort) physique; (needs) matériel(le) ▷ *adv* (carry, lift) dans ses bras

body ['bɒdɪ] *n* corps *m*; (of car) carrosserie *f*; (of plane) fuselage *m*; (also: **~ stocking**) body *m*, justaucorps *m*; (fig: society) organe *m*, organisme *m*; (: quantity) ensemble *m*, masse *f*; (of wine) corps *m*; **~ ruling** organe directeur; **in a ~** en masse, ensemble; (speak) comme un seul et même homme

body-building ['bɔdɪbɪldɪŋ] n body-building m, culturisme m

bodyguard ['bɔdɪgɑːd] n garde m du corps

bodywork ['bɔdɪwɜːk] n carrosserie f

bog [bɔg] n tourbière f ⊳ vt: **to get ~ged down (in)** (fig) s'enliser (dans)

bogus ['bəugəs] adj bidon inv; fantôme

boil [bɔɪl] vt (faire) bouillir ⊳ vi bouillir ⊳ n (Med) furoncle m; **to come to the** or (US) **a ~** bouillir; **to bring to the** or (US) **a ~** porter à ébullition; **boil down** vi (fig): **to ~ down to** se réduire or ramener à; **boil over** vi déborder

boiled egg n œuf m à la coque

boiler ['bɔɪləʳ] n chaudière f

boiling ['bɔɪlɪŋ] adj: **I'm ~ (hot)** (inf) je crève de chaud

boiling point n point m d'ébullition

boisterous ['bɔɪstərəs] adj bruyant(e), tapageur(-euse)

bold [bəuld] adj hardi(e), audacieux(-euse); (pej) effronté(e); (outline, colour) franc/franche, tranché(e), marqué(e)

bollard ['bɔləd] n (Naut) bitte f d'amarrage; (Brit Aut) borne lumineuse or de signalisation

bolt [bəult] n verrou m, (with nut) boulon m ⊳ adv: **~ upright** droit(e) comme un piquet ⊳ vt (door) verrouiller; (food) engloutir ⊳ vi se sauver, filer (comme une flèche); **a ~ from the blue** (horse) s'emballer; (fig) un coup de tonnerre dans un ciel bleu

bomb [bɔm] n bombe f ⊳ vt bombarder

bombard [bɔm'bɑːd] vt bombarder

bomb disposal n: **~ unit** section f de déminage; **~ expert** artificier m

bomber ['bɔməʳ] n (Aviat) caporal m d'artillerie; (Aviat) bombardier m; (terrorist) poseur m de bombes

bombing ['bɔmɪŋ] n bombardement m

bomb scare n alerte f à la bombe

bombshell ['bɔmʃɛl] n obus m; (fig) bombe f

bond [bɔnd] n lien m; (binding promise) engagement m, obligation f; (Finance) obligation; **bonds** npl (chains) chaînes fpl; **in ~** (of goods) en entrepôt

bondage ['bɔndɪdʒ] n esclavage m

bone [bəun] n os m; (of fish) arête f ⊳ vt désosser; ôter les arêtes de

bone-dry ['bəun'draɪ] adj absolument sec/sèche

bone idle adj fainéant(e)

bone marrow n moelle osseuse

bonfire ['bɔnfaɪəʳ] n feu m (de joie); (for rubbish) feu

bonnet ['bɔnɪt] n bonnet m; (Brit: of car) capot m

bonus ['bəunəs] n (money) prime f; (advantage) avantage m

bony ['bəunɪ] adj (arm, face: Med: tissue) osseux(-euse); (thin: person) squelettique; (meat) plein(e) d'os; (fish) plein d'arêtes

boo [buː] excl hou!, peuh! ⊳ vt huer ⊳ n huée f

booby trap ['buːbɪ-] n guet-apens m

book [buk] n livre m; (of stamps, tickets etc) carnet m; (Comm): **books** npl comptes mpl, comptabilité f ⊳ vt (ticket) prendre; (seat, room) réserver; (driver) dresser un procès-verbal à; (football player) prendre le nom de, donner un carton à; **I ~ed a table in the name of ...** j'ai réservé une table au nom de ...; **to keep the ~s** tenir la comptabilité; **by the ~** à la lettre, selon les règles; **to throw the ~ at sb** passer un savon à qn; **book in** vi (Brit: at hotel) prendre sa chambre; **book up** vt réserver; **all seats are ~ed up** tout est pris, c'est complet; **the hotel is ~ed up** l'hôtel est complet

bookcase ['bukkeɪs] n bibliothèque f (meuble)

booking ['bukɪŋ] n (Brit) réservation f; **I confirmed my fax/email** j'ai confirmé ma réservation par fax/e-mail

booking office n (Brit) bureau m de location

book-keeping ['buk'kiːpɪŋ] n comptabilité f

booklet ['buklɪt] n brochure f

bookmaker ['bukmeɪkəʳ] n bookmaker m

bookmark ['bukmɑːk] n (for book) marque-page m; (Comput) signet m

bookseller ['bukselər] n libraire m/f

bookshelf ['bukʃɛlf] n (single) étagère f (à livres); (bookcase) bibliothèque f; **bookshelves** rayons mpl (de bibliothèque)

bookshop ['bukʃɔp], **bookstore** ['bukstɔːʳ] n librairie f

book store n = **bookshop**

boom [buːm] n (noise) grondement m; (in prices, population) forte augmentation; (busy period) boom m, vague f de prospérité f ⊳ vi gronder; prospérer

boon [buːn] n bénédiction f, grand avantage

boost [buːst] n stimulant m, remontant m ⊳ vt stimuler; **to give a ~ to sb's spirits** or **to sb** remonter le moral à qn

booster ['buːstəʳ] n (TV) amplificateur m (de signal); (Elec) survolteur m; (also: **~ rocket**) booster m; (Med: vaccine) rappel m

boot [buːt] n botte f; (for hiking) chaussure f (de marche); (ankle boot) bottine f; (Brit: of car) coffre m ⊳ vt (Comput) lancer, mettre en route; **to ~** (in addition) par-dessus le marché, en plus; **to give sb the ~** (inf) flanquer qn dehors, virer qn

booth [buːð] n (at fair) baraque (foraine); (of telephone etc) cabine f; (also: **voting ~**) isoloir m

booze [buːz] (inf) n boissons fpl alcooliques, alcool m ⊳ vi boire, picoler

border ['bɔːdəʳ] n bordure f; bord m; (of a country) frontière f; **the B~s** la région frontière entre l'Écosse et l'Angleterre; **border on** vt fus être voisin(e) de, toucher à

borderline ['bɔːdəlaɪn] n (fig) ligne f de démarcation ⊳ adj: **~ case** cas m limite

bore [bɔːʳ] pt of **bear** ⊳ vt (person) ennuyer, raser; (hole) percer; (well, tunnel) creuser ⊳ n (person) raseur(-euse); (boring thing) barbe f; (of gun) calibre m

bored ['bɔːd] adj: **to be ~** s'ennuyer; **he's ~ to tears** or **to death** or **stiff** il s'ennuie à mourir

boredom ['bɔːdəm] n ennui m

boring ['bɔːrɪŋ] adj ennuyeux(-euse)

born [bɔːn] adj: **to be ~** naître; **I was ~ in 1960** je suis né en 1960; **~ blind** aveugle de naissance; **a ~ comedian** un comédien-né

borne [bɔːn] pp of **bear**

borough ['bʌrə] n municipalité f

borrow ['bɔrəu] vt: **to ~ sth (from sb)** emprunter qch (à qn); **may I ~ your car?** est-ce que je peux vous emprunter votre voiture?

Bosnian ['bɔznɪən] adj bosniaque, bosnien(ne) ▷ n Bosniaque m/f, Bosnien(ne)

bosom ['buzəm] n poitrine f; (fig) sein m

boss [bɔs] n patron(ne) ▷ vt (also: **~ about, ~ around**) mener à la baguette

bossy ['bɔsɪ] adj autoritaire

bosun ['bəusn] n maître m d'équipage

botany ['bɔtənɪ] n botanique f

botch [bɔtʃ] vt (also: **~ up**) saboter, bâcler

both [bəuθ] adj: les deux, l'un(e) et l'autre ▷ pron: **~ (of them)** les deux, tous/toutes (les) deux, l'un(e) et l'autre; **~ of us went, we ~ went** nous y sommes allés tous les deux ▷ adv: **~ A and B** A et B; **they sell ~ the fabric and the finished curtains** ils vendent (et) le tissu et les rideaux (finis), ils vendent à la fois le tissu et les rideaux (finis)

bother ['bɔðəʳ] vt (worry) tracasser; (needle, bait) importuner, ennuyer; (disturb) déranger ▷ vi (also: **~ o.s.**) se tracasser, se faire du souci ▷ n (trouble) ennuis mpl; **it is a ~ to have to do** c'est vraiment ennuyeux d'avoir à faire ▷ excl zut!; **to ~ doing** prendre la peine de faire; **I'm sorry to ~ you** excusez-moi de vous déranger; **please don't ~** ne vous dérangez pas; **don't ~** ce n'est pas la peine; **it's no ~** aucun problème

bottle ['bɔtl] n bouteille f; (baby's) biberon m; (of perfume, medicine) flacon m ▷ vt mettre en bouteille(s); **~ of wine/milk** bouteille de vin/lait; **wine/milk ~** bouteille à vin/lait; **bottle up** vt refouler, contenir

bottle bank n conteneur m (de bouteilles)

bottleneck ['bɔtlnɛk] n (in traffic) bouchon m; (in production) goulet m d'étranglement

bottle-opener ['bɔtləupnəʳ] n ouvre-bouteille m

bottom ['bɔtəm] n (of container, sea etc) fond m; (buttocks) derrière m; (of page, list) bas m; (of chair) siège m; (of mountain, tree, hill) pied m ▷ adj (shelf, step) du bas; **to get to the ~ of sth** (fig) découvrir le fin fond de qch

bough [bau] n branche f, rameau m

bought [bɔːt] pt, pp of **buy**

boulder ['bəuldəʳ] n gros rocher (gén lisse, arrondi)

bounce [bauns] vi (ball) rebondir; (cheque) être refusé (étant sans provision); (also: **to ~ forward/out etc**) bondir, s'élancer ▷ vt faire rebondir ▷ n (rebound) rebond m; **he's got plenty of ~** (fig) il est plein d'entrain or d'allant

bouncer ['baunsəʳ] n (inf: at dance, club) videur m

bound [baund] pt, pp of **bind** ▷ n (gen pl) limite f; (leap) bond m ▷ vi (leap) bondir ▷ vt (limit) borner ▷ adj: **to be ~ to do sth** (obliged) être obligé(e) or avoir obligation de faire qch; **he's ~ to fail** (likely) il est sûr d'échouer, son échec est inévitable or assuré; **~ by** (law, regulation) engagé(e) par; **~ for** à destination de; **out of ~s** dont l'accès est interdit

boundary ['baundrɪ] n frontière f

bouquet ['bukeɪ] n bouquet m

bourbon ['buəbən] n (US: also: **~ whiskey**) bourbon m

bout [baut] n période f; (of malaria etc) accès m, crise f, attaque f; (Boxing etc) combat m, match m

boutique [buːˈtiːk] n boutique f

bow¹ [bəu] n nœud m; (weapon) arc m; (Mus) archet m

bow² [bau] n (with body) révérence f, inclination f (du buste or corps); (Naut: also: **~s**) proue f ▷ vi faire une révérence, s'incliner; (yield): **to ~ to** or **before** s'incliner devant, se soumettre à; **to ~ to the inevitable** accepter l'inévitable or l'inéluctable

bowels [bauəlz] npl intestins mpl; (fig) entrailles fpl

bowl [bəul] n (for eating) bol m; (for washing) cuvette f; (ball) boule f; (of pipe) fourneau m ▷ vi (Cricket) lancer (la balle); **bowl over** vt (fig) renverser

bow-legged ['bəuˈlɛgɪd] adj aux jambes arquées

bowler ['bəuləʳ] n joueur m de boules; (Cricket) lanceur m (de la balle); (Brit: also: **~ hat**) (chapeau m) melon m

bowling ['bəulɪŋ] n (game) jeu m de boules, jeu de quilles

bowling alley n bowling m

bowling green n terrain m de boules (gazonné et carré)

bowls [bəulz] n (jeu m de) boules fpl

bow tie [bəu-] n nœud m papillon

box [bɔks] n (also: **cardboard ~**) carton m; (crate) caisse f; (Theat) loge f ▷ vt mettre en boîte; (Sport) boxer avec ▷ vi boxer, faire de la boxe

boxer ['bɔksəʳ] n (person) boxeur m; (dog) boxer m

boxer shorts npl caleçon m

boxing ['bɔksɪŋ] n (sport) boxe f

Boxing Day n (Brit) le lendemain de Noël; voir article

⟡ **BOXING DAY**

Boxing Day est le lendemain de Noël, férié en Grande-Bretagne. Ce nom vient d'une coutume du XIXe siècle qui consistait à donner des cadeaux de Noël (dans des boîtes) à ses employés etc le 26 décembre.

boxing gloves *npl* gants *mpl* de boxe
boxing ring *n* ring *m*
box office *n* bureau *m* de location
box room *n* débarras *m*; chambrette *f*
boy [bɔɪ] *n* garçon *m*
boy band *n* boys band *m*
boycott ['bɔɪkɒt] *n* boycottage *m* ▷ *vt* boycotter
boyfriend ['bɔɪfrɛnd] *n* (petit) ami
boyish ['bɔɪʃ] *adj* d'enfant, de garçon; **to look ~** (*man: appear youthful*) faire jeune
BR *abbr* = **British Rail**
bra [brɑː] *n* soutien-gorge *m*
brace [breɪs] *n* (*support*) attache *f*, agrafe *f*; (*Brit: also:* **~s:** *on teeth*) appareil *m* (dentaire); (*tool*) vilebrequin *m*; (*Typ: also:* **~ bracket**) accolade *f* ▷ *vt* (*support*) consolider, soutenir; **braces** *npl* (*Brit: for trousers*) bretelles *fpl*; **to ~ o.s.** (*fig*) se préparer mentalement
bracelet ['breɪslɪt] *n* bracelet *m*
bracing ['breɪsɪŋ] *adj* tonifiant(e), tonique
bracket ['brækɪt] *n* (*Tech*) tasseau *m*, support *m*; (*group*) classe *f*, tranche *f*; (*also:* **brace ~**) accolade *f*; (*also:* **round ~**) parenthèse *f*; (*also:* **square ~**) crochet *m* ▷ *vt* mettre entre parenthèses; (*fig: also:* **~ together**) regrouper; **income ~** tranche *f* des revenus; **in ~s** entre parenthèses *or* crochets
brag [bræg] *vi* se vanter
braid [breɪd] *n* (*trimming*) galon *m*; (*of hair*) tresse *f*, natte *f*
brain [breɪn] *n* cerveau *m*; **brains** *npl* (*intellect, food*) cervelle *f*; **he's got ~s** il est intelligent
brainwash ['breɪnwɒʃ] *vt* faire subir un lavage de cerveau à
brainwave ['breɪnweɪv] *n* idée *f* de génie
brainy ['breɪnɪ] *adj* intelligent(e), doué(e)
braise [breɪz] *vt* braiser
brake [breɪk] *n* frein *m* ▷ *vt*, *vi* freiner
brake light *n* feu *m* de stop
bran [bræn] *n* son *m*
branch [brɑːntʃ] *n* branche *f*; (*Comm*) succursale *f*; (*: of bank*) agence *f*; (*of association*) section locale ▷ *vi* bifurquer; **branch off** *vi* (*road*) bifurquer; **branch out** *vi* diversifier ses activités; **to ~ out into** étendre ses activités à
brand [brænd] *n* marque (commerciale) ▷ *vt* (*cattle*) marquer (au fer rouge); (*fig: pej*): **to ~ sb a communist** *etc* traiter *or* qualifier qn de communiste *etc*
brand name *n* nom *m* de marque
brand-new ['brænd'njuː] *adj* tout(e) neuf/neuve, flambant neuf/neuve
brandy ['brændɪ] *n* cognac *m*, fine *f*

brash [bræʃ] *adj* effronté(e)
brass [brɑːs] *n* cuivre *m* (jaune), laiton *m*; **the ~** (*Mus*) les cuivres
brass band *n* fanfare *f*
brat [bræt] *n* (*pej*) mioche *m/f*, môme *m/f*
brave [breɪv] *adj* courageux(-euse), brave ▷ *n* guerrier indien ▷ *vt* braver, affronter
bravery ['breɪvərɪ] *n* bravoure *f*, courage *m*
brawl [brɔːl] *n* rixe *f*, bagarre *f* ▷ *vi* se bagarrer
brazen ['breɪzn] *adj* impudent(e), effronté(e) ▷ *vt*: **to ~ it out** payer d'effronterie, crâner
brazier ['breɪzɪə'] *n* brasero *m*
Brazil [brə'zɪl] *n* Brésil *m*
Brazilian [brə'zɪljən] *adj* brésilien(ne) ▷ *n* Brésilien(ne)
breach [briːtʃ] *vt* ouvrir une brèche dans ▷ *n* (*gap*) brèche *f*; (*estrangement*) brouille *f*; (*breaking*): **~ of contract** rupture *f* de contrat; **~ of the peace** attentat *m* à l'ordre public; **~ of trust** abus *m* de confiance
bread [brɛd] *n* pain *m*; (*inf: money*) fric *m*; **~ and butter** tartines (beurrées); (*fig*) subsistance *f*; **to earn one's daily ~** gagner son pain; **to know which side one's ~ is buttered (on)** savoir où est son avantage *or* intérêt
breadbin ['brɛdbɪn] *n* (*Brit*) boîte *f or* huche *f* à pain
breadbox ['brɛdbɒks] *n* (*US*) boîte *f or* huche *f* à pain
breadcrumbs ['brɛdkrʌmz] *npl* miettes *fpl* de pain; (*Culin*) chapelure *f*, panure *f*
breadline ['brɛdlaɪn] *n*: **to be on the ~** être sans le sou *or* dans l'indigence
breadth [brɛtθ] *n* largeur *f*
breadwinner ['brɛdwɪnə'] *n* soutien *m* de famille
break [breɪk] (*pt* **broke**, *pp* **broken**) [brəuk, 'brəukən] *vt* casser, briser; (*promise*) rompre; (*law*) violer ▷ *vi* se casser, se briser; (*weather*) tourner; (*storm*) éclater; (*day*) se lever ▷ *n* (*gap*) brèche *f*; (*fracture*) cassure *f*; (*rest*) interruption *f*, arrêt *m*; (*: short*) pause *f*; (*: at school*) récréation *f*; (*chance*) chance *f*, occasion *f* favorable; **to ~ one's leg** *etc* se casser la jambe *etc*; **to ~ a record** battre un record; **to ~ the news to sb** annoncer la nouvelle à qn; **to ~ with sb** rompre avec qn; **to ~ even** *vi* rentrer dans ses frais; **to ~ free** *or* **loose** *vi* se dégager, s'échapper; **to take a ~** (*few minutes*) faire une pause, s'arrêter cinq minutes; (*holiday*) prendre un peu de repos; **without a ~** sans interruption, sans arrêt; **break down** *vt* (*door etc*) enfoncer; (*resistance*) venir à bout de; (*figures, data*) décomposer, analyser ▷ *vi* s'effondrer; (*Med*) faire une dépression (nerveuse); (*Aut*) tomber en panne; **my car has broken down** ma voiture est en panne; **break in** *vt* (*horse etc*) dresser ▷ *vi* (*burglar*) entrer par effraction; (*interrupt*) interrompre; **break into** *vt fus* (*house*) s'introduire *or* pénétrer par effraction dans; **break off** *vi*

(*speaker*) s'interrompre; (*branch*) se rompre ▷ vt (*talks, engagement*) rompre; **break open** vt (*door etc*) forcer, fracturer; **break out** vi éclater, se déclarer; (*prisoner*) s'évader; **to ~ out in spots** se couvrir de boutons; **break through** vi: **the sun broke through** le soleil a fait son apparition ▷ vt fus (*defences, barrier*) franchir; (*crowd*) se frayer un passage à travers; **break up** vi (*partnership*) cesser, prendre fin; (*marriage*) se briser; (*crowd, meeting*) se séparer; (*ship*) se disloquer; (*Scol: pupils*) être en vacances; (*line*) couper; **the line's** or **you're ~ing up** ça coupe ▷ vt fracasser, casser; (*fight etc*) interrompre, faire cesser; (*marriage*) désunir

breakage ['breɪkɪdʒ] n casse f; **to pay for ~s** payer la casse

breakdown ['breɪkdaun] n (*Aut*) panne f; (*in communications, marriage*) rupture f; (*Med: also:* **nervous ~**) dépression (nerveuse); (*of figures*) ventilation f, répartition f

breakdown truck, (*US*) **breakdown van** n dépanneuse f

breaker ['breɪkəʳ] n brisant m

breakfast ['brɛkfəst] n petit déjeuner m; **what time is ~?** le petit déjeuner est à quelle heure?

break-in ['breɪkɪn] n cambriolage m

breaking and entering n (*Law*) effraction f

breakthrough ['breɪkθru:] n percée f

breakwater ['breɪkwɔ:təʳ] n brise-lames m inv, digue f

breast [brɛst] n (*of woman*) sein m; (*chest*) poitrine f; (*of chicken, turkey*) blanc m

breast-feed ['brɛstfi:d] vt, vi (*irreg like:* **feed**) allaiter

breast-stroke ['brɛststrəuk] n brasse f

breath [brɛθ] n haleine f, souffle m; **to go out for a ~ of air** sortir prendre l'air; **to take a deep ~** respirer à fond; **out of ~** à bout de souffle, essoufflé(e)

Breathalyser® ['brɛθəlaɪzəʳ] n (*Brit*) alcootest m

breathe [bri:ð] vt, vi respirer; **I won't ~ a word about it** je n'en soufflerai pas mot, je n'en dirai rien à personne; **breathe in** vi inspirer ▷ vt aspirer; **breathe out** vt, vi expirer

breather ['bri:ðəʳ] n moment m de repos or de répit

breathing ['bri:ðɪŋ] n respiration f

breathless ['brɛθlɪs] adj essoufflé(e), haletant(e), oppressé(e); **~ with excitement** le souffle coupé par l'émotion

breathtaking ['brɛθteɪkɪŋ] adj stupéfiant(e), à vous couper le souffle

breath test n alcootest m

bred [brɛd] pt, pp of **breed**

breed [bri:d] (pt, pp **bred**) [brɛd] vt élever, faire l'élevage de; (*fig: hate, suspicion*) engendrer ▷ vi se reproduire ▷ n race f, variété f

breeding ['bri:dɪŋ] n reproduction f; élevage m; (*upbringing*) éducation f

breeze [bri:z] n brise f

breezy ['bri:zɪ] adj (*day, weather*) venteux(-euse); (*manner*) désinvolte; (*person*) jovial(e)

brevity ['brɛvɪtɪ] n brièveté f

brew [bru:] vt (*tea*) faire infuser; (*beer*) brasser; (*plot*) tramer, préparer ▷ vi (*tea*) infuser; (*beer*) fermenter; (*fig*) se préparer, couver

brewery ['bru:ərɪ] n brasserie f (*fabrique*)

bribe [braɪb] n pot-de-vin m ▷ vt acheter; soudoyer; **to ~ sb to do sth** soudoyer qn pour qu'il fasse qch

bribery ['braɪbərɪ] n corruption f

bric-a-brac ['brɪkəbræk] n bric-à-brac m

brick [brɪk] n brique f

bricklayer ['brɪkleɪəʳ] n maçon m

bridal ['braɪdl] adj nuptial(e); **~ party** noce f

bride [braɪd] n mariée f, épouse f

bridegroom ['braɪdgru:m] n marié m, époux m

bridesmaid ['braɪdzmeɪd] n demoiselle f d'honneur

bridge [brɪdʒ] n pont m; (*Naut*) passerelle f (de commandement); (*of nose*) arête f; (*Cards, Dentistry*) bridge m ▷ vt (*river*) construire un pont sur; (*gap*) combler

bridle ['braɪdl] n bride f ▷ vt refréner, mettre la bride à; (*horse*) brider

bridle path n piste or allée cavalière

brief [bri:f] adj bref/brève ▷ n (*Law*) dossier m, cause f; (*gen*) tâche f ▷ vt mettre au courant; (*Mil*) donner des instructions à; **briefs** npl slip m; **in ~ ...** (en) bref ...

briefcase ['bri:fkeɪs] n serviette f; porte-documents m inv

briefing ['bri:fɪŋ] n instructions fpl; (*Press*) briefing m

briefly ['bri:flɪ] adv brièvement; (*visit*) en coup de vent; **to glimpse ~** entrevoir

brigadier [brɪgə'dɪəʳ] n brigadier général

bright [braɪt] adj brillant(e); (*room, weather*) clair(e); (*person: clever*) intelligent(e), doué(e); (*: cheerful*) gai(e); (*idea*) génial(e); (*colour*) vif/vive; **to look on the ~ side** regarder le bon côté des choses

brighten ['braɪtn] (*also:* **~ up**) vt (*room*) éclaircir; égayer ▷ vi s'éclaircir; (*person*) retrouver un peu de sa gaieté

brilliance ['brɪljəns] n éclat m; (*fig: of person*) brio m

brilliant ['brɪljənt] adj brillant(e); (*light, sunshine*) éclatant(e); (*inf: great*) super

brim [brɪm] n bord m

brine [braɪn] n eau salée; (*Culin*) saumure f

bring (pt, pp **brought**) [brɪŋ, brɔ:t] vt (*thing*) apporter; (*person*) amener; **to ~ sth to an end** mettre fin à qch; **I can't ~ myself to fire him** je ne peux me résoudre à le mettre à la porte; **bring about** vt provoquer, entraîner;

bring back vt rapporter; (*person*) ramener; **bring down** vt (*lower*) abaisser; (*shoot down*) abattre; (*government*) faire s'effondrer; **bring forward** vt avancer; (*Book-keeping*) reporter; **bring in** vt (*person*) faire entrer; (*object*) rentrer; (*Pol: legislation*) introduire; (*Law: verdict*) rendre; (*produce: income*) rapporter; **bring off** vt (*task, plan*) réussir, mener à bien; (*deal*) mener à bien; **bring on** vt (*illness, attack*) provoquer; (*player, substitute*) amener; **bring out** vt sortir; (*meaning*) faire ressortir, mettre en relief; (*new product, book*) sortir; **bring round, bring to** vt (*unconscious person*) ranimer; **bring up** vt élever; (*carry up*) monter; (*question*) soulever; (*food: vomit*) vomir, rendre

brink [brɪŋk] n bord m; **on the ~ of doing** sur le point de faire, à deux doigts de faire; **she was on the ~ of tears** elle était au bord des larmes

brisk [brɪsk] adj vif/vive; (*abrupt*) brusque; (*trade etc*) actif(-ive); **to go for a ~ walk** se promener d'un bon pas; **business is ~** les affaires marchent (bien)

bristle ['brɪsl] n poil m ▷ vi se hérisser; **bristling with** hérissé(e) de

Brit [brɪt] n abbr (*inf: = British person*) Britannique m/f

Britain ['brɪtən] n (*also: Great ~*) la Grande-Bretagne; **in ~** en Grande-Bretagne

British ['brɪtɪʃ] adj britannique ▷ npl: **the ~** les Britanniques mpl

British Isles npl: **the ~** les îles fpl Britanniques

British Rail n compagnie ferroviaire britannique, ≈ SNCF f

Briton ['brɪtən] n Britannique m/f

Brittany ['brɪtənɪ] n Bretagne f

brittle ['brɪtl] adj cassant(e), fragile

broach [brəʊtʃ] vt (*subject*) aborder

B road n (*Brit*) ≈ route départementale

broad [brɔːd] adj large; (*distinction*) général(e); (*accent*) prononcé(e) ▷ n (*US inf*) nana f; **~ hint** allusion transparente; **in ~ daylight** en plein jour; **the ~ outlines** les grandes lignes

broadband ['brɔːdbænd] n transmission f à haut débit

broad bean n fève f

broadcast ['brɔːdkɑːst] (*pt, pp broadcast*) n émission f ▷ vt (*Radio*) radiodiffuser; (*TV*) téléviser ▷ vi émettre

broaden ['brɔːdn] vt élargir; **to ~ one's mind** élargir ses horizons ▷ vi s'élargir

broadly ['brɔːdlɪ] adv en gros, généralement

broad-minded ['brɔːd'maɪndɪd] adj large d'esprit

broccoli ['brɒkəlɪ] n brocoli m

brochure ['brəʊʃjʊər] n prospectus m, dépliant m

broil [brɔɪl] (*US*) vt rôtir

broke [brəʊk] pt of **break** ▷ adj (*inf*) fauché(e); **to go ~** (*business*) faire faillite

broken ['brəʊkn] pp of **break** ▷ adj (*stick, leg etc*) cassé(e); (*machine: also: ~ down*) fichu(e); (*promise, vow*) rompu(e); **a ~ marriage** un couple dissocié; **a ~ home** un foyer désuni; **in ~ French/English** dans un français/anglais approximatif or hésitant

broken-hearted ['brəʊkn'hɑːtɪd] adj (ayant) le cœur brisé

broker ['brəʊkər] n courtier m

brolly ['brɒlɪ] n (*Brit inf*) pépin m, parapluie m

bronchitis [brɒŋ'kaɪtɪs] n bronchite f

bronze [brɒnz] n bronze m

brooch [brəʊtʃ] n broche f

brood [bruːd] n couvée f ▷ vi (*hen, storm*) couver; (*person*) méditer (sombrement), ruminer

broom [brum] n balai m; (*Bot*) genêt m

broomstick ['brumstɪk] n manche m à balai

Bros. abbr (*Comm*: = brothers) Frères

broth [brɒθ] n bouillon m de viande et de légumes

brothel ['brɒθl] n maison close, bordel m

brother ['brʌðər] n frère m

brother-in-law ['brʌðərɪn'lɔːr] n beau-frère m

brought [brɔːt] pt, pp of **bring**

brow [brau] n front m; (*rare: gen: eyebrow*) sourcil m; (*of hill*) sommet m

brown [braun] adj brun(e), marron inv; (*hair*) châtain inv; (*tanned*) bronzé(e); (*rice, bread, flour*) complet(-ète) ▷ n (*colour*) brun m, marron m ▷ vt brunir; (*Culin*) faire dorer, faire roussir; **to go ~** (*person*) bronzer; (*leaves*) jaunir

brown bread n pain m bis

Brownie ['braunɪ] n jeannette f éclaireuse (cadette)

brown paper n papier m d'emballage, papier kraft

brown rice n riz m complet

brown sugar n cassonade f

browse [brauz] vi (*in shop*) regarder (*sans acheter*); (*among books*) bouquiner, feuilleter les livres; (*animal*) paître; **to ~ through a book** feuilleter un livre

browser ['brauzər] n (*Comput*) navigateur m

bruise [bruːz] n bleu m, ecchymose f, contusion f ▷ vt contusionner, meurtrir ▷ vi (*fruit*) se taler, se meurtrir; **to ~ one's arm** se faire un bleu au bras

brunette [bruː'net] n (*femme*) brune

brunt [brʌnt] n: **the ~ of** (*attack, criticism etc*) le plus gros de

brush [brʌʃ] n brosse f; (*for painting*) pinceau m; (*for shaving*) blaireau m; (*quarrel*) accrochage m, prise f de bec ▷ vt brosser; (*also: ~ past, ~ against*) effleurer, frôler; **to have a ~ with sb** s'accrocher avec qn; **to have a ~ with the police** avoir maille à partir avec la police; **brush aside** vt écarter, balayer; **brush up** vt (*knowledge*) rafraîchir, réviser

brushwood ['brʌʃwud] n broussailles fpl, taillis m

Brussels ['brʌslz] n Bruxelles

Brussels sprout n chou m de Bruxelles

brutal ['bru:tl] adj brutal(e)

brute [bru:t] n brute f ▷ adj: **by ~ force** par la force

B.Sc. n abbr = **Bachelor of Science**

BSE n abbr (= bovine spongiform encephalopathy) ESB f, BSE f

bubble ['bʌbl] n bulle f ▷ vi bouillonner, faire des bulles; (sparkle, fig) pétiller

bubble bath n bain moussant

bubble gum n chewing-gum m

bubblejet printer ['bʌbldʒet-] n imprimante f à bulle d'encre

buck [bʌk] n mâle m (d'un lapin, lièvre, daim etc); (US inf) dollar m ▷ vi ruer, lancer une ruade; **to pass the ~ (to sb)** se décharger de la responsabilité (sur qn); **buck up** vi (cheer up) reprendre du poil de la bête, se remonter ▷ vt: **to ~ one's ideas up** se reprendre

bucket ['bʌkɪt] n seau m ▷ vi (Brit inf): **the rain is ~ing (down)** il pleut à verse

Buckingham Palace ['bʌkɪŋhəm-] n le palais de Buckingham; voir article

buckle ['bʌkl] n boucle f ▷ vt (belt etc) boucler, attacher ▷ vi (warp) tordre, gauchir; (: wheel) se voiler; **buckle down** vi s'y mettre

bud [bʌd] n bourgeon m; (of flower) bouton m ▷ vi bourgeonner; (flower) éclore

Buddhism ['budɪzəm] n bouddhisme m

Buddhist ['budɪst] adj bouddhiste ▷ n Bouddhiste m/f

budding ['bʌdɪŋ] adj (flower) en bouton; (poet etc) en herbe; (passion etc) naissant(e)

buddy ['bʌdɪ] n (US) copain m

budge [bʌdʒ] vt faire bouger ▷ vi bouger

budgerigar ['bʌdʒərɪgɑ:'] n perruche f

budget ['bʌdʒɪt] n budget m ▷ vi: **to ~ for sth** inscrire qch au budget; **I'm on a tight ~** je dois faire attention à mon budget

budgie ['bʌdʒɪ] n = **budgerigar**

buff [bʌf] adj (couleur f) chamois m ▷ n (inf: enthusiast) mordu(e)

buffalo (pl **buffalo** or **buffaloes**) ['bʌfələu] n (Brit) buffle m; (US) bison m

buffer ['bʌfə'] n tampon m; (Comput) mémoire f tampon ▷ vti (Comput) mettre en mémoire tampon

buffering ['bʌfərɪŋ] n (Comput) mise f en mémoire tampon

buffet n ['bufeɪ] (food Brit: bar) buffet m ▷ vt ['bʌfɪt] gifler, frapper; secouer, ébranler

buffet car n (Brit Rail) voiture-bar f

bug [bʌg] n (bedbug etc) punaise f; (esp US: any insect) insecte m, bestiole f; (fig: germ) virus m, microbe m; (spy device) dispositif m d'écoute (électronique), micro clandestin; (Comput: of program) erreur f; (: of equipment) défaut m ▷ vt (room) poser des micros dans; (inf: annoy) embêter; **I've got the travel ~** (fig) j'ai le virus du voyage

buggy ['bʌgɪ] n poussette f

bugle ['bju:gl] n clairon m

build [bɪld] n (of person) carrure f, charpente f ▷ vt (pt, pp **built**) [bɪlt] construire, bâtir; **build on** vt fus (fig) tirer parti de, partir de; **build up** vt accumuler, amasser; (business) développer; (reputation) bâtir

builder ['bɪldə'] n entrepreneur m

building ['bɪldɪŋ] n (trade) construction f; (structure) bâtiment m, construction f; (: residential, offices) immeuble m

building site n chantier m (de construction)

building society n (Brit) société f de crédit immobilier; voir article

built [bɪlt] pt, pp of **build**

built-in ['bɪlt'ɪn] adj (cupboard) encastré(e); (device) incorporé(e); intégré(e)

built-up ['bɪlt'ʌp] adj: **~ area** agglomération (urbaine); zone urbanisée

bulb [bʌlb] n (Bot) bulbe m, oignon m; (Elec) ampoule f

Bulgaria [bʌl'gɛərɪə] n Bulgarie f

Bulgarian [bʌl'gɛərɪən] adj bulgare ▷ n Bulgare m/f; (Ling) bulgare m

bulge [bʌldʒ] n renflement m, gonflement m; (in birth rate, sales) brusque augmentation f ▷ vi faire saillie; présenter un renflement; (pocket, file): **to be bulging with** être plein(e) à craquer de

bulimia [bə'lɪmɪə] n boulimie f

bulimic [bju:'lɪmɪk] adj, n boulimique m/f

bulk [bʌlk] n masse f, volume m; **in ~** (Comm) en gros, en vrac; **the ~ of** la plus grande or grosse partie de

bulky ['bʌlkɪ] adj volumineux(-euse), encombrant(e)

bull [bul] n taureau m; (male elephant, whale) mâle m; (Stock Exchange) haussier m; (Rel) bulle f

bulldog ['buldɔg] n bouledogue m

bulldozer ['buldəuzəʳ] n bulldozer m

bullet ['bulɪt] n balle f (de fusil etc)

bulletin ['bulɪtɪn] n bulletin m, communiqué m; (also: **news ~**) (bulletin d')informations fpl

bulletin board n (Comput) messagerie f (électronique)

bulletproof ['bulɪtpruːf] adj à l'épreuve des balles; **~ vest** gilet m pare-balles

bullfight ['bulfaɪt] n corrida f, course f de taureaux

bullfighter ['bulfaɪtəʳ] n torero m

bullfighting ['bulfaɪtɪŋ] n tauromachie f

bullion ['buljən] n or m or argent m en lingots

bullock ['bulək] n bœuf m

bullring ['bulrɪŋ] n arène f

bull's-eye ['bulzaɪ] n centre m (de la cible)

bully ['bulɪ] n brute f, tyran m ▷ vt tyranniser, rudoyer; (frighten) intimider

bum [bʌm] n (inf: Brit: backside) derrière m; (: esp US: tramp) vagabond(e), traîne-savates m/f inv; (: idler) glandeur m; **bum around** vi (inf) vagabonder

bumblebee ['bʌmblbiː] n bourdon m

bump [bʌmp] n (blow) coup m, choc m; (jolt) cahot m; (on road etc, on head) bosse f ▷ vt heurter, cogner; (car) emboutir; **bump along** vi avancer en cahotant; **bump into** vt fus rentrer dans, tamponner; (inf: meet) tomber sur

bumper ['bʌmpəʳ] n pare-chocs m inv ▷ adj: **~ crop/harvest** récolte/moisson exceptionnelle

bumper cars npl (US) autos tamponneuses

bumpy ['bʌmpɪ] adj (road) cahoteux(-euse); **it was a ~ flight/ride** on a été secoués dans l'avion/la voiture

bun [bʌn] n (cake) petit gâteau; (bread) petit pain au lait; (of hair) chignon m

bunch [bʌntʃ] n (of flowers) bouquet m; (of keys) trousseau m; (of bananas) régime m; (of people) groupe m; **bunches** npl (in hair) couettes fpl; **~ of grapes** grappe f de raisin

bundle ['bʌndl] n paquet m ▷ vt (also: **~ up**) faire un paquet de; (put): **to ~ sth/sb into** fourrer or enfourner qch/qn dans; **bundle off** vt (person) faire sortir (en toute hâte); expédier; **bundle out** vt éjecter, sortir (sans ménagements)

bungalow ['bʌŋgələu] n bungalow m

bungee jumping ['bʌndʒiː'dʒʌmpɪŋ] n saut m à l'élastique

bungle ['bʌŋgl] vt bâcler, gâcher

bunion ['bʌnjən] n oignon m (au pied)

bunk [bʌŋk] n couchette f; (Brit inf): **to do a ~** mettre les bouts or les voiles; **bunk off** vi (Brit inf: Scol) sécher (les cours); **I'll ~ off at 3 o'clock this afternoon** je vais mettre les bouts or les voiles à 3 heures cet après-midi

bunk beds npl lits superposés

bunker ['bʌŋkəʳ] n (coal store) soute f à charbon; (Mil, Golf) bunker m

bunny ['bʌnɪ] n (also: **~ rabbit**) lapin m

bunting ['bʌntɪŋ] n pavoisement m, drapeaux mpl

buoy [bɔɪ] n bouée f; **buoy up** vt faire flotter; (fig) soutenir, épauler

buoyant ['bɔɪənt] adj (ship) flottable; (carefree) gai(e), plein(e) d'entrain; (Comm: market, economy) actif(-ive); (: prices, currency) soutenu(e)

burden ['bəːdn] n fardeau m, charge f ▷ vt charger; (oppress) accabler, surcharger; **to be a ~ to sb** être un fardeau pour qn

bureau (pl **bureaux**) ['bjuərəu, -z] n (Brit: writing desk) bureau m, secrétaire m; (US: chest of drawers) commode f; (office) bureau, office m

bureaucracy [bjuə'rɔkrəsɪ] n bureaucratie f

bureaucrat ['bjuərəkræt] n bureaucrate m/f, rond-de-cuir m

bureau de change [-də'ʃɑːʒ] (pl **bureaux de change**) n bureau m de change

bureaux ['bjuərəuz] npl of **bureau**

burger ['bəːgəʳ] n hamburger m

burglar ['bəːgləʳ] n cambrioleur m

burglar alarm n sonnerie f d'alarme

burglary ['bəːglərɪ] n cambriolage m

Burgundy ['bəːgəndɪ] n Bourgogne f

burial ['bɛrɪəl] n enterrement m

burly ['bəːlɪ] adj de forte carrure, costaud(e)

Burma ['bəːmə] n Birmanie f; see also **Myanmar**

burn [bəːn] vt, vi (pt, pp **burned** or **burnt** [bəːnt]) brûler ▷ n brûlure f; **the cigarette ~t a hole in her dress** la cigarette a fait un trou dans sa robe; **I've ~t myself!** je me suis brûlé(e)!; **burn down** vt incendier, détruire par le feu; **burn out** vt (writer etc): **to ~ o.s. out** s'user (à force de travailler)

burner ['bəːnəʳ] n brûleur m

burning ['bəːnɪŋ] adj (building, forest) en flammes; (issue, question) brûlant(e); (ambition) dévorant(e)

Burns' Night [bəːnz-] n fête écossaise à la mémoire du poète Robert Burns; voir article

◈ BURNS' NIGHT

◈ Burns' Night est une fête qui a lieu le 25 janvier, à la mémoire du poète écossais Robert Burns (1759–1796), à l'occasion de laquelle les Écossais partout dans le monde organisent un souper, en général arrosé de whisky. Le plat principal est toujours le haggis, servi avec de la purée de pommes de terre et de la purée de rutabagas. On apporte le haggis au son des cornemuses et au cours du repas on lit des poèmes de Burns et on chante ses chansons.

burnt [bə:nt] *pt, pp of* **burn**

burp [bə:p] *(inf) n* rot *m* ▷ *vi* roter

burrow ['bʌrəu] *n* terrier *m* ▷ *vt* creuser ▷ *vi (rabbit)* creuser un terrier; *(rummage)* fouiller

bursary ['bə:səri] *n (Brit)* bourse *f* (d'études)

burst [bə:st] *(pt, pp* **burst**) *vt* faire éclater; *(river: banks etc)* rompre ▷ *vi* éclater; *(tyre)* crever ▷ *n* explosion *f*; *(also:* **~ pipe**) fuite *f* *(due à une rupture)*; **a ~ of enthusiasm/energy** un accès d'enthousiasme/d'énergie; **~ of laughter** éclat *m* de rire; **a ~ of applause** une salve d'applaudissement; **a ~ of gunfire** une rafale de tir; **a ~ of speed** une pointe de vitesse; **~ blood vessel** rupture *f* de vaisseau sanguin; **the river has ~ its banks** le cours d'eau est sorti de son lit; **to ~ into flames** s'enflammer soudainement; **to ~ out laughing** éclater de rire; **to ~ into tears** fondre en larmes; **to ~ open** *vi* s'ouvrir violemment *or* soudainement; **to be ~ing with** *(container)* être plein(e) (à craquer) de, regorger de; *(fig)* être débordant(e) de; **burst into** *vt fus (room etc)* faire irruption dans; **burst out of** *vt fus* sortir précipitamment de

bury ['berɪ] *vt* enterrer; **to ~ one's face in one's hands** se couvrir le visage de ses mains; **to ~ one's head in the sand** *(fig)* pratiquer la politique de l'autruche; **to ~ the hatchet** *(fig)* enterrer la hache de guerre

bus *(pl* **buses**) [bʌs, 'bʌsɪz] *n* (auto) bus *m*

bus conductor *n* receveur(-euse) *m/f* de bus

bush [buʃ] *n* buisson *m*; *(scrub land)* brousse *f*; **to beat about the ~** tourner autour du pot

bushy ['buʃɪ] *adj* broussailleux(-euse), touffu(e)

busily ['bɪzɪlɪ] *adv:* **to be ~ doing sth** s'affairer à faire qch

business ['bɪznɪs] *n (matter, firm)* affaire *f*; *(trading)* affaires *fpl*; *(job, duty)* travail *m*; **to be away on ~** être en déplacement d'affaires; **I'm here on ~** je suis là pour affaires; **he's in the insurance ~** il est dans les assurances; **to do ~ with sb** traiter avec qn; **it's none of my ~** cela ne me regarde pas, ce ne sont pas mes affaires; **he means ~** il ne plaisante pas, il est sérieux

business class *n (on plane)* classe *f* affaires

businesslike ['bɪznɪslaɪk] *adj* sérieux(-euse), efficace

businessman ['bɪznɪsmən] *(irreg) n* homme *m* d'affaires

business trip *n* voyage *m* d'affaires

businesswoman ['bɪznɪswumən] *(irreg) n* femme *f* d'affaires

busker ['bʌskəʳ] *n (Brit)* artiste ambulant(e)

bus pass *n* carte *f* de bus

bus shelter *n* abribus *m*

bus station *n* gare routière

bus stop *n* arrêt *m* d'autobus

bust [bʌst] *n* buste *m*; *(measurement)* tour *m* de poitrine ▷ *adj (inf: broken)* fichu(e), fini(e) ▷ *vt (inf: Police: arrest)* pincer; **to go ~** faire faillite

bustle ['bʌsl] *n* remue-ménage *m*, affairement *m* ▷ *vi* s'affairer, se démener

bustling ['bʌslɪŋ] *adj (person)* affairé(e); *(town)* très animé(e)

busy ['bɪzɪ] *adj* occupé(e); *(shop, street)* très fréquenté(e); *(US: telephone, line)* occupé ▷ *vt:* **to ~ o.s.** s'occuper; **he's a ~ man** *(normally)* c'est un homme très pris; *(temporarily)* il est très pris

busybody ['bɪzɪbɒdɪ] *n* mouche *f* du coche, âme *f* charitable

busy signal *n (US)* tonalité *f* occupé *inv*

 KEYWORD

but [bʌt] *conj* mais; **I'd love to come, but I'm busy** j'aimerais venir mais je suis occupé; **he's not English but French** il n'est pas anglais mais français; **but that's far too expensive!** mais c'est bien trop cher!
▷ *prep (apart from, except)* sauf, excepté; **nothing but** rien d'autre que; **we've had nothing but trouble** nous n'avons eu que des ennuis; **no-one but him can do it** lui seul peut le faire; **who but a lunatic would do such a thing?** qui sinon un fou ferait une chose pareille?; **but for you/your help** sans toi/ton aide; **anything but that** tout sauf *or* excepté ça, tout mais pas ça; **the last but one** *(Brit)* l'avant-dernier(-ère)
▷ *adv (just, only)* ne ... que; **she's but a child** elle n'est qu'une enfant; **had I but known** si seulement j'avais su; **I can but try** je peux toujours essayer; **all but finished** pratiquement terminé; **anything but finished** tout sauf fini, très loin d'être fini

butcher ['butʃəʳ] *n* boucher *m* ▷ *vt* massacrer; *(cattle etc for meat)* tuer

butcher's ['butʃəz], **butcher's shop** *n* boucherie *f*

butler ['bʌtləʳ] *n* maître *m* d'hôtel

butt [bʌt] *n (cask)* gros tonneau; *(thick end)* (gros) bout; *(of gun)* crosse *f*; *(of cigarette)* mégot *m*; *(Brit fig: target)* cible *f* ▷ *vt* donner un coup de tête à; **butt in** *vi (interrupt)* interrompre

butter ['bʌtəʳ] *n* beurre *m* ▷ *vt* beurrer

buttercup ['bʌtəkʌp] *n* bouton *m* d'or

butterfly ['bʌtəflaɪ] *n* papillon *m*; *(Swimming: also:* **~ stroke**) brasse *f* papillon

buttocks ['bʌtəks] *npl* fesses *fpl*

button ['bʌtn] *n* bouton *m*; *(US: badge)* pin *m* ▷ *vt (also:* **~ up**) boutonner ▷ *vi* se boutonner

buttress ['bʌtrɪs] *n* contrefort *m*

buy [baɪ] *(pt, pp* **bought**) [bɔ:t] *vt* acheter; *(Comm: company)* (r)acheter ▷ *n* achat *m*; **that**

was a good/bad ~ c'était un bon/mauvais achat; **to ~ sth/sth from sb** acheter qch à qn; **to ~ sb a drink** offrir un verre *or* à boire à qn; **can I ~ you a drink?** je vous offre un verre?; **where can I ~ some postcards?** où est-ce que je peux acheter des cartes postales?; **buy back** *vt* racheter; **buy in** *vt* (*Brit*: *goods*) acheter, faire venir; **buy into** *vt fus* (*Brit Comm*) acheter des actions de; **buy off** *vt* (*bribe*) acheter; **buy out** *vt* (*partner*) désintéresser; (*business*) racheter; **buy up** *vt* acheter en bloc, rafler

buyer ['baɪə^r] *n* acheteur(-euse) *m/f*; **~'s market** marché *m* favorable aux acheteurs

buzz [bʌz] *n* bourdonnement *m*; (*inf: phone call*): **to give sb a ~** passer un coup de fil à qn ▷ *vi* bourdonner ▷ *vt* (*call on intercom*) appeler; (*with buzzer*) sonner; (*Aviat*: *plane, building*) raser; **my head is ~ing** j'ai la tête qui bourdonne; **buzz off** *vi* (*inf*) s'en aller, ficher le camp

buzzer ['bʌzə^r] *n* timbre *m* électrique

buzz word *n* (*inf*) mot *m* à la mode *or* dans le vent

 KEYWORD

by [baɪ] *prep* **1** (*referring to cause, agent*) par, de; **killed by lightning** tué par la foudre; **surrounded by a fence** entouré d'une barrière; **a painting by Picasso** un tableau de Picasso

2 (*referring to method, manner, means*): **by bus/car** en autobus/voiture; **by train** par le *or* en train; **to pay by cheque** payer par chèque; **by moonlight/candlelight** à la lueur de la lune/d'une bougie; **by saving hard, he ...** à force d'économiser, il ...

3 (*via, through*) par; **we came by Dover** nous sommes venus par Douvres

4 (*close to, past*) à côté de; **the house by the school** la maison à côté de l'école; **a holiday by the sea** des vacances au bord de la mer; **she sat by his bed** elle était assise à son chevet; **she went by me** elle est passée à côté de moi; **I go by the post office every day** je passe devant la poste tous les jours

5 (*with time: not later than*) avant; (*: during*): **by daylight** à la lumière du jour; **by night** la nuit, de nuit; **by 4 o'clock** avant 4 heures; **by this time tomorrow** d'ici demain à la même heure; **by the time I got here it was too late** lorsque je suis arrivé il était déjà trop tard

6 (*amount*) à; **by the kilo/metre** au kilo/au mètre; **paid by the hour** payé à l'heure; **to increase** *etc* **by the hour** augmenter *etc* d'heure en heure

7 (*Math: measure*): **to divide/multiply by 3** diviser/multiplier par 3; **a room 3 metres by 4** une pièce de 3 mètres sur 4; **it's broader by a metre** c'est plus large d'un mètre; **the**

bullet missed him by inches la balle est passée à quelques centimètres de lui; **one by one** un à un; **little by little** petit à petit, peu à peu

8 (*according to*) d'après, selon; **it's 3 o'clock by my watch** il est 3 heures à ma montre; **it's all right by me** je n'ai rien contre

9: (all) by oneself *etc* tout(e) seul(e) ▷ *adv* **1** *see* **go**; **pass** *etc*

2: by and by un peu plus tard, bientôt; **by and large** dans l'ensemble

bye ['baɪ], **bye-bye** ['baɪ'baɪ] *excl* au revoir!, salut!

bye-law ['baɪlɔː] *n* = **by-law**

by-election ['baɪɪlɛkʃən] *n* (*Brit*) élection (législative) partielle

bygone ['baɪgɒn] *adj* passé(e) ▷ *n*: **let ~s be ~s** passons l'éponge, oublions le passé

by-law ['baɪlɔː] *n* arrêté municipal

bypass ['baɪpɑːs] *n* rocade *f*; (*Med*) pontage *m* ▷ *vt* éviter

by-product ['baɪprɒdʌkt] *n* sous-produit *m*, dérivé *m*; (*fig*) conséquence *f* secondaire, retombée *f*

bystander ['baɪstændə^r] *n* spectateur(-trice), badaud(e)

byte [baɪt] *n* (*Comput*) octet *m*

byword ['baɪwəːd] *n*: **to be a ~ for** être synonyme de (*fig*)

C¹, c¹ [siː] *n* (*letter*) C, c *m*; (*Scol: mark*) C; (*Mus*): C do *m*; **C for Charlie** C comme Célestin

C² *abbr* (= Celsius, centigrade) C

c² *abbr* (= century) s.; (= circa) v.; (*US etc*) = **cent(s)**

CA *n abbr* = **Central America**; (*Aviat*) équipage *m*

cab [kæb] *n* taxi *m*; (*of train, truck*) cabine *f*; (*horse-drawn*) fiacre *m*

cabaret ['kæbəreɪ] *n* attractions *fpl*; (*show*) spectacle *m* de cabaret

cabbage ['kæbɪdʒ] *n* chou *m*

cabin ['kæbɪn] *n* (*house*) cabane *f*, hutte *f*; (*on ship*) cabine *f*; (*on plane*) compartiment *m*

cabin crew *n* équipage *m*

cabin cruiser *n* yacht *m* (à moteur)

cabinet ['kæbɪnɪt] *n* (*Pol*) cabinet *m*; (*furniture*) petit meuble à tiroirs et rayons; (*also: display ~*) vitrine *f*, petite armoire vitrée

cabinet minister *n* ministre *m* (*membre du cabinet*)

cable ['keɪbl] *n* câble *m* ▷ *vt* câbler, télégraphier

cable car ['keɪblkɑːʳ] *n* téléphérique *m*

cable television *n* télévision *f* par câble

cache [kæʃ] *n* cachette *f*; **a ~ of food** *etc* un dépôt secret de provisions *etc*, une cachette contenant des provisions *etc*

cackle ['kækl] *vi* caqueter

cactus (*pl* **cacti**) ['kæktəs, -taɪ] *n* cactus *m*

cadet [kə'dɛt] *n* (*Mil*) élève *m* officier; **police ~** élève agent de police

cadge [kædʒ] *vt* (*inf*) se faire donner; **to ~ a meal (off sb)** se faire inviter à manger (par qn)

Caesarean, (*US*) **Cesarean** [siːˈzɛərɪən] *adj*: **~ (section)** césarienne *f*

café ['kæfeɪ] *n* ≈ café(-restaurant) *m* (*sans alcool*)

cafeteria [kæfɪ'tɪərɪə] *n* cafétéria *f*

caffeine ['kæfiːn] *n* caféine *f*

cage [keɪdʒ] *n* cage *f* ▷ *vt* mettre en cage

cagey ['keɪdʒɪ] *adj* (*inf*) réticent(e), méfiant(e)

cagoule [kə'guːl] *n* K-way® *m*

Cairo ['kaɪərəʊ] *n* le Caire

cajole [kə'dʒəʊl] *vt* couvrir de flatteries *or* de gentillesses

cake [keɪk] *n* gâteau *m*; **~ of soap** savonnette *f*; **it's a piece of ~** (*inf*) c'est un jeu d'enfant; **he wants to have his ~ and eat it (too)** (*fig*) il veut tout avoir

caked [keɪkt] *adj*: **~ with** raidi(e) par, couvert(e) d'une croûte de

calcium ['kælsɪəm] *n* calcium *m*

calculate ['kælkjuleɪt] *vt* calculer; (*estimate: chances, effect*) évaluer; **calculate on** *vt fus*: **to ~ on sth/on doing sth** compter sur qch/ faire qch

calculation [kælkju'leɪʃən] *n* calcul *m*

calculator ['kælkjuleɪtəʳ] *n* machine *f* à calculer, calculatrice *f*

calendar ['kæləndəʳ] *n* calendrier *m*

calendar year *n* année civile

calf (*pl* **calves**) [kɑːf, kɑːvz] *n* (*of cow*) veau *m*; (*of other animals*) petit *m*; (*also: ~skin*) veau *m*, vachette *f*; (*Anat*) mollet *m*

calibre, (*US*) **caliber** ['kælɪbəʳ] *n* calibre *m*

call [kɔːl] *vt* (*gen, also Tel*) appeler; (*announce: flight*) annoncer; (*meeting*) convoquer; (*strike*) lancer ▷ *vi* appeler; (*visit: also: ~ in, ~ round*) passer ▷ *n* (*shout*) appel *m*, cri *m*; (*summons: for flight etc, fig: lure*) appel; (*visit*) visite *f*; (*also: telephone ~*) coup *m* de téléphone; communication *f*; **to be on ~** être de permanence; **to be ~ed** s'appeler; **she's ~ed Suzanne** elle s'appelle Suzanne; **who is ~ing?** (*Tel*) qui est à l'appareil?; **London ~ing** (*Radio*) ici Londres; **please give me a ~ at 7** appelez-moi à 7 heures; **to make a ~** téléphoner, passer un coup de fil; **can I make a ~ from here?** est-ce que je peux téléphoner d'ici?; **to pay a ~ on sb** rendre visite à qn, passer voir qn; **there's not much ~ for these items** ces articles ne sont pas très demandés; **call at** *vt fus* (*ship*) faire escale à; (*train*) s'arrêter à; **call back** *vi* (*return*) repasser; (*Tel*) rappeler ▷ *vt* (*Tel*) rappeler; **can you ~ back later?** pouvez-vous rappeler plus tard?; **call for** *vt fus* (*demand*) demander; (*fetch*) passer prendre; **call in** *vt* (*doctor, expert, police*) appeler, faire venir; **call off** *vt* annuler; **the strike was ~ed off** l'ordre de grève a été rapporté; **call on** *vt fus* (*visit*) rendre visite à, passer voir; (*request*): **to ~ on**

sb **to do** inviter qn à faire; **call out** vi
pousser un cri ou des cris ▷ vt (doctor, police,
troops) appeler; **call up** vt (Mil) appeler,
mobiliser; (Tel) appeler

call box ['kɔːlbɒks] n (Brit) cabine f
téléphonique

call centre, (US) **call center** n centre m
d'appels

caller ['kɔːlər] n (Tel) personne f qui appelle;
(visitor) visiteur m; **hold the line, ~!** (Tel) ne
quittez pas, Monsieur (or Madame)!

call girl n call-girl f

call-in ['kɔːlɪn] n (US Radio, TV) programme m
à ligne ouverte

calling ['kɔːlɪŋ] n vocation f; (trade, occupation)
état m

calling card n (US) carte f de visite

callous ['kæləs] adj dur(e), insensible

calm [kɑːm] adj calme ▷ n calme m ▷ vt
calmer, apaiser; **calm down** vi se calmer,
s'apaiser ▷ vt calmer, apaiser

calmly ['kɑːmlɪ] adv calmement, avec calme

Calor gas® ['kælər-] n (Brit) butane m,
butagaz® m

calorie ['kælərɪ] n calorie f; **low ~ product**
produit m pauvre en calories

calves [kɑːvz] npl of **calf**

camber ['kæmbər] n (of road) bombement m

Cambodia [kæm'bəʊdɪə] n Cambodge m

camcorder ['kæmkɔːdər] n caméscope m

came [keɪm] pt of **come**

camel ['kæməl] n chameau m

camera ['kæmərə] n appareil photo m; (Cine,
TV) caméra f; **digital ~** appareil numérique;
in ~ à huis clos, en privé

cameraman ['kæmərəmæn] (irreg) n
caméraman m

camera phone n téléphone m avec appareil
photo

camouflage ['kæməflɑːʒ] n camouflage m
▷ vt camoufler

camp [kæmp] n camp m ▷ vi camper ▷ adj
(man) efféminé(e)

campaign [kæm'peɪn] n (Mil, Pol) campagne
f ▷ vi (also fig) faire campagne; **to ~ for/
against** militer pour/contre

campaigner [kæm'peɪnər] n: **~ for**
partisan(e) de; **~ against** opposant(e) à

camp bed ['kæmp'bɛd] n (Brit) lit m de camp

camper ['kæmpər] n campeur(-euse); (vehicle)
camping-car m

camping ['kæmpɪŋ] n camping m; **to go ~**
faire du camping

camping gas® n butane m

campsite ['kæmpsaɪt] n (terrain m de)
camping m

campus ['kæmpəs] n campus m

can¹ [kæn] n (of milk, oil, water) bidon m; (tin)
boîte f (de conserve) ▷ vt mettre en conserve;
a ~ of beer une canette de bière; **he had to
carry the ~** (Brit inf) on lui a fait porter le
chapeau; see also **keyword**

KEYWORD

can² [kæn] (negative **cannot** or **can't**, conditional
and pt **could**) aux vb **1** (be able to) pouvoir; **you
can do it if you try** vous pouvez le faire si
vous essayez; **I can't hear you** je ne
t'entends pas

2 (know how to) savoir; **I can swim/play
tennis/drive** je sais nager/jouer au tennis/
conduire; **can you speak French?** parlez-
vous français?

3 (may) pouvoir; **can I use your phone?** puis-
je me servir de votre téléphone?

4 (expressing disbelief, puzzlement etc): **it can't be
true!** ce n'est pas possible!; **what CAN he
want?** qu'est-ce qu'il peut bien vouloir?

5 (expressing possibility, suggestion etc): **he could
be in the library** il est peut-être dans la
bibliothèque; **she could have been delayed**
il se peut qu'elle ait été retardée; **they could
have forgotten** ils ont pu oublier

Canada ['kænədə] n Canada m

Canadian [kə'neɪdɪən] adj canadien(ne) ▷ n
Canadien(ne)

canal [kə'næl] n canal m

canary [kə'nɛərɪ] n canari m, serin m

cancel ['kænsəl] vt annuler; (train)
supprimer; (party, appointment)
décommander; (cross out) barrer, rayer;
(stamp) oblitérer; (cheque) faire opposition à;
I would like to ~ my booking je voudrais
annuler ma réservation; **cancel out** vt
annuler; **they ~ each other out** ils
s'annulent

cancellation [kænsə'leɪʃən] n annulation f;
suppression f; oblitération f; (Tourism)
réservation annulée, client etc qui s'est
décommandé

Cancer ['kænsər] n (Astrology) le Cancer; **to
be ~** être du Cancer

cancer ['kænsər] n cancer m

candid ['kændɪd] adj (très) franc/franche,
sincère

candidate ['kændɪdeɪt] n candidat(e)

candle ['kændl] n bougie f; (of tallow)
chandelle f; (in church) cierge m

candlelight ['kændllaɪt] n: **by ~** à la lumière
d'une bougie; (dinner) aux chandelles

candlestick ['kændlstɪk] n (also: **candle
holder**) bougeoir m; (bigger, ornate)
chandelier m

candour, (US) **candor** ['kændər] n (grande)
franchise or sincérité

candy ['kændɪ] n sucre candi; (US) bonbon m

candy bar (US) n barre f chocolatée

candyfloss ['kændɪflɒs] n (Brit) barbe f à papa

cane [keɪn] n canne f; (for baskets, chairs etc)
rotin m ▷ vt (Brit Scol) administrer des coups
de bâton à

canister ['kænɪstər] n boîte f (gén en métal); (of
gas) bombe f

cannabis ['kænəbɪs] n (drug) cannabis m; (cannabis plant) chanvre indien

canned ['kænd] adj (food) en boîte, en conserve; (inf: music) enregistré(e); (Brit inf: drunk) bourré(e); (US inf: worker) mis(e) à la porte

cannon (pl cannon or cannons) ['kænən] n (gun) canon m

cannot ['kænɔt] = **can not**

canoe [kə'nu:] n pirogue f; (Sport) canoë m

canoeing [kə'nu:ɪŋ] n (sport) canoë m

canon ['kænən] n (clergyman) chanoine m; (standard) canon m

can-opener [-'əupnər] n ouvre-boîte m

canopy ['kænəpɪ] n baldaquin m; dais m

can't [kɑ:nt] = **can not**

canteen [kæn'ti:n] n (eating place) cantine f; (Brit: of cutlery) ménagère f

canter ['kæntər] n petit galop ▷ vi aller au petit galop

canvas ['kænvəs] n (gen) toile f; **under ~** (camping) sous la tente; (Naut) toutes voiles dehors

canvass ['kænvəs] vi (Pol): **to ~ for** faire campagne pour ▷ vt (Pol: district) faire la tournée électorale dans; (: person) solliciter le suffrage de; (Comm: district) prospecter; (citizens, opinions) sonder

canyon ['kænjən] n cañon m, gorge f (profonde)

cap [kæp] n casquette f; (for swimming) bonnet m de bain; (of pen) capuchon m; (of bottle) capsule f; (Brit: contraceptive: also: **Dutch ~**) diaphragme m; (Football) sélection f pour l'équipe nationale ▷ vt capsuler; (outdo) surpasser; (put limit on) plafonner; **~ped with** coiffé(e) de; **and to ~ it all, he ...** (Brit) pour couronner le tout, il ...

capability [keɪpə'bɪlɪtɪ] n aptitude f, capacité f

capable ['keɪpəbl] adj capable; **~ of** (interpretation etc) susceptible de

capacity [kə'pæsɪtɪ] n (of container) capacité f, contenance f; (ability) aptitude f; **filled to ~** plein(e); **in his ~ as** en sa qualité de; **in an advisory ~** à titre consultatif; **to work at full ~** travailler à plein rendement

cape [keɪp] n (garment) cape f; (Geo) cap m

caper ['keɪpər] n (Culin: gen pl) câpre f; (prank) farce f

capital ['kæpɪtl] n (also: **~ city**) capitale f; (money) capital m; (also: **~ letter**) majuscule f

capital gains tax n impôt m sur les plus-values

capitalism ['kæpɪtəlɪzəm] n capitalisme m

capitalist ['kæpɪtəlɪst] adj, n capitaliste m/f

capitalize ['kæpɪtəlaɪz] vt (provide with capital) financer; **capitalize on** vt fus (fig) profiter de

capital punishment n peine capitale

Capitol ['kæpɪtl] n: **the ~** le Capitole; voir article

CAPITOL

Le Capitol est le siège du "Congress", à Washington. Il est situé sur Capitol Hill.

Capricorn ['kæprɪkɔ:n] n le Capricorne; **to be ~** être du Capricorne

capsize [kæp'saɪz] vt faire chavirer ▷ vi chavirer

capsule ['kæpsju:l] n capsule f

captain ['kæptɪn] n capitaine m ▷ vt commander, être le capitaine de

caption ['kæpʃən] n légende f

captive ['kæptɪv] adj, n captif(-ive)

captivity [kæp'tɪvɪtɪ] n captivité f

capture ['kæptʃər] vt (prisoner, animal) capturer; (town) prendre; (attention) capter; (Comput) saisir ▷ n capture f; (of data) saisie f de données

car [kɑ:r] n voiture f, auto f; (US Rail) wagon m, voiture; **by ~** en voiture

carafe [kə'ræf] n carafe f

caramel ['kærəməl] n caramel m

carat ['kærət] n carat m; **18 ~ gold** or m à 18 carats

caravan ['kærəvæn] n caravane f

caravan site n (Brit) camping m pour caravanes

carbohydrate [kɑ:bəu'haɪdreɪt] n hydrate m de carbone; (food) féculent m

carbon ['kɑ:bən] n carbone m

carbon dioxide [-daɪ'ɔksaɪd] n gaz m carbonique, dioxyde m de carbone

carbon footprint n empreinte f carbone

carbon monoxide [-mɔ'nɔksaɪd] n oxyde m de carbone

carbon paper n papier m carbone

car boot sale n voir article

CAR BOOT SALE

Type de brocante très populaire, où chacun vide sa cave ou son grenier. Les articles sont présentés dans des coffres de voitures et la vente a souvent lieu sur un parking ou dans un champ. Les brocanteurs d'un jour doivent s'acquitter d'une petite contribution pour participer à la vente.

carburettor, (US) **carburetor** [kɑ:bju'retər] n carburateur m

card [kɑ:d] n carte f; (material) carton m; (membership card) carte d'adhérent; **to play ~s** jouer aux cartes

cardboard ['kɑ:dbɔ:d] n carton m

card game n jeu m de cartes

cardiac ['kɑ:dɪæk] adj cardiaque

cardigan ['kɑ:dɪgən] n cardigan m

cardinal ['kɑ:dɪnl] adj cardinal(e); (importance) capital(e) ▷ n cardinal m

card index n fichier m (alphabétique)

cardphone ['kɑ:dfəun] n téléphone m à carte (magnétique)

care [keə˚] n soin m, attention f; (worry) souci m ▷ vi: **to ~ about** (feel interest for) se soucier de, s'intéresser à; (person: love) être attaché(e) à; **in sb's ~** à la garde de qn, confié à qn; **~ of** (on letter) chez; **"with ~"** "fragile"; **to take ~ (to do)** faire attention (à faire); **to take ~ of** vt s'occuper de; **the child has been taken into ~** l'enfant a été placé en institution; **would you ~ to/for ...?** voulez-vous ...?; **I wouldn't ~ to do it** je n'aimerais pas le faire; **I don't ~** ça m'est bien égal, peu m'importe; **I couldn't ~ less** cela m'est complètement égal, je m'en fiche complètement; **care for** vt fus s'occuper de; (like) aimer

career [kə'rɪə˚] n carrière f ▷ vi (also: **~ along**) aller à toute allure

career woman irreg n femme ambitieuse

carefree ['keəfri:] adj sans souci, insouciant(e)

careful ['keəful] adj soigneux(-euse); (cautious) prudent(e); **(be) ~!** (fais) attention!; **to be ~ with one's money** regarder à la dépense

carefully ['keəfəlɪ] adv avec soin, soigneusement; prudemment

caregiver ['keəgɪvə˚] (US) n (professional) travailleur social; (unpaid) personne qui s'occupe d'un proche qui est malade

careless ['keəlɪs] adj négligent(e); (heedless) insouciant(e)

carelessness ['keəlɪsnɪs] n manque m de soin, négligence f; insouciance f

carer ['keərə˚] n (professional) travailleur social; (unpaid) personne qui s'occupe d'un proche qui est malade

caress [kə'rɛs] n caresse f ▷ vt caresser

caretaker ['keəteɪkə˚] n gardien(ne), concierge m/f

car-ferry ['kɑ:fɛrɪ] n (on sea) ferry(-boat) m; (on river) bac m

cargo (pl **cargoes**) ['kɑ:gəu] n cargaison f, chargement m

car hire n (Brit) location f de voitures

Caribbean [kærɪ'bi:ən] adj, n: **the ~ (Sea)** la mer des Antilles or des Caraïbes

caring ['keərɪŋ] adj (person) bienveillant(e); (society, organization) humanitaire

carnation [kɑ:'neɪʃən] n œillet m

carnival ['kɑ:nɪvl] n (public celebration) carnaval m; (US: funfair) fête foraine

carol ['kærəl] n: **(Christmas) ~** chant m de Noël

carousel [kærə'sɛl] n (for luggage) carrousel m; (US) manège m

carp [kɑ:p] n (fish) carpe f; **carp at** vt fus critiquer

car park (Brit) n parking m, parc m de stationnement

carpenter ['kɑ:pɪntə˚] n charpentier m; (joiner) menuisier m

carpentry ['kɑ:pɪntrɪ] n charpenterie f, métier m de charpentier; (woodwork: at school etc) menuiserie f

carpet ['kɑ:pɪt] n tapis m ▷ vt recouvrir (d'un tapis); **fitted ~** (Brit) moquette f

carpet sweeper [-'swi:pə˚] n balai m mécanique

car phone n téléphone m de voiture

car rental n (US) location f de voitures

carriage ['kærɪdʒ] n (Brit Rail) wagon m; (horse-drawn) voiture f; (of goods) transport m; (: cost) port m; (of typewriter) chariot m; (bearing) maintien m, port m; **~ paid** port dû; **~ free** franco de port; **~ paid** (en) port payé

carriageway ['kærɪdʒweɪ] n (Brit: part of road) chaussée f

carrier ['kærɪə˚] n transporteur m, camionneur m; (company) entreprise f de transport; (Med) porteur(-euse); (Naut) porte-avions m inv

carrier bag n (Brit) sac m en papier or en plastique

carrot ['kærət] n carotte f

carry ['kærɪ] vt (subj: person) porter; (: vehicle) transporter; (a motion, bill) voter, adopter; (Math: figure) retenir; (Comm: interest) rapporter; (involve: responsibilities etc) comporter, impliquer; (Med: disease) être porteur de ▷ vi (sound) porter; **to get carried away** (fig) s'emballer, s'enthousiasmer; **this loan carries 10% interest** ce prêt est à 10% (d'intérêt); **carry forward** vt (gen, Book-keeping) reporter; **carry on** vi (continue) continuer; (inf: make a fuss) faire des histoires ▷ vt (conduct: business) diriger; (: conversation) entretenir; (continue: business, conversation) continuer; **to ~ on with sth/doing** continuer qch/à faire; **carry out** vt (orders) exécuter; (investigation) effectuer; (idea, threat) mettre à exécution

carrycot ['kærɪkɔt] n (Brit) porte-bébé m

carry-on ['kærɪ'ɔn] n (inf: fuss) histoires fpl; (: annoying behaviour) cirque m, cinéma m

cart [kɑ:t] n charrette f ▷ vt (inf) transporter

carton ['kɑ:tən] n (box) carton m; (of yogurt) pot m (en carton); (of cigarettes) cartouche f

cartoon [kɑ:'tu:n] n (Press) dessin m (humoristique); (satirical) caricature f; (comic strip) bande dessinée; (Cine) dessin animé

cartridge ['kɑ:trɪdʒ] n (for gun, pen) cartouche f; (for camera) chargeur m; (music tape) cassette f; (of record player) cellule f

carve [kɑ:v] vt (meat: also: **~ up**) découper; (wood, stone) tailler, sculpter

carving ['kɑ:vɪŋ] n (in wood etc) sculpture f

carving knife n couteau m à découper

car wash n station f de lavage (de voitures)

case [keɪs] n cas m; (Law) affaire f, procès m; (box) caisse f, boîte f; (for glasses) étui m; (Brit: also: **suit~**) valise f; (Typ): **lower/upper ~**

minuscule f/majuscule f; **to have a good ~** avoir de bons arguments; **there's a strong ~ for reform** il y aurait lieu d'engager une réforme; **in ~ of** en cas de; **in ~ he** au cas où il; **just in ~** à tout hasard; **in any ~** en tout cas, de toute façon

cash [kæʃ] n argent m; (Comm) (argent m) liquide m, numéraire m; liquidités fpl; (: in payment) argent comptant, espèces fpl ▷ vt encaisser; **to pay (in) ~** payer (en argent) comptant or en espèces; **~ with order/on delivery** (Comm) payable or paiement à la commande/livraison; **to be short of ~** être à court d'argent; **I haven't got any ~** je n'ai pas de liquide; **cash in** vt (insurance policy etc) toucher; **cash in on** vt fus profiter de

cashback ['kæʃbæk] n (discount) remise f; (at supermarket etc) retrait m (à la caisse)
cashbook ['kæʃbuk] n livre m de caisse
cash card n carte f de retrait
cash desk n (Brit) caisse f
cash dispenser n distributeur m automatique de billets
cashew [kæ'ʃu:] n (also: **~ nut**) noix f de cajou
cashier [kæ'ʃɪə'] n caissier-(ère) ▷ vt (Mil) destituer, casser
cashmere ['kæʃmɪə'] n cachemire m
cash point n distributeur m automatique de billets
cash register n caisse enregistreuse
casing ['keɪsɪŋ] n revêtement (protecteur), enveloppe (protectrice)
casino [kə'si:nəu] n casino m
casket ['kɑ:skɪt] n coffret m; (US: coffin) cercueil m
casserole ['kæsərəul] n (pot) cocotte f; (food) ragoût m (en cocotte)
cassette [kæ'set] n cassette f
cassette player n lecteur m de cassettes
cassette recorder n magnétophone m à cassettes
cast [kɑ:st] (vb: pt, pp **cast**) vt (throw) jeter; (shadow: lit) projeter; (: fig) jeter; (glance) jeter; (shed) perdre; se dépouiller de; (metal) couler, fondre ▷ n (Theat) distribution f; (mould) moule m; (also: **plaster ~**) plâtre m; **to ~ sb as Hamlet** attribuer à qn le rôle d'Hamlet; **to ~ one's vote** voter, exprimer son suffrage; **to ~ doubt on** jeter un doute sur; **cast aside** vt (reject) rejeter; **cast off** vi (Naut) larguer les amarres; (Knitting) arrêter les mailles ▷ vt (Knitting) arrêter; **cast on** (Knitting) vt monter ▷ vi monter les mailles
castanets [kæstə'nɛts] npl castagnettes fpl
castaway ['kɑ:stəweɪ] n naufragé(e)
caster sugar ['kɑ:stə-] n (Brit) sucre m semoule
casting vote ['kɑ:stɪŋ-] n (Brit) voix f prépondérante (pour départager)
cast-iron ['kɑ:staɪən] adj (lit) de or en fonte; (fig: will) de fer; (alibi) en béton
cast iron n fonte f

castle ['kɑ:sl] n château m; (fortress) château-fort m; (Chess) tour f
castor ['kɑ:stə'] n (wheel) roulette f
castor oil n huile f de ricin
castrate [kæs'treɪt] vt châtrer
casual ['kæʒjul] adj (by chance) de hasard, fait(e) au hasard, fortuit(e); (irregular: work etc) temporaire; (unconcerned) désinvolte; **~ wear** vêtements mpl sport inv
casually ['kæʒjulɪ] adv avec désinvolture, négligemment; (by chance) fortuitement
casualty ['kæʒjultɪ] n accidenté(e), blessé(e); (dead) victime f, mort(e); (Brit: Med: department) urgences fpl; **heavy casualties** lourdes pertes
cat [kæt] n chat m
Catalan ['kætəlæn] adj catalan(e)
catalogue, (US) **catalog** ['kætəlɔg] n catalogue m ▷ vt cataloguer
catalyst ['kætəlɪst] n catalyseur m
catalytic converter [kætə'lɪtɪkkən'və:tə'] n pot m catalytique
catapult ['kætəpʌlt] n lance-pierres m inv, fronde f; (Hist) catapulte f
cataract ['kætərækt] n (also Med) cataracte f
catarrh [kə'tɑ:'] n rhume m chronique, catarrhe f
catastrophe [kə'tæstrəfɪ] n catastrophe f
catch [kætʃ] (pt, pp **caught**) [kɔ:t] vt (ball, train, thief, cold) attraper; (person: by surprise) prendre, surprendre; (understand) saisir; (get entangled) accrocher ▷ vi (fire) prendre; (get entangled) s'accrocher ▷ n (fish etc) prise f; (thief etc) capture f; (hidden problem) attrape f; (Tech) loquet m; cliquet m; **to ~ sb's attention** or **eye** attirer l'attention de qn; **to ~ fire** prendre feu; **to ~ sight of** apercevoir; **to play ~** jouer à chat; (with ball) jouer à attraper le ballon; **catch on** vi (become popular) prendre; (understand): **to ~ on (to sth)** saisir (qch); **catch out** vt (Brit: fig: with trick question) prendre en défaut; **catch up** vi (with work) rattraper, combler son retard ▷ vt (also: **~ up with**) rattraper
catching ['kætʃɪŋ] adj (Med) contagieux(-euse)
catchment area ['kætʃmənt-] n (Brit Scol) aire f de recrutement; (Geo) bassin m hydrographique
catch phrase n slogan m, expression toute faite
catchy ['kætʃɪ] adj (tune) facile à retenir
category ['kætɪgərɪ] n catégorie f
cater ['keɪtə'] vi: **to ~ for** (Brit: needs) satisfaire, pourvoir à; (: readers, consumers) s'adresser à, pourvoir aux besoins de; (Comm: parties etc) préparer des repas pour
caterer ['keɪtərə'] n traiteur m; fournisseur m
catering ['keɪtərɪŋ] n restauration f; approvisionnement m, ravitaillement m
caterpillar ['kætəpɪlə'] n chenille f ▷ cpd (vehicle) à chenille; **~ track** n chenille f

cathedral [kə'θiːdrəl] *n* cathédrale *f*
Catholic ['kæθəlɪk] (Rel) *adj* catholique ▷ *n* catholique *m/f*
catholic ['kæθəlɪk] *adj* (wide-ranging) éclectique; universel(le); libéral(e)
cattle ['kætl] *npl* bétail *m*, bestiaux *mpl*
catty ['kætɪ] *adj* méchant(e)
catwalk ['kætwɔːk] *n* passerelle *f*; (for models) podium *m* (de défilé de mode)
caucus ['kɔːkəs] *n* (US Pol) comité électoral (pour désigner des candidats); *voir article*; (Brit Pol: group) comité local (d'un parti politique)

⬙ **CAUCUS**

⬙ Un *caucus* aux États-Unis est une réunion
⬙ restreinte des principaux dirigeants d'un
⬙ parti politique, précédant souvent une
⬙ assemblée générale, dans le but de
⬙ choisir les candidats ou de définir une
⬙ ligne d'action. Par extension, ce terme
⬙ désigne également l'état-major d'un
⬙ parti politique.

caught [kɔːt] *pt, pp of* catch
cauliflower ['kɒlɪflauə'] *n* chou-fleur *m*
cause [kɔːz] *n* cause *f* ▷ *vt* causer; **there is no ~ for concern** il n'y a pas lieu de s'inquiéter; **to ~ sth to be done** faire faire qch; **to ~ sb to do sth** faire faire qch à qn
caution ['kɔːʃən] *n* prudence *f*; (warning) avertissement *m* ▷ *vt* avertir, donner un avertissement à
cautious ['kɔːʃəs] *adj* prudent(e)
cavalry ['kævəlrɪ] *n* cavalerie *f*
cave [keɪv] *n* caverne *f*, grotte *f* ▷ *vi*: **to go caving** faire de la spéléo(logie); **cave in** *vi* (roof etc) s'effondrer
caveman ['keɪvmæn] *irreg n* homme *m* des cavernes
caviar, caviare ['kævɪɑː'] *n* caviar *m*
cavity ['kævɪtɪ] *n* cavité *f*; (Med) carie *f*
CB *n abbr* (= Citizens' Band (Radio)) CB *f*; (Brit: = Companion of (the Order of) the Bath) titre honorifique
CBI *n abbr* (= Confederation of British Industry) ≈ MEDEF *m* (= Mouvement des entreprises de France)
cc *abbr* (= cubic centimetre) cm³; (on letter etc) = **carbon copy**
CCTV *n abbr* = **closed-circuit television**
CD *n abbr* (= compact disc) CD *m*; (Mil: Brit) = **Civil Defence (Corps)**; (: US) = **Civil Defense** ▷ *abbr* (Brit: = Corps Diplomatique) CD
CD burner *n* graveur *m* de CD
CD player *n* platine *f* laser
CD-ROM [siːdiːˈrɒm] *n abbr* (= compact disc read-only memory) CD-ROM *m inv*
CD writer *n* graveur *m* de CD
cease [siːs] *vt, vi* cesser
ceasefire ['siːsfaɪə'] *n* cessez-le-feu *m*
ceaseless ['siːslɪs] *adj* incessant(e), continuel(le)

cedar ['siːdə'] *n* cèdre *m*
ceilidh ['keɪlɪ] *n* bal *m* folklorique écossais *or* irlandais
ceiling ['siːlɪŋ] *n* (also fig) plafond *m*
celebrate ['sɛlɪbreɪt] *vt, vi* célébrer
celebrated ['sɛlɪbreɪtɪd] *adj* célèbre
celebration [sɛlɪˈbreɪʃən] *n* célébration *f*
celebrity [sɪˈlɛbrɪtɪ] *n* célébrité *f*
celery ['sɛlərɪ] *n* céleri *m* (en branches)
cell [sɛl] *n* (gen) cellule *f*; (Elec) élément *m* (de pile)
cellar ['sɛlə'] *n* cave *f*
cello ['tʃɛləu] *n* violoncelle *m*
Cellophane® ['sɛləfeɪn] *n* cellophane® *f*
cellphone ['sɛlfəun] *n* (téléphone *m*) portable *m*, mobile *m*
Celsius ['sɛlsɪəs] *adj* Celsius *inv*
Celt [kɛlt, sɛlt] *n* Celte *m/f*
Celtic ['kɛltɪk, 'sɛltɪk] *adj* celte, celtique ▷ *n* (Ling) celtique *m*
cement [sə'mɛnt] *n* ciment *m* ▷ *vt* cimenter
cement mixer *n* bétonnière *f*
cemetery ['sɛmɪtrɪ] *n* cimetière *m*
censor ['sɛnsə'] *n* censeur *m* ▷ *vt* censurer
censorship ['sɛnsəʃɪp] *n* censure *f*
censure ['sɛnʃə'] *vt* blâmer, critiquer
census ['sɛnsəs] *n* recensement *m*
cent [sɛnt] *n* (unit of dollar, euro) cent *m* (= un centième du dollar, de l'euro); *see also* **per**
centenary [sɛn'tiːnərɪ], (US) **centennial** [sɛn'tɛnɪəl] *n* centenaire *m*
center ['sɛntə'] *n, vt* (US) = **centre**
centigrade ['sɛntɪgreɪd] *adj* centigrade
centimetre, (US) **centimeter** ['sɛntɪmiːtə'] *n* centimètre *m*
centipede ['sɛntɪpiːd] *n* mille-pattes *m inv*
central ['sɛntrəl] *adj* central(e)
Central America *n* Amérique centrale
central heating *n* chauffage central
central reservation *n* (Brit Aut) terre-plein central
centre, (US) **center** ['sɛntə'] *n* centre *m* ▷ *vt* centrer; (Phot) cadrer; (concentrate): **to ~ (on)** centrer (sur)
centre-forward ['sɛntəˈfɔːwəd] *n* (Sport) avant-centre *m*
centre-half ['sɛntəˈhɑːf] *n* (Sport) demi-centre *m*
century ['sɛntjurɪ] *n* siècle *m*; **in the twentieth ~** au vingtième siècle
CEO *n abbr* (US) = **chief executive officer**
ceramic [sɪ'ræmɪk] *adj* céramique
cereal ['sɪːrɪəl] *n* céréale *f*
ceremony ['sɛrɪmənɪ] *n* cérémonie *f*; **to stand on ~** faire des façons
certain ['səːtən] *adj* certain(e); **to make ~ of** s'assurer de; **for ~** certainement, sûrement
certainly ['səːtənlɪ] *adv* certainement
certainty ['səːtəntɪ] *n* certitude *f*
certificate [sə'tɪfɪkɪt] *n* certificat *m*
certify ['səːtɪfaɪ] *vt* certifier; (award diploma to) conférer un diplôme *etc* à; (declare insane)

déclarer malade mental(e) ▷ vi: **to ~ to** attester

cervical ['sə:vɪkl] adj: ~ **cancer** cancer m du col de l'utérus; ~ **smear** frottis vaginal

cervix ['sə:vɪks] n col m de l'utérus

cf. abbr (= compare) cf., voir

CFC n abbr (= chlorofluorocarbon) CFC m

ch. abbr (= chapter) chap

chafe [tʃeɪf] vt irriter, frotter contre ▷ vi (fig): **to ~ against** se rebiffer contre, regimber contre

chain [tʃeɪn] n (gen) chaîne f ▷ vt (also: ~ **up**) enchaîner, attacher (avec une chaîne)

chain reaction n réaction f en chaîne

chain-smoke ['tʃeɪnsməuk] vi fumer cigarette sur cigarette

chain store n magasin m à succursales multiples

chair [tʃeə'] n chaise f; (armchair) fauteuil m; (of university) chaire f; (of meeting) présidence f ▷ vt (meeting) présider; **the ~** (US: electric chair) la chaise électrique

chairlift ['tʃeəlɪft] n télésiège m

chairman ['tʃeəmən] irreg n président m

chairperson ['tʃeəpə:sn] irreg n président(e)

chairwoman ['tʃeəwumən] n présidente f

chalet ['ʃæleɪ] n chalet m

chalk [tʃɔ:k] n craie f; **chalk up** vt écrire à la craie; (fig: success etc) remporter

challenge ['tʃælɪndʒ] n défi m ▷ vt défier; (statement, right) mettre en question, contester; **to ~ sb to a fight/game** inviter qn à se battre/à jouer (sous forme d'un défi); **to ~ sb to do** mettre qn au défi de faire

challenging ['tʃælɪndʒɪŋ] adj (task, career) qui représente un défi or une gageure; (tone, look) de défi, provocateur(-trice)

chamber ['tʃeɪmbə'] n chambre f; (Brit Law: gen pl) cabinet m; ~ **of commerce** chambre de commerce

chambermaid ['tʃeɪmbəmeɪd] n femme f de chambre

chamber music n musique f de chambre

champagne [ʃæm'peɪn] n champagne m

champion ['tʃæmpɪən] n (also of cause) champion(ne) ▷ vt défendre

championship ['tʃæmpɪənʃɪp] n championnat m

chance [tʃɑ:ns] n (luck) hasard m; (opportunity) occasion f, possibilité f; (hope, likelihood) chance f; (risk) risque m ▷ vt (risk) risquer; (happen): **to ~ to do** faire par hasard ▷ adj fortuit(e), de hasard; **there is little ~ of his coming** il est peu probable or il y a peu de chances qu'il vienne; **to take a ~** prendre un risque; **it's the ~ of a lifetime** c'est une occasion unique; **by ~** par hasard; **to ~ doing sth** se risquer à faire qch; **to ~ it** risquer le coup, essayer; **chance on, chance upon** vt fus (person) tomber sur, rencontrer par hasard; (thing) trouver par hasard

chancellor ['tʃɑ:nsələ'] n chancelier m

Chancellor of the Exchequer [-ɪks'tʃekə'] (Brit) n chancelier m de l'Échiquier

chandelier [ʃændə'lɪə'] n lustre m

change [tʃeɪndʒ] vt (alter, replace: Comm: money) changer; (switch, substitute: hands, trains, clothes, one's name etc) changer de; (transform): **to ~ sb into** changer or transformer qn en ▷ vi (gen) changer; (change clothes) se changer; (be transformed): **to ~ into** se changer or transformer en ▷ n changement m; (money) monnaie f; **to ~ gear** (Aut) changer de vitesse; **to ~ one's mind** changer d'avis; **she ~d into an old skirt** elle (s'est changée et) a enfilé une vieille jupe; **a ~ of clothes** des vêtements de rechange; **for a ~** pour changer; **small ~** petite monnaie; **to give sb ~ for** or **of £10** faire à qn la monnaie de 10 livres; **do you have ~ for £10?** vous avez la monnaie de 10 livres?; **where can I ~ some money?** où est-ce que je peux changer de l'argent?; **keep the ~!** gardez la monnaie!; **change over** vi (swap) échanger; (change: drivers etc) changer; (change sides: players etc) changer de côté; **to ~ over from sth to sth** passer de qch à qch

changeable ['tʃeɪndʒəbl] adj (weather) variable; (person) d'humeur changeante

change machine n distributeur m de monnaie

changeover ['tʃeɪndʒəuvə'] n (to new system) changement m, passage m

changing ['tʃeɪndʒɪŋ] adj changeant(e)

changing room n (Brit: in shop) salon m d'essayage m; (: Sport) vestiaire m

channel ['tʃænl] n (TV) chaîne f; (waveband, groove, fig: medium) canal m; (of river, sea) chenal m ▷ vt canaliser; (fig: interest, energies): **to ~** into diriger vers; **through the usual ~s** en suivant la filière habituelle; **green/red ~** (Customs) couloir m or sortie f "rien à déclarer"/"marchandises à déclarer"; **the (English) C~** la Manche

channel-hopping ['tʃænl'hɔpɪŋ] n (TV) zapping m

Channel Islands npl: **the ~** les îles fpl Anglo-Normandes

Channel Tunnel n: **the ~** le tunnel sous la Manche

chant [tʃɑ:nt] n chant m; mélopée f; (Rel) psalmodie f ▷ vt chanter, scander; psalmodier

chaos ['keɪɔs] n chaos m

chaotic [keɪ'ɔtɪk] adj chaotique

chap [tʃæp] n (Brit inf: man) type m; (term of address): **old ~** mon vieux ▷ vt (skin) gercer, crevasser

chapel ['tʃæpl] n chapelle f

chaplain ['tʃæplɪn] n aumônier m

chapped [tʃæpt] adj (skin, lips) gercé(e)

chapter ['tʃæptə'] n chapitre m

char [tʃɑ:'] vt (burn) carboniser ▷ vi (Brit: cleaner) faire des ménages ▷ n (Brit) = **charlady**

character ['kærıktə'] n caractère m; (in novel, film) personnage m; (eccentric person) numéro m, phénomène m; **a person of good ~** une personne bien

characteristic ['kærıktə'rıstık] adj, n caractéristique (f)

characterize ['kærıktəraız] vt caractériser; **to ~ (as)** définir (comme)

charcoal ['tʃɑ:kəul] n charbon m de bois; (Art) charbon

charge [tʃɑ:dʒ] n (accusation) accusation f; (Law) inculpation f; (cost) prix (demandé); (of gun, battery, Mil: attack) charge f ⊳ vt (gun, battery, Mil: enemy) charger; (customer, sum) faire payer ⊳ vi (gen with: up, along etc) foncer; **charges** npl (costs) frais mpl, (Brit Tel): **to reverse the ~s** téléphoner en PCV; **bank/ labour ~s** frais mpl de banque/main-d'œuvre; **is there a ~?** doit-on payer?; **there's no ~** c'est gratuit, on ne fait pas payer; **extra ~** supplément m; **to take ~ of** se charger de; **to be in ~ of** être responsable de, s'occuper de; **to ~ in/out** entrer/sortir en trombe; **to ~ down/up** dévaler/ grimper à toute allure; **to ~ sb (with)** (Law) inculper qn (de); **they ~d us £10 for the meal** ils nous ont fait payer le repas 10 livres, ils nous ont compté 10 livres pour le repas; **how much do you ~ for this repair?** combien demandez-vous pour cette réparation?; **to ~ an expense (up) to sb** mettre une dépense sur le compte de qn; **~ it to my account** facturez-le sur mon compte

charge card n carte f de client (émise par un grand magasin)

charger ['tʃɑ:dʒə'] n (also: **battery ~**) chargeur m; (old: warhorse) cheval m de bataille

charismatic [kærız'mætık] adj charismatique

charity ['tʃærıtı] n charité f; (organization) institution f charitable or de bienfaisance, œuvre f (de charité)

charity shop n (Brit) boutique vendant des articles d'occasion au profit d'une organisation caritative

charm [tʃɑ:m] n charme m; (on bracelet) breloque f ⊳ vt charmer, enchanter

charming ['tʃɑ:mıŋ] adj charmant(e)

chart [tʃɑ:t] n tableau m, diagramme m; graphique m; (map) carte marine; (weather chart) carte f du temps ⊳ vt dresser or établir la carte de; (sales, progress) établir la courbe de; **charts** npl (Mus) hit-parade m; **to be in the ~s** (record, pop group) figurer au hit-parade

charter ['tʃɑ:tə'] vt (plane) affréter ⊳ n (document) charte f; **on ~** (plane) affrété(e)

chartered accountant ['tʃɑ:təd-] n (Brit) expert-comptable m

charter flight n charter m

chase [tʃeıs] vt poursuivre, pourchasser; (also: **~ away**) chasser ⊳ n poursuite f,

chasse f; **chase down** vt (US) = **chase up**; **chase up** vt (Brit: person) relancer; (: information) rechercher

chasm ['kæzəm] n gouffre m, abîme m

chat [tʃæt] vi (also: **have a ~**) bavarder, causer; (on Internet) chatter ⊳ n conversation f; (on Internet) chat m; **chat up** vt (Brit inf: girl) baratiner

chat room n (Internet) salon m de discussion

chat show n (Brit) talk-show m

chatter ['tʃætə'] vi (person) bavarder, papoter ⊳ n bavardage m, papotage m; **my teeth are ~ing** je claque des dents

chatterbox ['tʃætəbɔks] n moulin m à paroles, babillard(e)

chatty ['tʃætı] adj (style) familier(-ière); (person) enclin(e) à bavarder or au papotage

chauffeur ['ʃəufə'] n chauffeur m (de maître)

chauvinist ['ʃəuvınıst] n (also: **male ~**) phallocrate m, macho m; (nationalist) chauvin(e)

cheap [tʃi:p] adj bon marché inv, pas cher/ chère; (reduced: ticket) à prix réduit; (: fare) réduit(e); (joke) facile, d'un goût douteux; (poor quality) à bon marché, de qualité médiocre ⊳ adv à bon marché, pour pas cher; **~er** adj moins cher/chère; **can you recommend a ~ hotel/restaurant, please?** pourriez-vous m'indiquer un hôtel/ restaurant bon marché?

cheap day return n billet m d'aller et retour réduit (valable pour la journée)

cheaply ['tʃi:plı] adv à bon marché, à bon compte

cheat [tʃi:t] vi tricher; (in exam) copier ⊳ vt tromper, duper; (rob): **to ~ sb out of sth** escroquer qch à qn ⊳ n tricheur(-euse) m/f; escroc m; (trick) duperie f, tromperie f; **cheat on** vt fus tromper

Chechnya [tʃıtʃ'njɑ:] n Tchétchénie f

check [tʃɛk] vt vérifier; (passport, ticket) contrôler; (halt) enrayer; (restrain) maîtriser ⊳ vi (official etc) se renseigner ⊳ n vérification f; contrôle m; (curb) frein m; (Brit: bill) addition f; (US) = **cheque**; (pattern: gen pl) carreaux mpl ⊳ adj (also: **~ed: pattern, cloth**) à carreaux; **to ~ with sb** demander à qn; **to keep a ~ on sb/sth** surveiller qn/qch; **check in** vi (in hotel) remplir sa fiche (d'hôtel); (at airport) se présenter à l'enregistrement ⊳ vt (luggage) (faire) enregistrer; **check off** vt (tick off) cocher; **check out** vi (in hotel) régler sa note ⊳ vt (luggage) retirer; (investigate: story) vérifier; (person) prendre des renseignements sur; **check up** vi: **to ~ up (on sth)** vérifier (qch); **to ~ up on sb** se renseigner sur le compte de qn

checkbook ['tʃɛkbuk] n (US) = **chequebook**

checked ['tʃɛkt] adj (pattern, cloth) à carreaux

checkered ['tʃɛkəd] adj (US) = **chequered**

checkers ['tʃɛkəz] n (US) jeu m de dames

check-in ['tʃɛkin] n (also: ~ desk: at airport) enregistrement m

checking account ['tʃɛkɪŋ-] n (US) compte courant

checklist ['tʃɛklɪst] n liste f de contrôle

checkmate ['tʃɛkmeɪt] n échec et mat m

checkout ['tʃɛkaut] n (in supermarket) caisse f

checkpoint ['tʃɛkpɔɪnt] n contrôle m

checkroom ['tʃɛkru:m] (US) n consigne f

checkup ['tʃɛkʌp] n (Med) examen médical, check-up m

cheddar ['tʃɛdəʳ] n (also: ~ cheese) cheddar m

cheek [tʃi:k] n joue f; (impudence) toupet m, culot m; **what a ~!** quel toupet!

cheekbone ['tʃi:kbəun] n pommette f

cheeky ['tʃi:kɪ] adj effronté(e), culotté(e)

cheep [tʃi:p] n (of bird) piaulement m ▷ vi piauler

cheer [tʃɪəʳ] vt acclamer, applaudir; (gladden) réjouir, réconforter ▷ vi applaudir ▷ n (gen pl) acclamations fpl, applaudissements mpl; bravos mpl, hourras mpl; **~s!** à la vôtre!; **cheer on** vt encourager (par des cris etc); **cheer up** vi se dérider, reprendre courage ▷ vt remonter le moral à or de, dérider, égayer

cheerful ['tʃɪəful] adj gai(e), joyeux(-euse)

cheerio ['tʃɪərɪ'əu] excl (Brit) salut!, au revoir!

cheerleader ['tʃɪəli:dəʳ] n membre d'un groupe de majorettes qui chantent et dansent pour soutenir leur équipe pendant les matchs de football américain

cheese [tʃi:z] n fromage m

cheeseboard ['tʃi:zbɔ:d] n plateau m à fromages; (with cheese on it) plateau m de fromages

cheeseburger ['tʃi:zbə:gəʳ] n cheeseburger m

cheesecake ['tʃi:zkeɪk] n tarte f au fromage

cheetah ['tʃi:tə] n guépard m

chef [ʃɛf] n chef (cuisinier)

chemical ['kɛmɪkl] adj chimique ▷ n produit m chimique

chemist ['kɛmɪst] n (Brit: pharmacist) pharmacien(ne); (scientist) chimiste m/f

chemistry ['kɛmɪstrɪ] n chimie f

chemist's ['kɛmɪsts], **chemist's shop** n (Brit) pharmacie f

cheque, (US) **check** [tʃɛk] n chèque m; **to pay by ~** payer par chèque

chequebook, (US) **checkbook** ['tʃɛkbuk] n chéquier m, carnet m de chèques

cheque card n (Brit) carte f (d'identité) bancaire

chequered, (US) **checkered** ['tʃɛkəd] adj (fig) varié(e)

cherish ['tʃɛrɪʃ] vt chérir; (hope etc) entretenir

cherry ['tʃɛrɪ] n cerise f; (also: ~ tree) cerisier m

chess [tʃɛs] n échecs mpl

chessboard ['tʃɛsbɔ:d] n échiquier m

chest [tʃɛst] n poitrine f; (box) coffre m, caisse f; **to get sth off one's ~** (inf) vider son sac

chestnut ['tʃɛsnʌt] n châtaigne f; (also: ~ tree) châtaignier m; (colour) châtain m ▷ adj (hair) châtain inv; (horse) alezan

chest of drawers n commode f

chew [tʃu:] vt mâcher

chewing gum ['tʃu:ɪŋ-] n chewing-gum m

chic [ʃi:k] adj chic inv, élégant(e)

chick [tʃɪk] n poussin m; (inf) pépée f

chicken ['tʃɪkɪn] n poulet m; (inf: coward) poule mouillée; **chicken out** vi (inf) se dégonfler

chickenpox ['tʃɪkɪnpɔks] n varicelle f

chickpea ['tʃɪkpi:] n pois m chiche

chicory ['tʃɪkərɪ] n chicorée f; (salad) endive f

chief [tʃi:f] n chef m ▷ adj principal(e); **C~ of Staff** (Mil) chef d'État-major

chief executive, (US) **chief executive officer** n directeur(-trice) général(e)

chiefly ['tʃi:flɪ] adv principalement, surtout

chiffon ['ʃɪfɔn] n mousseline f de soie

chilblain ['tʃɪlbleɪn] n engelure f

child (pl **children**) [tʃaɪld, 'tʃɪldrən] n enfant m/f

child abuse n maltraitance f d'enfants; (sexual) abus mpl sexuels sur des enfants

child benefit n (Brit) ≈ allocations familiales

childbirth ['tʃaɪldbə:θ] n accouchement m

childcare ['tʃaɪldkɛəʳ] n (for working parents) garde f des enfants (pour les parents qui travaillent)

childhood ['tʃaɪldhud] n enfance f

childish ['tʃaɪldɪʃ] adj puéril(e), enfantin(e)

childlike ['tʃaɪldlaɪk] adj innocent(e), pur(e)

child minder n (Brit) garde f d'enfants

children ['tʃɪldrən] npl of **child**

Chile ['tʃɪlɪ] n Chili m

chill [tʃɪl] n (of water) froid m; (of air) fraîcheur f; (Med) refroidissement m, coup m de froid ▷ adj froid(e), glacial(e) ▷ vt (person) faire frissonner; refroidir; (Culin) mettre au frais, rafraîchir; **"serve -ed"** "à servir frais"; **chill out** vi (inf: esp US) se relaxer

chilli, chili ['tʃɪlɪ] n piment m (rouge)

chilly ['tʃɪlɪ] adj froid(e), glacé(e); (sensitive to cold) frileux(-euse); **to feel ~** avoir froid

chime [tʃaɪm] n carillon m ▷ vi carillonner, sonner

chimney ['tʃɪmnɪ] n cheminée f

chimney sweep n ramoneur m

chimpanzee [tʃɪmpæn'zi:] n chimpanzé m

chin [tʃɪn] n menton m

China ['tʃaɪnə] n Chine f

china ['tʃaɪnə] n (material) porcelaine f; (crockery) vaisselle f en f porcelaine

Chinese [tʃaɪ'ni:z] adj chinois(e) ▷ n (pl inv) Chinois(e); (Ling) chinois m

chink [tʃɪŋk] n (opening) fente f, fissure f; (noise) tintement m

chip [tʃɪp] n (gen pl: Culin: Brit) frite f; (: US: also: **potato ~**) chip m; (of wood) copeau m; (of glass, stone) éclat m; (also: **micro~**) puce f; (in gambling) fiche f ▷ vt (cup, plate) ébrécher; **when the ~s are down** (fig) au moment critique; **chip in** vi (inf) mettre son grain de sel

chip shop n (Brit) friterie f; voir article

chiropodist [kɪˈrɒpədɪst] n (Brit) pédicure m/f

chirp [tʃə:p] n pépiement m, gazouillis m;
(of crickets) stridulation f ▷ vi pépier,
gazouiller; chanter, striduler

chisel [ˈtʃɪzl] n ciseau m

chit [tʃɪt] n mot m, note f

chitchat [ˈtʃɪttʃæt] n bavardage m,
papotage m

chivalry [ˈʃɪvəlrɪ] n chevalerie f; esprit m
chevaleresque

chives [tʃaɪvz] npl ciboulette f, civette f

chlorine [ˈklɔ:ri:n] n chlore m

choc-ice [ˈtʃɒkaɪs] n (Brit) esquimau® m

chock-a-block [ˈtʃɒkəˈblɒk], **chock-full**
[tʃɔk'ful] adj plein(e) à craquer

chocolate [ˈtʃɒklɪt] n chocolat m

choice [tʃɔɪs] n choix m ▷ adj de choix; **by** or
from ~ par choix; **a wide ~** un grand choix

choir [ˈkwaɪər] n chœur m, chorale f

choirboy [ˈkwaɪəˈbɔɪ] n jeune choriste m,
petit chanteur

choke [tʃəuk] vi étouffer ▷ vt étrangler;
étouffer; (block) boucher, obstruer ▷ n (Aut)
starter m

cholesterol [kəˈlestərəl] n cholestérol m

choose (pt chose, pp chosen) [tʃu:z, tʃəuz,
ˈtʃəuzn] vt choisir ▷ vi: **to ~ between** choisir
entre; **to ~ from** choisir parmi; **to ~ to do**
décider de faire, juger bon de faire

choosy [ˈtʃu:zɪ] adj: **(to be) ~** (faire le) difficile

chop [tʃɒp] vt (wood) couper (à la hache);
(Culin: also: **~ up**) couper (fin), émincer,
hacher (en morceaux) ▷ n coup m (de hache, du
tranchant de la main); (Culin) côtelette f; **to get
the ~** (Brit inf: project) tomber à l'eau; (: person:
be sacked) se faire renvoyer; **chop down** vt
(tree) abattre; **chop off** vt trancher

chopper [ˈtʃɒpər] n (helicopter) hélicoptère m,
hélico m

choppy [ˈtʃɒpɪ] adj (sea) un peu agité(e)

chopsticks [ˈtʃɒpstɪks] npl baguettes fpl

chord [kɔ:d] n (Mus) accord m

chore [tʃɔ:ʳ] n travail m de routine;
household ~s travaux mpl du ménage

chortle [ˈtʃɔ:tl] vi glousser

chorus [ˈkɔ:rəs] n chœur m; (repeated part of
song, also fig) refrain m

chose [tʃəuz] pt of **choose**

chosen [ˈtʃəuzn] pp of **choose**

chowder [ˈtʃaudəʳ] n soupe f de poisson

Christ [kraɪst] n Christ m

christen [ˈkrɪsn] vt baptiser

christening [ˈkrɪsnɪŋ] n baptême m

Christian [ˈkrɪstɪən] adj, n chrétien(ne)

Christianity [krɪstɪˈænɪtɪ] n christianisme m

Christian name n prénom m

Christmas [ˈkrɪsməs] n Noël m or f; **happy** or
merry ~! joyeux Noël!

Christmas card n carte f de Noël

Christmas carol n chant m de Noël

Christmas Day n le jour de Noël

Christmas Eve n la veille de Noël; la nuit de
Noël

Christmas pudding n (esp Brit) Christmas m
pudding

Christmas tree n arbre m de Noël

chrome [krəum] n chrome m

chromium [ˈkrəumɪəm] n chrome m; (also:
~ plating) chromage m

chronic [ˈkrɒnɪk] adj chronique; (fig: liar,
smoker) invétéré(e)

chronicle [ˈkrɒnɪkl] n chronique f

chronological [krɒnəˈlɒdʒɪkl] adj
chronologique

chrysanthemum [krɪˈsænθəməm] n
chrysanthème m

chubby [ˈtʃʌbɪ] adj potelé(e), rondelet(te)

chuck [tʃʌk] vt (inf) lancer, jeter; (Brit: also:
~ up: job) lâcher; (: person) plaquer; **chuck out**
vt (inf: person) flanquer dehors or à la porte;
(: rubbish etc) jeter

chuckle [ˈtʃʌkl] vi glousser

chug [tʃʌg] vi faire teuf-teuf; souffler

chum [tʃʌm] n copain/copine

chunk [tʃʌŋk] n gros morceau; (of bread)
quignon m

church [tʃə:tʃ] n église f; **the C~ of England**
l'Église anglicane

churchyard [ˈtʃə:tʃjɑ:d] n cimetière m

churn [tʃə:n] n (for butter) baratte f; (also:
milk ~) (grand) bidon à lait; **churn out** vt
débiter

chute [ʃu:t] n goulotte f; (also: **rubbish ~**)
vide-ordures m inv; (Brit: children's slide)
toboggan m

chutney [ˈtʃʌtnɪ] n chutney m

CIA n abbr (= Central Intelligence Agency) CIA f

CID n abbr (= Criminal Investigation Department)
≈ P.J. f

cider [ˈsaɪdəʳ] n cidre m

cigar [sɪˈgɑːʳ] n cigare m

cigarette [sɪgəˈret] n cigarette f

cigarette case n étui m à cigarettes

cigarette end n mégot m

cigarette lighter n briquet m

Cinderella [sɪndəˈrelə] n Cendrillon

cine-camera [ˈsɪnɪˈkæmərə] n (Brit) caméra f

cinema ['sɪnəmə] n cinéma m
cinnamon ['sɪnəmən] n cannelle f
circle ['sɜːkl] n cercle m; (in cinema) balcon m ▷ vi faire or décrire des cercles ▷ vt (surround) entourer, encercler; (move round) faire le tour de, tourner autour de
circuit ['sɜːkɪt] n circuit m; (lap) tour m
circuitous [sə'kjuːɪtəs] adj indirect(e), qui fait un détour
circular ['sɜːkjuləʳ] adj circulaire ▷ n circulaire f; (as advertisement) prospectus m
circulate ['sɜːkjuleɪt] vi circuler ▷ vt faire circuler
circulation [sɜːkju'leɪʃən] n circulation f; (of newspaper) tirage m
circumflex ['sɜːkəmfleks] n (also: ~ accent) accent m circonflexe
circumstances ['sɜːkəmstænsɪz] npl circonstances fpl; (financial condition) moyens mpl, situation financière; **in** or **under the ~** dans ces conditions; **under no ~** en aucun cas, sous aucun prétexte
circus ['sɜːkəs] n cirque m; (also: **C~**: in place names) place f
CIS n abbr (= Commonwealth of Independent States) CEI f
cistern ['sɪstən] n réservoir m (d'eau); (in toilet) réservoir de la chasse d'eau
cite [saɪt] vt citer
citizen ['sɪtɪzn] n (Pol) citoyen(ne); (resident): **the ~s of this town** les habitants de cette ville
citizenship ['sɪtɪznʃɪp] n citoyenneté f; (Brit: Scol) = éducation f civique
citrus fruits ['sɪtrəs-] npl agrumes mpl
city ['sɪtɪ] n (grande) ville f; **the C~** la Cité de Londres (centre des affaires)
city centre n centre ville m
city technology college n (Brit) établissement m d'enseignement technologique (situé dans un quartier défavorisé)
civic ['sɪvɪk] adj civique; (authorities) municipal(e)
civic centre n (Brit) centre administratif (municipal)
civil ['sɪvɪl] adj civil(e); (polite) poli(e), civil(e)
civil engineer n ingénieur civil
civilian [sɪ'vɪlɪən] adj, n civil(e)
civilization [sɪvɪlaɪ'zeɪʃən] n civilisation f
civilized ['sɪvɪlaɪzd] adj civilisé(e); (fig) où règnent les bonnes manières, empreint(e) d'une courtoisie de bon ton
civil law n code civil; (study) droit civil
civil rights npl droits mpl civiques
civil servant n fonctionnaire m/f
Civil Service n fonction publique, administration f
civil war n guerre civile
CJD n abbr (= Creutzfeldt-Jakob disease) MCJ f
clad [klæd] adj: ~ **(in)** habillé(e) de, vêtu(e) de
claim [kleɪm] vt (rights etc) revendiquer; (compensation) réclamer; (assert) déclarer,

prétendre ▷ vi (for insurance) faire une déclaration de sinistre ▷ n revendication f; prétention f; (right) droit m; (for expenses) note f de frais; **(insurance)** ~ demande f d'indemnisation, déclaration f de sinistre; **to put in a ~ for** (pay rise etc) demander
claimant ['kleɪmənt] n (Admin, Law) requérant(e)
claim form n (gen) formulaire m de demande
clairvoyant [kleə'vɔɪənt] n voyant(e), extra-lucide m/f
clam [klæm] n palourde f; **clam up** vi (inf) la boucler
clamber ['klæmbəʳ] vi grimper, se hisser
clammy ['klæmɪ] adj humide et froid(e) (au toucher), moite
clamour, (US) **clamor** ['klæməʳ] n (noise) clameurs fpl; (protest) protestations bruyantes ▷ vi: **to ~ for sth** réclamer qch à grands cris
clamp [klæmp] n crampon m; (on workbench) valet m; (on car) sabot m de Denver ▷ vt attacher; (car) mettre un sabot à; **clamp down on** vt fus sévir contre, prendre des mesures draconiennes à l'égard de
clan [klæn] n clan m
clang [klæŋ] n bruit m or fracas m métallique ▷ vi émettre un bruit or fracas métallique
clap [klæp] vi applaudir ▷ vt: **to ~ (one's hands)** battre des mains ▷ n claquement m; tape f; **a ~ of thunder** un coup de tonnerre
clapping ['klæpɪŋ] n applaudissements mpl
claret ['klærət] n (vin m de) bordeaux m (rouge)
clarify ['klærɪfaɪ] vt clarifier
clarinet [klærɪ'nɛt] n clarinette f
clarity ['klærɪtɪ] n clarté f
clash [klæʃ] n (sound) choc m, fracas m; (with police) affrontement m; (fig) conflit m ▷ vi se heurter; être or entrer en conflit; (colours) jurer; (dates, events) tomber en même temps
clasp [klɑːsp] n (of necklace, bag) fermoir m ▷ vt serrer, étreindre
class [klɑːs] n (gen) classe f; (group, category) catégorie f ▷ vt classer, classifier
classic ['klæsɪk] adj classique ▷ n (author, work) classique m; (race etc) classique f
classical ['klæsɪkl] adj classique
classification [klæsɪfɪ'keɪʃən] n classification f
classified ['klæsɪfaɪd] adj (information) secret(-ète); ~ **ads** petites annonces
classify ['klæsɪfaɪ] vt classifier, classer
classmate ['klɑːsmeɪt] n camarade m/f de classe
classroom ['klɑːsrum] n (salle f de) classe f
classroom assistant n assistant(-e) d'éducation
classy ['klɑːsɪ] (inf) adj classe (inf)
clatter ['klætəʳ] n cliquetis m ▷ vi cliqueter
clause [klɔːz] n clause f; (Ling) proposition f

claustrophobic [klɔːstrəˈfəubɪk] *adj* (*person*) claustrophobe; (*place*) où l'on se sent claustrophobe

claw [klɔː] *n* griffe *f*; (*of bird of prey*) serre *f*; (*of lobster*) pince *f* ▷ *vt* griffer; déchirer

clay [kleɪ] *n* argile *f*

clean [kliːn] *adj* propre; (*clear, smooth*) net(te); (*record, reputation*) sans tache; (*joke, story*) correct(e) ▷ *vt* nettoyer ▷ *adv*: **he ~ forgot** il a complètement oublié; **to come ~** (*inf*: *admit guilt*) se mettre à table; **to ~ one's teeth** se laver les dents; **~ driving licence** or (*US*) **record** permis où n'est portée aucune indication de contravention; **clean off** *vt* enlever; **clean out** *vt* nettoyer (à fond); **clean up** *vt* nettoyer; (*fig*) remettre de l'ordre dans ▷ *vi* (*fig*: *make profit*): **to ~ up on** faire son beurre avec

clean-cut [ˈkliːnˈkʌt] *adj* (*man*) soigné; (*situation etc*) bien délimité(e), net(te), clair(e)

cleaner [ˈkliːnəʳ] *n* (*person*) nettoyeur(-euse), femme *f* de ménage; (*also:* **dry ~**) teinturier(-ière); (*product*) détachant *m*

cleaner's [ˈkliːnəz] *n* (*also:* **dry ~**) teinturier *m*

cleaning [ˈkliːnɪŋ] *n* nettoyage *m*

cleanliness [ˈklɛnlɪnɪs] *n* propreté *f*

cleanse [klɛnz] *vt* nettoyer; purifier

cleanser [ˈklɛnzəʳ] *n* détergent *m*; (*for face*) démaquillant *m*

clean-shaven [ˈkliːnˈʃeɪvn] *adj* rasé(e) de près

cleansing department [ˈklɛnzɪŋ-] *n* (*Brit*) service *m* de voirie

clear [klɪəʳ] *adj* clair(e); (*glass, plastic*) transparent(e); (*road, way*) libre, dégagé(e); (*profit, majority*) net(te); (*conscience*) tranquille; (*skin*) frais/fraîche; (*sky*) dégagé(e) ▷ *vt* (*road*) dégager, déblayer; (*table*) débarrasser; (*room etc: of people*) faire évacuer; (*woodland*) défricher; (*cheque*) compenser; (*Comm*: *goods*) liquider; (*Law*: *suspect*) innocenter; (*obstacle*) franchir or sauter sans heurter ▷ *vi* (*weather*) s'éclaircir; (*fog*) se dissiper ▷ *adv*: **~ of** à distance de, à l'écart de ▷ *n*: **to be in the ~** (*out of debt*) être dégagé(e) de toute dette; (*out of suspicion*) être lavé(e) de tout soupçon; (*out of danger*) être hors de danger; **to ~ the table** débarrasser la table, desservir; **to ~ one's throat** s'éclaircir la gorge; **to ~ a profit** faire un bénéfice net; **to make it ~ to sb that ...** bien faire comprendre à qn que ...; **I have a ~ day tomorrow** (*Brit*) je n'ai rien de prévu demain; **to keep ~ of sb/sth** éviter qn/qch; **clear away** *vt* (*things, clothes etc*) enlever, retirer; **to ~ away the dishes** débarrasser la table; **clear off** *vi* (*inf*: *leave*) dégager; **clear up** *vi* s'éclaircir, se dissiper ▷ *vt* ranger, mettre en ordre; (*mystery*) éclaircir, résoudre

clearance [ˈklɪərəns] *n* (*removal*) déblayage *m*; (*free space*) dégagement *m*; (*permission*) autorisation *f*

clear-cut [ˈklɪəˈkʌt] *adj* précis(e), nettement défini(e)

clearing [ˈklɪərɪŋ] *n* (*in forest*) clairière *f*; (*Brit Banking*) compensation *f*, clearing *m*

clearing bank *n* (*Brit*) banque *f* qui appartient à une chambre de compensation

clearly [ˈklɪəlɪ] *adv* clairement; (*obviously*) de toute évidence

clearway [ˈklɪəweɪ] *n* (*Brit*) route *f* à stationnement interdit

clef [klɛf] *n* (*Mus*) clé *f*

cleft [klɛft] *n* (*in rock*) crevasse *f*, fissure *f*

clementine [ˈklɛməntaɪn] *n* clémentine *f*

clench [klɛntʃ] *vt* serrer

clergy [ˈkləːdʒɪ] *n* clergé *m*

clergyman [ˈkləːdʒɪmən] *irreg n* ecclésiastique *m*

clerical [ˈklɛrɪkl] *adj* de bureau, d'employé de bureau; (*Rel*) clérical(e), du clergé

clerk [klɑːk] *n* (*Brit*) employé(e) de bureau; (*US*: *salesman/woman*) vendeur(-euse); **C~ of Court** (*Law*) greffier *m* (du tribunal)

clever [ˈklɛvəʳ] *adj* (*intelligent*) intelligent(e); (*skilful*) habile, adroit(e); (*device, arrangement*) ingénieux(-euse), astucieux(-euse)

cliché [ˈkliːʃeɪ] *n* cliché *m*

click [klɪk] *vi* faire un bruit sec or un déclic; (*Comput*) cliquer ▷ *vt*: **to ~ one's tongue** faire claquer sa langue; **to ~ one's heels** claquer des talons; **to ~ on an icon** cliquer sur une icône

client [ˈklaɪənt] *n* client(e)

cliff [klɪf] *n* falaise *f*

climate [ˈklaɪmɪt] *n* climat *m*

climate change *n* changement *m* climatique

climax [ˈklaɪmæks] *n* apogée *m*, point culminant *m*; (*sexual*) orgasme *m*

climb [klaɪm] *vi* grimper, monter; (*plane*) prendre de l'altitude ▷ *vt* (*stairs*) monter; (*mountain*) escalader; (*tree*) grimper à ▷ *n* montée *f*, escalade *f*; **to ~ over a wall** passer par dessus un mur; **climb down** *vi* (re)descendre; (*Brit fig*) rabattre de ses prétentions

climb-down [ˈklaɪmdaun] *n* (*Brit*) reculade *f*

climber [ˈklaɪməʳ] *n* (*also:* **rock ~**) grimpeur(-euse), varappeur(-euse); (*plant*) plante grimpante

climbing [ˈklaɪmɪŋ] *n* (*also:* **rock ~**) escalade *f*, varappe *f*

clinch [klɪntʃ] *vt* (*deal*) conclure, sceller

cling (*pt, pp* **clung**) [klɪŋ, klʌŋ] *vi*: **to ~ (to)** se cramponner (à), s'accrocher (à); (*clothes*) coller (à)

Clingfilm® [ˈklɪŋfɪlm] *n* film *m* alimentaire

clinic [ˈklɪnɪk] *n* clinique *f*; centre médical; (*session*: *Med*) consultation(s) *f(pl)*, séance(s) *f(pl)*; (*Sport*) séance(s) de perfectionnement

clinical [ˈklɪnɪkl] *adj* clinique; (*fig*) froid(e)

clink [klɪŋk] *vi* tinter, cliqueter

clip [klɪp] n (for hair) barrette f; (also: **paper ~**) trombone m; (Brit: also: **bulldog ~**) pince f de bureau; (holding hose etc) collier m or bague f (métallique) de serrage; (TV, Cine) clip m ▷ vt (also: **~ together**: papers) attacher; (hair, nails) couper; (hedge) tailler

clippers ['klɪpəz] npl tondeuse f; (also: **nail ~**) coupe-ongles m inv

clipping ['klɪpɪŋ] n (from newspaper) coupure f de journal

cloak [kləuk] n grande cape ▷ vt (fig) masquer, cacher

cloakroom ['kləukrum] n (for coats etc) vestiaire m; (Brit: W.C.) toilettes fpl

clock [klɔk] n (large) horloge f; (small) pendule f; **round the ~** (work etc) vingt-quatre heures sur vingt-quatre; **to sleep round the ~** or **the ~ round** faire le tour du cadran; **30,000 on the ~** (Brit Aut) 30 000 milles au compteur; **to work against the ~** faire la course contre la montre; **clock in** or **on** (Brit) vi (with card) pointer (en arrivant); (start work) commencer à travailler; **clock off** or **out** (Brit) vi (with card) pointer (en partant); (leave work) quitter le travail; **clock up** vt (miles, hours etc) faire

clockwise ['klɔkwaɪz] adv dans le sens des aiguilles d'une montre

clockwork ['klɔkwə:k] n rouages mpl, mécanisme m; (of clock) mouvement m (d'horlogerie) ▷ adj (toy, train) mécanique

clog [klɔg] n sabot m ▷ vt boucher, encrasser ▷ vi (also: **~ up**) se boucher, s'encrasser

cloister ['klɔɪstər] n cloître m

clone [kləun] n clone m ▷ vt cloner

close¹ [kləus] adj (near): ~ **(to)** près (de), proche (de); (writing, texture) serré(e); (contact, link, watch) étroit(e); (examination) attentif(-ive), minutieux(-euse); (contest) très serré(e); (weather) lourd(e), étouffant(e); (room) mal aéré(e) ▷ adv près, à proximité; ~ **to** prep près de; ~ **by**, ~ **at hand** adj, adv tout(e) près; **how ~ is Edinburgh to Glasgow?** combien de kilomètres y-a-t-il entre Édimbourg et Glasgow?; **a ~ friend** un ami intime; **to have a ~ shave** (fig) l'échapper belle; **at ~ quarters** tout près, à côté

close² [kləuz] vt fermer; (bargain, deal) conclure ▷ vi (shop etc) fermer; (lid, door etc) se fermer; (end) se terminer, se conclure ▷ n (end) conclusion f; **to bring sth to a ~** mettre fin à qch; **what time do you ~?** à quelle heure fermez-vous?; **close down** vt, vi fermer (définitivement); **close in** vi (hunters) approcher; (night, fog) tomber; **the days are closing in** les jours raccourcissent; **to ~ in on sb** cerner qn; **close up** vt (area) boucler

closed [kləuzd] adj (shop etc) fermé(e); (road) fermé à la circulation

closed shop n organisation f qui n'admet que des travailleurs syndiqués

close-knit ['kləus'nɪt] adj (family, community) très uni(e)

closely ['kləuslɪ] adv (examine, watch) de près; **we are ~ related** nous sommes proches parents; **a ~ guarded secret** un secret bien gardé

closet ['klɔzɪt] n (cupboard) placard m, réduit m

close-up ['kləusʌp] n gros plan

closing time n heure f de fermeture

closure ['kləuʒər] n fermeture f

clot [klɔt] n (of blood, milk) caillot m; (inf: person) ballot m ▷ vi (blood) former des caillots; (: external bleeding) se coaguler

cloth [klɔθ] n (material) tissu m, étoffe f; (Brit: also: **tea ~**) torchon m; lavette f; (also: **table~**) nappe f

clothe [kləuð] vt habiller, vêtir

clothes [kləuðz] npl vêtements mpl, habits mpl; **to put one's ~ on** s'habiller; **to take one's ~ off** enlever ses vêtements

clothes brush n brosse f à habits

clothes line n corde f (à linge)

clothes peg, (US) **clothes pin** n pince f à linge

clothing ['kləuðɪŋ] n = **clothes**

cloud [klaud] n nuage m ▷ vt (liquid) troubler; **to ~ the issue** brouiller les cartes; **every ~ has a silver lining** (proverb) à quelque chose malheur est bon (proverbe); **cloud over** vi se couvrir; (fig) s'assombrir

cloudburst ['klaudbə:st] n violente averse

cloudy ['klaudɪ] adj nuageux(-euse), couvert(e); (liquid) trouble

clout [klaut] n (blow) taloche f; (fig) pouvoir m ▷ vt flanquer une taloche à

clove [kləuv] n clou m de girofle; **a ~ of garlic** une gousse d'ail

clover ['kləuvər] n trèfle m

clown [klaun] n clown m ▷ vi (also: **~ about**, **~ around**) faire le clown

cloying ['klɔɪɪŋ] adj (taste, smell) écœurant(e)

club [klʌb] n (society) club m; (weapon) massue f, matraque f; (also: **golf ~**) club ▷ vt matraquer ▷ vi: **to ~ together** s'associer; **clubs** npl (Cards) trèfle m

club class n (Aviat) classe f club

clubhouse ['klʌbhaus] n pavillon m

cluck [klʌk] vi glousser

clue [klu:] n indice m; (in crosswords) définition f; **I haven't a ~** je n'en ai pas la moindre idée

clump [klʌmp] n: **~ of trees** bouquet m d'arbres

clumsy ['klʌmzɪ] adj (person) gauche, maladroit(e); (object) malcommode, peu maniable

clung [klʌŋ] pt, pp of **cling**

cluster ['klʌstər] n (petit) groupe m; (of flowers) grappe f ▷ vi se rassembler

clutch [klʌtʃ] n (Aut) embrayage m; (grasp): **~es** étreinte f, prise f ▷ vt (grasp) agripper; (hold tightly) serrer fort; (hold on to) se cramponner à

clutter ['klʌtər] vt (also: **~ up**) encombrer ▷ n désordre m, fouillis m

cm *abbr* (= *centimetre*) cm
CND *n abbr* = **Campaign for Nuclear Disarmament**
Co. *abbr* = **company, county**
c/o *abbr* (= *care of*) c/o, aux bons soins de
coach [kəutʃ] *n* (*bus*) autocar *m*; (*horse-drawn*) diligence *f*; (*of train*) voiture *f*, wagon *m*; (*Sport: trainer*) entraîneur(-euse); (*school: tutor*) répétiteur(-trice) ▷ *vt* (*Sport*) entraîner; (*student*) donner des leçons particulières à
coach station (*Brit*) *n* gare routière
coach trip *n* excursion *f* en car
coal [kəul] *n* charbon *m*
coal face *n* front *m* de taille
coalfield ['kəulfiːld] *n* bassin houiller
coalition [kəuə'lɪʃən] *n* coalition *f*
coalman ['kəulmən] *irreg n* charbonnier *m*, marchand *m* de charbon
coal mine *n* mine *f* de charbon
coarse [kɔːs] *adj* grossier(-ère), rude; (*vulgar*) vulgaire
coast [kəust] *n* côte *f* ▷ *vi* (*car, cycle*) descendre en roue libre
coastal ['kəustl] *adj* côtier(-ère)
coastguard ['kəustgaːd] *n* garde-côte *m*
coastline ['kəustlaɪn] *n* côte *f*, littoral *m*
coat [kəut] *n* manteau *m*; (*of animal*) pelage *m*, poil *m*; (*of paint*) couche *f* ▷ *vt* couvrir, enduire; **~ of arms** blason *m*, armoiries *fpl*
coat hanger *n* cintre *m*
coating ['kəutɪŋ] *n* couche *f*, enduit *m*
coax [kəuks] *vt* persuader par des cajoleries
cob [kɔb] *n see* **corn**
cobbled ['kɔbld] *adj* pavé(e)
cobbler ['kɔblə'] *n* cordonnier *m*
cobbles, cobblestones ['kɔblz, 'kɔblstəunz] *npl* pavés (ronds)
cobweb ['kɔbweb] *n* toile *f* d'araignée
cocaine [kə'keɪn] *n* cocaïne *f*
cock [kɔk] *n* (*rooster*) coq *m*; (*male bird*) mâle *m* ▷ *vt* (*gun*) armer; **to ~ one's ears** (*fig*) dresser l'oreille
cockerel ['kɔkərl] *n* jeune coq *m*
cockle ['kɔkl] *n* coque *f*
cockney ['kɔknɪ] *n* cockney *m/f* (*habitant des quartiers populaires de l'East End de Londres*), ≈ faubourien(ne)
cockpit ['kɔkpɪt] *n* (*in aircraft*) poste *m* de pilotage, cockpit *m*
cockroach ['kɔkrəutʃ] *n* cafard *m*, cancrelat *m*
cocktail ['kɔkteɪl] *n* cocktail *m*; **prawn ~**, (*US*) **shrimp ~** cocktail de crevettes
cocktail cabinet *n* (*meuble-*)bar *m*
cocktail party *n* cocktail *m*
cocoa ['kəukəu] *n* cacao *m*
coconut ['kəukənʌt] *n* noix *f* de coco
C.O.D. *abbr* = **cash on delivery**; (*US*) = **collect on delivery**
cod [kɔd] *n* morue fraîche, cabillaud *m*
code [kəud] *n* code *m*; (*Tel: area code*) indicatif *m*; **~ of behaviour** règles *fpl* de conduite; **~ of practice** déontologie *f*

cod-liver oil ['kɔdlɪvər-] *n* huile *f* de foie de morue
coeducational ['kəuedju'keɪʃənl] *adj* mixte
coercion [kəu'əːʃən] *n* contrainte *f*
coffee ['kɔfɪ] *n* café *m*; **white ~**, (*US*) **~ with cream** (café-)crème *m*
coffee bar *n* (*Brit*) café *m*
coffee bean *n* grain *m* de café
coffee break *n* pause-café *f*
coffee maker *n* cafetière *f*
coffeepot ['kɔfɪpɔt] *n* cafetière *f*
coffee shop *n* café *m*
coffee table *n* (petite) table basse
coffin ['kɔfɪn] *n* cercueil *m*
cog [kɔg] *n* (*wheel*) roue dentée; (*tooth*) dent *f* (d'engrenage)
cogent ['kəudʒənt] *adj* puissant(e), convaincant(e)
cognac ['kɔnjæk] *n* cognac *m*
coherent [kəu'hɪərənt] *adj* cohérent(e)
coil [kɔɪl] *n* rouleau *m*, bobine *f*; (*one loop*) anneau *m*, spire *f*; (*of smoke*) volute *f*; (*contraceptive*) stérilet *m* ▷ *vt* enrouler
coin [kɔɪn] *n* pièce *f* (de monnaie) ▷ *vt* (*word*) inventer
coinage ['kɔɪnɪdʒ] *n* monnaie *f*, système *m* monétaire
coinbox ['kɔɪnbɔks] *n* (*Brit*) cabine *f* téléphonique
coincide [kəuɪn'saɪd] *vi* coïncider
coincidence [kəu'ɪnsɪdəns] *n* coïncidence *f*
Coke® [kəuk] *n* coca *m*
coke [kəuk] *n* (*coal*) coke *m*
colander ['kɔləndər] *n* passoire *f* (à légumes)
cold [kəuld] *adj* froid(e) ▷ *n* froid *m*; (*Med*) rhume *m*; **it's ~** il fait froid; **to be ~** (*person*) avoir froid; **to catch ~** prendre *or* attraper froid; **to catch a ~** s'enrhumer, attraper un rhume; **in ~ blood** de sang-froid; **to have ~ feet** avoir froid aux pieds; (*fig*) avoir la frousse *or* la trouille; **to give sb the ~ shoulder** battre froid à qn
cold sore *n* bouton *m* de fièvre
coleslaw ['kəulslɔː] *n* sorte de salade de chou cru
colic ['kɔlɪk] *n* colique(s) *f(pl)*
collaborate [kə'læbəreɪt] *vi* collaborer
collapse [kə'læps] *vi* s'effondrer, s'écrouler; (*Med*) avoir un malaise ▷ *n* effondrement *m*, écroulement *m*; (*of government*) chute *f*
collapsible [kə'læpsəbl] *adj* pliant(e), télescopique
collar ['kɔlər] *n* (*of coat, shirt*) col *m*; (*for dog*) collier *m*; (*Tech*) collier, bague *f* ▷ *vt* (*inf: person*) pincer
collarbone ['kɔləbəun] *n* clavicule *f*
collateral [kə'lætərl] *n* nantissement *m*
colleague ['kɔliːg] *n* collègue *m/f*
collect [kə'lekt] *vt* rassembler; (*pick up*) ramasser; (*as a hobby*) collectionner; (*Brit: call for*) (passer) prendre; (*mail*) faire la levée de, ramasser; (*money owed*) encaisser; (*donations, subscriptions*) recueillir ▷ *vi* (*people*) se

rassembler; (dust, dirt) s'amasser; **to ~ one's thoughts** réfléchir, réunir ses idées; **~ on delivery (COD)** (US Comm) payable or paiement à la livraison; **to call ~** (US Tel) téléphoner en PCV

collection [kə'lekʃən] n collection f; (of mail) levée f; (for money) collecte f, quête f

collective [kə'lektɪv] adj collectif(-ive) ▷ n collectif m

collector [kə'lektə'] n collectionneur m; (of taxes) percepteur m; (of rent, cash) encaisseur m; **~'s item** or **piece** pièce f de collection

college ['kɔlɪdʒ] n collège m; (of technology, agriculture etc) institut m; **to go to ~** faire des études supérieures; **~ of education** = école normale

collide [kə'laɪd] vi: **to ~ (with)** entrer en collision (avec)

colliery ['kɔlɪərɪ] n (Brit) mine f de charbon, houillère f

collision [kə'lɪʒən] n collision f, heurt m; **to be on a ~ course** aller droit à la collision; (fig) aller vers l'affrontement

colloquial [kə'ləukwɪəl] adj familier(-ère)

cologne [kə'ləun] n (also: **eau de ~**) eau f de cologne

colon ['kəulən] n (sign) deux-points mpl; (Med) côlon m

colonel ['kə:nl] n colonel m

colonial [kə'ləunɪəl] adj colonial(e)

colony ['kɔlənɪ] n colonie f

colour, (US) **color** ['kʌlə'] n couleur f ▷ vt colorer; (dye) teindre; (paint) peindre; (with crayons) colorier; (news) fausser, exagérer ▷ vi (blush) rougir ▷ cpd (film, photograph, television) en couleur; **colours** npl (of party, club) couleurs fpl; **I'd like a different ~** je le voudrais dans un autre coloris; **colour in** vt colorier

colour bar, (US) **color bar** n discrimination raciale (dans un établissement etc)

colour-blind, (US) **color-blind** ['kʌləblaɪnd] adj daltonien(ne)

coloured, (US) **colored** ['kʌləd] adj coloré(e); (photo) en couleur

colour film, (US) **color film** n (for camera) pellicule f (en) couleur

colourful, (US) **colorful** ['kʌləful] adj coloré(e), vif/vive; (personality) pittoresque, haut(e) en couleurs

colouring, (US) **coloring** ['kʌlərɪŋ] n colorant m; (complexion) teint m

colour scheme, (US) **color scheme** n combinaison f de(s) couleur(s)

colour television, (US) **color television** n télévision f (en) couleur

colt [kəult] n poulain m

column ['kɔləm] n colonne f; (fashion column, sports column etc) rubrique f; **the editorial ~** l'éditorial m

columnist ['kɔləmnɪst] n rédacteur(-trice) d'une rubrique

coma ['kəumə] n coma m

comb [kəum] n peigne m ▷ vt (hair) peigner; (area) ratisser, passer au peigne fin

combat ['kɔmbæt] n combat m ▷ vt combattre, lutter contre

combination [kɔmbɪ'neɪʃən] n (gen) combinaison f

combine [kəm'baɪn] vt combiner ▷ vi s'associer; (Chem) se combiner ▷ n ['kɔmbaɪn] association f; (Econ) trust m; (also: **~ harvester**) moissonneuse-batteuse (-lieuse) f; **to ~ sth with sth** (one quality with another) joindre ou allier qch à qch; **a ~d effort** un effort conjugué

combine harvester n moissonneuse-batteuse(-lieuse) f

KEYWORD

come (pt **came**, pp **come**) [kʌm, keɪm] vi **1** (movement towards) venir; **to come running** arriver en courant; **he's come here to work** il est venu ici pour travailler; **come with me** suivez-moi; **to come into sight** or **view** apparaître

2 (arrive) arriver; **to come home** rentrer (chez soi ou à la maison); **we've just come from Paris** nous arrivons de Paris; **coming!** j'arrive!

3 (reach): **to come to** (decision etc) parvenir à, arriver à; **the bill came to £40** la note s'est élevée à 40 livres; **if it comes to it** s'il le faut, dans le pire des cas

4 (occur): **an idea came to me** il m'est venu une idée; **what might come of it** ce qui pourrait en résulter, ce qui pourrait advenir or se produire

5 (be, become): **to come loose/undone** se défaire/desserrer; **I've come to like him** j'ai fini par bien l'aimer

6 (inf: sexually) jouir

come about vi se produire, arriver

come across vt fus rencontrer par hasard, tomber sur ▷ vi: **to come across well/badly** faire une bonne/mauvaise impression

come along vi (Brit: pupil, work) faire des progrès, avancer; **come along!** viens!; allons!, allez!

come apart vi s'en aller en morceaux; se détacher

come away vi partir, s'en aller; (become detached) se détacher

come back vi revenir; (reply): **can I come back to you on that one?** est-ce qu'on peut revenir là-dessus plus tard?

come by vt fus (acquire) obtenir, se procurer

come down vi descendre; (prices) baisser; (buildings) s'écrouler; (: be demolished) être démoli(e)

come forward vi s'avancer; (make o.s. known) se présenter, s'annoncer

come from vt fus (source) venir de; (place) venir de, être originaire de

come in vi entrer; (train) arriver; (fashion) entrer en vogue; (on deal etc) participer

come in for vt fus (criticism etc) être l'objet de

come into vt fus (money) hériter de

come off vi (button) se détacher; (attempt) réussir

come on vi (lights, electricity) s'allumer; (central heating) se mettre en marche; (pupil, work, project) faire des progrès, avancer; **come on!** viens!; allons!, allez!

come out vi sortir; (sun) se montrer; (book) paraître; (stain) s'enlever; (strike) cesser le travail, se mettre en grève

come over vt fus: **I don't know what's come over him!** je ne sais pas ce qui lui a pris!

come round vi (after faint, operation) revenir à soi, reprendre connaissance

come through vi (survive) s'en sortir; (telephone call): **the call came through** l'appel est bien parvenu

come to vi revenir à soi ▷ vt (add up to: amount): **how much does it come to?** ça fait combien?

come under vt fus (heading) se trouver sous; (influence) subir

come up vi monter; (sun) se lever; (problem) se poser; (event) survenir; (in conversation) être soulevé

come up against vt fus (resistance, difficulties) rencontrer

come upon vt fus tomber sur

come up to vt fus arriver à; **the film didn't come up to our expectations** le film nous a déçu

come up with vt fus (money) fournir; **he came up with an idea** il a eu une idée, il a proposé quelque chose

comeback ['kʌmbæk] n (Theat) rentrée f; (reaction) réaction f; (response) réponse f

comedian [kə'miːdɪən] n (comic) comique m; (Theat) comédien m

comedy ['kɒmɪdɪ] n comédie f; (humour) comique m

comet ['kɒmɪt] n comète f

comeuppance [kʌm'ʌpəns] n: **to get one's ~** recevoir ce qu'on mérite

comfort ['kʌmfət] n confort m, bien-être m; (solace) consolation f, réconfort m ▷ vt consoler, réconforter

comfortable ['kʌmfətəbl] adj confortable; (person) à l'aise; (financially) aisé(e); (patient) dont l'état est stationnaire; **I don't feel very ~ about it** cela m'inquiète un peu

comfortably ['kʌmfətəblɪ] adv (sit) confortablement; (live) à l'aise

comfort station n (US) toilettes fpl

comic ['kɒmɪk] adj (also: **~al**) comique ▷ n (person) comique m; (Brit: magazine: for children) magazine m de bandes dessinées or de BD; (: for adults) illustré m

comic book (US) n (for children) magazine m de bandes dessinées or de BD; (for adults) illustré m

comic strip n bande dessinée

coming ['kʌmɪŋ] n arrivée f ▷ adj (next) prochain(e); (future) à venir; **in the ~ weeks** dans les prochaines semaines

comma ['kɒmə] n virgule f

command [kə'mɑːnd] n ordre m, commandement m; (Mil: authority) commandement; (mastery) maîtrise f; (Comput) commande f ▷ vt (troops) commander; (be able to get) (pouvoir) disposer de, avoir à sa disposition; (deserve) avoir droit à; **to ~ sb to do** donner l'ordre or commander à qn de faire; **to have/take ~ of** avoir/prendre le commandement de; **to have at one's ~** (money, resources etc) disposer de

commandeer [kɒmən'dɪər] vt réquisitionner (par la force)

commander [kə'mɑːndər] n chef m; (Mil) commandant m

commando [kə'mɑːndəu] n commando m; membre m d'un commando

commemorate [kə'meməreɪt] vt commémorer

commence [kə'mens] vt, vi commencer

commend [kə'mend] vt louer; (recommend) recommander

commensurate [kə'menʃərɪt] adj: **~ with/to** en rapport avec/selon

comment ['kɒment] n commentaire m ▷ vi faire des remarques or commentaires; **to ~ on** faire des remarques sur; **to ~ that** faire remarquer que; **"no ~"** "je n'ai rien à déclarer"

commentary ['kɒmentərɪ] n commentaire m; (Sport) reportage m (en direct)

commentator ['kɒmenteɪtər] n commentateur m; (Sport) reporter m

commerce ['kɒməːs] n commerce m

commercial [kə'məːʃəl] adj commercial(e) ▷ n (Radio, TV) annonce f publicitaire, spot m (publicitaire)

commercial break n (Radio, TV) spot m (publicitaire)

commiserate [kə'mɪzəreɪt] vi: **to ~ with sb** témoigner de la sympathie pour qn

commission [kə'mɪʃən] n (committee, fee) commission f; (order for work of art etc) commande f ▷ vt (Mil) nommer (à un commandement); (work of art) commander, charger un artiste de l'exécution de; **out of ~** (Naut) hors de service; (machine) hors service; **I get 10%** ~ je reçois une commission de 10%; **~ of inquiry** (Brit) commission d'enquête

commissionaire [kəmɪʃə'nɛər] n (Brit: at shop, cinema etc) portier m (en uniforme)

commissioner [kə'mɪʃənər] n membre m d'une commission; (Police) préfet m (de police)

commit [kə'mɪt] vt (act) commettre;
(resources) consacrer; (to sb's care) confier (à); **to
~ o.s. (to do)** s'engager (à faire); **to ~ suicide**
se suicider; **to ~ to writing** coucher par écrit;
to ~ sb for trial traduire qn en justice

commitment [kə'mɪtmənt] n engagement
m; (obligation) responsabilité(s) (fpl)

committee [kə'mɪtɪ] n comité m;
commission f; **to be on a ~** siéger dans un
comité or une commission)

commodity [kə'mɔdɪtɪ] n produit m,
marchandise f, article m; (food) denrée f

common ['kɔmən] adj (gen) commun(e);
(usual) courant(e) ▷ n terrain communal; **in ~**
en commun; **in ~ use** d'un usage courant;
it's ~ knowledge that il est bien connu or
notoire que; **to the ~ good** pour le bien de
tous, dans l'intérêt général

commoner ['kɔmənəʳ] n roturier(-ière)

common law n droit coutumier

commonly ['kɔmənlɪ] adv communément,
généralement; couramment

Common Market n Marché commun

commonplace ['kɔmənpleɪs] adj banal(e),
ordinaire

common room n salle commune; (Scol) salle
des professeurs

Commons ['kɔmənz] npl (Brit Pol): **the
(House of) ~** la chambre des Communes

common sense n bon sens

Commonwealth ['kɔmənwɛlθ] n: **the ~** le
Commonwealth; voir article

commotion [kə'məuʃən] n désordre m,
tumulte m

communal ['kɔmju:nl] adj (life)
communautaire; (for common use) commun(e)

commune ['kɔmju:n] n (group)
communauté f ▷ vi [kə'mju:n]: **to ~ with**
(nature) converser intimement avec;
communier avec

communicate [kə'mju:nɪkeɪt] vt
communiquer, transmettre ▷ vi: **to ~ (with)**
communiquer (avec)

communication [kəmju:nɪ'keɪʃən] n
communication f

communication cord n (Brit) sonnette f
d'alarme

communion [kə'mju:nɪən] n (also: **Holy C~**)
communion f

communism ['kɔmjunɪzəm] n
communisme m

communist ['kɔmjunɪst] adj, n
communiste m/f

community [kə'mju:nɪtɪ] n communauté f

community centre, (US) **community
center** n foyer socio-éducatif, centre m de
loisirs

community chest n (US) fonds commun

community service n ≈ travail m d'intérêt
général, TIG m

commutation ticket [kɔmju'teɪʃən-] n (US)
carte f d'abonnement

commute [kə'mju:t] vi faire le trajet
journalier (de son domicile à un lieu de travail assez
éloigné) ▷ vt (Law) commuer; (Math: terms etc)
opérer la commutation de

commuter [kə'mju:təʳ] n banlieusard(e) (qui
fait un trajet journalier pour se rendre à son travail)

compact adj [kəm'pækt] compact(e) ▷ n
['kɔmpækt] contrat m, entente f; (also:
powder ~) poudrier m

compact disc n disque compact

compact disc player, n lecteur m de disques
compacts

companion [kəm'pænjən] n compagnon/
compagne

companionship [kəm'pænjənʃɪp] n
camaraderie f

company ['kʌmpənɪ] n (also Comm, Mil, Theat)
compagnie f; **he's good ~** il est d'une
compagnie agréable; **we have ~** nous avons
de la visite; **to keep sb ~** tenir compagnie à
qn; **to part ~ with** se séparer de; **Smith and
C~** Smith et Compagnie

company car n voiture f de fonction

company director n administrateur(-trice)

company secretary n (Brit Comm) secrétaire
général (d'une société)

comparable ['kɔmpərəbl] adj comparable

comparative [kəm'pærətɪv] adj (study)
comparatif(-ive); (relative) relatif(-ive)

comparatively [kəm'pærətɪvlɪ] adv
(relatively) relativement

compare [kəm'pɛəʳ] vt: **to ~ sth/sb with** or **to**
comparer qch/qn avec or à ▷ vi: **to ~ (with)** se
comparer (à); être comparable (à); **how do
the prices ~?** comment sont les prix?, est-ce
que les prix sont comparables?; **~d with** or **to**
par rapport à

comparison [kəm'pærɪsn] n comparaison f;
in ~ (with) en comparaison (de)

compartment [kəm'pɑ:tmənt] n (also Rail)
compartiment m; **a non-smoking ~** un
compartiment non-fumeurs

compass ['kʌmpəs] n boussole f; **compasses**
npl (Math) compas m; **within the ~ of** dans
les limites de

compassion [kəm'pæʃən] n compassion f,
humanité f

compassionate [kəm'pæʃənɪt] adj
accessible à la compassion, au cœur
charitable et bienveillant; **on ~ grounds**
pour raisons personnelles or de famille

compatible [kəm'pætɪbl] adj compatible

compel [kəm'pɛl] vt contraindre, obliger

compelling [kəm'pɛlɪŋ] adj (fig: argument)
irrésistible

compensate ['kɔmpənseɪt] vt indemniser,
dédommager ▷ vi: **to ~ for** compenser

compensation [kɔmpən'seɪʃən] n
compensation f; (money) dédommagement
m, indemnité f

compere ['kɔmpɛəʳ] n présentateur(-trice),
animateur(-trice)

compete [kəm'pi:t] vi (take part) concourir; (vie): **to ~ (with)** rivaliser (avec), faire concurrence (à)

competent ['kɔmpɪtənt] adj compétent(e), capable

competition [kɔmpɪ'tɪʃən] n (contest) compétition f, concours m; (Econ) concurrence f; **in ~ with** en concurrence avec

competitive [kəm'pɛtɪtɪv] adj (Econ) concurrentiel(le); (sports) de compétition; (person) qui a l'esprit de compétition

competitor [kəm'pɛtɪtər] n concurrent(e)

complacency [kəm'pleɪsnsɪ] n contentement m de soi, autosatisfaction f

complacent [kəm'pleɪsnt] adj (trop) content(e) de soi

complain [kəm'pleɪn] vi: **to ~ (about)** se plaindre (de); (in shop etc) réclamer (au sujet de); **complain of** vt fus (Med) se plaindre de

complaint [kəm'pleɪnt] n plainte f; (in shop etc) réclamation f; (Med) affection f

complement ['kɔmplɪmənt] n complément m; (esp of ship's crew etc) effectif complet ▷ vt (enhance) compléter

complementary [kɔmplɪ'mɛntərɪ] adj complémentaire

complete [kəm'pli:t] adj complet(-ète); (finished) achevé(e) ▷ vt achever, parachever; (set, group) compléter; (a form) remplir

completely [kəm'pli:tlɪ] adv complètement

completion [kəm'pli:ʃən] n achèvement m; (of contract) exécution f; **to be nearing ~** être presque terminé

complex ['kɔmplɛks] adj complexe ▷ n (Psych, buildings etc) complexe m

complexion [kəm'plɛkʃən] n (of face) teint m; (of event etc) aspect m, caractère m

compliance [kəm'plaɪəns] n (submission) docilité f; (agreement): **~ with** le fait de se conformer à; **in ~ with** en conformité avec, conformément à

complicate ['kɔmplɪkeɪt] vt compliquer

complicated ['kɔmplɪkeɪtɪd] adj compliqué(e)

complication [kɔmplɪ'keɪʃən] n complication f

compliment n ['kɔmplɪmənt] compliment m ▷ vt ['kɔmplɪmɛnt] complimenter; **compliments** npl compliments mpl, hommages mpl; vœux mpl; **to pay sb a ~** faire or adresser un compliment à qn; **to ~ sb (on sth/on doing sth)** féliciter qn (pour qch/de faire qch)

complimentary [kɔmplɪ'mɛntərɪ] adj flatteur(-euse); (free) à titre gracieux

complimentary ticket n billet m de faveur

comply [kəm'plaɪ] vi: **to ~ with** se soumettre à, se conformer à

component [kəm'pəunənt] adj composant(e), constituant(e) ▷ n composant m, élément m

compose [kəm'pəuz] vt composer; (form): **to be ~d of** se composer de; **to ~ o.s.** se calmer, se maîtriser; **to ~ one's features** prendre une contenance

composed [kəm'pəuzd] adj calme, posé(e)

composer [kəm'pəuzər] n (Mus) compositeur m

composition [kɔmpə'zɪʃən] n composition f

composure [kəm'pəuʒər] n calme m, maîtrise f de soi

compound ['kɔmpaund] n (Chem, Ling) composé m; (enclosure) enclos m, enceinte f ▷ adj composé(e); (fracture) compliqué(e) ▷ vt [kəm'paund] (fig: problem etc) aggraver

compound fracture n fracture compliquée

compound interest n intérêt composé

comprehend [kɔmprɪ'hɛnd] vt comprendre

comprehension [kɔmprɪ'hɛnʃən] n compréhension f

comprehensive [kɔmprɪ'hɛnsɪv] adj (très) complet(-ète); **~ policy** (Insurance) assurance f tous risques

comprehensive [kɔmprɪ'hɛnsɪv], **comprehensive school** n (Brit) école secondaire non sélective avec libre circulation d'une section à l'autre, ≈ CES m

compress vt [kəm'prɛs] comprimer; (text, information) condenser ▷ n ['kɔmprɛs] (Med) compresse f

comprise [kəm'praɪz] vt (also: **be ~d of**) comprendre; (constitute) constituer, représenter

compromise ['kɔmprəmaɪz] n compromis m ▷ vt compromettre ▷ vi transiger, accepter un compromis ▷ cpd (decision, solution) de compromis

compulsion [kəm'pʌlʃən] n contrainte f, force f; **under ~** sous la contrainte

compulsive [kəm'pʌlsɪv] adj (Psych) compulsif(-ive); (book, film etc) captivant(e); **he's a ~ smoker** c'est un fumeur invétéré

compulsory [kəm'pʌlsərɪ] adj obligatoire

computer [kəm'pju:tər] n ordinateur m; (mechanical) calculatrice f

computer game n jeu m vidéo

computer-generated [kəm'pju:tə-'dʒɛnəreɪtɪd] adj de synthèse

computerize [kəm'pju:təraɪz] vt (data) traiter par ordinateur; (system, office) informatiser

computer programmer n programmeur(-euse)

computer programming n programmation f

computer science n informatique f

computer studies npl informatique f

computing [kəm'pju:tɪŋ] n informatique f

comrade ['kɔmrɪd] n camarade m/f

con [kɔn] vt duper; (cheat) escroquer ▷ n escroquerie f; **to ~ sb into doing sth** tromper qn pour lui faire faire qch

conceal [kən'si:l] vt cacher, dissimuler

concede [kən'si:d] vt concéder ▷ vi céder
conceit [kən'si:t] n vanité f, suffisance f, prétention f
conceited [kən'si:tɪd] adj vaniteux(-euse), suffisant(e)
conceive [kən'si:v] vt, vi concevoir; **to ~ of sth/of doing sth** imaginer qch/de faire qch
concentrate ['kɔnsəntreɪt] vi se concentrer ▷ vt concentrer
concentration [kɔnsən'treɪʃən] n concentration f
concentration camp n camp m de concentration
concept ['kɔnsɛpt] n concept m
concern [kən'sə:n] n affaire f, (Comm) entreprise f, firme f, (anxiety) inquiétude f, souci m ▷ vt (worry) inquiéter; (involve) concerner; (relate to) se rapporter à; **to be ~ed (about)** s'inquiéter (de), être inquiet(-ète) (au sujet de); **"to whom it may ~"** "à qui de droit"; **as far as I am ~ed** en ce qui me concerne; **to be ~ed with** (person: involved with) s'occuper de; **the department ~ed** (under discussion) le service en question; (involved) le service concerné
concerning [kən'sə:nɪŋ] prep en ce qui concerne, à propos de
concert ['kɔnsət] n concert m; **in ~** à l'unisson, en chœur; ensemble
concerted [kən'sə:tɪd] adj concerté(e)
concert hall n salle f de concert
concerto [kən'tʃə:təu] n concerto m
concession [kən'sɛʃən] n (compromise) concession f; (reduced price) réduction f; **tax ~** dégrèvement fiscal; **"~s"** tarif réduit
concise [kən'saɪs] adj concis(e)
conclude [kən'klu:d] vt conclure ▷ vi (speaker) conclure; (events): **to ~ (with)** se terminer (par)
conclusion [kən'klu:ʒən] n conclusion f; **to come to the ~ that** (en) conclure que
conclusive [kən'klu:sɪv] adj concluant(e), définitif(-ive)
concoct [kən'kɔkt] vt confectionner, composer
concoction [kən'kɔkʃən] n (food, drink) mélange m
concourse ['kɔŋkɔ:s] n (hall) hall m, salle f des pas perdus; (crowd) affluence f; multitude f
concrete ['kɔŋkri:t] n béton m ▷ adj concret(-ète); (Constr) en béton
concur [kən'sə:r] vi être d'accord
concurrently [kən'kʌrntlɪ] adv simultanément
concussion [kən'kʌʃən] n (Med) commotion (cérébrale)
condemn [kən'dɛm] vt condamner
condensation [kɔndɛn'seɪʃən] n condensation f
condense [kən'dɛns] vi se condenser ▷ vt condenser

condensed milk [kən'dɛnst-] n lait concentré (sucré)
condition [kən'dɪʃən] n condition f; (disease) maladie f ▷ vt déterminer, conditionner; **in good/poor ~** en bon/mauvais état; **a heart ~** une maladie cardiaque; **weather ~s** conditions fpl météorologiques; **on ~ that** à condition que + sub, à condition de
conditional [kən'dɪʃənl] adj conditionnel(le); **to be ~ upon** dépendre de
conditioner [kən'dɪʃənər] n (for hair) baume démêlant; (for fabrics) assouplissant m
condo ['kɔndəu] n (US inf) = condominium
condolences [kən'dəulənsɪz] npl condoléances fpl
condom ['kɔndəm] n préservatif m
condominium [kɔndə'mɪnɪəm] n (US: building) immeuble m (en copropriété); (: rooms) appartement m (dans un immeuble en copropriété)
condone [kən'dəun] vt fermer les yeux sur, approuver (tacitement)
conducive [kən'dju:sɪv] adj: **~ to** favorable à, qui contribue à
conduct n ['kɔndʌkt] conduite f ▷ vt [kə n'dʌkt] conduire; (manage) mener, diriger; (Mus) diriger; **to ~ o.s.** se conduire, se comporter
conductor [kən'dʌktər] n (of orchestra) chef m d'orchestre; (on bus) receveur m; (US: on train) chef m de train; (Elec) conducteur m
conductress [kən'dʌktrɪs] n (on bus) receveuse f
cone [kəun] n cône m; (for ice-cream) cornet m; (Bot) pomme f de pin, cône
confectioner [kən'fɛkʃənər] n (of cakes) pâtissier(-ière); (of sweets) confiseur(-euse); **~'s (shop)** confiserie(-pâtisserie) f
confectionery [kən'fɛkʃənrɪ] n (sweets) confiserie f; (cakes) pâtisserie f
confer [kən'fə:r] vt: **to ~ sth on** conférer qch à ▷ vi conférer, s'entretenir; **to ~ (with sb about sth)** s'entretenir (de qch avec qn)
conference ['kɔnfərns] n conférence f; **to be in ~** être en réunion or en conférence
confess [kən'fɛs] vt confesser, avouer ▷ vi (admit sth) avouer; (Rel) se confesser
confession [kən'fɛʃən] n confession f
confetti [kən'fɛti] n confettis mpl
confide [kən'faɪd] vi: **to ~ in** s'ouvrir à, se confier à
confidence ['kɔnfɪdns] n confiance f; (also: **self-~**) assurance f, confiance en soi; (secret) confidence f; **to have (every) ~ that** être certain que; **motion of no ~** motion f de censure; **in ~** (speak, write) en confidence, confidentiellement; **to tell sb sth in strict ~** dire qch à qn en toute confidence
confidence trick n escroquerie f
confident ['kɔnfɪdənt] adj (self-assured) sûr(e) de soi; (sure) sûr

confidential [kɒnfɪ'dɛnʃəl] *adj*
confidentiel(le); (*secretary*) particulier(-ère)

confine [kən'faɪn] *vt* limiter, borner; (*shut up*)
confiner, enfermer; **to ~ o.s. to doing sth/to
sth** se contenter de faire qch/se limiter à qch

confined [kən'faɪnd] *adj* (*space*) restreint(e),
réduit(e)

confinement [kən'faɪnmənt] *n*
emprisonnement *m*, détention *f*; (*Mil*)
consigne *f* (au quartier); (*Med*)
accouchement *m*

confines ['kɒnfaɪnz] *npl* confins *mpl*,
bornes *fpl*

confirm [kən'fə:m] *vt* (*report, Rel*) confirmer;
(*appointment*) ratifier

confirmation [kɒnfə'meɪʃən] *n*
confirmation *f*; ratification *f*

confirmed [kən'fə:md] *adj* invétéré(e),
incorrigible

confiscate ['kɒnfɪskeɪt] *vt* confisquer

conflict *n* ['kɒnflɪkt] conflit *m*, lutte *f* ⊳ *vi*
[kən'flɪkt] être *or* entrer en conflit; (*opinions*)
s'opposer, se heurter

conflicting [kən'flɪktɪŋ] *adj* contradictoire

conform [kən'fɔ:m] *vi*: **to ~ (to)** se
conformer (à)

confound [kən'faund] *vt* confondre; (*amaze*)
rendre perplexe

confront [kən'frʌnt] *vt* (*two people*)
confronter; (*enemy, danger*) affronter, faire
face à; (*problem*) faire face à

confrontation [kɒnfrən'teɪʃən] *n*
confrontation *f*

confuse [kən'fju:z] *vt* (*person*) troubler;
(*situation*) embrouiller; (*one thing with another*)
confondre

confused [kən'fju:zd] *adj* (*person*) dérouté(e),
désorienté(e); (*situation*) embrouillé(e)

confusing [kən'fju:zɪŋ] *adj* peu clair(e),
déroutant(e)

confusion [kən'fju:ʒən] *n* confusion *f*

congeal [kən'dʒi:l] *vi* (*oil*) se figer; (*blood*) se
coaguler

congenial [kən'dʒi:nɪəl] *adj* sympathique,
agréable

congested [kən'dʒɛstɪd] *adj* (*Med*)
congestionné(e); (*fig*) surpeuplé(e);
congestionné; bloqué(e); (*telephone lines*)
encombré(e)

congestion [kən'dʒɛstʃən] *n* (*Med*)
congestion *f*; (*fig: traffic*) encombrement *m*

congratulate [kən'grætjuleɪt] *vt*: **to ~ sb
(on)** féliciter qn (de)

congratulations [kəngrætju'leɪʃənz] *npl*:
~ (on) félicitations *fpl* (pour) ⊳ *excl*: **~!** (toutes
mes) félicitations!

congregate ['kɒŋgrɪgeɪt] *vi* se rassembler,
se réunir

congregation [kɒŋgrɪ'geɪʃən] *n* assemblée *f*
(des fidèles)

congress ['kɒŋgrɛs] *n* congrès *m*; (*Pol*):
C~ Congrès *m*; *voir article*

◈ **CONGRESS**
◈
◈ Le *Congress* est le parlement des États-
◈ Unis. Il comprend la "House of
◈ Representatives" et le "Senate".
◈ Représentants et sénateurs sont élus au
◈ suffrage universel direct. Le Congrès se
◈ réunit au "Capitol", à Washington.

congressman ['kɒŋgrɛsmən] *irreg n* membre
m du Congrès

congresswoman ['kɒŋgrɛswumən] *irreg n*
membre *m* du Congrès

conifer ['kɒnɪfə'] *n* conifère *m*

conjugate ['kɒndʒugeɪt] *vt* conjuguer

conjugation [kɒndʒə'geɪʃən] *n*
conjugaison *f*

conjunction [kən'dʒʌŋkʃən] *n* conjonction *f*;
in ~ with (conjointement) avec

conjunctivitis [kəndʒʌŋktɪ'vaɪtɪs] *n*
conjonctivite *f*

conjure ['kʌndʒə'] *vt* faire apparaître (par la
prestidigitation); [kən'dʒuə'] conjurer,
supplier ⊳ *vi* faire des tours de passe-passe;
conjure up *vt* (*ghost, spirit*) faire apparaître;
(*memories*) évoquer

conjurer ['kʌndʒərə'] *n* prestidigitateur *m*,
illusionniste *m/f*

conman ['kɒnmæn] *irreg n* escroc *m*

connect [kə'nɛkt] *vt* joindre, relier; (*Elec*)
connecter; (*Tel: caller*) mettre en connexion;
(: *subscriber*) brancher; (*fig*) établir un rapport
entre, faire un rapprochement entre ⊳ *vi*
(*train*): **to ~ with** assurer la correspondance
avec; **to be ~ed with** avoir un rapport avec;
(*have dealings with*) avoir des rapports avec,
être en relation avec; **I am trying to ~ you**
(*Tel*) j'essaie d'obtenir votre communication

connecting flight *n* (vol *m* de)
correspondance *f*

connection [kə'nɛkʃən] *n* relation *f*, lien *m*;
(*Elec*) connexion *f*; (*Tel*) communication *f*;
(*train etc*) correspondance *f*; **in ~ with** à propos
de; **what is the ~ between them?** quel est le
lien entre eux?; **business ~s** relations
d'affaires; **to miss/get one's ~** (*train etc*)
rater/avoir sa correspondance

connive [kə'naɪv] *vi*: **to ~ at** se faire le
complice de

conquer ['kɒŋkə'] *vt* conquérir; (*feelings*)
vaincre, surmonter

conquest ['kɒŋkwɛst] *n* conquête *f*

cons [kɒnz] *npl see* **convenience**; **pro**

conscience ['kɒnʃəns] *n* conscience *f*; **in all ~**
en conscience

conscientious [kɒnʃɪ'ɛnʃəs] *adj*
consciencieux(-euse); (*scruple, objection*) de
conscience

conscious ['kɒnʃəs] *adj* conscient(e);
(*deliberate: insult, error*) délibéré(e); **to
become ~ of sth/that** prendre conscience
de qch/que

consciousness ['kɒnʃəsnɪs] *n* conscience *f*; (*Med*) connaissance *f*; **to lose/regain ~** perdre/reprendre connaissance

conscript ['kɒnskrɪpt] *n* conscrit *m*

consecutive [kən'sɛkjutɪv] *adj* consécutif(-ive); **on three ~ occasions** trois fois de suite

consensus [kən'sɛnsəs] *n* consensus *m*; **the ~ (of opinion)** le consensus (d'opinion)

consent [kən'sɛnt] *n* consentement *m* ▷ *vi*: **to ~ (to)** consentir (à); **age of ~** âge nubile (légal); **by common ~** d'un commun accord

consequence ['kɒnsɪkwəns] *n* suites *fpl*, conséquence *f*; (*significance*) importance *f*; **in ~** en conséquence, par conséquent

consequently ['kɒnsɪkwəntlɪ] *adv* par conséquent, donc

conservation [kɒnsə'veɪʃən] *n* préservation *f*, protection *f*; (*also*: **nature ~**) défense *f* de l'environnement; **energy ~** économies *fpl* d'énergie

conservative [kən'sə:vətɪv] *adj* conservateur(-trice); (*cautious*) prudent(e)

Conservative [kən'sə:vətɪv] *adj, n* (*Brit Pol*) conservateur(-trice); **the ~ Party** le parti conservateur

conservatory [kən'sə:vətrɪ] *n* (*room*) jardin *m* d'hiver; (*Mus*) conservatoire *m*

conserve [kən'sə:v] *vt* conserver, préserver; (*supplies, energy*) économiser ▷ *n* confiture *f*, conserve *f* (de fruits)

consider [kən'sɪdə*] *vt* (*study*) considérer, réfléchir à; (*take into account*) penser à, prendre en considération; (*regard, judge*) considérer, estimer; **to ~ doing sth** envisager de faire qch; **~ yourself lucky** estimez-vous heureux; **all things ~ed** (toute) réflexion faite

considerable [kən'sɪdərəbl] *adj* considérable

considerably [kən'sɪdərəblɪ] *adv* nettement

considerate [kən'sɪdərɪt] *adj* prévenant(e), plein(e) d'égards

consideration [kənsɪdə'reɪʃən] *n* considération *f*; (*reward*) rétribution *f*, rémunération *f*; **out of ~ for** par égard pour; **under ~** à l'étude; **my first ~ is my family** ma famille passe avant tout le reste

considering [kən'sɪdərɪŋ] *prep*: **~ (that)** étant donné (que)

consign [kən'saɪn] *vt* expédier, livrer

consignment [kən'saɪnmənt] *n* arrivage *m*, envoi *m*

consist [kən'sɪst] *vi*: **to ~ of** consister en, se composer de

consistency [kən'sɪstənsɪ] *n* (*thickness*) consistance *f*; (*fig*) cohérence *f*

consistent [kən'sɪstənt] *adj* logique, cohérent(e); **~ with** compatible avec, en accord avec

consolation [kɒnsə'leɪʃən] *n* consolation *f*

console¹ [kən'səul] *vt* consoler

console² ['kɒnsəul] *n* console *f*

consonant ['kɒnsənənt] *n* consonne *f*

conspicuous [kən'spɪkjuəs] *adj* voyant(e), qui attire l'attention; **to make o.s. ~** se faire remarquer

conspiracy [kən'spɪrəsɪ] *n* conspiration *f*, complot *m*

constable ['kʌnstəbl] *n* (*Brit*) ≈ agent *m* de police, gendarme *m*; **chief ~** ≈ préfet *m* de police

constabulary [kən'stæbjulərɪ] *n* ≈ police *f*, gendarmerie *f*

constant ['kɒnstənt] *adj* constant(e); incessant(e)

constantly ['kɒnstəntlɪ] *adv* constamment, sans cesse

constipated ['kɒnstɪpeɪtɪd] *adj* constipé(e)

constipation [kɒnstɪ'peɪʃən] *n* constipation *f*

constituency [kən'stɪtjuənsɪ] *n* (*Pol: area*) circonscription électorale; (*: electors*) électorat *m*; *voir article*

CONSTITUENCY

Une *constituency* est à la fois une région qui élit un député au parlement et l'ensemble des électeurs dans cette région. En Grande-Bretagne, les députés font régulièrement des "permanences" dans leur circonscription électorale lors desquelles les électeurs peuvent venir les voir pour parler de leurs problèmes de logement etc.

constituent [kən'stɪtjuənt] *n* électeur(-trice); (*part*) élément constitutif, composant *m*

constitute ['kɒnstɪtju:t] *vt* constituer

constitution [kɒnstɪ'tju:ʃən] *n* constitution *f*

constitutional [kɒnstɪ'tju:ʃənl] *adj* constitutionnel(le)

constraint [kən'streɪnt] *n* contrainte *f*; (*embarrassment*) gêne *f*

construct [kən'strʌkt] *vt* construire

construction [kən'strʌkʃən] *n* construction *f*; (*fig: interpretation*) interprétation *f*; **under ~** (*building etc*) en construction

constructive [kən'strʌktɪv] *adj* constructif(-ive)

consul ['kɒnsl] *n* consul *m*

consulate ['kɒnsjulɪt] *n* consulat *m*

consult [kən'sʌlt] *vt* consulter; **to ~ sb (about sth)** consulter qn (à propos de qch)

consultant [kən'sʌltənt] *n* (*Med*) médecin consultant; (*other specialist*) consultant *m*, (*expert-*)conseil *m* ▷ *cpd*: **~ engineer** *n* ingénieur-conseil *m*; **~ paediatrician** *n* pédiatre *m*; **legal/management ~** conseiller *m* juridique/en gestion

consultation [kɒnsəl'teɪʃən] *n* consultation *f*; **in ~ with** en consultation avec

consulting room [kən'sʌltɪŋ-] n (Brit)
cabinet m de consultation

consume [kən'sjuːm] vt consommer; (subj:
flames, hatred, desire) consumer; **to be ~d with
hatred** être dévoré par la haine; **to be ~d
with desire** brûler de désir

consumer [kən'sjuːməʳ] n
consommateur(-trice); (of electricity, gas etc)
usager m

consumer goods npl biens mpl de
consommation

consumer society n société f de
consommation

consummate ['kɒnsʌmeɪt] vt consommer

consumption [kən'sʌmpʃən] n
consommation f; **not fit for human ~** non
comestible

cont. abbr (= continued) suite

contact ['kɒntækt] n contact m; (person)
connaissance f, relation f ▷ vt se mettre en
contact or en rapport avec; **to be in ~ with
sb/sth** être en contact avec qn/qch;
business ~s relations fpl d'affaires,
contacts mpl

contact lenses npl verres mpl de contact

contagious [kən'teɪdʒəs] adj
contagieux(-euse)

contain [kən'teɪn] vt contenir; **to ~ o.s.** se
contenir, se maîtriser

container [kən'teɪnəʳ] n récipient m; (for
shipping etc) conteneur m

contaminate [kən'tæmɪneɪt] vt contaminer

cont'd abbr (= continued) suite

contemplate ['kɒntəmpleɪt] vt contempler;
(consider) envisager

contemporary [kən'tempərərɪ] adj
contemporain(e); (design, wallpaper) moderne
▷ n contemporain(e)

contempt [kən'tempt] n mépris m,
dédain m; **~ of court** (Law) outrage m à
l'autorité de la justice

contemptuous [kən'temptjuəs] adj
dédaigneux(-euse), méprisant(e)

contend [kən'tend] vt: **to ~ that** soutenir or
prétendre que ▷ vi: **to ~ with** (compete)
rivaliser avec; (struggle) lutter avec; **to have
to ~ with** (be faced with) avoir affaire à, être
aux prises avec

contender [kən'tendəʳ] n prétendant(e);
candidat(e)

content [kən'tent] adj content(e), satisfait(e)
▷ vt contenter, satisfaire ▷ n ['kɒntent]
contenu m; (of fat, moisture) teneur f; **contents**
npl (of container etc) contenu m; **(table of) ~s**
table f des matières; **to be ~ with** se
contenter de; **to ~ o.s. with sth/with doing
sth** se contenter de qch/de faire qch

contented [kən'tentɪd] adj content(e),
satisfait(e)

contention [kən'tenʃən] n dispute f,
contestation f; (argument) assertion f,
affirmation f; **bone of ~** sujet m de discorde

contest n ['kɒntest] combat m, lutte f;
(competition) concours m ▷ vt [kən'test]
contester, discuter; (compete for) disputer;
(Law) attaquer

contestant [kən'testənt] n concurrent(e);
(in fight) adversaire m/f

context ['kɒntekst] n contexte m; **in/out of ~**
dans le/hors contexte

continent ['kɒntɪnənt] n continent m; **the
C~** (Brit) l'Europe continentale; **on the C~** en
Europe (continentale)

continental [kɒntɪ'nentl] adj continental(e)
▷ n (Brit) Européen(ne) (continental(e))

continental breakfast n café (or thé)
complet

continental quilt n (Brit) couette f

contingency [kən'tɪndʒənsɪ] n éventualité f,
événement imprévu

continual [kən'tɪnjuəl] adj continuel(le)

continually [kən'tɪnjuəlɪ] adv
continuellement, sans cesse

continuation [kəntɪnju'eɪʃən] n
continuation f; (after interruption) reprise f;
(of story) suite f

continue [kən'tɪnjuː] vi continuer ▷ vt
continuer; (start again) reprendre; **to be ~d**
(story) à suivre; **~d on page 10** suite page 10

continuity [kɒntɪ'njuːɪtɪ] n continuité f;
(TV) enchaînement m; (Cine) script m

continuous [kən'tɪnjuəs] adj continu(e),
permanent(e); (Ling) progressif(-ive);
~ performance (Cine) séance permanente;
~ stationery (Comput) papier m en continu

continuous assessment (Brit) n contrôle
continu

continuously [kən'tɪnjuəslɪ] adv (repeatedly)
continuellement; (uninterruptedly) sans
interruption

contort [kən'tɔːt] vt tordre, crisper

contour ['kɒntuəʳ] n contour m, profil m;
(also: **~ line**) courbe f de niveau

contraband ['kɒntrəbænd] n contrebande f
▷ adj de contrebande

contraception [kɒntrə'sepʃən] n
contraception f

contraceptive [kɒntrə'septɪv] adj
contraceptif(-ive), anticonceptionnel(le) ▷ n
contraceptif m

contract n ['kɒntrækt] contrat m ▷ cpd (price,
date) contractuel(le); (work) contractuel(le) ▷ vi [kə
n'trækt] (become smaller) se contracter, se
resserrer ▷ vt contracter; (Comm): **to ~ to do
sth** s'engager (par contrat) à faire qch; **~ of
employment/service** contrat de travail/de
service; **contract in** vi s'engager (par
contrat); (Brit Admin) s'affilier au régime de
retraite complémentaire; **contract out** vi
se dégager, (Brit Admin) opter pour la non-
affiliation au régime de retraite
complémentaire

contraction [kən'trækʃən] n contraction f;
(Ling) forme contractée

contractor [kən'træktə^r] n entrepreneur m
contradict [kɔntrə'dıkt] vt contredire; (be contrary to) démentir, être en contradiction avec
contradiction [kɔntrə'dıkʃən] n contradiction f; **to be in ~ with** contredire, être en contradiction avec
contraflow ['kɔntrəfləu] n (Aut): **~ lane** voie f à contresens; **there's a ~ system in operation on ...** une voie a été mise en sens inverse sur ...
contraption [kən'træpʃən] n (pej) machin m, truc m
contrary[1] ['kɔntrərı] adj contraire, opposé(e) ▷ n contraire m; **on the ~** au contraire; **unless you hear to the ~** sauf avis contraire; **~ to what we thought** contrairement à ce que nous pensions
contrary[2] [kən'trɛərı] adj (perverse) contrariant(e), entêté(e)
contrast n ['kɔntra:st] contraste m ▷ vt [kən'tra:st] mettre en contraste, contraster; **in ~ to** or **with** contrairement à, par opposition à
contravene [kɔntrə'vi:n] vt enfreindre, violer, contrevenir à
contribute [kən'trıbju:t] vi contribuer ▷ vt: **to ~ £10/an article to** donner 10 livres/un article à; **to ~ to** (gen) contribuer à; (newspaper) collaborer à; (discussion) prendre part à
contribution [kɔntrı'bju:ʃən] n contribution f; (Brit: for social security) cotisation f; (to publication) article m
contributor [kən'trıbjutə^r] n (to newspaper) collaborateur(-trice); (of money, goods) donateur(-trice)
contrive [kən'traıv] vt combiner, inventer ▷ vi: **to ~ to do** s'arranger pour faire, trouver le moyen de faire
control [kən'trəul] vt (process, machinery) commander; (temper) maîtriser; (disease) enrayer; (check) contrôler ▷ n maîtrise f; (power) autorité f; **controls** npl (of machine etc) commandes fpl; (on radio) boutons mpl de réglage; **to take ~** se rendre maître de; (Comm) acquérir une participation majoritaire dans; **to be in ~ of** être maître de, maîtriser; (in charge of) être responsable de; **to ~ o.s.** se contrôler; **everything is under ~** j'ai (or il a etc) la situation en main; **the car went out of ~** j'ai (or il a etc) perdu le contrôle du véhicule; **beyond our ~** indépendant(e) de notre volonté
control panel n (on aircraft, ship, TV etc) tableau m de commandes
control room n (Naut Mil) salle f des commandes; (Radio, TV) régie f
control tower n (Aviat) tour f de contrôle
controversial [kɔntrə'və:ʃl] adj discutable, controversé(e)
controversy ['kɔntrəvə:sı] n controverse f, polémique f

convalesce [kɔnvə'lɛs] vi relever de maladie, se remettre (d'une maladie)
convector [kən'vɛktə^r] n radiateur m à convection, appareil m de chauffage par convection
convene [kən'vi:n] vt convoquer, assembler ▷ vi se réunir, s'assembler
convenience [kən'vi:nıəns] n commodité f; **at your ~** quand or comme cela vous convient; **at your earliest ~** (Comm) dans les meilleurs délais, le plus tôt possible; **all modern ~s, all mod cons** (Brit) avec tout le confort moderne, tout confort
convenient [kən'vi:nıənt] adj commode; **if it is ~ to you** si cela vous convient, si cela ne vous dérange pas
convent ['kɔnvənt] n couvent m
convention [kən'vɛnʃən] n convention f; (custom) usage m
conventional [kən'vɛnʃənl] adj conventionnel(le)
convent school n couvent m
conversant [kən'və:snt] adj: **to be ~ with** s'y connaître en; être au courant de
conversation [kɔnvə'seıʃən] n conversation f
converse ['kɔnvə:s] n contraire m, inverse m ▷ vi [kən'və:s]: **to ~ (with sb about sth)** s'entretenir (avec qn de qch)
conversely [kɔn'və:slı] adv inversement, réciproquement
conversion [kən'və:ʃən] n conversion f; (Brit: of house) transformation f, aménagement m; (Rugby) transformation f
convert vt [kən'və:t] (Rel, Comm) convertir; (alter) transformer; (house) aménager; (Rugby) transformer ▷ n ['kɔnvə:t] converti(e)
convertible [kən'və:təbl] adj convertible ▷ n (voiture f) décapotable f
convey [kən'veı] vt transporter; (thanks) transmettre; (idea) communiquer
conveyor belt [kən'veıə^r-] n convoyeur m, tapis roulant
convict vt [kən'vıkt] déclarer (or reconnaître) coupable ▷ n ['kɔnvıkt] forçat m, convict m
conviction [kən'vıkʃən] n (Law) condamnation f; (belief) conviction f
convince [kən'vıns] vt convaincre, persuader; **to ~ sb (of sth/that)** persuader qn (de qch/que)
convinced [kən'vınst] adj: **~ of/that** convaincu(e) de/que
convincing [kən'vınsıŋ] adj persuasif(-ive), convaincant(e)
convoluted ['kɔnvəlu:tıd] adj (shape) tarabiscoté(e); (argument) compliqué(e)
convoy ['kɔnvɔı] n convoi m
convulse [kən'vʌls] vt ébranler; **to be ~d with laughter** se tordre de rire
cook [kuk] vt (faire) cuire ▷ vi cuire; (person) faire la cuisine ▷ n cuisinier(-ière); **cook up** vt (inf: excuse, story) inventer

cookbook ['kʊkbʊk] n livre m de cuisine
cooker ['kʊkə^r] n cuisinière f
cookery ['kʊkərɪ] n cuisine f
cookery book n (Brit) = **cookbook**
cookie ['kʊkɪ] n (US) biscuit m, petit gâteau sec; (Comput) cookie m, témoin m de connexion
cooking ['kʊkɪŋ] n cuisine f ▷ cpd (apples, chocolate) à cuire; (utensils, salt) de cuisine
cool [kuːl] adj frais/fraîche; (not afraid) calme; (unfriendly) froid(e); (impertinent) effronté(e); (inf: trendy) cool inv (inf); (: great) super inv (inf) ▷ vt, vi rafraîchir, refroidir; **it's ~** (weather) il fait frais; **to keep sth ~** or **in a ~ place** garder or conserver qch au frais; **cool down** vi refroidir; (fig: person, situation) se calmer; **cool off** vi (become calmer) se calmer; (lose enthusiasm) perdre son enthousiasme
coop [kuːp] n poulailler m ▷ vt: **to ~ up** (fig) cloîtrer, enfermer
cooperate [kəʊ'ɔpəreɪt] vi coopérer, collaborer
cooperation [kəʊɔpə'reɪʃən] n coopération f, collaboration f
cooperative [kəʊ'ɔpərətɪv] adj coopératif(-ive) ▷ n coopérative f
coordinate vt [kəʊ'ɔːdɪneɪt] coordonner ▷ n [kəʊ'ɔːdɪnət] (Math) coordonnée f; **coordinates** npl (clothes) ensemble m, coordonnés mpl
co-ownership ['kəʊ'əʊnəʃɪp] n copropriété f
cop [kɔp] n (inf) flic m
cope [kəʊp] vi s'en sortir, tenir le coup; **to ~ with** (problem) faire face à; (take care of) s'occuper de
copper ['kɔpə^r] n cuivre m; (Brit: inf: policeman) flic m; **coppers** npl petite monnaie
copy ['kɔpɪ] n copie f; (book etc) exemplaire m; (material: for printing) copie ▷ vt copier; (imitate) imiter; **rough ~** (gen) premier jet; (Scol) brouillon m; **fair ~** version définitive; propre m; **to make good ~** (Press) faire un bon sujet d'article; **copy out** vt copier
copyright ['kɔpɪraɪt] n droit m d'auteur, copyright m; **~ reserved** tous droits (de reproduction) réservés
coral ['kɔrəl] n corail m
cord [kɔːd] n corde f; (fabric) velours côtelé, whipcord m; corde f; (Elec) cordon m (d'alimentation), fil m (électrique); **cords** npl (trousers) pantalon m de velours côtelé
cordial ['kɔːdɪəl] adj cordial(e), chaleureux(-euse) ▷ n sirop m; cordial m
cordless ['kɔːdlɪs] adj sans fil
cordon ['kɔːdn] n cordon m; **cordon off** vt (area) interdire l'accès à; (crowd) tenir à l'écart
corduroy ['kɔːdərɔɪ] n velours côtelé
core [kɔː^r] n (of fruit) trognon m, cœur m; (Tech: also of earth) noyau m; (of nuclear reactor, fig: of problem etc) cœur ▷ vt enlever le trognon or le cœur de; **rotten to the ~** complètement pourri

coriander [kɔrɪ'ændə^r] n coriandre f
cork [kɔːk] n (material) liège m; (of bottle) bouchon m
corkscrew ['kɔːkskruː] n tire-bouchon m
corn [kɔːn] n (Brit: wheat) blé m; (US: maize) maïs m; (on foot) cor m; **~ on the cob** (Culin) épi m de maïs au naturel
corned beef ['kɔːnd-] n corned-beef m
corner ['kɔːnə^r] n coin m; (in road) tournant m, virage m; (Football: also: **~ kick**) corner m ▷ vt (trap: prey) acculer; (fig) coincer; (Comm: market) accaparer ▷ vi prendre un virage; **to cut ~s** (fig) prendre des raccourcis
corner shop (Brit) n magasin m du coin
cornerstone ['kɔːnəstəʊn] n pierre f angulaire
cornet ['kɔːnɪt] n (Mus) cornet m à pistons; (Brit: of ice-cream) cornet (de glace)
cornflakes ['kɔːnfleɪks] npl cornflakes mpl
cornflour ['kɔːnflaʊə^r] n (Brit) farine f de maïs, maïzena® f
cornstarch ['kɔːnstɑːtʃ] n (US) farine f de maïs, maïzena® f
Cornwall ['kɔːnwəl] n Cournouailles f
corny ['kɔːnɪ] adj (inf) rebattu(e), galvaudé(e)
coronary ['kɔrənərɪ] n: **~ (thrombosis)** infarctus m (du myocarde), thrombose f coronaire
coronation [kɔrə'neɪʃən] n couronnement m
coroner ['kɔrənə^r] n coroner m, officier de police judiciaire chargé de déterminer les causes d'un décès
corporal ['kɔːpərl] n caporal m, brigadier m ▷ adj: **~ punishment** châtiment corporel
corporate ['kɔːpərɪt] adj (action, ownership) en commun; (Comm) de la société
corporation [kɔːpə'reɪʃən] n (of town) municipalité f, conseil municipal; (Comm) société f
corps [kɔː^r] (pl **corps**) [kɔːz] n corps m; **the diplomatic ~** le corps diplomatique; **the press ~** la presse
corpse [kɔːps] n cadavre m
correct [kə'rekt] adj (accurate) correct(e), exact(e); (proper) correct, convenable ▷ vt corriger; **you are ~** vous avez raison
correction [kə'rekʃən] n correction f
correspond [kɔrɪs'pɔnd] vi correspondre; **to ~ to sth** (be equivalent to) correspondre à qch
correspondence [kɔrɪs'pɔndəns] n correspondance f
correspondence course n cours m par correspondance
correspondent [kɔrɪs'pɔndənt] n correspondant(e)
corresponding [kɔrɪs'pɔndɪŋ] adj correspondant(e)
corridor ['kɔrɪdɔː^r] n couloir m, corridor m
corrode [kə'rəʊd] vt corroder, ronger ▷ vi se corroder
corrugated ['kɔrəgeɪtɪd] adj plissé(e); ondulé(e)
corrugated iron n tôle ondulée

corrupt [kəˈrʌpt] *adj* corrompu(e); (*Comput*) altéré(e) ▷ *vt* corrompre; (*Comput*) altérer; ~ **practices** (*dishonesty, bribery*) malversation *f*
corruption [kəˈrʌpʃən] *n* corruption *f*; (*Comput*) altération *f* (de données)
Corsica [ˈkɔːsɪkə] *n* Corse *f*
cosmetic [kɔzˈmetɪk] *n* produit *m* de beauté, cosmétique *m* ▷ *adj* (*preparation*) cosmétique; (*fig: reforms*) symbolique, superficiel(le)
cosmetic surgery *n* chirurgie *f* esthétique
cosmopolitan [kɔzməˈpɔlɪtn] *adj* cosmopolite
cost [kɔst] (*pt, pp* **cost**) *n* coût *m* ▷ *vi* coûter ▷ *vt* établir *or* calculer le prix de revient de; **costs** *npl* (*Comm*) frais *mpl*; (*Law*) dépens *mpl*; **how much does it ~?** combien ça coûte?; **it ~s £5/too much** cela coûte 5 livres/trop cher; **what will it ~ to have it repaired?** combien cela coûtera de le faire réparer?; **to ~ sb time/effort** demander du temps/un effort à qn; **it ~ him his life/job** ça lui a coûté la vie/son emploi; **at all ~s** coûte que coûte, à tout prix
co-star [ˈkəʊstɑːʳ] *n* partenaire *m/f*
cost-effective [ˈkɔstɪˈfektɪv] *adj* rentable
costly [ˈkɔstlɪ] *adj* coûteux(-euse)
cost of living [ˈkɔstəvˈlɪvɪŋ] *n* coût *m* de la vie ▷ *adj*: ~ **allowance** indemnité *f* de vie chère; ~ **index** indice *m* du coût de la vie
cost price *n* (*Brit*) prix coûtant *or* de revient
costume [ˈkɔstjuːm] *n* costume *m*; (*lady's suit*) tailleur *m*; (*Brit: also:* **swimming ~**) maillot *m* (de bain)
costume jewellery *n* bijoux *mpl* de fantaisie
cosy, (*US*) **cozy** [ˈkəʊzɪ] *adj* (*room, bed*) douillet(te); (*scarf, gloves*) bien chaud(e); (*atmosphere*) chaleureux(-euse); **to be ~** (*person*) être bien (au chaud)
cot [kɔt] *n* (*Brit: child's*) lit *m* d'enfant, petit lit; (*US: campbed*) lit de camp
cottage [ˈkɔtɪdʒ] *n* petite maison (à la campagne), cottage *m*
cottage cheese *n* fromage blanc (*maigre*)
cotton [ˈkɔtn] *n* coton *m*; (*thread*) fil *m* (de coton); ~ **dress** *etc* robe *etc* en *or* de coton; **cotton on** *vi* (*inf*): **to ~ on (to sth)** piger (qch)
cotton bud (*Brit*) *n* coton-tige® *m*
cotton candy (*US*) *n* barbe *f* à papa
cotton wool *n* (*Brit*) ouate *f*, coton *m* hydrophile
couch [kautʃ] *n* canapé *m*; divan *m*; (*doctor's*) table *f* d'examen; (*psychiatrist's*) divan ▷ *vt* formuler, exprimer
couchette [kuːˈʃet] *n* couchette *f*
cough [kɔf] *vi* tousser ▷ *n* toux *f*; **I've got a ~** j'ai la toux
cough mixture, cough syrup *n* sirop *m* pour la toux
cough sweet *n* pastille *f* pour *or* contre la toux
could [kud] *pt of* **can²**
couldn't [ˈkudnt] = **could not**

council [ˈkaunsl] *n* conseil *m*; **city** *or* **town ~** conseil municipal; **C~ of Europe** Conseil de l'Europe
council estate *n* (*Brit*) (quartier *m* *or* zone *f* de) logements loués à/par la municipalité
council house *n* (*Brit*) maison *f* (à loyer modéré) louée par la municipalité
councillor, (*US*) **councilor** [ˈkaunsləʳ] *n* conseiller(-ère)
council tax *n* (*Brit*) impôts locaux
counsel [ˈkaunsl] *n* conseil *m*; (*lawyer*) avocat(e) ▷ *vt*: **to ~ (sb to do sth)** conseiller (à qn de faire qch); ~ **for the defence/the prosecution** (avocat de la) défense/ avocat du ministère public
counselling, (*US*) **counseling** [ˈkaunslɪŋ] *n* (*Psych*) aide psychosociale
counsellor, (*US*) **counselor** [ˈkaunsləʳ] *n* conseiller(-ère); (*US Law*) avocat *m*
count [kaunt] *vt, vi* compter ▷ *n* compte *m*; (*nobleman*) comte *m*; **to ~ (up) to 10** compter jusqu'à 10; **to keep ~ of sth** tenir le compte de qch; **not ~ing the children** sans compter les enfants; **10 ~ing him** 10 avec lui, 10 en le comptant; **to ~ the cost of** établir le coût de; **it ~s for very little** cela n'a pas beaucoup d'importance; ~ **yourself lucky** estimez-vous heureux; **count in** *vt* (*inf*): **to ~ sb in on sth** inclure qn dans qch; **count on** *vt fus* compter sur; **to ~ on doing sth** compter faire qch; **count up** *vt* compter, additionner
countdown [ˈkauntdaun] *n* compte *m* à rebours
countenance [ˈkauntɪnəns] *n* expression *f* ▷ *vt* approuver
counter [ˈkauntəʳ] *n* comptoir *m*; (*in post office, bank*) guichet *m*; (*in game*) jeton *m* ▷ *vt* aller à l'encontre de, opposer; (*blow*) parer ▷ *adv*: ~ **to** à l'encontre de; contrairement à; **to buy under the ~** (*fig*) acheter sous le manteau *or* en sous-main; **to ~ sth with sth/ by doing sth** contrer *or* riposter à qch par qch/en faisant qch
counteract [ˈkauntərˈækt] *vt* neutraliser, contrebalancer
counterclockwise [ˈkauntəˈklɔkwaɪz] (*US*) *adv* en sens inverse des aiguilles d'une montre
counterfeit [ˈkauntəfɪt] *n* faux *m*, contrefaçon *f* ▷ *vt* contrefaire ▷ *adj* faux/ fausse
counterfoil [ˈkauntəfɔɪl] *n* talon *m*, souche *f*
counterpart [ˈkauntəpɑːt] *n* (*of document etc*) double *m*; (*of person*) homologue *m/f*
countess [ˈkauntɪs] *n* comtesse *f*
countless [ˈkauntlɪs] *adj* innombrable
country [ˈkʌntrɪ] *n* pays *m*; (*native land*) patrie *f*; (*as opposed to town*) campagne *f*; (*region*) région *f*, pays; **in the ~** à la campagne; **mountainous ~** pays de montagne, région montagneuse

**country and western, country and
western music** n musique f country

country dancing n (Brit) danse f folklorique

country house n manoir m, (petit) château

countryman ['kʌntrɪmən] irreg n (national)
compatriote m; (rural) habitant m de la
campagne, campagnard m

countryside ['kʌntrɪsaɪd] n campagne f

county ['kaʊntɪ] n comté m

coup [kuː] (pl coups) [kuː] n (achievement)
beau coup; (also: ~ **d'état**) coup d'État

couple ['kʌpl] n couple m ▷ vt (carriages)
atteler; (Tech) coupler; (ideas, names) associer;
a ~ of (two) deux; (a few) deux ou trois

coupon ['kuːpɔn] n (voucher) bon m de
réduction; (detachable form) coupon m
détachable, coupon-réponse m; (Finance)
coupon

courage ['kʌrɪdʒ] n courage m

courageous [kə'reɪdʒəs] adj
courageux(-euse)

courgette [kuə'ʒet] n (Brit) courgette f

courier ['kurɪə'] n messager m, courrier m;
(for tourists) accompagnateur(-trice)

course [kɔːs] n cours m; (of ship) route f;
(for golf) terrain m; (part of meal) plat m;
first ~ entrée f; **of** ~ adv bien sûr; **(no,) of ~
not!** bien sûr que non!, évidemment que
non!; **in the** ~ **of** au cours de ...; **in the** ~ **of the
next few days** au cours des prochains jours;
in due ~ en temps utile or voulu; ~ **(of action)**
parti m, ligne f de conduite; **the best** ~ **would
be to** ... le mieux serait de ...; **we have no
other** ~ **but to** ... nous n'avons pas d'autre
solution que de ...; ~ **of lectures** série f de
conférences; ~ **of treatment** (Med)
traitement m

court [kɔːt] n cour f; (Law) tribunal m;
(Tennis) court m ▷ vt (woman) courtiser, faire
la cour à; (fig: favour, popularity) rechercher;
(: death, disaster) courir après, flirter avec; **out
of** ~ (Law: settle) à l'amiable; **to take to** ~
actionner or poursuivre en justice; ~ **of
appeal** cour d'appel

courteous ['kəːtɪəs] adj courtois(e), poli(e)

courtesy ['kəːtəsɪ] n courtoisie f, politesse f;
(by) ~ **of** avec l'aimable autorisation de

courtesy bus, courtesy coach n navette
gratuite

court-house ['kɔːthaʊs] n (US) palais m de
justice

courtier ['kɔːtɪə'] n courtisan m, dame f de
cour

court martial (pl courts martial) n cour
martiale, conseil m de guerre

courtroom ['kɔːtruːm] n salle f de tribunal

courtyard ['kɔːtjɑːd] n cour f

cousin ['kʌzn] n cousin(e); **first** ~ cousin(e)
germain(e)

cove [kəʊv] n petite baie, anse f

covenant ['kʌvənənt] n contrat m,
engagement m ▷ vt: **to ~ £200 per year to a**

charity s'engager à verser 200 livres par an à
une œuvre de bienfaisance

cover ['kʌvə'] vt couvrir; (Press: report on) faire
un reportage sur; (feelings, mistake) cacher;
(include) englober; (discuss) traiter ▷ n (of book,
Comm) couverture f; (of pan) couvercle m; (over
furniture) housse f; (shelter) abri m; **covers** npl
(on bed) couvertures; **to take** ~ se mettre à
l'abri; **under** ~ à l'abri; **under** ~ **of darkness**
à la faveur de la nuit; **under separate** ~
(Comm) sous pli séparé; **£10 will** ~ **everything**
10 livres suffiront (pour tout payer); **cover
up** vt (person, object): **to** ~ **up (with)** couvrir
(de); (fig: truth, facts) occulter ▷ vi: **to** ~ **up for
sb** (fig) couvrir qn

coverage ['kʌvərɪdʒ] n (in media) reportage m;
(Insurance) couverture f

cover charge n couvert m (supplément à payer)

covering ['kʌvərɪŋ] n couverture f,
enveloppe f

covering letter, (US) **cover letter** n lettre
explicative

cover note n (Insurance) police f provisoire

covert ['kʌvət] adj (threat) voilé(e), caché(e);
(attack) indirect(e); (glance) furtif(-ive)

cover-up ['kʌvərʌp] n tentative f pour
étouffer une affaire

covet ['kʌvɪt] vt convoiter

cow [kaʊ] n vache f ▷ cpd femelle ▷ vt
effrayer, intimider

coward ['kaʊəd] n lâche m/f

cowardice ['kaʊədɪs] n lâcheté f

cowardly ['kaʊədlɪ] adj lâche

cowboy ['kaʊbɔɪ] n cow-boy m

cower ['kaʊə'] vi se recroqueviller; trembler

coy [kɔɪ] adj faussement effarouché(e) or
timide

cozy ['kəʊzɪ] adj (US) = **cosy**

CPA n abbr (US) = **certified public accountant**

crab [kræb] n crabe m

crab apple n pomme f sauvage

crack [kræk] n (split) fente f, fissure f; (in cup,
bone) fêlure f; (in wall) lézarde f; (noise)
craquement m, coup (sec); (joke) plaisanterie
f; (inf: attempt): **to have a** ~ **(at sth)** essayer
(qch); (Drugs) crack m ▷ vt fendre, fissurer;
fêler; lézarder; (whip) faire claquer; (nut)
casser; (problem) résoudre, trouver la clef de;
(code) déchiffrer ▷ cpd (athlete) de première
classe, d'élite; **to get** ~**ing** (inf) s'y mettre, se
magner; **crack down on** vt fus (crime) sévir
contre, réprimer; (spending) mettre un frein
à; **crack up** vi être au bout de son rouleau,
flancher

cracked [krækt] adj (cup, bone) fêlé(e); (broken)
cassé(e); (wall) lézardé(e); (surface)
craquelé(e); (inf) toqué(e), timbré(e)

cracker ['krækə'] n (also: **Christmas** ~)
pétard m; (biscuit) biscuit (salé), craquelin m;
a ~ **of a ...** (Brit inf) un(e) ... formidable; **he's** ~**s**
(Brit inf) il est cinglé

crackle ['krækl] *vi* crépiter, grésiller

cradle ['kreɪdl] *n* berceau *m* ▷ *vt* (*child*) bercer; (*object*) tenir dans ses bras

craft [krɑːft] *n* métier (*artisanal*); (*cunning*) ruse *f*, astuce *f*; (*boat: pl inv*) embarcation *f*, barque *f*; (*plane: pl inv*) appareil *m*

craftsman (*irreg*) ['krɑːftsmən] *irreg n* artisan *m* ouvrier (*qualifié*)

craftsmanship ['krɑːftsmənʃɪp] *n* métier *m*, habileté *f*

crafty ['krɑːftɪ] *adj* rusé(e), malin(-igne), astucieux(-euse)

crag [kræg] *n* rocher escarpé

cram [kræm] *vt* (*fill*): **to ~ sth with** bourrer qch de; (*put*): **to ~ sth into** fourrer qch dans ▷ *vi* (*for exams*) bachoter

cramp [kræmp] *n* crampe *f* ▷ *vt* gêner, entraver; **I've got ~ in my leg** j'ai une crampe à la jambe

cramped [kræmpt] *adj* à l'étroit, très serré(e)

cranberry ['krænbərɪ] *n* canneberge *f*

crane [kreɪn] *n* grue *f* ▷ *vt, vi*: **to ~ forward**, **to ~ one's neck** allonger le cou

crank [kræŋk] *n* manivelle *f*; (*person*) excentrique *m/f*

cranny ['krænɪ] *n see* **nook**

crap [kræp] *n* (*inf!: nonsense*) conneries *fpl* (!); (: *excrement*) merde *f* (!); **the party was ~** la fête était merdique (!); **to have a ~** chier (!)

crash [kræʃ] *n* (*noise*) fracas *m*; (*of car, plane*) collision *f*; (*of business*) faillite *f*; (*Stock Exchange*) krach *m* ▷ *vt* (*plane*) écraser ▷ *vi* (*plane*) s'écraser; (*two cars*) se percuter, s'emboutir; (*business*) s'effondrer; **to ~ into** se jeter or se fracasser contre; **he ~ed the car into a wall** il s'est écrasé contre un mur avec sa voiture

crash course *n* cours intensif

crash helmet *n* casque (*protecteur*)

crash landing *n* atterrissage forcé or en catastrophe

crate [kreɪt] *n* cageot *m*; (*for bottles*) caisse *f*

cravat [krə'væt] *n* foulard (*noué autour du cou*)

crave [kreɪv] *vt, vi*: **to ~ (for)** désirer violemment, avoir un besoin physiologique de, avoir une envie irrésistible de

crawl [krɔːl] *vi* ramper; (*vehicle*) avancer au pas ▷ *n* (*Swimming*) crawl *m*; **to ~ on one's hands and knees** aller à quatre pattes; **to ~ to sb** (*inf*) faire de la lèche à qn

crayfish ['kreɪfɪʃ] *n* (*pl inv: freshwater*) écrevisse *f*; (*saltwater*) langoustine *f*

crayon ['kreɪən] *n* crayon *m* (*de couleur*)

craze [kreɪz] *n* engouement *m*

crazy ['kreɪzɪ] *adj* fou/folle; **to go ~** devenir fou; **to be ~ about sb/sth** (*inf*) être fou de qn/qch

creak [kriːk] *vi* (*hinge*) grincer; (*floor, shoes*) craquer

cream [kriːm] *n* crème *f* ▷ *adj* (*colour*) crème *inv*; **whipped ~** crème fouettée; **cream off** *vt* (*fig*) prélever

cream cake *n* (*petit*) gâteau à la crème

cream cheese *n* fromage *m* à la crème, fromage blanc

creamy ['kriːmɪ] *adj* crémeux(-euse)

crease [kriːs] *n* pli *m* ▷ *vt* froisser, chiffonner ▷ *vi* se froisser, se chiffonner

create [kriː'eɪt] *vt* créer; (*impression, fuss*) faire

creation [kriː'eɪʃən] *n* création *f*

creative [kriː'eɪtɪv] *adj* créatif(-ive)

creator [kriː'eɪtəʳ] *n* créateur(-trice)

creature ['kriːtʃəʳ] *n* créature *f*

crèche [krɛʃ] *n* garderie *f*, crèche *f*

credence ['kriːdns] *n* croyance *f*, foi *f*

credentials [krɪ'dɛnʃlz] *npl* (*references*) références *fpl*; (*identity papers*) pièces *f* d'identité; (*letters of reference*) pièces justificatives

credibility [krɛdɪ'bɪlɪtɪ] *n* crédibilité *f*

credible ['krɛdɪbl] *adj* digne de foi, crédible

credit ['krɛdɪt] *n* crédit *m*; (*recognition*) honneur *m*; (*Scol*) unité *f* de valeur ▷ *vt* (*Comm*) créditer; (*believe: also*: **give ~ to**) ajouter foi à, croire; **credits** *npl* (*Cine*) générique *m*; **to be in ~** (*person, bank account*) être créditeur(-trice); **on ~** à crédit; **to one's ~** à son honneur; à son actif; **to take the ~ for** s'attribuer le mérite de; **it does him ~** cela lui fait honneur; **to ~ sb with** (*fig*) prêter or attribuer à qn; **to ~ £5 to sb** créditer (le compte de) qn de 5 livres

credit card *n* carte *f* de crédit; **do you take ~s?** acceptez-vous les cartes de crédit?

credit crunch *n* crise *f* du crédit

creditor ['krɛdɪtəʳ] *n* créancier(-ière)

creed [kriːd] *n* croyance *f*, credo *m*, principes *mpl*

creek [kriːk] *n* (*inlet*) crique *f*, anse *f*; (*US: stream*) ruisseau *m*, petit cours d'eau

creep [kriːp] (*pt, pp* **crept**) [kriːp, krɛpt] *vi* ramper; (*silently*) se faufiler, se glisser; (*plant*) grimper ▷ *n* (*inf: flatterer*) lèche-botte *m*; **he's a ~** c'est un type puant; **it gives me the ~s** cela me fait froid dans le dos; **to ~ up on sb** s'approcher furtivement de qn

creeper ['kriːpəʳ] *n* plante grimpante

creepy ['kriːpɪ] *adj* (*frightening*) qui fait frissonner, qui donne la chair de poule

cremate [krɪ'meɪt] *vt* incinérer

crematorium (*pl* **crematoria**) [krɛmə'tɔːrɪəm, -'tɔːrɪə] *n* four *m* crématoire

crepe [kreɪp] *n* crêpe *m*

crepe bandage *n* (*Brit*) bande *f* Velpeau®

crept [krɛpt] *pt, pp of* **creep**

crescent ['krɛsnt] *n* croissant *m*; (*street*) rue *f* (*en arc de cercle*)

cress [krɛs] *n* cresson *m*

crest [krɛst] *n* crête *f*; (*of helmet*) cimier *m*; (*of coat of arms*) timbre *m*

crestfallen ['krɛstfɔːlən] *adj* déconfit(e), découragé(e)

Crete ['kriːt] *n* Crète *f*

crevice ['krɛvɪs] *n* fissure *f*, lézarde *f*, fente *f*

crew [kru:] n équipage m; (Cine) équipe f (de tournage); (gang) bande f

crew-cut ['kru:kʌt] n: **to have a ~** avoir les cheveux en brosse

crew-neck ['kru:nek] n col ras

crib [krɪb] n lit m d'enfant; (for baby) berceau m ▷ vt (inf) copier

crick [krɪk] n crampe f; **~ in the neck** torticolis m

cricket ['krɪkɪt] n (insect) grillon m, cri-cri m inv; (game) cricket m

cricketer ['krɪkɪtə'] n joueur m de cricket

crime [kraɪm] n crime m; **minor ~** délit mineur, infraction mineure

criminal ['krɪmɪnl] adj, n criminel(le)

crimson ['krɪmzn] adj cramoisi(e)

cringe [krɪndʒ] vi avoir un mouvement de recul; (fig) s'humilier, ramper

crinkle ['krɪŋkl] vt froisser, chiffonner

cripple ['krɪpl] n boiteux(-euse), infirme m/f ▷ vt (person) estropier, paralyser; (ship, plane) immobiliser; (production, exports) paralyser; **~d with rheumatism** perclus(e) de rhumatismes

crisis (pl **crises**) ['kraɪsɪs, -si:z] n crise f

crisp [krɪsp] adj croquant(e); (weather) vif/ vive; (manner etc) brusque

crisps [krɪsps] (Brit) npl (pommes fpl) chips fpl

crispy ['krɪspɪ] adj croustillant(e)

crisscross ['krɪskrɔs] adj entrecroisé(e), en croisillons ▷ vt sillonner; **~ pattern** croisillons mpl

criterion (pl **criteria**) [kraɪ'tɪərɪən, -'tɪərɪə] n critère m

critic ['krɪtɪk] n critique m/f

critical ['krɪtɪkl] adj critique; **to be ~ of sb/ sth** critiquer qn/qch

critically ['krɪtɪklɪ] adv (examine) d'un œil critique; (speak) sévèrement; **~ ill** gravement malade

criticism ['krɪtɪsɪzəm] n critique f

criticize ['krɪtɪsaɪz] vt critiquer

croak [krəuk] vi (frog) coasser; (raven) croasser

Croat ['krəuæt] adj, n = **Croatian**

Croatia [krəu'eɪʃə] n Croatie f

Croatian [krəu'eɪʃən] adj croate ▷ n Croate m/f; (Ling) croate m

crochet ['krəuʃeɪ] n travail m au crochet

crockery ['krɔkərɪ] n vaisselle f

crocodile ['krɔkədaɪl] n crocodile m

crocus ['krəukəs] n crocus m

croft [krɔft] n (Brit) petite ferme

croissant ['krwasɑ̃] n croissant m

crony ['krəunɪ] n copain/copine f

crook [kruk] n escroc m; (of shepherd) houlette f

crooked ['krukɪd] adj courbé(e), tordu(e); (action) malhonnête

crop [krɔp] n (produce) culture f; (amount produced) récolte f; (riding crop) cravache f; (of bird) jabot m ▷ vt (hair) tondre; (animals:

grass) brouter; **crop up** vi surgir, se présenter, survenir

cross [krɔs] n croix f; (Biol) croisement m ▷ vt (street etc) traverser; (arms, legs, Biol) croiser; (cheque) barrer; (thwart: person, plan) contrarier ▷ vi: **the boat ~es from ... to ...** le bateau fait la traversée de ... à ... ▷ adj en colère, fâché(e); **to ~ o.s.** se signer, faire le signe de (la) croix; **we have a ~ed line** (Brit: on telephone) il y a des interférences; **they've got their lines ~ed** (fig) il y a un malentendu entre eux; **to be/ get ~ with sb (about sth)** être en colère/(se) fâcher contre qn (à propos de qch); **cross off** or **out** vt barrer, rayer; **cross over** vi traverser

crossbar ['krɔsbɑ:'] n barre transversale

cross-Channel ferry ['krɔs'tʃænl-] n ferry m qui fait la traversée de la Manche

cross-country ['krɔs'kʌntrɪ], **cross-country race** n cross(-country) m

cross-examine ['krɔsɪg'zæmɪn] vt (Law) faire subir un examen contradictoire à

cross-eyed ['krɔsaɪd] adj qui louche

crossfire ['krɔsfaɪə'] n feux croisés

crossing ['krɔsɪŋ] n croisement m, carrefour m; (sea passage) traversée f; (also: **pedestrian ~**) passage clouté; **how long does the ~ take?** combien de temps dure la traversée?

crossing guard (US) n contractuel qui fait traverser la rue aux enfants

cross-purposes ['krɔs'pə:pəsɪz] npl: **to be at ~ with sb** comprendre qn de travers; **we're (talking) at ~** on ne parle pas de la même chose

cross-reference ['krɔs'refrəns] n renvoi m, référence f

crossroads ['krɔsrəudz] n carrefour m

cross section n (Biol) coupe transversale; (in population) échantillon m

crosswalk ['krɔswɔ:k] n (US) passage clouté

crosswind ['krɔswɪnd] n vent m de travers

crossword ['krɔswə:d] n mots mpl croisés

crotch [krɔtʃ] n (of garment) entrejambe m; (Anat) entrecuisse f

crouch [krautʃ] vi s'accroupir; (hide) se tapir; (before springing) se ramasser

crouton ['kru:tɔn] n croûton m

crow [krəu] n (bird) corneille f; (of cock) chant m du coq, cocorico m ▷ vi (cock) chanter; (fig) pavoiser, chanter victoire

crowbar ['krəubɑ:'] n levier m

crowd [kraud] n foule f ▷ vt bourrer, remplir ▷ vi affluer, s'attrouper, s'entasser; **~s of people** une foule de gens

crowded ['kraudɪd] adj bondé(e), plein(e); **~ with** plein de

crown [kraun] n couronne f; (of head) sommet m de la tête, calotte crânienne; (of hat) fond m; (of hill) sommet m ▷ vt (also tooth) couronner

crown jewels npl joyaux mpl de la Couronne

crow's-feet ['krəuzfiːt] npl pattes fpl d'oie (fig)

crucial ['kruːʃl] adj crucial(e), décisif(-ive); (also: ~ **to**) essentiel(le) à

crucifix ['kruːsɪfɪks] n crucifix m

crucifixion [kruːsɪˈfɪkʃən] n crucifiement m, crucifixion f

crude [kruːd] adj (materials) brut(e); non raffiné(e); (basic) rudimentaire, sommaire; (vulgar) cru(e), grossier(-ière) ▷ n (also: ~ oil) (pétrole m) brut m

cruel ['kruəl] adj cruel(le)

cruelty ['kruəltɪ] n cruauté f

cruise [kruːz] n croisière f ▷ vi (ship) croiser; (car) rouler; (aircraft) voler; (taxi) être en maraude

cruiser ['kruːzə'] n croiseur m

crumb [krʌm] n miette f

crumble ['krʌmbl] vt émietter ▷ vi s'émietter; (plaster etc) s'effriter; (land, earth) s'ébouler; (building) s'écrouler, crouler; (fig) s'effondrer

crumbly ['krʌmblɪ] adj friable

crumpet ['krʌmpɪt] n petite crêpe (épaisse)

crumple ['krʌmpl] vt froisser, friper

crunch [krʌntʃ] vt croquer; (underfoot) faire craquer, écraser; faire crisser ▷ n (fig) instant m or moment m critique, moment de vérité

crunchy ['krʌntʃɪ] adj croquant(e), croustillant(e)

crusade [kruːˈseɪd] n croisade f ▷ vi (fig): **to ~ for/against** partir en croisade pour/contre

crush [krʌʃ] n (crowd) foule f, cohue f; (love): **to have a ~ on sb** avoir le béguin pour qn; (drink): **lemon ~** citron pressé m ▷ vt écraser; (crumple) froisser; (grind, break up: garlic, ice) piler; (: grapes) presser; (hopes) anéantir

crust [krʌst] n croûte f

crusty ['krʌstɪ] adj (bread) croustillant(e); (inf: person) revêche, bourru(e); (: remark) irrité(e)

crutch [krʌtʃ] n béquille f; (Tech) support m; (also: **crotch**) entrejambe m

crux [krʌks] n point crucial

cry [kraɪ] vi pleurer; (shout: also: ~ **out**) crier ▷ n cri m; **why are you ~ing?** pourquoi pleures-tu?; **to ~ for help** appeler à l'aide; **she had a good ~** - elle a pleuré un bon coup; **it's a far ~ from ...** (fig) on est loin de ...; **cry off** vi se dédire; se décommander; **cry out** vi (call out, shout) pousser un cri ▷ vt crier

cryptic ['krɪptɪk] adj énigmatique

crystal ['krɪstl] n cristal m

crystal-clear ['krɪstl'klɪə'] adj clair(e) comme de l'eau de roche

CSA n abbr = **Confederate States of America**; (Brit: = Child Support Agency) organisme pour la protection des enfants de parents séparés, qui contrôle le versement des pensions alimentaires.

CTC n abbr (Brit) = **city technology college**

cub [kʌb] n petit m (d'un animal); (also: ~ **scout**) louveteau m

Cuba ['kjuːbə] n Cuba m

cube [kjuːb] n cube m ▷ vt (Math) élever au cube

cubic ['kjuːbɪk] adj cubique; ~ **metre** etc mètre m etc cube; ~ **capacity** (Aut) cylindrée f

cubicle ['kjuːbɪkl] n (in hospital) box m; (at pool) cabine f

cuckoo ['kukuː] n coucou m

cuckoo clock n (pendule f à) coucou m

cucumber ['kjuːkʌmbə'] n concombre m

cuddle ['kʌdl] vt câliner, caresser ▷ vi se blottir l'un contre l'autre

cue [kjuː] n queue f de billard; (Theat etc) signal m

cuff [kʌf] n (Brit: of shirt, coat etc) poignet m, manchette f; (US: on trousers) revers m; (blow) gifle f ▷ vt gifler; **off the ~** adv à l'improviste

cufflinks ['kʌflɪŋks] n boutons m de manchette

cuisine [kwɪˈziːn] n cuisine f, art m culinaire

cul-de-sac ['kʌldəsæk] n cul-de-sac m, impasse f

cull [kʌl] vt sélectionner; (kill selectively) pratiquer l'abattage sélectif de ▷ n (of animals) abattage sélectif

culminate ['kʌlmɪneɪt] vi: **to ~ in** finir or se terminer par; (lead to) mener à

culmination [kʌlmɪˈneɪʃən] n point culminant

culottes [kjuːˈlɔts] npl jupe-culotte f

culprit ['kʌlprɪt] n coupable m/f

cult [kʌlt] n culte m

cultivate ['kʌltɪveɪt] vt (also fig) cultiver

cultivation [kʌltɪˈveɪʃən] n culture f

cultural ['kʌltʃərəl] adj culturel(le)

culture ['kʌltʃə'] n (also fig) culture f

cultured ['kʌltʃəd] adj cultivé(e) (fig)

cumbersome ['kʌmbəsəm] adj encombrant(e), embarrassant(e)

cumin ['kʌmɪn] n (spice) cumin m

cunning ['kʌnɪŋ] n ruse f, astuce f ▷ adj rusé(e), malin(-igne); (clever: device, idea) astucieux(-euse)

cup [kʌp] n tasse f; (prize, event) coupe f; (of bra) bonnet m; **a ~ of tea** une tasse de thé

cupboard ['kʌbəd] n placard m

cup final n (Brit Football) finale f de la coupe

cup tie ['kʌptaɪ] n (Brit Football) match m de coupe

curate ['kjuərɪt] n vicaire m

curator [kjuəˈreɪtə'] n conservateur m (d'un musée etc)

curb [kəːb] vt refréner, mettre un frein à; (expenditure) limiter, juguler ▷ n (fig) frein m; (US) bord m du trottoir

curdle ['kəːdl] vi (se) cailler

cure [kjuə'] vt guérir; (Culin: salt) saler; (: smoke) fumer; (: dry) sécher ▷ n remède m; **to be ~d of sth** être guéri de qch

curfew ['kəːfjuː] n couvre-feu m

curiosity [kjuərɪˈɔsɪtɪ] n curiosité f

curious ['kjuərɪəs] adj curieux(-euse); **I'm ~ about him** il m'intrigue

curl [kə:l] n boucle f (de cheveux); (of smoke etc) volute f ▷ vt, vi boucler; (tightly) friser; **curl up** vi s'enrouler; (person) se pelotonner

curler ['kə:lə'] n bigoudi m, rouleau m; (Sport) joueur(-euse) de curling

curly ['kə:lɪ] adj bouclé(e); (tightly curled) frisé(e)

currant ['kʌrnt] n raisin m de Corinthe, raisin sec; (fruit) groseille f

currency ['kʌrnsɪ] n monnaie f; **foreign ~** devises étrangères, monnaie étrangère; **to gain ~** (fig) s'accréditer

current ['kʌrnt] n courant m ▷ adj (common) courant(e); (tendency, price, event) actuel(le); **direct/alternating ~** (Elec) courant continu/ alternatif; **the ~ issue of a magazine** le dernier numéro d'un magazine; **in ~ use** d'usage courant

current account n (Brit) compte courant

current affairs npl (questions fpl d')actualité f

currently ['kʌrntlɪ] adv actuellement

curriculum (pl **curriculums** or **curricula**) [kə'rɪkjuləm, -lə] n programme m d'études

curriculum vitae [-'vi:taɪ] n curriculum vitae (CV) m

curry ['kʌrɪ] n curry m ▷ vt: **to ~ favour with** chercher à gagner la faveur or à s'attirer les bonnes grâces de; **chicken ~** curry de poulet, poulet m au curry

curry powder n poudre f de curry

curse [kə:s] vi jurer, blasphémer ▷ vt maudire ▷ n (spell) malédiction f; (problem, scourge) fléau m; (swearword) juron m

cursor ['kə:sə'] n (Comput) curseur m

cursory ['kə:sərɪ] adj superficiel(le), hâtif(-ive)

curt [kə:t] adj brusque, sec(-sèche)

curtail [kə:'teɪl] vt (visit etc) écourter; (expenses etc) réduire

curtain ['kə:tn] n rideau m; **to draw the ~s** (together) fermer or tirer les rideaux; (apart) ouvrir les rideaux

curtsey, curtsy ['kə:tsɪ] n révérence f ▷ vi faire une révérence

curve [kə:v] n courbe f; (in the road) tournant m, virage m ▷ vt courber ▷ vi se courber; (road) faire une courbe

curved [kə:vd] adj courbe

cushion ['kʊʃən] n coussin m ▷ vt (seat) rembourrer; (fall, shock) amortir

custard ['kʌstəd] n (for pouring) crème anglaise

custody ['kʌstədɪ] n (of child) garde f; (for offenders) détention préventive; **to take sb into ~** placer qn en détention préventive; **in the ~ of** sous la garde de

custom ['kʌstəm] n coutume f, usage m; (Law) droit coutumier, coutume f; (Comm) clientèle f

customary ['kʌstəmərɪ] adj habituel(le); **it is ~ to do it** l'usage veut qu'on le fasse

customer ['kʌstəmə'] n client(e); **he's an awkward ~** (inf) ce n'est pas quelqu'un de facile

customized ['kʌstəmaɪzd] adj personnalisé(e); (car etc) construit(e) sur commande

custom-made ['kʌstəm'meɪd] adj (clothes) fait(e) sur mesure; (other goods: also: **custom-built**) hors série, fait(e) sur commande

customs ['kʌstəmz] npl douane f; **to go through (the) ~** passer la douane

customs officer n douanier m

cut [kʌt] (pt, pp cut) vt couper; (meat) découper; (shape, make) tailler; couper; creuser; graver; (reduce) réduire; (inf: lecture, appointment) manquer ▷ vi couper; (intersect) se couper ▷ n (gen) coupure f; (of clothes) coupe f; (of jewel) taille f; (in salary etc) réduction f; (of meat) morceau m; **to ~ teeth** (baby) faire ses dents; **to ~ a tooth** percer une dent; **to ~ one's finger** se couper le doigt; **to get one's hair ~** se faire couper les cheveux; **I've ~ myself** je me suis coupé; **to ~ sth short** couper court à qch; **to ~ sb dead** ignorer (complètement) qn; **cut back** vt (plants) tailler; (production, expenditure) réduire; **cut down** vt (tree) abattre; (reduce) réduire; **to ~ sb down to size** (fig) remettre qn à sa place; **cut down on** vt fus réduire; **cut in** vi (interrupt: conversation): **to ~ in (on)** couper la parole (à); (Aut) faire une queue de poisson; **cut off** vt couper; (fig) isoler; **we've been ~ off** (Tel) nous avons été coupés; **cut out** vt (picture etc) découper; (remove) supprimer; **cut up** vt découper

cutback ['kʌtbæk] n réduction f

cute [kju:t] adj mignon(ne), adorable; (clever) rusé(e), astucieux(-euse)

cutlery ['kʌtlərɪ] n couverts mpl; (trade) coutellerie f

cutlet ['kʌtlɪt] n côtelette f

cutout ['kʌtaʊt] n coupe-circuit m inv; (paper figure) découpage m

cut-price ['kʌt'praɪs], (US) **cut-rate** ['kʌt'reɪt] adj au rabais, à prix réduit

cut-throat ['kʌtθrəʊt] n assassin m ▷ adj: **~ competition** concurrence f sauvage

cutting ['kʌtɪŋ] adj tranchant(e), coupant(e); (fig) cinglant(e) ▷ n (Brit: from newspaper) coupure f (de journal); (from plant) bouture f; (Rail) tranchée f; (Cine) montage m

CV n abbr = **curriculum vitae**

cwt abbr = **hundredweight**

cyanide ['saɪənaɪd] n cyanure m

cyberspace ['saɪbəspeɪs] n cyberespace m

cycle ['saɪkl] n cycle m; (bicycle) bicyclette f, vélo m ▷ vi faire de la bicyclette

cycle hire n location f de vélos

cycle lane, cycle path n piste f cyclable

cycling ['saɪklɪŋ] n cyclisme m; **to go on a ~ holiday** (Brit) faire du cyclotourisme

cyclist ['saɪklɪst] n cycliste m/f

cyclone ['saɪkləʊn] n cyclone m

cygnet ['sɪgnɪt] n jeune cygne m

cylinder ['sɪlɪndə'] n cylindre m

cymbals ['sɪmblz] *npl* cymbales *fpl*

cynic ['sɪnɪk] *n* cynique *m/f*

cynical ['sɪnɪkl] *adj* cynique

cynicism ['sɪnɪsɪzəm] *n* cynisme *m*

Cypriot ['sɪprɪət] *adj* cypriote, chypriote ▷ *n* Cypriote *m/f*, Chypriote *m/f*

Cyprus ['saɪprəs] *n* Chypre *f*

cyst [sɪst] *n* kyste *m*

cystitis [sɪs'taɪtɪs] *n* cystite *f*

czar [zɑː] *n* tsar *m*

Czech [tʃɛk] *adj* tchèque ▷ *n* Tchèque *m/f*; (*Ling*) tchèque *m*

Czechoslovak [tʃɛkə'sləuvæk] *adj, n* = **Czechoslovakian**

Czechoslovakia [tʃɛkəslə'vækɪə] *n* Tchécoslovaquie *f*

Czechoslovakian [tʃɛkəslə'vækɪən] *adj* tchécoslovaque ▷ *n* Tchécoslovaque *m/f*

Czech Republic *n*: **the ~** la République tchèque

d

D¹, d¹ [diː] *n* (letter) D, d *m*; (*Mus*): **D** ré *m*; **D for David**, (*US*) **D for Dog** D comme Désirée

D² *abbr* (*US Pol*) = **democrat; democratic**

d *abbr* (*Brit: old*) = **penny**

dab [dæb] *vt* (*eyes, wound*) tamponner; (*paint, cream*) appliquer (par petites touches *or* rapidement); **a ~ of paint** un petit coup de peinture

dabble ['dæbl] *vi*: **to ~ in** faire *or* se mêler *or* s'occuper un peu de

dad, daddy [dæd, 'dædɪ] *n* papa *m*

daffodil ['dæfədɪl] *n* jonquille *f*

daft [dɑːft] *adj* (*inf*) idiot(e), stupide; **to be ~ about** être toqué(e) *or* mordu(e) de

dagger ['dægə'] *n* poignard *m*; **to be at ~s drawn with sb** être à couteaux tirés avec qn; **to look ~s at sb** foudroyer qn du regard

daily ['deɪlɪ] *adj* quotidien(ne), journalier(-ière) ▷ *n* quotidien *m*; (*Brit: servant*) femme *f* de ménage (*à la journée*) ▷ *adv* tous les jours; **twice ~** deux fois par jour

dainty ['deɪntɪ] *adj* délicat(e), mignon(ne)

dairy ['dɛərɪ] *n* (*shop*) crémerie *f*, laiterie *f*; (*on farm*) laiterie ▷ *adj* laitier(-ière)

dairy produce *n* produits laitiers

dairy products *npl* produits laitier

daisy ['deɪzɪ] *n* pâquerette *f*

dale [deɪl] *n* vallon *m*

dam [dæm] *n* (*wall*) barrage *m*; (*water*) réservoir *m*, lac *m* de retenue ▷ *vt* endiguer

damage ['dæmɪdʒ] *n* dégâts *mpl*, dommages *mpl*; (*fig*) tort *m* ▷ *vt* endommager, abîmer;

(fig) faire du tort à; **damages** *npl (Law)* dommages-intérêts *mpl*; **to pay £5000 in ~s** payer 5000 livres de dommages- intérêts; **~ to property** dégâts matériels

damn [dæm] *vt* condamner; *(curse)* maudire ▷ *n (inf)*: **I don't give a ~** je m'en fous ▷ *adj (inf: also: ~ed)*: **this ~ ...** ce sacré *or* foutu ...; **~ (it)!** zut!

damning ['dæmɪŋ] *adj (evidence)* accablant(e)

damp [dæmp] *adj* humide ▷ *n* humidité *f* ▷ *vt (also: ~en: cloth, rag)* humecter; *(: enthusiasm etc)* refroidir

damson ['dæmzən] *n* prune *f* de Damas

dance [dɑːns] *n* danse *f*; *(ball)* bal *m* ▷ *vi* danser; **to ~ about** sautiller, gambader

dance floor *n* piste *f* de danse

dance hall *n* salle *f* de bal, dancing *m*

dancer ['dɑːnsəʳ] *n* danseur(-euse)

dancing ['dɑːnsɪŋ] *n* danse *f*

dandelion ['dændɪlaɪən] *n* pissenlit *m*

dandruff ['dændrəf] *n* pellicules *fpl*

D & T *n abbr (Brit: Scol)* = **design and technology**

Dane [deɪn] *n* Danois(e)

danger ['deɪndʒəʳ] *n* danger *m*; **~!** *(on sign)* danger!; **there is a ~ of fire** il y a (un) risque d'incendie; **in ~** en danger; **he was in ~ of falling** il risquait de tomber; **out of ~** hors de danger

dangerous ['deɪndʒrəs] *adj* dangereux(-euse)

dangle ['dæŋgl] *vt* balancer; *(fig)* faire miroiter ▷ *vi* pendre, se balancer

Danish ['deɪnɪʃ] *adj* danois(e) ▷ *n (Ling)* danois *m*

dare [dɛəʳ] *vt*: **to ~ sb to do** défier qn *or* mettre qn au défi de faire ▷ *vi*: **to ~ (to) do sth** oser faire qch; **I ~n't tell him** *(Brit)* je n'ose pas le lui dire; **I ~ say he'll turn up** il est probable qu'il viendra

daring ['dɛərɪŋ] *adj* hardi(e), audacieux(-euse) ▷ *n* audace *f*, hardiesse *f*

dark [dɑːk] *adj (night, room)* obscur(e), sombre; *(colour, complexion)* foncé(e), sombre; *(fig)* sombre ▷ *n*: **in the ~** dans le noir; **to be in the ~ about** *(fig)* ignorer tout de; **after ~** après la tombée de la nuit; **it is/is getting ~** il fait nuit/commence à faire nuit

darken ['dɑːkn] *vt* obscurcir, assombrir ▷ *vi* s'obscurcir, s'assombrir

dark glasses *npl* lunettes noires

darkness ['dɑːknɪs] *n* obscurité *f*

darkroom ['dɑːkrum] *n* chambre noire

darling ['dɑːlɪŋ] *adj, n* chéri(e)

darn [dɑːn] *vt* repriser

dart [dɑːt] *n* fléchette *f*; *(in sewing)* pince *f* ▷ *vi*: **to ~ towards** *(also:* **make a ~ towards***)* se précipiter *or* s'élancer vers; **to ~ away/along** partir/passer comme une flèche

dartboard ['dɑːtbɔːd] *n* cible *f* (de jeu de fléchettes)

darts [dɑːts] *n* jeu *m* de fléchettes

dash [dæʃ] *n (sign)* tiret *m*; *(small quantity)* goutte *f*, larme *f* ▷ *vt (throw)* jeter *or* lancer violemment; *(hopes)* anéantir ▷ *vi*: **to ~ towards** *(also:* **make a ~ towards***)* se précipiter *or* se ruer vers; **a ~ of soda** un peu d'eau gazeuse; **dash away** *vi* partir à toute allure; **dash off** *vi* = **dash away**

dashboard ['dæʃbɔːd] *n (Aut)* tableau *m* de bord

dashing ['dæʃɪŋ] *adj* fringant(e)

data ['deɪtə] *npl* données *fpl*

database ['deɪtəbeɪs] *n* base *f* de données

data processing *n* traitement *m* des données

date [deɪt] *n* date *f*; *(with sb)* rendez-vous *m*; *(fruit)* datte *f* ▷ *vt* dater; *(person)* sortir avec; **what's the ~ today?** quelle date sommes- nous aujourd'hui?; **~ of birth** date de naissance; **closing ~** date de clôture; **to ~** *adv* à ce jour; **out of ~** périmé(e); **up to ~** à la page, mis(e) à jour, moderne; **to bring up to ~** *(correspondence, information)* mettre à jour; *(method)* moderniser; *(person)* mettre au courant; **letter ~d 5th July** *or (US)* **July 5th** lettre (datée) du 5 juillet

dated ['deɪtɪd] *adj* démodé(e)

date rape *n* viol *m* (à l'issue d'un rendez-vous galant)

daub [dɔːb] *vt* barbouiller

daughter ['dɔːtəʳ] *n* fille *f*

daughter-in-law ['dɔːtərɪnlɔː] *n* belle-fille *f*, bru *f*

daunting ['dɔːntɪŋ] *adj* décourageant(e), intimidant(e)

dawdle ['dɔːdl] *vi* traîner, lambiner; **to ~ over one's work** traînasser *or* lambiner sur son travail

dawn [dɔːn] *n* aube *f*, aurore *f* ▷ *vi* (*day*) se lever, poindre; *(fig)* naître, se faire jour; **at ~** à l'aube; **from ~ to dusk** du matin au soir; **it ~ed on him that ...** il lui vint à l'esprit que ...

day [deɪ] *n* jour *m*; *(as duration)* journée *f*; *(period of time, age)* époque *f*, temps *m*; **the ~ before** la veille, le jour précédent; **the ~ after, the following ~** le lendemain, le jour suivant; **the ~ before yester~** avant-hier; **the ~ after tomorrow** après-demain; **(on) the ~ that ...** le jour où ...; **~ by ~** jour après jour; **by ~** de jour; **paid by the ~** payé(e) à la journée; **these ~s, in the present ~** de nos jours, à l'heure actuelle

daybreak ['deɪbreɪk] *n* point *m* du jour

day-care centre ['deɪkɛə-] *n (for elderly etc)* centre *m* d'accueil de jour; *(for children)* garderie *f*

daydream ['deɪdriːm] *n* rêverie *f* ▷ *vi* rêver (tout éveillé)

daylight ['deɪlaɪt] *n* (lumière *f* du) jour *m*

day return *n (Brit)* billet *m* d'aller-retour *(valable pour la journée)*

daytime ['deɪtaɪm] *n* jour *m*, journée *f*

day-to-day ['deɪtə'deɪ] *adj* (*routine, expenses*) journalier(-ière); **on a ~ basis** au jour le jour

day trip *n* excursion *f* (d'une journée)

daze [deɪz] *vt* (*drug*) hébéter; (*blow*) étourdir ▷ *n*: **in a ~** hébété(e), étourdi(e)

dazed [deɪzd] *adj* abruti(e)

dazzle ['dæzl] *vt* éblouir, aveugler

dazzling ['dæzlɪŋ] *adj* (*light*) aveuglant(e), éblouissant(e); (*fig*) éblouissant(e)

DC *abbr* (*Elec*) = **direct current**; (*US*) = **District of Columbia**

D-day ['diːdeɪ] *n* le jour J

dead [dɛd] *adj* mort(e); (*numb*) engourdi(e), insensible; (*battery*) à plat ▷ *adv* (*completely*) absolument, complètement; (*exactly*) juste; **the dead** *npl* les morts; **he was shot ~** il a été tué d'un coup de revolver; **~ on time** à l'heure pile; **~ tired** éreinté(e), complètement fourbu(e); **to stop ~** s'arrêter pile *or* net; **the line is ~** (*Tel*) la ligne est coupée

deaden [dɛdn] *vt* (*blow, sound*) amortir; (*make numb*) endormir, rendre insensible

dead end *n* impasse *f*

dead heat *n* (*Sport*): **to finish in a ~** terminer ex aequo

deadline ['dɛdlaɪn] *n* date *f or* heure *f* limite; **to work to a ~** avoir des délais stricts à respecter

deadlock ['dɛdlɔk] *n* impasse *f* (*fig*)

dead loss *n* (*inf*): **to be a ~** (*person*) n'être bon/ bonne à rien; (*thing*) ne rien valoir

deadly ['dɛdlɪ] *adj* mortel(le); (*weapon*) meurtrier(-ière); **~ dull** ennuyeux(-euse) à mourir, mortellement ennuyeux

deadpan ['dɛdpæn] *adj* impassible; (*humour*) pince-sans-rire *inv*

Dead Sea *n*: **the ~** la mer Morte

deaf [dɛf] *adj* sourd(e); **to turn a ~ ear to sth** faire la sourde oreille à qch

deafen ['dɛfn] *vt* rendre sourd(e); (*fig*) assourdir

deafening ['dɛfnɪŋ] *adj* assourdissant(e)

deaf-mute ['dɛfmjuːt] *n* sourd-e-muet/te

deafness ['dɛfnɪs] *n* surdité *f*

deal [diːl] *n* affaire *f*, marché *m* ▷ *vt* (*pt, pp* **dealt**) [dɛlt] (*blow*) porter; (*cards*) donner, distribuer; **to strike a ~ with sb** faire *or* conclure un marché avec qn; **it's a ~!** (*inf*) marché conclu!, tope-là!, topez-là!; **he got a bad ~ from them** ils ont mal agi envers lui; **he got a fair ~ from them** ils ont agi loyalement envers lui; **a good ~** (*a lot*) beaucoup; **a good ~ of**, **a great ~ of** beaucoup de, énormément de; **deal in** *vt fus* (*Comm*) faire le commerce de, être dans le commerce de; **deal with** *vt fus* (*Comm*) traiter avec; (*handle*) s'occuper *or* se charger de; (*be about: book etc*) traiter de

dealer ['diːlə'] *n* (*Comm*) marchand *m*; (*Cards*) donneur *m*

dealings ['diːlɪŋz] *npl* (*in goods, shares*) opérations *fpl*, transactions *fpl*; (*relations*) relations *fpl*, rapports *mpl*

dealt [dɛlt] *pt, pp of* **deal**

dean [diːn] *n* (*Rel, Brit Scol*) doyen *m*; (*US Scol*) conseiller principal/conseillère principale d'éducation

dear [dɪə'] *adj* cher/chère; (*expensive*) cher, coûteux(-euse) ▷ *n*: **my ~** mon cher/ma chère ▷ *excl*: **~ me!** mon Dieu!; **D~ Sir/Madam** (*in letter*) Monsieur/Madame; **D~ Mr/Mrs X** Cher Monsieur/Chère Madame X

dearly ['dɪəlɪ] *adv* (*love*) tendrement; (*pay*) cher

death [dɛθ] *n* mort *f*; (*Admin*) décès *m*

death certificate *n* acte *m* de décès

deathly ['dɛθlɪ] *adj* de mort ▷ *adv* comme la mort

death penalty *n* peine *f* de mort

death rate *n* taux *m* de mortalité

death sentence *n* condamnation *f* à mort

death toll *n* nombre *m* de morts

debase [dɪ'beɪs] *vt* (*currency*) déprécier, dévaloriser; (*person*) abaisser, avilir

debatable [dɪ'beɪtəbl] *adj* discutable, contestable; **it is ~ whether ...** il est douteux que ...

debate [dɪ'beɪt] *n* discussion *f*, débat *m* ▷ *vt* discuter, débattre ▷ *vi* (*consider*): **to ~ whether** se demander si

debit ['dɛbɪt] *n* débit *m* ▷ *vt*: **to ~ a sum to sb** *or* **to sb's account** porter une somme au débit de qn, débiter qn d'une somme

debit card *n* carte *f* de paiement

debris ['dɛbriː] *n* débris *mpl*, décombres *mpl*

debt [dɛt] *n* dette *f*; **to be in ~** avoir des dettes, être endetté(e); **bad ~** créance *f* irrécouvrable

debtor ['dɛtə'] *n* débiteur(-trice)

debug [diː'bʌg] *vt* (*Comput*) déboguer

debut ['deɪbjuː] *n* début(s) *m(pl)*

Dec. *abbr* (= *December*): déc

decade ['dɛkeɪd] *n* décennie *f*, décade *f*

decadence ['dɛkədəns] *n* décadence *f*

decaf ['diːkæf] *n* (*inf*) déca *m*

decaffeinated [dɪ'kæfɪneɪtɪd] *adj* décaféiné(e)

decanter [dɪ'kæntə'] *n* carafe *f*

decay [dɪ'keɪ] *n* (*of food, wood etc*) décomposition *f*, pourriture *f*; (*of building*) délabrement *m*; (*fig*) déclin *m*; (*also: tooth ~*) carie *f* (dentaire) ▷ *vi* (*rot*) se décomposer, pourrir; (: *teeth*) se carier; (*fig: city, district, building*) se délabrer; (: *civilization*) décliner; (: *system*) tomber en ruine

deceased [dɪ'siːst] *n*: **the ~** le/la défunt(e)

deceit [dɪ'siːt] *n* tromperie *f*, supercherie *f*

deceitful [dɪ'siːtful] *adj* trompeur(-euse)

deceive [dɪ'siːv] *vt* tromper; **to ~ o.s.** s'abuser

December [dɪ'sɛmbə'] *n* décembre *m*; *see also* **July**

decency ['diːsənsɪ] *n* décence *f*

decent ['di:sənt] *adj* (*proper*) décent(e), convenable; **they were very ~ about it** ils se sont montrés très chics

deception [dɪ'sepʃən] *n* tromperie *f*

deceptive [dɪ'septɪv] *adj* trompeur(-euse)

decide [dɪ'saɪd] *vt* (*subj: person*) décider; (*question, argument*) trancher, régler ▷ *vi* se décider, décider; **to ~ to do/that** décider de faire/que; **to ~ on** décider, se décider pour; **to ~ on doing** décider de faire; **to ~ against doing** décider de ne pas faire

decided [dɪ'saɪdɪd] *adj* (*resolute*) résolu(e), décidé(e); (*clear, definite*) net(te), marqué(e)

decidedly [dɪ'saɪdɪdlɪ] *adv* résolument; incontestablement, nettement

deciduous [dɪ'sɪdjuəs] *adj* à feuilles caduques

decimal ['desɪməl] *adj* décimal(e) ▷ *n* décimale *f*; **to three ~ places** (jusqu')à la troisième décimale

decimal point *n* = virgule *f*

decipher [dɪ'saɪfə'] *vt* déchiffrer

decision [dɪ'sɪʒən] *n* décision *f*; **to make a ~** prendre une décision

decisive [dɪ'saɪsɪv] *adj* décisif(-ive); (*influence*) décisif, déterminant(e); (*manner, person*) décidé(e), catégorique; (*reply*) ferme, catégorique

deck [dek] *n* (*Naut*) pont *m*; (*of cards*) jeu *m*; (*record deck*) platine *f*; (*of bus*): **top ~** impériale *f*; **to go up on ~** monter sur le pont; **below ~** dans l'entrepont

deckchair ['dektʃeə'] *n* chaise longue

declaration [deklə'reɪʃən] *n* déclaration *f*

declare [dɪ'klεə'] *vt* déclarer

decline [dɪ'klaɪn] *n* (*decay*) déclin *m*; (*lessening*) baisse *f* ▷ *vt* refuser, décliner ▷ *vi* décliner; (*business*) baisser; **~ in living standards** baisse du niveau de vie; **to ~ to do sth** refuser (poliment) de faire qch

decoder [di:'kəudə'] *n* (*Comput, TV*) décodeur *m*

decorate ['dekəreɪt] *vt* (*adorn, give a medal to*) décorer; (*paint and paper*) peindre et tapisser

decoration [dekə'reɪʃən] *n* (*medal etc, adornment*) décoration *f*

decorator ['dekəreɪtə'] *n* peintre *m* en bâtiment

decoy ['di:kɔɪ] *n* piège *m*; **they used him as a ~ for the enemy** ils se sont servis de lui pour attirer l'ennemi

decrease *n* ['di:kri:s] diminution *f* ▷ *vt, vi* [di:'kri:s] diminuer; **to be on the ~** diminuer, être en diminution

decree [dɪ'kri:] *n* (*Pol, Rel*) décret *m*; (*Law*) arrêt *m*, jugement *m* ▷ *vt*: **to ~ (that)** décréter (que), ordonner (que); **~ absolute** jugement définitif (de divorce); **~ nisi** jugement provisoire de divorce

dedicate ['dedɪkeɪt] *vt* consacrer; (*book etc*) dédier

dedicated ['dedɪkeɪtɪd] *adj* (*person*) dévoué(e); (*Comput*) spécialisé(e), dédié(e); **~ word processor** station *f* de traitement de texte

dedication [dedɪ'keɪʃən] *n* (*devotion*) dévouement *m*; (*in book*) dédicace *f*

deduce [dɪ'dju:s] *vt* déduire, conclure

deduct [dɪ'dʌkt] *vt*: **to ~ sth (from)** déduire qch (de), retrancher qch (de); (*from wage etc*) prélever qch (sur), retenir qch (sur)

deduction [dɪ'dʌkʃən] *n* (*deducting, deducing*) déduction *f*; (*from wage etc*) prélèvement *m*, retenue *f*

deed [di:d] *n* action *f*, acte *m*; (*Law*) acte notarié, contrat *m*; **~ of covenant** (acte *m* de) donation *f*

deem [di:m] *vt* (*formal*) juger, estimer; **to ~ it wise to do** juger bon de faire

deep [di:p] *adj* (*water, sigh, sorrow, thoughts*) profond(e); (*voice*) grave ▷ *adv*: **~ in snow** recouvert(e) d'une épaisse couche de neige; **spectators stood 20 ~** il y avait 20 rangs de spectateurs; **knee-~ in water** dans l'eau jusqu'aux genoux; **4 metres ~** de 4 mètres de profondeur; **how ~ is the water?** l'eau a quelle profondeur?; **he took a ~ breath** il inspira profondément, il prit son souffle

deepen [di:pn] *vt* (*hole*) approfondir ▷ *vi* s'approfondir; (*darkness*) s'épaissir

deepfreeze ['di:p'fri:z] *n* congélateur *m* ▷ *vt* surgeler

deep-fry ['di:p'fraɪ] *vt* faire frire (dans une friteuse)

deeply ['di:plɪ] *adv* profondément; (*dig*) en profondeur; (*regret, interested*) vivement

deep-sea ['di:p'si:] *adj*: **~ diver** plongeur sous-marin; **~ diving** plongée sous-marine; **~ fishing** pêche hauturière

deep-seated ['di:p'si:tɪd] *adj* (*belief*) profondément enraciné(e)

deer [dɪə'] *n pl inv*: **the ~** les cervidés *mpl*; (*Zool*): **(red) ~** cerf *m*; **(fallow) ~** daim *m*; **(roe) ~** chevreuil *m*

deerskin ['dɪəskɪn] *n* peau *f* de daim

deface [dɪ'feɪs] *vt* dégrader; barbouiller; rendre illisible

default [dɪ'fɔ:lt] *vi* (*Law*) faire défaut; (*gen*) manquer à ses engagements ▷ *n* (*Comput: also*: **~ value**) valeur *f* par défaut; **by ~** (*Law*) par défaut, par contumace; (*Sport*) par forfait; **to ~ on a debt** ne pas s'acquitter d'une dette

defeat [dɪ'fi:t] *n* défaite *f* ▷ *vt* (*team, opponents*) battre; (*fig: plans, efforts*) faire échouer

defect *n* ['di:fekt] *n* défaut *m* ▷ *vi* [dɪ'fekt]: **to ~ to the enemy/the West** passer à l'ennemi/l'Ouest; **physical ~** malformation *f*, vice *m* de conformation; **mental ~** anomalie *or* déficience mentale

defective [dɪ'fektɪv] *adj* défectueux(-euse)

defence, (*US*) **defense** [dɪ'fens] *n* défense *f*; **in ~ of** pour défendre; **witness for the ~** témoin *m* à décharge; **the Ministry of D~**,

(US) **the Department of Defense** le ministère de la Défense nationale

defenceless [dɪˈfɛnslɪs] *adj* sans défense

defend [dɪˈfɛnd] *vt* défendre; (*decision, action, opinion*) justifier, défendre

defendant [dɪˈfɛndət] *n* défendeur(-deresse); (*in criminal case*) accusé(e), prévenu(e)

defender [dɪˈfɛndər] *n* défenseur *m*

defense [dɪˈfɛns] *n* (US) = **defence**

defensive [dɪˈfɛnsɪv] *adj* défensif(-ive) ▷ *n* défensive *f*; **on the ~** sur la défensive

defer [dɪˈfəːr] *vt* (*postpone*) différer, ajourner ▷ *vi* (*submit*): **to ~ to sb/sth** déférer à qn/qch, s'en remettre à qn/qch

defiance [dɪˈfaɪəns] *n* défi *m*; **in ~ of** au mépris de

defiant [dɪˈfaɪənt] *adj* provocant(e), de défi; (*person*) rebelle, intraitable

deficiency [dɪˈfɪʃənsɪ] *n* (*lack*) insuffisance *f*; (: *Med*) carence *f*; (*flaw*) faiblesse *f*; (*Comm*) déficit *m*, découvert *m*

deficient [dɪˈfɪʃənt] *adj* (*inadequate*) insuffisant(e); (*defective*) défectueux(-euse); **to be ~ in** manquer de

deficit [ˈdɛfɪsɪt] *n* déficit *m*

define [dɪˈfaɪn] *vt* définir

definite [ˈdɛfɪnɪt] *adj* (*fixed*) défini(e), (bien) déterminé(e); (*clear, obvious*) net(te), manifeste; (*Ling*) défini(e); (*certain*) sûr(e); **he was ~ about it** il a été catégorique; il était sûr de son fait

definitely [ˈdɛfɪnɪtlɪ] *adv* sans aucun doute

definition [dɛfɪˈnɪʃən] *n* définition *f*; (*clearness*) netteté *f*

deflate [diːˈfleɪt] *vt* dégonfler; (*pompous person*) rabattre le caquet à; (*Econ*) provoquer la déflation de; (: *prices*) faire tomber or baisser

deflect [dɪˈflɛkt] *vt* détourner, faire dévier

deformed [dɪˈfɔːmd] *adj* difforme

defraud [dɪˈfrɔːd] *vt* frauder; **to ~ sb of sth** soutirer qch malhonnêtement à qn; escroquer qch à qn, frustrer qn de qch

defrost [diːˈfrɒst] *vt* (*fridge*) dégivrer; (*frozen food*) décongeler

deft [dɛft] *adj* adroit(e), preste

defunct [dɪˈfʌŋkt] *adj* défunt(e)

defuse [diːˈfjuːz] *vt* désamorcer

defy [dɪˈfaɪ] *vt* défier; (*efforts etc*) résister à; **it defies description** cela défie toute description

degenerate *vi* [dɪˈdʒɛnəreɪt] dégénérer ▷ *adj* [dɪˈdʒɛnərɪt] dégénéré(e)

degree [dɪˈgriː] *n* degré *m*; (*Scol*) diplôme *m* (universitaire); **10 ~s below (zero)** 10 degrés au-dessous de zéro; **a (first) ~ in maths** (*Brit*) une licence en maths; **a considerable ~ of risk** un considérable facteur or élément de risque; **by ~s** (*gradually*) par degrés; **to some ~, to a certain ~** jusqu'à un certain point, dans une certaine mesure

dehydrated [diːhaɪˈdreɪtɪd] *adj* déshydraté(e); (*milk, eggs*) en poudre

de-ice [ˈdiːˈaɪs] *vt* (*windscreen*) dégivrer

de-icer [ˈdiːˈaɪsər] *n* dégivreur *m*

deign [deɪn] *vi*: **to ~ to do** daigner faire

dejected [dɪˈdʒɛktɪd] *adj* abattu(e), déprimé(e)

delay [dɪˈleɪ] *vt* (*journey, operation*) retarder, différer; (*traveller, train*) retarder; (*payment*) différer ▷ *vi* s'attarder ▷ *n* délai *m*, retard *m*; **to be ~ed** être en retard; **without ~** sans délai, sans tarder

delectable [dɪˈlɛktəbl] *adj* délicieux(-euse)

delegate *n* [ˈdɛlɪgɪt] délégué(e) ▷ *vt* [ˈdɛlɪgeɪt] déléguer; **to ~ sth to sb/to do sth** déléguer qch à qn/qn pour faire qch

delete [dɪˈliːt] *vt* rayer, supprimer; (*Comput*) effacer

deli [ˈdɛlɪ] *n* épicerie fine

deliberate *adj* [dɪˈlɪbərɪt] (*intentional*) délibéré(e); (*slow*) mesuré(e) ▷ *vi* [dɪˈlɪbəreɪt] délibérer, réfléchir

deliberately [dɪˈlɪbərɪtlɪ] *adv* (*on purpose*) exprès, délibérément

delicacy [ˈdɛlɪkəsɪ] *n* délicatesse *f*; (*choice food*) mets fin or délicat, friandise *f*

delicate [ˈdɛlɪkɪt] *adj* délicat(e)

delicatessen [dɛlɪkəˈtɛsn] *n* épicerie fine

delicious [dɪˈlɪʃəs] *adj* délicieux(-euse), exquis(e)

delight [dɪˈlaɪt] *n* (grande) joie, grand plaisir ▷ *vt* enchanter; **she's a ~ to work with** c'est un plaisir de travailler avec elle; **a ~ to the eyes** un régal or plaisir pour les yeux; **to take ~ in** prendre grand plaisir à; **to be the ~ of** faire les délices or la joie de

delighted [dɪˈlaɪtɪd] *adj*: **~ (at or with sth)** ravi(e) (de qch); **to be ~ to do sth/that** être enchanté(e) or ravi(e) de faire qch/que; **I'd be ~** j'en serais enchanté or ravi

delightful [dɪˈlaɪtful] *adj* (*person*) absolument charmant(e), adorable; (*meal, evening*) merveilleux(-euse)

delinquent [dɪˈlɪŋkwənt] *adj, n* délinquant(e)

delirious [dɪˈlɪrɪəs] *adj* (*Med: fig*) délirant(e); **to be ~** délirer

deliver [dɪˈlɪvər] *vt* (*mail*) distribuer; (*goods*) livrer; (*message*) remettre; (*speech*) prononcer; (*warning, ultimatum*) lancer; (*free*) délivrer; (*Med: baby*) mettre au monde; (: *woman*) accoucher; **to ~ the goods** (*fig*) tenir ses promesses

delivery [dɪˈlɪvərɪ] *n* (*of mail*) distribution *f*; (*of goods*) livraison *f*; (*of speaker*) élocution *f*; (*Med*) accouchement *m*; **to take ~ of** prendre livraison de

delude [dɪˈluːd] *vt* tromper, leurrer; **to ~ o.s.** se leurrer, se faire des illusions

delusion [dɪˈluːʒən] *n* illusion *f*; **to have ~s of grandeur** être un peu mégalomane

de luxe [dəˈlʌks] *adj* de luxe

delve [dɛlv] vi: **to ~ into** fouiller dans

demand [dɪ'mɑːnd] vt réclamer, exiger; (need) exiger, requérir ▷ n exigence f; (claim) revendication f; (Econ) demande f; **to ~ sth (from** or **of sb)** exiger qch (de qn), réclamer qch (à qn); **in ~** demandé(e), recherché(e); **on ~** sur demande

demanding [dɪ'mɑːndɪŋ] adj (person) exigeant(e); (work) astreignant(e)

demean [dɪ'miːn] vt: **to ~ o.s.** s'abaisser

demeanour, (US) **demeanor** [dɪ'miːnəʳ] n comportement m, maintien m

demented [dɪ'mɛntɪd] adj dément(e), fou/folle

demise [dɪ'maɪz] n décès m

demister [diː'mɪstəʳ] n (Brit Aut) dispositif m anti-buée inv

demo ['dɛməu] n abbr (inf: = demonstration) (protest) manif f; (Comput) démonstration f

democracy [dɪ'mɔkrəsɪ] n démocratie f

democrat ['dɛməkræt] n démocrate m/f

democratic [dɛmə'krætɪk] adj démocratique; **the D~ Party** (US) le parti démocrate

demolish [dɪ'mɔlɪʃ] vt démolir

demolition [dɛmə'lɪʃən] n démolition f

demon ['diːmən] n démon m ▷ cpd: **a ~ squash player** un crack en squash; **a ~ driver** un fou du volant

demonstrate ['dɛmənstreɪt] vt démontrer, prouver; (show) faire une démonstration de ▷ vi: **to ~ (for/against)** manifester (en faveur de/contre)

demonstration [dɛmən'streɪʃən] n démonstration f; (Pol etc) manifestation f; **to hold a ~** (Pol etc) organiser une manifestation, manifester

demonstrator ['dɛmənstreɪtəʳ] n (Pol etc) manifestant(e); (Comm: sales person) vendeur(-euse); (: car, computer etc) modèle m de démonstration

demote [dɪ'məut] vt rétrograder

demure [dɪ'mjuəʳ] adj sage, réservé(e), d'une modestie affectée

den [dɛn] n (of lion) tanière f; (room) repaire m

denial [dɪ'naɪəl] n (of accusation) démenti m; (of rights, guilt, truth) dénégation f

denim ['dɛnɪm] n jean m; **denims** npl (blue-)jeans mpl

Denmark ['dɛnmɑːk] n Danemark m

denomination [dɪnɔmɪ'neɪʃən] n (money) valeur f; (Rel) confession f, culte m

denounce [dɪ'nauns] vt dénoncer

dense [dɛns] adj dense; (inf: stupid) obtus(e), dur(e) or lent(e) à la comprenette

densely ['dɛnslɪ] adv: **~ wooded** couvert(e) d'épaisses forêts; **~ populated** à forte densité (de population), très peuplé(e)

density ['dɛnsɪtɪ] n densité f

dent [dɛnt] n bosse f ▷ vt (also: **make a ~ in**) cabosser; **to make a ~ in** (fig) entamer

dental ['dɛntl] adj dentaire

dental floss [-flɔs] n fil m dentaire

dental surgeon n (chirurgien(ne)) dentiste

dental surgery n cabinet m de dentiste

dentist ['dɛntɪst] n dentiste m/f; **~'s surgery** (Brit) cabinet m de dentiste

dentures ['dɛntʃəz] npl dentier msg

deny [dɪ'naɪ] vt nier; (refuse) refuser; (disown) renier; **he denies having said it** il nie l'avoir dit

deodorant [diː'əudərənt] n désodorisant m, déodorant m

depart [dɪ'pɑːt] vi partir; **to ~ from** (leave) quitter, partir de; (fig: differ from) s'écarter de

department [dɪ'pɑːtmənt] n (Comm) rayon m; (Scol) section f; (Pol) ministère m, département m; **that's not my ~** (fig) ce n'est pas mon domaine or ma compétence, ce n'est pas mon rayon; **D~ of State** (US) Département d'État

department store n grand magasin

departure [dɪ'pɑːtʃəʳ] n départ m; (fig): **~ from** écart m par rapport à; **a new ~** une nouvelle voie

departure lounge n salle f de départ

depend [dɪ'pɛnd] vi: **to ~ (up)on** dépendre de; (rely on) compter sur; (financially) dépendre (financièrement) de, être à la charge de; **it ~s** cela dépend; **~ing on the result ...** selon le résultat ...

dependable [dɪ'pɛndəbl] adj sûr(e), digne de confiance

dependant [dɪ'pɛndənt] n personne f à charge

dependent [dɪ'pɛndənt] adj: **to be ~ (on)** dépendre (de) ▷ n = **dependant**

depict [dɪ'pɪkt] vt (in picture) représenter; (in words) (dé)peindre, décrire

depleted [dɪ'pliːtɪd] adj (considérablement) réduit(e) or diminué(e)

deport [dɪ'pɔːt] vt déporter, expulser

deposit [dɪ'pɔzɪt] n (Chem, Comm, Geo) dépôt m; (of ore, oil) gisement m; (part payment) arrhes fpl, acompte m; (on bottle etc) consigne f; (for hired goods etc) cautionnement m, garantie f ▷ vt déposer; (valuables) mettre or laisser en dépôt; **to put down a ~ of £50** verser 50 livres d'arrhes or d'acompte; laisser 50 livres en garantie

deposit account n compte m sur livret

depot ['dɛpəu] n dépôt m; (US: Rail) gare f

depreciate [dɪ'priːʃɪeɪt] vt déprécier ▷ vi se déprécier, se dévaloriser

depress [dɪ'prɛs] vt déprimer; (press down) appuyer sur, abaisser; (wages etc) faire baisser

depressed [dɪ'prɛst] adj (person) déprimé(e), abattu(e); (area) en déclin, touché(e) par le sous-emploi; (Comm: market, trade) maussade; **to get ~** se démoraliser, se laisser abattre

depressing [dɪ'prɛsɪŋ] adj déprimant(e)

depression [dɪ'prɛʃən] n (Econ) dépression f

deprivation [dɛprɪ'veɪʃən] n privation f; (loss) perte f

deprive [dɪ'praɪv] vt: **to ~ sb of** priver qn de
deprived [dɪ'praɪvd] adj déshérité(e)
dept. abbr (= department) dép, dépt
depth [dɛpθ] n profondeur f; **in the ~s of** au fond de; au cœur de; au plus profond de; **to be in the ~s of despair** être au plus profond du désespoir; **at a ~ of 3 metres** à 3 mètres de profondeur; **to be out of one's ~** (Brit: swimmer) ne plus avoir pied; (fig) être dépassé(e), nager; **to study sth in ~** étudier qch en profondeur
deputize ['dɛpjutaɪz] vi: **to ~ for** assurer l'intérim de
deputy ['dɛpjutɪ] n (replacement) suppléant(e), intérimaire m/f; (second in command) adjoint(e); (Pol) député m; (US: also: **~ sheriff**) shérif adjoint ▷ adj: **~ chairman** vice-président m; **~ head** (Scol) directeur(-trice) adjoint(e), sous-directeur(-trice); **~ leader** (Brit Pol) vice-président(e), secrétaire adjoint(e)
derail [dɪ'reɪl] vt faire dérailler; **to be ~ed** dérailler
deranged [dɪ'reɪndʒd] adj: **to be (mentally) ~** avoir le cerveau dérangé
derby ['də:rbɪ] n (US) (chapeau m) melon m
derelict ['dɛrɪlɪkt] adj abandonné(e), à l'abandon
derisory [dɪ'raɪsərɪ] adj (sum) dérisoire; (smile, person) moqueur(-euse), railleur(-euse)
derive [dɪ'raɪv] vt: **to ~ sth from** tirer qch de; trouver qch dans ▷ vi: **to ~ from** provenir de, dériver de
derogatory [dɪ'rɔgətərɪ] adj désobligeant(e), péjoratif(-ive)
descend [dɪ'sɛnd] vt, vi descendre; **to ~ from** descendre de, être issu(e) de; **to ~ to** s'abaisser à; **in ~ing order of importance** par ordre d'importance décroissante; **descend on** vt fus (enemy, angry person) tomber or sauter sur; (misfortune) s'abattre sur; (gloom, silence) envahir; **visitors ~ed (up)on us** des gens sont arrivés chez nous à l'improviste
descendant [dɪ'sɛndənt] n descendant(e)
descent [dɪ'sɛnt] n descente f; (origin) origine f
describe [dɪs'kraɪb] vt décrire
description [dɪs'krɪpʃən] n description f; (sort) sorte f, espèce f; **of every ~** de toutes sortes
desecrate ['dɛsɪkreɪt] vt profaner
desert [n 'dɛzət n désert m ▷ vt [dɪ'zə:t] déserter, abandonner ▷ vi (Mil) déserter
deserted [dɪ'zə:tɪd] adj désert(e)
deserter [dɪ'zə:təʳ] n déserteur m
desertion [dɪ'zə:ʃən] n désertion f
desert island n île déserte
deserve [dɪ'zə:v] vt mériter
deserving [dɪ'zə:vɪŋ] adj (person) méritant(e); (action, cause) méritoire
design [dɪ'zaɪn] n (sketch) plan m, dessin m;

(layout, shape) conception f, ligne f; (pattern) dessin, motif(s) m(pl); (of dress, car) modèle m; (art) design m, stylisme m; (intention) dessein m ▷ vt dessiner; (plan) concevoir; **to have ~s on** avoir des visées sur; **well-~ed** adj bien conçu(e); **industrial ~** esthétique industrielle
design and technology n (Brit: Scol) technologie f
designate vt ['dɛzɪgneɪt] désigner ▷ adj ['dɛzɪgnɪt] désigné(e)
designer [dɪ'zaɪnəʳ] n (Archit, Art) dessinateur(-trice); (Industry) concepteur m, designer m; (Fashion) styliste m/f
desirable [dɪ'zaɪərəbl] adj (property, location, purchase) attrayant(e); **it is ~ that** il est souhaitable que
desire [dɪ'zaɪəʳ] n désir m ▷ vt désirer, vouloir; **to ~ to do sth/that** désirer faire qch/que
desk [dɛsk] n (in office) bureau m; (for pupil) pupitre m; (Brit: in shop, restaurant) caisse f; (in hotel, at airport) réception f
desk-top publishing ['dɛsktɔp-] n publication assistée par ordinateur, PAO f
desolate ['dɛsəlɪt] adj désolé(e)
despair [dɪs'pɛəʳ] n désespoir m ▷ vi: **to ~ of** désespérer de; **to be in ~** être au désespoir
despatch [dɪs'pætʃ] n, vt = **dispatch**
desperate ['dɛspərɪt] adj désespéré(e); (fugitive) prêt(e) à tout; (measures) désespéré, extrême; **to be ~ for sth/to do sth** avoir désespérément besoin de qch/de faire qch; **we are getting ~** nous commençons à désespérer
desperately ['dɛspərɪtlɪ] adv désespérément; (very) terriblement, extrêmement; **~ ill** très gravement malade
desperation [dɛspə'reɪʃən] n désespoir m; **in (sheer) ~** en désespoir de cause
despicable [dɪs'pɪkəbl] adj méprisable
despise [dɪs'paɪz] vt mépriser, dédaigner
despite [dɪs'paɪt] prep malgré, en dépit de
despondent [dɪs'pɔndənt] adj découragé(e), abattu(e)
dessert [dɪ'zə:t] n dessert m
dessertspoon [dɪ'zə:tspu:n] n cuiller f à dessert
destination [dɛstɪ'neɪʃən] n destination f
destined ['dɛstɪnd] adj: **to be ~ to do sth** être destiné(e) à faire qch; **~ for London** à destination de Londres
destiny ['dɛstɪnɪ] n destinée f, destin m
destitute ['dɛstɪtju:t] adj indigent(e), dans le dénuement; **~ of** dépourvu(e) or dénué(e) de
destroy [dɪs'trɔɪ] vt détruire; (injured horse) abattre; (dog) faire piquer
destroyer [dɪs'trɔɪəʳ] n (Naut) contre-torpilleur m
destruction [dɪs'trʌkʃən] n destruction f
destructive [dɪs'trʌktɪv] adj destructeur(-trice)

detach [dɪ'tætʃ] vt détacher
detached [dɪ'tætʃt] adj (attitude) détaché(e)
detached house n pavillon m maison(nette) (individuelle)
detachment [dɪ'tætʃmənt] n (Mil) détachement m; (fig) détachement, indifférence f
detail ['di:teɪl] n détail m; (Mil) détachement m ▷ vt raconter en détail, énumérer; (Mil): to ~ sb (for) affecter qn (à), détacher qn (pour); in ~ en détail; to go into ~(s) entrer dans les détails
detailed ['di:teɪld] adj détaillé(e)
detain [dɪ'teɪn] vt retenir; (in captivity) détenir; (in hospital) hospitaliser
detect [dɪ'tɛkt] vt déceler, percevoir; (Med, Police) dépister; (Mil, Radar, Tech) détecter
detection [dɪ'tɛkʃən] n découverte f; (Med, Police) dépistage m; (Mil, Radar, Tech) détection f; to escape ~ échapper aux recherches, éviter d'être découvert(e); (mistake) passer inaperçu(e); crime ~ le dépistage des criminels
detective [dɪ'tɛktɪv] n agent m de la sûreté, policier m; private ~ détective privé
detective story n roman policier
detention [dɪ'tɛnʃən] n détention f; (Scol) retenue f, consigne f
deter [dɪ'tə:ʳ] vt dissuader
detergent [dɪ'tə:dʒənt] n détersif m, détergent m
deteriorate [dɪ'tɪərɪəreɪt] vi se détériorer, se dégrader
determination [dɪtə:mɪ'neɪʃən] n détermination f
determine [dɪ'tə:mɪn] vt déterminer; to ~ to do résoudre de faire, se déterminer à faire
determined [dɪ'tə:mɪnd] adj (person) déterminé(e), décidé(e); (quantity) déterminé, établi(e); (effort) très gros(se); ~ to do bien décidé à faire
deterrent [dɪ'tɛrənt] n effet m de dissuasion; force f de dissuasion; to act as a ~ avoir un effet dissuasif
detest [dɪ'tɛst] vt détester, avoir horreur de
detonate ['dɛtəneɪt] vi exploser ▷ vt faire exploser or détoner
detour ['di:tuəʳ] n détour m; (US Aut: diversion) déviation f
detract [dɪ'trækt] vt: to ~ from (quality, pleasure) diminuer; (reputation) porter atteinte à
detriment ['dɛtrɪmənt] n: to the ~ of au détriment de, au préjudice de; without ~ to sans porter atteinte or préjudice à, sans conséquences fâcheuses pour
detrimental [dɛtrɪ'mɛntl] adj: ~ to préjudiciable or nuisible à
devaluation [dɪvælju'eɪʃən] n dévaluation f
devastate ['dɛvəsteɪt] vt dévaster; he was ~d by the news cette nouvelle lui a porté un coup terrible

devastating ['dɛvəsteɪtɪŋ] adj dévastateur(-trice); (news) accablant(e)
develop [dɪ'vɛləp] vt (gen) développer; (disease) commencer à souffrir de; (habit) contracter; (resources) mettre en valeur, exploiter; (land) aménager ▷ vi se développer; (situation, disease: evolve) évoluer; (facts, symptoms: appear) se manifester, se produire; can you ~ this film? pouvez-vous développer cette pellicule?; to ~ a taste for sth prendre goût à qch; to ~ into devenir
developer [dɪ'vɛləpəʳ] n (Phot) révélateur m; (of land) promoteur m; (also: property ~) promoteur immobilier
developing country [dɪ'vɛləpɪŋ-] n pays m en voie de développement
development [dɪ'vɛləpmənt] n développement m; (of land) exploitation f; (new fact, event) rebondissement m, fait(s) nouveau(x)
device [dɪ'vaɪs] n (scheme) moyen m, expédient m; (apparatus) appareil m, dispositif m; explosive ~ engin explosif
devil ['dɛvl] n diable m; démon m
devious ['di:vɪəs] adj (means) détourné(e); (person) sournois(e), dissimulé(e)
devise [dɪ'vaɪz] vt imaginer, concevoir
devoid [dɪ'vɔɪd] adj: ~ of dépourvu(e) de, dénué(e) de
devolution [di:və'lu:ʃən] n (Pol) décentralisation f
devote [dɪ'vəut] vt: to ~ sth to consacrer qch à
devoted [dɪ'vəutɪd] adj dévoué(e); to be ~ to être dévoué(e) or très attaché(e) à; (book etc) être consacré(e) à
devotee [dɛvəu'ti:] n (Rel) adepte m/f; (Mus, Sport) fervent(e)
devotion [dɪ'vəuʃən] n dévouement m, attachement m; (Rel) dévotion f, piété f
devour [dɪ'vauəʳ] vt dévorer
devout [dɪ'vaut] adj pieux(-euse), dévot(e)
dew [dju:] n rosée f
diabetes [daɪə'bi:ti:z] n diabète m
diabetic [daɪə'bɛtɪk] n diabétique m/f ▷ adj (person) diabétique; (chocolate, jam) pour diabétiques
diabolical [daɪə'bɔlɪkl] adj diabolique; (inf: dreadful) infernal(e), atroce
diagnose [daɪəg'nəuz] vt diagnostiquer
diagnosis (pl **diagnoses**) [daɪəg'nəusɪs, -si:z] n diagnostic m
diagonal [daɪ'ægənl] adj diagonal(e) ▷ n diagonale f
diagram ['daɪəgræm] n diagramme m, schéma m
dial ['daɪəl] n cadran m ▷ vt (number) faire, composer; to ~ a wrong number faire un faux numéro; can I ~ London direct? puis-je or est-ce-que je peux avoir Londres par l'automatique?
dialect ['daɪəlɛkt] n dialecte m

dialling code ['daɪəlɪŋ-], (US) **dial code** n indicatif m (téléphonique); **what's the ~ for Paris?** quel est l'indicatif de Paris?

dialling tone ['daɪəlɪŋ-], (US) **dial tone** n tonalité f

dialogue, (US) **dialog** ['daɪəlɒg] n dialogue m

diameter [daɪ'æmɪtər] n diamètre m

diamond ['daɪəmənd] n diamant m; (shape) losange m; **diamonds** npl (Cards) carreau m

diaper ['daɪəpər] n (US) couche f

diaphragm ['daɪəfræm] n diaphragme m

diarrhoea, (US) **diarrhea** [daɪə'riːə] n diarrhée f

diary ['daɪərɪ] n (daily account) journal m; (book) agenda m; **to keep a ~** tenir un journal

dice [daɪs] n (pl inv) dé m ▷ vt (Culin) couper en dés or en cubes

dictate vt [dɪk'teɪt] dicter ▷ vi: **to ~ to** (person) imposer sa volonté à, régenter; **I won't be ~d to** je n'ai d'ordres à recevoir de personne ▷ n ['dɪkteɪt] injonction f

dictation [dɪk'teɪʃən] n dictée f; **at ~ speed** à une vitesse de dictée

dictator [dɪk'teɪtər] n dictateur m

dictatorship [dɪk'teɪtəʃɪp] n dictature f

dictionary ['dɪkʃənrɪ] n dictionnaire m

did [dɪd] pt of **do**

didn't ['dɪdnt] = **did not**

die [daɪ] n (pl **dice**) dé m; (pl **dies**) coin m; matrice f; étampe f ▷ vi mourir; **to ~ of** or **from** mourir de; **to be dying** être mourant(e); **to be dying for sth** avoir une envie folle de qch; **to be dying to do sth** mourir d'envie de faire qch; **die away** vi s'éteindre; **die down** vi se calmer, s'apaiser; **die out** vi disparaître, s'éteindre

diesel ['diːzl] n (vehicle) diesel m; (also: **~ oil**) carburant m diesel, gas-oil m

diesel engine n moteur m diesel

diet ['daɪət] n alimentation f; (restricted food) régime m ▷ vi (also: **be on a ~**) suivre un régime; **to live on a ~ of** se nourrir de

differ ['dɪfər] vi: **to ~ from sth** (be different) être différent(e) de qch, différer de qch; **to ~ from sb over sth** ne pas être d'accord avec qn au sujet de qch

difference ['dɪfrəns] n différence f; (quarrel) différend m, désaccord m; **it makes no ~ to me** cela m'est égal, cela m'est indifférent; **to settle one's ~s** résoudre la situation

different ['dɪfrənt] adj différent(e)

differentiate [dɪfə'renʃɪeɪt] vt différencier ▷ vi se différencier; **to ~ between** faire une différence entre

differently ['dɪfrəntlɪ] adv différemment

difficult ['dɪfɪkəlt] adj difficile; **~ to understand** difficile à comprendre

difficulty ['dɪfɪkəltɪ] n difficulté f; **to have difficulties with** avoir des ennuis or problèmes avec; **to be in ~** avoir des difficultés, avoir des problèmes

diffident ['dɪfɪdənt] adj qui manque de confiance or d'assurance, peu sûr(e) de soi

dig [dɪg] vt (pt, pp **dug**) [dʌg] (hole) creuser; (garden) bêcher ▷ n (prod) coup m de coude; (fig: remark) coup de griffe or de patte; (Archaeology) fouille f; **to ~ into** (snow, soil) creuser; **to ~ into one's pockets for sth** fouiller dans ses poches pour chercher or prendre qch; **to ~ one's nails into** enfoncer ses ongles dans; **dig in** vi (also: **o.s. in**: Mil) se retrancher; (: fig) tenir bon, se braquer; (inf: eat) attaquer (un repas or un plat etc) ▷ vt (compost) bien mélanger à la bêche; (knife, claw) enfoncer; **to ~ in one's heels** (fig) se braquer, se buter; **dig out** vt (survivors, car from snow) sortir or dégager (à coups de pelles or pioches); **dig up** vt déterrer

digest vt [daɪ'dʒɛst] digérer ▷ n ['daɪdʒɛst] sommaire m, résumé m

digestion [dɪ'dʒɛstʃən] n digestion f

digit ['dɪdʒɪt] n (number) chiffre m (de 0 à 9); (finger) doigt m

digital ['dɪdʒɪtl] adj (system, recording, radio) numérique, digital(e); (watch) à affichage numérique or digital

digital camera n appareil m photo numérique

digital TV n télévision f numérique

dignified ['dɪgnɪfaɪd] adj digne

dignity ['dɪgnɪtɪ] n dignité f

digress [daɪ'grɛs] vi: **to ~ from** s'écarter de, s'éloigner de

digs [dɪgz] npl (Brit inf) piaule f, chambre meublée

dilapidated [dɪ'læpɪdeɪtɪd] adj délabré(e)

dilemma [daɪ'lɛmə] n dilemme m; **to be in a ~** être pris dans un dilemme

diligent ['dɪlɪdʒənt] adj appliqué(e), assidu(e)

dill [dɪl] n aneth m

dilute [daɪ'luːt] vt diluer ▷ adj dilué(e)

dim [dɪm] adj (light, eyesight) faible; (memory, outline) vague, indécis(e); (room) sombre; (inf: stupid) borné(e), obtus(e) ▷ vt (light) réduire, baisser; (US Aut) mettre en code, baisser; **to take a ~ view of sth** voir qch d'un mauvais œil

dime [daɪm] n (US) pièce f de 10 cents

dimension [daɪ'mɛnʃən] n dimension f

diminish [dɪ'mɪnɪʃ] vt, vi diminuer

diminutive [dɪ'mɪnjutɪv] adj minuscule, tout(e) petit(e) ▷ n (Ling) diminutif m

dimmer ['dɪmər] n (also: **~ switch**) variateur m; **dimmers** npl (US Aut: dipped headlights) phares mpl, code inv; (parking lights) feux mpl de position

dimple ['dɪmpl] n fossette f

din [dɪn] n vacarme m ▷ vt: **to ~ sth into sb** (inf) enfoncer qch dans la tête or la caboche de qn

dine [daɪn] vi dîner

diner ['daɪnəʳ] n (person) dîneur(-euse); (Rail) = dining car; (US: eating place) petit restaurant

dinghy ['dɪŋgɪ] n youyou m; (inflatable) canot m pneumatique; (also: **sailing ~**) voilier m, dériveur m

dingy ['dɪndʒɪ] adj miteux(-euse), minable

dining car ['daɪnɪŋ-] n (Brit) voiture-restaurant f, wagon-restaurant m

dining room ['daɪnɪŋ-] n salle f à manger

dining table [daɪnɪŋ-] n table f de (la) salle à manger

dinner ['dɪnəʳ] n (evening meal) dîner m; (lunch) déjeuner m; (public) banquet m; **~'s ready!** à table!

dinner jacket n smoking m

dinner party n dîner m

dinner time n (evening) heure f du dîner; (midday) heure du déjeuner

dinosaur ['daɪnəsɔːʳ] n dinosaure m

dip [dɪp] n (slope) déclivité f; (in sea) baignade f, bain m; (Culin) = sauce f ▷ vt tremper, plonger; (Brit Aut: lights) mettre en code, baisser ▷ vi plonger

diploma [dɪ'pləʊmə] n diplôme m

diplomacy [dɪ'pləʊməsɪ] n diplomatie f

diplomat ['dɪpləmæt] n diplomate m

diplomatic [dɪplə'mætɪk] adj diplomatique; **to break off ~ relations (with)** rompre les relations diplomatiques (avec)

dipstick ['dɪpstɪk] n (Brit Aut) jauge f de niveau d'huile

dipswitch ['dɪpswɪtʃ] n (Brit Aut) commutateur m de code

dire [daɪəʳ] adj (poverty) extrême; (awful) affreux(-euse)

direct [daɪ'rekt] adj direct(e); (manner, person) direct, franc/franche ▷ vt (tell way) diriger, orienter; (letter, remark) adresser; (Cine, TV) réaliser; (Theat) mettre en scène; (order): **to ~ sb to do sth** ordonner à qn de faire qch ▷ adv directement; **can you ~ me to ...?** pouvez-vous m'indiquer le chemin de ...?

direct debit n (Brit Banking) prélèvement m automatique

direction [dɪ'rekʃən] n direction f; (Theat) mise f en scène; (Cine, TV) réalisation f; **directions** npl (to a place) indications fpl; **~s for use** mode m d'emploi; **to ask for ~s** demander sa route or son chemin; **sense of ~** sens m de l'orientation; **in the ~ of** dans la direction de, vers

directly [dɪ'rektlɪ] adv (in straight line) directement, tout droit; (at once) tout de suite, immédiatement

director [dɪ'rektəʳ] n directeur m; (board member) administrateur m; (Theat) metteur m en scène; (Cine, TV) réalisateur(-trice); **D~ of Public Prosecutions** (Brit) = procureur général

directory [dɪ'rektərɪ] n annuaire m; (also: **street ~**) indicateur m de rues; (also: **trade ~**) annuaire du commerce; (Comput) répertoire m

directory enquiries, (US) **directory assistance** n (Tel: service) renseignements mpl

dirt [dəːt] n saleté f; (mud) boue f; **to treat sb like ~** traiter qn comme un chien

dirt-cheap ['dəːt'tʃiːp] adj (ne) coûtant presque rien

dirty ['dəːtɪ] adj sale; (joke) cochon(ne) ▷ vt salir; **~ story** histoire cochonne; **~ trick** coup tordu

disability [dɪsə'bɪlɪtɪ] n invalidité f, infirmité f

disabled [dɪs'eɪbld] adj handicapé(e); (maimed) mutilé(e); (through illness, old age) impotent(e)

disadvantage [dɪsəd'vɑːntɪdʒ] n désavantage m, inconvénient m

disagree [dɪsə'griː] vi (differ) ne pas concorder; (be against, think otherwise): **to ~ (with)** ne pas être d'accord (avec); **garlic ~s with me** l'ail ne me convient pas, je ne supporte pas l'ail

disagreeable [dɪsə'griːəbl] adj désagréable

disagreement [dɪsə'griːmənt] n désaccord m, différend m

disallow ['dɪsə'lau] vt rejeter, désavouer; (Brit Football: goal) refuser

disappear [dɪsə'pɪəʳ] vi disparaître

disappearance [dɪsə'pɪərəns] n disparition f

disappoint [dɪsə'pɔɪnt] vt décevoir

disappointed [dɪsə'pɔɪntɪd] adj déçu(e)

disappointing [dɪsə'pɔɪntɪŋ] adj décevant(e)

disappointment [dɪsə'pɔɪntmənt] n déception f

disapproval [dɪsə'pruːvəl] n désapprobation f

disapprove [dɪsə'pruːv] vi: **to ~ of** désapprouver

disarm [dɪs'ɑːm] vt désarmer

disarmament [dɪs'ɑːməmənt] n désarmement m

disarray [dɪsə'reɪ] n désordre m, confusion f; **in ~** (troops) en déroute; (thoughts) embrouillé(e); (clothes) en désordre; **to throw into ~** semer la confusion or le désordre dans (or parmi)

disaster [dɪ'zɑːstəʳ] n catastrophe f, désastre m

disastrous [dɪ'zɑːstrəs] adj désastreux(-euse)

disband [dɪs'bænd] vt démobiliser; disperser ▷ vi se disperser; se disperser

disbelief ['dɪsbə'liːf] n incrédulité f; **in ~** avec incrédulité

disc [dɪsk] n disque m; (Comput) = disk

discard [dɪs'kɑːd] vt (old things) se débarrasser de, mettre au rancart or au rebut; (fig) écarter, renoncer à

discern [dɪ'səːn] vt discerner, distinguer

discerning [dɪ'səːnɪŋ] adj judicieux(-euse), perspicace

discharge vt [dɪs'tʃɑːdʒ] (duties) s'acquitter de; (settle: debt) s'acquitter de, régler; (waste etc) déverser; décharger; (Elec, Med) émettre; (patient) renvoyer (chez lui); (employee, soldier) congédier, licencier; (defendant) relaxer, élargir ▷ n [ˈdɪstʃɑːdʒ] (Elec, Med) émission f; (also: **vaginal ~**) pertes blanches; (dismissal) renvoi m; licenciement m; élargissement m; **to ~ one's gun** faire feu; **~d bankrupt** failli(e), réhabilité(e).

discipline [ˈdɪsɪplɪn] n discipline f ▷ vt discipliner; (punish) punir; **to ~ o.s. to do sth** s'imposer or s'astreindre à une discipline pour faire qch.

disc jockey n disque-jockey m (DJ)

disclaim [dɪs'kleɪm] vt désavouer, dénier

disclose [dɪs'kləuz] vt révéler, divulguer

disclosure [dɪs'kləuʒəʳ] n révélation f, divulgation f

disco [ˈdɪskəu] n abbr discothèque f

discoloured, (US) **discolored** [dɪs'kʌləd] adj décoloré(e), jauni(e)

discomfort [dɪs'kʌmfət] n malaise m, gêne f; (lack of comfort) manque m de confort

disconcert [dɪskən'sɜːt] vt déconcerter, décontenancer

disconnect [dɪskə'nɛkt] vt détacher; (Elec, Radio) débrancher; (gas, water) couper

discontent [dɪskən'tɛnt] n mécontentement m

discontented [dɪskən'tɛntɪd] adj mécontent(e)

discontinue [dɪskən'tɪnjuː] vt cesser, interrompre; **"-d"** (Comm) "fin de série"

discord [ˈdɪskɔːd] n discorde f, dissension f; (Mus) dissonance f

discount n [ˈdɪskaunt] remise f, rabais m ▷ vt [dɪs'kaunt] (report etc) ne pas tenir compte de; **to give sb a ~ on sth** faire une remise or un rabais à qn sur qch; **~ for cash** escompte f au comptant; **~ at a ~** avec une remise or réduction, au rabais

discourage [dɪs'kʌrɪdʒ] vt décourager; (dissuade, deter) dissuader, décourager

discover [dɪs'kʌvəʳ] vt découvrir

discovery [dɪs'kʌvərɪ] n découverte f

discredit [dɪs'krɛdɪt] vt (idea) mettre en doute; (person) discréditer ▷ n discrédit m

discreet [dɪs'kriːt] adj discret(-ète)

discrepancy [dɪ'skrɛpənsɪ] n divergence f, contradiction f

discretion [dɪ'skrɛʃən] n discrétion f; **at the ~ of** à la discrétion de; **use your own ~** à vous de juger

discriminate [dɪ'skrɪmɪneɪt] vi: **to ~ between** établir une distinction entre, faire la différence entre; **to ~ against** pratiquer une discrimination contre

discriminating [dɪ'skrɪmɪneɪtɪŋ] adj qui a du discernement

discrimination [dɪskrɪmɪ'neɪʃən] n discrimination f; (judgment) discernement m;

racial/sexual ~ discrimination raciale/sexuelle

discuss [dɪ'skʌs] vt discuter de; (debate) discuter

discussion [dɪ'skʌʃən] n discussion f; **under ~** en discussion

disdain [dɪs'deɪn] n dédain m

disease [dɪ'ziːz] n maladie f

disembark [dɪsɪm'bɑːk] vt, vi débarquer

disentangle [dɪsɪn'tæŋgl] vt démêler

disfigure [dɪs'fɪgəʳ] vt défigurer

disgrace [dɪs'greɪs] n honte f; (disfavour) disgrâce f ▷ vt déshonorer, couvrir de honte

disgraceful [dɪs'greɪsful] adj scandaleux(-euse), honteux(-euse)

disgruntled [dɪs'grʌntld] adj mécontent(e)

disguise [dɪs'gaɪz] n déguisement m ▷ vt déguiser; (voice) déguiser, contrefaire; (feelings etc) masquer, dissimuler; **in ~** déguisé(e); **to ~ o.s. as** se déguiser en; **there's no disguising the fact that ...** on ne peut pas se dissimuler que ...

disgust [dɪs'gʌst] n dégoût m, aversion f ▷ vt dégoûter, écœurer

disgusted [dɪs'gʌstɪd] adj dégoûté(e), écœuré(e)

disgusting [dɪs'gʌstɪŋ] adj dégoûtant(e), révoltant(e)

dish [dɪʃ] n plat m; **to do** or **wash the ~es** faire la vaisselle; **dish out** vt distribuer; **dish up** vt servir; (facts, statistics) sortir, débiter

dishcloth [ˈdɪʃklɔθ] n (for drying) torchon m; (for washing) lavette f

dishearten [dɪs'hɑːtn] vt décourager

dishevelled, (US) **disheveled** [dɪ'ʃɛvəld] adj ébouriffé(e), décoiffé(e), débraillé(e)

dishonest [dɪs'ɔnɪst] adj malhonnête

dishonour, (US) **dishonor** [dɪs'ɔnəʳ] n déshonneur m

dishonourable, (US) **dishonorable** [dɪs'ɔnərəbl] adj déshonorant(e)

dishtowel [ˈdɪʃtauəl] n (US) torchon m (à vaisselle)

dishwasher [ˈdɪʃwɔʃəʳ] n lave-vaisselle m; (person) plongeur(-euse)

disillusion [dɪsɪ'luːʒən] vt désabuser, désenchanter ▷ n désenchantement m; **to become ~ed (with)** perdre ses illusions (en ce qui concerne)

disinfect [dɪsɪn'fɛkt] vt désinfecter

disinfectant [dɪsɪn'fɛktənt] n désinfectant m

disintegrate [dɪs'ɪntɪgreɪt] vi se désintégrer

disinterested [dɪs'ɪntrəstɪd] adj désintéressé(e)

disjointed [dɪs'dʒɔɪntɪd] adj décousu(e), incohérent(e)

disk [dɪsk] n (Comput) disquette f; **single-/double-sided ~** disquette une face/double face

disk drive n lecteur m de disquette

diskette [dɪs'kɛt] n (Comput) disquette f

dislike [dɪsˈlaɪk] n aversion f, antipathie f ▷ vt ne pas aimer; **to take a ~ to sb/sth** prendre qn/qch en grippe; **I ~ the idea** l'idée me déplaît

dislocate [ˈdɪsləkeɪt] vt disloquer, déboîter; (services etc) désorganiser; **he has ~d his shoulder** il s'est disloqué l'épaule

dislodge [dɪsˈlɔdʒ] vt déplacer, faire bouger; (enemy) déloger

disloyal [dɪsˈlɔɪəl] adj déloyal(e)

dismal [ˈdɪzml] adj (gloomy) lugubre, maussade; (very bad) lamentable

dismantle [dɪsˈmæntl] vt démonter; (fort, warship) démanteler

dismay [dɪsˈmeɪ] n consternation f ▷ vt consterner; **much to my ~** à ma grande consternation, à ma grande inquiétude

dismiss [dɪsˈmɪs] vt congédier, renvoyer; (idea) écarter; (Law) rejeter ▷ vi (Mil) rompre les rangs

dismissal [dɪsˈmɪsl] n renvoi m

dismount [dɪsˈmaunt] vi mettre pied à terre

disobedient [dɪsəˈbiːdɪənt] adj désobéissant(e), indiscipliné(e)

disobey [dɪsəˈbeɪ] vt désobéir à; (rule) transgresser, enfreindre

disorder [dɪsˈɔːdəʳ] n désordre m; (rioting) désordres mpl; (Med) troubles mpl

disorderly [dɪsˈɔːdəlɪ] adj (room) en désordre; (behaviour, retreat, crowd) désordonné(e)

disorganized [dɪsˈɔːgənaɪzd] adj désorganisé(e)

disorientated [dɪsˈɔːrɪɛnteɪtɪd] adj désorienté(e)

disown [dɪsˈəun] vt renier

disparaging [dɪsˈpærɪdʒɪŋ] adj désobligeant(e); **to be ~ about sb/sth** faire des remarques désobligeantes sur qn/qch

dispassionate [dɪsˈpæʃənət] adj calme, froid(e), impartial(e), objectif(-ive)

dispatch [dɪsˈpætʃ] vt expédier, envoyer; (deal with: business) régler, en finir avec ▷ n envoi m, expédition f; (Mil, Press) dépêche f

dispel [dɪsˈpɛl] vt dissiper, chasser

dispense [dɪsˈpɛns] vt distribuer, administrer; (medicine) préparer (et vendre); **to ~ sb from** dispenser qn de; **dispense with** vt fus se passer de; (make unnecessary) rendre superflu(e)

dispenser [dɪsˈpɛnsəʳ] n (device) distributeur m

dispensing chemist [dɪsˈpɛnsɪŋ-] n (Brit) pharmacie f

disperse [dɪsˈpəːs] vt disperser; (knowledge) disséminer ▷ vi se disperser

dispirited [dɪsˈpɪrɪtɪd] adj découragé(e), déprimé(e)

displace [dɪsˈpleɪs] vt déplacer

display [dɪsˈpleɪ] n (of goods etc) étalage m; affichage m; (Comput: information) visualisation f; (: device) visuel m; (of feeling) manifestation f; (pej) ostentation f; (show, spectacle) spectacle m; (military display) parade f militaire ▷ vt montrer; (goods) mettre à l'étalage, exposer; (results, departure times) afficher; (pej) faire étalage de; **on ~** (exhibits) exposé(e), exhibé(e); (goods) à l'étalage

displease [dɪsˈpliːz] vt mécontenter, contrarier; **~d with** mécontent(e) de

displeasure [dɪsˈplɛʒəʳ] n mécontentement m

disposable [dɪsˈpəuzəbl] adj (pack etc) jetable; (income) disponible; **~ nappy** (Brit) couche f à jeter, couche-culotte f

disposal [dɪsˈpəuzl] n (of rubbish) évacuation f, destruction f; (of property etc: by selling) vente f; (: by giving away) cession f; (availability, arrangement) disposition f; **at one's ~** à sa disposition; **to put sth at sb's ~** mettre qch à la disposition de qn

dispose [dɪsˈpəuz] vt disposer ▷ vi: **to ~ of** (time, money) disposer de; (unwanted goods) se débarrasser de, se défaire de; (Comm: stock) écouler, vendre; (problem) expédier

disposed [dɪsˈpəuzd] adj: **~ to do** disposé(e) à faire

disposition [dɪspəˈzɪʃən] n disposition f; (temperament) naturel m

disproportionate [dɪsprəˈpɔːʃənət] adj disproportionné(e)

disprove [dɪsˈpruːv] vt réfuter

dispute [dɪsˈpjuːt] n discussion f; (also: **industrial ~**) conflit m ▷ vt (question) contester; (matter) discuter; (victory) disputer; **to be in** or **under ~** (matter) être en discussion; (territory) être contesté(e)

disqualify [dɪsˈkwɔlɪfaɪ] vt (Sport) disqualifier; **to ~ sb for sth/from doing** (status, situation) rendre qn inapte à qch/à faire; (authority) signifier à qn l'interdiction de faire; **to ~ sb (from driving)** (Brit) retirer à qn son permis (de conduire)

disquiet [dɪsˈkwaɪət] n inquiétude f, trouble m

disregard [dɪsrɪˈgɑːd] vt ne pas tenir compte de ▷ n (indifference): **~ (for)** (feelings) indifférence f (pour), insensibilité f (à); (danger, money) mépris m (pour)

disrepair [dɪsrɪˈpɛəʳ] n mauvais état; **to fall into ~** (building) tomber en ruine; (street) se dégrader

disreputable [dɪsˈrɛpjutəbl] adj (person) de mauvaise réputation, peu recommandable; (behaviour) déshonorant(e); (area) mal famé(e), louche

disrespectful [dɪsrɪˈspɛktful] adj irrespectueux(-euse)

disrupt [dɪsˈrʌpt] vt (plans, meeting, lesson) perturber, déranger

disruption [dɪsˈrʌpʃən] n perturbation f, dérangement m

dissatisfaction [dɪssætɪsˈfækʃən] n mécontentement m, insatisfaction f

dissatisfied [dɪs'sætɪsfaɪd] *adj*: ~ **(with)** insatisfait(e) (de)

dissect [dɪ'sɛkt] *vt* disséquer; *(fig)* disséquer, éplucher

dissent [dɪ'sɛnt] *n* dissentiment *m*, différence *f* d'opinion

dissertation [dɪsə'teɪʃən] *n (Scol)* mémoire *m*

disservice [dɪs'sə:vɪs] *n*: **to do sb a ~** rendre un mauvais service à qn; desservir qn

dissimilar [dɪ'sɪmɪlə'] *adj*: ~ **(to)** dissemblable (à), différent(e) (de)

dissipate ['dɪsɪpeɪt] *vt* dissiper; *(energy, efforts)* disperser

dissolute ['dɪsəlu:t] *adj* débauché(e), dissolu(e)

dissolve [dɪ'zɔlv] *vt* dissoudre ▷ *vi* se dissoudre, fondre; *(fig)* disparaître; **to ~ in(to) tears** fondre en larmes

distance ['dɪstns] *n* distance *f*; **what's the ~ to London?** à quelle distance se trouve Londres?; **it's within walking ~** on peut y aller à pied; **in the ~** au loin

distant ['dɪstnt] *adj* lointain(e), éloigné(e); *(manner)* distant(e), froid(e)

distaste [dɪs'teɪst] *n* dégoût *m*

distasteful [dɪs'teɪstful] *adj* déplaisant(e), désagréable

distended [dɪs'tɛndɪd] *adj (stomach)* dilaté(e)

distil, *(US)* **distill** [dɪs'tɪl] *vt* distiller

distillery [dɪs'tɪlərɪ] *n* distillerie *f*

distinct [dɪs'tɪŋkt] *adj* distinct(e); *(clear)* marqué(e); **as ~ from** par opposition à, en contraste avec

distinction [dɪs'tɪŋkʃən] *n* distinction *f*; *(in exam)* mention *f* très bien; **to draw a ~ between** faire une distinction entre; **a writer of ~** un écrivain réputé

distinctive [dɪs'tɪŋktɪv] *adj* distinctif(-ive)

distinguish [dɪs'tɪŋgwɪʃ] *vt* distinguer ▷ *vi*: **to ~ between** *(concepts)* distinguer entre, faire une distinction entre; **to ~ o.s.** se distinguer

distinguished [dɪs'tɪŋgwɪʃt] *adj (eminent, refined)* distingué(e); *(career)* remarquable, brillant(e)

distinguishing [dɪs'tɪŋgwɪʃɪŋ] *adj (feature)* distinctif(-ive), caractéristique

distort [dɪs'tɔ:t] *vt* déformer

distract [dɪs'trækt] *vt* distraire, déranger

distracted [dɪs'træktɪd] *adj (not concentrating)* distrait(e); *(worried)* affolé(e)

distraction [dɪs'trækʃən] *n* distraction *f*, dérangement *m*; **to drive sb to ~** rendre qn fou/folle

distraught [dɪs'trɔ:t] *adj* éperdu(e)

distress [dɪs'trɛs] *n* détresse *f*; *(pain)* douleur *f* ▷ *vt* affliger; **in ~** *(ship)* en perdition; *(plane)* en détresse; **~ed area** *(Brit)* zone sinistrée

distressing [dɪs'trɛsɪŋ] *adj* douloureux(-euse), pénible, affligeant(e)

distribute [dɪs'trɪbju:t] *vt* distribuer

distribution [dɪstrɪ'bju:ʃən] *n* distribution *f*

distributor [dɪs'trɪbjutə'] *n (gen: Tech)* distributeur *m*; *(Comm)* concessionnaire *m/f*

district ['dɪstrɪkt] *n (of country)* région *f*; *(of town)* quartier *m*; *(Admin)* district *m*

district attorney *n (US)* = procureur *m* de la République

district nurse *n (Brit)* infirmière visiteuse

distrust [dɪs'trʌst] *n* méfiance *f*, doute *m* ▷ *vt* se méfier de

disturb [dɪs'tə:b] *vt* troubler; *(inconvenience)* déranger; **sorry to ~ you** excusez-moi de vous déranger

disturbance [dɪs'tə:bəns] *n* dérangement *m*; *(political etc)* troubles *mpl*; *(by drunks etc)* tapage *m*; **to cause a ~** troubler l'ordre public; **~ of the peace** *(Law)* tapage injurieux *or* nocturne

disturbed [dɪs'tə:bd] *adj (worried, upset)* agité(e), troublé(e); **to be emotionally ~** avoir des problèmes affectifs

disturbing [dɪs'tə:bɪŋ] *adj* troublant(e), inquiétant(e)

disuse [dɪs'ju:s] *n*: **to fall into ~** tomber en désuétude

disused [dɪs'ju:zd] *adj* désaffecté(e)

ditch [dɪtʃ] *n* fossé *m*; *(for irrigation)* rigole *f* ▷ *vt (inf)* abandonner; *(person)* plaquer

dither ['dɪðə'] *vi* hésiter

ditto ['dɪtəu] *adv* idem

dive [daɪv] *n* plongeon *m*; *(of submarine)* plongée *f*; *(Aviat)* piqué *m*; *(pej: café, bar etc)* bouge *m* ▷ *vi* plonger; **to ~ into** *(bag etc)* plonger la main dans; *(place)* se précipiter dans

diver ['daɪvə'] *n* plongeur *m*

diverse [daɪ'və:s] *adj* divers(e)

diversion [daɪ'və:ʃən] *n (Brit Aut)* déviation *f*; *(distraction, Mil)* diversion *f*

diversity [daɪ'və:sɪtɪ] *n* diversité *f*, variété *f*

divert [daɪ'və:t] *vt (Brit: traffic)* dévier; *(plane)* dérouter; *(train, river)* détourner; *(amuse)* divertir

divide [dɪ'vaɪd] *vt* diviser; *(separate)* séparer ▷ *vi* se diviser; **to ~ (between** *or* **among)** répartir *or* diviser (entre); **40 ~d by 5** 40 divisé par 5; **divide out** *vt*: **to ~ out (between** *or* **among)** distribuer *or* répartir (entre)

divided highway *(US)* *n* route *f* à quatre voies

dividend ['dɪvɪdɛnd] *n* dividende *m*

divine [dɪ'vaɪn] *adj* divin(e) ▷ *vt (future)* prédire; *(truth)* deviner, entrevoir; *(water, metal)* détecter la présence de *(par l'intermédiaire de la radiesthésie)*

diving ['daɪvɪŋ] *n* plongée (sous-marine)

diving board *n* plongeoir *m*

divinity [dɪ'vɪnɪtɪ] *n* divinité *f*; *(as study)* théologie *f*

division [dɪ'vɪʒən] *n* division *f*; *(Brit: Football)* division *f*; *(separation)* séparation *f*; *(Comm)* service *m*; *(Brit: Pol)* vote *m*; *(also: ~ of labour)* division du travail

divorce [dɪ'vɔːs] *n* divorce *m* ▷ *vt* divorcer d'avec

divorced [dɪ'vɔːst] *adj* divorcé(e)

divorcee [dɪvɔː'siː] *n* divorcé(e)

DIY *adj, n abbr* (Brit) = **do-it-yourself**

dizzy ['dɪzɪ] *adj* (height) vertigineux(-euse); **to make sb ~** donner le vertige à qn; **I feel ~** la tête me tourne, j'ai la tête qui tourne

DJ *n abbr* = **disc jockey**

DNA *n abbr* (= deoxyribonucleic acid) ADN *m*

DNA fingerprinting [-'fɪŋɡəprɪntɪŋ] *n* technique *f* des empreintes génétiques

do *abbr* (= ditto) d

KEYWORD

do [duː] (*pt* **did**, *pp* **done**) *n* (*inf*: party etc) soirée *f*, fête *f*; (: formal gathering) réception *f* ▷ *vb* **1** (*in negative constructions*) non traduit; **I don't understand** je ne comprends pas **2** (*to form questions*) non traduit; **didn't you know?** vous ne le saviez pas?; **what do you think?** qu'en pensez-vous?; **why didn't you come?** pourquoi n'êtes-vous pas venu? **3** (*for emphasis, in polite expressions*): **people do make mistakes sometimes** on peut toujours se tromper; **she does seem rather late** je trouve qu'elle est bien en retard; **do sit down/help yourself** asseyez-vous/servez-vous je vous en prie; **do take care!** faites bien attention à vous!; **I DO wish I could go** j'aimerais tant y aller; **but I DO like it!** mais si, je l'aime! **4** (*used to avoid repeating vb*): **she swims better than I do** elle nage mieux que moi; **do you agree? — yes, I do/no I don't** vous êtes d'accord? — oui/non; **she lives in Glasgow — so do I** elle habite Glasgow — moi aussi; **he didn't like it and neither did we** il n'a pas aimé ça, et nous non plus; **who broke it? — I did** qui l'a cassé? — c'est moi; **he asked me to help him and I did** il m'a demandé de l'aider, et c'est ce que j'ai fait **5** (*in question tags*): **you like him, don't you?** vous l'aimez bien, n'est-ce pas?; **he laughed, didn't he?** il a ri, n'est-ce pas?; **I don't know him, do I?** je ne crois pas le connaître ▷ *vt* **1** (*gen*: carry out, perform etc) faire; (*visit*: city, museum) faire, visiter; **what are you doing tonight?** qu'est-ce que vous faites ce soir?; **what do you do?** (*job*) que faites-vous dans la vie?; **what did he do with the cat?** qu'a-t-il fait du chat?; **what can I do for you?** que puis-je faire pour vous?; **to do the cooking/washing-up** faire la cuisine/la vaisselle; **to do one's teeth/hair/nails** se brosser les dents/se coiffer/se faire les ongles **2** (*Aut etc*: distance) faire; (: speed) faire du; **we've done 200 km already** nous avons déjà fait 200 km; **the car was doing 100** la

voiture faisait du 100 (à l'heure); **he can do 100 in that car** il peut faire du 100 (à l'heure) dans cette voiture-là ▷ *vi* **1** (*act, behave*) faire; **do as I do** faites comme moi **2** (*get on, fare*) marcher; **the firm is doing well** l'entreprise marche bien; **he's doing well/badly at school** ça marche bien/mal pour lui à l'école; **how do you do?** comment allez-vous?; (*on being introduced*) enchanté(e)! **3** (*suit*) aller; **will it do?** est-ce que ça ira? **4** (*be sufficient*) suffire, aller; **will £10 do?** est-ce que 10 livres suffiront?; **that'll do** ça suffit, ça ira; **that'll do!** (*in annoyance*) ça va or suffit comme ça!; **to make do (with)** se contenter (de)

do away with *vt fus* abolir; (*kill*) supprimer

do for *vt fus* (Brit inf: clean for) faire le ménage chez

do up *vt* (laces, dress) attacher; (buttons) boutonner; (zip) fermer; (renovate: room) refaire; (: house) remettre à neuf; **to do o.s. up** se faire beau/belle

do with *vt fus* (need): **I could do with a drink/some help** quelque chose à boire/un peu d'aide ne serait pas de refus; **it could do with a wash** ça ne lui ferait pas de mal d'être lavé; (be connected with): **that has nothing to do with you** cela ne vous concerne pas; **I won't have anything to do with it** je ne veux pas m'en mêler; **what has that got to do with it?** quel est le rapport?, qu'est-ce que cela vient faire là-dedans?

do without *vi* s'en passer; **if you're late for tea then you'll do without** si vous êtes en retard pour le dîner il faudra vous en passer ▷ *vt fus* se passer de; **I can do without a car** je peux me passer de voiture

dock [dɔk] *n* dock *m*; (wharf) quai *m*; (Law) banc *m* des accusés ▷ *vi* se mettre à quai; (Space) s'arrimer ▷ *vt*: **they ~ed a third of his wages** ils lui ont retenu or décompté un tiers de son salaire; **docks** *npl* (Naut) docks

docker ['dɔkə'] *n* docker *m*

dockyard ['dɔkjɑːd] *n* chantier *m* de construction navale

doctor ['dɔktə'] *n* médecin *m*, docteur *m*; (PhD etc) docteur *m* ▷ *vt* (cat) couper; (interfere with: food) altérer; (: drink) frelater; (: text, document) arranger; **~'s office** (US) cabinet *m* de consultation; **call a ~!** appelez un docteur or un médecin!

Doctor of Philosophy *n* (degree) doctorat *m*; (person) titulaire *m/f* d'un doctorat

document ['dɔkjumənt] *n* document *m* ▷ *vt* ['dɔkjument] documenter

documentary [dɔkju'mɛntərɪ] *adj, n* documentaire (*m*)

documentation [dɔkjumən'teɪʃən] *n* documentation *f*

dodge [dɒdʒ] n truc m; combine f ▷ vt
esquiver, éviter ▷ vi faire un saut de côté;
(*Sport*) faire une esquive; **to ~ out of the way**
s'esquiver; **to ~ through the traffic** se
faufiler *or* faire de savantes manœuvres
entre les voitures

dodgems [dɒdʒəmz] npl (*Brit*) autos
tamponneuses

dodgy [dɒdʒɪ] adj (inf: *uncertain*)
douteux(-euse); (: *shady*) louche

doe [dəu] n (*deer*) biche f; (*rabbit*) lapine f

does [dʌz] vb see **do**

doesn't [dʌznt] = **does not**

dog [dɒg] n chien(ne) ▷ vt (*follow closely*)
suivre de près, ne pas lâcher d'une semelle;
(*fig: memory etc*) poursuivre, harceler; **to go to
the ~s** (*nation etc*) aller à vau-l'eau

dog collar n collier m de chien; (*fig*)
faux-col m d'ecclésiastique

dog-eared [dɒgɪəd] adj corné(e)

dogged [dɒgɪd] adj obstiné(e), opiniâtre

doggy bag [dɒgɪ-] n petit sac pour emporter
les restes

dogsbody [dɒgzbɒdɪ] n (*Brit*) bonne f à tout
faire, tâcheron m

doings [duːɪŋz] npl activités fpl

do-it-yourself [duːɪtjɔːˈself] n bricolage m

doldrums [dɒldrəmz] npl: **to be in the ~**
avoir le cafard; être dans le marasme

dole [dəul] n (*Brit: payment*) allocation f de
chômage; **on the ~** au chômage; **dole out** vt
donner au compte-goutte

doll [dɒl] n poupée f; **doll up** vt: **to ~ o.s. up** se
faire beau/belle

dollar [dɒlər] n dollar m

dolphin [dɒlfɪn] n dauphin m

dome [dəum] n dôme m

domestic [dəˈmɛstɪk] adj (*duty, happiness*)
familial(e); (*policy, affairs, flight*) intérieur(e);
(*news*) national(e); (*animal*) domestique

domesticated [dəˈmɛstɪkeɪtɪd] adj
domestiqué(e); (*pej*) d'intérieur; **he's very ~**
il participe volontiers aux tâches
ménagères; question ménage, il est très
organisé

dominant [dɒmɪnənt] adj dominant(e)

dominate [dɒmɪneɪt] vt dominer

domineering [dɒmɪˈnɪərɪŋ] adj
dominateur(-trice), autoritaire

dominion [dəˈmɪnɪən] n domination f;
territoire m; dominion m

domino [dɒmɪnəu] (*pl* **dominoes**) n
domino m

dominoes [dɒmɪnəuz] n (*game*) dominos mpl

don [dɒn] n (*Brit*) professeur m d'université
▷ vt revêtir

donate [dəˈneɪt] vt faire don de, donner

donation [dəˈneɪʃən] n donation f, don m

done [dʌn] pp of **do**

donkey [dɒŋkɪ] n âne m

donor [dəunər] n (*of blood etc*) donneur(-euse);
(*to charity*) donateur(-trice)

donor card n carte f de don d'organes

don't [dəunt] = **do not**

donut [dəunʌt] (*US*) n = **doughnut**

doodle [duːdl] n griffonnage m, gribouillage m
▷ vi griffonner, gribouiller

doom [duːm] n (*fate*) destin m; (*ruin*) ruine f
▷ vt: **to be ~ed to failure** être voué(e) à
l'échec

door [dɔːr] n porte f; (*Rail, car*) portière f; **to go
from ~ to ~** aller de porte en porte

doorbell [dɔːbɛl] n sonnette f

door handle n poignée f de porte; (*of car*)
poignée de portière

doorknob [dɔːnɔb] n poignée f *or* bouton m
de porte

doorman [dɔːmən] irreg n (*in hotel*) portier m;
(*in block of flats*) concierge m

doormat [dɔːmæt] n paillasson m

doorstep [dɔːstɛp] n pas m de (la) porte,
seuil m

doorway [dɔːweɪ] n embrasure f de) porte f

dope [dəup] n (inf: *drug*) drogue f; (: *person*)
andouille f; (: *information*) tuyaux mpl,
rancards mpl ▷ vt (*horse etc*) doper

dormant [dɔːmənt] adj assoupi(e), en
veilleuse; (*rule, law*) inappliqué(e)

dormitory [dɔːmɪtrɪ] n (*Brit*) dortoir m;
(*US: hall of residence*) résidence f universitaire

dormouse (*pl* **dormice**) [dɔːmaus, -maɪs] n
loir m

DOS [dɒs] n abbr (= *disk operating system*) DOS m

dosage [dəusɪdʒ] n dose f; dosage m; (*on label*)
posologie f

dose [dəus] n dose f; (*Brit: bout*) attaque f ▷ vt:
to ~ o.s. se bourrer de médicaments; **a ~ of
flu** une belle *or* bonne grippe

dosh [dɒʃ] (*inf*) n fric m

doss house [dɒs-] n (*Brit*) asile m de nuit

dot [dɔt] n point m; (*on material*) pois m ▷ vt:
~ted with parsemé(e) de; **on the ~** à l'heure
tapante

dotcom [dɔtˈkɔm] n point com m,
pointcom m

dotted line [dɔtɪd-] n ligne pointillée; (*Aut*)
ligne discontinue; **to sign on the ~** signer à
l'endroit indiqué *or* sur la ligne pointillée;
(*fig*) donner son consentement

double [dʌbl] adj double ▷ adv (*fold*) en deux;
(*twice*): **to cost ~ (sth)** coûter le double (de
qch) *or* deux fois plus (que qch) ▷ n double m;
(*Cine*) doublure f ▷ vt doubler; (*fold*) plier en
deux ▷ vi doubler; (*have two uses*): **to ~ as**
servir aussi de; **~ five two six (5526)** (*Brit Tel*)
cinquante-cinq – vingt-six; **it's spelt with a
~ "l"** ça s'écrit avec deux "l"; **on the ~, at
the ~** au pas de course; **double back** vi
(*person*) revenir sur ses pas; **double up** vi (*bend
over*) se courber, se plier; (*share room*) partager
la chambre

double bass n contrebasse f

double bed n grand lit

double-breasted [dʌblˈbrɛstɪd] adj croisé(e)

double-check ['dʌbl'tʃɛk] vt, vi revérifier

double-click ['dʌbl'klɪk] vi (Comput) double-cliquer

double-cross ['dʌbl'krɔs] vt doubler, trahir

double-decker ['dʌbl'dɛkəʳ] n autobus m à impériale

double glazing n (Brit) double vitrage m

double room n chambre f pour deux

doubles ['dʌblz] n (Tennis) double m

double yellow lines npl (Brit: Aut) double bande jaune marquant l'interdiction de stationner

doubly ['dʌblɪ] adv doublement, deux fois plus

doubt [daut] n doute m ▷ vt douter de; **no ~** sans doute; **without (a) ~** sans aucun doute; **beyond ~** adv indubitablement ▷ adj indubitable; **to ~ that** douter que + sub; **I ~ it very much** j'en doute fort

doubtful ['dautful] adj douteux(-euse); (person) incertain(e); **to be ~ about sth** avoir des doutes sur qch, ne pas être convaincu de qch; **I'm a bit ~** je n'en suis pas certain or sûr

doubtless ['dautlɪs] adv sans doute, sûrement

dough [dəu] n pâte f; (inf: money) fric m, pognon m

doughnut ['dəunʌt], (US) **donut** n beignet m

dove [dʌv] n colombe f

Dover ['dəuvəʳ] n Douvres

dovetail ['dʌvteɪl] n: **~ joint** assemblage m à queue d'aronde ▷ vi (fig) concorder

dowdy ['daudɪ] adj démodé(e), mal fagoté(e)

down [daun] n (fluff) duvet m; (hill) colline (dénudée) ▷ adv en bas, vers le bas; (on the ground) par terre ▷ prep en bas de; (along) le long de ▷ vt (enemy) abattre; (inf: drink) siffler; **to fall ~** tomber; **she's going ~ to Bristol** elle descend à Bristol; **to write sth ~** écrire qch; **~ there** là-bas (en bas), là au fond; **~ here** ici en bas; **the price of meat is ~** le prix de la viande a baissé; **I've got it ~ in my diary** c'est inscrit dans mon agenda; **to pay £2 ~** verser 2 livres d'arrhes or en acompte; **England is two goals ~** l'Angleterre a deux buts de retard; **to walk ~ a hill** descendre une colline; **to run ~ the street** descendre la rue en courant; **~ tools** (Brit) cesser le travail; **~ with X!** à bas X!

down-and-out ['daunəndaut] n (tramp) clochard(e)

down-at-heel ['daunət'hi:l] adj (fig) miteux(-euse)

downcast ['daunka:st] adj démoralisé(e)

downfall ['daunfɔ:l] n chute f; ruine f

downhearted ['daun'hɑ:tɪd] adj découragé(e)

downhill ['daun'hɪl] adv (face, look) en aval, vers l'aval; (roll, go) vers le bas, en bas ▷ n (Ski: also: **~ race**) descente f; **to go ~** descendre; (business) péricliter, aller à vau-l'eau

Downing Street ['daunɪŋ-] n (Brit): **10 ~** résidence du Premier ministre; voir article

download ['daunləud] n téléchargement m ▷ vt (Comput) télécharger

downloadable [daun'ləudəbl] adj (Comput) téléchargeable

down payment n acompte m

downpour ['daunpɔ:ʳ] n pluie torrentielle, déluge m

downright ['daunraɪt] adj (lie etc) effronté(e); (refusal) catégorique

downsize [daun'saɪz] vt réduire l'effectif de

Down's syndrome [daunz-] n mongolisme m, trisomie f; **a ~ baby** un bébé mongolien or trisomique

downstairs ['daun'stɛəz] adv (on or to ground floor) au rez-de-chaussée; (on or to floor below) à l'étage inférieur; **to come ~, to go ~** descendre (l'escalier)

downstream ['daunstri:m] adv en aval

down-to-earth ['dauntu'ə:θ] adj terre à terre inv

downtown ['daun'taun] adv en ville ▷ adj (US): **~ Chicago** le centre commerçant de Chicago

down under adv en Australie or Nouvelle Zélande

downward ['daunwəd] adj, adv vers le bas; **a ~ trend** une tendance à la baisse, une diminution progressive

downwards ['daunwədz] adv vers le bas

dowry ['dauri] n dot f

doz. abbr = **dozen**

doze [dauz] vi sommeiller; **doze off** vi s'assoupir

dozen ['dʌzn] n douzaine f; **a ~ books** une douzaine de livres; **80p a ~** 80p la douzaine; **~s of** des centaines de

Dr. abbr (= doctor) Dr; (in street names) = **drive**

drab [dræb] adj terne, morne

draft [drɑ:ft] n (of letter, school work) brouillon m; (of literary work) ébauche f; (of contract, document) version f préliminaire; (Comm) traite f; (US Mil) contingent m; (: call-up) conscription f ▷ vt faire le brouillon de; (document, report) rédiger une version préliminaire de; (Mil: send) détacher; see also **draught**

drag [dræg] vt traîner; (river) draguer ▷ vi traîner ▷ n (Aviat, Naut) résistance f; (inf) casse-pieds m/f; (women's clothing): **in ~** (en) travesti; **to ~ and drop** (Comput) glisser-poser; **drag away** vt: **to ~ away (from)** arracher or emmener de force (de); **drag on** vi s'éterniser

dragon ['drægn] n dragon m

dragonfly ['drægənflaɪ] n libellule f

drain [dreɪn] n égout m; (on resources) saignée f ▷ vt (land, marshes) drainer, assécher; (vegetables) égoutter; (reservoir etc) vider ▷ vi (water) s'écouler; **to feel ~ed** (of energy or emotion) être miné(e)

drainage ['dreɪnɪdʒ] n (system) système m d'égouts; (act) drainage m

draining board (US) ['dreɪnɪŋ-], **drainboard** ['dreɪnbɔːd] n égouttoir m

drainpipe ['dreɪnpaɪp] n tuyau m d'écoulement

drama ['drɑːmə] n (art) théâtre m, art m dramatique; (play) pièce f; (event) drame m

dramatic [drəˈmætɪk] adj (Theat) dramatique; (impressive) spectaculaire

dramatist ['dræmətɪst] n auteur m dramatique

dramatize ['dræmətaɪz] vt (events etc) dramatiser; (adapt) adapter pour la télévision (or pour l'écran)

drank [dræŋk] pt of drink

drape [dreɪp] vt draper; **drapes** npl (US) rideaux mpl

drastic ['dræstɪk] adj (measures) d'urgence, énergique; (change) radical(e)

draught (US) **draft** [drɑːft] n courant m d'air; (of chimney) tirage m; (Naut) tirant m d'eau; **on ~** (beer) à la pression

draught beer n bière f (à la) pression

draughtboard ['drɑːftbɔːd] n (Brit) damier m

draughts [drɑːfts] n (Brit: game) (jeu m de) dames fpl

draughtsman, (US) **draftsman** ['drɑːftsmən] irreg n dessinateur(-trice) (industriel(le))

draw [drɔː] (vb: pt **drew**, pp **drawn**) [druː, drɔːn] vt tirer; (picture) dessiner; (attract) attirer; (line, circle) tracer; (money) retirer; (wages) toucher; (comparison, distinction): **to ~ (between)** faire (entre) ▷ vi (Sport) faire match nul ▷ n match nul; (lottery) loterie f; (: picking of ticket) tirage m au sort; **to ~ to a close** toucher à or tirer à sa fin; **to ~ near** vi s'approcher; approcher; **draw back** vi (move back): **to ~ back (from)** reculer (de); **draw in** vi (Brit: car) s'arrêter le long du trottoir; (: train) entrer en gare or dans la station; **draw on** vt (resources) faire appel à; (imagination, person) avoir recours à, faire appel à; **draw out** vi (lengthen) s'allonger ▷ vt (money) retirer; **draw up** vi (stop) s'arrêter ▷ vt (document) établir, dresser; (plan) formuler, dessiner; (chair) approcher

drawback ['drɔːbæk] n inconvénient m, désavantage m

drawbridge ['drɔːbrɪdʒ] n pont-levis m

drawer [drɔːʳ] n tiroir m; ['drɔːəʳ] (of cheque) tireur m

drawing ['drɔːɪŋ] n dessin m

drawing board n planche f à dessin

drawing pin n (Brit) punaise f

drawing room n salon m

drawl [drɔːl] n accent traînant

drawn [drɔːn] pp of draw ▷ adj (haggard) tiré(e), crispé(e)

dread [dred] n épouvante f, effroi m ▷ vt redouter, appréhender

dreadful ['dredful] adj épouvantable, affreux(-euse)

dream [driːm] n rêve m ▷ vt, vi (pt, pp dreamed or dreamt) [dremt] rêver; **to have a ~ about sb/sth** rêver à qn/qch; **sweet ~s!** faites de beaux rêves!; **dream up** vt inventer

dreamer ['driːməʳ] n rêveur(-euse)

dreamt [dremt] pt, pp of dream

dreamy ['driːmɪ] adj (absent-minded) rêveur(-euse)

dreary ['drɪərɪ] adj triste; monotone

dredge [dredʒ] vt draguer; **dredge up** vt draguer; (fig: unpleasant facts) (faire) ressortir

dregs [dregz] npl lie f

drench [drentʃ] vt tremper; **~ed to the skin** trempé(e) jusqu'aux os

dress [dres] n robe f; (clothing) habillement m, tenue f ▷ vt habiller; (wound) panser; (food) préparer ▷ vi: **she ~es very well** elle s'habille très bien; **to ~ o.s., to get ~ed** s'habiller; **to ~ a shop window** faire l'étalage or la vitrine; **dress up** vi s'habiller; (in fancy dress) se déguiser

dress circle n (Brit) premier balcon

dresser ['dresəʳ] n (Theat) habilleur(-euse); (also: **window ~**) étalagiste m/f; (furniture) vaisselier m; (: US) coiffeuse f, commode f

dressing ['dresɪŋ] n (Med) pansement m; (Culin) sauce f, assaisonnement m

dressing gown n (Brit) robe f de chambre

dressing room n (Theat) loge f; (Sport) vestiaire m

dressing table n coiffeuse f

dressmaker ['dresmeɪkəʳ] n couturière f

dress rehearsal n (répétition f) générale f

drew [druː] pt of draw

dribble ['drɪbl] vi tomber goutte à goutte; (baby) baver ▷ vt (ball) dribbler

dried [draɪd] adj (fruit, beans) sec/sèche; (eggs, milk) en poudre

drier ['draɪəʳ] n = dryer

drift [drɪft] n (of current etc) force f; direction f; (of sand etc) amoncellement m; (of snow) rafale f; coulée f; (: on ground) congère f; (general meaning) sens général ▷ vi (boat) aller à la dérive, dériver; (sand, snow) s'amonceler, s'entasser; **to let things ~** laisser les choses aller à la dérive; **to ~ apart** (friends, lovers) s'éloigner l'un de l'autre; **I get** or **catch your ~** je vois en gros ce que vous voulez dire

driftwood ['drɪftwud] n bois flotté

drill [drɪl] n foret m; (bit) foret m; (of dentist) roulette f, fraise f; (Mil) exercice m ▷ vt percer; (troops) entraîner; (pupils: in grammar)

faire faire des exercices à ▷ *vi* (*for oil*) faire un
or des forage(s)

drink [drɪŋk] *n* boisson *f*; (*alcoholic*) verre *m*
▷ *vt, vi* (*pt* **drank**, *pp* **drunk**) [dræŋk, drʌŋk]
boire; **to have a ~** boire quelque chose, boire
un verre; **a ~ of water** un verre d'eau; **would
you like a ~?** tu veux boire quelque chose?;
we had ~s before lunch on a pris l'apéritif;
drink in *vt* (*fresh air*) inspirer profondément;
(*story*) avaler, ne pas perdre une miette de;
(*sight*) se remplir la vue de

drink-driving ['drɪŋk'draɪvɪŋ] *n* conduite *f*
en état d'ivresse

drinker ['drɪŋkə^r] *n* buveur(-euse)

drinking water *n* eau *f* potable

drip [drɪp] *n* (*drop*) goutte *f*; (*sound: of water etc*)
bruit *m* de l'eau qui tombe goutte à goutte;
(*Med: device*) goutte-à-goutte *m inv*; (*: liquid*)
perfusion *f*; (*inf: person*) lavette *f*, nouille *f* ▷ *vi*
tomber goutte à goutte; (*tap*) goutter;
(*washing*) s'égoutter; (*wall*) suinter

drip-dry ['drɪp'draɪ] *adj* (*shirt*) sans repassage

dripping ['drɪpɪŋ] *n* graisse *f* de rôti ▷ *adj*:
~ wet trempé(e)

drive [draɪv] (*pt* **drove**, *pp* **driven**) [drəuv,
'drɪvn] *n* promenade *f* or trajet *m* en voiture;
(*also:* **~way**) allée *f*; (*energy*) dynamisme *m*,
énergie *f*; (*Psych*) besoin *m*; pulsion *f*; (*push*)
effort (concerté); càmpagne *f*; (*Sport*) drive *m*;
(*Tech*) entraînement *m*; traction *f*;
transmission *f*; (*Comput: also:* **disk~**) lecteur
m de disquette ▷ *vt* conduire; (*nail*) enfoncer;
(*push*) chasser, pousser; (*Tech: motor*)
actionner; entraîner ▷ *vi* (*be at the wheel*)
conduire; (*travel by car*) aller en voiture; **to go
for a ~** aller faire une promenade en voiture;
it's 3 hours' ~ from London Londres est à
3 heures de route; **left-/right-hand ~** (*Aut*)
conduite *f* à gauche/droite; **front-/rear-
wheel ~** (*Aut*) traction *f* avant/arrière; **to ~ sb
to (do) sth** pousser or conduire qn à (faire)
qch; **to ~ sb mad** rendre qn fou/folle; **drive
at** *vt fus* (*fig: intend, mean*) vouloir dire, en
venir à; **drive on** *vi* poursuivre sa route,
continuer; (*after stopping*) reprendre sa route,
repartir ▷ *vt* (*incite, encourage*) inciter; **drive
out** *vt* (*force out*) chasser

drive-by ['draɪvbaɪ] *n* (*also:* **~ shooting**)
tentative d'assassinat par coups de feu tirés d'une
voiture

drive-in ['draɪvɪn] *adj, n* (*esp US*) drive-in *m*

drivel ['drɪvl] *n* (*inf*) idioties *fpl*,
imbécillités *fpl*

driven ['drɪvn] *pp* of **drive**

driver ['draɪvə^r] *n* conducteur(-trice); (*of taxi,
bus*) chauffeur *m*

driver's license *n* (*US*) permis *m* de conduire

driveway ['draɪvweɪ] *n* allée *f*

driving ['draɪvɪŋ] *adj*: **~ rain** *n* pluie battante
▷ *n* conduite *f*

driving instructor *n* moniteur *m* d'auto-
école

driving lesson *n* leçon *f* de conduite

driving licence *n* (*Brit*) permis *m* de conduire

driving school *n* auto-école *f*

driving test *n* examen *m* du permis de
conduire

drizzle ['drɪzl] *n* bruine *f*, crachin *m* ▷ *vi*
bruiner

drool [dru:l] *vi* baver; **to ~ over sb/sth** (*fig*)
baver d'admiration or être en extase devant
qn/qch

droop [dru:p] *vi* (*flower*) commencer à se
faner; (*shoulders, head*) tomber

drop [drɔp] *n* (*of liquid*) goutte *f*; (*fall*) baisse *f*;
(*: in salary*) réduction *f*; (*also:* **parachute ~**)
saut *m*; (*of cliff*) dénivellation *f*; à-pic *m* ▷ *vt*
laisser tomber; (*voice, eyes, price*) baisser;
(*passenger*) déposer ▷ *vi* (*wind, temperature, price,
voice*) tomber; (*numbers, attendance*) diminuer;
drops *npl* (*Med*) gouttes; **cough ~s** pastilles
fpl pour la toux; **a ~ of 10%** une baisse or
réduction de 10%; **to ~ anchor** jeter l'ancre;
to ~ sb a line mettre un mot à qn; **drop in** *vi*
(*inf: visit*): **to ~ in (on)** faire un saut (chez),
passer (chez); **drop off** *vi* (*sleep*) s'assoupir
▷ *vt* (*passenger*) déposer; **to ~ sb off** déposer
qn; **drop out** *vi* (*withdraw*) se retirer; (*student
etc*) abandonner, décrocher

dropout ['drɔpaut] *n* (*from society*)
marginal(e); (*from university*) drop-out *m/f*,
dropé(e)

dropper ['drɔpə^r] *n* (*Med etc*) compte-gouttes
m inv

droppings ['drɔpɪŋz] *npl* crottes *fpl*

drought [draut] *n* sécheresse *f*

drove [drəuv] *pt* of **drive** ▷ *n*: **~s of people**
une foule de gens

drown [draun] *vt* noyer; (*also:* **~ out:** *sound*)
couvrir, étouffer ▷ *vi* se noyer

drowsy ['drauzɪ] *adj* somnolent(e)

drug [drʌg] *n* médicament *m*; (*narcotic*)
drogue *f* ▷ *vt* droguer; **to be on ~s** se droguer;
he's on ~s il se drogue; (*Med*) il est sous
médication

drug addict *n* toxicomane *m/f*

drug dealer *n* revendeur(-euse) de drogue

druggist ['drʌgɪst] *n* (*US*) pharmacien(ne)-
droguiste

drugstore ['drʌgstɔ:^r] *n* (*US*) pharmacie-
droguerie *f*, drugstore *m*

drum [drʌm] *n* tambour *m*; (*for oil, petrol*)
bidon *m* ▷ *vt*: **to ~ one's fingers on the
table** pianoter or tambouriner sur la table;
drums *npl* (*Mus*) batterie *f*; **drum up** *vt*
(*enthusiasm, support*) susciter, rallier

drummer ['drʌmə^r] *n* (joueur *m* de)
tambour *m*

drunk [drʌŋk] *pp* of **drink** ▷ *adj* ivre, soûl(e)
▷ *n* (*also:* **~ard**) ivrogne *m/f*; **to get ~** s'enivrer,
se soûler

drunken ['drʌŋkən] *adj* ivre, soûl(e); (*rage,
stupor*) ivrogne, d'ivrogne; **~ driving** conduite
f en état d'ivresse

dry [draɪ] *adj* sec/sèche; (*day*) sans pluie; (*humour*) pince-sans-rire; (*uninteresting*) aride, rébarbatif(-ive) ▷ *vt* sécher; (*clothes*) faire sécher ▷ *vi* sécher; **on ~ land** sur la terre ferme; **to ~ one's hands/hair/eyes** se sécher les mains/les cheveux/les yeux; **dry off** *vi, vt* sécher; **dry up** *vi* (*river, supplies*) se tarir; (: *speaker*) sécher, rester sec

dry-cleaner's ['draɪ'kliːnəz] *n* teinturerie *f*

dry-cleaning ['draɪ'kliːnɪŋ] *n* (*process*) nettoyage *m* à sec

dryer ['draɪə^r] *n* (*tumble-dryer*) sèche-linge *m inv*; (*for hair*) sèche-cheveux *m inv*

dryness ['draɪnɪs] *n* sécheresse *f*

dry rot *n* pourriture sèche (*du bois*)

DSS *n abbr* (*Brit*) = **Department of Social Security**

DTP *n abbr* (= *desktop publishing*) PAO *f*

dual ['djuəl] *adj* double

dual carriageway *n* (*Brit*) route *f* à quatre voies

dual-purpose ['djuəl'pəːpəs] *adj* à double emploi

dubbed [dʌbd] *adj* (*Ciné*) doublé(e); (*nicknamed*) surnommé(e)

dubious ['djuːbɪəs] *adj* hésitant(e), incertain(e); (*reputation, company*) douteux(-euse); (*also*: **I'm very ~ about it**) j'ai des doutes sur la question, je n'en suis pas sûr du tout

duchess ['dʌtʃɪs] *n* duchesse *f*

duck [dʌk] *a* canard *m* ▷ *vi* se baisser vivement, baisser subitement la tête ▷ *vt* plonger dans l'eau

duckling ['dʌklɪŋ] *n* caneton *m*

duct [dʌkt] *n* conduite *f*, canalisation *f*; (*Anat*) conduit *m*

dud [dʌd] *n* (*shell*) obus non éclaté; (*object, tool*): **it's a ~** c'est de la camelote, ça ne marche pas ▷ *adj* (*Brit*: *cheque*) sans provision; (: *note, coin*) faux/fausse

due [djuː] *adj* (*money, payment*) dû/due; (*expected*) attendu(e); (*fitting*) qui convient ▷ *n* dû *m* ▷ *adv*: **~ north** droit vers le nord; **dues** *npl* (*for club, union*) cotisation *f*; (*in harbour*) droits *mpl* (de port); **~ to** (*because of*) en raison de; (*caused by*) dû à; **in ~ course** en temps utile *ou* voulu; (*in the end*) finalement; **the rent is ~ on the 30th** il faut payer le loyer le 30; **the train is ~ at 8 a.m.** le train est attendu à 8 h; **she is ~ back tomorrow** elle doit rentrer demain; **he is ~ £10** on lui doit 10 livres; **I am ~ 6 days' leave** j'ai droit à 6 jours de congé; **to give sb his** *or* **her ~** être juste envers qn

duel ['djuəl] *n* duel *m*

duet [djuːˈɛt] *n* duo *m*

duffel bag, duffle bag ['dʌfl-] *n* sac marin

duffel coat, duffle coat ['dʌfl-] *n* duffel-coat *m*

dug [dʌɡ] *pt, pp of* **dig**

duke [djuːk] *n* duc *m*

dull [dʌl] *adj* (*boring*) ennuyeux(-euse); (*slow*) borné(e); (*not bright*) morne, terne; (*sound, pain*) sourd(e); (*weather, day*) gris(e), maussade; (*blade*) émoussé(e) ▷ *vt* (*pain, grief*) atténuer; (*mind, senses*) engourdir

duly ['djuːlɪ] *adv* (*on time*) en temps voulu; (*as expected*) comme il se doit

dumb [dʌm] *adj* muet(te); (*stupid*) bête; **to be struck ~** (*fig*) rester abasourdi(e), être sidéré(e)

dumbfounded [dʌmˈfaʊndɪd] *adj* sidéré(e)

dummy ['dʌmɪ] *n* (*tailor's model*) mannequin *m*; (*mock-up*) factice *m*, maquette *f*; (*Sport*) feinte *f*; (*Brit*: *for baby*) tétine *f* ▷ *adj* faux/fausse, factice

dump [dʌmp] *n* tas d'ordures; (*also*: **rubbish ~**) décharge (publique); (*Mil*) dépôt *m*; (*Comput*) listage *m* (de la mémoire); (*inf*: *place*) trou *m* ▷ *vt* (*put down*) déposer; déverser; (*get rid of*) se débarrasser de; (*Comput*) lister; (*Comm*: *goods*) vendre à perte (*sur le marché extérieur*); **to be (down) in the ~s** (*inf*) avoir le cafard, broyer du noir

dumpling ['dʌmplɪŋ] *n* boulette *f* (de pâte)

dumpy ['dʌmpɪ] *adj* courtaud(e), boulot(te)

dunce [dʌns] *n* âne *m*, cancre *m*

dune [djuːn] *n* dune *f*

dung [dʌŋ] *n* fumier *m*

dungarees [dʌŋɡəˈriːz] *npl* bleu(s) *m(pl)*; (*for child, woman*) salopette *f*

dungeon ['dʌndʒən] *n* cachot *m*

duplex ['djuːplɛks] *n* (*US*: *also*: **~ apartment**) duplex *m*

duplicate *n* ['djuːplɪkət] double *m*, copie exacte; (*copy of letter etc*) duplicata *m* ▷ *adj* (*copy*) en double ▷ *vt* ['djuːplɪkeɪt] faire un double de; (*on machine*) polycopier; **in ~** en deux exemplaires, en double; **~ key** double *m* de la (*ou* d'une) clé

durable ['djuərəbl] *adj* durable; (*clothes, metal*) résistant(e), solide

duration [djuəˈreɪʃən] *n* durée *f*

during ['djuərɪŋ] *prep* pendant, au cours de

dusk [dʌsk] *n* crépuscule *m*

dust [dʌst] *n* poussière *f* ▷ *vt* (*furniture*) essuyer, épousseter; (*cake etc*): **to ~ with** saupoudrer de; **dust off** *vt* (*also fig*) dépoussiérer

dustbin ['dʌstbɪn] *n* (*Brit*) poubelle *f*

duster ['dʌstə^r] *n* chiffon *m*

dustman ['dʌstmən] *irreg n* (*Brit*) boueux *m*, éboueur *m*

dustpan ['dʌstpæn] *n* pelle *f* à poussière

dusty ['dʌstɪ] *adj* poussiéreux(-euse)

Dutch [dʌtʃ] *adj* hollandais(e), néerlandais(e) ▷ *n* (*Ling*) hollandais *m*, néerlandais *m* ▷ *adv*: **to go ~** *ou* **dutch** (*inf*) partager les frais; **the Dutch** *npl* les Hollandais, les Néerlandais

Dutchman ['dʌtʃmən] *irreg n* Hollandais *m*

Dutchwoman ['dʌtʃwumən] *irreg n* Hollandaise *f*

duty ['dju:tɪ] n devoir m; (tax) droit m, taxe f;
duties npl fonctions fpl; **to make it one's ~
to do sth** se faire un devoir de faire qch; **to
pay ~ on sth** payer un droit or une taxe sur
qch; **on ~** de service; (at night etc) de garde; **off
~** libre, pas de service or de garde

duty-free ['dju:tɪ'fri:] adj exempté(e) de
douane, hors-taxe; **~ shop** boutique f hors-
taxe

duvet ['du:veɪ] n (Brit) couette f

DVD n abbr (= digital versatile or video disc) DVD m

DVD burner n graveur m de DVD

DVD player n lecteur m de DVD

DVD writer n graveur m de DVD

dwarf (pl **dwarves**) [dwɔ:f, dwɔ:vz] n nain(e)
▷ vt écraser

dwell (pt, pp **dwelt**) [dwɛl, dwɛlt] vi
demeurer; **dwell on** vt fus s'étendre sur

dwelt [dwɛlt] pt, pp of **dwell**

dwindle ['dwɪndl] vi diminuer, décroître

dye [daɪ] n teinture f ▷ vt teindre; **hair ~**
teinture pour les cheveux

dying ['daɪɪŋ] adj mourant(e), agonisant(e)

dyke [daɪk] n (embankment) digue f

dynamic [daɪ'næmɪk] adj dynamique

dynamite ['daɪnəmaɪt] n dynamite f ▷ vt
dynamiter, faire sauter à la dynamite

dynamo ['daɪnəməʊ] n dynamo f

dyslexia [dɪs'lɛksɪə] n dyslexie f

dyslexic [dɪs'lɛksɪk] adj, n dyslexique m/f

E¹, e [i:] n (letter) E, e m; (Mus): **E** mi m; **E for
Edward**, (US) **E for Easy** E comme Eugène

E² abbr (= east) E ▷ n abbr (Drugs) = **ecstasy**

each [i:tʃ] adj chaque ▷ pron chacun(e); **~ one**
chacun(e); **~ other** l'un l'autre; **they hate ~
other** ils se détestent (mutuellement); **you
are jealous of ~ other** vous êtes jaloux l'un
de l'autre; **~ day** chaque jour, tous les jours;
they have 2 books ~ ils ont 2 livres chacun;
they cost £5 ~ ils coûtent 5 livres (la) pièce;
~ of us chacun(e) de nous

eager ['i:ɡər] adj (person, buyer) empressé(e);
(lover) ardent(e), passionné(e); (keen: pupil,
worker) enthousiaste; **to be ~ to do sth**
(impatient) brûler de faire qch; (keen) désirer
vivement faire qch; **to be ~ for** (event) désirer
vivement; (vengeance, affection, information)
être avide de

eagle ['i:ɡl] n aigle m

ear [ɪər] n oreille f; (of corn) épi m; **up to one's
~s in debt** endetté(e) jusqu'au cou

earache ['ɪəreɪk] n mal m aux oreilles

eardrum ['ɪədrʌm] n tympan m

earl [ə:l] n comte m

earlier ['ə:lɪər] adj (date etc) plus rapproché(e);
(edition etc) plus ancien(ne), antérieur(e) ▷ adv
plus tôt

early ['ə:lɪ] adv tôt, de bonne heure; (ahead of
time) en avance; (near the beginning) au début
▷ adj précoce, qui se manifeste (or se fait) tôt
or de bonne heure; (Christians, settlers)
premier(-ière); (reply) rapide; (death)

prématuré(e); (*work*) de jeunesse; **to have an ~ night/start** se coucher/partir tôt *or* de bonne heure; **take the ~ train** prenez le premier train; **in the ~** *or* **~ in the spring/19th century** au début *or* commencement du printemps/19ème siècle; **you're ~!** tu es en avance!; **~ in the morning** tôt le matin; **she's in her ~ forties** elle a un peu plus de quarante ans *or* de la quarantaine; **at your earliest convenience** (*Comm*) dans les meilleurs délais

early retirement *n* retraite anticipée

earmark ['ɪəmɑːk] *vt*: **to ~ sth for** réserver *or* destiner qch à

earn [əːn] *vt* gagner; (*Comm: yield*) rapporter; **to ~ one's living** gagner sa vie; **this ~ed him much praise, he ~ed much praise for this** ceci lui a valu de nombreux éloges; **he's ~ed his rest/reward** il mérite *or* a bien mérité *or* a bien gagné son repos/sa récompense

earnest ['əːnɪst] *adj* sérieux(-euse) ▷ *n* (*also:* **~ money**) acompte *m*, arrhes *fpl*; **in ~** *adv* sérieusement, pour de bon

earnings ['əːnɪŋz] *npl* salaire *m*; gains *mpl*; (*of company etc*) profits *mpl*, bénéfices *mpl*

earphones ['ɪəfəunz] *npl* écouteurs *mpl*

earplugs ['ɪəplʌgz] *npl* boules *fpl* Quiès®; (*to keep out water*) protège-tympans *mpl*

earring ['ɪərɪŋ] *n* boucle *f* d'oreille

earshot ['ɪəʃɔt] *n*: **out of/within ~** hors de portée/à portée de voix

earth [əːθ] *n* (*gen, also Brit Elec*) terre *f*; (*of fox etc*) terrier *m* ▷ *vt* (*Brit Elec*) relier à la terre

earthenware ['əːθnwɛə*] *n* poterie *f*; faïence *f* ▷ *adj* de *or* en faïence

earthquake ['əːθkweɪk] *n* tremblement *m* de terre, séisme *m*

earthy ['əːθɪ] *adj* (*fig*) terre à terre *inv*, truculent(e)

ease [iːz] *n* facilité *f*, aisance *f*; (*comfort*) bien-être *m* ▷ *vt* (*soothe: mind*) tranquilliser; (*reduce: pain, problem*) atténuer; (*: tension*) réduire; (*loosen*) relâcher, détendre; (*help pass*): **to ~ sth in/out** faire pénétrer/sortir qch délicatement *or* avec douceur, faciliter la pénétration/la sortie de qch ▷ *vi* (*situation*) se détendre; **with ~** sans difficulté, aisément; **life of ~** vie oisive; **at ~** à l'aise; (*Mil*) au repos; **ease off, ease up** *vi* diminuer, (*slow down*) ralentir; (*relax*) se détendre

easel ['iːzl] *n* chevalet *m*

easily ['iːzɪlɪ] *adv* facilement; (*by far*) de loin

east [iːst] *n* est *m* ▷ *adj* (*wind*) d'est; (*side*) est *inv* ▷ *adv* à l'est, vers l'est; **the E~** l'Orient *m*; (*Pol*) les pays *mpl* de l'Est

eastbound ['iːstbaund] *adj* en direction de l'est; (*carriageway*) est *inv*

Easter ['iːstə*] *n* Pâques *fpl* ▷ *adj* (*holidays*) de Pâques, pascal(e)

Easter egg *n* œuf *m* de Pâques

easterly ['iːstəlɪ] *adj* d'est

eastern ['iːstən] *adj* de l'est, oriental(e); **E~ Europe** l'Europe de l'Est; **the E~ bloc** (*Pol*) les pays *mpl* de l'Est

Easter Sunday *n* le dimanche de Pâques

eastward ['iːstwəd], **eastwards** ['iːstwədz] *adv* vers l'est, à l'est

easy ['iːzɪ] *adj* facile; (*manner*) aisé(e) ▷ *adv*: **to take it** *or* **things ~** (*rest*) ne pas se fatiguer; (*not worry*) ne pas (trop) s'en faire; **to have an ~ life** avoir la vie facile; **payment on ~ terms** (*Comm*) facilités *fpl* de paiement; **that's easier said than done** c'est plus facile à dire qu'à faire, c'est vite dit; **I'm ~** (*inf*) ça m'est égal

easy chair *n* fauteuil *m*

easy-going ['iːzɪ'gəuɪŋ] *adj* accommodant(e), facile à vivre

eat (*pt* **ate**, *pp* **eaten**) [iːt, eɪt, 'iːtn] *vt, vi* manger; **can we have something to ~?** est-ce qu'on peut manger quelque chose?; **eat away** *vt* (*sea*) saper, éroder; (*acid*) corroder; **eat away at, eat into** *vt fus* ronger, attaquer; **eat out** *vi* manger au restaurant; **eat up** *vt* (*food*) finir (de manger); **it ~s up electricity** ça bouffe du courant, ça consomme beaucoup d'électricité

eaten ['iːtn] *pp* of **eat**

eaves [iːvz] *npl* avant-toit *m*

eavesdrop ['iːvzdrɔp] *vi*: **to ~ (on)** écouter de façon indiscrète

ebb [ɛb] *n* reflux *m* ▷ *vi* refluer; (*fig: also*: **~ away**) décliner; **the ~ and flow** le flux et le reflux; **to be at a low ~** (*fig*) être bien bas(se), ne pas aller bien fort

ebony ['ɛbənɪ] *n* ébène *f*

e-book ['iːbuk] *n* livre *m* électronique

e-business ['iːbɪznɪs] *n* (*company*) entreprise *f* électronique; (*commerce*) commerce *m* électronique

ECB *n abbr* (= *European Central Bank*) BCE *f* (= *Banque centrale européenne*)

eccentric [ɪk'sɛntrɪk] *adj, n* excentrique *m/f*

echo ['ɛkəu] (*pl* **echoes**) *n* écho *m* ▷ *vt* répéter; faire chorus avec ▷ *vi* résonner; faire écho

eclipse [ɪ'klɪps] *n* éclipse *f* ▷ *vt* éclipser

eco-friendly [iːkəu'frɛndlɪ] *adj* non nuisible à *or* qui ne nuit pas à l'environnement

ecological [iːkə'lɔdʒɪkəl] *adj* écologique

ecology [ɪ'kɔlədʒɪ] *n* écologie *f*

e-commerce [iːkəmɑːs] *n* commerce *m* électronique

economic [iːkə'nɔmɪk] *adj* économique; (*profitable*) rentable

economical [iːkə'nɔmɪkl] *adj* économique; (*person*) économe

economics [iːkə'nɔmɪks] *n* (*Scol*) économie *f* politique ▷ *npl* (*of project etc*) côté *m or* aspect *m* économique

economist [ɪ'kɔnəmɪst] *n* économiste *m/f*

economize [ɪ'kɔnəmaɪz] *vi* économiser, faire des économies

economy [ɪ'kɔnəmɪ] *n* économie *f*;
  economies of scale économies d'échelle
economy class *n* (*Aviat*) classe *f* touriste
economy class syndrome *n* syndrome *m*
  de la classe économique
economy size *n* taille *f* économique
ecstasy ['ekstəsɪ] *n* extase *f*; (*Drugs*) ecstasy
  m; **to go into ecstasies over** s'extasier sur
ecstatic [eks'tætɪk] *adj* extatique, en extase
eczema ['eksɪmə] *n* eczéma *m*
edge [edʒ] *n* bord *m*; (*of knife etc*) tranchant *m*,
  fil *m* ▷ *vt* border ▷ *vi*: **to ~ forward** avancer
  petit à petit; **to ~ away from** s'éloigner
  furtivement de; **on ~** (*fig*) crispé(e), tendu(e);
  to have the ~ on (*fig*) l'emporter (de justesse)
  sur, être légèrement meilleur que
edgeways ['edʒweɪz] *adv* latéralement; **he
  couldn't get a word in ~** il ne pouvait pas
  placer un mot
edgy ['edʒɪ] *adj* crispé(e), tendu(e)
edible ['edɪbl] *adj* comestible; (*meal*)
  mangeable
Edinburgh ['edɪnbərə] *n* Édimbourg; *voir
  article*

◈ **EDINBURGH FESTIVAL**

  Le Festival d'Édimbourg, qui se tient
  chaque année durant trois semaines au
  mois d'août, est l'un des grands festivals
  européens. Il est réputé pour son
  programme officiel mais aussi pour son
  festival "off" (the Fringe) qui propose des
  spectacles aussi bien traditionnels que
  résolument d'avant-garde. Pendant la
  durée du Festival se tient par ailleurs, sur
  l'esplanade du château, un grand
  spectacle de musique militaire, le
  "Military Tattoo".

edit ['edɪt] *vt* (*text, book*) éditer; (*report*)
  préparer; (*film*) monter; (*broadcast*) réaliser;
  (*magazine*) diriger; (*newspaper*) être le
  rédacteur *or* la rédactrice en chef de
edition [ɪ'dɪʃən] *n* édition *f*
editor ['edɪtə'] *n* (*of newspaper*)
  rédacteur(-trice), rédacteur(-trice) en chef;
  (*of sb's work*) éditeur(-trice); (*also*: **film ~**)
  monteur(-euse); **political/ foreign ~**
  rédacteur politique/au service étranger
editorial [edɪ'tɔːrɪəl] *adj* de la rédaction,
  éditorial(e) ▷ *n* éditorial *m*; **the ~ staff** la
  rédaction
educate ['edjukeɪt] *vt* (*teach*) instruire; (*bring
  up*) éduquer; **~d at ...** qui a fait ses études à ...
educated ['edjukeɪtɪd] *adj* (*person*) cultivé(e)
education [edju'keɪʃən] *n* éducation *f*;
  (*studies*) études *fpl*; (*teaching*) enseignement *m*,
  instruction *f*; (*at university: subject etc*)
  pédagogie *f*; **primary** *or* (*US*) **elementary/
  secondary ~** instruction *f* primaire/
  secondaire

educational [edju'keɪʃənl] *adj* pédagogique;
  (*institution*) scolaire; (*useful*) instructif(-ive);
  (*game, toy*) éducatif(-ive); **~ technology**
  technologie *f* de l'enseignement
eel [iːl] *n* anguille *f*
eerie ['ɪərɪ] *adj* inquiétant(e), spectral(e),
  surnaturel(le)
effect [ɪ'fekt] *n* effet *m* ▷ *vt* effectuer;
  effects *npl* (*Theat*) effets *mpl*; (*property*) effets,
  affaires *fpl*; **to take ~** (*Law*) entrer en vigueur,
  prendre effet; (*drug*) agir, faire son effet; **to
  put into ~** (*plan*) mettre en application *or* à
  exécution; **to have an ~ on sb/sth** avoir *or*
  produire un effet sur qn/qch; **in ~** en fait;
  his letter is to the ~ that ... sa lettre nous
  apprend que ...
effective [ɪ'fektɪv] *adj* efficace; (*striking:
  display, outfit*) frappant(e), qui produit *or* fait
  de l'effet; (*actual*) véritable; **to become ~**
  (*Law*) entrer en vigueur, prendre effet; **~ date**
  date *f* d'effet *or* d'entrée en vigueur
effectively [ɪ'fektɪvlɪ] *adv* efficacement;
  (*strikingly*) d'une manière frappante, avec
  beaucoup d'effet; (*in reality*) effectivement,
  en fait
effectiveness [ɪ'fektɪvnɪs] *n* efficacité *f*
effeminate [ɪ'femɪnɪt] *adj* efféminé(e)
effervescent [efə'vesnt] *adj* effervescent(e)
efficiency [ɪ'fɪʃənsɪ] *n* efficacité *f*; (*of machine,
  car*) rendement *m*
efficient [ɪ'fɪʃənt] *adj* efficace; (*machine, car*)
  d'un bon rendement
efficiently [ɪ'fɪʃəntlɪ] *adv* efficacement
effort ['efət] *n* effort *m*; **to make an ~ to do
  sth** faire *or* fournir un effort pour faire qch
effortless ['efətlɪs] *adj* sans effort, aisé(e);
  (*achievement*) facile
effusive [ɪ'fjuːsɪv] *adj* (*person*) expansif(-ive);
  (*welcome*) chaleureux(-euse)
e.g. *adv abbr* (= *exempli gratia*) par exemple,
  p. ex.
egg [eg] *n* œuf *m*; **hard-boiled/soft-boiled ~**
  œuf dur/à la coque; **egg on** *vt* pousser
eggcup ['egkʌp] *n* coquetier *m*
egg plant ['egplɑːnt] (*US*) *n* aubergine *f*
eggshell ['egʃel] *n* coquille *f* d'œuf ▷ *adj*
  (*colour*) blanc cassé *inv*
egg white *n* blanc *m* d'œuf
egg yolk *n* jaune *m* d'œuf
ego ['iːgəu] *n* (*self-esteem*) amour-propre *m*;
  (*Psych*) moi *m*
egotism ['egəutɪzəm] *n* égotisme *m*
egotist ['egəutɪst] *n* égocentrique *m/f*
Egypt ['iːdʒɪpt] *n* Égypte *f*
Egyptian [ɪ'dʒɪpʃən] *adj* égyptien(ne) ▷ *n*
  Égyptien(ne)
eiderdown ['aɪdədaun] *n* édredon *m*
Eiffel Tower ['aɪfəl-] *n* tour *f* Eiffel
eight [eɪt] *num* huit
eighteen [eɪ'tiːn] *num* dix-huit
eighteenth [eɪ'tiːnθ] *num* dix-huitième
eighth [eɪtθ] *num* huitième

eightieth ['eɪtɪɪθ] *num* quatre-vingtième

eighty ['eɪtɪ] *num* quatre-vingt(s)

Eire ['ɛərə] *n* République *f* d'Irlande

either ['aɪðəʳ] *adj* l'un ou l'autre; *(both, each)* chaque ▷ *pron*: ~ **(of them)** l'un ou l'autre ▷ *adv* non plus ▷ *conj*: ~ **good or bad** ou bon ou mauvais, soit bon soit mauvais; **I haven't seen ~ one or the other** je n'ai vu ni l'un ni l'autre; **on ~ side** de chaque côté; **I don't like ~** je n'aime ni l'un ni l'autre; **no, I don't ~** moi non plus; **which bike do you want? — ~ will do** quel vélo voulez-vous? — n'importe lequel; **answer with ~ yes or no** répondez par oui ou par non

eject [ɪ'dʒɛkt] *vt (tenant etc)* expulser; *(object)* éjecter ▷ *vi (pilot)* s'éjecter

elaborate *adj* [ɪ'læbərɪt] compliqué(e), recherché(e), minutieux(-euse) ▷ *vt* [ɪ'læbəreɪt] élaborer ▷ *vi* entrer dans les détails

elastic [ɪ'læstɪk] *adj, n* élastique (*m*)

elastic band *n (Brit)* élastique *m*

elated [ɪ'leɪtɪd] *adj* transporté(e) de joie

elation [ɪ'leɪʃən] *n* (grande) joie, allégresse *f*

elbow ['ɛlbəu] *n* coude *m* ▷ *vt*: **to ~ one's way through the crowd** se frayer un passage à travers la foule (en jouant des coudes)

elder ['ɛldəʳ] *adj* aîné(e) ▷ *n (tree)* sureau *m*; **one's ~s** ses aînés

elderly ['ɛldəlɪ] *adj* âgé(e) ▷ *npl*: **the ~** les personnes âgées

eldest ['ɛldɪst] *adj, n*: **the ~ (child)** l'aîné(e) (des enfants)

elect [ɪ'lɛkt] *vt* élire; *(choose)*: **to ~ to do** choisir de faire ▷ *adj*: **the president ~** le président désigné

election [ɪ'lɛkʃən] *n* élection *f*; **to hold an ~** procéder à une élection

electioneering [ɪlɛkʃə'nɪərɪŋ] *n* propagande électorale, manœuvres électorales

elector [ɪ'lɛktəʳ] *n* électeur(-trice)

electoral [ɪ'lɛktərəl] *adj* électoral(e)

electorate [ɪ'lɛktərɪt] *n* électorat *m*

electric [ɪ'lɛktrɪk] *adj* électrique

electrical [ɪ'lɛktrɪkl] *adj* électrique

electric blanket *n* couverture chauffante

electric fire *n (Brit)* radiateur *m* électrique

electrician [ɪlɛk'trɪʃən] *n* électricien *m*

electricity [ɪlɛk'trɪsɪtɪ] *n* électricité *f*; **to switch on/off the ~** rétablir/couper le courant

electric shock *n* choc *m* or décharge *f* électrique

electrify [ɪ'lɛktrɪfaɪ] *vt (Rail)* électrifier; *(audience)* électriser

electronic [ɪlɛk'trɔnɪk] *adj* électronique

electronic mail *n* courrier *m* électronique

electronics [ɪlɛk'trɔnɪks] *n* électronique *f*

elegance ['ɛlɪɡəns] *n* élégance *f*

elegant ['ɛlɪɡənt] *adj* élégant(e)

element ['ɛlɪmənt] *n (gen)* élément *m*; *(of heater, kettle etc)* résistance *f*

elementary [ɛlɪ'mɛntərɪ] *adj* élémentaire; *(school, education)* primaire

elementary school *n (US)* école *f* primaire; *voir article*

⬡ **ELEMENTARY SCHOOL**

⬡ Aux États-Unis et au Canada, une
⬡ *elementary school* (également appelée
⬡ "grade school" ou "grammar school" aux
⬡ États-Unis) est une école publique où les
⬡ enfants passent les six à huit premières
⬡ années de leur scolarité.

elephant ['ɛlɪfənt] *n* éléphant *m*

elevate ['ɛlɪveɪt] *vt* élever

elevation [ɛlɪ'veɪʃən] *n* élévation *f*; *(height)* altitude *f*

elevator ['ɛlɪveɪtəʳ] *n (in warehouse etc)* élévateur *m*, monte-charge *m inv*; *(US: lift)* ascenseur *m*

eleven [ɪ'lɛvn] *num* onze

elevenses [ɪ'lɛvnzɪz] *npl (Brit)* ≈ pause-café *f*

eleventh [ɪ'lɛvnθ] *num* onzième; **at the ~ hour** *(fig)* à la dernière minute

elicit [ɪ'lɪsɪt] *vt*: **to ~ (from)** obtenir (de); tirer (de)

eligible ['ɛlɪdʒəbl] *adj* éligible; *(for membership)* admissible; **an ~ young man** un beau parti; **to be ~ for sth** remplir les conditions requises pour qch; **~ for a pension** ayant droit à la retraite

eliminate [ɪ'lɪmɪneɪt] *vt* éliminer

elm [ɛlm] *n* orme *m*

elongated ['iːlɔŋɡeɪtɪd] *adj* étiré(e), allongé(e)

elope [ɪ'ləup] *vi (lovers)* s'enfuir (ensemble)

eloquent ['ɛləkwənt] *adj* éloquent(e)

else [ɛls] *adv* d'autre; **something ~** quelque chose d'autre, autre chose; **somewhere ~** ailleurs, autre part; **everywhere ~** partout ailleurs; **everyone ~** tous les autres; **nothing ~** rien d'autre; **is there anything ~ I can do?** est-ce que je peux faire quelque chose d'autre?; **where ~?** à quel autre endroit?; **little ~** pas grand-chose d'autre

elsewhere [ɛls'wɛəʳ] *adv* ailleurs, autre part

elude [ɪ'luːd] *vt* échapper à; *(question)* éluder

elusive [ɪ'luːsɪv] *adj* insaisissable; *(answer)* évasif(-ive)

emaciated [ɪ'meɪsɪeɪtɪd] *adj* émacié(e), décharné(e)

email ['iːmeɪl] *n abbr (= electronic mail)* (e-)mail *m*, courriel *m* ▷ *vt*: **to ~ sb** envoyer un (e-)mail or un courriel à qn

email account *n* compte *m* (e-)mail

email address *n* adresse *f* (e-)mail or électronique

emancipate [ɪ'mænsɪpeɪt] *vt* émanciper

embankment [ɪm'bæŋkmənt] *n (of road, railway)* remblai *m*, talus *m*; *(of river)* berge *f*, quai *m*; *(dyke)* digue *f*

embargo [ɪm'bɑːgəu] (pl **embargoes**) n (Comm, Naut) embargo m; (prohibition) interdiction f ▷ vt frapper d'embargo, mettre l'embargo sur; **to put an ~ on sth** mettre l'embargo sur qch

embark [ɪm'bɑːk] vi embarquer; **to ~ on** (s')embarquer à bord de or sur ▷ vt embarquer; **to ~ on** (journey etc) commencer, entreprendre; (fig) se lancer or s'embarquer dans

embarkation [ɛmbɑː'keɪʃən] n embarquement m

embarrass [ɪm'bærəs] vt embarrasser, gêner

embarrassed [ɪm'bærəst] adj gêné(e); **to be ~** être gêné(e)

embarrassing [ɪm'bærəsɪŋ] adj gênant(e), embarrassant(e)

embarrassment [ɪm'bærəsmənt] n embarras m, gêne f; (embarrassing thing, person) source f d'embarras

embassy ['ɛmbəsɪ] n ambassade f; **the French E~** l'ambassade de France

embellish [ɪm'bɛlɪʃ] vt embellir; enjoliver

embers ['ɛmbəz] npl braise f

embezzle [ɪm'bɛzl] vt détourner

embezzlement [ɪm'bɛzlmənt] n détournement m (de fonds)

embitter [ɪm'bɪtər] vt aigrir; envenimer

embody [ɪm'bɔdɪ] vt (features) réunir, comprendre; (ideas) formuler, exprimer

embossed [ɪm'bɔst] adj repoussé(e), gaufré(e); **~ with** où figure(nt) en relief

embrace [ɪm'breɪs] vt embrasser, étreindre; (include) embrasser, couvrir, comprendre ▷ vi s'embrasser, s'étreindre ▷ n étreinte f

embroider [ɪm'brɔɪdər] vt broder; (fig: story) enjoliver

embroidery [ɪm'brɔɪdərɪ] n broderie f

embryo ['ɛmbrɪəu] n (also fig) embryon m

emerald ['ɛmərəld] n émeraude f

emerge [ɪ'məːdʒ] vi apparaître; (from room, car) surgir; (from sleep, imprisonment) sortir; **it ~s that** (Brit) il ressort que

emergency [ɪ'məːdʒənsɪ] n (crisis) cas m d'urgence; (Med) urgence f; **in an ~** en cas d'urgence; **state of ~** état m d'urgence

emergency brake (US) n frein m à main

emergency exit n sortie f de secours

emergency landing n atterrissage forcé

emergency room n (US: Med) urgences fpl

emergency services npl: **the ~** (fire, police, ambulance) les services mpl d'urgence

emery board ['ɛmərɪ-] n lime f à ongles (en carton émerisé)

emigrate ['ɛmɪgreɪt] vi émigrer

emigration [ɛmɪ'greɪʃən] n émigration f

eminent ['ɛmɪnənt] adj éminent(e)

emissions [ɪ'mɪʃənz] npl émissions fpl

emit [ɪ'mɪt] vt émettre

emoticon [ɪ'məutɪkən] n (Comput) émoticone m

emotion [ɪ'məuʃən] n sentiment m; (as opposed to reason) émotion f, sentiments

emotional [ɪ'məuʃənl] adj (person) émotif(-ive), très sensible; (needs) affectif(-ive); (scene) émouvant(e); (tone, speech) qui fait appel aux sentiments

emotive [ɪ'məutɪv] adj émotif(-ive); **~ power** capacité f d'émouvoir or de toucher

emperor ['ɛmpərər] n empereur m

emphasis (pl **emphases**) ['ɛmfəsɪs, -siːz] n accent m; **to lay** or **place ~ on sth** (fig) mettre l'accent sur, insister sur; **the ~ is on reading** la lecture tient une place primordiale, on accorde une importance particulière à la lecture

emphasize ['ɛmfəsaɪz] vt (syllable, word, point) appuyer or insister sur; (feature) souligner, accentuer

emphatic [ɛm'fætɪk] adj (strong) énergique, vigoureux(-euse); (unambiguous, clear) catégorique

empire ['ɛmpaɪər] n empire m

employ [ɪm'plɔɪ] vt employer; **he's ~ed in a bank** il est employé de banque, il travaille dans une banque

employee [ɪmplɔɪ'iː] n employé(e)

employer [ɪm'plɔɪər] n employeur(-euse)

employment [ɪm'plɔɪmənt] n emploi m; **to find ~** trouver un emploi or du travail; **without ~** au chômage, sans emploi; **place of ~** lieu m de travail

employment agency n agence f or bureau m de placement

empower [ɪm'pauər] vt: **to ~ sb to do** autoriser or habiliter qn à faire

empress ['ɛmprɪs] n impératrice f

emptiness ['ɛmptɪnɪs] n vide m; (of area) aspect m désertique

empty ['ɛmptɪ] adj vide; (street, area) désert(e); (threat, promise) en l'air, vain(e) ▷ n (bottle) bouteille f vide ▷ vt vider; se vider; (liquid) s'écouler; **on an ~ stomach** à jeun; **to ~ into** (river) se jeter dans, se déverser dans

empty-handed ['ɛmptɪ'hændɪd] adj les mains vides

EMU n abbr (= European Monetary Union) UME f

emulate ['ɛmjuleɪt] vt rivaliser avec, imiter

emulsion [ɪ'mʌlʃən] n émulsion f; (also: **~ paint**) peinture mate

enable [ɪ'neɪbl] vt: **to ~ sb to do** permettre à qn de faire, donner à qn la possibilité de faire

enamel [ɪ'næməl] n émail m; (also: **~ paint**) (peinture f) laque f

enchant [ɪn'tʃɑːnt] vt enchanter

enchanting [ɪn'tʃɑːntɪŋ] adj ravissant(e), enchanteur(-eresse)

encl. abbr (on letters etc: = enclosed) ci-joint(e); (= enclosure) PJ f

enclose [ɪn'kləuz] vt (land) clôturer; (space, object) entourer; (letter etc): **to ~ (with)** joindre (à); **please find ~d** veuillez trouver ci-joint

enclosure [ɪnˈkləʊʒəʳ] n enceinte f; (in letter etc) annexe f

encompass [ɪnˈkʌmpəs] vt encercler, entourer; (include) contenir, inclure

encore [ɒŋˈkɔːʳ] excl, n bis (m)

encounter [ɪnˈkaʊntəʳ] n rencontre f ▷ vt rencontrer

encourage [ɪnˈkʌrɪdʒ] vt encourager; (industry, growth) favoriser; **to ~ sb to do sth** encourager qn à faire qch

encouragement [ɪnˈkʌrɪdʒmənt] n encouragement m

encouraging [ɪnˈkʌrɪdʒɪŋ] adj encourageant(e)

encroach [ɪnˈkrəʊtʃ] vi: **to ~ (up)on** empiéter sur

encyclopaedia, encyclopedia [ɛnsaɪkləʊˈpiːdɪə] n encyclopédie f

end [ɛnd] n fin f; (of table, street, rope etc) bout m, extrémité f; (of pointed object) pointe f; (of town) bout m; (Sport) côté m ▷ vt terminer; (also: **bring to an ~, put an ~ to**) mettre fin à ▷ vi se terminer, finir; **from ~ to ~** d'un bout à l'autre; **to come to an ~** prendre fin; **to be at an ~** être fini(e), être terminé(e); **in the ~** finalement; **on ~** (object) debout, dressé(e); **to stand on ~** (hair) se dresser sur la tête; **for 5 hours on ~** durant 5 heures d'affilée or de suite; **for hours on ~** pendant des heures (et des heures); **at the ~ of the day** (Brit fig) en fin de compte; **to this ~, with this ~ in view** à cette fin, dans ce but; **end up** vi: **to ~ up in** (condition) finir or se terminer par; (place) finir or aboutir à

endanger [ɪnˈdeɪndʒəʳ] vt mettre en danger; **an ~ed species** une espèce en voie de disparition

endearing [ɪnˈdɪərɪŋ] adj attachant(e)

endeavour, (US) **endeavor** [ɪnˈdɛvəʳ] n effort m; (attempt) tentative f ▷ vt: **to ~ to do** tenter or s'efforcer de faire

ending [ˈɛndɪŋ] n dénouement m, conclusion f; (Ling) terminaison f

endive [ˈɛndaɪv] n (curly) chicorée f; (smooth, flat) endive f

endless [ˈɛndlɪs] adj sans fin, interminable; (patience, resources) inépuisable, sans limites; (possibilities) illimité(e)

endorse [ɪnˈdɔːs] vt (cheque) endosser; (approve) appuyer, approuver, sanctionner

endorsement [ɪnˈdɔːsmənt] n (approval) appui m, aval m; (signature) endossement m; (Brit: on driving licence) contravention f (portée au permis de conduire)

endurance [ɪnˈdjuərəns] n endurance f

endure [ɪnˈdjuəʳ] vt (bear) supporter, endurer ▷ vi (last) durer

enemy [ˈɛnəmɪ] adj, n ennemi(e); **to make an ~ of sb** se faire un(e) ennemi(e) de qn, se mettre qn à dos

energetic [ɛnəˈdʒɛtɪk] adj énergique; (activity) très actif(-ive), qui fait se dépenser (physiquement)

energy [ˈɛnədʒɪ] n énergie f; **Department of E~** ministère m de l'Énergie

enforce [ɪnˈfɔːs] vt (law) appliquer, faire respecter

engage [ɪnˈgeɪdʒ] vt engager; (Mil) engager le combat avec; (lawyer) prendre ▷ vi (Tech) s'enclencher, s'engrener; **to ~ in** se lancer dans; **to ~ sb in conversation** engager la conversation avec qn

engaged [ɪnˈgeɪdʒd] adj (Brit: busy, in use) occupé(e); (betrothed) fiancé(e); **to get ~** se fiancer; **the line's ~** la ligne est occupée; **he is ~ in research/a survey** il fait de la recherche/une enquête

engaged tone n (Brit Tel) tonalité f occupé inv

engagement [ɪnˈgeɪdʒmənt] n (undertaking) obligation f, engagement m; (appointment) rendez-vous m inv; (to marry) fiançailles fpl; (Mil) combat m; **I have a previous ~** j'ai déjà un rendez-vous, je suis déjà pris(e)

engagement ring n bague f de fiançailles

engaging [ɪnˈgeɪdʒɪŋ] adj engageant(e), attirant(e)

engine [ˈɛndʒɪn] n (Aut) moteur m; (Rail) locomotive f

engine driver n (Brit: of train) mécanicien m

engineer [ɛndʒɪˈnɪəʳ] n ingénieur m; (Brit: repairer) dépanneur m; (Navy, US Rail) mécanicien m; **civil/mechanical ~** ingénieur des Travaux Publics or des Ponts et Chaussées/mécanicien

engineering [ɛndʒɪˈnɪərɪŋ] n engineering m, ingénierie f; (of bridges, ships) génie m; (of machine) mécanique f ▷ cpd: **~ works** or **factory** atelier m de construction mécanique

England [ˈɪŋglənd] n Angleterre f

English [ˈɪŋglɪʃ] adj anglais(e) ▷ n (Ling) anglais m; **the ~** npl les Anglais; **an ~ speaker** un anglophone

English Channel n: **the ~** la Manche

Englishman [ˈɪŋglɪʃmən] irreg n Anglais m

Englishwoman [ˈɪŋglɪʃwumən] irreg n Anglaise f

engrave [ɪnˈgreɪv] vt graver

engraving [ɪnˈgreɪvɪŋ] n gravure f

engrossed [ɪnˈgrəʊst] adj: **~ in** absorbé(e) par, plongé(e) dans

engulf [ɪnˈgʌlf] vt engloutir

enhance [ɪnˈhɑːns] vt rehausser, mettre en valeur; (position) améliorer; (reputation) accroître

enjoy [ɪnˈdʒɔɪ] vt aimer, prendre plaisir à; (have benefit of: health, fortune) jouir de; (: success) connaître; **to ~ o.s.** s'amuser

enjoyable [ɪnˈdʒɔɪəbl] adj agréable

enjoyment [ɪnˈdʒɔɪmənt] n plaisir m

enlarge [ɪnˈlɑːdʒ] vt accroître; (Phot) agrandir ▷ vi: **to ~ on** (subject) s'étendre sur

enlargement [ɪnˈlɑːdʒmənt] n (Phot) agrandissement m

enlighten [ɪnˈlaɪtn] vt éclairer

enlightened [ɪnˈlaɪtnd] *adj* éclairé(e)

enlightenment [ɪnˈlaɪtnmənt] *n* édification *f*; éclaircissements *mpl*; (*Hist*): **the E~** = le Siècle des lumières

enlist [ɪnˈlɪst] *vt* recruter; (*support*) s'assurer ▷ *vi* s'engager; **~ed man** (*US Mil*) simple soldat *m*

enmity [ˈenmɪtɪ] *n* inimitié *f*

enormous [ɪˈnɔːməs] *adj* énorme

enough [ɪˈnʌf] *adj*: **~ time/books** assez *or* suffisamment de temps/livres ▷ *adv*: **big ~** assez *or* suffisamment grand ▷ *pron*: **have you got ~?** (en) avez-vous assez?; **will five be ~?** est-ce que cinq suffiront?, est-ce qu'il y en aura assez avec cinq?; **~ to eat** assez à manger; **that's ~!** ça suffit!, assez!; **that's ~, thanks** cela suffit *or* c'est assez, merci; **I've had ~!** je n'en peux plus!; **I've had ~ of him** j'en ai assez de lui; **he has not worked ~** il n'a pas assez *or* suffisamment travaillé, il n'a pas travaillé assez *or* suffisamment; **~! assez!**, ça suffit!; **it's hot ~ (as it is)!** il fait assez chaud comme ça!; **he was kind ~ to lend me the money** il a eu la gentillesse de me prêter l'argent; **... which, funnily** *or* **oddly ~, ...** qui, chose curieuse, ...

enquire [ɪnˈkwaɪəʳ] *vt, vi* = **inquire**

enquiry [ɪnˈkwaɪərɪ] *n* = **inquiry**

enrage [ɪnˈreɪdʒ] *vt* mettre en fureur *or* en rage, rendre furieux(-euse)

enrich [ɪnˈrɪtʃ] *vt* enrichir

enrol, (*US*) **enroll** [ɪnˈrəul] *vt* inscrire ▷ *vi* s'inscrire

enrolment, (*US*) **enrollment** [ɪnˈrəulmənt] *n* inscription *f*

en route [ɔnˈruːt] *adv* en route, en chemin; **~ for** *or* **to** en route vers, à destination de

en suite [ˈɒnswiːt] *adj*: **with ~ bathroom** avec salle de bains en attenante

ensure [ɪnˈʃuəʳ] *vt* assurer, garantir; **to ~ that** s'assurer que

entail [ɪnˈteɪl] *vt* entraîner, nécessiter

entangle [ɪnˈtæŋgl] *vt* emmêler, embrouiller; **to become ~d in sth** (*fig*) se laisser entraîner *or* empêtrer dans qch

enter [ˈentəʳ] *vt* (*room*) entrer dans, pénétrer dans; (*club, army*) entrer à; (*profession*) embrasser; (*competition*) s'inscrire à *or* pour; (*sb for a competition*) (faire) inscrire; (*write down*) inscrire, noter; (*Comput*) entrer, introduire ▷ *vi* entrer; **enter for** *vt fus* s'inscrire à, se présenter pour *or* à; **enter into** *vt fus* (*explanation*) se lancer dans; (*negotiations*) entamer; (*debate*) prendre part à; (*agreement*) conclure; **enter on** *vt fus* commencer; **enter up** *vt* inscrire; **enter upon** *vt fus* = **enter on**

enterprise [ˈentəpraɪz] *n* (*company, undertaking*) entreprise *f*; (*initiative*) (esprit *m* d')initiative *f*; **free ~** libre entreprise; **private ~** entreprise privée

enterprising [ˈentəpraɪzɪŋ] *adj* entreprenant(e), dynamique; (*scheme*) audacieux(-euse)

entertain [entəˈteɪn] *vt* amuser, distraire; (*invite*) recevoir (à dîner); (*idea, plan*) envisager

entertainer [entəˈteɪnəʳ] *n* artiste *m/f* de variétés

entertaining [entəˈteɪnɪŋ] *adj* amusant(e), distrayant(e) ▷ *n*: **to do a lot of ~** beaucoup recevoir

entertainment [entəˈteɪnmənt] *n* (*amusement*) distraction *f*, divertissement *m*, amusement *m*; (*show*) spectacle *m*

enthralled [ɪnˈθrɔːld] *adj* captivé(e)

enthusiasm [ɪnˈθuːzɪæzəm] *n* enthousiasme *m*

enthusiast [ɪnˈθuːzɪæst] *n* enthousiaste *m/f*; **a jazz** *etc* **~** un fervent *or* passionné du jazz *etc*

enthusiastic [ɪnθuːzɪˈæstɪk] *adj* enthousiaste; **to be ~ about** être enthousiasmé(e) par

entire [ɪnˈtaɪəʳ] *adj* (tout) entier(-ère)

entirely [ɪnˈtaɪəlɪ] *adv* entièrement, complètement

entirety [ɪnˈtaɪərətɪ] *n*: **in its ~** dans sa totalité

entitle [ɪnˈtaɪtl] *vt* (*allow*): **to ~ sb to do** donner (le) droit à qn de faire; **to ~ sb to sth** donner droit à qch à qn

entitled [ɪnˈtaɪtld] *adj* (*book*) intitulé(e); **to be ~ to do** avoir le droit de faire

entrance *n* [ˈentrns] entrée *f* ▷ *vt* [ɪnˈtrɑːns] enchanter, ravir; **where's the ~?** où est l'entrée?; **to gain ~ to** (*university etc*) être admis à

entrance examination *n* examen *m* d'entrée *or* d'admission

entrance fee *n* (*to museum etc*) prix *m* d'entrée; (*to join club etc*) droit *m* d'inscription

entrance ramp *n* (*US Aut*) bretelle *f* d'accès

entrant [ˈentrnt] *n* (*in race etc*) participant(e), concurrent(e); (*Brit: in exam*) candidat(e)

entrenched [enˈtrentʃt] *adj* retranché(e)

entrepreneur [ˈɒntrəprəˈnəːʳ] *n* entrepreneur *m*

entrust [ɪnˈtrʌst] *vt*: **to ~ sth to** confier qch à

entry [ˈentrɪ] *n* entrée *f*; (*in register, diary*) inscription *f*; (*in ledger*) écriture *f*; **"no ~"** "défense d'entrer", "entrée interdite"; (*Aut*) "sens interdit"; **single/double ~ book-keeping** comptabilité *f* en partie simple/double

entry form *n* feuille *f* d'inscription

entry phone *n* (*Brit*) interphone *m* (à l'entrée d'un immeuble)

envelop [ɪnˈveləp] *vt* envelopper

envelope [ˈenvələup] *n* enveloppe *f*

envious [ˈenvɪəs] *adj* envieux(-euse)

environment [ɪnˈvaɪrnmənt] *n* (*social, moral*) milieu *m*; (*natural world*): **the ~** l'environnement *m*; **Department of the E~** (*Brit*) *ministère de l'Équipement et de l'Aménagement du territoire*

environmental [ɪnvaɪərn'mɛntl] *adj* (*of surroundings*) du milieu; (*issue, disaster*) écologique; **~ studies** (*in school etc*) écologie *f*

environmentally [ɪnvaɪərn'mɛntlɪ] *adv*: **~ sound/friendly** qui ne nuit pas à l'environnement

envisage [ɪn'vɪzɪdʒ] *vt* (*imagine*) envisager; (*foresee*) prévoir

envoy ['ɛnvɔɪ] *n* envoyé(e); (*diplomat*) ministre *m* plénipotentiaire

envy ['ɛnvɪ] *n* envie *f* ▷ *vt* envier; **to ~ sb sth** envier qch à qn

epic ['ɛpɪk] *n* épopée *f* ▷ *adj* épique

epidemic [ɛpɪ'dɛmɪk] *n* épidémie *f*

epilepsy ['ɛpɪlɛpsɪ] *n* épilepsie *f*

epileptic [ɛpɪ'lɛptɪk] *adj, n* épileptique *m/f*

epileptic fit [ɛpɪ'lɛptɪk-] *n* crise *f* d'épilepsie

episode ['ɛpɪsəud] *n* épisode *m*

epitome [ɪ'pɪtəmɪ] *n* (*fig*) quintessence *f*, type *m*

epitomize [ɪ'pɪtəmaɪz] *vt* (*fig*) illustrer, incarner

equal ['i:kwl] *adj* égal(e) ▷ *n* égal(e) ▷ *vt* égaler; **~ to** (*task*) à la hauteur de; **~ to doing** de taille à *or* capable de faire

equality [i:'kwɔlɪtɪ] *n* égalité *f*

equalize ['i:kwəlaɪz] *vt, vi* (*Sport*) égaliser

equally ['i:kwəlɪ] *adv* également; (*share*) en parts égales; (*treat*) de la même façon; (*pay*) autant; (*just as*) tout aussi; **they are ~ clever** ils sont tout aussi intelligents

equanimity [ɛkwə'nɪmɪtɪ] *n* égalité *f* d'humeur

equate [ɪ'kweɪt] *vt*: **to ~ sth with** comparer qch à; assimiler qch à; **to ~ sth to** mettre qch en équation avec; égaler qch à

equation [ɪ'kweɪʃən] *n* (*Math*) équation *f*

equator [ɪ'kweɪtə'] *n* équateur *m*

equilibrium [i:kwɪ'lɪbrɪəm] *n* équilibre *m*

equip [ɪ'kwɪp] *vt* équiper; **to ~ sb/sth with** équiper *or* munir qn/qch de; **he is well ~ped for the job** il a les compétences *or* les qualités requises pour ce travail

equipment [ɪ'kwɪpmənt] *n* équipement *m*; (*electrical etc*) appareillage *m*, installation *f*

equities ['ɛkwɪtɪz] *npl* (*Brit Comm*) actions cotées en Bourse

equivalent [ɪ'kwɪvəlnt] *adj* équivalent(e) ▷ *n* équivalent *m*; **to be ~ to** équivaloir à, être équivalent(e) à

ER *abbr* (*Brit*: = *Elizabeth Regina*) la reine Élisabeth; (*US*: *Med*: = *emergency room*) urgences *fpl*

era ['ɪərə] *n* ère *f*, époque *f*

eradicate [ɪ'rædɪkeɪt] *vt* éliminer

erase [ɪ'reɪz] *vt* effacer

eraser [ɪ'reɪzə'] *n* gomme *f*

erect [ɪ'rɛkt] *adj* droit(e) ▷ *vt* construire; (*monument*) ériger, élever; (*tent etc*) dresser

erection [ɪ'rɛkʃən] *n* (*Physiol*) érection *f*; (*of building*) construction *f*; (*of machinery etc*) installation *f*

ERM *n abbr* (= *Exchange Rate Mechanism*) mécanisme *m* des taux de change

erode [ɪ'rəud] *vt* éroder; (*metal*) ronger

erosion [ɪ'rəuʒən] *n* érosion *f*

erotic [ɪ'rɔtɪk] *adj* érotique

errand ['ɛrnd] *n* course *f*, commission *f*; **to run ~s** faire des courses; **~ of mercy** mission *f* de charité, acte *m* charitable

erratic [ɪ'rætɪk] *adj* irrégulier(-ière), inconstant(e)

error ['ɛrə'] *n* erreur *f*; **typing/spelling ~** faute *f* de frappe/d'orthographe; **in ~** par erreur, par méprise; **~s and omissions excepted** sauf erreur ou omission

erupt [ɪ'rʌpt] *vi* entrer en éruption; (*fig*) éclater, exploser

eruption [ɪ'rʌpʃən] *n* éruption *f*; (*of anger, violence*) explosion *f*

escalate ['ɛskəleɪt] *vi* s'intensifier; (*costs*) monter en flèche

escalator ['ɛskəleɪtə'] *n* escalier roulant

escapade [ɛskə'peɪd] *n* fredaine *f*, équipée *f*

escape [ɪ'skeɪp] *n* évasion *f*, fuite *f*; (*of gas etc*) fuite; (*Tech*) échappement *m* ▷ *vi* s'échapper, fuir; (*from jail*) s'évader; (*fig*) s'en tirer, en réchapper; (*leak*) fuir; s'échapper ▷ *vt* échapper à; **to ~ from** (*person*) échapper à; (*place*) s'échapper de; (*fig*) fuir; **to ~ to** (*another place*) fuir à, s'enfuir à; **to ~ to safety** se réfugier dans *or* gagner un endroit sûr; **to ~ notice** passer inaperçu(e); **his name ~s me** son nom m'échappe

escapism [ɪ'skeɪpɪzəm] *n* évasion *f* (*fig*)

escort *vt* [ɪ'skɔ:t] escorter ▷ *n* ['ɛskɔ:t] (*Mil*) escorte *f*; (*to dance etc*): **her ~** son compagnon *or* cavalier; **his ~** sa compagne

Eskimo ['ɛskɪməu] *adj* esquimau(de), eskimo ▷ *n* Esquimau(de); (*Ling*) esquimau *m*

especially [ɪ'spɛʃlɪ] *adv* (*particularly*) particulièrement; (*above all*) surtout

espionage ['ɛspɪənɑːʒ] *n* espionnage *m*

Esquire [ɪ'skwaɪə'] *n* (*Brit*: *abbr* **Esq.**): **J. Brown, ~** Monsieur J. Brown

essay ['ɛseɪ] *n* (*Scol*) dissertation *f*; (*Literature*) essai *m*; (*attempt*) tentative *f*

essence ['ɛsns] *n* essence *f*; (*Culin*) extrait *m*; **in ~** en substance; **speed is of the ~** l'essentiel, c'est la rapidité

essential [ɪ'sɛnʃl] *adj* essentiel(le); (*basic*) fondamental(e); **essentials** *npl* éléments essentiels; **it is ~ that** il est essentiel *or* primordial que

essentially [ɪ'sɛnʃlɪ] *adv* essentiellement

establish [ɪ'stæblɪʃ] *vt* établir; (*business*) fonder, créer; (*one's power etc*) asseoir, affirmer

established [ɪ'stæblɪʃt] *adj* bien établi(e)

establishment [ɪ'stæblɪʃmənt] *n* établissement *m*; (*founding*) création *f*; (*institution*) établissement; **the E~** les pouvoirs établis; l'ordre établi

estate [ɪ'steɪt] *n* (*land*) domaine *m*,
propriété *f*; (*Law*) biens *mpl*, succession *f*;
(*Brit: also:* **housing ~**) lotissement *m*

estate agent *n* (*Brit*) agent immobilier

estate car *n* (*Brit*) break *m*

esteem [ɪ'stiːm] *n* estime *f* ▷ *vt* estimer;
apprécier; **to hold sb in high ~** tenir qn en
haute estime

esthetic [ɪs'θetɪk] *adj* (*US*) = **aesthetic**

estimate [n 'estɪmət] estimation *f*; (*Comm*)
devis *m* *vt* ['estɪmeɪt] estimer ▷ *vi* (*Brit Comm*):
to ~ for estimer, faire une estimation de;
(*bid for*) faire un devis pour; **to give sb an ~ of**
faire *or* donner un devis à qn pour; **at a
rough ~** approximativement

estimation [estɪ'meɪʃən] *n* opinion *f*;
estime *f*; **in my ~** à mon avis, selon moi

estranged [ɪs'treɪndʒd] *adj* (*couple*) séparé(e);
(*husband, wife*) dont on s'est séparé(e)

etc *abbr* (= *et cetera*) etc

eternal [ɪ'təːnl] *adj* éternel(le)

eternity [ɪ'təːnɪtɪ] *n* éternité *f*

ethical ['eθɪkl] *adj* moral(e)

ethics ['eθɪks] *n* éthique *f* ▷ *npl* moralité *f*

Ethiopia [iːθɪ'əʊpɪə] *n* Éthiopie *f*

ethnic ['eθnɪk] *adj* ethnique; (*clothes, food*)
folklorique, exotique, *propre aux minorités
ethniques non-occidentales*

ethnic minority *n* minorité *f* ethnique

ethos ['iːθɔs] *n* (*système m de*) valeurs *fpl*

e-ticket ['iːtɪkɪt] *n* billet *m* électronique

etiquette ['etɪket] *n* convenances *fpl*,
étiquette *f*

EU *n* *abbr* (= *European Union*) UE *f*

euro ['juərəʊ] *n* (*currency*) euro *m*

Euroland ['juərəʊlænd] *n* Euroland *m*

Europe ['juərəp] *n* Europe *f*

European [juərə'piːən] *adj* européen(ne) ▷ *n*
Européen(ne)

European Community *n* Communauté
européenne

European Union *n* Union européenne

Eurostar® ['juərəʊstaːʳ] *n* Eurostar® *m*

evacuate [ɪ'vækjueɪt] *vt* évacuer

evade [ɪ'veɪd] *vt* échapper à; (*question etc*)
éluder; (*duties*) se dérober à

evaluate [ɪ'væljueɪt] *vt* évaluer

evaporate [ɪ'væpəreɪt] *vi* s'évaporer; (*fig:
hopes, fear*) s'envoler; (*anger*) se dissiper ▷ *vt*
faire évaporer

evaporated milk [ɪ'væpəreɪtɪd-] *n* lait
condensé (non sucré)

evasion [ɪ'veɪʒən] *n* dérobade *f*; (*excuse*) faux-
fuyant *m*

eve [iːv] *n*: **on the ~ of** à la veille de

even ['iːvn] *adj* (*level, smooth*) régulier(-ière);
(*equal*) égal(e); (*number*) pair(e) ▷ *adv* même;
~ if même si + *indic*; **~ though** quand (bien)
même + *cond*; alors même que + *cond*; **~ more**
encore plus; **~ faster** encore plus vite; **~ so**
quand même; **not ~** pas même; **~ he was
there** même lui était là; **~ on Sundays**
même le dimanche; **to break ~** s'y retrouver,
équilibrer ses comptes; **to get ~ with sb**
prendre sa revanche sur qn; **even out** *vi*
s'égaliser

evening ['iːvnɪŋ] *n* soir *m*; (*as duration, event*)
soirée *f*; **in the ~** le soir; **this ~** ce soir;
tomorrow/yesterday ~ demain/hier soir

evening class *n* cours *m* du soir

evening dress *n* (*man's*) tenue *f* de soirée,
smoking *m*; (*woman's*) robe *f* de soirée

event [ɪ'vent] *n* événement *m*; (*Sport*) épreuve
f; **in the course of ~s** par la suite; **in the ~ of**
en cas de; **in the ~** en réalité, en fait; **at all ~s**,
(*Brit*) **in any ~** en tout cas, de toute manière

eventful [ɪ'ventful] *adj* mouvementé(e)

eventual [ɪ'ventʃuəl] *adj* final(e)

eventuality [ɪventʃu'ælɪtɪ] *n* possibilité *f*,
éventualité *f*

eventually [ɪ'ventʃuəlɪ] *adv* finalement

ever ['evəʳ] *adv* jamais; (*at all times*) toujours;
(*in questions*): **why ~ not?** mais enfin,
pourquoi pas?; **the best ~** le meilleur qu'on
ait jamais vu; **have you ~ seen it?** l'as-tu
déjà vu?, as-tu eu l'occasion *or* t'est-il arrivé
de le voir?; **did you ~ meet him?** est-ce qu'il
vous est arrivé de le rencontrer?; **have you ~
been there?** y êtes-vous déjà allé?; **for ~** pour
toujours; **hardly ~** ne … presque jamais; **~
since** (*as adv*) depuis; (*as conj*) depuis que; **~ so
pretty** si joli; **thank you ~ so much** merci
mille fois

evergreen ['evəɡriːn] *n* arbre *m* à feuilles
persistantes

everlasting [evə'laːstɪŋ] *adj* éternel(le)

KEYWORD

every ['evrɪ] *adj* **1** (*each*) chaque; **every one of
them** tous (sans exception); **every shop in
town was closed** tous les magasins en ville
étaient fermés

2 (*all possible*) tous/toutes les; **I gave you
every assistance** j'ai fait tout mon possible
pour vous aider; **I have every confidence in
him** j'ai entièrement *or* pleinement
confiance en lui; **we wish you every
success** nous vous souhaitons beaucoup
de succès

3 (*showing recurrence*) tous les; **every day** tous
les jours, chaque jour; **every other car** une
voiture sur deux; **every other/third day**
tous les deux/trois jours; **every now and
then** de temps en temps

everybody ['evrɪbɔdɪ] *pron* = **everyone**

everyday ['evrɪdeɪ] *adj* (*expression*) courant(e),
d'usage courant; (*use*) courant; (*clothes, life*)
de tous les jours; (*occurrence, problem*)
quotidien(ne)

everyone ['evrɪwʌn] *pron* tout le monde, tous
pl; **~ knows about it** tout le monde le sait; **~
else** tous les autres

everything ['εvrιθιη] *pron* tout; ~ **is ready** tout est prêt; **he did ~ possible** il a fait tout son possible

everywhere ['εvrιwεə'] *adv* partout; ~ **you go you meet ...** où qu'on aille on rencontre ...

evict [ι'vιkt] *vt* expulser

eviction [ι'vιkʃən] *n* expulsion *f*

evidence ['εvιdns] *n* (*proof*) preuve(s) *f(pl)*; (*of witness*) témoignage *m*; (*sign*) signe *m*; **to show ~ of** donner des signes de; **to give ~** témoigner, déposer; **in ~** (*obvious*) en évidence; en vue

evident ['εvιdnt] *adj* évident(e)

evidently ['εvιdntlι] *adv* de toute évidence; (*apparently*) apparemment

evil ['i:vl] *adj* mauvais(e) ▷ *n* mal *m*

evoke [ι'vəuk] *vt* évoquer; (*admiration*) susciter

evolution [i:və'lu:ʃən] *n* évolution *f*

evolve [ι'vɔlv] *vt* élaborer ▷ *vi* évoluer, se transformer

ewe [ju:] *n* brebis *f*

ex [εks] *n* (*inf*): **my ex** mon ex

ex- [εks] *prefix* (*former: husband, president etc*) ex-; (*out of*): **the price ~works** le prix départ usine

exact [ιg'zækt] *adj* exact(e) ▷ *vt*: **to ~ sth (from)** (*signature, confession*) extorquer qch (à); (*apology*) exiger qch (de)

exacting [ιg'zæktιη] *adj* exigeant(e); (*work*) fatigant(e)

exactly [ιg'zæktlι] *adv* exactement; **~!** parfaitement!, précisément!

exaggerate [ιg'zædʒəreιt] *vt, vi* exagérer

exaggeration [ιgzædʒə'reιʃən] *n* exagération *f*

exalted [ιg'zɔ:ltιd] *adj* (*rank*) élevé(e); (*person*) haut placé(e); (*elated*) exalté(e)

exam [ιg'zæm] *n abbr* (*Scol*) = **examination**

examination [ιgzæmι'neιʃən] *n* (*Scol, Med*) examen *m*; **to take** *or* **sit an ~** (*Brit*) passer un examen; **the matter is under ~** la question est à l'examen

examine [ιg'zæmιn] *vt* (*gen*) examiner; (*Scol, Law: person*) interroger; (*inspect: machine, premises*) inspecter; (*passport*) contrôler; (*luggage*) fouiller

examiner [ιg'zæmιnə'] *n* examinateur(-trice)

example [ιg'zα:mpl] *n* exemple *m*; **for ~** par exemple; **to set a good/bad ~** donner le bon/mauvais exemple

exasperate [ιg'zα:spəreιt] *vt* exaspérer, agacer

exasperated [ιg'zα:spəreιtιd] *adj* exaspéré(e)

exasperation [ιgzα:spə'reιʃən] *n* exaspération *f*, irritation *f*

excavate ['εkskəveιt] *vt* (*site*) fouiller, excaver; (*object*) mettre au jour

excavation [εkskə'veιʃən] *n* excavation *f*

exceed [ιk'si:d] *vt* dépasser; (*one's powers*) outrepasser

exceedingly [ιk'si:dιηlι] *adv* extrêmement

excel [ιk'sεl] *vi* exceller ▷ *vt* surpasser; **to ~ o.s.** se surpasser

excellence ['εksələns] *n* excellence *f*

excellent ['εksələnt] *adj* excellent(e)

except [ιk'sεpt] *prep* (*also*: ~ **for, ~ing**) sauf, excepté, à l'exception de ▷ *vt* excepter; ~ **if/ when** sauf si/quand; ~ **that** excepté que, si ce n'est que

exception [ιk'sεpʃən] *n* exception *f*; **to take ~ to** s'offusquer de; **with the ~ of** à l'exception de

exceptional [ιk'sεpʃənl] *adj* exceptionnel(le)

exceptionally [ιk'sεpʃənəlι] *adv* exceptionnellement

excerpt ['εksə:pt] *n* extrait *m*

excess [ιk'sεs] *n* excès *m*; **in ~ of** plus de

excess baggage *n* excédent *m* de bagages

excess fare *n* supplément *m*

excessive [ιk'sεsιv] *adj* excessif(-ive)

exchange [ιks'tʃeιndʒ] *n* échange *m*; (*also*: **telephone ~**) central *m* ▷ *vt*: **to ~ (for)** échanger (contre); **could I ~ this, please?** est-ce que je peux échanger ceci, s'il vous plaît?; **in ~ for** en échange de; **foreign ~** (*Comm*) change *m*

exchange rate *n* taux *m* de change

excise *n* ['εksaιz] taxe *f* ▷ *vt* [εk'saιz] exciser

excite [ιk'saιt] *vt* exciter

excited [ιk'saιtəd] *adj* (tout/toute) excité(e); **to get ~** s'exciter

excitement [ιk'saιtmənt] *n* excitation *f*

exciting [ιk'saιtιη] *adj* passionnant(e)

exclaim [ιk'skleιm] *vi* s'exclamer

exclamation [εksklə'meιʃən] *n* exclamation *f*

exclamation mark, (US) exclamation point *n* point *m* d'exclamation

exclude [ιk'sklu:d] *vt* exclure

excluding [ιk'sklu:dιη] *prep*: ~ **VAT** la TVA non comprise

exclusion [ιk'sklu:ʒən] *n* exclusion *f*; **to the ~ of** à l'exclusion de

exclusion zone *n* zone interdite

exclusive [ιk'sklu:sιv] *adj* exclusif(-ive); (*club, district*) sélect(e); (*item of news*) en exclusivité ▷ *adv* (*Comm*) exclusivement, non inclus; ~ **of VAT** TVA non comprise; ~ **of postage** (les) frais de poste non compris; **from 1st to 15th March** ~ du 1er au 15 mars exclusivement *or* exclu; ~ **rights** (*Comm*) exclusivité *f*

exclusively [ιk'sklu:sιvlι] *adv* exclusivement

excruciating [ιk'skru:ʃιeιtιη] *adj* (*pain*) atroce, déchirant(e); (*embarrassing*) pénible

excursion [ιk'skə:ʃən] *n* excursion *f*

excuse *n* [ιk'skju:s] excuse *f* ▷ *vt* [ιk'skju:z] (*forgive*) excuser; (*justify*) excuser, justifier; **to ~ sb from** (*activity*) dispenser qn de; ~ **me!** excusez-moi!, pardon!; **now if you will ~ me, ...** maintenant, si vous (le) permettez ...; **to make ~s for sb** trouver des excuses à qn; **to ~ o.s. for sth/for doing sth** s'excuser de/d'avoir fait qch

ex-directory ['ɛksdɪ'rɛktərɪ] adj (Brit) sur la liste rouge

execute ['ɛksɪkju:t] vt exécuter

execution [ɛksɪ'kju:ʃən] n exécution f

executive [ɪg'zɛkjutɪv] n (person) cadre m; (managing group) bureau m; (Pol) exécutif m ▷ adj exécutif(-ive); (position, job) de cadre; (secretary) de direction; (offices) de la direction; (car, plane) de fonction

exemplify [ɪg'zɛmplɪfaɪ] vt illustrer

exempt [ɪg'zɛmpt] adj: ~ from exempté(e) or dispensé(e) de ▷ vt: to ~ sb from exempter or dispenser qn de

exercise ['ɛksəsaɪz] n exercice m ▷ vt exercer; (patience etc) faire preuve de; (dog) promener ▷ vi (also: to take ~) prendre de l'exercice

exercise book n cahier m

exert [ɪg'zə:t] vt exercer, employer; (strength, force) employer; to ~ o.s. se dépenser

exertion [ɪg'zə:ʃən] n effort m

exhale [ɛks'heɪl] vt (breathe out) expirer; exhaler ▷ vi expirer

exhaust [ɪg'zɔ:st] n (also: ~ fumes) gaz mpl d'échappement; (also: ~ pipe) tuyau m d'échappement ▷ vt épuiser; to ~ o.s. s'épuiser

exhausted [ɪg'zɔ:stɪd] adj épuisé(e)

exhaustion [ɪg'zɔ:stʃən] n épuisement m; nervous ~ fatigue nerveuse

exhaustive [ɪg'zɔ:stɪv] adj très complet(-ète)

exhibit [ɪg'zɪbɪt] n (Art) objet exposé, pièce exposée; (Law) pièce à conviction ▷ vt (Art) exposer; (courage, skill) faire preuve de

exhibition [ɛksɪ'bɪʃən] n exposition f; ~ of temper manifestation f de colère

exhilarating [ɪg'zɪləreɪtɪŋ] adj grisant(e), stimulant(e)

ex-husband ['ɛks'hʌzbənd] n ex-mari m

exile ['ɛksaɪl] n exil m; (person) exilé(e) f ▷ vt exiler; in ~ en exil

exist [ɪg'zɪst] vi exister

existence [ɪg'zɪstəns] n existence f; to be in ~ exister

existing [ɪg'zɪstɪŋ] adj (laws) existant(e); (system, regime) actuel(le)

exit ['ɛksɪt] n sortie f ▷ vi (Comput, Theat) sortir; where's the ~? où est la sortie?

exit poll n sondage m (fait à la sortie de l'isoloir)

exit ramp n (US Aut) bretelle f d'accès

exodus ['ɛksədəs] n exode m

exonerate [ɪg'zɔnəreɪt] vt: to ~ from disculper de

exotic [ɪg'zɔtɪk] adj exotique

expand [ɪk'spænd] vt (area) agrandir; (quantity) accroître; (influence etc) étendre ▷ vi (population, production) s'accroître; (trade, etc) se développer, s'accroître; (gas, metal) se dilater, dilater; to ~ on (notes, story etc) développer

expanse [ɪk'spæns] n étendue f

expansion [ɪk'spænʃən] n (territorial, economic) expansion f; (of trade, influence etc) développement m; (of production)

accroissement m; (of population) croissance f; (of gas, metal) expansion, dilatation f

expect [ɪk'spɛkt] vt (anticipate) s'attendre à, s'attendre à ce que + sub; (count on) compter sur, escompter; (hope for) espérer; (require) demander, exiger; (suppose) supposer; (await: also baby) attendre ▷ vi: to be ~ing (pregnant woman) être enceinte; to ~ sb to do (anticipate) s'attendre à ce que qn fasse; (demand) attendre de qn qu'il fasse; to ~ to do sth penser or compter faire qch, s'attendre à faire qch; as ~ed comme prévu; I ~ so je crois que oui, je crois bien

expectancy [ɪks'pɛktənsɪ] n attente f; life ~ espérance f de vie

expectant [ɪk'spɛktənt] adj qui attend (quelque chose); ~ mother future maman

expectation [ɛkspɛk'teɪʃən] n (hope) attente f, espérance(s) f(pl); (belief) attente; in ~ of dans l'attente de, en prévision de; against or contrary to all ~(s) contre toute attente, contrairement à ce qu'on attendait; to come or live up to sb's ~s répondre à l'attente or aux espérances de qn

expedient [ɪk'spi:dɪənt] adj indiqué(e), opportun(e), commode ▷ n expédient m

expedition [ɛkspə'dɪʃən] n expédition f

expel [ɪk'spɛl] vt chasser, expulser; (Scol) renvoyer, exclure

expend [ɪk'spɛnd] vt consacrer; (use up) dépenser

expenditure [ɪk'spɛndɪtʃə'] n (act of spending) dépense f; (money spent) dépenses fpl

expense [ɪk'spɛns] n (high cost) coût m; (spending) dépense f, frais mpl; expenses npl frais mpl; dépenses; to go to the ~ of faire la dépense de; at great/little ~ à grands/ peu de frais; at the ~ of aux frais de; (fig) aux dépens de

expense account n (note f de) frais mpl

expensive [ɪk'spɛnsɪv] adj cher/chère, coûteux(-euse); to be ~ coûter cher; it's too ~ ça coûte trop cher; ~ tastes goûts mpl de luxe

experience [ɪk'spɪərɪəns] n expérience f ▷ vt connaître; (feeling) éprouver; to know by ~ savoir par expérience

experienced [ɪk'spɪərɪənst] adj expérimenté(e)

experiment [ɪk'spɛrɪmənt] n expérience f ▷ vi faire une expérience; to ~ with expérimenter; to perform or carry out an ~ faire une expérience; as an ~ à titre d'expérience

experimental [ɪkspɛrɪ'mɛntl] adj expérimental(e)

expert ['ɛkspə:t] adj expert(e) ▷ n expert m; ~ in or at doing sth spécialiste de qch; an ~ on sth un spécialiste de qch; ~ witness (Law) expert m

expertise [ɛkspə:'ti:z] n (grande) compétence

expire [ɪk'spaɪə'] vi expirer

expiry [ɪkˈspaɪərɪ] n expiration f
expiry date n date f d'expiration; (on label) à utiliser avant ...
explain [ɪkˈspleɪn] vt expliquer; **explain away** vt justifier, excuser
explanation [ekspləˈneɪʃən] n explication f; **to find an ~ for sth** trouver une explication à qch
explanatory [ɪkˈsplænətrɪ] adj explicatif(-ive)
explicit [ɪkˈsplɪsɪt] adj explicite; (definite) formel(le)
explode [ɪkˈspləʊd] vi exploser ▷ vt faire exploser; (fig: theory) démolir; **to ~ a myth** détruire un mythe
exploit n [ˈeksplɔɪt] exploit m ▷ vt [ɪkˈsplɔɪt] exploiter
exploitation [eksplɔɪˈteɪʃən] n exploitation f
exploratory [ɪkˈsplɔrətrɪ] adj (fig: talks) préliminaire; **~ operation** (Med) intervention f (à visée) exploratrice
explore [ɪkˈsplɔːʳ] vt explorer; (possibilities) étudier, examiner
explorer [ɪkˈsplɔːrəʳ] n explorateur(-trice)
explosion [ɪkˈspləʊʒən] n explosion f
explosive [ɪkˈspləʊsɪv] adj explosif(-ive) ▷ n explosif m
exponent [ɪkˈspəʊnənt] n (of school of thought etc) interprète m, représentant m; (Math) exposant m
export vt [ekˈspɔːt] exporter ▷ n [ˈekspɔːt] exportation f ▷ cpd [ˈekspɔːt] d'exportation
exporter [ekˈspɔːtəʳ] n exportateur m
expose [ɪkˈspəʊz] vt exposer; (unmask) démasquer, dévoiler; **to ~ o.s.** (Law) commettre un outrage à la pudeur
exposed [ɪkˈspəʊzd] adj (land, house) exposé(e); (Elec: wire) à nu; (pipe, beam) apparent(e)
exposure [ɪkˈspəʊʒəʳ] n exposition f; (publicity) couverture f; (Phot: speed) (temps m de) pose f; (: shot) pose; **suffering from ~** (Med) souffrant des effets du froid et de l'épuisement; **to die of ~** (Med) mourir de froid
exposure meter n posemètre m
express [ɪkˈspres] adj (definite) formel(le), exprès(-esse); (Brit: letter etc) exprès inv ▷ n (train) rapide m ▷ adv (send) exprès ▷ vt exprimer; **to ~ o.s.** s'exprimer
expression [ɪkˈspreʃən] n expression f
expressly [ɪkˈspreslɪ] adv expressément, formellement
expressway [ɪkˈspreswei] n (US) voie f express (à plusieurs files)
exquisite [ekˈskwɪzɪt] adj exquis(e)
extend [ɪkˈstend] vt (visit, street) prolonger; (deadline) reporter, remettre; (building) agrandir; (offer) présenter, offrir; (Comm: credit) accorder; (hand, arm) tendre ▷ vi (land) s'étendre

extension [ɪkˈstenʃən] n (of visit, street) prolongation f; (of building) agrandissement m; (building) annexe f; (to wire, table) rallonge f; (telephone: in offices) poste m; (: in private house) téléphone m supplémentaire; **~ 3718** (Tel) poste 3718
extension cable, extension lead n (Elec) rallonge f
extensive [ɪkˈstensɪv] adj étendu(e), vaste; (damage, alterations) considérable; (inquiries) approfondi(e); (use) largement répandu(e)
extensively [ɪkˈstensɪvlɪ] adv considérablement; **he's travelled ~** il a beaucoup voyagé
extent [ɪkˈstent] n étendue f; (degree: of damage, loss) importance f; **to some ~** dans une certaine mesure; **to a certain ~** dans une certaine mesure, jusqu'à un certain point; **to a large ~** en grande partie; **to the ~ of ...** au point de ...; **to what ~?** dans quelle mesure?, jusqu'à quel point?; **to such an ~ that ...** à tel point que ...
extenuating [ɪkˈstenjueɪtɪŋ] adj: **~ circumstances** circonstances atténuantes
exterior [ekˈstɪərɪəʳ] adj extérieur(e) ▷ n extérieur m
external [ekˈstəːnl] adj externe ▷ n: **the ~s** les apparences fpl; **for ~ use only** (Med) à usage externe
extinct [ɪkˈstɪŋkt] adj (volcano) éteint(e); (species) disparu(e)
extinction [ɪkˈstɪŋkʃən] n extinction f
extinguish [ɪkˈstɪŋgwɪʃ] vt éteindre
extort [ɪkˈstɔːt] vt: **to ~ sth (from)** extorquer qch (à)
extortionate [ɪkˈstɔːʃnɪt] adj exorbitant(e)
extra [ˈekstrə] adj supplémentaire, de plus ▷ adv (in addition) en plus ▷ n supplément m; (perk) à-coté m; (Cine, Theat) figurant(e); **wine will cost ~** le vin sera en supplément; **~ large sizes** très grandes tailles
extract vt [ɪkˈstrækt] extraire; (tooth) arracher; (money, promise) soutirer ▷ n [ˈekstrækt] extrait m
extracurricular [ˈekstrəkəˈrɪkjuləʳ] adj (Scol) parascolaire
extradite [ˈekstrədaɪt] vt extrader
extramarital [ˈekstrəˈmærɪtl] adj extraconjugal(e)
extramural [ˈekstrəˈmjuərl] adj hors-faculté inv
extraordinary [ɪkˈstrɔːdnrɪ] adj extraordinaire; **the ~ thing is that ...** le plus étrange or étonnant c'est que ...
extravagance [ɪkˈstrævəgəns] n (excessive spending) prodigalités fpl; (thing bought) folie f, dépense excessive
extravagant [ɪkˈstrævəgənt] adj extravagant(e); (in spending: person) prodigue, dépensier(-ière); (: tastes) dispendieux(-euse)
extreme [ɪkˈstriːm] adj, n extrême (m); **the ~ left/right** (Pol) l'extrême gauche f/droite f; **~s**

of temperature différences *fpl* extrêmes de température

extremely [ɪkˈstriːmlɪ] *adv* extrêmement

extremist [ɪkˈstriːmɪst] *adj, n* extrémiste *m/f*

extricate [ˈɛkstrɪkeɪt] *vt*: **to ~ sth (from)** dégager qch (de)

extrovert [ˈɛkstrəvɜːt] *n* extraverti(e)

ex-wife [ˈɛkswaɪf] *n* ex-femme *f*

eye [aɪ] *n* œil *m*; (*of needle*) trou *m*, chas *m* ▷ *vt* examiner; **as far as the ~ can see** à perte de vue; **to keep an ~ on** surveiller; **to have an ~ for sth** avoir l'œil pour qch; **in the public ~** en vue; **with an ~ to doing sth** (*Brit*) en vue de faire qch; **there's more to this than meets the ~** ce n'est pas aussi simple que cela paraît

eyeball [ˈaɪbɔːl] *n* globe *m* oculaire

eyebrow [ˈaɪbraʊ] *n* sourcil *m*

eye drops [ˈaɪdrɒps] *npl* gouttes *fpl* pour les yeux

eyelash [ˈaɪlæʃ] *n* cil *m*

eyelid [ˈaɪlɪd] *n* paupière *f*

eyeliner [ˈaɪlaɪnəʳ] *n* eye-liner *m*

eye-opener [ˈaɪəʊpnəʳ] *n* révélation *f*

eye shadow [ˈaɪʃædəʊ] *n* ombre *f* à paupières

eyesight [ˈaɪsaɪt] *n* vue *f*

eyesore [ˈaɪsɔːʳ] *n* horreur *f*, chose *f* qui dépare *or* enlaidit

eye witness *n* témoin *m* oculaire

F¹, f [ɛf] *n* (*letter*) F, f *m*; (*Mus*): **F** fa *m*; **F for Frederick**, (*US*) **F for Fox** F comme François

F² *abbr* (= *Fahrenheit*) F

fable [ˈfeɪbl] *n* fable *f*

fabric [ˈfæbrɪk] *n* tissu *m* ▷ *cpd*: **~ ribbon** (*for typewriter*) ruban *m* (en) tissu

fabulous [ˈfæbjʊləs] *adj* fabuleux(-euse); (*inf: super*) formidable, sensationnel(le)

face [feɪs] *n* visage *m*, figure *f*; (*expression*) air *m*; grimace *f*; (*of clock*) cadran *m*; (*of cliff*) paroi *f*; (*of mountain*) face *f*; (*of building*) façade *f*; (*side, surface*) face *f* ▷ *vt* faire face à; (*facts etc*) accepter; **~ down** (*person*) à plat ventre; (*card*) face en dessous; **to lose/save ~** perdre/sauver la face; **to pull a ~** faire une grimace; **in the ~ of** (*difficulties etc*) face à, devant; **on the ~ of it** à première vue; **~ to ~** face à face; **face up to** *vt fus* faire face à, affronter

face cloth *n* (*Brit*) gant *m* de toilette

face cream *n* crème *f* pour le visage

face lift *n* lifting *m*; (*of façade etc*) ravalement *m*, retapage *m*

face pack *n* (*Brit*) masque *m* (de beauté)

face powder *n* poudre *f* (pour le visage)

face value [ˈfeɪsˈvæljuː] *n* (*of coin*) valeur nominale; **to take sth at ~** (*fig*) prendre qch pour argent comptant

facial [ˈfeɪʃl] *adj* facial(e) ▷ *n* soin complet du visage

facilitate [fəˈsɪlɪteɪt] *vt* faciliter

facilities [fəˈsɪlɪtɪz] *npl* installations *fpl*,

équipement m; **credit** ~ facilités de paiement
facility [fə'sɪlɪtɪ] n facilité f
facing ['feɪsɪŋ] prep face à, en face de ▷ n (of wall etc) revêtement m; (Sewing) revers m
facsimile [fæk'sɪmɪlɪ] n (exact replica) facsimilé m; (also: ~ **machine**) télécopieur m; (transmitted document) télécopie f
fact [fækt] n fait m; **in** ~ en fait; **to know for a** ~ **that** ... savoir pertinemment que ...
faction ['fækʃən] n faction f
factor ['fæktə^r] n facteur m; (of sun cream) indice m (de protection); (Comm) factor m, société f d'affacturage; (: agent) dépositaire m/f ▷ vi faire du factoring; **safety** ~ facteur de sécurité; **I'd like a** ~ **15 suntan lotion** je voudrais une crème solaire d'indice 15
factory ['fæktərɪ] n usine f, fabrique f
factual ['fæktjuəl] adj basé(e) sur les faits
faculty ['fækəltɪ] n faculté f; (US: teaching staff) corps enseignant
fad [fæd] n (personal) manie f; (craze) engouement m
fade [feɪd] vi se décolorer, passer; (light, sound) s'affaiblir, disparaître; (flower) se faner; **fade away** vi (sound) s'affaiblir; **fade in** vt (picture) ouvrir en fondu; (sound) monter progressivement; **fade out** vt (picture) fermer en fondu; (sound) baisser progressivement
fag [fæg] n (Brit inf: cigarette) clope f; (: chore): **what a** ~! quelle corvée!; (US inf: homosexual) pédé m
Fahrenheit ['fɑːrənhaɪt] n Fahrenheit m inv
fail [feɪl] vt (exam) échouer à; (candidate) recaler; (subj: courage, memory) faire défaut à ▷ vi échouer; (supplies) manquer; (eyesight, health, light: also: **be ~ing**) baisser, s'affaiblir; (brakes) lâcher; **to** ~ **to do sth** (neglect) négliger de or ne pas faire qch; (be unable) ne pas arriver or parvenir à faire qch; **without** ~ à coup sûr; sans faute
failing ['feɪlɪŋ] n défaut m ▷ prep faute de; ~ **that** à défaut, sinon
failure ['feɪljə^r] n échec m; (person) raté(e); (mechanical etc) défaillance f; **his** ~ **to turn up** le fait de n'être pas venu or qu'il ne soit pas venu
faint [feɪnt] adj faible; (recollection) vague; (mark) à peine visible; (smell, breeze, trace) léger(-ère) ▷ n évanouissement m ▷ vi s'évanouir; **to feel** ~ défaillir
faintest ['feɪntɪst] adj: **I haven't the** ~ **idea** je n'en ai pas la moindre idée
faintly ['feɪntlɪ] adv faiblement; (vaguely) vaguement
fair [fɛə^r] adj équitable, juste; (reasonable) correct(e), honnête; (hair) blond(e); (skin, complexion) pâle, blanc/blanche; (weather) beau/belle; (good enough) assez bon(ne); (sizeable) considérable ▷ adv: **to play** ~ jouer franc jeu ▷ n foire f; (Brit: funfair) fête (foraine); (also: **trade** ~) foire(-exposition)

commerciale; **it's not** ~! ce n'est pas juste!; **a** ~ **amount of** une quantité considérable de
fairground ['fɛəgraʊnd] n champ m de foire
fair-haired [fɛə'hɛəd] adj (person) aux cheveux clairs, blond(e)
fairly ['fɛəlɪ] adv (justly) équitablement; (quite) assez; **I'm** ~ **sure** j'en suis quasiment or presque sûr
fairness ['fɛənɪs] n (of trial etc) justice f, équité f; (of person) sens m de la justice; **in all** ~ en toute justice
fair trade n commerce m équitable
fairway ['fɛəweɪ] n (Golf) fairway m
fairy ['fɛərɪ] n fée f
fairy tale n conte m de fées
faith [feɪθ] n foi f; (trust) confiance f; (sect) culte m, religion f; **to have** ~ **in sb/sth** avoir confiance en qn/qch
faithful ['feɪθful] adj fidèle
faithfully ['feɪθfəlɪ] adv fidèlement; **yours** ~ (Brit: in letters) veuillez agréer l'expression de mes salutations les plus distinguées
fake [feɪk] n (painting etc) faux m; (photo) trucage m; (person) imposteur m ▷ adj faux/fausse ▷ vt (emotions) simuler; (painting) faire un faux de; (photo) truquer; (story) fabriquer; **his illness is a** ~ sa maladie est une comédie or de la simulation
falcon ['fɔːlkən] n faucon m
fall [fɔːl] n chute f; (decrease) baisse f; (US: autumn) automne m ▷ vi (pt fell, pp fallen) [fɛl, 'fɔːlən] tomber; (price, temperature, dollar) baisser; **falls** npl (waterfall) chute f d'eau, cascade f; **to** ~ **flat** vi (on one's face) tomber de tout son long, s'étaler; (joke) tomber à plat; (plan) échouer; **to** ~ **short of** (sb's expectations) ne pas répondre à; **a** ~ **of snow** (Brit) une chute de neige; **fall apart** vi (object) tomber en morceaux; (inf: emotionally) craquer; **fall back** vi reculer, se retirer; **fall back on** vt fus se rabattre sur; **to have something to** ~ **back on** (money etc) avoir quelque chose en réserve; (job etc) avoir une solution de rechange; **fall behind** vi prendre du retard; **fall down** vi (person) tomber; (building) s'effondrer, s'écrouler; **fall for** vt fus (trick) se laisser prendre à; (person) tomber amoureux(-euse) de; **fall in** vi s'effondrer; (Mil) se mettre en rangs; **fall in with** vt fus (sb's plans etc) accepter; **fall off** vi tomber; (diminish) baisser, diminuer; **fall out** vi (friends etc) se brouiller; (hair, teeth) tomber; **fall over** vi tomber (par terre); **fall through** vi (plan, project) tomber à l'eau
fallacy ['fæləsɪ] n erreur f, illusion f
fallen ['fɔːlən] pp of **fall**
fallout ['fɔːlaʊt] n retombées (radioactives)
fallow ['fæləʊ] adj en jachère; en friche
false [fɔːls] adj faux/fausse; **under** ~ **pretences** sous un faux prétexte
false alarm n fausse alerte

false teeth *npl* (Brit) fausses dents, dentier *m*

falter ['fɔːltə'] *vi* chanceler, vaciller

fame [feɪm] *n* renommée *f*, renom *m*

familiar [fə'mɪlɪə'] *adj* familier(-ière); **to be ~ with sth** connaître qch; **to make o.s. ~ with sth** se familiariser avec qch; **to be on ~ terms with sb** bien connaître qn

familiarize [fə'mɪlɪəraɪz] *vt* familiariser; **to ~ o.s. with** se familiariser avec

family ['fæmɪlɪ] *n* famille *f*

family doctor *n* médecin *m* de famille

family planning *n* planning familial

famine ['fæmɪn] *n* famine *f*

famished ['fæmɪʃt] *adj* affamé(e); **I'm ~!** (*inf*) je meurs de faim!

famous ['feɪməs] *adj* célèbre

famously ['feɪməslɪ] *adv* (*get on*) fameusement, à merveille

fan [fæn] *n* (*folding*) éventail *m*; (*Elec*) ventilateur *m*; (*person*) fan *m*, admirateur(-trice); (*Sport*) supporter *m/f* ▷ *vt* éventer; (*fire, quarrel*) attiser; **fan out** *vi* se déployer (en éventail)

fanatic [fə'nætɪk] *n* fanatique *m/f*

fan belt *n* courroie *f* de ventilateur

fan club *n* fan-club *m*

fancy ['fænsɪ] *n* (*whim*) fantaisie *f*, envie *f*; (*imagination*) imagination *f* ▷ *adj* (*luxury*) de luxe; (*elaborate: jewellery, packaging*) fantaisie *inv*; (*showy*) tape-à-l'œil *inv*; (*pretentious: words*) recherché(e) ▷ *vt* (*feel like, want*) avoir envie de; (*imagine*) imaginer; **to take a ~ to** se prendre d'affection pour; s'enticher de; **it took** *or* **caught my ~** ça m'a plu; **when the ~ takes him** quand ça lui prend; **to ~ that** ... se figurer *or* s'imaginer que ...; **he fancies her** elle lui plaît

fancy dress *n* déguisement *m*, travesti *m*

fancy-dress ball [fænsɪ'drɛs-] *n* bal masqué *or* costumé

fang [fæŋ] *n* croc *m*; (*of snake*) crochet *m*

fan heater *n* (Brit) radiateur *m* soufflant

fantasize ['fæntəsaɪz] *vi* fantasmer

fantastic [fæn'tæstɪk] *adj* fantastique

fantasy ['fæntəsɪ] *n* imagination *f*, fantaisie *f*; (*unreality*) fantasme *m*

fanzine ['fænziːn] *n* fanzine *m*

FAQ *n abbr* (= *frequently asked question*) FAQ *f inv*, faq *f inv* ▷ *abbr* (= *free alongside quay*) FLQ

far [fɑː'] *adj* (*distant*) lointain(e), éloigné(e) ▷ *adv* loin; **the ~ side/end** l'autre côté/bout; **the ~ left/right** (Pol) l'extrême gauche *f*/droite *f*; **is it ~ to London?** est-ce qu'on est loin de Londres?; **it's not ~ (from here)** ce n'est pas loin (d'ici); **~ away, ~ off** au loin, dans le lointain; **~ better** bien mieux; **~ from** loin de; **by ~** de loin, de beaucoup; **as ~ back as the 13th century** dès le 13e siècle; **go as ~ as the bridge** allez jusqu'au pont; **as ~ as I know** pour autant que je sache; **how ~ is it to ...?** combien y a-t-il jusqu'à ...?; **as ~ as**

possible dans la mesure du possible; **how ~ have you got with your work?** où en êtes-vous dans votre travail?

faraway ['fɑːrəweɪ] *adj* lointain(e); (*look*) absent(e)

farce [fɑːs] *n* farce *f*

fare [fɛə'] *n* (*on trains, buses*) prix *m* du billet; (*in taxi*) prix de la course; (*passenger in taxi*) client *m*; (*food*) table *f*, chère *f* ▷ *vi* se débrouiller; **half ~** demi-tarif; **full ~** plein tarif

Far East *n*: **the ~** l'Extrême-Orient *m*

farewell [fɛə'wɛl] *excl, n* adieu *m* ▷ *cpd* (*party etc*) d'adieux

farm [fɑːm] *n* ferme *f* ▷ *vt* cultiver; **farm out** *vt* (*work etc*) distribuer

farmer ['fɑːmə'] *n* fermier(-ière), cultivateur(-trice)

farmhand ['fɑːmhænd] *n* ouvrier(-ière) agricole

farmhouse ['fɑːmhaus] *n* (maison *f* de) ferme *f*

farming ['fɑːmɪŋ] *n* agriculture *f*; (*of animals*) élevage *m*; **intensive ~** culture intensive; **sheep ~** élevage du mouton

farmland ['fɑːmlænd] *n* terres cultivées *or* arables

farm worker *n* = **farmhand**

farmyard ['fɑːmjɑːd] *n* cour *f* de ferme

far-reaching ['fɑː'riːtʃɪŋ] *adj* d'une grande portée

fart [fɑːt] (*inf!*) *n* pet *m* ▷ *vi* péter

farther ['fɑːðə'] *adv* plus loin ▷ *adj* plus éloigné(e), plus lointain(e)

farthest ['fɑːðɪst] *superlative of* **far**

fascinate ['fæsɪneɪt] *vt* fasciner, captiver

fascinating ['fæsɪneɪtɪŋ] *adj* fascinant(e)

fascination [fæsɪ'neɪʃən] *n* fascination *f*

fascism ['fæʃɪzəm] *n* fascisme *m*

fascist ['fæʃɪst] *adj, n* fasciste *m/f*

fashion ['fæʃən] *n* mode *f*; (*manner*) façon *f*, manière *f* ▷ *vt* façonner; **in ~** à la mode; **out of ~** démodé(e); **in the Greek ~** à la grecque; **after a ~** (*finish, manage etc*) tant bien que mal

fashionable ['fæʃnəbl] *adj* à la mode

fashion show *n* défilé *m* de mannequins *or* de mode

fast [fɑːst] *adj* rapide; (*clock*): **to be ~** avancer; (*dye, colour*) grand *or* bon teint *inv* ▷ *adv* vite, rapidement; (*stuck, held*) solidement ▷ *n* jeûne *m* ▷ *vi* jeûner; **my watch is 5 minutes ~** ma montre avance de 5 minutes; **~ asleep** profondément endormi; **as ~ as I can** aussi vite que je peux; **to make a boat ~** (Brit) amarrer un bateau

fasten ['fɑːsn] *vt* attacher, fixer; (*coat*) attacher, fermer ▷ *vi* s'attacher; **fasten on, fasten upon** *vt fus* (*idea*) se cramponner à

fastener ['fɑːsnə'], **fastening** ['fɑːsnɪŋ] *n* fermeture *f*, attache *f*; (Brit: *zip fastener*) fermeture éclair® *inv* *or* à glissière

fast food n fast food m, restauration f rapide

fastidious [fæs'tɪdɪəs] adj exigeant(e), difficile

fat [fæt] adj gros(se) ▷ n graisse f; (on meat) gras m; (for cooking) matière grasse; **to live off the ~ of the land** vivre grassement

fatal ['feɪtl] adj (mistake) fatal(e); (injury) mortel(le)

fatality [fə'tælɪtɪ] n (road death etc) victime f, décès m

fatally ['feɪtəlɪ] adv fatalement; (injured) mortellement

fate [feɪt] n destin m; (of person) sort m; **to meet one's ~** trouver la mort

fateful ['feɪtful] adj fatidique

father ['fɑːðər] n père m

Father Christmas n le Père Noël

father-in-law ['fɑːðərɪnlɔː] n beau-père m

fatherly ['fɑːðəlɪ] adj paternel(le)

fathom ['fæðəm] n brasse f (= 1828 mm) ▷ vt (mystery) sonder, pénétrer

fatigue [fə'tiːg] n fatigue f; (Mil) corvée f; **metal ~** fatigue du métal

fatten ['fætn] vt, vi engraisser

fattening ['fætnɪŋ] adj (food) qui fait grossir; **chocolate is ~** le chocolat fait grossir

fatty ['fætɪ] adj (food) gras(se) ▷ n (inf) gros/grosse

fatuous ['fætjuəs] adj stupide

faucet ['fɔːsɪt] n (US) robinet m

fault [fɔːlt] n faute f; (defect) défaut m; (Geo) faille f ▷ vt trouver des défauts à, prendre en défaut; **it's my ~** c'est ma faute; **to find ~ with** trouver à redire or à critiquer à; **at ~** fautif(-ive), coupable; **to a ~** à l'excès

faulty ['fɔːltɪ] adj défectueux(-euse)

fauna ['fɔːnə] n faune f

favour, (US) **favor** ['feɪvər] n faveur f; (help) service m ▷ vt (proposition) être en faveur de; (pupil etc) favoriser; (team, horse) donner gagnant; **to do sb a ~** rendre un service à qn; **in ~ of** en faveur de; **to be in ~ of sth/of doing sth** être partisan de qch/de faire qch; **to find ~ with sb** trouver grâce aux yeux de qn

favourable, (US) **favorable** ['feɪvrəbl] adj favorable; (price) avantageux(-euse)

favourite, (US) **favorite** ['feɪvrɪt] adj, n favori(te)

fawn [fɔːn] n (deer) faon m ▷ adj (also: **~-coloured**) fauve ▷ vi: **to ~ (up)on** flatter servilement

fax [fæks] n (document) télécopie f; (machine) télécopieur m ▷ vt envoyer par télécopie

FBI n abbr (US: = Federal Bureau of Investigation) FBI m

fear [fɪər] n crainte f, peur f ▷ vt craindre ▷ vi: **to ~ for** craindre pour; **to ~ that** craindre que; **~ of heights** vertige m; **for ~ of** de peur que + sub or de + infinitive

fearful ['fɪəful] adj craintif(-ive); (sight, noise) affreux(-euse), épouvantable; **to be ~ of** avoir peur de, craindre

fearless ['fɪəlɪs] adj intrépide, sans peur

feasible ['fiːzəbl] adj faisable, réalisable

feast [fiːst] n festin m, banquet m; (Rel: also: **~ day**) fête f ▷ vi festoyer; **to ~ on** se régaler de

feat [fiːt] n exploit m, prouesse f

feather ['feðər] n plume f ▷ vt: **to ~ one's nest** (fig) faire sa pelote ▷ cpd (bed etc) de plumes

feature ['fiːtʃər] n caractéristique f; (article) chronique f, rubrique f ▷ vt (film) avoir pour vedette(s) ▷ vi figurer (en bonne place); **features** npl (of face) traits mpl; **a (special) ~ on sth/sb** un reportage sur qch/qn; **it ~d prominently in ...** cela a figuré en bonne place sur or dans ...

feature film n long métrage

Feb. abbr (= February) fév

February ['fɛbruərɪ] n février m; see also **July**

fed [fɛd] pt, pp of **feed**

federal ['fɛdərəl] adj fédéral(e)

federation [fɛdə'reɪʃən] n fédération f

fed up [fɛd'ʌp] adj: **to be ~ (with)** en avoir marre or plein le dos (de)

fee [fiː] n rémunération f; (of doctor, lawyer) honoraires mpl; (of school, college etc) frais mpl de scolarité; (for examination) droits mpl; **entrance/membership ~** droit d'entrée/d'inscription; **for a small ~** pour une somme modique

feeble ['fiːbl] adj faible; (attempt, excuse) pauvre; (joke), piteux(-euse)

feed [fiːd] n (of baby) tétée f; (of animal) nourriture f, pâture f; (on printer) mécanisme m d'alimentation ▷ vt (pt, pp **fed**) [fɛd] (person) nourrir; (Brit: baby: breastfeed) allaiter; (: with bottle) donner le biberon à; (horse etc) donner à manger à; (machine) alimenter; (data etc): **to ~ sth into** enregistrer qch dans; **feed back** vt (results) donner en retour; **feed on** vt fus se nourrir de

feedback ['fiːdbæk] n (Elec) effet m Larsen; (from person) réactions fpl

feel [fiːl] n (sensation) sensation f; (impression) impression f ▷ vt (pt, pp **felt**) [fɛlt] (touch) toucher; (explore) tâter, palper; (cold, pain) sentir; (grief, anger) ressentir, éprouver; (think, believe): **to ~ (that)** trouver que; **I ~ that you ought to do it** il me semble que vous devriez le faire; **to ~ hungry/cold** avoir faim/froid; **to ~ lonely/better** se sentir seul/mieux; **I don't ~ well** je ne me sens pas bien; **to ~ sorry for** avoir pitié de; **it ~s soft** c'est doux au toucher; **it ~ colder here** je trouve qu'il fait plus froid ici; **it ~s like velvet** on dirait du velours, ça ressemble au velours; **to ~ like** (want) avoir envie de; **to ~ about** or **around** fouiller, tâtonner; **to get the ~ of sth** (fig) s'habituer à qch

feeler ['fiːləʳ] n (of insect) antenne f; (fig):
to put out a ~ or ~s tâter le terrain

feeling ['fiːlɪŋ] n (physical) sensation f;
(emotion, impression) sentiment m; to hurt sb's
~s froisser qn; ~s ran high about it cela a
déchaîné les passions; what are your ~s
about the matter? quel est votre sentiment
sur cette question?; my ~ is that ... j'estime
que ...; I have a ~ that ... j'ai l'impression
que ...

feet [fiːt] npl of foot

feign [feɪn] vt feindre, simuler

fell [fɛl] pt of fall ▷ vt (tree) abattre ▷ n
(Brit: mountain) montagne f; (: moorland):
the ~s la lande ▷ adj: with one ~ blow d'un
seul coup

fellow ['fɛləu] n type m; (comrade)
compagnon m; (of learned society) membre m;
(of university) universitaire m/f; (membre du
conseil) ▷ cpd: their ~ prisoners/students
leurs camarades prisonniers/étudiants;
his ~ workers ses collègues mpl (de travail)

fellow citizen n concitoyen(ne)

fellow countryman irreg n compatriote m

fellow men npl semblables mpl

fellowship ['fɛləuʃɪp] n (society) association f;
(comradeship) amitié f, camaraderie f; (Scol)
sorte de bourse universitaire

felony ['fɛlənɪ] n crime m, forfait m

felt [fɛlt] pt, pp of feel ▷ n feutre m

felt-tip ['fɛlttɪp-] n (also: ~ pen) stylo-feutre m

female ['fiːmeɪl] n (Zool) femelle f; (pej:
woman) bonne femme ▷ adj (Biol, Elec)
femelle; (sex, character) féminin(e); (vote etc)
des femmes; (child etc) du sexe féminin;
male and ~ students étudiants et
étudiantes

feminine ['fɛmɪnɪn] adj féminin(e) ▷ n
féminin m

feminist ['fɛmɪnɪst] n féministe m/f

fence [fɛns] n barrière f; (Sport) obstacle m;
(inf: person) receleur(-euse) ▷ vt (also: ~ in)
clôturer ▷ vi faire de l'escrime; to sit on
the ~ (fig) ne pas se mouiller

fencing ['fɛnsɪŋ] n (Sport) escrime m

fend [fɛnd] vi: to ~ for o.s. se débrouiller
(tout seul); fend off vt (attack etc) parer;
(questions) éluder

fender ['fɛndəʳ] n garde-feu m inv; (on boat)
défense f; (US: of car) aile f

fennel ['fɛnl] n fenouil m

ferment vi [fə'mɛnt] fermenter ▷ n ['fɜːmɛnt]
(fig) agitation f, effervescence f

fern [fɜːn] n fougère f

ferocious [fə'rəuʃəs] adj féroce

ferret ['fɛrɪt] n furet m; ferret about, ferret
around vi fureter; ferret out vt dénicher

ferry ['fɛrɪ] n (small) bac m; (large: also: ~boat)
ferry(-boat m) m ▷ vt transporter; to ~ sth/sb
across or over faire traverser qch/qn

fertile ['fɜːtaɪl] adj fertile; (Biol) fécond(e);
~ period période f de fécondité

fertilize ['fɜːtɪlaɪz] vt fertiliser; (Biol)
féconder

fertilizer ['fɜːtɪlaɪzəʳ] n engrais m

fester ['fɛstəʳ] vi suppurer

festival ['fɛstɪvəl] n (Rel) fête f; (Art, Mus)
festival m

festive ['fɛstɪv] adj de fête; the ~ season
(Brit: Christmas) la période des fêtes

festivities [fɛs'tɪvɪtɪz] npl réjouissances fpl

festoon [fɛs'tuːn] vt: to ~ with orner de

fetch [fɛtʃ] vt aller chercher; (Brit: sell for)
rapporter; how much did it ~? ça a atteint
quel prix?; fetch up vi (Brit) se retrouver

fête [feɪt] n fête f, kermesse f

fetus ['fiːtəs] n (US) = foetus

feud [fjuːd] n querelle f, dispute f ▷ vi se
quereller, se disputer; a family ~ une
querelle de famille

fever ['fiːvəʳ] n fièvre f; he has a ~ il a de la
fièvre

feverish ['fiːvərɪʃ] adj fiévreux(-euse), fébrile

few [fjuː] adj (not many) peu de ▷ pron peu;
~ succeed il y en a peu qui réussissent,
(bien) peu réussissent; they were ~ ils
étaient peu (nombreux), il y en avait peu;
a ~ (as adj) quelques; (as pron) quelques-
uns(-unes); I know a ~ j'en connais
quelques-uns; quite a ~ ... adj un certain
nombre de ..., pas mal de ...; in the next ~
days dans les jours qui viennent; in the past
~ days ces derniers jours; every ~ days/
months tous les deux ou trois jours/mois;
a ~ more ... encore quelques ..., quelques ...
de plus

fewer ['fjuːəʳ] adj moins de ▷ pron moins;
they are ~ now il y en a moins maintenant,
ils sont moins (nombreux) maintenant

fewest ['fjuːɪst] adj le moins nombreux

fiancé [fɪ'ɑːnseɪ] n fiancé m

fiancée [fɪ'ɑːnseɪ] n fiancée f

fiasco [fɪ'æskəu] n fiasco m

fib [fɪb] n bobard m

fibre, (US) **fiber** ['faɪbəʳ] n fibre f

fibreglass, Fiberglass® (US) ['faɪbəglɑːs] n
fibre f de verre

fickle ['fɪkl] adj inconstant(e), volage,
capricieux(-euse)

fiction ['fɪkʃən] n romans mpl, littérature f
romanesque; (invention) fiction f

fictional ['fɪkʃənl] adj fictif(-ive)

fictitious [fɪk'tɪʃəs] adj fictif(-ive),
imaginaire

fiddle ['fɪdl] n (Mus) violon m; (cheating)
combine f; escroquerie f ▷ vt (Brit: accounts)
falsifier, maquiller; tax ~ fraude fiscale,
combine f pour échapper au fisc; to work a ~
traficoter; fiddle with vt fus tripoter

fidelity [fɪ'dɛlɪtɪ] n fidélité f

fidget ['fɪdʒɪt] vi se trémousser, remuer

field [fiːld] n champ m; (fig) domaine m,
champ; (Sport: ground) terrain m; (Comput)
champ, zone f; to lead the ~ (Sport, Comm)

dominer; **the children had a ~ day** (fig)
c'était un grand jour pour les enfants
field marshal n maréchal m
fieldwork ['fiːldwɜːk] n travaux mpl
pratiques (or recherches fpl) sur le terrain
fiend [fiːnd] n démon m
fierce [fɪəs] adj (look, animal) féroce, sauvage;
(wind, attack, person) (très) violent(e); (fighting,
enemy) acharné(e)
fiery ['faɪərɪ] adj ardent(e), brûlant(e),
fougueux(-euse)
fifteen [fɪf'tiːn] num quinze
fifteenth [fɪf'tiːnθ] num quinzième
fifth [fɪfθ] num cinquième
fiftieth ['fɪftɪɪθ] num cinquantième
fifty ['fɪftɪ] num cinquante
fifty-fifty ['fɪftɪ'fɪftɪ] adv moitié-moitié; **to
share ~ with sb** partager moitié-moitié avec
qn ▷ adj: **to have a ~ chance (of success)**
avoir une chance sur deux (de réussir)
fig [fɪg] n figue f
fight [faɪt] (pt, pp fought) [fɔːt] n (between
persons) bagarre f; (argument) dispute f; (Mil)
combat m; (against cancer etc) lutte f ▷ vt se
battre contre; (cancer, alcoholism, emotion)
combattre, lutter contre; (election) se
présenter à; (Law: case) défendre ▷ vi se
battre; (argue) se disputer; (fig): **to ~ (for/
against)** lutter (pour/contre); **fight back** vi
rendre les coups; (after illness) reprendre le
dessus ▷ vt (tears) réprimer; **fight off** vt
repousser; (disease, sleep, urge) lutter contre
fighter ['faɪtər] n lutteur m; (fig: plane)
chasseur m
fighting ['faɪtɪŋ] n combats mpl; (brawls)
bagarres fpl
figment ['fɪgmənt] n: **a ~ of the
imagination** une invention
figurative ['fɪgjʊrətɪv] adj figuré(e)
figure ['fɪgər] n (Drawing, Geom) figure f;
(number) chiffre m; (body, outline) silhouette f;
(person's shape) ligne f, formes fpl; (person)
personnage m ▷ vt (US: think) supposer ▷ vi
(appear) figurer; (US: make sense) s'expliquer;
public ~ personnalité f; **~ of speech** figure f
de rhétorique; **figure on** vt fus (US): **to ~ on
doing** compter faire; **figure out** vt
(understand) arriver à comprendre; (plan)
calculer
figurehead ['fɪgəhɛd] n (Naut) figure f de
proue; (pej) prête-nom m
file [faɪl] n (tool) lime f; (dossier) dossier m;
(folder) dossier, chemise f; (: binder) classeur m;
(Comput) fichier m; (row) file f ▷ vt (nails, wood)
limer; (papers) classer; (Law: claim) faire
enregistrer; déposer ▷ vi: **to ~ in/out** entrer/
sortir l'un derrière l'autre; **to ~ past** défiler
devant; **to ~ a suit against sb** (Law) intenter
un procès à qn
filing cabinet n classeur m (meuble)
Filipino [fɪlɪ'piːnəʊ] adj philippin(e) ▷ n
(person) Philippin(e); (Ling) tagalog m

fill [fɪl] vt remplir; (vacancy) pourvoir à ▷ n: **to
eat one's ~** manger à sa faim; **to ~ with**
remplir de; **fill in** vt (hole) boucher; (form)
remplir; (details, report) compléter; **fill out** vt
(form, receipt) remplir; **fill up** vt remplir ▷ vi
(Aut) faire le plein; **~ it up, please** (Aut) le
plein, s'il vous plaît
fillet ['fɪlɪt] n filet m ▷ vt préparer en filets
fillet steak n filet m de bœuf, tournedos m
filling ['fɪlɪŋ] n (Culin) garniture f, farce f;
(for tooth) plombage m
filling station n station-service f, station f
d'essence
film [fɪlm] n film m; (Phot) pellicule f, film;
(of powder, liquid) couche f, pellicule ▷ vt
(scene) filmer ▷ vi tourner; **I'd like a
36-exposure ~** je voudrais une pellicule
de 36 poses
film star n vedette f de cinéma
filter ['fɪltər] n filtre m ▷ vt filtrer
filter lane n (Brit Aut: at traffic lights) voie f de
dégagement; (: on motorway) voie f de sortie
filter tip n bout m filtre
filth [fɪlθ] n saleté f
filthy ['fɪlθɪ] adj sale, dégoûtant(e); (language)
ordurier(-ière), grossier(-ière)
fin [fɪn] n (of fish) nageoire f; (of shark)
aileron m; (of diver) palme f
final ['faɪnl] adj final(e), dernier(-ière);
(decision, answer) définitif(-ive) ▷ n (Brit Sport)
finale f; **finals** npl (Scol) examens mpl de
dernière année; (US Sport) finale f; **~ demand**
(on invoice etc) dernier rappel
finale [fɪ'nɑːlɪ] n finale m
finalist ['faɪnəlɪst] n (Sport) finaliste m/f
finalize ['faɪnəlaɪz] vt mettre au point
finally ['faɪnəlɪ] adv (eventually) enfin,
finalement; (lastly) en dernier lieu;
(irrevocably) définitivement
finance [faɪ'næns] n finance f ▷ vt financer;
finances npl finances fpl
financial [faɪ'nænʃəl] adj financier(-ière);
~ statement bilan m, exercice financier
financial year n année f budgétaire
find [faɪnd] vt (pt, pp found) [faʊnd] trouver;
(lost object) retrouver ▷ n trouvaille f,
découverte f; **to ~ sb guilty** (Law) déclarer qn
coupable; **to ~ (some) difficulty in doing
sth** avoir du mal à faire qch; **find out** vt se
renseigner sur; (truth, secret) découvrir;
(person) démasquer ▷ vi: **to ~ out about**
(make enquiries) se renseigner sur; (by chance)
apprendre
findings ['faɪndɪŋz] npl (Law) conclusions fpl,
verdict m; (of report) constatations fpl
fine [faɪn] adj (weather) beau/belle; (excellent)
excellent(e); (thin, subtle, not coarse) fin(e);
(acceptable) bien inv ▷ adv (well) très bien;
(small) fin, finement ▷ n (Law) amende f;
contravention f ▷ vt (Law) condamner à une
amende; donner une contravention à; **he's ~**
il va bien; **the weather is ~** il fait beau;

you're doing ~ c'est bien, vous vous débrouillez bien; **to cut it ~** calculer un peu juste

fine arts *npl* beaux-arts *mpl*

finery ['faɪnərɪ] *n* parure *f*

finger ['fɪŋgə'] *n* doigt *m* ▷ *vt* palper, toucher; **index ~** index *m*

fingernail ['fɪŋgəneɪl] *n* ongle *m* (de la main)

fingerprint ['fɪŋgəprɪnt] *n* empreinte digitale ▷ *vt* (*person*) prendre les empreintes digitales de

fingertip ['fɪŋgətɪp] *n* bout *m* du doigt; (*fig*): **to have sth at one's ~s** avoir qch à sa disposition; (*knowledge*) savoir qch sur le bout du doigt

finish ['fɪnɪʃ] *n* fin *f*; (*Sport*) arrivée *f*; (*polish etc*) finition *f* ▷ *vt* finir, terminer ▷ *vi* finir, se terminer; (*session*) s'achever; **to ~ doing sth** finir de faire qch; **to ~ third** arriver *or* terminer troisième; **when does the show ~?** quand est-ce que le spectacle se termine?; **finish off** *vt* finir, terminer; (*kill*) achever; **finish up** *vi, vt* finir

finishing line ['fɪnɪʃɪŋ-] *n* ligne *f* d'arrivée

finite ['faɪnaɪt] *adj* fini(e); (*verb*) conjugué(e)

Finland ['fɪnlənd] *n* Finlande *f*

Finn [fɪn] *n* Finnois(e), Finlandais(e)

Finnish ['fɪnɪʃ] *adj* finnois(e), finlandais(e) ▷ *n* (*Ling*) finnois *m*

fir [fə:'] *n* sapin *m*

fire ['faɪə'] *n* feu *m*; (*accidental*) incendie *m*; (*heater*) radiateur *m* ▷ *vt* (*discharge*): **to ~ a gun** tirer un coup de feu; (*fig*: *interest*) enflammer, animer; (*inf*: *dismiss*) mettre à la porte, renvoyer ▷ *vi* (*shoot*) tirer, faire feu ▷ *cpd*: **~ hazard**, **~ risk**: **that's a fire hazard or risk** cela présente un risque d'incendie; **~! au feu!**; **on ~** en feu; **to set ~ to sth**, **set sth on ~** mettre le feu à qch; **insured against ~** assuré contre l'incendie

fire alarm *n* avertisseur *m* d'incendie

firearm ['faɪərɑːm] *n* arme *f* à feu

fire brigade *n* (régiment *m* de sapeurs-) pompiers *mpl*

fire department *n* (*US*) = **fire brigade**

fire engine *n* (*Brit*) pompe *f* à incendie

fire escape *n* escalier *m* de secours

fire exit *n* issue *f* or sortie *f* de secours

fire extinguisher *n* extincteur *m*

fireman *irreg* ['faɪəmən] *n* pompier *m*

fireplace ['faɪəpleɪs] *n* cheminée *f*

fireside ['faɪəsaɪd] *n* foyer *m*, coin *m* du feu

fire station *n* caserne *f* de pompiers

fire truck *n* (*US*) = **fire engine**

firewall ['faɪəwɔːl] *n* (*Internet*) pare-feu *m*

firewood ['faɪəwud] *n* bois *m* de chauffage

fireworks ['faɪəwəːks] *npl* (*display*) feu(x) *m*(*pl*) d'artifice

firing squad *n* peloton *m* d'exécution

firm [fə:m] *adj* ferme ▷ *n* compagnie *f*, firme *f*; **it is my ~ belief that …** je crois fermement que …

firmly ['fə:mlɪ] *adv* fermement

first [fə:st] *adj* premier(-ière) ▷ *adv* (*before other people*) le premier, la première; (*before other things*) en premier, d'abord; (*when listing reasons etc*) en premier lieu, premièrement; (*in the beginning*) au début ▷ *n* (*person*: *in race*) premier(-ière); (*Brit Scol*) mention *f* très bien; (*Aut*) première *f*; **the ~ of January** le premier janvier; **at ~** au commencement, au début; **~ of all** tout d'abord, pour commencer; **in the ~ instance** en premier lieu; **I'll do it ~ thing tomorrow** je le ferai tout de suite demain matin

first aid *n* premiers secours *or* soins

first-aid kit [fə:st'eɪd-] *n* trousse *f* à pharmacie

first-class ['fə:st'klɑːs] *adj* (*ticket etc*) de première classe; (*excellent*) excellent(e), exceptionnel(le); (*post*) en tarif prioritaire

first-hand ['fə:st'hænd] *adj* de première main

first lady *n* (*US*) femme *f* du président

firstly ['fə:stlɪ] *adv* premièrement, en premier lieu

first name *n* prénom *m*

first-rate ['fə:st'reɪt] *adj* excellent(e)

fiscal ['fɪskl] *adj* fiscal(e)

fiscal year *n* exercice financier

fish [fɪʃ] *n* (*pl inv*) poisson *m*; poissons *mpl* ▷ *vt*, *vi* pêcher; **to ~ a river** pêcher dans une rivière; **~ and chips** poisson frit et frites

fisherman *irreg* ['fɪʃəmən] *n* pêcheur *m*

fish farm *n* établissement *m* piscicole

fish fingers *npl* (*Brit*) bâtonnets *mpl* de poisson (congelés)

fishing ['fɪʃɪŋ] *n* pêche *f*; **to go ~** aller à la pêche

fishing boat *n* barque *f* de pêche

fishing line *n* ligne *f* (de pêche)

fishing rod *n* canne *f* à pêche

fishing tackle *n* attirail *m* de pêche

fishmonger ['fɪʃmʌŋgə'] *n* (*Brit*) marchand *m* de poisson

fishmonger's ['fɪʃmʌŋgəz], **fishmonger's shop** *n* (*Brit*) poissonnerie *f*

fish slice *n* (*Brit*) pelle *f* à poisson

fish sticks *npl* (*US*) = **fish fingers**

fishy ['fɪʃɪ] *adj* (*inf*) suspect(e), louche

fist [fɪst] *n* poing *m*

fit [fɪt] *adj* (*Med, Sport*) en (bonne) forme; (*proper*) convenable; approprié(e) ▷ *vt* (*subj*: *clothes*) aller à; (*adjust*) ajuster; (*put in, attach*) installer, poser; adapter; (*equip*) équiper, garnir, munir; (*suit*) convenir à ▷ *vi* (*clothes*) aller; (*parts*) s'adapter; (*in space, gap*) entrer, s'adapter ▷ *n* (*Med*) accès *m*, crise *f*; (*of anger*) accès; (*of hysterics, jealousy*) crise; **~ to** (*ready to*) en état de; **~ for** (*worthy*) digne de; (*capable*) apte à; **to keep ~** se maintenir en forme; **this dress is a tight/good ~** cette robe est un peu juste/(me) va très bien; **a ~ of coughing** une quinte de toux; **to have a ~**

(Med) faire or avoir une crise; (inf) piquer une crise; **by ~s and starts** par à-coups; **fit in** vi (add up) cadrer; (integrate) s'intégrer; (to new situation) s'adapter; **fit out** vt (Brit: also: **~ up**) équiper

fitful ['fitful] adj intermittent(e)

fitment ['fitmənt] n meuble encastré, élément m

fitness ['fitnis] n (Med) forme f physique; (of remark) à-propos m, justesse f

fitted ['fitid] adj (jacket, shirt) ajusté(e)

fitted carpet ['fitid-] n moquette f

fitted kitchen ['fitid-] n (Brit) cuisine équipée

fitted sheet ['fitid-] n drap-housse m

fitter ['fitə^r] n monteur m; (Dressmaking) essayeur(-euse)

fitting ['fitiŋ] adj approprié(e) ▷ n (of dress) essayage m; (of piece of equipment) pose f, installation f

fitting room n (in shop) cabine f d'essayage

fittings ['fitiŋz] npl installations fpl

five [faiv] num cinq

fiver ['faivə^r] n (inf: Brit) billet m de cinq livres; (: US) billet de cinq dollars

fix [fiks] vt (date, amount etc) fixer; (sort out) arranger; (mend) réparer; (make ready: meal, drink) préparer; (inf: game etc) truquer ▷ n: **to be in a ~** être dans le pétrin; **fix up** vt (meeting) arranger; **to ~ sb up with sth** faire avoir qch à qn

fixation [fik'seiʃən] n (Psych) fixation f; (fig) obsession f

fixed [fikst] adj (prices etc) fixe; **there's a ~ charge** il y a un prix forfaitaire; **how are you ~ for money?** (inf) question fric, ça va?

fixture ['fikstʃə^r] n installation f (fixe); (Sport) rencontre f (au programme)

fizzy ['fizi] adj pétillant(e), gazeux(-euse)

flabbergasted ['flæbəgɑːstid] adj sidéré(e), ahuri(e)

flabby ['flæbi] adj mou/molle

flag [flæg] n drapeau m; (also: **~stone**) dalle f ▷ vi faiblir; fléchir; **~ of convenience** pavillon m de complaisance; **flag down** vt héler, faire signe (de s'arrêter) à

flagpole ['flægpəul] n mât m

flagship ['flægʃip] n vaisseau m amiral; (fig) produit m vedette

flair [flεə^r] n flair m

flak [flæk] n (Mil) tir antiaérien; (inf: criticism) critiques fpl

flake [fleik] n (of rust, paint) écaille f; (of snow, soap powder) flocon m ▷ vi (also: **~ off**) s'écailler

flamboyant [flæm'bɔiənt] adj flamboyant(e), éclatant(e); (person) haut(e) en couleur

flame [fleim] n flamme f

flamingo [flə'miŋgəu] n flamant m (rose)

flammable ['flæməbl] adj inflammable

flan [flæn] n (Brit) tarte f

flank [flæŋk] n flanc m ▷ vt flanquer

flannel ['flænl] n (Brit: also: **face ~**) gant m de toilette; (fabric) flanelle f; (Brit inf) baratin m; **flannels** npl pantalon m de flanelle

flap [flæp] n (of pocket, envelope) rabat m ▷ vt (wings) battre (de) ▷ vi (sail, flag) claquer; (inf: also: **be in a ~**) paniquer

flare [flεə^r] n (signal) signal lumineux; (Mil) fusée éclairante; (in skirt etc) évasement m; **flares** npl (trousers) pantalon m à pattes d'éléphant; **flare up** vi s'embraser; (fig: person) se mettre en colère, s'emporter; (: revolt) éclater

flash [flæʃ] n éclair m; (also: **news ~**) flash m (d'information); (Phot) flash ▷ vt (switch on) allumer (brièvement); (direct): **to ~ sth at** braquer qch sur; (flaunt) étaler, exhiber; (send: message) câbler; (smile) lancer ▷ vi briller; jeter des éclairs; (light on ambulance etc) clignoter; **a ~ of lightning** un éclair; **in a ~** en un clin d'œil; **to ~ one's headlights** faire un appel de phares; **he ~ed by** or **past** il passa (devant nous) comme un éclair

flashback ['flæʃbæk] n flashback m, retour m en arrière

flashbulb ['flæʃbʌlb] n ampoule f de flash

flashcube ['flæʃkjuːb] n cube-flash m

flashlight ['flæʃlait] n lampe f de poche

flashy ['flæʃi] adj (pej) tape-à-l'œil inv, tapageur(-euse)

flask [flɑːsk] n flacon m, bouteille f; (Chem) ballon m; (also: **vacuum ~**) bouteille f thermos®

flat [flæt] adj plat(e); (tyre) dégonflé(e), à plat; (beer) éventé(e); (battery) à plat; (denial) catégorique; (Mus) bémol inv; (: voice) faux/fausse ▷ n (Brit: apartment) appartement m; (Aut) crevaison f, pneu crevé; (Mus) bémol m; **~ out** (work) sans relâche; (race) à fond; **~ rate of pay** (Comm) salaire m fixe

flatly ['flætli] adv catégoriquement

flatten ['flætn] vt (also: **~ out**) aplatir; (crop) coucher; (house, city) raser

flatter ['flætə^r] vt flatter

flattering ['flætəriŋ] adj flatteur(-euse); (clothes etc) seyant(e)

flattery ['flætəri] n flatterie f

flaunt [flɔːnt] vt faire étalage de

flavour, (US) **flavor** ['fleivə^r] n goût m, saveur f; (of ice cream etc) parfum m ▷ vt parfumer, aromatiser; **vanilla-~ed** à l'arôme de vanille, vanillé(e); **what ~s do you have?** quels parfums avez-vous?; **to give** or **add ~ to** donner du goût à, relever

flavouring, (US) **flavoring** ['fleivəriŋ] n arôme m (synthétique)

flaw [flɔː] n défaut m

flawless ['flɔːlis] adj sans défaut

flax [flæks] n lin m

flea [fliː] n puce f

flea market n marché m aux puces

fleck [flεk] n (of dust) particule f; (of mud, paint, colour) tacheture f, moucheture f ▷ vt tacher, éclabousser; **brown ~ed with white** brun moucheté de blanc

fled [flɛd] *pt, pp* of **flee**

flee (*pt, pp* **fled**) [fli:, flɛd] *vt* fuir, s'enfuir de ▷ *vi* fuir, s'enfuir

fleece [fli:s] *n* (*of sheep*) toison *f*; (*top*) (laine *f*) polaire *f* ▷ *vt* (*inf*) voler, filouter

fleet [fli:t] *n* flotte *f*; (*of lorries, cars etc*) parc *m*; convoi *m*

fleeting ['fli:tɪŋ] *adj* fugace, fugitif(-ive); (*visit*) très bref/brève

Flemish ['flɛmɪʃ] *adj* flamand(e) ▷ *n* (*Ling*) flamand *m*; **the ~** *npl* les Flamands

flesh [flɛʃ] *n* chair *f*

flesh wound [-wu:nd] *n* blessure superficielle

flew [flu:] *pt* of **fly**

flex [flɛks] *n* fil *m* or câble *m* électrique (souple) ▷ *vt* (*knee*) fléchir; (*muscles*) bander

flexibility [flɛksɪ'bɪlɪtɪ] *n* flexibilité *f*

flexible ['flɛksəbl] *adj* flexible; (*person, schedule*) souple

flexitime ['flɛksɪtaɪm], (*US*) **flextime** ['flɛkstaɪm] *n* horaire *m* variable or à la carte

flick [flɪk] *n* petit coup; (*with finger*) chiquenaude *f* ▷ *vt* donner un petit coup à; (*switch*) appuyer sur; **flick through** *vt fus* feuilleter

flicker ['flɪkə'] *vi* (*light, flame*) vaciller ▷ *n* vacillement *m*; **a ~ of light** une brève lueur

flier ['flaɪə'] *n* aviateur *m*

flies [flaɪz] *npl* of **fly**

flight [flaɪt] *n* vol *m*; (*escape*) fuite *f*; (*also:* **~ of steps**) escalier *m*; **to take ~** prendre la fuite; **to put to ~** mettre aux fuite

flight attendant *n* steward *m*, hôtesse *f* de l'air

flight deck *n* (*Aviat*) poste *m* de pilotage; (*Naut*) pont *m* d'envol

flimsy ['flɪmzɪ] *adj* peu solide; (*clothes*) trop léger(-ère); (*excuse*) pauvre, mince

flinch [flɪntʃ] *vi* tressaillir; **to ~ from** se dérober à, reculer devant

fling [flɪŋ] *vt* (*pt, pp* **flung**) [flʌŋ] jeter, lancer ▷ *n* (*love affair*) brève liaison, passade *f*

flint [flɪnt] *n* silex *m*; (*in lighter*) pierre *f* (à briquet)

flip [flɪp] *n* chiquenaude *f* ▷ *vt* (*throw*) donner une chiquenaude à; (*switch*) appuyer sur; (*US: pancake*) faire sauter; **to ~ sth over** retourner qch ▷ *vi*: **to ~ for sth** (*US*) jouer qch à pile ou face; **flip through** *vt fus* feuilleter

flip-flops ['flɪpflɔps] *npl* (*esp Brit*) tongs *fpl*

flippant ['flɪpənt] *adj* désinvolte, irrévérencieux(-euse)

flipper ['flɪpə'] *n* (*of animal*) nageoire *f*; (*for swimmer*) palme *f*

flirt [flə:t] *vi* flirter ▷ *n* flirteur(-euse)

float [fləut] *n* flotteur *m*; (*in procession*) char *m*; (*sum of money*) réserve *f* ▷ *vi* flotter; (*bather*) flotter, faire la planche ▷ *vt* faire flotter; (*loan, business, idea*) lancer

flock [flɔk] *n* (*of sheep*) troupeau *m*; (*of birds*) vol *m*; (*of people*) foule *f*

flog [flɔg] *vt* fouetter

flood [flʌd] *n* inondation *f*; (*of letters, refugees etc*) flot *m* ▷ *vt* inonder; (*Aut: carburettor*) noyer ▷ *vi* (*place*) être inondé; (*people*): **to ~ into** envahir; **to ~ the market** (*Comm*) inonder le marché; **in ~** en crue

flooding ['flʌdɪŋ] *n* inondation *f*

floodlight ['flʌdlaɪt] *n* projecteur *m* ▷ *vt* éclairer aux projecteurs, illuminer

floor [flɔ:'] *n* sol *m*; (*storey*) étage *m*; (*of sea, valley*) fond *m*; (*fig: at meeting*): **the ~** l'assemblée *f*, les membres *mpl* de l'assemblée ▷ *vt* (*knock down*) terrasser; (*baffle*) désorienter; **on the ~** par terre; **ground ~,** (*US*) **first ~** rez-de-chaussée *m*; **first ~,** (*US*) **second ~** premier étage; **top ~** dernier étage; **what ~ is it on?** c'est à quel étage?; **to have the ~** (*speaker*) avoir la parole

floorboard ['flɔ:bɔ:d] *n* planche *f* (*du plancher*)

flooring ['flɔ:rɪŋ] *n* sol *m*; (*wooden*) plancher *m*; (*material to make floor*) matériau(x) *m(pl)* pour planchers; (*covering*) revêtement *m* de sol

floor show *n* spectacle *m* de variétés

flop [flɔp] *n* fiasco *m* ▷ *vi* (*fail*) faire fiasco; (*fall*) s'affaler, s'effondrer

floppy ['flɔpɪ] *adj* lâche, flottant(e) ▷ *n* (*Comput: also:* **~ disk**) disquette *f*; **~ hat** chapeau *m* à bords flottants

flora ['flɔ:rə] *n* flore *f*

floral ['flɔ:rl] *adj* floral(e); (*dress*) à fleurs

florid ['flɔrɪd] *adj* (*complexion*) fleuri(e); (*style*) plein(e) de fioritures

florist ['flɔrɪst] *n* fleuriste *m/f*

florist's ['flɔrɪsts], **florist's shop** *n* magasin *m* or boutique *f* de fleuriste

flotation [fləu'teɪʃən] *n* (*of shares*) émission *f*; (*of company*) lancement *m* (en Bourse)

flounder ['flaundə'] *n* (*Zool*) flet *m* ▷ *vi* patauger

flour ['flauə'] *n* farine *f*

flourish ['flʌrɪʃ] *vi* prospérer ▷ *vt* brandir ▷ *n* (*gesture*) moulinet *m*; (*decoration*) fioriture *f*; (*of trumpets*) fanfare *f*

flout [flaut] *vt* se moquer de, faire fi de

flow [fləu] *n* (*of water, traffic etc*) écoulement *m*; (*tide, influx*) flux *m*; (*of orders, letters etc*) flot *m*; (*of blood, Elec*) circulation *f*; (*of river*) courant *m* ▷ *vi* couler; (*traffic*) s'écouler; (*robes, hair*) flotter

flow chart, flow diagram *n* organigramme *m*

flower ['flauə'] *n* fleur *f* ▷ *vi* fleurir; **in ~** en fleur

flower bed *n* plate-bande *f*

flowerpot ['flauəpɔt] *n* pot *m* (à fleurs)

flowery ['flauərɪ] *adj* fleuri(e)

flown [fləun] *pp* of **fly**

fl. oz. *abbr* = **fluid ounce**

flu [flu:] *n* grippe *f*

fluctuate ['flʌktjueɪt] vi varier, fluctuer

fluent ['fluːənt] adj (speech, style) coulant(e), aisé(e); **he's a ~ speaker/reader** il s'exprime/lit avec aisance or facilité; **he speaks ~ French, he's ~ in French** il parle le français couramment

fluff [flʌf] n duvet m; (on jacket, carpet) peluche f

fluffy ['flʌfɪ] adj duveteux(-euse); (jacket, carpet) pelucheux(-euse); (toy) en peluche

fluid ['fluːɪd] n fluide m; (in diet) liquide m ▷ adj liquide

fluid ounce n (Brit) = 0.028 l; 0.05 pints

fluke [fluːk] n coup m de veine

flung [flʌŋ] pt, pp of **fling**

fluorescent [fluəˈresnt] adj fluorescent(e)

fluoride ['fluəraɪd] n fluor m

flurry ['flʌrɪ] n (of snow) rafale f, bourrasque f; **a ~ of activity** un affairement soudain; **a ~ of excitement** une excitation soudaine

flush [flʌʃ] n (on face) rougeur f; (fig: of youth etc) éclat m; (of blood) afflux m ▷ vt nettoyer à grande eau; (also: ~ **out**) débusquer ▷ vi rougir ▷ adj (inf) en fonds; (level): ~ **with** au ras de, de niveau avec; **to ~ the toilet** tirer la chasse (d'eau); **hot ~es** (Med) bouffées fpl de chaleur

flushed ['flʌʃt] adj (tout(e)) rouge

flustered ['flʌstəd] adj énervé(e)

flute [fluːt] n flûte f

flutter ['flʌtə'] n (of panic, excitement) agitation f; (of wings) battement m ▷ vi (bird) battre des ailes, voleter; (person) aller et venir dans une grande agitation

flux [flʌks] n: **in a state of ~** fluctuant sans cesse

fly [flaɪ] (pt **flew**, pp **flown**) [fluː, fləʊn] n (insect) mouche f; (on trousers: also: **flies**) braguette f ▷ vt (plane) piloter; (passengers, cargo) transporter (par avion); (distance) parcourir ▷ vi voler; (passengers) aller en avion; (escape) s'enfuir, fuir; (flag) se déployer; **to ~ open** s'ouvrir brusquement; **to ~ off the handle** s'énerver, s'emporter; **fly away, fly off** vi s'envoler; **fly in** vi (plane) atterrir; **he flew in yesterday** il est arrivé hier (par avion); **fly out** vi partir (par avion)

fly-drive ['flaɪdraɪv] n formule f avion plus voiture

flying ['flaɪɪŋ] n (activity) aviation f; (action) vol m ▷ adj: ~ **visit** visite f éclair inv; **with ~ colours** haut la main; **he doesn't like ~** il n'aime pas voyager en avion

flying saucer n soucoupe volante

flying start n: **to get off to a ~** faire un excellent départ

flyover ['flaɪəʊvə'] n (Brit: overpass) pont routier, saut-de-mouton m (Canada)

flysheet ['flaɪʃiːt] n (for tent) double toit m

FM abbr (Brit Mil) = **field marshal**; (Radio: = frequency modulation) FM

foal [fəʊl] n poulain m

foam [fəʊm] n écume f; (on beer) mousse f; (also: ~ **rubber**) caoutchouc m mousse; (also: **plastic ~**) mousse cellulaire or de plastique ▷ vi (liquid) écumer; (soapy water) mousser

fob [fɔb] n (also: **watch ~**) chaîne f, ruban m ▷ vt: **to ~ sb off with sth** refiler qch à qn

focal point n foyer m; (fig) centre m de l'attention, point focal

focus ['fəʊkəs] n (pl **focuses**) foyer m; (of interest) centre m ▷ vt (field glasses etc) mettre au point; (light rays) faire converger ▷ vi: **to ~ (on)** (with camera) régler la mise au point (sur); (with eyes) fixer son regard (sur); (fig: concentrate) se concentrer; **out of/in ~** (picture) flou(e)/net(te); (camera) pas au point/au point

fodder ['fɔdə'] n fourrage m

foe [fəʊ] n ennemi m

foetus, (US) **fetus** ['fiːtəs] n fœtus m

fog [fɔg] n brouillard m

foggy ['fɔgɪ] adj: **it's ~** il y a du brouillard

fog lamp, (US) **fog light** n (Aut) phare m anti-brouillard

foil [fɔɪl] vt déjouer, contrecarrer ▷ n feuille f de métal; (kitchen foil) papier m d'alu(minium); (Fencing) fleuret m; **to act as a ~ to** (fig) servir de repoussoir or de faire-valoir à

fold [fəʊld] n (bend, crease) pli m; (Agr) parc m à moutons; (fig) bercail m ▷ vt plier; **to ~ one's arms** croiser les bras; **fold up** vi (map etc) se plier, se replier; (business) fermer boutique ▷ vt (map etc) plier, replier

folder ['fəʊldə'] n (for papers) chemise f; (: binder) classeur m; (brochure) dépliant m; (Comput) dossier m

folding ['fəʊldɪŋ] adj (chair, bed) pliant(e)

foliage ['fəʊlɪɪdʒ] n feuillage m

folk [fəʊk] npl gens mpl ▷ cpd folklorique; **folks** npl (inf: parents) famille f, parents mpl

folklore ['fəʊklɔː'] n folklore m

folk music n musique f folklorique; (contemporary) musique folk, folk m

folk song ['fəʊksɔŋ] n chanson f folklorique; (contemporary) chanson folk inv

follow ['fɔləʊ] vt suivre ▷ vi suivre; (result) s'ensuivre; **to ~ sb's advice** suivre les conseils de qn; **I don't quite ~ you** je ne vous suis plus; **to ~ in sb's footsteps** emboîter le pas à qn; (fig) suivre les traces de qn; **it ~s that ...** de ce fait, il s'ensuit que ...; **to ~ suit** (fig) faire de même; **follow out** vt (idea, plan) poursuivre, mener à terme; **follow through** vt = **follow out**; **follow up** vt (victory) tirer parti de; (letter, offer) donner suite à; (case) suivre

follower ['fɔləʊə'] n disciple m/f, partisan(e)

following ['fɔləʊɪŋ] adj suivant(e) ▷ n partisans mpl, disciples mpl

follow-up ['fɔləʊʌp] n suite f; (on file, case) suivi m

folly ['fɒlɪ] n inconscience f; sottise f; (building) folie f

fond [fɒnd] adj (memory, look) tendre, affectueux(-euse); (hopes, dreams) un peu fou/folle; **to be ~ of** aimer beaucoup

fondle ['fɒndl] vt caresser

font [fɒnt] n (Rel) fonts baptismaux; (Typ) police f de caractères

food [fu:d] n nourriture f

food mixer n mixeur m

food poisoning n intoxication f alimentaire

food processor n robot m de cuisine

food stamp n (US) bon m de nourriture (pour indigents)

foodstuffs ['fu:dstʌfs] npl denrées fpl alimentaires

fool [fu:l] n idiot(e); (Hist: of king) bouffon m, fou m; (Culin) mousse f de fruits ▷ vt berner, duper ▷ vi (also: ~ around) faire l'idiot or l'imbécile; **to make a ~ of sb** (ridicule) ridiculiser qn; (trick) berner qn; **to make a ~ of o.s.** se couvrir de ridicule; **you can't ~ me** vous (ne) me la ferez pas, on (ne) me la fait pas; **fool about, fool around** vi (pej: waste time) traînailler, glandouiller; (: behave foolishly) faire l'idiot or l'imbécile

foolhardy ['fu:lha:dɪ] adj téméraire, imprudent(e)

foolish ['fu:lɪʃ] adj idiot(e), stupide; (rash) imprudent(e)

foolproof ['fu:lpru:f] adj (plan etc) infaillible

foot (pl **feet**) [fut, fi:t] n pied m; (of animal) patte f; (measure) pied (= 30.48 cm; 12 inches) ▷ vt (bill) casquer, payer; **on ~** à pied; **to find one's feet** (fig) s'acclimater; **to put one's ~ down** (Aut) appuyer sur le champignon; (say no) s'imposer

footage ['fʊtɪdʒ] n (Cine: length) ≈ métrage m; (: material) séquences fpl

foot-and-mouth [fʊtənd'maʊθ], **foot-and-mouth disease** n fièvre aphteuse

football ['fʊtbɔ:l] n (ball) ballon m (de football); (sport: Brit) football m; (: US) football américain

footballer ['fʊtbɔ:lər] n (Brit) = **football player**

football match n (Brit) match m de foot(ball)

football player n footballeur(-euse), joueur(-euse) de football; (US) joueur(-euse) de football américain

football pools npl (US) ≈ loto m sportif, ≈ pronostics mpl (sur les matchs de football)

footbrake ['fʊtbreɪk] n frein m à pédale

footbridge ['fʊtbrɪdʒ] n passerelle f

foothills ['fʊthɪlz] npl contreforts mpl

foothold ['fʊthəʊld] n prise f (de pied)

footing ['fʊtɪŋ] n (fig) position f; **to lose one's ~** perdre pied; **on an equal ~** sur pied d'égalité

footlights ['fʊtlaɪts] npl rampe f

footnote ['fʊtnəʊt] n note f (en bas de page)

footpath ['fʊtpɑ:θ] n sentier m; (in street) trottoir m

footprint ['fʊtprɪnt] n trace f (de pied)

footstep ['fʊtstɛp] n pas m

footwear ['fʊtwɛər] n chaussures fpl

 KEYWORD

for [fɔ:r] prep **1** (indicating destination, intention, purpose) pour; **the train for London** le train pour (or à destination de) Londres; **he left for Rome** il est parti de Hove; **he went for the paper** il est allé chercher le journal; **is this for me?** c'est pour moi?; **it's time for lunch** c'est l'heure du déjeuner; **what's it for?** ça sert à quoi?; **what for?** (why) pourquoi?; (to what end) pour quoi faire?, à quoi bon?; **for sale** à vendre; **to pray for peace** prier pour la paix

2 (on behalf of, representing) pour; **the MP for Hove** le député de Hove; **to work for sb/sth** travailler pour qn/qch; **I'll ask him for you** je vais lui demander pour toi; **G for George** G comme Georges

3 (because of) pour; **for this reason** pour cette raison; **for fear of being criticized** de peur d'être critiqué

4 (with regard to) pour; **it's cold for July** il fait froid pour juillet; **a gift for languages** un don pour les langues

5 (in exchange for): **I sold it for £5** je l'ai vendu 5 livres; **to pay 50 pence for a ticket** payer un billet 50 pence

6 (in favour of) pour; **are you for or against us?** êtes-vous pour ou contre nous?; **I'm all for it** je suis tout à fait pour; **vote for X** votez pour X

7 (referring to distance) pendant, sur; **there are roadworks for 5 km** il y a des travaux sur or pendant 5 km; **we walked for miles** nous avons marché pendant des kilomètres

8 (referring to time) pendant; depuis; pour; **he was away for 2 years** il a été absent pendant 2 ans; **she will be away for a month** elle sera absente (pendant) un mois; **it hasn't rained for 3 weeks** ça fait 3 semaines qu'il ne pleut pas, il ne pleut pas depuis 3 semaines; **I have known her for years** je la connais depuis des années; **can you do it for tomorrow?** est-ce que tu peux le faire pour demain?

9 (with infinitive clauses): **it is not for me to decide** ce n'est pas à moi de décider; **it would be best for you to leave** le mieux serait que vous partiez; **there is still time for you to do it** vous avez encore le temps de le faire; **for this to be possible ...** pour que cela soit possible ..

10 (in spite of): **for all that** malgré cela, néanmoins; **for all his work/efforts** malgré tout son travail/tous ses efforts; **for all his complaints, he's very fond of her** il a beau

forage ['fɒrɪdʒ] n fourrage m ▷ vi fourrager, fouiller

foray ['fɒreɪ] n incursion f

forbid (pt **forbad** or **forbade**, pp **forbidden**) [fə'bɪd, -'bæd, -'bɪdn] vt défendre, interdire; **to ~ sb to do** défendre or interdire à qn de faire

forbidden [fə'bɪdn] adj défendu(e)

forbidding [fə'bɪdɪŋ] adj d'aspect or d'allure sévère or sombre

force [fɔːs] n force f ▷ vt forcer; (push) pousser (de force); **Forces** npl: **the F~s** (Brit Mil) les forces armées; **to ~ o.s. to do** se forcer à faire; **to ~ sb to do sth** forcer qn à faire qch; **in ~** (being used: rule, law, prices) en vigueur; (in large numbers) en force; **to come into ~** entrer en vigueur; **a ~ 5 wind** un vent de force 5; **the sales** ~ (Comm) la force de vente; **to join ~s** unir ses forces; **force back** vt (crowd, enemy) repousser; (tears) refouler; **force down** vt (food) se forcer à manger

forced [fɔːst] adj forcé(e)

force-feed ['fɔːsfiːd] vt nourrir de force

forceful ['fɔːsful] adj énergique

forcibly ['fɔːsəblɪ] adv par la force, de force; (vigorously) énergiquement

ford [fɔːd] n gué m ▷ vt passer à gué

fore [fɔːr] n: **to the ~** en évidence; **to come to the ~** se faire remarquer

forearm ['fɔːrɑːm] n avant-bras m inv

foreboding [fɔː'bəudɪŋ] n pressentiment m (néfaste)

forecast ['fɔːkɑːst] n prévision f; (also: **weather ~**) prévisions fpl météorologiques, météo f ▷ vt (irreg like: **cast**) prévoir

forecourt ['fɔːkɔːt] n (of garage) devant m

forefinger ['fɔːfɪŋgər] n index m

forefront ['fɔːfrʌnt] n: **in the ~ of** au premier rang or plan de

foregone ['fɔːgɒn] adj: **it's a ~ conclusion** c'est à prévoir, c'est couru d'avance

foreground ['fɔːgraund] n premier plan m ▷ cpd (Comput) prioritaire

forehead ['fɒrɪd] n front m

foreign ['fɒrɪn] adj étranger(-ère); (trade) extérieur(e); (travel) à l'étranger

foreign currency n devises étrangères

foreigner ['fɒrɪnər] n étranger(-ère) m/f

foreign exchange n (system) change m; (money) devises fpl

Foreign Office n (Brit) ministère m des Affaires étrangères

Foreign Secretary n (Brit) ministre m des Affaires étrangères

foreleg ['fɔːleg] n patte f de devant, jambe antérieure

foreman irreg ['fɔːmən] n (in construction) contremaître m; (Law: of jury) président m (du jury)

foremost ['fɔːməust] adj le/la plus en vue, premier(-ière) ▷ adv: **first and ~** avant tout, tout d'abord

forename ['fɔːneɪm] n prénom m

forensic [fə'rɛnsɪk] adj: **~ medicine** médecine légale; **~ expert** expert m de la police, expert légiste

forerunner ['fɔːrʌnər] n précurseur m

foresee (pt **foresaw**, pp **foreseen**) [fɔː'siː, -'sɔː, -'siːn] vt prévoir

foreseeable [fɔː'siːəbl] adj prévisible

foreseen [fɔː'siːn] pp of **foresee**

foreshadow [fɔː'ʃædəu] vt présager, annoncer, laisser prévoir

foresight ['fɔːsaɪt] n prévoyance f

forest ['fɒrɪst] n forêt f

forestry ['fɒrɪstrɪ] n sylviculture f

foretaste ['fɔːteɪst] n avant-goût m

foretell (pt, pp **foretold**) [fɔː'tɛl, -'təuld] vt prédire

foretold [fɔː'təuld] pt, pp of **foretell**

forever [fə'rɛvər] adv pour toujours; (fig: endlessly) continuellement

foreword ['fɔːwəːd] n avant-propos m inv

forfeit ['fɔːfɪt] n prix m, rançon f ▷ vt perdre; (one's life, health) payer de

forgave [fə'geɪv] pt of **forgive**

forge [fɔːdʒ] n forge f ▷ vt (signature) contrefaire; (wrought iron) forger; **to ~ documents/a will** fabriquer de faux papiers/un faux testament; **to ~ money** (Brit) fabriquer de la fausse monnaie; **forge ahead** vi pousser de l'avant, prendre de l'avance

forged [fɔːdʒd] adj faux/fausse

forger ['fɔːdʒər] n faussaire m

forgery ['fɔːdʒərɪ] n faux m, contrefaçon f

forget (pt **forgot**, pp **forgotten**) [fə'gɛt, -'gɒt, -'gɒtn] vt, vi oublier; **to ~ to do sth** oublier de faire qch; **to ~ about sth** (accidentally) oublier qch; (on purpose) ne plus penser à qch; **I've forgotten my key/passport** j'ai oublié ma clé/mon passeport

forgetful [fə'gɛtful] adj distrait(e), étourdi(e); **~ of** oublieux(-euse) de

forget-me-not [fə'gɛtmɪnɒt] n myosotis m

forgive (pt **forgave**, pp **forgiven**) [fə'gɪv, -'geɪv, -'gɪvn] vt pardonner; **to ~ sb for sth/for doing sth** pardonner qch à qn/à qn de faire qch

forgiveness [fə'gɪvnɪs] n pardon m

forgo (pt **forwent**, pp **forgone**) [fɔː'gəu, -'wɛnt, -'gɒn] vt = **forego**

forgot [fə'gɒt] pt of **forget**

forgotten [fə'gɒtn] pp of **forget**

fork [fɔːk] n (for eating) fourchette f; (for gardening) fourche f; (of roads) bifurcation f; (of railways) embranchement m ▷ vi (road) bifurquer; **fork out** (inf: pay) vt allonger, se fendre de ▷ vi casquer

fork-lift truck ['fɔːklɪft-] *n* chariot élévateur
forlorn [fə'lɔːn] *adj* (*person*) délaissé(e);
(*deserted*) abandonné(e); (*hope, attempt*)
désespéré(e)
form [fɔːm] *n* forme *f*; (*Scol*) classe *f*;
(*questionnaire*) formulaire *m* ▷ *vt* former;
(*habit*) contracter; **in the ~ of** sous forme de;
to ~ part of sth faire partie de qch; **to be on
good ~** (*Sport: fig*) être en forme; **on top ~** en
pleine forme
formal ['fɔːməl] *adj* (*offer, receipt*) en bonne et
due forme; (*person*) cérémonieux(-euse), à
cheval sur les convenances; (*occasion, dinner*)
officiel(le); (*garden*) à la française; (*Art,
Philosophy*) formel(le); (*clothes*) de soirée
formality [fɔː'mælɪtɪ] *n* formalité *f*,
cérémonie(s) *f(pl)*
formally ['fɔːməlɪ] *adv* officiellement;
formellement; cérémonieusement
format ['fɔːmæt] *n* format *m* ▷ *vt* (*Comput*)
formater
formation [fɔː'meɪʃən] *n* formation *f*
formative ['fɔːmətɪv] *adj*: **~ years** années *fpl*
d'apprentissage (*fig*) or de formation (*d'un
enfant, d'un adolescent*)
former ['fɔːmə'] *adj* ancien(ne); (*before n*)
précédent(e); **the ~ ... the latter** le premier
... le second, celui-là ... celui-ci; **the ~
president** l'ex-président; **the ~ Yugoslavia/
Soviet Union** l'ex Yougoslavie/Union
Soviétique
formerly ['fɔːməlɪ] *adv* autrefois
formidable ['fɔːmɪdəbl] *adj* redoutable
formula ['fɔːmjulə] *n* formule *f*; **F~ One** (*Aut*)
Formule un
forsake (*pt* **forsook**, *pp* **forsaken**)
[fə'seɪk, -'suk, -'seɪkən] *vt* abandonner
fort [fɔːt] *n* fort *m*; **to hold the ~** (*fig*) assurer
la permanence
forte ['fɔːtɪ] *n* (point) fort *m*
forth [fɔːθ] *adv* en avant; **to go back and ~**
aller et venir; **and so ~** et ainsi de suite
forthcoming [fɔːθ'kʌmɪŋ] *adj* qui va paraître
or avoir lieu prochainement; (*character*)
ouvert(e), communicatif(-ive); (*available*)
disponible
forthright ['fɔːθraɪt] *adj* franc/franche,
direct(e)
forthwith ['fɔːθ'wɪθ] *adv* sur le champ
fortieth ['fɔːtɪɪθ] *num* quarantième
fortify ['fɔːtɪfaɪ] *vt* (*city*) fortifier; (*person*)
remonter
fortitude ['fɔːtɪtjuːd] *n* courage *m*, force *f*
d'âme
fortnight ['fɔːtnaɪt] *n* (*Brit*) quinzaine *f*,
quinze jours *mpl*; **it's a ~ since ...** il y a quinze
jours que ...
fortnightly ['fɔːtnaɪtlɪ] *adj* bimensuel(le)
▷ *adv* tous les quinze jours
fortress ['fɔːtrɪs] *n* forteresse *f*
fortunate ['fɔːtʃənɪt] *adj* heureux(-euse);
(*person*) chanceux(-euse); **to be ~** avoir de la

chance; **it is ~ that** c'est une chance que, il
est heureux que
fortunately ['fɔːtʃənɪtlɪ] *adv* heureusement,
par bonheur
fortune ['fɔːtʃən] *n* chance *f*; (*wealth*) fortune
f; **to make a ~** faire fortune
fortune-teller ['fɔːtʃəntelə'] *n* diseuse *f* de
bonne aventure
forty ['fɔːtɪ] *num* quarante
forum ['fɔːrəm] *n* forum *m*, tribune *f*
forward ['fɔːwəd] *adj* (*movement, position*) en
avant, vers l'avant; (*not shy*) effronté(e); (*in
time*) en avance; (*Comm: delivery, sales, exchange*)
à terme ▷ *adv* (*also:* **~s**) en avant ▷ *n* (*Sport*)
avant *m* ▷ *vt* (*letter*) faire suivre; (*parcel, goods*)
expédier; (*fig*) promouvoir, favoriser; **to look
~ to sth** attendre qch avec impatience; **to
move ~** avancer; **"please ~"** "prière de faire
suivre"; **~ planning** planification *f* à long
terme
forwarding address *n* adresse *f* de
réexpédition
forward slash *n* barre *f* oblique
fossil ['fɔsl] *adj, n* fossile *m*; **~ fuel**
combustible *m* fossile
foster ['fɔstə'] *vt* (*encourage*) encourager,
favoriser; (*child*) élever
foster child *n* enfant élevé dans une famille
d'accueil
foster parent *n* parent qui élève un enfant sans
l'adopter
fought [fɔːt] *pt, pp* of **fight**
foul [faul] *adj* (*weather, smell, food*) infect(e);
(*language*) ordurier(-ière); (*deed*) infâme ▷ *n*
(*Football*) faute *f* ▷ *vt* (*dirty*) salir, encrasser;
(*football player*) commettre une faute sur;
(*entangle: anchor, propeller*) emmêler; **he's got
a ~ temper** il a un caractère de chien
foul play *n* (*Sport*) jeu déloyal; (*Law*) acte
criminel; **~ is not suspected** la mort (*or*
l'incendie *etc*) n'a pas de causes suspectes, on
écarte l'hypothèse d'un meurtre (*or* d'un acte
criminel)
found [faund] *pt, pp* of **find** ▷ *vt* (*establish*)
fonder
foundation [faun'deɪʃən] *n* (*act*) fondation *f*;
(*base*) fondement *m*; (*also:* **~ cream**) fond *m* de
teint; **foundations** *npl* (*of building*) fondations
fpl; **to lay the ~s** (*fig*) poser les fondements
founder ['faundə'] *n* fondateur *m* ▷ *vi* couler,
sombrer
foundry ['faundrɪ] *n* fonderie *f*
fountain ['fauntɪn] *n* fontaine *f*
fountain pen *n* stylo *m* (à encre)
four [fɔː'] *num* quatre; **on all ~s** à quatre
pattes
four-letter word ['fɔːletə-'] *n* obscénité *f*,
gros mot
four-poster ['fɔː'pəustə-'] *n* (*also:* **~ bed**) lit *m* à
baldaquin
fourteen ['fɔː'tiːn] *num* quatorze
fourteenth ['fɔː'tiːnθ] *num* quatorzième

fourth [fɔːθ] num quatrième ▷ n (Aut: also: **~ gear**) quatrième f

four-wheel drive [fɔː'wiːl-] n (Aut: car) voiture f à quatre roues motrices; **with ~** à quatre roues motrices

fowl [faul] n volaille f

fox [fɒks] n renard m ▷ vt mystifier

foyer ['fɔɪeɪ] n (in hotel) vestibule m; (Theat) foyer m

fraction ['frækʃən] n fraction f

fracture ['fræktʃəʳ] n fracture f ▷ vt fracturer

fragile ['frædʒaɪl] adj fragile

fragment ['frægmənt] n fragment m

fragrance ['freɪgrəns] n parfum m

fragrant ['freɪgrənt] adj parfumé(e), odorant(e)

frail [freɪl] adj fragile, délicat(e); (person) frêle

frame [freɪm] n (of building) charpente f; (of human, animal) charpente, ossature f; (of picture) cadre m; (of door, window) encadrement m, chambranle m; (of spectacles: also: **~s**) monture f ▷ vt (picture) encadrer; (theory, plan) construire, élaborer; **to ~ sb** (inf) monter un coup contre qn; **~ of mind** disposition f d'esprit

framework ['freɪmwɜːk] n structure f

France [frɑːns] n la France; **in ~** en France

franchise ['fræntʃaɪz] n (Pol) droit m de vote; (Comm) franchise f

frank [fræŋk] adj franc/franche ▷ vt (letter) affranchir

frankly ['fræŋklɪ] adv franchement

frantic ['fræntɪk] adj (hectic) frénétique; (need, desire) effréné(e); (distraught) hors de soi

fraternity [frə'tɜːnɪtɪ] n (club) communauté f, confrérie f; (spirit) fraternité f

fraud [frɔːd] n supercherie f, fraude f, tromperie f; (person) imposteur m

fraught [frɔːt] adj (tense: person) très tendu(e); (: situation) pénible; **~ with** (difficulties etc) chargé(e), plein(e) de

fray [freɪ] n bagarre f; (Mil) combat m ▷ vt effilocher ▷ vi s'effilocher; **tempers were ~ed** les gens commençaient à s'énerver; **her nerves were ~ed** elle était à bout de nerfs

freak [friːk] n (eccentric person) phénomène m; (unusual event) hasard m extraordinaire; (pej: fanatic): **health food ~** fana m/f ou obsédé(e) de l'alimentation saine ▷ adj (storm) exceptionnel(le); (accident) bizarre; **freak out** vi (inf: drop out) se marginaliser; (: on drugs) se défoncer

freckle ['frɛkl] n tache f de rousseur

free [friː] adj libre; (gratis) gratuit(e); (liberal) généreux(-euse), large ▷ vt (prisoner etc) libérer; (jammed object or person) dégager; **is this seat ~?** la place est libre?; **to give sb a ~ hand** donner carte blanche à qn; **~ and easy** sans façon, décontracté(e); **admission ~** entrée libre; **~ (of charge)** gratuitement

freedom ['friːdəm] n liberté f

Freefone® ['friːfəun] n numéro vert

free-for-all ['friːfərɔːl] n mêlée générale

free gift n prime f

freehold ['friːhəuld] n propriété foncière libre

free kick n (Sport) coup franc

freelance ['friːlɑːns] adj (journalist etc) indépendant(e), free-lance inv; (work) en free-lance ▷ adv en free-lance

freely ['friːlɪ] adv librement; (liberally) libéralement

freemason ['friːmeɪsn] n franc-maçon m

Freepost® ['friːpəust] n (Brit) port payé

free-range ['friːreɪndʒ] adj (egg) de ferme; (chicken) fermier

free trade n libre-échange m

freeway ['friːweɪ] n (US) autoroute f

free will n libre arbitre m; **of one's own ~** de son plein gré

freeze [friːz] (pt **froze**, pp **frozen**) [frəuz, 'frəuzn] vi geler ▷ vt geler; (food) congeler; (prices, salaries) bloquer, geler ▷ n gel m; (of prices, salaries) blocage m; **freeze over** vi (river) geler; (windscreen) se couvrir de givre ou de glace; **freeze up** vi geler

freeze-dried ['friːzdraɪd] adj lyophilisé(e)

freezer ['friːzəʳ] n congélateur m

freezing ['friːzɪŋ] adj: **~ (cold)** (room etc) glacial(e); (person, hands) gelé(e), glacé(e) ▷ n: **3 degrees below ~** 3 degrés au-dessous de zéro; **it's ~** il fait un froid glacial

freezing point n point m de congélation

freight [freɪt] n (goods) fret m, cargaison f; (money charged) fret, prix m du transport; **~ forward** port dû; **~ inward** port payé par le destinataire

freight train n (US) train m de marchandises

French [frɛntʃ] adj français(e) ▷ n (Ling) français m; the **~** npl les Français; **what's the ~ (word) for ...?** comment dit-on ... en français?

French bean n (Brit) haricot vert

French bread n pain m français

French dressing n (Culin) vinaigrette f

French fried potatoes, (French fries) (US) npl (pommes de terre fpl) frites fpl

French horn n (Mus) cor m (d'harmonie)

French kiss n baiser profond

French loaf n = pain m, = parisien m

Frenchman irreg ['frɛntʃmən] n Français m

French stick n = baguette f

French window n porte-fenêtre f

Frenchwoman irreg ['frɛntʃwumən] n Française f

frenzy ['frɛnzɪ] n frénésie f

frequency ['friːkwənsɪ] n fréquence f

frequent adj ['friːkwənt] fréquent(e) ▷ vt [frɪ'kwɛnt] fréquenter

frequently ['friːkwəntlɪ] adv fréquemment

fresh [frɛʃ] adj frais/fraîche; (new) nouveau/ nouvelle; (cheeky) familier(-ière), culotté(e); **to make a ~ start** prendre un nouveau départ

freshen ['frɛʃən] vi (wind, air) fraîchir; **freshen up** vi faire un brin de toilette

fresher ['frɛʃə'] n (Brit University: inf) bizuth m, étudiant(e) de première année

freshly ['frɛʃlɪ] adv nouvellement, récemment

freshman (US) irreg ['frɛʃmən] n = **fresher**

freshness ['frɛʃnɪs] n fraîcheur f

freshwater ['frɛʃwɔ:tə'] adj (fish) d'eau douce

fret [frɛt] vi s'agiter, se tracasser

friar ['fraɪə'] n moine m, frère m

friction ['frɪkʃən] n friction f, frottement m

Friday ['fraɪdɪ] n vendredi m; see also **Tuesday**

fridge [frɪdʒ] n (Brit) frigo m, frigidaire® m

fried [fraɪd] pt, pp of **fry** ▷ adj frit(e); **~ egg** œuf m sur le plat

friend [frɛnd] n ami(e) ▷ vt (Internet) ajouter comme ami(e); **to make ~s with** se lier (d'amitié) avec

friendly ['frɛndlɪ] adj amical(e); (kind) sympathique, gentil(le); (place) accueillant(e); (Pol: country) ami(e) ▷ n (also: **~ match**) match amical; **to be ~ with** être ami(e) avec; **to be ~ to** être bien disposé(e) à l'égard de

friendship ['frɛndʃɪp] n amitié f

fries [fraɪz] (esp US) npl = **chips**

frieze [fri:z] n frise f, bordure f

frigate ['frɪgɪt] n (Naut: modern) frégate f

fright [fraɪt] n peur f, effroi m; **to give sb a ~** faire peur à qn; **to take ~** prendre peur, s'effrayer; **she looks a ~** elle a l'air d'un épouvantail

frighten ['fraɪtn] vt effrayer, faire peur à; **frighten away, frighten off** vt (birds, children etc) faire fuir, effaroucher

frightened ['fraɪtnd] adj: **to be ~ (of)** avoir peur (de)

frightening ['fraɪtnɪŋ] adj effrayant(e)

frightful ['fraɪtful] adj affreux(-euse)

frigid ['frɪdʒɪd] adj frigide

frill [frɪl] n (of dress) volant m; (of shirt) jabot m; **without ~s** (fig) sans manières

fringe [frɪndʒ] n (Brit: of hair) frange f; (edge: of forest etc) bordure f; (fig): **on the ~** en marge

fringe benefits npl avantages sociaux or en nature

Frisbee® ['frɪzbɪ] n Frisbee® m

frisk [frɪsk] vt fouiller

fritter ['frɪtə'] n beignet m; **fritter away** vt gaspiller

frivolous ['frɪvələs] adj frivole

frizzy ['frɪzɪ] adj crépu(e)

fro [frəʊ] adv see **to**

frock [frɔk] n robe f

frog [frɔg] n grenouille f; **to have a ~ in one's throat** avoir un chat dans la gorge

frogman irreg ['frɔgmən] n homme-grenouille m

frolic ['frɔlɪk] n ébats mpl ▷ vi folâtrer, batifoler

 KEYWORD

from [frɔm] prep **1** (indicating starting place, origin etc) de; **where do you come from?, where are you from?** d'où venez-vous?; **where has he come from?** d'où arrive-t-il?; **from London to Paris** de Londres à Paris; **to escape from sb/sth** échapper à qn/qch; **a letter/telephone call from my sister** une lettre/un appel de ma sœur; **to drink from the bottle** boire à (même) la bouteille; **tell him from me that ...** dites-lui de ma part que ...

2 (indicating time) (à partir) de; **from one o'clock to or until or till two** d'une heure à deux heures; **from January (on)** à partir de janvier

3 (indicating distance) de; **the hotel is one kilometre from the beach** l'hôtel est à un kilomètre de la plage

4 (indicating price, number etc) de; **prices range from £10 to £50** les prix varient entre 10 livres et 50 livres; **the interest rate was increased from 9% to 10%** le taux d'intérêt est passé de 9% à 10%

5 (indicating difference) de; **he can't tell red from green** il ne peut pas distinguer le rouge du vert; **to be different from sb/sth** être différent de qn/qch

6 (because of, on the basis of): **from what he says** d'après ce qu'il dit; **weak from hunger** affaibli par la faim

front [frʌnt] n (of house, dress) devant m; (of coach, train) avant m; (of book) couverture f; (promenade: also: **sea ~**) bord m de mer; (Mil, Pol, Meteorology) front m; (fig: appearances) contenance f, façade f ▷ adj de devant; (page, row) premier(-ière); (seat, wheel) avant inv ▷ vi: **to ~ onto sth** donner sur qch; **in ~ (of)** devant

frontage ['frʌntɪdʒ] n façade f; (of shop) devanture f

front door n porte f d'entrée; (of car) portière f avant

frontier ['frʌntɪə'] n frontière f

front page n première page

front room n (Brit) pièce f de devant, salon m

front-wheel drive ['frʌntwi:l-] n traction f avant

frost [frɔst] n gel m, gelée f; (also: **hoar~**) givre m

frostbite ['frɔstbaɪt] n gelures fpl

frosted ['frɔstɪd] adj (glass) dépoli(e); (esp US: cake) glacé(e)

frosting ['frɔstɪŋ] n (esp US: on cake) glaçage m

frosty ['frɔstɪ] adj (window) couvert(e) de givre; (weather, welcome) glacial(e)

froth [frɔθ] n mousse f; écume f

frown [fraʊn] n froncement m de sourcils ▷ vi froncer les sourcils; **frown on** vt (fig) désapprouver

froze [frəuz] *pt of* **freeze**

frozen ['frəuzn] *pp of* **freeze** ▷ *adj* (*food*) congelé(e); (*very cold: person: Comm: assets*) gelé(e)

fruit [fru:t] *n* (*pl inv*) fruit *m*

fruiterer ['fru:tərə^r] *n* fruitier *m*, marchand(e) de fruits; **~'s** (**shop**) fruiterie *f*

fruitful ['fru:tful] *adj* fructueux(-euse); (*plant, soil*) fécond(e)

fruition [fru:'ɪʃən] *n*: **to come to ~** se réaliser

fruit juice *n* jus *m* de fruit

fruit machine *n* (*Brit*) machine *f* à sous

fruit salad *n* salade *f* de fruits

frustrate [frʌs'treɪt] *vt* frustrer; (*plot, plans*) faire échouer

frustrated [frʌs'treɪtɪd] *adj* frustré(e)

fry (*pt, pp* **fried**) [fraɪ, -d] *vt* (faire) frire ▷ *n*: **small ~** le menu fretin

frying pan ['fraɪɪŋ-] *n* poêle *f* (à frire)

ft. *abbr* = **foot; feet**

fudge [fʌdʒ] *n* (*Culin*) sorte de confiserie à base de sucre, de beurre et de lait ▷ *vt* (*issue, problem*) esquiver

fuel [fjuəl] *n* (*for heating*) combustible *m*; (*for engine*) carburant *m*

fuel oil *n* mazout *m*

fuel poverty pauvreté *f* énergétique

fuel tank *n* cuve *f* à mazout, citerne *f*; (*in vehicle*) réservoir *m* de or à carburant

fugitive ['fju:dʒɪtɪv] *n* fugitif(-ive)

fulfil, (*US*) **fulfill** [ful'fɪl] *vt* (*function, condition*) remplir; (*order*) exécuter; (*wish, desire*) satisfaire, réaliser

fulfilment, (*US*) **fulfillment** [ful'fɪlmənt] *n* (*of wishes*) réalisation *f*

full [ful] *adj* plein(e); (*details, hotel, bus*) complet(-ète); (*price*) fort(e), normal(e); (*busy: day*) chargé(e); (*skirt*) ample, large ▷ *adv*: **to know ~ well that** savoir fort bien que; **~ (up)** (*hotel etc*) complet(-ète); **I'm ~ (up)** j'ai bien mangé; **~ employment/fare** plein emploi/tarif; **a ~ two hours** deux bonnes heures; **at ~ speed** à toute vitesse; **in ~** (*reproduce, quote, pay*) intégralement; (*write name etc*) en toutes lettres

full-length ['ful'leŋθ] *adj* (*portrait*) en pied; (*coat*) long(ue); **~ film** long métrage

full moon *n* pleine lune

full-scale ['fulskeɪl] *adj* (*model*) grandeur nature *inv*; (*search, retreat*) complet(-ète), total(e)

full stop *n* point *m*

full-time ['ful'taɪm] *adj, adv* (*work*) à plein temps ▷ *n* (*Sport*) fin *f* du match

fully ['fulɪ] *adv* entièrement, complètement; (*at least*): **~ as big** au moins aussi grand

fully-fledged ['fulɪ'fledʒd] *adj* (*teacher, barrister*) diplômé(e); (*citizen, member*) à part entière

fumble ['fʌmbl] *vi* fouiller, tâtonner ▷ *vt* (*ball*) mal réceptionner, cafouiller; **fumble with** *vt fus* tripoter

fume [fju:m] *vi* (*rage*) rager

fumes [fju:mz] *npl* vapeurs *fpl*, émanations *fpl*, gaz *mpl*

fun [fʌn] *n* amusement *m*, divertissement *m*; **to have ~** s'amuser; **for ~** pour rire; **it's not much ~** ce n'est pas très drôle *or* amusant; **to make ~ of** se moquer de

function ['fʌŋkʃən] *n* fonction *f*; (*reception, dinner*) cérémonie *f*, soirée officielle ▷ *vi* fonctionner; **to ~ as** faire office de

functional ['fʌŋkʃənl] *adj* fonctionnel(le)

fund [fʌnd] *n* caisse *f*, fonds *m*; (*source, store*) source *f*, mine *f*; **funds** *npl* (*money*) fonds *mpl*

fundamental [fʌndə'mentl] *adj* fondamental(e); **fundamentals** *npl* principes *mpl* de base

funeral ['fju:nərəl] *n* enterrement *m*, obsèques *fpl* (*more formal occasion*)

funeral director *n* entrepreneur *m* des pompes funèbres

funeral parlour *n* (*Brit*) dépôt *m* mortuaire

funeral service *n* service *m* funèbre

funfair ['fʌnfeə^r] *n* (*Brit*) fête (foraine)

fungus (*pl* **fungi**) ['fʌŋgəs, -gaɪ] *n* champignon *m*; (*mould*) moisissure *f*

funnel ['fʌnl] *n* entonnoir *m*; (*of ship*) cheminée *f*

funny ['fʌnɪ] *adj* amusant(e), drôle; (*strange*) curieux(-euse), bizarre

fur [fə:^r] *n* fourrure *f*; (*Brit: in kettle etc*) (dépôt *m* de) tartre *m*

fur coat *n* manteau *m* de fourrure

furious ['fjuərɪəs] *adj* furieux(-euse); (*effort*) acharné(e); **to be ~ with sb** être dans une fureur noire contre qn

furlong ['fə:lɔŋ] *n* = 201.17 m (*terme d'hippisme*)

furnace ['fə:nɪs] *n* fourneau *m*

furnish ['fə:nɪʃ] *vt* meubler; (*supply*) fournir; **~ed flat** *or* (*US*) **apartment** meublé *m*

furnishings ['fə:nɪʃɪŋz] *npl* mobilier *m*, articles *mpl* d'ameublement

furniture ['fə:nɪtʃə^r] *n* meubles *mpl*, mobilier *m*; **piece of ~** meuble *m*

furrow ['fʌrəu] *n* sillon *m*

furry ['fə:rɪ] *adj* (*animal*) à fourrure; (*toy*) en peluche

further ['fə:ðə^r] *adj* supplémentaire, autre; nouveau/nouvelle ▷ *adv* plus loin; (*more*) davantage; (*moreover*) de plus ▷ *vt* faire avancer *or* progresser, promouvoir; **how much ~ is it?** quelle distance *or* combien reste-t-il à parcourir?; **until ~ notice** jusqu'à nouvel ordre *or* avis; **~ to your letter of ...** (*Comm*) suite à votre lettre du ...

further education *n* enseignement *m* postscolaire (*recyclage, formation professionnelle*)

furthermore [fə:ðə'mɔ:^r] *adv* de plus, en outre

furthest ['fə:ðɪst] *superlative of* **far**

fury ['fjuərɪ] *n* fureur *f*

fuse, (US) **fuze** [fjuːz] n fusible m; (for bomb etc) amorce f, détonateur m ▷ vt, vi (metal) fondre; (fig) fusionner; (Brit: Elec): **to ~ the lights** faire sauter les fusibles or les plombs; **a ~ has blown** un fusible a sauté

fuse box n boîte f à fusibles

fusion ['fjuːʒən] n fusion f

fuss [fʌs] n (anxiety, excitement) chichis mpl, façons fpl; (commotion) tapage m; (complaining, trouble) histoire(s) f(pl) ▷ vi faire des histoires ▷ vt (person) embêter; **to make a ~** faire des façons (or des histoires); **to make a ~ of sb** dorloter qn; **fuss over** vt fus (person) dorloter

fussy ['fʌsɪ] adj (person) tatillon(ne), difficile, chichiteux(-euse); (dress, style) tarabiscoté(e); **I'm not ~** (inf) ça m'est égal

future ['fjuːtʃə'] adj futur(e) ▷ n avenir m; (Ling) futur m; **futures** npl (Comm) opérations fpl à terme; **in (the) ~** à l'avenir; **in the near/ immediate ~** dans un avenir proche/ immédiat

fuze [fjuːz] n, vt, vi (US) = **fuse**

fuzzy ['fʌzɪ] adj (Phot) flou(e); (hair) crépu(e)

FYI abbr = **for your information**

g

G¹, g [dʒiː] n (letter) G, g m; (Mus): **G** sol m; **G for George** G comme Gaston

G² n abbr (Brit Scol: = good) b (= bien); (US Cine: = general (audience)) ≈ tous publics; (Pol: = G8) G8 m

g. abbr (= gram) g; (= gravity) g

gabble ['gæbl] vi bredouiller; jacasser

gable ['geɪbl] n pignon m

gadget ['gædʒɪt] n gadget m

Gaelic ['geɪlɪk] adj, n (Ling) gaélique (m)

gag [gæg] n (on mouth) bâillon m; (joke) gag m ▷ vt (prisoner etc) bâillonner ▷ vi (choke) étouffer

gaiety ['geɪɪtɪ] n gaieté f

gain [geɪn] n (improvement) gain m; (profit) gain, profit m ▷ vt gagner ▷ vi (watch) avancer; **to ~ from/by** gagner de/à; **to ~ on sb** (catch up) rattraper qn; **to ~ 3lbs (in weight)** prendre 3 livres; **to ~ ground** gagner du terrain

gal. abbr = **gallon**

gala ['gaːlə] n gala m; **swimming ~** grand concours de natation

galaxy ['gæləksɪ] n galaxie f

gale [geɪl] n coup m de vent; **~ force 10** vent m de force 10

gallant ['gælənt] adj vaillant(e), brave; (towards ladies) empressé(e), galant(e)

gall bladder ['gɔːl-] n vésicule f biliaire

gallery ['gælərɪ] n galerie f; (also: **art ~**) musée m; (: private) galerie; (for spectators) tribune f; (: in theatre) dernier balcon

gallon ['gæln] n gallon m (Brit = 4.543 l; US = 3.785 l), = 8 pints

gallop ['gæləp] n galop m ▷ vi galoper; **~ing inflation** inflation galopante

gallows ['gæləuz] n potence f

gallstone ['gɔːlstəun] n calcul m (biliaire)

galore [gə'lɔːʳ] adv en abondance, à gogo

Gambia ['gæmbɪə] n Gambie f

gambit ['gæmbɪt] n (fig): **(opening) ~** manœuvre f stratégique

gamble ['gæmbl] n pari m, risque calculé ▷ vt, vi jouer; **to ~ on the Stock Exchange** jouer en or à la Bourse; **to ~ on** (fig) miser sur

gambler ['gæmbləʳ] n joueur m

gambling ['gæmblɪŋ] n jeu m

game [geɪm] n jeu m; (event) match m; (of tennis, chess, cards) partie f; (Hunting) gibier m ▷ adj brave; (willing): **to be ~ (for)** être prêt(e) (à or pour); **a ~ of football/tennis** une partie de football/tennis; **big ~** gros gibier; **games** npl (Scol) sport m; (sport event) jeux

gamekeeper ['geɪmkiːpəʳ] n garde-chasse m

gamer ['geɪməʳ] n joueur(-euse) de jeux vidéos

games console ['geɪmz-] n console f de jeux vidéo

game show ['geɪmʃəu] n jeu télévisé

gaming ['geɪmɪŋ] n (video games) jeux mpl vidéos

gammon ['gæmən] n (bacon) quartier m de lard fumé; (ham) jambon fumé or salé

gamut ['gæmət] n gamme f

gang [gæŋ] n bande f, groupe m; (of workmen) équipe f; **gang up** vi: **to ~ up on sb** se liguer contre qn

gangster ['gæŋstəʳ] n gangster m, bandit m

gangway ['gæŋweɪ] n passerelle f; (Brit: of bus) couloir central

gaol [dʒeɪl] n, vt (Brit) = **jail**

gap [gæp] n trou m; (in time) intervalle m; (fig) lacune f; vide m; (difference): **~ (between)** écart m (entre)

gape [geɪp] vi (person) être or rester bouche bée; (hole, shirt) être ouvert(e)

gaping ['geɪpɪŋ] adj (hole) béant(e)

gap year n année que certains étudiants prennent pour voyager ou pour travailler avant d'entrer à l'université

garage ['gærɑːʒ] n garage m

garage sale n vide-grenier m

garbage ['gɑːbɪdʒ] n (US: rubbish) ordures fpl, détritus mpl; (inf: nonsense) âneries fpl

garbage can n (US) poubelle f, boîte f à ordures

garbage collector n (US) éboueur m

garbled ['gɑːbld] adj déformé(e), faussé(e)

garden ['gɑːdn] n jardin m ▷ vi jardiner; **gardens** npl (public) jardin public; (private) parc m

garden centre (Brit) n pépinière f, jardinerie f

gardener ['gɑːdnəʳ] n jardinier m

gardening ['gɑːdnɪŋ] n jardinage m

gargle ['gɑːgl] vi se gargariser ▷ n gargarisme m

garish ['gɛərɪʃ] adj criard(e), voyant(e)

garland ['gɑːlənd] n guirlande f; couronne f

garlic ['gɑːlɪk] n ail m

garment ['gɑːmənt] n vêtement m

garnish ['gɑːnɪʃ] (Culin) vt garnir ▷ n décoration f

garrison ['gærɪsn] n garnison f ▷ vt mettre en garnison, stationner

garter ['gɑːtəʳ] n jarretière f; (US: suspender) jarretelle f

gas [gæs] n gaz m; (used as anaesthetic): **to be given ~** se faire endormir; (US: gasoline) essence f ▷ vt asphyxier; (Mil) gazer; **I can smell ~** ça sent le gaz

gas cooker n (Brit) cuisinière f à gaz

gas cylinder n bouteille f de gaz

gas fire n (Brit) radiateur m à gaz

gash [gæʃ] n entaille f; (on face) balafre f ▷ vt taillader; balafrer

gasket ['gæskɪt] n (Aut) joint m de culasse

gas mask n masque m à gaz

gas meter n compteur m à gaz

gasoline ['gæsəliːn] n (US) essence f

gasp [gɑːsp] n halètement m; (of shock etc): **she gave a small ~ of pain** la douleur lui coupa le souffle ▷ vi haleter; (fig) avoir le souffle coupé; **gasp out** vt (say) dire dans un souffle or d'une voix entrecoupée

gas pedal n (US) accélérateur m

gas ring n brûleur m

gas station n (US) station-service f

gas tank n (US Aut) réservoir m d'essence

gas tap n bouton m (de cuisinière à gaz); (on pipe) robinet m à gaz

gastric ['gæstrɪk] adj gastrique

gate [geɪt] n (of garden) portail m; (of field, at level crossing) barrière f; (of building, town, at airport) porte f; (of lock) vanne f

gateau (pl **gateaux**) ['gætəu, -z] n gros gâteau à la crème

gatecrash ['geɪtkræʃ] vt s'introduire sans invitation dans

gateway ['geɪtweɪ] n porte f

gather ['gæðəʳ] vt (flowers, fruit) cueillir; (pick up) ramasser; (assemble: objects) rassembler; (: people) réunir; (: information) recueillir; (understand) comprendre; (Sewing) froncer ▷ vi (assemble) se rassembler; (dust) s'amasser; (clouds) s'amonceler; **to ~ (from/that)** conclure or déduire (de/que); **as far as I can ~** d'après ce que je comprends; **to ~ speed** prendre de la vitesse

gathering ['gæðərɪŋ] n rassemblement m

gaudy ['gɔːdɪ] adj voyant(e)

gauge [geɪdʒ] n (standard measure) calibre m; (Rail) écartement m; (instrument) jauge f ▷ vt jauger; (fig: sb's capabilities, character) juger de; **to ~ the right moment** calculer le moment propice; **petrol ~**, (US) **gas ~** jauge d'essence

gaunt [gɔ:nt] adj décharné(e); (grim, desolate) désolé(e)

gauntlet ['gɔ:ntlɪt] n (fig): **to throw down the ~** jeter le gant; **to run the ~ through an angry crowd** se frayer un passage à travers une foule hostile or entre deux haies de manifestants etc hostiles

gauze [gɔ:z] n gaze f

gave [geɪv] pt of **give**

gay [geɪ] adj (homosexual) homosexuel(le); (slightly old-fashioned: cheerful) gai(e), réjoui(e); (colour) gai, vif/vive

gaze [geɪz] n regard m fixe ▷ vi: **to ~ at** vt fixer du regard

gazump [gə'zʌmp] vi (Brit) revenir sur une promesse de vente pour accepter un prix plus élevé

GB abbr = **Great Britain**

GCE n abbr (Brit) = **General Certificate of Education**

GCSE n abbr (Brit: = General Certificate of Secondary Education) examen passé à l'âge de 16 ans sanctionnant les connaissances de l'élève; **she's got eight ~s** elle a réussi dans huit matières aux épreuves du GCSE

gear [gɪər] n matériel m, équipement m; (Tech) engrenage m; (Aut) vitesse f ▷ vt (fig: adapt) adapter; **top** or (US) **high/low** = quatrième (or cinquième)/première vitesse; **in** = en prise; **out of ~** au point mort; **our service is ~ed to meet the needs of the disabled** notre service répond de façon spécifique aux besoins des handicapés; **gear up** vi: **to ~ up (to do)** se préparer (à faire)

gear box n boîte f de vitesse

gear lever n levier m de vitesse

gear shift (US) n = **gear lever**

gear stick (Brit) n = **gear lever**

geese [gi:s] npl of **goose**

gel [dʒɛl] n gelée f; (Chem) colloïde m

gem [dʒɛm] n pierre précieuse

Gemini ['dʒɛmɪnaɪ] n les Gémeaux mpl; **to be ~** être des Gémeaux

gender ['dʒɛndər] n genre m; (person's sex) sexe m

gene [dʒi:n] n (Biol) gène m

general ['dʒɛnərl] n général m ▷ adj général(e); **in ~** en général; **the ~ public** le grand public; **~ audit** (Comm) vérification f annuelle

general anaesthetic, (US) **general anesthetic** n anesthésie générale

general delivery n poste restante

general election n élection(s) législative(s)

generalize ['dʒɛnrəlaɪz] vi généraliser

general knowledge n connaissances générales

generally ['dʒɛnrəlɪ] adv généralement

general practitioner n généraliste m/f

general store n épicerie f

generate ['dʒɛnəreɪt] vt engendrer; (electricity) produire

generation [dʒɛnə'reɪʃən] n génération f; (of electricity etc) production f

generator ['dʒɛnəreɪtər] n générateur m

generosity [dʒɛnə'rɔsɪtɪ] n générosité f

generous ['dʒɛnərəs] adj généreux(-euse); (copious) copieux(-euse)

genetic [dʒɪ'nɛtɪk] adj génétique; **~ engineering** ingénierie m génétique; **~ fingerprinting** système m d'empreinte génétique

genetically modified adj (food etc) génétiquement modifié(e)

genetics [dʒɪ'nɛtɪks] n génétique f

Geneva [dʒɪ'ni:və] n Genève; **Lake ~** le lac Léman

genial ['dʒi:nɪəl] adj cordial(e), chaleureux(-euse); (climate) clément(e)

genitals ['dʒɛnɪtlz] npl organes génitaux

genius ['dʒi:nɪəs] n génie m

gent [dʒɛnt] n abbr (Brit inf) = **gentleman**

genteel [dʒɛn'ti:l] adj de bon ton, distingué(e)

gentle ['dʒɛntl] adj doux/douce; (breeze, touch) léger(-ère)

gentleman irreg ['dʒɛntlmən] n monsieur m; (well-bred man) gentleman m; **~'s agreement** gentleman's agreement m

gently ['dʒɛntlɪ] adv doucement

gentry ['dʒɛntrɪ] n petite noblesse

gents [dʒɛnts] n W.-C. mpl (pour hommes)

genuine ['dʒɛnjuɪn] adj véritable, authentique; (person, emotion) sincère

genuinely ['dʒɛnjuɪnlɪ] adv sincèrement, vraiment

geographic [dʒɪə'græfɪk], **geographical** [dʒɪə'græfɪkl] adj géographique

geography [dʒɪ'ɔgrəfɪ] n géographie f

geology [dʒɪ'ɔlədʒɪ] n géologie f

geometric [dʒɪə'mɛtrɪk], **geometrical** [dʒɪə'mɛtrɪkl] adj géométrique

geometry [dʒɪ'ɔmətrɪ] n géométrie f

geranium [dʒɪ'reɪnɪəm] n géranium m

geriatric [dʒɛrɪ'ætrɪk] adj gériatrique ▷ n patient(e) gériatrique

germ [dʒə:m] n (Med) microbe m; (Biol: fig) germe m

German ['dʒə:mən] adj allemand(e) ▷ n Allemand(e); (Ling) allemand m

German measles n rubéole f

Germany ['dʒə:mənɪ] n Allemagne f

gesture ['dʒɛstjər] n geste m; **as a ~ of friendship** en témoignage d'amitié

 KEYWORD

get [gɛt] (pt, pp **got**, US: pp **gotten**) vi **1** (become, be) devenir; **to get old/tired** devenir vieux/fatigué, vieillir/se fatiguer; **to get drunk** s'enivrer; **to get ready/washed/shaved** etc se préparer/laver/raser etc; **to get killed** se faire tuer; **to get dirty** se salir; **to get married** se marier; **when do I get paid?**

quand est-ce que je serai payé?; **it's getting late** il se fait tard

2 (*go*): **to get to/from** aller à/de; **to get home** rentrer chez soi; **how did you get here?** comment es-tu arrivé ici?; **he got across the bridge/under the fence** il a traversé le pont/est passé au-dessous de la barrière

3 (*begin*) commencer or se mettre à; **to get to know sb** apprendre à connaître qn; **I'm getting to like him** je commence à l'apprécier; **let's get going** or **started** allons-y

4 (*modal aux vb*): **you've got to do it** il faut que vous le fassiez; **I've got to tell the police** je dois le dire à la police

▷ *vt* **1**: **to get sth done** (*do*) faire qch; (*have done*) faire faire qch; **to get sth/sb ready** préparer qch/qn; **to get one's hair cut** se faire couper les cheveux; **to get the car going** or **to go** (faire) démarrer la voiture; **to get sb to do sth** faire faire qch à qn; **to get sb drunk** enivrer qn

2 (*obtain*: *money, permission, results*) obtenir, avoir; (*buy*) acheter; (*find*: *job, flat*) trouver; (*fetch*: *person, doctor, object*) aller chercher; **to get sth for sb** procurer qch à qn; **get me Mr Jones, please** (*on phone*) passez-moi Mr Jones, s'il vous plaît; **can I get you a drink?** est-ce que je peux vous servir à boire?

3 (*receive*: *present, letter*) recevoir, avoir; (*acquire*: *reputation*) avoir; (*prize*) obtenir; **what did you get for your birthday?** qu'est-ce que tu as eu pour ton anniversaire?; **how much did you get for the painting?** combien avez-vous vendu le tableau?

4 (*catch*) prendre, saisir, attraper; (*hit*: *target etc*) atteindre; **to get sb by the arm/throat** prendre or saisir or attraper qn par le bras/à la gorge; **get him!** arrête-le!; **the bullet got him in the leg** il a pris la balle dans la jambe; **he really gets me!** il me porte sur les nerfs!

5 (*take, move*): **to get sth to sb** faire parvenir qch à qn; **do you think we'll get it through the door?** on arrivera à le faire passer par la porte?; **I'll get you there somehow** je me débrouillerai pour t'y emmener

6 (*catch, take*: *plane, bus etc*) prendre; **where do I get the train for Birmingham?** où prend-on le train pour Birmingham?

7 (*understand*) comprendre, saisir; (*hear*) entendre; **I've got it!** j'ai compris!; **I don't get your meaning** je ne vois or comprends pas ce que vous voulez dire; **I didn't get your name** je n'ai pas entendu votre nom

8 (*have, possess*): **to have got** avoir; **how many have you got?** vous en avez combien?

9 (*illness*) avoir; **I've got a cold** j'ai le rhume; **she got pneumonia and died** elle a fait une pneumonie et elle en est morte

get about *vi* se déplacer; (*news*) se répandre

get across *vt*: **to get across (to)** (*message, meaning*) faire passer (à)

▷ *vi*: **to get across (to)** (*speaker*) se faire comprendre (par)

get along *vi* (*agree*) s'entendre; (*depart*) s'en aller; (*manage*) = **get by**

get at *vt fus* (*attack*) s'en prendre à; (*reach*) attraper, atteindre; **what are you getting at?** à quoi voulez-vous en venir?

get away *vi* partir, s'en aller; (*escape*) s'échapper

get away with *vt fus* (*punishment*) en être quitte pour; (*crime etc*) se faire pardonner

get back *vi* (*return*) rentrer

▷ *vt* récupérer, recouvrer; **to get back to** (*start again*) retourner or revenir à; (*contact again*) recontacter; **when do we get back?** quand serons-nous de retour?

get back at *vt fus* (*inf*): **to get back at sb** rendre la monnaie de sa pièce à qn

get by *vi* (*pass*) passer; (*manage*) se débrouiller; **I can get by in Dutch** je me débrouille en hollandais

get down *vi, vt fus* descendre

▷ *vt* descendre; (*depress*) déprimer

get down to *vt fus* (*work*) se mettre à (faire); **to get down to business** passer aux choses sérieuses

get in *vi* entrer; (*arrive home*) rentrer; (*train*) arriver

▷ *vt* (*bring in*: *harvest*) rentrer; (: *coal*) faire rentrer; (: *supplies*) faire des provisions de

get into *vt fus* entrer dans; (*car, train etc*) monter dans; (*clothes*) mettre, enfiler, endosser; **to get into bed/a rage** se mettre au lit/en colère

get off *vi* (*from train etc*) descendre; (*depart*: *person, car*) s'en aller; (*escape*) s'en tirer

▷ *vt* (*remove*: *clothes, stain*) enlever; (*send off*) expédier; (*have as leave*: *day, time*): **we got 2 days off** nous avons eu 2 jours de congé

▷ *vt fus* (*train, bus*) descendre de; **where do I get off?** où est-ce que je dois descendre?; **to get off to a good start** (*fig*) prendre un bon départ

get on *vi* (*at exam etc*) se débrouiller; (*agree*): **to get on (with)** s'entendre (avec); **how are you getting on?** comment ça va?

▷ *vt fus* monter dans; (*horse*) monter sur

get on to *vt fus* (*Brit*: *deal with*: *problem*) s'occuper de; (*contact*: *person*) contacter

get out *vi* sortir; (*of vehicle*) descendre; (*news etc*) s'ébruiter

▷ *vt* sortir

get out of *vt fus* sortir de; (*duty etc*) échapper à, se soustraire à

get over *vt fus* (*illness*) se remettre de

▷ *vt* (*communicate*: *idea etc*) communiquer; (*finish*): **let's get it over (with)** finissons-en

get round *vi*: **to get round to doing sth** se mettre (finalement) à faire qch

▷ *vt fus* contourner; (*fig*: *person*) entortiller

get through vi (Tel) avoir la communication; **to get through to sb** atteindre qn
▷ vt fus (finish: work, book) finir, terminer
get together vi se réunir
▷ vt rassembler
get up vi (rise) se lever
▷ vt fus monter
get up to vt fus (reach) arriver à; (prank etc) faire

getaway ['gɛtəweɪ] n fuite f
geyser ['giːzəʳ] n chauffe-eau m inv; (Geo) geyser m
Ghana ['gɑːnə] n Ghana m
ghastly ['gɑːstlɪ] adj atroce, horrible; (pale) livide, blême
gherkin ['gəːkɪn] n cornichon m
ghetto ['gɛtəu] n ghetto m
ghetto blaster [-blɑːstəʳ] n (inf) gros radiocassette
ghost [gəust] n fantôme m, revenant m ▷ vt (sb else's book) écrire
giant ['dʒaɪənt] n géant(e) ▷ adj géant(e), énorme; (size) packet géant
gibberish ['dʒɪbərɪʃ] n charabia m
giblets ['dʒɪblɪts] npl abats mpl
Gibraltar [dʒɪ'brɔːltəʳ] n Gibraltar m
giddy ['gɪdɪ] adj (dizzy): **to be** (or **feel**) ~ avoir le vertige; (height) vertigineux(-euse); (thoughtless) sot(te), étourdi(e)
gift [gɪft] n cadeau m, présent m; (donation, talent) don m; (Comm: also: **free ~**) cadeau(-réclame) m; **to have a ~ for sth** avoir des dons pour or le don de qch
gifted ['gɪftɪd] adj doué(e)
gift shop, (US) **gift store** n boutique f de cadeaux
gift token, gift voucher n chèque-cadeau m
gig [gɪg] n (inf: concert) concert m
gigabyte ['dʒɪgəbaɪt] n gigaoctet m
gigantic [dʒaɪ'gæntɪk] adj gigantesque
giggle ['gɪgl] vi pouffer, ricaner sottement ▷ n petit rire sot, ricanement m
gill [dʒɪl] n (measure) = 0.25 pints (Brit = 0.148 l; US = 0.118 l)
gills [gɪlz] npl (of fish) ouïes fpl, branchies fpl
gilt [gɪlt] n dorure f ▷ adj doré(e)
gilt-edged ['gɪltedʒd] adj (stocks, securities) de premier ordre
gimmick ['gɪmɪk] n truc m; **sales ~** offre promotionnelle
gin [dʒɪn] n gin m
ginger ['dʒɪndʒəʳ] n gingembre m; **ginger up** vt secouer; animer
ginger ale, ginger beer n boisson gazeuse au gingembre
gingerbread ['dʒɪndʒəbred] n pain m d'épices
gingerly ['dʒɪndʒəlɪ] adv avec précaution
gipsy ['dʒɪpsɪ] n = **gypsy**
giraffe [dʒɪ'rɑːf] n girafe f

girder ['gəːdəʳ] n poutrelle f
girl [gəːl] n fille f, fillette f; (young unmarried woman) jeune fille; (daughter) fille; **an English ~** une jeune Anglaise; **a little English ~** une petite Anglaise
girl band n girls band m
girlfriend ['gəːlfrend] n (of girl) amie f; (of boy) petite amie
Girl Guide n (Brit) éclaireuse f; (Roman Catholic) guide f
girlish ['gəːlɪʃ] adj de jeune fille
Girl Scout n (US) = **Girl Guide**
giro ['dʒaɪrəu] n (bank giro) virement m bancaire; (post office giro) mandat m
gist [dʒɪst] n essentiel m
give [gɪv] (pt **gave**, pp **given**) (geɪv, 'gɪvn] n (of fabric) élasticité f ▷ vt donner ▷ vi (break) céder; (stretch: fabric) se prêter; **to ~ sb sth, ~ sth to sb** donner qch à qn; (gift) offrir qch à qn; (message) transmettre qch à qn; **to ~ sb a call/kiss** appeler/embrasser qn; **to ~ a cry/sigh** pousser un cri/un soupir; **how much did you ~ for it?** combien (l')avez-vous payé?; **12 o'clock, ~ or take a few minutes** midi, à quelques minutes près; **to ~ way** céder; (Brit Aut) donner la priorité; **give away** vt donner; (give free) faire cadeau de; (betray) donner, trahir; (disclose) révéler; (bride) conduire à l'autel; **give back** vt rendre; **give in** vi céder ▷ vt donner; **give off** vt dégager; **give out** vt (food etc) distribuer; (news) annoncer ▷ vi (be exhausted: supplies) s'épuiser; (fail) lâcher; **give up** vi renoncer ▷ vt renoncer à; **to ~ up smoking** arrêter de fumer; **to ~ o.s. up** se rendre
given ['gɪvn] pp of **give** ▷ adj (fixed: time, amount) donné(e), déterminé(e) ▷ conj: **~ the circumstances ...** étant donné les circonstances ..., vu les circonstances ...; **~ that ...** étant donné que ...
glacier ['glæsɪəʳ] n glacier m
glad [glæd] adj content(e); **to be ~ about sth/that** être heureux(-euse) or bien content de qch/que; **I was ~ of his help** j'étais bien content de (pouvoir compter sur) son aide or qu'il m'aide
gladly ['glædlɪ] adv volontiers
glamorous ['glæmərəs] adj (person) séduisant(e); (job) prestigieux(-euse)
glamour, (US) **glamor** ['glæməʳ] n éclat m, prestige m
glance [glɑːns] n coup m d'œil ▷ vi: **to ~ at** jeter un coup d'œil à; **glance off** vt fus (bullet) ricocher sur
glancing ['glɑːnsɪŋ] adj (blow) oblique
gland [glænd] n glande f
glare [glɛəʳ] n (of anger) regard furieux; (of light) lumière éblouissante; (of publicity) feux mpl ▷ vi briller d'un éclat aveuglant; **to ~ at** lancer un regard or des regards furieux à
glaring ['glɛərɪŋ] adj (mistake) criant(e), qui saute aux yeux

glass [glɑ:s] *n* verre *m*; (*also*: **looking ~**) miroir *m*; **glasses** *npl* (*spectacles*) lunettes *fpl*

glasshouse ['glɑ:shaus] *n* serre *f*

glassware ['glɑ:swɛəᵉ] *n* verrerie *f*

glaze [gleɪz] *vt* (*door*) vitrer; (*pottery*) vernir; (*Culin*) glacer ▷ *n* vernis *m*; (*Culin*) glaçage *m*

glazed [gleɪzd] *adj* (*eye*) vitreux(-euse); (*pottery*) verni(e); (*tiles*) vitrifié(e)

glazier ['gleɪzɪəᵉ] *n* vitrier *m*

gleam [gli:m] *n* lueur *f* ▷ *vi* luire, briller; **a ~ of hope** une lueur d'espoir

glean [gli:n] *vt* (*information*) recueillir

glee [gli:] *n* joie *f*

glen [glɛn] *n* vallée *f*

glib [glɪb] *adj* qui a du bagou; facile

glide [glaɪd] *vi* glisser; (*Aviat*, *bird*) planer ▷ *n* glissement *m*; vol plané

glider ['glaɪdəᵉ] *n* (*Aviat*) planeur *m*

gliding ['glaɪdɪŋ] *n* (*Aviat*) vol *m* à voile

glimmer ['glɪməᵉ] *vi* luire ▷ *n* lueur *f*

glimpse [glɪmps] *n* vision passagère, aperçu *m* ▷ *vt* entrevoir, apercevoir; **to catch a ~ of** entrevoir

glint [glɪnt] *n* éclair *m* ▷ *vi* étinceler

glisten ['glɪsn] *vi* briller, luire

glitter ['glɪtəᵉ] *vi* scintiller, briller ▷ *n* scintillement *m*

gloat [gləʊt] *vi*: **to ~ (over)** jubiler (à propos de)

global ['gləʊbl] *adj* (*world-wide*) mondial(e); (*overall*) global(e)

globalization [gləʊblaɪz'eɪʃən] *n* mondialisation *f*

global warming [-'wɔ:mɪŋ] *n* réchauffement *m* de la planète

globe [gləʊb] *n* globe *m*

gloom [glu:m] *n* obscurité *f*; (*sadness*) tristesse *f*, mélancolie *f*

gloomy ['glu:mɪ] *adj* (*person*) morose; (*place*, *outlook*) sombre; **to feel ~** avoir *or* se faire des idées noires

glorious ['glɔ:rɪəs] *adj* glorieux(-euse); (*beautiful*) splendide

glory ['glɔ:rɪ] *n* gloire *f*; splendeur *f* ▷ *vi*: **to ~ in** se glorifier de

gloss [glɔs] *n* (*shine*) brillant *m*, vernis *m*; (*also*: **~ paint**) peinture brillante *or* laquée; **gloss over** *vt fus* glisser sur

glossary ['glɔsərɪ] *n* glossaire *m*, lexique *m*

glossy ['glɔsɪ] *adj* brillant(e), luisant(e) ▷ *n* (*also*: **~ magazine**) revue *f* de luxe

glove [glʌv] *n* gant *m*

glove compartment *n* (*Aut*) boîte *f* à gants, vide-poches *m inv*

glow [gləʊ] *vi* rougeoyer; (*face*) rayonner; (*eyes*) briller ▷ *n* rougeoiement *m*

glower ['glauəᵉ] *vi* lancer des regards mauvais

glucose ['glu:kəʊs] *n* glucose *m*

glue [glu:] *n* colle *f* ▷ *vt* coller

glum [glʌm] *adj* maussade, morose

glut [glʌt] *n* surabondance *f* ▷ *vt* rassasier; (*market*) encombrer

glutton ['glʌtn] *n* glouton(ne); **a ~ for work** un bourreau de travail

GM *abbr* (= genetically modified) génétiquement modifié(e)

gm *abbr* (= gram) g

GMO *n abbr* (= genetically modified organism) OGM *m*

GMT *abbr* (= Greenwich Mean Time) GMT

gnat [næt] *n* moucheron *m*

gnaw [nɔ:] *vt* ronger

go [gəʊ] (*pt* **went**, *pp* **gone**) [wɛnt, gɔn] *vi* aller; (*depart*) partir, s'en aller; (*work*) marcher; (*break*) céder; (*time*) passer; (*be sold*): **to go for £10** se vendre 10 livres; (*become*): **to go pale/mouldy** pâlir/moisir ▷ *n* (*pl* **goes**); **to have a go (at)** essayer (de faire); **to be on the go** être en mouvement; **whose go is it?** à qui est-ce de jouer?; **to go by car/on foot** aller en voiture/à pied; **he's going to do it** il va le faire, il est sur le point de le faire; **to go for a walk** aller se promener; **to go dancing/shopping** aller danser/faire les courses; **to go looking for sb/sth** aller *or* partir à la recherche de qn/qch; **to go to sleep** s'endormir; **to go and see sb, go to see sb** aller voir qn; **how is it going?** comment ça marche?; **how did it go?** comment est-ce que ça s'est passé?; **to go round the back/by the shop** passer par derrière/devant le magasin; **my voice has gone** j'ai une extinction de voix; **the cake is all gone** il n'y a plus de gâteau; **I'll take whatever is going** (*Brit*) je prendrai ce qu'il y a (*or ce que vous avez*); **... to go** (*US*: *food*) ... à emporter; **go about** *vi* (*also*: **go around**) aller çà et là; (*rumour*) se répandre ▷ *vt fus*: **how do I go about this?** comment dois-je m'y prendre (pour faire ceci)?; **to go about one's business** s'occuper de ses affaires; **go after** *vt fus* (*pursue*) poursuivre, courir après; (*job*, *record etc*) essayer d'obtenir; **go against** *vt fus* (*be unfavourable to*) être défavorable à; (*be contrary to*) être contraire à; **go ahead** *vi* (*make progress*) avancer; (*take place*) avoir lieu; (*get going*) y aller; **go along** *vi* aller, avancer ▷ *vt fus* longer, parcourir; **as you go along** (*with your work*) au fur et à mesure (de votre travail); **to go along with** (*accompany*) accompagner; (*agree with*: *idea*) être d'accord sur; (: *person*) suivre; **go away** *vi* partir, s'en aller; **go back** *vi* rentrer; revenir; (*go again*) retourner; **go back on** *vt fus* (*promise*) revenir sur; **go by** *vi* (*years*, *time*) passer, s'écouler ▷ *vt fus* s'en tenir à; (*believe*) en croire; **go down** *vi* descendre; (*number*, *price*, *amount*) baisser; (*ship*) couler; (*sun*) se coucher ▷ *vt fus* descendre; **that should go down well with him** (*fig*) ça devrait lui plaire; **go for** *vt fus* (*fetch*) aller chercher; (*like*) aimer; (*attack*) s'en prendre à; attaquer; **go in** *vi* entrer;

go in for vt fus (competition) se présenter à; (like) aimer; **go into** vt fus entrer dans; (investigate) étudier, examiner; (embark on) se lancer dans; **go off** vi partir, s'en aller; (food) se gâter; (milk) tourner; (bomb) sauter; (alarm clock) sonner; (alarm) se déclencher; (lights etc) s'éteindre; (event) se dérouler ▷ vt fus ne plus aimer, ne plus avoir envie de; **the gun went off** le coup est parti; **to go off to sleep** s'endormir; **the party went off well** la fête s'est bien passée or était très réussie; **go on** vi continuer; (happen) se passer; (lights) s'allumer ▷ vt fus (be guided by: evidence etc) se fonder sur; **to go on doing** continuer à faire; **what's going on here?** qu'est-ce qui se passe ici?; **go on at** vt fus (nag) tomber sur le dos de; **go on with** vt fus poursuivre, continuer; **go out** vi sortir; (fire, light) s'éteindre; (tide) descendre; **to go out with sb** sortir avec qn; **go over** vi (ship) chavirer ▷ vt fus (check) revoir, vérifier; **to go over sth in one's mind** repasser qch dans son esprit; **go past** vt fus: **to go past sth** passer devant qch; **go round** vi (circulate: news, rumour) circuler; (revolve) tourner; (suffice) suffire (pour tout le monde); (visit): **to go round to sb's** passer chez qn; aller chez qn; (make a detour): **to go round (by)** faire un détour (par); **go through** vt fus (town etc) traverser; (search through) fouiller; (suffer) subir; (examine: list, book) lire or regarder en détail, éplucher; (perform: lesson) réciter; (: formalities) remplir; (: programme) exécuter; **go through with** vt fus (plan, crime) aller jusqu'au bout de; **go under** vi (sink: also fig) couler; (: person) succomber; **go up** vi monter; (price) augmenter ▷ vt fus gravir; (also: **go up in flames**) flamber, s'enflammer brusquement; **go with** vt fus aller avec; **go without** vt fus se passer de
goad [gəud] vt aiguillonner
go-ahead ['gəuəhɛd] adj dynamique, entreprenant(e) ▷ n feu vert
goal [gəul] n but m
goalkeeper ['gəulki:pəʳ] n gardien m de but
goal-post ['gəulpəust] n poteau m de but
goat [gəut] n chèvre f
gobble ['gɔbl] vt (also: **~ down**, **~ up**) engloutir
go-between ['gəubitwi:n] n médiateur m
god [gɔd] n dieu m; **G~** Dieu
godchild ['gɔdtʃaild] n filleul(e)
goddaughter ['gɔddɔ:təʳ] n filleule f
goddess ['gɔdis] n déesse f
godfather ['gɔdfɑ:ðəʳ] n parrain m
god-forsaken ['gɔdfəseikən] adj maudit(e)
godmother ['gɔdmʌðəʳ] n marraine f
godsend ['gɔdsend] n aubaine f
godson ['gɔdsʌn] n filleul m
goggles ['gɔglz] npl (for skiing etc) lunettes (protectrices); (for swimming) lunettes de piscine
going ['gəuiŋ] n (conditions) état m du terrain ▷ adj: **the ~ rate** le tarif (en vigueur); **a ~**

concern une affaire prospère; **it was slow ~** les progrès étaient lents, ça n'avançait pas vite
gold [gəuld] n or m ▷ adj en or; (reserves) d'or
golden ['gəuldən] adj (made of gold) en or; (gold in colour) doré(e)
goldfish ['gəuldfiʃ] n poisson m rouge
goldmine ['gəuldmain] n mine f d'or
gold-plated ['gəuld'pleitid] adj plaqué(e) or inv
goldsmith ['gəuldsmiθ] n orfèvre m
golf [gɔlf] n golf m
golf ball n balle f de golf; (on typewriter) boule f
golf club n club m de golf; (stick) club m, crosse f de golf
golf course n terrain m de golf
golfer ['gɔlfəʳ] n joueur(-euse) de golf
gone [gɔn] pp of **go** ▷ adj parti(e)
gong [gɔŋ] n gong m
good [gud] adj bon(ne); (kind) gentil(le); (child) sage; (weather) beau/belle ▷ n bien m; **goods** npl marchandise f, articles mpl; (Comm etc) marchandises; **~!** bon!, très bien!; **to be ~ at** être bon en; **to be ~ for** être bon pour; **it's ~ for you** c'est bon pour vous; **it's a ~ thing you were there** heureusement que vous étiez là; **she is ~ with children/her hands** elle sait bien s'occuper des enfants/sait se servir de ses mains; **to feel ~** se sentir bien; **it's ~ to see you** ça me fait plaisir de vous voir, je suis content de vous voir; **he's up to no ~** il prépare quelque mauvais coup; **it's no ~ complaining** cela ne sert à rien de se plaindre; **to make ~** (deficit) combler; (losses) compenser; **for the common ~** dans l'intérêt commun; **for ~** (for ever) pour de bon, une fois pour toutes; **would you be ~ enough to …?** auriez-vous la bonté or l'amabilité de …?; **that's very ~ of you** c'est très gentil de votre part; **is this any ~?** (will it do?) est-ce que ceci fera l'affaire?, est-ce que cela peut vous rendre service?; (what's it like?) qu'est-ce que ça vaut?; **~s and chattels** biens mpl et effets mpl; **a ~ deal (of)** beaucoup (de); **a ~ many** beaucoup (de); **~ morning/afternoon!** bonjour!; **~ evening!** bonsoir!; **~ night!** bonsoir!; (on going to bed) bonne nuit!
goodbye [gud'bai] excl au revoir!; **to say ~ to sb** dire au revoir à qn
Good Friday n Vendredi saint
good-looking ['gud'lukiŋ] adj beau/belle, bien inv
good-natured ['gud'neitʃəd] adj (person) qui a un bon naturel; (discussion) enjoué(e)
goodness ['gudnis] n (of person) bonté f; **for ~ sake!** je vous en prie!; **~ gracious!** mon Dieu!
goods train n (Brit) train m de marchandises
goodwill [gud'wil] n bonne volonté f; (Comm) réputation f (auprès de la clientèle)
goose (pl **geese**) [gu:s, gi:s] n oie f
gooseberry ['guzbəri] n groseille f à maquereau; **to play ~** (Brit) tenir la chandelle

goose bumps, goose pimples npl chair f
de poule
gooseflesh ['guːsfleʃ] n, **goosepimples**
['guːspɪmplz] npl chair f de poule
gore [gɔːʳ] vt encorner ▷ n sang m
gorge [gɔːdʒ] n gorge f ▷ vt: **to ~ o.s. (on)** se
gorger (de)
gorgeous ['gɔːdʒəs] adj splendide, superbe
gorilla [gə'rɪlə] n gorille m
gorse [gɔːs] n ajoncs mpl
gory ['gɔːrɪ] adj sanglant(e)
gosh [gɔʃ] (inf) excl mince alors!
go-slow ['gəu'sləu] n (Brit) grève perlée
gospel ['gɔspl] n évangile m
gossip ['gɔsɪp] n (chat) bavardages mpl;
(malicious) commérage m, cancans mpl;
(person) commère f ▷ vi bavarder; cancaner,
faire des commérages; **a piece of ~** un ragot,
un racontar
gossip column n (Press) échos mpl
got [gɔt] pt, pp of **get**
gotten ['gɔtn] (US) pp of **get**
gourmet ['guəmeɪ] n gourmet m,
gastronome m/f
gout [gaut] n goutte f
govern ['gʌvən] vt (gen: Ling) gouverner;
(influence) déterminer
governess ['gʌvənɪs] n gouvernante f
government ['gʌvnmənt] n gouvernement m;
(Brit: ministers) ministère m ▷ cpd de l'État
governor ['gʌvənəʳ] n (of colony, state, bank)
gouverneur m; (of school, hospital etc)
administrateur(-trice); (Brit: of prison)
directeur(-trice)
gown [gaun] n robe f; (of teacher, Brit: of judge)
toge f
GP n abbr (Med) = **general practitioner; who's
your GP?** qui est votre médecin traitant?
GPS n abbr (= global positioning system) GPS m
grab [græb] vt saisir, empoigner; (property,
power) se saisir de ▷ vi: **to ~ at** essayer de
saisir
grace [greɪs] n grâce f ▷ vt (honour) honorer;
(adorn) orner; **5 days' ~** un répit de 5 jours; **to
say ~** dire le bénédicité; (after meal) dire les
grâces; **with a good/bad ~** de bonne/
mauvaise grâce; **his sense of humour is his
saving ~** il se rachète par son sens de
l'humour
graceful ['greɪsful] adj gracieux(-euse),
élégant(e)
gracious ['greɪʃəs] adj (kind) charmant(e),
bienveillant(e); (elegant) plein(e) d'élégance,
d'une grande élégance; (formal: pardon etc)
miséricordieux(-euse) ▷ excl: **(good) ~!** mon
Dieu!
grade [greɪd] n (Comm: quality) qualité f; (size)
calibre m; (type) catégorie f; (in hierarchy) grade
m, échelon m; (Scol) note f; (US: school class)
classe f; (: gradient) pente f ▷ vt classer; (by
size) calibrer; graduer; **to make the ~** (fig)
réussir

grade crossing n (US) passage m à niveau
grade school n (US) école f primaire
gradient ['greɪdɪənt] n inclinaison f, pente f;
(Geom) gradient m
gradual ['grædjuəl] adj graduel(le),
progressif(-ive)
gradually ['grædjuəlɪ] adv peu à peu,
graduellement
graduate n ['grædjuɪt] diplômé(e)
d'université; (US: of high school) diplômé(e)
de fin d'études ▷ vi ['grædjueɪt] obtenir un
diplôme d'université (or de fin d'études)
graduation [grædju'eɪʃən] n cérémonie f de
remise des diplômes
graffiti [grə'fiːtɪ] n, npl graffiti mpl
graft [grɑːft] n (Agr, Med) greffe f; (bribery)
corruption f ▷ vt greffer; **hard ~** (Brit: inf)
boulot acharné
grain [greɪn] n (single piece) grain m; (no pl:
cereals) céréales fpl; (US: corn) blé m; (of wood)
fibre f; **it goes against the ~** cela va à
l'encontre de sa (or ma etc) nature
gram [græm] n gramme m
grammar ['græməʳ] n grammaire f
grammar school n (Brit) ≈ lycée m
grammatical [grə'mætɪkl] adj
grammatical(e)
gramme [græm] n = **gram**
gran [græn] (inf) n (Brit) mamie f (inf), mémé f
(inf); **my ~** (young child speaking) ma mamie or
mémé; (older child or adult speaking) ma grand-
mère
grand [grænd] adj magnifique, splendide;
(terrific) magnifique, formidable; (gesture etc)
noble ▷ n (inf: thousand) mille livres fpl (or
dollars mpl)
grandad ['grændæd] (inf) n = **granddad**
grandchild (pl **grandchildren**) ['græntʃaɪld,
'græntʃɪldrən] n petit-fils m, petite-fille f;
grandchildren npl petits-enfants
granddad ['grændæd] n (inf) papy m (inf),
papi m (inf), pépé m (inf); **my ~** (young child
speaking) mon papy or papi or pépé; (older child
or adult speaking) mon grand-père
granddaughter ['grændɔːtəʳ] n petite-fille f
grandfather ['grændfɑːðəʳ] n grand-père m
grandma ['grænmɑː] n (inf) = **gran**
grandmother ['grænmʌðəʳ] n grand-mère f
grandpa ['grænpɑː] n (inf) = **granddad**
grandparents ['grændpɛərənts] npl grands-
parents mpl
grand piano n piano m à queue
Grand Prix ['grɑ̃ː'priː] n (Aut) grand prix
automobile
grandson ['grænsʌn] n petit-fils m
grandstand ['grændstænd] n (Sport)
tribune f
granite ['grænɪt] n granit m
granny ['grænɪ] n (inf) = **gran**
grant [grɑːnt] vt accorder; (a request) accéder
à; (admit) concéder ▷ n (Scol) bourse f; (Admin)
subside m, subvention f; **to take sth for ~ed**

considérer qch comme acquis; **to take sb for ~ed** considérer qn comme faisant partie du décor; **to ~ that** admettre que

granulated ['grænjuleɪtɪd] *adj*: **~ sugar** sucre *m* en poudre

grape [greɪp] *n* raisin *m*; **a bunch of ~s** une grappe de raisin

grapefruit ['greɪpfruːt] *n* pamplemousse *m*

graph [grɑːf] *n* graphique *m*, courbe *f*

graphic ['græfɪk] *adj* graphique; (*vivid*) vivant(e)

graphics ['græfɪks] *n* (*art*) arts *mpl* graphiques; (*process*) graphisme *m* ▷ *npl* (*drawings*) illustrations *fpl*

grapple ['græpl] *vi*: **to ~ with** être aux prises avec

grasp [grɑːsp] *vt* saisir, empoigner; (*understand*) saisir, comprendre ▷ *n* (*grip*) prise *f*; (*fig*) compréhension *f*, connaissance *f*; **to have sth within one's ~** avoir qch à sa portée; **to have a good ~ of sth** (*fig*) bien comprendre qch; **grasp at** *vt fus* (*rope etc*) essayer de saisir; (*fig*: *opportunity*) sauter sur

grasping ['grɑːspɪŋ] *adj* avide

grass [grɑːs] *n* herbe *f*; (*lawn*) gazon *m*; (*Brit inf*: *informer*) mouchard(e); (: *ex-terrorist*) balanceur(-euse)

grasshopper ['grɑːshɒpəʳ] *n* sauterelle *f*

grass roots *npl* (*fig*) base *f*

grate [greɪt] *n* grille *f* de cheminée ▷ *vi* grincer ▷ *vt* (*Culin*) râper

grateful ['greɪtful] *adj* reconnaissant(e)

grater ['greɪtəʳ] *n* râpe *f*

gratifying ['grætɪfaɪɪŋ] *adj* agréable, satisfaisant(e)

grating ['greɪtɪŋ] *n* (*iron bars*) grille *f* ▷ *adj* (*noise*) grinçant(e)

gratitude ['grætɪtjuːd] *n* gratitude *f*

gratuity [grə'tjuːɪtɪ] *n* pourboire *m*

grave [greɪv] *n* tombe *f* ▷ *adj* grave, sérieux(-euse)

gravel ['grævl] *n* gravier *m*

gravestone ['greɪvstəun] *n* pierre tombale

graveyard ['greɪvjɑːd] *n* cimetière *m*

gravity ['grævɪtɪ] *n* (*Physics*) gravité *f*; pesanteur *f*; (*seriousness*) gravité, sérieux *m*

gravy ['greɪvɪ] *n* jus *m* (de viande), sauce *f* (au jus de viande)

gray [greɪ] *adj* (*US*) = **grey**

graze [greɪz] *vi* paître, brouter ▷ *vt* (*touch lightly*) frôler, effleurer; (*scrape*) écorcher ▷ *n* écorchure *f*

grease [griːs] *n* (*fat*) graisse *f*; (*lubricant*) lubrifiant *m* ▷ *vt* graisser; lubrifier; **to ~ the skids** (*US*: *fig*) huiler les rouages

greaseproof paper ['griːspruːf-] *n* (*Brit*) papier sulfurisé

greasy ['griːsɪ] *adj* gras(se), graisseux(-euse); (*hands, clothes*) graisseux; (*Brit*: *road, surface*) glissant(e)

great [greɪt] *adj* grand(e); (*heat, pain etc*) très fort(e), intense; (*inf*) formidable; **they're ~**

friends ils sont très amis, ce sont de grands amis; **we had a ~ time** nous nous sommes bien amusés; **it was ~!** c'était fantastique *or* super!; **the ~ thing is that ...** ce qu'il y a de vraiment bien c'est que ...

Great Britain *n* Grande-Bretagne *f*

great-grandfather [greɪt'grænfɑːðəʳ] *n* arrière-grand-père *m*

great-grandmother [greɪt'grænmʌðəʳ] *n* arrière-grand-mère *f*

greatly ['greɪtlɪ] *adv* très, grandement; (*with verbs*) beaucoup

greatness ['greɪtnɪs] *n* grandeur *f*

Greece [griːs] *n* Grèce *f*

greed [griːd] *n* (*also*: **~iness**) avidité *f*; (*for food*) gourmandise *f*

greedy ['griːdɪ] *adj* avide; (*for food*) gourmand(e)

Greek [griːk] *adj* grec/grecque ▷ *n* Grec/Grecque; (*Ling*) grec *m*; **ancient/modern ~** grec classique/moderne

green [griːn] *adj* vert(e); (*inexperienced*) (bien) jeune, naïf(-ïve); (*ecological*: *product etc*) écologique ▷ *n* (*colour*) vert *m*; (*on golf course*) green *m*; (*stretch of grass*) pelouse *f*; (*also*: **village ~**) ≈ place *f* du village; **greens** *npl* (*vegetables*) légumes verts; **to have ~ fingers** *or* (*US*) **a ~ thumb** (*fig*) avoir le pouce vert; **G~** (*Pol*) écologiste *m/f*; **the G~ Party** le parti écologiste

green belt *n* (*round town*) ceinture verte

green card *n* (*Aut*) carte verte; (*US*: *work permit*) permis *m* de travail

greenery ['griːnərɪ] *n* verdure *f*

greengage ['griːngeɪdʒ] *n* reine-claude *f*

greengrocer ['griːngrəusəʳ] *n* (*Brit*) marchand *m* de fruits et légumes

greengrocer's ['griːngrəusəz], **greengrocer's shop** *n* magasin *m* de fruits et légumes

greenhouse ['griːnhaus] *n* serre *f*

greenhouse effect *n*: **the ~** l'effet *m* de serre

greenhouse gas *n* gaz *m* contribuant à l'effet de serre

greenish ['griːnɪʃ] *adj* verdâtre

Greenland ['griːnlənd] *n* Groenland *m*

green salad *n* salade verte

greet [griːt] *vt* accueillir

greeting ['griːtɪŋ] *n* salutation *f*; **Christmas/ birthday ~s** souhaits *mpl* de Noël/de bon anniversaire

greeting card, greetings card *n* carte *f* de vœux

gregarious [grə'gɛərɪəs] *adj* grégaire; sociable

grenade [grə'neɪd] *n* (*also*: **hand ~**) grenade *f*

grew [gruː] *pt of* **grow**

grey, (*US*) **gray** [greɪ] *adj* gris(e); (*dismal*) sombre; **to go ~** (*commencer à*) grisonner

grey-haired, (*US*) **gray-haired** [greɪ'hɛəd] *adj* aux cheveux gris

greyhound ['greɪhaund] *n* lévrier *m*

grid [grɪd] n grille f; (Elec) réseau m; (US Aut) intersection f (matérialisée par des marques au sol)

gridlock ['grɪdlɒk] n (traffic jam) embouteillage m

gridlocked ['grɪdlɒkt] adj: **to be ~** (roads) être bloqué par un embouteillage; (talks etc) être suspendu

grief [griːf] n chagrin m, douleur f; **to come to ~** (plan) échouer; (person) avoir un malheur

grievance ['griːvəns] n doléance f, grief m; (cause for complaint) grief

grieve [griːv] vi avoir du chagrin; se désoler ▷ vt faire de la peine à, affliger; **to ~ for sb** pleurer qn; **to ~ at** se désoler de; pleurer

grievous ['griːvəs] adj grave, cruel(le); **~ bodily harm** (Law) coups mpl et blessures fpl

grill [grɪl] n (on cooker) gril m; (also: **mixed ~**) grillade(s) f(pl); (also: **~room**) rôtisserie f ▷ vt (Brit) griller; (inf: question) interroger longuement, cuisiner

grille [grɪl] n grillage m; (Aut) calandre f

grillroom ['grɪlrum] n rôtisserie f

grim [grɪm] adj sinistre, lugubre; (serious, stern) sévère

grimace [grɪ'meɪs] n grimace f ▷ vi grimacer, faire une grimace

grime [graɪm] n crasse f

grin [grɪn] n large sourire m ▷ vi sourire; **to ~ (at)** faire un grand sourire (à)

grind [graɪnd] (pt, pp **ground**) [graund] vt écraser; (coffee, pepper etc) moudre; (US: meat) hacher; (make sharp) aiguiser; (polish: gem, lens) polir ▷ vi (car gears) grincer ▷ n (work) corvée f; **to ~ one's teeth** grincer des dents; **to ~ to a halt** (vehicle) s'arrêter dans un grincement de freins; (fig) s'arrêter, s'immobiliser; **the daily ~** (inf) le train-train quotidien

grip [grɪp] n (handclasp) poigne f; (control) prise f; (handle) poignée f; (holdall) sac m de voyage ▷ vt saisir, empoigner; (viewer, reader) captiver; **to come to ~s with** se colleter avec, en venir aux prises avec; **to ~ the road** (Aut) adhérer à la route; **to lose one's ~** lâcher prise; (fig) perdre les pédales, être dépassé(e)

gripping ['grɪpɪŋ] adj prenant(e), palpitant(e)

grisly ['grɪzlɪ] adj sinistre, macabre

gristle ['grɪsl] n cartilage m (de poulet etc)

grit [grɪt] n gravillon m; (courage) cran m ▷ vt (road) sabler; **to ~ one's teeth** serrer les dents; **to have a piece of ~ in one's eye** avoir une poussière or saleté dans l'œil

grits [grɪts] npl (US) gruau m de maïs

groan [grəun] n (of pain) gémissement m; (of disapproval, dismay) grognement m ▷ vi gémir; grogner

grocer ['grəusə*] n épicier m

groceries ['grəusərɪz] npl provisions fpl

grocer's ['grəusəz], **grocer's shop, grocery** ['grəusərɪ] n épicerie f

groin [grɔɪn] n aine f

groom [gruːm] n (for horses) palefrenier m; (also: **bride~**) marié m ▷ vt (horse) panser; (fig): **to ~ sb for** former qn pour

groove [gruːv] n sillon m, rainure f

grope [grəup] vi tâtonner; **to ~ for** chercher à tâtons

gross [grəus] adj grossier(-ière); (Comm) brut(e) ▷ n pl inv (twelve dozen) grosse f ▷ vt (Comm): **to ~ £500,000** gagner 500 000 livres avant impôt

grossly ['grəuslɪ] adv (greatly) très, grandement

grotesque [grə'tɛsk] adj grotesque

grotto ['grɒtəu] n grotte f

grotty ['grɒtɪ] adj (Brit inf) minable

ground [graund] pt, pp of **grind** ▷ n sol m, terre f; (land) terrain m, terres fpl; (Sport) terrain; (reason: gen pl) raison f; (US: also: **~ wire**) terre f ▷ vt (plane) empêcher de décoller, retenir au sol; (US Elec) équiper d'une prise de terre, mettre à la terre ▷ vi (ship) s'échouer ▷ adj (coffee etc) moulu(e); (US: meat) haché(e); **grounds** npl (gardens etc) parc m, domaine m; (of coffee) marc m; **on the ~, to the ~** par terre; **below ~** sous terre; **to gain/lose ~** gagner/perdre du terrain; **common ~** terrain d'entente; **he covered a lot of ~ in his lecture** sa conférence a traité un grand nombre de questions or la question en profondeur

ground cloth n (US) = **groundsheet**

ground floor n (Brit) rez-de-chaussée m

grounding ['graundɪŋ] n (in education) connaissances fpl de base

groundless ['graundlɪs] adj sans fondement

groundsheet ['graundʃiːt] n (Brit) tapis m de sol

ground staff n équipage m au sol

groundwork ['graundwəːk] n préparation f

group [gruːp] n groupe m ▷ vt (also: **~ together**) grouper ▷ vi (also: **~ together**) se grouper

grouse [graus] n pl inv (bird) grouse f (sorte de coq de bruyère) ▷ vi (complain) rouspéter, râler

grove [grəuv] n bosquet m

grovel ['grɒvl] vi (fig): **to ~ (before)** ramper (devant)

grow (pt **grew**, pp **grown**) [grəu, gruː, grəun] vi (plant) pousser, croître; (person) grandir; (increase) augmenter, se développer; (become) devenir; **to ~ rich/weak** s'enrichir/s'affaiblir ▷ vt cultiver, faire pousser; (hair, beard) laisser pousser; **grow apart** vi (fig) se détacher (l'un de l'autre); **grow away from** vt fus (fig) s'éloigner de; **grow on** vt fus: **that painting is ~ing on me** je finirai par aimer ce tableau; **grow out of** vt fus (clothes) devenir trop grand pour; (habit) perdre (avec le temps); **he'll ~ out of it** ça lui passera; **grow up** vi grandir

grower ['grəuə*] n producteur m; (Agr) cultivateur(-trice)

growing ['grəuɪŋ] adj (fear, amount)

croissant(e), grandissant(e); **~ pains** (*Med*) fièvre *f* de croissance; (*fig*) difficultés *fpl* de croissance

growl [graul] *vi* grogner

grown [grəun] *pp of* **grow** ▷ *adj* adulte

grown-up [grəun'ʌp] *n* adulte *m/f*, grande personne

growth [grəuθ] *n* croissance *f*, développement *m*; (*what has grown*) pousse *f*; poussée *f*; (*Med*) grosseur *f*, tumeur *f*

grub [grʌb] *n* larve *f*; (*inf: food*) bouffe *f*

grubby [grʌbɪ] *adj* crasseux(-euse)

grudge [grʌdʒ] *n* rancune *f* ▷ *vt*: **to ~ sb sth** (*in giving*) donner qch à qn à contre-cœur; (*resent*) reprocher qch à qn; **to bear sb a ~ (for)** garder rancune *or* en vouloir à qn (de); **he ~s spending** il rechigne à dépenser

gruelling, (*US*) **grueling** ['gruəlɪŋ] *adj* exténuant(e)

gruesome ['gru:səm] *adj* horrible

gruff [grʌf] *adj* bourru(e)

grumble ['grʌmbl] *vi* rouspéter, ronchonner

grumpy ['grʌmpɪ] *adj* grincheux(-euse)

grunt [grʌnt] *vi* grogner ▷ *n* grognement *m*

G-string ['dʒi:strɪŋ] *n* (*garment*) cache-sexe *m inv*

guarantee [gærən'ti:] *n* garantie *f* ▷ *vt* garantir; **he can't ~ (that) he'll come** il n'est pas absolument certain de pouvoir venir

guard [gɑ:d] *n* garde *f*, surveillance *f*; (*squad: Boxing, Fencing*) garde *f*; (*one man*) garde *m*; (*Brit Rail*) chef *m* de train; (*safety device: on machine*) dispositif *m* de sûreté; (*also:* **fire~**) garde-feu *m inv* ▷ *vt* garder, surveiller; (*protect*): **to ~ sb/ sth (against** *or* **from**) protéger qn/qch (contre); **to be on one's ~** (*fig*) être sur ses gardes; **guard against** *vi*: **to ~ against doing sth** se garder de faire qch

guarded ['gɑ:dɪd] *adj* (*fig*) prudent(e)

guardian ['gɑ:dɪən] *n* gardien(ne); (*of minor*) tuteur(-trice)

guard's van ['gɑ:dz-] *n* (*Brit Rail*) fourgon *m*

guerrilla [gə'rɪlə] *n* guérillero *m*

guess [ges] *vi* deviner; (*estimate*) évaluer; (*US*) croire, penser ▷ *n* supposition *f*, hypothèse *f*; **to take** *or* **have a ~** essayer de deviner; **to keep sb ~ing** laisser qn dans le doute *or* l'incertitude, tenir qn en haleine

guesswork ['geswə:k] *n* hypothèse *f*; **I got the answer by ~** j'ai deviné la réponse

guest [gest] *n* invité(e); (*in hotel*) client(e); **be my ~** faites comme chez vous

guest house ['gesthaus] *n* pension *f*

guest room *n* chambre *f* d'amis

guffaw [gʌ'fɔ:] *n* gros rire ▷ *vi* pouffer de rire

guidance ['gaɪdəns] *n* (*advice*) conseils *mpl*; **under the ~ of** conseillé(e) *or* encadré(e) par, sous la conduite de; **vocational ~** orientation professionnelle; **marriage ~** conseils conjugaux

guide [gaɪd] *n* (*person*) guide *m/f*; (*book*) guide *m*; (*also:* **Girl G~**) éclaireuse *f*; (*Roman*

Catholic) guide *f* ▷ *vt* guider; **to be ~d by sb/ sth** se laisser guider par qn/qch; **is there an English-speaking ~?** est-ce que l'un des guides parle anglais?

guidebook ['gaɪdbuk] *n* guide *m*; **do you have a ~ in English?** est-ce que vous avez un guide en anglais?

guide dog *n* chien *m* d'aveugle

guided tour *n* visite guidée; **what time does the ~ start?** la visite guidée commence à quelle heure?

guidelines ['gaɪdlaɪnz] *npl* (*advice*) instructions générales, conseils *mpl*

guild [gɪld] *n* (*Hist*) corporation *f*; (*sharing interests*) cercle *m*, association *f*

guillotine ['gɪləti:n] *n* guillotine *f*; (*for paper*) massicot *m*

guilt [gɪlt] *n* culpabilité *f*

guilty ['gɪltɪ] *adj* coupable; **to plead ~/not ~** plaider coupable/non coupable; **to feel ~ about doing sth** avoir mauvaise conscience à faire qch

guinea pig ['gɪnɪ-] *n* cobaye *m*

guise [gaɪz] *n* aspect *m*, apparence *f*

guitar [gɪ'tɑ:ʳ] *n* guitare *f*

guitarist [gɪ'tɑ:rɪst] *n* guitariste *m/f*

gulf [gʌlf] *n* golfe *m*; (*abyss*) gouffre *m*; **the (Persian) G~** le golfe Persique

gull [gʌl] *n* mouette *f*

gullible ['gʌlɪbl] *adj* crédule

gully ['gʌlɪ] *n* ravin *m*; ravine *f*; couloir *m*

gulp [gʌlp] *vi* avaler sa salive; (*from emotion*) avoir la gorge serrée, s'étrangler ▷ *vt* (*also:* **~ down**) avaler ▷ *n* (*of drink*) gorgée *f*; **at one ~** d'un seul coup

gum [gʌm] *n* (*Anat*) gencive *f*; (*glue*) colle *f*; (*sweet*) boule *f* de gomme; (*also:* **chewing-~**) chewing-gum *m* ▷ *vt* coller

gumboots ['gʌmbu:ts] *npl* (*Brit*) bottes *fpl* en caoutchouc

gun [gʌn] *n* (*small*) revolver *m*, pistolet *m*; (*rifle*) fusil *m*, carabine *f*; (*cannon*) canon *m* ▷ *vt* (*also:* **~ down**) abattre; **to stick to one's ~s** (*fig*) ne pas en démordre

gunboat ['gʌnbəut] *n* canonnière *f*

gunfire ['gʌnfaɪəʳ] *n* fusillade *f*

gunman *irreg* ['gʌnmən] *n* bandit armé

gunpoint ['gʌnpɔɪnt] *n*: **at ~** sous la menace du pistolet (*or* fusil)

gunpowder ['gʌnpaudəʳ] *n* poudre *f* à canon

gunshot ['gʌnʃɔt] *n* coup *m* de feu; **within ~** à portée de fusil

gurgle ['gə:gl] *n* gargouillis *m* ▷ *vi* gargouiller

gush [gʌʃ] *n* jaillissement *m*, jet *m* ▷ *vi* jaillir; (*fig*) se répandre en effusions

gust [gʌst] *n* (*of wind*) rafale *f*; (*of smoke*) bouffée *f*

gusto ['gʌstəu] *n* enthousiasme *m*

gut [gʌt] *n* intestin *m*, boyau *m*; (*Mus etc*) boyau ▷ *vt* (*poultry, fish*) vider; (*building*) ne laisser que les murs de; **guts** *npl* (*Anat*) boyaux *mpl*; (*inf: courage*) cran *m*; **to hate sb's**

~s ne pas pouvoir voir qn en peinture *or* sentir qn

gutter ['gʌtə'] *n* (*of roof*) gouttière *f*; (*in street*) caniveau *m*; (*fig*) ruisseau *m*

guy [gaɪ] *n* (*inf: man*) type *m*; (*also:* **~rope**) corde *f*; (*figure*) effigie de Guy Fawkes

Guy Fawkes' Night [gaɪ'fɔːks-] *n voir article*

guzzle ['gʌzl] *vi* s'empiffrer ▷ *vt* avaler gloutonnement

gym [dʒɪm] *n* (*also:* **gymnasium**) gymnase *m*; (*also:* **gymnastics**) gym *f*

gymnasium [dʒɪm'neɪzɪəm] *n* gymnase *m*

gymnast ['dʒɪmnæst] *n* gymnaste *m/f*

gymnastics [dʒɪm'næstɪks] *n, npl* gymnastique *f*

gym shoes *npl* chaussures *fpl* de gym(nastique)

gynaecologist, (*US*) **gynecologist** [gaɪnɪ'kɔlədʒɪst] *n* gynécologue *m/f*

gypsy ['dʒɪpsɪ] *n* gitan(e), bohémien(ne) ▷ *cpd:* **~ caravan** *n* roulotte *f*

haberdashery [hæbə'dæʃərɪ] *n* (*Brit*) mercerie *f*

habit ['hæbɪt] *n* habitude *f*; (*costume: Rel*) habit *m*; (*for riding*) tenue *f* d'équitation; **to get out of/into the ~ of doing sth** perdre/prendre l'habitude de faire qch

habitat ['hæbɪtæt] *n* habitat *m*

habitual [hə'bɪtjuəl] *adj* habituel(le); (*drinker, liar*) invétéré(e)

hack [hæk] *vt* hacher, tailler ▷ *n* (*cut*) entaille *f*; (*blow*) coup *m*; (*pej: writer*) nègre *m*; (*old horse*) canasson *m*

hacker ['hækə'] *n* (*Comput*) pirate *m* (informatique); (*: enthusiast*) passionné(e) *m/f* des ordinateurs

hackneyed ['hæknɪd] *adj* usé(e), rebattu(e)

had [hæd] *pt, pp of* **have**

haddock (*pl* **haddock** *or* **haddocks**) ['hædək] *n* églefin *m*; **smoked ~** haddock *m*

hadn't ['hædnt] = **had not**

haemorrhage, (*US*) **hemorrhage** ['hɛmərɪdʒ] *n* hémorragie *f*

haemorrhoids, (*US*) **hemorrhoids** ['hɛmərɔɪdz] *npl* hémorroïdes *fpl*

haggle ['hægl] *vi* marchander; **to ~ over** chicaner sur

Hague [heɪg] *n:* **The ~** La Haye

hail [heɪl] *n* grêle *f* ▷ *vt* (*call*) héler; (*greet*) acclamer ▷ *vi* grêler; (*originate*): **he ~s from Scotland** il est originaire d'Écosse

hailstone ['heɪlstəun] *n* grêlon *m*

hair [hɛə^r] n cheveux mpl; (on body) poils mpl, pilosité f; (of animal) pelage m; (single hair: on head) cheveu m; (: on body, of animal) poil m; **to do one's ~** se coiffer

hairband ['hɛəbænd] n (elasticated) bandeau m; (plastic) serre-tête m

hairbrush ['hɛəbrʌʃ] n brosse f à cheveux

haircut ['hɛəkʌt] n coupe f (de cheveux)

hairdo ['hɛəduː] n coiffure f

hairdresser ['hɛədrɛsə^r] n coiffeur(-euse)

hairdresser's ['hɛədrɛsəz] n salon m de coiffure, coiffeur m

hair dryer ['hɛədraɪə^r] n sèche-cheveux m, séchoir m

hair gel n gel m pour cheveux

hairgrip ['hɛəgrɪp] n pince f à cheveux

hairnet ['hɛənɛt] n résille f

hairpiece ['hɛəpiːs] n postiche m

hairpin ['hɛəpɪn] n épingle f à cheveux

hairpin bend, (US) **hairpin curve** n virage m en épingle à cheveux

hair-raising ['hɛəreɪzɪŋ] adj à (vous) faire dresser les cheveux sur la tête

hair removing cream n crème f dépilatoire

hair spray n laque f (pour les cheveux)

hairstyle ['hɛəstaɪl] n coiffure f

hairy ['hɛərɪ] adj poilu(e), chevelu(e); (inf: frightening) effrayant(e)

hake (pl **hake** or **hakes**) [heɪk] n colin m, merlu m

half [haːf] n (pl **halves**) [haːvz] moitié f; (of beer: also: **~ pint**) ≈ demi m; (Rail, bus: also: **~ fare**) demi-tarif m; (Sport: of match) mi-temps f; (: of ground) moitié (du terrain) ▷ adj demi(e) ▷ adv (à) moitié, à demi; **~ an hour** une demi-heure; **~ a dozen** une demi-douzaine; **~ a pound** une demi-livre, ≈ 250 g; **two and a ~** deux et demi; **a week and a ~** une semaine et demie; **~ (of it)** la moitié; **~ (of)** la moitié de; **~ the amount of** la moitié de; **to cut sth in ~** couper qch en deux; **~ past three** trois heures et demie; **empty/closed** à moitié vide/fermé; **to go halves (with sb)** se mettre de moitié avec qn

half board n (Brit: in hotel) demi-pension f

half-brother ['haːfbrʌðə^r] n demi-frère m

half-caste ['haːfkaːst] n (pej) métis(se)

half day n demi-journée f

half fare n demi-tarif m

half-hearted ['haːf'haːtɪd] adj tiède, sans enthousiasme

half-hour ['haːf'auə^r] n demi-heure f

half-mast ['haːf'maːst] n: **at ~** (flag) en berne, à mi-mât

halfpenny ['heɪpnɪ] n demi-penny m

half-price ['haːf'praɪs] adj à moitié prix ▷ adv (also: **at ~**) à moitié prix

half term n (Brit Scol) vacances fpl (de demi-trimestre)

half-time ['haːf'taɪm] n mi-temps f

halfway ['haːf'weɪ] adv à mi-chemin; **to meet sb ~** (fig) parvenir à un compromis avec

qn; **~ through sth** au milieu de qch

hall [hɔːl] n salle f; (entrance way: big) hall m; (small) entrée f; (: US: corridor) couloir m; (mansion) château m, manoir m

hallmark ['hɔːlmaːk] n poinçon m; (fig) marque f

hallo [hə'ləu] excl = **hello**

hall of residence n (Brit) pavillon m or résidence f universitaire

Hallowe'en, Halloween ['hæləu'iːn] n veille f de la Toussaint; voir article

✷ HALLOWE'EN

Selon la tradition, Hallowe'en est la nuit des fantômes et des sorcières. En Écosse et aux États-Unis surtout (et de plus en plus en Angleterre) les enfants, pour fêter Hallowe'en, se déguisent ce soir-là et ils vont ainsi de porte en porte en demandant de petits cadeaux (du chocolat, etc).

hallucination [həluːsɪ'neɪʃən] n hallucination f

hallway ['hɔːlweɪ] n (entrance) vestibule m; (corridor) couloir m

halo ['heɪləu] n (of saint etc) auréole f; (of sun) halo m

halt [hɔːlt] n halte f, arrêt m ▷ vt faire arrêter; (progress etc) interrompre ▷ vi faire halte, s'arrêter; **to call a ~ to sth** (fig) mettre fin à qch

halve [haːv] vt (apple etc) partager or diviser en deux; (reduce by half) réduire de moitié

halves [haːvz] npl of **half**

ham [hæm] n jambon m; (inf: also: **radio ~**) radio-amateur m; (also: **~ actor**) cabotin(e)

hamburger ['hæmbəːgə^r] n hamburger m

hamlet ['hæmlɪt] n hameau m

hammer ['hæmə^r] n marteau m ▷ vt (nail) enfoncer; (fig) éreinter, démolir ▷ vi (at door) frapper à coups redoublés; **to ~ a point home to sb** faire rentrer qch dans la tête de qn; **hammer out** vt (metal) étendre au marteau; (fig: solution) élaborer

hammock ['hæmək] n hamac m

hamper ['hæmpə^r] vt gêner ▷ n panier m (d'osier)

hamster ['hæmstə^r] n hamster m

hamstring ['hæmstrɪŋ] n (Anat) tendon m du jarret

hand [hænd] n main f; (of clock) aiguille f; (handwriting) écriture f; (at cards) jeu m; (measurement: of horse) paume f; (worker) ouvrier(-ière) ▷ vt passer, donner; **to give sb a ~** donner un coup de main à qn; **at ~** à portée de la main; **in ~** (situation) en main; (work) en cours; **we have the situation in ~** nous avons la situation bien en main; **to be on ~** (person) être disponible; (emergency services) se tenir prêt(e) (à intervenir); **to ~**

(*information etc*) sous la main, à portée de la main; **to force sb's ~** forcer la main à qn; **to have a free ~** avoir carte blanche; **to have sth in one's ~** tenir qch à la main; **on the one ~ ..., on the other ~** d'une part ..., d'autre part; **hand down** *vt* passer; (*tradition, heirloom*) transmettre; (*US: sentence, verdict*) prononcer; **hand in** *vt* remettre; **hand out** *vt* distribuer; **hand over** *vt* remettre; (*powers etc*) transmettre; **hand round** *vt* (*Brit: information*) faire circuler; (*: chocolates etc*) faire passer

handbag ['hændbæg] *n* sac *m* à main
hand baggage *n* = **hand luggage**
handbook ['hændbuk] *n* manuel *m*
handbrake ['hændbreɪk] *n* frein *m* à main
handcuffs ['hændkʌfs] *npl* menottes *fpl*
handful ['hændful] *n* poignée *f*
handicap ['hændɪkæp] *n* handicap *m* ▷ *vt* handicaper; **mentally/physically ~ped** handicapé(e) mentalement/physiquement
handicraft ['hændɪkrɑːft] *n* travail *m* d'artisanat, technique artisanale
handiwork ['hændɪwəːk] *n* ouvrage *m*; **this looks like his ~** (*pej*) ça a tout l'air d'être son œuvre
handkerchief ['hæŋkətʃɪf] *n* mouchoir *m*
handle ['hændl] *n* (*of door etc*) poignée *f*; (*of cup etc*) anse *f*; (*of knife etc*) manche *m*; (*of saucepan*) queue *f*; (*for winding*) manivelle *f* ▷ *vt* toucher, manier; (*deal with*) s'occuper de; (*treat: people*) prendre; **"~ with care" "**fragile"; **to fly off the ~** s'énerver
handlebar ['hændlbɑː] *n*, **handlebars** ['hændlbɑːz] *npl* guidon *m*
hand luggage ['hændlʌɡɪdʒ] *n* bagages *mpl* à main; **one item of ~** un bagage à main
handmade ['hænd'meɪd] *adj* fait(e) à la main
handout ['hændaut] *n* (*money*) aide *f*, don *m*; (*leaflet*) prospectus *m*; (*press handout*) communiqué *m* de presse; (*at lecture*) polycopié *m*
handrail ['hændreɪl] *n* (*on staircase etc*) rampe *f*, main courante
handset ['hændset] *n* (*Tel*) combiné *m*
hands-free ['hændz'friː] *adj* mains libres *inv* ▷ *n* (*also: ~ kit*) kit *m* mains libres *inv*
handshake ['hændʃeɪk] *n* poignée *f* de main; (*Comput*) établissement *m* de la liaison
handsome ['hænsəm] *adj* beau/belle; (*gift*) généreux(-euse); (*profit*) considérable
handwriting ['hændraɪtɪŋ] *n* écriture *f*
handy ['hændɪ] *adj* (*person*) adroit(e); (*close at hand*) sous la main; (*convenient*) pratique; **to come in ~** être *or* s'avérer) utile
hang (*pt, pp* **hung**) [hæŋ, hʌŋ] *vt* accrocher; (*criminal*) (*pt, pp* **hanged**) pendre ▷ *vi* pendre; (*hair, drapery*) tomber ▷ *n*: **to get the ~ of (doing) sth** (*inf*) attraper le coup pour faire qch; **hang about, hang around** *vi* flâner, traîner; **hang back** *vi* (*hesitate*): **to ~ back**

(from doing) être réticent(e) (pour faire); **hang down** *vi* pendre; **hang on** *vi* (*wait*) attendre ▷ *vt fus* (*depend on*) dépendre de; **~ on to** (*keep hold of*) ne pas lâcher; (*keep*) garder; **hang out** *vt* (*washing*) étendre (dehors) ▷ *vi* pendre; (*inf: live*) habiter, percher; (*: spend time*) traîner; **hang round** *vi* = **hang around**; **hang together** *vi* (*argument etc*) se tenir, être cohérent(e); **hang up** *vi* (*Tel*) raccrocher ▷ *vt* (*coat, painting etc*) accrocher, suspendre; **to ~ up on sb** (*Tel*) raccrocher au nez de qn
hangar ['hæŋə'] *n* hangar *m*
hanger ['hæŋə'] *n* cintre *m*, portemanteau *m*
hanger-on [hæŋər'ɔn] *n* parasite *m*
hang-gliding ['hæŋɡlaɪdɪŋ] *n* vol *m* libre *or* sur aile delta
hangover ['hæŋəuvə'] *n* (*after drinking*) gueule *f* de bois
hang-up ['hæŋʌp] *n* complexe *m*
hanker ['hæŋkə'] *vi*: **to ~ after** avoir envie de
hankie, hanky ['hæŋkɪ] *n abbr* = **handkerchief**
haphazard [hæp'hæzəd] *adj* fait(e) au hasard, fait(e) au petit bonheur
happen ['hæpən] *vi* arriver, se passer, se produire; **what's ~ing?** que se passe-t-il?; **she ~ed to be free** il s'est trouvé (or se trouvait) qu'elle était libre; **if anything ~ed to him** s'il lui arrivait quoi que ce soit; **as it ~s** justement; **happen on, happen upon** *vt fus* tomber sur
happening ['hæpnɪŋ] *n* événement *m*
happily ['hæpɪlɪ] *adv* heureusement; (*cheerfully*) joyeusement
happiness ['hæpɪnɪs] *n* bonheur *m*
happy ['hæpɪ] *adj* heureux(-euse); **~ with** (*arrangements etc*) satisfait(e) de; **to be ~ to do** faire volontiers; **yes, I'd be ~** to oui, avec plaisir *or* (bien) volontiers; **~ birthday!** bon anniversaire!; **~ Christmas/New Year!** joyeux Noël/bonne année!
happy-go-lucky ['hæpɪɡəu'lʌkɪ] *adj* insouciant(e)
happy hour *n* l'heure *f* de l'apéritif, *heure pendant laquelle les consommations sont à prix réduit*
harass ['hærəs] *vt* accabler, tourmenter
harassment ['hærəsmənt] *n* tracasseries *fpl*; **sexual ~** harcèlement sexuel
harbour, (*US*) **harbor** ['hɑːbə'] *n* port *m* ▷ *vt* héberger, abriter; (*hopes, suspicions*) entretenir; **to ~ a grudge against sb** en vouloir à qn
hard [hɑːd] *adj* dur(e); (*question, problem*) difficile; (*facts, evidence*) concret(-ète) ▷ *adv* (*work*) dur; (*think, try*) sérieusement; **to look ~ at** regarder fixement; (*thing*) regarder de près; **to drink ~** boire sec; **~ luck!** pas de veine!; **no ~ feelings!** sans rancune!; **to be ~ of hearing** être dur(e) d'oreille; **to be ~ done by** être traité(e) injustement; **to be ~ on sb** être dur(e) avec qn; **I find it ~ to believe that ...** je n'arrive pas à croire que ...

h

hardback ['hɑːdbæk] n livre relié
hardboard ['hɑːdbɔːd] n Isorel® m
hard cash n espèces fpl
hard disk n (Comput) disque dur
harden ['hɑːdn] vt durcir; (steel) tremper; (fig) endurcir ▷ vi (substance) durcir
hard-headed ['hɑːd'hedɪd] adj réaliste, décidé(e)
hard labour n travaux forcés
hardly ['hɑːdlɪ] adv (scarcely) à peine; (harshly) durement; **it's ~ the case** ce n'est guère le cas; **~ anywhere/ever** presque nulle part/ jamais; **I can ~ believe it** j'ai du mal à le croire
hardship ['hɑːdʃɪp] n (difficulties) épreuves fpl; (deprivation) privations fpl
hard shoulder n (Brit Aut) accotement stabilisé
hard-up [hɑːd'ʌp] adj (inf) fauché(e)
hardware ['hɑːdwɛəʳ] n quincaillerie f; (Comput, Mil) matériel m
hardware shop, (US) **hardware store** n quincaillerie f
hard-wearing [hɑːd'wɛərɪŋ] adj solide
hard-working [hɑːd'wɜːkɪŋ] adj travailleur(-euse), consciencieux(-euse)
hardy ['hɑːdɪ] adj robuste; (plant) résistant(e) au gel
hare [hɛəʳ] n lièvre m
hare-brained ['hɛəbreɪnd] adj farfelu(e), écervelé(e)
harm [hɑːm] n mal m; (wrong) tort m ▷ vt (person) faire du mal or du tort à; (thing) endommager; **to mean no ~** ne pas avoir de mauvaises intentions; **there's no ~ in trying** on peut toujours essayer; **out of ~'s way** à l'abri du danger, en lieu sûr
harmful ['hɑːmful] adj nuisible
harmless ['hɑːmlɪs] adj inoffensif(-ive)
harmony ['hɑːmənɪ] n harmonie f
harness ['hɑːnɪs] n harnais m ▷ vt (horse) harnacher; (resources) exploiter
harp [hɑːp] n harpe f ▷ vi: **to ~ on about** revenir toujours sur
harrowing ['hærəuɪŋ] adj déchirant(e)
harsh [hɑːʃ] adj (hard) dur(e); (severe) sévère; (rough: surface) rugueux(-euse); (unpleasant: sound) discordant(e); (: light) cru(e); (: taste) âpre
harvest ['hɑːvɪst] n (of corn) moisson f; (of fruit) récolte f; (of grapes) vendange f ▷ vi, vt moissonner; récolter; vendanger
has [hæz] vb see **have**
hash [hæʃ] n (Culin) hachis m; (fig: mess) gâchis m
hasn't ['hæznt] = **has not**
hassle ['hæsl] n (inf: fuss) histoire(s) f(pl)
haste [heɪst] n hâte f, précipitation f; **in ~** à la hâte, précipitamment
hasten ['heɪsn] vt hâter, accélérer ▷ vi se hâter, s'empresser; **I ~ to add that ...** je m'empresse d'ajouter que ...

hastily ['heɪstɪlɪ] adv à la hâte; (leave) précipitamment
hasty ['heɪstɪ] adj (decision, action) hâtif(-ive); (departure, escape) précipité(e)
hat [hæt] n chapeau m
hatch [hætʃ] n (Naut: also: **~way**) écoutille f; (Brit: also: **service ~**) passe-plats m inv ▷ vi éclore ▷ vt faire éclore; (fig: scheme) tramer, ourdir
hatchback ['hætʃbæk] n (Aut) modèle m avec hayon arrière
hatchet ['hætʃɪt] n hachette f
hate [heɪt] vt haïr, détester ▷ n haine f; **to ~ to do** or **doing** détester faire; **I ~ to trouble you, but ...** désolé de vous déranger, mais ...
hateful ['heɪtful] adj odieux(-euse), détestable
hatred ['heɪtrɪd] n haine f
haughty ['hɔːtɪ] adj hautain(e), arrogant(e)
haul [hɔːl] vt traîner, tirer; (by lorry) camionner; (Naut) haler ▷ n (of fish) prise f; (of stolen goods etc) butin m
haulage ['hɔːlɪdʒ] n transport routier
haulier ['hɔːlɪəʳ], (US) **hauler** ['hɔːləʳ] n transporteur (routier), camionneur m
haunch [hɔːntʃ] n hanche f; **~ of venison** cuissot m de chevreuil
haunt [hɔːnt] vt (subj: ghost, fear) hanter; (: person) fréquenter ▷ n repaire m
haunted ['hɔːntɪd] adj (castle etc) hanté(e); (look) égaré(e), hagard(e)

 KEYWORD

have [hæv] (pt, pp **had**) aux vb **1** (gen) avoir; être; **to have eaten/slept** avoir mangé/dormi; **to have arrived/gone** être arrivé(e)/allé(e); **he has been promoted** il a eu une promotion; **having finished** or **when he had finished, he left** quand il a eu fini, il est parti; **we'd already eaten** nous avions déjà mangé
2 (in tag questions): **you've done it, haven't you?** vous l'avez fait, n'est-ce pas?
3 (in short answers and questions): **no I haven't!/ yes we have!** mais non!/mais si!; **so I have!** ah oui!, oui c'est vrai!; **I've been there before, have you?** j'y suis déjà allé, et vous?
▷ modal aux vb (be obliged): **to have (got) to do sth** devoir faire qch, être obligé(e) de faire qch; **she has (got) to do it** elle doit le faire, il faut qu'elle le fasse; **you haven't to tell her** vous n'êtes pas obligé de le lui dire; (must not) ne le lui dites surtout pas; **do you have to book?** il faut réserver?
▷ vt **1** (possess) avoir; **he has (got) blue eyes/ dark hair** il a les yeux bleus/les cheveux bruns
2 (referring to meals etc): **to have breakfast** prendre le petit déjeuner; **to have dinner/ lunch** dîner/déjeuner; **to have a drink** prendre un verre; **to have a cigarette** fumer une cigarette

3 (*receive*) avoir, recevoir; (*obtain*) avoir; **may I have your address?** puis-je avoir votre adresse?; **you can have it for £5** vous pouvez l'avoir pour 5 livres; **I must have it for tomorrow** il me le faut pour demain; **to have a baby** avoir un bébé

4 (*maintain, allow*): **I won't have it!** ça ne se passera pas comme ça!; **we can't have that** nous ne tolérerons pas ça

5 (*by sb else*): **to have sth done** faire faire qch; **to have one's hair cut** se faire couper les cheveux; **to have sb do sth** faire faire qch à qn

6 (*experience, suffer*) avoir; **to have a cold/flu** avoir un rhume/la grippe; **to have an operation** se faire opérer; **she had her bag stolen** elle s'est fait voler son sac

7 (*+noun*): **to have a swim/walk** nager/se promener; **to have a bath/shower** prendre un bain/une douche; **let's have a look** regardons; **to have a meeting** se réunir; **to have a party** organiser une fête; **let me have a try** laissez-moi essayer

8 (*inf: dupe*) avoir; **he's been had** il s'est fait avoir or rouler

have out vt: **to have it out with sb** (*settle a problem etc*) s'expliquer (franchement) avec qn

haven ['heɪvn] n port m; (*fig*) havre m

haven't ['hævnt] = **have not**

havoc ['hævək] n ravages mpl, dégâts mpl; **to play ~ with** (*fig*) désorganiser complètement; détraquer

Hawaii [hə'waɪ:] n (îles fpl) Hawaï m

hawk [hɔ:k] n faucon m ▷ vt (*goods for sale*) colporter

hawthorn ['hɔ:θɔ:n] n aubépine f

hay [heɪ] n foin m

hay fever n rhume m des foins

haystack ['heɪstæk] n meule f de foin

haywire ['heɪwaɪəʳ] adj (*inf*): **to go ~** perdre la tête; mal tourner

hazard ['hæzəd] n (*risk*) danger m, risque m; (*chance*) hasard m, chance f ▷ vt risquer, hasarder; **to be a health/fire ~** présenter un risque pour la santé/d'incendie; **to ~ a guess** émettre or hasarder une hypothèse

hazardous ['hæzədəs] adj hasardeux(-euse), risqué(e)

hazard warning lights npl (Aut) feux mpl de détresse

haze [heɪz] n brume f

hazel ['heɪzl] n (*tree*) noisetier m ▷ adj (*eyes*) noisette inv

hazelnut ['heɪzlnʌt] n noisette f

hazy ['heɪzɪ] adj brumeux(-euse); (*idea*) vague; (*photograph*) flou(e)

HD abbr (= high definition) HD (= haute définition)

HDTV n abbr (= high definition television) TVHD f (= télévision haute-définition)

he [hi:] pron il; **it is he who ...** c'est lui qui ...; **here he is** le voici; **he-bear** etc ours etc mâle

head [hɛd] n tête f; (*leader*) chef m; (*of school*) directeur(-trice); (*of secondary school*) proviseur m ▷ vt (*list*) être en tête de; (*group, company*) être à la tête de; **heads** pl (*on coin*) (le côté) face; **~s or tails** pile ou face; **~ first** la tête la première; **~ over heels in love** follement or éperdument amoureux(-euse); **to ~ the ball** faire une tête; **10 euros a** or **per ~** 10 euros par personne; **to sit at the ~ of the table** présider la tablée; **to have a ~ for business** avoir des dispositions pour les affaires; **to have no ~ for heights** être sujet(te) au vertige; **to come to a ~** (*fig: situation etc*) devenir critique; **head for** vt fus se diriger vers; (*disaster*) aller à; **head off** vt (*threat, danger*) détourner

headache ['hɛdeɪk] n mal m de tête; **to have a ~** avoir mal à la tête

headaddress ['hɛddrɛs] n coiffure f

heading ['hɛdɪŋ] n titre m; (*subject title*) rubrique f

headlamp ['hɛdlæmp] (Brit) n = **headlight**

headland ['hɛdlənd] n promontoire m, cap m

headlight ['hɛdlaɪt] n phare m

headline ['hɛdlaɪn] n titre m

headlong ['hɛdlɔŋ] adv (*fall*) la tête la première; (*rush*) tête baissée

headmaster [hɛd'mɑ:stəʳ] n directeur m, proviseur m

headmistress [hɛd'mɪstrɪs] n directrice f

head office n siège m, bureau m central

head-on [hɛd'ɔn] adj (*collision*) de plein fouet

headphones ['hɛdfəʊnz] npl casque m (à écouteurs)

headquarters ['hɛdkwɔ:təz] npl (*of business*) bureau or siège central; (Mil) quartier général

headrest ['hɛdrɛst] n appui-tête m

headroom ['hɛdrum] n (*in car*) hauteur f de plafond; (*under bridge*) hauteur limite; dégagement m

headscarf (pl **headscarves**) ['hɛdskɑ:f, -skɑ:vz] n foulard m

headset ['hɛdsɛt] n = **headphones**

headstrong ['hɛdstrɔŋ] adj têtu(e), entêté(e)

headteacher [hɛd'ti:tʃəʳ] n directeur(-trice); (*of secondary school*) proviseur m

head waiter n maître m d'hôtel

headway ['hɛdweɪ] n: **to make ~** avancer, faire des progrès

headwind ['hɛdwɪnd] n vent m contraire

heady ['hɛdɪ] adj capiteux(-euse), enivrant(e)

heal [hi:l] vt, vi guérir

health [hɛlθ] n santé f; **Department of H~** (Brit, US) = ministère m de la Santé

health care n services médicaux

health centre n (Brit) centre m de santé

health food n aliment(s) naturel(s)

health food shop n magasin m diététique

Health Service n: **the ~** (Brit) = la Sécurité Sociale

healthy ['hɛlθɪ] adj (*person*) en bonne santé; (*climate, food, attitude etc*) sain(e)

heap [hiːp] n tas m, monceau m ▷ vt (also: ~ up) entasser, amonceler; **she ~ed her plate with cakes** elle a chargé son assiette de gâteaux; **~s (of)** (inf: lots) des tas (de); **to ~ favours/praise/gifts etc on sb** combler qn de faveurs/d'éloges/de cadeaux etc

hear (pt, pp **heard**) [hɪəʳ, həːd] vt entendre; (news) apprendre; (lecture) assister à, écouter ▷ vi entendre; **to ~** (have news of) avoir des nouvelles de; **did you ~ about the move?** tu es au courant du déménagement?; **to ~ from sb** recevoir des nouvelles de qn; **I've never ~d of that book** je n'ai jamais entendu parler de ce livre; **hear out** vt écouter jusqu'au bout

heard [həːd] pt, pp of **hear**

hearing [ˈhɪərɪŋ] n (sense) ouïe f; (of witnesses) audition f; (of a case) audience f; (of committee) séance f; **to give sb a ~** (Brit) écouter ce que qn a à dire

hearing aid n appareil m acoustique

hearsay [ˈhɪəseɪ] n on-dit mpl, rumeurs fpl; **by ~** adv par ouï-dire

hearse [həːs] n corbillard m

heart [hɑːt] n cœur m; **hearts** npl (Cards) cœur m; **at ~** au fond; **by ~** (learn, know) par cœur; **to have a weak ~** avoir le cœur malade, avoir des problèmes de cœur; **to lose/take ~** perdre/prendre courage; **to set one's ~ on sth/on doing sth** vouloir absolument qch/faire qch; **the ~ of the matter** le fond du problème

heart attack n crise f cardiaque

heartbeat [ˈhɑːtbiːt] n battement m de cœur

heartbreaking [ˈhɑːtbreɪkɪŋ] adj navrant(e), déchirant(e)

heartbroken [ˈhɑːtbrəukən] adj: **to be ~** avoir beaucoup de chagrin

heartburn [ˈhɑːtbəːn] n brûlures fpl d'estomac

heart disease n maladie f cardiaque

heart failure n (Med) arrêt m du cœur

heartfelt [ˈhɑːtfɛlt] adj sincère

hearth [hɑːθ] n foyer m, cheminée f

heartily [ˈhɑːtɪlɪ] adv chaleureusement; (laugh) de bon cœur; (eat) de bon appétit; **to agree ~** être entièrement d'accord; **to be ~ sick of** (Brit) en avoir ras le bol de

heartless [ˈhɑːtlɪs] adj (person) sans cœur, insensible; (treatment) cruel(le)

hearty [ˈhɑːtɪ] adj chaleureux(-euse); (appetite) solide; (dislike) cordial(e); (meal) copieux(-euse)

heat [hiːt] n chaleur f; (fig) ardeur f; feu m; (Sport: also: **qualifying ~**) éliminatoire f; (Zool): **in** or **on ~** (Brit) en chaleur ▷ vt chauffer; **heat up** vi (liquid) chauffer; (room) se réchauffer ▷ vt réchauffer

heated [ˈhiːtɪd] adj chauffé(e); (fig) passionné(e), échauffé(e), excité(e)

heater [ˈhiːtəʳ] n appareil m de chauffage; radiateur m; (in car) chauffage m; (water heater) chauffe-eau m

heath [hiːθ] n (Brit) lande f

heather [ˈhɛðəʳ] n bruyère f

heating [ˈhiːtɪŋ] n chauffage m

heatstroke [ˈhiːtstrəuk] n coup m de chaleur

heatwave [ˈhiːtweɪv] n vague f de chaleur

heave [hiːv] vt soulever (avec effort) ▷ vi se soulever; (retch) avoir des haut-le-cœur ▷ n (push) poussée f; **to ~ a sigh** pousser un gros soupir

heaven [ˈhɛvn] n ciel m, paradis m; (fig) paradis; **~ forbid!** surtout pas!; **thank ~!** Dieu merci!; **for ~'s sake!** (pleading) je vous en prie!; (protesting) mince alors!

heavenly [ˈhɛvnlɪ] adj céleste, divin(e)

heavily [ˈhɛvɪlɪ] adv lourdement; (drink, smoke) beaucoup; (sleep, sigh) profondément

heavy [ˈhɛvɪ] adj lourd(e); (work, rain, user, eater) gros(se); (drinker, smoker) grand(e); (schedule, week) chargé(e); **it's too ~** c'est trop lourd; **it's ~ going** ça ne va pas tout seul, c'est pénible

heavy goods vehicle n (Brit) poids lourd m

heavyweight [ˈhɛvɪweɪt] n (Sport) poids lourd

Hebrew [ˈhiːbruː] adj hébraïque ▷ n (Ling) hébreu m

Hebrides [ˈhɛbrɪdiːz] npl: **the ~** les Hébrides fpl

heckle [ˈhɛkl] vt interpeller (un orateur)

hectare [ˈhɛktɑːʳ] n (Brit) hectare m

hectic [ˈhɛktɪk] adj (schedule) très chargé(e); (day) mouvementé(e); (activity) fiévreux(-euse); (lifestyle) trépidant(e)

he'd [hiːd] = **he would; he had**

hedge [hɛdʒ] n haie f ▷ vi se dérober ▷ vt: **to ~ one's bets** (fig) se couvrir; **as a ~ against inflation** pour se prémunir contre l'inflation; **hedge in** vt entourer d'une haie

hedgehog [ˈhɛdʒhɔg] n hérisson m

heed [hiːd] vt (also: **take ~ of**) tenir compte de, prendre garde à

heedless [ˈhiːdlɪs] adj insouciant(e)

heel [hiːl] n talon m ▷ vt (shoe) retalonner; **to bring to ~** (dog) faire venir à ses pieds; (fig: person) rappeler à l'ordre; **to take to one's ~s** prendre ses jambes à son cou

hefty [ˈhɛftɪ] adj (person) costaud(e); (parcel) lourd(e); (piece, price) gros(se)

heifer [ˈhɛfəʳ] n génisse f

height [haɪt] n (of person) taille f, grandeur f; (of object) hauteur f; (of plane, mountain) altitude f; (high ground) hauteur, éminence f; (fig: of glory, fame, power) sommet m; (: of luxury, stupidity) comble m; **at the ~ of summer** au cœur de l'été; **what ~ are you?** combien mesurez-vous?, quelle est votre taille?; **of average ~** de taille moyenne; **to be afraid of ~s** être sujet(te) au vertige; **it's the ~ of fashion** c'est le dernier cri

heighten [ˈhaɪtn] vt hausser, surélever; (fig) augmenter

heir [ɛəʳ] n héritier m

heiress ['ɛərɛs] n héritière f

heirloom ['ɛəlu:m] n meuble m (or bijou m or tableau m) de famille

held [hɛld] pt, pp of **hold**

helicopter ['hɛlɪkɔptər] n hélicoptère m

hell [hɛl] n enfer m; **a ~ of a ...** (inf) un(e) sacré(e) ...; **oh ~!** (inf) merde!

he'll [hi:l] = **he will; he shall**

hellish ['hɛlɪʃ] adj infernal(e)

hello [hə'ləu] excl bonjour!; (to attract attention) hé!; (surprise) tiens!

helm [hɛlm] n (Naut) barre f

helmet ['hɛlmɪt] n casque m

help [hɛlp] n aide f; (cleaner etc) femme f de ménage; (assistant etc) employé(e) ▷ vt, vi aider; **~!** au secours!; **~ yourself** servez-vous; **can you ~ me?** pouvez-vous m'aider?; **can I ~ you?** (in shop) vous désirez?; **with the ~ of** (person) avec l'aide de; (tool etc) à l'aide de; **to be of ~ to sb** être utile à qn; **to ~ sb (to) do sth** aider qn à faire qch; **I can't ~ saying** je ne peux pas m'empêcher de dire; **he can't ~ it** il n'y peut rien; **help out** vi aider ▷ vt: **to ~ sb out** aider qn

helper ['hɛlpər] n aide m/f, assistant(e)

helpful ['hɛlpful] adj serviable, obligeant(e); (useful) utile

helping ['hɛlpɪŋ] n portion f

helpless ['hɛlplɪs] adj impuissant(e); (baby) sans défense

helpline ['hɛlplaɪn] n service m d'assistance téléphonique; (free) ≈ numéro vert

hem [hɛm] n ourlet m ▷ vt ourler; **hem in** vt cerner; **to feel ~med in** (fig) avoir l'impression d'étouffer, se sentir oppressé(e) or écrasé(e)

hemisphere ['hɛmɪsfɪər] n hémisphère m

hemorrhage ['hɛmərɪdʒ] n (US) = **haemorrhage**

hemorrhoids ['hɛmərɔɪdz] npl (US) = **haemorrhoids**

hen [hɛn] n poule f; (female bird) femelle f

hence [hɛns] adv (therefore) d'où, de là; **2 years ~** d'ici 2 ans

henceforth [hɛns'fɔ:θ] adv dorénavant

hen night, hen party n soirée f entre filles (avant le mariage de l'une d'elles)

hepatitis [hɛpə'taɪtɪs] n hépatite f

her [hə:r] pron (direct) la, l' + vowel or h mute; (indirect) lui; (stressed, after prep) elle ▷ adj son/ sa, ses pl; **I see ~** je la vois; **give ~ a book** donne-lui un livre; **after ~** après elle; see also **me; my**

herald ['hɛrəld] n héraut m ▷ vt annoncer

heraldry ['hɛrəldrɪ] n héraldique f; (coat of arms) blason m

herb [hə:b] n herbe f; **herbs** npl fines herbes

herbal ['hə:bl] adj à base de plantes

herbal tea n tisane f

herd [hə:d] n troupeau m; (of wild animals, swine) troupeau, troupe f ▷ vt (drive: animals, people) mener, conduire; (gather) rassembler; **~ed together** parqués (comme du bétail)

here [hɪər] adv ici; (time) alors ▷ excl tiens!, tenez!; **~!** (present) présent!; **~ is, ~ are** voici; **~'s my sister** voici ma sœur; **~ he/she is** le/la voici; **~ she comes** la voici qui vient; **come ~!** viens ici!; **~ and there** ici et là

hereafter [hɪər'ɑ:ftər] adv après, plus tard; ci-après ▷ n: **the ~** l'au-delà m

hereby [hɪə'baɪ] adv (in letter) par la présente

hereditary [hɪ'rɛdɪtrɪ] adj héréditaire

heresy ['hɛrəsɪ] n hérésie f

heritage ['hɛrɪtɪdʒ] n héritage m, patrimoine m; **our national ~** notre patrimoine national

hermit ['hə:mɪt] n ermite m

hernia ['hə:nɪə] n hernie f

hero ['hɪərəu] (pl **heroes**) n héros m

heroic [hɪ'rəuɪk] adj héroïque

heroin ['hɛrəuɪn] n héroïne f (drogue)

heroine ['hɛrəuɪn] n héroïne f (femme)

heron ['hɛrən] n héron m

herring ['hɛrɪŋ] n hareng m

hers [hə:z] pron le/la sien(ne), les siens/ siennes; **a friend of ~** un(e) ami(e) à elle, un(e) de ses ami(e)s; see also **mine'**

herself [hə:'sɛlf] pron (reflexive) se; (emphatic) elle-même; (after prep) elle; see also **oneself**

he's [hi:z] = **he is; he has**

hesitant ['hɛzɪtənt] adj hésitant(e), indécis(e); **to be ~ about doing sth** hésiter à faire qch

hesitate ['hɛzɪteɪt] vi: **to ~ (about/to do)** hésiter (sur/à faire)

hesitation [hɛzɪ'teɪʃən] n hésitation f; **I have no ~ in saying (that) ...** je n'hésiterais pas à dire (que) ...

heterosexual ['hɛtərəu'sɛksjuəl] adj, n hétérosexuel(le)

hexagon ['hɛksəgən] n hexagone m

hey [heɪ] excl hé!

heyday ['heɪdeɪ] n: **the ~ of** l'âge m d'or de, les beaux jours de

HGV n abbr = **heavy goods vehicle**

hi [haɪ] excl salut!; (to attract attention) hé!

hiatus [haɪ'eɪtəs] n trou m, lacune f; (Ling) hiatus m

hibernate ['haɪbəneɪt] vi hiberner

hiccough, hiccup ['hɪkʌp] vi hoqueter ▷ n hoquet m; **to have (the) ~s** avoir le hoquet

hid [hɪd] pt of **hide**

hidden ['hɪdn] pp of **hide** ▷ adj: **there are no ~ extras** absolument tout est compris dans le prix; **~ agenda** intentions non déclarées

hide [haɪd] (pt **hid**, pp **hidden**) n (skin) peau f ▷ vt cacher; (feelings, truth) dissimuler; **to ~ sth from sb** cacher qch à qn ▷ vi: **to ~ (from sb)** se cacher (de qn)

hide-and-seek ['haɪdən'si:k] n cache-cache m

hideous ['hɪdɪəs] adj hideux(-euse), atroce

hiding ['haɪdɪŋ] n (beating) correction f, volée f de coups; **to be in ~** (concealed) se tenir caché(e)

hierarchy [ˈhaɪərɑːkɪ] n hiérarchie f

hi-fi [ˈhaɪfaɪ] adj, n abbr (= high fidelity)
hi-fi f inv

high [haɪ] adj haut(e); (speed, respect, number)
grand(e); (price) élevé(e); (wind) fort(e),
violent(e); (voice) aigu(ë); (inf: person: on drugs)
défoncé(e), fait(e); (: on drink) soûl(e),
bourré(e); (Brit Culin: meat, game) faisandé(e);
(: spoilt) avarié(e) ▷ adv haut, en haut ▷ n
(weather) zone f de haute pression; **exports
have reached a new ~** les exportations ont
atteint un nouveau record; **20 m ~** haut(e) de
20 m; **to pay a ~ price for sth** payer cher
pour qch; **~ in the air** haut dans le ciel

highbrow [ˈhaɪbrau] adj, n intellectuel(le)

highchair [ˈhaɪtʃɛər] n (child's) chaise haute

high-class [ˈhaɪˈklɑːs] adj (neighbourhood, hotel)
chic inv, de grand standing; (performance etc)
de haut niveau

higher education n études supérieures

high-handed [haɪˈhændɪd] adj très
autoritaire; très cavalier(-ière)

high-heeled [haɪˈhiːld] adj à hauts talons

high heels npl talons hauts, hauts talons

high jump n (Sport) saut m en hauteur

highlands [ˈhaɪləndz] npl région
montagneuse; **the H~** (in Scotland) les
Highlands mpl

highlight [ˈhaɪlaɪt] n (fig: of event) point
culminant ▷ vt (emphasize) faire ressortir,
souligner; **highlights** npl (in hair) reflets mpl

highlighter [ˈhaɪlaɪtər] n (pen) surligneur
(lumineux)

highly [ˈhaɪlɪ] adv extrêmement, très;
(unlikely) fort; (recommended, skilled, qualified)
hautement; **~ paid** très bien payé(e); **to
speak ~ of** dire beaucoup de bien de

highly strung adj nerveux(-euse), toujours
tendu(e)

highness [ˈhaɪnɪs] n hauteur f; **His/Her H~**
son Altesse f

high-pitched [haɪˈpɪtʃt] adj aigu(ë)

high-rise [ˈhaɪraɪz] n (also: **~ block,
~ building**) tour f (d'habitation)

high school n lycée m; (US) établissement m
d'enseignement supérieur; voir article

HIGH SCHOOL

Une high school est un établissement
d'enseignement secondaire. Aux États-
Unis, il y a la "Junior High School", qui
correspond au collège, et la "Senior High
School", qui correspond au lycée. En
Grande-Bretagne, c'est un nom que l'on
donne parfois aux écoles secondaires;
voir "elementary school".

high season n (Brit) haute saison

high street n (Brit) grand-rue f

high-tech [ˈhaɪˈtɛk] (inf) adj de pointe

highway [ˈhaɪweɪ] n (Brit) route f; (US) route
nationale; **the information ~** l'autoroute f
de l'information

Highway Code n (Brit) code m de la route

hijack [ˈhaɪdʒæk] vt détourner (par la force) ▷ n
(also: **~ing**) détournement m (d'avion)

hijacker [ˈhaɪdʒækər] n auteur m d'un
détournement d'avion, pirate m de l'air

hike [haɪk] vi faire des excursions à pied ▷ n
excursion f à pied, randonnée f; (inf: in prices
etc) augmentation f ▷ vt (inf) augmenter

hiker [ˈhaɪkər] n promeneur(-euse),
excursionniste m/f

hiking [ˈhaɪkɪŋ] n excursions fpl à pied,
randonnée f

hilarious [hɪˈlɛərɪəs] adj (behaviour, event)
désopilant(e)

hill [hɪl] n colline f; (fairly high) montagne f;
(on road) côte f

hillside [ˈhɪlsaɪd] n (flanc m de) coteau m

hill walking [ˈhɪlˈwɔːkɪŋ] n randonnée f
de basse montagne

hilly [ˈhɪlɪ] adj vallonné(e),
montagneux(-euse); (road) à fortes côtes

hilt [hɪlt] n (of sword) garde f; **to the ~** (fig:
support) à fond

him [hɪm] pron (direct) le, l' + vowel or h mute;
(stressed, indirect, after prep) lui; **I see ~** je le vois;
give ~ a book donne-lui un livre; **after ~**
après lui; see also **me**

himself [hɪmˈsɛlf] pron (reflexive) se;
(emphatic) lui-même; (after prep) lui; see
also **oneself**

hind [haɪnd] adj de derrière ▷ n biche f

hinder [ˈhɪndər] vt gêner; (delay) retarder;
(prevent): **to ~ sb from doing** empêcher qn de
faire

hindrance [ˈhɪndrəns] n gêne f, obstacle m

hindsight [ˈhaɪndsaɪt] n bon sens après
coup; **with (the benefit of) ~** avec du recul,
rétrospectivement

Hindu [ˈhɪnduː] n Hindou(e)

Hinduism [ˈhɪnduːɪzəm] n (Rel)
hindouisme m

hinge [hɪndʒ] n charnière f ▷ vi (fig): **to ~ on**
dépendre de

hint [hɪnt] n allusion f; (advice) conseil m;
(clue) indication f ▷ vt: **to ~ that** insinuer que
▷ vi: **to ~ at** faire une allusion à; **to drop a ~**
faire une allusion or insinuation; **give me a ~**
(clue) mettez-moi sur la voie, donnez-moi
une indication

hip [hɪp] n hanche f; (Bot) fruit m de
l'églantier or du rosier

hippie, hippy [ˈhɪpɪ] n hippie m/f

hippo [ˈhɪpəu] (pl **hippos**) n hippopotame m

hippopotamus [hɪpəˈpɔtəməs]
(pl **hippopotamuses** or **hippopotami**
[hɪpəˈpɔtəmaɪ]) n hippopotame m

hippy [ˈhɪpɪ] n = **hippie**

hire [ˈhaɪər] vt (Brit: car, equipment) louer;
(worker) embaucher, engager ▷ n location f;
for ~ à louer; (taxi) libre; **on ~** en location;

I'd like to ~ a car je voudrais louer une voiture; **hire out** vt louer

hire car, hired car [haɪəd-] n (Brit) voiture f de location

hire purchase n (Brit) achat m (or vente f) à tempérament or crédit; **to buy sth on ~** acheter qch en location-vente

his [hɪz] pron le/la sien(ne), les siens/siennes ▷ adj son/sa, ses pl; **this is ~** c'est à lui, c'est le sien; **a friend of ~** un(e) de ses ami(e)s, un(e) ami(e) à lui; see also **mine¹** see also **my**

Hispanic [hɪs'pænɪk] adj (in US) hispano-américain(e) ▷ n Hispano-Américain(e)

hiss [hɪs] vi siffler ▷ n sifflement m

historian [hɪ'stɔːrɪən] n historien(ne)

historic [hɪ'stɔrɪk], **historical** [hɪ'stɔrɪkl] adj historique

history ['hɪstərɪ] n histoire f; **medical ~** (of patient) passé médical

hit [hɪt] vt (pt, pp **hit**) frapper; (knock against) cogner; (reach: target) atteindre, toucher; (collide with: car) entrer en collision avec, heurter; (fig: affect) toucher; (find) tomber sur ▷ n coup m; (success) coup réussi; succès m; (song) chanson f à succès, tube m; (to website) visite f; (on search engine) résultat m de recherche; **to ~ it off with sb** bien s'entendre avec qn; **to ~ the headlines** être à la une des journaux; **to ~ the road** (inf) se mettre en route; **hit back** vi: **to ~ back at sb** prendre sa revanche sur qn; **hit on** vt fus (answer) trouver (par hasard); (solution) tomber sur (par hasard); **hit out at** vt fus envoyer un coup à; (fig) attaquer; **hit upon** vt fus = **hit on**

hit-and-run driver ['hɪtænd'rʌn-] n chauffard m

hitch [hɪtʃ] vt (fasten) accrocher, attacher; (also: ~ **up**) remonter d'un saccade ▷ vi faire de l'autostop ▷ n (knot) nœud m; (difficulty) anicroche f, contretemps m; **to ~ a lift** faire du stop; **technical ~** incident m technique; **hitch up** vt (horse, cart) atteler; see also **hitch**

hitch-hike ['hɪtʃhaɪk] vi faire de l'auto-stop

hitch-hiker ['hɪtʃhaɪkəʳ] n auto-stoppeur(-euse)

hitch-hiking ['hɪtʃhaɪkɪŋ] n auto-stop m, stop m (inf)

hi-tech ['haɪ'tɛk] adj de pointe ▷ n high-tech m

hitherto [hɪðə'tuː] adv jusqu'ici, jusqu'à présent

hitman ['hɪtmæn] irreg n (inf) tueur m à gages

HIV n abbr (= human immunodeficiency virus) HIV m, VIH m; **~-negative/positive** séronégatif(-ive)/positif(-ive)

hive [haɪv] n ruche f; **the shop was a ~ of activity** (fig) le magasin était une véritable ruche; **hive off** vt (inf) mettre à part, séparer

HMS abbr (Brit) = **His** or **Her Majesty's Ship**

hoard [hɔːd] n (of food) provisions fpl, réserves fpl; (of money) trésor m ▷ vt amasser

hoarding ['hɔːdɪŋ] n (Brit) panneau m d'affichage or publicitaire

hoarse [hɔːs] adj enroué(e)

hoax [həʊks] n canular m

hob [hɔb] n plaque chauffante

hobble ['hɔbl] vi boitiller

hobby ['hɔbɪ] n passe-temps favori

hobo ['həʊbəʊ] n (US) vagabond m

hockey ['hɔkɪ] n hockey m

hockey stick n crosse f de hockey

hog [hɔg] n porc (châtré) m ▷ vt (fig) accaparer; **to go the whole ~** aller jusqu'au bout

Hogmanay [hɔgmə'neɪ] n réveillon m du jour de l'An, Saint-Sylvestre f; voir article

HOGMANAY

La Saint-Sylvestre ou "New Year's Eve" se nomme *Hogmanay* en Écosse. En cette occasion, la famille et les amis se réunissent pour entendre sonner les douze coups de minuit et pour fêter le "first-footing", une coutume qui veut qu'on se rende chez ses amis et voisins en apportant quelque chose à boire (du whisky en général) et un morceau de charbon en gage de prospérité pour la nouvelle année.

hoist [hɔɪst] n palan m ▷ vt hisser

hold [həʊld] (pt, pp **held**) [hɛld] vt tenir; (contain) contenir; (meeting) tenir; (keep back) retenir; (believe) maintenir, considérer; (possess) avoir; détenir ▷ vi (withstand pressure) tenir (bon); (be valid) valoir; (on telephone) attendre ▷ n prise f; (fig) influence f; (Naut) cale f; **to catch** or **get (a) ~ of** saisir; **to get ~ of** (find) trouver; **to get ~ of o.s.** se contrôler; **~ the line!** (Tel) ne quittez pas!; **to ~ one's own** (fig) (bien) se défendre; **to ~ office** (Pol) avoir un portefeuille; **to ~ firm** or **fast** tenir bon; **he ~s the view that ...** il pense or estime que ..., d'après lui ...; **to ~ sb responsible for sth** tenir qn pour responsable de qch; **hold back** vt retenir; (secret) cacher; **to ~ sb back from doing sth** empêcher qn de faire qch; **hold down** vt (person) maintenir à terre; (job) occuper; **hold forth** vi pérorer; **hold off** vt tenir à distance ▷ vi: **if the rain ~s off** s'il ne pleut pas, s'il ne se met pas à pleuvoir; **hold on** vi tenir bon; (wait) attendre; **~ on!** (Tel) ne quittez pas!; **to ~ on to sth** (grasp) se cramponner à qch; (keep) conserver or garder qch; **hold out** vt offrir ▷ vi (resist): **to ~ out (against)** résister (devant), tenir bon (devant); **hold over** vt (meeting etc) ajourner, reporter; **hold up** vt (raise) lever; (support) soutenir; (delay) retarder; (: traffic) ralentir; (rob) braquer

holdall ['həʊldɔːl] n (Brit) fourre-tout m inv

holder ['həuldə'] n (container) support m; (of ticket, record) détenteur(-trice); (of office, title, passport etc) titulaire m/f

holding ['həuldɪŋ] n (share) intérêts mpl; (farm) ferme f

hold-up ['həuldʌp] n (robbery) hold-up m; (delay) retard m; (Brit: in traffic) embouteillage m

hole [həul] n trou m ▷ vt trouer, faire un trou dans; **~ in the heart** (Med) communication f interventriculaire; **to pick ~s (in)** (fig) chercher des poux (dans); **hole up** vi se terrer

holiday ['hɔlədɪ] n (Brit: vacation) vacances fpl; (day off) jour m de congé; (public) jour férié; **to be on ~** être en vacances; **I'm here on ~** je suis ici en vacances; **tomorrow is a ~** demain c'est fête, on a congé demain

holiday camp n (Brit: for children) colonie f de vacances; (also: **holiday centre**) camp m de vacances

holiday home n (rented) location f de vacances; (owned) résidence f secondaire

holiday job n (Brit) boulot m (inf) de vacances

holiday-maker ['hɔlədɪmeɪkə'] n (Brit) vacancier(-ière)

holiday resort n centre m de villégiature or de vacances

Holland ['hɔlənd] n Hollande f

hollow ['hɔləu] adj creux(-euse); (fig) faux/fausse ▷ n creux m; (in land) dépression f (de terrain), cuvette f ▷ vt: **to ~ out** creuser, évider

holly ['hɔlɪ] n houx m

holocaust ['hɔləkɔ:st] n holocauste m

holster ['həulstə'] n étui m de revolver

holy ['həulɪ] adj saint(e); (bread, water) bénit(e); (ground) sacré(e)

Holy Ghost, Holy Spirit n Saint-Esprit m

homage ['hɔmɪdʒ] n hommage m; **to pay ~ to** rendre hommage à

home [həum] n foyer m, maison f; (country) pays natal, patrie f; (institution) maison ▷ adj de famille; (Econ, Pol) national(e), intérieur(e); (Sport: team) qui reçoit; (: match, win) sur leur (or notre) terrain ▷ adv chez soi, à la maison; au pays natal; (right in: nail etc) à fond; **at ~** = chez soi, à la maison; to go (or come) rentrer (chez soi), rentrer à la maison (or au pays); **I'm going ~ on Tuesday** je rentre mardi; **make yourself at ~** faites comme chez vous; **near my ~** près de chez moi; **home in on** vt fus (missile) se diriger automatiquement vers or sur

home address n domicile permanent

homeland ['həumlænd] n patrie f

homeless ['həumlɪs] adj sans foyer, sans abri; **the homeless** npl les sans-abri mpl

homely ['həumlɪ] adj (plain) simple, sans prétention; (welcoming) accueillant(e)

home-made [həum'meɪd] adj fait(e) à la maison

home match n match m à domicile

Home Office n (Brit) ministère m de l'Intérieur

homeopathy etc [həumɪ'ɔpəθɪ] (US) n = **homoeopathy** etc

home owner ['həuməunə'] n propriétaire occupant

home page n (Comput) page f d'accueil

home rule n autonomie f

Home Secretary n (Brit) ministre m de l'Intérieur

homesick ['həumsɪk] adj: **to be ~** avoir le mal du pays; (missing one's family) s'ennuyer de sa famille

home town n ville natale

homeward ['həumwəd] adj (journey) du retour ▷ adv = **homewards**

homework ['həumwə:k] n devoirs mpl

homicide ['hɔmɪsaɪd] n (US) homicide m

homoeopathic, (US) **homeopathic** [həumɪ'pæθɪk] adj (medicine) homéopathique; (doctor) homéopathe

homoeopathy, (US) **homeopathy** [həumɪ'ɔpəθɪ] n homéopathie f

homogeneous [hɔməu'dʒi:nɪəs] adj homogène

homosexual [hɔməu'sɛksjuəl] adj, n homosexuel(le)

honest ['ɔnɪst] adj honnête; (sincere) franc/franche; **to be quite ~ with you ...** à dire vrai ...

honestly ['ɔnɪstlɪ] adv honnêtement; franchement

honesty ['ɔnɪstɪ] n honnêteté f

honey ['hʌnɪ] n miel m; (inf: darling) chéri(e)

honeycomb ['hʌnɪkəum] n rayon m de miel; (pattern) nid m d'abeilles, motif alvéolé ▷ vt (fig): **to ~ with** cribler de

honeymoon ['hʌnɪmu:n] n lune f de miel, voyage m de noces; **we're on ~** nous sommes en voyage de noces

honeysuckle ['hʌnɪsʌkl] n chèvrefeuille m

Hong Kong ['hɔŋ'kɔŋ] n Hong Kong

honk [hɔŋk] n (Aut) coup m de klaxon ▷ vi klaxonner

honorary ['ɔnərərɪ] adj honoraire; (duty, title) honorifique; **~ degree** diplôme m honoris causa

honour, (US) **honor** ['ɔnə'] vt honorer ▷ n honneur m; **in ~ of** en l'honneur de; **to graduate with ~s** obtenir sa licence avec mention

honourable, (US) **honorable** ['ɔnərəbl] adj honorable

honours degree ['ɔnəz-] n (Scol) = licence f avec mention

hood [hud] n capuchon m; (of cooker) hotte f; (Brit Aut) capote f; (US Aut) capot m; (inf) truand m

hoodie ['hudɪ] n (top) sweat m à capuche

hoof (pl hoofs or hooves) [hu:f, hu:vz] n sabot m

hook [huk] n crochet m; (on dress) agrafe f; (for fishing) hameçon m ▷ vt accrocher; (dress) agrafer; **off the ~** (Tel) décroché; **~ and eye** agrafe; **by ~ or by crook** de gré ou de force, coûte que coûte; **to be ~ed (on)** (inf) être accroché(e) (par); (person) être dingue (de); **hook up** vt (Radio, TV etc) faire un duplex entre

hooligan ['huːlɪgən] n voyou m

hoop [huːp] n cerceau m; (of barrel) cercle m

hoot [huːt] vi (Brit: Aut) klaxonner; (siren) mugir; (owl) hululer ▷ vt (jeer at) huer ▷ n huée f; coup m de klaxon; mugissement m; hululement m; **to ~ with laughter** rire aux éclats

hooter ['huːtər] n (Brit Aut) klaxon m; (Naut, factory) sirène f

Hoover® ['huːvər] n (Brit) aspirateur m ▷ vt: **to hoover** (room) passer l'aspirateur dans; (carpet) passer l'aspirateur sur

hooves [huːvz] npl of **hoof**

hop [hɔp] vi sauter; (on one foot) sauter à cloche-pied; (bird) sautiller ▷ n saut m

hope [həup] vt, vi espérer ▷ n espoir m; **I ~ so** je l'espère; **I ~ not** j'espère que non

hopeful ['həupful] adj (person) plein(e) d'espoir; (situation) prometteur(-euse), encourageant(e); **I'm ~ that she'll manage to come** j'ai bon espoir qu'elle pourra venir

hopefully ['həupfulɪ] adv (expectantly) avec espoir, avec optimisme; (one hopes) avec un peu de chance; **~, they'll come back** espérons bien qu'ils reviendront

hopeless ['həuplɪs] adj désespéré(e), sans espoir; (useless) nul(le)

hops [hɔps] npl houblon m

horizon [hə'raɪzn] n horizon m

horizontal [hɔrɪ'zɔntl] adj horizontal(e)

hormone ['hɔːməun] n hormone f

horn [hɔːn] n corne f; (Mus) cor m; (Aut) klaxon m

hornet ['hɔːnɪt] n frelon m

horoscope ['hɔrəskəup] n horoscope m

horrendous [hə'rɛndəs] adj horrible, affreux(-euse)

horrible ['hɔrɪbl] adj horrible, affreux(-euse)

horrid ['hɔrɪd] adj (person) détestable; (weather, place, smell) épouvantable

horrific [hɔ'rɪfɪk] adj horrible

horrify ['hɔrɪfaɪ] vt horrifier

horrifying ['hɔrɪfaɪɪŋ] adj horrifiant(e)

horror ['hɔrər] n horreur f

horror film n film m d'épouvante

hors d'œuvre [ɔː'dəːvrə] n hors d'œuvre m

horse [hɔːs] n cheval m

horseback ['hɔːsbæk]: **on ~** adj, adv à cheval

horse chestnut n (nut) marron m (d'Inde); (tree) marronnier m (d'Inde)

horseman ['hɔːsmən] irreg n cavalier m

horsepower ['hɔːspauər] n puissance f (en chevaux); (unit) cheval-vapeur m (CV)

horse-racing ['hɔːsreɪsɪŋ] n courses fpl de chevaux

horseradish ['hɔːsrædɪʃ] n raifort m

horse riding n (Brit) équitation f

horseshoe ['hɔːsʃuː] n fer m à cheval

hose [həuz] n (also: **~pipe**) tuyau m; (in garden) tuyau d'arrosage; **hose down** vt laver au jet

hosepipe ['həuzpaɪp] n tuyau m; (in garden) tuyau d'arrosage; (for fire) tuyau d'incendie

hospitable ['hɔspɪtəbl] adj hospitalier(-ière)

hospital ['hɔspɪtl] n hôpital m; **in ~**, (US) **in the ~** à l'hôpital; **where's the nearest ~?** où est l'hôpital le plus proche?

hospitality [hɔspɪ'tælɪtɪ] n hospitalité f

host [həust] n hôte m; (in hotel etc) patron m; (TV, Radio) présentateur(-trice), animateur(-trice); (large number): **a ~ of** une foule de; (Rel) hostie f ▷ vt (TV programme) présenter, animer

hostage ['hɔstɪdʒ] n otage m

hostel ['hɔstl] n foyer m; (also: **youth ~**) auberge f de jeunesse

hostess ['həustɪs] n hôtesse f; (Brit: also: **air ~**) hôtesse de l'air; (TV, Radio) présentatrice f; (in nightclub) entraîneuse f

hostile ['hɔstaɪl] adj hostile

hostility [hɔ'stɪlɪtɪ] n hostilité f

hot [hɔt] adj chaud(e); (as opposed to only warm) très chaud; (spicy) fort(e); (fig: contest) acharné(e); (topic) brûlant(e); (temper) violent(e), passionné(e); **to be ~** (person) avoir chaud; (thing) être (très) chaud; (weather) faire chaud; **hot up** (Brit inf) vi (situation) devenir tendu(e); (party) s'animer ▷ vt (pace) accélérer, forcer; (engine) gonfler

hotbed ['hɔtbɛd] n (fig) foyer m, pépinière f

hot dog n hot-dog m

hotel [həu'tɛl] n hôtel m

hothouse ['hɔthaus] n serre chaude

hotline ['hɔtlaɪn] n (Pol) téléphone m rouge, ligne directe

hotly ['hɔtlɪ] adv passionnément, violemment

hotplate ['hɔtpleɪt] n (on cooker) plaque chauffante

hotpot ['hɔtpɔt] n (Brit Culin) ragoût m

hotspot ['hɔtspɔt] n (Comput: also: **wireless ~**) borne f wifi, hotspot m

hot-water bottle [hɔt'wɔːtə-] n bouillotte f

hound [haund] vt poursuivre avec acharnement ▷ n chien courant; **the ~s** la meute

hour ['auər] n heure f; **at 30 miles an ~ =** à 50 km à l'heure; **lunch ~** heure du déjeuner; **to pay sb by the ~** payer qn à l'heure

hourly ['auəlɪ] adj toutes les heures; (rate) horaire; **~ paid** adj payé(e) à l'heure

house n (pl **houses**) [haus, 'hauzɪz] n maison f; (Pol) chambre f; (Theat) salle f; auditoire m ▷ vt [hauz] (person) loger, héberger; **at (or to)**

my ~ chez moi; **the H~ of Commons/of Lords** (Brit) la Chambre des communes/des lords; *voir article;* **the H~ (of Representatives)** (US) la Chambre des représentants; *voir article;* **on the ~** (fig) aux frais de la maison

house arrest *n* assignation *f* à domicile

houseboat ['hausbəut] *n* bateau (aménagé en habitation)

housebound ['hausbaund] *adj* confiné(e) chez soi

housebreaking ['hausbreikıŋ] *n* cambriolage *m* (avec effraction)

household ['haushəuld] *n* (*Admin etc*) ménage *m*; (*people*) famille *f*, maisonnée *f*; **~ name** nom connu de tout le monde

householder ['haushəuldəʳ] *n* propriétaire *m/f*; (*head of house*) chef *m* de famille

housekeeper ['hauski:pəʳ] *n* gouvernante *f*

housekeeping ['hauski:pıŋ] *n* (*work*) ménage *m*; (*also:* **~ money**) argent *m* du ménage; (*Comput*) gestion *f* (des disques)

house-warming ['hauswɔːmıŋ] *n* (*also:* **~ party**) pendaison *f* de crémaillère

housewife (*irreg*) ['hauswaıf] *n* ménagère *f*; femme *f* au foyer

house wine *n* cuvée *f* maison *or* du patron

housework ['hauswəːk] *n* (travaux *mpl* du) ménage *m*

housing ['hauzıŋ] *n* logement *m* ▷ *cpd* (*problem, shortage*) de *or* du logement

housing development, housing estate (Brit) *n* (*blocks of flats*) cité *f*; (*houses*) lotissement *m*

hovel ['hɔvl] *n* taudis *m*

hover ['hɔvəʳ] *vi* planer; **to ~ round sb** rôder *or* tourner autour de qn

hovercraft ['hɔvəkrɑːft] *n* aéroglisseur *m*, hovercraft *m*

how [hau] *adv* comment; **~ are you?** comment allez-vous?; **~ do you do?** bonjour; (*on being introduced*) enchanté(e); **~ far is it to ...?** combien y a-t-il jusqu'à ...?; **~ long have you been here?** depuis combien de temps êtes-vous là?; **~ lovely/awful!** que *or* comme c'est joli/affreux!; **~ many/much?** combien?; **~ much time/many people?** combien de temps/gens?; **~ much does it cost?** ça coûte combien?; **~ old are you?** quel âge avez-vous?; **~ tall is he?** combien mesure-t-il?; **~ is school?** ça va à l'école?; **~ was the film?** comment était le film?; **~'s life?** (*inf*) comment ça va?; **~ about a drink?** si on buvait quelque chose?; **~ is it that ...?** comment se fait-il que ... +*sub*?

however [hau'evəʳ] *conj* pourtant, cependant ▷ *adv* de quelque façon *or* manière que +*sub*; (+*adjective*) quelque *or* si ... que +*sub*; (*in questions*) comment; **~ I do it** de quelque manière que je m'y prenne; **~ cold it is** même s'il fait très froid; **~ did you do it?** comment y êtes-vous donc arrivé?

howl [haul] *n* hurlement *m* ▷ *vi* hurler; (*wind*) mugir

H.P. *n abbr* (Brit) = **hire purchase**

h.p. *abbr* (*Aut*) = **horsepower**

HQ *n abbr* (= *headquarters*) QG *m*

hr *abbr* (= *hour*) h

hrs *abbr* (= *hours*) h

HTML *n abbr* (= *hypertext markup language*) HTML *m*

hub [hʌb] *n* (*of wheel*) moyeu *m*; (*fig*) centre *m*, foyer *m*

hubcap [hʌbkæp] *n* (*Aut*) enjoliveur *m*

huddle ['hʌdl] *vi*: **to ~ together** se blottir les uns contre les autres

hue [hju:] *n* teinte *f*, nuance *f*; **~ and cry** *n* tollé (général), clameur *f*

huff [hʌf] *n*: **in a ~** fâché(e); **to take the ~** prendre la mouche

hug [hʌg] *vt* serrer dans ses bras; (*shore, kerb*) serrer ▷ *n* étreinte *f*; **to give sb a ~** serrer qn dans ses bras

huge [hju:dʒ] *adj* énorme, immense

hulk [hʌlk] *n* (*ship*) vieux rafiot; (*car, building*) carcasse *f*; (*person*) mastodonte *m*, malabar *m*

hull [hʌl] *n* (*of ship*) coque *f*; (*of nuts*) coque, (*of peas*) cosse *f*

hullo [hə'ləu] *excl* = **hello**

hum [hʌm] *vt* (*tune*) fredonner ▷ *vi* fredonner; (*insect*) bourdonner; (*plane, tool*) vrombir ▷ *n* fredonnement *m*; bourdonnement *m*; vrombissement *m*

human ['hju:mən] *adj* humain(e) ▷ *n* (*also:* **~ being**) être humain

humane [hju:'meın] *adj* humain(e), humanitaire

humanitarian [hju:mænı'tɛərıən] *adj* humanitaire

humanity [hju:'mænıtı] *n* humanité *f*

human rights *npl* droits *mpl* de l'homme

humble ['hʌmbl] *adj* humble, modeste ▷ *vt* humilier

humdrum ['hʌmdrʌm] *adj* monotone, routinier(-ière)

humid ['hju:mıd] *adj* humide

humidity [hju:'mıdıtı] *n* humidité *f*

humiliate [hju:'mılıeıt] *vt* humilier

humiliating [hju:'mılıeıtıŋ] *adj* humiliant(e)

humiliation [hju:mılı'eıʃən] *n* humiliation *f*

hummus ['huməs] *n* houm(m)ous *m*

humorous ['hju:mərəs] *adj* humoristique; (*person*) plein(e) d'humour

humour, (US) humor ['hju:məʳ] *n* humour *m*; (*mood*) humeur *f* ▷ *vt* (*person*) faire plaisir à; se prêter aux caprices de; **sense of ~** sens *m* de l'humour; **to be in a good/bad ~** être de bonne/mauvaise humeur

hump [hʌmp] *n* bosse *f*

hunch [hʌntʃ] *n* bosse *f*; (*premonition*) intuition *f*; **I have a ~ that** j'ai (comme une vague) idée que

hunchback ['hʌntʃbæk] *n* bossu(e)

hunched [hʌntʃt] adj arrondi(e), voûté(e)
hundred ['hʌndrəd] num cent; **about a ~ people** une centaine de personnes; **~s of** des centaines de; **I'm a ~ per cent sure** j'en suis absolument certain
hundredth ['hʌndrɪdθ] num centième
hundredweight ['hʌndrɪdweɪt] n (Brit) =50.8 kg; 112 lb; (US) = 45.3 kg; 100 lb
hung [hʌŋ] pt, pp of **hang**
Hungarian [hʌŋ'gɛərɪən] adj hongrois(e) ▷ n Hongrois(e); (Ling) hongrois m
Hungary ['hʌŋgərɪ] n Hongrie f
hunger ['hʌŋgə^r] n faim f ▷ vi: **to ~ for** avoir faim de, désirer ardemment
hungry ['hʌŋgrɪ] adj affamé(e); **to be ~** avoir faim; **~ for** (fig) avide de
hunk [hʌŋk] n gros morceau; (inf: man) beau mec
hunt [hʌnt] vt (seek) chercher; (criminal) pourchasser; (Sport) chasser ▷ vi (search): **to ~ for** chercher (partout); (Sport) chasser ▷ n (Sport) chasse f; **hunt down** vt pourchasser
hunter ['hʌntə^r] n chasseur m; (Brit: horse) cheval m de chasse
hunting ['hʌntɪŋ] n chasse f
hurdle ['hə:dl] n (for fences) claie f; (Sport) haie f; (fig) obstacle m
hurl [hə:l] vt lancer (avec violence); (abuse, insults) lancer
hurrah, hurray [hu'rɑ:, hu'reɪ] excl hourra!
hurricane ['hʌrɪkən] n ouragan m
hurried ['hʌrɪd] adj pressé(e), précipité(e); (work) fait(e) à la hâte
hurriedly ['hʌrɪdlɪ] adv précipitamment, à la hâte
hurry ['hʌrɪ] n hâte f, précipitation f ▷ vi se presser, se dépêcher ▷ vt (person) faire presser, faire se dépêcher; (work) presser; **to be in a ~** être pressé(e); **to do sth in a ~** faire qch en vitesse; **to ~ in/out** entrer/sortir précipitamment; **to ~ home** se dépêcher de rentrer; **hurry along** vi marcher d'un pas pressé; **hurry away, hurry off** vi partir précipitamment; **hurry up** vi se dépêcher
hurt [hə:t] (pt, pp **hurt**) vt (cause pain to) faire mal à; (injure, fig) blesser; (damage: business, interests etc) nuire à; faire du tort à ▷ vi faire mal ▷ adj blessé(e); **my arm ~s** j'ai mal au bras; **I ~ my arm** je me suis fait mal au bras; **to ~ o.s.** se faire mal; **where does it ~?** où avez-vous mal?, où est-ce que ça vous fait mal?
hurtful ['hə:tful] adj (remark) blessant(e)
hurtle ['hə:tl] vt lancer (de toutes ses forces) ▷ vi: **to ~ past** passer en trombe; **to ~ down** dégringoler
husband ['hʌzbənd] n mari m
hush [hʌʃ] n calme m, silence m ▷ vt faire taire; **~!** chut!; **hush up** vt (fact) étouffer
husk [hʌsk] n (of wheat) balle f; (of rice, maize) enveloppe f; (of peas) cosse f
husky ['hʌskɪ] adj (voice) rauque; (burly)

costaud(e) ▷ n chien m esquimau or de traîneau
hustle ['hʌsl] vt pousser, bousculer ▷ n bousculade f; **~ and bustle** n tourbillon m (d'activité)
hut [hʌt] n hutte f; (shed) cabane f
hutch [hʌtʃ] n clapier m
hyacinth ['haɪəsɪnθ] n jacinthe f
hydrant ['haɪdrənt] n prise f d'eau; (also: **fire ~**) bouche f d'incendie
hydraulic [haɪ'drɔ:lɪk] adj hydraulique
hydroelectric ['haɪdrəʊɪ'lɛktrɪk] adj hydro-électrique
hydrofoil ['haɪdrəfɔɪl] n hydrofoil m
hydrogen ['haɪdrədʒən] n hydrogène m
hyena [haɪ'i:nə] n hyène f
hygiene ['haɪdʒi:n] n hygiène f
hygienic [haɪ'dʒi:nɪk] adj hygiénique
hymn [hɪm] n hymne m; cantique m
hype [haɪp] n (inf) matraquage m publicitaire or médiatique
hyperlink ['haɪpəlɪŋk] n hyperlien m
hypermarket ['haɪpəmɑ:kɪt] (Brit) n hypermarché m
hypertext ['haɪpətɛkst] n (Comput) hypertexte m
hyphen ['haɪfn] n trait m d'union
hypnotize ['hɪpnətaɪz] vt hypnotiser
hypocrisy [hɪ'pɔkrɪsɪ] n hypocrisie f
hypocrite ['hɪpəkrɪt] n hypocrite m/f
hypocritical [hɪpə'krɪtɪkl] adj hypocrite
hypothesis (pl **hypotheses**) [haɪ'pɔθɪsɪs, -si:z] n hypothèse f
hysterical [hɪ'stɛrɪkl] adj hystérique; (funny) hilarant(e); **to become ~** avoir une crise de nerfs
hysterics [hɪ'stɛrɪks] npl (violente) crise de nerfs; (laughter) crise de rire; **to be in/have ~** (anger, panic) avoir une crise de nerfs; (laughter) attraper un fou rire

h

I¹, i [aɪ] n (letter) I, i m; **I for Isaac,** (US) **I for Item** I comme Irma

I² [aɪ] pron je; (before vowel) j'; (stressed) moi ▷ abbr (= island, isle) I

ice [aɪs] n glace f; (on road) verglas m ▷ vt (cake) glacer; (drink) faire rafraîchir ▷ vi (also: **~ over**) geler; (also: **~ up**) se givrer; **to put sth on ~** (fig) mettre qch en attente

iceberg ['aɪsbə:g] n iceberg m; **the tip of the ~** (also fig) la partie émergée de l'iceberg

icebox ['aɪsbɔks] n (US) réfrigérateur m; (Brit) compartiment m à glace; (insulated box) glacière f

ice cream n glace f

ice cube n glaçon m

iced [aɪst] adj (drink) frappé(e); (coffee, tea, also cake) glacé(e)

ice hockey n hockey m sur glace

Iceland ['aɪslənd] n Islande f

Icelander ['aɪsləndər] n Islandais(e)

Icelandic [aɪs'lændɪk] adj islandais(e) ▷ n (Ling) islandais m

ice lolly n (Brit) esquimau m

ice rink n patinoire f

ice skating ['aɪsskeɪtɪŋ] n patinage m (sur glace)

icicle ['aɪsɪkl] n glaçon m (naturel)

icing ['aɪsɪŋ] n (Aviat etc) givrage m; (Culin) glaçage m

icing sugar n (Brit) sucre m glace

icon ['aɪkɔn] n icône f

ICT n abbr (Brit: Scol: = information and communications technology) TIC fpl

icy ['aɪsɪ] adj glacé(e); (road) verglacé(e); (weather, temperature) glacial(e)

I'd [aɪd] = **I would; I had**

ID card n carte f d'identité

idea [aɪ'dɪə] n idée f; **good ~!** bonne idée!; **to have an ~ that ...** avoir idée que ...; **I have no ~** je n'ai pas la moindre idée

ideal [aɪ'dɪəl] n idéal m ▷ adj idéal(e)

ideally [aɪ'dɪəlɪ] adv (preferably) dans l'idéal; (perfectly): **he is ~ suited to the job** il est parfait pour ce poste; **~ the book should have ...** l'idéal serait que le livre ait ...

identical [aɪ'dɛntɪkl] adj identique

identification [aɪdɛntɪfɪ'keɪʃən] n identification f; **means of ~** pièce f d'identité

identify [aɪ'dɛntɪfaɪ] vt identifier ▷ vi: **to ~ with** s'identifier à

Identikit® [aɪ'dɛntɪkɪt] n: **~ (picture)** portrait-robot m

identity [aɪ'dɛntɪtɪ] n identité f

identity card n carte f d'identité

identity theft n usurpation f d'identité

ideology [aɪdɪ'ɔlədʒɪ] n idéologie f

idiom ['ɪdɪəm] n (language) langue f, idiome m; (phrase) expression f idiomatique; (style) style m

idiosyncrasy [ɪdɪəu'sɪŋkrəsɪ] n particularité f, caractéristique f

idiot ['ɪdɪət] n idiot(e), imbécile m/f

idiotic [ɪdɪ'ɔtɪk] adj idiot(e), bête, stupide

idle ['aɪdl] adj (doing nothing) sans occupation, désœuvré(e); (lazy) oisif(-ive), paresseux(-euse); (unemployed) au chômage; (machinery) au repos; (question, pleasures) vain(e), futile ▷ vi (engine) tourner au ralenti; **to lie ~** être arrêté, ne pas fonctionner; **idle away** vt: **to ~ away one's time** passer son temps à ne rien faire

idol ['aɪdl] n idole f

idolize ['aɪdəlaɪz] vt idolâtrer, adorer

idyllic [ɪ'dɪlɪk] adj idyllique

i.e. abbr (= id est: that is) c. à d., c'est-à-dire

if [ɪf] conj si ▷ n: **there are a lot of ifs and buts** il y a beaucoup de si mpl et de mais mpl; **I'd be pleased if you could do it** je serais très heureux si vous pouviez le faire; **if necessary** si nécessaire, le cas échéant; **if so** si c'est le cas; **if not** sinon; **if only I could!** si seulement je pouvais!; **if only he were here** si seulement il était là; **if only to show him my gratitude** ne serait-ce que pour lui témoigner ma gratitude; see also **as**; **even**

ignite [ɪg'naɪt] vt mettre le feu à, enflammer ▷ vi s'enflammer

ignition [ɪg'nɪʃən] n (Aut) allumage m; **to switch on/off the ~** mettre/couper le contact

ignition key n (Aut) clé f de contact

ignorance ['ɪgnərəns] n ignorance f; **to keep**

sb in ~ of sth tenir qn dans l'ignorance de qch

ignorant ['ɪgnərənt] *adj* ignorant(e); **to be ~ of** (*subject*) ne rien connaître en; (*events*) ne pas être au courant de

ignore [ɪg'nɔːʳ] *vt* ne tenir aucun compte de; (*mistake*) ne pas relever; (*person: pretend to not see*) faire semblant de ne pas reconnaître; (*: pay no attention to*) ignorer

ill [ɪl] *adj* (*sick*) malade; (*bad*) mauvais(e) ▷ *n* mal *m* ▷ *adv*: **to speak/think ~ of sb** dire/penser du mal de qn; **to be taken ~** tomber malade

I'll [aɪl] = **I will; I shall**

ill-advised [ɪləd'vaɪzd] *adj* (*decision*) peu judicieux(-euse); (*person*) malavisé(e)

ill-at-ease [ɪlət'iːz] *adj* mal à l'aise

illegal [ɪ'liːgl] *adj* illégal(e)

illegible [ɪ'lɛdʒɪbl] *adj* illisible

illegitimate [ɪlɪ'dʒɪtɪmət] *adj* illégitime

ill-fated [ɪl'feɪtɪd] *adj* malheureux(-euse); (*day*) néfaste

ill feeling *n* ressentiment *m*, rancune *f*

ill health *n* mauvaise santé

illiterate [ɪ'lɪtərət] *adj* illettré(e); (*letter*) plein(e) de fautes

ill-mannered [ɪl'mænəd] *adj* impoli(e), grossier(-ière)

illness ['ɪlnɪs] *n* maladie *f*

ill-treat [ɪl'triːt] *vt* maltraiter

illuminate [ɪ'luːmɪneɪt] *vt* (*room, street*) éclairer; (*for special effect*) illuminer; **~d sign** enseigne lumineuse

illumination [ɪluːmɪ'neɪʃən] *n* éclairage *m*; illumination *f*

illusion [ɪ'luːʒən] *n* illusion *f*; **to be under the ~ that** avoir l'illusion que

illustrate ['ɪləstreɪt] *vt* illustrer

illustration [ɪlə'streɪʃən] *n* illustration *f*

ill will *n* malveillance *f*

IM *n abbr* (= *instant messaging*) messagerie *f* instantanée ▷ *vt* envoyer un message instantané à

I'm [aɪm] = **I am**

image ['ɪmɪdʒ] *n* image *f*; (*public face*) image de marque

imagery ['ɪmɪdʒərɪ] *n* images *fpl*

imaginary [ɪ'mædʒɪnərɪ] *adj* imaginaire

imagination [ɪmædʒɪ'neɪʃən] *n* imagination *f*

imaginative [ɪ'mædʒɪnətɪv] *adj* imaginatif(-ive); (*person*) plein(e) d'imagination

imagine [ɪ'mædʒɪn] *vt* s'imaginer; (*suppose*) imaginer, supposer

imbalance [ɪm'bæləns] *n* déséquilibre *m*

imitate ['ɪmɪteɪt] *vt* imiter

imitation [ɪmɪ'teɪʃən] *n* imitation *f*

immaculate [ɪ'mækjulət] *adj* impeccable; (*Rel*) immaculé(e)

immaterial [ɪmə'tɪərɪəl] *adj* sans importance, insignifiant(e)

immature [ɪmə'tjuəʳ] *adj* (*fruit*) qui n'est pas mûr(e); (*person*) qui manque de maturité

immediate [ɪ'miːdɪət] *adj* immédiat(e)

immediately [ɪ'miːdɪətlɪ] *adv* (*at once*) immédiatement; **~ next to** juste à côté de

immense [ɪ'mɛns] *adj* immense, énorme

immerse [ɪ'məːs] *vt* immerger, plonger; **to ~ sth in** plonger qch dans; **to be ~d in** (*fig*) être plongé dans

immersion heater [ɪ'məːʃən-] *n* (*Brit*) chauffe-eau *m* électrique

immigrant ['ɪmɪgrənt] *n* immigrant(e); (*already established*) immigré(e)

immigration [ɪmɪ'greɪʃən] *n* immigration *f*

imminent ['ɪmɪnənt] *adj* imminent(e)

immoral [ɪ'mɔrl] *adj* immoral(e)

immortal [ɪ'mɔːtl] *adj, n* immortel(le)

immune [ɪ'mjuːn] *adj*: **~ (to)** immunisé(e) (contre)

immune system *n* système *m* immunitaire

immunity [ɪ'mjuːnɪtɪ] *n* immunité *f*; **diplomatic ~** immunité diplomatique

immunize ['ɪmjunaɪz] *vt* immuniser

impact ['ɪmpækt] *n* choc *m*, impact *m*; (*fig*) impact

impair [ɪm'pɛəʳ] *vt* détériorer, diminuer

impart [ɪm'pɑːt] *vt* (*make known*) communiquer, transmettre; (*bestow*) confier, donner

impartial [ɪm'pɑːʃl] *adj* impartial(e)

impassable [ɪm'pɑːsəbl] *adj* infranchissable; (*road*) impraticable

impassive [ɪm'pæsɪv] *adj* impassible

impatience [ɪm'peɪʃəns] *n* impatience *f*

impatient [ɪm'peɪʃənt] *adj* impatient(e); **to get** *or* **grow ~** s'impatienter

impatiently [ɪm'peɪʃəntlɪ] *adv* avec impatience

impeccable [ɪm'pɛkəbl] *adj* impeccable, parfait(e)

impede [ɪm'piːd] *vt* gêner

impediment [ɪm'pɛdɪmənt] *n* obstacle *m*; (*also:* **speech ~**) défaut *m* d'élocution

impending [ɪm'pɛndɪŋ] *adj* imminent(e)

imperative [ɪm'pɛrətɪv] *adj* nécessaire; (*need*) urgent(e), pressant(e); (*tone*) impérieux(-euse) ▷ *n* (*Ling*) impératif *m*

imperfect [ɪm'pəːfɪkt] *adj* imparfait(e); (*goods etc*) défectueux(-euse) ▷ *n* (*Ling: also*: **~ tense**) imparfait *m*

imperial [ɪm'pɪərɪəl] *adj* impérial(e); (*Brit: measure*) légal(e)

impersonal [ɪm'pəːsənl] *adj* impersonnel(le)

impersonate [ɪm'pəːsəneɪt] *vt* se faire passer pour; (*Theat*) imiter

impertinent [ɪm'pəːtɪnənt] *adj* impertinent(e), insolent(e)

impervious [ɪm'pəːvɪəs] *adj* imperméable; (*fig*): **~ to** insensible à; inaccessible à

impetuous [ɪm'pɛtjuəs] *adj* impétueux(-euse), fougueux(-euse)

impetus ['ɪmpɪtəs] n impulsion f; (of runner)
élan m

impinge [ɪm'pɪndʒ]: **to ~ on** vt fus (person)
affecter, toucher; (rights) empiéter sur

implant [ɪm'plɑːnt] vt (Med) implanter; (fig:
idea, principle) inculquer

implement n ['ɪmplɪmənt] outil m,
instrument m; (for cooking) ustensile m ▷ vt
['ɪmplɪmɛnt] exécuter, mettre à effet

implicate ['ɪmplɪkeɪt] vt impliquer,
compromettre

implication [ɪmplɪ'keɪʃən] n implication f;
by ~ indirectement

implicit [ɪm'plɪsɪt] adj implicite; (complete)
absolu(e), sans réserve

imply [ɪm'plaɪ] vt (hint) suggérer, laisser
entendre; (mean) indiquer, supposer

impolite [ɪmpə'laɪt] adj impoli(e)

import vt [ɪm'pɔːt] importer ▷ n ['ɪmpɔːt]
(Comm) importation f; (meaning) portée f,
signification f ▷ cpd ['ɪmpɔːt] (duty, licence etc)
d'importation

importance [ɪm'pɔːtns] n importance f;
to be of great/little ~ avoir beaucoup/peu
d'importance

important [ɪm'pɔːtnt] adj important(e); **it is
~ that** il importe que, il est important que;
it's not ~ c'est sans importance, ce n'est pas
important

importer [ɪm'pɔːtər] n importateur(-trice)

impose [ɪm'pəuz] vt imposer ▷ vi: **to ~ on sb**
abuser de la gentillesse de qn

imposing [ɪm'pəuzɪŋ] adj imposant(e),
impressionnant(e)

imposition [ɪmpə'zɪʃən] n (of tax etc)
imposition f; **to be an ~ on** (person) abuser de
la gentillesse or la bonté de

impossible [ɪm'pɔsɪbl] adj impossible; **it is ~
for me to leave** il m'est impossible de partir

impotent ['ɪmpətnt] adj impuissant(e)

impound [ɪm'paund] vt confisquer, saisir

impoverished [ɪm'pɔvərɪʃt] adj pauvre,
appauvri(e)

impractical [ɪm'præktɪkl] adj pas pratique;
(person) qui manque d'esprit pratique

impregnable [ɪm'pregnəbl] adj (fortress)
imprenable; (fig) inattaquable, irréfutable

impress [ɪm'pres] vt impressionner, faire
impression sur; (mark) imprimer, marquer;
to ~ sth on sb faire bien comprendre qch
à qn

impressed [ɪm'prest] adj impressionné(e)

impression [ɪm'preʃən] n impression f;
(of stamp, seal) empreinte f; (imitation)
imitation f; **to make a good/bad ~ on sb**
faire bonne/mauvaise impression sur qn;
to be under the ~ that avoir l'impression
que

impressionist [ɪm'preʃənɪst] n
impressionniste m/f

impressive [ɪm'presɪv] adj
impressionnant(e)

imprint ['ɪmprɪnt] n empreinte f; (Publishing)
notice f; (: label) nom m (de collection or
d'éditeur)

imprison [ɪm'prɪzn] vt emprisonner, mettre
en prison

imprisonment [ɪm'prɪznmənt] n
emprisonnement m; (period): **to sentence sb
to 10 years' ~** condamner qn à 10 ans de
prison

improbable [ɪm'prɔbəbl] adj improbable;
(excuse) peu plausible

improper [ɪm'prɔpər] adj (wrong) incorrect(e);
(unsuitable) déplacé(e), de mauvais goût;
(indecent) indécent(e); (dishonest)
malhonnête

improve [ɪm'pruːv] vt améliorer ▷ vi
s'améliorer; (pupil etc) faire des progrès;
improve on, improve upon vt fus (offer)
enchérir sur

improvement [ɪm'pruːvmənt] n
amélioration f; (of pupil etc) progrès m; **to
make ~s to** apporter des améliorations à

improvise ['ɪmprəvaɪz] vt, vi improviser

impudent ['ɪmpjudnt] adj impudent(e)

impulse ['ɪmpʌls] n impulsion f; **on ~**
impulsivement, sur un coup de tête

impulsive [ɪm'pʌlsɪv] adj impulsif(-ive)

◯ **KEYWORD**

in [ɪn] prep **1** (indicating place, position) dans;
in the house/the fridge dans la maison/
le frigo; **in the garden** dans le or au jardin;
in town en ville; **in the country** à la
campagne; **in school** à l'école; **in here/
there** ici/là

2 (with place names: of town, region, country): **in
London** à Londres; **in England** en
Angleterre; **in Japan** au Japon; **in the
United States** aux États-Unis

3 (indicating time: during): **in spring** au
printemps; **in summer** en été; **in May/2005**
en mai/2005; **in the afternoon** (dans)
l'après-midi; **at 4 o'clock in the afternoon**
à 4 heures de l'après-midi

4 (indicating time: in the space of) en; (: future)
dans; **I did it in 3 hours/days** je l'ai fait en
3 heures/jours; **I'll see you in 2 weeks** or **in
2 weeks' time** je te verrai dans 2 semaines;
once in a hundred years une fois tous les
cent ans

5 (indicating manner etc) à; **in a loud/soft voice**
à voix haute/basse; **in pencil** au crayon; **in
writing** par écrit; **in French** en français; **to
pay in dollars** payer en dollars; **the boy in
the blue shirt** le garçon à or avec la chemise
bleue

6 (indicating circumstances): **in the sun** au
soleil; **in the shade** à l'ombre; **in the rain**
sous la pluie; **a change in policy** un
changement de politique

7 (indicating mood, state): **in tears** en larmes;

in anger sous le coup de la colère; **in despair** au désespoir; **in good condition** en bon état; **to live in luxury** vivre dans le luxe
8 (*with ratios, numbers*): **1 in 10 households, 1 household in 10** 1 ménage sur 10; **20 pence in the pound** 20 pence par livre sterling; **they lined up in twos** ils se mirent en rangs (deux) par deux; **in hundreds** par centaines
9 (*referring to people, works*) chez; **the disease is common in children** c'est une maladie courante chez les enfants; **in (the works of) Dickens** chez Dickens, dans (l'œuvre de) Dickens
10 (*indicating profession etc*) dans; **to be in teaching** être dans l'enseignement
11 (*after superlative*) de; **the best pupil in the class** le meilleur élève de la classe
12 (*with present participle*): **in saying this** en disant ceci
▷ *adv*: **to be in** (*person: at home, work*) être là; (*train, ship, plane*) être arrivé(e); (*in fashion*) être à la mode; **to ask sb in** inviter qn à entrer; **to run/limp** *etc* **in** entrer en courant/boitant *etc*; **their party is in** leur parti est au pouvoir
▷ *n*: **the ins and outs (of)** (*of proposal, situation etc*) les tenants et aboutissants (de)

in. *abbr* = **inch; inches**
inability [ɪnəˈbɪlɪtɪ] *n* incapacité *f*; **~ to pay** incapacité de payer
inaccurate [ɪnˈækjurət] *adj* inexact(e); (*person*) qui manque de précision
inadequate [ɪnˈædɪkwət] *adj* insuffisant(e), inadéquat(e)
inadvertently [ɪnədˈvəːtntlɪ] *adv* par mégarde
inadvisable [ɪnədˈvaɪzəbl] *adj* à déconseiller; **it is ~ to** il est déconseillé de
inane [ɪˈneɪn] *adj* inepte, stupide
inanimate [ɪnˈænɪmət] *adj* inanimé(e)
inappropriate [ɪnəˈprəuprɪət] *adj* inopportun(e), mal à propos; (*word, expression*) impropre
inarticulate [ɪnɑːˈtɪkjulət] *adj* (*person*) qui s'exprime mal; (*speech*) indistinct(e)
inasmuch [ɪnəzˈmʌtʃ] *adv*: **~ as** vu que, en ce sens que
inaugurate [ɪˈnɔːgjureɪt] *vt* inaugurer; (*president, official*) investir de ses fonctions
inauguration [ɪnɔːgjuˈreɪʃən] *n* inauguration *f*; investiture *f*
inborn [ɪnˈbɔːn] *adj* (*feeling*) inné(e); (*defect*) congénital(e)
inbred [ɪnˈbred] *adj* inné(e), naturel(le); (*family*) consanguin(e)
Inc. *abbr* = **incorporated**
incapable [ɪnˈkeɪpəbl] *adj*: **~ (of)** incapable (de)
incapacitate [ɪnkəˈpæsɪteɪt] *vt*: **to ~ sb from doing** rendre qn incapable de faire
incense *n* [ˈɪnsens] encens *m* ▷ *vt* [ɪnˈsens] (*anger*) mettre en colère

incentive [ɪnˈsentɪv] *n* encouragement *m*, raison *f* de se donner de la peine
incessant [ɪnˈsesnt] *adj* incessant(e)
incessantly [ɪnˈsesntlɪ] *adv* sans cesse, constamment
inch [ɪntʃ] *n* pouce *m* (=25 mm; 12 in a foot); **within an ~ of** à deux doigts de; **he wouldn't give an ~** (*fig*) il n'a pas voulu céder d'un pouce; **inch forward** *vi* avancer petit à petit
incidence [ˈɪnsɪdns] *n* (*of crime, disease*) fréquence *f*
incident [ˈɪnsɪdnt] *n* incident *m*; (*in book*) péripétie *f*
incidental [ɪnsɪˈdentl] *adj* accessoire; (*unplanned*) accidentel(le); **~ to** qui accompagne; **~ expenses** faux frais *mpl*
incidentally [ɪnsɪˈdentəlɪ] *adv* (*by the way*) à propos
inclination [ɪnklɪˈneɪʃən] *n* inclination *f*; (*desire*) envie *f*
incline *n* [ˈɪnklaɪn] pente *f*, plan incliné ▷ *vt* [ɪnˈklaɪn] incliner ▷ *vi* (*surface*) s'incliner; **to ~ to** avoir tendance à; **to be ~d to do** (*want to*) être enclin(e) à faire; (*have a tendency to do*) avoir tendance à faire; **to be well ~d towards sb** être bien disposé(e) à l'égard de qn
include [ɪnˈkluːd] *vt* inclure, comprendre; **service is/is not ~d** le service est compris/n'est pas compris
including [ɪnˈkluːdɪŋ] *prep* y compris; **~ service** service compris
inclusion [ɪnˈkluːʒən] *n* inclusion *f*
inclusive [ɪnˈkluːsɪv] *adj* inclus(e), compris(e); **~ of tax** taxes comprises; **£50 ~ of all surcharges** 50 livres tous frais compris
income [ˈɪnkʌm] *n* revenu *m*; (*from property etc*) rentes *fpl*; **gross/net ~** revenu brut/net; **~ and expenditure account** compte *m* de recettes et de dépenses
income support *n* (*Brit*) ≈ revenu *m* minimum d'insertion, RMI *m*
income tax *n* impôt *m* sur le revenu
incoming [ˈɪnkʌmɪŋ] *adj* (*passengers, mail*) à l'arrivée; (*government, tenant*) nouveau/nouvelle; **~ tide** marée montante
incompatible [ɪnkəmˈpætɪbl] *adj* incompatible
incompetence [ɪnˈkɔmpɪtns] *n* incompétence *f*, incapacité *f*
incompetent [ɪnˈkɔmpɪtnt] *adj* incompétent(e), incapable
incomplete [ɪnkəmˈpliːt] *adj* incomplet(-ète)
incongruous [ɪnˈkɔŋgruəs] *adj* peu approprié(e); (*remark, act*) incongru(e), déplacé(e)
inconsiderate [ɪnkənˈsɪdərət] *adj* (*action*) inconsidéré(e); (*person*) qui manque d'égards
inconsistency [ɪnkənˈsɪstənsɪ] *n* (*of actions etc*) inconséquence *f*; (*of work*) irrégularité *f*; (*of statement etc*) incohérence *f*

inconsistent [ɪnkən'sɪstnt] *adj* qui manque de constance; (*work*) irrégulier(-ière); (*statement*) peu cohérent(e); **~ with** en contradiction avec

inconspicuous [ɪnkən'spɪkjuəs] *adj* qui passe inaperçu(e); (*colour, dress*) discret(-ète); **to make o.s. ~** ne pas se faire remarquer

inconvenience [ɪnkən'viːnjəns] *n* inconvénient *m*; (*trouble*) dérangement *m* ▷ *vt* déranger; **don't ~ yourself** ne vous dérangez pas

inconvenient [ɪnkən'viːnjənt] *adj* malcommode; (*time, place*) mal choisi(e), qui ne convient pas; (*visitor*) importun(e); **that time is very ~ for me** c'est un moment qui ne me convient pas du tout

incorporate [ɪn'kɔːpəreɪt] *vt* incorporer; (*contain*) contenir ▷ *vi* fusionner; (*two firms*) se constituer en société

incorporated [ɪn'kɔːpəreɪtɪd] *adj*: **~ company** (*US*) ≈ société *f* anonyme

incorrect [ɪnkə'rekt] *adj* incorrect(e); (*opinion, statement*) inexact(e)

increase *n* ['ɪnkriːs] augmentation *f* ▷ *vi, vt* [ɪn'kriːs] augmenter; **an ~ of 5%** une augmentation de 5%; **to be on the ~** être en augmentation

increasing [ɪn'kriːsɪŋ] *adj* croissant(e)

increasingly [ɪn'kriːsɪŋlɪ] *adv* de plus en plus

incredible [ɪn'kredɪbl] *adj* incroyable

incredibly [ɪn'kredɪblɪ] *adv* incroyablement

incubator ['ɪnkjubeɪtə'] *n* incubateur *m*; (*for babies*) couveuse *f*

incumbent [ɪn'kʌmbənt] *adj*: **it is ~ on him to ...** il lui appartient de ... ▷ *n* titulaire *m/f*

incur [ɪn'kəː'] *vt* (*expenses*) encourir; (*anger, risk*) s'exposer à; (*debt*) contracter; (*loss*) subir

indebted [ɪn'detɪd] *adj*: **to be ~ to sb (for)** être redevable à qn (de)

indecent [ɪn'diːsnt] *adj* indécent(e), inconvenant(e)

indecent assault *n* (*Brit*) attentat *m* à la pudeur

indecent exposure *n* outrage *m* public à la pudeur

indecisive [ɪndɪ'saɪsɪv] *adj* indécis(e); (*discussion*) peu concluant(e)

indeed [ɪn'diːd] *adv* (*confirming, agreeing*) en effet, effectivement; (*for emphasis*) vraiment; (*furthermore*) d'ailleurs; **yes ~!** certainement!

indefinitely [ɪn'defɪnɪtlɪ] *adv* (*wait*) indéfiniment; (*speak*) vaguement, avec imprécision

indemnity [ɪn'dɛmnɪtɪ] *n* (*insurance*) assurance *f*, garantie *f*; (*compensation*) indemnité *f*

independence [ɪndɪ'pɛndns] *n* indépendance *f*

Independence Day *n* (*US*) fête de l'Indépendance américaine; *voir article*

▓ INDEPENDENCE DAY

L'*Independence Day* est la fête nationale aux États-Unis, le 4 juillet. Il commémore l'adoption de la déclaration d'Indépendance, en 1776, écrite par Thomas Jefferson et proclamant la séparation des 13 colonies américaines de la Grande-Bretagne.

independent [ɪndɪ'pɛndnt] *adj* indépendant(e); (*radio*) libre; **to become ~** s'affranchir

independent school *n* (*Brit*) école privée

index ['ɪndɛks] *n* (*pl* **indexes**) (*in book*) index *m*; (*: in library etc*) catalogue *m*; (*pl* **indices**) ['ɪndɪsiːz] (*ratio, sign*) indice *m*

index card *n* fiche *f*

index finger *n* index *m*

index-linked ['ɪndɛks'lɪŋkt], (*US*) **indexed** ['ɪndɛkst] *adj* indexé(e) (sur le coût de la vie *etc*)

India ['ɪndɪə] *n* Inde *f*

Indian ['ɪndɪən] *adj* indien(ne) ▷ *n* Indien(ne); (**American**) **~** Indien(ne) (d'Amérique)

Indian Ocean *n*: **the ~** l'océan Indien

indicate ['ɪndɪkeɪt] *vt* indiquer ▷ *vi* (*Brit Aut*): **to ~ left/right** mettre son clignotant à gauche/à droite

indication [ɪndɪ'keɪʃən] *n* indication *f*, signe *m*

indicative [ɪn'dɪkətɪv] *adj* indicatif(-ive); **to be ~ of sth** être symptomatique de qch ▷ *n* (*Ling*) indicatif *m*

indicator ['ɪndɪkeɪtə'] *n* (*sign*) indicateur *m*; (*Aut*) clignotant *m*

indices ['ɪndɪsiːz] *npl of* **index**

indict [ɪn'daɪt] *vt* accuser

indictment [ɪn'daɪtmənt] *n* accusation *f*

indifference [ɪn'dɪfrəns] *n* indifférence *f*

indifferent [ɪn'dɪfrənt] *adj* indifférent(e); (*poor*) médiocre, quelconque

indigenous [ɪn'dɪdʒɪnəs] *adj* indigène

indigestion [ɪndɪ'dʒɛstʃən] *n* indigestion *f*, mauvaise digestion

indignant [ɪn'dɪgnənt] *adj*: **~ (at sth/ with sb)** indigné (e) (de qch/contre qn)

indignity [ɪn'dɪgnɪtɪ] *n* indignité *f*, affront *m*

indirect [ɪndɪ'rekt] *adj* indirect(e)

indiscreet [ɪndɪ'skriːt] *adj* indiscret(-ète); (*rash*) imprudent(e)

indiscriminate [ɪndɪ'skrɪmɪnət] *adj* (*person*) qui manque de discernement; (*admiration*) aveugle; (*killings*) commis(e) au hasard

indispensable [ɪndɪ'spɛnsəbl] *adj* indispensable

indisputable [ɪndɪ'spjuːtəbl] *adj* incontestable, indiscutable

individual [ɪndɪ'vɪdjuəl] *n* individu *m* ▷ *adj* individuel(le); (*characteristic*) particulier(-ière), original(e)

individually [ɪndɪ'vɪdjuəlɪ] adv
individuellement

indoctrination [ɪndɔktrɪ'neɪʃən] n
endoctrinement m

Indonesia [ɪndə'ni:zɪə] n Indonésie f

indoor ['ɪndɔ:ʳ] adj d'intérieur; (plant)
d'appartement; (swimming pool) couvert(e);
(sport, games) pratiqué(e) en salle

indoors [ɪn'dɔ:z] adv à l'intérieur; (at home)
à la maison

induce [ɪn'dju:s] vt (persuade) persuader; (bring
about) provoquer; (labour) déclencher; **to ~ sb
to do sth** inciter or pousser qn à faire qch

inducement [ɪn'dju:smənt] n incitation f;
(incentive) but m; (pej: bribe) pot-de-vin m

indulge [ɪn'dʌldʒ] vt (whim) céder à,
satisfaire; (child) gâter ▷ vi: **to ~ in sth**
(luxury) s'offrir qch, se permettre qch;
(fantasies etc) se livrer à qch

indulgence [ɪn'dʌldʒəns] n fantaisie f (que
l'on s'offre); (leniency) indulgence f

indulgent [ɪn'dʌldʒənt] adj indulgent(e)

industrial [ɪn'dʌstrɪəl] adj industriel(le);
(injury) du travail; (dispute) ouvrier(-ère)

industrial action n action revendicative

industrial estate n (Brit) zone industrielle

industrialist [ɪn'dʌstrɪəlɪst] n industriel m

industrial park n (US) zone industrielle

industrious [ɪn'dʌstrɪəs] adj
travailleur(-euse)

industry ['ɪndəstrɪ] n industrie f; (diligence)
zèle m, application f

inebriated [ɪ'ni:brɪeɪtɪd] adj ivre

inedible [ɪn'edɪbl] adj immangeable; (plant
etc) non comestible

ineffective [ɪnɪ'fektɪv], **ineffectual**
[ɪnɪ'fektʃuəl] adj inefficace; incompétent(e)

inefficient [ɪnɪ'fɪʃənt] adj inefficace

inequality [ɪnɪ'kwɔlɪtɪ] n inégalité f

inescapable [ɪnɪ'skeɪpəbl] adj inéluctable,
inévitable

inevitable [ɪn'evɪtəbl] adj inévitable

inevitably [ɪn'evɪtəblɪ] adv inévitablement,
fatalement

inexpensive [ɪnɪk'spɛnsɪv] adj bon marché inv

inexperienced [ɪnɪk'spɪərɪənst] adj
inexpérimenté(e); **to be ~ in sth** manquer
d'expérience dans qch

inexplicable [ɪnɪk'splɪkəbl] adj inexplicable

infallible [ɪn'fælɪbl] adj infaillible

infamous ['ɪnfəməs] adj infâme,
abominable

infancy ['ɪnfənsɪ] n petite enfance, bas âge;
(fig) enfance, débuts mpl

infant ['ɪnfənt] n (baby) nourrisson m; (young
child) petit(e) enfant

infantry ['ɪnfəntrɪ] n infanterie f

infant school n (Brit) classes fpl préparatoires
(entre 5 et 7 ans)

infatuated [ɪn'fætjueɪtɪd] adj: **~ with**
entiché(e) de; **to become ~ (with sb)**
s'enticher (de qn)

infatuation [ɪnfætju'eɪʃən] n toquade f;
engouement m

infect [ɪn'fekt] vt (wound) infecter; (person,
blood) contaminer; (fig: pej) corrompre; **~ed
with** (illness) atteint(e) de; **to become ~ed**
(wound) s'infecter

infection [ɪn'fekʃən] n infection f; (contagion)
contagion f

infectious [ɪn'fekʃəs] adj infectieux(-euse);
(also fig) contagieux(-euse)

infer [ɪn'fəːʳ] vt: **to ~ (from)** conclure (de),
déduire (de)

inferior [ɪn'fɪərɪəʳ] adj inférieur(e); (goods)
de qualité inférieure ▷ n inférieur(e); (in
rank) subalterne m/f; **to feel ~** avoir un
sentiment d'infériorité

inferiority [ɪnfɪərɪ'ɔrətɪ] n infériorité f

infertile [ɪn'fə:taɪl] adj stérile

infertility [ɪnfə:'tɪlɪtɪ] n infertilité f,
stérilité f

infested [ɪn'festɪd] adj: **~ (with)** infesté(e) (de)

in-fighting ['ɪnfaɪtɪŋ] n querelles fpl internes

infinite ['ɪnfɪnɪt] adj infini(e); (time, money)
illimité(e)

infinitely ['ɪnfɪnɪtlɪ] adv infiniment

infinitive [ɪn'fɪnɪtɪv] n infinitif m

infinity [ɪn'fɪnɪtɪ] n infinité f; (also Math)
infini m

infirmary [ɪn'fə:mərɪ] n hôpital m; (in school,
factory) infirmerie f

inflamed [ɪn'fleɪmd] adj enflammé(e)

inflammable [ɪn'flæməbl] adj (Brit)
inflammable

inflammation [ɪnflə'meɪʃən] n
inflammation f

inflatable [ɪn'fleɪtəbl] adj gonflable

inflate [ɪn'fleɪt] vt (tyre, balloon) gonfler; (fig:
exaggerate) grossir, gonfler; (: increase) gonfler

inflation [ɪn'fleɪʃən] n (Econ) inflation f

inflationary [ɪn'fleɪʃənərɪ] adj inflationniste

inflexible [ɪn'fleksɪbl] adj inflexible, rigide

inflict [ɪn'flɪkt] vt: **to ~ on** infliger à

influence ['ɪnfluəns] n influence f ▷ vt
influencer; **under the ~ of** sous l'effet de;
under the ~ of alcohol en état d'ébriété

influential [ɪnflu'enʃl] adj influent(e)

influenza [ɪnflu'enzə] n grippe f

influx ['ɪnflʌks] n afflux m

info (inf) ['ɪnfəu] n (= information)
renseignements mpl

infomercial ['ɪnfəuməːʃl] (US) n (for product)
publi-information f; (Pol) émission où un
candidat présente son programme électoral

inform [ɪn'fɔ:m] vt: **to ~ sb (of)** informer or
avertir qn (de) ▷ vi: **to ~ on sb** dénoncer qn,
informer contre qn; **to ~ sb about** renseigner
qn sur, mettre qn au courant de

informal [ɪn'fɔ:ml] adj (person, manner, party)
simple, sans cérémonie; (visit, discussion)
dénué(e) de formalités; (announcement,
invitation) non officiel(le); (colloquial)
familier(-ère); **"dress ~"** "tenue de ville"

informality [ɪnfɔːˈmælɪtɪ] *n* simplicité *f*, absence *f* de cérémonie; caractère non officiel

informant [ɪnˈfɔːmənt] *n* informateur(-trice)

information [ɪnfəˈmeɪʃən] *n* information(s) *f(pl)*; renseignements *mpl*; (*knowledge*) connaissances *fpl*; **to get ~ on** se renseigner sur; **a piece of ~** un renseignement; **for your ~** à titre d'information

information desk *n* accueil *m*

information office *n* bureau *m* de renseignements

information technology *n* informatique *f*

informative [ɪnˈfɔːmətɪv] *adj* instructif(-ive)

informer [ɪnˈfɔːməʳ] *n* dénonciateur(-trice); (*also: police ~*) indicateur(-trice)

infra-red [ɪnfrəˈred] *adj* infrarouge

infrastructure [ˈɪnfrəstrʌktʃəʳ] *n* infrastructure *f*

infrequent [ɪnˈfriːkwənt] *adj* peu fréquent(e), rare

infringe [ɪnˈfrɪndʒ] *vt* enfreindre ▷ *vi*: **to ~ on** empiéter sur

infringement [ɪnˈfrɪndʒmənt] *n*: **~ (of)** infraction *f* (à)

infuriate [ɪnˈfjuərɪeɪt] *vt* mettre en fureur

infuriating [ɪnˈfjuərɪeɪtɪŋ] *adj* exaspérant(e)

ingenious [ɪnˈdʒiːnjəs] *adj* ingénieux(-euse)

ingenuity [ɪndʒɪˈnjuːɪtɪ] *n* ingéniosité *f*

ingenuous [ɪnˈdʒɛnjuəs] *adj* franc/franche, ouvert(e)

ingot [ˈɪŋɡət] *n* lingot *m*

ingrained [ɪnˈɡreɪnd] *adj* enraciné(e)

ingratiate [ɪnˈɡreɪʃɪeɪt] *vt*: **to ~ o.s. with** s'insinuer dans les bonnes grâces de, se faire bien voir de

ingredient [ɪnˈɡriːdɪənt] *n* ingrédient *m*; (*fig*) élément *m*

inhabit [ɪnˈhæbɪt] *vt* habiter

inhabitant [ɪnˈhæbɪtnt] *n* habitant(e)

inhale [ɪnˈheɪl] *vt* inhaler; (*perfume*) respirer; (*smoke*) avaler ▷ *vi* (*breathe in*) aspirer; (*in smoking*) avaler la fumée

inhaler [ɪnˈheɪləʳ] *n* inhalateur *m*

inherent [ɪnˈhɪərənt] *adj*: **~ (in or to)** inhérent(e) (à)

inherit [ɪnˈherɪt] *vt* hériter (de)

inheritance [ɪnˈherɪtəns] *n* héritage *m*; (*fig*): **the situation that was his ~ as president** la situation dont il a hérité en tant que président; **law of ~** droit *m* de la succession

inhibit [ɪnˈhɪbɪt] *vt* (*Psych*) inhiber; (*growth*) freiner; **to ~ sb from doing** empêcher or retenir qn de faire

inhibition [ɪnhɪˈbɪʃən] *n* inhibition *f*

inhuman [ɪnˈhjuːmən] *adj* inhumain(e)

initial [ɪˈnɪʃl] *adj* initial(e) ▷ *n* initiale *f* ▷ *vt* parafer; **initials** *npl* initiales *fpl*; (*as signature*) parafe *m*

initially [ɪˈnɪʃəlɪ] *adv* initialement, au début

initiate [ɪˈnɪʃɪeɪt] *vt* (*start*) entreprendre; amorcer; (*enterprise*) lancer; (*person*) initier;

to ~ sb into a secret initier qn à un secret; **to ~ proceedings against sb** (*Law*) intenter une action à qn, engager des poursuites contre qn

initiative [ɪˈnɪʃətɪv] *n* initiative *f*; **to take the ~** prendre l'initiative

inject [ɪnˈdʒekt] *vt* (*liquid, fig: money*) injecter; (*person*): **to ~ sb with sth** faire une piqûre de qch à qn

injection [ɪnˈdʒekʃən] *n* injection *f*, piqûre *f*; **to have an ~** se faire faire une piqûre

injure [ˈɪndʒəʳ] *vt* blesser; (*wrong*) faire du tort à; (*damage: reputation etc*) compromettre; (*feelings*) heurter; **to ~ o.s.** se blesser

injured [ˈɪndʒəd] *adj* (*person, leg etc*) blessé(e); (*tone, feelings*) offensé(e); **~ party** (*Law*) partie lésée

injury [ˈɪndʒərɪ] *n* blessure *f*; (*wrong*) tort *m*; **to escape without ~** s'en sortir sain et sauf

injury time *n* (*Sport*) arrêts *mpl* de jeu

injustice [ɪnˈdʒʌstɪs] *n* injustice *f*; **you do me an ~** vous êtes injuste envers moi

ink [ɪŋk] *n* encre *f*

ink-jet printer [ˈɪŋkdʒet-] *n* imprimante *f* à jet d'encre

inkling [ˈɪŋklɪŋ] *n* soupçon *m*, vague idée *f*

inlaid [ˈɪnleɪd] *adj* incrusté(e); (*table etc*) marqueté(e)

inland *adj* [ˈɪnlənd] intérieur(e) ▷ *adv* [ɪnˈlænd] à l'intérieur, dans les terres; **~ waterways** canaux *mpl* et rivières *fpl*

Inland Revenue *n* (*Brit*) fisc *m*

in-laws [ˈɪnlɔːz] *npl* beaux-parents *mpl*; belle famille

inlet [ˈɪnlet] *n* (*Geo*) crique *f*

inmate [ˈɪnmeɪt] *n* (*in prison*) détenu(e); (*in asylum*) interné(e)

inn [ɪn] *n* auberge *f*

innate [ɪˈneɪt] *adj* inné(e)

inner [ˈɪnəʳ] *adj* intérieur(e)

inner city *n* centre *m* urbain (*souffrant souvent de délabrement, d'embouteillages etc*)

inner-city [ˈɪnəˈsɪtɪ] *adj* (*schools, problems*) de quartiers déshérités

inner tube *n* (*of tyre*) chambre *f* à air

inning [ˈɪnɪŋ] *n* (*US: Baseball*) tour *m* de batte; **innings** *npl* (*Cricket*) tour de batte; (*Brit fig*): **he has had a good ~s** il (en) a bien profité

innocence [ˈɪnəsns] *n* innocence *f*

innocent [ˈɪnəsnt] *adj* innocent(e)

innocuous [ɪˈnɔkjuəs] *adj* inoffensif(-ive)

innovation [ɪnəʊˈveɪʃən] *n* innovation *f*

innovative [ˈɪnəʊˈveɪtɪv] *adj* novateur(-trice); (*product*) innovant(e)

innuendo [ɪnjuˈendəʊ] (*pl* **innuendoes**) *n* insinuation *f*, allusion *f*

innumerable [ɪˈnjuːmrəbl] *adj* innombrable

in-patient [ˈɪnpeɪʃənt] *n* malade hospitalisé(e)

input [ˈɪnput] *n* (*contribution*) contribution *f*; (*resources*) ressources *fpl*; (*Elec*) énergie *f*, puissance *f*; (*of machine*) consommation *f*;

(*Comput*) entrée *f* (de données); (: *data*) données *fpl* ▷ *vt* (*Comput*) introduire, entrer
inquest ['ɪnkwɛst] *n* enquête (criminelle); (*coroner's*) enquête judiciaire
inquire [ɪn'kwaɪə'] *vi* demander ▷ *vt* demander, s'informer de; **to ~ about** s'informer de, se renseigner sur; **to ~ when/where/whether** demander quand/ où/si; **inquire after** *vt fus* demander des nouvelles de; **inquire into** *vt fus* faire une enquête sur
inquiry [ɪn'kwaɪərɪ] *n* demande *f* de renseignements; (*Law*) enquête *f*, investigation *f*; **"inquiries" "renseignements"; to hold an ~ into sth** enquêter sur qch
inquisitive [ɪn'kwɪzɪtɪv] *adj* curieux(-euse)
ins. *abbr* = **inches**
insane [ɪn'seɪn] *adj* fou/folle; (*Med*) aliéné(e)
insanity [ɪn'sænɪtɪ] *n* folie *f*; (*Med*) aliénation (mentale)
inscription [ɪn'skrɪpʃən] *n* inscription *f*; (*in book*) dédicace *f*
inscrutable [ɪn'skru:təbl] *adj* impénétrable
insect ['ɪnsɛkt] *n* insecte *m*
insecticide [ɪn'sɛktɪsaɪd] *n* insecticide *m*
insect repellent *n* crème *f* anti-insectes
insecure [ɪnsɪ'kjuə'] *adj* (*person*) anxieux(-euse); (*job*) précaire; (*building etc*) peu sûr(e)
insecurity [ɪnsɪ'kjuərɪtɪ] *n* insécurité *f*
insensitive [ɪn'sɛnsɪtɪv] *adj* insensible
insert *vt* [ɪn'sə:t] insérer ▷ *n* ['ɪnsə:t] insertion *f*
insertion [ɪn'sə:ʃən] *n* insertion *f*
in-service ['ɪn'sə:vɪs] *adj* (*training*) continu(e); (*course*) d'initiation; de perfectionnement; de recyclage
inshore *adj* ['ɪnʃɔ:'] côtier(-ière) ▷ *adv* [ɪn'ʃɔ:'] près de la côte; vers la côte
inside ['ɪn'saɪd] *n* intérieur *m*; (*of road: Brit*) côté *m* gauche (*de la route*); (: *US, Europe etc*) côté droit (*de la route*) ▷ *adj* intérieur(e) ▷ *adv* à l'intérieur, dedans ▷ *prep* à l'intérieur de; (*of time*): **~ 10 minutes** en moins de 10 minutes; **insides** *npl* (*inf*) intestins *mpl*; **~ information** renseignements *mpl* à la source; **~ story** histoire racontée par un témoin; **to go ~** rentrer
inside lane *n* (*Aut: in Britain*) voie *f* de gauche; (: *in US, Europe*) voie *f* de droite
inside out *adv* à l'envers; (*know*) à fond; **to turn sth ~** retourner qch
insider dealing, insider trading *n* (*Stock Exchange*) délit *m* d'initiés
insight ['ɪnsaɪt] *n* perspicacité *f*; (*glimpse, idea*) aperçu *m*; **to gain (an) ~ into** parvenir à comprendre
insignificant [ɪnsɪg'nɪfɪknt] *adj* insignifiant(e)
insincere [ɪnsɪn'sɪə'] *adj* hypocrite
insinuate [ɪn'sɪnjueɪt] *vt* insinuer

insist [ɪn'sɪst] *vi* insister; **to ~ on doing** insister pour faire; **to ~ on sth** exiger qch; **to ~ that** insister pour que + *sub*; (*claim*) maintenir *or* soutenir que
insistent [ɪn'sɪstənt] *adj* insistant(e), pressant(e); (*noise, action*) ininterrompu(e)
insole ['ɪnsəul] *n* semelle intérieure; (*fixed part of shoe*) première *f*
insolent ['ɪnsələnt] *adj* insolent(e)
insolvent [ɪn'sɔlvənt] *adj* insolvable; (*bankrupt*) en faillite
insomnia [ɪn'sɔmnɪə] *n* insomnie *f*
inspect [ɪn'spɛkt] *vt* inspecter; (*Brit: ticket*) contrôler
inspection [ɪn'spɛkʃən] *n* inspection *f*; (*Brit: of tickets*) contrôle *m*
inspector [ɪn'spɛktə'] *n* inspecteur(-trice); (*Brit: on buses, trains*) contrôleur(-euse)
inspiration [ɪnspə'reɪʃən] *n* inspiration *f*
inspire [ɪn'spaɪə'] *vt* inspirer
inspiring [ɪn'spaɪərɪŋ] *adj* inspirant(e)
instability [ɪnstə'bɪlɪtɪ] *n* instabilité *f*
install, (*US*) **instal** [ɪn'stɔ:l] *vt* installer
installation [ɪnstə'leɪʃən] *n* installation *f*
instalment, (*US*) **installment** [ɪn'stɔ:lmənt] *n* (*payment*) acompte *m*, versement partiel; (*of TV serial etc*) épisode *m*; **in ~s** (*pay*) à tempérament; (*receive*) en plusieurs fois
instance ['ɪnstəns] *n* exemple *m*; **for ~** par exemple; **in many ~s** dans bien des cas; **in that ~** dans ce cas; **in the first ~** tout d'abord, en premier lieu
instant ['ɪnstənt] *n* instant *m* ▷ *adj* immédiat(e), urgent(e); (*coffee, food*) instantané(e), en poudre; **the 10th ~** le 10 courant
instantly ['ɪnstəntlɪ] *adv* immédiatement, tout de suite
instant messaging *n* messagerie *f* instantanée
instead [ɪn'stɛd] *adv* au lieu de cela; **~ of** au lieu de; **~ of sb** à la place de qn
instep ['ɪnstɛp] *n* cou-de-pied *m*; (*of shoe*) cambrure *f*
instigate ['ɪnstɪgeɪt] *vt* (*rebellion, strike, crime*) inciter à; (*new ideas etc*) susciter
instil [ɪn'stɪl] *vt*: **to ~ (into)** inculquer (à); (*courage*) insuffler (à)
instinct ['ɪnstɪŋkt] *n* instinct *m*
instinctive [ɪn'stɪŋktɪv] *adj* instinctif(-ive)
institute ['ɪnstɪtju:t] *n* institut *m* ▷ *vt* instituer, établir; (*inquiry*) ouvrir; (*proceedings*) entamer
institution [ɪnstɪ'tju:ʃən] *n* institution *f*; (*school*) établissement *m* (scolaire); (*for care*) établissement (psychiatrique *etc*)
instruct [ɪn'strʌkt] *vt* instruire, former; **to ~ sb in sth** enseigner qch à qn; **to ~ sb to do** charger qn *or* ordonner à qn de faire
instruction [ɪn'strʌkʃən] *n* instruction *f*; **instructions** *npl* (*orders*) directives *fpl*; **~s for use** mode *m* d'emploi

instructor [ɪnˈstrʌktəʳ] *n* professeur *m*; (*for skiing, driving*) moniteur *m*
instrument [ˈɪnstrəmənt] *n* instrument *m*
instrumental [ɪnstruˈmentl] *adj* (*Mus*) instrumental(e); **to be ~ in sth/in doing sth** contribuer à qch/à faire qch
instrument panel *n* tableau *m* de bord
insufficient [ɪnsəˈfɪʃənt] *adj* insuffisant(e)
insular [ˈɪnsjuləʳ] *adj* insulaire; (*outlook*) étroit(e); (*person*) aux vues étroites
insulate [ˈɪnsjuleɪt] *vt* isoler; (*against sound*) insonoriser
insulation [ɪnsjuˈleɪʃən] *n* isolation *f*; (*against sound*) insonorisation *f*
insulin [ˈɪnsjulɪn] *n* insuline *f*
insult *n* [ˈɪnsʌlt] insulte *f*, affront *m* ▷ *vt* [ɪnˈsʌlt] insulter, faire un affront à
insulting [ɪnˈsʌltɪŋ] *adj* insultant(e), injurieux(-euse)
insurance [ɪnˈʃuərəns] *n* assurance *f*; **fire/ life ~** assurance-incendie/-vie; **to take out ~ (against)** s'assurer (contre)
insurance company *n* compagnie *f* or société *f* d'assurances
insurance policy *n* police *f* d'assurance
insure [ɪnˈʃuəʳ] *vt* assurer; **to ~ (o.s.) against** (*fig*) parer à; **to ~ sb/sb's life** assurer qn/la vie de qn; **to be ~d for £5000** être assuré(e) pour 5000 livres
intact [ɪnˈtækt] *adj* intact(e)
intake [ˈɪnteɪk] *n* (*Tech*) admission *f*; (*consumption*) consommation *f*; (*Brit Scol*): **an ~ of 200 a year** 200 admissions par an
integral [ˈɪntɪgrəl] *adj* (*whole*) intégral(e); (*part*) intégrant(e)
integrate [ˈɪntɪgreɪt] *vt* intégrer ▷ *vi* s'intégrer
integrity [ɪnˈtɛgrɪtɪ] *n* intégrité *f*
intellect [ˈɪntəlɛkt] *n* intelligence *f*
intellectual [ɪntəˈlɛktjuəl] *adj, n* intellectuel(le)
intelligence [ɪnˈtɛlɪdʒəns] *n* intelligence *f*; (*Mil*) informations *fpl*, renseignements *mpl*
Intelligence Service *n* services *mpl* de renseignements
intelligent [ɪnˈtɛlɪdʒənt] *adj* intelligent(e)
intend [ɪnˈtɛnd] *vt* (*gift etc*): **to ~ sth for** destiner qch à; **to ~ to do** avoir l'intention de faire
intense [ɪnˈtɛns] *adj* intense; (*person*) véhément(e)
intensely [ɪnˈtɛnslɪ] *adv* intensément; (*moving*) profondément
intensify [ɪnˈtɛnsɪfaɪ] *vt* intensifier
intensity [ɪnˈtɛnsɪtɪ] *n* intensité *f*
intensive [ɪnˈtɛnsɪv] *adj* intensif(-ive)
intensive care *n*: **to be in ~** être en réanimation
intensive care unit *n* service *m* de réanimation
intent [ɪnˈtɛnt] *n* intention *f* ▷ *adj* attentif(-ive), absorbé(e); **to all ~s and**

purposes en fait, pratiquement; **to be ~ on doing sth** être (bien) décidé à faire qch
intention [ɪnˈtɛnʃən] *n* intention *f*
intentional [ɪnˈtɛnʃənl] *adj* intentionnel(le), délibéré(e)
intently [ɪnˈtɛntlɪ] *adv* attentivement
interact [ɪntərˈækt] *vi* avoir une action réciproque; (*people*) communiquer
interaction [ɪntərˈækʃən] *n* interaction *f*
interactive [ɪntərˈæktɪv] *adj* (*group*) interactif(-ive); (*Comput*) interactif, conversationnel(le)
intercept [ɪntəˈsɛpt] *vt* intercepter; (*person*) arrêter au passage
interchange *n* [ˈɪntətʃeɪndʒ] (*exchange*) échange *m*; (*on motorway*) échangeur *m* ▷ *vt* [ɪntəˈtʃeɪndʒ] échanger; mettre à la place l'un(e) de l'autre
interchangeable [ɪntəˈtʃeɪndʒəbl] *adj* interchangeable
intercom [ˈɪntəkɔm] *n* interphone *m*
intercourse [ˈɪntəkɔːs] *n* rapports *mpl*; **sexual ~** rapports sexuels
interest [ˈɪntrɪst] *n* intérêt *m*; (*Comm: stake, share*) participation *f*, intérêts *mpl* ▷ *vt* intéresser; **compound/simple ~** intérêt composé/simple; **British ~s in the Middle East** les intérêts britanniques au Moyen-Orient; **his main ~ is ...** ce qui l'intéresse le plus est ...
interested [ˈɪntrɪstɪd] *adj* intéressé(e); **to be ~ in sth** s'intéresser à qch; **I'm ~ in going** ça m'intéresse d'y aller
interesting [ˈɪntrɪstɪŋ] *adj* intéressant(e)
interest rate *n* taux *m* d'intérêt
interface [ˈɪntəfeɪs] *n* (*Comput*) interface *f*
interfere [ɪntəˈfɪəʳ] *vi*: **to ~ in** (*quarrel*) s'immiscer dans; (*other people's business*) se mêler de; **to ~ with** (*object*) tripoter, toucher à; (*plans*) contrecarrer; (*duty*) être en conflit avec; **don't ~** mêlez-vous de vos affaires
interference [ɪntəˈfɪərəns] *n* (*gen*) ingérence *f*; (*Physics*) interférence *f*; (*Radio, TV*) parasites *mpl*
interim [ˈɪntərɪm] *adj* provisoire; (*post*) intérimaire ▷ *n*: **in the ~** dans l'intérim
interior [ɪnˈtɪərɪəʳ] *n* intérieur *m* ▷ *adj* intérieur(e); (*minister, department*) de l'intérieur
interior decorator, interior designer *n* décorateur(-trice) d'intérieur
interior design *n* architecture *f* d'intérieur
interjection [ɪntəˈdʒɛkʃən] *n* interjection *f*
interlock [ɪntəˈlɔk] *vi* s'enclencher ▷ *vt* enclencher
interlude [ˈɪntəluːd] *n* intervalle *m*; (*Theat*) intermède *m*
intermediate [ɪntəˈmiːdɪət] *adj* intermédiaire; (*Scol: course, level*) moyen(ne)
intermission [ɪntəˈmɪʃən] *n* pause *f*; (*Theat, Cine*) entracte *m*

intern vt [ɪn'tə:n] interner ▷ n ['ɪntə:n] (US)
interne m/f

internal [ɪn'tə:nl] adj interne; (dispute, reform
etc) intérieur(e); **~ injuries** lésions fpl
internes

internally [ɪn'tə:nəlɪ] adv intérieurement;
"not to be taken ~" "pour usage externe"

Internal Revenue Service n (US) fisc m

international [ɪntə'næʃənl] adj
international(e) ▷ n (Brit Sport)
international m

Internet ['ɪntənet] n: **the ~** l'Internet m

Internet café n cybercafé m

Internet Service Provider n fournisseur m
d'accès à Internet

Internet user n internaute m/f

interplay ['ɪntəpleɪ] n effet m réciproque,
jeu m

interpret [ɪn'tə:prɪt] vt interpréter ▷ vi
servir d'interprète

interpretation [ɪntə:prɪ'teɪʃən] n
interprétation f

interpreter [ɪn'tə:prɪtər] n interprète m/f;
could you act as an ~ for us? pourriez-vous
nous servir d'interprète?

interrelated [ɪntərɪ'leɪtɪd] adj en
corrélation, en rapport étroit

interrogate [ɪn'terəugeɪt] vt interroger;
(suspect etc) soumettre à un interrogatoire

interrogation [ɪnterəu'geɪʃən] n
interrogation f; (by police) interrogatoire m

interrogative [ɪntə'rɒgətɪv] adj
interrogateur(-trice) ▷ n (Ling)
interrogatif m

interrupt [ɪntə'rʌpt] vt, vi interrompre

interruption [ɪntə'rʌpʃən] n interruption f

intersect [ɪntə'sekt] vt couper, croiser;
(Math) intersecter ▷ vi se croiser, se couper;
s'intersecter

intersection [ɪntə'sekʃən] n intersection f;
(of roads) croisement m

intersperse [ɪntə'spə:s] vt: **to ~ with**
parsemer de

interstate [ɪntə'steɪt] (US) n autoroute f
(qui relie plusieurs États)

intertwine [ɪntə'twaɪn] vt entrelacer ▷ vi
s'entrelacer

interval ['ɪntəvl] n intervalle m; (Brit: Theat)
entracte m; (: Sport) mi-temps f; **bright ~s** (in
weather) éclaircies fpl; **at ~s** par intervalles

intervene [ɪntə'vi:n] vi (time) s'écouler
(entre-temps); (event) survenir; (person)
intervenir

intervention [ɪntə'venʃən] n intervention f

interview ['ɪntəvju:] n (Radio, TV) interview f;
(for job) entrevue f ▷ vt interviewer, avoir une
entrevue avec

interviewer ['ɪntəvjuər] n (Radio, TV)
interviewer m

intestine [ɪn'testɪn] n intestin m; **large ~**
gros intestin; **small ~** intestin grêle

intimacy ['ɪntɪməsɪ] n intimité f

intimate adj ['ɪntɪmət] intime; (friendship)
profond(e); (knowledge) approfondi(e) ▷ vt
['ɪntɪmeɪt] suggérer, laisser entendre;
(announce) faire savoir

intimidate [ɪn'tɪmɪdeɪt] vt intimider

intimidating [ɪn'tɪmɪdeɪtɪŋ] adj
intimidant(e)

into ['ɪntu] prep dans; **~ pieces/French**
en morceaux/français; **to change pounds ~**
dollars changer des livres en dollars; **3 ~ 9**
goes 3 9 divisé par 3 donne 3; **she's ~ opera**
c'est une passionnée d'opéra

intolerant [ɪn'tɒlərnt] adj: **~ (of)**
intolérant(e) (de); (Med) intolérant (à)

intoxicated [ɪn'tɒksɪkeɪtɪd] adj ivre

intractable [ɪn'træktəbl] adj (child, temper)
indocile, insoumis(e); (problem) insoluble;
(illness) incurable

intranet [ɪn'trænet] n intranet m

intransitive [ɪn'trænsɪtɪv] adj
intransitif(-ive)

intravenous [ɪntrə'vi:nəs] adj
intraveineux(-euse)

in-tray ['ɪntreɪ] n courrier m "arrivée"

intricate ['ɪntrɪkət] adj complexe,
compliqué(e)

intrigue [ɪn'tri:g] n intrigue f ▷ vt intriguer
▷ vi intriguer, comploter

intriguing [ɪn'tri:gɪŋ] adj fascinant(e)

intrinsic [ɪn'trɪnsɪk] adj intrinsèque

introduce [ɪntrə'dju:s] vt introduire;
(TV show etc) présenter; **to ~ sb (to sb)**
présenter qn (à qn); **to ~ sb to** (pastime,
technique) initier qn à; **may I ~ ...?** je vous
présente ...

introduction [ɪntrə'dʌkʃən] n introduction
f; (of person) présentation f; (to new experience)
initiation f; **a letter of ~** une lettre de
recommandation

introductory [ɪntrə'dʌktərɪ] adj
préliminaire, introductif(-ive); **~ remarks**
remarques fpl liminaires; **an ~ offer** une
offre de lancement

intrude [ɪn'tru:d] vi (person) être importun(e);
to ~ on or **into** (conversation etc) s'immiscer
dans; **am I intruding?** est-ce que je vous
dérange?

intruder [ɪn'tru:dər] n intrus(e)

intuition [ɪntju:'ɪʃən] n intuition f

inundate ['ɪnʌndeɪt] vt: **to ~ with** inonder de

invade [ɪn'veɪd] vt envahir

invalid n ['ɪnvəlɪd] malade m/f; (with disability)
invalide m/f ▷ adj [ɪn'vælɪd] (not valid)
invalide, non valide

invaluable [ɪn'væljuəbl] adj inestimable,
inappréciable

invariably [ɪn'veərɪəblɪ] adv invariablement;
she is ~ late elle est toujours en retard

invasion [ɪn'veɪʒən] n invasion f

invent [ɪn'vent] vt inventer

invention [ɪn'venʃən] n invention f

inventive [ɪn'ventɪv] adj inventif(-ive)

inventor [ɪn'vɛntə'] n inventeur(-trice)

inventory ['ɪnvəntrɪ] n inventaire m

invert [ɪn'vɜːt] vt intervertir; (cup, object) retourner

inverted commas [ɪn'vɜːtɪd-] npl (Brit) guillemets mpl

invest [ɪn'vɛst] vt investir; (endow): **to ~ sb with sth** conférer qch à qn ▷ vi faire un investissement, investir; **to ~ in** placer de l'argent or investir dans; (fig: acquire) s'offrir, faire l'acquisition de

investigate [ɪn'vɛstɪgeɪt] vt étudier, examiner; (crime) faire une enquête sur

investigation [ɪnvɛstɪ'geɪʃən] n examen m; (of crime) enquête f, investigation f

investigator [ɪn'vɛstɪgeɪtə'] n investigateur(-trice); **private ~** détective privé

investment [ɪn'vɛstmənt] n investissement m, placement m

investor [ɪn'vɛstə'] n épargnant(e); (shareholder) actionnaire m/f

invigilator [ɪn'vɪdʒɪleɪtə'] n (Brit) surveillant m (d'examen)

invigorating [ɪn'vɪgəreɪtɪŋ] adj vivifiant(e), stimulant(e)

invisible [ɪn'vɪzɪbl] adj invisible

invitation [ɪnvɪ'teɪʃən] n invitation f; **by ~ only** sur invitation; **at sb's ~** à la demande de qn

invite [ɪn'vaɪt] vt inviter; (opinions etc) demander; (trouble) chercher; **to ~ sb (to do)** inviter qn (à faire); **to ~ sb to dinner** inviter qn à dîner; **invite out** vt inviter (à sortir); **invite over** vt inviter (chez soi)

inviting [ɪn'vaɪtɪŋ] adj engageant(e), attrayant(e); (gesture) encourageant(e)

invoice ['ɪnvɔɪs] n facture f ▷ vt facturer; **to ~ sb for goods** facturer des marchandises à qn

involuntary [ɪn'vɒləntrɪ] adj involontaire

involve [ɪn'vɒlv] vt (entail) impliquer; (concern) concerner; (require) nécessiter; **to ~ sb in** (theft etc) impliquer qn dans; (activity, meeting) faire participer qn à

involved [ɪn'vɒlvd] adj (complicated) complexe; **to be ~ in** (take part) participer à; (be engrossed) être plongé(e) dans; **to feel ~** se sentir concerné(e); **to become ~ (in love etc)** s'engager

involvement [ɪn'vɒlvmənt] n (personal role) rôle m; (participation) participation f; (enthusiasm) enthousiasme m; (of resources, funds) mise f en jeu

inward ['ɪnwəd] adj (movement) vers l'intérieur; (thought, feeling) profond(e), intime ▷ adv = **inwards**

inwards ['ɪnwədz] adv vers l'intérieur

I/O abbr (Comput: = input/output) E/S

iodine ['aɪədiːn] n iode m

IOM abbr = **Isle of Man**

iota [aɪ'əutə] n (fig) brin m, grain m

IOU n abbr (= I owe you) reconnaissance f de dette

iPod® ['aɪpɒd] n iPod® m

IQ n abbr (= intelligence quotient) Q.I. m

IRA n abbr (= Irish Republican Army) IRA f; (US) = **individual retirement account**

Iran [ɪ'rɑːn] n Iran m

Iranian [ɪ'reɪnɪən] adj iranien(ne) ▷ n Iranien(ne); (Ling) iranien m

Iraq [ɪ'rɑːk] n Irak m

Iraqi [ɪ'rɑːkɪ] adj irakien(ne) ▷ n Irakien(ne)

irate [aɪ'reɪt] adj courroucé(e)

Ireland ['aɪələnd] n Irlande f; **Republic of ~** République f d'Irlande

iris, irises ['aɪrɪs, -ɪz] n iris m

Irish ['aɪrɪʃ] adj irlandais(e) ▷ npl: **the ~** les Irlandais ▷ n (Ling) irlandais m; **the Irish** npl les Irlandais

Irishman ['aɪrɪʃmən] irreg n Irlandais m

Irish Sea n: **the ~** la mer d'Irlande

Irishwoman ['aɪrɪʃwumən] irreg n Irlandaise f

iron ['aɪən] n fer m; (for clothes) fer m à repasser ▷ adj de or en fer ▷ vt (clothes) repasser; **irons** npl (chains) fers mpl, chaînes fpl; **iron out** vt (crease) faire disparaître au fer; (fig) aplanir; faire disparaître

ironic [aɪ'rɒnɪk], **ironical** [aɪ'rɒnɪkl] adj ironique

ironically [aɪ'rɒnɪklɪ] adv ironiquement

ironing ['aɪənɪŋ] n (activity) repassage m; (clothes: ironed) linge repassé; (: to be ironed) linge à repasser

ironing board n planche f à repasser

ironmonger ['aɪənmʌŋgə'] n (Brit) quincaillier m; **~'s (shop)** quincaillerie f

irony ['aɪrənɪ] n ironie f

irrational [ɪ'ræʃənl] adj irrationnel(le); (person) qui n'est pas rationnel

irregular [ɪ'regjulə'] adj irrégulier(-ière); (surface) inégal(e); (action, event) peu orthodoxe

irrelevant [ɪ'reləvənt] adj sans rapport, hors de propos

irresistible [ɪrɪ'zɪstɪbl] adj irrésistible

irrespective [ɪrɪ'spɛktɪv]: **~ of** prep sans tenir compte de

irresponsible [ɪrɪ'spɒnsɪbl] adj (act) irréfléchi(e); (person) qui n'a pas le sens des responsabilités

irrigate ['ɪrɪgeɪt] vt irriguer

irrigation [ɪrɪ'geɪʃən] n irrigation f

irritable ['ɪrɪtəbl] adj irritable

irritate ['ɪrɪteɪt] vt irriter

irritating ['ɪrɪteɪtɪŋ] adj irritant(e)

irritation [ɪrɪ'teɪʃən] n irritation f

IRS n abbr (US) = **Internal Revenue Service**

is [ɪz] vb see **be**

ISDN n abbr (= Integrated Services Digital Network) RNIS m

Islam ['ɪzlɑːm] n Islam m

Islamic [ɪz'lɑːmɪk] adj islamique;

~ fundamentalists intégristes *mpl* musulmans

island ['aɪlənd] *n* île *f*; (*also*: **traffic ~**) refuge *m* (pour piétons)

islander ['aɪləndəʳ] *n* habitant(e) d'une île, insulaire *m/f*

isle [aɪl] *n* île *f*

isn't ['ɪznt] = **is not**

isolate ['aɪsəleɪt] *vt* isoler

isolated ['aɪsəleɪtɪd] *adj* isolé(e)

isolation [aɪsə'leɪʃən] *n* isolement *m*

ISP *n abbr* = **Internet Service Provider**

Israel ['ɪzreɪl] *n* Israël *m*

Israeli [ɪz'reɪlɪ] *adj* israélien(ne) ▷ *n* Israélien(ne)

issue ['ɪʃuː] *n* question *f*, problème *m*; (*outcome*) résultat *m*, issue *f*; (*of banknotes*) émission *f*; (*of newspaper*) numéro *m*; (*of book*) publication *f*, parution *f*; (*offspring*) descendance *f* ▷ *vt* (*rations, equipment*) distribuer; (*orders*) donner; (*statement*) publier, faire; (*certificate, passport*) délivrer; (*book*) faire paraître; publier; (*banknotes, cheques, stamps*) émettre, mettre en circulation ▷ *vi*: **to ~ from** provenir de; **at ~** en jeu, en cause; **to avoid the ~** éluder le problème; **to take ~ with sb (over sth)** exprimer son désaccord avec qn (sur qch); **to make an ~ of sth** faire de qch un problème; **to confuse** *or* **obscure the ~** embrouiller la question

IT *n abbr* = **information technology**

KEYWORD

it [ɪt] *pron* **1** (*specific: subject*) il/elle; (: *direct object*) le/la, l'; (: *indirect object*) lui; **it's on the table** c'est *or* il (*or* elle) est sur la table; **I can't find it** je n'arrive pas à le trouver; **give it to me** donne-le-moi

2 (*after prep*): **about/from/of it** en; **I spoke to him about it** je lui en ai parlé; **what did you learn from it?** qu'est-ce que vous en avez retiré?; **I'm proud of it** j'en suis fier; **I've come from it** j'en viens; **in/to it** y; **put the book in it** mettez-y le livre; **it's on it** c'est dessus; **he agreed to it** il y a consenti; **did you go to it?** (*party, concert etc*) est-ce que vous y êtes allé(s)?; **above it, over it** (au-)dessus; **below it, under it** (en-)dessous; **in front of/behind it** devant/derrière

3 (*impersonal*) il; ce, cela, ça; **it's raining** il pleut; **it's Friday tomorrow** demain, c'est vendredi *or* nous sommes, vendredi; **it's 6 o'clock** il est 6 heures; **how far is it? — it's 10 miles** c'est loin? — c'est à 10 miles; **it's 2 hours by train** c'est à 2 heures de train; **who is it? — it's me** qui est-ce? — c'est moi

Italian [ɪ'tæljən] *adj* italien(ne) ▷ *n* Italien(ne); (*Ling*) italien *m*

italic [ɪ'tælɪk] *adj* italique

italics [ɪ'tælɪks] *npl* italique *m*

Italy ['ɪtəlɪ] *n* Italie *f*

itch [ɪtʃ] *n* démangeaison *f* ▷ *vi* (*person*) éprouver des démangeaisons; (*part of body*) démanger; **I'm ~ing to do** l'envie me démange de faire

itchy ['ɪtʃɪ] *adj* qui démange; **my back is ~** j'ai le dos qui me démange

it'd ['ɪtd] = **it would; it had**

item ['aɪtəm] *n* (*gen*) article *m*; (*on agenda*) question *f*, point *m*; (*in programme*) numéro *m*; (*also*: **news ~**) nouvelle *f*; **~s of clothing** articles vestimentaires

itemize ['aɪtəmaɪz] *vt* détailler, spécifier

itinerary [aɪ'tɪnərərɪ] *n* itinéraire *m*

it'll ['ɪtl] = **it will; it shall**

its [ɪts] *adj* son/sa, ses *pl* ▷ *pron* le/la sien(ne), les siens/siennes

it's [ɪts] = **it is; it has**

itself [ɪt'sɛlf] *pron* (*reflexive*) se; (*emphatic*) lui-même/elle-même

ITV *n abbr* (*Brit*: = *Independent Television*) chaîne de télévision commerciale

IUD *n abbr* = **intra-uterine device**

I've [aɪv] = **I have**

ivory ['aɪvərɪ] *n* ivoire *m*

ivy ['aɪvɪ] *n* lierre *m*

J

jab [dʒæb] *vt*: **to ~ sth into** enfoncer *or* planter qch dans ▷ *n* coup *m*; (*Med: inf*) piqûre *f*

jack [dʒæk] *n* (*Aut*) cric *m*; (*Bowls*) cochonnet *m*; (*Cards*) valet *m*; **jack in** *vt* (*inf*) laisser tomber; **jack up** *vt* soulever (au cric)

jackal ['dʒækl] *n* chacal *m*

jacket ['dʒækɪt] *n* veste *f*, veston *m*; (*of boiler etc*) enveloppe *f*; (*of book*) couverture *f*, jaquette *f*

jacket potato *n* pomme *f* de terre en robe des champs

jackknife ['dʒæknaɪf] *n* couteau *m* de poche ▷ *vi*: **the lorry ~d** la remorque (du camion) s'est mise en travers

jack plug *n* (*Brit*) jack *m*

jackpot ['dʒækpɒt] *n* gros lot

Jacuzzi® [dʒə'kuːzɪ] *n* jacuzzi® *m*

jaded ['dʒeɪdɪd] *adj* éreinté(e), fatigué(e)

jagged ['dʒægɪd] *adj* dentelé(e)

jail [dʒeɪl] *n* prison *f* ▷ *vt* emprisonner, mettre en prison

jail sentence *n* peine *f* de prison

jam [dʒæm] *n* confiture *f*; (*of shoppers etc*) cohue *f*; (*also*: **traffic ~**) embouteillage *m* ▷ *vt* (*passage etc*) encombrer, obstruer; (*mechanism, drawer etc*) bloquer, coincer; (*Radio*) brouiller ▷ *vi* (*mechanism, sliding part*) se coincer, se bloquer; (*gun*) s'enrayer; **to be in a ~** (*inf*) être dans le pétrin; **to get sb out of a ~** (*inf*) sortir qn du pétrin; **to ~ sth into** (*stuff*) entasser *or* comprimer qch dans; (*thrust*) enfoncer qch

dans; **the telephone lines are ~med** les lignes (téléphoniques) sont encombrées

Jamaica [dʒə'meɪkə] *n* Jamaïque *f*

jam jar *n* pot *m* à confiture

jammed [dʒæmd] *adj* (*window etc*) coincé(e)

jam-packed [dʒæm'pækt] *adj*: **~ (with)** bourré(e) (de)

jangle ['dʒæŋgl] *vi* cliqueter

janitor ['dʒænɪtə^r] *n* (*caretaker*) concierge *m*

January ['dʒænjuərɪ] *n* janvier *m*; *see also* **July**

Japan [dʒə'pæn] *n* Japon *m*

Japanese [dʒæpə'niːz] *adj* japonais(e) ▷ *n pl inv* Japonais(e); (*Ling*) japonais *m*

jar [dʒɑː^r] *n* (*stone, earthenware*) pot *m*; (*glass*) bocal *m* ▷ *vi* (*sound*) produire un son grinçant *or* discordant; (*colours etc*) détonner, jurer ▷ *vt* (*shake*) ébranler, secouer

jargon ['dʒɑːgən] *n* jargon *m*

jaundice ['dʒɔːndɪs] *n* jaunisse *f*

javelin ['dʒævlɪn] *n* javelot *m*

jaw [dʒɔː] *n* mâchoire *f*

jay [dʒeɪ] *n* geai *m*

jaywalker ['dʒeɪwɔːkə^r] *n* piéton indiscipliné

jazz [dʒæz] *n* jazz *m*; **jazz up** *vt* animer, égayer

jealous ['dʒɛləs] *adj* jaloux(-ouse)

jealousy ['dʒɛləsɪ] *n* jalousie *f*

jeans [dʒiːnz] *npl* jean *m*

jeer [dʒɪə^r] *vi*: **to ~ (at)** huer; se moquer cruellement (de), railler

Jehovah's Witness [dʒɪ'həʊvəz-] *n* témoin *m* de Jéhovah

Jello® ['dʒɛləʊ] (*US*) *n* gelée *f*

jelly ['dʒɛlɪ] *n* (*dessert*) gelée *f*; (*US: jam*) confiture *f*

jellyfish ['dʒɛlɪfɪʃ] *n* méduse *f*

jeopardize ['dʒɛpədaɪz] *vt* mettre en danger *or* péril

jeopardy ['dʒɛpədɪ] *n*: **in ~** en danger *or* péril

jerk [dʒəːk] *n* secousse *f*, saccade *f*; (*of muscle*) spasme *m*; (*inf*) pauvre type *m* ▷ *vt* (*shake*) donner une secousse à; (*pull*) tirer brusquement ▷ *vi* (*vehicles*) cahoter

jersey ['dʒəːzɪ] *n* tricot *m*; (*fabric*) jersey *m*

Jesus ['dʒiːzəs] *n* Jésus *m*; **~ Christ** Jésus-Christ

jet [dʒɛt] *n* (*of gas, liquid*) jet *m*; (*Aut*) gicleur *m*; (*Aviat*) avion *m* à réaction, jet *m*

jet-black ['dʒɛt'blæk] *adj* (d'un noir) de jais

jet engine *n* moteur *m* à réaction

jet lag *n* décalage *m* horaire

jet-ski *vi* faire du jet-ski *or* scooter des mers

jettison ['dʒɛtɪsn] *vt* jeter par-dessus bord

jetty ['dʒɛtɪ] *n* jetée *f*, digue *f*

Jew [dʒuː] *n* Juif *m*

jewel ['dʒuːəl] *n* bijou *m*, joyau *m*; (*in watch*) rubis *m*

jeweller, (*US*) **jeweler** ['dʒuːələ^r] *n* bijoutier(-ière), joaillier *m*

jeweller's, **jeweller's shop** *n* (*Brit*) bijouterie *f*, joaillerie *f*

jewellery, (*US*) **jewelry** ['dʒuːəlrɪ] *n* bijoux *mpl*

Jewess ['dʒuːɪs] n Juive f
Jewish ['dʒuːɪʃ] adj juif/juive
jibe [dʒaɪb] n sarcasme m
jiffy ['dʒɪfɪ] n (inf): **in a ~** en un clin d'œil
jigsaw ['dʒɪgsɔː] n (also: **~ puzzle**) puzzle m; (tool) scie sauteuse
jilt [dʒɪlt] vt laisser tomber, plaquer
jingle ['dʒɪŋgl] n (advertising jingle) couplet m publicitaire ▷ vi cliqueter, tinter
jinx [dʒɪŋks] n (inf) (mauvais) sort
jitters ['dʒɪtəz] npl (inf): **to get the ~** avoir la trouille or la frousse
job [dʒɔb] n (chore, task) travail m, tâche f; (employment) emploi m, poste m, place f; **a part-time/full-time ~** un emploi à temps partiel/à plein temps; **he's only doing his ~** il fait son boulot; **it's a good ~ that ...** c'est heureux or c'est une chance que ...+ sub; **just the ~!** (c'est) juste or exactement ce qu'il faut!
job centre ['dʒɔbsɛntə'] (Brit) n ≈ ANPE f, ≈ Agence nationale pour l'emploi
jobless ['dʒɔblɪs] adj sans travail, au chômage ▷ npl: **the ~** les sans-emploi m inv, les chômeurs mpl
jockey ['dʒɔkɪ] n jockey m ▷ vi: **to ~ for position** manœuvrer pour être bien placé
jog [dʒɔg] vt secouer ▷ vi (Sport) faire du jogging; **to ~ along** cahoter; trotter; **to ~ sb's memory** rafraîchir la mémoire de qn
jogging ['dʒɔgɪŋ] n jogging m
join [dʒɔɪn] vt (put together) unir, assembler; (become member of) s'inscrire à; (meet) rejoindre, retrouver; (queue) se joindre à ▷ vi (roads, rivers) se rejoindre, se rencontrer ▷ n raccord m; **will you ~ us for dinner?** vous dînerez avec nous?; **I'll ~ you later** je vous rejoindrai plus tard; **to ~ forces (with)** s'associer (à); **join in** vi se mettre de la partie ▷ vt fus se mêler à; **join up** vi (meet) se rejoindre; (Mil) s'engager
joiner ['dʒɔɪnə'] (Brit) n menuisier m
joint [dʒɔɪnt] n (Tech) jointure f, joint m; (Anat) articulation f, jointure f; (Brit Culin) rôti m; (inf: place) boîte f; (of cannabis) joint ▷ adj commun(e); (committee) mixte, paritaire; (winner) ex aequo; **~ responsibility** coresponsabilité f
joint account n compte joint
jointly ['dʒɔɪntlɪ] adv ensemble, en commun
joke [dʒəuk] n plaisanterie f; (also: **practical ~**) farce f ▷ vi plaisanter; **to play a ~ on** jouer un tour à, faire une farce à
joker ['dʒəukə'] n plaisantin m, blagueur(-euse); (Cards) joker m
jolly ['dʒɔlɪ] adj gai(e), enjoué(e); (enjoyable) amusant(e), plaisant(e) ▷ adv (Brit inf) rudement, drôlement ▷ vt (Brit): **to ~ sb along** amadouer qn, convaincre or entraîner qn à force d'encouragements; **~ good!** (Brit) formidable!

jolt [dʒəult] n cahot m, secousse f; (shock) choc m ▷ vt cahoter, secouer
Jordan [dʒɔːdən] n (country) Jordanie f; (river) Jourdain m
jostle ['dʒɔsl] vt bousculer, pousser ▷ vi jouer des coudes
jot [dʒɔt] n: **not one ~** pas un brin; **jot down** vt inscrire rapidement, noter
jotter ['dʒɔtə'] (Brit) n cahier m (de brouillon); bloc-notes m
journal ['dʒəːnl] n journal m
journalism ['dʒəːnəlɪzəm] n journalisme m
journalist ['dʒəːnəlɪst] n journaliste m/f
journey ['dʒəːnɪ] n voyage m; (distance covered) trajet m ▷ vi voyager; **the ~ takes two hours** le trajet dure deux heures; **a 5-hour ~** un voyage de 5 heures; **how was your ~?** votre voyage s'est bien passé?
joy [dʒɔɪ] n joie f
joyful ['dʒɔɪful], **joyous** ['dʒɔɪəs] adj joyeux(-euse)
joyrider ['dʒɔɪraɪdə'] n voleur(-euse) de voiture (qui fait une virée dans le véhicule volé)
joy stick ['dʒɔɪstɪk] n (Aviat) manche m à balai; (Comput) manche à balai, manette f (de jeu)
JP n abbr = **Justice of the Peace**
Jr abbr = **junior**
jubilant ['dʒuːbɪlnt] adj triomphant(e), réjoui(e)
judge [dʒʌdʒ] n juge m ▷ vt juger; (estimate: weight, size etc) apprécier; (consider) estimer ▷ vi: **judging or to ~ by his expression** d'après son expression; **as far as I can ~** autant que je puisse en juger
judgment, judgement ['dʒʌdʒmənt] n jugement m; (punishment) châtiment m; **in my ~** à mon avis; **to pass ~ on** (Law) prononcer un jugement (sur)
judicial [dʒuː'dɪʃl] adj judiciaire; (fair) impartial(e)
judiciary [dʒuː'dɪʃɪərɪ] n (pouvoir m) judiciaire n
judo ['dʒuːdəu] n judo m
jug [dʒʌg] n pot m, cruche f
juggernaut ['dʒʌgənɔːt] n (Brit: huge truck) mastodonte m
juggle ['dʒʌgl] vi jongler
juggler ['dʒʌglə'] n jongleur m
juice [dʒuːs] n jus m; (inf: petrol): **we've run out of ~** c'est la panne sèche
juicy ['dʒuːsɪ] adj juteux(-euse)
jukebox ['dʒuːkbɔks] n juke-box m
July [dʒuː'laɪ] n juillet m; **the first of ~** le premier juillet; **(on) the eleventh of ~** le onze juillet; **in the month of ~** au mois de juillet; **at the beginning/end of ~** au début/ à la fin (du mois) de juillet, début/fin juillet; **in the middle of ~** au milieu (du mois) de juillet, à la mi-juillet; **during ~** pendant le mois de juillet; **in ~ of next year** en juillet de l'année prochaine; **each or every ~** tous les

ans or chaque année en juillet; **~ was wet this year** il a beaucoup plu cette année en juillet

jumble ['dʒʌmbl] n fouillis m ▷ vt (also: **~ up, ~ together**) mélanger, brouiller

jumble sale n (Brit) vente f de charité; voir article

JUMBLE SALE

Les jumble sales ont lieu dans les églises, salles des fêtes ou halls d'écoles, et l'on y vend des articles de toutes sortes, en général bon marché et surtout d'occasion, pour collecter des fonds pour une œuvre de charité, une école (par exemple, pour acheter des ordinateurs), ou encore une église (pour réparer un toit etc).

jumbo ['dʒʌmbəʊ] adj (also: **~ jet**) (avion) gros porteur (à réaction); **~ size** format maxi or extra-grand

jump [dʒʌmp] vi sauter, bondir; (with fear etc) sursauter; (increase) monter en flèche ▷ vt sauter, franchir ▷ n saut m, bond m; (with fear etc) sursaut m; (fence) obstacle m; **to ~ the queue** (Brit) passer avant son tour; **jump about** vi sautiller; **jump at** vt fus (fig) sauter sur; **he ~ed at the offer** il s'est empressé d'accepter la proposition; **jump down** vi sauter (pour descendre); **jump up** vi se lever (d'un bond)

jumper ['dʒʌmpə'] n (Brit: pullover) pull-over m; (US: pinafore dress) robe-chasuble f; (Sport) sauteur(-euse)

jump leads, (US) **jumper cables** npl câbles mpl de démarrage

jumpy ['dʒʌmpɪ] adj nerveux(-euse), agité(e)

Jun. abbr = **June; junior**

junction ['dʒʌŋkʃən] n (Brit: of roads) carrefour m; (of rails) embranchement m

juncture ['dʒʌŋktʃə'] n: **at this ~** à ce moment-là, sur ces entrefaites

June [dʒuːn] n juin m; see also **July**

jungle ['dʒʌŋgl] n jungle f

junior ['dʒuːnɪə'] adj, n: **he's ~ to me (by two years), he's my ~ (by two years)** il est mon cadet (de deux ans), il est plus jeune que moi (de deux ans); **he's ~ to me** (seniority) il est en dessous de moi (dans la hiérarchie), j'ai plus d'ancienneté que lui

junior high school n (US) = collège m d'enseignement secondaire; see also **high school**

junior school n (Brit) école f primaire

junk [dʒʌŋk] n (rubbish) camelote f; (cheap goods) bric-à-brac m inv; (ship) jonque f ▷ vt (inf) abandonner, mettre au rancart

junk food n snacks vite prêts (sans valeur nutritive)

junkie ['dʒʌŋkɪ] n (inf) junkie m, drogué(e)

junk mail n prospectus mpl; (Comput) messages mpl publicitaires

junk shop n (boutique f de) brocanteur m

Junr abbr = **junior**

Jupiter ['dʒuːpɪtə'] n (planet) Jupiter f

jurisdiction [dʒʊərɪs'dɪkʃən] n juridiction f; **it falls or comes within/outside our ~** cela est/n'est pas de notre compétence or ressort

juror ['dʒʊərə'] n juré m

jury ['dʒʊərɪ] n jury m

just [dʒʌst] adj juste ▷ adv: **he's ~ done it/ left** il vient de le faire/partir; **~ as I expected** exactement or précisément comme je m'y attendais; **~ right/two o'clock** exactement or juste ce qu'il faut/deux heures; **we were ~ going** nous partions; **I was ~ about to phone** j'allais téléphoner; **~ as he was leaving** au moment or à l'instant précis où il partait; **~ before/enough/here** juste avant/ assez/là; **it's ~ me/a mistake** ce n'est que moi/(rien) qu'une erreur; **~ missed/caught** manqué/attrapé de justesse; **~ listen to this!** écoutez un peu ça!; **~ ask someone the way** vous n'avez qu'à demander votre chemin à quelqu'un; **it's ~ as good** c'est (vraiment) aussi bon; **she's ~ as clever as you** elle est tout aussi intelligente que vous; **it's ~ as well that you ...** heureusement que vous ...; **not ~ now** pas tout de suite; **~ a minute!, ~ one moment!** un instant (s'il vous plaît)!

justice ['dʒʌstɪs] n justice f; (US: judge) juge m de la Cour suprême; **Lord Chief J~** (Brit) premier président de la cour d'appel; **this photo doesn't do you ~** cette photo ne vous avantage pas

Justice of the Peace n juge m de paix

justification [dʒʌstɪfɪ'keɪʃən] n justification f

justify ['dʒʌstɪfaɪ] vt justifier; **to be justified in doing sth** être en droit de faire qch

jut [dʒʌt] vi (also: **~ out**) dépasser, faire saillie

juvenile ['dʒuːvənaɪl] adj juvénile; (court, books) pour enfants ▷ n adolescent(e)

K

K, k [keɪ] n (letter) K, k m; **K for King** K comme
Kléber ▷ abbr (= one thousand) K; (Brit: = Knight)
titre honorifique

kangaroo [kæŋɡəˈruː] n kangourou m

karaoke [kɑːrəˈəʊkɪ] n karaoké m

karate [kəˈrɑːtɪ] n karaté m

kebab [kəˈbæb] n kebab m

keel [kiːl] n quille f; **on an even ~** (fig) à flot;
keel over vi (Naut) chavirer, dessaler; (person)
tomber dans les pommes

keen [kiːn] adj (eager) plein(e)
d'enthousiasme; (interest, desire, competition)
vif/vive; (eye, intelligence) pénétrant(e); (edge)
effilé(e); **to be ~ to do** or **on doing sth** désirer
vivement faire qch, tenir beaucoup à faire
qch; **to be ~ on sth/sb** aimer beaucoup qch/
qn; **I'm not ~ on going** je ne suis pas chaud
pour y aller, je n'ai pas très envie d'y aller

keep [kiːp] (pt, pp **kept**) [kɛpt] vt (retain,
preserve) garder; (hold back) retenir; (shop,
accounts, promise, diary) tenir; (support) (a
promise) tenir; (chickens, bees, pigs etc) élever ▷ vi
(food) se conserver; (remain: in a certain state or
place) rester ▷ n (of castle) donjon m; (food etc):
enough for his ~ assez pour (assurer) sa
subsistance; **to ~ doing sth** (continue)
continuer à faire qch; (repeatedly) ne pas
arrêter de faire qch; **to ~ sb from doing/sth
from happening** empêcher qn de faire or
que qn (ne) fasse/que qch (n')arrive; **to ~ sb
happy/a place tidy** faire que qn soit content/
qu'un endroit reste propre; **to ~ sb waiting**
faire attendre qn; **to ~ an appointment** ne
pas manquer un rendez-vous; **to ~ a record
of sth** prendre note de qch; **to ~ sth to o.s.**
garder qch pour soi, tenir qch secret; **to ~ sth
from sb** cacher qch à qn; **to ~ time** (clock) être
à l'heure, ne pas retarder; **for ~s** (inf) pour de
bon, pour toujours; **keep away** vt: **to ~ sth/
sb away from sb** tenir qch/qn éloigné de qn
▷ vi: **to ~ away (from)** ne pas s'approcher
(de); **keep back** vt (crowds, tears, money)
retenir; (conceal: information): **to ~ sth back
from sb** cacher qch à qn ▷ vi rester en
arrière; **keep down** vt (control: prices, spending)
empêcher d'augmenter, limiter; (retain: food)
garder ▷ vi (person) rester assis(e); rester par
terre; **keep in** vt (invalid, child) garder à la
maison; (Scol) consigner ▷ vi (inf): **to ~ in
with sb** rester en bons termes avec qn; **keep
off** vt (dog, person) éloigner ▷ vi ne pas
s'approcher; **if the rain ~s off** s'il ne pleut
pas; **~ your hands off!** pas touche! (inf);
"~ off the grass" "pelouse interdite"; **keep
on** vi continuer; **to ~ on doing** continuer à
faire; **don't ~ on about it!** arrête (d'en
parler)!; **keep out** vt empêcher d'entrer ▷ vi
(stay out) rester en dehors; **"~ out"** "défense
d'entrer"; **keep up** vi (fig: in comprehension)
suivre ▷ vt continuer, maintenir; **to ~ up
with sb** (in work etc) se maintenir au même
niveau que qn; (in race etc) aller aussi vite
que qn

keeper [ˈkiːpəʳ] n gardien(ne)

keep-fit [ˈkiːpˈfɪt] n gymnastique f
(d'entretien)

keeping [ˈkiːpɪŋ] n (care) garde f; **in ~ with** en
harmonie avec

keepsake [ˈkiːpseɪk] n souvenir m

kennel [ˈkɛnl] n niche f; **kennels** npl (for
boarding) chenil m

Kenya [ˈkɛnjə] n Kenya m

kept [kɛpt] pt, pp of **keep**

kerb [kəːb] n (Brit) bordure f du trottoir

kernel [ˈkəːnl] n amande f; (fig) noyau m

kerosene [ˈkɛrəsiːn] n kérosène m

ketchup [ˈkɛtʃəp] n ketchup m

kettle [ˈkɛtl] n bouilloire f

key [kiː] n (gen, Mus) clé f; (of piano, typewriter)
touche f; (on map) légende f ▷ adj (factor, role,
area) clé inv ▷ cpd (-)clé ▷ vt (also: **~ in**: text)
saisir; **can I have my ~?** je peux avoir ma clé?;
a ~ issue un problème fondamental

keyboard [ˈkiːbɔːd] n clavier m ▷ vt (text)
saisir

keyed up [kiːdˈʌp] adj: **to be (all) ~** être
surexcité(e)

keyhole [ˈkiːhəʊl] n trou m de la serrure

keyhole surgery n chirurgie très minutieuse où
l'incision est minimale

keynote [ˈkiːnəʊt] n (Mus) tonique f; (fig)
note dominante

keyring [ˈkiːrɪŋ] n porte-clés m

k

kg *abbr* (= *kilogram*) K
khaki [ˈkɑːkɪ] *adj, n* kaki *m*
kick [kɪk] *vt* donner un coup de pied à ▷ *vi* (*horse*) ruer ▷ *n* coup *m* de pied; (*of rifle*) recul *m*; (*inf: thrill*): **he does it for ~s** il le fait parce que ça l'excite, il le fait pour le plaisir; **to ~ the habit** (*inf*) arrêter; **kick around** *vi* (*inf*) traîner; **kick off** *vi* (*Sport*) donner le coup d'envoi
kick-off [ˈkɪkɔf] *n* (*Sport*) coup *m* d'envoi
kid [kɪd] *n* (*inf: child*) gamin(e), gosse *m/f*; (*animal, leather*) chevreau *m* ▷ *vi* (*inf*) plaisanter, blaguer
kidnap [ˈkɪdnæp] *vt* enlever, kidnapper
kidnapper [ˈkɪdnæpəʳ] *n* ravisseur(-euse)
kidnapping [ˈkɪdnæpɪŋ] *n* enlèvement *m*
kidney [ˈkɪdnɪ] *n* (*Anat*) rein *m*; (*Culin*) rognon *m*
kidney bean *n* haricot *m* rouge
kill [kɪl] *vt* tuer; (*fig*) faire échouer; détruire; supprimer ▷ *n* mise *f* à mort; **to ~ time** tuer le temps; **kill off** *vt* exterminer; (*fig*) éliminer
killer [ˈkɪləʳ] *n* tueur(-euse); (*murderer*) meurtrier(-ière)
killing [ˈkɪlɪŋ] *n* meurtre *m*; (*of group of people*) tuerie *f*, massacre *m*; (*inf*): **to make a ~** se remplir les poches, réussir un beau coup ▷ *adj* (*inf*) tordant(e)
killjoy [ˈkɪldʒɔɪ] *n* rabat-joie *m inv*
kiln [kɪln] *n* four *m*
kilo [ˈkiːləu] *n* kilo *m*
kilobyte [ˈkiːləubaɪt] *n* (*Comput*) kilo-octet *m*
kilogram, kilogramme [ˈkɪləugræm] *n* kilogramme *m*
kilometre, (US) kilometer [ˈkɪləmiːtəʳ] *n* kilomètre *m*
kilowatt [ˈkɪləuwɔt] *n* kilowatt *m*
kilt [kɪlt] *n* kilt *m*
kin [kɪn] *n* see **next-of-kin**
kind [kaɪnd] *adj* gentil(le), aimable ▷ *n* sorte *f*, espèce *f*; (*species*) genre *m*; **would you be ~ enough to ...?, would you be so ~ as to ...?** auriez-vous la gentillesse *or* l'obligeance de ...?; **it's very ~ of you (to do)** c'est très aimable à vous (de faire); **to be two of a ~** se ressembler; **in ~** (*Comm*) en nature; (*fig*): **to repay sb in ~** rendre la pareille à qn; **~ of** (*inf: rather*) plutôt; **a ~ of** une sorte de; **what ~ of ...?** quelle sorte de ...?
kindergarten [ˈkɪndəɡɑːtn] *n* jardin *m* d'enfants
kind-hearted [kaɪndˈhɑːtɪd] *adj* bon/bonne
kindle [ˈkɪndl] *vt* allumer, enflammer
kindly [ˈkaɪndlɪ] *adj* bienveillant(e), plein(e) de gentillesse ▷ *adv* avec bonté; **will you ~ ...** auriez-vous la bonté *or* l'obligeance de ...; **he didn't take it ~** il l'a mal pris
kindness [ˈkaɪndnɪs] *n* (*quality*) bonté *f*, gentillesse *f*
king [kɪŋ] *n* roi *m*
kingdom [ˈkɪŋdəm] *n* royaume *m*

kingfisher [ˈkɪŋfɪʃəʳ] *n* martin-pêcheur *m*
king-size [ˈkɪŋsaɪz], **king-sized** [ˈkɪŋsaɪzd] *adj* (*cigarette*) (*format*) extra-long/longue
king-size bed, king-sized bed *n* grand lit (*de 1,95 m de large*)
kiosk [ˈkiːɔsk] *n* kiosque *m*; (*Brit: also:* **telephone ~**) cabine *f* (téléphonique); (*also:* **newspaper ~**) kiosque à journaux
kipper [ˈkɪpəʳ] *n* hareng fumé et salé
kiss [kɪs] *n* baiser *m* ▷ *vt* embrasser; **to ~ (each other)** s'embrasser; **to ~ sb goodbye** dire au revoir à qn en l'embrassant
kiss of life *n* (*Brit*) bouche à bouche *m*
kit [kɪt] *n* équipement *m*, matériel *m*; (*set of tools etc*) trousse *f*; (*for assembly*) kit *m*; **tool ~** nécessaire *m* à outils; **kit out** *vt* (*Brit*) équiper
kitchen [ˈkɪtʃɪn] *n* cuisine *f*
kitchen sink *n* évier *m*
kite [kaɪt] *n* (*toy*) cerf-volant *m*; (*Zool*) milan *m*
kitten [ˈkɪtn] *n* petit chat, chaton *m*
kitty [ˈkɪtɪ] *n* (*money*) cagnotte *f*
kiwi [ˈkiːwiː] *n* (*also:* **~ fruit**) kiwi *m*
km *abbr* (= *kilometre*) km
km/h *abbr* (= *kilometres per hour*) km/h
knack [næk] *n*: **to have the ~ (of doing)** avoir le coup (pour faire); **there's a ~** il y a un coup à prendre *or* une combine
knapsack [ˈnæpsæk] *n* musette *f*
knead [niːd] *vt* pétrir
knee [niː] *n* genou *m*
kneecap [ˈniːkæp] *n* rotule *f* ▷ *vt* tirer un coup de feu dans la rotule de
kneel [niːl] (*pt, pp* **knelt**) [niːl, nɛlt] *vi* (*also:* **~ down**) s'agenouiller
knelt [nɛlt] *pt, pp of* **kneel**
knew [njuː] *pt of* **know**
knickers [ˈnɪkəz] *npl* (*Brit*) culotte *f* (de femme)
knife (*pl* **knives**) [naɪf, naɪvz] *n* couteau *m* ▷ *vt* poignarder, frapper d'un coup de couteau; **~, fork and spoon** couvert *m*
knight [naɪt] *n* chevalier *m*; (*Chess*) cavalier *m*
knighthood [ˈnaɪthud] *n* chevalerie *f*; (*title*): **to get a ~** être fait chevalier
knit [nɪt] *vt* tricoter; (*fig*): **to ~ together** unir ▷ *vi* tricoter; (*broken bones*) se ressouder; **to ~ one's brows** froncer les sourcils
knitting [ˈnɪtɪŋ] *n* tricot *m*
knitting needle *n* aiguille *f* à tricoter
knitwear [ˈnɪtwɛəʳ] *n* tricots *mpl*, lainages *mpl*
knives [naɪvz] *npl of* **knife**
knob [nɔb] *n* bouton *m*; (*Brit*): **a ~ of butter** une noix de beurre
knock [nɔk] *vt* frapper; (*bump into*) heurter; (*make: hole etc*): **to ~ a hole in** faire un trou dans, trouer; (*force: nail etc*): **to ~ a nail into** enfoncer un clou dans; (*fig: col*) dénigrer ▷ *vi* (*engine*) cogner; (*at door etc*): **to ~ at/on** frapper à/sur ▷ *n* coup *m*; **he ~ed at the door** il frappa à la porte; **knock down** *vt* renverser; (*price*) réduire; **knock off** *vi* (*inf: finish*) s'arrêter (de travailler) ▷ *vt* (*vase, object*) faire

tomber; (inf: steal) piquer; (fig: from price etc):
to ~ off £10 faire une remise de 10 livres;
knock out vt assommer; (Boxing) mettre
k.-o.; (in competition) éliminer; **knock over** vt
(object) faire tomber; (pedestrian) renverser
knocker ['nɔkəʳ] n (on door) heurtoir m
knockout ['nɔkaut] n (Boxing) knock-out m,
K.-O. m; **~ competition** (Brit) compétition f
avec épreuves éliminatoires
knot [nɒt] n (gen) nœud m ▷ vt nouer; **to tie
a ~** faire un nœud
know [nəu] vt (pt knew, pp known) [njuː, nə
un] savoir; (person, place) connaître; **to ~ that**
savoir que; **to ~ how to do** savoir faire; **to ~
how to swim** savoir nager; **to ~ about/of sth**
(event) être au courant de qch; (subject)
connaître qch; **to get to ~ sth** (fact)
apprendre qch; (place) apprendre à connaître
qch; **I don't ~** je ne sais pas; **I don't ~ him** je
ne le connais pas; **do you ~ where I can ...?**
savez-vous où je peux ...?; **to ~ right from
wrong** savoir distinguer le bon du mauvais;
as far as I ~ ... ... à ma connaissance ..., autant
que je sache ...
know-all ['nəuɔːl] n (Brit pej) je-sais-tout m/f
know-how ['nəuhau] n savoir-faire m,
technique f, compétence f
knowing ['nəuɪŋ] adj (look etc) entendu(e)
knowingly ['nəuɪŋlɪ] adv (on purpose)
sciemment; (smile, look) d'un air entendu
know-it-all ['nəuɪtɔːl] n (US) = **know-all**
knowledge ['nɔlɪdʒ] n connaissance f;
(learning) connaissances, savoir m; **to have no
~ of** ignorer; **not to my ~** pas à ma
connaissance; **without my ~** à mon insu;
to have a working ~ of French se
débrouiller en français; **it is common ~ that
...** chacun sait que ...; **it has come to my ~
that ...** j'ai appris que ...
knowledgeable ['nɔlɪdʒəbl] adj bien
informé(e)
known [nəun] pp of know ▷ adj (thief, facts)
notoire; (expert) célèbre
knuckle ['nʌkl] n articulation f (des
phalanges), jointure f; **knuckle down** vi (inf)
s'y mettre; **knuckle under** vi (inf) céder
koala [kəuˈɑːlə] n (also: ~ bear) koala m
Koran [kɔˈrɑːn] n Coran m
Korea [kəˈrɪə] n Corée f; **North/South ~** Corée
du Nord/Sud
Korean [kəˈrɪən] adj coréen(ne) ▷ n
Coréen(ne)
kosher ['kəuʃəʳ] adj kascher inv
Kosovar, Kosovan ['kɔsəvaːʳ, 'kɔsəvən] adj
kosovar(e)
Kosovo ['kɔsəvəu] n Kosovo m
Kuwait [ku'weɪt] n Koweït m

I

L¹, l [ɛL] n (letter) L, l m; **L for Lucy**, (US) **L for
Love** L comme Louis
L² abbr (= lake, large) L; (= left) g; (Brit Aut:
= learner) signale un conducteur débutant
l. abbr (= litre) l
lab [læb] n abbr (= laboratory) labo m
label ['leɪbl] n étiquette f; (brand: of record)
marque f ▷ vt étiqueter; **to ~ sb a ...** qualifier
qn de ...
labor etc ['leɪbəʳ] (US) n = **labour** etc
laboratory [ləˈbɔrətərɪ] n laboratoire m
Labor Day n (US, Canada) fête f du travail
(le premier lundi de septembre); voir article

⬦ **LABOR DAY**
⬦
⬦ Labor Day aux États-Unis et au Canada est
⬦ fixée au premier lundi de septembre.
⬦ Instituée par le Congrès en 1894 après
⬦ avoir été réclamée par les mouvements
⬦ ouvriers pendant douze ans, elle a perdu
⬦ une grande partie de son caractère
⬦ politique pour devenir un jour férié assez
⬦ ordinaire et l'occasion de partir pour un
⬦ long week-end avant la rentrée des classes.

labor union n (US) syndicat m
Labour ['leɪbəʳ] n (Brit Pol: also: **the ~ Party**)
le parti travailliste, les travaillistes mpl
labour, (US) **labor** ['leɪbəʳ] n (work) travail m;
(workforce) main-d'œuvre f; (Med) travail,
accouchement m ▷ vi: **to ~ (at)** travailler dur

(à), peiner (sur) ▷ vt: **to ~ a point** insister sur un point; **in ~** (Med) en travail

laboured, (US) **labored** ['leɪbəd] adj lourd(e), laborieux(-euse); (breathing) difficile, pénible; (style) lourd, embarrassé(e)

labourer, (US) **laborer** ['leɪbərəʳ] n manœuvre m; **farm ~** ouvrier m agricole

lace [leɪs] n dentelle f; (of shoe etc) lacet m ▷ vt (shoe: also: **~ up**) lacer; (drink) arroser, corser

lack [læk] n manque m ▷ vt manquer de; **through** or **for ~ of** faute de, par manque de; **to be ~ing** manquer, faire défaut; **to be ~ing in** manquer de

lacquer ['lækəʳ] n laque f

lacy ['leɪsɪ] adj (made of lace) en dentelle; (like lace) comme de la dentelle, qui ressemble à de la dentelle

lad [læd] n garçon m, gars m; (Brit: in stable etc) lad m

ladder ['lædəʳ] n échelle f; (Brit: in tights) maille filée ▷ vt, vi (Brit: tights) filer

laden ['leɪdn] adj: **~ (with)** chargé(e) (de); **fully ~** (truck, ship) en pleine charge

ladle ['leɪdl] n louche f

lady ['leɪdɪ] n dame f; **"ladies and gentlemen ..."** "Mesdames ... Messieurs ..."; **young ~** jeune fille f; (married) jeune femme f; **L- Smith** lady Smith; **the ladies' (room)** les toilettes fpl des dames; **a ~ doctor** une doctoresse, une femme médecin

ladybird ['leɪdɪbəːd], (US) **ladybug** ['leɪdɪbʌg] n coccinelle f

ladylike ['leɪdɪlaɪk] adj distingué(e)

ladyship ['leɪdɪʃɪp] n: **your L-** Madame la comtesse (or la baronne etc)

lag [læg] n retard m ▷ vi (also: **~ behind**) rester en arrière, traîner; (fig) rester à la traîne ▷ vt (pipes) calorifuger

lager ['laːgəʳ] n bière blonde

lagoon [lə'guːn] n lagune f

laid [leɪd] pt, pp of **lay**

laid back adj (inf) relaxe, décontracté(e)

laid up adj alité(e)

lain [leɪn] pp of **lie**

lake [leɪk] n lac m

lamb [læm] n agneau m

lamb chop n côtelette f d'agneau

lame [leɪm] adj (also fig) boiteux(-euse); **~ duck** (fig) canard boiteux

lament [lə'mɛnt] n lamentation f ▷ vt pleurer, se lamenter sur

laminated ['læmɪneɪtɪd] adj laminé(e); (windscreen) (en vefre) feuilleté

lamp [læmp] n lampe f

lamppost ['læmppəust] n (Brit) réverbère m

lampshade ['læmpʃeɪd] n abat-jour m inv

lance [laːns] n lance f ▷ vt (Med) inciser

land [lænd] n (as opposed to sea) terre f (ferme); (country) pays m; (soil) terre; (piece of land) terrain m; (estate) terre(s), domaine(s) m(pl) ▷ vi (from ship) débarquer; (Aviat) atterrir; (fig: fall) (re)tomber ▷ vt (passengers, goods)

débarquer; (obtain) décrocher; **to go/travel by ~** se déplacer par voie de terre; **to own ~** être propriétaire foncier; **to ~ on one's feet** (also fig) retomber sur ses pieds; **to ~ sb with sth** (inf) coller qch à qn; **land up** vi atterrir, (finir par) se retrouver

landfill site ['lændfɪl-] n centre m d'enfouissement des déchets

landing ['lændɪŋ] n (from ship) débarquement m; (Aviat) atterrissage m; (of staircase) palier m

landing card n carte f de débarquement

landing strip n piste f d'atterrissage

landlady ['lændleɪdɪ] n propriétaire f, logeuse f; (of pub) patronne f

landlocked ['lændlɔkt] adj entouré(e) de terre(s), sans accès à la mer

landlord ['lændlɔːd] n propriétaire m, logeur m; (of pub etc) patron m

landmark ['lændmaːk] n (point m de) repère m; **to be a ~** (fig) faire date or époque

landowner ['lændəunəʳ] n propriétaire foncier or terrien

landscape ['lænskeɪp] n paysage m

landscape architect, landscape gardener n paysagiste m/f

landslide ['lændslaɪd] n (Geo) glissement m (de terrain); (fig: Pol) raz-de-marée (électoral)

lane [leɪn] n (in country) chemin m; (in town) ruelle f; (Aut: of road) voie f; (: line of traffic) file f; (in race) couloir m; **shipping ~** route f maritime or de navigation

language ['læŋgwɪdʒ] n langue f; (way one speaks) langage m; **what ~s do you speak?** quelles langues parlez-vous?; **bad ~** grossièretés fpl, langage grossier

language laboratory n laboratoire m de langues

language school n école f de langue

lank [læŋk] adj (hair) raide et terne

lanky ['læŋkɪ] adj grand(e) et maigre, efflanqué(e)

lantern ['læntn] n lanterne f

lap [læp] n (of track) tour m (de piste); (of body): **in** or **on one's ~** sur les genoux ▷ vt (also: **~ up**) laper ▷ vi (waves) clapoter; **lap up** vt (fig) boire comme du petit-lait, se gargariser de; (: lies etc) gober

lapel [lə'pɛl] n revers m

Lapland ['læplænd] n Laponie f

lapse [læps] n défaillance f; (in behaviour) écart m (de conduite) ▷ vi (Law) cesser d'être en vigueur; (contract) expirer; (pass) être périmé; (subscription) prendre fin; **to ~ into bad habits** prendre de mauvaises habitudes; **~ of time** laps m de temps, intervalle m; **a ~ of memory** un trou de mémoire

laptop ['læptɔp], **laptop computer** n (ordinateur m) portable m

larceny ['laːsənɪ] n vol m

larch [laːtʃ] n mélèze m

lard [laːd] n saindoux m

larder ['laːdəʳ] n garde-manger m inv

large [lɑːdʒ] adj grand(e); (person, animal) gros/grosse; **to make ~r** agrandir; **a ~ number of people** beaucoup de gens; **by and ~** en général; **on a ~ scale** sur une grande échelle; **at ~** (free) en liberté; (generally) en général; pour la plupart; see also **by**

largely ['lɑːdʒlɪ] adv en grande partie; (principally) surtout

large-scale ['lɑːdʒ'skeɪl] adj (map, drawing etc) à grande échelle; (fig) important(e)

lark [lɑːk] n (bird) alouette f; (joke) blague f, farce f; **lark about** vi faire l'idiot, rigoler

laryngitis [lærɪn'dʒaɪtɪs] n laryngite f

lasagne [lə'zænjə] n lasagne f

laser ['leɪzə'] n laser m

laser printer n imprimante f laser

lash [læʃ] n coup m de fouet; (also: **eye~**) cil m ⊳ vt fouetter; (tie) attacher; **lash down** vt attacher; amarrer; arrimer ⊳ vi (rain) tomber avec violence; **lash out** vi: **to ~ out** (at or against sb/sth) attaquer violemment (qn/qch); **to ~ out** (on sth) (inf: spend) se fendre (de qch)

lass [læs] (Brit) n (jeune) fille f

lasso [læ'suː] n lasso m ⊳ vt prendre au lasso

last [lɑːst] adj (not time) dernier(-ière) ⊳ adv en dernier; (most recently) la dernière fois; (finally) finalement ⊳ vi durer; **~ week** la semaine dernière; **~ night** (evening) hier soir; (night) la nuit dernière; **at ~** enfin; **~ but one** avant-dernier(-ière); **the ~ time** la dernière fois; **it ~s** (for) **2 hours** ça dure 2 heures

last-ditch ['lɑːst'dɪtʃ] adj ultime, désespéré(e)

lasting ['lɑːstɪŋ] adj durable

lastly ['lɑːstlɪ] adv en dernier lieu, pour finir

last-minute ['lɑːstmɪnɪt] adj de dernière minute

latch [lætʃ] n loquet m; **latch onto** vt fus (cling to: person, group) s'accrocher à; (idea) se mettre en tête

late [leɪt] adj (not on time) en retard; (far on in day etc) tardif(-ive); (: edition, delivery) dernier(-ière); (recent) récent(e), dernier; (former) ancien(ne); (dead) défunt(e) ⊳ adv tard; (behind time, schedule) en retard; **to be ~** avoir du retard; **to be 10 minutes ~** avoir 10 minutes de retard; **sorry I'm ~** désolé d'être en retard; **it's too ~** il est trop tard; **to work ~** travailler tard; **~ in life** sur le tard, à un âge avancé; **of ~** dernièrement; **in ~ May** vers la fin (du mois) de mai, fin mai; **the ~ Mr X** feu M. X

latecomer ['leɪtkʌmə'] n retardataire m/f

lately ['leɪtlɪ] adv récemment

later ['leɪtə'] adj (date etc) ultérieur(e); (version etc) plus récent(e) ⊳ adv plus tard; **~ on today** plus tard dans la journée

latest ['leɪtɪst] adj tout(e) dernier(-ière); **the ~ news** les dernières nouvelles; **at the ~** au plus tard

lathe [leɪð] n tour m

lather ['lɑːðə'] n mousse f (de savon) ⊳ vt savonner ⊳ vi mousser

Latin ['lætɪn] n latin m ⊳ adj latin(e)

Latin America n Amérique latine

Latin American adj latino-américain(e), d'Amérique latine ⊳ n Latino-Américain(e)

latitude ['lætɪtjuːd] n (also fig) latitude f

latter ['lætə'] adj deuxième, dernier(-ière) ⊳ n: **the ~** ce dernier, celui-ci

latterly ['lætəlɪ] adv dernièrement, récemment

laudable ['lɔːdəbl] adj louable

laugh [lɑːf] n rire m ⊳ vi rire; **(to do sth) for a ~** (faire) qch pour rire; **laugh at** vt fus se moquer de; (joke) rire de; **laugh off** vt écarter or rejeter par une plaisanterie or par une boutade

laughable ['lɑːfəbl] adj risible, ridicule

laughing stock n: **the ~ of** la risée de

laughter ['lɑːftə'] n rire m; (of several people) rires mpl

launch [lɔːntʃ] n lancement m; (boat) chaloupe f; (also: **motor ~**) vedette f ⊳ vt (ship, rocket, plan) lancer; **launch into** vt fus se lancer dans; **launch out** vi: **to ~ out** (into) se lancer (dans)

launder ['lɔːndə'] vt laver; (fig: money) blanchir

Launderette® ['lɔːn'drɛt], (US) **Laundromat®** ['lɔːndrəmæt] n laverie f (automatique)

laundry ['lɔːndrɪ] n (clothes) linge m; (business) blanchisserie f; (room) buanderie f; **to do the ~** faire la lessive

laurel ['lɔrl] n laurier m; **to rest on one's ~s** se reposer sur ses lauriers

lava ['lɑːvə] n lave f

lavatory ['lævətərɪ] n toilettes fpl

lavender ['lævəndə'] n lavande f

lavish ['lævɪʃ] adj (amount) copieux(-euse); (meal) somptueux(-euse); (hospitality) généreux(-euse); (person: giving freely): **~ with** prodigue de ⊳ vt: **to ~ sth on sb** prodiguer qch à qn; (money) dépenser qch sans compter pour qn

law [lɔː] n loi f; (science) droit m; **against the ~** contraire à la loi; **to study ~** faire du droit; **to go to ~** (Brit) avoir recours à la justice; **~ and order** n l'ordre public

law-abiding ['lɔːəbaɪdɪŋ] adj respectueux(-euse) des lois

law court n tribunal m, cour f de justice

lawful ['lɔːful] adj légal(e), permis(e)

lawless ['lɔːlɪs] adj (action) illégal(e); (place) sans loi

lawn [lɔːn] n pelouse f

lawnmower ['lɔːnməuə'] n tondeuse f à gazon

lawn tennis n tennis m

law school n faculté f de droit

lawsuit ['lɔːsuːt] n procès m; **to bring a ~ against** engager des poursuites contre

lawyer ['lɔːjə'] n (consultant, with company) juriste m; (for sales, wills etc) ≈ notaire m; (partner, in court) ≈ avocat m

lax [læks] *adj* relâché(e)

laxative ['læksətɪv] *n* laxatif *m*

lay [leɪ] *pt of* **lie** ▷ *adj* laïque; (*not expert*) profane ▷ *vt* (*pt, pp* **laid**) [leɪd] poser, mettre; (*eggs*) pondre; (*trap*) tendre; (*plans*) élaborer; **to ~ the table** mettre la table; **to ~ the facts/one's proposals before sb** présenter les faits/ses propositions à qn; **to get laid** (*inf!*) baiser (!), se faire baiser (!); **lay aside, lay by** *vt* mettre de côté; **lay down** *vt* poser; (*rules etc*) établir; **to ~ down the law** (*fig*) faire la loi; **lay in** *vt* accumuler, s'approvisionner en; **lay into** *vi* (*inf: attack*) tomber sur; (: *scold*) passer une engueulade à; **lay off** *vt* (*workers*) licencier; **lay on** *vt* (*water, gas*) mettre, installer; (*provide: meal etc*) fournir; (*paint*) étaler; **lay out** *vt* (*design*) dessiner, concevoir; (*display*) disposer; (*spend*) dépenser; **lay up** *vt* (*store*) amasser; (*car*) remiser; (*ship*) désarmer; (*illness*) forcer à s'aliter

layabout ['leɪəbaʊt] *n* fainéant(e)

lay-by ['leɪbaɪ] *n* (*Brit*) aire *f* de stationnement (sur le bas-côté)

layer ['leɪə*] *n* couche *f*

layman ['leɪmən] *irreg n* (*Rel*) laïque *m*; (*non-expert*) profane *m*

layout ['leɪaʊt] *n* disposition *f*, plan *m*, agencement *m*; (*Press*) mise *f* en page

laze [leɪz] *vi* paresser

lazy ['leɪzɪ] *adj* paresseux(-euse)

lb. *abbr* (*weight*) = **pound**

lead¹ [liːd] (*pt, pp* **led**) [lɛd] *n* (*front position*) tête *f*; (*distance, time ahead*) avance *f*; (*clue*) piste *f*; (*to battery*) raccord *m*; (*Elec*) fil *m*; (*for dog*) laisse *f*; (*Theat*) rôle principal ▷ *vt* (*guide*) mener, conduire; (*induce*) amener; (*be leader of*) être à la tête de; (*Sport*) être en tête de; (*orchestra: Brit*) être le premier violon de; (: *US*) diriger ▷ *vi* (*Sport*) mener, être en tête; **to ~ to** (*road, pipe*) mener à, conduire à; (*result in*) conduire à; aboutir à; **to ~ sb astray** détourner qn du droit chemin; **to be in the ~** (*Sport: in race*) mener, être en tête; (: *in match*) mener (à la marque); **to take the ~** (*Sport*) passer en tête, prendre la tête; mener; (*fig*) prendre l'initiative; **to ~ sb to believe that ...** amener qn à croire que ...; **to ~ sb to do sth** amener qn à faire qch; **to ~ the way** montrer le chemin; **lead away** *vt* emmener; **lead back** *vt* ramener; **lead off** *vi* (*in game etc*) commencer; **lead on** *vt* (*tease*) faire marcher; **to ~ sb on to** (*induce*) amener qn à; **lead up to** *vt* conduire à; (*in conversation*) en venir à

lead² [lɛd] *n* (*metal*) plomb *m*; (*in pencil*) mine *f*

leaded petrol *n* essence *f* au plomb

leaden ['lɛdn] *adj* de or en plomb

leader ['liːdə*] *n* (*of team*) chef *m*; (*of party etc*) dirigeant(e), chef *m*; (*Sport: in league*) leader *m*; (: *in race*) coureur *m* de tête; (*in newspaper*) éditorial *m*; **they are ~s in their field** (*fig*) ils sont à la pointe du progrès dans leur domaine; **the L~ of the House** (*Brit*) le chef de la majorité ministérielle

leadership ['liːdəʃɪp] *n* (*position*) direction *f*; **under the ~ of ...** sous la direction de ...; **qualities of ~** qualités *fpl* de chef or de meneur

lead-free ['lɛdfriː] *adj* sans plomb

leading ['liːdɪŋ] *adj* de premier plan; (*main*) principal(e); (*in race*) de tête; **a ~ question** une question tendancieuse; **~ role** rôle prépondérant or de premier plan

leading lady *n* (*Theat*) vedette (féminine)

leading light *n* (*person*) sommité *f*, personnalité *f* de premier plan

leading man *irreg n* (*Theat*) vedette (masculine)

lead singer [liːd-] *n* (*in pop group*) (chanteur *m*) vedette *f*

leaf (*pl* **leaves**) [liːf, liːvz] *n* feuille *f*; (*of table*) rallonge *f*; **to turn over a new ~** (*fig*) changer de conduite or d'existence; **to take a ~ out of sb's book** (*fig*) prendre exemple sur qn; **leaf through** *vt* (*book*) feuilleter

leaflet ['liːflɪt] *n* prospectus *m*, brochure *f*; (*Pol, Rel*) tract *m*

league [liːg] *n* ligue *f*; (*Football*) championnat *m*; (*measure*) lieue *f*; **to be in ~ with** avoir partie liée avec, être de mèche avec

leak [liːk] *n* (*out: also fig*) fuite *f*; (*in*) infiltration *f* ▷ *vi* (*pipe, liquid etc*) fuir; (*shoes*) prendre l'eau; (*ship*) faire eau ▷ *vt* (*liquid*) répandre; (*information*) divulguer; **leak out** *vi* fuir; (*information*) être divulgué(e)

lean [liːn] (*pt, pp* **leaned** or **leant**) [lɛnt] *adj* maigre ▷ *n* (*of meat*) maigre *m* ▷ *vt*: **to ~ sth on** appuyer qch sur ▷ *vi* (*slope*) pencher; (*rest*): **to ~ against** s'appuyer contre; être appuyé(e) contre; **to ~ on** s'appuyer sur; **lean back** *vi* se pencher en arrière; **lean forward** *vi* se pencher en avant; **lean out** *vi*: **to ~ out (of)** se pencher au dehors (de); **lean over** *vi* se pencher

leaning ['liːnɪŋ] *adj* penché(e) ▷ *n*: **~ (towards)** penchant *m* (pour); **the L~ Tower of Pisa** la tour penchée de Pise

leant [lɛnt] *pt, pp of* **lean**

leap [liːp] *n* bond *m*, saut *m* ▷ *vi* (*pt, pp* **leaped** or **leapt**) [lɛpt] bondir, sauter; **to ~ at an offer** saisir une offre; **leap up** *vi* (*person*) faire un bond; se lever d'un bond

leapfrog ['liːpfrɔg] *n* jeu *m* de saute-mouton

leapt [lɛpt] *pt, pp of* **leap**

leap year *n* année *f* bissextile

learn (*pt, pp* **learned** or **learnt**) [ləːn, -t] *vt, vi* apprendre; **to ~ (how) to do sth** apprendre à faire qch; **we were sorry to ~ that ...** nous avons appris avec regret que ...; **to ~ about sth** (*Scol*) étudier qch; (*hear, read*) apprendre qch

learned ['ləːnɪd] *adj* érudit(e), savant(e)

learner ['ləːnə*] *n* débutant(e); (*Brit: also:* **~ driver**) (conducteur(-trice)) débutant(e)

learning ['lə:nɪŋ] n savoir m
learnt [lə:nt] pt, pp of **learn**
lease [li:s] n bail m ▷ vt louer à bail; **on** ~ en
location; **lease back** vt vendre en cession-
bail
leash [li:ʃ] n laisse f
least [li:st] adj: **the** ~ (+noun) le/la plus
petit(e), le/la moindre; (smallest amount of)
le moins de ▷ pron: **(the)** ~ le moins ▷ adv
(+verb) le moins ▷ adj: **the** ~ le/la moins; **the**
~ **money** le moins d'argent; **the** ~ **expensive**
le/la moins cher/chère; **the** ~ **possible effort**
le moins d'effort possible; **at** ~ au moins; (or
rather) du moins; **you could at** ~ **have
written** tu aurais au moins pu écrire; **not in
the** ~ pas le moins du monde
leather ['lɛðəʳ] n cuir m ▷ cpd en or de cuir;
~ **goods** maroquinerie f
leave [li:v] (pt, pp left) [lɛft] vt laisser; (go
away from) quitter; (forget) oublier ▷ vi partir,
s'en aller ▷ n (time off) congé m; (Mil, also:
consent) permission f; **what time does the
train/bus** ~? le train/le bus part à quelle
heure?; **to** ~ **sth to sb** (money etc) laisser qch à
qn; **to be left** rester; **there's some milk left
over** il reste du lait; **to** ~ **school** quitter
l'école, terminer sa scolarité; ~ **it to me!**
laissez-moi faire!, je m'en occupe!; **on** ~ en
permission; **to take one's** ~ **of** prendre
congé de; ~ **of absence** n congé
exceptionnel; (Mil) permission spéciale;
leave behind vt (also fig) laisser; (opponent in
race) distancer; (forget) laisser, oublier; **leave
off** vt (cover, lid, heating) ne pas (re)mettre;
(light) ne pas (r)allumer, laisser éteint(e);
(Brit inf: stop): **to** ~ **off (doing sth)** s'arrêter
(de faire qch); **leave on** vt (coat etc) garder,
ne pas enlever; (lid) laisser dessus; (light, fire,
cooker) laisser allumé(e); **leave out** vt
oublier, omettre
leaves [li:vz] npl of **leaf**
Lebanon ['lɛbənən] n Liban m
lecherous ['lɛtʃərəs] adj lubrique
lecture ['lɛktʃəʳ] n conférence f; (Scol) cours
(magistral) ▷ vi donner des cours; enseigner
▷ vt (scold) sermonner, réprimander; **to**
faire un cours (or son cours) sur; **to give a** ~
(on) faire une conférence (sur), faire un
cours (sur)
lecture hall n amphithéâtre m
lecturer ['lɛktʃərəʳ] n (speaker)
conférencier(-ière); (Brit: at university)
professeur m (d'université), prof m/f de fac
(inf); **assistant** ~ (Brit) ≈ assistant(e); **senior** ~
(Brit) ≈ chargé(e) d'enseignement
lecture theatre n = **lecture hall**
led [lɛd] pt, pp of **lead**[1]
ledge [lɛdʒ] n (of window, on wall) rebord m;
(of mountain) saillie f, corniche f
ledger ['lɛdʒəʳ] n registre m, grand livre
leech [li:tʃ] n sangsue f
leek [li:k] n poireau m

leer [lɪəʳ] vi: **to** ~ **at sb** regarder qn d'un air
mauvais or concupiscent, lorgner qn
leeway ['li:weɪ] n (fig): **to make up** ~
rattraper son retard; **to have some** ~ avoir
une certaine liberté d'action
left [lɛft] pt, pp of **leave** ▷ adj gauche ▷ adv
à gauche ▷ n gauche f; **there are two** ~ il en
reste deux; **on the** ~, **to the** ~ à gauche;
the L- (Pol) la gauche
left-hand ['lɛfthænd] adj: **the** ~ **side** la
gauche, le côté gauche
left-hand drive ['lɛfthænd-] n (Brit)
conduite f à gauche; (vehicle) véhicule m avec
la conduite à gauche
left-handed [lɛft'hændɪd] adj gaucher(-ère);
(scissors etc) pour gauchers
left-luggage [lɛft'lʌgɪdʒ], **left-luggage
office** n (Brit) consigne f
left-luggage locker [lɛft'lʌgɪdʒ-] n (Brit)
(casier m à) consigne f automatique
left-overs ['lɛftəʊvəz] npl restes mpl
left wing n (Mil, Sport) aile f gauche; (Pol)
gauche f
left-wing ['lɛft'wɪŋ] adj (Pol) de gauche
leg [lɛg] n jambe f; (of animal) patte f; (of
furniture) pied m; (Culin: of chicken) cuisse f;
(of journey) étape f; **1st/2nd** ~ (Sport) match m
aller/retour; (of journey) 1ère/2ème étape; ~ **of
lamb** (Culin) gigot m d'agneau; **to stretch
one's** ~**s** se dégourdir les jambes
legacy ['lɛgəsɪ] n (also fig) héritage m, legs m
legal ['li:gl] adj (permitted by law) légal(e);
(relating to law) juridique; **to take** ~ **action** or
proceedings against sb poursuivre qn en
justice
legal holiday (US) n jour férié
legalize ['li:gəlaɪz] vt légaliser
legally ['li:gəlɪ] adv légalement; ~ **binding**
juridiquement contraignant(e)
legal tender n monnaie légale
legend ['lɛdʒənd] n légende f
legendary ['lɛdʒəndərɪ] adj légendaire
leggings ['lɛgɪnz] npl caleçon m
legible ['lɛdʒəbl] adj lisible
legislation [lɛdʒɪs'leɪʃən] n législation f;
a piece of ~ un texte de loi
legislative ['lɛdʒɪslətɪv] adj législatif(-ive)
legislature ['lɛdʒɪslətʃəʳ] n corps législatif
legitimate [lɪ'dʒɪtɪmət] adj légitime
leg-room ['lɛgru:m] n place f pour les jambes
leisure ['lɛʒəʳ] n (free time) temps libre,
loisirs mpl; **at** ~ (tout) à loisir; **at your** ~ (later)
à tête reposée
leisure centre n (Brit) centre m de loisirs
leisurely ['lɛʒəlɪ] adj tranquille, fait(e) sans
se presser
lemon ['lɛmən] n citron m
lemonade [lɛmə'neɪd] n (fizzy) limonade f
lemon tea n thé m au citron
lend (pt, pp lent) [lɛnd, lɛnt] vt: **to** ~ **sth (to
sb)** prêter qch (à qn); **could you** ~ **me some
money?** pourriez-vous me prêter de

l'argent?; **to ~ a hand** donner un coup de main

length [lɛŋθ] n longueur f; (section: of road, pipe etc) morceau m, bout m; **~ of time** durée f; **what ~ is it?** quelle longueur fait-il?; **it is 2 metres in ~** cela fait 2 mètres de long; **to fall full ~** tomber de tout son long; **at ~** (at last) enfin, à la fin; (lengthily) longuement; **to go to any ~(s) to do sth** faire n'importe quoi pour faire qch, ne reculer devant rien pour faire qch

lengthen [ˈlɛŋθən] vt allonger, prolonger ▷ vi s'allonger

lengthways [ˈlɛŋθweɪz] adv dans le sens de la longueur, en long

lengthy [ˈlɛŋθɪ] adj (très) long/longue

lenient [ˈliːnɪənt] adj indulgent(e), clément(e)

lens [lɛnz] n lentille f; (of spectacles) verre m; (of camera) objectif m

Lent [lɛnt] n carême m

lent [lɛnt] pt, pp of **lend**

lentil [ˈlɛntl] n lentille f

Leo [ˈliːəu] n le Lion; **to be ~** être du Lion

leopard [ˈlɛpəd] n léopard m

leotard [ˈliːətɑːd] n justaucorps m

leprosy [ˈlɛprəsɪ] n lèpre f

lesbian [ˈlɛzbɪən] n lesbienne f ▷ adj lesbien(ne)

less [lɛs] adj moins de ▷ pron, adv moins ▷ prep: **~ tax/10% discount** avant impôt/ moins 10% de remise; **~ than that/you** moins que cela/vous; **~ than half** moins de la moitié; **~ than one/a kilo/3 metres** moins de un/d'un kilo/de 3 mètres; **~ than ever** moins que jamais; **~ and ~** de moins en moins; **the ~ he works ...** moins il travaille ...

lessen [ˈlɛsn] vi diminuer, s'amoindrir, s'atténuer ▷ vt diminuer, réduire, atténuer

lesser [ˈlɛsəʳ] adj moindre; **to a ~ extent** or **degree** à un degré moindre

lesson [ˈlɛsn] n leçon f; **a maths ~** une leçon or un cours de maths; **to give ~s in** donner des cours de; **to teach sb a ~** (fig) donner une bonne leçon à qn; **it taught him a ~** (fig) cela lui a servi de leçon

let (pt, pp **let**) [lɛt] vt laisser; (Brit: lease) louer; **to ~ sb do sth** laisser qn faire qch; **to ~ sb know sth** faire savoir qch à qn, prévenir qn de qch; **he ~ me go** il m'a laissé partir; **~ the water boil and ...** faites bouillir l'eau et ...; **to ~ go** lâcher prise; **to ~ go of sth, to ~ sth go** lâcher qch; **~'s go** allons-y; **~ him come** qu'il vienne; **"to ~"** (Brit) "à louer"; **let down** vt (lower) baisser; (dress) rallonger; (hair) défaire; (Brit: tyre) dégonfler; (disappoint) décevoir; **let go** vi lâcher prise ▷ vt lâcher; **let in** vt laisser entrer; (visitor etc) faire entrer; **what have you ~ yourself in for?** à quoi t'es-tu engagé?; **let off** vt (allow to leave) laisser partir; (not punish) ne pas punir; (taxi driver, bus driver) déposer; (firework etc) faire

partir; (bomb) faire exploser; (smell etc) dégager; **to ~ off steam** (fig: inf) se défouler, décharger sa rate or bile; **let on** vi (inf): **to ~ on that ....** révéler que ..., dire que ...; **let out** vt laisser sortir; (dress) élargir; (scream) laisser échapper; (Brit: rent out) louer; **let up** vi diminuer, s'arrêter

lethal [ˈliːθl] adj mortel(le), fatal(e); (weapon) meurtrier(-ère)

letter [ˈlɛtəʳ] n lettre f; **letters** npl (Literature) lettres; **small/capital ~** minuscule f/ majuscule f; **~ of credit** lettre f de crédit

letter bomb n lettre piégée

letterbox [ˈlɛtəbɔks] n (Brit) boîte f aux or à lettres

lettering [ˈlɛtərɪŋ] n lettres fpl; caractères mpl

lettuce [ˈlɛtɪs] n laitue f, salade f

let-up [ˈlɛtʌp] n répit m, détente f

leukaemia, (US) **leukemia** [luːˈkiːmɪə] n leucémie f

level [ˈlɛvl] adj (flat) plat(e), plan(e), uni(e); (horizontal) horizontal(e) ▷ n niveau m; (flat place) terrain plat; (also: **spirit ~**) niveau à bulle ▷ vt niveler, aplanir; (gun) pointer, braquer; (accusation): **to ~ (against)** lancer or porter (contre) ▷ vi (inf): **to ~ with sb** être franc/franche avec qn; **"A" ~s** npl (Brit) ≈ baccalauréat m; **"O" ~s** npl (Brit: formerly) examens passés à l'âge de 16 ans sanctionnant les connaissances de l'élève; ≈ brevet m des collèges; **a ~ spoonful** (Culin) une cuillerée rase; **to be ~ with** être au même niveau que; **to draw ~ with** (team) arriver à égalité de points avec, égaliser avec; arriver au même classement que; (runner, car) arriver à la hauteur de, rattraper; **on the ~** à l'horizontale; (fig: honest) régulier(-ière); **level off, level out** vi (prices etc) se stabiliser ▷ vt (ground) aplanir, niveler

level crossing n (Brit) passage m à niveau

level-headed [lɛvlˈhɛdɪd] adj équilibré(e)

lever [ˈliːvəʳ] n levier m ▷ vt: **to ~ up/out** soulever/extraire au moyen d'un levier

leverage [ˈliːvərɪdʒ] n (influence): **~ (on** or **with)** prise f (sur)

levy [ˈlɛvɪ] n taxe f, impôt m ▷ vt (tax) lever; (fine) infliger

lewd [luːd] adj obscène, lubrique

liability [laɪəˈbɪlətɪ] n responsabilité f; (handicap) handicap m

liable [ˈlaɪəbl] adj (subject): **~ to** sujet(te) à, passible de; (responsible): **~ (for)** responsable (de); (likely): **~ to do** susceptible de faire; **to be ~ to a fine** être passible d'une amende

liaise [liːˈeɪz] vi: **to ~ with** assurer la liaison avec

liaison [liːˈeɪzɔn] n liaison f

liar [ˈlaɪəʳ] n menteur(-euse)

libel [ˈlaɪbl] n diffamation f; (document) écrit m diffamatoire ▷ vt diffamer

liberal [ˈlɪbərl] adj libéral(e); (generous): **~ with** prodigue de, généreux(-euse) avec ▷ n: **L~** (Pol) libéral(e)

Liberal Democrat n (Brit) libéral(e)-démocrate m/f

liberate ['lɪbəreɪt] vt libérer

liberation [lɪbə'reɪʃən] n libération f

liberty ['lɪbətɪ] n liberté f; **to be at ~** (criminal) être en liberté; **at ~ to do** libre de faire; **to take the ~ of** prendre la liberté de, se permettre de

Libra ['li:brə] n la Balance; **to be ~** être de la Balance

librarian [laɪ'brɛərɪən] n bibliothécaire m/f

library ['laɪbrərɪ] n bibliothèque f

libretto [lɪ'bretəʊ] n livret m

Libya ['lɪbɪə] n Libye f

lice [laɪs] npl of **louse**

licence, (US) **license** ['laɪsns] n autorisation f, permis m; (Comm) licence f; (Radio, TV) redevance f; (also: **driving ~**: US: also: **driver's license**) permis m (de conduire); (excessive freedom) licence; **import ~** licence d'importation; **produced under ~** fabriqué(e) sous licence

licence number n (Brit Aut) numéro m d'immatriculation

license ['laɪsns] n (US) = **licence** ▷ vt donner une licence à; (car) acheter la vignette de; délivrer la vignette de

licensed ['laɪsnst] adj (for alcohol) patenté(e) pour la vente des spiritueux, qui a une patente de débit de boissons; (car) muni(e) de la vignette

license plate n (US Aut) plaque f minéralogique

licensing hours (Brit) npl heures fpl d'ouvertures (des pubs)

lick [lɪk] vt lécher; (inf: defeat) écraser, flanquer une piquette or raclée à ▷ n coup m de langue; **a ~ of paint** un petit coup de peinture; **to ~ one's lips** (fig) se frotter les mains

licorice ['lɪkərɪʃ] n = **liquorice**

lid [lɪd] n couvercle m; (eyelid) paupière f; **to take the ~ off sth** (fig) exposer or étaler qch au grand jour

lie [laɪ] n mensonge m ▷ vi (pt, pp **lied**) (tell lies) mentir; (pt **lay**, pp **lain**) [leɪ, leɪn] (rest) être étendu(e) or allongé(e) or couché(e); (in grave) être enterré(e), reposer; (object: be situated) se trouver, être; **to ~ low** (fig) se cacher, rester caché(e); **to tell ~s** mentir; **lie about, lie around** vi (things) traîner; (Brit: person) traînasser, flemmarder; **lie back** vi se renverser en arrière; **lie down** vi se coucher, s'étendre; **lie up** vi (hide) se cacher

Liechtenstein ['lɪktənstaɪn] n Liechtenstein m

lie-down ['laɪdaʊn] n (Brit): **to have a ~** s'allonger, se reposer

lie-in ['laɪɪn] n (Brit): **to have a ~** faire la grasse matinée

lieutenant [lɛf'tɛnənt, US: lu:'tɛnənt] n lieutenant m

life (pl **lives**) [laɪf, laɪvz] n vie f; **to come to ~** (fig) ▷ cpd de vie; à vie; la vie; à vie; **true to ~** réaliste, fidèle à la réalité; **to paint from ~** peindre d'après nature; **to be sent to prison for ~** être condamné(e) (à la réclusion criminelle) à perpétuité; **country/city ~** la vie à la campagne/à la ville

life assurance n (Brit) = **life insurance**

lifebelt ['laɪfbɛlt] n (Brit) bouée f de sauvetage

lifeboat ['laɪfbəʊt] n canot m or chaloupe f de sauvetage

lifebuoy ['laɪfbɔɪ] n bouée f de sauvetage

lifeguard ['laɪfgɑːd] n surveillant m de baignade

life insurance n assurance-vie f

life jacket n gilet m or ceinture f de sauvetage

lifeless ['laɪflɪs] adj sans vie, inanimé(e); (dull) qui manque de vie or de vigueur

lifelike ['laɪflaɪk] adj qui semble vrai(e) or vivant(e), ressemblant(e); (painting) réaliste

lifelong ['laɪflɔŋ] adj de toute une vie, de toujours

life preserver [-prɪ'zɜːvə'] n (US) gilet m or ceinture f de sauvetage

life-saving ['laɪfseɪvɪŋ] n sauvetage m

life sentence n condamnation f à vie or à perpétuité

life-size ['laɪfsaɪz], **life-sized** ['laɪfsaɪzd] adj grandeur nature

life span n (durée f de) vie f

lifestyle ['laɪfstaɪl] n style m de vie

life-support system n (Med) respirateur artificiel

lifetime ['laɪftaɪm] n: **in his ~** de son vivant; **the chance of a ~** la chance de ma (or sa etc) vie, une occasion unique

lift [lɪft] vt soulever, lever; (end) supprimer, lever; (steal) prendre, voler ▷ vi (fog) se lever ▷ n (Brit: elevator) ascenseur m; **to give sb a ~** (Brit) emmener or prendre qn en voiture; **can you give me a ~ to the station?** pouvez-vous m'emmener à la gare?; **lift off** vi (rocket, helicopter) décoller; **lift out** vt sortir; (troops, evacuees etc) évacuer par avion or hélicoptère; **lift up** vt soulever

lift-off ['lɪftɔf] n décollage m

light [laɪt] n lumière f; (daylight) lumière, jour m; (lamp) lampe f; (Aut: rear light) feu m; (: headlamp) phare m; (for cigarette etc): **have you got a ~?** avez-vous du feu? ▷ vt (pt, pp **lighted** or **lit**) [lɪt] (candle, cigarette, fire) allumer; (room) éclairer ▷ adj (room, colour) clair(e); (not heavy, also fig) léger(-ère); (not strenuous) peu fatigant(e) ▷ adv (travel) avec peu de bagages; **lights** npl (traffic lights) feux mpl; **to turn the ~ on/off** allumer/éteindre; **to cast or shed or throw ~ on** éclaircir; **to come to ~** être dévoilé(e) or découvert(e); **in the ~ of** à la lumière de; étant donné; **to make ~ of sth** (fig) prendre qch à la légère, faire peu de cas de qch; **light up** vi s'allumer; (face) s'éclairer; (smoke) allumer une cigarette *or* une pipe *etc* ▷ *vt* (*illuminate*) éclairer, illuminer

light bulb *n* ampoule *f*

lighten ['laɪtn] *vi* s'éclairer ▷ *vt* (*light up*) éclairer; (*make lighter*) éclaircir; (*make less heavy*) alléger

lighter ['laɪtə'] *n* (*also*: **cigarette ~**) briquet *m*; (: *in car*) allume-cigare *m inv*; (*boat*) péniche *f*

light-headed [laɪt'hedɪd] *adj* étourdi(e), écervelé(e)

light-hearted [laɪt'hɑːtɪd] *adj* gai(e), joyeux(-euse), enjoué(e)

lighthouse ['laɪthaus] *n* phare *m*

lighting ['laɪtɪŋ] *n* éclairage *m*; (*in theatre*) éclairages

lightly ['laɪtlɪ] *adv* légèrement; **to get off ~** s'en tirer à bon compte

lightness ['laɪtnɪs] *n* clarté *f*; (*in weight*) légèreté *f*

lightning ['laɪtnɪŋ] *n* foudre *f*; (*flash*) éclair *m*

lightning conductor, (US) **lightning rod** *n* paratonnerre *m*

light pen *n* crayon *m* optique

lightweight ['laɪtweɪt] *adj* (*suit*) léger(-ère) ▷ *n* (*Boxing*) poids léger

like [laɪk]` *vt* aimer (bien) ▷ *prep* comme ▷ *adj* semblable, pareil(le) ▷ *n*: **the ~** un(e) pareil(le) *or* semblable; le/la pareil(le); (*pej*) (d')autres du même genre *or* acabit; **his ~s and dislikes** ses goûts *mpl* *or* préférences *fpl*; **I would ~**, **I'd ~** je voudrais, j'aimerais; **would you ~ a coffee?** voulez-vous du café?; **to be/look ~ sb/sth** ressembler à qn/qch; **what's he ~?** comment est-il?; **what's the weather ~?** quel temps fait-il?; **what does it look ~?** de quoi est-ce que ça a l'air?; **what does it taste ~?** quel goût est-ce que ça a?; **that's just ~ him** c'est bien de lui, ça lui ressemble; **something ~ that** quelque chose comme ça; **do it ~ this** fais-le comme ceci; **I feel ~ a drink** je boirais bien quelque chose; **if you ~** si vous voulez; **it's nothing ~ ...** ce n'est pas du tout comme ...; **there's nothing ~ ...** il n'y a rien de tel que ...

likeable ['laɪkəbl] *adj* sympathique, agréable

likelihood ['laɪklɪhud] *n* probabilité *f*; **in all ~** selon toute vraisemblance

likely ['laɪklɪ] *adj* (*result, outcome*) probable; (*excuse*) plausible; **he's ~ to leave** il va sûrement partir, il risque fort de partir; **not ~!** (*inf*) pas de danger!

likeness ['laɪknɪs] *n* ressemblance *f*

likewise ['laɪkwaɪz] *adv* de même, pareillement

liking ['laɪkɪŋ] *n* (*for person*) affection *f*; (*for thing*) penchant *m*, goût *m*; **to take a ~ to sb** se prendre d'amitié pour qn; **to be to sb's ~** être au goût de qn, plaire à qn

lilac ['laɪlək] *n* lilas *m* ▷ *adj* lilas *inv*

Lilo® ['laɪləu] *n* matelas *m* pneumatique

lily ['lɪlɪ] *n* lis *m*; **~ of the valley** muguet *m*

limb [lɪm] *n* membre *m*; **to be out on a ~** (*fig*) être isolé(e)

limber ['lɪmbə']: **to ~ up** *vi* se dégourdir, se mettre en train

limbo ['lɪmbəu] *n*: **to be in ~** (*fig*) être tombé(e) dans l'oubli

lime [laɪm] *n* (*tree*) tilleul *m*; (*fruit*) citron vert, lime *f*; (*Geo*) chaux *f*

limelight ['laɪmlaɪt] *n*: **in the ~** (*fig*) en vedette, au premier plan

limerick ['lɪmərɪk] *n* petit poème humoristique

limestone ['laɪmstəun] *n* pierre *f* à chaux; (*Geo*) calcaire *m*

limit ['lɪmɪt] *n* limite *f* ▷ *vt* limiter; **weight/speed ~** limite de poids/de vitesse

limited ['lɪmɪtɪd] *adj* limité(e), restreint(e); **~ edition** édition *f* à tirage limité; **to be ~ to** se limiter à, ne concerner que

limited company, limited liability company *n* (*Brit*) ≈ société *f* anonyme

limousine ['lɪməziːn] *n* limousine *f*

limp [lɪmp] *n*: **to have a ~** boiter ▷ *vi* boiter ▷ *adj* mou/molle

limpet ['lɪmpɪt] *n* patelle *f*; **like a ~** (*fig*) comme une ventouse

line [laɪn] *n* (*gen*) ligne *f*; (*stroke*) trait *m*; (*wrinkle*) ride *f*; (*rope*) corde *f*; (*wire*) fil *m*; (*of poem*) vers *m*; (*row, series*) rangée *f*; (*of people*) file *f*, queue *f*; (*railway track*) voie *f*; (*Comm*: *series of goods*) article(s) *m(pl)*, ligne de produits; (*work*) métier *m* ▷ *vt*: **to ~ (with)** (*clothes*) doubler (de); (*box*) garnir *or* tapisser (de); (*subj*: *trees, crowd*) border; **to stand in ~** (*US*) faire la queue; **to cut in ~** (*US*) passer avant son tour; **in his ~ of business** dans sa partie, dans son rayon; **on the right ~s** sur la bonne voie; **a new ~ in cosmetics** une nouvelle ligne de produits de beauté; **hold the ~ please** (*Brit Tel*) ne quittez pas; **to be in ~ for sth** (*fig*) être en lice pour qch; **in ~ with** en accord avec, en conformité avec; **in a ~** aligné(e); **to bring sth into ~ with sth** aligner qch sur qch; **to draw the ~ at (doing) sth** (*fig*) se refuser à (faire) qch; ne pas tolérer *or* admettre (qu'on fasse) qch; **to take the ~ that ...** être d'avis *or* de l'opinion que ...; **line up** *vi* s'aligner, se mettre en rang(s); (*in queue*) faire la queue ▷ *vt* aligner; (*event*) prévoir; (*find*) trouver; **to have sb/sth ~d up** avoir qn/qch en vue *or* de prévu(e)

linear ['lɪnɪə'] *adj* linéaire

lined [laɪnd] *adj* (*paper*) réglé(e); (*face*) marqué(e), ridé(e); (*clothes*) doublé(e)

linen ['lɪnɪn] *n* linge *m* (de corps *or* de maison); (*cloth*) lin *m*

liner ['laɪnə'] *n* (*ship*) paquebot *m* de ligne; (*for bin*) sac-poubelle *m*

linesman ['laɪnzmən] *irreg n* (*Tennis*) juge *m* de ligne; (*Football*) juge de touche

line-up ['laɪnʌp] *n* (*US*: *queue*) file *f*; (*also*: **police ~**) parade *f* d'identification; (*Sport*) (composition *f* de l')équipe *f*

linger ['lɪŋgə'] *vi* s'attarder; traîner; (*smell, tradition*) persister

lingerie ['lænʒəri:] n lingerie f
linguist ['lɪŋgwɪst] n linguiste m/f; **to be a good ~** être doué(e) pour les langues
linguistic [lɪŋ'gwɪstɪk] adj linguistique
linguistics [lɪŋ'gwɪstɪks] n linguistique f
lining ['laɪnɪŋ] n doublure f; (Tech) revêtement m; (: of brakes) garniture f
link [lɪŋk] n (connection) lien m, rapport m; (Internet) lien; (of a chain) maillon m ▷ vt relier, lier, unir; **links** npl (Golf) (terrain m de) golf m; **rail ~** liaison f ferroviaire; **link up** vt relier ▷ vi (people) se rejoindre; (companies etc) s'associer
lino ['laɪnəʊ] n = **linoleum**
linoleum [lɪ'nəʊlɪəm] a linoléum m
lion ['laɪən] n lion m
lioness ['laɪənɪs] n lionne f
lip [lɪp] n lèvre f; (of cup etc) rebord m; (insolence) insolences fpl
liposuction ['lɪpəʊsʌkʃən] n liposuccion f
lip-read ['lɪpriːd] vi (irreg like: **read**) lire sur les lèvres
lip salve [-sælv] n pommade f pour les lèvres, pommade rosat
lip service n: **to pay ~ to sth** ne reconnaître le mérite de qch que pour la forme or qu'en paroles
lipstick ['lɪpstɪk] n rouge m à lèvres
liqueur [lɪ'kjʊəʳ] n liqueur f
liquid ['lɪkwɪd] n liquide m ▷ adj liquide
liquidize ['lɪkwɪdaɪz] vt (Brit Culin) passer au mixer
liquidizer ['lɪkwɪdaɪzəʳ] n (Brit Culin) mixer m
liquor ['lɪkəʳ] n spiritueux m, alcool m
liquorice ['lɪkərɪʃ] n (Brit) réglisse m
liquor store (US) n magasin m de vins et spiritueux
Lisbon ['lɪzbən] n Lisbonne
lisp [lɪsp] n zézaiement m ▷ vi zézayer
list [lɪst] n liste f; (of ship) inclinaison f ▷ vt (write down) inscrire; (make list of) faire la liste de; (enumerate) énumérer; (Comput) lister ▷ vi (ship) gîter, donner de la bande; **shopping ~** liste des courses
listed building ['lɪstɪd-] n (Archit) monument classé
listen ['lɪsn] vi écouter; **to ~ to** écouter
listener ['lɪsnəʳ] n auditeur(-trice)
listless ['lɪstlɪs] adj indolent(e), apathique
lit [lɪt] pt, pp of **light**
liter ['liːtəʳ] n (US) = **litre**
literacy ['lɪtərəsɪ] n degré m d'alphabétisation, fait m de savoir lire et écrire; (Brit: Scol) enseignement m de la lecture et de l'écriture
literal ['lɪtərl] adj littéral(e)
literally ['lɪtrəlɪ] adv littéralement; (really) réellement
literary ['lɪtərərɪ] adj littéraire
literate ['lɪtərət] adj qui sait lire et écrire; (educated) instruit(e)
literature ['lɪtrɪtʃəʳ] n littérature f; (brochures etc) copie f publicitaire, prospectus mpl

lithe [laɪð] adj agile, souple
litigation [lɪtɪ'geɪʃən] n litige m; contentieux m
litre, (US) **liter** ['liːtəʳ] n litre m
litter ['lɪtəʳ] n (rubbish) détritus mpl; (dirtier) ordures fpl; (young animals) portée f ▷ vt éparpiller; laisser des détritus dans; **~ed with** jonché(e) de, couvert(e) de
litter bin n (Brit) poubelle f
little ['lɪtl] adj (small) petit(e); (not much): **~ milk** peu de lait ▷ adv peu; **a ~** un peu (de); **a ~ milk** un peu de lait; **a ~ bit** un peu; **for a ~ while** pendant un petit moment; **with difficulty** sans trop de difficulté; **as ~ as possible** le moins possible; **~ by ~** petit à petit, peu à peu; **to make ~ of** faire peu de cas de
little finger n auriculaire m, petit doigt
live¹ [laɪv] adj (animal) vivant(e), en vie; (wire) sous tension; (broadcast) (transmis(e)) en direct; (issue) d'actualité, brûlant(e); (unexploded) non explosé(e); **~ ammunition** munitions fpl de combat
live² [lɪv] vi (reside) vivre, habiter; **to ~ in London** habiter (à) Londres; **where do you ~?** où habitez-vous?; **live down** vt faire oublier (avec le temps); **live in** vi être logé(e) et nourri(e); être interne; **live off** vt (land, fish etc) vivre de; (pej: parents etc) vivre aux crochets de; **live on** vt fus (food) vivre de ▷ vi survivre; **to ~ on £50 a week** vivre avec 50 livres par semaine; **live out** vi (Brit: students) être externe ▷ vt: **to ~ out one's days** or **life** passer sa vie; **live together** vi vivre ensemble, cohabiter; **live up** vt: **to ~ it up** (inf) faire la fête; mener la grande vie; **live up to** vt fus se montrer à la hauteur de
livelihood ['laɪvlɪhud] n moyens mpl d'existence
lively ['laɪvlɪ] adj vif/vive, plein(e) d'entrain; (place, book) vivant(e)
liven up ['laɪvn-] vt (room etc) égayer; (discussion, evening) animer ▷ vi s'animer
liver ['lɪvəʳ] n foie m
lives [laɪvz] npl of **life**
livestock ['laɪvstɔk] n cheptel m, bétail m
livid ['lɪvɪd] adj livide, blafard(e); (furious) furieux(-euse), furibond(e)
living ['lɪvɪŋ] adj vivant(e), en vie ▷ n: **to earn** or **make a ~** gagner sa vie; **within ~ memory** de mémoire d'homme
living conditions npl conditions fpl de vie
living room n salle f de séjour
living standards npl niveau m de vie
living wage n salaire m permettant de vivre (décemment)
lizard ['lɪzəd] n lézard m
load [ləud] n (weight) poids m; (thing carried) chargement m, charge f; (Elec, Tech) charge ▷ vt: **to ~ (with)** (also: **~ up: lorry, ship**) charger (de); (gun, camera) charger (avec); (Comput) charger; **a ~ of**, **~s of** (fig) un or des tas de, des

masses de; **to talk a ~ of rubbish** (inf) dire des bêtises

loaded ['ləʊdɪd] adj (dice) pipé(e); (question) insidieux(-euse); (inf: rich) bourré(e) de fric; (: drunk) bourré

loaf (pl **loaves**) [ləʊf, ləʊvz] n pain m, miche f ▷ vi (also: **~ about, ~ around**) fainéanter, traîner

loan [ləʊn] n prêt m ▷ vt prêter; **on ~** prêté(e), en prêt; **public ~** emprunt public

loath [ləʊθ] adj: **to be ~ to do** répugner à faire

loathe [ləʊð] vt détester, avoir en horreur

loaves [ləʊvz] npl of **loaf**

lobby ['lɒbɪ] n hall m, entrée f; (Pol) groupe m de pression, lobby m ▷ vt faire pression sur

lobster ['lɒbstə'] n homard m

local ['ləʊkl] adj Local(e) ▷ n (Brit: pub) pub m or café m du coin; **the locals** npl les gens mpl du pays or du coin

local anaesthetic, (US) **local anesthetic** n anesthésie locale

local authority n collectivité locale, municipalité f

local call n (Tel) communication urbaine

local government n administration locale or municipale

locality [ləʊ'kælɪtɪ] n région f, environs mpl; (position) lieu m

locally ['ləʊkəlɪ] adv localement; dans les environs or la région

locate [ləʊ'keɪt] vt (find) trouver, repérer; (situate) situer; **to be ~d in** être situé à or en

location [ləʊ'keɪʃən] n emplacement m; **on ~** (Cine) en extérieur

loch [lɒx] n lac m, loch m

lock [lɒk] n (of door, box) serrure f; (of canal) écluse f; (of hair) mèche f, boucle f ▷ vt (with key) fermer à clé; (immobilize) bloquer ▷ vi (door etc) fermer à clé; (wheels) se bloquer; **~ stock and barrel** (fig) en bloc; **on full ~** (Brit Aut) le volant tourné à fond; **lock away** vt (valuables) mettre sous clé; (criminal) mettre sous les verrous, enfermer; **lock in** vt enfermer; **lock out** vt enfermer dehors; (on purpose) mettre à la porte; (: workers) lock-outer; **lock up** vt (person) enfermer; (house) fermer à clé ▷ vi lui fermer (à clé)

locker ['lɒkə'] n casier m; (in station) consigne f automatique

locker-room ['lɒkəru:m] (US) n (Sport) vestiaire m

locket ['lɒkɪt] n médaillon m

locksmith ['lɒksmɪθ] n serrurier m

lock-up ['lɒkʌp] n (prison) prison f; (cell) cellule f provisoire; (also: **~ garage**) box m

locomotive [ləʊkə'məʊtɪv] n locomotive f

locum ['ləʊkəm] n (Med) suppléant(e) de médecin etc

lodge [lɒdʒ] n pavillon m (de gardien); (also: **hunting ~**) pavillon de chasse; (Freemasonry) loge f ▷ vi (person): **to ~ with** être logé(e) chez,

être en pension chez; (bullet) se loger ▷ vt (appeal etc) présenter; déposer; **to ~ a complaint** porter plainte; **to ~ (itself) in/ between** se loger dans/entre

lodger ['lɒdʒə'] n locataire m/f; (with room and meals) pensionnaire m/f

lodging ['lɒdʒɪŋ] n logement m; see also **board**

lodgings ['lɒdʒɪŋz] npl chambre f, meublé m

loft [lɒft] n grenier m; (apartment) grenier aménagé (en appartement) (gén dans ancien entrepôt ou fabrique)

lofty ['lɒftɪ] adj élevé(e); (haughty) hautain(e); (sentiments, aims) noble

log [lɒg] n (of wood) bûche f; (Naut) livre m or journal m de bord; (of car) ≈ carte grise ▷ n abbr (= logarithm) log m ▷ vt enregistrer; **log in, log on** vi (Comput) ouvrir une session, entrer dans le système; **log off, log out** vi (Comput) clore une session, sortir du système

logbook ['lɒgbuk] n (Naut) livre m or journal m de bord; (Aviat) carnet m de vol; (of lorry driver) carnet de route; (of movement of goods etc) registre m; (of car) ≈ carte grise

loggerheads ['lɒgəhɛdz] npl: **at ~ (with)** à couteaux tirés (avec)

logic ['lɒdʒɪk] n logique f

logical ['lɒdʒɪkl] adj logique

login ['lɒgɪn] n (Comput) identifiant m

logo ['ləʊgəʊ] n logo m

loin [lɔɪn] n (Culin) filet m, longe f; **loins** npl reins mpl

Loire [lwa:] n: **the (River) ~** la Loire

loiter ['lɔɪtə'] vi s'attarder; **to ~ (about)** traîner, musarder; (pej) rôder

loll [lɒl] vi (also: **~ about**) se prélasser, fainéanter

lollipop ['lɒlɪpɒp] n sucette f

lollipop man/lady (Brit) irreg n contractuel(le) qui fait traverser la rue aux enfants; voir article

⁂ **LOLLIPOP MEN/LADIES**

⁂
⁂ Les lollipop men/ladies sont employés pour
⁂ aider les enfants à traverser la rue à
⁂ proximité des écoles à l'heure où ils
⁂ entrent en classe et à la sortie. On les
⁂ repère facilement à cause de leur long
⁂ ciré jaune et ils portent une pancarte
⁂ ronde pour faire signe aux
⁂ automobilistes de s'arrêter. On les
⁂ appelle ainsi car la forme circulaire
⁂ de cette pancarte rappelle une sucette.

lolly ['lɒlɪ] n (inf: ice) esquimau m; (: lollipop) sucette f; (: money) fric m

London ['lʌndən] n Londres

Londoner ['lʌndənə'] n Londonien(ne)

lone [ləʊn] adj solitaire

loneliness ['ləʊnlɪnɪs] n solitude f, isolement m

lonely ['ləʊnlɪ] adj seul(e); (childhood etc) solitaire; (place) solitaire, isolé(e)

long [lɔŋ] *adj* long/longue ▷ *adv* longtemps ▷ *n*: **the ~ and the short of it is that ...** (*fig*) le fin mot de l'histoire c'est que ... ▷ *vi*: **to ~ for sth/to do sth** avoir très envie de qch/de faire qch, attendre qch avec impatience/attendre avec impatience de faire qch; **he had ~ understood that ...** il avait compris depuis longtemps que ...; **how ~ is this river/course?** quelle est la longueur de ce fleuve/la durée de ce cours?; **6 metres ~** (long) de 6 mètres; **6 months ~** qui dure 6 mois, de 6 mois; **all night ~** toute la nuit; **he no ~er comes** il ne vient plus; **I can't stand it any ~er** je ne peux plus le supporter; **~ before** longtemps avant; **before ~** (+ *future*) avant peu, dans peu de temps; (+ *past*) peu de temps après; **~ ago** il y a longtemps; **don't be ~!** fais vite!, dépêche-toi!; **I shan't be ~** je n'en ai pas pour longtemps; **at ~ last** enfin; **in the ~ run** à la longue; finalement; **so** *or* **as ~ as** à condition que + *sub*

long-distance [lɔŋ'dɪstəns] *adj* (*race*) de fond; (*call*) interurbain(e)

longer ['lɔŋgə^r] *adv see* **long**

longhand ['lɔŋhænd] *n* écriture normale *or* courante

long-haul ['lɔŋhɔ:l] *adj* (*flight*) long-courrier

longing ['lɔŋɪŋ] *n* désir *m*, envie *f*; (*nostalgia*) nostalgie *f* ▷ *adj* plein(e) d'envie *or* de nostalgie

longitude ['lɔŋgɪtju:d] *n* longitude *f*

long jump *n* saut *m* en longueur

long-life [lɔŋ'laɪf] *adj* (*batteries etc*) longue durée *inv*; (*milk*) longue conservation

long-lost ['lɔŋlɔst] *adj* perdu(e) depuis longtemps

long-range ['lɔŋ'reɪndʒ] *adj* à longue portée; (*weather forecast*) à long terme

long-sighted ['lɔŋ'saɪtɪd] *adj* (*Brit*) presbyte; (*fig*) prévoyant(e)

long-standing ['lɔŋ'stændɪŋ] *adj* de longue date

long-suffering [lɔŋ'sʌfərɪŋ] *adj* empreint(e) d'une patience résignée; extrêmement patient(e)

long-term ['lɔŋtə:m] *adj* à long terme

long wave *n* (*Radio*) grandes ondes, ondes longues

long-winded [lɔŋ'wɪndɪd] *adj* intarissable, interminable

loo [lu:] *n* (*Brit inf*) w.-c *mpl*, petit coin

look [luk] *vi* regarder; (*seem*) sembler, paraître, avoir l'air; (*building etc*): **to ~ south/on to the sea** donner au sud/sur la mer ▷ *n* regard *m*; (*appearance*) air *m*, allure *f*, aspect *m*; **looks** *npl* (*good looks*) physique *m*, beauté *f*; **to ~ like** ressembler à; **it ~s like him** on dirait que c'est lui; **it ~s about 4 metres long** je dirais que ça fait 4 mètres de long; **it ~s all right to me** ça me paraît bien; **to have a ~** regarder; **to have a ~ at sth** jeter un coup d'œil à qch; **to have a ~ for sth** chercher qch; **to ~ ahead** regarder devant soi; (*fig*) envisager l'avenir; **~ (here)!** (*annoyance*) écoutez!; **look after** *vt fus* s'occuper de, prendre soin de; (*luggage etc*: *watch over*) garder, surveiller; **look around** *vi* regarder autour de soi; **look at** *vt fus* regarder; (*problem etc*) examiner; **look back** *vi*: **to ~ back at sth/sb** se retourner pour regarder qch/qn; **to ~ back on** (*event, period*) évoquer, repenser à; **look down on** *vt fus* (*fig*) regarder de haut, dédaigner; **look for** *vt fus* chercher; **we're ~ing for a hotel/restaurant** nous cherchons un hôtel/restaurant; **look forward to** *vt fus* attendre avec impatience; **I'm not ~ing forward to it** cette perspective ne me réjouit guère; **~ing forward to hearing from you** (*in letter*) dans l'attente de vous lire; **look in** *vi*: **to ~ in on sb** passer voir qn; **look into** *vt fus* (*matter, possibility*) examiner, étudier; **look on** *vi* regarder (en spectateur); **look out** *vi* (*beware*): **to ~ out (for)** prendre garde (à), faire attention (à); **~ out!** attention!; **look out for** *vt fus* (*seek*) être à la recherche de; (*try to spot*) guetter; **look over** *vt* (*essay*) jeter un coup d'œil à; (*town, building*) visiter (rapidement); (*person*) jeter un coup d'œil à; examiner de la tête aux pieds; **look round** *vt fus* (*house, shop*) faire le tour de ▷ *vi* (*turn*) regarder derrière soi, se retourner; **to ~ round for sth** chercher qch; **look through** *vt fus* (*papers, book*) examiner; (: *briefly*) parcourir; (*telescope*) regarder à travers; **look to** *vt fus* veiller à; (*rely on*) compter sur; **look up** *vi* lever les yeux; (*improve*) s'améliorer ▷ *vt* (*word*) chercher; (*friend*) passer voir; **look up to** *vt fus* avoir du respect pour

lookout ['lukaut] *n* (*tower etc*) poste *m* de guet; (*person*) guetteur *m*; **to be on the ~ (for)** guetter

loom [lu:m] *n* métier *m* à tisser ▷ *vi* (*also*: **~ up**) surgir; (*event*) paraître imminent(e); (*threaten*) menacer

loony ['lu:nɪ] *adj*, *n* (*inf*) timbré(e), cinglé(e) *m/f*

loop [lu:p] *n* boucle *f*; (*contraceptive*) stérilet *m* ▷ *vt*: **to ~ sth round sth** passer qch autour de qch

loophole ['lu:phəul] *n* (*fig*) porte *f* de sortie; échappatoire *f*

loose [lu:s] *adj* (*knot, screw*) desserré(e); (*stone*) branlant(e); (*clothes*) vague, ample, lâche; (*hair*) dénoué(e), épars(e); (*not firmly fixed*) pas solide; (*animal*) en liberté, échappé(e); (*life*) dissolu(e); (*morals, discipline*) relâché(e); (*thinking*) peu rigoureux(-euse), vague; (*translation*) approximatif(-ive) ▷ *n*: **to be on the ~** être en liberté ▷ *vt* (*free*: *animal*) lâcher; (: *prisoner*) relâcher, libérer; (*slacken*) détendre, relâcher; desserrer; défaire; donner du mou a; donner du ballant à; (*Brit*: *arrow*) tirer; **~ connection** (*Elec*) mauvais contact; **to be at**

a ~ end *or* (US) **at ~ ends** (*fig*) ne pas trop savoir quoi faire; **to tie up ~ ends** (*fig*) mettre au point *or* régler les derniers détails

loose change *n* petite monnaie

loose chippings [-'tʃɪpɪŋz] *npl* (*on road*) gravillons *mpl*

loosely ['luːslɪ] *adv* sans serrer; (*imprecisely*) approximativement

loosen ['luːsn] *vt* desserrer, relâcher, défaire; **loosen up** *vi* (*before game*) s'échauffer; (*inf: relax*) se détendre, se laisser aller

loot [luːt] *n* butin *m* ▷ *vt* piller

lop-sided ['lɔp'saɪdɪd] *adj* de travers, asymétrique

lord [lɔːd] *n* seigneur *m*; **L~ Smith** lord Smith; **the L~** (*Rel*) le Seigneur; **my L~** (*to noble*) Monsieur le comte/le baron; (*to judge*) Monsieur le juge; (*to bishop*) Monseigneur; **good L~!** mon Dieu!

Lords ['lɔːdz] *npl* (*Brit: Pol*): **the (House of) ~** (*Brit*) la Chambre des Lords

lordship ['lɔːdʃɪp] *n* (*Brit*): **your L~** Monsieur le comte (*or* le baron *or* le Juge)

lore [lɔːʳ] *n* tradition(s) *f(pl)*

lorry ['lɔrɪ] *n* (*Brit*) camion *m*

lorry driver *n* (*Brit*) camionneur *m*, routier *m*

lose (*pt, pp* **lost**) [luːz, lɔst] *vt* perdre; (*opportunity*) manquer, perdre; (*pursuers*) distancer, semer ▷ *vi* perdre; **I've lost my wallet/passport** j'ai perdu mon portefeuille/passeport; **to ~** (*time*) (*clock*) retarder; **to ~ no time** (**in doing sth**) ne pas perdre de temps (à faire qch); **to get lost** *vi* (*person*) se perdre; **my watch has got lost** ma montre est perdue; **lose out** *vi* être perdant(e)

loser ['luːzəʳ] *n* perdant(e); **to be a good/ bad ~** être beau/mauvais joueur

loss [lɔs] *n* perte *f*; **to cut one's ~es** limiter les dégâts; **to make a ~** enregistrer une perte; **to sell sth at a ~** vendre qch à perte; **to be at a ~** être perplexe *or* embarrassé(e); **to be at a ~ to do** se trouver incapable de faire

lost [lɔst] *pt, pp of* **lose** perdu(e); **to get ~** *vi* se perdre; **I'm ~** je me suis perdu; **~ in thought** perdu dans ses pensées; **~ and found property** *n* (US) objets trouvés; **~ and found** *n* (US) bureau *m* des objets trouvés

lost property *n* (*Brit*) objets trouvés; **~ office** *or* **department** (*bureau m des*) objets trouvés

lot [lɔt] *n* (*at auctions, set*) lot *m*; (*destiny*) sort *m*, destinée *f*; **the ~** (*everything*) le tout; (*everyone*) tous *mpl*, toutes *fpl*; **a ~** beaucoup; **a ~ of** beaucoup de; **~s of** des tas de; **to draw ~s** (**for sth**) tirer (qch) au sort

lotion ['ləʊʃən] *n* lotion *f*

lottery ['lɔtərɪ] *n* loterie *f*

loud [laʊd] *adj* bruyant(e), sonore; (*voice*) fort(e); (*condemnation etc*) vigoureux(-euse); (*gaudy*) voyant(e), tapageur(-euse) ▷ *adv* (*speak etc*) fort; **out ~** tout haut

loud-hailer [laʊd'heɪləʳ] *n* porte-voix *m inv*

loudly ['laʊdlɪ] *adv* fort, bruyamment

loudspeaker [laʊd'spiːkəʳ] *n* haut-parleur *m*

lounge [laʊndʒ] *n* salon *m*; (*of airport*) salle *f*; (*Brit: also:* **~ bar**) (salle de) café *m or* bar *m* ▷ *vi* (*also:* **~ about, ~ around**) se prélasser, paresser

lounge suit *n* (*Brit*) complet *m*; (: *on invitation*) "tenue de ville"

louse (*pl* **lice**) [laʊs, laɪs] *n* pou *m*; **louse up** [lauz-] *vt* (*inf*) gâcher

lousy ['laʊzɪ] (*inf*) *adj* (*bad quality*) infect(e), moche; **I feel ~** je suis mal fichu(e)

lout [laʊt] *n* rustre *m*, butor *m*

lovable ['lʌvəbl] *adj* très sympathique; adorable

love [lʌv] *n* amour *m* ▷ *vt* aimer; (*caringly, kindly*) aimer beaucoup; **I ~ chocolate** j'adore le chocolat; **to ~ to do** aimer beaucoup *or* adorer faire; **I'd ~ to come** cela me ferait très plaisir (de venir); **"15 ~"** (*Tennis*) "15 à rien *or* zéro"; **to be/fall in ~ with** être/tomber amoureux(-euse) de; **to make ~** faire l'amour; **~ at first sight** le coup de foudre; **to send one's ~ to** sb adresser ses amitiés à qn; **~ from Anne, ~, Anne** affectueusement, Anne; **I ~ you** je t'aime

love affair *n* liaison (amoureuse)

love life *n* vie sentimentale

lovely ['lʌvlɪ] *adj* (*pretty*) ravissant(e); (*friend, wife*) charmant(e); (*holiday, surprise*) très agréable, merveilleux(-euse); **we had a ~ time** c'était vraiment très bien, nous avons eu beaucoup de plaisir

lover ['lʌvəʳ] *n* amant *m*; (*person in love*) amoureux(-euse); (*amateur*): **a ~ of** un(e) ami(e) de, un(e) amoureux(-euse) de

loving ['lʌvɪŋ] *adj* affectueux(-euse), tendre, aimant(e)

low [ləʊ] *adj* bas/basse; (*quality*) mauvais(e), inférieur(e) ▷ *adv* bas ▷ *n* (*Meteorology*) dépression *f* ▷ *vi* (*cow*) mugir; **to feel ~** se sentir déprimé(e); **he's very ~** (*ill*) il est bien bas *or* très affaibli; **to turn (down) ~** *vt* baisser; **to be ~ on** (*supplies etc*) être à court de; **to reach a new** *or* **an all-time ~** tomber au niveau le plus bas

low-alcohol [ləʊ'ælkəhɔl] *adj* à faible teneur en alcool, peu alcoolisé(e)

low-calorie ['ləʊ'kælərɪ] *adj* hypocalorique

low-cut ['ləʊkʌt] *adj* (*dress*) décolleté(e)

lower *adj* ['ləʊəʳ] inférieur(e) ▷ *vt* ['ləʊəʳ] baisser; (*resistance*) diminuer ▷ *vi* ['laʊəʳ] (*person*): **to ~ at sb** jeter un regard mauvais *or* noir à qn; (*sky, clouds*) être menaçant(e); **to ~ o.s. to** s'abaisser à

lower sixth (*Brit*) *n* (*Scol*) première *f*

low-fat ['ləʊ'fæt] *adj* maigre

lowland, lowlands ['ləʊlənd(z)] *n(pl)* plaine(s) *f(pl)*

lowly ['ləʊlɪ] *adj* humble, modeste

loyal ['lɔɪəl] *adj* loyal(e), fidèle

loyalty ['lɔɪəltɪ] *n* loyauté *f*, fidélité *f*

loyalty card n carte f de fidélité
lozenge ['lɒzɪndʒ] n (Med) pastille f; (Geom) losange m
L-plates ['εlpleɪts] npl (Brit) plaques fpl (obligatoires) d'apprenti conducteur
Lt abbr (= lieutenant) Lt.
Ltd abbr (Comm: company: = limited) ≈ S.A.
lubricant ['lu:brɪkənt] n lubrifiant m
lubricate ['lu:brɪkeɪt] vt lubrifier, graisser
luck [lʌk] n chance f; **bad** ~ malchance f, malheur m; **to be in** ~ avoir de la chance; **to be out of** ~ ne pas avoir de chance; **good** ~! bonne chance!; **bad** or **hard** or **tough** ~! pas de chance!
luckily ['lʌkɪlɪ] adv heureusement, par bonheur
lucky ['lʌkɪ] adj (person) qui a de la chance; (coincidence) heureux(-euse); (number etc) qui porte bonheur
lucrative ['lu:krətɪv] adj lucratif(-ive), rentable, qui rapporte
ludicrous ['lu:dɪkrəs] adj ridicule, absurde
lug [lʌg] vt traîner, tirer
luggage ['lʌgɪdʒ] n bagages mpl; **our** ~ **hasn't arrived** nos bagages ne sont pas arrivés; **could you send someone to collect our** ~? pourriez-vous envoyer quelqu'un chercher nos bagages?
luggage rack n (in train) porte-bagages m inv; (: made of string) filet m à bagages; (on car) galerie f
lukewarm ['lu:kwɔ:m] adj tiède
lull [lʌl] n accalmie f; (in conversation) pause f ▷ vt: **to** ~ **sb to sleep** bercer qn pour qu'il s'endorme; **to be** ~**ed into a false sense of security** s'endormir dans une fausse sécurité
lullaby ['lʌləbaɪ] n berceuse f
lumbago [lʌm'beɪgəʊ] n lumbago m
lumber ['lʌmbə'] n (wood) bois m de charpente; (junk) bric-à-brac m inv ▷ vt (Brit inf): **to** ~ **sb with sth/sb** coller or refiler qch/qn à qn ▷ vi (also: ~ **about,** ~ **along**) marcher pesamment
lumberjack ['lʌmbədʒæk] n bûcheron m
luminous ['lu:mɪnəs] adj lumineux(-euse)
lump [lʌmp] n morceau m; (in sauce) grumeau m; (swelling) grosseur f ▷ vt (also: ~ **together**) réunir, mettre en tas
lump sum n somme globale or forfaitaire
lumpy ['lʌmpɪ] adj (sauce) qui a des grumeaux; (bed) défoncé(e), peu confortable
lunar ['lu:nə'] adj lunaire
lunatic ['lu:nətɪk] n fou/folle, dément(e) ▷ adj fou/folle, dément(e)
lunch [lʌntʃ] n déjeuner m ▷ vi déjeuner; **it is his** ~ **hour** c'est l'heure où il déjeune; **to invite sb to** or **for** ~ inviter qn à déjeuner
lunch break, lunch hour n pause f de midi, heure f du déjeuner
luncheon ['lʌntʃən] n déjeuner m
luncheon meat n sorte de saucisson

luncheon voucher n chèque-repas m, ticket-repas m
lunchtime ['lʌntʃtaɪm] n: **it's** ~ c'est l'heure du déjeuner
lung [lʌŋ] n poumon m
lunge [lʌndʒ] vi (also: ~ **forward**) faire un mouvement brusque en avant; **to** ~ **at sb** envoyer or assener un coup à qn
lurch [lə:tʃ] vi vaciller, tituber ▷ n écart m brusque, embardée f; **to leave sb in the** ~ laisser qn se débrouiller or se dépêtrer tout(e) seul(e)
lure [luə'] n (attraction) attrait m, charme m; (in hunting) appât m, leurre m ▷ vt attirer or persuader par la ruse
lurid ['luərɪd] adj affreux(-euse), atroce
lurk [lə:k] vi se tapir, se cacher
luscious ['lʌʃəs] adj succulent(e), appétissant(e)
lush [lʌʃ] adj luxuriant(e)
lust [lʌst] n (sexual) désir (sexuel); (Rel) luxure f; (fig): ~ **for** soif f de; **lust after** vt fus convoiter, désirer
lusty ['lʌstɪ] adj vigoureux(-euse), robuste
Luxembourg ['lʌksəmbə:g] n Luxembourg m
luxurious [lʌg'zjuərɪəs] adj luxueux(-euse)
luxury ['lʌkʃərɪ] n luxe m ▷ cpd de luxe
Lycra® ['laɪkrə] n Lycra® m
lying ['laɪɪŋ] n mensonge(s) m(pl) ▷ adj (statement, story) mensonger(-ère), faux/fausse; (person) menteur(-euse)
Lyons ['ljɔ̃] n Lyon
lyric ['lɪrɪk] adj lyrique
lyrical ['lɪrɪkl] adj lyrique
lyrics ['lɪrɪks] npl (of song) paroles fpl

m

m. *abbr* (= *metre*) m; (= *million*) M; (= *mile*) mi

M.A. *n abbr* (*Scol*) = **Master of Arts** ▷ *abbr* (*US*) = **military academy**; (*US*) = **Massachusetts**

ma [mɑː] (*inf*) *n* maman *f*

mac [mæk] *n* (*Brit*) imper(méable *m*) *m*

macaroni [mækə'rəʊnɪ] *n* macaronis *mpl*

Macedonia [mæsɪ'dəʊnɪə] *n* Macédoine *f*

Macedonian [mæsɪ'dəʊnɪən] *adj* macédonien(ne) ▷ *n* Macédonien(ne); (*Ling*) macédonien *m*

machine [mə'ʃiːn] *n* machine *f* ▷ *vt* (*dress etc*) coudre à la machine; (*Tech*) usiner

machine gun *n* mitrailleuse *f*

machine language *n* (*Comput*) langage *m* machine

machinery [mə'ʃiːnərɪ] *n* machinerie *f*, machines *fpl*; (*fig*) mécanisme(s) *m*(*pl*)

machine washable *adj* (*garment*) lavable en machine

macho ['mætʃəʊ] *adj* macho *inv*

mackerel ['mækrɪ] *n* (*pl inv*) maquereau *m*

mackintosh ['mækɪntɒʃ] *n* (*Brit*) imperméable *m*

mad [mæd] *adj* fou/folle; (*foolish*) insensé(e); (*angry*) furieux(-euse); **to go ~** devenir fou; **to be ~ (keen) about** *or* **on sth** (*inf*) être follement passionné de qch, être fou de qch

Madagascar [mædə'gæskəʳ] *n* Madagascar *m*

madam ['mædəm] *n* madame *f*; **yes ~** oui Madame; **M~ Chairman** Madame la Présidente

mad cow disease *n* maladie *f* des vaches folles

madden ['mædn] *vt* exaspérer

made [meɪd] *pt, pp of* **make**

Madeira [mə'dɪərə] *n* (*Geo*) Madère *f*; (*wine*) madère *m*

made-to-measure ['meɪdtə'mɛʒəʳ] *adj* (*Brit*) fait(e) sur mesure

made-up ['meɪdʌp] *adj* (*story*) inventé(e), fabriqué(e)

madly ['mædlɪ] *adv* follement; **~ in love** éperdument amoureux(-euse)

madman ['mædmən] *irreg n* fou *m*, aliéné *m*

madness ['mædnɪs] *n* folie *f*

Madrid [mə'drɪd] *n* Madrid

Mafia ['mæfɪə] *n* maf(f)ia *f*

mag [mæg] *n abbr* (*Brit inf:* = *magazine*) magazine *m*

magazine [mægə'ziːn] *n* (*Press*) magazine *m*, revue *f*; (*Radio, TV*) magazine; (*Mil: store*) dépôt *m*, arsenal *m*; (*of firearm*) magasin *m*

maggot ['mægət] *n* ver *m*, asticot *m*

magic ['mædʒɪk] *n* magie *f* ▷ *adj* magique

magical ['mædʒɪkl] *adj* magique; (*experience, evening*) merveilleux(-euse)

magician [mə'dʒɪʃən] *n* magicien(ne)

magistrate ['mædʒɪstreɪt] *n* magistrat *m*; juge *m*; **~s' court** (*Brit*) ≈ tribunal *m* d'instance

magnet ['mægnɪt] *n* aimant *m*

magnetic [mæg'nɛtɪk] *adj* magnétique

magnificent [mæg'nɪfɪsnt] *adj* superbe, magnifique; (*splendid: robe, building*) somptueux(-euse), magnifique

magnify ['mægnɪfaɪ] *vt* grossir; (*sound*) amplifier

magnifying glass ['mægnɪfaɪɪŋ-] *n* loupe *f*

magnitude ['mægnɪtjuːd] *n* ampleur *f*

magpie ['mægpaɪ] *n* pie *f*

mahogany [mə'hɒgənɪ] *n* acajou *m* ▷ *cpd* en (bois d')acajou

maid [meɪd] *n* bonne *f*; (*in hotel*) femme *f* de chambre; **old ~** (*pej*) vieille fille

maiden ['meɪdn] *n* jeune fille *f* ▷ *adj* (*aunt etc*) non mariée; (*speech, voyage*) inaugural(e)

maiden name *n* nom *m* de jeune fille

mail [meɪl] *n* poste *f*; (*letters*) courrier *m* ▷ *vt* envoyer (par la poste); **by ~** par la poste

mailbox ['meɪlbɒks] *n* (*US: also Comput*) boîte *f* aux lettres

mailing list ['meɪlɪŋ-] *n* liste *f* d'adresses

mailman ['meɪlmæn] *irreg n* (*US*) facteur *m*

mail-order ['meɪlɔːdəʳ] *n* vente *f* or achat *m* par correspondance ▷ *cpd*: **~ firm** or **house** maison *f* de vente par correspondance

maim [meɪm] *vt* mutiler

main [meɪn] *adj* principal(e) ▷ *n* (*pipe*) conduite principale, canalisation *f*; **the ~s** (*Elec*) le secteur; **the ~ thing** l'essentiel *m*; **in the ~** dans l'ensemble

main course *n* (*Culin*) plat *m* de résistance

mainframe ['meɪnfreɪm] n (also: ~ **computer**) (gros) ordinateur, unité centrale

mainland ['meɪnlənd] n continent m

mainly ['meɪnlɪ] adv principalement, surtout

main road n grand axe, route nationale

mainstay ['meɪnsteɪ] n (fig) pilier m

mainstream ['meɪnstriːm] n (fig) courant principal

main street n rue f principale

maintain [meɪn'teɪn] vt entretenir; (continue) maintenir, préserver; (affirm) soutenir; **to ~ that ...** soutenir que ...

maintenance ['meɪntənəns] n entretien m; (Law: alimony) pension f alimentaire

maisonette [meɪzə'net] n (Brit) appartement m en duplex

maize [meɪz] n (Brit) maïs m

majestic [mə'dʒestɪk] adj majestueux(-euse)

majesty ['mædʒɪstɪ] n majesté f; (title): **Your M~** Votre Majesté

major ['meɪdʒəʳ] n (Mil) commandant m ▷ adj (important) important(e); (most important) principal(e); (Mus) majeur(e) ▷ vi (US Scol): **to ~ (in)** se spécialiser (en); **a ~ operation** (Med) une grosse opération

Majorca [mə'jɔːkə] n Majorque f

majority [mə'dʒɔrɪtɪ] n majorité f ▷ cpd (verdict, holding) majoritaire

make [meɪk] vt (pt, pp **made**) [meɪd] faire; (manufacture) faire, fabriquer; (earn) gagner; (decision) prendre; (friend) se faire; (speech) faire, prononcer; (cause to be): **to ~ sb sad** etc rendre qn triste etc; (force): **to ~ sb do sth** obliger qn à faire qch, faire faire qch à qn; (equal): **2 and 2 ~ 4** 2 et 2 font 4 ▷ n (manufacture) fabrication f; (brand) marque f; **to ~ the bed** faire le lit; **to ~ a fool of sb** (ridicule) ridiculiser qn; (trick) avoir ou duper qn; **to ~ a profit** faire un ou des bénéfice(s); **to ~ a loss** essuyer une perte; **to ~ it** (in time etc) y arriver; (succeed) réussir; **what time do you ~ it?** quelle heure avez-vous?; **I ~ it £249** d'après mes calculs ça fait 249 livres; **to be made of** être en; **to ~ good** (succeed) faire son chemin, réussir ▷ vt (deficit) combler; (losses) compenser; **to ~ do with** se contenter de; se débrouiller avec; **make for** vt fus (place) se diriger vers; **make off** vi filer; **make out** vt (write out: cheque) faire; (decipher) déchiffrer; (understand) comprendre; (see) distinguer; (claim, imply) prétendre, vouloir faire croire; **to ~ out a case for sth** présenter des arguments solides en faveur de qch; **make over** vt (assign): **to ~ over (to)** céder (à), transférer (au nom de); **make up** vt (invent) inventer, imaginer; (constitute) constituer; (parcel, bed) faire ▷ vi se réconcilier; (with cosmetics) se maquiller, se farder; **to be made up of** se composer de; **make up for** vt fus compenser; (lost time) rattraper

make-believe ['meɪkbɪliːv] n: **a world of ~** un monde de chimères or d'illusions; **it's**

just ~ c'est de la fantaisie; c'est une illusion

makeover ['meɪkəʊvəʳ] n (by beautician) soins mpl de maquillage; (change of image) changement m d'image; **to give sb a ~** relooker qn

maker ['meɪkəʳ] n fabricant m; (of film, programme) réalisateur(-trice)

makeshift ['meɪkʃɪft] adj provisoire, improvisé(e)

make-up ['meɪkʌp] n maquillage m

making ['meɪkɪŋ] n (fig): **in the ~** en formation or gestation; **to have the ~s of** (actor, athlete) avoir l'étoffe de

malaria [mə'leərɪə] n malaria f, paludisme m

Malaysia [mə'leɪzɪə] n Malaisie f

male [meɪl] n (Biol, Elec) mâle m ▷ adj (sex, attitude) masculin(e); (animal) mâle; (child etc) du sexe masculin; **~ and female students** étudiants et étudiantes

malevolent [mə'levələnt] adj malveillant(e)

malfunction [mæl'fʌŋkʃən] n fonctionnement défectueux

malice ['mælɪs] n méchanceté f, malveillance f

malicious [mə'lɪʃəs] adj méchant(e), malveillant(e); (Law) avec intention criminelle

malignant [mə'lɪgnənt] adj (Med) malin(-igne)

mall [mɔːl] n (also: **shopping ~**) centre commercial

mallet ['mælɪt] n maillet m

malnutrition [mælnjuː'trɪʃən] n malnutrition f

malpractice [mæl'præktɪs] n faute professionnelle; négligence f

malt [mɔːlt] n malt m ▷ cpd (whisky) pur malt

Malta ['mɔːltə] n Malte f

Maltese [mɔːl'tiːz] adj maltais(e) ▷ n (pl inv) Maltais(e); (Ling) maltais m

mammal ['mæml] n mammifère m

mammoth ['mæməθ] n mammouth m ▷ adj géant(e), monstre

man (pl **men**) [mæn, mɛn] n homme m; (Sport) joueur m; (Chess) pièce f; (Draughts) pion m ▷ vt (Naut: ship) garnir d'hommes; (machine) assurer le fonctionnement de; (Mil: gun) servir; (: post) être de service à; **an old ~** un vieillard; **~ and wife** mari et femme

manage ['mænɪdʒ] vi se débrouiller; (succeed) y arriver, réussir ▷ vt (business) gérer; (team, operation) diriger; (control: ship) manier, manœuvrer; (: person) savoir s'y prendre avec; (device, things to do, carry etc) arriver à se débrouiller avec, s'en tirer avec; **to ~ to do** se débrouiller pour faire; (succeed) réussir à faire

manageable ['mænɪdʒəbl] adj maniable; (task etc) faisable; (number) raisonnable

management ['mænɪdʒmənt] n (running) administration f, direction f; (people in charge: of business, firm) dirigeants mpl, cadres mpl; (: of hotel, shop, theatre) direction; **"under new ~"**

"changement de gérant", "changement de propriétaire"

manager ['mænɪdʒəʳ] *n* (*of business*) directeur *m*; (*of institution etc*) administrateur *m*; (*of department, unit*) responsable *m/f*, chef *m*; (*of hotel etc*) gérant *m*; (*Sport*) manager *m*; (*of artist*) impresario *m*; **sales** ~ responsable *or* chef des ventes

manageress [mænɪdʒə'rɛs] *n* directrice *f*; (*of hotel etc*) gérante *f*

managerial [mænɪ'dʒɪərɪəl] *adj* directorial(e); (*skills*) de cadre, de gestion; ~ **staff** cadres *mpl*

managing director ['mænɪdʒɪŋ-] *n* directeur général

mandarin ['mændərɪn] *n* (*also:* ~ **orange**) mandarine *f*; (*person*) mandarin *m*

mandate ['mændeɪt] *n* mandat *m*

mandatory ['mændətərɪ] *adj* obligatoire; (*powers etc*) mandataire

mane [meɪn] *n* crinière *f*

maneuver [mə'nu:vəʳ] (*US*) *n* = **manoeuvre**

manfully ['mænfəlɪ] *adv* vaillamment

mangetout ['mɒnʒ'tu:] *n* mange-tout *m inv*

mangle ['mæŋgl] *vt* déchiqueter; mutiler ▷ *n* essoreuse *f*; calandre *f*

mango (*pl* **mangoes**) ['mæŋgəu] *n* mangue *f*

mangy ['meɪndʒɪ] *adj* galeux(-euse)

manhandle ['mænhændl] *vt* (*mistreat*) maltraiter, malmener; (*move by hand*) manutentionner

manhole ['mænhəul] *n* trou *m* d'homme

manhood ['mænhud] *n* (*age*) âge *m* d'homme; (*manliness*) virilité *f*

man-hour ['mænauəʳ] *n* heure-homme *f*, heure *f* de main-d'œuvre

manhunt ['mænhʌnt] *n* chasse *f* à l'homme

mania ['meɪnɪə] *n* manie *f*

maniac ['meɪnɪæk] *n* maniaque *m/f*; (*fig*) fou/folle

manic ['mænɪk] *adj* maniaque

manicure ['mænɪkjuəʳ] *n* manucure *f* ▷ *vt* (*person*) faire les mains à

manifest ['mænɪfɛst] *vt* manifester ▷ *adj* manifeste, évident(e) ▷ *n* (*Aviat, Naut*) manifeste *m*

manifesto [mænɪ'fɛstəu] *n* (*Pol*) manifeste *m*

manipulate [mə'nɪpjuleɪt] *vt* manipuler; (*system, situation*) exploiter

mankind [mæn'kaɪnd] *n* humanité *f*, genre humain

manly ['mænlɪ] *adj* viril(e)

man-made ['mæn'meɪd] *adj* artificiel(le); (*fibre*) synthétique

manner ['mænəʳ] *n* manière *f*, façon *f*; (*behaviour*) attitude *f*, comportement *m*; **manners** *npl*: (**good**) ~**s** (bonnes) manières; **bad** ~**s** mauvaises manières; **all** ~ **of** toutes sortes de

mannerism ['mænərɪzəm] *n* particularité *f* de langage (*or* de comportement), tic *m*

manoeuvre, (*US*) **maneuver** [mə'nu:vəʳ] *vt*

(*move*) manœuvrer; (*manipulate: person*) manipuler; (: *situation*) exploiter ▷ *n* manœuvre *f*; **to** ~ **sb into doing sth** manipuler qn pour lui faire faire qch

manor ['mænəʳ] *n* (*also:* ~ **house**) manoir *m*

manpower ['mænpauəʳ] *n* main-d'œuvre *f*

mansion ['mænʃən] *n* château *m*, manoir *m*

manslaughter ['mænslɔːtəʳ] *n* homicide *m* involontaire

mantelpiece ['mæntlpiːs] *n* cheminée *f*

manual ['mænjuəl] *adj* manuel(le) ▷ *n* manuel *m*

manufacture [mænju'fæktʃəʳ] *vt* fabriquer ▷ *n* fabrication *f*

manufacturer [mænju'fæktʃərəʳ] *n* fabricant *m*

manure [mə'njuəʳ] *n* fumier *m*; (*artificial*) engrais *m*

manuscript ['mænjuskrɪpt] *n* manuscrit *m*

many ['mɛnɪ] *adj* beaucoup de, de nombreux(-euses) ▷ *pron* beaucoup, un grand nombre; **how** ~? combien?; **a great** ~ un grand nombre (de); **too** ~ **difficulties** trop de difficultés; **twice as** ~ deux fois plus; ~ **a** ... bien des ..., plus d'un(e) ...

map [mæp] *n* carte *f*; (*of town*) plan *m* ▷ *vt* dresser la carte de; **can you show it to me on the** ~? pouvez-vous me l'indiquer sur la carte?; **map out** *vt* tracer; (*fig: task*) planifier; (*career, holiday*) organiser, préparer (à l'avance); (: *essay*) faire le plan de

maple ['meɪpl] *n* érable *m*

mar [mɑːʳ] *vt* gâcher, gâter

marathon ['mærəθən] *n* marathon *m* ▷ *adj*: **a** ~ **session** une séance-marathon

marble ['mɑːbl] *n* marbre *m*; (*toy*) bille *f*; **marbles** *npl* (*game*) billes

March [mɑːtʃ] *n* mars *m*; *see also* **July**

march [mɑːtʃ] *vi* marcher au pas; (*demonstrators*) défiler ▷ *n* marche *f*; (*demonstration*) manifestation *f*; **to** ~ **out of into** *etc* sortir de/entrer dans *etc* (*de manière décidée ou impulsive*)

mare [mɛəʳ] *n* jument *f*

margarine [mɑːdʒə'riːn] *n* margarine *f*

margin ['mɑːdʒɪn] *n* marge *f*

marginal ['mɑːdʒɪnl] *adj* marginal(e); ~ **seat** (*Pol*) siège disputé

marginally ['mɑːdʒɪnəlɪ] *adv* très légèrement, sensiblement

marigold ['mærɪɡəuld] *n* souci *m*

marijuana [mærɪ'wɑːnə] *n* marijuana *f*

marina [mə'riːnə] *n* marina *f*

marinade *n* [mærɪ'neɪd] marinade *f* ▷ *vt* ['mærɪneɪd] = **marinate**

marinate ['mærɪneɪt] *vt* (faire) mariner

marine [mə'riːn] *adj* marin(e) ▷ *n* fusilier marin; (*US*) marine *m*

marital ['mærɪtl] *adj* matrimonial(e)

marital status *n* situation *f* de famille

maritime ['mærɪtaɪm] *adj* maritime

marjoram ['mɑːdʒərəm] *n* marjolaine *f*

mark [mɑːk] n marque f; (of skid etc) trace f; (Brit Scol) note f; (Sport) cible f; (currency) mark m; (Brit Tech): **M~ 2/3** 2ème/3ème série f or version f; (oven temperature): **(gas) ~ 4** thermostat m 4 ▷ vt (also Sport: player) marquer; (stain) tacher; (Brit Scol) corriger, noter; (also: **punctuation ~s**) signes mpl de ponctuation; **to ~ time** marquer le pas; **to be quick off the ~ (in doing)** (fig) ne pas perdre de temps (pour faire); **up to the ~** (in efficiency) à la hauteur; **mark down** vt (prices, goods) démarquer, réduire le prix de; **mark off** vt (tick off) cocher, pointer; **mark out** vt désigner; **mark up** vt (price) majorer

marked [mɑːkt] adj (obvious) marqué(e), net(te)

marker ['mɑːkəʳ] n (sign) jalon m; (bookmark) signet m

market ['mɑːkɪt] n marché m ▷ vt (Comm) commercialiser; **to be on the ~** être sur le marché; **on the open ~** en vente libre; **to play the ~** jouer à la or spéculer en Bourse

market garden n (Brit) jardin maraîcher

marketing ['mɑːkɪtɪŋ] n marketing m

marketplace ['mɑːkɪtpleɪs] n place f du marché; (Comm) marché m

market research n étude f de marché

marksman ['mɑːksmən] irreg n tireur m d'élite

marmalade ['mɑːməleɪd] n confiture f d'oranges

maroon [məˈruːn] vt: **to be ~ed** être abandonné(e); (fig) être bloqué(e) ▷ adj (colour) bordeaux inv

marquee [mɑːˈkiː] n chapiteau m

marriage ['mærɪdʒ] n mariage m

marriage certificate n extrait m d'acte de mariage

married ['mærɪd] adj marié(e); (life, love) conjugal(e)

marrow ['mærəu] n (of bone) moelle f; (vegetable) courge f

marry ['mærɪ] vt épouser, se marier avec; (subj: father, priest etc) marier ▷ vi (also: **get married**) se marier

Mars [mɑːz] n (planet) Mars f

Marseilles [mɑːˈseɪ] n Marseille

marsh [mɑːʃ] n marais m, marécage m

marshal ['mɑːʃl] n maréchal m; (US: fire, police) ≈ capitaine m; (for demonstration, meeting) membre m du service d'ordre ▷ vt rassembler

marshy ['mɑːʃɪ] adj marécageux(-euse)

martyr ['mɑːtəʳ] n martyr(e) ▷ vt martyriser

martyrdom ['mɑːtədəm] n martyre m

marvel ['mɑːvl] n merveille f ▷ vi: **to ~ (at)** s'émerveiller (de)

marvellous, (US) **marvelous** ['mɑːvləs] adj merveilleux(-euse)

Marxism ['mɑːksɪzəm] n marxisme m

Marxist ['mɑːksɪst] adj, n marxiste (m/f)

marzipan ['mɑːzɪpæn] n pâte f d'amandes

mascara [mæsˈkɑːrə] n mascara m

mascot ['mæskət] n mascotte f

masculine ['mæskjulɪn] adj masculin(e) ▷ n masculin m

mash [mæʃ] vt (Culin) faire une purée de

mashed potato n, **mashed potatoes** npl purée f de pommes de terre

mask [mɑːsk] n masque m ▷ vt masquer

mason ['meɪsn] n (also: **stone~**) maçon m; (also: **free~**) franc-maçon m

masonry ['meɪsnrɪ] n maçonnerie f

masquerade [mæskəˈreɪd] n bal masqué; (fig) mascarade f ▷ vi: **to ~ as** se faire passer pour

mass [mæs] n multitude f, masse f; (Physics) masse; (Rel) messe f ▷ cpd (communication) de masse; (unemployment) massif(-ive) ▷ vi se masser; **masses** npl: **the ~es** les masses; **~es of** (inf) des tas de; **to go to ~** aller à la messe

massacre ['mæsəkəʳ] n massacre m ▷ vt massacrer

massage ['mæsɑːʒ] n massage m ▷ vt masser

massive ['mæsɪv] adj énorme, massif(-ive)

mass media npl mass-media mpl

mass-produce ['mæsprəˈdjuːs] vt fabriquer en série

mass production n fabrication f en série

mast [mɑːst] n mât m; (Radio, TV) pylône m

master ['mɑːstəʳ] n maître m; (in secondary school) professeur m; (in primary school) instituteur m; (title for boys): **M~ X** Monsieur X ▷ vt maîtriser; (learn) apprendre à fond; (understand) posséder parfaitement or à fond; **~ of ceremonies (MC)** n maître des cérémonies; **M~ of Arts/Science (MA/MSc)** n ≈ titulaire m/f d'une maîtrise (en lettres/science); **M~ of Arts/Science degree (MA/MSc)** n ≈ maîtrise f

masterly ['mɑːstəlɪ] adj magistral(e)

mastermind ['mɑːstəmaɪnd] n esprit supérieur m ▷ vt diriger, être le cerveau de

masterpiece ['mɑːstəpiːs] n chef-d'œuvre m

master plan n stratégie f d'ensemble

mastery ['mɑːstərɪ] n maîtrise f; connaissance parfaite

masturbate ['mæstəbeɪt] vi se masturber

mat [mæt] n petit tapis; (also: **door~**) paillasson m; (also: **table~**) set m de table ▷ adj = **matt**

match [mætʃ] n allumette f; (game) match m, partie f; (fig) égal(e); mariage m; parti m ▷ vt (also: **~ up**) assortir; (go well with) aller bien avec, s'assortir à; (equal) égaler, valoir ▷ vi être assorti(e); **to be a good ~** être bien assorti(e); **match up** vt assortir

matchbox ['mætʃbɒks] n boîte f d'allumettes

matching ['mætʃɪŋ] adj assorti(e)

mate [meɪt] n camarade m/f de travail; (inf) copain/copine; (animal) partenaire m/f, mâle/femelle; (in merchant navy) second m ▷ vi s'accoupler ▷ vt accoupler

material [məˈtɪərɪəl] n (substance) matière f, matériau m; (cloth) tissu m, étoffe f; (information, data) données fpl ▷ adj matériel(le); (*relevant: evidence*) pertinent(e); (*important*) essentiel(le); **materials** *npl* (*equipment*) matériaux *mpl*; **reading** ~ de quoi lire, de la lecture

materialize [mə'tɪərɪəlaɪz] *vi* se matérialiser, se réaliser

maternal [mə'tə:nl] *adj* maternel(le)

maternity [mə'tə:nɪtɪ] *n* maternité *f* ▷ *cpd* de maternité, de grossesse

maternity dress *n* robe *f* de grossesse

maternity hospital *n* maternité *f*

maternity leave *n* congé *m* de maternité

math [mæθ] *n* (*US: = mathematics*) maths *fpl*

mathematical [mæθə'mætɪkl] *adj* mathématique

mathematician [mæθəmə'tɪʃən] *n* mathématicien(ne)

mathematics [mæθə'mætɪks] *n* mathématiques *fpl*

maths [mæθs] *n abbr* (*Brit: = mathematics*) maths *fpl*

matinée ['mætɪneɪ] *n* matinée *f*

mating call *n* appel *m* du mâle

matrices ['meɪtrisi:z] *npl of* **matrix**

matriculation [mətrɪkju'leɪʃən] *n* inscription *f*

matrimonial [mætrɪ'məʊnɪəl] *adj* matrimonial(e), conjugal(e)

matrimony ['mætrɪmənɪ] *n* mariage *m*

matrix (*pl* **matrices**) ['meɪtrɪks, 'meɪtrisi:z] *n* matrice *f*

matron ['meɪtrən] *n* (*in hospital*) infirmière-chef *f*; (*in school*) infirmière *f*

matt [mæt] *adj* mat(e)

matted ['mætɪd] *adj* emmêlé(e)

matter ['mætə*] *n* question *f*; (*Physics*) matière *f*, substance *f*; (*content*) contenu *m*, fond *m*; (*Med: pus*) pus *m* ▷ *vi* importer; **matters** *npl* (*affairs, situation*) la situation; **it doesn't ~** cela n'a pas d'importance; (*I don't mind*) cela ne fait rien; **what's the ~?** qu'est-ce qu'il y a?, qu'est-ce qui ne va pas?; **no ~ what** quoi qu'il arrive; **that's another ~** c'est une autre affaire; **as a ~ of course** tout naturellement; **as a ~ of fact** en fait; **it's a ~ of habit** c'est une question d'habitude; **printed ~** imprimés *mpl*; **reading ~** (*Brit*) de quoi lire, de la lecture

matter-of-fact ['mætərəv'fækt] *adj* terre à terre, neutre

mattress ['mætrɪs] *n* matelas *m*

mature [mə'tjuə*] *adj* mûr(e); (*cheese*) fait(e); (*wine*) arrive(e) à maturité ▷ *vi* mûrir; (*cheese, wine*) se faire

mature student *n* étudiant(e) plus âgé(e) que la moyenne

maturity [mə'tjuərɪtɪ] *n* maturité *f*

maul [mɔ:l] *vt* lacérer

mauve [məʊv] *adj* mauve

max *abbr* = **maximum**

maximize ['mæksɪmaɪz] *vt* (*profits etc, chances*) maximiser

maximum ['mæksɪməm] (*pl* **maxima**) ['mæksɪmə] *adj* maximum ▷ *n* maximum *m*

May [meɪ] *n* mai *m*; *see also* **July**

may [meɪ] (*conditional* **might**) *vi* (*indicating possibility*): **he ~ come** il se peut qu'il vienne; (*be allowed to*): ~ **I smoke?** puis-je fumer?; (*wishes*): ~ **God bless you!** (que) Dieu vous bénisse!; ~ **I sit here?** vous permettez que je m'assoie ici?; **he might be there** il pourrait bien y être, il se pourrait qu'il y soit; **you ~ as well go** vous feriez aussi bien d'y aller; **I might as well go** je ferais aussi bien d'y aller, autant y aller; **you might like to try** vous pourriez (peut-être) essayer

maybe ['meɪbɪ] *adv* peut-être; ~ **he'll ...** peut-être qu'il ...; ~ **not** peut-être pas

May Day *n* le Premier mai

mayday ['meɪdeɪ] *n* S.O.S *m*

mayhem ['meɪhem] *n* grabuge *m*

mayonnaise [meɪə'neɪz] *n* mayonnaise *f*

mayor [mɛə*] *n* maire *m*

mayoress ['mɛərɛs] *n* (*female mayor*) maire *m*; (*wife of mayor*) épouse *f* du maire

maze [meɪz] *n* labyrinthe *m*, dédale *m*

MD *n abbr* (*= Doctor of Medicine*) titre universitaire; (*Comm*) = **managing director**

me [mi:] *pron* me, m' + *vowel or h mute*; (*stressed, after prep*) moi; **it's me** c'est moi; **he heard me** il m'a entendu; **give me a book** donnez-moi un livre; **it's for me** c'est pour moi

meadow ['medəʊ] *n* prairie *f*, pré *m*

meagre, (*US*) **meager** ['mi:gə*] *adj* maigre

meal [mi:l] *n* repas *m*; (*flour*) farine *f*; **to go out for a ~** sortir manger

mealtime ['mi:ltaɪm] *n* heure *f* du repas

mean [mi:n] *adj* (*with money*) avare, radin(e); (*unkind*) mesquin(e), méchant(e); (*shabby*) misérable; (*US inf: animal*) méchant, vicieux(-euse); (: *person*) vache; (*average*) moyen(ne) ▷ *vt* (*pt, pp* **meant**) [ment] (*signify*) signifier, vouloir dire; (*refer to*) faire allusion à, parler de; (*intend*): **to ~ to do** avoir l'intention de faire ▷ *n* moyenne *f*; **means** *npl* (*way, money*) moyens *mpl*; **by ~s of** (*instrument*) au moyen de; **by all ~s** je vous en prie; **to be ~t for** être destiné(e) à; **do you ~ it?** vous êtes sérieux?; **what do you ~?** que voulez-vous dire?

meander [mɪ'ændə*] *vi* faire des méandres; (*fig*) flâner

meaning ['mi:nɪŋ] *n* signification *f*, sens *m*

meaningful ['mi:nɪŋful] *adj* significatif(-ive); (*relationship*) valable

meaningless ['mi:nɪŋlɪs] *adj* dénué(e) de sens

meanness ['mi:nnɪs] *n* avarice *f*; mesquinerie *f*

meant [ment] *pt, pp of* **mean**

meantime ['mi:ntaɪm] *adv* (*also:* **in the ~**) pendant ce temps

meanwhile ['mi:nwaɪl] *adv* = **meantime**

measles ['mi:zlz] *n* rougeole *f*

measure ['mɛʒə'] vt, vi mesurer ▷ n mesure f;
(ruler) règle (graduée); **a litre ~** un litre; **some
~ of success** un certain succès; **to take ~s
to do sth** prendre des mesures pour faire
qch; **measure up** vi: **to ~ up (to)** être à la
hauteur (de)
measurements ['mɛʒəməntz] npl mesures
fpl; **chest/hip ~** tour m de poitrine/hanches;
to take sb's ~ prendre les mesures de qn
meat [mi:t] n viande f; **I don't eat ~** je ne
mange pas de viande; **cold ~s** (Brit) viandes
froides; **crab ~** crabe f
meatball ['mi:tbɔ:l] n boulette f de viande
Mecca ['mɛkə] n la Mecque; (fig): **a ~ (for)** la
Mecque (de)
mechanic [mɪ'kænɪk] n mécanicien m; **can
you send a ~?** pouvez-vous nous envoyer un
mécanicien?
mechanical [mɪ'kænɪkl] adj mécanique
mechanics [mə'kænɪks] n mécanique f ▷ npl
mécanisme m
mechanism ['mɛkənɪzəm] n mécanisme m
medal ['mɛdl] n médaille f
medallion [mɪ'dæljən] n médaillon m
medallist, (US) **medalist** ['mɛdlɪst] n (Sport)
médaillé(e)
meddle ['mɛdl] vi: **to ~ in** se mêler de,
s'occuper de; **to ~ with** toucher à
media ['mi:dɪə] npl media mpl ▷ npl of
medium
mediaeval [mɛdɪ'i:vl] adj = **medieval**
median ['mi:dɪən] n (US: also: **~ strip**) bande
médiane
mediate ['mi:dɪeɪt] vi servir d'intermédiaire
Medicaid ['mɛdɪkeɪd] n (US) assistance médicale
aux indigents
medical ['mɛdɪkl] adj médical(e) ▷ n (also:
~ examination) visite médicale; (private)
examen médical
medical certificate n certificat médical
Medicare ['mɛdɪkɛə'] n (US) régime d'assurance
maladie
medicated ['mɛdɪkeɪtɪd] adj traitant(e),
médicamenteux(-euse)
medication [mɛdɪ'keɪʃən] n (drugs etc)
médication f
medicine ['mɛdsɪn] n médecine f; (drug)
médicament m
medieval [mɛdɪ'i:vl] adj médiéval(e)
mediocre [mi:dɪ'əukə'] adj médiocre
meditate ['mɛdɪteɪt] vi: **to ~ (on)** méditer
(sur)
meditation [mɛdɪ'teɪʃən] n méditation f
Mediterranean [mɛdɪtə'reɪnɪən] adj
méditerranéen(ne); **the ~ (Sea)** la (mer)
Méditerranée
medium ['mi:dɪəm] adj moyen(ne) ▷ n (pl
media) (means) moyen m; (pl **mediums**)
(person) médium m; **the happy ~** le juste
milieu
medium-sized ['mi:dɪəm'saɪzd] adj de taille
moyenne

medium wave n (Radio) ondes moyennes,
petites ondes
medley ['mɛdlɪ] n mélange m
meek [mi:k] adj doux/douce, humble
meet (pt, pp met) [mi:t, mɛt] vt rencontrer;
(by arrangement) retrouver, rejoindre; (for the
first time) faire la connaissance de; (go and
fetch): **I'll ~ you at the station** j'irai te
chercher à la gare; (opponent, danger, problem)
faire face à; (requirements) satisfaire à,
répondre à; (bill, expenses) régler, honorer ▷ vi
(friends) se rencontrer; se retrouver; (in session)
se réunir; (join: lines, roads) se joindre ▷ n (Brit
Hunting) rendez-vous m de chasse; (US Sport)
rencontre f, meeting m; **pleased to ~ you!**
enchanté!; **nice ~ing you** ravi d'avoir fait
votre connaissance; **meet up** vi: **to ~ up
with sb** rencontrer qn; **meet with** vt fus
(difficulty) rencontrer; **to ~ with success** être
couronné(e) de succès
meeting ['mi:tɪŋ] n (of group of people)
réunion f; (between individuals) rendez-vous m;
(formal) assemblée f; (Sport: rally) rencontre,
meeting m; (interview) entrevue f; **she's at** or
in a ~ (Comm) elle est en réunion; **to call a ~**
convoquer une réunion
meeting place n lieu m de (la) réunion;
(for appointment) lieu de rendez-vous
mega ['mɛgə] (inf) adv: **he's ~ rich** il est
hyper-riche
megabyte ['mɛgəbaɪt] n (Comput) méga-
octet m
megaphone ['mɛgəfəun] n porte-voix m inv
megapixel ['mɛgəpɪksl] ɡ mégapixel m
meh [mɛ] excl bof
melancholy ['mɛlənkəlɪ] n mélancolie f
▷ adj mélancolique
mellow ['mɛləu] adj velouté(e), doux/douce;
(colour) riche et profond(e); (fruit) mûr(e) ▷ vi
(person) s'adoucir
melody ['mɛlədɪ] n mélodie f
melon ['mɛlən] n melon m
melt [mɛlt] vi fondre; (become soft) s'amollir;
(fig) s'attendrir ▷ vt faire fondre; **melt away**
vi fondre complètement; **melt down** vt
fondre
meltdown ['mɛltdaun] n fusion f (du cœur
d'un réacteur nucléaire)
melting pot ['mɛltɪŋ-] n (fig) creuset m; **to be
in the ~** être encore en discussion
member ['mɛmbə'] n membre m; (of club,
political party) membre, adhérent(e) ▷ cpd:
~ country/state n pays m/état m membre
membership ['mɛmbəʃɪp] n (becoming a
member) adhésion f; admission f; (being a
member) qualité f de membre, fait m d'être
membre; (members) membres mpl, adhérents
mpl; (number of members) nombre m des
membres or adhérents
membership card n carte f de membre
memento [mə'mɛntəu] n souvenir m
memo ['mɛməu] n note f (de service)

memoir ['mɛmwɑːʳ] n mémoire m, étude f;
memoirs npl mémoires

memorable ['mɛmərəbl] adj mémorable

memorandum (pl **memoranda**)
[mɛmə'rændəm, -də] n note f (de service);
(Diplomacy) mémorandum m

memorial [mɪ'mɔːrɪəl] n mémorial m ▷ adj
commémoratif(-ive)

memorize ['mɛməraɪz] vt apprendre or
retenir par cœur

memory ['mɛmərɪ] n (also Comput) mémoire f;
(recollection) souvenir m; **to have a good/bad ~**
avoir une bonne/mauvaise mémoire; **loss of
~** perte f de mémoire; **in ~ of** à la mémoire de

memory card n (for digital camera) carte f
mémoire

memory stick n (Comput: flash pen) clé f USB;
(: card) carte f mémoire

men [mɛn] npl of **man**

menace ['mɛnɪs] n menace f; (inf: nuisance)
peste f, plaie f ▷ vt menacer; **a public ~** un
danger public

menacing ['mɛnɪsɪŋ] adj menaçant(e)

mend [mɛnd] vt réparer; (darn)
raccommoder, repriser ▷ n reprise f; **on the ~**
en voie de guérison; **to ~ one's ways**
s'amender

mending ['mɛndɪŋ] n raccommodages mpl

menial ['miːnɪəl] adj de domestique,
inférieur(e); subalterne

meningitis [mɛnɪn'dʒaɪtɪs] n méningite f

menopause ['mɛnəupɔːz] n ménopause f

men's room (US) n: **the ~** les toilettes fpl pour
hommes

menstruation [mɛnstru'eɪʃən] n
menstruation f

menswear ['mɛnzwɛəʳ] n vêtements mpl
d'hommes

mental ['mɛntl] adj mental(e); **~ illness**
maladie mentale

mental hospital n hôpital m psychiatrique

mentality [mɛn'tælɪtɪ] n mentalité f

mentally ['mɛntlɪ] adv: **to be ~ handicapped**
être handicapé(e) mental(e); **the ~ ill** les
malades mentaux

menthol ['mɛnθɒl] n menthol m

mention ['mɛnʃən] n mention f ▷ vt
mentionner, faire mention de; **don't ~ it!**
je vous en prie, il n'y a pas de quoi!; **I need
hardly ~ that ...** est-il besoin de rappeler
que ...?; **not to ~ ..., without ~ing ...** sans
parler de ..., sans compter ...

menu ['mɛnjuː] n (set menu, Comput) menu m;
(list of dishes) carte f; **could we see the ~?**
est-ce qu'on peut voir la carte?

MEP n abbr = **Member of the European
Parliament**

mercenary ['məːsɪnərɪ] adj (person)
intéressé(e), mercenaire m ▷ n mercenaire m

merchandise ['məːtʃəndaɪz] n
marchandises fpl ▷ vt commercialiser

merchant ['məːtʃənt] n négociant m,

marchand m; **timber/wine ~** négociant en
bois/vins, marchand de bois/vins

merchant bank n (Brit) banque f d'affaires

merchant navy, (US) **merchant marine** n
marine marchande

merciful ['məːsɪful] adj
miséricordieux(-euse), clément(e)

merciless ['məːsɪlɪs] adj impitoyable, sans
pitié

mercury ['məːkjʊrɪ] n mercure m

mercy ['məːsɪ] n pitié f, merci f; (Rel)
miséricorde f; **to have ~ on sb** avoir pitié de
qn; **at the ~ of** à la merci de

mere [mɪəʳ] adj simple; (chance) pur(e); **a ~
two hours** seulement deux heures

merely ['mɪəlɪ] adv simplement, purement

merge [məːdʒ] vt unir; (Comput) fusionner,
interclasser ▷ vi (colours, shapes, sounds) se
mêler; (roads) se joindre; (Comm) fusionner

merger ['məːdʒəʳ] n (Comm) fusion f

meringue [mə'ræŋ] n meringue f

merit ['mɛrɪt] n mérite m, valeur f ▷ vt
mériter

mermaid ['məːmeɪd] n sirène f

merry ['mɛrɪ] adj gai(e); **M~ Christmas!**
joyeux Noël!

merry-go-round ['mɛrɪgəuraund] n
manège m

mesh [mɛʃ] n mailles fpl ▷ vi (gears)
s'engrener; **wire ~** grillage m (métallique),
treillis m (métallique)

mesmerize ['mɛzməraɪz] vt hypnotiser;
fasciner

mess [mɛs] n désordre m, fouillis m, pagaille f;
(muddle: of life) gâchis m; (: of economy) pagaille f;
(dirt) saleté f; (Mil) mess m, cantine f; **to be
(in) a ~** être en désordre; **to be/get o.s. in a ~**
(fig) être/se mettre dans le pétrin; **mess
about** or **around** (inf) vi perdre son temps;
mess about or **around with** vt fus (inf)
chambarder, tripoter; **mess up** vt (dirty)
salir; (spoil) gâcher; **mess with** (inf) vt fus
(challenge, confront) se frotter à; (interfere with)
toucher à

message ['mɛsɪdʒ] n message m; **can I leave
a ~?** est-ce que je peux laisser un message?;
are there any ~s for me? est-ce que j'ai des
messages?; **to get the ~** (fig: inf) saisir, piger

messenger ['mɛsɪndʒəʳ] n messager m

Messrs, Messrs. ['mɛsəz] abbr (on letters:
= messieurs) MM

messy ['mɛsɪ] adj (dirty) sale; (untidy) en
désordre

met [mɛt] pt, pp of **meet** ▷ adj abbr
(= meteorological) météo inv

metabolism [mɛ'tæbəlɪzəm] n
métabolisme m

metal ['mɛtl] n métal m ▷ cpd en métal ▷ vt
empierrer

metallic [mɛ'tælɪk] adj métallique

metaphor ['mɛtəfəʳ] n métaphore f

meteor ['miːtɪəʳ] n météore m

meteorite ['miːtɪəraɪt] n météorite m or f
meteorology [miːtɪə'rɔlədʒɪ] n
météorologie f
meter ['miːtə'] n (instrument) compteur m;
(also: **parking ~**) parc(o)mètre m; (US: unit)
= **metre** ▷ vt (US Post) affranchir à la
machine
method ['mɛθəd] n méthode f; **~ of payment**
mode m or modalité f de paiement
methodical [mɪ'θɔdɪkl] adj méthodique
Methodist ['mɛθədɪst] adj, n méthodiste (m/f)
methylated spirit ['mɛθɪleɪtɪd-] n (Brit: also:
meths) alcool m à brûler
meticulous [me'tɪkjuləs] adj
méticuleux(-euse)
metre, (US) **meter** ['miːtə'] n mètre m
metric ['mɛtrɪk] adj métrique; **to go ~**
adopter le système métrique
metro ['mɛtrəu] n métro m
metropolitan [mɛtrə'pɔlɪtən] adj
métropolitain(e); **the M~ Police** (Brit) la
police londonienne
mettle ['mɛtl] n courage m
mew [mjuː] vi (cat) miauler
mews [mjuːz] n (Brit): **~ cottage** maisonnette
aménagée dans une ancienne écurie ou remise
Mexican ['mɛksɪkən] adj mexicain(e) ▷ n
Mexicain(e)
Mexico ['mɛksɪkəu] n Mexique m
mg abbr (= milligram) mg
miaow [miːˈau] vi miauler
mice [maɪs] npl of **mouse**
micro ['maɪkrəu] n (also: **~computer**)
micro(-ordinateur m) m
micro... [maɪkrəu] prefix micro...
microchip ['maɪkrəutʃɪp] n (Elec) puce f
microcomputer ['maɪkrəukəm'pjuːtə'] n
micro-ordinateur m
microphone ['maɪkrəfəun] n microphone m
microscope ['maɪkrəskəup] n microscope m;
under the ~ au microscope
mid [mɪd] adj: **~ May** la mi-mai; **~ afternoon**
le milieu de l'après-midi; **in ~ air** en plein
ciel; **he's in his ~ thirties** il a dans les
trente-cinq ans
midday [mɪd'deɪ] n midi m
middle ['mɪdl] n milieu m; (waist) ceinture f,
taille f ▷ adj du milieu; (average) moyen(ne);
in the ~ of the night au milieu de la nuit;
I'm in the ~ of reading it je suis (justement)
en train de le lire
middle-aged [mɪdl'eɪdʒd] adj d'un certain
âge, ni vieux ni jeune; (pej: values, outlook)
conventionnel(le), rassis(e)
Middle Ages npl: **the ~** le moyen âge
middle-class [mɪdl'klɑːs] adj bourgeois(e)
middle class n, **middle classes** npl: **the
~(es)** = les classes moyennes
Middle East n: **the ~** le Proche-Orient, le
Moyen-Orient
middleman ['mɪdlmæn] irreg n
intermédiaire m

middle name n second prénom
middle-of-the-road ['mɪdləvðə'rəud] adj
(policy) modéré(e), du juste milieu; (music etc)
plutôt classique, assez traditionnel(le)
middle school n (US) école pour les enfants de
12 à 14 ans, ≈ collège m; (Brit) école pour les enfants
de 8 à 14 ans
middleweight ['mɪdlweɪt] n (Boxing) poids
moyen
middling ['mɪdlɪŋ] adj moyen(ne)
midge [mɪdʒ] n moucheron m
midget ['mɪdʒɪt] n nain(e) ▷ adj minuscule
Midlands ['mɪdləndz] npl comtés du centre de
l'Angleterre
midnight ['mɪdnaɪt] n minuit m; **at ~** à
minuit
midriff ['mɪdrɪf] n estomac m, taille f
midst [mɪdst] n: **in the ~ of** au milieu de
midsummer [mɪd'sʌmə'] n milieu m de l'été
midway [mɪd'weɪ] adj, adv: **~ (between)** à
mi-chemin (entre); **~ through ...** au milieu
de ..., en plein(e) ...
midweek [mɪd'wiːk] adj du milieu de la
semaine ▷ adv au milieu de la semaine, en
pleine semaine
midwife (pl **midwives**) ['mɪdwaɪf, -vz] n
sage-femme f
midwinter [mɪd'wɪntə'] n milieu m de l'hiver
might [maɪt] vb see **may** ▷ n puissance f,
force f
mighty ['maɪtɪ] adj puissant(e) ▷ adv (inf)
rudement
migraine ['miːgreɪn] n migraine f
migrant ['maɪgrənt] n (bird, animal) migrateur
m; (person) migrant(e); nomade m/f ▷ adj
migrateur(-trice); migrant(e); nomade;
(worker) saisonnier(-ière)
migrate [maɪ'greɪt] vi migrer
migration [maɪ'greɪʃən] n migration f
mike [maɪk] n abbr (= microphone) micro m
mild [maɪld] adj doux/douce; (reproach,
infection) léger(-ère); (illness) bénin(-igne);
(interest) modéré(e); (taste) peu relevé(e) ▷ n
bière légère
mildly ['maɪldlɪ] adv doucement; légèrement;
to put it ~ (inf) c'est le moins qu'on puisse
dire
mile [maɪl] n mil(l)e m (= 1609 m); **to do 30 ~s
per gallon** = faire 9, 4 litres aux cent
mileage ['maɪlɪdʒ] n distance f en milles,
= kilométrage m
mileometer [maɪ'lɔmɪtə'] n compteur m
kilométrique
milestone ['maɪlstəun] n borne f; (fig)
jalon m
militant ['mɪlɪtnt] adj, n militant(e)
military ['mɪlɪtərɪ] adj militaire ▷ n: **the ~**
l'armée f, les militaires mpl
militia [mɪ'lɪʃə] n milice f
milk [mɪlk] n lait m ▷ vt (cow) traire; (fig:
person) dépouiller, plumer; (: situation)
exploiter à fond

milk chocolate n chocolat m au lait
milkman ['mɪlkmən] n irreg laitier m
milk shake n milk-shake m
milky ['mɪlkɪ] adj (drink) au lait; (colour) laiteux(-euse)
Milky Way n Voie lactée
mill [mɪl] n moulin m; (factory) usine f, fabrique f; (spinning mill) filature f; (flour mill) minoterie f; (steel mill) aciérie f ▷ vt moudre, broyer ▷ vi (also: ~ about) grouiller
millennium (pl millenniums or millennia) [mɪˈlɛnɪəm, -ˈlɛnɪə] n millénaire m
millennium bug n bogue m or bug m de l'an 2000
miller ['mɪləʳ] n meunier m
milli... ['mɪlɪ] prefix milli...
milligram, milligramme ['mɪlɪɡræm] n milligramme m
millilitre, (US) **milliliter** ['mɪlɪliːtəʳ] n millilitre m
millimetre, (US) **millimeter** ['mɪlɪmiːtəʳ] n millimètre m
million ['mɪljən] n million m; a ~ pounds un million de livres sterling
millionaire [mɪljəˈnɛəʳ] n millionnaire m
millionth [mɪljənθ] num millionième
milometer [maɪˈlɒmɪtəʳ] n = **mileometer**
mime [maɪm] n mime m ▷ vt, vi mimer
mimic ['mɪmɪk] n imitateur(-trice) ▷ vt, vi imiter, contrefaire
min. abbr (= minute(s)) mn.; (= minimum) min.
mince [mɪns] vt hacher ▷ vi (in walking) marcher à petits pas maniérés ▷ n (Brit Culin) viande hachée, hachis m; he does not ~ (his) words il ne mâche pas ses mots
mincemeat ['mɪnsmiːt] n hachis de fruits secs utilisés en pâtisserie; (US) viande hachée, hachis m
mince pie n sorte de tarte aux fruits secs
mincer ['mɪnsəʳ] n hachoir m
mind [maɪnd] n esprit m ▷ vt (attend to, look after) s'occuper de; (be careful) faire attention à; (object to): I don't ~ the noise je ne crains pas le bruit, le bruit ne me dérange pas; it is on my ~ cela me préoccupe; to change one's ~ changer d'avis; to be in two ~s about sth (Brit) être indécis(e) or irrésolu(e) en ce qui concerne qch; to my ~ à mon avis, selon moi; to be out of one's ~ ne plus avoir toute sa raison; to keep sth in ~ ne pas oublier qch; to bear sth in ~ tenir compte de qch; to have sb/sth in ~ avoir qn/qch en tête; to have in ~ to do avoir l'intention de faire; it went right out of my ~ ça m'est complètement sorti de la tête; to bring or call sth to ~ se rappeler qch; to make up one's ~ se décider; do you ~ if ...? est-ce que cela vous gêne si ...?; I don't ~ cela ne me dérange pas; (don't care) ça m'est égal; ~ you, ... remarquez, ...; never ~ peu importe, ça ne fait rien; (don't worry) ne vous en faîtes pas; "~ the step" "attention à la marche"

minder ['maɪndəʳ] n (child minder) gardienne f; (bodyguard) ange gardien (fig)
mindful ['maɪndful] adj: ~ of attentif(-ive) à, soucieux(-euse) de
mindless ['maɪndlɪs] adj irréfléchi(e); (violence, crime) insensé(e); (boring: job) idiot(e)
mine¹ [maɪn] pron le/la mien(ne), les miens/miennes; a friend of ~ un de mes amis, un ami à moi; this book is ~ ce livre est à moi
mine² [maɪn] n mine f ▷ vt (coal) extraire; (ship, beach) miner
minefield ['maɪnfiːld] n champ m de mines
miner ['maɪnəʳ] n mineur m
mineral ['mɪnərəl] adj minéral(e) ▷ n minéral m; **minerals** npl (Brit: soft drinks) boissons gazeuses (sucrées)
mineral water n eau minérale
mingle ['mɪŋɡl] vt mêler, mélanger ▷ vi: to ~ with se mêler à
miniature ['mɪnətʃəʳ] adj (en) miniature ▷ n miniature f
minibar ['mɪnɪbɑːʳ] n minibar m
minibus ['mɪnɪbʌs] n minibus m
minicab ['mɪnɪkæb] n (Brit) taxi m indépendant
minimal ['mɪnɪml] adj minimal(e)
minimize ['mɪnɪmaɪz] vt (reduce) réduire au minimum; (play down) minimiser
minimum ['mɪnɪməm] n (pl minima) ['mɪnɪmə] minimum m ▷ adj minimum; to reduce to a ~ réduire au minimum
mining ['maɪnɪŋ] n exploitation minière ▷ adj minier(-ière); de mineurs
miniskirt ['mɪnɪskəːt] n mini-jupe f
minister ['mɪnɪstəʳ] n (Brit Pol) ministre m; (Rel) pasteur m ▷ vi: to ~ to sb donner ses soins à qn; to ~ to sb's needs pourvoir aux besoins de qn
ministerial [mɪnɪsˈtɪərɪəl] adj (Brit Pol) ministériel(le)
ministry ['mɪnɪstrɪ] n (Brit Pol) ministère m; (Rel): to go into the ~ devenir pasteur
mink [mɪŋk] n vison m
minor ['maɪnəʳ] adj petit(e), de peu d'importance; (Mus, poet, problem) mineur(e) ▷ n (Law) mineur(e)
minority [maɪˈnɒrɪtɪ] n minorité f; to be in a ~ être en minorité
mint [mɪnt] n (plant) menthe f; (sweet) bonbon m à la menthe ▷ vt (coins) battre; the (Royal) M~, the (US) M~ l'hôtel m de la Monnaie; in ~ condition à l'état de neuf
minus ['maɪnəs] n (also: ~ sign) signe m moins ▷ prep moins; 12 - 6 equals 6 12 moins 6 égal 6; ~ 24°C moins 24°C
minute¹ n ['mɪnɪt] minute f; (official record) procès-verbal m, compte rendu; **minutes** npl (of meeting) procès-verbal m, compte rendu; it is 5 ~s past 3 il est 3 heures 5; wait a ~! (attendez) un instant!; at the last ~ à la dernière minute; up to the ~ (fashion) dernier cri; (news) de dernière minute; (machine, technology) de pointe

minute² adj [maɪˈnjuːt] minuscule; (detailed) minutieux(-euse); **in ~ detail** par le menu
miracle [ˈmɪrəkl] n miracle m
miraculous [mɪˈrækjuləs] adj miraculeux(-euse)
mirage [ˈmɪrɑːʒ] n mirage m
mirror [ˈmɪrəʳ] n miroir m, glace f; (in car) rétroviseur m ▷ vt refléter
mirth [mə:θ] n gaieté f
misadventure [mɪsədˈventʃəʳ] n mésaventure f; **death by ~** (Brit) décès accidentel
misapprehension [ˈmɪsæprɪˈhenʃən] n malentendu m, méprise f
misappropriate [mɪsəˈprəuprɪeɪt] vt détourner
misbehave [mɪsbɪˈheɪv] vi mal se conduire
misc. abbr = miscellaneous
miscalculate [mɪsˈkælkjuleɪt] vt mal calculer
miscarriage [ˈmɪskærɪdʒ] n (Med) fausse couche f; **~ of justice** erreur f judiciaire
miscellaneous [mɪsɪˈleɪnɪəs] adj (items, expenses) divers(es); (selection) varié(e)
mischief [ˈmɪstʃɪf] n (naughtiness) sottises fpl; (fun) farce f; (playfulness) espièglerie f; (harm) mal m, dommage m; (maliciousness) méchanceté f
mischievous [ˈmɪstʃɪvəs] adj (playful, naughty) coquin(e), espiègle; (harmful) méchant(e)
misconception [ˈmɪskənˈsepʃən] n idée fausse
misconduct [mɪsˈkɒndʌkt] n inconduite f; **professional ~** faute professionnelle
misdemeanour, (US) **misdemeanor** [mɪsdɪˈmiːnəʳ] n écart m de conduite; infraction f
miser [ˈmaɪzəʳ] n avare m/f
miserable [ˈmɪzərəbl] adj (person, expression) malheureux(-euse); (conditions) misérable; (weather) maussade; (offer, donation) minable; (failure) pitoyable; **to feel ~** avoir le cafard
miserly [ˈmaɪzəlɪ] adj avare
misery [ˈmɪzərɪ] n (unhappiness) tristesse f; (pain) souffrances fpl; (wretchedness) misère f
misfire [mɪsˈfaɪəʳ] vi rater; (car engine) avoir des ratés
misfit [ˈmɪsfɪt] n (person) inadapté(e)
misfortune [mɪsˈfɔːtʃən] n malchance f, malheur m
misgiving [mɪsˈgɪvɪŋ] n (apprehension) craintes fpl; **to have ~s about sth** avoir des doutes quant à qch
misguided [mɪsˈgaɪdɪd] adj malavisé(e)
mishandle [mɪsˈhændl] vt (treat roughly) malmener; (mismanage) mal s'y prendre pour faire or résoudre etc
mishap [ˈmɪshæp] n mésaventure f
misinform [mɪsɪnˈfɔːm] vt mal renseigner
misinterpret [mɪsɪnˈtəːprɪt] vt mal interpréter
misjudge [mɪsˈdʒʌdʒ] vt méjuger, se méprendre sur le compte de

mislay [mɪsˈleɪ] vt (irreg like: lay) égarer
mislead [mɪsˈliːd] vt (irreg like: lead) induire en erreur
misleading [mɪsˈliːdɪŋ] adj trompeur(-euse)
mismanage [mɪsˈmænɪdʒ] vt mal gérer; mal s'y prendre pour faire or résoudre etc
misplace [mɪsˈpleɪs] vt égarer; **to be ~d** (trust etc) être mal placé(e)
misprint [ˈmɪsprɪnt] n faute f d'impression
misrepresent [mɪsreprɪˈzent] vt présenter sous un faux jour
Miss [mɪs] n Mademoiselle; **Dear ~ Smith** Chère Mademoiselle Smith
miss [mɪs] vt (fail to get, attend, see) manquer, rater; (appointment, class) manquer; (escape, avoid) échapper à, éviter; (notice loss of: money etc) s'apercevoir de l'absence de; (regret the absence of): **I ~ him/it** il/cela me manque ▷ vi manquer ▷ n (shot) coup manqué; **we ~ed our train** nous avons raté notre train; **the bus just ~ed the wall** le bus a évité le mur de justesse; **you're ~ing the point** vous êtes à côté de la question; **you can't ~ it** vous ne pouvez pas vous tromper; **miss out** vt (Brit) oublier; **miss out on** vt fus (fun, party) rater, manquer; (chance, bargain) laisser passer
misshapen [mɪsˈʃeɪpən] adj difforme
missile [ˈmɪsaɪl] n (Aviat) missile m; (object thrown) projectile m
missing [ˈmɪsɪŋ] adj manquant(e); (after escape, disaster: person) disparu(e); **to go ~** disparaître; **~ person** personne disparue, disparu(e); **~ in action** (Mil) porté(e) disparu(e)
mission [ˈmɪʃən] n mission f; **on a ~ to sb** en mission auprès de qn
missionary [ˈmɪʃənrɪ] n missionnaire m/f
mission statement n déclaration f d'intention
misspell [mɪsˈspel] vt (irreg like: spell) mal orthographier
mist [mɪst] n brume f ▷ vi (also: ~ over, ~ up) devenir brumeux(-euse); (Brit: windows) s'embuer
mistake [mɪsˈteɪk] n erreur f, faute f ▷ vt (irreg like: take) (meaning) mal comprendre; (intentions) se méprendre sur; **to ~ for** prendre pour; **by ~** par erreur, par inadvertance; **to make a ~** (in writing) faire une faute; (in calculating etc) faire une erreur; **there must be some ~** il doit y avoir une erreur, se tromper; **to make a ~ about sb/sth** se tromper sur le compte de qn/sur qch
mistaken [mɪsˈteɪkən] pp of **mistake** ▷ adj (idea etc) erroné(e); **to be ~** faire erreur, se tromper
mister [ˈmɪstəʳ] n (inf) Monsieur m; see **Mr**
mistletoe [ˈmɪsltəu] n gui m
mistook [mɪsˈtuk] pt of **mistake**
mistress [ˈmɪstrɪs] n maîtresse f; (Brit: in primary school) institutrice f; (: in secondary school) professeur m

mistrust [mɪs'trʌst] vt se méfier de ▷ n: ~ **(of)** méfiance f (à l'égard de)

misty ['mɪstɪ] adj brumeux(-euse); (glasses, window) embué(e)

misunderstand [mɪsʌndə'stænd] vt, vi (irreg like: **stand**) mal comprendre

misunderstanding ['mɪsʌndə'stændɪŋ] n méprise f, malentendu m; **there's been a ~** il y a eu un malentendu

misunderstood [mɪsʌndə'stud] pt, pp of **misunderstand** ▷ adj (person) incompris(e)

misuse n [mɪs'juːs] mauvais emploi; (of power) abus m ▷ vt [mɪs'juːz] mal employer; abuser de

mitigate ['mɪtɪgeɪt] vt atténuer; **mitigating circumstances** circonstances atténuantes

mitt ['mɪt], **mitten** ['mɪtn] n moufle f; (fingerless) mitaine f

mix [mɪks] vt mélanger; (sauce, drink etc) préparer ▷ vi se mélanger; (socialize): **he doesn't ~ well** il est peu sociable ▷ n mélange m; **to ~ sth with sth** mélanger qch à qch; **to ~ business with pleasure** unir l'utile à l'agréable; **cake ~** préparation f pour gâteau; **mix in** vt incorporer, mélanger; **mix up** vt mélanger; (confuse) confondre; **to be ~ed up in sth** être mêlé(e) à qch or impliqué(e) dans qch

mixed [mɪkst] adj (feelings, reactions) contradictoire; (school, marriage) mixte

mixed grill n (Brit) assortiment m de grillades

mixed salad n salade f de crudités

mixed-up [mɪkst'ʌp] adj (person) désorienté(e), embrouillé(e)

mixer ['mɪksə'] n (for food) batteur m, mixeur m; (drink) boisson gazeuse (servant à couper un alcool); (person): **he is a good ~** il est très sociable

mixture ['mɪkstʃə'] n assortiment m, mélange m; (Med) préparation f

mix-up ['mɪksʌp] n: **there was a ~** il y a eu confusion

ml abbr (= millilitre(s)) ml

mm abbr (= millimetre) mm

moan [məun] n gémissement m ▷ vi gémir; (inf: complain): **to ~ (about)** se plaindre (de)

moat [məut] n fossé m, douves fpl

mob [mɔb] n foule f; (disorderly) cohue f; (pej): **the ~** la populace ▷ vt assaillir

mobile ['məubaɪl] adj mobile ▷ n (Art) mobile m; (Brit inf: mobile phone) (téléphone m) portable m, mobile m; **applicants must be ~** (Brit) les candidats devront être prêts à accepter tout déplacement

mobile home n caravane f

mobile phone n (téléphone m) portable m, mobile m

mobility [məu'bɪlɪtɪ] n mobilité f

mobilize ['məubɪlaɪz] vt, vi mobiliser

mock [mɔk] vt ridiculiser; (laugh at) se moquer de ▷ adj faux/fausse; **mocks** npl (Brit: Scol) examens blancs

mockery ['mɔkərɪ] n moquerie f, raillerie f; **to make a ~ of** ridiculiser, tourner en dérision

mock-up ['mɔkʌp] n maquette f

mod [mɔd] adj see **convenience**

mod cons ['mɔd'kɔnz] npl abbr (Brit) = **modern conveniences**; see **convenience**

mode [məud] n mode m; (of transport) moyen m

model ['mɔdl] n modèle m; (person: for fashion) mannequin m; (: for artist) modèle ▷ vt (with clay etc) modeler ▷ vi travailler comme mannequin ▷ adj (railway: toy) modèle réduit inv; (child, factory) modèle; **to ~ clothes** présenter des vêtements; **to ~ o.s. on** imiter; **to ~ sb/sth on** modeler qn/qch sur

modem ['məudɛm] n modem m

moderate [adj [n'mɔdərət, vb'mɔdəreɪt] adj modéré(e); (amount, change) peu important(e) ▷ n (Pol) modéré(e) ▷ vi se modérer, se calmer ▷ vt modérer

moderation [mɔdə'reɪʃən] n modération f, mesure f; **in ~** à dose raisonnable, pris(e) or pratiqué(e) modérément

modern ['mɔdən] adj moderne

modernize ['mɔdənaɪz] vt moderniser

modern languages npl langues vivantes

modest ['mɔdɪst] adj modeste

modesty ['mɔdɪstɪ] n modestie f

modification [mɔdɪfɪ'keɪʃən] n modification f; **to make ~s** faire or apporter des modifications

modify ['mɔdɪfaɪ] vt modifier

module ['mɔdjuːl] n module m

mogul ['məugl] n (fig) nabab m; (Ski) bosse f

mohair ['məuhɛə'] n mohair m

Mohammed [mə'hæmɛd] n Mahomet m

moist [mɔɪst] adj humide, moite

moisten ['mɔɪsn] vt humecter, mouiller légèrement

moisture ['mɔɪstʃə'] n humidité f; (on glass) buée f

moisturizer ['mɔɪstʃəraɪzə'] n crème hydratante

molar ['məulə'] n molaire f

molasses [məu'læsɪz] n mélasse f

mold etc [məuld] (US) n = **mould** etc

mole [məul] n (animal, spy) taupe f; (spot) grain m de beauté

molecule ['mɔlɪkjuːl] n molécule f

molest [məu'lɛst] vt (assault sexually) attenter à la pudeur de; (attack) molester; (harass) tracasser

mollycoddle ['mɔlɪkɔdl] vt chouchouter, couver

molt [məult] vi (US) = **moult**

molten ['məultən] adj fondu(e); (rock) en fusion

mom [mɔm] n (US) = **mum**

moment ['məumənt] n moment m, instant m; (importance) importance f; **at the ~** en ce moment; **for the ~** pour l'instant; **in**

a ~ dans un instant; **"one ~ please"** (Tel) "ne quittez pas"

momentarily ['məuməntrili] adv momentanément; (US: soon) bientôt

momentary ['məuməntəri] adj momentané(e), passager(-ère)

momentous [məu'mentəs] adj important(e), capital(e)

momentum [məu'mentəm] n élan m, vitesse acquise; (fig) dynamique f; **to gather ~** prendre de la vitesse; (fig) gagner du terrain

mommy ['mɔmɪ] n (US: mother) maman f

Monaco ['mɔnəkəu] n Monaco f

monarch ['mɔnək] n monarque m

monarchy ['mɔnəkɪ] n monarchie f

monastery ['mɔnəstəri] n monastère m

Monday ['mʌndɪ] n lundi m; see also **Tuesday**

monetary ['mʌnɪtəri] adj monétaire

money ['mʌnɪ] n argent m; **to make ~** (person) gagner de l'argent; (business) rapporter; **I've got no ~ left** je n'ai plus d'argent, je n'ai plus un sou

money belt n ceinture-portefeuille f

money order n mandat m

money-spinner ['mʌnɪspɪnər] n (inf) mine f d'or (fig)

mongrel ['mʌŋgrəl] n (dog) bâtard m

monitor ['mɔnɪtər] n (TV, Comput) écran m, moniteur m; (Brit Scol) chef m de classe; (US Scol) surveillant m (d'examen) ▷ vt contrôler; (foreign station) être à l'écoute de; (progress) suivre de près

monk [mʌŋk] n moine m

monkey ['mʌŋkɪ] n singe m

monkey nut n (Brit) cacahuète f

monologue ['mɔnəlɔg] n monologue m

monopoly [mə'nɔpəlɪ] n monopole m; **Monopolies and Mergers Commission** (Brit) commission britannique d'enquête sur les monopoles

monosodium glutamate [mɔnə'səudɪəm 'glu:təmeɪt] n glutamate m de sodium

monotone ['mɔnətəun] n ton m (or voix f) monocorde; **to speak in a ~** parler sur un ton monocorde

monotonous [mə'nɔtənəs] adj monotone

monsoon [mɔn'su:n] n mousson f

monster ['mɔnstər] n monstre m

monstrous ['mɔnstrəs] adj (huge) gigantesque; (atrocious) monstrueux(-euse), atroce

month [mʌnθ] n mois m; **every ~** tous les mois; **300 dollars a ~** 300 dollars par mois

monthly ['mʌnθlɪ] adj mensuel(le) ▷ adv mensuellement ▷ n (magazine) mensuel m, publication mensuelle; **twice ~** deux fois par mois

Montreal [mɔntrɪ'ɔ:l] n Montréal f

monument ['mɔnjumənt] n monument m

moo [mu:] vi meugler, beugler

mood [mu:d] n humeur f, disposition f; **to be in a good/bad ~** être de bonne/mauvaise humeur; **to be in the ~ for** être d'humeur à, avoir envie de

moody ['mu:dɪ] adj (variable) d'humeur changeante, lunatique; (sullen) morose, maussade

moon [mu:n] n lune f

moonlight ['mu:nlaɪt] n clair m de lune ▷ vi travailler au noir

moonlighting ['mu:nlaɪtɪŋ] n travail m au noir

moonlit ['mu:nlɪt] adj éclairé(e) par la lune; **a ~ night** une nuit de lune

moor [muər] n lande f ▷ vt (ship) amarrer ▷ vi mouiller

moorland ['muələnd] n lande f

moose [mu:s] n (pl inv) élan m

mop [mɔp] n balai m à laver; (for dishes) lavette f à vaisselle ▷ vt éponger, essuyer; **~ of hair** tignasse f; **mop up** vt éponger

mope [məup] vi avoir le cafard, se morfondre; **mope about, mope around** vi broyer du noir, se morfondre

moped ['məuped] n cyclomoteur m

moral ['mɔrl] adj moral(e) ▷ n morale f; **morals** npl moralité f

morale [mɔ'rɑ:l] n moral m

morality [mə'rælɪtɪ] n moralité f

morass [mə'ræs] n marais m, marécage m

morbid ['mɔ:bɪd] adj morbide

 KEYWORD

more [mɔ:r] adj **1** (greater in number etc) plus (de), davantage (de); **more people/work (than)** plus de gens/de travail (que) **2** (additional) encore (de); **do you want (some) more tea?** voulez-vous encore du thé?; **is there any more wine?** reste-t-il du vin?; **I have no** or **I don't have any more money** je n'ai plus d'argent; **it'll take a few more weeks** ça prendra encore quelques semaines ▷ pron plus, davantage; **more than 10** plus de 10; **it cost more than we expected** cela a coûté plus que prévu; **I want more** j'en veux plus or davantage; **is there any more?** est-ce qu'il en reste?; **there's no more** il n'y en a plus; **a little more** un peu plus; **many/much more** beaucoup plus, bien davantage ▷ adv plus; **more dangerous/easily (than)** plus dangereux/facilement (que); **more and more expensive** de plus en plus cher; **more or less** plus ou moins; **more than ever** plus que jamais; **once more** encore une fois, une fois de plus; **and what's more ...** et de plus ..., et qui plus est ...

moreover [mɔ:'rəuvər] adv de plus

morgue [mɔ:g] n morgue f

morning ['mɔ:nɪŋ] n matin m; (as duration) matinée f ▷ cpd matinal(e); (paper) du matin; **in the ~** le matin; **7 o'clock in the ~** 7 heures du matin; **this ~** ce matin

morning sickness n nausées matinales
Moroccan [mə'rɔkən] adj marocain(e) ▷ n Marocain(e)
Morocco [mə'rɔkəu] n Maroc m
moron ['mɔːrɔn] n idiot(e), minus m/f
morphine ['mɔːfiːn] n morphine f
morris dancing ['mɔrɪs-] (Brit) danses folkloriques anglaises; voir article

◈ **MORRIS DANCING**
◈
◈ Le morris dancing est une danse folklorique
◈ anglaise traditionnellement réservée
◈ aux hommes. Habillés tout en blanc et
◈ portant des clochettes, ils exécutent
◈ différentes figures avec des mouchoirs et
◈ de longs bâtons. Cette danse est très
◈ populaire dans les fêtes de village.

Morse [mɔːs] n (also: ~ code) morse m
morsel ['mɔːsl] n bouchée f
mortal ['mɔːtl] adj, n mortel(le)
mortar ['mɔːtəʳ] n mortier m
mortgage ['mɔːgɪdʒ] n hypothèque f; (loan) prêt m (or crédit m) hypothécaire ▷ vt hypothéquer; **to take out a ~** prendre une hypothèque, faire un emprunt
mortgage company n (US) société f de crédit immobilier
mortician [mɔː'tɪʃən] n (US) entrepreneur m de pompes funèbres
mortified ['mɔːtɪfaɪd] adj mort(e) de honte
mortuary ['mɔːtjuərɪ] n morgue f
mosaic [məu'zeɪɪk] n mosaïque f
Moscow ['mɔskəu] n Moscou
Moslem ['mɔzləm] adj, n = **Muslim**
mosque [mɔsk] n mosquée f
mosquito (pl **mosquitoes**) [mɔs'kiːtəu] n moustique m
moss [mɔs] n mousse f
most [məust] adj (majority of) la plupart de; (greatest amount of) le plus de ▷ pron la plupart ▷ adv le plus; (very) très, extrêmement; **the ~** le plus; **~ fish** la plupart des poissons; **the ~ beautiful woman in the world** la plus belle femme du monde; **~ of** (with plural) la plupart de; (with singular) la plus grande partie de; **~ of them** la plupart d'entre eux; **~ of the time** la plupart du temps; **I saw ~** (a lot but not all) j'en ai vu la plupart; (more than anyone else) c'est moi qui en ai vu le plus; **at the (very) ~** au plus; **to make the ~ of** profiter au maximum de
mostly ['məustlɪ] adv (chiefly) surtout, principalement; (usually) généralement
MOT n abbr (Brit: = Ministry of Transport): **the ~ (test)** visite technique (annuelle) obligatoire des véhicules à moteur
motel [məu'tel] n motel m
moth [mɔθ] n papillon m de nuit; (in clothes) mite f
mother ['mʌðəʳ] n mère f ▷ vt (pamper, protect) dorloter

motherhood ['mʌðəhud] n maternité f
mother-in-law ['mʌðərɪnlɔː] n belle-mère f
motherly ['mʌðəlɪ] adj maternel(le)
mother-of-pearl ['mʌðərəv'pɜːl] n nacre f
Mother's Day n fête f des Mères
mother-to-be ['mʌðətə'biː] n future maman
mother tongue n langue maternelle
motif [məu'tiːf] n motif m
motion ['məuʃən] n mouvement m; (gesture) geste m; (at meeting) motion f; (Brit: also: **bowel ~**) selles fpl ▷ vt, vi: **to ~ (to) sb to do** faire signe à qn de faire; **to be in ~** (vehicle) être en marche; **to set in ~** mettre en marche; **to go through the ~s of doing sth** (fig) faire qch machinalement or sans conviction
motionless ['məuʃənlɪs] adj immobile, sans mouvement
motion picture n film m
motivate ['məutɪveɪt] vt motiver
motivated ['məutɪveɪtɪd] adj motivé(e)
motivation [məutɪ'veɪʃən] n motivation f
motive ['məutɪv] n motif m, mobile m ▷ adj moteur(-trice); **from the best (of) ~s** avec les meilleures intentions (du monde)
motley ['mɔtlɪ] adj hétéroclite; bigarré(e), bariolé(e)
motor ['məutəʳ] n moteur m; (Brit inf: vehicle) auto f ▷ adj moteur(-trice)
motorbike ['məutəbaɪk] n moto f
motorboat ['məutəbəut] n bateau m à moteur
motorcar ['məutəkɑː] n (Brit) automobile f
motorcycle ['məutəsaɪkl] n moto f
motorcycle racing n course f de motos
motorcyclist ['məutəsaɪklɪst] n motocycliste m/f
motoring ['məutərɪŋ] (Brit) n tourisme m automobile ▷ adj (accident) de voiture, de la route; **~ holiday** vacances fpl en voiture; **~ offence** infraction f au code de la route
motorist ['məutərɪst] n automobiliste m/f
motor mechanic n mécanicien m garagiste
motor racing n (Brit) course f automobile
motor trade n secteur m de l'automobile
motorway ['məutəweɪ] n (Brit) autoroute f
mottled ['mɔtld] adj tacheté(e), marbré(e)
motto (pl **mottoes**) ['mɔtəu] n devise f
mould, (US) **mold** [məuld] n moule m; (mildew) moisissure f ▷ vt mouler, modeler; (fig) façonner
mouldy, (US) **moldy** ['məuldɪ] adj moisi(e); (smell) de moisi
moult, (US) **molt** [məult] vi muer
mound [maund] n monticule m, tertre m
mount [maunt] n (hill) mont m, montagne f; (horse) monture f; (for jewel etc) carton m de montage; (for picture) carton m ▷ vt monter; (horse) monter à; (bike) monter sur; (exhibition) organiser, monter; (picture) monter sur carton; (stamp) coller dans un album ▷ vi (inflation, tension) augmenter; **mount up** vi

s'élever, monter; (bills, problems, savings) s'accumuler

mountain ['mauntɪn] n montagne f ▷ cpd de (la) montagne; **to make a ~ out of a molehill** (fig) se faire une montagne d'un rien

mountain bike n VTT m, vélo m tout terrain

mountaineer [mauntɪ'nɪəʳ] n alpiniste m/f

mountaineering [mauntɪ'nɪərɪŋ] n alpinisme m; **to go ~** faire de l'alpinisme

mountainous ['mauntɪnəs] adj montagneux(-euse)

mountain range n chaîne f de montagnes

mountain rescue team n colonne f de secours

mountainside ['mauntɪnsaɪd] n flanc m or versant m de la montagne

mourn [mɔːn] vt pleurer ▷ vi: **to ~ for sb** pleurer qn; **to ~ for sth** se lamenter sur qch

mourner ['mɔːnəʳ] n parent(e) or ami(e) du défunt; personne f en deuil or venue rendre hommage au défunt

mourning ['mɔːnɪŋ] n deuil m ▷ cpd (dress) de deuil; **in ~** en deuil

mouse (pl **mice**) [maus, maɪs] n (also Comput) souris f

mouse mat n (Comput) tapis m de souris

mousetrap ['maustræp] n souricière f

moussaka [mu'sɑːkə] n moussaka f

mousse [muːs] n mousse f

moustache, (US) **mustache** [məs'tɑːʃ] n moustache(s) f(pl)

mousy ['mausɪ] adj (person) effacé(e); (hair) d'un châtain terne

mouth [mauθ, pl mauðz] n bouche f; (of dog, cat) gueule f; (of river) embouchure f; (of hole, cave) ouverture f; (of bottle) goulot m; (opening) orifice m

mouthful ['mauθful] n bouchée f

mouth organ n harmonica m

mouthpiece ['mauθpiːs] n (of musical instrument) bec m, embouchure f; (spokesperson) porte-parole m inv

mouthwash ['mauθwɔʃ] n eau f dentifrice

mouth-watering ['mauθwɔːtərɪŋ] adj qui met l'eau à la bouche

movable ['muːvəbl] adj mobile

move [muːv] n (movement) mouvement m; (in game) coup m; (: turn to play) tour m; (change of house) déménagement m; (change of job) changement m d'emploi ▷ vt déplacer, bouger; (emotionally) émouvoir; (Pol: resolution etc) proposer ▷ vi (gen) bouger, remuer; (traffic) circuler; (also: ~ house) déménager; (in game) jouer; **can you ~ your car, please?** pouvez-vous déplacer votre voiture, s'il vous plaît?; **to ~ towards** se diriger vers; **to ~ to do sth** pousser or inciter qn à faire qch; **to get a ~ on** se dépêcher, se remuer; **move about** vi (fidget) remuer; (travel) voyager, se déplacer; **move along** vi se pousser; **move away** vi s'en aller,

s'éloigner; **move back** vi revenir, retourner; **move forward** vi avancer ▷ vt avancer; (people) faire avancer; **move in** vi (to a house) emménager; (police, soldiers) intervenir; **move off** vi s'éloigner, s'en aller; **move on** vi se remettre en route ▷ vt (onlookers) faire circuler; **move out** vi (of house) déménager; **move over** vi se pousser, se déplacer; **move up** vi avancer; (employee) avoir de l'avancement; (pupil) passer dans la classe supérieure

moveable [muːvəbl] adj = **movable**

movement ['muːvmənt] n mouvement m; **~ (of the bowels)** (Med) selles fpl

movie ['muːvi] n film m; **movies** npl: **the ~s** le cinéma

movie theater (US) n cinéma m

moving ['muːvɪŋ] adj en mouvement; (touching) émouvant(e) ▷ n (US) déménagement m

mow (pt **mowed**, pp **mowed** or **mown**) [məu, -d, -n] vt faucher; (lawn) tondre; **mow down** vt faucher

mower ['məuəʳ] n (also: **lawn~**) tondeuse f à gazon

mown [məun] pp of **mow**

Mozambique [məuzəm'biːk] n Mozambique m

MP n abbr (= Military Police) PM; (Brit) = **Member of Parliament**; (Canada) = **Mounted Police**

MP3 n mp3 m

MP3 player n baladeur m numérique, lecteur m mp3

mpg n abbr (= miles per gallon) (30 mpg = 9,4 l. aux 100 km)

m.p.h. abbr (= miles per hour) (60 mph = 96 km/h)

Mr, (US) **Mr.** ['mɪstəʳ] n: **Mr X** Monsieur X, M. X

Mrs, (US) **Mrs.** ['mɪsɪz] n: **~ X** Madame X, Mme X

Ms, (US) **Ms.** [mɪz] n (Miss or Mrs): **Ms X** Madame X, Mme X; voir article

  Ms

  Ms est un titre utilisé à la place de "Mrs"
  (Mme) ou de "Miss" (Mlle) pour éviter la
  distinction traditionnelle entre femmes
  mariées et femmes non mariées.

MSc n abbr = **Master of Science**

MSP n abbr (= Member of the Scottish Parliament) député m au Parlement écossais

Mt abbr (Geo: = mount) Mt

much [mʌtʃ] adj beaucoup de ▷ adv, n or pron beaucoup; **~ milk** beaucoup de lait; **we don't have ~ time** nous n'avons pas beaucoup de temps; **how ~ is it?** combien est-ce que ça coûte?; **it's not ~** ce n'est pas beaucoup; **too ~** trop (de); **so ~** tant (de); **I like it ~** j'aime beaucoup/tellement ça; **as ~ as** autant de; **thank you very ~** merci beaucoup; **that's**

~ better c'est beaucoup mieux; **~ to my amazement ...** à mon grand étonnement ...

muck [mʌk] n (mud) boue f; (dirt) ordures fpl; **muck about** vi (inf) faire l'imbécile; (: waste time) traînasser; (: tinker) bricoler; tripoter; **muck in** vi (Brit inf) donner un coup de main; **muck out** vt (stable) nettoyer; **muck up** vt (inf: ruin) gâcher, esquinter; (: dirty) salir; (: exam, interview) se planter à

mucky ['mʌkɪ] adj (dirty) boueux(-euse), sale

mucus ['mjuːkəs] n mucus m

mud [mʌd] n boue f

muddle ['mʌdl] n (mess) pagaille f, fouillis m; (mix-up) confusion f ▷ vt (also: ~ up) brouiller, embrouiller; **to be in a ~** (person) ne plus savoir où l'on en est; **to get in a ~** (while explaining etc) s'embrouiller; **muddle along** vi aller son chemin tant bien que mal; **muddle through** vi se débrouiller

muddy ['mʌdɪ] adj boueux(-euse)

mudguard ['mʌdɡɑːd] n garde-boue m inv

muesli ['mjuːzlɪ] n muesli m

muffin ['mʌfɪn] n (roll) petit pain rond et plat; (cake) petit gâteau au chocolat ou aux fruits

muffle ['mʌfl] vt (sound) assourdir, étouffer; (against cold) emmitoufler

muffled ['mʌfld] adj étouffé(e), voilé(e)

muffler ['mʌflər] n (scarf) cache-nez m inv; (US Aut) silencieux m

mug [mʌɡ] n (cup) tasse f (sans soucoupe); (: for beer) chope f; (inf: face) bouille f; (: fool) poire f ▷ vt (assault) agresser; **it's a ~'s game** (Brit) c'est bon pour les imbéciles; **mug up** vt (Brit inf: also: ~ up on) bosser, bûcher

mugger ['mʌɡər] n agresseur m

mugging ['mʌɡɪŋ] n agression f

muggy ['mʌɡɪ] adj lourd(e), moite

mule [mjuːl] n mule f

multicoloured, (US) **multicolored** ['mʌltɪkʌləd] adj multicolore

multi-level ['mʌltɪlevl] adj (US) = **multistorey**

multimedia ['mʌltɪ'miːdɪə] adj multimédia inv

multinational [mʌltɪ'næʃənl] n multinationale f ▷ adj multinational(e)

multiple ['mʌltɪpl] adj multiple ▷ n multiple m; (Brit: also: ~ store) magasin m à succursales (multiples)

multiple choice, **multiple choice test** n QCM m, questionnaire m à choix multiple

multiple sclerosis [-sklɪ'rəusɪs] n sclérose f en plaques

multiplex ['mʌltɪpleks], **multiplex cinema** n (cinéma m) multisalles m

multiplication [mʌltɪplɪ'keɪʃən] n multiplication f

multiply ['mʌltɪplaɪ] vt multiplier ▷ vi se multiplier

multistorey ['mʌltɪ'stɔːrɪ] adj (Brit: building) à étages; (: car park) à étages or niveaux multiples

mum [mʌm] n (Brit) maman f ▷ adj: **to keep ~** ne pas souffler mot; **~'s the word!** motus et bouche cousue!

mumble ['mʌmbl] vt, vi marmotter, marmonner

mummy ['mʌmɪ] n (Brit: mother) maman f; (embalmed) momie f

mumps [mʌmps] n oreillons mpl

munch [mʌntʃ] vt, vi mâcher

mundane [mʌn'deɪn] adj banal(e), terre à terre inv

municipal [mjuː'nɪsɪpl] adj municipal(e)

mural ['mjuərl] n peinture murale

murder ['məːdər] n meurtre m, assassinat m ▷ vt assassiner; **to commit ~** commettre un meurtre

murderer ['məːdərər] n meurtrier m, assassin m

murderous ['məːdərəs] adj meurtrier(-ière)

murky ['məːkɪ] adj sombre, ténébreux(-euse); (water) trouble

murmur ['məːmər] n murmure m ▷ vt, vi murmurer; **heart ~** (Med) souffle m au cœur

muscle ['mʌsl] n muscle m; (fig) force f; **muscle in** vi s'imposer, s'immiscer

muscular ['mʌskjulər] adj musculaire; (person, arm) musclé(e)

muse [mjuːz] vi méditer, songer ▷ n muse f

museum [mjuː'zɪəm] n musée m

mushroom ['mʌʃrum] n champignon m ▷ vi (fig) pousser comme un (or des) champignon(s)

music ['mjuːzɪk] n musique f

musical ['mjuːzɪkl] adj musical(e); (person) musicien(ne) ▷ n (show) comédie musicale

musical instrument n instrument m de musique

music centre n chaîne compacte

musician [mjuː'zɪʃən] n musicien(ne)

Muslim ['mʌzlɪm] adj, n musulman(e)

muslin ['mʌzlɪn] n mousseline f

mussel ['mʌsl] n moule f

must [mʌst] aux vb (obligation): **I ~ do it** je dois le faire, il faut que je le fasse; (probability): **he ~ be there by now** il doit y être maintenant, il y est probablement maintenant; (suggestion, invitation): **you ~ come and see me** il faut que vous veniez me voir ▷ n nécessité f, impératif m; **it's a ~** c'est indispensable; **I ~ have made a mistake** j'ai dû me tromper

mustache ['mʌstæʃ] n (US) = **moustache**

mustard ['mʌstəd] n moutarde f

muster ['mʌstər] vt rassembler; (also: ~ up: strength, courage) rassembler

mustn't ['mʌsnt] = **must not**

mute [mjuːt] adj, n muet(te)

muted ['mjuːtɪd] adj (noise) sourd(e), assourdi(e); (criticism) voilé(e); (Mus) en sourdine; (: trumpet) bouché(e)

mutilate ['mjuːtɪleɪt] vt mutiler

mutiny ['mjuːtɪnɪ] n mutinerie f ▷ vi se mutiner

mutter ['mʌtər] *vt, vi* marmonner, marmotter

mutton ['mʌtn] *n* mouton *m*

mutual ['mju:tʃuəl] *adj* mutuel(le), réciproque; (*benefit, interest*) commun(e)

mutually ['mju:tʃuəlɪ] *adv* mutuellement, réciproquement

muzzle ['mʌzl] *n* museau *m*; (*protective device*) muselière *f*; (*of gun*) gueule *f* ▷ *vt* museler

my [maɪ] *adj* mon/ma, mes *pl*; **my house/car/gloves** ma maison/ma voiture/mes gants; **I've washed my hair/cut my finger** je me suis lavé les cheveux/coupé le doigt; **is this my pen or yours?** c'est mon stylo ou c'est le vôtre?

myself [maɪ'sɛlf] *pron* (*reflexive*) me; (*emphatic*) moi-même; (*after prep*) moi; *see also* **oneself**

mysterious [mɪs'tɪərɪəs] *adj* mystérieux(-euse)

mystery ['mɪstərɪ] *n* mystère *m*

mystical ['mɪstɪkl] *adj* mystique

mystify ['mɪstɪfaɪ] *vt* (*deliberately*) mystifier; (*puzzle*) ébahir

myth [mɪθ] *n* mythe *m*

mythology [mɪ'θɒlədʒɪ] *n* mythologie *f*

n/a *abbr* (= *not applicable*) n.a.; (*Comm etc*) = **no account**

naff [næf] (*Brit: inf*) *adj* nul(le)

nag [næg] *vt* (*scold*) être toujours après, reprendre sans arrêt ▷ *n* (*pej: horse*) canasson *m*; (*person*): **she's an awful ~** elle est constamment après lui (*or* eux *etc*), elle est très casse-pieds

nagging ['nægɪŋ] *adj* (*doubt, pain*) persistant(e) ▷ *n* remarques continuelles

nail [neɪl] *n* (*human*) ongle *m*; (*metal*) clou *m* ▷ *vt* clouer; **to ~ sth to sth** clouer qch à qch; **to ~ sb down to a date/price** contraindre qn à accepter *or* donner une date/un prix; **to pay cash on the ~** (*Brit*) payer rubis sur l'ongle

nailbrush ['neɪlbrʌʃ] *n* brosse *f* à ongles

nailfile ['neɪlfaɪl] *n* lime *f* à ongles

nail polish *n* vernis *m* à ongles

nail polish remover *n* dissolvant *m*

nail scissors *npl* ciseaux *mpl* à ongles

nail varnish *n* (*Brit*) = **nail polish**

naïve [naɪ'i:v] *adj* naïf(-ïve)

naked ['neɪkɪd] *adj* nu(e); **with the ~ eye** à l'œil nu

name [neɪm] *n* nom *m*; (*reputation*) réputation *f* ▷ *vt* nommer; (*identify: accomplice etc*) citer; (*price, date*) fixer, donner; **by ~** par son nom; de nom; **in the ~ of** au nom de; **what's your ~?** comment vous appelez-vous?, quel est votre nom?; **my ~ is Peter** je m'appelle Peter; **to take sb's ~ and address** relever l'identité de qn *or* les nom et adresse de qn; **to make a ~ for o.s.** se faire un nom; **to get (o.s.) a bad ~** se faire une mauvaise réputation; **to call sb ~s** traiter qn de tous les noms

nameless ['neɪmlɪs] *adj* sans nom; (*witness, contributor*) anonyme

namely ['neɪmlɪ] *adv* à savoir

namesake ['neɪmseɪk] *n* homonyme *m*

nanny ['nænɪ] *n* bonne *f* d'enfants

nap [næp] *n* (*sleep*) (petit) somme ▷ *vi*: **to be caught ~ping** être pris(e) à l'improviste *or* en défaut

nape [neɪp] *n*: **~ of the neck** nuque *f*

napkin ['næpkɪn] *n* serviette *f* (de table)

nappy ['næpɪ] *n* (*Brit*) couche *f*

nappy rash *n*: **to have ~** avoir les fesses rouges

narcissus (*pl* **narcissi**) [nɑːˈsɪsəs, -saɪ] *n* narcisse *m*

narcotic [nɑːˈkɔtɪk] *n* (*Med*) narcotique *m*

narcotics [nɑːˈkɔtɪkz] *npl* (*illegal drugs*) stupéfiants *mpl*

narrative ['nærətɪv] *n* récit *m* ▷ *adj* narratif(-ive)

narrator [nəˈreɪtəʳ] *n* narrateur(-trice)

narrow ['nærəu] *adj* étroit(e); (*fig*) restreint(e), limité(e) ▷ *vi* (*road*) devenir plus étroit, se rétrécir; (*gap, difference*) se réduire; **to have a ~ escape** l'échapper belle; **narrow down** *vt* restreindre

narrowly ['nærəulɪ] *adv*: **he ~ missed injury/the tree** il a failli se blesser/rentrer dans l'arbre; **he only ~ missed the target** il a manqué la cible de peu *or* de justesse

narrow-minded [nærəuˈmaɪndɪd] *adj* à l'esprit étroit, borné(e); (*attitude*) borné(e)

nasal ['neɪzl] *adj* nasal(e)

nasty ['nɑːstɪ] *adj* (*person: malicious*) méchant(e); (: *rude*) très désagréable; (*smell*) dégoûtant(e); (*wound, situation*) mauvais(e), vilain(e); (*weather*) affreux(-euse); **to turn ~** (*situation*) mal tourner; (*weather*) se gâter; (*person*) devenir méchant; **it's a ~ business** c'est une sale affaire

nation ['neɪʃən] *n* nation *f*

national ['næʃənl] *adj* national(e) ▷ *n* (*abroad*) ressortissant(e); (*when home*) national(e)

national anthem *n* hymne national

national dress *n* costume national

National Health Service *n* (*Brit*) *service national de santé*, ≈ Sécurité Sociale

National Insurance *n* (*Brit*) ≈ Sécurité Sociale

nationalism ['næʃnəlɪzəm] *n* nationalisme *m*

nationalist ['næʃnəlɪst] *adj, n* nationaliste *m/f*

nationality [næʃəˈnælɪtɪ] *n* nationalité *f*

nationalize ['næʃnəlaɪz] *vt* nationaliser

nationally ['næʃnəlɪ] *adv* du point de vue national; dans le pays entier

national park *n* parc national

National Trust *n* (*Brit*) ≈ Caisse *f* nationale des monuments historiques et des sites; *voir article*

⟐ **NATIONAL TRUST**

⟐ Le *National Trust* est un organisme
⟐ indépendant, à but non lucratif, dont la
⟐ mission est de protéger et de mettre en
⟐ valeur les monuments et les sites
⟐ britanniques en raison de leur intérêt
⟐ historique ou de leur beauté naturelle.

nationwide ['neɪʃənwaɪd] *adj* s'étendant à l'ensemble du pays; (*problem*) à l'échelle du pays entier ▷ *adv* à travers *or* dans tout le pays

native ['neɪtɪv] *n* habitant(e) du pays, autochtone *m/f*; (*in colonies*) indigène *m/f* ▷ *adj* du pays, indigène; (*country*) natal(e); (*language*) maternel(le); (*ability*) inné(e); **a ~ of Russia** une personne originaire de Russie; **a ~ speaker of French** une personne de langue maternelle française

Native American *n* Indien(ne) d'Amérique ▷ *adj* amérindien(ne)

native speaker *n* locuteur natif; *see also* **native**

NATO ['neɪtəu] *n abbr* (= *North Atlantic Treaty Organization*) OTAN *f*

natural ['nætʃrəl] *adj* naturel(le); **to die of ~ causes** mourir d'une mort naturelle

natural gas *n* gaz naturel

natural history *n* histoire naturelle

naturalist ['nætʃrəlɪst] *n* naturaliste *m/f*

naturally ['nætʃrəlɪ] *adv* naturellement

natural resources *npl* ressources naturelles

nature ['neɪtʃəʳ] *n* nature; **by ~** par tempérament, de nature; **documents of a confidential ~** documents à caractère confidentiel

nature reserve *n* (*Brit*) réserve naturelle

naught [nɔːt] *n* = **nought**

naughty ['nɔːtɪ] *adj* (*child*) vilain(e), pas sage; (*story, film*) grivois(e)

nausea ['nɔːsɪə] *n* nausée *f*

naval ['neɪvl] *adj* naval(e)

naval officer *n* officier *m* de marine

nave [neɪv] *n* nef *f*

navel ['neɪvl] *n* nombril *m*

navigate ['nævɪgeɪt] *vt* (*steer*) diriger, piloter ▷ *vi* naviguer; (*Aut*) indiquer la route à suivre

navigation [nævɪˈgeɪʃən] *n* navigation *f*

navvy ['nævɪ] *n* (*Brit*) terrassier *m*

navy ['neɪvɪ] *n* marine *f*; **Department of the N~** (*US*) ministère *m* de la Marine

navy-blue ['neɪvɪ'bluː] *adj* bleu marine *inv*

Nazi ['nɑːtsɪ] *adj* nazi(e) ▷ *n* Nazi(e)

NB *abbr* (= *nota bene*) NB; (*Canada*) = **New Brunswick**

near [nɪəʳ] *adj* proche ▷ *adv* près ▷ *prep* (*also*: **~ to**) près de ▷ *vt* approcher de; **~ here/there** près d'ici/non loin de là; **£25,000 or ~est**

offer (Brit) 25 000 livres à débattre; **in the ~ future** dans un proche avenir; **to come ~** vi s'approcher

nearby ['nɪə'baɪ] adj proche ▷ adv tout près, à proximité

nearly ['nɪəlɪ] adv presque; **I ~ fell** j'ai failli tomber; **it's not ~ big enough** ce n'est vraiment pas assez grand, c'est loin d'être assez grand

near miss n collision évitée de justesse; (when aiming) coup manqué de peu or de justesse

nearside ['nɪəsaɪd] (Aut) n (right-hand drive) côté m gauche; (left-hand drive) côté droit ▷ adj de gauche; de droite

near-sighted [nɪə'saɪtɪd] adj myope

neat [niːt] adj (person, work) soigné(e); (room etc) bien tenu(e) or rangé(e); (solution, plan) habile; (spirits) pur(e); **I drink it ~** je le bois sec or sans eau

neatly ['niːtlɪ] adv avec soin or ordre; (skilfully) habilement

necessarily ['nesɪsrɪlɪ] adv nécessairement; **not ~** pas nécessairement or forcément

necessary ['nesɪsrɪ] adj nécessaire; **if ~** si besoin est, le cas échéant

necessity [nɪ'sesɪtɪ] n nécessité f; chose nécessaire or essentielle; **in case of ~** en cas d'urgence

neck [nɛk] n cou m; (of horse, garment) encolure f; (of bottle) goulot m ▷ vi (inf) se peloter; **~ and ~** à égalité; **to stick one's ~ out** (inf) se mouiller

necklace ['nɛklɪs] n collier m

neckline ['nɛklaɪn] n encolure f

necktie ['nɛktaɪ] n (esp US) cravate f

nectarine ['nɛktərɪn] n brugnon m, nectarine f

need [niːd] n besoin m ▷ vt avoir besoin de; **to ~ to do** devoir faire; avoir besoin de faire; **you don't ~ to go** vous n'avez pas besoin or vous n'êtes pas obligé de partir; **a signature is ~ed** il faut une signature; **to be in ~ of** or **have ~ of** avoir besoin de; **£10 will meet my immediate ~s** 10 livres suffiront pour mes besoins immédiats; **in case of ~** en cas de besoin, au besoin; **there's no ~ to do ....** il n'y a pas lieu de faire ..., il n'est pas nécessaire de faire ...; **there's no ~ for that** ce n'est pas la peine, cela n'est pas nécessaire

needle ['niːdl] n aiguille f; (on record player) saphir m ▷ vt (inf) asticoter, tourmenter

needless ['niːdlɪs] adj inutile; **~ to say, ...** inutile de dire que ...

needlework ['niːdlwəːk] n (activity) travaux mpl d'aiguille; (object) ouvrage m

needn't ['niːdnt] = **need not**

needy ['niːdɪ] adj nécessiteux(-euse)

negative ['nɛgətɪv] n (Phot, Elec) négatif m; (Ling) terme m de négation ▷ adj négatif(-ive); **to answer in the ~** répondre par la négative

neglect [nɪ'glɛkt] vt négliger; (garden) ne pas entretenir; (duty) manquer à ▷ n (of person, duty, garden) le fait de négliger; (state of) ~ abandon m; **to ~ to do sth** négliger or omettre de faire qch; **to ~ one's appearance** se négliger

neglected [nɪ'glɛktɪd] adj négligé(e), à l'abandon

negligee ['nɛglɪʒeɪ] n déshabillé m

negotiate [nɪ'gəʊʃɪeɪt] vi négocier ▷ vt négocier; (Comm) négocier; (obstacle) franchir, négocier; (bend in road) négocier; **to ~ with sb for sth** négocier avec qn en vue d'obtenir qch

negotiation [nɪgəʊʃɪ'eɪʃən] n négociation f, pourparlers mpl; **to enter into ~s with sb** engager des négociations avec qn

negotiator [nɪ'gəʊʃɪeɪtəʳ] n négociateur(-trice)

neigh [neɪ] vi hennir

neighbour, neighbor (US) ['neɪbəʳ] n voisin(e)

neighbourhood, neighborhood (US) ['neɪbəhud] n (place) quartier m; (people) voisinage m

neighbouring, neighboring (US) ['neɪbərɪŋ] adj voisin(e), avoisinant(e)

neighbourly, neighborly (US) ['neɪbəlɪ] adj obligeant(e); (relations) de bon voisinage

neither ['naɪðəʳ] adj, pron aucun(e) (des deux), ni l'un(e) ni l'autre ▷ conj: **~ do I** moi non plus; **I didn't move and ~ did Claude** je n'ai pas bougé, (et) Claude non plus ▷ adv: **~ good nor bad** ni bon ni mauvais; **~ did I refuse** (et or mais) je n'ai pas non plus refusé; **~ of them** ni l'un ni l'autre

neon ['niːɔn] n néon m

neon light n lampe f au néon

Nepal [nɪ'pɔːl] n Népal m

nephew ['nevjuː] n neveu m

nerve [nəːv] n nerf m; (bravery) sang-froid m, courage m; (cheek) aplomb m, toupet m; **nerves** npl (nervousness) nervosité f; **he gets on my ~s** il m'énerve; **to have a fit of ~s** avoir le trac; **to lose one's ~** (self-confidence) perdre son sang-froid

nerve-racking ['nəːvrækɪŋ] adj angoissant(e)

nervous ['nəːvəs] adj nerveux(-euse); (anxious) inquiet(-ète), plein(e) d'appréhension; (timid) intimidé(e)

nervous breakdown n dépression nerveuse

nest [nɛst] n nid m ▷ vi (se) nicher, faire son nid; **~ of tables** table f gigogne

nest egg n (fig) bas m de laine, magot m

nestle ['nɛsl] vi se blottir

Net [nɛt] n (Comput): **the ~** (Internet) le Net

net [nɛt] n filet m; (fabric) tulle f ▷ adj net(te) ▷ vt (fish etc) prendre au filet; (money: person) toucher; (: deal, sale) rapporter; **~ of tax** net d'impôt; **he earns £10,000 ~ per year** il gagne 10 000 livres net par an

netball ['nɛtbɔ:l] n netball m
Netherlands ['nɛðələndz] npl: **the ~** les Pays-Bas mpl
nett [nɛt] adj = **net**
netting ['nɛtɪŋ] n (for fence etc) treillis m, grillage m; (fabric) voile m
nettle ['nɛtl] n ortie f
network ['nɛtwə:k] n réseau m ▷ vt (Radio, TV) diffuser sur l'ensemble du réseau; (computers) interconnecter; **there's no ~ coverage here** (Tel) il n'y a pas de réseau ici
neurotic [njuə'rɔtɪk] adj, n névrosé(e)
neuter ['nju:təʳ] adj neutre ▷ n neutre m ▷ vt (cat etc) châtrer, couper
neutral ['nju:trəl] adj neutre ▷ n (Aut) point mort
neutralize ['nju:trəlaɪz] vt neutraliser
never ['nɛvəʳ] adv (ne ...) jamais; **I ~ went** je n'y suis pas allé; **I've ~ been to Spain** je ne suis jamais allé en Espagne; **~ again** plus jamais; **~ in my life** jamais de ma vie; see also **mind**
never-ending [nɛvər'ɛndɪŋ] adj interminable
nevertheless [nɛvəðə'lɛs] adv néanmoins, malgré tout
new [nju:] adj nouveau/nouvelle; (brand new) neuf/neuve; **as good as ~** comme neuf
New Age n New Age m
newbie ['nju:bɪ] n (beginner) newbie mf; (on forum) nouveau(-elle)
newborn ['nju:bɔ:n] adj nouveau-né(e)
newcomer ['nju:kʌməʳ] n nouveau venu/ nouvelle venue
new-fangled ['nju:fæŋgld] adj (pej) ultramoderne (et farfelu(e))
new-found ['nju:faund] adj de fraîche date; (friend) nouveau/nouvelle
newly ['nju:lɪ] adv nouvellement, récemment
newly-weds ['nju:lɪwɛdz] npl jeunes mariés mpl
news [nju:z] n nouvelle(s) f(pl); (Radio, TV) informations fpl, actualités fpl; **a piece of ~** une nouvelle; **good/bad ~** bonne/mauvaise nouvelle; **financial ~** (Press, Radio, TV) page financière
news agency n agence f de presse
newsagent ['nju:zeɪdʒənt] n (Brit) marchand m de journaux
newscaster ['nju:zkɑ:stəʳ] n (Radio, TV) présentateur(-trice)
news flash n flash m d'information
newsletter ['nju:zlɛtəʳ] n bulletin m
newspaper ['nju:zpeɪpəʳ] n journal m; **daily ~** quotidien m; **weekly ~** hebdomadaire m
newsprint ['nju:zprɪnt] n papier m (de) journal
newsreader ['nju:zri:dəʳ] n = **newscaster**
newsreel ['nju:zri:l] n actualités (filmées)
news stand n kiosque m à journaux
newt [nju:t] n triton m

New Year n Nouvel An; **Happy ~!** Bonne Année!; **to wish sb a happy ~** souhaiter la Bonne Année à qn
New Year's Day n le jour de l'An
New Year's Eve n la Saint-Sylvestre
New York [-'jɔ:k] n New York; (also: **~ State**) New York m
New Zealand [-'zi:lənd] n Nouvelle-Zélande f ▷ adj néo-zélandais(e)
New Zealander [-'zi:ləndəʳ] n Néo-Zélandais(e)
next [nɛkst] adj (in time) prochain(e); (seat, room) voisin(e), d'à côté; (meeting, bus stop) suivant(e) ▷ adv la fois suivante; la prochaine fois; (afterwards) ensuite; **~ to** prep à côté de; **~ to nothing** presque rien; **~ time** adv la prochaine fois; **the ~ day** le lendemain, le jour suivant or d'après; **~ week** la semaine prochaine; **the ~ week** la semaine suivante; **~ year** l'année prochaine; **"turn to the ~ page"** "voir page suivante"; **~ please!** (at doctor's etc) au suivant!; **who's ~?** c'est à qui?; **the week after ~** dans deux semaines; **when do we meet ~?** quand nous revoyons-nous?
next door adv à côté ▷ adj (neighbour) d'à côté
next-of-kin ['nɛkstəv'kɪn] n parent m le plus proche
NHS n abbr (Brit) = **National Health Service**
nib [nɪb] n (of pen) (bec m de) plume f
nibble ['nɪbl] vt grignoter
nice [naɪs] adj (holiday, trip, taste) agréable; (flat, picture) joli(e); (person) gentil(le); (distinction, point) subtil(e)
nicely ['naɪslɪ] adv agréablement; joliment; gentiment; subtilement; **that will do ~** ce sera parfait
niceties ['naɪsɪtɪz] npl subtilités fpl
niche [ni:ʃ] n (Archit) niche f
nick [nɪk] n (indentation) encoche f; (wound) entaille f; (Brit inf): **in good ~** en bon état ▷ vt (cut): **to ~ o.s.** se couper; (inf: steal) faucher, piquer; (: Brit: arrest) choper, pincer; **in the ~ of time** juste à temps
nickel ['nɪkl] n nickel m; (US) pièce f de 5 cents
nickname ['nɪkneɪm] n surnom m ▷ vt surnommer
nicotine ['nɪkəti:n] n nicotine f
nicotine patch n timbre m anti-tabac, patch m
niece [ni:s] n nièce f
Nigeria [naɪ'dʒɪərɪə] n Nigéria m or f
niggling ['nɪglɪŋ] adj tatillon(ne); (detail) insignifiant(e); (doubt, pain) persistant(e)
night [naɪt] n nuit f; (evening) soir m; **at ~** la nuit; **by ~** de nuit; **in the ~, during the ~** pendant la nuit; **last ~** (evening) hier soir; (night-time) la nuit dernière; **the ~ before last** avant-hier soir
nightcap ['naɪtkæp] n boisson prise avant le coucher
night club n boîte f de nuit

nightdress ['naɪtdrɛs] n chemise f de nuit

nightfall ['naɪtfɔːl] n tombée f de la nuit

nightie ['naɪtɪ] n chemise f de nuit

nightingale ['naɪtɪŋgeɪl] n rossignol m

nightlife ['naɪtlaɪf] n vie f nocturne

nightly ['naɪtlɪ] adj (news) du soir; (by night) nocturne ▷ adv (every evening) tous les soirs; (every night) toutes les nuits

nightmare ['naɪtmɛəʳ] n cauchemar m

night porter n gardien m de nuit, concierge m de service la nuit

night school n cours mpl du soir

night shift ['naɪtʃɪft] n équipe f de nuit

night-time ['naɪttaɪm] n nuit f

night watchman irreg n veilleur m de nuit; poste m de nuit

nil [nɪl] n rien m; (Brit Sport) zéro m

Nile [naɪl] n: **the ~** le Nil

nimble ['nɪmbl] adj agile

nine [naɪn] num neuf

nineteen [naɪn'tiːn] num dix-neuf

nineteenth [naɪn'tiːnθ] num dix-neuvième

ninetieth ['naɪntɪɪθ] num quatre-vingt-dixième

ninety ['naɪntɪ] num quatre-vingt-dix

ninth [naɪnθ] num neuvième

nip [nɪp] vt pincer ▷ vi (Brit inf): **to ~ out/down/up** sortir/descendre/monter en vitesse ▷ n pincement m; (drink) petit verre; **to ~ into a shop** faire un saut dans un magasin

nipple ['nɪpl] n (Anat) mamelon m, bout m du sein

nitrogen ['naɪtrədʒən] n azote m

 KEYWORD

no [nəʊ] (pl **noes**) adv (opposite of "yes") non; **are you coming? — no (I'm not)** est-ce que vous venez? — non; **would you like some more? — no thank you** vous en voulez encore? — non merci

▷ adj (not any) (ne ...) pas de, (ne ...) aucun(e); **I have no money/books** je n'ai pas d'argent/ de livres; **no student would have done it** aucun étudiant ne l'aurait fait; **"no smoking"** "défense de fumer"; **"no dogs"** "les chiens ne sont pas admis"

▷ n non m; **I won't take no for an answer** il n'est pas question de refuser

nobility [nəʊ'bɪlɪtɪ] n noblesse f

noble ['nəʊbl] adj noble

nobody ['nəʊbədɪ] pron (ne ...) personne

nod [nɔd] vi faire un signe de (la) tête (affirmatif ou amical); (sleep) somnoler ▷ vt: **to ~ one's head** faire un signe de (la) tête; (in agreement) faire signe que oui ▷ n signe m de (la) tête; **they ~ded their agreement** ils ont acquiescé d'un signe de la tête; **nod off** vi s'assoupir

noise [nɔɪz] n bruit m; **I can't sleep for the ~** je n'arrive pas à dormir à cause du bruit

noisy ['nɔɪzɪ] adj bruyant(e)

nominal ['nɔmɪnl] adj (rent, fee) symbolique; (value) nominal(e)

nominate ['nɔmɪneɪt] vt (propose) proposer; (appoint) nommer

nomination [nɔmɪ'neɪʃən] n nomination f

nominee [nɔmɪ'niː] n candidat agréé; personne nommée

non- [nɔn] prefix non-

nonalcoholic [nɔnælkə'hɔlɪk] adj non alcoolisé(e)

noncommittal [nɔnkə'mɪtl] adj évasif(-ive)

nondescript ['nɔndɪskrɪpt] adj quelconque, indéfinissable

none [nʌn] pron aucun(e); **~ of you** aucun d'entre vous, personne parmi vous; **I have ~ left** je n'en ai plus; **~ at all** (not one) aucun(e); **how much milk? — ~ at all** combien de lait? — pas du tout; **he's ~ the worse for it** il ne s'en porte pas plus mal

nonentity [nɔ'nɛntɪtɪ] n personne insignifiante

nonetheless ['nʌnðə'lɛs] adv néanmoins

nonexistent [nɔnɪg'zɪstənt] adj inexistant(e)

non-fiction [nɔn'fɪkʃən] n littérature f non romanesque

nonplussed [nɔn'plʌst] adj perplexe

nonsense ['nɔnsəns] n absurdités fpl, idioties fpl; **~! ne dites pas d'idioties!; it is ~ to say that ...** il est absurde de dire que ....

non-smoker ['nɔn'sməʊkəʳ] n non-fumeur m

non-smoking ['nɔn'sməʊkɪŋ] adj non-fumeur

non-stick ['nɔn'stɪk] adj qui n'attache pas

nonstop ['nɔn'stɔp] adj direct(e), sans arrêt (or escale) ▷ adv sans arrêt

noodles ['nuːdlz] npl nouilles fpl

nook [nuk] n: **~s and crannies** recoins mpl

noon [nuːn] n midi m

no-one ['nəʊwʌn] pron = **nobody**

noose [nuːs] n nœud coulant; (hangman's) corde f

nor [nɔːʳ] conj = **neither** ▷ adv see **neither**

norm [nɔːm] n norme f

normal ['nɔːml] adj normal(e) ▷ n: **to return to ~** redevenir normal(e)

normally ['nɔːməlɪ] adv normalement

Normandy ['nɔːməndɪ] n Normandie f

north [nɔːθ] n nord m ▷ adj nord inv; (wind) du nord ▷ adv au or vers le nord

North Africa n Afrique f du Nord

North African adj nord-africain(e), d'Afrique du Nord ▷ n Nord-Africain(e)

North America n Amérique f du Nord

North American n Nord-Américain(e) ▷ adj nord-américain(e), d'Amérique du Nord

northbound ['nɔːθbaʊnd] adj (traffic) en direction du nord; (carriageway) nord inv

north-east [nɔːθˈiːst] n nord-est m

northerly ['nɔːðəlɪ] adj (wind, direction) du nord

northern ['nɔːðən] adj du nord, septentrional(e)

Northern Ireland n Irlande f du Nord

North Korea n Corée f du Nord

North Pole n: the ~ le pôle Nord

North Sea n: the ~ la mer du Nord

northward ['nɔːθwəd], **northwards** ['nɔːθwədz] adv vers le nord

north-west [nɔːθˈwɛst] n nord-ouest m

Norway ['nɔːweɪ] n Norvège f

Norwegian [nɔːˈwiːdʒən] adj norvégien(ne) ▷ n Norvégien(ne); (Ling) norvégien m

nose [nəuz] n nez m; (of dog, cat) museau m; (fig) flair m ▷ vi (also: ~ one's way) avancer précautionneusement; **to pay through the ~ (for sth)** (inf) payer un prix excessif (pour qch); **nose about, nose around** vi fouiner or fureter (partout)

nosebleed ['nəuzbliːd] n saignement m de nez

nose-dive ['nəuzdaɪv] n (descente f en) piqué m

nosey ['nəuzɪ] adj (inf) curieux(-euse)

nostalgia [nɔsˈtældʒə] n nostalgie f

nostalgic [nɔsˈtældʒɪk] adj nostalgique

nostril ['nɔstrɪl] n narine f; (of horse) naseau m

nosy ['nəuzɪ] (inf) adj = **nosey**

not [nɔt] adv (ne ...) pas; **he is ~** or **isn't here** il n'est pas ici; **you must ~** or **mustn't do that** tu ne dois pas faire ça; **I hope ~** j'espère que non; **~ at all** pas du tout; (after thanks) de rien; **it's too late, isn't it?** c'est trop tard, n'est-ce pas?; **~ yet/now** pas encore/maintenant; see also **only**

notable ['nəutəbl] adj notable

notably ['nəutəblɪ] adv (particularly) en particulier; (markedly) spécialement

notary ['nəutərɪ] n (also: ~ public) notaire m

notch [nɔtʃ] n encoche f; **notch up** vt (score) marquer; (victory) remporter

note [nəut] n note f; (letter) mot m; (banknote) billet m ▷ vt (also: ~ down) noter; (notice) constater; **just a quick ~ to let you know ...** juste un mot pour vous dire ...; **to take ~s** prendre des notes; **to compare ~s** (fig) échanger des (or leurs etc) impressions; **to take ~ of** prendre note de; **a person of ~** une personne éminente

notebook ['nəutbuk] n carnet m; (for shorthand etc) bloc-notes m

noted ['nəutɪd] adj réputé(e)

notepad ['nəutpæd] n bloc-notes m

notepaper ['nəutpeɪpə'] n papier m à lettres

nothing ['nʌθɪŋ] n rien m; **he does ~** il ne fait rien; **~ new** rien de nouveau; **for ~** (free) pour rien, gratuitement; (in vain) pour rien; **~ at all** rien du tout; **~ much** pas grand-chose

notice ['nəutɪs] n (announcement, warning) avis m; (of leaving) congé m; (Brit: review: of play etc) critique f, compte rendu m ▷ vt

remarquer, s'apercevoir de; **without ~** sans préavis; **advance ~** préavis m; **to give sb ~ of sth** notifier qn de qch; **at short ~** dans un délai très court; **until further ~** jusqu'à nouvel ordre; **to give ~, hand in one's ~** (employee) donner sa démission, démissionner; **to take ~ of** prêter attention à; **to bring sth to sb's ~** porter qch à la connaissance de qn; **it has come to my ~ that ...** on m'a signalé que ...; **to escape** or **avoid ~** (essayer de) passer inaperçu or ne pas se faire remarquer

noticeable ['nəutɪsəbl] adj visible

notice board n (Brit) panneau m d'affichage

notify ['nəutɪfaɪ] vt: **to ~ sth to sb** notifier qch à qn; **to ~ sb of sth** avertir qn de qch

notion ['nəuʃən] n idée f; (concept) notion f; **notions** npl (US: haberdashery) mercerie f

notorious [nəuˈtɔːrɪəs] adj notoire (souvent en mal)

notwithstanding [nɔtwɪθˈstændɪŋ] adv néanmoins ▷ prep en dépit de

nought [nɔːt] n zéro m

noun [naun] n nom m

nourish ['nʌrɪʃ] vt nourrir

nourishing ['nʌrɪʃɪŋ] adj nourrissant(e)

nourishment ['nʌrɪʃmənt] n nourriture f

Nov. abbr (= November) nov

novel ['nɔvl] n roman m ▷ adj nouveau/ nouvelle, original(e)

novelist ['nɔvəlɪst] n romancier m

novelty ['nɔvəltɪ] n nouveauté f

November [nəuˈvɛmbə'] n novembre m; see also **July**

novice ['nɔvɪs] n novice m/f

now [nau] adv maintenant ▷ conj: **~ (that)** maintenant (que); **right ~** tout de suite; **by ~** à l'heure qu'il est; **just ~**: **that's the fashion just now** c'est la mode en ce moment or maintenant; **I saw her just ~** je viens de la voir, je l'ai vue à l'instant; **I'll read it just ~** je vais le lire à l'instant or dès maintenant; **~ and then, ~ and again** de temps en temps; **from ~ on** dorénavant; **in 3 days from ~** dans or d'ici trois jours; **between ~ and Monday** d'ici (à) lundi; **that's all for ~** c'est tout pour l'instant

nowadays ['nauədeɪz] adv de nos jours

nowhere ['nəuwɛə'] adv (ne ...) nulle part; **~ else** nulle part ailleurs

nozzle ['nɔzl] n (of hose) jet m, lance f; (of vacuum cleaner) suceur m

nr abbr (Brit) = **near**

nuclear ['njuːklɪə'] adj nucléaire

nucleus (pl **nuclei**) ['njuːklɪəs, 'njuːklɪaɪ] n noyau m

nude [njuːd] adj nu(e) ▷ n (Art) nu m; **in the ~** (tout(e)) nu(e)

nudge [nʌdʒ] vt donner un (petit) coup de coude à

nudist ['njuːdɪst] n nudiste m/f

nudity ['njuːdɪtɪ] n nudité f

nuisance ['nju:sns] *n*: **it's a ~** c'est (très) ennuyeux *or* gênant; **he's a ~** il est assommant *or* casse-pieds; **what a ~!** quelle barbe!

null [nʌl] *adj*: **~ and void** nul(le) et non avenu(e)

numb [nʌm] *adj* engourdi(e); *(with fear)* paralysé(e) ▷ *vt* engourdir; **~ with cold** engourdi(e) par le froid, transi(e) (de froid); **~ with fear** transi de peur, paralysé(e) par la peur

number ['nʌmbəʳ] *n* nombre *m*; *(numeral)* chiffre *m*; *(of house, car, telephone, newspaper)* numéro *m* ▷ *vt* numéroter; *(amount to)* compter; **a ~ of** un certain nombre de; **they were seven in ~** ils étaient (au nombre de) sept; **to be ~ed among** compter parmi; **the staff ~s 20** le nombre d'employés s'élève à *or* est de 20; **wrong ~** *(Tel)* mauvais numéro

number plate *n* (Brit Aut) plaque *f* minéralogique *or* d'immatriculation

Number Ten *n* (Brit: 10 Downing Street) *résidence du Premier ministre*

numeral ['nju:mərəl] *n* chiffre *m*

numerate ['nju:mərɪt] *adj* (Brit): **to be ~** avoir des notions d'arithmétique

numerical [nju:'mɛrɪkl] *adj* numérique

numerous ['nju:mərəs] *adj* nombreux(-euse)

nun [nʌn] *n* religieuse *f*, sœur *f*

nurse [nə:s] *n* infirmière *f*; *(also:* **~maid**) bonne *f* d'enfants ▷ *vt* (patient, cold) soigner; (baby: Brit) bercer (dans ses bras); (: US) allaiter, nourrir; (hope) nourrir

nursery ['nə:sərɪ] *n* (room) nursery *f*; (institution) crèche *f*, garderie *f*; (for plants) pépinière *f*

nursery rhyme *n* comptine *f*, chansonnette *f* pour enfants

nursery school *n* école maternelle

nursery slope *n* (Brit Ski) piste *f* pour débutants

nursing ['nə:sɪŋ] *n* (profession) profession *f* d'infirmière; (care) soins *mpl* ▷ *adj* (mother) qui allaite

nursing home *n* clinique *f*; (for convalescence) maison *f* de convalescence *or* de repos; (for old people) maison de retraite

nurture ['nə:tʃəʳ] *vt* élever

nut [nʌt] *n* (of metal) écrou *m*; (fruit: walnut) noix *f*; (: hazelnut) noisette *f*; (: peanut) cacahuète *f* (terme générique en anglais) ▷ *adj* (chocolate etc) aux noisettes; **he's ~s** (inf) il est dingue

nutcrackers ['nʌtkrækəz] *npl* casse-noix *m inv*, casse-noisette(s) *m*

nutmeg ['nʌtmɛg] *n* (noix *f*) muscade *f*

nutrient ['nju:trɪənt] *adj* nutritif(-ive) ▷ *n* substance nutritive

nutrition [nju:'trɪʃən] *n* nutrition *f*, alimentation *f*

nutritious [nju:'trɪʃəs] *adj* nutritif(-ive), nourrissant(e)

nuts [nʌts] (inf) *adj* dingue

nutshell ['nʌtʃɛl] *n* coquille *f* de noix; **in a ~** en un mot

nutter ['nʌtəʳ] (Brit: inf) *n*: **he's a complete ~** il est complètement cinglé

NVQ *n abbr* (Brit) = **National Vocational Qualification**

nylon ['naɪlɔn] *n* nylon *m* ▷ *adj* de *or* en nylon; **nylons** *npl* bas *mpl* nylon

n

O

oak [əuk] *n* chêne *m* ▷ *cpd* de or en (bois de) chêne
O.A.P. *n abbr* (*Brit*) = **old age pensioner**
oar [ɔːʳ] *n* aviron *m*, rame *f*; **to put** or **shove one's ~ in** (*fig: inf*) mettre son grain de sel
oasis (*pl* **oases**) [əuˈeɪsɪs, əuˈeɪsiːz] *n* oasis *f*
oath [əuθ] *n* serment *m*; (*swear word*) juron *m*; **to take the ~** prêter serment; **on** (*Brit*) or **under ~** sous serment; assermenté(e)
oatmeal [ˈəutmiːl] *n* flocons *mpl* d'avoine
oats [əuts] *n* avoine *f*
obedience [əˈbiːdɪəns] *n* obéissance *f*; **in ~ to** conformément à
obedient [əˈbiːdɪənt] *adj* obéissant(e); **to be ~ to sb/sth** obéir à qn/qch
obese [əuˈbiːs] *adj* obèse
obesity [əuˈbiːsɪtɪ] *n* obésité *f*
obey [əˈbeɪ] *vt* obéir à; (*instructions, regulations*) se conformer à ▷ *vi* obéir
obituary [əˈbɪtjuərɪ] *n* nécrologie *f*
object *n* [ˈɔbdʒɪkt] objet *m*; (*purpose*) but *m*, objet; (*Ling*) complément *m* d'objet ▷ *vi* [əbˈdʒɛkt]: **to ~ to** (*attitude*) désapprouver; (*proposal*) protester contre, élever une objection contre; **I ~!** je proteste!; **he ~ed that ...** il a fait valoir or a objecté que ...; **do you ~ to my smoking?** est-ce que cela vous gêne si je fume?; **what's the ~ of doing that?** quel est l'intérêt de faire cela?; **money is no ~** l'argent n'est pas un problème
objection [əbˈdʒɛkʃən] *n* objection *f*; (*drawback*) inconvénient *m*; **if you have no ~**

si vous n'y voyez pas d'inconvénient; **to make** or **raise an ~** élever une objection
objectionable [əbˈdʒɛkʃənəbl] *adj* très désagréable; choquant(e)
objective [əbˈdʒɛktɪv] *n* objectif *m* ▷ *adj* objectif(-ive)
obligation [ɔblɪˈɡeɪʃən] *n* obligation *f*, devoir *m*; (*debt*) dette *f* (de reconnaissance); **"without ~"** "sans engagement"
obligatory [əˈblɪɡətərɪ] *adj* obligatoire
oblige [əˈblaɪdʒ] *vt* (*force*): **to ~ sb to do** obliger or forcer qn à faire; (*do a favour*) rendre service à, obliger; **to be ~d to sb for sth** être obligé(e) à qn de qch; **anything to ~!** (*inf*) (toujours prêt à rendre) service!
obliging [əˈblaɪdʒɪŋ] *adj* obligeant(e), serviable
oblique [əˈbliːk] *adj* oblique; (*allusion*) indirect(e) ▷ *n* (*Brit Typ*): **~ (stroke)** barre *f* oblique
obliterate [əˈblɪtəreɪt] *vt* effacer
oblivion [əˈblɪvɪən] *n* oubli *m* ~
oblivious [əˈblɪvɪəs] *adj*: **~ of** oublieux(-euse) de
oblong [ˈɔblɔŋ] *adj* oblong(ue) ▷ *n* rectangle *m*
obnoxious [əbˈnɔkʃəs] *adj* odieux(-euse); (*smell*) nauséabond(e)
oboe [ˈəubəu] *n* hautbois *m*
obscene [əbˈsiːn] *adj* obscène
obscure [əbˈskjuəʳ] *adj* obscur(e) ▷ *vt* obscurcir; (*hide: sun*) cacher
observant [əbˈzəːvnt] *adj* observateur(-trice)
observation [ɔbzəˈveɪʃən] *n* observation *f*; (*by police etc*) surveillance *f*
observatory [əbˈzəːvətrɪ] *n* observatoire *m*
observe [əbˈzəːv] *vt* observer; (*remark*) faire observer or remarquer
observer [əbˈzəːvəʳ] *n* observateur(-trice)
obsess [əbˈsɛs] *vt* obséder; **to be ~ed by** or **with sb/sth** être obsédé(e) par qn/qch
obsession [əbˈsɛʃən] *n* obsession *f*
obsessive [əbˈsɛsɪv] *adj* obsédant(e)
obsolete [ˈɔbsəliːt] *adj* dépassé(e), périmé(e)
obstacle [ˈɔbstəkl] *n* obstacle *m*
obstacle race *n* course *f* d'obstacles
obstinate [ˈɔbstɪnɪt] *adj* obstiné(e); (*pain, cold*) persistant(e)
obstruct [əbˈstrʌkt] *vt* (*block*) boucher, obstruer; (*halt*) arrêter; (*hinder*) entraver
obstruction [əbˈstrʌkʃən] *n* obstruction *f*; (*to plan, progress*) obstacle *m*
obtain [əbˈteɪn] *vt* obtenir ▷ *vi* avoir cours
obvious [ˈɔbvɪəs] *adj* évident(e), manifeste
obviously [ˈɔbvɪəslɪ] *adv* manifestement; (*of course*): **~, he ...** or **he ~ ...** il est bien évident qu'il ...; **~!** bien sûr!; **~ not!** évidemment pas!, bien sûr que non!
occasion [əˈkeɪʒən] *n* occasion *f*; (*event*) événement *m* ▷ *vt* occasionner, causer; **on that ~** à cette occasion; **to rise to the ~** se montrer à la hauteur de la situation

occasional [ə'keɪʒənl] *adj* pris(e) (*or* fait(e) *etc*) de temps en temps; (*worker, spending*) occasionnel(le)

occasionally [ə'keɪʒənəlɪ] *adv* de temps en temps, quelquefois; **very ~** (*assez*) rarement

occult [ɔ'kʌlt] *adj* occulte ⊳ *n*: **the ~** le surnaturel

occupant ['ɔkjupənt] *n* occupant *m*

occupation [ɔkju'peɪʃən] *n* occupation *f*; (*job*) métier *m*, profession *f*; **unfit for ~** (*house*) impropre à l'habitation

occupational hazard *n* risque *m* du métier

occupier ['ɔkjupaɪə'] *n* occupant(e)

occupy ['ɔkjupaɪ] *vt* occuper; **to ~ o.s. with** *or* **by doing** s'occuper à faire; **to be occupied with sth** être occupé avec qch

occur [ə'kə:'] *vi* se produire; (*difficulty, opportunity*) se présenter; (*phenomenon, error*) se rencontrer; **to ~ to sb** venir à l'esprit de qn

occurrence [ə'kʌrəns] *n* (*existence*) présence *f*, existence *f*; (*event*) cas *m*, fait *m*

ocean ['əuʃən] *n* océan *m*; **~s of** (*inf*) des masses de

o'clock [ə'klɔk] *adv*: **it is 5 ~** il est 5 heures

OCR *n abbr* = **optical character reader; optical character recognition**

Oct. *abbr* (= **October**) oct

October [ɔk'təubə'] *n* octobre *m*; *see also* **July**

octopus ['ɔktəpəs] *n* pieuvre *f*

odd [ɔd] *adj* (*strange*) bizarre, curieux(-euse); (*number*) impair(e); (*left over*) qui reste, en plus; (*not of a set*) dépareillé(e); **60 ~** 60 et quelques; **at ~ times** de temps en temps; **the ~ one out** l'exception *f*

oddity ['ɔdɪtɪ] *n* bizarrerie *f*; (*person*) excentrique *m/f*

odd-job man [ɔd'dʒɔb-] *irreg n* homme *m* à tout faire

odd jobs *npl* petits travaux divers

oddly ['ɔdlɪ] *adv* bizarrement, curieusement

oddments ['ɔdmənts] *npl* (*Brit Comm*) fins *fpl* de série

odds [ɔdz] *npl* (*in betting*) cote *f*; **the ~ are against his coming** il y a peu de chances qu'il vienne; **it makes no ~** cela n'a pas d'importance; **to succeed against all the ~** réussir contre toute attente; **~ and ends** de petites choses; **at ~** en désaccord

odometer [ɔ'dɔmɪtə'] *n* (*US*) odomètre *m*

odour, **odor** (*US*) ['əudə'] *n* odeur *f*

⊙ **KEYWORD**

of [ɔv, əv] *prep* **1** (*gen*) de; **a friend of ours** un de nos amis; **a boy of 10** un garçon de 10 ans; **that was kind of you** c'était gentil de votre part

2 (*expressing quantity, amount, dates etc*) de; **a kilo of flour** un kilo de farine; **how much of this do you need?** combien vous en faut-il?; **there were three of them** (*people*) ils étaient 3; (*objects*) il y en avait 3; **three of us went**

3 d'entre nous y sont allé(e)s; **the 5th of July** le 5 juillet; **a quarter of 4** (*US*) 4 heures moins le quart

3 (*from, out of*) en, de; **a statue of marble** une statue de *or* en marbre; **made of wood** (fait) en bois

off [ɔf] *adj, adv* (*engine*) coupé(e); (*light, TV*) éteint(e); (*tap*) fermé(e); (*Brit: food*) mauvais(e), avancé(e); (*: milk*) tourné(e); (*absent*) absent(e); (*cancelled*) annulé(e); (*removed*): **the lid was ~** le couvercle était retiré *or* n'était pas mis; (*away*): **to run/drive ~** partir en courant/en voiture ⊳ *prep* de; **to be ~** (*to leave*) partir, s'en aller; **I must be ~** il faut que je file; **to be ~ sick** être absent pour cause de maladie; **a day ~** un jour de congé; **to have an ~ day** n'être pas en forme; **he had his coat ~** il avait enlevé son manteau; **the hook is ~** le crochet s'est détaché; le crochet n'est pas mis; **10% ~** (*Comm*) 10% de rabais; **5 km ~ (the road)** à 5 km (de la route); **~ the coast** au large de la côte; **a house ~ the main road** une maison à l'écart de la grand-route; **it's a long way ~** c'est loin (d'ici); **I'm ~ meat** je ne mange plus de viande; je n'aime plus la viande; **on the ~ chance** à tout hasard; **to be well/badly ~** être bien/mal loti; (*financially*) être aisé/dans la gêne; **~ and on, on and ~** de temps à autre; **I'm afraid the chicken is ~** (*Brit: not available*) je regrette, il n'y a plus de poulet; **that's a bit ~** (*fig: inf*) c'est un peu fort

offal ['ɔfl] *n* (*Culin*) abats *mpl*

off-colour ['ɔf'kʌlə'] *adj* (*Brit: ill*) malade, mal fichu(e); **to feel ~** être mal fichu

offence, (*US*) **offense** [ə'fens] *n* (*crime*) délit *m*, infraction *f*; **to give ~ to** blesser, offenser; **to take ~ at** se vexer de, s'offenser de; **to commit an ~** commettre une infraction

offend [ə'fend] *vt* (*person*) offenser, blesser ⊳ *vi*: **to ~ against** (*law, rule*) contrevenir à, enfreindre

offender [ə'fendə'] *n* délinquant(e); (*against regulations*) contrevenant(e)

offense [ə'fens] *n* (*US*) = **offence**

offensive [ə'fensɪv] *adj* offensant(e), choquant(e); (*smell etc*) très déplaisant(e); (*weapon*) offensif(-ive) ⊳ *n* (*Mil*) offensive *f*

offer ['ɔfə'] *n* offre *f*, proposition *f* ⊳ *vt* offrir, proposer; **to make an ~ for sth** faire une offre pour qch; **to ~ sth to sb, ~ sb sth** offrir qch à qn; **to ~ to do sth** proposer de faire qch; **"on ~"** (*Comm*) "en promotion"

offering ['ɔfərɪŋ] *n* offrande *f*

offhand [ɔf'hænd] *adj* désinvolte ⊳ *adv* spontanément; **I can't tell you ~** je ne peux pas vous le dire comme ça

office ['ɔfɪs] *n* (*place*) bureau *m*; (*position*) charge *f*, fonction *f*; **doctor's ~** (*US*) cabinet (médical); **to take ~** entrer en fonctions; **through his good ~s** (*fig*) grâce à ses bons

o

offices; **O~ of Fair Trading** (Brit) organisme de protection contre les pratiques commerciales abusives
office automation n bureautique f
office block, (US) **office building** n immeuble m de bureaux
office hours npl heures fpl de bureau; (US Med) heures de consultation
officer ['ɔfɪsəʳ] n (Mil etc) officier m; (also: **police ~**) agent m (de police); (of organization) membre m du bureau directeur
office worker n employé(e) de bureau
official [ə'fɪʃl] adj (authorized) officiel(le) ▷ n officiel m; (civil servant) fonctionnaire m/f; (of railways, post office, town hall) employé(e)
officiate [ə'fɪʃɪeɪt] vi (Rel) officier; **to ~ as Mayor** exercer les fonctions de maire; **to ~ at a marriage** célébrer un mariage
officious [ə'fɪʃəs] adj trop empressé(e)
offing ['ɔfɪŋ] n: **in the ~** (fig) en perspective
off-licence ['ɔflaɪsns] n (Brit: shop) débit m de vins et de spiritueux
off-line [ɔf'laɪn] adj (Comput) (en mode) autonome; (: switched off) non connecté(e)
off-peak [ɔf'piːk] adj aux heures creuses; (electricity, ticket) au tarif heures creuses
off-putting ['ɔfputɪŋ] adj (Brit: remark) rébarbatif(-ive); (person) rebutant(e), peu engageant(e)
off-road vehicle ['ɔfrəud-] n véhicule m tout-terrain
off-season ['ɔf'siːzn] adj, adv hors-saison inv
offset ['ɔfset] vt (irreg like: **set**) (counteract) contrebalancer, compenser ▷ n (also: **~ printing**) offset m
offshoot ['ɔfʃuːt] n (fig) ramification f, antenne f; (: of discussion etc) conséquence f
offshore [ɔf'ʃɔːʳ] adj (breeze) de terre; (island) proche du littoral; (fishing) côtier(-ière); **~ oilfield** gisement m pétrolifère en mer
offside ['ɔf'saɪd] n (Aut: with right-hand drive) côté droit; (: with left-hand drive) côté gauche ▷ adj (Sport) hors jeu; (Aut: in Britain) de droite; (: in US, Europe) de gauche
offspring ['ɔfsprɪŋ] n progéniture f
offstage [ɔf'steɪdʒ] adv dans les coulisses
off-the-peg ['ɔfðə'peg], (US) **off-the-rack** ['ɔfðə'ræk] adv en prêt-à-porter
off-white ['ɔfwaɪt] adj blanc cassé inv
often ['ɔfn] adv souvent; **how ~ do you go?** vous y allez tous les combien?; **every so ~** de temps en temps, de temps à autre; **as ~ as not** la plupart du temps
Ofwat ['ɔfwɔt] n abbr (Brit: = Office of Water Services) organisme qui surveille les activités des compagnies des eaux
oh [əu] excl ô!, oh!, ah!
oil [ɔɪl] n huile f; (petroleum) pétrole m; (for central heating) mazout m ▷ vt (machine) graisser
oilcan ['ɔɪlkæn] n burette f de graissage; (for storing) bidon m à huile

oilfield ['ɔɪlfiːld] n gisement m de pétrole
oil filter n (Aut) filtre m à huile
oil painting n peinture f à l'huile
oil refinery n raffinerie f de pétrole
oil rig n derrick m; (at sea) plate-forme pétrolière
oil slick n nappe f de mazout
oil tanker n (ship) pétrolier m; (truck) camion-citerne m
oil well n puits m de pétrole
oily ['ɔɪlɪ] adj huileux(-euse); (food) gras(se)
ointment ['ɔɪntmənt] n onguent m
O.K., okay ['əu'keɪ] (inf) excl d'accord! ▷ vt approuver, donner son accord à ▷ n: **to give sth one's ~** donner son accord à qch ▷ adj (not bad) pas mal, en règle; en bon état; sain et sauf; acceptable; **is it ~?, are you ~?** ça va?; **are you ~ for money?** ça va or ira question argent?; **it's ~ with** or **by me** ça me va, c'est d'accord en ce qui me concerne
old [əuld] adj vieux/vieille; (person) vieux, âgé(e); (former) ancien(ne), vieux; **how ~ are you?** quel âge avez-vous?; **he's 10 ~: to** **years ~** il a 10 ans, il est âgé de 10 ans; **~er brother/sister** frère/sœur aîné(e); **any ~ thing will do** n'importe quoi fera l'affaire
old age n vieillesse f
old-age pensioner n (Brit) retraité(e)
old-fashioned ['əuld'fæʃnd] adj démodé(e); (person) vieux jeu inv
old people's home n (esp Brit) maison f de retraite
olive ['ɔlɪv] n (fruit) olive f; (tree) olivier m ▷ adj (also: **~-green**) (vert) olive inv
olive oil n huile f d'olive
Olympic [əu'lɪmpɪk] adj olympique; **the ~ Games, the ~s** les Jeux mpl olympiques
omelette, omelet ['ɔmlɪt] n omelette f; **ham/cheese omelet(te)** omelette au jambon/fromage
omen ['əumən] n présage m
ominous ['ɔmɪnəs] adj menaçant(e), inquiétant(e); (event) de mauvais augure
omit [əu'mɪt] vt omettre; **to ~ to do sth** négliger de faire qch

---

KEYWORD

on [ɔn] prep **1** (indicating position) sur; **on the table** sur la table; **on the wall** sur le or au mur; **on the left** à gauche; **I haven't any money on me** je n'ai pas d'argent sur moi
2 (indicating means, method, condition etc): **on foot** à pied; **on the train/plane** (be) dans le train/l'avion; (go) en train/avion; **on the telephone/radio/television** au téléphone/à la radio/à la télévision; **to be on drugs** se droguer; **on holiday**, Brit **on vacation** (US) en vacances; **on the continent** sur le continent
3 (referring to time): **on Friday** vendredi; **on Fridays** le vendredi; **on June 20th** le 20 juin; **a week on Friday** vendredi en huit; **on arrival**

à l'arrivée; **on seeing this** en voyant cela
4 (about, concerning) sur, de; **a book on Balzac/physics** un livre sur Balzac/de physique
5 (at the expense of): **this round is on me** c'est ma tournée
▷ adv **1** (referring to dress): **to have one's coat on** avoir (mis) son manteau; **to put one's coat on** mettre son manteau; **what's she got on?** qu'est-ce qu'elle porte?
2 (referring to covering): **screw the lid on tightly** vissez bien le couvercle
3 (further, continuously): **to walk** etc **on** continuer à marcher etc; **on and off** de temps à autre; **from that day on** depuis ce jour
▷ adj **1** (in operation: machine) en marche; (: radio, TV, light) allumé(e); (: tap, gas) ouvert(e); (: brakes) mis(e); **is the meeting still on?** (not cancelled) est-ce que la réunion a bien lieu?; **it was well on in the evening** c'était tard dans la soirée; **when is this film on?** quand passe ce film?
2 (inf): **that's not on!** (not acceptable) cela ne se fait pas!; (not possible) pas question!

once [wʌns] adv une fois; (formerly) autrefois
▷ conj une fois que + sub; **I've had left/it was done** une fois qu'il fut parti/ que ce fut terminé; **at** ~ tout de suite, immédiatement; (simultaneously) à la fois; **all at** ~ adv tout d'un coup; **a week** une fois par semaine; **more** encore une fois; **I knew him** ~ je l'ai connu autrefois; **and for all** une fois pour toutes; **upon a time there was …** il y avait une fois …, il était une fois …

oncoming ['ɒnkʌmɪŋ] adj (traffic) venant en sens inverse

one [wʌn] num un(e); **one hundred and fifty** cent cinquante; **one by one** un(e) à or par un(e); **one day** un jour
▷ adj **1** (sole) seul(e), unique; **the one book which** l'unique or le seul livre qui; **the one man who** le seul (homme) qui
2 (same) même; **they came in the one car** ils sont venus dans la même voiture
▷ pron **1**: **this one** celui-ci/celle-ci; **that one** celui-là/celle-là; **I've already got one/a red one** j'en ai déjà un(e)/un(e) rouge; **which one do you want?** lequel voulez-vous?
2: **one another** l'un(e) l'autre; **to look at one another** se regarder
3 (impersonal) on; **one never knows** on ne sait jamais; **to cut one's finger** se couper le doigt; **one needs to eat** il faut manger
4 (phrases): **to be one up on sb** avoir l'avantage sur qn; **to be at one (with sb)** être d'accord (avec qn)

one-day excursion ['wʌndeɪ-] n (US) billet m d'aller-retour (valable pour la journée)

one-man ['wʌn'mæn] adj (business) dirigé(e) etc par un seul homme

one-man band n homme-orchestre m

one-off [wʌn'ɒf] n (Brit inf) exemplaire m unique ▷ adj unique

oneself [wʌn'sɛlf] pron se; (after prep, also emphatic) soi-même; **to hurt** ~ se faire mal; **to keep sth for** ~ garder qch pour soi; **to talk to** ~ se parler à soi-même; **by** ~ tout seul

one-shot [wʌn'ʃɒt] (US) n = **one-off**

one-sided [wʌn'saɪdɪd] adj (argument, decision) unilatéral(e); (judgment, account) partial(e); (contest) inégal(e)

one-to-one ['wʌntəwʌn] adj (relationship) univoque

one-way ['wʌnweɪ] adj (street, traffic) à sens unique

ongoing ['ɒngəʊɪŋ] adj en cours; (relationship) suivi(e)

onion ['ʌnjən] n oignon m

on-line ['ɒnlaɪn] adj (Comput) en ligne; (: switched on) connecté(e)

onlooker ['ɒnlʊkər] n spectateur(-trice)

only ['əʊnlɪ] adv seulement ▷ adj seul(e), unique ▷ conj seulement, mais; **an** ~ **child** un enfant unique; **not** ~ … **but also** non seulement … mais aussi; **I** ~ **took one** j'en ai seulement pris un, je n'en ai pris qu'un; **I saw her** ~ **yesterday** je l'ai vue hier encore; **I'd be** ~ **too pleased to help** je ne serais que trop content de vous aider; **I would come,** ~ **I'm very busy** je viendrais bien mais j'ai beaucoup à faire

on-screen [ɒn'skriːn] adj à l'écran

onset ['ɒnsɛt] n début m; (of winter, old age) approche f

onshore ['ɒnʃɔːr] adj (wind) du large

onslaught ['ɒnslɔːt] n attaque f, assaut m

onto ['ɒntu] prep = **on to**

onward ['ɒnwəd], **onwards** ['ɒnwədz] adv (move) en avant; **from that time** ~**s** à partir de ce moment

oops [ups] excl houp!; ~**-a-daisy!** houp-là!

ooze [uːz] vi suinter

opaque [əʊ'peɪk] adj opaque

OPEC ['əʊpɛk] n abbr (= Organization of Petroleum-Exporting Countries) OPEP f

open ['əʊpn] adj ouvert(e); (car) découvert(e); (road, view) dégagé(e); (meeting) public(-ique); (admiration) manifeste; (question) non résolu(e); (enemy) déclaré(e) ▷ vt ouvrir ▷ vi (flower, eyes, door, debate) s'ouvrir; (shop, bank, museum) ouvrir; (book etc: commence) commencer, débuter; **is it** ~ **public?** est-ce ouvert au public?; **what time do you** ~? à quelle heure ouvrez-vous?; **in the** ~ **(air)** en plein air; **the** ~ **sea** le large; ~ **ground** (among trees) clairière f; (waste ground) terrain m vague; **to have an** ~ **mind (on sth)** avoir l'esprit ouvert (sur qch); **open on to** vt fus (room, door) donner sur; **open out** vt ouvrir ▷ vi s'ouvrir; **open up** vt ouvrir; (blocked road) dégager ▷ vi s'ouvrir

open-air [əupnˈɛəʳ] *adj* en plein air
opening [ˈəupnɪŋ] *n* ouverture *f*; *(opportunity)* occasion *f*; *(work)* débouché *m*; *(job)* poste vacant
opening hours *npl* heures *fpl* d'ouverture
open learning *n* enseignement universitaire à la carte, notamment par correspondance; *(distance learning)* télé-enseignement *m*
openly [ˈəupnlɪ] *adv* ouvertement
open-minded [əupnˈmaɪndɪd] *adj* à l'esprit ouvert
open-necked [ˈəupnnɛkt] *adj* à col ouvert
open-plan [ˈəupnˈplæn] *adj* sans cloisons
Open University *n* (Brit) *cours universitaires par correspondance; voir article*

> ● **OPEN UNIVERSITY**
>
> ● L'*Open University* a été fondée en 1969.
> ● L'enseignement comprend des cours
> ● (certaines plages horaires sont réservées
> ● à cet effet à la télévision et à la radio), des
> ● devoirs qui sont envoyés par l'étudiant à
> ● son directeur ou sa directrice d'études, et
> ● un séjour obligatoire en université d'été.
> ● Il faut préparer un certain nombre
> ● d'unités de valeur pendant une période
> ● de temps déterminée et obtenir la
> ● moyenne à un certain nombre d'entre
> ● elles pour recevoir le diplôme visé.

opera [ˈɔpərə] *n* opéra *m*
opera house *n* opéra *m*
opera singer *n* chanteur(-euse) d'opéra
operate [ˈɔpəreɪt] *vt* (machine) faire marcher, faire fonctionner; *(system)* pratiquer ▷ *vi* fonctionner; *(drug)* faire effet; **to ~ on sb (for)** *(Med)* opérer qn (de)
operatic [ɔpəˈrætɪk] *adj* d'opéra
operating [ˈɔpəreɪtɪŋ] *adj* (Comm: costs, profit) d'exploitation; *(Med)*: **~ table** table *f* d'opération
operating room *n* (US: Med) salle *f* d'opération
operating theatre *n* (Brit: Med) salle *f* d'opération
operation [ɔpəˈreɪʃən] *n* opération *f*; *(of machine)* fonctionnement *m*; **to have an ~ (for)** se faire opérer (de); **to be in ~** (machine) être en service; *(system)* être en vigueur
operational [ɔpəˈreɪʃənl] *adj* opérationnel(le); *(ready for use)* en état de marche; **when the service is fully ~** lorsque le service fonctionnera pleinement
operative [ˈɔpərətɪv] *adj* (measure) en vigueur ▷ *n* (in factory) ouvrier(-ière); **the ~ word** le mot clef
operator [ˈɔpəreɪtəʳ] *n* (of machine) opérateur(-trice); *(Tel)* téléphoniste *m/f*
opinion [əˈpɪnjən] *n* opinion *f*, avis *m*; **in my ~** à mon avis; **to seek a second ~** demander un deuxième avis

opinionated [əˈpɪnjəneɪtɪd] *adj* aux idées bien arrêtées
opinion poll *n* sondage *m* d'opinion
opponent [əˈpəunənt] *n* adversaire *m/f*
opportunity [ɔpəˈtjuːnɪtɪ] *n* occasion *f*; **to take the ~ to do** *or* **of doing** profiter de l'occasion pour faire
oppose [əˈpəuz] *vt* s'opposer à; **to be ~d to sth** être opposé(e) à qch; **as ~d to** par opposition à
opposing [əˈpəuzɪŋ] *adj* (side) opposé(e)
opposite [ˈɔpəzɪt] *adj* opposé(e); *(house etc)* d'en face ▷ *adv* en face ▷ *prep* en face de ▷ *n* opposé *m*, contraire *m*; *(of word)* contraire; **"see ~ page"** "voir ci-contre"
opposition [ɔpəˈzɪʃən] *n* opposition *f*
oppress [əˈprɛs] *vt* opprimer
oppressive [əˈprɛsɪv] *adj* oppressif(-ive)
opt [ɔpt] *vi*: **to ~ for** opter pour; **to ~ to do** choisir de faire; **opt out** *vi* (school, hospital) devenir autonome; *(health service)* devenir privé(e); **to ~ out of** choisir de ne pas participer à *or* de ne pas faire
optical [ˈɔptɪkl] *adj* optique; *(instrument)* d'optique
optical character reader *n* lecteur *m* optique
optical character recognition *n* lecture *f* optique
optician [ɔpˈtɪʃən] *n* opticien(ne)
optimism [ˈɔptɪmɪzəm] *n* optimisme *m*
optimist [ˈɔptɪmɪst] *n* optimiste *m/f*
optimistic [ɔptɪˈmɪstɪk] *adj* optimiste
optimum [ˈɔptɪməm] *adj* optimum
option [ˈɔpʃən] *n* choix *m*, option *f*; *(Scol)* matière *f* à option; *(Comm)* option; **to keep one's ~s open** *(fig)* ne pas s'engager; **I have no ~** je n'ai pas le choix
optional [ˈɔpʃənl] *adj* facultatif(-ive); *(Comm)* en option; **~ extras** accessoires *mpl* en option, options *fpl*
or [ɔːʳ] *conj* ou; *(with negative)*: **he hasn't seen or heard anything** il n'a rien vu ni entendu; **or else** sinon; ou bien
oral [ˈɔːrəl] *adj* oral(e) ▷ *n* oral *m*
orange [ˈɔrɪndʒ] *n* (fruit) orange *f* ▷ *adj* orange *inv*
orange juice *n* jus *m* d'orange
orbit [ˈɔːbɪt] *n* orbite *f* ▷ *vt* graviter autour de; **to be in/go into ~ (round)** être/entrer en orbite (autour de)
orchard [ˈɔːtʃəd] *n* verger *m*; **apple ~** verger de pommiers
orchestra [ˈɔːkɪstrə] *n* orchestre *m*; *(US: seating)* (fauteuils *mpl* d')orchestre
orchid [ˈɔːkɪd] *n* orchidée *f*
ordain [ɔːˈdeɪn] *vt* (Rel) ordonner; *(decide)* décréter
ordeal [ɔːˈdiːl] *n* épreuve *f*
order [ˈɔːdəʳ] *n* ordre *m*; *(Comm)* commande *f* ▷ *vt* ordonner; *(Comm)* commander; **in ~** en ordre; *(of document)* en règle; **out of ~** (not in

correct order) en désordre; (*machine*) hors service; (*telephone*) en dérangement; **a machine in working** – une machine en état de marche; **in ~ of size** par ordre de grandeur; **in ~ to do/ that** pour faire/que + *sub*; **to place an ~ for sth with sb** commander qch auprès de qn, passer commande de qch à qn; **could I ~ now, please?** je peux commander, s'il vous plaît?; **to be on ~** être en commande; **made to ~** fait sur commande; **to be under ~s to do sth** avoir ordre de faire qch; **a point of ~** un point de procédure; **to the ~ of** (*Banking*) à l'ordre de; **to ~ sb to do** ordonner à qn de faire

order form *n* bon *m* de commande

orderly ['ɔːdəlɪ] *n* (*Mil*) ordonnance *f*; (*Med*) garçon *m* de salle ▷ *adj* (*room*) en ordre; (*mind*) méthodique; (*person*) qui a de l'ordre

ordinary ['ɔːdnrɪ] *adj* ordinaire, normal(e); (*pej*) ordinaire, quelconque; **out of the ~** exceptionnel(le)

Ordnance Survey map *n* (*Brit*) ≈ carte *f* d'État-major

ore [ɔː*r*] *n* minerai *m*

oregano [ɒrɪ'gɑːnəʊ] *n* origan *m*

organ ['ɔːgən] *n* organe *m*; (*Mus*) orgue *m*, orgues *fpl*

organic [ɔː'gænɪk] *adj* organique; (*crops etc*) biologique, naturel(le)

organism ['ɔːgənɪzəm] *n* organisme *m*

organization [ɔːgənaɪ'zeɪʃən] *n* organisation *f*

organize ['ɔːgənaɪz] *vt* organiser; **to get ~d** s'organiser

organized ['ɔːgənaɪzd] *adj* (*planned*) organisé(e); (*efficient*) bien organisé

organizer ['ɔːgənaɪzə*r*] *n* organisateur(-trice)

orgasm ['ɔːgæzəm] *n* orgasme *m*

orgy ['ɔːdʒɪ] *n* orgie *f*

Orient ['ɔːrɪənt] *n*: **the ~** l'Orient *m*

oriental [ɔːrɪ'entl] *adj* oriental(e) ▷ *n* Oriental(e)

orientation [ɔːrɪen'teɪʃən] *n* (*attitudes*) tendance *f*; (*in job*) orientation *f*; (*of building*) orientation, exposition *f*

origin ['ɔrɪdʒɪn] *n* origine *f*; **country of ~** pays *m* d'origine

original [ə'rɪdʒɪnl] *adj* original(e); (*earliest*) originel(le) ▷ *n* original *m*

originally [ə'rɪdʒɪnəlɪ] *adv* (*at first*) à l'origine

originate [ə'rɪdʒɪneɪt] *vi*: **~ from** être originaire de; (*suggestion*) provenir de; **to ~ in** (*custom*) prendre naissance dans, avoir son origine dans

Orkney ['ɔːknɪ] *n* (*also*: **the ~s, the ~ Islands**) les Orcades *fpl*

ornament ['ɔːnəmənt] *n* ornement *m*; (*trinket*) bibelot *m*

ornamental [ɔːnə'mentl] *adj* décoratif(-ive); (*garden*) d'agrément

ornate [ɔː'neɪt] *adj* très orné(e)

orphan ['ɔːfn] *n* orphelin(e) ▷ *vt*: **to be ~ed** devenir orphelin

orthodox ['ɔːθədɔks] *adj* orthodoxe

orthopaedic, (US) **orthopedic** [ɔːθə'piːdɪk] *adj* orthopédique

ostensibly [ɔs'tensɪblɪ] *adv* en apparence

ostentatious [ɔsten'teɪʃəs] *adj* prétentieux(-euse); ostentatoire

osteopath ['ɔstɪəpæθ] *n* ostéopathe *m/f*

ostracize ['ɔstrəsaɪz] *vt* frapper d'ostracisme

ostrich ['ɔstrɪtʃ] *n* autruche *f*

other ['ʌðə*r*] *adj* autre ▷ *pron*: **the ~ (one)** l'autre; **~s** (*other people*) d'autres ▷ *adv*: **~ than** autrement que; à part; **some actor or ~** un certain acteur, je ne sais quel acteur; **somebody or ~** quelqu'un; **some ~ people have still to arrive** on attend encore quelques personnes; **the ~ day** l'autre jour; **the car was none ~ than John's** la voiture n'était autre que celle de John

otherwise ['ʌðəwaɪz] *adv, conj* autrement; **an ~ good piece of work** par ailleurs, un beau travail

Ottawa ['ɔtəwə] *n* Ottawa

otter ['ɔtə*r*] *n* loutre *f*

ouch [autʃ] *excl* aïe!

ought (*pt* **ought**) [ɔːt] *aux vb*: **I ~ to do it** je devrais le faire, il faudrait que je le fasse; **this ~ to have been corrected** cela aurait dû être corrigé; **he ~ to win** (*probability*) il devrait gagner; **you ~ to go and see it** vous devriez aller le voir

ounce [auns] *n* once *f* (28.35g; 16 in a pound)

our ['auə*r*] *adj* notre, nos *pl*; *see also* **my**

ours [auəz] *pron* le/la nôtre, les nôtres; *see also* **mine**¹

ourselves [auə'selvz] *pron pl* (*reflexive, after preposition*) nous; (*emphatic*) nous-mêmes; **we did it (all) by ~** nous avons fait ça tous seuls; *see also* **oneself**

oust [aust] *vt* évincer

out [aut] *adv* dehors; (*published, not at home etc*) sorti(e); (*light, fire*) éteint(e); (*on strike*) en grève ▷ *vt*: **to ~ sb** révéler l'homosexualité de qn; **~ here** ici; **~ there** là-bas; **he's ~** (*absent*) il est sorti; (*unconscious*) il est sans connaissance; **to be ~ in one's calculations** s'être trompé dans ses calculs; **to run/back** *etc* **~** sortir en courant/en reculant *etc*; **to be ~ and ab~** *or* (*US*) **around again** être de nouveau sur pied; **before the week was ~** avant la fin de la semaine; **the journey ~** l'aller *m*; **the boat was 10 km ~** le bateau était à 10 km du rivage; **~ loud** *adv* à haute voix; **~ of** *prep* (*outside*) en dehors de; (*because of*: *anger etc*) par; (*from among*): **10 ~ of 10** 10 sur 10; (*without*): **~ of petrol** sans essence, à court d'essence; **made ~ of wood** en or de bois; **~ of order** (*machine*) en panne; (*Tel*: *line*) en dérangement; **~ of stock** (*Comm*: *article*) épuisé(e); (: *shop*) en rupture de stock

out-and-out ['autəndaut] *adj* véritable

outback ['autbæk] *n* campagne isolée; (*in Australia*) intérieur *m*

outboard ['autbɔːd] n: **~ (motor)** (moteur m) hors-bord m

outbound ['autbaund] adj: **~ (from/for)** en partance (de/pour)

outbreak ['autbreɪk] n (of violence) éruption f, explosion f; (of disease) de nombreux cas; **the ~ of war south of the border** la guerre qui s'est déclarée au sud de la frontière

outburst ['autbɜːst] n explosion f, accès m

outcast ['autkɑːst] n exilé(e); (socially) paria m

outcome ['autkʌm] n issue f, résultat m

outcrop ['autkrɔp] n affleurement m

outcry ['autkraɪ] n tollé (général)

outdated [aut'deɪtɪd] adj démodé(e)

outdo [aut'duː] vt (irreg like: **do**) surpasser

outdoor [aut'dɔːʳ] adj de or en plein air

outdoors [aut'dɔːz] adv dehors; au grand air

outer ['autəʳ] adj extérieur(e); **~ suburbs** grande banlieue

outer space n espace m cosmique

outfit ['autfɪt] n équipement m; (clothes) tenue f; (inf: Comm) organisation f, boîte f

outgoing ['autgəuɪŋ] adj (president, tenant) sortant(e); (character) ouvert(e), extraverti(e)

outgoings ['autgəuɪŋz] npl (Brit: expenses) dépenses fpl

outgrow [aut'grəu] vt (irreg like: **grow**) (clothes) devenir trop grand(e) pour

outhouse ['authaus] n appentis m, remise f

outing ['autɪŋ] n sortie f; excursion f

outlaw ['autlɔː] n hors-la-loi m inv ▷ vt (person) mettre hors la loi; (practice) proscrire

outlay ['autleɪ] n dépenses fpl; (investment) mise f de fonds

outlet ['autlɛt] n (for liquid etc) issue f, sortie f; (for emotion) exutoire m; (for goods) débouché m; (also: **retail ~**) point m de vente; (US: Elec) prise f de courant

outline ['autlaɪn] n (shape) contour m; (summary) esquisse f, grandes lignes ▷ vt (fig: theory, plan) exposer à grands traits

outlive [aut'lɪv] vt survivre à

outlook ['autluk] n perspective f; (point of view) attitude f

outlying ['autlaɪɪŋ] adj écarté(e)

outmoded [aut'məudɪd] adj démodé(e); dépassé(e)

outnumber [aut'nʌmbəʳ] vt surpasser en nombre

out-of-date [autəv'deɪt] adj (passport, ticket) périmé(e); (theory, idea) dépassé(e); (custom) désuet(-ète); (clothes) démodé(e)

out-of-doors ['autəv'dɔːz] adv = **outdoors**

out-of-the-way ['autəvðə'weɪ] adj loin de tout; (fig) insolite

out-of-town [autəv'taun] adj (shopping centre etc) en périphérie

outpatient ['autpeɪʃənt] n malade m/f en consultation externe

outpost ['autpəust] n avant-poste m

output ['autput] n rendement m, production f; (Comput) sortie f ▷ vt (Comput) sortir

outrage ['autreɪdʒ] n (anger) indignation f; (violent act) atrocité f, acte m de violence; (scandal) scandale m ▷ vt outrager

outrageous [aut'reɪdʒəs] adj atroce; (scandalous) scandaleux(-euse)

outright adv [aut'raɪt] complètement; (deny, refuse) catégoriquement; (ask) carrément; (kill) sur le coup ▷ adj ['autraɪt] complet(-ète); catégorique

outset ['autsɛt] n début m

outside [aut'saɪd] n extérieur m ▷ adj extérieur(e); (remote, unlikely): **an ~ chance** une (très) faible chance ▷ adv (au) dehors, à l'extérieur ▷ prep hors de, à l'extérieur de; (in front of) devant; **at the ~** (fig) au plus or maximum; **~ left/right** (Football) ailier gauche/droit

outside lane n (Aut: in Britain) voie f de droite; (: in US, Europe) voie de gauche

outside line n (Tel) ligne extérieure

outsider [aut'saɪdəʳ] n (in race etc) outsider m; (stranger) étranger(-ère)

outsize ['autsaɪz] adj énorme; (clothes) grande taille inv

outskirts ['autskɜːts] npl faubourgs mpl

outspoken [aut'spəukən] adj très franc/franche

outstanding [aut'stændɪŋ] adj remarquable, exceptionnel(le); (unfinished: work, business) en suspens, en souffrance; (debt) impayé(e); (problem) non réglé(e); **your account is still ~** vous n'avez pas encore tout remboursé

outstay [aut'steɪ] vt: **to ~ one's welcome** abuser de l'hospitalité de son hôte

outstretched [aut'strɛtʃt] adj (hand) tendu(e); (body) étendu(e)

outstrip [aut'strɪp] vt (also fig) dépasser

out-tray ['auttreɪ] n courrier m "départ"

outward ['autwəd] adj (sign, appearances) extérieur(e); (journey) (d')aller

outwards ['autwədz] adv (esp Brit) = **outward**

outweigh [aut'weɪ] vt l'emporter sur

outwit [aut'wɪt] vt se montrer plus malin que

oval ['əuvl] adj, n ovale m

Oval Office n (US: Pol) voir article

⬦ **OVAL OFFICE**

L'*Oval Office* est le bureau personnel du président des États-Unis à la Maison-Blanche, ainsi appelé du fait de sa forme ovale. Par extension, ce terme désigne la présidence elle-même.

ovary ['əuvərɪ] n ovaire m

oven ['ʌvn] n four m

oven glove n gant m de cuisine

ovenproof ['ʌvnpruːf] adj allant au four

oven-ready ['ʌvnrɛdɪ] adj prêt(e) à cuire

over ['əuvəʳ] adv (par-)dessus; (excessively) trop ▷ adj (or adv) (finished) fini(e), terminé(e); (too *much*) en plus ▷ *prep* sur; par-dessus; (*above*) au-dessus de; (*on the other side of*) de l'autre côté de; (*more than*) plus de; (*during*) pendant; (*about, concerning*): **they fell out ~ money/her** ils se sont brouillés pour des questions d'argent/à cause d'elle; **~ here** ici; **~ there** là-bas; **all ~** (*everywhere*) partout; (*finished*) fini(e); **~ and ~ (again)** à plusieurs reprises; **and above** en plus de; **to ask sb ~** inviter qn (à passer); **to go ~ to sb's** passer chez qn; **to fall ~** tomber; **to turn sth ~** retourner qch; **now ~ to our Paris correspondent** nous passons l'antenne à notre correspondant à Paris; **the world ~** dans le monde entier; **she's not ~ intelligent** (*Brit*) elle n'est pas particulièrement intelligente

overall ['əʊvərɔːl] *adj* (*length*) total(e); (*study, impression*) d'ensemble ▷ *n* (*Brit*) blouse *f* ▷ *adv* [əʊvər'ɔːl] dans l'ensemble, en général; **overalls** *npl* (*boiler suit*) bleus *mpl* (de travail)

overawe [əʊvər'ɔː] *vt* impressionner

overbalance [əʊvə'bæləns] *vi* basculer

overboard ['əʊvəbɔːd] *adv* (*Naut*) par-dessus bord; **to go ~ for sth** (*fig*) s'emballer (pour qch)

overbook [əʊvə'bʊk] *vi* faire du surbooking

overcame [əʊvə'keɪm] *pt of* **overcome**

overcast ['əʊvəkɑːst] *adj* couvert(e)

overcharge [əʊvə'tʃɑːdʒ] *vt*: **to ~ sb for sth** faire payer qch trop cher à qn

overcoat ['əʊvəkəʊt] *n* pardessus *m*

overcome [əʊvə'kʌm] *vt* (*irreg like*: **come**) (*defeat*) triompher de; (*difficulty*) surmonter ▷ *adj* (*emotionally*) bouleversé(e); **~ with grief** accablé(e) de douleur

overcrowded [əʊvə'kraʊdɪd] *adj* bondé(e); (*city, country*) surpeuplé(e)

overdo [əʊvə'duː] *vt* (*irreg like*: **do**) exagérer; (*overcook*) trop cuire; **to ~ it, to ~ things** (*work too hard*) en faire trop, se surmener

overdone [əʊvə'dʌn] *adj* (*vegetables, steak*) trop cuit(e)

overdose ['əʊvədəʊs] *n* dose excessive

overdraft ['əʊvədrɑːft] *n* découvert *m*

overdrawn [əʊvə'drɔːn] *adj* (*account*) à découvert

overdue [əʊvə'djuː] *adj* en retard; (*bill*) impayé(e); (*change*) qui tarde; **that change was long ~** ce changement n'avait que trop tardé

overestimate [əʊvər'estɪmeɪt] *vt* surestimer

overflow *vi* [əʊvə'fləʊ] déborder ▷ *n* ['əʊvəfləʊ] trop-plein *m*; (*also*: **~ pipe**) tuyau *m* d'écoulement, trop-plein *m*

overgrown [əʊvə'grəʊn] *adj* (*garden*) envahi(e) par la végétation; **he's just an ~ schoolboy** (*fig*) c'est un écolier attardé

overhaul *vt* [əʊvə'hɔːl] réviser ▷ *n* ['əʊvəhɔːl] révision *f*

overhead [*adv* əʊvə'hɛd, *adj, n* 'əʊvəhɛd] *adv* au-dessus ▷ *adj* aérien(ne); (*lighting*) vertical(e) ▷ *n* (*US*) = **overheads**

overhead projector *n* rétroprojecteur *m*

overheads ['əʊvəhɛdz] *npl* (*Brit*) frais généraux

overhear [əʊvə'hɪər] *vt* (*irreg like*: **hear**) entendre (par hasard)

overheat [əʊvə'hiːt] *vi* devenir surchauffé(e); (*engine*) chauffer

overjoyed [əʊvə'dʒɔɪd] *adj* ravi(e), enchanté(e)

overland ['əʊvəlænd] *adj, adv* par voie de terre

overlap *vi* [əʊvə'læp] se chevaucher ▷ *n* ['əʊvəlæp] chevauchement *m*

overleaf [əʊvə'liːf] *adv* au verso

overload [əʊvə'ləʊd] *vt* surcharger

overlook [əʊvə'lʊk] *vt* (*have view of*) donner sur; (*miss*) oublier, négliger; (*forgive*) fermer les yeux sur

overnight *adv* [əʊvə'naɪt] (*happen*) durant la nuit; (*fig*) soudain ▷ *adj* ['əʊvənaɪt] d'une (or de) nuit; soudain(e); **to stay ~ (with sb)** passer la nuit (chez qn); **he stayed there ~** il y a passé la nuit; **if you travel ~ ...** si tu fais le voyage de nuit ...; **he'll be away ~** il ne rentrera pas ce soir

overnight bag *n* nécessaire *m* de voyage

overpass ['əʊvəpɑːs] *n* (*US: for cars*) pont autoroutier; (*: for pedestrians*) passerelle *f*, pont *m*

overpower [əʊvə'paʊər] *vt* vaincre; (*fig*) accabler

overpowering [əʊvə'paʊərɪŋ] *adj* irrésistible; (*heat, stench*) suffocant(e)

overrate [əʊvə'reɪt] *vt* surestimer

overreact [əʊvəriːˈækt] *vi* réagir de façon excessive

override [əʊvə'raɪd] *vt* (*irreg like*: **ride**) (*order, objection*) passer outre à; (*decision*) annuler

overriding [əʊvə'raɪdɪŋ] *adj* prépondérant(e)

overrule [əʊvə'ruːl] *vt* (*decision*) annuler; (*claim*) rejeter; (*person*) rejeter l'avis de

overrun [əʊvə'rʌn] *vt* (*irreg like*: **run**) (*Mil: country etc*) occuper; (*time limit etc*) dépasser ▷ *vi* dépasser le temps imparti; **the town is ~ with tourists** la ville est envahie de touristes

overseas [əʊvə'siːz] *adv* outre-mer; (*abroad*) à l'étranger ▷ *adj* (*trade*) extérieur(e); (*visitor*) étranger(-ère)

oversee [əʊvə'siː] *vt* (*irreg like*: **see**) surveiller

overshadow [əʊvə'ʃædəʊ] *vt* (*fig*) éclipser

oversight ['əʊvəsaɪt] *n* omission *f*, oubli *m*; **due to an ~** par suite d'une inadvertance

oversleep [əʊvə'sliːp] *vi* (*irreg like*: **sleep**) se réveiller (trop) tard

overspend [əʊvə'spɛnd] *vi* (*irreg like*: **spend**) dépenser de trop; **we have overspent by 5,000 dollars** nous avons dépassé notre budget de 5 000 dollars, nous avons dépensé 5 000 dollars de trop

overstep [əʊvə'stɛp] *vt*: **to ~ the mark** dépasser la mesure

o

overt [əʊ'vɜːt] *adj* non dissimulé(e)

overtake [əʊvə'teɪk] *vt* (*irreg like:* **take**) dépasser; (*Brit: Aut*) dépasser, doubler

overthrow [əʊvə'θrəʊ] *vt* (*irreg like:* **throw**) (*government*) renverser

overtime ['əʊvətaɪm] *n* heures *fpl* supplémentaires; **to do** *or* **work ~** faire des heures supplémentaires

overtone ['əʊvətəʊn] *n* (*also:* **~s**) note *f*, sous-entendus *mpl*

overtook [əʊvə'tʊk] *pt of* **overtake**

overture ['əʊvətʃʊə'] *n* (*Mus, fig*) ouverture *f*

overturn [əʊvə'tɜːn] *vt* renverser; (*decision, plan*) annuler ▷ *vi* se retourner

overweight [əʊvə'weɪt] *adj* (*person*) trop gros(se); (*luggage*) trop lourd(e)

overwhelm [əʊvə'wɛlm] *vt* (*subj: emotion*) accabler, submerger; (*enemy, opponent*) écraser

overwhelming [əʊvə'wɛlmɪŋ] *adj* (*victory, defeat*) écrasant(e); (*desire*) irrésistible; **one's ~ impression is of heat** on a une impression dominante de chaleur

overwrought [əʊvə'rɔːt] *adj* excédé(e)

owe [əʊ] *vt* devoir; **to ~ sb sth, to ~ sth to sb** devoir qch à qn; **how much do I ~ you?** combien est-ce que je vous dois?

owing to ['əʊɪŋtuː] *prep* à cause de, en raison de

owl [aʊl] *n* hibou *m*

own [əʊn] *vt* posséder ▷ *vi* (*Brit*) **to ~ to sth** reconnaître *or* avouer qch; **to ~ to having done sth** avouer avoir fait qch ▷ *adj* propre; **a room of my ~** une chambre à moi, ma propre chambre; **can I have it for my (very) ~?** puis-je l'avoir pour moi (tout) seul?; **to get one's ~ back** prendre sa revanche; **on one's ~** tout(e) seul(e); **to come into one's ~** trouver sa voie; trouver sa justification; **own up** *vi* avouer

owner ['əʊnə'] *n* propriétaire *m/f*

ownership ['əʊnəʃɪp] *n* possession *f*; **it's under new ~** (*shop etc*) il y a eu un changement de propriétaire

ox (*pl* **oxen**) [ɔks, 'ɔksn] *n* bœuf *m*

Oxbridge ['ɔksbrɪdʒ] *n* (*Brit*) *les universités d'Oxford et de Cambridge; voir article*

⁂ **OXBRIDGE**

Oxbridge, nom formé à partir des mots Ox(ford) et (Cam)bridge, s'utilise pour parler de ces deux universités comme formant un tout, dans la mesure où elles sont toutes deux les universités britanniques les plus prestigieuses et mondialement connues.

oxen ['ɔksən] *npl of* **ox**

oxtail ['ɔksteɪl] *n*: **~ soup** soupe *f* à la queue de bœuf

oxygen ['ɔksɪdʒən] *n* oxygène *m*

oyster ['ɔɪstə'] *n* huître *f*

oz. *abbr* = **ounce; ounces**

ozone ['əʊzəʊn] *n* ozone *m*

ozone friendly ['əʊzəʊnfrɛndlɪ] *adj* qui n'attaque pas *or* qui préserve la couche d'ozone

ozone hole *n* trou *m* d'ozone

ozone layer *n* couche *f* d'ozone

p

p *abbr* (= *page*) p; (*Brit*) = **penny; pence**

P.A. *n abbr* = **personal assistant; public address system** ▷ *abbr* (*US*) = **Pennsylvania**

pa [pɑː] *n* (*inf*) papa *m*

p.a. *abbr* = **per annum**

pace [peɪs] *n* pas *m*; (*speed*) allure *f*; vitesse *f* ▷ *vi*: **to ~ up and down** faire les cent pas; **to keep ~ with** aller à la même vitesse que; (*events*) se tenir au courant de; **to set the ~** (*running*) donner l'allure; (*fig*) donner le ton; **to put sb through his ~s** (*fig*) mettre qn à l'épreuve

pacemaker ['peɪsmeɪkə'] *n* (*Med*) stimulateur *m* cardiaque; (*Sport: also:* **pacesetter**) meneur(-euse) de train

Pacific [pə'sɪfɪk] *n*: **the ~ (Ocean)** le Pacifique, l'océan *m* Pacifique

pacifier ['pæsɪfaɪə'] *n* (*US: dummy*) tétine *f*

pack [pæk] *n* paquet *m*; (*bundle*) ballot *m*; (*of hounds*) meute *f*; (*of thieves, wolves etc*) bande *f*; (*of cards*) jeu *m*; (*US: of cigarettes*) paquet; (*back pack*) sac *m* à dos ▷ *vt* (*goods*) empaqueter, emballer; (*in suitcase etc*) emballer; (*box*) remplir; (*cram*) entasser; (*press down*) tasser; damer; (*Comput*) grouper, tasser ▷ *vi*: **to ~ (one's bags)** faire ses bagages; **to ~ into** (*room, stadium*) s'entasser dans; **to send sb ~ing** (*inf*) envoyer promener qn; **pack in** (*Brit inf*) *vi* (*machine*) tomber en panne ▷ *vt* (*boyfriend*) plaquer; **~ it in!** laisse tomber!; **pack off** *vt*: **to ~ sb off to** expédier qn à; **pack up** *vi* (*Brit inf: machine*) tomber en panne; (: *person*) se tirer ▷ *vt* (*belongings*) ranger; (*goods, presents*) empaqueter, emballer

package ['pækɪdʒ] *n* paquet *m*; (*of goods*) emballage *m*, conditionnement *m*; (*also:* **~ deal**: *agreement*) marché global; (: *purchase*) forfait *m*; (*Comput*) progiciel *m* ▷ *vt* (*goods*) conditionner

package holiday *n* (*Brit*) vacances organisées

package tour *n* voyage organisé

packaging ['pækɪdʒɪŋ] *n* (*wrapping materials*) emballage *m*; (*of goods*) conditionnement *m*

packed [pækt] *adj* (*crowded*) bondé(e)

packed lunch (*Brit*) *n* repas froid

packet ['pækɪt] *n* paquet *m*

packing ['pækɪŋ] *n* emballage *m*

packing case *n* caisse *f* (d'emballage)

pact [pækt] *n* pacte *m*, traité *m*

pad [pæd] *n* bloc(-notes *m*) *m*; (*to prevent friction*) tampon *m*; (*for inking*) tampon *m* encreur; (*inf: flat*) piaule *f* ▷ *vt* rembourrer ▷ *vi*: **to ~ in/about** *etc* entrer/aller et venir *etc* à pas feutrés

padded ['pædɪd] *adj* (*jacket*) matelassé(e); (*bra*) rembourré(e); **~ cell** cellule capitonnée

padding ['pædɪŋ] *n* rembourrage *m*; (*fig*) délayage *m*

paddle ['pædl] *n* (*oar*) pagaie *f*; (*US: for table tennis*) raquette *f* de ping-pong ▷ *vi* (*with feet*) barboter, faire trempette ▷ *vt*: **to ~ a canoe** *etc* pagayer

paddling pool ['pædlɪŋ-] *n* petit bassin

paddock ['pædək] *n* enclos *m*; (*Racing*) paddock *m*

padlock ['pædlɔk] *n* cadenas *m* ▷ *vt* cadenasser

paediatrics, (*US*) **pediatrics** [piːdɪ'ætrɪks] *n* pédiatrie *f*

paedophile, pedophile (*US*) ['piːdəufaɪl] *n* pédophile *m*

pagan ['peɪgən] *adj, n* païen(ne)

page [peɪdʒ] *n* (*of book*) page *f*; (*also:* **~ boy**) groom *m*, chasseur *m*; (*at wedding*) garçon *m* d'honneur ▷ *vt* (*in hotel etc*) (faire) appeler

pageant ['pædʒənt] *n* spectacle *m* historique; grande cérémonie

pageantry ['pædʒəntrɪ] *n* apparat *m*, pompe *f*

pager ['peɪdʒə'] *n* bip *m* (*inf*), Alphapage® *m*

paid [peɪd] *pt, pp* of **pay** ▷ *adj* (*work, official*) rémunéré(e); (*holiday*) payé(e); **to put ~ to** (*Brit*) mettre fin à, mettre par terre

pail [peɪl] *n* seau *m*

pain [peɪn] *n* douleur *f*; (*inf: nuisance*) plaie *f*; **to be in ~** souffrir, avoir mal; **to have a ~ in** avoir mal à *or* une douleur à *or* dans; **to take ~s to do** se donner du mal pour faire; **on ~ of death** sous peine de mort

pained ['peɪnd] *adj* peiné(e), chagrin(e)

painful ['peɪnful] *adj* douloureux(-euse); (*difficult*) difficile, pénible

painfully ['peɪnfəlɪ] *adv* (*fig: very*) terriblement

painkiller ['peɪnkɪlə'] n calmant m,
analgésique m

painless ['peɪnlɪs] adj indolore

painstaking ['peɪnzteɪkɪŋ] adj (person)
soigneux(-euse); (work) soigné(e)

paint [peɪnt] n peinture f ▷ vt peindre; (fig)
dépeindre; **to ~ the door blue** peindre la
porte en bleu; **to ~ in oils** faire de la peinture
à l'huile

paintbrush ['peɪntbrʌʃ] n pinceau m

painter ['peɪntə'] n peintre m

painting ['peɪntɪŋ] n peinture f; (picture)
tableau m

paintwork ['peɪntwə:k] n (Brit) peintures fpl;
(: of car) peinture f

pair [peə'] n (of shoes, gloves etc) paire f; (of
people) couple m; (twosome) duo m; **~ of
scissors** (paire de) ciseaux mpl; **~ of
trousers** pantalon m; **pair off** vi se mettre
par deux

pajamas [pə'dʒɑ:məz] npl (US) pyjama(s)
m(pl)

Pakistan [pɑ:kɪ'stɑ:n] n Pakistan m

Pakistani [pɑ:kɪ'stɑ:nɪ] adj pakistanais(e)
▷ n Pakistanais(e)

pal [pæl] n (inf) copain/copine

palace ['pæləs] n palais m

palatable ['pælɪtəbl] adj bon/bonne,
agréable au goût

palate ['pælɪt] n palais m (Anat)

pale [peɪl] adj pâle ▷ vi pâlir ▷ n: **to be
beyond the ~** être au ban de la société; **to
grow** or **turn ~** (person) pâlir; **~ blue** adj
bleu pâle inv; **to ~ into insignificance
(beside)** perdre beaucoup d'importance
(par rapport à)

Palestine ['pælɪstaɪn] n Palestine f

Palestinian [pælɪs'tɪnɪən] adj
palestinien(ne) ▷ n Palestinien(ne)

palette ['pælɪt] n palette f

pall [pɔ:l] n (of smoke) voile m ▷ vi: **to ~ (on)**
devenir lassant (pour)

pallet ['pælɪt] n (for goods) palette f

pallid ['pælɪd] adj blême

palm [pɑ:m] n (Anat) paume f; (also: **~ tree**)
palmier m; (leaf, symbol) palme f ▷ vt: **to ~ sth
off on sb** (inf) refiler qch à qn

Palm Sunday n le dimanche des Rameaux

paltry ['pɔ:ltrɪ] adj dérisoire; piètre

pamper ['pæmpə'] vt gâter, dorloter

pamphlet ['pæmflət] n brochure f; (political
etc) tract m

pan [pæn] n (also: **sauce~**) casserole f;
(also: **frying ~**) poêle f; (of lavatory) cuvette f
▷ vi (Cine) faire un panoramique ▷ vt (inf:
book, film) éreinter; **to ~ for gold** laver du
sable aurifère

pancake ['pænkeɪk] n crêpe f

panda ['pændə] n panda m

pandemic [pæn'dɛmɪk] n pandémie f

pandemonium [pændɪ'məunɪəm] n
tohu-bohu m

pander ['pændə'] vi: **to ~ to** flatter
bassement; obéir servilement à

pane [peɪn] n carreau m (de fenêtre), vitre f

panel ['pænl] n (of wood, cloth etc) panneau m;
(Radio, TV) panel m, invités mpl; (for interview,
exams) jury m; (official: of experts) table ronde,
comité m

panelling, paneling (US) ['pænəlɪŋ] n
boiseries fpl

pang [pæŋ] n: **~s of remorse** pincements mpl
de remords; **~s of hunger/conscience**
tiraillements mpl d'estomac/de la conscience

panhandler ['pænhændlə'] n (US inf)
mendiant(e)

panic ['pænɪk] n panique f, affolement m ▷ vi
s'affoler, paniquer

panicky ['pænɪkɪ] adj (person) qui panique or
s'affole facilement

panic-stricken ['pænɪkstrɪkən] adj affolé(e)

panorama [pænə'rɑ:mə] n panorama m

pansy ['pænzɪ] n (Bot) pensée f; (inf) tapette f,
pédé m

pant [pænt] vi haleter

panther ['pænθə'] n panthère f

panties ['pæntɪz] npl slip m, culotte f

pantihose ['pæntɪhəuz] n (US) collant m

pantomime ['pæntəmaɪm] n (Brit)
spectacle m de Noël; voir article

⬡ **PANTOMIME**
⬡
⬡ Une pantomime (à ne pas confondre avec
⬡ le mot tel qu'on l'utilise en français,
⬡ que l'on appelle également de façon
⬡ familière "panto", est un genre de farce
⬡ où le personnage principal est souvent
⬡ un jeune garçon et où il y a toujours une
⬡ "dame", c'est-à-dire une vieille femme
⬡ jouée par un homme, et un méchant.
⬡ La plupart du temps, l'histoire est basée
⬡ sur un conte de fées comme Cendrillon
⬡ ou Le Chat botté, et le public est
⬡ encouragé à participer en prévenant le
⬡ héros du danger imminent. Ce genre
⬡ de spectacle, qui s'adresse surtout aux
⬡ enfants, vise également un public
⬡ d'adultes au travers des nombreuses
⬡ plaisanteries faisant allusion à des faits
⬡ d'actualité.

pantry ['pæntrɪ] n garde-manger m inv;
(room) office m

pants [pænts] n (Brit: woman's) culotte f, slip m;
(: man's) slip m, caleçon m; (US: trousers)
pantalon m

pantyhose ['pæntɪhəuz] (US) npl collant m

paper ['peɪpə'] n papier m; (also: **wall~**) papier
peint; (also: **news~**) journal m; (academic essay)
article m; (exam) épreuve écrite ▷ adj en or de
papier ▷ vt tapisser (de papier peint); **papers**
npl (also: **identity ~s**) papiers mpl (d'identité);
a piece of ~ (odd bit) un bout de papier; (sheet)

une feuille de papier; **to put sth down on ~** mettre qch par écrit

paperback ['peɪpəbæk] *n* livre broché *or* non relié; (*small*) livre *m* de poche ▷ *adj*: **~ edition** édition brochée

paper bag *n* sac *m* en papier

paper clip *n* trombone *m*

paper handkerchief, paper hankie *n* (*inf*) mouchoir *m* en papier

paper shop *n* (*Brit*) marchand *m* de journaux

paperweight ['peɪpəweɪt] *n* presse-papiers *m inv*

paperwork ['peɪpəwə:k] *n* papiers *mpl*; (*pej*) paperasserie *f*

paprika ['pæprɪkə] *n* paprika *m*

par [pɑ:ʳ] *n* pair *m*; (*Golf*) normale *f* du parcours; **on a ~ with** à égalité avec, au même niveau que; **at ~** au pair; **above/below ~** au-dessus/au-dessous du pair; **to feel below** *or* **under** *or* **not up to ~** ne pas se sentir en forme

paracetamol [pærə'si:təmɔl] (*Brit*) *n* paracétamol *m*

parachute ['pærəʃu:t] *n* parachute *m* ▷ *vi* sauter en parachute

parade [pə'reɪd] *n* défilé *m*; (*inspection*) revue *f*; (*street*) boulevard *m* ▷ *vt* (*fig*) faire étalage de ▷ *vi* défiler; **a fashion ~** (*Brit*) un défilé de mode

paradise ['pærədaɪs] *n* paradis *m*

paradox ['pærədɔks] *n* paradoxe *m*

paradoxically [pærə'dɔksɪklɪ] *adv* paradoxalement

paraffin ['pærəfɪn] *n* (*Brit*): **~ (oil)** pétrole (lampant); **liquid ~** huile *f* de paraffine

paragon ['pærəgən] *n* parangon *m*

paragraph ['pærəgrɑ:f] *n* paragraphe *m*; **to begin a new ~** aller à la ligne

parallel ['pærəlɛl] *adj*: **~ (with** *or* **to)** parallèle (à); (*fig*) analogue (à) ▷ *n* (*line*) parallèle *f*; (*fig, Geo*) parallèle *m*

paralysed ['pærəlaɪzd] *adj* paralysé(e)

paralysis (*pl* **paralyses**) [pə'rælɪsɪs, -si:z] *n* paralysie *f*

paralyze ['pærəlaɪz] *vt* paralyser

paramedic [pærə'mɛdɪk] *n* auxiliaire *m/f* médical(e)

paramount ['pærəmaunt] *adj*: **of ~ importance** de la plus haute *or* grande importance

paranoid ['pærənɔɪd] *adj* (*Psych*) paranoïaque; (*neurotic*) paranoïde

paraphernalia [pærəfə'neɪlɪə] *n* attirail *m*, affaires *fpl*

parasite ['pærəsaɪt] *n* parasite *m*

parasol ['pærəsɔl] *n* ombrelle *f*; (*at café etc*) parasol *m*

paratrooper ['pærətru:pəʳ] *n* parachutiste *m* (*soldat*)

parcel ['pɑ:sl] *n* paquet *m*, colis *m* ▷ *vt* (*also*: **~ up**) empaqueter; **parcel out** *vt* répartir

parchment ['pɑ:tʃmənt] *n* parchemin *m*

pardon ['pɑ:dn] *n* pardon *m*; (*Law*) grâce *f* ▷ *vt* pardonner à; (*Law*) gracier; **~! pardon!**; **~ me!** (*after burping etc*) excusez-moi!; **I beg your ~!** (*I'm sorry*) pardon!, je suis désolé!; **(I beg your) ~?, (US) ~ me?** (*what did you say?*) pardon?

parent ['pɛərənt] *n* (*father*) père *m*; (*mother*) mère *f*; **parents** *npl* parents *mpl*

parental [pə'rɛntl] *adj* parental(e), des parents

Paris ['pærɪs] *n* Paris

parish ['pærɪʃ] *n* paroisse *f*; (*Brit: civil*) ≈ commune *f* ▷ *adj* paroissial(e)

Parisian [pə'rɪzɪən] *adj* parisien(ne), de Paris ▷ *n* Parisien(ne)

park [pɑ:k] *n* parc *m*, jardin public ▷ *vt* garer ▷ *vi* se garer; **can I ~ here?** est-ce que je peux me garer ici?

parking ['pɑ:kɪŋ] *n* stationnement *m*; **"no ~"** "stationnement interdit"

parking lot *n* (*US*) parking *m*, parc *m* de stationnement

parking meter *n* parc(o)mètre *m*

parking ticket *n* P.-V. *m*

parkway ['pɑ:kweɪ] *n* (*US*) route *f* express (*en site vert ou aménagé*)

parliament ['pɑ:ləmənt] *n* parlement *m*

parliamentary [pɑ:lə'mɛntərɪ] *adj* parlementaire

parlour, (*US*) **parlor** ['pɑ:ləʳ] *n* salon *m*

Parmesan [pɑ:mɪ'zæn] *n* (*also*: **~ cheese**) Parmesan *m*

parochial [pə'rəukɪəl] *adj* paroissial(e); (*pej*) à l'esprit de clocher

parole [pə'rəul] *n*: **on ~** en liberté conditionnelle

parrot ['pærət] *n* perroquet *m*

parry ['pærɪ] *vt* esquiver, parer à

parsley ['pɑ:slɪ] *n* persil *m*

parsnip ['pɑ:snɪp] *n* panais *m*

parson ['pɑ:sn] *n* ecclésiastique *m*; (*Church of England*) pasteur *m*

part [pɑ:t] *n* partie *f*; (*of machine*) pièce *f*; (*Theat*) rôle *m*; (*Mus*) voix *f*; partie; (*of serial*) épisode *m*; (*US: in hair*) raie *f* ▷ *adj* partiel(le) ▷ *adv* = **partly** ▷ *vt* séparer ▷ *vi* (*people*) se séparer; (*crowd*) s'ouvrir; (*roads*) se diviser; **to take ~ in** participer à, prendre part à; **to take sb's ~** prendre le parti de qn, prendre parti pour qn; **on his ~** de sa part; **for my ~** en ce qui me concerne; **for the most ~** en grande partie; dans la plupart des cas; **for the better ~ of the day** pendant la plus grande partie de la journée; **to be ~ and parcel of** faire partie de; **in ~** en partie; **to take sth in good/bad** prendre qch du bon/mauvais côté; **part with** *vt fus* (*person*) se séparer de; (*possessions*) se défaire de

part exchange *n* (*Brit*): **in ~** en reprise

partial ['pɑ:ʃl] *adj* (*incomplete*) partiel(le); (*unjust*) partial(e); **to be ~ to** aimer, avoir un faible pour

P

participant [pɑːˈtɪsɪpənt] n (in competition, campaign) participant(e)
participate [pɑːˈtɪsɪpeɪt] vi: **to ~ (in)** participer (à), prendre part (à)
participation [pɑːtɪsɪˈpeɪʃən] n participation f
participle [ˈpɑːtɪsɪpl] n participe m
particle [ˈpɑːtɪkl] n particule f; (of dust) grain m
particular [pəˈtɪkjulə*] adj (specific) particulier(-ière); (special) particulier, spécial(e); (fussy) difficile, exigeant(e); (careful) méticuleux(-euse); **in ~** en particulier, surtout
particularly [pəˈtɪkjuləlɪ] adv particulièrement; (in particular) en particulier
particulars [pəˈtɪkjuləz] npl détails mpl; (information) renseignements mpl
parting [ˈpɑːtɪŋ] n séparation f; (Brit: in hair) raie f ▷ adj d'adieu; **his ~ shot was ...** il lança en partant ....
partisan [pɑːtɪˈzæn] n partisan(e) ▷ adj partisan(e); de parti
partition [pɑːˈtɪʃən] n (Pol) partition f, division f; (wall) cloison f
partly [ˈpɑːtlɪ] adv en partie, partiellement
partner [ˈpɑːtnə*] n (Comm) associé(e); (Sport) partenaire m/f; (spouse) conjoint(e); (lover) ami(e); (at dance) cavalier(-ière) ▷ vt être l'associé or le partenaire or le cavalier de
partnership [ˈpɑːtnəʃɪp] n association f; **to go into ~ (with), form a ~ (with)** s'associer (avec)
partridge [ˈpɑːtrɪdʒ] n perdrix f
part-time [pɑːˈtaɪm] adj, adv à mi-temps, à temps partiel
party [ˈpɑːtɪ] n (Pol) parti m; (celebration) fête f; (: formal) réception f; (: in evening) soirée f; (team) équipe f; (group) groupe m; (Law) partie f; **dinner ~** dîner m; **to give** or **throw a ~** donner une réception; **we're having a ~ next Saturday** nous organisons une soirée or réunion entre amis samedi prochain; **it's for our son's birthday** - c'est pour la fête (or le goûter) d'anniversaire de notre garçon; **to be a ~ to a crime** être impliqué(e) dans un crime
party dress n robe habillée
pass [pɑːs] vt (time, object) passer; (place) passer devant; (friend) croiser; (exam) être reçu(e) à, réussir; (candidate) admettre; (overtake) dépasser; (approve) approuver, accepter; (law) promulguer ▷ vi passer; (Scol) être reçu(e) or admis(e), réussir ▷ n (permit) laissez-passer m inv; (membership card) carte f d'accès or d'abonnement; (in mountains) col m; (Sport) passe f; (Scol: also: ~ mark): **to get a ~** être reçu(e) (sans mention); **to ~ sb sth** passer qch à qn; **could you ~ the salt/oil, please?** pouvez-vous me passer le sel/l'huile, s'il vous plaît?; **she could ~ for 25** on lui donnerait 25 ans; **to ~ sth through a ring** etc

(faire) passer qch dans un anneau etc; **could you ~ the vegetables round?** pourriez-vous faire passer les légumes?; **things have come to a pretty ~** (Brit) voilà où on en est!; **to make a ~ at sb** (inf) faire des avances à qn
pass away vi mourir; **pass by** vi passer ▷ vt (ignore) négliger; **pass down** vt (customs, inheritance) transmettre; **pass on** vi (die) s'éteindre, décéder ▷ vt (hand on): **to ~ on (to)** transmettre (à); (: illness) passer (à); (: price rises) répercuter (sur); **pass out** vi s'évanouir; (Brit Mil) sortir (d'une école militaire); **pass over** vt (ignore) passer sous silence; **pass up** vt (opportunity) laisser passer
passable [ˈpɑːsəbl] adj (road) praticable; (work) acceptable
passage [ˈpæsɪdʒ] n (also: ~**way**) couloir m; (gen, in book) passage m; (by boat) traversée f
passbook [ˈpɑːsbuk] n livret m
passenger [ˈpæsɪndʒə*] n passager(-ère)
passer-by [pɑːsəˈbaɪ] n passant(e)
passing [ˈpɑːsɪŋ] adj (fig) passager(-ère); **in ~** en passant
passing place n (Aut) aire f de croisement
passion [ˈpæʃən] n passion f; **to have a ~ for sth** avoir la passion de qch
passionate [ˈpæʃənɪt] adj passionné(e)
passion fruit n fruit m de la passion
passive [ˈpæsɪv] adj (also Ling) passif(-ive)
passive smoking n tabagisme passif
Passover [ˈpɑːsəuvə*] n Pâque juive
passport [ˈpɑːspɔːt] n passeport m
passport control n contrôle m des passeports
passport office n bureau m de délivrance des passeports
password [ˈpɑːswəːd] n mot m de passe
past [pɑːst] prep (in front of) devant; (further than) au delà de, plus loin que; après; (later than) après ▷ adv: **to run ~** passer en courant ▷ adj passé(e); (president etc) ancien(ne) ▷ n passé m; **he's ~ forty** il a dépassé la quarantaine, il a plus de or passé quarante ans; **ten/quarter ~ eight** huit heures dix/un or et quart; **it's ~ midnight** il est plus de minuit, il est passé minuit; **he ran ~ me** il m'a dépassé en courant, il a passé devant moi en courant; **for the ~ few/3 days** depuis quelques/3 jours; ces derniers/3 derniers jours; **in the ~** (gen) dans le temps, autrefois; (Ling) au passé; **I'm ~ caring** je ne m'en fais plus; **to be ~ it** (Brit inf: person) avoir passé l'âge
pasta [ˈpæstə] n pâtes fpl
paste [peɪst] n pâte f; (Culin: meat) pâté m (à tartiner); (: tomato) purée f, concentré m; (glue) colle f (de pâte); (jewellery) strass m ▷ vt coller
pastel [ˈpæstl] adj pastel inv ▷ n (Art: pencil) (crayon m) pastel m; (: drawing) (dessin m au) pastel; (colour) ton m pastel inv
pasteurized [ˈpæstəraɪzd] adj pasteurisé(e)

pastille ['pæstl] n pastille f
pastime ['pɑːstaɪm] n passe-temps m inv, distraction f
pastor ['pɑːstə'] n pasteur m
pastry ['peɪstrɪ] n pâte f; (cake) pâtisserie f
pasture ['pɑːstʃə'] n pâturage m
pasty¹ n ['pæstɪ] petit pâté (en croûte)
pasty² ['peɪstɪ] adj pâteux(-euse); (complexion) terreux(-euse)
pat [pæt] vt donner une petite tape à; (dog) caresser ▷ n: **a ~ of butter** une noisette de beurre; **to give sb/o.s. a ~ on the back** (fig) congratuler qn/se congratuler; **he knows it (off) ~**, (US) **he has it down ~** il sait cela sur le bout des doigts
patch [pætʃ] n (of material) pièce f; (eye patch) cache m; (spot) tache f; (of land) parcelle f; (on tyre) rustine f ▷ vt (clothes) rapiécer; **a bad ~** (Brit) une période difficile; **patch up** vt réparer
patchy ['pætʃɪ] adj inégal(e); (incomplete) fragmentaire
pâté ['pæteɪ] n pâté m, terrine f
patent ['peɪtnt] (US) ['pætnt] n brevet m (d'invention) ▷ vt faire breveter ▷ adj patent(e), manifeste
patent leather n cuir verni
paternal [pə'tə:nl] adj paternel(le)
paternity leave [pə'tə:nɪtɪ-] n congé m de paternité
path [pɑːθ] n chemin m, sentier m; (in garden) allée f; (of planet) course f; (of missile) trajectoire f
pathetic [pə'θetɪk] adj (pitiful) pitoyable; (very bad) lamentable, minable; (moving) pathétique
pathological [pæθə'lɔdʒɪkl] adj pathologique
pathway ['pɑːθweɪ] n chemin m, sentier m; (in garden) allée f
patience ['peɪʃns] n patience f; (Brit: Cards) réussite f; **to lose (one's) ~** perdre patience
patient ['peɪʃnt] n malade m/f; (of dentist etc) patient(e) ▷ adj patient(e)
patio ['pætɪəu] n patio m
patriotic [pætrɪ'ɔtɪk] adj patriotique; (person) patriote
patrol [pə'trəul] n patrouille f ▷ vt patrouiller dans; **to be on ~** être de patrouille
patrol car n voiture f de police
patrolman [pə'trəulmən] irreg n (US) agent m de police
patron ['peɪtrən] n (in shop) client(e); (of charity) patron(ne); **~ of the arts** mécène m
patronize ['pætrənaɪz] vt être (un) client or un habitué de; (fig) traiter avec condescendance
patronizing ['pætrənaɪzɪŋ] adj condescendant(e)
patter ['pætə'] n crépitement m, tapotement m; (sales talk) boniment m ▷ vi crépiter, tapoter

pattern ['pætən] n modèle m; (Sewing) patron m; (design) motif m; (sample) échantillon m; **behaviour ~** mode m de comportement
patterned ['pætənd] adj à motifs
pauper ['pɔːpə'] n indigent(e); **~'s grave** fosse commune
pause [pɔːz] n pause f, arrêt m; (Mus) silence m ▷ vi faire une pause, s'arrêter; **to ~ for breath** reprendre son souffle; (fig) faire une pause
pave [peɪv] vt paver, daller; **to ~ the way for** ouvrir la voie à
pavement ['peɪvmənt] n (Brit) trottoir m; (US) chaussée f
pavilion [pə'vɪlɪən] n pavillon m; tente f; (Sport) stand m
paving ['peɪvɪŋ] n (material) pavé m, dalle f; (area) pavage m, dallage m
paving stone n pavé m
paw [pɔː] n patte f ▷ vt donner un coup de patte à; (person: pej) tripoter
pawn [pɔːn] n gage m; (Chess, also fig) pion m ▷ vt mettre en gage
pawnbroker ['pɔːnbrəukə'] n prêteur m sur gages
pawnshop ['pɔːnʃɔp] n mont-de-piété m
pay [peɪ] (pt, pp **paid**) [peɪd] n salaire m; (of manual worker) paie f ▷ vt payer; (be profitable to: also fig) rapporter à ▷ vi payer; (be profitable) être rentable; **how much did you ~ for it?** combien l'avez-vous payé?, vous l'avez payé combien?; **I paid £5 for that ticket** j'ai payé ce billet 5 livres; **can I ~ by credit card?** est-ce que je peux payer par carte de crédit?; **to ~ one's way** payer sa part; (company) couvrir ses frais; **to ~ dividends** (fig) porter ses fruits, s'avérer rentable; **it won't ~ you to do that** vous ne gagnerez rien à faire cela; **to ~ attention (to)** prêter attention (à); **to ~ sb a visit** rendre visite à qn; **to ~ one's respects to sb** présenter ses respects à qn; **pay back** vt rembourser; **pay for** vt fus payer; **pay in** vt verser; **pay off** vt (debts) régler, acquitter; (person) rembourser; (workers) licencier ▷ vi (scheme, decision) se révéler payant(e); **to ~ sth off in instalments** payer qch à tempérament; **pay out** vt (money) payer, sortir de sa poche; (rope) laisser filer; **pay up** vt (debts) régler; (amount) payer
payable ['peɪəbl] adj payable; **to make a cheque ~ to sb** établir un chèque à l'ordre de qn
pay-as-you-go [peɪəzjə'gəu] adj (mobile phone) à carte prépayée
payday n jour m de paie
payee [peɪ'iː] n bénéficiaire m/f
pay envelope n (US) paie f
payment ['peɪmənt] n paiement m; (of bill) règlement m; (of deposit, cheque) versement m; **advance ~** (part sum) acompte m; (total sum) paiement anticipé; **deferred ~, ~ by**

instalments paiement par versements échelonnés; **monthly ~** mensualité f; **in ~ for, in ~ of** en règlement; **on ~ of £5** pour 5 livres

payout ['peɪaʊt] n (from insurance) dédommagement m; (in competition) prix m

pay packet n (Brit) paie f

pay phone n cabine f téléphonique, téléphone public

pay raise n (US) = **pay rise**

pay rise n (Brit) augmentation f (de salaire)

payroll ['peɪrəʊl] n registre m du personnel; **to be on a firm's ~** être employé par une entreprise

pay slip n (Brit) bulletin m de paie, feuille f de paie

pay television n chaînes fpl payantes

PC n abbr = **personal computer**; (Brit) = **police constable** ▷ adj abbr = **politically correct** ▷ abbr (Brit) = **Privy Councillor**

p.c. abbr = **per cent**; **postcard**

pcm n abbr (= per calender month) par mois

PDA n abbr (= personal digital assistant) agenda m électronique

PE n abbr (= physical education) EPS f ▷ abbr (Canada) = **Prince Edward Island**

pea [pi:] n (petit) pois

peace [pi:s] n paix f; (calm) calme m, tranquillité f; **to be at ~ with sb/sth** être en paix avec qn/qch; **to keep the ~** (policeman) assurer le maintien de l'ordre; (citizen) ne pas troubler l'ordre

peaceful ['pi:sful] adj paisible, calme

peach [pi:tʃ] n pêche f

peacock ['pi:kɔk] n paon m

peak [pi:k] n (mountain) pic m, cime f; (of cap) visière f; (fig: highest level) maximum m; (: of career, fame) apogée m

peak hours npl heures fpl d'affluence or de pointe

peal [pi:l] n (of bells) carillon m; **~s of laughter** éclats mpl de rire

peanut ['pi:nʌt] n arachide f, cacahuète f

peanut butter n beurre m de cacahuète

pear [pɛər] n poire f

pearl [pə:l] n perle f

peasant ['pɛznt] n paysan(ne)

peat [pi:t] n tourbe f

pebble ['pɛbl] n galet m, caillou m

peck [pɛk] vt (also: **~ at**) donner un coup de bec à; (food) picorer ▷ n coup m de bec; (kiss) bécot m

pecking order ['pɛkɪŋ-] n ordre m hiérarchique

peckish ['pɛkɪʃ] adj (Brit inf): **I feel ~** je mangerais bien quelque chose, j'ai la dent

peculiar [prˈkju:lɪər] adj (odd) étrange, bizarre, curieux(-euse); (particular) particulier(-ière); **~ to** particulier à

pedal ['pɛdl] n pédale f ▷ vi pédaler

pedantic [prˈdæntɪk] adj pédant(e)

peddler ['pɛdlər] n colporteur m; camelot m

pedestal ['pɛdəstl] n piédestal m

pedestrian [prˈdɛstrɪən] n piéton m ▷ adj piétonnier(-ière); (fig) prosaïque, terre à terre inv

pedestrian crossing n (Brit) passage clouté

pedestrianized [prˈdɛstrɪənaɪzd] adj: **a ~ street** une rue piétonne

pedestrian precinct, (US) **pedestrian zone** n (Brit) zone piétonne

pediatrics [pi:dɪˈætrɪks] n (US) = **paediatrics**

pedigree ['pɛdɪgri:] n ascendance f; (of animal) pedigree m ▷ cpd (animal) de race

pedophile ['pi:dəʊfaɪl] (US) n = **paedophile**

pee [pi:] vi (inf) faire pipi, pisser

peek [pi:k] vi jeter un coup d'œil (furtif)

peel [pi:l] n pelure f, épluchure f; (of orange, lemon) écorce f ▷ vt peler, éplucher ▷ vi (paint etc) s'écailler; (wallpaper) se décoller; (skin) peler; **peel back** vt décoller

peep [pi:p] n (look) coup d'œil furtif; (sound) pépiement m ▷ vi (Brit) jeter un coup d'œil (furtif); **peep out** vi (Brit) se montrer (furtivement)

peephole ['pi:phəʊl] n judas m

peer [pɪər] vi: **to ~ at** regarder attentivement, scruter ▷ n (noble) pair m; (equal) pair, égal m

peerage ['pɪərɪdʒ] n pairie f

peeved [pi:vd] adj irrité(e), ennuyé(e)

peg [pɛg] n cheville f; (for coat etc) patère f; (Brit: also: **clothes ~**) pince f à linge ▷ vt (clothes) accrocher; (Brit: groundsheet) fixer (avec des piquets); (fig: prices, wages) contrôler, stabiliser

Pekinese, Pekingese [pi:kɪˈni:z] n pékinois m

pelican ['pɛlɪkən] n pélican m

pelican crossing n (Brit Aut) feu m à commande manuelle

pellet ['pɛlɪt] n boulette f; (of lead) plomb m

pelt [pɛlt] vt: **to ~ sb (with)** bombarder qn (de) ▷ vi (rain) tomber à seaux; (inf: run) courir à toutes jambes ▷ n peau f

pelvis ['pɛlvɪs] n bassin m

pen [pɛn] n (for writing) stylo m; (for sheep) parc m; (US inf: prison) taule f; **to put ~ to paper** prendre la plume

penal ['pi:nl] adj pénal(e)

penalize ['pi:nəlaɪz] vt pénaliser; (fig) désavantager

penalty ['pɛnltɪ] n pénalité f; sanction f; (fine) amende f; (Sport) pénalisation f; (also: **~ kick**: Football) penalty m; (: Rugby) pénalité f; **to pay the ~ for** être pénalisé(e) pour

penance ['pɛnəns] n pénitence f

pence [pɛns] npl of **penny**

pencil ['pɛnsl] n crayon m; **pencil in** vt noter provisoirement

pencil case n trousse f (d'écolier)

pencil sharpener n taille-crayon(s) m inv

pendant ['pɛndnt] n pendentif m

pending ['pɛndɪŋ] prep en attendant ▷ adj en suspens

pendulum ['pɛndjuləm] n pendule m; (of clock) balancier m

penetrate ['pɛnɪtreɪt] vt pénétrer dans; (enemy territory) entrer en; (sexually) pénétrer

pen friend n (Brit) correspondant(e)

penguin ['pɛŋgwɪn] n pingouin m

penicillin [ˌpɛnɪ'sɪlɪn] n pénicilline f

peninsula [pə'nɪnsjulə] n péninsule f

penis ['pi:nɪs] n pénis m, verge f

penitentiary [ˌpɛnɪ'tɛnʃərɪ] n (US) prison f

penknife ['pɛnnaɪf] n canif m

pen name n nom m de plume, pseudonyme m

penniless ['pɛnɪlɪs] adj sans le sou

penny (pl **pennies** or **pence**) ['pɛnɪ, 'pɛnɪz, pɛns] n (Brit) penny m; (US) cent m

pen pal n correspondant(e)

pension ['pɛnʃən] n (from company) retraite f; (Mil) pension f; **pension off** vt mettre à la retraite

pensioner ['pɛnʃənə'] n (Brit) retraité(e)

pension fund n caisse f de retraite

pension plan n plan m de retraite

pentagon ['pɛntəgən] n pentagone m; **the P~** (US Pol) le Pentagone; voir article

⊜ **PENTAGON**

⊜ Le Pentagon est le nom donné aux bureaux
⊜ du ministère de la Défense américain,
⊜ situés à Arlington en Virginie, à cause de
⊜ la forme pentagonale du bâtiment dans
⊜ lequel ils se trouvent. Par extension, ce
⊜ terme est également utilisé en parlant du
⊜ ministère lui-même.

pentathlon [pɛn'tæθlən] n pentathlon m

Pentecost ['pɛntɪkɔst] n Pentecôte f

penthouse ['pɛnthaus] n appartement m (de luxe) en attique

pent-up ['pɛntʌp] adj (feelings) refoulé(e)

penultimate [pɪ'nʌltɪmət] adj pénultième, avant-dernier(-ière)

people ['pi:pl] npl gens mpl; personnes fpl; (inhabitants) population f; (Pol) peuple m ⊳ n (nation, race) peuple m ⊳ vt peupler; **I know ~ who ...** je connais des gens qui ...; **the room was full of ~** la salle était pleine de monde or de gens; **several ~ came** plusieurs personnes sont venues; **~ say that ...** on dit or les gens disent que ...; **old ~** les personnes âgées; **young ~** les jeunes; **a man of the ~** un homme du peuple

pepper ['pɛpə'] n poivre m; (vegetable) poivron m ⊳ vt (Culin) poivrer

pepper mill n moulin m à poivre

peppermint ['pɛpəmɪnt] n (plant) menthe poivrée; (sweet) pastille f de menthe

pep talk ['pɛptɔ:k] n (inf) (petit) discours d'encouragement

per [pə:'] prep par; **~ hour** (miles etc) à l'heure; (fee) (de) l'heure; **~ kilo** etc le kilo etc;

~ day/~son par jour/personne; **~ annum** per an; **as ~ your instructions** conformément à vos instructions

perceive [pə'si:v] vt percevoir; (notice) remarquer, s'apercevoir de

per cent adv pour cent; **a 20 ~ discount** une réduction de 20 pour cent

percentage [pə'sɛntɪdʒ] n pourcentage m; **on a ~ basis** au pourcentage

perception [pə'sɛpʃən] n perception f; (insight) sensibilité f

perceptive [pə'sɛptɪv] adj (remark, person) perspicace

perch [pə:tʃ] n (fish) perche f; (for bird) perchoir m ⊳ vi (se) percher

percolator ['pə:kəleɪtə'] n percolateur m; cafetière f électrique

percussion [pə'kʌʃən] n percussion f

perennial [pə'rɛnɪəl] adj perpétuel(le); (Bot) vivace ⊳ n (Bot) (plante f) vivace f, plante pluriannuelle

perfect ['pə:fɪkt] adj parfait(e) ⊳ n (also: **~ tense**) parfait m ⊳ vt [pə'fɛkt] (technique, skill, work of art) parfaire; (method, plan) mettre au point; **he's a ~ stranger to me** il m'est totalement inconnu

perfection [pə'fɛkʃən] n perfection f

perfectly ['pə:fɪktlɪ] adv parfaitement; **I'm ~ happy with the situation** cette situation me convient parfaitement; **you know ~ well** vous le savez très bien

perforate ['pə:fəreɪt] vt perforer, percer

perforation [ˌpə:fə'reɪʃən] n perforation f; (line of holes) pointillé m

perform [pə'fɔ:m] vt (carry out) exécuter, remplir; (concert etc) donner ⊳ vi (actor, musician) jouer; (machine, car) marcher, fonctionner; (company, economy): **to ~ well/badly** produire de bons/mauvais résultats

performance [pə'fɔ:məns] n représentation f, spectacle m; (of an artist) interprétation f; (Sport: of car, engine) performance f; (of company, economy) résultats mpl; **the team put up a good ~** l'équipe a bien joué

performer [pə'fɔ:mə'] n artiste m/f

perfume ['pə:fju:m] n parfum m ⊳ vt parfumer

perhaps [pə'hæps] adv peut-être; **~ he'll ...** peut-être qu'il ...; **~ so/not** peut-être que oui/que non

peril ['pɛrɪl] n péril m

perimeter [pə'rɪmɪtə'] n périmètre m

period ['pɪərɪəd] n période f; (Hist) époque f; (Scol) cours m; (full stop) point m; (Med) règles fpl ⊳ adj (costume, furniture) d'époque; **for a ~ of three weeks** pour (une période de) trois semaines; **the holiday ~** (Brit) la période des vacances

periodical [ˌpɪərɪ'ɔdɪkl] adj périodique ⊳ n périodique m

periodically [pɪərɪˈɔdɪklɪ] *adv*
périodiquement

peripheral [pəˈrɪfərəl] *adj* périphérique ▷ *n*
(*Comput*) périphérique *m*

perish [ˈpɛrɪʃ] *vi* périr, mourir; (*decay*) se
détériorer

perishable [ˈpɛrɪʃəbl] *adj* périssable

perjury [ˈpəːdʒərɪ] *n* (*Law: in court*)
faux témoignage; (*breach of oath*)
parjure *m*

perk [pəːk] *n* (*inf*) avantage *m*, à-côté *m*; **perk
up** *vi* (*inf: cheer up*) se ragaillardir

perky [ˈpəːkɪ] *adj* (*cheerful*) guilleret(te), gai(e)

perm [pəːm] *n* (*for hair*) permanente *f* ▷ *vt*: **to
have one's hair ~ed** se faire faire une
permanente

permanent [ˈpəːmənənt] *adj* permanent(e);
(*job, position*) permanent, fixe; (*dye, ink*)
indélébile; **I'm not ~ here** je ne suis pas ici à
titre définitif; **~ address** adresse habituelle

permanently [ˈpəːmənəntlɪ] *adv* de façon
permanente; (*move abroad*) définitivement;
(*open, closed*) en permanence; (*tired, unhappy*)
constamment

permeate [ˈpəːmɪeɪt] *vi* s'infiltrer ▷ *vt*
s'infiltrer dans; pénétrer

permissible [pəˈmɪsɪbl] *adj* permis(e),
acceptable

permission [pəˈmɪʃən] *n* permission *f*,
autorisation *f*; **to give sb ~ to do sth** donner
à qn la permission de faire qch

permissive [pəˈmɪsɪv] *adj* tolérant(e); **the ~
society** la société de tolérance

permit *n* [ˈpəːmɪt] permis *m*; (*entrance pass*)
autorisation *f*, laissez-passer *m*; (*for goods*)
licence *f* ▷ *vt* [pəˈmɪt] permettre; **to ~ sb to
do** autoriser qn à faire, permettre à qn de
faire; **weather ~ting** si le temps le permet

perpendicular [pəːpənˈdɪkjuləʳ] *adj, n*
perpendiculaire *f*

perplex [pəˈplɛks] *vt* (*person*) rendre perplexe;
(*complicate*) embrouiller

persecute [ˈpəːsɪkjuːt] *vt* persécuter

persecution [pəːsɪˈkjuːʃən] *n* persécution *f*

persevere [pəːsɪˈvɪəʳ] *vi* persévérer

Persian [ˈpəːʃən] *adj* persan(e) ▷ *n* (*Ling*)
persan *m*; **the ~ Gulf** le golfe Persique

persist [pəˈsɪst] *vi*: **to ~ (in doing)** persister
(à faire), s'obstiner (à faire)

persistent [pəˈsɪstənt] *adj* persistant(e),
tenace; (*lateness, rain*) persistant; **~ offender**
(*Law*) multirécidiviste *m/f*

person [ˈpəːsn] *n* personne *f*; **in ~** en
personne; **on** *or* **about one's ~** sur soi; **to ~
call** (*Tel*) appel *m* avec préavis

personal [ˈpəːsnl] *adj* personnel(le);
~ belongings, **~ effects** effets personnels;
~ hygiene hygiène *f* intime; **a ~ interview**
un entretien

personal assistant *n* secrétaire
personnel(le)

personal column *n* annonces personnelles

personal computer *n* ordinateur
individuel, PC *m*

personality [pəːsəˈnælɪtɪ] *n* personnalité *f*

personally [ˈpəːsnəlɪ] *adv* personnellement;
to take sth ~ se sentir visé(e) par qch

personal organizer *n* agenda (personnel);
(*electronic*) agenda électronique

personal stereo *n* Walkman® *m*,
baladeur *m*

personnel [pəːsəˈnɛl] *n* personnel *m*

perspective [pəˈspɛktɪv] *n* perspective *f*; **to
get sth into ~** ramener qch à sa juste mesure

perspex® [ˈpəːspɛks] *n* (*Brit*) Plexiglas® *m*

perspiration [pəːspɪˈreɪʃən] *n* transpiration *f*

persuade [pəˈsweɪd] *vt*: **to ~ sb to do sth**
persuader qn de faire qch, amener *or* décider
qn à faire qch; **to ~ sb of sth/that** persuader
qn de qch/que

persuasion [pəˈsweɪʒən] *n* persuasion *f*;
(*creed*) conviction *f*

persuasive [pəˈsweɪsɪv] *adj* persuasif(-ive)

perverse [pəˈvəːs] *adj* pervers(e); (*contrary*)
entêté(e), contrariant(e)

pervert *n* [ˈpəːvəːt] perverti(e) ▷ *vt* [pəˈvəːt]
pervertir; (*words*) déformer

pessimism [ˈpɛsɪmɪzəm] *n* pessimisme *m*

pessimist [ˈpɛsɪmɪst] *n* pessimiste *m/f*

pessimistic [pɛsɪˈmɪstɪk] *adj* pessimiste

pest [pɛst] *n* animal *m* (*or* insecte *m*) nuisible;
(*fig*) fléau *m*

pester [ˈpɛstəʳ] *vt* importuner, harceler

pesticide [ˈpɛstɪsaɪd] *n* pesticide *m*

pet [pɛt] *n* animal familier; (*favourite*)
chouchou *m* ▷ *cpd* (*favourite*) favori(e) ▷ *vt*
choyer; (*stroke*) caresser, câliner ▷ *vi* (*inf*) se
peloter; **~ lion** *etc* lion *etc* apprivoisé;
teacher's ~ chouchou *m* du professeur;
~ hate bête noire

petal [ˈpɛtl] *n* pétale *m*

peter [ˈpiːtəʳ]: **to ~ out** *vi* s'épuiser; s'affaiblir

petite [pəˈtiːt] *adj* menu(e)

petition [pəˈtɪʃən] *n* pétition *f* ▷ *vt* adresser
une pétition à ▷ *vi*: **to ~ for divorce**
demander le divorce

petrified [ˈpɛtrɪfaɪd] *adj* (*fig*) mort(e) de peur

petrol [ˈpɛtrəl] *n* (*Brit*) essence *f*; **I've run out
of ~** je suis en panne d'essence

petrol can *n* (*Brit*) bidon *m* à essence

petroleum [pəˈtrəulɪəm] *n* pétrole *m*

petrol pump *n* (*Brit: in car, at garage*) pompe *f*
à essence

petrol station *n* (*Brit*) station-service *f*

petrol tank *n* (*Brit*) réservoir *m* d'essence

petticoat [ˈpɛtɪkəut] *n* jupon *m*

petty [ˈpɛtɪ] *adj* (*mean*) mesquin(e);
(*unimportant*) insignifiant(e), sans
importance

petty cash *n* caisse *f* des dépenses courantes,
petite caisse

petty officer *n* second-maître *m*

petulant [ˈpɛtjulənt] *adj* irritable

pew [pjuː] *n* banc *m* (d'église)

pewter ['pju:tə'] n étain m

phantom ['fæntəm] n fantôme m; (vision) fantasme m

pharmacist ['fɑ:məsɪst] n pharmacien(ne)

pharmacy ['fɑ:məsɪ] n pharmacie f

phase [feɪz] n phase f, période f; **phase in** vt introduire progressivement; **phase out** vt supprimer progressivement

Ph.D. abbr = **Doctor of Philosophy**

pheasant ['feznt] n faisan m

phenomena [fə'nɒmɪnə] npl of **phenomenon**

phenomenal [fɪ'nɒmɪnl] adj phénoménal(e)

phenomenon (pl **phenomena**) [fə'nɒmɪnən, -nə] n phénomène m

Philippines ['fɪlɪpi:nz] npl (also: **Philippine Islands**): **the ~** les Philippines fpl

philosopher [fɪ'lɒsəfə'] n philosophe m

philosophical [fɪlə'sɒfɪkl] adj philosophique

philosophy [fɪ'lɒsəfɪ] n philosophie f

phlegm [flem] n flegme m

phobia ['fəubjə] n phobie f

phone [fəun] n téléphone m ▷ vt téléphoner à ▷ vi téléphoner; **to be on the ~** avoir le téléphone; (be calling) être au téléphone; **phone back** vt, vi rappeler; **phone up** vt téléphoner à ▷ vi téléphoner

phone bill n facture f de téléphone

phone book n annuaire m

phone box, (US) **phone booth** n cabine f téléphonique

phone call n coup m de fil or de téléphone

phonecard ['fəunkɑ:d] n télécarte f

phone-in ['fəunɪn] n (Brit Radio, TV) programme m à ligne ouverte

phone number n numéro m de téléphone

phonetics [fə'netɪks] n phonétique f

phoney ['fəunɪ] adj faux/fausse, factice; (person) pas franc/franche ▷ n (person) charlatan m; fumiste m/f

photo ['fəutəu] n photo f; **to take a ~ of** prendre en photo

photo album n album m de photos

photocopier ['fəutəukɒpɪə'] n copieur m

photocopy ['fəutəukɒpɪ] n photocopie f ▷ vt photocopier

photograph ['fəutəgræf] n photographie f ▷ vt photographier; **to take a ~ of sb** prendre qn en photo

photographer [fə'tɒgrəfə'] n photographe m/f

photography [fə'tɒgrəfɪ] n photographie f

phrase [freɪz] n expression f; (Ling) locution f ▷ vt exprimer; (letter) rédiger

phrase book n recueil m d'expressions (pour touristes)

physical ['fɪzɪkl] adj physique; **~ examination** examen médical; **~ exercises** gymnastique f

physical education n éducation f physique

physically ['fɪzɪklɪ] adv physiquement

physician [fɪ'zɪʃən] n médecin m

physicist ['fɪzɪsɪst] n physicien(ne)

physics ['fɪzɪks] n physique f

physiotherapist [fɪzɪəu'θerəpɪst] n kinésithérapeute m/f

physiotherapy [fɪzɪəu'θerəpɪ] n kinésithérapie f

physique [fɪ'zi:k] n (appearance) physique m; (health etc) constitution f

pianist ['pi:ənɪst] n pianiste m/f

piano [pɪ'ænəu] n piano m

pick [pɪk] n (tool: also: **~-axe**) pic m, pioche f ▷ vt choisir; (gather) cueillir; (remove) prendre; (lock) forcer; (scab, spot) gratter, écorcher; **take your ~** faites votre choix; **the ~ of** le/la meilleur(e) de; **to ~ a bone** ronger un os; **to ~ one's nose** se mettre les doigts dans le nez; **to ~ one's teeth** se curer les dents; **to ~ sb's brains** faire appel aux lumières de qn; **to ~ pockets** pratiquer le vol à la tire; **to ~ a quarrel with sb** chercher noise à qn; **pick at** vt fus: **to ~ at one's food** manger du bout des dents, chipoter; **pick off** vt (kill) (viser soigneusement et) abattre; **pick on** vt fus (person) harceler; **pick out** vt choisir; (distinguish) distinguer; **pick up** vi (improve) remonter, s'améliorer ▷ vt ramasser; (telephone) décrocher; (collect) passer prendre; (Aut) prendre; (learn) apprendre; (Radio) capter; **to ~ up speed** prendre de la vitesse; **to ~ o.s. up** se relever; **to ~ up where one left off** reprendre là où l'on s'est arrêté

picket ['pɪkɪt] n (in strike) gréviste m/f participant à un piquet de grève; piquet m de grève ▷ vt mettre un piquet de grève devant

pickle ['pɪkl] n (also: **~s**: as condiment) pickles mpl ▷ vt conserver dans du vinaigre ou dans de la saumure; **in a ~** (fig) dans le pétrin

pickpocket ['pɪkpɒkɪt] n pickpocket m

pick-up ['pɪkʌp] n (also: **~ truck**) pick-up m inv; (Brit: on record player) bras m pick-up

picnic ['pɪknɪk] n pique-nique m ▷ vi piqueniquer

picnic area n aire f de pique-nique

picture ['pɪktʃə'] n (also TV) image f; (painting) peinture f, tableau m; (photograph) photo(graphie) f; (drawing) dessin m; (film) film m; (fig: description) description f ▷ vt (imagine) se représenter; (describe) dépeindre, représenter; **pictures** npl: **the ~s** (Brit) le cinéma; **to take a ~ of sb/sth** prendre qn/ qch en photo; **would you take a ~ of us, please?** pourriez-vous nous prendre en photo, s'il vous plaît?; **the overall ~** le tableau d'ensemble; **to put sb in the ~** mettre qn au courant

picture book n livre m d'images

picture frame n cadre m

picture messaging n picture messaging m, messagerie f d'images

picturesque [pɪktʃə'resk] adj pittoresque

pie [paɪ] n tourte f; (of fruit) tarte f; (of meat) pâté m en croûte

piece [piːs] n morceau m; (of land) parcelle f; (item): **a ~ of furniture/advice** un meuble/conseil; (Draughts) pion m ▷ vt: **to ~ together** rassembler; **in ~s** (broken) en morceaux, en miettes; (not yet assembled) en pièces détachées; **to take to ~s** démonter; **in one ~** (object) intact(e); **to get back all in one ~** (person) rentrer sain et sauf; **a 10p ~** (Brit) une pièce de 10p; **~ by ~** morceau par morceau; **a six-~ band** un orchestre de six musiciens; **to say one's ~** réciter son morceau

piecemeal ['piːsmiːl] adv par bouts

piecework ['piːswəːk] n travail m aux pièces or à la pièce

pie chart n graphique m à secteurs, camembert m

pier [pɪəʳ] n jetée f; (of bridge etc) pile f

pierce [pɪəs] vt percer, transpercer; **to have one's ears ~d** se faire percer les oreilles

pierced [pɪəst] adj (ears) percé(e)

pig [pɪg] n cochon m, porc m; (pej: unkind person) mufle m; (: greedy person) goinfre m

pigeon ['pɪdʒən] n pigeon m

pigeonhole ['pɪdʒənhəul] n casier m

piggy bank ['pɪgɪ-] n tirelire f

pigheaded ['pɪg'hɛdɪd] adj entêté(e), têtu(e)

piglet ['pɪglɪt] n petit cochon, porcelet m

pigskin ['pɪgskɪn] n (peau f de) porc m

pigsty ['pɪgstaɪ] n porcherie f

pigtail ['pɪgteɪl] n natte f, tresse f

pike [paɪk] n (spear) pique f; (fish) brochet m

pilchard ['pɪltʃəd] n pilchard m (sorte de sardine)

pile [paɪl] n (pillar, of books) pile f; (heap) tas m; (of carpet) épaisseur f; **in a ~** en tas; **pile on** vt: **to ~ it on** (inf) exagérer; **pile up** vi (accumulate) s'entasser, s'accumuler ▷ vt (put in heap) empiler, entasser; (accumulate) accumuler

piles [paɪlz] npl hémorroïdes fpl

pile-up ['paɪlʌp] n (Aut) télescopage m, collision f en série

pilfering ['pɪlfərɪŋ] n chapardage m

pilgrim ['pɪlgrɪm] n pèlerin m; voir article

---

pilgrimage ['pɪlgrɪmɪdʒ] n pèlerinage m

pill [pɪl] n pilule f; **the ~** la pilule; **to be on the ~** prendre la pilule

pillage ['pɪlɪdʒ] vt piller

pillar ['pɪləʳ] n pilier m

pillar box n (Brit) boîte f aux lettres (publique)

pillion ['pɪljən] n (of motor cycle) siège m arrière; **to ride ~** être derrière; (on horse) être en croupe

pillow ['pɪləu] n oreiller m

pillowcase ['pɪləukeɪs], **pillowslip** ['pɪləuslɪp] n taie f d'oreiller

pilot ['paɪlət] n pilote m ▷ cpd (scheme etc) pilote, expérimental(e) ▷ vt piloter

pilot light n veilleuse f

pimp [pɪmp] n souteneur m, maquereau m

pimple ['pɪmpl] n bouton m

PIN n abbr (= personal identification number) code m confidentiel

pin [pɪn] n épingle f; (Tech) cheville f; (Brit: drawing pin) punaise f; (in grenade) goupille f; (Brit Elec: of plug) broche f ▷ vt épingler; **~s and needles** fourmis fpl; **to ~ sb against/to** clouer qn contre/à; **to ~ sb down** (fig) coincer qn; **to ~ sth on sb** (fig) mettre qch sur le dos de qn; **pin down** vt (fig): **to ~ sb down** obliger qn à répondre; **there's something strange here but I can't quite ~ it down** il y a quelque chose d'étrange ici, mais je n'arrive pas exactement à savoir quoi

pinafore ['pɪnəfɔːʳ] n tablier m

pinball ['pɪnbɔːl] n flipper m

pincers ['pɪnsəz] npl tenailles fpl

pinch [pɪntʃ] n pincement m; (of salt etc) pincée f ▷ vt pincer; (inf: steal) piquer, chiper ▷ vi (shoe) serrer; **at a ~** à la rigueur; **to feel the ~** (fig) se ressentir des restrictions (or de la récession etc)

pincushion ['pɪnkuʃən] n pelote f à épingles

pine [paɪn] n (also: **~ tree**) pin m ▷ vi: **to ~ for** aspirer à, désirer ardemment; **pine away** vi dépérir

pineapple ['paɪnæpl] n ananas m

ping [pɪŋ] n (noise) tintement m

ping-pong® ['pɪŋpɔŋ] n ping-pong® m

pink [pɪŋk] adj rose ▷ n (colour) rose m; (Bot) œillet m, mignardise f

pinpoint ['pɪnpɔɪnt] vt indiquer (avec précision)

pint [paɪnt] n pinte f (Brit = 0,57 l; US = 0,47 l); (Brit inf) ≈ demi m, ≈ pot m

pioneer [paɪə'nɪəʳ] n explorateur(-trice); (early settler) pionnier m; (fig) pionnier, précurseur m ▷ vt être un pionnier de

pious ['paɪəs] adj pieux(-euse)

pip [pɪp] n (seed) pépin m; **pips** npl: **the ~s** (Brit: time signal on radio) le top

pipe [paɪp] n tuyau m, conduite f; (for smoking) pipe f; (Mus) pipeau m ▷ vt amener par tuyau; **pipes** npl (also: **bag~s**) cornemuse f; **pipe down** vi (inf) se taire

pipe cleaner n cure-pipe m

pipe dream n chimère f, utopie f

pipeline ['paɪplaɪn] n (for gas) gazoduc m,

pipeline m; (for oil) oléoduc m, pipeline; **it is in the ~** (fig) c'est en route, ça va se faire

piper ['paɪpə'] n (flautist) joueur(-euse) de pipeau; (of bagpipes) joueur(-euse) de cornemuse

piping ['paɪpɪŋ] adv: **~ hot** très chaud(e)

pique [piːk] n dépit m

pirate ['paɪərət] n pirate m ▷ vt (CD, video, book) pirater

pirated ['paɪərətɪd] adj pirate

Pisces ['paɪsiːz] n les Poissons mpl; **to be ~** être des Poissons

piss [pɪs] vi (inf!) pisser (!); **~ off!** tire-toi! (!)

pissed [pɪst] (inf!) adj (Brit: drunk) bourré(e); (US: angry) furieux(-euse)

pistol ['pɪstl] n pistolet m

piston ['pɪstən] n piston m

pit [pɪt] n trou m, fosse f; (also: **coal ~**) puits m de mine; (also: **orchestra ~**) fosse d'orchestre; (US: fruit stone) noyau m ▷ vt: **to ~ sb against sb** opposer qn à qn; **to ~ o.s. against** se mesurer à; **pits** npl (in motor racing) aire f de service

pitch [pɪtʃ] n (Brit Sport) terrain m; (throw) lancement m; (Mus) ton m; (of voice) hauteur f; (fig: degree) degré m; (also: **sales ~**) baratin m, boniment m; (Naut) tangage m; (tar) poix f ▷ vt (throw) lancer; (tent) dresser; (set: price, message) adapter, positionner ▷ vi (Naut) tanguer; (fall): **to ~ into/off** tomber dans/de; **to be ~ed forward** être projeté(e) en avant; **at this ~** à ce rythme

pitch-black ['pɪtʃ'blæk] adj noir(e) comme poix

pitched battle [pɪtʃ-] n bataille rangée

pitfall ['pɪtfɔːl] n trappe f, piège m

pith [pɪθ] n (of plant) moelle f; (of orange etc) intérieur m de l'écorce; (fig) essence f; vigueur f

pithy ['pɪθɪ] adj piquant(e); vigoureux(-euse)

pitiful ['pɪtɪful] adj (touching) pitoyable; (contemptible) lamentable

pitiless ['pɪtɪlɪs] adj impitoyable

pittance ['pɪtns] n salaire m de misère

pity ['pɪtɪ] n pitié f ▷ vt plaindre; **what a ~!** quel dommage!; **it is a ~ that you can't come** c'est dommage que vous ne puissiez venir; **to have** or **take ~ on sb** avoir pitié de qn

pizza ['piːtsə] n pizza f

placard ['plækɑːd] n affiche f; (in march) pancarte f

placate [plə'keɪt] vt apaiser, calmer

place [pleɪs] n endroit m, lieu m; (proper position, job, rank, seat) place f; (house) maison f, logement m; (in street names): **Laurel ~ ~** rue des Lauriers; (home): **at/to his ~** chez lui ▷ vt (position) placer, mettre; (identify) situer; reconnaître; **to take ~** avoir lieu; (occur) se produire; **to take sb's ~** remplacer qn; **to change ~s with sb** changer de place avec qn; **from ~ to ~** d'un endroit à l'autre; **all over**

the **~** partout; **out of ~** (not suitable) déplacé(e), inopportun(e); **I feel out of ~ here** je ne me sens pas à ma place ici; **in the first ~** d'abord, en premier; **to put sb in his ~** (fig) remettre qn à sa place; **he's going ~s** (fig: inf) il fait son chemin; **it is not my ~ to do it** ce n'est pas à moi de le faire; **to ~ an order with sb (for)** (Comm) passer commande à qn (de); **to be ~d** (in race, exam) se placer; **how are you ~d next week?** comment ça se présente pour la semaine prochaine?

place mat n set m de table; (in linen etc) napperon m

placement ['pleɪsmənt] n placement m; (during studies) stage m

placid ['plæsɪd] adj placide

plague [pleɪg] n fléau m; (Med) peste f ▷ vt (fig) tourmenter; **to ~ sb with questions** harceler qn de questions

plaice [pleɪs] n (pl inv) carrelet m

plaid [plæd] n tissu écossais

plain [pleɪn] adj (in one colour) uni(e); (clear) clair(e), évident(e); (simple) simple, ordinaire; (frank) franc/franche; (not handsome) quelconque, ordinaire; (cigarette) sans filtre; (without seasoning etc) nature inv ▷ adv franchement, carrément ▷ n plaine f; **in ~ clothes** (police) en civil; **to make sth ~ to sb** faire clairement comprendre qch à qn

plain chocolate n chocolat m à croquer

plainly ['pleɪnlɪ] adv clairement; (frankly) carrément, sans détours

plaintiff ['pleɪntɪf] n plaignant(e)

plait [plæt] n tresse f, natte f ▷ vt tresser, natter

plan [plæn] n plan m; (scheme) projet m ▷ vt (think in advance) projeter; (prepare) organiser ▷ vi faire des projets; **to ~ to do** projeter de faire; **how long do you ~ to stay?** combien de temps comptez-vous rester?

plane [pleɪn] n (Aviat) avion m; (also: **~ tree**) platane m; (tool) rabot m; (Art, Math etc) plan m; (fig) niveau m, plan ▷ adj plan(e); plat(e) ▷ vt (with tool) raboter

planet ['plænɪt] n planète f

plank [plæŋk] n planche f; (Pol) point m d'un programme

planner ['plænə'] n planificateur(-trice); (chart) planning m; **town** or (US) **city ~** urbaniste m/f

planning ['plænɪŋ] n planification f; **family ~** planning familial

planning permission n (Brit) permis m de construire

plant [plɑːnt] n plante f; (machinery) matériel m; (factory) usine f ▷ vt planter; (bomb) déposer, poser; (microphone, evidence) cacher

plantation [plæn'teɪʃən] n plantation f

plaque [plæk] n plaque f

plaster ['plɑːstə^r] n plâtre m; (also: ~ **of Paris**) plâtre à mouler; (Brit: also: **sticking ~**) pansement adhésif ▷ vt plâtrer; (cover): **to ~ with** couvrir de; **in ~** (Brit: leg etc) dans le plâtre

plaster cast n (Med) plâtre m; (model, statue) moule m

plastered ['plɑːstəd] adj (inf) soûl(e)

plastic ['plæstɪk] n plastique m ▷ adj (made of plastic) en plastique; (flexible) plastique, malléable; (art) plastique

plastic bag n sac m en plastique

plasticine® ['plæstɪsiːn] n pâte f à modeler

plastic surgery n chirurgie f esthétique

plate [pleɪt] n (dish) assiette f; (sheet of metal, on door: Phot) plaque f; (Typ) cliché m; (in book) gravure f; (dental) dentier m; (Aut: number plate) plaque minéralogique; **gold/silver ~** (dishes) vaisselle f d'or/d'argent

plateau (pl **plateaus** or **plateaux**) ['plætəu, -z] n plateau m

plate glass n verre m à vitre, vitre f

platform ['plætfɔːm] n (at meeting) tribune f; (Brit: of bus) plate-forme f; (stage) estrade f; (Rail^y) quai m; (Pol) plateforme f; **the train leaves from ~ 7** le train part de la voie 7

platinum ['plætɪnəm] n platine m

platoon [plə'tuːn] n peloton m

platter ['plætə^r] n plat m

plausible ['plɔːzɪbl] adj plausible; (person) convaincant(e)

play [pleɪ] n jeu m; (Theat) pièce f (de théâtre) ▷ vt (game) jouer à; (team, opponent) jouer contre; (instrument) jouer de; (part, piece of music, note) jouer; (CD etc) passer ▷ vi jouer; **to bring** or **call into ~** faire entrer en jeu; **to ~ safe** ne prendre aucun risque; **to ~ a trick on sb** jouer un tour à qn; **they're ~ing at soldiers** ils jouent aux soldats; **to ~ for time** (fig) chercher à gagner du temps; **to ~ into sb's hands** (fig) faire le jeu de qn; **play about, play around** vi (person) s'amuser; **play along** vi (fig): **to ~ along with** (person) entrer dans le jeu de ▷ vt (fig): **to ~ sb along** faire marcher qn; **play back** vt repasser, réécouter; **play down** vt minimiser; **play on** vt fus (sb's feelings, credulity) jouer sur; **to ~ on sb's nerves** porter sur les nerfs de qn; **play up** vi (cause trouble) faire des siennes

playboy ['pleɪbɔɪ] n playboy m

player ['pleɪə^r] n joueur(-euse); (Theat) acteur(-trice); (Mus) musicien(ne)

playful ['pleɪful] adj enjoué(e)

playground ['pleɪgraund] n cour f de récréation; (in park) aire f de jeux

playgroup ['pleɪgruːp] n garderie f

playing card ['pleɪɪŋ-] n carte f à jouer

playing field ['pleɪɪŋ-] n terrain m de sport

playmate ['pleɪmeɪt] n camarade m/f, copain/copine

play-off ['pleɪɔf] n (Sport) belle f

playpen ['pleɪpɛn] n parc m (pour bébé)

playschool ['pleɪskuːl] n = **playgroup**

plaything ['pleɪθɪŋ] n jouet m

playtime ['pleɪtaɪm] n (Scol) récréation f

playwright ['pleɪraɪt] n dramaturge m

plc abbr (Brit: = public limited company) ≈ SARL f

plea [pliː] n (request) appel m; (excuse) excuse f; (Law) défense f

plead [pliːd] vt plaider; (give as excuse) invoquer ▷ vi (Law) plaider; (beg): **to ~ with sb (for sth)** implorer qn (d'accorder qch); **to ~ for sth** implorer qch; **to ~ guilty/not guilty** plaider coupable/non coupable

pleasant ['plɛznt] adj agréable

pleasantry ['plɛzntrɪ] n (joke) plaisanterie f; **pleasantries** npl (polite remarks) civilités fpl

please [pliːz]-excl s'il te (or vous) plaît ▷ vt plaire à ▷ vi (think fit): **do as you ~** faites comme il vous plaira; **my bill, ~** l'addition, s'il vous plaît; **~ don't cry!** je t'en prie, ne pleure pas!; **~ yourself!** (inf) (faites) comme vous voulez!

pleased [pliːzd] adj: **~ (with)** content(e) (de); **~ to meet you** enchanté (de faire votre connaissance); **we are ~ to inform you that …** nous sommes heureux de vous annoncer que …

pleasing ['pliːzɪŋ] adj plaisant(e), qui fait plaisir

pleasure ['plɛʒə^r] n plaisir m; **"it's a ~"** "je vous en prie"; **with ~** avec plaisir; **is this trip for business or ~?** est-ce un voyage d'affaires ou d'agrément?

pleat [pliːt] n pli m

pledge [plɛdʒ] n gage m; (promise) promesse f ▷ vt engager; promettre; **to ~ support for sb** s'engager à soutenir qn; **to ~ sb to secrecy** faire promettre à qn de garder le secret

plentiful ['plɛntɪful] adj abondant(e), copieux(-euse)

plenty ['plɛntɪ] n abondance f; **~ of** beaucoup de; (sufficient) (bien) assez de; **we've got ~ of time** nous avons largement le temps

pliable ['plaɪəbl] adj flexible; (person) malléable

pliers ['plaɪəz] npl pinces fpl

plight [plaɪt] n situation f critique

plimsolls ['plɪmsəlz] npl (Brit) (chaussures fpl) tennis fpl

plinth [plɪnθ] n socle m

PLO n abbr (= Palestine Liberation Organization) OLP f

plod [plɔd] vi avancer péniblement; (fig) peiner

plonk [plɔŋk] (inf) n (Brit: wine) pinard m, piquette f ▷ vt: **to ~ sth down** poser brusquement qch

plot [plɔt] n complot m, conspiration f; (of story, play) intrigue f; (of land) lot m de terrain, lopin m ▷ vt (mark out) tracer point par point; (Naut) pointer; (make graph of) faire le graphique de; (conspire) comploter ▷ vi comploter; **a vegetable ~** (Brit) un carré de légumes

plough, plow (US) [plau] n charrue f ▷ vt (earth) labourer; **to ~ money into** investir dans; **plough back** vt (Comm) réinvestir; **plough through** vt fus (snow etc) avancer péniblement dans

ploughman, plowman (US) ['plaumən] irreg n laboureur m

plow [plau] (US) n = **plough**

ploy [plɔi] n stratagème m

pls abbr (= please) SVP m

pluck [plʌk] vt (fruit) cueillir; (musical instrument) pincer; (bird) plumer ▷ n courage m, cran m; **to ~ one's eyebrows** s'épiler les sourcils; **to ~ up courage** prendre son courage à deux mains

plug [plʌg] n (stopper) bouchon m, bonde f; (Elec) prise f de courant; (Aut: also: **spark(ing) ~**) bougie f ▷ vt (hole) boucher; (inf: advertise) faire du battage pour, matraquer; **to give sb/ sth a ~** (inf) faire de la pub pour qn/qch; **plug in** vt (Elec) brancher ▷ vi (Elec) se brancher

plughole ['plʌghəul] n (Brit) trou m (d'écoulement)

plum [plʌm] n (fruit) prune f ▷ adj: **~ job** (inf) travail m en or

plumb [plʌm] adj vertical(e) ▷ n plomb m ▷ adv (exactly) en plein ▷ vt sonder; **plumb in** vt (washing machine) faire le raccordement de

plumber ['plʌmə^r] n plombier m

plumbing ['plʌmɪŋ] n (trade) plomberie f; (piping) tuyauterie f

plummet ['plʌmɪt] vi (person, object) plonger; (sales, prices) dégringoler

plump [plʌmp] adj rondelet(te), dodu(e), bien en chair ▷ vt: **to ~ sth (down) on** laisser tomber qch lourdement sur; **plump for** vt fus (inf: choose) se décider pour; **plump up** vt (cushion) battre (pour lui redonner forme)

plunder ['plʌndə^r] n pillage m ▷ vt piller

plunge [plʌndʒ] n plongeon m; (fig) chute f ▷ vt plonger ▷ vi (fall) tomber, dégringoler; (dive) plonger; **to take the ~** se jeter à l'eau

plunging ['plʌndʒɪŋ] adj (neckline) plongeant(e)

pluperfect [plu:'pə:fɪkt] n (Ling) plus-que-parfait m

plural ['pluərl] adj pluriel(le) ▷ n pluriel m

plus [plʌs] n (also: **~ sign**) signe m plus; (advantage) atout m ▷ prep plus; **ten/twenty ~** plus de dix/vingt; **it's a ~** c'est un atout

plush [plʌʃ] adj somptueux(-euse) ▷ n peluche f

ply [plaɪ] n (of wool) fil m; (of wood) feuille f, épaisseur f ▷ vt (tool) manier; (a trade) exercer ▷ vi (ship) faire la navette; **three ~ (wool)** laine f à trois fils; **to ~ sb with drink** donner continuellement à boire à qn

plywood ['plaɪwud] n contreplaqué m

P.M. n abbr (Brit) = **prime minister**

p.m. adv abbr (= post meridiem) de l'après-midi

PMS n abbr (= premenstrual syndrome) syndrome prémenstruel

PMT n abbr (= premenstrual tension) syndrome prémenstruel

pneumatic [nju:'mætɪk] adj pneumatique

pneumatic drill [nju:'mætɪk-] n marteau-piqueur m

pneumonia [nju:'məunɪə] n pneumonie f

poach [pəutʃ] vt (cook) pocher; (steal) pêcher (or chasser) sans permis ▷ vi braconner

poached [pəutʃt] adj (egg) poché(e)

poacher ['pəutʃə^r] n braconnier m

P.O. Box n abbr = **post office box**

pocket ['pɔkɪt] n poche f ▷ vt empocher; **to be (£5) out of ~** (Brit) en être de sa poche (pour 5 livres)

pocketbook ['pɔkɪtbuk] n (notebook) carnet m; (US: wallet) portefeuille m; (: handbag) sac m à main

pocket knife n canif m

pocket money n argent m de poche

pod [pɔd] n cosse f ▷ vt écosser

podcast ['pɔdkɑːst] n podcast m ▷ vi podcaster

podgy ['pɔdʒɪ] adj rondelet(te)

podiatrist [pɔ'di:ətrɪst] n (US) pédicure m/f

podium ['pəudɪəm] n podium m

poem ['pəuɪm] n poème m

poet ['pəuɪt] n poète m

poetic [pəu'ɛtɪk] adj poétique

poetry ['pəuɪtrɪ] n poésie f

poignant ['pɔɪnjənt] adj poignant(e); (sharp) vif/vive

point [pɔɪnt] n (Geom, Scol, Sport, on scale) point m; (tip) pointe f; (in time) moment m; (in space) endroit m; (subject, idea) point, sujet m; (purpose) but m; (also: **decimal ~**): **2 ~ 3 (2.3)** 2 virgule 3 (2,3); (Brit Elec: also: **power ~**) prise f (de courant) ▷ vt (show) indiquer; (wall, window) jointoyer; (gun etc): **to ~ sth at** braquer or diriger qch sur ▷ vi: **to ~ at** montrer du doigt; **points** npl (Aut) vis platinées; (Rail) aiguillage m; **good ~s** qualités fpl; **the train stops at Carlisle and all ~s south** le train dessert Carlisle et toutes les gares vers le sud; **to make a ~** faire une remarque; **to make a ~ of doing sth** ne pas manquer de faire qch; **to make one's ~** se faire comprendre; **to get/ miss the ~** comprendre/ne pas comprendre; **to come to the ~** en venir au fait; **when it comes to the ~** le moment venu; **there's no ~ (in doing)** cela ne sert à rien (de faire); **to be on the ~ of doing sth** être sur le point de faire qch; **that's the whole ~!** précisément!; **to be beside the ~** être à côté de la question; **you've got a ~ there!** (c'est) juste!; **in ~ of fact** en fait, en réalité; **~ of departure** (also fig) point de départ; **~ of order** point de procédure; **~ of sale** (Comm) point de vente; **to ~ to sth** (fig) signaler; **point out** vt (show) montrer, indiquer; (mention) faire remarquer, souligner

point-blank ['pɔɪnt'blæŋk] adv (fig) catégoriquement; (also: **at ~ range**) à bout portant ▷ adj (fig) catégorique

pointed ['pɔɪntɪd] adj (shape) pointu(e); (remark) plein(e) de sous-entendus

pointer ['pɔɪntəʳ] n (stick) baguette f; (needle) aiguille f; (dog) chien m d'arrêt; (clue) indication f; (advice) tuyau m

pointless ['pɔɪntlɪs] adj inutile, vain(e)

point of view n point m de vue

poise [pɔɪz] n (balance) équilibre m; (of head, body) port m; (calmness) calme m ▷ vt placer en équilibre; **to be ~d for** (fig) être prêt à

poison ['pɔɪzn] n poison m ▷ vt empoisonner

poisonous ['pɔɪznəs] adj (snake) venimeux(-euse); (substance, plant) vénéneux(-euse); (fumes) toxique; (fig) pernicieux(-euse)

poke [pəuk] vt (fire) tisonner; (jab with finger, stick etc) piquer; pousser du doigt; (put): **to ~ sth in(to)** fourrer or enfoncer qch dans ▷ n (jab) (petit) coup; (to fire) coup m de tisonnier; **to ~ fun at sb** se moquer de qn; **poke about** vi fureter; **poke out** vi (stick out) sortir ▷ vt: **to ~ one's head out of the window** passer la tête par la fenêtre

poker ['pəukəʳ] n tisonnier m; (Cards) poker m

poky ['pəukɪ] adj exigu(ë)

Poland ['pəulənd] n Pologne f

polar ['pəuləʳ] adj polaire

polar bear n ours blanc

Pole [pəul] n Polonais(e)

pole [pəul] n (of wood) mât m, perche f; (Elec) poteau m; (Geo) pôle m

pole bean n (US) haricot m (à rames)

pole vault ['pəulvɔːlt] n saut m à la perche

police [pə'liːs] npl police f ▷ vt maintenir l'ordre dans; **a large number of ~ were hurt** de nombreux policiers ont été blessés

police car n voiture f de police

police constable n (Brit) agent m de police

police force n police f, forces fpl de l'ordre

policeman [pə'liːsmən] irreg n agent m de police, policier m

police officer n agent m de police

police station n commissariat m de police

policewoman [pə'liːswumən] irreg n femme-agent f

policy ['pɔlɪsɪ] n politique f; (also: **insurance ~**) police f (d'assurance); (of newspaper, company) politique générale; **to take out a ~** (Insurance) souscrire une police d'assurance

polio ['pəulɪəu] n polio f

Polish ['pəulɪʃ] adj polonais(e) ▷ n (Ling) polonais m

polish ['pɔlɪʃ] n (for shoes) cirage m; (for floor) cire f, encaustique f; (for nails) vernis m; (shine) éclat m, poli m; (fig: refinement) raffinement m ▷ vt (put polish on: shoes, wood) cirer; (make shiny) astiquer, faire briller; (fig: improve) perfectionner; **polish off** vt (work) expédier; (food) liquider

polished ['pɔlɪʃt] adj (fig) raffiné(e)

polite [pə'laɪt] adj poli(e); **it's not ~ to do that** ça ne se fait pas

politely [pə'laɪtlɪ] adv poliment

politeness [pə'laɪtnɪs] n politesse f

political [pə'lɪtɪkl] adj politique

politically [pə'lɪtɪklɪ] adv politiquement; **~ correct** politiquement correct(e)

politician [pɔlɪ'tɪʃən] n homme/femme politique, politicien(ne)

politics ['pɔlɪtɪks] n. politique f

poll [pəul] n scrutin m, vote m; (also: **opinion ~**) sondage m (d'opinion) ▷ vt (votes) obtenir; **to go to the ~s** (voters) aller aux urnes; (government) tenir des élections

pollen ['pɔlən] n pollen m

polling day n (Brit) jour m des élections

polling station n (Brit) bureau m de vote

pollute [pə'luːt] vt polluer

pollution [pə'luːʃən] n pollution f

polo ['pəuləu] n polo m

polo-neck ['pəuləunɛk] adj à col roulé ▷ n (sweater) pull m à col roulé

polo shirt n polo m

polyester [pɔlɪ'ɛstəʳ] n polyester m

polystyrene [pɔlɪ'staɪriːn] n polystyrène m

polythene ['pɔlɪθiːn] n (Brit) polyéthylène m

polythene bag n sac m en plastique

pomegranate ['pɔmɪgrænɪt] n grenade f

pomp [pɔmp] n pompe f, faste m, apparat m

pompous ['pɔmpəs] adj pompeux(-euse)

pond [pɔnd] n étang m; (stagnant) mare f

ponder ['pɔndəʳ] vi réfléchir ▷ vt considérer, peser

ponderous ['pɔndərəs] adj pesant(e), lourd(e)

pong [pɔŋ] (Brit inf) n puanteur f ▷ vi schlinguer

pony ['pəunɪ] n poney m

ponytail ['pəunɪteɪl] n queue f de cheval

pony trekking [-trɛkɪŋ] n (Brit) randonnée f équestre or à cheval

poodle ['puːdl] n caniche m

pool [puːl] n (of rain) flaque f; (pond) mare f; (artificial) bassin m; (also: **swimming ~**) piscine f; (sth shared) fonds commun; (money at cards) cagnotte f; (billiards) poule f; (Comm: consortium) pool m; (US: monopoly trust) trust m ▷ vt mettre en commun; **pools** npl (football) ≈ loto sportif; **typing ~**, (US) **secretary ~** pool m dactylographique; **to do the (football) ~s** (Brit) ≈ jouer au loto sportif; see also **football pools**

poor [puəʳ] adj pauvre; (mediocre) médiocre, faible, mauvais(e) ▷ npl: **the ~** les pauvres mpl

poorly ['puəlɪ] adv pauvrement; (badly) mal, médiocrement ▷ adj souffrant(e), malade

pop [pɔp] n (noise) bruit sec; (Mus) musique f pop; (inf: drink) soda m; (US inf: father) papa m ▷ vt (put) fourrer, mettre (rapidement) ▷ vi éclater; (cork) sauter; **she ~ped her head out of the window** elle passa la tête par la fenêtre; **pop in** vi entrer en passant; **pop out** vi sortir; **pop up** vi apparaître, surgir

popcorn ['pɒpkɔːn] n pop-corn m

pope [pəup] n pape m

poplar ['pɒplə] n peuplier m

popper ['pɒpə] n (Brit) bouton-pression m

poppy ['pɒpɪ] n (wild) coquelicot m; (cultivated) pavot m

Popsicle® ['pɒpsɪkl] n (US) esquimau m (glace)

pop star n pop star f

popular ['pɒpjulə] adj populaire; (fashionable) à la mode; **to be ~ (with)** (person) avoir du succès (auprès de); (decision) être bien accueilli(e) (par)

popularity [pɒpju'lærɪtɪ] n popularité f

population [pɒpju'leɪʃən] n population f

pop-up adj (Comput: menu, window) pop up inv ▷ n pop up m inv, fenêtre f pop up

porcelain ['pɔːslɪn] n porcelaine f

porch [pɔːtʃ] n porche m; (US) véranda f

porcupine ['pɔːkjupaɪn] n porc-épic m

pore [pɔː] n pore m ▷ vi: **to ~ over** s'absorber dans, être plongé(e) dans

pork [pɔːk] n porc m

pork chop n côte f de porc

pork pie n pâté m de porc en croûte

porn [pɔːn] adj (inf) porno ▷ n (inf) porno m

pornographic [pɔːnə'græfɪk] adj pornographique

pornography [pɔː'nɒgrəfɪ] n pornographie f

porpoise ['pɔːpəs] n marsouin m

porridge ['pɒrɪdʒ] n porridge m

port [pɔːt] n (harbour) port m; (opening in ship) sabord m; (Naut: left side) bâbord m; (wine) porto m; (Comput) port m, accès m ▷ cpd portuaire, du port; **to ~** (Naut) à bâbord; **~ of call** (port d')escale f

portable ['pɔːtəbl] adj portatif(-ive)

porter ['pɔːtə] n (for luggage) porteur m; (doorkeeper) gardien(ne); portier m

portfolio [pɔːt'fəuljəu] n portefeuille m; (of artist) portfolio m

porthole ['pɔːthəul] n hublot m

portion ['pɔːʃən] n portion f, part f

portrait ['pɔːtreɪt] n portrait m

portray [pɔː'treɪ] vt faire le portrait de; (in writing) dépeindre, représenter; (subj: actor) jouer

Portugal ['pɔːtjugl] n Portugal m

Portuguese [pɔːtju'giːz] adj portugais(e) ▷ n (pl inv) Portugais(e); (Ling) portugais m

pose [pəuz] n pose f; (pej) affectation f ▷ vi poser; (pretend): **to ~ as** se faire passer pour ▷ vt poser; (problem) créer; **to strike a ~** poser (pour la galerie)

posh [pɒʃ] adj (inf) chic inv; **to talk ~** parler d'une manière affectée

position [pə'zɪʃən] n position f; (job, situation) situation f ▷ vt mettre en place or en position; **to be in a ~ to do sth** être en mesure de faire qch

positive ['pɒzɪtɪv] adj positif(-ive); (certain) sûr(e), certain(e); (definite) formel(le), catégorique; (clear) indéniable, réel(le)

positively ['pɒzɪtɪvlɪ] adv (affirmatively, enthusiastically) de façon positive; (inf: really) carrément; **to think ~** être positif(-ive)

possess [pə'zes] vt posséder; **like one ~ed** comme un fou; **whatever can have ~ed you?** qu'est-ce qui vous a pris?

possession [pə'zeʃən] n possession f; **possessions** npl (belongings) affaires fpl; **to take ~ of sth** prendre possession de qch

possessive [pə'zesɪv] adj possessif(-ive)

possibility [pɒsɪ'bɪlɪtɪ] n possibilité f; (event) éventualité f; **he's a ~ for the part** c'est un candidat possible pour le rôle

possible ['pɒsɪbl] adj possible; (solution) envisageable, éventuel(le); **it is ~ to do it** il est possible de le faire; **as far as ~** dans la mesure du possible, autant que possible; **if ~** si possible; **as big as ~** aussi gros que possible

possibly ['pɒsɪblɪ] adv (perhaps) peut-être; **if you ~ can** si cela vous est possible; **I cannot ~ come** il m'est impossible de venir

post [pəust] n (Brit: mail) poste f; (: collection) levée f; (: letters, delivery) courrier m; (job, situation) poste m; (pole) poteau m; (trading post) comptoir (commercial); (on internet forum) billet m, post m ▷ vt (to internet) poster; (Brit: send by post, Mil) poster; (: appoint): **to ~** affecter à; (notice) afficher; **by ~** (Brit) par la poste; **by return of ~** (Brit) par retour du courrier; **where can I ~ these cards?** où est-ce que je peux poster ces cartes postales?; **to keep sb ~ed** tenir qn au courant

postage ['pəustɪdʒ] n tarifs mpl d'affranchissement; **~ paid** port payé; **~ prepaid** (US) franco de port

postal ['pəustl] adj postal(e)

postal order n mandat(-poste m) m

postbox ['pəustbɒks] n (Brit) boîte f aux lettres (publique)

postcard ['pəustkɑːd] n carte postale

postcode ['pəustkəud] n (Brit) code postal

poster ['pəustə] n affiche f

poste restante [pəust'restɑ̃ːnt] n (Brit) poste restante

postgraduate ['pəust'grædjuət] n =étudiant(e) de troisième cycle

posthumous ['pɒstjuməs] adj posthume

postman ['pəustmən] (Brit) irreg n facteur m

postmark ['pəustmɑːk] n cachet m (de la poste)

post-mortem [pəust'mɔːtəm] n autopsie f

post office n (building) poste f; (organization): **the Post Office** les postes fpl

post office box n boîte postale

postpone [pəs'pəun] vt remettre (à plus tard), reculer

P

posture ['pɒstʃə'] n posture f; (fig) attitude f
▷ vi poser

postwar [pəust'wɔː'] adj d'après-guerre

postwoman [pəust'wumən] (Brit) irreg n
factrice f

posy ['pəuzi] n petit bouquet

pot [pɒt] n (for cooking) marmite f; casserole f;
(teapot) théière f; (for coffee) cafetière f; (for
plants, jam) pot m; (piece of pottery) poterie f;
(inf: marijuana) herbe f ▷ vt (plant) mettre en
pot; **to go to ~** (inf) aller à vau-l'eau; **~s of**
(Brit inf) beaucoup de, plein de

potato (pl **potatoes**) [pə'teɪtəu] n pomme f
de terre

potato peeler n épluche-légumes m

potent ['pəutnt] adj puissant(e); (drink)
fort(e), très alcoolisé(e); (man) viril

potential [pə'tɛnʃl] adj potentiel(le) ▷ n
potentiel m; **to have ~** être
prometteur(-euse); ouvrir des possibilités

pothole ['pɒthəul] n (in road) nid m de poule;
(Brit: underground) gouffre m, caverne f

potholing ['pɒthəulɪŋ] n (Brit): **to go ~** faire
de la spéléologie

potluck [pɒt'lʌk] n: **to take ~** tenter sa
chance

pot plant n plante f d'appartement

potted ['pɒtɪd] adj (food) en conserve; (plant)
en pot; (fig: shortened) abrégé(e)

potter ['pɒtə'] n potier m ▷ vi (Brit): **to ~
around** or **about** bricoler; **~'s wheel** tour m
de potier

pottery ['pɒtərɪ] n poterie f; **a piece of ~** une
poterie

potty ['pɒtɪ] adj (Brit inf: mad) dingue ▷ n
(child's) pot m

pouch [pautʃ] n (Zool) poche f; (for tobacco)
blague f; (for money) bourse f

poultry ['pəultrɪ] n volaille f

pounce [pauns] vi: **to ~ (on)** bondir (sur),
fondre (sur) ▷ n bond m, attaque f

pound [paund] n livre f (weight = 453g, 16 ounces;
money = 100 pence); (for dogs, cars) fourrière f ▷ vt
(beat) bourrer de coups, marteler; (crush)
piler, pulvériser; (with guns) pilonner ▷ vi
(heart) battre violemment, taper; **half a ~ (of)**
une demi-livre (de); **a five-~ note** un billet de
cinq livres

pound sterling n livre f sterling

pour [pɔː'] vt verser ▷ vi couler à flots; (rain)
pleuvoir à verse; **to ~ sb a drink** verser or
servir à boire à qn; **to come ~ing in** (water)
entrer à flots; (letters) arriver par milliers;
(cars, people) affluer; **pour away, pour off** vt
vider; **pour in** vi (people) affluer, se précipiter;
(news, letters) arriver en masse; **pour out** vi
(people) sortir en masse ▷ vt vider; (fig)
déverser; (serve: a drink) verser

pouring ['pɔːrɪŋ] adj: **~ rain** pluie
torrentielle

pout [paut] n moue f ▷ vi faire la moue

poverty ['pɒvətɪ] n pauvreté f, misère f

poverty-stricken ['pɒvətɪstrɪkn] adj pauvre,
déshérité(e)

powder ['paudə'] n poudre f ▷ vt poudrer; **to
~ one's nose** se poudrer; (euphemism) aller à la
salle de bain

powder compact n poudrier m

powdered milk n lait m en poudre

powder room n toilettes fpl (pour dames)

power ['pauə'] n (strength, nation) puissance f,
force f; (ability, Pol: of party, leader) pouvoir m;
(Math) puissance; (of speech, thought) faculté f;
(Elec) courant m ▷ vt faire marcher,
actionner; **to do all in one's ~ to help sb**
faire tout ce qui est en son pouvoir pour aider
qn; **the world ~s** les grandes puissances; **to
be in ~** être au pouvoir

power cut n (Brit) coupure f de courant

powered ['pauəd] adj: **~ by** actionné(e) par,
fonctionnant à; **nuclear-~ submarine** sous-
marin m (à propulsion) nucléaire

power failure n panne f de courant

powerful ['pauəful] adj puissant(e);
(performance etc) très fort(e)

powerless ['pauəlɪs] adj impuissant(e)

power point n (Brit) prise f de courant

power station n centrale f électrique

power struggle n lutte f pour le pouvoir

p.p. n abbr (= per procurationem: by proxy) p.p.

PR n abbr = **proportional representation;
public relations** ▷ abbr (US) = **Puerto Rico**

practical ['præktɪkl] adj pratique

practicality [præktɪ'kælɪtɪ] n (of plan)
aspect m pratique; (of person) sens m pratique;
practicalities npl détails mpl pratiques

practical joke n farce f

practically ['præktɪklɪ] adv (almost)
pratiquement

practice ['præktɪs] n pratique f; (of profession)
exercice m; (at football etc) entraînement m;
(business) cabinet m; clientèle f ▷ vt, vi (US)
= **practise; in ~** (in reality) en pratique; **out of ~**
rouillé(e); **2 hours' piano ~** 2 heures de
travail or d'exercices au piano; **target ~**
exercices de tir; **it's common ~** c'est courant,
ça se fait couramment; **to put sth into ~**
mettre qch en pratique

practise, (US) **practice** ['præktɪs] vt (work at:
piano, backhand etc) s'exercer à, travailler; (train
for: sport) s'entraîner à; (a sport, religion, method)
pratiquer; (profession) exercer ▷ vi s'exercer,
travailler; (train) s'entraîner; (lawyer, doctor)
exercer; **to ~ for a match** s'entraîner pour
un match

practising, (US) **practicing** ['præktɪsɪŋ] adj
(Christian etc) pratiquant(e); (lawyer) en
exercice; (homosexual) déclaré

practitioner [præk'tɪʃənə'] n praticien(ne)

pragmatic [præg'mætɪk] adj pragmatique

prairie ['prɛərɪ] n savane f; (US): **the ~s** la
Prairie

praise [preɪz] n éloge(s) m(pl), louange(s) f(pl)
▷ vt louer, faire l'éloge de

praiseworthy ['preɪzwɜːðɪ] *adj* digne de louanges

pram [præm] *n* (*Brit*) landau *m*, voiture *f* d'enfant

prance [prɑːns] *vi* (*horse*) caracoler

prank [præŋk] *n* farce *f*

prawn [prɔːn] *n* crevette *f* (rose)

prawn cocktail *n* cocktail *m* de crevettes

pray [preɪ] *vi* prier

prayer [prɛəʳ] *n* prière *f*

preach [priːtʃ] *vt*, *vi* prêcher; **to ~ at sb** faire la morale à qn

preacher ['priːtʃəʳ] *n* prédicateur *m*; (*US*: *clergyman*) pasteur *m*

precarious [prɪ'kɛərɪəs] *adj* précaire

precaution [prɪ'kɔːʃən] *n* précaution *f*

precede [prɪ'siːd] *vt*, *vi* précéder

precedent ['presɪdənt] *n* précédent *m*; **to establish** *or* **set a ~** créer un précédent

preceding [prɪ'siːdɪŋ] *adj* qui précède (*or* précédait)

precinct ['priːsɪŋkt] *n* (*round cathedral*) pourtour *m*, enceinte *f*; (*US*: *district*) circonscription *f*, arrondissement *m*; **precincts** *npl* (*neighbourhood*) alentours *mpl*, environs *mpl*; **pedestrian ~** (*Brit*) zone piétonnière; **shopping ~** (*Brit*) centre commercial

precious ['preʃəs] *adj* précieux(-euse) ▷ *adv* (*inf*): **~ little** *or* **few** fort peu; **your ~ dog** (*ironic*) ton chien chéri, ton chéri chien

precipitate [prɪ'sɪpɪtɪt] *adj* (*hasty*) précipité(e) ▷ *vt* [prɪ'sɪpɪteɪt] précipiter

precise [prɪ'saɪs] *adj* précis(e)

precisely [prɪ'saɪslɪ] *adv* précisément

precision [prɪ'sɪʒən] *n* précision *f*

precocious [prɪ'kəʊʃəs] *adj* précoce

precondition ['priːkən'dɪʃən] *n* condition *f* nécessaire

predator ['predətəʳ] *n* prédateur *m*, rapace *m*

predecessor ['priːdɪsɛsəʳ] *n* prédécesseur *m*

predicament [prɪ'dɪkəmənt] *n* situation *f* difficile

predict [prɪ'dɪkt] *vt* prédire

predictable [prɪ'dɪktəbl] *adj* prévisible

prediction [prɪ'dɪkʃən] *n* prédiction *f*

predominantly [prɪ'dɒmɪnəntlɪ] *adv* en majeure partie; (*especially*) surtout

pre-empt [priː'emt] *vt* (*Brit*) acquérir par droit de préemption; (*fig*) anticiper sur; **to ~ the issue** conclure avant même d'ouvrir les débats

preen [priːn] *vt*: **to ~ itself** (*bird*) se lisser les plumes; **to ~ o.s.** s'admirer

prefab ['priːfæb] *n abbr* (= *prefabricated building*) bâtiment préfabriqué

preface ['prefəs] *n* préface *f*

prefect ['priːfekt] *n* (*Brit*: *in school*) élève chargé de certaines fonctions de discipline; (*in France*) préfet *m*

prefer [prɪ'fɜːʳ] *vt* préférer; (*Law*): **to ~ charges** procéder à une inculpation; **to ~ coffee to tea** préférer le café au thé; **to ~ doing** *or* **to do sth** préférer faire qch

preferable ['prefrəbl] *adj* préférable

preferably ['prefrəblɪ] *adv* de préférence

preference ['prefrəns] *n* préférence *f*; **in ~ to sth** plutôt que qch, de préférence à qch

preferential [prefə'renʃəl] *adj* préférentiel(le); **~ treatment** traitement *m* de faveur

prefix ['priːfɪks] *n* préfixe *m*

pregnancy ['pregnənsɪ] *n* grossesse *f*

pregnant ['pregnənt] *adj* enceinte *adj f*; (*animal*) pleine; **3 months ~** enceinte de 3 mois

prehistoric ['priːhɪs'tɒrɪk] *adj* préhistorique

prejudice ['predʒudɪs] *n* préjugé *m*; (*harm*) tort *m*, préjudice *m* ▷ *vt* porter préjudice à; (*bias*): **to ~ sb in favour of/against** prévenir qn en faveur de/contre; **racial ~** préjugés raciaux

prejudiced ['predʒudɪst] *adj* (*person*) plein(e) de préjugés; (*in a matter*) partial(e); (*view*) préconçu(e), partial(e); **to be ~ against sb/sth** avoir un parti-pris contre qn/qch; **to be racially ~** avoir des préjugés raciaux

preliminary [prɪ'lɪmɪnərɪ] *adj* préliminaire

prelude ['preljuːd] *n* prélude *m*

premarital ['priː'mærɪtl] *adj* avant le mariage; **~ contract** contrat *m* de mariage

premature ['premətʃʊəʳ] *adj* prématuré(e); **to be ~ (in doing sth)** aller un peu (trop) vite (en faisant qch)

premier ['premɪəʳ] *adj* premier(-ière), principal(e) ▷ *n* (*Pol*: *Prime Minister*) premier ministre; (*Pol*: *President*) chef *m* de l'État

premiere ['premɪɛəʳ] *n* première *f*

Premier League *n* première division

premise ['premɪs] *n* prémisse *f*

premises ['premɪsɪz] *n* locaux *mpl*; **on the ~** sur les lieux; sur place; **business ~** locaux commerciaux

premium ['priːmɪəm] *n* prime *f*; **to be at a ~** (*fig*: *housing etc*) être très demandé(e), être rarissime; **to sell at a ~** (*shares*) vendre au-dessus du pair

premium bond *n* (*Brit*) obligation *f* à prime, bon *m* à lots

premonition [premə'nɪʃən] *n* prémonition *f*

preoccupied [priː'ɒkjupaɪd] *adj* préoccupé(e)

prep [prep] *adj abbr*: **~ school** = **preparatory school** ▷ *n abbr* (= *preparation*) étude *f*

prepaid [priː'peɪd] *adj* payé(e) d'avance

preparation [prepə'reɪʃən] *n* préparation *f*; **preparations** *npl* (*for trip, war*) préparatifs *mpl*; **in ~ for** en vue de

preparatory [prɪ'pærətərɪ] *adj* préparatoire; **~ to sth/to doing sth** en prévision de qch/ avant de faire qch

preparatory school *n* (*Brit*) école primaire privée; (*US*) lycée privé; *voir article*

En Grande-Bretagne, une *preparatory school* – ou, plus familièrement, une *prep school* – est une école payante qui prépare les enfants de 7 à 13 ans aux "public schools".

prepare [prɪ'pɛəʳ] *vt* préparer ▷ *vi*: **to ~ for** se préparer à

prepared [prɪ'pɛəd] *adj*: **~ for** préparé(e) à; **~ to** prêt(e) à

preposition [prɛpə'zɪʃən] *n* préposition f

preposterous [prɪ'pɔstərəs] *adj* ridicule, absurde

prep school *n* = **preparatory school**

prerequisite [priː'rɛkwɪzɪt] *n* condition f préalable

presbyterian [prɛzbɪ'tɪərɪən] *adj, n* presbytérien(ne)

preschool ['priː'skuːl] *adj* préscolaire; *(child)* d'âge préscolaire

prescribe [prɪ'skraɪb] *vt* prescrire; **~d books** *(Brit Scol)* œuvres *fpl* au programme

prescription [prɪ'skrɪpʃən] *n* prescription f; *(Med)* ordonnance f; (: *medicine*) médicament m (obtenu sur ordonnance); **to make up** or *(US)* **fill a ~** faire une ordonnance; **could you write me a ~?** pouvez-vous me faire une ordonnance?; **"only available on ~"** "uniquement sur ordonnance"

presence ['prɛzns] *n* présence f; **in sb's ~** en présence de qn; **~ of mind** présence d'esprit

present ['prɛznt] *adj* présent(e); *(current)* présent, actuel(le) ▷ *n* cadeau m; *(actuality, also*: **~ tense**) présent m ▷ *vt* [prɪ'zɛnt] présenter; *(prize, medal)* remettre; *(give)*: **to ~ sb with sth** offrir qch à qn; **to be ~ at** assister à; **those ~** les présents; **at ~** ce moment; **to give sb a ~** offrir un cadeau à qn; **to ~ sb (to sb)** présenter qn (à qn)

presentable [prɪ'zɛntəbl] *adj* présentable

presentation [prɛzn'teɪʃən] *n* présentation f; *(gift)* cadeau m, présent m; *(ceremony)* remise f du cadeau (or de la médaille *etc*); **on ~ of** *(voucher etc)* sur présentation de

present-day ['prɛzntdeɪ] *adj* contemporain(e), actuel(le)

presenter [prɪ'zɛntəʳ] *n* (Brit Radio, TV) présentateur(-trice)

presently ['prɛzntlɪ] *adv (soon)* tout à l'heure, bientôt; *(with verb in past)* peu après; *(at present)* en ce moment; *(US: now)* maintenant

preservation [prɛzə'veɪʃən] *n* préservation f, conservation f

preservative [prɪ'zəːvətɪv] *n* agent m de conservation

preserve [prɪ'zəːv] *vt (keep safe)* préserver, protéger; *(maintain)* conserver, garder; *(food)* mettre en conserve ▷ *n (for game, fish)* réserve f; *(often pl: jam)* confiture f; (: *fruit*) fruits *mpl* en conserve

preside [prɪ'zaɪd] *vi* présider

president ['prɛzɪdənt] *n* président(e); (US: *of company*) président-directeur général, PDG *m*

presidential [prɛzɪ'dɛnʃl] *adj* présidentiel(le)

press [prɛs] *n (tool, machine, newspapers)* presse f; *(for wine)* pressoir m; *(crowd)* cohue f, foule f ▷ *vt (push)* appuyer sur; *(squeeze)* presser, serrer; *(clothes: iron)* repasser; *(pursue)* talonner; *(insist)*: **to ~ sth on sb** presser qn d'accepter qch; *(urge, entreat)*: **to ~ sb to do** or **into doing sth** pousser qn à faire qch ▷ *vi* appuyer, peser; se presser; **we are ~ed for time** le temps nous manque; **to ~ for sth** faire pression pour obtenir qch; **to ~ sb for an answer** presser qn de répondre; **to ~ charges against sb** *(Law)* engager des poursuites contre qn; **to go to ~** *(newspaper)* aller à l'impression; **to be in the ~** *(being printed)* être sous presse; *(in the newspapers)* être dans le journal; **press ahead** *vi* = **press on**; **press on** *vi* continuer

press conference *n* conférence f de presse

pressing ['prɛsɪŋ] *adj* urgent(e), pressant(e) ▷ *n* repassage m

press stud *n* (Brit) bouton-pression m

press-up ['prɛsʌp] *n* (Brit) traction f

pressure ['prɛʃəʳ] *n* pression f; *(stress)* tension f ▷ *vt* = **to put pressure on**; **to put ~ on sb (to do sth)** faire pression sur qn (pour qu'il fasse qch)

pressure cooker *n* cocotte-minute® f

pressure gauge *n* manomètre m

pressure group *n* groupe m de pression

prestige [prɛs'tiːʒ] *n* prestige m

prestigious [prɛs'tɪdʒəs] *adj* prestigieux(-euse)

presumably [prɪ'zjuːməblɪ] *adv* vraisemblablement; **~ he did it** c'est sans doute lui (qui a fait cela)

presume [prɪ'zjuːm] *vt* présumer, supposer; **to ~ to do** *(dare)* se permettre de faire

pretence, (US) **pretense** [prɪ'tɛns] *n (claim)* prétention f; *(pretext)* prétexte m; **she is devoid of all ~** elle n'est pas du tout prétentieuse; **to make a ~ of doing** faire semblant de faire; **on** or **under the ~ of doing sth** sous prétexte de faire qch; **under false ~s** sous des prétextes fallacieux

pretend [prɪ'tɛnd] *vt (feign)* feindre, simuler ▷ *vi (feign)* faire semblant; *(claim)*: **to ~ to sth** prétendre à qch; **to ~ to do** faire semblant de faire

pretense [prɪ'tɛns] *n* (US) = **pretence**

pretentious [prɪ'tɛnʃəs] *adj* prétentieux(-euse)

pretext ['priːtɛkst] *n* prétexte m; **on** or **under the ~ of doing sth** sous prétexte de faire qch

pretty ['prɪtɪ] *adj* joli(e) ▷ *adv* assez

prevail [prɪ'veɪl] *vi (win)* l'emporter, prévaloir; *(be usual)* avoir cours; *(persuade)*: **to ~ (up)on sb to do** persuader qn de faire

prevailing [prɪˈveɪlɪŋ] *adj* (*widespread*) courant(e), répandu(e); (*wind*) dominant(e)

prevalent [ˈprevələnt] *adj* répandu(e), courant(e); (*fashion*) en vogue

prevent [prɪˈvent] *vt*: **to ~ (from doing)** empêcher (de faire)

preventative [prɪˈventətɪv] *adj* préventif(-ive)

prevention [prɪˈvenʃən] *n* prévention *f*

preventive [prɪˈventɪv] *adj* préventif(-ive)

preview [ˈpriːvjuː] *n* (*of film*) avant-première *f*; (*fig*) aperçu *m*

previous [ˈpriːvɪəs] *adj* (*last*) précédent(e); (*earlier*) antérieur(e); (*question, experience*) préalable; **I have a ~ engagement** je suis déjà pris(e); **~ to doing** avant de faire

previously [ˈpriːvɪəslɪ] *adv* précédemment, auparavant

prewar [ˈpriːˈwɔːˈ] *adj* d'avant-guerre

prey [preɪ] *n* proie *f* ▷ *vi*: **to ~ on** s'attaquer à; **it was ~ing on his mind** ça le rongeait *or* minait

price [praɪs] *n* prix *m*; (*Betting: odds*) cote *f* ▷ *vt* (*goods*) fixer le prix de; tarifer; **what is the ~ of …?** combien coûte …?, quel est le prix de …?; **to go up** *or* **rise in ~** augmenter; **to put a ~ on sth** chiffrer qch; **to be ~d out of the market** (*article*) être trop cher pour soutenir la concurrence; (*producer, nation*) ne pas pouvoir soutenir la concurrence; **what ~ his promises now?** (*Brit*) que valent maintenant toutes ses promesses?; **he regained his freedom, but at a ~** il a retrouvé sa liberté, mais cela lui a coûté cher

priceless [ˈpraɪslɪs] *adj* sans prix, inestimable; (*inf: amusing*) impayable

price list *n* tarif *m*

prick [prɪk] *n* (*sting*) piqûre *f*; (*inf!*) bitte *f* (!); connard *m* (!) ▷ *vt* piquer; **to ~ up one's ears** dresser *or* tendre l'oreille

prickle [ˈprɪkl] *n* (*of plant*) épine *f*; (*sensation*) picotement *m*

prickly [ˈprɪklɪ] *adj* piquant(e), épineux(-euse); (*fig: person*) irritable

prickly heat *n* fièvre *f* miliaire

pride [praɪd] *n* (*feeling proud*) fierté *f*; (*pej*) orgueil *m*; (*self-esteem*) amour-propre *m* ▷ *vt*: **to ~ o.s. on** se flatter de; s'enorgueillir de; **to take (a) ~ in** être (très) fier(-ère) de; **to take a ~ in doing** mettre sa fierté à faire; **to have ~ of place** (*Brit*) avoir la place d'honneur

priest [priːst] *n* prêtre *m*

priesthood [ˈpriːsthud] *n* prêtrise *f*, sacerdoce *m*

prim [prɪm] *adj* collet monté *inv*, guindé(e)

primarily [ˈpraɪmərɪlɪ] *adv* principalement, essentiellement

primary [ˈpraɪmərɪ] *adj* primaire; (*first in importance*) premier(-ière), primordial(e) ▷ *n* (*US: election*) (élection *f*) primaire *f*

primary school *n* (*Brit*) école *f* primaire; *voir article*

PRIMARY SCHOOL

Les *primary schools* en Grande-Bretagne accueillent les enfants de 5 à 11 ans. Elles marquent le début du cycle scolaire obligatoire et elles comprennent deux sections: la section des petits ("infant school") et la section des grands ("junior school"); voir "secondary school".

prime [praɪm] *adj* primordial(e), fondamental(e); (*excellent*) excellent(e) ▷ *vt* (*gun, pump*) amorcer; (*fig*) mettre au courant ▷ *n*: **in the ~ of life** dans la fleur de l'âge

Prime Minister *n* Premier ministre

primeval [praɪˈmiːvl] *adj* primitif(-ive)

primitive [ˈprɪmɪtɪv] *adj* primitif(-ive)

primrose [ˈprɪmrəuz] *n* primevère *f*

primus® [ˈpraɪməs], **primus® stove** *n* (*Brit*) réchaud *m* de camping

prince [prɪns] *n* prince *m*

princess [prɪnˈses] *n* princesse *f*

principal [ˈprɪnsɪpl] *adj* principal(e) ▷ *n* (*head teacher*) directeur *m*, principal *m*; (*in play*) rôle principal; (*money*) principal *m*

principally [ˈprɪnsɪplɪ] *adv* principalement

principle [ˈprɪnsɪpl] *n* principe *m*; **in ~** en principe; **on ~** par principe

print [prɪnt] *n* (*mark*) empreinte *f*; (*letters*) caractères *mpl*; (*fabric*) imprimé *m*; (*Art*) gravure *f*, estampe *f*; (*Phot*) épreuve *f* ▷ *vt* imprimer; (*publish*) publier; (*write in capitals*) écrire en majuscules; **out of ~** épuisé(e); **▸ print out** *vt* (*Comput*) imprimer

printed matter [ˈprɪntɪd-] *n* imprimés *mpl*

printer [ˈprɪntəˈ] *n* (*machine*) imprimante *f*; (*person*) imprimeur *m*

printing [ˈprɪntɪŋ] *n* impression *f*

printout [ˈprɪntaut] *n* (*Comput*) sortie *f* imprimante

prior [ˈpraɪəˈ] *adj* antérieur(e), précédent(e); (*more important*) prioritaire ▷ *n* (*Rel*) prieur *m* ▷ *adv*: **~ to doing** avant de faire; **without ~ notice** sans préavis; **to have a ~ claim to sth** avoir priorité pour qch

priority [praɪˈɒrɪtɪ] *n* priorité *f*; **to have** *or* **take ~ over sth/sb** avoir la priorité sur qch/qn

prise [praɪz] *vt*: **to ~ open** forcer

prison [ˈprɪzn] *n* prison *f* ▷ *cpd* pénitentiaire

prisoner [ˈprɪznəˈ] *n* prisonnier(-ière); **the ~ at the bar** l'accusé(e); **to take sb ~** faire qn prisonnier

prisoner of war *n* prisonnier(-ière) de guerre

pristine [ˈprɪstiːn] *adj* virginal(e)

privacy [ˈprɪvəsɪ] *n* intimité *f*, solitude *f*

private [ˈpraɪvɪt] *adj* (*not public*) privé(e); (*personal*) personnel(le); (*house, car, lesson*) particulier(-ière); (*quiet: place*) tranquille ▷ *n* soldat *m* de deuxième classe; **"~"** (*on envelope*) "personnelle"; (*on door*) "privé"; **in ~** en privé;

in (his) ~ life dans sa vie privée; **he is a very ~ person** il est très secret; **to be in ~ practice** être médecin (*or* dentiste *etc*) non conventionné; **~ hearing** (*Law*) audience *f* à huis-clos

private detective *n* détective privé

private enterprise *n* entreprise privée

privately ['praɪvɪtlɪ] *adv* en privé; (*within oneself*) intérieurement

private property *n* propriété privée

private school *n* école privée

privatize ['praɪvɪtaɪz] *vt* privatiser

privet ['prɪvɪt] *n* troène *m*

privilege ['prɪvɪlɪdʒ] *n* privilège *m*

privy ['prɪvɪ] *adj*: **to be ~ to** être au courant de

prize [praɪz] *n* prix *m* ▷ *adj* (*example, idiot*) parfait(e); (*bull, novel*) primé(e) ▷ *vt* priser, faire grand cas de

prize-giving ['praɪzgɪvɪŋ] *n* distribution *f* des prix

prizewinner ['praɪzwɪnə^r] *n* gagnant(e)

pro [prəu] *n* (*inf: Sport*) professionnel(le) ▷ *prep* pro; **pros** *npl*: **the ~s and cons** le pour et le contre

probability [prɔbə'bɪlɪtɪ] *n* probabilité *f*; **in all ~** très probablement

probable ['prɔbəbl] *adj* probable; **it is ~/ hardly ~ that …** il est probable/peu probable que …

probably ['prɔbəblɪ] *adv* probablement

probation [prə'beɪʃən] *n* (*in employment*) (période *f* d')essai *m*; (*Law*) liberté surveillée; (*Rel*) noviciat *m*, probation *f*; **on ~** (*employee*) à l'essai; (*Law*) en liberté surveillée

probe [prəub] *n* (*Med, Space*) sonde *f*; (*enquiry*) enquête *f*, investigation *f* ▷ *vt* sonder, explorer

problem ['prɔbləm] *n* problème *m*; **to have ~s with the car** avoir des ennuis avec la voiture; **what's the ~?** qu'y a-t-il?, quel est le problème?; **I had no ~ in finding her** je n'ai pas eu de mal à la trouver; **no ~!** pas de problème!

procedure [prə'siːdʒə^r] *n* (*Admin, Law*) procédure *f*; (*method*) marche *f* à suivre, façon *f* de procéder

proceed [prə'siːd] *vi* (*go forward*) avancer; (*act*) procéder; (*continue*): **to ~ (with)** continuer, poursuivre; **to ~ to** aller à; passer à; **to ~ to do** se mettre à faire; **I am not sure how to ~** je ne sais pas exactement comment m'y prendre; **to ~ against sb** (*Law*) intenter des poursuites contre qn

proceedings [prə'siːdɪŋz] *npl* (*measures*) mesures *fpl*; (*Law: against sb*) poursuites *fpl*; (*meeting*) réunion *f*, séance *f*; (*records*) compte rendu; actes *mpl*

proceeds ['prəusiːdz] *npl* produit *m*, recette *f*

process ['prəuses] *n* processus *m*; (*method*) procédé *m* ▷ *vt* traiter ▷ *vi* [prə'ses] (*Brit formal: go in procession*) défiler; **in ~** en cours;

we are in the ~ of doing nous sommes en train de faire

processing ['prəusesɪŋ] *n* traitement *m*

procession [prə'seʃən] *n* défilé *m*, cortège *m*; **funeral ~** (*on foot*) cortège funèbre; (*in cars*) convoi *m* mortuaire

proclaim [prə'kleɪm] *vt* déclarer, proclamer

procrastinate [prəu'kræstɪneɪt] *vi* faire traîner les choses, vouloir tout remettre au lendemain

procure [prə'kjuə^r] *vt* (*for o.s.*) se procurer; (*for sb*) procurer

prod [prɔd] *vt* pousser ▷ *n* (*push, jab*) petit coup, poussée *f*

prodigal ['prɔdɪgl] *adj* prodigue

prodigy ['prɔdɪdʒɪ] *n* prodige *m*

produce *n* ['prɔdjuːs] (*Agr*) produits *mpl* ▷ *vt* [prə'djuːs] produire; (*show*) présenter; (*cause*) provoquer, causer; (*Theat*) monter, mettre en scène; (*TV: programme*) réaliser; (: *play, film*) mettre en scène; (*Radio: programme*) réaliser; (: *play*) mettre en ondes

producer [prə'djuːsə^r] *n* (*Theat*) metteur *m* en scène; (*Agr, Comm, Cine*) producteur *m*; (*TV: of programme*) réalisateur *m*; (: *of play, film*) metteur en scène; (*Radio: of programme*) réalisateur; (: *of play*) metteur en ondes

product ['prɔdʌkt] *n* produit *m*

production [prə'dʌkʃən] *n* production *f*; (*Theat*) mise en scène; **to put into ~** (*goods*) entreprendre la fabrication de

production line *n* chaîne *f* (de fabrication)

productive [prə'dʌktɪv] *adj* productif(-ive)

productivity [prɔdʌk'tɪvɪtɪ] *n* productivité *f*

Prof. [prɔf] *abbr* (= *professor*) Prof

profession [prə'feʃən] *n* profession *f*; **the ~s** les professions libérales

professional [prə'feʃənl] *n* professionnel(le) ▷ *adj* professionnel(le); (*work*) de professionnel; **he's a ~ man** il exerce une profession libérale; **to take ~ advice** consulter un spécialiste

professionally [prə'feʃnəlɪ] *adv* professionnellement; (*Sport: play*) en professionnel; **I only know him ~** je n'ai avec lui que des relations de travail

professor [prə'fesə^r] *n* professeur *m* (*titulaire d'une chaire*); (*US: teacher*) professeur *m*

proficiency [prə'fɪʃənsɪ] *n* compétence *f*, aptitude *f*

profile ['prəufaɪl] *n* profil *m*; **to keep a high/ low ~** (*fig*) rester *or* être très en évidence/ discret(-ète)

profit ['prɔfɪt] *n* (*from trading*) bénéfice *m*; (*advantage*) profit *m* ▷ *vi*: **to ~ (by *or* from)** profiter (de); **~ and loss account** compte *m* de profits et pertes; **to make a ~** faire un *or* des bénéfice(s); **to sell sth at a ~** vendre qch à profit

profitable ['prɔfɪtəbl] *adj* lucratif(-ive), rentable; (*fig: beneficial*) avantageux(-euse); (: *meeting*) fructueux(-euse)

profound [prə'faʊnd] *adj* profond(e)
profusely [prə'fju:slɪ] *adv* abondamment;
(*thank etc*) avec effusion
prognosis [prɒg'nəʊsɪs] (*pl* **prognoses**) *n*
pronostic *m*
programme, (*US*) **program** ['prəʊgræm] *n*
(*Comput: also Brit*) programme *m*; (*Radio, TV*)
émission *f* ▷ *vt* programmer
programmer ['prəʊgræmə'] *n*
programmeur(-euse)
programming, (*US*) **programing**
['prəʊgræmɪŋ] *n* programmation *f*
progress *n* ['prəʊgres] progrès *m*(*pl*) ▷ *vi*
[prə'gres] progresser, avancer; **in ~** en cours;
to make ~ progresser, faire des progrès, être
en progrès; **as the match ~ed** au fur et à
mesure que la partie avançait
progressive [prə'gresɪv] *adj* progressif(-ive);
(*person*) progressiste
prohibit [prə'hɪbɪt] *vt* interdire, défendre;
to ~ sb from doing sth défendre *or* interdire
à qn de faire qch; **"smoking ~ed"** "défense
de fumer"
project [*n* 'prɒdʒekt, *vb* prə'dʒekt] *n* (*plan*)
projet *m*, plan *m*; (*venture*) opération *f*,
entreprise *f*; (*Scol: research*) étude *f*, dossier *m*
▷ *vt* projeter ▷ *vi* (*stick out*) faire saillie,
s'avancer
projection [prə'dʒekʃən] *n* projection *f*;
(*overhang*) saillie *f*
projector [prə'dʒektə'] *n* (*Cine etc*)
projecteur *m*
prolific [prə'lɪfɪk] *adj* prolifique
prolong [prə'lɒŋ] *vt* prolonger
prom [prɒm] *n abbr* = **promenade**;
promenade concert; (*US: ball*) bal *m*
d'étudiants; **the P~s** *série de concerts de musique
classique; voir article*

⚫ **PROM**

⚫ En Grande-Bretagne, un *promenade concert*
⚫ ou *prom* est un concert de musique
⚫ classique, ainsi appelé car, à l'origine,
⚫ le public restait debout et se promenait
⚫ au lieu de rester assis. De nos jours, une
⚫ partie du public reste debout, mais il y
⚫ a également des places assises (plus
⚫ chères). Les *Proms* les plus connus sont
⚫ les Proms londoniens. La dernière séance
⚫ (the "Last Night of the Proms") est un
⚫ grand événement médiatique où se
⚫ jouent des airs traditionnels et
⚫ patriotiques.

⚫ Aux États-Unis et au Canada, le *prom* ou
⚫ *promenade* est un bal organisé par le lycée.

promenade [prɒmə'nɑːd] *n* (*by sea*)
esplanade *f*, promenade *f*
promenade concert *n* concert *m* (de
musique classique)

prominent ['prɒmɪnənt] *adj* (*standing out*)
proéminent(e); (*important*) important(e);
he is ~ in the field of ... il est très connu
dans le domaine de ...
promiscuous [prə'mɪskjʊəs] *adj* (*sexually*) de
mœurs légères
promise ['prɒmɪs] *n* promesse *f* ▷ *vt, vi*
promettre; **to make sb a ~** faire une
promesse à qn; **a young man of ~** un jeune
homme plein d'avenir; **to ~ well** *vi*
promettre
promising ['prɒmɪsɪŋ] *adj* prometteur(-euse)
promote [prə'məʊt] *vt* promouvoir; (*venture,
event*) organiser, mettre sur pied; (*new product*)
lancer; **the team was ~d to the second
division** (*Brit Football*) l'équipe est montée en
2ᵉ division
promoter [prə'məʊtə'] *n* (*of event*)
organisateur(-trice)
promotion [prə'məʊʃən] *n* promotion *f*
prompt [prɒmpt] *adj* rapide ▷ *n* (*Comput*)
message *m* (de guidage) ▷ *vt* inciter; (*cause*)
entraîner, provoquer; (*Theat*) souffler (son
rôle *or* ses répliques) à; **they're very ~**
(*punctual*) ils sont ponctuels; **at 8 o'clock ~**
à 8 heures précises; **he was ~ to accept** il a
tout de suite accepté; **to ~ sb to do** inciter *or*
pousser qn à faire
promptly ['prɒmptlɪ] *adv* (*quickly*)
rapidement, sans délai; (*on time*)
ponctuellement
prone [prəʊn] *adj* (*lying*) couché(e) (face
contre terre); (*liable*): **~ to** enclin(e) à; **to be ~
to illness** être facilement malade; **to be ~ to
an illness** être sujet à une maladie; **she is ~
to burst into tears if ...** elle a tendance à
tomber en larmes si ...
prong [prɒŋ] *n* pointe *f*; (*of fork*) dent *f*
pronoun ['prəʊnaʊn] *n* pronom *m*
pronounce [prə'naʊns] *vt* prononcer ▷ *vi*: **to
~ (up)on** se prononcer sur; **how do you ~ it?**
comment est-ce que ça se prononce?; **they ~d
him unfit to drive** ils l'ont déclaré inapte à
la conduite
pronunciation [prənʌnsɪ'eɪʃən] *n*
prononciation *f*
proof [pruːf] *n* preuve *f*; (*test, of book, Phot*)
épreuve *f*; (*of alcohol*) degré *n* ▷ *adj*: **~ against**
à l'épreuve de ▷ *vt* (*Brit: tent, anorak*)
imperméabiliser; **to be 70° ~** ≈ titrer 40
degrés
prop [prɒp] *n* support *m*, étai *m*; (*fig*) soutien
m ▷ *vt* (*also*: **~ up**) étayer, soutenir; **props** *npl*
accessoires *mpl*; (*lean*): **to ~ sth against**
appuyer qch contre *or* à
propaganda [prɒpə'gændə] *n* propagande *f*
propel [prə'pel] *vt* propulser, faire avancer
propeller [prə'pelə'] *n* hélice *f*
propensity [prə'pensɪtɪ] *n* propension *f*
proper ['prɒpə'] *adj* (*suited, right*) approprié(e),
bon/bonne; (*seemly*) correct(e), convenable;
(*authentic*) vrai(e), véritable; (*inf: real*) fini(e),

p

vrai(e); (*referring to place*): **the village ~**
le village proprement dit; **to go through
the ~ channels** (*Admin*) passer par la voie
officielle
properly ['prɒpəlɪ] adv correctement,
convenablement; (*really*) bel et bien
proper noun n nom m propre
property ['prɒpətɪ] n (*possessions*) biens mpl;
(*house etc*) propriété f; (*land*) terres fpl,
domaine m; (*Chem etc: quality*) propriété f;
it's their ~ cela leur appartient, c'est leur
propriété
prophecy ['prɒfɪsɪ] n prophétie f
prophesy ['prɒfɪsaɪ] vt prédire ▷ vi
prophétiser
prophet ['prɒfɪt] n prophète m
proportion [prə'pɔːʃən] n proportion f;
(*share*) part f, partie f ▷ vt proportionner;
proportions npl (*size*) dimensions fpl; **to be
in/out of ~ to** or **with sth** être à la mesure
de/hors de proportion avec qch; **to see sth
in ~** (*fig*) ramener qch à de justes proportions
proportional [prə'pɔːʃənl], **proportionate**
[prə'pɔːʃənɪt] adj proportionnel(le)
proposal [prə'pəuzl] n proposition f, offre f;
(*plan*) projet m; (*of marriage*) demande f en
mariage
propose [prə'pəuz] vt proposer, suggérer;
(*have in mind*): **to ~ sth/to do** or **doing sth**
envisager qch/de faire qch ▷ vi faire sa
demande en mariage; **to ~ to do** avoir
l'intention de faire
proposition [prɒpə'zɪʃən] n proposition f; **to
make sb a ~** faire une proposition à qn
proprietor [prə'praɪətər] n propriétaire m/f
propriety [prə'praɪətɪ] n (*seemliness*)
bienséance f, convenance f
prose [prəuz] n prose f; (*Scol: translation*)
thème m
prosecute ['prɒsɪkjuːt] vt poursuivre
prosecution [prɒsɪ'kjuːʃən] n poursuites fpl
judiciaires; (*accusing side: in criminal case*)
accusation f; (: *in civil case*) la partie
plaignante
prosecutor ['prɒsɪkjuːtər] n (*lawyer*)
procureur m; (*also: public ~*) ministère public;
(*US: plaintiff*) plaignant(e)
prospect n ['prɒspekt] perspective f; (*hope*)
espoir m, chances fpl ▷ vt, vi [prə'spekt]
prospecter; **prospects** npl (*for work etc*)
possibilités fpl d'avenir, débouchés mpl; **we
are faced with the ~ of leaving** nous
risquons de devoir partir; **there is every ~ of
an early victory** tout laisse prévoir une
victoire rapide
prospecting [prə'spektɪŋ] n prospection f
prospective [prə'spektɪv] adj (*possible*)
éventuel(le); (*future*) futur(e)
prospectus [prə'spektəs] n prospectus m
prosper ['prɒspər] vi prospérer
prosperity [prɒ'sperɪtɪ] n prospérité f
prosperous ['prɒspərəs] adj prospère

prostitute ['prɒstɪtjuːt] n prostituée f;
male ~ prostitué m
protect [prə'tekt] vt protéger
protection [prə'tekʃən] n protection f; **to be
under sb's ~** être sous la protection de qn
protective [prə'tektɪv] adj protecteur(-trice);
(*clothing*) de protection; **~ custody** (*Law*)
détention préventive
protein ['prəutiːn] n protéine f
protest [n 'prəutest, vb prə'test] n
protestation f ▷ vi: **to ~ against/about**
protester contre/à propos de ▷ vt protester
de; **to ~ (that)** protester que
Protestant ['prɒtɪstənt] adj, n protestant(e)
protester, protestor [prə'testər] n (*in
demonstration*) manifestant(e)
protracted [prə'træktɪd] adj prolongé(e)
protractor [prə'træktər] n (*Geom*)
rapporteur m
protrude [prə'truːd] vi avancer, dépasser
proud [praud] adj fier(-ère); (*pej*)
orgueilleux(-euse); **to be ~ to do sth** être fier
de faire qch; **to do sb ~** (*inf*) faire honneur
à qn; **to do sb ~** (*inf*) ne se priver de rien
prove [pruːv] vt prouver, démontrer ▷ vi:
to ~ correct etc s'avérer juste etc; **to ~ o.s.**
montrer ce dont on est capable; **to ~ o.s./
itself (to be) useful etc** se montrer or se
révéler utile etc; **he was ~d right in the end**
il s'est avéré qu'il avait raison
proverb ['prɒvɜːb] n proverbe m
provide [prə'vaɪd] vt fournir; **to ~ sb with
sth** fournir qch à qn; **to be ~d with** (*person*)
disposer de; (*thing*) être équipé(e) or
muni(e) de; **provide for** vt fus (*person*)
subvenir aux besoins de; (*future event*)
prévoir
provided [prə'vaɪdɪd] conj: **~ (that)** à
condition que + sub
providing [prə'vaɪdɪŋ] conj à condition
que + sub
province ['prɒvɪns] n province f; (*fig*)
domaine m
provincial [prə'vɪnʃəl] adj provincial(e)
provision [prə'vɪʒən] n (*supply*) provision f;
(*supplying*) fourniture f; approvisionnement m;
(*stipulation*) disposition f; **provisions** npl (*food*)
provisions fpl; **to make ~ for** (*one's future*)
assurer; (*one's family*) assurer l'avenir de;
there's no ~ for this in the contract
le contrat ne prévoit pas cela
provisional [prə'vɪʒənl] adj provisoire ▷ n:
P~ (*Irish Pol*) Provisional m (*membre de la
tendance activiste de l'IRA*)
proviso [prə'vaɪzəu] n condition f; **with the ~
that** à la condition (expresse) que
provocative [prə'vɒkətɪv] adj
provocateur(-trice), provocant(e)
provoke [prə'vəuk] vt provoquer; **to ~ sb to
sth/to do** or **into doing sth** pousser qn à
qch/à faire qch
prowess ['prauɪs] n prouesse f

prowl [praul] vi (also: ~ **about, ~ around**)
rôder ▷ n: **to be on the** ~ rôder
prowler ['praulə'] n rôdeur(-euse)
proximity [prɔk'sɪmɪtɪ] n proximité f
proxy ['prɔksɪ] n procuration f; **by** ~ par
procuration
prudent ['pru:dnt] adj prudent(e)
prune [pru:n] n pruneau m ▷ vt élaguer
pry [praɪ] vi: **to ~ into** fourrer son nez dans
PS n abbr (= postscript) PS m
psalm [sɑ:m] n psaume m
pseudonym ['sju:dənɪm] n pseudonyme m
PSHE n abbr (Brit: Scol: = personal, social and health
education) cours d'éducation personnelle, sanitaire et
sociale préparant à la vie adulte
psyche ['saɪkɪ] n psyché m
psychiatric [saɪkɪ'ætrɪk] adj psychiatrique
psychiatrist [saɪ'kaɪətrɪst] n psychiatre m/f
psychic ['saɪkɪk] adj (also: **~al**) (méta)
psychique; (person) doué(e) de télépathie or
d'un sixième sens
psychoanalysis (pl **psychoanalyses**)
[saɪkəʊ'nælɪsɪs, -si:z] n psychanalyse f
psychoanalyst [saɪkəʊ'ænəlɪst] n
psychanalyste m/f
psychological [saɪkə'lɔdʒɪkl] adj
psychologique
psychologist [saɪ'kɔlədʒɪst] n
psychologue m/f
psychology [saɪ'kɔlədʒɪ] n psychologie f
psychotherapy [saɪkəʊ'θerəpɪ] n
psychothérapie f
pt abbr = **pint; pints; point; points**
PTO abbr (= please turn over) TSVP
PTV abbr (US) = **pay television**
pub [pʌb] n abbr (= public house) pub m
puberty ['pju:bətɪ] n puberté f
public ['pʌblɪk] adj public(-ique) ▷ n
public m; **in ~** en public; **the general** ~ le
grand public; **to be ~ knowledge** être de
notoriété publique; **to go ~** (Comm) être
coté(e) en Bourse; **to make ~** rendre public
public address system n (système m de)
sonorisation f, sono f (col)
publican ['pʌblɪkən] n patron or gérant m
de pub
publication [pʌblɪ'keɪʃən] n publication f
public company n société f anonyme
public convenience n (Brit) toilettes fpl
public holiday n (Brit) jour férié
public house n (Brit) pub m
publicity [pʌb'lɪsɪtɪ] n publicité f
publicize ['pʌblɪsaɪz] vt (make known) faire
connaître, rendre public; (advertise) faire de
la publicité pour
public limited company n ≈ société f
anonyme (SA) (cotée en Bourse)
publicly ['pʌblɪklɪ] adv publiquement,
en public
public opinion n opinion publique
public relations n or npl relations publiques
(RP)

public school n (Brit) école privée; (US) école
publique; voir article

⬡ **PUBLIC SCHOOL**
⬡
⬡ Une public school est un établissement
⬡ d'enseignement secondaire privé.
⬡ Bon nombre d'entre elles sont des
⬡ pensionnats. Beaucoup ont également
⬡ une école primaire qui leur est rattachée
⬡ (une "prep" ou "preparatory school")
⬡ pour préparer les élèves au cycle
⬡ secondaire. Ces écoles sont en général
⬡ prestigieuses, et les frais de scolarité sont
⬡ très élevés dans les plus connues
⬡ (Westminster, Eton, Harrow). Beaucoup
⬡ d'élèves vont ensuite à l'université,
⬡ et un grand nombre entre à Oxford ou
⬡ à Cambridge. Les grands industriels,
⬡ les députés et les hauts fonctionnaires
⬡ sortent souvent de ces écoles.
⬡ Aux États-Unis, le terme "public school"
⬡ désigne tout simplement une école
⬡ publique gratuite.

public-spirited [pʌblɪk'spɪrɪtɪd] adj qui fait
preuve de civisme
public transport, (US) **public
transportation** n transports mpl en
commun
publish ['pʌblɪʃ] vt publier
publisher ['pʌblɪʃə'] n éditeur m
publishing ['pʌblɪʃɪŋ] n (industry) édition f;
(of a book) publication f
pub lunch n repas m de bistrot
pucker ['pʌkə'] vt plisser
pudding ['pudɪŋ] n (Brit: dessert) dessert m,
entremets m; (sweet dish) pudding m,
gâteau m; (sausage) boudin m; **rice** ~ ≈ riz m
au lait; **black** ~, (US) **blood** ~ boudin (noir)
puddle ['pʌdl] n flaque f d'eau
puff [pʌf] n bouffée f ▷ vt: **to ~ one's pipe**
tirer sur sa pipe; (also: **~ out**: sails, cheeks)
gonfler ▷ vi sortir par bouffées; (pant)
haleter; **to ~ out smoke** envoyer des
bouffées de fumée
puff pastry, (US) **puff paste** n pâte
feuilletée
puffy ['pʌfɪ] adj bouffi(e), boursouflé(e)
pull [pul] n (tug): **to give sth a** ~ tirer sur
qch; (of moon, magnet, the sea etc) attraction f;
(fig) influence f ▷ vt tirer; (trigger) presser;
(strain: muscle, tendon) se claquer ▷ vi tirer;
to ~ a face faire une grimace; **to ~ to pieces**
mettre en morceaux; **to ~ one's punches**
(also fig) ménager son adversaire; **to ~ one's
weight** y mettre du sien; **to ~ o.s. together**
se ressaisir; **to ~ sb's leg** (fig) faire marcher
qn; **to ~ strings (for sb)** intervenir (en faveur
de qn); **pull about** vt (Brit: handle roughly:
object) maltraiter; (: person) malmener;
pull apart vt séparer; (break) mettre en

pièces, démantibuler; **pull away** vi (vehicle: move off) partir; (draw back) s'éloigner; **pull back** vt (lever etc) tirer sur; (curtains) ouvrir ▷ vi (refrain) s'abstenir; (Mil: withdraw) se retirer; **pull down** vt baisser, abaisser; (house) démolir; (tree) abattre; **pull in** vi (Aut) se ranger; (Rail) entrer en gare; **pull off** vt enlever, ôter; (deal etc) conclure; **pull out** vi démarrer, partir; (withdraw) se retirer; (Aut: come out of line) déboîter ▷ vt (from bag, pocket) sortir; (remove) arracher; (withdraw) retirer; **pull over** vi (Aut) se ranger; **pull round** vi (unconscious person) revenir à soi; (sick person) se rétablir; **pull through** vi s'en sortir; **pull up** vi (stop) s'arrêter ▷ vt remonter; (uproot) déraciner, arracher; (stop) arrêter

pulley ['pʊlɪ] n poulie f

pullover ['pʊləʊvəʳ] n pull-over m, tricot m

pulp [pʌlp] n (of fruit) pulpe f; (for paper) pâte f à papier; (pej: also: ~ **magazines** etc) presse f à sensation or de bas étage; **to reduce sth to (a)** ~ réduire qch en purée

pulpit ['pʊlpɪt] n chaire f

pulsate [pʌl'seɪt] vi battre, palpiter; (music) vibrer

pulse [pʌls] n (of blood) pouls m; (of heart) battement m; (of music, engine) vibrations fpl; **pulses** npl (Culin) légumineuses fpl; **to feel** or **take sb's** ~ prendre le pouls à qn

puma ['pjuːmə] n puma m

pump [pʌmp] n pompe f; (shoe) escarpin m ▷ vt pomper; (fig: inf) faire parler; **to ~ sb for information** essayer de soutirer des renseignements à qn; **pump up** vt gonfler

pumpkin ['pʌmpkɪn] n potiron m, citrouille f

pun [pʌn] n jeu de mots, calembour m

punch [pʌntʃ] n (blow) coup m de poing; (fig: force) vivacité f, mordant m; (tool) poinçon m; (drink) punch m ▷ vt (make a hole in) poinçonner, perforer; (hit): **to ~ sb/sth** donner un coup de poing à qn/sur qch; **to ~ a hole (in)** faire un trou (dans); **punch in** vi (US) pointer (en arrivant); **punch out** vi (US) pointer (en partant)

punch line n (of joke) conclusion f

punch-up ['pʌntʃʌp] n (Brit inf) bagarre f

punctual ['pʌŋktjuəl] adj ponctuel(le)

punctuation [pʌŋktju'eɪʃən] n ponctuation f

puncture ['pʌŋktʃəʳ] n (Brit) crevaison f ▷ vt crever; **I have a** ~ (Aut) j'ai (un pneu) crevé

pundit ['pʌndɪt] n individu m qui pontifie, pontife m

pungent ['pʌndʒənt] adj piquant(e); (fig) mordant(e), caustique

punish ['pʌnɪʃ] vt punir; **to ~ sb for sth/for doing sth** punir qn de qch/d'avoir fait qch

punishment ['pʌnɪʃmənt] n punition f, châtiment m; (fig: inf): **to take a lot of** ~ (boxer) encaisser; (car, person etc) être mis(e) à dure épreuve

punk [pʌŋk] n (person: also: ~ **rocker**) punk m/f;

(music: also: ~ **rock**) le punk; (US inf: hoodlum) voyou m

punt [pʌnt] n (boat) bachot m; (Irish) livre irlandaise ▷ vi (Brit: bet) parier

punter ['pʌntəʳ] n (Brit: gambler) parieur(-euse); (: inf) Monsieur m tout le monde; type m

puny ['pjuːnɪ] adj chétif(-ive)

pup [pʌp] n chiot m

pupil ['pjuːpl] n, élève m/f; (of eye) pupille f

puppet ['pʌpɪt] n marionnette f, pantin m

puppy ['pʌpɪ] n chiot m, petit chien

purchase ['pəːtʃɪs] n achat m; (grip) prise f ▷ vt acheter; **to get a ~ on** trouver appui sur

purchaser ['pəːtʃɪsəʳ] n acheteur(-euse)

pure [pjʊəʳ] adj pur(e); **a ~ wool jumper** un pull en pure laine; **~ and simple** pur(e) et simple

purely ['pjʊəlɪ] adv purement

purge [pəːdʒ] n (Med) purge f; (Pol) épuration f, purge ▷ vt purger; (fig) épurer, purger

purify ['pjʊərɪfaɪ] vt purifier, épurer

purity ['pjʊərɪtɪ] n pureté f

purple ['pəːpl] adj violet(te); (face) cramoisi(e)

purpose ['pəːpəs] n intention f, but m; **on ~** exprès; **for illustrative ~s** à titre d'illustration; **for teaching ~s** dans un but pédagogique; **for the ~s of this meeting** pour cette réunion; **to no ~** en pure perte

purposeful ['pəːpəsful] adj déterminé(e), résolu(e)

purr [pəːʳ] n ronronnement m ▷ vi ronronner

purse [pəːs] n (Brit: for money) porte-monnaie m inv, bourse f; (US: handbag) sac m (à main) ▷ vt serrer, pincer

purser ['pəːsəʳ] n (Naut) commissaire m du bord

pursue [pə'sjuː] vt poursuivre; (pleasures) rechercher; (inquiry, matter) approfondir

pursuit [pə'sjuːt] n poursuite f; (occupation) occupation f, activité f; **scientific ~s** recherches fpl scientifiques; **in (the) ~ of sth** à la recherche de qch

pus [pʌs] n pus m

push [pʊʃ] n poussée f; (effort) gros effort; (drive) énergie f ▷ vt pousser; (button) appuyer sur; (thrust): **to ~ sth (into)** enfoncer qch (dans); (fig: product) mettre en avant, faire de la publicité pour ▷ vi pousser; appuyer; **to ~ a door open/shut** pousser une porte (pour l'ouvrir/pour la fermer); **"~"** (on door) "pousser"; (on bell) "appuyer"; **to ~ for** (better pay, conditions) réclamer; **to be ~ed for time/ money** être à court de temps/d'argent; **she is ~ing fifty** (inf) elle frise la cinquantaine; **at a ~** (Brit inf) à la limite, à la rigueur; **push aside** vt écarter; **push in** vi s'introduire de force; **push off** vi (inf) filer, ficher le camp; **push on** vi (continue) continuer; **push over** vt renverser; **push through** vt (measure) faire

voter ▷ vi (in crowd) se frayer un chemin;
push up vt (total, prices) faire monter
pushchair ['pʊʃtʃɛəˀ] n (Brit) poussette f
pusher ['pʊʃəˀ] n (also: **drug ~**)
revendeur(-euse) (de drogue),
ravitailleur(-euse) (en drogue)
pushover ['pʊʃəʊvəˀ] n (inf): **it's a ~** c'est un
jeu d'enfant
push-up ['pʊʃʌp] n (US) traction f
pushy ['pʊʃɪ] adj (pej) arriviste
pussy ['pʊsɪ], **pussy-cat** n (inf) minet m
put (pt, pp put) [pʊt] vt mettre; (place)
placer; (say) dire, exprimer; (a question)
poser; (case, view) exposer, présenter; (estimate)
estimer; **to ~ sb in a good/bad mood** mettre
qn de bonne/mauvaise humeur; **to ~ sb to**
bed mettre qn au lit, coucher qn; **to ~ sb to a**
lot of trouble déranger qn; **how shall I ~ it?**
comment dirais-je?, comment dire?; **to ~ a**
lot of time into sth passer beaucoup de
temps à qch; **to ~ money on a horse** miser
sur un cheval; **I ~ it to you that ...** (Brit) je
(vous) suggère que ..., je suis d'avis que ...;
to stay ~ ne pas bouger; **put about** vi (Naut)
virer de bord ▷ vt (rumour) faire courir; **put**
across vt (ideas etc) communiquer; faire
comprendre; **put aside** vt mettre de côté;
put away vt (store) ranger; **put back** vt
(replace) remettre, replacer; (postpone)
remettre; (delay, watch, clock) retarder; **this**
will ~ us back ten years cela nous ramènera
dix ans en arrière; **put by** vt (money) mettre
de côté, économiser; **put down** vt (parcel etc)
poser, déposer; (pay) verser; (in writing) mettre
par écrit, inscrire; (suppress: revolt etc)
réprimer, écraser; (attribute) attribuer;
(animal) abattre; (cat, dog) faire piquer; **put**
forward vt (ideas) avancer, proposer; (date,
watch, clock) avancer; **put in** vt (gas, electricity)
installer; (complaint) soumettre; (time, effort)
consacrer; **put in for** vt fus (job) poser sa
candidature pour; (promotion) solliciter; **put**
off vt (light etc) éteindre; (postpone) remettre
à plus tard, ajourner; (discourage) dissuader;
put on vt (clothes, lipstick, CD) mettre; (light etc)
allumer; (play etc) monter; (extra bus, train etc)
mettre en service; (food, meal: provide) servir;
(: cook) mettre à cuire or à chauffer; (weight)
prendre; (assume: accent, manner) prendre;
(: airs) se donner, prendre; (inf: tease) faire
marcher; (inform, indicate): **to ~ sb on to sb/**
sth indiquer qn/qch à qn; **to ~ the brakes on**
freiner; **put out** vt (take outside) mettre
dehors; (one's hand) tendre; (news, rumour)
faire courir, répandre; (light etc) éteindre;
(person: inconvenience) déranger, gêner; (Brit:
dislocate) se démettre ▷ vi (Naut): **to ~ out to**
sea prendre le large; **to ~ out from**
Plymouth quitter Plymouth; **put through**
vt (Tel: caller) mettre en communication;
(: call) passer; (plan) faire accepter; **~ me**
through to Miss Blair passez-moi Miss

Blair; **put together** vt mettre ensemble;
(assemble: furniture) monter, assembler; (meal)
préparer; **put up** vt (raise) lever, relever,
remonter; (pin up) afficher; (hang) accrocher;
(build) construire, ériger; (tent) monter;
(umbrella) ouvrir; (increase) augmenter;
(accommodate) loger; (incite): **to ~ sb up to**
doing sth pousser qn à faire qch; **to ~ sth up**
for sale mettre qch en vente; **put upon** vt fus:
to be ~ upon (imposed on) se laisser faire; **put**
up with vt fus supporter
putt [pʌt] vt, vi putter ▷ n putt m
putting green ['pʌtɪŋ-] n green m
putty ['pʌtɪ] n mastic m
put-up ['pʊtʌp] adj: **~ job** coup monté
puzzle ['pʌzl] n énigme f, mystère m; (game)
jeu m, casse-tête m; (jigsaw) puzzle m; (also:
crossword ~) mots croisés ▷ vt intriguer,
rendre perplexe ▷ vi se creuser la tête; **to ~**
over chercher à comprendre
puzzled ['pʌzld] adj perplexe; **to be ~ about**
sth être perplexe au sujet de qch
puzzling ['pʌzlɪŋ] adj déconcertant(e),
inexplicable
pyjamas [pɪ'dʒɑːməz] npl (Brit) pyjama m;
a pair of ~ un pyjama
pylon ['paɪlən] n pylône m
pyramid ['pɪrəmɪd] n pyramide f
Pyrenees [pɪrə'niːz] npl Pyrénées fpl

q

quack [kwæk] n (of duck) coin-coin m inv; (pej: doctor) charlatan m ▷ vi faire coin-coin

quad [kwɔd] n abbr = **quadruplet**; **quadrangle**

quadrangle ['kwɔdræŋgl] n (Math) quadrilatère m; (courtyard: abbr: quad) cour f

quadruple [kwɔ'dru:pl] adj, n quadruple m ▷ vt, vi quadrupler

quadruplet [kwɔ'dru:plɪt] n quadruplé(e)

quail [kweɪl] n (Zool) caille f ▷ vi: **to ~ at** or **before** reculer devant

quaint [kweɪnt] adj bizarre; (old-fashioned) désuet(-ète); (picturesque) au charme vieillot, pittoresque

quake [kweɪk] vi trembler ▷ n abbr = **earthquake**

qualification [kwɔlɪfɪ'keɪʃən] n (often pl: degree etc) diplôme m; (training) qualification(s) f(pl); (ability) compétence(s) f(pl); (limitation) réserve f, restriction f; **what are your ~s?** qu'avez-vous comme diplômes?; quelles sont vos qualifications?

qualified ['kwɔlɪfaɪd] adj (trained) qualifié(e); (professionally) diplômé(e); (fit, competent) compétent(e), qualifié(e); (limited) conditionnel(le); **it was a ~ success** ce fut un succès mitigé; **~ for/to do** qui a les diplômes requis pour/pour faire; qualifié pour/pour faire

qualify ['kwɔlɪfaɪ] vt qualifier; (modify) atténuer, nuancer; (limit: statement) apporter des réserves à ▷ vi: **to ~ (as)** obtenir son diplôme (de); **to ~ (for)** remplir les conditions requises (pour); (Sport) se qualifier (pour)

quality ['kwɔlɪtɪ] n qualité f ▷ cpd de qualité; **of good/poor ~** de bonne/mauvaise qualité

quality press n (Brit): **the ~** la presse d'information; voir article

quality time n moments privilégiés

qualm [kwɑ:m] n doute m; scrupule m; **to have ~s about sth** avoir des doutes sur qch; éprouver des scrupules à propos de qch

quandary ['kwɔndrɪ] n: **in a ~** devant un dilemme, dans l'embarras

quantify ['kwɔntɪfaɪ] vt quantifier

quantity ['kwɔntɪtɪ] n quantité f; **in ~** en grande quantité

quantity surveyor n (Brit) métreur vérificateur

quarantine ['kwɔrnti:n] n quarantaine f

quarrel ['kwɔrl] n querelle f, dispute f ▷ vi se disputer, se quereller; **to have a ~ with sb** se quereller avec qn; **I've no ~ with him** je n'ai rien contre lui; **I can't ~ with that** je ne vois rien à redire à cela

quarry ['kwɔrɪ] n (for stone) carrière f; (animal) proie f, gibier m ▷ vt (marble etc) extraire

quart [kwɔ:t] n ≈ litre m

quarter ['kwɔ:tə*] n quart m; (of year) trimestre m; (district) quartier m; (US, Canada: 25 cents) (pièce f de) vingt-cinq cents mpl ▷ vt partager en quartiers or en quatre; (Mil) caserner, cantonner; **quarters** npl logement m; (Mil) quartiers mpl, cantonnement m; **a ~ of an hour** un quart d'heure; **it's a ~ to 3, (US) it's a ~ of 3** il est 3 heures moins le quart; **it's a ~ past 3, (US) it's a ~ after 3** il est 3 heures et quart; **from all ~s** de tous côtés

quarter final n quart m de finale

quarterly ['kwɔ:təlɪ] adj trimestriel(le) ▷ adv tous les trois mois ▷ n (Press) revue trimestrielle

quartet, quartette [kwɔ:'tɛt] n quatuor m; (jazz players) quartette m

quartz [kwɔ:ts] n quartz m ▷ cpd de or en quartz; (watch, clock) à quartz

quash [kwɔʃ] vt (verdict) annuler, casser

quaver ['kweɪvə^r] n (Brit Mus) croche f ▷ vi trembler

quay [ki:] n (also: **~side**) quai m

queasy ['kwi:zɪ] adj (stomach) délicat(e); **to feel ~** avoir mal au cœur

Quebec [kwɪ'bɛk] n (city) Québec; (province) Québec m

queen [kwi:n] n (gen) reine f; (Cards etc) dame f

queen mother n reine mère f

queer [kwɪə^r] adj étrange, curieux(-euse); (suspicious) louche; (Brit: sick): **I feel ~** je ne me sens pas bien ▷ n (inf: highly offensive) homosexuel m

quell [kwɛl] vt réprimer, étouffer

quench [kwɛntʃ] vt (flames) éteindre; **to ~ one's thirst** se désaltérer

query ['kwɪərɪ] n question f; (doubt) doute m; (question mark) point m d'interrogation ▷ vt (disagree with, dispute) mettre en doute, questionner

quest [kwɛst] n recherche f, quête f

question ['kwɛstʃən] n question f ▷ vt (person) interroger; (plan, idea) mettre en question or en doute; **to ask sb a ~**, **to put a ~ to sb** poser une question à qn; **to bring** or **call sth into ~** remettre qch en question; **the ~ is ...** la question est de savoir ...; **it's a ~ of doing** il s'agit de faire; **there's some ~ of doing** il est question de faire; **beyond ~** sans aucun doute; **out of the ~** hors de question

questionable ['kwɛstʃənəbl] adj discutable

question mark n point m d'interrogation

questionnaire [kwɛstʃə'nɛə^r] n questionnaire m

queue [kju:] (Brit) n queue f, file f ▷ vi (also: **~ up**) faire la queue; **to jump the ~** passer avant son tour

quibble ['kwɪbl] vi ergoter, chicaner

quiche [ki:ʃ] n quiche f

quick [kwɪk] adj rapide; (reply) prompt(e), rapide; (mind) vif/vive; (agile) agile, vif/vive ▷ adv vite, rapidement ▷ n: **cut to the ~** (fig) touché(e) au vif; **be ~!** dépêche-toi!; **to be ~ to act** agir tout de suite

quicken ['kwɪkən] vt accélérer, presser; (rouse) stimuler ▷ vi s'accélérer, devenir plus rapide

quickly ['kwɪklɪ] adv (fast) vite, rapidement; (immediately) tout de suite

quicksand ['kwɪksænd] n sables mouvants

quick-witted [kwɪk'wɪtɪd] adj à l'esprit vif

quid [kwɪd] n pl inv (Brit inf) livre f

quiet ['kwaɪət] adj tranquille, calme; (not noisy: engine) silencieux(-euse); (reserved) réservé(e); (voice) bas(se); (not busy: day, ceremony, colour) calme; (silence) silence m ▷ n tranquillité f, calme m; (silence) silence m ▷ vt, vi (US) = **quieten**; **keep ~!** tais-toi!; **on the ~** en secret, discrètement; **I'll have a ~ word with him** je lui en parlerai discrètement

quieten ['kwaɪətn] (also: **~ down**) vi se calmer, s'apaiser ▷ vt calmer, apaiser

quietly ['kwaɪətlɪ] adv tranquillement; (silently) silencieusement; (discreetly) discrètement

quietness ['kwaɪətnɪs] n tranquillité f, calme m; silence m

quilt [kwɪlt] n édredon m; (continental quilt) couette f

quin [kwɪn] n abbr = **quintuplet**

quintuplet [kwɪn'tju:plɪt] n quintuplé(e)

quip [kwɪp] n remarque piquante or spirituelle, pointe f ▷ vt: **... he quipped ...** lança-t-il

quirk [kwə:k] n bizarrerie f; **by some ~ of fate** par un caprice du hasard

quirky ['kwə:kɪ] adj singulier(-ère)

quit [kwɪt] (pt, pp quit or quitted) vt quitter ▷ vi (give up) abandonner, renoncer; (resign) démissionner; **to ~ doing** arrêter de faire; **~ stalling!** (US inf) arrête de te dérober!; **notice to ~** (Brit) congé m (signifié au locataire)

quite [kwaɪt] adv (rather) assez, plutôt; (entirely) complètement, tout à fait; **~ new** plutôt neuf; tout à fait neuf; **she's ~ pretty** elle est plutôt jolie; **I ~ understand** je comprends très bien; **~ a few of them** un assez grand nombre d'entre eux; **that's not ~ right** ce n'est pas tout à fait juste; **not ~ as many as last time** pas tout à fait autant que la dernière fois; **~ (so)!** exactement!

quits [kwɪts] adj: **~ (with)** quitte (envers); **let's call it ~** restons-en là

quiver ['kwɪvə^r] vi trembler, frémir ▷ n (for arrows) carquois m

quiz [kwɪz] n (on TV) jeu-concours m (télévisé); (in magazine etc) test m de connaissances ▷ vt interroger

quizzical ['kwɪzɪkl] adj narquois(e)

quota ['kwəutə] n quota m

quotation [kwəu'teɪʃən] n citation f; (of shares etc) cote f, cours m; (estimate) devis m

quotation marks npl guillemets mpl

quote [kwəut] n citation f; (estimate) devis m ▷ vt (sentence, author) citer; (price) donner, soumettre; (shares) coter ▷ vi: **to ~ from** citer; **to ~ for a job** établir un devis pour des travaux; **quotes** npl (inverted commas) guillemets mpl; **in ~s** entre guillemets; **~ ... unquote** (in dictation) ouvrez les guillemets ... fermez les guillemets

r

Rabat [rə'bɑːt] *n* Rabat
rabbi ['ræbaɪ] *n* rabbin *m*
rabbit ['ræbɪt] *n* lapin *m* ▷ *vi*: **to ~ (on)** (Brit)
parler à n'en plus finir
rabbit hutch *n* clapier *m*
rabble ['ræbl] *n* (pej) populace *f*
rabies ['reɪbiːz] *n* rage *f*
RAC *n abbr* (Brit: = Royal Automobile Club)
≈ ACF *m*
raccoon, racoon [rə'kuːn] *n* raton *m* laveur
race [reɪs] *n* (species) race *f*; (competition, rush)
course *f* ▷ *vt* (person) faire la course avec;
(horse) faire courir; (engine) emballer ▷ *vi*
(compete) faire la course, courir; (hurry) aller
à toute vitesse, courir; (engine) s'emballer;
(pulse) battre très vite; **the human ~** la race
humaine; **to ~ in/out** *etc* entrer/sortir *etc* à
toute vitesse
race car *n* (US) = **racing car**
race car driver *n* (US) = **racing driver**
racecourse ['reɪskɔːs] *n* champ *m* de courses
racehorse ['reɪshɔːs] *n* cheval *m* de course
racer ['reɪsə'] *n* (bike) vélo *m* de course
racetrack ['reɪstræk] *n* piste *f*
racial ['reɪʃl] *adj* racial(e)
racing ['reɪsɪŋ] *n* courses *fpl*
racing car *n* (Brit) voiture *f* de course
racing driver *n* (Brit) pilote *m* de course
racism ['reɪsɪzəm] *n* racisme *m*
racist ['reɪsɪst] *adj*, *n* raciste *m/f*
rack [ræk] *n* (for guns, tools) râtelier *m*; (for
clothes) portant *m*; (for bottles) casier *m*; (also:

luggage ~) filet *m* à bagages; (also: **roof ~**)
galerie *f*; (also: **dish ~**) égouttoir *m* ▷ *vt*
tourmenter; **magazine ~** porte-revues *m inv*;
shoe ~ étagère *f* à chaussures; **toast ~** porte-
toast *m*; **to ~ one's brains** se creuser la
cervelle; **to go to ~ and ruin** (building) tomber
en ruine; (business) péricliter; **rack up** *vt*
accumuler
racket ['rækɪt] *n* (for tennis) raquette *f*; (noise)
tapage *m*, vacarme *m*; (swindle) escroquerie *f*;
(organized crime) racket *m*
racquet ['rækɪt] *n* raquette *f*
racy ['reɪsɪ] *adj* plein(e) de verve, osé(e)
radar ['reɪdɑː'] *n* radar *m* ▷ *cpd* radar *inv*
radial ['reɪdɪəl] *adj* (also: **~-ply**) à carcasse
radiale
radiant ['reɪdɪənt] *adj* rayonnant(e); (Physics)
radiant(e)
radiate ['reɪdɪeɪt] *vt* (heat) émettre, dégager
▷ *vi* (lines) rayonner
radiation [reɪdɪ'eɪʃən] *n* rayonnement *m*;
(radioactive) radiation *f*
radiator ['reɪdɪeɪtə'] *n* radiateur *m*
radical ['rædɪkl] *adj* radical(e)
radii ['reɪdɪaɪ] *npl of* radius
radio ['reɪdɪəu] *n* radio *f* ▷ *vi*: **to ~ to sb**
envoyer un message radio à qn ▷ *vt*
(information) transmettre par radio; (one's
position) signaler par radio; (person) appeler
par radio; **on the ~** à la radio
radioactive ['reɪdɪəu'æktɪv] *adj*
radioactif(-ive)
radio cassette *n* radiocassette *m*
radio-controlled ['reɪdɪəukən'trəuld] *adj*
radioguidé(e)
radio station *n* station *f* de radio
radish ['rædɪʃ] *n* radis *m*
radius (*pl* **radii**) ['reɪdɪəs, -ɪaɪ] *n* rayon *m*;
(Anat) radius *m*; **within a ~ of 50 miles** dans
un rayon de 50 milles
RAF *n abbr* (Brit) = **Royal Air Force**
raffle ['ræfl] *n* tombola *f* ▷ *vt* mettre comme
lot dans une tombola
raft [rɑːft] *n* (craft: also: **life ~**) radeau *m*; (logs)
train *m* de flottage
rafter ['rɑːftə'] *n* chevron *m*
rag [ræg] *n* chiffon *m*; (pej: newspaper) feuille *f*,
torchon *m*; (for charity) attractions organisées par
les étudiants au profit d'œuvres de charité ▷ *vt* (Brit)
chahuter, mettre en boîte; **rags** *npl* haillons
mpl; **in ~s** (person) en haillons; (clothes) en
lambeaux
rag doll *n* poupée *f* de chiffon
rage [reɪdʒ] *n* (fury) rage *f*, fureur *f* ▷ *vi* (person)
être fou/folle de rage; (storm) faire rage, être
déchaîné(e); **to fly into a ~** se mettre en rage;
it's all the ~ cela fait fureur
ragged ['rægɪd] *adj* (edge) inégal(e), qui
accroche; (clothes) en loques; (cuff)
effiloché(e); (appearance) déguenillé(e)
raid [reɪd] *n* (Mil) raid *m*; (criminal) hold-up *m*
inv; (by police) descente *f*, rafle *f* ▷ *vt* faire un

raid sur or un hold-up dans or une descente dans

rail [reɪl] n (on stair) rampe f; (on bridge, balcony) balustrade f; (of ship) bastingage m; (for train) rail m; **rails** npl rails mpl, voie ferrée; **by** ~ en train, par le train

railcard ['reɪlkɑːd] n (Brit) carte f de chemin de fer; **young person's** ~ carte f jeune

railing ['reɪlɪŋ] n, **railings** ['reɪlɪŋz] npl grille f

railway ['reɪlweɪ], (US) **railroad** ['reɪlrəʊd] n chemin m de fer; (track) voie f ferrée

railway line n (Brit) ligne f de chemin de fer; (track) voie ferrée

railwayman ['reɪlweɪmən] irreg n cheminot m

railway station n (Brit) gare f

rain [reɪn] n pluie f ▷ vi pleuvoir; **in the** ~ sous la pluie; **it's** ~**ing** il pleut; **it's** ~**ing cats and dogs** il pleut à torrents

rainbow ['reɪnbəʊ] n arc-en-ciel m

raincoat ['reɪnkəʊt] n imperméable m

raindrop ['reɪndrɔp] n goutte f de pluie

rainfall ['reɪnfɔːl] n chute f de pluie; (measurement) hauteur f des précipitations

rainforest ['reɪnfɔrɪst] n forêt tropicale

rainy ['reɪnɪ] adj pluvieux(-euse)

raise [reɪz] n augmentation f ▷ vt (lift) lever; hausser; (end: siege, embargo) lever; (build) ériger; (increase) augmenter; (morale) remonter; (standards) améliorer; (a protest, doubt) provoquer, causer; (a question) soulever; (cattle, family) élever; (crop) faire pousser; (army, funds) rassembler; (loan) obtenir; **to** ~ **one's glass to sb/sth** porter un toast en l'honneur de qn/qch; **to** ~ **one's voice** élever la voix; **to** ~ **sb's hopes** donner de l'espoir à qn; **to** ~ **a laugh/a smile** faire rire/sourire

raisin ['reɪzn] n raisin sec

rake [reɪk] n (tool) râteau m; (person) débauché m ▷ vt (garden) ratisser; (fire) tisonner; (with machine gun) balayer ▷ vi: **to** ~ **through** (fig: search) fouiller (dans)

rally ['rælɪ] n (Pol etc) meeting m, rassemblement m; (Aut) rallye m; (Tennis) échange m ▷ vt rassembler, rallier; (support) gagner ▷ vi se rallier; (sick person) aller mieux; (Stock Exchange) reprendre; **rally round** vi venir en aide ▷ vt fus se rallier à; venir en aide à

RAM [ræm] n abbr (Comput: = random access memory) mémoire vive

ram [ræm] n bélier m ▷ vt (push) enfoncer; (soil) tasser; (crash into: vehicle) emboutir; (: lamppost etc) percuter; (in battle) éperonner

Ramadan [ræmə'dæn] n Ramadan m

ramble ['ræmbl] n randonnée f ▷ vi (walk) se promener, faire une randonnée; (pej: also: ~ **on**) discourir, pérorer

rambler ['ræmblə'] n promeneur(-euse), randonneur(-euse); (Bot) rosier grimpant

rambling ['ræmblɪŋ] adj (speech) décousu(e); (house) plein(e) de coins et de recoins; (Bot) grimpant(e)

ramp [ræmp] n (incline) rampe f; (Aut) dénivellation f; (in garage) pont m; **on/off** ~ (US Aut) bretelle f d'accès

rampage ['ræmpeɪdʒ] n: **to be on the** ~ se déchaîner ▷ vi [ræm'peɪdʒ]: **they went rampaging through the town** ils ont envahi les rues et ont tout saccagé sur leur passage

rampant ['ræmpənt] adj (disease etc) qui sévit

ram raiding [-reɪdɪŋ] n pillage d'un magasin en enfonçant la vitrine avec une voiture volée

ramshackle ['ræmʃækl] adj (house) délabré(e); (car etc) déglingué(e)

ran [ræn] pt of **run**

ranch [rɑːntʃ] n ranch m

rancher ['rɑːntʃə'] n (owner) propriétaire m de ranch; (ranch hand) cowboy m

rancid ['rænsɪd] adj rance

rancour, (US) **rancor** ['ræŋkə'] n rancune f, rancœur f

random ['rændəm] adj fait(e) or établi(e) au hasard; (Comput, Math) aléatoire ▷ n: **at** ~ au hasard

random access memory n (Comput) mémoire vive, RAM f

randy ['rændɪ] adj (Brit inf) excité(e); lubrique

rang [ræŋ] pt of **ring**

range [reɪndʒ] n (of mountains) chaîne f; (of missile, voice) portée f; (of products) choix m, gamme f; (also: **shooting** ~) champ m de tir; (: indoor) stand m de tir; (also: **kitchen** ~) fourneau m (de cuisine) ▷ vt (place) mettre en rang, placer; (roam) parcourir ▷ vi: **to** ~ **over** couvrir; **to** ~ **from ... to** aller de ... à; **price** ~ éventail m des prix; **do you have anything else in this price** ~? avez-vous autre chose dans ces prix?; **within** (firing) ~ à portée (de tir); ~**d left/right** (text) justifié à gauche/à droite

ranger ['reɪndʒə'] n garde m forestier

rank [ræŋk] n rang m; (Mil) grade m; (Brit: also: **taxi** ~) station f de taxis ▷ vi: **to** ~ **among** compter or se classer parmi ▷ vt: **I** - **him sixth** je le place sixième ▷ adj (smell) nauséabond(e); (hypocrisy, injustice etc) flagrant(e); **he's a** ~ **outsider** il n'est vraiment pas dans la course; **the** ~**s** (Mil) la troupe; **the** ~ **and file** (fig) la masse, la base; **to close** ~**s** (Mil: fig) serrer les rangs

ransack ['rænsæk] vt fouiller (à fond); (plunder) piller

ransom ['rænsəm] n rançon f; **to hold sb to** ~ (fig) exercer un chantage sur qn

rant [rænt] vi fulminer

rap [ræp] n petit coup sec; tape f; (music) rap m ▷ vt (door) frapper sur or à; (table etc) taper sur

rape [reɪp] n viol m; (Bot) colza m ▷ vt violer

rape oil, rapeseed oil ['reɪp(siːd)-] n huile f de colza

rapid ['ræpɪd] adj rapide

rapidly ['ræpɪdlɪ] adv rapidement

rapids ['ræpɪdz] npl (Geo) rapides mpl

rapist ['reɪpɪst] n auteur m d'un viol

rapport [ræ'pɔːʳ] n entente f

rapturous ['ræptʃərəs] adj extasié(e);
frénétique

rare [reəʳ] adj rare; (Culin: steak) saignant(e)

rarely ['reəlɪ] adv rarement

raring ['reərɪŋ] adj: **to be ~ to go** (inf) être très
impatient(e) de commencer

rascal ['rɑːskl] n vaurien m

rash [ræʃ] adj imprudent(e), irréfléchi(e) ▷ n
(Med) rougeur f, éruption f; (of events) série f
(noire); **to come out in a ~** avoir une
éruption

rasher ['ræʃəʳ] n fine tranche (de lard)

raspberry ['rɑːzbərɪ] n framboise f

raspberry bush n framboisier m

rasping ['rɑːspɪŋ] adj: **~ noise** grincement m

rat [ræt] n rat m

rate [reɪt] n (ratio) taux m, pourcentage m;
(speed) vitesse f, rythme m; (price) tarif m ▷ vt
(price) évaluer, estimer; (people) classer;
(deserve) mériter; **rates** npl (Brit: property tax)
impôts locaux; **to ~ sb/sth as** considérer qn/
qch comme; **to ~ sb/sth among** classer qn/
qch parmi; **to ~ sb/sth highly** avoir une
haute opinion de qn/qch; **at a ~ of 60 kph**
à une vitesse de 60 km/h; **at any ~** en tout
cas; **~ of exchange** taux or cours m du change;
~ of flow débit m; **~ of return** (taux de)
rendement m; **pulse ~** fréquence f des
pulsations

rateable value ['reɪtəbl-] n (Brit) valeur
locative imposable

ratepayer ['reɪtpeɪəʳ] n (Brit) contribuable
m/f (payant les impôts locaux)

rather ['rɑːðəʳ] adv (somewhat) assez, plutôt;
(to some extent) un peu; **it's ~ expensive** c'est
assez cher; (too much) c'est un peu cher;
there's ~ a lot il y en a beaucoup; **I would** or
I'd ~ go j'aimerais mieux or je préférerais
partir; **I had ~ go** il vaudrait mieux que je
parte; **I'd ~ not leave** j'aimerais mieux ne
pas partir; **or ~** (more accurately) ou plutôt;
I ~ think he won't come je crois bien qu'il
ne viendra pas

rating ['reɪtɪŋ] n (assessment) évaluation f;
(score) classement m; (Finance) cote f;
(Naut: category) classe f; (: sailor: Brit)
matelot m; **ratings** npl (Radio) indice(s) m(pl)
d'écoute; (TV) Audimat® m

ratio ['reɪʃɪəʊ] n proportion f; **in the ~ of**
100 to 1 dans la proportion de 100 contre 1

ration ['ræʃən] n ration f ▷ vt rationner;
rations npl (food) vivres mpl

rational ['ræʃənl] adj raisonnable, sensé(e);
(solution, reasoning) logique; (Med: person)
lucide

rationale [ræʃə'nɑːl] n raisonnement m;
justification f

rationalize ['ræʃnəlaɪz] vt rationaliser;

(conduct) essayer d'expliquer or de motiver

rat race n foire f d'empoigne

rattle ['rætl] n (of door, window) battement m;
(of coins, chain) cliquetis m; (of train, engine)
bruit m de ferraille; (for baby) hochet m;
(of sports fan) crécelle f ▷ vi cliqueter; (car, bus)
to ~ along rouler en faisant un bruit de
ferraille ▷ vt agiter (bruyamment); (inf:
disconcert) décontenancer; (: annoy) embêter

rattlesnake ['rætlsneɪk] n serpent m à
sonnettes

raucous ['rɔːkəs] adj rauque

rave [reɪv] vi (in anger) s'emporter; (with
enthusiasm) s'extasier; (Med) délirer ▷ n
(inf: party) rave f, soirée f techno ▷ adj (scene,
culture, music) rave, techno ▷ cpd: **~ review** (inf)
critique f dithyrambique

raven ['reɪvən] n grand corbeau

ravenous ['rævənəs] adj affamé(e)

ravine [rə'viːn] n ravin m

raving ['reɪvɪŋ] adj: **he's ~ mad** il est
complètement cinglé

ravishing ['rævɪʃɪŋ] adj enchanteur(-eresse)

raw [rɔː] adj (uncooked) cru(e); (not processed)
brut(e); (sore) à vif, irrité(e); (inexperienced)
inexpérimenté(e); (weather, day) froid(e) et
humide; **~ deal** (inf: bad bargain) sale coup m;
(: unfair treatment): **to get a ~ deal** être traité(e)
injustement; **~ materials** matières
premières

raw material n matière première

ray [reɪ] n rayon m; **~ of hope** lueur f d'espoir

raze [reɪz] vt (also: **~ to the ground**) raser

razor ['reɪzəʳ] n rasoir m

razor blade n lame f de rasoir

Rd abbr = **road**

RE n abbr (Brit: = religious education) instruction
religieuse; (Brit Mil: = Royal Engineers)

re [riː] prep concernant

reach [riːtʃ] n portée f, atteinte f; (of river etc)
étendue f ▷ vt atteindre, arriver à; (conclusion,
decision) parvenir à ▷ vi s'étendre; (stretch out
hand): **to ~ up/down** etc (for sth) lever/
baisser etc le bras (pour prendre qch); **to ~ sb**
by phone joindre qn par téléphone; **out of/**
within ~ (object) hors de/à portée; **within**
easy ~ (of) (place) à proximité (de), proche
(de); **reach out** vt tendre ▷ vi:
allonger le bras (pour prendre)

react [riː'ækt] vi réagir

reaction [riː'ækʃən] n réaction f

reactor [riː'æktəʳ] n réacteur m

read (pt, pp **read**) [riːd, rɛd] vi lire ▷ vt lire;
(understand) comprendre, interpréter; (study)
étudier; (meter) relever; (subj: instrument etc)
indiquer, marquer; **to take sth as ~** (fig)
considérer qch comme accepté; **do you ~**
me? (Tel) est-ce que vous me recevez?; **read**
out vt lire à haute voix; **read over** vt relire;
read through vt (quickly) parcourir;
(thoroughly) lire jusqu'au bout; **read up** vt,
read up on vt fus étudier

readable ['riːdəbl] adj facile or agréable à lire

reader ['riːdəʳ] n lecteur(-trice); (book) livre m de lecture; (Brit: at university) maître m de conférences

readership ['riːdəʃɪp] n (of paper etc) (nombre m de) lecteurs mpl

readily ['redɪlɪ] adv volontiers, avec empressement; (easily) facilement

readiness ['redɪnɪs] n empressement m; **in ~** (prepared) prêt(e)

reading ['riːdɪŋ] n lecture f; (understanding) interprétation f; (on instrument) indications fpl

ready ['redɪ] adj prêt(e); (willing) prêt, disposé(e); (quick) prompt(e); (available) disponible ▷ n: **at the ~** (Mil) prêt à faire feu; (fig) tout(e) prêt(e); **~ for use** prêt à l'emploi; **to be ~ to do sth** être prêt à faire qch; **when will my photos be ~?** quand est-ce que mes photos seront prêtes?; **to get ~** (as vi) se préparer; (as vt) préparer

ready-cooked ['redɪ'kʊkd] adj précuit(e)

ready-made ['redɪ'meɪd] adj tout(e) faite(e)

ready-to-wear ['redɪtə'wɛəʳ] adj (en) prêt-à-porter

real [rɪəl] adj (world, life) réel(le); (genuine) véritable; (proper) vrai(e) ▷ adv (US inf: very) vraiment; **in ~ life** dans la réalité

real ale n bière traditionnelle

real estate n biens fonciers or immobiliers

realistic [rɪə'lɪstɪk] adj réaliste

reality [riː'ælɪtɪ] n réalité f; **in ~** en réalité, en fait

reality TV n téléréalité f

realization [rɪəlaɪ'zeɪʃən] n (awareness) prise f de conscience; (fulfilment: also: of asset) réalisation f

realize ['rɪəlaɪz] vt (understand) se rendre compte de, prendre conscience de; (a project, Comm: asset) réaliser

really ['rɪəlɪ] adv vraiment; **~?** vraiment?, c'est vrai?

realm [relm] n royaume m; (fig) domaine m

realtor ['rɪəltɔːʳ] n (US) agent immobilier

reap [riːp] vt moissonner; (fig) récolter

reappear [riːə'pɪəʳ] vi réapparaître, reparaître

rear [rɪəʳ] adj de derrière, arrière inv; (Aut: wheel etc) arrière ▷ n arrière m, derrière m ▷ vt (cattle, family) élever ▷ vi (also: **~ up**: animal) se cabrer

rearguard ['rɪəgɑːd] n arrière-garde f

rearrange [rɪːə'reɪndʒ] vt réarranger

rear-view mirror n (Aut) rétroviseur m

rear-wheel drive n (Aut) traction f arrière

reason ['riːzn] n raison f ▷ vi: **to ~ with sb** raisonner qn, faire entendre raison à qn; **the ~ for/why** la raison de/pour laquelle; **to have ~ to think** avoir lieu de penser; **it stands to ~ that** il va sans dire que; **she claims with good ~ that ...** elle affirme à juste titre que ...; **all the more ~ why** raison

de plus pour + infinitive or pour que + sub; **within ~** dans les limites du raisonnable

reasonable ['riːznəbl] adj raisonnable; (not bad) acceptable

reasonably ['riːznəblɪ] adv (behave) raisonnablement; (fairly) assez; **one can ~ assume that ...** on est fondé à or il est permis de supposer que ...

reasoning ['riːznɪŋ] n raisonnement m

reassurance [riːə'ʃuərəns] n (factual) assurance f, garantie f; (emotional) réconfort m

reassure [riːə'ʃuəʳ] vt rassurer; **to ~ sb of** donner à qn l'assurance répétée de

rebate ['riːbeɪt] n (on product) rabais m; (on tax etc) dégrèvement m; (repayment) remboursement m

rebel n ['rɛbl] rebelle m/f ▷ vi [rɪ'bɛl] se rebeller, se révolter

rebellion [rɪ'bɛljən] n rébellion f, révolte f

rebellious [rɪ'bɛljəs] adj rebelle

rebound vi [rɪ'baund] (ball) rebondir ▷ n ['riːbaund] rebond m

rebuff [rɪ'bʌf] n rebuffade f ▷ vt repousser

rebuild [riː'bɪld] vt (irreg like: **build**) reconstruire

rebuke [rɪ'bjuːk] n réprimande f, reproche m ▷ vt réprimander

rebut [rɪ'bʌt] vt réfuter

recall vt [rɪ'kɔːl] rappeler; (remember) se rappeler, se souvenir de ▷ n ['riːkɔl] rappel m; (ability to remember) mémoire f; **beyond ~** adj irrévocable

recant [rɪ'kænt] vi se rétracter; (Rel) abjurer

recap ['riːkæp] n récapitulation f ▷ vt, vi récapituler

recede [rɪ'siːd] vi s'éloigner; reculer

receding [rɪ'siːdɪŋ] adj (forehead, chin) fuyant(e); **~ hairline** front dégarni

receipt [rɪ'siːt] n (document) reçu m; (for parcel etc) accusé m de réception; (act of receiving) réception f; **receipts** npl (Comm) recettes fpl; **to acknowledge ~ of** accuser réception de; **we are in ~ of ...** nous avons reçu ...; **can I have a ~, please?** je peux avoir un reçu, s'il vous plaît?

receive [rɪ'siːv] vt recevoir; (guest) recevoir, accueillir; **"~d with thanks"** (Comm) "pour acquit"; **R~d Pronunciation** voir article

receiver [rɪ'siːvəʳ] n (Tel) récepteur m, combiné m; (Radio) récepteur; (of stolen goods) receleur m; (for bankruptcies) administrateur m judiciaire

recent ['ri:snt] adj récent(e); **in ~ years** au cours de ces dernières années

recently ['ri:sntli] adv récemment; **as ~ as** pas plus tard que; **until ~** jusqu'à il y a peu de temps encore

receptacle [rɪ'septɪkl] n récipient m

reception [rɪ'sepʃən] n réception f; (welcome) accueil m, réception

reception desk n réception f

receptionist [rɪ'sepʃənɪst] n réceptionniste m/f

recess [rɪ'ses] n (in room) renfoncement m; (for bed) alcôve f; (secret place) recoin m; (Pol etc: holiday) vacances fpl; (US Law: short break) suspension f d'audience; (Scol: esp US) récréation f

recession [rɪ'seʃən] n (Econ) récession f

recharge [ri:'tʃɑːdʒ] vt (battery) recharger

recipe ['resɪpɪ] n recette f

recipient [rɪ'sɪpɪənt] n (of payment) bénéficiaire m/f; (of letter) destinataire m/f

recital [rɪ'saɪtl] n récital m

recite [rɪ'saɪt] vt (poem) réciter; (complaints etc) énumérer

reckless ['rekləs] adj (driver etc) imprudent(e); (spender etc) insouciant(e)

reckon ['rekən] vt (count) calculer, compter; (consider) considérer, estimer; (think): **I ~ (that)** ... je pense (que) ..., j'estime (que) ... ▷ vi: **he is somebody to be ~ed with** il ne faut pas le sous-estimer; **to ~ without sb/ sth** ne pas tenir compte de qn/qch; **reckon on** vt fus compter sur, s'attendre à

reckoning ['rekniŋ] n compte m, calcul m; estimation f; **the day of ~** le jour du Jugement

reclaim [rɪ'kleɪm] vt (land: from sea) assécher; (: from forest) défricher; (: with fertilizer) amender; (demand back) réclamer (le remboursement or la restitution de); (waste materials) récupérer

recline [rɪ'klaɪn] vi être allongé(e) or étendu(e)

reclining [rɪ'klaɪnɪŋ] adj (seat) à dossier réglable

recluse [rɪ'klu:s] n reclus(e), ermite m

recognition [rekəg'nɪʃən] n reconnaissance f; **in ~ of** en reconnaissance de; **to gain ~** être reconnu(e); **transformed beyond ~** méconnaissable

recognizable ['rekəgnaɪzəbl] adj: ~ (by) reconnaissable (à)

recognize ['rekəgnaɪz] vt: **to ~ (by/as)** reconnaître (à/comme étant)

recoil [rɪ'kɔɪl] vi (person): **to ~ (from)** reculer (devant) ▷ n (of gun) recul m

recollect [rekə'lekt] vt se rappeler, se souvenir de

recollection [rekə'lekʃən] n souvenir m;

to the best of my ~ autant que je m'en souvienne

recommend [rekə'mend] vt recommander; **can you ~ a good restaurant?** pouvez-vous me conseiller un bon restaurant?; **she has a lot to ~ her** elle a beaucoup de choses en sa faveur

recommendation [rekəmen'deɪʃən] n recommandation f

reconcile ['rekənsaɪl] vt (two people) réconcilier; (two facts) concilier, accorder; **to ~ o.s. to** se résigner à

recondition [ri:kən'dɪʃən] vt remettre à neuf; réviser entièrement

reconnoitre, (US) **reconnoiter** [rekə'nɔɪtər] (Mil) vt reconnaître ▷ vi faire une reconnaissance

reconsider [ri:kən'sɪdər] vt reconsidérer

reconstruct [ri:kən'strʌkt] vt (building) reconstruire; (crime, system) reconstituer

record n ['rekɔːd] rapport m, récit m; (of meeting etc) procès-verbal m; (register) registre m; (file) dossier m; (Comput) article m; (also: **police ~**) casier m judiciaire; (Mus: disc) disque m; (Sport) record m ▷ adj record inv ▷ vt [rɪ'kɔːd] (set down) noter; (relate) rapporter; (Mus: song etc) enregistrer; **public ~s** archives fpl; **to keep a ~ of** noter; **to keep the ~ straight** (fig) mettre les choses au point; **he is on ~ as saying that ...** il a déclaré en public que ...; **Italy's excellent ~** les excellents résultats obtenus par l'Italie; **off the ~** adj officieux(-euse) ▷ adv officieusement; **in ~ time** dans un temps record

record card n (in file) fiche f

recorded delivery [rɪ'kɔːdɪd-] n (Brit Post): **to send sth ~** = envoyer qch en recommandé

recorded delivery letter [rɪ'kɔːdɪd-] n (Brit Post) = lettre recommandée

recorder [rɪ'kɔːdər] n (Law) avocat nommé à la fonction de juge; (Mus) flûte f à bec

record holder n (Sport) détenteur(-trice) du record

recording [rɪ'kɔːdɪŋ] n (Mus) enregistrement m

record player n tourne-disque m

recount [rɪ'kaʊnt] vt raconter

re-count n ['ri:kaʊnt] (Pol: of votes) nouveau décompte (des suffrages) ▷ vt [ri:'kaʊnt] recompter

recoup [rɪ'ku:p] vt: **to ~ one's losses** récupérer ce qu'on a perdu, se refaire

recourse [rɪ'kɔːs] n recours m; expédient m; **to have ~ to** recourir à, avoir recours à

recover [rɪ'kʌvər] vt récupérer ▷ vi (from illness) se rétablir; (from shock) se remettre; (country) se redresser

recovery [rɪ'kʌvərɪ] n récupération f; rétablissement m; (Econ) redressement m

recreate [ri:krɪ'eɪt] vt recréer

recreation [rekrɪ'eɪʃən] n (leisure) récréation f, détente f

recreational [rekrɪ'eɪʃənl] adj pour la détente, récréatif(-ive)

recreational drug [rekrɪ'eɪʃənl-] n drogue récréative

recreational vehicle [rekrɪ'eɪʃənl-] n (US) camping-car m

recruit [rɪ'kruːt] n recrue f ▷ vt recruter

recruitment [rɪ'kruːtmənt] n recrutement m

rectangle ['rektæŋgl] n rectangle m

rectangular [rek'tæŋgjuləʳ] adj rectangulaire

rectify ['rektɪfaɪ] vt (error) rectifier, corriger; (omission) réparer

rector ['rektəʳ] n (Rel) pasteur m; (in Scottish universities) personnalité élue par les étudiants pour les représenter

recuperate [rɪ'kjuːpəreɪt] vi (from illness) se rétablir

recur [rɪ'kəːʳ] vi se reproduire; (idea, opportunity) se retrouver; (symptoms) réapparaître

recurrence [rɪ'kəːrns] n répétition f; réapparition f

recurrent [rɪ'kəːrnt] adj périodique, fréquent(e)

recurring [rɪ'kəːrɪŋ] adj (problem) périodique, fréquent(e); (Math) périodique

recyclable [riː'saɪkləbl] adj recyclable

recycle [riː'saɪkl] vt, vi recycler

recycling [riː'saɪklɪŋ] n recyclage m

red [red] n rouge m; (Pol: pej) rouge m/f ▷ adj rouge; (hair) roux/rousse; **in the ~** (account) à découvert; (business) en déficit

red carpet treatment n réception f en grande pompe

Red Cross n Croix-Rouge f

redcurrant ['redkʌrənt] n groseille f (rouge)

redden ['redn] vt, vi rougir

redecorate [riː'dekəreɪt] vt refaire à neuf, repeindre et retapisser

redeem [rɪ'diːm] vt (debt) rembourser; (sth in pawn) dégager; (fig, also Rel) racheter

redeeming [rɪ'diːmɪŋ] adj (feature) qui sauve, qui rachète (le reste)

redeploy [riːdɪ'plɔɪ] vt (Mil) redéployer; (staff, resources) reconvertir

red-haired [red'heəd] adj roux/rousse

red-handed [red'hændɪd] adj: **to be caught ~** être pris(e) en flagrant délit or la main dans le sac

redhead ['redhed] n roux/rousse

red herring n (fig) diversion f, fausse piste

red-hot [red'hɒt] adj chauffé(e) au rouge, brûlant(e)

redirect [riːdaɪ'rekt] vt (mail) faire suivre

red light n: **to go through a ~** (Aut) brûler un feu rouge

red-light district ['redlaɪt-] n quartier mal famé

red meat n viande f rouge

redo [riː'duː] vt (irreg like: **do**) refaire

redress [rɪ'dres] n réparation f ▷ vt redresser; **to ~ the balance** rétablir l'équilibre

Red Sea n: **the ~** la mer Rouge

redskin ['redskɪn] n Peau-Rouge m/f

red tape n (fig) paperasserie f (administrative)

reduce [rɪ'djuːs] vt réduire; (lower) abaisser; **"~ speed now"** (Aut) "ralentir"; **to ~ sth by/to** réduire qch de/à; **to ~ sb to tears** faire pleurer qn

reduced [rɪ'djuːst] adj réduit(e); **"greatly ~ prices"** "gros rabais"; **at a ~ price** (goods) au rabais; (ticket etc) à prix réduit

reduction [rɪ'dʌkʃən] n réduction f; (of price) baisse f; (discount) rabais m; réduction; **is there a ~ for children/students?** y a-t-il une réduction pour les enfants/les étudiants?

redundancy [rɪ'dʌndənsɪ] n (Brit) licenciement m, mise f au chômage; **compulsory ~** licenciement; **voluntary ~** départ m volontaire

redundant [rɪ'dʌndnt] adj (Brit: worker) licencié(e), mis(e) au chômage; (detail, object) superflu(e); **to be made ~** (worker) être licencié, être mis au chômage

reed [riːd] n (Bot) roseau m; (Mus: of clarinet etc) anche f

reef [riːf] n (at sea) récif m, écueil m

reek [riːk] vi: **to ~ (of)** puer, empester

reel [riːl] n bobine f; (Tech) dévidoir m; (Fishing) moulinet m; (Cine) bande f; (dance) quadrille écossais ▷ vt (Tech) bobiner; (also: ~ up) enrouler ▷ vi (sway) chanceler; **my head is ~ing** j'ai la tête qui tourne; **reel in** vt (fish, line) ramener; **reel off** vt (say) énumérer, débiter

ref [ref] n abbr (inf: = referee) arbitre m

refectory [rɪ'fektərɪ] n réfectoire m

refer [rɪ'fəːʳ] vt: **to ~ sth to** (dispute, decision) soumettre qch à; **to ~ sb to** (inquirer, patient) adresser qn à; (reader: to text) renvoyer qn à ▷ vi: **to ~ to** (allude to) parler de, faire allusion à; (consult) se reporter à; (apply to) s'appliquer à; **~ring to your letter** (Comm) en réponse à votre lettre; **he ~red me to the manager** il m'a dit de m'adresser au directeur

referee [refə'riː] n arbitre m; (Tennis) juge-arbitre m; (Brit: for job application) répondant(e) ▷ vt arbitrer

reference ['refrəns] n référence f, renvoi m; (mention) allusion f, mention f; (for job application: letter) références; lettre f de recommandation; (: person) répondant(e); **with ~ to** en ce qui concerne; (Comm: in letter) me référant à; **"please quote this ~"** (Comm) "prière de rappeler cette référence"

reference book n ouvrage m de référence

reference number n (Comm) numéro m de référence

refill vt [riː'fɪl] remplir à nouveau; (pen, lighter etc) recharger ▷ n ['riːfɪl] (for pen etc) recharge f

refine [rɪ'faɪn] *vt* (*sugar, oil*) raffiner; (*taste*) affiner; (*idea, theory*) peaufiner

refined [rɪ'faɪnd] *adj* (*person, taste*) raffiné(e)

refinery [rɪ'faɪnərɪ] *n* raffinerie *f*

reflect [rɪ'flɛkt] *vt* (*light, image*) réfléchir, refléter; (*fig*) refléter ▷ *vi* (*think*) réfléchir, méditer; **it ~s badly on him** cela le discrédite; **it ~s well on him** c'est tout à son honneur

reflection [rɪ'flɛkʃən] *n* réflexion *f*; (*image*) reflet *m*; (*criticism*): **~ on** critique *f* de; atteinte *f* à; **on ~** réflexion faite

reflex ['ri:flɛks] *adj, n* réflexe (*m*)

reflexive [rɪ'flɛksɪv] *adj* (Ling) réfléchi(e)

reform [rɪ'fɔ:m] *n* réforme *f* ▷ *vt* réformer

reformatory [rɪ'fɔ:mətərɪ] *n* (US) centre *m* d'éducation surveillée

refrain [rɪ'freɪn] *vi*: **to ~ from doing** s'abstenir de faire ▷ *n* refrain *m*

refresh [rɪ'frɛʃ] *vt* rafraîchir; (*subj: food, sleep etc*) redonner des forces à

refresher course [rɪ'frɛʃə-] *n* (Brit) cours *m* de recyclage

refreshing [rɪ'frɛʃɪŋ] *adj* (*drink*) rafraîchissant(e); (*sleep*) réparateur(-trice); (*fact, idea etc*) qui réjouit par son originalité or sa rareté

refreshment [rɪ'frɛʃmənt] *n*: **for some ~** (*eating*) pour se restaurer *or* sustenter; **in need of ~** (*resting etc*) ayant besoin de refaire ses forces

refreshments [rɪ'frɛʃmənts] *npl* rafraîchissements *mpl*

refrigerator [rɪ'frɪdʒəreɪtə'] *n* réfrigérateur *m*, frigidaire *m*

refuel [ri:'fjuəl] *vt* ravitailler en carburant ▷ *vi* se ravitailler en carburant

refuge ['rɛfju:dʒ] *n* refuge *m*; **to take ~ in** se réfugier dans

refugee [rɛfju'dʒi:] *n* réfugié(e)

refund *n* ['ri:fʌnd] remboursement *m* ▷ *vt* [rɪ'fʌnd] rembourser

refurbish [ri:'fə:bɪʃ] *vt* remettre à neuf

refusal [rɪ'fju:zəl] *n* refus *m*; **to have first ~ on sth** avoir droit de préemption sur qch

refuse¹ ['rɛfju:s] *n* ordures *fpl*, détritus *mpl*

refuse² [rɪ'fju:z] *vt, vi* refuser; **to ~ to do sth** refuser de faire qch

refuse collection *n* ramassage *m* d'ordures

regain [rɪ'geɪn] *vt* (*lost ground*) regagner; (*strength*) retrouver

regal ['ri:gl] *adj* royal(e)

regard *n* [rɪ'gɑ:d] *n* respect *m*, estime *f*, considération *f* ▷ *vt* considérer; **to give one's ~s to** faire ses amitiés à; **"with kindest ~s"** "bien amicalement"; **as ~s, with ~ to** en ce qui concerne

regarding [rɪ'gɑ:dɪŋ] *prep* en ce qui concerne

regardless [rɪ'gɑ:dlɪs] *adv* quand même; **~ of** sans se soucier de

regenerate [rɪ'dʒɛnəreɪt] *vt* régénérer ▷ *vi* se régénérer

reggae ['rɛgeɪ] *n* reggae *m*

régime [reɪ'ʒi:m] *n* régime *m*

regiment *n* ['rɛdʒɪmənt] *n* régiment *m* ▷ *vt* ['rɛdʒɪmɛnt] imposer une discipline trop stricte à

regimental [rɛdʒɪ'mɛntl] *adj* d'un régiment

region ['ri:dʒən] *n* région *f*; **in the ~ of** (*fig*) aux alentours de

regional ['ri:dʒənl] *adj* régional(e)

register ['rɛdʒɪstə'] *n* registre *m*; (*also:* **electoral ~**) liste électorale ▷ *vt* enregistrer, inscrire; (*birth*) déclarer; (*vehicle*) immatriculer; (*luggage*) enregistrer; (*letter*) envoyer en recommandé; (*subj: instrument*) marquer ▷ *vi* s'inscrire; (*at hotel*) signer le registre; (*make impression*) être (bien) compris(e); **to ~ for a course** s'inscrire à un cours; **to ~ a protest** protester

registered ['rɛdʒɪstəd] *adj* (*design*) déposé(e); (*Brit: letter*) recommandé(e); (*student, voter*) inscrit(e)

registered trademark *n* marque déposée

registrar ['rɛdʒɪstrɑ:'] *n* officier *m* de l'état civil; secrétaire *m/f* général

registration [rɛdʒɪs'treɪʃən] *n* (*act*) enregistrement *m*; (*of student*) inscription *f*; (*Brit Aut: also:* **~ number**) numéro *m* d'immatriculation

registry ['rɛdʒɪstrɪ] *n* bureau *m* de l'enregistrement

registry office ['rɛdʒɪstrɪ-] *n* (Brit) bureau *m* de l'état civil; **to get married in a ~** ≈ se marier à la mairie

regret [rɪ'grɛt] *n* regret *m* ▷ *vt* regretter; **to ~ that** regretter que + *sub*; **we ~ to inform you that ...** nous sommes au regret de vous informer que ...

regretfully [rɪ'grɛtfəlɪ] *adv* à *or* avec regret

regrettable [rɪ'grɛtəbl] *adj* regrettable, fâcheux(-euse)

regular ['rɛgjulə'] *adj* régulier(-ière); (*usual*) habituel(le), normal(e); (*listener, reader*) fidèle; (*soldier*) de métier; (Comm: *size*) ordinaire ▷ *n* (*client etc*) habitué(e)

regularly ['rɛgjuləlɪ] *adv* régulièrement

regulate ['rɛgjuleɪt] *vt* régler

regulation [rɛgju'leɪʃən] *n* (*rule*) règlement *m*; (*adjustment*) réglage *m* ▷ *cpd* réglementaire

rehabilitation ['ri:əbɪlɪ'teɪʃən] *n* (*of offender*) réhabilitation *f*; (*of addict*) réadaptation *f*; (*of disabled*) rééducation *f*, réadaptation *f*

rehearsal [rɪ'hə:səl] *n* répétition *f*; **dress ~** (*répétition*) générale *f*

rehearse [rɪ'hə:s] *vt* répéter

reign [reɪn] *n* règne *m* ▷ *vi* régner

reimburse [ri:ɪm'bə:s] *vt* rembourser

rein [reɪn] *n* (*for horse*) rêne *f*; **to give sb free ~** (*fig*) donner carte blanche à qn

reincarnation [ri:ɪnkɑː'neɪʃən] *n* réincarnation *f*

reindeer ['reɪndɪə'] *n* (*pl inv*) renne *m*

reinforce [riːɪnˈfɔːs] vt renforcer
reinforced concrete [riːɪnˈfɔːst-] n béton armé
reinforcement [riːɪnˈfɔːsmənt] n (action) renforcement m
reinforcements [riːɪnˈfɔːsmənts] npl (Mil) renfort(s) m(pl)
reinstate [riːɪnˈsteɪt] vt rétablir, réintégrer
reject n [ˈriːdʒekt] (Comm) article m de rebut ▷ vt [rɪˈdʒekt] refuser; (Comm: goods) mettre au rebut; (idea) rejeter
rejection [rɪˈdʒekʃən] n rejet m, refus m
rejoice [rɪˈdʒɔɪs] vi: **to ~ (at or over)** se réjouir (de)
rejuvenate [rɪˈdʒuːvəneɪt] vt rajeunir
relapse [rɪˈlæps] n (Med) rechute f
relate [rɪˈleɪt] vt (tell) raconter; (connect) établir un rapport entre ▷ vi: **to ~ to** (connect) se rapporter à; **to ~ to sb** (interact) entretenir des rapports avec qn
related [rɪˈleɪtɪd] adj apparenté(e); **~ to** (subject) lié(e) à
relating to [rɪˈleɪtɪŋ-] prep concernant
relation [rɪˈleɪʃən] n (person) parent(e); (link) rapport m, lien m; **relations** npl (relatives) famille f; **diplomatic/international ~s** relations diplomatiques/internationales; **in ~ to** en ce qui concerne; par rapport à; **to bear no ~ to** être sans rapport avec
relationship [rɪˈleɪʃənʃɪp] n rapport m, lien m; (personal ties) relations fpl, rapports; (also: **family ~**) lien de parenté; (affair) liaison f; **they have a good ~** ils s'entendent bien
relative [ˈrelətɪv] n parent(e) ▷ adj relatif(-ive); (respective) respectif(-ive); **all her ~s** toute sa famille
relatively [ˈrelətɪvlɪ] adv relativement
relax [rɪˈlæks] vi (muscle) se relâcher; (person: unwind) se détendre; (calm down) se calmer ▷ vt relâcher; (mind, person) détendre
relaxation [riːlækˈseɪʃən] n relâchement m; (of mind) détente f; (recreation) détente, délassement m; (entertainment) distraction f
relaxed [rɪˈlækst] adj relâché(e); détendu(e)
relaxing [rɪˈlæksɪŋ] adj délassant(e)
relay [ˈriːleɪ] n (Sport) course f de relais ▷ vt (message) retransmettre, relayer
release [rɪˈliːs] n (from prison, obligation) libération f; (of gas etc) émission f; (of film etc) sortie f; (new recording) disque m; (device) déclencheur m ▷ vt (prisoner) libérer; (book, film) sortir; (report, news) rendre public, publier; (gas etc) émettre, dégager; (free: from wreckage etc) dégager; (Tech: catch, spring etc) déclencher; (let go: person, animal) relâcher; (: hand, object) lâcher; (: grip, brake) desserrer; **to ~ one's grip** or **hold** lâcher prise; **to ~ the clutch** (Aut) débrayer
relegate [ˈreləgeɪt] vt reléguer; (Brit Sport): **to be ~d** descendre dans une division inférieure

relent [rɪˈlent] vi se laisser fléchir
relentless [rɪˈlentlɪs] adj implacable; (non-stop) continuel(le)
relevant [ˈreləvənt] adj (question) pertinent(e); (corresponding) approprié(e); (fact) significatif(-ive); (information) utile; **~ to** ayant rapport à, approprié à
reliable [rɪˈlaɪəbl] adj (person, firm) sérieux(-euse), fiable; (method, machine) fiable; (news, information) sûr(e)
reliably [rɪˈlaɪəblɪ] adv: **to be ~ informed** savoir de source sûre
reliance [rɪˈlaɪəns] n: **~ (on)** (trust) confiance f (en); (dependence) besoin m (de), dépendance f (de)
relic [ˈrelɪk] n (Rel) relique f; (of the past) vestige m
relief [rɪˈliːf] n (from pain, anxiety) soulagement m; (help, supplies) secours m(pl); (of guard) relève f; (Art, Geo) relief m; **by way of light** ~ pour faire diversion
relieve [rɪˈliːv] vt (pain, patient) soulager; (fear, worry) dissiper; (bring help) secourir; (take over from: gen) relayer; (: guard) relever; **to ~ sb of sth** débarrasser qn de qch; **to ~ sb of his command** (Mil) relever qn de ses fonctions; **to ~ o.s.** (euphemism) se soulager, faire ses besoins
relieved [rɪˈliːvd] adj soulagé(e); **to be ~ that ...** être soulagé que ...; **I'm ~ to hear it** je suis soulagé de l'entendre
religion [rɪˈlɪdʒən] n religion f
religious [rɪˈlɪdʒəs] adj religieux(-euse); (book) de piété
religious education n instruction religieuse
relinquish [rɪˈlɪŋkwɪʃ] vt abandonner; (plan, habit) renoncer à
relish [ˈrelɪʃ] n (Culin) condiment m; (enjoyment) délectation f ▷ vt (food etc) savourer; **to ~ doing** se délecter à faire
relocate [riːləʊˈkeɪt] vt (business) transférer ▷ vi se transférer, s'installer or s'établir ailleurs; **to ~ in** (dépménager et) s'installer or s'établir à, se transférer à
reluctance [rɪˈlʌktəns] n répugnance f
reluctant [rɪˈlʌktənt] adj peu disposé(e), qui hésite; **to be ~ to do sth** hésiter à faire qch
reluctantly [rɪˈlʌktəntlɪ] adv à contrecœur, sans enthousiasme
rely on [rɪˈlaɪ-] vt fus (be dependent on) dépendre de; (trust) compter sur
remain [rɪˈmeɪn] vi rester; **to ~ silent** garder le silence; **I ~, yours faithfully** (Brit: in letters) je vous prie d'agréer, Monsieur etc l'assurance de mes sentiments distingués
remainder [rɪˈmeɪndəʳ] n reste m; (Comm) fin f de série
remaining [rɪˈmeɪnɪŋ] adj qui reste
remains [rɪˈmeɪnz] npl restes mpl
remake [ˈriːmeɪk] n (Cine) remake m

r

remand [rɪ'mɑːnd] n: **on ~** en détention
préventive ▷ vt: **to be ~ed in custody** être
placé(e) en détention préventive

remark [rɪ'mɑːk] n remarque f, observation f
▷ vt (faire) remarquer, dire; (notice)
remarquer; **to ~ on sth** faire une or des
remarque(s) sur qch

remarkable [rɪ'mɑːkəbl] adj remarquable

remarkably [rɪ'mɑːkəblɪ] adv
remarquablement

remarry [riː'mærɪ] vi se remarier

remedial [rɪ'miːdɪəl] adj (tuition, classes) de
rattrapage

remedy ['rɛmədɪ] n: **~ (for)** remède m (contre
or à) ▷ vt remédier à

remember [rɪ'mɛmbəʳ] vt se rappeler, se
souvenir de; (send greetings): **~ me to him**
saluez-le de ma part; **I ~ seeing it, I ~ having
seen it** je me rappelle l'avoir vu or que je l'ai
vu; **she ~ed to do it** elle a pensé à le faire; **~
me to your wife** rappelez-moi au bon
souvenir de votre femme

remembrance [rɪ'mɛmbrəns] n souvenir m;
mémoire f

Remembrance Day n (Brit) ≈ (le jour de)
l'Armistice m, ≈ le 11 novembre; voir article

◈ **REMEMBRANCE DAY**

◈ Remembrance Day ou Remembrance Sunday est
◈ le dimanche le plus proche du 11
◈ novembre, jour où la Première Guerre
◈ mondiale a officiellement pris fin. Il rend
◈ hommage aux victimes des deux guerres
◈ mondiales. À cette occasion, on observe
◈ deux minutes de silence à 11h, heure de la
◈ signature de l'armistice avec l'Allemagne
◈ en 1918; certaines membres de la famille
◈ royale et du gouvernement déposent des
◈ gerbes de coquelicots au cénotaphe de
◈ Whitehall, et des couronnes sont placées
◈ sur les monuments aux morts dans toute
◈ la Grande-Bretagne; par ailleurs, les gens
◈ portent des coquelicots artificiels
◈ fabriqués et vendus par des membres de
◈ la légion britannique blessés au combat,
◈ au profit des blessés de guerre et de leur
◈ famille.

remind [rɪ'maɪnd] vt: **to ~ sb of sth** rappeler
qch à qn; **to ~ sb to do** faire penser à qn à
faire, rappeler à qn qu'il doit faire; **that ~s
me!** j'y pense!

reminder [rɪ'maɪndəʳ] n (Comm: letter)
rappel m; (note etc) pense-bête m; (souvenir)
souvenir m

reminisce [rɛmɪ'nɪs] vi: **to ~ (about)** évoquer
ses souvenirs (de)

reminiscent [rɛmɪ'nɪsnt] adj: **~ of** qui
rappelle, qui fait penser à

remiss [rɪ'mɪs] adj négligent(e); **it was ~ of
me** c'était une négligence de ma part

remission [rɪ'mɪʃən] n rémission f; (of debt,
sentence) remise f; (of fee) exemption f

remit [rɪ'mɪt] vt (send: money) envoyer

remittance [rɪ'mɪtns] n envoi m,
paiement m

remnant ['rɛmnənt] n reste m, restant m;
(of cloth) coupon m; **remnants** npl (Comm) fins
fpl de série

remorse [rɪ'mɔːs] n remords m

remorseful [rɪ'mɔːsful] adj plein(e) de
remords

remorseless [rɪ'mɔːslɪs] adj (fig) impitoyable

remote [rɪ'məut] adj éloigné(e), lointain(e);
(person) distant(e); (possibility) vague; **there is
a ~ possibility that …** il est tout juste
possible que …

remote control n télécommande f

remotely [rɪ'məutlɪ] adv au loin; (slightly)
très vaguement

remould ['riːməuld] n (Brit: tyre) pneu m
rechapé

removable [rɪ'muːvəbl] adj (detachable)
amovible

removal [rɪ'muːvəl] n (taking away)
enlèvement m; suppression f; (Brit: from
house) déménagement m; (from office: dismissal)
renvoi m; (of stain) nettoyage m; (Med)
ablation f

removal man irreg n (Brit) déménageur m

removal van n (Brit) camion m de
déménagement

remove [rɪ'muːv] vt enlever, retirer;
(employee) renvoyer; (stain) faire partir; (abuse)
supprimer; (doubt) chasser; **first cousin
once ~d** cousin(e) au deuxième degré

Renaissance [rɪ'neɪsɑ̃s] n: **the ~** la
Renaissance

rename [riː'neɪm] vt rebaptiser

render ['rɛndəʳ] vt rendre; (Culin: fat) clarifier

rendering ['rɛndərɪŋ] n (Mus etc)
interprétation f

rendezvous ['rɔndɪvuː] n rendez-vous m inv
▷ vi opérer une jonction, se rejoindre; **to ~
with sb** rejoindre qn

renew [rɪ'njuː] vt renouveler; (negotiations)
reprendre; (acquaintance) renouer

renewable [rɪ'njuːəbl] adj (energy)
renouvelable; **~s** énergies renouvelables

renewal [rɪ'njuːəl] n renouvellement m;
reprise f

renounce [rɪ'nauns] vt renoncer à; (disown)
renier

renovate ['rɛnəveɪt] vt rénover; (work of art)
restaurer

renown [rɪ'naun] n renommée f

renowned [rɪ'naund] adj renommé(e)

rent [rɛnt] pt, pp of **rend** ▷ n loyer m ▷ vt
louer; (car, TV) louer, prendre en location;
(also: **~ out:** car, TV) louer, donner en location

rental ['rɛntl] n (for television, car) (prix m de)
location f

reorganize [riː'ɔːgənaɪz] vt réorganiser

rep [rɛp] n abbr (Comm) = **representative**; (Theat) = **repertory**

repair [rɪ'pɛə²] n réparation f ▷ vt réparer; **in good/bad ~** en bon/mauvais état; **under ~** en réparation; **where can I get this ~ed?** où est-ce que je peux faire réparer ceci?

repair kit n trousse f de réparations

repatriate [ri:'pætrɪeɪt] vt rapatrier

repay [ri:'peɪ] vt (irreg like: **pay**) (money, creditor) rembourser; (sb's efforts) récompenser

repayment [ri:'peɪmənt] n remboursement m; récompense f

repeal [rɪ'pi:l] n (of law) abrogation f; (of sentence) annulation f ▷ vt abroger; annuler

repeat [rɪ'pi:t] n (Radio, TV) reprise f ▷ vt répéter; (pattern) reproduire; (promise, attack, also Comm: order) renouveler; (Scol: a class) redoubler ▷ vi répéter; **can you ~ that, please?** pouvez-vous répéter, s'il vous plaît?

repeatedly [rɪ'pi:tɪdlɪ] adv souvent, à plusieurs reprises

repeat prescription n (Brit): **I'd like a ~** je voudrais renouveler mon ordonnance

repel [rɪ'pɛl] vt repousser

repellent [rɪ'pɛlənt] adj repoussant(e) ▷ n: **insect ~** insectifuge m; **moth ~** produit m antimite(s)

repent [rɪ'pɛnt] vi: **to ~ (of)** se repentir (de)

repentance [rɪ'pɛntəns] n repentir m

repercussions [ri:pə'kʌʃənz] npl répercussions fpl

repertory ['rɛpətərɪ] n (also: **~ theatre**) théâtre m de répertoire

repetition [rɛpɪ'tɪʃən] n répétition f

repetitive [rɪ'pɛtɪtɪv] adj (movement, work) répétitif(-ive); (speech) plein(e) de redites

replace [rɪ'pleɪs] vt (put back) remettre, replacer; (take the place of) remplacer; (Tel): **"~ the receiver"** "raccrochez"

replacement [rɪ'pleɪsmənt] n replacement m; (substitution) remplacement m; (person) remplaçant(e)

replay ['ri:pleɪ] n (of match) match rejoué; (of tape, film) répétition f

replenish [rɪ'plɛnɪʃ] vt (glass) remplir (de nouveau); (stock etc) réapprovisionner

replica ['rɛplɪkə] n réplique f, copie exacte

reply [rɪ'plaɪ] n réponse f ▷ vi répondre; **in ~ (to)** en réponse (à); **there's no ~** (Tel) ça ne répond pas

report [rɪ'pɔ:t] n rapport m; (Press etc) reportage m; (Brit: also: **school ~**) bulletin m (scolaire); (of gun) détonation f ▷ vt rapporter, faire un compte rendu de; (Press etc) faire un reportage sur; (notify: accident) signaler; (: culprit) dénoncer ▷ vi (make a report) faire un rapport; (for newspaper) faire un reportage (sur); **I'd like to ~ a theft** je voudrais signaler un vol; (present o.s.): **to ~ (to sb)** se présenter (chez qn); **it is ~ed that** on dit ou annonce que; **it is ~ed from Berlin that** on nous apprend de Berlin que

report card n (US, Scottish) bulletin m (scolaire)

reportedly [rɪ'pɔ:tɪdlɪ] adv: **she is ~ living in Spain** elle habiterait en Espagne; **he ~ told them to ...** il leur aurait dit de ...

reporter [rɪ'pɔ:tə²] n reporter m

repose [rɪ'pəuz] n: **in ~** en ou au repos

represent [rɛprɪ'zɛnt] vt représenter; (view, belief) présenter, expliquer; (describe): **to ~ sth as** présenter or décrire qch comme; **to ~ to sb that** expliquer à qn que

representation [rɛprɪzɛn'teɪʃən] n représentation f; **representations** npl (protest) démarche f

representative [rɛprɪ'zɛntətɪv] n représentant(e); (Comm) représentant(e) (de commerce); (US Pol) député m ▷ adj représentatif(-ive), caractéristique

repress [rɪ'prɛs] vt réprimer

repression [rɪ'prɛʃən] n répression f

reprieve [rɪ'pri:v] n (Law) grâce f; (fig) sursis m, délai m ▷ vt gracier; accorder un sursis or un délai à

reprimand ['rɛprɪmɑ:nd] n réprimande f ▷ vt réprimander

reprisal [rɪ'praɪzl] n représailles fpl; **to take ~s** user de représailles

reproach [rɪ'prəutʃ] n reproche m ▷ vt: **to ~ sb with sth** reprocher qch à qn; **beyond ~** irréprochable

reproachful [rɪ'prəutʃful] adj de reproche

reproduce [ri:prə'dju:s] vt reproduire ▷ vi se reproduire

reproduction [ri:prə'dʌkʃən] n reproduction f

reproof [rɪ'pru:f] n reproche m

reptile ['rɛptaɪl] n reptile m

republic [rɪ'pʌblɪk] n république f

republican [rɪ'pʌblɪkən] adj, n républicain(e)

repudiate [rɪ'pju:dɪeɪt] vt (ally, behaviour) désavouer; (accusation) rejeter; (wife) répudier

repulsive [rɪ'pʌlsɪv] adj repoussant(e), répulsif(-ive)

reputable ['rɛpjutəbl] adj de bonne réputation; (occupation) honorable

reputation [rɛpju'teɪʃən] n réputation f; **to have a ~ for** être réputé(e) pour; **he has a ~ for being awkward** il a la réputation de ne pas être commode

reputed [rɪ'pju:tɪd] adj réputé(e); **he is ~ to be rich/intelligent** etc on dit qu'il est riche/intelligent etc

reputedly [rɪ'pju:tɪdlɪ] adv d'après ce qu'on dit

request [rɪ'kwɛst] n demande f; (formal) requête f ▷ vt: **to ~ (of or from sb)** demander (à qn); **at the ~ of** à la demande de

request stop n (Brit: for bus) arrêt facultatif

require [rɪ'kwaɪə²] vt (need: subj: person) avoir besoin de; (: thing, situation) nécessiter, demander; (want) exiger; (order): **to ~ sb to do sth/sth of sb** exiger que qn fasse qch/qch

r

de qn; **if ~d** s'il le faut; **what qualifications are ~d?** quelles sont les qualifications requises?; **~d by law** requis par la loi

requirement [rɪˈkwaɪəmənt] n (need) exigence f; besoin m; (condition) condition f (requise)

requisition [rɛkwɪˈzɪʃən] n: **~ (for)** demande f (de) ▷ vt (Mil) réquisitionner

resat [riːˈsæt] pt, pp of **resit**

rescue [ˈrɛskjuː] n (from accident) sauvetage m; (help) secours mpl ▷ vt sauver; **to come to sb's ~** venir au secours de qn

rescue party n équipe f de sauvetage

rescuer [ˈrɛskjuəʳ] n sauveteur m

research [rɪˈsɜːtʃ] n recherche(s) f(pl) ▷ vt faire des recherches sur ▷ vi: **to ~ (into sth)** faire des recherches (sur qch); **a piece of ~** un travail de recherche; **~ and development (R & D)** recherche-développement (R-D)

resemblance [rɪˈzɛmbləns] n ressemblance f; **to bear a strong ~ to** ressembler beaucoup à

resemble [rɪˈzɛmbl] vt ressembler à

resent [rɪˈzɛnt] vt éprouver du ressentiment de, être contrarié(e) par

resentful [rɪˈzɛntful] adj irrité(e), plein(e) de ressentiment

resentment [rɪˈzɛntmənt] n ressentiment m

reservation [rɛzəˈveɪʃən] n (booking) réservation f; (doubt, protected area) réserve f; (Brit Aut: also: **central ~**) bande médiane; **to make a ~ (in an hotel/a restaurant/on a plane)** réserver or retenir une chambre/une table/une place; **with ~s** (doubts) avec certaines réserves

reservation desk n (US: in hotel) réception f

reserve [rɪˈzəːv] n réserve f; (Sport) remplaçant(e) ▷ vt (seats etc) réserver, retenir; **reserves** npl (Mil) réservistes mpl; **in ~** en réserve

reserved [rɪˈzəːvd] adj réservé(e)

reservoir [ˈrɛzəvwɑːʳ] n réservoir m

reshuffle [riːˈʃʌfl] n: **Cabinet ~** (Pol) remaniement ministériel

residence [ˈrɛzɪdəns] n résidence f; **to take up ~** s'installer; **in ~** (queen etc) en résidence; (doctor) résidant(e)

residence permit n (Brit) permis m de séjour

resident [ˈrɛzɪdənt] n (of country) résident(e); (of area, house) habitant(e); (in hotel) pensionnaire m ▷ adj résident(e)

residential [rɛzɪˈdɛnʃəl] adj de résidence; (area) résidentiel(le); (course) avec hébergement sur place

residential school n internat m

residue [ˈrɛzɪdjuː] n reste m; (Chem, Physics) résidu m

resign [rɪˈzaɪn] vt (one's post) se démettre de ▷ vi démissionner; **to ~ o.s. to** (endure) se résigner à

resignation [rɛzɪɡˈneɪʃən] n (from post) démission f; (state of mind) résignation f; **to tender one's ~** donner sa démission

resigned [rɪˈzaɪnd] adj résigné(e)

resilient [rɪˈzɪlɪənt] adj (person) qui réagit, qui a du ressort

resin [ˈrɛzɪn] n résine f

resist [rɪˈzɪst] vt résister à

resistance [rɪˈzɪstəns] n résistance f

resit vt [riːˈsɪt] (Brit pt, pp **resat**) (exam) repasser ▷ n [ˈriːsɪt] deuxième session f (d'un examen)

resolution [rɛzəˈluːʃən] n résolution f; **to make a ~** prendre une résolution

resolve [rɪˈzɒlv] n résolution f ▷ vt (decide): **to ~ to do** résoudre or décider de faire; (problem) résoudre

resort [rɪˈzɔːt] n (seaside town) station f balnéaire; (for skiing) station de ski; (recourse) recours m ▷ vi: **to ~ to** avoir recours à; **in the last ~** en dernier ressort

resounding [rɪˈzaundɪŋ] adj retentissant(e)

resource [rɪˈsɔːs] n ressource f; **resources** npl ressources; **natural ~s** ressources naturelles; **to leave sb to his (or her) own ~s** (fig) livrer qn à lui-même (or elle-même)

resourceful [rɪˈsɔːsful] adj ingénieux(-euse), débrouillard(e)

respect [rɪsˈpɛkt] n respect m; (point, detail): **in some ~s** à certains égards ▷ vt respecter; **respects** npl respects, hommages mpl; **to have** or **show ~ for sb/sth** respecter qn/qch; **out of ~ for** par respect pour; **with ~ to** en ce qui concerne; **in ~ of** sous le rapport de, quant à; **in this ~** sous ce rapport, à cet égard; **with due ~ I ...** malgré le respect que je vous dois, je ...

respectable [rɪsˈpɛktəbl] adj respectable; (quite good: result etc) honorable; (player) assez bon/bonne

respectful [rɪsˈpɛktful] adj respectueux(-euse)

respective [rɪsˈpɛktɪv] adj respectif(-ive)

respectively [rɪsˈpɛktɪvlɪ] adv respectivement

respite [ˈrɛspaɪt] n répit m

respond [rɪsˈpɒnd] vi répondre; (react) réagir

response [rɪsˈpɒns] n réponse f; (reaction) réaction f; **in ~ to** en réponse à

responsibility [rɪspɒnsɪˈbɪlɪtɪ] n responsabilité f; **to take ~ for sth/sb** accepter la responsabilité de qch/d'être responsable de qn

responsible [rɪsˈpɒnsɪbl] adj (liable): **~ (for)** responsable (de); (person) digne de confiance; (job) qui comporte des responsabilités; **to be ~ to sb (for sth)** être responsable devant qn (de qch)

responsibly [rɪsˈpɒnsɪblɪ] adv avec sérieux

responsive [rɪsˈpɒnsɪv] adj (student, audience) réceptif(-ive); (brakes, steering) sensible

rest [rɛst] n repos m; (stop) arrêt m, pause f; (Mus) silence m; (support) support m, appui m; (remainder) reste m; (be supported): **to ~ on** appuyer or reposer sur; (remain) rester ▷ vt (lean): **to ~ sth on/against**

appuyer qch sur/contre; **the ~ of them** les autres; **to set sb's mind at ~** tranquilliser qn; **it ~s with him to** c'est à lui de; **~ assured that ...** soyez assuré que ...

restaurant ['rɛstərɔ̃] n restaurant m

restaurant car n (Brit Rail) wagon-restaurant m

restful ['rɛstful] adj reposant(e)

restive ['rɛstɪv] adj agité(e), impatient(e); (horse) rétif(-ive)

restless ['rɛstlɪs] adj agité(e); **to get ~** s'impatienter

restoration [rɛstə'reɪʃən] n (of building) restauration f; (of stolen goods) restitution f

restore [rɪ'stɔːʳ] vt (building) restaurer; (sth stolen) restituer; (peace, health) rétablir; **to ~ to** (former state) ramener à

restrain [rɪs'treɪn] vt (feeling) contenir; (person): **to ~ (from doing)** retenir (de faire)

restrained [rɪs'treɪnd] adj (style) sobre; (manner) mesuré(e)

restraint [rɪs'treɪnt] n (restriction) contrainte f; (moderation) retenue f; (of style) sobriété f; **wage ~** limitations salariales

restrict [rɪs'trɪkt] vt restreindre, limiter

restriction [rɪs'trɪkʃən] n restriction f, limitation f

rest room n (US) toilettes fpl

restructure [riː'strʌktʃəʳ] vt restructurer

result [rɪ'zʌlt] n résultat m ⊳ vi: **to ~ (from)** résulter (de); **to ~ in** aboutir à, se terminer par; **as a ~ it is too expensive** il en résulte que c'est trop cher; **as a ~ of** à la suite de

resume [rɪ'zjuːm] vt (work, journey) reprendre; (sum up) résumer ⊳ vi (work etc) reprendre

résumé ['reɪzjuːmeɪ] n (summary) résumé m; (US: curriculum vitae) curriculum vitae m inv

resumption [rɪ'zʌmpʃən] n reprise f

resurgence [rɪ'sɔːdʒəns] n réapparition f

resurrection [rɛzə'rɛkʃən] n résurrection f

resuscitate [rɪ'sʌsɪteɪt] vt (Med) réanimer

retail ['riːteɪl] n (vente f au) détail m ⊳ adj de or au détail ⊳ adv au détail ⊳ vt vendre au détail ⊳ vi: **to ~ at 10 euros** se vendre au détail à 10 euros

retailer ['riːteɪləʳ] n détaillant(e)

retail price n prix m de détail

retain [rɪ'teɪn] vt (keep) garder, conserver; (employ) engager

retainer [rɪ'teɪnəʳ] n (servant) serviteur m; (fee) acompte m, provision f

retaliate [rɪ'tælɪeɪt] vi: **to ~ (against)** se venger (de); **to ~ (on sb)** rendre la pareille (à qn)

retaliation [rɪtælɪ'eɪʃən] n représailles fpl, vengeance f; **in ~ for** par représailles pour

retarded [rɪ'tɑːdɪd] adj retardé(e)

retch [rɛtʃ] vi avoir des haut-le-cœur

retentive [rɪ'tɛntɪv] adj: **~ memory** excellente mémoire

retina ['rɛtɪnə] n rétine f

retire [rɪ'taɪəʳ] vi (give up work) prendre sa retraite; (withdraw) se retirer, partir; (go to bed) (aller) se coucher

retired [rɪ'taɪəd] adj (person) retraité(e)

retirement [rɪ'taɪəmənt] n retraite f

retiring [rɪ'taɪərɪŋ] adj (person) réservé(e); (chairman etc) sortant(e)

retort [rɪ'tɔːt] n (reply) riposte f; (container) cornue f ⊳ vi riposter

retrace [riː'treɪs] vt reconstituer; **to ~ one's steps** revenir sur ses pas

retract [rɪ'trækt] vt (statement, claws) rétracter; (undercarriage, aerial) rentrer, escamoter ⊳ vi se rétracter; rentrer

retrain [riː'treɪn] vt recycler ⊳ vi se recycler

retread vt [riː'trɛd] (Aut: tyre) rechaper ⊳ n ['riːtrɛd] pneu rechapé

retreat [rɪ'triːt] n retraite f ⊳ vi battre en retraite; (flood) reculer; **to beat a hasty ~** (fig) partir avec précipitation

retribution [rɛtrɪ'bjuːʃən] n châtiment m

retrieval [rɪ'triːvəl] n récupération f; réparation f; recherche f et extraction f

retrieve [rɪ'triːv] vt (sth lost) récupérer; (situation, honour) sauver; (error, loss) réparer; (Comput) rechercher

retriever [rɪ'triːvəʳ] n chien m d'arrêt

retrospect ['rɛtrəspɛkt] n: **in ~** rétrospectivement, après coup

retrospective [rɛtrə'spɛktɪv] adj rétrospectif(-ive); (law) rétroactif(-ive) ⊳ n (Art) rétrospective f

return [rɪ'tɜːn] n (going or coming back) retour m; (of sth stolen etc) restitution f; (recompense) récompense f; (Finance: from land, shares) rapport m; (report) relevé m, rapport m ⊳ cpd (journey) de retour; (Brit: ticket) aller et retour; (match) retour ⊳ vi (person etc: come back) revenir; (: go back) retourner ⊳ vt rendre; (bring back) rapporter; (send back) renvoyer; (put back) remettre; (Pol: candidate) élire; **returns** npl (Comm) recettes fpl; (Finance) bénéfices mpl; (: returned goods) marchandises renvoyées; **many happy ~s (of the day)!** bon anniversaire!; **by ~ (of post)** par retour (du courrier); **in ~ (for)** en échange (de); **a ~ (ticket) for ...** un billet aller et retour pour ...

return ticket n (esp Brit) billet m aller-retour

reunion [riː'juːnɪən] n réunion f

reunite [riːjuː'naɪt] vt réunir

reuse [riː'juːz] vt réutiliser

rev [rɛv] n abbr (= revolution) (Aut) tour m ⊳ vt (also: ~ up) emballer ⊳ vi (also: ~ up) s'emballer

revamp [riː'væmp] vt (house) retaper; (firm) réorganiser

reveal [rɪ'viːl] vt (make known) révéler; (display) laisser voir

revealing [rɪ'viːlɪŋ] adj révélateur(-trice); (dress) au décolleté généreux or suggestif

revel ['rɛvl] vi: **to ~ in sth/in doing** se délecter de qch/à faire

revelation [rɛvə'leɪʃən] n révélation f

revenge [rɪ'vendʒ] n vengeance f; (in game etc) revanche f ▷ vt venger; **to take ~ (on)** se venger (sur)

revenue ['revənju:] n revenu m

reverberate [rɪ'və:bəreɪt] vi (sound) retentir, se répercuter; (light) se réverbérer

reverence ['revərəns] n vénération f, révérence f

Reverend ['revərənd] adj vénérable; (in titles): **the ~ John Smith** (Anglican) le révérend John Smith; (Catholic) l'abbé (John) Smith; (Protestant) le pasteur (John) Smith

reversal [rɪ'və:sl] n (of opinion) revirement m; (of order) renversement m; (of direction) changement m

reverse [rɪ'və:s] n contraire m, opposé m; (back) dos m, envers m; (of paper) verso m; (of coin) revers m; (Aut: also: **~ gear**) marche f arrière ▷ adj (order, direction) opposé(e), inverse ▷ vt (order, position) changer, inverser; (direction, policy) changer complètement de; (decision) annuler; (roles) renverser; (car) faire marche arrière avec; (Law: judgment) réformer ▷ vi (Brit Aut) faire marche arrière; **to go into ~** faire marche arrière; **in ~ order** en ordre inverse

reversing lights [rɪ'və:sɪŋ-] npl (Brit Aut) feux mpl de marche arrière or de recul

revert [rɪ'və:t] vi: **to ~ to** revenir à, retourner à

review [rɪ'vju:] n revue f; (of book, film) critique f; (of situation, policy) examen m, bilan m; (US: examination) examen ▷ vt passer en revue; faire la critique de; examiner; **to come under ~** être révisé(e)

reviewer [rɪ'vju:ə'] n critique m

revise [rɪ'vaɪz] vt réviser, modifier; (manuscript) revoir, corriger ▷ vi (study) réviser; **~d edition** édition revue et corrigée

revision [rɪ'vɪʒən] n révision f; (revised version) version corrigée

revival [rɪ'vaɪvəl] n reprise f; (recovery) rétablissement m; (of faith) renouveau m

revive [rɪ'vaɪv] vt (person) ranimer; (custom) rétablir; (economy) relancer; (hope, courage) raviver, faire renaître; (play, fashion) reprendre ▷ vi (person) reprendre connaissance; (: from ill health) se rétablir; (hope etc) renaître; (activity) reprendre

revoke [rɪ'vəuk] vt révoquer; (promise, decision) revenir sur

revolt [rɪ'vəult] n révolte f ▷ vi se révolter, se rebeller ▷ vt révolter, dégoûter

revolting [rɪ'vəultɪŋ] adj dégoûtant(e)

revolution [revə'lu:ʃən] n révolution f; (of wheel etc) tour m, révolution

revolutionary [revə'lu:ʃənrɪ] adj, n révolutionnaire (m/f)

revolve [rɪ'vɔlv] vi tourner

revolver [rɪ'vɔlvə'] n revolver m

revolving [rɪ'vɔlvɪŋ] adj (chair) pivotant(e); (light) tournant(e)

revolving door n (porte f à) tambour m

revulsion [rɪ'vʌlʃən] n dégoût m, répugnance f

reward [rɪ'wɔ:d] n récompense f ▷ vt: **to ~ (for)** récompenser (de)

rewarding [rɪ'wɔ:dɪŋ] adj (fig) qui (en) vaut la peine, gratifiant(e); **financially ~** financièrement intéressant(e)

rewind [ri:'waɪnd] vt (irreg like: **wind**) (watch) remonter; (tape) réembobiner

rewire [ri:'waɪə'] vt (house) refaire l'installation électrique de

rewritable [ri:'raɪtəbl] adj (CD, DVD) réinscriptible

rewrite [ri:'raɪt] (pt **rewrote**, pp **rewritten**) vt récrire

rheumatism ['ru:mətɪzəm] n rhumatisme m

Rhine [raɪn] n: **the (River) ~** le Rhin

rhinoceros [raɪ'nɔsərəs] n rhinocéros m

rhubarb ['ru:bɑ:b] n rhubarbe f

rhyme [raɪm] n rime f; (verse) vers mpl ▷ vi: **to ~ (with)** rimer (avec); **without ~ or reason** sans rime ni raison

rhythm ['rɪðm] n rythme m

rib [rɪb] n (Anat) côte f ▷ vt (mock) taquiner

ribbon ['rɪbən] n ruban m; **in ~s** (torn) en lambeaux

rice [raɪs] n riz m

rice pudding n riz m au lait

rich [rɪtʃ] adj riche; (gift, clothes) somptueux(-euse); **the ~** npl les riches mpl; **riches** npl richesses fpl; **to be ~ in sth** être riche en qch

richly ['rɪtʃlɪ] adv richement; (deserved, earned) largement, grandement

rickets ['rɪkɪts] n rachitisme m

rid [rɪd] (pt, pp **rid**) vt: **to ~ sb of** débarrasser qn de; **to get ~ of** se débarrasser de

riddle ['rɪdl] n (puzzle) énigme f ▷ vt: **to be ~d with** être criblé(e) de; (fig) être en proie à

ride [raɪd] (pt **rode**, pp **ridden**) [rəud, 'rɪdn] n promenade f, tour m; (distance covered) trajet m ▷ vi (as sport) monter (à cheval), faire du cheval; (go somewhere: on horse, bicycle) aller (à cheval or bicyclette etc); (travel: on bicycle, motor cycle, bus) rouler ▷ vt (horse) monter; (distance) parcourir, faire; **we rode all day/all the way** nous sommes restés toute la journée en selle/avons fait tout le chemin en selle or à cheval; **to ~ a horse/bicycle** monter à cheval/à bicyclette; **can you ~ a bike?** est-ce que tu sais monter à bicyclette?; **to ~ at anchor** (Naut) être à l'ancre; **horse/car ~** promenade or tour à cheval/en voiture; **to go for a ~** faire une promenade en voiture or à bicyclette etc); **to take sb for a ~** (fig) faire marcher qn; (cheat) rouler qn; **ride out** vt: **to ~ out the storm** (fig) surmonter les difficultés

rider ['raɪdə'] n cavalier(-ière) f; (in race) jockey m; (on bicycle) cycliste m/f; (on

motorcycle) motocycliste *m/f*; (*in document*)
annexe *f*, clause additionnelle

ridge [rɪdʒ] *n* (*of hill*) faîte *m*; (*of roof, mountain*)
arête *f*; (*on object*) strie *f*

ridicule ['rɪdɪkjuːl] *n* ridicule *m*; dérision *f*
▷ *vt* ridiculiser, tourner en dérision; **to hold
sb/sth up to ~** tourner qn/qch en ridicule

ridiculous [rɪ'dɪkjuləs] *adj* ridicule

riding ['raɪdɪŋ] *n* équitation *f*

riding school *n* manège *m*, école *f*
d'équitation

rife [raɪf] *adj* répandu(e); **~ with** abondant(e) en

riffraff ['rɪfræf] *n* racaille *f*

rifle ['raɪfl] *n* fusil *m* (à canon rayé) ▷ *vt* vider,
dévaliser; **rifle through** *vt fus* fouiller dans

rifle range *n* champ *m* de tir; (*indoor*) stand *m*
de tir

rift [rɪft] *n* fente *f*, fissure *f*; (*fig: disagreement*)
désaccord *m*

rig [rɪg] *n* (*also*: **oil ~**: *on land*) derrick *m*; (: *at
sea*) plate-forme pétrolière *f* ▷ *vt* (*election etc*)
truquer; **rig out** *vt* (*Brit*) habiller; (: *pej*)
fringuer, attifer; **rig up** *vt* arranger, faire
avec des moyens de fortune

rigging ['rɪgɪŋ] *n* (*Naut*) gréement *m*

right [raɪt] *adj* (*true*) juste, exact(e); (*correct*)
bon/bonne; (*suitable*) approprié(e),
convenable; (*just*) juste, équitable; (*morally
good*) bien *inv*; (*not left*) droit(e) ▷ *n* (*moral good*)
bien *m*; (*title, claim*) droit *m*; (*not left*) droite *f*
▷ *adv* (*answer*) correctement; (*treat*) bien,
comme il faut; (*not on the left*) à droite ▷ *vt*
redresser ▷ *excl* bon!; **rights** *npl* (*Comm*)
droits *mpl*; **the ~ time** (*precise*) l'heure exacte;
(*not wrong*) la bonne heure; **do you have the ~
time?** avez-vous l'heure juste or exacte?;
to be ~ (*person*) avoir raison; (*answer*) être
juste or correct(e); **to get sth ~** ne pas se
tromper sur qch; **let's get it ~ this time!**
essayons de ne pas nous tromper cette fois-
ci!; **you did the ~ thing** vous avez bien fait;
to put a mistake ~ (*Brit*) rectifier une erreur;
by ~s en toute justice; **on the ~** à droite; **~
and wrong** le bien et le mal; **to be in the ~**
avoir raison; **film ~s** droits d'adaptation
cinématographique; **~ now** en ce moment
même; (*immediately*) tout de suite; **~ before/
after** juste avant/après; **~ against the wall**
tout contre le mur; **~ ahead** tout droit; droit
devant; **~ in the middle** en plein milieu;
~ away immédiatement; **to go ~ to the end
of sth** aller jusqu'au bout de qch

right angle *n* (*Math*) angle droit

righteous ['raɪtʃəs] *adj* droit(e),
vertueux(-euse); (*anger*) justifié(e)

rightful ['raɪtful] *adj* (*heir*) légitime

right-hand ['raɪthænd] *adj*: **the ~ side** la
droite

right-hand drive *n* (*Brit*) conduite *f* à droite; (*vehicle*) véhicule *m* avec la conduite à droite

right-handed [raɪt'hændɪd] *adj* (*person*)
droitier(-ière)

right-hand man ['raɪthænd-] *irreg n* bras
droit (*fig*)

rightly ['raɪtlɪ] *adv* bien, correctement; (*with
reason*) à juste titre; **if I remember ~** (*Brit*) si
je me souviens bien

right of way *n* (*on path etc*) droit *m* de passage;
(*Aut*) priorité *f*

right wing *n* (*Mil, Sport*) aile droite; (*Pol*)
droite *f*

right-wing [raɪt'wɪŋ] *adj* (*Pol*) de droite

rigid ['rɪdʒɪd] *adj* rigide; (*principle, control*)
strict(e)

rigmarole ['rɪgmərəʊl] *n* galimatias *m*,
comédie *f*

rigorous ['rɪgərəs] *adj* rigoureux(-euse)

rile [raɪl] *vt* agacer

rim [rɪm] *n* bord *m*; (*of spectacles*) monture *f*;
(*of wheel*) jante *f*

rind [raɪnd] *n* (*of bacon*) couenne *f*; (*of lemon etc*)
écorce *f*, zeste *m*; (*of cheese*) croûte *f*

ring [rɪŋ] (*pt* rang, *pp* rung) [ræŋ, rʌŋ] *n*
anneau *m*; (*on finger*) bague *f*; (*also*: **wedding ~**)
alliance *f*; (*for napkin*) rond *m*; (*of people, objects*)
cercle *m*; (*of spies*) réseau *m*; (*of smoke etc*) rond
m; (*arena*) piste *f*, arène *f*; (*for boxing*) ring *m*;
(*sound of bell*) sonnerie *f*; (*telephone call*) coup *m*
de téléphone ▷ *vi* (*telephone, bell*) sonner;
(*person: by telephone*) téléphoner; (*ears*)
bourdonner; (*also*: **~ out**: *voice, words*) retentir
▷ *vt* (*Brit Tel*: *also*: **~ up**) téléphoner à, appeler;
to ~ the bell sonner; **to give sb a ~** (*Tel*)
passer un coup de téléphone or de fil à qn;
that has the ~ of truth about it cela sonne
vrai; **the name doesn't ~ a bell (with me)**
ce nom ne me dit rien; **ring back** *vt, vi* (*Brit
Tel*) rappeler; **ring off** *vi* (*Brit Tel*) raccrocher;
ring up (*Brit*) *vt* (*Tel*) téléphoner à, appeler

ring binder *n* classeur *m* à anneaux

ringing ['rɪŋɪŋ] *n* (*of bell*) tintement *m*; (*louder:
also*: **of telephone**) sonnerie *f*; (*in ears*)
bourdonnement *m*

ringing tone *n* (*Brit Tel*) tonalité *f* d'appel

ringleader ['rɪŋliːdə'] *n* (*of gang*) chef *m*,
meneur *m*

ringlets ['rɪŋlɪts] *npl* anglaises *fpl*

ring road *n* (*Brit*) rocade *f*; (*motorway*)
périphérique *m*

ringtone ['rɪŋtəʊn] *n* (*on mobile*) sonnerie *f*
(*de téléphone portable*)

rink [rɪŋk] *n* (*also*: **ice ~**) patinoire *f*; (*for roller-
skating*) skating *m*

rinse [rɪns] *n* rinçage *m* ▷ *vt* rincer

riot ['raɪət] *n* émeute *f*, bagarres *fpl* ▷ *vi*
(*demonstrators*) manifester avec violence;
(*population*) se soulever, se révolter; **a ~ of
colours** une débauche or orgie de couleurs;
to run ~ se déchaîner

riotous ['raɪətəs] *adj* tapageur(-euse);
tordant(e)

rip [rɪp] *n* déchirure *f* ▷ *vt* déchirer ▷ *vi* se
déchirer; **rip off** *vt* (*inf: cheat*) arnaquer; **rip
up** *vt* déchirer

r

ripcord ['rɪpkɔːd] n poignée f d'ouverture
ripe [raɪp] adj (fruit) mûr(e); (cheese) fait(e)
ripen ['raɪpn] vt mûrir ▷ vi mûrir; se faire
rip-off ['rɪpɔf] n (inf): **it's a ~!** c'est du vol manifeste!, c'est de l'arnaque!
ripple ['rɪpl] n ride f, ondulation f; (of applause, laughter) cascade f ▷ vi se rider, onduler ▷ vt rider, faire onduler
rise [raɪz] n (slope) côte f, pente f; (hill) élévation f; (increase: in wages: Brit) augmentation f; (: in prices, temperature) hausse f, augmentation; (fig: to power etc) ascension f ▷ vi (pt **rose**, pp **risen**) [rəuz, rɪzn] s'élever, monter; (prices, numbers) augmenter, monter; (waters, river) monter; (sun, wind, person: from chair, bed) se lever; (also: ~ **up**: tower, building) s'élever; (: rebel) se révolter; se rebeller; (in rank) s'élever; ~ **to power** montée f au pouvoir; **to give ~ to** donner lieu à; **to ~ to the occasion** se montrer à la hauteur
risen ['rɪzn] pp of **rise**
rising ['raɪzɪŋ] adj (increasing: number, prices) en hausse; (tide) montant(e); (sun, moon) levant(e) ▷ n (uprising) soulèvement m, insurrection f
risk [rɪsk] n risque m, danger m; (deliberate) risque ▷ vt risquer; **to take** or **run the ~ of doing** courir le risque de faire; **at ~** en danger; **at one's own ~** à ses risques et périls; **it's a fire/health ~** cela présente un risque d'incendie/pour la santé; **I'll ~ it** je vais risquer le coup
risky ['rɪskɪ] adj risqué(e)
rissole ['rɪsəul] n croquette f
rite [raɪt] n rite m; **the last ~s** les derniers sacrements
ritual ['rɪtjuəl] adj rituel(le) ▷ n rituel m
rival ['raɪvl] n rival(e); (in business) concurrent(e) ▷ adj rival(e); qui fait concurrence ▷ vt (match) égaler; (compete with) être en concurrence avec; **to ~ sb/sth in** rivaliser avec qn/qch in
rivalry ['raɪvlrɪ] n rivalité f; (in business) concurrence f
river ['rɪvə'] n rivière f; (major: also fig) fleuve m ▷ cpd (port, traffic) fluvial(e); **up/down ~** en amont/aval
riverbank ['rɪvəbæŋk] n rive f, berge f
riverbed ['rɪvəbed] n lit m (de rivière or de fleuve)
rivet ['rɪvɪt] n rivet m ▷ vt riveter; (fig) river, fixer
Riviera [rɪvɪ'ɛərə] n: **the (French) ~** la Côte d'Azur; **the Italian ~** la Riviera (italienne)
road [rəud] n route f; (in town) rue f; (fig) chemin, voie f ▷ cpd (accident) de la route; **main ~** grande route; **major/minor ~** route principale or à priorité/voie secondaire; **it takes four hours by ~** il y a quatre heures de route; **which ~ do I take for …?** quelle route dois-je prendre pour aller à …?; **"~ up"** (Brit) "attention travaux"

road accident n accident m de la circulation
roadblock ['rəudblɔk] n barrage routier
roadhog ['rəudhɔg] n chauffard m
road map n carte routière
road rage n comportement très agressif de certains usagers de la route
road safety n sécurité routière
roadside ['rəudsaɪd] n bord m de la route, bas-côté m ▷ cpd (situé(e) etc) au bord de la route; **by the ~** au bord de la route
road sign ['rəudsaɪn] n panneau m de signalisation
road tax n (Brit Aut) taxe f sur les automobiles
roadway ['rəudweɪ] n chaussée f
roadworks ['rəudwəːks] npl travaux mpl (de réfection des routes)
roadworthy ['rəudwəːðɪ] adj en bon état de marche
roam [rəum] vi errer, vagabonder ▷ vt parcourir, errer par
roar [rɔː'] n rugissement m; (of crowd) hurlements mpl; (of vehicle, thunder, storm) grondement m ▷ vi rugir; hurler; gronder; **to ~ with laughter** rire à gorge déployée
roast [rəust] n rôti m ▷ vt (meat) (faire) rôtir; (coffee) griller, torréfier
roast beef n rôti m de bœuf, rosbif m
rob [rɔb] vt (person) voler; (bank) dévaliser; **to ~ sb of sth** voler or dérober qch à qn; (fig: deprive) priver qn de qch
robber ['rɔbə'] n bandit m, voleur m
robbery ['rɔbərɪ] n vol m
robe [rəub] n (for ceremony etc) robe f; (also: **bath~**) peignoir m; (US: rug) couverture f ▷ vt revêtir (d'une robe)
robin ['rɔbɪn] n rouge-gorge m
robot ['rəubɔt] n robot m
robust [rəu'bʌst] adj robuste; (material, appetite) solide
rock [rɔk] n (substance) roche f, roc m; (boulder) rocher m, roche; (US: small stone) caillou m; (Brit: sweet) ≈ sucre m d'orge (swing gently: cradle) balancer; (: child) bercer; (shake) ébranler, secouer ▷ vi se balancer, être ébranlé(e) or secoué(e); **on the ~s** (drink) avec des glaçons; (ship) sur les écueils; (marriage etc) en train de craquer; **to ~ the boat** (fig) jouer les trouble-fête
rock and roll n rock (and roll) m, rock'n'roll m
rock-bottom ['rɔk'bɔtəm] n (fig) niveau le plus bas ▷ adj (fig: prices) sacrifié(e); **to reach** or **touch ~** (price, person) tomber au plus bas
rock climbing n varappe f
rockery ['rɔkərɪ] n (jardin m de) rocaille f
rocket ['rɔkɪt] n fusée f; (Mil) fusée, roquette f; (Culin) roquette ▷ vi (prices) monter en flèche
rocking chair ['rɔkɪŋ-] n fauteuil m à bascule
rocking horse ['rɔkɪŋ-] n cheval m à bascule
rocky ['rɔkɪ] adj (hill) rocheux(-euse); (path) rocailleux(-euse); (unsteady: table) branlant(e)
rod [rɔd] n (metallic) tringle f; (Tech) tige f; (wooden) baguette f; (also: **fishing ~**) canne f à pêche

rode [rəʊd] *pt of* **ride**

rodent ['rəʊdnt] *n* rongeur *m*

rodeo ['rəʊdɪəʊ] *n* rodéo *m*

roe [rəʊ] *n* (*species: also:* **~ deer**) chevreuil *m*; (*of fish: also:* **hard ~**) œufs *mpl* de poisson; **soft ~** laitance *f*

rogue [rəʊg] *n* coquin(e)

role [rəʊl] *n* rôle *m*

role-model ['rəʊlmɒdl] *n* modèle *m* à émuler

role play, role playing *n* jeu *m* de rôle

roll [rəʊl] *n* rouleau *m*; (*of banknotes*) liasse *f*; (*also:* **bread ~**) petit pain; (*register*) liste *f*; (*sound: of drums etc*) roulement *m*; (*movement: of ship*) roulis *m* ▷ *vt* rouler; (*also:* **~ up:** *string*) enrouler; (*also:* **~ out:** *pastry*) étendre au rouleau, abaisser ▷ *vi* rouler; (*wheel*) tourner; **cheese ~** ≈ sandwich *m* au fromage (*dans un petit pain*); **roll about, roll around** *vi* rouler çà et là; (*person*) se rouler par terre; **roll by** *vi* (*time*) s'écouler, passer; **roll in** *vi* (*mail, cash*) affluer; **roll over** *vi* se retourner; **roll up** *vi* (*inf: arrive*) arriver, s'amener ▷ *vt* (*carpet, cloth, map*) rouler; (*sleeves*) retrousser; **to ~ o.s. up into a ball** se rouler en boule

roll call *n* appel *m*

roller ['rəʊlə'] *n* rouleau *m*; (*wheel*) roulette *f*; (*for road*) rouleau compresseur; (*for hair*) bigoudi *m*

Rollerblades® ['rəʊləbleɪdz] *npl* patins *mpl* en ligne

roller coaster *n* montagnes *fpl* russes

roller skates *npl* patins *mpl* à roulettes

roller-skating ['rəʊləskeɪtɪŋ] *n* patin *m* à roulettes; **to go ~** faire du patin à roulettes

rolling ['rəʊlɪŋ] *adj* (*landscape*) onduleux(-euse)

rolling pin *n* rouleau *m* à pâtisserie

rolling stock *n* (*Rail*) matériel roulant

ROM [rɒm] *n abbr* (*Comput:* = *read-only memory*) mémoire morte, ROM *f*

Roman ['rəʊmən] *adj* romain(e) ▷ *n* Romain(e)

Roman Catholic *adj, n* catholique (*m/f*)

romance [rə'mæns] *n* (*love affair*) idylle *f*; (*charm*) poésie *f*; (*novel*) roman *m* à l'eau de rose

Romania [rəʊ'meɪnɪə] *n* = **Rumania**

Romanian [rəʊ'meɪnɪən] *adj, n see* **Rumanian**

Roman numeral *n* chiffre romain

romantic [rə'mæntɪk] *adj* romantique; (*novel, attachment*) sentimental(e)

Rome [rəʊm] *n* Rome

romp [rɒmp] *n* jeux bruyants ▷ *vi* (*also:* **~ about**) s'ébattre, jouer bruyamment; **to ~ home** (*horse*) arriver bon premier

rompers ['rɒmpəz] *npl* barboteuse *f*

roof [ru:f] *n* toit *m*; (*of tunnel, cave*) plafond *m* ▷ *vt* couvrir (d'un toit); **the ~ of the mouth** la voûte du palais

roofing ['ru:fɪŋ] *n* toiture *f*

roof rack *n* (*Aut*) galerie *f*

rook [ruk] *n* (*bird*) freux *m*; (*Chess*) tour *f* ▷ *vt* (*inf: cheat*) rouler, escroquer

room [ru:m] *n* (*in house*) pièce *f*; (*also:* **bed~**) chambre *f* (à coucher); (*in school etc*) salle *f*; (*space*) place *f*; **rooms** *npl* (*lodging*) meublé *m*; **"~s to let", (*US*) "~s for rent"** chambres à louer"; **is there ~ for this?** est-ce qu'il y a de la place pour ceci?; **to make ~ for sb** faire de la place à qn; **there is ~ for improvement** on peut faire mieux

rooming house ['ru:mɪŋ-] *n* (*US*) maison *f* de rapport

roommate ['ru:mmeɪt] *n* camarade *m/f* de chambre

room service *n* service *m* des chambres (*dans un hôtel*)

roomy ['ru:mɪ] *adj* spacieux(-euse); (*garment*) ample

roost [ru:st] *n* juchoir *m* ▷ *vi* se jucher

rooster ['ru:stə'] *n* coq *m*

root [ru:t] *n* (*Bot, Math*) racine *f*; (*fig: of problem*) origine *f*, fond *m* ▷ *vi* (*plant*) s'enraciner; **to take ~** (*plant, idea*) prendre racine; **root about** *vi* (*fig*) fouiller; **root for** *vt fus* (*inf*) applaudir; **root out** *vt* extirper

rope [rəʊp] *n* corde *f*; (*Naut*) cordage *m* ▷ *vt* (*box*) corder; (*tie up or together*) attacher; (*climbers: also:* **~ together**) encorder; (*area: also:* **~ off**) interdire l'accès de; (: *divide off*) séparer; **to ~ sb in** (*fig*) embringuer qn; **to know the ~s** (*fig*) être au courant, connaître les ficelles

rosary ['rəʊzərɪ] *n* chapelet *m*

rose [rəʊz] *pt of* **rise** ▷ *n* rose *f*; (*also:* **~bush**) rosier *m*; (*on watering can*) pomme *f* ▷ *adj* rose

rosé ['rəʊzeɪ] *n* rosé *m*

rosebud ['rəʊzbʌd] *n* bouton *m* de rose

rosemary ['rəʊzmərɪ] *n* romarin *m*

roster ['rɒstə'] *n:* **duty ~** tableau *m* de service

rostrum ['rɒstrəm] *n* tribune *f* (*pour un orateur etc*)

rosy ['rəʊzɪ] *adj* rose; **a ~ future** un bel avenir

rot [rɒt] *n* (*decay*) pourriture *f*; (*fig: pej: nonsense*) idioties *fpl*, balivernes *fpl* ▷ *vt, vi* pourrir; **to stop the ~** (*Brit fig*) rétablir la situation; **dry ~** pourriture sèche (*du bois*); **wet ~** pourriture (du bois)

rota ['rəʊtə] *n* liste *f*, tableau *m* de service; **on a ~ basis** par roulement

rotary ['rəʊtərɪ] *adj* rotatif(-ive)

rotate [rəʊ'teɪt] *vt* (*revolve*) faire tourner; (*change round: crops*) alterner; (: *jobs*) faire à tour de rôle ▷ *vi* (*revolve*) tourner

rotating [rəʊ'teɪtɪŋ] *adj* (*movement*) tournant(e)

rotten ['rɒtn] *adj* (*decayed*) pourri(e); (*dishonest*) corrompu(e); (*inf: bad*) mauvais(e), moche; **to feel ~** (*ill*) être mal fichu(e)

rotund [rəʊ'tʌnd] *adj* rondelet(te); arrondi(e)

rough [rʌf] *adj* (*cloth, skin*) rêche, rugueux(-euse); (*terrain*) accidenté(e); (*path*) rocailleux(-euse); (*voice*) rauque, rude;

(*person, manner: coarse*) rude, fruste; (: *violent*) brutal(e); (*district, weather*) mauvais(e); (*sea*) houleux(-euse); (*plan*) ébauché(e); (*guess*) approximatif(-ive) ▷ *n* (*Golf*) rough *m* ▷ *vt*: **to ~ it** vivre à la dure; **the sea is ~ today** la mer est agitée aujourd'hui; **to have a ~ time (of it)** en voir de dures; **~ estimate** approximation *f*; **to play ~** jouer avec brutalité; **to sleep ~** (*Brit*) coucher à la dure; **to feel ~** (*Brit*) être mal fichu(e); **rough out** *vt* (*draft*) ébaucher

roughage ['rʌfɪdʒ] *n* fibres *fpl* diététiques

rough-and-ready ['rʌfən'redɪ] *adj* (*accommodation, method*) rudimentaire

rough copy, rough draft *n* brouillon *m*

roughly ['rʌflɪ] *adv* (*handle*) rudement, brutalement; (*speak*) avec brusquerie; (*make*) grossièrement; (*approximately*) à peu près, en gros; **~ speaking** en gros

roulette [ru:'lɛt] *n* roulette *f*

Roumania *etc* [ru:'meɪnɪə] *n* = **Romania** *etc*

round [raund] *adj* rond(e) ▷ *n* rond *m*, cercle *m*; (*Brit: of toast*) tranche *f*; (*duty: of policeman, milkman etc*) tournée *f*; (: *of doctor*) visites *fpl*; (*game: of cards, in competition*) partie *f*; (*Boxing*) round *m*; (*of talks*) série *f* ▷ *vt* (*corner*) tourner; (*bend*) prendre; (*cape*) doubler ▷ *prep* autour de ▷ *adv*: **right ~, all ~** tout autour; **in ~ figures** en chiffres ronds; **to go the ~s** (*disease, story*) circuler; **the daily ~** (*fig*) la routine quotidienne; **~ of ammunition** cartouche *f*; **~ of applause** applaudissements *mpl*; **~ of drinks** tournée *f*; **~ of sandwiches** (*Brit*) sandwich *m*; **the long way ~** (par) le chemin le plus long; **all (the) year ~** toute l'année; **it's just ~ the corner** c'est juste après le coin; (*fig*) c'est tout près; **to ask sb ~** inviter qn (chez soi); **I'll be ~ at 6 o'clock** je serai là à 6 heures; **to go ~** faire le tour ou un détour; **to go ~ to sb's (house)** aller chez qn; **to go ~ an obstacle** contourner un obstacle; **go ~ the back** passez par derrière; **to go ~ a house** visiter une maison, faire le tour d'une maison; **enough to go ~** assez pour tout le monde; **she arrived ~ (about) noon** (*Brit*) elle est arrivée vers midi; **~ the clock** 24 heures sur 24; **round off** *vt* (*speech etc*) terminer; **round up** *vt* rassembler; (*criminals*) effectuer une rafle de; (*prices*) arrondir (au chiffre supérieur)

roundabout ['raundəbaut] *n* (*Brit Aut*) rond-point *m* (à sens giratoire); (*at fair*) manège *m* (de chevaux de bois) ▷ *adj* (*route, means*) détourné(e)

rounders ['raundəz] *npl* (*game*) ≈ balle *f* au camp

roundly ['raundlɪ] *adv* (*fig*) tout net, carrément

round trip *n* (*voyage m*) aller et retour *m*

roundup ['raundʌp] *n* rassemblement *m*; (*of criminals*) rafle *f*; **a ~ of the latest news** un rappel des derniers événements

rouse [rauz] *vt* (*wake up*) réveiller; (*stir up*) susciter, provoquer; (*interest*) éveiller; (*suspicions*) susciter, éveiller

rousing ['rauzɪŋ] *adj* (*welcome*) enthousiaste

route [ru:t] *n* itinéraire *m*; (*of bus*) parcours *m*; (*of trade, shipping*) route *f*; **"all ~s"** (*Aut*) "toutes directions"; **the best ~ to London** le meilleur itinéraire pour aller à Londres

routine [ru:'ti:n] *adj* (*work*) ordinaire, courant(e); (*procedure*) d'usage ▷ *n* (*habits*) habitudes *fpl*; (*pej*) train-train *m*; (*Theat*) numéro *m*; **daily ~** occupations journalières

row¹ [rəu] *n* (*line*) rangée *f*; (*of people, seats, Knitting*) rang *m*; (*behind one another: of cars, people*) file *f* ▷ *vi* (*in boat*) ramer; (*as sport*) faire de l'aviron ▷ *vt* (*boat*) faire aller à la rame *or* à l'aviron; **in a ~** (*fig*) d'affilée

row² [rau] *n* (*noise*) vacarme *m*; (*dispute*) dispute *f*, querelle *f*; (*scolding*) réprimande *f*, savon *m* ▷ *vi* (*also*: **to have a ~**) se disputer, se quereller

rowboat ['rəubəut] *n* (*US*) canot *m* (à rames)

rowdy ['raudɪ] *adj* chahuteur(-euse); bagarreur(-euse) ▷ *n* voyou *m*

rowing ['rəuɪŋ] *n* canotage *m*; (*as sport*) aviron *m*

rowing boat *n* (*Brit*) canot *m* (à rames)

royal ['rɔɪəl] *adj* royal(e)

Royal Air Force *n* (*Brit*) armée de l'air britannique

royalty ['rɔɪəltɪ] *n* (*royal persons*) (membres *mpl* de la) famille royale; (*payment: to author*) droits *mpl* d'auteur; (: *to inventor*) royalties *fpl*

rpm *abbr* (= *revolutions per minute*) t/mn (= = *tours/minute*)

R.S.V.P. *abbr* (= *répondez s'il vous plaît*) RSVP

Rt. Hon. *abbr* (*Brit*: = *Right Honourable*) titre donné aux députés de la Chambre des communes

rub [rʌb] *vt* (*with cloth*) coup *m* de chiffon *or* de torchon; (*on person*) friction *f*; **to give sth a ~** donner un coup de chiffon *or* de torchon à qch ▷ *vt* frotter; (*person*) frictionner; (*hands*) se frotter; **to ~ sb up** (*Brit*) *or* **to ~ sb** (*US*) **the wrong way** prendre qn à rebrousse-poil; **rub down** *vt* (*body*) frictionner; (*horse*) bouchonner; **rub in** *vt* (*ointment*) faire pénétrer; **rub off** *vi* partir; **to ~ off on** déteindre sur; **rub out** *vt* effacer ▷ *vi* s'effacer

rubber ['rʌbə'] *n* caoutchouc *m*; (*Brit: eraser*) gomme *f* (à effacer)

rubber band *n* élastique *m*

rubber gloves *npl* gants *mpl* en caoutchouc

rubber plant *n* caoutchouc *m* (*plante verte*)

rubbish ['rʌbɪʃ] *n* (*from household*) ordures *fpl*; (*fig: pej*) choses *fpl* sans valeur; camelote *f*; (*nonsense*) bêtises *fpl*, idioties *fpl* ▷ *vt* (*Brit inf*) dénigrer, rabaisser; **what you've just said is ~** tu viens de dire une bêtise

rubbish bin *n* (*Brit*) boîte *f* à ordures, poubelle *f*

rubbish dump *n* (*Brit: in town*) décharge publique, dépotoir *m*

rubble ['rʌbl] n décombres mpl; (smaller) gravats mpl; (Constr) blocage m

ruby ['ru:bɪ] n rubis m

rucksack ['rʌksæk] n sac m à dos

rudder ['rʌdə'] n gouvernail m

ruddy ['rʌdɪ] adj (face) coloré(e); (inf: damned) sacré(e), fichu(e)

rude [ru:d] adj (impolite: person) impoli(e); (: word, manners) grossier(-ière); (shocking) indécent(e), inconvenant(e); **to be ~ to sb** être grossier envers qn

ruffle ['rʌfl] vt (hair) ébouriffer; (clothes) chiffonner; (water) agiter; (fig: person) émouvoir, faire perdre son flegme à; **to get ~d** s'énerver

rug [rʌg] n petit tapis; (Brit: blanket) couverture f

rugby ['rʌgbɪ] n (also: **~ football**) rugby m

rugged ['rʌgɪd] adj (landscape) accidenté(e); (features, character) rude; (determination) farouche

ruin ['ru:ɪn] n ruine f ▷ vt ruiner; (spoil: clothes) abîmer; (: event) gâcher; **ruins** npl (of building) ruine(s); **in ~s** en ruine

rule [ru:l] n règle f; (regulation) règlement m; (government) autorité f, gouvernement m; (dominion etc): **under British ~** sous l'autorité britannique ▷ vt (country) gouverner; (person) dominer; (decide) décider ▷ vi commander; décider; (Law): **to ~ against/in favour of/on** statuer contre/au règlement/de; **to ~ that** (umpire, judge etc) décider que; **it's against the ~s** c'est contraire au règlement; **by ~ of thumb** à vue de nez; **as a ~** normalement, en règle générale; **rule out** vt exclure; **murder cannot be ~d out** l'hypothèse d'un meurtre ne peut être exclue

ruled [ru:ld] adj (paper) réglé(e)

ruler ['ru:lə'] n (sovereign) souverain(e); (leader) chef m (d'État); (for measuring) règle f

ruling ['ru:lɪŋ] adj (party) au pouvoir; (class) dirigeant(e) ▷ n (Law) décision f

rum [rʌm] n rhum m ▷ adj (Brit inf) bizarre

Rumania [ru:'meɪnɪə] n Roumanie f

Rumanian [ru:'meɪnɪən] adj roumain(e) ▷ n Roumain(e); (Ling) roumain m

rumble ['rʌmbl] n grondement m; (of stomach, pipe) gargouillement m ▷ vi gronder; (stomach, pipe) gargouiller

rummage ['rʌmɪdʒ] vi fouiller

rumour, (US) **rumor** ['ru:mə'] n rumeur f, bruit m (qui court) ▷ vt: **it is ~ed that** le bruit court que

rump [rʌmp] n (of animal) croupe f

rump steak n romsteck m

rumpus ['rʌmpəs] n (inf) tapage m, chahut m; (quarrel) prise f de bec; **to kick up a ~** faire toute une histoire

run [rʌn] (pt **ran**, pp **run**) [ræn, rʌn] n (race) course f; (outing) tour m or promenade f (en voiture); (distance travelled) parcours m, trajet m; (series) suite f, série f; (Theat) série de représentations; (Ski) piste f; (Cricket, Baseball) point m; (in tights, stockings) maille filée, échelle f ▷ vt (business) diriger; (competition, course) organiser; (hotel, house) tenir; (race) participer à; (Comput: program) exécuter; (force through: rope, pipe): **to ~ sth through** faire passer qch à travers; (to pass: hand, finger): **to ~ sth over** promener or passer qch sur; (water, bath) faire couler; (Press: feature) publier ▷ vi courir; (pass: road etc) passer; (work: machine, factory) marcher; (bus, train) circuler; (play) se jouer, être à l'affiche; (: contract) être valide or en vigueur; (slide: drawer etc) glisser; (flow: river, bath, nose) couler; (colours, washing) déteindre; (in election) être candidat, se présenter; **at a ~** au pas de course; **to go for a ~** aller courir or faire un peu de course à pied; (in car) faire un tour or une promenade (en voiture); **to break into a ~** se mettre à courir; **a ~ of luck** une série de coups de chance; **to have the ~ of sb's house** avoir la maison de qn à sa disposition; **there was a ~ on** (meat, tickets) les gens se sont rués sur; **in the long ~** à la longue, à longue échéance; **in the short ~** à brève échéance, à court terme; **on the ~** en fuite; **to make a ~ for it** s'enfuir; **I'll ~ you to the station** je vais vous emmener or conduire à la gare; **to ~ errands** faire des commissions; **the train ~s between Gatwick and Victoria** le train assure le service entre Gatwick et Victoria; **the bus ~s every 20 minutes** il y a un autobus toutes les 20 minutes; **it's very cheap to ~** (car, machine) c'est très économique; **to ~ on petrol** or (US) **gas/on batteries** marcher à l'essence/au diesel/sur piles; **to ~ for president** être candidat à la présidence; **to ~ a risk** courir un risque; **their losses ran into millions** leurs pertes se sont élevées à plusieurs millions; **to be ~ off one's feet** (Brit) ne plus savoir où donner de la tête; **run about** vi (children) courir çà et là; **run across** vt fus (find) trouver par hasard; **run after** vt fus (to catch up) courir après; (chase) poursuivre; **run around** vi = **run about**; **run away** vi s'enfuir; **run down** vi (clock) s'arrêter (faute d'avoir été remonté) ▷ vt (Aut: knock over) renverser; (Brit: reduce: production) réduire progressivement; (: factory/shop) réduire progressivement la production/l'activité de; (criticize) critiquer, dénigrer; **to be ~ down** (tired) être fatigué(e) or à plat; **run in** vt (Brit: car) roder; **run into** vt fus (meet: person) rencontrer par hasard; (: trouble) se heurter à; (collide with) heurter; **to ~ into debt** contracter des dettes; **run off** vi s'enfuir ▷ vt (water) laisser s'écouler; (copies) tirer; **run out** vi (person) sortir en courant; (liquid) couler; (lease) expirer; (money) être épuisé(e); **run out of** vt fus se trouver à court de; **I've ~ out of petrol** or (US)

gas je suis en panne d'essence; **run over** vt (Aut) écraser ▷ vt fus (revise) revoir, reprendre; **run through** vt fus (recap) reprendre, revoir; (play) répéter; **run up** vi: **to ~ up against** (difficulties) se heurter à ▷ vt: **to ~ up a debt** s'endetter

runaway ['rʌnəweɪ] adj (horse) emballé(e); (truck) fou/folle; (person) fugitif(-ive); (child) fugueur(-euse); (inflation) galopant(e)

rung [rʌŋ] pp of **ring** ▷ n (of ladder) barreau m

runner ['rʌnər] n (in race: person) coureur(-euse); (: horse) partant m; (on sledge) patin m; (for drawer etc) coulisseau m; (carpet: in hall etc) chemin m

runner bean n (Brit) haricot m (à rames)

runner-up [rʌnər'ʌp] n second(e)

running ['rʌnɪŋ] n (in race etc) course f; (of business, organization) direction f, gestion f; (of event) organisation f; (of machine etc) marche f, fonctionnement m ▷ adj (water) courant(e); (commentary) suivi(e); **6 days ~** 6 jours de suite; **to be in/out of the ~ for sth** être/ne pas être sur les rangs pour qch

running commentary n commentaire détaillé

running costs npl (of business) frais mpl de gestion; (of car): **the ~ are high** elle revient cher

runny ['rʌnɪ] adj qui coule

run-of-the-mill ['rʌnəvðə'mɪl] adj ordinaire, banal(e)

runt [rʌnt] n avorton m

run-up ['rʌnʌp] n (Brit): **~ to sth** période f précédant qch

runway ['rʌnweɪ] n (Aviat) piste f (d'envol or d'atterrissage)

rupture ['rʌptʃər] n (Med) hernie f ▷ vt: **to ~ o.s.** se donner une hernie

rural ['ruərl] adj rural(e)

rush [rʌʃ] n course précipitée; (of crowd, Comm: sudden demand) ruée f; (hurry) hâte f; (of anger, joy) accès m; (current) flot m; (Bot) jonc m; (for chair) paille f ▷ vt (hurry) transporter or envoyer d'urgence; (attack: town etc) prendre d'assaut; (Brit inf: overcharge) estamper; faire payer ▷ vi se précipiter; **don't ~ me!** laissez-moi le temps de souffler!; **to ~ sth off** (do quickly) faire qch à la hâte; (send) envoyer qch d'urgence; **is there any ~ for this?** est-ce urgent?; **we've had a ~ of orders** nous avons reçu une avalanche de commandes; **I'm in a ~ (to do)** je suis vraiment pressé (de faire); **gold ~** ruée vers l'or; **rush through** vt fus (work) exécuter à la hâte ▷ vt (Comm: order) exécuter d'urgence

rush hour n heures fpl de pointe or d'affluence

rusk [rʌsk] n biscotte f

Russia ['rʌʃə] n Russie f

Russian ['rʌʃən] adj russe ▷ n Russe m/f; (Ling) russe m

rust [rʌst] n rouille f ▷ vi rouiller

rustic ['rʌstɪk] adj rustique ▷ n (pej) rustaud(e)

rustle ['rʌsl] vi bruire, produire un bruissement ▷ vt (paper) froisser; (US: cattle) voler

rustproof ['rʌstpruːf] adj inoxydable

rusty ['rʌstɪ] adj rouillé(e)

rut [rʌt] n ornière f; (Zool) rut m; **to be in a ~** (fig) suivre l'ornière, s'encroûter

ruthless ['ruːθlɪs] adj sans pitié, impitoyable

RV abbr (= revised version) traduction anglaise de la Bible de 1885 ▷ n abbr (US) = **recreational vehicle**

rye [raɪ] n seigle m

S

Sabbath ['sæbəθ] *n* (*Jewish*) sabbat *m*;
(*Christian*) dimanche *m*
sabotage ['sæbətɑːʒ] *n* sabotage *m* ▷ *vt*
saboter
saccharin, saccharine ['sækərɪn] *n*
saccharine *f*
sachet ['sæʃeɪ] *n* sachet *m*
sack [sæk] *n* (*bag*) sac *m* ▷ *vt* (*dismiss*) renvoyer,
mettre à la porte; (*plunder*) piller, mettre à
sac; **to give sb the ~** renvoyer qn, mettre qn
à la porte; **to get the ~** être renvoyé(e) or
mis(e) à la porte
sacking ['sækɪŋ] *n* toile *f* à sac; (*dismissal*)
renvoi *m*
sacrament ['sækrəmənt] *n* sacrement *m*
sacred ['seɪkrɪd] *adj* sacré(e)
sacrifice ['sækrɪfaɪs] *n* sacrifice *m* ▷ *vt*
sacrifier; **to make ~s (for sb)** se sacrifier or
faire des sacrifices (pour qn)
sad [sæd] *adj* (*unhappy*) triste; (*deplorable*)
triste, fâcheux(-euse); (*inf: pathetic: thing*)
triste, lamentable; (: *person*) minable
saddle ['sædl] *n* selle *f* ▷ *vt* (*horse*) seller; **to be
~d with sth** (*inf*) avoir qch sur les bras
saddlebag ['sædlbæg] *n* sacoche *f*
sadistic [sə'dɪstɪk] *adj* sadique
sadly ['sædlɪ] *adv* tristement; (*unfortunately*)
malheureusement; (*seriously*) fort
sadness ['sædnɪs] *n* tristesse *f*
s.a.e. *n abbr* (*Brit*: = *stamped addressed envelope*)
enveloppe affranchie pour la réponse
safari [sə'fɑːrɪ] *n* safari *m*

safe [seɪf] *adj* (*out of danger*) hors de danger, en
sécurité; (*not dangerous*) sans danger;
(*cautious*) prudent(e); (*sure: bet*) assuré(e) ▷ *n*
coffre-fort *m*; **~ from** à l'abri de; **~ and sound**
sain(e) et sauf/sauve; **(just) to be on the ~
side** pour plus de sûreté, par précaution; **to
play ~** ne prendre aucun risque; **it is ~ to say
that ...** on peut dire sans crainte que ...;
~ journey! bon voyage!
safe-conduct [seɪf'kɔndʌkt] *n* sauf-
conduit *m*
safe-deposit ['seɪfdɪpɔzɪt] *n* (*vault*) dépôt *m*
de coffres-forts; (*box*) coffre-fort *m*
safeguard ['seɪfgɑːd] *n* sauvegarde *f*,
protection *f* ▷ *vt* sauvegarder, protéger
safekeeping ['seɪf'kiːpɪŋ] *n* bonne garde
safely ['seɪflɪ] *adv* (*assume, say*) sans risque
d'erreur; (*drive, arrive*) sans accident; **I can ~
say ...** je peux dire à coup sûr ...
safe sex *n* rapports sexuels protégés
safety ['seɪftɪ] *n* sécurité *f*; **~ first!** la sécurité
d'abord!
safety belt *n* ceinture *f* de sécurité
safety pin *n* épingle *f* de sûreté or de nourrice
safety valve *n* soupape *f* de sûreté
saffron ['sæfrən] *n* safran *m*
sag [sæg] *vi* s'affaisser, fléchir; (*hem, breasts*)
pendre
sage [seɪdʒ] *n* (*herb*) sauge *f*; (*person*) sage *m*
Sagittarius [sædʒɪ'tɛərɪəs] *n* le Sagittaire;
to be ~ être du Sagittaire
Sahara [sə'hɑːrə] *n*: **the ~ (Desert)** le (désert
du) Sahara *m*
said [sɛd] *pt, pp of* **say**
sail [seɪl] *n* (*on boat*) voile *f*; (*trip*): **to go for a ~**
faire un tour en bateau ▷ *vt* (*boat*)
manœuvrer, piloter ▷ *vi* (*travel: ship*) avancer,
naviguer; (: *passenger*) aller or se rendre
(en bateau); (*set off*) partir, prendre la mer;
(*Sport*) faire de la voile; **they ~ed into
Le Havre** ils sont entrés dans le port du
Havre; **sail through** *vi, vt fus* (*fig*) réussir
haut la main
sailboat ['seɪlbəut] *n* (*US*) bateau *m* à voiles,
voilier *m*
sailing ['seɪlɪŋ] *n* (*Sport*) voile *f*; **to go ~** faire de
la voile
sailing boat *n* bateau *m* à voiles, voilier *m*
sailing ship *n* grand voilier
sailor ['seɪləʳ] *n* marin *m*, matelot *m*
saint [seɪnt] *n* saint(e)
sake [seɪk] *n*: **for the ~ of** (*out of concern for*)
pour (l'amour de), dans l'intérêt de; (*out of
consideration for*) par égard pour; (*in order to
achieve*) pour plus de, par souci de; **arguing
for arguing's ~** discuter pour (le plaisir de)
discuter; **for heaven's ~!** pour l'amour du
ciel!; **for the ~ of argument** à titre
d'exemple
salad ['sæləd] *n* salade *f*; **tomato ~** salade de
tomates
salad bowl *n* saladier *m*

salad cream n (Brit) (sorte f de) mayonnaise f

salad dressing n vinaigrette f

salami [sə'lɑːmɪ] n salami m

salary ['sælərɪ] n salaire m, traitement m

sale [seɪl] n vente f; (at reduced prices) soldes mpl; **sales** npl (total amount sold) chiffre m de ventes; **"for ~"** "à vendre"; **on ~** en vente; **on ~ or return** vendu(e) avec faculté de retour; **closing-down** or **liquidation ~** (US) liquidation f (avant fermeture); **~ and lease back** n cession-bail f

saleroom ['seɪlruːm] n salle f des ventes

sales assistant, (US) **sales clerk** n vendeur(-euse)

salesman ['seɪlzmən] irreg n (in shop) vendeur m; (representative) représentant m de commerce

salesperson ['seɪlzpəːsn] irreg n (in shop) vendeur(-euse)

sales rep n (Comm) représentant(e) m/f

saleswoman ['seɪlzwumən] irreg n (in shop) vendeuse f

saline ['seɪlaɪn] adj salin(e)

saliva [sə'laɪvə] n salive f

salmon ['sæmən] n (pl inv) saumon m

salon ['sælɔn] n salon m

saloon [sə'luːn] n (US) bar m; (Brit Aut) berline f; (ship's lounge) salon m

salt [sɔːlt] n sel m ▷ vt saler ▷ cpd de sel; (Culin) salé(e); **an old ~** un vieux loup de mer; **salt away** vt mettre de côté

salt cellar n salière f

saltwater ['sɔːltwɔːtər] adj (fish etc) (d'eau) de mer

salty ['sɔːltɪ] adj salé(e)

salute [sə'luːt] n salut m; (of guns) salve f ▷ vt saluer

salvage ['sælvɪdʒ] n (saving) sauvetage m; (things saved) biens sauvés or récupérés ▷ vt sauver, récupérer

salvation [sæl'veɪʃən] n salut m

Salvation Army [sæl'veɪʃən-] n Armée f du Salut

same [seɪm] adj même ▷ pron: **the ~** le/la même, les mêmes; **the ~ book as** le même livre que; **on the ~ day** le même jour; **at the ~ time** en même temps; (yet) néanmoins; **all** or **just the ~** tout de même, quand même; **they're one and the ~** (person/thing) c'est une seule et même personne/chose; **to do the ~** faire de même, en faire autant; **to do the ~ as sb** faire comme qn; **and the ~ to you!** et à vous de même!; (after insult) toi-même!; **~ here!** moi aussi!; **the ~ again!** (in bar etc) la même chose!

sample ['sɑːmpl] n échantillon m; (Med) prélèvement m ▷ vt (food, wine) goûter; **to take a ~** prélever un échantillon; **free ~** échantillon gratuit

sanction ['sæŋkʃən] n approbation f, sanction f ▷ vt cautionner, sanctionner; **sanctions** npl (Pol) sanctions; **to impose**

economic ~s on or **against** prendre des sanctions économiques contre

sanctity ['sæŋktɪtɪ] n sainteté f, caractère sacré

sanctuary ['sæŋktjuərɪ] n (holy place) sanctuaire m; (refuge) asile m; (for wildlife) réserve f

sand [sænd] n sable m ▷ vt sabler; (also: **~ down:** wood etc) poncer

sandal ['sændl] n sandale f

sandbox ['sændbɔks] n (US: for children) tas m de sable

sand castle ['sændkɑːsl] n château m de sable

sand dune n dune f de sable

sandpaper ['sændpeɪpər] n papier m de verre

sandpit ['sændpɪt] n (Brit: for children) tas m de sable

sands [sændz] npl plage f (de sable)

sandstone ['sændstəun] n grès m

sandwich ['sændwɪtʃ] n sandwich m ▷ vt (also: **~ in**) intercaler; **~ed between** pris en sandwich entre; **cheese/ham ~** sandwich au fromage/jambon

sandwich course n (Brit) cours m de formation professionnelle

sandy ['sændɪ] adj sablonneux(-euse); couvert(e) de sable; (colour) sable inv, blond roux inv

sane [seɪn] adj (person) sain(e) d'esprit; (outlook) sensé(e), sain(e)

sang [sæŋ] pt of **sing**

sanitary ['sænɪtərɪ] adj (system, arrangements) sanitaire; (clean) hygiénique

sanitary towel, (US) **sanitary napkin** ['sænɪtərɪ-] n serviette f hygiénique

sanitation [sænɪ'teɪʃən] n (in house) installations fpl sanitaires; (in town) système m sanitaire

sanitation department n (US) service m de voirie

sanity ['sænɪtɪ] n santé mentale; (common sense) bon sens

sank [sæŋk] pt of **sink**

Santa Claus [sæntə'klɔːz] n le Père Noël

sap [sæp] n (of plants) sève f ▷ vt (strength) saper, miner

sapling ['sæplɪŋ] n jeune arbre m

sapphire ['sæfaɪər] n saphir m

sarcasm ['sɑːkæzm] n sarcasme m, raillerie f

sarcastic [sɑː'kæstɪk] adj sarcastique

sardine [sɑː'diːn] n sardine f

Sardinia [sɑː'dɪnɪə] n Sardaigne f

SASE n abbr (US: = self-addressed stamped envelope) enveloppe affranchie pour la réponse

sash [sæʃ] n écharpe f

sat [sæt] pt, pp of **sit**

Sat. abbr (= Saturday) sa

satchel ['sætʃl] n cartable m

satellite ['sætəlaɪt] adj, n satellite m

satellite dish n antenne f parabolique

satellite navigation system n système m de navigation par satellite

satellite television n télévision f par satellite

satin ['sætɪn] n satin m ▷ adj en or de satin, satiné(e); **with a ~ finish** satiné(e)

satire ['sætaɪəʳ] n satire f

satisfaction [sætɪs'fækʃən] n satisfaction f

satisfactory [sætɪs'fæktərɪ] adj satisfaisant(e)

satisfied ['sætɪsfaɪd] adj satisfait(e); **to be ~ with sth** être satisfait de qch

satisfy ['sætɪsfaɪ] vt satisfaire, contenter; (convince) convaincre, persuader; **to ~ the requirements** remplir les conditions; **to ~ sb (that)** convaincre qn (que); **to ~ o.s. of sth** vérifier qch, s'assurer de qch

satisfying ['sætɪsfaɪɪŋ] adj satisfaisant(e)

Saturday ['sætədɪ] n samedi m; see also **Tuesday**

sauce [sɔ:s] n sauce f

saucepan ['sɔ:spən] n casserole f

saucer ['sɔ:səʳ] n soucoupe f

Saudi Arabia n Arabie f Saoudite

Saudi (Arabian) ['saudɪ] adj saoudien(ne) ▷ n Saoudien(ne)

sauna ['sɔ:nə] n sauna m

saunter ['sɔ:ntəʳ] vi: **to ~ along** aller en flânant or se balader jusqu'à

sausage ['sɔsɪdʒ] n saucisse f; (salami etc) saucisson m

sausage roll n friand m

sautéed ['səuteɪd] adj sauté(e)

savage ['sævɪdʒ] adj (cruel, fierce) brutal(e), féroce; (primitive) primitif(-ive), sauvage ▷ n sauvage m/f ▷ vt attaquer férocement

save [seɪv] vt (person, belongings) sauver; (money) mettre de côté, économiser; (time) (faire) gagner; (keep) garder; (Comput) sauvegarder; (Sport: stop) arrêter; (avoid: trouble) éviter ▷ vi (also: ~ up) mettre de l'argent de côté ▷ n (Sport) arrêt m (du ballon) ▷ prep sauf, à l'exception de; **it will ~ me an hour** ça me fera gagner une heure; **to ~ face** sauver la face; **God ~ the Queen!** vive la Reine!

saving ['seɪvɪŋ] n économie f ▷ adj: **the ~ grace of** ce qui rachète; **savings** npl économies fpl; **to make ~s** faire des économies

savings account n compte m d'épargne

savings and loan association (US) n ≈ société f de crédit immobilier

savings bank n caisse f d'épargne

saviour, (US) **savior** ['seɪvjəʳ] n sauveur m

savour, (US) **savor** ['seɪvəʳ] n saveur f, goût m ▷ vt savourer

savoury, (US) **savory** ['seɪvərɪ] adj savoureux(-euse); (dish: not sweet) salé(e)

saw [sɔ:] pt of **see** ▷ n (tool) scie f ▷ vt (pt sawed, pp sawed or sawn) [sɔ:n] scier; **to ~ sth up** débiter qch à la scie

sawdust ['sɔ:dʌst] n sciure f

sawmill ['sɔ:mɪl] n scierie f

sawn [sɔ:n] pp of **saw**

sawn-off ['sɔ:nɔf], (US) **sawed-off** ['sɔ:dɔf] adj: **~ shotgun** carabine f à canon scié

sax [sæks] (inf) n saxo m

saxophone ['sæksəfəun] n saxophone m

say [seɪ] n: **to have one's ~** dire ce qu'on a à dire ▷ vt (pt, pp said) [sed] dire; **to have a ~** avoir voix au chapitre; **could you ~ that again?** pourriez-vous répéter ce que vous venez de dire?; **to ~ yes/no** dire oui/non; **she said (that) I was to give you this** elle m'a chargé de vous remettre ceci; **my watch ~s 3 o'clock** ma montre indique 3 heures, il est 3 heures à ma montre; **shall we ~ Tuesday?** disons mardi?; **that doesn't ~ much for him** ce n'est pas vraiment à son honneur; **when all is said and done** en fin de compte, en définitive; **there is something or a lot to be said for it** cela a des avantages; **that is to ~** c'est-à-dire; **to ~ nothing of** sans compter; **~ that ...** mettons or disons que ...; **that goes without ~ing** cela va sans dire, cela va de soi

saying ['seɪɪŋ] n dicton m, proverbe m

scab [skæb] n croûte f; (pej) jaune m

scaffold ['skæfəld] n échafaud m

scaffolding ['skæfəldɪŋ] n échafaudage m

scald [skɔ:ld] n brûlure f ▷ vt ébouillanter

scale [skeɪl] n (of fish) écaille f; (Mus) gamme f; (of ruler, thermometer etc) graduation f, échelle (graduée); (of salaries, fees etc) barème m; (of map, also size, extent) échelle f ▷ vt (mountain) escalader; (fish) écailler; **scales** npl balance f; (larger) bascule f; (also: **bathroom ~s**) pèse-personne m inv; **pay ~** échelle des salaires; **~ of charges** tableau m des tarifs; **on a large ~** sur une grande échelle, en grand; **to draw sth to ~** dessiner qch à l'échelle; **small-~ model** modèle réduit; **scale down** vt réduire

scallion ['skæljən] n oignon m; (US: salad onion) ciboule f; (: shallot) échalote f; (: leek) poireau m

scallop ['skɔləp] n coquille f Saint-Jacques; (Sewing) feston m

scalp [skælp] n cuir chevelu ▷ vt scalper

scalpel ['skælpl] n scalpel m

scam [skæm] n (inf) arnaque f

scampi ['skæmpɪ] npl langoustines (frites), scampi mpl

scan [skæn] vt (examine) scruter, examiner; (glance at quickly) parcourir; (poetry) scander; (TV, Radar) balayer ▷ n (Med) scanographie f

scandal ['skændl] n scandale m; (gossip) ragots mpl

Scandinavia [skændɪ'neɪvɪə] n Scandinavie f

Scandinavian [skændɪ'neɪvɪən] adj scandinave ▷ n Scandinave m/f

scanner ['skænəʳ] n (Radar, Med) scanner m, scanographe m; (Comput) scanner

scant [skænt] adj insuffisant(e)

scanty ['skæntɪ] *adj* peu abondant(e), insuffisant(e), maigre

scapegoat ['skeɪpgəʊt] *n* bouc *m* émissaire

scar [skɑːʳ] *n* cicatrice *f* ▷ *vt* laisser une cicatrice *or* une marque à

scarce [skɛəs] *adj* rare, peu abondant(e); **to make o.s. ~** (*inf*) se sauver

scarcely ['skɛəslɪ] *adv* à peine, presque pas; **~ anybody** pratiquement personne; **I can ~ believe it** j'ai du mal à le croire

scarcity ['skɛəsɪtɪ] *n* rareté *f*, manque *m*, pénurie *f*

scare [skɛəʳ] *n* peur *f*, panique *f* ▷ *vt* effrayer, faire peur à; **to ~ sb stiff** faire une peur bleue à qn; **bomb ~** alerte *f* à la bombe; **scare away, scare off** *vt* faire fuir

scarecrow ['skɛəkrəʊ] *n* épouvantail *m*

scared [skɛəd] *adj*: **to be ~** avoir peur

scarf (*pl* **scarves**) [skɑːf, skɑːvz] *n* (*long*) écharpe *f*; (*square*) foulard *m*

scarlet ['skɑːlɪt] *adj* écarlate

scarlet fever *n* scarlatine *f*

scarves [skɑːvz] *npl of* **scarf**

scary ['skɛərɪ] *adj* (*inf*) effrayant(e); (*film*) qui fait peur

scathing ['skeɪðɪŋ] *adj* cinglant(e), acerbe; **to be ~ about sth** être très critique vis-à-vis de qch

scatter ['skætəʳ] *vt* éparpiller, répandre; (*crowd*) disperser ▷ *vi* se disperser

scatterbrained ['skætəbreɪnd] *adj* écervelé(e), étourdi(e)

scavenger ['skævɪndʒəʳ] *n* éboueur *m*

scenario [sɪ'nɑːrɪəʊ] *n* scénario *m*

scene [siːn] *n* (*Theat, fig etc*) scène *f*; (*of crime, accident*) lieu(x) *m(pl)*, endroit *m*; (*sight, view*) spectacle *m*, vue *f*; **behind the ~s** (*also fig*) dans les coulisses; **to make a ~** (*inf: fuss*) faire une scène *or* toute une histoire; **to appear on the ~** (*also fig*) faire son apparition, arriver; **the political ~** la situation politique

scenery ['siːnərɪ] *n* (*Theat*) décor(s) *m(pl)*; (*landscape*) paysage *m*

scenic ['siːnɪk] *adj* scénique; offrant de beaux paysages *or* panoramas

scent [sɛnt] *n* parfum *m*, odeur *f*; (*fig: track*) piste *f*; (*sense of smell*) odorat *m* ▷ *vt* parfumer; (*smell: also fig*) flairer; (*also*: **to put** *or* **throw sb off the ~**: *fig*) mettre qn sur une mauvaise piste

sceptical, (*US*) **skeptical** ['skɛptɪkl] *adj* sceptique

schedule ['ʃɛdjuːl, *US*: 'skɛdjuːl] *n* programme *m*, plan *m*; (*of trains*) horaire *m*; (*of prices etc*) barème *m*, tarif *m* ▷ *vt* prévoir; **as ~d** comme prévu; **on ~** à l'heure (prévue); à la date prévue; **to be ahead of/behind ~** avoir de l'avance/du retard; **we are working to a very tight ~** notre programme de travail est très serré *or* intense; **everything went according to ~** tout s'est passé comme prévu

scheduled flight *n* vol régulier

scheme [skiːm] *n* plan *m*, projet *m*; (*method*) procédé *m*; (*plot*) complot *m*, combine *f*; (*arrangement*) arrangement *m*, classification *f*; (*pension scheme etc*) régime *m* ▷ *vt, vi* comploter, manigancer; **colour ~** combinaison *f* de(s) couleurs

scheming ['skiːmɪŋ] *adj* rusé(e), intrigant(e) ▷ *n* manigances *fpl*, intrigues *fpl*

schizophrenic [skɪtsə'frɛnɪk] *adj* schizophrène

scholar ['skɔləʳ] *n* érudit(e); (*pupil*) boursier(-ère)

scholarship ['skɔləʃɪp] *n* érudition *f*; (*grant*) bourse *f* (d'études)

school [skuːl] *n* (*gen*) école *f*; (*secondary school*) collège *m*; lycée *m*; (*in university*) faculté *f*; (*US: university*) université *f*; (*of fish*) banc *m* ▷ *cpd* scolaire ▷ *vt* (*animal*) dresser

schoolbook ['skuːlbʊk] *n* livre *m* scolaire *or* de classe

schoolboy ['skuːlbɔɪ] *n* écolier *m*; (*at secondary school*) collégien *m*; lycéen *m*

schoolchildren ['skuːltʃɪldrən] *npl* écoliers *mpl*; (*at secondary school*) collégiens *mpl*; lycéens *mpl*

schoolgirl ['skuːlgəːl] *n* écolière *f*; (*at secondary school*) collégienne *f*; lycéenne *f*

schooling ['skuːlɪŋ] *n* instruction *f*, études *fpl*

schoolmaster ['skuːlmɑːstəʳ] *n* (*primary*) instituteur *m*; (*secondary*) professeur *m*

schoolmistress ['skuːlmɪstrɪs] *n* (*primary*) institutrice *f*; (*secondary*) professeur *m*

schoolteacher ['skuːltiːtʃəʳ] *n* (*primary*) instituteur(-trice); (*secondary*) professeur *m*

science ['saɪəns] *n* science *f*; **the ~s** les sciences; (*Scol*) les matières *fpl* scientifiques

science fiction *n* science-fiction *f*

scientific [saɪən'tɪfɪk] *adj* scientifique

scientist ['saɪəntɪst] *n* scientifique *m/f*; (*eminent*) savant *m*

sci-fi ['saɪfaɪ] *n abbr* (*inf*: = *science fiction*) SF *f*

scissors ['sɪzəz] *npl* ciseaux *mpl*; **a pair of ~** une paire de ciseaux

scoff [skɔf] *vt* (*Brit inf: eat*) avaler, bouffer ▷ *vi*: **to ~ (at)** (*mock*) se moquer (de)

scold [skəʊld] *vt* gronder, attraper, réprimander

scone [skɔn] *n* sorte de petit pain rond au lait

scoop [skuːp] *n* pelle *f* (à main); (*for ice cream*) boule *f* à glace; (*Press*) reportage exclusif *or* à sensation; **scoop out** *vt* évider, creuser; **scoop up** *vt* ramasser

scooter ['skuːtəʳ] *n* (*motor cycle*) scooter *m*; (*toy*) trottinette *f*

scope [skəʊp] *n* (*capacity: of plan, undertaking*) portée *f*, envergure *f*; (: *of person*) compétence *f*, capacités *fpl*; (*opportunity*) possibilités *fpl*; **within the ~ of** dans les limites de; **there is plenty of ~ for improvement** (*Brit*) cela pourrait être beaucoup mieux

scorch [skɔːtʃ] *vt* (*clothes*) brûler (légèrement), roussir; (*earth, grass*) dessécher, brûler

scorching ['skɔːtʃɪŋ] *adj* torride, brûlant(e)

score [skɔːʳ] *n* score *m*, décompte *m* des points; (*Mus*) partition *f* ▷ *vt* (*goal, point*) marquer; (*success*) remporter; (*cut: leather, wood, card*) entailler, inciser ▷ *vi* marquer des points; (*Football*) marquer un but; (*keep score*) compter les points; **on that ~** sur ce chapitre, à cet égard; **to have an old ~ to settle with sb** (*fig*) avoir un (vieux) compte à régler avec qn; **a ~ of** (*twenty*) vingt; **~s of** (*fig*) des tas de; **to ~ 6 out of 10** obtenir 6 sur 10; **score out** *vt* rayer, barrer, biffer

scoreboard ['skɔːbɔːd] *n* tableau *m*

scorer ['skɔːrəʳ] *n* (*Football*) auteur *m* du but; buteur *m*; (*keeping score*) marqueur *m*

scorn [skɔːn] *n* mépris *m*, dédain *m* ▷ *vt* mépriser, dédaigner

Scorpio ['skɔːpɪəu] *n* le Scorpion; **to be ~** être du Scorpion

scorpion ['skɔːpɪən] *n* scorpion *m*

Scot [skɔt] *n* Écossais(e)

Scotch [skɔtʃ] *n* whisky *m*, scotch *m*

scotch [skɔtʃ] *vt* faire échouer; enrayer; étouffer

Scotch tape® (*US*) *n* scotch® *m*, ruban adhésif

scot-free ['skɔt'friː] *adj*: **to get off ~** s'en tirer sans être puni(e); s'en sortir indemne

Scotland ['skɔtlənd] *n* Écosse *f*

Scots [skɔts] *adj* écossais(e)

Scotsman ['skɔtsmən] *irreg n* Écossais *m*

Scotswoman ['skɔtswumən] *irreg n* Écossaise *f*

Scottish ['skɔtɪʃ] *adj* écossais(e); **the ~ National Party** le parti national écossais; **the ~ Parliament** le Parlement écossais

scoundrel ['skaundrl] *n* vaurien *m*

scour ['skauəʳ] *vt* (*clean*) récurer; frotter; décaper; (*search*) battre, parcourir

scout [skaut] *n* (*Mil*) éclaireur *m*; (*also*: **boy ~**) scout *m*; **girl ~** (*US*) guide *f*; **scout around** *vi* chercher

scowl [skaul] *vi* se renfrogner, avoir l'air maussade; **to ~ at** regarder de travers

scrabble ['skræbl] *vi* (*claw*): **to ~ (at)** gratter; **to ~ about** *or* **around for sth** chercher qch à tâtons ▷ *n*: **S~®** Scrabble® *m*

scram [skræm] *vi* (*inf*) ficher le camp

scramble ['skræmbl] *n* (*rush*) bousculade *f*, ruée *f* ▷ *vi* grimper/descendre tant bien que mal; **to ~ for** se bousculer *or* se disputer pour (avoir); **to go scrambling** (*Sport*) faire du trial

scrambled eggs ['skræmbld-] *npl* œufs brouillés

scrap [skræp] *n* bout *m*, morceau *m*; (*fight*) bagarre *f*; (*also*: **~ iron**) ferraille *f* ▷ *vt* jeter, mettre au rebut; (*fig*) abandonner, laisser tomber ▷ *vi* se bagarrer; **scraps** *npl* (*waste*) déchets *mpl*; **to sell sth for ~** vendre qch à la casse *or* à la ferraille

scrapbook ['skræpbuk] *n* album *m*

scrap dealer *n* marchand *m* de ferraille

scrape [skreɪp] *vt*, *vi* gratter, racler ▷ *n*: **to get into a ~** s'attirer des ennuis; **scrape through** *vi* (*exam etc*) réussir de justesse; **scrape together** *vt* (*money*) racler ses fonds de tiroir pour réunir

scrap heap *n* tas *m* de ferraille; (*fig*): **on the ~** au rancart *or* rebut

scrap merchant *n* (*Brit*) marchand *m* de ferraille

scrap paper *n* papier *m* brouillon

scratch [skrætʃ] *n* égratignure *f*, rayure *f*; (*on paint*) éraflure *f*; (*from claw*) coup *m* de griffe ▷ *adj*: **~ team** équipe de fortune *or* improvisée ▷ *vt* (*rub*) (se) gratter; (*record*) rayer; (*paint etc*) érafler; (*with claw, nail*) griffer; (*Comput*) effacer ▷ *vi* (se) gratter; **to start from ~** partir de zéro; **to be up to ~** être à la hauteur

scratch card *n* carte *f* à gratter

scrawl [skrɔːl] *n* gribouillage *m* ▷ *vi* gribouiller

scrawny ['skrɔːnɪ] *adj* décharné(e)

scream [skriːm] *n* cri perçant, hurlement *m* ▷ *vi* crier, hurler; **to be a ~** (*inf*) être impayable; **to ~ at sb to do sth** crier *or* hurler à qn de faire qch

screech [skriːtʃ] *n* cri strident, hurlement *m*; (*of tyres, brakes*) crissement *m*, grincement *m* ▷ *vi* hurler; crisser, grincer

screen [skriːn] *n* écran *m*; (*in room*) paravent *m*; (*Cine, TV*) écran; (*fig*) écran, rideau *m* ▷ *vt* masquer, cacher; (*from the wind etc*) abriter, protéger; (*film*) projeter; (*candidates etc*) filtrer; (*for illness*): **to ~ sb for sth** faire subir un test de dépistage de qch à qn

screening ['skriːnɪŋ] *n* (*of film*) projection *f*; (*Med*) test *m* (*or* tests) de dépistage; (*for security*) filtrage *m*

screenplay ['skriːnpleɪ] *n* scénario *m*

screen saver *n* (*Comput*) économiseur *m* d'écran

screw [skruː] *n* vis *f*; (*propeller*) hélice *f* ▷ *vt* (*also*: **~ in**) visser; (*inf!: woman*) baiser (!); **to ~ sth to the wall** visser qch au mur; **to have one's head ~ed on** (*fig*) avoir la tête sur les épaules; **screw up** *vt* (*paper etc*) froisser; (*inf: ruin*) bousiller; **to ~ up one's eyes** se plisser les yeux; **to ~ up one's face** faire la grimace

screwdriver ['skruːdraɪvəʳ] *n* tournevis *m*

scribble ['skrɪbl] *n* gribouillage *m* ▷ *vt* gribouiller, griffonner; **to ~ sth down** griffonner qch

script [skrɪpt] *n* (*Cine etc*) scénario *m*, texte *m*; (*in exam*) copie *f*; (*writing*) (écriture *f*) script *m*

Scripture ['skrɪptʃəʳ] *n* Écriture sainte

scroll [skrəul] *n* rouleau *m* ▷ *vt* (*Comput*) faire défiler (sur l'écran)

scrounge [skraundʒ] (*inf*) *vt*: **to ~ sth (off** *or* **from sb)** se faire payer qch (par qn), emprunter qch (à qn) ▷ *vi*: **to ~ on sb** vivre aux crochets de qn

scrounger ['skraundʒəʳ] *n* parasite *m*

scrub [skrʌb] n (clean) nettoyage m (à la brosse); (land) broussailles fpl ▷ vt (floor) nettoyer à la brosse; (pan) récurer; (washing) frotter; (reject) annuler

scruff [skrʌf] n: **by the ~ of the neck** par la peau du cou

scruffy ['skrʌfɪ] adj débraillé(e)

scrum [skrʌm], **scrummage** ['skrʌmɪdʒ] n mêlée f

scruple ['skru:pl] n scrupule m; **to have no ~s about doing sth** n'avoir aucun scrupule à faire qch

scrutiny ['skru:tɪnɪ] n examen minutieux; **under the ~ of sb** sous la surveillance de qn

scuba diving ['sku:bə-] n plongée sous-marine

scuff [skʌf] vt érafler

scuffle ['skʌfl] n échauffourée f, rixe f

sculptor ['skʌlptə'] n sculpteur m

sculpture ['skʌlptʃə'] n sculpture f

scum [skʌm] n écume f, mousse f; (pej: people) rebut m, lie f

scurry ['skʌrɪ] vi filer à toute allure; **to ~ off** détaler, se sauver

scuttle ['skʌtl] n (Naut) écoutille f; (also: **coal ~**) seau m (à charbon) ▷ vt (ship) saborder ▷ vi (scamper): **to ~ away, ~ off** détaler

scythe [saɪð] n faux f

sea [si:] n mer f ▷ cpd marin(e), de (la) mer, maritime; **on the ~** (boat) en mer; (town) au bord de la mer; **by** or **beside the ~** (holiday, town) au bord de la mer; **by ~** par mer, en bateau; **out to ~** au large; **(out) at ~** en mer; **heavy** or **rough ~(s)** grosse mer, mer agitée; **a ~ of faces** (fig) une multitude de visages; **to be all at ~** (fig) nager complètement

seaboard ['si:bɔ:d] n côte f

seafood ['si:fu:d] n fruits mpl de mer

sea front ['si:frʌnt] n bord m de mer

seagoing ['si:gəuɪŋ] adj (ship) de haute mer

seagull ['si:gʌl] n mouette f

seal [si:l] n (animal) phoque m; (stamp) sceau m, cachet m; (impression) cachet, estampille f ▷ vt sceller; (envelope) coller; (: with seal) cacheter; (decide: sb's fate) décider (de); (: bargain) conclure; **~ of approval** approbation f; **seal off** vt (close) condamner; (forbid entry to) interdire l'accès de

sea level n niveau m de la mer

sea lion n lion m de mer

seam [si:m] n couture f; (of coal) veine f, filon m; **the hall was bursting at the ~s** la salle était pleine à craquer

seaman ['si:mən] irreg n marin m

seance ['seɪɔns] n séance f de spiritisme

seaplane ['si:pleɪn] n hydravion m

search [sə:tʃ] n (for person, thing, Comput) recherche(s) f(pl); (of drawer, pockets) fouille f; (Law: at sb's home) perquisition f ▷ vt fouiller; (examine) examiner minutieusement; scruter ▷ vi: **to ~ for** chercher; **in ~ of** à la recherche de; **search through** vt fus fouiller

search engine n (Comput) moteur m de recherche

searching ['sə:tʃɪŋ] adj (look, question) pénétrant(e); (examination) minutieux(-euse)

searchlight ['sə:tʃlaɪt] n projecteur m

search party n expédition f de secours

search warrant n mandat m de perquisition

seashore ['si:ʃɔ:'] n rivage m, plage f, bord m de (la) mer; **on the ~** sur le rivage

seasick ['si:sɪk] adj: **to be ~** avoir le mal de mer

seaside ['si:saɪd] n bord m de mer

seaside resort n station f balnéaire

season ['si:zn] n saison f ▷ vt assaisonner, relever; **to be in/out of ~** être/ne pas être de saison; **the busy ~** (for shops) la période de pointe; (for hotels etc) la pleine saison; **the open ~** (Hunting) la saison de la chasse

seasonal ['si:zənl] adj saisonnier(-ière)

seasoned ['si:znd] adj (wood) séché(e); (fig: worker, actor, troops) expérimenté(e); **a ~ campaigner** un vieux militant, un vétéran

seasoning ['si:znɪŋ] n assaisonnement m

season ticket n carte f d'abonnement

seat [si:t] n siège m; (in bus, train: place) place f; (Parliament) siège; (buttocks) postérieur m; (of trousers) fond m ▷ vt faire asseoir, placer; (have room for) avoir des places assises pour, pouvoir accueillir; **are there any ~s left?** est-ce qu'il reste des places?; **to take one's ~** prendre place; **to be ~ed** être assis; **please be ~ed** veuillez vous asseoir

seat belt n ceinture f de sécurité

seating ['si:tɪŋ] n sièges fpl, places assises

sea water n eau f de mer

seaweed ['si:wi:d] n algues fpl

seaworthy ['si:wə:ðɪ] adj en état de naviguer

sec. abbr (= second) sec

secluded [sɪ'klu:dɪd] adj retiré(e), à l'écart

seclusion [sɪ'klu:ʒən] n solitude f

second¹ ['sɛkənd] num deuxième, second(e) ▷ adv (in race etc) en seconde position ▷ n (unit of time) seconde f; (Aut: also: **~ gear**) seconde; (in series, position) deuxième m/f, second(e); (Comm: imperfect) article m de second choix; (Brit Scol) ≈ licence f avec mention ▷ vt (motion) appuyer; **seconds** npl (inf: food) rab m (inf); **Charles the S~** Charles II; **just a ~!** une seconde!, un instant!; (stopping sb) pas si vite!; **~ floor** (Brit) deuxième (étage) m; (US) premier (étage) m; **to ask for a ~ opinion** (Med) demander l'avis d'un autre médecin

second² [sɪ'kɔnd] vt (employee) détacher, mettre en détachement

secondary ['sɛkəndərɪ] adj secondaire

secondary school n (age 11 to 15) collège m; (age 15 to 18) lycée m

second-class ['sɛkənd'klɑ:s] adj de deuxième classe; (Rail) de seconde (classe); (Post) au tarif réduit; (pej) de qualité inférieure ▷ adv (Rail) en seconde; (Post) au tarif réduit; ~ **citizen** citoyen(ne) de deuxième classe

second hand n (on clock) trotteuse f
secondhand ['sɛkənd'hænd] adj d'occasion; (information) de seconde main ▷ adv (buy) d'occasion; **to hear sth** ~ apprendre qch indirectement

secondly ['sɛkəndlɪ] adv deuxièmement; **firstly** ... ~ ... d'abord ... ensuite ... or de plus ...

secondment [sɪ'kɔndmənt] n (Brit) détachement m

second-rate ['sɛkənd'reɪt] adj de deuxième ordre, de qualité inférieure

second thoughts npl: **to have** ~ changer d'avis; **on** ~ or **thought** (US) à la réflexion

secrecy ['si:krəsɪ] n secret m; **in** ~ en secret

secret ['si:krɪt] adj secret(-ète) ▷ n secret m; **in** ~ adv en secret, secrètement, en cachette; **to keep sth** ~ **from sb** cacher qch à qn, ne pas révéler qch à qn; **to make no** ~ **of sth** ne pas cacher qch; **keep it** ~ n'en parle à personne

secretary ['sɛkrətrɪ] n secrétaire m/f; (Comm) secrétaire général; **S**~ **of State** (US Pol) ≈ ministre m des Affaires étrangères; **S**~ **of State (for)** (Brit Pol) ministre m (de)

secretive ['si:krətɪv] adj réservé(e); (pej) cachottier(-ière), dissimulé(e)

secretly ['si:krɪtlɪ] adv en secret, secrètement, en cachette

secret service n services secrets

sect [sɛkt] n secte f

sectarian [sɛk'tɛərɪən] adj sectaire

section ['sɛkʃən] n section f; (department) section; (Comm) rayon m; (of document) section, article m, paragraphe m; (cut) coupe f ▷ vt sectionner; **the business** etc ~ (Press) la page des affaires etc

sector ['sɛktə'] n secteur m

secular ['sɛkjulə'] adj laïque

secure [sɪ'kjuə'] adj (free from anxiety) sans inquiétude, sécurisé(e); (firmly fixed) solide, bien attaché(e) (or fermé(e) etc); (in safe place) en lieu sûr, en sûreté ▷ vt (fix) fixer, attacher; (get) obtenir, se procurer; (Comm: loan) garantir; **to make sth** ~ bien fixer or attacher qch; **to** ~ **sth for sb** obtenir qch pour qn, procurer qch à qn

security [sɪ'kjuərɪtɪ] n sécurité f, mesures fpl de sécurité; (for loan) caution f, garantie f; **securities** npl (Stock Exchange) valeurs fpl, titres mpl; **to increase** or **tighten** ~ renforcer les mesures de sécurité; ~ **of tenure** stabilité f d'un emploi, titularisation f

security guard n garde chargé de la sécurité; (transporting money) convoyeur m de fonds

sedan [sə'dæn] n (US Aut) berline f

sedate [sɪ'deɪt] adj calme; posé(e) ▷ vt donner des sédatifs à

sedative ['sɛdɪtɪv] n calmant m, sédatif m

seduce [sɪ'dju:s] vt séduire

seduction [sɪ'dʌkʃən] n séduction f

seductive [sɪ'dʌktɪv] adj séduisant(e); (smile) séducteur(-trice); (fig: offer) alléchant(e)

see [si:] (pt **saw**, pp **seen**) [sɔ:, si:n] vt (gen) voir; (accompany): **to** ~ **sb to the door** reconduire or raccompagner qn jusqu'à la porte ▷ vi voir ▷ n évêché m; **to** ~ **that** (ensure) veiller à ce que + sub, faire en sorte que + sub, s'assurer que; **there was nobody to be** ~**n** il n'y avait pas un chat; **let me** ~ (show me) fais(-moi) voir; (let me think) voyons (un peu); **to go and** ~ **sb** aller voir qn; ~ **for yourself** voyez vous-même; **I don't know what she** ~**s in him** je ne sais pas ce qu'elle lui trouve; **as far as I can** ~ pour autant que je puisse en juger; ~ **you!** au revoir!, à bientôt!; ~ **you soon/later/tomorrow!** à bientôt/plus tard/demain!; **see about** vt fus (deal with) s'occuper de; **see off** vt accompagner (à l'aéroport etc); **see out** vt (take to door) raccompagner à la porte; **see through** vt mener à bonne fin ▷ vt fus voir clair dans; **see to** vt fus s'occuper de, se charger de

seed [si:d] n graine f; (fig) germe m; (Tennis etc) tête f de série; **to go to** ~ (plant) monter en graine; (fig) se laisser aller

seedling ['si:dlɪŋ] n jeune plant m, semis m

seedy ['si:dɪ] adj (shabby) minable, miteux(-euse)

seeing ['si:ɪŋ] conj: ~ **(that)** vu que, étant donné que

seek [si:k] (pt, pp **sought**) [sɔ:t] vt chercher, rechercher; **to** ~ **advice/help from sb** demander conseil/de l'aide à qn; **seek out** vt (person) chercher

seem [si:m] vi sembler, paraître; **there** ~**s to be** ... il semble qu'il y a ..., on dirait qu'il y a ...; **it** ~**s (that)** ... il semble que ...; **what** ~**s to be the trouble?** qu'est-ce qui ne va pas?

seemingly ['si:mɪŋlɪ] adv apparemment

seen [si:n] pp of **see**

seep [si:p] vi suinter, filtrer

seesaw ['si:sɔ:] n (jeu m de) bascule f

seethe [si:ð] vi être en effervescence; **to** ~ **with anger** bouillir de colère

see-through ['si:θru:] adj transparent(e)

segment ['sɛgmənt] n segment m; (of orange) quartier m

segregate ['sɛgrɪgeɪt] vt séparer, isoler

Seine [seɪn] n: **the (River)** ~ la Seine

seize [si:z] vt (grasp) saisir, attraper; (take possession of) s'emparer de; (opportunity) saisir; (Law) saisir; **seize on** vt fus saisir, sauter sur; **seize up** vi (Tech) se gripper; **seize upon** vt fus = **seize on**

seizure ['si:ʒə'] n (Med) crise f, attaque f; (of power) prise f; (Law) saisie f

seldom ['sɛldəm] adv rarement

select [sɪ'lɛkt] adj choisi(e), d'élite; (hotel, restaurant, club) chic inv, sélect inv ▷ vt

sélectionner, choisir; **a ~ few** quelques
privilégiés

selection [sɪˈlɛkʃən] *n* sélection *f*, choix *m*

selective [sɪˈlɛktɪv] *adj* sélectif(-ive); (*school*)
à recrutement sélectif

self (*pl* **selves**) [sɛlf, sɛlvz] *n*: **the ~** le moi *inv*
▷ *prefix* auto-

self-assured [sɛlfəˈʃʊəd] *adj* sûr(e) de soi,
plein(e) d'assurance

self-catering [sɛlfˈkeɪtərɪŋ] *adj* (*Brit: flat*)
avec cuisine, où l'on peut faire sa cuisine;
(*: holiday*) en appartement (*or* chalet *etc*) loué

self-centred, (*US*) **self-centered**
[sɛlfˈsɛntəd] *adj* égocentrique

self-confidence [sɛlfˈkɒnfɪdns] *n* confiance
f en soi

self-confident [sɛlfˈkɒnfɪdnt] *adj* sûr(e) de
soi, plein(e) d'assurance

self-conscious [sɛlfˈkɒnʃəs] *adj* timide, qui
manque d'assurance

self-contained [sɛlfkənˈteɪnd] *adj* (*Brit: flat*)
avec entrée particulière, indépendant(e)

self-control [sɛlfkənˈtrəʊl] *n* maîtrise *f* de
soi

self-defence, (*US*) **self-defense** [sɛlfdɪˈfɛns]
n autodéfense *f*; (*Law*) légitime défense *f*

self-discipline [sɛlfˈdɪsɪplɪn] *n* discipline
personnelle

self-drive [sɛlfˈdraɪv] *adj* (*Brit*): **~ car** voiture *f*
de location

self-employed [sɛlfɪmˈplɔɪd] *adj* qui
travaille à son compte

self-esteem [sɛlfɪˈstiːm] *n* amour-propre *m*

self-evident [sɛlfˈɛvɪdnt] *adj* évident(e), qui
va de soi

self-governing [sɛlfˈɡʌvənɪŋ] *adj* autonome

self-indulgent [sɛlfɪnˈdʌldʒənt] *adj* qui ne se
refuse rien

self-interest [sɛlfˈɪntrɪst] *n* intérêt
personnel

selfish [ˈsɛlfɪʃ] *adj* égoïste

selfishness [ˈsɛlfɪʃnɪs] *n* égoïsme *m*

selfless [ˈsɛlflɪs] *adj* désintéressé(e)

self-pity [sɛlfˈpɪtɪ] *n* apitoiement *m* sur soi-
même

self-possessed [sɛlfpəˈzɛst] *adj* assuré(e)

self-preservation [ˈsɛlfprɛzəˈveɪʃən] *n*
instinct *m* de conservation

self-raising [sɛlfˈreɪzɪŋ], (*US*) **self-rising**
[sɛlfˈraɪzɪŋ] *adj*: **~ flour** farine *f* pour gâteaux
(*avec levure incorporée*)

self-respect [sɛlfrɪsˈpɛkt] *n* respect *m* de soi,
amour-propre *m*

self-righteous [sɛlfˈraɪtʃəs] *adj* satisfait(e)
de soi, pharisaïque

self-sacrifice [sɛlfˈsækrɪfaɪs] *n* abnégation *f*

self-satisfied [sɛlfˈsætɪsfaɪd] *adj* content(e)
de soi, suffisant(e)

self-service [sɛlfˈsəːvɪs] *adj, n* libre-service
(*m*), self-service (*m*)

self-sufficient [sɛlfsəˈfɪʃnt] *adj*
indépendant(e)

self-taught [sɛlfˈtɔːt] *adj* autodidacte

sell (*pt, pp* **sold**) [sɛl, səʊld] *vt* vendre ▷ *vi* se
vendre; **to ~ at** *or* **for 10 euros** se vendre 10
euros; **to ~ sb an idea** (*fig*) faire accepter une
idée à qn; **sell off** *vt* liquider; **sell out** *vi*: **to ~
out (of sth)** (*use up stock*) vendre tout son
stock (de qch); ▷ *vt* **to ~ out (to)** (*Comm*) vendre
son fonds *or* son affaire (à) ▷ *vt* vendre tout
son stock de; **the tickets are all sold out** il
ne reste plus de billets; **sell up** *vi* vendre son
fonds *or* son affaire

sell-by date [ˈsɛlbaɪ-] *n* date *f* limite de vente

seller [ˈsɛlə^r] *n* vendeur(-euse), marchand(e);
~'s market marché *m* à la hausse

selling price [ˈsɛlɪŋ-] *n* prix *m* de vente

Sellotape® [ˈsɛləʊteɪp] *n* (*Brit*) scotch® *m*

selves [sɛlvz] *npl of* **self**

semblance [ˈsɛmblns] *n* semblant *m*

semen [ˈsiːmən] *n* sperme *m*

semester [sɪˈmɛstə^r] *n* (*esp US*) semestre *m*

semi... [ˈsɛmɪ] *prefix* semi-, demi-; à demi, à
moitié ▷ *n*: **semi = semidetached house**

semicircle [ˈsɛmɪsəːkl] *n* demi-cercle *m*

semicolon [sɛmɪˈkəʊlən] *n* point-virgule *m*

semidetached [sɛmɪdɪˈtætʃt],
semidetached house *n* (*Brit*) maison
jumelée *or* jumelle

semi-final [sɛmɪˈfaɪnl] *n* demi-finale *f*

seminar [ˈsɛmɪnɑː^r] *n* séminaire *m*

seminary [ˈsɛmɪnərɪ] *n* (*Rel: for priests*)
séminaire *m*

semiskilled [sɛmɪˈskɪld] *adj*: **~ worker**
ouvrier(-ière) spécialisé(e)

semi-skimmed [ˈsɛmɪˈskɪmd] *adj* demi-
écrémé(e)

senate [ˈsɛnɪt] *n* sénat *m*; (*US*): **the S~** le
Sénat; *voir article*

⊚ **SENATE**

⊚ Le *Senate* est la chambre haute du
⊚ "Congress", le parlement des États-Unis.
⊚ Il est composé de 100 sénateurs, 2 par
⊚ État, élus au suffrage universel direct
⊚ tous les 6 ans, un tiers d'entre eux étant
⊚ renouvelé tous les 2 ans.

senator [ˈsɛnɪtə^r] *n* sénateur *m*

send (*pt, pp* **sent**) [sɛnd, sɛnt] *vt* envoyer; **to ~
by post** *or* (*US*) **mail** envoyer *or* expédier par
la poste; **to ~ sb for sth** envoyer qn chercher
qch; **to ~ word that ...** faire dire que ...; **she
~s (you) her love** elle vous adresse ses
amitiés; **to ~ sb to Coventry** (*Brit*) mettre qn
en quarantaine; **to ~ sb to sleep** endormir
qn; **to ~ sb into fits of laughter** faire rire qn
aux éclats; **to ~ sth flying** envoyer valser qch;
send away *vt* (*letter, goods*) envoyer, expédier;
send away for *vt fus* commander par
correspondance, se faire envoyer; **send back**
vt renvoyer; **send for** *vt fus* envoyer chercher;
faire venir; (*by post*) se faire envoyer,

commander par correspondance; **send in** vt (*report, application, resignation*) remettre; **send off** vt (*goods*) envoyer, expédier; (*Brit Sport: player*) expulser or renvoyer du terrain; **send on** vt (*Brit: letter*) faire suivre; (*luggage etc: in advance*) (faire) expédier à l'avance; **send out** vt (*invitation*) envoyer (par la poste); (*emit: light, heat, signal*) émettre; **send round** vt (*letter, document etc*) faire circuler; **send up** vt (*person, price*) faire monter; (*Brit: parody*) mettre en boîte, parodier

sender ['sɛndər] n expéditeur(-trice)

send-off ['sɛndɔf] n: **a good ~** des adieux chaleureux

senile ['si:naɪl] adj sénile

senior ['si:nɪər] adj (*older*) aîné(e), plus âgé(e); (*high-ranking*) de haut niveau; (*of higher rank*): **to be ~ to sb** être le supérieur de qn ▷ n (*older*): **she is 15 years his ~** elle est son aînée de 15 ans, elle est plus âgée que lui de 15 ans; (*in service*) personne f qui a plus d'ancienneté; **P. Jones ~** P. Jones père

senior citizen n personne f du troisième âge

senior high school n (*US*) ≈ lycée m

seniority [si:nɪˈɔrɪti] n priorité f d'âge, ancienneté f; (*in rank*) supériorité f (hiérarchique)

sensation [sɛnˈseɪʃən] n sensation f; **to create a ~** faire sensation

sensational [sɛnˈseɪʃənl] adj qui fait sensation; (*marvellous*) sensationnel(le)

sense [sɛns] n sens m; (*feeling*) sentiment m; (*meaning*) sens, signification f; (*wisdom*) bon sens ▷ vt sentir, pressentir; **senses** npl raison f; **it makes ~** c'est logique; **there is no ~ in (doing) that** cela n'a pas de sens; **to come to one's ~s** (*regain consciousness*) reprendre conscience; (*become reasonable*) revenir à la raison; **to take leave of one's ~s** perdre la tête

senseless ['sɛnslɪs] adj insensé(e), stupide; (*unconscious*) sans connaissance

sense of humour, (*US*) **sense of humor** n sens m de l'humour

sensible ['sɛnsɪbl] adj sensé(e), raisonnable; (*shoes etc*) pratique

sensitive ['sɛnsɪtɪv] adj: **~ (to)** sensible (à); **he is very ~ about it** c'est un point très sensible (chez lui)

sensual ['sɛnsjuəl] adj sensuel(le)

sensuous ['sɛnsjuəs] adj voluptueux(-euse), sensuel(le)

sent [sɛnt] pt, pp of **send**

sentence ['sɛntns] n (*Ling*) phrase f; (*Law: judgment*) condamnation f, sentence f; (*: punishment*) peine f ▷ vt: **to ~ sb to death/to 5 years** condamner qn à mort/à 5 ans; **to pass ~ on sb** prononcer une peine contre qn

sentiment ['sɛntɪmənt] n sentiment m; (*opinion*) opinion f, avis m

sentimental [sɛntɪˈmɛntl] adj sentimental(e)

sentry ['sɛntrɪ] n sentinelle f, factionnaire m

separate [adj 'sɛprɪt, vb 'sɛpəreɪt] adj séparé(e); (*organization*) indépendant(e); (*day, occasion, issue*) différent(e) ▷ vt séparer; (*distinguish*) distinguer ▷ vi se séparer; **~ from** distinct(e) de; **under ~ cover** (*Comm*) sous pli séparé; **to ~ into** diviser en

separately ['sɛprɪtlɪ] adv séparément

separates ['sɛprɪts] npl (*clothes*) coordonnés mpl

separation [sɛpəˈreɪʃən] n séparation f

September [sɛpˈtɛmbər] n septembre m; see also **July**

septic ['sɛptɪk] adj septique; (*wound*) infecté(e); **to go ~** s'infecter

septic tank n fosse f septique

sequel ['si:kwl] n conséquence f; séquelles fpl; (*of story*) suite f

sequence ['si:kwəns] n ordre m, suite f; (*in film*) séquence f; (*dance*) numéro m; **in ~** par ordre, dans l'ordre, les uns après les autres; **~ of tenses** concordance f des temps

sequin ['si:kwɪn] n paillette f

Serb [sə:b] adj, n = **Serbian**

Serbia ['sə:bɪə] n Serbie f

Serbian ['sə:bɪən] adj serbe ▷ n Serbe m/f; (*Ling*) serbe m

serene [sɪˈri:n] adj serein(e), calme, paisible

sergeant ['sɑ:dʒənt] n sergent m; (*Police*) brigadier m

serial ['sɪərɪəl] n feuilleton m ▷ adj (*Comput: interface, printer*) série inv; (*: access*) séquentiel(le)

serial killer n meurtrier m tuant en série

serial number n numéro m de série

series ['sɪərɪz] n série f; (*Publishing*) collection f

serious ['sɪərɪəs] adj sérieux(-euse); (*accident etc*) grave; **are you ~ (about it)?** parlez-vous sérieusement?

seriously ['sɪərɪəslɪ] adv sérieusement; (*hurt*) gravement; **~ rich/difficult** (*inf: extremely*) drôlement riche/difficile; **to take sth/sb ~** prendre qch/qn au sérieux

sermon ['sə:mən] n sermon m

serrated [sɪˈreɪtɪd] adj en dents de scie

servant ['sə:vənt] n domestique m/f; (*fig*) serviteur/servante

serve [sə:v] vt (*employer etc*) servir, être au service de; (*purpose*) servir à; (*customer, food, meal*) servir; (*subj: train*) desservir; (*apprenticeship*) faire, accomplir; (*prison term*) faire; purger ▷ vi (*Tennis*) servir; (*be useful*): **to ~ as/for/to do** servir de/à/à faire ▷ n (*Tennis*) service m; **are you being ~d?** est-ce qu'on s'occupe de vous?; **to ~ on a committee/jury** faire partie d'un comité/jury; **it ~s him right** c'est bien fait pour lui; **it ~s my purpose** cela fait mon affaire; **serve out**, **serve up** vt (*food*) servir

server [sə:və'] n (*Comput*) serveur m

service ['sə:vɪs] n (*gen*) service m; (*Aut*) révision f; (*Rel*) office m ▷ vt (*car etc*) réviser;

services npl (Econ: tertiary sector) (secteur m) tertiaire m, secteur des services; (Brit: on motorway) station-service f; (Mil): **the S~s** npl les forces armées; **to be of ~ to sb, to do sb a ~** rendre service à qn; **~ included/not included** service compris/non compris; **to put one's car in for ~** donner sa voiture à réviser; **dinner ~** service de table

serviceable ['sə:vɪsəbl] adj pratique, commode

service area n (on motorway) aire f de services

service charge n (Brit) service m

serviceman ['sə:vɪsmən] irreg n militaire m

service station n station-service f

serviette [sə:vɪ'ɛt] n (Brit) serviette f (de table)

session ['sefən] n (sitting) séance f; (Scol) année f scolaire (or universitaire); **to be in ~** siéger, être en session or en séance

set [sɛt] (pt, pp set) n série f, assortiment m; (of tools etc) jeu m; (Radio, TV) poste m; (Tennis) set m; (group of people) cercle m, milieu m; (Cine) plateau m; (Theat: stage) scène f; (: scenery) décor m; (Math) ensemble m; (Hairdressing) mise f en plis ▷ adj (fixed) fixe, déterminé(e); (ready) prêt(e) ▷ vt (place) mettre, poser, placer; (fix, establish) fixer; (: record) établir; (assign: task, homework) donner; (exam) composer; (adjust) régler; (decide: rules etc) fixer, choisir; (Typ) composer ▷ vi (sun) se coucher; (jam, jelly, concrete) prendre; (bone) se ressouder; **to be ~ on doing** être résolu(e) à faire; **to be all ~ to do** être (fin) prêt(e) pour faire; **to be (dead) ~ against** être (totalement) opposé à; **he's ~ in his ways** il n'est pas très souple, il tient à ses habitudes; **to ~ to music** mettre en musique; **to ~ on fire** mettre le feu à; **to ~ free** libérer; **to ~ sth going** déclencher qch; **to ~ the alarm clock for seven o'clock** mettre le réveil à sonner à sept heures; **to ~ sail** partir, prendre la mer; **a ~ phrase** une expression toute faite, une locution; **a ~ of false teeth** un dentier; **a ~ of dining-room furniture** une salle à manger; **set about** vt fus (task) entreprendre, se mettre à; **to ~ about doing sth** se mettre à faire qch; **set aside** vt mettre de côté; (time) garder; **set back** vt (in time): **to ~ back (by)** retarder (de); (place): **a house ~ back from the road** une maison située en retrait de la route; **set down** vt (subj: bus, train) déposer; **set in** vi (infection, bad weather) s'installer; (complications) survenir, surgir; **the rain has ~ in for the day** c'est parti pour qu'il pleuve toute la journée; **set off** vi se mettre en route, partir ▷ vt (bomb) faire exploser; (cause to start) déclencher; (show up well) mettre en valeur, faire valoir; **set out** vi: **to ~ out (from)** partir (de) ▷ vt (arrange) disposer; (state) présenter, exposer; **to ~ out to do** entreprendre de faire; avoir pour but or intention de faire; **set up** vt (organization)

fonder, créer; (monument) ériger; **to ~ up shop** (fig) s'établir, s'installer

setback ['sɛtbæk] n (hitch) revers m, contretemps m; (in health) rechute f

set menu n menu m

settee [sɛ'ti:] n canapé m

setting ['sɛtɪŋ] n cadre m; (of jewel) monture f; (position: of controls) réglage m

settle ['sɛtl] vt (argument, matter, account) régler; (problem) résoudre; (Med: calm) calmer; (colonize: land) coloniser ▷ vi (bird, dust etc) se poser; (sediment) se déposer; **to ~ to sth** se mettre sérieusement à qch; **to ~ for sth** accepter qch, se contenter de qch; **to ~ on sth** opter or se décider pour qch; **that's ~d then** alors, c'est d'accord!; **to ~ one's stomach** calmer des maux d'estomac; **settle down** vi (get comfortable) s'installer; (become calmer) se calmer; se ranger; **settle in** vi s'installer; **settle up** vi: **to ~ up with sb** régler (ce que l'on doit à) qn

settlement ['sɛtlmənt] n (payment) règlement m; (agreement) accord m; (colony) colonie f; (village etc) village m, hameau m; **in ~ of our account** (Comm) en règlement de notre compte

settler ['sɛtlə'] n colon m

setup ['sɛtʌp] n (arrangement) manière f dont les choses sont organisées; (situation) situation f, allure f des choses

seven ['sɛvn] num sept

seventeen [sɛvn'ti:n] num dix-sept

seventeenth [sɛvn'ti:nθ] num dix-septième

seventh ['sɛvnθ] num septième

seventieth ['sɛvntɪɪθ] num soixante-dixième

seventy ['sɛvntɪ] num soixante-dix

sever ['sɛvə'] vt couper, trancher; (relations) rompre

several ['sɛvərl] adj, pron plusieurs pl; **~ of us** plusieurs d'entre nous; **~ times** plusieurs fois

severance ['sɛvərəns] n (of relations) rupture f

severance pay n indemnité f de licenciement

severe [sɪ'vɪə'] adj (stern) sévère, strict(e); (serious) grave, sérieux(-euse); (hard) rigoureux(-euse), dur(e); (plain) sévère, austère

severity [sɪ'vɛrɪtɪ] n sévérité f; gravité f; rigueur f

sew (pt **sewed**, pp **sewn**) [səu, səud, səun] vt, vi coudre; **sew up** vt (re)coudre; **it is all ~n up** (fig) c'est dans le sac or dans la poche

sewage ['su:ɪdʒ] n vidange(s) f(pl)

sewer ['su:ə'] n égout m

sewing ['səuɪŋ] n couture f; (item(s)) ouvrage m

sewing machine n machine f à coudre

sewn [səun] pp of **sew**

sex [sɛks] n sexe m; **to have ~ with** avoir des rapports (sexuels) avec

sexism ['sɛksɪzəm] n sexisme m

sexist ['sɛksɪst] adj sexiste

sexual ['sɛksjuəl] adj sexuel(le); **~ assault** attentat m à la pudeur; **~ harassment** harcèlement sexuel

sexual intercourse n rapports sexuels

sexuality [sɛksjuˈælɪtɪ] n sexualité f

sexy ['sɛksɪ] adj sexy inv

shabby ['ʃæbɪ] adj miteux(-euse); (behaviour) mesquin(e), méprisable

shack [ʃæk] n cabane f, hutte f

shackles ['ʃæklz] npl chaînes fpl, entraves fpl

shade [ʃeɪd] n ombre f; (for lamp) abat-jour m inv; (of colour) nuance f, ton m; (US: window shade) store m; (small quantity): **a ~ of** un soupçon de + abater du soleil, ombrager; **shades** npl (US: sunglasses) lunettes fpl de soleil; **in the ~** à l'ombre; **a ~ smaller** un tout petit peu plus petit

shadow ['ʃædəu] n ombre f ▷ vt (follow) filer; **without** or **beyond a ~ of** doubt sans l'ombre d'un doute

shadow cabinet n (Brit Pol) cabinet parallèle formé par le parti qui n'est pas au pouvoir

shadowy ['ʃædəu] adj ombragé(e); (dim) vague, indistinct(e)

shady ['ʃeɪdɪ] adj ombragé(e); (fig: dishonest) louche, véreux(-euse)

shaft [ʃɑːft] n (of arrow, spear) hampe f; (Aut, Tech) arbre m; (of mine) puits m; (of lift) cage f; (of light) rayon m, trait m; **ventilator ~** conduit m d'aération or de ventilation

shaggy ['ʃægɪ] adj hirsute; en broussaille

shake [ʃeɪk] (pt **shook**, pp **shaken**) [ʃuk, 'ʃeɪkn] vt secouer; (bottle, cocktail) agiter; (house, confidence) ébranler ▷ vi trembler ▷ n secousse f; **to ~ one's head** (in refusal etc) dire or faire non de la tête; (in dismay) secouer la tête; **to ~ hands with sb** serrer la main à qn; **shake off** vt secouer; (pursuer) se débarrasser de; **shake up** vt secouer

shaky ['ʃeɪkɪ] adj (hand, voice) tremblant(e); (building) branlant(e), peu solide; (memory) chancelant(e); (knowledge) incertain(e)

shall [ʃæl] aux vb: **I ~ go** j'irai; **~ I open the door?** j'ouvre la porte?; **I'll get the coffee, ~ I?** je vais chercher le café, d'accord?

shallow ['ʃæləu] adj peu profond(e); (fig) superficiel(le), qui manque de profondeur

sham [ʃæm] n frime f, (jewellery, furniture) imitation f ▷ adj feint(e), simulé(e) ▷ vt feindre, simuler

shambles ['ʃæmblz] n confusion f, pagaïe f, fouillis m; **the economy is (in) a complete ~** l'économie est dans la confusion la plus totale

shame [ʃeɪm] n honte f ▷ vt faire honte à; **it is a ~ (that/to do)** c'est dommage (que + sub/de faire); **what a ~!** quel dommage!; **to put sb/sth to ~** (fig) faire honte à qn/qch

shameful ['ʃeɪmful] adj honteux(-euse), scandaleux(-euse)

shameless ['ʃeɪmlɪs] adj éhonté(e), effronté(e); (immodest) impudique

shampoo [ʃæm'puː] n shampooing m ▷ vt faire un shampooing à; **~ and set** shampooing et mise f en plis

shamrock ['ʃæmrɔk] n trèfle m (emblème national de l'Irlande)

shandy ['ʃændɪ] n bière panachée

shan't [ʃɑːnt] = **shall not**

shantytown ['ʃæntɪtaun] n bidonville m

shape [ʃeɪp] n forme f ▷ vt façonner, modeler; (clay, stone) donner forme à; (statement) formuler; (sb's ideas, character) former; (sb's life) déterminer; (course of events) influer sur le cours de ▷ vi (also: **~ up**: events) prendre tournure; (: person) faire des progrès, s'en sortir; **to take ~** prendre forme or tournure; **in the ~ of a heart** en forme de cœur; **I can't bear gardening in any ~ or form** je déteste le jardinage sous quelque forme que ce soit; **to get o.s. into ~** (re)trouver la forme

-shaped [ʃeɪpt] suffix: **heart-** en forme de cœur

shapeless ['ʃeɪplɪs] adj informe, sans forme

shapely ['ʃeɪplɪ] adj bien proportionné(e), beau/belle

share [ʃɛər] n (thing received, contribution) part f; (Comm) action f ▷ vt partager; (have in common) avoir en commun; **to ~ out (among** or **between)** partager (entre); **to ~ in** (joy, sorrow) prendre part à; (profits) participer à, avoir part à; (work) partager

shareholder ['ʃɛəhəuldər] n (Brit) actionnaire m/f

shark [ʃɑːk] n requin m

sharp [ʃɑːp] adj (razor, knife) tranchant(e), bien aiguisé(e); (point, voice) aigu(ë); (nose, chin) pointu(e); (outline, increase) net(te); (curve, bend) brusque; (cold, pain) vif/vive; (taste) piquant(e), âcre; (Mus) dièse; (person: quick-witted) vif/vive, éveillé(e); (: unscrupulous) malhonnête ▷ n (Mus) dièse m ▷ adv: **at 2 o'clock ~** à 2 heures pile or tapantes; **turn ~ left** tournez immédiatement à gauche; **to be ~ with sb** être brusque avec qn; **look ~!** dépêche-toi!

sharpen ['ʃɑːpn] vt aiguiser; (pencil) tailler; (fig) aviver

sharpener ['ʃɑːpnər] a (also: **pencil ~**) taille-crayon(s) m inv; (also: **knife ~**) aiguisoir m

sharp-eyed [ʃɑːp'aɪd] adj à qui rien n'échappe

sharply ['ʃɑːplɪ] adv (turn, stop) brusquement; (stand out) nettement; (criticize, retort) sèchement, vertement

shatter ['ʃætər] vt fracasser, briser, faire voler en éclats; (fig: upset) bouleverser; (: ruin) briser, ruiner ▷ vi voler en éclats, se briser, se fracasser

shattered ['ʃætəd] adj (overwhelmed, grief-stricken) bouleversé(e); (inf: exhausted) éreinté(e)

shave [ʃeɪv] vt raser ▷ vi se raser ▷ n: **to have a ~** se raser

shaver ['ʃeɪvə'] n (also: **electric ~**) rasoir m électrique

shaving ['ʃeɪvɪŋ] n (action) rasage m

shaving brush n blaireau m

shaving cream n crème f à raser

shaving foam n mousse f à raser

shavings ['ʃeɪvɪŋz] npl (of wood etc) copeaux mpl

shawl [ʃɔːl] n châle m

she [ʃiː] pron elle; **there ~ is** la voilà; **she-elephant** etc éléphant m etc femelle

sheaf (pl **sheaves**) [ʃiːf, ʃiːvz] n gerbe f

shear [ʃɪə'] vt (pt **sheared**, pp **sheared** or **shorn**) [ʃɔːn] (sheep) tondre; **shear off** vt tondre; (branch) élaguer

shears ['ʃɪəz] npl (for hedge) cisaille(s) f(pl)

sheath [ʃiːθ] n gaine f, fourreau m, étui m; (contraceptive) préservatif m

shed [ʃed] n remise f, resserre f; (Industry, Rail) hangar m ▷ vt (pt, pp **shed**) (leaves, fur etc) perdre; (tears) verser, répandre; (workers) congédier; **to ~ light on** (problem, mystery) faire la lumière sur

she'd [ʃiːd] = **she had**; **she would**

sheen [ʃiːn] n lustre m

sheep [ʃiːp] n (pl inv) mouton m

sheepdog ['ʃiːpdɔg] n chien m de berger

sheepskin ['ʃiːpskɪn] n peau f de mouton

sheer [ʃɪə'] adj (utter) pur(e), pur et simple; (steep) à pic, abrupt(e); (almost transparent) extrêmement fin(e) ▷ adv à pic, abruptement; **by ~ chance** par pur hasard

sheet [ʃiːt] n (on bed) drap m; (of paper) feuille f; (of glass, metal etc) feuille f, plaque f

sheik, sheikh [ʃeɪk] n cheik m

shelf (pl **shelves**) [ʃelf, ʃelvz] n étagère f, rayon m; **set of shelves** rayonnage m

shell [ʃel] n (on beach) coquillage m; (of egg, nut etc) coquille f; (explosive) obus m; (of building) carcasse f ▷ vt (crab, prawn etc) décortiquer; (peas) écosser; (Mil) bombarder (d'obus); **shell out** vi (inf): **to ~ out (for)** casquer (pour)

she'll [ʃiːl] = **she will**; **she shall**

shellfish ['ʃelfɪʃ] n (pl inv: crab etc) crustacé m; (: scallop etc) coquillage m ▷ npl (as food) fruits mpl de mer

shell suit n survêtement m

shelter ['ʃeltə'] n abri m, refuge m ▷ vt abriter, protéger; (give lodging to) donner asile à ▷ vi s'abriter, se mettre à l'abri; **to take ~ (from)** s'abriter (de)

sheltered ['ʃeltəd] adj (life) retiré(e), à l'abri des soucis; (spot) abrité(e)

sheltered housing n foyers mpl (pour personnes âgées ou handicapées)

shelve [ʃelv] vt (fig) mettre en suspens or en sommeil

shelves ['ʃelvz] npl of **shelf**

shelving ['ʃelvɪŋ] n (shelves) rayonnage(s) m(pl)

shepherd ['ʃepəd] n berger m ▷ vt (guide) guider, escorter

shepherd's pie ['ʃepədz-] n ≈ hachis m Parmentier

sheriff ['ʃerɪf] (US) n shérif m

sherry ['ʃerɪ] n xérès m, sherry m

she's [ʃiːz] = **she is**; **she has**

Shetland ['ʃetlənd] n (also: **the ~s, the ~ Isles** or **Islands**) les îles fpl Shetland

shield [ʃiːld] n bouclier m; (protection) écran m de protection ▷ vt: **to ~ (from)** protéger (de or contre)

shift [ʃɪft] n (change) changement m; (work period) période f de travail; (of workers) équipe f, poste m ▷ vt déplacer, changer de place; (remove) enlever ▷ vi changer de place, bouger; **the wind has ~ed to the south** le vent a tourné au sud; **a ~ in demand** (Comm) un déplacement de la demande

shift work n travail m par roulement; **to do ~** travailler par roulement

shifty ['ʃɪftɪ] adj sournois(e); (eyes) fuyant(e)

shimmer ['ʃɪmə'] n miroitement m, chatoiement m ▷ vi miroiter, chatoyer

shin [ʃɪn] n tibia m ▷ vi: **to ~ up/down a tree** grimper dans un/descendre d'un arbre

shine [ʃaɪn] n (pt, pp **shone**) [ʃɔn] n éclat m, brillant m ▷ vi briller ▷ vt (torch): **to ~ on** braquer sur; (polish) (pt, pp **shined**) faire briller or reluire

shingle ['ʃɪŋgl] n (on beach) galets mpl; (on roof) bardeau m

shingles ['ʃɪŋglz] n (Med) zona m

shiny ['ʃaɪnɪ] adj brillant(e)

ship [ʃɪp] n bateau m; (large) navire m ▷ vt transporter (par mer); (send) expédier (par mer); (load) charger, embarquer; **on board ~** à bord

shipbuilding ['ʃɪpbɪldɪŋ] n construction navale

shipment ['ʃɪpmənt] n cargaison f

shipping ['ʃɪpɪŋ] n (ships) navires mpl; (traffic) navigation f; (the industry) industrie navale; (transport) transport m

shipwreck ['ʃɪprek] n épave f; (event) naufrage m ▷ vt: **to be ~ed** faire naufrage

shipyard ['ʃɪpjɑːd] n chantier naval

shire ['ʃaɪə'] n (Brit) comté m

shirt [ʃəːt] n chemise f; (woman's) chemisier m; **in ~ sleeves** en bras de chemise

shit [ʃɪt] excl (inf!) merde (!)

shiver ['ʃɪvə'] n frisson m ▷ vi frissonner

shoal [ʃəul] n (of fish) banc m

shock [ʃɔk] n (impact) choc m, heurt m; (Elec) secousse f, décharge f; (emotional) choc m; (Med) commotion f, choc m ▷ vt (scandalize) choquer, scandaliser; (upset) bouleverser; **suffering from ~** (Med) commotionné(e); **it gave us a ~** ça nous a fait un choc; **it came as a ~ to hear that ...** nous avons appris avec stupeur que ...

shock absorber [-əbzɔːbə'] n amortisseur m

shocking ['ʃɔkɪŋ] *adj* (*outrageous*) choquant(e), scandaleux(-euse); (*awful*) épouvantable

shoddy ['ʃɔdɪ] *adj* de mauvaise qualité, mal fait(e)

shoe [ʃu:] *n* chaussure *f*, soulier *m*; (*also:* **horse~**) fer *m* à cheval; (*also:* **brake ~**) mâchoire *f* de frein ▷ *vt* (*pt, pp* **shod**) [ʃɔd] (*horse*) ferrer

shoelace ['ʃu:leɪs] *n* lacet *m* (de soulier)

shoe polish *n* cirage *m*

shoeshop ['ʃu:ʃɔp] *n* magasin *m* de chaussures

shoestring ['ʃu:strɪŋ] *n*: **on a ~** (*fig*) avec un budget dérisoire; avec des moyens très restreints

shone [ʃɔn] *pt, pp of* **shine**

shook [ʃuk] *pt of* **shake**

shoot [ʃu:t] (*pt, pp* **shot**) [ʃɔt] *n* (*on branch, seedling*) pousse *f*; (*shooting party*) partie *f* de chasse ▷ *vt* (*game: hunt*) chasser; (: *aim at*) tirer; (: *kill*) abattre; (*person*) blesser/tuer d'un coup de fusil (*or de revolver*); (*execute*) fusiller; (*arrow*) tirer; (*gun*) tirer un coup de; (*Cine*) tourner ▷ *vi* (*with gun, bow*): **to ~ (at)** tirer (sur); (*Football*) shooter, tirer; **to ~ past sb** passer en flèche devant qn; **to ~ in/out** entrer/sortir comme une flèche; **shoot down** *vt* (*plane*) abattre; **shoot up** *vi* (*fig: prices etc*) monter en flèche

shooting ['ʃu:tɪŋ] *n* (*shots*) coups *mpl* de feu; (*attack*) fusillade *f*; (*murder*) homicide *m* (à l'aide d'une arme à feu); (*Hunting*) chasse *f*; (*Cine*) tournage *m*

shooting star *n* étoile filante

shop [ʃɔp] *n* magasin *m*; (*workshop*) atelier *m* ▷ *vi* (*also:* **go ~ping**) faire ses courses *or* ses achats; **repair ~** atelier de réparations; **to talk ~** (*fig*) parler boutique; **shop around** *vi* faire le tour des magasins (pour comparer les prix); (*fig*) se renseigner avant de choisir *or* décider

shop assistant *n* (*Brit*) vendeur(-euse)

shop floor *n* (*Brit: fig*) ouvriers *mpl*

shopkeeper ['ʃɔpkiːpəᴿ] *n* marchand(e), commerçant(e)

shoplifting ['ʃɔplɪftɪŋ] *n* vol *m* à l'étalage

shopper ['ʃɔpəᴿ] *n* personne *f* qui fait ses courses, acheteur(-euse)

shopping ['ʃɔpɪŋ] *n* (*goods*) achats *mpl*, provisions *fpl*

shopping bag *n* sac *m* (à provisions)

shopping centre, (*US*) **shopping center** *n* centre commercial

shopping mall *n* centre commercial

shopping trolley *n* (*Brit*) Caddie® *m*

shop-soiled ['ʃɔpsɔɪld] *adj* défraîchi(e), qui a fait la vitrine

shop window *n* vitrine *f*

shore [ʃɔːᴿ] *n* (*of sea, lake*) rivage *m*, rive *f* ▷ *vt*: **to ~ (up)** étayer; **on ~** à terre

shorn [ʃɔːn] *pp of* **shear** ▷ *adj*: **~ of** dépouillé(e) de

short [ʃɔːt] *adj* (*not long*) court(e); (*soon finished*) court, bref/brève; (*person, step*) petit(e); (*curt*) brusque, sec/sèche; (*insufficient*) insuffisant(e) ▷ *n* (*also:* **~ film**) court métrage; (*Elec*) court-circuit *m*; **to be ~ of sth** être à court de *or* manquer de qch; **to be in ~ supply** manquer, être difficile à trouver; **I'm 3 ~** il m'en manque 3; **in ~** bref; en bref; **~ of doing** à moins de faire; **everything ~ of** tout sauf; **it is ~ for** c'est l'abréviation *or* le diminutif de; **a ~ time ago** il y a peu de temps; **in the ~ term** à court terme; **to cut ~** (*speech, visit*) abréger, écourter; (*person*) couper la parole à; **to fall ~ of** ne pas être à la hauteur de; **to run ~ of** arriver à court de, venir à manquer de; **to stop ~** s'arrêter net; **to stop ~ of** ne pas aller jusqu'à

shortage ['ʃɔːtɪdʒ] *n* manque *m*, pénurie *f*

shortbread ['ʃɔːtbred] *n* ≈ sablé *m*

short-change [ʃɔːt'tʃeɪndʒ] *vt*: **to ~ sb** ne pas rendre assez à qn

short-circuit [ʃɔːt'səːkɪt] *n* court-circuit *m* ▷ *vt* court-circuiter ▷ *vi* se mettre en court-circuit

shortcoming ['ʃɔːtkʌmɪŋ] *n* défaut *m*

shortcrust pastry ['ʃɔːtkrʌst-], **short pastry** *n* (*Brit*) pâte brisée

shortcut ['ʃɔːtkʌt] *n* raccourci *m*

shorten ['ʃɔːtn] *vt* raccourcir; (*text, visit*) abréger

shortfall ['ʃɔːtfɔːl] *n* déficit *m*

shorthand ['ʃɔːthænd] *n* (*Brit*) sténo(graphie) *f*; **to take sth down in ~** prendre qch en sténo

shorthand typist *n* (*Brit*) sténodactylo *m/f*

shortlist ['ʃɔːtlɪst] *n* (*Brit: for job*) liste *f* des candidats sélectionnés

short-lived ['ʃɔːt'lɪvd] *adj* de courte durée

shortly ['ʃɔːtlɪ] *adv* bientôt, sous peu

short notice *n*: **at ~** au dernier moment

shorts [ʃɔːts] *npl*: (**a pair of**) **~** un short

short-sighted [ʃɔːt'saɪtɪd] *adj* (*Brit*) myope; (*fig*) qui manque de clairvoyance

short-sleeved [ʃɔːt'sliːvd] *adj* à manches courtes

short-staffed [ʃɔːt'stɑːft] *adj* à court de personnel

short-stay [ʃɔːt'steɪ] *adj* (*car park*) de courte durée

short story *n* nouvelle *f*

short-tempered [ʃɔːt'tempəd] *adj* qui s'emporte facilement

short-term ['ʃɔːttəːm] *adj* (*effect*) à court terme

short wave *n* (*Radio*) ondes courtes

shot [ʃɔt] *pt, pp of* **shoot** ▷ *n* coup *m* (de feu); (*shotgun pellets*) plombs *mpl*; (*try*) coup, essai *m*; (*injection*) piqûre *f*; (*Phot*) photo *f*; **to be a good/poor ~** (*person*) tirer bien/mal; **to fire a ~ at sb/sth** tirer sur qn/qch; **to have a ~ at (doing) sth** essayer de faire qch; **like a ~** comme une flèche; (*very readily*) sans hésiter;

to get ~ of sb/sth (*inf*) se débarrasser de qn/ qch; **a big ~** (*inf*) un gros bonnet

shotgun ['ʃɔtgʌn] *n* fusil *m* de chasse

should [ʃud] *aux vb*: **I ~ go now** je devrais partir maintenant; **he ~ be there now** il devrait être arrivé maintenant; **I ~ go if I were you** si j'étais vous j'irais; **I ~ like to** volontiers, j'aimerais bien; **~ he phone ...** si jamais il téléphone ...

shoulder ['ʃəuldəʳ] *n* épaule *f*; (*Brit: of road*): **hard ~** accotement *m* ▷ *vt* (*fig*) endosser, se charger de; **to look over one's ~** regarder derrière soi (en tournant la tête); **to rub ~s with sb** (*fig*) côtoyer qn; **to give sb the cold ~** (*fig*) battre froid à qn

shoulder bag *n* sac *m* à bandoulière

shoulder blade *n* omoplate *f*

shouldn't ['ʃudnt] = **should not**

shout [ʃaut] *n* cri *m* ▷ *vt* crier ▷ *vi* crier, pousser des cris; **to give sb a ~** appeler qn; **shout down** *vt* huer

shouting ['ʃautɪŋ] *n* cris *mpl*

shove [ʃʌv] *vt* pousser; (*inf: put*): **to ~ sth in** fourrer or ficher qch dans ▷ *n* poussée *f*; **he ~d me out of the way** il m'a écarté en me poussant; **shove off** *vi* (*Naut*) pousser au large; (*fig: col*) ficher le camp

shovel ['ʃʌvl] *n* pelle *f* ▷ *vt* pelleter, enlever (*or* enfourner) à la pelle

show [ʃəu] (*pt* **showed**, *pp* **shown**) [ʃəun] *n* (*of emotion*) manifestation *f*, démonstration *f*; (*semblance*) semblant *m*, apparence *f*; (*exhibition*) exposition *f*, salon *m*; (*Theat, TV*) spectacle *m*; (*Cine*) séance *f* ▷ *vt* montrer; (*film*) passer; (*courage etc*) faire preuve de, manifester; (*exhibit*) exposer ▷ *vi* se voir, être visible; **can you ~ me where it is, please?** pouvez-vous me montrer où c'est?; **to ask for a ~ of hands** demander que l'on vote à main levée; **to be on ~** être exposé(e); **it's just for ~** c'est juste pour l'effet; **who's running the ~ here?** (*inf*) qui est-ce qui commande ici?; **to ~ sb to his seat/to the door** accompagner qn jusqu'à sa place/la porte; **to ~ a profit/loss** (*Comm*) indiquer un bénéfice/une perte; **it just goes to ~ that ...** ça prouve bien que ...; **show in** *vt* (*stand out*) faire entrer; **show off** *vi* (*pej*) crâner ▷ *vt* (*display*) faire valoir; (*pej*) faire étalage de; **show out** *vt* reconduire à la porte; **show up** *vi* (*stand out*) ressortir; (*inf: turn up*) se montrer ▷ *vt* démontrer; (*unmask*) démasquer, dénoncer; (*flaw*) faire ressortir

show business *n* le monde du spectacle

showdown ['ʃəudaun] *n* épreuve *f* de force

shower ['ʃauəʳ] *n* (*for washing*) douche *f*; (*rain*) averse *f*; (*of stones etc*) pluie *f*, grêle *f*; (*US: party*) réunion organisée pour la remise de cadeaux ▷ *vi* prendre une douche, se doucher ▷ *vt*: **to ~ sb with** (*gifts etc*) combler qn de; (*abuse etc*) accabler qn de; (*missiles*) bombarder qn de; **to have** *or* **take a ~** prendre une douche, se doucher

shower cap *n* bonnet *m* de douche

shower gel *n* gel *m* douche

showerproof ['ʃauəpru:f] *adj* imperméable

showing ['ʃəuɪŋ] *n* (*of film*) projection *f*

show jumping [-dʒʌmpɪŋ] *n* concours *m* hippique

shown [ʃəun] *pp of* **show**

show-off ['ʃəuɔf] *n* (*inf: person*) crâneur(-euse), m'as-tu-vu(e)

showpiece ['ʃəupi:s] *n* (*of exhibition etc*) joyau *m*, clou *m*; **that hospital is a ~** cet hôpital est un modèle du genre

showroom ['ʃəurum] *n* magasin *m* or salle *f* d'exposition

shrank [ʃræŋk] *pt of* **shrink**

shrapnel ['ʃræpnl] *n* éclats *mpl* d'obus

shred [ʃred] *n* (*gen pl*) lambeau *m*, petit morceau; (*fig: of truth, evidence*) parcelle *f* ▷ *vt* mettre en lambeaux, déchirer; (*documents*) détruire; (*Culin: grate*) râper; (: *lettuce etc*) couper en lanières

shredder ['ʃredəʳ] *n* (*for vegetables*) râpeur *m*; (*for documents, papers*) déchiqueteuse *f*

shrewd [ʃru:d] *adj* astucieux(-euse), perspicace; (*business person*) habile

shriek [ʃri:k] *n* cri perçant *or* aigu; hurlement *m* ▷ *vt*, *vi* hurler, crier

shrill [ʃrɪl] *adj* perçant(e), aigu(ë), strident(e)

shrimp [ʃrɪmp] *n* crevette grise

shrine [ʃraɪn] *n* châsse *f*; (*place*) lieu *m* de pèlerinage

shrink (*pt* **shrank**, *pp* **shrunk**) [ʃrɪŋk, ʃræŋk, ʃrʌŋk] *vi* rétrécir; (*fig*) diminuer; (*also*: **~ away**) reculer ▷ *vt* (*wool*) (faire) rétrécir ▷ *n* (*inf: pej*) psychanalyste *m/f*; **to ~ from (doing) sth** reculer devant (la pensée de faire) qch

shrink-wrap ['ʃrɪŋkræp] *vt* emballer sous film plastique

shrivel ['ʃrɪvl] (*also*: **~ up**) *vt* ratatiner, flétrir ▷ *vi* se ratatiner, se flétrir

shroud [ʃraud] *n* linceul *m* ▷ *vt*: **~ed in mystery** enveloppé(e) de mystère

Shrove Tuesday ['ʃrəuv-] *n* (le) Mardi gras

shrub [ʃrʌb] *n* arbuste *m*

shrubbery ['ʃrʌbərɪ] *n* massif *m* d'arbustes

shrug [ʃrʌg] *n* haussement *m* d'épaules ▷ *vt*, *vi*: **to ~ (one's shoulders)** hausser les épaules; **shrug off** *vt* faire fi de; (*cold, illness*) se débarrasser de

shrunk [ʃrʌŋk] *pp of* **shrink**

shudder ['ʃʌdəʳ] *n* frisson *m*, frémissement *m* ▷ *vi* frissonner, frémir

shuffle ['ʃʌfl] *vt* (*cards*) battre; **to ~ (one's feet)** traîner les pieds

shun [ʃʌn] *vt* éviter, fuir

shunt [ʃʌnt] *vt* (*Rail: direct*) aiguiller; (: *divert*) détourner ▷ *vi*: **to ~ (to and fro)** faire la navette

shut (*pt*, *pp* **shut**) [ʃʌt] *vt* fermer ▷ *vi* (se) fermer; **shut down** *vt* fermer définitivement; (*machine*) arrêter ▷ *vi* fermer définitivement; **shut off** *vt* couper, arrêter;

shut out vt (person, cold) empêcher d'entrer; (noise) éviter d'entendre; (block: view) boucher; (: memory of sth) chasser de son esprit; **shut up** vi (inf: keep quiet) se taire ▷ vt (close) fermer; (silence) faire taire

shutter ['ʃʌtə^r] n volet m; (Phot) obturateur m

shuttle ['ʃʌtl] n navette f; (also: **~ service**) (service m de) navette f ▷ vi (vehicle, person) faire la navette ▷ vt (passengers) transporter par un système de navette

shuttlecock ['ʃʌtlkɔk] n volant m (de badminton)

shuttle diplomacy n navettes fpl diplomatiques

shy [ʃaɪ] adj timide; **to fight ~ of** se dérober devant; **to be ~ of doing sth** hésiter à faire qch, ne pas oser faire qch ▷ vi: **to ~ away from doing sth** (fig) craindre de faire qch

Siberia [saɪ'bɪərɪə] n Sibérie f

siblings ['sɪblɪŋz] npl (formal) frères et sœurs mpl (de mêmes parents)

Sicily ['sɪsɪlɪ] n Sicile f

sick [sɪk] adj (ill) malade; (Brit: vomiting): **to be ~** vomir; (humour) noir(e), macabre; **to feel ~** avoir envie de vomir, avoir mal au cœur; **to fall ~** tomber malade; **to be (off) ~** être absent(e) pour cause de maladie; **a ~ person** un(e) malade; **to be ~ of** (fig) en avoir assez de

sick bay n infirmerie f

sicken ['sɪkn] vt écœurer ▷ vi: **to be ~ing for sth** (cold, flu etc) couver qch

sickening ['sɪknɪŋ] adj (fig) écœurant(e), révoltant(e), répugnant(e)

sickle ['sɪkl] n faucille f

sick leave n congé m de maladie

sickly ['sɪklɪ] adj maladif(-ive), souffreteux(-euse); (causing nausea) écœurant(e)

sickness ['sɪknɪs] n maladie f; (vomiting) vomissement(s) m(pl)

sick note n (from parents) mot m d'absence; (from doctor) certificat médical

sick pay n indemnité f de maladie (versée par l'employeur)

side [saɪd] n côté m; (of animal) flanc m; (of lake, road) bord m; (of mountain) versant m; (fig: aspect) côté, aspect m; (team: Sport) équipe f; (TV: channel) chaîne f ▷ adj (door, entrance) latéral(e) ▷ vi: **to ~ with sb** prendre le parti de qn, se ranger du côté de qn; **by the ~ of** au bord de; **~ by ~** côte à côte; **the right/wrong ~** le bon/mauvais côté, l'endroit/l'envers m; **they are on our ~** ils sont avec nous; **from all ~s** de tous côtés; **to rock from ~ to ~** se balancer; **to take ~s (with)** prendre parti (pour); **a ~ of beef** = un quartier de bœuf

sideboard ['saɪdbɔːd] n buffet m

sideboards (Brit) ['saɪdbɔːdz], **sideburns** ['saɪdbəːnz] npl (whiskers) pattes fpl

side drum n (Mus) tambour plat, caisse claire

side effect n effet m secondaire

sidelight ['saɪdlaɪt] n (Aut) veilleuse f

sideline ['saɪdlaɪn] n (Sport) (ligne f de) touche f; (fig) activité f secondaire

sidelong ['saɪdlɔŋ] adj: **to give sb a ~ glance** regarder qn du coin de l'œil

side order n garniture f

side road n petite route, route transversale

sideshow ['saɪdʃəu] n attraction f

sidestep ['saɪdstɛp] vt (question) éluder; (problem) éviter ▷ vi (Boxing etc) esquiver

side street n rue transversale

sidetrack ['saɪdtræk] vt (fig) faire dévier de son sujet

sidewalk ['saɪdwɔːk] n (US) trottoir m

sideways ['saɪdweɪz] adv de côté

siding ['saɪdɪŋ] n (Rail) voie f de garage

siege [siːdʒ] n siège m; **to lay ~ to** assiéger

sieve [sɪv] n tamis m, passoire f ▷ vt tamiser, passer (au tamis)

sift [sɪft] vt passer au tamis or au crible; (fig) passer au crible ▷ vi (fig): **to ~ through** passer en revue

sigh [saɪ] n soupir m ▷ vi soupirer, pousser un soupir

sight [saɪt] n (faculty) vue f; (spectacle) spectacle m; (on gun) mire f ▷ vt apercevoir; **in ~** visible; (fig) en vue; **out of ~** hors de vue; **at ~** (Comm) à vue; **at first ~** à première vue, au premier abord; **I know her by ~** je la connais de vue; **to catch ~ of sb/sth** apercevoir qn/qch; **to lose ~ of sb/sth** perdre qn/qch de vue; **to set one's ~s on sth** jeter son dévolu sur qch

sightseeing ['saɪtsiːɪŋ] n tourisme m; **to go ~** faire du tourisme

sign [saɪn] n (gen) signe m; (with hand etc) signe, geste m; (notice) panneau m, écriteau m; (also: **road ~**) panneau de signalisation ▷ vt signer; **as a ~ of** en signe de; **it's a good/bad ~** c'est bon/mauvais signe; **plus/minus ~** signe plus/moins; **there's no ~ of a change of mind** rien ne laisse présager un revirement; **he was showing ~s of improvement** il commençait visiblement à faire des progrès; **to ~ one's name** signer; **where do I ~?** où dois-je signer?; **sign away** vt (rights etc) renoncer officiellement à; **sign for** vt fus (item) signer le reçu pour; **sign in** vi signer le registre (en arrivant); **sign off** vi (Radio, TV) terminer l'émission; **sign on** vi (Mil) s'engager; (Brit: as unemployed) s'inscrire au chômage; (enrol) s'inscrire ▷ vt (Mil) engager; (employee) embaucher; **to ~ on for a course** s'inscrire pour un cours; **sign out** vi signer le registre (en partant); **sign over** vt: **to ~ sth over to sb** céder qch par écrit à qn; **sign up** vt (Mil) engager ▷ vi (Mil) s'engager; (for course) s'inscrire

signal ['sɪgnl] n signal m ▷ vi (Aut) mettre son clignotant ▷ vt (person) faire signe à; (message) communiquer par signaux; **to ~ a**

left/right turn (*Aut*) indiquer *or* signaler que l'on tourne à gauche/droite; **to ~ to sb (to do sth)** faire signe à qn (de faire qch)

signalman ['sɪgnlmən] *n* (*Rail*) aiguilleur *m*

signature ['sɪgnətʃəʳ] *n* signature *f*

signature tune *n* indicatif musical

signet ring ['sɪgnət-] *n* chevalière *f*

significance [sɪg'nɪfɪkəns] *n* signification *f*; importance *f*; **that is of no ~** ceci n'a pas d'importance

significant [sɪg'nɪfɪkənt] *adj* significatif(-ive); (*important*) important(e), considérable

signify ['sɪgnɪfaɪ] *vt* signifier

sign language *n* langage *m* par signes

signpost ['saɪnpəust] *n* poteau indicateur

Sikh [si:k] *adj, n* Sikh *m/f*

silence ['saɪlns] *n* silence *m* ▷ *vt* faire taire, réduire au silence

silencer ['saɪlənsəʳ] *n* (*Brit: on gun, Aut*) silencieux *m*

silent ['saɪlnt] *adj* silencieux(-euse); (*film*) muet(te); **to keep** *or* **remain ~** garder le silence, ne rien dire

silent partner *n* (*Comm*) bailleur *m* de fonds, commanditaire *m*

silhouette [sɪlu:'et] *n* silhouette *f* ▷ *vt*: **~d against** se profilant sur, se découpant contre

silicon chip ['sɪlɪkən-] *n* puce *f* électronique

silk [sɪlk] *n* soie *f* ▷ *cpd* de *or* en soie

silky ['sɪlkɪ] *adj* soyeux(-euse)

silly ['sɪlɪ] *adj* stupide, sot(te), bête; **to do something ~** faire une bêtise

silt [sɪlt] *n* vase *f*; limon *m*

silver ['sɪlvəʳ] *n* argent *m*; (*money*) monnaie *f* (en pièces d'argent); (*also*: **~ware**) argenterie *f* ▷ *adj* (*made of silver*) d'argent, en argent; (*in colour*) argenté(e); (*car*) gris métallisé *inv*

silver-plated [sɪlvə'pleɪtɪd] *adj* plaqué(e) argent

silversmith ['sɪlvəsmɪθ] *n* orfèvre *m/f*

silvery ['sɪlvrɪ] *adj* argenté(e)

SIM card ['sɪm-] *abbr* (*Tel*) carte *f* SIM

similar ['sɪmɪləʳ] *adj*: **~ (to)** semblable (à)

similarity [sɪmɪ'lærɪtɪ] *n* ressemblance *f*, similarité *f*

similarly ['sɪmɪləlɪ] *adv* de la même façon, de même

simmer ['sɪməʳ] *vi* cuire à feu doux, mijoter; **simmer down** *vi* (*fig: inf*) se calmer

simple ['sɪmpl] *adj* simple; **the ~ truth** la vérité pure et simple

simplicity [sɪm'plɪsɪtɪ] *n* simplicité *f*

simplify ['sɪmplɪfaɪ] *vt* simplifier

simply ['sɪmplɪ] *adv* simplement; (*without fuss*) avec simplicité; (*absolutely*) absolument

simulate ['sɪmjuleɪt] *vt* simuler, feindre

simultaneous [sɪmǝl'teɪnɪǝs] *adj* simultané(e)

simultaneously [sɪmǝl'teɪnɪǝslɪ] *adv* simultanément

sin [sɪn] *n* péché *m* ▷ *vi* pécher

since [sɪns] *adv, prep* depuis ▷ *conj* (*time*) depuis que; (*because*) puisque, étant donné que, comme; **~ then, ever ~** depuis ce moment-là; **~ Monday** depuis lundi; **(ever) ~ I arrived** depuis mon arrivée, depuis que je suis arrivé

sincere [sɪn'sɪǝʳ] *adj* sincère

sincerely [sɪn'sɪǝlɪ] *adv* sincèrement; **Yours ~** (*at end of letter*) veuillez agréer, Monsieur (*or* Madame) l'expression de mes sentiments distingués *or* les meilleurs

sincerity [sɪn'serɪtɪ] *n* sincérité *f*

sinew ['sɪnju:] *n* tendon *m*; **sinews** *npl* muscles *mpl*

sing (*pt* **sang**, *pp* **sung**) [sɪŋ, sæŋ, sʌŋ] *vt, vi* chanter

Singapore [sɪŋgǝ'pɔ:ʳ] *n* Singapour *m*

singe [sɪndʒ] *vt* brûler légèrement; (*clothes*) roussir

singer ['sɪŋǝʳ] *n* chanteur(-euse)

singing ['sɪŋɪŋ] *n* (*of person, bird*) chant *m*; façon *f* de chanter; (*of kettle, bullet, in ears*) sifflement *m*

single ['sɪŋgl] *adj* seul(e), unique; (*unmarried*) célibataire; (*not double*) simple ▷ *n* (*Brit: also*: **~ ticket**) aller *m* (simple); (*record*) 45 tours *m*; **singles** *npl* (*Tennis*) simple *m*; (*US: single people*) célibataires *m/fpl*; **not a ~ one was left** il n'en est pas resté un(e), seul(e); **every ~ day** chaque jour sans exception; **single out** *vt* choisir; (*distinguish*) distinguer

single bed *n* lit *m* d'une personne *or* à une place

single-breasted ['sɪŋglbrestɪd] *adj* droit(e)

single file *n*: **in ~** en file indienne

single-handed [sɪŋgl'hændɪd] *adv* tout(e) seul(e), sans (aucune) aide

single-minded [sɪŋgl'maɪndɪd] *adj* résolu(e), tenace

single parent *n* parent unique (*or* célibataire); **single-parent family** famille monoparentale

single room *n* chambre *f* à un lit *or* pour une personne

single-track road [sɪŋgl'træk-] *n* route *f* à voie unique

singly ['sɪŋglɪ] *adv* séparément

singular ['sɪŋgjulǝʳ] *adj* singulier(-ière); (*odd*) singulier, étrange; (*outstanding*) remarquable; (*Ling*) (au) singulier, du singulier ▷ *n* (*Ling*) singulier *m*; **in the feminine ~** au féminin singulier

sinister ['sɪnɪstǝʳ] *adj* sinistre

sink [sɪŋk] (*pt* **sank**, *pp* **sunk**) [sæŋk, sʌŋk] *n* évier *m*; (*washbasin*) lavabo *m* ▷ *vt* (*ship*) (faire) couler, faire sombrer; (*foundations*) creuser; (*piles etc*): **to ~ sth into** enfoncer qch dans ▷ *vi* couler, sombrer; (*ground etc*) s'affaisser; **to ~ into sth** (*chair*) s'enfoncer dans qch; **he sank into a chair/the mud** il s'est enfoncé dans un fauteuil/la boue; **a ~ing feeling** un serrement de cœur; **sink in** vi s'enfoncer, pénétrer; (*explanation*) rentrer (inf), être compris; **it took a long time to ~ in** il a fallu longtemps pour que ça rentre

sinner ['sɪnə'] n pécheur(-eresse)

sinus ['saɪnəs] n (*Anat*) sinus m inv

sip [sɪp] n petite gorgée ▷ vt boire à petites gorgées

siphon ['saɪfən] n siphon m ▷ vt (*also*: **~ off**) siphonner; (: *fig*: *funds*) transférer; (: *illegally*) détourner

sir [sə'] n monsieur m; **S~ John Smith** sir John Smith; **yes ~** oui Monsieur; **Dear S~** (*in letter*) Monsieur

siren ['saɪərn] n sirène f

sirloin ['sə:lɔɪn] n (*also*: **~ steak**) aloyau m

sissy ['sɪsɪ] n (*inf*: *coward*) poule mouillée

sister ['sɪstə'] n sœur f; (*nun*) religieuse f, (*Brit*: *nurse*) infirmière f en chef ▷ cpd: **~ organization** organisation f sœur; **~ ship** (sister(-)ship m

sister-in-law ['sɪstərɪnlɔ:] n belle-sœur f

sit (*pt, pp* **sat**) [sɪt, sæt] vi s'asseoir; (*be sitting*) être assis(e); (*assembly*) être en séance, siéger; (*for painter*) poser; (*dress etc*) tomber ▷ vt (*exam*) passer, se présenter à; **to ~ tight** ne pas bouger; **sit about**, **sit around** vi être assis(e) or rester à ne rien faire; **sit back** vi (*in seat*) bien s'installer, se carrer; **sit down** vi s'asseoir; **to be ~ting down** être assis(e); **sit in** vi: **to ~ in on a discussion** assister à une discussion; **sit on** vt fus (*jury, committee*) faire partie de; **sit up** vi s'asseoir, (*straight*) se redresser; (*not go to bed*) rester debout, ne pas se coucher

sitcom ['sɪtkɔm] n abbr (TV: = *situation comedy*) sitcom f, comédie f de situation

site [saɪt] n emplacement m, site m; (*also*: **building ~**) chantier m ▷ vt placer

sit-in ['sɪtɪn] n (*demonstration*) sit-in m inv, occupation f de locaux

sitting ['sɪtɪŋ] n (*of assembly etc*) séance f; (*in canteen*) service m

sitting room n salon m

situated ['sɪtjueɪtɪd] adj situé(e)

situation [sɪtju'eɪʃən] n situation f; **"~s vacant/wanted"** (*Brit*) "offres/demandes d'emploi"

six [sɪks] num six

sixteen [sɪks'ti:n] num seize

sixteenth [sɪks'ti:nθ] num seizième

sixth [sɪksθ] num sixième ▷ n: **the upper/lower ~** (*Brit Scol*) la terminale/la première

sixth form n (*Brit*) ≈ classes fpl de première et de terminale

sixth-form college n lycée n'ayant que des classes de première et de terminale

sixtieth ['sɪkstɪɪθ] num soixantième

sixty ['sɪkstɪ] num soixante

size [saɪz] n dimensions fpl; (*of person*) taille f; (*of clothing*) taille; (*of shoes*) pointure f; (*of estate, area*) étendue f; (*of problem*) ampleur f;

(*of company*) importance f; (*glue*) colle f; **I take ~ 14** (*of dress etc*) ≈ je prends du 42 or la taille 42; **the small/large ~** (*of soap powder etc*) le petit/grand modèle; **it's the ~ of ...** c'est de la taille (or grosseur) de ..., c'est grand (or gros) comme ...; **cut to ~** découpé(e) aux dimensions voulues; **size up** vt juger, jauger

sizeable ['saɪzəbl] adj (*object, building, estate*) assez grand(e); (*amount, problem, majority*) assez important(e)

sizzle ['sɪzl] vi grésiller

skate [skeɪt] n patin m; (*fish*: *pl inv*) raie f ▷ vi patiner; **skate over**, **skate around** vt (*problem, issue*) éluder

skateboard ['skeɪtbɔ:d] n skateboard m, planche f à roulettes

skateboarding ['skeɪtbɔ:dɪŋ] n skateboard m

skater ['skeɪtə'] n patineur(-euse)

skating ['skeɪtɪŋ] n patinage m

skating rink n patinoire f

skeleton ['skɛlɪtn] n squelette m; (*outline*) schéma m

skeleton staff n effectifs réduits

skeptical ['skɛptɪkl] (US) adj = **sceptical**

sketch [skɛtʃ] n (*drawing*) croquis m, esquisse f; (*outline plan*) aperçu m; (*Theat*) sketch m, saynète f ▷ vt esquisser, faire un croquis or une esquisse de; (*plan etc*) esquisser

sketch book n carnet m à dessin

sketchy ['skɛtʃɪ] adj incomplet(-ète), fragmentaire

skewer ['skju:ə'] n brochette f

ski [ski:] n ski m ▷ vi skier, faire du ski

ski boot n chaussure f de ski

skid [skɪd] n dérapage m ▷ vi déraper; **to go into a ~** déraper

skier ['ski:ə'] n skieur(-euse)

skiing ['ski:ɪŋ] n ski m; **to go ~** (aller) faire du ski

ski jump n (*ramp*) tremplin m; (*event*) saut m à skis

skilful, (US) **skillful** ['skɪlful] adj habile, adroit(e)

ski lift n remonte-pente m inv

skill [skɪl] n (*ability*) habileté f, adresse f, talent m; (*requiring training*) compétences fpl

skilled [skɪld] adj habile, adroit(e); (*worker*) qualifié(e)

skim [skɪm] vt (*milk*) écrémer; (*soup*) écumer; (*glide over*) raser, effleurer ▷ vi: **to ~ through** (*fig*) parcourir

skimmed milk [skɪmd-], (US) **skim milk** n lait écrémé

skimp [skɪmp] vt (*work*) bâcler, faire à la va-vite; (*cloth etc*) lésiner sur

skimpy ['skɪmpɪ] adj étriqué(e); maigre

skin [skɪn] n peau f ▷ vt (*fruit etc*) éplucher; (*animal*) écorcher; **wet** or **soaked to the ~** trempé(e) jusqu'aux os

skin cancer n cancer m de la peau

skin-deep ['skɪn'di:p] adj superficiel(le)

S

skin diving n plongée sous-marine
skinhead ['skɪnhɛd] n skinhead m
skinny ['skɪnɪ] adj maigre, maigrichon(ne)
skintight ['skɪntaɪt] adj (dress etc) collant(e),
ajusté(e)
skip [skɪp] n petit bond or saut; (Brit: container)
benne f ▷ vi gambader, sautiller; (with rope)
sauter à la corde ▷ vt (pass over) sauter; **to ~
school** (esp US) faire l'école buissonnière
ski pass n forfait-skieur(s) m
ski pole n bâton m de ski
skipper ['skɪpə'] n (Naut, Sport) capitaine m;
(in race) skipper m ▷ vt (boat) commander;
(team) être le chef de
skipping rope ['skɪpɪŋ-], (US) **skip rope** n
corde f à sauter
skirmish ['skə:mɪʃ] n escarmouche f,
accrochage m
skirt [skə:t] n jupe f ▷ vt longer, contourner
skirting board ['skə:tɪŋ-] n (Brit) plinthe f
ski slope n piste f de ski
ski suit n combinaison f de ski
ski tow n = **ski lift**
skittle ['skɪtl] n quille f; **skittles** (game) (jeu m
de) quilles fpl
skive [skaɪv] vi (Brit inf) tirer au flanc
skull [skʌl] n crâne m
skunk [skʌŋk] n mouffette f; (fur) sconse m
sky [skaɪ] n ciel m; **to praise sb to the skies**
porter qn aux nues
skylight ['skaɪlaɪt] n lucarne f
skyscraper ['skaɪskreɪpə'] n gratte-ciel m inv
slab [slæb] n plaque f; (of stone) dalle f; (of
wood) bloc m; (of meat, cheese) tranche épaisse
slack [slæk] adj (loose) lâche, desserré(e);
(slow) stagnant(e); (careless) négligent(e), peu
sérieux(-euse) or conscientieux(-euse); (Comm:
market) peu actif(-ive); (: demand)
faible; (period) creux(-euse) ▷ n (in rope etc)
mou m; **business is ~** les affaires vont mal
slacken ['slækn] (also: **~ off**) vi ralentir,
diminuer ▷ vt relâcher
slacks [slæks] npl pantalon m
slag heap n crassier m
slag off (Brit: inf) vt dire du mal de
slain [sleɪn] pp of **slay**
slam [slæm] vt (door) (faire) claquer; (throw)
jeter violemment, flanquer; (inf: criticize)
éreinter, démolir ▷ vi claquer
slander ['slɑ:ndə'] n calomnie f; (Law)
diffamation f ▷ vt calomnier; diffamer
slang [slæŋ] n argot m
slant [slɑ:nt] n inclinaison f; (fig) angle m,
point m de vue
slanted ['slɑ:ntɪd] adj tendancieux(-euse)
slanting ['slɑ:ntɪŋ] adj en pente, incliné(e);
couché(e)
slap [slæp] n claque f, gifle f; (on the back)
tape f ▷ vt donner une claque or une gifle
(or une tape) à; **to ~ on** (paint) appliquer
rapidement ▷ adv (directly) tout droit,
en plein

slapdash ['slæpdæʃ] adj (work) fait(e) sans
soin or à la va-vite; (person) insouciant(e),
négligent(e)
slapstick ['slæpstɪk] n (comedy) grosse farce
(style tarte à la crème)
slap-up ['slæpʌp] adj (Brit): **a ~ meal** un repas
extra or fameux
slash [slæʃ] vt entailler, taillader; (fig: prices)
casser
slat [slæt] n (of wood) latte f, lame f
slate [sleɪt] n ardoise f ▷ vt (fig: criticize)
éreinter, démolir
slaughter ['slɔ:tə'] n carnage m, massacre m;
(of animals) abattage m ▷ vt (animal) abattre;
(people) massacrer
slaughterhouse ['slɔ:təhaus] n abattoir m
Slav [slɑ:v] adj slave
slave [sleɪv] n esclave m/f ▷ vi (also: **~ away**)
trimer, travailler comme un forçat; **to ~
(away) at sth/at doing sth** se tuer à qch/à
faire qch
slavery ['sleɪvərɪ] n esclavage m
slay (pt **slew**, pp **slain**) [sleɪ, slu:, sleɪn] vt
(literary) tuer
sleazy ['sli:zɪ] adj miteux(-euse), minable
sled [slɛd] (US) = **sledge**
sledge [slɛdʒ] n luge f
sledgehammer ['slɛdʒhæmə'] n marteau m
de forgeron
sleek [sli:k] adj (hair, fur) brillant(e),
luisant(e); (car, boat) aux lignes pures or
élégantes
sleep [sli:p] n sommeil m ▷ vi (pt, pp **slept**)
[slɛpt] dormir; (spend night) dormir, coucher
▷ vt: **we can ~ 4** on peut coucher or loger 4
personnes; **to go to ~** s'endormir; **to have a
good night's ~** passer une bonne nuit; **to
put to ~** (patient) endormir; (animal:
euphemism: kill) piquer; **to ~ lightly** avoir le
sommeil léger; **to ~ with sb** (have sex) coucher
avec qn; **sleep around** vi coucher à droite et
à gauche; **sleep in** vi (oversleep) se réveiller
trop tard; (on purpose) faire la grasse matinée;
sleep together vi (have sex) coucher
ensemble
sleeper ['sli:pə'] n (person) dormeur(-euse);
(Brit Rail: on track) traverse f; (: train)
train-couchettes m; (: carriage)
wagon-lits m, voiture-lits f; (: berth)
couchette f
sleeping bag ['sli:pɪŋ-] n sac m de couchage
sleeping car ['sli:pɪŋ-] n wagon-lits m,
voiture-lits f
sleeping partner ['sli:pɪŋ-] n (Brit Comm)
= **silent partner**
sleeping pill ['sli:pɪŋ-] n somnifère m
sleepless ['sli:plɪs] adj: **a ~ night** une nuit
blanche
sleepover ['sli:pəuvə'] n nuit f chez un
copain or une copine; **we're having a ~ at
Jo's** nous allons passer la nuit chez Jo
sleepwalk ['sli:pwɔ:k] vi marcher en dormant

sleepwalker ['sli:pwɔ:kəʳ] n somnambule m/f

sleepy ['sli:pɪ] adj qui a envie de dormir; (fig) endormi(e); **to be** or **feel ~** avoir sommeil, avoir envie de dormir

sleet [sli:t] n neige fondue

sleeve [sli:v] n manche f; (of record) pochette f

sleeveless ['sli:vlɪs] adj (garment) sans manches

sleigh [sleɪ] n traîneau m

sleight [slaɪt] n: **~ of hand** tour m de passe-passe

slender ['slendəʳ] adj svelte, mince; (fig) faible, ténu(e)

slept [slɛpt] pt, pp of **sleep**

slew [slu:] vi (also: **~ round**) virer, pivoter ⊳ pt of **slay**

slice [slaɪs] n tranche f; (round) rondelle f; (utensil) spatule f; (also: **fish ~**) pelle f à poisson ⊳ vt couper en tranches (or en rondelles); **~d bread** pain m en tranches

slick [slɪk] adj (skilful) bien ficelé(e); (salesperson) qui a du bagout, mielleux(-euse) ⊳ n (also: **oil ~**) nappe f de pétrole, marée noire

slide [slaɪd] (pt, pp **slid**) [slɪd] n (in playground) toboggan m; (Phot) diapositive f; (Brit: also: **hair ~**) barrette f; (microscope slide) (lame f) porte-objet m; (in prices) chute f, baisse f ⊳ vt (faire) glisser ⊳ vi glisser; **to let things ~** (fig) laisser les choses aller à la dérive

sliding ['slaɪdɪŋ] adj (door) coulissant(e); **~ roof** (Aut) toit ouvrant

sliding scale n échelle f mobile

slight [slaɪt] adj (slim) mince, menu(e); (frail) frêle; (trivial) faible, insignifiant(e); (small) petit(e), léger(-ère) (before n) ⊳ n offense f, affront m ⊳ vt (offend) blesser, offenser; **the ~est** le (or la) moindre; **not in the ~est** pas le moins du monde, pas du tout

slightly ['slaɪtlɪ] adv légèrement, un peu; **~ built** fluet(te)

slim [slɪm] adj mince ⊳ vi maigrir; (diet) suivre un régime amaigrissant

slime [slaɪm] n vase f; substance visqueuse

slimming ['slɪmɪŋ] n amaigrissement m ⊳ adj (diet, pills) amaigrissant(e), pour maigrir; (food) qui ne fait pas grossir

slimy ['slaɪmɪ] adj visqueux(-euse), gluant(e); (covered with mud) vaseux(-euse)

sling [slɪŋ] n (Med) écharpe f; (for baby) porte-bébé m; (weapon) fronde f, lance-pierre m ⊳ vt (pt **slung**, pp [slʌŋ]) lancer, jeter; **to have one's arm in a ~** avoir le bras en écharpe

slip [slɪp] n faux pas; (mistake) erreur f, bévue f; (underskirt) combinaison f; (of paper) petite feuille, fiche f ⊳ vt (slide) glisser ⊳ vi (slide) glisser; (decline) baisser; (move smoothly): **to ~ into/out of** se glisser or se faufiler dans/hors de; **to let a chance ~ by** laisser passer une occasion; **to ~ sth on/off** enfiler/enlever qch; **it ~ped from her hand** cela lui a glissé des mains; **to give sb the ~** fausser

compagnie à qn; **a ~ of the tongue** un lapsus; **slip away** vi s'esquiver; **slip in** vt glisser; **slip out** vi sortir; **slip up** vi faire une erreur, gaffer

slipped disc [slɪpt-] n déplacement m de vertèbre

slipper ['slɪpəʳ] n pantoufle f

slippery ['slɪpərɪ] adj glissant(e); (fig: person) insaisissable

slip road n (Brit: to motorway) bretelle f d'accès

slip-up ['slɪpʌp] n bévue f

slipway ['slɪpweɪ] n cale f (de construction or de lancement)

slit [slɪt] n fente f; (cut) incision f; (tear) déchirure f ⊳ vt (pt, pp **slit**) fendre; couper, inciser; déchirer; **to ~ sb's throat** trancher la gorge à qn

slither ['slɪðəʳ] vi glisser, déraper

sliver ['slɪvəʳ] n (of glass, wood) éclat m; (of cheese, sausage) petit morceau

slob [slɔb] n (inf) rustaud(e)

slog [slɔg] n (Brit: effort) gros effort; (: work) tâche fastidieuse ⊳ vi travailler très dur

slogan ['sləugən] n slogan m

slope [sləup] n pente f, côte f; (side of mountain) versant m; (slant) inclinaison f ⊳ vi: **to ~ down** être or descendre en pente; **to ~ up** monter

sloping ['sləupɪŋ] adj en pente, incliné(e); (handwriting) penché(e)

sloppy ['slɔpɪ] adj (work) peu soigné(e), bâclé(e); (appearance) négligé(e), débraillé(e); (film etc) sentimental(e)

slot [slɔt] n fente f; (fig: in timetable, Radio, TV) créneau m, plage f ⊳ vt: **to ~ sth into** encastrer or insérer qch dans ⊳ vi: **to ~ into** s'encastrer or s'insérer dans

sloth [sləuθ] n (vice) paresse f; (Zool) paresseux m

slot machine n (Brit: vending machine) distributeur m (automatique), machine f à sous; (for gambling) appareil m or machine à sous

slouch [slautʃ] vi avoir le dos rond, être voûté(e); **slouch about, slouch around** vi traîner à ne rien faire

Slovakia [sləu'vækɪə] n Slovaquie f

Slovene [sləu'vi:n] adj slovène ⊳ n Slovène m/f; (Ling) slovène m

Slovenia [sləu'vi:nɪə] n Slovénie f

Slovenian [sləu'vi:nɪən] adj, n = **Slovene**

slovenly ['slʌvənlɪ] adj sale, débraillé(e), négligé(e)

slow [sləu] adj lent(e); (watch): **to be ~** retarder ⊳ adv lentement ⊳ vt, vi ralentir; **"~"** (road sign) "ralentir"; **at a ~ speed** à petite vitesse; **to be ~ to act/decide** être lent à agir/décider; **my watch is 20 minutes ~** ma montre retarde de 20 minutes; **business is ~** les affaires marchent au ralenti; **to go ~** (driver) rouler lentement; (in industrial dispute) faire la grève perlée; **slow down** vi ralentir

S

slowly ['sləulɪ] *adv* lentement

slow motion *n*: **in ~** au ralenti

sludge [slʌdʒ] *n* boue *f*

slug [slʌg] *n* limace *f*; (*bullet*) balle *f*

sluggish ['slʌgɪʃ] *adj* (*person*) mou/molle, lent(e); (*stream, engine, trading*) lent(e); (*business, sales*) stagnant(e)

sluice [slu:s] *n* écluse *f*; (*also*: **~ gate**) vanne *f* ▷ *vt*: **to ~ down** *or* **out** laver à grande eau

slum [slʌm] *n* (*house*) taudis *m*; **slums** *npl* (*area*) quartiers *mpl* pauvres

slump [slʌmp] *n* baisse soudaine, effondrement *m*; (*Econ*) crise *f* ▷ *vi* s'effondrer, s'affaisser

slung [slʌŋ] *pt, pp of* **sling**

slur [slɜːʳ] *n* bredouillement *m*; (*smear*): **~ (on)** atteinte *f* (à); insinuation *f* (contre) ▷ *vt* mal articuler; **to be a ~ on** porter atteinte à

slush [slʌʃ] *n* neige fondue

slut [slʌt] *n* souillon *f*

sly [slaɪ] *adj* (*person*) rusé(e); (*smile, expression, remark*) sournois(e); **on the ~** en cachette

smack [smæk] *n* (*slap*) tape *f*; (*on face*) gifle *f* ▷ *vt* donner une tape à; (*on face*) gifler; (*on bottom*) donner la fessée à ▷ *vi*: **to ~ of** avoir des relents de, sentir ▷ *adv* (*inf*): **it fell ~ in the middle** c'est tombé en plein milieu *or* en plein dedans; **to ~ one's lips** se lécher les babines

small [smɔːl] *adj* petit(e); (*letter*) minuscule ▷ *n*: **the ~ of the back** le creux des reins; **to get** *or* **grow ~er** diminuer; **to make ~er** (*amount, income*) diminuer; (*object, garment*) rapetisser; **a ~ shopkeeper** un petit commerçant

small ads *npl* (*Brit*) petites annonces

small change *n* petite *or* menue monnaie

smallholder ['smɔːlhəuldəʳ] *n* (*Brit*) petit cultivateur

small hours *npl*: **in the ~** au petit matin

smallpox ['smɔːlpɒks] *n* variole *f*

small talk *n* menus propos

smart [smɑːt] *adj* élégant(e), chic *inv*; (*clever*) intelligent(e), (*pej*) futé(e); (*quick*) vif/vive, prompt(e) ▷ *vi* faire mal, brûler; **the ~ set** le beau monde; **to look ~** être élégant(e); **my eyes are ~ing** j'ai les yeux irrités *or* qui me piquent

smart card ['smɑːt'kɑːd] *n* carte *f* à puce

smarten up ['smɑːtn-] *vi* devenir plus élégant(e), se faire beau/belle ▷ *vt* rendre plus élégant(e)

smart phone *n* smartphone *m*

smash [smæʃ] *n* (*also*: **~-up**) collision *f*, accident *m*; (*Mus*) succès foudroyant; (*sound*) fracas *m* ▷ *vt* casser, briser, fracasser; (*opponent*) écraser; (*hopes*) ruiner, détruire; (*Sport: record*) pulvériser ▷ *vi* se briser, se fracasser; s'écraser; **smash up** *vt* (*car*) bousiller; (*room*) tout casser dans

smashing ['smæʃɪŋ] *adj* (*inf*) formidable

smattering ['smætərɪŋ] *n*: **a ~ of** quelques notions de

smear [smɪəʳ] *n* (*stain*) tache *f*; (*mark*) trace *f*; (*Med*) frottis *m*; (*insult*) calomnie *f* ▷ *vt* enduire; (*make dirty*) salir; (*fig*) porter atteinte à; **his hands were ~ed with oil/ink** il avait les mains maculées de cambouis/d'encre

smear campaign *n* campagne *f* de dénigrement

smear test *n* (*Brit Med*) frottis *m*

smell [smɛl] (*pt, pp* **smelt** *or* **smelled**) [smɛlt, smɛld] *n* odeur *f*; (*sense*) odorat *m* ▷ *vt* sentir ▷ *vi* (*pej*) sentir mauvais; (*food etc*): **to ~ (of)** sentir; **it ~s good** ça sent bon

smelly ['smɛlɪ] *adj* qui sent mauvais, malodorant(e)

smelt [smɛlt] *pt, pp of* **smell** ▷ *vt* (*ore*) fondre

smile [smaɪl] *n* sourire *m* ▷ *vi* sourire

smirk [smɜːk] *n* petit sourire suffisant *or* affecté

smock [smɒk] *n* blouse *f*, sarrau *m*

smog [smɒg] *n* brouillard mêlé de fumée

smoke [sməuk] *n* fumée *f* ▷ *vt, vi* fumer; **to have a ~** fumer une cigarette; **do you ~?** est-ce que vous fumez?; **do you mind if I ~?** ça ne vous dérange pas que je fume?; **to go up in ~** (*house etc*) brûler; (*fig*) partir en fumée

smoke alarm *n* détecteur *m* de fumée

smoked ['sməukt] *adj* (*bacon, glass*) fumé(e)

smoker ['sməukəʳ] *n* (*person*) fumeur(-euse); (*Rail*) wagon *m* fumeurs

smoke screen *n* rideau *m or* écran *m* de fumée; (*fig*) paravent *m*

smoking ['sməukɪŋ] *n*: **"no ~"** (*sign*) "défense de fumer"; **to give up ~** arrêter de fumer

smoking compartment, (*US*) **smoking car** *n* wagon *m* fumeurs

smoky ['sməukɪ] *adj* enfumé(e); (*taste*) fumé(e)

smolder ['sməuldəʳ] *vi* (*US*) = **smoulder**

smooth [smu:ð] *adj* lisse; (*sauce*) onctueux(-euse); (*flavour, whisky*) moelleux(-euse); (*cigarette*) doux/douce; (*movement*) régulier(-ière), sans à-coups *or* heurts; (*landing, takeoff*) en douceur; (*flight*) sans secousses; (*pej: person*) doucereux(-euse), mielleux(-euse) ▷ *vt* (*also*: **~ out**) lisser, défroisser; (*creases, difficulties*) faire disparaître; **smooth over** *vt*: **to ~ things over** (*fig*) arranger les choses

smother ['smʌðəʳ] *vt* étouffer

smoulder, (*US*) **smolder** ['sməuldəʳ] *vi* couver

SMS *n abbr* (= *short message service*) SMS *m*

SMS message *n* (*message m*) SMS *m*

smudge [smʌdʒ] *n* tache *f*, bavure *f* ▷ *vt* salir, maculer

smug [smʌg] *adj* suffisant(e), content(e) de soi

smuggle ['smʌgl] *vt* passer en contrebande *or* en fraude; **to ~ in/out** (*goods etc*) faire entrer/sortir clandestinement *or* en fraude

smuggler ['smʌgləʳ] *n* contrebandier(-ière)

smuggling ['smʌglɪŋ] n contrebande f

smutty ['smʌtɪ] adj (fig) grossier(-ière), obscène

snack [snæk] n casse-croûte m inv; **to have a ~** prendre un en-cas, manger quelque chose (de léger)

snack bar n snack(-bar) m

snag [snæg] n inconvénient m, difficulté f

snail [sneɪl] n escargot m

snake [sneɪk] n serpent m

snap [snæp] n (sound) claquement m, bruit sec; (photograph) photo f, instantané m; (game) sorte de jeu de bataille ▷ adj subit(e), fait(e) sans réfléchir ▷ vt (fingers) faire claquer; (break) casser net; (photograph) prendre un instantané de ▷ vi se casser net or avec un bruit sec; (fig: person) craquer; (speak sharply) parler d'un ton brusque; **to ~ open/shut** s'ouvrir/se refermer brusquement; **to ~ one's fingers at** (fig) se moquer de; **a cold ~** (of weather) un refroidissement soudain de la température; **snap at** vt fus (subj: dog) essayer de mordre; **snap off** vt (break) casser net; **snap up** vt sauter sur, saisir

snappy ['snæpɪ] adj prompt(e); (slogan) qui a du punch; **make it ~!** (inf: hurry up) grouille-toi!, magne-toi!

snapshot ['snæpʃɔt] n photo f, instantané m

snare [snɛəʳ] n piège m ▷ vt attraper, prendre au piège

snarl [snɑːl] n grondement m or grognement m féroce ▷ vi gronder ▷ vt: **to get ~ed up** (wool, plans) s'emmêler; (traffic) se bloquer

snatch [snætʃ] n (fig) vol m; (small amount): **~es of** des fragments mpl or bribes fpl de ▷ vt saisir (d'un geste vif); (steal) voler ▷ vi: **don't ~!** doucement!; **to ~ a sandwich** manger or avaler un sandwich à la hâte; **to ~ some sleep** arriver à dormir un peu; **snatch up** vt saisir, s'emparer de

sneak [sniːk] (US pt **snuck**) vi: **to ~ in/out** entrer/sortir furtivement or à la dérobée ▷ vt: **to ~ a look at sth** regarder furtivement qch ▷ n (inf: pej: informer) faux jeton; **to ~ up on sb** s'approcher de qn sans faire de bruit

sneakers ['sniːkəz] npl tennis mpl, baskets fpl

sneer [snɪəʳ] n ricanement m ▷ vi ricaner, sourire d'un air sarcastique; **to ~ at sb/sth** se moquer de qn/qch avec mépris

sneeze [sniːz] n éternuement m ▷ vi éternuer

sniff [snɪf] n reniflement m ▷ vi renifler ▷ vt renifler, flairer; (glue, drug) sniffer, respirer; **sniff at** vt fus: **it's not to be ~ed at** il ne faut pas cracher dessus, ce n'est pas à dédaigner

snigger ['snɪgəʳ] n ricanement m; rire moqueur ▷ vi ricaner

snip [snɪp] n (cut) entaille f; (piece) petit bout; (Brit: inf: bargain) (bonne) occasion or affaire ▷ vt couper

sniper ['snaɪpəʳ] n (marksman) tireur embusqué

snippet ['snɪpɪt] n bribes fpl

snob [snɔb] n snob m/f

snobbish ['snɔbɪʃ] adj snob inv

snooker ['snuːkəʳ] n sorte de jeu de billard

snoop [snuːp] vi: **to ~ on sb** espionner qn; **to ~ about** fureter

snooze [snuːz] n petit somme ▷ vi faire un petit somme

snore [snɔːʳ] vi ronfler ▷ n ronflement m

snorkel ['snɔːkl] n (of swimmer) tuba m

snort [snɔːt] n grognement m ▷ vi grogner; (horse) renâcler ▷ vt (inf: drugs) sniffer

snout [snaut] n museau m

snow [snəu] n neige f ▷ vi neiger ▷ vt: **to be ~ed under with work** être débordé(e) de travail

snowball ['snəubɔːl] n boule f de neige

snowbound ['snəubaund] adj enneigé(e), bloqué(e) par la neige

snowdrift ['snəudrɪft] n congère f

snowdrop ['snəudrɔp] n perce-neige f

snowfall ['snəufɔːl] n chute f de neige

snowflake ['snəufleɪk] n flocon m de neige

snowman ['snəumæn] irreg n bonhomme m de neige

snowplough, (US) **snowplow** ['snəuplau] n chasse-neige m inv

snowshoe ['snəuʃuː] n raquette f (pour la neige)

snowstorm ['snəustɔːm] n tempête f de neige

snub [snʌb] vt repousser, snober ▷ n rebuffade f

snub-nosed [snʌb'nəuzd] adj au nez retroussé

snuck [snʌk] (US) pt, pp of **sneak**

snuff [snʌf] n tabac m à priser ▷ vt (also: **~ out**: candle) moucher

snug [snʌg] adj douillet(te), confortable; (person) bien au chaud; **it's a ~ fit** c'est bien ajusté(e)

snuggle ['snʌgl] vi: **to ~ down in bed/up to sb** se pelotonner dans son lit/contre qn

KEYWORD

so [səu] adv **1** (thus, likewise) ainsi, de cette façon; **if so** si oui; **so do** or **have I** moi aussi; **it's 5 o'clock — so it is!** il est 5 heures — en effet! or c'est vrai!; **I hope/think so** je l'espère/le crois; **so far** jusqu'ici, jusqu'à maintenant; (in past) jusque-là; **quite so!** exactement!, c'est bien ça!; **even so** quand même, tout de même

2 (in comparisons etc: to such a degree) si, tellement; **so big (that)** si or tellement grand (que); **she's not so clever as her brother** elle n'est pas aussi intelligente que son frère

3: **so much** adj, adv tant (de); **I've got so much work** j'ai tant de travail; **I love you so much** je vous aime tant; **so many** tant (de)

4 (phrases): **10 or so** à peu près or environ 10; **so long!** (inf: goodbye) au revoir!, à un de ces jours!; **so to speak** pour ainsi dire; **so (what)?** (*inf*) (bon) et alors?, et après? ▷ *conj* **1** (*expressing purpose*): **so as to do** pour faire, afin de faire; **so (that)** pour que *or* afin que + *sub* **2** (*expressing result*) donc, par conséquent; **so that** si bien que, de (telle) sorte que; **so that's the reason!** c'est donc (pour) ça!; **so you see, I could have gone** alors tu vois, j'aurais pu y aller

soak [səʊk] *vt* faire *or* laisser tremper; (*drench*) tremper ▷ *vi* tremper; **to be ~ed through** être trempé jusqu'aux os; **soak in** *vi* pénétrer, être absorbé(e); **soak up** *vt* absorber

soaking ['səʊkɪŋ] *adj* (*also*: **~ wet**) trempé(e)

so-and-so ['səʊənsəʊ] *n* (*somebody*) un(e) tel(le)

soap [səʊp] *n* savon *m*

soapflakes ['səʊpfleɪks] *npl* paillettes *fpl* de savon

soap opera *n* feuilleton télévisé (*quotidienneté réaliste ou embellie*)

soap powder *n* lessive *f*, détergent *m*

soapy ['səʊpɪ] *adj* savonneux(-euse)

soar [sɔːʳ] *vi* monter (en flèche), s'élancer; (*building*) s'élancer; **~ing prices** prix qui grimpent

sob [sɔb] *n* sanglot *m* ▷ *vi* sangloter

sober ['səʊbəʳ] *adj* qui n'est pas (*or* plus) ivre; (*serious*) sérieux(-euse), sensé(e); (*moderate*) mesuré(e); (*colour, style*) sobre, discret(-ète); **sober up** *vt* dégriser ▷ *vi* se dégriser

so-called ['səʊ'kɔːld] *adj* soi-disant *inv*

soccer ['sɔkəʳ] *n* football *m*

sociable ['səʊʃəbl] *adj* sociable

social ['səʊʃl] *adj* social(e); (*sociable*) sociable ▷ *n* (petite) fête

social club *n* amicale *f*, foyer *m*

socialism ['səʊʃəlɪzəm] *n* socialisme *m*

socialist ['səʊʃəlɪst] *adj*, *n* socialiste (*m/f*)

socialize ['səʊʃəlaɪz] *vi* voir *or* rencontrer des gens, se faire des amis; **to ~ with** (*meet often*) fréquenter; (*get to know*) lier connaissance *or* parler avec

social life *n* vie sociale; **how's your ~?** est-ce que tu sors beaucoup?

socially ['səʊʃəlɪ] *adv* socialement, en société

social networking [-'nɛtwəːkɪŋ] *n* réseaux *mpl* sociaux

social security *n* aide sociale

social services *npl* services sociaux

social work *n* assistance sociale

social worker *n* assistant(e) sociale(e)

society [sə'saɪətɪ] *n* société *f*; (*club*) société *f*, association *f*; (*also*: **high ~**) (haute) société, grand monde ▷ *cpd* (*party*) mondain(e)

sociology [səʊsɪ'ɔlədʒɪ] *n* sociologie *f*

sock [sɔk] *n* chaussette *f* ▷ *vt* (*inf*: *hit*) flanquer un coup à; **to pull one's ~s up** (*fig*) se secouer (les puces)

socket ['sɔkɪt] *n* cavité *f*; (*Elec: also*: **wall ~**) prise *f* de courant; (*: for light bulb*) douille *f*

sod [sɔd] *n* (*of earth*) motte *f*; (*Brit inf!*) con *m* (!), salaud *m* (!); **sod off** *vi*: **~ off!** (*Brit inf!*) fous le camp!, va te faire foutre! (!)

soda ['səʊdə] *n* (*Chem*) soude *f*; (*also*: **~ water**) eau *f* de Seltz; (*US: also*: **~ pop**) soda *m*

sodium ['səʊdɪəm] *n* sodium *m*

sofa ['səʊfə] *n* sofa *m*, canapé *m*

sofa bed *n* canapé-lit *m*

soft [sɔft] *adj* (*not rough*) doux/douce; (*not hard*) doux, mou/molle; (*not loud*) doux, léger(-ère); (*kind*) doux, gentil(le); (*weak*) indulgent(e); (*stupid*) stupide, débile

soft drink *n* boisson non alcoolisée

soft drugs *npl* drogues douces

soften ['sɔfn] *vt* (r)amollir; (*fig*) adoucir ▷ *vi* se ramollir; (*fig*) s'adoucir

softly ['sɔftlɪ] *adv* doucement; (*touch*) légèrement; (*kiss*) tendrement

softness ['sɔftnɪs] *n* douceur *f*

software ['sɔftwɛəʳ] *n* logiciel *m*, software *m*

soggy ['sɔgɪ] *adj* (*clothes*) trempé(e); (*ground*) détrempé(e)

soil [sɔɪl] *n* (*earth*) sol *m*, terre *f* ▷ *vt* salir; (*fig*) souiller

solar ['səʊləʳ] *adj* solaire

solar panel *n* panneau *m* solaire

solar power *n* énergie *f* solaire

solar system *n* système *m* solaire

sold [səʊld] *pt, pp of* **sell**

solder ['səʊldəʳ] *vt* souder (*au fil à souder*) ▷ *n* soudure *f*

soldier ['səʊldʒəʳ] *n* soldat *m*, militaire *m* ▷ *vi*: **to ~ on** persévérer, s'accrocher; **toy ~** petit soldat

sold out *adj* (*Comm*) épuisé(e)

sole [səʊl] *n* (*of foot*) plante *f*; (*of shoe*) semelle *f*; (*fish: pl inv*) sole *f* ▷ *adj* seul(e), unique; **the ~ reason** la seule et unique raison

solely ['səʊllɪ] *adv* seulement, uniquement; **I will hold you ~ responsible** je vous en tiendrai pour seul responsable

solemn ['sɔləm] *adj* solennel(le); (*person*) sérieux(-euse), grave

sole trader *n* (*Comm*) chef *m* d'entreprise individuelle

solicit [sə'lɪsɪt] *vt* (*request*) solliciter ▷ *vi* (*prostitute*) racoler

solicitor [sə'lɪsɪtəʳ] *n* (*Brit: for wills etc*) ≈ notaire *m*; (*: in court*) ≈ avocat *m*

solid ['sɔlɪd] *adj* (*strong, sound, reliable: not liquid*) solide; (*not hollow: mass*) compact(e); (*: metal, rock, wood*) massif(-ive); (*meal*) consistant(e), substantiel(le); (*vote*) unanime ▷ *n* solide *m*; **to be on ~ ground** être sur la terre ferme; (*fig*) être en terrain sûr; **we waited two ~ hours** nous avons attendu deux heures entières

solidarity [sɔlɪ'dærɪtɪ] *n* solidarité *f*

solitary ['sɔlɪtərɪ] *adj* solitaire
solitary confinement *n* (*Law*) isolement *m* (cellulaire)
solitude ['sɔlɪtju:d] *n* solitude *f*
solo ['səuləu] *n* solo *m* ▷ *adv* (*fly*) en solitaire
soloist ['səuləuɪst] *n* soliste *m/f*
soluble ['sɔljubl] *adj* soluble
solution [sə'lu:ʃən] *n* solution *f*
solve [sɔlv] *vt* résoudre
solvent ['sɔlvənt] *adj* (*Comm*) solvable ▷ *n* (*Chem*) (dis)solvant *m*
sombre, (*US*) **somber** ['sɔmbə'] *adj* sombre, morne

○ KEYWORD

some [sʌm] *adj* **1** (*a certain amount or number of*): **some tea/water/ice cream** du thé/de l'eau/ de la glace; **some children/apples** des enfants/pommes; **I've got some money but not much** j'ai de l'argent mais pas beaucoup
2 (*certain: in contrasts*): **some people say that ...** il y a des gens qui disent que ...; **some films were excellent, but most were mediocre** certains films étaient excellents, mais la plupart étaient médiocres
3 (*unspecified*): **some woman was asking for you** il y avait une dame qui vous demandait; **he was asking for some book (or other)** il demandait un livre quelconque; **some day** un de ces jours; **some day next week** un jour la semaine prochaine; **after some time** après un certain temps; **at some length** assez longuement; **in some form or other** sous une forme ou une autre, sous une forme quelconque
▷ *pron* **1** (*a certain number*) quelques-un(e)s, certain(e)s; **I've got some** (*books etc*) j'en ai (quelques-uns); **some (of them) have been sold** certains ont été vendus
2 (*a certain amount*) un peu; **I've got some** (*money, milk*) j'en ai (un peu); **would you like some?** est-ce que vous en voulez?, en voulez-vous?; **could I have some of that cheese?** pourrais-je avoir un peu de ce fromage?; **I've read some of the book** j'ai lu une partie du livre
▷ *adv*: **some 10 people** quelque 10 personnes, 10 personnes environ

somebody ['sʌmbədɪ] *pron* = **someone**
somehow ['sʌmhau] *adv* d'une façon ou d'une autre; (*for some reason*) pour une raison ou une autre
someone ['sʌmwʌn] *pron* quelqu'un; **~ or other** quelqu'un, je ne sais qui
someplace ['sʌmpleɪs] *adv* (*US*) = **somewhere**
somersault ['sʌməsɔ:lt] *n* culbute *f*, saut périlleux ▷ *vi* faire la culbute *or* un saut périlleux; (*car*) faire un tonneau

something ['sʌmθɪŋ] *pron* quelque chose *m*; **~ interesting** quelque chose d'intéressant; **~ to do** quelque chose à faire; **he's ~ like me** il est un peu comme moi; **it's ~ of a problem** il y a là un problème
sometime ['sʌmtaɪm] *adv* (*in future*) un de ces jours, un jour ou l'autre; (*in past*): **~ last month** au cours du mois dernier
sometimes ['sʌmtaɪmz] *adv* quelquefois, parfois
somewhat ['sʌmwɔt] *adv* quelque peu, un peu
somewhere ['sʌmweə'] *adv* quelque part; **~ else** ailleurs, autre part
son [sʌn] *n* fils *m*
song [sɔŋ] *n* chanson *f*; (*of bird*) chant *m*
son-in-law ['sʌnɪnlɔ:] *n* gendre *m*, beau-fils *m*
soon [su:n] *adv* bientôt; (*early*) tôt; **~ afterwards** peu après; **quite ~** sous peu; **how ~ can you do it?** combien de temps vous faut-il pour le faire, au plus pressé?; **how ~ can you come back?** quand *or* dans combien de temps pouvez-vous revenir, au plus tôt?; **see you ~!** à bientôt!; *see also* **as**
sooner ['su:nə'] *adv* (*time*) plus tôt; (*preference*): **I would ~ do that** j'aimerais autant or je préférerais faire ça; **~ or later** tôt ou tard; **no ~ said than done** sitôt dit, sitôt fait; **the ~ the better** le plus tôt sera le mieux; **no ~ had we left than ...** à peine étions-nous partis que ...
soot [sut] *n* suie *f*
soothe [su:ð] *vt* calmer, apaiser
sophisticated [sə'fɪstɪkeɪtɪd] *adj* raffiné(e), sophistiqué(e); (*machinery*) hautement perfectionné(e), très complexe; (*system etc*) très perfectionné(e), sophistiqué
sophomore ['sɔfəmɔ:'] *n* (*US*) étudiant(e) de seconde année
sopping ['sɔpɪŋ] *adj* (*also*: **~ wet**) tout(e) trempé(e)
soppy ['sɔpɪ] *adj* (*pej*) sentimental(e)
soprano [sə'prɑ:nəu] *n* (*voice*) soprano *m*; (*singer*) soprano *m/f*
sorbet ['sɔ:beɪ] *n* sorbet *m*
sorcerer ['sɔ:sərə'] *n* sorcier *m*
sordid ['sɔ:dɪd] *adj* sordide
sore [sɔ:'] *adj* (*painful*) douloureux(-euse), sensible; (*offended*) contrarié(e), vexé(e) ▷ *n* plaie *f*; **to have a ~ throat** avoir mal à la gorge; **it's a ~ point** (*fig*) c'est un point délicat
sorely ['sɔ:lɪ] *adv* (*tempted*) fortement
sorrow ['sɔrəu] *n* peine *f*, chagrin *m*
sorry ['sɔrɪ] *adj* désolé(e); (*condition, excuse, tale*) triste, déplorable; (*sight*) désolant(e); **~!** pardon!, excusez-moi!; **~?** pardon?; **to feel ~ for sb** plaindre qn; **I'm ~ to hear that ...** je suis désolé(e) *or* navré(e) d'apprendre que ...; **to be ~ about sth** regretter qch

S

sort [sɔːt] n genre m, espèce f, sorte f; (make: of coffee, car etc) marque f ⊳ vt (also: ~ out: select which to keep) trier; (classify) classer; (tidy) ranger; (letters etc) trier; (Comput) trier; **what ~ do you want?** quelle sorte or quel genre voulez-vous?; **what ~ of car?** quelle marque de voiture?; **I'll do nothing of the ~!** je ne ferai rien de tel!; **it's ~ of awkward** (inf) c'est plutôt gênant; **sort out** vt (problem) résoudre, régler

sorting office ['sɔːtɪŋ-] n (Post) bureau m de tri

SOS n SOS m

so-so ['səʊsəʊ] adv comme ci comme ça

sought [sɔːt] pt, pp of **seek**

soul [səʊl] n âme f; **the poor ~ had nowhere to sleep** le pauvre n'avait nulle part où dormir; **I didn't see a ~** je n'ai vu (absolument) personne

soulful ['səʊlful] adj plein(e) de sentiment

sound [saʊnd] adj (healthy) en bonne santé, sain(e); (safe, not damaged) solide, en bon état; (reliable, not superficial) sérieux(-euse), solide; (sensible) sensé(e) ⊳ adv: **~ asleep** profondément endormi(e) ⊳ n (noise, volume) son m; (louder) bruit m; (Geo) détroit m, bras m de mer ⊳ vt (alarm) sonner; (also: **~ out**: opinions) sonder ⊳ vi sonner, retentir; (fig: seem) sembler (être); **to be of ~ mind** être sain(e) d'esprit; **it doesn't ~ right** ça ne me dit rien qui vaille; **to ~ one's horn** (Aut) klaxonner, actionner son avertisseur; **to ~ like** ressembler à; **it ~s as if ...** il semblerait que ..., j'ai l'impression que ...; **sound off** vi (inf): **to ~ off (about)** la ramener (sur)

sound barrier n mur m du son

sound bite n phrase toute faite (pour être citée dans les médias)

sound effects npl bruitage m

soundly ['saʊndlɪ] adv (sleep) profondément; (beat) complètement, à plate couture

soundproof ['saʊndpruːf] vt insonoriser ⊳ adj insonorisé(e)

soundtrack ['saʊndtræk] n (of film) bande f sonore

soup [suːp] n soupe f, potage m; **in the ~** (fig) dans le pétrin

soup plate n assiette creuse or à soupe

soupspoon ['suːpspuːn] n cuiller f à soupe

sour ['saʊər] adj aigre, acide; (milk) tourné(e), aigre; (fig) acerbe, aigre; revêche; **to go or turn ~** (milk, wine) tourner; (fig: relationship, plans) mal tourner; **it's ~ grapes** c'est du dépit

source [sɔːs] n source f; **I have it from a reliable ~ that** je sais de source sûre que

south [saʊθ] n sud m ⊳ adj sud inv, (du) sud ⊳ adv au sud, vers le sud; **(to the) ~ of** au sud de; **to travel ~** aller en direction du sud

South Africa n Afrique f du Sud

South African adj sud-africain(e) ⊳ n Sud-Africain(e)

South America n Amérique f du Sud

South American adj sud-américain(e) ⊳ n Sud-Américain(e)

southbound ['saʊθbaʊnd] adj en direction du sud; (carriageway) sud inv

south-east [saʊθ'iːst] n sud-est m

southerly ['sʌðəlɪ] adj du sud; au sud

southern ['sʌðən] adj (du) sud; méridional(e); **with a ~ aspect** orienté(e) or exposé(e) au sud; **the ~ hemisphere** l'hémisphère sud or austral

South Korea n Corée f du Sud

South of France n: **the ~** le Sud de la France, le Midi

South Pole n Pôle m Sud

South Wales n sud m du Pays de Galles

southward ['saʊθwəd], **southwards** ['saʊθwədz] adv vers le sud

south-west [saʊθ'wɛst] n sud-ouest m

souvenir [suːvə'nɪər] n souvenir m (objet)

sovereign ['sɔvrɪn] adj, n souverain(e)

soviet ['səʊvɪət] adj soviétique

sow[1] [səʊ] (pt sowed, pp sown) [səʊn] vt semer

sow[2] [saʊ] truie f

soya ['sɔɪə], (US) **soy** [sɔɪ] n: **~ bean** graine f de soja; **~ sauce** sauce f au soja

spa [spɑː] n (town) station thermale; (US: also: **health ~**) établissement m de cure de rajeunissement

space [speɪs] n (gen) espace m; (room) place f, espace; (length of time) laps m de temps ⊳ cpd spatial(e) ⊳ vt (also: **~ out**) espacer; **to clear a ~ for sth** faire de la place pour qch; **in a confined ~** dans un espace réduit or restreint; **in a short ~ of time** dans peu de temps; **(with)in the ~ of an hour** en l'espace d'une heure

spacecraft ['speɪskrɑːft] n engin or vaisseau spatial

spaceman ['speɪsmæn] irreg n astronaute m, cosmonaute m

spaceship ['speɪsʃɪp] n = **spacecraft**

spacing ['speɪsɪŋ] n espacement m; **single/double ~** (Typ etc) interligne m simple/double

spacious ['speɪʃəs] adj spacieux(-euse), grand(e)

spade [speɪd] n (tool) bêche f, pelle f; (child's) pelle; **spades** npl (Cards) pique m

spaghetti [spə'gɛtɪ] n spaghetti mpl

Spain [speɪn] n Espagne f

spam [spæm] n (Comput) pourriel m

span [spæn] n (of bird, plane) envergure f; (of arch) portée f; (in time) espace m de temps, durée f ⊳ vt enjamber, franchir; (fig) couvrir, embrasser

Spaniard ['spænjəd] n Espagnol(e)

spaniel ['spænjəl] n épagneul m

Spanish ['spænɪʃ] adj espagnol(e), d'Espagne ⊳ n (Ling) espagnol m; **the Spanish** npl les Espagnols; **~ omelette** omelette f à l'espagnole

spank [spæŋk] vt donner une fessée à

spanner ['spænə^r] n (Brit) clé f (de mécanicien)

spare [spɛə^r] adj de réserve, de rechange; (surplus) de or en trop, de reste ▷ n (part) pièce f de rechange, pièce détachée ▷ vt (do without) se passer de; (afford to give) donner, accorder, passer; (not hurt) épargner; (not use) ménager; **to ~** (surplus) en surplus, de trop; **there are 2 going** (Brit) il y en a 2 de disponible; **to ~ no expense** ne pas reculer devant la dépense; **can you ~ the time?** est-ce que vous avez le temps?; **there is no time to ~** il n'y a pas de temps à perdre; **I've a few minutes to ~** je dispose de quelques minutes

spare part n pièce f de rechange, pièce détachée

spare room n chambre f d'ami

spare time n moments mpl de loisir

spare tyre, (US) **spare tire** n (Aut) pneu m de rechange

spare wheel n (Aut) roue f de secours

sparingly ['spɛərɪŋlɪ] adv avec modération

spark [spɑːk] n étincelle f; (fig) étincelle, lueur f

sparkle ['spɑːkl] n scintillement m, étincellement m, éclat m ▷ vi étinceler, scintiller; (bubble) pétiller

sparkling ['spɑːklɪŋ] adj étincelant(e), scintillant(e); (wine) mousseux(-euse), pétillant(e); (water) pétillant(e), gazeux(-euse)

spark plug n bougie f

sparrow ['spærəu] n moineau m

sparse [spɑːs] adj clairsemé(e)

spartan ['spɑːtən] adj (fig) spartiate

spasm ['spæzəm] n (Med) spasme m; (fig) accès m

spasmodic [spæz'mɔdɪk] adj (fig) intermittent(e)

spastic ['spæstɪk] n handicapé(e) moteur

spat [spæt] pt, pp of **spit** ▷ n (US) prise f de bec

spate [speɪt] n (fig): **~ of** avalanche f or torrent m de; **in ~** (river) en crue

spatula ['spætjulə] n spatule f

spawn [spɔːn] vt pondre; (pej) engendrer ▷ vi frayer ▷ n frai m

speak (pt **spoke**, pp **spoken**) [spiːk, spəuk, 'spəukn] vt (language) parler; (truth) dire ▷ vi parler; (make a speech) prendre la parole; **to ~ to sb/of** or **about sth** parler à qn/de qch; **I don't ~ French** je ne parle pas français; **do you ~ English?** parlez-vous anglais?; **can I ~ to ...?** est-ce que je peux parler à ...?; **~ing!** (on telephone) c'est moi-même!; **to ~ one's mind** dire ce que l'on pense; **it ~s for itself** c'est évident; **~ up!** parle plus fort!; **he has no money to ~ of** il n'a pas d'argent; **speak for** vt fus: **to ~ for sb** parler pour qn; **that picture is already spoken for** (in shop) ce tableau est déjà réservé

speaker ['spiːkə^r] n (in public) orateur m; (also: **loud~**) haut-parleur m; (for stereo etc) baffle m, enceinte f; (Pol): **the S~** (Brit) le président de la Chambre des communes or des représentants; (US) le président de la Chambre; **are you a Welsh ~?** parlez-vous gallois?

spear [spɪə^r] n lance f ▷ vt transpercer

spearhead ['spɪəhɛd] n fer m de lance; (Mil) colonne f d'attaque ▷ vt (attack etc) mener

spec [spɛk] n (Brit inf): **on ~** à tout hasard; **to buy on ~** acheter avec l'espoir de faire une bonne affaire

special ['spɛʃl] adj spécial(e) ▷ n (train) train spécial; **take ~ care** soyez particulièrement prudents; **nothing ~** rien de spécial; **today's ~** (at restaurant) le plat du jour

special delivery n (Post): **by ~** en express

special effects npl (Cine) effets spéciaux

specialist ['spɛʃəlɪst] n spécialiste m/f; **heart ~** cardiologue m/f

speciality [spɛʃɪ'ælɪtɪ] n (Brit) spécialité f

specialize ['spɛʃəlaɪz] vi: **to ~ (in)** se spécialiser (dans)

specially ['spɛʃlɪ] adv spécialement, particulièrement

special needs npl (Brit) difficultés fpl d'apprentissage scolaire

special offer n (Comm) réclame f

special school n (Brit) établissement m d'enseignement spécialisé

specialty ['spɛʃəltɪ] n (US) = **speciality**

species ['spiːʃiːz] n (pl inv) espèce f

specific [spə'sɪfɪk] adj (not vague) précis(e), explicite; (particular) particulier(-ière); (Bot, Chem etc) spécifique; **to be ~ to** être particulier à, être le or un caractère (or les caractères) spécifique(s) de

specifically [spə'sɪfɪklɪ] adv explicitement, précisément; (intend, ask, design) expressément, spécialement; (exclusively) exclusivement, spécifiquement

specification [spɛsɪfɪ'keɪʃən] n spécification f; stipulation f; **specifications** npl (of car, building etc) spécification

specify ['spɛsɪfaɪ] vt spécifier, préciser; **unless otherwise specified** sauf indication contraire

specimen ['spɛsɪmən] n spécimen m, échantillon m; (Med: of blood) prélèvement m; (: of urine) échantillon m

speck [spɛk] n petite tache, petit point; (particle) grain m

speckled ['spɛkld] adj tacheté(e), moucheté(e)

specs [spɛks] npl (inf) lunettes fpl

spectacle ['spɛktəkl] n spectacle m; **spectacles** npl (Brit) lunettes fpl

spectacular [spɛk'tækjulə^r] adj spectaculaire ▷ n (Cine etc) superproduction f

spectator [spɛk'teɪtə^r] n spectateur(-trice)

spectrum (pl **spectra**) ['spɛktrəm, -rə] n spectre m; (fig) gamme f

speculate ['spekjuleɪt] vi spéculer; *(try to guess)*: **to ~ about** s'interroger sur

speculation [spekju'leɪʃən] n spéculation f; conjectures fpl

speech [spiːtʃ] n *(faculty)* parole f; *(talk)* discours m, allocution f; *(manner of speaking)* façon f de parler, langage m; *(language)* langage m; *(enunciation)* élocution f

speechless ['spiːtʃlɪs] adj muet(te)

speed [spiːd] n vitesse f; *(promptness)* rapidité f ▷ vi *(pt, pp sped)* [sped] *(Aut: exceed speed limit)* faire un excès de vitesse; **to ~ along/by** etc aller/passer etc à toute vitesse; **at ~** *(Brit)* rapidement; **at full or top ~** à toute vitesse or allure; **at a ~ of 70 km/h** à une vitesse de 70 km/h; **shorthand/typing ~s** nombre m de mots à la minute en sténographie/dactylographie; **a five-~ gearbox** une boîte cinq vitesses; **speed up** *(pt, pp speeded up)* vi aller plus vite, accélérer ▷ vt accélérer

speedboat ['spiːdbəut] n vedette f, hors-bord m inv

speedily ['spiːdɪlɪ] adv rapidement, promptement

speeding ['spiːdɪŋ] n *(Aut)* excès m de vitesse

speed limit n limitation f de vitesse, vitesse maximale permise

speedometer [spɪ'dɔmɪtər] n compteur m (de vitesse)

speedway n *(Sport)* piste f de vitesse pour motos; *(also: ~ racing)* épreuve(s) f(pl) de vitesse de motos

speedy ['spiːdɪ] adj rapide, prompt(e)

spell [spel] n *(also: magic ~)* sortilège m, charme m; *(period of time)* (courte) période ▷ vt *(pt, pp spelt or spelled)* [spelt, speld] *(in writing)* écrire, orthographier; *(aloud)* épeler; *(fig)* signifier; **to cast a ~ on sb** jeter un sort à qn; **he can't ~** il fait des fautes d'orthographe; **how do you ~ your name?** comment écrivez-vous votre nom?; **can you ~ it for me?** pouvez-vous me l'épeler?; **spell out** vt *(explain)*: **to ~ sth out for sb** expliquer qch clairement à qn

spellbound ['spelbaund] adj envoûté(e), subjugué(e)

spellchecker ['speltʃekər] n *(Comput)* correcteur m or vérificateur m orthographique

spelling ['spelɪŋ] n orthographe f

spelt [spelt] pt, pp of **spell**

spend *(pt, pp spent)* [spend, spent] vt *(money)* dépenser; *(time, life)* passer; *(devote)* consacrer; **to ~ time/money/effort on sth** consacrer du temps/de l'argent/de l'énergie à qch

spending ['spendɪŋ] n dépenses fpl; **government ~** les dépenses publiques

spendthrift ['spendθrɪft] n dépensier(-ière)

spent [spent] pt, pp of **spend** ▷ adj *(patience)*

épuisé(e), à bout; *(cartridge, bullets)* vide; **~ matches** vieilles allumettes

sperm [spəːm] n spermatozoïde m; *(semen)* sperme m

sphere [sfɪər] n sphère f; *(fig)* sphère, domaine m

spice [spaɪs] n épice f ▷ vt épicer

spicy ['spaɪsɪ] adj épicé(e), relevé(e); *(fig)* piquant(e)

spider ['spaɪdər] n araignée f; **~'s web** toile f d'araignée

spike [spaɪk] n pointe f; *(Elec)* pointe de tension; *(Bot)* épi m; **spikes** npl *(Sport)* chaussures fpl à pointes

spill *(pt, pp spilt or spilled)* [spɪl, -t, -d] vt renverser; répandre ▷ vi se répandre; **to ~ the beans** *(inf)* vendre la mèche; *(: confess)* lâcher le morceau; **spill out** vi sortir à flots, se répandre; **spill over** vi déborder

spilt [spɪlt] pt, pp of **spill**

spin [spɪn] *(pt, pp spun)* [spʌn] n *(revolution of wheel)* tour m; *(Aviat)* (chute f en) vrille f; *(trip in car)* petit tour, balade f; *(on ball)* effet m ▷ vt *(wool etc)* filer; *(Brit: clothes)* essorer ▷ vi *(turn)* tourner, tournoyer; **to ~ a yarn** débiter une longue histoire; **to ~ a coin** *(Brit)* jouer à pile ou face; **spin out** vt faire durer

spinach ['spɪnɪtʃ] n épinard m; *(as food)* épinards mpl

spinal ['spaɪnl] adj vertébral(e), spinal(e)

spinal cord n moelle épinière

spin doctor n *(inf)* personne employée pour présenter un parti politique sous un jour favorable

spin-dryer [spɪn'draɪər] n *(Brit)* essoreuse f

spine [spaɪn] n colonne vertébrale; *(thorn)* épine f, piquant m

spineless ['spaɪnlɪs] adj invertébré(e); *(fig)* mou/molle, sans caractère

spinning ['spɪnɪŋ] n *(of thread)* filage m; *(by machine)* filature f

spinning top n toupie f

spin-off ['spɪnɔf] n sous-produit m; avantage inattendu

spinster ['spɪnstər] n célibataire f; vieille fille

spiral ['spaɪərl] n spirale f ▷ adj en spirale ▷ vi *(fig: prices etc)* monter en flèche; **the inflationary ~** la spirale inflationniste

spiral staircase n escalier m en colimaçon

spire ['spaɪər] n flèche f, aiguille f

spirit ['spɪrɪt] n *(soul)* esprit m, âme f; *(ghost)* esprit, revenant m; *(mood)* esprit, état m d'esprit; *(courage)* courage m, énergie f; **spirits** npl *(drink)* spiritueux mpl, alcool m; **in good ~s** de bonne humeur; **in low ~s** démoralisé(e); **community ~** solidarité f; **public ~** civisme m

spirited ['spɪrɪtɪd] adj vif/vive, fougueux(-euse), plein(e) d'allant

spiritual ['spɪrɪtjuəl] adj spirituel(le); *(religious)* religieux(-euse) ▷ n *(also: Negro ~)* spiritual m

spit [spɪt] n (for roasting) broche f; (spittle) crachat m; (saliva) salive f ▷ vi (pt, pp **spat**) [spæt] cracher; (sound) crépiter; (rain) crachiner

spite [spaɪt] n rancune f, dépit m ▷ vt contrarier, vexer; **in ~ of** en dépit de, malgré

spiteful ['spaɪtful] adj malveillant(e), rancunier(-ière)

spittle ['spɪtl] n salive f; bave f; crachat m

splash [splæʃ] n (sound) plouf m; (of colour) tache f ▷ vt éclabousser ▷ vi (also: **~ about**) barboter, patauger; **splash out** vi (Brit) faire une folie

spleen [spli:n] n (Anat) rate f

splendid ['splɛndɪd] adj splendide, superbe, magnifique

splint [splɪnt] n attelle f, éclisse f

splinter ['splɪntəʳ] n (wood) écharde f; (metal) éclat m ▷ vi (wood) se fendre; (glass) se briser

split [splɪt] (pt, pp **split**) n fente f, déchirure f; (fig: Pol) scission f ▷ vt fendre, déchirer; (party) diviser; (work, profits) partager, répartir ▷ vi (break) se fendre, se briser; (divide) se diviser; **let's ~ the difference** coupons la poire en deux; **to do the ~s** faire le grand écart; **split up** vi (couple) se séparer, rompre; (meeting) se disperser

spoil (pt, pp **spoiled** or **spoilt**) [spɔɪl, -d, -t] vt (damage) abîmer; (mar) gâcher; (child) gâter; (ballot paper) rendre nul ▷ vi: **to be ~ing for a fight** chercher la bagarre

spoils [spɔɪlz] npl butin m

spoilsport ['spɔɪlspɔːt] n trouble-fête m/f inv, rabat-joie m inv

spoilt [spɔɪlt] pt, pp of **spoil** ▷ adj (child) gâté(e); (ballot paper) nul(le)

spoke [spəuk] pt of **speak** ▷ n rayon m

spoken ['spəukn] pp of **speak**

spokesman ['spəuksmən] irreg n porte-parole m inv

spokesperson ['spəukspɜːsn] irreg n porte-parole m inv

spokeswoman ['spəukswumən] (irreg) n porte-parole m inv

sponge [spʌndʒ] n éponge f; (Culin: also: **~ cake**) ≈ biscuit m de Savoie ▷ vt éponger ▷ vi: **to ~ off** or **on** vivre aux crochets de

sponge bag n (Brit) trousse f de toilette

sponsor ['spɒnsəʳ] n (Radio, TV, Sport) sponsor m; (for application) parrain m, marraine f; (Brit: for fund-raising event) donateur(-trice) ▷ vt (programme, competition etc) parrainer, patronner, sponsoriser; (Pol: bill) présenter; (new member) parrainer; (fund-raiser) faire un don à; **I ~ed him at 3p a mile** (in fund-raising race) je me suis engagé à lui donner 3p par mile

sponsorship ['spɒnsəʃɪp] n sponsoring m; patronage m, parrainage m; dons mpl

spontaneous [spɒn'teɪnɪəs] adj spontané(e)

spooky ['spu:kɪ] adj (inf) qui donne la chair de poule

spool [spu:l] n bobine f

spoon [spu:n] n cuiller f

spoon-feed ['spu:nfi:d] vt nourrir à la cuiller; (fig) mâcher le travail à

spoonful ['spu:nful] n cuillerée f

sport [spɔ:t] n sport m; (amusement) divertissement m; (person) chic type m/chic fille f ▷ vt (wear) arborer; **indoor/outdoor ~s** sports en salle/de plein air; **to say sth in ~** dire qch pour rire

sporting ['spɔ:tɪŋ] adj sportif(-ive); **to give sb a ~ chance** donner sa chance à qn

sport jacket n (US) = **sports jacket**

sports car n voiture f de sport

sports centre (Brit) n centre sportif

sports jacket n (Brit) veste f de sport

sportsman ['spɔ:tsmən] irreg n sportif m

sportsmanship ['spɔ:tsmənʃɪp] n esprit sportif, sportivité f

sports utility vehicle n véhicule m de loisirs (de type SUV)

sportswear ['spɔ:tswɛəʳ] n vêtements mpl de sport

sportswoman ['spɔ:tswumən] irreg n sportive f

sporty ['spɔ:tɪ] adj sportif(-ive)

spot [spɒt] n tache f; (dot: on pattern) pois m; (pimple) bouton m; (place) endroit m, coin m; (also: **~ advertisement**) message m publicitaire; (small amount): **a ~** un peu de ▷ vt (notice) apercevoir, repérer; **on the ~** sur place, sur les lieux; (immediately) sur le champ; **to put sb on the ~** (fig) mettre qn dans l'embarras; **to come out in ~s** se couvrir de boutons, avoir une éruption de boutons

spot check n contrôle intermittent

spotless ['spɒtlɪs] adj immaculé(e)

spotlight ['spɒtlaɪt] n projecteur m; (Aut) phare m auxiliaire

spotted ['spɒtɪd] adj tacheté(e), moucheté(e); à pois; **~ with** tacheté(e) de

spotty ['spɒtɪ] adj (face) boutonneux(-euse)

spouse [spauz] n époux/épouse

spout [spaut] n (of jug) bec m; (of liquid) jet m ▷ vi jaillir

sprain [spreɪn] n entorse f, foulure f ▷ vt: **to ~ one's ankle** se fouler or se tordre la cheville

sprang [spræŋ] pt of **spring**

sprawl [sprɔ:l] vi s'étaler ▷ n: **urban ~** expansion urbaine; **to send sb ~ing** envoyer qn rouler par terre

spray [spreɪ] n jet m (en fines gouttelettes); (from sea) embruns mpl; (aerosol) vaporisateur m, bombe f; (for garden) pulvérisateur m; (of flowers) petit bouquet m ▷ vt vaporiser, pulvériser; (crops) traiter ▷ cpd (deodorant etc) en bombe or atomiseur

spread [sprɛd] n (pt, pp **spread**) (distribution) répartition f; (Culin) pâte f à tartiner; (inf: meal) festin m; (Press, Typ: two pages) double page f ▷ vt (paste, contents) étendre, étaler;

(*rumour, disease*) répandre, propager; (*repayments*) échelonner, étaler; (*wealth*) répartir ▷ *vi* s'étendre; se répandre; se propager; (*stain*) s'étaler; **middle-age ~** embonpoint *m* (pris avec l'âge); **spread out** *vi* (*people*) se disperser

spread-eagled ['spredi:gld] *adj*: **to be** *or* **lie ~** être étendu(e) bras et jambes écartés

spreadsheet ['spredʃi:t] *n* (*Comput*) tableur *m*

spree [spri:] *n*: **to go on a ~** faire la fête

sprightly ['spraitli] *adj* alerte

spring [sprɪŋ] (*pt* **sprang**, *pp* **sprung**) [spræŋ, sprʌŋ] *n* (*season*) printemps *m*; (*leap*) bond *m*, saut *m*; (*coiled metal*) ressort *m*; (*bounciness*) élasticité *f*; (*of water*) source *f* ▷ *vi* bondir, sauter ▷ *vt*: **to ~ a leak** (*pipe etc*) se mettre à fuir; **he sprang the news on me** il m'a annoncé la nouvelle de but en blanc; **in ~, in the ~** au printemps; **to ~ from** provenir de; **to ~ into action** passer à l'action; **to walk with a ~ in one's step** marcher d'un pas souple; **spring up** *vi* (*problem*) se présenter, surgir; (*plant, buildings*) surgir de terre

springboard ['sprɪŋbɔ:d] *n* tremplin *m*

spring-clean [sprɪŋ'kli:n] *n* (*also*: **~ing**) grand nettoyage de printemps

spring onion *n* (*Brit*) ciboule *f*, cive *f*

springtime ['sprɪŋtaɪm] *n* printemps *m*

sprinkle ['sprɪŋkl] *vt* (*pour*) répandre; verser; **to ~ water** *etc* **on, ~ with water** *etc* asperger d'eau *etc*; **to ~ sugar** *etc* **on, ~ with sugar** *etc* saupoudrer de sucre *etc*; **~d with** (*fig*) parsemé(e) de

sprinkler ['sprɪŋklə'] *n* (*for lawn etc*) arroseur *m*; (*to put out fire*) diffuseur *m* d'extincteur automatique d'incendie

sprint [sprɪnt] *n* sprint *m* ▷ *vi* courir à toute vitesse; (*Sport*) sprinter

sprinter ['sprɪntə'] *n* sprinteur(-euse)

sprout [spraut] *vi* germer, pousser

sprouts [sprauts] *npl* (*also*: **Brussels ~**) choux *mpl* de Bruxelles

spruce [spru:s] *n* épicéa *m* ▷ *adj* net(te), pimpant(e); **spruce up** *vt* (*smarten up*: *room etc*) apprêter; **to ~ o.s. up** se faire beau/belle

sprung [sprʌŋ] *pp of* **spring**

spun [spʌn] *pt, pp of* **spin**

spur [spə:'] *n* éperon *m*; (*fig*) aiguillon *m* ▷ *vt* (*also*: **~ on**) éperonner; aiguillonner; **on the ~ of the moment** sous l'impulsion du moment

spurious ['spjuəriəs] *adj* faux/fausse

spurn [spə:n] *vt* repousser avec mépris

spurt [spə:t] *n* jet *m*; (*of blood*) jaillissement *m*; (*of energy*) regain *m*, sursaut *m* ▷ *vi* jaillir, gicler; **to put in** *or* **on a ~** (*runner*) piquer un sprint; (*fig*: *in work etc*) donner un coup de collier

spy [spaɪ] *n* espion(ne) ▷ *vi*: **to ~ on** espionner, épier ▷ *vt* (*see*) apercevoir ▷ *cpd* (*film, story*) d'espionnage

spying ['spaɪɪŋ] *n* espionnage *m*

sq. *abbr* (*Math etc*) = **square**

squabble ['skwɔbl] *n* querelle *f*, chamaillerie *f* ▷ *vi* se chamailler

squad [skwɔd] *n* (*Mil, Police*) escouade *f*, groupe *m*; (*Football*) contingent *m*; **flying ~** (*Police*) brigade volante

squadron ['skwɔdrn] *n* (*Mil*) escadron *m*; (*Aviat, Naut*) escadrille *f*

squalid ['skwɔlɪd] *adj* sordide, ignoble

squall [skwɔ:l] *n* rafale *f*, bourrasque *f*

squalor ['skwɔlə'] *n* conditions *fpl* sordides

squander ['skwɔndə'] *vt* gaspiller, dilapider

square [skwɛə'] *n* carré *m*; (*in town*) place *f*; (*US: block of houses*) îlot *m*, pâté *m* de maisons; (*instrument*) équerre *f* ▷ *adj* carré(e); (*honest*) honnête, régulier(-ière); (*inf: ideas, tastes*) vieux jeu *inv*, qui retarde ▷ *vt* (*arrange*) régler; arranger; (*Math*) élever au carré; (*reconcile*) concilier ▷ *vi* (*agree*) cadrer, s'accorder; **all ~** quitte; à égalité; **a ~ meal** un repas convenable; **2 metres ~** 2 mètres sur 2; **1 ~ metre** 1 mètre carré; **we're back to ~ one** (*fig*) on se retrouve à la case départ; **square up** *vi* (*Brit*: *settle*) régler; **to ~ up with sb** régler ses comptes avec qn

squarely ['skwɛəlɪ] *adv* carrément; (*honestly, fairly*) honnêtement, équitablement

square root *n* racine carrée

squash [skwɔʃ] *n* (*Brit: drink*): **lemon/orange ~** citronnade *f*/orangeade *f*; (*Sport*) squash *m*; (*US: vegetable*) courge *f* ▷ *vt* écraser

squat [skwɔt] *adj* petit(e) et épais(se), ramassé(e) ▷ *vi* (*also*: **~ down**) s'accroupir; (*on property*) squatter, squattériser

squatter ['skwɔtə'] *n* squatter *m*

squeak [skwi:k] *n* (*of hinge, wheel etc*) grincement *m*; (*of shoes*) craquement *m*; (*of mouse etc*) petit cri aigu ▷ *vi* (*hinge, wheel*) grincer; (*mouse*) pousser un petit cri

squeal [skwi:l] *vi* pousser un *or* des cri(s) aigu(s) *or* perçant(s); (*brakes*) grincer

squeamish ['skwi:mɪʃ] *adj* facilement dégoûté(e); facilement scandalisé(e)

squeeze [skwi:z] *n* pression *f*; (*also*: **credit ~**) encadrement *m* du crédit, restrictions *fpl* de crédit ▷ *vt* presser; (*hand, arm*) serrer ▷ *vi*: **to ~ past/under sth** se glisser avec (beaucoup de) difficulté devant/sous qch; **a ~ of lemon** quelques gouttes de citron; **squeeze out** *vt* exprimer; (*fig*) soutirer

squelch [skwɛltʃ] *vi* faire un bruit de succion; patauger

squid [skwɪd] *n* calmar *m*

squiggle ['skwɪgl] *n* gribouillis *m*

squint [skwɪnt] *vi* loucher ▷ *n*: **he has a ~** il louche, il souffre de strabisme; **to ~ at sth** regarder qch du coin de l'œil; (*quickly*) jeter un coup d'œil à qch

squirm [skwə:m] *vi* se tortiller

squirrel ['skwɪrəl] *n* écureuil *m*

squirt [skwə:t] *n* jet *m* ▷ *vi* jaillir, gicler ▷ *vt* faire gicler

Sr *abbr* = **senior**; *(Rel)* = **sister**
Sri Lanka [srɪ'læŋkə] *n* Sri Lanka *m*
St *abbr* = **saint**; **street**
stab [stæb] *n* (*with knife etc*) coup *m* (de couteau *etc*); (*of pain*) lancée *f*; (*inf*: *try*): **to have a ~ at (doing) sth** s'essayer à (faire) qch ▷ *vt* poignarder; **to ~ sb to death** tuer qn à coups de couteau
stability [stə'bɪlɪtɪ] *n* stabilité *f*
stable ['steɪbl] *n* écurie *f* ▷ *adj* stable; **riding ~s** centre *m* d'équitation
stack [stæk] *n* tas *m*, pile *f* ▷ *vt* empiler, entasser; **there's ~s of time** (*Brit inf*) on a tout le temps
stadium ['steɪdɪəm] *n* stade *m*
staff [stɑ:f] *n* (*work force*) personnel *m*; (*Brit Scol*: *also*: **teaching ~**) professeurs *mpl*, enseignants *mpl*, personnel enseignant; (*servants*) domestiques *mpl*; (*Mil*) état-major *m*; (*stick*) perche *f*, bâton *m* ▷ *vt* pourvoir en personnel
stag [stæg] *n* cerf *m*; (*Brit Stock Exchange*) loup *m*
stage [steɪdʒ] *n* scène *f*; (*platform*) estrade *f*; (*point*) étape *f*, stade *m*; (*profession*): **the ~** le théâtre ▷ *vt* (*play*) monter, mettre en scène; (*demonstration*) organiser; (*fig*: *recovery etc*) effectuer; **in ~s** par étapes, par degrés; **to go through a difficult ~** traverser une période difficile; **in the early ~s** au début; **in the final ~s** à la fin
stagecoach ['steɪdʒkəʊtʃ] *n* diligence *f*
stage manager *n* régisseur *m*
stagger ['stægə*] *vi* chanceler, tituber ▷ *vt* (*person*: *amaze*) stupéfier; bouleverser; (*hours, holidays*) étaler, échelonner
staggering ['stægərɪŋ] *adj* (*amazing*) stupéfiant(e), renversant(e)
stagnant ['stægnənt] *adj* stagnant(e)
stagnate [stæg'neɪt] *vi* stagner, croupir
stag night, stag party *n* enterrement *m* de vie de garçon
staid [steɪd] *adj* posé(e), rassis(e)
stain [steɪn] *n* tache *f*; (*colouring*) colorant *m* ▷ *vt* tacher; (*wood*) teindre
stained glass [steɪnd-] *n* (*decorative*) verre coloré; (*in church*) vitraux *mpl*; **~ window** vitrail *m*
stainless ['steɪnlɪs] *adj* (*steel*) inoxydable
stainless steel *n* inox *m*, acier *m* inoxydable
stain remover *n* détachant *m*
stair [steə*] *n* (*step*) marche *f*
staircase ['steəkeɪs] *n* = **stairway**
stairs [steəz] *npl* escalier *m*; **on the ~** dans l'escalier
stairway ['steəweɪ] *n* escalier *m*
stake [steɪk] *n* pieu *m*, poteau *m*; (*Comm*: *interest*) intérêts *mpl*; (*Betting*) enjeu *m* ▷ *vt* risquer, jouer; (*also*: **~ out**: *area*) marquer, délimiter; **to be at ~** être en jeu; **to have a ~ in sth** avoir des intérêts (en jeu) dans qch; **to ~ a claim (to sth)** revendiquer (qch)

stale [steɪl] *adj* (*bread*) rassis(e); (*food*) pas frais/fraîche; (*beer*) éventé(e); (*smell*) de renfermé; (*air*) confiné(e)
stalemate ['steɪlmeɪt] *n* pat *m*; (*fig*) impasse *f*
stalk [stɔ:k] *n* tige *f* ▷ *vt* traquer ▷ *vi*: **to ~ out/off** sortir/partir d'un air digne
stall [stɔ:l] *n* (*Brit*: *in street, market etc*) éventaire *m*, étal *m*; (*in stable*) stalle *f* ▷ *vt* (*Aut*) caler; (*fig*: *delay*) retarder ▷ *vi* (*Aut*) caler; (*fig*) essayer de gagner du temps; **stalls** *npl* (*Brit*: *in cinema, theatre*) orchestre *m*; **a newspaper/flower ~** un kiosque à journaux/de fleuriste
stallion ['stæljən] *n* étalon *m* (*cheval*)
stamina ['stæmɪnə] *n* vigueur *f*, endurance *f*
stammer ['stæmə*] *n* bégaiement *m* ▷ *vi* bégayer
stamp [stæmp] *n* timbre *m*; (*also*: **rubber ~**) tampon *m*; (*mark, also fig*) empreinte *f*; (*on document*) cachet *m* ▷ *vi* (*also*: **~ one's foot**) taper du pied ▷ *vt* (*letter*) timbrer; (*with rubber stamp*) tamponner; **stamp out** *vt* (*fire*) piétiner; (*crime*) éradiquer; (*opposition*) éliminer
stamp album *n* album *m* de timbres(-poste)
stamp collecting [-kəlεktɪŋ] *n* philatélie *f*
stamped addressed envelope *n* (*Brit*) enveloppe affranchie pour la réponse
stampede [stæm'pi:d] *n* ruée *f*; (*of cattle*) débandade *f*
stance [stæns] *n* position *f*
stand [stænd] (*pt, pp* **stood**) [stʊd] *n* (*position*) position *f*; (*for taxis*) station *f* (de taxis); (*Mil*) résistance *f*; (*structure*) guéridon *m*; support *m*; (*Comm*) étalage *m*, stand *m*; (*Sport*: *also*: **~s**) tribune *f*; (*also*: **music ~**) pupitre *m* ▷ *vi* être or se tenir (debout); (*rise*) se lever, se mettre debout; (*be placed*) se trouver; (*remain*: *offer etc*) rester valable ▷ *vt* (*place*) mettre, poser; (*tolerate, withstand*) supporter; (*treat, invite*) offrir, payer; **to make a ~** prendre position; **to take a ~ on an issue** prendre position sur un problème; **to ~ for parliament** (*Brit*) se présenter aux élections (*comme candidat à la députation*); **to ~ guard** or **watch** (*Mil*) monter la garde; **it ~s to reason** c'est logique; cela va de soi; **as things ~** dans l'état actuel des choses; **to ~ sb a drink/meal** payer à boire/à manger à qn; **I can't ~ him** je ne peux pas le voir; **stand aside** *vi* s'écarter; **stand back** *vi* (*move back*) reculer, s'écarter; **stand by** *vi* (*be ready*) se tenir prêt(e) ▷ *vt fus* (*opinion*) s'en tenir à; (*person*) ne pas abandonner, soutenir; **stand down** *vi* (*withdraw*) se retirer; (*Law*) renoncer à ses droits; **stand for** *vt fus* (*signify*) représenter, signifier; (*tolerate*) supporter, tolérer; **stand in for** *vt fus* remplacer; **stand out** *vi* (*be prominent*) ressortir; **stand up** *vi* (*rise*) se lever, se mettre debout; **stand up for** *vt fus* défendre; **stand up to** *vt fus* tenir tête à, résister à
standard ['stændəd] *n* (*norm*) norme *f*, étalon *m*; (*level*) niveau *m* (voulu); (*criterion*)

critère m; (flag) étendard m ▷ adj (size etc)
ordinaire, normal(e); (model, feature) standard
inv; (practice) courant(e); (text) de base;
standards npl (morals) morale f, principes
mpl; **to be** or **come up to** ~ être du niveau
voulu or à la hauteur; **to apply a double** ~
avoir or appliquer deux poids deux mesures

standard lamp n (Brit) lampadaire m

standard of living n niveau m de vie

stand-by ['stændbaɪ] n remplaçant(e) ▷ adj
(provisions) de réserve; **to be on** ~ se tenir
prêt(e) (à intervenir); (doctor) être de garde

stand-by ticket n (Aviat) billet m stand-by

stand-in ['stændɪn] n remplaçant(e); (Cine)
doublure f

standing ['stændɪŋ] adj debout inv;
(permanent) permanent(e); (rule) immuable;
(army) de métier; (grievance) constant(e), de
longue date ▷ n réputation f, rang m,
standing m; (duration): **of 6 months'** ~ qui
dure depuis 6 mois; **of many years'** ~ qui
dure or existe depuis longtemps; **he was
given a** ~ **ovation** on s'est levé pour
l'acclamer; **it's a** ~ **joke** c'est un vieux sujet
de plaisanterie; **a man of some** ~ un homme
estimé

standing order n (Brit: at bank) virement m
automatique, prélèvement m bancaire;
standing orders npl (Mil) règlement m

standing room n places fpl debout

standpoint ['stændpɔɪnt] n point m de vue

standstill ['stændstɪl] n: **at a** ~ à l'arrêt; (fig)
au point mort; **to come to a** ~ s'immobiliser,
s'arrêter

stank [stæŋk] pt of **stink**

staple ['steɪpl] n (for papers) agrafe f; (chief
product) produit m de base ▷ adj (food, crop,
industry etc) de base principal(e) ▷ vt agrafer

stapler ['steɪplər] n agrafeuse f

star [stɑːr] n étoile f; (celebrity) vedette f ▷ vi:
to ~ (**in**) être la vedette (de) ▷ vt (Cine) avoir
pour vedette; **4-**~ **hotel** hôtel m 4 étoiles; **2-**~
petrol (Brit) essence f ordinaire; **4-**~ **petrol**
(Brit) super m; **stars** npl: **the** ~**s** (Astrology)
l'horoscope m

starboard ['stɑːbəd] n tribord m; **to** ~ à
tribord

starch [stɑːtʃ] n amidon m; (in food) fécule f

stardom ['stɑːdəm] n célébrité f

stare [stɛər] n regard m fixe ▷ vi: **to** ~ **at**
regarder fixement

starfish ['stɑːfɪʃ] n étoile f de mer

stark [stɑːk] adj (bleak) désolé(e), morne;
(simplicity, colour) austère; (reality, poverty) nu(e)
▷ adv: ~ **naked** complètement nu(e)

starling ['stɑːlɪŋ] n étourneau m

starry ['stɑːrɪ] adj étoilé(e)

starry-eyed [stɑːrɪ'aɪd] adj (innocent)
ingénu(e)

start [stɑːt] n commencement m, début m; (of
race) départ m; (sudden movement) sursaut m;
(advantage) avance f, avantage m ▷ vt

commencer; (cause: fight) déclencher;
(rumour) donner naissance à; (fashion) lancer;
(found: business, newspaper) lancer, créer;
(engine) mettre en marche ▷ vi (begin)
commencer; (begin journey) partir, se mettre
en route; (jump) sursauter; **when does the
film** ~? à quelle heure est-ce que le film
commence?; **at the** ~ au début; **for a** ~
d'abord, pour commencer; **to make an early**
~ partir or commencer de bonne heure; **to** ~
doing or **to do sth** se mettre à faire qch; **to** ~
(**off**) **with ...** (firstly) d'abord ...; (at the
beginning) au commencement ...; **start off** vi
commencer; (leave) partir; **start out** vi (begin)
commencer; (set out) partir; **start over** vi
(US) recommencer; **start up** vi commencer;
(car) démarrer ▷ vt (fight) déclencher;
(business) créer; (car) mettre en marche

starter ['stɑːtər] n (Aut) démarreur m; (Sport:
official) starter m; (: runner, horse) partant m;
(Brit Culin) entrée f

starting point ['stɑːtɪŋ-] n point m de départ

startle ['stɑːtl] vt faire sursauter; donner un
choc à

startling ['stɑːtlɪŋ] adj surprenant(e),
saisissant(e)

starvation [stɑː'veɪʃən] n faim f, famine f; **to
die of** ~ mourir de faim or d'inanition

starve [stɑːv] vi mourir de faim ▷ vt laisser
mourir de faim; **I'm starving** je meurs de
faim

state [steɪt] n état m; (Pol) État; (pomp): **in** ~
en grande pompe ▷ vt (declare) déclarer,
affirmer; (specify) indiquer, spécifier; **States**
npl: **the S~s** les États-Unis; **to be in a** ~ être
dans tous ses états; ~ **of emergency** état
d'urgence; ~ **of mind** état d'esprit; **the** ~ **of
the art** l'état actuel de la technologie (or des
connaissances)

stately ['steɪtlɪ] adj majestueux(-euse),
imposant(e)

stately home n manoir m or château m
(ouvert au public)

statement ['steɪtmənt] n déclaration f;
(Law) déposition f; (Econ) relevé m; **official** ~
communiqué officiel; ~ **of account, bank** ~
relevé m de compte

state school n école publique

statesman ['steɪtsmən] irreg n homme m
d'État

static ['stætɪk] n (Radio) parasites mpl; (also:
~ **electricity**) électricité f statique ▷ adj
statique

station ['steɪʃən] n gare f; (also: **police** ~)
poste m or commissariat m (de police); (Mil)
poste m (militaire); (rank) condition f, rang m
▷ vt placer, poster; **action** ~**s** postes de
combat; **to be** ~**ed in** (Mil) être en garnison à

stationary ['steɪʃnərɪ] adj à l'arrêt, immobile

stationer ['steɪʃənər] n papetier(-ière)

stationer's, stationer's shop n (Brit)
papeterie f

stationery ['steɪʃnəri] n papier m à lettres, petit matériel de bureau

station wagon n (US) break m

statistic [stə'tɪstɪk] n statistique f

statistics [stə'tɪstɪks] n (science) statistique f

statue ['stætjuː] n statue f

stature ['stætʃə²] n stature f; (fig) envergure f

status ['steɪtəs] n position f, situation f; (prestige) prestige m; (Admin, official position) statut m

status quo [-'kwəu] n: **the ~** le statu quo

status symbol n marque f de standing, signe extérieur de richesse

statute ['stætjuːt] n loi f; **statutes** npl (of club etc) statuts mpl

statutory ['stætjutri] adj statutaire, prévu(e) par un article de loi; **~ meeting** assemblée constitutive or statutaire

staunch [stɔːntʃ] adj sûr(e), loyal(e) ▷ vt étancher

stay [steɪ] n (period of time) séjour m; (Law): **~ of execution** sursis m à statuer ▷ vi rester; (reside) loger; (spend some time) séjourner; **to ~ put** ne pas bouger; **to ~ with friends** loger chez des amis; **to ~ the night** passer la nuit; **stay away** vi (from person, building) ne pas s'approcher; (from event) ne pas venir; **stay behind** vi rester en arrière; **stay in** vi (at home) rester à la maison; **stay on** vi rester; **stay out** vi (of house) ne pas rentrer; (strikers) rester en grève; **stay up** vi (at night) ne pas se coucher

staying power ['steɪɪŋ-] n endurance f

stead [stɛd] n (Brit): **in sb's ~** à la place de qn; **to stand sb in good ~** être très utile or servir beaucoup à qn

steadfast ['stɛdfɑːst] adj ferme, résolu(e)

steadily ['stɛdɪlɪ] adv (regularly) progressivement; (firmly) fermement; (walk) d'un pas ferme; (fixedly: look) sans détourner les yeux

steady ['stɛdɪ] adj stable, solide, ferme; (regular) constant(e), régulier(-ière); (person) calme, pondéré(e) ▷ vt assurer, stabiliser; (nerves) calmer; (voice) assurer; **a ~ boyfriend** un petit ami; **to ~ oneself** reprendre son aplomb

steak [steɪk] n (meat) bifteck m, steak m; (fish, pork) tranche f

steal (pt **stole**, pp **stolen**) [stiːl, stəul, 'stəuln] vt, vi voler; (move) se faufiler, se déplacer furtivement; **my wallet has been stolen** on m'a volé mon portefeuille; **steal away, steal off** vi s'esquiver

stealth [stɛlθ] n: **by ~** furtivement

steam [stiːm] n vapeur f ▷ vt passer à la vapeur; (Culin) cuire à la vapeur ▷ vi fumer; (ship) avancer à la vapeur; **under one's own ~** (fig) par ses propres moyens; **to run out of ~** (fig: person) caler; être à bout; **to let off ~** (fig: inf) se défouler; **steam up** vi (window) se couvrir de buée; **to get ~ed up about sth** (fig: inf) s'exciter à propos de qch

steam engine n locomotive f à vapeur

steamer ['stiːmə²] n (bateau m à) vapeur m; (Culin) ≈ couscoussier m

steamship ['stiːmʃɪp] n = **steamer**

steamy ['stiːmɪ] adj humide; (window) embué(e); (sexy) torride

steel [stiːl] n acier m ▷ cpd d'acier

steelworks ['stiːlwəːks] n aciérie f

steep [stiːp] adj raide, escarpé(e); (price) très élevé(e), excessif(-ive) ▷ vt (faire) tremper

steeple ['stiːpl] n clocher m

steer [stɪə²] n bœuf m ▷ vt diriger; (boat) gouverner; (lead: person) guider, conduire ▷ vi tenir le gouvernail; **to ~ clear of sb/sth** (fig) éviter qn/qch

steering ['stɪərɪŋ] n (Aut) conduite f

steering wheel n volant m

stem [stɛm] n (of plant) tige f; (of leaf, fruit) queue f; (of glass) pied m ▷ vt contenir, endiguer; (attack, spread of disease) juguler; **stem from** vt fus provenir de, découler de

stench [stɛntʃ] n puanteur f

stencil ['stɛnsl] n stencil m; pochoir m ▷ vt polycopier

stenographer [stɛ'nɔɡrəfə²] n (US) sténographe m/f

step [stɛp] n pas m; (stair) marche f; (action) mesure f, disposition f ▷ vi: **to ~ forward/back** faire un pas en avant/arrière, avancer/reculer; **steps** npl (Brit) = **stepladder**; **~ by ~** pas à pas; (fig) petit à petit; **to be in/out of ~ (with)** (fig) aller dans le sens (de)/être déphasé(e) (par rapport à); **step down** vi (fig) se retirer, se désister; **step in** vi (fig) intervenir; **step off** vt fus descendre de; **step over** vt fus enjamber; **step up** vt (production, sales) augmenter; (campaign, efforts) intensifier

stepbrother ['stɛpbrʌðə²] n demi-frère m

stepchild ['stɛptʃaɪld] (pl **stepchildren**) n beau-fils m, belle-fille f

stepdaughter ['stɛpdɔːtə²] n belle-fille f

stepfather ['stɛpfɑːðə²] n beau-père m

stepladder ['stɛplædə²] n (Brit) escabeau m

stepmother ['stɛpmʌðə²] n belle-mère f

stepping stone ['stɛpɪŋ-] n pierre f de gué; (fig) tremplin m

stepsister ['stɛpsɪstə²] n demi-sœur f

stepson ['stɛpsʌn] n beau-fils m

stereo ['stɛrɪəu] n (sound) stéréo f; (hi-fi) chaîne f stéréo ▷ adj (also: **~phonic**) stéréo(phonique); **in ~** en stéréo

stereotype ['stɛrɪətaɪp] n stéréotype m ▷ vt stéréotyper

sterile ['stɛraɪl] adj stérile

sterilize ['stɛrɪlaɪz] vt stériliser

sterling ['stəːlɪŋ] adj sterling inv; (silver) de bon aloi, fin(e); (fig) à toute épreuve, excellent(e) ▷ n (currency) livre f sterling inv; **a pound ~** une livre sterling

stern [stəːn] adj sévère ▷ n (Naut) arrière m, poupe f

S

steroid ['stɪərɔɪd] n stéroïde m
stew [stju:] n ragoût m ▷ vt, vi cuire à la casserole; **~ed tea** thé trop infusé; **~ed fruit** fruits cuits or en compote
steward ['stju:əd] n (Aviat, Naut, Rail) steward m; (in club etc) intendant m; (also: **shop ~**) délégué syndical
stewardess ['stju:ədɛs] n hôtesse f
stick [stɪk] (pt, pp **stuck**) [stʌk] n bâton m; (for walking) canne f; (of chalk etc) morceau m ▷ vt (glue) coller; (thrust): **to ~ sth into** piquer or planter or enfoncer qch dans; (inf: put) mettre, fourrer; (: tolerate) supporter ▷ vi (adhere) tenir, coller; (remain) rester; (get jammed: door, lift) se bloquer; **to get hold of the wrong end of the ~** (Brit fig) comprendre de travers; **to ~ to** (one's promise) s'en tenir à; (principles) rester fidèle à; **stick around** vi (inf) rester (dans les parages); **stick out** vi dépasser, sortir ▷ vt: **to ~ it out** (inf) tenir le coup; **stick up** vi dépasser, sortir; **stick up for** vt fus défendre
sticker ['stɪkə'] n auto-collant m
sticking plaster ['stɪkɪŋ-] n sparadrap m, pansement adhésif
stick insect n phasme m
stick shift n (US Aut) levier m de vitesses
stick-up ['stɪkʌp] n (inf) braquage m, hold-up m
sticky ['stɪkɪ] adj poisseux(-euse); (label) adhésif(-ive); (fig: situation) délicat(e)
stiff [stɪf] adj (gen) raide, rigide; (door, brush) dur(e); (difficult) difficile, ardu(e); (cold) froid(e), distant(e); (strong, high) fort(e), élevé(e) ▷ adv: **to be bored/scared/frozen ~** s'ennuyer à mourir/être mort(e) de peur/froid; **to be** or **feel ~** (person) avoir des courbatures; **to have a ~ back** avoir mal au dos; **~ upper lip** (Brit: fig) flegme m (typiquement britannique)
stiffen ['stɪfn] vt raidir, renforcer ▷ vi se raidir; se durcir
stiff neck n torticolis m
stifle ['staɪfl] vt étouffer, réprimer
stifling ['staɪflɪŋ] adj (heat) suffocant(e)
stigma ['stɪgmə] n (Bot, Med, Rel) (pl **stigmata**) [stɪg'mɑːtə] (fig), **stigmas** n stigmate m
stile [staɪl] n échalier m
stiletto [stɪ'lɛtəu] n (Brit: also: **~ heel**) talon m aiguille
still [stɪl] adj (motionless) immobile; (calm) calme, tranquille; (Brit: mineral water etc) non gazeux(-euse) ▷ adv (up to this time) encore, toujours; (even) encore; (nonetheless) quand même, tout de même ▷ n (Cine) photo f; **to stand ~** rester immobile, ne pas bouger; **keep ~!** ne bouge pas!; **he ~ hasn't arrived** il n'est pas encore arrivé, il n'est toujours pas arrivé
stillborn ['stɪlbɔːn] adj mort-né(e)
still life n nature morte
stilt [stɪlt] n échasse f; (pile) pilotis m

stilted ['stɪltɪd] adj guindé(e), emprunté(e)
stimulate ['stɪmjuleɪt] vt stimuler
stimulus (pl **stimuli**) ['stɪmjuləs, 'stɪmjulaɪ] n stimulant m; (Biol, Psych) stimulus m
sting [stɪŋ] n piqûre f; (organ) dard m; (inf: confidence trick) arnaque m ▷ vt, vi (pt, pp **stung**) [stʌŋ] piquer; **my eyes are ~ing** j'ai les yeux qui piquent
stingy ['stɪndʒɪ] adj avare, pingre, chiche
stink [stɪŋk] n puanteur f ▷ vi (pt **stank**, pp **stunk**) [stæŋk, stʌŋk] puer, empester
stinking ['stɪŋkɪŋ] adj (fig: inf) infect(e); **~ rich** bourré(e) de pognon
stint [stɪnt] n part f de travail ▷ vi: **to ~ on** lésiner sur, être chiche de
stir [stə:'] n agitation f, sensation f ▷ vt remuer ▷ vi remuer, bouger; **to give sth a ~** remuer qch; **to cause a ~** faire sensation; **stir up** vt exciter; (trouble) fomenter, provoquer
stir-fry ['stə:'fraɪ] vt faire sauter ▷ n: **~ vegetable** légumes sautés à la poêle
stirrup ['stɪrəp] n étrier m
stitch [stɪtʃ] n (Sewing) point m; (Knitting) maille f; (Med) point de suture; (pain) point de côté ▷ vt coudre, piquer; (Med) suturer
stoat [stəut] n hermine f (avec son pelage d'été)
stock [stɔk] n réserve f, provision f; (Comm) stock m; (Agr) cheptel m, bétail m; (Culin) bouillon m; (Finance) valeurs fpl, titres mpl; (Rail: also: **rolling ~**) matériel roulant; (descent, origin) souche f ▷ adj (fig: reply etc) courant(e); classique ▷ vt (have in stock) avoir, vendre; **well-~ed** bien approvisionné(e) or fourni(e); **in ~** en stock, en magasin; **out of ~** épuisé(e); **to take ~** (fig) faire le point; **~s and shares** valeurs (mobilières), titres; **government ~** fonds publics; **stock up** vi: **to ~ up (with)** s'approvisionner (en)
stockbroker ['stɔkbrəukə'] n agent m de change
stock cube n (Brit Culin) bouillon-cube m
stock exchange n Bourse f (des valeurs)
stockholder ['stɔkhəuldə'] n (US) actionnaire m/f
stocking ['stɔkɪŋ] n bas m
stock market n Bourse f, marché financier
stockpile ['stɔkpaɪl] n stock m, réserve f ▷ vt stocker, accumuler
stocktaking ['stɔkteɪkɪŋ] n (Brit Comm) inventaire m
stocky ['stɔkɪ] adj trapu(e), râblé(e)
stodgy ['stɔdʒɪ] adj bourratif(-ive), lourd(e)
stoke [stəuk] vt garnir, entretenir; chauffer
stole [stəul] pt of **steal** ▷ n étole f
stolen ['stəuln] pp of **steal**
stomach ['stʌmək] n estomac m; (abdomen) ventre m ▷ vt digérer, supporter
stomachache ['stʌməkeɪk] n mal m à l'estomac or au ventre
stone [stəun] n pierre f; (pebble) caillou m, galet m; (in fruit) noyau m; (Med) calcul m; (Brit: weight) = 6.348 kg; 14 pounds ▷ cpd de or en

pierre ▷ vt (*person*) lancer des pierres sur, lapider; (*fruit*) dénoyauter; **within a ~'s throw of the station** à deux pas de la gare

stone-cold ['stəʊn'kəʊld] *adj* complètement froid(e)

stone-deaf ['stəʊn'dɛf] *adj* sourd(e) comme un pot

stonework ['stəʊnwəːk] *n* maçonnerie *f*

stood [stud] *pt, pp of* **stand**

stool [stuːl] *n* tabouret *m*

stoop [stuːp] *vi* (*also*: **have a ~**) être voûté(e); (*also*: **~ down**: *bend*) se baisser, se courber; (*fig*): **to ~ to sth/doing sth** s'abaisser jusqu'à qch/jusqu'à faire qch

stop [stɔp] *n* arrêt *m*; (*short stay*) halte *f*; (*in punctuation*) point *m* ▷ vt arrêter; (*break off*) interrompre; (*also*: **put a ~ to**) mettre fin à; (*prevent*) empêcher ▷ vi s'arrêter; (*rain, noise etc*) cesser, s'arrêter; **could you ~ here/at the corner?** arrêtez-vous ici/au coin, s'il vous plaît; **to ~ doing sth** cesser *or* arrêter de faire qch; **to ~ sb (from) doing sth** empêcher qn de faire qch; **to ~ dead** *vi* s'arrêter net; **~ it!** arrête!; **stop by** *vi* s'arrêter (au passage); **stop off** *vi* faire une courte halte; **stop up** *vt* (*hole*) boucher

stopgap ['stɔpgæp] *n* (*person*) bouche-trou *m*; (*also*: **~ measure**) mesure *f* intérimaire

stopover ['stɔpəʊvə'] *n* halte *f*; (*Aviat*) escale *f*

stoppage ['stɔpɪdʒ] *n* arrêt *m*; (*of pay*) retenue *f*; (*strike*) arrêt *m* de travail; (*obstruction*) obstruction *f*

stopper ['stɔpə'] *n* bouchon *m*

stop press *n* nouvelles *fpl* de dernière heure

stopwatch ['stɔpwɔtʃ] *n* chronomètre *m*

storage ['stɔːrɪdʒ] *n* emmagasinage *m*; (*of nuclear waste etc*) stockage *m*; (*in house*) rangement *m*; (*Comput*) mise *f* en mémoire *or* réserve

storage heater *n* (*Brit*) radiateur *m* électrique par accumulation

store [stɔː'] *n* (*stock*) provision *f*, réserve *f*; (*depot*) entrepôt *m*; (*Brit: large shop*) grand magasin; (*US: shop*) magasin *m* ▷ vt emmagasiner; (*nuclear waste etc*) stocker; (*information*) enregistrer; (*in filing system*) classer, ranger; (*Comput*) mettre en mémoire; **stores** *npl* (*food*) provisions; **who knows what is in ~ for us?** qui sait ce que l'avenir nous réserve *or* ce qui nous attend?; **to set great/little ~ by sth** faire grand cas/peu de cas de qch; **store up** *vt* mettre en réserve, emmagasiner

storekeeper ['stɔːkiːpə'] *n* (*US*) commerçant(e)

storeroom ['stɔːruːm] *n* réserve *f*, magasin *m*

storey, (*US*) **story** ['stɔːrɪ] *n* étage *m*

stork [stɔːk] *n* cigogne *f*

storm [stɔːm] *n* tempête *f*; (*thunderstorm*) orage *m* ▷ vi (*fig*) fulminer ▷ vt prendre d'assaut

stormy ['stɔːmɪ] *adj* orageux(-euse)

story ['stɔːrɪ] *n* histoire *f*; récit *m*; (*Press: article*) article *m*; (: *subject*) affaire *f*; (*US*) = **storey**

storybook ['stɔːrɪbuk] *n* livre *m* d'histoires *or* de contes

stout [staut] *adj* (*strong*) solide; (*brave*) intrépide; (*fat*) gros(se), corpulent(e) ▷ *n* bière brune

stove [stəʊv] *n* (*for cooking*) fourneau *m*; (: *small*) réchaud *m*; (*for heating*) poêle *m*; **gas/electric ~** (*cooker*) cuisinière *f* à gaz/électrique

stow [stəʊ] *vt* ranger; cacher

stowaway ['stəʊəweɪ] *n* passager(-ère) clandestin(e)

straddle ['strædl] *vt* enjamber, être à cheval sur

straggle ['strægl] *vi* être (*or* marcher) en désordre; **~d along the coast** disséminé(e) tout au long de la côte

straight [streɪt] *adj* droit(e); (*hair*) raide; (*frank*) honnête, franc/franche; (*simple*) simple; (*Theat: part, play*) sérieux(-euse); (*inf: heterosexual*) hétéro *inv* ▷ *adv* (*tout*) droit; (*drink*) sec, sans eau ▷ *n*: **the ~** (*Sport*) la ligne droite; **to put** *or* **get ~** mettre en ordre, mettre de l'ordre dans; (*fig*) mettre au clair; **let's get this ~** mettons les choses au point; **10 ~ wins** 10 victoires d'affilée; **to go ~ home** rentrer directement à la maison; **~ away, ~ off** (*at once*) tout de suite; **~ off, ~ out** sans hésiter

straighten ['streɪtn] *vt* ajuster; (*bed*) arranger; **straighten out** *vt* (*fig*) débrouiller; **to ~ things out** arranger les choses; **straighten up** *vi* (*stand up*) se redresser; (*tidy*) ranger

straighteners ['streɪtnəz] *npl* (*for hair*) lisseur *msg*

straight-faced [streɪt'feɪst] *adj* impassible ▷ *adv* en gardant son sérieux

straightforward [streɪt'fɔːwəd] *adj* simple; (*frank*) honnête, direct(e)

strain [streɪn] *n* (*Tech*) tension *f*; pression *f*; (*physical*) effort *m*; (*mental*) tension (nerveuse); (*Med*) entorse *f*; (*streak, trace*) tendance *f*; élément *m*; (*breed: of plants*) variété *f*; (: *of animals*) race *f*; (*of virus*) souche *f* ▷ vt (*stretch*) tendre fortement; (*fig: resources etc*) mettre à rude épreuve, grever; (*hurt: back etc*) se faire mal à; (*filter*) passer, filtrer; (*vegetables*) égoutter ▷ *vi* peiner, fournir un gros effort; **strains** *npl* (*Mus*) accords *mpl*, accents *mpl*; **he's been under a lot of ~** il a traversé des moments difficiles, il est très éprouvé nerveusement

strained [streɪnd] *adj* (*muscle*) froissé(e); (*laugh etc*) forcé(e), contraint(e); (*relations*) tendu(e)

strainer ['streɪnə'] *n* passoire *f*

strait [streɪt] *n* (*Geo*) détroit *m*; **straits** *npl*: **to be in dire ~s** (*fig*) avoir de sérieux ennuis

straitjacket ['streɪtdʒækɪt] *n* camisole *f* de force

S

strait-laced ['streɪt'leɪst] *adj* collet monté *inv*

strand [strænd] *n* (*of thread*) fil *m*, brin *m*; (*of rope*) toron *m*; (*of hair*) mèche *f* ▷ *vt* (*boat*) échouer

stranded ['strændɪd] *adj* en rade, en plan

strange [streɪndʒ] *adj* (*not known*) inconnu(e); (*odd*) étrange, bizarre

strangely ['streɪndʒlɪ] *adv* étrangement, bizarrement; *see also* **enough**

stranger ['streɪndʒəʳ] *n* (*unknown*) inconnu(e); (*from somewhere else*) étranger(-ère); **I'm a ~ here** je ne suis pas d'ici

strangle ['stræŋgl] *vt* étrangler

stranglehold ['stræŋglhəʊld] *n* (*fig*) emprise totale, mainmise *f*

strap [stræp] *n* lanière *f*, courroie *f*, sangle *f*; (*of slip, dress*) bretelle *f* ▷ *vt* attacher (avec une courroie *etc*)

strappy [stræpɪ] *adj* (*dress*) à bretelles; (*sandals*) à lanières

strategic [strə'ti:dʒɪk] *adj* stratégique

strategy ['strætɪdʒɪ] *n* stratégie *f*

straw [strɔː] *n* paille *f*; **that's the last ~!** ça c'est le comble!

strawberry ['strɔːbərɪ] *n* fraise *f*; (*plant*) fraisier *m*

stray [streɪ] *adj* (*animal*) perdu(e), errant(e); (*scattered*) isolé(e) ▷ *vi* s'égarer; **~ bullet** balle perdue

streak [stri:k] *n* bande *f*, filet *m*; (*in hair*) raie *f*; (*fig: of madness etc*): **a ~ of** une ou des tendance(s) à ▷ *vt* zébrer, strier ▷ *vi*: **to ~ past** passer à toute allure; **to have ~s in one's hair** s'être fait faire des mèches; **a winning/losing ~** une bonne/mauvaise série ou période

stream [stri:m] *n* (*brook*) ruisseau *m*; (*current*) courant *m*, flot *m*; (*of people*) défilé ininterrompu, flot ▷ *vt* (*Scol*) répartir par niveau ▷ *vi* ruisseler; **to ~ in/out** entrer/sortir à flots; **against the ~** à contre courant; **on ~** (*new power plant etc*) en service

streamer ['stri:məʳ] *n* serpentin *m*, banderole *f*

streamlined ['stri:mlaɪnd] *adj* (*Aviat*) fuselé(e), profilé(e); (*Aut*) aérodynamique; (*fig*) rationalisé(e)

street [stri:t] *n* rue *f*; **the back ~s** les quartiers pauvres; **to be on the ~s** (*homeless*) être à la rue ou sans abri

streetcar ['stri:tkɑːʳ] *n* (*US*) tramway *m*

street lamp *n* réverbère *m*

street light *n* réverbère *m*

street map, street plan *n* plan *m* des rues

streetwise ['stri:twaɪz] *adj* (*inf*) futé(e), réaliste

strength [streŋθ] *n* force *f*; (*of girder, knot etc*) solidité *f*; (*of chemical solution*) titre *m*; (*of wine*) degré *m* d'alcool; **on the ~ of** en vertu de; **at full ~** au grand complet; **below ~** à effectifs réduits

strengthen ['streŋθn] *vt* renforcer; (*muscle*) fortifier; (*building, Econ*) consolider

strenuous ['strenjuəs] *adj* vigoureux(-euse), énergique; (*tiring*) ardu(e), fatigant(e)

stress [stres] *n* (*force, pressure*) pression *f*; (*mental strain*) tension (nerveuse), stress *m*; (*accent*) accent *m*; (*emphasis*) insistance *f* ▷ *vt* insister sur, souligner; (*syllable*) accentuer; **to lay great ~ on sth** insister beaucoup sur qch; **to be under ~** être stressé(e)

stressed [strest] *adj* (*tense*) stressé(e); (*syllable*) accentué(e)

stressful ['stresful] *adj* (*job*) stressant(e)

stretch [stretʃ] *n* (*of sand etc*) étendue *f*; (*of time*) période *f* ▷ *vi* s'étirer; (*extend*): **to ~ to** *ou* **as far as** s'étendre jusqu'à; (*be enough: money, food*): **to ~ to** aller pour ▷ *vt* tendre, étirer; (*spread*) étendre; (*fig*) pousser (au maximum); **at a ~** d'affilée; **to ~ a muscle** se distendre un muscle; **to ~ one's legs** se dégourdir les jambes; **stretch out** *vi* s'étendre ▷ *vt* (*arm etc*) allonger, tendre; (*to spread*) étendre; **to ~ out for sth** allonger la main pour prendre qch

stretcher ['stretʃəʳ] *n* brancard *m*, civière *f*

stretchy ['stretʃɪ] *adj* élastique

strewn [stru:n] *adj*: **~ with** jonché(e) de

stricken ['strɪkən] *adj* très éprouvé(e); dévasté(e); (*ship*) très endommagé(e); **~ with** frappé(e) *ou* atteint(e) de

strict [strɪkt] *adj* strict(e); **in ~ confidence** tout à fait confidentiellement

strictly ['strɪktlɪ] *adv* strictement; **~ confidential** strictement confidentiel(le); **~ speaking** à strictement parler

stride [straɪd] *n* grand pas, enjambée *f* ▷ *vi* (*pt* **strode**) [strəʊd] marcher à grands pas; **to take in one's ~** (*fig: changes etc*) accepter sans sourciller

strife [straɪf] *n* conflit *m*, dissensions *fpl*

strike [straɪk] (*pt, pp* **struck**) [strʌk] *n* grève *f*; (*of oil etc*) découverte *f*; (*attack*) raid *m* ▷ *vt* frapper; (*oil etc*) trouver, découvrir; (*make: agreement, deal*) conclure ▷ *vi* faire grève; (*attack*) attaquer; (*clock*) sonner; **to go on** *ou* **come out on ~** se mettre en grève, faire grève; **to ~ a match** frotter une allumette; **to ~ a balance** (*fig*) trouver un juste milieu; **strike back** *vi* (*Mil, fig*) contre-attaquer; **strike down** *vt* (*fig*) terrasser; **strike off** *vt* (*from list*) rayer; (*doctor etc*) radier; **strike out** *vt* rayer; **strike up** (*Mus*) se mettre à jouer; **to ~ up a friendship with** se lier d'amitié avec

striker ['straɪkəʳ] *n* gréviste *m/f*; (*Sport*) buteur *m*

striking ['straɪkɪŋ] *adj* frappant(e), saisissant(e); (*attractive*) éblouissant(e)

string [strɪŋ] *n* ficelle *f*, fil *m*; (*row: of beads*) rang *m*; (: *of onions, excuses*) chapelet *m*; (: *of people, cars*) file *f*; (*Mus*) corde *f*; (*Comput*) chaîne *f* ▷ *vt* (*pt, pp* **strung**) [strʌŋ]: **to ~ out**

échelonner; **to ~ together** enchaîner; **the strings** npl (Mus) les instruments mpl à cordes; **to pull ~s** (fig) faire jouer le piston; **to get a job by pulling ~s** obtenir un emploi en faisant jouer le piston; **with no ~s attached** (fig) sans conditions

stringed instrument, string instrument [striŋ(d)-] n (Mus) instrument m à cordes

stringent ['strindʒənt] adj rigoureux(-euse); (need) impérieux(-euse)

strip [strip] n bande f; (Sport) tenue f ▷ vt (undress) déshabiller; (paint) décaper; (fig) dégarnir, dépouiller; (also: ~ down: machine) démonter ▷ vi se déshabiller; **wearing the Celtic** ~ en tenue du Celtic; **strip off** vt (paint etc) décaper ▷ vi (person) se déshabiller

strip cartoon n bande dessinée

stripe [straip] n raie f, rayure f; (Mil) galon m

striped ['straipt] adj rayé(e), à rayures

stripper ['stripər] n strip-teaseuse f

strip-search ['stripsə:tʃ] n fouille corporelle (en faisant se déshabiller la personne) ▷ vt: **to ~ sb** fouiller qn (en le faisant se déshabiller)

stripy ['straipi] adj rayé(e)

strive (pt **strove**, pp **striven**) [straiv, strəuv, 'strivn] vi: **to ~ to do/for sth** s'efforcer de faire/d'obtenir qch

strode [strəud] pt of **stride**

stroke [strəuk] n coup m; (Med) attaque f; (caress) caresse f; (Swimming: style) (sorte f de) nage f; (of piston) course f ▷ vt caresser; **at a ~** d'un (seul) coup; **on the ~ of 5** à 5 heures sonnantes; **a 2-~ engine** un moteur à 2 temps

stroll [strəul] n petite promenade ▷ vi flâner, se promener nonchalamment; **to go for a ~** aller se promener or faire un tour

stroller ['strəulər] n (US: for child) poussette f

strong [strɔŋ] adj (gen) fort(e); (healthy) vigoureux(-euse); (heart, nerves) solide; (distaste, desire) vif/vive; (drugs, chemicals) puissant(e) ▷ adv: **to be going ~** (company) marcher bien; (person) être toujours solide; **they are 50 ~** ils sont au nombre de 50

stronghold ['strɔŋhəuld] n forteresse f, fort m; (fig) bastion m

strongly ['strɔŋli] adv fortement, avec force; vigoureusement; solidement; **I feel ~ about it** c'est une question qui me tient particulièrement à cœur; (negatively) j'y suis profondément opposé(e)

strongroom ['strɔŋru:m] n chambre forte

strove [strəuv] pt of **strive**

struck [strʌk] pt, pp of **strike**

structural ['strʌktʃrəl] adj structural(e); (Constr) de construction; affectant les parties portantes

structure ['strʌktʃər] n structure f; (building) construction f

struggle ['strʌgl] n lutte f ▷ vi lutter, se battre; **to have a ~ to do sth** avoir beaucoup de mal à faire qch

strum [strʌm] vt (guitar) gratter de

strung [strʌŋ] pt, pp of **string**

strut [strʌt] n étai m, support m ▷ vi se pavaner

stub [stʌb] n (of cigarette) bout m, mégot m; (of ticket etc) talon m ▷ vt: **to ~ one's toe (on sth)** se heurter le doigt de pied (contre qch); **stub out** vt écraser

stubble ['stʌbl] n chaume m; (on chin) barbe f de plusieurs jours

stubborn ['stʌbən] adj têtu(e), obstiné(e), opiniâtre

stuck [stʌk] pt, pp of **stick** ▷ adj (jammed) bloqué(e), coincé(e); **to get ~** se bloquer or coincer

stuck-up [stʌk'ʌp] adj prétentieux(-euse)

stud [stʌd] n (on boots etc) clou m; (collar stud) bouton m de col; (earring) petite boucle d'oreille; (of horses: also: ~ farm) écurie f, haras m; (also: ~ horse) étalon m ▷ vt (fig): **~ded with** parsemé(e) or criblé(e) de

student ['stju:dənt] n étudiant(e) ▷ adj (life) estudiantin(e), étudiant(e), d'étudiant; (residence, restaurant) universitaire; (loan, movement) étudiant, universitaire d'étudiant; **law/medical ~** étudiant en droit/médecine

student driver n (US) (conducteur(-trice)) débutant(e)

students' union n (Brit: association) ≈ union f des étudiants; (: building) ≈ foyer m des étudiants

studio ['stju:diəu] n studio m, atelier m; (TV etc) studio

studio flat, (US) **studio apartment** n studio m

studious ['stju:diəs] adj studieux(-euse), appliqué(e); (studied) étudié(e)

studiously ['stju:diəsli] adv (carefully) soigneusement

study ['stʌdi] n étude f; (room) bureau m ▷ vt étudier; (examine) examiner ▷ vi étudier, faire ses études; **to make a ~ of sth** étudier qch, faire une étude de qch; **to ~ for an exam** préparer un examen

stuff [stʌf] n (gen) chose(s) f(pl), truc m; (belongings) affaires fpl, trucs; (substance) substance f ▷ vt rembourrer; (Culin) farcir; (inf: push) fourrer; (animal: for exhibition) empailler; **my nose is ~ed up** j'ai le nez bouché; **get ~ed!** (inf!) va te faire foutre! (!); **~ed toy** jouet m en peluche

stuffing ['stʌfiŋ] n bourre f, rembourrage m; (Culin) farce f

stuffy ['stʌfi] adj (room) mal ventilé(e) or aéré(e); (ideas) vieux jeu inv

stumble ['stʌmbl] vi trébucher; **to ~ across** or **on** (fig) tomber sur

stumbling block ['stʌmbliŋ-] n pierre f d'achoppement

stump [stʌmp] n souche f; (of limb) moignon m ▷ vt: **to be ~ed** sécher, ne pas savoir que répondre

S

stun [stʌn] vt (blow) étourdir; (news) abasourdir, stupéfier

stung [stʌŋ] pt, pp of **sting**

stunk [stʌŋk] pp of **stink**

stunned [stʌnd] adj assommé(e); (fig) sidéré(e)

stunning ['stʌnɪŋ] adj (beautiful) étourdissant(e); (news etc) stupéfiant(e)

stunt [stʌnt] n tour m de force; (in film) cascade f, acrobatie f; (publicity) truc m publicitaire; (Aviat) acrobatie f ▷ vt retarder, arrêter

stuntman ['stʌntmæn] irreg n cascadeur m

stupendous [stju:'pɛndəs] adj prodigieux(-euse), fantastique

stupid ['stju:pɪd] adj stupide, bête

stupidity [stju:'pɪdɪtɪ] n stupidité f, bêtise f

sturdy ['stə:dɪ] adj (person, plant) robuste, vigoureux(-euse); (object) solide

stutter ['stʌtə'] n bégaiement m ▷ vi bégayer

sty [staɪ] n (of pigs) porcherie f

stye [staɪ] n (Med) orgelet m

style [staɪl] n style m; (of dress etc) genre m; (distinction) allure f, cachet m, style; (design) modèle m; **in the latest ~** à la dernière mode; **hair ~** coiffure f

stylish ['staɪlɪʃ] adj élégant(e), chic inv

stylist ['staɪlɪst] n (hair stylist) coiffeur(-euse); (literary stylist) styliste m/f

stylus (pl **styli** or **styluses**) ['staɪləs, -laɪ] n (of record player) pointe f de lecture

suave [swɑ:v] adj doucereux(-euse), onctueux(-euse)

sub... [sʌb] prefix sub..., sous-

subconscious [sʌb'kɔnʃəs] adj subconscient(e) ▷ n subconscient m

subcontract n ['sʌb'kɔntrækt] contrat m de sous-traitance ▷ vt [sʌbkən'trækt] sous-traiter

subdue [səb'dju:] vt subjuguer, soumettre

subdued [səb'dju:d] adj calme, atténué(e); (light) tamisé(e); (person) qui a perdu de son entrain

subject n ['sʌbdʒɪkt] sujet m; (Scol) matière f ▷ vt [səb'dʒɛkt]: **to ~ to** soumettre à; exposer à; **to be ~ to** (law) être soumis(e) à; (disease) être sujet(te) à; **~ to confirmation in writing** sous réserve de confirmation écrite; **to change the ~** changer de conversation

subjective [səb'dʒɛktɪv] adj subjectif(-ive)

subject matter n sujet m; (content) contenu m

subjunctive [səb'dʒʌŋktɪv] adj subjonctif(-ive) ▷ n subjonctif m

sublet [sʌb'lɛt] vt sous-louer

submarine [sʌbmə'ri:n] n sous-marin m

submerge [səb'mə:dʒ] vt submerger; immerger ▷ vi plonger

submission [səb'mɪʃən] n soumission f; (to committee etc) présentation f

submissive [səb'mɪsɪv] adj soumis(e)

submit [səb'mɪt] vt soumettre ▷ vi se soumettre

subnormal [sʌb'nɔ:ml] adj au-dessous de la normale; (person) arriéré(e)

subordinate [sə'bɔ:dɪnət] adj (junior) subalterne; (Grammar) subordonné(e) ▷ n subordonné(e)

subpoena [səb'pi:nə] (Law) n citation f, assignation f ▷ vt citer or assigner (à comparaître)

subscribe [səb'skraɪb] vi cotiser; **to ~ to** (opinion, fund) souscrire à; (newspaper) s'abonner à; être abonné(e) à

subscriber [səb'skraɪbə'] n (to periodical, telephone) abonné(e)

subscription [səb'skrɪpʃən] n (to fund) souscription f; (to magazine etc) abonnement m; (membership dues) cotisation f; **to take out a ~ to** s'abonner à

subsequent ['sʌbsɪkwənt] adj ultérieur(e), suivant(e); **~ to** prep à la suite de

subsequently ['sʌbsɪkwəntlɪ] adv par la suite

subside [səb'saɪd] vi (land) s'affaisser; (flood) baisser; (wind, feelings) tomber

subsidence [səb'saɪdns] n affaissement m

subsidiary [səb'sɪdɪərɪ] adj subsidiaire, accessoire; (Brit Scol: subject) complémentaire ▷ n filiale f

subsidize ['sʌbsɪdaɪz] vt subventionner

subsidy ['sʌbsɪdɪ] n subvention f

substance ['sʌbstəns] n substance f; (fig) essentiel m; **a man of ~** un homme jouissant d'une certaine fortune; **to lack ~** être plutôt mince (fig)

substantial [səb'stænʃl] adj substantiel(le); (fig) important(e)

substantially [səb'stænʃəlɪ] adv considérablement; en grande partie

substantiate [səb'stænʃɪeɪt] vt étayer, fournir des preuves à l'appui de

substitute ['sʌbstɪtju:t] n (person) remplaçant(e); (thing) succédané m ▷ vt: **to ~ sth/sb for** substituer qch/qn à, remplacer par qch/qn

substitution [sʌbstɪ'tju:ʃən] n substitution f

subterranean [sʌbtə'reɪnɪən] adj souterrain(e)

subtitled ['sʌbtaɪtld] adj sous-titré(e)

subtitles ['sʌbtaɪtlz] npl (Cine) sous-titres mpl

subtle ['sʌtl] adj subtil(e)

subtotal [sʌb'təutl] n total partiel

subtract [səb'trækt] vt soustraire, retrancher

subtraction [səb'trækʃən] n soustraction f

suburb ['sʌbə:b] n faubourg m; **the ~s** la banlieue

suburban [sə'bə:bən] adj de banlieue, suburbain(e)

suburbia [sə'bə:bɪə] n la banlieue

subway ['sʌbweɪ] n (Brit: underpass) passage souterrain; (US: railway) métro m

succeed [sək'si:d] vi réussir ▷ vt succéder à;
to ~ in doing réussir à faire

succeeding [sək'si:dɪŋ] adj suivant(e), qui
suit (or suivent or suivront etc)

success [sək'sɛs] n succès m; réussite f

successful [sək'sɛsful] adj qui a du succès;
(candidate) choisi(e), agréé(e); (business)
prospère, qui réussit; (attempt) couronné(e)
de succès; **to be ~ (in doing)** réussir (à faire)

successfully [sək'sɛsfəlɪ] adv avec succès

succession [sək'sɛʃən] n succession f; **in ~**
successivement; **3 years in ~** 3 ans de suite

successive [sək'sɛsɪv] adj successif(-ive);
on 3 ~ days 3 jours de suite or consécutifs

successor [sək'sɛsə^r] n successeur m

succumb [sə'kʌm] vi succomber

such [sʌtʃ] adj tel/telle; (of that kind): **~ a book**
un livre de ce genre or pareil, un tel livre;
(so much): **~ courage** un tel courage ▷ adv si;
~ books des livres de ce genre or pareils, de
tels livres; **~ a long trip** un si long voyage;
~ good books de si bons livres; **~ a long trip
that** un voyage si or tellement long que;
~ a lot of tellement or tant de; **making ~ a
noise that** faisant un tel bruit que or
tellement de bruit que; **~ a long time ago** il y
a si or tellement longtemps; **~ as** (like) tel/
telle que, comme; **a noise ~ as to** un bruit de
nature à; **~ books as I have** les quelques
livres que j'ai; **as ~** adv en tant que tel/telle,
à proprement parler

such-and-such ['sʌtʃənsʌtʃ] adj tel ou tel/
telle ou telle

suck [sʌk] vt sucer; (breast, bottle) téter; (pump,
machine) aspirer

sucker ['sʌkə^r] n (Bot, Zool, Tech) ventouse f;
(inf) naïf(-ïve), poire f

suction ['sʌkʃən] n succion f

Sudan [su'dɑ:n] n Soudan m

sudden ['sʌdn] adj soudain(e), subit(e); **all
of a ~** soudain, tout à coup

suddenly ['sʌdnlɪ] adv brusquement, tout à
coup, soudain

sudoku [su'dəuku:] n sudoku m

suds [sʌdz] npl eau savonneuse

sue [su:] vt poursuivre en justice, intenter un
procès à ▷ vi: **to ~ (for)** intenter un procès
(pour); **to ~ for divorce** engager une
procédure de divorce; **to ~ sb for damages**
poursuivre qn en dommages-intérêts

suede [sweɪd] n daim m, cuir suédé ▷ cpd de
daim

suet ['suɪt] n graisse f de rognon or de bœuf

suffer ['sʌfə^r] vt souffrir, subir; (bear) tolérer,
supporter, subir ▷ vi souffrir; **to ~ from**
(illness) souffrir de, avoir; **to ~ from the
effects of alcohol/a fall** se ressentir des
effets de l'alcool/des conséquences d'une
chute

sufferer ['sʌfərə^r] n malade m/f; victime m/f

suffering ['sʌfərɪŋ] n souffrance(s) f(pl)

suffice [sə'faɪs] vi suffire

sufficient [sə'fɪʃənt] adj suffisant(e);
~ money suffisamment d'argent

sufficiently [sə'fɪʃəntlɪ] adv suffisamment,
assez

suffocate ['sʌfəkeɪt] vi suffoquer; étouffer

sugar ['ʃugə^r] n sucre m ▷ vt sucrer

sugar beet n betterave sucrière

sugar cane n canne f.à sucre

suggest [sə'dʒɛst] vt suggérer, proposer;
(indicate) sembler indiquer; **what do you ~ I
do?** que vous me suggérez de faire?

suggestion [sə'dʒɛstʃən] n suggestion f

suicide ['suɪsaɪd] n suicide m; **to commit ~**
se suicider; **~ bombing** attentat m suicide; see
also **commit**

suicide bomber n kamikaze m/f

suit [su:t] n (man's) costume m, complet m;
(woman's) tailleur m, ensemble m; (Cards)
couleur f; (lawsuit) procès m ▷ vt (subj: clothes,
hairstyle) aller à; (be convenient for) convenir à;
(adapt): **to ~ sth to** adapter or approprier qch
à; **to be ~ed to sth** (suitable for) être adapté(e)
or approprié(e) à qch; **well ~ed** (couple) faits
l'un pour l'autre, très bien assortis; **to bring
a ~ against sb** intenter un procès contre qn;
to follow ~ (fig) faire de même

suitable ['su:təbl] adj qui convient;
approprié(e), adéquat(e); **would tomorrow
be ~?** est-ce que demain vous conviendrait?;
we found somebody ~ nous avons trouvé la
personne qu'il nous faut

suitably ['su:təblɪ] adv comme il se doit (or se
devait etc), convenablement

suitcase ['su:tkeɪs] n valise f

suite [swi:t] n (of rooms, also Mus) suite f;
(furniture): **bedroom/dining room ~**
(ensemble m de) chambre f à coucher/salle f
à manger; **a three-piece ~** un salon (canapé
et deux fauteuils)

suitor ['su:tə^r] n soupirant m, prétendant m

sulfur ['sʌlfə^r] (US) n = **sulphur**

sulk [sʌlk] vi bouder

sulky ['sʌlkɪ] adj boudeur(-euse), maussade

sullen ['sʌlən] adj renfrogné(e), maussade;
morne

sulphur, (US) **sulfur** ['sʌlfə^r] n soufre m

sultana [sʌl'tɑ:nə] n (fruit) raisin (sec) de
Smyrne

sultry ['sʌltrɪ] adj étouffant(e)

sum [sʌm] n somme f; (Scol) calcul m; **sum
up** vt résumer; (evaluate rapidly) récapituler
▷ vi résumer

summarize ['sʌməraɪz] vt résumer

summary ['sʌmərɪ] n résumé m ▷ adj (justice)
sommaire

summer ['sʌmə^r] n été m ▷ cpd d'été,
estival(e); **in (the) ~** en été, pendant l'été

summer holidays npl grandes vacances

summerhouse ['sʌməhaus] n (in garden)
pavillon m

summertime ['sʌmətaɪm] n (season) été m

summer time n (by clock) heure f d'été

summit ['sʌmɪt] n sommet m; (also: ~ **conference**) (conférence f au) sommet m

summon ['sʌmən] vt appeler, convoquer; **to ~ a witness** citer or assigner un témoin; **summon up** vt rassembler, faire appel à

summons ['sʌmənz] n citation f, assignation f ▷ vt citer, assigner; **to serve a ~ on sb** remettre une assignation à qn

Sun. abbr (= Sunday) dim

sun [sʌn] n soleil m; **in the ~** au soleil; **to catch the ~** prendre le soleil; **everything under the ~** absolument tout

sunbathe ['sʌnbeɪð] vi prendre un bain de soleil

sunbed ['sʌnbɛd] n lit pliant; (with sun lamp) lit à ultra-violets

sunblock ['sʌnblɒk] n écran m total

sunburn ['sʌnbə:n] n coup m de soleil

sunburned ['sʌnbə:nd], **sunburnt** ['sʌnbə:nt] adj bronzé(e), hâlé(e); (painfully) brûlé(e) par le soleil

Sunday ['sʌndɪ] n dimanche m; see also **Tuesday**

Sunday school n ≈ catéchisme m

sundial ['sʌndaɪəl] n cadran m solaire

sundown ['sʌndaun] n coucher m du soleil

sundries ['sʌndrɪz] npl articles divers

sundry ['sʌndrɪ] adj divers(e), différent(e); **all and ~** tout le monde, n'importe qui

sunflower ['sʌnflauə'] n tournesol m

sung [sʌŋ] pp of **sing**

sunglasses ['sʌnglɑ:sɪz] npl lunettes fpl de soleil

sunk [sʌŋk] pp of **sink**

sunlight ['sʌnlaɪt] n (lumière f du) soleil m

sunlit ['sʌnlɪt] adj ensoleillé(e)

sun lounger n chaise longue

sunny ['sʌnɪ] adj ensoleillé(e); (fig) épanoui(e), radieux(-euse); **it is ~** il fait (du) soleil, il y a du soleil

sunrise ['sʌnraɪz] n lever m du soleil

sun roof n (Aut) toit ouvrant

sunscreen ['sʌnskri:n] n crème f solaire

sunset ['sʌnsɛt] n coucher m du soleil

sunshade ['sʌnʃeɪd] n (lady's) ombrelle f; (over table) parasol m

sunshine ['sʌnʃaɪn] n (lumière f du) soleil m

sunstroke ['sʌnstrəuk] n insolation f, coup m de soleil

suntan ['sʌntæn] n bronzage m

suntan lotion n lotion f or lait m solaire

suntan oil n huile f solaire

super ['su:pə'] adj (inf) formidable

superannuation [su:pərænju'eɪʃən] n cotisations fpl pour la pension

superb [su:'pə:b] adj superbe, magnifique

supercilious [su:pə'sɪlɪəs] adj hautain(e), dédaigneux(-euse)

superficial [su:pə'fɪʃəl] adj superficiel(le)

superimpose ['su:pərɪm'pəuz] vt superposer

superintendent [su:pərɪn'tɛndənt] n directeur(-trice); (Police) ≈ commissaire m

superior [su'pɪərɪə'] adj supérieur(e); (Comm: goods, quality) de qualité supérieure; (smug) condescendant(e), méprisant(e) ▷ n supérieur(e); **Mother S~** (Rel) Mère supérieure

superiority [supɪərɪ'ɔrɪtɪ] n supériorité f

superlative [su'pə:lətɪv] adj sans pareil(le), suprême ▷ n (Ling) superlatif m

superman ['su:pəmæn] irreg n surhomme m

supermarket ['su:pəmɑ:kɪt] n supermarché m

supernatural [su:pə'nætʃərəl] adj surnaturel(le) ▷ n: **the ~** le surnaturel

superpower ['su:pəpauə'] n (Pol) superpuissance f

supersede [su:pə'si:d] vt remplacer, supplanter

superstition [su:pə'stɪʃən] n superstition f

superstitious [su:pə'stɪʃəs] adj superstitieux(-euse)

superstore ['su:pəstɔ:'] n (Brit) hypermarché m, grande surface

supervise ['su:pəvaɪz] vt (children etc) surveiller; (organization, work) diriger

supervision [su:pə'vɪʒən] n surveillance f; (monitoring) contrôle m; (management) direction f; **under medical ~** sous contrôle du médecin

supervisor ['su:pəvaɪzə'] n surveillant(e); (in shop) chef m de rayon; (Scol) directeur(-trice) de thèse

supper ['sʌpə'] n dîner m; (late) souper m; **to have ~** dîner; souper

supple ['sʌpl] adj souple

supplement n ['sʌplɪmənt] supplément m ▷ vt [sʌplɪ'mɛnt] ajouter à, compléter

supplementary [sʌplɪ'mɛntərɪ] adj supplémentaire

supplementary benefit n (Brit) allocation f supplémentaire d'aide sociale

supplier [sə'plaɪə'] n fournisseur m

supply [sə'plaɪ] vt (provide) fournir; (equip): **to ~ (with)** approvisionner or ravitailler (en); fournir (en); (system, machine): **to ~ sth (with sth)** alimenter qch (en qch); (a need) répondre à ▷ n provision f, réserve f; (supplying) approvisionnement m; (Tech) alimentation f; **supplies** npl (food) vivres mpl; (Mil) subsistances fpl; **office supplies** fournitures fpl de bureau; **to be in short ~** être rare, manquer; **the electricity/water/gas ~** l'alimentation f en électricité/eau/gaz; **~ and demand** l'offre f et la demande; **it comes supplied with an adaptor** il (or elle) est pourvu(e) d'un adaptateur

supply teacher n (Brit) suppléant(e)

support [sə'pɔ:t] n (moral, financial etc) soutien m, appui m; (Tech) support m, soutien ▷ vt soutenir, supporter; (financially) subvenir aux besoins de; (uphold) être pour, être partisan de, appuyer; (Sport: team) être pour; **to ~ o.s.** (financially) gagner sa vie

supporter [səˈpɔːtəʳ] n (Pol etc) partisan(e); (Sport) supporter m

suppose [səˈpəuz] vt, vi supposer; imaginer; **to be ~d to do/be** être censé(e) faire/être; **I don't ~ she'll come** je suppose qu'elle ne viendra pas, cela m'étonnerait qu'elle vienne

supposedly [səˈpəuzɪdlɪ] adv soi-disant

supposing [səˈpəuzɪŋ] conj si, à supposer que + sub

suppress [səˈpres] vt (revolt, feeling) réprimer; (information) faire disparaître; (scandal, yawn) étouffer

supreme [suˈpriːm] adj suprême

surcharge [ˈsəːtʃaːdʒ] n surcharge f; (extra tax) surtaxe f

sure [ʃuəʳ] adj (gen) sûr(e); (definite, convinced) sûr, certain(e) ▷ adv (inf: US): **that ~ is pretty, that's ~ pretty** c'est drôlement joli(e); **~!** (of course) bien sûr!; **~ enough** effectivement; **I'm not ~ how/why/when** je ne sais pas très bien comment/pourquoi/quand; **to be ~ of o.s.** être sûr de soi; **to make ~ of sth/that** s'assurer de qch/que, vérifier qch/que

surely [ˈʃuəlɪ] adv sûrement; certainement; **~ you don't mean that!** vous ne parlez pas sérieusement!

surf [səːf] n (waves) ressac m ▷ vt: **to ~ the Net** surfer sur Internet, surfer sur le net

surface [ˈsəːfɪs] n surface f ▷ vt (road) poser un revêtement sur ▷ vi remonter à la surface; (fig) faire surface; **on the ~** (fig) au premier abord; **by ~ mail** par voie de terre, (by sea) par voie maritime

surface mail n courrier m par voie de terre (or maritime)

surfboard [ˈsəːfbɔːd] n planche f de surf

surfeit [ˈsəːfɪt] n: **a ~ of** un excès de; une indigestion de

surfer [ˈsəːfəʳ] n (in sea) surfeur(-euse); **web** or **net ~** internaute m/f

surfing [ˈsəːfɪŋ] n surf m

surge [səːdʒ] n (of emotion) vague f; (Elec) pointe f de courant ▷ vi déferler; **to ~ forward** se précipiter (en avant)

surgeon [ˈsəːdʒən] n chirurgien m

surgery [ˈsəːdʒərɪ] n chirurgie f; (Brit: room) cabinet m (de consultation); (also: **~ hours**) heures fpl de consultation; (of MP etc) permanence f (où le député reçoit les électeurs etc); **to undergo ~** être opéré(e)

surgical [ˈsəːdʒɪkl] adj chirurgical(e)

surgical spirit n (Brit) alcool m à 90°

surname [ˈsəːneɪm] n nom m de famille

surpass [səːˈpɑːs] vt surpasser, dépasser

surplus [ˈsəːpləs] n surplus m, excédent m ▷ adj en surplus, de trop; (Comm) excédentaire; **it is ~ to our requirements** cela dépasse nos besoins; **~ stock** surplus m

surprise [səˈpraɪz] n (gen) surprise f; (astonishment) étonnement m ▷ vt surprendre, étonner; **to take by ~** (person) prendre au dépourvu; (Mil: town, fort) prendre par surprise

surprised [səˈpraɪzd] adj (look, smile) surpris(e), étonné(e); **to be ~** être surpris

surprising [səˈpraɪzɪŋ] adj surprenant(e), étonnant(e)

surprisingly [səˈpraɪzɪŋlɪ] adv (easy, helpful) étonnamment, étrangement; (somewhat) **~, he agreed** curieusement, il a accepté

surrender [səˈrendəʳ] n reddition f, capitulation f ▷ vi se rendre, capituler ▷ vt (claim, right) renoncer à

surreptitious [sʌrəpˈtɪʃəs] adj subreptice, furtif(-ive)

surrogate [ˈsʌrəgɪt] n (Brit: substitute) substitut m ▷ adj de substitution, de remplacement; **a food ~** un succédané alimentaire; **~ coffee** ersatz m or succédané m de café

surrogate mother n mère porteuse or de substitution

surround [səˈraund] vt entourer; (Mil etc) encercler

surrounding [səˈraundɪŋ] adj environnant(e)

surroundings [səˈraundɪŋz] npl environs mpl, alentours mpl

surveillance [səːˈveɪləns] n surveillance f

survey n [ˈsəːveɪ] enquête f, étude f; (in house buying etc) inspection f, (rapport m d') expertise f; (of land) levé m; (comprehensive view: of situation etc) vue f d'ensemble ▷ vt [səːˈveɪ] (situation) passer en revue; (examine carefully) inspecter; (building) expertiser; (land) faire le levé de; (look at) embrasser du regard

surveyor [səˈveɪəʳ] n (of building) expert m; (of land) (arpenteur m) géomètre m

survival [səˈvaɪvl] n survie f; (relic) vestige m ▷ cpd (course, kit) de survie

survive [səˈvaɪv] vi survivre; (custom etc) subsister ▷ vt (accident etc) survivre à, réchapper de; (person) survivre à

survivor [səˈvaɪvəʳ] n survivant(e)

susceptible [səˈseptəbl] adj: **~ (to)** sensible (à); (disease) prédisposé(e) (à)

suspect adj, n [ˈsʌspɛkt] suspect(e) ▷ vt [səsˈpɛkt] soupçonner, suspecter

suspend [səsˈpend] vt suspendre

suspended sentence [səsˈpendɪd-] n (Law) condamnation f avec sursis

suspender belt [səsˈpendə-] n (Brit) porte-jarretelles m inv

suspenders [səsˈpendəz] npl (Brit) jarretelles fpl; (US) bretelles fpl

suspense [səsˈpens] n attente f, incertitude f; (in film etc) suspense m; **to keep sb in ~** tenir qn en suspens, laisser qn dans l'incertitude

suspension [səsˈpenʃən] n (gen, Aut) suspension f; (of driving licence) retrait m provisoire

suspension bridge n pont suspendu

suspicion [səs'pɪʃən] n soupçon(s) m(pl); **to be under ~** être considéré(e) comme suspect(e), être suspecté(e); **arrested on ~ of murder** arrêté sur présomption de meurtre

suspicious [səs'pɪʃəs] adj (suspecting) soupçonneux(-euse), méfiant(e); (causing suspicion) suspect(e); **to be ~ of** or **about sb/ sth** avoir des doutes à propos de qn/sur qch, trouver qn/qch suspect(e)

sustain [səs'teɪn] vt soutenir; supporter; corroborer; (subj: food) nourrir, donner des forces à; (damage) subir; (injury) recevoir

sustainable [səs'teɪnəbl] adj (rate, growth) qui peut être maintenu(e); (development) durable

sustained [səs'teɪnd] adj (effort) soutenu(e), prolongé(e)

sustenance ['sʌstɪnəns] n nourriture f; moyens mpl de subsistance

SUV n abbr (esp US: = sports utility vehicle) SUV m, véhicule m de loisirs

swab [swɔb] n (Med) tampon m; prélèvement m ⊳ vt (Naut: also: **~ down**) nettoyer

swagger ['swægəʳ] vi plastronner, parader

swallow ['swɔləu] n (bird) hirondelle f; (of food etc) gorgée f ⊳ vt avaler; (fig: story) gober; **swallow up** vt engloutir

swam [swæm] pt of **swim**

swamp [swɔmp] n marais m, marécage m ⊳ vt submerger

swan [swɔn] n cygne m

swap [swɔp] n échange m, troc m ⊳ vt: **to ~ (for)** échanger (contre), troquer (contre)

swarm [swɔ:m] n essaim m ⊳ vi (bees) essaimer; (people) grouiller; **to be ~ing with** grouiller de

swastika ['swɔstɪkə] n croix gammée

swat [swɔt] vt écraser ⊳ n (Brit: also: **fly ~**) tapette f

sway [sweɪ] vi se balancer, osciller; tanguer ⊳ vt (influence) influencer ⊳ n (rule, power): **~ (over)** emprise f (sur); **to hold ~ over sb** avoir de l'emprise sur qn

swear [swɛəʳ] (pt **swore**, pp **sworn**) [swɔ:ʳ, swɔ:n] vt, vi jurer; **to ~ to sth** jurer de qch; **to ~ an oath** prêter serment; **swear in** vt assermenter

swearword ['swɛəwə:d] n gros mot, juron f

sweat [swɛt] n sueur f, transpiration f ⊳ vi suer; **in a ~** en sueur

sweater ['swɛtəʳ] n tricot m, pull m

sweatshirt ['swɛtʃə:t] n sweat-shirt m

sweaty ['swɛtɪ] adj en sueur, moite or mouillé(e) de sueur

Swede [swi:d] n Suédois(e)

swede [swi:d] n (Brit) rutabaga m

Sweden ['swi:dn] n Suède f

Swedish ['swi:dɪʃ] adj suédois(e) ⊳ n (Ling) suédois m

sweep [swi:p] (pt, pp **swept**) [swɛpt] n coup m de balai; (curve) grande courbe; (range) champ m; (also: **chimney ~**) ramoneur m ⊳ vt balayer; (subj: current) emporter; (subj: fashion, craze) se répandre dans ⊳ vi avancer majestueusement or rapidement; s'élancer; s'étendre; **sweep away** vt balayer; entraîner; emporter; **sweep past** vi passer majestueusement or rapidement; **sweep up** vt, vi balayer

sweeping ['swi:pɪŋ] adj (gesture) large, circulaire; (changes, reforms) radical(e); **a ~ statement** une généralisation hâtive

sweet [swi:t] n (Brit: pudding) dessert m; (candy) bonbon m ⊳ adj doux/douce; (not savoury) sucré(e); (fresh) frais/fraîche, pur(e); (kind) gentil(le); (baby) mignon(ne) ⊳ adv: **to smell ~** sentir bon; **to taste ~** avoir un goût sucré; **~ and sour** adj aigre-doux/douce

sweetcorn ['swi:tkɔ:n] n maïs doux

sweeten ['swi:tn] vt sucrer; (fig) adoucir

sweetener ['swi:tnəʳ] n (Culin) édulcorant m

sweetheart ['swi:thɑ:t] n amoureux(-euse)

sweetness ['swi:tnɪs] n douceur f; (of taste) goût sucré

sweet pea n pois m de senteur

sweetshop ['swi:tʃɔp] n (Brit) confiserie f

swell [swɛl] (pt **swelled**, pp **swollen** or **swelled**) ['swəulən] n (of sea) houle f ⊳ adj (US: inf: excellent) chouette ⊳ vt (increase) grossir, augmenter ⊳ vi (increase) grossir, augmenter; (sound) s'enfler; (Med: also: **~ up**) enfler

swelling ['swɛlɪŋ] n (Med) enflure f; (: lump) grosseur f

sweltering ['swɛltərɪŋ] adj étouffant(e), oppressant(e)

swept [swɛpt] pt, pp of **sweep**

swerve [swə:v] vi (to avoid obstacle) faire une embardée or un écart; (off the road) dévier

swift [swɪft] n (bird) martinet m ⊳ adj rapide, prompt(e)

swig [swɪg] n (inf: drink) lampée f

swill [swɪl] n pâtée f ⊳ vt (also: **~ out, ~ down**) laver à grande eau

swim [swɪm] (pt **swam**, pp **swum**) [swæm, swʌm] n: **to go for a ~** aller nager or se baigner ⊳ vi nager; (Sport) faire de la natation; (fig: head, room) tourner ⊳ vt traverser (à la nage); (distance) faire (à la nage); **to ~ a length** nager une longueur; **to go ~ming** aller nager

swimmer ['swɪməʳ] n nageur(-euse)

swimming ['swɪmɪŋ] n nage f, natation f

swimming cap n bonnet m de bain

swimming costume n (Brit) maillot m (de bain)

swimming pool n piscine f

swimming trunks npl maillot m de bain

swimsuit ['swɪmsu:t] n maillot m (de bain)

swindle ['swɪndl] n escroquerie f ⊳ vt escroquer

swine [swaɪn] n (pl inv) pourceau m, porc m; (inf!) salaud m (!)

swine flu n grippe f porcine

swing [swɪŋ] (pt, pp **swung**) [swʌŋ] n (in

playground) balançoire f; (*movement*) balancement m, oscillations fpl; (*change in opinion etc*) revirement m; (*Mus*) swing m; rythme m ▷ vt balancer, faire osciller; (*also:* ~ **round**) tourner, faire virer ▷ vi se balancer, osciller; (*also:* ~ **round**) virer, tourner; **a ~ to the left** (*Pol*) un revirement en faveur de la gauche; **to be in full ~** battre son plein; **to get into the ~ of things** se mettre dans le bain; **the road ~s south** la route prend la direction sud

swing bridge n pont tournant

swing door n (*Brit*) porte battante

swingeing ['swɪndʒɪŋ] adj (*Brit*) écrasant(e); considérable

swipe [swaɪp] n grand coup; gifle f ▷ vt (*hit*) frapper à toute volée; gifler; (*inf: steal*) piquer; (*credit card etc*) faire passer (dans la machine)

swipe card n carte f magnétique

swirl [swəːl] n tourbillon m ▷ vi tourbillonner, tournoyer

Swiss [swɪs] adj suisse ▷ n (pl inv) Suisse(-esse)

switch [swɪtʃ] n (*for light, radio etc*) bouton m; (*change*) changement m, revirement m ▷ vt (*change*) changer; (*exchange*) intervertir; (*invert*): **to ~** (**round** or **over**) changer de place; **switch off** vt éteindre; (*engine, machine*) arrêter; **could you ~ off the light?** pouvez-vous éteindre la lumière?; **switch on** vt allumer; (*engine, machine*) mettre en marche; (*Brit: water supply*) ouvrir

switchboard ['swɪtʃbɔːd] n (*Tel*) standard m

Switzerland ['swɪtsələnd] n Suisse f

swivel ['swɪvl] vi (*also:* ~ **round**) pivoter, tourner

swollen ['swəʊlən] pp of **swell** ▷ adj (*ankle etc*) enflé(e)

swoon [swuːn] vi se pâmer

swoop [swuːp] n (*by police etc*) rafle f, descente f; (*of bird etc*) descente f en piqué ▷ vi (*bird: also:* ~ **down**) descendre en piqué, piquer

swop [swɒp] n, vt = **swap**

sword [sɔːd] n épée f

swordfish ['sɔːdfɪʃ] n espadon m

swore [swɔːʳ] pt of **swear**

sworn [swɔːn] pp of **swear** ▷ adj (*statement, evidence*) donné(e) sous serment; (*enemy*) juré(e)

swot [swɒt] vt, vi bûcher, potasser

swum [swʌm] pp of **swim**

swung [swʌŋ] pt, pp of **swing**

syllable ['sɪləbl] n syllabe f

syllabus ['sɪləbəs] n programme m; **on the ~** au programme

symbol ['sɪmbl] n symbole m

symbolic [sɪmˈbɒlɪk], **symbolical** [sɪmˈbɒlɪkl] adj symbolique

symmetrical [sɪˈmɛtrɪkl] adj symétrique

symmetry ['sɪmɪtrɪ] n symétrie f

sympathetic [sɪmpəˈθɛtɪk] adj (*showing pity*) compatissant(e); (*understanding*) bienveillant(e), compréhensif(-ive); ~ **towards** bien disposé(e) envers

sympathize ['sɪmpəθaɪz] vi: **to ~ with sb** plaindre qn; (*in grief*) s'associer à la douleur de qn; **to ~ with sth** comprendre qch

sympathizer ['sɪmpəθaɪzəʳ] n (*Pol*) sympathisant(e)

sympathy ['sɪmpəθɪ] n (*pity*) compassion f; **sympathies** npl (*support*) soutien m; **in ~ with** en accord avec; (*strike*) en or par solidarité avec; **with our deepest ~** en vous priant d'accepter nos sincères condoléances

symphony ['sɪmfənɪ] n symphonie f

symptom ['sɪmptəm] n symptôme m; indice m

synagogue ['sɪnəgɒg] n synagogue f

syndicate ['sɪndɪkɪt] n syndicat m, coopérative f; (*Press*) agence f de presse

syndrome ['sɪndrəʊm] n syndrome m

synonym ['sɪnənɪm] n synonyme m

synopsis (pl **synopses**) [sɪˈnɒpsɪs, -siːz] n résumé m, synopsis m

synthetic [sɪnˈθɛtɪk] adj synthétique ▷ n matière f synthétique; **synthetics** npl textiles artificiels

syphon ['saɪfən] n, vb = **siphon**

Syria ['sɪrɪə] n Syrie f

syringe [sɪˈrɪndʒ] n seringue f

syrup ['sɪrəp] n sirop m; (*Brit: also:* **golden ~**) mélasse raffinée

system ['sɪstəm] n système m; (*order*) méthode f; (*Anat*) organisme m

systematic [sɪstəˈmætɪk] adj systématique; méthodique

system disk n (*Comput*) disque m système

systems analyst n analyste-programmeur m/f

S

style très concis. Ce type de journaux vise des lecteurs s'intéressant aux faits divers ayant un parfum de scandale; voir "quality press"

taboo [tə'bu:] *adj, n* tabou (*m*)

tack [tæk] *n* (*nail*) petit clou; (*stitch*) point *m* de bâti; (*Naut*) bord *m*, bordée *f*; (*fig*) direction *f* ▷ *vt* (*nail*) clouer; (*sew*) bâtir ▷ *vi* (*Naut*) tirer un *or* des bord(s); **to change ~** virer de bord; **on the wrong ~** (*fig*) sur la mauvaise voie; **to ~ sth on to (the end of) sth** (*of letter, book*) rajouter qch à la fin de qch

tackle ['tækl] *n* matériel *m*, équipement *m*; (*for lifting*) appareil *m* de levage; (*Football, Rugby*) plaquage *m* ▷ *vt* (*difficulty, animal, burglar*) s'attaquer à; (*person: challenge*) s'expliquer avec; (*Football, Rugby*) plaquer

tacky ['tækɪ] *adj* collant(e); (*paint*) pas sec/ sèche; (*inf: shabby*) moche; (*pej: poor-quality*) minable; (: *showing bad taste*) ringard(e)

tact [tækt] *n* tact *m*

tactful ['tæktful] *adj* plein(e) de tact

tactical ['tæktɪkl] *adj* tactique; **~ error** erreur *f* de tactique

tactics ['tæktɪks] *n, npl* tactique *f*

tactless ['tæktlɪs] *adj* qui manque de tact

tadpole ['tædpəul] *n* têtard *m*

taffy ['tæfɪ] *n* (*US*) (bonbon *m* au) caramel *m*

tag [tæg] *n* étiquette *f*; **price/name ~** étiquette (portant le prix/le nom); **tag along** *vi* suivre

tail [teɪl] *n* queue *f*; (*of shirt*) pan *m* ▷ *vt* (*follow*) suivre, filer; **tails** *npl* (*suit*) habit *m*; **to turn ~** se sauver à toutes jambes; *see also* **head**; **tail away, tail off** *vi* (*in size, quality etc*) baisser peu à peu

tailback ['teɪlbæk] *n* (*Brit*) bouchon *m*

tail end *n* bout *m*, fin *f*

tailgate ['teɪlgeɪt] *n* (*Aut*) hayon *m* arrière

tailor ['teɪləʳ] *n* tailleur *m* (*artisan*) ▷ *vt*: **to ~ sth (to)** adapter qch exactement (à); **~'s (shop)** (boutique *f* de) tailleur *m*

tailoring ['teɪlərɪŋ] *n* (*cut*) coupe *f*

tailor-made ['teɪlə'meɪd] *adj* fait(e) sur mesure; (*fig*) conçu(e) spécialement

tailwind ['teɪlwɪnd] *n* vent *m* arrière *inv*

tainted ['teɪntɪd] *adj* (*food*) gâté(e); (*water, air*) infecté(e); (*fig*) souillé(e)

Taiwan ['taɪ'wɑːn] *n* Taïwan (*no article*)

Taiwanese [taɪwə'niːz] *adj* taïwanais(e) ▷ *n inv* Taïwanais(e)

take [teɪk] (*pt* **took**, *pp* **taken**) [tuk, 'teɪkn] *vt* prendre; (*gain: prize*) remporter; (*require: effort, courage*) demander; (*tolerate*) accepter, supporter; (*hold: passengers etc*) contenir; (*accompany*) emmener, accompagner; (*bring, carry*) apporter, emporter; (*exam*) passer, se présenter à; (*conduct: meeting*) présider ▷ *vi* (*dye, fire etc*) prendre ▷ *n* (*Cine*) prise *f* de vues; **to ~ sth from** (*drawer etc*) prendre qch dans; (*person*) prendre qch à; **I ~ it that** je suppose

---

ta [tɑ:] *excl* (*Brit inf*) merci!

tab [tæb] *n* (*loop on coat etc*) attache *f*; (*label*) étiquette *f*; (*on drinks can etc*) languette *f*; **to keep ~s on** (*fig*) surveiller

tabby ['tæbɪ] *n* (*also:* **~ cat**) chat(te) tigré(e)

table ['teɪbl] *n* table *f* ▷ *vt* (*Brit: motion etc*) présenter; **to lay** *or* **set the ~** mettre le couvert *or* la table; **to clear the ~** débarrasser la table; **league ~** (*Brit Football, Rugby*) classement *m* (du championnat); **~ of contents** table des matières

tablecloth ['teɪblklɔθ] *n* nappe *f*

table d'hôte [tɑ:bl'dəut] *adj* (*meal*) à prix fixe

table lamp *n* lampe décorative *or* de table

tablemat ['teɪblmæt] *n* (*for plate*) napperon *m*, set *m*; (*for hot dish*) dessous-de-plat *m inv*

tablespoon ['teɪblspu:n] *n* cuiller *f* de service; (*also:* **~ful:** *as measurement*) cuillerée *f* à soupe

tablet ['tæblɪt] *n* (*Med*) comprimé *m*; (: *for sucking*) pastille *f*; (*of stone*) plaque *f*; **~ of soap** (*Brit*) savonnette *f*

table tennis *n* ping-pong *m*, tennis *m* de table

table wine *n* vin *m* de table

tabloid ['tæblɔɪd] *n* (*newspaper*) quotidien *m* populaire; *voir article*

◈ **TABLOID PRESS**

◈ Le terme *tabloid press* désigne les journaux populaires de demi-format où l'on trouve beaucoup de photos et qui adoptent un

que; **I took him for a doctor** je l'ai pris pour un docteur; **to ~ sb's hand** prendre qn par la main; **to ~ for a walk** (*child, dog*) emmener promener; **to be ~n ill** tomber malade; **to ~ it upon o.s. to do sth** prendre sur soi de faire qch; **~ the first (street) on the left** prenez la première à gauche; **it won't ~ long** ça ne prendra pas longtemps; **I was quite ~n with her/it** elle/cela m'a beaucoup plu; **take after** *vt fus* ressembler à; **take apart** *vt* démonter; **take away** *vt* (*carry off*) emporter; (*remove*) enlever; (*subtract*) soustraire ▷ *vi*: **to ~ away from** diminuer; **take back** *vt* (*return*) rendre, rapporter; (*one's words*) retirer; **take down** *vt* (*building*) démolir; (*dismantle: scaffolding*) démonter; (*letter etc*) prendre, écrire; **take in** *vt* (*deceive*) tromper, rouler; (*understand*) comprendre, saisir; (*include*) couvrir, inclure; (*lodger*) prendre; (*orphan, stray dog*) recueillir; (*dress, waistband*) reprendre; **take off** *vi* (*Aviat*) décoller ▷ *vt* (*remove*) enlever; (*imitate*) imiter, pasticher; **take on** *vt* (*work*) accepter, se charger de; (*employee*) prendre, embaucher; (*opponent*) accepter de se battre contre; **take out** *vt* sortir; (*remove*) enlever; (*invite*) sortir avec; (*licence*) se procurer; **to ~ sth out of** enlever qch de; (*out of drawer etc*) prendre qch dans; **don't ~ it out on me!** ne t'en prends pas à moi!; **to ~ sb out to a restaurant** emmener qn au restaurant; **take over** *vt* (*business*) reprendre ▷ *vi*: **to ~ over from sb** prendre la relève de qn; **take to** *vt fus* (*person*) se prendre d'amitié pour; (*activity*) prendre goût à; **to ~ to doing sth** prendre l'habitude de faire qch; **take up** *vt* (*one's story*) reprendre; (*dress*) raccourcir; (*occupy: time, space*) prendre, occuper; (*engage in: hobby etc*) se mettre à; (*accept: offer, challenge*) accepter; (*absorb: liquids*) absorber ▷ *vi*: **to ~ up with sb** se lier d'amitié avec qn

takeaway ['teɪkəweɪ] (*Brit*) *adj* (*food*) à emporter ▷ *n* (*shop, restaurant*) = magasin *m* qui vend des plats à emporter

taken ['teɪkən] *pp of* **take**

takeoff ['teɪkɔf] *n* (*Aviat*) décollage *m*

takeout ['teɪkaʊt] *adj, n* (*US*) = **takeaway**

takeover ['teɪkəʊvə^r] *n* (*Comm*) rachat *m*

takings ['teɪkɪŋz] *npl* (*Comm*) recette *f*

talc [tælk] *n* (*also:* **~um powder**) talc *m*

tale [teɪl] *n* (*story*) conte *m*, histoire *f*; (*account*) récit *m*; (*pej*) histoire; **to tell ~s** (*fig*) rapporter

talent ['tælnt] *n* talent *m*, don *m*

talented ['tæləntɪd] *adj* doué(e), plein(e) de talent

talk [tɔːk] *n* (*a speech*) causerie *f*, exposé *m*; (*conversation*) discussion *f*; (*interview*) entretien *m*, propos *mpl*; (*gossip*) racontars *mpl* (*péj*) ▷ *vi* parler; (*chatter*) bavarder; **talks** *npl* (*Pol etc*) entretiens *mpl*; conférence *f*; **to give a ~** faire un exposé; **to ~ about** parler de; (*converse*) s'entretenir *or* parler de; **~ing of films, have**

you seen ...? à propos de films, as-tu vu ...?; **to ~ sb out of/into doing** persuader qn de ne pas faire/de faire; **to ~ shop** parler métier *or* affaires; **talk over** *vt* discuter (de)

talkative ['tɔːkətɪv] *adj* bavard(e)

talk show *n* (*TV, Radio*) émission-débat *f*

tall [tɔːl] *adj* (*person*) grand(e); (*building, tree*) haut(e); **to be 6 feet ~** = mesurer 1 mètre 80; **how ~ are you?** combien mesurez-vous?

tall story *n* histoire *f* invraisemblable

tally ['tælɪ] *n* compte *m* ▷ *vi*: **to ~ (with)** correspondre (à); **to keep a ~ of sth** tenir le compte de qch

talon ['tælən] *n* griffe *f*; (*of eagle*) serre *f*

tambourine [tæmbə'riːn] *n* tambourin *m*

tame [teɪm] *adj* apprivoisé(e); (*fig: story, style*) insipide

tamper ['tæmpə^r] *vi*: **to ~ with** toucher à (*en cachette ou sans permission*)

tampon ['tæmpən] *n* tampon *m* hygiénique *or* périodique

tan [tæn] *n* (*also:* **sun~**) bronzage *m* ▷ *vt, vi* bronzer, brunir ▷ *adj* (*colour*) marron clair *inv*; **to get a ~** bronzer

tandem ['tændəm] *n* tandem *m*

tang [tæŋ] *n* odeur (*or* saveur) piquante

tangent ['tændʒənt] *n* (*Math*) tangente *f*; **to go off at a ~** (*fig*) partir dans une digression

tangerine [tændʒə'riːn] *n* mandarine *f*

tangle ['tæŋgl] *n* enchevêtrement *m* ▷ *vt* enchevêtrer; **to get in(to) a ~** s'emmêler

tank [tæŋk] *n* réservoir *m*; (*for processing*) cuve *f*; (*for fish*) aquarium *m*; (*Mil*) char *m* d'assaut, tank *m*

tanker ['tæŋkə^r] *n* (*ship*) pétrolier *m*; tanker *m*; (*truck*) camion-citerne *m*; (*Rail*) wagon-citerne *m*

tankini [tæn'kiːnɪ] *n* tankini *m*

tanned [tænd] *adj* bronzé(e)

tantalizing ['tæntəlaɪzɪŋ] *adj* (*smell*) extrêmement appétissant(e); (*offer*) terriblement tentant(e)

tantamount ['tæntəmaunt] *adj*: **~ to** qui équivaut à

Tanzania [tænzə'nɪə] *n* Tanzanie *f*

tap [tæp] *n* (*on sink etc*) robinet *m*; (*gentle blow*) petite tape ▷ *vt* frapper *or* taper légèrement; (*resources*) exploiter, utiliser; (*telephone*) mettre sur écoute; **on ~** (*beer*) en tonneau; (*fig: resources*) disponible

tap dancing ['tæpdɑːnsɪŋ] *n* claquettes *fpl*

tape [teɪp] *n* (*for tying*) ruban *m*; (*also:* **magnetic ~**) bande *f* (magnétique); (*cassette*) cassette *f*; (*sticky*) Scotch® *m* ▷ *vt* (*record*) enregistrer (au magnétoscope *or* sur cassette); (*stick*) coller avec du Scotch®; **on ~** (*song etc*) enregistré(e)

tape deck *n* platine *f* d'enregistrement

tape measure *n* mètre *m* à ruban

taper ['teɪpə^r] *n* cierge *m* ▷ *vi* s'effiler

t

tape recorder *n* magnétophone *m*

tapestry ['tæpɪstrɪ] *n* tapisserie *f*

tar [tɑː] *n* goudron *m*; **low-/middle--cigarettes** cigarettes *fpl* à faible/moyenne teneur en goudron

target ['tɑːgɪt] *n* cible *f*; (*fig: objective*) objectif *m*; **to be on ~** (*project*) progresser comme prévu

tariff ['tærɪf] *n* (*Comm*) tarif *m*; (*taxes*) tarif douanier

tarmac ['tɑːmæk] *n* (*Brit: on road*) macadam *m*; (*Aviat*) aire *f* d'envol ▷ *vt* (*Brit*) goudronner

tarnish ['tɑːnɪʃ] *vt* ternir

tarpaulin [tɑːˈpɔːlɪn] *n* bâche goudronnée

tarragon ['tærəgən] *n* estragon *m*

tart [tɑːt] *n* (*Culin*) tarte *f*; (*Brit inf: pej: prostitute*) poule *f* ▷ *adj* (*flavour*) âpre, aigrelet(te); **tart up** *vt* (*inf*): **to ~ o.s. up** se faire beau/belle; (: *pej*) s'attifer

tartan ['tɑːtn] *n* tartan *m* ▷ *adj* écossais(e)

tartar ['tɑːtəʳ] *n* (*on teeth*) tartre *m*

tartar sauce, tartare sauce *n* sauce *f* tartare

task [tɑːsk] *n* tâche *f*; **to take to ~** prendre à partie

task force *n* (*Mil, Police*) détachement spécial

tassel ['tæsl] *n* gland *m*; pompon *m*

taste [teɪst] *n* goût *m*; (*fig: glimpse, idea*) idée *f*, aperçu *m* ▷ *vt* goûter ▷ *vi*: **to ~ of** (*fish etc*) avoir le *or* un goût de; **it ~s like fish** ça a un *or* le goût de poisson, on dirait du poisson; **what does it ~ like?** quel goût ça a?; **you can ~ the garlic (in it)** on sent bien l'ail; **to have a ~ of sth** goûter (à) qch; **can I have a ~?** je peux goûter?; **to have a ~ for sth** aimer qch, avoir un penchant pour qch; **to be in good/bad** *or* **poor ~** être de bon/mauvais goût

tasteful ['teɪstful] *adj* de bon goût

tasteless ['teɪstlɪs] *adj* (*food*) insipide; (*remark*) de mauvais goût

tasty ['teɪstɪ] *adj* savoureux(-euse), délicieux(-euse)

tatters ['tætəz] *npl*: **in ~** (*also*: **tattered**) en lambeaux

tattoo [təˈtuː] *n* tatouage *m*; (*spectacle*) parade *f* militaire ▷ *vt* tatouer

tatty ['tætɪ] *adj* (*Brit inf*) défraîchi(e), en piteux état

taught [tɔːt] *pt, pp of* **teach**

taunt [tɔːnt] *n* raillerie *f* ▷ *vt* railler

Taurus ['tɔːrəs] *n* le Taureau; **to be ~** être du Taureau

taut [tɔːt] *adj* tendu(e)

tax [tæks] *n* (*on goods etc*) taxe *f*; (*on income*) impôts *mpl*, contributions *fpl* ▷ *vt* taxer; imposer; (*fig: patience etc*) mettre à l'épreuve; **before/after ~** avant/après l'impôt; **free of ~** exonéré(e) d'impôt

taxable ['tæksəbl] *adj* (*income*) imposable

taxation [tækˈseɪʃən] *n* taxation *f*; impôts *mpl*, contributions *fpl*; **system of ~** système fiscal

tax avoidance *n* évasion fiscale

tax disc *n* (*Brit Aut*) vignette *f* (automobile)

tax evasion *n* fraude fiscale

tax-free ['tæksfriː] *adj* exempt(e) d'impôts

taxi ['tæksɪ] *n* taxi *m* ▷ *vi* (*Aviat*) rouler (lentement) au sol

taxi driver *n* chauffeur *m* de taxi

taxi rank, (*Brit*) **taxi stand** *n* station *f* de taxis

tax payer [-peɪəʳ] *n* contribuable *m/f*

tax relief *n* dégrèvement *or* allègement fiscal, réduction *f* d'impôt

tax return *n* déclaration *f* d'impôts *or* de revenus

TB *n abbr* = **tuberculosis**

tbc *abbr* = **to be confirmed**

tea [tiː] *n* thé *m*; (*Brit: snack: for children*) goûter *m*; **high ~** (*Brit*) collation combinant goûter et dîner

tea bag *n* sachet *m* de thé

tea break *n* (*Brit*) pause-thé *f*

teach (*pt, pp* **taught**) [tiːtʃ, tɔːt] *vt*: **to ~ sb sth, to ~ sth to sb** apprendre qch à qn; (*in school etc*) enseigner qch à qn ▷ *vi* enseigner; **it taught him a lesson** (*fig*) ça lui a servi de leçon

teacher ['tiːtʃəʳ] *n* (*in secondary school*) professeur *m*; (*in primary school*) instituteur(-trice); **French ~** professeur de français

teaching ['tiːtʃɪŋ] *n* enseignement *m*

tea cosy *n* couvre-théière *m*

teacup ['tiːkʌp] *n* tasse *f* à thé

teak [tiːk] *n* teck *m* ▷ *adj* en *or* de teck

tea leaves *npl* feuilles *fpl* de thé

team [tiːm] *n* équipe *f*; (*of animals*) attelage *m*; **team up** *vi*: **to ~ up (with)** faire équipe (avec)

teamwork ['tiːmwəːk] *n* travail *m* d'équipe

teapot ['tiːpɔt] *n* théière *f*

tear¹ ['tɪəʳ] *n* larme *f*; **in ~s** en larmes; **to burst into ~s** fondre en larmes

tear² [tɛəʳ] (*pt* **tore**, *pp* **torn**) [tɔːʳ, tɔːn] *n* déchirure *f* ▷ *vt* déchirer ▷ *vi* se déchirer; **to ~ to pieces** *or* **to bits** *or* **to shreds** mettre en pièces; (*fig*) démolir; **tear along** *vi* (*rush*) aller à toute vitesse; **tear apart** *vt* (*also fig*) déchirer; **tear away** *vt*: **to ~ o.s. away (from sth)** (*fig*) s'arracher (de qch); **tear down** *vt* (*building, statue*) démolir; (*poster, flag*) arracher; **tear off** *vt* (*sheet of paper etc*) arracher; (*one's clothes*) enlever à toute vitesse; **tear out** *vt* (*sheet of paper, cheque*) arracher; **tear up** *vt* (*sheet of paper etc*) déchirer, mettre en morceaux *or* pièces

tearful ['tɪəful] *adj* larmoyant(e)

tear gas ['tɪə] *n* gaz *m* lacrymogène

tearoom ['tiːruːm] *n* salon *m* de thé

tease [tiːz] *n* taquin *m* ▷ *vt* taquiner; (*unkindly*) tourmenter

tea set *n* service *m* à thé

teaspoon ['tiːspuːn] *n* petite cuiller; (*also*: **~ful**: *as measurement*) = cuillerée *f* à café

teat [tiːt] n tétine f
teatime ['tiːtaɪm] n l'heure f du thé
tea towel n (Brit) torchon m (à vaisselle)
technical ['tɛknɪkl] adj technique
technicality [tɛknɪ'kælɪtɪ] n technicité f; (detail) détail m technique; **on a legal ~** à cause de (or grâce à) l'application à la lettre d'une subtilité juridique; pour vice de forme
technically ['tɛknɪklɪ] adv techniquement; (strictly speaking) en théorie, en principe
technician [tɛk'nɪʃən] n technicien(ne)
technique [tɛk'niːk] n technique f
techno ['tɛknəʊ] n (Mus) techno f
technological [tɛknə'lɒdʒɪkl] adj technologique
technology [tɛk'nɒlədʒɪ] n technologie f
teddy ['tɛdɪ], **teddy bear** n ours m (en peluche)
tedious ['tiːdɪəs] adj fastidieux(-euse)
tee [tiː] n (Golf) tee m
teem [tiːm] vi: **to ~ (with)** grouiller (de); **it is ~ing (with rain)** il pleut à torrents
teen [tiːn] adj = **teenage** ▷ n (US) = **teenager**
teenage ['tiːneɪdʒ] adj (fashions etc) pour jeunes, pour adolescents; (child) qui est adolescent(e)
teenager ['tiːneɪdʒəʳ] n adolescent(e)
teens [tiːnz] npl: **to be in one's ~** être adolescent(e)
tee-shirt ['tiːʃəːt] n = **T-shirt**
teeter ['tiːtəʳ] vi chanceler, vaciller
teeth [tiːθ] npl of **tooth**
teethe [tiːð] vi percer ses dents
teething troubles ['tiːðɪŋ-] npl (fig) difficultés initiales
teetotal ['tiː'təʊtl] adj (person) qui ne boit jamais d'alcool
telecommunications ['tɛlɪkəmjuːnɪ'keɪʃənz] n télécommunications fpl
teleconferencing [tɛlɪ'kɒnfərənsɪŋ] n téléconférence(s) f(pl)
telegram ['tɛlɪɡræm] n télégramme m
telegraph ['tɛlɪɡrɑːf] n télégraphe m
telegraph pole ['tɛlɪɡrɑːf-] n poteau m télégraphique
telephone ['tɛlɪfəʊn] n téléphone m ▷ vt (person) téléphoner à; (message) téléphoner; **to have a ~** (Brit), **to be on the ~** (subscriber) être abonné(e) au téléphone; **to be on the ~** (be speaking) être au téléphone
telephone book n = **telephone directory**
telephone booth, (Brit) **telephone box** n cabine f téléphonique
telephone call n appel m téléphonique
telephone directory n annuaire m (du téléphone)
telephone number n numéro m de téléphone
telephonist [tə'lɛfənɪst] n (Brit) téléphoniste m/f
telesales ['tɛlɪseɪlz] npl télévente f

telescope ['tɛlɪskəʊp] n télescope m ▷ vi se télescoper ▷ vt télescoper
televise ['tɛlɪvaɪz] vt téléviser
television ['tɛlɪvɪʒən] n télévision f; **on ~** à la télévision
television programme n émission f de télévision
television set n poste m de télévision, téléviseur m
telex ['tɛlɛks] n télex m ▷ vt (message) envoyer par télex; (person) envoyer un télex à ▷ vi envoyer un télex
tell (pt, pp **told**) [tɛl, təʊld] vt dire; (relate: story) raconter; (distinguish): **to ~ sth from** distinguer qch de ▷ vi (talk): **to ~ of** parler de; (have effect) se faire sentir, se voir; **to ~ sb to do** dire à qn de faire; **to ~ sb about sth** (place, object etc) parler de qch à qn; (what happened etc) raconter qch à qn; **to ~ the time** (know how to) savoir lire l'heure; **can you ~ me the time?** pourriez-vous me dire l'heure?; **(I) ~ you what, ...** écoute, ...; **I can't ~ them apart** je n'arrive pas à les distinguer; **tell off** vt réprimander, gronder; **tell on** vt fus (inform against) dénoncer, rapporter contre
teller ['tɛləʳ] n (in bank) caissier(-ière)
telling ['tɛlɪŋ] adj (remark, detail) révélateur(-trice)
telltale ['tɛlteɪl] n rapporteur(-euse) ▷ adj (sign) éloquent(e), révélateur(-trice)
telly ['tɛlɪ] n abbr (Brit inf: = television) télé f
temp [tɛmp] n (Brit: = temporary worker) intérimaire m/f ▷ vi travailler comme intérimaire
temper ['tɛmpəʳ] n (nature) caractère m; (mood) humeur f; (fit of anger) colère f ▷ vt (moderate) tempérer, adoucir; **to be in a ~** être en colère; **to lose one's ~** se mettre en colère; **to keep one's ~** rester calme
temperament ['tɛmprəmənt] n (nature) tempérament m
temperamental [tɛmprə'mɛntl] adj capricieux(-euse)
temperate ['tɛmprət] adj modéré(e); (climate) tempéré(e)
temperature ['tɛmprətʃəʳ] n température f; **to have** or **run a ~** avoir de la fièvre
temple ['tɛmpl] n (building) temple m; (Anat) tempe f
temporary ['tɛmpərərɪ] adj temporaire, provisoire; (job, worker) temporaire; **~ secretary** (secrétaire f) intérimaire f; **a ~ teacher** un professeur remplaçant or suppléant
tempt [tɛmpt] vt tenter; **to ~ sb into doing** induire qn à faire; **to be ~ed to do sth** être tenté(e) de faire qch
temptation [tɛmp'teɪʃən] n tentation f
tempting ['tɛmptɪŋ] adj tentant(e); (food) appétissant(e)
ten [tɛn] num dix ▷ n: **~s of thousands** des dizaines fpl de milliers

tenacity [tə'næsɪtɪ] n ténacité f
tenancy ['tenənsɪ] n location f; état m de
locataire
tenant ['tenənt] n locataire m/f
tend [tend] vt s'occuper de; (sick etc) soigner
▷ vi: **to ~ to do** avoir tendance à faire; (colour):
to ~ to tirer sur
tendency ['tendənsɪ] n tendance f
tender ['tendə'] adj tendre; (delicate)
délicat(e); (sore) sensible; (affectionate) tendre,
doux/douce ▷ n (Comm: offer) soumission f;
(money): **legal ~** cours légal ▷ vt offrir; **to ~
one's resignation** donner sa démission; **to
put in a ~ (for)** faire une soumission (pour);
to put work out to ~ (Brit) mettre un contrat
en adjudication
tendon ['tendən] n tendon m
tenement ['tenəmənt] n immeuble m (de
rapport)
tenner ['tenə'] n (Brit inf) billet m de dix livres
tennis ['tenɪs] n tennis m ▷ cpd (club, match,
racket, player) de tennis
tennis ball n balle f de tennis
tennis court n (court m de) tennis m
tennis match n match m de tennis
tennis player n joueur(-euse) de tennis
tennis racket n raquette f de tennis
tennis shoes npl (chaussures fpl de)
tennis mpl
tenor ['tenə'] n (Mus) ténor m; (of speech etc)
sens général
tenpin bowling ['tenpɪn-] n (Brit) bowling m
(à 10 quilles)
tense [tens] adj tendu(e); (person) tendu,
crispé(e) ▷ n (Ling) temps m ▷ vt (tighten:
muscles) tendre
tension ['tenʃən] n tension f
tent [tent] n tente f
tentative ['tentətɪv] adj timide, hésitant(e);
(conclusion) provisoire
tenterhooks ['tentəhuks] npl: **on ~** sur des
charbons ardents
tenth [tenθ] num dixième
tent peg n piquet m de tente
tent pole n montant m de tente
tenuous ['tenjuəs] adj ténu(e)
tenure ['tenjuə'] n (of property) bail m; (of job)
période f de jouissance; statut m de titulaire
tepid ['tepɪd] adj tiède
term [tə:m] n (limit) terme m; (word) terme,
mot m; (Scol) trimestre m; (Law) session f ▷ vt
appeler; **terms** npl (conditions) conditions fpl;
(Comm) tarif m; **~ of imprisonment** période f
de prison; **his ~ of office** la période où il était
en fonction; **in the short/long ~** à court/
long terme; **"easy ~s"** (Comm) "facilités de
paiement"; **to come to ~s with** (problem)
faire face à; **to be on good ~s with** bien
s'entendre avec, être en bons termes avec
terminal ['tə:mɪnl] adj terminal(e); (disease)
dans sa phase terminale; (patient) incurable
▷ n (Elec) borne f; (for oil, ore etc, also Comput)

terminal m; (also: **air ~**) aérogare f; (Brit: also:
coach ~) gare routière
terminally ['tə:mɪnlɪ] adv: **to be ~ ill** être
condamné(e)
terminate ['tə:mɪneɪt] vt mettre fin à;
(pregnancy) interrompre ▷ vi: **to ~ in** finir en
or par
termini ['tə:mɪnaɪ] npl of **terminus**
terminology [tə:mɪ'nɔlədʒɪ] n
terminologie f
terminus (pl **termini**) ['tə:mɪnəs, 'tə:mɪnaɪ] n
terminus m inv
terrace ['terəs] n terrasse f; (Brit: row of houses)
rangée f de maisons (attenantes les unes aux
autres); **the ~s** (Brit Sport) les gradins mpl
terraced ['terəst] adj (garden) en terrasses;
(in a row: house) attenant(e) aux maisons
voisines
terracotta ['terə'kɔtə] n terre cuite
terrain [te'reɪn] n terrain m (sol)
terrestrial [tɪ'restrɪəl] adj terrestre
terrible ['terɪbl] adj terrible, atroce; (weather,
work) affreux(-euse), épouvantable
terribly ['terɪblɪ] adv terriblement; (very badly)
affreusement mal
terrier ['terɪə'] n terrier m (chien)
terrific [tə'rɪfɪk] adj (very great) fantastique,
incroyable, terrible; (wonderful) formidable,
sensationnel(le)
terrified ['terɪfaɪd] adj terrifié(e); **to be ~ of
sth** avoir très peur de qch
terrify ['terɪfaɪ] vt terrifier
terrifying ['terɪfaɪɪŋ] adj terrifiant(e)
territorial [terɪ'tɔ:rɪəl] adj territorial(e)
territory ['terɪtərɪ] n territoire m
terror ['terə'] n terreur f
terrorism ['terərɪzəm] n terrorisme m
terrorist ['terərɪst] n terroriste m/f
terrorist attack n attentat m terroriste
test [test] n (trial, check) essai m; (: of goods in
factory) contrôle m; (of courage etc) épreuve f;
(Med) examen m; (Chem) analyse f; (exam:
of intelligence etc) test m (d'aptitude); (Scol)
interrogation f de contrôle; (also: **driving ~**)
(examen du) permis m de conduire ▷ vt
essayer; contrôler; mettre à l'épreuve;
examiner; analyser; tester; faire subir une
interrogation à; **to put sth to the ~** mettre
qch à l'épreuve
testament ['testəmənt] n testament m;
the Old/New T~ l'Ancien/le Nouveau
Testament
testicle ['testɪkl] n testicule m
testify ['testɪfaɪ] vi (Law) témoigner, déposer;
to ~ to sth (Law) attester qch; (gen)
témoigner de qch
testimony ['testɪmənɪ] n (Law) témoignage m,
déposition f
test match n (Cricket, Rugby) match m
international
test tube n éprouvette f
tetanus ['tetənəs] n tétanos m

tether ['tɛðəʳ] vt attacher ▷ n: **at the end of one's ~** à bout (de patience)

text [tɛkst] n texte m; (on mobile phone) SMS m inv, texto® m ▷ vt (inf) envoyer un SMS or texto® à

textbook ['tɛkstbuk] n manuel m

textile ['tɛkstaɪl] n textile m

text message n SMS m inv, texto® m

text messaging [-'mɛsɪdʒɪŋ] n messagerie textuelle

texture ['tɛkstʃəʳ] n texture f; (of skin, paper etc) grain m

Thai [taɪ] adj thaïlandais(e) ▷ n Thaïlandais(e); (Ling) thaï m

Thailand ['taɪlænd] n Thaïlande f

Thames [tɛmz] n: **the (River) ~** la Tamise

than [ðæn, ðən] conj que; (with numerals): **more ~ 10/once** plus de 10/d'une fois; **I have more/less ~ you** j'en ai plus/moins que toi; **she has more apples ~ pears** elle a plus de pommes que de poires; **it is better to phone ~ to write** il vaut mieux téléphoner (plutôt) qu'écrire; **she is older ~ you think** elle est plus âgée que tu le crois; **no sooner did he leave ~ the phone rang** il venait de partir quand le téléphone a sonné

thank [θæŋk] vt remercier, dire merci à; **thanks** npl remerciements mpl ▷ excl merci!; **~ you (very much)** merci (beaucoup); **~ heavens, ~ God** Dieu merci; **~s to** prep grâce à

thankful ['θæŋkful] adj: **~ (for)** reconnaissant(e) (de); **~ for/that** (relieved) soulagé(e) de/que

thankfully ['θæŋkfəlɪ] adv avec reconnaissance; avec soulagement; (fortunately) heureusement; **~ there were few victims** il y eut fort heureusement peu de victimes

thankless ['θæŋklɪs] adj ingrat(e)

Thanksgiving ['θæŋksgɪvɪŋ], **Thanksgiving Day** n jour m d'action de grâce; voir article

 THANKSGIVING (DAY)

Thanksgiving (Day) est un jour de congé aux États-Unis, le quatrième jeudi du mois de novembre, commémorant la bonne récolte que les Pèlerins venus de Grande-Bretagne ont eue en 1621; traditionnellement, c'était un jour où l'on remerciait Dieu et où l'on organisait un grand festin. Une fête semblable, mais qui n'a aucun rapport avec les Pères Pèlerins, a lieu au Canada le deuxième lundi d'octobre.

 KEYWORD

that [ðæt] adj (demonstrative) (pl **those**) ce, cet + vowel or h mute, cette f; **that man/woman/ book** cet homme/cette femme/ce livre; (not this) cet homme-là/cette femme-là/ce livre-là; **that one** celui-là/celle-là

▷ pron **1** (demonstrative) (pl **those**) ce; (not this one) cela, ça; (that one) celui/celle; **who's that?** qui est-ce?; **what's that?** qu'est-ce que c'est?; **is that you?** c'est toi?; **I prefer this to that** je préfère ceci à cela or ça; **that's what he said** c'est or voilà ce qu'il a dit; **will you eat all that?** tu vas manger tout ça?; **that is (to say)** c'est-à-dire, à savoir; **at or with that, he ...** là-dessus, il ...; **do it like that** fais-le comme ça

2 (relative: subject) qui; (: object) que; (: after prep) lequel/laquelle, lesquels/lesquelles pl; **the book that I read** le livre que j'ai lu; **the books that are in the library** les livres qui sont dans la bibliothèque; **all that I have** tout ce que j'ai; **the box that I put it in** la boîte dans laquelle je l'ai mis; **the people that I spoke to** les gens auxquels or à qui j'ai parlé; **not that I know of** pas à ma connaissance

3 (relative: of time) où; **the day that he came** le jour où il est venu

▷ conj que; **he thought that I was ill** il pensait que j'étais malade

▷ adv (demonstrative): **I don't like it that much** ça ne me plaît pas tant que ça; **I didn't know it was that bad** je ne savais pas que c'était si or aussi mauvais; **that high** aussi haut; si haut; **it's about that high** c'est à peu près de cette hauteur

thatched [θætʃt] adj (roof) de chaume; **~ cottage** chaumière f

thaw [θɔː] n dégel m ▷ vi (ice) fondre; (food) dégeler ▷ vt (food) (faire) dégeler; **it's ~ing** (weather) il dégèle

 KEYWORD

the [ðiː, ðə] def art **1** (gen) le, la f, l' + vowel or h mute, les pl (NB: à + le(s) = **au(x)**; de + le = **du**; de + les = **des**); **the boy/girl/ink** le garçon/la fille/ l'encre; **the children** les enfants; **the history of the world** l'histoire du monde; **give it to the postman** donne-le au facteur; **to play the piano/flute** jouer du piano/de la flûte

2 (+ adj to form n) le, la f, l' + vowel or h mute, les pl; **the rich and the poor** les riches et les pauvres; **to attempt the impossible** tenter l'impossible

3 (in titles): **Elizabeth the First** Elisabeth première; **Peter the Great** Pierre le Grand

4 (in comparisons): **the more he works, the more he earns** plus il travaille, plus il gagne de l'argent; **the sooner the better** le plus tôt sera le mieux

theatre, (US) **theater** ['θɪətəʳ] n théâtre m; (also: **lecture ~**) amphithéâtre m, amphi m (inf); (Med: also: **operating ~**) salle f d'opération

theatre-goer, (US) **theater-goer**
['θɪətəgəʊəʳ] n habitué(e) du théâtre
theatrical [θɪ'ætrɪkl] adj théâtral(e); ~
company troupe f de théâtre
theft [θɛft] n vol m (larcin)
their [ðɛəʳ] adj leur, leurs pl; see also **my**
theirs [ðɛəz] pron le/la leur, les leurs; **it is ~**
c'est à eux; **a friend of ~** un de leurs amis;
see also **mine¹**
them [ðɛm, ðəm] pron (direct) les; (indirect)
leur; (stressed, after prep) eux/elles; **I see ~** je les
vois; **give ~ the book** donne-leur le livre;
give me a few of ~ donnez m'en quelques
uns (or quelques unes); see also **me**
theme [θiːm] n thème m
theme park n parc m à thème
theme song n chanson principale
themselves [ðəm'sɛlvz] pl pron (reflexive) se;
(emphatic, after prep) eux-mêmes/elles-mêmes;
between ~ entre eux/elles; see also **oneself**
then [ðɛn] adv (at that time) alors, à ce
moment-là; (next) puis, ensuite; (and also) et
puis ▷ conj (therefore) alors, dans ce cas ▷ adj:
the ~ president le président d'alors or de
l'époque; **by ~** (past) à ce moment-là; (future)
d'ici là; **from ~ on** dès lors; **before ~** avant;
until ~ jusqu'à ce moment-là, jusque-là; **and
~ what?** et puis après?; **what do you want
me to do ~?** (afterwards) que veux-tu que je
fasse ensuite?; (in that case) bon alors, qu'est-
ce que je fais?
theology [θɪ'ɔlədʒɪ] n théologie f
theoretical [θɪə'rɛtɪkl] adj théorique
theory ['θɪərɪ] n théorie f
therapist ['θɛrəpɪst] n thérapeute m/f
therapy ['θɛrəpɪ] n thérapie f

 KEYWORD

there [ðɛəʳ] adv 1: **there is**, **there are** il y a;
there are 3 of them (people, things) il y en a 3;
there is no-one here/no bread left il n'y a
personne/il n'y a plus de pain; **there has
been an accident** il y a eu un accident
2 (referring to place) là, là-bas; **it's there** c'est
là(-bas); **in/on/up/down there** là-dedans/
là-dessus/là-haut/en bas; **he went there on
Friday** il y est allé vendredi; **to go there and
back** faire l'aller-retour; **I want that book
there** je veux ce livre-là; **there he is!** le voilà!
3: **there, there** (esp to child) allons, allons!

thereabouts ['ðɛərə'bauts] adv (place) par là,
près de là; (amount) environ, à peu près
thereafter [ðɛər'ɑːftəʳ] adv par la suite
thereby ['ðɛəbaɪ] adv ainsi
therefore ['ðɛəfɔːʳ] adv donc, par conséquent
there's ['ðɛəz] = **there is**; **there has**
thermal ['θəːml] adj thermique; ~ **paper/
printer** papier m/imprimante f thermique;
~ **underwear** sous-vêtements mpl en
Thermolactyl®

thermometer [θə'mɔmɪtəʳ] n
thermomètre m
Thermos® ['θəːmɔs] n (also: ~ **flask**)
thermos m or f inv
thermostat ['θəːməustæt] n thermostat m
thesaurus [θɪ'sɔːrəs] n dictionnaire m
synonymique
these [ðiːz] pl pron ceux-ci/celles-ci ▷ pl adj
ces; (not those): ~ **books** ces livres-ci
thesis (pl **theses**) ['θiːsɪs, 'θiːsiːz] n thèse f
they [ðeɪ] pl pron ils/elles; (stressed) eux/elles;
~ **say that ...** (it is said that) on dit que ...
they'd [ðeɪd] = **they had**; **they would**
they'll [ðeɪl] = **they shall**; **they will**
they're [ðɛəʳ] = **they are**
they've [ðeɪv] = **they have**
thick [θɪk] adj épais(se); (crowd) dense; (stupid)
bête, borné(e) ▷ n: **in the ~ of** au beau milieu
de, en plein cœur de; **it's 20 cm ~** ça a 20 cm
d'épaisseur
thicken ['θɪkn] vi s'épaissir ▷ vt (sauce etc)
épaissir
thickness ['θɪknɪs] n épaisseur f
thickset [θɪk'sɛt] adj trapu(e), costaud(e)
thief (pl **thieves**) [θiːf, θiːvz] n voleur(-euse)
thigh [θaɪ] n cuisse f
thimble ['θɪmbl] n dé m (à coudre)
thin [θɪn] adj mince; (skinny) maigre; (soup)
peu épais(se); (hair, crowd) clairsemé(e); (fog)
léger(-ère) ▷ vt (hair) éclaircir; (also: ~ **down**:
sauce, paint) délayer ▷ vi (fog) s'éclaircir; (also:
~ **out**: crowd) se disperser; **his hair is ~ning** il
se dégarnit
thing [θɪŋ] n chose f; (object) objet m;
(contraption) truc m; **things** npl (belongings)
affaires fpl; **first ~ (in the morning)** à la
première heure, tout de suite (le matin); **last
~ (at night), he ...** juste avant de se coucher,
il ...; **the ~ is ...** c'est que ...; **for one ~** d'abord;
the best ~ would be to le mieux serait de;
how are ~s? comment ça va?; **to have a ~
about** (be obsessed by) être obsédé(e) par; (hate)
détester; **poor ~!** le (or la) pauvre!
think (pt, pp **thought**) [θɪŋk, θɔːt] vi penser,
réfléchir ▷ vt penser, croire; (imagine)
s'imaginer; **to ~ of** penser à; **what do you ~
of it?** qu'en pensez-vous?; **what did you ~ of
them?** qu'avez-vous pensé d'eux?; **to ~
about sth/sb** penser à qch/qn; **I'll ~ about it**
je vais y réfléchir; **to ~ of doing** avoir l'idée
de faire; **I ~ so/not** je crois or pense que oui/
non; **to ~ well of** avoir une haute opinion de;
~ **again!** attention, réfléchis bien!; **to ~ aloud**
penser tout haut; **think out** vt (plan) bien
réfléchir à; (solution) trouver; **think over** vt
bien réfléchir à; **I'd like to ~ things over**
(offer, suggestion) j'aimerais bien y réfléchir un
peu; **think through** vt étudier dans tous les
détails; **think up** vt inventer, trouver
think tank n groupe m de réflexion
thinly ['θɪnlɪ] adv (cut) en tranches fines;
(spread) en couche mince

third [θəːd] num troisième ▷ n troisième m/f;
(fraction) tiers m; (Aut) troisième (vitesse) f;
(Brit Scol: degree) ≈ licence f avec mention
passable; **a ~ of** le tiers de

thirdly ['θəːdlɪ] adv troisièmement

third party insurance n (Brit) assurance f
au tiers

third-rate ['θəːd'reɪt] adj. de qualité médiocre

Third World n: **the ~** le Tiers-Monde

thirst [θəːst] n soif f

thirsty ['θəːstɪ] adj qui a soif, assoiffé(e);
(work) qui donne soif; **to be ~** avoir soif

thirteen [θəː'tiːn] num treize

thirteenth [θəː'tiːnθ] num treizième

thirtieth ['θəːtɪɪθ] num trentième

thirty ['θəːtɪ] num trente

🔵 **KEYWORD**

this [ðɪs] adj (demonstrative) (pl **these**) ce, cet +
vowel or h mute, cette f; **this man/woman/
book** cet homme/cette femme/ce livre; (not
that) cet homme-ci/cette femme-ci/ce livre-
ci; **this one** celui-ci/celle-ci; **this time** cette
fois-ci; **this time last year** l'année dernière
à la même époque; **this way** (in this direction)
par ici; (in this fashion) de cette façon, ainsi
▷ pron (demonstrative) (pl **these**) ce; (not that
one) celui-ci/celle-ci, ceci; **who's this?** qui
est-ce?; **what's this?** qu'est-ce que c'est?;
I prefer this to that je préfère ceci à cela;
they were talking of this and that ils
parlaient de choses et d'autres; **this is
where I live** c'est ici que j'habite; **this is
what he said** voici ce qu'il a dit; **this is Mr
Brown** (in introductions) je vous présente Mr
Brown; (in photo) c'est Mr Brown; (on
telephone) ici Mr Brown
▷ adv (demonstrative): **it was about this big**
c'était à peu près de cette grandeur or grand
comme ça; **I didn't know it was this bad** je
ne savais pas que c'était si or aussi mauvais

thistle ['θɪsl] n chardon m

thorn [θɔːn] n épine f

thorough ['θʌrə] adj (search) minutieux(-euse);
(knowledge, research) approfondi(e); (work, person)
consciencieux(-euse); (cleaning) à fond

thoroughbred ['θʌrəbred] n (horse)
pur-sang m inv

thoroughfare ['θʌrəfeər] n rue f; **"no ~"** (Brit)
"passage interdit"

thoroughly ['θʌrəlɪ] adv (search)
minutieusement; (study) en profondeur;
(clean) à fond; (very) tout à fait; **he ~ agreed** il
était tout à fait d'accord

those [ðəuz] pl pron ceux-là/celles-là ▷ pl adj
ces; (not these): **~ books** ces livres-là

though [ðəu] conj bien que + sub, quoique + sub
▷ adv pourtant; **even ~** quand bien même +
conditional; **it's not easy, ~** pourtant, ce n'est
pas facile

thought [θɔːt] pt, pp of **think** ▷ n pensée f;
(idea) idée f; (opinion) avis m; (intention)
intention f; **after much ~** après mûre
réflexion; **I've just had a ~** je viens de penser
à quelque chose; **to give sth some ~** réfléchir
à qch

thoughtful ['θɔːtful] adj (deep in thought)
pensif(-ive); (serious) réfléchi(e); (considerate)
prévenant(e)

thoughtless ['θɔːtlɪs] adj qui manque de
considération

thousand ['θauzənd] num mille; **one ~** mille;
two ~ deux mille; **~s of** des milliers de

thousandth ['θauzəntθ] num millième

thrash [θræʃ] vt rouer de coups; (as
punishment) donner une correction à;
(inf: defeat) battre à plate(s) couture(s);
thrash about vi se débattre; **thrash out** vt
débattre de

thread [θred] n fil m; (of screw) pas m, filetage
m ▷ vt (needle) enfiler; **to ~ one's way
between** se faufiler entre

threadbare ['θredbeər] adj râpé(e), élimé(e)

threat [θret] n menace f; **to be under ~ of**
être menacé(e) de

threaten ['θretn] vi (storm) menacer ▷ vt: **to ~
sb with sth/to do** menacer qn de qch/de
faire

threatening ['θretnɪŋ] adj menaçant(e)

three [θriː] num trois

three-dimensional [θriːdɪ'menʃənl] adj à
trois dimensions; (film) en relief

three-piece suit ['θriːpiːs-] n complet m
(avec gilet)

three-piece suite n salon m (canapé et deux
fauteuils)

three-ply [θriː'plaɪ] adj (wood) à trois
épaisseurs; (wool) trois fils inv

three-quarters [θriː'kwɔːtəz] npl trois-
quarts mpl; **~ full** aux trois-quarts plein

threshold ['θreʃhəuld] n seuil m; **to be on
the ~ of** (fig) être au seuil de

threw [θruː] pt of **throw**

thrifty ['θrɪftɪ] adj économe

thrill [θrɪl] n (excitement) émotion f, sensation
forte; (shudder) frisson m ▷ vi tressaillir,
frissonner ▷ vt (audience) électriser

thrilled [θrɪld] adj: **~ (with)** ravi(e) de

thriller ['θrɪlər] n film m or roman m or pièce f)
à suspense

thrilling ['θrɪlɪŋ] adj (book, play etc)
saisissant(e); (news, discovery) excitant(e)

thrive (pt **thrived** or **throve**, pp **thrived** or
thriven) [θraɪv, θrəuv, 'θrɪvn] vi pousser or
se développer bien; (business) prospérer; **he ~s
on it** cela lui réussit

thriving ['θraɪvɪŋ] adj vigoureux(-euse);
(business, community) prospère

throat [θrəut] n gorge f; **to have a sore ~**
avoir mal à la gorge

throb [θrɔb] n (of heart) pulsation f; (of engine)
vibration f; (of pain) élancement m ▷ vi (heart)

t

palpiter; (engine) vibrer; (pain) lanciner; (wound) causer des élancements; **my head is ~bing** j'ai des élancements dans la tête

throes [θrəʊz] npl: **in the ~ of** au beau milieu de; en proie à; **in the ~ of death** à l'agonie

throne [θrəʊn] n trône m

throng ['θrɒŋ] n foule f ▷ vt se presser dans

throttle ['θrɒtl] n (Aut) accélérateur m ▷ vt étrangler

through [θruː] prep à travers; (time) pendant, durant; (by means of) par, par l'intermédiaire de; (owing to) à cause de ▷ adj (ticket, train, passage) direct(e) ▷ adv à travers; **(from) Monday ~ Friday** (US) de lundi à vendredi; **to let sb ~** laisser passer qn; **to put sb ~ to sb** (Tel) passer qn à qn; **to be ~** (Brit: : Tel) avoir la communication; (esp US: have finished) avoir fini; **"no ~ traffic"** (US) "passage interdit"; **"no ~ road"** (Brit) "impasse"

throughout [θruː'aʊt] prep (place) partout dans; (time) durant tout(e) le/la ▷ adv partout

throw [θrəʊ] n jet m; (Sport) lancer m ▷ vt (pt threw, pp thrown) [θruː, θrəʊn] lancer, jeter; (Sport) lancer; (rider) désarçonner; (fig) déconcerter; (pottery) tourner; **to ~ a party** donner une réception; **throw about; throw around** vt (litter etc) éparpiller; **throw away** vt jeter; (money) gaspiller; **throw in** (Sport: ball) remettre en jeu; (include) ajouter; **throw off** vt se débarrasser de; **throw out** vt jeter; (reject) rejeter; (person) mettre à la porte; **throw together** vt (clothes, meal etc) assembler à la hâte; (essay) bâcler; **throw up** vi vomir

throwaway ['θrəʊəweɪ] adj à jeter

throw-in ['θrəʊɪn] n (Sport) remise f en jeu

thrown [θrəʊn] pp of **throw**

thru [θruː] (US) prep = **through**

thrush [θrʌʃ] n (Zool) grive f; (Med: esp in children) muguet m; (: in women: Brit) muguet vaginal

thrust [θrʌst] n (Tech) poussée f ▷ vt (pt, pp thrust) pousser brusquement; (push in) enfoncer

thud [θʌd] n bruit sourd

thug [θʌg] n voyou m

thumb [θʌm] n (Anat) pouce m ▷ vt (book) feuilleter; **to ~ a lift** faire de l'auto-stop, arrêter une voiture; **to give sb/sth the ~s up/~s down** donner/refuser de donner le feu vert à qn/qch; **thumb through** vt (book) feuilleter

thumbtack ['θʌmtæk] n (US) punaise f (clou)

thump [θʌmp] n grand coup; (sound) bruit sourd ▷ vt cogner sur ▷ vi cogner, frapper

thunder ['θʌndə*] n tonnerre m ▷ vi tonner; (train etc): **to ~ past** passer dans un grondement or un bruit de tonnerre

thunderbolt ['θʌndəbəʊlt] n foudre f

thunderclap ['θʌndəklæp] n coup m de tonnerre

thunderstorm ['θʌndəstɔːm] n orage m

thundery ['θʌndərɪ] adj orageux(-euse)

Thursday ['θɜːzdɪ] n jeudi m; see also **Tuesday**

thus [ðʌs] adv ainsi

thwart [θwɔːt] vt contrecarrer

thyme [taɪm] n thym m

tiara [tɪ'ɑːrə] n (woman's) diadème m

Tibet [tɪ'bɛt] n Tibet m

tick [tɪk] n (sound: of clock) tic-tac m; (mark) coche f; (Zool) tique f; (Brit inf): **in a ~** dans un instant; (Brit inf: credit): **to buy sth on ~** acheter qch à crédit ▷ vi faire tic-tac ▷ vt (item on list) cocher; **to put a ~ against sth** cocher qch; **tick off** vt (item on list) cocher; (person) réprimander, attraper; **tick over** vi (Brit: engine) tourner au ralenti; (: fig) aller or marcher doucettement

ticket ['tɪkɪt] n billet m; (for bus, tube) ticket m; (in shop: on goods) étiquette f; (for library) carte f; (also: **parking ~**) contravention f, p.-v. m; (US Pol) liste électorale (soutenue par un parti); **to get a (parking) ~** (Aut) attraper une contravention (pour stationnement illégal)

ticket barrier n (Brit: Rail) portillon m automatique

ticket collector n contrôleur(-euse)

ticket inspector n contrôleur(-euse)

ticket machine n billetterie f automatique

ticket office n guichet m, bureau m de vente des billets

tickle ['tɪkl] n chatouillement m ▷ vi chatouiller ▷ vt chatouiller; (fig) plaire à; faire rire

ticklish ['tɪklɪʃ] adj (person) chatouilleux(-euse); (which tickles: blanket) qui chatouille; (: cough) qui irrite; (problem) épineux(-euse)

tidal ['taɪdl] adj (river) à marée

tidal wave n raz-de-marée m inv

tidbit ['tɪdbɪt] n (esp US) = **titbit**

tiddlywinks ['tɪdlɪwɪŋks] n jeu m de puce

tide [taɪd] n marée f; (fig: of events) cours m ▷ vt: **to ~ sb over** dépanner qn; **high/low ~** marée haute/basse

tidy ['taɪdɪ] adj (room) bien rangé(e); (dress, work) net/nette, soigné(e); (person) ordonné(e), qui a de l'ordre; (: in character) soigneux(-euse); (mind) méthodique ▷ vt (also: **~ up**) ranger; **to ~ o.s. up** s'arranger

tie [taɪ] n (string etc) cordon m; (Brit: also: **neck~**) cravate f; (fig: link) lien m; (Sport: draw) égalité f de points; match nul; (: match) rencontre f; (US Rail) traverse f ▷ vt (parcel) attacher; (ribbon) nouer ▷ vi (Sport) faire match nul; finir à égalité de points; **"black/white ~"** "smoking/habit de rigueur"; **family ~s** liens de famille; **to ~ sth in a bow** faire un nœud à or avec qch; **to ~ a knot in sth** faire un nœud à qch; **tie down** vt attacher; (fig): **to ~ sb down to** contraindre qn à accepter; **to feel ~d down** (by relationship) se sentir coincé(e); **tie in** vi: **to ~ in (with)** (correspond) correspondre (à); **tie on** vt (Brit: label etc) attacher (avec une ficelle); **tie up** vt (parcel) ficeler; (dog, boat) attacher; (prisoner) ligoter; (arrangements) conclure; **to be ~d up** (busy) être pris(e) or occupé(e)

tier [tɪəʳ] n gradin m; (of cake) étage m

tiger ['taɪgəʳ] n tigre m

tight [taɪt] adj (rope) tendu(e), raide; (clothes) étroit(e), très juste; (budget, programme, bend) serré(e); (control) strict(e), sévère; (inf: drunk) ivre, rond(e) ▷ adv (squeeze) très fort; (shut) à bloc, hermétiquement; **to be packed ~** (suitcase) être bourré(e); (people) être serré(e); **hold ~!** accrochez-vous bien!

tighten ['taɪtn] vt (rope) tendre; (screw) resserrer; (control) renforcer ▷ vi se tendre; se resserrer

tightfisted [taɪt'fɪstɪd] adj avare

tightly ['taɪtlɪ] adv (grasp) bien, très fort

tightrope ['taɪtrəup] n corde f raide

tights [taɪts] npl (Brit) collant m

tile [taɪl] n (on roof) tuile f; (on wall or floor) carreau m ▷ vt (floor, bathroom etc) carreler

tiled [taɪld] adj en tuiles; carrelé(e)

till [tɪl] n caisse (enregistreuse) ▷ vt (land) cultiver ▷ prep, conj = **until**

tiller ['tɪləʳ] n (Naut) barre f (du gouvernail)

tilt [tɪlt] vt pencher, incliner ▷ vi pencher, être incliné(e) ▷ n (slope) inclinaison f; **to wear one's hat at a ~** porter son chapeau incliné sur le côté; **(at) full ~** à toute vitesse

timber ['tɪmbəʳ] n (material) bois m de construction; (trees) arbres mpl

time [taɪm] n temps m; (epoch: often pl) époque f, temps; (by clock) heure f; (moment) moment m; (occasion, also Math) fois f; (Mus) mesure f ▷ vt (race) chronométrer; (programme) minuter; (visit) fixer; (remark etc) choisir le moment de; **a long ~** un long moment, longtemps; **four at a ~** quatre à la fois; **for the ~ being** pour le moment; **from ~ to ~** de temps en temps; **~ after ~, ~ and again** bien des fois; **at ~s** parfois; **in ~** (soon enough) à temps; (after some time) avec le temps, à la longue; (Mus) en mesure; **in a week's ~** dans une semaine; **in no ~** en un rien de temps; **any ~** n'importe quand; **on ~** à l'heure; **to be 30 minutes behind/ahead of ~** avoir 30 minutes de retard/d'avance; **by the ~ he arrived** quand il est arrivé, le temps qu'il arrive + sub; **5 ~s 5** 5 fois 5; **what ~ is it?** quelle heure est-il?; **what ~ do you make it?** quelle heure avez-vous?; **what ~ is the museum/shop open?** à quelle heure ouvre le musée/magasin?; **to have a good ~** bien s'amuser; **we (or they etc) had a hard ~** ça a été difficile or pénible; **~'s up!** c'est l'heure!; **I've no ~ for it** (fig) cela m'agace; **he'll do it in his own (good) ~** (without being hurried) il le fera quand il en aura le temps; **he'll do it in** or (US) **on his own ~** (out of working hours) il le fera à ses heures perdues; **to be behind the ~s** retarder (sur son temps)

time bomb n bombe f à retardement

time lag n (Brit) décalage m; (: in travel) décalage horaire

timeless ['taɪmlɪs] adj éternel(le)

time limit n limite f de temps, délai m

timely ['taɪmlɪ] adj opportun(e)

time off n temps m libre

timer ['taɪməʳ] n (in kitchen) compte-minutes m inv; (Tech) minuteur m

timescale ['taɪmskeɪl] n délais mpl

time-share ['taɪmʃɛəʳ] n maison f/ appartement m en multipropriété

time switch n (Brit) minuteur m; (: for lighting) minuterie f

timetable ['taɪmteɪbl] n (Rail) (indicateur m) horaire m; (Scol) emploi m du temps; (programme of events etc) programme m

time zone n fuseau m horaire

timid ['tɪmɪd] adj timide; (easily scared) peureux(-euse)

timing ['taɪmɪŋ] n minutage m; (Sport) chronométrage m; **the ~ of his resignation** le moment choisi pour sa démission

timpani ['tɪmpənɪ] npl timbales fpl

tin [tɪn] n étain m; (also: **~ plate**) fer-blanc m; (Brit: can) boîte f (de conserve); (: for baking) moule m (à gâteau); (for storage) boîte f; **a ~ of paint** un pot de peinture

tinfoil ['tɪnfɔɪl] n papier m d'étain or d'aluminium

tinge [tɪndʒ] n nuance f ▷ vt: **~d with** teinté(e) de

tingle ['tɪŋgl] n picotement m; frisson m ▷ vi picoter; (person) avoir des picotements

tinker ['tɪŋkəʳ] n rétameur ambulant; (gipsy) romanichel m; **tinker with** vt fus bricoler, rafistoler

tinkle ['tɪŋkl] vi tinter ▷ n (inf): **to give sb a ~** passer un coup de fil à qn

tinned [tɪnd] adj (Brit: food) en boîte, en conserve

tin opener [-'əupnəʳ] n (Brit) ouvre-boîte(s) m

tinsel ['tɪnsl] n guirlandes fpl de Noël (argentées)

tint [tɪnt] n teinte f; (for hair) shampooing colorant ▷ vt (hair) faire un shampooing colorant à

tinted ['tɪntɪd] adj (hair) teint(e); (spectacles, glass) teinté(e)

tiny ['taɪnɪ] adj minuscule

tip [tɪp] n (end) bout m; (protective: on umbrella etc) embout m; (gratuity) pourboire m; (Brit: for coal) terril m; (Brit: for rubbish) décharge f; (advice) tuyau m ▷ vt (waiter) donner un pourboire à; (tilt) incliner; (overturn: also: **~ over**) renverser; (empty: also: **~ out**) déverser; (predict: winner etc) pronostiquer; **he ~ped out the contents of the box** il a vidé le contenu de la boîte; **how much**

should I ~? combien de pourboire est-ce qu'il faut laisser?; **tip off** vt prévenir, avertir

tip-off ['tɪpɔf] n (hint) tuyau m

tipped ['tɪpt] adj (Brit: cigarette) (à bout) filtre inv; **steel-~** à bout métallique, à embout de métal

tipsy ['tɪpsɪ] adj un peu ivre, éméché(e)

tiptoe ['tɪptəʊ] n: **on ~** sur la pointe des pieds

tiptop ['tɪptɔp] adj: **in ~ condition** en excellent état

tire ['taɪə'] n (US) = **tyre** ▷ vt fatiguer ▷ vi se fatiguer; **tire out** vt épuiser

tired ['taɪəd] adj fatigué(e); **to be/feel/look ~** être/se sentir/avoir l'air fatigué; **to be ~ of** en avoir assez de, être las/lasse de

tireless ['taɪəlɪs] adj infatigable, inlassable

tire pressure (US) = **tyre pressure**

tiresome ['taɪəsəm] adj ennuyeux(-euse)

tiring ['taɪərɪŋ] adj fatigant(e)

tissue ['tɪʃuː] n tissu m; (paper handkerchief) mouchoir m en papier, kleenex® m

tissue paper n papier m de soie

tit [tɪt] n (bird) mésange f; (inf: breast) nichon m; **to give ~ for tat** rendre coup pour coup

titbit ['tɪtbɪt] n (food) friandise f; (before meal) amuse-gueule m inv; (news) potin m

title ['taɪtl] n titre m; (Law: right): **~ (to)** droit m (à)

title deed n (Law) titre (constitutif) de propriété

title role n rôle principal

T-junction ['tiː'dʒʌŋkʃən] n croisement m en T

TM n abbr = **trademark**; **transcendental meditation**

 KEYWORD

to [tuː, tə] prep (with noun/pronoun) **1** (direction) à; (towards) vers; envers; **to go to France/ Portugal/London/school** aller en France/au Portugal/à Londres/à l'école; **to go to Claude's/the doctor's** aller chez Claude/le docteur; **the road to Edinburgh** la route d'Édimbourg

2 (as far as) (jusqu')à; **to count to 10** compter jusqu'à 10; **from 40 to 50 people** de 40 à 50 personnes

3 (with expressions of time): **a quarter to 5** 5 heures moins le quart; **it's twenty to 3** il est 3 heures moins vingt

4 (for, of) de; **the key to the front door** la clé de la porte d'entrée; **a letter to his wife** une lettre (adressée) à sa femme

5 (expressing indirect object) à; **to give sth to sb** donner qch à qn; **to talk to sb** parler à qn; **it belongs to him** cela lui appartient, c'est à lui; **to be a danger to sb** être dangereux(-euse) pour qn

6 (in relation to) à; **3 goals to 2** (buts) à 2; **30 miles to the gallon** ≈ 9,4 litres aux cent (km)

7 (purpose, result): **to come to sb's aid** venir au secours de qn, porter secours à qn; **to sentence sb to death** condamner qn à mort; **to my surprise** à ma grande surprise

▷ prep (with vb) **1** (simple infinitive): **to go/eat** aller/manger

2 (following another vb): **to want/try/start to do** vouloir/essayer de/commencer à faire

3 (with vb omitted): **I don't want to** je ne veux pas

4 (purpose, result) pour; **I did it to help you** je l'ai fait pour vous aider

5 (equivalent to relative clause): **I have things to do** j'ai des choses à faire; **the main thing is to try** l'important est d'essayer

6 (after adjective etc): **ready to go** prêt(e) à partir; **too old/young to ...** trop vieux/jeune pour ...

▷ adv: **push/pull the door to** tirez/poussez la porte; **to go to and fro** aller et venir

toad [təʊd] n crapaud m

toadstool ['təʊdstuːl] n champignon (vénéneux)

toast [təʊst] n (Culin) pain grillé, toast m; (drink, speech) toast ▷ vt (Culin) faire griller; (drink to) porter un toast à; **a piece** or **slice of ~** un toast

toaster ['təʊstə'] n grille-pain m inv

tobacco [tə'bækəʊ] n tabac m; **pipe ~** tabac à pipe

tobacconist [tə'bækənɪst] n marchand(e) de tabac; **~'s (shop)** (bureau m de) tabac m

toboggan [tə'bɔgən] n toboggan m; (child's) luge f

today [tə'deɪ] adv, n (also fig) aujourd'hui (m); **what day is it ~?** quel jour sommes-nous aujourd'hui?; **what date is it ~?** quelle est la date aujourd'hui?; **~ is the 4th of March** aujourd'hui nous sommes le 4 mars; **a week ago** ~ il y a huit jours aujourd'hui

toddler ['tɔdlə'] n enfant m/f qui commence à marcher, bambin m

toe [təʊ] n doigt m de pied, orteil m; (of shoe) bout m ▷ vt: **to ~ the line** (fig) obéir, se conformer; **big ~** gros orteil; **little ~** petit orteil

toenail ['təʊneɪl] n ongle m de l'orteil

toffee ['tɔfɪ] n caramel m

toffee apple n (Brit) pomme caramélisée

together [tə'geðə'] adv ensemble; (at same time) en même temps; **~ with** prep avec

toil [tɔɪl] n dur travail, labeur m ▷ vi travailler dur; peiner

toilet ['tɔɪlət] n (Brit: lavatory) toilettes fpl, cabinets mpl ▷ cpd (bag, soap etc) de toilette; **to go to the ~** aller aux toilettes; **where's the ~?** où sont les toilettes?

toilet bag n (Brit) nécessaire m de toilette

toilet paper n papier m hygiénique

toiletries ['tɔɪlətrɪz] npl articles mpl de toilette

toilet roll n rouleau m de papier hygiénique

token ['təukən] n (sign) marque f, témoignage m; (metal disc) jeton m; (voucher) bon m, coupon m ▷ adj (fee, strike) symbolique; **by the same ~** (fig) de même; **book/record ~** (Brit) chèque-livre/-disque m

Tokyo ['təukjəu] n Tokyo

told [təuld] pt, pp of **tell**

tolerable ['tɔlərəbl] adj (bearable) tolérable; (fairly good) passable

tolerant ['tɔlərnt] adj: **~ (of)** tolérant(e) (à l'égard de)

tolerate ['tɔləreɪt] vt supporter; (Med,: Tech) tolérer

toll [təul] n (tax, charge) péage m ▷ vi (bell) sonner; **the accident ~ on the roads** le nombre des victimes de la route

toll call n (US Tel) appel m (à) longue distance

toll-free ['təul'fri:] adj (US) gratuit(e) ▷ adv gratuitement

tomato [tə'mɑːtəu] (pl **tomatoes**) n tomate f

tomato sauce n sauce f tomate

tomb [tu:m] n tombe f

tomboy ['tɔmbɔɪ] n garçon manqué

tombstone ['tu:mstəun] n pierre tombale

tomcat ['tɔmkæt] n matou m

tomorrow [tə'mɔrəu] adv, n (of radio, Brit Tel) demain (m); **the day after ~** après-demain; **a week ~** demain en huit; **~ morning** demain matin

ton [tʌn] n tonne f (Brit: = 1016 kg; US = 907 kg; metric = 1000 kg); (Naut: also: **register ~**) tonneau m (= 2.83 cu.m); **~s of** (inf) des tas de

tone [təun] n ton m; (of radio, Brit Tel) tonalité f ▷ vi (also: **~ in**) s'harmoniser; **tone down** vt (colour, criticism) adoucir; (sound) baisser; **tone up** vt (muscles) tonifier

tone-deaf [təun'def] adj qui n'a pas d'oreille

tongs [tɔŋz] npl pinces fpl; (for coal) pincettes fpl; (for hair) fer m à friser

tongue [tʌŋ] n langue f; **~ in cheek** adv ironiquement

tongue-tied ['tʌŋtaɪd] adj (fig) muet(te)

tonic ['tɔnɪk] n (Med) tonique m; (Mus) tonique f; (also: **~ water**) Schweppes® m

tonight [tə'naɪt] adv, n cette nuit; (this evening) ce soir; **(I'll) see you ~!** à ce soir!

tonne [tʌn] n (Brit: metric ton) tonne f

tonsil ['tɔnsl] n amygdale f; **to have one's ~s out** se faire opérer des amygdales

tonsillitis [tɔnsɪ'laɪtɪs] n amygdalite f; **to have ~** avoir une angine or une amygdalite

too [tu:] adv (excessively) trop; (also) aussi; **it's ~ sweet** c'est trop sucré; **I went ~** moi aussi, j'y suis allé; **~ much** (as adv) trop; (as adj) trop de; **~ many** adj trop de; **~ bad!** tant pis!

took [tuk] pt of **take**

tool [tu:l] n outil m; (fig) instrument m ▷ vt travailler, ouvrager

tool box n boîte f à outils

tool kit n trousse f à outils

toot [tu:t] n coup m de sifflet (or de klaxon) ▷ vi siffler; (with car-horn) klaxonner

tooth (pl **teeth**) [tu:θ, ti:θ] n (Anat, Tech) dent f; **to have a ~ out** or (US) **pulled** se faire arracher une dent; **to brush one's teeth** se laver les dents; **by the skin of one's teeth** (fig) de justesse

toothache ['tu:θeɪk] n mal m de dents; **to have ~** avoir mal aux dents

toothbrush ['tu:θbrʌʃ] n brosse f à dents

toothpaste ['tu:θpeɪst] n (pâte f) dentifrice m

toothpick ['tu:θpɪk] n cure-dent m

top [tɔp] n (of mountain, head) sommet m; (of page, ladder) haut m; (of list, queue) commencement m; (of box, cupboard, table) dessus m; (lid: of box, jar) couvercle m; (: of bottle) bouchon m; (toy) toupie f; (Dress: blouse etc) haut; (: of pyjamas) veste f ▷ adj du haut; (in rank) premier(-ière); (best) meilleur(e) ▷ vt (exceed) dépasser; (be first in) être en tête de; **the ~ of the milk** (Brit) la crème du lait; **at the ~ of the stairs/page/street** en haut de l'escalier/de la page/de la rue; **from ~ to bottom** de fond en comble; **on ~ of** sur; (in addition to) en plus de; **from ~ to toe** (Brit) de la tête aux pieds; **at the ~ of the list** en tête de liste; **at the ~ of one's voice** à tue-tête; **at ~ speed** à toute vitesse; **over the ~** (inf: behaviour etc) qui dépasse les limites; **top up**, (US) **top off** vt (bottle) remplir; (salary) compléter; **to ~ up one's mobile (phone)** recharger son compte

top floor n dernier étage

top hat n haut-de-forme m

top-heavy [tɔp'hevɪ] adj (object) trop lourd(e) du haut

topic ['tɔpɪk] n sujet m, thème m

topical ['tɔpɪkl] adj d'actualité

topless ['tɔplɪs] adj (bather etc) aux seins nus; **~ swimsuit** monokini m

top-level ['tɔplevl] adj (talks) à l'échelon le plus élevé

topmost ['tɔpməust] adj le/la plus haut(e)

topping ['tɔpɪŋ] n (Culin) couche de crème, fromage etc qui recouvre un plat

topple ['tɔpl] vt renverser, faire tomber ▷ vi basculer; tomber

top-secret ['tɔp'si:krɪt] adj ultra-secret(-ète)

topsy-turvy ['tɔpsɪ'tə:vɪ] adj, adv sens dessus-dessous

top-up ['tɔpʌp] n (for mobile phone) recharge f, minutes fpl; **would you like a ~?** je vous en remets or rajoute?

top-up card n (for mobile phone) recharge f

torch [tɔ:tʃ] n torche f; (Brit: electric) lampe f de poche

tore [tɔ:ʳ] pt of **tear²**

torment n ['tɔ:mɛnt] tourment m ▷ vt [tɔ:'mɛnt] tourmenter; (fig: annoy) agacer

torn [tɔ:n] pp of **tear²** ▷ adj: **~ between** (fig) tiraillé(e) entre

tornado [tɔ:'neɪdəu] (pl **tornadoes**) n tornade f

torpedo [tɔːˈpiːdəu] (pl **torpedoes**) n torpille f

torrent ['tɔrnt] n torrent m

torrential [tɔˈrɛnʃl] adj torrentiel(le)

tortoise ['tɔːtəs] n tortue f

tortoiseshell ['tɔːtəʃɛl] adj en écaille

torture ['tɔːtʃəʳ] n torture f ▷ vt torturer

Tory ['tɔːrɪ] adj, n (Brit Pol) tory m/f, conservateur(-trice)

toss [tɔs] vt lancer, jeter; (Brit: pancake) faire sauter; (head) rejeter en arrière ▷ vi: **to ~ up for sth** (Brit) jouer qch à pile ou face ▷ n (movement: of head etc) mouvement soudain; (of coin) tirage m à pile ou face; **to ~ a coin** jouer à pile ou face; **to ~ and turn** (in bed) se tourner et se retourner; **to win/lose the ~** gagner/perdre à pile ou face; (Sport) gagner/ perdre le tirage au sort

tot [tɔt] n (Brit: drink) petit verre; (child) bambin m; **tot up** vt (Brit: figures) additionner

total ['təutl] adj total(e) ▷ n total m ▷ vt (add up) faire le total de, additionner; (amount to) s'élever à; **in ~** au total

totalitarian [təutælɪˈtɛərɪən] adj totalitaire

totally ['təutəlɪ] adv totalement

totter ['tɔtəʳ] vi chanceler; (object, government) être chancelant(e)

touch [tʌtʃ] n contact m, toucher m; (sense, skill: of pianist etc) toucher; (fig: note, also Football) touche f ▷ vt (gen) toucher; (tamper with) toucher à; **the personal ~** la petite note personnelle; **to put the finishing ~es to sth** mettre la dernière main à qch; **a ~ of** (fig) un petit peu de; une touche de; **in ~ with** en contact or rapport avec; **to get in ~ with** prendre contact avec; **I'll be in ~** je resterai en contact; **to lose ~** (friends) se perdre de vue; **to be out of ~ with events** ne pas être au courant de ce qui se passe; **touch down** vi (Aviat) atterrir; (on sea) amerrir; **touch on** vt fus (topic) effleurer, toucher; **touch up** vt (paint) retoucher

touch-and-go ['tʌtʃən'gəu] adj incertain(e); **it was ~ whether we did it** nous avons failli ne pas le faire

touchdown ['tʌtʃdaun] n (Aviat) atterrissage m; (on sea) amerrissage m; (US Football) essai m

touched [tʌtʃt] adj (moved) touché(e); (inf) cinglé(e)

touching ['tʌtʃɪŋ] adj touchant(e), attendrissant(e)

touchline ['tʌtʃlaɪn] n (Sport) (ligne f de) touche f

touch screen n (Tech) écran tactile; **~ mobile** (téléphone) portable m à écran tactile; **~ technology** technologie f à écran tactile

touch-sensitive ['tʌtʃsɛnsɪtɪv] adj (keypad) à effleurement; (screen) tactile

touchy ['tʌtʃɪ] adj (person) susceptible

tough [tʌf] adj dur(e); (resistant) résistant(e),

solide; (meat) dur, coriace; (firm) inflexible; (journey) pénible; (task, problem, situation) difficile; (rough) dur ▷ n (gangster etc) dur m; **~ luck!** pas de chance!; tant pis!

toughen ['tʌfn] vt rendre plus dur(e) (or plus résistant(e) or plus solide)

toupee ['tuːpeɪ] n postiche m

tour ['tuəʳ] n voyage m; (also: **package ~**) voyage organisé; (of town, museum) tour m, visite f; (by band) tournée f ▷ vt visiter; **to go on a ~ of** (museum, region) visiter; **to go on ~** partir en tournée

tour guide n (person) guide m/f

tourism ['tuərɪzm] n tourisme m

tourist ['tuərɪst] n touriste m/f ▷ adv (travel) en classe touriste ▷ cpd touristique; **the ~ trade** le tourisme

tourist office n syndicat m d'initiative

tournament ['tuənəmənt] n tournoi m

tour operator n (Brit) organisateur m de voyages, tour-opérateur m

tousled ['tauzld] adj (hair) ébouriffé(e)

tout [taut] vi: **to ~ for** essayer de raccrocher, racoler; **to ~ sth (around)** (Brit) essayer de placer or (re)vendre qch ▷ n (Brit: ticket tout) revendeur m de billets

tow [təu] n: **to give sb a ~** (Aut) remorquer ▷ vt remorquer; (caravan, trailer) tracter; **"on ~"**, (US) **"in ~"** (Aut) "véhicule en remorque"; **tow away** vt (subj: police) emmener à la fourrière; (: breakdown service) remorquer

toward [təˈwɔːd], **towards** [təˈwɔːdz] prep vers; (of attitude) envers, à l'égard de; (of purpose) pour; **~(s) noon/the end of the year** vers midi/la fin de l'année; **to feel friendly ~(s) sb** être bien disposé envers qn

towel ['tauəl] n serviette f (de toilette); (also: **tea ~**) torchon m; **to throw in the ~** (fig) jeter l'éponge

towelling ['tauəlɪŋ] n (fabric) tissu-éponge m

towel rail, (US) **towel rack** n porte-serviettes m inv

tower ['tauəʳ] n tour f ▷ vi (building, mountain) se dresser (majestueusement); **to ~ above** or **over sb/sth** dominer qn/qch

tower block n (Brit) tour f (d'habitation)

towering ['tauərɪŋ] adj très haut(e), imposant(e)

town [taun] n ville f; **to go to ~** aller en ville; (fig) y mettre le paquet; **in the ~** dans la ville, en ville; **to be out of ~** (person) être en déplacement

town centre n (Brit) centre m de la ville, centre-ville m

town council n conseil municipal

town hall n ≈ mairie f

town plan n plan m de ville

town planning n urbanisme m

towrope ['təurəup] n (câble m de) remorque f

tow truck n (US) dépanneuse f

toxic ['tɔksɪk] adj toxique

toxic asset n (Econ) actif m toxique

toy [tɔɪ] n jouet m; **toy with** vt fus jouer avec; (idea) caresser

toyshop ['tɔɪʃɒp] n magasin m de jouets

trace [treɪs] n trace f ▷ vt (draw) tracer, dessiner; (follow) suivre la trace de; (locate) retrouver; **without ~** (disappear) sans laisser de traces; **there was no ~ of it** il n'y en avait pas trace

tracing paper ['treɪsɪŋ-] n papier-calque m

track [træk] n (mark) trace f; (path: gen) chemin m, piste f; (: of bullet etc) trajectoire f; (: of suspect, animal) piste f, (Rail) voie ferrée, rails mpl; (on tape, Comput, Sport) piste f; (on CD) piste f; (on record) plage f ▷ vt suivre la trace or la piste de; **to keep ~ of** suivre; **to be on the right ~** (fig) être sur la bonne voie; **track down** vt (prey) trouver et capturer; (sth lost) finir par retrouver

tracksuit ['træksuːt] n survêtement m

tract [trækt] n (Geo) étendue f, zone f; (pamphlet) tract m; **respiratory ~** (Anat) système m respiratoire

traction ['trækʃən] n traction f

tractor ['træktər] n tracteur m

trade [treɪd] n commerce m; (skill, job) métier m ▷ vi faire du commerce ▷ vt (exchange): **to ~ sth (for sth)** échanger qch (contre qch); **to ~ with/in** faire du commerce avec/le commerce de; **foreign ~** commerce extérieur; **trade in** vt (old car etc) faire reprendre

trade fair n foire(-exposition) commerciale

trade-in price n prix m à la reprise

trademark ['treɪdmɑːk] n marque f de fabrique

trade name n marque déposée

trader ['treɪdər] n commerçant(e), négociant(e)

tradesman ['treɪdzmən] irreg n (shopkeeper) commerçant m; (skilled worker) ouvrier qualifié

trade union n syndicat m

trade unionist [-'juːnjənɪst] n syndicaliste m/f

trading ['treɪdɪŋ] n affaires fpl, commerce m

tradition [trə'dɪʃən] n tradition f; **traditions** npl coutumes fpl, traditions

traditional [trə'dɪʃənl] adj traditionnel(le)

traffic ['træfɪk] n trafic m; (cars) circulation f ▷ vi: **to ~ in** (pej: liquor, drugs) faire le trafic de

traffic calming [-'kɑːmɪŋ] n ralentissement m de la circulation

traffic circle n (US) rond-point m

traffic island n refuge m (pour piétons)

traffic jam n embouteillage m

traffic lights npl feux mpl (de signalisation)

traffic warden n contractuel(le)

tragedy ['trædʒədɪ] n tragédie f

tragic ['trædʒɪk] adj tragique

trail [treɪl] n (tracks) trace f, piste f; (path) chemin m, piste f; (of smoke etc) traînée f ▷ vt (drag) traîner, tirer; (follow) suivre ▷ vi traîner; (in game, contest) être en retard; **to be on sb's ~** être sur la piste de qn; **trail away**, **trail off** vi (sound, voice) s'évanouir; (interest) disparaître; **trail behind** vi traîner, être à la traîne

trailer ['treɪlər] n (Aut) remorque f; (US) caravane f; (Cine) bande-annonce f

trailer truck n (US) (camion m) semi-remorque m

train [treɪn] n train m; (in underground) rame f; (of dress) traîne f; (Brit: series): **~ of events** série f d'événements ▷ vt (apprentice, doctor etc) former; (Sport) entraîner; (dog) dresser; (memory) exercer; (point: gun etc): **to ~ sth on** braquer qch sur ▷ vi recevoir sa formation; (Sport) s'entraîner; **one's ~ of thought** le fil de sa pensée; **to go by ~** voyager par le train or en train; **what time does the ~ from Paris get in?** à quelle heure arrive le train de Paris?; **is this the ~ for ...?** c'est bien le train pour ...?; **to ~ sb to do sth** apprendre à qn à faire qch; (employee) former qn à faire qch

trained [treɪnd] adj qualifié(e), qui a reçu une formation; dressé(e)

trainee [treɪ'niː] n stagiaire m/f; (in trade) apprenti(e)

trainer ['treɪnər] n (Sport) entraîneur(-euse); (of dogs etc) dresseur(-euse); **trainers** npl (shoes) chaussures fpl de sport

training ['treɪnɪŋ] n formation f; (Sport) entraînement m; (of dog etc) dressage m; **in ~** (Sport) à l'entraînement; (fit) en forme

training college n école professionnelle; (for teachers) ≈ école normale

training course n cours m de formation professionnelle

training shoes npl chaussures fpl de sport

trait [treɪt] n trait m (de caractère)

traitor ['treɪtər] n traître m

tram [træm] n (Brit: also: **~car**) tram(way) m

tramp [træmp] n (person) vagabond(e), clochard(e); (inf: pej: woman): **to be a ~** être coureuse ▷ vi marcher d'un pas lourd ▷ vt (walk through: town, streets) parcourir à pied

trample ['træmpl] vt: **to ~ (underfoot)** piétiner; (fig) bafouer

trampoline ['træmpəliːn] n trampoline m

tranquil ['træŋkwɪl] adj tranquille

tranquillizer, (US) **tranquilizer** ['træŋkwɪlaɪzər] n (Med) tranquillisant m

transact [træn'zækt] vt (business) traiter

transaction [træn'zækʃən] n transaction f; **transactions** npl (minutes) actes mpl; **cash ~** transaction au comptant

transatlantic ['trænzət'læntɪk] adj transatlantique

transcript ['trænskrɪpt] n transcription f (texte)

transfer n ['trænsfər] (gen, also Sport) transfert m; (Pol: of power) passation f;

(*of money*) virement *m*; (*picture, design*)
décalcomanie *f*; (: *stick-on*) autocollant *m* ▷ *vt*
[træns'fəː'] transférer; passer; virer;
décalquer; **to ~ the charges** (*Brit Tel*)
téléphoner en P.C.V.; **by bank ~** par virement
bancaire

transfer desk *n* (*Aviat*) guichet *m* de transit

transform [træns'fɔːm] *vt* transformer

transformation [trænsfə'meɪʃən] *n*
transformation *f*

transfusion [træns'fjuːʒən] *n* transfusion *f*

transient ['trænzɪənt] *adj* transitoire,
éphémère

transistor [træn'zɪstə'] *n* (*Elec: also:* **~ radio**)
transistor *m*

transit ['trænzɪt] *n*: **in ~** en transit

transition [træn'zɪʃən] *n* transition *f*

transitive ['trænzɪtɪv] *adj* (*Ling*)
transitif(-ive)

transit lounge *n* (*Aviat*) salle *f* de transit

translate [trænz'leɪt] *vt*: **to ~ (from/into)**
traduire (du/en); **can you ~ this for me?**
pouvez-vous me traduire ceci?

translation [trænz'leɪʃən] *n* traduction *f*;
(*Scol: as opposed to prose*) version *f*

translator [trænz'leɪtə'] *n* traducteur(-trice)

transmission [trænz'mɪʃən] *n*
transmission *f*

transmit [trænz'mɪt] *vt* transmettre; (*Radio,
TV*) émettre

transmitter [trænz'mɪtə'] *n* émetteur *m*

transparency [træns'pɛərnsɪ] *n* (*Brit Phot*)
diapositive *f*

transparent [træns'pærnt] *adj* transparent(e)

transpire [træns'paɪə'] *vi* (*become known*): **it
finally ~d that ...** on a finalement appris
que ...; (*happen*) arriver

transplant *vt* [træns'plɑːnt] transplanter;
(*seedlings*) repiquer ▷ *n* ['trænsplɑːnt] (*Med*)
transplantation *f*; **to have a heart ~** subir
une greffe du cœur

transport *n* ['trænspɔːt] transport *m* ▷ *vt*
[træns'pɔːt] transporter; **public ~** transports
en commun; **Department of T~** (*Brit*)
ministère *m* des Transports

transportation [trænspɔː'teɪʃən] *n*
(*moyen m de*) transport *m*; (*of prisoners*)
transportation *f*; **Department of T~** (*US*)
ministère *m* des Transports

transport café *n* (*Brit*) ≈ routier *m*

transvestite [trænz'vɛstaɪt] *n* travesti(e)

trap [træp] *n* (*snare, trick*) piège *m*; (*carriage*)
cabriolet *m* ▷ *vt* prendre au piège; (*immobilize*)
bloquer; (*confine*) coincer; **to set** *or* **lay a ~
(for sb)** tendre un piège (à qn); **to shut
one's ~** (*inf*) la fermer

trap door *n* trappe *f*

trapeze [trə'piːz] *n* trapèze *m*

trappings ['træpɪŋz] *npl* ornements *mpl*;
attributs *mpl*

trash [træʃ] *n* (*pej: goods*) camelote *f*;
(: *nonsense*) sottises *fpl*; (*US: rubbish*) ordures *fpl*

trash can *n* (*US*) poubelle *f*

trashy ['træʃɪ] *adj* (*inf*) de camelote, qui ne
vaut rien

trauma ['trɔːmə] *n* traumatisme *m*

traumatic [trɔː'mætɪk] *adj* traumatisant(e)

travel ['trævl] *n* voyage(s) *m(pl)* ▷ *vi* voyager;
(*move*) aller, se déplacer; (*news, sound*) se
propager ▷ *vt* (*distance*) parcourir; **this wine
doesn't ~ well** ce vin voyage mal

travel agency *n* agence *f* de voyages

travel agent *n* agent *m* de voyages

travel insurance *n* assurance-voyage *f*

traveller, (*US*) **traveler** ['trævlə'] *n*
voyageur(-euse); (*Comm*) représentant *m*
de commerce

traveller's cheque, (*US*) **traveler's check** *n*
chèque *m* de voyage

travelling, (*US*) **traveling** ['trævlɪŋ] *n*
voyage(s) *m(pl)* ▷ *adj* (*circus, exhibition*)
ambulant(e) ▷ *cpd* (*bag, clock*) de voyage;
(*expenses*) de déplacement

travel-sick ['trævlsɪk] *adj*: **to get ~** avoir le
mal de la route (*or de mer or de l'air*)

travel sickness *n* mal *m* de la route (*or de
mer or de l'air*)

trawler ['trɔːlə'] *n* chalutier *m*

tray [treɪ] *n* (*for carrying*) plateau *m*; (*on desk*)
corbeille *f*

treacherous ['trɛtʃərəs] *adj* traître(sse);
(*ground, tide*) dont il faut se méfier; **road
conditions are ~** l'état des routes est
dangereux

treacle ['triːkl] *n* mélasse *f*

tread [trɛd] *n* (*step*) pas *m*; (*sound*) bruit *m* de
pas; (*of tyre*) chape *f*, bande *f* de roulement
▷ *vi* (*pt* **trod**, *pp* **trodden**) [trɔd, 'trɔdn]
marcher; **tread on** *vt fus* marcher sur

treason ['triːzn] *n* trahison *f*

treasure ['trɛʒə'] *n* trésor *m* ▷ *vt* (*value*)
tenir beaucoup à; (*store*) conserver
précieusement

treasurer ['trɛʒərə'] *n* trésorier(-ière)

treasury ['trɛʒərɪ] *n* trésorerie *f*; **the T~**, (*US*)
the T~ Department ≈ le ministère des
Finances

treat [triːt] *n* petit cadeau, petite surprise
▷ *vt* traiter; **it was a ~** ça m'a (*or nous a etc*)
vraiment fait plaisir; **to ~ sb to sth** offrir qch
à qn; **to ~ sth as a joke** prendre qch à la
plaisanterie

treatment ['triːtmənt] *n* traitement *m*;
to have ~ for sth (*Med*) suivre un traitement
pour qch

treaty ['triːtɪ] *n* traité *m*

treble ['trɛbl] *adj* triple ▷ *n* (*Mus*) soprano *m*
▷ *vt*, *vi* tripler

treble clef *n* clé *f* de sol

tree [triː] *n* arbre *m*

trek [trɛk] *n* (*long walk*) randonnée *f*; (*tiring
walk*) longue marche, trotte *f* ▷ *vi* (*as holiday*)
faire de la randonnée

tremble ['trɛmbl] *vi* trembler

tremendous [trɪ'mɛndəs] *adj* (*enormous*) énorme; (*excellent*) formidable, fantastique

tremor ['trɛməʳ] *n* tremblement *m*; (*also:* **earth ~**) secousse *f* sismique

trench [trɛntʃ] *n* tranchée *f*

trend [trɛnd] *n* (*tendency*) tendance *f*; (*of events*) cours *m*; (*fashion*) mode *f*; **~ towards/away from doing** tendance à faire/à ne pas faire; **to set the ~** donner le ton; **to set a ~** lancer une mode

trendy ['trɛndɪ] *adj* (*idea, person*) dans le vent; (*clothes*) dernier cri *inv*

trespass ['trɛspəs] *vi*: **to ~ on** s'introduire sans permission dans; (*fig*) empiéter sur; **"no ~ing"** "propriété privée", "défense d'entrer"

trestle ['trɛsl] *n* tréteau *m*

trial ['traɪəl] *n* (*Law*) procès *m*, jugement *m*; (*test: of machine etc*) essai *m*; (*worry*) souci *m*; **trials** *npl* (*unpleasant experiences*) épreuves *fpl*; (*Sport*) épreuves éliminatoires; **horse ~s** concours *m* hippique; **~ by jury** jugement par jury; **to be sent for ~** être traduit(e) en justice; **to be on ~** passer en jugement; **by ~ and error** par tâtonnements

trial period *n* période *f* d'essai

triangle ['traɪæŋgl] *n* (*Math, Mus*) triangle *m*

triangular [traɪ'æŋgjuləʳ] *adj* triangulaire

tribe [traɪb] *n* tribu *f*

tribesman ['traɪbzmən] *n* membre *m* de la tribu

tribunal [traɪ'bjuːnl] *n* tribunal *m*

tributary ['trɪbjutərɪ] *n* (*river*) affluent *m*

tribute ['trɪbjuːt] *n* tribut *m*, hommage *m*; **to pay ~ to** rendre hommage à

trick [trɪk] *n* (*magic*) tour *m*; (*joke, prank*) tour, farce *f*; (*skill, knack*) astuce *f*; (*Cards*) levée *f* ▷ *vt* attraper, rouler; **to play a ~ on sb** jouer un tour à qn; **to ~ sb into doing sth** persuader qn par la ruse de faire qch; **to ~ sb out of sth** obtenir qch de qn par la ruse; **it's a ~ of the light** c'est une illusion d'optique causée par la lumière; **that should do the ~** (*fam*) ça devrait faire l'affaire

trickery ['trɪkərɪ] *n* ruse *f*

trickle ['trɪkl] *n* (*of water etc*) filet *m* ▷ *vi* couler en un filet or goutte à goutte; **to ~ in/out** (*people*) entrer/sortir par petits groupes

tricky ['trɪkɪ] *adj* difficile, délicat(e)

tricycle ['traɪsɪkl] *n* tricycle *m*

trifle ['traɪfl] *n* bagatelle *f*; (*Culin*) = diplomate *m* ▷ *adv*: **a ~ long** un peu long ▷ *vi*: **to ~ with** traiter à la légère

trifling ['traɪflɪŋ] *adj* insignifiant(e)

trigger ['trɪgəʳ] *n* (*of gun*) gâchette *f*; **trigger off** *vt* déclencher

trim [trɪm] *adj* net(te); (*house, garden*) bien tenu(e); (*figure*) svelte ▷ *n* (*haircut etc*) légère coupe; (*embellishment*) finitions *fpl*; (*on car*) garnitures *fpl* ▷ *vt* (*cut*) couper légèrement; (*decorate*): **to ~ (with)** décorer (de); (*Naut: a sail*) gréer; **to keep in (good) ~** maintenir en (bon) état

trimmings ['trɪmɪŋz] *npl* décorations *fpl*; (*extras: gen Culin*) garniture *f*

trinket ['trɪŋkɪt] *n* bibelot *m*; (*piece of jewellery*) colifichet *m*

trio ['triːəu] *n* trio *m*

trip [trɪp] *n* voyage *m*; (*excursion*) excursion *f*; (*stumble*) faux pas ▷ *vi* faire un faux pas, trébucher; (*go lightly*) marcher d'un pas léger; **on a ~** en voyage; **trip up** *vi* trébucher ▷ *vt* faire un croc-en-jambe à

tripe [traɪp] *n* (*Culin*) tripes *fpl*; (*pej: rubbish*) idioties *fpl*

triple ['trɪpl] *adj* triple ▷ *adv*: **~ the distance/the speed** trois fois la distance/la vitesse

triplets ['trɪplɪts] *npl* triplés(-ées)

triplicate ['trɪplɪkət] *n*: **in ~** en trois exemplaires

tripod ['traɪpɔd] *n* trépied *m*

trite [traɪt] *adj* banal(e)

triumph ['traɪʌmf] *n* triomphe *m* ▷ *vi*: **to ~ (over)** triompher (de)

triumphant [traɪ'ʌmfənt] *adj* triomphant(e)

trivia ['trɪvɪə] *npl* futilités *fpl*

trivial ['trɪvɪəl] *adj* insignifiant(e); (*commonplace*) banal(e)

trod [trɔd] *pt of* **tread**

trodden ['trɔdn] *pp of* **tread**

trolley ['trɔlɪ] *n* chariot *m*

trombone [trɔm'bəun] *n* trombone *m*

troop [truːp] *n* bande *f*, groupe *m* ▷ *vi*: **to ~ in/ out** entrer/sortir en groupe; **troops** *npl* (*Mil*) troupes *fpl*; (*: men*) hommes *mpl*, soldats *mpl*; **~ing the colour** (*Brit: ceremony*) le salut au drapeau

trophy ['trəufɪ] *n* trophée *m*

tropic ['trɔpɪk] *n* tropique *m*; **in the ~s** sous les tropiques; **T~ of Cancer/Capricorn** tropique du Cancer/Capricorne

tropical ['trɔpɪkl] *adj* tropical(e)

trot [trɔt] *n* trot *m* ▷ *vi* trotter; **on the ~** (*Brit: fig*) d'affilée; **trot out** *vt* (*excuse, reason*) débiter; (*names, facts*) réciter les uns après les autres

trouble ['trʌbl] *n* difficulté(s) *f(pl)*, problème(s) *m(pl)*; (*worry*) ennuis *mpl*, soucis *mpl*; (*bother, effort*) peine *f*; (*Pol*) conflit(s) *m(pl)*, troubles *mpl*; (*Med*): **stomach** *etc* **~** troubles gastriques *etc* ▷ *vt* (*disturb*) déranger, gêner; (*worry*) inquiéter ▷ *vi*: **to ~ to do** prendre la peine de faire; **troubles** *npl* (*Pol etc*) troubles; (*personal*) ennuis, soucis; **to be in ~** avoir des ennuis; (*ship, climber etc*) être en difficulté; **to have ~ doing sth** avoir du mal à faire qch; **to go to the ~ of doing** se donner le mal de faire; **it's no ~!** je vous en prie!; **please don't ~ yourself** je vous en prie, ne vous dérangez pas!; **the ~ is ...** le problème, c'est que ...; **what's the ~?** qu'est-ce qui ne va pas?

troubled ['trʌbld] *adj* (*person*) inquiet(-ète); (*times, life*) agité(e)

troublemaker ['trʌblmeɪkə'] n élément perturbateur, fauteur m de troubles

troubleshooter ['trʌblʃu:tə'] n (in conflict) conciliateur m

troublesome ['trʌblsəm] adj (child) fatigant(e), difficile; (cough) gênant(e)

trough [trɒf] n (also: **drinking ~**) abreuvoir m; (also: **feeding ~**) auge f; (depression) creux m; (channel) chenal m; **~ of low pressure** (Meteorology) dépression f

trousers ['trauzəz] npl pantalon m; **short ~** (Brit) culottes courtes

trout [traut] n (pl inv) truite f

trowel ['trauəl] n truelle f; (garden tool) déplantoir m

truant ['truənt] n: **to play ~** (Brit) faire l'école buissonnière

truce [tru:s] n trêve f

truck [trʌk] n camion m; (Rail) wagon m à plate-forme; (for luggage) chariot m (à bagages)

truck driver n camionneur m

truck farm n (US) jardin maraîcher

true [tru:] adj vrai(e); (accurate) exact(e); (genuine) vrai, véritable; (faithful) fidèle; (wall) d'aplomb; (beam) droit(e); (wheel) dans l'axe; **to come ~** se réaliser; **~ to life** réaliste

truffle ['trʌfl] n truffe f

truly ['tru:lɪ] adv vraiment, réellement; (truthfully) sans mentir; (faithfully) fidèlement; **yours ~** (in letter) je vous prie d'agréer, Monsieur (or Madame etc), l'expression de mes sentiments respectueux

trump [trʌmp] n atout m; **to turn up ~s** (fig) faire des miracles

trumpet ['trʌmpɪt] n trompette f

truncheon ['trʌntʃən] n bâton m (d'agent de police); matraque f

trundle ['trʌndl] vt, vi: **to ~ along** rouler bruyamment

trunk [trʌŋk] n (of tree, person) tronc m; (of elephant) trompe f; (case) malle f; (US Aut) coffre m; **trunks** npl (also: **swimming ~s**) maillot m or slip m de bain

truss [trʌs] n (Med) bandage m herniaire ▷ vt: **to ~ (up)** (Culin) brider

trust [trʌst] n confiance f; (responsibility): **to place sth in sb's ~** confier la responsabilité de qch à qn; (Law) fidéicommis m; (Comm) trust m ▷ vt (rely on) avoir confiance en; (entrust): **to ~ sth to sb** confier qch à qn; (hope): **to ~ (that)** espérer (que); **to take sth on ~** accepter qch les yeux fermés; **in ~** (Law) par fidéicommis

trusted ['trʌstɪd] adj en qui l'on a confiance

trustee [trʌs'ti:] n (Law) fidéicommissaire m/f; (of school etc) administrateur(-trice)

trustful ['trʌstful] adj confiant(e)

trustworthy ['trʌstwə:ðɪ] adj digne de confiance

truth [tru:θ, pl tru:ðz] n vérité f

truthful ['tru:θful] adj (person) qui dit la vérité; (answer) sincère; (description) exact(e), vrai(e)

try [traɪ] n essai m, tentative f; (Rugby) essai ▷ vt (attempt) essayer, tenter; (test: sth new: also: **~ out**) éprouver ▷ vi essayer; **to ~ to do** essayer de faire; (seek) chercher à faire; **to ~ one's (very) best** or **one's (very) hardest** faire de son mieux; **to give sth a ~** essayer qch; **try on** vt (clothes) essayer; **to ~ it on** (fig) tenter le coup, bluffer; **try out** vt essayer, mettre à l'essai

trying ['traɪɪŋ] adj pénible

T-shirt ['ti:ʃə:t] n tee-shirt m

T-square ['ti:skwɛə'] n équerre f en T

tsunami [tsu'nɑ:mɪ] n tsunami m

tub [tʌb] n cuve f; (for washing clothes) baquet m; (bath) baignoire f

tubby ['tʌbɪ] adj rondelet(te)

tube [tju:b] n tube m; (Brit: underground) métro m; (for tyre) chambre f à air; (inf: television): **the ~** la télé

tuberculosis [tjubə:kju'ləusɪs] n tuberculose f

tube station n (Brit) station f de métro

TUC n abbr (Brit: = Trades Union Congress) confédération f des syndicats britanniques

tuck [tʌk] n (Sewing) pli m, rempli m ▷ vt (put) mettre; **tuck away** vt cacher, ranger; (money) mettre de côté; (building): **to be ~ed away** être caché(e); **tuck in** vt rentrer; (child) border ▷ vi (eat) manger de bon appétit; attaquer le repas; **tuck up** vt (child) border

tuck shop n (Brit Scol) boutique f à provisions

Tuesday ['tju:zdɪ] n mardi m; **(the date) today is ~ 23rd March** nous sommes aujourd'hui le mardi 23 mars; **on ~** mardi; **on ~s** le mardi; **every ~** tous les mardis, chaque mardi; **every other ~** un mardi sur deux; **last/next ~** mardi dernier/prochain; **~ next** mardi qui vient; **the following ~** le mardi suivant; **a week/fortnight on ~**, **~ week/fortnight** mardi en huit/quinze; **the ~ before last** l'autre mardi; **the ~ after next** mardi en huit; **~ morning/lunchtime/afternoon/evening** mardi matin/midi/après-midi/soir; **~ night** mardi soir; (overnight) la nuit de mardi (à mercredi); **~'s newspaper** le journal de mardi

tuft [tʌft] n touffe f

tug [tʌg] n (ship) remorqueur m ▷ vt tirer (sur)

tug-of-war [tʌgəv'wɔ:'] n lutte f à la corde

tuition [tju:'ɪʃən] n (Brit: lessons) leçons fpl; (: private) cours particuliers; (US: fees) frais mpl de scolarité

tulip ['tju:lɪp] n tulipe f

tumble ['tʌmbl] n (fall) chute f, culbute f ▷ vi tomber, dégringoler; (somersault) faire une or des culbute(s) ▷ vt renverser, faire tomber; **to ~ to sth** (inf) réaliser qch

tumbledown ['tʌmbldaun] adj délabré(e)

tumble dryer n (Brit) séchoir m (à linge) à air chaud

tumbler ['tʌmblə'] n verre (droit), gobelet m

tummy ['tʌmɪ] n (inf) ventre m

tumour, (US) **tumor** ['tju:mə'] n tumeur f

tuna ['tju:nə] n (pl inv: also: ~ **fish**) thon m

tune [tju:n] n (melody) air m ▷ vt (Mus) accorder; (Radio, TV, Aut) régler, mettre au point; **to be in/out of ~** (instrument) être accordé/désaccordé; (singer) chanter juste/faux; **to be in/out of ~ with** (fig) être en accord/désaccord avec; **she was robbed to the ~ of £30,000** (fig) on lui a volé la jolie somme de 10 000 livres; **tune in** vi (Radio, TV): **to ~ in (to)** se mettre à l'écoute (de); **tune up** vi (musician) accorder son instrument

tuneful ['tju:nful] adj mélodieux(-euse)

tuner ['tju:nə'] n (radio set) tuner m; **piano ~** accordeur m de pianos

tunic ['tju:nɪk] n tunique f

Tunis ['tju:nɪs] n Tunis

Tunisia [tju:'nɪzɪə] n Tunisie f

Tunisian [tju:'nɪzɪən] adj tunisien(ne) ▷ n Tunisien(ne)

tunnel ['tʌnl] n tunnel m; (in mine) galerie f ▷ vi creuser un tunnel (or une galerie)

turbulence ['tə:bjuləns] n (Aviat) turbulence f

tureen [tə'ri:n] n soupière f

turf [tə:f] n gazon m; (clod) motte f (de gazon) ▷ vt gazonner; **the T~** le turf, les courses fpl; **turf out** vt (inf) jeter; jeter dehors

Turk [tə:k] n Turc/Turque

Turkey ['tə:kɪ] n Turquie f

turkey ['tə:kɪ] n dindon m, dinde f

Turkish ['tə:kɪʃ] adj turc/turque ▷ n (Ling) turc m

turmoil ['tə:mɔɪl] n trouble m, bouleversement m

turn [tə:n] n tour m; (in road) tournant m; (tendency: of mind, events) tournure f; (performance) numéro m; (Med) crise f, attaque f ▷ vt tourner; (collar, steak) retourner; (age) atteindre; (shape: wood, metal) tourner; (milk) faire tourner; (change): **to ~ sth into** changer qch en ▷ vi (object, wind, milk) tourner; (person: look back) se (re)tourner; (reverse direction) faire demi-tour; (change) changer; (become) devenir; **to ~ into** se changer en, se transformer en; **a good ~** un service; **a bad ~** un mauvais tour; **it gave me quite a ~** ça m'a fait un coup; **"no left ~"** (Aut) "défense de tourner à gauche"; **~ left/right at the next junction** tournez à gauche/droite au prochain carrefour; **it's your ~** c'est (à) votre tour; **in ~** à son tour; à tour de rôle; **to take ~s** se relayer; **to take ~s at** faire à tour de rôle; **at the ~ of the year/century** à la fin de l'année/du siècle; **to take a ~ for the worse** (situation, events) empirer; **his health** or **he has taken a ~ for the worse**

son état s'est aggravé; **turn about** vi faire demi-tour; faire un demi-tour; **turn around** vi (person) se retourner ▷ vt (object) tourner; **turn away** vi se détourner, tourner la tête ▷ vt (reject: person) renvoyer; (: business) refuser; **turn back** vi revenir, faire demi-tour; **turn down** vt (refuse) rejeter, refuser; (reduce) baisser; (fold) rabattre; **turn in** vi (inf: go to bed) aller se coucher ▷ vt (fold) rentrer; **turn off** vi (from road) tourner ▷ vt (light, radio etc) éteindre; (tap) fermer; (engine) arrêter; **I can't ~ the heating off** je n'arrive pas à éteindre le chauffage; **turn on** vt (light, radio etc) allumer; (tap) ouvrir; (engine) mettre en marche; **I can't ~ the heating on** je n'arrive pas à allumer le chauffage; **turn out** vt (light, gas) éteindre; (produce: goods, novel, good pupils) produire ▷ vi (voters, troops) se présenter; **to ~ out to be ...** s'avérer ..., se révéler ...; **turn over** vi (person) se retourner ▷ vt (object) retourner; (page) tourner; **turn round** vi faire demi-tour; (rotate) tourner; **turn to** vt fus: **to ~ to sb** s'adresser à qn; **turn up** vi (person) arriver, se pointer (inf); (lost object) être retrouvé(e) ▷ vt (collar) remonter; (radio, heater) mettre plus fort

turning ['tə:nɪŋ] n (in road) tournant m; **the first ~ on the right** la première (rue or route) à droite

turning point n (fig) tournant m, moment m décisif

turnip ['tə:nɪp] n navet m

turnout ['tə:naut] n (nombre m de personnes dans l')assistance f; (of voters) taux m de participation

turnover ['tə:nəuvə'] n (Comm: amount of money) chiffre m d'affaires; (: of goods) roulement m; (of staff) renouvellement m, changement m; (Culin) sorte de chausson; **there is a rapid ~ in staff** le personnel change souvent

turnpike ['tə:npaɪk] n (US) autoroute f à péage

turnstile ['tə:nstaɪl] n tourniquet m (d'entrée)

turntable ['tə:nteɪbl] n (on record player) platine f

turn-up ['tə:nʌp] n (Brit: on trousers) revers m

turpentine ['tə:pəntaɪn] n (also: **turps**) (essence f de) térébenthine f

turquoise ['tə:kwɔɪz] n (stone) turquoise f ▷ adj turquoise inv

turret ['tʌrɪt] n tourelle f

turtle ['tə:tl] n tortue marine

turtleneck ['tə:tlnɛk], **turtleneck sweater** n pullover m à col montant

tusk [tʌsk] n défense f (d'éléphant)

tutor ['tju:tə'] n (Brit Scol: in college) directeur(-trice) d'études; (private teacher) précepteur(-trice)

tutorial [tju:'tɔ:rɪəl] n (Scol) (séance f de) travaux mpl pratiques

tuxedo [tʌk'si:dəu] n (US) smoking m

TV [ti:'vi:] n abbr (= television) télé f, TV f

twang [twæŋ] n (of instrument) son vibrant; (of voice) ton nasillard ▷ vi vibrer ▷ vt (guitar) pincer les cordes de

tweed [twi:d] n tweed m

tweezers ['twi:zəz] npl pince f à épiler

twelfth [twelfθ] num douzième

twelve [twelv] num douze; **at ~ (o'clock)** à midi; (midnight) à minuit

twentieth ['twentiiθ] num vingtième

twenty ['twenti] num vingt

twice [twais] adv deux fois; **~ as much** deux fois plus; **~ a week** deux fois par semaine; **she is ~ your age** elle a deux fois ton âge

twiddle ['twidl] vt, vi: **to ~ (with) sth** tripoter qch; **to ~ one's thumbs** (fig) se tourner les pouces

twig [twig] n brindille f ▷ vt, vi (inf) piger

twilight ['twailait] n crépuscule m; (morning) aube f; **in the ~** dans la pénombre

twin [twin] adj, n jumeau(-elle) ▷ vt jumeler

twin-bedded room ['twin'bɛdid-] n = **twin room**

twin beds npl lits mpl jumeaux

twine [twain] n ficelle f ▷ vi (plant) s'enrouler

twinge [twindʒ] n (of pain) élancement m; (of conscience) remords m

twinkle ['twiŋkl] n scintillement m; pétillement m ▷ vi scintiller; (eyes) pétiller

twin room n chambre f à deux lits

twirl [twə:l] n tournoiement m ▷ vt faire tournoyer ▷ vi tournoyer

twist [twist] n torsion f, tour m; (in wire, flex) tortillon m; (bend: in road) tournant m; (in story) coup m de théâtre ▷ vt tordre; (weave) entortiller; (roll around) enrouler; (fig) déformer ▷ vi s'entortiller; s'enrouler; (road, river) serpenter; **to ~ one's ankle/wrist** (Med) se tordre la cheville/le poignet

twit [twit] n (inf) crétin(e)

twitch [twitʃ] n (pull) coup sec, saccade f; (nervous) tic m ▷ vi se convulser; avoir un tic

two [tu:] num deux; **~ by ~, in ~s** par deux; **to put ~ and ~ together** (fig) faire le rapprochement

two-door [tu:'dɔ:'] adj (Aut) à deux portes

two-faced [tu:'feist] adj (pej: person) faux/ fausse

twofold ['tu:fəuld] adv: **to increase ~** doubler ▷ adj (increase) de cent pour cent; (reply) en deux parties

two-piece ['tu:'pi:s] n (also: **~ suit**) (costume m) deux-pièces m inv; (also: **~ swimsuit**) (maillot m de bain) deux-pièces

twosome ['tu:səm] n (people) couple m

two-way ['tu:wei] adj (traffic) dans les deux sens; **~ radio** émetteur-récepteur m

tycoon [tai'ku:n] n: **(business) ~** gros homme d'affaires

type [taip] n (category) genre m, espèce f; (model) modèle m; (example) type m; (Typ) type, caractère m ▷ vt (letter etc) taper (à la machine); **what ~ do you want?** quel genre voulez-vous?; **in bold/italic ~** en caractères gras/en italiques

typecast ['taipkɑ:st] adj condamné(e) à toujours jouer le même rôle

typeface ['taipfeis] n police f (de caractères)

typescript ['taipskript] n texte dactylographié

typewriter ['taipraitə'] n machine f à écrire

typewritten ['taipritn] adj dactylographié(e)

typhoid ['taifɔid] n typhoïde f

typhoon [tai'fu:n] n typhon m

typical ['tipikl] adj typique, caractéristique

typically ['tipikli] adv (as usual) comme d'habitude; (characteristically) typiquement

typing ['taipiŋ] n dactylo(graphie) f

typist ['taipist] n dactylo m/f

tyrant ['taiərənt] n tyran m

tyre, (US) **tire** ['taiə'] n pneu m

tyre pressure n (Brit) pression f (de gonflage)

u

U-bend ['juːbɛnd] *n* (*Brit Aut*) coude *m*, virage *m* en épingle à cheveux; (*in pipe*) coude

ubiquitous [juːˈbɪkwɪtəs] *adj* doué(e) d'ubiquité, omniprésent(e)

udder ['ʌdəʳ] *n* pis *m*, mamelle *f*

UFO ['juːfəʊ] *n abbr* (= *unidentified flying object*) ovni *m*

Uganda [juːˈgændə] *n* Ouganda *m*

ugh [əːh] *excl* pouah!

ugly ['ʌɡlɪ] *adj* laid(e), vilain(e); (*fig*) répugnant(e)

UHT *adj abbr* (= *ultra-heat treated*); **~ milk** lait *m* UHT *or* longue conservation

UK *n abbr* = **United Kingdom**

ulcer ['ʌlsəʳ] *n* ulcère *m*; **mouth ~** aphte *f*

Ulster ['ʌlstəʳ] *n* Ulster *m*

ulterior [ʌlˈtɪərɪəʳ] *adj* ultérieur(e); **~ motive** arrière-pensée *f*

ultimate ['ʌltɪmət] *adj* ultime, final(e); (*authority*) suprême ▷ *n*: **the ~ in luxury** le summum du luxe

ultimately ['ʌltɪmətlɪ] *adv* (*at last*) en fin de compte; (*fundamentally*) finalement; (*eventually*) par la suite

ultimatum (*pl* **ultimatums** *or* **ultimata**) [ʌltɪˈmeɪtəm, -tə] *n* ultimatum *m*

ultrasound ['ʌltrəsaʊnd] *n* (*Med*) ultrason *m*

ultraviolet ['ʌltrəˈvaɪəlɪt] *adj* ultraviolet(te)

umbilical [ʌmbɪˈlaɪkl] *adj*: **~ cord** cordon ombilical

umbrella [ʌmˈbrɛlə] *n* parapluie *m*; (*for sun*) parasol *m*; (*fig*): **under the ~ of** sous les auspices de; chapeauté(e) par

umpire ['ʌmpaɪəʳ] *n* arbitre *m*; (*Tennis*) juge *m* de chaise ▷ *vt* arbitrer

umpteen [ʌmpˈtiːn] *adj* je ne sais combien de; **for the umpteeth time** pour la nième fois

UN *n abbr* = **United Nations**

unable [ʌnˈeɪbl] *adj*: **to be ~ to** ne (pas) pouvoir, être dans l'impossibilité de; (*not capable*) être incapable de

unacceptable [ʌnəkˈsɛptəbl] *adj* (*behaviour*) inadmissible; (*price, proposal*) inacceptable

unaccompanied [ʌnəˈkʌmpənɪd] *adj* (*child, lady*) non accompagné(e); (*singing, song*) sans accompagnement

unaccustomed [ʌnəˈkʌstəmd] *adj* inaccoutumé(e), inhabituel(le); **to be ~ to sth** ne pas avoir l'habitude de qch

unanimous [juːˈnænɪməs] *adj* unanime

unanimously [juːˈnænɪməslɪ] *adv* à l'unanimité

unarmed [ʌnˈɑːmd] *adj* (*person*) non armé(e); (*combat*) sans armes

unattached [ʌnəˈtætʃt] *adj* libre, sans attaches

unattended [ʌnəˈtɛndɪd] *adj* (*car, child, luggage*) sans surveillance

unattractive [ʌnəˈtræktɪv] *adj* peu attrayant(e); (*character*) peu sympathique

unauthorized [ʌnˈɔːθəraɪzd] *adj* non autorisé(e), sans autorisation

unavailable [ʌnəˈveɪləbl] *adj* (*article, room, book*) (qui n'est) pas disponible; (*person*) (qui n'est) pas libre

unavoidable [ʌnəˈvɔɪdəbl] *adj* inévitable

unaware [ʌnəˈwɛəʳ] *adj*: **to be ~ of** ignorer, ne pas savoir, être inconscient(e) de

unawares [ʌnəˈwɛəz] *adv* à l'improviste, au dépourvu

unbalanced [ʌnˈbælənst] *adj* déséquilibré(e)

unbearable [ʌnˈbɛərəbl] *adj* insupportable

unbeatable [ʌnˈbiːtəbl] *adj* imbattable

unbeknown [ʌnbɪˈnəun], **unbeknownst** [ʌnbɪˈnəunst] *adv*: **~ to** à l'insu de

unbelievable [ʌnbɪˈliːvəbl] *adj* incroyable

unbend [ʌnˈbɛnd] (*irreg like*: **bend**) *vi* se détendre ▷ *vt* (*wire*) redresser, détordre

unbiased, unbiassed [ʌnˈbaɪəst] *adj* impartial(e)

unborn [ʌnˈbɔːn] *adj* à naître

unbreakable [ʌnˈbreɪkəbl] *adj* incassable

unbroken [ʌnˈbrəukn] *adj* intact(e); (*line*) continu(e); (*record*) non battu(e)

unbutton [ʌnˈbʌtn] *vt* déboutonner

uncalled-for [ʌnˈkɔːldfɔːʳ] *adj* déplacé(e), injustifié(e)

uncanny [ʌnˈkænɪ] *adj* étrange, troublant(e)

unceremonious [ʌnsɛrɪˈməunɪəs] *adj* (*abrupt, rude*) brusque

uncertain [ʌnˈsəːtn] *adj* incertain(e); (*hesitant*) hésitant(e); **we were ~ whether ...** nous ne savions pas vraiment si ...; **in no ~ terms** sans équivoque possible

uncertainty [ʌn'sə:tntɪ] n incertitude f, doutes mpl

unchanged [ʌn'tʃeɪndʒd] adj inchangé(e)

uncivilized [ʌn'sɪvɪlaɪzd] adj non civilisé(e); (fig) barbare

uncle ['ʌŋkl] n oncle m

unclear [ʌn'klɪər] adj (qui n'est) pas clair(e) or évident(e); **I'm still ~ about what I'm supposed to do** je ne sais pas encore exactement ce que je dois faire

uncomfortable [ʌn'kʌmfətəbl] adj inconfortable, peu confortable; (uneasy) mal à l'aise, gêné(e); (situation) désagréable

uncommon [ʌn'kɔmən] adj rare, singulier(-ière), peu commun(e)

uncompromising [ʌn'kɔmprəmaɪzɪŋ] adj intransigeant(e), inflexible

unconcerned [ʌnkən'sə:nd] adj (unworried): **to be ~ (about)** ne pas s'inquiéter (de)

unconditional [ʌnkən'dɪʃənl] adj sans conditions

unconscious [ʌn'kɔnʃəs] adj sans connaissance, évanoui(e); (unaware): **~ (of)** inconscient(e) (de) ▷ n: **the ~** l'inconscient m; **to knock sb ~** assommer qn

unconsciously [ʌn'kɔnʃəslɪ] adv inconsciemment

uncontrollable [ʌnkən'trəuləbl] adj (child, dog) indiscipliné(e); (temper, laughter) irrépressible

unconventional [ʌnkən'vɛnʃənl] adj peu conventionnel(le)

uncouth [ʌn'ku:θ] adj grossier(-ière), fruste

uncover [ʌn'kʌvər] vt découvrir

undecided [ʌndɪ'saɪdɪd] adj indécis(e), irrésolu(e)

undeniable [ʌndɪ'naɪəbl] adj indéniable, incontestable

under ['ʌndər] prep sous; (less than) (de) moins de; au-dessous de; (according to) selon, en vertu de ▷ adv au-dessous; en dessous; **from ~ sth** de dessous or de sous qch; **~ there** là-dessous; **in ~ 2 hours** en moins de 2 heures; **~ anaesthetic** sous anesthésie; **~ discussion** en discussion; **~ the circumstances** étant donné les circonstances; **~ repair** en (cours de) réparation

underage [ʌndər'eɪdʒ] adj qui n'a pas l'âge réglementaire

undercarriage ['ʌndəkærɪdʒ] n (Brit Aviat) train m d'atterrissage

undercharge [ʌndə'tʃɑ:dʒ] vt ne pas faire payer assez à

undercoat ['ʌndəkəut] n (paint) couche f de fond

undercover [ʌndə'kʌvər] adj secret(-ète), clandestin(e)

undercurrent ['ʌndəkʌrnt] n courant sous-jacent

undercut [ʌndə'kʌt] vt (irreg like: **cut**) vendre moins cher que

underdog ['ʌndədɔg] n opprimé m

underdone [ʌndə'dʌn] adj (Culin) saignant(e); (: pej) pas assez cuit(e)

underestimate ['ʌndər'estɪmeɪt] vt sous-estimer, mésestimer

underfed [ʌndə'fed] adj sous-alimenté(e)

underfoot [ʌndə'fut] adv sous les pieds

undergo [ʌndə'gəu] vt (irreg like: **go**) subir; (treatment) suivre; **the car is ~ing repairs** la voiture est en réparation

undergraduate [ʌndə'grædjuɪt] n étudiant(e) (qui prépare la licence) ▷ cpd: **~ courses** cours mpl préparant à la licence

underground ['ʌndəgraund] adj souterrain(e); (fig) clandestin(e) ▷ n (Brit: railway) métro m; (Pol) clandestinité f

undergrowth ['ʌndəgrəuθ] n broussailles fpl, sous-bois m

underhand [ʌndə'hænd], **underhanded** [ʌndə'hændɪd] adj (fig) sournois(e), en dessous

underlie [ʌndə'laɪ] vt (irreg like: **lie**) être à la base de; **the underlying cause** la cause sous-jacente

underline [ʌndə'laɪn] vt souligner

undermine [ʌndə'maɪn] vt saper, miner

underneath [ʌndə'ni:θ] adv (en) dessous ▷ prep sous, au-dessous de

underpaid [ʌndə'peɪd] adj sous-payé(e)

underpants ['ʌndəpænts] npl caleçon m, slip m

underpass ['ʌndəpɑ:s] n (Brit: for pedestrians) passage souterrain; (: for cars) passage inférieur

underprivileged [ʌndə'prɪvɪlɪdʒd] adj défavorisé(e)

underrate [ʌndə'reɪt] vt sous-estimer, mésestimer

underscore [ʌndə'skɔ:r] vt souligner

undershirt ['ʌndəʃə:t] n (US) tricot m de corps

undershorts ['ʌndəʃɔ:ts] npl (US) caleçon m, slip m

underside ['ʌndəsaɪd] n dessous m

underskirt ['ʌndəskə:t] n (Brit) jupon m

understand [ʌndə'stænd] vt, vi (irreg like: **stand**) comprendre; **I don't ~** je ne comprends pas; **I ~ that ...** je me suis laissé dire que ..., je crois comprendre que ...; **to make o.s. understood** se faire comprendre

understandable [ʌndə'stændəbl] adj compréhensible

understanding [ʌndə'stændɪŋ] adj compréhensif(-ive) ▷ n compréhension f; (agreement) accord m; **to come to an ~ with sb** s'entendre avec qn; **on the ~ that ...** à condition que ...

understatement ['ʌndəsteɪtmənt] n: **that's an ~** c'est (bien) peu dire, le terme est faible

understood [ʌndə'stud] pt, pp of **understand** ▷ adj entendu(e); (implied) sous-entendu(e)

understudy ['ʌndəstʌdɪ] n doublure f

undertake [ʌndə'teɪk] vt (irreg like: **take**) (job,

task) entreprendre; (*duty*) se charger de; **to ~ to do sth** s'engager à faire qch
undertaker ['ʌndəteɪkə'] *n* (*Brit*) entrepreneur *m* des pompes funèbres, croque-mort *m*
undertaking ['ʌndəteɪkɪŋ] *n* entreprise *f*; (*promise*) promesse *f*
undertone ['ʌndətəʊn] *n* (*low voice*): **in an ~** à mi-voix; (*of criticism etc*) nuance cachée
underwater [ʌndə'wɔːtə'] *adv* sous l'eau ▷ *adj* sous-marin(e)
underway [ʌndə'weɪ] *adj*: **to be ~** (*meeting, investigation*) être en cours
underwear ['ʌndəwɛə'] *n* sous-vêtements *mpl*; (*women's only*) dessous *mpl*
underwent [ʌndə'wɛnt] *pt of* **undergo**
underworld ['ʌndəwɜːld] *n* (*of crime*) milieu *m*, pègre *f*
underwrite [ʌndə'raɪt] *vt* (*Finance*) garantir; (*Insurance*) souscrire
undesirable [ʌndɪ'zaɪərəbl] *adj* peu souhaitable; (*person, effect*) indésirable
undies ['ʌndɪz] *npl* (*inf*) dessous *mpl*, lingerie *f*
undiplomatic ['ʌndɪplə'mætɪk] *adj* peu diplomatique, maladroit(e)
undisputed ['ʌndɪs'pjuːtɪd] *adj* incontesté(e)
undo [ʌn'duː] *vt* (*irreg like:* **do**) défaire
undoing [ʌn'duːɪŋ] *n* ruine *f*, perte *f*
undone [ʌn'dʌn] *pp of* **undo** ▷ *adj*: **to come ~** se défaire
undoubted [ʌn'dautɪd] *adj* indubitable, certain(e)
undoubtedly [ʌn'dautɪdlɪ] *adv* sans aucun doute
undress [ʌn'drɛs] *vi* se déshabiller ▷ *vt* déshabiller
undue [ʌn'djuː] *adj* indu(e), excessif(-ive)
undulating ['ʌndjuleɪtɪŋ] *adj* ondoyant(e), onduleux(-euse)
unduly [ʌn'djuːlɪ] *adv* trop, excessivement
unearth [ʌn'ɜːθ] *vt* déterrer; (*fig*) dénicher
unearthly [ʌn'ɜːθlɪ] *adj* surnaturel(le); (*hour*) indu(e), impossible
uneasy [ʌn'iːzɪ] *adj* mal à l'aise, gêné(e); (*worried*) inquiet(-ète); (*feeling*) désagréable; (*peace, truce*) fragile; **to feel ~ about doing sth** se sentir mal à l'aise à l'idée de faire qch
uneconomic ['ʌniːkə'nɔmɪk], **uneconomical** ['ʌniːkə'nɔmɪkl] *adj* peu économique; peu rentable
uneducated [ʌn'ɛdjukeɪtɪd] *adj* sans éducation
unemployed [ʌnɪm'plɔɪd] *adj* sans travail, au chômage ▷ *n*: **the ~** les chômeurs *mpl*
unemployment [ʌnɪm'plɔɪmənt] *n* chômage *m*
unemployment benefit, (*US*) **unemployment compensation** *n* allocation *f* de chômage
unending [ʌn'ɛndɪŋ] *adj* interminable
unequal [ʌn'iːkwəl] *adj* inégal(e)
unerring [ʌn'ɜːrɪŋ] *adj* infaillible, sûr(e)

uneven [ʌn'iːvn] *adj* inégal(e); (*quality, work*) irrégulier(-ière)
unexpected [ʌnɪk'spɛktɪd] *adj* inattendu(e), imprévu(e)
unexpectedly [ʌnɪk'spɛktɪdlɪ] *adv* (*succeed*) contre toute attente; (*arrive*) à l'improviste
unfailing [ʌn'feɪlɪŋ] *adj* inépuisable; infaillible
unfair [ʌn'fɛə'] *adj*: **~ (to)** injuste (envers); **it's ~ that ...** il n'est pas juste que ...
unfaithful [ʌn'feɪθful] *adj* infidèle
unfamiliar [ʌnfə'mɪlɪə'] *adj* étrange, inconnu(e); **to be ~ with sth** mal connaître qch
unfashionable [ʌn'fæʃnəbl] *adj* (*clothes*) démodé(e); (*place*) peu chic *inv*; (*district*) déshérité(e), pas à la mode
unfasten [ʌn'fɑːsn] *vt* défaire; (*belt, necklace*) détacher; (*open*) ouvrir
unfavourable, (*US*) **unfavorable** [ʌn'feɪvrəbl] *adj* défavorable
unfeeling [ʌn'fiːlɪŋ] *adj* insensible, dur(e)
unfinished [ʌn'fɪnɪʃt] *adj* inachevé(e)
unfit [ʌn'fɪt] *adj* (*physically: ill*) en mauvaise santé; (: *out of condition*) pas en forme; (*incompetent*): **~ (for)** impropre (à); (*work, service*) inapte (à)
unfold [ʌn'fəuld] *vt* déplier; (*fig*) révéler, exposer ▷ *vi* se dérouler
unforeseen ['ʌnfɔː'siːn] *adj* imprévu(e)
unforgettable [ʌnfə'gɛtəbl] *adj* inoubliable
unfortunate [ʌn'fɔːtʃnət] *adj* malheureux(-euse); (*event, remark*) malencontreux(-euse)
unfortunately [ʌn'fɔːtʃnətlɪ] *adv* malheureusement
unfounded [ʌn'faundɪd] *adj* sans fondement
unfriendly [ʌn'frɛndlɪ] *adj* peu aimable, froid(e), inimical(e)
unfurnished [ʌn'fɜːnɪʃt] *adj* non meublé(e)
ungainly [ʌn'geɪnlɪ] *adj* gauche, dégingandé(e)
ungodly [ʌn'gɔdlɪ] *adj* impie; **at an ~ hour** à une heure indue
ungrateful [ʌn'greɪtful] *adj* qui manque de reconnaissance, ingrat(e)
unhappiness [ʌn'hæpɪnɪs] *n* tristesse *f*, peine *f*
unhappy [ʌn'hæpɪ] *adj* triste, malheureux(-euse); (*unfortunate: remark etc*) malheureux(-euse); (*not pleased*): **~ with** mécontent(e) de, peu satisfait(e) de
unharmed [ʌn'hɑːmd] *adj* indemne, sain(e) et sauf/sauve
UNHCR *n abbr* (= *United Nations High Commission for Refugees*) HCR *m*
unhealthy [ʌn'hɛlθɪ] *adj* (*gen*) malsain(e); (*person*) maladif(-ive)
unheard-of [ʌn'hɜːdɔv] *adj* inouï(e), sans précédent
unhelpful [ʌn'hɛlpful] *adj* (*person*) peu serviable; (*advice*) peu utile

unhurt [ʌn'hə:t] *adj* indemne, sain(e) et sauf/sauve

unidentified [ʌnaɪ'dɛntɪfaɪd] *adj* non identifié(e); *see also* **UFO**

uniform ['ju:nɪfɔ:m] *n* uniforme *m* ▷ *adj* uniforme

unify ['ju:nɪfaɪ] *vt* unifier

unimportant [ʌnɪm'pɔ:tənt] *adj* sans importance

uninhabited [ʌnɪn'hæbɪtɪd] *adj* inhabité(e)

unintentional [ʌnɪn'tɛnʃənəl] *adj* involontaire

union ['ju:njən] *n* union *f*; (*also*: **trade ~**) syndicat *m* ▷ *cpd* du syndicat, syndical(e)

Union Jack *n* drapeau du Royaume-Uni

unique [ju:'ni:k] *adj* unique

unisex ['ju:nɪsɛks] *adj* unisexe

unison ['ju:nɪsn] *n*: **in ~** à l'unisson, en chœur

unit ['ju:nɪt] *n* unité *f*; (*section: of furniture etc*) élément *m*, bloc *m*; (*team, squad*) groupe *m*, service *m*; **production ~** atelier *m* de fabrication; **kitchen ~** élément de cuisine; **sink ~** bloc-évier *m*

unite [ju:'naɪt] *vt* unir ▷ *vi* s'unir

united [ju:'naɪtɪd] *adj* uni(e); (*country, party*) unifié(e); (*efforts*) conjugué(e)

United Kingdom *n* Royaume-Uni *m*

United Nations, United Nations Organization *n* (Organisation *f* des) Nations unies

United States, United States of America *n* États-Unis *mpl*

unit trust *n* (*Brit Comm*) fonds commun de placement, FCP *m*

unity ['ju:nɪtɪ] *n* unité *f*

universal [ju:nɪ'və:sl] *adj* universel(le)

universe ['ju:nɪvə:s] *n* univers *m*

university [ju:nɪ'və:sɪtɪ] *n* université *f* ▷ *cpd* (*student, professor*) d'université; (*education, year, degree*) universitaire

unjust [ʌn'dʒʌst] *adj* injuste

unkempt [ʌn'kɛmpt] *adj* mal tenu(e), débraillé(e); mal peigné(e)

unkind [ʌn'kaɪnd] *adj* peu gentil(le), méchant(e)

unknown [ʌn'nəun] *adj* inconnu(e); **~ to me** sans que je le sache; **~ quantity** (*Math, fig*) inconnue *f*

unlawful [ʌn'lɔ:ful] *adj* illégal(e)

unleaded [ʌn'lɛdɪd] *n* (*also*: **~ petrol**) essence *f* sans plomb

unleash [ʌn'li:ʃ] *vt* détacher; (*fig*) déchaîner, déclencher

unless [ʌn'lɛs] *conj*: **~ he leaves** à moins qu'il (ne) parte; **~ we leave** à moins de partir, à moins que nous (ne) partions; **~ otherwise stated** sauf indication contraire; **~ I am mistaken** si je ne me trompe

unlike [ʌn'laɪk] *adj* dissemblable, différent(e) ▷ *prep* à la différence de, contrairement à

unlikely [ʌn'laɪklɪ] *adj* (*result, event*) improbable; (*explanation*) invraisemblable

unlimited [ʌn'lɪmɪtɪd] *adj* illimité(e)

unlisted ['ʌn'lɪstɪd] *adj* (*US Tel*) sur la liste rouge; (*Stock Exchange*) non coté(e) en Bourse

unload [ʌn'ləud] *vt* décharger

unlock [ʌn'lɔk] *vt* ouvrir

unlucky [ʌn'lʌkɪ] *adj* (*person*) malchanceux(-euse); (*object, number*) qui porte malheur; **to be ~** (*person*) ne pas avoir de chance

unmarried [ʌn'mærɪd] *adj* célibataire

unmistakable, unmistakeable [ʌnmɪs'teɪkəbl] *adj* indubitable; qu'on ne peut pas ne pas reconnaître

unmitigated [ʌn'mɪtɪgeɪtɪd] *adj* non mitigé(e), absolu(e), pur(e)

unnatural [ʌn'nætʃrəl] *adj* non naturel(le); (*perversion*) contre nature

unnecessary [ʌn'nɛsəsərɪ] *adj* inutile, superflu(e)

unnoticed [ʌn'nəutɪst] *adj* inaperçu(e); **to go ~** passer inaperçu

UNO ['ju:nəu] *n abbr* = **United Nations Organization**

unobtainable [ʌnəb'teɪnəbl] *adj* (*Tel*) impossible à obtenir

unobtrusive [ʌnəb'tru:sɪv] *adj* discret(-ète)

unofficial [ʌnə'fɪʃl] *adj* (*news*) officieux(-euse), non officiel(le); (*strike*) ≈ sauvage

unorthodox [ʌn'ɔ:θədɔks] *adj* peu orthodoxe

unpack [ʌn'pæk] *vi* défaire sa valise, déballer ses affaires ▷ *vt* (*suitcase*) défaire; (*belongings*) déballer

unpaid [ʌn'peɪd] *adj* (*bill*) impayé(e); (*holiday*) non-payé(e), sans salaire; (*work*) non rétribué(e); (*worker*) bénévole

unpalatable [ʌn'pælətəbl] *adj* (*truth*) désagréable (à entendre)

unparalleled [ʌn'pærəlɛld] *adj* incomparable, sans égal

unpleasant [ʌn'plɛznt] *adj* déplaisant(e), désagréable

unplug [ʌn'plʌg] *vt* débrancher

unpopular [ʌn'pɔpjulə*r*] *adj* impopulaire; **to make o.s. ~ (with)** se rendre impopulaire (auprès de)

unprecedented [ʌn'prɛsɪdɛntɪd] *adj* sans précédent

unpredictable [ʌnprɪ'dɪktəbl] *adj* imprévisible

unprofessional [ʌnprə'fɛʃənl] *adj* (*conduct*) contraire à la déontologie

UNPROFOR [ʌn'prəufɔ:*r*] *n abbr* (= *United Nations Protection Force*) FORPRONU *f*

unprotected ['ʌnprə'tɛktɪd] *adj* (*sex*) non protégé(e)

unqualified [ʌn'kwɔlɪfaɪd] *adj* (*teacher*) non diplômé(e), sans titres; (*success*) sans réserve, total(e); (*disaster*) total(e)

unquestionably [ʌn'kwɛstʃənəblɪ] *adv* incontestablement

unravel [ʌn'rævl] *vt* démêler

unreal [ʌnˈrɪəl] adj irréel(le); (extraordinary) incroyable

unrealistic [ˈʌnrɪəˈlɪstɪk] adj (idea) irréaliste; (estimate) peu réaliste

unreasonable [ʌnˈriːznəbl] adj qui n'est pas raisonnable; **to make ~ demands on sb** exiger trop de qn

unrelated [ʌnrɪˈleɪtɪd] adj sans rapport; (people) sans lien de parenté

unreliable [ʌnrɪˈlaɪəbl] adj sur qui (or quoi) on ne peut pas compter, peu fiable

unremitting [ʌnrɪˈmɪtɪŋ] adj inlassable, infatigable, acharné(e)

unreservedly [ʌnrɪˈzɜːvɪdlɪ] adv sans réserve

unrest [ʌnˈrest] n agitation f, troubles mpl

unroll [ʌnˈrəʊl] vt dérouler

unruly [ʌnˈruːlɪ] adj indiscipliné(e)

unsafe [ʌnˈseɪf] adj (in danger) en danger; (journey, car) dangereux(-euse); (method) hasardeux(-euse); **~ to drink/eat** non potable/comestible

unsaid [ʌnˈsed] adj: **to leave sth ~** passer qch sous silence

unsatisfactory [ˈʌnsætɪsˈfæktərɪ] adj peu satisfaisant(e), qui laisse à désirer

unsavoury, (US) **unsavory** [ʌnˈseɪvərɪ] adj (fig) peu recommandable, répugnant(e)

unscathed [ʌnˈskeɪðd] adj indemne

unscrew [ʌnˈskruː] vt dévisser

unscrupulous [ʌnˈskruːpjʊləs] adj sans scrupules

unsettled [ʌnˈsetld] adj (restless) perturbé(e); (unpredictable) instable; incertain(e); (not finalized) non résolu(e)

unsettling [ʌnˈsetlɪŋ] adj qui a un effet perturbateur

unshaven [ʌnˈʃeɪvn] adj non or mal rasé(e)

unsightly [ʌnˈsaɪtlɪ] adj disgracieux(-euse), laid(e)

unskilled [ʌnˈskɪld] adj: **~ worker** manœuvre m

unspeakable [ʌnˈspiːkəbl] adj indicible; (awful) innommable

unspoiled [ˈʌnˈspɔɪld], **unspoilt** [ˈʌnˈspɔɪlt] adj (place) non dégradé(e)

unstable [ʌnˈsteɪbl] adj instable

unsteady [ʌnˈstedɪ] adj mal assuré(e), chancelant(e), instable

unstuck [ʌnˈstʌk] adj: **to come ~** se décoller; (fig) faire fiasco

unsuccessful [ʌnsəkˈsesful] adj (attempt) infructueux(-euse); (writer, proposal) qui n'a pas de succès; (marriage) malheureux(-euse), qui ne réussit pas; **to be ~** (in attempting sth) ne pas réussir; ne pas avoir de succès; (application) ne pas être retenu(e)

unsuitable [ʌnˈsuːtəbl] adj qui ne convient pas, peu approprié(e); (time) inopportun(e)

unsure [ʌnˈʃʊəʳ] adj pas sûr(e); **to be ~ of o.s.** ne pas être sûr de soi, manquer de confiance en soi

unsuspecting [ʌnsəˈspektɪŋ] adj qui ne se méfie pas

unsympathetic [ˈʌnsɪmpəˈθetɪk] adj hostile; (unpleasant) antipathique; **~ to** indifférent(e) à

untapped [ʌnˈtæpt] adj (resources) inexploité(e)

unthinkable [ʌnˈθɪŋkəbl] adj impensable, inconcevable

untidy [ʌnˈtaɪdɪ] adj (room) en désordre; (appearance, person) débraillé(e); (person: in character) sans ordre, désordonné; débraillé; (work) peu soigné(e)

untie [ʌnˈtaɪ] vt (knot, parcel) défaire; (prisoner, dog) détacher

until [ənˈtɪl] prep jusqu'à; (after negative) avant ▷ conj jusqu'à ce que+sub, en attendant que+sub; (in past, after negative) avant que+sub; **~ he comes** jusqu'à ce qu'il vienne, jusqu'à son arrivée; **~ now** jusqu'à présent, jusqu'ici; **~ then** jusque-là; **from morning ~ night** du matin au soir or jusqu'au soir

untimely [ʌnˈtaɪmlɪ] adj inopportun(e); (death) prématuré(e)

untold [ʌnˈtəʊld] adj incalculable; indescriptible

untoward [ʌntəˈwɔːd] adj fâcheux(-euse), malencontreux(-euse)

untrue [ʌnˈtruː] adj (statement) faux/fausse

unused¹ [ʌnˈjuːzd] adj (new) neuf/neuve

unused² [ʌnˈjuːst] adj: **to be ~ to sth/to doing sth** ne pas avoir l'habitude de qch/de faire qch

unusual [ʌnˈjuːʒʊəl] adj insolite, exceptionnel(le), rare

unusually [ʌnˈjuːʒʊəlɪ] adv exceptionnellement, particulièrement

unveil [ʌnˈveɪl] vt dévoiler

unwanted [ʌnˈwɒntɪd] adj (child, pregnancy) non désiré(e); (clothes etc) à donner

unwelcome [ʌnˈwelkəm] adj importun(e); **to feel ~** se sentir de trop

unwell [ʌnˈwel] adj indisposé(e), souffrant(e); **to feel ~** ne pas se sentir bien

unwieldy [ʌnˈwiːldɪ] adj difficile à manier

unwilling [ʌnˈwɪlɪŋ] adj: **to be ~ to do** ne pas vouloir faire

unwillingly [ʌnˈwɪlɪŋlɪ] adv à contrecœur, contre son gré

unwind [ʌnˈwaɪnd] (irreg like: **wind**) vt dérouler ▷ vi (relax) se détendre

unwise [ʌnˈwaɪz] adj imprudent(e), peu judicieux(-euse)

unwitting [ʌnˈwɪtɪŋ] adj involontaire

unwittingly [ʌnˈwɪtɪŋlɪ] adv involontairement

unworkable [ʌnˈwɜːkəbl] adj (plan etc) inexploitable

unworthy [ʌnˈwɜːðɪ] adj indigne

unwrap [ʌnˈræp] vt défaire; ouvrir

unwritten [ʌnˈrɪtn] adj (agreement) tacite

unzip [ʌnˈzɪp] vt ouvrir (la fermeture éclair de); (Comput) dézipper

u

KEYWORD

up [ʌp] *prep*: **he went up the stairs/the hill** il a monté l'escalier/la colline; **the cat was up a tree** le chat était dans un arbre; **they live further up the street** ils habitent plus haut dans la rue; **go up that road and turn left** remontez la rue et tournez à gauche
▷ *vi* (*inf*): **she upped and left** elle a fichu le camp sans plus attendre
▷ *adv* **1** en haut; en l'air; (*upwards, higher*): **up in the sky/the mountains** (là-haut) dans le ciel/les montagnes; **put it a bit higher up** mettez-le un peu plus haut; **to stand up** (*get up*) se lever, se mettre debout; (*be standing*) être debout; **up there** là-haut; **up above** au-dessus; **"this side up"** "haut"
2: **to be up** (*out of bed*) être levé(e); (*prices*) avoir augmenté or monté; (*finished*): **when the year was up** à la fin de l'année; **time's up** c'est l'heure
3: **up to** (*as far as*) jusqu'à; **up to now** jusqu'à présent
4: **to be up to** (*depending on*): **it's up to you** c'est à vous de décider; (*equal to*): **he's not up to it** (*job, task etc*) il n'en est pas capable; (*inf: be doing*): **what is he up to?** qu'est-ce qu'il peut bien faire?
5 (*phrases*): **he's well up in** or **on ...** (*Brit: knowledgeable*) il s'y connaît en ...; **up with Leeds United!** vive Leeds United!; **what's up?** (*inf*) qu'est-ce qui ne va pas?; **what's up with him?** (*inf*) qu'est-ce qui lui arrive?
▷ *n*: **ups and downs** hauts et bas *mpl*

up-and-coming [ʌpənd'kʌmɪŋ] *adj* plein(e) d'avenir or de promesses
upbringing ['ʌpbrɪŋɪŋ] *n* éducation *f*
update [ʌp'deɪt] *vt* mettre à jour
upfront [ʌp'frʌnt] *adj* (*open*) franc/franche ▷ *adv* (*pay*) d'avance; **to be ~ about sth** ne rien cacher de qch
upgrade [ʌp'greɪd] *vt* (*person*) promouvoir; (*job*) revaloriser; (*property, equipment*) moderniser
upheaval [ʌp'hiːvl] *n* bouleversement *m*; (*in room*) branle-bas *m*; (*event*) crise *f*
uphill [ʌp'hɪl] *adj* difficile, pénible; (*fig: task*) difficile, pénible ▷ *adv* (*face, look*) en amont, vers l'amont; (*go, move*) vers le haut, en haut; **to go ~ monter**
uphold [ʌp'həʊld] *vt* (*irreg like:* **hold**) maintenir; soutenir
upholstery [ʌp'həʊlstərɪ] *n* rembourrage *m*; (*cover*) tissu *m* d'ameublement; (*of car*) garniture *f*
upkeep ['ʌpkiːp] *n* entretien *m*
upmarket [ʌp'mɑːkɪt] *adj* (*product*) haut de gamme *inv*; (*area*) chic *inv*
upon [ə'pɒn] *prep* sur
upper ['ʌpə*] *adj* supérieur(e); du dessus ▷ *n* (*of shoe*) empeigne *f*

upper class *n*: **the ~ =** la haute bourgeoisie
upper-class [ʌpə'klɑːs] *adj* de la haute société, aristocratique; (*district*) élégant(e), huppé(e); (*accent, attitude*) caractéristique des classes supérieures
upper hand *n*: **to have the ~** avoir le dessus
uppermost ['ʌpəməʊst] *adj* le/la plus haut(e), en dessus; **it was ~ in my mind** j'y pensais avant tout autre chose
upper sixth *n* terminale *f*
upright ['ʌpraɪt] *adj* droit(e); (*fig*) droit, honnête ▷ *n* montant *m*
uprising ['ʌpraɪzɪŋ] *n* soulèvement *m*, insurrection *f*
uproar ['ʌprɔː*] *n* tumulte *m*, vacarme *m*; (*protests*) protestations *fpl*
uproot [ʌp'ruːt] *vt* déraciner
upset *n* ['ʌpsɛt] dérangement *m* ▷ *vt* [ʌp'sɛt] (*irreg like:* **set**) (*glass etc*) renverser; (*plan*) déranger; (*person: offend*) contrarier; (*: grieve*) faire de la peine à; bouleverser ▷ *adj* [ʌp'sɛt] contrarié(e); peiné(e); (*stomach*) détraqué(e), dérangé(e); **to get ~** (*sad*) devenir triste; (*offended*) se vexer; **to have a stomach ~** (*Brit*) avoir une indigestion
upshot ['ʌpʃɒt] *n* résultat *m*; **the ~ of it all was that ...** il a résulté de tout cela que ...
upside down [ʌpsaɪd-] *adv* à l'envers; **to turn sth ~** (*fig: place*) mettre sens dessus dessous
upstairs [ʌp'stɛəz] *adv* en haut ▷ *adj* (*room*) du dessus, d'en haut ▷ *n*: **the ~** l'étage *m*; **there's no ~** il n'y a pas d'étage
upstart ['ʌpstɑːt] *n* parvenu(e)
upstream [ʌp'striːm] *adv* en amont
uptake ['ʌpteɪk] *n*: **he is quick/slow on the ~** il comprend vite/est lent à comprendre
uptight [ʌp'taɪt] *adj* (*inf*) très tendu(e), crispé(e)
up-to-date [ʌptə'deɪt] *adj* moderne; (*information*) très récent(e)
upturn ['ʌptəːn] *n* (*in economy*) reprise *f*
upward ['ʌpwəd] *adj* ascendant(e); vers le haut ▷ *adv* vers le haut; (*more than*): **~ of** plus de; **and ~** et plus, et au-dessus
upwards ['ʌpwədz] *adv* vers le haut; (*more than*): **~ of** plus de; **and ~** et plus, et au-dessus
uranium [juə'reɪnɪəm] *n* uranium *m*
Uranus [juə'reɪnəs] *n* Uranus *f*
urban ['əːbən] *adj* urbain(e)
urban clearway *n* rue *f* à stationnement interdit
urbane [əː'beɪn] *adj* urbain(e), courtois(e)
urchin ['əːtʃɪn] *n* gosse *m*, garnement *m*
urge [əːdʒ] *n* besoin (impératif), envie (pressante) ▷ *vt* (*caution etc*) recommander avec insistance; (*person*): **to ~ sb to do** exhorter qn à faire, pousser qn à faire, recommander vivement à qn de faire; **urge on** *vt* pousser, presser
urgency ['əːdʒənsɪ] *n* urgence *f*; (*of tone*) insistance *f*

urgent ['əːdʒənt] *adj* urgent(e); (*plea, tone*) pressant(e)

urinal ['juərɪnl] *n* (*Brit: place*) urinoir *m*

urinate ['juərɪneɪt] *vi* uriner

urine ['juərɪn] *n* urine *f*

URL *abbr* (= *uniform resource locator*) URL *f*

urn [əːn] *n* urne *f*; (*also*: **tea ~**) fontaine *f* à thé

US *n abbr* = **United States**

us [ʌs] *pron* nous; *see also* **me**

USA *n abbr* = **United States of America**; (*Mil*) = **United States Army**

use *n* [juːs] emploi *m*, utilisation *f*; usage *m*; (*usefulness*) utilité *f* ▷ *vt* [juːz] se servir de, utiliser, employer; **in ~** en usage; **out of ~** hors d'usage; **to be of ~** servir, être utile; **to make ~ of sth** utiliser qch; **ready for ~** prêt à l'emploi; **it's no ~** ça ne sert à rien; **to have the ~ of** avoir l'usage de; **what's this ~d for?** à quoi est-ce que ça sert?; **she ~d to do it** elle le faisait (autrefois), elle avait coutume de le faire; **to be ~d to** avoir l'habitude de, être habitué(e) à; **to get ~d to** s'habituer à; **use up** *vt* finir, épuiser; (*food*) consommer

used [juːzd] *adj* (*car*) d'occasion

useful ['juːsful] *adj* utile; **to come in ~** être utile

usefulness ['juːsfəlnɪs] *n* utilité *f*

useless ['juːslɪs] *adj* inutile; (*inf: person*) nul(le)

user ['juːzəʳ] *n* utilisateur(-trice), usager *m*

user-friendly ['juːzə'frendlɪ] *adj* convivial(e), facile d'emploi

username ['juːzəneɪm] *n* nom *m* d'utilisateur

usher [ʌʃəʳ] *n* placeur *m* ▷ *vt*: **to ~ sb in** faire entrer qn

usherette [ʌʃə'rɛt] *n* (*in cinema*) ouvreuse *f*

usual ['juːʒuəl] *adj* habituel(le); **as ~** comme d'habitude

usually ['juːʒuəlɪ] *adv* d'habitude, d'ordinaire

utensil [juː'tɛnsl] *n* ustensile *m*; **kitchen ~s** batterie *f* de cuisine

uterus ['juːtərəs] *n* utérus *m*

utility [juː'tɪlɪtɪ] *n* utilité *f*; (*also*: **public ~**) service public

utility room *n* buanderie *f*

utilize ['juːtɪlaɪz] *vt* utiliser; (*make good use of*) exploiter

utmost ['ʌtməust] *adj* extrême, le/la plus grand(e) ▷ *n*: **to do one's ~** faire tout son possible; **of the ~ importance** d'une importance capitale, de la plus haute importance

utter ['ʌtəʳ] *adj* total(e), complet(-ète) ▷ *vt* prononcer, proférer; (*sounds*) émettre

utterance ['ʌtrns] *n* paroles *fpl*

utterly ['ʌtəlɪ] *adv* complètement, totalement

U-turn ['juː'təːn] *n* demi-tour *m*; (*fig*) volte-face *f inv*

v. *abbr* = **verse**; (= *vide*) v.; (= *versus*) vs; (= *volt*) V

vacancy ['veɪkənsɪ] *n* (*Brit: job*) poste vacant; (*room*) chambre *f* disponible; **"no vacancies"** "complet"

vacant ['veɪkənt] *adj* (*post*) vacant(e); (*seat etc*) libre, disponible; (*expression*) distrait(e)

vacate [və'keɪt] *vt* quitter

vacation [və'keɪʃən] *n* (*esp US*) vacances *fpl*; **to take a ~** prendre des vacances; **on ~** en vacances

vacationer [və'keɪʃənəʳ], (*US*) **vacationist** [və'keɪʃənɪst] *n* vacancier(-ière)

vaccinate ['væksɪneɪt] *vt* vacciner

vaccination [væksɪ'neɪʃən] *n* vaccination *f*

vaccine ['væksiːn] *n* vaccin *m*

vacuum ['vækjum] *n* vide *m*

vacuum cleaner *n* aspirateur *m*

vacuum-packed ['vækjumpækt] *adj* emballé(e) sous vide

vagina [və'dʒaɪnə] *n* vagin *m*

vagrant ['veɪgrənt] *n* vagabond(e), mendiant(e)

vague [veɪg] *adj* vague, imprécis(e); (*blurred: photo, memory*) flou(e); **I haven't the ~st idea** je n'en ai pas la moindre idée

vaguely ['veɪglɪ] *adv* vaguement

vain [veɪn] *adj* (*useless*) vain(e); (*conceited*) vaniteux(-euse); **in ~** en vain

valentine ['væləntaɪn] *n* (*also*: **~ card**) carte *f* de la Saint-Valentin

Valentine's Day ['væləntaɪnz-] *n* Saint-Valentin *f*

valiant ['væliənt] *adj* vaillant(e),
courageux(-euse)

valid ['vælid] *adj* (*document*) valide, valable;
(*excuse*) valable

valley ['væli] *n* vallée *f*

valour, (US) **valor** ['vælə^r] *n* courage *m*

valuable ['væljuəbl] *adj* (*jewel*) de grande
valeur; (*time, help*) précieux(-euse)

valuables ['væljuəblz] *npl* objets *mpl* de
valeur

valuation [vælju'eiʃən] *n* évaluation *f*,
expertise *f*

value ['vælju:] *n* valeur *f* ▷ *vt* (*fix price*)
évaluer, expertiser; (*appreciate*) apprécier;
(*cherish*) tenir à; **values** *npl* (*principles*)
valeurs *fpl*; **you get good ~ (for money) in
that shop** vous en avez pour votre argent
dans ce magasin; **to lose (in) ~** (*currency*)
baisser; (*property*) se déprécier; **to gain (in) ~**
(*currency*) monter; (*property*) prendre de la
valeur; **to be of great ~ to sb** (*fig*) être très
utile à qn

value added tax [-'ædid-] *n* (*Brit*) taxe *f* à la
valeur ajoutée

valued ['vælju:d] *adj* (*appreciated*) estimé(e)

valve [vælv] *n* (*in machine*) soupape *f*; (*on tyre*)
valve *f*; (*in radio*) lampe *f*; (*Med*) valve, valvule *f*

vampire ['væmpaiə^r] *n* vampire *m*

van [væn] *n* (*Aut*) camionnette *f*; (*Brit Rail*)
fourgon *m*

vandal ['vændl] *n* vandale *m/f*

vandalism ['vændəlizəm] *n* vandalisme *m*

vandalize ['vændəlaiz] *vt* saccager

vanguard ['vænga:d] *n* avant-garde *m*

vanilla [və'nilə] *n* vanille *f* ▷ *cpd* (*ice cream*) à la
vanille

vanish ['væniʃ] *vi* disparaître

vanity ['væniti] *n* vanité *f*

vantage ['vɑ:ntidʒ] *n*: **~ point** bonne
position

vapour, (US) **vapor** ['veipə^r] *n* vapeur *f*;
(*on window*) buée *f*

variable ['vɛəriəbl] *adj* variable; (*mood*)
changeant(e) ▷ *n* variable *f*

variance ['vɛəriəns] *n*: **to be at ~ (with)** être
en désaccord (avec); (*facts*) être en
contradiction (avec)

variant ['vɛəriənt] *n* variante *f*

variation [vɛəri'eiʃən] *n* variation *f*; (*in
opinion*) changement *m*

varicose ['værikəus] *adj*: **~ veins** varices *fpl*

varied ['vɛərid] *adj* varié(e), divers(e)

variety [və'raiəti] *n* variété *f*; (*quantity*)
nombre *m*, quantité *f*; **a wide ~ of ...** une
quantité *or* un grand nombre de ...
(différent(e)s *or* divers(es)); **for a ~ of
reasons** pour diverses raisons

variety show *n* (spectacle *m* de) variétés *fpl*

various ['vɛəriəs] *adj* divers(e), différent(e);
(*several*) divers, plusieurs; **at ~ times** (*different*)
en diverses occasions; (*several*) à plusieurs
reprises

varnish ['vɑ:niʃ] *n* vernis *m*; (*for nails*) vernis
(à ongles) ▷ *vt* vernir; **to ~ one's nails** se
vernir les ongles

vary ['vɛəri] *vt, vi* varier, changer; **to ~ with *or*
according to** varier selon

vase [vɑ:z] *n* vase *m*

Vaseline® ['væsili:n] *n* vaseline *f*

vast [vɑ:st] *adj* vaste, immense; (*amount,
success*) énorme

VAT [væt] *n abbr* (*Brit*: = value added tax) TVA *f*

vat [væt] *n* cuve *f*

vault [vɔ:lt] *n* (*of roof*) voûte *f*; (*tomb*) caveau *m*;
(*in bank*) salle *f* des coffres; chambre forte;
(*jump*) saut *m* ▷ *vt* (*also*: **~ over**) sauter (d'un
bond)

vaunted ['vɔ:ntid] *adj*: **much-~** tant
célébré(e)

VCR *n abbr* = **video cassette recorder**

VD *n abbr* = **venereal disease**

VDU *n abbr* = **visual display unit**

veal [vi:l] *n* veau *m*

veer [viə^r] *vi* tourner; (*car, ship*) virer

vegan ['vi:gən] *n* végétalien(ne)

vegeburger ['vedʒibə:gə^r] *n* burger
végétarien

vegetable ['vedʒtəbl] *n* légume *m* ▷ *adj*
végétal(e)

vegetarian [vedʒi'tɛəriən] *adj, n*
végétarien(ne); **do you have any ~ dishes?**
avez-vous des plats végétariens?

vegetation [vedʒi'teiʃən] *n* végétation *f*

vehement ['vi:imənt] *adj* violent(e),
impétueux(-euse); (*impassioned*) ardent(e)

vehicle ['vi:ikl] *n* véhicule *m*

veil [veil] *n* voile *m* ▷ *vt* voiler; **under a ~ of
secrecy** (*fig*) dans le plus grand secret

vein [vein] *n* veine *f*; (*on leaf*) nervure *f*; (*fig:
mood*) esprit *m*

Velcro® ['velkrəu] *n* velcro® *m*

velocity [vi'lɔsiti] *n* vitesse *f*, vélocité *f*

velvet ['velvit] *n* velours *m*

vending machine ['vendiŋ-] *n* distributeur
m automatique

vendor ['vendə^r] *n* vendeur(-euse); **street ~**
marchand ambulant

veneer [və'niə^r] *n* placage *m* de bois; (*fig*)
vernis *m*

venereal [vi'niəriəl] *adj*: **~ disease** maladie
vénérienne

Venetian blind [vi'ni:ʃən-] *n* store vénitien

vengeance ['vendʒəns] *n* vengeance *f*; **with
a ~** (*fig*) vraiment, pour de bon

venison ['venisn] *n* venaison *f*

venom ['venəm] *n* venin *m*

vent [vent] *n* conduit *m* d'aération; (*in dress,
jacket*) fente *f* ▷ *vt* (*fig: one's feelings*) donner
libre cours à

ventilation [venti'leiʃən] *n* ventilation *f*,
aération *f*

ventilator ['ventileitə^r] *n* ventilateur *m*

ventriloquist [ven'triləkwist] *n*
ventriloque *m/f*

venture ['vɛntʃəʳ] n entreprise f ▷ vt risquer, hasarder ▷ vi s'aventurer, se risquer; **a business ~** une entreprise commerciale; **to ~ to do sth** se risquer à faire qch

venue ['vɛnjuː] n lieu m; (of conference etc) lieu de la réunion (or manifestation etc); (of match) lieu de la rencontre

Venus ['viːnəs] n (planet) Vénus f

verb [vəːb] n verbe m

verbal ['vəːbl] adj verbal(e); (translation) littéral(e)

verbatim [vəː'beɪtɪm] adj, adv mot pour mot

verdict ['vəːdɪkt] n verdict m; **~ of guilty/not guilty** verdict de culpabilité/de non-culpabilité

verge [vəːdʒ] n bord m; **"soft ~s"** (Brit) "accotements non stabilisés"; **on the ~ of doing** sur le point de faire; **verge on** vt fus approcher de

verify ['vɛrɪfaɪ] vt vérifier

vermin ['vəːmɪn] npl animaux mpl nuisibles; (insects) vermine f

vermouth ['vəːməθ] n vermouth m

versatile ['vəːsətaɪl] adj polyvalent(e)

verse [vəːs] n vers mpl; (stanza) strophe f; (in Bible) verset m; **in ~** en vers

version ['vəːʃən] n version f

versus ['vəːsəs] prep contre

vertical ['vəːtɪkl] adj vertical(e) ▷ n verticale f

vertigo ['vəːtɪɡəu] n vertige m; **to suffer from ~** avoir des vertiges

verve [vəːv] n brio m; enthousiasme m

very ['vɛrɪ] adv très ▷ adj: **the ~ book which** le livre même que; **the ~ thought (of it) ...** rien que d'y penser ...; **at the ~ end** tout à la fin; **the ~ last** tout dernier; **at the ~ least** au moins; **~ well** très bien; **~ little** très peu; **~ much** beaucoup

vessel ['vɛsl] n (Anat, Naut) vaisseau m; (container) récipient m; see also **blood**

vest [vɛst] n (Brit: underwear) tricot m de corps; (US: waistcoat) gilet m ▷ vt: **to ~ sb with sth, to ~ sth in sb** investir qn de qch

vested interest n: **to have a ~ in doing** avoir tout intérêt à faire; **vested interests** npl (Comm) droits acquis

vet [vɛt] n abbr (Brit: = veterinary surgeon) vétérinaire m/f; (US: = veteran) ancien(ne) combattant(e) ▷ vt examiner minutieusement; (text) revoir; (candidate) se renseigner soigneusement sur, soumettre à une enquête approfondie

veteran ['vɛtərn] n vétéran m; (also: **war ~**) ancien combattant ▷ adj: **she's a ~ campaigner for ...** cela fait très longtemps qu'elle lutte pour ...

veterinary surgeon ['vɛtrɪnərɪ-] (Brit) n vétérinaire m/f

veto ['viːtəu] n (pl vetoes) veto m ▷ vt opposer son veto à; **to put a ~ on** mettre (or opposer) son veto à

vex [vɛks] vt fâcher, contrarier

vexed [vɛkst] adj (question) controversé(e)

via ['vaɪə] prep par, via

viable ['vaɪəbl] adj viable

vibrate [vaɪ'breɪt] vi: **to ~ (with)** vibrer (de); (resound) retentir (de)

vibration [vaɪ'breɪʃən] n vibration f

vicar ['vɪkəʳ] n pasteur m (de l'Église anglicane)

vicarage ['vɪkərɪdʒ] n presbytère m

vicarious [vɪ'kɛərɪəs] adj (pleasure, experience) indirect(e)

vice [vaɪs] n (evil) vice m; (Tech) étau m

vice- [vaɪs] prefix vice-

vice-chairman [vaɪs'tʃɛəmən] irreg n vice-président(e)

vice squad n ≈ brigade mondaine

vice versa ['vaɪsɪ'vəːsə] adv vice versa

vicinity [vɪ'sɪnɪtɪ] n environs mpl, alentours mpl

vicious ['vɪʃəs] adj (remark) cruel(le), méchant(e); (blow) brutal(e); (dog) méchant(e), dangereux(-euse); **a ~ circle** un cercle vicieux

victim ['vɪktɪm] n victime f; **to be the ~ of** être victime de

victor ['vɪktəʳ] n vainqueur m

Victorian [vɪk'tɔːrɪən] adj victorien(ne)

victorious [vɪk'tɔːrɪəs] adj victorieux(-euse)

victory ['vɪktərɪ] n victoire f; **to win a ~ over sb** remporter une victoire sur qn

video ['vɪdɪəu] n (video film) vidéo f; (also: **~ cassette**) vidéocassette f; (also: **~ cassette recorder**) magnétoscope m ▷ vt (with recorder) enregistrer; (with camera) filmer ▷ cpd vidéo inv

video camera n caméra f vidéo inv

video cassette recorder n = **video recorder**

video game n jeu m vidéo inv

videophone n vidéophone m

video recorder n magnétoscope m

video shop n vidéoclub m

video tape n bande f vidéo inv; (cassette) vidéocassette f

video wall n mur m d'images vidéo

vie [vaɪ] vi: **to ~ with** lutter avec, rivaliser avec

Vienna [vɪ'ɛnə] n Vienne

Vietnam, Viet Nam ['vjɛt'næm] n Viêt-nam or Vietnam m

Vietnamese [vjɛtnə'miːz] adj vietnamien(ne) ▷ n (pl inv) Vietnamien(ne); (Ling) vietnamien m

view [vjuː] n vue f; (opinion) avis m, vue ▷ vt voir, regarder; (situation) considérer; (house) visiter; **on ~** (in museum etc) exposé(e); **in full ~ of sb** sous les yeux de qn; **to be within ~ (of sth)** être à portée de vue (de qch); **an overall ~ of the situation** une vue d'ensemble de la situation; **in my ~** à mon avis; **in ~ of the fact that** étant donné que; **with a ~ to doing sth** dans l'intention de faire qch

viewer ['vjuːəʳ] n (viewfinder) viseur m; (small projector) visionneuse f; (TV) téléspectateur(-trice)

viewfinder ['vjuːfaɪndə'] *n* viseur *m*
viewpoint ['vjuːpɔɪnt] *n* point *m* de vue
vigilant ['vɪdʒɪlənt] *adj* vigilant(e)
vigorous ['vɪgərəs] *adj* vigoureux(-euse)
vile [vaɪl] *adj* (*action*) vil(e); (*smell, food*) abominable; (*temper*) massacrant(e)
villa ['vɪlə] *n* villa *f*
village ['vɪlɪdʒ] *n* village *m*
villager ['vɪlɪdʒə'] *n* villageois(e)
villain ['vɪlən] *n* (*scoundrel*) scélérat *m*; (*Brit: criminal*) bandit *m*; (*in novel etc*) traître *m*
vinaigrette [vɪneɪ'grɛt] *n* vinaigrette *f*
vindicate ['vɪndɪkeɪt] *vt* défendre avec succès; justifier
vindictive [vɪn'dɪktɪv] *adj* vindicatif(-ive), rancunier(-ière)
vine [vaɪn] *n* vigne *f*; (*climbing plant*) plante grimpante
vinegar ['vɪnɪgə'] *n* vinaigre *m*
vineyard ['vɪnjɑːd] *n* vignoble *m*
vintage ['vɪntɪdʒ] *n* (*year*) année *f*, millésime *m* ▷ *cpd* (*car*) d'époque; (*wine*) de grand cru; **the 1970 ~** le millésime 1970
vinyl ['vaɪnl] *n* vinyle *m*
viola [vɪ'əulə] *n* alto *m*
violate ['vaɪəleɪt] *vt* violer
violation [vaɪə'leɪʃən] *n* violation *f*; **in ~ of** (*rule, law*) en infraction à, en violation de
violence ['vaɪələns] *n* violence *f*; (*Pol etc*) incidents violents
violent ['vaɪələnt] *adj* violent(e); **a ~ dislike of sb/sth** une aversion profonde pour qn/qch
violet ['vaɪələt] *adj* (*colour*) violet(te) ▷ *n* (*plant*) violette *f*
violin [vaɪə'lɪn] *n* violon *m*
violinist [vaɪə'lɪnɪst] *n* violoniste *m/f*
VIP *n abbr* (= *very important person*) VIP *m*
virgin ['vəːdʒɪn] *n* vierge *f* ▷ *adj* vierge; **she is a ~** elle est vierge; **the Blessed V~** la Sainte Vierge
Virgo ['vəːgəu] *n* la Vierge; **to be ~** être de la Vierge
virile ['vɪraɪl] *adj* viril(e)
virtual ['vəːtjuəl] *adj* (*Comput, Physics*) virtuel(le); (*in effect*): **it's a ~ impossibility** c'est quasiment impossible; **the ~ leader** le chef dans la pratique
virtually ['vəːtjuəlɪ] *adv* (*almost*) pratiquement; **it is ~ impossible** c'est quasiment impossible
virtual reality *n* (*Comput*) réalité virtuelle
virtue ['vəːtjuː] *n* vertu *f*; (*advantage*) mérite *m*, avantage *m*; **by ~ of** en vertu *or* raison de
virtuous ['vəːtjuəs] *adj* vertueux(-euse)
virus ['vaɪərəs] *n* (*Med, Comput*) virus *m*
visa ['viːzə] *n* visa *m*
vise [vaɪs] *n* (*US Tech*) = **vice**
visibility [vɪzɪ'bɪlɪtɪ] *n* visibilité *f*
visible ['vɪzəbl] *adj* visible; **~ exports/imports** exportations/importations *fpl* visibles
vision ['vɪʒən] *n* (*sight*) vue *f*, vision *f*; (*foresight, in dream*) vision

visit ['vɪzɪt] *n* visite *f*; (*stay*) séjour *m* ▷ *vt* (*person; US: also: ~ with*) rendre visite à; (*place*) visiter; **on a private/official ~** en visite privée/officielle
visiting hours *npl* heures *fpl* de visite
visitor ['vɪzɪtə'] *n* visiteur(-euse); (*to one's house*) invité(e); (*in hotel*) client(e)
visitor centre, visitor center (*US*) *n* hall *m* or centre *m* d'accueil
visor ['vaɪzə'] *n* visière *f*
vista ['vɪstə] *n* vue *f*, perspective *f*
visual ['vɪzjuəl] *adj* visuel(le)
visual aid *n* support visuel (pour l'enseignement)
visual display unit *n* console *f* de visualisation, visuel *m*
visualize ['vɪzjuəlaɪz] *vt* se représenter; (*foresee*) prévoir
visually-impaired ['vɪzjuəlɪɪm'pɛəd] *adj* malvoyant(e)
vital ['vaɪtl] *adj* vital(e); **of ~ importance (to sb/sth)** d'une importance capitale (pour qn/qch)
vitality [vaɪ'tælɪtɪ] *n* vitalité *f*
vitally ['vaɪtəlɪ] *adv* extrêmement
vital statistics *npl* (*of population*) statistiques *fpl* démographiques; (*inf: woman's*) mensurations *fpl*
vitamin ['vɪtəmɪn] *n* vitamine *f*
vivacious [vɪ'veɪʃəs] *adj* animé(e), qui a de la vivacité
vivid ['vɪvɪd] *adj* (*account*) frappant(e), vivant(e); (*light, imagination*) vif/vive
vividly ['vɪvɪdlɪ] *adv* (*describe*) d'une manière vivante; (*remember*) de façon précise
V-neck ['viːnɛk] *n* décolleté *m* en V
vocabulary [vəu'kæbjulərɪ] *n* vocabulaire *m*
vocal ['vəukl] *adj* vocal(e); (*articulate*) qui n'hésite pas à s'exprimer, qui sait faire entendre ses opinions; **vocals** *npl* voix *fpl*
vocal cords *npl* cordes vocales
vocation [vəu'keɪʃən] *n* vocation *f*
vocational [vəu'keɪʃənl] *adj* professionnel(le); **~ guidance/training** orientation/formation professionnelle
vociferous [və'sɪfərəs] *adj* bruyant(e)
vodka ['vɔdkə] *n* vodka *f*
vogue [vəug] *n* mode *f*; (*popularity*) vogue *f*; **to be in ~** être en vogue *or* à la mode
voice [vɔɪs] *n* voix *f*; (*opinion*) avis *m* ▷ *vt* (*opinion*) exprimer, formuler; **in a loud/soft ~** à voix haute/basse; **to give ~ to** exprimer
voice mail *n* (*system*) messagerie *f* vocale, boîte *f* vocale; (*device*) répondeur *m*
void [vɔɪd] *n* vide *m* ▷ *adj* (*invalid*) nul(le); (*empty*): **~ of** vide de, dépourvu(e) de
volatile ['vɔlətaɪl] *adj* volatil(e); (*fig: person*) versatile; (: *situation*) explosif(-ive)
volcano (*pl* **volcanoes**) [vɔl'keɪnəu] *n* volcan *m*
volition [və'lɪʃən] *n*: **of one's own ~** de son propre gré

volley ['vɒlɪ] n (of gunfire) salve f; (of stones etc) pluie f, volée f; (Tennis etc) volée

volleyball ['vɒlɪbɔːl] n volley(-ball) m

volt [vəʊlt] n volt m

voltage ['vəʊltɪdʒ] n tension f, voltage m; **high/low ~** haute/basse tension

volume ['vɒljuːm] n volume m; (of tank) capacité f; **~ one/two** (of book) tome un/deux; **his expression spoke ~s** son expression en disait long

voluntarily ['vɒləntrɪlɪ] adv volontairement; bénévolement

voluntary ['vɒləntərɪ] adj volontaire; (unpaid) bénévole

volunteer [vɒlən'tɪər] n volontaire m/f ▷ vt (information) donner spontanément ▷ vi (Mil) s'engager comme volontaire; **to ~ to do** se proposer pour faire

vomit ['vɒmɪt] n vomissure f ▷ vt, vi vomir

vote [vəʊt] n vote m, suffrage m; (votes cast) voix f, vote; (franchise) droit m de vote ▷ vt (bill) voter; (chairman) élire; (propose): **to ~ that** proposer que +sub ▷ vi voter; **to put sth to the ~, to take a ~ on sth** mettre qch aux voix, procéder à un vote sur qch; **~ for** or **in favour of/against** vote pour/contre; **to ~ to do sth** voter en faveur de faire qch; **~ of censure** motion f de censure; **~ of thanks** discours m de remerciement

voter ['vəʊtər] n électeur(-trice)

voting ['vəʊtɪŋ] n scrutin m, vote m

vouch [vaʊtʃ]: **to ~ for** vt fus se porter garant de

voucher ['vaʊtʃər] n (for meal, petrol, gift) bon m; (receipt) reçu m; **travel ~** bon m de transport

vow [vaʊ] n vœu m, serment m ▷ vi jurer; **to take** or **make a ~ to do sth** faire le vœu de faire qch

vowel ['vaʊəl] n voyelle f

voyage ['vɔɪɪdʒ] n voyage m par mer, traversée f; (by spacecraft) voyage

vulgar ['vʌlgər] adj vulgaire

vulnerable ['vʌlnərəbl] adj vulnérable

vulture ['vʌltʃər] n vautour m

W

wad [wɒd] n (of cotton wool, paper) tampon m; (of banknotes etc) liasse f

waddle ['wɒdl] vi se dandiner

wade [weɪd] vi: **to ~ through** marcher dans, patauger dans; (fig: book) venir à bout de ▷ vt passer à gué

wafer ['weɪfər] n (Culin) gaufrette f; (Rel) pain m d'hostie; (Comput) tranche f (de silicium)

waffle ['wɒfl] n (Culin) gaufre f; (inf) rabâchage m; remplissage m ▷ vi parler pour ne rien dire; faire du remplissage

waft [wɒft] vt porter ▷ vi flotter

wag [wæg] vt agiter, remuer ▷ vi remuer; **the dog ~ged its tail** le chien a remué la queue

wage [weɪdʒ] n (also: ~s) salaire m, paye f ▷ vt: **to ~ war** faire la guerre; **a day's ~s** un jour de salaire

wage earner [-əːnər] n salarié(e); (breadwinner) soutien m de famille

wage packet n (Brit) (enveloppe f de) paye f

wager ['weɪdʒər] n pari m ▷ vt parier

wagon, waggon ['wægən] n (horse-drawn) chariot m; (Brit Rail) wagon m (de marchandises)

wail [weɪl] n gémissement m; (of siren) hurlement m ▷ vi gémir; (siren) hurler

waist [weɪst] n taille f, ceinture f

waistcoat ['weɪskəʊt] n (Brit) gilet m

waistline ['weɪstlaɪn] n (tour m de) taille f

wait [weɪt] n attente f ▷ vi attendre; **to ~ for sb/sth** attendre qn/qch; **to keep sb ~ing**

faire attendre qn; **~ for me, please** attendez-moi, s'il vous plaît; **~ a minute!** un instant!; **"repairs while you ~"** "réparations minute"; **I can't ~ to ...** (fig) je meurs d'envie de ...; **to lie in ~ for** guetter; **wait behind** vi rester (à attendre); **wait on** vt fus servir; **wait up** vi attendre, ne pas se coucher; **don't ~ up for me** ne m'attendez pas pour aller vous coucher

waiter ['weɪtə'] n garçon m (de café), serveur m

waiting ['weɪtɪŋ] n: **"no ~"** (Brit Aut) "stationnement interdit"

waiting list n liste f d'attente

waiting room n salle f d'attente

waitress ['weɪtrɪs] n serveuse f

waive [weɪv] vt renoncer à, abandonner

wake [weɪk] (pt **woke** or **waked**, pp **woken** or **waked**) [wəuk, 'wəukn] vt (also: **~ up**) réveiller ▷ vi (also: **~ up**) se réveiller ▷ n (for dead person) veillée f mortuaire; (Naut) sillage m; **to ~ up to sth** (fig) se rendre compte de qch; **in the ~ of** (fig) à la suite de; **to follow in sb's ~** (fig) marcher sur les traces de qn

Wales [weɪlz] n pays m de Galles; **the Prince of ~** le prince de Galles

walk [wɔːk] n promenade f; (short) petit tour; (gait) démarche f; (path) chemin m; (in park etc) allée f; (pace): **at a quick ~** d'un pas rapide ▷ vi marcher; (for pleasure, exercise) se promener ▷ vt (distance) faire à pied; (dog) promener; **10 minutes' ~ from** à 10 minutes de marche de; **to go for a ~** se promener; faire un tour; **from all ~s of life** de toutes conditions sociales; **I'll ~ you home** je vais vous raccompagner chez vous; **walk out** vi (go out) sortir; (as protest) partir (en signe de protestation); (strike) se mettre en grève; **to ~ out on sb** quitter qn

walker ['wɔːkə'] n (person) marcheur(-euse)

walkie-talkie ['wɔːkɪ'tɔːkɪ] n talkie-walkie m

walking ['wɔːkɪŋ] n marche f à pied; **it's within ~ distance** on peut y aller à pied

walking shoes npl chaussures fpl de marche

walking stick n canne f

Walkman® ['wɔːkmən] n Walkman® m

walkout ['wɔːkaut] n (of workers) grève-surprise f

walkover ['wɔːkəuvə'] n (inf) victoire f or examen m etc facile

walkway ['wɔːkweɪ] n promenade f, cheminement piéton

wall [wɔːl] n mur m; (of tunnel, cave) paroi f; **to go to the ~** (fig: firm etc) faire faillite; **wall in** vt (garden etc) entourer d'un mur

walled [wɔːld] adj (city) fortifié(e)

wallet ['wɔlɪt] n portefeuille m; **I can't find my ~** je ne retrouve plus mon portefeuille

wallflower ['wɔːlflauə'] n giroflée f; **to be a ~** (fig) faire tapisserie

wallow ['wɔləu] vi se vautrer; **to ~ in one's grief** se complaire à sa douleur

wallpaper ['wɔːlpeɪpə'] n papier peint ▷ vt tapisser

walnut ['wɔːlnʌt] n noix f; (tree, wood) noyer m

walrus (pl **walrus** or **walruses**) ['wɔːlrəs] n morse m

waltz [wɔːlts] n valse f ▷ vi valser

wand [wɔnd] n (also: **magic ~**) baguette f (magique)

wander ['wɔndə'] vi (person) errer, aller sans but; (thoughts) vagabonder; (river) serpenter ▷ vt errer dans

wane [weɪn] vi (moon) décroître; (reputation) décliner

wangle ['wæŋgl] (Brit inf) vt se débrouiller pour avoir; carotter ▷ n combine f, magouille f

want [wɔnt] vt vouloir; (need) avoir besoin de; (lack) manquer de ▷ n (poverty) pauvreté f, besoin m; **wants** npl (needs) besoins mpl; **to ~ to do** vouloir faire; **to ~ sb to do** vouloir que qn fasse; **you're ~ed on the phone** on vous demande au téléphone; **"cook ~ed"** "on demande un cuisinier"; **for ~ of** par manque de, faute de

wanted ['wɔntɪd] adj (criminal) recherché(e) par la police

wanting ['wɔntɪŋ] adj: **to be ~ (in)** manquer (de); **to be found ~** ne pas être à la hauteur

war [wɔː'] n guerre f; **to go to ~** se mettre en guerre; **to make ~ (on)** faire la guerre (à)

ward [wɔːd] n (in hospital) salle f; (Pol) section électorale; (Law: child: also: **~ of court**) pupille m/f; **ward off** vt parer, éviter

warden ['wɔːdn] n (Brit: of institution) directeur(-trice); (of park, game reserve) gardien(ne); (Brit: also: **traffic ~**) contractuel(le); (of youth hostel) responsable m/f

warder ['wɔːdə'] n (Brit) gardien m de prison

wardrobe ['wɔːdrəub] n (cupboard) armoire f; (clothes) garde-robe f; (Theat) costumes mpl

warehouse ['wɛəhaus] n entrepôt m

wares [wɛəz] npl marchandises fpl

warfare ['wɔːfɛə'] n guerre f

warhead ['wɔːhɛd] n (Mil) ogive f

warily ['wɛərɪlɪ] adv avec prudence, avec précaution

warm [wɔːm] adj chaud(e); (person, thanks, welcome, applause) chaleureux(-euse); (supporter) ardent(e), enthousiaste; **it's ~** il fait chaud; **I'm ~** j'ai chaud; **to keep sth ~** tenir qch au chaud; **with my ~est thanks/congratulations** avec mes remerciements/mes félicitations les plus sincères; **warm up** vi (person, room) se réchauffer; (water) chauffer; (athlete, discussion) s'échauffer ▷ vt (food) (faire) réchauffer; (water) (faire) chauffer; (engine) faire chauffer

warm-hearted [wɔːm'hɑːtɪd] adj affectueux(-euse)

warmly ['wɔːmlɪ] adv (dress) chaudement; (thank, welcome) chaleureusement

warmth [wɔːmθ] n chaleur f

warn [wɔːn] vt avertir, prévenir; **to ~ sb (not) to do** conseiller à qn de (ne pas) faire

warning [wɔːnɪŋ] n avertissement m; (notice) avis m; (signal) avertisseur m; **without (any) ~** (suddenly) inopinément; (without notifying) sans prévenir; **gale ~** (Meteorology) avis de grand vent

warning light n avertisseur lumineux

warning triangle n (Aut) triangle m de présignalisation

warp [wɔːp] n (Textiles) chaîne f ▷ vi (wood) travailler, se voiler or gauchir ▷ vt voiler; (fig) pervertir

warrant [wɔrnt] n (guarantee) garantie f; (Law: to arrest) mandat m d'arrêt; (: to search) mandat de perquisition ▷ vt (justify, merit) justifier

warranty [wɔrəntɪ] n garantie f; **under ~** (Comm) sous garantie

warren [wɔrən] n (of rabbits) terriers mpl, garenne f

warrior [wɔrɪəʳ] n guerrier(-ière)

Warsaw [wɔːsɔː] n Varsovie

warship [wɔːʃɪp] n navire m de guerre

wart [wɔːt] n verrue f

wartime [wɔːtaɪm] n: **in ~** en temps de guerre

wary [wɛərɪ] adj prudent(e); **to be ~ about** or **of doing sth** hésiter beaucoup à faire qch

was [wɔz] pt of **be**

wash [wɔʃ] vt laver; (sweep, carry: sea etc) emporter, entraîner; (: ashore) rejeter ▷ vi se laver; (sea): **to ~ over/against sth** inonder/ baigner qch ▷ n (paint) badigeon m; (clothes) lessive f; (washing programme) lavage m; (of ship) sillage m; **to give sth a ~** laver qch; **to have a ~** se laver, faire sa toilette; **he was ~ed overboard** il a été emporté par une vague; **wash away** vt (stain) enlever au lavage; (subj: river etc) emporter; **wash down** vt laver; laver à grande eau; **wash off** vi partir au lavage; **wash up** vi (Brit) faire la vaisselle; (US: have a wash) se débarbouiller

washable [wɔʃəbl] adj lavable

washbasin [wɔʃbeɪsn] n lavabo m

washer [wɔʃəʳ] n (Tech) rondelle f, joint m

washing [wɔʃɪŋ] n (Brit: linen etc: dirty) linge m; (: clean) lessive f

washing line n (Brit) corde f à linge

washing machine n machine f à laver

washing powder n (Brit) lessive f (en poudre)

Washington [wɔʃɪŋtən] n (city, state) Washington m

washing-up [wɔʃɪŋʌp] n (Brit) vaisselle f

washing-up liquid n (Brit) produit m pour la vaisselle

wash-out [wɔʃaut] n (inf) désastre m

washroom [wɔʃrum] n (US) toilettes fpl

wasn't [wɔznt] = **was not**

wasp [wɔsp] n guêpe f

wastage [weɪstɪdʒ] n gaspillage m; (in manufacturing, transport etc) déchet m

waste [weɪst] n gaspillage m; (of time) perte f; (rubbish) déchets mpl; (also: **household ~**) ordures fpl ▷ adj (energy, heat) perdu(e); (food) inutilisé(e); (land, ground: in city) à l'abandon; (: in country) inculte, en friche; (leftover): **~ material** déchets ▷ vt gaspiller; (time, opportunity) perdre; **wastes** npl étendue f désertique; **it's a ~ of money** c'est de l'argent jeté en l'air; **to go to ~** être gaspillé(e); **to lay ~** (destroy) dévaster; **waste away** vi dépérir

waste disposal, waste disposal unit n (Brit) broyeur m d'ordures

wasteful [weɪstful] adj gaspilleur(-euse); (process) peu économique

waste ground n (Brit) terrain m vague

wastepaper basket [weɪstpeɪpə-] n corbeille f à papier

watch [wɔtʃ] n montre f; (act of watching) surveillance f; (guard: Mil) sentinelle f; (: Naut) homme m de quart; (Naut: spell of duty) quart m ▷ vt (look at) observer; (: match, programme) regarder; (spy on, guard) surveiller; (be careful of) faire attention à ▷ vi regarder; (keep guard) monter la garde; **to keep a close ~ on sb/sth** surveiller qn/qch de près; **to keep ~** faire le guet; **~ what you're doing** fais attention à ce que tu fais; **watch out** vi faire attention

watchdog [wɔtʃdɔg] n chien m de garde; (fig) gardien(ne)

watchful [wɔtʃful] adj attentif(-ive), vigilant(e)

watchmaker [wɔtʃmeɪkəʳ] n horloger(-ère)

watchman [wɔtʃmən] irreg n gardien m; (also: **night ~**) veilleur m de nuit

watch strap [wɔtʃstræp] n bracelet m de montre

water [wɔːtəʳ] n eau f ▷ vt (plant, garden) arroser ▷ vi (eyes) larmoyer; **a drink of ~** un verre d'eau; **in British ~s** dans les eaux territoriales Britanniques; **to pass ~** uriner; **to make sb's mouth ~** mettre l'eau à la bouche de qn; **water down** vt (milk etc) couper avec de l'eau; (fig: story) édulcorer

watercolour, (US) **watercolor** [wɔːtəkʌləʳ] n aquarelle f; **watercolours** npl couleurs fpl pour aquarelle

watercress [wɔːtəkrɛs] n cresson m (de fontaine)

waterfall [wɔːtəfɔːl] n chute f d'eau

water heater n chauffe-eau m

watering can [wɔːtərɪŋ-] n arrosoir m

water lily n nénuphar m

waterline [wɔːtəlaɪn] n (Naut) ligne f de flottaison

waterlogged [wɔːtəlɔgd] adj détrempé(e); imbibé(e) d'eau

water main n canalisation f d'eau

watermelon [wɔːtəmɛlən] n pastèque f

W

waterproof ['wɔːtəpruːf] *adj* imperméable

watershed ['wɔːtəʃed] *n* (*Geo*) ligne *f* de partage des eaux; (*fig*) moment *m* critique, point décisif

water-skiing ['wɔːtəskiːɪŋ] *n* ski *m* nautique

watertight ['wɔːtətaɪt] *adj* étanche

waterway ['wɔːtəweɪ] *n* cours *m* d'eau navigable

waterworks ['wɔːtəwɜːks] *npl* station *f* hydraulique

watery ['wɔːtərɪ] *adj* (*colour*) délavé(e); (*coffee*) trop faible

watt [wɒt] *n* watt *m*

wave [weɪv] *n* vague *f*; (*of hand*) geste *m*, signe *m*; (*Radio*) onde *f*; (*in hair*) ondulation *f*; (*fig: of enthusiasm, strikes etc*) vague ▸ *vi* faire signe de la main; (*flag*) flotter au vent; (*grass*) ondoyer ▸ *vt* (*handkerchief*) agiter; (*stick*) brandir; (*hair*) onduler; **short/medium ~** (*Radio*) ondes courtes/moyennes; **long ~** (*Radio*) grandes ondes; **the new ~** (*Cine, Mus*) la nouvelle vague; **to ~ goodbye to sb** dire au revoir de la main à qn; **wave aside**, **wave away** *vt* (*fig: suggestion, objection*) rejeter, repousser; (*: doubts*) chasser; (*person*): **to ~ sb aside** faire signe à qn de s'écarter

wavelength ['weɪvleŋθ] *n* longueur *f* d'ondes

waver ['weɪvə'] *vi* vaciller; (*voice*) trembler; (*person*) hésiter

wavy ['weɪvɪ] *adj* (*hair, surface*) ondulé(e); (*line*) onduleux(-euse)

wax [wæks] *n* cire *f*; (*for skis*) fart *m* ▸ *vt* cirer; (*car*) lustrer; (*skis*) farter ▸ *vi* (*moon*) croître

waxworks ['wækswɜːks] *npl* personnages *mpl* de cire; musée *m* de cire

way [weɪ] *n* chemin *m*, voie *f*; (*path, access*) passage *m*; (*distance*) distance *f*; (*direction*) chemin, direction *f*; (*manner*) façon *f*, manière *f*; (*habit*) habitude *f*, façon; (*condition*) état *m*; **which ~?** – **this ~/that ~** par où *or* de quel côté? – par ici/par là; **to crawl one's ~ to ...** ramper jusqu'à ...; **to lie one's ~ out of it** s'en sortir par un mensonge; **to lose one's ~** perdre son chemin; **on the ~** (*to*) en route (pour); **to be on one's ~** être en route; **to be in the ~** bloquer le passage; (*fig*) gêner; **to keep out of sb's ~** éviter qn; **it's a long ~ away** c'est loin d'ici; **the village is rather out of the ~** le village est plutôt à l'écart *or* isolé; **to go out of one's ~ to do** (*fig*) se donner beaucoup de mal pour faire; **to be under ~** (*work, project*) être en cours; **to make ~ (for sb/sth)** faire place (à qn/qch); (*fig*) s'écarter pour laisser passer (qn/qch); **to get one's own ~** arriver à ses fins; **put it the right ~ up** (*Brit*) mettez-le dans le bon sens; **to be the wrong ~ round** être à l'envers, ne pas être dans le bon sens; **he's in a bad ~** il va mal; **in a ~** dans un sens; **by the ~** à propos; **in some ~s** à certains égards; d'un côté, dans **in the ~ of** en fait de, comme; **by ~ of** (*through*) en passant

par, via; (*as a sort of*) en guise de; **"~ in"** (*Brit*) "entrée"; **"~ out"** (*Brit*) "sortie"; **the ~ back** le chemin du retour; **this ~ and that** par-ci par-là; **"give ~"** (*Brit Aut*) "cédez la priorité"; **no ~!** (*inf*) pas question!

waylay [weɪ'leɪ] *vt* (*irreg like*: **lay**) attaquer; (*fig*): **I got waylaid** quelqu'un m'a accroché

wayward ['weɪwəd] *adj* capricieux(-euse), entêté(e)

W.C. *n abbr* (*Brit*: = *water closet*) w.-c. *mpl*, waters *mpl*

we [wiː] *pl pron* nous

weak [wiːk] *adj* faible; (*health*) fragile; (*beam etc*) peu solide; (*tea, coffee*) léger(-ère); **to grow ~(er)** s'affaiblir, faiblir

weaken ['wiːkn] *vi* faiblir ▸ *vt* affaiblir

weakling ['wiːklɪŋ] *n* gringalet *m*; faible *m/f*

weakness ['wiːknɪs] *n* faiblesse *f*; (*fault*) point *m* faible

wealth [welθ] *n* (*money, resources*) richesse(s) *f(pl)*; (*of details*) profusion *f*

wealthy ['welθɪ] *adj* riche

wean [wiːn] *vt* sevrer

weapon ['wepən] *n* arme *f*; **~s of mass destruction** armes *fpl* de destruction massive

wear [weə'] (*pt* **wore**, *pp* **worn**) ['wɔː', wɔːn] *n* (*use*) usage *m*; (*deterioration through use*) usure *f* ▸ *vt* (*clothes*) porter; (*put on*) mettre; (*beard etc*) avoir; (*damage: through use*) user ▸ *vi* (*last*) faire de l'usage; (*rub etc through*) s'user; **sports/baby~** vêtements *mpl* de sport/pour bébés; **evening ~** tenue *f* de soirée; **~ and tear** usure *f*; **to ~ a hole in sth** faire (à la longue) un trou dans qch; **wear away** *vt* user, ronger ▸ *vi* s'user, être rongé(e); **wear down** *vt* user; (*strength*) épuiser; **wear off** *vi* disparaître; **wear on** *vi* se poursuivre; passer; **wear out** *vt* user; (*person, strength*) épuiser

weary ['wɪərɪ] *adj* (*tired*) épuisé(e); (*dispirited*) las/lasse; abattu(e) ▸ *vt* lasser ▸ *vi*: **to ~ of** se lasser de

weasel ['wiːzl] *n* (*Zool*) belette *f*

weather ['weðə'] *n* temps *m* ▸ *vt* (*wood*) faire mûrir; (*storm: lit, fig*) essuyer; (*crisis*) survivre à; **what's the ~ like?** quel temps fait-il?; **under the ~** (*fig: ill*) mal fichu(e)

weather-beaten ['weðəbiːtn] *adj* (*person*) hâlé(e); (*building*) dégradé(e) par les intempéries

weather forecast *n* prévisions *fpl* météorologiques, météo *f*

weatherman ['weðəmæn] *irreg n* météorologue *m*

weather vane [-veɪn] *n* = **weather cock**

weave (*pt* **wove**, *pp* **woven**) [wiːv, wəuv, 'wəuvn] *vt* (*cloth*) tisser; (*basket*) tresser ▸ *vi* (*fig*) (*pt, pp* **weaved**) (*move in and out*) se faufiler

weaver ['wiːvə'] *n* tisserand(e)

web [web] *n* (*of spider*) toile *f*; (*on duck's foot*) palmure *f*; (*fig*) tissu *m*; (*Comput*): **the (World-Wide) W~** le Web

web address n adresse f Web
webcam ['webkæm] n webcam f
weblog ['weblɒg] n blog m, blogue m
web page n (Comput) page f Web
website ['websaɪt] n (Comput) site m web
wed [wed] (pt, pp **wedded**) vt épouser ⊳ vi se marier ⊳ n: **the newly--s** les jeunes mariés
we'd [wi:d] = **we had; we would**
wedding ['wedɪŋ] n mariage m
wedding anniversary n anniversaire m de mariage; **silver/golden ~** noces fpl d'argent/d'or
wedding day n jour m du mariage
wedding dress n robe f de mariée
wedding ring n alliance f
wedge [wedʒ] n (of wood etc) coin m; (under door etc) cale f; (of cake) part f ⊳ vt (fix) caler; (push) enfoncer, coincer
Wednesday ['wednzdɪ] n mercredi m; see also **Tuesday**
wee [wi:] adj (Scottish) petit(e); tout(e) petit(e)
weed [wi:d] n mauvaise herbe f ⊳ vt désherber; **weed out** vt éliminer
weedkiller ['wi:dkɪlə'] n désherbant m
weedy ['wi:dɪ] adj (man) gringalet
week [wi:k] n semaine f; **once/twice a ~** une fois/deux fois par semaine; **in two ~s' time** dans quinze jours; **a ~ today/on Tuesday** aujourd'hui/mardi en huit
weekday ['wi:kdeɪ] n jour m de semaine; (Comm) jour ouvrable; **on ~s** en semaine
weekend [wi:k'end] n week-end m
weekly ['wi:klɪ] adv une fois par semaine, chaque semaine ⊳ adj, n hebdomadaire (m)
weep [wi:p] (pt, pp **wept**) [wept] vi (person) pleurer; (Med: wound etc) suinter
weeping willow ['wi:pɪŋ-] n saule pleureur
weigh [weɪ] vt, vi peser; **to ~ anchor** lever l'ancre; **to ~ the pros and cons** peser le pour et le contre; **weigh down** vt (branch) faire plier; (fig: with worry) accabler; **weigh out** vt (goods) peser; **weigh up** vt examiner
weight [weɪt] n poids m ⊳ vt alourdir; (fig: factor) pondérer; **sold by ~** vendu au poids; **to put on/lose ~** grossir/maigrir; **~s and measures** poids et mesures
weighting ['weɪtɪŋ] n: **~ allowance** indemnité f de résidence
weightlifter ['weɪtlɪftə'] n haltérophile m
weightlifting ['weɪtlɪftɪŋ] n haltérophilie f
weighty ['weɪtɪ] adj lourd(e)
weir [wɪə'] n barrage m
weird [wɪəd] adj bizarre; (eerie) surnaturel(le)
welcome ['welkəm] adj bienvenu(e) ⊳ n accueil m ⊳ vt accueillir; (also: **bid ~**) souhaiter la bienvenue à; (be glad of) se réjouir de; **to be ~** être le/la bienvenu(e); **to make sb ~** faire bon accueil à qn; **you're ~ to try** vous pouvez essayer si vous voulez; **you're ~!** (after thanks) de rien, il n'y a pas de quoi
weld [weld] n soudure f ⊳ vt souder

welder ['weldə'] n (person) soudeur m
welfare ['welfeə'] n (wellbeing) bien-être m; (social aid) assistance sociale
welfare state n État-providence m
well [wel] n puits m ⊳ adv bien ⊳ adj: **to be ~** aller bien ⊳ excl eh bien!; (relief also) bon!; (resignation) enfin!; **~ done!** bravo!; **I don't feel ~** je ne me sens pas bien; **get ~ soon!** remets-toi vite!; **to do ~** bien réussir; (business) prospérer; **to think ~ of sb** penser du bien de qn; **as ~** (in addition) aussi, également; **you might as ~ tell me** tu ferais aussi bien de me le dire; **as ~ as** aussi bien que or de; en plus de; **~, as I was saying ...** donc, comme je disais ...; **well up** vi (tears, emotions) monter
we'll [wi:l] = **we will; we shall**
well-behaved ['welbɪ'heɪvd] adj sage, obéissant(e)
well-being ['wel'bi:ɪŋ] n bien-être m
well-built ['wel'bɪlt] adj (house) bien construit(e); (person) bien bâti(e)
well-deserved ['weldɪ'zə:vd] adj (bien) mérité(e)
well-dressed ['wel'drest] adj bien habillé(e), bien vêtu(e)
well-groomed ['-gru:md] adj très soigné(e)
well-heeled ['wel'hi:ld] adj (inf: wealthy) fortuné(e), riche
wellies ['welɪz] (inf) npl (Brit) = **wellingtons**
wellingtons ['welɪŋtənz] npl (also: **wellington boots**) bottes fpl en caoutchouc
well-known ['wel'nəun] adj (person) bien connu(e)
well-mannered ['wel'mænəd] adj bien élevé(e)
well-meaning ['wel'mi:nɪŋ] adj bien intentionné(e)
well-off ['wel'ɔf] adj aisé(e), assez riche
well-paid [wel'peɪd] adj bien payé(e)
well-read ['wel'red] adj cultivé(e)
well-to-do ['weltə'du:] adj aisé(e), assez riche
well-wisher ['welwɪʃə'] n ami(e), admirateur(-trice); **scores of ~s had gathered** de nombreux amis et admirateurs s'étaient rassemblés; **letters from ~s** des lettres d'encouragement
Welsh [welʃ] adj gallois(e) ⊳ n (Ling) gallois m; **the Welsh** npl (people) les Gallois
Welsh Assembly n Parlement gallois
Welshman ['welʃmən] irreg n Gallois m
Welshwoman ['welʃwumən] irreg n Galloise f
went [went] pt of **go**
wept [wept] pt, pp of **weep**
were [wə:'] pt of **be**
we're [wɪə'] = **we are**
weren't [wə:nt] = **were not**
west [west] n ouest m ⊳ adj ⊳ adj (wind) d'ouest; (side) ouest inv ⊳ adv à or vers l'ouest; **the W** l'Occident m, l'Ouest

westbound ['wɛstbaund] adj en direction de l'ouest; (carriageway) ouest inv

westerly ['wɛstəlɪ] adj (situation) à l'ouest; (wind) d'ouest

western ['wɛstən] adj occidental(e), de or à l'ouest ▷ n (Cine) western m

West Indian adj antillais(e) ▷ n Antillais(e)

West Indies [-'ɪndɪz] npl Antilles fpl

westward ['wɛstwəd], **westwards** ['wɛstwədz] adv vers l'ouest

wet [wɛt] adj mouillé(e); (damp) humide; (soaked: also: **~ through**) trempé(e); (rainy) pluvieux(-euse) ▷ vt: **to ~ one's pants** or **o.s.** mouiller sa culotte, faire pipi dans sa culotte; **to get ~** se mouiller; **"~ paint"** "attention peinture fraîche"

wetsuit ['wɛtsuːt] n combinaison f de plongée

we've [wiːv] = **we have**

whack [wæk] vt donner un grand coup à

whale [weɪl] n (Zool) baleine f

wharf (pl **wharves**) [wɔːf, wɔːvz] n quai m

⬤ **KEYWORD**

what [wɔt] adj 1 (in questions) quel(le); **what size is he?** quelle taille fait-il?; **what colour is it?** de quelle couleur est-ce?; **what books do you need?** quels livres vous faut-il?
2 (in exclamations): **what a mess!** quel désordre!; **what a fool I am!** que je suis bête!
▷ pron 1 (interrogative) que; de/à/en etc quoi; **what are you doing?** que faites-vous?, qu'est-ce que vous faites?; **what is happening?** qu'est-ce qui se passe?, que se passe-t-il?; **what are you talking about?** de quoi parlez-vous?; **what are you thinking about?** à quoi pensez-vous?; **what is it called?** comment ça s'appelle?; **what about me?** et moi?; **what about doing ...?** et si on faisait ...?
2 (relative: subject) ce qui; (: direct object) ce que; (: indirect object) ce à quoi, ce dont; **I saw what you did/was on the table** j'ai vu ce que vous avez fait/ce qui était sur la table; **tell me what you remember** dites-moi ce dont vous vous souvenez; **what I want is a cup of tea** ce que je veux, c'est une tasse de thé
▷ excl (disbelieving) quoi!, comment!

whatever [wɔt'ɛvər] adj: **take ~ book you prefer** prenez le livre que vous préférez, peu importe lequel; **~ book you take** quel que soit le livre que vous preniez ▷ pron: **do ~ is necessary** faites (tout) ce qui est nécessaire; **~ happens** quoi qu'il arrive; **no reason ~** or **~soever** pas la moindre raison; **nothing ~soever** rien du tout

~~~~~~~ [wɔtsəu'ɛvər] adj see **whatever**
~~~blé m~~, froment m
~~~l] vt: **to ~ sb into doing sth**
~~~ôler qn pour qu'il fasse qch; **to ~**

sth out of sb obtenir qch de qn par des cajoleries

wheel [wiːl] n roue f; (Aut: also: **steering ~**) volant m; (Naut) gouvernail m ▷ vt (pram etc) pousser, rouler ▷ vi (birds) tournoyer; (also: **~ round:** person) se retourner, faire volte-face

wheelbarrow ['wiːlbærəu] n brouette f

wheelchair ['wiːltʃɛər] n fauteuil roulant

wheel clamp n (Aut) sabot m (de Denver)

wheeze [wiːz] n respiration bruyante (d'asthmatique) ▷ vi respirer bruyamment

⬤ **KEYWORD**

when [wɛn] adv quand; **when did he go?** quand est-ce qu'il est parti?
▷ conj 1 (at, during, after the time that) quand, lorsque; **she was reading when I came in** elle lisait quand or lorsque je suis entré
2 (on, at which): **on the day when I met him** le jour où je l'ai rencontré
3 (whereas) alors que; **I thought I was wrong when in fact I was right** j'ai cru que j'avais tort alors qu'en fait j'avais raison

whenever [wɛn'ɛvər] adv quand donc ▷ conj quand; (every time that) chaque fois que; **I go ~ I can** j'y vais quand or chaque fois que je le peux

where [wɛər] adv, conj où; **this is ~** c'est là que; **~ are you from?** d'où venez vous?

whereabouts ['wɛərəbauts] adv où donc ▷ n: **nobody knows his ~** personne ne sait où il se trouve

whereas [wɛər'æz] conj alors que

whereby [wɛər'baɪ] adv (formal) par lequel (or laquelle etc)

wherever [wɛər'ɛvər] adv où donc ▷ conj où que + sub; **sit ~ you like** asseyez-vous (là) où vous voulez

wherewithal ['wɛəwɪðɔːl] n: **the ~ (to do sth)** les moyens mpl (de faire qch)

whether ['wɛðər] conj si; **I don't know ~ to accept or not** je ne sais pas si je dois accepter ou non; **it's doubtful ~** il est peu probable que + sub; **~ you go or not** que vous y alliez ou non

⬤ **KEYWORD**

which [wɪtʃ] adj 1 (interrogative: direct, indirect) quel(le); **which picture do you want?** quel tableau voulez-vous?; **which one?** lequel/laquelle?
2: **in which case** auquel cas; **we got there at 8pm, by which time the cinema was full** quand nous sommes arrivés à 20h, le cinéma était complet
▷ pron 1 (interrogative) lequel/laquelle, lesquels/lesquelles pl; **I don't mind which** peu importe lequel; **which (of these) are yours?** lesquels sont à vous?; **tell me which**

you want dites-moi lesquels or ceux que vous voulez

2 (relative: subject) qui; (: object) que; sur/vers etc lequel/laquelle (NB: à + lequel = **auquel**; de + lequel = **duquel**); **the apple which you ate/ which is on the table** la pomme que vous avez mangée/qui est sur la table; **the chair on which you are sitting** la chaise sur laquelle vous êtes assis; **the book of which you spoke** le livre dont vous avez parlé; **he said he knew, which is true/I was afraid of** il a dit qu'il le savait, ce qui est vrai/ce que je craignais; **after which** après quoi

whichever [wɪtʃ'evər] adj: **take ~ book you prefer** prenez le livre que vous préférez, peu importe lequel; **~ book you take** quel que soit le livre que vous preniez; **~ way you** de quelque façon que vous + sub

while [waɪl] n moment m ▷ conj pendant que; (as long as) tant que; (as, whereas) alors que; (though) bien que + sub, quoique + sub; **for a ~** pendant quelque temps; **in a ~** dans un moment; **all the ~** pendant tout ce temps-là; **we'll make it worth your ~** nous vous récompenserons de votre peine; **while away** vt (time) (faire) passer

whilst [waɪlst] conj = **while**

whim [wɪm] n caprice m

whimper ['wɪmpər] n geignement m ▷ vi geindre

whimsical ['wɪmzɪkl] adj (person) capricieux(-euse); (look) étrange

whine [waɪn] n gémissement m; (of engine, siren) plainte stridente ▷ vi gémir, geindre, pleurnicher; (dog, engine, siren) gémir

whip [wɪp] n fouet m; (for riding) cravache f; (Pol: person) chef m de file (assurant la discipline dans son groupe parlementaire) ▷ vt fouetter; (snatch) enlever (or sortir) brusquement; **whip up** vt (cream) fouetter; (inf: meal) préparer en vitesse; (stir up: support) stimuler; (: feeling) attiser, aviver; voir article

◈ **WHIP**

◈ Un whip est un député dont le rôle est,
◈ entre autres, de s'assurer que les
◈ membres de son parti sont régulièrement
◈ présents à la "House of Commons",
◈ surtout lorsque les votes ont lieu.
◈ Les convocations que les whips envoient
◈ se distinguent, selon leur degré
◈ d'importance, par le fait qu'elles sont
◈ soulignées 1, 2 ou 3 fois (les "1-, 2-, ou
◈ 3-line whips").

whipped cream [wɪpt-] n crème fouettée

whip-round ['wɪpraund] n (Brit) collecte f

whirl [wəːl] n tourbillon m ▷ vi tourbillonner; (dancers) tournoyer ▷ vt faire tourbillonner; faire tournoyer

whirlpool ['wəːlpuːl] n tourbillon m

whirlwind ['wəːlwɪnd] n tornade f

whirr [wəːr] vi bruire; ronronner; vrombir

whisk [wɪsk] n (Culin) fouet m ▷ vt (eggs) fouetter, battre; **to ~ sb away or off** emmener qn rapidement

whiskers ['wɪskəz] npl (of animal) moustaches fpl; (of man) favoris mpl

whisky, (Irish, US) **whiskey** ['wɪskɪ] n whisky m

whisper ['wɪspər] n chuchotement m; (fig: of leaves) bruissement m; (rumour) rumeur f ▷ vt, vi chuchoter

whistle ['wɪsl] n (sound) sifflement m; (object) sifflet m ▷ vi siffler ▷ vt siffler, siffloter

white [waɪt] adj blanc/blanche; (with fear) blême ▷ n blanc m; (person) blanc/blanche; **to turn** or **go ~** (person) pâlir, blêmir; (hair) blanchir; **the ~s** (washing) le linge blanc; **tennis ~s** tenue f de tennis

whiteboard ['waɪtbɔːd] n tableau m blanc; **interactive ~** tableau m (blanc) interactif

white coffee n (Brit) café m au lait, (café) crème m

white-collar worker ['waɪtkɔlə-] n employé(e) de bureau

white elephant n (fig) objet dispendieux et superflu

White House n (US): **the ~** la Maison-Blanche; voir article

◈ **WHITE HOUSE**

◈ La White House est un grand bâtiment
◈ blanc situé à Washington D.C. où réside
◈ le Président des États-Unis. Par
◈ extension, ce terme désigne l'exécutif
◈ américain.

white lie n pieux mensonge

white paper n (Pol) livre blanc

whitewash ['waɪtwɔʃ] n (paint) lait m de chaux ▷ vt blanchir à la chaux; (fig) blanchir

whiting ['waɪtɪŋ] n (pl inv: fish) merlan m

Whitsun ['wɪtsn] n la Pentecôte

whittle ['wɪtl] vt: **to ~ away, to ~ down** (costs) réduire, rogner

whizz [wɪz] vi aller (or passer) à toute vitesse

whizz kid n (inf) petit prodige

who [huː] pron qui

whodunit [huː'dʌnɪt] n (inf) roman policier

whoever [huː'evər] pron: **~ finds it** celui/celle qui le trouve (, qui que ce soit), quiconque le trouve; **ask ~ you like** demandez à qui vous voulez; **~ he marries** qui que ce soit or quelle que soit la personne qu'il épouse; **~ told you that?** qui a bien pu vous dire ça?, qui donc vous a dit ça?

whole [həul] adj (complete) entier(-ière), tout(e); (not broken) intact(e), complet(-ète) ▷ n (entire unit) tout m; (all): **the ~ of** la totalité de, tout(e) le/la; **the ~ lot (of it)** tout; **the ~**

lot (of them) tous (sans exception); **the ~ of the time** tout le temps; **the ~ of the town** la ville tout entière; **on the ~, as a ~** dans l'ensemble

wholefood ['həulfu:d] *n*, **wholefoods** ['həulfu:dz] *npl* aliments complets

wholehearted [həul'hɑ:tɪd] *adj* sans réserve(s), sincère

wholeheartedly [həul'hɑ:tɪdlɪ] *adv* sans réserve; **to agree ~** être entièrement d'accord

wholemeal ['həulmi:l] *adj* (*Brit: flour, bread*) complet(-ète)

wholesale ['həulseɪl] *n* (*vente f en*) gros *m* ▷ *adj* (*price*) de gros; (*destruction*) systématique

wholesaler ['həulseɪlə¹] *n* grossiste *m/f*

wholesome ['həulsəm] *adj* sain(e); (*advice*) salutaire

wholewheat ['həulwi:t] *adj* = **wholemeal**

wholly ['həulɪ] *adv* entièrement, tout à fait

⬤ KEYWORD

whom [hu:m] *pron* **1** (*interrogative*) qui; **whom did you see?** qui avez-vous vu?; **to whom did you give it?** à qui l'avez-vous donné? **2** (*relative*) que; à/de *etc* qui; **the man whom I saw/to whom I spoke** l'homme que j'ai vu/à qui j'ai parlé

whooping cough ['hu:pɪŋ-] *n* coqueluche *f*

whore [hɔ:¹] *n* (*inf: pej*) putain *f*

⬤ KEYWORD

whose [hu:z] *adj* **1** (*possessive: interrogative*): **whose book is this?, whose is this book?** à qui est ce livre?; **whose pencil have you taken?** à qui est le crayon que vous avez pris?, c'est le crayon de qui que vous avez pris?; **whose daughter are you?** de qui êtes-vous la fille? **2** (*possessive: relative*): **the man whose son I rescued** l'homme dont *or* de qui vous avez sauvé le fils; **the girl whose sister you were speaking to** la fille à la sœur de qui *or* de laquelle vous parliez; **the woman whose car was stolen** la femme dont la voiture a été volée ▷ *pron* à qui; **whose is this?** à qui est ceci?; **I know whose it is** je sais à qui c'est

⬤ KEYWORD

why [waɪ] *adv* pourquoi; **why is he late?** pourquoi est-il en retard?; **why not?** pourquoi pas? ▷ *conj*: **I wonder why he said that** je me demande pourquoi il a dit ça; **that's not why I'm here** ce n'est pas pour ça que je suis là; **the reason why** la raison pour laquelle ▷ *excl* eh bien!, tiens!; **why, it's you!** tiens,

c'est vous!; **why, that's impossible!** voyons, c'est impossible!

wicked ['wɪkɪd] *adj* méchant(e); (*mischievous: grin, look*) espiègle, malicieux(-euse); (*crime*) pervers(e); (*terrible: prices, weather*) épouvantable; (*inf: very good*) génial(e) (*inf*)

wicket ['wɪkɪt] *n* (*Cricket: stumps*) guichet *m*; (*: grass area*) espace compris entre les deux guichets

wide [waɪd] *adj* large; (*area, knowledge*) vaste, très étendu(e); (*choice*) grand(e) ▷ *adv*: **to open ~** ouvrir tout grand; **to shoot ~** tirer à côté; **it is 3 metres ~** cela fait 3 mètres de large

wide-awake [waɪdə'weɪk] *adj* bien éveillé(e)

widely ['waɪdlɪ] *adv* (*different*) radicalement; (*spaced*) sur une grande étendue; (*believed*) généralement; (*travel*) beaucoup; **to be ~ read** (*author*) être beaucoup lu(e); (*reader*) avoir beaucoup lu, être cultivé(e)

widen ['waɪdn] *vt* élargir ▷ *vi* s'élargir

wide open *adj* grand(e) ouvert(e)

widespread ['waɪdspred] *adj* (*belief etc*) très répandu(e)

widget ['wɪdʒɪt] *n* (*Comput*) widget *m*

widow ['wɪdəu] *n* veuve *f*

widowed ['wɪdəud] *adj* (*qui est devenu(e)*) veuf/veuve

widower ['wɪdəuə¹] *n* veuf *m*

width [wɪdθ] *n* largeur *f*; **it's 7 metres in ~** cela fait 7 mètres de large

wield [wi:ld] *vt* (*sword*) manier; (*power*) exercer

wife (*pl* **wives**) [waɪf, waɪvz] *n* femme *f*, épouse *f*

Wi-Fi *n* wifi *m*

wig [wɪg] *n* perruque *f*

wiggle ['wɪgl] *vt* agiter, remuer ▷ *vi* (*loose screw etc*) branler; (*worm*) se tortiller

wild [waɪld] *adj* sauvage; (*sea*) déchaîné(e); (*idea, life*) fou/folle; (*behaviour*) déchaîné(e), extravagant(e); (*inf: angry*) hors de soi, furieux(-euse); (*: enthusiastic*): **to be ~ about** être fou/folle or dingue de ▷ *n*: **the ~** la nature; **wilds** *npl* régions *fpl* sauvages

wild card *n* (*Comput*) caractère *m* de remplacement

wilderness ['wɪldənɪs] *n* désert *m*, région *f* sauvage

wildlife ['waɪldlaɪf] *n* faune *f* (et flore *f*)

wildly ['waɪldlɪ] *adv* (*behave*) de manière déchaînée; (*applaud*) frénétiquement; (*hit, guess*) au hasard; (*happy*) follement

wilful, (*US*) **willful** ['wɪlful] *adj* (*person*) obstiné(e); (*action*) délibéré(e); (*crime*) prémédité(e)

⬤ KEYWORD

will [wɪl] *aux vb* **1** (*forming future tense*): **I will finish it tomorrow** je le finirai demain;

I will have finished it by tomorrow je l'aurai fini d'ici demain; **will you do it? — yes I will/no I won't** le ferez-vous? — oui/non; **you won't lose it, will you?** vous ne le perdrez pas, n'est-ce pas?
2 (*in conjectures, predictions*): **he will** or **he'll be there by now** il doit être arrivé à l'heure qu'il est; **that will be the postman** ça doit être le facteur
3 (*in commands, requests, offers*): **will you be quiet!** voulez-vous bien vous taire!; **will you help me?** est-ce que vous pouvez m'aider?; **will you have a cup of tea?** voulez-vous une tasse de thé?; **I won't put up with it!** je ne le tolérerai pas!
▷ *vt* (*pt, pp* **willed**); **to will sb to do** souhaiter ardemment que qn fasse; **he willed himself to go on** par un suprême effort de volonté, il continua
▷ *n* volonté *f*; (*document*) testament *m*; **to do sth of one's own free will** faire qch de son propre gré; **against one's will** à contre-cœur

willing ['wɪlɪŋ] *adj* de bonne volonté, serviable ▷ *n*: **to show ~** faire preuve de bonne volonté; **he's ~ to do it** il est disposé à le faire, il veut bien le faire
willingly ['wɪlɪŋlɪ] *adv* volontiers
willingness ['wɪlɪŋnɪs] *n* bonne volonté
willow ['wɪləu] *n* saule *m*
willpower ['wɪl'pauə'] *n* volonté *f*
willy-nilly ['wɪlɪ'nɪlɪ] *adv* bon gré mal gré
wilt [wɪlt] *vi* dépérir
win [wɪn] (*pt, pp* **won**) [wʌn] *n* (*in sports etc*) victoire *f* ▷ *vt* (*battle, money*) gagner; (*prize, contract*) remporter; (*popularity*) acquérir ▷ *vi* gagner; **win over** *vt* convaincre; **win round** *vt* gagner, se concilier
wince [wɪns] *n* tressaillement *m* ▷ *vi* tressaillir
winch [wɪntʃ] *n* treuil *m*
wind[1] [wɪnd] *n* (*also Med*) vent *m*; (*breath*) souffle *m* ▷ *vt* (*take breath away*) couper le souffle à; **the ~(s)** (*Mus*) les instruments *mpl* à vent; **into** or **against the ~** contre le vent; **to get ~ of sth** (*fig*) avoir vent de qch; **to break ~** avoir des gaz
wind[2] [waɪnd] (*pt, pp* **wound**) [waund] *vt* enrouler; (*wrap*) envelopper; (*clock, toy*) remonter ▷ *vi* (*road, river*) serpenter; **wind down** *vt* (*car window*) baisser; (*fig: production, business*) réduire progressivement; **wind up** *vt* (*clock*) remonter; (*debate*) terminer, clôturer
windfall ['wɪndfɔ:l] *n* coup *m* de chance
wind farm *n* ferme *f* éolienne
winding ['waɪndɪŋ] *adj* (*road*) sinueux(-euse); (*staircase*) tournant(e)
wind instrument *n* (*Mus*) instrument *m* à vent
windmill ['wɪndmɪl] *n* moulin *m* à vent

window ['wɪndəu] *n* fenêtre *f*; (*in car, train: also*: **~pane**) vitre *f*; (*in shop etc*) vitrine *f*
window box *n* jardinière *f*
window cleaner *n* (*person*) laveur(-euse) de vitres
window ledge *n* rebord *m* de la fenêtre
window pane *n* vitre *f*, carreau *m*
window seat *n* (*on plane*) place *f* côté hublot
window-shopping ['wɪndəuʃɔpɪŋ] *n*: **to go ~** faire du lèche-vitrines
windowsill ['wɪndəusɪl] *n* (*inside*) appui *m* de la fenêtre; (*outside*) rebord *m* de la fenêtre
windpipe ['wɪndpaɪp] *n* gosier *m*
wind power *n* énergie éolienne
windscreen ['wɪndskri:n] *n* pare-brise *m inv*
windscreen washer *n* lave-glace *m inv*
windscreen wiper ['waɪpə'] (US) **windshield wiper** [-waɪpə'] *n* essuie-glace *m inv*
windshield ['wɪndfi:ld] (US) *n* = **windscreen**
windsurfing ['wɪndsə:fɪŋ] *n* planche *f* à voile
windswept ['wɪndswɛpt] *adj* balayé(e) par le vent
windy ['wɪndɪ] *adj* (*day*) de vent, venteux(-euse); (*place, weather*) venteux; **it's ~** il y a du vent
wine [waɪn] *n* vin *m* ▷ *vt*: **to ~ and dine sb** offrir un dîner bien arrosé à qn
wine bar *n* bar *m* à vin
wine cellar *n* cave *f* à vins
wine glass *n* verre *m* à vin
wine list *n* carte *f* des vins
wine tasting [-teɪstɪŋ] *n* dégustation *f* (de vins)
wine waiter *n* sommelier *m*
wing [wɪŋ] *n* aile *f*; (*in air force*) groupe *m* d'escadrilles; **wings** *npl* (*Theat*) coulisses *fpl*
winger ['wɪŋə'] *n* (*Sport*) ailier *m*
wing mirror *n* (*Brit*) rétroviseur latéral
wink [wɪŋk] *n* clin *m* d'œil ▷ *vi* faire un clin d'œil; (*blink*) cligner des yeux
winner ['wɪnə'] *n* gagnant(e)
winning ['wɪnɪŋ] *adj* (*team*) gagnant(e); (*goal*) décisif(-ive); (*charming*) charmeur(-euse)
winnings ['wɪnɪŋz] *npl* gains *mpl*
winter ['wɪntə'] *n* hiver *m* ▷ *vi* hiverner; **in ~** en hiver
winter sports *npl* sports *mpl* d'hiver
wintertime ['wɪntətaɪm] *n* hiver *m*
wintry ['wɪntrɪ] *adj* hivernal(e)
wipe [waɪp] *n* coup *m* de torchon (*or* de chiffon *or* d'éponge); **to give sth a ~** donner un coup de torchon/de chiffon/d'éponge à qch ▷ *vt* essuyer; (*erase: tape*) effacer; **to ~ one's nose** se moucher; **wipe off** *vt* essuyer; **wipe out** *vt* (*debt*) éteindre, amortir; (*memory*) effacer; (*destroy*) anéantir; **wipe up** *vt* essuyer
wire ['waɪə'] *n* fil *m* (de fer); (*Elec*) fil électrique; (*Tel*) télégramme *m* ▷ *vt* (*fence*) grillager; (*house*) faire l'installation électrique de; (*also*: **~ up**) brancher; (*person: send telegram to*) télégraphier à

W

wireless ['waɪəlɪs] n (Brit) télégraphie f sans fil; (set) T.S.F. f

wiring ['waɪərɪŋ] n (Elec) installation f électrique

wiry ['waɪərɪ] adj noueux(-euse), nerveux(-euse)

wisdom ['wɪzdəm] n sagesse f; (of action) prudence f

wisdom tooth n dent f de sagesse

wise [waɪz] adj sage, prudent(e); (remark) judicieux(-euse); **I'm none the ~r** je ne suis pas plus avancé(e) pour autant; **wise up** vi (inf): **to ~ up to** commencer à se rendre compte de

wish [wɪʃ] n (desire) désir m; (specific desire) souhait m, vœu m ▷ vt souhaiter, désirer, vouloir; **best ~es** (on birthday etc) meilleurs vœux; **with best ~es** (in letter) bien amicalement; **give her my best ~es** faites-lui mes amitiés; **to ~ sb goodbye** dire au revoir à qn; **he ~ed me well** il m'a souhaité bonne chance; **to ~ to do/sb to do** désirer or vouloir faire/que qn fasse; **to ~ for** souhaiter; **to ~ sth on sb** souhaiter qch à qn

wishful ['wɪʃful] adj: **it's ~ thinking** c'est prendre ses désirs pour des réalités

wistful ['wɪstful] adj mélancolique

wit [wɪt] n (also: ~s: intelligence) intelligence f, esprit m; (presence of mind) présence f d'esprit; (wittiness) esprit; (person) homme/femme d'esprit; **to be at one's ~s' end** (fig) ne plus savoir que faire; **to have one's ~s about one** avoir toute sa présence d'esprit, ne pas perdre la tête; **to ~** adv à savoir

witch [wɪtʃ] n sorcière f

witchcraft ['wɪtʃkrɑːft] n sorcellerie f

 KEYWORD

with [wɪð, wɪθ] prep **1** (in the company of) avec; (at the home of) chez; **we stayed with friends** nous avons logé chez des amis; **I'll be with you in a minute** je suis à vous dans un instant

2 (descriptive): **a room with a view** une chambre avec vue; **the man with the grey hat/blue eyes** l'homme au chapeau gris/aux yeux bleus

3 (indicating manner, means, cause): **with tears in her eyes** les larmes aux yeux; **to walk with a stick** marcher avec une canne; **red with anger** rouge de colère; **to shake with fear** trembler de peur; **to fill sth with water** remplir qch d'eau

4 (in phrases): **I'm with you** (I understand) je vous suis; **to be with it** (inf: up-to-date) être dans le vent

withdraw [wɪð'drɔː] vt (irreg like: draw) retirer ▷ vi se retirer; (go back on promise) se rétracter; **to ~ into o.s.** se replier sur soi-même

withdrawal [wɪð'drɔːəl] n retrait m; (Med) état m de manque

withdrawal symptoms npl: **to have ~** être en état de manque, présenter les symptômes mpl de sevrage

withdrawn [wɪð'drɔːn] pp of **withdraw** ▷ adj (person) renfermé(e)

withdrew [wɪð'druː] pt of **withdraw**

wither ['wɪðə'] vi se faner

withhold [wɪð'həuld] vt (irreg like: hold) (money) retenir; (decision) remettre; **to ~ (from)** (permission) refuser (à); (information) cacher (à)

within [wɪð'ɪn] prep à l'intérieur de ▷ adv à l'intérieur; **~ his reach** à sa portée; **~ sight of** en vue de; **~ a mile of** à moins d'un mille de; **~ the week** avant la fin de la semaine; **~ an hour from now** d'ici une heure; **to be ~ the law** être légal(e) or dans les limites de la légalité

without [wɪð'aut] prep sans; **~ a coat** sans manteau; **~ speaking** sans parler; **~ anybody knowing** sans que personne le sache; **to go or do ~ sth** se passer de qch

withstand [wɪð'stænd] vt (irreg like: stand) résister à

witness ['wɪtnɪs] n (person) témoin m; (evidence) témoignage m ▷ vt (event) être témoin de; (document) attester l'authenticité de; **to bear ~ to sth** témoigner de qch; **~ for the prosecution/defence** témoin à charge/à décharge; **to ~ to sth/having seen sth** témoigner de qch/d'avoir vu qch

witness box, (US) **witness stand** n barre f des témoins

witty ['wɪtɪ] adj spirituel(le), plein(e) d'esprit

wives [waɪvz] npl of **wife**

wizard ['wɪzəd] n magicien m

wk abbr = **week**

wobble ['wɔbl] vi trembler; (chair) branler

woe [wəu] n malheur m

woke [wəuk] pt of **wake**

woken ['wəukn] pp of **wake**

wolf (pl wolves) [wulf, wulvz] n loup m

woman (pl women) ['wumən, 'wɪmɪn] n femme f ▷ cpd: **~ doctor** femme f médecin; **~ friend** amie f; **~ teacher** professeur m femme; **young ~** jeune femme; **women's page** (Press) page f des lectrices

womanly ['wumənlɪ] adj féminin(e)

womb [wuːm] n (Anat) utérus m

women ['wɪmɪn] npl of **woman**

won [wʌn] pt, pp of **win**

wonder ['wʌndə'] n merveille f, miracle m; (feeling) émerveillement m ▷ vi: **to ~ whether/why** se demander si/pourquoi; **to ~ at** (surprise) s'étonner de; (admiration) s'émerveiller de; **to ~ about** songer à; **it's no ~ that** il n'est pas étonnant que + sub

wonderful ['wʌndəful] adj merveilleux(-euse)

won't [wəunt] = **will not**

wood [wud] *n* (*timber, forest*) bois *m* ▷ *cpd* de bois, en bois

wood carving *n* sculpture *f* en *or* sur bois

wooded ['wudɪd] *adj* boisé(e)

wooden ['wudn] *adj* en bois; (*fig: actor*) raide; (: *performance*) qui manque de naturel

woodpecker ['wudpɛkəʳ] *n* pic *m* (*oiseau*)

woodwind ['wudwɪnd] *n* (*Mus*) bois *m*; **the ~** les bois *mpl*

woodwork ['wudwə:k] *n* menuiserie *f*

woodworm ['wudwə:m] *n* ver *m* du bois; **the table has got ~** la table est piquée des vers

wool [wul] *n* laine *f*; **to pull the ~ over sb's eyes** (*fig*) en faire accroire à qn

woollen, (*US*) **woolen** ['wulən] *adj* de *or* en laine; (*industry*) lainier(-ière) ▷ *n*: **~s** lainages *mpl*

woolly, (*US*) **wooly** ['wulɪ] *adj* laineux(-euse); (*fig: ideas*) confus(e)

word [wə:d] *n* mot *m*; (*spoken*) mot, parole *f*; (*promise*) parole; (*news*) nouvelles *fpl* ▷ *vt* rédiger, formuler; **~ for ~** (*repeat*) mot pour mot; (*translate*) mot à mot; **what's the ~ for "pen" in French?** comment dit-on "pen" en français?; **to put sth into ~s** exprimer qch; **in other ~s** en d'autres termes; **to have a ~ with sb** toucher un mot à qn; **to have ~s with sb** (*quarrel*) avoir des mots avec qn; **to break/keep one's ~** manquer à sa parole/ tenir (sa) parole; **I'll take your ~ for it** je vous crois sur parole; **to send ~ of** prévenir de; **to leave ~ (with sb/for sb) that ...** laisser un mot (à qn/pour qn) disant que ...

wording ['wə:dɪŋ] *n* termes *mpl*, langage *m*; (*of document*) libellé *m*

word processing *n* traitement *m* de texte

word processor [-prəusesəʳ] *n* machine *f* de traitement de texte

wore [wɔ:ʳ] *pt of* **wear**

work [wə:k] *n* travail *m*; (*Art, Literature*) œuvre *f* ▷ *vi* travailler; (*mechanism*) marcher, fonctionner; (*plan etc*) marcher; (*medicine*) agir ▷ *vt* (*clay, wood etc*) travailler; (*mine etc*) exploiter; (*machine*) faire marcher *or* fonctionner; (*miracles etc*) faire; **works** *n*. (*Brit: factory*) usine *f* ▷ *npl* (*of clock, machine*) mécanisme *m*; **how does this ~?** comment est-ce que ça marche?; **the TV isn't ~ing** la télévision est en panne *or* ne marche pas; **to go to ~** aller travailler; **to set to ~**, **to start ~** se mettre à l'œuvre; **to be at ~ (on sth)** travailler (sur qch); **to be out of ~** être au chômage *or* sans emploi; **to ~ hard** travailler dur; **to ~ loose** se défaire, se desserrer; **road ~s** travaux *mpl* (d'entretien des routes); **work on** *vt fus* travailler à; (*principle*) se baser sur; **work out** *vi* (*plans etc*) marcher; (*Sport*) s'entraîner ▷ *vt* (*problem*) résoudre; (*plan*) élaborer; **it ~s out at £100** ça fait 100 livres; **work up** *vt*: **to get ~ed up** se mettre dans tous ses états

workable ['wə:kəbl] *adj* (*solution*) réalisable

workaholic [wə:kə'hɔlɪk] *n* bourreau *m* de travail

worker ['wə:kəʳ] *n* travailleur(-euse), ouvrier(-ière); **office ~** employé(e) de bureau

work experience *n* stage *m*

workforce ['wə:kfɔ:s] *n* main-d'œuvre *f*

working ['wə:kɪŋ] *adj* (*day, tools etc, conditions*) de travail; (*wife*) qui travaille; (*partner, population*) actif(-ive); **in ~ order** en état de marche; **a ~ knowledge of English** une connaissance toute pratique de l'anglais

working class *n* classe ouvrière ▷ *adj*: **working-class** ouvrier(-ière), de la classe ouvrière

working week *n* semaine *f* de travail

workman ['wə:kmən] *irreg n* ouvrier *m*

workmanship ['wə:kmənʃɪp] *n* métier *m*, habileté *f*; facture *f*

work of art *n* œuvre *f* d'art

workout ['wə:kaut] *n* (*Sport*) séance *f* d'entraînement

work permit *n* permis *m* de travail

workplace ['wə:kpleɪs] *n* lieu *m* de travail

worksheet ['wə:kʃi:t] *n* (*Scol*) feuille *f* d'exercices; (*Comput*) feuille *f* de programmation

workshop ['wə:kʃɔp] *n* atelier *m*

work station *n* poste *m* de travail

work surface *n* plan *m* de travail

worktop ['wə:ktɔp] *n* plan *m* de travail

work-to-rule ['wə:ktə'ru:l] *n* (*Brit*) grève *f* du zèle

world [wə:ld] *n* monde *m* ▷ *cpd* (*champion*) du monde; (*power, war*) mondial(e); **all over the ~** dans le monde entier, partout dans le monde; **to think the ~ of sb** (*fig*) ne jurer que par qn; **what in the ~ is he doing?** qu'est-ce qu'il peut bien être en train de faire?; **to do sb a ~ of good** faire le plus grand bien à qn; **W~ War One/Two**, **the First/Second W~ War** la Première/ Deuxième Guerre mondiale; **out of this ~** *adj* extraordinaire

World Cup *n*: **the ~** (*Football*) la Coupe du monde

worldly ['wə:ldlɪ] *adj* de ce monde

world-wide ['wə:ld'waɪd] *adj* universel(le) ▷ *adv* dans le monde entier

World-Wide Web *n*: **the ~** le Web

worm [wə:m] *n* (*also:* **earth~**) ver *m*

worn [wɔ:n] *pp of* **wear** ▷ *adj* usé(e)

worn-out ['wɔ:naut] *adj* (*object*) complètement usé(e); (*person*) épuisé(e)

worried ['wʌrɪd] *adj* inquiet(-ète); **to be ~ about sth** être inquiet au sujet de qch

worry ['wʌrɪ] *n* souci *m* ▷ *vt* inquiéter ▷ *vi* s'inquiéter, se faire du souci; **to ~ about** *or* **over sth/sb** se faire du souci pour *or* à propos de qch/qn

worrying ['wʌrɪɪŋ] *adj* inquiétant(e)

worse [wə:s] *adj* pire, plus mauvais(e) ▷ *adv* plus mal ▷ *n* pire *m*; **to get ~** (*condition,*

w

situation) empirer, se dégrader; **a change for the ~** une détérioration; **he is none the ~ for it** il ne s'en porte pas plus mal; **so much the ~ for you!** tant pis pour vous!

worsen ['wə:sn] vt, vi empirer

worse off adj moins à l'aise financièrement; (fig): **you'll be ~ this way** ça ira moins bien de cette façon; **he is now ~ than before** il se retrouve dans une situation pire qu'auparavant

worship ['wə:ʃɪp] n culte m ⊳ vt (God) rendre un culte à; (person) adorer; **Your W~** (Brit: to mayor) Monsieur le Maire; (: to judge) Monsieur le Juge

worst [wə:st] adj le/la pire, le/la plus mauvais(e) ⊳ adv le plus mal ⊳ n pire m; **at ~** au pis aller; **if the ~ comes to the ~** si le pire doit arriver

worth [wə:θ] n valeur f ⊳ adj: **to be ~** valoir; **how much is it ~?** ça vaut combien?; **it's ~ it** cela en vaut la peine, ça vaut la peine; **it is ~ one's while (to do)** ça vaut le coup (inf) (de faire); **50 pence ~ of apples** (pour) 50 pence de pommes

worthless ['wə:θlɪs] adj qui ne vaut rien

worthwhile ['wə:θ'waɪl] adj (activity) qui en vaut la peine; (cause) louable; **a ~ book** un livre qui vaut la peine d'être lu

worthy ['wə:ðɪ] adj (person) digne; (motive) louable; **~ of** digne de

KEYWORD

would [wud] aux vb **1** (conditional tense): **if you asked him he would do it** si vous le lui demandiez, il le ferait; **if you had asked him he would have done it** si vous le lui aviez demandé, il l'aurait fait

2 (in offers, invitations, requests): **would you like a biscuit?** voulez-vous un biscuit?; **would you close the door please?** voulez-vous fermer la porte, s'il vous plaît?

3 (in indirect speech): **I said I would do it** j'ai dit que je le ferais

4 (emphatic): **it WOULD have to snow today!** naturellement il neige aujourd'hui! or il fallait qu'il neige aujourd'hui!

5 (insistence): **she wouldn't do it** elle n'a pas voulu or elle a refusé de le faire

6 (conjecture): **it would have been midnight** il devait être minuit; **it would seem so** on dirait bien

7 (indicating habit): **he would go there on Mondays** il y allait le lundi

would-be ['wudbi:] adj (pej) soi-disant

wouldn't ['wudnt] = **would not**

wound¹ [wu:nd] n blessure f ⊳ vt blesser; **~ed in the leg** blessé à la jambe

wound² [waund] pt, pp of **wind²**

wove [wəuv] pt of **weave**

woven ['wəuvn] pp of **weave**

wrap [ræp] n (stole) écharpe f; (cape) pèlerine f ⊳ vt (also: **~ up**) envelopper; (parcel) emballer; (wind) enrouler; **under ~s** (fig: plan, scheme) secret(-ète)

wrapper ['ræpər] n (on chocolate etc) papier m; (Brit: of book) couverture f

wrapping ['ræpɪŋ] n (of sweet, chocolate) papier m; (of parcel) emballage m

wrapping paper n papier m d'emballage; (for gift) papier cadeau

wreak [ri:k] vt (destruction) entraîner; **to ~ havoc** faire des ravages; **to ~ vengeance on** se venger de, exercer sa vengeance sur

wreath [ri:θ, pl ri:ðz] n couronne f

wreck [rɛk] n (sea disaster) naufrage m; (ship) épave f; (vehicle) véhicule accidenté; (pej: person) loque (humaine) ⊳ vt démolir; (ship) provoquer le naufrage de; (fig) briser, ruiner

wreckage ['rɛkɪdʒ] n débris mpl; (of building) décombres mpl; (of ship) naufrage m

wren [rɛn] n (Zool) troglodyte m

wrench [rɛntʃ] n (Tech) clé f (à écrous); (tug) violent mouvement de torsion; (fig) déchirement m ⊳ vt tirer violemment sur, tordre; **to ~ sth from** arracher qch (violemment) à or de

wrestle ['rɛsl] vi: **to ~ (with sb)** lutter (avec qn); **to ~ with** (fig) se débattre avec, lutter contre

wrestler ['rɛslər] n lutteur(-euse)

wrestling ['rɛslɪŋ] n lutte f; (also: **all-in ~:** Brit) catch m

wretched ['rɛtʃɪd] adj misérable; (inf) maudit(e)

wriggle ['rɪgl] n tortillement m ⊳ vi (also: **~ about**) se tortiller

wring [rɪŋ] (pt, pp **wrung**) [rɪŋ, rʌŋ] vt tordre; (wet clothes) essorer; (fig): **to ~ sth out of** arracher qch à

wrinkle ['rɪŋkl] n (on skin) ride f; (on paper etc) pli m ⊳ vt rider, plisser ⊳ vi se plisser

wrinkled ['rɪŋkld], **wrinkly** ['rɪŋklɪ] adj (fabric, paper) froissé(e), plissé(e); (surface) plissé; (skin) ridé(e), plissé

wrist [rɪst] n poignet m

wrist watch ['rɪstwɔtʃ] n montre-bracelet f

writ [rɪt] n acte m judiciaire; **to issue a ~ against sb, to serve a ~ on sb** assigner qn en justice

write (pt **wrote**, pp **written**) [raɪt, rəut, 'rɪtn] vt, vi écrire; (prescription) rédiger; **to ~ sb a letter** écrire une lettre à qn; **write away** vi: **to ~ away for** (information) (écrire pour) demander; (goods) (écrire pour) commander; **write down** vt noter; (put in writing) mettre par écrit; **write off** vt (debt) passer aux profits et pertes; (project) mettre une croix sur; (depreciate) amortir; (smash up: car etc) démolir complètement; **write out** vt écrire; (copy) recopier; **write up** vt rédiger

write-off ['raɪtɔf] n perte totale; **the car is a ~** la voiture est bonne pour la casse

writer ['raɪtəʳ] *n* auteur *m*, écrivain *m*
writhe [raɪð] *vi* se tordre
writing ['raɪtɪŋ] *n* écriture *f*; (*of author*) œuvres *fpl*; **in ~** par écrit; **in my own ~** écrit(e) de ma main
writing paper *n* papier *m* à lettres
written ['rɪtn] *pp of* **write**
wrong [rɒŋ] *adj* (*incorrect*) faux/fausse; (*incorrectly chosen: number, road etc*) mauvais(e); (*not suitable*) qui ne convient pas; (*wicked*) mal; (*unfair*) injuste ▷ *adv* mal ▷ *n* tort *m* ▷ *vt* faire du tort à, léser; **to be ~** (*answer*) être faux/fausse; (*in doing/saying*) avoir tort (de dire/faire); **you are ~ to do it** tu as tort de le faire; **it's ~ to steal, stealing is ~** c'est mal de voler; **you are ~ about that, you've got it ~** tu te trompes; **to be in the ~** avoir tort; **what's ~?** qu'est-ce qui ne va pas?; **there's nothing ~** tout va bien; **what's ~ with the car?** qu'est-ce qu'elle a, la voiture?; **to go ~** (*person*) se tromper; (*plan*) mal tourner; (*machine*) se détraquer; **I took a ~ turning** je me suis trompé de route
wrongful ['rɒŋful] *adj* injustifié(e); **~ dismissal** (*Industry*) licenciement abusif
wrongly ['rɒŋlɪ] *adv* à tort; (*answer, do, count*) mal, incorrectement; (*treat*) injustement
wrong number *n* (*Tel*): **you have the ~** vous vous êtes trompé de numéro
wrong side *n* (*of cloth*) envers *m*
wrote [rəʊt] *pt of* **write**
wrought [rɔːt] *adj*: **~ iron** fer forgé
wrung [rʌŋ] *pt, pp of* **wring**
wt. *abbr* (= *weight*) pds.
WWW *n abbr* = **World-Wide Web**

X

XL *abbr* (= *extra large*) XL
Xmas ['ɛksməs] *n abbr* = **Christmas**
X-ray ['ɛksreɪ] *n* (*ray*) rayon *m* X; (*photograph*) radio(graphie) *f* ▷ *vt* radiographier
xylophone ['zaɪləfəʊn] *n* xylophone *m*

Yellow Pages® *npl* (*Tel*) pages *fpl* jaunes

yelp [jɛlp] *n* jappement *m*; glapissement *m*
▷ *vi* japper; glapir

yes [jɛs] *adv* oui; (*answering negative question*) si
▷ *n* oui *m*; **to say ~ (to)** dire oui (à)

yesterday ['jɛstədɪ] *adv, n* hier (*m*);
~ morning/evening hier matin/soir; **the
day before ~** avant-hier; **all day ~** toute la
journée d'hier

yet [jɛt] *adv* encore; (*in questions*) déjà ▷ *conj*
pourtant, néanmoins; **it is not finished ~** ce
n'est pas encore fini *or* toujours pas fini;
must you go just ~? dois-tu déjà partir?;
have you eaten ~? vous avez déjà mangé?;
the best ~ le meilleur jusqu'ici *or* jusque-là;
as ~ jusqu'ici, encore; **a few days ~** encore
quelques jours; **~ again** une fois de plus

yew [ju:] *n* if *m*

Yiddish ['jɪdɪʃ] *n* yiddish *m*

yield [ji:ld] *n* production *f*, rendement *m*;
(*Finance*) rapport *m* ▷ *vt* produire, rendre,
rapporter; (*surrender*) céder ▷ *vi* céder; (*US
Aut*) céder la priorité; **a ~ of 5%** un rendement
de 5%

YMCA *n abbr* (= *Young Men's Christian Association*)
≈ union chrétienne de jeunes gens (UCJG)

yob ['jɔb], **yobbo** ['jɔbəu] *n* (*Brit inf*)
loubar(d) *m*

yoga ['jəugə] *n* yoga *m*

yoghurt, yogurt ['jɔgət] *n* yaourt *m*

yoke [jəuk] *n* joug *m* ▷ *vt* (*also:* **~ together**:
oxen) accoupler

yolk [jəuk] *n* jaune *m* (d'œuf)

 KEYWORD

you [ju:] *pron* **1** (*subject*) tu; (*polite form*) vous;
(*plural*) vous; **you are very kind** vous êtes très
gentil; **you French enjoy your food** vous
autres Français, vous aimez bien manger;
you and I will go toi et moi *or* vous et moi,
nous irons; **there you are!** vous voilà!
2 (*object: direct, indirect*) te, t' + *vowel*; vous;
I know you je te *or* vous connais; **I gave it
to you** je te l'ai donné, je vous l'ai donné
3 (*stressed*) toi; vous; **I told you to do it** c'est
à toi *or* vous que j'ai dit de le faire
4 (*after prep, in comparisons*) toi; vous; **it's for
you** c'est pour toi *or* vous; **she's younger
than you** elle est plus jeune que toi *or* vous
5 (*impersonal: one*) on; **fresh air does you
good** l'air frais fait du bien; **you never know**
on ne sait jamais; **you can't do that!** ça ne se
fait pas!

you'd [ju:d] = **you had**; **you would**

you'll [ju:l] = **you will**; **you shall**

young [jʌŋ] *adj* jeune ▷ *npl* (*of animal*) petits
mpl; (*people*): **the ~** les jeunes, la jeunesse;
a ~ man un jeune homme; **a ~ lady**
(*unmarried*) une jeune fille, une demoiselle;
(*married*) une jeune femme *or* dame; **my ~er**

---

y

yacht [jɔt] *n* voilier *m*; (*motor, luxury yacht*)
yacht *m*

yachting ['jɔtɪŋ] *n* yachting *m*, navigation *f*
de plaisance

yachtsman ['jɔtsmən] *irreg n* yacht(s)man *m*

Yank [jæŋk], **Yankee** ['jæŋkɪ] *n* (*pej*)
Amerloque *m/f*, Ricain(e)

yank [jæŋk] *vt* tirer d'un coup sec

yap [jæp] *vi* (*dog*) japper

yard [jɑ:d] *n* (*of house etc*) cour *f*; (*US: garden*)
jardin *m*; (*measure*) yard *m* (= 914 mm; 3 feet);
builder's ~ chantier *m*

yard sale *n* (*US*) brocante *f* (dans son propre
jardin)

yardstick ['jɑ:dstɪk] *n* (*fig*) mesure *f*, critère *m*

yarn [jɑ:n] *n* fil *m*; (*tale*) longue histoire

yawn [jɔ:n] *n* bâillement *m* ▷ *vi* bâiller

yawning ['jɔ:nɪŋ] *adj* (*gap*) béant(e)

yd. *abbr* = **yard**; **yards**

yeah [jɛə] *adv* (*inf*) ouais

year [jɪə*] *n* an *m*, année *f*; **every ~** tous les ans, chaque année; **this ~**
cette année; **a** *or* **per ~** par an; **~ in, ~ out**
année après année; **to be 8 ~s old** avoir 8 ans;
an eight-~-old child un enfant de huit ans

yearly ['jɪəlɪ] *adj* annuel(le) ▷ *adv*
annuellement; **twice ~** deux fois par an

yearn [jə:n] *vi*: **to ~ for sth/to do** aspirer à
qch/à faire

yeast [ji:st] *n* levure *f*

yell [jɛl] *n* hurlement *m*, cri *m* ▷ *vi* hurler

yellow ['jɛləu] *adj, n* jaune (*m*)

brother mon frère cadet; **the ~er generation** la jeune génération

younger [ˈjʌŋɡəʳ] *adj* (*brother etc*) cadet(te)

youngster [ˈjʌŋstəʳ] *n* jeune *m/f*; (*child*) enfant *m/f*

your [jɔːʳ] *adj* ton/ta, tes *pl*; (*polite form, pl*) votre, vos *pl*; *see also* **my**

you're [juəʳ] = **you are**

yours [jɔːz] *pron* le/la tien(ne), les tiens/tiennes; (*polite form, pl*) le/la vôtre, les vôtres; **is it ~?** c'est à toi (*or* à vous)?; **a friend of ~** un(e) de tes (*or* de vos) amis; *see also* **faithfully; sincerely**

yourself [jɔːˈsɛlf] *pron* (*reflexive*) te; (: *polite form*) vous; (*after prep*) toi; vous; (*emphatic*) toi-même; vous-même; **you ~ told me** c'est vous qui me l'avez dit, vous me l'avez dit vous-même; *see also* **oneself**

yourselves [jɔːˈsɛlvz] *pl pron* vous; (*emphatic*) vous-mêmes; *see also* **oneself**

youth [juːθ] *n* jeunesse *f*; (*young man*) (*pl* **youths**) [juːðz] jeune homme *m*; **in my ~** dans ma jeunesse, quand j'étais jeune

youth club *n* centre *m* de jeunes

youthful [ˈjuːθfʊl] *adj* jeune; (*enthusiasm etc*) juvénile; (*misdemeanour*) de jeunesse

youth hostel *n* auberge *f* de jeunesse

you've [juːv] = **you have**

Yugoslav [ˈjuːɡəʊslaːv] *adj* (*Hist*) yougoslave ▷ *n* Yougoslave *m/f*

Yugoslavia [juːɡəʊˈslaːvɪə] *n* (*Hist*) Yougoslavie *f*

yuppie [ˈjʌpɪ] *n* yuppie *m/f*

YWCA *n abbr* (= *Young Women's Christian Association*) union chrétienne féminine

Z

zany [ˈzeɪnɪ] *adj* farfelu(e), loufoque

zap [zæp] *vt* (*Comput*) effacer

zeal [ziːl] *n* (*revolutionary etc*) ferveur *f*; (*keenness*) ardeur *f*, zèle *m*

zebra [ˈziːbrə] *n* zèbre *m*

zebra crossing *n* (*Brit*) passage clouté *or* pour piétons

zero [ˈzɪərəʊ] *n* zéro *m* ▷ *vi*: **to ~ in on** (*target*) se diriger droit sur; **5° below ~** 5 degrés au-dessous de zéro

zest [zɛst] *n* entrain *m*, élan *m*; (*of lemon etc*) zeste *m*

zigzag [ˈzɪgzæg] *n* zigzag *m* ▷ *vi* zigzaguer, faire des zigzags

Zimbabwe [zɪmˈbaːbwɪ] *n* Zimbabwe *m*

Zimmer® [ˈzɪməʳ] *n* (*also*: **~ frame**) déambulateur *m*

zinc [zɪŋk] *n* zinc *m*

zip [zɪp] *n* (*also*: **~ fastener**) fermeture *f* éclair® *or* à glissière; (*energy*) entrain *m* ▷ *vt* (*file*) zipper; (*also*: **~ up**) fermer (avec une fermeture éclair®)

zip code *n* (*US*) code postal

zip file *n* (*Comput*) fichier *m* zip *inv*

zipper [ˈzɪpəʳ] *n* (*US*) = **zip**

zit [zɪt] (*inf*) *n* bouton *m*

zodiac [ˈzəʊdɪæk] *n* zodiaque *m*

zone [zəʊn] *n* zone *f*

zoo [zuː] *n* zoo *m*

zoology [zuːˈɒlədʒɪ] *n* zoologie *f*

zoom [zuːm] *vi*: **to ~ past** passer en

trombe; **to ~ in (on sb/sth)** (*Phot, Cine*) zoomer (sur qn/qch)

zoom lens *n* zoom *m*, objectif *m* à focale variable

zucchini [zuːˈkiːnɪ] *n* (*US*) courgette *f*